D1158022

# Modern
# Black
# Writers

# Modern Black Writers

*Second Edition*
*Edited by Manitou Wordworks*

## St. James Press

AN IMPRINT OF THE GALE GROUP

DETROIT • SAN FRANCISCO • LONDON
BOSTON • WOODBRIDGE, CT

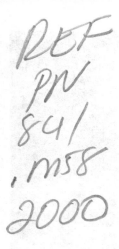

Manitou Wordworks, *Editors*

Joann Cerrito, *Project Coordinator*

Laura Standley Berger, David Collins, Stephen Cusack, Nicolet V. Elert, Miranda Ferrara, Jamie C. FitzGerald, Kristin Hart, Laura S. Kryhoski, Margaret Mazurkiewicz, Michael J. Tyrkus, *St. James Press Staff*

Peter M. Gareffa, *Managing Editor, St. James Press*

Mary Beth Trimper, *Composition Manager*
Dorothy Maki, *Manufacturing Manger*
Wendy Blurton, *Senior Buyer*

Cynthia Baldwin, *Product Design Manager*
Martha Schiebold, *Art Director*

Maria L. Franklin, *Permissions Manager*
Kimberly F. Smilay, *Permissions Specialist*

Modern black writers—2nd ed.
    p. cm.
    Includes bibliographical references (p.) and index
    ISBN 1-55862-436-8 (hardcover)
    1. Literature—Black authors—Dictionaries. 2. Blacks in literature—Dictionaries.
    PN841.M58 1999                              99-048501

Printed in the United States of America

St. James Press is an imprint of Gale Group

Gale Group and Design is a trademark used herein under license

10 9 8 7 6 5 4 3 2 1

# INTRODUCTION

When he was invited to participate on the advisory board for this new edition of *Modern Black Writers*, Richard Yarborough, coeditor of the *Norton Anthology of African-American Literature* and Associate Professor of African-American Literature at the University of California, Los Angeles, accepted enthusiastically—noting that he had used *Modern Black Writers* when he was a student. That example of continuity is appropriate to consider while discussing the purpose of this new edition, which expands upon a rich and now traditional source for the study of black writers from around the world.

Building upon the earlier volumes of *Modern Black Writers*, advisers and editors for this edition outlined three major goals to expand the usefulness of this reference source: 1) represent significant writers who have emerged during the last two decades of the twentieth century; 2) update entries on authors who continue to publish new works; 3) provide significant end-of-the-century analyses of writers who lived earlier in the twentieth century. Accordingly, users of this new edition will find entries on more recently established novelists (Edwidge Danticat, Tsitsi Dangarembga), poets (Yusef Komunyakaa, Dionne Brand), and dramatists (Adrienne Kennedy, Tess Onwueme), as well as some previously neglected authors, like Ann Petry, who have had a resurgence of critical attention in the 1990s.

The scope of *Modern Black Writers* has been expanded to include popular writers of such subgenres as speculative/science fiction (Samuel R. Delany and Octavia Butler) and detective fiction (Walter Mosley). Additionally, important new pieces bring further insight into works by Langston Hughes, Zora Neale Hurston, and many other major authors from earlier in the century.

Finally, the new edition continues coverage of major authors of the present day—Nobel Laureates Toni Morrison, Wole Soyinka, and Derek Walcott among them. Researchers will also discover that reprinted criticism in this edition is more generous in length, providing space for more extensive analyses to complement reviews and shorter excerpts that highlight a major theme of an essay. We trust these approaches will expand on the tradition of *Modern Black Writers*, just as contemporary black writers expand on the literary riches of their forebears.

# EDITOR'S NOTE

For this new edition, two important enhancements have been made to the text. First, citations for periodical articles have been expanded to include the full title of the magazine or journal, eliminating the need for a separate key to abbreviations. Second, full bibliographies have been added to the entries, replacing the shorter lists of works mentioned in the text which were appended to the first two volumes. For those works originally published in a language other than English, the titles of published translations are also given. Free translations of non-English language titles appear, in roman type, when no published translation exists or when the title of the published translation differs markedly from the original.

As in the previous edition, a dagger following the citation for an article indicates that the excerpt has been translated for use in *Modern Black Writers*. Excerpts which originally appeared in volume one of the previous edition were translated by editor Michael Popkin in collaboration with Debra Popkin; excerpts from volume two, a supplement to the first edition, were translated by Sharada Krishnamurthy.

# ADVISERS

Ali Jimale Ahmed
*Queen's College*
*City University of New York*

Cecil Abrahams
*Brock University*
*St. Catherines, Ontario*
*Canada*

Jason Berner
*Hunter College*
*City University of New York*

Charlotte H. Bruner
*Iowa State University*

Lucy Z. Dlamini
*University of Swaziland*
*Kwaluseni, Swaziland*

Dorothy Driver
*University of Cape Town*
*South Africa*

Babafemi Folorunso
*Obafemi Awolowo University*
*Ile-Ife, Nigeria*

Evelyn J. Hawthorne
*Howard University*

W. P. Kenney
*Manhattan College*

Renée Larrier
*Rutgers University*

Wole Ogundele
*Obafemi Awolowo University*
*Ile-Ife, Nigeria*

Tejumola Olaniyan
*University of Virginia*

Oyekan Owomoyela
*University of Nebraska Lincoln*

Reinhard Sander
*Amherst College*

Eric Sellin
*Tulane University*

Juris Silenieks
*Carnegie Mellon University*

Janice Spleth
*West Virginia University*

Michael Thorpe
*Mount Allison University*
*Sackville, New Brunswick*
*Canada*

Richard Yarborough
*University of California, Los Angeles*

Hal Wylie
*University of Texas at Austin*

# LIST OF ENTRANTS

Peter Abrahams
Chinua Achebe
Ama Ata Aidoo
Opal Palmer Adisa
Jacques-Stéphen Alexis
T. M. Aluko
Elechi Amadi
Maya Angelou
Michael Anthony
Kofi Anyidoho
Ayi Kwei Armah
William Attaway
Kofi Awoonor

Miriama Bâ
Seydou Badian
James Baldwin
Toni Cade Bambara
Amiri Baraka
Francis Bebey
Sylvain Bemba
Louise Bennet
Mongo Beti
Olympe Bhêly-Quénum
Arna Bontemps
David Bradley
Dionne Brand
Edward Kamau Brathwaite
Erna Brodber
Gwendolyn Brooks
Sterling A. Brown
Dennis Brutus
Ed Bullins
Octavia Butler

Camara Laye
Aimé Césaire
Patrick Chamoiseau
Syl Cheney-Coker
Charles W. Chestnutt
Alice Childress
John Pepper Clark
Austin C. Clarke
Michelle Cliff
Lucille Clifton
Merle Collins
Maryse Condé
Countee Cullen

Bernard Binlin Dadié
Léon-Gontran Damas
Tsitsi Dangarembga
Edwige Danticat
Samuel Delany
William Demby

René Depestre
Nafissatou Niang Diallo
Birago Diop
David Diop
Rita Dove
Paul Laurence Dunbar

Zee Edgell
Cyprian Ekwensi
Ralph Ellison
Buchi Emecheta

Nuruddin Farah
Jessie Fauset

Ernest J. Gaines
Beryl Gilroy
Nikki Giovanni
Edouard Glissant
Lorna Goodison

Lorraine Hansberry
Michael S. Harper
Wilson Harris
Robert Hayden
Bessie Head
John Hearne
Roy A. K. Heath
Chester Himes
Merle Hodge
Langston Hughes
Zora Neale Hurston

Festus Iyayi

C. L. R. James
Charles Johnson
James Weldon Johnson
Gayl Jones
A. C. Jordan
Bertène Juminer

Cheikh Hamidou Kane
William Melvin Kelley
Adrienne Kennedy
John Oliver Killens
Jamaica Kincaid
Yusef Komunyakaa
Ahmadou Kourouma
Mazisi Kunene

Sony Labou Tansi
Alex La Guma
Kojo Laing

George Lamming
Werewere Liking
Henri Lopes
Audre Lorde
Earl Lovelace

David Maillu
Roger Mais
Jack Mapanje
René Maran
Dambudzo Marechera
Paule Marshall
Daniel Maximin
Claude McKay
Terry McMillan
Jean Métellus
Edgar Mittelholzer
Thomas Mofolo
Toni Morrison
Walter Mosley
Es'kai (Ezekiel) Mphahlele
S. E. K. Mqhayi
Oswald Mtshali
V. Y. Mudimbe
Micere Githae Mugo
John Munonye
Albert Murray
Meja Mwangi

Gloria Naylor
Cheik Aliou Ndao
Njabulo Ndebele
Agostinho Neto
Ngugi wa Thiong'o
Richard Ntiru
Flora Nwapa
Onuora Nzekwu

Grace Ogot
Gabriel Okaral
Christopher Okigbo
Ben Okri
Tess Onwueme
Femi Osofisan
Niyi Osundare
Yambo Ouologuem
Ferdinand Oyono

Okot p'Bitek
Lenrie Peters
Ann Petry
Anthony Phelps
Marlene Nourbese Philip
Caryl Phillips

Sol T. Plaatje

Jean-Joseph Rabéarivelo
Ishmael Reed
V. S. Reid
Richard Rive
Shaaban Robert
Ola Rotimi
Jacques Roumain
David Rubadiri

Andrew Salkey
Sonia Sanchez
Ken Saro Wiwa
Simone Schwarz-Bart
Sembène Ousmane
Léopold Sédar Senghor
Olive Senior

Sipho Sepamla
Mongane (Wally) Serote
Robert Serumaga
Ntozake Shange
Bode Sowande
Aminata Sow Fall
Wole Soyinka
Garth St. Omer
Efua Sutherland

Taban lo Liyong
Jean Baptiste Tati-Loutard
Tchicaya U Tam'si
Philippe Thoby-Marcelin
    and Pierre Marcelin
Wallace Thurman
Miriam Tlali
Melvin B. Tolson

Jean Toomer
Amos Tutuola

B. W. Vilakazi

Derek Walcott
Alice Walker
Margaret Walker
Myriam Warner-Vieyra
John Edgar Wideman
John A. Williams
August Wilson
Richard Wright
Sylvia Wynter

Bernard Zadi Zaourou
Joseph Zobel

# ENTRANTS BY COUNTRY

**ANGOLA**
Agostinho Neto

**ANTIGUA**
Jamaica Kincaid

**BARBADOS**
Edward Brathwaite
Austin C. Clarke
George Lamming
Paule Marshall

**BELIZE**
Zee Edgell

**BENIN**
Olympe Bhély-Quénum

**CAMEROON**
Francis Bebey
Mongo Beti
Werewere Liking
Ferdinand Oyono

**CONGO**
Sylvain Bemba
Sony Labou Tansi
Henri Lopes
Jean Baptiste Tati-Loutard
Tchicaya U Tam'si

**COTE D'IVOIRE**
Bernard Binlin Dadié
Ahmadou Kourouma
Bernard Zadi Zaourou

**FRENCH GUIANA**
Léon-Gontran Damas
Bertène Juminer

**GAMBIA**
Lenrie Peters

**GHANA**
Ama Ata Aidoo
Kofi Anyidoho
Ayi Kwei Armah
Kofi Awoonor
Kojo Laing
Efua Sutherland

**GRENADA**
Merle Collins

**GUADELOUPE**
Maryse Condé
Daniel Maximin
Simone Schwarz-Bart
Myriam Warner-Vieyra

**GUINEA**
Camara Laye

**GUYANA**
Beryl Gilroy
Wilson Harris
Roy A. K. Heath
Edgar Mittelholzer

**HAITI**
Jacques-Stéphen Alexis
Edwige Danticat
René Depestre
Jean Métellus
Anthony Phelps
Jacques Roumain
Philippe Thoby-Marcelin
    and Pierre Marcelin

**JAMAICA**
Opal Palmer Adisa
Louise Bennet
Erna Brodber
Michelle Cliff
Lorna Goodison
John Hearne
Roger Mais
Claude McKay
Marlene Nourbese Philip
V. S. Reid
Andrew Salkey
Olive Senior
Sylvia Wynter

**KENYA**
David Maillu
Micere Githae Mugo
Meja Mwangi
Ngugi wa Thiong'o
Grace Okot

**LESOTHO**
Thomas Mofolo

**MADAGASCAR**
Jean-Joseph Rabéarivelo

**MALAWI**
Jack Mapanje
David Rubadiri

**MALI**
Seydou Badian
Yambo Ouologuem

**MARTINIQUE**
Aimé Césaire
Patrick Chamoiseau
Edouard Glissant
René Maran
Joseph Zobel

**NIGERIA**
Chinua Achebe
Timothy Aluko
Elechi Amadi
John Pepper Clark
Cyprian Ekwensi
Buchi Emecheta
Festus Iyayi
John Munonye
Flora Nwapa
Onuora Nzekwu
Gabriel Okara
Christopher Okigbo
Ben Okri
Tess Onwueme
Femi Osofisan
Niyi Osundare
Ola Rotimi
Ken Saro Wiwa
Bode Sowande
Wole Soyinka
Amos Tutuola

**SENEGAL**
Mariama Bâ
Nafissatou Niang Diallo
Birago Diop
David Diop
Cheikh Hamidou Kane
Cheik Aliou Ndao
Sembène Ousmane
Léopold Sédar Senghor
Aminata Sow Fall

**SIERRA LEONE**
Syl Cheney-Coker

**SOMALIA**
Nuruddin Farah

**SOUTH AFRICA**
Peter Abrahams
Dennis Brutus
Bessie Head
A. C. Jordan
Mazisi Kunene
Alex La Guma
Es'kai (Ezekiel) Mphahlele
S. E. K. Mqhayi
Oswald Mtshali
Njabulo Ndebele
Sol T. Plaatje
Richard Rive
Sipho Sepamla
Mongane (Wally) Serote
Miriam Tlali
B. W. Vilakazi

**ST. KITTS**
Caryl Phillips

**ST. LUCIA**
Garth St. Omer
Derek Walcott

**TANZANIA**
Shabaan Robert

**TRINIDAD AND
  TOBAGO**
Michael Anthony
Dionne Brand
Merle Hodge
C. L. R James
Earl Lovelace

**UGANDA**
Richard Ntiru
Okot p'Bitek
Robert Serumaga
Taban lo Liyong

**UNITED STATES**
Maya Angelou
William Attaway
James Baldwin
Toni Cade Bambara
Amiri Baraka
Arna Bontemps
David Bradley
Gwendolyn Brooks
Sterling A. Brown
Ed Bullins
Octavia Butler
Charles W. Chestnutt
Alice Childress
Lucille Clifton
Countee Cullen
Samuel Delany
William Demby
Rita Dove
Paul Laurence Dunbar
Ralph Ellison
Jessie Fauset
Ernest J. Gaines
Nikki Giovanni
Lorraine Hansberry
Michael S. Harper
Robert Hayden
Chester Himes
Langston Hughes

Zora Neale Hurston
Charles Johnson
James Weldon Johnson
Gayl Jones
William Melvin Kelley
Adrienne Kennedy
John Oliver Killens
Yusef Komunyakaa
Audre Lorde
Terry McMillan
Toni Morrison
Walter Mosley
Albert Murray
Gloria Naylor
Ann Petry
Ishmael Reed
Sonia Sanchez
Ntozake Shange
Wallace Thurman
Melvin B. Tolson
Jean Toomer
Alice Walker
Margaret Walker
John Edgar Wideman
John A. Williams
August Wilson
Richard Wright

**ZAIRE**
V. Y. Mudimbe

**ZIMBABWE**
Tsitsi Dangarembga
Dambudzo Marchera

# A

## ABRAHAMS, Peter (1919–)
### South Africa

Mr. Peter Abrahams is a South African native. This fact dominates whatever he writes. In South Africa, as you travel by train, you look out of the window and see, in that large, empty land, a solitary native walking delicately, in his ochre-coloured blanket, across the red earth dotted with scrubby trees of an incredible apple-green. It makes a fine picture, and then you forget it. Or if you have a house you have also a native "boy," or, in the Cape, a coloured maid. Then it is a case of the servant question, which, from the master's point of view, is the same everywhere. And sometimes, in very liberal company, you discuss the native problem, generally with the feeling it is our problem, not his. Altogether it is high time Mr. Abrahams came along to remind us that ultimately it is not a matter of pictures or servants or political embarrassments but of a backward society that must eventually be educated and given generous opportunity.

*Dark Testament* is a miscellany—scenes from the author's life and two or three short stories, also largely from life though much influenced by the writing of Mr. William Saroyan. Naturally it is an emotional book, but it is first of all a book—in spite of alien influences and the author's melancholy cast of mind the most honest piece of literature that has come out of Africa for years. The reader will find that familiar scenes have taken on strange shapes. This is not the polite Cape Town (for instance) of Malay flowerwomen still sitting in the urban principal street or of parties at Kelvin Grove: this is District Six and the region round Roeland Street as seen by those who must live in them. This is the outlook of those whose life is squalor and poverty and nothing whatever to look forward to. On the spot it is as easy to see things too large as it is, with laziness or lack of conscience, to ignore them. But if Mr. Abrahams can presently add humour, to forestall the charge that he has no sense of proportion, he will have provided exactly the loud, deep, moving voice his nation sorely needs.

*Times Literary Supplement.* January 16, 1943, p. 34

*Wild Conquest*, which is a story of the Great Trek, has a special interest, for its author, Mr. Peter Abrahams, is a South African Negro. He writes with vividness and great dignity. He is just to the Boers, and his picture of the Matabele, about to be crushed, moves one with its restraint and suppressed emotion. This is a good novel in its own right, and it may be the forerunner of an entire school of African literary art.

C. P. Snow. *The Sunday Times.* May 20, 1951, p. 3

Undoubtedly *Black Boy* is only one daguerreotype of the South as it was in Richard Wright's youth. There are other, fairer pictures just as true. No one book, no one individual, has ever told all there is to tell about our home. But *Black Boy* is not, therefore, to be waved airily aside. It reveals too much about an effect, the effect of a system upon a person sensitive enough to produce some of the most valuable writing in this our time.

Now, from one of South Africa's Coloured people comes a book which it is hard not to compare with *Black Boy*. Like Richard Wright, Peter Abrahams is a foremost voice of a distressed group. Like *Black Boy*, Abrahams' *Tell Freedom* covers the years of boyhood and youth its author spent in an environment that galled him to the quick. Like *Black Boy, Tell Freedom* ends with its author on his way to what he hopes will be a freer life.

But *Tell Freedom* is a tenderer record than *Black Boy*. That is, however, only because Peter Abrahams is a gentler spirit than Richard Wright. It has nothing to do with the picture of South Africa he paints or with its racial tensions between whites, Coloured, natives and Orientals. Much of this recital is played out against the background of Johannesburg, in a racial slum—named Vrededorp— in which Peter Abrahams spent his youth. It shifts in brief episodes to the country, to the missionary college he attended, and finally, first, to Cape Town and at last to Durban, whence he embarks at the book's end for England. And yet, in a sense, the scene never shifts. Wherever it takes us, the great, unforgettable features are the virulence and the obduracy of South African color caste.

Blyden Jackson. *Phylon.* 15, 4, 1954, pp. 410–11

Had [*Mine Boy*] not been about a South African Negro, I dare say no one would pay it much attention, for it clearly lacks distinction of any sort, though the subject leads one to expect vastly more of the sociological and the melodramatic than actually emerges. The story of Xuma, the young Negro who comes to work in the mines and runs up against the racial problem, has possibilities that we who have had our proletarian novel could face with equanimity.

Mr. Abrahams has not focused his lens. He does not decide, at any point, whether he is writing a picaresque novel, a tract, a love story, or a kind of *Bildungsroman*. Nor does Mr. Abrahams have the novelist's eye, the eye for detail which reveals a way of life and a society. His people drink beer, dance, fight, and love rather in the style of Catfish Row, and although the author tells us how warmly human everybody is, and how deeply everyone feels for everyone else, there doesn't seem to be any particular reason why they should. As for the characters themselves, they are shadows. We have no sense of their blackness as a race nor of their essence as individuals, and again I suggest that this lack derives from the author's uncertainty as to his own intention: neither he nor the reader is ever sure of just how to take the story. Is this a call to arms? to empathy? to esthetic appreciation?

The ending of the book provides the gauge of the extent of Mr. Abrahams' confusion: Xuma goes rigorously off to jail in support of his white friend, for a reason surely, but not, as it works out in this story, for a reason cogent enough to move us to full sympathy. One simply says to oneself, Life is not, cannot be, like that. Xuma learns that the black man must not lust after the goods of the white man, that white and black must love one another or die, but we see only in the haziest, most sentimental way that this is true. Who on earth would quarrel with the notion? I think I would, when it gets mixed up with art, and in the inevitable confusion, art and life vitiate one another.

All this seems to me as much as to say that Mr. Abrahams has not mastered the two most telling techniques of the novelist: dramatization and expression.

Louis O. Coxe. *The Yale Review.* September, 1955, pp. 154–55

The first half of [*A Wreath for Udomo*] slowly meanders, its water touching every nook, so that we intimately know the minutest details about the actors involved. . . .

When the reality comes—when Udomo has to go out to Panafrica for the cause—sacrificing his English girl whom he loves and who has helped to make him—romantic dalliance gives way to ruthless action. The contrast in mood is so striking that the writing could have been done by a different Peter Abrahams, the same one who wrote *Mine Boy* and *Wild Conquest*. Tension mounts all the time. The Africans, not fully realised in the first part of the book, suddenly come into their own. The white men on the coast are handled with a touch of ironic humour.

One feels a genuine involvement in the fates of the actors of this fevered drama and each one comes to an end at once unexpected and dramatic but thoroughly in character. The climax of the story, achieved by a kind of poetic montage, is grand and leaves a lasting impression on the mind.

If only the same man had written both parts of the book, charging even the dream with a suggestion of the tension to come, the effect would have been better sustained and the book would have lost nothing either artistically or in political intention.

Cyprian Ekwensi. *West African Review.* June 1956, p. 603

Peter Abrahams's *Wild Conquest* is one of the few novels that try to go back to the beginning of the great moral dilemma of black and white. In his story Peter Abrahams (who is himself a black South African) shows how a double burden of savagery and guilt on the part of both black and white bred hatred, and he takes as his starting point the day when the British decreed the freeing of slaves. Out of fear, the Boer masters of a band of black men who have been their slaves precipitate a killing of both black and white. The slaves had intended to leave peaceably the land they had tilled and the homestead that they had built for their masters. But the Boers fear that their ex-slaves will try to take the farm and homestead, as has happened elsewhere, and they kill one of the slaves as a gesture; there is a fight and the Boer family leaves to join the Great Trek to the hinterland, away from the jurisdiction and administration of the British. They set the homestead on fire behind them.

This novel gives us, too, an idea of what the trek meant to the forebears of those who make up the great majority of the nation— the Africans themselves. The wise man of the Matabele says that the coming of the white man deep into the interior meant "the end of living by the spear and the beginning of living by the head." The book ends at the great clash between black and white, when the Matabele were defeated. It is "the point between yesterday and tomorrow. The old ends here; the new starts here. This is the end of a lifetime. The beginning of a lifetime.". . .

*A Wreath for Udomo* . . . is about the sort of problems ex-victims have to face when they are freed of an imposed system, and have to work out a discipline and morality of their own.

Nadine Gordimer. *Times Literary Supplement.* August 11, 1961, p. 522

[Abrahams] is a classicist who takes less from Europe than from Africa. In Black Africa ancient tales are striking in their *concision*; contemporary tales, in their verbosity. The modern ones can get lost in details and commentaries; the ancient ones are firmly based on *facts*. The fact is an image, which has symbolic value; reasoning cuts off the roots of facts, of *life*. Abrahams has rediscovered the *style* of the ancient tales, thus confirming that there is no truth—or art—but the general.

Let us only compare him to the other South African novelists and story-tellers, who live their stories by presenting them to us under a magnifying-glass, which prevents these writers from *bringing their stories to life*. It is true that *A Wreath for Udomo* was written after a trip to South Africa, but from a distance, with a degree of physical and moral perspective. . . .

The lesson I learn from *A Wreath for Udomo* is the following. Negritude, to express itself, must go beyond itself by going beyond folklore and exoticism. It will do so by returning to the very sources of Negritude: to our ancient art, which is *art* because its subject is *Man* and because its rhythm is marked not by *abundance* but by *restraint*, the very restraint that gives everything its proper place. This is why I say that Peter Abrahams is the *classicist of Negritude*. [1963]

Léopold Sédar Senghor. *Liberté I: Négritude et humanisme* (Paris, Éditions du Seuil, 1964), pp. 427–28, 430†

On the African side in South Africa Peter Abrahams stands high on the list. His early novels, *Dark Testament, Song of the City, Mine Boy*, are all in the Richard Wright tradition. One of his most successful novels though is *Wild Conquest*, a novel based on the story of the Great Trek. The urgency in this novel at times makes the style erratic and patchy, but he gives us introspection and characters who have lives of their own, capable of expansion. But even Abrahams does bother us in some of his passages . . . [when he writes the] kind of protest which limits the emotional and intellectual range of characterization. The total framework of the novel has been chalked out for us; the situations are familiar. We know we are in a country which considers it a crime for two people with different pigmentation to fall in love with each other. The temptations to overplay the situation somehow detract from the impact of the characters.

Abrahams overplays in this novel the ready-made group attitudes and responses. There is an excessive play of fate in the lives of the characters and, as a result, their experience becomes a minute fraction of life. On the other hand, however, Fieta, the coloured woman who emerges from a dissipated life and grows to know and accept the importance of her love for crippled Mad Sam whose own life is perpetual pain, is interesting as a character. The image of Fieta is not limited by any impending disaster from outside herself or from Mad Sam, although these impending disasters loom large and engulf the total lives of these two people. Their image is capable of development. Here again we know that they are under-dogs and this makes them vulnerable. There is a wide area of self-response open to them and to the reader. Their conception has no bounds.

David Rubadiri. *Transition*. No. 15, 1964, p. 40

In this autobiographical statement, *Tell Freedom*, where colors and races collide and clash, where social circumstances are fat with poverty and suffering, [Abrahams] moves from the dream within a drop of rain through an ever-increasing, darkening awareness to the point of departure, where the "long night" comes to an end.

From the very beginning of the book, Abrahams sets its basic tonality—the contrapuntal interplay between illusion and reality, between fantasy and actuality—the juxtaposition of the warm security of the author's inner being with the threatening harshness of the outer world. . . .

Christianity had failed him; his love-making had gone awry. He was moving away from his family. He realized that to many whites he seemed as filth, when he was physically flung onto the floor by a shop-keeper who was "near the point of nausea through touching human waste," while another customer boomed something about his being a "black baboon." Even though he was becoming increasingly conscious that many international ideologies and credoes did not extend to the black and Colored man's situation, yet he still attempted to grasp at one of these, Communism. But there, too, the equation did not work; the egalitarian illusion proved fraudulent. To Abrahams, it was ideology without humanity.

And so Peter Abrahams, like so many black writers, has no recourse but to flee from a land which is both tender and austere, for he could not bridge the distance between the open landscape and the closed social reality. In the claustrophobic actuality of South Africa he could not feed the fantasy imagination so necessary to him as a writer.

But any flight by black writers creates another paradox since it is their intelligence and vision which must be called upon to carve freedom for their people, to lead to the justice and dignity which the land itself breathes.

Wilfred Cartey. Introduction to Peter Abrahams, *Tell Freedom* (New York, Macmillan, 1970), pp. vii, xiv

[In *The Path of Thunder*] Abrahams made a bold venture into the complex racial patterns of his early experience. This novel is a tale of melodramatic violence set in the northern Cape Province, the Karroo. In form it is not unlike novels such as [Dickens's] *Little Dorrit*, [Hardy's] *The Return of the Native* and [Faulkner's] *Light in August*. A mystery about paternity is solved across the colour line (also the line of social class) and the pattern of a dangerous society is exposed by a near blind old woman. . . .

The strong central hero gives cohesion to the work. We are never far from the circle of Lanny's thoughts, which give a focus to the action rather like those of other radical heroes in novels of the 1950s such as [Kingsley Amis's] *Lucky Jim* and [John Wain's] *Hurry on Down*. Like the heroes of Lawrence and Thomas Hardy, Lanny feels with his blood and sees the landscape as an extension of personal experience. . . .

From the widening horizons of London, and doubtless stimulated by his acquaintance with [the Caribbean intellectual and activist] George Padmore and others of his circle, Abrahams attempted increasingly ambitious themes in his next four novels. *Wild Conquest* is a South African's view of the Great Trek without the conventional northwards slant. Abrahams looks southwards as well and shows the process of expansion and invasion from both sides. *A Night of Their Own* is a fragment, again showing both sides, from the modern politics of subversion and mass imprisonment in South Africa. *A Wreath for Udomo* shows the rise to power and betrayal of his aides and a South African confederate by a modern African political leader. *This Island Now* sketches the rise to power and the enfeebled tyranny of a black nationalist party in a Caribbean island. Despite their flaws these are works which provided a new impetus in writing about African subjects.

Christopher Heywood. In Christopher Heywood, ed., *Perspectives on African Literature* (New York, Africana, 1971), pp. 165, 167–68

The most prolific novelist from South Africa is Peter Abrahams; and his early novel, *Mine Boy*, which was published in 1946 . . . is representative of the South African novel as a whole. The story itself is relatively uncomplicated—an account of a young man's exposure to life in Johannesburg and his work as leader of one of the work crews in a gold mine. The concentration, however, is on life in Johannesburg itself; thus *Mine Boy* is a novel with urbanization as its theme. . . .

There is little plot in *Mine Boy*. Rather, Abrahams' story is one of character and atmosphere, for, like Cyprian Ekwensi's Lagos, Abrahams' picture of Johannesburg's Malay Camp is in many ways the prime concern of his novel. Blacks, Coloureds, and whites are all in the novel but it is only the sections of the story that are set in the Malay Camp among the African characters that are truly alive. The brief sojourns that Xuma makes in the segregated white areas of the city are flat and considerably less realistically drawn; Abrahams' white characters are often given to mouthing ideas of racial equality—rather than living these ideas as the African characters do. . . .

If Xuma is lonely and isolated because of his unfulfilled love and the debilitating life in Johannesburg, there is still companionship. Again and again Abrahams illustrates the growing friendship Xuma shares with Leah, Ma Plank, and Marsy. This is of crucial importance since *Mine Boy* differs so greatly from other African fiction where the family still plays a significant part. In *Mine Boy* the family has been completely destroyed, there is no sense of the communal consciousness. People band together out of a common need. There is no sense of the basic filial unit which plays such an important function in tropical African fiction. Nor are there any children to give the novel warmth and humor and the happiness we have seen in other African novels. Abrahams has created an adult world instead—in a city which eventually destroys its inhabitants. The strong characters, other than Xuma, are all women, and in spite of the optimistic and overly didactic ending, one cannot foresee much of a future for Xuma. He is still young; the city will eventually count him in its toll.

Charles R. Larson. *The Emergence of African Fiction* (Bloomington, Indiana University Press, 1971), pp. 162–63, 165–66

Peter Abrahams is a novelist of ideas. He writes about the machinery of politics and power, but he uses his considerable grasp of this area of activity to serve his central interest, which is the problem of individual freedom in contemporary human affairs. . . .

It should be stated at the outset that Abrahams' ability as a writer of fiction is in the middle range, and the grandiose claims made for his work from time to time by propagandists of African literary culture have been misguided. He is a skilful, if flawed, writer, and there is evidence that he finds the writing of fiction arduous. What is most apparent about his fiction is the complete sincerity and honesty of the author. He has not chosen an easy path; he feels every word he writes and seems incapable of writing conscious pot-boilers. The subjects he returns to again and again in his fiction are the problems which have most exercised—and come near to paralysing in the process—the liberal mind in the West since the end of the second world war. They are the problems of how to reconcile the liberal conscience to the unpleasant consequences of necessary action; how to resist inroads made into the integrity of the individual, especially where these inroads are the results of justified attempts to set others free, to put them on the road to the liberal goal of individual fulfilment. Abrahams invokes and even to some extent typifies the liberal dilemma of the twentieth century.

Michael Wade. *Peter Abrahams* (London, Evans Brothers, 1972), pp. 4–5

*This Island Now* is the climax of Abrahams' examination of the ways in which the blacks hope to attain freedom and achieve their racial identity. Published barely a year after *A Night of Their Own*, its dominant mood is urgency, as the title of the book indicates well enough. Thus, although one might have assumed that Abrahams had been working on the novel and laid it aside in 1963–64 to write *A Night*, it appears that in fact most of *This Island Now* was not written until the earlier book was published. Either Abrahams was dissatisfied with the conclusions reached in the earlier novel or he found the problem too pressing to be dealt with in one book. Abrahams, never a good artist except when on familiar grounds, has transferred the setting from Africa to the West Indies where he now lives. There is no doubt that the physical terrain of *This Island Now* is largely that of Jamaica as described in his essay, ''The Real Jamaica,'' and the political terrain that of Haiti. Yet the book is a serious political novel precisely because it avoids the easy banalities that its theme and facile analogy with, say, Dr Duvalier might provoke.

The over-riding quality of *This Island Now* is its simplicity. It is partly an epic simplicity, the subject of the novel being the efforts of an individual to revolutionise the power structure of his society. In addition, it is a simplicity which allows the novel's political theme, free from the accretion of confusing details, to be transferred from its peculiar geographical setting. The problems which confront President Albert Josiah are more than those of a tiny island in the Caribbean; they are problems which face the developing countries in general and which have threatened to embroil the big powers in a global war. At the beginning of his revolution, Josiah threatens that if the foreign mercantile companies attempt to buck him, he will 'nationalise everything, beat the racialist drum, drive all capitalists out of the country, and ask for help from the communist world.'

One effect of the novel's simplicity is the lack of any details of social living. More than in *A Night of Their Own*, Abrahams is so preoccupied with the political conflict that everything else recedes to the background. This includes the mass of the people. Society in *This Island Now* operates like an iceberg: a glittering speck dominates the landscape while the vast bulk remains invisible. True, the people are present throughout the novel, the continuity of their lives providing a kind of stable background, but they are largely mute, passive, and helpless; instead of forming a live background which will provide the plot with genuine action, they constitute the clay from which Josiah wants to mould a revolutionary society. What makes the conflicts within the novel so intense is that the stakes are so high: no less than the destiny of the three million people of the island and—beyond them, what we are never allowed to forget throughout the narrative—the fate of the whole black race. . . .

The simplicity of *This Island Now* is most evident in its characterisation. There are no complexities of character. Each individual is used to represent a concept, usually the guiding principle of his profession. 'Cannibalism is part of business,' says Old Nathan Isaacs, the head of the Isaacs' family empire, as he closes his deal with Josiah. According to John Stanhope, the head of the civil service, 'no area of the life of a good public servant, especially a very senior one, could ever be wholly private or personal.' Maxwell Johnson, the editor of the island's main newspaper, gives the classic interpretation of the journalist's duty: 'Our business is to get the news and when we go beyond the getting and presenting of the news then our so-called commitment goes to hell.' Justice Wright, setting himself on a collision course with Josiah, intones: 'The rule of law must never depend on the strength or weakness of the position of any ruler. It must be constant, above person and position.' There can be no real complexities where characters stand for and represent such sure and simple concepts as professional ethics.

Abrahams further simplifies the picture by dividing his characters into black and white—along racial lines. A critic has complained of Abrahams' 'infuriating habit of telling us the exact colour of every character he introduces.' The novelist's answer would be that he is describing a society stratified along racial lines. However, division into black and white not only simplifies, but also polarises, issues. While all the whites oppose Josiah, practically no black man supports his opponents. Even the 'fiercely independent' Miss Martha Lee, a compound mixture of so many races, is forced to take a position on the colour spectrum on the island; a black sergeant silently compliments her: 'big job and all and pretty enough to claim to be Chinese; but no she doesn't claim to be coloured or Chinese coloured or any of those fancy ways of denying the blackness in her. She comes straight out with the blackness in her.' Josiah, who is strikingly light brown, 'had projected so strongly the image of himself as a black man that everybody accepted him as a black man.'

A novelist who is less concerned with individuals but uses people to represent or personify concepts cannot give a satisfactory treatment of society. Abrahams seems to be dealing less with people in society than with society as illustrated in certain abstracted characteristics. This is what makes it so easy for Josiah to accomplish his revolution. By making each character stand for a concept, the defeat of the character is made to look like the overthrow of that concept. . . .

A general characteristic of this novel is that all the characters dwell in almost complete isolation. The only person who tries to reach out to another person is Andrew (Andy) Simpson, but his love affair with Sarah, the Chief Justice's daughter, is blighted by her father's refusal to go along with the socio-political revolution. Otherwise no other character has connections beyond his professional interests. Having buried his wife and child on the island (in circumstances which suggest that Abrahams merely copied Jones' family misfortunes from *A Wreath*), Johnson's life is his newspaper. Stanhope dines out occasionally, but his constant companion is his dog, given to him by the late President, whose wife receives only a passing mention in the story, but who otherwise has left no children or friends behind.

It is difficult to imagine a satisfactory public drama where characters are not seen in their relationships with each other. . . . However, there is no doubt that Abrahams engineers this deliberately. Its epic and archetypal simplicities, which give *This Island Now* the character of a fable or a parable, strengthen it as a political novel. We are not witnessing private quarrels, motivated by personal vendetta.

*This Island Now* leaves us in no doubt about the extremely heavy cost and the wide array of people paying it. 'In our context,' Andy had confidently predicted to Martha at the beginning, 'to act in the interest of the people is to offend someone, some special interest. No matter what we do, someone will cry tyranny.' By the end of the story, but put at the beginning of the novel—a successful attempt to portray the irony of fortune that is such a strong theme in the novel—the people are mumbling tyranny against a revolution designed for their own good. Adds Abrahams: 'Once this earth had communicated a high sense of freedom to its children, especially in the years immediately after the withdrawal of the occupying power. Now fear was a long shadow over the land and its children.' A novelist more knowledgeable in the ways of revolutions has written: 'Hopes grotesquely betrayed, ideals caricatured—that is the definition of revolutionary success.'

Could Abrahams, by using more complex characters instead of fable figures, have more convincingly argued his case that modernisation must be inevitably accompanied by dictatorship? It is probable that a political point of view can be argued only in the simplicity of the black-and-white characters that he has used. Could he have reached different conclusions if he had created a sense of society complete with the continuities of social living? *This Island Now* fails as a first-class political novel because it does not maintain a balance of interrelation between character, psychology, political ideas and political actions, because it does not allow a variety of personal political motives. On the other hand, by including such details, the novel would have lost the intensity of its conflicts and the poignancy of its dilemma. Indeed, both its strengths and weaknesses are inseparably interwoven.

> Kolawole Ogungbesan. *The Writings of Peter Abrahams* (New York: Africana Publishing Company, 1979), pp. 131–45.

BIBLIOGRAPHY
*Dark Testament*, 1942; *Song of the City*, 1945; *Mine Boy*, 1946; *The Path of Thunder*, 1948; *Wild Conquest*, 1950; *Return to Goli*, 1953; *Tell Freedom* (autobiography), 1954; *A Wreath for Udomo*, 1956; *Jamaica: An Island Mosaic*, 1957; *A Night of Their Own*, 1965; *This Island Now*, 1966; *Tongues of Fire*, 1985; *The View from Coyaba*, 1985; *A Blackman Speaks of Freedom*, 1985; *Hard Rain*, 1988; *Pressure Drop*, 1989

# ACHEBE, Chinua (1930–)

## Nigeria

In powerfully realistic prose [Achebe] sets out [in *Things Fall Apart*] to write a fictional but almost documentary account of the day to day happenings in a small Nigerian village without evasion, sophistry or apology. Fascinated one reads about the customs, the culture, and the strange rituals, the fearful hazards of the yam harvest, and the bewildered downfall of our hero Okonkwo, the great wrestler and successful farmer. There is horror in some of the ritual and the superstition, but somehow they are less fearful when simply and naturally described by a writer who clearly has some recollection of them himself. In the same way the Spanish Inquisition is not as horrifying to Roman Catholic zealots as it is to Protestants or even Pagans. There is plenty of humour too, especially in the description of the first two missionaries on the scene, one liberal and gentle and understanding, and the next attacking his problems with fundamentalist rage and zeal. Even a Christian reader must surely compare this last unfavourably with the simple and human medicine man, although the author makes no effort to force any such conclusion.

Altogether the African villagers appear as happy, self-contained people, who like most men, blame or praise the Gods for their sorrows and pleasures. Village discipline was stern, even harsh, but its very inescapability makes nonsense of some of the early descriptions of these villages by explorers and missionaries. Many books and anthropological treatises have told about the power of religious superstition, but here is one which forcefully but impartially gives us the reasons for both.

> Mercedes Mackay. *African Affairs*. July 1958, p. 243

It is a credit to Mr. Achebe's judgement that he has constructed his first novel [*Things Fall Apart*] along very simple lines but I think it possible to find it too simple. Art is, of course, all selection, yet one cannot help remarking that the subject which he tackles in a short novel cannot be exhausted in a twenty-volume anthropological treatise. And although as novel readers we may be interested in anthropological data, we are even more interested in the shifting relations between these data and the adventures of the individual, the modes of thought which produce them and are produced by them. It also seems to me that for the implicit assertion that West Africa has a culture of its own to have its fullest effect, the form of the novel ought to have shown some awareness of the art of this culture. We do not have the novel form, of course, but there are implications in our music, sculpture and folklore which the West African novelist cannot neglect if he wishes to do more than merely imitate a European fashion. (Civilisation is, after all, an integration of diverse regional elements, and we shall not be justified to make use of its resources unless we are prepared to add to them.)

I am in particular disappointed that there is in *Things Fall Apart* so little of the lyricism which marks our village life. So pronounced is this quality that Joyce Cary, an acute observer quite incapable, unfortunately, of interpreting his observations, repeatedly portrayed Nigerian life as a musical farce, and the typical Nigerian as a lyrical half-wit. Mr. Achebe was probably inhibited by the difficulty he experiences in writing passable verse. All the same, I suspect that his sensitivity to "dark" Africa (of the late nineteenth century) is insufficient—and not surprisingly, because his generation did not know the life he is out to present.

Ben Obumselu. *Ibadan*. February, 1959, p. 38

Mr. Chinua Achebe is the young Nigerian writer who made something of a name for himself with a first novel called *Things Fall Apart*, which portrayed the collapse of tribal life through the story of one Okonkwo of the Obi tribe. The hero of Mr. Achebe's new novel [*No Longer at Ease*] is the grandson of Okonkwo: Obi Okonkwo who leaves his village to be educated in England. He returns after four years and takes a job as a civil servant in Lagos. He acquires a girl friend. He buys a car. He pays his mother's hospital bills and his brother's school bills. He lends small amounts of money to uneducated Africans. He has trouble repaying the money which the Umuofia Progressive Union raised to send him to London. He has to pay for an abortion. He accepts a bribe. He is arrested. And that is all. His white boss, Mr. Green, says, "I'm all for equality and all that. I for one would hate to live in South Africa. But equality won't alter facts." Another breath of the wind of change has been charted.

It is usual, almost traditional, to pay tribute to the simplicity of style of novels such as this. We tend to harp on about it, as if short words were something new in fiction. I suppose the fact of the matter is that simplicity is all we ask for in the African novel. We want a lucid, uncluttered account of the way life is changing in these territories. We want sound, competent craftsmen to put up the framework; later, when the chronicles of change are more or less complete, some very fortunate writers indeed will be able to fill the framework in, wallowing in the new luxuries of characterisation, motivation, depth, psychology and all the rest of it. Meanwhile we are grateful to such as Mr. Achebe for such unadorned tales as *No Longer at Ease*.

Keith Waterhouse. *New Statesman*. September 17, 1960, p. 398

*No Longer at Ease* is bound to create a certain sense of diffuseness and slackness after the austere tragic dignity of *Things Fall Apart*, a dignity which recalls Conrad, who is in fact one of Chinua Achebe's mentors. The fluid world of Obi Okonkwo is simply not susceptible of the same classic treatment, and to have captured it at all is an achievement of sympathy and imagination. Achebe measures the decline in the simple contrast of Obi and his grandfather; the grandson has more humanity, more gentleness, a wider awareness, but he lacks the force and integrity of his ancestor. . . .

If *No Longer at Ease* is something less than a tragedy, it is because Achebe does not see Obi Okonkwo as a tragic hero. The pressures that pull and mould him are all pressures making for compromise and accommodation; these are not the stuff of tragedy but of failure and decline. The alien forces that destroyed old Okonkwo were mysterious and inexorable, but still largely external and dramatic. He could see his enemies and die fighting them, even without comprehending them. But Obi is destroyed by "doing what everyone does"; by running away from scandal, living above his income, taking bribes. The enemies of his integrity are all-pervasive and do not dramatize themselves.

Gerald Moore. *Seven African Writers* (London, Oxford University Press, 1962), pp. 68–71

Chinua Achebe chose to bring out his back cloth in relief at the areas of tension. In a sense—not a pejorative one—he is a chronicler, content to follow creases and stress lines, not to impose his own rearrangement on them. That this can be a creative process is demonstrated by the inexorable fate that overtakes his hero, Okonkwo, in *Things Fall Apart*. The demand we make of an expressed way of life is, first and foremost, reality. The writer must impress an acceptance. Enactments of tribal peculiarities must emerge from characters in that society, not interfere with our recognition of basic humanity, not be just a concession to quaintness-mongers. Why, for instance, do we accept so easily and unreservedly the accident of the hero's exploded gun especially as a prelude to the final downfall of one of the village elite? Dissected coldly, events that are not part of the dramatic progression of character or other events are instantly suspect. But Achebe has established another pattern, a rhythm compounded not merely of motives but of understated mysteries—mysteries as much to the characters as to their remote observer—of psychical influences on daily routine, of a man's personal *chi*, of initiations, of guilt and purifications whose ethics are not those of a court of law but of the forces of Nature cycle, of the living and the dead. It is a subtle process, and its first principle, faithfully observed by the author, is the philosophy of acceptance. Not blind, slavish acceptance but a positive faith, an acceptance of forces that begin where the physical leaves off. . . .

Language lends nobility to the life and downfall of Okonkwo; the same language in *No Longer at Ease* merely rebukes the author, as if he has taken his main character too seriously. It is doubtful if Achebe's forte lies in the ability to spit occasionally, or to laugh from the belly when the situation demands it, but he must learn at least to be less prodigal with his stance of a lofty equipoise. For this has bred the greatest objection to his work, this feeling of unrelieved competence, of a lack of the active spark, inspiration.

Wole Soyinka. *American Scholar*. Summer 1963, pp. 392–94

Upon reading Chinua Achebe's two novels, *Things Fall Apart*, and its sequel, *No Longer at Ease*, one encounters an interesting structure of tragic characters in the Okonkwo family, intriguing one to seek a means of explaining the situation. . . .

What precisely accounts for the fact that each of these characters in the lineage depicted in the novels was a failure? Achebe himself is probably inclined to think that the *ndi-ocha* (white men) caused it all, and in some respects he could be partially correct. Others might find that the causes of the several failures are ascertainable only because each particular character has such and such a temperament and was faced with certain difficulties which would "naturally" bring about his downfall. I believe that the explanation, if one exists, lies in the fact that Okonkwo severely antagonized the *ndichie* (ancestors) and *Chukwu* (Chineke, Eze Chitoke, Eze-Binigwe, etc.—the High God, Creator, and Giver of all life and power) by killing Ikemefuna, the boy who called Okonkwo ''father.'' Okonkwo thus alienated his *chi* (*God Within*, not ''personal god'' as Achebe blasphemously refers to *chi*, reflecting possibly a jaundiced attitude toward his own people's religion). . . .

Achebe makes a vainglorious attempt in these two books—and I suspect he will continue so in *Arrow of God*—to ascribe all the evils which occurred in Ibo society to the coming of the white men. But he stacks the cards in the novels, hinting here and there at the truth, yet not explaining fully the substratum of divine forces working to influence the characters. His own motives perhaps are linked with his patent desire to indicate that outsiders can never understand the works of Igbo-speaking writers (whose novels are in English), although one must properly leave the subject of authors' motivations to psychiatrists. Whatever the case may be, however, what caused ''things'' to ''fall apart'' and what made the Ibo man ''no longer at ease'' in the case of Achebe's works were the evil actions of Okonkwo, who brought the wrath of Chukwu, the *alusi* [spirits], and the *ndichie* upon his own lineage.

> Austin J. Shelton. *Transition*. March-April, 1964, pp. 36–37

In a recent interview, Achebe said that having ''learned a lot more about these particular people, you know, my ancestors,'' he had himself come to think of his first book as no longer adequate. Such a writer as he does not have to do research. As he himself admits, when he was born in 1930 things had not changed that much, and as he grew up he was able to talk freely with those whom he now remotely refers to as ''ancestors''; ceremonies were still celebrated, with less intensity perhaps than in the old days, but their original meaning could be inferred by a mind mature enough to grasp the significance of their forms. But this is the point: As the author's own imaginative life has thickened with awareness, so the society he writes about—Umuofia in another guise—has also become more complicated, the forces and characters surrounding the central consciousness of the hero standing out in a sharper, more radical relief.

Ezeulu, the hero of Achebe's *Arrow of God*, bears a certain resemblance to Okonkwo of *Things Fall Apart*. Again we are confronted with an old man's personal struggle with the undeniable facts of Christianity and colonialism, a struggle exacerbated by tensions and loyalties within the self, and within the clan as related to the self. But here we have the further complication of a god, Ulu, whose agent, or ''arrow,'' this grand old Ezeulu effectively is. And in making Ezeulu the vehicle of a god, Achebe begins to ask a series of psychological and moral questions, questions which we Westerners usually discuss in connection with the exceptional, the fanatical (like Luther or Joan of Arc), but which in the Nigerian context are associated with the deepest common proprieties. What is it like being in a society where *all* men act in the company of the unseen as a real presence, as a plurality of presences whose influences are immediately felt, exploited, and perhaps misinterpreted or dangerously gainsaid?

> Judith Illsley Gleason. *This Africa* (Evanston, Ill., Northwestern University Press, 1965), pp. 86–87

In two previous novels, *Things Fall Apart* and *No Longer at Ease*, the young Nigerian writer Chinua Achebe performed a difficult task with skill and ease. In each, he played one theme against another to produce a work of fiction that, while striking in the simplicity of both style and story, projects a sense of the complex realities—the passion and the tragedy of change and adjustment, of cultural death and revival, of social disorganization and rebuilding—that only an African who stands astride the two worlds of present-day Africa can truly know. In *Arrow of God*, Achebe has done it again. The new novel is not without faults, but it is a tribute to Achebe's growth as an artist and a man to say that he now commands even greater skill and a deeper compassion than he did before. . . .

As moving as the story itself is, *Arrow of God* is perhaps more remarkable for its vividly pictorial descriptions of tribal village life in eastern Nigeria, and for its insights into the workings of the African mind. The rituals and ceremonies, the logic and passion behind them, all come clear, and we know more of humanity, which has nothing to do with time and place and states imposed upon the soul by the artifices of a social order. *Arrow of God* combines imaginative power with literary gifts that much older and more sophisticated (Western) writers might well envy.

> Saunders Redding. *African Forum*. Summer 1965, pp. 142–43

At first it would seem as though in *Arrow of God*, Achebe is giving us the mixture as before, in *Things Fall Apart*. Several images, proverbs and devices from the old novel reappear. The python is once again a symbol of the Igbo-Christian conflict. The bird *Enekenti-Oba* who wrestled with his *chi* appears again to underline a philosophical idea which by its persistence seems central to Achebe's writing. Winterbottom's complete failure to understand the thinking of his subjects or to treat them as human beings instead of administrative pawns, reminds us of the earlier D.O. *Arrow of God* is nevertheless essentially different in conception. While the central conflict in *Things Fall Apart* has been between traditional Igbo civilization and Christian imperialism, the conflict in *Arrow of God* is really within Igbo society itself. . . .

[*Arrow of God*] is more substantial than either of Achebe's two earlier works—more complex than *Things Fall Apart* and hence lacking the endearing simplicity of that novel. Its great contribution is its shift of emphasis from the clash of Africa with the outside world to the internal tensions of Africa itself, a clash which seems to be absent in much African writing. We had this in the urban setting of *No Longer at Ease*, here we have it in an unidealized rural setting.

Achebe neither idealizes nor patronizes the Africa of yesterday. His villages are not paradises. They are the scenes of love as well as hatred, goodwill and envy, peace and war. Thus his novel is a human novel. His success in bringing out the general humanity above the Africanness of his themes is what gives him a high place among African writers.

> Eldred Jones. *Journal of Commonwealth Literature*. September 1965, pp. 176, 178

Chinua Achebe is well known as a writer throughout Africa and even beyond. His fame rests on solid personal achievements. As a young man of twenty-eight he brought honour to his native Nigeria by writing *Things Fall Apart*, the first novel of unquestioned literary merit from English-speaking West Africa. Critics tend to agree that no African novelist writing in English has yet surpassed

Achebe's achievement in *Things Fall Apart*, except perhaps Achebe himself. It was written nine years ago, and since then Achebe has written three novels and won several literary prizes. During this time his reputation has grown like a bush-fire in the harmattan. Today he is regarded by many as Africa's finest novelist.

If ever a man of letters deserved his success, that man is Achebe. He is a careful and fastidious artist in full control of his art, a serious craftsman who disciplines himself not only to write regularly but to write well. He has that sense of decorum, proportion and design lacked by many contemporary novelists, African and non-African alike. He is also a committed writer who believes that it is his duty to serve his society. . . .

What gives each of Achebe's novels an air of historical authenticity is his use of the English language. He has developed not one prose style but several, and in each novel he is careful to select the style or styles that will best suit his subject. In dialogue, for example, a westernized African character will never speak exactly like a European character nor will he speak like an illiterate village elder. Achebe, a gifted ventriloquist, is able to individualize his characters by differentiating their speech. . . . Achebe has devised an African vernacular style which simulates the idiom of Ibo, his native tongue.

> Bernth Lindfors. *African Literature Today.* No. 1, 1968, pp. 3–4

To interpret Achebe's work as mere explication of the Nigerian scene, either that of his grandfather's or his own generation, is to mistake his intention and his achievement. In kind with most writers of his generation, he has shown in his published novels and short stories a pre-occupation with certain basic themes, of which the legacy of colonial rule is the central core. It is true that the novels reveal the destructive consequences of the rule of the colonial period. But these are not displayed for their own sake. They are there because they arise out of and reflect to a sensitive mind a manifest indifference and caprice which mirrors life itself. This pre-occupation is found in each of the novels as Achebe explores its meaning and seeks to accommodate himself to it. The heroes of the first three novels have their origins in this. These heroes, conceived in tragic terms, are men in varying degrees conscious of the fact that life turns out to be less manageable and less perfect than they had expected, they react to life in various ways—with courage, honesty and generosity, with pessimism and cynicism—in their attempts to get through life with honour and reward.

It can be argued that for Achebe the principal virtue is to accept stoically what life serves up. But his pre-occupation is more than this: it is the plight of the individual in a world characterized by uncertainty, pain and violence. Achebe is essentially a moralist, concerned with considerations of right and wrong as they are revealed by the individual's responses to the circumstances which surround him.

> G. D. Killam. *The Novels of Chinua Achebe* (New York, Africana, 1969), p. 11

*No Longer at Ease* seems to be too socially satirical to be able to carry off convincingly the tragic effect Achebe gives us reason to think he is striving for. What one misses is the artistically cohesive

tension between chief character and setting that occurs in *Things Fall Apart*. The setting is as economically and convincingly created, but is felt to be almost incidental to the story of Obi. Like one of the magi, Obi returns from abroad, having caught the flavour of a different—an efficient, rational—dispensation. His mind is packed full of elevated notions of public service, and he is determined to play his full part in reinvigorating the Nigerian civil service and stamping out all the old corruption that so ill befits a new nation. The story records his failure. It is an attempt at a tale of muted tragedy, told laconically rather than with detachment.

Achebe's method is clearly hinted at in the account of Obi's interview for his job. During a discussion of Graham Greene's *The Heart of the Matter*, Obi says that life is "like a bowl of wormwood which one sips a little at a time world without end." "A real tragedy," he asserts, "takes place in a corner, in an untidy spot." It would seem that Achebe intends Obi's story to be tragic in this sort of Audenesque way, a view confirmed by the very banal level at which Obi's defeat takes place. He succumbs because loans have to be repaid, money sent home, expenses accounted for. For this effect to be produced Obi has to be made so naïve and self-deluded that he comes close to appearing merely childish. While his story can also be read partly as a paradigm of a man caught between the irreconcilable values of different ways of life, his enmeshment happens too easily to win our sympathetic involvement. As the catalogue of debts and expenditure mounts, one becomes too aware of the cards being stacked against him. It is a very simple-minded young man indeed who does not expect to receive a demand for income tax or an electricity bill.

> Arthur Ravenscroft. *Chinua Achebe* (London, Longmans, Green, 1969), pp. 20–21

Although every piece tells its story, the stories [in *Girls at War, and Other Stories*] are slight and, except for one or two imponderably African twists, more or less predictable. The book is chiefly memorable for its vivid sketches of African life, especially where new ideas of religion and social custom or new political upheavals infringe upon the settled life of the village.

More scholarly hands than mine will one day attempt a critical assessment of the extent to which the extreme differences of cultural background between, for instance, a Yoruba writer like Soyinka and an Ibo writer like Achebe have influenced their art. My own feeling is that the village community of Ibo tradition provides the ideal setting for almost any sort of novel, and I should be surprised if the literary world is not soon assailed by a great flood of Ibo writings now that the surviving Ibos are shut up in the tiny enclave prepared for them, with nothing else to do.

But the overwhelming impression one receives from Achebe's writing—more strongly, I think, than from any other African writer—is one of anger against those who speak of tribalism as something to be disparaged, something impeding Africa's advancement to the delights of Coventry, Slough, and Detroit.

> Auberon Waugh. *Spectator.* March 11, 1972, p. 397

*A Man of the People* is very likely a slighter thing than the sturdy, plodding, much better-known *Things Fall Apart*; but what it lacks in massive solidity of structure, *A Man of the People* more than makes up in technical refinement: in flexibility of characterization and subtlety and delicate assurance of tone. The nature of Achebe's achievement might be made clearer if one imagined a new generic name for such a work as *Things Fall Apart*: an historical/cultural fiction, perhaps, or a sociological presentation, or a ritual, anthropological drama. (This novel, for good reason, is most popular with ethnologists and anthropologists, with social scientists in general, and with "African studies" experts.) *A Man of the People*, on the other hand, is pre-eminently a "novel," with all the dramatized complexity of human relations implied by the tradition of the novel.

While the satire of *A Man of the People* rejects, there is a parallel movement, focussing on Odili and his moral growth, that makes discoveries and accepts, that integrates experience around a new personal center and asserts this individual personality as a replacement for the village code of conduct that has been violated and destroyed. *A Man of the People* takes place in a world much worse off, much more corrupt and cynical and generally nasty, than the world of *Things Fall Apart*, yet Achebe, or at least his hero, finds in this wretched world a life that is both meaningful and possible. *A Man of the People* does not merely show that a certain world of grace is lost forever—of course it is—but takes that loss for granted and attempts to say what there may be of value in this world without innocence that lies about us.

> James Olney. *Tell Me Africa* (Princeton, New Jersey, Princeton University Press, 1973), pp. 202–3

[*A Man of the People*] is doubly significant, for apart from confirming the author's mastery of technique and his succinct use of language (this time it has a relaxed warm flow), it marks a break with his earlier attitude. He has turned his back on the European presence. He no longer feels the need to explain, or point out mistakes, by merely re-creating. The process, I believe, started with *Arrow of God*. But even there (though the teacher is not reacting to the colonizer's view of Africa he is in fact more interested in problems of power and responsibility) the teacher took his time, was patient with his pupils. What has happened in *A Man of the People*—the change in attitude to his audience—is something which can only be felt by following, through the earlier novels, Achebe's creative response to a rapidly changing society.

Now, in the new novel, the teacher talks to his pupils, directly. He has lost patience. He retains self-control in that he does not let anger drive him into incoherent rage and wild lashing. Instead he takes his satirical whip and raps his pupils—with anger, of course, sometimes with pathos verging on tears, but often with bitterness, though this is hardly discernible because below it flow compassion and a zest for life. His pupils are—or ought to be—disturbed. For in *A Man of the People* the teacher accuses them all of complicity in the corruption that has beset our society. *Your* indifference and cynicism has given birth to and nurtured Chief Nanga, he says. . . .

What Achebe has done in *A Man of the People* is to make it impossible or inexcusable for other African writers to do other than address themselves directly to their audiences in Africa—not in a comforting spirit—and tell them that such problems are their concern. The teacher no longer stands apart to contemplate. He has moved with a whip among the pupils, flagellating himself as well as them. He is now the true man of the people. [1966]

> Ngugi wa Thiong'o. *Homecoming* (New York, Lawrence Hill, 1973), pp. 52, 54

*Arrow of God* is decidedly Achebe's most balanced and finished novel. The theme of conflict between two cultures is not here exploited per se. Around this theme, however, and operating at a more dramatic level is the theme of man and god. This theme, as indicated, is borrowed entirely from the African theological thinking. The Europeans are also instruments in the hands of the gods; each moment of Ezeulu's confrontation with his enemies, his friends, and his god breathes the authenticity of that history and that past whose dignity Achebe has promised to restore. But as an artist, he goes beyond the mere restoration, creating a story of tragic grandeur, based firmly in a culture and owing its strength to the re-creation of the very idiom and language of that culture.

Achebe's latest novel, *A Man of the People*, owes very little to any theme or principle derived wholly or in part from his African world. It is the story of African decline, the collapse of those dreams raised by the dawn of independence. What marks it is its satirical quality, its journalistic accuracy, and its peculiarly restless inability or refusal to confront the heart of the political malaise by creating an almost hopeless political situation and a group of naïve leftists who mistake their own self-interest for political motivation. *A Man of the People* is a modern novel that points to the larger questions of the future, especially as it deals with the theme of political growth and direction. It points to the future both in theme and style more than any of the earlier novels, with the exception of *No Longer at Ease* with which it shares a common ground. More realistic, it ushers the reader into the contemporary African predicament.

> Kofi Awoonor. *The Breast of the Earth* (Garden City, New York, Doubleday, 1975), p. 279

Named by Christianized parents after Queen Victoria's beloved; master of the colonial master's tongue, splendidly appropriating it to interpret his country's and people's past; bold user of freedom won by Africa against white domination; Albert Chinualumogu become Chinua Achebe is himself the definitive African experience. It is not a *linear* one. The importance of his book of essays, *Morning Yet on Creation Day*, is that in an unpretentious hundred-odd pages it establishes this so impressively. . . .

Achebe writes of having lived, as an Igbo child born in 1930 in Eastern Nigeria, at the crossroads of cultures. He adds of Africa: "We still do today." But unlike most contemporary black writers and thinkers, he does not see this circumstance as fission and refraction. He regards the inheritance of many cultures as his risk and right. To him the criss-cross of Africa and Euroamerica is a place of a "certain dangerous potency; dangerous because a man might perish there wrestling with multiple-headed spirits, but also he might be lucky and return to his people with the boon of prophetic vision." Achebe himself has done so with—to borrow an irresistible Achebean phrase from elsewhere in the book—"unfair insights." This book brings us the benefit. In his sanity and shrewd sagacity he is like the market town in his essay "Onitsha, Gift of the Niger," to which the great river brings the people and produce of the 2,600-mile journey it makes from its source: "Because Onitsha sees everything it has come to distrust single-mindedness."

> Nadine Gordimer. *Times Literary Supplement*. October 17, 1975, p. 1227

Chinua Achebe's *Things Fall Apart* demonstrates a mastery of plot and structure, strength of characterization, competence in the manipulation of language, and consistency and depth of thematic exploration which is rarely found in a first novel. Although he has never quite been able to sustain this exceptionally high standard in subsequent novels, the general level of performance remains consistently impressive and he assuredly deserves his place as one of the most accomplished African writers. In the history of the anglophone novel, Achebe comes next to [Cyprian] Ekwensi in chronological importance, but his work is much more comprehensive in scope than that of the latter, who confines himself almost entirely to contemporary situations. All the shaping forces which combined to stimulate the growth of modern African literature in the 1950s are discernible in Achebe's work. . . .

Novels like *Things Fall Apart* and *Arrow of God* in which the author sets out to demonstrate the beauty and validity of traditional life and its destruction by an alien civilization must inevitably have a very high sociological content, since the nature of the society must be thoroughly documented before its collapse is shown. This need partly dictates the structure of *Things Fall Apart* and *Arrow of God*, the first parts of both novels being comparatively leisurely portrayals of Igbo society, whereas the second halves move much more rapidly, showing the forces which bring about the collapse. It also accounts for the high sociological content of the earliest African novels. However, a novel is not a sociological document; readers go to novels not for sociological information, but for impressions of life powerfully realized. Sociological information will therefore appear tedious to most readers unless it is expertly handled in the novel, that is, unless it is made to appear part of the vibrant life of the people the author is describing and does not seem to be sociological lore per se. Novelists like Achebe and [Elechi] Amadi have proved themselves very adept at the incorporation of sociological material. Again and again we ask ourselves why it is that after reading hosts of novels which have been made tedious because of the preponderance of unassimilated sociological material, we can come back to Achebe's *Things Fall Apart*, half of which consists of sociological lore, and still be captivated by it. The answer is simply that in this novel the sociological does not call attention to itself as being purely sociological; it is presented as part of the life and activity of the people and is almost always related to some aspect of human character. At times the sociological is introduced as part of the detail which makes the book realistic and interesting. In chapter two for instance, the traditional fear of the darkness and of dangerous animals, and the various superstitions concerning them, are incorporated into the general tension of the announcement of the meeting. When in chapter three Nwakibie invites his wives to drink Okonkwo's palm-wine in their due order, the process is saved from looking like pure sociological information by the attention to detail and the concentration on the words and gestures of the participants, so that a sense of drama is generated and the whole seems to be part of life as it is lived among the Igbos. Even the songs have a relevance they do not have in the works of less accomplished novelists. For instance, the song the women sing after Okonkwo's success in the wrestling match is relevant to that contest and to Okonkwo's character, and the contest is itself presented as part of the lives and feelings of the people. Then the childhood song Ikemefuna remembers as he is on his way to his death heightens the poignancy of the events all the more.

In fact, in *Things Fall Apart* the presentation of the sociological goes hand in hand with the development of Okonkwo's character.

In the very deepest sense of the words, *Things Fall Apart* is a novel which shows the interrelationship of environment and character, one of Achebe's main aims being to demonstrate the way in which Okonkwo's character has been molded by his environment. At every single point in the narrative, Achebe tries to relate every belief, every activity of his society to some aspect of Okonkwo's character. If the novel is structured in such a way that at the end of the first part we have a powerful picture of the society that will collapse in the second part, it is also structured so that at the end of the first part the growth of Okonkwo's character has been perfectly traced and his personality established as one of the leading men in his clan; and it is that personality which will be largely in decline in the second. In this novel there is a masterly manipulation of plot and structure and a judicious deployment of the sociological, which ensures that the development of Okonkwo's character and the presentation of his society are coextensive and contemporaneous.

Eustace Palmer. *The Growth of the African Novel* (London: Heinemann, 1979), pp. 63, 72–73

In depicting the disintegration of Igbo culture in both *Things Fall Apart* and *Arrow of God*, Achebe does not give us a partial or biased view of the historical epoch he is dealing with. He makes use of a wide variety of characters to represent different points of view and social groups. In *Arrow of God*, for instance, Ezeulu, Nwaka, and Akuebue represent the chief priest and elders of traditional society; Captain Winterbottom and Clarke are representatives of colonial administrators with different personalities, while Brown, Goodcountry, and Onachukwu stand for various approaches to the evangelization of Africans. Thus we are able to see how political, religious, tribal, and personal factors all contributed to the crumbling of the traditional social structure. Although the encroachment of the white man's civilization and political power features as the principal catalyst in this change, Achebe does not exonerate his ancestors from blame. Ezeulu's pride and unbending character and his personal conflicts with Nwaka are partly responsible for what happens. The author consequently succeeds in presenting a truthful and balanced account of reality and is able to capture the mood of the epoch. His method is that of objective realism.

Achebe typifies what has become the commonest version of African realism. His linear plots are not only an imitation of the African traditional story, but also coincide with the structure of nineteenth-century European realist fiction. And, just as the nineteenth-century European realists presented a critique of capitalism in non-Marxist terms, Achebe attacks cultural imperialism and postindependence corruption in what may be termed "moderate" terms. He certainly presents a progressive view of history. He aligns himself with anticolonialist forces in *Arrow of God* and *Things Fall Apart* and is critical of the rampant corruption and misdemeanors of the emerging African ruling class in *No Longer at Ease* and *A Man of the People*, but he only goes so far and no further. He does not present a Marxist or in any way radical view of social problems, but he succeeds in giving us a truthful account of what he portrays. His characters are typical and the circumstances under which they operate are natural and convincing. In the two "Old World" novels where he gives a truthful account of Igbo society without glossing over its weaknesses and despite his declared intention to dispose of "the fundamental theme," his art becomes a model of the triumph of realism over the claims of nationalism.

> Emmanuel Ngara. *Art and Ideology in the African Novel* (London: Heinemann, 1985), pp. 111–12

[Achebe's] novels either deal with the African past or refer to the presence of the so-called dark continent. They attack the colonist's view that the "blackman . . . had slept in a dark continent until the Livingstones and Stanleys woke him into history," without idealizing the precolonial era. According to a statement in the *Times Literary Supplement* in 1965, "*Things Fall Apart* is probably already as big a factor in the formation of a young West African's picture of his past, and of his relation to it, as any of the still rather distorted teachings of the pulpit and the primary school." As becomes evident in *A Man of the People*, Achebe is nevertheless also highly critical of the political and social development in postindependent Africa. . . .

Reflecting the social and political reality in postcolonial Africa, *A Man of the People* discloses in literary terms that the federal system installed by the British colonial government was too shaky to guarantee the necessary stability for the independent African nations. . . .

While Achebe's earlier works expose the author's concern for a revaluation of the African past and the search for a national identity, consequently conveying a rather constructive spirit, *A Man of the People* shows an entirely different Achebe. The novel can both be understood as the literary expression of historical change and the changed historical perspective of the author. The "national movement" which was based on the ideological alliance of the masses and the new African elite falls apart immediately after independence. Now it is no longer the opposition between the colonial power and the African population which dominates the political scene but the diverging interests of the black bourgeoisie and the mass of the people. Under these circumstances Achebe's sympathy for the underprivileged among his countrymen seems the only adequate reaction of a writer who claims to be a social critic, the highly negative presentation of Africa's new rulers in *A Man of the People* the only appropriate expression of his critical awareness. This is also mirrored in a change of the narrative perspective. In his last novel, Achebe introduces the first person narrative which implies a greater, if not even more skeptical, distance between the author and his character. . . .

In *A Man of the People* the situation is profoundly changed by the intervention of the military which may be regarded as Achebe's fictitious solution to a problem that many Nigerian intellectuals actually hoped for. How closely Achebe had anticipated the political development became evident when, only nine days after *A Man of the People* was published in 1966, a real, but in the end unsuccessful, coup d'état created further political chaos in Nigeria. Achebe, accused of having supported the rebels, was put into prison. Considering these circumstances, it may not be a surprise that a great number of critics have only praised the anticipatory quality of *A Man of the People* while they have at the same time overlooked its literary merits.

> Wolfgang Klooss. In Hedwig Bock and Albert Wertheim, eds. *Essays on Contemporary Post-Colonial Fiction* (Munich: Max Hueber, 1986), pp. 24, 38–40

*Anthills of the Savannah* is as different a novel as each of Achebe's has been from the one preceding it, or others that have come after it. But this [one] is tidier, with a narrative structure that is earthly, and a language which, on the whole, is spare, and a telling that is direct. Now and again, there is a stylistic stutter. Often the points in the novel are made in a roundabout way or else in a cryptic manner, and sometimes the reader becomes the proverbial man who's lost a camel for which he looks in a milk container. Nevertheless, this is a most charming novel, a book of metonyms, a rich treasure of transferred meanings.

We're back to where the story of *A Man of the People* was interrupted, in 1966, by the army takeover of power in Nigeria. Only we are not in Nigeria, but in a fictitious country called Kangan Republic, where in a recent popular referendum, the head of state, an army general, has failed to be elected president-for-life, because one of the provinces of which the land comprises says "no." The name of this province will ring hatefully in the general's ears, and Abazon will have become his obsession. Anyway, the Kangan Republic is much smaller than Nigeria and is misruled by a general with the abbreviated name of Sam, a general who has the touch of the clown, and the wit of a simpleton, and who . . . refers to himself as the Big Mouth, literally a translation of the Somali nickname for Siyad Barre, Somalia's generalissimo for the past seventeen-plus years. There are endless references to other African tyrants, some by name, some not. . . .

Abazon may be seen as a symbol of dissent to a dictatorship, but it is also a rural Africa which has no muscle to show to the metropolis-concentrated form of bourgeois authoritarianism. In fact, it is much more that. In Somalia, we know what happens when a given province challenges Siyad Barre's authority: the lifeline to the region is severed, no boreholes are dug, no development projects are financed, no teachers are any longer transferred to this area, etc., etc., etc., precisely the very measures described in *Anthills*.

> Nuruddin Farah. *West Africa*. September 21, 1987, pp. 1828, 1830

More people have read Chinua Achebe than any other African writer. This is no less true outside the continent than it is within it. And this is constantly reflected in the fact that more critical attention is paid to his novels than to the work of any other writer. Find someone who has read but one African literary work, and the odds are that the work will be Achebe's *Things Fall Apart*. The reasons for this are not hard to surmise. Achebe writes in a style that is at once accessible to the individual who knows nothing of Africa and intensely compelling to even the most knowledgeable Africanist. He was one of the first writers to effectively dramatize the most important historical, political, and cultural issues facing Africa, and he has remained among the best. Moreover, he is a consummate artist; he always tells a good story. . . .

By turns Achebe has been both praised and condemned for his didacticism. Regardless of how it is judged, perhaps the least controversial statement anyone could make in the field of African literature is that Chinua Achebe is a didactic writer. By his own statements and through his work, Achebe clearly shows his belief in the role of the artist as teacher. The pejoration of the word "didactic" in Western criticism, however, makes this statement rather misleading for many readers. Achebe's artistic concerns are with presenting a holistic view of the ethos of his people in an entirely vital, dynamic mode that is expressive of his culture in terms of form no less than content. His works progress in a linear manner and are set in an historical framework that reveals the persistence of cultural continuity despite internal and external threats to the society. Yet, as [Wole] Soyinka noted, there is never a mere photographic rendering of the world he gives us. We confront an ethical consciousness, an authorial presence that leads us into the societal structures of Igbo life and proceeds in a realistic, linear, and historical manner, while revealing the depth and breadth of strategies open to the individual and society for coping with reality. Achebe's works are didactic, but not in the manner of a facile, two-dimensional realism where all ethical choices are clear cut.

Richard K. Priebe. *Myth, Realism, and the West African Writer* (Trenton: Africa World Press, 1988), pp. 47–48

Achebe is ... not exclusively a narrator of a nation's course through history and its individuals' personal destinies, but he also delightfully, if thoughtfully, offers us an insight into the inevitable relationship between folklore and literature, between African and European—specifically, Nigerian and British—values, and the tragic consequences of such a relationship. For those individuals who are caught up in this conflicting relationship, life offers no ease; for them, things fall apart. The center cannot hold.

The clash of traditional and modern values is easily plotted in Achebe. What is less evident, and therefore needs our focus, is that for Achebe's characters, the tragic choice between opposing values inevitably turns out to be a conflict between the spoken and the written word, between the folklore of the clan and the literature of the foreigner. This clash does not result in a simple victory or defeat. Achebe is too sensitive to the general ironies and ambiguities of life to offer a clear black-and-white solution. The conflict produces, instead, something akin to Greek tragedy: the rise and tragic fall of an individual caught between two impossible choices. . . .

Abdul R. JanMohamed, in his recent study, *Manichean Aesthetics: The Politics of Literature in Colonial Africa*, concludes that a basic ideological function of African literature is to negate European influences and thus restore the old culture. Achebe, in my opinion, does this by juxtaposing the two cultures in such a way as to reduce them to their most basic level—the word either sung, spoken, or written. The final word on the clash of cultures is not yet in, and may never be in; meanwhile, Achebe shows, that those who must make peace with the past and the present and the future, must not lose sight of the word. For, in the beginning was the word. And in the end too.

Raman Singh. *Neohelicon*. 16, 2 (1989), pp. 159–60, 167

Chinua Achebe dedicated his first three novels, *Things Fall Apart*, *No Longer at Ease*, and *Arrow of God* to helping the African people regain their sense of personal dignity, which they lost in their contact with colonialism. In the process of demonstrating such a fundamental commitment, he took a historical look back to the pattern of life in his characters before and after their confrontation with Europe. The internal weaknesses of their society are also exposed in order to present a balanced picture of that confrontation. The tragic flaws of old Okonkwo and Ezeulu, and the moral vacillation of Obi Okonkwo are sympathetically portrayed by the author, although these characters are held responsible for their contributory roles in their individual tragedies. But despite the

instances of human weakness, miscalculations, power tussle, and clashes between human wills and the dictates of the gods, the prevailing tone of these works is still that of the type of optimism that follows well-wrought tragic work. The human errors responsible for the tragedies are restricted to the tragic heroes and a few identifiable characters whose corporate errors do not contribute to a sense of total loss and doom. Rather, there is hope that a new society will be built from the broken pieces of the past. Despite Ezeulu's sad end, traditional sanctions remain operative and continue to judge the actions of men.

The apparent tone of pessimism for which Achebe has been accused begins with *A Man of the People*, which is set in postindependence Nigeria. Like Achebe's former novels, it is deeply analytical. It mercilessly exposes the nature and roots of the bribery, corruption, and apathy which had come to typify Nigeria of the 1960s. Despite its comic exterior, the author's disillusionment is the most consistent aspect of the novel. Neither Nanga the crook nor Odili the idealist is spared Achebe's biting satire. Achebe's commitment resides exactly in his concern for the society and his criticism of all segments of it, both the corrupt and those who condone their corruption through general apathy. Such criticism constitutes the negative form of commitment, the type which exposes and criticizes in order to effect change. This mood dominates most of Achebe's later works, both poetry and criticism, written after the Nigerian Civil War.

Virginia U. Ola. In Jonathan A. Peters, Mildred P. Mortimer, and Russell V. Linnemann, eds. *Literature of Africa and the African Continuum* (Washington, D. C.: Three Continents Press, 1989), pp. 133–34

Twenty-two years have elapsed since *A Man of the People*: years that have seen worse things in Africa than that book prophesied. And then, in 1987, Achebe published *Anthills of the Savannah*. Set in an African country whose young, recently established military ruler has just sought confirmation from the people in his aim to become president-for-life, it seems to take up just where *A Man of the People* left off. Technically, too, it pursues the development already evident in the other books: it is as different from them, that is to say, as they are from each other. Indeed in this difference lies its continuity. . . .

Achebe's commitment here is to a history made vital and actual in language, and aware of itself as such. History is not, as it was in *Things Fall Apart*, there in the past to be known and told about: it comes into being in the minds and feelings of those involved in it. It is the product of the words which form it. That, I think, is why there is no fixed standpoint in *Anthills*, no single storyteller and no single story: the face of history has become a crowd snapshot, with its own very real claim to objectivity. And this takes us back to *Things Fall Apart*. For if there is an important linear development in Achebe's attitude to history, a movement from involved detachment to detached involvement, the more important development is circular. *Things Fall Apart* was also, it will be remembered, a mixed, imbalanced form.

*Anthills of the Savannah* is involved in the genesis of history. What takes place here does so inside the characters who tell their story. They, mentally and emotionally, are struggling to find guidelines through the morass of violence and fear which has taken the place of corruption in their society. . . .

For the anthills [of the title] are symbols, things which speak and, speaking, link past and future: " . . . like anthills surviving to tell the new grass of the savannah about last year's brush fires." And the novel itself is now symbol, not discourse. It is not about anything, nor does it have any purpose, beyond itself; it *is*, it has become, history. A history neither reported now, nor interpreted, but presented as the thing-in-language of a high objectivity. . . . History, we are told in this novel, is learning a language; it is learning that one is not alone. For in it we assimilate the events that made and make us. History and myth have been deconstructed: they have once again been liberated into language.

> Joseph Swann. In Geoffrey V. Davis and Hena Maes-Jelinek, eds. *Crisis and Creativity in the New Literatures in English* (Amsterdam: Rodopi, 1990), pp. 197–98, 200–1, 203

Achebe is read and discussed more than any other African novelist, and his works have come to constitute important interpretative spaces in the development and critique of the postcolonial condition and its aesthetic. Nevertheless, Achebe has suffered the misfortune of being taken for granted: the intricate and deep structures that inform his narratives are rarely examined, except on an elementary introductory level, and the ideologies that inform his narratives and his theoretical reflections rarely seem to have the influence one would expect from Africa's leading novelist. . . . [His] writings and thought must be placed in their proper perspective, placed in relation to both some important literary precursors and within the nationalist tradition that produced him. Only then can we begin to understand why the kinds of narratives Achebe inaugurated have acquired so much ideological import, why he is indispensable to understanding the colonial and postcolonial condition in Africa. . . .

Achebe's seminal status in the history of African literature lies precisely in his ability to have realized that the novel provided a new way of reorganizing African cultures, especially in the crucial juncture of transition from colonialism to national independence, and his fundamental belief that narrative can indeed propose alternative worlds beyond the realities imprisoned in colonial and postcolonial relations of power. In other words, Achebe was possibly the first of our writers to recognize the function of the novel not solely as a mode of representing reality, but one which had limitless possibilities of inventing a new national community. In Achebe's works, questions of national identity are closely related to narrative strategies; fiction allows the writer to express a different vision and perspective. . . .

Indeed, the historical significance of Achebe's works lies in his ability to evolve narrative procedures through which the colonial language, which was previously intended to designate and reproduce the colonial ideology, now evokes new forms of expression, proffers a new oppositional discourse, thereby countering the "permanence of vision" embedded in colonialist discourse. . . . And in seeking a new form of expressing African culture, Achebe and his contemporaries were also seeking a way out of the prisonhouse of colonialism. For these writers to evoke a new African identity—which is one of Achebe's declared goals and persistent themes—these writers had to take the colonial project into account; they had to interrogate its vision, ideologies, historical claims, and its theory of Africans. In Achebe's case, the imperative to confront the colonial project in its totality arises from the belief that "colonization was the most important event in our

history from all kinds of angles . . . most of the problems we see in our politics derive from the moment when we lost our initiative to other people, to colonizers." Significantly, Achebe's return to the colonial archive is motivated by the need to imagine the future: taking colonialism into account (both in terms of writing about it and interrogating its claims) "will help us to map out our plans for the future."

> Simon Gikandi. *Reading Chinua Achebe* (London: James Currey, 1991), pp. 1–4

Achebe's novels are replete with tragic events and generally end with the death or destruction of the protagonist. *Things Fall Apart* ends with the tragic death of Okonkwo, an Oedipal tragedy, reinforced by the irony of circumstance in which Okonkwo, desperately fleeing from the fate of his father, finally meets his fate in the evil forest. He rose very high in his community, but he was to be buried like a dog. In *Arrow of God*, the Chief Priest of Ulu, having "sacrificed" two of his sons (Oduche and Obika) to save his god and the traditional system, is himself "sacrificed" in the end, while his god loses to the Christian God. Achebe's most recent novel, *Anthills of the Savannah*, ends with the total elimination of the key figures, including Chris who dies under extremely absurd circumstances after Sam's dictatorship is overthrown. With his vision based on these and more tragic incidents, Achebe seems to be a pessimist, and we wonder how that position might affect his redemptive role in society. In *Critics on Chinua Achebe*, Agetua has noted that some critics believe that Achebe's first three novels "contain very little sunshine and hope" and that his main characters often "come to grief under circumstances which emphasize the cruel futility of things." Is Achebe, therefore, a pessimist?

Achebe is certainly not a pessimist, for pessimism implies hopelessness and total darkness at the end of the tunnel, both of which are not reflected in his novels. As a realist interested in presenting both sides of the picture, Achebe explores the bright and the dark aspects of the human condition with no suggestion whatsoever that the dark experience is irremediable. Still, we have to contend with the fact that all his novels end unhappily. To begin with, an unhappy ending does not prove pessimism, just as a happy resolution might ultimately not indicate optimism. Nevertheless, Achebe's primary subject is Africa's past and present, and judging from the social and political condition of Africa as he realistically portrays it, a happy ending would sound absurd and illogical. "What about *Anthills of the Savannah*," an objector might argue, "it ends on a note of celebration of life." The resolution of this novel, no doubt, is controversial; however, it seems that in spite of the last chapter, the novel still ends as a tragedy. The deaths of Ikem and Chris overshadow the celebration scene in the last chapter. More importantly, we are uneasily aware, that the celebration notwithstanding, the military is still in power, and the murderer of Chris and his type still loom large in Kangan. It is remarkable that after the naming ceremony in the last chapter, the group conversation winds up on the death of Chris, and the novel finally closes on that sad note. Structurally, therefore, the bright picture of the naming ceremony is parenthetically and paradigmatically sandwiched between two Chris episodes, one about his actual death (chapter seventeen) and the other about a powerful recall of his death. However, our position is that even the unhappy resolutions do not undercut the optimism in Achebe.

Achebe's optimism is revealed in his open—ended conclusions with a suggestion of action continuing with greater sunshine in the future. It is remarkable that each of his novels ends with an opening for a new beginning, thus confirming Achebe's firm belief in the strength of man's resilience. In *Things Fall Apart*, Okonkwo dies and his attempt to resist change fails, but the white man introduces the bible, Western technology, and new commerce, which signify a new beginning. In *Arrow of God*, Ulu yields his authority to the Christian God, and parents harvest their crops in the name of their sons who have embraced Western education and the Christian religion. This, too, is indicative of a new beginning. *No Longer at Ease* closes with a remorseful protagonist, a moral change that reveals self-knowledge and the possibility of future improvement. The fall of the politicians and the advent of the military in *A Man of the People* create grounds for a new attempt at nation building. In *Anthills of the Sayannah*, a new order could result from the ecumenical group. Although the sky is overcast with the continuing presence of the military; some brightness is already envisioned in the horizon.

Romanus Okey Muoneke. *Art, Rebellion, and Redemption: A Reading of The Novels of Chinua Achebe* (New York: Peter Lang Publishing, 1994

In Chinua Achebe's fifth novel, *Anthills of the Savannah* (1987), a wise old man insists that storytelling is more important to a community than drumming or fighting a war:

> Why? Because it is only the story that can continue beyond the war and the warrior. It is the story that outlives the sound of war-drums and the exploits of brave fighters. It is the story . . . that saves our progeny from blundering like blind beggars into the spikes of the cactus fence. The story is our escort; without it, we are blind. Does the blind man own his escort? No, neither do we the story; rather it is the story that owns us and directs us.

Over the last century Africa has experienced a great deal of turmoil, has heard many war-drums and seen many battles. Initially these were colonial conflicts; today they tend to be civil wars or struggles between unelected leaders and the people they misrule. The stories of these turbulent years have not been easy to tell, but many writers have taken a stab at it, putting on record at least a small portion of Africa's contemporary history in instructive fictional terms.

Of these storytellers no one has been more successful than Chinua Achebe. His novels have offered us not just lucid instruction but also profound enlightenment, enabling us to see more clearly what has happened in Africa and why. His stories have been our escort, our most reliable guide to that continent's troubled past and troubling present. He has made it impossible for us to remain blind to African realities.

Achebe's first novel, *Things Fall Apart* (1958), was set in a traditional Ibo village community in eastern Nigeria at the turn of the century, when the first missionaries and colonial administrative officials were beginning to penetrate inland. Its hero was Okonkwo, a famous warrior and expert farmer who had risen to become a wealthy and respected leader of his clan.

Achebe's rich portrayal of traditional Ibo society glowed with compassion. The customs, rituals, beliefs and institutions that regulated the lives of villagers before the arrival of the white man were sympathetically depicted and shown to be worthy of our respect. Okonkwo and his people were obviously not living in a state of wild savagery and barbarism. Theirs was a well-ordered society adapted to its environment.

But at the same time Achebe made no attempt to conceal some bad features of traditional Ibo life, including wife beating, caste taboos and infanticide. He also recognized that among Ibo men a very heavy emphasis was placed on proving oneself a man by displays of extraordinary strength or courage; this was partly what ultimately brought Okonkwo down when he tried singlehandedly to halt the encroachments Europeans had made on his community. In order to help us understand the full dimensions of Okonkwo's tragedy, Achebe tried to present a balanced view of Ibo society that took into account its internal weaknesses as well as its strengths.

When the two cultures eventually collided, the weaker one gave way. Achebe was careful to show that the collapse of traditional African society was due as much to internal infirmity as to external force, that the society unwilling to bend must eventually break. But he also demonstrated quite convincingly that this particular African society would have been able to survive quite a long time had it not been for Europe's sudden intrusion into its midst. His novel revealed that Ibo villages were well organized and democratically governed, that there were religious and legal constraints on an individual's behavior and that achievement was prized, making it possible for a hard-working man to rise to a high position in the clan regardless of his parentage.

Ibo society, to put it briefly, was civilized and stable, not primitive and chaotic. Then, with the coming of the white man, things fell apart, and anarchy was loosed upon the Ibo world. The white men, in other words, were not bringers of light to a dark continent, as was popularly supposed, and their ''civilizing mission'' did not result in peace, order and harmony. Rather, they were ignorant servants of a powerful English queen who disrupted a well-ordered, cohesive, pacific society by imposing on it their own forms of government and religious worship. Achebe thus reinterpreted African history, seeing it through African eyes.

His interpretation was objective, honest and fair to all sides. Although his sympathies were primarily with the Ibo villagers, he understood the colonial mentality of his European characters well enough to portray them not as villains or monsters but as convincing human beings whose actions were motivated by dedication to an ideal. His purpose was to examine Africa's first confrontation with Europe from an African point of view, yet he managed to stand sufficiently aloof from the encounter so that his vision was not blurred by emotion. He saw and made us see the misunderstandings that precipitated conflict, the chain of events that inevitably led to tragedy. And because he never lost sight of the larger dimensions of his story, specific actions always took on a wider significance that gave them paradigmatic value. Achebe evidently was talking not just about Okonkwo and Iboland but also about other Africans elsewhere and indeed about all colonized people wherever they happened to be.

This novel, which has sold in the millions all over the world, has probably done more to reshape the image of Africa in colonial times than any other single book. It enabled everyone—Africans as well as non-Africans—to view African experience from an indigenous perspective, and it did this in a wholly satisfactory artistic manner, persuading us as much by its aesthetic elegance as by its powerful argument. It was Africa's first modern classic.

Part of what distinguished this novel was the limpid and versatile style in which it was written. Instead of having his British and Ibo characters speak in the same idiom, Achebe devised for his kinsmen an African vernacular style that simulated expression in his native tongue. Ibo words, figures of speech and proverbs were translated virtually verbatim and introduced into appropriate passages of dialogue and exposition. These expressions were inserted so skillfully that they served not as exotic verbal ornaments but as functional agents of characterization and cultural description. Achebe thus succeeded in giving the English language a new prose style, an African style that perfectly suited his African message.

His next novel, *No Longer at Ease* (1960), intended as a sequel to *Things Fall Apart*, was set in the capital of Nigeria in the late 1950's and had as its hero Okonkwo's grandson, Obi Okonkwo, a young, Westernized bureaucrat who finds himself torn between two cultures—the old and new. Although he comes back from his university studies in England with high ideals and a determination to prove himself an honest, hard-working civil servant, he eventually slides into corruption because he is unable to reconcile the remands placed upon him by his Westernized girlfriend and his tradition-bound parents. Like his grandfather, Obi was another victim of cultural conflict, the major difference being that now the conflict was psychological rather than physical. Obi had been weaned away from traditional values but had not fully assimilated Western ideals; having no firm moral convictions, he was confused by his predicament and fell.

But again, as in *Things Fall Apart*, Achebe did not try to blame this fall entirely on Europe. He acknowledged the weaknesses within traditional society as well as the human frailty of his hero. His intention was simply to show us what his people had lost during the colonial encounter, and he felt that one of their greatest misfortunes was their forfeiture of a clear code of moral values. It is this spiritual loss that left Obi and his society no longer at ease in the modern world.

In his next novel, *Arrow of God* (1964), Achebe turned back to the 1920's to fill in the temporal gap between his first two works. This time he chose as his hero a headstrong chief priest of an Ibo snake cult who fell victim to the changing times and to his own towering pride. Ezeulu attempted to come to terms with the innovations introduced into his world by the church and the colonial administration, and this angered some of his followers and rivals. In the end he was destroyed by his compromise with Europe, for this undermined his position in the community. When Europe later betrayed him, he chose to take a foolishly proud stand in an effort to reestablish his authority, but he had already lost too much ground with his people, so he quickly fell, descending finally into isolation and madness.

*Arrow of God* was Achebe's longest, most complex and most successful novel, possessing a richness of texture, depth of characterisation and ambiguity that cannot be found in his other fiction. The ambiguity derived from Achebe's enigmatical depiction of Ezeulu. Was the priest merely an "arrow in the bow of his god," was he the victim of hubris, or was he mad? The novel provided no clear answer to this question, leaving readers to ponder the nature of the perplexing relationship between a priest and his god.

The religious drama in *Arrow of God* was played out against the backdrop of the colonial drama in Nigeria. Achebe was actually telling two stories at once, interweaving them with such skill that they could not be separated. Ezeulu, a guardian of the old order, must be destroyed before the new order can firmly establish itself in Iboland. Missionaries and European administrative officials subvert the old priest's authority in the clan and thereby precipitate his fall. The forces of change, which Ezeulu had hoped to forestall, thus overwhelm him and transform his society. The battle of cultures is once again won by Europe.

In his fourth novel, *A Man of the People* (1966), Achebe brought the historical record right up to contemporary times. Indeed, this novel, published only nine days after Nigeria experienced its first military coup, even ended with a military coup. It appeared that Achebe had predicted with uncanny accuracy the end of his country's first republic.

But the novel no doubt was intended as a political parable, not as a prophecy. It had as its central character a corrupt politician who had elbowed his way into prominence and power. But M. A. Nanga, one of the finest rogues in African fiction, was only a symptom of a sick postcolonial African society; one needed to look into the very heart of the body politic to account for such a diseased member. Achebe's diagnosis was that people who had recently passed through a period of colonial rule adopted a rather cynical attitude toward political corruption. They were willing to excuse the extravagances of their leaders because they believed that these men who had led the struggle for political independence now had a right to eat "the national cake." They also believed that a well-fed M.P. might let a few crumbs fall to his constituents. Such cynicism kept hungry men like Nanga in power and perpetuated a tradition of corruption in government. The sick society had to undergo a major political convulsion before such cynicism was transmuted into hope.

Although *A Man of the People* was a comedy and ended happily with Nanga's removal from government, it remained, like Achebe's other novels, a disturbingly pessimistic work. While censuring Africa for allowing itself to be corrupted by forces from within and without. Achebe again indicted Europe for contributing to the moral confusion and political chaos that beset independent African states. His characters were representative men and women of their time, yet emblematic of the ills and malaise that afflicted modem African society. Nothing seemed completely right in so debauched a world.

In Nigeria that confusion and chaos were to lead first to military rule and then to full-fledged civil war. During this period Achebe stopped writing novels altogether, but in the aftermath of the war he turned his hand to poetry, short fiction, essays and speech-writing. It was not until 1987, a full 21 years after *A Man of the People*, that he published another novel, *Anthills of the Savannah*. In this new work he picked up more or less where he had left off, focusing a sharp eye on the military elite that had ruled Nigeria and many other African countries after the collapse of democratically elected regimes.

The focal character, a Sanhurst graduate who has risen to the top position in his nation after a military coup and who clearly relishes being called "Your Excellency," wishes to be proclaimed President-for-Life. When his ambitions are frustrated, he feels insecure and angry and seeks to punish those he perceives as his foes, including two of his closest school buddies. In the end all three men are killed, and their friends, associates and lovers are left to pick up the pieces. There is a suggestion that out of this new-found unity among the long-suffering masses in Africa something positive will emerge, but one of the central questions raised in the course of the narrative—"What must a people do to appease an embittered history?"—remains unanswered. Perhaps things have fallen so far apart in modern Africa there is little that can be done by the powerless except to form alliances among themselves and hope that one day their suffering will end. But their future does not look particularly bright.

Throughout his career Achebe has kept pace with the times by responding to the changing preoccupations of his society. Forty years ago he was a reconstructionist dedicated to creating a dignified image of the African past; today he is an angry reformer crusading against the immorality and injustices of the African present. His novels thus not only chronicle 100 years of Nigerian history but also reflect the dominant African intellectual concerns of the past four decades.

For this reason one suspects his novels will have enduring significance. Later generations of readers will find in them an interpretation of African experience that is characteristic of its time. The compassionate evocations of Ibo village life, the graphic depictions of modern city life, the brilliantly drawn characters will probably speak with as much power then as they do today, eloquently recalling crucial moments in that confused era in Nigeria's past that began with the arrival of the first white men and ended with the imposition and perpetuation of indigenous military rule. Tomorrow as well as today, Achebe's novels will remain our trusty escorts, guiding us to a better understanding of an eventful century in African history.

Bernth Lindfors. *America*. 175, 2 (July 20, 1996), pp. 23–25.

[At first glance, *Things Fall Apart*] appears to have a perfectly transparent narrative line: it tells the tragic story of Okonkwo's rise and fall among the Igbo people, concluding with that least ambiguous of all endings, the death of the hero. With only a few exceptions, critics have understood the novel in precisely these terms, seeing its closing pages as entirely unproblematic. Yet any straight forward reading of Achebe's ending must reconcile itself with the fact that the novel describes a situation of profound cultural entropy, a society in which the norms of conduct and institutions of governance are in the process of "falling apart." What is more, while Achebe's novel movingly elegizes the passing away of traditional Igbo culture, the long view it adopts—looking ahead to the future establishment of Nigeria—suggests that Achebe's own position on the modernization of Africa is, at the very least, complicated. Given the subject of Achebe's novel and his own divided response to it, we would expect a fairly open-ended conclusion, one that acknowledges its own closure as tentative, even contingent. . . .

*Things Fall Apart* resists the idea of a single or simple resolution by providing three distinct endings, three different ways of reading the events that conclude the novel. [At the same time, these endings relate] to three different conceptions of history, especially as it is produced within a postcolonial context. First, Achebe writes a form of nationalist history. Here the interest is essentially reconstructive and centers on recovering an Igbo past that has been neglected or suppressed by historians who would not or could not write from an African perspective. As Achebe observed in 1964, four years after Nigerian independence: "Historians everywhere are re-writing the stories of the new nations—replacing short, garbled, despised history with a more sympathetic account" [Chinua Achebe, "The Role of the Writer in a New Nation," *African Writers on African Writing*, 1973]. Nationalist history tends to emphasize what other histories have either glossed over or flatly denied—namely that "African people did not hear of culture for the first time from Europeans; that their societies were not mindless

but frequently had a philosophy of great depth and value and beauty, that they had poetry and, above all, they had dignity." Second, Achebe writes a form of adversarial history. Here the emphasis falls not on the reconstruction of an authentic past that has been lost, but on the deconstruction of a counterfeit past that has been imposed. Adversarial history enables Achebe to write against what he himself has called "colonialist" discourse, against the attitudes and assumptions, the language and rhetoric that characterized British colonial rule in Nigeria. Third, Achebe writes a form of metahistory. This kind of history calls attention to itself as a piece of writing, a narrative construction that depends on principles of selection (what material will be included?), emphasis (what importance will be attached to it?) and shaping (how will it be organized and arranged?).

Yet *Things Fall Apart* is concerned not only with writing history, but also with fashioning tragedy. Achebe himself made this point in an interview with Robert Serumaga, in which he discussed the political implications of tragedy and explicitly referred to his novel as an example of that genre. A good deal of the critical literature has focused on this issue, addressing the question of whether the novel is indeed a tragedy and, if so, what kind of tragedy. . . . It will be my contention that much of the disagreement over generic classification has resulted from a failure to identify Achebe's multi-perspectival approach to the problem—a failure to recognize that he has written three distinct endings. Hence, I also want to argue that the novel offers us a variety of responses to tragedy, as well as history. According to the model I shall develop, nationalist history is associated with classical or Artistotelian tragedy; adversarial history is associated with modern or ironic tragedy; and metahistory is associated with critical discourse. My larger purpose in pursuing this line of analysis is to suggest that *Things Fall Apart* demands what is, in effect, a palimpsestic reading, a kind of historical and generic archaeology, which is designed to uncover, layer by layer, those experiences that have accreted around colonialism and its protracted aftermath. . . .

The crisis of the novel comes in the penultimate chapter when an impudent messenger, sent by the colonial authorities, orders a tribal meeting to disband. Okonkwo the warrior is moved to action. . . .

The scene is presented with a devastating simplicity. From the perspective of the first ending, the people of Umuofia have deserted Okonkwo and in the process betrayed themselves, but the wiping of the machete is the only eloquence he permits himself. It is an ordinary and everyday gesture, yet in the present context it acquires special significance: Okonkwo remains true to the martial ethos that his people have abandoned, here represented by the warrior's care of his weapon; at the same time, he symbolically dissolves his connection with his people, wiping away the blood bond that has joined them. This gesture is especially resonant because, as critics have pointed out, in killing the messenger he is shedding the blood of a fellow Igbo.

The suicide that follows is itself a profound violation of Igbo law, which strictly prohibits acts of self-destruction. The question of how we should respond to Okonkwo's final deed has been examined in detail by Kalu Ogbaa and Damian Opata, but with strikingly different results [see Kalu Ogbaa's "A Cultural Note on Okonkwo's Suicide," pp. 126–34, and Damian Opata's "The Sudden End of Alienation: A Reconsideration of Okonkwo's Suicide in Chinua Achebe's *Things Fall Apart*," *African Marburgensia* 22.2 (1989)]. For Ogbaa the suicide grows out of Okonkwo's failure to act with sufficient piety toward the Igbo gods and traditions, while for Opata it is a consequence of the Igbos' refusal to rally around Okonkwo and join him in resisting the British. As was the case with discussions of the novel's tragedy, the disagreement arises in the first place because the reader has difficulty establishing Achebe's position on a number of issues—difficulty knowing, for example, where he stands on the question of violent resistance to the British. Of course, this interpretive problem largely disappears once we begin to read the novel palimpsestically as a layering of diverse perspectives on history and tragedy. Hence, understood within the terms of the novel's first ending, Okonkwo's suicide is the logical and necessary consequence of an idealistic and absolutist position. Both nationalist history and heroic tragedy demand that he remain unyielding and that the Igbos honor their cultural heritage by refusing assimilation. Even in this final gesture, then, Okonkwo functions as the true representative of his people. For, as he sees it, Igbo culture has willingly succumbed to its own annihilation, committing what is a form of collective suicide by submitting to the British. In taking his own life, Okonkwo has simply preceded his people in their communal destruction. Once again he has led the way.

The novel's second ending, which I associate with adversarial history, views events from the heavily ironized perspective of the District Commissioner. Igbo culture is now presented not from the inside as vital and autonomous, but from the outside as an object of anthropological curiosity, and its collapse is understood not as an African tragedy but as a European triumph. As the final scene of the novel unfolds, the Igbos take the District Commissioner to the place where the suicide was committed. . . .

What is particularly noteworthy in this episode is the way the District Commissioner effortlessly shifts from the "resolute administrator" to the "student of primitive customs." Here Achebe demonstrates that, within a colonial context, the Foucauldian power-knowledge nexus is much more than a speculative theory—it is an inescapable and omnipresent reality. Thus, those who wrote historical and anthropological accounts of the Igbos were typically either representatives of the British government or their semi-official guests, and the colonial administration not only helped to enable such research by "opening up" various regions, but also relied upon it in determining local policy. . . .

What the District Commissioner ultimately achieves is not genuine understanding but the illusion of understanding that comes with the power to control:

> Every day brought him some new material. The story of this man who had killed a messenger and hanged himself Would make interesting reading. One could almost write a whole chapter on him. Perhaps not a whole chapter but a reasonable paragraph, at any rate. There was so much else to include, and one must be firm in cutting out details. He had already chosen the title of the book, after much thought: The Pacification of the Primitive Tribes of the Lower Niger.

With these words, *Things Fall Apart* completes its passage from the heroic tragedy of the first ending to the biting irony of the second ending. In his well-known essay on *Heart of Darkness*, Achebe argues against European accounts of Africa that have reduced its people to—I quote Achebe quoting Conrad—"rudimentary souls" capable only of "a violent babble of uncouth sounds." In presenting Okonkwo's epic story, epitomized by the first ending, Achebe offers a powerful counter-statement to the

"dark continent" idea of Africa. But with the second ending he does something more. By ironically undermining the perspective of the District Commissioner, by exposing the latter's personal ignorance (not a "whole chapter" but a "reasonable paragraph") and political interests (the "pacification" of the Lower Niger), Achebe seeks to confront and finally to discredit the entire discourse of colonialism, those quasi-historical, quasi-anthropological writings that have treated Africa as nothing more than—again I quote Achebe—"a foil to Europe, a place of negations."

At the same time, the second ending begins to redefine our point of view on the tragic events of the novel. Although this ending is clearly meant to undermine the District Commissioner's position, indeed to portray him as a fool, it nevertheless substantially alters the tone and mood of Achebe's resolution. Obviously the novel would read very differently—and its tragedy function very differently—if it concluded with, say, a heroic recitation of Okonkwo's suicide by Obeirika. In other words, the final chapter of *Things Fall Apart* serves not as a simple denouement—one that helps us sort out a rather messy climax—but as a significant qualification of what has gone before, a distinctly new ending that complicates our sense of Achebe's approach to both history and tragedy. . . .

What I shall identify as the third ending is located in *No Longer At Ease*, the sequel to *Things Fall Apart*. No doubt, the assertion that one text contains the ending of another will immediately strike some readers as dubious. Such a claim begins to gain credibility, however, when we remember that Achebe originally conceived of his two novels as the first and third sections of a single work. In other words, the compositional history of *Things Fall Apart* and *No Longer* At Ease provides some justification for treating the latter as a continuation of the former, an extension that qualifies Okonkwo's story, even redirects its course. Indeed, there is good reason to argue that *No Longer At Ease* is not only a continuation of *Things Fall Apart* but also a rewriting of it, one that essentially recapitulates the action of the earlier novel, though in a markedly different setting. Hence, both novels tell the story of a representative of the Igbo people who takes a stand on a question of principle and is destroyed in the ensuing collision between African and European values. . . .

The point of intersection between the two novels, the scene in which I locate the third ending of *Things Fall Apart*, occurs when Okonkwo's grandson, Obi, a university-educated civil servant, finds himself discussing tragedy with a British colonial officer. Obi advances the opinion—of special interest given the first ending of *Things Fall Apart*—that suicide ruins a tragedy. . . .

Obi draws a distinction in this passage between two kinds of tragedy. In traditional or Aristotelian tragedy, there is a clear resolution, an aesthetic pay-off that comes in the form of catharsis; but in modern or ironic tragedy, the tragedy described in Auden's "Musee des Beaux Arts," the fall from a high place is likened to Brueghel's famous painting of Icarus. In the foreground the ploughman ploughs his field; in the background a ship sails on its way. And it is only after careful inspection that we are able to discover the place of tragedy: there in the corner, barely perceptible, we see Icarus's two legs breaking the surface of the water, sole testimony of his personal catastrophe.

While the point of departure for Obi's discussion of tragedy is Graham Greene's *The Heart of the Matter*, his observations have an obvious application to *Things Fall Apart*. Okonkwo's story as viewed from the Igbo perspective presents history in the form of classical or heroic tragedy. Okonkwo's story as viewed from the

District Commissioner's perspective presents history in the form of modern or ironic tragedy. One of Obi's remarks is particularly apposite: there is no purging of the emotions in modern tragedy, because "we are not there." These words perfectly describe the situation of the District Commissioner. He "was not there" in the sense that he was never in a position genuinely to understand Okonkwo, to appreciate who he was and what he represented.

It is important to stress, however, that the novel's first ending is not in some way compromised because it is associated with the "conventional," while the novel's second ending is in some way enhanced because it is associated with the "real." Indeed, if Achebe provides us with any controlling point of view, it comes with the third ending, which illustrates the vexed and ambiguous relation in which the postcolonial stands to its own past. For with his remarks on tragedy, Obi is offering a narrative analysis of what is literally his own past. In describing a tragedy that ends in suicide, he is describing his grandfather's tragic fall and its significance for Igbo culture after it was lost, after "things fell apart"

What the novel's third ending illustrates, then, is that the boundaries between the "conventional" and the "real," the heroic and the ironic, are not clearly or cleanly drawn. From Obi's perspective—and, for that matter, the reader's—Okonkwo functions both as a literary persona and a living person, an epic hero and an historical anachronism. Yet the novel does not invite us to select one of these alternatives so much as to understand the various, though decidedly distinctive, truths they articulate. In other words, we are not meant to choose from among three possible endings, but to read all of them, as it were, simultaneously and palimpsestically. If we are able to do this, we shall see how Achebe's sense of an ending is intimately bound up with his sense of cultural loss; how the tragedy of the past necessarily depends on the perspective of the present; and how history is inevitably written for both the "they who were there" and the "we who are not there."

Richard Begam. *Studies in the Novel.* 29, 3 (Fall 1997), pp. 396–411.

BIBLIOGRAPHY
*Things Fall Apart*, 1958; *No Longer At Ease*, 1960; *Arrow of God*, 1964; *A Man of the People*, 1966; *Beware Soul-Brother, and Other Poems*, 1971; *Girls at War, and Other Stories*, 1972; *Christmas in Biafra and Other Poems*, 1973; *How the Leopard Got His Claws*, 1973; *Morning Yet on Creation Day*, 1975; "Onitsha, Gift of the Niger," 1975; *The Drum: A Children's Story*, 1977; *The Flute*, 1979; *The Trouble with Nigeria*, 1983; *Anthills of the Savannah*, 1987; *The University and the Leadership Factor in Nigerian Politics*, 1988; *Another Africa,* 1997

# ADISA, Opal Palmer (1954–)
**Jamaica**

Opal Palmer Adisa is a Jamaican woman writer. The four stories she has collected in [*Bake Face & Other Guava Stories*] are about her sisters, contemporary Jamaican women. Not the ones you might see on TV travel ads, who are eternally smiling as they serve you, but women who must struggle to maintain their integrity, as much as their physical survival, in a society plagued for centuries by slavery, colonialism and poverty. These women are descendants of African slaves, and the reality of their lives has been camouflaged by the perennial image the Caribbean evokes for outsiders—an image that merges, paradoxically, paradise and servitude.

But Adisa's women do not see themselves as things created for use. Although constrained by social conditions, they have inner lives that sometimes even they cannot understand, and a sense of a particular way of life to which they can refer. They reach for self-expression in a world which offers them little access to literacy, far less education and self-cultivation, but a world which values the spoken word, an art in which they naturally participate.

In writing about her sisters who still live in the Jamaican countryside, Opal Adisa gives voice to their pleasures, conflicts and feelings as few Jamaican writers before her have done. Her stories are about a plantation worker, a domestic, a village wife, and a fisherman's wife, women who constitute the majority of Jamaican women but who seldom appear as central in even their countrymen's works. Just the existence of this collection, then, is significant, for seldom have we heard the voices of Jamaican rural women who have yet to be directed to the cities, to the metropolises of the world, women who defy our version of who a contemporary woman should be. In refusing to idealize them either as overt rebels or content earth mothers, Adisa attempts to express their complexity.

Not surprisingly, the central character in each of these stories is a mother or a mother-to-be, the one role all Jamaican women are expected to play, whether they live in the town or the country, whether they are middle-class or working-class. Motherhood for these women is the inevitable result of sex, to which they know they have a natural right. Yet each of Adisa's four protagonists relates quite differently to motherhood. Lilly, the domestic in "Duppy Get Her," must have her baby at home, in the land of her mother and mother's mother; the child belongs to her maternal ancestors regardless of where she or the father might be. In contrast, Bake-Face leaves her daughter and husband for part of each year to live with her love Mr. Johnson. Denise MacFarlane, the major character in "Me Man Angel," resents the younger seven of her nine children, for she feels that they "forced themselves on her without giving her time to prepare for them" and that their very existence has distorted her husband's relationship to her. However, in "Widows' Walk," June-Plum enjoys her four children but doesn't want any more, as times are hard. For these four mothers, the experience of motherhood is as varied as the shapes of their bodies, the contours of their personalities. Unlike the smiling nannies' on TV, their attitude towards their children, and therefore themselves, is affected by their bonds with other people, sometimes with their men, often with their own mothers.

In fact, a thread that runs throughout these stories is these women's relationship to *their* mothers and to other women. If they have any telling relationship, either satisfactory or not, it is their sense of their maternal forebears. In "Duppy Get Her" that relationship is central, for Lilly is possessed by her grandmother's call to come home to have her baby. For Bake-Face, the death of her parents at a tender age leaves her uncared for and vulnerable to the harsh male world. The lack of a mother will affect the way her personality develops. In contrast, the sweet and prickly June-Plum remembers her mother with fondness.

Along with their mothers, other women provide solace, advice, care, sometimes grief, to these women. It is the strong women's community of the plantation which helps Bake-Face to feel more at ease with herself; still, it is other women who cause her confusion and whom she tries to understand. In ''Widows' Walk,'' the complexity of a woman's relationship with herself is heightened, for it is Yemoja, the female West African loa of the ocean still revered by New World blacks, whom June-Plum must come to know. June-Plum's growing understanding of the goddess Yemoja is as much the major theme of this story as the woman's wait for her fisherman husband.

The ties between these women and the men they love or marry are also critical to these stories. As for women throughout the world who live in societies where survival is a struggle, cooperation between the sexes or the lack of it can gravely affect the quality of life.

Barbara Christian. Introduction to *Bake Face & Other Guava Stories*, by Opal Palmer Adisa (Berkeley: Kelsey St. Press, 1986), pp. ix–xii

As a girl I often scraped my knee, not because I had poor balance or tripped over my feet but because I dared to be more or other than what good girls were supposed to be. I was never a good girl, and I passionately disliked those girls who displayed such behavior and loathed their dull expressions. Nice girls never scraped their knees.

As a woman I am often scraping my knee, sometimes without even falling. Perhaps it is because I dare to demand that the way be cleared for me or that I insist on leading the line at times. My choice. Always. Now as I reflect, I see that there is much in common between the little girl who frequently scraped her knee and has scars to prove it and this woman, me, who must often walk stiff-legged in defiance of the scrapes that are inflicted, often by the insensitive, the blind, the upholders of norms, traditions, and antiquated values that I had no part in setting and by which I will not abide. I scrape my knee.

I have found that among my female friends, knee scrapers tip the scale. We are so abundant with our songs, our plays, our poems, our paintings, our research, our cameras, and our children that all of us continuously scrape our knees and will not stop, even though we are not masochistic. But doing what we do, in the society in which we live, demands payment for our disregard of the law—Women, know thy place and thy place is often in the kitchen or horizontally disposed. Let me hasten to add that I find both positions appealing at times, but option is the operative mode in this regard. So we scrape our knees. . . .

My writing is an attempt to grapple with what it means to be a woman, black, Caribbean, conscious. These are not different realities; they are integrated. I cannot emphasize the wholeness enough. Too often nothing gets accomplished because we separate into camps and compartmentalize our experiences based on an internalization of our Euro-American education. I am symphonic, and whatever I process is integrated in myself as a woman, a person of African descent, a Caribbean. Like the tree of which I am a branch, I am perennial. I am certain of my continuation even though the form might alter to adapt to a new climate. I/we will be around because we are knee scrapers, survivors of the seas and wind, reapers of cane and banana, makers of history.

I am a delphinium, partly through heritage but mostly by example, and I must admit that my examples were almost women who never showed any diffidence in the face of adversaries. I associate the carnival colors of my girlhood with these women, who were as captivating as the yellow poui blossoms, breathtaking

as the flame-red flamboyant, and bittersweet like sugarcane. My short story collection, *Bake-Face and Other Guava Stories*, is a tribute to those women who never have access to microphones, who carry their madness sewed into their skirt hems and tied in their hand-kerchieves buried in their bosoms. Giving voice to this madness that besieges us, giving voice to the celebration of our lives, giving voice to our quiet fears and invisible tears, giving voice to our struggles, our victories, our determination, I scrape my knee, she scrapes her knee, we all scrape our knees.

Who are these women, Bake-Face, Lilly, Denise, and June-Plum? They are women who are always waiting for some man to enter their lives and change them until they realize that their knees are connected to feet that move, to eyes that show them themselves, to a spirit that guides them. Guava is a fruit that grew in my backyard. Often when it was ripe the exterior skin remained green and rough, unappealing, but when I bit into the pinky meat, I was overwhelmed by the soft-sweet taste. So, too, these women, if simply judged by their physical appearance, seem unflattering, but once you enter them, allow them to tell their stories, the wealth and breadth of their lives assail you like a spider's web. That is why they are presented in my collection, *Bake-Face and Other Guava Stories*; more likely than not you would walk by them without even inquiring if their knees are healed yet. Bake-Face scrapes her knees because she chooses herself over her only love, Mr. Johnson; Lilly scrapes her knee because she cohabits with Richard, who cannot accept himself, so her deceased grandmother has to come and reclaim her by guiding her back to the protection of her mother; Denise scrapes her knee because she loves her nephew Perry to distraction, believing that to be needed completely is the ultimate achievement of womanhood; and June-Plum stumbles and gnashes both knees because she makes another woman, Yemoja, her alter ego, her competitor, rather than recognizing her need simply to be a woman, beautiful and free from the demands and inquiries of children. So they all scrape their knees many times and learn from their injury to walk with themselves. They stumble, but they continue on.

Opal Palmer Adisa. In Selwyn R. Cudjoe, ed. *Caribbean Women Writers: Essays from the First International Conference* (Wellesley: Calaleux Publications, 1990), pp. 145–50

BIBLIOGRAPHY
*Bake Face & Other Guava Stories*, 1986; *Traveling Women*, 1989; *Tamarind and Mango Women*, 1995; *It Begins with Tears*, 1998

# AIDOO, Ama Ata (1942–)
**Ghana**

Miss Christina Ama Aidoo's play, *The Dilemma of a Ghost* . . . was performed by Theatre Workshop of Lagos from January 26th to 28th. This play takes off where Lorraine Hansberry's *Raisin in the Sun* left off, with Assegai the African on the brink of marrying an American Negro girl. That play has given a glimpse of the extraordinary vision of their ''homeland'' prevalent among less informed American Negroes. This vision was the result of little knowledge and much romance.

Miss Aidoo's play explores the situation in which an American Negro bride returns "home" with her Ghanaian husband, to find herself a complete stranger, colour not withstanding. The agonising situation is portrayed with the kind of humour that is next door to tears. The crux of the play is the differing attitudes to childbearing. . . .

Miss Aidoo displays a gift—very useful to a social dramatist—of showing both sides of the coin at the same time. She shows the reverence of African village society towards motherhood while at the same time exposing the inherent cruelty of a system which makes the childless woman utterly miserable.

The play has a hopeful end. Not the rather doubtful hope that black people, whatever their background, can always understand each other, but the more universal one that there is common underlying essential humanity, which, given certain conditions, can come to the surface. In this play, motherhood, suppressed in one person, gratefully welcomed by another, and agonisingly unavailable to a third, is the unifying link.

Eldred Jones. *Bulletin of the Association of African Literature in English.* No. 2, 1965, p. 33

Since she has only one play and two short stories so far published, it is perhaps too early to herald [Aidoo] as a pathfinder; but she clearly represents a movement that is gathering force among the younger writers. In her story "No Sweetness Here," published in the *Black Orpheus Anthology*, she describes with tenderness and compassion a woman's love for her child. To an American or European reader, this story might seem charming if not particularly unusual in form. In African writing, however, the story is quite unique, for it explores with convincing legitimacy the intensity of individual emotional experience. Now, to show that she can turn to wider issues, Miss Aidoo has given us *The Dilemma of a Ghost*, a play that has already been performed in Accra, Lagos, and Ibadan. . . .

*The Dilemma of a Ghost* is a delightful piece of writing, simple, delicate, and containing much wisdom. The dialog has authenticity, as well as sparkle and wit, though there are occasional failures in the use of American slang. It is less successful as a play, because Miss Aidoo lacked an experienced stage director to help her work out a final version before publication. In this she suffers the same lack as all dramatists in West Africa, where there is no professional English-language theater group. . . .

Since Miss Aidoo wrote *The Dilemma of a Ghost* when she was still an undergraduate at the University of Ghana, it may seem churlish to draw attention to weaknesses in the dramatic construction. On the other hand, she is an artist exploring new realities with skill and distinction, and a patronizing accolade would be out of place. We look forward to seeing developments in Miss Aidoo's dialectic skill and personal insight, for she is among the first of a growing literary line of Africans unburdened, at least in part, by the problem of the color line, beneath which has always lain the problem of the culture line. And there are many more ghosts needing this kind of exorcism.

C. J. Rea. *African Forum.* Summer 1965, pp. 112–13

The play *Anowa* cries out to be performed. The story is simple enough, of the life of a girl in "the state of Abura" in the 1870s, a strange girl, too advanced for her time, whose father felt should perhaps have been a priestess. Instead, being a progressive woman,

Anowa chooses her own husband, Kofi Ako, and they go to the coast where the husband grows rich on the palm oil trade. But Anowa is barren, and slowly becomes ghost-like, trying to persuade her husband to take another wife. The climax is a great quarrel between the two, following which they both commit suicide. Although there is a certain Greek starkness about it, the language switches easily from the folksy-conversational to the apocalyptic. . . .

The short stories [in *No Sweetness Here*], like the play, are simple and direct, being concerned with the real problems of ordinary people. There is a certain social consciousness, in some of them, a burning desire to point a lesson, such as in the tale of the woman who worries that her sister is the mistress of a politician. With the coup she hopes the situation will change, but then her sister comes home with a highly placed army captain. Ama Ata writes with transparent honesty: behind it there is the feeling, the same as in the novels of Ayi Kwei Armah, of being near to tears. She and Armah are in the front rank of the literary talents that have come to the fore in recent years in Ghana.

K. W. *West Africa.* January 30-February 5, 1971, p. 133

[In *No Sweetness Here*] Ama Ata Aidoo celebrates womanhood in general and motherhood in particular. She stands up for the woman who must go and protect her own; who must go through "pregnancy and birth and death and pain, and death again." There will always be a fresh corpse and she will weep all over again. The woman who, even while she is nursing an infant, must lose her husband to the south, where there will be better money for one's work. And it will still be the woman—the mother—who must receive the news first that her son is going to leave his wife and child. . . . The woman who watches over a sick child. . . . The mother who waits for the man who never returns—son or lover or husband. . . . The mother who knows that she is giving birth for the second time when she launches her son on the road to higher education. . . .

The men in Miss Aidoo's fiction are mere shadows or voices or just "fillers." Somewhere, quietly, they seem to be manipulating the woman's life or negatively controlling it or simply having a good time, knowing that they are assured of something like a divine top-dog position in life. Given this premise the woman, without worrying about her traditional place, simply gets up on her feet and asserts not her importance in relation to the male, but her motherhood.

Ezekiel Mphahlele. Introduction to Ama Ata Aidoo, *No Sweetness Here* (Garden City, New York, Doubleday, 1972), pp. xix–xx

Various African writers have depicted the conditions and quality of life of traditional and modern African womanhood. . . . Still, it seems to me that the Ghanaian writer Ama Ata Aidoo is unique for she almost exclusively rivets attention on black African womanhood of the village and the city. And because she is a woman, Miss Aidoo is able to view the plight of African women from a natural and familiar vantage point.

In *No Sweetness Here*, a collection of eleven short stories, the male characters generally play a peripheral role. They are frequently in the background, usually managing directly or indirectly to bring about the suffering of women. In those allusions to life in

Accra and other urban centers of Ghana Miss Aidoo depicts the moral failings of young women who become prostitutes or mistresses of wealthy men in order to enjoy the material opportunities offered in a city. On the other hand, the stories set in villages do not offer a particularly pleasant alternative for the African woman, especially if she is the least respected wife in a polygamous household. In such a case the wife asserts her identity as a woman through her love of her children. A tragic situation occurs if she can have no children or her single child dies. Such is the case in the title story "No Sweetness Here."...

Does Miss Aidoo offer a solution to the dilemma of the modern urban African woman? Not directly. However, she does suggest that education offers a chance for a woman to develop herself independently of the pressures placed upon her by men. Otherwise she must be content to exploit her body and be exploited.

Donald Bayer Burness. *Studies in Black Literature.* Summer 1973, pp. 21, 23

Among contemporary Ghanaian dramatists, male and female, only Ama Ata Aidoo compares with [Efua] Sutherland in exploiting oral literature, especially folk drama, in modern theater. Like ... Sutherland, Aidoo has taught extensively in her field. She graduated from the University of Ghana in 1964, and subsequently attended a creative writing program at Stanford University in the United States. Since then she has taught as a research fellow at the Institute of African Studies in the University of Ghana, and as visiting lecturer in other African universities and in American colleges. Both as writer and teacher she has always demonstrated a special interest in the kind of oral literary traditions that so strongly influence her own plays.

As Aidoo has remarked, her ideal form of theater is one that capitalizes on the dramatic art of storytelling. This kind of theater, she feels, would actually be a complete environment in which the usual amenities of eating and drinking would be combined with storytelling, poetry-reading, and plays. In Aidoo one encounters a tremendous confidence in the integrity and inclusiveness of the oral tradition. She perceives the tradition of storytelling as one that actually combines techniques and conventions that are often separated into distinctive genres, especially in the Western literary tradition. The storyteller's art is therefore a synthesis of poetry, dramatic play-acting, and narrative plot. This art is social in the most literal sense. The artist is physically and morally located in the center of her, or his, audience, and the story itself reflects and perpetuates the moral and cultural values of the audience. Consequently when Aidoo talks of a theater that, ideally, duplicates the oral tradition, she is emphasizing the inclusiveness of that oral tradition—and the extent to which the art and function of the storyteller's performance become direct extensions of the storyteller's society....

Each Aidoo story bears the idiosyncracies of her protagonist and reflects the manner in which each protagonist is conceived as a performer offering judgments and justifying actions by way of a personal performance. Thus even in a rare Aidoo poem we can see her consistent strategy as a short story writer at work. For example, in "Last of the Proud Ones" the language is carefully subordinated to the powerful personality and voice of the old woman who speaks in the work. As the last survivor of her generation, she is contemptuous of the new-fangled ways, and the strange inventions, of the modern (Westernized) world. A diet of bread and cheese is

therefore an unspeakable abomination, and she will have nothing to do with it. The stuff, she snorts, "reeks, reeks/the odor of stinking fish!"

It is important to emphasize that Aidoo consistently applies this technique—the short story as oral performance—to all of her short stories, irrespective of whether or not they are drawn directly from the nonliterate milieu of her rural characters or from the literate and literary traditions of Western narrative forms. This consistency suggests that she is able to apply a method that she cultivates out of her own oral tradition to a modern, literate medium. This ability is significant because it represents an achievement that is often discussed but rarely achieved in African literature—the integration of traditional oral techniques with Western literary forms.

Lloyd W. Brown. *Women Writers in Black Africa* (Westport, Connecticut: Greenwood Press, 1981), pp. 84–85, 100–1

The play *Anowa* is set in what is now Ghana a hundred years ago, in about 1870. It tells the story of an exceptional woman who had an inquiring and willful mind, as well as insights and an understanding well beyond that of her peers. Neighbors said that she should have been apprenticed to the priestesses of the local cult; but since she was the only child of her parents, they hoped for a normal married life for her and a continuation of the family. Against her mother's wishes she willfully marries Kofi Ako, the young man of her own choice, and walks out of her parent's home swearing never to return....

*Anowa* is a traditional tale, a legend of the Akan. Aidoo has returned to the folk story to find what might be meaningful in it for contemporary society. She brings to the story, as she considers it again, issues which she sees as crucial for any thinking African today: exploitation of men, of women; concepts of personal responsibility, in general, and of the intellectual in particular. Can the old tale particularize any of these issues? And once she has found meaning, she can then try to reach the form that will give that meaning substance. It is the very opposite to Sutherland's approach to the oral tradition.

*Anowa* must surely be one of the most profound African plays to have been written so far. And yet it is not popular, in my experience, even among students, especially men, who insist that Anowa herself is a witch and needs to be slapped by her husband. Ama Ata Aidoo's reputation as a dramatist rests upon her earlier and much less complex play, *[The] Dilemma of a Ghost*, which is about a young professional Ghanaian who returns from the United States with a black American wife. She is a child of slaves, say the women of the community, and they intend to shun her.

Michael Etherton. *The Development of African Drama* (London: Hutchinson University Library for Africa, 1982), pp. 227–28, 237–38

In *No Sweetness Here*, [Aidoo] addresses the theme of the African and African-American relationship in the short story entitled "Other Versions." While the tale actually concerns the bond of love between a young Ghanaian student, Kofi, and his mother, who has been a significant influence in his being able to continue his education, the young man also comes to realize that he shares an affinity with black Americans and, even more, that many African-American women are of the same pattern as many African women: they are lovely in their selflessness, sharing, and caring.

The beginning of ''Other Versions'' recounts Kofi's unhappiness over his mother's insisting that he should give a portion of his money to his father whenever he receives any. Our protagonist believes that if anyone shared his money, it should be his mother because she is the one who has made all the sacrifices. But his mother never accepts money for herself. As the story progresses, Kofi is successful in his studies. Consequently, he is awarded a scholarship to America to further his education.

Shortly after arriving in the United States, he is invited by a white family for dinner. While at the home of this family, our narrator is jolted into the realization that he feels more akin to the black cook whom he meets when Mr. Merrow, his host, is taking the two of them home, than he does to the white family: ''You know what sometimes your heart does? Mine did that just then. Kind of turned itself round in a funny way.'' Kofi achieves a shock of recognition.

His consciousness grows when, as the young student tells us on another occasion (perhaps the next evening or two), he is on his way home by subway. He sees another black woman and he associates her with the cook who had been in Mrs. Merrow's kitchen. The young Ghanaian says that he became confused but, at any rate, he put his hands in his pocket, took out his scholarship dollars, crumpled them up and passed them to her, saying: ''Eh . . . eh . . . I come from Africa and you remind me of my mother. Please would you take this from me?'' Just as his mother who had been so unselfish, the black woman motions him to sit down beside her and she says: ''Son, keep them dollars, I sure know you need them more than I do.'' The young student then reflects: ''Of course, she was mother. And so there was no need to see. But now I could openly look at her beautiful face.'' The story ends with the emphasis on the mother-son relationship, and although the young narrator says ''there was no need to see,'' he *has* seen. He has recognized some specific commonalities between Africans and African-Americans.

Mildred A. Hill-Lubin. *Presence Africaine.* 124 (1982), pp. 195–97

*Our Sister Killjoy*, like Aidoo's short stories, deals with so many problems. . . . [Its] success depends largely on the ability of the author to lend all the problems equal spikes. In that regard Ngugi [wa Thiong'o] and Sembène [Ousmane] come to mind—writers who are fully aware in their works that a campaign for social justice is meaningful only when all disadvantaged people in human society receive undiscriminating attention. It is that same principle which makes Aidoo's works feminist literature with a difference. . . .

The three major sections of *Our Sister Killjoy* merge into each other in whorls. The concerns are the same and the examples used to support those concerns are similar as we shift from one geographical focus to the other. In the final major section, there is greater introspection because of the literary approach—a confrontational ''love letter'' from Sissie to an imaginary male partner. The letter suggests a way out of the morass—communication between man and woman. . . . Such dialogue based on a mutually comprehensible language would then form the secret springboard for the solution of *all* the spiritual and material problems bedeviling the black world.

Aidoo has dealt with women's problems with arresting wisdom and grace. The conservative dissenter and the radical sympathizer will probably find her approach stimulating. Aidoo's forte is her tremendous *feeling* and honesty of sentiment in expressing those issues. Her works ring like the unimpugnable scold of a justly aggravated parent. . . . Aidoo's identification extends beyond ''underprivileged womanhood and the arrogance of manhood'' to include a variety of social problems across geographical boundaries. Without doubt, like her feminist mouthpiece in her play, *Anowa*, Aidoo has learnt and heard that ''in other lands a woman is nothing.'' Despite that knowledge, ''everything counts'' in the way she assembles her materials in her short stories and novel, *Our Sister Killjoy*, to register a feminism reasonably in tune with social realities.

Chimalum Nwankwo. In Carole Boyce Davies and Anne Adams Graves, eds. *Ngambika: Studies of Women in African Literature* (Trenton, New Jersey: Africa World Press, 1986), pp. 155, 158

Certainly there is much to recognize and approve of in the stories collected in *No Sweetness Here and Other Stories*. Aidoo uses her dramatist's skills to create an immediacy of environment and experience into which the reader is drawn, almost as participant rather than observer. The emotional lives of characters are conveyed palpably, making us share in their confusions and sorrows born of repeated failures and defeats as well as occasional joys and triumphs. Huge themes of personal and political betrayal, modernity versus tradition, changing gender roles and the impact of colonialism on African (Ghanaian) culture, relationships between women and between women and the men in their lives, as well as intergenerational conflicts and resolutions—all these figure prominently in the eleven stories. Yet, for all of their complexity, there is nothing heavy-handed about the stories. Rather, these are tales that deliberately evoke the so-called simplicity of an oral culture, but do so with an irony aimed at the smugly sophisticated (read: western/ized) reader as well as at many of the characters and conventions represented in the stories. Thus, Setu's repeated refrain to her husband—''I do not know, Zirigu, I do not know, my husband''—whenever she is about to contradict him sets the stage for the multiple ironies being explored in the story ''For Whom Things Did Not Change.'' In her case, she knows only too well that her husband is wrong in his resigned attitude toward the fate of poor people like himself in the wake of Ghana's supposed ''independence.'' Yet, aware of the subservient role she is supposed to play as wife, she must be careful how she couches her opinions. The rest of the story explores the ironies of postcolonialism, in which corrupt native elites have replaced the former colonial masters. The capping irony—and emblematic of the tone set by the rest of the collection—is that when Zirigu finally exhibits some spark of rebellion against the ruling order that can't see fit to provide folks like him with even a proper toilet, it is Setu who counsels resignation, accepting defeat.

In the title story a woman who decides to challenge the patriarchal codes and sue for divorce, even if it means giving up her beloved son to the boy's father, ends up broken by the sudden death of this son, killed by the bite of a poisonous snake. It seems that even nature will punish a woman who tries to be strong and fly in the face of convention. The majority of stories in this collection tell similar tales, where women learn to be strong in response to men's fickleness and abuse. The men are portrayed as generally weak of character, most often as corrupt "big men" of the cities or aspiring to that status. The women who succumb to their lust are not simplistically portrayed as innocent victims, yet in their collusion with the (anti) values of avarice and consumption, they become part of the generalized landscape of moral decay, corruption, and increasing inequity of life which Aidoo portrays. No one seems capable of voicing a challenge to such a system. It is therefore difficult, at least for me, to agree with Katrak's assessment that "even as she honestly faces the many sociocultural situations where 'sweetness' has vanished, Aidoo finds a way to retain a sympathetic and loving concern for the people who inhabit her world." For some of those belonging to a vanishing past, perhaps; for most of those representing Ghana's (and, by extension, Africa's) present and future.

Fawzia Afzal-Khan. *World Literature Today.* 71, 1 (Winter 1997), p. 71

[[*Our Sister Killjoy or Reflections from a Black-eyed Squint* (1979)] utilizes the very devices of Ghanaian oral literature to suggest that colonialism has fractured African society so severely that art is no longer both 'a form of aesthetic expression and a mode of communication', solidly rooted in 'underlying social, cultural and religious values', as J.H. Kwabena Nketia describes traditional drama. Instead, the contemporary African artist, in Aidoo's view, is unsure of, even rebuffed by, his audience. His attempts at communal expression are stifled; his fate, ironically, is like that of his Western counterpart: to speak in isolation, most often in defiance and frustration. It is nothing less than a tour de force that Aidoo successfully employs traditional oral techniques to present us with such a non-traditional conclusion.

The book jacket announces that *Our Sister Killjoy* is a novel, but at first glance, it appears to be a mélange of fictional episodes in both prose and verse mixed with sections of political speculation and social criticism. The book is divided into four parts: "Into A Bad Dream', 'The Plums', 'From Our Sister Killjoy', and 'A Love Letter'. Briefly, the story is of 'our Sister', Sissie, who is selected by officials in Ghana to accompany other young Africans to a youth hostel in Germany. There, she develops a troubling relationship with a discontented and lonely German housewife and learns something about connections between women and, particularly, about her own predicament as an African woman. She then travels to London and comes face-to-face with others like herself who had left Africa for the promises of Western education. In the end, she returns to Africa, but only after arguing with her compatriots and alienating her lover because of her outspoken political beliefs.

Aidoo tells this story in the third-person, using the omniscient narrator common to many Western novels, but the narrative proper does not begin until page 8. Preceding the story are several pages of curiously spaced, conversational observations about neo-colonial, 'moderate' blacks and, 'academic-pseudo-intellectuals' (p. 6). Page 6 is only three-quarters filled with prose; pages 5 and 7 are shaped like poems; and pages 3 and 4 consist of only one line apiece.

In addition to this unusual typography, the feature that suggests that Aidoo has something other than the conventional novel in mind is the conversational nature of these passages. She begins with the reassurance, 'Things are working out' (p. 3), as though the reader already knows what these 'Things' are. This casual, imprecise beginning establishes a dynamic between reader and writer essential to Aidoo's overall goal.

First, as every good story-teller must, she whets her reader's curiosity to discover what has been happening to her speaker, what it is that might be in doubt of 'working out'. Second, by beginning in the middle of the action, she establishes a bond of prior acquaintanceship with her reader. When the narrator then calls him, 'my brother' (p. 7), he is transformed from a stranger, a distant reader of a novel on a cold, printed page, interested privately in a good story, perhaps, into a member of her community involved in the very situation confronting the main character. Moreover, the style in these first pages tends toward the epistolary, a technique she will make explicit in the fourth section, thus enhancing the intimacy between writer and reader, between speaker and listener. In a very real sense, because Aidoo has defined her audience so carefully, both by the conversational style and by the designation, 'my brother', we, as readers, become participants and, at least temporarily, part of her society, confronting the dilemmas of one of our own kind whose experiences and decisions hold meaning for our own lives. Such is the traditional dynamic between the African poet and his audience.

Arlene Elder. Elder D. Jones ed. *Women in African Literature Today.*Trenton: Africa World Press, Inc., 1987, pp. 109–11

*The Dilemma of a Ghost* is a domestic comedy dramatizing the well-known literary theme of the cultural complex of the African been-to, that is, the African who has been overseas. Ato Yawson, the hero, a young Ghanaian man, returns home from America after his education with an Afro-American wife, and the problem that arises is that of reconciling his acquired Western way of life with that of his native home. By his education and marriage, Ato's life and that of his relations have become diametrical, and it becomes his responsibility to harmonize the two.

The two outstanding areas where conflict arises are the rites of stool veneration and the childbearing ideal of marriage perpetuated by Ato's relations. He can no longer regard these ideals in the same light as his relations, but even when he wants to pay lip service to them, his wife pulls him to the opposite stand. Moreover, he lacks enough tact to handle the situation, showing himself utterly unequal to the challenge. At the end of the play it is his mother who leads Eulalie, his wife, into the old section of the house while he remains dazed and unreconciled.

The physical setting reflects the opposing poles of the drama. It is an old family house with a new annex. The illiterate, traditionalist members of the family live in the old section while the annex is reserved for Ato, the new man. This device is not a mere dramatic fancy, but a true reflection of similar situations that arise in Ghanaian life. The ambivalence of the plot is dramatically clinched at the end of the play when Ato, in his bewilderment, is torn between going to the annex and going to the old section. This is symbolic of his inability to resolve his dilemma. Another device to dramatize the theme is the underlying dream-story of the ghost, derived from Fanti folklore, which parodies the story of Ato; for

Ato has become a ghost, his true native personality having been negated by his Westernization.

Richard K. Priebe. *Ghanaian Literatures* (New York: Greenwood Press, 1988), p. 178

[*Our Sister Killjoy*] traces the experience of Sissie, an African student in Europe. Her realization of the damage the West has inflicted on her culture is foregrounded in the text. At the end of the novel, Sissie returns from Europe to Ghana, confident in her anti-Western nationalism, although she is stigmatized for her stance by her own peer group, who belong to a culturally disaffected, Westernized elite.

The second part of the novel is dominated by Aidoo's account of the friendship between Sissie and the German lesbian Marija. Although when Sissie first meets Marija it is immediately apparent that the German woman is married and has a child, it is also clear that Marija's approach to Sissie is neither casual nor disinterested. . . .

As the friendship grows, Aidoo indicates the comfort it offers Sissie, who is otherwise socially isolated in the West. In Marija's house Sissie talks about Africa, or each sits with [her] own thoughts. Marija gives Sissie plums from her garden, and Aidoo invests this gift with symbolic resonance. The physical appearance of the fruit is stressed, with their feminine shape and smoothness and skin color "almost like [Sissie's] own." . . . For Marija, the plums are a way of reaching Sissie, of touching her sensibility, and in their physical appearance, they are a homage. For Sissie the gift represents what the friendship gives more generally, a validation of female qualities in which she can find comfort and self-substantiation. . . .

Aidoo's account of a homosexual relationship differs from that in many African novels because it is so detailed and avoids a monothematic, pejorative treatment. It is closely related to the novel's primary thematic development, in that it shows Sissie—black and heterosexual—still able to maintain sympathy for Marija and to perceive common ground between Marija's position and her own. . . .

There are, then, two elements here: Sissie empathizing with Marija as female; Sissie seeing her own stigmatization reflected in Marija's. The relationship between these two factors is made clearer in the last section of the novel. Having been abandoned in London by a man she loves—and who loves her, but is alienated by her "anti-Western neurosis," Sissie comments: "I shall be lonely again. O yes, everyone gets lonely some time or other. After all, if we look closer into ourselves, shall we not admit that the warmth from other people comes so sweet to us when it comes, because we always carry with us the knowledge of the cold loneliness of death?" In the end Sissie's loneliness derives from her stigmatization not only by the West but, more damagingly, by her peers in her own society. Marija's loneliness, meanwhile, is that of a lesbian, who must seek relationships with other women outside the margins of her community. While Aidoo's approach is nonpejorative, it is predicated on the assumption that Marija's condition is a marked terms, that it is defined by what, in the context of African literature, must be read as highly nonrepresentative characteristics. As for Sissie, the disadvantage she faces is more acute than that faced by a black man or even by a more representative black woman. She is a black woman isolated from her community because of her political

convictions. Her loneliness is similar to Marija's then, in having a double origin, the result of a very narrowly determined condition.

Chris Dunton. *Research in African Literatures.* 20, 3 (Fall 1989), pp. 431–34

There is much to be said for Ama Ata Aidoo's latest book, *Changes [A Love Story]*, and the way in which she brings out the cultural complexities of this love story based in Ghana. Her heroine Esi brings to the fore the dilemmas faced by women whose education and Western influences conflict with their cultural background. The issues of marital rape, the struggle for independence, jealousy and tradition, are all featured in this [consciousness] raising novel. Yet while the story possesses all the ingredients for a riveting read, this is hindered by Aidoo's rather ponderous and cumbersome style, which prevents it from realizing its full potential.

Esi, a slim, attractive, well-educated woman, is clearly seen by her close friend and family to have made a drastic and foolish decision when she leaves her husband. The constant pressure he inflicts on her to leave the job she loves, have more children and become a "proper wife," represent some of the common dilemmas faced by the modern African woman. As a result, Esi feels suffocated and trapped, unable to make him understand her feelings. Aidoo tentatively raises the issue of marital rape, which prompts Esi's separation from her husband, but never really dwells on the subject. It is as if both Esi and the author realize that in an African society there could not possibly be an "indigenous word or phrase for it."

What Aidoo does tackle particularly well is the complexity and potential danger in trying to fuse modern ideas with traditional methods. When Esi later meets and falls in love with Ali, an intelligent, successful, and married man, she decides to become his second wife. Ironically it is her traditionalist family and friend who try to dissuade her, but to Esi the position of second wife appears to be the perfect way to continue her independent lifestyle as a career woman without the burden of a full-time husband and household to look after. Unfortunately as she later finds out, the reality of her situation is far different.

Bola Makanjuola. *West Africa.* April 1–7, 1991, p. 474

In 1985 the College Press of Zimbabwe published the first collection of Aidoo's poetry, *Someone Talking to Sometime*, which contains some of her older poems that have appeared in anthologies and other poetry collections and some new ones. The two parts of the collection—"Of Love and Commitment" and "Someone Talking to Sometime"—total forty-four poems. . . .

*Someone Talking to Sometime* reiterates various themes articulated in Aidoo's other works. In characteristic Aidoo fashion, criticism is blended with affirmation, and tragedy and pain are toned down with wit and humor. Political corruption is humorously depicted in "From the Only Speech That Was Not Delivered at the Rally": the insanity and collapse of order in contemporary Africa are suggested by the image of being overtaken "by / winter at the height of an / equatorial noon." Highly condemnatory poems, such as "Nation Building" and "A Salute to African Universities" and those in the "Routine Drug" sequence, are balanced by more affirmative poems—"Of Love and Commitment," "Lorisnrudi," and "For Kinna II." Aidoo employs a conversational style to lend humor to the essentially tragic nature of existence and to invest the poems with the enduring quality of the blues.

Ama Ata Aidoo has established herself as a versatile and impressive writer for adults, and she has also written stories and poetry for children [*The Eagle and the Chickens and Other Stories* and *Birds and Other Poems*]. Her most recent work, *Changes: A Love Story*, is a novel that presents a critical look at options in love and marriage for contemporary African women. Through the female character Esi, who is an educated, ambitious, career-oriented Ghanaian, Aidoo explores such issues as marital rape and career choices, and their impact on love and marital relationships, highlighting the role of compromise. She scrutinizes through fiction the age-old institutions of monogamy and polygamy.

> Naana Banyiwa Horne. In Bernth Lindfors and Reinhard Sander, eds. *Dictionary of Literary Biography* Vol. 117 (Detroit: Gale Research, 1992), pp. 38–39

In "For Whom Things Did Not Change," the second story in Ama Ata Aidoo's collection *No Sweetness Here*, a young man recounts the tale of a bad yam. In it he tells how Nanaa cuts a slice of a large yam; it is rotten. Then she cuts another slice, and another, and another. All are rotten. Finally, she gouges out the head of the yam. It is brown and soft. Rotten. The young man, Kobina, draws from the childhood parable a significance for the corrupt social context of modern Ghana:

"What was it that ate it up so completely? And yet, here I go again, old yam has to rot in order that new yam can grow. Where is the earth? Who is going to do the planting? Certainly not us—too full with drink, eyes clouded in smoke and heads full of women.

The image of soil and regrowth, here stated emphatically and then rejected as implausible, goes to the heart of a good deal of Africa's writing. . . .

But the agrarian attachments of the so called "first generation" of African writers are not shared by Aidoo. Her preoccupation with "land" and "growth" is not primarily linked to a postcolonial discourse on agricultural, or cultural, or religious —though these issues certainly inform the background of her perceptions. She makes relatively little of the image of "earth" and "planting" in *No Sweetness Here*. It is a minor issue in the collection's title story; there is only occasional mention elsewhere. More directly, she is concerned with what Homi Bhabha has described as "the cultural and historical hybridity of the postcolonial world . . . as the paradigmatic place of departure." It is the immediate predicament of Ghana's cultural and political hegemony that defines the context of her discussion, and her narrative affinity is with a present-future nexus rather than with retracing an indigene-colonial hypothesis. In effect, she shifts the emphasis of her discourse away from explication of why things came to be as they are toward speculation as to how things may be altered. In Bhabha's terms, Aidoo takes as her paradigmatic starting point the experience of the present, without in any way disavowing the past as the informer of present consciousness, and strives to re-evaluate and re-define the aspirations of the future in relation to a present dystopian actuality. . . .

The definitiveness of Aidoo's "Certainly not us" in the yam allegory carries the caustic import of her compatriot Ayi Kwei Armah's *The Beautiful Ones Are Not Yet Born*—the suggestion that the present means to remedy present circumstances simply do not exist. The conundrum of hopelessness in the present, but

hopefulness in the future (those who are as yet unborn), is one shared by both writers.

Ama Ata Aidoo's Ghana, like that of Ayi Kwei Armah, is a place of unenviable suffering, a world without sweetness or even the prospect of it. . . .

In fact, Aidoo has regretted titling the collection *No Sweetness Here*, and has admitted that she seriously considered changing the name for the most recent reprint of the work. It is interesting that she views a change of the collective title of the anthology as a possible remedy to the charge of "pessimism." This could be construed as misguided, since accusations of pessimism have emerged from textual rather than titular perspectives. On the other hand, the line she may be taking implicitly is that the title tends to lay a false trail of gloom—one that critics have been all too willing to follow. The truth is that just as Armah's title of *The Beautyful Ones Are Not Yet Born* is illusory in its suggestion of the absolute barrenness of current human worth, so *No Sweetness Here* is misleading in its insinuation of an absolute lack of sweetness.

The point is well illustrated in the fable of the bad yam. The diction is absolute and inflexible: "ate it up so completely"; "Certainly not us"; "too full with drink . . . ." And yet the fact that Kobina, the young man who tells the yam parable, even exists is surely a signal of hope? He demonstrates by his very being that it is possible to nurture values of integrity and egalitarianism even within an all-pervading context of greed, dishonesty and elitism. Further, both before and after the yam parable, Kobina shows himself to be more than a decorative ornament of goodness. He acts upon his goodness. Immediately before, he requests that the servants, Zirigu and Setu, call him "Kobina, not Master"; immediately after, we are reminded of the excitement at the Rest House because of his insistence that he should eat with the servants. Kobina's internalized question "Who is going to do the planting?" is sandwiched between its obvious answer: people like Kobina.

This is an intriguing narrative technique—the juxtaposition of antithetical statements of promise and despair. The polarities are not, however, balanced in emphasis, and this may well lead to undue distortions in critical judgments about Aidoo's pessimism as a writer. Aidoo tends to articulate the absolute of hopelessness more forthrightly than she does the recurrent indicators of the benign. In the tale of the yam, we tend rather to listen to what the storyteller says than to weigh the worth and import of the man who is saying it.

Of course, it is one thing to avow that there are signs of sweetness in *No Sweetness Here*, but quite another to argue that they are meaningful or that they temper the overwhelming bitterness ranged against them. So what if Kobina is a nice young man who likes to treat people equally? The facts are that colonial Ghana has simply become neocolonial Ghana. Kobina may be different from the typical run of well-to-do young men, but most are not. And those whom he would wish to treat differently have become so attuned to the normative social structuring of things that they themselves demonstrate a manifest conservatism to change, even when Kobina, and perhaps the reader, would identify change as beneficial to them. There may be the isolated Kobina, the occasional M'ma Asana of "Certain Winds from the South," the rare Connie of "Two Sisters"—but these are solitary exemplars of perception and virtue, locked apparently helplessly in the maelstrom of decay and decadence that envelops their world. Good they may be, but what chance have they of changing things?

Aidoo's paradox of subtle virtue amidst obvious despair may demand a more accurate reformulation of the issues critics have raised about Aidoo's authorial pessimism, but it does not necessarily demand hope. The binary duality established in *For Whom Things Did Not Change,* the tension between institutionalized decay and individualized purity, stands as an untenable modus operandi for the amelioration of society. The author herself has been troubled by the prospect of progress from a position of debilitating social stagnancy.

"One has to go on. If one refuses to survive, if one refuses to 'manage', one has given in to despair. And I don't think anybody has a right to despair, because it is not possible for any one person to have all the variables to give an answer to a particular situation. So we do the best we can and move on from day to day" [she told Adeola James, *In Their Own Voices: African Women Writers Talk*].

But what is the purpose of "going on"? Individual perseverance and goodness may be a hopeful sign, but a hopeful sign of what? Pitting a few disparate, pure individuals against what Barbara Harlow, with reference to *The Beautyful Ones Are Not Yet Born,* has described as "a society which is portrayed as surviving on nothing but the offal of its own corruption" is hardly an encouraging harbinger of change.

A partial solution may lie in a movement beyond the moral/immoral binary configuration that a story like *For Whom Things Did Not Change* establishes, for this kind of thesis constantly formulates the issue of changing society on win/lose terms. Human affairs are rarely so clear-cut or amenable. In fact, several of the stories in *No Sweetness Here* offer a philosophic structuring that is more subtle than a simple opposition of ethical polarities, and seek to locate issues of societal worth within a different, and possibly more pragmatic, argumentative framework. . . .

There is certainly an oracular quality to the writing of Ama Ata Aidoo. Like Ayi Kwei Armah, she feels a compulsion to express her distaste for aspects of Ghanaian society in the most absolute terms. The rhetorical extravagance is a response to the level of societal malaise she perceives - an invective born of the imperative need to make people listen and take note.

It is not, however, the invective of hopelessness. That benign, principled characters walk her Ghanaian streets is in itself encouraging. For all of society's pervasive decay, the inherent goodness of some individuals remains unsilted by its irksome flow. But the ability of their goodness, of itself, to change things significantly is not evidenced in Armah's narrative nor does it seem plausible in the face of such a mortifying literary portraiture of Ghanaian societal decay. In her depiction of the continuum of female experience, there seems greater cause for optimism. By identifying the commonalities of female experience in a degrading context of patriarchal behavioral imperatives, Aidoo moves beyond the possibility of individual goodness toward the speculative realms of a collective female moral entrenchment against the decadence of a given, masculinized world.

> Clayton G. MacKenzie. *Studies in Short Fiction.* 32, 2 (Spring 1995)

BIBLIOGRAPHY

*"No Sweetness Here,"* 1963; *"Last of the Proud Ones,"* 1964; *The Dilemma of a Ghost,* 1965; *Anowa,* 1970; *No Sweetness Here,* 1970; *Our Sister Killjoy,* 1977; *Someone Talking to Sometime,* 1985; *The Eagle and the Chickens and Other Stories,* 1986; *Birds and Other Poems,* 1987; *Changes: A Love Story,* 1991; *An Angry Letter in January and Other Poems,* 1992; *The Girl Who Can and Other Stories,* 1997

# ALEXIS, Jacques-Stéphen (1922–1961)
## Haiti

[In *Comrade General Sun*] Alexis tells the story of Hilarion and Claire-Heureuse, who are poor blacks in Haiti in the prewar years. The novel is primarily a love story, for Hilarion and Claire-Heureuse love each other, love the joy of the sun and the peacefulness of conversations and the beach; they love life. But the novel is also a story of poverty and hatred, for the protagonists are hungry; Hilarion has stolen in order to eat. He has been locked up, beaten, and humiliated, and he has come out of prison a communist. . . .

This long, sumptuously colored romantic chronicle, which combines evocations of Caribbean family life and political demands, and which uses the resources of the art of the popular tale and the richness, preciosity, and naïveté of the Creole dialect, reveals the power of a literature that is nourished by the folklore, the language, and the passions of a country that is still innocent of "western" literature. In this respect, Alexis's novel seems much more promising than, for example, Aimé Césaire's poetry, which is all too full of surrealist memories and is too Europeanized. . . .

Throughout *Comrade General Sun* there run a force and a lyric freedom that unify the love story, the exoticism, and the political message. The message thus appears as a necessary metamorphosis of the storyteller's sensibility, not as the result of a deliberate choice among several ways of telling the story. Alexis's achievement is that he does not in any way give the impression of having written the novel out of his convictions as a Haitian communist; instead, his work suggests that there is no other way to speak about the Caribbean people today. Passages as different as Paco's death and his immediate assumption of a symbolic function, scenes of labor in the sugar-cane fields, and the love of the young couple all become simultaneous moments—the colorful, violent, and tender scenes of a single painting illuminated by the rays of "Comrade Sun," who is the great joyful source of strength for the men tied to poverty and to hope for their land.

> François Nourissier. *La nouvelle revue francaise.* October, 1955, pp. 787–88†

*In the Blink of an Eye* revives the sentimental theme, made fashionable by Hugo and Alexandre Dumas *fils,* of the fallen woman who is redeemed by love. But the story of the woman's fall is very long in Alexis's novel. The details about La Nina Estrellita's "profession" and her vices recall the climate of crudeness that reigns in Zola's *Nana.* And yet, despite the evidence of La Nina's moral debasement, she is the woman whom El Caucho has chosen. Around this couple there is an indefinable halo which indicates the similarity of their souls and which is the sign of the eternal promises inscribed in their flesh. . . .

Is *In the Blink of an Eye* Jacques Alexis's best novel? Perhaps so, if one shares the novelist's own conviction. In any case, this novel is the book in which he accomplished his mission. The characterization of El Caucho is indeed the culmination of an undertaking begun with Hilarion. . . . El Caucho is a true proletarian. He does not have to be trained: his training has been completed. He is the worker who is conscious of his role in society and of his importance in the struggle that is being waged. . . .

Yet the character of El Caucho does not entirely account for Alexis's preference for this novel. In *In the Blink of an Eye* he not only accomplished his mission but he also liberated himself [from his obsession with the bourgeoisie]. *Comrade General Sun* is overloaded with criticism of society. It is the story of a revolt against God and against the capitalistic organization of man's work. The description of the strikes that stand out in the narrative and the murders that are committed has the appearance of protest writing. And the moral of *The Musical Trees*, whereby the earth takes revenge and triumphs over the greed of the authorities, has no other meaning than its protest.

*In the Blink of an Eye*, on the other hand, calmly asserts refusal by creating a universe outside the bounds of bourgeois virtue and the demands of conventional morality. The milieu in which the novel takes place, the atmosphere of vice, perversion, and obscenity in which it is clothed, is itself a defiance of the bourgeoisie. But that is not all. La Nina's rehabilitation is a symbol, as is El Caucho's natural chivalry. This book is a vision that contrasts with the portrait drawn elsewhere by the novelist of a bourgeois society in which everything is borrowed, falsely enlightening, and obscurely corrupt.

Ghislain Gouraige. *Histoire de la littérature haïtienne* (Port-au-Prince, Imprimerie H. A. Théodore, 1960), pp. 293–97†

As a novelist Alexis is similar to the unanimist Jules Romains. Like the author of *Men of Good Will*, Alexis wished to express life in all its multiplicity and movement during an era of his country's history. A panorama of Haitian life from 1934 to 1942 is presented in *Comrade General Sun* and *The Musical Trees*.

Alexis does not construct his works around a single plot. . . . The life of Hilarion and that of Gonaïbo [the hero of *The Musical Trees*] are only secondary to an immense documentary fresco composed of descriptions, portraits, various peasant scenes, and psychological analyses. The danger of this style is quite evident: it diffuses the reader's interest.

Like Voltaire and Anatole France, Alexis has made his ideas explicit in his various works. It is easy to discover his political and social thoughts and his religious ideas in his writing.

In politics he leans toward communism. His liking for Pierre Roumel and Doctor Jean-Michel and for his hero Hilarion, who has been indoctrinated by these two militants, is clear. The message left by the dying Hilarion leaves no doubt about this point.

It must be added that Alexis is profoundly nationalist. The narrative of *The Musical Trees* is in itself enough proof of Alexis's nationalism. He also seems anti-bourgeois—which is explained by his socialism. His depictions of Port-au-Prince society are often satirical. On the other hand, Alexis loves the common people: he commiserates with their poverty and defends their customs and traditions.

It cannot be said that Alexis is indifferent to religion. He favors a national Catholic clergy and also the Catholic Church. But he would like Haitian priests to be more attentive to the voices of the native land and to the voices of the ancestors. Thus, people came to believe that he was urging the Haitian clergy to practice an impossible "mixture" [of Christianity and voodooism]. . . .

He chooses images that are sometimes realistic, sometimes ethereal, sometimes grandiose, and sometimes pretty. It is evident that Alexis possesses an extraordinary, marvelous imagination, a gift that had never been granted to a Haitian novelist before him.

*Manuel illustré d'histoire de la littérature haïtienne* (Port-au-Prince: Éditions Henri Deschamps, 1961), pp. 487–88†

Jacques Alexis was born on April 22, 1922, in the city of Gonaives. He studied medicine in Paris. His admiration for Jacques Roumain is well known. A writer and a political militant, Alexis was the cofounder in 1959 of a Haitian communist party, the Entente Populaire. To carry out a secret mission, he landed surreptitiously on the northwest coast of Haiti. There he was spotted, seized, and executed. That was in April, 1961.

Direct political activity was not the only field on which Jacques Alexis struggled. He also fought on the literary battlefield for the development of his country. A struggle for development was indeed the way in which he conceived of his mission as a novelist. . . .

The novel *The Musical Trees* is an analysis of the situation in Haiti in 1941–42. At that time the rural world of the Haitian peasants was under attack on two fronts, economic and religious: an American rubber company was setting up a plantation on land stolen from the peasants, and the Catholics were campaigning against the voodoo religion. This intertwining, this overlapping, this intersecting of events, provides the author with an opportunity to develop his views on the role of the Catholic religion in the development of rural Haiti. What, in Jacques Alexis's opinion, is the role played by the Catholic religion? His negative attitude toward the Church is very close to that of Jacques Roumain. Indeed, Roumain himself is present in the novel under the name Pierre Roumel, a journalist defending the peasants' cause. When Alexis attacks the Church, he uses almost the same arguments Roumain used.

Claude Souffrant. *Europe*. January 1971, pp. 34–35†

Alexis took advantage of his exile in France to continue his medical studies. He specialized in neurology. His innate restlessness led him to frequent the numerous intellectual circles that blossomed in Paris right after the war. He got to know Césaire, Senghor, and all the exponents of Negritude. He was drawn to existentialism. He became friendly with Aragon and the most advanced of the progressive intellectuals. He immersed himself in social realism, which dates back to Zola and Anatole France; he discovered socialist realism, Gorki and Ehrenburg. A need, an impulse, a new passion then arose, and took form through these new aesthetic prisms. Between his busy hours at the hospital, Alexis the neurologist wanted to write, to re-create the distant image of his fatherland by harmonizing the flow of images that besieged his mind despite the years of exile and separation. . . .

Alexis's first two novels, as well as his collection of stories [*Romancero in the Stars*], explored the unlimited field of traditions, legends, and beliefs of rural life in Haiti. "If the zombi stories are legends," insists Alexis, "happy are those whose legends are so great and alive!" Thus, the artist's imagination and the multicolored marvels of social reality intertwine to the point at which it is difficult to distinguish one from the other. Then a new dimension of realism is born: "magic realism," which suffuses Alexis's literary works. His characters seem to spring from the most authentic tableaux in Haitian primitive painting. They arise from real life as well. Their lives are shaped by the lush tropical vegetation, the tribulations of peasant life, the mysteries and rites of voodoo, and the serene desire for improvement characteristic of the Haitian people.

Gérard Pierre-Charles. *Europe*. January 1971, pp. 67–68

BIBLIOGRAPHY
Comrade General Sun (*Compère Général Soleil*, 1955); The Musical Trees (*Les arbres musiciens*, 1957); In the Blink of an Eye (*L'espace d'un cillement*, 1959); Romancero in the Stars (*Romancero aux étoiles*, 1960)

# ALUKO, T. M. (1918– )
## Nigeria

[Aluko] has attempted to do for Yorubaland what [Achebe] has done for Iboland, namely to present an image of the past at that point where the civilisation of the Western world came into contact with it. But whereas Mr. Achebe assesses the two civilisations objectively, writing from the inside at the same time, Mr. Aluko attitudinises and, what is more, does on the whole lack that empathy which is so necessary if a historical novel is to rise above the level of bald observation. The result is that [*One Man, One Wife*] convinces only in patches, and that his interpretation of the past appears to suffer from bias and preconceptions. His is almost a total rejection of the past.

He imposes a sort of Manichaean division. It is acceptable that the pastor should regard his mission as bringing light into the darkness of the Yoruba religion; but from cover to cover the impression is given that this is also the author's standpoint. Thus the indigenous religion means for him as it does for the pastor nothing more than ''the worship of streams and trees.'' He fails to see it as a philosophy of life or as a social system; and so, looking back, he sees only its inadequacies. For children it is only the fear of evil spirits in the dark; for adults the fear of a god of smallpox, and so on. One is tempted to say that if the author's comprehension and interpretation of Yoruba life did not exceed that of the Rev. David, the latter should have been the mouthpiece of the story. To put it differently, one expects of a novelist that his view of things be larger and more comprehensive than the sum total of the views of his characters.

One is not here concerned with whether this interpretation of the past is right or wrong. The point is that it is too limited and biased to serve as a basis for the imaginative truth which we demand of fiction. Polygamy emerges as an institution without a single creditable feature. Indeed, the clash between it and Christian monogamy hardly appears to be a clash between two approaches to life; even for the author it is simply a clash between light and darkness.

Arthur D. Drayton. *Ibadan*. November 1960, p. 29

The main strength of *One Man, One Matchet* lies not so much in the plot as in the magnificent characterisation. There is a fascinating interplay of character and motivation. The characters are drawn with warmth and sympathy and at no point does the author try to manipulate them for his own ends. Mr. Aluko has a sharp eye for human foibles and even the most dignified of his people are not above ridiculousness. The characters are memorable: flamboyant Benjamin Benjamin; irascible old Chief Momo; rich, vain and gullible Olowekere, jockeying for a chieftaincy; meek and mild Reverend Josiah Olaiya, anxious to divert some of the streams of campaign money into his church. But they are lovable people— even the unworthiest of them. And in the unhurried, rural tempo of the book they play out their individual dramas under the author's kindly but ever-watchful eye. Life is charmingly inconclusive and here and there Mr. Aluko gracefully squanders an incident which promised possibilities. But the sure touch is always there, evoking the smell of life.

In an age of axe-grinding it is remarkable that Mr. Aluko does not seem to have an axe of his own to grind. There is an absence of posturing: that is left to his characters. Mr. Aluko, too, never passes judgment: that is left to his readers. And neither does he explain his characters to potential foreign readers: there is no need because his characters are universal. The writing is clear, with many a sudden comic turn. Perhaps the book could have done without the last chapter which is explanatory, for by then the drama has been well and truly played out. *One Man, One Matchet* is a significant contribution not only to African writing but to the world's writing and one looks forward to this talented Nigerian writer's next book.

Alfred Hutchinson. *The New African*. July 1965, p. 114

There is not much difference between the situation in [*Kinsman and Foreman*] and the situation in Aluko's second novel, *One Man, One Matchet*; an honest man and a rogue are in conflict, and the rogue eventually loses out. What gives *Kinsman and Foreman* an interesting twist is the family connection between the honest man and the rogue. . . .

Taken as it is, the novel has several good points. Amusing incidents are skillfully strung together and knotted at the end into a hilarious climax. The narrative moves along unfettered by the distracting irrelevancies and digressions that crippled Aluko's earlier novels. Aluko's characterization has improved too. Major figures are well-defined and minor figures sketched in a variety of gay colors. Each character has a particular role to play in the parade of comic events. Also, Aluko's satirical thrusts are sharper and more widely distributed than in his previous novels. He slashes with vigor at church, state, family and individual. Even the follies of British justice and American philanthropy receive a few pertinent jabs. If one compares *Kinsman and Foreman* with Aluko's formless first novel, *One Man, One Wife*, one can see quite clearly that Aluko has come a long way in seven years. He still has a good distance to go before he will be close to front-runners like Achebe, but at least he is moving in the right direction and making better progress than Ekwensi. . . .

Bernth Lindfors. *Africa Today*. October 1967, p. 29

*One Man, One Matchet* is a more ambitious novel than *One Man, One Wife*. The clash of concepts is once again the theme. This novel should be required reading for every European or American technician and teacher involved in aid schemes in Africa, as well as for every African government official dealing with development projects, for Aluko sees clearly the heartbreaking difficulties which such projects inevitably entail, and he manages to make comprehensible the genuinely held and diametrically opposed views of the old chiefs and the new young men of government. . . .

Aluko displays great talent in catching the individuals' voices and the general tone of village meetings—the Yoruba love of words, the lengthy speeches and interminable preliminary greetings, the unhurried way in which everyone is allowed his say and yet the way in which this age-old tribal method now impedes action. . . .

The ending, with Udo's resignation and his discussion of the country's problems with his successor, is flat and too theoretical. Nevertheless, for its incisive irony, perceptive social analysis and convincing character portrayals, *One Man, One Matchet* will remain worth reading for a long time to come.

Margaret Laurence. *Long Drums and Cannons* (London: Macmillan, 1968), pp. 171–72, 175–76

*Chief the Honourable Minister* is a bad, a very bad, piece of writing. Indeed, Mr. Aluko cannot be serious. Life is just too short to spend on either writing or reading such nonsense. This light pile of numbered pages reminds me of the "plot" cards I discovered as a freshman in college: the penurious yet budding writer could arrange and rearrange them in geometric manner for plot, subplot, counterplot, and so forth. He would then send the fleshed-out result to the Western and detective pulp story publishers. Mr. Aluko's listless tale is reminiscent of just this. His heroes, villains, mistresses, expatriate midget brains in the imaginary African state of Afromacoland have absolutely no pretense at depth or dimension. The story—of governmental corruption and incompetence—reads like an editorial from the *Daily Times* of Lagos, Nigeria, in the worst days of that nation's strife. . . .

The author of this tale should tell us why Moses is a good guy, why Dauda is a bad guy, why bribery, corruption, incompetence exist. These things do not happen from nowhere, just as men are not born good guys, bad guys, or even bumbling guys. At the outset of this book all the characters, undimensional, are, as it were, poised at the starting line. They have no substance; they are just *faits accomplis*. The book then goes on as if the characters and events were wound up and let go in some elementary good-bad-bumbling dialectic.

J. Dennis Delaney. *African Studies Review.* September 1971, p. 329

*Chief the Honourable Minister* is a satire of the national "democratic" government, the "Freedom for All Party," which is established at the end of British colonial rule. The story is set in an imaginary state called Afromacoland. Throughout the novel, attention is directed not at the people of the state, but at the government officials. Hardly any mention is made of there even being people over which the officials rule. Each official is titled a minister in charge of a department, but it is never established what the function or purpose of each department is in regard to the people. The people of Afromacoland are not served by the government; they are only used by the government officials to support their selfish gains.

Aluko's failure to portray each minister in detail does not weaken the book's impact; rather it highlights the meaninglessness of the government and contributes to the general satirical nature of the novel. Actually, the ministers are not individuals; they are stereotyped as selfish, ridiculous, fat men. Their actions, judgments, and minds are all one. Their lengthy, meaningless titles are the only identity they possess; never do they identify with the country or people they control.

Aluko was always a social satirist, but his early novels were in a light vein. Now as an outsider, he is able to treat seriously the plight of the ordinary man, surrounded by self-seeking politicians. The laughter in the last two novels is not merely laughter for its own sake but laughter directed at reforming society. This was the function of masquerade verse in traditional Yoruba society, and, as has been seen, Aluko has moved strongly in this direction.

O. R. Dathorne. *The Black Mind* (Minneapolis: University of Minnesota Press, 1974), pp. 168–69

Aluko is now one of the most prolific novelists in West Africa, yet his fifth novel is not essentially very different from his first. In *His Worshipful Majesty* we find the same type of thin plot, the same weakly developed characters and the same bombastic language juxtaposed with the same kind of overbearingly moralistic theme that runs through all his work. In his early novels of culture conflict, as well as in his more recent one about a political coup, we find much that has been derived from Achebe; in this novel with its attempts to incorporate Yoruba festivals and Yoruba praise poetry, we hear echoes of Soyinka. Such derivation is legitimate, but Aluko never seems to go beyond, or even come up to, his models. In short, one is tempted to dismiss him as a second rate novelist.

However, despite his lack of originality there are both literary and extra-literary reasons that make Aluko's novels, and in particular *His Worshipful Majesty*, worthwhile reading. . . . Though the work as a whole may not be a finely wrought novel, Aluko has again shown himself to be a master of hyperbole and an important chronicler of the cultural changes in West Africa that were brought about by European colonialism.

Richard Priebe. *Books Abroad.* Spring 1974, p. 412

In *One Man, One Matchet* Aluko shows himself to possess the enlightened, progressive yet practical attitudes which the more thoughtful colonial administrators wished to instil into their black successors. Indeed the novel, set in 1949, concerns the handing on of authority by a white colonial administrator, Stanfield, favourably portrayed by Aluko, to a black successor. . . .

Aluko's portrayal of the villagers of Ipaja shows a lively grasp of communal psychology and a talent for neat and telling caricature. The villagers show all the selfish shortsightedness of children, and something also of the child's exasperating innocence. Indeed if Aluko were white he would certainly be accused of a patronising and racist condescension towards them! Chief Momo's speech on the taxation issue which follows Akpan's (but which, being in Yoruba Akpan cannot understand) illustrates this.

'Who in Ipaja does not know that the first assessment is always too high? When the Clerk first writes down three pounds for you, do you not go to beg the Chiefs and do you not go to see the Clerk at home? When you do this, do they not have mercy on you and do they not ask you to pay fifteen shillings instead of the original three pounds? And after paying the Kola for the Oba and Chiefs and the

Clerk, you still pay less than the original three pounds which the Clerk first writes against your name. And everyone is happy—you, the Oba and Chiefs—and is the Clerk not happy?' and he looked at that worthy who in his embarrassment was scribbling nonsense on the foolscap sheet before him.

'Now because we have a black District Officer, we must pay oppressive taxes. . . .'

Momo simply has no conception that there is anything improper in the state of affairs he is describing. He has no notion of corruption or misappropriation of public funds. For him taxation is simply an arbitrary imposition from above, to be evaded as far as possible, or complied with under sufferance. Even the limited compliance which the villagers do afford to the authorities is not an encouraging sign. When they are obedient to the administration this is not out of responsible public spirit, but out of an abject and servile fear of the white man, as exasperating to Aluko (and the reader) as their stubborn defiance: 'We must do whatever the White Man says. He now owns Ipaja. He owns the world,' one Elder observed.' And later Momo remarks: 'One more step and the White Man would become God'. The villagers accord Akpan grudging respect because he is identified in their minds with the all-powerful whites. Indeed they constantly refer to him as 'the black White Man'.

Aluko thus, through vigorous caricature and broad comedy, highlights the key political problem facing Nigeria during this transition period. The old small-scale village system of responsibilities and loyalties has become inadequate in the context of the modern, impersonal nation-state which is in the process of being born. The people, however, particularly the older men, still cannot help seeing the world in terms of local customs and allegiances. And the situation is growing worse with the gradual withdrawal of the white man. At least the whites could impose an external, impartial and efficient order on society, by brute force if necessary. When the 'black white men' begin to take over, with the confusion of response this inevitably evokes in the people, chaos seems virtually inevitable. The analysis seems to lead to the conclusion that the British democratic system simply cannot work in the Nigeria of Aluko's day, or that it can be made to work only by the use of greater coercion than would be tolerated in Britain—in other words by ceasing to be democracy.

It is characteristic of Aluko that this problem should be seen in terms of comedy and satire, rather than tragedy. This is ensured by the drastic simplifications of focus which are central to Aluko's technique. By refusing to permit any dignity or pathos to the elders of Ipaja he excludes the more complex human dimensions of the situation which might interfere with his straightforwardly progressive and enlightened political interpretation. As it is, the villagers (with the partial exception of Ajayi, who is treated sketchily and killed off as soon as possible) remain delightfully exasperating caricatures, whose childlike antics continually interfere with Akpan's efforts to improve their lot.

James Booth. *Writers and Politics in Nigeria* (New York: Africana Publishing Company, 1981), pp. 82–7

BIBLIOGRAPHY
*One Man, One Wife*, 1959; *One Man, One Matchet*, 1964; *Kinsman and Foreman*, 1966; *Chief the Honourable Minister*, 1970; *His Worshipful Majesty*, 1973; *Wrong Ones in the Dock*, 1982; *State of Our Own*, 1986; *Conduct Unbecoming*, 1993; *My Years of Service*, 1994

# AMADI, Elechi (1934– )
## Nigeria

Novels about daily life in Eastern Nigerian villages by past or present inhabitants of them now appear almost weekly. [*The Concubine*], the latest, is particularly interesting for two reasons. First, Elechi Amadi, whose first published work this is, was educated at Government College, Umuahia, and the former University College, Ibadan, and is now a captain in the Nigerian army, attached to the Military School in Zaria. He took a degree in mathematics and physics and did not take his commission until he had spent some time land surveying and teaching. One knew that Nigerian army officers were versatile, in view of their role in running their country now: but Captain Amadi is probably the only novelist among them.

The other point of interest in the book is that this is not a novel of conflict. No Europeans, or even European influences, disturb the village scene. The writing is clear, simple and economical although some of the dialogue is rather stilted—not because it uses traditional Ibo forms of address, but because it is not always all in "key.". . .

One is tempted to speak of a "classical tragedy," with the gods ever at hand to demand allegiance and to punish remorselessly human offences and frailties. But the figures are not of the stature demanded by classical tragedy.

The pace is slow, one is spared few details. But this is a story told for its own sake and is not a substitute for an anthropological treatise or a political manifesto. Captain Amadi's people still lack sufficient depth. If they acquired that his work would acquire a new dimension.

D. B. *West Africa (London)* June 11, 1966, p. 657

Amadi goes even further than Chinua Achebe in portraying traditional religious concepts, for the Ibo society about which Achebe is writing was already affected and altered by life-views dissimilar to its own. Amadi's Ibo villages in *The Concubine* represent a society which had not yet fallen prey to self-doubts. Its gods could be cruel, but they were real, and they affected the lives of mortals in real and inexplicable ways. Strangely, what at first appears to be a limitation of the novel—the single viewpoint, as contrasted with Achebe's ability to grasp and convey a multiplicity of viewpoints—turns out to be a type of strength, for Amadi's effect ultimately depends upon the extent to which he can convey the gods as actual and potent. He is not writing primarily about people's relationships with one another, although these provide much of the novel's substance. The underlying theme is always man's fate, to what extent he can change it, and how he chooses to face the inevitable. In this respect, Amadi's writing has something in common with that of John Pepper Clark, who is also concerned with destiny in very similar ways. . . .

*The Concubine* expresses in admirably simple poetic prose the age-old conflict of man with his gods, his awe of them and at the same time his proud attempts to bind them, to make them do his will. Although Amadi differs sharply from Wole Soyinka in that *The Concubine* does not offer alternative and contemporary interpretations to the struggle between men and gods, he resembles Soyinka in another way, for most definitely neither writer is a liberal humanist. Amadi, like Soyinka, does not ever suggest that man is improving and will ultimately be able to direct wisely and knowingly every facet of his life. On the contrary, *The Concubine* expresses the mystery at the centre of being. Amadi's is an essentially sombre view of life, and his novel contains an acute awareness of fate's ironies, for at the exact moment when we think the prize is within our grasp, the gods cut the thread. This outlook is reminiscent of the references Achebe makes to Chukwu, the supreme God, who severs a man's life when it is sweetest to him.

> Margaret Laurence. *Long Drums and Cannons* (London, Macmillan, 1968), pp. 182–84

It would . . . be very naïve to think that [*The Great Ponds*] is simply the account, powerful as it might be, of a feud between two tribes, and of their ultimate destruction. . . . The second level of the story is implied in the final laconic sentence: "Wonjo, as the villagers called the Great Influenza of 1918, was to claim a grand total of some twenty million lives all over the world." Thus is explained the death of the inhabitants of both Chiolu and Aliakoro, wrongly attributed to the blind rage of Ogbunabali "executing judgment, killing off both parties to a dispute. . . ." Thus is made clear the weakness of Man. Limited as he is in his comprehension and knowledge, he does not understand how derisive are his quarrels and vain his victories. He pitiably tries to give a meaning to things far above his reach and opposes events which cannot be opposed. He passes away without ever realizing that he is a mere dot in the intricate pattern of mankind.

*The Great Ponds* is a lesson in humility. The simplicity of the style and the minute selection of detail further enhance the dramatic aspect. Amadi is a master at rendering the innermost feelings of his characters. Olumba, the great warrior from Chiolu, is the anti-hero *par excellence*, because of the multiplicity of questions he asks himself and the gulf of doubt he vainly attempts to conceal in his soul. But at the same time and owing to his very ambiguity, he is one of the finest portraits ever drawn by an African writer. Critics will not fail to draw a parallel between the story which is told here and recent events in Africa. Amadi might well have been inspired by the bloody Civil War in Nigeria; however, to explain the book in this light will not do justice to its power and tragic value. It is a tale of human fragility, stubbornness and despair. The characters are not so much Nigerians, or Africans, but Men, victims of their own limitations, unable to grasp the tragedy of the world.

Elechi Amadi opens new roads to the African novelist. He leaves aside the purely grand essays in homage to the past; he is not concerned with the satire of modern Africa; he forces the reader to search for the very meaning of life.

> Maryse Conde. *Presence africaine.* No. 80, 1971, pp. 164–65

Although many readers applaud Elechi Amadi's *The Concubine*, quite a few have grave reservations about the novel. While praising the novelist's presentation of his society and his powers of characterization, they are unable to accept his portrayal of the supernatural. They compare him with Hardy, and deplore his attempt to attribute responsibility to the gods, when their experience shows that the motivations of conduct and the agents of destiny are strictly sociological. On the other hand, I have met many students who frankly admitted that of all the African novels they have read, *The Concubine* was the only one they could respond to fully, because it

presented an almost exact copy of village life as they knew it. This conflict of opinion presents a very interesting problem. On the one hand, the strictures against the novel are honest and serious, and have to be seriously considered; but on the other hand, one has to be careful about denigrating a work which elicits such a powerful response, precisely because of its especial relevance to people's lives. I rather suspect that some people condemn the novel as a reflex action, simply because they do not believe in the supernatural at all, and not because of any stylistic defect. . . .

Amadi is not conducting a rational argument to prove the existence of supernatural forces. He may not even believe in the supernatural himself; there is no evidence in the novel that he does. He merely presents to us a group of people for whom the supernatural is important, and he tries to make their way of life as realistic as possible.

> Eustace Palmer. *An Introduction to the African Novel* (New York, Africana, 1972), pp. 117, 128

*The Great Ponds*, by Elechi Amadi, not only gives a Homeric nobility to the tiny war between Nigerian villages but recovers, in its acceptance of magic as a fact, the power the Greek dramatists had—of making mental acts seem momentous. . . .

At a symposium in Lagos a year ago, I heard a dazzling variety of literary tactics enunciated by a dozen Nigerian writers and critics. Elechi Amadi (addressed as "Captain Amadi," in deference to the Army years of his varied career) put forward with an arresting earnestness the opinion that supernatural reality should play its part in a narrative whose characters believe in magic. The first question from the audience challenged this notion, or, rather, asked that it be clarified to mean that such belief should be shown to be *subjectively* influencing the characters. Captain Amadi, a slender, gracious, and handsome figure in a white robe, appeared to consent to the modification, there in the juju-proof setting of the university auditorium, amid the steel chairs and the flexnecked microphones and the beaming pink faces of U.S.I.S. officials, with the metropolis of Lagos clattering beyond the windows. But it seemed to me that Captain Amadi did not in fact mean anything quite so reasonable as the proposition that believers believe, but something more supernatural, and his novel confirms my impression. . . .

The suspense of Olumba's struggle not to die is frightful. The motions of his morale feel immense. We see life as pre-scientific man saw it—as a spiritual liquid easily spilled. The invisible forces pressing upon Olumba are totally plausible. The novel treats magic respectfully, as something that usually works. The recipes of witchery are matter-of-factly detailed, as are the fevers and divinations they inarguably produce. But Olumba's heroic battle is against a force deeper than magic—the death wish itself, the urge toward osmotic reabsorption into the encircling ocean of darkness wherein life is a precarious, thin-walled epiphenomenon. [Jan. 21, 1974]

> John Updike. *Picked-Up Pieces* (New York, Alfred A. Knopf, 1975), pp. 327–29, 331–32

Elechi Amadi's treatment of the supernatural is remarkable but not unique. Nearly all African novelists portray man as existing in mutual cooperation with other men, and in communion with the gods. This communion and cooperation between the human and the divine is important, and indeed, indispensable, for the realization of what [Wole] Soyinka describes as "cosmic totality," a relationship compounded by fellow men and supernatural essences, a relationship that is particularly vital for the African world-view.

However, in no other Nigerian novels have the gods been more dominant than in those of Amadi. Here the gods, uncanny, implacable, and ubiquitous, are not only an essence but a presence, woven as it were into every aspect of human relationship. In *The Concubine*, the sea-king intervenes even before the beginning of the story, and throughout remains the paramount but unseen force manipulating human life and orchestrating the painful course of men's tragic drama. The dreaded Ogbunabali breaks in halfway through *The Great Ponds*, and thereafter his power dominates human thought and action and pilots the very movement of the story. Consequently, in a vein reminiscent of early Greek tragedy and Victorian fiction, fatalism and its episodic surrogates of coincidence, omens, and premonitions loom large in the narrative.

> Niyi Osundare. In Eldred Durosimi Jones, ed. *African Literature Today*. 11 (1980), p. 97

Amadi's *The Slave* explores that which is central, relevant, and essential in the reclamation of black history and rehabilitation of black dignity, the presentation of a community pulsating with life of a self-sufficient and rich culture. . . .

In *The Slave*, form and content are both mutually expressive of the whole with the language as the abstract vehicle for expressing the myths, legends, art, and a whole way of life of a people. My interest is to see how Amadi presents through African aesthetics the complex interplay between the individual and his community. *The Slave* narrates the story of Olumati, grandson of the late village wrestling champion, Wakwakata, who returns to Aliji from Amadioha's shrine to reclaim his father's deserted inheritance. He struggles very hard to make a living and win recognition through palm-wine tapping and trapping. What success he experiences is largely due to the love of his sister Aleru, the constant help of his friend and brother-in-law Nyeche, and his own secret ambition to succeed and marry Enaa, the village beauty, whose *mgbede* or traditional seclusion parallels the duration of the novel. Aleru dies in her first pregnancy and sorrow devastates her brother and husband alike. His handicaps are many, and the last straw for Olumati is to learn of Enaa's betrothal to the village carver, Wizo, at the *mgbede* outing. Heartbroken and disconsolate, Olumati gives up the struggle and flees back to Amadioha's shrine at Isiala.

Amadi's language as vehicle for articulating the artifacts of a rich culture exhibits a remarkable fresh and symbolic texture, full of imagery, allusions to legends, to gods, feasts and festivals. . . .

Art in African aesthetics gives concreteness to religious beliefs and attitudes. Art in all its forms: music, dancing, carving, painting, and decorating are all collective and utilitarian, expressing collective emotions, enhancing the communal and corporate, celebrating communal beauty and creativity, and together heightening the aesthetic quality of life. In *The Slave*, Amadi skillfully welds together all the artistic tendencies and creativity of his community around the unifying traditional rite of puberty or *mgbede*. Since marriage and procreation are so central to communal survival, it is little wonder that the entire community is involved with Enaa's *mgbede*. She is the image of African beauty: tall, stately, graceful,

and a virgin. Nyeche, Eze Minikwe's son, who refuses Enaa because she is taller than him, admits that she is "a formidable girl, an Eze's daughter in style if not in fact."

Amadi is careful, not just to describe for us the beauty of *mgbede* but by weaving exciting natural dialogues between Enaa and the various visitors to her *mgbede* hut, we not only learn more about each character, but also through their eyes, gaze our fill at the intricate and delicate woman's world. Above all, the *mgbede* is but a physical symbol of communality. Enaa's girlfriends and age-mates have decorated the *mgbede*; age-mates of her brother have helped in rethatching the roof; everyone seems to have contributed gifts and food towards giving Enaa a two-year luxury treatment before marriage. In addition, the carver, Wizo, has spared no efforts nor talent in carving, free of charge, the best of stools and masks for Enaa's *mgbede*. . . .

African aesthetics becomes flesh and blood in Enaa. There is in her beauty a smoothness of skin, a joy of living, a lightness of heart, a grace and a style, that is in a special way African, superb in its uniqueness, excellent in its grandeur.

> Ebele Keo. *The Literary Criterion*. 23, 1–2 (1988), pp. 145–46, 148–49

The perpetual thwarting of man's most cherished desires and the disjunction between intention, action, and result; the role of chance and the gods in the affairs of men; man's mistaken understanding of his relationship with that which is other-than-man; and his helplessness before an overwhelming, blank, cosmos; these are the themes that all Elechi Amadi's three novels, *The Concubine*, *The Great Ponds*, and *The Slave*, explore. All three have the same large subject of past rural life in the southernmost part of Nigeria (the author's own area), a life that knew nothing about the white race. In this rural world, life is tranquil and moves on an even, traditional keel. But "even keel" only in the sense that it had yet to experience the disruptive presence of the missionary or colonist, for there abound frictions between one villager and another or a god, and between two neighboring villages. Except in the second novel, Amadi places such frictions within the fictional context of an unchanging universe.

The three novels are simple in construction, the stories told in the stark manner of mythical narratives. They convey the mystery at the core of human existence, once and for all foreclosed to man and always defeating his efforts at self-realization. This vision is manifested in the ironic plot of each novel and complemented by the enigmatic standpoint of the omniscient narrator. The cosmic blankness and the author's strict objectivity combine to limit any critic's effort at interpreting the novels; but if only for the evocation of pristine African life, their unusual thematic focus and ironic plots, Amadi's novels deserve more critical attention than they have so far received. Equally important is his smooth blending of elements from oral forms of narrative—myth, romance, folktale, legend—with that most characteristic mode of the novel, realism. . . .

Elechi Amadi's novels remain neglected and, when remembered, misinterpreted. If the neglect is understandable on account of their not contributing to the great debate on Africa's political present or future, the misinterpretation is harder to explain. In plot manipulation, narrative technique, and language, Amadi's art is a model of simplicity, while the stories themselves have the uncomplicated movement and clarity of daylight. Paradoxically, these qualities have misled his few critics into imposing their own, oftentimes arbitrary, meanings. No wonder that no two of Amadi's few critics agree on the meaning of any of his works.

Wole Ogundele. *World Literature Written in English*. 28, 2 (Autumn 1988), pp. 189–90

In Elechi Amadi's first two novels, *The Concubine* and *The Great Ponds*, myth enjoys only a haphazard relationship with history. Myth combines forcefully with mores to create an African ahistorical world that must delight every anthropological critic. . . .

One crucial aspect of Amadi's work that also deserves close attention is the activities of those ubiquitous beings in the traditional African landscape, the medicine men—recognized as *dibias* in the Igbo world-view. Their absence would vitiate the power of any claims to the ambience of a traditional African society. . . . In *The Great Ponds* and *The Concubine* these *dibias* live up to their position in traditional African societies. They attempt always to reinforce in various ways the occult vitality in nature, especially when human life is at stake. It is in these efforts that we also sometimes find those disagreeable elements that readers find unacceptable in Amadi's works.

There is something about Amadi's not talking about errors of government in his first two novels. This is not to say that there is something intrinsically wrong in an artist adopting that posture; however, sometimes (because of the nature of subject matter) it becomes imperative for an artist to recognize the necessity for some kind of ideological matrix or historicity in favor of the society whose mores are being represented. With reference to Amadi's *dibias*, the degree to which they succeed in manipulating nature and the critical and derisive comments attendant on their visions, practices, and failures suggest a certain kind of artistic levity with negative effects on the pictures being painted. Even though everything points to the practices of these *dibias* being cosmologically related to the outlook of the society, their exposure to crucial circumstances that challenge the veracity of their practices would not recommend them positively to any reader's judgement.

Chimalum Nwankwo. In A. L. McLeod, ed. *Subjects Worthy Fame* (New Delhi: Sterling Publishers, 1989), pp. 88, 91

Many critics have underlined Amadi's mastery of the English language and his skill in representing the supernatural in his novels. But few have studied the interaction between theme and style. Amadi's first three novels are set in traditional Africa before the coming of the white man. The supernatural is often introduced as one of the possible causes for the mysterious events that take place. Yet there is always more than one possible interpretation. Doubts remain concerning the natural, supernatural, rational, or irrational nature of the causes for these happenings. The reader has difficulty choosing between different explanations. . . .

It may appear that the notions of fantasy and realism are antithetical for the very reason that fantasy allows for the presence of doubts and maintains some hesitation in the reader, while ''realism'' aims at stating some ''truth.'' Yet, if we take the example of Amadi's novels, fantasy and realism are not incompatible. The writer merely diversifies the values and meanings of the world he describes, thus multiplying levels of reading. Amadi works from the inside and leaves the reader free to pick up the

contradictions and ambiguities in the events presented to him. Through using realism, he prevents the reader from relegating the characters to mere objects of superstition. In fact realism conditions the reader's hesitation between the natural and the supernatural. . . . Amadi does not try to make a stand against the rational skepticism of any reader. Instead he tries to present events as they appear to the characters in the society and at the moment in time concerned. He allies realism and fantasy and, thanks to the coherence of his style and themes, creates the illusion of the plausible.

Alfred Kiema. *Commonwealth Essays & Studies*. 12, 2 (Spring 1990), pp. 86, 89–90

*Sunset in Biafra* is a personal account of [Amadi's] experiences as a detainee during the [Nigerian Civil War], having been branded a saboteur and imprisoned by the Biafran forces. Through his chronicle we are provided a portrait of the experiences of non-Igbo minorities residing in Biafra: the repression, the abuses, the dangers of being too slow and unenthusiastic to embrace the cause. Whereas Amadi's civil war diary basically portrays the secessionist leaders as a militarily incompetent and intransigent group leading young Igbos to their slaughter, his portrait certainly seems to legitimize the horror which appears as a backdrop in [Flora] Nwapa's works.

The fear of voicing one's opinions about the war because of the threat of detention, of being branded a saboteur—the experience of the protagonist in Nwapa's *Never Again*—was only too real for Amadi. . . . The abuses that civilians suffered occurred on both sides of the conflict, and in the aftermath of the war, somehow lives had to be pieced together again, if at all possible. This concern is the theme of Amadi's civil war novel *Estrangement*.

The backdrop for this novel is the early days after the war has ended and Nigerians are returning to the cities they had fled earlier. Although the defeat of Biafra is not mentioned, we know by reference the historical context for the novel. *Estrangement* is a love story played out in the ruins not only of cities and villages but of lives irreparably damaged during those thirty months. A husband returns to Port Harcourt from refuge in Biafra only to find that his wife has been involved with a soldier and has given birth to this other man's child. The permanent estrangement that occurs when the husband rejects his wife is symbolic of the gulf between the pre- and postwar lives. For although each searches for a familiar place in previously abandoned homes, picking up where they left off is virtually impossible. Too much has changed the players in the drama. . . .

Although much of the novel reflects the efforts of ordinary people getting back to business as usual, for Ibekwe and Alekiri, their lives will not cross again. The activity of those surrounding them as well as their own efforts to salvage the rest of their lives apart from each other only heightens the gulf that wartime circumstances created, a permanent estrangement.

Maxine Sample. *Modern Fiction Studies*. 37, 3 (Autumn 1991), pp. 452–53

BIBLIOGRAPHY

*The Concubine*, 1966; *The Great Ponds*, 1969; *Isiburu; a play*, 1973; *Sunset in Biafra*, 1973; *Peppersoup; and, The Road to Ibadan*, 1977; *Dancer of Johannesburg*, 1978; *The Slave*, 1978;

*Ethics in Nigerian Culture*, 1982; *Estrangement*, 1986; *Elechi Amadi at 55: Poems, Short Stories, and Papers*, 1994

# ANGELOU, Maya (1928–)
**United States**

Maya Angelou's autobiography [*I Know Why the Caged Bird Sings*] . . . opens with a primal childhood scene that brings into focus the nature of the imprisoning environment from which the self will seek escape. The black girl child is trapped within the cage of her own diminished self-image around which interlock the bars of natural and social forces. The oppression of natural forces, of physical appearance and processes, foists a self-consciousness on all young girls who must grow from children into women. . . . The self-critical process is incessant, a driving demon. But in the black girl child's experience these natural bars are reinforced with the rusted iron social bars of racial subordination and impotence. Being born black is itself a liability in a world ruled by white standards of beauty which imprison the child a priori in a cage of ugliness. . . . I'm my own mistake. I haven't dreamed myself hard enough. I'll try again. The black and blue bruises of the soul multiply and compound as the caged bird flings herself against these bars. . . . If the black man is denied his potency and his masculinity, if his autobiography narrates the quest of the black male after a ''place'' of full manhood, the black woman is denied her beauty and her quest is one after self-accepted black womanhood. Thus the discovered pattern of significant moments Maya Angelou superimposes on the experience of her life is a pattern of moments that trace the quest of the black female after a ''place,'' a place where a child no longer need ask self-consciously, ''What you looking at me for?'' but where a woman can declare confidently, ''I am a beautiful, black woman.''. . .

Maya Angelou's autobiography comes to a sense of an ending: the black American girl child has succeeded in freeing herself from the natural and social bars imprisoning her in the cage of her own diminished self-image by assuming control of her life and fully accepting her black womanhood. The displaced child has found a ''place.'' With the birth of her child Maya is herself born into a mature engagement with the forces of life. In welcoming that struggle she refuses to live a death of quiet acquiescence. . . .

Once [Angelou] accepted the challenge of recovering the lost years, she accepted the challenge of the process of self-discovery and reconfirmed her commitment to life's struggle. By the time she, as autobiographer, finished remembering the past and shaping it into a pattern of significant moments, she had imposed some sense of an ending upon it. And in imposing that ending upon it, she gave the experience distance and a context and thereby came to understand the past and ultimately to understand herself. . . .

Her genius as a writer is her ability to recapture the texture of the way of life in the texture of its idioms, its idiosyncratic vocabulary and especially in its process of image-making. The imagery holds the reality, giving it immediacy. That she chooses to re-create the past in its own sounds suggests to the reader that she accepts the past and recognizes its beauty and its ugliness, its assets and its liabilities, its strength and its weakness. Here we witness a return to and final acceptance of the past in the return to and full acceptance of its language, the language a symbolic construct of a way of life.

Ultimately Maya Angelou's style testifies to her reaffirmation of self-acceptance, the self-acceptance she achieves within the pattern of the autobiography.

Sidonie Ann Smith. *Southern Humanities Review.* 7 (Fall 1973), pp. 367–68, 374–75

In many ways, *I Know Why the Caged Bird Sings* resembles Richard Wright's *Black Boy*. The setting is a small segregated town in the rural South; the parents have sent the children to live with relatives, one of whom owns a general store; Maya and her brother are forced to attend church, where they amuse themselves by making fun of the more zealous members of the congregation; the preacher comes to dinner and eats all the chicken; there is constant friction between the blacks and the poor whites; the fact of her oppression gradually intrudes on the writer's consciousness when she observes what happens around her—the hypocritical speeches of the white superintendent in their segregated school, the refusal of a white dentist to fix her teeth after her grandmother had salvaged his business; her brother helps fish a decomposed Negro body out of the pond while whites stand around and tell malicious jokes; the local sheriff gives them casual warnings whenever the Klan is about to go on a rampage; and finally, she migrates to a Northern city. Maya Angelou's complex sense of humor and compassion for other people's defects, however, endow her work with a different quality of radiance; she does not have Wright's mortal seriousness, or his estrangement, and does not take his risks. . . .

The distance in Maya Angelou's work is achieved by her sense of humor. She has the power of joking at herself, of re-creating the past in a comic spirit without belittling the other people involved and of capturing the pathetic and tragic overtones of the laughter without being overwhelmed by them. Frightened of a ghost story about the dead Mrs. Taylor, a woman who had always screamed her orders in the store because she was half deaf, Angelou remarks, ''the thought of that voice coming out of the grave and all the way down the hill from the cemetery and hanging over my head was enough to straighten my hair.'' As in Langston Hughes, the humor is often a way of shattering racist images by using them. She knows that the ''superstitious'' dread Negroes are supposed to have for graveyards is the butt of racist jokes and has felt the perpetual torture of trying to make her hair conform to white standards of beauty; both experiences are subdued, and controlled, by the comic purpose. It is the fear, and the author's ability to laugh at her insecurities, that we remember most—the caged bird's mastery of her song.

Stephen Butterfield, *Black Autobiography in America* (Amherst: University of Massachusetts Press, 1974), pp. 203, 209

When Maya Angelou started her autobiographical series in 1970 with *I know Why the Caged Bird Sings*, she naturally chose her childhood as the organizing principle of her first volume. The story of *Caged Bird* begins when the three-year-old Angelou and her four-year-old brother, Bailey, are turned over to the care of their paternal grandmother in Stamps, Arkansas, and it ends with the birth of her son when she is seventeen years old. The next two volumes, *Gather Together in My Name* and *Singin' and Swingin' and Gettin' Merry Like Christmas*, narrate Angelou's life along chronological lines for the most part, and one would expect that her most recent addition to the autobiographical sequence, *The Heart of a Woman*, would proceed with the account of her career as entertainer, writer, and freedom fighter. In many ways, Angelou meets her readers' expectations as she follows her life forward chronologically in organizing the newest segment in the series. Yet it is interesting to note that at the beginning of *The Heart of a Woman*, as she continues the account of her son's youth, she returns to the story of her own childhood repeatedly. The references to her childhood serve partly to create a textual link for readers who might be unfamiliar with the earlier volumes and partly to emphasize the suggestive similarities between her own childhood and that of her son. Maya Angelou's overwhelming sense of displacement and instability is, ironically, her son's burden too. . . .

In *The Heart of a Woman*, Angelou deliberately strives to capture the individual conversational styles of her relatives and friends. In a sense, her friends and acquaintances become "characters" in the story of her life, and like any good writer of fiction, she attempts to make their conversations realistic and convincing. With some of the people who figure in her autobiography, there is no objective measure for credibility other than the reader's critical appreciation for life itself. If the conversant in question is not well-known beyond the scope of the autobiography, Angelou need only ensure that the dialogue attributed to the individual be consistent with his character as delineated in the text itself. Yet many of her friends and associates were either highly successful celebrities or popular political figures, and the conversations recorded in her life story have points of reference beyond the autobiographical text. In other words, readers can test the degree of verisimilitude in the recorded dialogues with either firsthand knowledge or secondhand sources of information about the celebrities' lives.

It is highly probable, for example, that many of Angelou's readers are already familiar with the rhetorical styles of Martin Luther King, Jr., and Malcolm X, and the popular lyrics of Billie Holiday. In fact the lives of these three people in such accounts as *Why We Can't Wait, The Autobiography of Malcolm X*, and *Lady Sings the Blues* have in many ways become part of our contemporary folk history. Angelou adds a personalized quality to her recollections of conversations with these individuals and many others. The record of their conversations in *The Heart of a Woman* brings them to life again, because the autobiographer is sensitive to and even somewhat self-conscious about the accurate reconstruction of their individual styles.

Since memory is not infallible, fictionalization comes into play whenever the autobiographer reconstructs or, perhaps more correctly, re-creates conversation. While the autobiographer relies on invention, he or she creates the illusion of an infallible memory that records exactly the feel of a place and the words spoken there.

Carol E. Neubauer. *Black American Literature Forum*. 17, 3 (Fall 1983), pp. 123–25

The first three days Angelou spends in Ghana serve as a microcosm for the dream-nightmare opposition at work in the book [*All God's Children Need Traveling Shoes*] as a whole. In 1962, at the age of thirty-three, Angelou and her seventeen-year-old son Guy arrive in Accra full of expectations. Suddenly, tragedy scuttles Guy's plans to begin attending the University of Ghana and Angelou's intentions to go on to a job in Liberia. . . . As a result Angelou stays in Ghana to care for Guy, getting a job as an administrative assistant at the university. *All God's Children* describes the two years she spent in Ghana before leaving to take a position as a coordinator for Malcolm X's Organization of Afro-American Unity. Two major topics dominate the book: first, the Afro-American expatriate community's relations with both Africans and the Black Movement in the United States; second, Angelou's personal quest for connection with Africa. The two topics occasion the use of a number of romantic images. . . . Angelou spends most of her time with the Afro-American community, whom she calls the "Revolutionary Returnees." These Afro-Americans view Africa romantically, as a home, a heaven, and a mother. For example, because of their African descent, the Returnees believe they have a filial claim to Africa. . . . However, very early in the book the possibility that the expatriates are living in a dream world, having to invent connections with Africans rather than actually experiencing them is suggested: "We had come home, and if home was not what we had expected, never mind, our need for belonging allowed us to ignore the obvious and to create real places or even illusory places, befitting our imagination.". . .

Thus it seems that the connection Angelou and other Afro-Americans in Ghana have sought will not be realized, that she will depart from Africa disillusioned and alienated. . . . But then, right before leaving, she has an experience that reverses everything. While driving near Keta, Angelou has presentiments of something strange attaching to the region. She refuses to drive over a bridge and later learns that bridges in the area a hundred years previously were so poorly constructed that many people lost their lives because of them. A little further on a woman addresses her in Ewe, begins to wail upon learning that Angelou is an American, and shows her to other women who react the same way when they hear where she is from. Not only do Angelou's face and voice resemble those of people in the area, but during the slave trade some of the inhabitants of the region were transported to the New World. Angelou clearly believes that the elusive connection has at last been made: "I had not consciously come to Ghana to find the roots of my beginnings, but I had continually and accidentally tripped over them or fallen upon them in my everyday life." This realization comes just in the nick of time, for her stay in Ghana and the book itself end soon afterward. Angelou closes *All God's Children* with sentences that imply that her romantic quest for an African homeland has been successful: "Many years earlier I, or rather someone very like me and certainly related to me, had been taken from Africa by force. This second leave-taking would not be so onerous, for now I knew my people had never completely left Africa."

Although not a lie . . . this ending seems too easily manufactured at the last minute to resolve the problem of the book. The fact that Afro-Americans came from Africa was never in question. Angelou and other black Africans journeyed to Africa to establish viable and ongoing connections; despite Angelou's memorable epiphany at Keta, this is not accomplished. . . . Angelou experiences disillusionment and alienation in Africa. However, instead of stressing the nightmare side of Africanist discourse as her predecessors do, Angelou represses these feelings, refuses to relinquish her romantic image of Africa, and opts for the dream side of Africanist discourse.

John C. Gruesser. *Black American Literature Forum*. 24, 1 (Spring 1990), pp. 15–16, 18

A study of the work of Maya Angelou, autobiographer and poet, shows how the writer uses autobiography to define her quest for human individuality, identifying her personal struggle with the general condition of black Americans and claiming a representative role not only in relation to black Americans, but also in relation to the idea of America. Thus, through a study of her work, one gains a closer access to American cultural history. I find no precedent in American letters for the role Angelou has chosen and developed for herself. That is to say, I know of no American writer who has decided to make her or his major literary and cultural contribution so predominately in autobiographical form.

Through the device of autobiography, Angelou has celebrated the richness and vitality of Southern black life and the sense of community that persists in the face of poverty and racial prejudice, initially revealing this celebration through a portrait of life as experienced by a black child in the Arkansas of the 1930s (*I Know Why the Caged Bird Sings*). The second delineates a young woman struggling to create an existence that provides security and love in post-World War II America (*Gather Together in My Name*). The third presents a young, married adult in the 1950s seeking a career in show business and experiencing her first amiable contacts with whites (*Singin' and Swingin' and Gettin' Merry Like Christmas*). The fourth volume (*The Heart of a Woman*) shows a wiser, more mature woman in the 1960s, examining the roles of being a woman and a mother. In her most recent volume, Angelou demonstrates that *All God's Children Need Traveling Shoes* to take them beyond familiar borders and to enable them to see and understand the world from another's vantage point. . . .

Maya Angelou's significance as an autobiographer rests upon her exceptional ability to narrate her life story as a human being and as a black American woman in the twentieth century. In doing so, as one critic has observed, Angelou is performing for contemporary black and white Americans many of the same functions that an escaped slave like [Frederick] Douglass performed for nineteenth-century audiences through his autobiographical writings and lectures. This is [to] say, both Douglass and Angelou function as articulators of the nature and validity of the collective heritage as they interpret the particulars of a culture for a wide audience of both black and white Americans. Moreover, Angelou illuminates the black experience in an American context and in meaningful relation to the parallel and converging experiences of white Americans. In doing so, she provides her audiences with a fuller realization of the black American consciousness within the larger context and demonstrates that, as people who have lived varied and vigorous lives, black Americans embody the quintessential experiences of their race and culture.

> Dolly A. McPherson. *Order Out of Chaos: The Autobiographical Works of Maya Angelou* (New York: Peter Lang, 1990), pp. 5–6, 128–29

It was the culmination of a number of factors at the end of the 1960s that led to the outpouring of writings by Afro-American women. First, the inherent short-comings of the nationalism of the Black Power Movement; second, the increased social and economic pressures that led to the rapid deterioration of the urban centers of America; third, the rise of the feminist movement that made Afro-American women more conscious of their particularity; and, fourth, the increasing tensions in black male-female relations. . . . All of these factors led to a special kind of problematic to which the Afro-American woman had to address herself, adding a new and dynamic dimension to American literature. . . .

It is out of these conditions and in response to these specific concerns that Maya Angelou offered her autobiographical statements: *I Know Why the Caged Bird Sings*, *Gather Together in My Name*, *Singin' and Swingin' and Gettin' Merry Like Christmas*, *The Heart of a Woman*, and *All God's Children Need Traveling Shoes*. Although her last two works examine the manner in which the events of the 1960s impacted upon her life, they were produced in a time when some of the social and political fervor of the 1970s had abated and thus allowed for a more sober assessment. Needless to say, the political currents of the time are more prominent in the last two segments of her statement. As a statement, Angelou presents a powerful, authentic, and profound signification of Afro-American life and the changing concerns of the Afro-American woman in her quest for personal autonomy, understanding, and love. Such a statement, because of the simple, forthright, and honest manner in which it is presented, is depicted against the larger struggle of Afro-American and African peoples for their liberation and triumphs. It is a celebration of the struggle, survival, and existence of Afro-American people.

> Selwyn R. Cudjoe. In Henry Louis Gates, Jr., ed. *Reading Black, Reading Feminist* (New York: Meridian, 1990), pp. 284–85

BIBLIOGRAPHY

*I Know Why the Caged Bird Sings*, 1970; *Just Give Me a Cool Drink of Water 'Fore I Diiie*, 1971; *Gather Together in My Name*, 1974; *Oh Pray My Wings Are Gonna Fit Me Well*, 1975; *Singin' and Swingin' and Gettin' Merry Like Christmas*, 1976; *And Still I Rise*, 1978; *The Heart of a Woman*, 1981; *Shaker, Why Don't You Sing?*, 1981; *All God's Children Need Traveling Shoes*, 1986; *Mrs. Flowers: A Moment of Friendship*, 1986; *Now Sheba Sings the Song*, 1987; *I Shall Not Be Moved*, 1990; *Life Doesn't Frighten Me*, 1993; *On the Pulse of Morning*, 1993; *Wouldn't Take Nothing for My Journey Now*, 1993; *The Complete Collected Poems of Maya Angelou*, 1994; *My Painted House, My Friendly Chicken, and Me*, 1994; *Phenomenal Woman: Four Poems Celebrating Women*, 1994; *A Brave and Startling Truth*, 1995; *Kofi and His Magic*, 1996; *Even the Stars Look Lonesome*, 1997

# ANTHONY, Michael (1932–)
## Trinidad and Tobago

*The Games Were Coming* suffers from a heavy dose of Hemingway, so much so that it is sometimes difficult to tell whether Mr. Anthony intends a parody. The centre of the story is the fifteen-mile bicycle race of the Trinidad Southern Games. Leon has given up everything, including his girl, to fulfil his dream of winning the race, and when the girl seeks distraction elsewhere she goes a little too far and becomes pregnant by her employer. Leon, all unknowing, has promised to marry her if he wins, and his victory therefore takes on a double meaning, for it will keep her from shame and the streets. This is a plain tale simply told, and it should have been more complicated; Mr. Anthony is quite good on Carnival, and on the actual running of the race. But too much stylistic understatement does not hold up the rather unsubstantial narrative.

Peter Cohen. *Spectator* November 22, 1963, p. 674

For his second novel Mr. Anthony, a West Indian writer, has set himself the difficult task of presenting adult relationships as seen through the eyes of a sensitive and reflective twelve-year-old boy. It is to his credit that *The Year in San Fernando* is a thoroughly convincing and pleasing book. The boy, Francis, is sent from his village in Trinidad to the town of San Fernando to act as the servant-companion of old Mrs. Chandles. Coming from the limited environment of his small village, he is at first overwhelmed by everything, by the town itself, and by the complexity of the relationships existing between the adults he meets—between Mrs. Chandles and her two sons, Linden and Edwin, and between Linden Chandles and the two women, Marva and Julia. The reader shares the transformation with Francis, as significant patterns gradually emerge from a kaleidoscope of general impressions, and as his awareness and understanding of these relationships grow.

In carefully maintaining the physical and social perspectives as they would be apprehended by a young boy, Mr. Anthony shows that he has an instinct for telling detail, seen to particular effect in the descriptions of the daily scene in San Fernando and in the development of Francis's friendship with Julia.

M. Macmillan. *Journal of Commonwealth Literature.* September 1965, p. 175

[Anthony] is no literary tyro awaiting discovery. On the contrary, he has already chalked up three novels of more than usual merit and one can only despair that they have not won him wider recognition. Possibly this is because the particular virtues of his work, a scrupulous regard for truth at the expense of false drama and a lucid unflamboyant style, no longer appeal to a reading public almost exclusively hooked on a diet of sex, fantasy and hokum. Even so, as a West Indian writing of his native Trinidad, he might well have expected more attention from those critics who once embraced the Caribbean cult as feverishly as they now swallow tales of proletarian lust and squalor. It was not to be, however, and in the face of their continued neglect, it seemed that at least one immigrant novelist had missed the boat, if not to England itself where he has now settled, certainly to the sort of critical acclaim scored by a number of his fellow expatriates. But this, I fancy, may have had less to do with a shift in fashion than with the fact that the books themselves, although touching on the most inflammatory issues, allowed little scope for the airing of those social and political shibboleths so beloved by progressive writers.

The truth is that Mr. Anthony seems blissfully unaware that the accepted role of the Negro writer in our society is to propagandize, scarify and aggravate that burden of guilt in which—or so it often appears—the truly dedicated White liberal takes such masochistic pleasure. Consequently it would seem that his work is not so much inspired by any deep sense of racial injustice as by the desire to celebrate the beauty of his country, illuminate its social and cultural features, and portray its people as they really are, not as so many symbols of colonial exploitation, but as ordinary human beings who, pigmentation aside, might also be the less privileged natives of Brixton or Huddersfield. The pity is that such a persuasive and

enlightened approach will be largely ignored by a society weaned on the notion that anger is the only effective weapon against ignorance and prejudice.

Frank McGuiness. *London.* April 1967, pp. 117–18

[Like George Lamming] Michael Anthony is another novelist in exile whose sustenance is back in the West Indies. Indeed, this is even truer of him than it is of George Lamming. For, whereas the latter's dialectical concern leads him to the *roman à thèse*, for which the highly conceptualised situation suffices, Anthony has been drawing on his childhood in South Trinidad. The differences between their work stem directly from this: Lamming's novels are involved in design and style, Anthony's are delicate and straightforward, written as it were for the finely attuned ear; Lamming's appeal is to the intellect, Anthony's to a discriminating sensibility. And in his delicate recall of West Indian rural childhood, Michael Anthony recaptures its innocence and its fragility, thus exploring a vital area of experience through which exploration the Trinidadian, and I believe the West Indian, is better able to understand the nature of his sensibility.

To the imaginative fund out of which he writes, his sojourn in England could add nothing new—save that it could make more compelling and etch into sharper focus those values which, in the author's view, informed that childhood. Nor, indeed, can such a fund be inexhaustible. One can only hazard guesses, but my own feeling is that as the moment of that exhaustion draws nearer Michael Anthony's peculiar genius would be better served if he were in the West Indies rather than outside. He has recently taken up residence in Brazil, and if it is true that that country still retains a quality of innocence, then it is sure to sustain the freshness of his imagination and keep him along congenial paths.

A. D. Drayton. *Literary Half-Yearly.* January 1970, pp. 77–78

The New World intellectual, according to the Argentinian writer, Ezequiel Martínez Estrada, lives even more divorced from the small sufferings and daily lives of the people than his European counterpart. He understands this suffering with his intellect. . . . In this sense, Michael Anthony, like Samuel Selvon, is of all the West Indian writers, the least "intellectual." As ethnically "negro" as Selvon is "East Indian," Anthony in his novels, as Selvon in his short stories, fulfils the potential of that *cultural* fusion which is the unique imperative of being a Trinidadian, a West Indian, a New World man, i.e. the inevitable prototype of man in the future; if that future survives. . . .

*Green Days by the River* portrays consciously this unconscious and unaware *creole* fusion. The book is a long short story rather than a novel. It is simple in style and at times its simplicity palls— people laugh too much, are amused too often. But these are irrelevant faults compared to the fact that the book is accessible to the people whom he writes about. Made into a film, *Green Days by the River* would draw the interest and involvement of the young generation of West Indians. One can envisage the camera evoking what Anthony calls the "strange world of forest and shade." The book is penetrated with sun, the river Ortoire, sluggish with alligators—real? or imagined?—the cashew trees under which the young boys gather; their rivalry as they pelt at the thick stems or circle Rosalie Gidharee at the dance.

Sylvia Wynter. *Caribbean Studies.* Jan., 1970, pp. 111–14

The boy's vision [in *The Year in San Fernando*] suffuses elements of experience which we are habituated to seeing as disparate or indeed as belonging to opposed categories, like nostalgia-anticipation, town-country, pure-sordid. . . . Anthony is committed in *The Year in San Fernando* to involving us in the feel of a peculiarly open state of consciousness; and this is achieved by a scrupulous adherence to the boy's point of view, in a deceptively easy style that carries the necessary sensuous burden as well as sustaining the illusion of adolescent reportage. . . .

We might say that *The Year in San Fernando* continuously leads us away from a settled notion of the person to a more liberal view of latent and only sporadically realized possibilities. As on the level of character, so with respect to object and event: one of the effects of Anthony's narrative technique in *The Year in San Fernando* is to promote a vision for the reader in which each ''known'' factor in experience is restored to a more primordial condition of latency.

It is here I think that the astonishing originality of *The Year in San Fernando* lies. The image of Francis, deprived, and tethered to the Chandles house (even to having a lair below the house), in a circumscribed world of which he is trying to make sense, is an image of the condition of the modern West Indian. But out of this distress, Anthony has created an archetypal situation. On the one hand, there is the pattern of growth and natural progression suggested by the spontaneous metaphorical activity of the novel's language. On the other, there is the narrator's extreme openness to the possibilities of experience, marked by Francis's capacity for shock. Through the boy's consciousness Anthony induces us to make the confession of weakness, of unknowing, by which an unstable world is transformed into the flux of re-creation.

Kenneth Ramchand. *The West Indian Novel and Its Background* (New York: Barnes & Noble, 1970), pp. 212, 221–22

Michael Anthony's stories [in *Cricket in the Road*] are rich in tropical atmosphere and most of them explore, with an ''innocent eye,'' the world as seen by the child. They are short and lyrical and are more concerned with pin-pointing perceptions and emotions than with developing character or a strong story-line. Feelings are described with great simplicity—sometimes, it seems, with deliberate naivety—and the storms of childhood rage gently within a rather frail, bone china cup. But this shouldn't lead one to underestimate them: frequently, in stories like ''The Valley of Cocoa'' and ''Cricket in the Road,'' the simplicity is both delicate and convincing.

Chris Waters. *New Statesman.* November 9, 1973, pp. 696–97

BIBLIOGRAPHY
*The Games Were Coming,* 1963; *The Year in San Fernando;* 1965; *Green Days by the River,* 1967; *Cricket in the Road, and Other Stories,* 1973; *Sandra Street, and Other Stories,* 1973; *King of the Masquerade,* 1974; *Streets of Conflict,* 1976; *All That Glitters,* 1981; *The Chieftain's Carnival and Other Stories,* 1993.

# ANYIDOHO, Kofi (1947–)
## Ghana

The creative writing clubs established in secondary schools and training colleges across Ghana in the 1960s, and the new avenue provided by public readings and recitals of poetry have together contributed to the emergence of many new poetic voices in Ghana. One of the most notable is the winner of the first prize in the 1976 VALCO Literary Awards contest, Kofi Anyidoho. Like Kofi Awoonor, an Ewe, Anyidoho has absorbed much traditional Ewe poetry; but they both constitute extensions of that mode, for their individual stamp is discernible in their verse. In the case of Anyidoho, this is represented by a toughness of texture, an ability to explore variations of a single theme. . . .

Anyidoho's is poetry of the speaking voice. More than Awoonor but definitely less than [E. Y.] Egblewogbe, he reveals a tendency to the elegiac. . . . The theme of death and destruction is pervasive; the mood is predominantly gloomy, the tone somber. But Anyidoho's treatment of funereal themes does incorporate sometimes a critical detachment from the subject, a hint almost of macabre humor and satire. . . .

Even in poems with foreign settings, Anyidoho shows little joy. Invariably, we are given tragic forebodings, a sadly depleted patrimony, the agony of a wanderer struggling to get back home. . . . Anyidoho leaves an impression of moroseness, although he is not as fatalistic as Egblewogbe. He lacks Awoonor's occasional explosions of joy, even in his lighthearted excursions into abuse.

Jawa Apronti. In Kolawole Ogungbesan, ed. *New West African Literature* (London: Heinemann, 1979), pp. 40–41

Kofi Anyidoho's letters from America are now reprinted as ''My Mailman Friend Was Here,'' part four of *A Harvest of Our Dreams,* his second volume of verse which Heinemann [has] recently issued. The book confirms one's impression of his stature. Anyidoho returned from America more than a year ago, was in London in November, but his chosen abode, his own plot of rootedness, is Ghana, where he now lectures in the English department at Legon. More precisely, however, it is Wheta, that village of talent which, in the Volta region, nudges Keta into the sea. It is here that his art begins, and, so he would have us believe, ends. . . .

Anyidoho belongs to a generation which has lived to see its political hopes betrayed again and again, by Kwame Nkrumah (who remains a beguiling memory) by [Colonel I. K.] Acheampong, possibly even by [Jerry J.] Rawlings. It is in a threadbare Ghana that he must now ply his craft, drawing deep at wells of disappointment fed, as he never ceases to remind us, by ancient springs. If Ayi Kwei Armah is the prose chronicler of Ghana's decline, Anyidoho is its pallbearer. The poignancy of his accompanying dirge is at times almost unbearable. . . .

This volume contains three principal groups of poems. ''Elegy for the Revolution,'' a sequence first published separately by the Greenfield Press in 1978, and here reprinted at the end of the book, recounts the fading hopes of the last years of the National Redemption Council. Immediately before it comes a group of poems from the [United States], many of them contrasting the Ghanaian and American revolutionary legacies, the dearth that lies at the foot of the Thanksgiving table.

Other revolutions make fleeting appearances, notably Iran's, thus occasioning an arguably misjudged salute to Khomenei. [It] is with the most recent pieces, however, that the volume begins, poems which address themselves to the current dilemma of a people plighting their last troth in a regime which has promised to pluck the talisman of regeneration even from the Devil's jaws. . . .

In the face of all discouragement, Anyidoho holds his vision steady. For behind the despair is a calm grounded on the bedrock of a tradition he will not forsake. And, if the future is hazy, here is a writer who knows that for him there is but one way through, guided by the elder poets of whose rippling chants *A Harvest of Our Dreams* can provide but a distant echo, dimmed by the perplexities of our time.

Robert Fraser. *West Africa.* March 4, 1985, pp. 420–21

Much of the funereal gravity of [Ayi Kwei] Armah's vision of history finds its way into the inflections of Anyidoho's [*Elegy for the Revolution*]. The "Revolution" of the title was the overthrow in January 1972 of the democratically elected civilian government of Dr. Kofi Busia by Colonel I. K. Acheampong, whose National Redemption Council had itself, six years later, lost every shred of credibility with which the Ghanaian people had once endowed it. . . .

The typographical highlighting of key phrases, the tone of curdled regret, the oblique use of autobiographical anecdote are all typical of the method of this first collection which shows Anyidoho, surely the brightest representative of his generation, still searching for an exact personal idiom in which to do lyrical justice to his sense of dereliction. In the meantime, the poem operates by brilliant flashes: the two dogs circling one another like politicians sniffing the rump of opportunity, the "young veteran," already senile in hopeful scheming, and the pig which serves as a sardonic sacrifice to the doomed journey ahead. It is the "old peasant hoe in hand," who has already lived through so many violent, remote changes and in whose name the insurrection has nominally been staged, however, who earths the poem. At the time of writing the poet was a mature student of linguistics at the University of Ghana, where he had gone after several years of teaching Ewe and English. The pieces which eventually found their way into *Elegy for the Revolution*, published during the author's postgraduate studies in Indiana, are hence Accra poems invoking a ruined urban landscape. It is from Anyidoho's home district of Wheta in the Volta region, towards which his art would increasingly turn, however, from which these pieces derive their value system and their stubborn independence of thought.

Anyidoho possesses what can only be called a subversively provincial eye. At the very moment when the metropolitan demagogues are at their most deceptively strident, his attention will fix itself on the despised, silent northern servant as he reports for duty from his rudimentary backyard quarters in order to dance attendance on the argumentative employer who takes himself for the vanguard of the new revolutionary elite. . . .

Like all of his contemporaries Anyidoho grew to maturity against the distant rumblings of the Algerian War of liberation and the independence struggles in Asia and Africa. By the age of twenty-nine, when the majority of these poems were written, he had already lived long enough to see most of these aspirations reduced to tatters. Under the first impact of disappointment, his early poetry veers between the satirical and elegiac in a way that is not always satisfactory. . . .

Much of Anyidoho's most potent verse evokes [a] sense of isolation among kinfolk, the knowledge that he will always bear the birthmark of a hounded destiny. . . .

But Anyidoho's poetry is only dissenting in the quite special sense allotted to those who know that all human hopes and designs are prey to inscrutable and divisive forces. In the strongest of his pieces, the sensation of being set apart by a remorseless inner mania nevertheless constantly seems to aspire toward definitive political declaration.

Robert Fraser. *West African Poetry* (Cambridge: Cambridge University Press, 1986), pp. 301, 303–4, 339

[Anyidoho] possesses a certain ardor of thought and feeling which is the result of a young mind with solid convictions, solid insights, and solid values. Perhaps this is why his poetry is dominated by a complex range of moods. One can say he writes "mood poetry," a concept not unrelated to mood expressions associated with jazz. It is not also by coincidence that "Earthchild" (the title poem in his third collection [*Earthchild with Brain Surgery*]) was written under the influence of jazz and expresses a variety of complex tones and moods. Similarly, in *A Harvest of Our Dreams*, the total atmosphere is dominated by shades of brooding cynicism. This edition, it must be pointed out, also incorporates his first collection of poems (*Elegy for the Revolution*), and therefore one can trace in it a certain development in the poet's consciousness of "mood poetry." . . .

[It] would be totally wrong to think that Anyidoho's poetry is all fire and storm. Certainly, it is not all anger and frustration, significant though these are in his works. There is a relieving dimension of serenity and quietude, a serenity which celebrates those quiet moments of the human frame and the tender emotions which possess it or give it life. Human emotions of love, tenderness, loneliness, and anxiety are depicted as potentially explosive, equally destabilizing. However, the difference here is that the poet exercises a control of craftsmanship in his shaping of ideas and emotion, particularly in bending these to the beauty of words.

Kofi Agovi. *Presence Africaine.* 142 (1987), pp. 168–70

Anyidoho's books of poems, *Elegy for the Revolution, A Harvest of Our Dreams*, and *Earthchild [with Brain Surgery]*, speak of and with sentiments and sensations that recall, to some extent, those of Ghana's older writers, like the poets Kwesi Brew, Kofi Awoonor, and Atukwei Okai, and the novelist Ayi Kwei Armah. In light of this, it is significant that Anyidoho includes in his texts epigrams from the writings of his older compatriots. . . .

In the aftermath of independence, poetic concepts of nationality would bring forth, first in Brew and Awoonor and, subsequently, in Anyidoho, a multiplicity of images of harvest. . . .

Whether one is reading the long poem "Soul in Birthwaters," "A Piece of Hope," "Festival of Hopes" [in *Elegy for the Revolution*], or "Seedtime," "A Harvest of Our Dreams," "Akofa," and "Moments" [in *A Harvest of Our Dreams*], or "My Song" and "The Rise of the New Patriot" [in *Earthchild*], one is confronted with a poetry that breathes with extraordinary metaphors of hope. Indeed . . . it is a poetry that brings a new dimension to the phenomenon of hope and the expression of it. Thus, to take examples at random from the poems "Back to Memory," "Upon the Harvest Moon," and "The Passion-Gulf," all from *Elegy*, which reader of English poetry ever heard of "a festival of hope," "once upon a hope," or "boatfuls of hope"? Yet these and similar linguistic surprises or transgressions abound in Anyidoho, and serve to enrich thought, sentiment, and expression: they enable a creative link to be established between poet and ancestral time, a time of freedom and of fulfillment. The essence of that Motherland time is continuingly underscored by other verbal innovations, namely a succession of images and metaphors: covenant, dawn, hunting, laughter, and umbilical cord. These and other figures of speech, essentially the heartland of Anyidoho's creativity, are ethnic-oriented and earthbound. In other words, they allow a certain textual delirium to prevail and to give the sensation of oneness with earth in general and with the natural, animistic elements and mythologies of the poet's [homeland] in particular.

> J. Bekunuru Kubayanda. *Legon Journal of the Humanities.*
> 3 (1987), pp. 63–64

*AncestralLogic & CaribbeanBlues* reinforces the qualities for which Anyidoho is well known. Focusing on Africa and Africans of the diaspora, the poet appropriately uses African folklore for the formal, linguistic, and imagistic reinforcement of his Afrocentric ideas. . . .

The poet's preface, "IntroBlues," sets the sad tone for poems about the condition of Africans both in the diaspora and on the home continent. The poems are divided into three major sections: "CaribbeanBlues," "AncestralLogic," and "Santrofi Anoma." They move from travel abroad to the African home, from the historical and geographic to the philosophical. This also corresponds with a movement from the past to contemporary issues.

The "CaribbeanBlues" section opens with a remembrance of the Taino, a native Caribbean group wiped out by the European settlers. Written in 1992 on the five-hundredth anniversary of the so-called discovery of the Arawaks by Christopher Columbus, these poems evoke memories of pain for both the native Caribbeans and the Africans brought there as slaves. Writing mainly travel poems, the poet moves through the Dominican Republic, Haiti, and Cuba. He says, "The Haitian *Batey* / Is a living Wound / In the throat of the Sugar Mill." In the Dominican Republic he hears a Bakongo voice in the drums. There is irony suggested in the discrepancy between the natural beauty of the Caribbean region and its turbulent, sad history. The poet pays tribute to the heroic struggle of the oppressed people of the area.

"AncestralLogic" contains perhaps the two most moving poems in the collection. The speaker of "Lolita Jones" is an African-American who chastises Africans for not acknowledging the great pan-African achievement of Kwame Nkrumah. This poem in black American English evokes strong pan-African sentiments. "Air Zimbabwe: En Route Victoria Falls" treats European colonization of Africa and its aftermath. The third and final section deals with topical issues ranging from "DesertStorm" to military rule and political development in contemporary Africa. The poems here do not move so much as do those of the two earlier sections, maybe because the events are still very close and also because there are many philosophical statements. Santrofi, the dilemma bird of Akan mythology, seems to reflect the current plight of Africans. Dedicated to Jack Mapanje, who was perhaps still in jail at the time the poem was written, "Santrofi" relates the dangers of being an

artist in Africa, a fate suffered by, among others, [Wole] Soyinka, Ngugi [wa Thiong'o], and [Kofi] Awoonor. "Husago Dance" deals on a personal level with the existential theme of life and death. . . .

The collection represents a major development in Anyidoho's poetic career. The language is witty and strong, the images drawn from African folklore and environment give concrete form to the poet's Pan-African ideas, and the expression of Pan-African experience and perspective is most fulfilling in its orality, passion, and use of African (Ewe) proverbial and other oratorical figures.

> Tanure Ojaide. *World Literature Today.* 68, 1 (Winter 1994), pp. 191–92

[The] Ewe dirge tradition is an intrinsic element of [Anyidoho's poems in *Earthchild*]. . . . Nevertheless, the dirge impulse proceeds beyond the fact of death, for it projects into what could be described as a synthesization of sadness and hope in terms of projecting beyond current sorrow into the future. The issues of sadness and hope in Anyidoho's collection of poems entitled *Earthchild* remind us of the themes of. . . . Osundare's *Waiting Laughters*. But Anyidoho subsumes his own laughter within the ambiance of sorrow, thus making the hope connotative rather than declamatory.

The opening poem, "Fertility Game," is a lament in the true Ewe dirge tradition as the persona insists with a refrain, "come back home Agbenoxevi come back home." The implication is that "Agbenoxevi" will return, and in the third stanza the hope in that expectation becomes symbolic. . . .

The voice of Agbenoxevi is expected to "rise deep across the years" and even "thunder through deserts and painfields." It is that reference to "pain fields" which highlights the trope of sadness, for it could be said to be a "field" where there was tremendous suffering or an image of the terrible tribulations of the people. However, the ideas that those "who died" would "live again" or that those who die "wake up with seeds of life sprouting from their graves" portray the poet's concept in the utilization of the Ewe dirge tradition to comment on present reality and generate hope. Anyidoho also strives to incorporate the varied mores and norms of the oral traditions in the bid to reflect both the orality and the thematic purposes in the poem. In the later segments of the poem, the persona indicates that "Each midnight moonlight night I walk naked / to the crossroads," and this reference recalls a traditional ritual of propitiation or even expiation that is expected to attract rewards. But more important, this poem illustrates what has been identified as the achievement of lyricism through "the organization of verse in such a way that it has an incantatory and mournful effect". This incantatory effect reveals the use of a persona from both the traditional angles of character and subject matter to create arresting poetry.

The sorrow prominent in Anyidoho's poetry is not an end in itself, for in the poem "Honeycomb for Bee children," the persona stresses that for "every dirge Adidi sang / I now must weave a song of new birth-cords" and reaffirms later in the same poem that "long before the reign of thunderclouds / we were rainbow's favoured child." This optimistic note and the theme of hope in the exploitation of the dirge tradition may not be clear to the reader who merely glances at the titles of some of the poems. Anyidoho, for instance, gives some poems such titles as "A Dirge for

Christmas,'' ''A Dirge for our Birth,'' and ''A Dirge of Joy,'' thus illustrating the possibilities in the utilization of paradox and irony in the exploration of the Ewe dirge tradition. Christmas, births, and joys are normally socially associated with happiness and merriment but in their association with the ''dirge'' in those poems Anyidoho is not only calling attention to the unreliable nature of contemporary reality but also to the fact that pleasure and pain, or sadness and hope, sometimes possess indistinct boundaries. The underlying elements of poetic objectives in these instances of paradox are thus portrayed through such statements as: ''so let alone our Poets / To mourn Christmas with chants of Easter songs'' (''A Dirge for Christmas'') and ''Now we ask our mothers to confirm / the things our grandmothers say. / We beg our children to tell us who we were'' (''A Dirge for our Birth''). The statements therefore generate the view that ''these dirges kill our little Joys'' (''A Dirge for Joy''), which confirms their ironic implications but not at the expense of hope. Anyidoho is clearly distinct in his use of this dirge tradition because he proceeds beyond the normal association of the dirge. . . .

In addition, the nature of these dirges reveals a poetic dimension that is significant. Eustace Palmer notes that Anyidoho's ''favourite themes are the brutality of regimes, social disintegration, the betrayal of the revolution, the destruction of optimism, the conflict between tradition and Christianity, the clash of contrasting life styles, social deprivation, persecution of innocence and injustice in general'' and he also adds that ''he can be personal too''. It is the use of this personal voice in a manner that widens its horizon which makes Anyidoho's poetry interesting. Thus the dirges could be interpreted to refer not only to Ghana but to humanity in general, although the basic inspirational incidents originated in Ghana. Kofi Awoonor confirms in his essay ''Three Young Ghanaian Poets'' that Anyidoho's ''clear understanding of Ewe dirge has widened his own primary appreciation of the substance of the lyrical form of lament as both a personal and a public statement.'' Thus in the poem ''The News From Home,'' the poet affirms hope when he states:

I have not come this far
only to sit by the roadside
and break into tears
I could have wept at home
without a journey of several thorns

The hope projected here by the dirge is related to the stubborn will for survival even in the midst of social devastations. Later in the same poem, the poet insists: ''And I am tired / tired of all these noises of / condolence from those who / love to look upon the anger of the hungry / nod their head and stroll back home.'' This attitude accounts for the view at the end of the poem that ''those who sent their funeral cloths / to the washerman / awaiting the mortuary men to come'' will ''wait for the next and next / season only to see how well earth children grow fruit and flower,'' which is a reiteration of the hope of survival in spite of sadness. The socio-political issues are clearly the substance of these dirges, and in this instance when the poet writes of the ability of ''earth children'' to ''grow fruit and flower,'' his reference could be extended communally to other societies, other groups, and other peoples who portray signs of survival in their cultures despite enormous disasters.

Ezenwa-Ohaeto. *Research in African Literatures*. 27, 2 (Summer 1996), pp. 70–83

BIBLIOGRAPHY
*Elegy for the Revolution*, 1978; *A Harvest of Our Dreams*, 1984; *Earthchild with Brain Surgery*, 1985; *The Pan African Ideal in Literatures of the Black World*, 1989; *AncestralLogic & CaribbeanBlues*, 1993

# ARMAH, Ayi Kwei (1939–)
## Ghana

*The Beautyful Ones Are Not Yet Born* turns on the purgatory of a railway clerk (we never learn his name) who will end his days as a railway clerk because he carries the terrible burden of principle in a climate of ethics that permits advancement only under the table. . . .

Armah's handling of the clerk's ordeal is, to put it mildly, unusual. In fact, quite a few readers are going to find it revolting. For his message almost seems to be that power corrupts while absolute power defecates. The extent to which Armah relies on human waste to symbolize the decay of personal integrity is all but breathtaking—and this can, if you wish, refer to holding the nose. In brief, it really hits the fan.

This is literary talent? You bet it is. And I say that as one who finds most scatalogical prose not only disgusting but badly written. It calls for no small gift to expound on excreta and neither offend nor bore, even greater ability if this unlovely topic is to be made valid within the context of a novel. Armah brings it off, his objective being, of course, to convey a moral lesson—by highlighting his protagonist's uncompromising ethical rectitude through personal fastidiousness. To the clerk, going to the toilet is a nightmare, not only because the public lavatories which he uses happen to violate every rule of hygiene but because they also represent, in a very physical sense, the moral contamination which surrounds him—sometimes even tempts him in its foul way—and against which he must always be on guard. Armah has treated a most indelicate function with remarkable skill—and force.

Charles Miller. *Saturday Review*. August 31, 1968, p. 24

One could say that perhaps Mr. Armah has allowed his revulsion [in *The Beautyful Ones Are Not Yet Born*] to influence his use of visible symbols to describe the less visible but general decay of the people and the country. Even a ''bad'' Ghanaian (one who does not believe in the national uniqueness in all things) could find it difficult to accept in physical terms the necessity for hammering on every page the shit and stink from people and the environment. One has encountered similar and even worse physical decay in other parts of the world. Though again, like the fate of the workers, this does not make it any easier to put up with. But somehow one feels a slight unease that the ordinary people should be subjected to the rather hyperbolical exposure which this book makes. There are quite a few angles from which one can judge cleanliness, including the emotional and clinical. For instance, quite a few people might prefer to live any day in the city or town which forms the background to the book than in Santa Monica, near Los Angeles, with its cold, sterilized cleanliness. The choice may be between a pigsty and an expensive mortuary, of course.

What is clear, then, is that whatever is beautiful and genuinely pleasing in Ghana or about Ghanaians seems to have gone unmentioned in *The Beautyful Ones Are Not Yet Born*. Yet, what kind of beauty is that which is represented by a human being like that avaricious tinsel of an Estella? Or what could be pleasing in the heartless betrayal of a people's hopes? And can there be anything at all beautiful about the generation which does this betraying? Is it not true also that, when an atmosphere is polluted anyway, nothing escapes the general foulness? Besides, one has to grant Mr. Armah that there is a nightmarish possibility that a full awareness of all this can become so crippling, that its effect on even a potentially active individual might be to make him want to withdraw completely into himself—a tendency the Teacher already betrays and which this rather obscure and almost redundant figure in the book imparts to "the man."

> Christina Ama Ata Aidoo. Introduction to Ayi Kwei Armah, *The Beautyful Ones Are Not Yet Born* (New York: Macmillan, 1969), pp. xi-xii

[The protagonist in *The Beautyful Ones Are Not Yet Born*] is an epitome of the pathos and despair of the African who is caught up in the situation that Franz Fanon has brilliantly dealt with in *The Wretched of the Earth*: the African revolution has been betrayed at every turn. The only thing that has changed is the internal composition of the class of political masters. The underdog still suffers because national resources have yet to be harnessed and redistributed in a way that would meaningfully improve the lot of the man in the street.

The translation of such a dialectic into imaginative literature is not easy, especially when one's hero is so shadowy that when he engages in dialogue with other nameless characters (for instance with the naked man in Chapter Five) the reader is exposed to a lot of potential confusion. But there is enough evidence of Ayi Kwei Armah's competence as a writer to make one believe that he could have made satisfactory literature out of this material. The atmosphere of gloom is quite convincing, as is the fundamental pessimism and cynicism. . . .

In the end, the reader joins the unheroic hero in pondering (Chapters Nine and Ten) over what the African Revolution has done to its promises. This is a question all right-thinking Africans should ask themselves. They should seriously examine Ayi Kwei Armah's attempt at an artistic appraisal of this theme and should on no account be put off merely by the superabundance of filth in it. For it is important to condemn the book solely on artistic grounds and to protest only where one finds some elements that have not been effectively pressed into the service of art.

> Jawa Apronti. *The Legon Observer*. March 14, 1969, p. 24

The hero of *Fragments* is a passive man. He is a "been-to," an African who has been abroad. He is returning from America, where he has studied, and where he decided to become a writer. He also has had a nervous breakdown in the States, and needs a special drug to counter any attack. Baako is a symbolic African figure, the educated young man torn between the values of the old and new. But the distinction that Armah brilliantly shows is that even the new values have turned. In early African novels of colonialist Africa when the educated hero returned to his country he was adrift. He belonged neither to his tribesmen nor the British who acknowledged his education but never accepted him socially and

personally. Such heroes, in African novels, usually ended in despair and often self-inflicted violence. Now the "been-to" returns to his own country but finds the corrupt bureaucracy has changed from a white British to a black Ghanaian skin. . . .

The novel, while a powerful moral indictment of the present state of his country, makes its force felt through symbolism, not direct propagandistic means. This use of symbology is both Armah's weakness and virtue. The killing of a dog, the capture of gulls, the unfinished house in the hills—all these take on added layers of sense, as in a tone poem or painting—and sometimes the result is a wonderfully sensuous appreciation of the dissociation of life, the inward nature of each individual, the ultimate unknowingness of things. Yet the technique is so richly used that it becomes a drug. The pictorials, the moments are resonant phrases tossing suggestively in a dream.

I think the novel fails of its promise—for [*The Beautyful Ones Are Not Yet Born*] promised more than fragments. It still succeeds as a tone poem of powerful allegorical force.

> Martin Tucker. *New Republic*. January 31, 1970, p. 26

A careful reading of [*The Beautyful Ones Are Not Yet Born*] will not sustain [Christina Ama Ata Aidoo's] generalization that there is Ghanaian excrement, filth, and stink on every page, not even if we expand the disgusting objects to include other kinds of painful and ugly sights and unpleasantnesses of various sorts. And it is *not* clear that "whatever is beautiful and genuinely pleasing in Ghana or about Ghanaians seems to go unmentioned." . . .

What keeps this novel, with its rather sad action and its multitude of images of excrement and nastiness, from giving an overall impression of disgust, or depression, or even from seeming ridiculous or incredible? Well, there are a number of qualifying elements in the novel, elements which make a chord with the sad events and the more repugnant images, which help to make much beauty out of the ugliness. First, there is the gentleness, the kindness, the self-critical lovingness of the man, at once the main character of the novel, and its central intelligence and reflector, in whose mind we stay continually throughout the novel. His kindly thoughts for his wife, his children, his Teacher, and the poor and wretched of Ghana permeate the novel. . . .

Another qualifier of the harshness of the events and the repugnant images is the style of the novel. It is not a colloquial style, as might seem appropriate for the low-colloquial level of much of the vocabulary. Neither is it a harsh, staccato style, which would perhaps seem to fit some of the excremental and nasty language. It is a style of high rhetoric, fairly formal, a distinctly literary style, with a rhythm that swells and soars a bit. It is a style with language generally elevated, with allusions and referents of considerable portentousness. . . .

Another qualification: the images of excrement and filth always cluster around the corrupt Ghanaians, the bribers and the crooks, the party men and the white men's apes, the calloused and the brutal. . . .

Every reader must decide for himself about the total effect of Armah's *The Beautyful Ones Are Not Yet Born* in accordance with his literary intuition, his taste, his reading experience. For one reader at least the novel is splendid, one of the two or three best to come out of Africa, one worthy of a place of honor among the novels of its time in the whole world. And the images of excrement and nastiness, which are so conspicuous in the novel, find their justification in the mode of fiction Armah has chosen to write in and in the fact that they are skillfully qualified by other elements. . . . Even if "the beautyful ones" are *never* born in his country, Armah has made from the dirt and the despair, from the corruption and the foulness of all sorts, a beautiful work of art.

Harold R. Collins. *World Literature Written in English.* November 1971, pp. 45–47, 49

*The Beautyful Ones Are Not Yet Born* is a symbolic moral fable. What strikes one most forcefully, is the strength of the author's moral earnestness. On almost every page, in unusually vigorous and realistic language, Armah expresses his nausea at the corruption he sees everywhere. The symbolic nature of the characters and the vagueness of the setting reinforce the impression of a moral fable. Indeed, the temptation to compare this work with *Everyman* or Bunyan's *Pilgrim's Progress* is very strong. The characters are important not for what they are in themselves, but for what they represent. Most of them are very vaguely particularized and indicated by generalized names. The hero himself is known only as "the man," and is referred to variously as "the watcher," "the giver" and "the silent one." His immediate dependants are called "the loved ones," and one of the most important characters is called "the teacher." Although Maanan, Oyo, and Koomson have names, it is clear that their function is mainly symbolic. Ghana is itself symbolically presented, one of the consequences being that Accra is much less vividly described than the Lagos of Achebe or Ekwensi. But this deliberate vagueness makes it similar to *Everyman's* "Field Full of Folk" or Tutuola's "Land of the Deads.". . .

At the centre of the novel is the hero—the man—whose anonymity represents everyman, the ordinary Ghanaian citizen. He is a man of unquestioned integrity. . . . Nevertheless, Armah, far from idealizing his hero, demonstrates his passive impotence, and weakness. . . .

Although there can be little doubt that Armah makes his point about corruption in Ghana, the novel is not without its weaknesses. *The Beautyful Ones Are Not Yet Born* consists largely of the man's reflections, and the various impressions which impinge on his senses. But these impressions and reflections are about one thing and one thing alone—corruption and the rottenness that goes with it. Consequently, the novel seems to have a peculiarly theoretical and didactic quality, with the doctrine about corruption being persistently hammered into the reader's brain.

Eustace Palmer. *An Introduction to the African Novel* (New York, Africana, 1972), pp. 129, 131, 141

*Why Are We So Blest?*, by Ayi Kwei Armah, is more of an inspired travelogue than a novel. The real journey that the author deals with, however, is an uneasy one taken by Modin, a young African intellectual, in and out of the peripheries of revolutionary involvement. Modin is a young man inspired not by hope but by a death wish. One of the revolutionary bureaucrats declares in his Algiers office after Modin's first visit with his white American mistress: "He is one of those intellectuals who wants to die. He should have the courage to do it himself."

There is an obsessive preoccupation with black-white sexual relations throughout the book and the author offers far too many unnecessary and repetitive clinical details, which in the end produce yawns instead of fresh insights. This novel, unlike the other two by Armah, is one bereft of genuine emotions. Somehow in dissecting characters, situations, settings, there is an absence of tension. It demonstrates the sterility of a purely intellectual involvement in revolution, sex or life itself.

Jan Carew. *New York Times Book Review.* April 2, 1972, p. 14

Armah has already established himself through his first two novels as one of the leading West African novelists. *Why Are We So Blest?* not only confirms that evaluation, but caps his earlier achievements with an even more brilliant work. He is still working with the same counters, his own very personal experiences and a resultant sense of almost over-whelming despair, but he continuously pushes these counters into a larger public arena. He is like one of his characters, looking for "the kind of truth which merges all things and reveals the day's solid rock as only the pliable clay in the larger changing patterns of ages."

Written as a journal, the novel is built around the lives of three central characters, Solo, Modin and Aimée. Solo, a disillusioned revolutionary, is living in the country of Afrasia (read Algeria) supporting himself as a translator and doing occasional work for a group concerned with the liberation of the African Portuguese colonies from which he himself has come. Alternating with sections from his journal are journals of Modin, an African educated in the United States at Harvard, and his white American girl friend, Aimée. Modin and Aimée come to Afrasia to work for the liberation group, meet Solo and are put off by his cynicism. As the novel progresses we see all three being trapped in the cages of racism they strove to avoid. . . .

Many will read anti-white sentiments into [Armah's] treatment of Aimée. But neither the individual characters nor the book as a whole should be seen in terms of a simple black-white dichotomy. On an ethical level we can in fact see it as a carefully planned attack on all racism, but esthetically we can also apprehend it as a sensitive exploration into the minds of three alienated individuals and the web of relationships which created their respective sensibilities.

Richard Priebe. *Books Abroad.* Autumn 1972, p. 724

Since the publication of his first novel, *The Beautyful Ones Are Not Yet Born*, in 1968, there has been little dispute that of all the younger African novelists, Ayi Kwei Armah is one of the most talented. Now six years later, with the publication of a fourth novel, *Two Thousand Seasons*, it is clear that Armah is not only one of the most prolific contemporary African novelists, but also one of the most highly original—certainly the major prose stylist from Anglophone Africa. . . .

*Two Thousand Seasons* is an unfinished chronicle of Africa's servitude—two thousand seasons (wet and dry), one thousand years of struggle—against the invaders from the north, first the Arabs and then the Europeans: "a thousand seasons wasted wandering amazed along alien roads, another thousand spent finding paths to the living way." It is also a parable of epic proportions—in many ways more like an oral tale told by a griot, a song of life and death, than a realistic story as Armah's earlier works have been. Or, to put it still another way, *Two Thousand Seasons* is the first African novel—the first novel an African would have written several hundred years ago if Africans were writing novels then, the African version of the initial meeting with the West. . . .

His temporal thrust is intentionally confusing. One thing is clear, however. The two thousand seasons are far from being completed. They didn't end with the 1960s when so many African nations became independent. They won't end in the 1970s or the 1980s. And that is another reason why *Two Thousand Seasons* is such a fascinating novel. I have called it the first African novel because, historically, it describes the initial African reaction to the West, but it is also a novel about Africa today. And tomorrow, regrettably.

For Armah himself this is all quite a change from his earlier works—a continuous evidence of his growth as a writer, his ability to strike into new areas and not to write the same novel over and over again as so many writers (not just African writers) do throughout their careers. Instead, Armah has written a totally original work, the most significant book of his career—a complete break from his earlier works.

Charles R. Larson. *Africa Today.* Spring 1974, pp. 117, 119

[*The Beautyful Ones Are Not Yet Born*] is a well-written book. Armah's command of language and imagery is of a very high order indeed. But it is a sick book. Sick, not with the sickness of Ghana, but with the sickness of the *human condition.* The hero, pale and passive and nameless—a creation in the best manner of existentialist writing—wanders through the story in an anguished half-sleep, neck-deep in despair and human excrement of which we see rather a lot in the book. Did I say he *refused* to be corrupted? He did not do anything as positive as refusing. He reminded me very strongly of that man and woman in a Jean-Paul Sartre novel who sit in anguished gloom in a restaurant and then in a sudden access of nihilistic energy seize table knives and stab their hands right through to the wood—to prove some very obscure point to each other. Except that Armah's hero would be quite incapable of suffering any seizure.

Ultimately the novel failed to convince me. And this was because Armah insists that this story is happening in Ghana and not in some modern, existentialist no man's land. . . . But his Ghana is unrecognizable. This aura of cosmic sorrow and despair is as foreign and unusable as those monstrous machines Nkrumah was said to have imported from Eastern European countries. Said, that is, by critics like Armah.

True, Ghana was sick. And what country is not? But everybody has his own brand of ailment. Ayi Kwei Armah imposes so much foreign metaphor on the sickness of Ghana that it ceases to be true. And finally, the suggestion (albeit existentially tentative) of the hero's personal justification without faith nor works is grossly inadequate in a society where even a lunatic walking stark naked through the highways of Accra has an extended family somewhere suffering vicarious shame.

Armah is clearly an alienated writer, a modern writer complete with all the symptoms. Unfortunately Ghana is not a modern existentialist country. It is just a Western African state struggling to become a nation. So there is enormous distance between Armah and Ghana. [1973]

Chinua Achebe. *Morning Yet on Creation Day* (Garden City, New York: Doubleday, 1975), pp. 39–40

Ayi Kwei Armah's first three novels, *The Beautyful Ones Are Not Yet Born, Fragments,* and *Why Are We So Blest?*, sought to expose political and social corruption not only in contemporary Ghana but in Africa as a whole. On the other hand, his fourth novel, *Two Thousand Seasons*, delves into the past and in one majestic sweep of Africa's history seeks to demonstrate how those pure African values and traditions which used to exist in an almost prehistoric past were destroyed through the exploits of Arab predators and European destroyers. The similarity with [Yambo] Ouologuem is obvious; but where the anti-Négritudist Malian author seeks to dispel all the myths about African history, declaring that black notables, no less than Arab and European conquerors and imperialists, were responsible for the historical degradation of the continent, Armah adopts an essentially Négritudist position, the net effect of his presentation being the total condemnation of the Arabs and Europeans as the destroyers of the pristine values of a pure Africa. It is true that even in Armah's work there are indications that the black people had started losing "the way" before the advent of the predators and destroyers; indeed there is a suggestion . . . that their subjugation by the imperialists was itself the consequence of the black people's loss of the way. But the venom Armah directs at the imperialists, a venom unequalled in African literature, and the constant reference to the imperialists as the destroyers, indicates that he lays the blame squarely at their door. It would be a remarkable twist of fate if the anglophone writers begin their flirtation with Négritude at precisely the moment when the francophones seem to be abandoning it; for this exercise in racial retrieval, this attempt to rediscover a glorious African past unadulterated by all those forces associated with the imperialists, is now to be detected, not just in Armah, but to a certain extent in Ngugi [wa Thiong'o] and in some of [Wole] Soyinka's recent pronouncements.

Eustace Palmer. *The Growth of the African Novel* (London: Heinemann, 1979), pp. 221–22

Armah's stance against corruption, neocolonialism, and imperialism is not couched in terms that can in any sense be called moderate. It is decidedly militant or radical in the sense that it is expressed in vigorous, harsh, passionate, and uncompromising terms. Armah is a revolutionary but he is not a Marxist writer. No informed reader can deny that *Two Thousand Seasons* is influenced by Marxism. . . . It can be argued, for instance, that his ideological stance is consonant with socialism insofar as he takes a clearly partisan line—he is decidedly on the side of the oppressed. It is also arguable that the view of African history presented in *Two Thousand Seasons* is consistent with historical materialism. According to the Marxist conception of history, man has passed through various stages of social development from primitive communalism through slave societies, feudalism, capitalism, and socialism to the highest and final stage which is yet to be achieved—communism. In Armah's book African history passes through similar phases. The first stage is marked by an idealized form of egalitarianism when the people followed the way—this is the phase which inspires the prophetess Anoa. She wants the African people to return to the values of that period. The next decisive stage follows the period of contact between Africans and the Arabs. It was this phase which marked the rise of zombis, askaris, and other forces of oppression. It was also through the influence of the Arabs that kings like Koranche arose to oppress the people. The period of contact with Arabs is followed by the coming of the destroyers from the sea who bring with them capitalism, colonialism, and the slave trade. This phase is followed by the neocolonial phase when leaders like Kamuzu have replaced colonial rulers. Then comes the stage of an armed liberation struggle which gives rise to hopes of a genuine return to the way. This final stage is the millennium which the African people should hope for and fight for. It is a stage which parallels [Karl] Marx's vision of a classless society under communism.

> Emmanuel Ngara. *Art and Ideology in the African Novel* (London: Heinemann, 1985), pp. 112–13

Looking at the portraits of the women and the roles they play [in his novels] is one way of tracing the measure of resolution Armah finds in each text as he moves towards a greater understanding, or a more articulate explication, of the central problems he is exploring in all his works. For Armah, all oppression (whether social, political, or cultural) is a form of disease, and the source of all division among mankind. In each of his texts the same two fundamental problems are explored—the conflict between the private and social worlds in modern Africa and the crisis of divided loyalties this creates, as well as the difficulty, for the sensitive individual, of ordering the oppression and chaos of contemporary life into a comprehensible framework which takes account of the past as well as the present.

So far as the portraits of women are concerned, in all five novels [*The Beautyful Ones Are Not Yet Born*, *Fragments*, *Why Are We So Blest?*, *Two Thousand Seasons*, and *The Healers*] the division between parasites and prophets is stark. True to Armah's equation of things white with evil, and black with spirituality, the parasites are either Westernized African women, or, as in the case of Amy Reitsch in *Why Are We So Blest?*, both Western and white. The prophets are those women who are seen as being true to the aspirations of black African people, true to the ancient "way" that has long since been forgotten. In the two earliest novels, the female parasites are the mothers, wives, and sisters of the heroes. That is, they are always attached to the hearth. [It] is these "loved ones," as they are called, who are portrayed as the burden on the soul of the struggling and suffering hero. They are, whether intentionally or not, seen as the oppressors. They make demands, generally material ones concerned with keeping up social appearances, which always provoke a storm of conflict in their men. Pitted against them are the liberating prophets. This conception of them springs primarily from the literal role they play in the fourth novel, *Two Thousand Seasons*, the only work in which women ever initiate any action. In that novel, the voices of the prophets are female, and, at several crucial moments in the history being recounted, it is the women who save the nation, often in battle against the men. Yet, though their roles are not always so prominent, the other novels do contain women who are, in great and small ways, contending with oppression—their role being to understand their men in adverse circumstances, and, wherever possible, guard them and give them solace. They are liberating prophets in the sense that, even when

powerless, they have a vision which can protect their men and at least steer them in the direction of some kind of salvation.

> Abena P. A. Busia. In Carole Boyce Davies and Anne Adams Graves, eds. *Ngambika: Studies of Women in African Literature* (Trenton, New Jersey: Africa World Press, 1986), pp. 90–91

To approach Armah's daring experimentation with the techniques of African oral narratives from the critical assumptions governing discussion of the European novel is to mistake both the formal design and the spirit of the book. Few novels create deliberately unmemorable characters who are merely functions of a collective will or ramble episodically over vast spans of time in pursuit of racial destinies. Even fewer novels start from the premise that certain groups, nations, or races and their colonial underlings have engrossed most of the human vices and are wholly predictable because helpless before the evil of their own natures. Abandoning critical investigation for partisan invective, Armah makes no claim to criticize his "destroyers" and "predators" and their African quislings but simply hurls abuse at them, more after the fashion of the Ewe *halo* than that of Western satire. These features are, more often, the stock-in-trade of epic, saga, and chronicle, both in the African oral tradition of the griot and in its written European equivalents: namely, those Homeric and Norse marathons which similarly trace the migrations of whole peoples and celebrate the founding of nations and empires. Doubtless, some Western scholars would claim, however, that the latter use stock epithets with more ironic discrimination and with a more novel-like, fair-minded openness to the variety of human experience than are to be found in *Two Thousand Seasons*.

Armah's self-consciously staged griotlike discourse is concerned to correct the method of narrating African history as well as the history itself. There are, therefore, some significant departures from storytelling traditions. The author's avowedly anti-elitist standpoint shuns the griot's customary glorification of the matchless deeds of past heroes, which is derisively parodied by [Yambo] Ouologuem and, as Isidore Okpewho has observed, rejects the supernatural along with the superhuman and denies the narrator's single creative personality any domineering proprietorship over the events narrated. Armah's discourse makes communal and egalitarian ideals not only potentially realizable in the contemporary world but so certain to be achieved that the goals can be described as having already been won. His world-view is essentially secular and humanist. His narrative strategy emphasizes the griot's self-effacing assumption of a common identity with both the specific audience which his tale is designed to educate and the characters of the tale itself. Thus *Two Thousand Seasons* is not only *about* reciprocity; its technique *enacts* reciprocity between the storyteller, his tale, and his listeners.

> Derek Wright. *Journal of Commonwealth Literature.* 23, 1 (1988), p. 95

Ayi Kwei Armah's novels . . . are built around historical frames, and thus we can easily move in the direction of an ethical, even a literal analysis of thematic structure. Essentially, all his novels deal with individuals caught in the web of economic, cultural, and political forces dominating colonial and postcolonial Africa. To the extent, however, that we try to see these forces in terms of some European-African axis, we oversimplify and misread what Armah is doing. . . .

Ayi Kwei Armah's second novel, *Fragments*, contains what appears to be a perversion of the monomyth. Baako, the hero, is educated in the United States, an area which his people see as "a region of supernatural wonder." He returns to them with "a decisive victory"—namely, his degree—which gives him "the power to bestow boons on his fellow man." Baako himself does not perceive his journey in this light, but his family and friends do. The power he sees himself as possessing is a spiritual one, having nothing directly to do with the material benefits his people desire. Simply recognizing variations of the monomyth in Armah's work is not a useful exercise, but it is significant that much of his writing deals with characters who live on the margins of society in opposition to the values by which those inside society live their lives. In *The Beautyful Ones Are Not Yet Born*, "the man" confronts the futility of being good in a corrupt world. In *Fragments*, Baako confronts the futility of existing as a bearer of a spirituality the world has lost, and Modin, in *Why Are We So Blest?*, confronts it in revolutionary action. To paraphrase James Joyce, each of these heroes goes forth to encounter the reality of experience and forge in his soul the uncreated mythos of his race. . . .

Leaving aside for the moment Armah's heroes, we can see that the structure, or more accurately, the anti-structure of the societies he has rendered in each of his novels is a photographic negative of a well-ordered society. Without any idealization, in *Arrow of God* and *Things Fall Apart*, Chinua Achebe has depicted societies in which we could conceive of living; in *The Beautyful Ones Are Not Yet Born* we see a society from which we could desire only to escape. . . .

Ultimately, of course, there is no way of proving that Armah should not be read literally, but to do so means we must deny not only the rich symbolic complexity of his work, and thus his poetic genius, but also his African sensibility, the very particular way in which he sees the world as dynamic configurations of complementary opposites. In other words, we can look at the landscape of the man, the madness of Baako, or the sadistic torture of Modin as correlating directly to the real world and inducing us to accept an essentially nihilistic philosophy; or, we can look at these negations as symbolic action directed against an existing order, as essentially revolutionary, and hence inducing us to accept an apocalyptic orientation. If we accept Armah's images as symbolic action, it does not mean that we must totally discount their literal implications. The torture of Modin at the hands of the French soldiers can, and in fact should, be seen as a very real extension of white racism. But if we simply look at these images without also rationally discounting their literal reality, understanding that the work is fiction and not life, we can see them only as a monotonous, though grotesque, catalogue of negatives and fail to catch the vitality they have on an artistic level.

> Richard K. Priebe. *Myth, Realism, and the West African Writer* (Trenton, New Jersey: Africa World Press, 1988), pp. 21–24, 30

[The] integral structure [of *The Healers*] is based on mythmaking, through which it attains symbolic proportions. In fact, Armah

superimposes on its history of the Asante Empire a mythic level which is crucial to a full understanding of the novel. Since "a myth always refers to events alleged to have taken place in time" and "explains the present and the past as well as the future," the two intentions of myth and history are compatible. *The Healers* demands mythic interpretation, but it is informed by no classical European myth. In fact, Armah had already used myth, on a limited basis, in his earlier novels. In *Two Thousand Seasons* and *The Healers*, however, he embarked on a full-scale program of mythmaking. *The Healers* makes several references to traditional beliefs and practices, and habits of thoughts or behavior, which derive their origins not from the Greco-Roman myth of course, but from the African background. The novelist's overt purpose in mythmaking is to offer a dynamic impetus to the formation of a new social order and a new political ideology in which the collectivity, as opposed to individual achievement, competition, or manipulation, plays a leading role. In the writing of *The Healers*, Armah's imagination was unmistakably mythopoeic; mythmaking serves as an intensification of mood, a clarification of characters, and as a form of perception which brings his material to artistic concentration and endows his scenes with depth and liquidity. Armah's mythmaking thus exhibits both the "philosophic" and the artistic properties of myth in general. It proposes an admittedly individualized version of a people's ethical and cosmic vision, and it does so with narrative forms typical of myth's arbitrary plot (here the journey or quest), characters of heroic grandeur, and nature's complicity in the drama.

Armah's mythic didacticism is governed by two complementary arguments, one destructive, the other constructive. The first is "demythification." In presenting the rivalry and fragmentation of the Asante Empire and its failure to prevent British conquest, Armah demolishes currently prevailing myths which eulogize the government and society of that period. For its purpose, the novel relies on history—recorded fact in abundant detail—for support.

The constructive or positive myth is illustrated by Armah's dexterous interjection of a new, idealized society in which the only path to a harmonious and lasting survival is that of a communal consciousness and the total integration of individual feelings with collective life. Such a society is represented by the community of "healers" and their inspirational work in the novel.

> Ahmed Saber. In Jonathan A. Peters, Mildred P. Mortimer, and Russell V. Linnemann, eds. *Literature of Africa and the African Continuum* (Washington, D.C.: Three Continents Press, 1989), pp. 5–6

Ayi Kwei Armah is a mythmaker. Mythmakers make myths. They do not tell of past actions: They create fables to explain the past. They reorder past events to become meaningful to a people. They create the past linking their history with it. . . .

If [the creative artist] is a mythmaker, he first creates a destiny for his people. Then all defeats are interpreted as battles lost during the course of the long way whose final victory would belong to his chosen people. His people could be as rude, uncivilized, as the Trojans. They could be chased out. And, after traveling the seas, some of them could land near Rome: fatherless and motherless. They could be bastards, outcasts, what-have-you. Wolves would be invented for their foster mothers. The future glory of Rome, at a later date, would be attributed to them. Destiny is the controlling theme: a future glory whose quest makes the momentary sufferings one goes through insignificant and bearable.

This is why *Two Thousand Seasons* was invented for us. African governments have failed us, every one of them. Those which were around when *The Beautyful Ones* was written, had failed us. Failed us in terms of not matching aspirations with performances. Now, twenty years later, they are none the wiser.

Taban lo Liyong. *Journal of Commonwealth Literature.* 26, 1 (1991), pp. 14–15

Armah may have learned in a roundabout way that African writers who discuss "their work and themselves quite willingly, sometimes even eagerly" seek for something far less trivial than fame and its privileges: they cry out for their message of hope, often the African point of view, to be heard in no uncertain terms. Armah, however, has properly taken his place among writers who, in [D.S.] Izevbaye's words, "create taste for [their] own type of literary compositions by prescribing literary criteria and standards which are often more valuable in the appreciation of [their] own works than for the criticism of other works." A possible grouping of Armah's work of this category could be: the review essays "The Definitive Chaka," "The Caliban Complex," and "Battle for the Mind of Africa"; incidental responses to criticism of his work, including "Larsony or Fiction as Criticism of Fiction" and "The Lazy School of Literary Criticism"; sociopolitical theories, as elaborated in "African Socialism: Utopian or Scientific?" and "The Festival Syndrome"; and such items as "One Writer's Education" and "Interview with Dimgba," which basically provide biographical insights on the writer.

Such a classification, though, is neat and simplistic; it is only valid as a convenient tool of analysis, because all the writings are linked by an obsessive preoccupation with the question of Africa's future. Armah isolates the colonization of the mind of the African—with all the attendant inferiority complexes—as the most devastating legacy of colonialism, an approach that is cultural, as opposed to the materialist view, which lays emphasis on economic exploitation. These are the issues with which the writer is concerned in his novels and short stories as well.

Ode S. Ogede. *World Literature Today.* 66, 3 (Summer 1992), p. 439

Most critics agree that Ayi Kwei Armah wrote his first three novels in a modernistic Western style. The protagonists are estranged individuals looking for footing in a postcolonial Africa; they want to change a society that meets them with indifference. The intertextual subtexts are traditional African myth and legend, but the technique is recognizable from *Ulysses* or *Under the Volcano*.

In his last two novels, *Two Thousand Seasons* and *The Healers*, Armah used an oral narrative strategy. . . .

If there is mimetic illusion in these novels, it is found on the level of the narrating. Just as in his third novel, *Why Are We So Blest? Armah* has gone to great length to give the fictive narrative situation an illusion of mimesis. Even if the situations in the later novels are very different from the earlier ones, the mimetic effort from the author is the same, or at least, its purpose is: to make the narrative situation as real or convincing as possible.

The story, on the other hand, never tries to be anything but the raconteur's individual retelling of already-known facts and events—according to the African concept of orature—as opposed to literature. Typical of that tradition, much explicit commentary on the story and the narrating by an overt narrator occurs in both late novels—unlike the early three novels, where the narrator only implicitly comments on the story and the storytelling. In *The Healers* the storyteller addresses his audience in this fashion: "Could it be true there really was an army of white soldiers, a ghostly army actually marching against Kumase the never violated city this time?". . . These kinds of explicit comments are far more frequent in *Two Thousand Seasons*, however.

Only *Two Thousand Seasons* is we-narrated; an individual narrative-voice is never discernible. The narrator is extremely evident throughout the text, but always narrating with a we. After a prologue, the first word of the text is "we.". . .

The narrator asks frequent rhetorical questions of a fictive audience: "How many died quieter deaths that night with daggers stuck in their throats? How many tried to vomit poison?" That technique is, of course, characteristic of oral storytelling, where audience participation is a necessary part of the performance. However, it is the ontological liberties this narrator allows himself that make this novel so unique.

He uses "we" not only in the situation he narrates but also for his own participation in the story-universe. Considering the story-time of this novel, that technique is more remarkable than it at first may seem. Following the prologue, the story commences with two Arabic invasions and the African people's escape from the terror. The reader is by then a third of the way into the novel, and some three hundred years of story-time have elapsed. In the next few pages the narrator, runs through some four hundred years before arriving at the coming of the white colonialists during the reign of the treacherous king Koranche. The rest of the novel tells of a group of freedom-fighters and their rebellion against their king and the white conquerors.

The novel initially appears to be told in an ordinary third person perspective, hetero-extradiegetic in Genette's terminology, even if the narrator refers to himself with a we, both in the narrating present and the story past. In the story of the past, the we first seems to be synonymous with the people of Africa, or at least the earliest members of the narrator's own tribe. "After a hundred seasons we were so reduced, so abject had we become, that the destroyers feared no revolt". In another passage from almost the same place in the novel it becomes more ambiguous to which time level the narrator refers: "Among us some in spite of the plethora of warnings laughed at the white predators from the desert". Some ten pages into the text and the story, a group of people decide, to emigrate and search for new land to settle in. Then the narrator clearly is referring not only to an ideological we but is actually a member of that migrating group. When the group separates, the narrator becomes part of one group: "Then we followed those gone ahead. We found them stopped at the foot of the hills."

But that peculiar narrator can also in the same sentence refer to himself in the first person plural, in the narrative past, as well as in the narrative present: "What we do know is that after the success of our escape the white predators executed another terrible slaughter among those who chose to stay." In the present tense "we" refers to the time of recent narration, whereas "our" belongs to the story level, the diegesis. The story teller accomplishes that shift between different ontological levels without any adverb of time as marker, only the shift in tense indicates a change in time to the reader.

In the later half of the novel the narrator seems to be one of twenty in the group of freedom-fighters; that some seven hundred years of story time has elapsed since his migration to the new land Anoa will not thwart Armah's daring narrator: "There were twenty of us: eleven girls growing into women, nine boys growing into men." Some pages later the narrator names the twenty, but although he appears to be one of them, he never reveals which one.

Use of the plural voice may of course suggest that the twenty are telling the story jointly. A closer look at the text disputes this: The king lures the group onto a slave ship and puts them in chains; they manage to liberate themselves and the other prisoners. The narrator is there in the middle of the action:

"At that sound it seemed as if all the white destroyers and all their askaris shot every gun they had into us. We halted and shrank back. Eight of us lay in the space still between us and the white destroyers and their askaris. Among us the fear of death rose and shook the courage of our recent preparation out of most. While we hesitated ten more bodies fell and those farthest forward hurled their weight backward against the rest of us."

Derek Wright has suggested that the plural voice includes, or rather implicates, only the avant-garde, not the masses, which fits well into his view of the novel. Although the above quotation may support such a notion, and even if the assessment is perhaps valid on the ideological level of the text, it does not hold true on a level of narration. The fact that the narrator also was present during the migration contradicts that idea. As in the migration section, it is clear here that the narrator does not just see himself as descendent of these freedom-fighters; he is one of them, if anonymous, in a specific temporal and spatial place in the story: he is a homodiegetic narrator, taking part in the story as a character.

The reader may have problems accepting him as such, and would be happier to view him as heterodiegetic, absent from this story as character. He is nameless and never individually visible, but a participant in the one thousand years long story, in the fictive world of his own narration. And he, of course, abandons every claim on mimetic verisimilitude. Yet this raconteur insists on referring to himself with the spacious we on both the level of the story and its surrounding narration: "Three of the captives we freed—two women, one man—joined us. The others heard calls from home. They went. But we should not stop the onward flow of work with overlong remembrance of single battles won."

As homodiegetic narrator, participating in his own story, the narrator nevertheless does this only as character of the story, never as narrator. He never narrates from inside the universe of the story, but solely from the narration of the present, outside the diegesis, although both hetero—and homodiegetic, he remains extradiegetic in his narrating, which of course is according to oral storytelling. Rarely, if ever, does anyone narrate orally from inside the world of the story (except perhaps television or radio commentators). So Armah's narrator in *Two Thousand Seasons* is not only an extra-homodiegetic, but in his first person plural voice is also a conventional extra-heterodiegetic narrator.

Like most heterodiegetic narrations, the story is zero-focalized, in that the narrator is omniscient—in this case very all-knowing. As would any true oral storyteller he knows the outcome of the story he tells and reveals it in so-called proleptic phrases: "The rest remained a mystery to us, till Isanusi opened our eyes." At that point, Isanusi has not yet appeared in the story and will not for some time. Not only does the narrator know the outcome of the story, he can even hear other characters' thoughts:

"The king's mind was troubled by an unsolicited image: these people can walk naked and not be ashamed. Words invaded his head: they give more than they receive. I, the king, only know how to take. They are full vessels overflowing. I am empty. In place of a bottom I have a hole.". . .

By allowing himself to hear the thoughts of other characters, Armah's narrator knows far more than any character should, more than a homodiegetic narrator could do with any credibility. But because this narrator, both homo-and heterodiegetic, remains as narrator outside the story, remains extradiegetic, he grants himself this remarkable privilege. It is thanks to his extradiegetic nature that he can allow himself that.

*Two Thousand Seasons* is quite unique because its we-narrator allows himself to participate throughout a story almost one thousand years long. It is that shift between story level and the level of the narrative situation that is so radical and distinctive in *Two Thousand Seasons*. Perhaps *Two Thousand Seasons* is the kind of novel a griot would write if he had access to a written language and a literary tradition.

Lief Lorentzon. *Critique: Studies in Contemporary Fiction.* 38, 3 (Spring 1997), pp. 22–35

BIBLIOGRAPHY
*"African Socialism: Utopian or Scientific?,"* 1967; *The Beautyful Ones Are Not Yet Born*, 1967; *Fragments*, 1970; *Why Are We So Blest?*, 1972; *Two Thousand Seasons*, 1973; "The Definitive Chaka," 1975–1976; "Larsony or Fiction as Criticism of Fiction," 1976; *The Healers*, 1978; "The Caliban Complex," 1985; "The Festival Syndrome," 1985; "The Lazy School of Literary Criticism," 1985; "One Writer's Education," 1985; "Interview with Dimgba," 1986; "Battle for the Mind of Africa," 1987; *Osiris Rising: A Novel of Africa Past, Present, and Future*, 1995

# ATTAWAY, William (1911–1986)
## United States

[*Blood on the Forge*] is a story of transition and contrasting values. In the first part of the novel we are shown the naïve, almost formless personalities of the farm workers in their "natural" sharecropper setting. While the main portion of the narrative centers in the mill town, where we see the quicksilver personalities caught within the hot, hard forge of industry. The boys' names— through which Attaway symbolizes three basic attitudes to the world of steel—now become meaningful: Melody embodies the artistic principle; Big Mat, the religious; and Chinatown, the pagan. We see the new routine of toil (product of a way of life technologically years ahead of that from which they've come), grinding down upon these boys. Under it Big Mat's vague religion and mythology become inadequate; Melody, whose relationship to his world has always been expressed through his guitar, gives musical utterance to a new attitude, the blues; and the "blow-top" Chinatown's life becomes a mad ritual of "whiskey, whores, and wheel-barrows." Thus in this world of changing values all the old rules of living are melted away. . . .

Conceptionally, Attaway grasped the destruction of the folk, but missed its rebirth on a higher level. The writer did not see that while the folk individual was being liquidated in the crucible of steel, he was also undergoing fusion with new elements. Nor did Attaway see that the individual which emerged, blended of old and new, was better fitted for the problems of the industrial environment. As a result the author is so struck by the despair in his material that he fails to see any ground for hope for his characters. . . .

Some [Negroes] found in unionism a large part of the answer to their suffering. It was these, at the beginning only a few, who by pursuing their vision despite the antipathy of some white unionists and bosses alike, established those values embraced by a growing number of Negroes today. Serious writing about the Negro must spread this hard won consciousness.

Ralph Ellison. *Negro Quarterly.* Spring 1942, pp. 88–91

The thesis in *Blood on the Forge* is that Negroes are objects of discrimination and injustice on the labor market, especially when they offer "competition to white men." Attaway develops this thesis around economic conditions in the steel mills of Pennsylvania after World War I when Negroes were brought from the South for scab labor purposes. . . .

Big Mat and his brothers are the victims of unsatisfactory labor union strategy, for they are employed to break a strike rather than to become members of the union. Big Mat is given the official role of strikebreaker deputy. In the labor battle which follows, Big Mat loses his life, and Chinatown and Melody are left blind and mutilated. . . .

Attaway follows the conventional approach which is essentially documentation of evils inherent in the social order with particular reference to the Negro. Usually, flagrant injustices, discriminatory practices, and oppression compose the framework of such a novel. The danger that a Negro writer has to avoid is being too reportorial and documentary. There is, of course, no room for sentimentality because this is the grim business of projecting incidents of real life truthfully yet with narrative skill. Again, the Negro author has to prevent himself from becoming tractish in his fervor for advocating change rather than remaining purely objective. Attaway achieves success in *Blood on the Forge.*

Carl Milton Hughes. *The Negro Novelist* (New York: Citadel, 1953), pp. 79–82

Ellison's comment notwithstanding, *Blood on the Forge* is more than a novel of dissolution. Counterposed to the Moss brothers is the figure of Zanski, an old Ukrainian steelworker who represents a superior adjustment to the new industrial environment. Confronted with similar problems of acculturation, the transplanted Ukrainian peasants have been quicker to put their roots down than the Negro migrants. Zanski, knowing instinctively that no peasant can be happy unless he is growing things, insists at least upon having kids growing in his yard. In addition to realizing the importance of family life, the Slavs are overwhelmingly pro-union. Since Attaway will eventually part company with the Moss brothers on ideological grounds, Zanski helps to prepare the ground for this decisive shift in tone. . . .

The Moss brothers see the strike strictly from a racial point of view; there is nothing in their experience which would cause them

to do otherwise. . . . It is clear from Attaway's tone, however, that he is playing devil's advocate; his aim is to discredit Negro nationalism, from a somewhat broader point of view. Ideologically speaking, *Blood on the Forge* represents the shift from race consciousness to class consciousness which so many Negro intellectuals experienced during the Red Decade.

Robert A. Bone. *The Negro Novel in America* (New Haven: Yale University Press, 1958), pp. 138–39

[*Let Me Breathe Thunder*, Attaway's first novel] celebrates the loyalty and decency of men on the move, and the essential virtues of the life of the soil. Attaway's Negro themes . . . are muted and disguised, which allows him to speak the language of protest without using its rhetoric. In shying away from making his main characters Negroes, Attaway was perhaps fearful of having his novel labeled protest fiction. The two Negro characters who do appear in the novel have no especial "Negro" traits, and although one of them is nearly lynched for the supposed attempted rape of a white girl, scarcely any allusion is made to his race. It appears as if Attaway were bending over backwards to assure his readers that he is not writing "sociology." Such a position is absurd, since any reader would naturally associate lynchings and imaginary sex crimes with race. The novel falters on other counts: the characters rarely spring to life, and their situations vaguely suggest those Steinbeck described two years earlier in *Of Mice and Men*. Yet for all that, the narrative does possess a certain verve, and the prose is economical and clean in the Hemingway manner—objective but replete with undertones of irony and sadness. . . .

His first novel . . . was promising; his second, a classic of its kind. Why then did Attaway stop writing fiction? He was only twenty-nine when *Blood on the Forge* appeared. . . . It is perhaps in the realm of ideas that we may look for the source of Attaway's arrested artistic development. Basically Attaway is a romantic. *Let Me Breathe Thunder*, for all its praise of stable family life and the virtues of farming, ultimately celebrates the free-wheeling bohemianism of hoboes—and Attaway, by manipulating his plot this way and that, manages to free his protagonists from any social and moral obligations. In another romantic vein, *Blood on the Forge* projects the myth of the "good" soil corrupted by man's greed, whose logical absurdity manifests itself in the manufacture of steel. While no one would deny that the excesses of American capitalism have produced cruel and dehumanizing injustices, it is hard, after Darwin, to ascribe moral virtues to nature. And since it is scarcely possible any longer to look to nature as something apart and holy, Attaway may well have written himself out of subject matter.

Edward Margolies. *Native Sons* (Philadelphia: J. B. Lippincott, 1968), pp. 52, 63–64

*Blood on the Forge* is a well-written novel. It deserved the plaudits of critics past and present. It is a structurally sounder novel than *Native Son*, and the inner mechanics—symbols and images of life, death, and destruction—work as effectively for Attaway as they do for Wright. Yet, Attaway, unlike Wright, has accepted the argument that themes of universal import take preference over those of more parochial import; that is, the conflict between man and the machine is more universal than that between black man and a racist society. . . .

This despite the fact that Attaway lives in a universe marred by turmoil and dissension. The depression, as he knows so well, has brought men to the brink of revolution, the migration made it impossible for people to survive by the patterns of old. In such a new world, Melody and Chinatown, of course, are doomed; hedonism and paganism, twin evils for black men, are useless in a world in which the race war is an eternal given. This is not so for Big Mat; in a world of violence and turmoil, violence is the norm, and the man who tempers it with the proper humanism has come close to constructing a new ethic. Attaway could not accept this idea. There is too much of the naturalist in him, too much of the sociologist; he adheres to a code that preaches universal brotherhood, yet one that refuses to acknowledge the historical fact that such has been achieved only when one man possessed guns as powerful as the other. When Big Mat exchanges the Bible for the sheriff's cudgeon, he has leaped across centuries of black history into the modern world. Attaway, however, cannot accept him, recoils in horror from his own creation, attempts to convince the reader that excessive rage and compulsive anger have driven Mat to become more insane than other men, that violence represents not redemption for him, but vengeance, and that the race war, unlike other wars, must be fought out on the high plane of moral niceties and meaningless epithets. . . .

Attaway backs away from Armageddon at sight of the flames. What might have become a novel representing man's courage and strength, becomes one instead which consigns him to doom and damnation.

Addison Gayle, Jr. *The Way of the New World* (Garden City, New York: Doubleday, 1975), pp. 164–66

The structure and narrative technique of *Blood on the Forge* are largely familiar—the third-person narrator with selective omniscience, the hope for a new and better way of life that meets with disappointment, the destructive cycle in which the present recapitulates the dispossession of the past, and a linear journey that ends where it began. Anna, the prostitute who becomes Mat's woman, has already been discussed as a Mammy-Wattah figure. But there is another facet to Attaway's novel—its jazzlike use of images of fragmentation. These images carry the thematic burden of the novel and provide a solution to the problem of characterization in a novel whose characters are largely inarticulate, incapable of verbal expression.

Melody provides an early clue to this aspect of Attaway's technique. He believes that "a man had oughta know book learnin—so's he kin know how to say what he's feeling." But earlier he has been described as never having had "a craving in him that he couldn't slick away on his guitar." For Melody, his guitar provides a substitute for words. As the narrative progresses, however, his capacity to give musical shape to his feelings is eroded. Early on, he admits that "every once in a while he would get filled up . . . with a feeling that was too big to turn into any kind of music." Later, in the mill town, his guitar playing changes, from the "slicking" that was "for back home and the distance in the hills" to "quick chords with the finger . . . right for that new place [but] nothin' like the blues that spread fan-wise from the banks of the Mississippi," a way of playing better suited to "the whirling lights and . . . the

heart of the great red ingots." The stasis of [Jean Toomer's] Cane gives way to movement, and the images of twilight to images of whirling lights and fragmentation—and this is the change one must imagine in Melody's guitar playing, as he gives voice to his feelings about the milltown and about Anna. His feelings, however, get "too big" for even this changed way of playing; more or less deliberately, he injures his hand and hangs up his guitar. His feelings cut off from their expression, he becomes one of the images of fragmentation in the novel. And it is as though Attaway takes up where Melody leaves off, using a counterpoint of images centering on animals and barrenness that taken together signal that the erosion of time apparent in Cane is here complete. In the imagery of fragmentation, time explodes.

Bonnie J. Barthold. *Black Time: Fiction of Africa, the Caribbean, and the United States* (New Haven: Yale University Press, 1981), pp. 164–68.

One element of black folk culture that plays an important part in William Attaway's novel *Blood on the Forge* (1941) is the wishing game. Early in Part I, Melody, one of three Moss brothers subsisting on a poor Kentucky farm in 1919, begins the game. His motive is distraction from hunger while awaiting Big Mat, the brother who sharecrops the farm and who may bring some food. In the call-and-response fashion characteristic of Afro-American culture, Melody involves his brother Chinatown in the game: "'China,' he half sang, 'you know where I wish I was at now?'" Chinatown needs no prodding because the brothers have often played this game, their wishes usually formed by the "grand places pictured in the old newspapers" lining the walls of their shack. Led on by the responses of Chinatown, Melody spins his narrative. He imagines himself in town on a Saturday noon, all dressed up in a "white-checkered vest and a ice-cream suit," with a gold watch chain and "yeller shoes with dimes in the toes, Man, man!". . .

Throughout the novel, Attaway shows the crucial yet ambiguous role of wishing in black life by juxtaposing playful and serious manifestations. At times, the reader cannot determine which of the two forms is being expressed by a character, and one senses that the characters themselves are sometimes equivocal. When Big Mat returns with the makings for chitterlings, the family happily awaits their preparation. The white landowner who has given Mat the food surprisingly has promised the use of a mule, too. Immediately, Hattie and Melody begin imagining what the increased productivity will buy—fresh tobacco and pork on Sunday. When Chinatown voices suspicion, Hattie, reluctant to forgo her dream, advises not looking a gift horse in the mouth. Chinatown replies, "'I'm pass the mouth now. I'm lookin' right down his throat.'" Such caution regarding the white world proves true when Big Mat recalls that as the landowner made the loan he warned of "jacklegs" coming into the area recruiting blacks to go North and work. The refusal to let dreams lead one permanently away from the reality of living in a white world seems instinctive as long as these people live in Kentucky. When the brothers are forced to take the jackleg's offer and go to work in the Pennsylvania steel mills, though, only Melody successfully resists the lure of destructive wishes.

By making wishing a key element in Blood on the Forge, Attaway conveys a major theme of the novel. The fuller life seemingly promised for blacks by life in the North proves to be an illusion. When the hopes contained while living in the South are given expression in the North, even greater pain and disillusionment result. For Attaway, the lesson of the Great Migration to the promised land is ironic indeed.

> Samuel B. Garren. *CLA Journal.* 32, 1 (September 1988), pp 10–22

BIBLIOGRAPHY
*Carnival* (play), 1935; *Let Me Breathe Thunder*, 1939; *Blood on the Forge*, 1941; *Hear America Singing*, 1967; *One Hundred Years of Laughter* (television script), 1967

# AWOONOR, Kofi (1935–)
## Ghana

Christophe Okigbo . . . passes through a succession of Heavensgates. [In *Rediscovery*] George Awoonor-Williams waits at "hellgate," not to pass through but to be "delivered" from his place of waiting to a pleasanter spot. The fascination that Awoonor-Williams has with things basic, mysterious, such as death or the ritual acts of love or worship leads him to the temporary rediscovery and fleeting recognitions that he desires. He reminds one of Okigbo because he goes on and on with the purifications and is as dissatisfied with the "purified" state as Okigbo. But, unlike Okigbo's poetic litanies, Awoonor-Williams' poems are single moments selected out of a pattern of rediscovery. The points of crystallisation are recorded—both low and high, the moments of inglorious desire, the moments of discovering the strengths that his own soul possesses. Okigbo presents the notes and feelings of the entire journey; Awoonor-Williams selects the moments of greatest importance, ones which have a significance beyond themselves. Awoonor-Williams' great achievement is his use of "extended rhythms" and, in this, he is as skilful as Ezra Pound or the William Carlos Williams of *Paterson*. . . .

Awoonor-Williams extends his rhythms by extending the lines into other poems. . . . He is not "writing the same thing" as the similar lines might lead one to believe, but enlarging his theme by repetition in depth. Anyone who has read the Bible knows that Awoonor-Williams was not the first to sit "by the rivers of Babylon," but he puts this theft to work for him. And this also adds to the symphonic effect of the body of poems.

> Paul Theroux. *Black Orpheus.* August 1966, pp. 47–49

Awoonor's first volume of poetry, *Rediscovery*, was published by Mbari Publications (of Mbari Writers and Artists Club in Ibadan). Since then he has grown from strength to strength. Throughout, his poetry is characterized by the aura of a sage's words: now pleading, now cautioning, now ruminating over the African's position in relation to the ancestors or his father's gods, now asserting his need to go out in search of a stabilizing agent. The sage's voice often seems to ramble, strike out in some direction and return to reassert what it said before. Consequently, Awoonor's poems supplement one another, and a continuity of theme is maintained. The lyricism seldom flags, however. . . .

Awoonor speaks with a quiet voice always. No ranting, no squirming. The voice comes through in the beat of his lines—a beat which, coupled with the simplicity of the diction, captures the mood and slow pace of African contemplative speech. . . .

Kofi Awoonor has a keen ear for verbal music. I do not know of any African poet who can, like Awoonor, compose a line of verse in English that rolls off the tongue with exquisite music and do it again and again. The late Christopher Okigbo also had a sharp ear for verbal music, but he exploited the music that is inherent in the English language which he had mastered so remarkably. Awoonor, on the other hand, seems to bring another element from outside of the English language. Ewe, his mother tongue, is a highly musical language, but the music of an African language cannot be translated into that of a European one. It is an unnameable element he brings to the music he replays. . . .

The elegiac mood that pervades Kofi Awoonor's poetry reaches its high water mark in his "Lament of the Silent Sister." The cry for what Africa has lost in her traditional values with the accompanying exhortation for us to take a grip of ourselves, to ask our fathers to "sew the old days" for us, finds in "Lament of the Silent Sister" a concrete and still elevating subject—that of Christopher Okigbo, who died in the Nigerian war in 1967. I consider this elegy to be the finest in African writing, one of the finest in the English-speaking world. It is truly African, taking us on a wave that rises and falls, rises and falls to the deep tones of a funeral drum. And from deep down there the voice of the mourner rides on a diction that comes straight to the heart. . . .

Although Kofi Awoonor's poetry is packed with ideas, his gentle diction carries us there with its emotional drive, its traditional speech patterns. For all that, the poetry stays on the ground, avoiding any intellectual horseplay.

> Ezekiel Mphahlele. Introduction to Kofi Awoonor, *Night of My Blood* (Garden City, New York: Doubleday, 1971), pp. 9–10, 15, 17–18

[As] Wole Soyinka did in his novel *The Interpreters*, Awoonor [in *This Earth, My Brother* . . .] uses the most advanced literary techniques of Western fiction to present the whole scale of an African society, from the most "primitive" to the most "advanced." His story takes a man from his birth in a back-country Ewe village through his education and his successful career at the bar in Accra to his mental and emotional breakdown and death.

The story is given to us in a series of scenes at crucial or at casual moments, interspersed with internal dreamlike monologues. Every one of these episodes or reveries is presented in such a brilliant light that at first the reader may have an impression of a glowing but disordered kaleidoscope. Actually, as the reader soon realizes, this is a very economical means of giving us, in a little over two hundred pages, a knowledge of the inner life of a man and of the society that drives such a man to his final despair.

The reveries, we soon see, are those of a man in a madhouse. They are wild and in the vein of poetry that we know often represents the eruption of the unconscious. . . .

We have now a few books like *This Earth, My Brother* . . . which are bound to stand, it seems to me, not only as chronicles of the first tragic era of African independence but as noble contributions to the art of the world.

> John Thompson. *New York Review of Books.* September 23, 1971, p. 4

Kofi Awoonor was known until now for his poetry—a strong, muscular, controlled poetry. With [*This Earth, My Brother . . .*] he makes a dramatic new appearance in the role of prose-writer— again strong in his accents and in full confidence.

He calls the book "an allegorical tale of Africa." An allegory is as good a name as one can call this rather unusual and highly personal form. It is in fact a medley of forms—intense and tight sequences of poetic prose alternating with more open stretches of realistic narrative and now and again broken by shots of running commentary, all moving sometimes forwards in time sometimes backwards or in circles and at yet another time completely flung outside our accustomed historical time-scale. . . .

Despite those laughing people, laughing with all their white teeth, Africa is a place of torment and ugliness. Being Ghanaian and Ghana being so central to modern Africa, Awoonor can sometimes particularise his Africa into his Ghana—a "revolting malevolence" he calls it, reminding us of that other Ghanaian writer, Ayi Kwei Armah, author of the novel, *The Beautyful Ones Are Not Yet Born.*

Awoonor's allegory teems with people, places, incidents, thoughts, emotions, actions, evasions. It follows (pursues may be more apt) the hero from the very orgasm of his conception through his feverish life. It takes off without warning to any part of the world and makes unscheduled stops where it pleases. Yet despite such wide ranging techniques Awoonor never falls into superficialities. What he unfolds before us may be fleeting but it is always sharp and never, one is convinced, unimportant. And it is not a succession of haphazard impressions either despite the seeming arbitrariness of its sequences. There is a cumulativeness, indeed an organic, albeit bizarre, development towards the ultimate failure. But here is no existential futility; at every stage there is a misty hint of a viable alternative, of a road that is not taken, of a possibility that fails to develop. The central failure is African independence whose early promise is like the butterfly that the child Amamu caught in the fields of yellow sunflower as the moon, and it flew away again. He searched for it for days and found others that looked like it; but no, it was gone. . . .

So the death of [British] Empire was not to be seriously lamented. Senile and absurd it no longer had the will to stand by and protect its very own. But at least it had its heyday, its years of honour. Its successor, Independence, did not even wait to grow old before turning betrayer.

Chinua Achebe. *Transition.* No. 41, 1972, p. 69

Even the title [*This Earth, My Brother . . .*] is an exhalation of frustration and despair. To the lament "This Earth, my brother . . ." I can almost hear the "boh, na wah!" of the listener. Because we are warned by the author that this is an allegory I do not waste effort trying to read it straight like a thriller. But then, by what code shall I decipher the encoded commentary on Africa? Taking my cue from the title I first read it as a disillusioned portrait of the times as observed through the eyes of a suffering innocent. I followed the milieu-painting to its end; went along on a guided tour of the stations of dislocation and the marshes of corruption; went along on this tour of the ruins till I came to the final ruin— Amamu's madness. But this device of insanity? Having paddled down the river of his consciousness, having shared his inner musings, I found myself asking: Did Amamu have to go mad? Are his experiences and visions far out of the ordinary? What is there in

them to justify his going mad? Yaro's troubles, Ibrahim's death, the disastrous party the night before, all being really peripheral to the core of Amamu's being, do not seem to be sufficient forces to finally shove him over the brink into insanity. And so I am led to a reconsideration. . . .

But whatever the case, let us remember that to ask for more and for better is not to belittle what we have been already given. As a novel which unearths issues of fictional craft, *This Earth, My Brother . . .* is certainly worthy of critical note. As a work which tackles problems of African reality today, it is also worthy of general note. And of course, passages of poetic delight run through the realistic and stream-of-consciousness sequences of which the work is composed. Whatever its failings, however much it portrays surfaces without revealing shadows from the depths, this book is certainly not a soporific.

Chinweizu. *Okike.* December 1974, pp. 88, 95–96

Primarily through his poetry, Awoonor has established himself as one of the most significant contemporary African writers. His first two books of poetry, *Rediscovery* and *Night of My Blood,* show a powerful progression from a fascination with his roots, through an uncertain poetic and cultural synthesis with the west, to a voice that is confidently his own. More than any other western-African poet, with the possible exceptions of Christopher Okigbo and Wole Soyinka, Awoonor has succeeded in transcending the raw tensions of culture conflict. His poetry should be read as a series of attempts to find in the history and poetry of his people correlatives to his own personal anguish as a modern African. Poems that serve to accentuate the anguish and give definition to the progression may appear to be difficult, or simply uneven and rough, when removed from this context.

In both form and imagery Awoonor's poetry has been heavily influenced by the Ewe dirge. According to traditional Ewe beliefs, those who have just died and are entering another existence represent potential danger to those left behind, for the physical loss interrupts the continuity of society and threatens it with dissolution. Yet, good may also come out of a death, for a successful transition ends with the dead individual becoming an ancestral being who can be a beneficial force in the community. The purpose of the Ewe dirge is to aid the individual in making this transition.

For Awoonor the dirge becomes symbolic not only of an individual and societal process but also of the poet's passage from insufficiency to fulfillment, from chaos to order, from alienation to integration. Death and anguish pervade his poetry as mediating agents that force the continual restructuring, refocusing, and revitalizing of individual and communal order. In effect, Awoonor explores the relationship between contemporary society and traditional myth and ritual.

Richard Priebe. In *Encyclopedia of World Literature in the 20th Century* (New York, Frederick Ungar, 1975), Vol. IV, pp. 28–29

The jacket and title page insist that *This Earth, My Brother . . .* be called "An Allegorical Tale of Africa," though it seems no more allegorical than any novel is; i.e., its hero represents many men and his plight illustrates an aspect of the human condition. The hero, Amamu, is a young Ghanian lawyer, who, through the alternation of objective and introspective chapters (set, I think too fussily, in different sizes of type), proceeds to nervous breakdown and death. The stress he suffers is presumably the inordinate gap (and here the typographic device may have a point) between his primitive, hopeful, partially idyllic past and the mediocre, nagging, disappointed present of his life in an African metropolis no better able to cope with corruption and pollution and poverty than any other modern city. . . . Awoonor's Ghana is familiarly dismal, except that all the faces are black and the problems of over-development experienced in America are matched by the not dissimilar embarrassments of underdevelopment. Amamu is a thorough bourgeois male—uneasy in his work, a witness to injustice yet a professional participant in it, a citizen perpetually testifying, inwardly, to his own puzzling incrimination in the venal, weary workings of a mercenary society. . . .

Viewed externally, Amamu is not very impressive or dynamic, and his fate is less tragic than damply sad, a shadow melting back into shadows. Yet the novel's strength is its refusal to be spectacular, to feign anger it doesn't feel, or to present Ghanian life as anything much more than a fumbling, disheartened extension of colonial rule, a blurred carbon. Humanity is not . . . locked out; there are pages of faithful, inconsequential dialogue, with a lilt never heard in the West, and perhaps it is this sense of voice and voices that makes *This Earth, My Brother* . . . aimiable, despite its allegorical grimace. [Nov. 13, 1971]

John Updike. *Picked-Up Pieces* (New York, Alfred A. Knopf, 1975), pp. 321, 323

In politics and philosophy, as well as in the theory and practice of literature, Kofi Awoonor is a syncretist. He amalgamates all experiences, whether personal ones or the collective experiences of Africa, in order to produce a single vortex of images. Africa for him is a continent and a notion that draws into itself, appropriating and adapting, the whole of human life and history. . . .

In a note in his first volume, *Rediscovery, and Other Poems*, Awoonor (or George Awoonor Williams as he was then) says that he began writing in 1949. The notion of cultural synthesis is, however, one that came gradually to him. His first published adult poetry, "The Sea Eats the Land at Home," "Songs of Sorrow," and "Song of War," was largely derived from Ewe dirges, laments, and battle songs, which he learned in part from his grandmother, Afedomeshi, and translated into English. "Songs of Sorrow" has many lines of virtual translation from the work of Henoga Vinoko Akpalu, the originator of the modern style of Ewe dirge. It begins by talking about Dzobese Lisa, the Creator God or Fate of Ewe belief. The immutable fate destined for each person is said by the Ewe to be like the chameleon, whose sudden changes and foul-smelling feces are a significant metaphor for fate. Obviously regarding these poems as apprentice work, he chose not to include them in *Rediscovery*. In that volume, however, and in his second, *Night of My Blood*, several poems draw on the two early "Songs," incorporating whole long passages from them. Some other poems, Awoonor tells us, were first written in Ewe and subsequently translated into English. . . .

The first stage of Awoonor's progress towards cultural synthesis was . . . to rely heavily on Ewe oral poetry as his main source. The second was the bringing together in a single poem of material from the Ewe tradition and the European tradition in which he had been educated. Material from the two strands is set down side by side to emphasize a clash of cultures. Gerard Manley Hopkins, W. B. Yeats (in mythic and political ideology as well as in the creation of a mysterious mood of cosmic immanence), and T. S. Eliot are the major modern writers from whom he draws, but there is also a pervasive influence of the Bible.

Awoonor's first and second volume both contain several examples of each of the first two stages of his work. . . .

*Night of My Blood* contains one long poem, "Hymn to My Dumb Earth," that Awoonor regards as representing a third phase in his development, the synthesis of cultures rather than the juxtaposition of them as in the second phase. Here the material from each culture reinforces rather than opposes that of the other. Bud Powell, the jazz pianist; the crucified Christ; the childless villager; the man saddened by the venal politics of independence all merge into one, in much the same way as several of the disparate characters in [T. S. Eliot's] *The Waste Land* merge into Tiresias.

K. L. Goodwin. *Understanding African Poetry* (London: Heinemann, 1982), pp. 93–95

When his apprentice volume *Rediscovery, and Other Poems* appeared under the Mbari imprint in 1964, many of the pieces were recognized by Ewe speakers as reworkings of Akpalu lyrics. In some quarters he was even accused unofficially of a mild form of plagiarism. The charge is unjust, since the book's title is clear acknowledgement of a debt owed to a long and distinguished tradition within which textual ownership has little meaning. When seven years later a selection from the pieces in *Rediscovery* was interspersed among other poems composed in the interval to form the volume *Night of My Blood*, Awoonor's intention became clearer. As a young poet he had sat at the feet of the Anlo masters, attempting to render the sentiments of their tonal verse in the strains of an imported, accentual tongue. Later he felt able to proceed beyond "rediscovery" and extend the dirge tradition into a medium for comment both political and private.

Though the Akpalu versions in *Rediscovery* were in some cases very close to the originals, their indebtedness to Ewe tradition was the result of influences imbibed during childhood rather than of deliberate research. It was not until after their publication and the inception of many of the poems included in *Night of My Blood*, that, in the rainy season of 1970, Awoonor was able to make a visit to Wheta systematically to investigate the sources of his own inspiration. The study which resulted, *Guardians of the Sacred Word*, is both a remarkable sourcebook and a prolonged meditation on the social position and skills of the vernacular Ewe poet or *heno*, translations from the work of three of whom he was able to include. Though a general reliance on an indigenous form has long been recognized as a feature of Awoonor's achievement, it was not until the comparison of related texts thus made possible that the exact extent of his indebtedness became clear. . . .

Awoonor's views as to the relationship between a modern artist and his community are explained with some care both in his historical survey *The Breast of the Earth* and in interviews which he has given from time to time. His statements here show him to be as wary of sentimental oversimplification as he is of a cynical denigration of tradition. Africa is involved in a continuous process of cultural transformation—she continues to "expand, change, adapt"—and yet the way in which she responds to these challenges reflects deeply her own complex personality. In the slow, unravelling process of "growth and elimination" undergone by every modern African community, the poet has a vital role to play, for it is only through the disruptive consciousness of the poet, revealed in blinding flashes, that the zigzagging direction of the future may be seen. Thus, though relating to a community in some respects more complicated than that of the village, the contemporary literary artist may revive within himself the function of the *heno*: he too may be scorned and ignored, but only through him, as through the indigenous cantor, may the community dimly define itself. . . .

*Ride Me, Memory*, the volume which he published while in the United States, contains a set of ''American Profiles'' to balance the ''African Memories'' with which the book closes. Prospect of return therefore balances retrospect, and the biting edge of the collection falls midway between the two. Awoonor was very far from the first West African poet to give us his verse impressions of God's Own Country. . . . But Awoonor's case was exceptional because he was in possession of an especially portable talent. Though emphatically grounded in a local tradition, Awoonor appears to carry his Ewe soul around with him in his hand luggage.

Robert Fraser. *West African Poetry* (Cambridge: Cambridge University Press, 1986), pp. 158–59, 161, 290–91

Like [Christopher] Okigbo, Awoonor writes from the perspective of the poet-prodigal and, therefore, from within the context of the psychological myth of the journey. In his first major collection, *Night of My Blood*, almost every poem explores some aspect or nuance of the journey. The sense of alienation is everywhere, beginning with the lament in the first poem that ''my god of songs was ill.'' It continues as the poet wonders in the middle of the collection ''why could I not eat with elders/though my hands are washed clean in the salt river.'' And it is there in the last poem, in which the poet, hearing the fetish drums in the distance, realizes that ''they do not sound for me.'' ''I Heard a Bird Cry'' is the major poem in the collection, and it confronts the central ironies in the myth. The poet regrets leaving the hearth although he would not have become the poet if he had not undertaken the journey. And he returns to find ''the fallen walls of my father's house,'' walls which he, the reluctant Westernizing voyager, must rebuild. Here and elsewhere the journey becomes Awoonor's African version of the doctrine of the fortunate fall. But the collection does not have an autobiographical design. The two subsequent volumes do.

*Ride Me, Memory* is a slight collection of very personal poems arranged around a specific point in the cyclical journey. That is, the poet speaks from America, the farthest outward point in the journey; his is the voice of exile, ''alien here among the muddied fields.'' The first section of the collection called ''American Profiles,'' explores the world to which the Westernized African is drawn. There are pictures of Harlem, ''the dark dirge of America,'' and of SUNY Stony Brook, where ineffectual white liberals appear as ''Joshuas without trumpet or song.'' Perhaps the most important lesson the exiled poet learns is the lesson of blackness, which is the lesson of past pain and future triumph—the historical myth, if you will. In ''An American Memory of Africa,'' the climactic poem of the collection, he discovers that Sharpeville and Memphis are the same in their suffering, their promise of ''the hurricanes and eagles of tomorrow,'' and their color. Cut off from the Gulf of Guinea, he becomes a different kind of African by discovering the larger Africa of the historical myth and by discovering his relationship to those who inhabit it: Dennis Brutus, the ''professional exile''; Maya Angelou, the ''large savannah princess with the voice of

thunder''; and Langston Hughes, ''bagman of black rebirth.'' The second section, ''African Memories,'' evokes the Africa to which the transformed African must return—an Africa of broken pots and ''our fallen homestead.'' Wandering ''here where there is winter / birdsong and a yellow moon,'' he realizes that his is the paternally bestowed mythic task; he is ''the one who must resurrect / ancient days.''. . . .

*The House by the Sea* continues the autobiographical design. It is divided into two sections: section one, ''Before the Journey,'' contains poems of and from America, continuing the mood and mode of *Ride Me, Memory*. Like the poet, the poems wander America restlessly recording passing experience. The personal twists and turns in exile as he encounters what he calls the ''gothic beds of American vulgarity.'' In the second section the poet returns home to Ghana and, in fairly short order, to Fort Ussher prison, the fort functioning as a powerful symbol of the dislocating and suffocating present in which the Westernized African is forced to dwell, cut off from the past and from nature—from what Awoonor calls ''the hills / and the sea nearby.'' In this confusing present he completes the cyclical journey—his and his generation's—by promising the future. He promises his condemned friend, Kojo Tsikata, ''a garland / for your wounded knees,'' and he promises Ghana and Africa to ''plait my hope / into poems.'' And then in ''The Wayfarer Comes Home,'' the last poem in the collection and one of the great mythic poems of modern Africa, he fulfills his promise. He completes the journey by recalling the past, reacting to the present, and prophesying a future. By promising to ''stalk the evil animal'' and by predicting victory, he reaffirms the historical myth. In this affirmation he *achieves* his past, his home, and his purpose.

Thomas R. Knipp. In Eileen Julien, Mildred Mortimer, and Curtis Schade, eds. *African Literature in Its Social and Political Dimensions* (Washington, D. C.: Three Continents Press, 1986), pp. 47–48

The formal structure of Kofi Awoonor's *This Earth, My Brother* is probably as puzzling to the African reader as it is to the non-African reader. In strictly formal terms the book is more like a prose poem than a novel, though for purposes of general discussion it is not worthwhile quibbling about the label. Despite the extremely thin narrative thread which runs through it, *This Earth* relates to a tradition of expressionistic experimentation that can be traced from James Joyce to the present, though it is questionable how far this alone would lead anyone. Nor is it necessarily helpful to learn that the author himself has insisted on his work being thought of as a poem. The final judgment will of course be left to the reader. But classification per se, whether by the artist or his critics, is a rather useless game if it fails to reveal perceptions into the situation the artist has presented, and there is little beyond the obvious that a formal analysis of this novel will yield to the critic who does not take into consideration the formal elements that come from Eweland as well as those which come from England. . . .

Yet in discussing his poetry, Awoonor has said that he has been influenced primarily by the tradition of the Ewe song, ''especially the Ewe dirge, the dirge form, the lament, and its lyrical structure with the repetition of sections, segments, lines, along with an enormous, a stark and at times almost naive quality which this poetry possessed.'' In fact, the images, motifs, and themes we find in the novel are very close to those Awoonor has employed in his poetry. . . . The assertion that *This Earth, My Brother* is a prose poem may thus have some critical relevance.

Richard K. Priebe. *Myth, Realism, and the West African Writer* (Trenton, New Jersey: Africa World Press, 1988), pp. 65–66

While he shows a deep interest in the oral tradition of African poetry, Awoonor has also enriched his work through his understanding of Western literature. Excerpts from Dante form an important motif in *This Earth, My Brother*, and many poems in *Night of My Blood* owe something to English writers from Shakespeare through T. S. Eliot. . . . Awoonor's poetry is exciting because it offers (at its best) the creative fusion of two cultures.

His poetry is also exciting because it transcends particular cultures. This universality is especially expressed in the recurring archetype at the core of *Night of My Blood* the journey, which as quest for meaning and identity is a pattern implicit in Western poetry since Homer. Awoonor develops the motif in several ways. There is the historical migration of the Ewe people chronicled and mythologized in "Night of My Blood," and there is the recent traumatic journey of the African people out of a technologically primitive culture of their own into the welter of modernization and Westernization. This development is viewed as a journey of the dispossessed in "Exiles." Conversely, there is the journey of "rediscovery" undertaken by those Africans who (like Awoonor, in "Desire") seek to regain the wisdom of their ancestors. The most important refinement in Awoonor's use of the motif involves the journey as voyage, with its cluster of associated symbols, the canoe, the river, the estuary, the sea. The boat as a symbol of the journeying soul is an archetype in the works of such English Romantics and moderns as [Percy Bysshe] Shelley, D. H. Lawrence, and Malcolm Lowry. We don't need to invoke the European tradition, though. The symbolism of the Ewe mythology of death and beyond is clearly the source of the boat image in many of Awoonor's poems.

L. R. Early. In Richard K. Priebe, ed. *Ghanaian Literatures* (New York: Greenwood Press, 1988), pp. 104–5

As the title page indicates, *Until the Morning After* is a selected volume of poems taken from four previously published collections: *Rediscovery*; *Night of My Blood*; *Ride Me, Memory*; and *The House by the Sea*. There are also nine new poems. The reader is thus provided with an overview of Kofi Awoonor's development as a poet and as a human being. His early lyrics invoking the mysteries of the natural world and welcoming the heritage of the Ewe people gradually give way to wider perspectives, but his early and eloquent "sorrow songs" continue, although they move into the dark world of power politics. . . .

Related to the urgency of freedom now is Awoonor's emphasis on brotherhood, perhaps best expressed in the poem "All Men Are Brothers." Doubtless his feelings about this fundamental need deepened when his brother writers and his brothers in Amnesty International succeeded in their efforts to obtain a trial for him after he had languished in prison for many months. Though convicted of harboring a fugitive, he was pardoned and freed. It seems evident that the "iron clang of door" still echoes in his thoughts, for there is genuine indignation in his new poems when he warns against

leaders like Idi Amin and the "leeches who live on the fat of a lean land." *Until the Morning After* should increase Awoonor's already large audience and further enhance his international stature.

Richard F. Bauerle. *World Literature Today*. 62, 4 (Autumn 1988), p. 715

Awoonor's allegory [*This Earth, My Brother*] teems with people, places, incidents, thoughts, emotions, actions, evasions. It follows (pursues may be more apt) the hero from the very orgasm of his conception through his feverish life. It takes off without warning to any part of the world and makes unscheduled stops where it pleases. Yet despite such wide-ranging techniques Awoonor never falls into preciousness or superficialities. What he unfolds before us may be fleeting but it is always sharp and never, one is convinced, unimportant. And it is not a succession of haphazard impressions either, despite the seeming arbitrariness of its sequences. There is a cumulativeness, indeed an organic, albeit bizarre, development towards the ultimate failure. But here is no existential futility; at every stage there is a misty hint of a viable alternative, of a road that is not taken, of a possibility that fails to develop. The central failure is African independence, whose early promise is like the butterfly that the child Amamu caught in the fields of yellow sunflowers wide as the moon, and it flew away again. He searched for it for days and found others that looked like it; but no, it was gone. Or his childhood love for the shadowy cousin who died at twelve of a mysterious pain that chewed her intestines, a love he was to spend his life searching for and not finding— certainly not from his been-to wife Alice, nor even from his more understanding mistress, though she tried harder. . . .

Through this teeming allegory we catch glimpses of the hero Amamu at significant moments in his life. The phrase "catch glimpses" is in fact misleading, since we know that even in those sequences that are most remote from him personally—for example, in the invocation of the poet killed in battle, [Christopher] Okigbo, or the assassinated freedom fighter, Eduardo Mondlane—it is Amamu who is stretched on the rack and also Africa, whose story his life parallels in its purposelessness and self-destructiveness.

The question that one must ask at the end of Awoonor's book is: What then? He hasn't given any answer, and doesn't have to. But of late, many writers have been asking such questions: What then? What does Africa do? A return journey womb-wards to a rendezvous with golden-age innocence is clearly inadequate. Amamu's father may have acted insensitively, but on balance he was right to show impatience at all the lachrymose farewells before the boy's first departure from his mother's hut to the greater world beyond. Shoving aside the wailing women, he had brusquely and with a curse hoisted the boy into the lorry waiting to take him on a dusty journey to the coast and the future. The future is unavoidable. It has to be met. What is not inevitable is malingering purposelessness.

Chinua Achebe. *Hopes and Impediments: Selected Essays* (New York: Doubleday, 1989), pp. 122, 125–26

Awoonor's recent book of poems *Until the Morning After*, which won the 1988 Commonwealth Poetry Prize for the African area, consists in part of selections from his earlier work, and in part of new poems, some of which are translations of works originally composed in Ewe. The nine works in this section titled "New

Poems,'' in theme, subject matter, style, technique, and language, reiterate many of Awoonor's basic preoccupations. The first few are in part laments over "life's tears" or "life's winds and fate." But as always with Awoonor and the Ewe dirge tradition, there is hope beyond death. . . .

Between the publication of *The House by the Sea* and that of *Until the Morning After* almost ten years elapsed. At least part of the explanation for the paucity of Awoonor's creative writing since his release from prison must be sought in a decisive change in his life, leading increasingly to direct participation in national politics. . . .

Whether Kofi Awoonor returns to his earlier preoccupation with imaginative writing or not, he has already secured a safe place within the canon of African literature, both for the quantity and the quality of his work. In particular his poetry is notable for its intense lyricism. He is classed with a select group of African poets who have been most successful in bringing African aesthetic norms to bear on their writing in English, a group that invariably includes Mazisi Kunene, Okot p'Bitek, and Christopher Okigbo. The contribution of these poets to world literature lies in the great poise and power with which they can take a second language with its own literary heritage and peculiar linguistic structures and yet use it so as to capture effectively the rhythms, the essential imagery, and the often elusive thought patterns of their first language and culture.

Kofi Anyidoho. In Bernth Lindfors and Reinhard Sander, eds. *Dictionary of Literary Biography,*. Vol.117. Detroit: Gale Research, 1992, pp. 89–90

Ghanaian novelists are notorious for their long absences from fiction, and the 1990s have seen the long-awaited return of some major talents. Kofi Awoonor and Ama Ata Aidoo allowed, respectively, 21 and 14 years to pass between the publication of their first and second novels, while 17 years separated the fifth and sixth works of Ayi Kwei Armah, the best-established writer of the three. Meanwhile, each has been active in other genres during the long intervals—poetry, short stories, essays—and none of them have fallen silent. Awoonor indicated, shortly after his experimental poetic first novel, *This Earth, My Brother* (1971), that he was at work on another, from which a lengthy extract was actually published in a journal [*Okike*] in 1975, and advance notices of the full version continued apace, even though it did not appear until 1992. . . .

[Comes the Voyager At Last] contains three parallel narratives. The first of these, written in a racy, vernacular jiveargot, is spoken by a poor black American whose 1950s experiences fall into the familiar pattern of social deprivation, wrongful arrest and imprisonment, followed by conversion to Black Islam and a return to Africa—experiences reminiscent of those of Malcom X, whose bodyguard he eventually becomes. The second narrator is a garrulous and facetious Ghanaian intellectual and poet-broadcaster cloned from Awoonor's own public career (his media work for Kwame Nkrumah's régime and demotion after its fall are directly autobiographical). The two men meet in an Accra nightclub, where the American, now called Brother Lumumba, gets into a fight over

a girl with two white expatriates and ends up knifing their African friend. The unnamed Ghanaian manages to spirit the fugitive away to his village in Eweland where, in a sentimental ending, he is adopted back into the ancestral African fold. In the novel's climactic vision of universal harmony, its twin-narratives of return—the American negro's to Africa and the Westernised African intellectual's to his native roots—converge in the black American's dream-consciousness and link up with a third narrative, that of the mythic southward journey of a slave caravan from desert to coast which is interspersed with the primary narratives throughout the book in a series of bardic interludes.

After the haunting elegiac beauty of *This Earth, My Brother*, Awoonor's new novel is disappointingly thin in texture, and his attempt to transfer the first book's black historical consciousness and motif of race-retrieval to the American context, without the aid of the earlier work's enriching poetic lyricism and visionary mythology, is largely unsuccessful. In the nightclub episode he handles well the tensions between the flippant, sophisticated cynicism of his swish Ghanaian and the raw racial polemics of the naïve American visitor, but does it perhaps too cleverly. The very distance between the two men makes their sudden assertion of racial solidarity and blood-brotherhood in the murder scene hard to accept. There has been little to prepare the reader for this mystic rapport: 'He swung around and aimed the knife at me. But in a split second he saw my face. He must have seen also the history of his sojourn and our common voyage in my eyes. He understood.'

When Brother Lumumba, during his initiation into village life, discovers in his race-memory vestiges of African ritual behaviour and instinctively embraces a lost heritage of celebratory dance and song—'soon he too joined in singing the words as if he had been familiar with them all his life'—the novel lapses into a shallow, simplistic *négritude* and the kind of sentimental fantasy indulged by writers like Alex Haley. In the manner of the latter's *Roots* (1976), the Ghanaian's village uncle muses on the miraculous likeness between his cousin and the visiting American: 'you would think they were twins who had slept in one womb'. At this point the reader is tempted to turn to two powerful studies of black Americans who are culturally isolated and painfully adrift in Africa—Aidoo's play, *The Dilemma of a Ghost* (1965), and Wole Soyinka's novel, *The Interpreters* (1965)—for a swift antidote.

Derek Wright. *The Journal of Modern African Studies*. 34, 1 (1996), pp. 179–92

BIBLIOGRAPHY
*Rediscovery, and Other Poems*, 1964; *Night of My Blood*, 1971; *This Earth, My Brother* . . . , 1971; *Ride Me, Memory*, 1973; *Guardians of the Sacred Word*, 1974; *The Breast of the Earth*, 1975; *The House by the Sea*, 1978; *The Ghana Revolution: Background Account from a Personal Perspective*, 1984; *Until the Morning After*, 1987; *Ghana: A Political History from Pre-European to Modern Times*, 1990; *Comes the Voyager At Last*, 1992; *Latin American and Caribbean Notebook*, 1992; *Africa, the Marginalized Continent*, 1994

# B

## BÂ, Mariama (1929–1981)
### Senegal

Her Western education notwithstanding, [Mariama Bâ] would like to be considered as an "average Senegalese woman," "a woman of the house." [*Une Si Longue Lettre*] is her first novel and it is filled with autobiographical elements, expressing as it does the novelist's desires and dilemmas, tracing her life in a society caught between the established order of the past and the exigencies of the present. A traditionalist at heart, Bâ aspires to be a revolutionary. A maternal retiring figure through and through, she aspires to be a pioneer in female emancipation. Her family upbringing and the Koranic training have imbued her with the absolute law of "divine wish": man is woman's overlord. Added to that is Bâ's fatalism. Destiny is a fixed reality, impossible to avoid.... However, such fatalistic tendencies are contradictory to the tenets of the white man's school where Bâ learned how to manipulate the French language. Submissiveness in the face of suffering is discouraged and the victim is told to demand total reform of the social order. Her "letter" is written in the form of a notebook kept by the heroine named Ramatoulaye. Married for thirty years to Modou by whom she has twelve children, Ramatoulaye has been separated for five years from her husband who repudiated her and left her for a much younger woman. Her "letter," ostensibly addressed to a bosom friend, a divorcee working as an interpreter in the Senegalese embassy in [the United States] and due to return home very soon, is written immediately after Modou's death. It is a reflection of life in a psychological ghetto of mental torture and social disorder, where woman is a slave and a beast of prey. Divorce is a rarity but separation and infidelity are common. The life of the couple, far from being a haven of contentment and consideration, is a hell of conniving criminals and common cretins. According to Bâ, two camps are precisely delineated: the victimizer, the slave-master, the ruler of this hell on earth, is Man; the victimized, the slave driven at times to the point of mental exhaustion, is Woman.

> Femi Ojo-Ade. In Eldred Durosimi Jones, ed. *African Literature Today*. 12 (1982), pp. 72–73

Ramatoulaye, the author of the long letter to her childhood friend Aïssatou, in Mariama Bâ's novel [*Une Si Longue Lettre*], presents [the] dilemma of a middle-aged woman in all its complex social, moral, and emotional implications.

She composes her letter over the first months following her husband's sudden death. During the compulsory seclusion imposed on a Muslim widow, she has time to review the thirty years of her married life and the formative years when she and Aïssatou were among the pioneers of girls' secondary school education. The epistolary form justifies the introspective analysis of the narrator's inner conflicts, lending authenticity to her honest heart-searchings. As the narrative progresses, we learn of the experiences of those two intelligent, responsible, generous-minded women, the impositions society has made on them, and the choices they make regarding their own destinies. Both defy convention and family opposition by marrying for love, without dowries, across caste barriers. Both women's happiness is suddenly disrupted by the introduction of a second wife. Aïssatou refuses the customary compromise, leaves her husband, and obtains a well-paid post at the Senegalese embassy in [the United States], enabling her to live independently and bring up her four sons. Then Ramatoulaye's husband casts an uxorious eye on his daughter's pretty school friend, Binetou, who is under pressure from her family to accept the "old man." He has bribed them with the offer of a new home in a smart suburb, a car, a monthly income, and a pilgrimage to Mecca. Binetou is thus presented, not only as Ramatoulaye's rival, but also as a victim, a sacrifice, on the altar of her parent's greed. After long and agonizing reflection, Ramatoulaye resolves to accept her husband's polygamy, much to the indignation of her eldest, emancipated daughter, who is horrified at her father's betrayal and her mother's obligation to share him with a seventeen-year-old. In spite of her education, her lucid intelligence, her love of life, Ramatoulaye retains a strong sense of the traditional role of Muslim women and the old moral values. She rejects Aïssatou's solution of divorce, partly because she still loves her husband and partly to maintain a stable home for her children. Five years later, she is a widow and discovers that her husband died penniless and deeply in debt, that her home is mortgaged, and that he had forgotten . . . all that he owed to her lifetime of devotion and had succumbed to the rapacity of his new in-laws and his adolescent bride. Only then does Ramatoulaye reflect bitterly on marriage, which for a woman means the amputation of her whole personality, her dignity, making her "an object to be used by the man she marries, his grandfather, grandmother, father, mother sister, brother, uncle, aunt, cousins and friends." But, in spite of disappointments and humiliations, although exploited by her husband and manipulated by his family, Ramatoulaye never loses her inner dignity, and she emerges from her anguish with her principles strengthened and her moral stature enhanced. We are sure she will succeed in shaping a life for herself....

*Une Si Longue Lettre* is the first truly feminist African novel, skillfully weaving the accounts of individual suffering and dilemmas into the exposition of her thesis: the issue of woman's status in Senegal today. Showing astonishing maturity of style and construction, it is a cry from the heart of a Muslim woman in a society in transition, voicing the social and religious constraints that weigh heavily on her. It also echoes women's protests against exploitation everywhere in the world and is a call to feminine solidarity.

> Dorothy S. Blair. *Senegalese Literature: A Critical History* (Boston: Twayne, 1984), pp. 137–39

Abandonment in the novels of Mariama Bâ is predominantly a female condition. It is both physical and psychological, and it transcends race, class, ethnicity, and caste.... The forces in society that set in motion the process that culminates in abandonment and the resultant impact of such a process on the abandoned female are conceived by Mariama Bâ to be enormously out of proportion to each other. The whim of accidental fancy of the male and the calculated machinations of a female elder, translated into reality either willingly or reluctantly by the male, place upon the female a burden infinitely heavier than the cause of that burden. The response to this unexpected burden takes one of two forms: reluctant surrender and bear the burden while lamenting and exposing social and other kinds of ills, or categorical refusal to shoulder the burden and opt for freedom through various means. In either case, the female will and determination to live and to retain the integrity of her moral principles usually predominate. Herein lies the faith and confidence of Mariama Bâ in a better future for women in particular, and humankind in general.

Posed in this manner, the problematic of abandonment in the novels of Mariama Bâ begins to take on the characteristics of a power struggle in which both sides, male as well as female, invoke canons of indigenous traditions as well as adopted on indigenous values (conceived of as "universal") to justify or contest attitudes, beliefs, and actions. More specifically, the novelist concentrates on the question of the misuse and distortion of power and privilege in a sociocultural milieu in which one segment of the population— male, acting independently or under pressure from outside forces (usually revenge or profit-motivated parents)—readily acknowledges but selfishly and deceptively perverts privileges bestowed upon it by tradition to the detriment and disadvantage of the female segment. The two possible responses to this selective adherence to tradition—selective because it acknowledges privileges yet shirks responsibilities and obligations that come with such privileges— defines the nature, the intensity, the parameters, and the outcome of this power struggle. In light of this, one can right away dismiss the stereotype of the docile traditional African woman who mutely and passively surrenders to the whims and dictates of the African man. The very idea of a response suggests some measure of consciousness, consciousness which, in the case of Mariama Bâ's heroines, is translated into various kinds of concrete actions designed, in most cases, to counteract the potentially devastating condition of physical and psychological abandonment.

Power struggle, then, is to be seen not so much in terms of victory/defeat, since it is the kind of struggle that yields a no win situation, but it is to be looked at from the perspective of the impact of the experience on the individual and the letter's ability to examine, articulate and utilize the transformative capabilities of such an experience of struggle. The heroines in *Une Si Longue Lettre*, Rama, Aïsatou, and Jacqueline, are a living testimony to the positive transformative capabilities of a negative experience born of the problematic of abandonment. Each one emerges from basically the same experience stronger and better placed to more clearly understand, cope with, analyze, and articulate the problems, challenges, and aspirations of not only women but of society. Such is the nature of the dialectical mind of Mariama Bâ. On the other hand, the white French heroine of *Un Chant écarlate*, Mireille de la Valée, exemplifies the tragedy and destruction attendant to the problematic of abandonment. Her response is qualitatively different from that of the heroines of *Une Si Longue Lettre* even though the experience that elicits the response is the same. Here, Mariama Bâ introduces the pivotal role of culture in response formulation and execution in the face of a given problematic.

Mbye Baboucar Cham. *Current Bibliography on African Affairs*. 17, 1 (1984–1985), pp. 30–31

One of the key concepts that emerges from Mariama Bâ's novels is that of choice. This is most striking in *Une Si Longue Lettre* where

the recurrence of words like . . . [the choice, to choose, I have chosen, I have decided, my decision, I wished, I did not wish to] is in itself indicative of the importance of choice for Mariama Bâ. In *Un Chant écarlate*, even though words pertaining to choice are less recurrent, crucial choices are constantly being made throughout the novel. The act of choosing is shown as being pivotal in human experience. It is indeed a powerful act which gives shape and direction to human existence. . . .

It is important to focus on the choices made by female characters in *Une Si Longue Lettre* because women are definitely at the center of the novel. . . . Ramatoulaye is portrayed as a strong, dignified woman who is confronted with a number of options throughout her life; she is therefore called upon to make vital choices. . . .

In this novel Mariama Bâ affirms that ["Each woman makes of her life what she wishes"]. This affirmation is very reminiscent of Jean-Paul Sartre's pronouncements on choice. Indeed, in *L'Être et le néant* and, in more simple terms in *L' Existentialisme best un humanisme* Sartre posits that human beings are nothing else than what they make of themselves. They are the sum total of their choices and through the act of choosing, they create themselves. Sartre, then, views choice as essential for the creation of self. Even though Mariama Bâ does not go as far as to make choice a metaphysical concept like Sartre who thinks that human beings are condemned to choose, she does consider choice to be of vital importance, to be the ultimate affirmation of self. It is indeed through choice that Ramatoulaye and Aïssatou find the strength and courage to face problems that overburden women, to overcome what threatens to deny the self. It is also through choice that they arrive at self-realization. However, this is not achieved without pain, without conflict. . . .

*Un Chant écarlate* deals with choice in a very different way. Here all the characters are called upon to make choices and they are all affected by each other's choices. . . .

All the characters in *Un Chant écarlate* make important choices, Ousmane chooses to marry Mireille, and to remain faithful to his culture. He also chooses to marry a second wife even though his father who is a staunch Muslim married only one wife. . . .

Mireille, on the other hand, chooses to study in Dakar so she can see Ousmane; she also chooses to be converted to Islam without measuring the implications of such a conversion. She also chooses to remain faithfull to her own culture. Her efforts of adaptation to Senegalese lifestyle are short-lived and frustrated by antagonistic forces. . . .

Even though the concept of choice underlies both novels, there is an essential difference in the way it is treated. In *Une Si Longue Lettre* there is no doubt that Modou, Binetou, Tante Nabou, and Mawdo make choices that affect others. However, the emphasis is clearly on the two main protagonists, Ramatoulaye and Aïssatou. Here, choice is essentially seen as it affects the individual lives of these two women, as it allows for growth, as it activates the development of consciousness. In *Un Chant écarlate*, on the other hand, choices affect not only the individuals who make them but also the people who are close to them.

Irène Assiba d' Almeida. In Carole Boyce Davies and Anne Adams Graves, eds. *Ngambika: Studies of Women in African Literature* (Trenton, New Jersey: Africa World Press, 1986), pp. 161–62, 165, 168–69

Mariama Bâ did not attack tradition and custom blatantly, but she expressed her disapproval of certain glaring abuses of tradition which impede progress. While she demonstrated an unflinching faith in the freedom of choice and the personal nature of marriage and romantic love, she also expressed her belief in the gain that the community in the modern context—the nation—would reap from the success and the attainment of happiness by individual couples. For her, family success depended on the harmony of the founding couple, and in turn, it was the grouping of all these successful and happy families that would constitute the nation. . . .

One could argue that there was nothing new in this idea in the African context, for it was in the interest of the community in general that the family would initiate ties that would ultimately lead to the union in marriage of young men and women. What was new, however, was the notion that marriage was above all based on the choice and initial attraction of the two principal partners. . . .

Bâ was the first African writer to stress unequivocally the strong desire of the new generation of Africans to break away from the age-old marriage customs and adopt a decidedly more modern approach based on free mutual choice and the equality of the two partners.

In her two novels, she pointedly showed that the extended family's action could invariably make such relationships fizzle out in bitter failure. And while never indulging in outright condemnation of the traditions of her society, she denounced the contemporary abuses of these traditions.

> Edris Makward. In Carole Boyce Davies and Anne Adams Graves, eds. *Ngambika: Studies of Women in African Literature* (Trenton, New Jersey: Africa World Press, 1986), pp. 274–75, 278

Mariama Bâ provides a positive model of the mother-in-law in the person of Rama in *Une si longue lettre*. Rama feels no urge to intervene in the affairs of her pregnant school-age daughter, Aissatou. Her main concern is with the unfairness of a system that will penalize a school-age girl for getting pregnant while leaving the other party, the male party, untouched. Faced with this situation, Rama's motherly instinct of support and protection for a child in trouble gets the better of her, and this is made easier by Ibrahima Sall's sense of respect and devotion to Aissatou and her family. She readily forgives her daughter's mistake and resolves to help them on the difficult road ahead. Most of all, she refuses to imprison her daughter in her own value system, realizing the limits of parental control over offspring in today's society: 'I accepted my subordinate role. The ripe fruit must fall from the tree.'

The phenomenon of women deliberately and maliciously sabotaging the happiness of other women in a male-dominated society is one that has come to be a major focal point in the work of Mariama Bâ and that of her compatriot, Aminata Sow-Fall. Daba's question to Dame Belle-Mère in *Une si longue lettre*, 'How can one woman destroy the happiness of another woman?' is constantly implied in *Un chant écarlate* where friends and colleagues of Ousmane, such as Rosalie, ponder over the implications of this phenomenon. What is the state of a society, the novelist seems to be asking, in which the likes of Oulaymatou Ngom fail, or do not even want, to question male vanity and excess, especially in the area of mate-sharing? Rosalie is even more disgusted at Oulaymatou's scheme: 'She waits for you to get married in order to throw herself

at him. What a spectacle! Her attitude is unworthy of a woman of this century. Women should unite.' In the absence of such female solidarity what hope is there for a change in the status quo of male domination, and what does this entail for the future of the institution of the family, marriage and society as a whole?

Our analysis of the role of the mother-in-law in the process of abandonment may convey the impression that the primary culprit here is the woman herself. However, the fact is that Mariama Bâ sees the vanity, lust and fickle-mindedness of the male as the greater decisive factor in this process. The novelist clearly sets the limits of the influence of the woman in the process without totally dismissing its negative effects. This sense of balance accounts for the writer's ability to penetrate beneath the surface reality of women and society to present the issue in all its complexity. Yaye khady may have set out to chase Mireille away, but it is really Ousmane who ultimately drives her insane and leads her to commit an act designed to be a final solution to her woes. Ousmane fails miserably to balance his loyalty to a scheming selfish mother with his own responsibilities as husband and partner of a woman in need of help in a new cultural environment. He becomes a prisoner and panders to the excesses of a value system whose distorted principles the so-called enlightened people of his generation are supposed to re-evaluate in the light of current realities and exigencies. Consequently, he gets caught in a web of distortion, deception and confusion which he adamantly, but clumsily, insists on rationalizing in the name of what his friends and contemporaries such as Lamine and Boly see as false négritude. His transformation from a hardworking youth full of respect, love and devotion to his parents and girlfriend, to a vain confused young man with distorted sociocultural values is a result of this failure. Rejected by Oulaymatou, he turns to Mireille for social and personal validation; challenged by Mireille to be responsible, he seeks escape in Oulaymatou who panders to his vanity and who now represents Africa and African culture in his eyes:

> 'Oulaymatou, double symbol in my life!' 'Symbol of the black woman' who it was his duty to liberate, 'symbol of Africa' one of whose 'enlightened sons' he was. In his mind, Oulaymatou was confused with Africa, 'an Africa to be reinstalled in her prerogatives, an Africa to be promoted.'

This sense of 'mission libératrice' becomes the spin that further turns Ousmane's mind and energy away from his obligations to his wife and son.

In both novels, Mariama Bâ examines the issue of intercaste, intercultural and interracial marriage and relationships, and she raises questions on whose satisfactory resolution will depend the stability and viability of much of the moral, political, social, economic and cultural fabric of her society. This issue is increasingly becoming a focal point for a number of African artists concerned about the nature and implications of personal and social relationships within and between societies in Africa, in particular. . . .

Although Mariama Bâ does not look at the currently topical issue of female excision and infibulation in these novels, her concern with the general issue of inequality puts her in the mainstream, if not the forefront, of contemporary feminine and African thought. In spite of awesome odds, her heroines are champions of change and justice and they inspire other women and people to live and carry on.

This affirmative attitude toward life that the novelist invests in her heroines and that she wants to inspire in all women is conveyed in a language and form that have few parallels in African literature. One of the distinguishing features of Mariama Bâ's language is its poetic majesty which effortlessly expresses the emotion and thoughts of her characters in ways that could come only from the imagination of an accomplished woman artist. The novelist is at her best in those instances when she takes us deep into the mind and feelings of mothers disappointed with the choice of mate of their offsprings, of mothers and other women scheming to undermine one another, of mothers on the joys, pains and challenges of motherhood, of women confiding in other women, of women concerned with the political and economic health of society, and of men trapped in a quagmire of vanity, lust and deception.

> Mbye B. Cham. Eldred Durosimi Jones, ed., *Women in African Literature Today* (Trenton: World Africa Press, 1987), pp. 98–100

A social history, [*Une Si Longue Lettre*, translated as *So Long a Letter*] deals very specifically with the struggle for social transformation. Ramatoulaye, the widow who writes, becomes conscious of the fact that, in the face of all the uncertainties and changes in her life, she is working out her salvation by addressing herself to a woman who is a sister spirit. In the course of the narrative, we watch a woman in her fifties being transformed, preparing to begin life anew.

The world of Mariama Bâ's novel is the contemporary African state, and her story takes place against the background of the creation of that civic state. Bâ gives us a Muslim woman living in a patriarchal culture whose religious tenets and social conventions, at least as they are institutionalized and practiced, serve to keep women subject. Bâ then creates for us a contemporary woman challenged by the impact of the modern city and state from whose debris she reclaims herself and her children; having helped build the still patriarchal state, she must reclaim herself from it. . . .

In this work Ramatoulaye shifts from a notion of woman as subject female to one of the *complementarity* of man and woman as the vital unit of that national whole in which she locates the liberated woman. In this movement, Bâ strikes at the heart of the motherhood issue . . . by placing mothering firmly *within* a definition of the liberated female self and symbolically rewriting the history of maternal alienation from the modern state. In the same way that griots draw us forward to the present in their narratives, Ramatoulaye recollects the histories of women from *her* perspective and finds a place for them in her account of their new world. This novel writes women back into history by making it her story also. It creates a heroine for whom the making of the modern state becomes also the making of a modern woman who survives and lives in that state and . . . becomes a mistress of her words, and worlds.

> Abena P. A. Busia. In Joe Weixlmann and Houston A. Baker, Jr., eds. *Studies in Black American Literature*, (Greenwood, Florida.: Penkevill, 1988), Vol. III, pp. 27–29

Setting her novel [*Une Si Longue Lettre*] in Dakar about twenty years after Senegal's independence from France, Bâ evaluates from a contemporary perspective the outcome of the nationalist and feminist movements of the late 1950s. The world of the novel is that of Dakar's established professional class, the members of which in their student days were in the vanguard of these progressive movements. What she reveals is the betrayal by this same privileged elite of the hopes and aspirations of both. While Bâ's focal concern is the female experience, the national fate that provides the backdrop enlarges the scope of the novel, and the undermining by bourgeois materialism of the nationalist ideals of liberty and equality serves as a vehicle to illuminate the compromising by women as well as men of the feminist ideal of a marriage contract based of parity between the sexes. . . . [The] unhappiness of Ramatoulaye, the work's central character, is a result not only of her victimization by the male social order but also of her continuing complicity in the process.

Crucial to an understanding and assessment of this novel is an appreciation of the narrative framework Bâ has so carefully and skillfully elaborated. The story is told in the first person by Ramatoulaye in the form of a letter-diary that she addresses to her friend Aïssatou and writes following the death of her husband Modou. Working within the genre of pseudo-autobiography, Bâ has her heroine tell her story, not directly, but with subconscious evasion and revelation. While Bâ's exploitation of the ironic possibilities of her narrative mode provides the novel with much of its meaning and flavor, it is in the narrative setting created for the telling that the informing force of the novel lies. Ramatoulaye writes her letter during the four months and ten days of secluded mourning prescribed by Islam for windows. In this Islamic practice, Bâ found her archetypical image of female experience. . . . Ramatoulaye's physical confinement during this period of mourning in the house she once shared with Modou replicates her psychological confinement in a debilitating stereotypical view of a woman's role.

> Florence Stratton. *Resarch in African Literatures.* 19, 1 (Summer 1988), p. 159

Ramatoulaye is a paradox, a conservative in revolt. She may endorse the European headmistress's exhortation to leave the bog of superstition, custom, and tradition, a call that equates African tradition with superstition and consigns both to the rubbish heap, but a part of her remains cautious, conservative, and ''patriotic.'' The harshness and contempt reserved for the lower class that Binetou and her mother represent, and the very different treatment accorded to Mawdo's royal mother and Nabou, has already been mentioned. The latter are associated with Africa's heroic past: the retributive violence of the warrior, his reckless courage, history combat, and thoroughbred horses. Of course, it is courage conceived of in aristocratic rather than in democratic terms. Like Camara Laye, Ramatoulaye regrets that traditional crafts decline into mere tourist art as the young artists choose European-run or European-modeled schools. In nonindustrialized countries, formal schooling and ''paper qualifications'' are sure avenues to well-paid jobs in the public sector. And as the individual rises, so does the extended family. Formal education is one means to an upward economic and social mobility, but traditional Ramatoulaye sees in young students only that lack of sensitivity to honor that leads to physical retaliation and assault. She who spoke about the bog of tradition also applauds the fierce resistance put up by old virtues against the inroads of imported vices. During the Algerian war of independence, the French attempted to compel Algerian women to discard their veils, but they clung to them: what was traditional was also national and, therefore, to be protected and preserved against foreign attack. Polygamy, which Ramatoulaye opposes, is sanctioned by Islam, a traditional religion, unlike Christianity. This is yet another contradiction and tension in devout, traditional, feminist Ramatoulaye. The conservative servative aspect of her character is also revealed in some of her opinions: for example, that cleanliness is one of the essential qualities of a women and that a woman's mouth should be fragrant: but don't these qualities apply to men as well? Unwittingly, she casts women in the role of sex objects, attracting and seducing men into marriage. In spite of the decline in the conduct of young women, Ramatoulaye will not give her daughters immunity in pleasure. The price of sin is an unwanted pregnancy; such a pregnancy indicates theft, theft of virginity and of family honor. A woman who exposes any part of her body, like a woman who smokes, exposes a jaunty shamelessness.

And so Ramatoulaye the rebel becomes afraid of progress. . . . Ramatoulaye's caution and skepticism seem to extend to Aïssatou, her dear and faithful friend: Has Aïssatou, because of her stay in the United States, become too Westernized? Will she insist on eating with a fork and knife, rather than with the hand? Will she wear trousers? And so Ramatoulaye continues to write her letter even after hearing that her old friends will return home on holiday, to write even on the very day before Aïssatou's arrival. The letter has now become a diary, a form suggesting greater loneliness, beginning and ending with oneself.

Charles Ponnuthurai Sarvan. *Modern Fiction Studies*. 34, 3 (Autumn 1988), pp. 459–60

[Marriage] remains a tangential concern in [Sembène Ousmane and Aminata Sow Fall] when compared with its place in the two novels Mariama Bâ wrote before her death in August, 1981. In the first novel, *So Long a Letter*, her protagonist, Ramatoulaye, "writes" a long letter to her friends Aïssatou—both of them victims of marriages that eventually went sour halfway. Ramatoulaye is shocked to learn of her husband's new desire for Binetou, their daughter's friend who used to spend part of her holidays with them. Part of the strangeness of Modou Fall's new appetite is located in the fact that the two of them had lived together as husband and wife for twenty-five years, and their marriage blessed them with twelve children. This horde of children and their mother are abandoned by Modou in preference for a younger woman. Aïssatou, on the other hand, considers her doctor-husband's second marriage as a breaking of faith in their relationship. She blames Mawdo for succumbing to his mother's long stratagem meant to humiliate her daughter-in-law by dangling before her son the sapling Nabou. Mawdo easily falls for this luscious bait, marries the teenage girl and expects Aïssatou to compromise and stay on. But she will not. Rather than accept Mawdo's second marriage, she decides to start life anew and alone. She will not bend her head in silence and accept a destiny that oppresses her. Aïssatou leaves with her four sons and takes to her studies, training as an interpreter and eventually finding a job at her country's embassy in America.

[*Un Chant écarlate*, translated as *Scarlet Song*] is a little variation of Bâ's concern in her first novel. Here the focus is still marriage, but this time it has been given a wider and more intensive scope. Two worlds—the worlds of the black man and that of the white—are brought together in a mixed marriage, which fails like the matrimonial unions of the African couples in *So Long a Letter* the Mawdo-Aïssatou, Modou-Ramatoulaye, and Samba-Jacqueline relationships. Ousmane Gueye and Mireille de la Vallé first met in a Dakar university when the latter's father was a French diplomat in the Senegalese capital. Monisieur de la Vallé who had been identified with moving speeches addressing the necessity to demolish racial barriers, has no problems in deciding Mireille's fate in Dakar as soon as he knows that she is cultivating the love of an African boy. He immediately flies his "adventurous" daughter to Paris, their home, where she continues her study. But Mireille will later marry this boy in Paris to the unrelenting anger of her parents. However, when the mixed couple return to Africa they discover too late that there is a wide hiatus between theory and practice, ideals and reality. The two come face-to-face with consuming cultural clashes that soon help to diminish the intensity of their original passion for each other. Unknown to Mireille, Ousmane makes plans for a second marriage, to a childhood friend called Ouleymatou. But when Mireille learns about the affair, she becomes schizophrenic, kills the only child of their marriage, Gorgui, and then attempts to murder her unfaithful husband.

In the two novels, Mariama Bâ consistently attacks the idea of polygyny, which is for her indeed a humiliation of women. None of her major female characters accepts it, and where it appears some of them do, it is because of the blind alley in which they find themselves—the confines of marriage or the limited opportunities available to them outside of it. Ramatoulaye and her co-wife Binetou in *So Long a Letter* and Ouleymatou in *Scarlet*, who are apparently undisturbed by the multiple marriages of their husbands, clearly bargain from weak positions.

J. O. J. Nwachukwu-Agbada. *Modern Fiction Studies*. 37, 3 (Autumn 1991), pp. 562–64

BIBLIOGRAPHY
*So Long a Letter* (*Une Si Longue Lettre*, 1980); A Scarlet Song (*Un Chant écarlate*, 1981)

# BADIAN, Seydou (1928– )
**Mali**

[Seydou Badian's first novel *Sous l'orage*, reissued as *Sous l'orage (Kany)*] was completed in Montpellier in 1954, and was published nine years later. . . .

The story itself is simple. . . . Kany, daughter of Benfa and Téné, is in love with a young man, Samou, who lives with his mother, Coumba. They are two childhood friends who went to the same school. But their love is opposed by their parents, who are bound to traditional customs: the father, Benfa, has decided long ago to marry his daughter to the old businessman Famagan. Obviously the young girl is supposed to blindly obey her father's wishes, which represent the ancestral wishes, but her personality and education prevent such a blind submission. She formally opposes Benfa, thereby creating a very serious conflict between father and daughter, a conflict of generations.

This pseudo-novel unfolds by using archetypes, therefore it is distracting to give room to a central character, since neither Benfa nor his daughter really occupy the foreground. Neither is described from the inside or the outside. Since one does not know Kany's exact age, her height, or her manner of dressing, and is thus deprived of any physical reference and of any emotional link with the past, . . . the reader concludes that by virtue of this deprivation, the author wanted to expose a character, not create a woman. . . .

[The themes] reflect the major preoccupations of the author, anxious about the destiny of his country as well as the upholding of the grand ancestral realities. Africa cannot remain as it is, nor can it reject the totality of its past. The difficult amalgamation cannot be achieved without problems. This is typified by the latent conflicts suggested in this novel, where tradition rules but where the opportunity of an outside pragmatism, necessary for a new lease of equilibrium, is also revealed.

S.M. Battestini. *Littérature Africaine Seydou Badian* (Paris: Fernard Nathan, 1968), pp. 32–33, 37†

Without being polemical, [*Sous l'orage*] is strongly didactic and it is a contribution to the literature of Négritude: devoid of satirical elements, it is a novel of ideas rather than of character and incident. . . .

The tone of the whole of Badian's novel is that of a moralizing tract addressed to the people of Sudan, with independence round the corner, and the responsibility for organizing their own society in sight. The situation of the action, and every episode is thus chosen with a view to exposing or illustrating an idea or principle. Badian places his characters first in a small town in the Sudan shortly after the end of World War II. On Kany's refusal to accept the marriage plans, she is banished with her sympathetic brother Birama to their father's distant birthplace. The journey in the train allows for a discussion between a carefully selected group of passengers, who express their grievances and points of view in a contrived academic dialogue. The sojourn in the primitive village brings the ''city youngsters'' into contact with African rural life, where they are taught by their uncle Djigui to understand and appreciate the best of the old traditions. There is also vague and inconclusive reference to the continued existence of secret societies, a pretext for a lesson in the ancient tribal beliefs. The melodramatic introduction of the epidemic of cerebrospinal meningitis, inadequately motivated, and unlinked to preceding or subsequent events, is used to show the reactions of the old and superstitious who think that disease is the result of a curse.

Seydou Badian clearly has an important message to convey to his compatriots and he has chosen the *roman à thèse* for the purpose. Although the novel will not have been read by large numbers of these, as it is written in a European tongue, he can justify himself by the fact that his lesson is addressed in the first instance to the young intellectuals, the product of Westernized schooling and white progress. As the ones who will take over responsibility when colonization comes to an end, they are advised to retain the best of the wisdom of Africa and keep a nice balance between the old and the new. The message comes over clearly; on this level the work is irreproachable. It is more open to criticism, if it is to be assessed as a contribution to original creative literature, in the genre that the author has adopted. The characters are not treated with profundity and so make little impact on the reader; the situations are contrived and the solution not psychologically motivated. But these reservations will fall away for those who place Badian's novel solely in the category of illustrative sociology.

Dorothy S. Blair. *African Literature in French* (London: Cambridge University Press, 1976), pp. 240–42

*Le Sang des masques* is an original work. Its originality resides primarily in the presentation of the subject and the perspective offered by Badian on contemporary African society. It is a novel of adventure, conflict, and dizzying intrigue.

In this novel, Seydou Badian is not attracted by traditional exoticism; but instead poses the everyday problems of Africa. The conflict of values constitutes the backdrop of the novel on which village and city intrigues are grafted. The universe of the two young heroes is divided into two distinct cultural zones. Will they succeed in bridging the gap that separates them? The two protagonists, Bakari and Nandi, originally in the camp of traditional culture, are literally thrown into the other cultural sphere by the pressure of events. Bakari goes to the city with his father's blessing. . . .

After an absence of three years, Bakari returns to the village. But the village has changed; indifference and hostility are prevalent. His childhood friends abandon him and he only encounters enemies. Veiled internal battles, for the conquest of power, place people in opposition to one another. Evil and greedy creatures like Bantji want to subjugate the others through words and magic. . . .

Bakari fights the forces of evil and conquers them thanks to the myth of courage and chivalrous virility still honored in the village. . . . And through dance, he wins the heart of Nandi. . . . The two are tied together by bonds of a loving friendship and spiritual complicity. . . . To assure his complete supremacy over the village, Bakari confronts and destroys the forces of deception and quackery represented by Bantji.

Bakari and Nandi meet in the city where they are torn from their milieu and their culture and assaulted by the values of the big city. . . .

And the only value the city holds is money. . . . Nandi is ill-treated and abandoned by her spouse . . . [and] finally returns to the village, disgusted by all that she saw and experienced in the city: a violent husband, women with loose morals, and the excessive power of money. The novel ends with the image of Nandi tracing in reverse the path taken by Bakari. She is in search of a more just and humane society, sheltered from violence, greed, and corruption. . . . Can the return of Nandi help preserve the purity and authenticity of ancient values? An element of doubt remains about this. One of the last sentences in the novel contains a message which is in effect an invitation to the creation of a new African culture. The co-penetration of ideas is inevitable in the real world. . . .

*Le Sang des masques* is a personal reflection by the author on the socio-cultural and economic upheavals that traverse modern Africa.

Christophe Dailly. *Presence Africaine.* 101–2 (1977), pp. 293–95†

After *Sous l'orage*, the . . . novel in which the solution to the problems of contemporary Africa was to be found in a slow and ever-negotiated collaboration between the young and old, Seydou Badian [released] in 1977 another novel, *Noces sacrées*, in which he unequivocally asserts the values of ancestral tradition. This work, set in the colonial period, might seem curiously backward and paradoxical if it did not express a concern increasingly shared at present by some African writers and critics: namely that of preserving endangered traditional values and ethos. . . .

*Noces sacrées* is essentially the story of the moral evolution of a Westernized African doctor—of note is the fact that Badian himself is a doctor—who is led by strange circumstances to rediscover the depths and intrinsic value of his traditional culture.

After numerous encounters which ultimately reveal to him the superiority of Africa over the West in matters of philosophy, religion, as well as technology, the hero returns willingly, through ritual initiation, to the world of his ancestry. . . .

*Noces sacrées* is particularly rich in accurate elements taken from the oral tradition. Even allowing for poetic license on the part of the author, this novel is unquestionably rooted in the Bambara magico-religious reality, as described by ethnographers. This aspect is indeed most significant for the message of the work: the Westernized African protagonist does undergo an initiatory return to the real, cultural sources of ancestral tradition and not merely the ever-archetypal return to the world of childhood. Moreover, the African tradition clearly demonstrates its universal relevance by receiving the two whites, Besnier and Mlle Baune, into its midst during an initiatory ceremony. This simple episode confirms the fact that the Western reader is equally and directly concerned by and implicated in the story. . . .

In conclusion, this novel, haunted by the N'domo and other occult powers, appears as an attempt to reassert a tradition and beliefs in danger of extinction. Like Birago Diop some twenty-five years earlier, Seydou Badian warns his compatriots against "the temptation of the West," the temptation to discard indiscriminately as obsolete the values and beliefs of the ancestral tradition. One may even wonder why Badian has chosen to set his novel in the colonial period rather than in the present. Might the author be suggesting that at the time of its most absolute supremacy, Europe was already supplanted, morally and technically—since precisely in the African view the moral and the technical go hand-in-hand by the specific nature of African power? As for the imposed involvement of the reader in the story, we would appear to be in the presence of yet another specifically African trait, transposed from the oral tradition: each listener/reader is an active witness, deeply committed by the word uttered by this descendant of the griot's Kouyate clan, whose name is Seydou Badian.

> Jacques Bourgeacq. *Pacific Moana Quarterly.* 6, 3–4 (July-October 1981), pp. 158–59, 161

[*La Mort de Chaka*, translated as *The Death of Chaka*] is a play of ideas rather than a comic entertainment with socially critical overtones. [Badian] had already served for nearly a year as minister of rural development and planning in Mali when he began writing it. Like many young intellectuals in Africa, Badian was a committed socialist who resented the humiliations imposed upon the continent by a history of colonialist oppression. To comprehend such feelings, one has merely to recall the disdain in which Europeans held African civilization until very recently. As late as 1962 [when *The Death of Chaka* was originally published as *La Mort de Chaka*], the well-known British historian Hugh Trevor-Roper publicly proclaimed that there was no history in Africa before the arrival of Europeans—only darkness. In view of such attitudes, Badian's preface takes on a heightened significance, for in referring to the historical Chaka, king of the Zulus in southern Africa and brilliant organizer of a 400,000-man army, he is offering evidence to support his conviction that there was not only history before the arrival of the white man but there were also great heroes who succeeded in forging political order from chaos. On one level, then, the play promotes an African sense of pride in history, for by depicting the Zulu leader as a noble idealist and linking him with the creation of a new nation, Badian is ascribing epic proportion to

a story that had been treated in a negative fashion by European historians, who tended to regard the historical Chaka as a bloodthirsty tyrant. Badian's choice of an historical subject thus reflects a desire to recover the truth and to refute ethnocentric commentators like Trevor-Roper. . . .

*The Death of Chaka* is essentially a dialogue of conflicting perspectives. First, Chaka is presented through the eyes of his rebellious generals. Although there is an undercurrent of recognition for his accomplishments, these men are disturbed by what they interpret as Chaka's arbitrary cruelty and self-aggrandizing tendencies. Beneath the surface of their comments, it becomes apparent that some of them are also jealous of him. And they are all tired of the continuous effort that he demands from them. The specific occasion for their discussion in the opening scenes is Chaka's announcement that the Zulu will attack a coalition of hostile tribes in the south in order to consolidate their previous victories and to remove the last major threat to their control in the area. In addition, the generals resent the fact that Chaka had recently removed them from their command of specific regiments (*impis*) and would henceforth assign them to their positions only shortly before the battle. The immediate objective of the generals is to prevent the battle from taking place, for they regard it as untimely and unreasonable.

As their conversations progress, however, they gradually persuade themselves that it is necessary to eliminate Chaka, whom they accuse of being mad and increasingly bloodthirsty. Their arguments appear credible, and the reader of the play is predisposed to judge Chaka unfavorably. Yet when Chaka himself appears on the stage relatively late in the play, their image of him is utterly discredited, and they themselves are revealed for what they are—petty, self-serving plotters against the legitimate authority of a genuine leader. Badian adopts this approach for a very good reason. Because the truly decisive socialist leaders of independent African nations are frequently maligned by local elites and by conservative interests in the industrialized world, he desires to make the case against such leaders appear plausible so that when it is revealed as fraudulent, the audience will gain insight into the way people are duped in the real world by similar, apparently valid arguments. The drama of Badian's play lies not in the action, but in the conflict of ideas. His major purpose in drawing upon the story of an early nineteenth-century African hero is to raise the level of consciousness about what needs to be done in the present.

> Richard Bjornson. Introduction to Guillaume Oyônô-Mbia and Seydou Badian. *Faces of African Independence: Three Plays* (Charlottesville: University Press of Virginia, 1988), pp. xxiv, xxvii–xxviii

Badian . . . presents, in *The Death of Chaka*, a tragedy of human nature unrelieved by any comic interludes and revealing the shattering interplay of self-confidence and jealousy on a patriot and nation-builder. . . .

Badian's Chaka is a patriot who is single-minded about the need to establish his people over other peoples in the area. He is conceived as gentle but very powerful, whether present or absent from the scene. Thus Badian does not deal with the controversial historical Chaka on whom many writers are so divided. The patriotism and commitment of Chaka is for Badian like the biblical Charity which "covereth a multitude of sins." "Hard" realism indicates that empires, civilization, and colonies have always been established at the cost of human lives and that the benefits of having them have invariably been reaped by the future generations. The play and its characters are hardly well developed but its message is unmistakably sympathetic to Chaka's patriotic leadership.

*The Death of Chaka* is a people's tragedy as much as it is that of the individual. The Zulu nation has lost the chance [of] political greatness and the struggle to regain it will never be easy for the descendants of Chaka. The voice of the people in the play is represented by that of a lone Zulu maiden, Notibel, who denounces her fiancé, Dingana, and pledges total allegiance to Chaka. As it were she is the ear of the people. In the first tableaux, when the mutiny against Chaka is being hatched, she enters uninvited. ''I have overheard everything. There has been talk of bloodshed,'' she says and warns the generals not to desert Chaka no matter what happens. Also in the second tableaux she comes in under similar circumstances saying ''Ndlebe, I overheard everything. I am disappointed,'' and thereafter she resolves: ''I was Mapo's sister. I was Dingana's fianceé. Now I am neither Mapo's sister nor Dingana's fianceé. I am Chaka's daughter. Like everyone else, I am a Zulu.'' Following this declaration of loyalty which is supposed to be that of other Zulus, Ntiobe's political commitment becomes complete. Like Ebrahim's Kinjekitile, the hero of the play of that name, the future now belongs to the people.

> J. Ndukaku Amankulor. *Ufahumu*. 17, 2 (Spring 1989), pp. 164, 168–169

BIBLIOGRAPHY

*Under the Storm* (*Sous l'orage*, 1957); The Death of Chaka (*La Mort de Chaka*, 1962); The Blood of the Masks (*Le Sang des masques*, 1976); Sacred Wedding (*Noces sacrées*, 1977); *Congo: terre généreuse, forêt féconde*, 1983

# BALDWIN, James (1924–1987)
**United States**

In his first novel [*Go Tell It on the Mountain*] James Baldwin has used the familiar story-within-a-story device to produce good entertainment—and something more: even the most insensitive of readers will put the book down with a troubled feeling of having ''looked on beauty bare.''

It is not, however, the kind of beauty to which lazy senses respond—no honeysuckle and moonlight, no pastoral charm or urban elegance, no pure young love, no soft, sweet lostness of the brave and the damned. Its beauty is the beauty of sincerity and of the courageous facing of hard subjective truth. This is not to say that there is nothing derivative—of what first novel can this be said?—but James Baldwin's critical judgments are perspicacious and his esthetic instincts sound, and he has read Faulkner and Richard Wright and, very notably, Dostoevski to advantage. A little of each is here—Faulkner in the style, Wright in the narrative, and the Russian in the theme. And yet style, story and theme are Baldwin's own, made so by the operation of the strange chemistry of talent which no one fully understands.

Baldwin's style is lucid and free-running but involved. It is a style that shows the man to be keenly sensitive to words. The frame story of *Go Tell It on the Mountain* is relatively slight. It is a simple account of what frustration does to an adolescent boy named John Grimes. The fact of his being a Negro has little significance other than as description. John could have been any susceptible fifteen-year-old, illegitimate boy, hated by his stepfather, estranged by younger children from his mother, and forced to live within himself. But living within oneself is unnatural for a physically healthy boy in Harlem, and John, in a violent burst of seeking for he knows not what, finds another world.

> J. Saunders Redding. *New York Herald Tribune Books*. May 17, 1953, p. 5

[In *Go Tell It on the Mountain*] John succumbs to his guilt and to his longings for reconciliation with his family, with his Negro-ness, and with God, and is seized by a religious convulsion. In submitting to it he chooses one of the two fates allowed the Negro. If he were to revolt, as so many in his family had done, the world would strike him down. If, on the other hand, he accepts the literal nothingness of what the world offers, and forfeits his hopes for a better life on earth, he will be accepting the burden of religion and of being a Negro. . . .

There are two ''mountains'' in this book. When, at the end, John is ''saved'' and has begun his tortured ascent of the mountain of Holiness, we feel that the injustice of his condition is subsumed for the moment in the larger, impersonal justice of the novel—the strange justice of tragedy. This is his doom, and there is a rightness about it if only because it is inevitable. But we recall that other ''mountain,'' the hill in Central Park from which John, at the beginning of the book, looked down beneath ''the brilliant sky, and beyond it, cloudy and far away, he saw the skyline of New York.'' It is the same kind of elevation from which, I am sure Mr. Baldwin wants us to remember, Eugène de Rastignac, at the close of [Balzac's] *Père Goriot*, surveys Paris. It is the prominence from which all the ''young men from the provinces'' catch their glimpse of the worlds they are to love and win. But for John Grimes there can be no winning; and when we realize this, that he can stand only on the mountain of Holiness, an otherworldly mountain made of bitterness and renunciation, a mountain where he finds his real identity, the poignancy of his earlier vision comes upon us with great force.

> Steven Marcus. *Commentary*. November 1953, pp. 460–61

James Baldwin writes down to nobody, and he is trying very hard to write up to himself. As an essayist he is thought-provoking, tantalizing, irritating, abusing and amusing. And he uses words as the sea uses waves, to flow and beat, advance and retreat, rise and take a bow in disappearing.

In *Notes of a Native Son*, James Baldwin surveys in pungent commentary certain phases of the contemporary scene as they relate to the citizenry of the United States, particularly Negroes. Harlem, the protest novel, bigoted religion, the Negro press and the student milieu of Paris are all examined in black and white, with alternate shutters clicking, for hours of reading interest. When the young man who wrote this book comes to a point where he can look at life purely as himself, and for himself, the color of his skin mattering not at all, when, as in his own words, he finds ''his birthright as a man no less than his birthright as a black man,'' America and the world might well have a major contemporary commentator.

Few American writers handle words more effectively in the essay form than James Baldwin. To my way of thinking, he is much better at provoking thought in the essay than he is in arousing emotion in fiction. I much prefer *Notes of a Native Son* to his novel, *Go Tell It on the Mountain*, where the surface excellence and poetry of his writing did not seem to me to suit the earthiness of his subject-matter. In his essays, words and material suit each other. The thought becomes poetry, and the poetry illuminates the thought.

Langston Hughes. *New York Times Book Review.* February 26, 1956, p. 26

*Giovanni's Room* is the best American novel dealing with homosexuality I have read. . . .

No one who has read any of James Baldwin's highly intelligent, clear-eyed essays—most recently, his quietly pitched reply in *Partisan Review* to William Faulkner's views on the desegregation problem—would expect him to treat so tangled a subject as homosexual relationships cheaply or too simply. He successfully avoids the cliché literary attitudes: overemphasis on the grotesque, and the use of homosexuality as a facile symbol for the estrangement which makes possible otherwise unavailable insights into the workings of ''normal'' society and ''normal'' people; in short, the Homosexual as Artist.

Not that *Giovanni's Room* is without faults. The novel's ending. . . is somewhat lame, his descriptions of the hero's emotions run too heavily to beating hearts, trembling, bright lights, overwhelming stirrings, falling, drowning, the bottom of the sea. Also, Baldwin's blond-athlete-type hero, like Norman Mailer's in *The Deer Park*, never wholly emerges from dimness.

Nevertheless, these shortcomings only slightly detract from the book's impact. If David, the American, remains even more lumpish than he is supposed to be, Giovanni, the experienced European more vulnerable than a child, is beautifully and economically realized. Baldwin insists on the painful, baffling complexity of things.

William Esty. *New Republic.* December 17, 1956, p. 26

When I read Baldwin's first collection of essays, *Notes of a Native Son*, I realized that the tortured intellectual consciousness I felt behind his fiction could be turned into the self-representation of an absolutely first-class essayist, reporter, and social critic. *Notes of a Native Son* is one of the two or three best books ever written about the Negro in America, and it is the work of an original literary talent who operates with as much power in the essay form as I've ever seen. I'm sure that Baldwin doesn't like to hear his essays praised at the expense (seemingly) of his fiction. And I'm equally sure that if Baldwin were not so talented a novelist he would not be so remarkable an essayist. But the great thing about his essays is that the form allows him to work out from all the conflicts raging in *him*, so that finally the ''I,'' the ''James Baldwin'' who is so sassy and despairing and bright, manages, without losing his authority as the central speaker, to show us all the different people hidden in him, all the voices for whom the ''I'' alone can speak.

Each of his essays in this new book [*Nobody Knows My Name*] is a facet of this different experience, each is a report from the battlefield that is himself, that he sometimes feels may be *only* himself. . . . No doubt other writers could have done all these pieces coolly, as correspondents from another shore to us; for Baldwin, each of his subjects represents a violent conflict in himself. . . .

What ultimately makes these essays so impressive and moving is not merely the *use* Baldwin makes of his conflicts but the fact that this personal form is an urgent necessity. This is the book of a deeply troubled man, the spiritual autobiography of someone who hopes, by confronting more than one beast on his way, to see whether his fear is entirely necessary. [1961]

Alfred Kazin. *Contemporaries* (Boston: Little, Brown, 1962), pp. 255–57

A lot of people would like to believe that [James Baldwin's writing is limited to his experience as a Negro] I suppose, because it makes it unnecessary to confront the reality of which Baldwin writes. Be that as it may, race is one of the major facts of our time and perhaps one reason it has become so explosive is precisely because it has been consciously ignored in literature. Besides, it is at least as important a theme as sex or dope, and if it moves Baldwin to expression, to eloquence, then our proper concern is with what he makes of it artistically. Undoubtedly he brings enough passion to it to indicate that the impact of race upon personality is a very important matter for him and he gives voice to it with impressive skill. On the other hand my own concerns with race are a bit muted and perhaps I am really more impatient, more concerned with putting race in a wider perspective. Perhaps matters which I work out in the silence of my room, Baldwin works out on the printed page; perhaps I have less hope, I don't know.

Ralph Ellison. *University of Chicago Magazine.* April 1962, p. 8

James Baldwin has quite literally been raising hell since he returned from a long European exile in the middle 1950's. . . .

From the Paris of Sartre, Beauvoir and Camus, from the expatriate Paris of Richard Wright, of the progenitors of the concept of ''Negritude,'' Senghor, Diop and Césaire, came Baldwin, cutting, slashing and stabbing his way onto the American literary scene. Just over thirty years old, he had a solid first novel under his belt, *Go Tell It on the Mountain*, a second one, *Giovanni's Room* (a little strong on homosexuality for most American stomachs), and a remarkable book of penetrating essays, *Notes of a Native Son*. In Europe he had certainly heard of Marx and Engels, imperialism and colonialism, but in his exile he had missed the day-to-day struggles (the Rosenbergs, Willie McGee, the Martinsville Seven) that had helped to shape his Afro-American contemporaries. Perhaps as a consequence, he was remarkably free of clichés, the bane of the creative writer, clichés not only of expression but of ideas. He had absolutely no gods, either of the Left or the Right. He seemed free, as dice-shooters say of the houseman, to call the shots the way he saw them. Naturally he was possessed of an outsized ego. One felt from the intensely personal nature of his work that he believed the earth had been created on the day he was born, and that the entire white power structure of the United States had been mobilized with the single purpose of oppressing *him*. . . .

Can one say precisely what has been Baldwin's achievement? I think it has been his ability to capture, in beautiful, passionate, and persuasive prose the essence of Negro determination to live in the American house as a free man or, failing that, to burn the American house down. I don't think Baldwin is himself yet willing to set the torch to the house. Other militant black intellectuals have, for the most part, broken off their dialogue with white America. As far as possible they address themselves only to their own people urging them to more aggressive levels of struggle. Baldwin, almost alone, still talks to the whites, in love and compassion, offering them a way out, if only they will listen.

Julian Mayfield. *Freedomways*. Spring 1963, pp. 148–50, 155

It is on the whole encouraging that James Baldwin should have become the voice of American Negroes, because he is also the voice of an American consciousness (conscience) which is not Negro. The word "home" occurs frequently in his writings, sometimes bitterly, sometimes quite ordinarily: and by it he means America, in spite of his being acutely aware that the white men of his country have never shared their home with the Negroes. James Baldwin is an American writer, regarded and criticized as such, one of the outstanding living writers in the English language. His very faults as a writer and a person—given the fact of his immense distinction as both—strengthen his position, because he can be criticized and argued with as a man who is neither black nor white, but who uses, and exists, within the English language.

As a writer, he has no color, but only mind and feelings as they are realized in words. One can quarrel, for example, with his misuse of words like "precisely" and "strictly" (usually introduced at a place where his argument is most blurred). James Baldwin is neither the golden-voiced god who sometimes descends on us from a black cloud—like those Negro athletes or Paul Robeson in his prime—nor is he a poet from another race and sphere of life—like Langston Hughes—for whom allowances have to be made. He is simply a writer in English who has had imposed on him by circumstances a point of view made tragic by those very circumstances. All his writings are speeches out of the play which is the tragedy of his race.

Stephen Spender. *Partisan Review*. Summer 1963, p. 256

Baldwin's intention [in *Another Country*] is to deny any moral significance whatever to the categories white and Negro, heterosexual and homosexual. He is saying that the terms white and Negro refer to two different conditions under which individuals live, but they are still individuals and their lives are still governed by the same fundamental laws of being. And he is saying, similarly, that the terms homosexuality and heterosexuality refer to two different conditions under which individuals pursue love, but they are still individuals and their pursuit of love is still governed by the same fundamental laws of being. Putting the two propositions together, he is saying, finally, that the only significant realities are individuals and love, and that anything which is permitted to

interfere with the free operation of this fact is evil and should be done away with.

Now, one might suppose that there is nothing particularly startling in this view of the world; it is, after all, only a form of the standard liberal attitude toward life. And indeed, stated as I have just stated it, and held with the mild attachment by which most liberal and enlightened Americans hold it, it is scarcely more shocking than the usual speech made at every convention of the American Society of Social Workers. But that is not the way James Baldwin holds it, and it is not the way he states it. He holds these attitudes with a puritanical ferocity, and he spells them out in such brutal and naked detail that one scarcely recognizes them any longer—and one is frightened by them, almost as though they implied a totally new, totally revolutionary, conception of the universe. And in a sense, of course, they do. For by taking these liberal pieties literally and by translating them into simple English, he puts the voltage back into them and they burn to the touch. [Oct., 1962]

Norman Podhoretz. *Doings and Undoings* (New York: Farrar, Straus, 1964), pp. 247–48

In the brief note James Baldwin has written as an introduction to the published version of *Blues for Mr. Charlie*, the only character he mentions at any length is the man appearing in the play as Lyle Britten, a white store-owner in a Southern town who murders a young Negro. Baldwin says of the killer, "We have the duty to try to understand this wretched man." But in the play that follows, the writer's sense of this particular duty seems to me to fail him. . . . I don't intend to hold a play deficient for failing an intention whose execution may properly have been thwarted in the act of writing, and is perhaps only recalled here in nostalgia for some purity of purpose. The deficiency is in the failure to be true not to the particular intention announced in the Introduction, but to those numerous intentions apparent in the first act, all most worthy, but none able to survive the unhealthy competition. . . .

In the remaining two acts of the play all the purposes of the first act collapse: indeed, everything collapses, sense, craft, and feeling. The duty to understand is replaced with a duty to do what is practically its opposite, to propagandize, or (reversing Blake's dictum) "to put off intellect and put on holiness." Hardly anything anyone has said or done to anyone else in Act One seems to have taken hold, and the not taking hold isn't what is made to seem the point, either. The point is that the writer has pronouncements to make which stand in the way of the play he began to write. . . .

If there is ever a Black Muslim nation, and if there is television in that nation, then something like Acts Two and Three of *Blues for Mr. Charlie* will probably be the kind of thing the housewives will watch on afternoon TV. It is soap opera designed to illustrate the superiority of blacks over whites.

Philip Roth. *New York Review of Books*. May 28, 1964, pp. 10–11

To a certain extent, Baldwin's work is the logical culmination of a literature that is conscious of its immersion in the absurd, rejecting any retreat even to an illuminated cellar, insisting upon the integrity of its characters, eager for human contacts, and determined, despite everything, to explore the world. The fervor shown by this young black writer to explain the condition of his brothers in his sparkling essays (*The Fire Next Time*) is the natural extension—or rather the concretization of the intentions—of the novelists of the possible. But Baldwin sometimes becomes so impassioned that his tone is reminiscent of that of the courtroom. Then the domain of literature is abandoned for that of the prosecution and the defense.

In his novels Baldwin attempts to be just as free from racial preoccupations as he is immersed in them in his essays. The themes of his novels are independent of skin color: the difficulty of loving, of penetrating another's universe (in *Another Country*), and the search for contact—even only physical contact—between two men who do not succeed in sharing ''Giovanni's room.'' The style of his novels is pallid, just as the novels themselves are colorless. The contradiction in Baldwin is that he writes ''white'' novels (by their style and subject), while his essays are ''black,'' profoundly committed, and written in flamboyant language.

Pierre Dommergues. *Les écrivains américvains d'aujourd'hui* (Paris, Presses Universitaries de France, 1965), pp. 109–10†

*Another Country* is a shocker. For the most part it is an abominably written book. It is sluggish in its prose, lifeless for its first hundred pages, stilted to despair in its dialogue. There are roles in plays called actor-proof. They are so conceived that even the worst actor will do fairly well. So *Another Country* is writer-proof. Its peculiar virtue is that Baldwin commits every *gaffe* in the art of novel writing and yet has a powerful book. . . .

It is at least a novel about matters which are important, but one can't let up on Baldwin for the way he wrote it. Years ago I termed him ''minor'' as a writer; I thought he was too smooth and too small. Now on his essays alone, on the long continuing line of poetic fire in his essays, one knows he has become one of the few writers of our time. But as a Negro novelist he could take lessons from a good journeyman like John Killens. Because *Another Country* is almost a major novel and yet it is far and away the weakest and worst near-major novel one has finished. It goes like the first draft of a first novelist who has such obvious stuff that one is ready, if an editor, to spend years guiding him into how to write, even as one winces at the sloppy company which must be kept.

Nobody has more elegance than Baldwin as an essayist, not one of us hasn't learned something about the art of the essay from him, and yet he can't even find a good prose for his novel. Maybe the form is not for him. He knows what he wants to say, and that is not the best condition for writing a novel. Novels go happiest when you discover something you did not know you knew. Baldwin's experience has shaped his tongue toward directness, for urgency—the honorable defense may be that he has not time nor patience to create characters, milieu, and mood for the revelation of important complexities he has already classified in his mind. [July, 1963]

Norman Mailer. *Cannibals and Christians* (New York: Dial, 1966), pp. 114–15

James Baldwin now belongs to The Establishment he continues to profane. Rich, famous, sometimes snarling, sometimes beguiling,

with a flat in Istanbul, a new apartment in Paris (''behind the Bastille, naturally'') and a newer house in New York, he is an essayist, novelist and play-wright esteemed on at least four continents, an American relatively secure in the literary firmament (yet sweating to stay there), the Negro author younger Negro authors must measure themselves against and—yes—occasionally try to put down.

He is a distillation of the nation's experience as well as his own. Talking of whites and Negroes, writing about them, he wavers between the first person plural and the third. But his duality reflects his country's. Growing up in a culture that is neither all white nor all black, he assimilated both parts. . . .

Inevitably, as the penalty of his success, he is castigated by many white Americans as an extremist and flailed by more radical Negroes as a moderate. A pamphlet published by a black nationalist satirized him with such viciousness that it made him weep. Yet at that very moment shoplifting drug addicts, desperate for a quick sale to finance their next fix, were hawking his books in Harlem's bars, perhaps the ultimate tribute to his popularity.

Fern Marja Eckman. *The Furious Passage of James Baldwin* (New York: M. Evans, 1966), pp. 239–41

I, as I imagine many others did and still do, lusted for anything that Baldwin had written. It would have been a gas for me to sit on a pillow beneath the womb of Baldwin's typewriter and catch each newborn page as it entered this world of ours. I was delighted that Baldwin, with those great big eyes of his, which one thought to be fixedly focused on the macrocosm, could also pierce the microcosm. And although he was so full of sound, he was not a noisy writer like Ralph Ellison. He placed so much of my own experience, which I thought I had understood, into new perspective.

Gradually, however, I began to feel uncomfortable about something in Baldwin. I was disturbed upon becoming aware of an aversion in my heart to part of the song he sang. Why this was so, I was unable at first to say. Then I read *Another Country*, and I knew why my love for Baldwin's vision had become ambivalent. . . .

There is a decisive quirk in Baldwin's vision which corresponds to his relationship to black people and to masculinity. It was this same quirk, in my opinion, that compelled Baldwin to slander Rufus Scott in *Another Country*, venerate André Gide, repudiate [Norman Mailer's] *The White Negro*, and drive the blade of Brutus into the corpse of Richard Wright. As Baldwin has said in *Nobody Knows My Name*, ''I think that I know something about the American masculinity which most men of my generation do not know because they have not been menaced by it in the way I have been.'' O.K., Sugar, but isn't it true that Rufus Scott, the weak, craven-hearted ghost of *Another Country*, bears the same relation to Bigger Thomas of *Native Son*, the black rebel of the ghetto and a man, as you yourself bore to the fallen giant, Richard Wright, a rebel and a man?

Eldridge Cleaver. *Soul on Ice* (New York, McGraw-Hill, 1968), pp. 97–98, 105–6

*Tell Me How Long the Train's Been Gone* is a remarkably bad novel, signaling the collapse of a writer of some distinction. . . .

Language rarely lies. It can reveal the insincerity of a writer's claims simply through a grating adjective or an inflated phrase. We come upon a frenzy of words and suspect it hides a paucity of feeling. In his new book Baldwin rarely settles into that controlled exactness of diction which shows the writer to have focused on the matter he wishes to describe or evoke; for Baldwin is now a writer systematically deceiving himself through rhetorical inflation and hysteria, whipping himself into postures of militancy and declarations of racial metaphysics which—for him, in *this* book—seem utterly inauthentic. One sign, a minor sign, of these troubles is Baldwin's compulsive obscenity. . . .

A much more important sign of difficulty is the abandon with which Baldwin opens wide the spigot of his rhetoric, that astonishing flow of high eloquence which served him so well in his later essays but is a style almost certain to entrap a novelist. For if you sound like the voice of doom, an avenging god proclaiming the fire next time, then you don't really have to bother yourself with the small business of the novelist, which is to convey how other, if imaginary, people talk and act. Baldwin seems to have lost respect for the novel as a form, and his great facility with language serves only to ease his violations of literary strictness.

There is still a third way in which Baldwin's language betrays him, perhaps most fundamentally of all. When he writes about Proudhammer's rise to fame and the adulation he receives from friends and public, Baldwin slips into the clichés of soap opera, for which he had already shown an alarming fondness in the past when dealing with homosexual love. Buried deep within this seemingly iconoclastic writer is a very conventional sensibility, perfectly attuned to the daydream of success. Now, if you add all these styles together, you get a weird mixture: the prose of *Redbook* (the magazine for young mamas) and the prose of *Evergreen Review* (the magazine for all them mothers).

Irving Howe. *Harper.* September 1968, pp. 95–97

The significance of *Another Country's* being a *regional* novel cannot be over-emphasized. The experience it describes is in many respects peculiarly New York, the conditions which operate are not to be found in quite the same way anywhere else in the country. This is the anxietyridden, abrasive, neurotic and merciless world of the artistic underground. What the characters seek is not simply love, and an end to loneliness, but to "make it." They are seeking to force the society to come to terms with their own existence, that is to say, seeking their public identity. So the natural insecurity of the modern human situation is for them heightened by the competitive and spiritually destructive hustle of New York's talent jungle. There are among the major characters, two writers, one actor, a singer and a T.V. producer. And as Truman Capote put it, "a boy's got to hustle." Their common enemy and the source of much of their neurosis, is anonymity and obscurity. They are all past the first flush of youth and some have begun to establish the basis of their fame and success. It is significant that the one character that seems to have established working terms on which to confront his own identity is Eric, the actor, who is "making it" on pretty much his own terms and without having done visible violence to his creative integrity. That he is also unrepentantly bi-sexual and appears to have made his personal peace with that reality also, is undoubtedly the cause of much of the heterosexual indignation that greeted the book. . . .

What this character represents is more subtle than simply an attack on the virility of the conventional American he-man. His ability to discover what and who he is, to accept this, and to be honest to his emotional impulses, however socially unacceptable they may be, is an expression of one of Baldwin's major insights.

Mike Thelwell. In C. W. E. Bigsby, ed., *The Black American Writer* (De Land, Florida: Everett/Edwards, 1969), Vol. I, pp. 189, 194

[One night in Paris in 1953] we hurried to the [Café des] Deux Magots and found Baldwin waiting for us at a table on the terrace across from the Église Saint-Germain. I was somewhat surprised to find Baldwin a small, intense young man of great excitability. Dick [Richard Wright] sat down in lordly fashion and started right off needling Baldwin, who defended himself with such intensity that he stammered, his body trembled, and his face quivered. I sat and looked from one to the other, Dick playing the fat cat and forcing Baldwin into the role of the quivering mouse. It wasn't particularly funny, but then Dick wasn't a funny man. I never found it easy to laugh with Dick; it was far easier to laugh at him on occasion. Dick accused Baldwin of showing his gratitude for all he had done for him by his scurrilous attacks. Baldwin defended himself by saying that Dick had written his story and hadn't left him, or any other American black writer, anything to write about. . . .

In the course of time [the others] left us to go to dinner, and still Baldwin and Dick carried on while I sat and watched the people come and go. Later we went down the boulevard to a Martiniquan café. It had grown later, close to midnight, and we had not eaten, but still the discussion went on. It seemed that Baldwin was wearing Dick down and I was getting quite drunk. The last I remember before I left them at it was Baldwin saying, "The sons must slay their fathers." . . . He was right. On the American literary scene, the powers that be have never admitted but one black at a time into the arena of fame, and to gain this coveted admission, the young writer must unseat the reigning deity. It's a pity but a reality as well.

Chester Himes. *The Quality of Hurt* (Garden City, New York: Doubleday, 1972), pp. 200–201

In his previous two novels [*Another Country* and *Tell Me How Long the Train's Been Gone*] Baldwin produced fantasies of black-white relationships in which various characters loved and lusted after one another seemingly *just because* they belonged to different races. In the process, he took very large liberties with the truth about such relationships as they normally exist in our society and, by so doing, may unwittingly have confirmed an impression which certain whites would be eager to embrace: that actually there is no race problem in America which cannot be solved by the application of a little tenderness and the recognition that what we all really want is to enjoy splendid sex together.

In *If Beale Street Could Talk* Baldwin has produced another fantasy of rather larger social implications, this time one in which the characters of black people living in contemporary Harlem are shown to be so noble and courageous that one is constrained to wonder how we ever imagined that conditions in the black urban ghettos are anything other than idyllic. If to be black is to be beautiful, to be poor and black is to be positively saintly. Yet another fiction of great attractiveness to the white mind is thus perpetrated: Ghetto blacks are very happy with their lot. In fact, they are just as simple and fun-loving as the grinning old darkies of southern legend.

To be sure, there is a good deal of adversity in Baldwin's story, but it is there just to demonstrate how well his characters can cope with it and come through with courage undaunted and hopes unsullied. . . .

It is extremely sad to see a writer of Baldwin's large gifts producing, in all seriousness, such junk. Yet it has been evident for some time that he is deteriorating as a novelist and becoming increasingly a victim of the vice of sentimentality. This seems a particular pity because Baldwin may have one great novel left within him which it would take the most radical courage to write, the story of a talented black writer who achieves worldwide success on the strength of his anger and, in succeeding, gradually loses his anger and comes to be loved by everybody. Clearly, such acceptance can be considered a triumph for a black man in America, but it can be death for a black writer in whom anger and talent are indivisible.

John W. Aldridge. *Saturday Review.* June 15, 1974, pp. 24–25

James Baldwin's late novel *If Beale Street Could Talk* . . . gives [a] graphic portrayal of the dread of intimacy. The work, a quasi-detective story on the surface, is divided into two parts, the first entitled "Troubled about My Soul," and the second, disproportionately short one, entitled "Zion." By virtue of such a structure, Baldwin suggests an introspective, even a spiritual bearing in the face of an action that is heavily social, with its exposé of police malice and its outcry against the destructive misery of the black and Puerto Rican poor.

But Baldwin earns his spiritual emphasis. Virtually every significant action in the text, except the rape which is falsely attributed to Fonny, the male protagonist, arises from an engagement of souls between two people. These engagements may be hostile, as is that between Fonny and the white policeman, Bell, who feels his power and life assumptions threatened by Fonny, and who accordingly contrives to pin the rape on Fonny.

The title of the second section, "Zion," suggesting recovery from the troubles of the soul and attainment of spiritual freedom, may be somewhat ironic. It seems evident that Fonny will be exonerated, on the grounds that the damning lineup was loaded against him (he was the only black man and the culprit was very dark in hue), and the victim cannot maintain her complaint, having at once lost her baby and her mind. But if we dwell a moment on this positive development, it gives rise to problems. The exoneration pivots on a technicality, and sustains itself on the destruction of another's spirit. The victim of the rape has looked into the same pit and mirror of vulnerability and violation as Fonny, and has been unable to stand it. She is the second minor character, Fonny's friend Daniel being the other, who comes too close to human cruelty, violation, and degradation. Whereas Fonny and the female narrator, Tish, prove that familiar, pedestrian life precludes ecstasy, Señora Sanchez (the rape victim) and Daniel find that the familiar preserves them from intimacy with horror.

The structure of the text, with a slow, tortured unfolding of social and spiritual distress giving way to a swift, revelatory brightness, tempts us to think of Fonny and Tish as looking into the pit of horror and, like the poet in [William] Blake's *Marriage of Heaven and Hell*, emerging not just unscathed but with a vision of heaven.

Michael G. Cooke. *Afro-American Literature in the Twentieth Century: The Achievement of Intimacy* (New Haven, Connecticut: Yale University Press, 1984), pp. 199–200

While exile constitutes a spiritual loss, chaos, and struggle, the African religious tradition also embodies within itself resources and renewal power. It is within this context that we look at James Baldwin's *Go Tell It on the Mountain*. One may question how this work can be cited as a continuation of African traditional religion when it reads so Christian and postulates the view that the primary concern of the characters is to get their souls "right" so they can meet God in Heaven. Nevertheless . . . it uncovers the African-American's adaptation of Christianity. James Baldwin himself, in writing this book and in many of his works, attests to his ambivalence about black religion. Because of his own search for identity and his earlier belief that when blacks were brought to America they were stripped of their cultural heritage, his earlier works attempt to place black religion solely in the area of Christianity. By doing so he is unable to accept black religion because he identifies Christianity with oppression and the lack of love in the world. However, when he does isolate aspects of black religion, as he does in *Go Tell It on the Mountain*, Baldwin realizes that there is something else in it. He sees a beauty, strength, morality which he finds difficult to repel.

Mildred A. Hill-Lubin. In Kofi Anyidoho, Abioseh M. Porter, Daniel Racine, and Janice Spleth, eds. *Interdisciplinary Dimensions of African Literature* (Washington, D.C.: Three Continents Press, 1985), pp. 204–5

Baldwin transmutes the messianic myth into that of an artist-priest whose visionary powers allow transcendence of oppression so that she or he can ultimately change history. To Baldwin, the personal and racial past are inseparable; therefore, to grasp racial history, one must first confront personal history. Beyond knowledge lies change, and within each sensitive intellectual lodge the tools for transforming history. *Go Tell It on the Mountain*, like [Ralph Ellison's] *Invisible Man*, exemplifies distrust of collective effort in favor of individual action. Moreover, although Baldwin's work anticipates the urge to explore and reconstruct history, an urge permeating Afro-American literature of the 1960s, 1970s, and 1980s, *Go Tell It on the Mountain* does not reckon with African history or culture.

The introspection Baldwin demands of his [readers] prohibits him from employing the romance, with its de-emphasis on subjectivity. Instead, he turns to the confessional mode to convey his protagonist's guilt, confession, and transcendence. By using flashbacks disguised as prayers to present personal histories, Baldwin underscores the spiritual dimensions of those histories, at the same time focusing on the points of congruence between the personal and racial past. Finally, one must applaud Baldwin's recognition of the centrality of religion in black life and his ingenuity in employing a fictional mode that clearly suggests spiritual and religious concerns.

> Jane Campbell. *Mythic Black Fiction: The Transformation of History* (Knoxville: University of Tennessee Press, 1986), p. 101

In truth, the way of life reconstructed in most of Baldwin's novels is informed by a biblical imagination that is almost as bleak as that in [Richard Wright's] *Native Son*. In *Go Tell It on the Mountain*, the Grimes family has only a tenuous grip on reality due to the religiosity of the storefront Pentecostal church. In *Giovanni's Room* the subject of black culture is displaced by the moral and social problems of white homosexuals in Europe. In *Another Country* a tortuous series of racial and sexual encounters—white vs. black, homosexual vs. heterosexual, North vs. South, European vs. American—drives jazz musician Rufus Scott to suicide but becomes the rite of passage to self-understanding for his jazz-singing sister Ida and the social rebels of modern America who affirm bisexuality as the highest form of love. In *Tell Me How Long the Train's Been Gone*, Leo Proudhammer contends with his private and public demons—heart condition, white mistress, black militant lover, racism, and the stultifying influence of his family—as he claws his way to salvation as a black actor. In *If Beale Street Could Talk*, Tish and Fonny, the blues protagonists, are able to endure and transcend the agony of harassment in the ghetto and prison through love (personal and familial) and art (black music and sculpture). And in *Just Above My Head*, Hall Montana, the first-person narrator-witness and older brother of the gospel-singing protagonist, testifies about the agonizing realities of human suffering and the ecstatic possibilities of love in the lives of those touched by his brother's journey on the gospel road.

As fascinating and ambitious as these novels are, only *Go Tell It on the Mountain*, *If Beale Street Could Talk*, and *Just Above My Head* illuminate the matrix of shared experience of black Americans. But like Wright, Baldwin focuses sharply on a single dimension of black culture. His emphasis, however, is not political but spiritual and sexual, not the terrifying possibilities of hatred, but the terrifying possibilities of love. In contrast to Wright's unrelenting narrative drive, Baldwin's short stories and novels are memorable for the soul-stirring eloquence and resonance of their pulpit oratory and black music as they plumb the depths of our suffering and the possibilities of our salvation.

> Bernard W. Bell. *The Afro-American Novel and Its Tradition* (Amherst: University of Massachusetts Press, 1987), p. 219

The attitudes of Baldwin's characters to the black church vary dramatically from novel to novel—from survival with a high price in *Go Tell It on the Mountain*, through social protest in *Another Country*, to all-out rejection in *Tell Me How Long the Train's Been Gone*, back to a saving or damning role, depending on the character, in *If Beale Street Could Talk*, to a decidedly political function in his last novel *Just Above My Head*. Despite these different viewpoints in the novels, James Baldwin the man knows that those who

hollered in black churches paid a price that began the liberation of the present generation, and his role as writer is to "excavate the role of the people who produced" him.

The final picture of *Go Tell It on the Mountain* is of an island of people united by their common faith in a God who promised to reward them for obeying His edicts. Around them is the sea of ghetto filth that threatens to engulf them with the "vices of perdition." They are returning home after an all night "tarry service" that had become an initiation ritual—a conversion event. The final picture encompasses the novel's principal preoccupations. During the hours preceding the "tarry service" we are witnesses to the Grimes' family battles that turn around guilt, poverty, wife-beating, and even sibling rivalry. These they leave to journey to the central location of "The Temple of Fire Baptized," to engage in rituals that affirm the beliefs that give meaning to their lives. The black church becomes a raft to which each of the characters clings. . . .

To date, Baldwin is the only black American novelist to write a serious novel exclusively around the rituals of the black church. For him as for [Arna] Bontemps and [Alice] Walker, the black church was a mystical body during slavery, but he goes beyond that to show that what was essentially beneficial in slavery had been transmitted unchanged to a nonslave era, with damaging results. The exorcism of pain and the promise of the glories of heaven treated in [Langston] Hughes and [Richard] Wright are also evident here. But the moral strength of a Vyry [in Margaret Walker's *Jubilee*] or an Aunt Hager [in Hughes's *Not Without Laughter*] is missing—even in a character like Deborah. Baldwin waited until *The Fire Next Time* and his later novels to express much of what he felt was negative about the black church. In *The Fire Next Time* he feels the black race would be better served if, instead of holding Sunday school classes and calling on the Lord, blacks organized rent strikes. Having been a preacher, he realized that what was deemed to be the Holy Spirit was simply theatrical conjuration; moreover the preachers knew it. It was only the congregation that was fooled. He chose, however, not to show these feelings in *Go Tell It on the Mountain*. In *Just Above My Head* Baldwin focuses on the political possibilities of the black church, especially in its use of the spirituals to strengthen the determination to fight injustice, just as in an earlier era those same spirituals had helped blacks to surmount injustice.

> H. Nigel Thomas. *From Folklore to Fiction: A Study of Folk Heroes and Rituals in the Black American Novel* (New York: Greenwood Press, 1988), pp. 143–44, 151

Since James Baldwin passed away in his adopted home, France, on the last day of November 1987, the many and varied tributes to him, like the blind men's versions of the elephant, have been consistent in one detail—the immensity, the sheer prodigality of endowment. . . .

When at last I met Jimmy in person in the jungles of Florida in 1980, I actually greeted him with *Mr. Baldwin, I presume*! You should have seen his eyes dancing, his remarkable face working in ripples of joyfulness. During the four days we spent down there I saw how easy it was to make Jimmy smile; and how the world he was doomed to inhabit would remorselessly deny him that simple benediction.

Baldwin and I were invited by the African Literature Association to open its annual conference in Gainesville with a public conversation. As we stepped into a tremendous ovation in the packed auditorium of the Holiday Inn, Baldwin was in particularly high spirits. I thought the old preacher in him was reacting to the multitude.

He went to the podium and began to make his opening statements. Within minutes a mystery voice came over the public address system and began to hurl racial insults at him and me. I will see that moment to the end of my life. The happiness brutally wiped off Baldwin's face; the genial manner gone; the eyes flashing in defiant combativeness; the voice incredibly calm and measured. And the words of remorseless prophecy began once again to flow. . . .

[Neither] history nor legend encourages us to believe that a man who sits on his fellow will some day climb down on the basis of sounds reaching him from below. And yet we must consider how so much more dangerous our already very perilous world would become if the oppressed everywhere should despair altogether of invoking reason and humanity to arbitrate their cause. This is the value and the relevance, into the foreseeable future, of James Baldwin.

Chinua Achebe. *Hopes and Impediments: Selected Essays* (New York: Doubleday, 1989), pp. 171, 173–76

The Library of America has issued a two-volume set of the works of James Baldwin, edited by Toni Morrison. Their appearance makes clear a fact little understood: Baldwin, as a social commentator, remains one of America's most unappreciated prophets. From his earliest essays and book reviews in magazines and journals such as the *Partisan Review, Harper's*, and the *New Leader*, Baldwin's taut, ironic clarity was a brisk breeze blowing through the literary world. His autobiographical novel, *Go Tell It on the Mountain*, published in 1953, painted a searing portrait of the claustrophobic worlds of fundamentalist religion, the post-World War II ghettos of African-Americans, the black family—indeed, the weight of history itself.

Baldwin's first book garnered significant praise, a harbinger, he hoped, of his future as a major American novelist. But that was never to be. With the 1955 publication of *Notes of a Native Son*, a collection of his early essays and reviews, Baldwin more fully revealed himself as the incisive, elegant essayist he would become. To be sure, this first collection was uneven—from the awkward self-consciousness of "Autobiographical Notes," to the bitter challenge to Richard Wright in "Everybody's Protest Novel" and "Many Thousands Gone." But what would linger for readers was the clear, pitiless vision of America's racial nightmare that Baldwin delineated with such precision.

In assuming the voice of an "objective" white American gazing at black Americans, Baldwin ran the risk of alienating the very people he hoped to represent. At the same time, he endeared himself to whites, who found in this literary device a safe space from which to regard the "Negro Problem." "Time has made some changes in the Negro face," he wrote in his essay "Many Thousands Gone." "Nothing has succeeded in making it exactly like our own, though the general desire seems to be to make it blank if one cannot make it white. When it has become blank, the past as thoroughly washed from the black face as it has been from ours, our guilt will be finished—at least it will have ceased to be visible, which we imagine to be much the same thing."

In some ways, the success of this early book was an old story—the often condescending acclaim of white readers amazed that someone black might function with authority and power in the territory of the mind (an attitude, sad to say, not limited to the mid-1950s). In truth, Baldwin not only functioned in such territory, he occupied it with enviable vigor and grace. His distracting affectation of a white persona notwithstanding, it is still a delight to read a writer who, more than forty years ago, put his finger on the pulse of our unresolved dilemma. In an era that has declared the end of racism, rereading Baldwin, following his merciless gaze across the American landscape, realizing how much has changed and how much has not, is a curious act of renewal.

It is a merciless gaze that continued through his subsequent essays, including "Nobody Knows My Name" (1961) and, most important, *The Fire Next Time* (1963), part manifesto, part plea, wholly American, and unforgettable. No African-American parents should fail to reread "My Dungeon Shook: Letter to My Nephew on the One Hundredth Anniversary of the Emancipation" and then save it for their children, to be read, I should think, at puberty. In that essay he wrote: "You were born into a society which spelled out with brutal clarity, and in as many ways as possible, that you were a worthless human being. . . . The details and symbols of your life have been deliberately constructed to make you believe what white people say about you. Please try to remember that what they believe, as well as what they do and cause you to endure, does not testify to your inferiority but to their inhumanity and fear."

Without Baldwin's voice to remind us, some of us might, in these waning days of the so-called American Century, believe that we had gone crazy, that the vast wasted space between black and white America was an illusion or an unrelinquished grudge. . . .

It would grieve Baldwin, who died in 1987, to discover that he is remembered primarily as one of the greatest essayists this country has produced. His heart belonged to fiction. To be sure, there is power in his novels and stories, rooted in the same bravery and clarity that distinguish his nonfiction. Included here are *Giovanni's Room*, the 1956 novel about a bisexual love affair, as well as *Another Country* (1962) and a collection of stories, *Going to Meet the Man* (1965). If his nonfiction work was strongest in its examination of race, Baldwin's fiction was marked by a deep hunger to dissect the complex patterns woven by race, gender, and sexuality. In some ways, that hunger was ahead of its time, perhaps even ahead of Baldwin's understanding. . . .

In these days of banned books and lowered educational expectations, it would be too much to hope that James Baldwin's work might become required reading, that people could never consider themselves well educated until they could discuss his precise, eloquent, often tragic vision of American life. But if we were that thoughtful a nation, Baldwin's work might not have been necessary at all. As it is, his voice is perhaps more vital to our nation's health than we know. This Library of America edition restores him to our consciousness.

Rosemary L. Bray. *American Scholar*. 67, 2 (Spring 1998), pp 162–64

BIBLIOGRAPHY
*Autobiographical Notes*, 1953; *Go Tell It on the Mountain*, 1953; *Notes of a Native Son*, 1955; *Giovanni's Room*, 1956; *Nobody Knows My Name*, 1961; *Another Country*, 1962; *The Fire Next Time*, 1963; *Blues for Mister Charlie* (play), 1964; *Going to Meet the Man* (short stories), 1965; *The Amen Corner* (play), 1968; *Tell Me How Long the Train's Been Gone*, 1968; *If Beale Street Could*

*Talk*, 1974; *Little Man, Little Man: A Story of Childhood* (juvenile), 1976; *Just Above My Head*, 1979; *Jimmy's Blues: Selected Poems*, 1983; *The Evidence of Things Not Seen*, 1985; *The Price of the Ticket: Collected Nonfiction 1948–1985*, 1985; *Harlem Quartet*, 1987; *The Welcome Table*, 1987; *Early Novels and Stories*, 1998; *Essays*, 1998

# BAMBARA, Toni Cade (1939–1995)
## United States

Contemporary black writers seem to view urban life as lovable only when the ancestor is there. The worst thing that can happen in a city is that the ancestor becomes merely a parent or an adult and is thereby seen as a betrayer—one who has abandoned his traditional role of adviser with a strong connection to the past.

Toni Cade Bambara has written two collections of short stories and one novel. She is a New Yorker, born and educated in that city with an intimate and fearless knowledge of it, and although the tone of most of her stories is celebratory, full of bravura, joyfully survivalist, the principal fear and grief of her characters is the betrayal of an adult who has abandoned not the role of providing for, but the role of adviser, competent protector. Of the sixteen stories in *Gorilla, My Love*, only two stories cannot fit that description. . . .

In her novel, *The Salt Eaters*, the theme is totally explicated. A would-be suicide is literally and metaphorically healed by the ancestor; the witch woman, the spiritual sage, the one who asks of this oh so contemporary and oh so urban daughter of the 1960s, "Are you sure you want to be well?" Here is the village, its values, its resources, its determination not to live, as Stevie Wonder has put it, "just enough for the city," and its requisites for survival only. The village is determined to flourish as well, and it is that factor that makes it possible for Velma to rise from the ancestor's shawl and drop it to the floor "like a cocoon."

> Toni Morrison. In Michael C. Jaye and Ann Chalmers Watts, eds. *Literature & the Urban Experience: Essays on the City and Literature* (New Brunswick, New Jersey: Rutgers University Press, 1981), pp. 40–41

*The Salt Eaters*, like one complex jazz symphony, orchestrates the chordal riffs introduced in the short stories of Toni Cade Bambara collected, so far, in two volumes: *Gorilla, My Love* and *The Sea Birds Are Still Alive*. The improvising, stylizing, vamping, re-creative method of the jazz composer is the formal method by which the narrative genius of Toni Cade Bambara evokes a usable past testing its values within an examined present moment while simultaneously exploring the recreative and transformative possibilities of experience. The method of the jazz composition informs the central themes and large revelation of the world of Bambara's fiction. In that world, time is not linear like clock time; rather, it is convergent. All time converges everywhere in that world in the immediate present; the contemporary, remote, or prehistorical past, and the incipient future are in constant fluid motion. Thus, a play of oppositions and the points of juncture between the past and present form a pattern of summons and response shaping the design of *Gorilla, My Love*, *The Sea Birds Are Still Alive*, and *The Salt Eaters*.

The meaning of ancestry and, consequently, the meaning of modernity is the primary focus of the Bambara narrator. The central vision of both the short and long fiction fixes a view of ancestry as the single most important inquiry of personhood and of community life. But ancestry, in the communities revealed in *Gorilla, My Love*, in *The Sea Birds Are Still Alive*, and in *The Salt Eaters* is no mere equivalent of the past. Rather, ancestry is the sum of the accumulated wisdom of the race, through time, as it manifests itself in the living, in the *e'gungun*, and in the yet unborn. Often, in the narrative world of Toni Cade Bambara, the search for ancestry is the unconscious quest of the central character as it is for Velma of *The Salt Eaters*, or it is the conscious quest as for Jewel in "The Survivor" of *Gorilla, My Love*. And, in the title story of *The Sea Birds Are Still Alive*, the ancestral theme and one of its sharpest images is sounded in the musings of a boat pilot: ". . . it's not the water in front that pulls the river along. It's the rear guard that is the driving force."

> Eleanor W. Traylor. In Mari Evans, ed. *Black Women Writers (1950–1980): A Critical Evaluation* (New York: Doubleday, 1984), pp. 65–66

Demonstrably, women are at the novel's [*The Salt Eaters*] center. Other aspects of it, too, are very *female*—references to "the moony womb," "the shedding of skin on schedule," and the synchrony of Palma's and Velma's menstrual clocks; the sister love between Nilda and Cecile who wear each other's hats; Obie's precise description of Velma's orgasm as "the particular spasm . . . the tremor begin[ning] at the tip of his joint" which it had taken him two years living with her to recognize; M'Dear's teaching that the "master brain" was in the "uterus, where all ideas sprung from and were nurtured and released to the lesser brain in the head." Such intimate attention parallels Bambara's larger interest in "black women and other women, particularly young women," in "that particular voice and stance that they're trying to find." . . . Like them, Bambara searches for a "new vocabulary of images" which, when found, is "stunning . . . very stunning."

First at the beginning, and then finally at the end, of studying the novel, one must reckon with its initially strange name. Of the three working titles which Bambara used to help her stay focused—"In the Last Quarter," "The Seven Sisters," and "The Salt Eaters"—this is the one she retained. . . . The title . . . calls into the subconscious images related to the folk concepts of "swallowing a bitter pill" and "breaking bread together." There are many allusions to salt in the novel, but they are not as numerous as references to some of the other major symbols. While the image of "The Salt Eaters" condenses the essence of this grand work, it does not reverberate all of its colors.

> Gloria T. Hull. In Marjorie Pryse and Hortense J. Spillers, eds. *Conjuring: Black Women, Fiction, and Literary Tradition* (Bloomington: Indiana University Press, 1985), pp. 230–31

Toni Cade Bambara's stories focus on the ways gender roles, ideology, family, and community condition the experiences of black women. She portrays initiation as a painful but frequently rewarding ritual. Like [James Alan] McPherson, she seeks to take her characters from a state of certainty to a state of doubt, but unlike him, she does not so clearly define the conventions of that certainty. She implies that the realm of woman is more organic and less overtly confrontational than that of man. Nonetheless, a dialectic is clearly at work, one that is in some ways more complex since it adds to generational, racial, and cultural oppositions the polarity of male-female. While Bambara says that she is ''much more concerned with the caring that lies beneath the antagonisms between black men and black women,'' she does repeatedly examine the nature of those antagonisms. Moreover, like [Ernest] Gaines and McPherson, she finds in folk material the means for her characters to resist fixed, dehumanizing identities, whether sexual, racial, or cultural. And also like these male writers, she tends to leave her characters at the edge of some new experience rather than with a sense of the completion of action and thus the resolution of oppositions. . . .

The stories of *Gorilla, My Love* are largely devoted to the lessons offered girls and young women within their local community or through representatives of the larger black folk community. Whether the lessons are learned or not, the tendency is to assume that the older members of the group have insights to pass along. Even in ''The Johnson Girls,'' where the women are all young, the forms they use to share their experiences are the traditional forms of black expression. What happens in *The Sea Birds Are Still Alive*, a second collection of stories, is that Bambara expresses some doubt about the validity of folk experience in the process of trying to link folk wisdom to feminist, and to some degree nationalist, ideology. This doubt grows out of a more overt ideological perspective in these stories. The central, often narrating characters are pitted on the one side against very hopeful political activists and on the other against the harsh conditions of the black community. Bambara moves the central figures from their doubt toward an acceptance of revolutionary action. But in the process her characters must raise important questions about ideology that cannot be easily answered. Ultimately, and despite the apparent intentions of the author, the acceptance of ambiguity, which is the condition of folk reality, seems a more powerful narrative force than the positive identity of ideological imposition. The results are uneasy narratives that sometimes must strain to make their points.

Keith E. Byerman. *Fingering the Jagged Grain: Tradition and Form in Recent Black Fiction* (Athens: University of Georgia Press, 1985), pp. 105, 114–15

Like her works in other genres, Bambara's short stories primarily aim at truth speaking, particularly as *truth* is related to the semiotic mediation of black existential modalities. Of primary importance are the construction and representation of an organic black community and the articulation of black nationalist ideology. Nevertheless, her two short story collections, *Gorilla, My Love* and *The Sea Birds Are Still Alive*, are marked by dissonance and ruptures; in both volumes, Bambara's insertion of themes related to the desires of black women and girls disrupts and often preempts the stories' primary focus on classic realism and nationalism.

In *Gorilla*, Bambara's use of the young girl Hazel as the primary narrator results in a decentering of the stories. In each narrative, a subtext focused on issues with which girls and women

are confronted threatens to displace the racial discourse that is in the dominant text. The stories in *Sea Birds*, which are generally more explicitly political than those in *Gorilla*, directly inscribe the tensions between racial and gender politics. The stories in *Sea Birds*, then, signal a pre-emergent feminist consciousness. In this collection, more complex development and representations of black women of ''the community,'' increased marginalization and deconstruction of mythologies centered on black males, and the general highlighting of feminine and feminist issues indicate a heightening of tensions between gender and racial politics.

Elliott Butler-Evans. *Race, Gender, and Desire* (Philadelphia: Temple University Press, 1989), pp. 92–93

The question of identity—of personal definition within the context of community—emerges as a central motif for Toni Cade Bambara's writing. Her female characters become as strong as they do, not because of some inherent ''eternal feminine'' quality granted at conception, but rather because of the lessons women learn from communal interaction. Identity is achieved, not bestowed. Bambara's short stories focus on such learning. Very careful to present situations in a highly orchestrated manner, Bambara describes the difficulties that her characters must overcome. . . .

Bambara's stories present a decided emphasis on the centrality of community. Many writers concentrate so specifically on character development or plot line that community seems merely a foil against which the characters react. For Bambara the community becomes essential as a locus for growth, not simply as a source of narrative tension. Thus, her characters and community do a circle dance around and within each other as learning and growth occur.

Bambara's women learn how to handle themselves within the divergent, often conflicting, strata that compose their communities. Such learning does not come easily; hard lessons result from hard knocks. Nevertheless, the women do not merely endure; they prevail, emerging from these situations more aware of their personal identities and of their potential for further self-actualization. More important, they guide others to achieve such awareness. . . .

Toni Cade Bambara's stories do more than paint a picture of black life in contemporary black settings. Many writers have done that, more or less successfully. Her stories portray women who struggle with issues and learn from them. Sometimes the lessons taste bitter and the women must accumulate more experience in order to gain perspective. By centering community in her stories, Bambara displays both the supportive and destructive aspects of communal interaction. Her stories do not describe a predictable, linear plot line; rather, the cyclic enfolding of characters and community produces the kind of tension missing in stories with a more episodic emphasis.

Her characters achieve a personal identity as a result of their participation in the human quest for knowledge, which brings power. Bambara's skill as a writer saves her characters from being stereotypic cutouts. Although her themes are universal, communities that Bambara describes rise above the generic. More fully delineated than her male characters, the women come across as specific people living in specific places. Bambara's best stories show her characters interacting within a political framework wherein the personal becomes political.

Martha M. Vertreace. In Mickey Pearlman, ed. *American Women Writing Fiction: Memory, Identity, Family, Space*

(Lexington: University Press of Kentucky, 1989), pp. 155–56, 165–66

One of the most arresting features of the short stories in Toni Cade Bambara's *The Sea Birds Are Still Alive* is their revolutionary thrust. The influence of the avenging Fury, revolution, upon the minds, hearts, and actions of the characters in the stories is manifested through the depiction of the characters' sense of time and through the prominence of descriptions of sound and motion.

One characteristic of the revolutionary is that he or she experiences the future as present. The expression, "revolution in my lifetime," which was the rallying cry of some radical black organizations of the sixties, is the embodiment of the spirit which governs many of the characters in *Sea Birds*. "Revolution" is future; "my lifetime," present. The expression conveys the hope and the expectation that the two time frames will congeal.

The revolutionary is always striving for a future in which current modes of action and thought are transformed or even obliterated as a result of the overthrow of "the system"—the government and its social, economic, and military apparatuses. The revolutionary welcomes—indeed, demands—the birth of a new man and a new woman to accompany the beginning of a new political and social order. Bambara's stories reveal characters who seek to be transformed during the revolutionary period so that they may be ready for the new order. The analogy that comes most readily to mind is that of the "born again" Christian, the believer who lives an exemplary life in order to be ready for the New Jerusalem. Although a revolutionary seeks a regeneration of secular, not of spiritual, existence, the revolutionaries in Bambara's stories display a fervor about their causes commensurate with the fervor of the devout.

Since a revolutionary lives by a sense of the presentness of the future, that person tries to create, either in his or her own mind, or in actuality, the environment which will take shape after the revolution. The militants in Sea Birds live in a state of readiness for social and political upheaval. They live in expectation of a time when poverty of pocket and spirit will disappear, so they attempt to create genuine sisterhood and brotherhood among their people. These are characters with eyes fixed on apocalypse.

One such character is Naomi in "The Apprentice." Although an indefatigable community organizer, she is not young, as might be expected; she is "salt and pepperish in the bush." Her collective feeds needy people and has a police watch to help forestall police brutality. She loves the masses and wants to spur them on to revolution; she dreams of how ideal people would be, once freed of their oppressors.

Naomi's statement, "It's just a matter of time, time and work . . . cause the revolution is here" implies that effort must be exerted so that the revolution can happen; yet, paradoxically, the revolution is happening. The confusion of present with future in Naomi's thinking suggests that working to create a revolution means immediate apprehension of revolution. . . .

"Broken Field Running" is a story about two teachers from a black "freedom school" and their charges. These teachers, like the protagonist of "The Apprentice," strive to bring the future to life now. "Broken Field Running" is set in the black ghetto of Cleveland, in winter, and the cold and snow create a harsh environment symbolic of the bitterness and omnipresence of white domination. The teachers and students of the story anticipate a postrevolutionary society devoid of bitterness because there will be no rich people and no poor people, only free people.

The teachers have names (Dada Lacey and Ndugu Jason) which are part African, part Western. These names suggest the transitional status of the adults, who were brought up in a Western tradition but who have embraced, at maturity, African ways. Some of the children at the school have Western names; a couple (Malaika and Kwane), non-Western. The non-Western names represent the hope that a new generation can be reared in non-Western ways. At the end of the story it is given to Malaika to present, in her innocent, endearing way, her vision of what a world of free people would be like:

> . . .everybody'll have warm clothes and we'll all trust each other and can stop at anybody's house for hot chocolate cause won't nobody be scared or selfish. Won't even be locks on the doors. And every sister will be my mother.

Malaika's vision of life after the revolution seems hopelessly ingenuous, yet pleads the case for revolution much better than could any strident harangue by an adult militant. It is a crime, as Malaika tells us her "nana" has said, that old people should have to eat dog food because that is all they can afford. It is a crime that poor people like those of "Broken Field Running" are forced to live in prison-like buildings, send their children to prison-like schools, shop in prison-like stores, and defend themselves both against a hostile white world and against their own black neighbors who steal from and assault them. Through Malaika, the voice of innocence appalled, we learn that we do need some kind of revolution to restore our humanity.

Dada Lacey, the freedom-school teacher, doubting that revolution will come to free the people, is trapped in the present—stymied in the gloom and degradation surrounding the slums near Hough Avenue. But Jason's words provide an answer to Lacey's despondency; Jason says that the revolutionary era is already here, "[b]ecause the new people, the new commitment, the new way is already here." Jason assures Malaika that the new era which she awaits is happening "in our lifetime."

Though Jason uses the phrase "in our lifetime" a few times, he never prefaces the expression with the word "revolution." He does not need to. The idea "revolution in our lifetime" is no deeply imprinted on the minds of all connected with his school that "revolution" is heard mentally as part of the slogan though the word is never said. For the freedom-school teachers and students, revolution, the future condition, is present existence.

The triumphant signs of this idea are the descriptions of circular movement at the end of the story. Jason whirls "around on his heel like he's executing a new figure." Malaika, using her arms as wings, glides around the teachers, who "stay put till she comes full circle." The circle is an image of revolution, a complete turn in law, behavior, custom, thought.

"Broken Field Running" shows a new generation being educated in communal values. The young, trained in liberation schools, will be the ones to single-mindedly carry out black nationalist goals. Their elders, like Dada Lacey, may tire of battling for freedom, but the young have the drive to pull the enervated through. The story concludes with Malaika and Ndugu Jason dragging the tired Dada Lacey along to Jason's home.

The revolution as a literal present, rather than the present-experienced-as-future, is illustrated by "The Sea Birds Are Still

Alive'' a story which has a central position and a central importance in the collection (as might be inferred from the use of the story's title as a title for the entire work). The three stories (''The Organizer's Wife,'' ''The Apprentice,'' and ''Broken Field Running'') which precede ''Sea Birds'' are about blacks who—thought not involved in violent conflict with the government, which they perceive as oppressive—await this conflict. However, the oppressed people depicted in ''Sea Birds'' are actually involved in a revolutionary struggle. For these people in an unnamed Asian country, war and death are everyday realities, and have been for decades. Thus, the word ''alive'' in the story's title has a powerful symbolism: in this world of carnage, where the common folk have been dying for generations in the attempt to rid themselves of a series of colonizers, the revolution will ultimately succeed and guarantee life where death has reigned omnipotent. Time in ''Sea Birds'' is demonstrated to be the revolutionary's strongest weapon, for with the patience born of a national tradition of struggle, the revolutionary will inevitably vanquish the ruling class. ''Sea Birds'' suggests a link between the African-American freedom movement and the worldwide movement of people of color fighting capitalism and imperialism. If Asians, like the Cubans mentioned in ''The Apprentice,'' can dare to work for their liberation, blacks, too, have this choice—this duty.

The rapid pace of ''The Apprentice,'' ''Broken Field Running,'' and ''The Long Night'' is a reminder that the person who demands ''revolution in my lifetime'' incessantly works toward that goal. It is no accident that a common synonym for the black civil rights struggle during its heyday was ''The Movement.'' A related expression, ''to move on,'' meant to act upon, to confront, or even to deal violently with an enemy.

''The Long Night,'' the fifth story in the collection, follows ''Sea Birds,'' a tale of the courage and persistence of Asian revolutionaries. The stories preceding ''Sea Birds'' are about blacks developing communal unity, organization, discipline—developing cultural awareness and political consciousness in preparation for a revolutionary era. The violent action of ''The Long Night'' is the climactic culmination of the lessons about building a revolution provided in the previous stories (especially ''Sea Birds,'' in which actual—not merely projected—violent struggle is represented).

''The Long Night,'' which describes a police raid on the headquarters of black revolutionaries, opens with a succession of noises. . . .

Despite its noisy beginning, ''The Long Night'' ends quietly. It ends with the mention of language. Language, the orderly patterning of meaningful sounds, is in decided contrast to the babel which opens the story. Thus an intimation is given of the state of order which will follow the revolution if the struggle is successful. . . .

After the long night comes day. The sound and the fury of revolution over, the people will be reborn with identities manifested to one another through the blood language linking ancestor and child in the knowledge of the struggle to be free.

Many of the characters in *Sea Birds* are conscious that, as Jason of ''Broken Field Running'' says, ''a whole new era is borning'' for the Third World. The birth of a new consciousness, in those seeking to midwife the new era is a precondition of that era's coming to light. In developing the new consciousness, which implies selfless dedication to renouncing materialism, bettering the lives of the poor, and building the community's resistance to oppression, the revolutionary has an eschatological awareness of inhabiting simultaneously the present and the future which he or she wants to bring about. Through the idea of embracing a ''home in the future,'' Bambara depicts the revolutionary's view of time as malleable, inevitably the servant of the Cause.

Just as time in the stories seems subject to the revolutionary will, so do motion and sound appear to be its agents. The birth of a new era is noisy and turbulent; fittingly, these qualities apply to the persistent images of motion and sound through which Bambara conveys the pell-mell haste, the catapulting drive of people consumed by the fury of revolution.

> Lois F. Lyles. *CLA Journal*, XXXVI, 2 (December 1992), pp. 134–44.

Toni Cade Bambara's short story ''My Man Bovanne,'' from her first collection of tales, *Gorilla, My Love* (1972), repudiates negative, trivializing, cultural stereotypes associated with age by presenting a female character who is independent and self-confident and thus counters the invisibility of older women in our society. The narrator, Hazel, introduces the theme of visibility at the beginning of the story, ''Blind people got a hummin jones if you notice,'' she observes. She sees that the blind man Bovanne goes unnoticed and is ignored. Visibility is recognized as a form of authority and power, which Hazel realizes Bovanne lacks (''and notice what no eyes will force you into to see people''). Whereas Bovanne is invisible due to his disability, Hazel is invisible as an older woman in a society that values youth and appearance. The younger generation stands for public opinion and is characterized through language and political speech. Hazel and Bovanne communicate with each other on the dance floor through body language and sensuality:

> And I press up close to dance with Bovanne who blind and
> I'm hummin and he hummin, chest to chest like talkin. . . .
> Touch talkin like the heel of the hand on the tambourine or
> on a drum.

Observing Bovanne in a wider social context, Hazel comes to see herself through the eyes of others, at first through the critical eyes of her children representing the social majority, who no longer perceive her as an individual, and then through Bovanne in his appreciation of her as a sexually attractive and ''very pretty woman.'' Hazel is presented through her perception of herself as a sensual being, which is supported by Bovanne, and through her children's perception of her as asexual and old.

Both Bovanne and Hazel have been invited to a party to serve a purpose: to win a certain vote and to represent the ''grass roots'' of the community. The children, who through their narrow definition of the black power movement demand a certain kind of black identity, are frustrated and angry at their mother because she does not fit their notion of how a woman of her age should behave. They reprimand Hazel for not being black enough, and her daughter accuses her of being apolitical and therefore invisible, Hazel performs a political act by asking Bovanne, who is being ignored, to dance. When her children take her to task for dancing with Bovanne, Hazel realizes that there is more at stake than simply the misperception of a blind man. She understands that her children no longer see her as an individual with needs of her own. . . .

In the encounter between Hazel and her children, Bambara shows the limitations of a political movement that merely allows for the binary distinction between black and white, young and old.

Hazel asks if the disagreement with her children is ''what they call a generation gap,'' and is reprimanded with rhetoric of the black power movement—''That's a white concept for a white phenomenon. There's no generation gap among Black people. The point is Mama . . . well it's pride. You embarrass yourself and us too dancin' like that''.

Hazel equates her children's condescending arrogance to the behavior of the police when they represent the power of a majority over a minority and discriminate on the basis of skin color. In this case, however, the issue is not race, but age—''Pullin me out of the party and hustlin me into some stranger's kitchen in the back of a bar just like the damn police. And ain't like I'm old old.'' When Hazel realizes that her children treat her the same way as Bovanne is treated by the community, she takes the empty rhetoric of her children (''old folks is the nation'') seriously and uses the political jargon to explain why she leaves the party with Bovanne. The title ''My Man Bovanne'' as an abridgment for the phrase ''that's my man, Bovanne,'' an expression of condescending praise and seeming acceptance that becomes in the course of the story the expression of the relationship between Hazel and Bovanne. . . .

Bovanne's ''blindness'' to social conventions and to stereotypical behavior toward older women allows him to ''see'' Hazel independent of social norms and opinions and to acknowledge her beauty.

Roberta Maierhafer. *Explicator*. 57, 1 (Fall 1998), p. 57–9

BIBLIOGRAPHY
*Zora* (screenplay), 1971; *Gorilla, My Love*, 1972; *The Johnson Girls* (screenplay), 1972; *The Sea Birds Are Still Alive*, 1977; *Transactions* (screenplay), 1979; *The Salt Eaters*, 1980; *The Long Night* (screenplay), 1981; *Epitaph for Willie* (screenplay), 1982; *Tar Baby* (screenplay, based on Toni Morrison's novel), 1984; *The Bombing of Osage* (screenplay), 1986; *Cecil B. Moore: Master Tactician of Direct Action* (screenplay), 1987; *If Blessing Comes*, 1987; *Raymond's Run*, 1990; *Deep Sightings and Rescue Missions: Fiction, Essays, and Conversations*, 1990

# BARAKA, Amiri (1934–)

## United States

In this first book [*Preface to a Twenty Volume Suicide Note*], where the poems are arranged chronologically, one can see even as the chaff flies that the grain is good. [LeRoi Jones's] special gift is an emotive music that might have made him predominantly a ''lyric poet,'' but his deeply felt preoccupation with more than personal issues enlarges the scope of his poems beyond what the term is often taken to mean. . . .

I feel that sometimes his work is muddled, and that after the event he convinces himself that it had to be that way; in other words, his conception of when a poem is ready to be printed differs from mine. But . . . he is developing swiftly and has a rich potential. Certain poems—especially ''The Clearing,'' ''The Turncoat,'' ''Notes for a Speech''—show what he can do. They are beautiful poems, and others that are less complete have passages of equal beauty.

Denise Levertov. *Nation*. Oct. 14, 1961, p. 252

*Blues People*, like much that is written by Negro Americans at the present moment, takes on an inevitable resonance from the Freedom Movement, but it is in itself characterized by a straining for a note of militancy which is, to say the least, distracting. Its introductory mood of scholarly analysis frequently shatters into a dissonance of accusation, and one gets the impression that while Jones wants to perform a crucial task which he feels *someone* should take on—as indeed someone should—he is frustrated by the restraint demanded of the critical pen and would like to pick up a club. . . .

Read as a record of an earnest young man's attempt to come to grips with his predicament as Negro American during a most turbulent period of our history, *Blues People* may be worth the reader's time. Taken as a theory of American Negro culture, it can only contribute more confusion than clarity. For Jones has stumbled over that ironic obstacle which lies in the path of any who would fashion a theory of American Negro culture while ignoring the intricate network of connections which binds Negroes to the larger society. To do so is to attempt a delicate brain surgery with a switch-blade. And it is possible that any viable theory of Negro American culture obligates us to fashion a more adequate theory of American culture as a whole.

Ralph Ellison. *Shadow and Act* (New York, Random House, 1964), pp. 248–253

I am not too happy to see Mr. Jones being hailed in the papers and on television for his anger; for it is not an anger of literary value, and he is a writer. Rather it is rage, it is blind, and, artistic considerations aside, it may well have made it nearly impossible for him to write an important play. The sad and depressing fact about *Dutchman* is that the writer so hates Lula, and so wants us to hate and detest her too, that he has not patience or strength enough to reveal the true nature of what it is she does.

I hesitate to make the chilling observation that perhaps Jones has not really interest enough at this point, and that like certain policemen or professional soldiers, he has come to hate the criminal more than he hates the crime. If only the playwright could have admitted not only to Negro anger, but to Negro dread and Negro lust. But instead of identifying the fear in the hero, he cleanses him of it by projecting the fear as a reality which is not even feared, and the lust is the lust of any healthy man. Jones seems unwilling, or unable, to believe that a crime more horrible than a crazy white woman killing an innocent Negro man with a knife is the crime committed against the spirit which causes it to imagine knives. To symbolize the attempt to murder a man's sexuality by having him actually murdered is to indulge a literary pretension at the expense of a human truth, to substitute false profundity for real sorrow.

The truth that *Dutchman* might have forced through our baffled sense of the racial nightmare is that the Negro humiliation has been so profound and so deep that a man as intelligent and educated and disciplined as Clay is supposed to be, living in a moment so full of possibility for Negroes as this one, cannot but be burdened with the most primal fears for his flesh. Ironically, in making Clay so badly innocent of his condition, and Lula so madly and viciously secret in her intention, Jones finally lets the white audience off much too easily. They may leave the theater saying, as in their genial and useless masochism they are more than willing to say, ''Yes, yes, we are guilty,'' but of what and why they cannot have much knowledge. And refusing them such knowledge, Mr. Jones, for all his anger, will never force their well-intentioned liberal ideas to be converted into feelings of compassionate suffering.

Philip Roth. *New York Review of Books.* May 28, 1964, p. 13

Mr. Jones is currently the white-haired black boy of American poetry. Talented in other forms of writing as well, particularly theater, Mr. Jones might become America's new Eugene O'Neill—provided he does not knock himself out with pure manure. His current offering, *The Toilet*, is full of verbal excrement. . . . So realistic is both acting and direction in this play that the leading white boy, beaten to his knees by a gang of Negroes, drools spittle upon the stage as he tries to rise. The triumphant black boys end up sticking the white student's head into a urinal. What all this does for race relations (as if it mattered at this late date) I do not know. . . .

For the sake of today's sensitive Negroes and battered white liberals, I would like to offer the producers at St. Mark's Playhouse a suggestion—double cast both [*The Toilet* and *The Slave*], and alternate performances racially. Every other night let all the present Negro characters be played by white actors, and vice versa. Four times a week I would like to see *white* school boys in *The Toilet* beating up a *colored* boy and sticking his head into a urinal. In *The Slave* let a bullying *white* man kick, curse, browbeat and shoot a nice liberal *black* professor and his wife in their suburban living room. To reverse the complexions on stage every other night by alternating casts would make for a very intriguing theatrical evening. Black would then be white—and white, black—which alternately would cancel out each other—since some critics (like the able Michael Smith in *The Village Voice*) claim that LeRoi Jones may not really be writing about color at all, but instead is concerned with no group ''smaller than mankind.'' God help us all!

Langston Hughes. *New York Post.* Jan. 15, 1965, p. 38

The war-cry [in *Dutchman*] does not really differ from those that whites hurl at one another. Just as Aimé Césaire's *The Tragedy of King Christophe* and, *a fortiori*, [Jean] Genet's *The Blacks* borrow European forms of art and thought to plead the cause of the blacks, so LeRoi Jones's Negritude seems to assert itself (especially as we see it from Paris) in the same forms the theme of bastardy takes in the white American writer Edward Albee. Lula's hysteria recalls Martha's in *Who's Afraid of Virginia Woolf?*, and Clay's demands those of the outcast in *The Zoo Story*.

The difference is that Albee feels a concern for his female characters approximating that of a son for his mother, even if she is only an adopted one, and a vague respect for the established order like that of a ward of the state who has difficulty becoming integrated into society; whereas LeRoi Jones spares nothing and no one. He has burned all his bridges, whence, from the same stylized naturalism, there arises an excess of crudeness, aggressiveness, and provocation. Because the notion of human solidarity itself is being contested, the white woman Lula is described with no more sense of decency or pity for her real disorder than if she were a dog; and Clay, once he has discovered his true feelings, ceases to place any limit on his scorn.

The result is a woman's being given a portrait marked by an indecorousness rarely encountered in the theater, and a spouting of invectives whose violence is no less unusual. But the play as a whole has more to it than the interest of a strange paroxysm. There is an obvious dramatic strength, and there are truths to meditate upon, in Clay's speech, which combines Bessie Smith's singing or Charlie Parker's music with cries of revulsion and racial hatred; and Lula's provocations have beauty in their mad obscenity.

Bertrand Poirot-Delpech. *Le monde.* November 6, 1965, p. 16†

If *The System of Dante's Hell* is a novel, then the *Divina Commedia* is a newspaper feature article in three installments. As eclectic as the novel is in both structure and content, it is not so indiscriminately inclusive as to accommodate a *collection* of impressionistic (and clearly) autobiographical sketches—particularly if the sketches do not add up to a story, nor to the development and revelation of character, not to a consistent illusion of reality and an intimation of truth. LeRoi Jones' assemblage of pieces does none of these. Excepting a short essay, disingenuously spun out of black nationalist platitudes, at the very end, *The System of Dante's Hell* closes with a section called ''The Heretics,'' which could have been a narration had it not been strained into an anagoge. And this piece about a Negro soldier's drunken weekend is as close to that succession of consequential events that we call a story—dramatic conflict, exposition, characterization, etc.—as Jones gets. In this piece, he tries to tell (say, show) something.

As for the rest, nothing. From the dust jacket you learn that the book is supposed to be ''an account of childhood and adolescence in the Negro slums of Newark,'' and you struggle with its unclosed parentheses, abrupt shifts in form and technique, sportive spellings and fragmented sentences. . . . The unexpected details, the far-fetched metaphors, the fantastic imagery lack integration and logic, and the result is a confirmation of the impression of pretentiousness—of fakery indeed!—that first strikes you in the symbolism of the title.

Saunders Redding. *Crisis.* January, 1966, p. 56

I went to see *The Toilet* and *Dutchman*, and a whole new world opened up to me. Until I saw *The Toilet*, I didn't realize how right I was in what I had done in *Clara's Ole Man*. I knew *Clara's Ole Man* was a radical departure from the work of those Black playwrights I had read. It was radical in its depiction of Black people, but I didn't realize how right it was in a deep and profoundly revolutionary sense, until I saw *The Toilet*. . . .

LeRoi has greatly influenced many young Black artists. I say without reservation that LeRoi is one of the most important, most significant figures in American theatre. Hardly anybody realizes this now except Black playwrights and artists. We know that the Man (LeRoi) has changed theatre in this country. His contribution to Black theatre will have a great effect on all theatre in this country. If people say that I'm the greatest American playwright, then they must also admit and acknowledge that LeRoi Jones is one of the most significant figures in American, world, and Black theatre.

Ed Bullins. In Ed Bullins, ed., *New Plays from the Black Theatre* (New York, Bantam, 1969), pp. xiv-xv

LeRoi Jones's *The System of Dante's Hell* . . . ostensibly consists of disconnected scenes and random thoughts or observations. Some early reviewers asserted that Jones used a pretentious title as an appeal to intellectuals. Yet, with meticulous precision, with broken but somehow poetic sentences, Jones does expose a Hell, a black ghetto thriving on incontinence, violence, and fraud, surrounded by "white monsters" who add to the torment of the Inferno and prevent escape. As his own protagonist, Jones . . . has penetrated the very depths of Hell—Newark Street: "This is the center I mean. Where it all, came on. The rest is suburb. The rest is outside this hole. Snakes die past this block. Flames subside."

Yet in a very real sense Jones believes that he belongs in the Inferno which he himself has helped to build. He has witnessed and participated in the basest evil. . . . In this urban Inferno the victims are not only tormented by their environment and their monsters but by each other, thereby removing the last trace of humanity. It is a city dominated by the Gorgon of Despair.

> Olga W. Vickery. In Melvin J. Friedman and John B. Vickery, eds., *The Shaken Realist* (Baton Rouge, Louisiana State University Press, 1970), p. 157

*Brooks*: I personally feel that [Jones] is one of the very good poets of today, and people hearing this who have no real knowledge of his work, but have seen merely a couple of "inflammatory" passages in the newspapers, might say, "Well, what in the world do you mean? That's no poet." But he is a most talented person. His work *works*.

*Stavros*: What do you feel makes Jones' the voice of his generation?

*Brooks*: Well, first of all he speaks to black people. They appreciate that. And he's uncompromising in his belief that the black people must subscribe to black solidarity and black self-consciousness.

*Stavros*: Is it his message or a poetic method that makes his poetry appeal particularly to blacks?

*Brooks*: If it is a "method," it comes just from the sincere interest in his own people and in his desire to reach them, to speak to them of what he believes is right.

*Stavros*: Is he employing any traditional forms, would you say, that may be associated with blacks, say, jazz rhythms?

*Brooks*: Yes, he and a number of the other black poets such as Larry Neal are interested in supplying black poetry with some strains of black music which they feel is the authentic art of the black people. They worship [John] Coltrane and Ornette Coleman, and whenever they can they try to push such music into their work. Sometimes the poetry seems to grow out of black music.

> Gwendolyn Brooks. Interviewed by George Stavros in Gwendolyn Brooks, *Report from Part One* (Detroit, Broadside, 1972), pp. 150–51

The characters in Baraka's early plays, particularly Clay [in *Dutchman*] and Walker [in *The Slave*], have all the fury of Bigger [in Richard Wright's *Native Son*] but it is their awareness, their ability to analyze and articulate their situation which is so terrible and shocking. Their fury and pain have been internalized to such an extent that even outward action, as in *The Slave*, brings no release and they, like Bigger, choke on their own rage. It is not without

significance that *The Slave* and *Dutchman* take the physical form of dialogues or conversations between a Black man and white people, for just as Wright abstracts the message of *Native Son* by putting into the mouth of Bigger's white lawyer a long analysis of the social context of Bigger's crimes and the subsequent appeal to the white jury (white society), Baraka seeks to educate white society to the feelings and situations of the collective Black man. All three works are addressed to the collective might and power of the white man. . . .

Walker and Clay are latter-day Bigger Thomases. They are viewed, it is true, from a different perspective, but Baraka's sights are trained on the same object as Wright's. And, while there is overstatement in Charles Gordone's view that "[Baraka] has said everything there is to be said in terms of Black and white relationships," it is certain that he has exhausted by thorough exploration in these and other plays Black/white conflict as a literary theme, leaving other artists the room to explore the Black heart.

> Sherley Anne Williams. *Give Birth to Brightness* (New York, Dial, 1972), pp. 103–4

The strongest piece of theatre I have seen in the past few years is *Slave Ship* by LeRoi Jones, as produced in 1969 at the Chelsea Theatre Center. Where [Richard] Wesley merely falls backward into racism [in his play *The Black Terror*] Jones leaps delightedly into it, face-forward. What is the white theatregoer to do? Stay away from Jones's play? Play at being black? That surely is an effort at identification with the victim which soon becomes ludicrous. Enjoy being put down by such a fanatic down-putter? That surely is an exercise in white masochism that only black sadists can contemplate with satisfaction. White middle-class liberals can be counted on for a goodly amount of breast beating, it is true, but not for this much.

As for myself, though I'm as guilt-ridden as the next man, I didn't really feel guiltier for seeing Jones's play, for, rightly or wrongly, I just didn't identify myself with the whites in it. How could one? They were monsters. Then I identified myself— sentimentally—with the blacks? Not that either. Not that *exactly*. Feeling detached from both groups, I found myself instinctively taking the play as an image of all such struggles. Finally, I did identify myself with the blacks but for me they weren't necessarily black. They were yellow, and from Vietnam. They were red, and from Manhattan. They were white-skinned and black with coal dust like the miners of Lancashire, where I come from. As a Socialist, I read LeRoi Jones's play as a series of extremely vivid images of capitalist exploitation, and this is not something I thought of later, it is only my later formulation of what I was actually feeling during the performance. So, as a Socialist, I got my consciousness raised by a writer who (I must assume) wants me liquidated as a carrier of the white plague; and whom I disapprove of as a racist.

> Eric Bentley. *Theatre of War* (New York, Viking, 1972), pp. 404–5

LeRoi Jones's early poetry is difficult. It even found its way into white American anthologies as a token Negro might be found in a white club. And after I have been struggling to decode his knotted language that darts in so many directions, the parentheses that run wild in much of the poetry—all in vain—I have no capacity for an emotional response for even the little I can understand. I feel as if I had been wading through a swamp the extent and shape of which I could not and cannot comprehend. What is often so exasperating about such poetry is that one suspects, and perhaps even *feels*, from the ring of the words that there is a coherent meaning here. . . .

But I know, from reading those poems I *do* understand and which therefore move me, I am prepared to take my chances with Jones and read him several times over. It is not a matter of allusions with him: it is another kind of intellectual complexity. He knows too that he is taking his chances when he writes a kind of poetry that several others besides me will not take the trouble to reread. If I were not teaching poetry, and were not also interested in black poetry in America, I do not think I should take so much trouble. Maybe he will say that's the people he writes for—those who are interested desperately enough. That is still taking a chance. Every so often I am happy to understand a poem of his. Because I find it is rich, it says a hell of a lot, it penetrates the blood. But I don't want to feel, as the old Browning Society used to feel, I belong to a coterie—the chosen ones who can enter LeRoi Jones's mental and spiritual workshop. I want to be able to shout and slap the back of a friend, shake him up and scream, "This is poetry, man!" and get a similar reaction from him.

Ezekiel Mphahlele. *Voices in the Whirlwind* (New York, Hill and Wang, 1972), pp. 33, 38

[Baraka] uses the theatre mainly as a political weapon, an extension of Black Power. To him, the theatre is not a medium of "protest," which Blacks see as a concession to the White world; it is rather an expression of Black culture, a mode of self-consciousness as well as of assault. Baraka's Revolutionary Theatre has only superficial resemblances to the Theatre of Cruelty of [Antonin] Artaud or Genet, which still adheres to formal art. Direct in its hatred, impatient with the obliqueness of drama, abusive and at times hysterical, the Revolutionary Theatre tends to draw energy from the passion of its audience rather than the imagination of its author. At its best, however, it draws also on the poetry, music, dance, on all the iconographies of Black culture. . . .

In *Slave Ship* Baraka resorts to a series of tableaux, a historical pageant of the Negro, a kind of "total theatre" that, although partial in its ideology, deploys in its "metalanguage" an experience larger than any of its verbal parts.

Ihab Hassan. *Contemporary American Literature* (New York, Frederick Ungar, 1973), pp. 166–68

In a general way, Jones is a romantic in the sense that many literary historians and scholars consider the post-Romantic Period symbolists, imagists, realists, naturalists, dadaists, impressionists, and other modern writers as latter day romantics or as part of a romantic continuum. He is a romantic in more specific ways as well. Like Emerson and certain other romantic writers, in a transcendentalistic way Jones places great faith in intuition, in feelings. As he applies this faith in an ethnocentric way, he would have blacks place faith in what he assumes to be their singular mystical impulses. He is

antirational in the way that romantics of Western European literature were opposed to the "cold" rationality of neoclassicism. Moreover, in connection with this reliance upon innate urgings and promptings, Jones inescapably asserts, as Blake and other romantic mystics contended, that man is divine, although, as Baraka, Jones would argue that the white man has perverted his, the white man's, divinity. Also, Jones is, like those romantics who would not conform to neoclassical religious dogma and traditions, romantic in that he is disdainful of the organized and orthodox religion of the majority and in that he has been himself a religious speculator and seeker. Next, Jones is romantic in his concern for the well-being, freedom, and dignity of the economically and politically weak, the dispossessed, the oppressed, and the downtrodden, as were the past century's romantic political and social libertarians and romantic champions of "humble" people. Further, Rousseau-like in his concern for the full development of man's potential, Jones sees his contemporary social, cultural, and political institutions as destructive of (black) man, so he would have man destroy, change, or control these institutions so that they, in his opinion, serve man rather than have man serve them. Further, Jones, like the Shelleys of the Romantic Period, is a visionary who sees creative artists as providers of philosophical and ideological bases for change. Next, in regard to technique, Jones, like many romantics of the past, will have little to do with conventional and prescribed forms and techniques, insists upon using the "language of the people," and constantly strives for new ways of writing, searching for what he calls a "post-American form." And it is obvious that Jones, as have countless romantics, uses his creative imagination to inform and shape his literary work.

Theodore R. Hudson. *From LeRoi Jones to Amiri Baraka: The Literary Works* (Durham, N.C., Duke University Press, 1973), pp. 179–80

A good many poets and critics don't like what's happened to the old LeRoi Jones, promising young Negro poet of *Preface to a Twenty Volume Suicide Note*. Baraka, obviously, is not interested in their opinions. Nevertheless, it is a mistake to dismiss him as an angry propagandist, as so many have done, because he appears to run against the literary grain. The old art of LeRoi Jones was written to be read. The new writing of Baraka is calculated to be heard—*how we sound*, he would say now—and his audience must have some sense of the Afro-American perspective from which his new writing issues.

The black aesthetic which shapes his writing is neither lacking in artistic taste (strident, anti-poetic, uncontrolled, say the critics) nor in itself startlingly new. It only appears that way from a literary point of view, one that is in many respects incongruous to the cultural context upon which his stylistic rationale is based. What is remarkable, from a literary standpoint, is the range of innovation his political ideology and altered cultural consciousness have required of him as a writer. For Baraka, though, it is not remarkable at all, but only the result of an inevitable artistic transformation, the sure spelling out of his specific placement in the world as a black writer. LeRoi Jones's *Preface to a Twenty Volume Suicide Note*, *Blues People*, and *The Dead Lecturer*, for all their apparent difficulties, lead comprehensively to the revolutionary identity of Imamu Amiri Baraka. And the transformation is not significant simply as a painful individual struggle, but more importantly represents the reintegration of the poet and his art into the stream of Afro-American culture.

William C. Fischer. *Massachusetts Review.* Spring, 1973, p. 305

The final rite [in *Slave Ship*], with its mimed cannibalistic aspect, is apocalyptic in both a mythical and a religious sense. In its mythical dimension, the ending completes the absorption of the natural, historical cycle into mythology. Its mythical movement is one of comic resurrection and integration, completed by the marriage of the spectator into community and the birth of the "old-new" black nation. This fertility ritual clearly has a religious dimension that has been prepared for by the continuous prayers to Obatala and Jesus, curses of the "Godless, white devil," and litanies such as "Rise, Rise, Rise, etc." Indeed, by creating basic images of resurrection with accompanying sensations of magic, charm, and incantation, Baraka returns the black audience to the most fundemental religious ground of tribal ceremony from which sprung the two greatest epochs of Western theatre (Greek and Christian), and which gave life to the archetypical African spirit. The spectators are as integral a part of the work as the congregation of a black Baptist church is of its service, and they function in much the same way. The nationalist myth of African-inspired renewal and Afro-American triumph is taken up by the audience because Baraka has called upon the community's shared aesthetic—the genius for musical improvisation. . . .

By claiming African roots in their totality, the black community controls its destiny as Clay, the middle-class greyboy [in *Dutchman*] could not. Now, Baraka's black heroes, not the witch-devil Lula, dance in triumph. The tragedy-burdened slave ship of *Dutchman* has become the dance-filled celebration of *Slave Ship*; musical transcendence has risen from the spirit of tragedy. . . .

Baraka's theatre, from *Dutchman* to *Slave Ship*, has clearly evolved from a concern with the individual cut loose from society to the community itself as victim, rebel, and, finally, triumphant hero.

Kimberly W. Benston. *Baraka: The Renegade and the Mask* (New Haven, Conn., Yale University Press, 1976), pp. 254–55

In [Amiri Baraka's] *Dutchman* the theme of the outsider has racial reverberations. The typical American outsider is the black educated man, difficult to place in the social ladder. He is doubly an outsider as he no longer belongs to the blacks, separated as he is in his aspirations and because of the potpourri nature of his culture, a factor that is reflected in the mythical and historical background of the play. Vis-à-vis the whites, he is considered an Uncle Tom, meek, aping white ways, and so desirous of their women. [Baraka] initially portrays this Uncle Tom stereotype in his portrayal of Clay, only to blast it in his exploration of the hidden aspect of the Uncle Tom—the revolutionary aspect. Thus, Lula and the American society which she represents experience a psychologically unbalancing phenomenon in [Baraka's] presentation of the erstwhile easygoing Uncle Tom. His Uncle Tom is an iceberg whose destructive potentialities are so well hidden that they take their victim by surprise. Lula the liberal thinks she knows Clay; but his tirade is unexpected, arousing primitive instincts for self-protection in her. For Lula and the society to maintain their equilibrium,

society must connive at getting rid of the outsider, as we see in Clay's instance. His character is not individualized, emphasizing the democratizing quality of black art. Clay is the chosen black representative, and his role, with its suffering and pain, is for the benefit of all black men. Indeed, one can envisage a black audience reacting to his tirade with punctuations of "say it, brother," "right on," "soul brother," etc., as he puts into words what had been in black minds. He is a typical black, educated middle-class man, one of many on the journey through American history. The antagonist is Lula, whose confrontation with Clay represents that great, unconsummated stereotypic romance between the white woman and the black American man. Receiving an inkling of the unseen reaches of this outsider, she unleashes her violence in typical frontier fashion, for these are the frontiers of the black-white relation, with its ignorance, its pretensions, its sexuality, its deceptiveness, its violence and blood bath.

Lula seems to have won this round but it is only seemingly so. Clay, however, has lived fully in his moment of outburst and, like [Ernest] Hemingway's Francis Macomber, he is a hero who has enjoyed a triumph though it is short-lived. Lula's murderous career indicates what she is—a mad criminal—as she waits to tackle her next victim. Her violence against Clay or all black men is a representation, from [Baraka's] point of view, of the emasculating nature of the relationship between white women and black men. Her use of a knife demonstrates symbolically black penis envy; it adequately illustrates the psychological and sexual undertones in the relationship. The disturbing nature of [Baraka's] portrayal is consequently obvious as he dismisses one popularly held opinion after the other.

Chikwenye Okonjo Ogunyemi. In Eldred Durosimi Jones, ed. *African Literature Today.* 9 (1978), pp. 29–30

The plays by Afro-American writer LeRoi Jones . . . who has used the African name Amiri Baraka ("blessed prince") in his civil and literary life since 1968, illustrate the political and artistic changes Baraka's writing underwent in the past twenty years. . . . The early works reflect, and in some ways herald, the gradual change in mood from the bohemian life of the Beat Generation in the 1950s to the new race consciousness and political flamboyance of the 1960s, the later plays show Baraka's commitment, first to black cultural nationalism and, in the case of the last play, to Maoism.

Baraka's first drama, *The Eighth Ditch (Is Drama)*, published and performed in 1961, is indicative of the interference of the "social" with the lyrical world of a poet's imagination who is obsessed with a narcissistic self-division into two personae, one "46," a young middle-class Negro boy scout, and his counterpart, guide, and seducer, "64," an older underprivileged black boy scout who introduces himself with the Melvillean salute "Call me Herman," and who is full of blues and allusions. The pure physical expression of which 64 and 46 seem capable in isolation is threatened and debased when other boy scouts in the camp find out about their homosexual affair.

This brief lyrical drama anticipates central structural elements of Baraka's later drama. Viewed on the literal level, the drama represents the two protagonists' inability to maintain a truly intimate sexual relationship, since they are confronted with the threatening presence of "others." At the end of the play, "46" is no longer a lover; for the benefit of the other boy scouts, he has been reduced to a commodity, an object. As in the later plays, *The Toilet* and *Dutchman*, the dramatic conflict originates with the assumed hostility of the not very well characterized ''others'' (boy scouts, classmates, or subway riders) toward the sensitive protagonists, a hostility which perverts love into abuse, into violence, or into the very act of killing. . . .

*The Toilet*, first performed in 1962, is set in an urban high school and deals again with loving self-expression in terms of homosexuality. The one-act play contrasts the homosexual relationship of two protagonists with the hostile and threatening, all-male outside world. Again, homosexuality is viewed positively by Baraka both as an outsider-situation analogous to, though now in conflict with, that of blackness, and as a possibility for the realization of ''love'' and ''beauty'' against the racial gang code of a hostile society. But there is also a new element of race consciousness in the play. . . .

Among Baraka's . . . plays performed at the Black Arts Repertory Theatre/School was *Experimental Death Unit No. 1.* . . . The play is a short ''black'' continuation of *Waiting for Godot*. Two white bums from the Theater of the Absurd, Duff and Loco, philosophize in Barakian lyricisms about life and art, beauty and intelligence, when a black prostitute appears on the Third Avenue scene. Duff and Loco make perverse propositions to the woman who is in need of money and entices the two men. The two men begin to make love to the woman in a hallway, when the black group for which the play is named comes marching in, behind a ''pike on the top of which is a white man's head still dripping blood.'' The group leader orders Loco, Duff, and the black woman killed; the white men's heads are cut off and fitted on two poles. The bodies are pushed into a heap, and the experimental death unit marches off. . . .

The difference between the play's decadent victims and their black executioners is further developed in the later play, *Home on the Range*. . . .

*Death Unit* and *Home on the Range* are attempts at debrainwashing a black audience, and at exorcising Baraka's literary past, by ridiculing absurdist drama as an expression of white degeneracy. Against this degenerate white world, Baraka poses the orderly military violence of the black execution squad and the power of black music and dance. The references to Robin Hood movies and to Frankenstein as well as the very title of *Home on the Range*, are indicative of another familiar technique, which Baraka now uses to reach black audiences: he continues his adaptations of American popular culture, even in the process of inverting its mythology.

The most famous example of a black nationalist popular culture play is *Jello*, a drama written for, and performed at, the Black Arts Repertory Theatre/School. *Jello* is a parody of the Jack Benny radio and television show; in the course of *Jello*, Eddie ''Rochester'' Anderson, Benny's chauffeur-servant, appears in a new, revolutionary role. Rochester lets his hair grow long, is ''postuncletom'' in appearance, and demands his ''back pay'' from Jack Benny. Although the miserly Benny does, eventually and reluctantly, part with his $300 in petty cash, Rochester still wants more: ''I want everything you got except the nasty parts.'' Perhaps as an elaboration of these ''nasty parts,'' Benny is later accused of advocating ''art for art's sake.'' While Rochester knows everything about Benny, Benny knows nothing about his chauffeur and ''friend.'' In the key speech of the play, Rochester almost becomes another Clay; he voices his moral grievance, which, of course, exceeds the demand for back pay, and criticizes the medium which the play parodies, that ''evil tube.'' . . .

*A Black Mass* continues the technique of inverting elements of American popular culture; it parodies *Frankenstein* as one-dimensionally as *Jello* parodied the Jack Benny show. *A Black Mass*, however, is also a black ritual which incorporates the mythology of the Nation of Islam into a black nationalist play which questions the functions of art and creativity. . . .

*Slave Ship: A Historical Pageant*, one of Baraka's most interesting plays of the black nationalist period, attempts to raise the political consciousness of black audiences by first showing historical models of black oppression and then breaking them on stage and inviting the audience to join in the ritual. Baraka's only endeavor to write a historical play—beyond the mythmaking of *A Black Mass*—interprets black history somewhat statically, as a chain of similar oppressive situations, in each of which blacks are the victimized group. On stage, the lower boat deck of the middle passage is transformed, first into slave market and ''quarters,'' and finally into a contemporary black ghetto. At the same time, the whites on the upper tier change their functions—from captain and sailors to slave dealers and plantation owners, and finally, to white business men. Between the two groups of white oppressors and black people is the middle-class Uncle Tom, who is at first a shuffling ''knee-grow'' aboard ship, later betrays Nat Turner's rebellion to his slave-master, and finally appears in a reverend's suit as a parody of Martin Luther King.

Werner Sollors. In Hedwig Bock and Albert Wertheim, eds. *Essays on Contemporary American Drama* (Munich: Hueber, 1981) pp. 105–6, 110–13, 117

It is difficult to find in [the so-called New Black Theater] a play which could be called an allegory in the strict sense; however, there are several that could be termed allegorical. [Amiri] Imamu Baraka's play, *Great Goodness of Life (A Coon Show)*, is an example. Reminiscent of [Franz] Kafka's *The Trial*, a middle-aged postal employee (bureaucrat) named Court Royal is arrested and charged by an anonymous voice (omnipotent Whiteman) which never reveals itself. The characters, some visible and some not, all represent something beyond their surface roles. Court's lawyer, for example, appears on stage with wires attached to his back and a huge wind-up key stuck in the side of his head. He babbles, slobbers, and grins as he recommends in exaggerated sheepishness that Court simply plead guilty and accept his fate without resistance. He is the overdrawn mimicked symbol of the Uncle Tom who stands ready to sell Court down the river at the mere suggestion of the anonymous White Voice. On the surface, he is a lawyer, but there is a second and more important meaning to be read beneath and concurrent with the surface story. This second meaning is made obvious to the audience through the use of blatant symbols like the wind-up key in the side of the lawyer's head, which tells us immediately that he is really the Uncle Tom of the story.

As the lawyer exits, another character variously named Young Voice, Young Boy, and Young Man enters. He is strong, young, and black, and speaks tough and cryptically. He wears only black. He, like the lawyer, demands that Court plead guilty, but for entirely different reasons. To Young Voice, Court is a ''guilty, stupid nigger'' because he has worked hard all his life and caused no trouble. Young Voice, who is obviously the play's militant antagonist, is also a captive of the unseen White Voice. In the end, Court is asked by that voice to shoot Young Voice in a blood rite that will set him free and turn his soul "white as snow." After only a brief hesitation, he shoots Young Voice, who dies, but not before saying in his last breath that Court is his "Papa." Court is stunned for a second, but quickly recovers, singing that his soul is "white as snow."

On the surface, we have the story of a weak man who kills his own son rather than resist the pressures of an evil power. In the second and concurrent meaning, we have a middle-aged black, a representative of an older generation, who is so intimidated and filled with fear of the white man that he is unable to stand up for the life of his own son. Filicide, an unthinkable sin, becomes preferable to resisting the omnipotent white man. Through allegory, the play achieves the suspense of drama as well as the implicit communication of a nationalistic value system.

> Shelby Steele. In Errol Hill, ed. *The Theatre of Black Americans* (New York: Applause, 1987), pp. 33–35

Baraka's revised aesthetic led him in at least two clear "social" directions, yielding first the agitprop dramas of *Four Black Revolutionary Plays* and *Jello*. With the exception of *A Black Mass*, these works conform closely to the requirements set forth in "The Revolutionary Theatre." In *Experimental Death Unit No. 1*, *Great Goodness of Life*, and *Madheart*, black victims are parodied, castigated, or shown in horrible deaths. Duff and Loco, the white characters of *Experimental Death Unit No. 1*, are appropriately crushed by the bullets of the Black Liberation Army—not before they have been rendered patently grotesque by their dialogue and actions, however. *A Black Mass* stands out from the company because its tone and language are elevated to match a sophisticated ideational framework. The conflict between Jacoub and his fellow "magicians" in the black arts is one between the restless, empirical inventor and the mystical artists who feel their oneness with all things. Finally, Jacoub creates both time and a hideous white beast who adores it under the following sanction: "Let us be fools. For creation is its own end." *A Black Mass* employs the demonology of the Nation of Islam, but in Baraka's hands its story takes on the character of a lyrical, mythopoeic exchange designed to guide the energies of the new Black Arts Movement. The play is dedicated to "the brothers and sisters of The Black Arts."

> Houston A. Baker, Jr. *Afro-American Poetics: Revisions of Harlem and the Black Aesthetic* (Madison: University of Wisconsin Press, 1988), pp. 131–32

Among contemporary writers, no one has been more provocative, politically and otherwise, than Amiri Baraka. . . . In the political sphere, Baraka has been as notorious for his radical transformations as for his radical stances. Bohemian aesthete, new left polemicist, black cultural nationalist, and Marxist-Leninist-Maoist, Baraka has declared his politics uncompromisingly at every phase of his career. More importantly . . . he has always insisted on an integral relationship between political and aesthetic commitments. I have written elsewhere on the major phases of Baraka's career and how his politics have shaped his creative work. The purpose of the present essay is to examine Baraka's use of popular cultural motifs and his understanding, at various points

of his career, of how political meaning imbues the icons of popular culture. . . .

Throughout *Preface to a Twenty Volume Suicide Note*, Baraka uses the icons of popular culture . . . both as objects of criticism and articles of faith. The same is true in his second collection of poems, *The Dead Lecturer*, except that these poems express the central existential crisis of Baraka's life, and his formulations present polarized extremes with a tone more shrill and less coy. He still sifts through the artifacts of popular culture in search of adequate articles of faith, but the sense of satisfactory resolution expressed in "In Memory of Radio" eludes him here. . . .

The turning point for Baraka came with his reinvestigation of Afro-American history, which helped him to transcend the dogmatic cultural nationalist assumption that the past offers only a dreary chronicle of abject slavery, cowardly capitulations, and false consciousness. At the same time, his study of Mao and rediscovery of Langston Hughes made him recognize the existence of a long and powerful international tradition of politicized art. These discoveries made it possible for Baraka to reconceive the relationship between the artist and existing culture. As a cultural nationalist, Baraka had assumed that the artist must destroy the corrupt existing culture in order to create a new, more humane culture. Now, he began to recognize the tradition of struggle embedded within existing culture, and this recognition entailed the possibility of an art grounded in that tradition of struggle. Such an art could celebrate as well as criticize; it could embody the complexities of real historical experience. Perhaps most importantly, it would allow the poet to write as a voice within a tradition and not just as a lonely pioneer, attempting by the naked force of rhetoric to lead his audience away from reality and into the promised land of utopian "blackness."

> David Lionel Smith. In Adam J. Sorkin, ed. *Politics and the Muse: Studies in the Politics of Recent American Literature* (Bowling Green, Ohio: Bowling Green State University Popular Press, 1989), pp.222, 225–26, 231–32

Baraka's deep concern with tradition is part of a pervasive concern among black intellectuals with identifying and codifying an existing tradition. . . .

Underlying or overt, the concern with tradition and traditions . . . counterpoints both political and aesthetic radicalism, and it locates unequivocally in Baraka's major poem *In the Tradition*, which he has both published and recorded (with music). Dedicating it to "Black Arthur Blythe," the alto saxophonist (whose 1979 record album lent the poem its title), Baraka calls it "a poem about African American history . . . a cultural history and political history." If a single work could sum him up "at a certain point," he says, it would probably be that poem. It incorporates his spirit, his energy, his musicality, all that he ever learned about and contributed to the visual and aural elements of modern poetry. . . .

Baraka's new book, *The Music*, clearly locates in its very title his focus for present and future. It is black music that has provided the lens, the cohesion, and the communication he has been pursuing as he "investigates the sun." This anthology of recent work, of [his wife] Amina's poetry and his own poetry, essays, and "antinuclear jazz musical," reveals a second and relatively new emphasis: Baraka as a poet/musician of praise—a lover of "The Music" (by which black music is understood) and the family of black musicians who create and interpret it, and a lover of his own family, itself consanguine within it.

D. H. Melhem. *Heroism in the New Black Poetry* (Lexington: University Press of Kentucky, 1990), pp. 220–21

Rebelling against conventional linguistics, Baraka's ''I Love Music'' uses no capital letters for proper nouns. This conscious subversion promotes a vision of freedom from stultifying categories of expression. Just as Baraka notes, in the essay ''Greenwich Village and the African-American Music,'' that the ''music was trying to get away from the restrictions of tradition without reason,'' so too his poetry was attempting, through subversion of conventional forms, to return to African rhythms, to reclaim the primacy of improvisation and the primordial construct. . . .

In the essay ''Expressive Language,'' Baraka articulates the need for a new speech to undermine hierarchies of Western meaning; and he searches for this voice in African rhythms. Baraka feels that the twisting of meanings by dominant language forms has been a cause of great confusion and ignorance, both on the part of the dominated and the dominator, the latter having convinced himself that his distortions are justified and are, in effect, solid reasoning and no distortion at all. The Slave Trade was blessed by the religious and political leaders in Europe because, to them, the African was a heathen whose enslavement was therefore a natural punishment by God for his sinful nature. Projective verse as used by Baraka . . . attempts to tear down the hierarchical language structures which have consolidated that illusory view of Western superiority by over-esteeming and inflating Western importance.

Anthony Kellman. *Ariel*. 21, 2 (April 1990), pp. 54–55

''The Screamers'' is like a free-form jazz solo. Many readers find it difficult because of its adroit blurring and blending of visual and temporal details, its shifts in time, setting, and emotional sequences; its fragments of biography, history, and sociopolitical commentary. Reading the story, then, is like solving a puzzle of space, time, character, chronology, event, and description. There are jazz-dada-surrealist shifts in accents; scenes and themes are introduced, reiterated, and amplified in solos within solos, where jazz is both meat and meteor, providing the substance and movement of the story. . . .

Although ''The Screamers'' challenges Western tradition in its obscuring and fragmenting of detail, it nevertheless maintains the complications of a traditional beginning: conflict and establishing the circumstances of character, society, and historical situation that must be resolved. As Baraka continues his jazz improvisations on divisiveness and solitude through the ''slow or jerked staccato,'' the narrator makes initial efforts at communion, but it is only a communion of perception and intellect, not of feeling; he like the others remains a ''valuable shadow, barely visible . . . Chanting at that dark crowd.'' Throughout the story, notes run together in a musical collage of identities and images: ''Big hats bent tight skirts'' in a ''mingled foliage of sweat and shadows.'' The narrator is aware of the poorer blacks' misperceptions of him as ''that same oppressor'' and acknowledges his own arrogant and disordered misinterpretations of their mystery. . . .

In his use of jazz as metaphor and model for narrative and dramatic strategies, Amiri Baraka in ''The Screamers'' fashions a form that shows the integration of the artistic and social imagination. The story doesn't entirely resolve social dilemmas and paradoxes of consciousness, but it is successful as a blending of aesthetic and moral function in a new mode, and it provides a breakthrough and a greater feeling of fictional boundaries through its use of jazz as subject, tonal structure, and aesthetic-ethical model.

Gayl Jones. *Liberating Voices: Oral Tradition in African American Literature* (Cambridge, Mass.: Harvard University Press, 1991), pp. 115–18, 122

As Leroi Jones, Baraka found himself out of his ethnie in a literary world that fetishized his ethnos. He never had a chance to view his ethnoculture with mere wonder, or nostalgia, or love. He found himself among a hundred white agents of articulation of a perceived black ethnoculture. Baraka's brief early years as a black bohemian are replete with this false agency. His ethnicization is directed by them—it is joyous, full of libido, and critical of the black bourgeoisie. Norman Mailer's ''White Negro'' lacked anger, sexual violence, black nationalism, or Marxism; he was a black man as the Beats wished to find him. The Beats wanted simply ''jazz as orgasm.'' At first Baraka provided it. Although the host society plays a role in the process from ethnogenesis to ethnicization in any ethnie, in the case of Baraka it is possible to say that attention was so great, and the black community so oppressed and silenced, that reverse ethnicization occurred, created by the Beats, in which Baraka was handed highly ideological material. In the beginning he takes an almost primordial approach to this manufactured culture. . . .

Thus Baraka confronts the pervasiveness of his ethnos in American culture and consciousness, as it is portrayed, sublimated, stolen, and examined by the majority. Baraka sees that blacks are, on the one hand, rendered historically inarticulate, and on the other, accorded by the majority with a deep and pivotal place in American culture. Baraka challenges, in these poems, the right of people outside the ethnos to influence ethnicization. He becomes an agent of articulation to challenge others who would claim the role; he becomes indeed a guerrilla of articulation.

Steve Harney. *Journal of American Studies*. 25, 3 (December 1991), pp. 371–72, 377

Deeply political, Amiri Baraka writes poems that have bothered many, reflecting as they do his dream of revolution, where the social orders will be recast, the races realigned. Much of his work is topical, written for the moment, and, as with agitprop verse, it's run the danger of becoming an historical footnote. Perhaps to consciously counter this eventuality, Baraka has placed musicality at the center of his efforts as a poet. He has often stated his aesthetic or purpose: ''The poetry I want to write is oral by tradition, mass aimed as its fundamental functional motive.''

Paul Vangelisti, the editor of [*Transbluency: The Selected Poems of Amiri Baraka/LeRoi Jones (1961–1995)*], divides the selected poetry into three periods, the Beat, Black Nationalism, and, finally, Third World Socialism. Baraka's ''lyrical realism'' is a stylistic constant, and his ''political avant-garde[ism]'' is the impulse that holds the work together. Almost from the beginning, the poetry is infused with the poet's emotional conflict between his racial culture and his self-recognition as an educated black man having come of age within a white culture. He copes with this dichotomy in a variety of ways, from expressions of rage to poses of cool detachment. In his best, most moving work, the "positions" are felt as coming not from the hardened heart or the fixed idea, but from the mind in flux, jockeying for a take on the particular situation at hand.

Marsilio Press deserves praise for bringing out this *Selected Poems*, an ample presentation from ten books. After the success of his first two books, *Preface to a Twenty Volume Suicide Note* (1961) and *The Dead Lecturer* (1964, the year of the *Dutchman*), came *Black Magic* (1969) itself a collection of three revolutionary books, *Sabotage, Target Study*, and *Black Art*, some of the most influential publications of the Black Arts Movement.

This book marked his nationalist phase, a period he'd look back on, not many years later, as "reactionary." However, passages abound that transcend the taint of narrow practicality. The first poem, "Three Modes of History and Culture," concludes:

I think about a time when I will be relaxed
When flames and non-specific passion wear themselves
away. And my eyes and hands and mind can turn
and soften, and my songs will be softer
and lightly weight the air.

Similarly, when he says in "Gatsby's Theory of Aesthetics" that "Poetry aims at difficult meanings," he is speaking about his personal response and understanding of the objective world: "I write poetry in order to feel, and that, finally, sensually, all the terms of my life. I write poetry to investigate my self, and my meaning and meanings." These are words of the artist superseding the polemicist.

Although *Black Magic* makes pronouncements and develops ideas about black nationalism, one finds further examples where poetry reaches inward: "I am real, and I can't say who / I am. Ask me if I know, I'll say / yes. I might say no. Still ask. / I'm Everett LeRoi Jones, 30 yrs old. / A black nigger in the universe. / A long breath singer, / wouldbe dancer, strong from years of fantasy, / and study."

Ultimately, he would like to be viewed as one speaking less for himself than the larger group his poems are intended for. One could imagine the following lines being issued from a soap box, an incendiary pulpit, or a hate rally. This is from "Black Art":

We want poems
like fists beating niggers out of Jocks
or dagger poems in the slimy bellies
of the owner-jews. Black poems to
smear on girdlemamma mulatto bitches
whose brains are red jelly stuck
between 'lizabeth taylor's toes. Stinking
Whores! We want 'poems that kill.'

The poem ends: "We want a black poem. And a / Black World. / Let the world be a Black Poem / And Let All Black People Speak This Poem / Silently / or LOUD." One might imagine a deeply sensitive man, one steeped in modernist literature, Kafka and so forth, finding a tormented comfort away from the subjective quarrels of the struggling self, comfort behind the "we" of his people's painful history and daily oppressions. By the early '70s he'd moved from the nationalist sentiments and strategies of *Black Magic* to the Marxist-Leninist investigations of *Hard Facts* (1972), where he still sees art, as did Vallejo, Aragon, and Aimé Césaire, as "a weapon of revolution."

Concurrent with Baraka's political/racial passions has been his commitment to jazz as a liberating force, as a balm and inspiration. Not only do his poems refer to music, players and songs, but the language and urban landscape of the poetry clearly have a jazz feel. He came of age during the bop revolution of the late 1940s and was involved in performing his poetry in jazz clubs and coffee houses. An exemplar of the Beat counterculture, Baraka's aesthetic includes emphasis on spontaneity, improvised structure, and the use of argot, and "natural" speech. Along with everything else wild and untethered, such as line breaks, punctuation, diction, and so forth.

In the 1960s Baraka wrote for *Downbeat* magazine and published two important books on jazz, *Blues People* (1963) and *Black Music* (1968). In his *Autobiography* (1984) he remembers: "Art Williams . . . also had poetry readings (at the Cellar) and I even read there myself one evening with a poet . . . Yusef Rahman. Yusef's poetry was a revelation to me. He was like Bird in his approach to poetry, seeming to scat and spit rapid-fire lines of eight notes at top speed. It was definitely speech musicked." His phrase is an updating of Emily Dickinson's famous definition of poetry as "language musically employed." Baraka has strengthened this emphasis throughout his career. "[We] were drenched in black music and wanted our poetry to be black music. Not only that, we wanted that poetry to be armed with the spirit of black revolution."

From the 1979 book, *Poetry for the Advanced*, is a good example of Baraka's jazz inspired poetry, "Pres Spoke in a Language" (dedicated to Lester Young): "Pres / had a language / and a life, like, / all his own, / but in the teeming whole of us he lived / tooting on his sideways horn." The poem evokes other classic players, "Bird's feathers / Trane's sinewy tracks / the slickster walking through the crowd / surviving on a terrifying wit / it's the jungle the jungle the jungle / we living in." At the end of this lyrical, controlled meditation on jazz and survival, Baraka reaches out to include his readers: "Save all that comrades, we need it."

More recent books go all out with Baraka's involvement in jazz. *In the Tradition* (1982), dedicated to "Black Arthur Blythe," the great alto player and exemplar of free jazz, is a long poem celebrating the heritage of black music. Lists of tunes are arranged along with jazz artists and political figures mixed in. It's an amazing performance piece that Baraka has chanted or half-sung around the world. "Speech #38," from *Wise, Why's, Y'z* (1995), is an example of Baraka's sound poetry and the sound is pure jazz. It opens, "OoBlahDee / Ooolyacoo / Bloomdido / OoBopShabam / Perdido Klackto-/ Veestedene / Salt Peanuts oroonie / McVouty / rebop," and continues for two pages that way.

In *The Selected Poems*, there are many poems that do not touch racial issues and do not make use of jazz idiom, but still demonstrate Baraka's individual voice. For instance, there are the "Crow Jane" poems from *The Dead Lecturer*, rich in literary reference, and then there is the opening of the famous "Black Dada Nihilismus." . . . The poem moves to elegy as it offers a list of black heroes who have absorbed the violence of racism and for whom suffering and resistance have been identical.

Viewing Baraka's work through a selected poem is a trip that inspires smiles (not always the comfortable kind) and admiration for qualities beyond the jazzy rhythms and the rage. There is restraint, sudden detachment, and technical control, often not noticed or mentioned in deference to the legend of poet as improvisor, poet as spontaneous bard. In "Balboa, The Entertainer," Baraka says: "Let my poems be a graph / of me." His is a complex graph, defying simple conclusions. His first book, *Preface to a Twenty Volume Suicide Note* has not yet been followed by the note, nor is the Preface finished.

Barry Wallenstein. *American Book Review*. 17, 3 (February-March 1996), pp. 7, 30

Houston A. Baker, Jr. has rightly observed [in *The Journey Back: Issues in Black Literature and Criticism*, 1980] that "the radical chic denizens of Bohemia [and] the casual liberals of the academy" have never recognized LeRoi Jones's/Amiri Baraka's achievement as a playwright and a poet because his "brilliantly projected conception of black as country—a separate and progressive nation with values antithetical to those of white America—stands in marked contrast to the ideas set forth by Baldwin, Wright, Ellison, and others in the fifties." That is, according to the integrationist politics that continue to dominate discussions of race in the United States, what we might in the 1990s call the "African-American problem" is indeed seen as the African-American's problem to examine and solve, not the white's. Baraka's Black Power political agenda, which perceives the United States as a society at least as black as it is white, a country built on "oppression and destruction," stands in marked contrast to the general integrationist bent of American radical politics. . . .

Baraka's one-act play *Dutchman* (1964) amply illustrates the persistence of racial tension in the United States in the 1960s and represents an emerging militant attitude on the part of American blacks, and on the part of black American playwrights. According to Samuel A. Hay [in *African/American Theatre: A Historical and Critical Analysis*, 1994], the African American Protest Drama of W.E.B. Du Bois, which viewed theatre as an integrationist "political weapon," was transformed by Baraka into the separatist Black Revolutionary Theatre of the 1960s, which "no longer represented appeals to share power," but depicted "seizures of power." Baraka himself has claimed that his play is an early example of "The Revolutionary Theatre," a theatre, like Artaud's "theatre of cruelty," that "should force change; it should be change" [Baraka, *Home: Social Essays*]. Baraka continues:

> The Revolutionary Theatre must EXPOSE! Show up the insides of these humans, look into black skulls. White men will cower before this theatre because it hates them. Because they themselves have been trained to hate. The Revolutionary Theatre must hate them for hating. For presuming with their technology to deny the supremacy of the Spirit. They will all die because of this.

Baraka's strong words point emphatically toward the end of this theatre: a revolutionary change in social structures. The idea that theatrical performance should attempt to force social change was initially articulated by Antonin Artaud in *The Theatre and Its Double*: "our present social state is iniquitous and should be destroyed. If this is a fact for the theater to be pre-occupied with, it is even more a matter for machine guns." Theatrical groups such as Julian Beck and Judith Malina's Living Theatre, founded in 1951, attempted to put Artaud's theories into practice. . . .

For Baraka, the theatre of which *Dutchman* is an example is centrally political; it will ultimately lead to the (at least) symbolic death of the white race. It is also, however, a psychological study, though one that exposes the limitations of the psychoanalytic

process. As Samuel Hay states it, "Black Revolutionary drama deconstructed both Outer Life and Inner Life." In *Dutchman*, Baraka attempts to psychoanalyze the black male in America, typified by the character Clay; his technique is meant to lay bare the social forces that make black men into neurotic subjects. His cure for their neurosis is race revolution and mass murder.

Frantz Fanon, in *Black Skin, White Masks*, extols the power of language rather than political activism to solve what he terms the "color problem," suggesting that this problem exists primarily in language itself: "From all sides dozens and hundreds of pages assail me and try to impose their wills on me. But a single line would be enough. Supply a single answer and the color problem would be stripped of all its importance." Fanon implies in this passage that if language is transformed—if the answer to this "problem" is found—the issue of race will simply disappear. This assumption is based on Fanon's naive trust in the Freudian psychoanalytic method. Freudian psychoanalysis asserts that one can solve psychological problems through language in a similar way, by making unconscious desires conscious through therapy. The surfacing of a psychological disorder in the conscious mind of the patient through the linguistic give-and-take of psychotherapy should, according to Freud, cure the disorder. . . .

Fanon's approach to the "color problem" reproduces Freud's method within a sociological frame: "I believe that only a psychoanalytical interpretation of the black problem can lay bare the anomalies of affect that are responsible for the structure of the complex." By applying the psychoanalytic process to the black man as an idea, Fanon hopes to "destroy" the "massive psychoexistential complex" that underlies "the juxtaposition of the white and black races. . . .by analyzing it" (emphasis mine). Like Freud, Fanon assumes that by making this "psychoexistential complex" conscious, he will eradicate it. *Dutchman* as historical text demonstrates that Fanon's solution was overly optimistic: the problems associated with black and white race relations did not evaporate in the decade between the publication *Peau Noire, Masques Blancs*, and the first performance of Baraka's play; indeed, they had multiplied and intensified. Baraka's text explores the psychology of race in the United States. . . .

However, Baraka, unlike Fanon, does not attempt to understand the "color problem" in order to solve it through a psychoanalytic sleight-of-hand; rather, his exposition of the situation of blacks in American culture is geared to an ultimate destruction of that culture: "The Revolutionary Theatre, which is now peopled with victims, will soon begin to be peopled with new kinds of heroes. . . .[T]hese will be new men, new heroes, and their enemies most of you who are reading this" [Baraka, *Home: Social Essays*]. *Dutchman's* Clay is presented as an example of the "victims" that people Revolutionary Theatre; he is identifiable as a Faustian anti-hero rather than a hero. But Baraka's intentions are clear: Clay, characterized primarily by his repressed desires to rape and murder whites, is martyred for the black revolutionary cause.

It is within the gothic, dreamlike atmosphere of *Dutchman* that the text's anti-hero, Clay, moves from a state of repression to one of acceptance of his unconscious desires. Indeed, the play encourages its black audience members to do likewise and warns its white viewers that the revolution is coming. Though he eventually expresses his desire to "[m]urder," Clay refuses to act on this impulse—indeed, it is Lula, the white villainess of the play, who will murder him. Clay dies at Lula's hands, then, as a self-aware but impotent and castrated subject. Lula functions in *Dutchman* as both Clay's mother and his demonic psychotherapist by bringing Clay's repressed desires to the surface of his consciousness. Through her verbal taunting she eventually peers into Clay's "black skull" and finds his murderous unconscious impulses.

A dutchman, "the theatrical term meaning a strip of cloth used to hid[e] the crack between the seams of flats, or, in a more general sense, a contrivance used to hide a defect of some kind" [Robert L. Tener, "Role Playing as a Dutchman," *Studies in Black Literature*, Vol. 3, No. 3, 1972], connotes something impermanently and fragilely held together that provides the illusion of solidity and permanence. The title *Dutchman* can be understood in this way as a metaphor for "the meretricious facade of civility" [George Ralph, "Jones's Dutchman," *The Explicator*, Vol. 43, No. 2, 1985] utilized by Clay both in his dress and his language to hide his murderous inner desires. It is this facade that Lula relentlessly strips away, as a psychoanalytic therapist might, attempting to access Clay's unconscious by getting behind "whatever surface his unconscious happens to be presenting to his notice at that moment," by asking him leading questions about his innermost thoughts. . . .

George Piggford. *Modern Drama*. XL, 1, (Spring 1997), pp. 74–82

BIBLIOGRAPHY
*The Eighth Ditch (Is Drama)*, 1961; *Preface to a Twenty Volume Suicide Note*, 1961; *Blues People: Negro Music in White America*, 1963; *The Baptism*, 1964; *The Dead Lecturer*, 1964; *Dutchman*, 1964; *The Slave*, 1964; *Experimental Death Unit No. 1*, 1965; *The System of Dante's Hell*, 1965; *Madheart*, 1966; *A Black Mass*, 1966; *Arm Yrself or Harm Yrself*, 1967; *Slave Ship*, 1967; *The Toilet*, 1967; *Black Art*, 1967; *Great Goodness of Life (A Coon Show)*, 1967; *Home on the Range*, 1968; *Four Black Revolutionary Plays*, 1969; *Jello*, 1970; *Junkies Are Full of (SHHH. . .)*, 1970; *In the Tradition*, 1982; *The Autobiography of LeRoi Jones/Amiri Baraka*, 1983; *The Music*, 1987; *Funk Lore*, 1996

# BEBEY, Francis (1929– )
**Cameroon**

Each of the short stories in the collection entitled *Embarras & Cie* is followed by a poem which echoes the theme, sometimes personal, sometimes traditional, in which fantasy, humor, reverie and serious reflections all meet. [Francis] Bebey is a very articulate artist, completely at home in a Western cultural environment in which he mainly lives. But he retains a deep loyalty to the artistic traditions of his origins in Cameroon. The humor, the fantasy and the lighthearted irony of much of his writing belie his seriousness as a disciple of an enlightened neo-Négritude school, less portentous than its predecessors and stripped of all militancy, which the situation in any case no longer demands. . . .

In the eight short stories of *Embarras & Cie* (the title comes from one of the poems inserted between the tales), the author speaks in his own name, sometimes recounting a brief personal

experience, sometimes an incident purporting to have occurred in his native Cameroonian village, or have been told to him by a fellow traveler. For the most part they are as light and transparent as gossamer and as smoothly textured as velvet—woven out of gentle raillery, mock self-deprecation, pseudo-naïveté, and disarming understatement. But under cover of this reassuring bonhomie, Bebey shoots off little barbed shafts and sometimes the gossamer is the web woven by a spider hidden in its heart to catch its prey. His exposition of a sorcerer's difficulties in making ends meet in this enlightened age is innocent enough, or his mockery of marriage customs and the one-up-manship of rural African society in "Le Mariage d'Edda," where the whole hierarchy of status symbols is revealed, ranging from a brick house to the ultimate in coveted possessions—a tropical pith helmet. But the dart sinks deeper in "Jimmy et l'égalité," aimed at the ambiguous position of the Westernized Negro—the "Black Frenchman"—and at the whole master-servant relationship of black Africa, inherited from the colonial era.

With only two works of fiction to his name, Bebey showed that he was an accomplished prose writer as well as a poet. With his sure sense of the ironic effects to be drawn from the simplest, colloquial language, with his humorous tolerance of human foibles, spiced at times with subtle malice, Francis Bebey's writing in his first novel [*Le Fils d'Agatha Moudio*] and short stories has the same impact of that of his countryman Bernard Dadié. Like him, too, he manages to imply criticism without dogmatism or any over attacks. If he trails a wisp of Négritude after him, it is a Négritude freed from any complexes, any protest, any hatred or even cynicism. It is compounded of a concern for honesty—which means for him writing as an African—and a preoccupation with getting through to his reader.

Dorothy S. Blair. *African Literature in French* (Cambridge: Cambridge University Press, 1976), pp. 171, 289–90

A Western reader, scrutinizing the novels of Francis Bebey, may be struck by their apparent lack of narrative consistency. It is as if the author had set out quite systematically to flout all the rules handed down by Flaubert, Henry James, and Ford Madox Ford. Objective narration and its attendant qualities of neutrality, impartiality, and *impassibilité* are thrown to the winds as Bebey's narrators become either his direct spokesmen or enjoy a bonanza of self-indulgence, interpreting the facts, pronouncing judgments, offering advice, and digressing at length on a host of subjects ranging from the trivial to the intellectually abstract. Far from adhering to the convention which requires that a story be told from one point of view, these same narrators adopt any stance convenient to their immediate purposes—omniscient author, author-participant, author-observer—within the confines of the same novel. In short, a dominant characteristic of Bebey's work is its polytonality.

Although familiar with Western novelistic techniques, having studied literature at two French *lycées* (La Rochelle and Louis le Grand) and at the Sorbonne, Bebey chooses quite consciously to discount them in favor of a more instinctive approach. . . . This insouciance produces a form of expression closely allied to that of the oral folktale as delivered by the traditional Doualan *conteur*. An examination of his three novels—*Le Fils d'Agatha Moudio, La Poupée ashanti* and *Le Roi Albert d'Effidi*—will demonstrate the point and highlight certain defects in Bebey's artistry.

*Le Fils d'Agatha Moudio* may be viewed as the unhappy tale of a simple, good-hearted young fisherman, Mbenda, who is constantly victimized by the social system and the mischievous appetites of those around him. He ends up saddled with two wives, both of whom have been unfaithful to him and may well continue to be so, and two children, neither of whom is his. To crown all, he seems perfectly resigned to his fate. A similar sense of tragedy hangs over *La Poupée ashanti*, set against the urban backdrop of Nkrumah's Accra. It is the drama of an attractive, intelligent and courageous girl who is seduced in primary school, denied an education, almost killed in a street demonstration, constantly badgered by her domineering grandmother, ultimately brainwashed into spending the rest of her life as a market vendor, and married to a husband whose values and educational level are so markedly different from her own that their future connubial happiness must be regarded at best as uncertain. Bebey's most recent novel, *Le Roi Albert d'Effidi*, brings us the bittersweet tale of a successful middle-aged businessman who is almost destroyed by his political and marital ambitions. Albert's new and dangerously young wife, Nani, is unfaithful to him. He loses an election after a particularly turbulent campaign involving the virtual destruction of his car and his self-respect. Finally, his wayward wife returns to him, and Albert, setting aside his political ambitions and some of his long-held beliefs, returns to his neglected shop.

In their sense of tragedy, these novels are worthy of Balzac. Yet Bebey, for all his cynicism, is basically an optimist in regard both to Africa and to humanity in general. And, equally important, he has a wry sense of humor. He could no more make tragedies out of his stories than could Molière out of *Le Tartuffe*. To have done so would have been to sacrifice their delightful irony, their lightness of tone, their earthiness and ring of truth. It would also have been to violate Bebey's own nature. Such considerations help explain his choice of narrative stance.

Norman Stokle. In Kolawole Ogungbesan, ed. *New West African Literature* (London: Heinemann, 1979), pp. 104–5

*La Poupée ashanti* is, at least on the surface, the most conventionally political of Bebey's works. Set in Accra, Ghana, shortly before Le Docteur's (read: Dr. Nkrumah) accession to the presidency of the new republic, it deals with the marketwomen and their political organization, with the country's leader himself, and includes a large political march and demonstration midway through the novel. And yet the main interest does not lie in politics. Despite the political background, it is essentially the love story of Edna, a young marketwoman, and Spio, a young and somewhat idealistic bureaucrat, which moves the plot. The political issue which is intertwined with this personal relationship centers on the marketwoman who has lost her seller's permit because the man to whom her daughter is engaged has been arrested for being a member of the opposition party in Parliament. This issue and, more generally, that of Le Docteur and the principle of his one-party state, are the subject of heated discussion between Edna, her aunt, and her grandmother, Mam, the leader of the Marketwomen's Association. These political issues are of serious interest now, and at the time Le Docteur (Nkrumah) was coming to real power, topical as well. But a close reading of the text produces two interesting discoveries: first, these key political issues are downplayed

by stylistic means and are thus shown to be of less than central importance; second, the novel never resolves these issues, an unusual situation in the highly polemic world of African fiction.

W. Curtis Schade. *Studies in Twentieth-Century Literature.* 4, 2 (Spring 1980), p. 163

In Francis Bebey's *Le Fils d'Agatha Moudio* we have a . . . humorous account of a love affair, opposed by the man's mother and, thus, by the village as a whole. Set in a fishing village during the colonial period, it offers its own version of the conflict between traditional and Western views of love and marriage. Agatha Moudio's love for Mbenda, a local fisherman, dates from the day when he forced the white monkey-hunters to pay for using the village's forest. By sprinkling salt on the fire, she causes a big rain storm, enabling her to spend the day undisturbed with Mbenda in his hut. They are in love, but Maa Médi, Mbenda's widowed mother, has no intention of allowing her son to fall into the clutches of a loose woman such as Agatha Moudio. As a way to block their relationship, Maa Médi prepares to marry her son to Fanny, whom his father had named, on his deathbed, as Mbenda's future bride. Powerless to oppose the will of his mother and the elders, he continues to see Agatha while the bargaining goes on with Fanny's people. In chapter seven Fanny becomes his wife, and in the next chapter we learn that she is pregnant—but Mbenda, thinking her too young, has never slept with her! Great commotion ensues as the truth is made known, but the birth of a daughter smooths things over. After further intrigues, including Agatha being driven to the city in the white monkey-hunter's car, we learn that Mbenda now has two wives, for Agatha, back in the village after her excursion to the city, has been installed in his hut by her aunt. The village is upset about this, feeling her to be a source of trouble, but, strangely enough, Fanny does not seem to mind at all.

Agatha Moudio is pregnant and is certain that it will be a boy. The village, joyous that some of its men who had been sent to prison are about to return, becomes kinder towards her. The child is born, a boy as predicted, but he is white. The reaction on Mbenda's part is first perplexity, but then joyful acceptance. . . .

While the central conflict is once again the question of who governs the marital relations of the younger generation, it is posed in a far more gentle, more humorous light than in the other works dealing with this theme. The traditional ways are upheld for only the best of motives, the central characters are all essentially likeable people, and the resolution at the end is a peaceful merging of the will of the village with the will of Mbenda and Agatha to love each other.

W. Curtis Schade. In Carolyn A. Parker and Stephen H. Arnold, eds. *When the Drumbeat Changes* (Washington, D. C.: Three Continents Press, 1981), pp. 49–50

Cameroon has had a tradition of producing fine satirists—Mongo Beti, Ferdinand Oyono—and now Francis Bebey, whose third novel is . . . now available in English translation. Warm, genial, comic, the book reflects Bebey's own humor and breadth. Bebey finds harmony in his own life as guitarist, poet, composer, novelist, and musicologist. [*Le Roi Albert d'Effidi*, translated as *King Albert*] reflects this balanced perspective. Set in the Cameroon of the late 1950s, the novel centers on the coming election of a delegate to represent three villages in a parliament for a newly independent nation. Each village claims supremacy for possessing either the highway or the church or the school. Village champions emerge: ''King'' Albert, successful, middle-aged merchant, hence capitalist; Toutouma, former railroad worker and trade-unionist, hence communist; and Bikounou, minor bureaucrat, the younger generation's upstart and individualist. . . .

Bebey keeps up plot suspense to the very end, for as one hilarious episode favors one champion, the next works to the advantage of another. Though all the principal characters suffer from their frailties, they are the more lovable by being so human. Bebey's sense of the ridiculous is most evident in dialogue, where often the seemingly naive comment contains an ironic twist. The villagers are proud to have learned church response in Latin. Accustomed to European visitors who are linguistically inept, they accommodate the white man's god in whose image he is made: ''God understands only Latin, and he never learned our language at school.''

The novel has depth: it presents not only delightful satire but also incisive commentary on cultural changes occurring in many Third World societies. The whimsy will amuse the Africanist and the newcomer to African literature alike.

> Charlotte H. Bruner. *World Literature Today.* 56, 3 (Summer 1982), 559–60

For Francis Bebey, change is necessary in African society today. But there is also need to control undesirable aspects of change in order to preserve certain desirable values in the traditional culture. This intention is reflected in the conciliatory measure which he proposes in his novel *Le Roi Albert d'Effidi*, in which traditional values are meaningfully adapted to serve the needs of modern Africa. The novel was published in 1976 by Editions CLE in Cameroon. *Le Roi Albert d'Effidi* attempts a reassessment of the African ancestral past showing its wealth and the extent to which tradition can be comfortably accommodated to the modern world. . . .

There is a conscious attempt in the novel to reaffirm African personality and culture. African food, hospitality, languages, music, and dance figure here prominently. The traditional set-up and beliefs which in the past secured peace, stability, and progress in the community are critically examined in the light of the needs of modern Africa. From an assessment of traditional standards in terms of such substantial goods as food, clothing, and shelter, the author passes to less tangible services such as those connected with education and social welfare. He extends his inquiry to the realm of the human spirit and shows the general sense of the individual and what constitutes social well-being in a traditional African society.

The author draws our attention to modern political campaigns, unheard of in the traditional past, marked by violence and conflicting ideologies which often end in disaster. The dangers of this unfortunate development in Africa in the name of modern politics are outlined by the author, and there is little consolation in telling the victims and the silent millions of modern Africans that the fire of discord has been lit by their own countrymen. *Le Roi Albert d'Effidi* pleads for a critical appraisal and rehabilitation of African traditional values. Francis Bebey appears convinced that traditional values are not necessarily incompatible with modern progress.

He calls for caution in matters of change and modernization. With him there is a great need to conduct careful research about the probable effects of alternative courses of action before taking a final decision on them.

> Elerius Edet John. *Language Quarterly.* 23, 3–4 (Spring-Summer 1985), pp. 42–43

Although Francis Bebey belongs to the same generation as Ferdinand Oyono and Mongo Beti, he did not begin to write seriously until the mid-1960s. His view of the world was shaped less by a resentment against colonialist oppression than by a desire for reconciliation, for he believed people could transcend the injustices of the past by accepting what cannot be changed and by committing themselves to a society based on love and productive work. Inspired partly by the Christian humanism he absorbed as the son of a Protestant pastor and partly by his respect for traditional African wisdom, Bebey's dream of reconciliation expresses his belief in a spiritual reality that gives meaning to human existence. When people lose contact with this reality, he contends, they begin to act in selfish, cruel, and hypocritical ways that prevent them from living in harmony with each other. Couched in a tone of comic irony, all his writings subtly reaffirm this sense of moral idealism.

All the major characters in his novels confront the opposition between modern and traditional values, and each of them ultimately synthesizes a hybrid world-view not altogether different from [Léopold Sédar] Senghor's ''*métissage cultural*.'' In fact, Senghor himself once told Bebey: ''you have done what I expect of an African artist—rooted yourself in the black African tradition while welcoming all available influences from abroad. This is how we shall develop from folklore to great works which are truly African.'' The traditional component of Bebey's world view is crucial to his synthesis of values, but it is not tied to outmoded beliefs, and he insists it must be freely chosen by Africans in response to their present needs, not imposed on them from the outside. . . .

This same impulse toward reconciliation is apparent in the balance Bebey seeks to strike between individual demands for self-realization and African principles of communal solidarity, between scientific knowledge and traditional wisdom, between productive work and the joy of living. It also emerges in the forgiveness and tolerance that allow the characters in his novels to overcome their resentments against each other and to establish relationships based on love and trust. In a sense, the dilemma they confront in defining their self-images is similar to that of newly independent African countries like Bebey's own Cameroon, and the endings of his novels suggest that these countries could articulate a viable sense of identity in the same way that his principal characters do—through hard work, willingness to accept what cannot be changed, forgiveness of past offenses, and commitment to a morally idealistic vision of peace and harmony.

> Richard Bjornson. In János Riesz and Alain Ricard, eds. *Semper Aliquid Novi: Littératures Comparée et Littératures d'Afrique* (Tübingen: Gunter Narr, 1990), pp. 205–6

Although couched in a tone of comic irony, [Bebey's] writings subtly affirm a moral idealism that reflects his faith in the spiritual dimension of human life while implicitly condemning those who turn their backs on it.

In traditional African society, an awareness of this higher reality was embedded in cultural practices and artifacts that Europeans transformed into museum pieces with economic value. However, as Bebey attempts to show in his long poem *Concert pour un vieux masque*, their real value lies in their ability to convey the communal spirit, the vitality, and the sense of awe with which Africans had traditionally confronted the harshness and mystery of life. One of the best-known Cameroonian singers and composers, he had originally presented *Concert* as a song, but when its message was misinterpreted by one of his listeners, he expanded it into a narrative poem that recounts the story of a mask that an old Angolan chief had presented as a token of friendship to a white Brazilian. Many years after returning to his homeland, the Brazilian forgot the chief's proviso that the mask not be sold or given to anyone else, and he allowed it to be exhibited in the local museum; however, during its first night in a display case, it mysteriously broke in half.

The mask in the poem symbolizes the human values that had found expression in African cultural practices. The old chief's generosity made these values accessible to the Brazilian, but because he lived in a materialistic society where people did not comprehend the real significance of the mask, he eventually betrayed its gift of knowledge. His betrayal denies the original function of the object that incarnates traditional spiritual insights, but it does not invalidate the insights themselves. In fact, the words of Bebey's poem endow them with new meaning and communicate them to a much larger audience.

> Richard Bjornson. *The African Quest for Freedom and Identity: Cameroonian Writing and the National Experience* (Bloomington: Indiana University Press, 1991), pp. 262–63

BIBLIOGRAPHY

*La radiodiffusion en Afrique noire*, 1963; The Son of Agatha Moudio (*Le Fils d'Agatha Moudio*, 1967): *Agatha Moudio's Son*, 1971; Embarrassment and Company (*Embarras & Cie*, 1968); *Musique de L'Afrique*, 1969; *Trois petits cireurs*, 1961; The Ashanti Doll (*La Poupée ashanti*, 1973): *The Ashanti Doll*, 1977; King Albert of Effidi (*Le Roi Albert d'Effidi*, 1974): *King Albert*, 1981; *La Musique africaine moderne*, 1975; *Le Petit Fumeur*, 1976; Concert for an Old Mask (*Concert pour un vieux masque*, 1980); *Nouvelle saison des fruits*, 1980; The Marriage of Edda (''Le Mariage d'Edda''), 1983; *Le ministre et le griot*, 1992; *L'enfant-pluie*, 1994

# BEMBA, Sylvain (1934–)
## Congo

[An] important dramatic procedure is borrowed from the tradition of the character *sine qua non* in oral literature, the griot or the singer of the tale as presenter of the performance. This character is frequently used in French-language theater.... [and Sylvain Bemba] makes use of this formal aspect in different ways in two of his plays. In *Un Foutu Monde pour un blanchisseur trop honnête* the griot's function is limited to providing a framework and an opening comment, and serving as a linking element between two acts of the play, a biting satire of the corruption that seems to have infected the whole population. The *blanchisseur*, Raphaël, embodies goodness and respectability, and is therefore alienated, since all the others are corrupt....

We do not encounter the presenter again [after the introductory passage] until the end of the first act. He remains outside developments on the stage. In another play by Bemba, this role does not remain restricted to that of providing a framework. In the character of the *amuseur public*, the storyteller is integrated *within* the action and he plays a considerable role. He continually comments on the action, followed by reactions from the public, in this case the other characters on the stage.... In *L'Homme qui tua le crocodile*, it is the rich N'Gandou, whose name means ''crocodile,'' who as a businessman terrorizes and exploits a whole district until a teacher from the local school rebels and the crocodile receives his just deserts. In this tragicomedy, as Bemba calls it, the *amuseur public* of the district where N'Gandou lives tells the people the fable of the crocodile who wants the river all to himself. It is clear to whom he is referring and the other characters, the people of the district, enthusiastically repeat certain sentences from the story-teller's tale at every turn, exactly as in a performance in the oral tradition.... In the ensuing scenes the actual struggle against N'Gandou unfolds. Here the teacher plays an important part. The *amuseur public* keeps the people (on stage and in the audience) informed about developments, and following the arrest of N'Gandou, warns them to remain alert because—and this is the moral—new N'Gandous can always appear, each exploiting the people in his own particular way.

In Bemba's play the *amuseur public* acts precisely as he has from time immemorial in Congolese ''reality.'' It begins with a death vigil (*veillée mortuaire*) at which a great number of people are present. The *amuseur public* is also there, as is customary. Cards or draughts are being played. The *amuseur* is the first character to speak; the group answers and already responds to his jokes and commentary.... Thus his role is clear from the beginning. He introduces the play, but does not stand outside the action: he functions on the same level as the other characters.

> Mineke Schipper. *Theatre Research International*. 9, 3 (1983–1984), pp. 226–28

In *Rêves portatifs*, the projectionist Ignace Kambéya, the unfortunate spouse of Marie Kabongo, is a twin who lost his brother when he was five years old. Responsible for a murder, imprisoned at the dawn of independence, he is the ''vanished one,'' the one who will return to haunt, divide, and separate the actors and players of the political debates that animate Inoco. His absence will have multiple repercussions.

Twins constitute a connection—a pair, a separation—that is concrete and alive. It is thanks to the character of Ignace Kambéya that Bemba can unfold in the novel connections of sequences, of characters, of actions, and of objects. Ignace is the one whose disastrous itinerary disrupts the sense of the festivities of independence, unties and divides the knot of ulterior events. Moudandou, on the other hand, is the one who never stops to bind, tie, chain, and trap.

We already know that in the first part of *Le Soleil est parti à M'Pemba*, Félix Gamboux kills N'Gampika, his younger brother. In the same first part we learn that Gamboux has become ''un tara bwolo, father of twins.'' It is these twins that we rediscover in the second part of the novel. All the connections (the groups of coincidences and the game of relations) gravitate around the theme of the destiny of the twin couple. Otto Rank explains, in *Don Juan et le double*, that the motif of twins is a concretization of the motif of the double—the twin couple, supernatural and heroic, appear to be united beyond life and death by the immortal connection which they incarnate. If in the first part of *Le Soleil est parti à M'Pemba* Félix Gamboux kills his brother, in the second part of the same novel, Albert N'Gambou and Ronald N'Gampika are twins whose relationship is that of two beings inaccessible to one another. . . .

The twin connection Ronald and Albert form leads them towards a dangerous meeting in a dangerous place. To some extent, this new death is only the recommencement (repetition, reiteration) of the murder perpetrated by Félix Gamboux in the first part of the novel. . . .

The narratives and plays of Sylvain Bemba (re)constitute a typology of characters, a typology of the forms of aggression and a typology of the systems of reading. The typology of the systems of reading discloses the links and divergences between reading methods. The typology of the forms of aggression reconstitutes . . . certain "independent forms of violent acquisition of living creatures: war, hunting, fishing." The typology of the forms of aggression is inseparable from a classification of techniques. The typology of characters reveals the different connections, like that of the role of doubles and of twins, distributions and incarnations of passions and forces. . . .

Sylvain Bemba establishes a constant interaction between the existence of machines and the theme of the double (the presence of twins). The twin has an extension beyond himself (he belongs to a human connection) and the machine is an extension of the human body. The machine (pole of an extension, or prosthesis) makes possible the doubling of the real, and provokes accidents and disappearances.

Ange-Séverin Malanda. *Presence Africaine*. 130 (1984), pp. 95–97, 100–1, 110

In Sylvain Bemba's *Une Eau dormante*, Olessou the fisherman, who dared to rise in protest against the village chief and the owner of the pond in which Olessou is fishing, is rescued from sure death by Ecombo-Veritas, a young man whom villagers consider to be half crazy and who is an allegory rather than a human character. In any case, he is the figure that the author needs to demonstrate the victory of justice and kindness over arbitrary acts, inequality, and evil. The author's move in this case is in consonance with the concept dating back to the Age of Enlightenment: it is possible to reorganize society through the favorable influence of an ideal character.

Bemba's comedy is extremely original because it offers two ways toward a happy outcome. The first way: Olessou, who is ordered by the chief to fight Sosso, the pond owner, in public, is saved from death by Ecombo-Veritas, who led the village youth to his rescue. The second version: Olessou overpowers Sosso in the fight. The melodrama of the situation is growing proportionately to Olessou's resistance to the efforts of Oluo, the village thief, and Sosso to subordinate him to their will. At first they try to talk the fisherman out of opposing them; then they intimidate him, abduct his wife, and finally decide to kill him. The features of "villains" in Oluo and Sosso, both of whom are retrogrades and selfish men,

are so overemphasized and pointed and the righteous Olessou is so lonely (the action takes place in the colonial period and the authorities are on the chief's side) that it requires a double happy ending to "justify" the survival of the protagonist: this does not arise from the development of the plot.

It is interesting to hear Bemba's arguments in justification of the obviously artificial character of the happy endings in his plays. On the one hand, he relies on the eternal moral code of the people: Olessou cannot be defeated because he embodies justice, kindness, and reason. On the other hand, the playwright explains the intervention of supernatural forces in the characters' struggle against evil by the fact that it reflects a psychological stereotype of mass consciousness—the popular belief in the presence of the irrational and magic in reality. "I am trying to express in a dramatic form what Congolese people hide under the cover of myth," Sylvain Bemba said in an interview with a Congolese literary journal in 1977. "If the fantastic did not combine with the real most closely, if it was not intertwined with the fiber of our social existence, I would never dream of introducing it into my plays."

Nina D. Lyakhovskaya. *Research in African Literatures*. 18, 4 (Winter 1987), pp. 464–65

In the works of Sylvain Bemba, the world of the imaginary is activated by elements like dream, the restoration of speech, and the meeting of the forbidden. The principal element is the voyage, the passage from one state to another, the ultimate test that leads to life. *L'Enfer, c'est Orféo* is the passage of the frontier, Orféo's voyage toward the maquis for regeneration. There, he rediscovers a sense of creatures and things. *Rêves portatifs* is the journey towards the life of others through image. Dreams are lived in an obscure room and projected on a white wall. The reinvented life unfolds to the rhythm of the salivation of Ignace the projectionist. It is a voyage through independence. *Le Dernier des cargonautes* is a novel of constant departure: departure from home for a rupture of moral values, departure for France to a confrontation of other battles, and expulsion for a return towards a collective village conscience. In *Léopolis*, the American Nora makes the cycle of return to the quest of a past prefiguring the future. She rediscovers *Léopolis*, the city of lions, and reconnects with the life of the great assassinated leader, Fabrice M'Pfum. It is the voyage towards the dimension of myth, similar to that of Patrice Lumumba. . . .

Bemba's narrative technique simultaneously incorporates several techniques of this sort. Man becomes the master of the universe when he dreams. If he stops dreaming, he dies. His literature appears like a transgression that destroys and creates at the same time. The work is then a product of diverse controlled circumstances, which the pathways of the imaginary allow to roam free, face to face with the self of the author, his biography, his story, his readings, his character, his habits, his human and ecological environment, and his philosophy. . . .

By an assiduous practice of the process of distancing, Sylvain Bemba has built some of his plays around pedagogical and demonstrative irony. *Une Eau dormante* provides the outline and *L'Homme qui tua le crocodile* is the perfect example. The urban decor covers the dealings of a usurer, with the symbolic name of the cayman, with Henri Balou the teacher, punctuated with the comments by a public entertainer. The author also rediscovers traditional, oral theatricality with this buffoon, philosopher, and implacable observer who enjoys the immunity of tolerance. This view of urban Africa is accentuated in *Embouteillage*, shown several times at Brazzaville, in *Un Foutu Monde pour un blanchisseur trop honnête*, *Eroshima*, and *L'Étrange Crime de Monsieur Pancrace Amadeus*. It is represented by the poetry of the social fantastic, popular language, satire and the detailed recreation of the jokes of the characters. . . .

The theater for Sylvain Bemba is, without contest, the nocturnal return to the community around the fire, replaced by projectors. It is the return to communion. With the principal protagonist, the community gets rid of its anxieties and, through a cultural identity, becomes a collective social character. . . .

For Sylvain Bemba, the novel today is the privileged space for the demonstration of the mechanisms of domination and exploitation through creatures of flesh and blood. . . .

All the characters in his novels live in a renewed state of solitude, because, often, the traveler finds himself alone, having left behind him his past experiences.

In Congolese literature, Sylvain Bemba's writings are probably the most prolific and also those in which social fantasy verges most directly with realism, and the magic of words is linked to that of things, in a rational didacticism. This type of writing revalorizes even more a culture made up of parables and a variety of bizarre and symbolic elements. The bizarre gives us a vantage point from which to view historic, political, and social truths. The characters glide through the bizarre with the weight of concrete, realistic truths in order to become transformed into living memories.

The work of Sylvain Bemba records the greatest tragic possibilities, from humor to death, thus summarizing our multidimensional dreams, whose dimensions become movements which contain the plenitude of body, time, space, and word.

Caya Makhélé. *Notre Librairie*. 92–93 (1988), pp. 97–99

Sylvain Bemba . . . is one of the most recent African writers to have achieved an international reputation, first in the theater, then through four novels that seem to puzzle readers. Critics also seem somewhat put off by his works, since they have received little sustained analysis, although Bemba's name is often seen in general discussions of the new African writing. Bemba mixes modern literary technique and complicated psychological and sociological concepts with elements drawn from African folklore, legend, tribal history, and religion in a quite original way. The supernatural aspects of African tradition are crossed with modern fantasy and science fiction in the manner of Third World "marvelous realism" to dig deeper into the double identity of the colonized person.

The theme of dancing masks provides a key to Bemba's main characters and to his literary methodology and style. The image of dancing masks is very close to the central concept behind all of Bemba's work. The masks worn by the characters, the roles they play, are less a disguise or protection than a symbol, a projection of the self, a label, an "identity," serving to relate the individual, especially the inner self (emotions, the subconscious), to the ideal self, the collective self, the historical self, the timeless self. Obviously masks are ambiguous, overdetermined, and kaleidoscopic, constantly shifting in valence, like the moods of the mythological gods with whom they are allied; but like all mythic elements they have a positive significance, weaving a web of references while educating those who witness their dance. . . .

Bemba is fascinated with the problem of identity and with central African history. There is always a doubling. In [*Le Soleil est parti à M'Pemba*] he presents two sets of twins, the second set sons of one of the brothers in the first. We can thereby contrast two generations and the difference between urban and rural settings. All Bemba's characters undergo striking transformations as we see them in different settings, playing different roles, assuming various identities, especially when they go to France. The Lumumba- and Schweitzer-like characters come to assume the mask of "hero" or ideal self; like the numerous political-leader characters, they come to represent the group and a kind of "collective self." In *Soleil* we are also given the classic case: the buffoon masker, playful, a clown, who uses a magic phonograph to do a rapid-rerun of recent African history to unmask the evils and distortions of colonialism and their vestiges in the postcolonial world. . . .

Bemba wrote his first novel, *Rêves portatifs*, at the age of forty, in 1979. The central concern is the relation of film to freedom. Bemba hangs all the diverse happenings on the story of a projectionist who has inadvertently gotten tangled up in drug dealing, just as the country of Palms is coming to independence. The rather rambling narration depicts not only the microcosm of the movies, but also nightclubs, jails, courts, journalism, politics, clinics, and bush hospitals. The author attacks all the cultural changes that accompany the birth of a new nation, which in itself might be seen as a manifestation of the mask theme; in running up the new flag the nation puts on a new mask. . . .

*Le Dernier des cargonautes*, the least substantial of Bemba's novels, relates to the mask theme in emphasizing changing identities in development of character. It combines the apparent simplicity of a Gidean récit with elements of medieval hagiography. It somewhat resembles [Albert] Camus's *Etranger* in focusing on the vicissitudes of the life of an exceptional Every man who is also something of a Christ figure; he resembles both [Patrice] Lumumba and [Albert] Schweitzer to some degree and is named "Emmanuel." . . .

Bemba's most recent novel, *Léopolis*, represents something of a new departure and demonstrates a new mastery. The fact that it was published in an inexpensive paperback edition indicates that the publisher believed it might attract a larger audience. This seems paradoxical, since the aspects that characterize the new "popular" literature in Africa have always been present in Bemba's work; but in this novel Bemba combines them with irony and some of the Brechtian distancing elements to create a work to be read on many levels. One may read it as a combination adventure tale, detective story, love story, and historical romance, or see it as a gentle mocking of the quest for the epic.

Hal Wylie. *World Literature Today*. 64, 1 (Winter 1990), pp. 20–23

BIBLIOGRAPHY

*Hell Is Orpheus* (*L'Enfer, c'est Orféo*, 1970); *The Man Who Killed the Crocodile* (*L'Homme qui tua le crocodile*, 1972); *Dormant Water* (*Une Eau dormante*, 1975); *Traffic Jam* (*Embouteillage*, 1975); *Tarentelle Noire et Diable Blanc*, 1976; *Portable Dreams* (*Rêves portatifs*, 1979); *A Screwed-Up World for a Too Honest Laundryman* (*Un Foutu Monde pour un blanchisseur trop honnête*, 1979); *The Sun Has Left for M'Pemba* (*Le Soleil est parti à M'Pemba*, 1982); *The Last of the Cargonauts* (*Le Dernier des cargonautes*, 1984); *Leopolis* (*Léopolis*, 1984); *The Strange Crime of Mr. Pancrace Amadeus* (*L'Étrange Crime de Monsieur Pancrace Amadeus*, 1986)

# BENNETT, Louise (1919–)
## Jamaica

Any discussion of Caribbean popular culture must notice the work of the Jamaican, Louise Bennett. Her unique gift is that she is both a folklore scholar and a brilliant popular entertainer, and while the qualities of Caribbean popular culture are evanescent before the recording of the conventional researcher, Bennett is able to physically recreate her findings in performances that reveal the idiom, the gestures, the stress and the flow of the personalities and private dramas of the people. Her use of dialect can be amusing, but is not necessarily so. In ''Bans O' Killing'' she places herself . . . in the tradition of poets who have used dialect for serious purposes, as the straightest route to the inner life of the ordinary people. Bennett would not claim either the depth of feeling or the lyrical impulse of the greatest dialect poets, and in a volume the length of her first major book of collected poems, *Jamaica Labrish*, there was inevitably some weak material. On the other hand her claim that dialect be taken seriously is not only valid, it is borne out by many of her own successful pieces. Through dialects she catches conversational tones that illuminate both individual and national character. . . .

Most of Bennett's verse is in a loose ballad form that focuses, without restricting, the rapidly shifting moods and attitudes of the character she assumes. . . .

Because Bennett uses essentially the natural speech idiom of the people, and because she is guarded from pretension by self-critical folk wit, she can . . . cover a range of subjects unrivalled by more conventional poets, without striking a false note. Further, her verse is a valuable aid to the social historian. Her selection of themes reflects the concerns of Jamaican life; the public ones—federation, street peddlers, bodybuilding contests, Paul Robeson's visit to Jamaica, emigration or an infuriating telephone system; and the private—the yard gossip or the death of a pet turkey watched by a hungry neighbor. More important, she approaches her theme by way of the attitude an ordinary person feels towards it, and it is this that makes an historical event meaningful. This is particularly important in the West Indies, where the private attitudes behind public events are so complex, a tension between national pride and self-satire, between knowledge, ignorance, and common sense.

Louis James. Introduction. *The Islands in Between: Essays on West Indian Literature* (London: Oxford University Press, 1968), pp. 15–17

I do not believe that Louise Bennett is a considerable poet. But a poet, and, in her best work, a better poet than most other Jamaican writers she certainly is. She does not offer her readers any great insight into the nature of life or human experience, but she recreates human experience vividly, delightfully, and intelligently. She is rarely pretentious—the most common fault in West Indian poetry; she is not derived from other poets—she has her own interesting voice; and she is invariably sane. . . .

I think her most central difficulty is choice of subject. Many of her poems are a sort of comic-verse journalism; she is quick to tackle the topical, which is only natural, as she published her early and some of her later poems in newspapers. One willingly says goodbye to numerous poems about new governors, new pantomimes, Paul Robeson's visit, a test match victory, and so on, where interest

has not survived the topicality of the subject. As in the same period of her topical poems she wrote others of more lasting interest, we can hardly complain: we can only regret that so much of the journalism has been published in book form. It would be a service to her readers if Bennett would present a *Collected Poems*, dropping all the ephemera and choosing the best of the others. . . .

Louise Bennett, then, is a poet of serious merit, although like all poets, she has her limitations. Like most poets she is . . . developing. And she is so much more rewarding a poet than many to whom we in Jamaica give the name, that it seems reasonable to expect more of those who claim an interest in poetry to give her more attention. She is sane; throughout, her poems imply that sound common sense and generous love and understanding of people are worthwhile assets. Jamaican dialect is, of course, limiting (in more senses than one); but within its limitations Louise Bennett works well. Hers is a precious talent.

Mervyn Morris. In Edward Baugh, ed. *Critics on Caribbean Literature: Readings in Literary Criticism* (New York: St. Martin's Press, 1978), pp. 137–38, 143, 147–48

In the case of Louise Bennett [the] performer's role has its source in her relatively early involvement in the theater. Hence during the late 1940s she studied at the Royal Academy of Dramatic Art, then worked with several repertory companies in England before returning to teach drama in Jamaica. As both performer and composer she is comparable with the calypsonian in that she relies less on the explicit statement about the ironic deception of the grinning mask, and more on the suggestive contrast between diction and rhythm, on the one hand, and on the other hand, the implications of her themes. But when she does offer explicit statement it does shed very useful light on the ironic import of those rhetorical devices which she and other artists in the oral tradition exploit.

Her most important, and comprehensive, collection of poems, *Jamaica Labrish*, offers several examples of such explicit statements. In ''War-Time Grocery,'' composed during World War II, the scarcity of food gives rise to the warning that ''happy'' talk and laughter among frustrated shoppers are definitely deceptive. And in ''My Dream'' the political unrest of those hard times and the resulting pressures for independence feed a discontent which is barely disguised: ''Dog a-sweat but long hair hide i' / Mout a laugh, but heart aleap!'' The witty, trenchant proverbs drawn from the colloquial language of the folk both explain and exemplify the idea of a mask. The proverb in ''My Dream'' is comparable in this regard with the very similar technique of ''Dutty Tough'' where wartime hardships persist, despite appearances to the contrary, like the dry toughness of rockhard dirt in drought: ''River flood but water scarce yaw, / Rain a-fall but dutty tuff!'' And in proverbs like these Louise Bennett . . . discovers the precise, built-in antitheses through which the folk verbalize their sense of conflict and social contradictions, and which the poet adopts as a ready-made mode of ironic statement.

But in developing the ironic implications of the performer's grinning mask Bennett goes beyond explicit statements of this kind. She also relies on the evocative contrast between her subject matter and her *manner* of statement. In ''Dutty Tough'' the elaboration on hard times lends itself to a raucous liveliness, even to farcical embellishment. . . . Altogether then, the playful raucousness of a Bennett poem is based on the same tactic which informs the calypsonian's irony—the traditional function of laughter and play as disguise and resistance in the language of the folk.

Lloyd W. Brown. *West Indian Poetry* (Boston: Twayne, 1978), pp. 106–7

The poems in Bennett's collection *Jamaica Labrish*, spanning approximately twenty-five years, cover a broad spectrum of dramatic personalities and events. The poems are classified in four groups: "City Life," "War-Time," "Politics," and "Jamaica—Now an' Then." Some of the subject matter is so topical that not all historical details are easily accessible to the contemporary reader. But the majority of poems constitute a kind of comedy of manners in which those recurring rascals of Caribbean societies—social climbers, petty crooks, displaced colonials, to name a few—come decidedly to grief.

One kind of social climber whom Bennett satirizes ruthlessly—for obvious reasons—is the character who feels impelled to deny any connections with the Creole culture. Several poems in the collection poke fun at this character type with varying degrees of gentleness. "Dry Foot Bwoy" satirizes a Jamaican of peasant stock who has travelled to England, perhaps to study, and has returned with an English accent and a bad case of linguistic amnesia. He can no longer converse with his former acquaintances, much to their annoyance, for he disclaims knowledge of Jamaican Creole. . . .

Similarly the poem "Noh Lickle Twang!" makes fun of a woman who is embarrassed because her son, newly returned from the United States after six months abroad, doesn't have even the slightest trace of an American accent. He cannot, therefore, be shown off to the discriminating neighbors, who, once he opens his mouth will think that he's surely been to Mocho—the archetypal Jamaican village that epitomizes social gaucheness. The depth of the young man's failure must be measured against his sister's success in acquiring the semblance of an American accent after having had only one week's exposure to American expatriates. The fact that her parents cannot understand her is the proof of her sophistication. So the poor mother bemoans her unhappy lot.

The tone of Bennett's satirical poems is not always as light as the poems cited above would suggest. In some poems in which Bennett confronts the demeaning poverty of the Jamaican worker—more often, nonworker—the comic vision seems inadequate to express the sustained pathos of intense poverty. The pain of deprivation cannot always be sublimated in laughter. The pair of poems . . . "Me Bredda" and "My Dream," demonstrate the differences of tone that Bennett can employ in examining the same subject matter. In both poems the persona is that of a female domestic servant, who, in Jamaica, has been a ubiquitous symbol of middle-class exploitation of cheap peasant labor. But whereas "Me Bredda," in true comic spirit, vigorously affirms the supremacy of Good over Evil, "My Dream" articulates the burgeoning political engagement over the oppressed in colonial Jamaica. . . .

The strength of Bennett's poetry . . . is the accuracy with which it depicts and attempts to correct through laughter the absurdities of Jamaican society. Its comic vision affirms a norm of common sense and good-natured decorum. The limitations of the poetry are partially the inevitable consequences of having used Jamaican Creole as a poetic medium. For what the experiments in Creole—whether St. Lucian, Trinidadian, or Barbadian, for example—have

indicated is that there are subtle nuances of thought and feeling that are at times best expressed in Creole, at times in English. The poet who relies exclusively on either medium reduces the expressive range of his/her art.

Louise Bennett, having chosen to write exclusively in Jamaican Creole, cannot easily answer the charge of parochialism and insularity. But what she loses in universality she gains in vivid particularity.

Carolyn Cooper. *World Literature Written in English.* 17, 1 (April 1978), pp. 322–25

Characteristically, the Louise Bennett poem is a comment in Creole on "the now" of Jamaican lives, often on something topical. It offers insight into, and corroborative evidence of, people's responses to particular events. To make sense of the poem, we sometimes need to know of the occasion that provoked it; and the topicality was often an important factor in the initial impact. Lloyd Brown makes the important point, however, that many of the poems survive their original contexts because "by virtue of their style their focus is less on the specific topics of the 1940s (food shortages, high prices, the war itself) and more on the continuing modes of perception they dramatize."

The modes of perception being dramatized are often themselves subjected to critical irony. The form most often employed by Louise Bennett is the dramatic monologue; and what Philip Drew wrote of [Robert] Browning's also applies to Louise Bennett's: "In poem after poem the vital point to observe is . . . that the speaker understands himself and his own situation less thoroughly than the reader, who nevertheless derived all his understanding from the poem." Poems by Louise Bennett often provoke in us that "combination of sympathy and judgment" which Robert Langbaum has identified as a common response to the dramatic monologue. . . .

Whether in print or in performance, many of the poems are remarkable as social commentary and as works of art. They deal with a variety of topics, including problems of colonial education, the vagaries of politics, economic hardship, bureaucratic humbug, strategies of survival. The poems in general promote acceptance of Jamaican culture; they draw on the customs, beliefs, language of ordinary Jamaicans, the living tissue of Jamaican life. They are critical of gossip. They expose people ashamed of being Jamaican or ashamed of being black. They ridicule class and color prejudice, but are more concerned to tackle black self-contempt or to express pride in being black. They undermine pretension of various kinds.

Mervyn Morris. In Daryl Cumber Dance, ed. *Fifty Caribbean Writers* (Westport, Connecticut.: Greenwood Press, 1986), pp. 37–38, 41

The work of Louise Bennett of Jamaica was . . . important in establishing a unique Caribbean literature and a distinctive woman's voice within it. The language and speech of Caribbean women had always played an important part in contesting slave and colonial domination and so was an important tool in the struggle for liberation. As a consequence, the articulation of the Jamaican experience in the exceptionally flexible and pliable medium of the dialect offered enormous possibilities for its use as a literary language. Because "all linguistic communities evolve systems of power relationships enforced by and repeated in language," it was not inconsistent that a great amount of interest was displayed in the literary possibilities of the dialect during the 1940s, when discontent with colonial rule in Jamaica reached new heights. Bennett's work challenged the privileged status accorded to the poetic tradition of white discourse in Caribbean letters, empowering the voices and expressions of the masses of Caribbean people. Bennett used the power of Jamaican speech to explore the complexity of the Jamaican experience and, in so doing, forced the members of the upper and middle classes to face their own linguistic and class biases. Her use of oral and scribal forms, as she forced the language to accommodate itself to express the poetic sentiments of the people, was an important breakthrough in Caribbean literature.

> Selwyn R. Cudjoe. Introduction. *Caribbean Women Writers* (Wellesley, Massachusetts.: Calaloux, 1990), pp. 25–26

Though Bennett maintains the old view of the working-class woman as more than a match for her oppressors at the level of language, her poems tend to show women using men as surrogates for their aggression and, at a first glance, she seems to follow the bias of Jamaican men in her presentation of women as apolitical. In ''Uriah Preach'' for example, Bennett recounts the vicarious pleasure taken by a Jamaican woman in the accomplishments of her children and especially in her son's ability to use his occasional ascent to the pulpit to lambast the family's enemies. . . . In ''Me Bredda,'' an irate woman who has failed to get a job as a domestic servant forces her would-be employer to placate her with two weeks' wages by threatening to call in her imaginary brother to settle the matter physically. . . . Here again the woman shifts the responsibility for physical confrontation to a male figure, implying that the woman herself no longer considers the threat of her own action sufficient to terrify the housewife she abuses.

Though Bennett often works through apolitical female figures who are more likely to react to the cut of a politician's clothes than what he says, she often expresses a womanist perspective on topical issues and her poems take note of social reforms intended to improve the position of women. In ''Bans O' Ooman!,'' for example, she celebrates the founding of the Jamaican Federation of Women in the 1940s aimed at bringing together women of all classes, describing the clothes and social status of the women who flock to support it as ''high and low, miggle suspended.'' Poems like ''Solja Work'' show the consequences of a local military presence for Jamaican women.

Bennett is one of the first creative writers to register the increase of female oppression which was one of the consequences of the male assertion of racial and political power during the nationalist movement of the 1940s and 1950s. Her poem ''Pinnacle'' satirizes the new chauvinism of men towards women as it manifested itself within the Rastafarian movement, which in other respects has had such a profound and in many ways beneficial effect on Jamaican attitudes to language, race, and spiritual values. Written after the brutal destruction of one of the first Rastafarian communities by the Jamaican government, the poem delights in the humiliation of one of the male members of the sect who had formerly used his Rastafarian convictions to terrorize his woman. . . . Bennett's satirical resources however are limited to what she can authentically express through the resonances of a specific social reality and way of speech, so that in her dramatic monologues she can only be

as positive about women as she thinks the character through whom she speaks is in real life. . . . This presentation of the female point of view elucidates Bennett's own method in her early poems, by which she is able to assert a sense of female strength under the guise of using male surrogates and seeming to acquiesce in ideas about female weakness. The fact that she feels constrained to work through such masks, however, gives an indication of the extent to which the attitude to women in Jamaican society had become that expressed in the song she quotes in her poem on Jamaican women: ''Oman a heaby load!''

> Rhonda Cobham. In Carole Boyce Davies and Elaine Savory Fido, eds. *Out of the Kumbla: Caribbean Women and Literature* (Trenton, New Jersey: Africa World Press, 1990), pp. 217–19

One of the most significant precedents for Caribbean women poets has been Louise Bennett, 'Miss Lou'. Born in Jamaica in 1919, Louise Bennett has achieved charismatic status for her work as a folklorist and performer. She has had a number of books published from the 1940s onwards, and her *Selected Poems* was published in 1982. But the best way to appreciate the extraordinary effervescence which she brings to her work is to hear her in performance, as in the 1983 live recording of her at the Lyric theater, *Yes M'Dear*. Her work derives much of its inspiration and material from the oral tradition in Jamaican culture, both in terms of content (stories, proverbs, street chants, children's games) and language (voices, intonations, idioms). The two are inevitably indistinguishable: it is the oral quality of Jamaican language in its tones, gestures and expressiveness which embodies the experience, attitudes and outlooks of the voices Louise Bennett creates and records. Many of her poems are dramatic monologues addressed by a character, sometimes through letter form, and not surprisingly many of these voices are women's. Anecdotal, immediate, full of humour and ironies, Miss Lou's poems 'generally comment on matters in hand, social and domestic. Their pronouncements are often self-ironising by virtue of the strategy of adopting a dramatic persona as the vehicle of the poem. Many of them are celebratory, so it is not unexpected to find her producing a poem like ''Jamaica Oman'':

> Neck an neck an foot an foot wid man
> She buckle hole her own;
> While man a call her 'so-so rib'
> Oman a ton backbone!
> An long before Oman Lib bruck out
> Over foreign lan
> Jamaica female wasa work
> Her liberated plan!

Louise Bennett's legacy has been widespread. The performance poet Mikey Smith acknowledged her as 'the mother' of 'dub' poetry, the performance form related to reggae. For women poets, her example has been vital. Later women performance poets have often added a more emphatic political dimension to their work, either covert or explicit, and this distinguishes them from Louise Bennett's more modulated satire. But they have carried on her pioneering use of 'nation language', Edward Kamau Brathwaite's coinage to replace the pejorative connotations of 'dialect' or 'creole'. And as part of this 'people speech', they have followed her emphasis upon oral delivery as essential to the experience of their work, a collective sharing which is quite distinctive in their view of cultural activity.

> Bruce Woodcock. In Gina Wisker, ed. *Black Women's Writing* (New York: St. Martin's Press, 1993)

More than any other single writer, Louise Bennett brought local language into the foreground of West Indian cultural life. From the 1940s, when she began contributing to the annual pantomime in Jamaica, Bennett's storytelling had a substantial influence on the literary credibility of dialect. But it was not an unqualified credibility. From the beginning, Bennett was aware that language is not a simple matter and that the unfamiliar has its own appeal—especially when linked with an assumed superiority. And she dealt with the equivocation of these attitudes with relentless irony. One of her poems tells of the dismay of a mother whose son has come back from the United States with no change in his speech, no heightening of his language. . . . The appeal of artifice, of strangeness—the superiority that distance or difference (in the right direction) generates—are satirized here even as the poem itself relies on this appeal, for its own cleverness is implicated in the satire. . . .

The acceptance of dialect in poetry, as in other forms of communication, was partly a matter of fashion. The popularity of Louise Bennett, whose work was on radio and in the newspapers as well as on stage and in books, helped create the fashion, and provided encouragement to other poets and storytellers.

> J. Edward Chamberlin. *Come Back to Me My Language: Poetry and the West Indies* (Urbana: University of Illinois Press, 1993), pp. 95–97

BIBLIOGRAPHY
*Dialect Verses*, 1940; *Jamaican Humour in Dialect*, 1943; *Lulu Sey: Dialect Verse*, 1943; *Miss Lulu Sez: A Collection of Dialect Poems*, 1948; *Folk Stories and Verses*, 1952; *Laugh with Louise: A Pot–pourri of Jamaican Folklore, Stories, Songs, Verses*, 1961; *Jamaica Labrish*, 1966; *Anancy and Miss Lou*, 1979; *Selected Poems*, 1982; *Aunty Roachy Seh*, 1993

# BETI, Mongo (1932– )
## Cameroon

In his novel [*The Poor Christ of Bomba*] Mongo Beti's central focus is the problem of the Christianization of the blacks. Father Drumont, a rough, determined missionary, thinks that after twenty years of work he has succeeded in driving Christ's message into Negro skulls. He is particularly proud of his *sixa*, which, as the author explains in a note, is a ''house that as a rule shelters young girls engaged to be married. Any native woman who wants to get married according to orthodox law has to stay in the *sixa* from two to four months.'' But one tour through the Catholic villages is all Father Drumont needs to measure his failure. The teachings he had bestowed upon the Negroes according to seemingly infallible methods turn out to have been useless. Baptism was only a means, thought the Africans, of taking over the power of the whites and

avoiding colonialist extortions. The girls in the *sixa*, who were supposed to be governed by a strict premarital control, were in fact taking great liberties with Christian morality. Indeed, the whole edifice that had been patiently constructed by the missionary crumbles within a few days. He leaves Africa, discouraged and gnawed at by doubt.

Through this personal failure, the failure of colonization itself becomes apparent. This priest, who thinks he knows the Africans and wants at all cost to impose upon them a behavior that conflicts with their habits and their conception of the world, is the administrator who, starting from prejudices set up as principles for action, persists in forcing the colonized people to enter a preestablished framework. He is the ethnologist who, after an ''educational'' trip to Africa, comes back with scholarly notes that would make an African villager laugh if he knew how to read French.

Like Ferdinand Oyono, Beti employs a humorous tone, and his racy conversations preclude any boredom. Perhaps this book, which is too full of facts for my taste, would have been improved by being more compressed and less loaded down with details. Nevertheless, Beti has given us incontestable proof of his talent as a novelist, and we can confidently await his next novel.

> David Diop. *Presence Africaine*. December 1956, pp. 126–27

At the age of twenty-two, while still a student at Aix, Mongo Beti offered his first novel to *Présence africaine*. After publishing a key chapter in the review, they decided to issue the whole book, though Beti himself already had doubts about it. *Cruel Town* was duly published by Éditions Africaines in 1954, under the name of Eza Boto. The author has since indicated his opinion of the novel by jettisoning this *nom de plume* and taking that of Mongo Beti for all his subsequent books.

*Cruel Town* is a bad novel; but it is manifestly not the work of a bad writer. Rather is it the trying out of a young talent, as yet loose and uncontrolled, but open and rich. If the book is sentimental, its very naïveté is often disarming; if its action is melodramatic, it bears everywhere the marks of feeling and experience.

The book begins rather well. The first chapter, in which the young hero Banda casually throws off his mistress and declares his intention of marrying a girl more acceptable to his dying mother, does not fully prepare us for the orgies of filial sentiment which are to follow. The next chapter, devoted to the cruel town itself, is certainly the best thing in the book. This, one of the few pieces of extended impersonal description in the novel, is beautifully built up and displays a gift of compassionate irony which is seldom apparent in the later pages. . . .

If [the] brilliance of observation [in this chapter] were maintained, *Cruel Town* would be a novel indeed. However, we are soon plunged into the raw and often tiresome emotions of young Banda, who now arrives in the town to sell his seasonal crop of cocoa. . . . All through [a] string of improbabilities runs the interior monologue of Banda. Often the naïve exclamations, repetitions and self-questionings of the hero are happily natural and unforced, but gradually they become tedious and, finally, infuriating. We have had enough of Banda. . . .

Strangely enough, it was precisely by the more controlled and skilful use of this exclamatory, naïve monologue that Mongo Beti developed some of the most effective passages in his second novel, *The Poor Christ of Bomba*. With this book, published only two years after *Cruel Town*, the writer emerged as a formidable satirist and one of the most percipient critics of European colonialism.

Gerald Moore. *Seven African Writers* (London: Oxford University Press, 1962), pp. 74–77

Compassion is the twin brother of Mongo Beti's grand iconoclasm (or perhaps what we are looking for is a word that combines the two). *Mission Accomplished*, bawdy, riotous, bursting on every page with sheer animal vitality, reads like that rare piece of studied artistry, an unpremeditated novel. In the literary effort to establish the African as, first before all else, a human being, Mongo Beti with this novel has leaped to the fore as the archpriest of the African's humanity. Mongo Beti takes the back cloth as he finds it, asserting simply that tradition is upheld not by one-dimensional innocents, but by cunning old codgers on chieftaincy stools, polygamous elders, watching hawklike the approach of young blood around their harem, by the eternal troublemaking females who plunge innocents, unaware, into memorable odysseys. Hospitality is not, as we are constantly romantically informed that it is, nearly so spontaneous. There is a mercenary edge, and this, alas, is not always traceable to that alien corrupt civilization!. . .

He has translated the slight alienation of his hero into village terms, with no condescension, no stances; the magnificent candor of the hero, Jean-Marie Medza, stranger to Kala, creates a vigorous clarity in characters, a precision of edges that Chinua Achebe, with no such uninhibited agent to hand, achieved in neither of his [first two] books. Sex is restored to its natural proportions, not a starting discovery made by the European every publishing day, nor a neo-Africanist venture sung by the apostles of Negritude and sanctified in shrines to puberty. Beti makes sex an unquestioned attitude; the result is that he demonstrates a truly idyllic love dignified by humor, by pathos, and crucial to the novel as a major factor in the development of a young, sensitive personality.

Wole Soyinka. *American Scholar.* Summer 1963, pp. 394–96

*Mission Accomplished* was published in Paris in 1957. It is the first novel by Mongo Beti to have been translated into English. . . . Because of a need to mystify the reader, which is characteristic of Beti's way of thinking, he took a title from detective and spy novels, a title pompous in its brevity, in order to point up everything grotesque about the celebrated ''mission,'' while describing it in a falsely smooth-spoken tone.

What is the book really about? A wife who fled (with her lover) in an attempt to free herself from her husband's rule must be brought back to her legal husband. Jean-Marie Medza, a high school student who has just failed the second part of his *baccalauréat* examination, is entrusted with this delicate mission, because he is a distant cousin of the husband. . . .

In this bush symphony, Jean-Marie Medza plays the solo part of the ''naïve'' boy, surrounded by a chorus of happy villagers. From beginning to end, Jean-Marie is the comic butt of the farce while acting as an accomplice. He accepts this adventure in Kala because he enjoys playing a country knight, but the ridiculous aspects of the situation at no time escape him. He enjoys telling us about them and stirring up a continuous flow of unrepressed laughter. He is not as foolish as he tries to appear, and the unexpected nature of the farce

delights him all the more since it protects him for a while from his father's anger. . . .

[Beti's] ''rebel's voice'' (as Gerald Moore called it) is fond of obscenity, which he claims is persuasive, and indecency, true or false. One can admire or criticize him for these penchants. At any rate, he can always take shelter behind his characters, who never attended any Academy, Parisian or Bantu.

Roger Mercier and M. and S. Battestini. *Mongo Beti* (Paris: Fernand Nathan, 1964), pp. 35–37

Beti is an experimenter, creating various situations and examining their evolution and the results. All the various side issues have equally to be analysed and occasionally—as with Kris in *The King Miraculously Healed*—a foreign element is added to give a little more spice to the brew. His novels are much more rambling than Oyono's. Many more aspects of colonial life among Africans are dealt with and the novels' effect, from the point of view of social criticism, is less direct, less forceful than those of Oyono. On the other hand, Beti's Europeans are not only the colonial ''type'' but also, and more especially, the kind who want to do good for the Africans but, unfortunately for them, start from the premise that all Africans are unable to organize their lives unless helped by Europeans. His favourite butts are, for this reason, missionaries and dedicated colonial administrators. . . . He shows how superficial Catholic influence is and how, if tribal customs and Catholicism exert conflicting pressures on the Africans in the backwoods, the former is the stronger. . . .

The characters of this novel have in fact much more importance in the novel and greater independence of action than those in [*The Poor Christ of Bomba* and *Mission Accomplished*]. Here, instead of being presented through the descriptions of a narrator, they are developed through their own words and acts, without a third person to interpret them. They are important because it is the interaction of their desires and interests which forms the basis of the comedy and satire of the novel. Because their motivations are an important factor in the novel Beti makes these characters much more definite as individuals. Their own personal interests are shown influencing every gesture and, in one case at least, the result is tragically grotesque rather than farcical. . . .

This novel is the last published by Beti. Like his others and those of Oyono it is, behind the humour, totally negative. The satirical attack on colonial Africa is totally destructive. This novel, with its emphasis on self-interest is, in this respect, Beti's most pessimistic.

A. C. Brench. *The Novelists' Inheritance in French Africa* (London: Oxford University Press, 1967), pp. 64, 68, 73–74

After *The King Miraculously Healed* Mongo Beti turned from literature to politics as Cameroon prepared for its independence. He returned from France to Cameroon in 1959, shortly before independence, as a sympathizer if not a partisan of the radical Union des Populations du Cameroun. He briefly landed in jail as a political suspect and after his release made his way back to France where he wrote a lively report on his experiences entitled ''Tumultuous Cameroon.'' In this satirical attack on the cooperation between the French colonial authorities and the future government of Cameroon he places his faith in the youth of Africa, without the doubts he had expressed in his novels, and confidently claims the leadership role for the young educated Africans. . . . But this revolution of youth has not yet materialized in Cameroon, the government he attacked so scathingly is still in power, and Mongo Beti has since 1959 lived in exile in France where he no longer writes but teaches French literature.

Mongo Beti's fiction is a record of failure, the failure to discern either the "intellectual direction" of the new Africa or the type of leader who can initiate the African into the mysteries of the modern world. But it is a successful record of failure. The author's ability to assume a multiplicity of frequently contradictory points of view, his capacity to bring out the humor in the contradictions and incongruities of modern Africa, as well as his realistic appraisal of African village society, indicate a critical detachment, an intellectual stance, which are rare in contemporary African literature. Mongo Beti has characterized himself as a "free traveler" whose writings are a running commentary on his native Cameroon. It is a pity that exile put such an early end to his journey.

Thomas Cassirer. *L'espirit createur.* Fall 1970, pp. 232–33

A careful reading of Mongo Beti's works reveals the writer's constant concern, his systematic desire, to dissociate himself from his fictional universe, to keep his distance from the characters and events that have sprung from his imagination. . . . Even when what happens in his novels is confirmed and strongly corroborated by real life, his subject is always the life of others and never his own. His own ideas are expressed only indirectly, only if another takes the responsibility for them and thus guarantees his safety.

This desire for camouflage and obvious distancing is immediately noticeable in his way of signing his works and taking legal responsibility for them. Alexandre Biyidi [his real name] never appears as such under his writings, except for his short story "Without Hate, Without Love" in which, by claiming to be disinterested, he offends nobody or irritates everybody, which actually amounts to the same thing. His rather personal diatribe against Laye Camara is signed "A. B.," and the initials are not immediately identifiable as his. His novels are always signed with a pseudonym. And for his explosive article "African Unity," he takes refuge behind the editorial board of the *Revue camerounaise.* This need of distancing does not mean only that Mongo Beti seeks to protect himself in public, to escape possible prosecution; it also reflects the very character of an ideologically repressive postcolonial police state, with its omnipresent censorship and its treacherous attacks on protesters who are isolated but too brazenly visible. And who could be more isolated and more visible in such circumstances than a distinctive artist?

Thomas Melone. *Mongo Béti: L'homme et le destin* (Paris: Présence Africaine, 1971), pp. 252–53

It has been rumored that Mongo Beti's *Plunder of Cameroun,* a searing criticism of government and politics in Cameroon published by F. Maspéro in Paris not long ago, has been banned in his country which in turn has succeeded in getting France to ban it also. And, so far, this writer has not been able to obtain a copy of the book in the United States. Nevertheless his most recent novel *Perpétue and the Habit of Unhappiness* is nonetheless a dramatic indictment of the ill-fated independence in his native land dominated by corrupt dictatorial power, as well as a forceful denunciation of the disgraceful status of African women in such regimes. With this novel Mongo Beti proves once again that he is one of the best of the contemporary Black African novelists, who seek to promote true liberty in Africa and to insure a lasting dignity for her.

With *Perpétue and the Habit of Unhappiness* the author's outstanding literary talent is again confirmed. The picturesque art of the story-teller is still there. Because of the seriousness of purpose and manner which the themes of politics and status of women demand of the author, one does not find an abundance of Mongo Beti's usual humor here and laughter does not dominate completely the various situations presented. Except for the doomed but sincere affection exchanged between Perpétue and Zeyang, tender love has no chance of survival in this novel. True friendship and camaraderie, as portrayed in the relationship between Perpétue and Anna-Marie her trusted and faithful companion, occupy great space in the book. The jealousy and treachery which Édouard unbridles against Perpétue never seem to be justified, but serve the author's purpose in dramatizing the status of African women.

Robert P. Smith, Jr. *CLA Journal.* March 1976, pp. 310–11

At the age of twenty-two, while still a student at [Aix-en-Provence], Mongo Beti [born Alexandre Biyidi-Awala] offered his first novel to *Présence Africaine.* After publishing a key chapter in the review, they decided to issue the whole book, though Beti himself already had doubts about it. *Ville cruelle* was duly published by Éditions Africaines in 1954, under the pen name of Eza Boto. The author has since indicated his opinion of the novel by jettisoning this nom de plume and taking that of Mongo Beti for all his subsequent books. . . .

*Ville cruelle . . .* combines a novelettish plot with a brilliance of observation and a quality of pain which we associate with a major novel. Strangely enough, it was precisely by the more controlled and skillful use of exclamatory, naïve monologue that Mongo Beti developed some of the most effective passages in his second novel, *Le Pauvre Christ de Bomba.* With this book, published only two years after *Ville cruelle,* the writer emerged as a formidable satirist and one of the most percipient critics of European colonialism. For now the naïvety of his hero, instead of being presented subjectively, becomes the pure mirror through which we see the greed, the folly and the tragic misunderstandings of a whole epoch in Africa's history. Used in this more distanced way, the monologue becomes a weapon of devastating satiric force.

*Le Pauvre Christ de Bomba* is written entirely in the form of a diary, the diary of an acolyte who accompanies his master, the Reverend Father Superior Drumont, on a missionary circuit through the land of Tala. Tala is a remote district of Cameroon which has been deliberately abandoned by Drumont for three whole years because of its "backsliding." He is now revisiting all the stations in the hope of finding the thirsty souls crying out for solace. In fact, of course, he finds nothing of the kind. The men of Tala have forgotten God and turned to bicycles. Even the women have fallen short on their cult payments. The churches are broken and empty, but the bars are full and the new money from cocoa is beginning to flow through the land, for we are now in the late 1930s. Drumont is an austere man of obstinate courage, choleric and impatient, moving with all the authority and confidence of twenty years' missionary work in Africa. But even his faith wavers before the spectacle of Tala. As the circuit progresses he questions himself and his purposes more and more deeply. For the first time he enters into dispute with his parishioners and listens to their arguments, instead of quelling them with his own energy and authority. Meanwhile the young administrator Vidal, who is also touring Tala, continually appeals to him as an ally. Is he not a fellow white and a Frenchman? Vidal assures him that all will soon be well, for a road is to be built through Tala by forced labor: The sufferings of the road gangs will soon fill the churches to bursting, as they have already done in those areas which lie along the main routes, under the heavy hand of the administration. The whole system of forced labor is a true friend of the Catholic Church, for is not contentment the great enemy of religion?

Gerald Moore. *Twelve African Writers* (Bloomington: Indiana University Press, 1980), pp. 194, 197–98

After a long period of silence, Mongo Beti published three novels within a short time. Seen together they convey the sense of an epic sweep materialized by their extension in time and space. The first novel, *Remember Ruben*, starts with a problem of genesis. Mor-Zamba, the hero of the novel, is a foundling. His quest for identity through the history of the Cameroonian people is partially fulfilled when, at the end of the novel, he learns from his friend Abena, that he is the son of the brutally deposed but long-lamented chief of Ekoundoum. He then decides to return to Ekoundoum to begin the work of transformation which the community yearns for. *Remember Ruben* covers forty years of the history of Cameroon, through World War II to independence in 1960.

*Perpétue [et l'habitude du malheur]*, the second novel, continues the story to the 1970s. The novel takes the form of an investigation into the causes of Perpétue's death. The investigation is conducted by her brother, Essola. Essola is a former militant of the Union des Populations du Cameroon a political party headed by the nationalist leader Ruben Um Nyobe, whose name provides the title for two of Beti's novels. After having served a long jail term in the prisons of the dictator Baba Tura, Essola is released on condition that he join the dictator's party.

Although [*La Ruine presque cocasse d'un polichinelle*] is a sequel of [*Remember Ruben*], it does not dwell in the semilegendary time of Mor-Zamba's childhood. It focuses on the first years of independence and shows an independent Cameroon caught in a total state of anarchy and violence. By responding to the popular call from Ekoundoum, Mor-Zamba acquires the ultimate characteristic of the epic hero. By liberating the people of Ekoundoum from a despotic chief he regains his full identity and returns to the community.

One of the pillars that sustain epic action is the reliance on myth as the leading light in the grand time swing proper to the epic narrative; *Remember Ruben* is an epic narrative both by the life it depicts and the style in which it does this. Time, as we shall see, is limitless, inexhaustible, and dense. The plot freely multiplies itself into a multitude of subplots born out of each other and resulting in an illusion of endlessness, through a psychological intensity that derives from the intensity of the life portrayed. Epic action develops into epic time; the action often plunges into the remote past, the apprehension of which is sometimes made possible through a name, a character who is both remote and close, and whose unmediated presence seems totally overwhelming. That character

whose existence finds a place in countless stories illustrating every moment in the life of the community is the link that bridges the gulf between history and the unfathomable time of origins.

While setting up the framework of the epic story the narrator of *Remember Ruben* appeals to Akomo, the ancestral creator of the Essazam nation: this he does in order to conjure up the most fundamental pillar of the community and bring forth a time span of unlimited extent. A careful reading will show that all the elements proper to the epic form the foundations of this narrative. These elements include a mystic reference, the characterization proper to the epic hero, and divine presence often expressed in prophetic terms throughout the narrative. It will also appear to the reader that all these three major elements which set the tone for epic action are structurally interrelated in the dynamic progression of the novel.

Kandioura Dramé. *Ufahumu*. 12, 2 (1983), pp. 45–46

Unlike Beti's other recent exile writing, *Les Deux Mères [de Guillaume Ismaël Dzewatama]* resembles the typical novel being written and published inside Africa today, studying marriage patterns and the evolving roles of women. Guillaume Ismaël has two mothers because his father, finding himself in a confused situation, tries to reconcile the two halves of his split personality by adding his French mistress as wife number two to his extended African family. Instead of bridging the gap, this aggravates all the problems. Seeing the tensions from the point of view of the African boy and his good-hearted, idealistic but naive white mother throws into relief the melodrama and pathos of modern Africa and all its ironies. The reader wonders who has the most colonized mentality in this swirl of alienations juxtaposing races, generations, classes, sexes, and roles.

Beti seems to be placing himself in the new ''popular'' literature in Africa. The psychological penetration and the realism seemingly derived from the autobiographical elements, however, plus the artistic use of ambiguity here, lend depth to the new genre. This is a curious love story, full of drama, harmonizing the political and literary in Beti.

Hal Wylie. *World Literature Today*. 58, 1 (Winter 1984), pp. 151–52

The early works of Mongo Beti with their biting satire and unrelenting criticism of the colonial situation in Africa, demonstrate a large degree of consistency in narrative tone. Detachment, cynicism, and distortion are features of that tone and the regularity of these features gives evidence of a patterning principle that blueprints these works. It circumscribes the relationships of characters who for the most part deal ineffectively with their changing environment. It also determines the manner and form of the narration, at times resulting in a narrative space literally charged with cynical distortions of the facts being related. The contours of this patterning principle, as it molds the reactions and movements of actors in the fictional realm, strongly evoke the paradigm of neurosis: Impulses to act get short-circuited or stem from invalid motivations. Works constructed in this way suggest a relationship between neurosis and the human potential for acting and reacting creatively. . . .

*Mission terminée* opens with the revelation that Medza has failed the oral examination for the *baccalauréat* degree. He masks his frustration and indignation with a cultivated response for anyone who might inquire: ''J'ai été recalé comme il se doit.'' It would be unacceptable for Medza to appear to have lost control of his situation, so he must remain flippant at all costs. This characteristic flippancy surfaces again when he engages in a brief sarcastic exchange with the driver of a transport vehicle. The agony in the faces of the other passengers mirrors the inappropriateness of Medza's remarks and laughter. For the moment he manages to retain mastery of his situation, but his sense of inadequacy becomes obvious as the novel progresses. Having been fueled by his most recent failure, it is not erased by the conscious efforts at nonchalance he displays. . . .

If neurotic responses can function creatively, as with Medza in *Mission terminée*, the creative impulse can also degenerate into a neurotic mockery of itself. We see examples of the latter in *Le Roi miraculé* where Beti deals with a society experiencing the most painful kind of cultural decline. Its members are forced to adjust as best they can, but suffer necessarily from an insecure ontological orientation: previously held practices and explanations (conventions) no longer make sense of life, and the resulting ontological insecurity breeds neurotic personalities, passive dependence, and confusion. All of the characters are in fact troubled, including the narrator. As Thomas Malone points out, these characters are caught up in a humiliating game with life. Beti heightens the effect this widespread neurotic anxiety will have on the reader by allowing it to permeate throughout all levels of the work. By exploring the neurotic potential of the creative function, he transforms neurosis into a creative tool.

> JoAnne Cornwell. *French Review*. 60, 5 (April 1987), pp. 644–45, 648–49

Although it is Mongo Beti's first novel and it is not difficult to point out its weaknesses, *Ville cruelle* is in fact a more substantial work than a cursory reading might suggest. On the surface the story line is strong and clear, although its components are often awkward and contrived. The hero, Banda, wishes to marry before his sick mother dies, so he goes to the nearby town of Tanga to sell his cocoa crop, intending to use the money he receives for it to pay the customary dowry. He is however cheated by the colonial officials who have to inspect the crop before it can be sold; they claim it is substandard and confiscate it in order to sell it for their own gain later. Banda then meets Odilia, whose brother Koumé is in hiding after taking the law into his own hands in an attempt to obtain his wages, which his white employer has not paid for months. Banda offers to hide Koumé in the forest, but Koumé is drowned while crossing the river separating Tanga from the forest. Banda takes Odilia to the safety of his own village, where he leaves her with his mother, while he returns to put Koumé's body where it will be quickly found by the police and so forestall any harassment of the dead man's family. Banda finds a large sum of money in Koumé's pocket which would more than compensate for his own loss that same morning. On his return home he decides it will be more honest to give the money to Odilia, who has a stronger claim to it. He then finds a suitcase lost by a Greek trader and his wife who have been driving up and down the countryside all day looking for

it. When he returns the case to them, Banda receives a reward exactly equivalent to what he expected to gain from his cocoa crop. So, in financial terms, all's well that ends well. With the blessing of his mother (who dies soon after), Banda marries Odilia, for whom he does not have to pay a dowry. Banda, who hates his village and had sworn to leave it when his mother died, now moves to Odilia's home village, where he is very happy, still dreaming of fulfilling his long-held ambition to work in the capital city, Fort-Negrè.

The plot is filled out with examples of the evils of colonialism, and it is here that the evocative quality of Beti's descriptions begins to reveal his talent as a writer. The second chapter, in which he describes the town of Tanga, is one of the most striking in the novel, and the only part of it translated so far into English. Beti portrays Tanga, and symbolically colonial life, as being divided in two—the two Tangas constitute two worlds and two destinies: on the one side of the town live the whites, whose world is that of the commercial center, while on the other side live the blacks, separate and exploited. The whole emphasis of the white world is on money, which takes precedence over all other considerations and which is slowly corrupting the moral values of the blacks who are themselves becoming obsessed with the same greed, expressed in the way the impoverished inhabitants of the shantytown of Tanga-Nord dream of the wealth that tomorrow will bring them; expressed in the dishonesty of the inspectors who condemn perfectly good cocoa beans to enrich themselves; . . . expressed above all through the novel's hero, who dreams of going to live in the town and who is obsessed by the need for money, so that his problems are only resolved when he is the lucky recipient of a windfall. On this level of the narrative, Beti seeks to show not only the injustices of colonial society, its hypocrisy and its morality based on self-interest, but also the total lack of concern for the welfare of the township blacks, the breakdown of social order, and the frightening instability of the world of the urban African. . . .

However, Beti is as critical of traditional society as he is of colonialism; he sees the former's male element as just another expression of the will to dominate. Indeed, Beti, through his hero Banda, stresses that male African society, typified by the elder, is even more repressive in its way than colonialism. . . . Banda has decided to leave his home village as soon as his mother dies and go to the town to escape the domination of the ''old men.'' The town, for all that it reflects the worst that is to be found in colonialism, is preferable to subjection to the authority of the ''old men'' of the village. The ''old men'' are the ''fathers'' of the community and individually and collectively act as the ''fathers'' of the orphaned Banda. Paternity and authority are associated in Banda's mind, and are together rejected, because the sole effect of authority is to give power to those who exercise it and to express the freedom of the individual. Beti's heroes cannot tolerate the loss of their personal freedom, even though acknowledgement of the collective will as expressed through the elders is widely held by African writers, particularly of Beti's generation, to be a fundamental value of traditional African society. Banda is therefore a ''loner''; he tries to justify this with the excuse that he is the victim of a will to exclude him, both on the part of the ''old men'' and of ''fate.''. . .

Beti equates the male, the paternal, with superficiality and with the clumsy verbal and physical bullying that accompanies authority founded on an absence of thought or feeling. The other side of the novel explores the female, the maternal, and sees it as exerting a different kind of authority which functions from within and is founded chiefly on the emotions. As far as the structure of the novel is concerned, the penetration beneath its surface-level criticism of colonial and African society coincides exactly with the contrast the author makes between the male and the female, the paternal and the maternal, external and internal authority, between gesture and emotion, speech and silence.

Clive Wake. In János Riesz and Alain Ricard, eds. *Semper Aliquid Novi: Littérature Comparée et Littératures d'Afrique* (Tübingen: Gunter Narr, 1990), pp. 297–300

After the appearance of *Main basse [sur le Cameroun]*, Beti published five novels, a documentary account of his difficulties with the Biya government, and countless articles. For more than a decade, he has kept alive *Peuples Noirs/Peuples Africains*, one of the few independent progressive journals with a focus on Africa. Throughout this flurry of publication, Beti was motivated by many of the same considerations that had prompted him to write *Mission terminée, Le Pauvre Christ de Bomba*, and his other preindependence novels. By juxtaposing the true historical situation with the self-serving myth that had been fabricated to disguise the beneficiaries of the collaboration between vested interests in France and Cameroon, Beti hoped to prod his readers into a critical consciousness that would enable them to liberate themselves from the new forms of oppression being imposed on them. As in his earlier work, he argued that Africans themselves must forge the image according to which they shall be known in the world, for only then will they be able to control their own destiny.

By repudiating the false images of Africa promulgated by a new alliance of oppressors, Beti contended, Africans could expose the fraud perpetrated on them by the illusory promises of political independence. Convinced that this alliance retains its power by cultivating a resigned acceptance among the people, he concluded that revolutionary social and political change is possible only if a heightened sense of awareness can be communicated to the general public in countries such as Cameroon. From this perspective, the act of writing becomes a gesture that sweeps away false images and lays the groundwork for a rational understanding of contemporary Africa in its socio-historical context. On the basis of this understanding, Africans can participate actively in this struggle for freedom and identity that, according to Beti, each people must undertake for itself.

The people in this case are the people who live within the boundaries of a single country. In contrast to Beti's earlier fiction, his writing after 1972 focuses on questions specifically related to national identity in Cameroon, although the situation there is sufficiently typical that his descriptions of corruption and oppression have considerable relevance to other African countries as well. Nevertheless, his allusions to people, places, and events in Cameroonian history make it evident that the novels, essays, and documentary exposés he wrote in the 1970s and 1980s are part of a larger attempt to reestablish the true story of Cameroonian independence and to offer it as a counterimage for the false one that had gained currency because the country's privileged class and its French allies controlled access to the mass media. His five novels from this period—*Perpétue et l'habitude du malheur, Remember Ruben, La Ruine presque cocasse d'un polichinelle, Les Deux Mères de Guillaume Ismaël Dzewatama*, and *La Revanche de Guillaume Ismaël Dzewatama*—are thus designed to provoke a

rethinking of what national identity might mean in a free and independent Cameroon.

Richard Bjornson. *The African Quest for Freedom and Identity: Cameroonian Writing and the National Experience* (Bloomington: Indiana University Press, 1991), p. 326

[Traditional] concepts of Fate exist in *Les deux mères* and in *La Revanche*. The most obvious example appears in the names given to the characters. In oral tales, the name of a character defined his personal disposition, thus predisposing him to a particular fate. In the novels, a number of characters bear a special name, for example, Baba Soulé, who represents the former president Ahmadou Ahidjo. "Baba" means father, and "Soulé" a drunkard. The name makes an obvious allusion to the alleged excessive drinking of Ahidjo, but more important, it suggests that this character will always act according to his two principal traits, and that he will never change. A name like Marie-Pierre evokes her kindness, her love, but also, with the homophone of Pierre (Peter; pierre: stone) it alludes to her strength and it symbolizes her future attitudes toward the events she will face.

Like Marie-Pierre, Guillaume Ismaël is given a double name to express the complexities of his personality; it also announces the future variations of his fate. The name Guillaume (William) calls to mind William the Conqueror or William Tell, suggesting aggressiveness and valor, while Ismaël—recalling Abraham's son or the character in *Moby Dick*—evokes painful experiences. Both names, however, promise a better future for the young hero.

Guillaume's trials and happy fate are both suggested by another traditional aspect of his character. His names and situation create a resemblance with the traditional literary type of the orphan, despite the fact that his parents are not dead. Guillaume's depiction as an orphan lets the reader know that the child will face a life full of difficulties. In fact, traditional tales show how people insult and mistreat orphans, and how, owing to their special place in society, the latter must accomplish formidable tasks during a painful journey. Nonetheless, the orphan overcomes all obstacles, and succeeds in his role as mediator between the two worlds of Life and Death.

[By] portraying Guillaume as an orphan, the author has given clues in advance about the child's fate. The path that he will follow is thus already mapped out.

Other aspects of traditional Bantu concepts of Fate appear when Mongo Beti alludes to "forces"; for example when one of his characters says that "Fate chooses us. . . . Fate is a terrible force, against which we are powerless, whoever we are." At another point the narrator declares that Guillaume feels so comfortable in his house since Marie-Pierre has repainted it that he considers it his "kingdom inaccessible to hostile forces" (*Les deux mères*). An unsuspecting reader would let this statement pass without weighing its implications. Yet according to the traditional way of thinking, such a statement informs us that the threats made by the chief of police, Alexandre Tientcheu, will have no effect as long as Guillaume stays in the house. . . .

It appears that a character cannot decide by himself to change the conduct expected of him. Yet his path can be changed by events. Such an approach shows man as a toy in the hands of Fate and is similar to the concepts traditionally held by Bantus. However, despite the sudden changes they can bring into someone's life, events do not always take place completely unannounced. From time to time, man receives some warning. In traditional oral literature, this happens often through a dream or premonition, and a number of Camerounian novelists have used these devices to announce future events. . . .

It is worth considering here a final traditional aspect of Fate that can be observed in attitudes toward money. In the customary setting, owning much more than the other villagers is frowned upon not only because people feared that only evil forces produce wealth, but also because richness irritates Fate. That is why the reader suspects that Jean-François will not long retain his new-found riches, and that for him, as for every man, life "will be marked by unforeseen and menacing bouncings, similar to the trajectory of a monstrously capricious soccerball."

Mongo Beti's characters behave thus according to traditional views about Fate. As these views are also represented in novels written by other Camerounian authors, one can safely say that Mongo Beti remains in accordance with his colleagues who live in Africa. Moreover, as they themselves have done, Mongo Beti includes in his novels Occidental beliefs adapted to the new urban culture of his native land. . . .

Mongo Beti's growing insistence on individual responsibility complements the views expressed by Camerounian writers living at home, such as Bernard Nanga in *Les Chauves-souris*, and Marie-Thérèse Assiga-Ahanda in *Sociétés africaines et "high society."* Both writers have insisted on individual rights as well as on the duty of every Camerounian to refuse to play the neo-colonialist game. Such an evolution in the thinking of Mongo Beti is consistent with his personal development; after all, he lives in France, a society that places a high value on individualism, a far cry from the communalism that characterized village life. Indeed, even a cursory glance at his earlier novels reveals his concept of Fate gradually changing in that direction.

We can follow this evolution from his first novel, *Ville cruelle*, in which his central character, Banda, loses the income of a whole year of work because he fails to follow the advice offered by his elders. Fate punishes him for that, but an ironic turn of events compensates him for his loss, when he discovers an important sum of money belonging to a Greek merchant. Justice is done in this bizarre way, but it does not happen because Banda had planned or acted in order to redress the situation. Considering that this character does not imagine a scheme or have precise intentions about his future, he resembles other principal characters from the next three novels by Mongo Beti: *Mission terminée, Le pauvre Christ de Bomba*, and *Le Roi miraculé*.

It is in *Perpétue*, however, that Mongo Beti's characters show a different attitude toward Fate. After being freed from a camp for political prisoners, Essola learns that his sister Perpétue has died, and he wants to know how it happened. The story focuses primarily on Essola's inquiry so that he plays mostly the part of a listener. His quest is thus a *prise de conscience*: he learns about the inequities women suffer in Camerounian society. Yet the ending contains other implications as well. Following rites reserved in the traditional Beti society for adulterous women, Essola murders his brother, whom he blames for not having taken good care of Perpétue. The sheer savagery of the act must not be considered as an indication of his depravity, but as a metaphor for the annihilation of his former passivity toward Fate.

Consequently, after *Perpétue*, Mongo Beti's characters are less passive than they once were. It is true to say that Fate still buffets them; nevertheless, they have learned to shape their fate to a certain

degree. The ideas the author expresses about Fate have thus evolved not only in a way that suits him personally, but also in accordance with the views of his colleagues who reside in Cameroun and who experience the latest changes in mental attitudes. In this manner, even if he does not reside in his native land, and even if he has not yet portrayed all the new aspects of contemporary society represented in his colleagues' novels, Mongo Beti has managed to keep his work relevant for his countrymen.

Claire L. Dehon. In Stephen H. Arnold, ed. *Critical Perspectives on Mongo Beti* (Boulder: Lynne Rienner Publishers, Inc., 1998), pp. 305–11

BIBLIOGRAPHY
*Ville cruelle*, 1954; *Le pauvre Christ de Bomba*, 1956 (*The Poor Christ of Bomba*), 1956; *Mission terminée*, (*Mission to Kala*), 1957; *Le roi miraculé* (*King Lazarus*), 1958; "Tumultueux Cameroun," 1959; "L'unité africaine," 1960); *Main basse sur le Cameroun*, 1972); *Perpétue et l'habitude de malheur*, 1974; *La ruine presque cocasse d'un polichinelle*, (*Lament for an African Pol*), 1979; *Les deux mères de Guillaume Ismael Dzewatama*, 1982; *Le revanche de Guillaume Ismael Dzewatama*, 1985; *L'histoire du fou*, 1994; *Trop de soleil tue l'amour*, 1999

# BHÊLY-QUÉNUM, Olympe (1928–)
## Benin

[*An Endless Trap*] is fiction, but one feels the reality of each detail so strongly that one has the impression of having lived the story—at first so beautiful, afterwards so tragic.

Ahouna lives with his parents, who are well-off peasants from the North of Dahomey. He tills the fields with his family and friends and this affords us very lively and beautiful descriptions. . . . Ahouna is also a poet. While tending his herds, his soul sings and the book often contains passages of tender and rustic poetry. His sensitive heart explodes with joy and happiness when he is loved by Anatou and the countryside echoes with sweet or passionate, nostalgic or animated music which he improvises. . . .

I think that [the] subtleties [in this novel] will be appreciated. In fact, the author is rarely violent, even in the second part of the book where Ahouna is in prison. I prefer not to tell how it came out in order to leave the full shock and horror of discovery to the reader. There are descriptions of "quarries" where the prisoners climbed down countless steps every day to find death under falling granite blocks, or madness under the implacable sun. I thought that I was reading a description of Mathausen concentration camp.

The author is an excellent painter of patriarchal scenes, and is just as good with tragic descriptions. A phrase or only single words recall how the Negroes see and feel and live under oppression and colonization. My ears can still hear their cries of rage. . . .

To sum up, this novel is a fresco from Dahomey, full of reality and lyricism. There are some delightful love-stories written in a very beautiful language which have the merit of "being seen from the inside" and described by a Dahomeian.

Andrée Clair. *Presence africaine*. (English ed.). 8, 1, 1961, pp. 170–71

Ahouna [the hero of *An Endless Trap*] combines within himself the values of life and death. The black Orpheus of the beginning of the novel becomes a black Orestes. . . . His is a drama of fate: a pastoral hero destined for happiness, he suddenly falls under the yoke of fetishes eager to destroy him: the *obas* [spirits that inhabit objects] stir up the vindictive hatred of the parents of the victim [who was murdered by Ahouna] in order to assure that Ahouna will disappear forever.

Born for simple happiness, Ahouna reaches the point of madness, horror, and panic. He does not understand why his destiny has abruptly changed course; he experiences the anger of the gods, of humans, and of objects, and when faced with the imminence of his own death, he will not utter one cry of hatred or make one move to rebel. Nor even, we should note, will he experience a feeling of Christian charity, an impulse that makes us forgive those who have injured us.

Ahouna's attitude is that of the fetishist (although he claims not to be one); despite the frequent references to Allah, the hero's attitude is related neither to Islam nor to Christianity (which is the religion practiced by Olympe Bhêly-Quénum himself). Ahouna's attitude is an unconditional surrender to the sovereign hidden powers, if that is their will. Although he does not recognize himself as completely guilty, he knows that he has unleashed the gods' anger and that only his immolation can appease them.

Roger Mercier and M. and S. Battestini. *Olympe Bhêly-Quénum* (Paris: Fernand Nathan, 1964), p. 8

As a youth, Ahouna [in *An Endless Trap*] lived the dreamy life of a herd boy with his flute, by means of which he called up visions of plenitude. But this northern harmony was destroyed by his wife's ill will, which triggered the spring, released what Ahouna calls "the monster within." Once freed, this spirit of destructiveness ravages him from within and without. From his home on the high plains of Baribaland, he is compulsively driven south, down the length of Dahomey to the lowlands of the Fon.

As the viciousness around and about him increases, the more despised he becomes, the closer he comes to the littoral. For the men of the south are subtle, he says, sullen and superstitious, corrupt products of a crossplay of influences from the sophisticated Yoruba and the wily traders from overseas. Everything is denser. The clenched fist thuds dully upon the earth's anvil, raging impotently over and over again. Exhausted, Ahouna finally falls victim to a clandestine ceremony of blood revenge. Thus the literature of the south, from the lower Niger to the lower Volta, seems inevitably linked to "the earth and dreams of the will" and that of the north, from the Senegal to the Upper Niger, to "the earth and dreams of repose."

Judith Gleason. *African Forum.* Spring 1966, pp. 82–83

*The Song of the Lake* . . . bears the message that traditional Africa, far from having to be rescued from oblivion, is very much alive and may have a more crucial role to play in the future of the continent than "modern" Africa. In Olympe Bhêly-Quénum's novels, the common themes of modern African literature—the impact of colonialism, the problem of acculturation, the social and political effects of modernization—usually appear as peripheral to the powerful influence of irrational supernatural forces. His first novel,

*An Endless Trap*, tells the story of one individual destroyed by an inexplicable fate; *The Song of the Lake*, set like the earlier novel in the author's native Dahomey, portrays an African community held in the grip of animism. The village of Wêsê, situated on the shore of a lake, is the focus of a tale in which political issues, the impact of Western rationalism, and the villagers' traditional fear of the man-eating gods of the lake are woven into a symbolic portrait of Africa as the battleground between the forces of enlightenment and those of fear. Using a narrative technique that seems alternatively inspired by the palaver and the adventure story, Bhêly-Quénum recounts a day of crisis on which this struggle reaches a climax in the village. . . .

*The Song of the Lake* is too short a novel to do full justice to the complexity of Olympe Bhêly-Quénum's conception. Themes and characters are at times outlined rather than fully developed, and the author is not entirely successful in weaving the many strands of his plot into a coherent whole. Yet this does not detract from the interest and value of the book. Bhêly-Quénum combines humor and psychological penetration with a talent for evocative description; and the extraordinary richness of levels in this novel—its blending of folk legend, social criticism, symbolism, and allegory—makes it stand out among modern African fiction.

Thomas Cassirer. *African Forum.* Spring 1967, pp. 135–36

The idea of the absurd is an obsession of the hero of Bhêly-Quénum's [*An Endless Trap*]. He assumes an attitude toward life that is both negative and pessimistic. . . .

The interest of *An Endless Trap* lies neither in its narrative, which is diffuse, nor in its formal unity, since there isn't any—in fact, some of the episodes and characters are incoherent and very poorly integrated into the work's thematic universe. The interest in Bhêly-Quénum's novel lies primarily in the vision . . . of the absurd as incarnated by its hero, Ahouna, a vision that imparts allegorical strength to the hero's situation.

The feeling of absurdity is first presented as a fundamental idea in the hero's consciousness. Ahouna's mind is shown to be particularly sensitive to the slightest disturbance in his inner life. Any phenomenon, even an atmospheric one, increases his feeling of ontological unbalance. . . . This feeling is accompanied by the awareness that life is completely devoid of meaning. . . .

For Ahouna, human existence is nothing but an "enormous trap set for man by Allah.". . . This causal reference to Allah, an absolute transcendental being, shows the extent to which the problematic individual's spirit tries to rationalize or to justify his downfall. . . . Is not the truly absurd or problematic man the one who, from the depths of his being, considers himself an absurdity, a meaningless being, yet who nevertheless clings to life with an unheard-of tenacity? In other words, however rational some of Ahouna's words may seem, they are less the result of a sober reflection on the overt world than the self-criticism of a psychological state mutilated by existential anxiety. It is in this anxiety that the real meaning and the motive of the hero's crime must be sought. And this crime, the murder of an innocent woman, can be considered here a gratuitous act. It has no other motivation than what can be furnished by a pathological neurosis. . . .

Sunday O. Anozie. *Sociologie du roman africain* (Paris: Éditions Aubier-Montaigne, 1970), pp. 161–62, 164–65

The writings of Olympe Bhely-Quenum are among the most tonic and independent-minded in the range of ''black francophone'' responses to the formal ending of colonialism and contain recurrent investigations of the ''couple domino'' (mixed-race, black/white couple). . . .

His first novel, *Un piege sans fin* [*Snares without end*], remains his best known and like many of his short stories, was written in the late 1950s. Ahouna, the narrator within the narration for the first nine chapters of the book in Genette's narratological scheme, and whose story lies at the heart of the novel, swiftly recalls a black/white marriage in his family, even though this emerges as being only incidental to the principal narrative. His sister Seitou attracted the attentions of a ''toubab'' (white man) called Tertullien. Ahouna records the initial innocence of the family's reactions:

> L'union libre de Tertullien et de Seitou avait introduit un Européen dans l'agglomeration de mon pere. Par je ne sais quoi encore quelle aberration, mon père, ma mère et moi nous nous croyions, de ce fait, a l'abri des mauvais traitements et des abus auxquels tous nos compatriotes étaient fréquemment soumis. Un toubab faisait partie de notre famille!
>
> The relationship between Tertullien and Seitou had brought a European into my father's compound. Through some aberration or other, my father, my mother, and I believed that by this fact alone we were shielded from the ill-treatment and abuse to which all our fellow-countrymen were frequently subjected. Our family included a white man as a member!

The couple went off to Cameroon and had first a son and then twins, but then Tertullien deserted Seitou, ''en colère parce qu'il ne pouvait faire l'amour avec elle sans consequences: ces gamins de sang mêlé'' ''angry because he could not make love to her without it having consequences: these half-caste children.'' Rather than delighting in such fecundity, he returned to France,

> sous pretexte qu'il detestait la honte et l'humiliation, selon son propre aveu. Car à l'entendre c'est, aussi bien dans son pays que dans sa race, une avanie que de s'unir à une negresse au point d'en avoir des enfants
>
> on the pretext that he detested shame and humiliation, on his own admission. For to listen to him you would think that, in his country and among his race, it is humiliating to go with a negress to the point of having children by her.

The villagers of Founkilla aligned themselves with the family's quite different initial reaction: they saw Bakari, Ahouna's father, who enjoyed the (sometimes doubtful) prestige of having fought as a tirailleur senegalais (West African soldier) in the First World War, as ''le beau-père d'un Européen, un Blanc était son gendre, il était le grand-père de trois métis. En vérite, il n'y avait plus de doute: Bakari était un homme heureux, comble'' 'the father-in-law of a European: a white man was his son-in-law, he was the grandfather of three half-caste children. Yes, there was no doubt about it: Bakari was a happy man, with everything he wanted'. . . . Other illusions will disappear in due course, and with them the family's ordered world. Bakari cannot bring himself to accept the humiliation of forced labor for the local French administrator, preferring to stab himself to death. Ahouna himself concludes his narration at the end of chapter nine with the account of an *acte gratuit* (gratuitous act), the murder of a woman he did not know.

Such violence prepares us for the violence of the nemesis that, eight chapters later, overwhelms him. . . .

''Liaison d'un été'' closes the collection of short stories to which it gives its name and is in certain respects the mirror image of ''Aventure africaine.'' Set in a resort in Normandy called Chanovre, it revolves around the close friendship between Cofi, a Ghanaian student, and Christa, an English girl staying with her family, the improbably named Gemcleaners, at the same guest house for a summer holiday. Cofi's ability to translate for the visitors puts him in a privileged position, and he finds Christa's auburn hair and tinkling laughter irresistible. Although the relationship blossoms discreetly, it comes to a sudden and tragic end when Christa is drowned. The tale nonetheless gives Bhely-Quenum the opportunity to present his essentially optimistic vision of race relations. . . .

Bhely-Quenum has stated: ''écrire la vie d'une Blanche qui aura vécu avec un Noir ou d'une Africaine et d'un Européen ne m'interesse pas. Trop de poncifs a ce sujet'' 'writing the story of a white woman who has lived with a Black or of an African woman with a European man doesn't interest me. There are too many stereotypes in that area.' Clearly, he wants to direct our attention to the imaginative stimulus of his writing rather than to relationships that, from being taboo, have become something of a totem. Yet his very return to the motif, firstly in the short stories we have recalled and then in two further novels, *L'initié* [*The initiate*] and the as yet unpublished *C'était a Tigony* [*Tigony*], suggests that he sees in it at least a fascinating nexus for the exploration of other issues. If race is not a problem, why does it figure so insistently? After *Un piège sans fin*, in which, as we have seen, things do not work out between Tertullien and Seitou, Bhely-Quenum's persistently positive and, in those novels where it figures, central representation of mixed-race marriages or intimate relationships contrasts starkly with that of the out-and-out racists (often but not exclusively European) who bring pressures to bear on the couple. So however, humanly, one might approve of an enlightened, liberal attitude, one cannot but regret, from a literary point of view, that the devil continues to have the best tunes. The intensity of racist passion felt by the Gemcleaner couple in ''Liaison d'un été'' and by the company bosses, both at Kariba and at Youngourou, in ''Aventure africaine,'' explodes in verbal and even physical assaults that are scarcely matched by the intensity of the discreet petting of Christa and Cofi and the even more discreetly veiled, if frequent, love-making of Julien and Gisele.

The longer form of the novel and the writer's growing experience conspire to help Bhely-Quenum avoid well-intentioned simplicities. *L'initié* enacts, rather than merely postulates, a successful mixed-race marriage. It becomes the most natural thing in the world simply because it is a given. The questions with which the novel deals lie elsewhere, notably in the exploration of the validity and nature of seemingly irrational forces welling up from powerful African traditions, in which good and evil are as central as in Western moral philosophies.

Skin color is not an issue in the book but a given, and while primary racism occurs sporadically around the ''couple domino,'' it is at a much deeper level that the novel makes its cultural exploration. Because of their shared personal and professional experiences, Marc and Corinne are not left on a naively optimistic threshold at the end, since their solidarity as a couple has been tested, their harmony and solidity proven, and their optimism at facing the future together well grounded. . . .

The increase of sophistication in Bhely-Quenum's novels *L'initié* and *C'était a Tigony* compared to the earlier short stories will be apparent even from their partial presentation in the present study. Nor should the above be considered more than a highly selective review of the author's work, since consideration of *Le chant du lac* [*The song of the lake*] and *Les appels du vodou* [*The calls of voodoo*], the former announced as "ce recit du monde negre" 'that narrative of the black world' and the latter as "un memorial de l'Afrique des profondeurs" 'a memorial to Africa's depths,' not to mention other short stories, whether collected, uncollected, or unpublished, would redress the balance firmly in favor of a profound exploration and representation of the "dark continent," notably in respect of those traditional rituals and mysteries so frequently dismissed by Europeans as mumbo-jumbo.

Even so, the motif of the "couple domino" recurs sufficiently often over forty years of writing to warrant our attention. Perhaps it should not surprise us coming from the pen of an African happily married to a Frenchwoman. As a focusing lens for interracial considerations, Bhely-Quenum's positive, nonracist representation of such couples through the eyes of the partners concerned (even Seitou's abandonment by Tertullien is recounted, not demonstrated, and no grudge seems to be held) nonetheless allows racists, more or less peripheral and passing in the narratives, to voice their entrenched opinions and so create a kaleidoscope of attitudes to lend density and texture to the writing. Racism, on the part of either whites or blacks, never wins the day in Bhely-Quenum; none of his heroes suffers the fate of Oumar in Sembene's *O pays, mon beau peuple!* [*Oh Country, My Beloved People*], and no half-caste child is killed in the atmosphere of bleak pessimism such as one finds in Mariama Ba's *Un chant ecarlate* [*The scarlet song*]. . . .

It is clear . . . that Bhely-Quenum is intent on persuading us to go beyond skin-deep color-blindness. Indeed, he takes that color-blindness for granted. Under his benign guidance, we are not simply initiated by proxy into the mysteries of Africa and encouraged not to impede its development any longer under the false colors of neocolonialism: we are invited to act more humanely and with greater tolerance toward our fellow human beings in general. Can there be a higher moral justification for engaging in the act of writing?

Roger Little. *Research in African Literatures*. 29, 1 (Spring 1998), pp. 66–86

BIBLIOGRAPHY
*Un piège sans fin*, 1960; *Liaison d'un été*, 1963; *Le chant du lac*, 1965; *L'Initié*, 1979; *Les appels du vodou*, 1994

# BONTEMPS, Arna (1902–1973)
## United States

Arna Bontemps' first venture in fiction [*God Sends Sunday*] is to me a profound disappointment. It is of the school of [Carl Van Vechten's] *Nigger Heaven* and [Claude McKay's] *Home to Harlem*. There is a certain pathetic touch to the painting of his poor little jockey hero, but nearly all else is sordid crime, drinking, gambling, whore-mongering, and murder. There is not a decent intelligent woman; not a single man with the slightest ambition or real

education, scarcely more than one human child in the whole book. Even the horses are drab. In the "Blues" alone Bontemps sees beauty. But in brown skins, frizzled hair and full contoured faces, there are to him nothing but ugly, tawdry, hateful things, which he describes with evident caricature.

One reads hurriedly on, waiting for a gleam of light, waiting for the Sunday that some poor ugly black God may send; but somehow it never comes; and if God appears at all it is in the form of a little drunken murderer riding South to Tia Juana on his back. . . .

Well—as I know I have said several times before—if you like this sort of thing, then this will be exactly the sort of thing you will especially like, and in that case you ought to run and read it.

W. E. B. Du Bois. *Crisis*. September 1931, p. 304

In that limited and almost barren field known as the Negro novel, Arna Bontemps's *Black Thunder* fills a yawning gap and fills it competently. Covering all those skimpy reaches of Negro letters I know, this is the only novel dealing forthrightly with the historical and revolutionary traditions of the Negro people.

*Black Thunder* is the true story of a slave insurrection that failed. But in his telling of the story of that failure Bontemps manages to reveal and dramatize through the character of his protagonist, Gabriel, a quality of folk courage unparalleled in the proletarian literature of this country. . . .

When considering Gabriel solely as an isolated individual, he seems sustained by an extremely foolish belief in himself; but when one remembers his slave state, when one realizes the extent to which he has made the wrongs of his people his wrongs, and the degree in which he has submerged his hopes in their hopes—when one remembers this, he appears logically and gloriously invincible.

The plan for the uprising is so simple and daring that when it is disclosed and tracked to its source, the fear-ridden whites can scarcely believe it. But Gabriel believes, he believes even when he is caught; even when the black cowl is capped about his head, even when the ax swings, he believes. Why?

For me the cardinal value of Bontemps's book, besides the fact that it is a thumping story well told, lies in the answer to that question. Perhaps I am straying further afield than the author did in search for an answer. If I do, it is because I believe we have in *Black Thunder* a revelation of the very origin and source of folk values in literature.

Even though Gabriel's character is revealed in terms of personal action and dialogue, I feel there is in him much more than mere personal dignity and personal courage. There is in his attitude something which transcends the limits of immediate consciousness. He is buoyed in his hope and courage by an optimism which takes no account of the appalling difficulties confronting him. He hopes when there are no objective reasons or grounds for hope; he fights when his fellow-slaves scamper for their lives. In doing so, he takes his place in that gallery of fictitious characters who exist on the plane of the ridiculous and the sublime. Bontemps endows Gabriel with a myth-like and deathless quality. And it is in this sense, I believe, that *Black Thunder* sounds a new note in Negro fiction, thereby definitely extending the boundaries and ideology of the Negro novel.

Richard Wright. *Partisan Review and Anvil*. April 1936, p. 31

*Black Thunder* is written with restraint and detachment. Bontemps portrays slaves, freedmen, planters, and French radicals with impartiality, showing no disposition to glorify pro-Negro nor to traduce anti-Negro characters in the book. Miscegenation on the Southern scene is not blinked. Furthermore, Bontemps succeeds in weaving Gabriel's uprising into the web of state and national life. We observe the Virginia legislature considering the sectional segregation of Negroes as an approach to the solution of racial difficulties and note the Federalist press, while championing a second term for John Quincy Adams, citing Gabriel's insurrection as an offshoot of the radicalism of Thomas Jefferson and his adherents. Although *Black Thunder* is not without blemish, A. B. Spingarn is quite correct in his observation that the book is "the best historical novel written by an American Negro.". . .

*Drums at Dusk*, a worthy successor to *Black Thunder*, is another vivid illustration of the richness of the Negro's past as a source for historical fiction.

> Hugh Gloster. *Negro Voices in American Fiction* (Chapel Hill: University of North Carolina Press, 1948), pp. 214–16

Arna Bontemps is a transitional figure whose novels bear the mark both of the Negro Renaissance and of the Depression years which follow. Born in Louisiana of Creole parentage, he moved to Los Angeles at an early age. He was educated at Pacific Union College and the University of Chicago; at present he is head librarian of Fisk University. A minor poet during the 1920's, Bontemps turned later to fiction, history, and books for children. He has written three novels, of which the first, *God Sends Sunday*, is an unadulterated product of the Negro Renaissance. The setting of the novel is the sporting world of racetrack men and gamblers, of jazz and the shimmy, of fights and razor carvings. His historical novels, however, which deal with slavery times, reflect the mood of the Depression era. By choosing slave insurrections as a basis for his plots, Bontemps stresses an aspect of slavery which was emotionally appealing to the rebellious thirties. . . .

It is Bontemps' intention in *Black Thunder* to credit the Negro slave with an obsessive love of freedom. The extent to which this interpretation is historically valid is a moot point. That some slaves felt an overwhelming desire to "go free" and acted upon it is certainly beyond dispute. In any case, complexity of characterization, together with a tone of restraint and a tendency to underwrite, combine to save *Black Thunder* from the worst features of a propaganda novel. What remains of protest and of race pride limits the book but does not destroy it.

Arna Bontemps' second historical novel, *Drums at Dusk*, is in every respect a retreat from the standards of *Black Thunder*. Deriving its plot from the Haitian slave rebellion which brought Toussaint l'Ouverture to power, the novel is unworthy of its subject. In writing of a successful rebellion, Bontemps is deprived of the dramatic power of tragedy, and he discovers no appropriate attitude to take its place. Upon a highly romantic plot he grafts a class analysis of society which is post-Marxian and flagrantly unhistorical. Frequently lapsing into crude melodrama, he embroiders his narrative with all of the sword-play, sex, and sadism of a Hollywood extravaganza.

> Robert A. Bone. *The Negro Novel in America* (New Haven: Yale University Press, 1958), pp. 120, 122–23

My ex-student and friend, Robert A. Bone, is at his critical poorest with Arna Bontemps' fiction. "*God Sends Sunday*," he writes, "is an unadulterated product of the Renaissance." This is an unadulterated lie. . . .

Arna Bontemps was not of the "Harlem Renaissance" . . . for seven good reasons. This is especially ironic, for at the close of his busy life he should have been tending to more important business than plaintively, nostalgically wailing them good old days (which Langston [Hughes], Wallace Thurman and Zora Neale Hurston later said never existed). Again, thanks to whatever gods may be, Arna, bless his aesthetic sensibility and his Christian heart was *not* a member of that motley crew. If he had tried to join that Mystic Order of the Sons of—Harlem, he would have been blackballed for the following cogent reasons:

1. He was born in Alexandria, La., or leastways "above Aleck" in the local parlance.

2. He was a painstaking writer, respecting the English language. He certainly did not write "Black," if there is such a monstrosity.

3. He knew a great deal about literature, foreign and domestic.

4. His first novel and his poems are all that he wrote during this nebulous period, and they all appeared just when the such-and-such hit the fan, and the Renaissance flopped.

5. His major accomplishment before 1930 was a good novel which later became a bad play (good only because it introduced us to that immortal Pearl Bailey). Well, this novel never mentions or touches upon Harlem or even New York life. The title of the play was *St. Louis Woman* (*Harlem* Renaissance?).

6. He was a sober, austere, melancholy, meditative, meticulous Christian gentleman, who was far from the hedonism blatant in the "Harlem Renaissance" credo. How far the lust for life credo went in actuality is an intriguing idea, later to be pursued.

7. He was a decent artist.

> Sterling A. Brown. *Black World.* September 1973, pp. 94–95

The poetry of Arna Bontemps has appeared in every major anthology of Negro writing since the Renaissance, but it was not until 1963 that he brought out a collection of his verse, *Personals*, a thin volume of only twenty-three poems published by Paul Bremen in London. . . .

Bontemps' poems make use of several recurring themes: the alien-and-exile allusions so often found in New Negro poetry; strong racial suggestiveness and applications; religious themes and imagery subtly used; and the theme of return to a former time, a former love, or a remembered place. On occasion he combines in a way common to lyrical writing the personal with the racial or the general. Many of these poems are protest poems; but the protest is oblique and suggestive rather than frontal. Over all of Bontemps' poetry there is a sad, brooding quality, a sombre "Il Penseroso" meditative cast. In *Personals* there are no obviously joyous or humorous pieces. . . .

The poems of Arna Bontemps lack the clear, unambiguous statement of those of his contemporaries: McKay, Cullen, Hughes. There is modern obscurity in these verses, and the so-called meaning often eludes the reader. Their craftsmanship, however, is impressive. The reader somehow feels a certain rightness in

Bontemps' lines, that what he has said could not be expressed otherwise. There is a quiet authority in these poems.

Arthur P. Davis. *From the Dark Tower* (Washington, D.C.: Howard University Press, 1974), pp. 84–86

In a letter dated March 2, 1955, Langston Hughes wrote his longtime friend Arna Bontemps to congratulate him on the publication of Bontemps's latest children's book: "*Lonesome Boy* is a perfectly charming and unusual book. I read it right off[;] it came in the mail today. I LOVE books that short and easy and pretty to read. It ought to make a wonderful gift book." Bontemps himself had written Hughes about the book a little more than a year earlier (on December 10, 1953): "This is the book I enjoyed writing, perhaps because I did it impulsively for myself, while editors hounded me for my misdeeds and threatened me if I did not deliver manuscripts I had contracted for. So I closed the door for two days and had myself a time." Another, perhaps more valid, reason he wrote this particular story about Bubber, a boy so lonesome he plays his trumpet whenever and wherever he can—ending up, as his grandfather subsequently explains, at a devil's ball—stems from Bontemps's own nostalgic feelings about his Louisiana heritage and, more specifically, about his own sense of being a lonesome boy.

A careful look at Bontemps's work shows the lonesome boy theme appearing over several years and in different forms. For example, Bontemps wrote a version of the story, "Lonesome Boy, Silver Trumpet," in the 1930s, but it was not published until his collection of short fiction *The Old South: "A Summer Tragedy" and Other Stories of the Thirties* appeared a few weeks after his death in 1973. And on May 5, 1966, he delivered a speech at the New York Public Library which was published in December of that year as "The Lonesome Boy Theme" in *The Horn Book* magazine. There, he states that he has often used the theme, particularly to reflect on himself, since he began writing fiction. . . .

Bontemps's use of the lonesome boy theme applies mainly to his children's literature, even though he clearly wrote *God Sends Sunday* for adult audiences.

While it would be facile to claim that all of his works—either for adults or children—reveal this autobiographical theme, his use of the theme suggests a reason behind the author's interest in writing for the young. A close examination of Bontemps's *Lonesome Boy,* therefore, can help explain his motivation to become one of the first authors of the twentieth century to write books for young African Americans. It can also explain some of his disillusionment with adult books and with the economics of the publishing world, which was still dominated by white publishers and white readers during the 1930s, even though the Harlem Renaissance would usher in permanent change.

*God Sends Sunday* (1931), *Black Thunder* (1936), and *Drums at Dusk* (1939) appeared during the Great Depression; none sold well. And even though he proposed several other novels and wrote at least one full-length, unpublished novel between 1939 and 1973, when he died, he did not publish an adult novel after *Drums at Dusk. Chariot in the Sky* (1951), Bontemps's semi-fictional account of the famous Fisk University Jubilee Singers, straddles the line between adolescent and adult material, although it was published as a book for older adolescents. As we shall see, economics as well as politics and autobiographical impulses motivated Bontemps to write for juvenile readers.

For public consumption, Bontemps justified his turn to juvenile writing from poetry and adult fiction with the claim that his novels were falling on blind eyes. Consider, for example, his "Introduction to the 1968 edition of Black Thunder," made more timely because of the Civil Rights Movement and the riotous explosions of anger in many American cities, including Watts, where Bontemps had lived as a child. Referring to the 1930s, he writes, "I began to suspect it was fruitless for a Negro in the United States to address serious writing to my generation, and I began to consider the alternative of trying to reach young readers not yet hardened or grown insensitive to man's inhumanity to man, as it is called.". . .

Bontemps revealed, albeit indirectly, another variation on these themes of his motivation for writing literature for African American children in his 1969 essay "The Slave Narrative: An American Genre," printed as an introduction to his selected *Great Slave Narratives* . These comments reflect Bontemps's unusual scholastic history of being one of a very few African Americans educated in the predominantly white, religiously conservative, Seventh-Day Adventist San Fernando Academy. Paradoxically, the comments also reflect both a powerful and deeply felt sense of injustice and an equally heartfelt nostalgic longing coalescing around his plans in the 1960s to write his autobiography (titled *A Man's Name*), but left unfinished at his death:

> When I was growing up, my teachers, as well as others unaware of what they were doing, gave me to understand that the only meaningful history of the Negro in the United States (possibly even in the world) began with the Emancipation Proclamation of 1863. In the half[-]century since my school days, I have had a chance to observe the tenacity of this assumption. As evidence to the contrary is disclosed, I begin to suspect that the colossal omissions they perpetuated were more than inadvertent. They were deliberate. Many may have been vindictive.

No wonder Bontemps wrote novels for adults about slave rebellions (*Black Thunder* and *Drums at Dusk* ), as well as nonfiction history like *The Story of the Negro and One Hundred Years of Negro Freedom.* No wonder he wrote *Chariot in the Sky* and edited *Golden Slippers* and *Hold Fast to Dreams* (poetry anthologies for young people). No wonder he wrote about Bubber, the lonesome boy; Slumber, the sad-faced boy; and several other young African American males in their callow youth or in their adolescent curiosity learning about life as African Americans, learning of both their heritage and their status in a predominantly white society. Earlier, he had publicly bemoaned the lack of diversity in his scholastic reading assignments and the effect on him as a minority student when he accepted the Jane Addams Award in 1956 (for the enlarged 1955 edition of *The Story of the Negro*): "These things I would like to have known as a school boy and as a college student in the integrated schools of California are also things I wish my classmates had learned on the same days when we were given the small fragments of generally uncomplimentary information about Negro Americans that was found in the texts and references then in use." In other words, we see Bontemps, over and over again, addressing the lack of stories, nonfiction and fiction, about African Americans. We also see Bontemps's recognition that all students suffer when schools socialize students in a monocultural context.

He set about remedying that no-longer-acceptable situation through his own literary production.

Joseph A. Alvarez. *African American Review*. 32, 1 (Spring 1998), pp. 23-32

BIBLIOGRAPHY
*God Sends Sunday*, 1931; *You Can't Pet a Possum*, 1934; *Black Thunder*, 1936; *Sad-Faced Boy*, 1937; *Drums at Dusk*, 1939; *We Have Tomorrow*, 1945; *Story of the Negro*, 1948; *Personals*, 1963

# BRADLEY, David (1950–)

## United States

David Bradley ranks among the most sophisticated literary stylists of his generation. His two novels present subtle and original perspectives on issues that traditionally have concerned significant Afro-American writers: the meaning of community, the effects of racism, the shape and substance of history. His first book *South Street*, went out of print soon after publication and has yet to receive the attention it merits. But his award-winning second novel, *The Chaneysville Incident*, has established Bradley's reputation among major contemporary authors. . . .

*South Street* explores the inner life of the Philadelphia ghetto, with particular emphasis on its three social and cultural centers: Lightnin' Ed's Bar and Grill (the corner dive owned and managed by genial but formidable Leo), the Elysium Hotel (headquarters of Leroy Briggs, a bloodthirsty, womanizing numbers runner), and the Word of Life (the nondenominational, theatrical showcase of a church over which a lecherous charlatan, the Reverend Mr. J. Peter Sloan, presides). With insightful characterizations, strikingly accurate dialogue, and irreverent wit, Bradley examines the kind of communal relationships that bind people of the street to each other. . . .

*The Chaneysville Incident* is the story of a young man's search for the meaning of his father's life and death. The protagonist, a young, black, Philadelphia-based professor of history named John Washington, does not know that this is what he is after when he returns home to western Pennsylvania to nurse (and then to bury) his ailing surrogate father, Old Jack Crawley. But Jack's death prompts him to visit his parents' home and study Moses's (his late father's) exhaustive collection of manuscripts and journals. This research helps him to understand his father's suicide and its relation to the death of . . . thirteen fugitive slaves years before. Moreover, the process of describing his findings to his white psychiatrist girlfriend, Judith, shows him what the true meaning of history is.

Valerie Smith. In Thadious M. Davis and Trudier Harris, eds. *Dictionary of Literary Biography*. Volume 33 (Detroit: Gale Research, 1984), pp. 28–31

It is as much a search for meaning as for being that inspires the trend toward reimmersion in Afro-American literature. The historian-protagonist in *The Chaneysville Incident* stands as a candid embodiment of this fact. John Washington's central act of closeting himself to study his dead father's carefully placed materials actually takes up the Afro-American motif of hibernation and makes it over into a preparation for understanding, not (as with [Ralph] Ellison) for action. . . .

The pressure toward understanding . . . precedes John's election of history as a career. It may indeed have caused it. In grade school he had discovered that ignorance equals humiliation, and that a little knowledge (outdoing [Alexander] Pope) comes close to being deadly, while total knowledge serves as a source of power. But the equation of understanding and power becomes less certain as the subject matter becomes larger and more complex. The only power John Washington really possesses at the end of his story is the power (admittedly not negligible) to shift the quest for understanding to Judith, and to us.

In effect Bradley has set up a circular reading of *The Chaneysville Incident*. The action ends by driving back to its beginning, to the aborted quest for knowledge of, and through, history, and to the surprise revelation of the will. Presumably, even though the "next man" cannot count on that prop, the cycle will somehow lead on to the dramatically vivid but intellectually irresolute fire in the snow and that to the thought of "someone else" who will "understand," and thus to the beginning again.

John Washington's reimmersion ends, but reimmersion must go on in perpetual resumption, at once revelatory and frustrating, at once emancipating and insufficient. The reader becomes John Washington's heir, the "next man" who however dares not burn the tools of his trade, having been enjoined to use them—that is, now, the book—in endless repetition. In this light, we might almost see Truman Held as immersing himself in Meridian's sleeping bag [in Alice Walker's *Meridian*] and then instantly making the reader his heir, with assurance no greater than John Washington holds out.

In the beautifully cadenced scene containing the pivotal quarrel between John and Judith . . . the latter all but enunciates the problematical status of understanding in the new concern with reimmersion in Afro-American literature.

Michael G. Cooke. *Afro-American Literature in the Twentieth Century: The Achievement of Intimacy* (New Haven: Yale University Press, 1984), pp. 214–16

Through use of the monomyth, Bradley . . . illustrates a firm conviction in the power one gains from personal history. His narrator, John Washington, leaves the urban North to return to the rural setting he came from. . . . John leaves home with a tangible goal: to bury his old friend, Jack; but he . . . finds himself completely obsessed by the desire to unbury his family history. During most of his quest, John's state of mind might be described as mad, in the sense of a transcendent awareness that ignores the distractions society attempts to impose. Bradley's opening passage suggests the Call to Adventure, as John receives a telephone call from his mother conveying John's boyhood mentor's wish that John come to his bedside before Jack dies. Lest the reader underestimate the nature of this call, John, the narrator, underlines its mythic significance: "Sometimes you can hear the [telephone] wire, hear it reaching out across the miles; whining with its own weight, crying out from the cold, panting at the distance, humming with the phantom sounds of someone else's conversation. . . . whining, crying, panting, humming, moaning like a live thing." With this haunting passage, reflective of Bradley's love of the oral narrative, John draws us into his vaguely supernatural vision. Ignoring, or perhaps compelled by, the midnight hour, he takes the next bus, thus beginning his quest; both reluctant to answer the Call to Adventure and driven to do so, John spurs himself on with hot toddies. John's departure from his adopted home, urban academia, takes him back to a region whose mythic significance is underlined by the names of its various locales: the County, the Town, the Hill.

After Jack's funeral, John realizes he has been summoned for reasons more complicated than a burial. He resists the wiles of three trickster figures: the Judge and his son, emblematic of the white power structure, who in archetypal fashion function to dissuade John from completing his journey, and John's mother, who has colluded with this white power structure. Returning to old Jack's cabin, and aided by the tools of historical scholarship, pens and notes that acquire a magical dimension because he believes they will help him untangle his personal history, he begins the second stage of his journey and the second major part of *The Chaneysville Incident*. Like Milkman [in Toni Morrison's *Song of Solomon*], John feels driven to merge himself with elemental reality; he abandons all but the most meager comforts Jack's dwelling provides. During this phase of his quest, John enters a state of mind akin to the holy madness of a mystic, leaving the corporal world almost entirely. Suffering through a number of grueling initiatory trials, including a deer hunt, John finally enters fully into the depths of the underworld: his creative imagination. The final section of *The Chaneysville Incident* begins when John emerges, having gained liberation as a result of immersing himself in his history and fusing that history with African philosophy. Finally, Bradley's hero returns to his urban community fortified with knowledge that transcends the historical facts that academia prizes. Until his quest, John Washington, an historian, has persistently avoided discussing the history of the region where he grew up, an area he has refused to visit for years. Before his quest, Milkman Dead has come to accept the notion that he is incapable of flight, a notion that denies his spiritual link with the past. Consequently, he has become shallow, inhibited, and incurious about his history. Both of these men, having spent years evading their personal histories, end up affirming them, typifying the strenuous journey from denial to celebration of Afro-American history.

> Jane Campbell. *Mythic Black Fiction: The Transformation of History* (Knoxville: University of Tennessee Press, 1986), pp. 139–40

In his second novel, *The Chaneysville Incident*, David Bradley has presented a narrative text in which authenticated historical material is so charged with the expressive claims of fiction as symbolic action that the book may today already claim a unique position within Afro-American fiction—a narrative tradition well-known for its concern with history. As Bradley's statements in the short preface to the novel make explicit, he places himself within a collective endeavor for the ten years it took him to conceptualize and finish the book. Bradley has drawn on archival research (his own and that of others) into family, community, and group history in order to invest the quest for personal and cultural self-definition of the central narrator John Washington with as much historical context as possible. . . .

In terms of the historical material, Bradley's novel tries to present a comprehensive perspective on the formative experience of black Americans (that is, on slavery and the desire for self-realization) and on the necessity of recapturing their past. On the

fictional level this quest is presented as a process of self-scrutiny and self-therapy for the precarious self-concept of a representative individual, John Washington. . . . The deliberate breaking-up of the narrative structure . . . points to Bradley's being heir to fictional techniques in the main-stream tradition of American literature. Bradley is trying to fuse not only black and white narrative traditions (thus claiming a non-segregated heritage), but also more fundamentally the documentary and imaginative reconstruction of the black experience in America, while at the same time raising positive questions about the interrelation of history and fiction. . . .

This is the main thrust of Bradley's novel: history can only become meaningful through active imaginative appropriation of its raw material, which is to say by an act of imaginative completion, by the fictional reconstruction of the unfinished story-line of history. The three major protagonists of the novel—C. K., Moses, and John Washington—together establish a fictional lineage with strong reference to factual history, but all enhanced and projected onto a more than life-size fictional screen in order to articulate central thematic concerns of Bradley's dramatized version of black history in the context of America. C. K. and Moses Washington are passionately concerned with defensive as well as offensive (or militant) social and political power, with survival as the prerequisite for an out-spoken (C. K.) or tacit (Moses) demand for gaining the power to have their say in shaping the national or local world they live in. Their heir John Washington has shifted his struggle for survival to the psychological and class level—he has to fend off both the destructive influence of white racism, and its equivalent of internalized self-hatred, as well as the suffocating norms of middle-class respectability embodied by his mother and her lineage. On the militant level, John (clad in the contemporary armor of the university professor) has shifted his ancestors' bid for power to the intellectual or cognitive sphere, with power becoming the control over and mediation of knowledge. As historian he partakes in exemplary fashion in the business of image-making and image control which has already been at the heart of black-white antagonism in America, and around which the novel in its continuing dialogical quest keeps moving, sometimes in contracting, sometimes in expanding circles, including a possible future as represented by Judith, and easily shifting from present to past since all time levels remain closely interconnected in the unremitting questioning attitude of John's mind.

> Klaus Ensslen. *Callaloo*. 11, 2 (Spring 1988), pp. 280–81, 286

The bodily locus in [*The Chaneysville Incident*] is the belly—the hero, John Washington, has a feeling of cold in his belly. The feeling of cold threatens, in dreams, to envelop him. I trace the formation—history, content, motivation—of that pain (the cold, frigidity) and its subsequent deformation or reformation. The cold is a bodily condition under tension, and in this case the tension is at least five generations old. The hero is offered and internalizes a sustained history of pain—slavery and its aftermath. He studies diligently, thoroughly, and extensively to find some missing piece of information, but he is off the track and he fails, which deeply grieves him. He suffers for what he does know as well as what he does not. He carries both the pain of history and the pain of failure in his belly, the locus of his coldness. What he eventually finds, he was not looking for; it provides a warmth that in turn allows him to understand something deeper than he could have anticipated, and it allows him be creative as a man and an artist. . . .

Bradley's novel builds on central themes in our separate and related American literary traditions; he creates a new dialectic both between and within the black and white traditions. We can see Bradley's relation to Faulkner's ''Bear,'' Melville's *Moby Dick*, and Hemingway's ''Old Man of the Sea'' in his use of the hunt as a way to explore the relation of man and nature and man to man. Bradley's hero, John Washington, a professor of history, is a contemporary descendant of Faulkner's Ikkemotubbe; he knows the primal relation of man and animal, hunter and hunted. As Faulkner writes in the opening page of ''The Bear'': ''It was of the men, not white not black not red but men, hunters, with the skill and hardihood to endure and the humility and skill to survive.'' But Bradley's hero also embodies a broader consciousness from other learning systems. Moreover, Bradley does not exclude women from his universe. And, of course, Bradley's metaphoric view on hunting has the perspective of historically being hunted. Bradley's hero, finally, wants more than what is considered in ''The Bear'' ''the best of all listening, the voices quiet and weighty and deliberate for retrospection and recollection and exactitude among the concrete trophies.'' For John Washington, the telling and listening to the telling of tales is a matter of life and death.

Bradley is also thematically related to black writers—James Baldwin, Ralph Ellison, and Alex Haley—in his hero's quest for identity as a black man in America. John Washington's situation, however, is complicated by his mixed genetic heritage, whose roots include African black, American Indian, and Anglo-Irish white, and his mixed education, apprenticed as a youngster to a black backwoodsman and later becoming a professor of history. John Washington confronts the issue of racism (white and black, external and internalized) through the family history he reconstructs and in his intimate relationships with his childhood mentor (a dying father) and the white woman with whom he has been living for five years. Bradley creates greater complexity than earlier writers (black and white) in his hero's search for identity. Bradley's hero endures new forms of alienation but gains new perspectives and offers new possibilities. . . .

The novel is epic—it has thematic concerns in common with the Iliad and *Odyssey*—the anger of Achilles and the necessity of Telemachos's search for his father. Bradley's mode of storytelling is also related to Homer's—it is highly embedded. The novel unfolds one new dimension after another—historical, political (micro and macro), linguistic, interpersonal, intrapsychic, spiritual. There is also an integral, unintrusive, and illuminating consciousness of the process of ''making'' with language. There is the history John tells us but also the histories of the history. Indeed, assembling and telling the history is what constitutes John's heroism. John's task involves all the processes of writing history—gathering and sorting information, reconstructing sequences and simultaneities, and confronting the gaps. The task also leads him to another modality of knowing, though to get there, he must drop his scientific/obsessional ways.

The focus of the history itself is on racial conflict from slavery to the present as seen through the microcosm of one line of descent—that of John's father, Moses Washington. A central concern of the history is with black heroism, rebellion, and subversion—the fight to be seen as autonomous. At the interpersonal level, the novel focuses on the tensions between generations, races, and sexes. The history and present moments of John's relationship to Judith has its own distinct tensions; and these tensions are brought up against the origins of John's side of the

antagonism and ambivalence: Jack Crawley, John's surrogate father, the last father in the line. Jack teaches John many invaluable skills; he tells two or three of the best stories in the novel (about the great trickster, Moses). At his funeral—in the belly of the text—we learn how generous he has been to the community. But he also prohibits John from the white world and the sexual world. John has entered both.

The world John grew up in, the one he now lives in, and the one he returns to are fraught with tension. The focus of this chapter is on how that tension manifests itself with the character, particularly how it is inscribed in the body and mapped out in the language. I specifically focus on the symptomatic pain in the belly of John Washington. The conflicts generating the pain and anxiety are rooted in the hero's historical quest, in the history he discerns, in the primal rage developed within his family with its rage, and in his fear of the gaps of history and relationships (and women). The resolution of the pain, the interpersonal knots, and the historical problems emerge almost most simultaneously, interdependently, precipitated by one another. The ending brings us to the birth of the narrative, the possible inception of new life, a new paternity, and an understanding of heroic suicide and spiritual birth. The hero, at least for the moment, succeeds in leaping the gaps between male and female, black and white, stories and history, past and present.

> Martin J. Gliserman. *Psychoanalysis, Language, and the Body of the Text* (Gainesville: University Press of Florida, 1996), pp. 150–54

BIBLIOGRAPHY
*South Street*, 1975; *The Chaneysville Incident*, 1981

# BRAND, Dionne (1953–)
## Trinidad

The collection of short stories *San Souci*, written between 1984 and 1988, pursues the narrative impulse to conventional communication, and [Brand's] early poetics begin to breathe more freely as the writer relaxes, albeit slightly, into prose. The stories present a mixture of voices or histories of the experiences of Black women in the Caribbean, and of those who have chosen to leave and go to Canada. The histories examine why they leave, looking at the structures and pressures of both societies, and why sometimes (rarely) the women return. These fables also look closely at the inhuman expectations of the people who employ the Black women, at the families they leave behind, the *other* children they care for instead, the abuse they receive, the fear they feel, their pride and the necessity / obstinacy of that pride. The writer makes her salient commentary on the cultures by taking epigrammatic density and extending a descriptive ground for it to build upon. The narrative structures are simple but the prose allows for an expansion of and anchoring in context. For example, 'Photograph' is a narrative excursion occasioned by looking at a faded photograph of her grandmother, which tersely put is saying that her grandmother acted as her mother for many years while her mother was 'away' earning money, and that on her mother's return her grandmother soon died. Phrased epigrammatically it is a story about the complications of familial love and power. The epigrammatic here is extended by a sequence of recountings, remembered incidents that emerge through analogical links. These inner stories or memories are not cumulative in the narrative sense; they do not lead to a conclusion about guilt or blame. Rather their procession accretes a verbal and literary density, in the initial descriptions of the speaker's relationship with her grandmother, that is disturbed and contorted upon the return of the mother. The resulting responses of both speaker and reader are complicated, intentionally and purposively difficult to analyse.

Similar expansive remedies of epigrammatic density are made possible throughout *Sans Souci*. The story 'I used to like the Dallas Cowboys' has a terse structure that runs like this: The speaker as a young girl used to like the Dallas Cowboys American football team, partly because football was *not* the local sport of cricket and partly because her in-depth knowledge of football proved her worth in a man's world. But she is later in Grenada at the time of the invasion and she recognizes in the American war machine many of the elements of the American football team. The concentration, the end-game direction, the ruthless beauty of their occupation with the game, all are transferred onto the precision of the military operation. The story then becomes a study in sport and war; it foregrounds the brief epigrammatic structure and contextualizes it, thereby regrounding the potential for cliché in the contingencies of an immediate rereading. The reader is encouraged to invert the parallels back onto the questions raised by cricket, which is the slave-master's game, played always at the ready for a riot, as well as onto the young girl's attempts to compete within a man's world. What happens is that the image begins to carry the larger ideological allusions along with it and the reader learns the social references.

These stories are skilfully executed essays in history, written to present the problems of marginalization as social and political, and as something that one must act on from the ground up. Their activity is underwritten by Brand's experience of grassroots community work, her writing on racism, and her studies at OISE. Her work is firmly assertive with an anger that readers either immediately recognize or need to make a place for: the necessity of voicing the fears, reactions, rejections that are tied up in the Black experience of Canada's racism.

*University of Toronto Quarterly.* 62, 2 (Winter 1992–93),
pp. 256–81

Several of Brand's most powerful images focus on the ability of the mind to delve into memory and invoke images that destroy and illumine. In "At the Lisbon Plate," the narrator's dreams contain fires that unleash global political revolutions and in "St. Mary's Estate" the narrator, in visiting the estate where her family worked as labourers, conjures an image of the still extant Great House and ignites it. These two brief examples highlight Brand's style that draws heavily on a woman's storytelling tradition to begin to refashion worlds disfigured by colonialism and neo-colonialism. . . .

["At the Lisbon Plate,"] explodes with postcolonial rage as Brand creates an iconoclastic revenge-seeking storyteller magician, a witch-figure who tells the collective story of the lost female and slave past while she comments upon contemporary social conditions that continue past oppression.

Similar to Jean Rhys's heroines, who often find solace in bars where they are anonymous and exiled, the narrator finds that the Lisbon Plate, a Portuguese bar located in the Kensington district of Toronto, is the perfect location for colonial exile. Here she can find

"refuge." This is where she "can be invisible or, if not invisible, at least drunk." In this setting, Brand brings the colonized, exiled woman in contact with the colonial forces that transfigured Trinidad and Tobago. In various ways, the setting is the meeting place for the Spaniards, French, and English, the forces that interchangeably conquered and ruled Trinidad and Tobago. It is also the nexus where the colonized woman discursively destroys and transforms the colonial past and acknowledges continuing oppression.

Even though the narrator feels "invisible," she cannot escape her colonial past and the past of her ancestors. The bar is owned by Rosa who had lived in "Angola and Mozambique." Rosa appears "accustomed to Black women" and she looks on the narrator "colonially." Patrons of the bar are men who are emblematic remnants of the colonial past: "Whip-handlers, skin-dealers," and a professor whose ethno-gaze classifies and appropriates native art. . . .

In addition to hearing stories of past colonial atrocities, the narrator hears contemporary stories of oppression that she feels Maria de Consecao, another bar patron, wanted to "get rid of." One story that Maria tells is the story of Rosa's brother, the priest who "gunned down" women and children in Angola. The narrator is also bitter when she sees in the newspaper that the press has "gone wild" about the murder of one Polish priest when, simultaneously, countless, but uncounted, "African laborers got killed and, besides that, fell to their deaths from third-floor police detention rooms in Johannesburg" (106).

As the narrator is bombarded with stories of oppression, she becomes introspective and sees herself from the "third-floor window of the furniture store across from the bar". . . .

As the narrator sits in drunken introspection, looking at her face inscribed with the painful past, the fantastic further enters the story and the "ordinary" disappears. As she imagines looking at herself from the third-floor window, she notes that she (the narrator) looks

> like a woman I met many years ago. As old as the dirt, she sat at the roadside waiting her time, an ivory pipe stuck in her withered lips and naked as she was born. That woman had stories, more lucid than mine and more frightening for that.

Indicating that this old woman unearths the buried past and "explodes" colonialism, the narrator describes her as the "old gravedigger"—whose "bones were black powder." This gravedigger returns to the Sargasso Sea every winter to "mine bones and suicides" (102), seemingly to "resurrect" the lives of the "living dead" buried in the landscape and the sea, those who have died but who cannot be obliterated from the land. This storytelling obeah woman, who has a "burning hand", promises the narrator her "memories and maps" and gives her a "juju belt full of perfidious mixtures, insolent smells and her secrets" (102), gifts that will provide the narrator with a way to subvert the Columbian era and to reach back to the Pre-Columbian past.

Although after the narrator meets and joins with the old "harridan," she warns the reader not to expect her storytelling to change, not to expect any old woman's tale, any "lies or fiction," the narrator's story becomes more magically fantastic after her encounter with the old woman. The narrator reveals the buried past and the conflict-fraught present as she tells the stories of various women in different eras: the story from the immediate past of her aunt who went mad from trying to pass by whitening her skin and masquerading as a Spanish woman, and the current story of her friend Elaine who thinks the "motherland is Africa" and who wants to be a "queen in ancient Mali" (99). Each of these stories reveals a Caribbean search for identity. . . .

The old woman's story that reveals the buried past and conflict-ridden present also transforms this fragmentation as it reveals it. The boundaries between the narrator and protagonist begin to dissolve as the narrator starts to resemble the old "bag of dust.". . .

Acting like a revenge-seeking riverain goddess, an ancient goddess of Africa, the old woman plans a course of retribution for colonial sins that first involves storytelling. Before participating in the old hag's plan, the narrator retells the [Albert Camus] narrative of the *Outsider*, from the Arab's point of view, an action that, like the stories of the insignificant women, reveals the perspective of the conquered. Her retelling of the story of the nameless Arab, now called Ahmed, shot by the European, first shows that "killing an Arab, pumping successive bullets into an Arab, is not and never has been an alienating experience for a European." It also demonstrates that the ultimate means of alienation is the murder of an individual of the "other" race and not the existential suffering of the white male.

After this retelling of the colonizer's discourse, the old hag gives the "go ahead" for her plan which represents a ritual retribution for colonial sins. The narrator and the old woman gather together all the oppressive colonial forces: the big white boy, the professor, the whiphandlers, the skindealers, and the moneychangers who frequent the Lisbon Plate. After defacing and "chewing" on the statue of Cristobal Colon that has been worshipped by the colonizers, the narrator/old woman chains her captives to the statue and sprays them with "oceans of blood" (114), the blood of generations of tortured colonized. The narrator recognizes the sins of Columbus, which Eric Williams reports included the maiming and murder of Amerindians. After the colonizing forces "choke" on the blood, the old woman and her companion, the narrator, "marinate" them in hot peppers, ironically acting like the cannibals the Europeans claimed the Caribs to be, and the old woman "laughs until her belly burst." This fantastical retribution . . . represents both a violent overturning of the colonizer's institutions and a visionary violence that unleashes the anger and pain that postcolonial societies still experience. Through drawing on a dissolution of boundaries inherent in the storytelling process, this narrative transforms the individual listener into a participant in the storytelling process.

In "Blossom: Priestess of Oya, Goddess of Winds, Storms, and Waterfall," Brand continues to express the rage of a woman oppressed by sexism and colourism, but in this magical story, she begins the process of creating, out of the ashes of this raging fire, a new narrative for postcolonial peoples. While not specifically about the storytelling process, "Blossom" is concerned with the way rage leads to a union with a transformative deity that results in a revised vision of the world. Working like the storyteller. . . . Brand begins to refashion the way the postcolonial subject conceives the world.

While "Blossom" and "At the Lisbon Plate" draw heavily on the destructive/enlightening aspects of the storytelling tradition, "Photograph" emphasizes the nurturing/protective aspects—the "protection and the cure" that forges a women's storytelling community.

In "Photograph," the grandmother, a figure of "ancestral story magic," is a storyteller who teaches her granddaughters how to cope with both tangible and intangible worlds, the intangible spirit world that Jamaica Kincaid notes was a reality in Caribbean life. . . .

The narrator of "Photograph" describes the storytelling atmosphere in which the granddaughters receive vital information about dealing with this world. . . .

The complex ritual is related in a way that combines practicality with immediate oral performance and sensual pleasure. The narrator also relates that the grandmother sat in her rocking chair, "the seat bursting from the weight of her hips," and spun stories that "languished over the darkness whose thickness we felt. . . . Some nights the darkness . . . would be suffused by the perfume of lady-of-the-night". The grandmother's stories, then, are associated with the fullness of the grandmother's body, and are transformed into material objects that float in the air around the children and create a way to control and manipulate the world.

The grandmother and her story become the world in which the children live. The narrator notes: "We dreamed in my grandmother and we woke up in her, bleary-eyed and gesturing for her arm, her elbows, her smell." Boundaries of "western" reality do not exist in this world, where the living and dead, the conscious and unconscious meet, and where waking and dreaming worlds intermingle. The story sucked at the grandmother's breast, the story which "suffused the night" and hung in the air like a sensual blanket, acts as both a protection and a cure. In passing it on to her granddaughters, the grandmother ensures the perpetuation and remembrance of the story of the people.

Brand's "words that burn," that "destroy and lighten," also "protect and cure." These narratives "destroy" and illumine colonial discourses that fuel the continuation of colonialism and neocolonial enterprises. In creating fictions that draw on the storytelling tradition, Brand discursively connects, across the imposed boundaries of time and geography, women and all postcolonial peoples; she also joins other writers in transforming the vision of the postcolonial subject. In hearing tales that are a "protection and a cure," the postcolonial subject begins to move closer to an era of true decolonization in which racism, colourism, sexism, and suffering are not accepted norms. In lighting "dreams that contain fires," Brand works discursive magic and offers hope to postcolonial worlds still burning in an inferno of oppression.

Kathleen J. Renk. *Ariel: A Review of International English Literature.* 27, 4 (October 1996), pp. 97–109

*In Another Place, Not Here*, Dionne Brand's first novel, explores the relationships between three women, set successively on an unnamed Caribbean island (Brand is from Trinidad), in Toronto, and on another nameless island, where an abortive "revolution" is crushed by American military intervention. Grenada, where Brand went in 1983 to "fling myself at the hope that the world could be upturned" (*Bread Out of Stone*, 1994), comes to mind. Inevitably, therefore, some readers will interpret the novel as fictionalized "herstory": most will find in it the anguish of colonial and postcolonial history, intensely projected through the three women's consciousness.

The first voice is that of Elizete, who has been a child abandoned by family, grudgingly adopted, then married off to an abusive husband. Though uneducated, she has developed a critical inner voice, for despised women—she desires to appease the spirit of her slave ancestor Adela, whose "sold" fate is linked with hers as oppressed woman and wife. Elizete's personal liberation, of dignity and sex, is promised through sudden attraction to Verlia, portrayed as "flying," "always coming apart"; but if their emotional and physical love redeems Elizete from negative "rage," Verlia's passionate revolutionary love divides them: "that was Verlia' [sic] love, the people buried in the field"—next to the sugar mills. . . .

Half the narrative is Verlia's, articulating an evolution and commitment seemingly close to Brand's and to many of her generation. This voice is fully convincing, whereas Elizete's fluctuates, sometimes falsified by authorial language and imagery. The young Verlia, rebelling against her people's resignation and internalized rage, must fly into and against the oppressive world out "there." When that becomes "here," after a discouraging encounter with Sudbury relatives anxiously seeking invisible "equality," she flies to Toronto's larger black community, to "grow into her Black Self": "she wants to be the kind of Black girl that is dangerous. Big-mouthed and dangerous." Self-hate is supplanted by hatred for whites: "She lives in this city for years without talking personably to a single white person or having one talk to her."

Verlia's loves, above all for "earthbound" Elizete—embodiment of the lost, loved place—are sacrificed to the "crucible of practice," the failed island revolutions precipitating her into "some other place . . . less tortuous, less fleshy." Between "retaliation or self-hatred" this relentless novel suggests no middle ground; yet Brand's "anointment" by a major publisher, for a novel whose writing was subsidized by a grant from the Ontario Arts Council, central to that "culture . . . organized around 'whiteness,'" must be bittersweet. Is it in Brand's eyes a form of appropriation she has turned to advantage? Surely it does not mean, against the novel's drift, that, in bell hooks's words, "white people can be anti-racist" (*Killing Rage*, 1995)? It is more fitting, perhaps, since Brand quotes Fanon on white transgression, to quote his *Black Skin, White Masks*. "I have no wish to be the victim of the fraud of a black world. My life should not be devoted to drawing up a balance-sheet of negro values."

There is no white world, there is no white ethic, any more than there is a white intelligence. There are in every part of the world men who search. And women too.

Michael Thorpe. *World Literature Today.* 71, 2 (Spring 1997), pp. 446–47

In her documentary films, Dionne Brand underscores the necessity for communal cohesion in and among Afro-Caribbean women and among women generally in the Canadian context. Her films exemplify the ways in which we might potentially defy barriers of race, class, sexuality, and nationality among ourselves through their presentation of candid interviews with Black women that reveal their struggles against multiple oppression in this alien landscape. Brand seeks, as she does in *No Burden to Carry*, to preserve the marginalized histories of Black women in Canada as well as those of Black women in the Caribbean at the same time she inserts her own life experiences in the public record. For Brand, it is clear that the personal, the political, and the historical are inextricably linked. . . .

*Older, Stronger, Wiser* (1989) is a short film, which showcases the lives of five Black women in Ontario. Each of these women has had to survive by working in various jobs, from domestic work, to farming, to politics. They have striven to better the lives of younger

generations of Black women by involving themselves in the struggle for Black rights in Canada and creating opportunities for change. Says Brand, in her narration, "If labor outside the home took the measure of these women's lives, leadership in the community was imperative.". . .

Dionne Brand's first film had a great impact in Black Canadian communities, as I noted when I attended a special screening of *Older, Stronger, Wiser* in Halifax, Nova Scotia in 1990. After Brand's brief introduction, a packed room of predominantly Black Haligonians viewed the film. I was surprised that so many of us had gathered to see a short film, a documentary at that, and that three generations of Nova Scotians were in attendance—the elderly, the middle-aged, the very young. As the film played, I heard many sighs of recognition, saw nods of approval, and the absorption of the engaged. I sat at the back of the room, not wanting to be too close to the screen in order to avoid showing disappointment, if I should feel any. But I was far from being disappointed and observed both the success of Brand's vision of rewriting history with our own words and the eagerness of the audience members to share their own experiences with Brand as well as with one another following the screening. Some women in the audience spoke of how they found the images of the Black women on the screen representative of their own life experiences; women behind me and in front of me leaned toward younger women and children to say, "Yes, I was in service and that was how it was." The experience for me was overwhelming. . . .

I was surprised to find out, years later, when reading "Bread Out of Stone" (1990), that the story behind the making of Brand's film was as heartbreaking as the Black women's stories she showcased. She writes in this essay of editing her film, "By now it's going on three years and it is actually torture, and I ask myself why did I start all this at all. Something about recovering history, history only important to me and women like me, so I couldn't just drop it, no matter how long it took". Of course, I should not have been surprised.

Brand's essay recounts the arduous process of turning the oral histories of Black women into a film and of how affected she was by her experiences with racism/sexism and with the homophobia that surrounded her as she brought the film into being. She remembers being asked by a white woman whether she thought of herself as "Black or woman," as if for a Black woman, the two identities could be separable. . . .

Brand's essay poignantly describes the choices that face a variety of Afro-Caribbean women in Canada struggling to affirm their own identities against the usual racial and sexist stereotypes that dominate their existence. She describes the resistance she encounters in areas where Black people, and Black women in particular, have been told they have no right to create a revolution, especially out of words and strips of film. Black women in Canada are continually told, as has been my experience as well, that they have no right to their own voices at the same time they are forced to survive by making the world habitable for others as cleaning women, child caretakers, office workers, cooks, and so on. . . .

Brand is suspect simply because she is a woman making a film about women. "Women are taught to abandon each other to the suffering of their sex, most of all Black women who have the hard white world in front of us so much the tyranny of sex is a small price, or so we think," writes Brand. For the Black woman, survival in a world that places our race before our sex while exploiting both often results in the decay of bonds between us: as women, we do not trust each other because we are told daily to pretend that we have no sex, or that we are ''superwomen,'' or that being Black means that we can only hold allegiances to Black men who (we are told) are far more oppressed than we are as (Black) women. . . . Homophobia surfaces from this divisive distrust. Brand continues: ''To prove that they are good women the conversation singes the borders of lesbian hate . . . plays at the burned edges, firing each other to the one point of unity between Black and white women—fear, contempt for women who love women''. Taught to fear each other, the women Brand describes form bridges out of contempt. Brand, like Lorde in her ''The Uses of Anger,'' suggests that bridges can alternatively be built out of understanding for the dis-similarities in our lives, as each of us struggles to survive in the face of a mysogynistic, racist, and homophobic patriarchal world order. By recuperating the lives of the Black women who created the paths on which we now wander, by affirming the experiences of our own individual travels, and by working together to define our own identities, we move closer to the bridge that will take us home. In this process, we enact the principles of Afro-Caribbean diasporic feminism in paying attention to those markers of status (race, sex, class, sexuality, and so on), which delimit the quality of our existence in this world, and move more swiftly toward a transformative progress that will better the condition of Black women's lives and of all others concurrently. By focusing on our personal existence and politicizing the parameters of that existence, we actively transform the terms of our exile and bring our alienation to an end.

> Myrian J. A. Chancy. *Searching for Safe Spaces: Afro-Caribbean Women Writers in Exile* (Philadelphia: Temple University Press, 1997)

*In Another Place, Not Here,* Dionne Brand's first novel tells the story of Elizete and Verlia, two Caribbean-born women, who meet on an unnamed island and enter into a brief, deeply sensual affair. Elizete is a rural sugarcane worker on the island of her birth. Verlia, who is educated and urban, fled the Caribbean for Canada as a teenager and returns years later to organize rural workers and take part in political revolution.

Brand's evocation of these women's lives depends less on the scaffolding of external event than on the distinctive rhythms of their speech and the looped paths of memory Divided in two parts, the novel first follows Elizete's journey from home to Canada and then charts Verlia's passage from the Caribbean to Toronto and back again, a return driven not just by political idealism but also by the missed taste and scent of tamarinds. Throughout, Brand employs a variety of fictional techniques. With hallucinatory verve, she pulls us between present and past, first person and third, incorporating voices that range from Elizete's potent island dialect to the terse, lucid diction of Verlia's diary entries.

For Elizete, Verlia becomes the catalyst who propels her out of her circumscribed existence: days in the fields, nights submitting to sex with a man named Isaiah. When Verlia disappears—she is last seen leaping from a cliff in a hail of gunfire—Elizete travels north to Toronto to search for some trace of her lover's former life.

Brand, who has written several highly acclaimed volumes of peotry was born in Trinidad and has lived in Canada since 1970. Like the Antigua born writer Jamaica Kincaid, she explores the political and psychological transit between the Caribbean and North America and, in the process, gives expression to the complicated negotiations of those whose interior landscape encompass both island and continent.

In Elizete, Brand offers us a character whose most urgent need is to acquire the words to describe the place in which she finds herself, as a means of claiming her history and making her own story real. As a child, Elizete was given away by her family to be raised by a meanspirited woman whose ancestor, Angela, was forcibly brought to the island from Africa. Adela was ''grieving, bad for where she came from,'' Elizete says. In despair and protest, Adela refused to learn the names of the plants around her, or even to name her own children. She called the island ''Nowhere,'' Elizete says. ''She insist so much is nowhere, she gone blind with not seeing.''

Both countering and appropriating Adela's history, Elizete invents a private language for the world she observes: ''tear up cloth flower, stinking fruit tree, draw blood bush monkey face flowers'' When she arrives, in Toronto, Elizete confronts another nowhere that she, too, cannot see clearly. The black realities of life as a black woman and illegal immigrant reach us through this blurred lens. Brand vividly conveys the impression of the city's wide streets and malls floating just out of reach.

By contrast, Verlia had embraced Toronto years earlier as the place where she would recreate herself. Politics—the black power movement of the 1970s—became her means of reinvention and also a way to slough off the weight of historical and familial suffering. Her yearning to transform herself is partly an attempt to escape a legacy of grief and fear. . . .

Passionate in its attention to emotional nuance and visual detail, *In Another Place, Not Here* weds beauty and a fierce intelligence in a work that offers a syncretic and multiple sense of place.

> Catherine Bush. *New York Times Book Review* (January 4, 1998), p. 12

BIBLIOGRAPHY
*Fore Day Morning*, 1978; *Earth Magic*, 1980; *Primitive Offensive*, 1982; *Winter Epigrams and Epigrams to Ernesto Cardenal in Defense of Claudia*, 1983; *Chronicles of the Hostile Sun*, 1984; *Sans Souci, and Other Stories*, 1989; *No Language Is Neutral*, 1990; *Bread Out of Stone*, 1994; *In Another Place, Not Here*, 1997; *Land to Light On*, 1997; *At the Full and Change of the Moon*, 1999

# BRATHWAITE, Edward Kamau (1930–)

## Barbados

West Indian poetry has suffered in locally edited anthologies from a total absence of critical standards. In fact, apart from the Martinique-based Césaire, who still awaits a good translation, there has up till now been virtually only Walcott. In the circumstances, perhaps, it is scarcely surprising, though set against West Indian prose and the liveliness of the best Calypso performers like Lord Beginner and Mighty Sparrow, disappointing. Neither the rich raciness of Caribbean idioms nor the spectacular conjunctions of visual images seem to have got into West Indian poetry, which as a genre exudes a technical timidity and general atmosphere of piety totally at odds with its political and social character.

Edward Brathwaite, in his *Rights of Passage*, makes an ambitious attempt to redress the balance. Eighty-six pages long, and the first part of a trilogy, it describes, in a variety of styles, a kind of double pilgrimage, personal and evolutionary; in private terms, the poet's travels from his birthplace to England and America before his final return home, in historical terms the long climb from slavery to independence.

It is altogether an impressive effort. . . . Making use of work-songs and blues, and alternating dense descriptive passages with short-lined and sharp résumés of local incident, Brathwaite builds up a coherent picture of contemporary Caribbean life. A Barbadian, he manages to achieve a balanced perspective without losing any of the historic thrust or sacrificing the native melancholy and nostalgia that underlie all West Indian exuberance. His poetic drive cannot always prevent drops into flatness but usually the sheer evocative power of place-names, and the sense of communities sustained by the shared rhythms of poverty, work and racial memory, keep the poem afloat.

Alan Ross. *London*. March 1967, pp. 96–97

[*Masks*] is the second in what is planned to be a trilogy. The first one was *Rights of Passage*. *Masks* deals with [Brathwaite's] eight-year sojourn in Ghana. By theme, idiom and rhythm he shows what excellence can emerge from an honest awareness and utilisation of one's inheritance. Even where the inheritance is on hand, Africa. He has done what other black writers have done, or tried, or should try, to do but never succeeded so well. This includes everyone from Césaire and Senghor to the contemporary young crop. I refer to, first, acceptance of Africa—our shame, our glories, past and present—not in defense or aggression, but quietly, as being us and all that is us: and that it is out of this that anything meaningful can come, including our "contribution to a universal culture." This is the awareness of the reality contained in his lines. . . .

There is a touching reverence in Edward Brathwaite for African usages, and this is quite obvious in his lines on libations and the sacrifice. However, what is really overwhelming about his poetic genius is what he makes English do for him. His language is sensitive to his awareness and his moods. . . .

His totally skilful use of the one African language he understands, Akan, in combination with English, makes some of us ashamedly envious and jealous. Naturally, non-Akan speakers, African and otherwise, would find the sections in the collection which are almost written entirely in Akan slightly irritating. But the book contains nothing but that which is alive and breathing, and anyone who cares would on second and third reading (which is only when it's possible to enjoy any poetry) find that the Akan bits, even when not understood literally, add to the beauty of the whole.

Ama Ata Aidoo. *West Africa*. September 21, 1968, p. 1099

Whereas Walcott is centrally concerned with Caribbean man, with his present and his island world, Brathwaite is haunted by a vision of the historic destiny of the negro race, not only in the Caribbean but everywhere. His poem [*Rights of Passage*] begins in the Sahara, all images of drought and sharp glitter, then moves into the damp silence of the forests, the savage encounter with the armed

intruders, the enslavement and the passage to the New World—the last a literal image of hell. Later it picks up the cyclical rhythm which seems to dominate the literature of the islands, the cycle of Discovery, Departure and Return upon which Book One of the present work is based. But Brathwaite's discovery of the new island home lacks the joy which Walcott imparts to it. The negro islander soon finds himself facing a new exile, to the urban slums and savage discrimination of America and England. Finally he returns to the islands, only to confront once more their poverty, hopelessness and squalor. The long shadow of the U.S. Marines now lies over the whole archipelago, inhibiting the process of revolution which can alone redeem them.

In his later poem *Masks*, Brathwaite does chronicle a kind of African homecoming, a personal exploration of what Africa was and is. But that poem . . . also ends upon a note of departure. The historical severance from Africa was, he implies, a final one. The West Indian can revisit it, draw strength and inspiration from it, but cannot, in the fullest sense, return.

Where Walcott, poet of seascape, rock and sunlight, cries "home is here!", Brathwaite, poet of voyages, train-whistles and quaysides, replies, "home is nowhere!" . . . If Walcott shows us how Caribbean man may learn to know and love his island, Brathwaite reminds us why he so often has to leave it. [1969]

Gerald Moore. *The Chosen Tongue* (New York: Harper & Row, 1970), pp. 28–29

Much of [Brathwaite's] poetry, especially in *Islands* and *Masks*, is an attempt to document in verse the historical experience of tribal Africa and of the deracinated African in the New World. When Brathwaite is successful a peculiar thing happens; not only is history compressed into poetry, but poetry finds its fulfilment in history. By this I mean that the poetry is so much an abstract of racial and historical experience, that significant events from contemporary history seem daily to reinforce and fulfil the poetry which then derives extra value from the hard clear light which it casts not only on the colonial past, but on our present historical moment. . . .

Brathwaite illustrates that the Black West Indian like his American counterpart does have an exceedingly rich, or at least a potentially rich, identity, but it is buried under centuries of slavery, colonialism and the self-contempt which goes with these. This is perhaps why *Islands* is saturated with the idea of death and rebirth. Brathwaite sees us as celebrating these two things in our every action. Death and rebirth are of course analogous to slavery and rebellion, or slavery and the independence which comes only when the slave consciously acts to free himself. Independence, like identity, cannot be given, it can only be asserted. So Brathwaite uses everything, Limbo, Cricket, politics, pocomania, steel-band, carnival, the wake, to explore these related themes of death and rebirth, slavery and rebellion. He seems to see us as perpetually wavering between the two states, always in danger of being sucked back into the womb-grave of the slave ship's hold.

G. Rohlehr. *Literary Half-Yearly*. July 1970, pp. 171–72, 175

Brathwaite, who is the foremost poet of the English-speaking Caribbean and at least in some sense a revolutionary, is never shrill, is always keen to the pathos of his people's plight, yet the basic

exuberance of his feeling cannot be doubted. In part it is revolutionary optimism, in part a closeness to his sources in folk culture.
Brathwaite has said that the chief literary influence on his work has
been the poetry of T. S. Eliot, but if this is so it has been an
influence almost entirely limited to matters of organization and
structure, and perhaps to Eliot's manner of rhyming, though this
could have come from anywhere. In texture, in verbal technique, in
almost everything, nothing could be further from Eliot's poetry
than Brathwaite's.

Brathwaite has made his reputation on three long poems, *Rights
of Passage*, *Masks*, and *Islands*. Now they have been published in
one volume, *The Arrivants: A New World Trilogy*, and it is a book
everyone should read. Brathwaite uses many voices, ranging from
standard English to dialects of several kinds, and in many rhythms,
from subdued free cadence to calypso. Not all passages are equally
successful; sometimes his jazz tempos remind us too much of
[Vachel] Lindsay's ''Congo'' or his dialect slips too far toward the
type of Auden's ballads. But in general he has been remarkably
successful in reproducing black speech patterns, both African and
Caribbean, in English syntax, using the standard techniques of
contemporary poetry, and he has been equally successful in suggesting to an international audience the cultural identities and
attitudes of his own people.

Hayden Carruth. *Hudson Review*. Summer 1974, p. 318

[Edward Kamau] Brathwaite's trilogy, *Rights of Passage*, *Masks*,
and *Islands*, constitutes an epic of sorts on the black West Indian's
history and culture. . . .

*Rights of Passage* concentrates on blacks in the Americas,
moving from the West Indies to the United States and back. The
second book, *Masks*, reverses the Middle Passage voyage by
returning the reader to Africa. Finally, *Islands* is both a return to the
contemporary West Indies and a symbolic retracing of the original
voyage of enslavement. The odyssey or journey motif of the trilogy
dramatizes the nature and function of the artistic imagination in the
black experience: art is a journey through time as well as space; it is
an act of memory, discovering and imitating the cycles of history,
and in the process both creating and demonstrating a heightened
new awareness of the past in the present. Consequently the work
song with which *Rights of Passage* opens exemplifies art as an act
of memory. . . .

[*Masks*] is also rooted in the strategy of developing a full
awareness through the cyclical course of memory and art. Here the
persistent journey motif describes the West Indian's cultural pilgrimage to West Africa. That pilgrimage is a literal and physical
one. But it is also psychic, linking the West Indian's modern return
to his Akan beginnings with the period in which his ancestors were
torn from West Africa by the slave trade and with that even earlier
period when those precolonial ancestors sought new homes for the
first time in West Africa. The total effect of this simultaneous
perception of time cycles is to reemphasize time itself as an
essentially cyclical, or circular whole. It is therefore appropriate
that the work opens with a ceremony of libation that celebrates the
cycle of time in the year that has ''come round / again.'' Moreover,
this impression of a cyclical wholeness also rests on the continental
dimensions of Africa, the cultural affinities between its distinctive
regions, and most important that cyclical perception of time and
experience which the poet shares with his Africans: ''all Africa / is
one, is whole.''. . .

The circular movement of art and memory also takes us back, in
the other direction, to the Caribbean starting point of *Rights of
Passage*. And this return is the main subject of *Islands*, the final
book of the trilogy. The major divisions of this work are centered
on the growing consciousness with which the West Indian returns
from the memories of, and journey to, Africa. . . . ''New World''
therefore represents both the New World ambience of the West
Indian and the new possibilities that are inherent in the West
Indian's recreated consciousness; ''Limbo'' recalls the legendary
roots of the dance as an exercise for slaves immediately after
disembarkation from the slaveships, and in so doing it celebrates
the West Indian endurance despite slavery; ''Rebellion'' offers
reminders of the old plantation systems, emphasizes their continuation under new, postcolonial disguises, into the present, and by
virtue of those reminders its title becomes a prophecy or threat;
''Possession'' picks up the rebellious, transforming energies of
''Rebellion'' by offering the contrast between islanders as possessions and islands as symbols of a new dignity or integrity: ''possession'' as spiritual possession (in the manner of folk religions from
Africa and the West) therefore celebrates the new, aggressive
consciousness within Brathwaite's West Indian. And in a fitting
conclusion to the circular structure of the trilogy as a whole, the
carnival dance of ''Beginnings'' recalls the folk songs and dance
with which *Rights of Passage* opens: in this concluding section the
dance celebrates the beginnings of a national consciousness that
has been derived from the total experience, or historical ''rites'' of
the Middle Passage.

Lloyd W. Brown. *West Indian Poetry* (Boston: Twayne,
1978), pp. 140–42, 149–50, 153

In his early work Brathwaite conceives of the poetic imagination as
a superior way of perceiving the world. The poetic reconstruction
of the world could redeem reality from its fallen state. In [an] early
poem in *Other Exiles* Brathwaite expresses the need for ''words to
refashion futures like a healer's hand.'' The same line recurs in
[*The Arrivants: A New World Trilogy*] . . . as the poet is attempting
to liberate the region from its sterile fallen state. The poet's public
voice has its roots in this early recognition of the role of art as a
means of discovering unconscious figurative meanings behind the
concrete and the visible. What was essentially a private literary
quest for the young Brathwaite later becomes the point of departure
for an aesthetic exploration of the Caribbean that transcends the
historical stereotype of pluralism and fragmentation.

Even though Brathwaite situates himself in a new vanguard of
West Indian writing, his actual career and experiences are not
unlike those of the generation of the ''first phase.'' Born in
Barbados in 1930 he follows the familiar pattern of metropolitan
exile and an eventual return to the West Indies. He receives his
higher education in Cambridge in the early 1950s and becomes in
his own words ''a roofless man of the world'' before returning to the
Caribbean. As is the case with most artists who underwent this
sequence of experiences, the odyssey served to heighten the poet's
sensitivity to the dilemma of alienation which plagued West Indian
intellectuals in exile.

During this period of exile Brathwaite's work reflects his
various experiences. For instance, ''The day the first snow fell'' is
basically about the poet's disappointment at discovering his estrangement in Britain from a world which he thought he could
possess. The frustration normally expected at this point in the

career of the exiled artist, when all worlds appear strange to him, never really emerges in Brathwaite's work. We have an important departure from the sense of dispossession that comes with exile, in the poet's eight-year stay in Ghana [from 1955 to 1962]. It is here that he discovers the sense of the sacred so crucial to the poetic imagination. He discovers a world which he cannot adopt but one which seems to retain a communion with the mysterious and numinous which is absent in the historically disadvantaged New World. His awareness of the customs and language of the Ghanaian people is seen in his adaptation of *Antigone* to a Ghanaian context in *Odale's Choice*. This does not represent an original project since the adaptation of classical drama to local situations was not unknown, but it does show a closeness to the environment in which he found himself, which is central to his dramatization of this experience in his trilogy.

> J. Michael Dash. In Bruce King, ed. *West Indian Literature*
> (Hamden, Connecticut: Archon Books, 1979), pp. 214–15

*The Arrivants* trilogy is essentially a record of the stages of Brathwaite's life from feelings of exile, through the years in Africa, to the discovery of his African heritage in the New World and the resulting sense of community. It is a creation of a mythology for the black West Indian to replace earlier images of the self created by white prejudice, colonialism, and European history. *Rights of Passage* . . . is a *Wasteland* based on the various roles and postures ("Uncle Tom," "Spider," "the Negro") of the descendants of Africans taken to the New World. It is partly a lament for a lost world: "We kept / our state on golden stools—remember?" It begins with an evocation of the past: "Drum skin whip / lash" and examines the life of the black man in the Americas and Europe.

The second part of the trilogy, *Masks*, celebrates the life Brathwaite found in Africa, particularly among the Akan in Ghana. Africa is a land of history remembered, music, dance, ancestors, customs and especially religion. The poem "The Making of the Drum" concerns the sacrifices that sacramentalize ordinary objects in African life. [The second section of the poem] "The Barrel of the Drum" is a catechism praising the holiness of the wood from which the drum will be made. [Sections 3–5] "The Two Curved Sticks of the Drummer," "Gourds and Rattles," [and] "The Gong-Gong" are among the various musical objects given a religious significance. The "Path-finders" poems treat of African heroes and places of the past. [The "Limits" poems recall] the movements of the West African tribes from their supposed home in Egypt, across the Sudan, until they settle on the coast, where the voyage to the New World and slavery will begin. "The Return" [poems treat] of Brathwaite himself in Africa. . . .

The poems in *Islands* . . . reject the imitation of European culture in the West Indies and treat of restoration, the recognition of African roots which will contribute towards the making of a new authenticity in the New World.

> Bruce King. *The New English Literatures: Cultural Nation-*
> *alism in a Changing World* (New York: St. Martin's Press,
> 1980), pp. 131–33

The load of black experience which is central to the thought in Brathwaite's trilogy as well as in his other volumes, *Other Exiles*, *Days & Nights*, *Black + Blues*, and his more recent volume *Mother*

*Poem*, is conveyed through sets of archetypal patterns which center around the sea as a redemptive as well as exiling elemental force, the journey which is at once specific and universal, and the earth as the base of cultural roots, the womb of life and the ultimate abode to which we retire at death. The result of this schematization of symbols and images is the constantly compelling concatenation of antithetical references to life and death, dryness and wetness, departure and arrival, exile and rediscovery, disintegration and restoration, hope and despair.

> Samuel Omo Asein. *World Literature Written in English.*
> 20, 1 (Spring 1981), p. 100

The first significations of the centrality of African deities in Brathwaite's poetry occur in his reference to fire and its associated images in *Rights of Passage*. . . . The recurrent images of fire in this first book point the way forward to the motif of Ogun (the Yoruba deity of war and creativity) in *Islands* while Anancy (the Akan creator god) who also becomes one of the prominent deities in the New World and, therefore, in *Islands*, is signalled through multifaceted allusions which recall the spider's (*anancy*) complex and intricate webs. Both Ogun and Anancy eventually emerge as the two presiding ancestral African deities in *Islands*, with the other African deities making infrequent but essential appearances. By choosing Ogun, the warrior and craftsman, and Anancy, the cunning spinner, as the expressive images of the New World situation, Brathwaite leaves us in no doubt as to the fact that he is set to articulate the spirit of creative struggle which has enabled the New World African to cope with and even overcome the debilitating effects of transplantation and enslavement.

*Islands* opens with a consideration of godhood in the New World. In "Jah," the first poem in *Islands*, Brathwaite focuses on both Western and African concepts of God and, in the process, establishes the tangible physical and subliminal links between Africa and the New World. He borrows organic and musical images (music is the intensive language of communication between man and the gods) to express these links: Nairobi's male elephant's trumpeting is taken up in the black music of Havana and Harlem; the orchestra of seven elephant-tusk horns used to relate history on state occasions in Africa (*Masks*) is echoed in the history-laden jazz of the black New World; and the slave ship's riggings are manifested in the new prisons of the steel bridges and skyscrapers of the white New World. The first part of this poem suggests that the Western god has become so debased and commercialized that he is synonymous with the cities' neon lights. The second part makes an almost equally devastating assessment of the African deities in the New World. In addition to being separated from Jah because there is "no sound . . . no ground to keep him down near the gods," Brathwaite suggests that the African deities "have been forgotten or hidden" because "the land has lost the memory of the most secret places." Anancy now prefers to peep "over the hills with the sunrise" and to "spin webs in the tree," and Ogun of the fiery temper is transformed into voiceless volcanoes. These views are, however, summations of the general views about African gods and cultures in the New World. Brathwaite is not necessarily in agreement and . . . he, at the worst, may be willing to concede only that the African deities are in a state of suspended animation. That he opens *Islands* with a consideration of the idea of godhead is in itself an indication that he considers it a very important index in any analysis of the New World African's psyche.

Funso Aiyejina. *World Literature Written in English.* 23, 2 (Spring 1984), pp. 398–99

For the poet Edward Brathwaite, himself a historian, history becomes a tool for the discovery of self. His trilogy, *The Arrivants*, focuses on the black man of the New World and defines his condition as "homeless" and "historyless." The European writers of West Indian history, far from having written for the black man, have vigorously suppressed his humanity and identity. Brathwaite is concerned therefore with the rediscovery of an African past and identity that will remove from the black man of the New World the sense of "loss" and dereliction which would be his lot from a different historical perspective.

The journey across Africa in *The Arrivants*, with its biblical echoes of the chosen people crossing the wilderness to the promised land, functions . . . by remaining, in image and symbol, central to our experience of literature. The African place names (Ougadongou, Chad, Timbuktu, Volta) ring like bells in the volume *Masks*, and create a sense of possession or repossession of a rich alternative historical reality. This sense is reinforced by rituals, such as the making of the drum, the dance of possession in "Adowa," the solemn dirge in Tano. . . .

History . . . which includes folk history and ritual, pervades Brathwaite's later volumes of poetry, imparting a distinct historical resonance to landscape, character and image in *Mother Poem* and *Sun Poem*. For Brathwaite, man's identity is determined by his past, but he must discover/re-create that past, rather than accept the crude "given" of the colonial tradition. In *Sun Poem* Brathwaite shows how this is accomplished, for even where the poetry appears lyrical and autobiographical, the historical resonances, as Gordon Rohlehr points out, are very much present.

Mark A. McWatt. *West Indian Literature and Its Social Context* (St. Michael, Barbados: Cave Hill, 1985), pp. 43–44

*Mother Poem* and *Sun Poem* are the first two poems in Edward Brathwaite's . . . poetic trilogy. Both poems are set in the post-Emancipation period on the island of Barbados. . . . Like *Rights of Passage*, *Masks*, and *Islands*—the poems of Brathwaite's first trilogy, *The Arrivants*—*Mother Poem* and *Sun Poem* are poems of multiple voices. *Mother Poem* traces the history of Barbados through the voices of working-class or folk women, a female slave, children, and a debt collector, agent of the capitalist merchant; these voices are interspersed with the at times ideologically committed descriptive, at times directly protesting voice of the visionary poet, evaluating the folk women's uncritical consumption of white bourgeois materialism, religion, and education (the last of these for their children), and the expedients associated with the socioeconomic conditions imposed on working-class married and family life by the plantation and its owner, the white mulatto merchant. The text is determined to give articulation to the often publicly silent dreaming of the folk women, to "slowly restore [their] silent gutters of word-fall" through the impersonations of art. *Sun Poem* traces the history of Barbados through the loss or perversion of male dreaming. The voices of the poem are many: the voice of the rainbow; the inner and speaking voices of Adam, the archetypal folk boy; the voices of Adam's sister, male playfellows and childhood sweetheart; the voice of an emasculated black male; the historical voices of a slaver and a follower of the slave rebellion leader, Bussa; and the at times ideologically committed descriptive, at times directly protesting voice of the visionary poet and historian. The poem carries in itself and in its connections with *Mother Poem* the implication that the plantation, the merchant, and female dreaming cause the loss or perversion of male dreaming and emasculation—as one male puts his dilemma in the poem: "i gettin smaller . . . is de sun dyein out of i vision." Both *Mother Poem* and *Sun Poem* close on a note of hope, with the rediscovery of the power of nam, the "soul, secret name, soul-source, connected with *nyam* (eat), yam (root food), *nyame* (name of god)," a rediscovery which the text insists will enable the present generations of black Bajans to find their Afro-West Indian roots, their folk/maroon heritage, and so become "the first potential parents" to "contain the ancestral house" threatened and made insecure by lack of solid foundations in the soil of landscape and history.

Sue Thomas. *Kunapipi.* 9, 1 (1987), pp. 33–34

Clearly the Afro-Caribbean writer who is most strongly influenced by black America is Edward Brathwaite. Born in Barbados and educated at Cambridge, he is a poet of international distinction. His formidable knowledge of the histories, cultures and literatures of the peoples of the African diaspora and his uncompromising cultural nationalism make him especially receptive to influences, both Afro-American and African. The elements of black American influence that are discernible in Brathwaite's poetry fall into two categories: allusions to aspects of Afro-American culture and incorporations of the blues forms and jazz techniques.

Brathwaite's intricately allusive poetry is replete with references to various aspects of black American culture, both classical and popular. A notable feature of his allusiveness is his frequent references to Afro-American cultural heroes. The evocations of those names not only constitute a leitmotif that reinforces his themes, but the individuals whose names are alluded to become symbols that undergird Brathwaite's concept of a Pan-African identity. For example, his anthology *Other Exiles*, has poems titled after Count Basie, Miles Davis, [John] Coltrane, and Charlie Parker; each of these poems provides a sensitive assessment of the titular hero's enriching contribution to the black musical tradition. To Brathwaite they are more than celebrities who represent the essence of black musical genius; they are spiritual guardians of the black civilization. In *Sun Poem*, for instance, he suggests that Aretha Franklin's voice, Coltrane's inventiveness, and Jesse Owens's athletic prowess are manifestations of Ogun, the Yoruba god of invention. In *X/Self*, his most recent volume of poetry, he has a poem titled "Julia." The title refers to the 1960s television series, "Julia," with Diahann Carroll, which was the first prime-time show in American television history with a black woman as a major character in a non-menial role. The poem contains allusions to Bill Cosby, [Muhammad] Ali, Tina Turner, the famed Apollo Theater of Harlem, and the Montgomery bus boycott that signaled the advent of the Civil Rights Movement in the South. In *The Arrivants* he employs innumerable Afro-American cultural referents—to Malcolm X, James Baldwin (whom he calls Jimmy Baldwin, with affectionate familiarity), Martin Luther King, Jr., Ralph Ellison, among many others.

Emmanuel S. Nelson. *Journal of American Culture.* 12, 4 (Winter 1989), pp. 55–56

In *Middle Passages*, as in much of the earlier work, it is not unexpected that Brathwaite would see the loss of self as the *X* or unknown quotient of personality; thus, the poetic effort becomes the dramatic quest to reclaim that self as personhood. In the end the *X* self becomes the dynamic and positive other half of the individual in the resulting flux originally cast in the form of placelessness: the void is then transformed through the sense of all the innate and inherent possibilities embedded in the human being as real *self* with one's dignity intact. Perhaps in so powerfully identifying this aspect of his poetic drive, Brathwaite curtails the purely intuitive self as imaginative expression. . . .

The various [poems] in *Middle Passages* attest to the range of history and ideas, beginning with the acknowledgment of language in "Word Making Man" and continuing with "Colombe," "Noom" (suggestive of African religion), "Duke" (Duke Ellington playing piano at seventy), "Flute(s)," "Veridian," "The Visibility Trigger," "How Europe underdeveloped Africa" (a familiar theme), "Stone" (for Mickey Smith, the dub poet), "The Sahell of Donatello," . . . "Soweto" (dedicated to the Mandelas), "Leopard," "Letter Sycorax," and "Irae." Although the sections are short, it is important to identify them as a way of tracing the organic poetic impulse, as the images flow and intertwine to reveal their inner selves through naming history with the voice of acknowledgment and protest.

Cyril Dabydeen. *World Literature Today.*, 2 (Spring 1993), p. 426

Brathwaite's second trilogy—*Mother Poem* (1977), *Sun Poem* (1982), and *X/Self* (1987)—centers around the island of Barbados, where he grew up. Brathwaite begins *Mother Poem* with an epigraph: "We're the first potential parents who can contain the ancestral house." It is from *The Whole Armour* (1962), a novel by Wilson Harris, who was a strong influence on Brathwaite in his early years as a poet. In a book of poems titled *Eternity to Season* (1954), Harris wrote of the exercise of the imagination as a weaving and unweaving of the self (and a convergence of linear and cyclical time), using as epigraph Penelope's account in the *Odyssey*: "In the daytime I would weave the mighty web and in the night unravel the same." . . . [The phrase] catches the indeterminacies of identity that Brathwaite cultivates in his work, usually by embracing the uncertainties and relativities of language. Brathwaite has often written about how West Indians have for so long had no language that derives from the experience of the land and of its people, and instead have had to rely on conventions that create discontinuities between experience and its expression or revelation in language. And so to make the connections possible he has developed strategies derived from the interactions of sound and sense and the patternings of speech and song. For example, in the following poem called "Nametracks" (from *Mother Poem*) he sets the proprieties of one type of language against the potentialities of another, in a voice that says "me" instead of "my," "mud," instead of "mother," and that also speaks the new word "nam."

The ancient mother who provides a kind of redemptive subversion here is Sycorax, Caliban's mother and Prospero's real antagonist, whose whispered words finally affirm who he really is ("you nam"), as the catlike images are transformed into "lion eye mane," the icon of Rastafarian pride, the conquering Lion of Judah.

*Sun Poem* moves from the landscape of Barbados to an account of the island turning around the poet's paternal ancestry. Among other things, it describes the familiar predicament of West Indians growing up in the 1930s and 1940s, "not knowing the names of our flowers and trees / scratchywhist womans tongue hogplum stinkin toe / we could only call our brothers robin hood or barnabas collins."

In the third book of the trilogy, *X/Self*, Brathwaite writes about spiritual discovery. As with many such adventures, this one begins with loss and bewilderment, a dark and negative time. The book opens with a question, posed in the epigraph (from an earlier poem by Brathwaite titled "The Dust," in *Rights of Passage*): "ev'rything look like it comin out wrong. / Why is dat? What it mean?"

*X/Self* tells of a journey home, a journey both geographical (from Africa and Europe to the West Indies) and psychological (from a diminished and distorted sense of self to a liberated one), and both linear and cyclical. There are accounts, occasionally polemical, about actions and events, causes and effects; and there are images of fulfilment and fatality, occasionally sentimental or melodramatic. All are represented in the journey that is *X/Self*.

The journey also portrays a movement from disbelief to belief in self and in society, as Brathwaite proposes what John Henry Newman once called a "grammar of assent," a way of getting from "no" to "yes," which is to say to an image of self (which for Newman was also an image of God) that can transcend the limitations of our everyday ways of seeing things and of talking about them.

The questing and questioning are obvious in the title itself, and in the use of the letter or prefix "x" in several of the individual poems. "X" has many associations, among them "x" as the unknown in the custom of mathematics. This fits with the riddling quality of the self that is at the center of the book. And there are further connotations, for "x" is routinely used in algebra both as an unknown—something you will discover; and as a variable, a symbol for whatever you want it to be—something you will invent, as it were, which makes it a nicely appropriate image for the voices in the poem and the selves they present.

This unknown, or undetermined, quality of "x" is important in another respect, related to the reluctance of many religions to name their God, since naming involves an act of power that is deemed to be the prerogative of God alone. Of course, this is precisely the power that poets sometimes claim, though often in a subordinate capacity; and it is a measure of how Brathwaite—whose namings are legion, and legendary—conceives the subject matter of this poem that he refrains from naming it.

"X" also marks the spot on the map where treasure is to be found, or where someone lives, as on maps we draw to guide a visitor to our home. And "x" was the mark used instead of a European-style signature by Indian chiefs to sign treaties, those oral agreements that only for the convenience of the Europeans were ever written down and that mapped out the dispossession of new-world nations by old-world newcomers.

The importance of exploring the land and the sea as well as the self is identified by Brathwaite right at the beginning of this trilogy, in *Mother Poem*, when he mentions the ancient watercourses, the rivers flowing to the sea. The word explore, in which another "x" is sounded, comes from the root word meaning to flow; it is intimately related to influence, and thereby to the continuities this trilogy celebrates. We are surely intended to carry this etymology over into the logic of *X/Self*; just as we are encouraged to link the prefix with the situation of ex-isle that conditions so many West Indian lives.

There are other dimensions to ''x.'' It is one of the least common letters in the English alphabet. But it has a special place in the Greek alphabet, to which our attention is drawn a number of times in Brathwaite's work. And it is prominent in several African languages, as Brathwaite makes apparent in the final poem of *X/Self* about the African god Shango (Xango), the god of thunder. There are also associations in the poem with the Black Muslim leader Malcolm X, and through this with the tradition of black liberation and power that goes back to Marcus Garvey and to Africa.

The particular Greek associations with the letter ''x'' are both general—most English words beginning with ''x'' derive from Greek roots—and specific—the letter ''x'' is often used as an emblem for Christ from the first letter of the Greek spelling (the writing of Christmas as Xmas being the most common instance of this). Furthermore, the Greek associations have to do with the perennial distinction between civilized and barbarian, or Prospero and Caliban. This brutal dichotomy is the element against which the self is protagonist in this book, engaged in the task of finding a language, a word, a letter which will be his own, with which he can identify himself, and by means of which he can transcend the debilitating antagonism that he experiences between the center and the margins, between those gathered within the walls of the city and those huddled or wandering outside.

''Rome burns / and our slavery begins.'' The Mediterranean and the Caribbean. The story starts with slavery and subjugation and starvation, the barbaric materialism of Europe and the apocalyptic desecration of Africa, the poet's spiritual homeland. Then a vision of the day of judgment, bringing together the heritage of slavery and the suffering of many other peoples and times and places. . . .

Brathwaite transforms European traditions into West Indian terms here. His poem is modeled after the medieval hymn ''Dies Irae,'' which in turn is drawn from a passage in the Old Testament Book of Zephaniah when the end of time is figured in ''the great day of the Lord. . . . even the voice of the day of the Lord. . . . That day is a day of wrath, a day of trouble and distress, a day of wasteness and desolation, a day of darkness and gloominess, a day of clouds and thick darkness, a day of the trumpet and alarm against the fenced cities, and against the high towers.''

But the difference in Brathwaite's poem is crucial, for he is not foretelling the day when time shall end, but instead is writing about a more intense awareness of time, of time's arrow and time's cycle—an awareness of the past and what it has done to his people. This is a poem about history, rather than about its obliteration in the apocalypse. Brathwaite signals this in several ways, among them by the title ''Dies Irie,'' a clever turn on ''Dies Irae'' that picks up the Rastafarian word *irie*, with its strongly positive meanings of powerful or stimulating (Brathwaite glosses it as ''high'' or ''happy''). This change draws our attention both to the difference and to the similarity, for the play on irie / irae also confirms the bond between the Old Testament and Rastafarianism.

Brathwaite's vision of this day is terrifying, but it is also filled with the eternal promise of revolution. This is celebrated in another poem in *X/Self* called ''The Visibility Trigger,'' a poem about the

poet's African inheritance and its arrival in the consciousness—the ways of seeing and saying—of West Indians with all the violence of surprise and revelation. . . .

Whether told about a people or an individual, whether an *Exodus* or a *Pilgrim's Progress* the story of leaving home and going back is a literary and spiritual inheritance that West Indians share with many others. Brathwaite's question—''where then is the nigger's home?''—both complicates and strengthens this bond, especially with one particular literary heritage. The story of Odysseus and his journey around the Mediterranean on his way home to Penelope from the Trojan Wars, that well-known tale of wandering and return, has a special place for West Indians. The Mediterranean is an African as well as a European sea, and so is the Caribbean; and both present images of home to their peoples, wherever they may be. Like Odysseus, Brathwaite journeys to take back what already belongs to him: his memories, his hopes, his language.

> J. Edward Chamberlain. *Come Back to Me My Language: Poetry and the West Indies.* (Champaign: University of Illinois Press, 1993)

In Brathwaite's poetry there is constant interaction between the poet's understanding of the history of creolization and the material, perspectives, and styles of poetry. His historical study of slave societies in the West Indies and his special researches into the development of Creole society in eighteenth-and nineteenth-century Jamaica gave him tremendous insights into the social and psychological processes involved in creolization. *The Development of Creole Society in Jamaica* not only unearths a British-American cultural link but also explains and describes the complex organization created around the planting of sugarcane and demonstrates its role in ''integrating'' separate classes of Jamaican society. Brathwaite's research reveals the slave's position in this structure. In delineating the various functional groups of slaves and their relation to other groups in the structure, he not only lifts the faceless mask of silence long placed on the slave's existence but also complicates the sociological paradigm of a plural society: ''Here, in Jamaica, fixed within the dehumanizing institution of slavery, were two cultures of people, having to adapt themselves to a new environment and to each other. The friction created by this confrontation was cruel, but it was also creative. The white plantations and social institutions described in this study reflect one aspect of this. The slaves' adaptation of their African culture to a new world reflects another.''

Brathwaite is aware, nevertheless, of the submerged existence of slave culture and of the possibilities that might have been achieved for Creole society had Jamaica recognized these elements of its creativity and integrated them more fully into the creolizing process. Such an awareness is undoubtedly an underlying factor in his relation to his material in *The Arrivants* and explains his conception of the imagination and of the artist's role as a myth maker and recoverer of ''history.''. . .

Brathwaite becomes identified with the ''authority'' of the submerged culture while at the same time elaborating a far-reaching order of the imagination. As a shaman figure he descends into the farthest reaches of memory, becoming the consciousness of his people at the same time as he unearths history and makes new myths. In such circumstances he does more than describe and illuminate: he appraises and draws out meaning; he bears witness and upholds. As his persona in ''Eating the Dead'' claims,

. . .I
can show
you what it means to eat
your god, drink his explosions of power
and from the slow sinking mud of your plunder, grow.

Brathwaite's move from history to art, from historical writing to poetry, must be seen in this context. History continually deals with the details and evidence of how things came to be. Its ordering impulse collates and structures available evidence to make an objective whole which it then encapsulates in a realistic narrative. Brathwaite's history of Creole society in Jamaica works within these structures, though it manages to transcend them: If his description and analysis of Jamaican institutions are systematically corroborated with data and evidence, his history of slave life and culture is necessarily anthropological, committed to uncovering what is concealed under the surface. Even as a historian, he writes with an artist's eye for possibility and the future, revealing a perspective that was to influence his mythical rearrangement of history in *The Arrivants*. Certainly only the imaginative leeway of the poet could have allowed him to link periods of African, Caribbean, and American history in the simultaneous presentations he achieves in sections of his trilogy. In poetry Brathwaite's purpose becomes more ambitious, intent on breaking the historical boundaries of space and time to offer West Indian man a wider conception of himself in history. The deliberate and epical arrangement of *The Arrivants* reflects this purpose, just as the multiplicity of points of view, moods, tone, and voice reflects the variety of historical experiences he draws upon.

> Nana Wilson-Tagoe. *Historical Thought and Literary Representation in West Indian Literature* (Gainesville: University of Florida Press, 1998)

BIBLIOGRAPHY
*"The day the first snow fell,"* 1953; *Odale's Choice*, 1967; *Rights of Passage*, 1967; *Masks*, 1968; *The People Who Came*, 1968–72; *Islands*, 1969; *Panda No. 349*, 1969; *Folk Culture of the Slaves in Jamaica*, 1970; *The Development of Creole Society in Jamaica, 1770–1820*, 1971; *The Arrivants: A New World Trilogy*, 1973; *Caribbean Man in Space and Time*, 1974; *Contradictory Omens: Cultural Diversity and Integration in the Caribbean*, 1974; *Days & Nights*, 1975; *Other Exiles*, 1975; *Black + Blue*, 1976; *Our Ancestral Heritage: A Bibliography of the Roots of Culture in the English-Speaking Caribbean*, 1976; *Mother Poem*, 1977; *Wars of Respect: Nanny, Sam Sharpe, and the Struggle for People's Liberation*, 1977; *Word Making Man: A Poem for Nicolas Guillen*, 1979; *Sun Poem*, 1982; *Third World Poems*, 1983; *The Colonial Encounter: Language*, 1984; *History of the Voice: The Development of Nation Language in Anglophone Caribbean Poetry*, 1984; *X/Self*, 1987; *Middle Passages*, 1992; *Trench Town Rock*, 1994

# BRODBER, Erna (1940– )
## Jamaica

Erna Brodber has, in a sense, *always* been a creative writer. Before starting secondary school, she had already earned the grand total of

seventeen shillings and sixpence in prize money for three short stories, published in the children's section of the Jamaican paper, the *Weekly Times*. Since then, she has been involved with theater, had poetry and short stories published in Caribbean journals, and written one acclaimed novel. . . .

The opening of *Jane and Louisa Will Soon Come Home* situates the reader in . . . [a] close-knit rural community, isolated but secure. "Mountains ring us round and cover us, banana leaves shelter us and sustain us." Here also is the extended family of small farmers, and here also "everybody is related," with the life of one impinging upon the life of others. The community is an entity in itself and, much like the "chorus of people in the lane" in Roger Mais's *Brother Man*, it speaks with one tongue: "the voice belongs to the family group dead and alive." That the dead ancestors are as vital a part of the community as the living is made clear early in the novel by the comparison of the white plantocracy's dead, safely "tombed and harmless" with the black peasant dead, imaged in terms of continual growth and influence on the living: "Our dead and living are shrouded together under zinc, sweet potato slips and thatch. Step warily—one body raises itself into a mountain of bodies which overtop to form a pit or a shelter for you." Community and communal ancestors, then, have power that can be positive ("a shelter") or negative ("a pit") for the individual. . . .

Despite the differing interpretations of a work that, by its very nature, invites complex and various readings, critical evaluation of *Jane and Louisa* has tended toward unanimous eulogy, particularly in its formal status as a new milestone in Caribbean creative writing. [Rhonda] Cobham hails the novel as "probably the most exciting piece of prose fiction by a West Indian author to appear in recent years," and [Jean Pierre] Durix makes the significant claim that "probably no one else in the West Indies, apart from Wilson Harris, has revolutionized the art of fiction as much as Erna Brodber in *Jane and Louisa*."

> Evelyn O'Callaghan. In Daryl Cumber Dance, ed. *Fifty Caribbean Writers* (Westport, Connecticut: Greenwood Press, 1986), pp. 73–74, 80–81

*Jane and Louisa Will Soon Come Home* makes selective use of the author's experience in mediating a variety of themes. Discussion of this novel so far has concentrated on Nellie's experience as a reflection of that of the Caribbean woman, with considerable attention also being given to stylistic and structural aspects of the novel and to the central image of the kumbla. Brodber's concern with communal ancestry has also been noted, and it has been generally recognized by her critics that Nellie's search for autonomy represents more than a search for a personal direction. The main purpose of this further examination is to show how she uses Nellie's experiences and those of other women whom she depicts to allude to specific incidents or events in her society's history, going back as far as the immediate postemancipation period. The portrait of the society is strengthened both by the parallel between Nellie's circumstances and those of the society and the way in which the outlook of the women portrayed relates to particular periods of Jamaican social history. The Caribbean woman's behavior, as Brodber has described it, has been formed very much in the same way as that of the slaves: to avoid conflict and to promote survival. In responding to experience in the way they do, she demonstrates, women become accomplices in their own oppression. Wittingly and unwittingly they create myths and perpetrate deceptions by which they are themselves controlled. Parallels with the colonial society caught up in the hoax of history are thus suggested. Furthermore, Nellie's attempt to free herself from the safe ''womb'' of inherited ideas evokes extreme schizophrenia comparable to the confusion and disaffection created within the social organism attempting to reorient itself. The new level of awareness which she achieves, through her re-examination of the past, is far removed from that of her grandmother, Granny Tucker. Nellie's changed outlook may be compared with that of the ex-colonial society in the 1970s, which has come to view its colonial heritage dispassionately.

Joyce Walker-Johnson. *Journal of West Indian Literature.* 3, 1 (January 1989), pp. 47–48

The landscape of Erna Brodber's *Jane and Louisa Will Soon Come Home* is largely that of rural Jamaica, a setting in which family ties are complicated by the sinuous bonds of color and class: a context within which an oral tradition of long-time story, family history, and pure gossip flourishes alongside the world of books and distant town. Brodber's narrative method exemplifies an interpretation of scribal and oral literary forms: a modernist, stream-of-consciousness narrative voice holds easy dialogue with the traditional teller of tales, the transmitter of [the Anancy] story, proverb, folk song, and dance.

Brodber's experiment in form is underscored by the writer's deliberately ingenuous assertion that *Jane and Louisa Will Soon Come Home* was not conceived as a novel: she set out to write a case study in abnormal psychology. But literary critics have appropriated the work, recognizing in its dense patterns of allusive imagery, its evocative language, and its carefully etched characterizations, the sensibility of the creative writer. The ''functionalist'' intention of the social psychologist appears divergent from the ''structuralist'' analysis of the literary critic. But Brodber's ''faction'' can be categorized within a neo-African folk aesthetic of functional form: literature as wordhoard, the repository of the accumulated wisdom of the community, the creative medium through which the norms of appropriate social behavior can be elaborated metaphorically.

The Afro-Jamaican folk ethos of *Jane and Louisa Will Soon Come Home* is evident in the organizing metaphors of the work, derived from the folk culture, and in its primary theme: the healing of the protagonist Nellie, who travels to ''foreign'' to study, and returns home to a profound sense of homelessness, from which she is redeemed only when she comes to understand the oral accounts of her fragmented family history, and the distorted perceptions of female identity and sexuality that she has internalized in childhood. The therapeutic power of the word is the subject and medium of Brodber's fictive art.

Carolyn Cooper. In Carole Boyce Davies and Elaine Savory Fido, eds. *Out of the Kumbla: Caribbean Women and Literature* (Trenton, New Jersey: Africa World Press, 1990), pp. 279–80

Erna Brodber did not set out to write a novel but rather to present a case study to teach the dissociative personality to her class in human growth and development. The case study incorporated some of the issues that concerned her and her students such as

male-female relations, black liberation, and the women's movement. The decision to publish this material was made by her sister, teacher-poet-critic Velma Pollard. . . .

Nellie Richmond, the protagonist of *Jane and Louisa Will Soon Come Home*, is born into a virtual Garden of Eden, where ''mountains ring us round and cover us, banana leaves shelter us and sustain us.'' Nellie's world is protected from everything; not even the sun can get in: ''Outside infiltrated our nest only as its weave allowed.'' But this Edenic existence is short-lived for growth brings with it a series of exposures and revelations that shatters Nellie's sense of herself. She becomes aware of color and class divisions in her family and in her community, recognizes the ''shame'' and ''filth'' and precariousness of being a female; has to face ''it'' (alternately menses, female sexuality, everything associated with being a woman), which sets her apart from everybody, including her favorite neighbor, Mass Stanley, and all the boys who had been her playmates; has to face physical development (''Have you ever seen a new sucker trying to grow out of a rotten banana root? My whole chest was that rotten banana root and there were two suckers''); has to submit to sex (recalled with shame and disgust in images of a ''long nasty snail,'' a ''mekke mekke thing''), simply because ''you want to be a woman; now you have a man. . . . Vomit and bear it''; has to accept that as a woman ''the world is waiting to drag you down: Woman luck de a dungle heap''; and has to acknowledge that ''the black womb is . . . an abominable scrap heap thing.''. . .

It adds up to more than our heroine can bear, and she suffers total psychic collapse. Her condition is sometimes described as a loss or lack of balance. Nellie's Aunt Becca warns her of the precarious position of women in the world, concluding, ''Learn that lest you be weighed in the balance and found wanting.'' Nellie's fear of losing the balance, of being found wanting, is a critical part of her dilemma and is reinforced in the many descriptions of her sensing herself spinning wildly; like Anancy caught in his own trap and convinced by his own words, ''spinning around in the woods,'' she is ''twirling madly in a still life.'' The importance of maintaining the balance is demonstrated in the experience of her neighbors: Mass Stanley's son David had to be cast out of his home because he disrupted the balance when he wanted to be a bull (man) in the same pen with his father. Mass Stanley's grandson Baba, on the other hand, ''never disturbed their balance.''

Nellie's ailment is frequently described as a cold, often icy, lump. This contrasts with the warmth of her original Eden: ''Ever see a fowl sitting on eggs in cold December rain. We knew the warmth and security of those eggs in the dark of her bottom.'' When, because of the onset of puberty, the boys in her neighborhood no longer tussle with her, she laments, ''What kind of coldness in this hot sun.'' After her first sexual experience she speaks of having to live in ''an ice cage'' and of the ''dry ice [that] works my body to a bloodless incision.'' She learns that displays of anger must be ''frozen with a compress of ice''; she characterizes her life as having ''passed through a seasoning of ice.''

Daryl Cumber Dance. In Selwyn R. Cudjoe, ed. *Caribbean Women Writers* (Wellesley, Massachusetts: Calaloux, 1990), pp. 170–71

*Jane and Louisa Will Soon Come Home* takes its title from a common children's song, the basis of a ring dance performed some evenings by little boys and girls in the yard or at the beach, anywhere outdoors, usually with adults helping out. Brodber takes the words and makes them into social commentary, then into talismans, then into mythic concentrations of the whole complex of Caribbean experience: childhood, city and country, the extended family, social mores and biases, sexual emergencies, political structures, and travel and study abroad (with all that these entail of culture shock and culture clarification and culture enlargement and culture reaffirmation). . . .

The text is replete with images of enclosure, refining, revising, compounding, enriching one another and the mind of the central speaker. We find enclosure as imprisonment (''I was being choked. . . . I needed out''), and as potential site of germination and growth (''immaculate egg,'' and the image of menstruation as a thing in its own space).

The kumbla is the ultimate image of enclosure in *Jane and Louisa*, and it is used with structural brilliance to resolve the contradictions and anxieties of the garden—the claustrophobia and paranoia and disgrace (since menstruation raises the danger of sexual capture and pregnancy, with its terminal confinement). The kumbla is the space of the self and space for the self, and is as versatile in form as our needs may be various: beachball, eggshell, light bulb, calabash, shell, parachute, womb, and, of course, the omnipresent ring of the title song. Where the garden gives space, the kumbla goes one better by giving both space and time—its only requirement is that one not stay in it too long, for fear of turning albino from lack of sun. The kumbla is the space-time for an apocalypse that is not yonder and happenstance in character, but the sum and product of experience that is illumined in our embrace.

> Michael G. Cooke. *Journal of West Indian Literature*. 4, 1 (January 1990), pp. 36–37

In Brodber's novel [*Myal*], the powerful grip of obeah—the debilitating obverse of therapeutic myal, is imaged most dramatically, and ironically, in the attempted theft of Anita's spirit by Mass Levi, a deacon in the Baptist church. Mass Levi, suddenly become impotent, appropriates the spirit of the young girl in order to regain sexual potency: a particularly perverse manifestation of the sexual exploitation of woman. The Kumina Queen, Miss Gatha (in collaboration with the Baptist minister, Simpson; the necromancer, Ole African, and somewhat surprisingly, the English wife of the white Jamaican Methodist minister, Brassington) draws the malevolent possessing spirit from the girl on to her own person.

Brodber's quiet shaping of this act of exorcism focuses on the intimate, human scale of this potentially sensationalist complex of circumstances. The spirit's power is manifest, but it is its containment (the healing) and the ordinariness of faith in the spirit world that is Brodber's point. This is not a lurid voodoo tale. . . .

There *is* a voodoo doll in Brodber's fiction . . . but its significance in the total architecture of the novel is not only that it is a literal artifact in the practice of obeah; rather, like the crumbling fertility doll that Baba mockingly carves for Nellie in *Jane and Louisa Will Soon Come Home* (Brodber's earlier novel), it becomes an icon of the zombification of diminished woman who is robbed of her possibilities: the alabaster baby. This is Ella's story, as well as Anita's. In Brodber's subtly shaded rural world, the reader focuses less on the ''strangeness'' of events and more on their import for characters who fully believe in a cosmology where

the natural and the supernatural, the demonic and the divine regularly consort.

> Carolyn Cooper. In Susheila Nasta, ed. *Motherlands* (New Brunswick: Rutgers University Press, 1992), pp. 71–74

In her essay ''Fiction in the Scientific Procedure,'' Brodber sees a continuity between her scientific and her literary projects. Both Brodber's social science and her fiction attempt to understand the social world as a *system* of relations. However, they differ from that ''objective'' narrative which [Edouard] Glissant condemns. For whereas the latter narrative erects binarisms, Brodber reveals a commitment to *overcoming* binarisms—notably the self/other, science/art, objectivity/subjectivity dualisms. Thus, she writes of a ''twinning of fiction and science.'' And her commitment to a realist epistemology also leads her away from formal realism. Like Glissant, then, Brodber doubles the meanings of objectivity, science, and realism.

In her attempt to understand Jamaican society, Brodber grapples with the bitter (post) colonial phenomenon of ''prejudice against blacks in a country of blacks. The enemy was a ghost that talked through black faces.'' Her novel, *Myal*, is in many ways a literalization of that metaphor. The novel is erected around the mulatto child Ella O'Grady. It spans the years 1913–1920, Ella's fourteenth to twenty-first year. As a story of education and coming to consciousness, the novel functions at least partly in the tradition of the *bildungsroman*. However, it does not proceed in the linear fashion of the traditional *bildungsroman*, but through a complex series of halvings and doublings. At the beginning of her story—though not at the beginning of the novel—we see Ella reciting [Rudyard] Kipling's ''The White Man's Burden.'' It is quite literally the colonizer's voice that speaks through her. At the time, she is unaware of the implications of a colonial text that describes her people, a colonized people, as ''half devil, half child.'' She does, however, know the pain of being a half-caste; like her mother, she knows what it is like to be a ''long face, thin lip, pointed nose soul in a round face, thick lip, big eye country.'' With her racial doubleness born of a forcible colonial coupling, Ella is not-quite-black-enough for most blacks to be comfortable with her; she is just-black-enough to be exotic and exciting to her white American husband; she is not-quite-white-enough to be worthy of carrying his children. We can reconstruct the novel as tracing Ella's development, from unconscious quiescence to the colonial text, through complicity with the text, and recognition that ''the half has not been told,'' to resistance to the text. . . .

[The] narrative strategy of doubling serves several purposes: it evokes the cultural and racial heterogeneity of Jamaica; it figures the reconnection of mind and body, the restoration to wholeness of people who have been split in half; it is the means by which texts are hybridized and appropriated; and it signals the possibility of reversal and renewal. *Myal* thus shares with postmodernism the vocabulary of doubleness, ambivalence, hybridity, and textual proliferation. However, unlike much postmodernist discourse, it retains a commitment to the categories of truth and error, knowledge and ignorance. . . . *Myal* dramatizes the difficulty of knowing; it does not assert the impossibility of knowing. The novel's suggestion that texts can yield knowledge about the world returns us to the metaphors of light and vision of Glissant's realism: ''And the draining brought clarity so that Ella could, after a time, see not only Mammy Mary and them people clearly but she could see the things around them." The "truth" towards which Ella moves is that the colonialist narratives offer an inadequate amount of reality: "It didn't go so," she realizes.

*Myal*'s proliferation of narratives does not, then, assert the equivalence of all texts. Its multiple narratives are not unconnected and discrete; they are related and conflicting. Indeed, doubling becomes a strategy for resisting and refusing colonialist narratives; it permits us to read the colonialist narrative in another light, as it were. The subjectification of the colonized depends on this ability to re-vision their reality, to provide an account of it which brings to light their possibilities. *Myal*'s project of reconstruction is thus tied to the project of recognition. The novel's faith in a poetics of doubleness, a "twilight poetics" that walks the border between obscurity and illumination, derives from the belief that it is at their borders that texts first fray, and it is there that the fabric of colonial narratives is most liable to be torn.

Shalini Puri. *Ariel*. 24, 3 (July 1993), pp. 98–99, 112

Recent West Indian literature by women offers a locus of debate over the retrieval of the body from and within western discursive erasure. This erasure of the female body and its possible reclamation is of course central to contemporary feminist debate, and has its own genealogy within feminist discourse. My interest in this question, however, is in the ways in which colonialism's discursive and institutional apparatuses obliterated and continue to obliterate the colonised (specifically female) body, and the counter-colonial strategies by which this "lost" body might be reclaimed. In their fiction Erna Brodber and Jamaica Kincaid anatomize the body's erasure under a colonialist scriptive drive and explore potentials for the re/cognition of corporeality and sexuality. . . .

Instructions as to the posture of pupils at desks, physical education and sport, marching formations, folk-dancing instruction, and, more cryptically but no less effectively, formal literary recitation, ensured the repression of the colonised and the reproduction of the English body through colonial subjects. The complex history of black-white sexuality within slave-plantation societies plus, in the nineteenth century, Victorian attitudes to sex, effected the particular repression of the black female body and female sexuality. Thus in the twentieth century, the library, the classroom and sexual relations remain the loci of continuing and complex colonialist erasure and repression.

Erna Brodber's "One Bubby Susan" takes anthropologist/historian Frank Cundall's account of an Arawak rock carving and "fleshes out" a counter-interpretation. In the narrator's tale of the origin of this petroglyph, the body of Arawak Susan is reanimated in Creole, instead of in "authoritative" Euro-historical discourse, and the tone is gossipy, not scholarly. In Brodber's version, Susan's history offers an allegory of the extirpation of the female fleshly body under colonialism—both in terms of military invasion and textual capture—leaving only a vague outline in rock. The outline was left by Susan's body when she was stoned to death by her own people for failing to save them from the tragic consequences of European invasion. Susan had earlier rejected her own culture's insistence on women's roles as exclusively those of child-rearer and home-maker and she had abandoned her group to pursue her own life. Alone in her cave, a retreat from the Arawak ideology of family, the solitary Susan ironically becomes an object of religious veneration. But

Mr Christopher Columbus come with him red rags and all abody . . . It was syphilis that time that come with the tourist rags. People start dropping dead like this and the bad treatment was something else. Man used as target practice!. . .
The whiteman was putting their hands and all where they should not be put and on top of that beating up the Arawak men and running their swords through them.

In an ironic combination of the sacred and the profanely-political, spirit and body, the embattled Arawaks begin to treat Susan's excrement as if it were the (mythical) gold the unscrupulous Europeans seek. Susan is denied any privacy and "decide that she not going to be no God with no privacy"; the narrative insists on the importance of the body, whatever the rewards of spiritual elevation. Susan plays dead, and in disappointment and frustration her people stone her. . . .

Susan's metonymic function in the story is further attested by her final erasure. Even when she is dead "them try to throw stones round what them think is the outline of her body". Her own people, now deeply interpellated by European representations of female corporeality and sexuality, make her shadowy outline the continuing object of their abuse.

The effects of European constructions of the female body within Caribbean communities are the subject of another short allegorical piece by Brodber entitled "Sleeping's Beauty and Prince Charming." Adapting the European fairytale and rewriting its terms and its language, Brodber investigates the legacy of European invasion/representation. The black female body is allegorised as lost through a European textuality so deeply interpellative that black "prince charmings" cannot conceive of or cope with Afro-Caribbean female bodies—their substance has been relegated to a legendary outline which is unseen, ignored, or still often the object of abuse, a fate similar to that of Arawak Susan.

Imaged as "a sightless Samson" Prince Charming of Brodber's parable first perceives Sleeping as simply a "disembodied voice". European textuality/slavery has rendered the black male unable to see black women who have been disembodied by that same history. References to Spenser, the Bible and the fairy tale of "Sleeping Beauty" emphasize the role of Euro-representation in this destructive disembodiment.

In response to historical/textual erasure, Brodber's parable interrogates these European fairy tales adopting (and adapting) the traditional Jamaican concluding formula: "Rastafari me nuh choose none." Invoking both a specifically Jamaican Rastafarian mode, and the notion of "Anancy stories"—an (oral) tradition of a different kind, attesting to the persistence of an Afro-Caribbean folk history/herstory which frequently (though not exclusively) was preserved and passed on by women—"Sleeping's Beauty and Prince Charming" rewrites the European script in a Caribbean narrative mode. The invocation of Anancy also conjures the pejorative relegation by the English colonisers of such Afro-Jamaican folk tales to the category of lies—dangerous lies outlawed in school curricula (and playground circulation) as disruptive of the middle-class English values such educational institutions sponsored. Thus, while Brodber's story inscribes and thematises the persisting effects in the Caribbean of a white education and reading practice (from the Bible and European "fairy tales" to contemporary writing by [interpellated] black male West Indians who are thus locked within that Anglo-Scribal tradition, and whose persisting author/ity provides the starting place for Brodber's narrative), it also suggests the possible retrieval, in time, of that lost female body.

Anglo-European textuality and its authoritative institutionalisation not only captured the Afro-Caribbean body within Euro-representation, but severed body from soul. Brodber's ''Sleeping'' is ''a black Ophelia sleeping for seven years''. But while her body is comatose/erased, Sleeping's ''soul'' wanders in search of her ''black knight.'' Though he can feel her eyes on him, can pick up her ''heavy vibrations,'' Charming cannot see her because there is ''nobody'' (no/body). By the conclusion of the parable, however, this Samson has regained his sight; he can now see black womanhood, though as yet he cannot fully accept her corporeality, her surprising re-embodiment after centuries of erasure; his conditioned apprehension of black woman as shadowy outlines, present only through European representation. . . .

As both these stories attest, the violence, *physical* and *textual*, of conquest and colonisation destroys cultures, but its impact, though always devastating, is uneven; there is a gender impact difference at the level of the victims. The violence done to others by colonial discourse is also a gendered technology, and gender matters at these moments of textual violence, where cultural genocide often produces a particular violence against women. Once the ''fairy tales'' of Europe have been internalised, there is often, as in ''One Bubby Susan'' and ''Sleeping's Beauty and Prince Charming,'' a continuation of colonialist power through local male agency. An inescapable aspect of that violence involves the erasure and abuse of female bodies and female sexuality.

In both Brodber's *Jane and Louisa Will Soon Come Home*, *Myal*, and in Kincaid's *Annie John* and *Lucy* there is an exploration of this erasure/abuse and the potential for retrieval of the colonised Caribbean body. All four texts trace the processes of female reembodiment and the retrieval of Caribbean voice and body from its entrapment/erasure within European script and from those Anglo-Victorian middle-class values with which an educated Caribbean middle-class were so deeply imbued.

Helen Tiffin. *Callaloo*. 16, 4 (Fall 1993), pp. 910–18

BIBLIOGRAPHY
*Abandonment of Children in Jamaica*, 1974; *Yards in the City of Kingston*, 1975; *Jane and Louisa Will Soon Come Home*, 1980; *Perceptions of Caribbean Women: Towards a Documentation of Stereotypes*, 1982; *Rural–Urban Migration and the Jamaican Child*, 1986; *Myal*, 1988; ''Fiction in the Scientific Procedure,'' 1990; *Louisiana: A Novel*, 1994

# BROOKS, Gwendolyn (1917–)
## United States

Two sections of [*A Street in Bronzeville*], including the one that gives it its title, represent rather unexciting vignettes of sentiment and character. They have, however, something of the spice and movement which many of the better Negro poets commonly lend to their work. No doubt a great bulk of the proficient and marketable poems written by poets of whatever color deal with such sure-fire or easy-mark situations as those in these groups. The good child envies the bad. Dreams are hard to sustain amid onion fumes or

where red fat roaches stroll up one's wall. God must be lonely. The hunchback speculates on heaven. Yet even these sketches are somewhat safeguarded in the present case by some actuality of detail, freshness of image, dryness of angle or flexibility of tempo. . . .

All in all, despite the fact that this first book has its share of unexciting verse, there are considerable resources evidenced for future work. Miss Brooks, to use one of her own phrases, ''scrapes life with a fine-tooth comb.'' And she shows a capacity to marry the special quality of her racial experience with the best attainments of our contemporary poetry tradition. Such compounding of resources out of varied stocks and traditions is the great hope of American art as it is of American life generally.

Amos N. Wilder. *Poetry*. December 1945, pp. 164, 166

Miss Brooks is a very accomplished poet indeed, often boiling her lines down to the sparsest expression of the greatest meaning, sometimes almost to a kind of word-shorthand that defies immediate grasp. Less simple and direct than the poems in her initial volume [*A Street in Bronzeville*], those in *Annie Allen* give, upon careful reading, as much interest and emotional impact. The book is a mood story in varying poetic forms of a girl's growth from childhood to the age of love, marriage, and motherhood.

There are sharp pictures of neighborhoods, relatives, friends, illnesses and deaths; of big city slums, cafes, and beauty shops. To me the third section, containing about half the poems in the book, ''The Womanhood,'' is its most effective. The qualms, the longings, the love of a poor mother for her child is here most movingly expressed. . . .

The people and the poems in Gwendolyn Brooks' book are alive, reaching, and very much of today.

Langston Hughes. *Voices*. Winter 1950, pp. 55–56

[Brooks] tends to use conventional forms with tightly locking rhymes that constrict her unduly, to fit an inappropriate vocabulary to a loose ballad rhythm, or to write poems of statement that would be more effective as poems of understatement. [*Annie Allen*] has the adventitious interest that attaches to relatively fresh subject matter, for Miss Brooks takes her themes chiefly from the world of the urban Negro. But she fails to make the most of her material. The intrinsic value of her work is the poet's prevailing attitude; here vitality and compassion are mingled in a manner not unique with Negroes but exhibited by them with remarkable frequency.

Babette Deutsch. *Yale Review*. Winter 1950, pp. 362–63

The fact that Miss Brooks displays an excellent knowledge of form, whether in the versatile handling of types of forms of poetry included in *Annie Allen* or in the metrical variations in the volume, can be readily seen as proof of [the] new emphasis upon conventional form. She skillfully handles a number of stanzaic forms including couplets, quatrains, the Italian Terza Rima, and even in ''The Anniad,'' the difficult rime-royal or the seven line stanza named for Chaucer. . . . In addition to these conventional forms she includes several poems written in free verse as well as occasional lines of blank verse. In regard to types she includes short lyrics, ballads, and sonnets written with veteran aplomb.

As a whole, *Annie Allen* is a fine delineation of the character of a young Negro woman from childhood through adolescence to complete maturity, but with slight racial exceptions it could apply to any female of a certain class and society. The entire volume is tinged with an highly sophisticated humor and is not only technically sure but also vindicates the promise of *A Street in Bronzeville*. Coming after the long hue and cry of white writers that Negroes as poets lack form and intellectual acumen, Miss Brooks' careful craftsmanship and sensitive understanding reflected in *Annie Allen* are not only personal triumphs but a racial vindication.

Margaret Walker. *Phylon*. 11, 4, 1950, pp. 351–52

There is every indication in *Maud Martha* that poetess Gwendolyn Brooks is capable of well rounded characterizations of which her heroine Maud is a finespun, fractional specimen. For what Miss Brooks presents in this slender volume are bright glimpses of a world turning upon Maud's soft meditations. Writing with the quiet charm and sparkling delicacy of tone which brought Emily Dickinson's bird down the walk to drink a dew, Miss Brooks has begat a kind of beauty upon ugliness by lighting up the humanity of her creation against the background of a Chicago slum area. . . .

Maud has not accepted herself with that unconscious assurance which makes her male counterpart, [Langston Hughes's] Jesse Simple, so articulate in his easy living with hard conditions. She finds herself too often wishing to be what her husband Paul, absorbed as he is in surface values, believes he wants her to be. For all practical purposes, this is as it should be, for what the author is dealing with from the inside of her creation are those very human hopes which grasp straw values in reaching very hungrily for real ones. In all this, Miss Brooks maintains a kind of subtle, close-lipped control over her style which so heightens its rich suggestiveness that one is led to believe he understands more for being told less.

Henry F. Winslow. *Crisis*. February 1954, p. 114

[In *The Bean Eaters* the] poems, generous and full of humanity, rattle with verbs and jangle with action. Their images are everyday; their subjects are poor people (often Negroes), the dreams of the downtrodden, the frustrations of the meek.

Yet, for all the worthiness of their themes and their aims, you will probably find them incomplete as poems. Miss Brooks appears more concerned to condemn social injustice and to draw sympathetic character portraits than to write poems that echo on every level, and as a result she repeats the same kind of statement too often for poetic truth.

The best poem in her book is a ballad of racial segregation [''The Ballad of Rudolph Reed''] with the stark rhythms and devices of the traditional ballad adapted to a theme that suits it perfectly. Most of this book, however, has the same virtues and faults as the title poem, which for the sake of journalistic realism ends in a catalogue that reminds the reader of nothing so much as Ogden Nash and destroys the poem's serious intent.

Peter Davison. *Atlantic*. September 1960, p. 93

When many of us think of protest poetry we tend to recall the fiery lines of ''If We Must Die,'' written by McKay during those

exciting days of the New Negro Movement. Moreover, we have somehow come to expect the same kind of bitterness and defiance in all poetry of this kind. But Miss Brooks's protest poems, written in an integration age, are usually quite different in spirit and approach from those of the New Negro generation. She has subtle irony, a quiet humor, and oftentimes a sense of pity, not only for the black victims of prejudice but also for the whites who are guilty. But her works as a rule are not fiery or defiant, and they are seldom bitter. . . .

When one compares Miss Brooks's racial problems with those of an earlier generation of Negro writers, he finds this significant difference. In most of the earlier poems, regardless of the bitterness expressed, there is an implied faith in a better day which will come either through the fulfillment of the American Dream or through the workings of a Just God. In these earlier works, there was also on occasion the kind of self-abasement one finds in [James David] Corrother's lines: ''To be a Negro in a day like this—/ Alas! Lord God, what evil have we done?'' There is no self-pity in Gwendolyn Brooks's racial poems and precious little optimism. She doesn't seem to have much faith in either the American Dream or a Just God. Expressing neither hope nor fear, she is content to describe conditions as they are in Bronzeville. She seems to be saying: these things are so, and they are bad; but modern men, white or black, are not heroic. One can't expect too much.

Arthur P. Davis. *CLA Journal*. December 1963, pp. 120, 125

It's too soon to say anything definitive about the work of Gwendolyn Brooks. Perhaps she hasn't yet written the poems that will stand out a hundred years from now as her major ones. But she has already written some that will undoubtedly be read so long as man cares about language and his fellows.

There have been no drastic changes in the tactics and subjects she has dealt with over the years. It's doubtful if future critics will talk about the early and the late Brooks, not unless she strikes out into much different territory after 1969. What one observes is a steady development of themes and types.

Her poetry is marked by a number of central concerns: black experience; the nature of greatness; the way in which man expresses his needs, makes do, or lashes out. Ordinarily the view is one of delicate balance, that of a passionate observer. The poems strike one as distinctly those of a woman but always muscled and precise, written from the pelvis rather than the biceps.

Dan Jaffe. In C. W. E. Bigsby, ed., *The Black American Writer* (De Land, Florida: Everett/Edwards, 1969), Vol. II, p. 93

When you view Gwendolyn Brooks's work in the pre-1967 period, you see a poet, a black poet in the actual (though still actively searching for her own definitions of blackness), on the roadway to becoming a conscious African poet or better yet a conscious African woman in America who chose poetry as her major craft. However, Gwendolyn Brooks describes her poetry prior to 1967 as ''work that was conditioned to the times and the people.'' In other words, poetry that leaped from the pages bringing forth ideas, definitions, images, reflections, forms, colors, etc., that were molded over a distance of many years—her poetry notebook started at the age of eleven—as a result of and as a reaction to the

American reality. And for black people, regardless of the level of their perception of the world, the American reality has always been a battle, a real alley fight. . . .

Gwendolyn Brooks's post 1967 poetry is fat-less. Her new work resembles a man getting off meat, turning to a vegetarian diet. What one immediately notices is that all the excess weight is quickly lost. Her work becomes extremely streamlined and to the point. . . .

We can see in the work of Gwendolyn Brooks of 1972 positive movement from that of the sayer to the doer, where she recognizes that *writing is not enough* for a people in a life and death struggle. For so few black writers to reflect the aspirations and needs of so many (there are about three hundred black writers who are published with any kind of regularity) is a responsibility that should not be taken lightly. Every word has to be considered and worked with so as to use it to its fullest potential.

Don L. Lee. Preface to Gwendolyn Brooks, *Report from Part One* (Detroit: Broadside, 1972), pp. 13–14, 22, 29

The world of white arts and letters has pointed to [Gwendolyn Brooks] with pride; it has bestowed kudos and a Pulitzer Prize [for *Annie Allen*]. The world of black arts and letters has looked on with mixed emotion, and pride has been only one part of the admixture. There have also been troubling questions about the poet's essential "blackness," her dedication to the melioration of the black American's social conditions. The real duality appears when we realize that Gwendolyn Brooks—though praised and awarded—does not appear on the syllabuses of most American literature courses, and her name seldom appears in the annual scholarly bibliographies of the academic world. She, it would seem, is a black writer after all, *not* an American writer. Yet when one listens to the voice of today's black revolutionary consciousness, one often hears that Miss Brooks' poetry fits the white, middle-class patterns that LeRoi Jones has seen as characteristic of "Negro literature.". . .

Gwendolyn Brooks represents a singular achievement. Beset by a double-consciousness, she has kept herself from being torn asunder by speaking the truth in poems that equal the best work in the black and white American literary traditions. Her characters are believable; her themes are manifold; and her technique is superb. The critic (whether white or black) who comes to her writing seeking only support for his ideology will be disappointed, for as Etheridge Knight has pointed out, she has ever spoken the truth. And truth, one likes to feel, always lies beyond the boundaries of any one ideology. Perhaps Miss Brooks' most significant achievement is her endorsement of this point of view, for from her hand and fertile imagination have come volumes of verse that transcend the dogma on either side of the American veil.

Houston A. Baker, Jr. *CLA Journal.* September 1972, pp. 24, 31

*Report from Part One* is a seemingly chunk and hunk assemblage of photographs, interviews, letters—backward glances on growing up in Chicago and coming of age in the Black Arts Movement. It is not a sustained dramatic narrative for the nosey, being neither the confessions of a private woman/poet or the usual sort of mahogany-desk memoir public personages inflict upon the populace at the first

sign of a cardiac. It is simply an extremely valuable book that is all of a piece and readable and memorable in unexpected ways. It documents the growth of Gwen Brooks. Documents that essentially lonely (no matter how close and numerous the friends who support, sustain and encourage you to stretch out and explore) process of opening the eyes, wrenching the self away from played-out modes, and finding new directions. It shows her reaching toward a perspective that reflects the recognition that the black artist is obliged to fashion an esthetic linked to the political dynamics of the community she serves. . . .

Like the younger black poets, Gwen Brooks since the late Sixties has been struggling for a cadence, style, idiom and content that will politicize and mobilize. Like the young black poets, her recent work is moving more toward gesture, sound, intonation, attitude and other characteristics that depend on oral presentation rather than private eyeballing. It is important to have the poet herself assess these moves in her own way so as to establish the ground for future critical biographies. But "change" and "shift" may be too heavy-handed, somewhat misleading; for in rereading the bulk of her work, which *Report from Part One* does prompt one to do, we see a continuum.

Toni Cade Bambara. *New York Times Book Review.* January 7, 1973, p. 1

[Gwendolyn Brooks's] *A Street in Bronzeville* and her *In the Mecca*, in all seriousness, could be used as reference works in sociology. Her *Annie Allen* quietly demonstrates the wealth of her observation of normal, not abnormal, psychology. She is at home with fact. Her alert mentality gathers in the evidence presented to the senses. But she is at home, also, with reflective thought. She sees not only the bare circumstance. She sees also its place in a rich context of fine relationships. Her craftsmanship is careful. Miss Brooks belongs to the school of writers who do not believe in wasting a single word. Selection and significance—one can divine in her diction how she has brooded over them, how every word has been chosen with due regard for the several functions it may be called upon to perform in the dispensation of a poem. But the brooding goes deep and it affects not only words. The words must be put together. And the principle of dire economy which governs her choice of diction disciplines severely all of her poetic maneuvers. Terseness, a judicious understatement combined with pregnant ellipses, often guides the reader into an adventure which permits a revelation of Miss Brooks's capacity for sensitive interpretations of the human comedy.

She never writes on "big" subjects. One finds on her agenda no librettos for Liberia [like Tolson's], no grand excursus into history like [Hayden's] "Middle Passage." *Annie Allen* typifies her method, the study, as it were, of the flower in the crannied wall. In such a method her genius operates within its area of greatest strength, the close inspection of a limited domain, to reap from that inspection, perhaps paradoxically, but still powerfully, a view of life in which one may see a microscopic portion of the universe intensely and yet, through that microscopic portion, see all truth for the human condition wherever it exists.

Blyden Jackson. In Blyden Jackson and Louis D. Rubin, Jr., *Black Poetry in America* (Baton Rouge: Louisiana State University Press, 1974), pp. 84–85

*Beckonings* exemplifies Brooks' movement toward her new style, which is characterized by a struggle between her normal tendency to make each word bear its full measure of weight and suggestion and an insistence upon directness and simplicity of diction. Actually, despite her reputation for complexity, there are already many poems across the body of her work which are simple and direct. *A Street in Bronzeville* contains a large number of simple poems, some of which become favorites with readers. I would suppose the main difficulties for the uninitiated readers in some earlier poems would be the presence of irony and understatement. *Beckonings* reduces the element of irony and often goes into direct statement. . . .

"Five Men against the Theme 'My Name Is Red Hot. Yo Name Ain Doodley Squat'" and "Sammy Chester Leaves 'Godspell' and Visits *Upward Bound* on a Lake Forest Lawn, Bringing West Afrika" use older techniques in a new way; that is, the unusual junction of words, the coinages, the sudden contrasts, and repetitions, remain within the bounds of a simplicity which is accessible to the pause for thought. There are other poems which make such combinations, and still others which move close to direct statement. "A Black Wedding Song" is a good example of this group.

The poems are evidence that the newer techniques will not sacrifice the complex rhythms of existence in their attempts to reach a wider audience.

George E. Kent. *Phylon.* Spring 1976, pp. 110–11

Gwendolyn Brooks is the only black woman poet to have achieved public and critical recognition before the 1960s. Her first book of poems, *A Street in Bronzeville*, was published in 1945. It was perhaps only "natural" that the white male literary establishment that published her, reviewed her, and gave her fame (poetry prizes, grants, and the Pulitzer Prize in 1949 for *Annie Allen*) should consider her an "exception," or, more commonly, should consider her neither black nor woman but poet: an American poet who happened to be Negro. Reviews of her work from that early period either ignore the question of race and sex . . . or take special issue with the matter of universality in poetry. . . .

It was only "natural" that Brooks's early poetry be largely defined by its acceptability. While she never whitewashed her subject matter (her poems have always been about black people, and frequently black women), her style—the manner in which she presented those subjects—was what [Don] Lee calls "European," demonstrating her preoccupation with a formal elegance and dexterity directly in the tradition of English literature. Brooks could always be topical or colloquial ("At Joe's Eats / You get your fish or chicken on meat platters"), but such localness was carefully embedded in the universal. . . .

Like the white women poets of her generation, Brooks may write about women, but rarely will she include herself among them. She never achieves either the personalism or the engagement that I have identified with the "feminine" poet. Yet there is a difference between her presentation of women and that of the white women poets who are her contemporaries: in Brooks's poetry—and, indeed, throughout the poetry of black women—there is a pride in womanhood that does not exist in the poetry of white women until recently. The white woman poet set herself apart from "women": she was special, because she was a poet. She was not and must not be like those motherly, housewifely, essentially weak creatures whose lifestyle she repudiated for the sake of her art. The black woman, on the other hand, as wife and mother has been many things but never weak. Her very strength has caused the black male of the 1960s and 1970s to label her Sapphire: to call her a cause of his own lack of manhood. Indeed! Gwendolyn Brooks, like the black women poets who have followed her, has always expressed pride in the black woman.

Suzanne Juhasz. *Naked and Fiery Forms: Modern American Poetry by Women. A New Tradition* (New York: Octagon Books, 1978), pp. 145, 149, 153–54

Gwendolyn Brooks's style of poetic realism has undergone developments that conform its use to her changes in both general and racial outlook, and to the evolving state of her consciousness. . . .

The consciousness producing *A Street in Bronzeville* was one making its first compassionate outreach to the broad range of humanity. On the one hand, it represented the mastered past: the author's old neighborhood and youth. On the other hand, it represented an intense getting acquainted with the present which was pressurized by the raw currents of Chicago's racial practices, and by World War II. Optimism prevailed, however, since the war situation had produced both threatening violence and some evidence that a broadened democracy would be born from it. In the poet's early work, one result is a deceptively simple surface. Syntax is most often either in close correlation with the usual subject plus verb plus object or complement pattern of a familiar prose sentence or within calling distance. Wielding this syntax is a friendly observer giving one a tour of the neighborhood or quick views of situations. Thus abrupt beginnings sound pretty much the way they do in our communications with friends with whom we share clarifying reference points. . . .

The style of *Annie Allen* emerges not only from the fact that the poet of the highly promising first book naturally expects to present greater mastery of craft in the second but also from a changed focus in consciousness. In her first book Brooks's emphasis had been upon community consciousness. In her second her emphasis is upon self-consciousness—an attempt to give artistic structure to tensions arising from the artist's experience in moving from the Edenic environment of her parents' home into the fallen world of Chicago tenement life in the roles of young wife, mother, and artist. Her efforts, however, were not an attempt to be confessional but an attempt to take advantage of the poetic form to move experiences immediately into symbols broader than the person serving as subject. A thoroughgoing search of the territory and the aspiration for still greater mastery of craft called for a struggle with language, a fact which would require the reader to make also a creative struggle. . . .

In *Bronzeville Boys and Girls*, a volume for juveniles, Brooks's skills effectively work together to comprise a language of poetry that describes for the child his or her experiences. Poems with bouncy rhymes are intermixed with those of more subtle and varied sound patterns. Emphasis upon the monosyllabic word at the end of end-stopped lines and other places, varying lengths of lines, repetition, and other devices sustain an interesting poetics which unpatronizingly presents the childhood world. "Ella" reveals something of the magic maintained, even down to a simple use of paradox in the first two lines: "Beauty has a coldness / That keeps you very warm. / 'If I run out to see the clouds, / That will be no harm!'"

In *The Bean Eaters* and certain of the new poems of *Selected Poems*, developments in style, for the most part, are responses to experimentations with loosened forms and the mileage one can gain from very simple statements. In *Annie Allen*, Brooks had loosened up the form of the sonnet in ''The Rites for Cousin Vit,'' with the use of elliptical syntax, the pressures of colloquial speech, and the cumulative capacity of all the poetic devices to create the impact of hyperbole. Cousin Vit was simply too vital to have died; thus Brooks interjects into the language of the sonnet the idiomatic swing and sensuality of the street: that Vit continued to do ''the snake-hips with a hiss. . . .'' In *The Bean Eaters* she again loosened up sonnet form in ''A Lovely Love'' by adapting the Petrarchan rhyme scheme to the situation of the tenement lovers, intermingling short and long complete statements with elliptical ones, and managing a nervous rhythm which imposes the illusion of being a one-to-one imitation of the behavior of lovers. The diction of the poem is a mixture of the romantic (''hyacinth darkness''), the realistic (''Let it be stairways, and a splintery box''), and the mythically religious (''birthright of our lovely love / In swaddling clothes. Not like that Other one''). Although the elliptical structures are more numerous and informal in ''Cousin Vit,'' the rhythm of ''A Lovely Love'' seems to make that poem the more complex achievement.

Another technical development is the poet's bolder movement into a free verse appropriate to the situation which she sometimes dots with rhyme. The technique will be more noticeable and surer in its achievement in the next volume, *In the Mecca*. But the poem ''A Bronzeville Mother Loiters in Mississippi. Meanwhile a Mississippi Mother Burns Bacon'' gives the technique full rein, except for the rhyming. The lines frequently move in the rhythms of easygoing conversation or in the loose patterns of stream-of-consciousness, as the poet portrays the movement from romantic notions to reality in the consciousness of the young white woman over whom a young black boy (reminiscent of the slain Emmett Till), has been lynched by her husband and his friend. The dramatic situation determines the length of lines, and the statements vary in form; short declarative sentences, simple sentences, phrase units understandable from their ties to preceding sentences, and long, complex structures. Additional sources of rhythm are repetition, parallel structures, and alliteration. . . .

With the publishing of *To Disembark*, it is apparent that Gwendolyn Brooks's change in outlook and consciousness has crystallized in an altered and distinctive style that offers the virtues of its own personality without denying its kinship with an earlier one. Most dramatic are the speaker's position in the center of her kinship group and the warmth and urgency of her speech. As indicated, the tendency of the language is toward a new simplicity. It can be seen in poems which, on the surface, remain very close to a traditional style of poetic realism but always evidence the fact that they proceed from an artist who is choosing from a wide range of resources. It can be seen in poems which will still, in particular passages, place language under great strain. Such patterns create also a recognizably new voice in the poetry.

> George Kent. In Mari Evans, ed. *Black Women Writers (1950–1980): A Critical Evaluation* (New York: Doubleday, 1984), pp. 88–89, 92, 96–97, 104

Brooks, in her poetry, seldom endows women with the power, integrity, or magnificence of her male figures. The passive and vulnerable Annie Allen, the heroine of her Pulitzer-Prize-winning poem [*Annie Allen*], is deserted by her soldier husband and left

pathetically mourning her fate in her little kitchenette, ''thoroughly / Derelict and dim and done.'' Sometimes Brooks's women manage to be ''decently wild'' as girls, but they grow up to be worried and fearful, or fretful over the loss of a man. They wither in back yards, afraid to tackle life; they are done in by dark skin; and, like ''estimable Mable,'' they are often incapable of estimating their worth without the tape measure of a man's interest in them. . . .

Rereading *Maud Martha* is a necessary step in revising the male-dominated Afro-American canon not only because this unusual text requires a different set of interpretative strategies but because it suggests a different set of rituals and symbols for Afro-American literature and a different set of progenitors. Current feminist theories which insist that we have to learn how to read the coded messages in women's texts—the silences, the evasions, the repression of female creativity—have helped me to reread *Maud Martha*, to read interiority in this text as one of the masks Maud uses to defend herself against rage. But if she cannot rely on the spoken word for help, she certainly appropriates power in more concealed ways—she writes her husband out of the text mid-way, she reduces her mother to a vain, pretentious fool, and she assigns her beautiful sister to a static end in a compromising marriage— thus the victim becomes superior to her victimizers. The reconstruction of scenes in which condescending others (white women and black and white men) are shown dominating Maud, while the reader is aware of her internal resistance, is another indirect way of giving Maud power. . . .

If *Maud Martha* is considered an integral part of the Afro-American canon, we will have to revise our conception of power and powerlessness, of heroism, of symbolic landscapes and ritual grounds. With his access to middle-class aspirations, to a public life and to male privilege, is the Invisible Man [in Ralph Ellison's *Invisible Man*] as easily defined out of existence as the physically vulnerable and speechless Maud? Yet, in spite of her greater powerlessness, she is not at the end of her text submerged in a dark hole, contemplating her invisibility in isolation. She is outside, in the light, with her daughter by the hand, exhilarated by the prospect of new life. Her ritual grounds are domestic enclosures, where we have rarely looked for heroic gestures; her most heroic act is one defiant declarative sentence; and yet she has changed in enough small ways for us to hope that ''these little promises, just under cover'' may, as she says earlier in the novel, in time, fulfill themselves.

> Mary Helen Washington. In Henry Louis Gates, Jr., ed. *Black Literature and Literary Theory* (New York: Methuen, 1984), pp. 255–56, 260

Gwendolyn Brooks has experimented with a variety of prosodic, syntactic, and narrative strategies. Her writing career has been remarkably rich in forms and ideas. Her creative practice has involved the ongoing articulation and formation of a variety of texts that express a shifting, exploratory, and ultimately performative consciousness. In terms of art, she has never been wary of ''the fascination of what's difficult''; but in terms of social justice, she has always addressed a range of America's social problems. In short, at the nexus of Brooks's art lies a fundamental commitment to both the modernist aesthetics of art and the common ideal of social justice.

Nowhere is this dual commitment more apparent than in the multiplicity of voices in her works. If the reader finds echoes of

T. S. Eliot and Countee Cullen in her poetry, there are also equally strong folk vernacular voices punctuating her forty-year literary career. Her three early works, *A Street in Bronzeville*, *Annie Allen*, and *The Bean Eaters*, present a wide range of poetic forms, including blues poems, ballads, experimental free verse, quatrains, Petrarchan sonnets, and Chaucerian stanzas. Her subsequent publications, *In the Mecca*, *Riot*, *Family Pictures*, *Beckonings*, and *To Disembark*, are written primarily in free verse and show her increasing concern with social issues, yet the variety of speakers continues. In fact, as the diversity of Brooks's achievement becomes apparent, our initial impression is one of a talent that does not need the unifying edge of a single, stylized voice or of a unique aesthetic with which to assert itself against tradition.

Yet Brooks's talent defines itself against the weight of tradition: She consistently utilizes the past while creating new constructs. Her variations on several traditions, several systems of values, give her poetry continuity within change, making it both difficult and original. She keeps before the reader that which is traditional at the same time that she modifies the tradition to accommodate her unique and developing sensibility.

Maria K. Mootry. In Maria K. Mootry and Gary Smith, eds. *A Life Distilled: Gwendolyn Brooks, Her Poetry and Fiction* (Urbana: University of Illinois Press, 1987), pp. 1–2

Although [Brooks] is currently serving as one of the most engaged artistic guides for a culture, she is more justly described as a herald than as an uninformed convert. She has mediated the dichotomy that left Paul Laurence Dunbar (whose *Complete Poems* she read at an early age) a torn and agonized man. Of course, she had the example of Dunbar, the Harlem Renaissance writers, and others to build upon, but at times even superior talents have been incapable of employing the accomplishments of the past for their own ends. Unlike the turn-of-the-century poet and a number of Renaissance writers, Brooks has often excelled the surrounding white framework, and she has been able to see clearly beyond it to the strengths and beauties of her own unique cultural tradition.

Gwendolyn Brooks represents a singular achievement. Beset by a double consciousness, she has kept herself from being torn asunder by crafting poems that equal the best in the black and white American literary traditions. Her characters are believable, her themes manifold, and her technique superb. The critic (whether black or white) who comes to her work seeking only support for his ideology will be disappointed for, as Etheridge Knight pointed out, she has ever spoken the truth. And truth, one likes to feel, always lies beyond the boundaries of any one ideology. Perhaps Brooks's most significant achievement is her endorsement of this point of view. From her hand and fertile imagination have come volumes that transcend the dogma on either side of the American veil. In their transcendence, they are fitting representatives of an "Effulgent lover of the Sun!"

Houston A. Baker, Jr. In Maria K. Mootry and Gary Smith, eds. *A Life Distilled: Gwendolyn Brooks, Her Poetry and Fiction* (Urbana: University of Illinois Press, 1987), p. 28

In contemporary poetry, the world of the poem is often conceived as a beleaguered fortress against the real world; to enter one is to depart from the other. This limits the material of reality for the

work and requires a choice between the two as means or end. Whether weighted toward solipsism or manipulation, the tendency results in an exclusive poetry, usually offered with matching poetics and criticism. The art of Gwendolyn Brooks makes no such dichotomy. It includes the world, its poetic emblems, and us. We are not merely to be ranked and shaped with the raw data of existence. We matter, in the vital properties of our thought, feeling, growth, and change, so that the poem becomes an interaction in a mutual process, socially resonant. . . .

Brooks's religious faith is ambivalent regarding the supernatural, yet it is deeply humanistic. Her apocalyptic imagery has a counterpart of stability, but its force is dynamic; its permanence, change. "Divorce"—from nature, as decried by [William Carlos] Williams and followers like Charles Olson; from God, as mourned in [T. S.] Eliot; from excellence in art, as scorned by [Ezra] Pound; from mind, as chided by [Wallace] Stevens—is transformed by Brooks into a concern with divorce from human dignity. Her work cries out against the subjugation of blacks, which may have inflicted more physical than spiritual damage, while it has hurt whites spiritually. Brooks embodies *caritas*, expressed in the poetic voice as it articulates a racial and communal vision. Hers is a unified sensibility, pragmatic and idealistic, shaped, in part, by the needs which it ventures to meet. . . .

[Brooks] belongs to that select category Pound called "the inventors," the highest classification of poets who create and expand formal limits and, thereby, taste itself. Development toward a genre of contemporary heroic poetry, offering distinctive style and language, may be considered Brooks's outstanding achievement. Various types of heroic, exemplified by several other black poets, are examined elsewhere. Yet Brooks's heroic, direct though subtle, comprehensive in sensibility and range, whether "grand" or "plain," socially responsive and evangelically fused, makes her work a paradigm of the genre. The unique authority with which she speaks to her people is based in mutual affection and esteem and a historically viable sense of kinship. Her call to black pride, even when chiding or dismayed, has a familial intimacy. This kind of rapport hovered over the Fireside Poets who supported the Union during the Civil War. For the earlier tradition of literature in English, the configuration is Miltonic and Romantic, the poet as artist and activist. For the native tradition of the American and African American folk preacher, it is sermonic and communal.

D. H. Melhem. *Gwendolyn Brooks: Poetry and the Heroic Voice* (Lexington: University Press of Kentucky, 1987), pp. 236–38

Gwendolyn Brooks's feminine landscape is clearly demarcated as heterosexual territory. Males are never far away from its female centers of attention, even when the male presence is overwhelmingly implicit and memorial, as it is in "The Anniad" and various other poems in the volume, *Annie Allen*. The poet's particular address to communities of women in her audience is persistent in the canon across four decades of work, reflecting the storm and stress of this period of African-American women's political consciousness with the 1981 publication, *Primer for Blacks: Three Preachments*, "To Those of My Sisters Who Kept Their Naturals." Brooks's work interweaves the female and her distinctive feelings into a delicate tissue of poetic response to the human situation, defined by a particular historical order—the African-American personality among the urban poor in the city of Chicago between World War II and the present of the poem. Within this body of work, the female voice, for all its poignant insistence, is a modified noun of vocality, danced through a range of appetite and desire that does not stand isolated from a masculine complement. If poetry is our teacher in this instance, not entirely estranged from theory, but subsuming it, then the "feminine" is manifest as an emphasis, neither hostile to "masculine" nor silenced by it. We are rather reminded now of an image of Jungian resolution with the circumferences of double circles overlapping to form an altered distance through the diameters of both. It is only by virtue of a perversion in the seeing that the overlapping circles can declare any independence whatsoever. They relinquish their imagined uniqueness to an enlarged order of circularity, as the peripheries of both now involve us at the center of each. Getting the point does not necessarily require that we embrace the idea, or the "man," but that we acknowledge it as a viable figure in the universe of female and "feminine" representability. This involved image of circularity renders a geometry for poets, and those are the depths and surfaces that claim our attention at the moment.

In Brooks's poetic order of things, the "feminine" is neither cause for particular celebration nor certain despair, but near to the "incandescent," it is analogous to that "wedge-shaped core of darkness," through which vision we see things in their fluid passage between dream and waking reality, as multiple meanings impinge on a central event. The poet's novelette *Maud Martha* does not exhaust Brooks's contemplation of the "feminine," but provides a point of illumination and departure concerning an important phase of her long and distinguished career as an American poet. If not chronologically central to the canon, *Maud Martha*, beside "The Anniad," is experienced by the reader as an "impression point.". . . *Maud Martha* brings to closure the poems in *A Street in Bronzeville* and *Annie Allen*, while it prepares the way for *The Bean Eaters* and, from the 1960s, the stunning poetry of *In the Mecca*.

> Hortense J. Spillers. In Henry Louis Gates, Jr., ed. *Reading Black, Reading Feminist* (New York: Meridian, 1990), pp. 249–50

In an unpublished handwritten and handbound collection of early poems entitled *Songs After Sunset* (1935–36), Gwendolyn Brooks begins and ends with an inscription to a cryptic figure named "Ima Twin." This figure may allude to a second volume of poems, as Erlene Stetson has suggested in an article on Brooks's unpublished poetry. . . . Or the figure may be self-referential, alluding to that sense of "twoness" or "double-consciousness" that W. E. B. DuBois described in 1903 as the governing trope of black American experience in *The Souls of Black Folk*: "One ever feels his twoness,—an American, a Negro, two souls, two thoughts, two unreconciled strivings; two warring ideals in one dark body, whose dogged strength alone keeps it from being torn asunder". Whatever its precise reference, the literary twin of Brooks's early poems serves as a fitting introduction to a black woman poet whose life and work might be read as a dynamic and continually self-transforming struggle to negotiate the conflicting demands of race, gender, and class, of aesthetics and politics, craft and commitment, modernism and populism, art and activism, black Americanism and black Africanism as she moved simultaneously toward an engagement with language as a form of social action—of guns and ammunition—in the making of an African-American poetics, and an assertion of the power of "The Womanhood"—and "the mother"—in the making of an African-American community.

As the inaugural and closing inscription of Brooks's early poems, "Ima Twin" also suggests the black woman poet's problematic relation not only to a white male but to a black male and white female literary tradition that has excluded her. At the time Brooks began to write, black creativity was in flower, but the black awakening that has come to be known as the "Harlem Renaissance" was a white-sponsored and black male-centered production, associated with the work of Langston Hughes, Countee Cullen, Claude McKay, and other male writers and artists. Although black women poets were writing and supporting each other in female literary networks during the "Renaissance" years, only the work of Georgia Douglas Johnson was published in book form.

It is in the context of black female absence from the literary tradition that the cryptic "Ima Twin" of Brooks's early poems begins to assume a culturally specific meaning. With no black female poetic tradition on which to draw, Brooks, in effect, invents a literary sister—black and female like herself—as the audience and muse for her earliest poems. This specifically black female inscription of *Songs After Sunset* is complemented visually by an ink drawing of a female singer with an open songbook who appears on the title page bearing the signature "Gwendolyn." The picture suggests the black female oral and folk culture from which Brooks drew in making herself the inaugural figure—the founder and inventor—of a black female poetic tradition in which she might muse and sing.

"You," Brooks's mother had early announced, "are going to be the lady Paul Laurence Dunbar." . . . The literary title conferred by her mother fostered Brooks's sense of commonality with the popular poet of the black people, at the same time that it marked the difference of the specifically female voice Brooks would bring to her representations of black life in America. "I believed every word she said and just kept on writing," Brooks remembers. "Sometimes I turned out two or three poems or a couple of stories in one day, all very, very, very bad".

In *Naked and Fiery Forms*, the feminist critic Suzanne Juhasz comments on the "triple bind" of "the black woman poet": "Being doubly oppressed, because of race and sex, she experiences conflict between being poet and woman, poet and black, black and woman". What is in fact striking about Brooks's life and work, however, is her relative lack of conflict between woman and poet compared with her white literary sisters; nor is there a particular conflict between Brooks's identity as black and poet. The actual site of Brooks's oppression is her existence—or lack of existence—as a black woman who is doubly invisible, effaced by both her race and her sex.

During Brooks's childhood and adolescence, the overwhelming fact of her existence was her race. As a child, Brooks remembers admiring her brown skin: "I had always considered it beautiful. I would stick out my arm, examine it, and smile. Charming! And convenient, for mud on my leg was not as annunciatory as was mud on the leg of light Rose Hurd." But Brooks's early delight in her color was not shared by her world, where racial codes of difference and inferiority were both inter- and intraracial. "One of the first 'world'-truths revealed to me when I at last became a member of SCHOOL," said Brooks, "was that, to be socially successful, a little girl must be Bright (of skin). It was better if your hair was curly, too—or at least Good Grade'' (Report from Part One). Forced to construct and measure herself within systems of value alien to herself—one male, the other white—Brooks felt alone, strange, ''inferior to everybody.'' Her sense of inferiority as a dark girl was reinforced by her inhibitions as a ''reserved, quiet child'': ''I was timid to the point of terror, silent, primly dressed. AND DARK. The boys did not mind telling me that this was the failing of failings.'' In the eyes of both light and dark men, she was either invisible or insignificant: ''the little Bright ones looked through me if I happened to inconvenience their vision, and those of my own hue rechristened me Ol' Black Gal''.

Later, in her poems, Brooks would become one of the first black women writers to record the emotional pain and complex psychic wounding of intraracial discrimination. The representation of black boys and later black men as instruments of intraracial oppression became a recurrent motif of Brooks's writing from ''The Ballad of Chocolate Mabbie'' and ''Ballad of Pearl May Lee'' in *A Street in Bronzeville* to ''The Anniad'' in *Annie Allen* and the rejection suffered by Maud as an ''Ol' Black Gal'' in Brooks's semi-autobiographical novel *Maud Martha*.

Whereas the ''sweet and chocolate'' girls of ''The Ballad of Chocolate Mabbie,'' ''The Anniad,'' and *Maud Martha* suffer in silence—''taming all that anger down''—in ''Ballad of Pearl May Lee,'' Brooks gives full voice to her own sense of personal rage in a fantasy of violence against the black man. The poem tells the story of a black man seduced by a white girl and then accused of rape and lynched by the white community. Told from the point of view of the black woman he betrayed, the poem expresses the paradoxical love/hate relationship between the black woman and the black man. Although Pearl May Lee loves Sammy, she is also enraged by the fact that in his eyes she is only ''dark meat''. . . .

The irony and tragedy of the poem is that Pearl May Lee's vindictive wish comes true, putting her paradoxically on the side of the black man's white killers. The poem registers the black woman's emotional turmoil and near insane breakdown, as her personal sense of love and loss are intercepted by violent feelings of rage and betrayal. . . .

As the story of a white girl's perfidy, ''Ballad of Pearl May Lee'' might be read as a parable of the black man's betrayal at the hands of the white community. But by locating the emotional effects of that betrayal in the damaged psyche of Pearl May Lee, the poem suggests the ricocheting effects of white violence and white hegemony in the black community as the black woman becomes both the agent and the victim of a killing urge directed simultaneously against white society, against the black man, and ultimately against herself.

Although Brooks speaks through the mask of Pearl May Lee, the poem articulates feelings of rage and betrayal that are clearly her own. ''I don't know whether you want to include woman rage in this discussion or not,'' she told Claudia Tate in a 1983 interview. ''But I hope you sense some real rage in 'The Ballad of Pearl May Lee.' The speaker is a very enraged person. I know because I consulted myself on how I felt. For instance, why in the world has it been that our men have preferred either white or that pigmentation which is as close to white as possible? That's all political'' (*Black Women Writers at Work*).

Betsy Erkkila. *The Wicked Sisters: Women Poets, a Literary History, and Discord* (New York: Oxford University Press 1997), pp. 186–90

BIBLIOGRAPHY

*A Street in Bronzeville*, 1945; ''The Anniad,'' 1949; *Annie Allen*, 1949; *Maud Martha*, 1953; *Bronzeville Boys and Girls*, 1956; ''The Ballad of Rudolph Reed,'' 1960; ''The Bean Eaters,'' 1960; *The Bean Eaters*, 1960; *A Catch of Shy Fish*, 1963; *Selected Poems*, 1963; *In the Time of Detachment, In the Time of Cold*, 1965; *For Illinois 1968: A Sesquicentennial Poem*, 1968; *In the Mecca*, 1968; *Riot*, 1969; *Family Pictures*, 1970; *Aloneness*, 1971; *The World of Gwendolyn Brooks*, 1971; *Aurora*, 1972; *Report from Part One: An Autobiography*, 1972; *The Tiger Who Wore White Gloves: Or You Are What You Are*, 1974; *Beckonings*, 1975; ''A Black Wedding Song,'' 1975; ''Five Men against the Theme 'My Name Is Red Hot. Yo Name Ain Doodley Squat,''' 1975; ''Sammy Chester Leaves 'Godspell' and Visits *Upward Bound* on a Lake Forest Lawn, Bringing West Afrika,'' 1975; *Primer for Blacks: Three Preachments*, 1980; *To Disembark*, 1981; *Young Poet's Primer*, 1981; *Black Love*, 1982; *Mayor Harold Washington [and] Chicago, The I Will City*, 1983; *Very Young Poets*, 1983; *Blacks*, 1987; *The Near–Johannesburg Boy, and Other Poems*, 1987; *Gottschalk and the Grande Tarantelle*, 1988; *Winnie*, 1988; *Children Coming Home*, 1991; *The Gwendolyn Brooks Library*, 1991; *Report from Part Two*, 1996; *Selected Poems*, 1999

# BROWN, Sterling A. (1901–)
**United States**

Mr. Brown's work is not only fine, it is also unique. He began writing just after the Negro poets had generally discarded conventionalized dialect, with its minstrel traditions of Negro life (traditions that had but slight relation, often no relation at all, to *actual* Negro life) with its artificial and false sentiment, its exaggerated geniality and optimism. He infused his poetry with genuine characteristic flavor by adopting as his medium the common, racy, living speech of the Negro in certain phases of *real* life. For his raw material he dug down into the deep mine of Negro folk poetry. He found the unfailing sources from which sprang the Negro folk epics and ballads such as ''Stagolee,'' ''John Henry,'' ''Casey Jones,'' ''Long Gone John'' and others.

But, as I said in commenting on his work in *The Book of American Negro Poetry*: he has made more than mere transcriptions of folk poetry, and he has done more than bring to it mere artistry; he has deepened its meanings and multiplied its implications. He has actually absorbed the spirit of his material, made it his own; and without diluting its primitive frankness and raciness, truly re-expressed it with artistry and magnified power. In a word, he has taken this raw material and worked it into original and authentic poetry.

James Weldon Johnson. Introduction to Sterling A. Brown, *Southern Road* (New York, Harcourt, Brace, 1932), pp. xiv-xv

Sterling Brown has penetrated the essence of Negro song, of folk song, and has utilized the expressiveness of dialect. But, the racial distinctiveness of his poetry does not depend exclusively on dialect; it also arises from the subtlest nuances of the ironic life of black men, from Brown's ability to plumb the depths of their feelings and pinpoint their psychology. . . .

Alain Locke, who has an admirable knowledge of the psychology of his race, tells us that the stereotyped black man is a clown, a buffoon, an easy smiler, a foolish weeper, and a credulous Christian, but that the real Black man is frequently a cynical fatalist, a sly pretender, and an impudent, whimsical pagan. Sterling Brown should be considered a rectifier of the false presentation of the black man, an excellent interpreter of the soul of his race who, in his songs, makes us familiar with all the subtleties of racial feelings. In the poem ''Children of the Mississippi'' he reaches the heights of poetic expression, in an orchestral harmony that arouses many deep feelings. The muddy, black flood waters of the Mississippi, with their hunger for death, overflow in the poem to sublime language, equal to that of the best poetry of any age.

> Ildefonso Pereda Valdés. In Ildefonso Pereda Valdés, ed., *Antología de la poesía negra americana* (Santiago, Chile: Ediciones Ercilla, 1936), pp. 12–13†

Through the Thirties and into the Forties there were three critics whose ideas on literature were dominant. These were Benjamin Brawley, Alain Locke, and Sterling Brown. . . .

Sterling Brown, the third and youngest of the formative critics of the Thirties, had barely begun his public career as critic when the Renaissance in its original form died away. Himself a poet, whose *Southern Road* appeared at the beginning of the Great Depression, he shared few of the urban delusions of the central figures of the Renaissance though he followed and understood them fully. Like Brawley, he was physically located away from the great Harlem metropolis during most of the Twenties but, unlike Brawley, he found the time and followed the urge to investigate more fully the Negro folk cultures of semi-rural Virginia, Missouri, and Tennessee while on teaching assignments in those regions. In both his poetry and in his criticism he therefore employed in greater depth a knowledge of the folk sources of literary expression. This knowledge was greater than that of prior and most contemporary interpreters of Negro expression; in addition it was buttressed by what most of his contemporaries also lacked: a thorough grounding in past and contemporary literatures. The newer traditions of realism and naturalism were not uncongenial to him and his studies in the Irish literary movement had convinced him that the major worth for the Negro literary movement lay in the life and expression of the people themselves. . . .

[His] credo is, essentially, that valid literary expression, in whatever form, must be true to its subject matter. The author must therefore forego all literary and social traditions which, either by softening sentimentally or exaggerating for effect, distort the substance for the sake of form, sales, conformity, or anything else which is properly extraneous to the subject matter at hand.

> Ulysses Lee. *Phylon*. 11, 4, 1950, pp. 330, 334–35

Many critics, writing in praise of Sterling Brown's first volume of verse, have seen fit to hail him as a significant new Negro poet. The discriminating few go further; they hail a new era in Negro poetry, for such is the deeper significance of this volume (*Southern Road*). Gauging the main objective of Negro poetry as the poetic portrayal of Negro folk-life true in both letter and spirit to the idiom of the folk's own way of feeling and thinking, we may say that here for

the first time is that much-desired and long-awaited acme attained or brought within actual reach. . . .

I do not mean to imply that Sterling Brown's art is perfect, or even completely mature. It is all the more promising that this volume represents the work of a young man just in his early thirties. But a Negro poet with almost complete detachment, yet with a tone of persuasive sincerity, whose muse neither clowns nor shouts, is indeed a promising and a grateful phenomenon. . . .

If we stop to inquire—as unfortunately the critic must—into the magic of [his] effects, we find the secret, I think, in this fact more than in any other: Sterling Brown has listened long and carefully to the folk in their intimate hours, when they were talking to themselves, not, so to speak, as in Dunbar, but actually as they do when the masks of protective mimicry fall. Not only has he dared to give quiet but bold expression to this private thought and speech, but he has dared to give the Negro peasant credit for thinking. In this way he has recaptured the shrewd Aesopian quality of the Negro folk-thought, which is more profoundly characteristic than their types of metaphors or their mannerisms of speech. They are, as he himself says, ''Illiterate, and somehow very wise,'' and it is this wisdom, bitter fruit of their suffering, combined with their characteristic fatalism and irony, which in this book gives a truer soul picture of the Negro than has ever yet been given poetically. [1934]

> Alain Locke. In Nancy Cunard, ed., *Negro: An Anthology* (New York, Frederick Ungar, 1970), pp. 88–90

*Southern Road* depicts the Negro as the victim not of the white man alone, but of all that surrounds him. He is enslaved by the land he cultivates, victimized by the lawless natural elements whose predilection it is to fall on him, as he is victimized by his own fear and that of others, and by his own ignorance and credulity. In short he is exposed to a terrible fate whose whole pitiless cruelty is sung in the blues and whose effects the people had always sought to ward off by means of superstitious precepts passed from generation to generation. . . .

The Negro's destiny, as presented in Brown's work, is ultimately a depressing one. But his outlook strikes us as significantly more pessimistic than that of his predecessors because he practically excludes the spiritual forces from his universe. In some obscure way, a vital bond still subsisted between the black man and God in the writings of James Weldon Johnson and Langston Hughes. Sterling Brown, on the contrary, makes the situation entirely clear: the black man suddenly finds himself isolated and must derive his whole strength from the people, who thus become the sole source of all true value. . . .

As for the poet himself, does he differ from them to any great extent? It would have been easy to understand, had the disillusioning portrait of the black man that he has painted for us ended in despair. The reason this does not occur is that he too has hit upon a way of escaping from an appalling reality. For it is an art of living that he has discovered in the humorous philosophy in which his race is steeped, and it may be more than a coincidence that Brown, the poet of the Negro Renaissance who most pitilessly excludes from his universe the whole range of religious forces, is at the same time the only truly humorous poet in the group. [1963]

> Jean Wagner. *Black Poets of the United States* (Urbana: University of Illinois Press, 1973), pp. 483, 496–98

*Southern Road*, the first collection of poems by Sterling A. Brown, was published in 1932, at the end of the New Negro Renaissance and the beginning of the Great Depression. Some time after the appearance of this small volume, which was generally favorably reviewed, Brown prepared for publication a second collection with the intriguing title *No Hiding Place*. This collection, however and regrettably, was never published. Meanwhile Brown's rising status as a poet was evidenced by occasional appearances of new poems of his in national periodicals and scholarly anthologies. No second collection of Brown's poems appeared, withal, until the recent publication of *The Last Ride of Wild Bill, and Eleven Narrative Poems*. The title poem in this collection is an excellent example of modern narrative folk poetry at its best. . . .

Contrary to Wagner's view, Brown's collections of poems can hardly be said to furnish proof that the dialect movement Johnson referred to has gone forward. Neither of them abounds in the mutilated English commonly called Negro dialect. Nor does it appear from them that Brown ever intended to indulge in—or perpetrate—that kind of writing. Rather he seems to have had his several characters employ only such illiterate and semiliterate usage as was expressive of their individuality. The substandard grammar and the comparatively few dialect spellings to which he resorted give the impression that he endeavored to represent without exaggeration illiterate and semiliterate usage as he had attentively heard it in his native Washington, D.C., in Lynchburg, Virginia; Jefferson City, Missouri; and Nashville, Tennessee, where he spent several years teaching college English; and in his travels elsewhere in the United States. Accordingly the usage in his poetry is at once radically different from what has been conventionally called Negro dialect and remarkably close to actual folk speech, as one would expect to find it in folk poetry.

W. Edward Farrison. *CLA Journal*. December 1975, pp. 286, 289

Sterling A. Brown was one of the few black writers of his generation who did not want to be part of the Harlem Renaissance. He was very proud that he had never shaken hands with Carl Van Vechten, who, he said, had done more than bad liquor to corrupt the Negro. The Harlem Renaissance was a publishers' gimmick, he said. It didn't last long enough to be called a renaissance, and very few Harlemites were in it. Black writers, he said, only went to Harlem for parties. Harlem was "the show-window, the cashier's till." While the young Niggerati were hovering around the tables of white patrons in Small's Paradise, Sterling himself was down in Lynchburg, Virginia, talking to a guitar player, Big Boy Davis, one of the rural characters whose ethos engaged Sterling's melancholy and rebellious sensibility, from which came a folk poetry of lasting originality. . . .

[Brown] spent his life talking—about folklore, stride piano, the shrewdness of the blues, A. E. Housman, Lena Horne, you name it. They used to say that every black in the United States knew every other black, and Sterling was one of those who had stories about everyone, from Jelly Roll Morton to a raconteur barber in Nashville. He was a connoisseur of black history and a guardian of its integrity. Volatile, ironic, and hopelessly genuine, he was in thrall to what he called the "mulch" of black culture. But black culture was also a text that he studied as no other black writer has before or since. He was the last of the New Negroes.

Sterling didn't mind being called a New Negro, though he said he'd been an old Negro for so long it was too late to do anything about it. During the New Negro movement in the early Twenties Sterling's poems began to appear in black magazines and anthologies, but his first collection of poems, *Southern Road*, wasn't published until 1932. The book that made his name came after the parties uptown ended and as the bread lines all over began, and that, as much as his nonconformist temperament, left him to go his own way. . . .

The historian Sterling Stuckey notes in his introduction to [*The Collected Poems of Sterling A. Brown*] that part of Sterling's achievement was to reclaim from stereotype such subjects as chain gangs, gamblers, cabarets, and crimes of passion. The itinerant entertainer who sticks his cigarette in his guitar before he sings his mother's favorite spiritual; the "golden, spacious grin" of Jack Johnson taking it like a man; a girl no longer recognizable under her streetwalker's paint; a disillusioned veteran who ends up buck-dancing on the midnight air; a woman who steals from the lady she works for "Cause what huh 'dear grandfawthaw' / Took from Mandy Jane's grandpappy" / Ain' no basket in de worl' / What kin tote all date away"—Sterling's poems reveal how in the struggle to exist the historic stands alongside the everyday. Several of his narrative poems involve self-defense, the faith that looks through death, or the fearless, manly man respected in hell. ("He said 'Come and get me' / They came and got him./ And they came by tens.") He had a vision of the folk as a subtle people at the mercy of what could jump out of the ordinary, and who take the tragic with uncommon understatement.

He carefully observed the Joe Meekses, Bessies, Big Jesses, Luther Johnsons, young Freds, Johnnies, and Sams, who abound in his poetry. He paid attention to their walks, their spare-ribbed yard dogs, silk shirts pink as sunsets, bulldog brogans, habits of mind ("Don't be no Chinaman, George"), and to their landscape of locust, flooding rivers, and cotton. He recognized the "folk eloquence" in everyday talk, understood how Ma Rainey could "jes' catch hold of us, somekindaway," but none of the characters in his ballads is treated sentimentally because his first duty was not to his sympathies but to the poem. He already trusted what they stood for, these railroad men highballing through the country, trying to "git de Jack," these lowlifes playing checkers with deacons, and placed the folk tradition of the black firmly within American poetry.

"Laughter is a vengeance," and as a poet Sterling was also a folklorist alive to the humor and paradoxes in his raw material. "Whuh folks, whuh folks; don't wuk muh brown too hahd! / Who's practisin' de Chahlston in yo' big backyahd." He told some tall tales or lies, as they are called, about a rascal, Slim Greer, who passes for white and courts a white woman only to be detected when he plays the piano as only a black can. In another, when "niggers" in Atlanta are forced to do their laughing in a telephone booth, Slim holds up the line because every time he looks at the hundreds of "shines" gripping their sides to keep from breaking the law he can't stop laughing. . . .

In his youth Sterling, like many other black writers of the period, was taken with the muckraking poetry of Carl Sandburg and the dramatic monologues of E. A. Robinson and especially with Frost, the speaking voice in modern poetry. But he has his own remarkable ability to fuse traditional meter with the natural rhythm of the speaker:

"No need in frettin'
Case good times go,

Things as dey happen
Jes' is so;
Nothin' las' always
Farz I know. . . .''
(''Old Man Buzzard'')

Sometimes he used the meter of the Methodist hymn, which lent a prayerful tone to his folk musing. . . .

Sterling wrote Petrarchan sonnets, free verse in standard English, blank verse, but he achieved his best poetic effects through his reinvention of dialect. He went beyond mimicry of broken English, or transcription of the blues line (''Leave 'is dirty city, take my foot up in my hand'') or imitations of folksy metaphor.

James Weldon Johnson once complained that dialect had only two stops, pathos and humor. Though Paul Laurence Dunbar had elevated the medium, young black poets after World War I were in revolt against Negro dialect poetry because of what Johnson saw as the artificiality of its subjects and ''exaggerated geniality,'' which had no relation to ''actual Negro life.'' Johnson believed that black poets had to find racial symbols from within, as Synge had done for the Irish. But *Southern Road* broke with the comic minstrel and plantation traditions. It made use of folk epics and ballads—like ''Stagolee,'' ''John Henry,'' ''Casey Jones,'' and ''Long Gone John''—to create what Johnson hailed as ''the common, racy, living speech of the Negro in certain parts of real life.'' Alain Locke pointed out that Sterling's portrayal of the Negro folk life succeeded not because it depended on being true to an idiom, but because in his psychological distance ''he dared to give the Negro credit for thinking.''

*Southern Road* was widely praised, yet trouble came. Sterling's second book of poems, *No Hiding Place*, was turned down by his publisher, Harcourt Brace, maybe for commercial reasons. Sterling never got over the rejection. He didn't publish another book of poems until 1975 when a black publisher issued *The Last Ride of Wild Bill*, a ballad from the 1930s about a numbers runner. The militant portraits of sharecroppers and ''niggrah'' clowns of *No Hiding Place* were later included in his *Collected Poems*.

Meanwhile, Sterling continued to produce reviews and essays on black literature, folklore, history, and music. He was a national editor of the Federal Writers Project from 1936 to 1939, and made important contributions to *Washington: City and Capital* (1937) and *The Negro in Virginia* (1940). He developed, with Alain Locke, a series for which he wrote the historical surveys *The Negro in American Fiction* (1937) and *Negro Poetry and Drama* (1937). He published, in the 1940s, unusually cool short stories about the South; traveled throughout the country as a kind of one-man department of black studies; and, of course, taught at Howard and at other universities as a visiting professor.

Sterling's readings were performances; between poems he would tell stories, and managed to be both down-home and as courtly as Duke Ellington. Someone told me he once demonstrated how to dance on a dime. Until I read Sterling's *The Negro Caravan*, dialect, to me, meant *Uncle Remus*, something to get over, just as stuck-up audiences had looked down their noses fifty years before. Sterling's 1941 anthology is still unsurpassed as a resource, even though black writing from Phyllis Wheatley and the slave narratives doesn't fit between the covers of one book anymore. I had never heard of novelists like J. A. Rogers and William Attaway, or

playwrights like Theodore Ward. Spirituals, work songs, tall tales, and the blues became an accessible literature.

Darryl Pinckney. *The New York Review of Books*. XXXVI, 4 (March 16, 1989), pp. 14–16

BIBLIOGRAPHY

*Outline for the Study of the Poetry of American Negroes*, 1930; ''Children of the Mississippi,'' 1932; *Southern Road*, 1932; *The Negro in American Fiction*, 1937; *Negro Poetry and Drama*, 1937; ''The Last Ride of Wild Bill,'' 1975; *The Last Ride of Wild Bill, and Eleven Narrative Poems*, 1975; *The Collected Poems of Sterling A. Brown*, 1980; *A Son's Return: Selected Essays of Sterling A. Brown*, 1996

# BRUTUS, Dennis (1924–)
## South Africa

Brutus's intellect is distinguished by its skill and intensity, certainly not . . . by depth. . . .

If Brutus is not a rare genius, he surely boasts a skillful, forceful, trained intelligence. The way he exercises his sure intellectual grip on his subjects calls to mind the method of John Donne and the Metaphysicals. A typical Dennis Brutus poem opens with a line or a couple of lines which holds in embryo the central motif of the piece. . . . Brutus then builds up his poem by developing this stated motif, arguing, describing, expounding, analysing, illustrating with vivid and living imagery, occasionally bolstering the argument with conceits, all the while echoing the opening lines either directly or through new images and descriptive details which embody the *idea* of the opening lines, and finally concluding in a dialectical and emotional point of rest in which the opening lines resound again.

Daniel Abasiekong. *Transition*. 23, 1965, p. 46

J. P. Clark, who has criticised Brutus, is right in saying that Nigerian poets do not write lines like ''obscene albinos''; but Nigerians are not murdered or imprisoned because they are black; they are not considered the black stinking lubrication that helps the huge cogs of the economy to run smoothly. Brutus is whipped and he lashes back furiously. It is true that sometimes his punches are wild, sometimes he misses, but he swings enough times for us to see what he is aiming at. Brutus, speaking for the millions of black South Africans, has been frustrated and turned away and confined and shot at and still nothing has changed. And so he continues to rage. . . .

There is horror in these poems [in *Sirens, Knuckles, Boots*], but it is not the horror of a man skittering in a high wind away from white ghosts stalking him with Sten-guns. It is rather the horror of a man seeing love nourished in bad soil, in a country made ugly by hatred. Perhaps Brutus likes to picture himself in flight, but I read these poems differently. He is not moving (living furiously does not mean bobbing around); he is staying, suffering the phantasms, and he is recording them faithfully. This takes great strength and dedication; he has escaped the decayed language of revolt, the clichés of the man oppressed. If the poems are depressive in their raging tenderness it is because Brutus is being hammered from within his soul and from without: the sirens in his ears, the knuckles and boots against his body.

Paul Theroux. *Black Orpheus.* August 1966, p. 43–45

Dennis Brutus is now living in exile in London. Were it not for the tragedy the last years have brought him and his family, one might think his situation part of some nightmarish Kafka farce. Yet its horror is only a bitter reflection of the edicts by which a ''coloured'' such as Brutus is forced to live in the Republic of South Africa. His poetry is denied publication in his country and only a slender volume published by the Mbari Writers and Artists Club of Nigeria [*Sirens, Knuckles, Boots*] is available to indicate the quality of both the spirit and poetry of this man. . . .

Throughout Brutus' poetry runs an infinite and continuous love for his sad yet beautiful country. Brutus never denies this affection. Replying to the newsman's inevitable question, he explained how he could feel affection for a country that treated him so viciously: ''It's a suffering people and a suffering land, assaulted, violated, raped, whatever you will, tremendously beautiful and I feel a great tenderness for it.'' This emotion shows in everything Brutus writes. . . .

Brutus affirms the hope that love and poetry, in mutual combination, can simultaneously reinforce the spirit. His lines take on an evocative lilt in their repetition:

Somehow we survive
and tenderness frustrated, does not wither . . .
But somehow we survive
Severance deprivation loss . . .
but somehow tenderness survives.

His assertion is vague. It is inexplicable but sure. How tenderness can survive, how even the very man can survive under such a dispensation we can hardly say. But Brutus affirms his own certainties. His attitude plays no heroics, though in avoiding that pose he is the more heroic. He answers oppression by the humane strength by which he lives—survives. Such strength is full enough; it even permits a little flamboyance in its confidence. . . .

Brutus once wrote ''under jackboots our bones and spirits crunch.'' The rest of his poetry contradicts this for it asserts the eventual triumph of spirits over jackboots. He rearticulates Orwell's view of the future of the jackboot stamping on the human face forever. But Brutus concludes with a courageous optimism that Orwell could not accept. His poetry convinces us that such optimism is not delusive. It is the source, not only of Brutus' capacity for survival, but of all hopes for equity in South Africa.

John Povey. *Journal of the New African Literature and the Arts.* Spring, 1967, pp. 95–96, 99–100

Dennis Brutus's first published poetry, *Sirens, Knuckles, Boots,* which came out in the early 1960's in Ibadan, displays the usual features of a beginner's work: brash, raw anger wielding the long thundering line and harsh sounds.

In *Letters to Martha,* the long thundering lines and awkward phraseology have given way to a subdued diction. And yet so much of the collection lapses into talkative verse which sounds like tired prose: like a guitar string that has lost its tension. One tends to condone this lapse because of the singleness of emotion and mood *Letters to Martha* represents. The impact is cumulative.

The promise one senses in *Letters to Martha* is certainly not anywhere near fulfillment in Brutus's later work. *Poems from Algiers. . .* is disappointing. There is nothing important the poems say, no specific emotion they can be said to be conveying. Only observational fragments. Two closely connected factors must account for this poverty: the poignant condition of exile that does not even have a base around which one's creative energies can regroup and rediscover their language; Brutus's ambivalence about the value of poetry or any other kind of creative writing in the present struggle against South African fascism. He has for ten years and more been at the head of a movement that is campaigning against racism in South African and international sport. . . . He feels the inner compulsion to write poetry, but he does not concede that it is important enough to warrant time off to organize his energies, to collect himself, and to hammer out a language that will match his sincerity of passion. And yet that impulse to communicate through the means of verse will not let him be. He feels guilty about not writing and yet will feel equally guilty for spending that much time writing.

Ezekiel Mphahlele. *Voices in the Whirlwind* (New York: Hill and Wang, 1972), pp. 91–92

The core of *Sirens, Knuckles, Boots* had been the love poems: each, while generally complete and satisfying, acquires additional force from its place in a closely linked sequence. A remarkable thoroughness is achieved mainly through a close application of imaginative and technical means; Brutus benefited from his reading of John Donne. Love inspires man's finest, most complete expression. And that expression, bred out of intense needs, assembles a language equal to the demands of feeling inspired by other experiences. Donne used it to chart his love for God: Brutus, his love for country. The language of love, by a semantic shift, is also the language of patriotism. . . .

His love for his wife is the base upon which [Brutus's] double-vision rests. And the double-vision, diffused throughout the poetry, adds a measure of variety and compensates for the relative narrowness of his subject-matter. Brutus must have seen the poetic advantages in such a move. By describing one, he describes the other. It is a double cropping of experience, compressing them to a point where they come to reside in a common vocabulary. . . .

How to restore love and loveliness, how to heal the rift in the feelings are recurring themes in Brutus's poetry. *Sirens, Knuckles, Boots* contains some of the most poignant pieces to come from Africa, contradicting those who allege that the ''situation of protest'' cannot yield vital, comprehensive poetry. They would be right if the protest submerges the poetry. Brutus's work, while narrow in range on account of its antecedents, is skilful and intelligent. The nature of his material lent itself to treatment in short lyrical poems, for which he developed a sharp, pungent style. The way he sets about a poem shows relentless logic. A quick glance at the first lines confirms that almost all those poems in *Sirens, Knuckles, Boots* start from specific moods and events, stated simply and concisely. He seems to know the limits, the emotional and mental area, within which the poem will find itself, and this enables him to maintain a firm grip as well as to construct his poem. While *Letters to Martha* adopts a loose, rambling discursive style, his first volume is reminiscent of metaphysical poetry, in the introspection, the combination of thought and feeling, tone, conceits, images and dialectical thrust.

> Edwin Thumboo. *Joliso*. 2, 2, 1974, pp. 36–38

Brutus's earlier verse explored the finest nuances of grammar, image and association; these poems [*China Poems*] achieve daring leaps of logic. They are exquisite and brief. Although inspired by haiku and *chüeh-chü*, they lack even the structural features of those forms which can be represented in English. Furthermore, their greatest success is in exactly the opposite effect of those genres: Brutus dictates the reader's response, both conceptual and affective. . . .

*Thoughts Abroad* displays Brutus's characteristic technique whereby involuted grammar and sound-play combine to accent each separate image, paradox and subtlety. Almost metrical, the rhythm creates an aura of Olympian remove while underscoring emotional and intellectual discords. Several poems maintain independent levels of meaning wherein, for example, a love lyric is addressed simultaneously to a woman and to his homeland. But the importance of the poems lies in the lucid, passionate reflections of a political exile in ironically greater comfort and distress, greater successes in vain, greater alienation in communing and commuting worldwide as he fights mankind's most vicious tyranny today.

> David Dorsey. *Books Abroad*. Spring 1976, pp. 459, 463

The poetry of Dennis Brutus is the reaction of one who is in mental agony, whether he is at home or abroad. This agony is partly caused by harassments, arrests, and imprisonment, and mainly by Brutus's concern for other suffering people. Thus Brutus feels psychically injured in some of his poems. When he traverses all his land as a "troubadour," finding wandering "motion sweeter far than rest," he is feeling the pinch of restiveness resulting from dislodgement. All the factors that make life uncomfortable are assembled . . . banning of "inquiry and movement," "Saracened arrest," and "the captor's hand"; and against them Brutus takes to roaming in freedom, "disdaining," "quixoting" (i.e. pursuing an ideal honor and devotion), singing all the time. His fight is purely psychological, not physical, for he puts up an attitude which his oppressors would least expect and which would disconcert them.

The emotional tension is palpable; to find "motion" sweeter than "rest" is in fact to have no rest. The conceit is as effective here as that used by John Donne when he wrote "Until I labor, I in labor lie," in the poem "Elegy: Going to Bed." Like W. B. Yeats, Brutus is pursuing his mask, his anti-self, or that which is least like him. His expression of love-emotions towards the land is a dramatization of his want of love. Thus instead of a "mistress-favor" he has "an arrow-brand" to adorn his breast. Brutus is therefore seeking for "something that is dear to him, but something that is out of reach."

> R. N. Egudu. *Modern African Poetry and the African Predicament* (New York: Barnes & Noble, 1978), pp. 53–54

Of the major [African] poets writing in English, the one who is least "Africanized" and the most alienated from the indigenous traditions of his homeland is Dennis Brutus. His style and tone, though they have shifted somewhat over his career, always draw on European rather than African models. His subjects, on the other hand, are largely drawn from experiences in South Africa, though they are seen as exemplifications of problems common to all humanity. . . .

The first poem of *Sirens, Knuckles, Boots*, "A troubadour, I traverse all my land," concerns the adventurous clandestine life he led before his arrest, defying banning orders, evading the Saracen scout cars used by the police, giving the African National Congress sign of the upraised thumb. It is a poem that, like "Nightsong: City," combines the political and the sexual: he is for instance, in the first quatrain, exploring and investigating both the land and the body of his mistress, or in the sestet being pulled away from his "service" of her by "the captor's hand." The troubadour image works well at the beginning, for medieval troubadours commonly engaged in illicit love affairs, spiced with the ever-present danger of discovery and punishment. Such an interruption to freedom and pleasure was, however, unlikely to be at the hands of the Saracens. The lord of the castle was the one likely to be captured by Saracens while he was away fighting in the Crusades; the troubadour was a minstrel who took advantage of the lord's absence at the wars to woo the castle ladies. To this extent, then, the troubadour image was suggestive of a life of pleasure during a state of war, or irresponsibility and fecklessness. This may be one reason why Brutus did not develop it fully: it held too many contradictions and unwanted overtones. In this poem, however, he ignores the problem and ends up with the troubadour snapped off like a frayed end . . . wearing no lady's favor but only [a] prison uniform branded with an arrow. . . .

The remaining early poems appended to the first section of *A Simple Lust* fall into the same categories as the poems of *Sirens, Knuckles, Boots*. There is a plangent elegy, "For a Dead African," more meditative than the somewhat brassy "At a Funeral," and opening with the memorable line "We have no heroes and no wars." The date of "Lutuli: 10 December 1961" is the day Chief Albert Luthuli, or former chief as the South African government would have it, was due to receive the Nobel Peace Prize in Oslo, after grave doubts that he would be permitted to leave South Africa. . . . Its imagery of the masterful African lion roaring might be compared with the autumn imagery of "Autumn comes here with ostentation." All but one of the other poems combine individual love with love for the country. The sense of love (both for a woman and for the land) easing his pain of loneliness and desperate, restless seeking is poignantly expressed here. In "I might be a better lover I believe," he yearns for a secure, lasting relationship, replacing the present situation where neither woman nor land can be Brutus's or the rightful owner's. In "When last I ranged and revelled," he admits, though "wryly," that he is now "the slave of an habituated love," irrespective of present appearances or conditions. Brutus's characteristic blue or green imagery for love continues to operate in these additional early poems. . . .

The original publication of *Letters to Martha [and Other Poems from a South African Prison]* included some early poems and some poems written after "Letters to Martha," without any clear indication of which were which. Several reviewers found the sequence confusing, with the result that the poems were rearranged in four more-or-less chronological groups in *A Simple Lust*. The first group, "Early Poems," ranges from the mid-1950s to the first half of 1963, before he was imprisoned. In style they range from the clotted polysyllables of "Longing" to the simple vignette of

"Train Journey." Brutus speaks of personal loneliness in "No, I do not brim with sorrow" and "Longing," and expresses the familiar need for comfort in "Nightsong: Country" and "The Mob." "The Mob," though occasioned by an attack by whites on a group of people demonstrating against the Sabotage Bill, is much more general in implication than the description "occasional" poem would suggest. Brutus has in fact said "I try to avoid 'occasional poetry,' because I have a guilt about it." The text of "The Mob" mourns his countrymen (in language drawn from biblical laments), and sketches the outline of a hostile mob of "faceless horrors," but it hardly alludes to the circumstances and not at all to the reason for protest and reaction. . . .

*Stubborn Hope* has poems from the years immediately before his imprisonment until well into the 1970s. "When they deprive me of the evenings" looks forward with apprehension to his inevitable imprisonment. "I remembered in the tranquil Sunday afternoon" refers to his imprisonment while awaiting trial. He thinks of Federico Garcia Lorca, the Spanish poet arrested and assassinated in 1936 who also liked to think of himself as a troubadour. The poem is suffused with typical Garcia Lorca images: plaza, church, bullring, tropic light, salt sea, wild orange, frangipani. . . .

Another theme continued in *Stubborn Hope* is that of elegies on the death of friends and admired leaders. The earliest in the volume is "I remember the simple practicality of your reminiscences," from the London years. It celebrates the life of Che Guevara, the freedom fighter in Cuba and South America. He was one of the eighty-two who, in November 1956, under Fidel Castro's leadership, sailed on the barely seaworthy yacht *Granma* to begin the Cuban revolution. Discovered by Batista's soldiers before they landed, only a remnant of the force remained to struggle to safety in the mountain chain of the Sierra Maestra. Though wounded in the landing, Guevara was one of only twelve survivors who reached the mountains and helped to set up the nucleus of a guerrilla army. His death in Bolivia in 1967 was greeted with dismay by radicals, especially youthful ones, throughout the world, and, as Brutus notes at the beginning, it produced some very emotive poetry in stark contrast to the "simple practicality" of Guevara's *Reminiscences of the Cuban Revolutionary War*. Brutus, always skeptical of claims to heroism, especially his own, characteristically speculates on whether this book is as "meretricious and falsified" as T. E. Lawrence's *Seven Pillars of Wisdom*, but decides that the undoubted sufferings of Guevara authenticate his account. . . .

Since the publication of *Stubborn Hope*, his published poetry has followed no new lines. There are, for instance, travel poems like "Berlin Notes" or "Crossing the Atlantic" and elegies like "In Memoriam: Solomon Mahlangu." Over the last thirty years, Brutus's poetry has in fact changed little. He began with a wide range of available styles and his career has concentrated at various times on one or another of them. His earliest poems are bejeweled metaphysical artifacts in imposed forms. His poems in the year after his release from Robben Island mostly adopt a rhetorically shaped simple style. And in 1973 he went to the extreme of minimalism. But he has always been able to write in various styles and his precepts have remained constant: determination, unremitting struggle, fortitude, patience, hope (both political and spiritual), tenderness, passion, vulnerability, and skeptical self-examination.

K. L. Goodwin. *Understanding African Poetry* (London: Heinemann, 1982), pp. 1, 4–5, 8–10, 23–25, 27

In his collection, *Letters to Martha*, Dennis Brutus gives a hint of his attitude towards his prison material: "I cut away the public trappings to assert / certain private essentialities." It is the private angle of prison life with its humanistic emphasis which the public figure, Brutus, examines urbanely and objectively and with a remarkable ironical distancing. This apparently calm exterior, a recognizable black South African pose in racial politics, covers up an inner turmoil and seething. In one dramatic vignette, he presents himself as unprotected, but we perceive an inner resilience that only the spiritually strong can possess when opposing a contemptible but powerful enemy. . . . His courage in the unequal struggle is the mark of his victory and heroism. He can therefore afford to be matter of fact when reporting the deplorable conditions under which he and the other prisoners find themselves on Robben Island. . . . [As if] indignities and deprivations are not enough, the prisoners, these descendants of a race of slaves, are psychologically demoralized by being chained together in pairs. Brutus's choice of aspects of prison life to emphasize demonstrates his acute awareness of the humiliating experience that is prison life, its emasculation of the black South African in a hideous system that remains apparently unchanging.

Brutus touches on the perennial conflict between the warder and the jailed, a relationship that the reader readily extends to the apartheid rulers and the black populace. . . . The factual reporting allows the reader to make even extreme associations, between the situation reported and the brutality of the Nazis towards the Jews, for example. It is intended to arouse the moral awareness of the international community, to get us to view seriously the individual scenarios that take place in South African prisons, and by extension, in South Africa itself. Brutus's strategy is to engage in a quiet, unobtrusive, and insistent attack on his enemies, in an approach that is compatible with Martin Luther King's philosophy of political nonviolence. Part of his attitude is a modesty and humility that will not jubilate over victory in any form. . . .

Brutus maintains a detached mood and achieves self-effacement with the use of imprecise pronouns like "one," "you," [and] "your" instead of "I." His objectivity lends an air of truth and sincerity to his account as he explores the degeneration of the human mind in prison through observing various prisoners and their ways of coping with their terrible status. Deprived of basic necessities of life like sex and music and prevented from watching objects of nature like stars and the carefree bird, some prisoners take recourse in psychosomatic illnesses or fantasizing. Others move towards "Coprophilism; necrophilism; fellatio; / penis amputation." Sodomy is rampant. Many find peace from their cares in the very private world of the insane. Yet through it all, with patience and without self-praise, Brutus not only survives the numerous hardships, the lot of the prisoner, but, like Malcolm X, matures through contact with so much hideousness and suffering. . . .

By handling the subject of prison life, mulling over it, seeing its corrosive effect on both the jailer and the jailed, Brutus grapples through it with the existential human predicament that man finds himself in. His message, even if ultimately didactic, as most good literature is, is humanistically convincing and artistically enunciated.

Chikwenye Okonjo Ogunyemi. *Ariel*. 13, 4 (October 1982), pp. 67–69, 71

Brutus has written few "militant" poems, or to be more precise, if he has written any, he has published very few of them. This is not surprising in a man who loves fine poetry and who has declared that it is immoral for the artist to introduce propaganda into his work: militant poems are often declamatory, or else they want to convince at all costs. But this is not Brutus's aim, and he has sometimes been reproached for it. Thus, during a public reading of his poetry (in Chelsea in August 1971), when he was criticized by a member of the audience for rarely writing "political" poems, Brutus retorted that it was true he had no intention of saying in so many words "apartheid is detestable," but: "This is apartheid as we live it; it is for you to draw the inescapable conclusions.". . .

*Poems from Algiers* is a slim volume comprising nine poems of varying length and a commentary running into several pages: the poems were written in Algeria during the first Pan-African Cultural Festival, the commentary a few months later. In a very significant way, the collection brings together Brutus's personal reflections, expressed with great frankness, and his self-questioning concerning his "representativeness" and hence his sense of belonging. But representative of what? And his belonging to what world? In this Mediterranean climate which is so close to that of the Cape, the thoughts he evokes mingle and become confused: does he belong to a clearly defined African or South African world? Or is he, in his fundamental solitariness, the unattached poet who is, by that fact, universal? Hence the poem that opens the collection, "And I am driftwood," a meditation on his destiny as an exile which opens out onto the mystery of man as a whole, and not only of the man Brutus. . . .

*Thoughts Abroad*, published in the same year but under a pseudonym to enable it to be sold in South Africa, opens with a very fine poem which, seven years after *Sirens [Knuckles, Boots]*, establishes the link between past and present. . . .

Indeed, it is in this collection that the song of exile comes across most powerfully, beneath the overcast skies of London or the bright skies of India with, at each stage and perhaps because of his freedom of movement, the memory of the men who are still in prison. . . .

The collection also reveals Brutus's wider commitment to the problems of his fellow men, whatever the color of their skin. The work of destroying deceptive appearances which so far he had restricted to South Africa he now carries out wherever he feels it necessary to dispel ambiguity. So, on a visit to Bristol, the former center of the slave trade, of the "triangular" trade which to a large extent made it possible for Britain to accumulate the capital necessary for its technological development, Brutus addresses [a] poem to the Quaker owners of Cadbury's. . . .

Since *A Simple Lust*, which essentially brings together the poems contained in *Sirens, Letters to Martha, Poems from Algiers*, and *Thoughts Abroad*, Brutus has published two slim volumes [*China Poems* and *Strains*]. . . .

In summarizing our view of this writer who is inseparable from the life of his country and his century and whose future development is difficult to predict (for Brutus is sixty), it may be best to stress those characteristics which show his originality.

As a man who has protested and as a poet, Brutus clearly deserves to be called a committed writer. With him, the marriage of poetry and commitment is possible and complete only because he is involved in two types of quite separate activity: political and parapolitical activities, and poetry. The former enable him to serve in his capacity as a citizen; they are the outlet for his need to act and to speak out. As a result, it has been possible for him to keep his

poetry relatively free of propaganda, since he has had the opportunity to make his ideals known in another way. It is no secret that Brutus dreams of being able to devote himself entirely to poetry: the fact that he has postponed the realization of this dream clearly shows that he gives his social and political responsibility priority.

It would, however, be to misunderstand him and the significance of his present struggle against the Nationalist government especially to view his commitment as a limited one.

Jacques Alvarez-Pereyre. *The Poetry of Commitment in South Africa* (London: Heinemann, 1984), pp. 138, 141–44

Much has been written about the poetry of Brutus, especially his images of pain, his prison poems, and his portrayal of the apartheid society. My aim . . . is to identify the poetic mask in the poems, describe it, and show its ramifications. . . .

The troubadour mask is extended and complicated after *Sirens, Knuckles, Boots; Letters to Martha*; and early exile poems. The later poems represent an alienated exile, still a troubadour in his being a poet of the open road. There is a close correlation between the poetic personality and the man in Brutus's poetry. The poet is familiar with his country and the world and speaks of human suffering because of sociopolitical injustice from the wealth of his individual experience as a sage and philosopher in his struggle to free the oppressed. Brutus uses this mask of a troubadour with ambivalence, but his position remains a valid poetic standpoint. . . .

*A Simple Lust* and *Stubborn Hope* clearly present the poet who is a fighter for justice at home and abroad, struggling to realize his poetic aims. The troubadour image is consistent in all of the poetry of Brutus. The poet is variously a wanderer, an exile, a dreamer, a bird, a sea-voyager; and in all these aspects he is pursuing an ideal. The poet is committed to his struggle and leaves no one in doubt as to which side he stands for: he fights as a spokesman and a representative of the oppressed and the victims of injustice in South Africa and elsewhere. As a troubadour he uses movement and the road to establish his wealth of experience and give credibility to his sayings. He is thus a witness and a victim of the injustice he fights against. The idea of being on the road has universal meaning as the road involves the quest for an ideal. The road also makes the experiences of the poet universal and human as it designates life. The poet's exile brought him the realization that there is evil everywhere, but there is an intensification of it in his country which he loves in spite of the apartheid system.

Tanure Ojaide. *Ariel*. 17, 1 (January 1986), pp. 55–56, 67–68

Brutus's peaceful response to the apartheid system is informed by a formidable academic intelligence which explores the possibilities of a more humane and passionate approach to the problems of existence. For instance: in "Postscripts," he speaks of the "mosaic of your calm and patient knowledge." In "For My Sons & Daughters," he says that despite "adult bitter years" and "loneliness," "my affection enables me to penetrate the decades and your minds / and . . . I hope to shape your better world." The spirit of love, forgiveness and fortitude, which Brutus evinces here, recalls the Biblical injunction which upholds "brotherly love" in the face of provocation and injustice. Although he has been misconstrued by some critics who think that this is a sign of weakness, the fact remains that the device enables him to come to terms with the conflicting emotions of ''love'' and ''hate'' in his poetry. On this score, Brutus deserves credit for writing with a rational intention and for making the objective reader perceive the serious purpose behind his irony.

Isaac I. Elimimian. *Literary Half-Yearly.* 28, 1 (January 1987), pp. 77–78

The poetry of Dennis Brutus is one more evidence that the ''artist has always functioned in African society as the recorder of mores and experiences of his society and as the voice of vision in his own time.'' The South African reality is one that cannot allow any sensitive writer in South Africa to remain aloof except, of course, as he wishes to be irrelevant. . . . It is no wonder then that the writings of not only Brutus but most other South African writers focus primarily on that monstrous epitome of man's inhumanity to man—the apartheid system in South Africa. For Brutus, ''a writer must write about what he sees around him and he must write truthfully about it; or he must come to terms with what is ugly in it and pretend that it is not there or that it is not bad.'' It is a happy thing that Brutus has chosen the first option. Because of this he has emerged as the foremost writer in Africa who has greatly contributed to that bid to overthrow the pernicious apartheid regime and white supremacy by the power of the pen. . . .

His poetry . . . is a direct response to the unsavory demands which a horrible sociopolitical situation makes on his personality. Every page of his poetry bristles with images of searing pain, spilling blood, contorting hearts or wracking nerves. In his poetry words are charged with lethal colors. From Brutus we read poetry that shocks, stimulates, agitates, activates and educates us about the South African society. In fact Dennis Brutus's poetry is inseparable from South African reality. He is the altruistic voice of the people, who has gone through all the experiences which any colored South African may undergo. To read his poetry is to read an artistic rendition of a sociopolitical discourse of the South African situation. . . . Brutus wants to say something and urgently too about the economic, social, residential, and educational deprivations meted to the South African majority in the civilized world and he feels that his life and the lives of millions of South African citizens depend on what he has to say.

Jasper A. Onuekwusi. *Literary Criterion.* 23, 1–2 (1988), pp. 59–60

The mines provide black South Africans with one common experience; the prisons with another. And a great deal of contemporary literature deals with the suffering experienced in the latter. Dennis Brutus' *Letters to Martha* consists of eighteen brief poems and six equally brief postscripts that we are to read as the progressively darker reflections of an imprisoned man addressed to his wife or lover outside. As Shava notes, the style of these poems was decidedly simpler than that Brutus had exhibited in earlier work. And, as Barnett observes, the simpler style was due to Brutus' conscious decision to try to reach a larger audience with *Letters to Martha* than with previous volumes of poetry.

The first poem presents mixed emotions—''sick relief'' (3); ''apprehension'' (4); ''exultation'' (8); ''vague heroism'' (11); ''self-pity'' (9); others. The prisoner does not yet know what to feel

or what to expect. The second and third poems bring him face to face with one prison reality: violence. In the second poem, he wonders at how knives find their way in; in the third, he reflects on the confused motives that cause prisoners to use these knives against each other.

In the fourth poem, Brutus' persona reflects on the various ways religion plays a role in prison life: one can pretend to be religious to curry favor; one can ''invoke divine revenge / against a rampaging injustice'' (12–13); one can talk to God ''in the grey silence of the empty afternoons'' (24).

In the next four poems, Brutus' persona turns from piety to perversion. Prisoners turn to behavior other than praying in their empty hours. They turn to ''Corpophilism; necrophilism; fellatio; / penis-amputation'' (5–6), as well as to ''suicide, self-damnation'' (9). They turn to demands for sodomy, and in the sixth poem, the prisoner talks about the three ways to deal with these demands: imagine ''romantic fantasies / or beautiful marriageable daughters'' (9–10), have ''fainting fits'' (12), or flee ''into insanity'' (13). Some prisoners even ''beg for sexual assault'' (2), and in the seventh poem, the prisoner tries to understand the state of mind that would lead one to desire what he terms ''absolute and ludicrous submission'' (9). In the eighth poem, the persona's tone curiously shifts. Now jaded, he can joke a bit about homosexuality in prison and talk about ''Blue champagne,'' ''the most popular 'girl' in the place'' (1–2).

The ninth poem shifts from inside to outside, as the prisoner reflects on how agonizing it must be for those outside not to know exactly what sufferings the men inside are enduring. The tenth poem presents another shift—from the sufferings of prison existence to the ''benefits.'' One acquires a deep understanding of ''one's fellow-men, / fellows, compeers'' (5–6); one acquires discipline; one acquires the rest that comes after ''honest toil'' (10). . . .

The sixteenth poem begins what seems to be the prisoner's withdrawal. He seems resigned to his situation; he seems to give up on defiance. And, in the last two poems, he turns to the birds, the clouds, and the stars. Unable to face (as well as name) the prison realities, he turns his eyes upward. Unfortunately, the prison authorities can deny him even these sights, as the conclusion to the eighteenth poem makes clear when ''anxious boots / and a warning barked / from the machine-gun post / on the catwalk'' (18–21) interrupt his star-gazing.

The postscripts continue this withdrawal. . . .

In the last postscript, the narrative perspective changes—from first person to third person. The prisoner has lost self-awareness; he now sees himself as an object. This self-objectification is described as offering him ''safety'' (8) ''from the battering importunities / of fists and genitals of sodomites'' (10–11). This self-objectification, we are told in the very last line, will lead to ''a maniac world'' in which ''he was safe'' (12).

Theodore F. Sheckels, *The Lion on the Freeway: A Thematic Introduction to Contemporary South African Literature in English* (New York: Peter Lang Publishing, 1996)

BIBLIOGRAPHY

*Sirens, Knuckles, Boots,* 1963; *Letters to Martha, and Other Poems from a South African Prison,* 1968; *Poems from Algiers,* 1970; *Thoughts Abroad,* 1970; *A Simple Lust,* 1973; *China Poems,* 1975;

*Strains*, 1975; *Stubborn Hope*, 1978; "Berlin Notes," 1979; "Cross-ing the Atlantic,"1979; "In Memoriam: Solomon Mahlangu," 1979; *Salutes and Censures*, 1984; *Airs and Tributes*, 1989; *Stubborn Hope: New Poems and Selections from China Poems and Strains*, 1991

# BULLINS, Ed (1935–)
## United States

Unlike the general run of young playwrights, Bullins does not spend most of his time showing what a whiz he is at creating monologists who gab endlessly in back rooms about their cranky existences. He gives his attention to the impact of one character on another, the blood of drama, not its gristle. . . .

*Clara's Ole Man* . . . is one of the best short American plays I have come across: realistic in manner yet throbbing with weirdness and driven by bursts of extravagant invention that make a definition by genre seem impertinent. Clara, a winsome young woman, invites an innocent fellow named Jack to her apartment. She shares the place with Big Girl, a huge rubbery male woman, and with Big Girl's sister, Baby Girl, a teenaged spastic who repeats any obscenity she hears in a croaking distortion.

The suspense grows out of the intimidation of Jack, who takes a long time to realize that he has landed in a lesbian nest and has unwittingly challenged Big Girl's ownership of Clara. All the characters are Negro, but I suspect the play would (and probably will) function almost as well with a German, Japanese or Turkish cast. . . .

Albert Bermel. *New Leader*. April 22, 1968, p. 28

The white problem in America is at the core of all Bullins's work. He denies being a working-class playwright: he is from the criminal class. All the other men in his family have been in prison. He is the only one who went to high school, who went to college; but he claims that working people in Harlem like his surrealist, intellectual plays.

*The Electronic Nigger* is not straight propaganda. An evening class in literary expression is being gently conducted by Mr. Jones, a novelist: the session is interrupted by a penologist, Mr. Carpentier, who spouts large generalisations in technical language—not unlike Marshall McLuhan's—and takes over the class, until Jones's head is full of noise and Carpentier is leading pupils in a mechanical goose-step, bawling abstract inanities. (All this is well staged, in-the-round, with life-like acting shifting slowly to an expressionist style, with a climax of disciplined noise and nightmare.) Neither Jones nor Carpentier is white. During the clash, Jones at one point appeals to Carpentier as his "black brother," but the latter denies being black. A white pupil calls him "Uncle Tom" and a black pupil says: "No. It's for me to say that."

D. A. N. Jones. *The Listener* Aug. 22, 1968, p. 253

*The Gentleman Caller* is a farce with a theme that recalls [Jean] Genet's *The Maids*. All the characters are symbolic. Madame, with a painted face, large pearl necklaces, and a blonde wig, is the white race. A black intellectual comes to read silently in her living room, and refuses her advances. Mamie, the huge black servant, who looks like a peasant, embodies the primitive wisdom of the masses. She kills the Gentleman, a ridiculously insignificant character dominated by his wife. She kills Madame, and, in the heat of the action, shoots the intellectual, who is doubtless guilty of preferring his books to guerrilla warfare. Mamie then dons a long African gown and answers the telephone with a revolutionary speech that greatly excited the young people in the audience at the Chelsea Theater, when the play was performed there on April 25, 1969: "Teach!" they shouted, laughing. . . .

Punch and Judy show, myth of Orpheus, minstrel show, electronic farce, humor, poetry, drama—Ed Bullins invents and masters different forms of action. His language, whether it is that of muggers or whether it parodies the whites, whether it speaks of electronics or of secret passions, is always theatrical. He is probably one of the best playwrights, white or black, of the new American theater.

Franck Jotterand. *Le nouveau théâtre américain* (Paris: Éditions du Seuil, 1970), pp. 206–7†

By saying that the oppressed are destroyed and debased by their experience, writers like Jones, Bullins, Franz Fanon, James Baldwin and [Eldridge] Cleaver expose themselves as apologists for imperialism. . . .

Ed Bullins' drama is one of despair and self-destruction. For him the enemy is other black men who are rapacious and irrational. His is a world of pimps and whores, criminals and junkies. In his *Goin' a Buffalo*, Bullins has a grim picture of these family and criminal relationships. Art who had supposedly saved Curt's life in a prison riot in *Goin' a Buffalo* insinuates himself into Curt's home and family and betrays him to the police in order to get his wife and money. In *Clara's Ole Man* nothing is possible for the people but parasitism; they live off each other's misfortune. Black people inflict violence, infidelity and betrayal on each other. In this psychological and social view of the blacks there is only self-destruction and soulfulness with which blacks can console themselves. . . .

The political line in dramatists like Jones, Bullins, Baldwin, [Douglas Turner] Ward and many others is the line of class collaboration and not struggle. This endears them to the monopoly capitalist class and wins them publicity and other forms of recognition from the class they serve. These dramatists are trying to mobilize political support for the decadent imperialists by saying that possibilities for change do not exist. The progressive dramatists create public opinion in favour of revolutionary change and present the black struggles as part of the worldwide united front against U.S. imperialism.

Mary Ellen Brooks. *Literature and Ideology*. No. 10, 1971, pp. 43–46

Beyond the political activism and the racial consciousness of his plays (which are, of course, what Bullins most values in them), there is another side. *In the Wine Time, In New England Winter, Goin' a Buffalo*, and other Bullins plays create a mood of lost innocence, purity and beauty that is universally meaningful. In fact, the dramatist creates in most of his work a counter-mood to that which dominates the actual dialogue—there is a sense of once-glimpsed loyalty, sensitivity, and romance which the ghetto reality of the setting makes impossible to attain. This obbligato of tenderness is so overpowered by the brutality of the ghetto that it exists in the plays as something once envisioned, but almost forgotten, by one or two main characters. . . .

That the reality of Black life in America perverts and destroys human dreams—whether of pure romance or of economic independence—and makes personal loyalty all but obsolete is Bullins' message. His technique is, through brutal dialogue and incident, to emphasize the grim reality of the ghetto; the better life his characters desire can be glimpsed in his plays as an increasingly remote ideal and finally only in the thwarted generosity of a few characters.

James R. Giles. *Players*. October–November 1972, pp. 32–33

Bullins' plays can generally be divided into two categories: satire and serious. But the line that divides them is sometimes very thin. Plays such as *The Electronic Nigger* and *The Pig Pen* are obviously satire. *The Electronic Nigger* is a scathing condemnation of the would-be black intellectual, and *The Pig Pen* is a laughing look at the world of so-called "revolutionary" integration (about eight black men and one white woman). This kind of satire is very explicit and the playwright's position is very clear on these subjects.

The serious plays, however, like *The Duplex*, *Clara's Ole Man*, and . . . *The Fabulous Miss Marie* . . . do not lend themselves to easy interpretations. *The Duplex* ends, for example, with the older woman, the landlady, going back downstairs in resignation to get her head-whipping from her man because of what she's done. And nobody moves to help her because supposedly anything her man does is within his right. But, we ask, will that help ease her loneliness? Will that prevent her from seeking out some other young man when things come down on her too hard again? Bullins doesn't say.

Clara is a young black girl living in a stifling tenement and her ole man turns out to be an older woman, the only one who seems to have cared enough, for whatever reason, to take her in and care for her. Is it wrong? Should Clara have tried to do something else? Bullins leaves it up to us to decide.

Perhaps it's only in *The Fabulous Miss Marie* that we see an exact blending of Bullins the satirist and Bullins the serious, for in "Miss Marie" we have a very skillfully drawn portrait of the Los Angeles bourgeoisie, with all its flaking superficialities and differing forms of greed. Near the end of the play a member of Miss Marie's clique remarks that none of them, the aging playboy teacher, his pill-popping wife, parasitic Miss Marie and her young boyfriends, or her castrated, overworked husband, have any children. They will not be perpetuated. Bullins is not elusive here. He shows a group of people that the audience clearly feels shouldn't be perpetuated. Here the lines are sharply drawn.

Lisbeth Gant. *The Drama Review*. December 1972, p. 52

*In the Wine Time* by Ed Bullins, author of *The Electronic Nigger*, unskins the exhaustion and hopelessness of the ghetto without any references to whites or to white racism—which are unnecessary. A simmering August night: on a worn wooden porch, a family marinates in cheap port, while a strolling cop swats his club against a wire fence, neighborhood voices yell down the block, their words

entangling many lives, and people mutter through screen doors. A husband bickers with his pregnant wife. She berates him for being jobless while *she* goes out to work: again and again, she says that he's not a man. . . . It's the recurrent theme of poverty: that women have the authority (which they also resent) because more jobs are open to them, and because whites have crippled the black male. At the same time, more and more black women are rebelling against this role casting—and against the accusations made against them by black men. . . .

Neighbors join the querulous porch life. People swear at each other for swearing, fight without meaning to, remark grimly on the numbing repetitions in their lives. Ed Bullins has distilled the language and the experience of the ghetto so magnificently that we learn more from this one mood play than from scores of sociological studies about growing up in the black slums, where the fatigue that oozes out of the suppression seems even stronger than despair. [Jan., 1969]

Nora Sayre. *Sixties Going on Seventies* (New York: Arbor House, 1973), pp. 345–46

[*The Reluctant Rapist*] has the tone and the content of the 19th century *Bildungsroman*, in which the youthful protagonist—in this case Steve Benson—is educated from innocence to experience. In the classic tradition, Steve is a loner, an outsider, and finally an outlaw. He rapes, dimly off in the background to the main action, but is "reluctant" to rape a woman he cannot love. Indeed, the reader is asked to believe that a mystical union is effected by that violation of another person's will, and that some of the women are bound to him for life. . . .

*The Reluctant Rapist* is a handbook to [Bullins's] plays. As a playwright, Bullins rips, tears, rapes; he blows apart black life. As a novelist, he explains what the ripping, tearing and raping are all about. They are the acts of a lover in deep need of blasting away the conventional laws and customs, the traditional faiths and beliefs to expose the truthful, irreducible center so that he and his beloved may at last be free. Steve Benson the rapist is a metaphor of Ed Bullins the playwright. And Steve's story is a reassembling of the bits from the exploded bombs and tearing beak. It is done through a reconstitution of time and a renewal of sex. Time unrolls and unwinds in this novel, opens out and folds back on itself, stops and starts. Pieces of Steve's life loom up before us as if cut loose from chronology. But the conventional order of events is one of those beliefs that has to be destroyed. And Bullins is successful in destroying it, in fusing the past with the present, in giving us the feeling of living the past again from the standpoint of the present and seeing the future infuse the past.

Jerry H. Bryant. *Nation*. Nov. 12, 1973, p. 504

For the critic, the value of this collection [of stories, *The Hungered One*] lies in its revelations about the early intellectual career of Bullins. For those familiar only with his later writing, and more particularly, the plays, this volume will remind them of the uncommon diversity of his early work. Yet, within this diversity and within this mixture of experimentation, the germ of the work that is later transformed into Bullins' realistic plays and stories can be discovered. Here, in this collection, we can find the early lineaments of some of his later characters waiting to be fleshed out. A few of the macabre themes that Bullins exploits later can be detected here, gradually merging. Testing narrative vehicles, for their limitations and merits, is present too. On the other hand, it is possible, through comparing Bullins' later work with this earlier material, to trace the shifts in his work—away from the symbolist mode and the metaphorical narrative. For all these reasons, it is valuable to have these stories.

However, these works raise a disquieting intellectual issue, one that relates to Bullins' later writing as well. Perhaps, only a very few Afro-American writers at work presently can equal the trained eye of Bullins. Seeing plainly and correctly is his great skill. Deploying these observations in economical, exceedingly lucid writing makes his work extremely accessible. Years from now, when his reputation is not so artificially inflated, his reports on Afro-American life will still constitute a major historical record of black society. It will be the fictional equivalent of an Afro-American *cinéma verité*. This is no ordinary achievement. And yet, it must be said that Bullins' eye is an extremely neutral one: he appears excessively timid about moving beyond mere observation, to insert himself in the record; he seems wary of structuring his perceptions into a definite intellectual format. Always, there is a hint that Bullins is verging on a political or ideological or strangely personal statement, but just as often, this energy is dissipated in verbal pyrotechnics, easy lampooning, or is reduced to a bare record of events and personalities. He proceeds along the smoothest course.

Kennell Jackson, Jr. *CLA Journal.* December 1974, pp. 297–98

In his dramas about Black life, Bullins generally suggests a vision by picturing the absence of vision. Love is a ruse for stealing a wife from a benefactor; it is adultery and lesbianism; it is abuse and betrayal. Manhood is the practice of Walter Younger's false dream [in *A Raisin in the Sun*]—to exploit others before they exploit you. And there is no good life. Bullins' vision is at best a dream which will never materialize, a nostalgia for what might have been. I have said that Black Arts drama assumes the responsibility of educating Black People to awareness of their needs for liberation. Bullins' dramas are educational primarily in the sense that they depict the sordid realities which must be transformed if Black life is to improve. . . .

Bullins' characters live in an all-Black world in which survival requires one to assume everyone else to be his enemy. Education is judged desirable, but crime provides more money. Whites who flutter through this world are not villains but alcoholics, dope addicts, prostitutes—as easily deceived as are the Blacks. Like Baldwin [in *The Amen Corner*], Bullins offers no problem to be solved by a White audience. If there is any significant difference between Baldwin and Bullins, it is that, whereas Baldwin rationalizes the behavior of a wandering musician who drinks liquor excessively, Bullins spares no feelings in portraying his protagonists as alcoholics, murderers, hypocrites, exploiters, bullies, and criminals who betray one another and even themselves. Pathetically, they succeed neither in self-improvement nor even in the crimes they attempt. The very multiplicity of examples of lack or loss of vision, I believe, suggests the need for vision and, thus, implies

Bullins' educational thesis—that such a world is salvageable only if it is supplied with visions of love, manhood, and a good life.

Darwin T. Turner. *Iowa Review.* Spring 1975, pp. 93–95

*The Duplex* is part of a cycle of twenty plays. I can only hope that future installments, or such past ones as I have missed, achieve more. For this is mere commercial theater, rather slow and faltering in the first two acts, quite slick in the second two, and brought to a sudden end without much of a resolution. It is, to be sure, *black* commercial theater, which in these confused times easily passes for art in both black and white circles. To me, it looks like second-rate William Inge, with the significant difference that Inge would not have required two acts for the kind of exposition that two scenes could have taken care of. . . .

There is nothing embarrassingly bad or unendurable about the play—with the possible exception of some of the old woman's maunderings; but neither its insight nor its language, neither its dramaturgy nor its perspective, is in any sustained way compelling. Its laughter is routine, and its poignancies, with one or two exceptions, are perfunctory. Yet there is a smooth functionalism about its better parts. . . . The chief virtue of Bullins' work is that black audiences can doubtless identify themselves with it wholeheartedly—as the black part of the openingnight audience noisily did—but here hides a danger. Recognition of yourself up there on the boards is not the end-all of art, at best the beginning. It is understandably satisfying for the audience of an emergent theater to see itself raised to the heights of the stage, with the social and cultural importance this implies. But for the work to become art, it must take the audience beyond mere self-recognition, identification with mirror images. It must do, say, envision things that in some profound sense have never been done, said, envisioned before, and this *The Duplex*, in terms other than its Negritude, fails to do. It is all basic minimums. [March 27, 1972]

John Simon. *Uneasy Stages* (New York: Random House, 1975), pp. 376–78

[*The Taking of Miss Janie*] devotes itself principally to black-white relations in the 1960's ("This tale is about the spirit of those times"), symbolized—or at least given some sort of framing device—by the ultimate rape of a naïve white girl by the black poet she wants simply as a "friend."

The rape opens the evening, with the toweled girl sobbing over the destruction of her dream, the cool and confident stripped male pointing out that it always had to come to this. The '60s, we gradually learn if we pay extremely close attention, were years of self-delusion: while blacks and whites, in the time of Kennedy and King, thought, through a marijuana haze, that they were "getting it all together," they were doing no such thing. Blacks, in the words of a cliché-spouting revolutionary who marches marionette-style to a drum in his head, were "still in love with their slave masters," were stupidly fighting a war "while loving the enemy." Whites were simply kidding themselves—pretending to understand black poetry, inventing Platonic social harmonies that didn't, couldn't, exist.

If I say that it takes extremely close attention to pick up this thread of meaning—provided I have myself got it straight—it's because author Bullins is so prodigal, not to say wandering, in his recall. . . . Most of the evening is flashback, the lion's share of it taken up by a black-white party in which sex and hostility give off approximately equal ''vibes.'' Mr. Bullins, as a writer, has a thing about parties. Play after play has made use of them—not so much dramatic as nearly stenographic use, as though the faithful recording of all that might be said and done in a casual, then hyped-up, personal and/or ethnic mix would surely end in some kind of intelligible patterning. A cat's-cradle formed of all those comings and goings must, in the end, convey *something*, mustn't it?. . .

Almost all of the best things [in the play] pull us away from Janie and her problem. The play's frame doesn't really contain or explain the things that shimmer inside it, and, quite apart from our losing the two principals for long stretches of time, we are left wondering why Janie's ''taking'' should be made to serve as summary of a decade's mishaps and misapprehensions. Is physical conquest the only answer to the thousand questions raised; was ''rape'' the resolution the '60s *ought* to have been seeking? Or is Janie no more than a nitwit, making impossibly childish demands in a situation too grave for children? The play's *structure* doesn't say, and we are forced to weave spider-webs of meaning for ourselves out of random snatches of biography, period echoes, interpolated monologues close to harangues.

Walter Kerr. *New York Times.* May 11, 1975, p. 5

BIBLIOGRAPHY

*How Do You Do?: A Nonsense Drama*, 1967; *A Son, Come Home* (play), 1968; *Clara's Ole Man* (play), 1968; *The Electronic Nigger* (play), 1969; *Goin' A Buffalo* (play), 1969; *In New England Winter*, 1969; *In the Wine Time* (play), 1969; *Ya Gonna Let Me Take You Out Tonight, Baby?* (play), 1969; *The Gentleman Caller* (play), 1970; *The Duplex: A Black Love Fable in Four Movements* (play), 1971; *The Hungered One: Early Writings* (collected short fiction), 1971; *The Pig Pen* (play), 1971; *The Fabulous Miss Marie*, 1972; *Four Dynamite Plays*, 1972; *The Theme Is Blackness: The Corner, and Other Plays*, 1972; *The Reluctant Rapist* (novel), 1973; *The Taking of Miss Janie* (play), 1981; *New/Lost Plays by Ed Bullins: An Anthology*, 1993

# BUTLER, Octavia E. (1947– )
## United States

The mythology that Octavia Butler creates in her first three books, *Patternmaster* (1976), *Mind of My Mind* (1977), and Survivor (1978), has elements of familiarity. She writes about a future society wherein a network of telepaths control the Earth and occasionally get out of control themselves. She writes of colonists who settle on an alien planet and battle hostile, furry creatures. She writes of strange, micro-organisms brought to Earth by astronauts that threaten the existence of human civilization. She writes of genetic evolution and selective breeding. Like most contemporary women authors, she writes of women in nontraditional roles.

[Reviewers] consider her a speculative fiction writer who is adequate, potentially outstanding, but at present neither particularly innovative nor interesting. However, Octavia Butler is not just another woman science fiction writer. Her major characters are black women, and through her characters and through the structure of her imagined social order, Butler consciously explores the impact of race and sex upon future society.

Ironically, many speculative fiction scholars have been lamenting the neglect of those very areas with which Butler has been dealing. Marilyn Hacker, for example, has declared it a ''serious drawback'' that speculative fiction has devoted so little attention to ''the vast area of human experience'' which includes ''family structures, child-rearing, and child-bearing, sexual relations—and relations between sexes (not, as some men would have it, the same topic at all).'' Ursula Le Guin is one who has decried the fact that ''in general, American sf has assumed a permanent hierarchy of superiors and inferiors, with rich, ambitious, aggressive males at the top, then a great gap, and then at the bottom the poor, the uneducated, the faceless masses, and all the women.'' And Pamela Sargent has mentioned, what most of us know, that ''the number of black sf writers can be counted on the fingers on one hand.'' Since Octavia Butler is a black woman who writes speculative fiction which is primarily concerned with social relationships, where rulers include women and nonwhites, the neglect of her work is startling.

Octavia Butler consciously chose to introduce the isms of race and sex into the genre and obviously did not set out to write ''fine, old fashioned sf.''. . .

One of Butler's major concerns is the possibility of a society in which males and females ''are honestly considered equal.'' This idea is developed by her manipulation of three major characters; however, it is important that she also creates several secondary female characters who are not identified by race. The reader can then assume that these characters are not necessarily black and therefore generalize about the position of all women in future society even as the levels of racial integration that Butler assumes are recognized. . . .

A brief analysis of the evolution of her three major women characters facilitates further understanding of Butler's speculations on the future. The first book, *Patternmaster*, gives us Amber as a significant and complex individual who functions as a symbol, a catalyst, and a mentor. The plot, however, centers around the struggle between an older brother, Coransee, and his younger brother, Teray, for the inheritance of the Pattern. Amber discerns in Teray a power to heal as well as to kill, and in teaching him to develop his humane tendencies, she teaches him the skills he needs to ultimately defeat his brother.

*In Mind of My Mind*, Mary gradually emerges as the protagonist; however, a central issue in this work concerns the effect of extraordinary mental powers upon individuals and their social relationships. Mary is the most developed of Doro's several children who people this book. She comes into her own when she overthrows her father; but Doro, his experiment, and his use of power are as much a focus of this work as Mary, who defines the limits of and represents an alternative to Doro's power.

It is not until the third novel, *Survivor*, that Butler presents a heroine. From beginning to end, *Survivor* is Alanna's story. Unlike Mary and Amber. Alanna has no extrasensory powers. Alanna . . . is an archetype, the kind of human who can survive in the future. Her attempts to overcome her weaknesses, to know and protect that which is vital, and to accept necessary changes inform our sensibilities concerning the potential of ordinary human beings and constitute the plot.

Each of these women is black. This is given as a fact, and it does, at times, affect their attitudes and influence their social situations: however, racial conflict or even racial tension is not the primary focus of the novels. Butler explains that she feels no particular need to champion black women, but that she writes from her own experience and sensitivities. . . . [She] affirms her place in Afro-American literary history without excluding her work from a larger context. Butler is theorizing upon the same questions that Ursula Le Guin, for example, has raised: "What about the cultural and the racial Other?" Like Butler, Le Guin affirms the inextricability of human kind. . . . Butler explores the future implications of racism and sexism by focusing upon relationships between powerful persons who are various kinds of Other.

Frances Smith Foster. *Extrapolation*. 23, 1 (Spring 1982), pp. 37–49

The combination of emotional power and conceptual complexity central to "Bloodchild" makes this, like all of Butler's fiction, an excellent example of literature which bridges the gap between "high" and popular culture in a manner as complex and unique as her position as science fiction's most prolific—if not only— African American feminist writer.

"Bloodchild" tells of a group of humans who escape antagonism on Earth to arrive on a planet where, generations later, their progeny become the valued property of a powerful alien species called the Tlic. Living on a protected Preserve, human families may be formed and children raised, but each family must offer at least one son to the Tlic. The young boy will serve as a host body for alien eggs which will grow to a potentially lethal larval stage within him before being removed by a female Tlic in a "blood ritual," a process in which the human is sliced open and the grubs are removed by probing Tlic limbs and mouth. The humans will never be free, but the current arrangements are better than those for the first generations, when the Tlic drugged humans and forced them to live in pens as no more than breeding stock.

The story centers on the complex relationship between T'Gatoi, the Tlic government official in charge of the Preserve, who struggles with her need to propagate and the simultaneous friendship with and enslavement of humans which such propagation necessitates; and Gan, the human boy raised from birth to carry T'Gatoi's eggs, who must face both his love for this maternal figure and his growing repulsion from her as a controlling alien being. Through these and other characters, and the setting in which Butler places them, we experience a text which simultaneously explores outer space—in its focus on extraterrestrials and human adventures beyond planet Earth—and inner space, through metaphoric figures which illustrate and invite comment upon the construction of identity. The inner space of "Bloodchild," like that in all of Butler's fiction, is filled with characters who highlight metaphoric considerations of gender, race, and species.

If Barbara Christian is right when she asserts that contemporary African American women write within a long tradition of struggles to represent the self in reaction to external conceptualizations, and Samuel Delany is right to consider science fiction an ideal genre through which to challenge traditional representations of subjectivity, then Butler is the writer to illustrate the best of both worlds. Because her black feminism appears solely in the highly metaphoric genre of science fiction, it is particularly through metaphors that her texts exemplify a meeting point between "high" and popular culture. And the metaphorization of identity, according to critical theorists such as Alice Jardine, Henry Louis Gates, Jr., and Mary

Midgley, is central to the postmodern condition, in its emphasis on addressing the tropes and gaps in traditional philosophy and the culture invoked through such discourse. . . .

Emphasis on the metaphoric impregnation of human males in "Bloodchild" makes the process of gynesis central to the story. In a 1986 article on Butler in *Ms.* magazine, Sherley Anne Williams reports that Butler "gleefully" describes "Bloodchild" as her "pregnant man story." Williams interprets the story as an exploration of "the paradoxes of power and inequality," as Butler portrays "the experience of a class who, like women throughout most of history, are valued chiefly for their reproductive capacities". I'd add that this "class" must be examined through issues of race and species as well as gender; however, Williams describes well the imaginative feminist space which makes the story so compelling a site for the study of gynesis in popular culture. Although human women tend to have more body fat—thus reducing their risk of damage or death at the bloodsucking mouths of the Tlic larvae—we learn that only men are "implanted." Human women are left to bear human children, especially sons for future Tlic usage and, at least superficially, human family bonding and happiness. Without such bonding, both species fear humans would become little more than pets or breeding stock.

One of the primary ways in which "Bloodchild" encourages a view of the Tlic power structure as a metaphor for human gender relations under patriarchy is through its depiction of men suffering the pains of childbearing (and when "birth" means removing grubs from around your internal organs, the pain can be intense). Even more powerful, however, is the suggestive complication of traditional gender roles during intercourse. . . .

The image of the female penetrating the male and impregnating him clearly complicates the traditional gendering of sexual imagery. The undulating body of T'Gatoi, forcing the egg into Gan's body, recalls human intercourse from both female and male positions: T'Gatoi's action embodies both possession of the female egg and male penetration and ejaculation. To this is added a representation of acquaintance rape in Gan's passivity, despite his agreement to be implanted. This example of popular cultural gynesis invites consideration of the gender complexity of the "pregnant man" and the "impregnating woman."

What we may learn from the story—that power relations ultimately determine the construction of identity, that how we see the world depends on how we are allowed or encouraged to see it— is related to but different from what we may feel. Butler manipulates her readers, emotionally even more than intellectually. As the story opens and we begin to read of sterile eggs and the velvet of alien skin, we are likely to be curious, though simultaneously disturbed by the alien's insistent attitude and watchful eye. We may experience further discomfort as we read of the alien female "caging" humans within her limbs to warm her body, and frustration as we watch a woman manipulated by an alien's power. Such reactions, which grow, as the story progresses, to invite feelings of fear, sorrow, and anger, encourage critical interpretation and explanation as we try to understand how and why we are pushed and pulled by Butler's subtle and evocative language.

Even as we reach the conclusion, after Gan has fought with T'Gatoi to reach what he considers a tolerable compromise, we may still feel ill at ease. T'Gatoi's final words, "'I'll take care of you,'" are an attempt to comfort Gan, Yet they only inspire further anxiety and distrust. And this is where Butler leaves her reader—in "Bloodchild" as in all of her fiction—in an uncomfortable, compromised space which offers only a superficial and unsatisfying closure. However, this is where she must leave us if our emotions are to support critical interpretation. If we are to leave the story with the disturbing awareness that our understanding of what we label gender, race, and species is entirely relative to the position from which we are permitted to understand these categories, we must feel as well as know it intellectually.

Elyce Rae Helford. *African American Review*. 28, 2 (Summer 1994), pp. 259–71

[Butler's work] is both fascinating and highly unusual, representing—not only in my mind, but to the growing number of critics and scholars being drawn to it—a richly rewarding and relatively rare fusion of sensibility, perception, and a driven, insightful intelligence.

That this is serious literature I have no doubt. But I must stress from the start that Butler is not, like some science fiction practitioners, overtly (and is never, like more than a few, over-bearingly) "literary." Her prose is crystalline, at its best, sensuous, sensitive, exact, but not in the least directed at calling attention to itself. The moving final paragraph of the *Xenogenesis* trilogy—the title signifying "the fancied projection of an organism altogether and permanently unlike the parent"—is thus a model of quietly passionate writing:

I chose a spot near the river. There I prepared the seed to go into the ground. I gave it a thick, nutritious coating, then brought it out of my body through my right sensory hand. I planted it deep in the rich soil of the riverbank. Seconds after I had expelled it, I felt it begin the tiny positioning movements of independent life.

Carefully, expertly crafted, deeply satisfying as it is to the reader of more than seven hundred preceding pages, and tautly, firmly resolving as it does the major plotline question, this is nevertheless determinedly functional, essentially unobtrusive prose. . . .

The passionate, abiding importance of the nurturing of new life, which clearly informs the *Xenogenesis* passage I have quoted, equally deeply informs the entire trilogy, as in every book of hers I have read. It seems to me feminist writing at its very best, writing which, like the poetry of Sheryl St. Germain . . . , proudly and utterly comfortably accepts itself as female. That strong, self-assured stance toward the fact of femaleness has been in Butler's work from the very first. The protagonist of *Pattern-Master* is, unlike the central figures in her other work, male. But he is quickly made to realize that the major female figure in the book, the woman "healer" with whom he binds himself, though clearly female and just as clearly both attractive and attracted to him, is "harder than she felt." Soon thereafter, he learns that her sexual interests are not limited to men. And some pages still further, when another female character makes the mistake of assuming that the healer is "his" woman, she is quickly, forcefully corrected. "I'm my own woman, Lady Darah. Now as before." (The two women have had prior contact, professional rather than sexual.) Finally, the protagonist asks the healer, bluntly, "Which do you prefer," men or women? She replies, "I'll tell you . . . But you won't like it. . . . When I meet a woman who attracts me, I prefer women . . . And when I meet a man who attracts me, I prefer men." The protagonist then effectively closes the discussion by announcing: "If that's the way you

are, I don't mind." Nor does he, even though, when he asks her to marry him, she refuses, once again for reasons of independence. "As my lead wife," he argues, "you'd have authority, freedom," but she swiftly responds, "How interested would you be in becoming my lead husband?"

For all its excellences, however, *Pattern-Master* is a smaller, less complex, less far-reaching fiction; in many ways it suggests the sweep and depth of *Xenogenesis* without quite achieving the trilogy's impact. Another striking precursor is *Wild Seed* (1980), which mythologizes Butler's black African heritage in an extraordinary fusion of both pre-slavery African and post-slavery American strands with what seems clearly the most urgent impulse behind all her writing, the drive to define, achieve, and nurture new life. "You steal, you kill," says the witch-like female protagonist, Anyanwu, to the even more wraith-like male protagonist, Doro. "What else do you do?" And he answers, speaking speech-words framed in Butler's beautifully calm prose, "'I build,' he said quietly. 'I search the land for people who are a little different—or very different. I search them out, I bring them together in groups, I begin to build them into a strong new people.'"

But Butler does not deal, as writers with lesser gifts so often do, with *themes*. Her novels teem with fully realized characters, male and female alike, who fascinatingly embody rather than merely represent ideas. Her fertile imagination throws up such intensely functioning, intricately enmeshed human beings that even minor personages take on vivid life—for yet another quality of a major fictive talent is a profound, virtually universal sympathy that permits imagined beings to be exactly what they in fact are, not idea-driven puppets who do only what their creators think the plot requires. The best writers are regularly, even easily, able to inhabit many skins, and to move and speak inside those superficially alien persons as if they were inside themselves. When a wondrously uncontrolled witch-like young woman leaps away from Doro, in terror, and falls heavily on a half-unconscious son of Doro, a man endowed with a propulsive power to move objects outside of his own body, the result is brilliantly, dramatically, tragically in character:

He gripped Nweke, threw her upward away from his painracked body—threw her upward with all the power he had used so many times to propel great ships out of storms. He did not know what he was doing any more than she did. He never saw her hit the ceiling, never saw her body flatten into it, distorted, crushed, never saw her head slam into one of the great beams and break and send down a grisly rain of blood and bits of bone and brain.

Again, this is not fancy writing; it is simply precise and tautly cadenced prose, forceful because it is focused, fictively superbly effective because it is in each and every detail true to the characters' lives. It is the furthest thing from accidental that the high point of such wonderfully accurate truthfulness, in the final pages, deals head-on with, and satisfyingly resolves, the novel's emotional and intellectual core. Anyanwu has fought, all along, to humanize Doro. She has sometimes seemed about to succeed, only again and again to fail. She therefore decides to commit suicide—and just when she is about to die, produces in Doro the reversion to human feeling for which she has so long struggled. But we are not told this in so many words, not at least right away. The novel's final words show us, first Doro's humanization, and then the success of what was not a strategy but Anyanwu's deep, thoroughly comprehensible decision. . . .

Butler does not need to resort to artificial icons or frantic adjectives. There is symbolism here, to be sure. But it is fully organic, neither laid on like icing nor, heavily, as with a trowel. . . .

I do not think, Butler being the kind of quietly powerful writer she is, that anything short of an attentive reading of *Xenogenesis* can convey anything like the book's multiple strengths. Not that it is deficient in either technical or substantive accomplishments. Each of the three component novels has a different though connected narrative point of view, the first using as its protagonist a black woman, Lilith Iyapo, the second using a part-human, Akin, and the third, told in the first person, experienced through the persona of Jodahs, also but markedly a part-human. Butler starts with the premise that humans have come very close to killing off one another, as well as destroying the earth humans have inhabited. An extra-terrestrial race, the Oankali, who speak of themselves, cryptically and rather oddly, as "traders," finds and preserves the few survivors. The how and why of that almost miraculous preservation, as also the full flowering of what it means that the Oankalis thus describe themselves, is what the three novels expose for us. The trilogy constitutes a remarkable exposition of eminently plausible emotional and genetic possibilities—imagined, from start to finish, in splendid detail, with a great range of characters both human and alien, and a fascinating unfolding of passionately felt, profoundly experienced events. More than all but a very small handful of "genre" books, *Xenogenesis* deals in basic wisdoms of a totally unparochial nature.

Burton Raffel. *The Literary Review.* 38, 3 (Spring 1995), pp. 454–61

Octavia E. Butler's fiction takes the African American journey motif one step further by projecting it quite literally into the future. Eight of her ten published novels are set in futuristic societies in which her heroic figures cope with and transcend various kinds of entrapment by undertaking an interesting assortment of open journeys.

*Patternmaster* (1976) describes a society that is controlled by an all-powerful ruler who dominates the inward and outward lives of his subjects by ruthlessly imposing a "pattern" of thought and behavior on them. Teray and Amber, the novel's dual heroes, seek to break away from this form of "physical slavery" and "mental slavery" by setting themselves in open motion. Amber, who is presented as an "independent" woman who is a "houseless wanderer," helps Teray overcome the tyranny of his brother Coransee by entering a liberating world of free space and motion. After killing Coransee, he breaks free of the "patterns" that have crippled him and he is able to experience physical and psychological freedom that is described in terms of open motion. . . .

All of Butler's patternist novels are centered in this quest to transcend the mental structures and social institutions that imprison people in roles defined by hierarchical societies that are essentially feudal in character. Anyanwu, the heroine of *Wild Seed*, escapes various forms of slavery in Africa and America by becoming a fugitive in search of free space. A "shapeshifter" who can, like the Greek god Proteus, always change her outward forms to escape the entrapments that authority figures design for her, she becomes at several points in the novel a bird flying away from danger or a dolphin who can be "cleansed" by swimming in the sea. Like Ellison's invisible man, her identity is essentially fluid and indeterminate, always moving to new stages of development. Her antagonist Doro, however, has a rigidly fixed personality and is described as "a tortoise encased in a shell that gets thicker and thicker each year." Whereas Anyanwu's function in the novel is to free herself and others from oppressive ideas and social structures, Doro is intent on building slave communities in Africa and America that give him absolute power over his subjects.

*Imago* (1989), likewise, presents two worlds in conflict, a "hierarchical" society that freezes people into static roles and a free society of Onkali, "space-going people" who envision life as a dynamic process of discovery and growth. While human beings dominate each other and kill those who do not fit into the "patterns" that they have constructed, the Onkali are engaged in an ongoing quest, a "long, long search for new species to combine with to construct new life forms." Fully intending "to leave the solar system in perhaps three centuries," they envision life as a colossal open journey, an ongoing search for fresh space providing new life.

Butler's fiction, therefore, clears new space for African American literature by using a science fiction mode in which black writers have rarely shown interest and infusing this mode with social and political themes that are relevant to contemporary black people. But her work is also in the main tradition of black American literature dating back to the slave narratives. In a 1984 interview with Margaret O'Connor she pointed out that much of her fiction was inspired by "the narratives of Frederick Douglass and others who endured slavery." Indeed, most of her work can be seen as signifying powerfully on the slave narratives, projecting them into the future and probing the residual effects of pre-Civil War slavery in present day and future America. Like the authors of nineteenth-century slave narratives, Butler envisions freedom as a radically open journey that must be experienced on physical, mental, and spiritual levels.

Robert Butler. *Contemporary African-American Fiction: The Open Journey* (Cranburg, New Jersey: Associated University Presses, 1998), pp. 133–43

BIBLIOGRAPHY

*Patternmaster*, 1976; *Mind of My Mind*, 1977; *Survivor,* 1978; *Wild Seed,* 1980; *Clay's Ark,* 1984; *Dawn: Xenogenesis,* 1987; *Adulthood Rites*, 1988; *Imago*, 1989; *The Evening and the Morning Light*, 1991; *Parable of the Sower*, 1993; *Bloodchild, and Other Stories, Four Walls Eight Windows*, 1995; *Parable of the Talents*, 1998

# C

## CAMARA Laye (1928–)
### Guinea

I am afraid that those who would open [*The Black Child*] with the thought of satisfying a hunger for the picturesque or escaping for a moment from the enervating condition of ''civilized'' man will be left unappeased. Unless they absolutely insist upon it, prejudice being stubborn, they will not find the classic ''darkest Africa'' nor the ''prelogical mentality'' so dear to the heart of the armchair traveler.

Of course, the book deals with animistic beliefs and practices, spirits intervene in the day-to-day life and a whole chapter is devoted to the rites of circumcision, but obviously the basis of the story is not to be found here. It is primarily universal man, man unqualified, with whom we are concerned. As a matter of fact, Camara was born at Kouroussa in French Guinea, a country with an old civilization. He is descended from the black Sudanese who in the Middle Ages founded the fabulously rich Mali Empire which was ruled for six centuries by the Moslem dynasty of the Keytas. . . .

Yet Camara does not speak to us of his people's past. He makes neither direct reference nor the slightest allusion to it, and he is content to evoke for us with emotional restraint the simple life of a dark child of the great plain of Guinea—a story told at first hand, since it is his own; but an awareness of this past helps us better to understand the psychology of the author and his characters. For me, this past—veiled as in a watermark—is always associated with the story.

> Philippe Thoby-Marcelin. Introduction to Camara Laye, *The Dark Child* (New York: Farrar, Straus, 1954), pp. 8, 11

All the poetry of [*The Black Child*] has flown away like feathers in the wind [from *The Gaze of the King*]. Therefore, the inadequacies of Camara as a novelist now stand out sharply: haphazard construction, uninteresting dialogue, none of the density fiction can have, no notion of how to present a climactic scene. Camara has not assimilated the technique of the novel! I could go on listing other defects.

After the black child, thoughtful and sensitive, we are presented a young king, slender and completely loaded down with gold. I am sure that Camara creates his characters in his own image. Perhaps he resembles this young king more than he thinks, this king who submits to the role he must play, who is elusive, and who has a rather limited capacity for judgment, since he seems hardly interested in worldly affairs. Like this king, under the cheap finery of elegant style, held by heavy conventional clasps, Camara allows us to perceive his skinny body. Like this king, he walks around like a somnambulist in a world which is ''such stuff as dreams are made on'' and which is carefully maintained by a ''judicious unconsciousness.'' Lastly, like his king he is an illusionist: he plays with mirages of hollow symbols and pretended richness. . . .

Sartre said somewhere that new ideas, since they are disconcerting and even shocking, necessarily displease. If Camara pleases people so easily, it is because he is reassuring; consequently, he offers us nothing really new. . . .

> A. B. (Mongo Beti). *Presence Africaine.* April-July 1955, pp. 143–44†

What first strikes the reader about *The Gaze of the King* is the ease and purity of the style. I am not speaking of grammar or punctuation; editors in publishing houses are paid for those things. I am speaking of the innate sense of the language, which is a gift; of the loving choice of the appropriate word, especially the manner of seizing words, of charging them with meaning and retaining their simplicity at the same time.

But Camara is more than a stylist; he is a novelist. In *The Gaze of the King*, the writer's imagination lies essentially in his ability to create characters and bring them to life. I am well aware that the subject of the novel was supplied by a dream. It could have been supplied by a news item. That Camara may have, as a starting point, borrowed some of Kafka's techniques does not bother me. Camara's symbolism is of the black-African variety. What makes it particularly black is that it opens the door to hope and that it is mystical. . . .

The African intelligentsia should not rush to condemn Camara once again, using the claim that his novel is not ''anti-colonialist.'' There are several ways of fighting colonialism. The writer could not follow the same route of commitment as the politician. French critics were right in being shocked (although they tried to hide it) at seeing Clarence, a fallen white man, try to find redemption through the Black King, who symbolizes the radiance of purity. [April 22, 1955]

> Léopold Sédar Senghor. *Liberté I: Négritude et humanisme* (Paris: Éditions du Seuil, 1964), pp. 173–74†

Camara, though being a school child, shared most of the experiences of the common village children, participating in their work and play and undergoing the traditional initiation rites. But as he grew older he was sent to a secondary school in Conakry and later he came to France to study engineering. When his money ran out he had to find work in a car factory. Lonely and depressed he sat down and wrote [*The Black Child*], this nostalgic book about his childhood. With great sensitivity the author describes his earliest memories and with infinite affection he builds up before our eyes the picture of his parents. . . .

Comparison springs to mind between Camara's *The Black Child* and the famous autobiography of an American Negro: Richard Wright's *Black Boy*. What a contrast between this gentle, nostalgic book and Richard Wright's bitter account of his stubborn childhood.

Camara's youth was happy, he was surrounded with love and affection and grew up in comparative security. Richard Wright's youth was all poverty and hunger and hatred. Camara describes his childhood with a touch of romanticism and he leaves the world of his parents with sadness and regret. Richard Wright describes his own youth with brutal realism and his whole effort is to cast off his past. Camara emerges from these experiences a deeply religious person. . . . Richard Wright emerges as a strict rationalist. . . . The immense difference in background and upbringing between these two writers symbolises the gulf that has arisen between the African and the American Negro and it may help us to understand the failure of Richard Wright to understand the people and the problems of Ghana about which he writes in his book *Black Power*.

Akanji. *Black Orpheus*. September 1957, pp. 47–48

Encountering Camara's *The Gaze of the King*, will the [European] critic not say, Why has this man not stuck to the simple, straightforward narrative of his *The Black Child*? For presumably the Western critic knows his Kafka. The cultivated naïveté of *The Black Child* charmed even the African reader. Even if it often grew precious, it carried an air of magic, of nostalgia, which worked through the transforming act of language. If the author was selective to the point of wish fulfillment, it was unimportant. That a reader could be so gracefully seduced into a village idyll is a tribute to the author.

But most intelligent readers like their Kafka straight, not geographically transposed. Even the character structure of Kafka's *The Castle* has been most blatantly retained—Clarence for Mr. K.; Kafka's Barnabas the Messenger becomes the Beggar Intermediary; Arthur and Jeremiah, the unpredictable assistants, are turned into Nagoa and Noaga. We are not even spared the role of the landlord—or innkeeper—take your choice! It is truly amazing that foreign critics have contented themselves with merely dropping an occasional ''Kafkaesque''—a feeble sop to integrity—since they cannot altogether ignore the more obvious imitativeness of Camara's technique. (I think we can tell when the line of mere ''influence'' has been crossed.) Even within the primeval pit of collective allegory-consciousness, it is self-delusive to imagine that the Progresses of these black and white pilgrims have sprung from independent creative stresses.

Wole Soyinka. *American Scholar*. Summer 1963, pp. 387–88

*Dramouss* leads us directly into the politics of Guinea, as seen and experienced by Fatoman, a native Guinean who has returned from Paris, where he completed his technical studies and worked at the Simca factory and even in Les Halles. . . .

*Dramouss* is primarily a political novel, directed at Sékou Touré, at a regime that had ''immolated democracy after the advent of the 'Defferre Law' and had begun to muzzle the naïve people of Guinea.'' To struggle against this state of affairs, one must first know what one wants for oneself before acting on behalf of the country. Fatoman, more a sentimentalist than a Muslim, says: ''What I do for my neighbor, I am also doing for myself and for God.'' But ''Dramouss,'' the female-symbol of Guinea, seen in a profoundly poetic dream, replies with common sense: ''Rather than serving others, you should tend to serving yourself.''

Fatoman flees his country after escaping from a Kafkaesque prison into which men are thrown without knowing why, then are judged and executed as in Kafka's *The Trial*. When he returns to his country, none of his friends are still alive: they have all been executed because they were against the regime.

Camara has painted a picture of Guinea under its present regime, where he himself has lived. The description of dreams and real events helps convey the authenticity of a situation that does not

do credit to Africa. ''The Black Child'' has grown up: he has learned to become aware of his milieu, and he speaks about it simply, even when rebellion seems to be crying out within him. He is a true writer.

Olympe Bhêly-Quénum. *L'Afrique actuelle*. November 1966, pp. 49–50†

The beauty of [*The Black Child*] is to be found in Camara's form and style, his deep understanding of people and, especially, of the mind of a growing child. He re-creates his childhood because he needs to understand why he has become the man he is, why so much that was precious had been irrevocably lost. His nostalgia, therefore, gives the novel meaning and continuity.

*The Black Child* is divided into twelve chapters. Each one of them is devoted to one particular event. Together, these represent the most important aspects of his childhood. Some events are unique, such as his circumcision, the conversation with his father about the little black snake, his first journey to Conakry. After this first separation from his family and Kouroussa such events predominate. Before it, however, they are deliberately balanced by descriptions of episodes which were repeated time and again during his early childhood; his father fashioning the gold ornament, holidays with his grandmother at Tindican, schooldays. . . .

[Camara] uses words to summon the meaning which lies behind his thoughts and emotions as a child, to evoke nostalgia. The descriptions are simple and unpretentious. At the same time they are complex, through the memories invoked by the re-creation of ordinary, day to day actions or the special events which changed his childhood. The deep meaning behind these simple descriptions is brought out by his use of repetition. A word is repeated, savoured almost, until its every implication, joyful and sad, has been extracted. . . .

A. C. Brench. *The Novelists' Inheritance in French Africa* (London: Oxford University Press, 1967), pp. 38–41

*Dramouss* is a sequel to *The Black Child*. The earlier book ends with the author's departure for Europe. Six years later Camara returns to Conakry and to his hometown of Kouroussa. He finds Guinea in the full effervescence of national liberation. There are, naturally, problems created by colonization and those concerning human relations as well as social and religious development. . . .

Dramouss is a woman, a divinity who reveals Guinea's future to the hero in a dream. First the present, with its cruel abominations; then the future, illuminated by the leadership of the ''black lion.'' . . .

[Camara] chooses to see human problems—both political and social—through [his parents'] religious concept of the world. The ''Black Lion,'' the symbol in the novel of the liberator Guinea is waiting for, is a religious animal: he is powerful yet pious, strong yet gentle. He is the ideal counterpart of the goddess Dramouss, the female savior. Camara dares to endure the life of his country because he is a believer.

But while it heartens him to place his hopes in the revelations of Dramouss, his contemplation of a brilliant world-to-come seems to make few demands on him. He does not show us the actual steps leading to the realization of that world in harsh everyday terms. His goal is that the ''incommunicable be communicated, and that

African thought, thus reintegrated and totally restored, be a nonaggressive but productive force.'' But to achieve this goal, to make our life of tomorrow more humane, is it necessary or is it enough for us to have a lovely poetic-religious flight of oratory?

Christophe Gudijiga. *Congo-Afrique*. May 1967, pp. 257–59†

An important notion suggested throughout [*The Gaze of the King*] is that the cultural superiority of the European depends upon the European's being in a control situation in which others must adapt to his culture; but that when the situation is reversed, the individual European is as much at a loss as the African when forced to adjust himself to European culture. Consequently, notions of cultural superiority and inferiority are invalid and at best superiority is relative to one's situation.

[A. C.] Brench has argued that Camara "alone has described the positive effect Africa can have on a white man in terms of assimilation, generally considered a problem to be faced exclusively by Africans in their contact with Europe.'' But this . . . misses the point. The problem does not concern *assimilation*, for Clarence—like Africans caught in European culture—doesn't *become* something else, but by ridding himself of evils makes himself worthy of *charitable acceptance* by the African king. The whole affair, by turning the tables, is a protest against such concepts as that of assimilation, in which one must give up one's own culture and blindly accept an alien culture. Camara is suggesting, rather, that although giving up error may be good, giving up one's culture for the sake of another is not.

Nor is it true, as [Gerald] Moore has said, that "quite as much as a search for God, Clarence's pilgrimage seems to be a search for identification.'' Clarence knows who he is, so there is no real problem of identification, but of his relationship with others, of his *relative worth*. As the African cannot be assimilated into European society, so the European cannot be assimilated into African society, although either can be accepted by performing certain approved actions. . . . To be assimilated by the alien society, Clarence must lose his original culture. This is the problem facing the African who succumbs to the hope of assimilation into French society: he will never become European at all. But Clarence is not destroyed: he is cleansed of evil; it is demonstrated that his worth is only relative to the culture in which he finds himself, so his notions of racial and cultural superiority were wrong and led to evil.

Austin J. Shelton. *L'espirit createur*. Fall 1970, pp. 216–17

In everything he has written—a more or less pure autobiography (*The Black Child*), a more or less pure novel (*The Gaze of the King*), and a book that is half-and-half (*Dramouss*)—different as the books may be formally, Camara develops a single theme that he works out in two opposed, complementary, and joined movements, movements that are the mirror opposites and the reversed images of one another. Separation and return, disunion and reunion—they are like the two sides of a single coin, or like an event and an image of that event reflected in the artist's eye. When Camara's father, in *The Black Child*, murmurs distractedly of "those far-off lands,'' he is thinking of the imminent separation that will take his son away to France, to Europe, to the non-African world; spiritually as well as physically the boy is about to depart, as his father recognizes, for a country that is distant in all ways from the country of his own being.

But when the young man sits down (as Camara has described himself doing) in a cold and cheerless hotel room in Paris to try to recapture his past experiences, a complete transformation has been effected: it is now Kouroussa, the African world of his father and mother and the town of his own childhood, that is "a far-off land.'' Through ambition he was separated, in nostalgia he returns. In *The Black Child* the two-fold theme revolves about the unified community on the one hand and the separated individual on the other; paradoxically it is the separated individual who recreates, in an act of memory and artistry, that world that in fact no longer exists—if it ever did exist in fact. . . .

This disunion and reunion, this separation and return, and the mystery wherein they are made one and the same, has been the theme of all of Camara's writing. In *The Black Child* the return is achieved through the artist's imagination; in *Dramouss* the return is literal (and disappointing); and in *The Gaze of the King* the return is symbolic and vicarious, the white man Clarence discovering in Africa the world of simplicity that Camara had lost through experience and had refound through art.

James Olney. *Tell Me Africa* (Princeton: Princeton University Press, 1973), pp. 126–27

All Laye's work can be seen as a continuing story of initiation into adult responsibility in this unstable world. This theme is evident in *L'Enfant noir*, in both the tribal rituals and the departures for school with which they are implicitly compared. One should also remember, however, the narrator's realisation that being initiated did not make him a 'man' and his deliberate attempt to separate himself from his own childhood when telling the story, in order to assert as forcefully as possible his passage to maturity. Clarence's experience in *Le Regard du roi* is an initiation in many ways similar to that of the African child. It is a personal test, necessitating a trip through the 'bush'. Like a tribal initiate, Clarence must become a member of a community. His initiation has a religious significance; he finds a new life with the King, in a way similar to the new life created through the shedding of blood in the Malinké ritual. *Dramouss* might be described as Fatoman's painful initiation into the nature of contemporary political reality. He remains for a long time rather childlike in his indignation, unwilling to recognise the facts, unable to take any responsible action concerning the way his country is developing. Perhaps the only successful initiation ceremony in *Dramouss* takes place in Fatoman's dream. *Le Maître de la parole* is largely about Soundiata's conception, childhood and initiation into adult responsibilities. He is still an adolescent when called to lead the army opposing the tyrant. Each of Laye's books is thus about tests of strength, the need to prove oneself when confronted with a difficult and changing external world. It is only after accepting this challenge that the hero may receive divine favour to aid him in his task.

When we look for a psychological unity in Laye's work we may find it in an extreme attachment to his mother-land. In *L'Enfant noir*, published six years after he left Guinea, Laye wrote: 'it was a terrible parting! I do not like to think of it. I can still hear my mother wailing. It was as if I was being torn apart.' Although he says that he worked out his anxiety about leaving Upper Guinea by describing his departure, it is probable that this traumatic event has provided the emotional charge behind all his work. Many years later he suggested that if *L'Enfant noir* is his most successful work, it is because 'one only has one childhood memory. It is always the best book.'

Whether or not *L'Enfant noir* is better than *Le Regard du roi*, the same experience of feeling uprooted from a childhood paradise, of feeling alienated in a foreign culture, directly expressed in *L'Enfant noir*, is transposed in the fiction of *Le Regard du roi*, and explains the emotional trauma of *Dramouss*, written when it was apparent that no return was possible and that exile was inevitable. This trauma is even apparent in *Le Maître de la parole*. Soundiata's exile often suggests a parallel to Laye's own; the triumphal return to Niani, described in other versions of the legend, is omitted.

Laye's life was in many ways an illustration of a moment in cultural history. He was representative of a kind of experience that is unlikely to recur at present. For him the normal problems of growing up were combined with the shock of a radical change in culture, a shock which—in the world of the transistor radio even in the poorest villages of West Africa—can never again be so powerful. Laye gave this experience perhaps its purest literary expression. In spite of the modesty of his background, in spite of the many obstacles to his desire to write, he managed to produce work of great interest at a moment when West Africa literature was in its infancy.

Adele King. *The Writings of Camara Laye* (London: Heinemann Educational Books Ltd., 1983), pp. 123–25

[Camara Laye] achieved world recognition for *The Dark Child*, a memoir of his childhood in Kouroussa, and *The Radiance of the King*, a surreal novel in which a white beggar wanders in search of a black king who will liberate him by the radiant smile that smites all sickness in a troubled soul. Laye's second work is allegorical, Kafkaesque and African in a unique way; it is a powerful and disturbing exploration of exile, quest and reconciliation with a power greater than logic or reason.

Although Laye's first book is often regarded as the perfect example of negritude—a work that illuminates the essence of African identity—he did not believe in the separatism the negritude movement spawned. His ideal was a unity of culture, just as the hero of his last work united the many kingdoms of the Upper Niger into the Mali empire.

Laye describes *The Guardian of the Word* as a "translation" of the legend "Kouma Lafolo Kouma," which he heard sung by the famed griot Babu Condé. The legend tells the history of the "great Sundiata, the son of the buffalo-panther and of the lion," who became the first Emperor of Mali and ruled from 1230 to 1255. In his rendering, Laye assumes the voice of a griot, who is the historian of his tribe as well as a performer and storyteller. In adopting this guise, Laye is adhering to a profound convention, for the traditionalist African writer did not claim individual authorship but considered himself a "keeper" of sacred words available to all. . . .

Some writers can criticize their society only indirectly—through legend. Laye had inveighed against the policies of [Guinean President] Sékou Touré in an autobiographical manuscript, *L'Exil*, but he could not publish it while his wife remained in a Guinean jail. . . . A careful reading of Laye's Sundiata epic, however, reveals that again he was hurling charges at his old adversary.

Laye's tale has dimensions beyond its relationship to specific history; he was attempting a revitalization of his work by returning to the basic resource of any literature—the springs of its traditions.

Still, his intent was not to preserve traditions; he was interested in nourishment and enrichment of contemporary life. Thus, although Laye's last work is filled with surrealist shades and European psychological insight, it is invigorated by the traditional African vision of the spiritual and historic. Camara Laye is saying that myth creates kinship among us all.

Martin Tucker. *New York Times Book Review*. June 24, 1984, p. 24

Camara Laye remains a controversial figure. He has been criticized by Mongo Beti for not addressing the issue of colonialism in his works. Lilyan Kestleloot claims that he did not write *Le Regard du roi*. This novel itself remains enigmatic, seeming to interrupt a continuum begun in *L'Enfant noir* and continued in *Dramouss*. This analysis, based on ethnographic research of Manding initiation rites, seeks to show, through Camara Laye's second novel, a logical sequence in his works. By founding evidence of such a continuum in the two-part Manding definition of action, in which spiritual reflection leads to political engagement, Laye's commitment first to spiritual and then to community values will not only offer support of his authorial claims to *Le Regard du roi*, but will also respond to Beti's criticism.

For the Manding, action is comprised of two parts: tama, which is characterized by reflection, exploration, and research, and kè, which is the realization and accomplishment of the knowledge acquired by this reflection. The four major works of Camara Laye can be divided into tama and kè in a way that emphasizes both his spiritual and his political determination. In *L'Enfant noir* and *Le Regard du roi*, the author's main goal is personal fulfillment and spiritual identity, embodying therefore the reflection and exploration characteristic of tama. *Dramouss* and *Le Maître de la parole*, on the other hand, reach outward to social concerns, and Laye, by his act of writing, takes action to shake up the status quo of an oppressive government (*Dramouss*) and to awaken his people to their heritage (*Le Maître de la parole*), thus fulfilling the second requirement of Manding action, kè.

Laye's first novel, *L'Enfant noir*, contains many themes, among them, his initiation into manhood. By consulting two of Dominique Zahan's ethnographic works, *Sociétés d'initiation Bambara* (published six years after *Le Regard du roi*) and *The Religion, Spirituality, and Thought of Traditional Africa*, along with other ethnographic studies, this initiation can be seen to be more than just a circumcision, rather, it is part of a vast network of secret male societies whose intricate philosophy forms the basis for Manding culture. According to Zahan, this network is organized into six dyow, six societies, each with their own initiations and specifications, through which the initiate passes respectively. Each dyow corresponds to certain body parts and certain senses, so that the six together create a full body with all its senses. The ultimate purpose then of the six initiation societies is to form a complete body capable of action. By passing through these societies, the initiate comes to recognize his full humanity in order to become more capable of acting upon it. The two-fold nature of this action, defined as tama and kè by these societies, is of special interest to this analysis, especially if we are to show that Camara Laye was a man of action, committed to social and political problems. . . .

According to Zahan, the n'domo creates a problem that the korè resolves. . . . [This] same relationship is present in Laye's first two novels; *L'Enfant noir*, with its many elements of the n'domo, asks a specific question which *Le Regard du roi*, embodying the korè, answers. This question concerns the role of women in the Manding male's quest for spirituality.

> Brenda Bertrand. *French Review.* 67, 4 (March 1994), p. 648

BIBLIOGRAPHY

*L'Enfant noir* (The African Child), 1953; *Le Regard du roi* (The Radiance of the King), 1954; *Dramouss* (A Dream of Africa), 1966; *Le Maitre de la parole* (The Guardian of the Word), 1978

# CÉSAIRE, Aimé (1913– )
**Martinique**

[In 1942] Aimé Césaire gave me a copy of his *Notebook on a Return to My Native Land*, which had been published in a limited edition by a Paris magazine in 1939. The poem, which must have gone unnoticed then, is nothing less than the greatest lyrical monument of our time. It brought me the richest certainty, the kind that one can never arrive at on one's own. Its author had gambled on everything I had ever believed was right, and he had incontestably won. What was at stake, with all due credit to Césaire's own genius, was our common conception of life.

Now that a bilingual edition in the United States has given this work wider circulation, people will see in it first its exceptionally rich movement, its exuberant flow, and a faculty of ceaselessly scanning the emotional world from top to bottom, to the point of turning it upside down. All these characteristics distinguish authentic poetry from the false, simulated poetry, of a venomous sort, that constantly proliferates around authentic poetry. "To sing or not to sing": that is the question, and there could be no salvation in poetry for anyone who does not "sing," although the poet must be asked to do *more* than sing. And I do not need to say that for those who do not sing, any recourse to rhyme, fixed meter, and other shoddy baggage could never deceive anyone's ears but those of Midas. Césaire is, before anything else, one who sings. . . .

Césaire's poetry, like all great poetry and all great art, has as its highest merit its power to transform what it uses; he begins with the most unlovely material, among which we have to include ugliness and servitude, and ends up producing the philosopher's stone, which we well know is no longer gold but freedom.

It would be useless to try to reduce Césaire's gift of song, his ability to reject what he does not need, and his power of magical transmutation . . . to a specific number of technical secrets. All one can validly say about these qualities is that all three contain a greater common denominator, which is an exceptional intensity of emotion in the face of the spectacle of life (leading to an impulse to act on life so as to change it) and, as such, this intensity will retain its full force until some new order comes into being.

> André Breton. *Hémisphères.* Fall-Winter, 1943–44, pp. 8–9†

The voice of Aimé Césaire, the black poet, which reached us right after the Liberation, was like a fresh breath; we heard tones that had never been sounded in French poetry. His first work, *Notebook on a Return to My Native Land*, a book woven of a single poem, seemed to obey no rule other than haste, as if it were appropriate to say everything at once, not omitting anything, as if it were necessary, here and now, to echo the most extreme urgency. This poem rose to the heights of French poetry like a meteor. What! A black voice finally refused to conform to our rhythms, to the rituals of our style, to the form we had imposed on the world—a form based on our landscape, our bearing, and our customs.

It seemed to me that this poem had been too quickly labeled as orthodoxy, surrealist orthodoxy, a literary preciosity of the same order as [André Breton's] *The White-Haired Revolver.* Césaire's poetry was quite a different matter: his revolt had a real basis; it was not related to any sort of ill humor or directed against a denigrated tradition. His revolt had its own sources . . . and its own mission [political freedom]. . . . It was marked by more haste, more determination, and more seriousness than the exercises of surrealism. Although we could become comfortable with surrealism—and we all got used to the *manifestos* of that school—we could not become comfortable with these cries, this long cry that was beginning to form its principles, to establish itself, and finally to bring in its wake things that were clearly going to threaten us. . . .

> Hubert Juin. *Aimé Césaire, poète noir* (Paris: Présence Africaine, 1956), pp. 19–20†

In Paris, at the Lycée Louis-le-Grand, Césaire met Léopold Sédar Senghor. This meeting led to a great friendship almost at once and to Césaire's discovery of Africa, the land of his heart, which he adopted immediately: "When I got to know Senghor [wrote Césaire], I called myself an African." . . .

In 1932 a little magazine called *Légitime défense* appeared; in it, communist and surrealist Caribbean students a few years older than Césaire violently denounced the corrupt society of Martinique, the misery of its people, and the ridiculous literary parrotry of its native writers. These were just the words that Césaire needed! For Césaire, Senghor, and Damas, that magazine was a true catalyst. The elders had their problems; they had to keep silent. That was not very important; a breach had been opened, and the three friends would make the roaring river of Negritude rush into that breach. . . .

Césaire, Senghor, and Damas began by founding a little newspaper, *L'étudiant noir*, which brought together the black students in Paris on the basis of color rather than country of origin. This new grouping meant a recognition of two obvious and essential facts: that a black man is not a white man, and that all blacks have certain problems in common. This was a healthy reaction against the attitude of those Caribbean students who had rejected their origins, had tried to act like whites and like Frenchmen, even more so in Paris than at home, and had tried to forget their color! This first stage of Negritude, this recognition of one-self, was followed, for Césaire and his companions, by an assumption of responsibility for their destiny as Negroes, for their history, and for their own culture. . . .

Instead of the classical French writers, *L'étudiant noir* set forth as models the spontaneity of black American writers, like Claude McKay and Langston Hughes, as well as the style of African sculpture, and the naturalness and humor of local tales, all of which were examples of a freedom of expression accordant with the original Negro temperament. . . .

For the first time, blacks spoke out to tell their fellow blacks "that instead of doing everything like a white man," they should, on the contrary, stay completely black, that their truth lay in their blackness and that it was beautiful. . . . Negritude was an enterprise undertaken to end the alienation of a whole race, and this movement laid the foundation on which the ideology of the decolonization of Africa would be built.

Lilyan Kesteloot. *Aimé Césaire* (Paris: Pierre Seghers, 1962), pp. 20–23†

A poem of Césaire . . . bursts and turns on itself as a fuse, as bursting suns which turn and explode in new suns, in a perpetual surpassing. It is not a question of meeting in a calm unity of opposites but rather a forced coupling, into a single sex, of black in its opposition to white. This dense mass of words, hurled into the air like rocks by a volcano is the Negritude which arrays itself against Europe and colonization. That which Césaire destroys is not all culture, it is the white culture; that which he conjures forth is not the desire of all, it is the revolutionary aspirations of the oppressed Negro; that which he touches in the depths of his being is not the soul, it is a certain form of humanity concrete and well determined. One can speak here of an automatic writing which is at the same time engaged and even directed; not that there is the intervention of reflection, but because the words and the images continually express the same torrid obsession. At the bottom of his soul, the white surrealist finds release; at the bottom of his soul, Césaire finds the fixed inflexibility of vindication and of resentment. . . .

In Césaire the great surrealist tradition is achieved, takes its definite sense, and destroys itself. Surrealism, European poetic movement, is stolen from the Europeans by a black who turns it against them and assigns it a rigorously prescribed function. . . . In Europe, surrealism, rejected by those who could have transfused it into their blood, languishes and expires. But at the moment it loses contact with the Revolution, here in the West Indies, it is grafted to another branch of the universal Revolution; here it unfolds itself into an enormous and sombre flower. The originality of Césaire is to have cast his direct and powerful concern for the Negro, for the oppressed and for the militant into the world of the most destructive, the freest and the most metaphysical poetry at a time when [Paul] Éluard and [Louis] Aragon were failing to give political content to their verse. And finally, that which tears itself from Césaire as a cry of grief, of love and of hate, is the *Negritude-object*. Here further, he follows the surrealist tradition which desires that the poem *objectivize*. The words of Césaire do not describe *Negritude*, they do not designate it, they do not copy it from outside as a painter does of a model; they *make* it; they compose it under our eyes. [1948]

Jean-Paul Sartre. *Black Orpheus* (Paris: Présence Africaine, 1963), pp. 36–39

This passage by Césaire [''those who have invented neither gunpowder nor the compass,'' in *Notebook on a Return to My Native Land*] is of crucial importance: it contrasts the spirit of Negro-African Civilization with that of the European world, the *farmer* with the *engineer*, to use Sartre's terms. We know that man's attitude toward nature is the essential problem, whose solution conditions man's destiny. ''Man's attitude toward nature'' contains both the essential *subject* and the essential *object*. The

European, *homo faber*, has to get to know nature so as to make it the instrument of his will for power: to *use* it. The European will give nature a fixed place through analysis, will make it a *dead* thing in order to dissect it. But how can one create life from a dead thing?

The Negro, on the contrary, subjective, ''impervious to all the winds of the world,'' discovers the object in its reality, in its *rhythm*. And he yields to it, following its living movement, going from the subject to the object, ''playing the game of the world.'' What does this mean except that, for the Negro, to know is to live— the life of the Other—by identifying with the object? To know [*con-naître*] means to be born to the Other by dying to the self: it is making love with the Other, it is dancing the Other. ''I feel, therefore I exist.'' Césaire writes: ''By thinking of the Congo/I became a Congo rustling with/forests and rivers.'' [1952]

Léopold Sédar Senghor. *Liberté I: Négritude et humanisme* (Paris: Éditions du Seuil, 1964), p. 141†

*The Tragedy of King Christophe* was published in 1963, two years after the death of Patrice Lumumba. Therefore, Césaire was aware of the circumstances of Lumumba's death when he wrote that play. But it was not until 1966, five years after Lumumba's murder, that Césaire finally decided, it seems, to deal directly with the African leader who was murdered in such a cowardly way.

Once again Césaire created a play about an African chief offered by destiny as a sacrifice to the Negro cause. *A Season in the Congo*, however, shows a development in Césaire's thesis about the Black Leader. In Christopher the portrait of the Leader was generally but not entirely clear. In Lumumba, who is closer to us, the portrait of the Black hero is made more precise. Césaire is able to repeat himself while renewing himself at the same time. *A Season in the Congo* presents the same theme as *And the Dogs Were Silent* and *The Tragedy of King Christophe*, yet the play is not the same. Even if the theme is the same, its presentation has evolved toward realism and precision. *A Season in the Congo* is also closer to historical truth than *The Tragedy of King Christophe* or *And the Dogs Were Silent*, whose stories are essentially invented.

The scenes of *A Season in the Congo* are short, quick, and, so to speak, choppy. The play is a kaleidoscope in which all of Patrice Lumumba's political life passes by. . . . Except for Lumumba and a very few others, the characters in *A Season in the Congo* are fragmented. This is as it should be, for, whether he is present or not, all the scenes center and converge on Lumumba.

Hénock Trouillot. *L'itinéraire d'Aimé Césaire* (Port-au-Prince: Imprimerie des Antilles, 1968), pp. 156, 158†

In 1942 André Breton, the leader of the French surrealist movement, in flight from the Nazis came to Martinique and there met Aimé Césaire. These two poets developed a strong friendship. It was an important event in Césaire's life. André Breton brought Césaire to the notice of important literary circles in France. By 1944 Aimé Césaire was back in Paris and received with great fanfare. In 1956, *Présence africaine*, a literary magazine founded in 1947 by Alioune Diop, reissued the *Notebook on a Return to My Native Land. Présence africaine* served as a forum for some of the most outstanding African and West Indian writers and intellectuals like Alioune Diop, Léopold Senghor, Césaire, Damas and many others who later played an important role in the African Independence movement.

In 1946 Césaire fought and won the election as Deputy to the French National Assembly for Martinique. He also became Mayor of Fort-de-France, a position he has occupied to this day. Martinique is a constituency of the French National Assembly and is represented by three deputies. Most of the deputies have always advocated association with France as the cornerstone of their politics. Césaire's election meant that for the first time a man who identified with the economic and political realities of Martinique was to become a voice in the French National Assembly. For Césaire, the scope for expressing his intense hostility against French domination and assimilation was widened. He was now not only the ideologist of the oppressed but their representative. Indeed he could rightly claim that he understood their needs and their demands because he was one of them. In spite of his educational achievements, he had refused to be assimilated. His position as Deputy demonstrated the extent to which Césaire had embraced his beliefs in active participation. He had realized that only by the exercise of power could what he considered better political and cultural values be implemented. He saw the position he occupied as Deputy as a power base from which he could effect the desired change.

Mazisi Kunene. Introduction to Aimé Césaire, *Return to My Native Land* (Baltimore: Penguin, 1969), pp. 25–26

The memory of having been torn from the maternal breast, from a culture and spirituality of the soil that were deeply rooted in the Negro soul, is present throughout Aimé Césaire's works. He cannot forget the extent of the looting of Africa, and the poet grieves for this violated Africa as much as he grieves for his native Martinique. . . .

The first European plunderers and exploiters were sure of their superiority over the inhabitants of the countries "liberated" from the darkness of ignorance. [In his *Discourse on Colonialism*] Césaire is persuaded that the "main responsibility in this area lies with Christian pedantry for having set forth dishonest equations: Christianity = civilization; paganism = savagery. These equations could lead only to abominable colonialist and racist consequences, whose victims were to be the Indians, the yellow-skinned peoples, and the Negroes.". . .

Basilio [the Belgian King in *A Season in the Congo*] recognizes that once Belgian domination will have ended in the Congo, the spirit of the Negroes, their own personality, will be reborn. What he calls the "barbarous root" is the vital essence of the Congolese. It is the negation of colonialist omnipotence and is the most dangerous threat to the Church, guardian of the established order. . . .

Africa hungers for itself because it has gone through the traumatic experience of having its own negation forced on it. For Césaire, this experience extends all the way to Martinique, for the experience is not rooted in the obscure mysticism of a place or continent, which has been humiliated, but in the spiritual condition of a whole people. The African and the Martinican share the same fate. The torture they suffer makes time and place relatively unimportant. Only details differentiate the Rebel [in *And the Dogs Were Silent*] and Lumumba [in *A Season in the Congo*], King Christophe [in *The Tragedy of King Christophe*] and Césaire. . . .

The Negro hero, aware of the role assigned to him by Western society, mocks the vain attempts to enslave him by force and to make him deny his brothers.

Frederick Ivor Case. *Essays in Criticism.* Fall 1970, pp. 242–44†

Against the backdrop of the magical, enchanting world of Shakespeare's *The Tempest*, Aimé Césaire [in his play *A Tempest*] recreates his vision of the black man's struggle against white tyranny. Original levels of metaphoric and thematic complexity recede to focus on the stark drama between oppressor and oppressed, between the desire for domination and the will to freedom. The setting is no longer a realm suspended in time and space where art and magic resolve the disorders and inequities of the temporal, political world. No longer can the play be considered in terms of spiritual and moral rebirth, as the movement from sin or crime through ordeal to contrition and forgiveness symbolized by the progression from tempest to the harmony of music. From the conflict between "civilization" and "primitive society," between colonizer and colonized, from the view of Caliban as "natural man"—all aspects of the play traditionally pointed out by critics—Césaire fashions a spectacle of racial conflict whose roots plunge deep into his own experience in colonial Martinique and whose chant echoes his early *Notebook on a Return to My Native Land*.

Césaire compresses the action into three acts and resolves the conflicts of Shakespeare's *Tempest* by the end of the second act: Ariel announces Prospero's forgiveness and the marriage of Ferdinand and Miranda. . . . The tension which has been building between Prospero and Caliban then intensifies freely. From Shakespeare to Césaire, Prospero evolves from the Renaissance symbol of Reason and what is best in man to the white colonizer whose very existence derives from power. Deposed not for his interest in the liberal arts but in a coup over his discovery of valuable new lands, Prospero rules over Caliban and Ariel as the colonial governor over native slaves. Usurping legitimate authority, as his brother did before him, he attempts to "teach" his values to the ignorant and resistant black indigene. But Caliban refuses the white culture as he rejects the white world's image of him as incorrigibly dirty and sexually obsessed. He will not deny his past and as a constant reminder of his disinheritance he will take the name X—as the Black Muslims do—to be "the man whose name has been stolen." Unlike Ariel, the non-violent mulatto integrationist who submits and seeks to stir Prospero's conscience, Caliban has become the black militant revolutionary whose cry, in English, "freedom now," links him to the universal struggle of his oppressed brothers. He prefers death with dignity: "death is better than humiliation and injustice."

Richard Regosin. *French Review.* April 1971, pp. 952–53

It has been noted that there is a fundamental unity among Césaire's heroes and that this unity arises from the author's presence in each of them. His presence is very apparent in the Rebel in *And the Dogs Were Silent*, who expresses Césaire's state of mind. He is doubly present in *The Tragedy of King Christophe*, speaking directly through the character of Metellus and showing his sympathy for one aspect of Christophe—his dream of grandeur for his people. In *A Season in the Congo* Patrice Lumumba's personality is too well known and his story is too recent for Césaire to transform them. The writer's voice, nevertheless, is often heard in the poetic and visionary remarks of his protagonist.

In his theater political questions have a central place, focusing on his greatest concern—the position of the black man in our era. But his theater is also "intentionally poetic." . . . Césaire's theater gives the spoken word, the dialogue, a special importance that stems from the lofty idea the author himself has about the power of language.

> Rodney E. Harris. *L'humanisme dans le théâtre d'Aimé Césaire* (Sherbrooke, Quebec: Éditions Naaman, 1973), p. 161†

Twenty years after [the] final edition appeared, forty years after [Aimé] Césaire began to write the poem, it is increasingly apparent that his *Cahier d'un retour au pays natal* is the product of a complex dialectic between the poet and his text, between the poet and his experience. In this sense, the poem appears not only as the beginning of the young writer's career, but also as a series of guideposts to his subsequent development. If we are to fully appreciate and understand this evolution from a personal to a more collectively oriented consciousness, we can do no worse than to follow the signs in the four versions of Césaire's most widely read work.

> Thomas A. Hale. In Carolyn A. Parker and Stephen H. Arnold, eds. *When the Drumbeat Changes* (Washington, D. C.: Three Continents Press, 1981), p. 192

The greatness of Césaire was not only that he stole his master's language and turned it into a weapon but that his long quest for a submerged identity gave him a deeper consciousness, enabling him to clearly understand the dialectics of master and slave. The true power of his miraculous weapon was that they gave the oppressed the warm vision of a possible humanism. . . .

Césaire says no to any kind of "racist anti-racism." He knows that racism is the logic of the exploiter and will be nothing but a mystification in the hands of the oppressed. He is against racist battle cries for he understands that the question is not so simple, that colonial problems cannot be analyzed in terms of color alone and that the instinctual "death to the whites" has to transcend itself in order to give way to a higher level of consciousness. . . . In his numerous collections of poems, essays, and particularly in his plays, Césaire has tried to study the painful process of decolonization with its pitfalls and tragedies. With [*La Tragédie du roi Christophe*, translated as *The Tragedy of King Christophe*] and [*Une Saison au Congo*, translated as *A Season in the Congo*], he has been searching for a solution to the chaos created by the neocolonial domination, for a lesson to learn from the tragic destinies of Christophe and Lumumba, for a philosophical and political understanding of decolonization seen in a global perspective. From his first work to his latest writing, we can observe a progression from the personal plane to the universal, from cultural to political consciousness and the beautiful metamorphosis of his Negro cry into a song, a love song for the whole human race, a song capable of forging a "blood transcending fraternity" rising from an immense "bush-fire of friendship."

> Guy Viêt Levilain. In Ileana Rodriguez and Marc Zimmerman, eds. *Process of Unity in Caribbean Society: Ideologies and Literature* (Minneapolis: Institute for the Study of Ideologies and Literatures, 1983), pp. 159–60

Like the laminaria, the algae that tenaciously cling to rock, Aimé Césaire, with his latest collection of poems [*Moi, Laminaire . . .*], reiterates his lifelong political and poetic commitments: Négritude, a name he coined designating one of the powerful ideas of the century; and surrealism, whose ideology and esthetics gave impetus to his writing and thought. There are of course new intonations too. Age, disillusionments, the wear and tear of living wedged between human wretchedness and the splendors of nature that mockingly promise happiness, violent destruction—all have taken their toll. . . . Departure, suffered and anticipated, its potential relief as well as affliction, is a much-modulated motif. There are homages to friends departed: Wifredo Lam, Léon Damas, Miguel Ángel Asturias. There are also old scores to be paid off, obsessions to be laid to rest. . . .

But if life takes away, it also enriches. . . . And indeed, the Césairean afflatus explodes with verbal energies, profuse vocabulary, tortuous syntax, startling images. But next to this intensity, there is also playfulness, sometimes a cheap jingling rhyme, sometimes a facetious wordplay. And as so often before, Césaire celebrates the Martinican landscape: the mountains, mangroves, ravines filled with marvels and significations, visited by the island's inevitable scourges, the hurricane and the earthquake. The volcano serves as a polysemous metaphor for the island, its people and the poet himself.

> Juris Silenieks. *World Literature Today*. 57, 4 (Autumn 1983), p. 678

As Césaire defines the past suffering of his people, the beauty and uniqueness of his land, and his dreams for both the people and the land, he experiences a catharsis which allows him to become the psychological leader of his people. He challenges himself to take on this role, he rejects hatred as a way of dealing with the white world, and he insists on love. . . .

In looking at the evolution of francophone poetry, and more particularly Caribbean poetry, it is clear that Césaire's is the voice of the awakener. He summons those who follow to act, to affirm their Négritude. He explores the negative emotions any victim feels for his oppressors, but he doesn't dwell on them. He dwells rather on the potential within the victims themselves, because he is eager to respond to the sense of humanity he has discovered, he is eager to press forward.

> Ann Armstrong Scarboro. *Concerning Poetry*. 17, 2 (Fall 1984) pp. 123–24

*Cahier d'un retour au pays natal* is admirable in the power of its images and in its inexorable movement from detached observation to commitment to struggle. A turning point occurs when Césaire turns from generalized description from on high (we can almost see him floating above Martinique in a French balloon) to a moving description of his own home and family. . . . And it is soon after this moving tableau that Césaire affirms that ''my tongue will serve those miseries which have no tongue, my voice the liberty of those who founder in the dungeons of despair.'' He goes on to affirm that ''life is not a spectacle, a sea of griefs is not a proscenium, a man who wails is not a dancing bear.''. . .

Throughout the [*Discours sur le colonialisme*, translated as *Discourse on Colonialism*], Césaire quotes at length from racist works by Christian humanists, but he either has not read or refuses to acknowledge the great socialist writers and philosophers of Europe. The only writer he speaks of with admiration is [Comte de] Lautréamont, a nineteenth-century poet and precursor of surrealism, known for a single work, *Chants de Maldoror*. Césaire admires his nightmare visions of the putrid capitalist system. Césaire's *Discourse* is grim and deeply pessimistic. This is not a dialectical analysis. The concluding paragraph on the mission of the proletariat seems tacked on; there is nothing in the rest of the work to indicate that the proletariat is developing and struggling or that the working class even exists.

> April Ane Knutson. *Ideology and Independence in the Americas* (Minneapolis: MEP Publications, 1989), pp. 47–48, 55

[Césaire] has made the study of international blackness his lifelong vocation. Léopold [Sédar] Senghor credits him for having articulated and defined the concept of Négritude, which concept, in spite of the attacks aimed at it today, essentially meant the understanding by blacks of the implications of their blackness. In 1939 Césaire pointed the way in his autobiographical poem, *Cahier d'un retour au pays natal*. In this outstanding work he unweaves the skeins of black suffering, vomits the self-hate that according to colonialism should have been his lot, and embraces his Africanness with a commitment to sing it, proclaim it, and beautify it. In so doing, he proclaimed himself the enemy of colonialism. In 1955 came the renowned masterpiece *Discours sur le colonialisme*. Moreover, Césaire was prepared to be more than a verbal antagonist: he became politically active. I feel that this experience with politics endowed him with many of the insights he brings to *A Season in the Congo*.

*A Season in the Congo* dramatizes several facets touching on the Congo in particular and Africa in general. The coming of the Belgians put an end to the great political and social traditions of the Congo. In their wake came social and ethical decay to the point that at independence colonialism had poisoned most of the leaders into believing that they were to be the new overlords to begin the oppression of their people exactly where the Belgians left off. In the case of the different ethnic groups, each felt that it alone should be the principal benefactor of independence. Because most of the characters are shown to be motivated by personal gain, men of Lumumba's vision and integrity, with a vocation to bring about African unity and restore African dignity, are a minuscule minority. But even such a character is insufficient, for leaders like Lumumba, granted the Machiavellian nature of the West, must be able to supersede the West in its political duplicity. (Perhaps a cunning leader had to be as ruthless and vain about power as Césaire portrays in another play, *La Tragédie du roi Christophe*.) Africa has the traditions, the wisdom, the structures for its potential unity, but does not have in place the altruistic leaders with a sufficiently broad vision to cement those structures. Finally, this

play demonstrates that a writer attempting to portray African reality can enrich his work significantly by incorporating into it many of the forms germane to African languages—the metaphor, the proverb, the fable, etc.

> Nigel Thomas. In Jonathan A. Peters, Mildred P. Mortimer, and Russell V. Linnemann, eds. *Literature of Africa and the African Continuum* (Washington, D.C.: Three Continents Press, 1989), p. 91

Césaire's Martinique background is just as germane to an understanding of his approach to escape as [V. S.] Naipaul's Indian affiliation is to his. The remnants of the once extensive French Caribbean empire have, in the twentieth century, been officially drawn into the political structure of the French republic. Martinique is an ''overseas department'' of France, and theoretically is on equal footing with other administrative regions of metropolitan France. Martinique is represented in the French National Assembly, and Césaire himself has served as a deputy. Again in theory, there is no racial discrimination in Martinican society, since all Martinicans are citizens of France. Indeed, ever since the heyday of colonialism, the French have held to the ideal of their ''mission civilisatrice,'' a movement to bring the ''natives'' the benefits of French culture. In the thinking of the French colonialist, even the blackest African could be considered French—and claim all the rights of a Frenchman—as long as he adopted French culture. Such a person was called an ''évolué'' as if to emphasize that, in assuming the mantle of Frenchness, he had become truly human.

On one level, this philosophy and the political integration it spawned were beacons of enlightenment. People in the British and Dutch West Indies could only look longingly at those in the French Antilles who seemed to have arrived at a plateau of metropolitan acceptance undreamed of in their own territories. But on the other hand, this policy, well intentioned though it may have been, had the vicious effect of relegating local culture ever further to the shadows. For the French West Indian, there *was* no culture but that of France. An English-island intellectual like Naipaul could *choose* to try to adopt English culture; a French-island intellectual was either French, or he was a savage.

For a self-aware Martinican of the late colonial period, this situation was intolerable. Césaire, for example, saw perfectly well that while he might be accorded an official status of Frenchman, he was certainly *not* French in the truest sense. His Frenchness was but a mask of culture. It is no accident that Martinique also produced the radical philosophy of Frantz Fanon. While Césaire, unlike Fanon, was able to play all along with the system for most of his long and productive career, he was never unaware that the mask of the évolué was a betrayal of his deepest self.

> Michael V. Angrosino. In Philip A. Dennis and Wendell Aycock, eds. *Literature and Anthropology* (Lubbock: Texas Tech University Press, 1989), pp. 122–23

Aimé Césaire's *Cahier d'un retour au pays natal* is one of the acknowledged masterpieces of francophone Caribbean literature. A great work seems to require a great man, a hero who can act and speak for an entire people, and indeed the period *Cahier* inhabits in Caribbean literary history has been referred to as an era of ''Heroic Negritude.'' There is scarcely any scholarship on the long poem which does not refer to it as ''epic'' and ''heroic.'' What I would like to argue, however, is that these terms are inappropriate, for two reasons. First, they function to smooth out the disruptive quality of the poem by couching it in comfortably traditional categories of genre. And second, since the epic hero is always male and the trajectory of his journey has traditionally been gendered as masculine, these generic labels also serve to thwart discussion of the poem's figuration of gender by suppressing the role the feminine plays and reading the poem's figuration of masculinity as ''natural.'' This ends up lending false coherence to the lyrical subject, suggesting an easily identifiable, active narrator moving through time and space, a notion Cahier d'un retour defies.

When one examines the way that the poem's complex imagery is gendered, one arrives at a point of reversal of terms, where what was once masculine (the sun) becomes feminine (the moon) and vice versa. This reversal is eventually overturned, yet a fundamental ambiguity remains and is never fully resolved. The poem's ending is both an attempt to rewrite the binary oppositions of masculine and feminine, vertical and horizontal, sun and moon, and a call to transcend a debilitating collective history. By unsettling this symbolic structure—what amounts to a ''colonial Imaginary.'' In Althusserian terms—the poem unsettles the ideology which strove to justify the wrenching history of the African diaspora.

Once the poem undermines its own binary imagery and starts to sketch in a third term, one can see that what has been viewed as a sort of phallic negritude, where ''negritude as phallus . . . revalorizes the black man,'' is nothing of the sort. The imposition of such Lacanian terms on the text leads to a reading of colonization and decolonization where the former is figured as emasculating and the latter as ''rephallicizing.'' What I would like to do is to provide a reading which both illuminates the construction of gender in the poem, and shows how attempts to fit the poem into traditional generic concepts (hero and epic) and Lacanian structures (by way of Althusser and Fanon) unintentionally acceptualize as a ''colonial Imaginary,'' then what is its own imaginary scheme?

I answer that question. I find it most useful to turn to the work of Luce Irigaray who has written lengthy critiques of Lacanian psychoanalytic theory and shown what a non-phallocentric entire Imaginary might look like, while still relying on Lacan's ideas. The most relevant aspect of Irigaray's work here is her insistence that Western philosophy is based on the ''logic of sameness.'' Psychoanalysis, starting with Freud, has defined sexual difference according to phallic logic:

> Patie prenante d'une idéologie qu'il ne remet pas en cause. [Freud] affirme que le ''masculin'' est le modele sequel, que toute représentation de désir ne peut ques'y étalonner. s'y soumettre.

By this masculine standard, the clitoris is a smaller version of the penis, and the little girl is a ''little man.'' This, of course allows women to be viewed as the same as men, but inferior. Extending this logic to wider philosophical terms, ''[c]ette domination du logos philosophique vient, pour une bonne part, de son pouvoir de réduire tout autre dans Economic du Même.'' This economy of the same is the engine which powers colonial discourse and colonial self-justification. When the standard of measure is the white European male, the resulting philosophy holds that Americans, including Africans of the diaspora, fall far short of that standard, which, not coincidentally, makes them ripe for the ''civilizing mission.'' From the insistent oppression of this colonial discourse

stems what Fanon calls the ''psychoexistential'' inferiority complex of blacks, the inter-realization, of racist ideology. Fanon's stated aim was to analyze the complex in order to destroy it.

Césaire, who was of course a great influence on Fanon, also has this destructive impulse as an aim; his text is linguistically disruptive in the same sense that Irigaray's is: ''Irigaray attempts to disrupt symbolic discourse . . . by reimagining the female Imaginary.'' Césaire's poem with its eruptive, disruptive denunciatory power aims to explode colonial discourse, the phallogocentric system on the other side of which lies a new map of the world, a different Imaginary. When the speaker of the poem associates himself with the masculine sun, he is filling in the role the colonizer had played. He is not upsetting the structure, but changing the players. In the historical context of the poem's production, this is an extraordinary move. . . . Césaire goes further than a reversal of terms: when the sun is removed from its privileged position, the rigid vertical-horizontal structure crumbles. The wind, which the speaker of the poem addresses throughout the last passage, serves as a new metaphor, one which, in this poem, defies being categorized or even defined since it can be felt but not touched, heard but not seen, spoken to as if it were listening. . . .

Is the wind a voice which can be heard around the world? Is it a reference to oral culture and oral art? A non-material response to the aggressive sharpness of colonizing technology? A holy spirit? A form of resistance which does not imply phallic logic?

It is the ''radical indeterminacy'' of the poem's final stretch which the reader is left with at the end, yet the outlines of something new are sketched in. The poem's troublesome conclusion, with its complexity of image and language, introduces a third and perhaps mediating term, suggesting a new Imaginary which remains to be fully articulated. If we return to L'Isolé soleil for a moment, it is interesting to see the way that Maximin reiterates a Caribbean landscape of three elements and insists on the triangularization of meaning and desire: the sun, the volcano and the sea make up the three terms in Maximin's geography. Towards the end of the book ''la voie lactée'' joins ''le soleil'' and ''la mer'' in a more feminized version of the threesome. This figuring and refiguring of three terms includes the play of characters who often comprise two men and a woman, reinscribing the threesome who founded ''Tropiques,'' Léon Damas. Aimé Césaire, and Suzanne Césaire. Maximin insists on the inclusion of a third term and of a female voice in what I would like to read as a novelistic continuation of Césaire's long poem. It is part of L'Isolé soleil's power that it recognizes the movement from two to three terms in Cahier, the triangularization of its imagery.

The poem's emphasis on vertical movement and insistence on masculinity should not, then, be read literally as the epic outpouring of a phallic leader, but rather as an attempt to subvert colonial discourse through reimagining the colonial Imaginary. The poem's blatant sexual images and gendered landscapes prove to be unstable and disruptive, suggesting a reading of the poem's masculinity that highlights its constructedness rather than its depiction of a natural process.

Hedy Kalikoff. *Callaloo*. 18, 2 (Spring 1995), pp. 492–05

To redefine Caribbean experience in Caribbean terms, [Césaire] founded his own socialist Progressive Party in 1958. From 1961 onward, he consistently advocated an autonomous federation of the D.O.M. in the Antilles and in Guyane. Throughout the 1960s, he attempted to prepare his constituents psychologically for self-rule and eventual nationhood through both political and cultural action.

As a form of cultural action, he wrote three plays that presented accessible, inspirational models of blacks' struggles for independence. The international context of the plays aimed to remind the Martinicans that morally, at least, they were not alone, and that their own striving for justice could in turn inspire others. Theater made Césaire's statements accessible to even the illiterate.

The last of these plays, *Une Tempête* (1969), parodies Shakespeare's original, satirizing the jarring contrast between the theory and practice of post-Shakespearean colonialism, between benevolent words and ready threats and uses of violence. It remains the only full-scale dramatic adaptation, and constitutes a detailed condemnation of imperialism and racism, rivaled in Césaire's career only by his masterpiece, the *Cahier*. Often studied, Césaire's parody deserves more attention than it has yet received, to explain the two added framing scenes, the landscape, and above all, the changes that transform Shakespeare's dreamlike drama into a vehicle for a satire of the Eurocentric, colonial imperialism articulated only after Shakespeare's time. Césaire's choice of a prestigious model also suggests that no corner of white culture should be immune to skeptical scrutiny. Césaire's intent is not to attack Shakespeare as a racist. He is protesting the derogatory stereotypes of ''natives'' that *The Tempest's* portrayal of a bestial Caliban clearly can be exploited to support—even though Caliban's mother herself came from Europe, so that he is only a second-generation settler. *The Tempest* itself implicitly evaluates the moral worth of each character according to the depth of his or her capacity to recognize Caliban as akin to the human. . . .

For Césaire's purposes, that Shakespeare's original version locates the action on an exotic island makes it well suited for adaptation as a political allegory of the Antilles. The marooned Prospero, the chief racist from Césaire's point of view, must have recalled to him the thousands of French sailors stranded in the Antilles for many months after the Nazi invasion of France. The islanders had to host and support these foreigners—many were ignorant and crudely prejudiced—while frequently receiving little but hostility and contempt in return.

Shakespeare's essentialist views, not necessarily racist themselves, can readily be used by racists concerned with preserving the status quo. In *The Tempest* Caliban's revolt is only a secondary disturbance of the social nexus, destined to be set right as are all such disturbances in Shakespeare's plays. The cast of characters foretells the outcome: Prospero's evil brother is styled ''the usurping Duke of Milan,'' and Prospero himself, ''the right Duke of Milan.'' That the first words of the text are ''The Scene, an uninhabited Island,'' underscores that Caliban and Ariel are not human to Shakespeare (Ariel himself acknowledges as much with his ''were I human'') and therefore possess no rights beyond those granted through the indulgence of Prospero. All of Shakespeare's story is told from Prospero's viewpoint—or more accurately, when other human characters' perceptions are directly presented, they are enchanted by love or magic, or deceived in the belief that they are the sole masters of their destiny.

Prospero assumes that because he has ''created'' Caliban as a civilized being, Caliban himself cannot be creative. Prospero's exclusive possession of ''magic'' (reaffirmed in Shakespeare, ultimately exposed as delusional in Césaire) betokens his (claim to a) monopoly on creativity. If Caliban defies him, it can only be as a fallen creature, a Galatea gone wrong.

To date, comparisons of Césaire and Shakespeare have limited themselves to content, neglecting the plays' overall form. By writing entirely in prose, Césaire removes the aestheticizing distraction of verse: he makes his text entirely businesslike, to function as a denunciation of colonialism. He thus also removes the hierarchical distinction, in Shakespeare, between those who speak in prose and those who speak in verse: the plebeian sailors, Stephano, and Trinculo, as opposed to the nobles. Erasing this invidious distinction, Césaire suggests that all have the same rights. In contrast, Shakespeare's and Césaire's Prosperos share the belief that Caliban is like an animal, has no language other than what Prospero taught him, and therefore, no valid viewpoint of his own. That Shakespeare's Ariel and Caliban often speak in verse, however, ennobles them linguistically and problematizes Prospero's elitist viewpoint.

The superficial significance of Césaire's leveling of language is that Prospero's claims to absolute superiority, in his confrontations with Caliban, are undercut by presenting the discourse of both on roughly the same level of elegance. The deeper implications, suggested by Caliban's occasional demonstrations of aesthetic and linguistic sensibilities in Shakespeare, are that, applied to drama, parody tends to flatten the text, whereas in lyric and narrative, it tends to enrich it. I mean that oppositional parody (German *Gegengesang* as distinguished from *Beigesang*) functions through a rhetoric that generates an intertextuality (as an awareness in the hearer or reader) calling into question the self-sufficient, absolute status of an original, either by confronting it with another, external text, or by exposing its own inner contradictions. Thus parody complicates. But drama, a medley of conflicting voices, forms a sort of *Sängerkrieg* in which each voice seeks to impose itself. To make its point, parody simplifies drama; it reduces these voices to two, in sharp contrast: here, racist authoritarianism versus liberationist protest. Thus Césaire, for example, eliminates the serene, loving side of Prospero, and the inquisitive, role-playing, sexually aware Miranda. He passes over the moment when Miranda is less accepting of Caliban than is Prospero, when she expresses great reluctance even to see him: ''Tis a villain, sir, / I do not love to look on,'' an exclamation that clearly prepares her ''Abhorred slave'' speech so often misattributed to Prospero, who at least wishes to tolerate Caliban's presence if only to exploit him. Césaire eliminates Miranda altogether from this confrontation with Caliban, so as to focus the racist voice in Prospero.

Both authors frame the play to emphasize its artificiality, but the respective effects are quite different. Shakespeare's frame glorifies Prospero: Césaire's diminishes him. The epilogue, a convention in Elizabethan plays though not in Shakespeare's, usually asks the indulgence and applause of the audience, in a deferred *captatio benevolentiae*. Shakespeare adopts it, for once, in this play, identifying himself with Prospero in a way that has been prepared throughout the final act. Thus he may be saying farewell to the magic of artistic creation and of the theater (after *The Tempest*, he was to write no more than, at most, and a few collaborations).

Césaire, in contrast, puts his framing scene at the beginning. In it an added character, ''Le Meneur du Jeu,'' urges everyone to don a mask corresponding to his or her chosen role. Only half a page long, this scene is fraught with suggestions. Most obviously, it demystifies Prospero as the imperialist magician who stages most of the events at will. No longer is it he who is the chief master of illusion; no longer does the colonial usurper exercise an almost unquestioned authority close to that of the playwright himself. It is the "Meneur du jeu" who actually summons the tempest, implicitly identified as a Yoruba god, Shango, although Prospero later thinks he is summoning it. The failure of Césaire's Prospero in his attempts to function as "meneur du jeu" appears most blatantly at two later moments in the play. During the wedding and at the end, Prospero cannot orchestrate the spectacle of the assimilated savage (this oxymoronic phrase betrays the unconscious bad faith of the white man's condescension) becoming gratefully subject to the authority of his colonial master.

Moreover, after having overtly subtitled his play "Adaptation pour un théâtre nègre," Césaire simultaneously introduces the racial differences that reflect the Caribbean social hierarchy of the colonial era, by specifying that Caliban is black and Ariel mulatto, and denounces these differences as superficial by using masks. Likewise, Jean Genet, for example, had a few years earlier exposed the speciousness of sociopolitical hierarchies in his anticolonial play *Les Paravants*. Two generations ago, at the height of the Négritude movement, or one generation ago, at the height of the assertions of black pride, one might have seen in such a gesture the dangerous, self-deluding effort to deny the reality of race and to forswear one's heritage, in a manner attacked by Frantz Fanon in Peau noire, masques blancs. With the hindsight of a quarter century, however, Césaire's ostensible masking of his multiracial cast of characters seems surprisingly modern, reflecting as it does a position lucidly articulated by Henry Louis Gates, Jr.: "'race' is a metaphor for something else and not an essence or a thing in itself, apart from its creation by an act of language . . . if we believe that races exist as things, as categories of being already 'there,' we cannot escape the danger of generalizing about observed differences between human beings as if these differences were consistent and determined, a priori . . . It is the penchant to generalize based upon essences perceived as biological which defines 'racism.'"

At the same time, Césaire's casting and costuming scene also militates against emotional identification with individual actors by members of the audience. Through the calculated artificiality of the masking, the spectators are distanced from the ensuing action, as they are in the epic theater of Bertholt Brecht, so that they will think rather than feel. Césaire seeks not catharsis, as an end in itself, but provocation and incitement to action.

Césaire then increases Caliban's stature by greatly reducing the two competing plots. In Shakespeare, the revenge plot is primary; the secondary plot, the idyll between Miranda and Ferdinand, then provides the occasion for a reconciliation; and Caliban serves mainly to enhance an atmosphere of fantasy and to glorify Prospero's clemency, which extends even to monsters. In Césaire, in contrast, it is Caliban's slave revolt, rather than the love story, that provides the principal motivation for the reconciliation: Prospero makes common cause with the other whites as natural allies who will protect him against Caliban in a racial conflict.

Laurence M. Porter. *Comparative Literature Studies*. 32, 3 (Summer, 1995), pp. 360–81

Two momentous events in the biography of Aimé Césaire—one literary, the other political—have converged to give the impression of a sense of closure to his dual career. The first was his abdication, so to speak, from electoral politics in Martinique in 1993; the second, the publication of his complete poetry in Paris in the following year. This sequence of events, whether coincidental or not, affords us a convenient vantage point from which to sketch an overview of his reception both locally and internationally.

To begin with the artistic horizon of reception: it is undeniable that, despite the apparent marginality of much postcolonial writing, Césaire's creative corpus places him securely within the central purview of the European poetic canon. Though (or more accurately, precisely because) his work is permeated by an indictment of Western imperialism and colonialism, its formal attributes no less than its subject-matter situate its author in an omnipresent dialogue with past representatives of that canon, such as Aeschylus, Shakespeare, Rousseau and Mallarmé. . . . [To] interpret Césaire's writing is to engage in an intertextual discourse that ranges from Greco-Roman to contemporary literatures. An inescapable consequence of this intertextual awareness is that his poetry is far more accessible to the sophisticated metropolitan French reader than it is to the local Caribbean audience. The exception that proves the rule may be the theatrical works; for the dramatic "triptych" on the black world comes closer than any of the author's other poetic compositions to being communicable to a less educated, popular audience. The varied reception accorded his most internationally known work, *Cahier*, is instructive in this regard. Because of its timing, no less than its patently anti-colonial message, the poem exerted a strong ideological impact on the postwar generation in the former French colonies, particularly in West Africa; whereas its local impact in Antillean francophone societies has been notoriously limited to a small intellectual elite. If this point be conceded in the case of *Cahier*, it is even more manifest with respect to the shorter lyric poems, which are composed in a dense, metaphorically laden style. For these reasons the question of the reception of the poetry may best be illuminated at the level of language. Since this is an issue that has aroused a great deal of controversy over the years, it is worth re-framing it succinctly in its cultural context.

Like the rest of the Caribbean archipelago, the island of Martinique is fundamentally bilingual. Alongside the standard languages of the European colonizers (e.g., English, French, Spanish, Dutch) there exist throughout the region various vernaculars that are now globally referred to as "creoles." Interestingly enough, these creole languages exhibit structural parallels that cut across national boundaries—parallels that probably are to be accounted for by a common base in certain recurrent West African linguistic features. Be that as it may, it is important to emphasize that Martinican creole is not to be dismissed in simplistic terms as a bastardized form of French (though it may have begun life as a so-called "pidgin" tongue), but is, in actual fact, a well-developed language in its own right, with a complex grammar and large lexicon. Though all the mature creoles of the region have by now been scientifically described by anthropological linguists, it remains the case that they are used almost exclusively in oral rather than written form. Since Césaire, however, like the vast majority of all published authors in the Caribbean, writes in the language of the former European master, he has from time to time been taken to task by latter-day champions of creole for devaluing the speech of the masses. Especially in the last decade or so, the French Caribbean movement that advocates "créolité" ("creoleness"—a concept that includes but is not limited to linguistics) has become increasingly strenuous in its denunciations of Césaire's adherence to French as his preferred literary medium. . . .

Within the acknowledged constraints of the colonizer's language, Césaire has consciously sought to occupy a linguistic space of his own making which is different from that staked out, at least rhetorically, by today's articulate champions of creole. . . .

The occasional deformations in syntax and vocabulary to which Césaire has subjected standard French do not, in the aggregate, bear out a strong claim for radical linguistic subversion. In short, his achievements as a poet are, as André Breton famously recognized, basically continuous with a metropolitan tradition of avant-garde writing.

The local reception of Césaire's ideology of racial identity, as summed up in the word négritude, has been no less mixed than that accorded to his poetic language. . . .

Césaire himself, in his well-known essay, "Culture and Colonization," had long since registered his rejection of the notion that a "mixed" culture in a postcolonial context could be integrated and harmonious rather than disjointed. Whatever side one may chose to take in the ongoing debate over how best to describe the enigma of Caribbean culture, it is a lasting merit of Césaire's outmoded formulation that it continues to inspire precisely the kind of self-reflection from generation to generation that has helped to generate the flowering of letters in the French Antilles.

If the ideological aspect of Césaire's multi-faceted legacy, as we have depicted it, has led to the insemination of a flourishing debate about the nature of postcolonial society, the strictly political aspect has had important ramifications that are all the more difficult to assess in view of their direct impact on the social and economic well-being of all Martinicans. I refer, of course, to Césaire's crucial role as midwife in bringing into being the constitutional status of the French Antilles as "overseas departments." From its very inception, "departmentalization" provoked sharp objections from those activists who contend that nothing short of full independence can prepare the ground for a thoroughgoing decolonization. By contrast, Césaire has never advocated an independence platform, even when it became clear to him that successive French governments were inclined to drag their feet on implementing the promise of a complete integration of the French Antilles into the nation of France. For his deep-seated reluctance to cut the umbilical cord with the Mother Country (in this case France rather than Africa) he has been roundly assailed by many younger critics who have appealed to the example of the independent countries of the former French West Africa. As with the question of the validity of the concept of négritude, however, "the jury is still out," as the saying goes, on the issue of whether political independence automatically leads to the elimination of economic dependence. . . .

When all is said and done, it is not Aimé Césaire the politician whom posterity will come to revere, but rather the extraordinary verbal artist who composed poems of the order of *Cahier* and dramas on the level of *Christophe*. This basic opinion is shared, on a more modest scale, by Césaire himself, who has registered the following trenchant exchange at the start of an interview with a noted American scholar:

ROWELL: In the United States we know you mainly as a poet and a playwright.
CÉSAIRE: The Americans know my better self.

Whatever judgment posterity may eventually pass on Aimé Césaire's protracted career as an elected politician—a career he has always seen as incidental to his role as a seminal thinker—it is certain that his exquisite poetry has earned him a well deserved place in the canon of major twentieth-century writers.

Gregson Davis. *Aimé Césaire*. (Cambridge: Cambridge University Press, 1997), pp. 178–84

BIBLIOGRAPHY
*Les armes miraculeuses,* 1946; *Soleil cou-coupe,* 1948; *Corps perdu,* 1949; *Discours sur le colonialisme,* 1950; *Lettre a Maurice Thorez,* 1956; *Cahier d'un retour au pays natal,* 1956; *Et les chiens se taisaient: tragedie,* 1956; *Toussaint L'Ouverture: La revolution francaise et le probleme coloniale,* 1960; *Ferrements,* 1960; *Cadastre,* 1961; *La tragedie du roi Christophe,* 1963; *Une saison au Congo,* 1966; *Une tempete: d'apres "le tempete" de Shakespeare. Adaptation pour un theatre 1969*; *Oeuvres completes,* 3 Vols., 1976; *Moi, Laminaire,* 1982; *Aime Cesaire: The Collected Poetry,* 1983; *Non-Vicious Circle: Twenty Poems,* 1985; *Lyric and Dramatic Poetry, 1946-82,* 1990

# CHAMOISEAU, Patrick (1953–)
## Martinique

Patrick Chamoiseau is emerging as one of the prominent writers and cultural leaders of Martinique today. Though his oeuvre, comprising poetry, drama, and fiction in French and in Creole, is not immense, it has earned him critical and popular acclaim. Chamoiseau is also a co-author [with Jean Bernabé and Raphaël Confiant] of a cultural manifesto of sorts, *Éloge de la créolité*, that proposes to dislodge Caribbean writing from the impasses of Négritude.

*Antan d'enfance*, dealing with childhood memories, is an illustration of some of the tenets of *créolité*. Recognizing the problematics of autobiographical writing, especially when the subject is early childhood, Chamoiseau settles for an interesting compromise: the point of reference is "le négrillon" (the little black boy), who is endowed, as it were, with an adult consciousness: "From our past nothing remains, yet we keep it all." In sequences both humorous and laden with feeling, Chamoiseau recreates childhood scenes from "the age of fire," when insect burning is the boy's principal preoccupation, to "the age of the tool," when the insects are mercilessly cut up. The little boy has a special relationship, defiant and affectionate, with Man Ninotte, his mother and the resourceful mistress of the household, whose courage and wisdom permit the family to survive the apocalypse of devastating hurricanes and stand firm on the treacherous grounds of the marketplace. Papa, on the other hand, is the "maître ès l'art créole" and the paragon of *créolité*, who easily orients himself among the various linguistic codes in the confluence of cultures of the region.

A rich panorama of sociocultural life in Fort-de-France is evoked with scenes from La Savane, the city's "Central Park," where politicians and merchants of love cross paths, and with scenes from the shops of the Syrians and the Chinese who ply their trade with pride and deceit. Chamoiseau arranges these scenes in a rich mosaic pattern, without chronological subordination, with different rhythms and tonalities, admixing French with suggestions of Creole vocabulary and syntax, thus demonstrating the vitality of cultures that thrive on intercontamination.

> Juris Silenieks. *World Literature Today.* 65, 3 (Summer 1991), p. 535

Chamoiseau takes liberties with French which not one of his French contemporaries could even imagine ever taking. It's like the license of a Brazilian using Portuguese, of a Latin American writer using Spanish—or, if you prefer, the freedom of a bilingual who refuses absolute authority to either of his languages and who has the courage to disobey them both. Chamoiseau does not compromise between French and Creole by mixing them up. His language is French, but French transformed—not creolized French (no Martiniquais speaks as he writes), but Chamoisified French: he endows his style with the casual charm of the rhythms and melody of speech (but not, please note, with its syntax or limited vocabulary); he grafts many Creole turns of phrase onto it: not for the sake of "naturalism" (to bring in "local color"), but for *aesthetic* reasons (for humor, quaintness, or for semantic precision). Above all, however, he takes the freedom to bring into French unaccustomed, unconventional, "impossible" expressions and neologisms (freedoms which French is less able to enjoy than many other languages). Chamoiseau effortlessly turns adjectives into nouns, nouns into adjectives, adjectives into adverbs, verbs into nouns, nouns into verbs, and so on. Yet none of these infringements leads to a reduction of the lexical and grammatical richness of French: there is no shortage of learned and rare words, and even that most academic of French verb forms, the past subjunctive, holds its own. . . .

At first glance, *Solibo Magnifique* may seem to be only an exotic novel of place, centered on a folktale-teller, a character that can only be imagined here. But it is not. Chamoiseau's latest novel deals with one of the major events in the history of culture: the meeting of oral literature in decline and of written literature in the making. In Europe, the place of this meeting is Boccaccio's *Decameron.* The first great work of European prose could not have come into being had there been no storytellers skilled at oral entertainment. . . .

"Hector Biancotti, this talk is for you," runs the dedication at the head of *Solibo Magnifique.* Chamoiseau underlines that it is *talk,* not writing. He sees himself as the direct descendant of the oral storytellers, and describes himself not as a writer, but as a "word-maker." On the supranational map of cultural history, he would place himself at the point where the spoken voice hands on the baton to literature. In this novel, the fictional storyteller called Solibo tells him: "I was a talker, but what you do is to write and to say that you come from talk." Chamoiseau is a writer come from talking.

But . . . Chamoiseau is not Boccaccio. He is a writer who has the sophistication of the modern novelists and it is from that position (as an heir of [James] Joyce and of [Franz] Kafka) that he holds out his hand to Solibo and to the oral prehistory of literature. *Solibo Magnifique* is thus a place where two times meet. "You give me your hand over a great distance," Solibo says to Chamoiseau.

The story: in a square called Savane, in Fort-de-France, Solibo is talking to a few chance listeners, among them Chamoiseau. In the middle of the talking, he drops dead. The aged Congo knows: he died of word-strangulation. The explanation hardly convinces the police, who seize upon the incident and labor hard to find the culprit. Interrogations of nightmarish cruelty ensue, during which the deceased storyteller's character is drawn and two suspects die under torture. In the end, the autopsy rules out murder. Solibo died inexplicably; maybe he really was strangled by a word.

The last pages of the book consist of what Solibo was saying when he dropped dead. This truly poetic, imaginary speech is an introduction to the aesthetics of orality: what Solibo tells is not a tale, but spoken words, fantasies, puns, jokes, it is freewheeling *automatic talking* (like automatic writing). And since it is talking, "language before writing," the rules of written language have no purchase here, so there is no punctuation: Solibo's talk is a flow without commas, periods, or paragraphs, like the poetry of Robert Desnos or Molly Bloom's monologue at the end of [Joyce's] *Ulysses,* like Philippe Sollers's *Paradis.* (Another example to show how at a particular point in history, popular and modern art can meet on the same path.)

> Milan Kundera. *New York Review of Books.* December 19, 1991, pp. 49–50

*Solibo Magnifique* establishes that the cultural dependence of the Caribbean people brought on the escheat of a tradition that is fundamental to their identity. As Paul Zweig writes in *The Adventurer,* the storyteller is the founder of civilization, and his disappearance puts the survival of the community in danger. That is why the recovery of the spoken, in one form or another, is indispensable and urgent to prevent its complete dissolution by exterior forces. "Collective memory is our emergency," declare the authors of the *Éloge de la créolité.* Chamoiseau not only saves it from ruin, but he perpetuates it in another form, walking on "the edge between the oral and the written," as Edouard Glissant so correctly emphasizes in the preface to *Chronique des sept misères.* Through the many narrative voices mixing French and Creole—a "linguistic space" that he manages remarkably well—Chamoiseau brings the Caribbean reality to life without complacency and with irresistible humor. Using a reworked syntax, he causes to emerge a new abundance of imagery, sonorities, metaphors, even a complete poetics of Creoleness. He also manages to impart to his discourse the verbal energy that attracted him so much to Solibo, because he anchors the "new" language to everyday reality, the movement of life experience.

The storyteller instinctively reveals the imaginary world of his community. "The writer" Chamoiseau, once his function as "marker" is complete, tries to consciously identify this imaginary realm; following the example of Solibo, he is "on alert." To capture the complexity of the cultural reality, he must free himself of the unicity of one linguistic practice; he therefore constructs his tale with the help of the French language, which he changes, enriches, and amplifies with the multilingualism that is Creole. "We believe that a creative use of intellect might lead to an order of reality capable of preserving for our Creoleness its fundamental complexity, its diffracted referential space" write [Jean] Bernabé, Chamoiseau and [Raphaël] Confiant. Chamoiseau splendidly communicates the complexity of his culture by exploding language.

> Marie-Agnès Sourieau. *Callaloo.* 15, 1 (Winter 1992), p. 136

*Texaco,* the third novel of Patrick Chamoiseau, traces the dual figures of a woman and a country: Marie-Sophie Laborieux (born around 1913, the daughter of a freed slave and founder of the Texaco district in Fort-de-France) and Martinique. The author of *Chronique des sept misères* and *Solibo Magnifique* has a grand ambition in this novel: to help the readers understand two centuries of the history of his country. . . .

One is carried by a tide of words and sensations. Wielding incantation as well as humor, having the sense of caricature as well as that of detailed descriptions, Chamoiseau narrates the story of an entire people. From this is derived the splendid portrait of Marie-Sophie, [a] "femme-matador" who knew to create a neighborhood in order to find an identity. . . .

*Texaco*, like any important novel, is a language, a style, and a reflection on literature. Chamoiseau defines himself clearly as a "keeper of words," situated near the complex and fragile frontier which separates oral and written literature. . . .

[To] love and defend Chamoiseau because of a penchant for the exotic . . . would be a serious mistake. Far from being a renewal of the French novel from the margins or from the outside . . . Chamoiseau's literature is an affirmation of belonging to French culture in all its diversity.

Who are the authors that Marie-Sophie reads and of whom she talks? Montaigne and Rabelais in the first place. And it is from their thoughts and their words that she draws her strength and her pugnacity. She learns very quickly, coming in contact with texts, to make a distinction between literature and the colonizer, between a culture that has always "welcomed" and a people—who, moreover, dislike their own culture—often sadly narrow-minded, revanchist, and hardened. To like Chamoiseau for the exotic is to perpetuate the mentality of the colonizer. It is to refuse this proclamation: "We declare ourselves Creoles. . . . Our history is a fabric of histories."

Josyane Savigneau. *Le Monde*. September 3–9, 1992, p. 12†

Chamoiseau's first published work, *Manman Dlo contre la fée Carabosse*, does seem to hold out the possibility of resistance. . . . The play dramatizes the conflict between the colonial powers and its culture, symbolized in the figure of the wicked fairy Carabosse taken from Creole folklore, and the dominated culture, symbolized by the water-spirit Manman Dlo and the forest-spirit Papa-Zombi, who, together with other denizens of forest and water, set out to counter the colonizing project of Carabosse and her assistant Balai. From the outset, Carabosse is associated with the written word and Manman Dlo and her allies with the spoken word (*la Parole*); Carabosse's initial effect is to reduce to silence all those spirits which previously had filled the island with unfettered speech and song. Gradually, however, Manman Dlo and Papa-Zombi muster the necessary resources of speech with which to confront Carabosse and her scribe Balai before unleashing the natural forces of wind and water which finally sweep her out of the island. On the surface, *Manman Dlo* is a straightforward nationalist allegory, notable for its optimistic assessment of the strengths of the dominated culture in the face of the dominant colonial system. Looked at more closely, however, the play reveals a fatal flaw which lies in the uncertainty of the origins and status of the Creole counterculture. By stressing Manman Dlo's African origins, the play seems to endow that counterculture with an identity anterior to and wholly separate from that of the colonial culture it is called upon to combat: it is as though Manman Dlo and her fellow spirits had

occupied the island for eons prior to the arrival of Carabosse and the written word. But, though they may be of African *origin*, Manman Dlo and Papa-Zombi are only in the Caribbean because Carabosse, in her guise as slave-trader, brought them there. Creole culture, like the Creole language itself, may be *anti*-colonial in character, but it is in no way *ante*-colonial. On the contrary, Créolité is a product and consequence of colonialism which, no matter how much it derives from non-European sources, is impregnated—some might say contaminated—at every point with the culture of the colonizer. It is different from, but in no way separate from, the dominant culture and, to that extent, is to be contrasted to the "traditional" cultures of black Africa or the Islamocentric cultures of the Maghreb which, for their part, are both anterior and exterior to the European colonial cultures superimposed upon them. Positing the Creole counterculture as entirely separate from the colonial culture certainly allows the play to be brought to a (wholly unhistorical) triumphant conclusion, but at the price of seriously distorting the relationship between "great" and "little" traditions in the French West Indies. Chamoiseau partially acknowledges that this is so in a final scene in which Manman Dlo hands over to her daughter Algoline the magic wand which Carabosse has left behind her in her flight from the island, urging her to *assimilate* the magic powers it embodies, including the formidable and enigmatic power of writing, with a view to transcending the opposition of Word and word, of speech and writing, that the play has dramatized. Where the writer himself stands in all this remains unclear. He is a son of the Word, dependent on it for his very being, but transcribing the spoken into the written exposes him to the charge of exploiting the very Word he would capture and celebrate. Like so much else, *Manman Dlo* raises this problem, the crucial theme of *Solibo Magnifique*, only to drop it: small wonder that, asked today about this product of his apprenticeship, Chamoiseau merely shrugs his shoulders and smiles.

Despite its simplistic and misleading presentation of the relationship between colonial culture and Creole counterculture, *Manman Dlo* clearly lays out the tripartite structure of Chamoiseau's imaginative universe. On the one hand, invariably associated with rationality, order, and the written word (French), is the world of the powerful who are not always necessarily white or French but can in assimilated Martinique include individuals of each and every racial category. Opposed to this, and commonly linked with fantasy, magic, the elemental forces of forest and water and, above all, with the spoken word (Creole), is the world of the powerless, usually men and women of African or Indian origin, who must somehow survive on terrain which, originally defined and regimented by the whites (*békés-France* and *békés-pays* alike), has progressively been invested by colored and black supporters of the dominant ideology of assimilationism. Straddling these two worlds and mediating between them is the writer or "marker of words" (*marqueur de paroles*) as Chamoiseau chooses to call himself, who belongs to neither world and both and whose interstitial position clearly resembles that of the *djobeurs* and other liminal figures whose lives form the subject of Chamoiseau's first novel *Chronique des sept misères*. The novel uses the vegetable market at Fort-de-France as a complex metaphor for the transformation of Martinican society from before World War II, through the three years of domination by the Vichy regime, to departmentalization in 1946 and the subsequent disintegration, becoming apparent in the early 1960s and accelerating in the 1970s, of the traditional Creole culture under the pressure of imported French goods, French lifestyles, French thought patterns, and, not least, of the French language itself.

Richard D. E. Burton. *Callaloo*. 16, 2 (Spring 1993), pp. 469–70

Nominally a novel, *Texaco* expands the traditional notions of the genre. It could qualify as an oral history of epic proportions. It is the narration by an African Martinican woman, Marie-Sophie Laborieux, to the author, who calls himself the "marqueur de paroles" but whom Marie-Sophie occasionally addresses, with obvious relish, as "Oiseau de Cham." The author, as he explains in the postface, first took copious notes, then resorted to a tape recorder, trying "to write life." The narrative, in mock imitation of archeological periodization, is divided into four epochs, which represent African Martinican building materials: straw, crate wood, fibrocement, and concrete. In terms of European historiography, the time span would encompass the years from circa 1823 to 1980. Biblical allusions enlarge the scope of the narrative. It begins with the sermon, not on the mount, but before old rum, and ends with resurrection—i.e., with the author's endeavor to resurrect life, "écrire la vie." . . .

Marie-Sophie, following a series of vicissitudes in her personal life, becomes willy-nilly the spokesperson for the slum dwellers. She pleads with the authorities (including "notre papa Césaire," then and still today the mayor of Fort-de-France), organizes demonstrations, and, when [Charles] De Gaulle comes to visit the former colony, prepares a sumptuous feast to show him how hospitable Martinicans can be. The general, perceived as a savior figure, does not come, however. Marie-Sophie engages in a titanic struggle against the owner of the land, a *béké*—i.e., a Frenchman born in the colonies. The people persevere, and in the end, as Christ makes another appearance, the authorities recognize the squatters, install electricity, and incorporate the settlement. Even the vicious *béké* is reconciled with his enemies.

Needless to say, the novel acquires epic dimensions. Fact and fiction intertwine to weave a narrative wherein myth and history complement each other. *Texaco* evokes an ethos and also a vision which, though localized, reaches out far beyond the region.

Juris Silenieks. *World Literature Today*. 67, 4 (Autumn 1993), pp. 877–78

As one might imagine, Chamoiseau the literary theorist seeks to practice what he preaches when he turns to writing fiction. As a writer, he consciously associates himself with the man on the plantation who, after the white master has gone to sleep, creeps out into the night and begins to tell tales. Chamoiseau the novelist is trying to make the oral (Creole) tradition of stories associated with Africa and slavery accessible to the written page, and at the same time he is trying to re-establish the central importance of the figure of the storyteller in the narrative life of the French Caribbean. As he observed in 1988, in an essay called "Les Contes de la survie": "Our stories and storytellers date from the period of slavery and colonialism. Their deepest meanings can be discerned only in reference to this fundamental epoch of French West Indian history. Our storyteller is the spokesman of a fettered, famished people, living in fear and in the various postures of survival."

*Texaco* spans the years 1823 to 1980, and it is divided into four "epochs," which represent the "African" Martinican building materials of the period: straw, crate wood, asbestos and concrete. The novel opens in the city of Saint-Pierre, the old cultural capital of the island, which was destroyed by a volcanic eruption in 1902. The location shifts to a place called Texaco, a classic shantytown of the African diaspora, peopled by former plantation slaves who are searching for urban employment. The township is located in the capital, Fort-de-France, near a petrochemical installation that is owned by the Texaco company. Texaco is considered an eyesore and an embarrassment by the authorities who wish to evict the "squatters" and to raze the place.

Chamoiseau situates himself as the recorder of the memories of Marie-Sophie Laborieux, a Creole woman largely responsible for the creation of the township. Utilizing a playful, witty device that is a part of the folklore tradition, the author is variously addressed by Marie-Sophie as "the Word Scratcher" (le Marqueur de paroles) or "Oiseau de Cham." Marie-Sophie recalls over a century and a half of her island's history, beginning with the story of her father, Esternome, all the while weaving into the fabric of her story the central events of Martinican history, including the abolition of slavery in 1848, the Vichy period during the Second World War, and De Gaulle's visit in 1964 to the island. At various times the novel introduces excerpts from Marie-Sophie's notebooks, Chamoiseau's letters to his "Source" (Marie-Sophie) and a government official's notes to "the Word Scratcher." Marie-Sophie struggles against the beke (white Frenchman born in the colonies) who owns the land, but eventually she triumphs and saves Texaco, extracting from the authorities the promise of decent roads and electricity for the township.

There are two refracting panes through which one can view this novel. There is the pane of allegory, as Chamoiseau demonstrates a great loyalty to the superstitions and the ancestral voices of those of African origin whose stories, beliefs and myths underpin the narrative framework. And there is the pane of language, as the author seeks to make something new out of the distinct languages. Joined together, the allegorical and the linguistic at times mystify the reader. Moreover, as the novel continually unfolds in a seemingly random fashion, one begins to search with increasing vigor for structural clues regarding closure. But Chamoiseau never promised a conventional narrative. In fact, in the introduction to his collection called *Creole Folktales* (1995), he reminds us that conventionality is the last thing we should anticipate from him: "I did not try to strip the tales you are about to read of all their mystery, nor did I append a glossary. Allow the strange words to work their secret magic, and above all, read these stories only at night."

Chamoiseau is a follower of Glissant's theories of marronage, which hold that the runaway slave who opposes the system is the archetypal Caribbean folk-hero. And yet, as I have noted, on these small islands the "maroon" can never truly escape and take to the hills and form self-determining, fully independent communities. The small-island rebel must remain, to some extent, dependent upon the plantation for food, women and friends. Out of this complex, ambivalent relationship to the power structure, the only way to resist and to affirm identity is to work with the system and against it at the same time, to undermine it from the inside and the outside.

What writers such as Patrick Chamoiseau, Raphael Confiant, Daniel Maximin and others are proposing is that this act of le petit marronage involves more than the "embracing of the amputated history" of Africa that was crucial for the avatars of "negritude," and it involves more than a Glissant-inspired refocusing of French Caribbean history. The act of literary petit marronage involves nothing less than the restructing of the French language. The revolutionary theories about the world of what Chamoiseau describes as ''Creolite'' advance the idea that French Caribbean national identity will be properly forged and preserved only by means of a balance of memory and language.

Being bilingual, the French Caribbean has traditionally offered its writers two options. The writer may produce a novel in polished French, perhaps adopting some Creole for the dialogue, to give a flavor of the region; this is the option favored by mainstream writers such as Maryse Conde or Simone Schwartz-Bart. Or the writer may choose to fully utilize Creole, as Raphael Confiant has done. By embarking upon this latter project, however, the writer risks losing a large part of his or her ''metropolitan'' readership, and perhaps local readers, too.

It is the achievement of Patrick Chamoiseau to have provided a third option. He moves fluidly between both languages, within paragraphs, within sentences even, and thereby forges a new ''French'' language out of the two, exploiting the space between the languages, developing illicit and unexpected fusions. They are oppositional and inclusive, for they depend upon a profound understanding of both French and Creole. And implicit in Chamoiseau's way is a full acknowledgement of the power of language. Marie-Sophie's notebooks refer to this idea: ''With their words, they would say: l'esclavage, slavery. But we would only hear l'estravaille, travail. When they found out and began to say Lestraville, to speak closer to us, we'd already cut the word down to travail, the idea of plain toil . . . ha ha ha, Sophie, the word cut across like a weapon. . . .''

Chamoiseau first demonstrated his new linguistic strategy in *Solibo Magnifique* (1988), the novel that preceded *Texaco*. The action begins in a square in Fort-de-France, where we find the central character, Solibo, talking to some people, among them the author. Suddenly Solibo drops dead. The police are called to investigate, two suspects die under torture and ultimately the cause of death remains a mystery. The conclusion of the novel is a narrative stream that flows without punctuation and recounts what Solibo was saying when he died. We ''hear'' Solibo's words; but this is written literature, not oral literature, and Chamoiseau is a writer. His task is to not only make his cultural and political point about language and the role of the storyteller, it is also to convince us that he has found a style that is faithful to the oral tradition. His narrator-hero reminds him of this problem: ''Solibo the Magnificent used to say to me: Cham Bird, you're a writer. O.K. Me, Solibo, I'm a talker. Do you see the distance between the two? . . . I'm going away, but you, you'll stay behind. I was a talker, but you write, telling people that you come from speech. You shake hands with me across the distance. That's fine, but the distance remains. . . .''

That distance, and the traversal of it, is Chamoiseau's method of addressing the problems of language and narrative, and it makes him a unique figure in French Caribbean literature. Chamoiseau's storyteller talks directly to the reader, insulting him, cajoling him, teasing him. He holds on to a rope that is looped through a ring in the reader's nose and he confidently leads him down an unpaved narrative highway. In the late nineteenth century, storyteller-writers stopped talking directly to readers. Sometime in the early twentieth century, such figures disappeared altogether, and abandoned their stories to the unchecked consciousness of their fictional

characters. Whatever one may think of Chamoiseau's ''revolutionary'' intentions, or the wisdom of his dropping a depth-charge into the heart of the French language, it is clear that this writer has not returned empty-handed to the oral tradition of Creole folktales. He has returned with the full armory of world literature, and a comprehensive knowledge of what has happened to the form of the novel in the twentieth century.

Caryl Phillips. *The New Republic*. 216, 17 (April 28, 1997), pp 45–50

In *School Days* Patrick Chamoiseau (winner of the 1992 Prix Goncourt) recounts with bitter charm his introduction to the Colonial education in the Martinique of the 1950s—the days when ''the blue-eyed Gaul with hair as yellow as wheat was everybody's ancestor.'' The child Chamoiseau, ''the little boy,'' desperately hungry for exploration of the outside world, latches onto school as the pathway to it, only to discover that this path demands the eradication of the ''barbarous,'' ''ol'-nigger ways'' of Creole. This is undertaken by the ''Teacher,'' a humorous exemplar of official culture with unhumorous methods of beating barbarity out of his students.

The little boy's induction into the confining, yet ultimately salvatory, horizon of language takes place under the shadows of two mentors: the Teacher, the enforcer of the written word, and Big Bellybutton, the class outcast, the unknowing preserver of the underground spoken word, and keeper of the Creole legend. It is this tension between improper Creole tongue and proper French text that defines much of Chamoiseau's work and provides much of this novel's humor and delightfully ribald episodes. Chamoiseau's writing, via Coverdale's charged and inventive translation, bristles with energy, opening up portals into the Creole dialect with Rabelaisian gusto.

The humor carries a weight, though. Chamoiseau's classmates are for the most part ostracized from any hope of a future in the colonies, and Big Bellybutton's inability to culturally assimilate ultimately crushes his spirit. It is left to the author to try to salvage whatever troubled identity is left to the Caribbean individual, an effort that takes up where Aimé Césaire's ''negritude'' left off. The novel locates a meeting point for speech and writing that should carry resonance for anyone concerned with the politics of identity and language.

Marc Lowenthal. *The Review of Contemporary Fiction*. 17, 3 (Fall 1997), p. 226

The original of *Solibo Magnificent* dates back to 1988, yet the intervening decade has not minimized the import of the work today. Reduced to a skeletal scheme, the novel could be considered a detective story—with a twist or two. Solibo Magnificent, an acclaimed but somewhat mysterious Martinican storyteller, is found dead in the Savanna, the central park of the island's capital, Fort-de-France. The police arrive in full force and, not believing that, according to the local bystanders, he died ''throat snickt by the word,'' launch into a full-scale French-style investigation of the event. They detain for interrogation as many people as they suspect may have witnessed the scene. A carnivalesque confrontation—since it is *Carnival time* arises between the representatives of the French administration, in the persons of the Chief Inspector and the

Chief Sergeant, and the detainees, who do not understand and sometimes just pretend not to understand—a form of dissent—French legalese. . . .

The carnivalesque scene, full of Eulenspiegels and pompous judges and those who arrive in "the van of the Law," turns into a nightmarish prosecution, as the two officials, frustrated by their failure to extract information that would promote their standing as relentless and ingenious upholders of civilization, law, and justice, resort to intimidation and torture to make witnesses confirm that Solibo's death was caused by some sinister deed, either poisoning or knifing. To escape the humiliation and pain, two detainees commit suicide by jumping out a window. The author, sometimes addressed as "Oiseau de Cham," who also witnesses the events—though not always from an omniscient perspective, but rather as a kind of collective consciousness—promises to record events in their entirety, an act which will not only chronicle the death of Solibo Magnificent, whose "throat was snickt by the word," but will also portend the death of orality in the face of the onslaught of a literal modus vivendi.

The novel, with its changing moods and its multitude of colorful characters, offers a rich tropical tapestry. It reads well, thanks to the efforts and resourcefulness of the translators, who had to cope with three linguistic modes: French, Creole, and that particular idiom somewhere between the two where those who call themselves Creolistes—among them most conspicuously Patrick Chamoiseau and Raphael Confiant—want to be found.

The question Patrick Chamoiseau poses is: how can one write in a land dominated by a foreign culture and ideology? In his *Ecrire en pays domine* he first tries to describe and analyze the domination, then elaborates a program to transcend it. . . .

*Ecrire* begins with a brief historical analysis of the three dominations the author feels have alienated his island of Martinique, the "brutal," the "silent," and the "furtive," which he sketches poetically and never makes clearly explicit. The book is divided into three parts, "Anagogie," "Anabase," and "Anabiose." Unfortunately, the logical progression of the argument is continually interrupted by entries into Chamoiseau's "sentimentheque," short tributes to his favorite writers and books, dumped into the text with no transition or effort to relate them to the flow of ideas. This supposedly shows the heterogeneity of his, and the island's, cultural background.

"Anabase" is subtitled "En digenese selon Glissant" and is further explained by "Ou l'ethnographe va devenir un Marqueur de Paroles." Here Chamoiseau descends into himself and into the soul of his country in a dream that can undo the colonial chains, a very Rimbaldian trip indeed. He imagines many variants of himself: as colonizer, African, Amerindian, Chinese, and ultimately "Moi-Creole," the synthesis and final term of the series. The writer pays tribute to several cultural types as precursors of the new Creolite writing, the storyteller, the voodoo magician, the driveur and major, as culture heroes of the resistance to outside domination.

"Anabiose" is explained by the phrase "Where the 'Marqueur de Paroles' starts to babble a strange poetics." The subdivisions here are "Political Mirage," "Languages," "Warrior Poetics," and "In the Stone World." Chamoiseau rather self-indulgently allows himself whimsical flights of fancy, imagining, and preaching, a vision of the future and utopian salvation. Armed with the Creole language, he goes to war, but it is a virtual war, a war of words and images. He believes that by linking the oral tradition to cyberspace, he, and the Martinicans, can transcend militancy,

political doctrine, and praxis to become masters of the ineffable. Allied with hackers and cyberpunks, he will sound the chaos and, through the alchemy of the word, replace the "Third" World with the World of the Philosopher's Stone ("Pierre Monde"). Chamoiseau imagines a "Meta-Nation" appearing through clouds of mysticism and wish-fulfillment—hardly a practical solution for the real problems of the people of his island.

Hal Wylie. *World Literature Today*. 72, 2 Spring 1998, p. 441

BIBLIOGRAPHY
*Manman Dlo contre la fee Carabosse: theatre contae*, 1982; *Chronique des sept miseres*, 1986; *Solibo Magnifique*, 1988; *Texaco*, 1992; *Antan d'enfance*, 1993; *Au temps de l'antan*, 1994; *Guyane: Traces-memoires du bagne*, 1994; *Chemin-d'ecole*, 1994; *L'esclave vieil homme et le molosse*, 1997

# CHENEY-COKER, Syl (1945–)
## Sierra Leone

The Creoles of Sierra Leone, who furnish their country with a disproportionate share of its cultural and political leaders, are descendants of the "recaptives" who were rescued from slave ships during the British suppression of the slave trade. The Creole ancestry of [Syl] Cheney-Coker is the source of much of the strength as well as many of the weaknesses of his poetry [in *Concerto for an Exile*]. Its rough rhythms, harsh diction, and extremes of self-revelation clearly reveal antecedents in [Arthur] Rimbaud, but its most important derivation is the ideal of Négritude. In his weaker poems Cheney-Coker's ambivalence about his Creole heritage betrays him into rhetorical rage against the Creole's oppression of the pure African, who personifies Négritude. . . . At worst, he falls into expressions of passionate self-loathing. But his best poems objectify a violent inner conflict between Africa ("the centrifugal mother") and his own feelings of unworthiness, stated in terms of his "foul genealogy," a Christian upbringing . . . and other "Afro-Saxon" impurities, including an unfortunate love affair with an Argentine woman "to whom I offered my Négritude / that señorita who tortured my heart." The sequence of poems leads finally to a breakthrough to a wisdom understood in terms of recovery from this romantic failure, a repudiation of exile ("agrophobia's sickness"), and a powerful affirmation of the value of poetry.

Robert L. Berner. *Books Abroad*. 48, 4 (Autumn 1974), pp. 835–36

Unlike [Sarif] Easmon who sees membership of the Creole group as a cause for congratulation, Cheney-Coker sees it as a cause for regret, since it reminds him of the Creole history of slavery, suggesting degradation of the black race and alienation from one's roots. The preface to his collection of poems subsumes his major themes—his sense of frustration and disillusionment, his rejection of institutionalized religion, the betrayal of his love, his disgust with himself, and his awareness of the erosion of his original black personality. A dominant motif in his poetry, which he claims is largely influenced by the Congolese poet Tchicaya U Tam'si, is the figure of the Argentinean woman with whom he fell disastrously in love. Since he sees the history and present predicament of Sierra Leone and Argentina as being basically similar, he had hoped, through his love, to bring the two continents together in a common cause. The woman therefore becomes the symbol of betrayal of love, personal despair, and loss of hope for the regeneration of an ailing Third World.

In poems such as "Hydropathy," "Freetown," "Absurdity," and "[The] Masochist," Cheney-Coker presents what he feels is the tragedy of his Creole ancestry. . . . His ancestry is one of the devastating effects of the slave trade and he sees himself as the polluted product of a violent and filthy rape. The consequence is a feeling of disgust with himself; he becomes "the running image" and "the foul progeny" of his race; the rot of his country, and even the vultures will be afraid of his corpse. But the meaning of their ancestry is lost on some of his countrymen who "plaster their skins with white cosmetics to look whiter than the snows of Europe" and who plead: "make us Black Englishmen decorated / Afro-Saxons / Creole masters leading native races." Several poems present his disgust with the Christian religion. He often refers to Christ as the Eunuch who lied to him at Calvary. . . . "Misery of the Converts" and "I Throw Myself to the Crocodiles" similarly present a Christianity that has taken sides with the oppressor against the downtrodden. Other poems, like "Toilers," consist of social comment pointing to the neglect of the toiling masses by the powers that be, and contrasting the opulence of the latter with the squalor of the former.

Eustace Palmer. In Bruce King and Kolawole Ogungbesan, eds. *A Celebration of Black and African Writing* (London: Oxford University Press, 1975), pp. 255–56

Cheney-Coker has provided us with a poetic preface to his volume *Concerto for an Exile*. He first describes his poems as "Venomous songs!," but later qualifies this statement by saying that "song by itself is no fertile language for death.". . . Personal and passionate poetry will investigate the poet's own mind; his feelings, beliefs, prejudices, and obsessions—what he calls the "tree of agony wickedly planted in my soul." It is a poetry which puts before us the history of the man and his society and which makes critical statements about that society. The poet's weapons—evolved as shock tactics—are violent words and violent, surrealist images. We are challenged to respond and, in our turn, we the readers challenge the poet to create art; poems, as opposed to verse and mere statements. . . .

Cheney-Coker is at his best, as a poet, in poems like "Toilers," "Freetown," "My Soul O Oasis!," "Environne," "Agony of the Dark Child," and "Myopia." He is at his best, that is to say, when he rigorously controls his poetic images and uses them organically in his poems. The poem "Environne" opens surrealistically and the surrealism is necessary in order to shock the readers out of a possible complacent attitude to the past history of Africa. . . . The poem "Storm" deals, in part, with the conflict between the privileged and underprivileged in modern African societies. The image of the storm is established in the poem as the image of revolt. The character of the storm is evoked economically, but powerfully. . . . The poem "Toilers" depends upon a contrast between the

inherent "fruitfulness" of Africa—especially traditional Africa—and the spiritual and physical blight which seems, to the poet, to affect most modern societies on the continent. What Cheney-Coker calls "black opulence" rules the roost to the detriment of the poor. The title of this poem is ironical; everyone is either toiling for nothing or for the wrong things.

All of these poems are intense and personal, but the best of them evoke feelings and aspirations common to all men. The poem "Freetown" works like this and so too does the poem "Guinea." Here, Cheney-Coker captures what we might call the spirit of revolutionary fervor.

M.J. Salt. In Eldred Durosimi Jones, ed. *African Literature Today*. 7 (1975), pp. 159–61

*The Graveyard Also Has Teeth* is a very edifying and interesting collection of poems of even texture and yet multifarious themes. This is the second book by [Cheney-Coker]. . . . The title derives from the Creole. In Sierra Leone, when mourners are deeply shocked by the death of a beloved, they show their sorrow and pain at the graveyard by shouting hysterically: "Eh, the grave yard bet (bites) me, eh, it bet (bites) me!" This title thus implies artistic creations of sadness, of agony, of pain full of cryptic and folded meanings.

The collection may be profitably viewed as a panorama of verse brilliantly folded with layers of diverse meanings, perceptions and sensibilities expressed within compressed images. The author obviously regards his poems as enigmas to be solved by the reader. These attributes might make the work appear too exacting but once the right intellectual effort is made, understanding comes easily and the reader sees the poet's landscape, shares in his creativity and in his experience. . . .

Bursting with creative energy, [Cheney-Coker] is sensitive and serious, bold and imaginative, speaking the voice of laughter through tears, of mourning, of anger, wisdom and truth. The collection consists of verse with familiar themes, situations and characters. The poems in this group, which include "Song for the Ravaged Country," "Talons in the Flesh of My Country," "The Executed," "Haemorrhage" and "Putrefaction," seem to be fairly direct descriptions or narratives with a delightful but modest poetic complexity. The themes and situations are easily reflected in the titles, making elaborate comments unnecessary. But lurking behind the paradoxical simplicity of the lines are strong, complex images of birth, initiation, growth and death.

These recurrent images, which help the poems in the collection to achieve an organic unity, seem to symbolize the human life cycle (including the poet's), its genesis, vicissitudes, fear, aspirations, and the search for the meaning of life or eternal good. It is in response to this that the poet embarks on his search, probing himself, the reality of his environment as well as that of our collective unconscious. . . .

Syl Cheney-Coker is a fascinating poet who blends theme, idiom, and syntax delightfully. The poems exude an admirable intricacy of language ordering. Significance is given to commonplace statements, events and situations through ironic emphasis. Over the years, the poet has tightened up his style and expression. His present collection is in places fierce, fluent, and tense. He is a nationalist, a poet of anger: he is angry with cheats, fakes, dupes, dictators, with life and death; angry with the world and with himself. . . .

Cheney-Coker's verse is powerful. Indeed, he is one of the best, if not the best poet that has come out of Africa in the last decade and is one of the most original and gifted African poets alive today.

Segun Dada. In Eldred Durosimi Jones, ed. *African Literature Today*. 13 (1983), pp. 240–41

In his third book of verse Syl Cheney-Coker devotes nearly all the fifty-plus poems to the development of a single theme. Whether the locale is his homeland of Sierra Leone or Chicago, his resonant voice speaks for the wretched of the world. He hears "a million muted cries" from Palestine, from Beirut, even from Japan, where babies are dying from mercury poisoning.

The unifying symbol of the collection is announced in the title, *The Blood in the Desert's Eyes*. These words become the title of the fourth poem, reappear in varied transformations now and again, and finally occur as the last line of the final poem. Literally, the desert is slowly encroaching on the fertile savanna of the poet's country, rendering the soil sterile and forcing the people from their homes. This deadly event is emblematic of the drying up of human concern for those in need the world over. In "Song on the Chinese Flute" Cheney-Coker speaks of the desert's eyes as "lenses" through which we can better see the hungry millions to whom we need to "hold the cup of hope."

Richard Bauerle. *World Literature Today*. 65, 2 (Spring 1991), p. 350

Divided into four books of four chapters each, *The Last Harmattan of Alusine Dunbar* sketches in broad historical strokes the founding of a West African settlement, the inevitable ramifications of development, and the devastating pains of growth when the idyllic is inevitably shattered by infiltration. The history of past and present "harmattans" is prefigured in the planetary movements of the visionary Alusine Dunbar's herniated testicles: the arrival of the black pioneers seeking freedom after the American revolution; the introduction of Christianity and Western education; the arrival of the British spoilers and the beginning of the "eruscient expropriation of land" for exclusive clubs where "Africans and dogs are not allowed"; the arrival of the Arabs and their cunning entrenchment (by the British) as major players in the settlement's economy in partial payment for their "accidental" discovery of the diamond; and finally, the evil of and destruction by black despots. Alas, the pathos which circumscribes life! Unrelenting harmattans with "the remorseless demons humans create in their lives," which allow "the leopards to go after the goats," will now replace the previous "harmattans" of historic and legendary kings.

Contrary to the criticism that character development is generally lacking in the African novel, Syl Cheney-Coker weds symbolism with humor and pathos to create memorable characterizations. There is Suleiman the Nubian (later Alusine Dunbar), the vagabond visionary whose herniated, optical testicles presage an age of endless bitter strife and colonial/neocolonial oppression. There are the revolutionaries—Thomas Bookerman, Sebastian Cromantine, Gustavius Martin, Emmanuel Cromantine, and Garbage—all pioneers of black freedom and witnesses to the historical force of the harmattan's ill omen.

Pamela J. Olubunmi Smith. *World Literature Today*. 65, 4 (Autumn 1991), pp. 755–56

*The Last Harmattan of Alusine Dunbar* encompasses in its epic sweep the African experience in slavery, colonialism, and neocolonialism. The world of its action stretches from the antebellum southern United States of America to an imaginary country in West Africa called "Malugueta," a thinly disguised present-day Sierra Leone, or even Liberia. . . .

The four books which constitute the core of this novel chronicle the futility and ephemeral character of human power as wave after wave of the slave master and slave transmutating into master to initiate and perpetuate oppression. From America to Africa, the story is the same. In a book teeming with a beautiful cast of well-realized characters, quite a few should be noteworthy, especially those whose pedigree constitute the fabric of what becomes, for Malagueta, a national heritage. . . .

*The Last Harmattan of Alusine Dunbar* is an unusual African novel with startling freshness, and there are a number of things which make it so. First, it is a novel of marvelous realism which comfortably takes a path most African writers have timidly avoided. And this is ironic because the African imagination powered with a unique cosmology and a dynamic eschatology appears more fertile for this kind of expression than that of any other culture. Second, even though the work is nationalistic in its ethnic sentiment, it is without that stridency and abrasion with which many activist writers mar their works. The novel is history, fantasy, magic, legend, and political testament unfolding before the eyes with the easy gait of the classic of adventure. Third, the author's intelligence and the intensity of verbal expression sustained for nearly 400 pages is no mean feat by any measure considering that in a work of that nature it is imperative for credibility to remain unflagging. And credibility does remain unflagging whether it is in the use of slave plantation Creole dialogue or in the clarity with which everything is described from the concrete to the sundry magical and inexplicable presences.

Chimalum Nwankwo. *African Studies Review*. 35, 1 (April 1992), pp. 134–35

BIBLIOGRAPHY

*Concerto for an Exile*, 1973; *The Graveyard Also Has Teeth*, 1980; *The Blood in the Desert's Eyes*, 1990; *The Last Harmattan of Alusine Dunbar*, 1990

# CHESNUTT, Charles W. (1858–1932)
**United States**

The critical reader of the story called "The Wife of His Youth," which appeared in these pages two years ago, must have noticed uncommon traits in what was altogether a remarkable piece of work. The first was the novelty of the material; for the writer dealt not only with people who were not white, but with people who were not black enough to contrast grotesquely with white people—who in fact were of that near approach to the ordinary American in race and color which leaves, at the last degree, every one but the connoisseur in doubt whether they are Anglo-Saxon or Anglo-African. Quite as striking as this novelty of the material was the author's thorough mastery of it, and his unerring knowledge of the life he had chosen in its peculiar racial characteristics. But above all, the story was notable for the passionless handling of a phase of our common life which is tense with potential tragedy; for the attitude, almost ironical, in which the artist observes the play of contesting emotions in the drama under his eyes; and for his apparently reluctant, apparently helpless consent to let the spectator know his real feeling in the matter. Any one accustomed to study methods in fiction, to distinguish between good and bad art, to feel the joy which the delicate skill possible only from a love of truth can give, must have known a high pleasure in the quiet self-restraint of the performance; and such a reader would probably have decided that the social situation in the piece was studied wholly from the outside, by an observer with special opportunities for knowing it, who was, as it were, surprised into final sympathy.

Now, however, it is known that the author of this story is of negro blood—diluted, indeed, in such measure that if he did not admit this descent few would imagine it, but still quite of that middle world which lies next, though wholly outside, our own. Since his first story appeared he has contributed several others to these pages, and he now makes a showing palpable to criticism in a volume called *The Wife of His Youth, and Other Stories of the Color Line*. . . .

He has sounded a fresh note, boldly, not blatantly, and he has won the ear of the more intelligent public.

W. D. Howells. *Atlantic*. May 1900, pp. 699–701

Nothing could exceed the tenderness with which the old and faithful figure of the wife is brought before us [in "The Wife of His Youth"], the soft dialect reproduced with indescribable art and charm. It is interesting to observe also that in this masterpiece of [Chesnutt's] accomplishment, as in much of his other work, we get the recurring note of comedy, suggesting that the farcical side of life is never wholly concealed from the writer's mental vision. At the most unexpected moments this capricious humor darts out at us, not always potent to amuse us, but always spontaneous and simple like the playfulness of a child. . . .

Closely allied to this purely humorous tendency is an inclination toward a more ironical banter, the subject of it always the idiosyncrasies of the negro race. We see their delight in posing, their easy irresponsibility in matters of veracity, their pompous snobbishness, their swift alternations of gayety and gloom, their thousand and one indications of imperfect development, as clearly as we see their gentleness and kindness, their luxuriant imagination, their amazing possibilities. In a word, we have in Mr. Chesnutt's three books [*The Wife of His Youth*, *The Conjure Woman*, *The House behind the Cedars*] . . . an ethnological study of extreme importance, such as only a peculiar union of two races and two historic periods could have made possible. Like Janus, the author turns his face toward the past, his vision embracing a drama that is over and never to be revived, and a still more mysterious drama that is hardly yet begun.

Elisabeth L. Cary. *The Book Buyer*. August 1901, pp. 27–28

Of [Chesnutt's] novels, *The House behind the Cedars* is commonly given first place. In the story of the heroine, Rena Walden, are treated some of the most subtle and searching questions raised by the color-line. Rena is sought in love by three men, George Tryon, a white man, whose love fails when put to the test; Jeff Wain, a coarse and brutal mulatto; and Frank Fowler, a devoted young Negro, who makes every sacrifice demanded by love. The novel, especially in its last pages, moves with an intensity that is an unmistakable sign of power. It is Mr. Chesnutt's most sustained treatment of the subject for which he has become best known, that is, the delicate and tragic situation of those who live on the borderline of the races; and it is the best work of fiction yet written by a member of the race in America.

In *The Marrow of Tradition* the main theme is the relations of two women, one white and one colored, whose father, the same white man, had in time been married to the mother of each. The novel touches upon most every phase of the Negro Problem. It is powerful plea, but perhaps too much a novel of purpose to satisfy the highest standards of art.

Benjamin Brawley. *The Negro in Literature and Art* (New York: Duffield, 1918), pp. 47–48

The struggle between Chesnutt the artist and Chesnutt the man (not immediately resolved) is evident in *The Wife of His Youth*. In these stories Chesnutt discards folk material to deal with the lives of a certain Negro type in Cleveland, the "Groveland" of his stories. These people represent the special and important group of Negroes with a large admixture of white blood. Because the peculiar situation of the near-whites was (and is) considered ideal for the purposes of propaganda, their lives had been used by nearly all the Negro novelists prior to Dunbar. This put upon such characters a certain stamp, and in that stamp lay danger for Chesnutt the artist.

The moods in which Chesnutt approaches his material are puzzling. In only a few of these stories is the reader sure of the author's point of view, his convictions. In "A Matter of Principle," for instance, a story of the color line in which the daughter of a well-to-do quadroon family loses a brilliant marriage because her father mistakes a stout, black gentleman for the lover whom he has never seen—what is the author's point of view? Based on the tragic absurdity of colorphobia, the story is a comedy of manners in the Molière sense. But what is Chesnutt's conviction as an artist? Does he sympathize with the existence of a color caste within the race? Is he holding his characters up to ridicule? Of what is he trying to convince us? In this and other stories one seems always at the point of making a discovery about the author, but the discovery never matures. The truth seems to be that in 1899, more than ten years after his return to Cleveland, Chesnutt's struggle was still in progress. He still was not sure what his attitude should be.

J. Saunders Redding. *To Make a Poet Black* (Chapel Hill: University of North Carolina Press, 1939), pp. 70–71

After *The Colonel's Dream* [in 1905] Chesnutt did not publish another book. A news article in *The Pittsburgh Courier* for June 30, 1928, announced a novel by Chesnutt which was to be published during the following winter, but this book did not appear. Chesnutt was quoted as having made the following statement concerning the volume: "The book is a novel dealing with Negro life of the present day, just as my former novels dealt with the same subject twenty-five years ago." Perhaps his silence was due, partly at least, to disappointment in the results of his campaign for the betterment of social conditions in the South.

Whether disappointed in his campaign or not, Chesnutt was an important trail-blazer in American Negro fiction. In his early stories of plantation life he not only made the folk tale a more faithful transcript of actual conditions but also became the first colored writer of fiction whose work was generally criticized without consideration of race. In *The Wife of His Youth, and Other Stories of the Color Line* he experimented with racial subject matter which he subsequently handled at greater length in *The House behind the Cedars*, *The Marrow of Tradition*, and *The Colonel's Dream*. All four of these books are favorably disposed toward the mulatto, who ostensibly represented for Chesnutt the most accomplished character in the Negro group. In treating the complexities of caste and color during the Reconstruction period, Chesnutt sometimes seems to accept the racial myths of his time; but he had a keen eye for social injustice and, before laying down his pen, he had either used or suggested many of the themes of the fiction of Negro life as we know it today.

> Hugh Gloster. *Negro Voices in American Fiction* (Chapel Hill: University of North Carolina Press, 1948), pp. 45–46

The tales of *The Conjure Woman* are all narrated by a white Northerner [John] who has gone South after the War in search of a suitable place of business for himself and a hospitable climate for his ailing wife. He settles on a plantation in North Carolina, where he hopes to develop a grape-growing industry. At the heart of each tale is a story within the story told by Uncle Julius, a shrewd old ex-slave who recalls pre-War incidents of conjuration. The white narrator retells these stories, always making clear to the reader that he is aware that Uncle Julius usually has a lurking personal interest in his entertaining tales. Julius probably profits from his employer's purchase of a worthless horse—a purchase prompted by Julius' conjure tale about a mule. Or Julius' church gains the use of a building which he has discouraged his employer from tearing down by a tale about the lumber from which it is made. The narrator, however, is paternalistically indulgent and good humored about Uncle Julius' motives. . . .

[But] as John patronizes Julius, he testifies to his own limitations and to the white world's fumbling inability to appreciate the wisdom, humor, and heart of a black man's experience, rooted in the cruelties of the slave experience. John's limited sympathy, his inability to fathom Julius' experience, is a hauntingly familiar projection of the white response to America's racial problem. Julius' various efforts to engage his employer's imagination, to arouse his sympathy, and to focus his indignation reflect Charles Chesnutt's own many-sided efforts to reach the imagination and the heart of his largely white audience.

> Robert M. Farnsworth. Introduction to Charles W. Chesnutt, *The Conjure Woman* (Ann Arbor: University of Michigan Press, 1969), pp. viii–ix, xvii

*The Conjure Woman* puts Joel Chandler Harris and Stephen Foster and all those dudes up to and including [William] Styron in their places. Uncle Julius is out to win. And he does. He convinces the cracker that the grapes have a spell on them and are therefore better left alone. He shows what would happen if the white man had to live in the Black man's shoes in ''Mars Jeems's Nightmare.'' And he keeps his nephew's job for him. He uses the white woman's

natural curiosity about Black men to his advantage. She always sympathizes with him while her husband is prone to back off. He is a good Black politician. The cracker gives the lumber that is ''Po' Sandy'' to the Black church. Uncle Julius is one of Black literature's most exciting characters precisely because he is so definite about his aims. He intends to see his people come out on top. John, the white voice, thought he could use Julius while it was the other way around. And Chesnutt drops a few gems on us dispelling the romantic theory about slavery's charms.

> Nikki Giovanni. *Gemini* (Indianapolis: Bobbs-Merrill, 1971), pp. 100–101

Dr. Miller [in *The Marrow of Tradition*] is Wellington's most successful Negro in the sense that he is as close to white as the town's written and unwritten laws will allow any black to be. His ''white'' appearance, his superior education, deportment, speech, wealth and social standing seem to place Miller in a class by himself, making him the classic ''middle man,'' neither fish nor fowl, whose existence both dramatizes the arbitrariness of distinctions based on race and simultaneously reinforces the absolute force of such distinctions.

The wealth of incidents and details contained in Helen Chesnutt's biography of her father indicates that much of Miller's personality was a projection of Charles Waddell Chesnutt. Chesnutt was a man who seemed extraordinarily in control of himself, stable, disciplined, capable of enormous sustained effort, a self-taught intellectual whose strivings for knowledge, culture and a career brought him into line with the Anglo-Saxon success model of his age. Like Miller, Chesnutt had learned to compartmentalize; the roles of professional man, father of a family, member of an oppressed minority, could be separated so that success in one area would not be undercut by insult or frustration in another. Chesnutt could view his writing as a business and give up a full-time commitment to it because the income from his books did not support his family in the style they were accustomed to. On one hand such compartmentalization is admirable and healthy, but taken to the extreme sanctioned by Western industrialized culture at the turn of the century, such an aptitude allowed Christian gentlemen to butcher and rob the nonwhite peoples of the earth. By forestalling an honest appraisal of the whole man, by resisting that long, hard look at the stresses and contradictions inherent in the multiplicity of ''faces'' he presented to Wellington, Miller was committing a perilous blunder. Chesnutt was serious enough, insightful enough, to realize that the individual will someday, somehow, be called upon to account for the arbitrary divisions by which he has shaped his life. . . .

The truth of the riot forces Wellington to recognize in itself *The Marrow of Tradition*, the bone-deep knowledge that men are either black or white and that nothing can occur between them that does not first take into account that dichotomy. This truth has stripped away the margin that Miller had believed supported his special kind of life.

> John Wideman. *American Scholar*. Winter 1972–73, pp. 130, 133

Perhaps the most impressive embodiment of Chesnutt's technical artistry was his last novel, *The Colonel's Dream*. The book's financial and popular failure at the hands of a biased, prejudiced readership should not blind us to its obvious artistic success when viewed by readers no longer caught up in the political and social narrowness of the early 1900s. . . .

The skeletal structure of *The Colonel's Dream* is a kind of missionary travel novel, which operates on the framework of a national allegory, as Colonel French travels South with Northern ideas and attempts an economic conversion. French himself is a national American hero "type": a figure of military bearing who is also a successful businessman. He is also a man who represents the "whole country," coupling a Southern past with a Northern present and attempting to unite the two under the banner of his industrial Northern way of life. The geographic movement and semiallegorical characterization are essential elements of the plot structure: both are important, not only for the traditional elements contained, but also for the innovations which Chesnutt added. . . .

French is a man with a tragic flaw stemming from his personality, and not just an allegorical hero who is defeated by a hostile, looming society. While he is partially the storybook hero of wealth, charm, money, ideals, and leisure, he is also the realistic product of his own past. Thus he brings to his crusade to the heathen South the same traits that made him successful in New York, and for that reason he is defeated. . . . The persistence and drive which have made French successful in the North now greatly harm him in Clarendon; and he is too insensitive to realize this fact. As Chesnutt realistically portrays him, the Colonel is not only too weak to be victorious everywhere, but he is even blind at times.

J. Noel Heermance. *Charles W. Chesnutt* (Hamden: Connecticut, Shoe String, 1974), pp. 184–86

BIBLIOGRAPHY

*"The Wife of His Youth,"* 1898; *The Conjure Woman*, 1899; *Frederick Douglass* (biography), 1899; *"Mars Jeems's Nightmare,"* 1899; *"A Matter of Principle,"* 1899; *"Po' Sandy,"* 1899; *The Wife of His Youth, and Other Stories of the Color Line*, 1899; *The House behind the Cedars*, 1900; *The Marrow of Tradition*, 1901; *The Colonel's Dream*, 1905; *The Short Fiction of Charles W. Chesnutt*, 1974; *Mandy Oxendine: A Novel*, 1997; *To Be an Author: Letters of Charles W. Chesnutt, 1898–1905*, 1997; *Paul Marchand, F.M.C.*, 1998

# CHILDRESS, Alice (1920–1994)
## United States

By using features from both written and oral traditions, Alice Childress is one black American writer who succeeds in adding a unique dimension to her work. In her collection *Like One of the Family: Conversations from a Domestic's Life*, Childress makes use of traditional metaphoric language and written form, but she uses the storytelling forms of black folk tradition to give Mildred, her major character, the means for telling her own stories and interacting with the audience. Usually in literary works in which the author relinquishes the reins of narration to a character, there is still a sense of an authorial presence. An author will create a semblance of removal for the purpose of evoking a particular response from readers, but [he or she] may still sense a direction for

[his or her] sympathies. In such cases, an author's ostensible absence from a scene suggests that the character has a life of his or her own, and a consciousness uncontrolled by the author. However, Childress's knowledge of folk forms allows her to succeed to a greater extent than most authors because she totally effaces herself from the narrative, and Mildred indeed seems to have a consciousness of her own.

Obviously we know that Alice Childress wrote a book called *Like One of the Family*. Beyond the title and the author's name, however, we never see the presiding presence of Childress. Once a reader opens the book, he or she ceases to be a reader and becomes a part of an audience. As members of that audience, we are never allowed to verbalize the fact that the author, Childress, is in control of the volume. We are simply confronted with a character, whose name we later learn is Mildred. We are never introduced to her or given any background information about her or presented with another character who tells us anything about her. The form of the collection allows us to see Mildred and no reality beyond that. We meet her, interact with her, and must rely upon her for whatever we experience in the book. As a character, Mildred completely controls her storytelling environment as well as the form in which her stories are presented. Mildred is not only the principal actor of the story, though; she quickly assumes the role of artist by embroidering the series of events in which she acts or has acted. She does her own kind of mythmaking without any apparent manipulation from Childress. While Mildred manages to incorporate forms of black folk storytelling, she nevertheless keeps her stories within the broad guidelines of the conscious creation of literature.

Trudier Harris. *Black American Literature Forum*. 14, 1 (Spring 1980), pp. 24–25

[In *Trouble in Mind*] Childress demonstrated a talent and ability to write humor that had social impact. Even though one laughed throughout the entire presentation, there was, inescapably, the understanding that although one was having an undeniably emotional and a profoundly intellectual experience, it was also political. One of Childress's great gifts: to have you laughing, not at the characters, but with them. It is a rare gift that does not come easily. Humor is of serious import, not a thing to take for granted. One gets the feeling that the writer loves the people she writes about. Love of life and people, accent on struggle, humor as a cultural weapon. . . .

Childress's drama *Wedding Band*, a play about an ailing white man and a black woman living together in a Carolina town, details the black woman's struggle against the racist attitudes of the town and against the members of the white man's middle-class family who are outraged by the relationship. Childress's other writings had seemed to have a total and timely relevance to the black experience in the [United States]; *Wedding Band* was a deviation. Perhaps the critic's own mood or bias was at fault. For one who was involved artistically, creatively, intellectually, and actively in the human rights struggle unfolding at the time, it is difficult, even in retrospect, to empathize or identify with the heroine's struggle for her relationship with the white man, symbolically the enemy incarnate of black hopes and aspirations. Nevertheless, again, at the heart of *Wedding Band* was the element of black struggle, albeit a struggle difficult to relate to. As usual, the art and craftsmanship were fine; the message, however, appeared out of sync with the times.

Her novel *A Hero Ain't Nothin' But a Sandwich* was adapted for a film production. It is the story of Benjie, a thirteen-year-old drug addict. There are some awesomely beautiful and powerful moments in this novel. One that comes immediately to mind is the poignant scene in which Butler Craig, the ''stepfather,'' saves spaced-out Benjie from falling from a Harlem rooftop, even as the boy begs his stepfather to let him go. '''Let go, Butler . . . let me die. Drop me, man!' He's flailing his legs, trying to work loose my hold, hollerin and fighting to die. 'Let me be dead!''' . . .

Alice Childress is a tremendously gifted artist who has consistently used her genius to effect a change in the world: to change the image we have of ourselves as human beings, black and white. Her primary and special concern has been the African image. She knew that black was beautiful when so many of us thought that Black Beauty was the name of a storybook horse, a figment of a writer's fantasy. Her gift has been used as an instrument against oppression; notwithstanding, she is always the consummate artist, telling her story powerfully and artistically. Her writing is always realistic, avoiding somehow the indulgence of wallowing in quagmires of despair and pessimism. After all, life is a short walk. There is so little time and so much living to achieve. Perhaps her greatest gift, along with her satiric bent and the thematic accent on struggle, is the leitmotif of love for people, particularly her own people. I have come away from most of her writing feeling mighty damn proud of the human race, especially the African aspect of it. Portraying it with great fidelity in all of its meanness, its pettiness, its prejudices, its superstitions. Childress captures most of all its capacity to overcome, to be better than it is, or ever could be, its monumental capacity for change.

> John O. Killens. In Mari Evans, ed. *Black Women Writers (1950–1980): A Critical Evaluation* (New York: Doubleday, 1984), pp. 129, 131–33

Alice Childress posits [an] idealized friendship between a black and a white woman in *A Short Walk*. The friendship between black Cora Green and white May Palmas happens simply and spontaneously because of the proximity of their apartments and because of the respect each has for the other. Cora says, ''May is my first close friend-girl of any race—my closest friend since Papa died. Like him, she also knows how to look at matters and trace meanings and feelings down to the core.'' Married to a Filipino and consequently ostracized by her mother, May is familiar with the pain caused by racial prejudice and counts on love, as she tells Cora, to conquer all. However as no racial tension exists between the two women, race is not a subject for discussion between them. Always supportive of each other, May sees Cora through her decision against abortion and through childbirth, and Cora sees May through [attempted] suicide and loneliness when her husband is jailed. They struggle together against their common poverty, and they take a common delight in food and music. Through the repeated exchange of gifts, Childress suggests that their friendship is ritualistically sealed forever. Although Childress confronts racist and sexist dilemmas in describing Cora's relationship with other characters in *A Short Walk*, the friendship between Cora and May, which continues until the end of Cora's life, in its lack of conflict and growth, might seem an unrealizable model. Yet in her representation of May's apartment as a meeting place for the countries and races of the world and of Cora's parties as a center for people from all walks of life, all

classes, and all sexual preferences, Childress seems to be emphatically suggesting that it is possible for human beings to accept their national, sexual, individual, and racial differences and to live together with peace and pleasure. The central theme of Childress's novel seems to be expressed in Cora's explanation of the basis of her friendship with May, ''. . . she's my friend. I love her for good and sufficient reason. It's not ever easy, but I try to accept people just as they come wrapped. . . . I treat white folks according to how they act, not by how they look.''

> Elizabeth [A.] Schultz. In Marjorie Pryse and Hortense J. Spillers, eds. *Conjuring: Black Women, Fiction, and Literary Tradition* (Bloomington: Indiana University Press, 1985), pp. 81–82

One very modern thing Childress did in her plays was to break down the binary oppositions so prevalent in Western society—black/white, male/female, North/South, artist/critic—with their implications that one is superior to the other. Such breaking of these categories is a major interest in much modern criticism as well as feminist theory today. . . .

By 1969 the racial situation in this country had shifted considerably, and *Wine in the Wilderness* reflects Childress's feelings about some of the new racial stereotypes. In the midst of a racial riot in Harlem, a black liberal couple brings Tommy, a thirty-year-old woman who works in a factory, to the apartment of Bill, a thirty-three-year-old artist, to serve as a model for the final panel of a triptych he is painting called ''Wine in the Wilderness,'' portraying three aspects of ''black womanhood.'' One painting is chaste ''black girlhood,'' the second is majestic ''Mother Africa,'' and the third will be a contemporary ''lost woman,'' a ''messed up chick'' to serve as warning to all ghetto women. Tommy warms up to Bill when she thinks he likes her, but when she finds out the kind of painting he is actually planning to make, she tells him that he likes blacks in the abstract but that ''[You] don't like flesh and blood niggers.'' Bill changes the triptych to embody more realistic images of the blacks he knows. . . .

Many of the characters and ideas in *Trouble in Mind* are as fresh as and perhaps more generally recognizable than they were thirty years ago. Both the character, Wiletta, and author Childress are actively protesting the few and false images of black women written by white men with ''blind spots.'' Wiletta, along with the other black actress in the play, Millie, jokes about the roles they have had to play. . . . In the second act, the director, Manners, is dissatisfied with Wiletta's performance and directs her by saying, ''We're dealing with simple, backward people but they're human beings.'' Wiletta quickly points out, '''Cause they colored, you tellin' me they're human bein's. . . . I know I'm a human bein'. . . .'' Childress, in writing the roles of Wiletta and Millie, has provided some alternative images of black women, three dimensional characters with weaknesses and strengths.

> Gayle Austin. *Southern Quarterly*. 25, 3 (Spring 1987), pp. 53, 55–57

In the first act of *Wedding Band*, a scene of reading and performance occurs that lies at the center of a feminist interpretation of the play. Mattie, a black woman who makes her living selling candy and caring for a little white girl, has received a letter from her husband in the Merchant Marine and needs a translator for it. Her new neighbor, Julia, the educated outsider trying to fit into working-class surroundings, reads the sentimental sailor's letter aloud. After her performance, in which the women listening have actively participated, Mattie tells Julia that, in addition to his love, her husband gives her what is more important, his *name and protection*. These two standards of conventional love are denied Julia because her lover of ten years is white; and even Mattie learns that because she never divorced her first husband, she is not now legally married and cannot receive marital war benefits. Neither woman enjoys a man's name or his protection, in part because the chivalry implied in such privilege was unattainable for blacks in the Jim Crow society of 1918 South Carolina. The women in *Wedding Band* learn to depend on themselves and each other rather than on absent men, a self-reliance born painfully through self-acceptance....

Set chronologically midway between the poles of Reconstruction and [the Civil Rights Movement], *Wedding Band* describes an era when lynching presented one answer to demands for equality in the South, while Harlem flowered as a mecca for black culture in the North. In the 1960s, white women and black men's sexual relations generated tension in the black community, but miscegenation as the white master's rape of his slave retains deeper historical ramifications for black women. Childress's drama, subtitled "a love/hate story in black and white," takes place on the tenth anniversary of Julia and her white lover in the backyard tenement to which Julia has moved after being evicted from countless other houses. Determined to get along with her nosy but well-meaning neighbors, Julia seems to have won a guarded acceptance until her lover, Herman, visits her. He has brought her a gold wedding band on a chain, and they plan to buy tickets on the Clyde Line to New York, where Julia will proudly and legally bear Herman's name. But Herman succumbs to the influenza epidemic, and in the second act he lies in Julia's bed waiting for his mother and sister to take him to a white doctor. Julia's landlady has refused to help because it is illegal for Herman to be in Julia's house, and she cannot appear to sanction Julia's immoral behavior. Herman's mother sides with the landlady in preserving respectability even at the cost of her son's life, and she will not carry him to the doctor until it grows dark enough to hide him. In the last scene, Herman returns to Julia with the boat tickets, which she refuses to take because his mother has convinced her that blacks and whites can never live together. Finally she appears to relent so that Herman can die believing that Julia, even without him, will go north.

The secondary characters, however, more than the two lovers, underscore the drama's didactic politics. They are types, but not stereotypes, and their separate dilemmas and personalities describe the injustices blacks have endured in the South. The landlady, Fanny, the neighbors Mattie and Lula, Lula's adopted son, Nelson, and the abusive white traveling salesman give the stage community a historic idiosyncrasy missing from Julia and Herman's relationship. Fanny has proudly joined the middle class by acquiring property and exploiting her tenants (in 1918 a relatively new possibility for black women) in the name of racial uplift. As homeworkers, Mattie and Lula exist bound to a variety of semi-skilled, low-paying jobs to feed their children. Nelson, as a soldier in the newly desegregated United States army, assumes that when the war is over he will be given the rights of a full citizen, even in South Carolina. He is a forerunner of the militant youth who would later provide the impatient voice to the nascent Civil Rights

Movement of the late 1940s, and whose dreams of integration would be realized only partially in the 1960s.

These characters who inhabit Miss Fanny's backyard tenement underscore the vexed issue of difference as explored by the feminist scholars cited above. Julia's problem throughout the play is less her white lover than her reluctance to see herself as a member of the black community. Although a mostly white theater audience would see her as a different sort of heroine because of race, her black neighbors perceive her as different from them for issues more complex than skin color. She assumes that her racial transgression with Herman will make her unwelcome among the women she wishes to confide in, but her aloofness from their day-to-day interests also serves as a protective shield. In this, Julia is similar to Lutie Johnson in Ann Petry's *The Street*, written in 1946. Both characters are ostensibly defined by their unequal relations with men, but their potential for salvation lies in the larger community that depends on the stability of its women. Lutie Johnson is so determined to move off "the street" in Harlem she thinks is pulling her down that she refuses to join the community Harlem offers her, a community that in some ways defies the white society keeping it poor. Neither poor nor uneducated, Julia finds herself defying the black community by asserting her right to love a white man, but this self-assertion is, in a larger sense, a more dangerous defiance of the white community. She wants her love story to be one of individual commitment and sacrifice, but it is that only in part. Julia's refinement in manners, education, and financial independence, which are middle-class, traditionally white attributes, make her and Herman available to each other. But theirs is, as the subtitle insists, a "love/hate" story, in which interracial love cannot be divorced from centuries of racial hate.

Catherine Wiley. In June Schlueter, ed. *Modern American Drama: The Female Canon* (Rutherford, New Jersey: Fairleigh Dickinson University Press, 1990), pp. 184, 187–89

BIBLIOGRAPHY

*Florence* (play), 1949; *Just a Little Simple* (play), 1950; *Gold through the Trees* (play), 1952; *Trouble in Mind* (play), 1955; *Like One of the Family: Conversations from a Domestic's Life*, 1956; *String* (play and screenplay), 1969 and 1979; *Wine in the Wilderness: A Comedy–Drama* (screenplay), 1969; *Mojo: A Black Love Story* (play), 1970; *A Hero Ain't Nothin' But a Sandwich* (novel and screenplay), 1973 and 1978; *Wedding Band* (play and screenplay), 1973; *When the Rattlesnake Sounds: A Play*, 1975; *Let's Hear It for the Queen: A Play*, 1976; *Sea Island Song* (play), 1977; *A Short Walk*, 1979; *Rainbow Jordan*, 1981; *Moms: A Praise Play for a Black Comedienne*, 1986; *Many Closets*, 1987; *These Other People*, 1989

# CLARK, John Pepper (1935–)
## Nigeria

What Ezra Pound is to Okigbo, Eliot and Hopkins are to Clark. As in the case of Okigbo one finds it occasionally disturbing to recognise the "ready made" language. But again we have to accept the fact that Eliot and Hopkins form a legitimate starting point for a young poet and that again we feel that the poet has often enough succeeded to burst out of the limitations set by the adopted language. Clark's *Poems* like Okigbo's *Heavensgate* gives us the immediate feeling that we are in the presence of a sincere, genuine poet. But that is where the similarity ends.

I have not observed either of them at work, but I am almost certain that they employ opposite techniques. I visualise Okigbo as a poet who gradually chisels away all the superfluous detail from a large chunk of experience. I see him filing away, balancing, reconstructing, until his verse has the hard edge and the transparency of a crystal. Clark on the other hand appears to me a more spontaneous poet. His writing is immediate. There is a feeling of urgency. He has so much to say, that he tries to cram more and more into the fragile form of his poem. His verse is packed with meaning; overloaded, bursting at the seams. One critic has said his poems are over-written. I should prefer to call them overcharged or over-powered. . . .

Clark's writing is extremely visual. One cannot fail to see that enormous rock on the sacred hill in Abeokuta boiling in the sun. But the visual experience leads the poet on to other thoughts basically quite unconnected. Yet this is no idle, aesthetic type of reflective poetry. In Clark's work we always feel that the poet is hard pressed, that he is writing under a form of compulsion, that he is himself like a ''pot all night on the boil,'' or a ''cauldron that cracks for heat.''

I cannot see Clark working for a long time on a poem. I imagine him writing in a kind of explosion, under the extreme pressure of experience, writing only if cornered by life, as it were, and then having got the thing off his chest losing interest and turning to the next thing.

The result is poetry that makes heavy reading, but which is moving, because it is always nourished by immediate experience and because the author's harassed, tormented and irrepressible personality is present in every line.

Ulli Beier. *Black Orpheus*. No. 12, 1963, pp. 47–48

John Pepper Clark, in the few poems he has in the [Langston] Hughes anthology [*Poems from Black Africa*], but more so because of his verse play *Song of a Goat*, convinces me that he is one of the most interesting Africans writing, English or French. Mr. Clark is a Nigerian, born in 1935, though I understand he is now in the graduate school at Princeton. For sure, nothing he could ever learn at Princeton would help him write so beautiful a work as *Song of a Goat*. It is English, but it is not. The tone, the references (immediate and accreted) belong to what I must consider an African experience. The English is pushed, as Senghor wished all Africans to do with European languages, past the immaculate boredom of the recent Victorians to a quality of experience that is non-European, though it is the European tongue which seems to shape it, externally. But Clark is after a specific emotional texture nowhere available in European literature or life. . . .

The play is about a traditional West African family split and destroyed by adultery. And the writing moves easily through the myth heart of African life, building a kind of ritual drama that depends as much on the writer's insides for its exactness and strength as it does on the narrating of formal ritualistic acts. The language is gentle and lyrical most of the time, but Clark's images and metaphors are strikingly and, I think, indigenously vivid. . . .

LeRoi Jones. *Poetry*. March 1964, p. 399

I confess readily that like everyone else (except perhaps the American) I had enjoyed the crude vigour of *America, Their America*. Stronger even than the feeling of antagonism which the American generates by his overt actions is the contempt which he arouses by his lack of self-knowledge, his blind displacement of a true image of himself. Any work which goes towards the destruction of the American self-image must enjoy an immediate validity and give a vindictive pleasure to all non-Americans, and even praise from what we hope will be a new generation of Americans.

So much for America, and so much for why *America, Their America* hit the easy chord of transferred enjoyment. Would that the appreciation of this book had been left purely on this level! But Nigeria would not be Nigeria and literary critics semi-literate if an attempt was not made to raise this book to some level of literary achievement to which even the author never aspired. Beginning with what could be shrugged off as the natural overspill of enthusiasm it has now reached the absurd proportions where a critic in the *Nigeria Magazine Literary Supplement* actually compares *America, Their America* to James Baldwin's *The Fire Next Time*.

On what level? Mr. Clark donned a pair of oversized gloves, shut his eyes tightly and delivered a wild-swinging, two-fisted clobbering attack with head for a battering ram and knees up in his opponent's crotch, relying on the principle that with so many random and energetic blows, the law of averages must ensure a hit. Each page of *America, Their America* reads exactly like that picture we see often in the Nigerian street, of a child fighting a man ten times his size who stands very still while the child's arms flail wildly over his head, crying all the time in frustration and self-pity.

Even this accompanying whine is not missing from Mr. Clark's book. His final interview with the Colonel which degenerates most strangely into a plea for human sympathy is the last act of the trouble-some child who is now faced with his punishment, but hopes to avoid it.

To compare the adult, perceptive analysis and the studied prose of James Baldwin with the catalogue of ''maverick'' reactions in *America, Their America* is not doing the author any good as it brings his work up for the kind of criticism which would normally be applied to a work of greater pretensions.

Wole Soyinka. *Ibadan*. June 1966, pp. 59–60

[Clark] has three plays to his credit—*Song of a Goat*, *The Masquerade* and *The Raft*. But it is as the author of *Song of a Goat* that he has made his reputation as a playwright. Clark's three plays are tragedies and critics have attempted to show how close to Greek tragedies they are. In each of these plays an individual is faced with some inexorable law of nature or unchangeable law of society. He tries his best to escape an impending woe. Perhaps in this sense the comparison with Greek tragedy is not irrelevant.

However, it should at once be stated that Clark's declared aim is to portray life in the Rivers as he knows and has observed it. Each of his plays deals with an aspect of life important to his people. Their social practices and beliefs, their shortcomings and difficulties are dramatised on the stage. This is why these plays have been so popular. That they all end in tragedy is not meant to be a reflection on their lives. This is the type of ending dictated by both the content of the plays and the approach of the playwright. . . .

J. P. Clark writes plays which depict a confrontation between an individual and forces much greater than himself. He has set a high standard for himself and it is a measure of his brilliance and literary competence that his plays are successful and well received by Nigerians and non-Nigerians alike. *Song of a Goat* is particularly widely acclaimed and has been staged many times in Nigeria, Africa and Europe. It was applauded at the Commonwealth Festival of the Arts not only for its dramatic excellence but also for the poetic language used to portray the overwhelmingly tragic atmosphere of the play.

Oladele Taiwo. *An Introduction to West African Literature* (London: Thomas Nelson, 1967), pp. 76–77

As a playwright Clark has seemed to suffer from a lack of familiarity with the demands of the theatre, and his plays have never fitted as comfortably on to the stage as have Soyinka's. The latter's craftsmanship stems from a close practical knowledge of the theatre as a director and actor, whereas Clark has no comparable experience. One result of this is that Clark's characters tend to talk where they might act, to recite where they should converse, and to remain static where they should move. Reported action has always been preponderant in his plays and the demands made upon his actors, directors and designers have tended to be unrealistic. A case in point, in *Song of a Goat*, is the decapitation of a goat, on stage, in order that its head can be thrust into a pot as a symbol of cuckoldry. The opening performance of a production of this play at Mbari, Ibadan (directed by Soyinka) tried to execute this instruction (without, for obvious reasons, adequate rehearsal), and the chastening experience upon actors and audience caused a symbolic gesture to be substituted on later nights. Similar appalling difficulties face the director in *The Raft*. To draw attention to this is not to ridicule Clark's dramatic aims, but rather to pinpoint what prevents the realization of his full potential as a playwright. For with *Ozidi* Clark has written a major piece for the theatre, of epic span and scope, and yet, once again, almost impossible to stage. . . .

On the modern stage and away from an Ijaw audience *Ozidi* will work effectively *only* if the director can return to the conditions in which the myth is at home, and make extensive use of dance and music (much of which is indicated in the text). *Ozidi* can become a most exciting dance-drama where the communication of mime and movement can overcome the limits of realism. It is in this form that one would like to see *Ozidi* tackled, for J. P. Clark has offered the theatre one of the most fascinating works to have been created in Nigeria in recent years.

Martin Banham. *Journal of Commonwealth Literature*. July 1969, pp. 132–33, 135

Neither Clark nor Okigbo is detained by [English] influences for very long. In fact Clark himself acquired the assurance and lyric power of his mature style rapidly, as a cursory glance through *Poems* and *A Reed in the Tide* would confirm.

Clark assumes—an assumption shared by Wole Soyinka, Lenrie Peters, Gabriel Okara, and Okigbo—that what he has to say is important. The change is not in the material out of which the poems are forged. It is demonstrably more fundamental, part of a new intellectual outlook based on a belief in the poet as a pioneer of a different kind. Poetry no longer catered for popular causes. The poet's sensibility is free and uncompromised, and functions as the focal point of his work, the still center of the turning world. . . .

As we should expect, Clark is conscious of the demands of his craft, aware that poetry is not a matter of popular sentiment alone; that the act of creation is critical in the best sense of the word. His own formal criticism is impressive for its perception and depth and the degree to which it supports and clarifies his practice as a poet and dramatist. . . . Taken in an African context, or the context of emerging nations where art is frequently tempted into propaganda, [his] priorities are eminently sensible. Clark's interests being what they should be, there is no tendency to classify experiences as suitable or unsuitable for poetry, or, what is more objectionable, to advocate set themes such as the "African personality." By saying that there is nothing special in the kind of experience a poet has, he places the impact and meaning, the *value* of a poem, squarely on the performance, not on the intrinsic attraction of the theme.

Edwin Thumboo. *Books Abroad.* Summer 1970, p. 388

Clark's success [as a poet] was due not only to [his] gift for recreating the local environment but also his genuine interest in the oral traditions which formed the only extant tradition. Clark was to complain later that Nigerians did not know as much about their oral traditions as they did about European mythologies. Apart from the absence of a written tradition which made the creation of a genuine national verse tradition a difficulty, the Nigerian poet also had to contend with the prejudice that the writer in a developing country is free from those sophisticated inhibitions which stifle the creative mind. Apparently he had only to look in his heart and write. Because of the spontaneous nature of his own verse Clark has had to contend with this prejudice in a greater measure than other writers. . . .

For the modern Nigerian poet writing in English, as for any other poet, a spontaneous outburst of emotion is inadequate, for the poet must not merely translate emotions or ideas from the life of one culture into the language of another, he must create a product that is a new whole in itself. He must not merely write as if so "hard pressed" that he is "writing in a kind of explosion, under the extreme pressure of experience" [Ulli Beier], but he must also ensure the quality of the expression. Mere reproduction of the experience could easily become sociological. So Clark attempts to escape from this through technique, first by experimenting with the techniques of other poets, then moving away from this pastiche making.

Dan Izevbaye. In Bruce King, ed., *Introduction to Nigerian Literature* (London: Evans Brothers, 1971), pp. 152–53, 157

The predicament [in *The Raft*] of the four men on the raft—Olotu, Kengide, Ogro, and Ibobo—drifting helplessly in the night, is meant to be taken as the predicament of the Nigerian nation as a whole as it looks for directions, searches for a teleology while floating about in the dangerous waters of the modern world. The raft is adrift, its moorings gone. Who or what cut it loose? Will anyone tell the four men where they are? Can anyone tell them where they are going? Without stars or moon to guide them (where Clark presumably means the certainties of the old order), they are lost. . . .

The raft floats helplessly on, until a big steamer passes. Ogro confidently swims to it for help; but he is beaten back into the water and drowns. Clearly this is a foreign vessel, a representation of the outside world, and the West in particular. The point of the incident is clear. Ogro, his friends, and their broken raft are not wanted by the crew of the passing ship; they receive no help in their calamitous situation. They are alone. They are powerless. Their situation, to use a happy phrase of Clark's that occurs here and as the title of his book of verse, is that of "a reed in the tide," moving at the mercy of forces beyond its control. There seems to be no hope. Even when, near the end of the play, the raft approaches Burutu, its destination, a brief eruption of hope is smothered by a blanket of fog. The two survivors can see nothing; they are drifting helplessly past Burutu towards the open sea. . . .

There is something approaching great art about the close of this play: two men, holding hands, shouting hopelessly in the night. They have no control over their situation; they drift on to an unknown fate. Even on land, at Burutu, the destination they had been happily anticipating, all is confusion and alarm, with the noise *of men crying and calling out to one another in fear.* A fact stressed at the close is the aloneness of Ibobo and Kengide now, an aloneness which stands out starkly as a modern feature against a traditional African background of family and tribal togetherness.

Adrian A. Roscoe. *Mother Is Gold* (Cambridge: Cambridge University Press, 1971), pp. 209–11

A vision of war. Four such words can only mock any attempt to describe J. P. Clark's latest book of poems [*Casualties: Poems 1966–68*]. Not content merely to elegize both the dead and living casualties of the Nigerian tragedy, Clark sets out to force the reader to actively participate in the human act of suffering. That he is remarkably successful in this despotic enforcement of the rites of Death is largely due to his decision to write in a style which, while closely paralleling the parable, often moves into an enigmatic tunnel vision. Clark watches the mindless destruction of both sides, "the roar of leopards amok from the forest," and manages to focus on individual acts of terror as well as the general state of fratricide; he does this by sculpturing *each* word as if it alone had to carry some two or three times its normal weight. . . .

Such a technique of arbitrarily holding us at arm's length, only to unexpectedly jerk us face to face with the realization that these symbols of death and chaos are no longer symbols but actual pain, demands our passage into Clark's world of frustrated despair. Even the second portion of the collection, "Incidental Songs for Several Persons," while not dealing with the horror of the Nigerian poems, is nevertheless dominated by a vision of ironic social decay.

R. Langenkamp. *World Literature Written in English.* November 1971, pp. 106–7

*The Wives' Revolt* is an economical comedy, with only three characters: Okoro; his wife, Koko; and Idama, his friend. At issue is money paid to the town Erhuwaren by "the oil company operating our land." One-third has been paid to the town elders, one-third to the other men in their age groups, and one-third similarly to the women. But the women object that the elders are all male, and the women desert the town. Okoro tries comically to contend with all the problems Koko has left behind, until she returns suffering from some sort of venereal infection. Okoro will

not hear any explanation, while he assumes the worst. As hard as Idama tries to intervene, Okoro will not stop talking long enough to hear, while Koko infuriates him with comments from the side. At last he swears to be silent: "There, I won't talk again. Yes; see I have stitched my lips from end to end. From now on, I'm the eunuch in service at the palace of the Oba of Benin—tongue pulled out by the root, eardrums punctured to the base, and therefore deaf, dumb from birth, and as the women will have it, completely without pestle." He is not silent of course, no more than a character in a medieval English interlude, or Hotspur. The interest of the play is not the novelty of the situation but Clark's witty display of Ijaw family and communal life through the old plot.

Ijaw life had long been Clark's great interest. In personal communication, Clark remarked that he did not know an uncle of his was a great poet until he began researching Urhobo poetry: "The point is that the poetry was already there. It was being sung and danced all around us. But we didn't know!"

Partly to correct this ignorance, Clark undertook to preserve the Ozidi saga, the hero tale he first published in dramatic form and then translated at length, in a volume that reproduces a transcription of an Ijaw recital of the story with Clark's translation in parallel columns. His research had found three versions, the festival performance that Clark and Speed filmed, a tale recited by the poet Afoluwa, and a full epic recited by another poet, Okabu Ojobolo. The third one was the version that Clark translated and published as *The Ozidi Saga.*

The saga was recorded in the sitting room of a lady in Ibadan, with an audience of enthusiastic listener-participants, mostly women, and with drumbeats as instrumental support. The saga is marked by repetition, prolixity, lapses of memory, and as Clark says in his introduction, "faults crying aloud in the frequent paratactic constructions." These very faults certify that the saga is, in the highest oral tradition, a unique thing, derived from but not identical with its predecessor renditions. Okabou learned the story from a professional storyteller, Atazi, for whom Okabou worked, apparently as a servant. That was many years earlier than the mid 1960s, when Okabou was already over seventy years old. *The Ozidi Saga* is a tale of Ado, the legendary city of Benin (not the real imperial city).

The water imagery shows that the saga is an indigenous work, though set in fictitious Ado. In the canon of Clark's work *The Ozidi Saga* is unusual in that it is so purely Ijaw. Clark labored to recreate, so far as the English language permitted, the Ijaw text. There is no verbal trickery, no oblique or cryptic allusion, no use of surprising rhythm, and no flamboyant imagery. Even Clark's wit and irony are reserved for the preface, the introductory essay, and the notes. The reader of the English text senses that he is as near the performance as print is likely to bring him.

The saga was told over the course of seven nights, each representing several hours of recitation, interspersed with songs, chants, comments, and responses. The alert reader can imagine Okabou's vigor at the start, his miming of the character Temugedege's cowardice, the spectator's delight and encouragement, the conscious directing of attention to the recorder, then the entry of the drumbeats and the mocking antiphonal song, followed by Temugedege's quavering fear and the laughter it provokes, and finally the teller describing and miming Ozidi's hyperbolic sword stroke. What makes this so important is that such liveliness has customarily been edited out of scholarly transcriptions of oral performances, making them more Homeric than alive. Clark is faithful to the tape recorder, not academic tradition. The result is both interesting and demanding—some would say too demanding. It is a work of literature more for study than entertainment.

The saga has much that Clark put into the play *Ozidi*, including the killing of Oreame by Ozidi. But one should not take this as seriously as Clark does; he sees it as retributive justice, but Okabou has the old witch appear to Ozidi in a dream and advise him how to bring her back to life.

The saga, taken in conjunction with the film and the play, makes for a grand, if sometimes ambiguous, achievement. The variety of forms provides an unprecedented sense of the whole. Nowhere else can the layman find so rounded and fully dimensioned a record of what is now a lost experience of epic. Not that Clark has been without his critics. Serious questions regarding the transcription and the translation have been raised. Clark, as an anthropologist and as a linguist, is but a talented amateur, and this fact shows.

He is more at home in literary criticism, his major work in this field being five essays that were collected as *The Example of Shakespeare*. "Themes of African Poetry of English Expression," for example, is an early (1964) review of the corpus of poetry from West, East, and South Africa. Clark takes into account the historical circumstances and the social context of African poets, while seeing the weaknesses of clichéd negritudist and resistance poetry and praising the successes of better poets. His point in the essay, however, is to refute the strictures of committed critics and anthologizers of bad poetry, such as some living in the West. In "The Communication Line between Poet and Public" (1966) he contrasts the immediate connection between writer and reader in the easy, often bombastic, old poetry celebrating Africa, with more interesting but difficult work of Okigbo. He sets himself (and Gabriel Okara) between the two extremes, noting, however, that some of his work gives readers trouble, as does the poetry of Soyinka. A gap, he says rightly, exists between poets and their public, widened by the training of some teachers, who appreciate only traditional English poetry and cannot accommodate modern poetry, whether Nigerian or British. . . .

[In] "The Hero as a Villain," Clark examines the great warrior-heroes of classical and English traditions—Achilles, Oedipus, Richard III, Othello, and Macbeth—along with Nigeria's Ozidi, to make a mild, ironic attack on recent Nigerian leadership. The warrior-hero often falls into error and wickedness, Clark says, and as a result needs cleansing. In Nigeria, "peace and justice" will not be possible, he suggests, until "society and the hero are purified of the villain within."

> Robert M. Wren. In Bernth Lindfors, and Reinhard Sander, editors. *Dictionary of Literary Biography, Volume 117: Twentieth-Century Caribbean and Black African Writers* (Detroit: Gale Research, 1992), pp. 112–133

BIBLIOGRAPHY
*Song of a Goat* (play), 1961; *Poems*, 1962; *America, Their America*, 1964; *The Masquerade*, 1964; *The Raft*, 1964; *Three Plays: Song of a Goat, The Masquerade, The Raft*, 1964; *A Reed in the Tide*, 1965; *Ozidi: A Play*, 1966; *Casualties: Poems 1966–68*, 1970; *The Example of Shakespeare: Critical Essays on African Literature*, 1970; *A Decade of Tongues: Selected Poems 1958–1968*, 1981; *State of the Union*, 1985; *The Bikoroa Plays*, 1985; *Mandela and Other Poems*, 1988; *Collected Plays and Poems: 1958-1988*, 1991; *The Wives' Revolt*, 1991

# CLARKE, Austin C. (1934–)
## Barbados

[Austin C.] Clarke's major themes are similar to those of most West Indian novels during the last thirty years—black awareness, national identity, the hateful ambiguities of the West, and the heroic potential of the black peasant. But the emphases and contexts through which he develops these topics are shaped by his experience of the Afro-American consciousness that has been gaining momentum during his stay in Canada and the United States. He has, in effect, helped to contribute a North American dimension to the characteristic identity motif of the West Indian novel; and as the major West Indian writer on the continent at the present time, he provides an invaluable perspective on an aspect of British Caribbean literature that has too often been minimized or ignored in the past. His significance in this respect is increased by the fact that he is among the few West Indian artists of any note to have lived and worked in North America, for any considerable time, since the beginning of the new "black revolution." In fact "revolution" is the major theme of his first novel, *[The] Survivors of the Crossing*. It presents the abortive attempts of Rufus, a sugar-plantation laborer, to effect an economic and political revolution in Barbados. He tries, unsuccessfully, to break the repressive powers of a white establishment by using the strike as his main weapon, and when that fails, resorts to equally ineffective terrorist tactics. But in spite of the very obvious political motif of the work, the real import of the revolution in *Survivors of the Crossing* is cultural and emotional, rather than constitutional. Hence the portrayal of Barbados in the mid-1960s as a politically deprived society, lacking even the fundamentals of a labor union movement, is an ironic rather than literal anachronism. All the constitutional, political, and economic trappings of the West Indian independence movement have been reduced, by Clarke, to the level of relative insignificance, in the face of the black apathy and self-hate that have traditionally stunted cultural and racial self-identity. The native government and its leaders are conspicuously absent from the main plot of *Survivors of the Crossing*, and are occasionally just referred to in passing as rather vague and irrelevant details of the background. The real powers in Rufus's world are the white plantation owner and a white-controlled police force, both exercising their influence through native sycophants. Rufus fails, then, not only because of his opponents' power and his own incapacities, but also because of the hostility or indifference of other blacks who actively or passively support the status quo. Whippetts, the black schoolteacher in Rufus's village, is a representative figure in this context; his violent hatred of Rufus and his contempt for members of his own race not only make him an effective opponent of the illfated revolution, but also demonstrate the educational and class barriers to an effective kind of racial self-identity in his society. . . .

The identity theme with its attendant conflicts also appears in Clarke's next novel, *Amongst Thistles and Thorns*. Both the coherent structure and psychological complexity of this work attest to the rapid development of Clarke's narrative techniques. He treats his racial and cultural subjects on a less exclusively external level than he has Rufus's political misadventures: the moral and emotional conflicts become more coherent and psychologically interesting by being presented as the experiences of a single character whose introspection provides the work with a kind of subjective unity.

*Amongst Thistles and Thorns* portrays a weekend in the life of Milton Sobers, a young schoolboy in Barbados, who runs away temporarily from both school and home. Milton's truancy is developed as a psychological quest, a search for identity that has racial as well as psychological overtones. He has run away from a sterile educational system represented by a servile and sadistic black teacher, an impersonal and detached white inspector, and the irrelevant offerings to a white "motherland" during the colonial rites of Empire Day. At the same time, he is detached from the society of his village, for only his father, Willy-Willy, shares his interest in the topic closest to his heart—Harlem. Milton's Harlem assumes the dominant symbolic proportions it has in [Claude] McKay's *Home to Harlem*, and his day-dreams of the famous black community at once testify to the importance of American symbolism in Clarke's fiction, and indicate the unifying subjectivity with which Clarke is developing his themes. . . .

Psychologically Clarke's themes evolve a stage further with the incisive irony of *The Meeting Point*. Familiar clashes with the external world of the status quo persist, but the more interesting conflicts are wholly internal: the actual process of self-identification is itself being more closely scrutinized, and is revealed as a painful, and often unresolved, series of conflicts *within* each awakening consciousness—the tension between nascent blackness on the one hand, and the old self-hate or apathy, on the other. Moreover, this is the fundamental ambiguity that proves to be the source of much of the novel's irony.

*The Meeting Point* is the story of Bernice Leach, a Barbadian immigrant working as the maid of the Burrmanns, a Jewish family in Toronto. The title of the work is itself ironic, for the novel dispels, rather than confirms, the optimistic connotations of the familiar phrase. "Meeting Point" really indicates, not reconciliation and harmony, but the collision of hostile attitudes: the black sensitivity of Bernice and her friends meeting the coldness and antipathy of Canadian society.

> Lloyd W. Brown. *Journal of Commonwealth Literature.* 9 (July 1970), pp. 90–91, 93, 95–96

Bertram Cumberbatch, better known as Boysie, the protagonist of *The Bigger Light*, has, after years of scrounging and scraping, achieved what by his standards is great material success. . . . Boysie's wife, Dots, has also progressed—from being a servant in a rich, suburban household to being a nurse's aide in a hospital. *Her* progress is not so much a case of material advancement as of a greater feeling of independence, of movement away from a servile condition. It is the nagging sense of servile status that, among other things, qualifies Boysie's success. For his "business," as he calls it grandly, is that of office cleaner, which he euphemistically refers to as "janitorial service"—and *he* is the only member of his so-called firm. His awareness that, in spite of his outward success, he has not essentially changed his condition of servility, is shown when he reflects: "Imagine! Most men and women too, go out every morning to work, wearing business clothes, nice clothes. And I go to work at night, wearing old clothes, as if I am a blasted cockroach!" In order to counteract this sense of inferiority, and to feel that he is truly a part of the country which has given him material security, Boysie tries to make himself over into a Canadian. This means denying his blackness and West Indianness. He stops going to the Mercury Club, a West Indian meeting place, and burns all his records of West Indian music and jazz, except for

Miles Davis's *Milestones*. His cultural and psychological confusion is further reflected in the fact that he later regrets, secretly, not having also kept back The Mighty Sparrow's "Congoman," a calypso about "three white women traveling through Africa" who are ambiguously eaten by savages, the savages thereby becoming the envy of the calypsonian. Boysie's attraction to this calypso shows that deep down inside him he still feels a need to assert himself as a black man, to enjoy a sense of "black power." And, of course, the meaning of the calypso for him and the sense of power which it gives him are inseparable from its language.

> Edward Baugh. *ACLALS Bulletin.* 5, 3 (December 1980), pp. 3–4

Clarke's closeness to [his protagonist, the poet-politician John] Moore in *The Prime Minister* creates some doubt as to how clearly he himself perceives Moore's failure. Yet Clarke raises some important issues through Moore. What is the poet's role in an ex-colony? Should he try to provide leadership through his poetry or through political action? Or should he divorce his writing from society entirely? *The Prime Minister* remains pessimistic about the ability of literature to effect change, though it is ambivalent about the power of the written word. No one reads John Moore's poetry, but the newspaper runs the country. Is Clarke suggesting that the writer who genuinely wishes to contribute to his country's real development (as opposed to the development of underdevelopment) should turn to journalism or music, to the popular forms that are reaching the people because they employ their language? But if he is, then why does he continue to write novels? Because he is trying to change the novel form, to make it more accessible as a popular genre, reflecting political concerns and challenging "literary standards of the colonization period." The powerful writing in *The Prime Minister* records the language of the people, particularly Kwame's speeches. As John Moore recognizes in a rare moment of insight: "The speech had ceased to be a political harangue and had become a work of art. . . ." Its strength mocks the false sentimentality of John Moore's lyrical evocations of "the blessed woman with her black beauty." If one could be sure that Clarke meant his readers to see John Moore as a false poet, then all would be well, but Clarke carries ambiguity to the point of confusion. . . .

Clarke's concern in *The Prime Minister* is to find a creatively violent language to challenge the old Miltonic rhythms that still hold John Moore's imagination in sway, but Clarke himself seems moved by some nostalgia for these European forms and by some fear of where violence in the language may lead him, so that *The Prime Minister* leaves us in limbo.

> Diana Brydon. *Canadian Literature.* 95 (Winter 1982), p. 184

In Austin Clarke's *Amongst Thistles and Thorns* a sonorous dialect is used simultaneously for comic effect and to register social protest. In one episode, Nathan feels that he is qualified to describe the limiting society to his woman Ruby: "I have come to a damn serious understanding during my travels in and around this blasted past tense village." The conversation occurs when Nathan and Ruby are considering sending their son to the high school. Nathan argues that there is no hope of any but the least-considered white-collar jobs for the educated black man. . . . The zest with which

Nathan puts this case and the rhythmic insistence of his language might be thought to distract from the force of the protest. But this would be true if direct protest were Clarke's sole intention. In fact, Nathan is an irresponsible character and his intention is to regain the favor of Ruby by attacking the things that threaten to thwart the boy. There is a protest element in his speech which is part of an authorial intention, but it is emphatically in the background.

> Kenneth Ramchand. *The West Indian Novel and Its Back-ground* (London: Heinemann, 1983), pp. 110–11

In Clarke, the realist and the idealist are always in a state of tension, comparable with the dual images of Canada and the Caribbean in his work. Indeed those dual images, those ironically balanced views of the real and the idealized, are themselves symptoms of the moral tension within Clarke's own artistic imagination. In essence, Clarke's art is rooted in tension, in his deep but inspired ambivalence towards his two societies—their myths, ideals, and cultural traditions. This all results in a network of finely balanced ironies in the comparison and contrast of the two, and in reenacting the conflicts within each of them. The complex of ironic analogies and contrasts goes beyond cultural groups as such. Clarke also focuses on individual attitudes and the relationships which symbolize their immediate cultural milieux while representing universal experiences—especially in matters of race, sex, material ambitions, and political power. . . .

The tensions between satiric outrage and idealistic vision have remained fairly constant throughout Clarke's career as a writer. From a moral point of view, the differences in tone and mood are often more apparent than real. Hence, the ebullient atmosphere that seems to characterize an early work like [*Amongst Thistles and Thorns*] does not really disguise the brooding tragedy of lost innocence. And the moral idealism which envisions the corruption of innocence as tragedy is identical to the grim short stories which have recently savaged Canadians; for the latter, too, have corrupted their own ideals. Given this basic constancy in Clarke's moral viewpoint, we must look to his choice of topics for a sense of overall pattern in his work. The pattern is basically chronological: the choice of topics shifts from peasant poverty in Barbados, in the earliest fiction, thence to immigrant experiences in Canada, and finally, the probing analysis of Canadian and Caribbean nationhood.

> Lloyd W. Brown. *El Dorado and Paradise: Canada and the Caribbean in Austin Clarke's Fiction* (Parkersburg, Iowa: Caribbean Books, 1989), pp. 7–8

After the publication of *The Prime Minister*, Clarke turned his hand to what he perceives to be the first volume of his memoirs, *Growing Up Stupid under the Union Jack*, in which he recounts his early experiences in rural Barbados, concluding with his leaving Combermere School for Harrison College, Barbados's prestigious senior high school. The many dramatic scenes, the lively dialogue, and the narrative pace invite the reader to parallel this memoir with Clarke's novels. Clarke renders vividly details of time, place, customs, and habits. And he evokes, not just recalls, his moods and feelings. The work points up how much *Amongst Thistles and Thorns* issued from Clarke's own boyhood experiences.

After a gap of five years, Clarke published in quick succession two volumes of stories: *When Women Rule* and *Nine Men Who*

*Laughed*. Of the eight stories in *When Women Rule*, five have the familiar working-class West Indian protagonist struggling to find his place in Canadian society. These stories are about men rendered impotent as much by their inhospitable environment as by wives, friends, and their own self-hatred. The other three are about working-class white Canadians, who, like the protagonist of ''The Collector,'' resent the incursion of immigrants, yearning for a time when Canada was ''pure.''. . .

Clarke's novel *Proud Empires* looks back at the Barbados politics of the 1950s. Boy, a thirteen-year-old high school student, prepares for a scholarship examination in the middle of a national election, which proves to be a rite of passage for him. It opens his eyes to the corruption and treachery of island politics. But Clarke is less concerned with Boy's development than with the reprehensible conduct of the politicians and the distorted values of the middle class. At the end of the novel Boy, who has gone to study in Toronto (where inevitably, like Clarke's other immigrant characters, he experiences racism), returns to the island and allows himself to be persuaded to enter politics. But Boy's experiences are so cursorily given and his character so sketchily portrayed that it is not clear exactly what he has learned about politics and what he can contribute politically. Characteristically *Proud Empires* has many fine episodes and scintillating dialogue, employing the rhythm and idiom of Barbados English, which helps considerably to bring the characters to life. The novel confirms that Clarke's strength as a novelist lies not so much in his probing the psyche and inner development of his protagonists as in capturing the subtleties of the social and political behavior of his Barbadian characters whether at home or abroad.

> Victor J. Ramraj. In Bernth Lindfors and Reinhard Sander, eds. *Dictionary of Literary Biography,* Vol 125 (Detroit: Gale Research, 1993), pp. 32–33

BIBLIOGRAPHY

*The Survivors of the Crossing*, 1964; *Amongst Thistles and Thorns*, 1965; *The Meeting Point*, 1967; *When He Was Free and Young and He Used to Wear Silks*, 1971; *Storm of Fortune*, 1973; *The Bigger Light*, 1975; *The Prime Minister*, 1977; *Growing Up Stupid under the Union Jack: A Memoir*, 1980; *Short Stories of Austin Clark*, 1984; *When Women Rule*, 1985; *The Confused Bewilderment of Martin Luther King & the Idea of Non-Violence as a Political Tactic*, 1986; *Nine Men Who Laughed*, 1986; *Proud Empires*, 1986; *In This City*, 1992; *There Are No Elders*, 1993; *A Passage Back Home: A Personal Reminiscence of Samuel Selvon*, 1994; *The Origin of Waves*, 1997

# CLIFF, Michelle (1946–)
## Jamaica

Michelle Cliff's *Claiming an Identity They Taught Me to Despise* deals head-on with the identity issue even to the expressive titling of her book. It is a lyrical, somewhat autobiographical exploration into identity with gender and heritage composing this identity. Landscape, history, family, events, places, all become features of her exploration. The movement of the book mirrors the migratory pattern, beginning in the Caribbean and childhood and moving to adulthood and America. The sections entitled ''Obsolete Geography'' and ''Filaments'' particularly typify this theme. In the first, we get an extended catalog of Caribbean fruits, vegetation, details of day-to-day experience like the waxing of parlor floors, the burying of umbilical cords, the slaughtering of domestic animals. Much of the identification with ''home'' comes from the rural grandmother who maintains continuity with homeland and whose entire being conveys the multifaceted composition of Caribbean society. We see her, however, caught up in the conflict of being privileged, yet poor, white-skinned but culturally Caribbean. Her mother is a distant, intangible, liminal presence in her life. The contradictions of surface appearance versus reality, of camouflage and passing are explored. . . . The hybrid Creoleness that is essentially the Caribbean, the necessity of accepting all facets of experience, history and personhood in the definition of a self become integrated in her consciousness of her own identity. Personal history, family history, and a people's history and culture all converge.

> Carole Boyce Davies. In Carole Boyce Davies and Elaine Savory Fido, eds. *Out of the Kumbla: Caribbean Women and Literature* (Trenton, New Jersey: Africa World Press, 1990), pp. 63–64

*Bodies of Water* is peopled with misfits, the lonely and forgotten, but the feel of [Cliff's] stories is more monotonous than [Pauline] Melville's [in *Shapeshifter*], and the cruelty of life more relentless. Her style is less quirky, but the stories are rich and sensual nonetheless, full of sights and sounds and smells: ''Her room, her pink expanse, smelled of urine and bay rum and the wet sugar which bound the tamarind balls. Ancestral scents.''

History, both personal and political, underpins many of the characters and their actions. ''A Hanged Man'' is a beautifully crafted evocation of the days of slavery and the human confusion engendered by brutality: a woman awaits ''fifty lashes and charge to account.'' The man to be paid for beating her has hung himself from his own whipping post—an incident Cliff has based on historical fact. In this story, as in others, the author abandons sequential narrative in a way that seems casual but is, in fact, minutely calculated. In ''Screen Memory,'' an actress recalls her upbringing in a series of bright, eclectic pictures. The thread is hard to follow but the style is apposite for a tale of remembrance and loss. The reader is left with strong visual images, and a vague impression of pain. Many of the protagonists are looking back at the past, towards the future or around the present. There are insights into life cycles; birth, aging, death; a young girl forced to care for her grandmother ''Resented the old woman as a portent—this is what little girls turn into.'' Alongside rich physical description, Cliff also uses scene setting as comment. ''Election Day'' shows two women in a queue for a polling booth as Ronald Reagan is about to be returned to office. The story has no overt political content, but the situation of the women is a wry note in the social tragedy they discuss.

> Louise Doughty. *Times Literary Supplement.* February 23, 1990. p. 203

From beginning to end, *Bodies of Water*, Michelle Cliff's first collection of short stories, is shadowed by dark but subtle images of

the child immigrant, sometimes the first-person narrator of these wonderfully rich and disturbing tales. This Jamaican-born author seems to understand, as perhaps only one who was a child immigrant herself can, the complex pain of the child whose parents have sent her away to another country for her own good. . . .

Each story in this collection tells a tale of abandonment, sometimes motivated purely by callousness, sometimes by racism, sexism, or homophobia, sometimes for the good of the child. Regardless of the reason, it is the abandonment that leaves such individuals damaged and scarred; these are the people Cliff celebrates. She presents them not as passive players in their dismal fates, but as people who struggle (though more quietly than not) to escape their condition even when escape is not possible. . . .

These bodies of water lapping against the shores of our common world remind us of human indifference and cruelty, but tell us too of the courage of those we would harm and of their will to survive. Michelle Cliff uses spare and taut language that sharply underscores the harsh realities of the worlds she recreates. *Bodies of Water* is a remarkable collection, a testimony to human endurance and the triumph of the spirit.

> Elizabeth Nunez-Harrell. *New York Times Book Review.* September 23, 1990, p. 22

A nun avenges seventy-five years of abuse by torching her family's Winnebago; a black woman bleaches herself into a checkerboard sideshow freak; a Vietnam vet wearing a hat of yesterday's news wanders in a forest of shell-shocked men: such is Michelle Cliff's landscape of fragmented souls in her short-story collection, *Bodies of Water.* . . .

Many of the stories feature abandoned children and disoriented adults, somehow set apart by a deeply wounding experience. Operating on a continually shifting foundation, where broken homes are more the rule than the exception, the characters often violate traditional social mores in their restless search for validation and wholeness. Rich intertextual references enliven the stories and illustrate how an individual's history can encompass many lives, as references from one ''life'' intrude into another. In ''A Woman Who Plays Trumpet Is Deported,'' set in the 1930s and 1940s, an African-American female musician travels to Paris, where ''They pay her to play. She stays in their hotel. Eats their food in a clean, well-lighted place. Pisses in their toilet. . . . No strange fruit hanging in the Tuileries.''

The narrative voices in *Bodies of Water* are quietly scattered, carefully avoiding certain disclosures, and Cliff's writing not only accommodates but even simulates this quality. Her sentences are choppy prose-poems, alternately flowing with the ease of free association and halting as pain becomes too sharp for conscious articulation: the effect is a sort of syntactical breakdown reflecting the internal state of her characters. If the reader is often puzzled and must struggle to piece together these narratives, it is a confirmation of Cliff's success at portraying characters who mystify even themselves.

> Laura Frost. *Review of Contemporary Fiction.* 11, 1 (Spring 1991), pp. 317–18

Cliff's first novel [*Abeng*] is concerned with the deconstruction of the Eurocentric phenomenon in Jamaica as a prelude to unearthing the repressed Afro-Caribbean experience in the island. Thus the reconstruction of elided black identities and African fragments long lost in the colonial archive is as urgent as the deconstruction of modernism and modernity. . . .

The uniqueness of Cliff's aesthetics lies in her realization that the fragmentation, silence, and repression that mark the life of the Caribbean subject under colonialism must be confronted not only as a problem to be overcome but also as a condition of possibility— as a license to dissimulate and to affirm difference—in which an identity is created out of the chaotic colonial and postcolonial history. In writing about the ways in which Caribbean subjects strive to subjectify themselves within the commodified space and time of colonial modernity, Cliff finds discursive value in the very fragmentation that other commentators have seen as the curse of West Indian history. According to Cliff, fragmentation can indeed function as a strategy of identity since the colonized writer struggles ''to get wholeness from fragmentation while working within fragmentation, producing work which may find its strength in its depiction of fragmentation, through form as well as content.'' . . .

Through deliberate strategies of intertextuality, Cliff reifies the linguistic and ideological conflicts that arise when colonialist discourse is challenged by the vernacular, when official versions of history are questioned by the silent history of the poor and powerless. By establishing the antagonistic relationship between linguistic forms (especially the oral and the written), and through the interpolation of time frames and the spatialization of historical events, she represents both the value and limits of fragmentation as a condition of history and as a strategy of representation. Furthermore, as a narrative of turbulence and crisis, *Abeng* is not intended simply to evoke the value of otherness, but also to provide a genealogy of the loss of value and speech in the colonial subject. By dispersing the historical narratives of colonialism, Cliff recenters, and gives value, to margins and edges. . . . [A] narrative whose goal is to disorient the reader from entrenched forms of modernism, *Abeng* finds its power in its parasitic and subversive relationship to previous texts, which it appropriates and then spits out, clearing a space for alternative systems of representation.

Simon Gikandi. *Writing in Limbo: Modernism and Caribbean Literature* (Ithaca, New York: Cornell University Press, 1992), pp. 233–36

Clare is clearly the protagonist of Michelle Cliff's 1987 novel *No Telephone to Heaven*, yet a large early section of the book focuses equally on Clare's mother Kitty who is Jamaican-born and never wants to live anywhere else. While still in Jamaica, Kitty marries Boy Savage and has two daughters. But then Kitty's mother, Miss Mattie, dies, and Boy seizes the opportunity to move his family to New York. For Kitty, the new life is a living death. She misses the climate, the foods, the music and patois, the customs and traditions of Jamaica. With no warning and no explanation, Kitty moves back to the islands, taking Clare's dark-skinned sister with her but leaving Clare and her father, both of whom can presumably make lives for themselves because they can ''pass for white.''

For Clare, however, Kitty's abrupt rejection is traumatic. She is left unmothered, while still a child, ''not feeling much of anything, except a vague dread that she belongs nowhere.'' Between Clare and her father a gulf exists that only widens with time, Boy Savage

having embraced his adopted country when he arrived in Brooklyn and completing his rejection of all things Jamaican by eventually marrying a white New Yorker of Italian descent. After Kitty dies, Clare's sister comes to visit in New York. But there is no bond between the two young women, and Clare is unable to find out from her sister why their mother took one of them and left the other, Clare, without so much as a word of farewell or explanation. Feeling rootless and alone, Clare begins an odyssey that takes her from New York to London and eventually across Europe, with intermittent returns to Jamaica. As Cliff writes about her protagonist, ''There are many bits and pieces to her, for she is composed of fragments. In this journey, she hopes, is her restoration.''

During her brief trips to Jamaica, Clare stays with relatives on her father's side of the family. These relatives are in fact quite proud of her when she moves to London and enrolls in university there, and they always encourage her to make the best of this wonderful opportunity. Clare, though, thinks sardonically of her motives: ''Choosing London with the logic of a Creole. This was the mother country. The country by whose grace her people existed in the first place.'' At the same time Clare's only true friend in Jamaica, a transvestite who calls himself Harry/Harriet, tries urgently to persuade Clare that she must return permanently to Jamaica, her true home. She resists Harry/Harriet's urging, yet she finds London no more hospitable than New York: ''I feel like a shadow,'' she says, ''like I could float through my days without ever touching . . . anyone.'' Still resisting a return to Jamaica, Clare becomes involved with a black man from Alabama, a Vietnam veteran who carries a leg wound that will never heal. Together, both of them fleeing demons that they can hardly name, they embark on a cross-European journey. As might be expected, they are unable to succor each other. After a miscarriage, and seriously ill from a resulting infection and fever, Clare returns to Jamaica for good. At this time, she is thirty-six years old.

The Jamaica to which Clare returns is ravaged by poverty, crime, and civil insurrection. Yet in the midst of all this, Clare begins to find her roots. She finds the way to her grandmother's house, now in ruins but also belonging to Clare. Nearby is a river where, as a child, she watched washerwomen at work, slapping the clothes on rocks worn as smooth as silk. Here, too, she often swam, and in remembrance she does so again: ''The importance of this water came back to her. Sweet on an island surrounded by salt. She shut her eyes and let the cool of it wash over her naked body, reaching up into her as she opened her legs. Rebaptism.''

This was not, though, a place where Clare came alone as a child. Thus she remembers that this river place was where her mother, Kitty, ''was alive, came alive,'' and Clare thinks, ''I was fortunate I knew her here.'' But then she stops, corrects herself: ''No, I was blessed to have her here. Her passion of place. Her sense of the people. Here is her; leave it at that.''

Indeed, ''here is her'' for Clare Savage. In returning to her mother's land, Clare finds her mother. Equally important, she finds herself. At one point an old island woman thinks that Clare *is* Kitty, and this seems to Clare an appropriate sign that the years and miles separating mother and daughter are diminished. In response to a question as to why she returned, Clare says, ''I returned to this island to mend . . . to bury . . . my mother. . . . I returned to this island because there was nowhere else. . . . I could live no longer in borrowed countries, on borrowed time.'' Having found her mother and herself, Clare goes on to make a personal and political commitment to Jamaica and its people. For the first time since leaving Kingston many years ago, Clare has found the place where she belongs.

Ann R. Morris and Margaret M. Dunn. In Susheila Nasta, ed. *Motherlands* (New Brunswick: Rutgers University Press, 1992), pp. 232–34

Michelle Cliff chooses the *abeng* as an emblem for her book [*Abeng*] because, like the conch, the book is an instrument of communication whose performative function seems to be valorized. The story she tells is meant to inform Jamaicans and non-Jamaicans alike, and she goes to great lengths to demystify the past in order to imagine, invent, and rewrite a different collective and personal history for the protagonist. The narrative weaves the personal and the political together, allowing the protagonist Clare Savage, who is but a thinly disguised alter ego of the author, to negotiate the conflicting elements of her cultural and familial background. She thus succeeds in reclaiming the multifaceted identity her family and society had "taught [her] to despise," namely, her mixed racial heritage, her femininity, and her homosexuality.

The narrative sets up an uneasy and duplicitous relationship with its audience. It begins with the standard disclaimer, "This work is a work of fiction, and any resemblance to persons alive or dead is entirely coincidental," despite its clearly autobiographical themes, which echo and repeat similar themes treated from a first-person perspective in Cliff's poetry and essays. But *Abeng* discloses far more about the author than does the poetry, while engaging the reader in a dialogue that confronts the fictions of self-representation. It would seem that, for Cliff, the third person is a self-protective device that creates sufficient distance, and thus helps her deal with the burden of history. Acts of disclosure are always painful, and since Cliff admits that she has labored "under the ancient taboos of the assimilated," the "hegemony of the past" cannot easily be broken by a straightforward act of self-portraiture. Like German writer Christa Wolf and Chinese-American writer Maxine Hong Kingston, Cliff uses postmodern fictional techniques that, in the words of Sidonie Smith, "challenge the ideology of individualism and with it the ideology of gender."

Françoise Lionnet. In Sidonie Smith and Julia Watson, eds. *De/Colonizing the Subject* (Minneapolis: University of Minnesota Press, 1992), pp. 323–24

The contemporary West Indian novel reflects a somewhat different sensibility than its predecessor: a significant percentage of today's West Indian writers are women, and they have recast the familiar project of articulating a national identity to reflect their specific experiences as women. Michelle Cliff's novels are critical to working out the problems of race and gender in this regard because they reflect her search for an Afrocentric identity through her planters and slave owners; thus, the search for a black history/identity is intimately bound up with a latent feminism as well as with a revolutionary social consciousness. . . .

*No Telephone to Heaven* builds upon *Abeng* by deconstructing the reductive gender/race ideology in the former so that it is not solely white, male, European culture which is the focal point of conflict but language itself, wherein gender and geopolitical categories are both created and fixed in memory. To attempt to imitate the "reality" of these categories thus becomes a futile project. In

the final analysis, it is discourse which creates meaning; by creating an alternative "reality" in a narrative structure which both extends and engages West Indian and European representations, the text attempts not an imaginary nor an imitation universe but a new kind of reality.

Belinda Edmondson. *Callaloo*. 16, 1 (Winter 1993), pp. 182, 190

Michelle Cliff's *No Telephone to Heaven* (1987) and Merle Collin's *Angel* (1987), like many other postcolonial novels, indirectly parallel the formation of the young self to that of the developing nation. *No Telephone to Heaven*, the story of Clare Savage's development into revolutionary consciousness and her involvement in a symbolic act of revolution in Michael Manley's Jamaica, and *Angel*, a novel about a girl growing up during the people's revolutionary government of Grenada, share a similar authorial project—the possibility of revolutionary social transformation. When Cliff and Collins attempt to figure this transformation through the reconceptualization of the established genre of the Bildungsroman, however, they textualize their projects in significantly different ways. Through playing off the conventions of the novel against those of several other genres—history, the epistolary, allegory, autobiography, testimonio—Cliff and Collins expose the complexity of the contradictions within generic conventions.

Precisely because *Angel* and *No Telephone to Heaven* are written for different audiences, from distinct class perspectives and historical contexts, they tell very different stories about the possibility of real social transformation. Cliff's text is predominantly allegorical while Collins structures her novel on a predominantly historical figuration. . . .

The issue of language choice is . . . central to postcolonial reconceptualizations and to any attempt at identifying an implied audience in the Caribbean context. What initially characterizes writing in the Caribbean is what George Steiner calls being "linguistically unhoused" for the writer must mediate between a "metropolitan" standard and the creole languages of her childhood and environment. Cliff's decision, then, to rely primarily on standard English and only cursorily to employ patois, not only marks the class/culture division between her narrator and the Jamaican characters who populate her fiction, but also signals the primary audience for whom the novel is written. Collins's choice of Grenadian creole, the language of the "subaltern" class, as the novel's language may also signify, among other purposes, her concern that the novel be accessible to those of that class who can read.

*Angel*, moreover, foregrounds the cautionary element inscribed in the original Bildungsroman, an aspect of the genre that is almost totally lost in the symbolism of *No Telephone to Heaven*. While *Angel* ultimately consists of a call to arms, *No Telephone to Heaven*, despite its critique of the People's National Party (PNP), does not want to bring Jamaicans together for another experiment in democratic socialism. . . .

When contrasted with Cliff's novel can be said to figure . . . class privilege by reinforcing the split in the linguistic practices which separate the "educated" from the "less cultured" classes. If the language choice Cliff makes signals her intended audience, then, we might say that she addresses very educated Caribbeans, at home or in exile (like herself) and a North-American readership.

Cliff's implied audience is also familiar with the European tradition of the *Bildungsroman*, for Clare, like Jamaica Kincaid's Annie John, exists in dialogue with *Jane Eyre*. Like Jane Eyre, Clare is motherless; she is solitary and left to wander, having "no relations to speak of except [like Jane Eyre] an uncle across the water." Cliff, however, goes a step further than Kincaid and incorporates Bertha Mason into Clare's intertextual identity: "Captive. Ragout. Mixture. Confused. Jamaican. Caliban. Carib. Cannibal. Cimarron. All Bertha. All Clare."

Clare feels closer to "wild-maned Bertha." She remembers how her father was forever trying to tame her hair: "she refused it; he called her Medusa. Do you intend to turn men to stone, daughter?" Centred on the figure of Medusa is the disclosure of Clare's internalization of sexual and racial oppression, the extent to which she has been forced to deny both her (homo) sexuality and her Africanness. As Susan Bowers points out, Medusa's mythical image has functioned like a magnifying mirror to reflect and focus Western thought as it relates to women, including how women think about themselves. Rediscovering and remembering the vitality and dark power of the mythological figure of Medusa, that primary trope of female sexuality, is as important for Cliff as Jamaica's revolutionary project itself. Attempting to trace the unconscious of the text, we might actually see these projects as related. By reworking the narratives that connect and separate mothers from daughters, moreover, Cliff's novel goes as far as to suggest that a return to a pre-oedipal, preverbal moment of origin can provide an instrument for binding the fragments of self.

Maria Helena Lima. *Ariel: A Review of International English Literature*. 24, 1 (January 1993), pp. 35–53

Much like some postmodern literature, Cliff's narratives combine multiple histories and places in order to imagine an alternative space in which different worlds coexist. The multiple components of Cliff's texts, picked up from her travels between nations, races, and cultures, refuse to fit into any *one* of the existing nations, races, and cultures. The question then inevitably arises: Does not fitting into one mean fitting into *many* or fitting into *none*? Cliff explores both possibilities.

In *The Land of Look Behind*, her 1985 collection of poetry and essays, Cliff describes the mulatto as living proof of interracial sex, usually the white man's transgressions outside the color line. Because of the prevalence of this narrative of rape and miscegenation, Cliff claims that many of the lighter fathers have broods of "outside" children who come and go by the back door. These darker children are "outside" because they are produced in extramarital alliances. They remain outside the realm of manners, outside the family—attending different schools, distanced from the light-skinned children in order to hide the shame of their father's border-crossing. This going "outside" is subversive in that it questions the superiority of white lovers, denies racist repulsion on the sexual level, and decenters white-centered power structures by exposing the center's involvement with "outsiders." Perhaps the outside is so fundamental to the status quo that the two are interdependent: The status quo is a product of their hidden proximity. In a racial materialization that prefigures the Derridean concept, the inside seems to be constructed by its relations with the outside.

Cliff analyzes the blurring lines of racial demarcation in Jamaica, as the light-skinned or "colored" Jamaicans take over the role of oppressor from the white British colonizers. In her well-known essay "If I Could Write This in Fire, I Would Write This in Fire," Cliff considers what happens when the "house nigger" assumes the position of master. In this changing of the guard, the biracial Jamaican crosses the traditional lines of correlation between (white) race and leadership, (European) nationality and conquest. Cliff claims that, at this point, "unreality overtook reality," meaning perhaps that biracial Jamaican "coloreds" constructed an image of the colonizer in themselves, and a simulation of white dominance overtook the authority of the "real" white colonizer (*Land*). Those with traces of both white and black racial origins also have the privilege to come and go between Jamaica, England, and the United States, replicating the triangular trade and reflecting the triangular patterns of cultural and economic neo-imperialism that exist in Jamaica today. The light-skinned middle class is endowed with a "double vision" much like W.E.B. Du Bois's "double-consciousness," but more complex in that it includes a view of colonization from both sides of a crumbling racial and national divide. Cliff concludes her essay with an evocation of the multiplicity of identities within Jamaican subjects: "We/they/I connect and disconnect," blurring like the Rasta "I and I," self with "Jah." Just as the Rastafarian conceives of his/her identity only in relation to "Jah," a transcendental or Godlike being, the biracial subject defines his/her identity in relation to another: an other race, an other self, an other being.

Within this affirmed duality, Cliff echoes Iola Leroy by subverting the traditional "colored" urge to emphasize the white and by wishing that she were darker. In "Artificial Skin," she expresses the wish that she could purchase "Artificial Skin" or melanin, casting racial identity as a surface that must be bought, rather than born into. Her desire to metamorphose would transform race into a mutable artifice, prefiguring postmodern identity yet differing from postmodernism by maintaining culturally, politically, and historically specific ties. Cliff notes the historic and demographic accuracy of her racial fluidity and multiplicity. Race is not decentered only in fiction, but in the "real" world, too. Her poem "Europe becomes blacker" claims that not only is the human makeup of contemporary Europe racially and nationally diverse, but it was "always dark" (*Land*). . . .

In her novel *Abeng* (1984), Cliff confronts the tragic mulatto narrative head-on and enacts in the realm of fiction those theories she avows in her essays. The Savage family is a racial and national hybrid, with origins scattered throughout the Miskito Indians, the Ashanti, and the British. The family even attends two different churches: Anglican and Baptist. Clare Savage, Cliff's semi-autobiographical heroine, is both black and white, pale and deeply colored. While her white friend Miss Winifred claims that "coons and buckra people were not meant to mix their blood" and "only sadness comes from mixture," Clare denies this pessimistic outlook. For Clare, everyone is mixed, and Jamaica is founded on "all kinds of mixture" (*Abeng*). Rather than fearing or attempting to hide this fact—as [Pauline] Hopkins's characters do in *Hagar's Daughter*—Clare, and Cliff, affirm this mixture as the true and empowering nature of Jamaican people. The origins of this culture are polyphonic: a multiracial and multinational subversion of singular notions of nationality and cultural origin. . . .

In *Free Enterprise* (1993), Cliff continues to explore the meaning of biracialism, to celebrate the Africanist elements within the mulatto tradition, to emphasize resistance (Granny Nanny, John Brown), and to criticize the bourgeois *gens inconnu* (unknown people) who deny their black ancestry and efface their own histories. Her light-skinned heroine Annie Christmas, like Clare Savage before her, rejects the European pretensions of her family and applies Mr. Bones's Liquid Blackener to "her carefully inbred skin." In the case of Annie, the rebellions of one daughter overturn the racial breeding of her ancestors. In this text, Cliff addresses the mulatto tradition directly: Annie echoes [William Wells] Brown's *Clotel* as she cross-dresses to help instrument a slave revolt. She meets Frances Harper face-to-face and criticizes her privileging of the "light-skinned female Christian octoroon" (Iola Leroy) because she ignores "the vast majority of our people." While Harper required recourse to the "exceptional" biracial subject in order to "wring hearts dry; white ones, at least," Cliff rejects this tendency. Annie denies these Iola-esque elements of her identity with skin blackener, "her back turned on *gens inconnu*," and a careful association with rebels and lepers, rather than the "Talented Tenth." Cliff favors those characters who, although they are "for all intents and purposes, white," seek out blacks and long for darker skin. She also emphasizes those elements of disguise that empower her characters and enable them to construct fluid identities. . . .

Cliff's collection of stories *Bodies of Water* (1990) also forces a reconceptualization of racial constitution, while remaining more clearly rooted in the tragic Zoe tradition. "Burning Bush" envisions a woman; the Girl from Martinique, who is biracial, black and white, because she paints patches on her body with whitewash in order to attract a crowd at the circus. Although she tries to pass her dual color off as an exotic practice from her native land, it is really a form of self-camouflage, designed to earn a livelihood. The "patchwork" woman considers this means of self-exhibition as a way to escape prostitution, as a more empowering form of economically motivated self-exploitation. The skin color is a way out for her. This "particolored" "checkerboard of a woman" produces a baby whose racial duality also reflects "certain practices of her native land." But these practices seem more real. The baby is born light-skinned, and the mother hopes that her skin will darken with age, perhaps to efface the traces of the "practice" of miscegenation. . . .

Cliff is never fully celebratory of biracialism, and her readers are unable to forget that racial mixture often began (and begins) with rape. Indeed, despite the foreground that imagines strategies for resistance, conquest remains in the background.

The repeated incidents of rape in these narratives make the story of the tragic mulatto a primary target for feminist analysis. Cliff returns to the tragic mulatto and criticizes the gendered oppressions of miscegenation, which targeted women as the objects of sexual desire and as the sources of "bastard" and "mixed-breed" reproduction. She also re-imagines the biracial woman, through both Clare and Zoe, as independent, empowered, resisting, and woman-loving. Their mothers are dark and teach them to love, rather than to feel alienated by, dark skin. Thus she exposes and condemns the tragedy, while envisioning a feminist alternative to tragedy. A feminist biracial subject would take advantage of her duality, her multiple potential, and play between different realms. Women like Clare use their biracial advantage to benefit the revolution with economic resources and knowledge from two cultures. In addition, they subvert singular categories of identity and chart new space for shifting, multiple, feminist subjectivities. . . .

If the interpenetration between races has lead to an erosion of racial differentiation, it has also caused an erosion of racial categories themselves. For example, "mulatto" has disappeared as a distinct identity category today and instead describes most African American identities, blending and destabilizing racial identification. It still holds power as a concept, however, and it carries a cultural memory that influences our perceptions of biracialism today. Once we get beyond the idea that biracialism is a tragedy, once we look forward to and imagine a future in which biracialism need not tell a story of rape and exclusion, we can develop new political strategies based on multiple identities. Biracial writers such as Cliff have access to multiple spheres of reference—languages (French, English, and patois), powerful traditions (obeah, African goddesses, Christianity), and histories of resistance (Granny Nanny's slave revolt, maroon colonies)—that are as yet unrecognized by most Americans. The non-singularity of biracial identity resists circumscription by a monocultural power structure that cannot accommodate multiplicity in a single subject, that does not attend to the actions of non-whites, and that cannot interpret the language and traditions of the "outside" group.

Cliff characterizes the Caribbean as "a confused universe, . . . with no center and no outward edge. Where almost everything was foreign" (*Free Enterprise*). In this vision, Caribbean culture is a composite of foreign cultures, with no governing center and no line of demarcation. In the Caribbean and in the U.S., the colonizer is at least as foreign as the darker-skinned peoples it has pushed to the margins. Cliff's paradigm forces us to rethink the history of cultural domination. The distinction between inside and outside becomes "confused" when no single culture can claim central status or delineate an outer boundary. The foreignness within problematizes the attempt to exclude "foreigners." Cliff bridges margin and center in her postcolonial universe (which exposes the exteriority of the dominant culture), in her transnational politics (which exceed singular concepts of the nation), and in her biracial characters (who subvert rigid concepts of racial identity). Looking backward, Cliff juxtaposes history and fiction, amplifying some events and decentering others.

Suzanne Bost. *African American Review*. 32, 4 (Winter 1998), pp. 673–86

BIBLIOGRAPHY
*Claiming an Identity They Taught Me to Despise*, 1980; *Abeng*, 1984; *The Land of Look Behind: Prose and Poetry*, 1985; *No Telephone to Heaven*, 1987; *Bodies of Water*, 1990; *Free Enterprise*, 1993; *The Store of a Million Items: Stories*, 1998

# CLIFTON, Lucille (1936–)
**United States**

There is a particular sort of movement rhetoric—it could belong either to the black movement or to the women's movement—which subverts the ambiguity of literature. Lucille Clifton avoids it much of the time. It must be a difficult thing to be a black writer in an age which demands political polarization of everyone—especially those who belong to oppressed groups. At times that demand for ideological clarification must interfere with a writer's freedom to be herself in all her complex selfhood. Lucille Clifton's definition of blackness is an organic part of her consciousness and therefore rightly pervades her work, but when she takes to self-conscious black mythmaking, she loses the subtlety which is her greatest strength. . . .

Whatever disappointments I have with *Good News about the Earth* spring mostly from that. Too many poems are agitprop, not art. Too much socialist realism. On second reading, when the shock of Lucille Clifton's perfect lines has been absorbed, some of the poems seem to collapse. The poems about the Panthers, Malcolm X, Eldridge Cleaver, Bobby Seale, Angela Davis, [and] Richard Penniman are artfully written, but they are not much more durable than the headlines which inspired them. They have practically no substance in and of themselves and rely principally upon the gut response of the reader. There is a place for writing like this—both as entertainment and as inspiration. Certainly it moves people, but then so do the most banal popular songs and so do angry slogans.

The question of politics and literature is ancient, and I do not pretend to be able to solve it here. I value Clifton and other black writers for reinterpreting black history, and thus reinterpreting American history, for daring to deal with their own internal racism and self-hatred, but I often feel they do not press their self-knowledge far enough. Surely there is *more* to say about the fantastic history of black/white relations in America (and the world over) than "white ways are the ways of death." A writer is supposed to be first of all a *knower* and a *self-knower*. If a poem contains no more *knowing* than an editorial, something is missing.

Erica Jong. *Parnassus.* 1, 1 (Fall-Winter 1972), pp. 86–87

Lucille Clifton, in her third collection of poems, *An Ordinary Woman*, plays on [a] collective sense of déjà vu, by using the power of everyday objects. She records the riddle of the ordinary with deliberate irony. In the first poem in the book, "In Salem," the "black witches know" that terror is not in weird phases of the moon or the witches' broom or the "wild clock face.". . . This is an extraordinary "ordinary" poem, a homely and particular source of history, of memory, the bread rising as the witch burns and the sinister association made and given its full measure of terror and truth in the emphasis on *ordinary*—the word and the state of mind. . . .

Lucille Clifton seems bent on examining in this book the states of mind, the personal commentary and paraphernalia that become momentous and historical. Her talent is for "news," facts that bloom into profundity or glamour, at best and worst respectively. Her language has flex and determination. She is an *intensifier*, steeped in what [Wallace] Stevens termed the "lentor and solemnity" of commonplace objects. In "At Last We Killed the Roaches," all these elements come together to render a poem like a scream sealed in the walls, a family curse falling with the dead roaches. . . . In one sense, the mnemonic becomes moral. Cleanliness instead of *reminding* us of godliness *is* godliness. Clifton knows this distortion well: if "such cleanliness is grace," then the slaughter of the roaches becomes the bondage and slaughter of the black race—the "tribe was broken" and it was "murder."

Yet despite this awareness, she occasionally, perversely, sets the same demon to work for her. The clock is thrown out the window, but we do not see time fly. It's just not enough, sometimes, the mnemonic: mentioning collard greens and Moses and Ms. Ann—although the words are touchstones and the phrases

reverberate with the authority of common use (the ordinary), they remain strung out and glittering in air like a failed incantation.

Carol Muske. *Parnassus.* 4, 2 (Spring-Summer 1976), pp. 111–13

Lucille Clifton is a soft-spoken poet. She writes verse that does not leap out at you, nor shout expletives and gimmicks to gain attention. A public poet whose use of concrete symbols and language is easily discernible, Lucille Clifton is guided by the dictates of her own consciousness rather than the dictates of form, structure, and audience. She is not an "intellectual" poet, although she does not disdain intellect. She simply prefers to write from her heart. Her poetry is concrete, often witty, sometimes didactic, yet it can be subtle and understated. Her short-lined economical verse is often a grand mixture of simplicity and wisdom. Repeated readings of her work show her to be a poet in control of her material and one who is capable of sustaining a controlling idea with seemingly little effort. Clifton is a poet of a literary tradition which includes such varied poets as Walt Whitman, Emily Dickinson, and Gwendolyn Brooks, who have inspired and informed her work.

Lucille Clifton writes with conviction; she always takes a moral and hopeful stance. She rejects the view that human beings are pawns in the hands of whimsical fate. She believes that we can shape our own destiny and right the wrongs by taking a moral stand. . . .

Her children's books are her most prolific literary product, and no analysis of her work could ignore their overall importance. Her books for children introduce themes, ideas, and points of view that may sometimes find their way into her poetry. It is important to note that she does not greatly alter her style as she moves from one genre to another. Her language remains direct, economical, and simply stated. She does not patronize the children for whom she writes. She gives them credit for being intelligent human beings who do not deserve to be treated differently because of their age. Being the mother of six children must certainly give her material for her books, but it is her respect for children as people and her finely tuned instincts about what is important to them—their fears, their joys—that make her a successful writer of children's literature.

Audrey T. McCluskey. In Mari Evans, ed. *Black Women Writers (1950–1980): A Critical Evaluation* (New York: Doubleday, 1984), pp. 139–40

[Clifton] is effective because, despite consciously limiting her vocabulary, she has defined her audience. She is not out to impress, or to showcase the scope of her lexicon. She is communicating ideas and concepts. She understands that precise communication is not an easy undertaking; language, at its root, seeks to express emotion, thought, action. Most poetry writing (other than the blues) is foreign to the black community. It is nearly impossible to translate to the page the changing linguistic nuances or the subtleties of body language blacks use in everyday conversation; the black writer's task is an extremely complicated and delicate one. But . . . Clifton does not write down to us, nor is she condescending or patronizing with her language. Most of her poems are short and tight, as is her language. Her poems are well-planned creations, and as small as some of them are, they are not cloudy nor rainy with words for words' sake. The task is not to fill the page with letters but to challenge the mind. . . .

Her originality is accomplished with everyday language and executed with musical percussion, pushed to the limits of poetic possibilities. Lucille Clifton is a lover of life, a person who feels her people. Her poems are messages void of didacticism and needless repetition. Nor does she shout or scream the language at you; her voice is birdlike but loud and high enough to pierce the ears of dogs. She is the quiet warrior, and, like the weapons of all good warriors, her weapons can hurt, kill, and protect.

Haki Madhubuti. In Mari Evans, ed. *Black Women Writers (1950–1980): A Critical Evaluation* (New York: Doubleday, 1984), p. 154

Despite the considerable achievements of *Good Times, Good News About the Earth,* and *Generations,* it is with the publication of *An Ordinary Woman* and *Two-Headed Woman* that Clifton strides to center stage among contemporary African-American poets. These two fine collections parse the female sector of African-American life and give vivid testimony to the terse brilliance which alerted readers of her early work to Clifton's enormous potential. Not only do they explore a broad swath of rarely examined experience; they do so in an appealing personal voice with an attractive infusion of self-revelation and wit. By now, all the major contemporary African-American women poets have written verse about women's lives: the mother-daughter dyad, heterosexual relations, oppressive standards of female beauty, and loneliness are common themes. The verse is often autobiographical, its saturation in African and African-American culture is explicit, and its tone varies from aggrieved to nostalgic to exultant. Several things set Clifton's work apart from the strophes of others. First, she has written more poems about women's lives than any other African-American poet except Gwendolyn Brooks. Second, she has consistently done so in the African-American demotic with sinewy diction, a confiding voice, and stark imagery.

With the Kali poems in *An Ordinary Woman,* Clifton makes a bold innovation in poetic presentation of African-American women. Rather than limning heroic embodiments of female power and triumph, or depicting lifelike women victimized by parents, racism, poverty, and sexism, Clifton invokes an aboriginal ebony-faced Indian goddess associated with blood, violence, and murder. Since the paternal slave ancestor Clifton celebrates in her memoir, *Generations,* came from Dahomey, with its well-known tradition of heroic women, Clifton could have crafted poems around an African-based tradition. In turning to Kali, however, she frees herself from the feminist tendency to see women as hapless victims and explores the psychic tensions of an introspective modern woman negotiating the dramatic changes in contemporary attitudes about culture, race, and gender at the same time that she juggles the roles of daughter, sister, artist, wife, and mother. Written in standard English, these lyrics differ from Clifton's earlier work in syntax and diction; they are also tighter and more forceful. Like her earlier work, however, they also employ short lines, few rhymes, brief stanzas, and recurring images of women's blood and bones. . . .

The thematic connections between *Two-Headed Woman* and Clifton's previous verse are immediately apparent. The opening "Homage to Mine" section demonstrates her continuing attention to family and friends and religious themes. In other ways, however, Clifton's latest volume of verse marks some sort of threshold

experience for her. Unlike most other African-American women poets of the 1960s and 1970s, Clifton's marriage has been stable, and she has had six children. None of her verse articulates either the strains between men and women or the loneliness which often characterizes the work of other female poets, and her sons and daughters have been sources of pleasure and affirmation for her.

Andrea Benton Rushing. In Diane Wood Middlebrook and Marilyn Yalom, eds. *Coming to Light: American Women Poets in the Twentieth Century* (Ann Arbor: University of Michigan Press, 1985), pp. 217–19

Fortunately for the world of young people's literature, there are those authors who broaden our realms of experience by representing and exploring African-American culture. Lucille Clifton is one of the most prolific and accomplished of this number. In this context, her work is especially impressive when viewed as an entire oeuvre. Each book works in concert with the others to illuminate aspects of the communities, largely African-American, in which the characters live their lives. Everett Anderson's is one of the lives which is documented through a series of books. An examination of the Everett Anderson stories reveals the range and richness of this youngster's life and of the series book itself. This is especially true when examined within the context of the secondary function (intentional or not) of Clifton's telling of story: the exploration of Afro-American community and consciousness.

Dianne Johnson-Feelings. *CLA Journal.* 14, 3 (Winter 1989), p. 174

Although Clifton, as a children's author, is perhaps best known for her Everett Anderson stories, I find her finest books to be *The Black BC's, The Times They Used to Be,* and *All Us Come Cross the Water.* The latter book, published in 1973, best demonstrates the fact that Clifton's ''children's'' writings are of a piece with her poetry, dignifying the lives of blacks through acts of memory and attention and through a well-wrought vernacular. *All Us Come Cross the Water* begins ''I got this teacher name Miss Wills. This day she come asking everybody to tell where they people come from.'' The main character of the story is called Jim by his teacher, but he calls himself Ujamaa. Like Clifton, he searches for information about his own lineage, consulting Big Mama: ''Big Mama is my Mama's Mama's Mama's Mama. She real old and she don't say much, but she see things cause she born with a veil over her face. That makes it so she can see spirits and things.'' Like Clifton's own family, Big Mama's family came over from Whyday in Dahomey. And like Clifton, whose own spare poetry requires careful attention, Big Mama can be cryptic. . . .

As both her poetry and *All Us Come Cross the Water* illustrate, ownership is linked to language and to naming. Telling the story, choosing the dialect, and picking the name are acts of power with direct consequences in terms of dignity and autonomy. Clifton's acts of naming are *not* the transcendental ''perfect fits'' imagined by Ralph Waldo Emerson, whose Adam-poet gives the ''true'' and ''original'' names to the creatures of the earth. It seems to me that Emerson's ideal is imaginable *only* from a position of power and privilege, not from within a family and a race where names are imposed as a brand and an exercise of power by someone else. Clifton's position as namer gets written in ''the making of poems.'' . . .

In her newest poems, Clifton's revisionary history focuses more insistently on women. In one poem, she rewrites woman's power relationship to God, concluding "i am the good daughter who stays at home / singing and sewing. / when i whisper He strains to hear me and / He does whatever i say." Earlier in her writing, Clifton found herself "turning out of the / white cage. turning out of the / lady cage.". . . Thus, her newest poems continue her work in defining and affirming "us."

Hank Lazer. *Southern Review.* 25, 3 (Summer 1989), pp. 766–69

Lucille Clifton's writing is deceptively simple. The poems are short, unrhymed, the lines typically between four and two beats. The sentences are usually declarative and direct, the punctuation light, the diction a smooth mix of standard English with varying styles and degrees of black vernacular. Almost nothing (including "i" and beginnings of sentences) is capitalized. Some poems have titles, other do not, a fact which may disconcert the reader, and is probably intended to. Marilyn Hacker has written that Clifton's poems remind her, in grace and deftness, of Japanese ink drawings. They remind me of a drum held in a woman's lap. The woman sits on a plain wooden chair, or on the earth. A community surrounds her. She slaps the drum with her bare hands. "Oh children," she says in the title poem of Clifton's first book, "think about the good times."

The work of a minimalist artist like Clifton makes empty space resonate. A spacious silence is not mere absence of noise, but locates us as it were on a cosmic stage. We are meant to understand the unsaid, to take our humble places with a sense of balance and belonging instead of the anxiety and alienation promoted by more conspicuously sublime and ambitious artistries. Omissions, as Marianne Moore remarks in quite another context, are not accidents; and as William Carlos Williams observes, in this mode, perfection is basic. Whatever the content of a particular piece, we should experience the craftsmanship of the minimalist as a set of unerring gestures governed by a constraining and shaping discipline, so habitual it seems effortless.

While the white space in such art stands for the largeness of space and time in which we human creatures find ourselves, the figured space stands for thick experience—experience which has been philosophically contemplated for an extended period. The artist, having patiently learned something quite exact about the dynamics of reality, offers it in concentrated form.

A byproduct of this concentration may be humor, the sacred levity associated with adepts in numerous traditions of religious art. Think of the Zen image of the laughing monk; John Cage's playfulness; the jokes of the thirteenth century Sufi poet Rumi, or those in the Chasidic stories told by Martin Buber; the trickster pranks of Coyote in Native American folktales, or Monkey King leaping to the end of the universe and peeing on the Buddha's little finger in a Chinese tale; remember the boyishly erotic mischievousness of the young Krishna in Hindu mythology. Then think of how Clifton fuses high comedy and high seriousness when she describes the poetic vocation, a topic most poets approach with a solemnity proportional to their/our insecurity. Clifton's "admonitions," the last poem in *good times*, ends:

children
when they ask you

why is your mama so funny
say
she is a poet
she don't have sense

Another early poem about her vocation is "prayer," which asks an unnamed listener to "lighten up," wonders why his hand is so heavy on "just poor/ me," and receives a response which makes this poem cunningly parallel John Milton's famous complaint of blindness:

answer
this is the stuff
i made the heroes out of
all the saints
and prophets and things
had to come by
this

Has Clifton read Milton's sonnet, which questions how God can exact the "day-labor" of poetry from a blind man, and ends in the famous "They also serve who only stand and wait"? Whether she has or not, what impresses me (and makes me laugh) is the identical structure of these two poems in which the poet interrogates God's fairness and gets fairly answered—and the marvelous freshness of Clifton's version. It thrills me as an American that this sacred conversation, this *de profundis*, can occur in my American language that, as Marianne Moore says, cats and dogs can read. I enjoy the down-home familiarity between Clifton and her God; I applaud a woman lining herself up with the heroes and prophets; and I feel, as well, for her struggle—which is not Milton's blindness, or Gerard Manley Hopkins's conviction of sin, but an American black woman's struggle which I can guess at. In a much later piece, "the making of poems," humility and comic afflatus again meet:

the reason why i do it
though i fail and fail
in the giving of true names
is i am adam and his mother
and these failures are my job.

What does it mean when a woman calls herself "adam and his mother?" The mother could be Eve, or a nameless pre-monotheistic goddess, or just any mother doing her homely work—and that conflation of myth and modernity is part of the joke. Making the poet double-gendered is another part. "True names" registers the archaic notion that language is not arbitrary, that poetry names essences of things—while the poet's failure, it seems to me conflates individual inadequacy with the imperfect meshing of signifiers and signified in a non-mythic world. How could "adam and his mother" find language for the way we live in the twentieth century? Still, they have to try. As with the simple double gesture of "this" to stand for the hardship God inflicts on saints and prophets, the idea of the poet's work as an impossible yet sacred task is effectively rendered in the plainest of language—right down to calling it not a task but a job. "The making of poems" demystifies poetic labor and dignifies maternal and manly labor. What these poems tell us is that high and low things can meet, along with the union of the holy and the comic, if one knows enough about both.

The source of Clifton's spiritual strength is black. It is also what she calls, punning on her own name, "the light." It comes, as she has her John the Baptist say in the "some jesus" poems, "in blackness like a star."

"Some jesus," the first of Clifton's revisionist religious sequences, begins like this:

adam and eve
the names
of the things
bloom in my mouth
my body opens
into brothers

You have to read that twice, I think, before you realize how simply and stunningly androgynous a poem it is—how lucidly it represents what Robert Hass, speaking of Rilke, calls "the pull inward, the erotic pull of the other we sense buried in the self," but represents it as achieved, not merely desired. The poet distinguishes male and female selves, voices, roles, but doesn't separate them from each other or from herself: she is both, they are both she. Casually proceeding then to inhabit the male personae of Cain, Moses, Solomon, Job, Daniel and Jonah, Clifton's voice in the New Testament section of this sequence section slides into the voice of a John who could be in Galilee or Philadelphia praising a savior. . . .

As her career proceeds, Clifton's spirituality grows bolder and more syncretic. In "to a dark moses" of Clifton's third book, an ordinary woman,

you are the one
i am lit for
come with your rod
that twists
and is a serpent.
i am the bush.
i am burning.
i am not consumed.

If we take this poem literally, and why should we not, God is a black woman who is also Lucille Clifton. In the sequence of Kali poems it is indeed "a woman god and terrible/ with her skulls and breasts," who pushes past the poet's fear and resistance, enters her bones, and forces her to say "i know i am your sister." Admitting the goddess of death as a portion of herself—of ourselves—is Clifton's most radical move in an ordinary woman. . . .

*Quilting: poems 1987–1990*, Clifton's boldest book, continues her meditations on history, loss, tragedy. Her affirmation of the body continues in two glorious poems on menstruation, "poem in praise of menstruation," and "to my last period," followed by the hilarious "wishes for sons," which fantasizes for them cramps, the last tampon, one week early, one week late, hot flashes and clots, and gynecologists resembling themselves.

Among the things of the spirit, her largest and loveliest work now is the ten-poem "Tree of Life" sequence, a lyric re-imagining of the role of Lucifer in Eden. "How art thou fallen from heaven, oh Lucifer, son of the morning," cries Isaiah. Clifton's version of the myth makes Lucifer (Lat. "light-bringer") at once light, lightning, and snake, servant of God, illuminator of mankind. As in the "some jesus" poems, the poet speaks through plural voices which seem to inhabit her. Hers is the voice of the mystified angels describing Lucifer's creation and fall in the first three poems, then woman's sensuous voice in "eve's version" and man's sensually and intellectually desperate one in "adam thinking." Most fascinatingly, her voice is also Lucifer's. . . .

In the penultimate poem, uncertainty moves toward certitude. Eve has whispered her knowledge of names to Adam, and the unidentified voice describes the threesome of "the story thus far." As in Clifton's earlier "creation," the time might be the year zero, or the day before yesterday: "so they went out/ clay and morning star/ following the bright back/ of the woman." (I recall, in this vista, Whitman's Adam with his Eve "by my side or back of me . . . or in front, and I following her.") As they pass the gate "into the unborn world," the imagery grows brighter, chaos falls away, "and everywhere seemed light/ seemed glorious/ seemed very eden." Again the fall is not a fall but a birth; the light of Eros and knowledge still surrounds the protagonists, or seems to. The "seemed," though inconspicuous, is crucial. Not until the final poem do uncertainties crown themselves assured. In the sequence's last poem, "lucifer speaks in his own voice," the light-bringer-snake knows he has done God's will and is

certain of a
graceful bed
and a soft caress
along my long belly
at endtime,

but only in the final lines does his voice finally merge with the poet's, as if to summarize her career so far:

illuminate i could
and so
illuminate i did.

That is the simplest possible description of Clifton's work.

Alicia Ostriker. *The American Poetry Review*. 22, 6 (November-December 1993), pp. 41–48

Lucille Clifton describes herself as a "big woman . . . rounder than the moon" (how round is that? Jolly round? Look-out-I'm-coming round?), and if her short, spindly poems didn't have such steel structures, they'd seem fearful of being whopped by an unstoppable force. In fact, a big, opened-up poem from Clifton, with rhythmic vigor and roll, might well prove a marvel. But we're not likely ever to see one; she long ago made her choice for the kind of mannerly reserve that, if hardly genteel, is politely cautious and which, because a little goes a long way, can leave, at the end of a volume, a hint of hollow silence in the air.

Not that Clifton always suppresses anger. Some of the poems in the middle section of *The Book of Light*, under the big-talking title "lightning bolt" (Clifton rejects capitals as if they were Establishment property), are even abusive. Her appropriation of the earth for her race in "the earth is a living thing" ("the earth . . . is a black shambling bear . . . a black hawk . . . a diamond blind in the black belly of coal") is only venial pride, a symbolic rite of reclaiming what was taken away, if not a revealing description of earth. But the racist innuendo of "crabbing" is something else. Here the "poet crab" says of the (doubtless white) crabbers,

this forward moving fingered thing inedible even to itself,
how can it understand the sweet sacred meat of others?

Here, Clifton uses the idea of difference as a ground for feeling superior. It's the old game of bias, but now judged as evil only in its white skin. As if taking turns on top could make matters right.

Clifton's politics of championing difference—except, of course, where the difference opposes her politics—finds an enemy in Wilson Goode, the black Philadelphia mayor who ordered the bombing of the building that housed "the Afrocentric back-to-nature group" called Move. . . .

The comic-book melodrama of "smoky finger" is only slightly less absurd than the suggestion that a Philadelphia black man might have "owned" Africa (based on the breathtaking equation of Africa with 6221 Osage Avenue, Philadelphia). The magnifying heat waves of the poet's anger show a Goode who is burning out, and betraying, an entire continent. . . .

Goode has moved away from "himself," which is his tribal fidelity to "africa." Ethnicity is an indelible, governing identity, inescapable except at the cost of loss of mind; mind itself is ethnic essence ("a mind / that would destroy itself"). The man is banished from the race forthwith. But this rhetorical triumph, this leave our presence—"move away"—rings hollow, since Goode, after all, has stayed and only "Move" has been removed—this last an outrage muffled by the poem's close, where even idiom ("stand fire / rather than difference") becomes diffused. At its fullest, the imagination is a curious blend of aggression and delicacy. Here it is merely aggressive.

Still other poems in "lightning bolt" wad themselves up in anger. "samson predicts from gaza the philadelphia fire" is as unconvincing as its title. "january 1991" implies that the Gulf War was about a refusal to recognize or tolerate difference, a "them and us" story, the ignorance all on our side, no economic motives in sight. "dear jesse helms" blames the senator himself for the same war's atrocities: "and jesse, / the smart bombs do not recognize the babies." The poem's criticism of government euphemisms ("civilian deaths have become / collateral damage, bullets / are anti-personnel") is effectively direct and simple, but I'd like to see it in a poem in which Helms is not so pat a straw villain, set up to endure the poet's flicking of matches at him. Several poems even scold Superman for failing to help a black woman named Clifton. There's heat in all this but little light, let alone a lightning flash. . . .

In the other two sections of the book, "reflection" and "splendor," contemplation prevails over anger, wisdom over a rough and righteous essay at power. If this poet's art has deepened since her 1969 debut volume, *Good Times*, it's in an increased capacity for quiet delicacy and fresh generalization. *The Book of Light* contains several poems that show Clifton's penchant and gift for lucid self-assessment, indeed a forbearance toward herself and her family like that of the moon for the earth. How take a cooler look at one's birth than "June 20" does? . . .

The poem's depth lies in the mysteriously successful, and just plain mysterious, barely specified other Clifton, the elementally ageless one (part child, part cyclically renewable rain) who nonetheless precedes the poet up the rope of her life. The other's superior position and her dangling rain-colored braids make up her entire description—that and everything not said about her, for instance, that she struggles or hungers. She seems to climb as a child does, not for reasons of necessity. In all, a poignant twist on certain old motifs—the double, the fata morgana, the guiding spirit. This is invention at its quiet best.

The other side of Clifton's political coin is idealization of black figures, especially family. In "daughters," this tendency hums agreeably. A great grandmother is "the arrow / that pierced our plain skin / and made us fancy women" (a trope that keeps folding up under scrutiny); "i like to think you gave us / extraordinary power . . . woman, i am / lucille, which stands for light, / daughter of thelma, daughter / of georgia, daughter of / dazzling you." But celebration seems forced in "my lost father," which kindly but

perhaps too conveniently ushers this troublesome individual into the heaven "of husbands fathers sons," safely segregated from wives and daughters. In "thel," the speaker's mother, her first landscape," sits "shy as a wren / . . . amid broken promises, / amid the sweet broken bodies / of birds"—this last phrase laid on with a butter knife. And politics and sentimentality merge in Clifton's portrayal of Sisyphus as a veritable "king" of power because he can always decide not to "allow / this myth to live." Can he? Yes, if crude expediency lifts him out of the classical tale, where he has no choice, and makes him a symbol of the oppressed.

Clifton's wisdom shows at its purest, on the other hand, in the splendid sequence of eight poems in which Lucifer and God are, of all things, "brothers"—akin: "that rib and rain and clay / in all its pride, "Lucifer says, "is what You are . . . all You / the loneliness, the perfect / imperfection." This is piercing and lovely writing. Entirely in Lucifer's voice, the sequence questions whether Adam's bruised heel allows Lucifer (here our spokesman) to credit, or enjoy, earthly beauty. Lucifer says:

i have grown old remembering this garden, the hum of the great cats moving into language, . . .

Again, the writing is magnificent. With these crisp sounds the poet rewrites *Genesis*, harmoniously merging the animal and the human ("hum" being the risky, magical, important connecting word, less problematical than "purr") and etherealizing Eve in the nonetheless dangerous word "fume." In all, and dizzyingly, the sweet and the feral intermingle, in what evades the extremes of anger and sentimentality. The answer to the question is: yes, beauty may be thrilled to.

This Lucifer tempts the reader, tempts God, but who can say he lacks wisdom? Indeed, it's God who is put on the defensive, being asked why, "in the confusion of a mountain of babies stacked like cord-wood, / . . . of tongues bitten through / by the language of assault," he neither raised His "hand / nor turned away." But "to ask You to explain," says the eighth poem (the sequence shiveringly grants God, at least, a capital), "is to deny You," and the seventh claims that there is mercy, there is grace," for "how otherwise / could i have come to this / marble spinning in space . . . how otherwise / could the two roads of this tongue / converge into a single / certitude?" Even if some readers may not accept Lucifer's theology (I do not), still his "single / certitude" is not arrived at by too simple a route. Such is the justice to experience and to ideas about experience that Clifton pays when, sans anger and sentimentality, she writes at her remarkable best.

Calvin Bedient. *Poetry*. 163, 6 (March 1994), pp. 344–49

That Lucille Clifton is one of the most engaging, gifted, and significant of contemporary poets is a critical evaluation more and more commonly held. Witness her inclusion in numerous anthologies, her nomination for the Pulitzer Prize, and her praises sung more frequently now than ever. Likewise, it is generally recognized that her poems offer an edifying personal wisdom, born of experience and deep thought, distilled by a keen and penetrating intelligence. The insights offered by her poems have attracted considerable critical appreciation. . . .

While her vision is thus appreciated, and its effects noticed, there has been little critical work that attempts to account for the *how* of Clifton's work, to explain her tremendous ability to use poetic discourse as an instrument for teaching. Perhaps this aspect of her poetry is overlooked as a critical focus because of persistent Anglo-American critical bias against the rhetorical in poetic discourse. Influenced by the expressivist tradition of romanticism, and beguiled by the formalist critical schools that react against romanticism, contemporary critics still tend to perceive poetry as primarily the expression of feeling and the making of meaning. This is often true even among those African-American and feminist critics who perceive literature as equipment for living. Such contemporary perceptions of poetry, and particularly lyric poetry, contrast with traditional African, European, and Asian conceptions of poetry that see it also as the product of rhetorical intention toward an audience, including the intention of teaching. . . .

[We] might expand our understanding and appreciation of her work by adding to our customary recognition of lyric as expressive of feeling and meaning also an understanding of lyric as rhetorical discourse, functioning to teach and thereby to alter the consciousness of its audience. . . .

Here, now, a poem from Clifton's *An Ordinary Woman*:

light
on my mother's tongue
breaks through her soft
extravagant hip
into life.
Lucille
she calls the light,
which was the name
of the grandmother
who waited by the crossroads
in Virginia
and shot the whiteman off his horse,
killing the killer of sons.
light breaks from her life
to her lives . . .
mine already is
an Afrikan name.

Perhaps the most striking characteristic of Clifton's poem is its structure, which functions to deny reader expectations, making the sequence of subject matter and of focus starkly surprising, especially the final lines. The relationship between the poem's four sentences is subtle, and even within one of the sentences, the second, the relationship of its clauses makes the ending a surprise completion of its beginning.

The poem begins with an image of birth that combines metonymic suggestions of joy and benediction associated with the word ''light,'' with a bodily and sensual metonymy for the poet's mother, giving the reader, through the phrase ''her soft / extravagant hip'' a sense of womanly form and of sensual, motherly warmth.

Clifton does not give this poem a conventional, separate title, so the word ''light'' derives emphasis not only from its being the first word of the poem and its occupying a line unto itself but also from its functioning for the reader as a de facto title; and like most titles it suggests a theme or focus. In the context of Clifton's oeurve the word ''light'' resonates with a rich variety of connotations. At times it is celestial and miraculous, or the presence of God, or a measure of consciousness, or, in the poem below, a complex combination of knowledge, self-knowledge, and compelling truth. . . .

In the section of *Two-headed Woman* titled ''the light that came to lucille clifton,'' several poems employ ''light'' as a metaphor for a spiritual presence of ancestors:

i
lucille clifton
hereby testify
that in that room
there was a light
and in that light
there was a voice
and in that voice
there was a sigh
and in that sigh
there was a world.
incandescence
formless form
and the soft
shuffle of sound
who are these strangers
peopleing this light?
lucille
we are
the Light
mother
someone calling itself Light
has opened my inside.
i am flooded with brilliance
mother,
someone of it is answering to
your name

A reader familiar with Clifton's work might intuitively experience the complex metaphoric resonance of the term, perceiving it as one node in a network of intertextual relationships. But I am most interested here in this individual poem and how Clifton creates the reader's experience through it, and this experience need not be diminished by lack of knowing Clifton's other work. In fact, her uses of the trope are so varied that one cannot presume from poem to poem exactly how she intends to use it. One only knows that it portends something significant, profound, and probably at least marvelous if not outright mystical. In ''light,'' Clifton emphasizes the significance and richness of the term, if not its approximate denotation, with clarity sufficient for even the first-time reader of her poetry to apprehend. In any case, because the initial reference to ''light'' in this poem is so abstract, the reader more likely focuses on the more visually concrete reference to the mother's hip.

This reference to hips also is significant, for Clifton often rhapsodizes about her body, celebrating not only her own beauty but also by extension the special beauty of all black women. As she pays homage to herself, her body and her ethos come to personify ''blackness blessed.'' Hips become a synecdoche, even a theme or motif, in Clifton, to suggest her own womanliness, the power of feminine form, and especially to celebrate the aesthetics of black women's bodies. . . .

In this lyric Clifton teaches by leading her reader to the discovery of a significant self-perception, by offering herself as an ethical exemplar, and by creating an imaginative experience for her audience to participate in. Her teaching by indirection calls for the reader to participate in the making of meaning and the discovery of the appropriate stance. As Madhubuti notes, Clifton ''is a writer of complexity, and she makes her readers work and think.'' The sense of revelation and discovery is all the stronger for the reader having had to share in the making of it. This dialogic strategy places her poem within the tradition of African-American communicative strategies such as signifyin', call and response, and teaching by parable, metaphor, and example.

Lucille Clifton, with her subtle virtuosity—as rhetorical as it is poetic, as functional as it is beautiful—fulfills one of the most faithfully pursued aspirations in the tradition of African-American poetics: She discovers and reveals beauty and dignity in the individual and the collective African-American self, and she teaches others to do likewise.

Mark Bernard White. *CLA Journal*. XL, 3 (March 1997), pp. 288–304

BIBLIOGRAPHY
*Good Times: Poems*, 1969; *The Black BCs*, 1970; *Some of the Days of Everett Anderson*, 1970; *Everett Anderson's Christmas Coming*, 1971; *Good News about the Earth: New Poems*, 1972; *All Us Come Cross the Water*, 1973; *The Boy Who Didn't Believe in Spring*, 1973; *Don't You Remember?*, 1973; *Good, Says Jerome*, 1973; *Everett Anderson's Year*, 1974; *An Ordinary Woman*, 1974; *The Times They Used to Be*, 1974; *My Brother Fine with Me*, 1975; *Everett Anderson's Friend*, 1976; *Generations: A Memoir*, 1976; *Three Wishes*, 1976; *Amifika*, 1977; *Everett Anderson's 1 2 3*, 1977; *Everett Anderson's Nine Month Long*, 1978; *The Lucky Stone*, 1979; *My Friend Jacob*, 1980; *Two-Headed Woman*, 1980; *Sonora Beautiful*, 1981; *Everett Anderson's Goodbye*, 1983; *Good Woman: Poems and a Memoir, 1969–1980*, 1987; *Next: New Poems*, 1987; *Ten Oxherding Pictures*, 1988; *Quilting: Poems 1987–1990*, 1991; *The Book of Light*, 1993; *The Terrible Stories: Poems*, 1996; *Dear Creator: A Week of Poems for Young People and Their Teachers*, 1997; *The Times They Used to Be*, 2000

# COLLINS, Merle (1950– )
## Grenada

The testimony of [Merle Collins's] poetry is one of transformation in attitudes, in ideas, and in language. A new freedom and love as woman, as Grenadian, as poet, flashes through her words. The joyous reception . . . given to such poems as "Callaloo" show how much she speaks for the people. The reflections on girlhood in the context of neocolonial cultural oppression, through the empathy with her grandmother in "The Lesson" and more directly in "The Butterfly Born," reflect the militancy of the Grenadian woman and her participation within the process of building the revolution. Yet the nourishment of the past is also acknowledged through the use of the patois, which is beginning to be legitimized and reincorporated into the language of the Grenada Revolution through the intervention of poets like Merle Collins.

Chris Searle. *Words Unchained: Language and Revolution in Grenada* (London: Zed Books, 1984), pp. 135–36

It is right and appropriate that this collection of poetry [*Because the Dawn Breaks!*] is dedicated to the Grenadian people. For the poems—their tone, language, content, and vibrant commitment—belong first and foremost to Grenada: the beauty of her landscape; the challenges of her history; and the grandeur of her people. So in the poems one hears not just the voice of Merle Collins, but that of the people of Grenada talking about their struggles, and in particular about their five years' experience of revolution and revolutionary transformation. The poems embody, and celebrate, the people's visions, dreams, and hopes during those momentous years of hovering on the brink of tremblingly new and full eternity. And above all is the celebration of beauty—the beauty of the *new* emerging from the *old*. I remember, says the poet, the form of the past foretelling the shape of things to come.

What is that past? It is one of slavery and colonialism and what goes with them: the exploitation, the oppression, the deformation of spirit. Blackness is denied: Africanism is denied; the very landscape of Grenada becomes a matter of shame. Blackness, Africanness, lower-class origins reflected in a mirror become, particularly for the petit bourgeois educated, a threat to the self-esteem of those "caught in the strange dilemma of non-belonging." The history celebrated in books and the media is that of the colonial conquerors. Gairyism perpetuated this and more. The meek, the exploited, and the oppressed were supposed to wait for compensation in heaven. Blessed are the meek. Deliverance will come from the big houses on the hill!

But that very past is one of continuous resistance by the meek, [Frantz] Fanon's wretched of the earth, for whom "struggle is the loudest song." It was out of that fierce and continuous struggle that came the 1979 Grenada Revolution. Merle Collins's poetry captures in telling images and clear languages the new horizons, the new possibilities opened up by the revolution. . . .

The revolution then embodies the dreams and visions of an awakened people. Not surprisingly, the image of the dream is the most dominant in the entire collection. In this Merle Collins joins another Caribbean revolutionary poet, Martin Carter, who celebrates the grandeur of all the struggling of the earth who sleep not to dream, but dream to change the world.

It is her consciousness that change is inevitable, that movement is not always along a straight line, and her commitment to the collective dream of Grenadian masses for a world in which they own the earth and the sweat that works the earth, that makes Merle Collins, the poet, not despair when the revolution suffers a double blow: the disintegration of the leadership and the invasion of Grenada by United States imperialist forces.

Ngugi wa Thiong'o. Introduction to Merle Collins. *Because the Dawn Breaks!* (London: Karia Press, 1985), pp. vi–viii, x–xi

Merle Collins's poetry identifies its constituency as the comrades in the struggle. It derives its artistic validity from its ability to inspire and support the revolutionary impulse. It is poetry to be read out loud to an audience that has shared the writer's private turmoil, if only at a distance. This sense of commitment to a cause that goes beyond aesthetic self-assertion has made the author ruthless in her exclusion of artistic extravagance. The poems' shared images are carefully chosen and sparingly used, giving a sense of unified purpose to the work as a whole—a quality that is often missing in poetry anthologies. One sees the influence of Edward Brathwaite in the poet's choice of rhyme scheme and line arrangement as well as the insistence of an oral dimension to the work. The influence of Ngugi [wa Thiong'o], with whom Merle has worked closely in her present exile, can also be traced in the clarity of her language and the unapologetically political dimension of her art. . . . This anthology establishes Merle Collins unequivocally as a poet deserving of a place among the poets of Caribbean heritage. She updates the political commitment of Martin Carter since she has at her command the oral and literary techniques that a new generation of poets since Brathwaite (Kwesi Johnson, Keens-Douglas, Grace Nichols, Michael Smith) have been developing. I can only hope that readers and educators inside and outside of the Caribbean will give this volume the attention it deserves both artistically and as a political statement. In an era of drowned dreams, [Collins's] poetry offers a lifeline.

Rhonda Cobham. *New Beacon Review.* 2–3 (November 1986), pp. 76–77

The novel [*Angel*] is set in Grenada and spans about thirty or forty years prior to and including the revolution of March 13, 1979 and its aftermath of the United States' invasion four years later. Collins traces the events in the life of Angel McAllister, a young black Grenadian woman whose parents work in the early years of their marriage, as agricultural laborers on the cocoa plantation of the DeLisles, members of the white planter elite. (The McAllisters had recently returned from Aruba to which they had earlier emigrated from Grenada to find work in the oil industry). Collins seldom clutters her narrative with dates, and one needs to have some knowledge of the chronology of historical currents in Grenada in order to place events in the novel properly in time. Angel's earliest memories are of the burning down of the DeLisle plantation sometime in the late 1940s or early 1950s. This event occurs during the activism of the fledgling labor movement which has been trying to secure more equitable remuneration and improved working conditions for agricultural laborers on the cocoa estates. There is repeated reference to a charismatic labor organizer named ''Leader'' (Collins's deliberately flimsy, pseudonymous allusion to Eric Gairy, later the Prime Minister overthrown in the revolution) who is the popular driving force behind the growing labor unrest, but who is dogged by rumors of dishonesty in his union's financial dealings. . . .

Perhaps the most compelling aspect of this novel is Merle Collins's willingness to reach deep down into the gut of the survival instinct often characteristic of the most desperately poor. That instinct manifests itself most clearly in her characters' readiness to work at all costs, even in the most humiliating conditions, at greatest inconvenience to themselves—often for the least remuneration. Both Doodsie and Allan go to Aruba to take advantage of labor opportunities presented there by the oil industry. When times are especially hard, Doodsie is prepared to engage in domestic labor, run a small goods shop, and plant her little plot. . . . Allan becomes part of the exploited migrant labor force in the United States, picking fruit and vegetables for meager wages, having to bear prolonged absence from his family, and missing the conviviality of native Grenadian life. In his loneliness, he writes Doodsie from Florida: ''We dont see a lot of people besides who we working with.'' Their friends, Ezra and her husband, are also migrant laborers, and as soon as he is old enough, Simon, Angel's younger brother, leaves the island to work in the United States.

Another strong point of the novel is that it reflects Collins's keen ear for her native Grenadian dialect, a talent which she uses to full narrative advantage in the work. The lilting cadence of the dialogue enters one's consciousness as much through the ear as through the mind. Collins is so accurate, so meticulous in her attention to the most minute details of phonetic reproduction that it is easy to imagine even the tone of voice accompanying the spoken words of the dialogue. At times, Collins's authorial voice merges with that of her characters, adopting the dialect form, and expertly submerging narrator and reader in the swirl of events taking place in the novel. . . .

The work's weakness derives from Collins's attempts to comment on too many aspects of Grenadian social oppression in too limited a narrative ambit. The novelist tries to address questions of racial inferiority, male domination, women's liberation, political oppression, and generational differences. The result is that the narrative pace lumbers as the author, somewhat gratuitously and heavy-handedly, injects an element of propaganda into Angel's utterances, Angel's education making her character a perfect vehicle for such talk. Thus, her remarks to her mother immediately prior to the invasion, manifest a hollow shrillness rather than the perceptive instruction which the author may have intended. . . .

These flaws apart, however, *Angel* is undeniably a literary hymn of praise to the ingenuity and survival skills of Grenada's working poor. In the final analysis, when politicians' promises ring hollow in the ears of the oppressed, as had happened so tragically in Grenada, there will be the comfort of storytellers like Merle Collins who record with love and respect for posterity the people's triumphs and tears.

Brenda DoHarris. *Zora Neale Hurston Forum.* 4, 1 (Fall 1989), pp. 25–28

In *Angel*, three generations of women experience the changes that Grenada undergoes under [Eric] Gairy's regime and the New Jewel Movement. ''The Revolution has given me a theme,'' Collins tells us, ''and has also developed a greater awareness of self and pride of being.'' The revolution was also instrumental in validating the Creole language and affirming its power through popular culture. It effected a reevaluation of the language and a reconceptualization of the curriculum which Grenadians initially resisted, as we see in the chapter that deals with the elections for the teachers' union, with secret campaigns ''to ensure that Angel and those who shared her views did not get on to the executive.''

Collins's novel explores the function of education, reading, and writing in nation formation and decolonization. The Caribbean child's encounter with language through the colonial school drove a wedge between the ''real'' world she saw about her and the world of the school and its curriculum. While the reality of the colonizers' books is made to supplant the reality of the island, Collins traces the evolution of Angel's consciousness until she ultimately rejects the world the colonial school has created. Like Annie John [in Jamaica Kincaid's *Annie John*], Angel devours Enid Blyton's adventures and the love stories her friends bring in. Angel's name is with time perceived as inadequate as she becomes darker, for in all books the children read ''angels [are] white.'' Rather than concentrating on Sunday service, Angel thinks up all sorts of stories about faraway places: ''In her mind, she went off sometimes by boat, sometimes by plane. . . . She never arrived anywhere in these daydreams; but she was often travelling.'' In Angel's case, however, the revolution creates a discursive space in which she can posit herself as a subject in the new Grenada, and she is able to see through the ''mist.'' . . .

The many different ways in which Collins conveys the evolution of both Angel's and Grenada's consciousness help create the documentary effect of the narrative—we get the truth from many angles of vision and through different channels—which makes the novel not only less teleological but more politically effective. Another evolutionary movement is figured in both the content and the form of the letters that the characters exchange throughout the novel. The epistolary validates Creole as a written language, and the letters ultimately serve to represent the unity of the Caribbean peoples in diaspora. As they trace the characters' movement among islands and to the United States, in search of better economic conditions, they ultimately help the reader to perceive them not only as an extended family, but as constituting a Caribbean community. The letters also allow Collins to articulate in the voice of the people the significance of the events that are occurring in the society: their own writing and interpretation of history. . . .

Providing a site of resistance to narrative closure, the female voices in the novel have their own genealogy in relation to the independence movement and the critical response to that movement articulated in the black power and socialist movements. But Angel's vision is not enough to maintain a critical distance from Party doctrine, whereas Doodsie knows better. . . . If the novel presents unity from a woman's perspective, it does not exclude men. The words and actions of Angel's brothers help us see that it is not only from a female perspective that totalitarian structures can be recognized. It is in the very paradox of unity and fragmentation that the novel reaches history, as [Patrick] Taylor suggests, neither as utopia, nor as tragic failure, but as the hope and possibility of a new future. . . .

It is also significant that Angel returns to Grenada to perform a ritual wake. Although she feels "a little bit stupid" about what she is going to do, to light a candle and sing the song they always sang at wakes, with her good eye, in "her mind's eye," Angel sees that the spirits are sympathetic. As a communal form, the wake is a way for the living people to deal with the reality of death and the loss of a loved one. Angel sees the "figures circling the room," and she tells her Sunday school teacher, who has been dead for ten years, that the spirits are "either gone, or they [are] sympathetic." The wake at the end of the novel functions as a symbol of past traditions which Angel must retain if she is to have an awareness of her community and her heritage. Angel is lighting a candle not only for the part of her self that was lost with the blinding of her left eye— the Angel that got carried away with party arrogance and detachment from the people they were supposed to be accountable to— but to all Grenadians who lost their lives trying to keep the revolution alive.

Maria Helena Lima. *Ariel.* 24, 1 (January 1993), pp. 45–48, 51–52

Merle Collins's second novel, *The Colour of Forgetting*, is a significant contribution to the recent body of African and diaspora literature that references the past to place the present in perspective. The inclination to forget a history, one of the characters reveals, is often tied to the shame of slavery. The book in part warns against internalizing that shame. In sum, *The Colour of Forgetting* blends oral-literature techniques and vernacular with masterful narrative control to yield impressive results.

The story is as much about a community as it is about a character. William Janvier (a.k.a. Thunder) is the hope of the community of Content in Grenada. He arrives from a long line of confused ancestry and tragedy: land disputes, family feuds, and conflicting political views. The troubled child is challenged to "walk back" over stories and histories to complement his formal education.

Separated into seventeen sections, the work draws on the cache of storytelling techniques in the oral tradition to provide its ordering. Collins deftly uses speakers to take control and order movement and content. The novel opens with the prophetic words, "Blood in the north, blood to come in the south, and the blue crying red in between." Carib, like her mother and grandmother before her, is the conscience of the community. The community "had grown up with Carib's voice and its endless effort to kick-start their memory.". . .

Mamag, the great-aunt, is as imposing a character as is Carib. Nearly a hundred years old by the time of the present story, she is the youngest sister of Thunder's grandfather, and she takes that responsibility seriously. In walking back over the Malheureuse story with Willive she admonishes: "Is not everything, everything people must tell children, but you have to know some things. You must know what happen in long time days, so you will expect the rough with the smooth, and it won't knock you down when it come." Similarly, Thunder's rather mute father Ned advises: "So now is the generations to come, like you and everybody who getting a education, have to write Ned name in the ground, have to say all the things that Ned couldn't say. Have to write thing down, since writing is the fashion these days." As Carib is the last in the lines of Caribs the exhorters, the hope is that the children will carry on the business of remembering. The novel cautions that the color of forgetting is red, as in the color of blood.

Collins's novel is a tribute to the Afro-Caribbean oral tradition, a vanishing landscape as well as an exploration in "life sense." Characters such as Carib, Mamag, and Willive struggle against forgetting the historical ties that have implications for the present. In the end Collins would have us understand that the humanity of a people, the survival of a people, rests with its young, the young's willful desire to present to its community what the textbooks do not: the history of ordinary people.

Adele S. Newson. *World Literature Today.* 70, 2 (Spring 1996), pp. 451–52

BIBLIOGRAPHY
*Because the Dawn Breaks!*, 1985; *Angel*, 1987; *Rain Darling: Stories*, 1990; *Rotten Pomerack*, 1992; *The Colour of Forgetting*, 1995

# CONDÉ, Maryse (1937–)
## Guadeloupe

[Maryse Condé's early plays *Dieu nous l'a donné* and *Mort d'Oluwémi d'Ajumako*] are concerned with the manipulation of social mores and myths by individuals seeking political power and influence. Her three novels, *Hérémakhonon*, *Une Saison à Rihata*, and *Ségou [les murailles de terre]*, attempt to make credible on an increasingly larger scale the personal human complexities involved in holy wars, national rivalries, and migrations of peoples. . . .

Condé, in her fiction as well as in her criticism, reflects her concern for the art of writing. Though her characters are not self-portraits, their remarks appear often to echo her experience and her critical opinions. For example, in her short story, ''Three Women in Manhattan,'' she sympathizes with each of three writer-characters. She finds irony in Eleanor's dislike of having to exploit the spurious antebellum glories of the Old South in order to please white critics in America. She understands Vera's frustration in finding no public for her romantic period novels of Haiti's glorious past. She recognizes Claude's frustration at having to address a foreign readership in a European tongue. . . .

It is not that there has been a change in Maryse Condé's basic understanding, nor even in her narrative skills, that one is impelled to view *Ségou*, her latest novel, as a truly remarkable book. . . . Indeed, the ability to make the truth of fiction compatible with the data of historical events is discernible in all her writing. . . . She is unwilling to accept a popular belief or to reject it just because it is popular, she is willing to refrain from drawing inferences and theorizing on the basis of inadequate or confusing evidence, and she has a persistent curiosity which sharpens her powers of observation. This same analytical intelligence and critical integrity are evident also in her many essays and scholarly critiques; they have often put her into bold relief against a popular attitude, as did her article ''Pourquoi la Négritude? Négritude ou r révolution?'' when presented to the colloquium in 1973. In that essay she refuted as ill-founded Léon Damas's enthusiastic perception of a healthy, triumphing Négritude, citing Haiti as a prime counterexample, among others. . . .

Upon reading *Ségou*, at least one difference from the two previous novels is immediately clear: its magnitude. The magnitude is not wholly one of the number of pages (nearly five hundred), but also of the years covered (sixty to eighty), of the localities involved (perhaps a dozen different nations or kingdoms), of the number of major historical and fictional characters extensively developed (over a dozen), of the major historical events integrally involved (the march of Islam over north central Africa, the later years of the slave trade, the ''repatriation'' in West Africa of Brazilian slaves, etc.).

Charlotte H. and David K. Bruner. *World Literature Today.*
59, 1 (Winter 1985), pp. 9–12

Maryse Condé's world of fiction possesses, besides its diversity, the quality of commanding attention by its power of conviction. The realism of the framework, the psychological verisimilitude, and the plausibility of the situations contribute to the development of a fiction which succeeds in creating the illusion of reality. The primary topics treated in these novels, such as cultural alienation, the political climate in young African nations, the penetration of Islam and European imperialism in the Sahel of the eighteenth century, link everything to a psychological, actual, or historic reality and by consequence to an easily identifiable referent.

Maryse Condé often uses the motif of alienation in her works; therefore, it is not surprising that exile, which is part of the same thematic, also occupies an important place. In *Hérémakhonon*, Veronica feels exiled from her native milieu in Guadeloupe, and from the cultural French milieu, in spite of successfully adopting its customs. And despite her ardent desire to be part of the African culture, she feels excluded from that culture too. Rihata, in *Une Saison à Rihata*, is perceived as the definitive, irremediable place of exile. In *Ségou: les murailles [de terre]*, the concept of exile is intrinsic to the very subject of the novel, which deals with a period of great mobility and cultural transition on the African continent. . . .

These are the direct, obvious, and literal expressions of exile. . . . In addition, certain techniques contribute equally to conveying this notion of exile; among them, three metaphors, that of the absent mother, the adoptive mother, and the seductress.

Maryse Condé frequently evokes the figure of the mother. This is not surprising considering the symbolic ties between the earth and the mother: the homeland and the mother both suggest the origin, the source of life, the first place of growth. However, in her works the theme of the mother presents a special interest, because of the perspective in which it is presented. In fact, the relationship of the child to the mother is, in the majority of the cases, marked by trauma. The mother is rarely the one who nourishes and protects the child, or whose presence and actions provide a safe haven for the child. On the contrary, the motifs of absence, death, defection, and ambiguity are most often associated with the maternal figure.

The theme of the mother is inscribed in a structure of absence-presence, which also dominates the organization of the motifs associated with exile, forced separation, regret for a lost homeland, recourse to the imaginary or to memory in order to try and re-create it, in short, conjuration of absence by the illusion of presence. In the eyes of her dispersed sons, Nya, the archetype of the mother, and Ségou, the cradle of the family, are closely linked. It is their combined memory that nourishes the nostalgia they feel and that revives their desire to return to the place of their origins.

There exists another figure, complementary to the previous one, that of the adoptive mother. . . . Both the adoptive mother and the land of exile shelter the exiled, the disinherited. However, an unalterable fact exists: being just adoptive mothers, they can only play a borrowed role.

Nevertheless, in *Ségou: les murailles*, the land of exile is endowed with different characteristics than those associated with the adoptive mother. It wears the traits of a seductress who uses her charms to attract the exiled. When the latter yields to his fascination and tries to be accepted by her, she rejects him by invoking his foreign origins, which she denigrates haughtily. The refusal which he suffers marks the perpetuation of his exclusion.

These three figures—the missing mother, the adoptive mother, and the seductress—are distinct from each other due to the nature of their representative content. However . . . these metaphors invite an identical interpretation by virtue of their antithetical structure whose respective poles are: absence and presence, identity and alterity, and attraction and rejection.

Arlette M. Smith. *French Review.* 62, 1 (October 1988), pp. 50–55†

The narrator in *Hérémakhonon*, Veronica, not only speaks incessantly of sex, it is her sexuality and her sexual activity that define her very essence. Moreover, the narrative act is inscribed within a masculine/feminine configuration of desire since it postulates a daughter-to-father or woman-to-lover discourse. In other words, the text is presented—at times alternately, at times simultaneously—as a conversation with and a search for the father (''le marabout mandingue'') and as a conversation with and a search for the lover. The father is, of course, the lover par excellence, the ultimate object of desire. . . .

Because of his attempts to deny her an active sexuality, the father, in addition to being her idol, is also Veronica's nemesis. This is because . . . Veronica, even as an adolescent, is conscious of her body as a locus for pleasure and of herself as a sexual being. . . . Because it is proscribed, Veronica, from the very beginning, imagines the sexual act as a liberating one and the sexual partner as giving access to a certain independence. Her first experience is then a deliberate act of defiance and separation from the family and especially from paternal restriction. . . .

She realizes that to make love is always to make a political choice. . . . As an adult, she continues to envision the sexual act as liberating. The African revolutions for independence, she contends, were in fact revolutions for sex. . . . Furthermore, revolutions and sex are so intertwined in her thinking that it is difficult for her to determine finally if, in general, one engages (in) sex in the name of the revolution or if one engages (in) the revolution in the name of sex. . . .

Veronica, who as an adolescent had been surprised ''en plein coit ou presque,'' is labeled by her father ''putain'' and, for different reasons, she is labeled ''intellectuelle de gauche''; but it is the first label only—the one with which, as an adult, she is insulted by her students—that she accepts and in which she gradually appears to take pride. For since she equates sexuality with (masculine) independence, Veronica esteems the prostitute for daring to attempt to usurp the masculine prerogative by striking a pose—albeit illusory—of independence and power.

Arthur Flannigan. *French Review*. 62, 2 (December 1988), pp. 306–8

Maryse Condé's novel, *Une Saison à Rihata*, set in a fictitious African country, opens with a description of the protagonist's house: it is cut off from the rest of the town, a picture of neglect and decay, damp, mildewed, a crumbling reflection of its former colonial glory. The appearance of the house offers a striking parallel to the situation of the family and in particular to that of its *Antillaise* mistress, Marie-Hélène—a stranger in exile and at odds with her surroundings in an alien and hostile society. A brilliant, middle-class woman, married to an African, she had hoped to heal the divisions in herself by a return to her ancestral homeland. Marie-Hélène's life in Africa, however, is characterized by shattered hopes and unfulfilled dreams. She finds herself banished to an isolated and stagnating provincial town and responds to being rejected by Africa by withdrawing from life and from those around her. The journey back has not recovered the lost mother, the mythical Africa, the ancestral homeland. Like [Aimé] Césaire's poet, the Antillean heroine fails to find what she expected. She becomes more cut off, more exiled from herself. The rejection of Africa leads to a corresponding withdrawal from all everyday reality, expressed metaphorically by her physical isolation: Her room becomes her refuge where she rejoins her rejected West Indian homeland through the medium of the dream and the imagination.

Elizabeth Wilson. In Carole Boyce Davies and Elaine Savory Fido, eds. *Out of the Kumbla: Caribbean Women and Literature* (Trenton, New Jersey: Africa World Press, 1990), p. 48

The story [of *Traversée de la mangrove*] is apparently simple. A dead man is discovered at Rivière au sel. This dead man is Francisco Alvarez Sanchez. He had landed in this part of Guadeloupe, reclaimed a house that everyone feared—one of those haunted houses that abound in Creole cultures of the Caribbean—and settled there, provoking the disruption of several lives. We will learn of these disruptions during his wake, as the people of Rivière au sel gather to contemplate his mysterious corpse and his equally mysterious death. And all those attending this dead man will, from chapter to chapter, tell about him, about their relationship with him, and about the part they played in his life—now gone. These recollections at the wake will reveal to us the multiple facets of Francisco Sanchez—subjective, incomplete, moving, and forgotten facets, even for the person recollecting them. And, slowly, these facets will reflect, not a character clear and sharp as in a Western novel, but a mysterious man who may have come from Cuba, or most certainly from Colombia; who was a son of Guadeloupe, though he really was not; and who feared something no one knew—maybe this very death that would mysteriously strike his lineage at a specific age. Through the testimony of Moise, Mira, Aristide, Mama Sonson, Carmélien, Désinor, Dinah, Dodose Pélagie, the historian Emile Etienne, and others, we see Francisco Sanchez foretell his own death, await and flee it at the same time, and also write about it—because he is a writer—in a novel that no one will read and which, of course, is entitled *Traversée de la mangrove*.

The wake is for us a melting pot of Creole culture, of its speech, of its orality, and it gave the extraordinary pretext that would allow plantation slaves to gather without spreading the fear that they were plotting to revolt or to burn down a plantation. I even have the feeling that the Creole language, in its whispers, that the Creole culture, in its ruses and detours, and that the Creole philosophy, in its underground, clandestine, and fatalist character, all were shaped in the wake's contours; there, too, was shaped our most painful subjectivity. The wake also is the space of the storyteller, our first literary figure, the one who, in the silence, gave us his voice, and who, facing death in the night, laughed, sang, challenged, as if to teach us how to resist our collective death and night. It is in this culturally powerful space, then, that Maryse Condé's novel evolves, revealing the mysterious reflections of Francisco Sanchez, a strange Caribbean vagabond. This revelation will not follow a straight narrative line, but rather the sinuous contours of the tale—or, more accurately, of several tales. It will not be traced in linear logic, but in the many detours and byroads constructed in the wandering utterances of each person at the wake—wandering and personal utterances, deeply rooted in a language to which we will return. It is difficult for the Creole language to ignore, in its growth, this space of the wake, and thus it is not surprising that Maryse Condé anchors her novel in this space, at the heart of our history and culture, and of our memory.

Patrick Chamoiseau. *Callaloo*. 14, 2 (Spring 1991), pp. 390–91

Maryse Conde's historical novel about the black witch of Salem [*Moi, Tituba, sorcière*, translated as *I, Tituba, Black Witch of Salem*] furnishes Tituba with a social consciousness as contemporary as the motivating impulse behind the novel, which drives Condé to retrieve fragments of an intentionally ignored history and to reshape them into a coherent, meaningful story. It is the same consciousness that has motivated contemporary women of African descent—both scholars and artists—to explore the infinite possibilities of our lost history.

As Condé offers to Tituba the possibility of filling the silence and voids with voice and presence, we who are Tituba's cultural kin experience the possibilities of our own history. Via an active, constitutive voice, Tituba leaps into history, shattering all the racist and misogynist misconceptions that have defined the place of black women. Tituba's revenge consists in having persuaded one of her descendants to rewrite her moment in history in her own African oral tradition. And when Tituba takes her place in the history of the Salem witch trials, the recorded history of that era—and indeed the entire history of the colonization process—is revealed to be seriously flawed.

> Angela Y. Davis. Foreword to Maryse Condé. *I, Tituba, Black Witch of Salem* (Charlottesville: University Press of Virginia, 1992), pp. xi–xii

In her newest novel, *Les Derniers Rois mages*, Condé tells the saga of three generations in the family of an African king exiled by the French from Benin to the island of Martinique but who ultimately returns to Africa—specifically, Algeria—to die. She skillfully interweaves the king's life, African customs, the past magnificence and grandeur of the king's panther clan, and the lives of his descendants, scarred by his majesty. The narrator is Djéré, the king's son by a local servant girl, who has been brought up at court, imbued with the legends and myths of Africa, and loved and pampered by all. That brief childhood spent with the exiled king casts its shadow over his entire life, and he cannot accept the fact that he and his mother are left behind when his "ancestor" goes back to Africa after six years. He resorts to writing a diary, recording like the griots of old all his reminiscences and the many stories and events told him by his father. This diary will later help his own offspring endure the daily hardship, poverty, disappointment, and scorn they will suffer from the inhabitants of Guadeloupe. . . .

Condé deftly interplays the various geographic settings of her novels—Martinique, Guadeloupe, America, and Africa—jumping from one continent to the other as her protagonists, from the former African ruler down to Spéro, muse about their lives. She provides her readers with descriptions of the local inhabitants, their way of life, their manner of spending time, their customs. The cultural clash which Spéro, the last of the "magician kings," experiences in the American South is subtly presented. The king's descendant becomes a looked-down-upon Negro in a milieu in which blacks, though officially equal, have yet to win truly equal footing with whites. An entire gallery of characters are sketched, both successes in life and failures, as Spéro comes in contact with them all. The relative material opulence of his domestic life, ensured by his industrious wife, does not satisfy him. He is emotionally dry and often longs for Guadeloupe, brooding about the past and his ancestors.

The novel is well written. The language is rich, and the text luxuriates in the islands' natural beauty, the blueness of the surrounding sea, the blooming of various tropical flowers and trees, and the variety of faces.

> Nadezda Obradović. *World Literature Today*. 66, 3 (Summer 1992), p. 564

As with [*Moi, Tituba, sorcière*], Condé opens *Les Derniers Rois mages* with a historical disclaimer to play upon readers' conventions of disbelief. When the French captured the last prince of the Fon dynasty of d'Abomey, known as Béhanzin, in early 1894, they were able to establish their protectorate of Dahomey. Béhanzin was deported to Martinique and died in Algeria in 1906. . . . Much as with Tituba, she thus assures us that, although we know the novel deals with an actual historical personality, the fiction will include conjecture and the imaginary. Condé again uses a multiple-point-of-view narration, concentrating primarily on the descendants of the African "king" but also on an African-American woman, Debbie. It is indeed Debbie's investigation into her African past that leads her to the French Caribbean and attracts her to Spéro, much as Veronica sought out her "nègre avec aïeux." The problem with Spéro's heritage, like that of his father Justin and grandfather Djéré (the child left behind in Martinique by the African king), is that the "royal" past provides neither glory nor power. The descendants of the original king have maintained only dreams of the past; they are, in fact, relatively lazy drunkards who "n'[ont] jamais rien fait de leurs deux mains." Exiled on his South Carolina island, Spéro epitomizes his ancestor's exile as well as that of African slaves exiled in the Caribbean. As she has remarked elsewhere, however, Condé affirms that, "Fait indéniable, l'exil crée des liens même factices." The spiritual link to his ancestor, both real and imaginary, offers him a fertile terrain for his primary activity: dreaming, as evidenced in both sections of the novel which open upon the supine Spéro, awaking from a recurrent dream. Whereas the women of the novel are active in their pursuits of the history of black people—his wife Debbie frenetically collects the oral histories of local African-Americans, and their daughter has left for the ancestral lands of Benin—one might wonder if, in portraying the young Anita (who echoes Veronica), Condé is not ultimately valorizing the role of men like Spéro. After all, she herself is "just a dreamer," she says, exploring "a certain past" and "a certain history" with her "imagination" and "intuition.". . .

The specificity of what Maryse Condé often portrays as a particularly Caribbean "identity problem" is emblematic of universal phenomena; through the "insular" realities of her characterized individuals, she presents in microcosm the universal conflicts of our splintered and multifaceted associations with and within the disparate elements of a modern, multicultural world. As exemplified by her transformation of the legacies of Tituba and Béhanzin, Condé shows us that a search for both individual and collective histories is limited only by the frontiers of our liberating imaginations.

> Thomas C. Spear. *World Literature Today*. 67, 4 (Autumn 1993), pp. 729–30

Francis Sancher, a k a Francisco Alvarez-Sanchez, lies snug in his coffin, his face framed by a glass window that allows friends and enemies one last look at the mystery man of Riviere au Sel, a country village on the Caribbean island of Guadeloupe.

Though we meet him first in death, Francis Sancher is quickly resurrected in the memories of those who are attending his wake at the house of Sylvestre Ramsaran, a local dignitary whose daughter, Vilma, was one of Francis' many conquests. Seeing such a crowd you might have concluded they were being hypocritical, notes the narrator of [*Crossing the Mangrove*]. For all of them, at one time or another, had called Francis a vagabond and a cur, and isn't the fate of a cur to die amid general indifference?

The contradictory answers to this question, presented in the speeches and internal monologues that make up *Crossing the Mangrove*, reveal images of a powerful and mysterious man who has liberated, oppressed, frightened and given solace to those who have gathered to bid him good-bye.

Elegantly translated into English by the author's husband, Richard Philcox, the narrative achieves its hypnotic effects through the intimate recollections of the villagers. They are a varied lot, ranging from Moise the postman to the old seer Mama Sonson, from the historian Emile Etienne to Xantippe, the village idiot.

These characters' memories of their sometimes painful encounters with Francis reveal a willful stranger who took control of the village through the force of his personality. At the same time, he was a man of deep melancholy, capable of recognizing their pain even before they themselves were aware of it.

Together, the villagers and the intruder inhabit a world of unstable facts. Francis is said to have fought with Castro in the Sierra Maestra. But after seeing his brother lying in his own blood, he hadn't had a minute's peace from all the suffering, accidents and deaths. Such agonies apparently forced him to lay his weapons aside and become a curandero, a wandering healer.

But there are other possibilities. Moise confidently asserts that Francis' family comes from here and he's trying to trace them. They were white Creoles who fled after abolition. This version of his story is put into question by Emile Etienne's wife when she asserts that Francis' planter ancestor might have been cursed by his slaves, and that Francis could be a ghost who had come back to haunt the scenes of his past crimes.

In the translator's preface, Mr. Philcox says that the model he had in mind for the tone and register of voice of *Crossing the Mangrove* was Virginia Woolf's *To the Lighthouse*. It is hard not to see his logic, since Ms. Conde (whose other novels include *Segu* and *Tree of Life*) manipulates her narrative in ways that are reminiscent of Woolf and moves almost as effortlessly into and out of her characters' minds.

Nevertheless, the structure as well as the tone of the novel seem closer to Gabriel Garcia Marquez's *Chronicle of a Death Foretold*, whose myriad voices reveal the fate of Santiago Nasar. There are also similarities between the effects Francis has on those who meet him and the reactions of the characters who encounter Kurtz in Conrad's *Heart of Darkness*.

All these protagonists are known to us from hearsay, revealed through the distorting lens of memory. This is not to say that Francis is a brother to Conrad's prince of the dark. Unlike Kurtz the destroyer, Francis is a healer, a man who tries to bring light and possibility into lives distorted by suffering and indifference.

In the end, of course, the villagers' recollections reveal more about Riviere au Sel than about Francis Sancher. The most intriguing image in *Crossing the Mangrove* is the window of the dead man's coffin, which reflects the storytellers' faces superimposed upon his. Everyone at the wake is bound by this doubleness, by this meeting in the glass. The multiple interpretations offered by the living reveal Riviere au Sel as a protean community, changed and changing still because of one man's brief sojourn there.

Lawrence Thornton. *New York Times Book Review*, July 16, 1995

Maryse Condé's sweeping, sometimes disjointed novel [*The Last of the African Kings*] follows the history of a fictional African royal family through forced exile to the Caribbean and eventual emigration to the United States, setting up a provocative critique of multiculturalism and modern race relations. Spero, the last remaining male descendant of ''the ancestor,'' is a painter and philanderer whose lack of ambition clashes with the grand plans of his wife, an African-American historian named Debbie Middleton. Debbie is a fervent believer in a unified black culture, seeing in a romantic vision of Africa, made flesh when she falls in love with Spero, the foundation of a future power base. But Spero's reality—backed by diaries written by his grandfather, Diéré, and influenced by the many stories and myths of his large family—cuts through simple generalizations. Condé's novel explores the complex interplay between America and Africa, symbolized in the cultural and racial jumble of the Caribbean Islands. For Spero, the Americans have ''made Africa into their carnival/their Mardi Grass procession whose rags they had looted. They did not attempt to understand either its sense or meaning.'' Condé's narrative, fluidly translated from the French by her husband, Richard Philcox, uses Irony and humor to portray travelers moving back and forth along the historic line between Africa, the Antilles and America, delivering a vision of the black diaspora that challenges stereotypes by celebrating individual differences.

Erik Burns. *New York Times Book Review* (February 8, 1998) p. 18

BIBLIOGRAPHY
*Dieu nous l'a donne*, 1973; *Mort d'Oluwemi d'Ajumako*, 1975; *Heremakhonon*, 1976; *La Civilisation du bossale*, 1978; *Le Profil d'une oeuvre: Cahier d'un retour au pays natal*, 1978; *La Parole des femmes*, 1979; *Une Saison a Rihata*, 1981; *Segou: Les Murailles de terre*, 1984; *Segou II: La Terre en miettes*, 1985; *Pays mele*, 1985; *Moi, Tituba, Sorciere Noire de Salem*, 1986; *La Vie scelerate*, 1987; *Haiti cherie*, 1987; *Pension les Alizes*, 1988; *An Tan Revolisyon*, 1989; *Victor et les barricades*, 1989; *Traversee de la mangrove*, 1990; *No Woman No Cry*, 1991; *Hugo le terrible*, 1991; *Les derniers rois mages*, 1992; *La Colonie du nouveau monde*, 1993; *The Last of the African Kings*, 1997

# CULLEN, Countee (1903–1946)
**United States**

This first volume of musical verses [*Color*] offers promise of distinction for its author, shows him to be a young poet of uncommon earnestness and diligence. Serious purpose and careful work are apparent in all of his poems. One feels that he will cultivate his fine talent with intelligence, and reap its full harvest. He has already developed a lyric idiom which is not, perhaps, very unusual or striking in itself, but which he has learned to employ with considerable virtuosity. To be sure, the many elements which have entered that reservoir below the threshold of his consciousness have undergone as yet no thorough chemistry. But although some of the poems are flagrantly reminiscent, not only in detail but in outline, one never catches him resting idly on his fulcrums. Indeed, he accepts them with such dignity and appreciation, and often uses them to such telling advantage, that one is inclined to call attention to them only by remarking that he "has taken his own where he has found it."

Perhaps the only protest to Mr. Cullen that one cares to insist on is against his frequent use of a rhetorical style, which is surely neither instinctive in origin nor agreeable in effect. "Yet do I marvel," he writes, instead of, "And yet I marvel," the natural and fitting phrase; and many of his poems are marred by similar distortions. Lofty diction in poetry, when it is unwarranted by feeling (and therefore, intermediately, by rhythm) is liable to seem only stilted and prosy. Neither can personal emotion survive conventional expression. It is because of this, I think, that I find Mr. Cullen's longest poem, "The Shroud of Color," the least moving of any he has written.

George H. Dillon. *Poetry.* April 1926, pp. 50–51

For two generations Negro poets have been trying to do what Mr. Cullen has succeeded in doing. First, trying to translate into lyric form the highly poetic urge to escape from the blatant realities of life in America into a vivid past, and, second, fleeing from the stigma of being called a *Negro* poet, by, as Dunbar so desired to do, ignoring folk material and writing of such abstractions as love and death.

There is hardly anyone writing poetry in America today who can make the banal sound as beautiful as does Mr. Cullen. He has an extraordinary ear for music, a most extensive and dexterous knowledge of words and their values, and an enviable understanding of conventional poetic forms. Technically, he is almost precocious, and never, it may be added, far from the academic; but he is also too steeped in tradition, too influenced mentally by certain conventions and taboos. When he does forget these things, as in his greatest poem, "Heritage" . . . he reaches heights no other Negro poet has ever reached, placing himself high among his contemporaries, both black or white. But he has not gone far enough. His second volume [*Copper Sun*] is not as lush with promise or as spontaneously moving as his first. There has been a marking time or side-stepping rather than a marching forward. If it seems we expect too much from this poet, we can only defend ourselves by saying that we expect no more than the poet's earlier work promises.

Mr. Cullen's love poems are too much made to order. His race poems, when he attempts to paint a moral, are inclined to be sentimental and stereotyped. It is when he gives vent to the pagan spirit and lets it inspire and dominate a poem's form and context that he does his most impressive work. His cleverly turned rebellious poems are also above the ordinary. But there are not enough of these in comparison to those poems which are banal, though beautiful.

Wallace Thurman. *Bookman.* July 1928, pp. 559–60

The danger of falling below expectations is especially great in the case of the poet who turns novelist. Mr. Cullen, whose poetry is admired by so many, and whose danger therefore is the greater, has nevertheless challenged fate successfully. His first novel [*One Way to Heaven*] goes over. . . .

Be not misled by the announcement that "this is a mad and witty modern picture of high life in Harlem." That part of it which portrays the "high life" of Harlem is not important and seems even less important than it might, because the effect is completely submerged in the larger and simpler realities of the rest of the book. This is because Mr. Cullen has chosen to change his method and his viewpoint in dealing with the upper level. Here he becomes a caricaturist, suppressing all his sympathies, sketching with a sharp and ungracious pen. But the less pretentious folk he has treated gently and delicately, in color. This juxtaposition of two so different subjects so differently handled is somehow like exhibiting a lovely pastel and a cartoon in the same frame.

Rudolph Fisher. *New York Herald Tribune Books.* February 28, 1932, p. 3

Mr. Cullen has rendered Euripides's best-known tragedy [*The Medea*] into living and utterable English. He has made little attempt to convey the poetry of the original, preferring to concentrate on dramatic situation and realistic portrayal of character. The result is a very forceful and poignant re-creation of the story of the barbarian sorceress whose fury against a faithless lover wins the tragic conflict with her love for her children. Only a few of the choruses have been put into lyrical form: the rest of the play has been cast in prose that is simple often to the point of baldness and, except for two or three incongruous lapses into slang, both colloquial and dignified. . . .

Perhaps fifty persons today read the classics in translation to one who reads them in the original; if there is to be a popular revival of interest in the Greek drama, it appears that this is more likely to originate in Harlem than in the universities.

Philip Blair Rice. *Nation.* September 18, 1935, p. 336

One important writer among the new Negroes stands out as having contributed nothing or little to this conglomeration [of vivid Negro characters]. That writer is the poet Countee Cullen. He for himself (as well as others for him) has written numerous disclaimers of an attitude narrowed by racial influence. He may be right. Certainly *Caroling Dusk*, his anthology of "verse by Negro poets," represents a careful culling of the less distinctive, that is to say, the less Negroid poetry of his most defiantly Negro contemporaries. Nevertheless it remains that when writing on race material Mr. Cullen is at his best. His is an unfortunate attitude, for it has been deliberately acquired and in that sense is artificial, tending to create a kind of effete and bloodless poetry in the manner of [William Stanley] Braithwaite. The essential quality of good poetry is utmost sincerity and earnestness of purpose. A poet untouched by his times, by his conditions, by his environment is only half a poet, for earnestness and sincerity grow in direct proportion as one feels intelligently the pressure of immediate life. One may not like the pressure and the necessities under which it forces one to labor, but one does not deny it. . . .

Now undoubtedly the biggest, single unalterable circumstance in the life of Mr. Cullen is his color. Most of the life he has lived has been influenced by it. And when he writes by it, he *writes*; but when this does not guide him, his pen trails faded ink across his pages.

J. Saunders Redding. *To Make a Poet Black* (Chapel Hill: University of North Carolina Press, 1939), pp. 108–9

About half of [Cullen's] "best poems" were written while he was a student of New York University, and it was during these years that he first came up for consideration as an authentic American writer, the goal to which he aspired. Up at "The Dark Tower," a gathering place of awakened Harlem, the very name of which was taken from one of Cullen's sonnets, there was never any doubt that he would make it. At the *Opportunity* banquets, where prizes were awarded by that once-influential magazine in order to encourage the efforts of new Negro writers, it was taken for granted that Cullen was in. Before he finished college, his poems had been published in a dozen or more magazines, including *The Nation, Poetry, The American Mercury*, and *Harper's. Color*, the first collection of these lyrics, made a solid impression in 1925, the year in which Cullen celebrated his twenty-second birthday.

*Copper Sun* and *The Ballad of the Brown Girl*, both presenting more of his undergraduate output, followed. . . . Meanwhile, the young poet went abroad on a Guggenheim Fellowship, perhaps, as much as anything else, to take stock. His stay in France was extended a year beyond his original plans, but even that wasn't long enough. His springtime leaves had fallen, and he was still waiting for a new season to bring another yield. He kept writing as a matter of habit, and the little shelf of his books increased steadily, but that wasn't the real thing; that wasn't what he was waiting for. A decade later he wrote to a friend, "My muse is either dead or taking a twenty-year sleep." . . .

Cullen did not live to see another springtime resurgence of his own creative powers comparable with the impulse that produced his first three books of poetry, the books which give his selected poems most of their lilt and brightness.

Arna Bontemps. *Saturday Review*. March 22, 1947, pp. 13, 44

Why did Countee Cullen drop racial poetry so suddenly and completely? What happened after the publication of *The Black Christ* to dry up the springs of racial verse? It has been argued that Cullen turned from racial themes because he came to feel too keenly the inner conflict which his status as poet and Negro imposed upon him. . . . Undeniably, Cullen the poet was disturbed by the added burden of race, but I am inclined to believe that he turned from racial themes for a much more realistic and down-to-earth cause; namely, a consciousness of waning powers in this particular area of poetry. He had worked the racial lode to depletion, and he realized it. . . .

Cullen's heart had had its say on the matter of race, and he preferred a "stony silence" to futile sound. We can easily understand his position. After all, there are only so many things that one can say on the race problem. The alien-and-exile theme with its glorification of Africa had become discredited even while Cullen was using it. Protest, like religion, is a very narrow subject for poetry. Cullen, a highly sensitive and intelligent artist, came to realize this and turned to greener pastures in children's literature.

Arthur P. Davis. *Phylon*. 14, 4, 1953, pp. 399–400

Cullen's satire [in *One Way to Heaven*] is friendly; Mrs. Brandon is never malicious and is a most likeable character. But it was satire directed towards Negroes, and doubtless some of Cullen's own

patrons, and such satire stands practically alone in the Harlem Renaissance. Perhaps most important is the relationship of the satire to Cullen's own career. From Harlem newspapers and from the portrayal of Mrs. Brandon and her friends, we can infer that the middle class Harlem reading public often bought Harlem Renaissance books without reading them, and were more concerned with the fact of a Negro literary renaissance than with the quality of the writings. Much of Cullen's own poetry, with its chauvinism and cloistered romanticism, seems to have been directed towards this group. And Cullen himself indulged almost as much as Mrs. Brandon in using high-sounding language where simple Anglo-Saxon words would suffice.

By 1932, judging from *One Way to Heaven*, Cullen was disillusioned, detached, and a little quizzical towards the Harlem Renaissance. Here he was breaking his own dictum that Negro writers should present only the appealing sides of Negro life to the white public. And he was ridiculing a main source of his own reputation, along with the excesses of chauvinism the Harlem Renaissance produced.

Stephen H. Bronz. *Roots of Negro Racial Consciousness* (New York: Libra, 1964), pp. 63–64

[Cullen] often tried out his verses [for children] by reading them to his cousin's little girls. Their greatest enjoyment came from the stories in verse about the strange animals he invented, such as the Wakeupworld with twelve eyes arranged clockwise in his head, the Lapalake that could never get enough to drink, and the proud Snakethatwalkeduponhistail. When the children demanded to know the origin of these amusing creatures, he had a ready answer. With a straight face he told them that Christopher, his cat (whom the youngsters knew and loved), had told him a long story about these unusual beasts. They were animals whose species are lost to us because they failed to get into Noah's Ark when the world was destroyed by the great flood. Each one had missed the boat because of a particular flaw in his character. Christopher had learned the story from his father through a long line of ancestors descended from the first Christopher, who had sailed on the Ark.

These stories in verse with prose interludes were later published as *The Lost Zoo*. . . . The love for his pets and his deep feeling for all animals gave this book a special place in Countee's affection.

Blanche E. Ferguson. *Countee Cullen and the Negro Renaissance* (New York: Dodd, Mead, 1966), pp. 155, 165

[Cullen] was, and probably still is, considered the least race-conscious of the Negro poets. . . . Nevertheless, it was because of the color of his skin that Countee Cullen was more aware of the racial poetry and could not be at all times "sheer poet." This was clearly a problem for Cullen—wanting to write lyrics on love, death, and beauty—always so consciously aware of his race. This can be seen, for instance, in his poem "Uncle Jim," where the struggle is neatly portrayed through the young boy, thinking of Keats, and his uncle, bitter with thoughts of the difference between being a black man or a white man in our society. . . .

For Cullen, then, the racial problem was always there, even when one was thinking of odes by Keats, and he was impelled—*in spite of everything I can do*—to write about this subject. This was the cause of much weakness in his writing, as well as some strength; for there are poems about race which have an emotional intensity that most of his white peers could not have matched.

Margaret Perry. *A Bio-Bibliography of Countee P. Cullen* (Westport, Connecticut, Greenwood, 1971), pp. 26–28

A significant writer—even a lyric poet—must perceive some truth, some reality which he wishes to reveal. It is the quality of this vision which elevates his song from the transitory to the memorable. In his earliest poems, Cullen sought such truth in a presumed affinity with Africa. He wanted to believe that impulses of his African heritage surged past his censoring consciousness and forced him to repudiate the white gods of Western Civilization. Cullen's Africa, however, was a utopia in which to escape from the harsh actualities of America, and the heritage a myth on which he hoped to erect a new faith to comfort himself in a world seemingly dedicated to furthering the interests of white men. . . .

As the African impulse waned, Cullen knelt before the altar of love, but there also false gods demanded sacrifices he would not offer. Like a wanderer disconsolate after a worldwide search, Cullen turned back to Christ. But he still could not rely upon the white god who governed the Methodist Church in which he had been reared; he could not believe a white god capable of comprehending the depths of a black man's suffering. Therefore, he fashioned for himself a black Christ with "dark, despairing features." This image, however, furnished scant comfort; Cullen knew that his own creation could not correct mankind's transgressions. Without faith, without vision, Cullen, whom Saunders Redding has compared with Shakespeare's ethereal Ariel, lost his power to sing and soar above the fleshly Calibans.

Darwin T. Turner. *In a Minor Chord: Three Afro-American Writers and Their Search for Identity* (Carbondale: Southern Illinois University Press, 1971), pp. 60–61

It is easy to understand why this long poem of 963 lines ["The Black Christ"] finally lost Cullen the sympathies of the black public. For the poem, with its mystical character, and despite the title and the theme of the narrative, is not essentially Negro in any way. Its very mysticism was condemned as childish [by J. Saunders Redding], and one critic [Benjamin Brawley] actually reproached the author for having dated the poem from Paris.

There may be more meaning in this reproof than might be thought, for "The Black Christ" has affinities with a type of literature that could scarcely arouse any echoes in an American reading public. It is, as we see it, something like the transposition into another setting of a French medieval miracle play with, at the same time, the character of a votive offering, on the lines of a well-known Passion play [that performed in Oberammergau, Bavaria] which was expressly composed to give thanks to heaven for having spared a whole population the horrors of the plague.

"The Black Christ" must be read as a poem of thanksgiving for the bestowal of the light of faith, as well as the translation into words of a contemplative experience. The religious exaltation that dictates the poem's entire structure bears the marks of the neophyte's sense of wonderment and his whole touching naïveté. With

such characteristics, however, "The Black Christ" was inevitably inaccessible to all but a handful of readers. [1963]

Jean Wagner. *Black Poets of the United States* (Urbana: University of Illinois Press, 1973), pp. 345–46

Most Anglo-American poetry tends to employ an iambic beat. In "Heritage" Cullen resorts to the use of a trochaic measure. It seems valid to assume that his choice of the descending line was no accident. Under such an assumption, it also seems highly possible that in the rhythms of "Heritage" Cullen hoped to suggest the throb of African drums, for certainly the percussive movement of a trochaic line may fall upon the ear like the big and small booms of tom-toms in the African bush. Moreover, if the trochees of "Heritage" are tom-toms, and especially if they are consciously so, they might be further proof of how un-African Cullen really was. They might tell us again that Cullen's Africa existed only when Cullen was able to put his mind on what he was doing, as he could put his mind on the *selection* of a beat. So it may be that his Africa was contrived and synthetic, not integral within him as it must have been to justify the claims he makes in "Heritage" of the presence of his forefathers' continent in his "blood." How significant, then, might be Cullen's allusion in "Heritage" to rain: "I can never rest at all when the rain begins to fall." The rain brings back, that is, so Cullen is implying, the drums and Africa. And very probably it did, at the literary level, the same level at which Eugene O'Neill could put his drums into *The Emperor Jones* or Somerset Maugham his rain into the play of the same name, with which almost surely Cullen was better acquainted than with Africa.

Blyden Jackson. In Blyden Jackson and Louis D. Rubin, Jr., *Black Poetry in America* (Baton Rouge: Louisiana State University Press, 1974), p. 49

Cullen was the most enchanting lyric voice of the Harlem Renaissance, far exceeding Claude McKay (by no means a poor singer himself), both of whom had been shaped by a youthful love for nineteenth-century English lyricism. But McKay's early encounter with that tradition had not discouraged his inclination to strong social and racial statement. He said once that when he read the great Victorian lyricists he could "feel their race, their class, their roots in the soil." And in one of his poems he prayed for "ancient music" to come to his "modern heart" and make him "the worthy singer of my world and race."

Cullen did not, could not, avoid entirely the question of race. But his view of himself as a poet did not permit him to make that question his main subject. Where McKay prayed to be a singer of his "world and race," Cullen aspired to sing more for "world" than for "race." To sing too much for the latter was, in his view, a form of social crusading, corrupting to the primary or essential function of poetry—or art, generally. Only occasionally was the sound of racial protest heard strongly in his work, as in his long poems "The Black Christ" and "The Shroud of Color," or in the much shorter "From the Dark Tower":

> We shall not always plant while others reap
> The golden increment of bursting fruit,
> Not always countenance, abject and mute,
> That lesser men should hold their brothers cheap;

The night whose sable breast relieves the stark,
White stars is no less lovely being dark,
And there are buds that cannot bloom at all
In light, but crumple, piteous, and fall;
So in the dark we hide the heart that bleeds,
And wait, and tend our agonizing seeds.

Usually, Cullen engaged the race problem obliquely—at times with deft jabs and glancing blows, as in ''For a Lady I Know'':

She even thinks that up in heaven
Her class lies late and snores
While poor black cherubs rise at seven
To do celestial chores.

At times with understated amusement, as in ''Incident'':

Once riding in old Baltimore,
Heart-filled, head-filled with glee
I saw a Baltimorean
Keep looking straight at me.
Now I was eight and very small,
And he was no whit bigger,
And so I smiled, but he poked
His tongue, and called me, ''Nigger.''
I saw the whole of Baltimore
From May until December;
Of all the things that happened there
That's all that I remember.

At other times with poignant irony, as in ''Yet Do I Marvel''. . . .

The larger portion of Cullen's poems (including some that made use of racial detail) were wry or plaintive commentaries on general experience: love, death, grief, yearning, nature, the passing of the seasons—and, of course, beauty,'' to which he was ''betrothed.'' He was among the three or four most quoted poets in America; for, as Calverton observed in 1929, Cullen wrote ''with an infectious beauty of rhythm.''. . .

To a number of Cullen's ambivalent colleagues in the Negro renaissance movement, it was indeed a curious thing that a black-born poet could so have learned to sing. Not even the race-conscious novelist Wallace Thurman could help praising Cullen's ''extraordinary ear for music,'' his ''extensive and dexterous knowledge of words and their values,'' his ''enviable understanding of conventional poetic forms.'' But Thurman, who seldom tossed a bouquet that wasn't followed by a brickbat, went on to criticize Cullen for being ''too steeped in tradition, too influenced mentally by certain conventions and taboos.'' Cullen, he added, was a bourgeois poet who ''never will seek the so-called lower elements of Negro life in his poetic rhythms and material.''

This quarrel was an echo, however faint, of the differing aesthetic programs favored by DuBois and Locke. Hughes (whose free conversational rhythms captured the moods of jazz and the ''so-called lower elements'' of Harlem life) also weighed in against Cullen's poetics. It was Cullen he had in mind in 1926 when he wrote:

One of the most promising of the young ''Negro'' poets said to me once, ''I want to be a poet—not a Negro poet''; meaning subconsciously, would like to be a white poet''; meaning behind that, ''I would like to be white.'' And I was very sorry the young man said that, for no great poet has ever been afraid of being himself. And I doubted then that, with

his desire to run away spiritually from his race, this boy would ever be a great poet.

Whether or not Hughes was correct in his psychoanalysis of Cullen, it would appear that the ''boy'' did gain recognition as a great poet. . . .

Harlem, where Cullen lived in the 1920s and beyond, was the paradigmatic black urban community of his time. Beneath the surface of its gaiety, it was the principal stage on which the dramas of black aspiration, self-discovery, and self-assertion were being enacted. Although Cullen's work was not without racial themes (however hard he may have tried to suppress them), it reflected no great absorption with the social styles, predicaments, and ambitions of those who formed the majority in the black population. This is surely not meant to suggest that as a black poet Cullen was obliged to limit his attention to the urgent affairs of skin color; he was as entitled as all artists are to follow the dictates of his imagination. But it is meant to suggest that an aesthete of his character—averse to direct social and racial confrontation in his work; reluctant to identify it too closely with black consciousness; feeling that such had no proper place in the life of poetry; even declining to regard himself as a ''Negro Poet''—a writer so aloof from the pressing issues and concerns of his people can scarcely have been the dominant and defining racial influence of his age. . . .

Still, if Cullen wasn't the first writer of color to identify the conundrum of blackness in American culture, he was certainly an outstanding example of it: a poet who desired to sing as he or his imagination pleased, uninhibited by the demanding subject matter of blackness. . . .

The problem that Cullen described, a problem of all black writers who shared his philosophy of art, was essentially the problem of artistic or cultural freedom—how to adjudicate the claims of personal imagination against the claims of racial community and political engagement. Cullen resolved those claims on the side of what was most animating to him, his imagination of himself as an artist, even if the melodies he sang were not so invigorating to the mass struggle for social change and racial progress.

Jervis Anderson. *The New Republic*. 204, 14 (April 8, 1991), pp. 27–33

Countee Cullen's best known poem, ''Yet Do I Marvel'' (1925), has been as widely misinterpreted as a poem as Cullen has been misunderstood as a poet. The sonnet seems to many readers and critics no more than the lament of a defeated soul, a complaint by a man unable to resolve the dilemma of being black and a poet. A reconsideration of the poem's structure and logic reveals that Cullen actually expresses the resolution of a paradox, rather than bemoaning his fate.

The poem comprises three quatrains and one couplet that mark off four specific examples of apparent injustice. These serve as preliminary illustrations of paradox, preceding irony of the climactic couplet:

I doubt not God is good, well-meaning, kind,
And did He stoop to quibble could tell why
The little buried mole continues blind,
Why flesh that mirrors Him must some day die,
Make plain the reason tortured Tantalus
Is baited by the fickle fruit, declare
If merely brute caprice dooms Sisyphus

To struggle up a never-ending stair.
Inscrutable His ways are, and immune
To catechism by a mind too strewn
With petty cares to slightly understand
What awful brain compels His awful hand.
Yet do I marvel at this curious thing:
To make a poet black, and bid him sing!

The speaker claims not to understand what appear to be unjust punishments, although he assumes these apparent injustices are explicable by God. Cullen selects and arranges these four examples strategically to emphasize his real point.

The first quatrain comprises two cases of seemingly cruel or undeserved punishment. When closely considered, however, these examples are neither unjust nor paradoxical. The ''little buried mole continues blind'' because he scarcely needs vision to thrive in his underground habitat; rather than being punished, the mole is perfectly equipped for survival. Certainly the mole does not perceive or experience his lot as a punishment. Similarly, man, whose ''flesh'' . . . mirrors God, will indeed die: but man as a spiritual reflection of his divine maker need die only physically in order to inherit eternal life of the spirit. According to the theology in which Cullen bases his poem, God made man in his image in a spiritual rather than in a physical sense; by so doing, God equipped man for survival beyond the grave. Rather than victims of ''brute caprice,'' mole and man are the recipients of natural and supernatural justice respectively.

With the two allusions to Greek mythology in the second quatrain, Cullen no doubt assumes that the reader will either recognize the references or discover the full stories; that so few readers have done so does not alter the implications of his use of these mythological subtexts. First, the poet pictures Tantalus eternally starving while food is just beyond his grasp. Tantalus, son of Zeus and king of Phrygia, was punished in such a manner for crimes against both mortals and gods. Accounts vary, but generally included among his offenses are stealing nectar and ambrosia from the gods and murdering his own son and serving him up as table food. In light of these crimes, the torture of Tantalus seems a symmetric example of the punishment fitting the offense, and no puzzle at all. The same is true of Cullen's reference to the Sisyphus myth in lines 8 and 9. . . .

Both the nature and sequence of these four examples clearly indicate that Cullen includes and designs them as preliminary to and analogous with his final paradox. He has included variety ranging from the most mundane of creatures (literally down-to-earth, one might add) to the spiritual disposition of mankind. He has spanned the real and the imaginary, the present natural world and the fictional past. Yet Cullen strings all this on one significant common thread—all four paradoxes are puzzles with built-in solutions. Through these carefully chosen examples the poet leads the reader to the recognition of the reconcilability of the ''curious thing'' he postulates in the concluding couplet.

There the speaker asserts, ''Yet do I marvel at this curious thing: / To make a poet black, and bid him sing!'' Note that ''this curious thing'' is not a dichotomy between being a poet and being black—as some readers are too quick to assume—but between being a black poet and being expected to ''sing.'' Cullen thus cites conditions of circumstance that are indeed difficult but not impossible to reconcile. Had he meant to conclude his sonnet by claiming that it is impossible to be both black and a poet, or for that matter, that it is impossible for a black poet to ''sing,'' he most certainly would not have led up to such assertions with specific self-reconcilable instances. Instead, these previous instances alert the reader that the climactic example is yet another paradox that is just that: a contradiction that is apparent rather than real.

The couplet (and the poem) turns on the connotation of the term ''sing.'' Cullen appropriately notes the difficulty of voicing lyric joy or of freely expressing artistic imagination at the exclusion of his racial status. Any African American poet writing in 1925 would have found it difficult to ignore the suffering of his race, or to ''sing'' of his blackness without an element of melancholy or rage in his song. Nonetheless, because to sing is so general, so expansive a term, rather than connoting isolation or exclusion, it more readily suggests inclusion, and perhaps even transcendence. Cullen acknowledges, even emphasizes, the difficulty for a black poet in answering that divine call to sing; but through the strategic presentation of precedent, he also claims that the black poet can still articulate his blackness and express his unique racial identity while singing his humanity.

Finally, the sonnet suggests possibility, just as the larger example of Countee Cullen's poetic canon more fully demonstrates that notion. Rather than evidence of his failure, the sonnet can be better and more accurately understood as an illustration of achievement.

Fred M. Fetrow. *The Explicator*. 56, 2 (Winter 1998), pp. 103–05

BIBLIOGRAPHY

*Color*, 1925; *The Ballad of the Brown Girl*, 1927; *Caroling Dusk*, 1927; *Copper Sun*, 1927; *The Black Christ, and Other Poems*, 1929; *One Way to Heaven*, 1932; *The Medea*, 1935; *The Lost Zoo*, 1940; *My Lives and How I Lost Them*, 1942; *On These I Stand: An Anthology of the Best Poems of Countee Cullen*, 1947

# D

## DADIÉ, Bernard Binlin (1916–)
### Ivory Coast

In *The Circle of Days* the lyrical movement is different [from that of David Diop's poetry]. Humor, tenderness, and harmony with life have a different density. *The Circle of Days* is more like a Negro spiritual than a message bearing vindictive fire. It expresses a more secretive consciousness and inner life. But Africa is equally present, and as sometimes in the works of Langston Hughes, it is colored with an evangelical humor: ''I thank you, God, for having created me Black,/for having made me/the sum of all sorrows. . . .''

Dadié's lyricism remains intimate and casual even when he makes accusations; he never appeals to the powers of hatred. . . . Besides a tender humor, a joy in living seems to me to best define Dadié's originality. It is a joy that defies death: ''Never a sad goodbye . . . Carry me/as if we were going to a celebration/hand in hand. . . .''

It is natural for the poet from the Ivory Coast to be sensitive to the magic of love. On this plane, Dadié attains the Dionysian fervor of David Diop. For Dadié, too, love is a participation in the elementary pulsations of life. . . .

The African charm that characterizes Dadié's stories also pervades his poetry, and leaves within us, as on his native sand, imprints of bare, agile feet!

René Depestre. *Presence Africaine.* December 1956, pp. 112–13†

Dadié belongs to the early post-First World War generation and for this reason his work reflects rather well the period of the true beginnings of the African evolution. Thus, he is a part of that group of intellectuals composed of doctors and teachers trained in Dakar who are commonly known as the ''educated persons'' of Negro Africa and who, to a large extent, make up our present-day governments. Consequently, he was caught up in the mesh of the movement, especially in politics, which shows us the constructive character of his book called *A Negro in Paris.* He thus follows the development of present-day Africa. . . .

His work is diverse and contrary and consists of legends, poems and novels, including [*A Negro in Paris*]. This book is splendid for its diversity of form: in some passages we find real poetic inspiration; in others, we have the impression that we are reading Voltaire or Montesquieu. It is well constructed and coherent, though in certain places the spirit of the work is somewhat lost.

I do not think this book seeks to transplant Western development—a part of whose culture we have acquired—into Africa. The issue is one involving her individual evolution confronted with Western culture, because it must be said that she can only evolve in terms of what she has received. This does not mean a mere copying but a synthesizing of her own in order to acquire her own individuality.

Joseph Miezan Bognini. *Presence Africaine* (English ed.). 8, 1, 1961, p. 156

As a counterpart of *Tales of Renart the Fox*, which belongs to the French Middle Ages, and the Cycle of Leuk the Hare, which belongs to the Senegalese soil, the Ivory Coast (together with [southern Togo and southern Dahomey]) offers us the Tales of the Spider.

Kacou Ananzè [in Dadié's *The Black Skirt*] personifies trickery, cleverness, and above all dishonesty and treachery, without the likeable and joyous traits that make Leuk and Renart so intensely vibrant. Kacou Ananzè incarnates the malicious spirit lying in wait for animals and men. Although surrounded by numerous other creatures, this character . . . creates the unifying element in this Book of Animals. Of the sixteen stories collected in *The Black Skirt*, ten are devoted to the spider. . . .

If Renart, Leuk, and their feathered and furry friends correspond approximately to their equivalents in nature, Kacou Ananzè, on the contrary, in no way shows the zoological features of the spider; he can reach the size of a man, bow down, stand up straight, and walk on two legs. His behavior is in every way reminiscent of that of the Ivory Coast peasant: he lives in a hut, cultivates his land, goes fishing, and does his shopping. Kacou Ananzè's anthropomorphism therefore precludes our classifying him as a zoological or mythical beast.

Roger Mercier and M. and S. Battestini. *Bernard Dadié* (Paris: Fernand Nathan, 1964), p. 7

[In *Boss of New York*] Dadié looks in an unusual way at ''surprising America,'' and this ''old west'' about which ''I thought everything had been said but which yielded things never revealed to anyone else.'' Dadié turns his gaze upon this land in which beauty and ugliness mingle without colliding. With a subtle knowledge of human psychology, he depicts this nation torn from a peaceful life by an infernal quest for supremacy. He explicitly describes this nation's shifting profile, letting America's whole ridiculous pretension be reflected through his naïveté.

Paris and New York do not make Dadié feel disillusioned, strangely uprooted, or sadly nostalgic. On the contrary, his trips allow him to observe minutely the ''immense absurdity'' surrounding him. From his deliberations there arises a grain of humor sufficient to set up that liberating distance which makes the ''Negro,'' formerly condemned to being observed and kept at a distance, into a human being who observes and judges in turn. Dadié is a remarkable manifestation in literature of the movement toward awareness as a prelude to liberation.

*Boss of New York*, for some readers a simple ''chronicle'' of a trip, is actually an amusing satire revealing the unknown, fragile underbelly of Yankee power.

C. Quillateau. *Bernard Binlin Dadié: L'homme et l'œuvre* (Paris, Présence Africaine, 1967), pp. 25–26†

[*A Negro in Paris*] is cast in the form of a traveler's book in which a foreign visitor writes a detailed and presumably ''objective'' description of the interesting customs and manners of his hosts. *A Negro in Paris* is extended irony, Dadié placing his main character, a West African, in the reverse role of many a rather smug European traveler to West Africa. Whereas the European would describe the quaint behavior of Africans for home consumption so that others might ''understand'' them, the narrator of this work describes Parisian mores with the same critical eye for relationships among minute, often ridiculous details. . . .

Dadié's basic theme seems to be that the Parisian is really a human being after all, and worthy of study, having a history and traditions which he reveres, gods whom he worships. And by drawing comparisons between the West African and the Parisian, the author suggests that Africans are as good as Europeans, or that Europeans are as bad as Africans, however the case might appear. The core problem is the understanding of persons of one culture by those of another.

Austin J. Shelton. *L'espirit createur.* Fall 1970, pp. 217, 219

Like so many other French-speaking Africans, Dadié is continuously asserting the beauty of African life as a constant reminder that colonialism cheated the black man out of his heritage. . . . *Climbié*, like the other prose works of its family, portrays the quality of African childhood experiences. The general outlines of the pattern are common: tough elementary education, dogged by poverty, sadistic schoolmastership, and so on; life among the many relatives in the African extended family; childhood ambitions; secondary education which is perpetually haunted by the fear of failure; the day one sets out in pursuit of one's vision; new experiences in the encounter with white authority that invariably suspects and fears the ''educated native.''

Nothing spectacular happens to Climbié until he has finished secondary school and is working—towards the end of the book.

His development is like the muted process of plant growth in which the seed germinates, pushes through, always in an upward thrust, until it blossoms and lays bare its foliage, now exposed to wind, sun, rain, insects that lie in wait for its juices, in a way it never happened before. As with the plant, things happen to Climbié; he never ''happens'' to them, until he reacts to white domination once he is back home from Senegal. His development is fully rendered by the marvellously subtle shift in Dadié's style, especially in Part II; the style ''grows up'' with Climbié. And yet, again, like a plant, he is part of the landscape which we view through him. Dadié has portrayed for us, often in a volatile idiom that reflects his mercurial personality, a human and physical landscape that is alive, at once friendly and hostile, and indifferent.

Ezekiel Mphahlele. Introduction to Bernard Dadié, *Climbié* (London: Heinemann Educational Books, 1971), pp. viii–ix

In effect [*Béâtrice du Congo* and *Iles de tempête*] insist on the presentation of a version of history other than the official one and the constitution of a memory different from the one constituted from a hegemonic position of the colonial or slave-trading power. This is a decentering of discourse that can be read as a form of resistance.

Two characters from Bernard Dadié's theater; Béâtrice du Congo and Toussaint Louverture, illustrate both political resistance and subversion of the discourse of power. In Dadié's plays, these characters are revived as charismatic individuals and revolutionary heroes. While their projects for society may bear a slight

resemblance, their destinies and their historical and literary legacies prove unequal. Toussaint, the male hero, has a visible presence in history and literature. While Béâtrice, the female character, has not been totally erased from African history, she has nevertheless been relegated to its margins. The history of African nationalism is written almost exclusively in the masculine.

In 1704, at the height of the evangelization of Central Africa, a young black prophetess appeared in the ancient kingdom of Kongo: Béâtrice Kimpa Vita, named ''la sainte Antoine congolaise'' 'the Congolese Saint Anthony' by the missionaries of the time because she claimed to be a reincarnation of Saint Anthony. Accused of heresy, she was arrested and sentenced by the Congolese political authorities and burned alive in 1706. . . .

In 1802, on the other side of the Atlantic, a free black man named Toussaint who had served as a French general led an army of slaves and freemen to rise up against both the existing order and the restoration of slavery in Saint-Domingue. This action marked the beginning of a war of independence. Arrested as a rebel and sent as a prisoner into exile in France, he was locked up in the Fort de Joux in the Jura, where he died in 1803. . . .

Bernard Dadié drew inspiration from the lives of the historical figures Béâtrice and Toussaint to create a nationalist theater. In the play *Béâtrice du Congo* (1970), Béâtrice is an ordinary woman in the Kingdom of Kongo. She had been baptized, like most of her peers, by the Capuchin missionaries, for the Manicongo, king of Kongo, had accepted the Christian faith and assimilation to the Bitanda ways of life, which henceforth directed the cultural and political life of the kingdom. It is in this context that Doña Béâtrice reveals herself as a prophetess, the bearer of a liberating mission. She begins to preach the creation of a national Congolese church and the restoration of the legitimate king in San Salvador, the capital. This outspokenness that calls religious ideology into question while contesting political power will lead to her condemnation.

Dadié's other play, *Iles de tempête* (1973), is also the literary symbol of a lived history, that of Toussaint, an ambiguous being, torn between two images: the poverty of his origins, on the one hand, and the opulence represented by Napoleon Bonaparte, on the other. Idealistic, he searches for a truth that would correspond to the one demanded by the liberation of a people whom he would like to make equal to those in Europe, particularly the France of Bonaparte. But he is also a man sensitive to power and demands of his people. By one of those ironies that are abundant in history, he is misunderstood by all and betrayed, and so will die in exile, far from the people and the land for which he had fought.

Dadié's two plays are not only a rereading and reinterpretation of the past, they also reveal a discourse that is both critical and self-critical: critical in its interpretation of colonization and slavery, both of which are fundamentally motivated by the desire for territorial conquest and the acquisition of material wealth; self-critical in its representation of a power with nationalist claims, but which is authoritarian, mimetic, and dominated by the West. In a remarkable way, these plays indicate a single paradigm: a catastrophe documented in history that has been recaptured in literature to present a means for rethinking the present and preparing for the future. . . .

It is evident that *Béâtrice du Congo* and *Iles de tempête* are directly inspired by historical reality. The major problem arising from a comparison between the historical figures and the literary characters is the credibility or truthfulness of their representations—the literary one that arises from a synchronic present, and the historic one that proceeds from a past reconstructed by a method aspiring to be objective and rigorous. For Béatrice and Toussaint, the question of credibility vanishes, or more precisely, it is articulated with the same conviction in both representations. In this way, the Béatrice of the eighteenth-century Capuchins, even if she appears more true to life, is just as much the result of an interpretation as the one proceeding from Dadié's imagination in our time. The same is true for the Toussaint of Haitian history in relation to the Toussaint of the literary text of Dadié, Césaire, or Glissant. In both the historical and the literary perspectives, representations are products of reconstruction. At this point, the real question becomes the relation between the extratextual historical reality and the textual content, produced by the literary or historical imagination of an author. . . .

The reconstruction of these two characters by Dadié is akin to Glissant's project to establish an ''histoire à faire'' 'history to be made,' which will be the counterpart to an ''histoire subie'' 'experienced history,' that is, history as reconstituted and written from the position of the colonial powers and the dominant cultures. Dadié's reconstruction is also in accord with the Césairean plan to construct a national memory through the resurrection of figures from the past who could then be referred to as national heroes. In the works of Glissant, Césaire, and Dadié, one finds the idea that a restoration of these figures to history constitutes an act of justice, which, as Nietzsche affirms in *The Use and Abuse of History*, establishes greatness in search of truth.

Calling into question official versions of history, Dadié's gaze toward the past also seeks to be a ''prophetic vision'' and a lesson on the use of the past. A victim of the different forms of violence accompanying colonization by the Bitanda and itself a source of violence, much like Toussaint in relation to the inhabitants of Saint-Domingue and to the French authority, the Congoloese government prefigures contemporary African politicians. Both, trained in the folly of grandeur and a mimetism of the West, come under the great temptation of power, which soon transforms them into authoritarian and autocratic leaders. Therefore, for Dadié, the past is neither a refuge nor the site of complacency in a nostalgic and narcissistic gaze. It functions, rather, to quote Michel de Certeau, as a ''processus de réemploi'' 'process of re-usage' to ''inventer le présent'' 'invent the present.'. . .

In sum, Béâtrice and Toussaint navigate between history and literature, inasmuch as Dadié exploits history in the name of literature in order to produce literary texts, and produces literary texts in order to rewrite history. Dadié's project is thus conceived as a contribution to the reconstitution of a collective experience rooted in violence and approached through two individual lives. In doing this, the historical perspective overlaps with the literary imagination, and literature with history. In the end, the discourse presented in Dadié's texts bears witness to two characters who, theoretically, are opposed to each other and whose opposition is summarized in binaries such as man and woman, African and Antillean, colonization and slavery. But in reality Toussaint and Béâtrice express the same signification and share a similar condition as dominated individuals without power or the right to speech, as well as the same quest involving alienation and the possibility for liberation. They also share the constitution of the text as a possible site for a political and ideological subversion whose essential tropes are inversion, irony, parallelism, and parody. . . .

At the same time it appropriates the repressed voices of the colonized, the slave, and the African woman, Dadié's literary imagination restores these figures to history and, in so doing, grounds them in the present. Literary imagination thus makes possible a rereading of the past and a reviving as exemplary heroes of those whom the official history of the conquerors had marked as negative signs and as examples of marginality. Dadié's plays assume an ideological function that consecrates the promotion of the colonial subject and the African woman as actors and agents in history. In the end, the literary text produced establishes itself as a space in which national history can be read.

> Elizabeth Mudimbe-Boyi. *Research in African Literatures.* 29, 3 (Fall 1998), pp. 98–103

BIBLIOGRAPHY

*Les Villes* (play), 1933; *Assemien Dehyle, roi du Sanwi: Precede de Mon pays et son theatre* (play), 1936; *Afrique debout*, 1950; *Legendes Africaines*, 1954; *Le Pagne noir*, 1955; *Climbié*, 1956; *La ronde des jours*, 1956; *Un Nègre à Paris*, 1959; *Patron de New York*, 1964; *Hommes de tous les continents*, 1967; *La Ville ou nul ne meurt*, 1968; *Beatrice du Congo: Piece en trois actes* (play), 1970; *Monsieur Thogo–gnini* (play), 1970; *Les Voix dans le vent* (play), 1970; *Iles de Tempete: Piece en sept tableaux* (play), 1973; *Papassidi, maitre–escroc* (play), 1975; *Mhoi–Ceul: Comedie en 5 tableaux* (play), 1979; *Commandant Taureault et ses negres*, 1980; *Les Jambes du fils de Dieu*, 1980; *Carnet de prison*, 1981; *Les Contes de Koutou–As–Samala*, 1982; *Ville ou nul ne meurt*, 1986

# DAMAS, Léon-Gontran (1912–)
**French Guiana**

For a long time I have hesitated to write about *Pigments*—not because its merits as poetry are negligible, but because it is primarily a testimony: a Negro poet tells us his reactions to White Society. . . . This point of view explains the tenseness of Damas's tone, the violence of an inspiration that makes the poet defend himself against others' curiosity and suffer the scars of his condition. These scars are also the reasons for his pride, since he feels he is a Negro and asserts himself as a Negro. Because of this self-assertion, Damas's lyricism coincides with his analysis of what it means to be a poet, a central theme in contemporary poetry. Damas—who has, so to speak, more enemies than anyone else because of his race—also nourishes a more forceful hatred of all forms of oppression. . . .

The Negro has been exploited and is no longer sure of having his own consciousness. What black intellectual has not been corrupted by a certain desire for ''assimilation,'' an attitude that disgusts Damas and makes him reject his childhood. . . . But the poet's very tragedy leads him to make protests that often go beyond his intentions: ''I always feel ready to foam with rage/against everything that surrounds me/against everything that prevents me from ever being/a man.'' Certainly I understand this language only too clearly. But listen, Damas, what prevents you from being a man is also what prevents me from being one, and the color of my skin or of yours is not really important! Your poems are ours, as is your sense of lost grandeur, a feeling that can be experienced by anyone, man or nation, who is sensitive enough. Is not the knowledge that we share the same enemies the most beautiful reason for us to like one another?

Léon Gabriel Gros. *Cahiers du sud.* September 1937, pp. 511–12†

For the most part, the French Negro poetry with which we are most familiar now (e.g., the recent work of Léopold Sédar Senghor and Aimé Césaire) is *engagée* [committed] in a European sense, supporting the Negro cause everywhere while often criticizing "white" civilization, and it owes a great debt to French culture and language; but it has its own idiom and standard of excellence that have developed from a new sense of Negritude bursting free. This poetry looks, at last, to Africa and speaks from an African heritage over the corpse, the still warm corpse, of colonialism.

However, *Pigments* is largely another thing, a little classic from another time. It is the poetry of a bitter Negro citizen of pre-war France—Damas, by the way, was among the first of the militant French Negro poets: Aimé Césaire, for instance, did not begin writing until the Forties. The result is often that kind of passionate social protest characteristic of the Thirties. . . . One is reminded more of Langston Hughes than of Senghor. But that is not necessarily bad, and besides, not all of the poems in [the present edition of *Pigments*] are products of the Thirties or a Thirties mind-set. Moreover, less subject to dating is the poet's art; it, like the whole idea of French Negro poetry or American jazz, is a product of a cultural blend; and the best analogy for Damas's art (and one that he insists on) is to jazz. That is, Damas's technique, whether his goal is direct social utterance or, just as characteristic, disinterested poetic utterance, or is a combination of the two, is best described as a jazz technique—endless theme and variation, incremental repetition, improvisation, and a kind of verbal counterpoint that adds up to a most impressive expression of a trapped man's Negritude. . . .

C. E. Nelson. *Books Abroad.* Autumn 1963, p. 476

Co-founder with Senghor and Césaire of the Negritude school, Léon-Gontran Damas was born in Cayenne, Guyane (French Guiana), South America. After completing his secondary studies at the Lycée Schoelcher in Fort-de-France, Martinique, he went on to Paris, where he studied law and met Césaire and Senghor. In Paris, Damas was an habitué of all the places frequented by blacks from many countries of the world who had been attracted to this intellectual "Mecca" and bastion of individual freedom. . . . Being a poor student, M. Damas lived intensely the intellectual and moral tragedy of his race, undergoing the identity crisis common to all his fellow blacks. His poetic sensitivity made him all the more vulnerable to that tragedy.

Damas's poetic works include *Pigments*, *Graffiti*, and *Black Label*. His poetry, in contrast to that of Césaire and Senghor, is unsophisticated. It finds expression through everyday words, common or noble, most often those words and expressions of the common people, colored at times by an outmoded gracefulness and the use of certain Creole terms, and all of it subjected to the rhythm of the *tam tam*, for with Damas, rhythm takes precedence over melody. Being unsophisticated, Damas's poetry is direct, brutish, and at times brutal; and not infrequently it is charged with an emotion disguised as humor, a characteristically Negro humor that

has been the black man's saving grace in a harsh and cruel world in which he has had, for years, no other defense or technique of survival.

Edward A. Jones. In Edward A. Jones, ed., *Voices of Négritude* (Valley Forge, Pennsylvania: Judson, 1971), pp. 63–64

When *Pigments* appeared in 1937, it caused a sensation. Claude McKay's lines, "Am I not Africa's son, Black of that black land where black deeds are done," which Damas used as an epigraph, and the title's unmistakable allusion to color, were underlined in Robert Desnos' introduction. . . . "With Damas, there is no question of his subject matter nor how he treats it, of the sharpness of his blade nor the status of his soul. Damas is Negro and insists on his Negro-ness and on his condition as a Negro. . . . These poems are . . . also a song of friendship offered in the name of his whole race by my friend, Damas the Negro, to all his white brothers.". . .

As for Desnos' characterizing *Pigments* as Damas' "song of friendship . . . to his white brothers," this is true only by the most generous extrapolation. Why sweeten the pill? The short poems of *Pigments* are a bitter testimony, variations on themes of *pain*. They do reveal compassion for fellow-sufferers other than the Black man (the Jews under Hitler, for example). But nowhere in these pages does this reader find, nor does she ask for, "a song of friendship." If anger, tenacity and a certain despair are the impact of this first book of poems, this first major work of the Negritude group, they are valid, sufficient and important in and by themselves. . . .

"Et Cetera," which ends the book *Pigments* . . . reflects its historical moment. Senegalese soldiers were long known as among the best in the French Army. Here the poet exhorts them to fight for their *own* independence, "to invade Senegal," rather than defend their colonial masters against the Germans. Doubtless this was among the Damas poems recited in Baoulé translation by rioting African draft resisters in the Ivory Coast in 1939. As a result, *Pigments* was quickly banned throughout French West Africa, an early indication of the revolutionary proclivities that the later poetry of Negritude, particularly Césaire's and David Diop's, would demonstrate even more.

Ellen Conroy Kennedy. *Black World.* January 1972, pp. 8–11

Damas's early poems struck a note of mockery, muffled laughter, irony. But in the three volumes following his first, one notices the intensity of violence that was found in Césaire. In them, however, we see more and more what becomes less and less apparent in Césaire—a definite rejection of the props of the white world and a turning toward the African continent which was to become *all* of him. . . .

The past in Césaire's poetry is one long, grim night and when he refers to the glory of Africa, he does so almost with the modesty of the stranger. Damas, on the other hand, recognizes a past within the disturbed environment, for he feels that the efforts of misdirected currents of history were responsible for his dilemma. With anguish therefore he exclaims in "Limbed" that he wishes to be given back the black dolls so that he could play games that would restore his world of instinct. . . .

Damas's anger is quieter, more reflective than Césaire's; he can look back on the centuries and forgive. Another interesting point of comparison between Damas and Césaire is that although they share in common the same subject matter, there is a different expression of tone. Whereas Damas laments in ''Reality'' that he is almost a negative person because he has accomplished nothing, Césaire ironically celebrates those who do not invent anything. In Damas's poetry little attempt is made to vaunt racial superiority by stating negative virtues. When he does attempt this kind of writing, he does not succeed. . . .

Damas is at his best when, as a participant in the culture, he can nevertheless strongly denounce it. When he goes completely over to the other side and writes semi-songs of mourning or praise, he does not succeed. He is too much the poet and person; the African oral tradition had spokesmen, never individualists.

O. R. Dathorne. *The Black Mind* (Minneapolis: University of Minnesota Press, 1974), pp. 315, 317–18

What is meant by the ''aesthetics of Léon-Gontran Damas'' is, as one may guess, his art as a writer. This art is discernible in both his prose and his verse. Within the limits of this presentation, it is not possible to describe the talent of the brilliant essayist of *Retour de Guyane*, ''Misère Noire'' [*Esprit* (June 1, 1939)] or ''*89 et nous les Noirs*'' [*Europe* (May-August 1939)] nor to demonstrate the art of the griot-like story-teller of *Veillées Noires*. I shall focus my remarks on the verse of the poet whose touch can be perceived anyhow in most of his prose works.

It is not difficult for a discriminating reader of Damas's poetry to detect some of his literary devices and techniques. But this can best be done in the light of what I would identify as Damas's manifesto of African poetry and which can actually be proved to be his own poetics.

[From his introduction to a small volume of verse entitled *Poènies, Nègres sur des airs africains* (later translated as *African Songs of Love, War, Grief and Abuse*)] one may summarize the chief articles of this profession of faith as follows:

a) African poetry is improvised and must be sung rather than recited:

b) the language of this poetry, which expresses everyday life, is colloquial; African poets do not improvise for scholars but for people; hence the use of mockeries, puns, plays upon words and simplicity in expression:

c) African poetry does not count on rhyme and meter but, rather, on tempo, melody and repetition that engender rhythm;

d) finally, antitheses and parallelisms of ideas are important parts of this poetry.

These features constitute for Damas the aesthetic cannons of black poetry and confer on it ''subtlety,'' ''delicacy'' and ''nuances.'' They are well illustrated in his own works.

In reviewing *African Songs* [in *Black Orpheus* (1962)], Professor Dathorne notes that ''these poems were not translated from any African language into French by Damas, but are obviously inspired by African verse.'' If so, Damas's art had reached a point where it could be assimilated with its actual source of inspiration. Even if this were not so, Damas still proved to be an excellent interpreter since the adaptations given us do not sound like narrow translations. In fact, he had shown his talent as a translator on several occasions. Veillées Noires is a volume of collected Guyanese folk-stories remarkably translated from Creole into French. Professor Cook, reviewing *Névralgies* [in *African Forum* (Spring 1967)], observes

For several years, Damas has been translating Langston Hughes's poetry: this reviewer has seen some of these translations in manuscript, and they are magnificent. This is not surprising not only because of Damas's talent, but also because they are kindred spirits.

A sample of these translations can be found in *Retour de Guyane* (1938) where Damas quotes and translates with savour ''I'm Makin' a Road,'' a poem improvised by L. white people.'' The same difficulty occurs with the phrase ''bon à rien'' used in the same poem, and which can be ''good for nothing'' or ''good Aryan.'' In both cases, the reader assumes the responsibility of transforming one interpretation into another.

This device may have been inspired by Claude McKay's *Banjo* but, here, the transformation is demanded by the writer. In a similar fashion, one of his characters transforms ''United States'' into ''United Snakes.''

Puns constitute one of the main elements of the humorous quality of this poetry which also consists of ellipses, allusions and unexpected associations. This aspect, which has been emphasized by many critics as one of the main characteristics of black poets in general and of Damas in particular, need not be insisted upon again here.

Finally, in his Introduction to *African Songs*, Damas referred to ''simplicity of expression.'' He is quite at home with this principle. His poetry uses plain speech, colloquial words, those of everyday conversation, which gives the impression that the poet is actually talking directly to us without academic concern. Many poems can be read like sentences improvised on the spur of the moment, as for example:

Pourquoi
Grands dieux
Pourquoi, pourquoi
faut-il que tout chante
fût-ce
l'amour
à tout jamais soudain
d'une pureté d'albâtre

If anything, the extreme simplicity which characterizes this poetry bears testimony to its authenticity and its pressing sincerity. What can be simpler and more sincere than this love poem?

Quand bien même
Je t'aimerais mal
en est-ce bien sûr
au point d'en avoir mal
pour sûr
tu sats que je t'aime
e'est sûr
au point d'en avoir mal
en est-ce bien sûr
toi qui m'aimes
toi qui m'aimes mal
c'est sûr

What a difference indeed with the elaborate, sophisticated, learned and sometimes hermetic poetry of his peers in Negritude—Césaire and Senghor. The latter humbly admitted the superiority of Damas as a black poet when he publicly declared in an American television interview in 1966:

> To a certain extent, Damas is the most Negro among us all. In fact, I studied the rhythm of his verse, it is exactly negro rhythm and it resembles that of Langston Hughes.

Césaire has expressed the same view on many occasions.

The question has been asked why Damas, for more authenticity, did not use his native Creole (which is a mixture of French and African) to write his poetry. He answered this question several times in interviews and writings. His argument was the following:

> We do not deny our native language while continuing to write in French, but our truth must be reflected in the European language that we had to learn and whose radiance is larger and may help to serve a better knowledge of man.

He also explained that

> Africans and West Indians have different languages complicated by countless dialects and a lack of a stable written literature. Thus, French like English for some and Portuguese or Spanish for others, offered itself as an excellent means for Negro expression. Like English, Portuguese and Spanish, French made it possible for all Negroes to communicate with some words and identifiable symbols.

Nevertheless, Damas was very often tempted to use Creole and one can find several passages where his native language will appear in his poetry even if he had to translate it into French such as in the following example:

> PIÈ PIÈ PIÈ
> PRIÈ Bondjé
> mon fi
> prié Bondjé
> Angou ka bouyi
> Angou ka bouyi
> Pierre Pierre
> Prie Dieu
> mon fiston
> prie Dieu
> mon fiston
> pour que soit fin prêt le maïs en crème
> à être savouré

He contended that Creole offers more rhythmic patterns, more affectivity and retains the linguistic memory of life on another continent at another time.

Damas is also said to have used surrealism as a means of access to identity. Because of his many connections with surrealist poets, one cannot deny some influences of this movement on his poetry, including a subrational layer of consciousness, dreams, fancies, snatches of incoherence and incongruous or gratuitous images. One may say, however, that Surrealism itself remains heavily endebted to Negro Art. What attracted Damas to this movement was precisely the possibility of aesthetic exchange between Blacks and Whites.

As a poet of Negritude, Damas made it a point to find out and express the essence of African aesthetics. He seems to have discovered an important part of it through African songs in different languages which he could learn, translate, interpret and assimilate to a point of identifying his own poetic expression with them. It was after their spontaneity in improvisation, their simplicity, their jocularity and their rhythmical patterns built up on repetitive segments that he created his song-like verse. By so doing he reached a coveted platform where his poetics became part and parcel of African aesthetics.

> Daniel L. Racine. *Présence Africaine*. 121 and 122 (1982), pp. 154–65

It is perhaps unfortunate that the name of Léon Damas is so often linked with those of Aimé Césaire and Léopold Senghor. The result is nearly always to the disadvantage of the French Guyanese poet, whose output is, to be candid, not as voluminous as that of the other two illustrious Negritude poets. The tendency seems to have been to study the various aspects of Césaire and Senghor while restricting analysis of Damas' works to his poems of protest in *Pigments*. This is not to imply that *Pigments* does not warrant analysis because of its great political and cultural impact, but those who examine Damas' poems solely for the Negritude manifesto they contain cut themselves off from some very refreshing aspects of the poems. Damas the fighter, the hater, the protester is well-documented, as are the reasons for the poet's wanting to fight, hate and protest. However, what about Damas the juggler of language, the subtle humorist, the singer of the blues, even the poet of love? It is thus interesting to examine these aspects of Damas along with the techniques and devices he used to achieve his aims.

In the years after the Second World War, and particularly in the theater in France, it became popular to show how writers were actually playing with the very language they were using. In this way, these authors showed how artificial language had become and also how modern man had ceased to fully appreciate the true impact of his language. Admittedly, the dramatists' use of language did vary from the poets', since, for the most part, their aim was not the same. The dramatists had other avenues open to them within the play, whereas the poets had to use the one poetic form, with only slight variations and innovations, whose very existence is its language. In the light of this, Damas must be credited with having had the foresight to re-direct our attention to the impact of language well-handled and to the vast potential of the ''word.'' When of Damas, Senghor said that his poetry was unsophisticated, direct and brutal, it was a recognition of the fact that there was indeed power and vitality behind the apparently simple, everyday style of the poems.

In an interview that he accorded the present author in June 1972, Damas admitted that when he started writing poetry, it was out of a sense of commitment. The aspiring poet had a cultural and political message to convey, for, as he says, one cannot separate politics from culture. . . .

Unlike the poetry of Senghor, with its long, flowing verset, full of images and explanations, Damas' poetry is almost abrupt, with frequent repetition, very short lines and numerous typographical variations. Damas' use of repetition goes beyond the normal desire for insistance or effect. He uses it as a potent linguistic weapon, elevating it to the level of a musical art form. The repetitions are of several types—of one word, of several words, of types of adverbs, adjectives, of whole stanzas, of nearly everything that catches the fancy of the poet at the moment of writing. . . .

Apart from what one could term the normal repetitive process, there seems to be a sort of charm exerted by the words on the poet, so that he continues to explore every possibility open to him while he is using them. He seems, too, to enjoy the elements of surprise that he is introducing. . . .

We find this process of re-introduction of elements already used in [the] poem, ''Bientôt'':

Bientòt
je n'aurai pas que dansé
bientòt
je n'aurai pas que chanté
bientòt
je n'aurai pas que frotté
bientòt
je n'aurai pas que trempé
bientòt
je n'aurai pas que dansé
chanté
frotté
trempé
frotté
chanté
dansé
Bientòt
Soon
I'll not only have danced
soon
I'll not only have sung
soon
I'll not only have rubbed
soon
I'll not only have soaked
soon
I'll not only have danced
sung
rubbed
soaked
rubbed
sung
danced
Soon

As can be seen, the entire poem is built on the repetitive form, which in turn gives it its circular movement, hence a feeling of completeness. For all this, the poem is extremely simple in form and once more manifests Damas' ability to juggle with the language he is using.

If we have dealt at such length with Damas use of repetition in the language of his poems, it is mainly because this process far surpasses the rest throughout Damas' poetry. But, as can be easily seen, there are in fact others—alliteration and pun among them. These all combine to produce a strain of humor which at times surprises the reader unfamiliar with Damas' techniques. One cannot escape the impression that in many of the poems, beneath all the suffering and pain, there still remains a sly dig at the enemy through more than a hint of a smile. This would indeed explain the surprising twist to so many of the poems. This is not to say that Damas takes his problems lightly, but he allows himself a degree of humor that the white enemy could not possibly attain or understand. In this he closely parallels the humor of early American blacks who for many years were forced, in the terms of Langston

Hughes, a great personal friend of Damas, to laugh in order to keep from crying. His is therefore a personal humor and one that fellow blacks can understand and share. The colonizer, for example, would see nothing humorous in the last line of the following:

Terrain privé
Domaine reservé
Defense d'enter
Ni chiens ni nègre sur le gazon
Private grounds
Guarded estate
No entry
No dogs or niggers on the grass

One has to be a part of the whole experience to fully appreciate how one could indeed view such (the lines actually represent warning signs) as something else beside insulting and tragic.

Perhaps the finest example of Damas' humor occurs in the poem ''Hoquet'' (Hiccups), which the poet says is his favorite. Here, all the techniques already mentioned blend to produce a neat indictment of the artificial upbringing that the Damas family strived for. There is repetition of the refrain ''Désastre/parlez-moi du désastre/parlez-m'en'' (Disaster/talk about disaster/tell me about it), a refrain in which the poet definitely has his tongue in his cheek as he breaks off from describing his mother's hypocritical admonitions. Damas resorts to some novel type lines as he pictures the mother extremely put out at the fact that her son should want to channel her precious music lessons into learning the banjo and guitar instead of the violin. . . .

Naturally, it would be false to give the impression that Damas sees himself as a humorist. The main claim here has been that the poet's humor is an integral part of the whole make-up of the poems, especially those in *Pigments*. Even in those poems in which Damas is being admittedly hard on those who were responsible for his condition and that of his fellow blacks, the poet often slips in a line or two showing that he is still able to smile under the suffering.

Another aspect of the poems that could well be re-examined is that of their music. It has often been pointed out that Damas' poetry is full of rhythm and that it evokes the world of jazz. One could add that many of the poems are reminiscent of the blues songs of the American blacks, as they do have many of the elements common to the blues—the nostalgic first person recollection of things past, suffering, problems with the loved one, the constant yearning for better things to come. Just as the blues singer finds some solace in singing about his plight, so too does Damas lighten his internal burdens by writing about them in words that have only to be set to music. One has only to go back to the discussion of the poet's constant use of repetition to realize that some of these have an air of a lament about them, as if the poet were slowly singing to the strumming of a guitar or to the beat of a drum. The poem ''Bientôt,'' already quoted, would be a good example of this, as is the poem ''Limbé'' (''Blues''), with its repetitive insistance ''Rendez-les moi mes poupees noires'' (Give me back my black dolls). There are poems in which the sound of the words have a definite melodious air:

Nuits sans nom
nuits sans lune
. . .
sans nom
sans lune

sans lune
sans nom
nuits sans lune
sans nom sans nom
Nights with no name
nights with no moon
no name
no moon
no moon
no name
nights with no moon
no name no name

It is apparent that Damas is here exploiting the musical aspect of the French to the fullest. Fortunately, on this occasion the English version does manage to re-capture some of the same musicality. Whether Damas would have been as musical had he been writing in another language is not really important. The fact remains that he had to use the only language he knew, and this he did with dexterity, exploring the full potential of a language that lends itself to musical interpretation.

There remains one final aspect of Damas' poetry that is hardly mentioned in most analyses—namely his variations on the theme of love, contained mainly in his collection *Névralgies*. Damas' poems of love show no trace of the poet's race, unlike those of Senghor which nearly always extol the virtues of the black woman. If, however, there is no trace of racial hatred or racial love, there is, nonetheless, the same technique that we have seen throughout the now typical Damas poem. This he uses to portray the universal lover in all his moods, happy when the loved one is near, sad when she is absent, jealous when he thinks that she is with someone else.

Damas' poetry, therefore, should not be seen merely as an incitement to black consciousness, though this remains a very important part of it. If one were to return for a while to the old argument over the separation of form and function, one would find that, in Damas' poems, the function is effective mainly because of the form; there can be no separation of the one from the other. As such, it is doing the poet a disservice to continue to look exclusively at what he achieved without also examining the way in which he set out to achieve it.

> Keith Q. Warner. *Critical Perspectives on Leon-Gontran Damas* (Washington, D. C.: Three Continents Press, 1988), pp. 87–98

BIBLIOGRAPHY
*Pigments*, 1937; *Veillees noires*, 1943; *Poems negres sur des airs africains*, 1948; *Graffiti*, 1952; *Black-Label*, 1956; *African Songs of Love, War, Grief, and Abuse*, 1961; *Nevralgies*, 1965

# DANGAREMBGA, Tsitsi (1959–)
## Zimbabwe

There is no doubt that approaches to *Nervous Conditions* which situate it within the frame of reference established by its epigraph [from Frante Faron] are both productive and illuminating. Yet there is another allusive moment in Dangarembga's text which is just as likely as the invocation of Fanon to attract the attentions of the postcolonial critic. This occurs in chapter five as Tambudzai, the novel's narrator, recalls her initial adolescent encounters with English literature, ''Plunging into [the] books'' contained in the ''various and extensive library'' belonging to Nyasha, her anglicized and slightly older cousin, reading ''everything from Enid Blyton to the Brontë sisters.'' The allusion here to ''the Brontë sisters''—if not Blyton—introduces the possibility for a reading of *Nervous Conditions* in terms of an alternative intertextual trajectory to that signalled so overtly by its epigraph: Tambudzai may read the Brontës but the novel in which she is located rewrites them for its own postcolonial purposes, and Charlotte Brontë's *Shirley* (1849) in particular. The central figure around which such a rewriting is performed is that of the female anorectic, textually embodied in the Nyasha of Dangarembga's novel, on the one hand, and the Caroline Helstone and Shirley Keeldar of Brontë's, on the other. . . .

While it is important to recall that anorexia does not enter Victorian medical discourses until the early 1870's, critics have nonetheless been inclined to read Brontë's *Shirley* as powerfully prefiguring those discourses.

Read as anorectics, the ''natives'' of Brontë's nineteenth-century Yorkshire—Caroline and Shirley—would thus appear to share the ''nervous condition'' that besets the Nyasha of Dangarembga's twentieth-century Rhodesia. By the same token, the somatic strategies deployed by their postcolonial counterpart function as a defiance of the patriarchal norm, figured preeminently, in Dangarembga's text, in the shape of Babamukuru, Nyasha's father. Babamukuru poses several problems for Nyasha which arise, in the first instance, from his ambiguously hybrid location between cultures—African and English—that are themselves in a direct colonial tension with one another. Even as he is ''revered patriarch,'' in Nyasha's scathing phrase, to his extended Shona family, Babamukuru is also what she astutely calls an ''historical artefact'': he is the product of a colonial/missionary education, at the hands of ''holy wizards'' followed by tertiary study in South Africa and then England and incorporated, as such, into the kind of black colonial elite which Fanon satirizes so heavily in the third chapter of *The Wretched of the Earth*. The contradictions and conflicts generated by Babamukuru's role as ''good African'' themselves find bodily or even hysterical expression: his ''nerves'' are said to be ''bad'' as a result of the hectic daily routines he carries out as family breadwinner and headmaster at the mission-school where Tambudzai and Nyasha both study.

In terms of gender and sexuality, however, the ''native''/Shona and colonial/missionary discourses regulating Babamukuru's subjectivity are not at odds, coalescing, as they do, around ideals of ''feminine decency, submissiveness and respect.'' These ideals are challenged and violated by Nyasha throughout the novel: she reads *Lady Chatterley's Lover*, ''forgetting to eat'' (p. 83) when her father slyly confiscates the book and she thinks she has mislaid it, dresses in a Western style that Babamukuru considers ''ungodly'' (p. 109) and returns late and unchaperoned from the mission-school Christmas dance because she has been dallying with a white boy. This last transgression precipitates what is quite literally the most striking scene in the novel. Babamukuru is scandalized and repeatedly accuses Nyasha of behaving like a ''whore.'' The violent verbal exchange between father and daughter rapidly escalates into bodily conflict as they flail and wrestle on Nyasha's bedroom-floor, threatening, as they always do, according to Maiguru, Nyasha's mother, to "tear [. . .] each other to pieces." While she is both silenced and physically worsted at the end of this scene, Nyasha is ultimately—as Tambudzai recognises—the "victim of her femaleness" or, more properly, the patriarchal codes by which that femaleness is circumscribed. Like Caroline and Shirley, however, Nyasha has developed alternative ways of continuing her struggle against Babamukuru and the patriarchal authority invested in him. Throughout the week after the fight, Nyasha grows increasingly vague and detached from those around her: she neither sees the hand that Tambudzai passes before her eyes nor hears her voice and, above all, "stop[s] eating again."

*Shirley's* disorderly female eaters cannot, however, be placed in straight-forward or unproblematic alliance with the Nyasha of *Nervous Conditions.* . . .

Nor does *Nervous Conditions* simply repeat or mirror Shirley's representation of disorderly female eating as patriarchal rebellion but supplements it with another meaning. Even as Nyasha's illness, following *Black Skin, White Masks,* would seem to imply a radical identification with white culture, it operates, simultaneously, as a medium for the articulation of a sustained resistance to colonialism and, in particular, the corpus of texts through which colonialism represents itself—to itself and to its others.

It is possible to read the anorectic body in *Nervous Conditions* in this way not least because of the novel's persistent figuration of the colonizers' texts in terms of food. One of the earliest examples of such a metaphorical linkage occurs in the third chapter of Dangarembga's novel as Babamukuru returns home from completing his education in England and is greeted by Jeremiah, Tambudzai's father. Babamukuru, Jeremiah admiringly exclaims:

"has returned appeased, having devoured English letters with a ferocious appetite! Did you think degrees were indigestible? If so, look at my brother. He has digested them! If you want to see an educated man, look at my brother, big brother to us all!"

Babamukuru's digestion of "English letters" renders him "Full of knowledge" in the words of one of Tambudzai's aunts. Yet while such epistemological repletion is the ground of Babamukuru's characteristically "grave and weighty" presence, the assimilation of colonial ideology produces the opposite effect upon Nyasha. As she crams for her Form Two examinations at Babamukuru's school, "reading and memorising all the time. To make sure [she gets] it all in," she suffers from "nerves" which manifest themselves in familiar ways:

She was working much harder than . . . ever . . . before, up long before her usual time, so that when breakfast was ready she had been studying in a concentrated state for an hour or more. At night it was the same: by eight o'clock she was curled up in bed with her books, but the light rarely went out before one. Everybody agreed that she was overdoing it. She was looking drawn and had lost so much of her appetite that it showed all over her body in the way the bones crept to the surface, but she did not seem to notice.

These disrupted temporal and bodily rhythms are not just the prosaic index of an anxious desire to excel academically, though Babamukuru certainly construes them in that way and is suitably "impressed by his daughter's industry." They constitute, rather,

the complex symptomatic expressions of a struggle—as "ferocious" as Babamukuru's reputed "appetite"—against the educational processes that are integral to Nyasha's anglicization and which she herself abets. As these expressions appear "all over her body" and creep to its "surface," it becomes evident that it is far more difficult for Nyasha than for her father to "stomach" the "Englishness" (p. 203) to which they are exposed alike.

By the final chapter of Nervous Conditions the staging of anorexia as a contestation of the "truths" incarnated in the texts of colonialism is at its most flamboyant. . . .

That *Nervous Conditions* should figure texts as food is entirely appropriate from the perspective of its intertextual relation to *Shirley,* since it is precisely in such terms that Brontë's novel offers itself to the reader—from as early on, indeed, as its second paragraph. . . .

*Shirley's* troping of itself as a "meal" whose "first dish" may well fail to sate the romance-hungry reader of *Jane Eyre,* published two years earlier, is doubly significant: it not only anticipates one of the most distinctive metaphorical strategies of *Nervous Conditions,* but also carries a certain historical—and indeed colonial—charge. For the text that represents itself as food is one that emerges in a context which is marked, precisely, by food's disastrous absence—the Irish Famine of 1845–50. . . .

The nature of the "nervous condition" with which representation might thus be said to be marked in *Shirley* accordingly necessitates a reconsideration or refocusing of the processes involved in Dangarembga's postcolonial rewriting of Brontë. *Nervous Conditions* reconfigures anorexia in Brontë's text in such a way as to extend its signifying range, as "Nyasha's rebellion" assumes a colonial as well as patriarchal dimension. At the same time, however, the gender-and class-conflicts which Brontë's text addresses cannot be disentangled from the specificities of the historical moment in which that text is produced. Appropriated and reinscribed by Dangarembga, Shirley's anorectic bodies—like those of its hungry and insurgent male workers—are freighted already with their own colonial burdens.

Carl Plasa. *Journal of Commonwealth Literature.* 33, 1 (Winter 1995), pp. 35–44

*Nervous Conditions* is meticulous in its attention to physical space, both geographical and bodily. The text details relentlessly the process of enculturation as a material process. Yet equally insistently, it deploys the category of a transcendent consciousness and refers to a liberated subjectivity. This ultimate gesture of reconciliation at the level of consciousness and its tortured syntax, read as an instance of postmodern reflexivity, remain unconvincing. And it may appear as a moment of narrative failure only if we invoke exclusively some rather arbitrary aesthetic criteria. It may be read, instead, more instructively, as a textual transaction, a cultural document that maps the institutional spaces through which the shifting positions of the transnational intellectual must be plotted. A formal problem, a specifically narrative difficulty, arises out of the materiality of the intellectual's position. . . .

In *Nervous Conditions,* Dangarembga articulates a tertiary space of the homestead, the mission, and the Convent. The relationship among the three spaces is fluid. The spaces, traversed by lines of force carrying their own intensities, are subject to constant and repeated deterritorializations and reterritorializations. Tambu moves through all three spaces as a figure of the transnational intellectual in the making; Nyasha, caught in the intermediate space, has travelled in the Western space and occasionally visits the ''native'' space of the homestead. Nhamo's movement from the homestead to the mission, though a relatively minor movement, anticipates these larger movements and their finely calibrated differences. Because of ''something that he saw at the mission,'' he ''refused to come home.'' A year later, ''no longer the same person,'' he was not only ''several tones lighter in complexion,'' but he ''had forgotten how to speak Shona.'' These details—such as his skin tone and his mother tongue—serve metonymically to signal the process of expatriation that is a central concern of the novel. Although we are informed rather humorously that Nhamo has not really forgotten Shona, we are told that ''he did not speak to [his mother] very often any more.'' Only his father is impressed: ''the more aphasic he became . . . the more my father was convinced that he was being educated.'' Whatever the ''something'' is that Nhamo sees at the mission, at his death, his mother is uncompromising in her indictment of it: ''First you took his tongue so that he could not speak to me. . . . You bewitched him and now he is dead. . . . You and your education have killed my son.''

This movement from the homestead to the mission, however, is enfolded in a simultaneous movement, that of Nyasha from the mission to the homestead. Her return to the homestead is exacerbated moreover by a long stay in England: ''I missed the bold, ebullient companion I had had who had gone to England but not returned from there.'' And Nyasha too has forgotten Shona, as Tambu registers indignantly: ''Shona was our language. What did people mean when they forgot it? . . . I remembered speaking freely and fluently before they went away, . . . Now they had turned into strangers.'' Even though Nhamo is disposed of fairly early in the novel and Nyasha's movements are mapped in detail, the same ''something'' that Nhamo sees is deployed in a series of statements both from and about Nyasha. Tambu, for example, tells us, ''I could not help wondering what my cousin had seen that I had not''; later he says, ''Nyasha gave me the impression of moving, always moving and striving towards some state that she had seen.'' Nyasha herself insists that ''when you're seen different things you want to be sure you're adjusting to the right thing.''. . .

Above all, Nyasha is mobilized against being ''trapped,'' against what she calls ''it'' in the passage above. The text does not simply oppose mobilization and fixity, dynamic and static. Rather, it posits the pairs as two types of movement. While the ''it'' may arguably have a direct reference to ''being an underdog,'' the progress from ''it'' to ''they control everything'' suggests a larger referential framework. What seems natural is the individual's subjection, the disciplining of the subject, and the normalization and routinization of disciplinary power. What individuals get used to is the stricter control; their internalization of discipline results in complete servitude. The novel documents the ways in which the body is implicated in the mechanisms of power, and to this end, it maintains a level of materiality, of corporality. The site of the most furious contention between Nyasha and her father, Babamukuru, is precisely the body. It often has to do with what she wears, how she talks, what she eats (or does not eat), and whether she dances (or whether she does not). The body is also the site on which Nyasha enacts her resistance. She wears short dresses, smokes cigarettes, and goes dancing. When forced to eat, she withdraws to the bathroom, ''gagging and choking,'' using her toothbrush to disgorge.

In the schizophrenic language of the climactic passage of the novel, the referential framework is completely dissipated. In spite of this referential slide, however, the moment is entirely lucid. If we extract a series of statements, represented in direct discourse, as Nyasha's speech, we have the following:

> I don't want to do it.
> They've done it to me.
> They did it to them too.
> Why do they do it . . . to me and to you and to him?
> Do you see what they've done?
> They've taken us away.

In spite of the rigid polarization of ''they'' and the progression, me-you-him-us, there is no identification between ''me'' and ''you'': ''but I'm not one of you.'' Rather, the sliding of references throughout the passage and the substitutions of pronouns serve as a mapping of the micropolitics of power. The disappearance of the ''brutal manifestations'' of power leaves only its circulation, the lines of which are marked along a series of innocuous pronouns. Even if there are certain moments of ostentatious brutality in the novel, Nyasha's resistance is directed not at the individual agent (''it's not his fault''), but at a structure of relations. Earlier in the novel, she says, ''It's not really him, you know. I mean not really the person. It's everything, it's everywhere.'' The lexicographical diffuseness in general and the referential obscurity suggest the nebulousness of agency and trace the circuits of power only by marking out its effects.

Biman Basu. *Ariel.* 28, 3 (July 1997), pp. 7–24

BIBLIOGRAPHY
*She No Longer Weeps*, 1987; *Nervous Condition*, 1988

# DANTICAT, Edwidge (1969–)
## Haiti

Edwidge Danticat dedicates her powerful first novel [*Breath, Eyes, Memory*] to ''The brave women of Haiti . . . on this shore and other shores. We have stumbled but we will not fall.'' Such optimism is extraordinary, given the everyday adversity faced by the women whose stories are interwoven with that of Sophie, the narrator.

Grandmother Ifé, mother Martine, aunt Atie, and daughter Sophie (and later Sophie's daughter, Brigitte) are rooted as firmly in their native Haitian soil as they are bound to one another, despite the ocean, experiences, and years that separate them. The ties to Haiti, the women's certainty of meeting there at the ''very end of each of our journeys,'' affords their only apparent security. ''Somehow, early on, our song makers and tale weavers had decided that we were all daughters of this land,'' Danticat writes. Structurally, the book reflects the centrality of Haiti: the longest of its four sections takes place there, although covering only a few days in a novel that covers years.

The story begins in Haiti. Through Sophie's 12-year-old eyes, the island seems a paradise of bougainvillea, poincianas, and the unconditional love of Tante Atie. Then Martine, the mother Sophie knew only as a photograph, sends for her from New York City. It seems a mean place that has worn out her mother: ''It was as though she had never stopped working in the cane fields after all.'' Sophie is haunted by the hardships of immigrant life, together with the ghosts from the past and the burdens of womanhood in a hostile world. She describes herself as a frightened insomniac, but somehow survives the test. Her older, jazz-musician husband, Joseph, one of the novel's few male characters and certainly the most loyal and gentle, gives her some strength. She copes through a resilient mélange of love, ties to home, and therapy. And when she returns to Haiti as an adult, she senses a sinister edge to the place, represented by the Tonton Macoutes (militiamen), the boat people, and her Tante Atie's bitterness.

"There is always a place where nightmares are passed on through generations like heirlooms," writes Danticat. In this book, one of those places is "testing," part of a "virginity cult, our mothers' obsession with keeping us pure and chaste," in which the mother probes her daughter's vagina (sometime violently) to see if she is still whole. She also listens to her daughter peeing to see if the sound suggests a deflowered, widened passage. Even rape has one positive result: the end of "testing" by an otherwise trusted mother. The invasiveness, pain, and humiliation turn daughter against mother generation after generation, Atie against Ifé, Sophie against Martine.

But there is reconciliation, too. As mothers and daughters, the women are bound in love as in hate. A mother may inflict on her daughter the same pain that drove her from her own mother. Why? "I did it because my mother had done it to me. I have no greater excuse." The book is a plea to end these divisive rituals. Mothers indeed long to break the cycle of pain, asking pointedly from beyond the grave, "'Ou libéré?' Are you free, my daughter?"

Suffering inflicted by a well-intentioned mother is all the more treacherous in a world where the birth of a girl child is marked by "no lamps, no candles, no more light." Danticat leaves the reader with no illusions as to why the welcome is so dark. As well as "testing," the women in this family endure rape, unwanted pregnancy, and violence that lead to mental illness, nightmares, sexual phobias, bulimia, and self-mutilation. Breast cancer seems almost benign in this context; being unmarried and childless does not.

Sophie wants and seems to be the hope for breaking with painful tradition. Returning to Haiti with her mother's body for burial, she reaches an important understanding: the testing was painful for Martine, too. Doing what she had to do as a Haitian woman, "My mother was as brave as stars at dawn." Sophie breaks free as she madly attacks the sugar cane in the midst of which her father had raped and impregnated her mother. We sense that Sophie—and Brigitte—are finally safe.

Despite all the suffering ("'Can one really die of chagrin?' I asked Tante Atie."), Danticat writes with a light and lyrical touch. Her characterization is vivid, her allusive language richly unembellished. Color (literal as well as linguistic) carries the reader from the daffodil yellow associated with Haiti and Sophie's early days in New York, to the more ominous red with which her mother surrounds herself in interior decoration as in death.

Occasionally Danticat devotes too many details to a banal incident or action, but this is a minor criticism for a first novel.

In a personal essay, Danticat calls Haiti a "rich landscape of memory." But she is afraid that female storytellers like herself may be Haiti's last surviving breath, eyes, and memory. In this compelling novel, the reader experiences the Haiti that Danticat fears will be lost.

Mary Mackay. *Belles Lettres: A Review of Books by Women.* 10, 1 (Fall 1994), pp. 36, 38

And over the years when you have needed us, you have always cried "Krik?" and we have answered "Krak!" and it has shown us that you have not forgotten us.

Edwidge Danticat's powerful collection of short stories, *Krik? Krak!* is a complicated, yet connected, chorus of Haitian voices affirming survival. Each one explores how memories of Haiti are passed on from one generation to the next—how Haiti will live on in the children of exiles in the United States, in the children of those who survived.

We know people by their stories.

Born in 1969 during the dictatorial regime of Papa Doc Duvalier, Danticat, author of the novel *Breath, Eyes, Memory*, was 4 years old when her parents emigrated to the United States and left her behind. She would not be able to join them until she was 12. The stories she tells—filled with such horrible details of rape, incest, extreme poverty, violent death—make you wonder what happened during those eight years of her development. But the awful-ness of the pain and the tragedy of Haitian poverty are not all Danticat has to tell. She weaves a rich web of remembered rituals and dream fragments that connects the first story to the last. As the stories progress from one to the next, we realize that Danticat is tracing a family lineage, a history of people related by circumstance.

They say behind the mountain are more mountains. Now I know it's true.

"Children of the Sea" is the first and most powerful story in the collection. A 20-year-old radio show host is hunted down by the military because he has spoken against its overthrow of the government. He (we never know his name) escapes the island, along with 36 others who are also fleeing political persecution and certain death, leaving behind the young woman he wants to marry. The story is told through their "letters": hers, from the midst of turmoil and violence in Haiti's cities and countryside; his from a makeshift raft in the middle of the Caribbean Sea. The cruel irony is that, of course, neither knows if the other is still alive. In the midst of such tragedy, the tale that sustains the young exile adrift at sea is of "the children of the deep blue sea, those who have escaped the chains of slavery to form a world beneath the heavens and the blood-drenched earth where you live."

Life is never lost, another one always comes up to replace the last.

In "Nineteen Thirty-Seven," Danticat takes us inside the walls of a Haitian prison. Images of shaven heads, torture and the burning of bodies are reminiscent of the Jewish holocaust. Told from the viewpoint of a daughter whose mother, a suspected witch, is imprisoned to keep her from "flying," we learn of ritual passed down from mother to daughter to protect them from the horrors of the present, the future, and most of all the past. Stories about the women's power became accusations of infanticide: "They were said to have been seen at night rising from the ground like birds on fire. . . . *Lougarou*, witch, criminal!" Danticat's stories often examine this fear of the female principle and its power of passing on stories, and consequently, culture.

What kind of legends will your daughters be told? What kind of charms will you give them to ward off evil?

Like the maternal power she invokes, Danticat's Haiti has a power to destroy and to create. Its people are caught between a place they want to be and the place they have to be. In her other stories set in Haiti, there are suicides, prostitution, miscarriages, murders. The sun shines while the people suffer. Her characters are individuals, not the indistinguishable masses of suffering Haitians featured in the Western media. Through her lens we hear the screaming, we see the blood, we smell the burning of human flesh. Danticat tells these stories as an act of recovery, to prevent the dismembering of the Haitian spirit for those who would have to leave Haiti and cross over to another side—the United States.

The last two stories in *Krik? Krak!* tell of Haitians who have made Brooklyn, New York, their home. In "New York Day Women," a young woman who works for a Madison Avenue advertising agency spots her mother on Fifth Avenue during her lunch break and observes her on her way to take care of rich white folks' children. "Caroline's Wedding" represents the last "crossing over": The American-born daughter of Haitian refugees chooses to marry someone who is not Haitian.

You have lived this long in this strange world, so far from home, because you remember.

Danticat's stories strongly reflect her desire to re-member and re-tell stories that have kept her Haitian spirit alive in the disjointed American landscape. She chronicles a people's spiritual resistance to oppression without exploring in any depth America's complicated and contradictory connection to it. Unlike her representations of Haitians under military rule and their conflicting desires to both stay and flee, Danticat's Haitian-American characters—those like herself who have been educated in the United States, who either have very remote memories of Haiti or none at all—have uncomplicated relationships to their "American" identity. Are there no "stories" to tell of America's reluctance to allow Haitians to enter Miami during the "AIDS scare"? Are there no "stories" of America leaving thousands of Haitians to drown in the Caribbean sea rather than give them political asylum? Are there no "stories" of the horror of America's earlier brutal occupation? These and other "stories" would surely problematize a second-generation Haitian-American's "American"-ness.

The stories that Edwidge Danticat has chosen to tell are deeply spiritual and ultimately disturbing. They are a powerful synthesis of the old with the new; the past with the present; a looking backward to go forward; a loud and powerful Krak! to her ancestors' spirit-giving Krik?

Kimberly Hébert. *Quarterly Black Review* (June 1995), p. 6

While a complicated relation to the mother tongue is an unspoken subtext in Edwidge Danticat's stories, her explicit subject is more often than not the complicated relations between flesh-and-blood mothers and their daughters, both in Haiti and in the diaspora. In *Krik? Krak!* (the title is a traditional call-and-response that begins a storytelling session), Danticat writes of a daughter visiting a jail in Port-au-Prince, where her mother has been sent under suspicion of witchcraft, she tells the story of a pair of daughters in Brooklyn preparing for the wedding of one of them to a Bahamian man, under the disapproving eye of their traditional mother. Danticat's first book, a novel entitled *Breath, Eyes, Memory*, which was published by Soho Press last year, charts the life of a young girl, Sophie, through her relationships with the women in her family: an aunt, her troubled mother, whom she joins in Brooklyn as she enters her teens, her grandmother, whose beliefs about raising daughters—including a practice called testing, in which a mother regularly checks with her own lingers to ensure that her adolescent daughter's hymen is intact—are family secrets painfully passed on through the generations; and her own daughter. Sophie's rebellion is chillingly depicted: To escape the testing, she breaks her own

hymen with a kitchen pestle, knowing that she will be thrown out of her mother's home. She must abandon her mother in order to escape her—though being motherless is virtually taboo in Haiti. (The Creole expression *san man-man*—literally, "motherless one"—is used to mean a person capable of any transgression, an outlaw or a vagabond: If he has no mother, there is no one to be shamed by his flouting of rules and customs.)

Though the content of her stories is often disturbing, Danticat's manner is warm and open, she is quick to point out that while, like Sophie, she was long separated from her own mother, the novel's more gruesome elements are not autobiographical. . . .

Danticat's stories are about what happens when it is revealed that the invincible mother is a fantasy: that mothers are sometimes absent and are often troubled daughters themselves. That Danticat has found a stepmother tongue in which to tell these tales suggests that realizing mothers are fallible need not be a catastrophe. Even when a mother, or a mother tongue, falls short, there are, after all, alternatives to becoming a *san man-man*.

Rebecca Mead. *New York Magazine* (2 November 20, 1995), p. 50

Danticat's personal background is as turbulent as one might expect from her writing. Born in 1969, in Port-au-Prince, Haiti, Danticat was separated from her father at age two, when he emigrated to the United States to work in a factory (he is currently a driver for a car service). Her mother, now retired, followed him when Danticat was four. Danticat and her younger brother, Eliab, were turned over to the care of her father's brother, a minister, who lived with his wife and grandson in Bel Air, a poor area of Port-au-Prince. At 12, Danticat finally rejoined her parents in Brooklyn, but had to struggle to remake her family ties (for starters, she had two new younger brothers). She also had to learn English from scratch (the family still speaks Creole at home) and endure epithets from public school classmates who mocked her as a "boat person." "My primary feeling the whole first year was one of loss," she recalls. "Loss of my childhood, and of the people I'd left behind—and also of being lost. It was like being a baby—learning everything for the first time."

But what Danticat had already learned in Haiti would prove a more valuable education. As a child in Bel Air, she received an enduring lesson in the power of storytelling at the feet of her aunt's grandmother, a woman whose long hair, with coins braided into it, the neighborhood children fought to comb. "She told stories when the people would gather—folk tales with her own spin on them, and stories about the family' says Danticat. "It was call-and-response—if the audience seemed bored, the story would speed up, and if they were participating, a song would go in. The whole interaction was exciting to me. These cross-generational exchanges didn't happen often, because children were supposed to respect their elders. But when you were telling stories, it was more equal, and fun." . . .

Danticat, who currently travels to Haiti as often as four times a year, has been researching *The Farming of Bones* since 1992. The novel takes as its historical background the reign of dictator Rafael Trujillo Molina, a period of rising Dominican nationalism and anti-immigrant sentiment (Haitians have been emigrating to the bordering Dominican Republic for work since the 19th century). In 1937, the anti-Haitian propaganda campaign flared into violence, resulting in the death of thousands of Haitians. An earlier story about a survivor of the massacre, "Nineteen ThirtySeven," is included in

*Krik? Krak!* But it wasn't until Danticat stood on the banks of the river Massacre itself, where the killings had taken place, that she fully realized that she wanted to make a novel out of the story. (The river is named after another 19th-century genocidal episode that had occurred on its banks.) "It was really strange to stand there—it was low tide, and people were bathing, and washing their clothes in the water," recalls Danticat. "There are no markers. I felt like I was standing on top of a huge mass grave, and just couldn't see the bodies. That's the first time I remember thinking, 'Nature has no memory—a line that later made its way into the book—and that's why we have to have memory.

*The Farming of Bones* is told from the perspective of Amabelle Desir, a young Haitian woman working as a servant on a sugar-cane plantation in the Dominican Republic in 1937. When the violence breaks out, Amabelle is maimed as she flees back into Haiti, but her lover, Sebastien, is murdered. The novel is more overtly historical than Danticat's previous writings. One senses that its author has laid to rest some of the personal issues that loom so large during the passage from adolescence to adulthood. These days, Danticat is focused instead on a mission of writing for the benefit of her community. "The massacre is not as well-known here as it is in Haiti," she says. "But I wasn't thinking so much I wanted to popularize it with a larger audience as with younger people, like my brothers, who didn't know about it at all. It's a part of our history, as Haitians, but it's also a part of the history of the world. Writing about it is an act of remembrance." . . .

"My characters are not representative of the community as a whole. As a writer, it's the person who is different from everybody else who might be interesting to you." Just as, one might argue, it is the writer who is different from everyone else—who, like Danticat, has a unique personal and historical legacy to share—who is most interesting readers.

Mallay Charters. *Publishers Weekly*. 245, 33 (August 17, 1998), p. 42

Hallucinatory vigor and a sense of mission—these are what, in her best moments, the Haitian-American writer Edwidge Danticat brings to her sobering novel[*The Farming of Bones*] about "two different peoples trying to share one tiny piece of land."

The setting is the border country of the Caribbean island of Hispaniola and the year is 1937, a place and time when the longstanding hostility between the Dominican Republic and its neighbor, Haiti, is about to erupt into bloodshed, carefully orchestrated by the Dominican dictator Rafael Trujillo Molina. But Amabelle Dèsir, the Haitian housemaid who is the novel's narrator, gives little credence to the rumors of imminent violence. Instead, her focus is on the worries of her immediate household. . . .

Danticat—the author of one earlier novel, *Breath, Eyes, Memory*, and a story collection, *Krik? Krak!*—capably evokes the shock with which a small personal world is disrupted by military mayhem. Even the title of *The Farming of Bones* reflects this duality, refering both to the grueling work that takes place on the sugar cane plantations and implicitly, the massacre to come. Despite this complex shading, the novel doesn't consistently achieve the nimble intensity of Danticat's strongest work in *Krik? Krak!*

The trouble, perhaps, is that Danticat's storytelling invention has been inhibited by the respect she has for her novel's historical sources. It is surely telling that the prickly yet affectionate servant-mistress bond between Amabelle and Seňora Valencia (Amabelle

always refers to her as "Seňora," even though the women grew up together) feels more astutely observed than the relationships among the Haitian characters, who are too uniformly noble to be entirely convincing. It also feels contrived when, in a flashback, Danticat orphans the young Amabelle on the Dominican-Haitian border during peace-time, although the account of her parents' death is unsettling enough to work.

There are technical oddities as well that detract from the power of Danticat's story. The novel opens with what appear to be two alternating narrators—suggested by different typefaces and contrasting prose styles. Yet it soon becomes clear that both voices belong to Amabelle, a device that seems miscalculated and unnecessary. More worrying are moments when the book's dialogue smacks of historical epic speak. ("Do you know that you can trust him who offered this place to you?")

Thankfully, there's no such creakiness in most of the descriptive prose. Danticat knows the value of under-statement in bringing nightmarish scenes to life, and a spare, searing poetry infuses many of the book's best passages. The randomness of death; the second guessing about where safety lies; the silence after an act of butchery in a remote mountain farm; all are eerily evoked, as is the fluid heedlessness of a crowd's hysteria when Trujillo appears in a border town at the height of the violence.

Some readers will wish that Danticat had supplied more information on the wider context of Haitian-Dominican animosity, including the two countries' long history of mutual invasion. But her primary concern is to depict the unfortunate lot of the Haitian migrant laborers who have only "the cane to curse, the harvest to dread, the future to fear," and who have no politics beyond an instinctive clan loyalty and the need to seek work wherever it might be. . . .

Not surprisingly, given her subject matter, Danticat's customary wry wit is present only in small doses—as when Amabelle, a spur-of-the-moment mid-wife helping to deliver Seňora Valencia's second twin, remarks. "I was feeling more experienced now." Later there is also a hideous dark humor in the absurd minutiae of persecution, the pronunciation test given to suspected Haitians whose inability to trill the Spanish "r" in "pereqd" ("parsley") could result in a death sentence.

In these and other passages, *The Farming of Bones* offers ample confirmation of Edwidge Danticat's considerable talents. Yet her finest work has led us to expect even more.

Michael Upchurch. *New York Times Book Review* (September 27, 1998), p.18

[The subject of *The Farming of Bones*] is the overnight massacre, in 1937, of between 15,000 and 18,000 Haitians, at the secret instructions of Gen. Rafael Trujillo Molina, the military dictator who ruled the Dominican Republic for thirty-one years. But because the large themes of trauma and collective memory are in the hands of a gifted fiction writer, the novel cannot be summarized by casual reference to genocidal fact. Indeed, some of the most interesting writers today—Toni Morrison in *Paradise*, Caryl Phillips in *Cambridge*—are blending history and fiction, imparting information, in the manner of nineteenth-century novelists, without seeming to.

*The Farming of Bones* opens with a fragment of intimacy, offset in bold, between the as-yet-unnamed narrator, Amabelle, and a young man named Sebastien Onius. The short sequence feels almost modern, Kundera-esque, except that its diction, with its lack of contractions, indicates that the novel is set in the historical past. Amabelle is having a recurring nightmare about her parents drowning in a river, an event, we later learn, that she witnessed at the age of 8; Sebastien, a Haitian sugarcane cutter whose father died in a hurricane, is trying to console her, almost like a therapist. In their enclosed space, he tells her: "Take off your nightdress and be naked for true. And when you are uncovered, you will know that you are fully awake." Their relationship is one of familiarity and trust. Amabelle tells him that she is "grieving for who I was, and even more for what I've become." Sebastien sees her as a "woman child, with deep black skin, all the shades of black in you." "I can still feel his lips," Amabelle says after he leaves, in what has become the author's signature poetic prose, which characterized her first novel, *Breath, Eyes, Memory,* and a short collection, *Krik? Krak!*—"the eggplant-violet gums that taste of greasy goat milk boiled to candied sweetness with mustard-colored potatoes."

Only with Sebastien does the narrator allow herself to be vulnerable, young; the next chapter reveals Amabelle to be sagacious, mature beyond her years of 25. We learn that she has been adopted by a Spanish family living in the Dominican Republic; her contemporary, Señora Valencia, is about to give birth. While they are waiting for the family doctor, Amabelle is unexpectedly called upon to deliver the baby. It's a boldly evoked, realistic scene: After a "coconut-cream colored" son is born, they await the birth of the placenta:

"What do you feel, Señora?"

"The birth pains again."

"It is your baby's old nest, forcing its way out," I said, remembering one of my mother's favorite expressions. The baby's old nest took its time coming out. It was like another child altogether.

But instead of the placenta, another head pops out: a baby girl's. Amabelle removes the umbilical cord from around the infant's neck, saving her life, something she learned from her parents— herb healers and midwives in Haiti.

The infant takes her "dusky rose" color "from the mere sight of your face," Señora Valencia lovingly tells Amabelle, but as she coos over her newborn, she worries: "Do you think my daughter will always be the color she is now? My poor love, what if she's mistaken for one of your people?"

The themes of class and race, and the history of the relationship between the third of the island that is Haiti and the rest that is the Dominican Republic, are thus gently introduced. When the Spanish conquered the island in the late eighteenth century, they ignored the Haitian side, which became a base for French and English buccaneers. By the seventeenth century the French had colonized Haiti, importing African slaves to cultivate their sugarcane plantations. Though 95 percent of Haiti was black, its dominant culture was French—its ruling elite, by the nineteenth century, mulatto. On the Dominican side, the dominant culture was Spanish, with a mixed population.

If "shade" is the issue among the Spanish-speaking, who want to keep their line light, there are subtle "shades" of difference between Amabelle and Señora Valencia: Though she has been adopted by Valencia's father, whom she intimately calls "Papi," she still calls Valencia "Señora." She has been raised almost as an equal, in that she is cherished; but "nearly everything I had was something Señora Valencia had once owned and no longer wanted." Because she is Haitian, Amabelle eats in the kitchen with

Haitian domestics and is akin to a servant: "Working for others, you learn to be, present and invisible at the same time, nearby when they needed you, far off when they didn't, but still close enough in case they changed their minds." Like Amabelle, Señora Valencia lost her mother long ago; they have grown up almost like sisters, except that Amabelle is both mother and father to herself.

These racial hierarchies are never rendered ideological in Danticat's prose; her characters are well rounded, varied. It is the Dominican family doctor, Doctor Javier, who suggests that he can find Amabelle well-paid work as a midwife at a clinic in Haiti, where he sometimes works; and it is Papi, Señora Valencia's father, with whom Amabelle feels most closely allied. He, like she, is a moral observer: "He felt himself the orphaned child of a now orphaned people. Perhaps this was why he often seemed more kindly disposed to the strangers for whom this side of the island had not always been home." Papi grew up poor in Valencia, Spain, the son of a baker: "There are times when he gave bread to everyone in our quarter to everyone for nothing," Papi says. "He would never let me eat until everyone else had eaten." Papi fought in Spain's wars over its colonies, but left for a more peaceful life because he didn't believe in them. Though he has allowed Valencia to marry a soldier, who has risen under Trujillo's increasingly ruthless dictatorship, he has little respect for the government and for his son-in-law: "Do I like the way things are conducted here now, everything run by military men?" He looks up at Señora Valencia's spectacularly large portrait of the Generalissimo. "No," Papi says. "I don't like any part of it."

Politics and personal lives soon become intertwined in *The Farming of Bones:* Valencia's husband, Señor Pico, while racing home to greet his newborn twins, hits a Haitian laborer on the road but does not bother to find out what happened to him; Sebastien, with his friend Yves, who was walking along with the laborer, now enters the main narrative, in the Spanish household, like an illegal alien. He tells Amabelle, with yams in his hands for her and bruises on his face, that their friend Joel is dead—he couldn't see who was driving. The passages among the Haitian sugarcane laborers, who work at a mill nearby, give us the title of the book: "the cane life, travay te pou zo, the farming of bones"—bare traces, in Danticat's prose, of African literature, of Achebe and Soyinka, in their choral sensibility, a respect for elders, a sense of belonging to a colonized class. Conflict and character are not defined solely in individual terms but as they relate to the larger community, trying to understand Joel's death. Bathing in a stream, using parsley to wash themselves, the youngsters speak in quiet, worried voices, and keep a respectful distance in the water from Kongo, Joel's mourning father. A feeling that the Dominicans are out for blood is growing; some of the cane workers band together to protect their people. As if by divine retribution, Señor Pico's twin boy dies and he can no longer bear the sight of his surviving, dark-skinned daughter; but he is soon called away to take part in a "new border control operation." The Haitians' premonitions have been both wrong and right: The unnamed operation is the killing of all Haitians on the Dominican side of the island.

Danticat's brilliance as a novelist is that she is able put this event into a credible, human context. In Amabelle's case, Doctor Javier warns her that the border patrol operation is genocidal. He and a leftist Haitian priest, Father Remain, are organizing to smuggle Haitian workers out of the Dominican Republic; Will she go? She, in turn, warns Sebastien and his sister, Mimi, who agree to meet at the chapel at the appointed hour. Others, like Yves, do not believe it, or choose not to see it; still others, like Kongo, prefer to die in their homes. Rumor becomes an invisible character. Truckloads of Haitians are rounded up, hurled from cliffs into the sea, shot by civilians, macheted. Poor Dominican peasants are asked to catch and bring Haitians to the soldiers. This we learn only indirectly, far later in the novel, through survivors and eyewitnesses, as they try to piece together what happened.

If one thinks of Nazi Germany, of Rwanda, Bosnia, Guatemala, East Timer, Cambodia—sites of genocide—in the end, mass slaughter comes down to individuals—luck, cunning, a critical word uttered or a silence kept—and the rest is a backward turning, a traumatized narrative to reconstruct events: where one was, who was there, what one saw, told over and over again, like a recurrent nightmare. The book's present now becomes its past, as the words ''farming the bones'' take on another meaning. . . .

The book has all along been a meditation on the effects of trauma. It began with a repeating nightmare—a child who had seen her parents drown, having crossed the river to the Dominican side to buy cooking pots. And it has been Amabelle's voice that has been the book's strength; but it also becomes its main flaw. She too often resembles an omniscient narrator; as a result, she is free to see believably, but not to act believably. Though Danticat conceived her as precocious—and as frozen by trauma from the beginning—one wonders if she might have had more force and credibility as a third-person character, a ''she.'' An inability to imagine Amabelle in three dimensions makes her choices—such as taking Odette's nose in her hand in the river—seem implausible. Amabelle sometimes also sounds too avuncular and stilted in her speech: ''You are a miracle, Father.'' ''Mimi's only a child,'' she says, speaking of a woman only four years younger than herself; ''Courage, dear one,'' she tells Joel's lover. She is the character—the ''shade''—who is hardest to grasp. Still, it is an interesting flaw, not a fatal flaw, in a beautifully conceived work, with monumental themes.

Zia Jaffrey. *The Nation* (November 16, 1998), p. 62

BIBLIOGRAPHY
*Breath, Eyes, Memory*, 1994; *Krik? Krak!*, 1995; *The Farming of Bones*, 1998

# DELANY, Samuel R. (1942– )
## United States

From the beginning, Delany has been noticed and praised as an important new talent in science fiction. *Babel-17* and *The Einstein Intersection* won Nebula Awards, as has some of his shorter fiction: one story, ''Time Considered as a Helix of Semi-Precious Stones,'' won both the Nebula and Hugo Awards. . . . As Judith Merril points out, Delany ''is in a unique position in science fiction today: everybody loves him. The 'solid core,' the casual readers, the literary dippers-in, the 'new-thing' crowd—Delany is all things to all readers.'' I believe Delany has earned such accolades.

Delany is not only a gifted writer, he is one of the most articulate theorists of science fiction to have emerged from the ranks of its writers. As the author of a number of important critical essays and an editor of the short-lived speculative quarterly, *Quark*, he has done much to open up critical discussion of science fiction as a genre, forcefully arguing its great potential as art.

Although his short stories reveal the same concern with craft as do his novels, and deal with the same basic themes, the novels provide the best guide to his development as a writer. I deal with them under four headings: the quest pattern: his use of the figures of the artist and the criminal; cultural invention; and style and structure, a large section dealing with his use of literary and mythological allusions, his continual concern to develop a poetic prose in which image and metaphor are of primary importance, and his slowly maturing vision of the novel as ''a monumental metaphor.'' Although Delany's early novels can be discussed under these headings, they are neither as complex nor as sophisticated as his later ones. Because *Empire Star* represents a sudden leap forward in terms of his handling of his diverse materials, it and the novels after it require a more thorough discussion than the earlier work. Furthermore, it can be argued that *Nova* represents the culmination of all the experiments with form and style that begin in *Empire Star*, although the concern with style is present in his work from the beginning.

One reason Delany is such a fine of writer is that, like Le Guin and Russ, he puts his characters in concrete cultural situations, in which they can be seen to act quite naturally. For his future human civilizations he invents a multitude of cultural possibilities. These depend on whether his outlook in a particular novel tends toward utopia or dystopia, whether he attempts to show progress or regress. Unlike Le Guin he does not posit a single future history stretching over a number of novels. In his early novels, he tends to use fairly ordinary methods to suggest the kinds of culture his characters represent; in the later galactic novels, he tends to use manners and mores to show up cultural differences, and to present a number of different cultures within a single system, usually galaxy-wide; this presentation of a whole scale of cultures within a single civilization is hinted at in *Empire Star* and presented in some depth in *Babel-17* and *Nova*. . . .

[Delany's work reveals that] he is by far the most self-conscious practitioner of his art. His own term ''multiplex'' probably best describes his work (attitudes, ideas, themes, craftsmanship, all their inter-relations, as well as his relation, as artist, to them all). A poet. . . . Delany is one of the finest wordsmiths in science fiction, a true ''maker.'' His great perseverance in continually developing his craft and never resting on his past achievements is revealed in the steady growth of artistry and multiplexity that can be traced through his first seven novels. His study of fictional craft has led him to the conclusion that fictions are ''models of reality'' whose relation to ''the real world'' is ambiguous and oblique, and totally unlike that of an historical report or newspaper article. As a result of this realization, he has become one of science fiction's most important experimenters, discovering, in the novels since *Empire Star*, new and exciting ways to use the forms of fiction in the creation of fictions.

Douglas Barbour. *Foundation*. 7 & 8 (March, 1975), pp. 105–21

Delany, in *Babel-17*, illustrates the realities of the black culture through the linguistic effects of double consciousness. When a person is exposed to two cultures, double consciousness evolves. A person, to survive, must be able to function in both cultures which means mastering both languages. A problem arises when two cultures, purportedly possessing identical languages, apply different meanings to some of their words. The importance of culture and the analogy of language and culture was stressed by Edward Sapir, one of the founders of the science of anthropological linguistics. He regarded a culture as that which a social group does and thinks, and regarded language as a way of thinking. Therefore, he posited that language is "the symbolic guide to culture."

The Sapir-Whorf hypothesis states that there is a "very close relationship between cultural categories and language." Whorf's contribution was that "meaning is essential to the study of linguistics, and the categories of meaning change from one cultural tradition to another." Therefore, the language one learns necessarily constrains and structures what it is that one says. It seems apparent, then, that language also has a direct effect on how one thinks, since the structure of the language influences the processes by which one formulates ideas. If the language does not contain words to symbolize certain ideas or concepts, it is impossible for a person to think about them.

Delany's employment of linguistics as the science and as the framework for the plot of *Babel-17* takes on added significance when the novel is analyzed as the product of a black writer who has fought the linguistic battle of double consciousness. Delany has survived as a black writer in a predominately white culture by mastering both white and black uses of similar languages and by adapting a predominately white literary genre to depict the conflicts between these two cultures and their psychological and linguistic affects on blacks. . . .

Delany posits the linguistic puzzle of "Babel-17," the language of the Invaders, as the framework for the novel. The power and effects of "Babel-17" are demonstrated within the plot: Rydra's sabotage of her own ship; the assassination of Ver Dorco, and the adventures of interstellar travel as Rydra searches for the key which will unlock the mysteries of "Babel-17."

Delany gives a general description of language and of the effects of an impersonal language, such as "Babel-17." "Babel-17" is used as a vehicle for exploring the function of language in controlling thought processes and individual actions. Since the language functions as a weapon, the setting must be placed in a time of warfare and the plot involves a mission to destroy that weapon. The plot and setting enable Delany to make social comments on the conservative (or anti-humanistic) paradigms of the anti-humanistic Alliance society and, by analogy, on our own current paradigms in reference to science and the individual.

Delany makes several statements on what a language is: "A language has its own internal logic, its own grammar, its own way of putting thoughts together with words that span various spectra of meaning." He contends that language is more than a mechanism for expressing thought: ". . . language is thought. Thought is information given form. The form is language."

The reader is never given a linguistic description of "Babel-17," although he is informed it is a computer-like language: "It's the most analytically exact language imaginable. But that's because everything is flexible, and ideas come in huge numbers of congruent sets, governed by the same words. This just means that the number of paradoxes you can come up with is staggering." Like a computer language, the elements of "Babel-17" have different meanings in different contexts.

"Babel-17's" one major disadvantage, however, is that it destroys the identity of the speaker. Just as a computer cannot correct its own programming or even be aware of the cause of any malfunctions in its programming, the "Babel-17" language is similarly structured: "The lack of an 'I' precludes any self-critical process. In fact it cuts out any awareness of the symbolic process at all—which is the way we distinguish between reality and our expression of reality." Rydra, as does any person living within the black culture, has two identities. She is, in one identity, a poetess, a space captain, and a loyal citizen of the Alliance. She is, in her other identity, a saboteur and unconsciously works against her native Alliance society. The latter identity is hidden from her by the amnesia instilled by the language "Babel-17." Similarly, the white culture exerts great influence because it can force stereotypic definitions on the black person. It is thus difficult for the black person to maintain his identity, and he frequently and unconsciously identifies himself as the whites portray him. The black person may find that he has succumbed to the white culture's expectations by accepting orders, by never questioning what is right for him, and by not causing trouble. If the black person capitulates to the definition imposed on him by a force outside of his culture, then, he is in danger of losing his identity. Similarly, Rydra struggles to maintain her identity against the power of "Babel-17," which contains no words for the concept of individuality.

Language, rather than science, is the instrument by which Rydra frees herself and Butcher from the power of "Babel-17." Rydra converts "Babel-17" into a weapon for the Alliance, thereby freeing the Alliance society from their war priorities. The novel can thus be interpreted as a statement by Delany that the arts are as important as the sciences. This is a comment on our educational priorities that promote science (which primarily perpetuates the value of things) at the expense of the humanities (which explores the understanding of ourselves).

Poetry meets these real needs and reveals knowledge of ourselves in terms of human values and purposes. It is used to transmit personal knowledge between the transmitter and the receiver. Poems reflect a cultural context as well as a personal message because they are created in an historical moment and are written in a language by an individual for an individual.

Delany uses poetry in three ways in his novel. First, the poems of Marilyn Hacker introduce each section of the novel. Secondly, the protagonist is a poetess which allows Delany to discuss the function and the development of a poet. Finally, a poem written by Delany is used to demonstrate the ordering power of "Babel-17" and to initiate the prevention of Jebel's assassination.

Delany presents the problem of identity in the black community through Rydra's search for selfhood. The poetry and explications on the role of the artist express the power of language in society. The psychological and sociological insights into how science is used to deprive and possibly destroy the individual argue against a prevailing paradigm in our modern technocratic society. Additionally, the struggle of minorities affected by double consciousness is recognizably described. Delany, through his discussion of language, questions such paradigms and dramatizes the power of the white culture over the black culture through his illustration of the effects of double consciousness in the black community.

Jane Weedman. *Samuel R. Delany* (Mercer Island, Washington: Starmount Press, 1982)

Even for a writer of such consistently high ambition and achievement as Samuel R. Delany, [*Stars in My Pocket Like Grains of*

*Sand*] represents a major step forward. It is a work of adult science fiction. Anyone who considers such a description inherently oxymoronic has only to open the book and start reading. But a word of caution: read slowly. This is not the science fiction of *Star Wars*, or even of *Dune*, which may be enjoyed—indeed, may be most enjoyable—when consumed at a breathless rate that hurries past any infelicities of plot or phrasing. Mr. Delany's fiction demands—and rewards—the kind of close reading that one ungrudgingly brings to *serious* novelists. His characters live complex emotional lives in complex societies. To unpack the layers of meaning in seemingly offhand remarks or exchanges of social pleasantries, the reader must be alert to small shifts in emphasis, repeated phrases or gestures that assume new significance in new contexts, patterns of behavior that only become apparent when the author supplies a crucial piece of information at just the proper moment.

What makes *Stars in My Pocket Like Grains of Sand* especially challenging—and satisfying—is that the complex society in which the characters move is one of the author's own imagining: a universe of the far future, which contains more than 6,000 inhabited worlds and a marvelously rich blend of cultures. The inhabitants of these worlds—both human and alien—relate to one another in ways that, however bizarre they may seem at first, are eventually seen to turn on such recognizable emotional fulcrums as love, loss and longing.

Mr. Delany is well aware of the demands his novel makes on the reader—especially the reader who is unfamiliar with the science fiction technique of revealing the nature of an imagined society through the words and actions of characters so thoroughly at home in the society that they never stop to contemplate the rules that govern their own behavior. In past novels, such as *Dhalgren* (1975), Mr. Delany showed himself capable of stylistic experimentation to convey an otherworldly ambiance. Here his goal is clarity—without sacrificing the complex vision that lies at the core of his work. . . .

*Stars in My Pocket Like Grains of Sand* is the first half of what Mr. Delany calls a diptych of novels. . . . But while this book ends without answering all the questions it raises, it does not feel ''incomplete.'' Sentence by sentence, phrase by phrase, it invites the reader to collaborate in the process of creation, in a way that few novels do. The reader who accepts this invitation has an extraordinarily satisfying experience in store for him/her.

Gerald Jonas. *New York Times Book Review*. (February 10, 1985), p. 15

[The shelf containing Delany's dozen-plus science fiction novels, holds as well] several collections of essays, a landmark autobiography, a series of sui generis postmodern fantasies praised by (among many others) Umberto Eco, short-story collections, finely wrought memories of growing up black and gay, addresses and polemics on gay affairs, pornographic novels, and hundreds upon hundreds of pages of criticism ranging from the abstract and theoretical (how do we go about, word by word, reconstructing a world in our language, in our thought?) to the most specific (as in his close readings of fellow science fiction writers or of Hart Crane).

From the first, Delany's reach has been encyclopedic. This shows in the scope and Balzacian inclusiveness of the initial epic, *The Fall of the Towers*, in his creation of a self-discrete universe-city in *Dhalgren*, in the social investigations of the Nevèrÿon tales

(a major theme of which is the change from barter to a money-based economy), in the epistemological underpinning of much of his later critical writing. . . .

Narrative, of course, is the method by which we most often negotiate that discriminatory plane. Delany is a great letter writer; sometimes running to forty or sixty pages, his letters are wonderfully turned stories, detailing the moments of his day, what he is reading and thinking, the people he meets, with a leisure and freedom he seldom allows himself in other writing. Yet even here the text is pushed intuitively, almost compulsively, toward patterns, toward meaning. He writes of ''the experiential stutter'' of shoes on a floor, notes that ''In the halls (not corridors) were rugs (not carpets).''

Self-examination is our other great bridge off that plane. ''Wherever we go, whatever we do, self is the sole object we study and learn,'' Emerson tells us—little difference if we travel to Concord or across galaxies. At first, in articles such as many of those collected in *The Jewel-Hinged Jaw*, Delany's self-examination took place apart from his fiction, on a kind of sidetrack. He had always put much of himself, re-imagined events from his own life, into his fiction. Then, in *The Einstein Intersection* the fiction itself became textually self-conscious. Excerpts from journals Delany kept while composing the novel and while traveling through Greece frame the novel's sections, reflecting, questioning. . . .

Delany's central characters are themselves likely to be storytellers—the poet of *Babel-17*, the singers of ''Time Considered as a Helix of Semiprecious Stones,'' Lobey with his musical machete in *The Einstein Intersection, Dhalgren's* Kid—even if inchoate ones. They are also likely to be outlaws, and in Delany outlaw and artist are often indistinguishable. He creates entire societies in order to depict those at society's margin. Outlaw, artist, the sexually unconstrained embody a revolutionary impulse at the heart of much of Delany's work.

All too often in science fiction, revolution (though a major theme) leads simply to inculcation or restoration of contemporary Western values to some land far removed in time or space. By contrast, Delany's revolutions—galactic, societal, personal, sexual, accomplished, or anticipated—like his own revolutionary work within the field, are real. These are the figures our lives make against the sky, he says again and again. . . .

In both its sexual preoccupations and its use of language (that is, in the sensual surface of the writing itself) Delany's work is sensual in a way little speculative fiction is; at the same time it is, again, unusually given to intellection. The fragments of the world float down to us in bits and pieces (this is sensation) and from them (by way of intellect, narrative, self-examination) we cobble together meaning. . . .

As one looks back on thirty-plus years of work, it becomes clear that all along Delany has searched for some ideal form, some mode of writing at once true and imagined, real and fictive, that might encompass it all, that might be able to contain the world's multifarious leanings, vectors, veerings, and prevarications. Once he thought that science fiction with its ready-made universals and symbolic potential might accomplish that. Further into his career he believed that ontological or epistemological criticism or the discipline of semiotics might. And if not those, then perhaps his Proustian incursions toward (always *toward*, for everything is approximation, everything is measured apprehension) autobiography. And still he longs to tell the true story of change, to say what would happen were *real* freedom ever rendered: to sketch out, from observing, from imagining, from living through its tatters, the lines of what true society might be.

James Sallis. *Review of Contemporary Fiction.* 16, 3 (Fall 1996), pp. 91–96

Samuel R. Delany is not only a celebrated and prolific author (more than thirty books to date), but he is also a very gifted thinker—a characteristic which (as we know) is not always associated with either success or productivity. It is very easy to imagine that in a parallel universe nearly contiguous with our own, Delany could have been a renowned mathematician or philosopher. As it is, math and philosophy are two of Delany's interests, two aspects of his wide-ranging erudition. His first claim to fame, of course, is being one of the most exciting and original science fiction writers of the second half of the twentieth century (and the first African American to explore this literary space), to which he has added deserved reputations as one of the most astute critics of SF and as a writer of a demanding form of fantasy that combines the subgenre of sword-and-sorcery with poststructuralist theory—what we might call a hybrid species of critical fiction. And increasingly, with books like Longer Views, Delany is garnering serious attention as an original critical mind, period.

*Longer Views,* which gathers together some of Delany's lengthier essays, poses a real challenge to any reviewer who isn't as much of a polymath as Delany is. Consider the contents: a piece, subtitled ''A Play of 19th and 20th Century Critical Fictions,'' that reads Richard Wagner and Antonin Artaud in relation to one another; a reading of Donna Haraway's ''Manifesto for Cyborgs''; an essay with the permutating title ''Aversion/Perversion/Diversion'' that deals with gay identity; ''Shadow and Ash,'' a multidiscursive piece that functions, I think, as a partial but perhaps typical itinerary of Delany's engaged and questing mind; an essay that describes itself as ''Some Notes on Hart Crane''; and, as an appendix, a meditation called ''Shadows,'' which Delany himself, in his preface, describes as follows: ''If 'Shadow and Ash' is the most important essay here, then 'Shadows' is its lengthy, chrestomathic preface.''

In the essay on Hart Crane, Delany's response to the sheer lyric power of Crane's language brought back my own response to his work when I first encountered him in my youth; moreover, his references to Novalis, James Thomson *(The City of Dreadful Night),* and Jean Toomer all evoked certain memories, sounded particular chords. Delany's particular take on Crane is persuasive to me, not because of the authority of his scholarship, but because I feel a kinship with the personal poetics of his experience with Crane's work.

If one were forced to select a single word to characterize Delany's writings in general, a logical choice would be *complexity.* Delany's work takes complexity in its various forms as its broad subject (whether he is talking about webs of worlds in a far-flung galactic future or the negotiations of identity experienced by a gay black man in late-twentieth-century America), and his work manifests complexity in style, structure, and vision. Another useful term would be *alterity.* (Complexity facilitates alterity, and vice versa.) Science fiction—and it is important to reiterate that Delany began as a science fiction writer, and remains one, whatever other avenues he has pursued—is all about alternatives, (im)possible worlds and adventures, *aliens.* It may have been essentially conservative for much of its history—an excess of technofetishism,

sexism, and xenophobia stalks the pages of many a science fiction tale—but it always had the potential, buoyed in part by its celebration of the imagination, to promote radical thinking, not just about the future, but about the present, which, some writers and critics would argue, is always (if only implicitly) SF's real subject. . . .

Although Delany is a black author, all of his work, whether fictional, autobiographical, or critical, serves to drive a postmodern stake through the heart of the undead notion that any identity—''black,'' ''gay,'' ''writer,'' what have you—is given and fully defining, rather than partial and contingent. (This includes our identity as readers, for, as Delany notes at the outset, ''reading is a multilayered process—like writing.'') But to describe Longer Views as a black text would, for most readers, be stretching the idea of blackness toward infinity—which might not be a bad thing (certainly someone like Sun Ra would have applauded it), though it surely would raise the hackles of folks for whom ''black'' / ''white'' / (name your perusasion) must be easily recognizable, nationalizable, and (intellectually or otherwise) commodifiable. The extent to which Delany's blackness suffuses his work, is always present, despite not being upside your head or in your face, will be a mystery to those still clinging to the old school of identity politics and its ready-to-wear, ready-to-bare essentialism.

Robert Elliot Fox. *African American Review.* 31, 1 (Spring 1999), pp. 173–74

BIBLIOGRAPHY

*The Jewels of Aptor,* abridged edition, 1962, complete edition 1976; *Captives of the Flame,* 1963, revised edition *Out of the Dead City,* 1968; *The Towers of Toron,* 1964; *City of a Thousand Suns,* 1965; *The Ballad of Beta-2,* 1965; *Empire Star,* 1966; *Babel-17,* 1966; *The Einstein Intersection,,* 1967; *Nova,* 1968; *Driftglass: Ten Tales of Speculative Fiction,* 1971; *The Tides of Lust,* 1973; *Dhalgren,* 1975; *Triton,* 1976; *Empire: A Visual Novel,* 1978; *Distant Stars,* 1981; *Stars in My Pocket Like Grains of Sand,* Bantam, 1984; *The Star Pits,* 1989; *They Fly at Ciron,* 1992; *Nevèrÿon, or, The Tale of Signs and Cities,* 1993; *Equinox,* 1994; *The Mad Man, Masquerade,* 1994; *Silent Interviews: On Language, Race, Sex, Science Fiction, and some Comics: A Collection of Written Interviews,* 1994; *Flight from Nevrongÿ,* 1994; *They Fly at Ciron,* 1995; *Atlantis: Three Tales,* 1995; *Trouble on Triton: An Ambiguous Heterotopia,* 1996; *Longer Views: Extended Essays,* 1996; *Bread & Wine: An Erotic Tale of New York City,* 1998; *Hogg,* 1998; *Times Square Red, Times Square Blue,* 1999; *Shorter Views: Queer Thoughts & the Politics of the Paraliterary,* 1999

# DEMBY, William (1922–)
## United States

Except that it is not deliberately complex and probing, *Beetlecreek* brings to mind Carson McCullers's *The Heart Is a Lonely Hunter;* for it is about the barriers—only temporarily surmountable—which separate human beings. The immediate foreground is the Negro quarter of a small town in West Virginia. The central figures are an old and half-crazed white man, a hermit tempted to give himself ''the right and power to reach out and touch people, to love,'' and a sensitive and imaginative adolescent Negro boy, the immediate cause of the temptation. The action the hermit takes, after a propitious beginning, is disastrous. The innocence of his feeling for the boy—he seeks a son as the boy a father—is beautifully conveyed. But to the Negro suburb he rapidly becomes a ''sex-fiend.'' Ultimately, in a fit of hysteria, the boy kills him, demonstrating Mr. Demby's gloomy views on the racial problem and the universal impossibility of any lasting communication between two human beings.

I like this novel very much, though it has an entirely predictable and banal ending. Unlike Langston Hughes and Richard Wright and William Gardiner Smith, Mr. Demby has avoided the inevitable pitfalls which beset the American Negro who writes out of his own experience. His book is only in a secondary sense about ''the Negro problem''; it is no *roman à thèse*, except for the general gloomy view about *all* human relationships. To put it very tritely, he is interested in his characters first as human beings and then as black or white. For all his painful awareness of what it means to be a Negro in a small Southern town, he never merely exploits his subject.

> Ernest Jones. *Nation*. February 11, 1950, pp. 138–39

Thematically [*Beetlecreek* moves] toward an existentialist definition of evil: if no other confirmation of his existence is possible, man will attempt to assert himself in negative and destructive ways. It is so with Bill Trapp, who even as a child preferred to be tormented than ignored; it is true of the townspeople, who find in their malicious persecution of Bill Trapp relief from their empty lives. It is true above all of David and Johnny, who suffer their creative powers to be perverted, rather than endure a spiritual vacuum. . . .

Recurrent images assume symbolic value and are used extensively to buttress the theme. The frantic, swooping birds, for example, provide an objective correlative to David's and Johnny's feelings of restlessness and dissatisfaction. The mirrors (each of the main characters studies himself in a mirror) underscore the problem of identity, while the swinging bridge suggests the social separation between colored and white in Beetlecreek. The season in which the action takes place (Indian summer) is converted into a particularly rich symbol. On one level, it helps to dramatize the necessity of choice, of decision: ''The birds swooped and swooped, all the time screaming, undecided what to do. The freak summer fooled everybody and everything.'' On another, it suggests that the crucial decisions faced by Bill Trapp, David, and Johnny represent their last chance for life.

> Robert A. Bone. *The Negro Novel in America* (New Haven: Yale University Press, 1958), pp. 195–96

*The Catacombs*, by William Demby, is in many ways an unusual novel. It purports to tell a story about a young Negro girl, Doris, but it is equally involved in telling the story of the writer, as well as recording snatches of news about the members of the bohemian circle in Rome to which the writer belongs. In addition, it details the major world news topics covered by the Italian press, events beside which the little personal dramas of the characters shrink into insignificance. The writer, a film script-writer and translator, makes use of the film technique of quick cuts and no continuity, a bold and frontal attack on narrative continuity. The action, if action it can be called, extends from 1961 to 1964, from the time Demby began to write the novel to the time he left Rome (where he had lived many years) to return to the United States. The focus of the novel is Doris's life in Rome as the dominant partner in a liaison with a weak-willed Italian count. Why Demby should decide to write a novel about Doris is not exactly clear. What is clear, however, is that she is a mere pretext.

The novelist, whose occupation and travels have no doubt made a cosmopolite of his psyche, succeeds very well in showing how insignificant the modern individual has become in the face of the larger issues that stir the world to its foundations. It is no wonder that the exploration of character in this novel comes flat and just short of the ridiculous. Doris is a mere representative of the rootless American adolescent found floating all over the world, especially in the exciting cities and bohemian centers of Europe. She patters philosophy, makes a show of cynicism and sophistication; but she is at bottom pathetically ignorant, completely confused, and given to outbursts of neurotic self-rejection. When the curtain falls, she is understandably lost in the dark maze of the Roman catacombs, while her Italian count prepares to follow his fortune to Hong Kong and his biographer to return with his wife and son to the United States.

> Emmanuel Obiechina. *African Forum*. Winter 1966, pp. 108–9

[*The Catacombs*] achieves something of a collage effect in which at odd moments the newspaper accounts Demby reads and quotes superimpose themselves, however precariously, on the narrative—the effect is a hovering sense of world and time on even the most private situations. But the various strands of the novel crisscross in other places as well. Demby may intrude on his story with seemingly vagrant thoughts of his own, with a letter someone is writing, with a street scene being played far outside the main arena of the drama by persons whom the reader does not know—or more frequently he may break into any dramatic action of his principals by projecting what some of the other major or minor characters may be doing or thinking at the precise moment.

This simultaneity of presentation is presumably what Demby means when he speaks somewhere of ''cubistic time.'' It is something almost animate—''time, always time, listening always listening, billions of years of imprisoned memory undistilled, electric-pointed stylus, plastic ballpoint pen.'' Actually, although the narrative generally unfolds in chronological order, Demby will, on occasion, shuttle back and forth in time in personal recollection or fantasy, or in a kind of Jungian race memory in which some odd newspaper item or disparate event suddenly assumes symbolic or archetypal importance. And yet the fragments do piece together. The novel begins and ends at the Easter season, the themes of death and resurrection become everywhere apparent like spirals within spirals.

If Demby's technique makes *The Catacombs* sound like something of a jigsaw, it is surprising to discover what intensely good reading the novel is.

> Edward Margolies. *Native Sons* (Philadelphia: J. B. Lippincott, 1968), pp. 182–83

Bill Trapp, Johnny, and David are the only ones [in *Beetlecreek*] in the swirl and mire of what is called life in Beetlecreek who have a

chance to pull themselves out. The others have long since succumbed to the disease of decay. But Trapp, the old "carny," and
his two new friends clearly see the options available to them. Trapp
can give up his solitary exile and, through Johnny, can allow his
trust in people and life to be restored. Johnny, can accept the old
man's friendship and thus repudiate the demands of the barber shop
crowd and the Nightriders that he stay away from the "queer"
hermit. And David, by abandoning his lifeless wife, Mary (whom
he married because she was pregnant and he wanted to "do the
right thing," and with whom he shares no love whatsoever), could
return to the city for which both his education and his temperament
make him better suited.

Demby sustains the drama of his plot with fine precision: Trapp
moves closer to accepting people; Johnny moves closer to accepting the friendship of the recluse which will give them both life; and
David seriously contemplates leaving Beetlecreek. But decay
wins out. . . .

Demby's characters, like Ellison's protagonist in *Invisible
Man*, are only incidentally black. While the black section of the
town of Beetlecreek is the setting of Demby's novel, there is little
significance in the author's focus on black life except, as Demby
suggests, that the inanity of this black community simply reflects
the corresponding inanity of the whole human community. It is this
human community that Demby is probing, with its death-sustain-
ing charade of organizations, rituals, and pettiness—a charade that
an individual, given the capacity and courage to make personal
moral choice, *can* repudiate, thereby redeeming himself for the *art*
of living.

Roger Whitlow. *Black American Literature* (Chicago: Nel-
son-Hall, 1973), pp. 123–25

*The Catacombs* draws on significant formal and thematic traditions
with a long history in Western literature. Within the specifically
African-American tradition, Demby engages the themes of freedom and literacy, which Stepto notes as the recurring hallmarks of
the African-American tradition; however, the modernist Demby
recasts the quest in light of the expatriate intellectual's relationship
to a worldwide struggle for national independence and civil rights.
In developing this theme, Demby employs as well as meditates on
the long tradition of the dialogue-debate in Western literature. In
particular, he formulates a significant part of the novel's argument
in terms similar to the poems and treatises on Christian principles
that were cast in the form of debate and dialogue. Especially in the
narrator's conversations with Doris, the imaginary protagonist of
the novel he is writing, and in her exchanges with the Count, her
fictional lover, *The Catacombs* reinvents the age-old dispute.
Demby does not employ the formal structure or terms of the debate,
but rather invents a series of scenarios that frame the issues within
the new, postmodern context. . . .

The most experimental characteristic of *The Catacombs* is its
mingling of texts derived from disparate planes of "reality." In an
interview, Demby noted that in *The Catacombs* he set himself the
challenge to write a novel in which "every page or every day's
work would reflect what has happened to me in my personal life
and the lives of the fictional characters who moved around at the
same time as the so-called real characters, the people in real life"
The protagonist and narrator, William Demby, who writes a journal
of his struggles to write a novel, inserts into his record (a)

newspaper clippings and summaries of news reports from the two-
year period covered by the novel (March 1962-April 1964), (b)
scenes from the novel he is writing about a young Black actress
named Doris and her liaison with an Italian count, (c) reports of
conversations with friends and family—including critiques of the
novel he is writing—and his participation in historical events like
the 1963 March on Washington, (d) fantasies in which he (as well
as, occasionally, his family) interacts with the fictional character
Doris, and (e) other texts he is creating, such as a letter to a friend in
Alabama and the ending to a screenplay. In practice the experiment
of reflecting "what has happened" in both fictional and real life
blurs the distinction between the author as he lives and the narrator-
protagonist that he constructs in his diary-form novel. Reality and
fiction intermingle and become indistinguishable.

The narrator-protagonist William Demby creates two characters who come to represent the traditional disputants in the Debate
of the Body and Soul. Doris, about whom the author says he is
writing a novel "with her permission," represents the Flesh. She
has a part as one of Elizabeth Taylor's slaves in *Antony and
Cleopatra*, which is being filmed in Rome during the first part of
the novel. The narrator-author delineates this character of his as a
woman of extraordinary physical appeal, a beauty specifically and
significantly African, "authentically ancient Egyptian." She is
associated with the earth and its promise of fertility; her hairdo
makes him "think of a black lacquered cone of spider webs, a
magical fertility symbol."

Representing the other term in the debate is the equally imaginary Count Raffaele. An Italian aristocrat from a decayed family,
he is cultivated and sensitive. It is also understood that he is
childless and had been impotent, but that his relationship with
Doris has revived his manhood and made him "a regular stallion."
Whereas Doris with her promise of fecundity stands for Body, the
Count, with his bureaucratic job in an airline office and his ancient
family, his learning and social connections, comes to represent
Soul, but specifically only the soul's faculty of Intellect. Soul, or
the complete soul, the vital or animating principle, remains the
elusive object of protagonist William Demby's quest, sought
sometimes in physical sensation, sometimes in dedication to ideals.
Ultimately the quest leads him to a female principle, and to Africa.
In the course of his journey the narrator re-formulates the debate
between the flesh and the spirit in historical and sociological as
well as psychological and religious terms: Africa and woman come
to stand roughly parallel with the Body, and Europe and colonialism are associated with aggressive, purely detached intellect.

Further complicating the debate is narrator-protagonist Demby's
own participation in it. He is a writer and self-conscious intellectual, a contributor of reviews to art magazines, a journalist, a
consultant to filmmakers; and he takes himself and his responsibility very seriously. Early in the book he assigns himself the role of
mentor to a writer friend, pontificating on the responsibility of a
Black writer in 1960s Alabama. On the other hand, an atavistic
yearning for the primeval and the purely physical frequently
overcomes him, and he questions the value of writing and the life of
the mind.

In her imaginary conversations with the narrator-protagonist,
Doris plays spokesperson for the anti-intellectual life of the senses,
often sharply criticizing the invasive and exploitive excesses of
intellectualism. She calls William Demby and all writers "vampires" and maintains that the writer's vision transforms real people
into mere material. Marilyn Monroe is the example she gives:

''The poor girl commits suicide out of love and you write it all down in your book and probably'll get rich and famous writing about other people's misery—!'' In Doris's view the writer visits a deadening and sterile attention on living beings. Doris's argument maintains that American Black author William Demby is the same sorry type as European Count Raffaele, Doris's other lover in the story: Demby finds himself lumped together in her mind with the sterile, the impotent, the lifeless. Finally, Doris maintains, Black people should not be writers at all: ''Let white people write things down.'' History itself, she implies, is part of the unhealthy burden of European culture.

William Demby, narrator and protagonist of *The Catacombs,* like William Demby the author, is an African-American bourgeois intellectual residing in Rome. A man educated in the European tradition, he lives the life of the mind as morally obligatory and psychologically satisfying. He is, inescapably, a member of a race that has been systematically excluded from education, and in the European imagination reduced to stereotypes of the ''merely'' physical. Yet he longs for the freedom, abandon, and joy he imagines in a life of the senses. He confronts the dilemma lamented by African-American writers from Phillis Wheatley to Countee Cullen: how to recover the positive values represented by Africa without acceding to the narrowing stereotype that would limit him as an African to only those characteristics. . . .

In striving toward simultaneity and a seamless integration of the various levels of reality that he was trying to organize—the impersonal world of history and news reports, the world of the imagination, the personal world of relationships and friends—Demby found to his astonishment ''that there was a real pattern that you perceived. What created this pattern, I don't know. Was it in the consciousness of the author, or was it that any event that you would see happening anywhere, were you to turn your consciousness on it, would fall into some kind of order?'' Speculating on the question, William Demby opts for a statement of faith in a meaningful—a moral—universe: ''I think that it gets to the deeper truth that there is no such thing as chaos perhaps. There may not be.'' The answer affirms the Christian view of an ordered universe, of the existence of an underlying ''Natural Law'' discoverable to the human mind; it runs counter to the modernist and postmodernist focus on the arbitrariness of system and law. It is the responsibility of the artist, Demby believes, to ''see connections,'' as well as ''to make some connection with the past.''

Hence the ending of *The Catacombs*: the allegorical baby, however satisfactory to the imagination, may not, finally, substitute for understanding and perception of the reality of things. It is true that Demby aims at synthesis and integration, rather than victory and domination as in the traditional rhetorical debate. In the modern world, merely winning is neither desirable nor functional. Neither, however, is the allegorical fantasy of romance and rebirth.

The ending of *The Catacombs* is ambiguous: Doris disappears in the catacomb of San Callisto and the Count, his eyes suddenly opened for the first time, wanders through the underground passageways calling out for her. Doris had embodied his illusion, the ''Idea of Africa'' that the Count and his father and the historical Europe stand for and had cherished for so long. Now, the illusion disappears with her. Count Raffaele confronts the opportunity to emulate his sister, Maria Novella, who has discovered in the real Africa a new humanity, a new model for human nature. The possibility remains open. Like the narrator, the reader is left to release fantasies of the ideal and to return to the real world to

seek—rather than to impose—a moral order that Demby believes underlies it.

In *The Catacombs* the debate between the Flesh and the Spirit is not resolved in the traditional academic intellectual mode, by means of a judgment on the correctness of one argument and the corresponding error of the other. Neither is it given a traditional mythic or comic resolution, a synthesis of opposites figured in sexual union with a fruitful outcome personified by a child. There is no conversion, either by force or by feeling. The ending is as puzzling and inconclusive as the entire novel is expansive in its embrace of contemporary life, history, myth, personal data, and intimate fantasies: the Count, his eyes opened, is still the Count, and nothing has changed except the ability to see. Dialogue itself, the process of coming to terms with the Other, appears to be the core of the novel's moral vision. It is precisely an ecumenical position and suggests a paradigm that protagonist-narrator-author William Demby offers to readers who themselves are engaged on the same search for meaning.

Helen Jaskoski. *Critique: Studies in Contemporary Fiction.* 35, 3 (Spring 1994), pp. 181–93

BIBLIOGRAPHY
*Beetlecreek*, 1950; *The Catacombs*, 1965; *Love Story Black*, 1978; *Blueboy*, 1979

# DEPESTRE, René (1926–)
## Haiti

René Depestre belongs to the second generation of Négritude poets. He was born in 1926 in the port town of Jacmel, in southern Haiti, and spent his early childhood there. Depestre's father died when he was a small child, leaving [his] widow to bring up a large family on slender means. For his secondary studies, Depestre went to the Ecole Tippenhauer in Port-au-Prince. As a teenager he met and much admired Jacques Roumain—both for his writings and the political ideals he represented. Depestre, who had known deprivation firsthand, wanted to see the continuing misery of his country and his people relieved. By the time he was twenty he had published two books of stirring, patriotic verse, *Etincelles* in 1945, and *Gerbe de sang* in 1946. He had also become editor-in-chief of a small, revolutionary newspaper, *La Ruche*, and was a leader of the group responsible for the overthrow of the Elie Lescot government in 1946. As a gesture of gratitude, the then new president of Haiti, Dumas Estimé, in 1947 awarded the young Depestre a scholarship to continue his education in France.

In 1950 the Estimé government fell, and was followed by the Magloire regime. Five years later, Duvalier took over the presidency and remained in power until his death in 1971, when he was succeeded by his son.

Depestre never returned to his homeland to live. In the 1950s he traveled a great deal in Europe, sojourning here and there on both sides of the Iron Curtain, frequently appearing at leftist-oriented international youth festivals, such as those in Berlin, Moscow, [and] Algiers, to speak and to read his poems. He also traveled widely in Central and South America, visiting Haiti briefly again in 1959. At least once, the intervention of a fellow poet of quite different political persuasion, Léopold [Sédar] Senghor, is said to have saved the "boilingly militant" Haitian—who had become a communist during his early years abroad—from being imprisoned for his political activities.

For some twenty years Depestre's poetry has continued to appear in France: *Végétations de clarté*, in 1951; *Traduit du grand large*, in 1952; and *Journal d'un animal marin*, in 1965—all published by Seghers. *Minerai noir* and *Un Arc-en-ciel pour l'occident chrétien* were published by Présence Africaine in 1957 and 1967 respectively. The last two books appeared since Depestre's emigration to Cuba.

> Ellen Conroy Kennedy. *The Négritude Poets* (New York: Thunder's Mouth Press, 1975), pp. 89–90

*Un Arc-en-ciel pour l'occident chrétien* [translated as *A Rainbow for the Christian West*], published in 1967, reveals the personal evolution of René Depestre as well as the synthesis of his poetic metamorphoses. Although it grows out of his earlier poetic collections . . . and although it reflects the bitterness of his exiles from Haiti and Cuba and then his joy on return, *Un Arc-en-ciel pour l'occident chrétien* has an intensity and a comprehensiveness of vision that mark it off from all his earlier works. Here he articulates a new humanism by transforming the dead past into living actuality. Traditionalism interacts with a prophetic, progressive impulse, and the facts of individual experience become expressive of larger, more universal possibilities. . . .

Seeking to join forces with world movements in revolutionary poetry, he creates a literature both rich in revolutionary action and in the spiritual qualities of his psychic inheritance. Through a confrontation of that past mythic tradition with the present, he aspires simultaneously to revitalize the past and transform the present.

The drama of *Un Arc-en-ciel pour l'occident chrétien* consists of this confrontation. The title itself is a key to Depestre's purpose. The symbol of the rainbow, connecting heaven to earth, dramatically embodies the interdependence of the earthly and the eternal. In the role of Haitian *houngan* (priest) he will descend to the dark stagnation of a sterile South (the parlor of an Alabama judge), steal the fire from the white man's "false gods," and, possessed by the sacred gods of voodoo, he will communicate their eternal truths to the alien white world. Within this work are gathered many connections. Relative to his previous poetry, it combines the black militancy of *Minerai noir* and the lyricism of *Journal d'un animal marin*. The constituent parts of his past creation are altogether transformed, yet never left behind. All that he articulated in his earlier poetry is now manifested through the essential, unifying elements of voodoo. It is through the external form of this indigenous dramatic rite that Depestre communicates that which acts in all traditions to liberate and he finally realizes his dream of twenty years. His last article during "The Debate over National Poetry" expresses his hope that he can create an original poetry, "a realism universal and human by content and Haitian as to its expressive contours." And, relevant to this debate, he rejects the supremacy of either the form or content, external tradition or individual freedom of inventiveness. For poetry, as ultimate synthesis, must unite and thus surpass these apparent contradictions. . . .

Although Depestre necessarily passes through annihilation and negation in his descent, the final shaping of the created mythology of *Un Arc-en-ciel pour l'occident chrétien* involves the revelation of both worlds, black and white, as mutually interrelated and interpenetrating. The structure of the entire work can be seen as the blacks' continuous movement forward: "I go forward barefoot/In the grass of my Négritude," passing through a transcendence of the limits of place in order to enter the civilization of the universal. Not content simply to delve into voodoo's past to find coherent, indigenous elements to countermand white attempts to falsify and dissociate, he also works to construct out of its basic principles a universal humanism. Thus, the dramatic phenomenon of continuous transformation, which is the major thrust of this collection, structurally manifests itself as a tense dialectic into which all stages of opposition finally disappear. Through self-transformation Depestre has articulated a new vision that completes the dramatic action of *Un Arc-en-ciel pour l'occident chrétien*. But in the "Prélude," the beginning of this collection, we get a fierce sense of the self that is to undergo this transformation—this "personal surpassing."

> Joan Dayan. Introduction to René Depestre. *A Rainbow for the Christian West* (Amherst: University of Massachusetts Press, 1977), pp. 3, 39–41

René Depestre is an essayist of the first rank. The essay in his hands successfully combines political immediacy and lasting literary values. [Karl] Marx's idea of human reality as essentially dialectical and historical is used as a base of vision of our times that is both analysis and synthesis, the creation of a jumping-off platform for Third World action. *Pour la révolution: pour la poésie* tries to rally Third World peoples by relating literary men to political leaders like Ho Chi Minh. Depestre works systematically to produce ideological "antibodies" (resistance to imperialism) and new myths to encourage and motivate Third World activists to seize the initiative from capitalistic media forces which impose alienated forms on colonized peoples. Battlefields for his essays include *Présence Africaine, Africasia, L'Action poétique, Casa de las Americas*, and other periodicals circulating in Africa and Latin America.

In poetry, short story, and now novel form, Depestre has effectively used imagination to inspire hope and faith in oppressed peoples, to pass on a vision of a better way of organizing society, a vision of a new culture and liberation. He has shown that revolt does not have to be sacrifice and pain, that activism and eros are related, that healthy sexuality involves commitment to ethical and political values. He struggles to demonstrate to Third World leaders that sexual revolution should be part of their anti-imperialistic struggle. Depestre uses fantasy in political writing in a new way, as in his new novel *El Palo Ensebado*, published originally in Spanish and later, in revised form in French as *Le Mât de cocagne*, where surrealism and social realism, sex and revolt are mixed in a most curious style. The protagonist, an ex-senator and leader of resistance forces in Haiti who was transformed into an impotent zombie after his partisans and relatives were tortured and killed, has decided to act, to "dezombify" himself after many years of tending a little shop in Port-au-Prince. He will prevail by climbing the *mât de cocagne*, the greased Maypole, and winning the national prize at the annual celebration used by the dictator and his *Tontons Macoutes* to further demonstrate that "dezombification" and revolt are still possible. In the ensuing cat and mouse game the ex-senator and the dictator use voodoo to strengthen their resolve, the dictator baptizing the *mât de cocagne* with his own blood to make it even more directly his phallic symbol "screwing" the people (Depestre's own characterization).

> Hal Wylie. In Carolyn A. Parker and Stephen H. Arnold, eds. *When the Drumbeat Changes* (Washington, D.C.: Three Continents Press, 1981), pp. 282–83

The most striking aspect of the novel [*Le Mât de cocagne*] is the use of the fantastic in what is essentially a realistic depiction of historical figures, set in a frame of real moral, social, and political problems. Surrealistic qualities are present, as is the influence of J. S. Alexis's theory of "Marvelous Realism." Depestre also reflects [Bertolt] Brecht's ideas on socialist writing. *Le Mât de cocagne* is a step forward in the evolution of a twentieth-century literary formula through which leftist writers can criticize and make political points while entertaining. Brecht's theories may perhaps be more easily applied in the Third World than to a capitalistic world where literature and entertainment are dominated by Hollywood and Madison Avenue. Theater (as [Antonin] Artaud and Brecht conceived it) is more alive in the "underdeveloped" world than in America or Europe, in the new countries where oral literature is still a living tradition, where there is still a feeling of community and where the village or town still has an organic quality. The "marvelous" has not been distorted by commercial interests and is still in touch with everyday life through myths and legends. The marvelous lives in the streets in a way the marvels of *The Exorcist* cannot. Depestre's brightly colored literary effects are analogous to those of Haitian "primitive" painting. Using voodoo and folklore that has an aura of the "sacred," Depestre creates modern fiction that reveals the exploitation of peoples and land produced by a regime which systematically sells out to outside financial interests. The rapaciousness of such regimes is evident in the trade in Haitian blood and cadavers dramatized in the novel.

> Hal Wylie. *World Literature Today.* 55, 1 (Winter 1981), p. 164

After publishing his earliest verse in Haiti in 1945–1946, Depestre was forced into exile by François Duvalier because of his political opposition to that dictator. He lived in Paris in the 1950s and in Cuba from after the revolution until recently, when he began to work for UNESCO in Paris and New York. All his poetry about the United States predates his residence there, however, so he does not write from firsthand experience. In his poetry, Depestre focuses on the manifestations of North American life most publicized in the Soviet and Cuban press which have touched him most deeply as a leftist, a Caribbean, and a black, namely racism, capitalism, imperialism, and militarism. . . .

Depestre identifies in the United States another variety of perversion, a collective sterility and alienation from the rest of humankind. In "Poème à hurler sous les fenêtres de la Maison Blanche," he probes North Americans' profound and neurotic desire for cleanliness, and discovers a need to cover corruption and callousness. . . . This black Haitian, writing in a Cuba sharply divided between the races in its prerevolutionary period, attributes white North America's moral insensitivity and hygienic compulsivity to guilt stemming from its role in the slave trade. The psychological portrayal elaborated by Depestre shows white America trapped in a syndrome of the denial of historical reality . . . and in a

desperate attempt to suppress its detractors who tell the painful truth. . . . Depestre's picture of the United States as monolithically racist seems to constitute an appeal to francophone "Third-Worlders" to mark that nation as a whole—not just a particular group or set of policies—as their inherent enemy, and as irremediably so. It has none of [Ernesto] Cardenal's subtlety, no sense of part of white America's being victimized by another segment of white America in the context of racism. That Depestre's racially based historical analysis flies in the face of Marxist theories of social science seems not to deter his pursuing that propagandistic course.

> Henry Cohen. *Revista/Review Interamericana.* 11, 2 (Summer 1981), pp. 220–21, 224–25

In the heart of *Un Arc-en-ciel pour l'occident chrétien*, Depestre exalts his Négritude by attacking the white colonial structure in a series of voodoo mystery poems. His use of the voodoo makes this work particularly relevant to Haitian culture today, because it "is the religion of the common people. It is a unifying force, an integrated system of beliefs, binding Haitians to their African heritage and creating a sense of collective responsibility to themselves—an indissoluble spirit of solidarity." The intensity created by the juxtaposition of the voodoo myths with the white culture is very powerful indeed.

Depestre thrusts the clichés whites have formulated about blacks into the intimate parlor of a "genteel" white family in Alabama, forcing the reader to acknowledge the existence of the clichés. He strips these scenes of the cloak of false courtesy sometimes characteristic of interaction between the races. There is a magnetism in the tension Depestre produces and a fascination in the horror of the prejudices he unveils for us.

> Ann Armstrong Scarboro. *Concerning Poetry.* 17, 2 (Fall 1984), p. 125

Depestre sees much good in Négritude. . . . But he also seems to be proposing an alternative, *le négrisme*, an interesting concept that may, however, be equally or more vague or confusing. Depestre presents it in the initial essay in *Bonjour et adieu[à la négritude]*: "Les Aventures du négrisme en Amérique latine." He cites Monica Mansour's book *La Poesia negrista* as the definitive source. It seems that Depestre may be stretching a concept which was a precise delineation in referring to a literary school in Spanish-and Portuguese-speaking Latin America, but which becomes amorphous when extended beyond Latin America. Depestre does not give a short, simple definition of *le négrisme*; instead he lists a number of defining factors. . . .

It seems that Depestre considers *négrisme* the dialectical gropings to counteract the racist definitions that developed out of the "colonial adventures of capitalism." It is a literature sympathetic to the plight of the enslaved or colonized black which attempted to humanize his image or identity by showing how the world looked from his point of view. The romantics, the abolitionists, and especially the avant-garde played an important role before black writers came to the fore.

Why does Depestre go to such length to further complicate an already confused conception by introducing yet another term to the francophone world? Besides the philosophical and political objections to Négritude already noted, he feels very ill at ease with any conception built on race. He feels that race is a delusion produced by the mystification used by the early stage of capitalism to justify the imposition of slavery and colonial conquest. He obviously feels that in the long run any philosophy built on race is counterproductive. He begins his book by stressing the need for a ''pan-human identity.'' He prefers ''Americology'' to Négritude, defining Americology as a study . . . that goes beyond race, culture, and language to demonstrate the creativity of *''créolité''* and *''marronnage''* or *''métissage''* (cultural cross pollination or hybridization) in producing American cultures. *Négrisme* offers several virtues or advantages. It is a historical reality that can be studied objectively, phenomenologically, independent of a priori definitions of race. It is open-ended in inviting all to participate. It relates well-known francophone and anglophone literary and philosophical events to those in the Hispanic Caribbean and in Latin America. It is necessarily dialectical and represents an effort to ''deracialize'' social relationships, so that political and economic factors can be seen. *Le négrisme* thus necessarily demands syntheses with political conceptions, and also philosophical and literary formulations, such as Marxism, socialism, surrealism. Depestre seems to feel it is less bound to the mid-twentieth-century moment of history and more future oriented.

> Hal Wylie. In Kofi Anyidoho, Abioseh M. Porter, Daniel Racine, and Janice Spleth, eds. *Interdisciplinary Dimensions of African Literature* (Washington, D. C.: Three Continents Press, 1985), pp. 47–48

Exiled from Haiti in 1946 at the age of twenty, [Depestre] writes a poetry that turns on the tension between an unattainable past and an unsatisfactory present. Depestre's transits through politics and places—a trek that takes him from Haiti to Paris to Cuba and then back to Paris—is most clearly conveyed by his presentations of woman. No matter where he is, his select muse remains the same: his chosen ''moyen de connaisance,'' she moves through these places with a peculiar redundancy. This redundancy becomes even more striking when the reader notes the poet's own progress from dream-dimmed Marxist adolescent (*Etincelles*) to the role of poet-houngan (*Un Arc-en-ciel pour l'occident chrétien*) to Cuban revolutionary (*Poète à Cuba*). But perhaps this progress is only apparent, for the series of poetic stances somehow land Depestre back in Paris (where he now works for UNESCO), still using the elusive idea of woman to gain a voice that expresses insurmountable longing but never assuages it, that claims a desire for change but never brings it about. In this strangely static ''progression,'' the very naming of woman becomes not an inspiration for revolutionary engagement, but an excuse for self-indulgence. We are left finally with a poet before his ''douce Hélène de la connaissance''—a revolutionary who has, perhaps unknowingly, crafted his own exclusive cult of Beauty.

Ostensibly in praise of women, Depestre writes *Alléluia pour une femmejardin*. . . . In this collection of stories, Depestre articulates the paradoxical use and abuse of woman's image in the Caribbean. . . . She is certainly not [W.B.] Yeats's ''white woman whom passion has worn'' nor that Hérodiade fashioned to embody the rigors of a [Stéphane] Mallarmé in pursuit of *poésie pure*. For

the black poet whose writing is determined by specific cultural and political constraints, the woman comes to be the muse of Négritude. She seems the means of transit from solitary thought to a poetic that promises to be at once lyrical and engaged; and she offers the poet the opportunity to turn personal love song into public exhortation. Yet like [Léopold Sédar] Senghor's famous ''Femme noire,'' who offers herself as the taut ''tamtam'' to be played upon by her ''vainqueur,'' Depestre's woman betrays something awry in this poet's apparently anti-idealizing thrust. Depestre has long argued against what he calls Senghor's ''totalitarian Négritude,'' his cult of a vague ''essence noire'' that mystifies the African people and serves the interests of a dominant social class. But in his attempt to recapture the singular identity of his Caribbean brothers, Depestre in fact dispossesses the female in his culture. The conversion of woman into motive for text exacts a cost on his poetry: the more Depestre uses the woman as conduit to revolt, the less ''revolutionary'' his poetry becomes. Whereas Depestre, the canny theorist of Négritude, demystifies the ''false identity'' determined by such taxonomic divisions as black or white—what he calls an ontological disguise—Depestre the lyricist remains trapped in a curious ''bovarysme.'' His desire to desire, turning his love objects into various images at his disposal, recolonizes the very semantic traps that colonial semiology has fabricated and that he has spent his life endeavoring to expose.

> Joan Dayan. *French Review.* 59, 4 (March 1986), pp. 582–83

Words like ''hope,'' ''future,'' and ''freedom'' acquire a new force in Depestre's triumphant vision of a world reborn. In presenting himself as a ''nègre aux vastes espoirs'' pursuing a dream of hope and freedom in *Etincelles*, Depestre indicates the scale of the political commitment envisaged by his generation. In presenting himself as an *enfant terrible* and acknowledging his debt to Arthur Rimbaud, Depestre clearly placed high value on the figure of the outsider, whether in the benign image of the child or that of the vengeful *poète maudit*. . . . In 1946 Depestre transformed Rimbaud's ''Mauvais sang'' into his *Gerbe de sang*. The pagan carnality already apparent in Depestre's early work is somewhat different from the earnest purposefulness of [Jacques] Roumain's poetic temperament. Nevertheless, the influence of Roumain's sensibility is unmistakable. This early verse anticipates the preoccupation in Depestre's entire oeuvre with a celebration of cultural encounters and a sustained assault on all systems that inhibit individual freedom, whether class, church, or state.

In inventing himself through his poetry, Depestre, whether as a ''petite lampe haitienne'' or ''animal marin'' in *Journal d'un animal marin* and *Poète à Cuba* or as virile hougan in *Un Arc-en-ciel pour l'occident chrétien*, projects himself as the marginalized figure ever watchful on the periphery and capable of brief moments of triumph against the forces of ''zombification.'' His poetic wanderings in Paris, Brazil, Cuba, and Jamaica are not construed as painful exile but rather as a ubiquitous adaptable self drawing on a cross-linguistic and cross-cultural reality. Depestre's ideal of ''geolibertinage'' is quite different from the idea of *marronnage* in the discourse of Négritude. The latter signifies individual salvation through escape. The former suggests a discovery of self through contact, in which the other becomes a liberating partner. In elaborating a poetics of rootlessness, in reacting against the inhibitions of Négritude's authenticity, Depestre had a liberating effect on poets in Haiti in the 1960s. . . .

Depestre's voice dominates Haitian poetry from the mid-1940s to the early 1960s. His continuous exile from Haiti, except for a brief period in 1958, and the terrors of [François] Duvalier's regime led him to despair for Haiti which he described in *Le Mât de cocagne* as a "zoocracy." Port-au-Prince emerges as a world of vermin and dust where only the living dead survive. His twenty years spent in Cuba would also lead to disappointment. Depestre became by the 1970s the incarnation of the poet as refugee, a condition shared by various writers who for various reasons are no longer rooted in a single community. This experience has led Depestre in recent times to rethink the whole question of exile. In favoring the word "errance" (errancy) over the word "exile" Depestre insists on the positive potential for self-transformation inherent in the condition of the poetic refugee.

J. Michael Dash. *Callaloo*. 15, 3 (Summer 1992), pp. 749–50

Determined by varying uses of exile, Depestre's writings can be read as a formidable tension between an unattainable past and an unsatisfactory present. His desire to make art out of a remembered Haiti, though sometimes imprisoned by memory, marks all of his works with a consistency that can only be called obsessive: a quest that keeps turning in on itself. As "navigator of forbidden seas"— with the slaves' sea journey from Africa to the New World ever in mind—Depestre journeys through a series of landscapes, increasingly solitary, from Dahomey to the United States, to South Africa, to Cuba, to Brazil, to France, all "far from Jacmel." . . .

When the metamorphoses of [*Hadriana dans tous mes rêves*] can be perceived as "mixing the horrors of death with the laughter of carnival," "blasphemous rites" and "saturnalia" coincident with "the vengeful magic of voodoo," then what kind of attitude or belief is formed about that land named Jacmel, Haiti? How can readers hearing news of another coup, another massacre, expect anything else from such a bizarre people? Some reviewers have stressed that the unbridled love-death scenes of this "crazy story" in the "hot tropics" are not to be found in "our pale, reasoning, Christian latitudes." "Too much, it's too much, will judge indomitable Cartesians! We are here in voodoo land." With such inevitable difference established, we need go no further. The phallic butterfly Balthazar can pierce sleeping virgins throughout Jacmel, Erzulie can lasciviously lift her dress, the black gods can copulate around Hadriana's coffin, but readers do not have to worry about the human context out of which these images are wrenched. For where are the humans in this "island of dreams"? One reviewer makes the link between the improbable and the actual. Talking of the strange life-in-death of Hadriana, whom Depestre describes as "the Creole fairy," "the white little angel," he writes: "Pseudodeath or pseudolife? Why look for an answer when the incredible belongs as naturally to the destiny of Haitians as the fatality of dictators."

Joan Dayan. *Yale French Studies*. 83, 2 (1993), pp. 157–58, 167–68

J.S. [Jasmina Sopova]: Your life as an adult and as a poet began with what you later called "a triple badge of rebellion"—proud

negritude, impassioned surrealism, and the idea of revolution. Today only the surrealism part seems to have survived.

R.D. [Rene Depestre]: It's a long story. When Andre Breton came to Haiti at the end of 1945, his visit coincided with an exhibition of the Cuban painter Wifredo Lam's paintings and a series of lectures given by the Martinique poet Aimé Césaire. This really fired the imagination of us young Haitian artists and writers. At that time we knew nothing about what was happening in the surrealist movement in France. For young people combatting President Elie Lescot's dreadful dictatorship, surrealism was the lifeblood of revolt. Contact with Breton had a contagious effect on us. After his first lecture in a Port-au-Prince cinema, we brought out a special issue of our new magazine *La Ruche* as a tribute to him. We went to prison for our pains and the magazine was banned.

What Breton discovered in Haiti, and made us discover too, was that surrealism wasn't just an aesthetic doctrine but something that could be part of a people's way of looking at the world; that there was a kind of grassroots surrealism. This restored our self-confidence. We saw that this sense of wonder we had secretly been a bit ashamed of and associated with a kind of underdevelopment was actually our weapon. Breton told us that in France "we launched surrealism as a movement based on intellectual foundations, you in Haiti learned all about it in the cradle." In other words, surrealism was something inherent in the Caribbean. Voodoo, a product of Franco-African syncretism, is an example of religious surrealism. The behaviour of the voodoo gods is supremely surrealist.

J.S.: So surrealism for you is much more than a literary movement.

R.D.: Much more. Many European writers, starting with the German Romantics and even before that, had a surrealist approach. I'm sure if you looked closely at Egyptian, Japanese or Chinese culture, you'd find surrealist elements there too. For me, surrealism is a way of injecting the supernatural into everyday life. You find it everywhere. But some people, like Haitians or Brazilians, display it more boldly than others. . . .

J.S.: You have celebrated the communist utopia in your poems.

R.D.: The Marxist utopia, with all its lies and repressive nightmares, took over my work and my life as a poet until the moment I broke with Stalinism. After living in places which had a huge "strategic" importance in the turmoil of our century— Moscow, Prague, Beijing, Hanoi and Havana—I realized that what was meant by "socialist revolution" in those places was not the opposite of the Haitian terror regime, but another form of the same perversion. Instead of promoting the heritage of the rights of man and the citizen, "the revolution" defiled the autonomy of women and men and carried out, at their expense, the most amazing hijack of ideals and dreams in all human history.

J.S.: What has become of the "revolutionary ideal" which drew you from Haiti to Europe and then on to Cuba?

R.D.: I ardently believed in revolution. For me it became a kind of natural state, like breathing, walking or swimming. And it nearly destroyed my integrity as a citizen and a writer. The ideal of revolution seriously impoverished my personal store of poetry and tenderness which, when I was twenty, made me think of my future work as a state of wonder and oneness with the world. It made my literary career that of a writer who performed psychological and intellectual somersaults and sudden existential about-turns—a kind of carnival of uncertainties and inconsistencies, adrift in the furious currents of the century's passions and ideals. The treasure islands invented by the utopias and mythologies of revolution went up in smoke with the great dreams of our youth—uniting the idea of transforming the world (Karl Marx) with that of changing life (Arthur Rimbaud).

J.S.: The word "utopia" as used by Marxists has a pejorative meaning for you. But doesn't the world need utopias?

R.D.: Octavio Paz has defined utopias as "the dreams of reason." We're just emerging from a terrible nightmare of reason. The nineteenth century, a critical age if ever there was one, gave birth to the idea of a revolutionary utopia. But the totally legitimate dream of earlier philosophers did not turn into the major transformation of human lives they had hoped for, nor into unprecedented progress for humankind. The generous aspirations of critical thought imposed on us, under the bogus label of "real socialism," an absolutism the like of which we had never seen before.

In saying this I do not wish to denigrate the idea of utopia as such. Old age reminds me these days that I don't have much time left and that I must hasten to express things I've kept to myself all my life. And hopefully express them with grace and maturity. So, in a way, I'm summing up my life's nomadic journey. And all self-criticism leads one to utopia. But hardened observer that I am, I deeply distrust a historical concept that this century's revolutions have debased. In place of the notion of realpolitik, which is at the root of most of the woes of people and societies and which still flourishes to an extraordinary degree in government, I offer the notion of realutopia.

J.S.: Could you explain what you mean by realutopia?

R.D.: It's an aesthetic concept which enables me to unite the various parts of my Franco-Haitian creole-ness as a writer. Doctors and physiologists call synergy the links between several elements which combine in a single function and a common effect. The idea of realutopia leads me to a kind of aesthetic and literary synergy which points in a single direction the multitude of experiences that I owe to magical reality, to negritude, to sun-kissed eroticism and to the creole fantasizing of Haitians, which is the surrealism of the humbled and the hurt.

J.S.: So you haven't entirely turned your back on negritude?

R.D.: I've always mistrusted the idea of negritude because I did not think it was possible to constitute an anthropology which is the exact opposite of the one which devalued us and downgraded us as "Blacks." You can't just transfer to a Black context what is said and done in terms of Whites. Aimé Césaire referred to this phenomenon as turning Gobineau upside down. I realized we had to create our own aesthetic and ideology without falling into "anti-racist racism." That's why I said goodbye to negritude at the same time as I dropped Marxism. I've only stuck with surrealism, which is still one of my working tools. I use both ends of the tool—the scholarly and the popular. But I mistrust surrealism too. Breton leaned towards the occult, trying to link surrealism with certain cabbalistic and Talmudic traditions—a shadowy area in the history of thought but no less interesting for that—which are the equivalent of looking for the philosopher's stone. I don't go along with that at all.

I've rejected the ideals of my youth and today I work with the tragic experiences which in my case they led to.

J.S.: How do you see the world these days?

R.D.: The idea of revolution has been buried and history marches on, with its media-fed procession of horrors and marvels. The myth of a great consummation of the body and the mind died of natural causes in a big Soviet-style bed. The corpse is still warm and already the spark of totalitarianism has reappeared in the shape of religious fundamentalism. All kinds of ethno-nationalist savagery, supposedly under the banner of a campaign to renew faithless societies, are building monuments to obscurantism, terrorism and new banditry by the state. On the borders of the West, the idea of a fundamentalist utopia has taken the place of a revolutionary one.

How can literature inspire people to embark on the adventure of a new renaissance?

R.D.: The answer to that is shaped by a context of fundamentalist horrors, inter-ethnic massacres and racist and nationalist violence. It's one of a planet completely ruled by market forces.

Thanks to the rational instruments of the rule of law and democracy, the institution of the market has survived all attacks on it. But most people now think the democracy of the market—its basis and the way it works—needs to be overhauled. Or else life in society is going to become a great planet-wide casino. So it's in the interests of the victorious marketplace to do something about the chaotic and aggressive conditions in which the globalization of human affairs is taking place.

Bold steps should be taken to make good use of the world's heritage of democratic experience, the rich store of rules of citizenship and the art of living together which is to be found in Western civil societies, the most developed and experienced in terms of law, liberties, justice and solidarity. We should be able to turn the current haphazard process of globalization into an unprecedented humanization of relations between individuals and nation-states. The international civil society which is growing up amid disorder and uncertainty needs the oxygen of world-wide public-spiritedness and the idea of solidarity that will be conducive to fair distribution of the values and principles which are now the shared property of the global village.

J.S.: Who could promote this global public-spiritedness?

R.D.: I see the bold imagination of poets and writers at the forefront of the values shared by the world's cultures. Our works, each with its own strictly aesthetic identity, should help scientists and politicians to revamp our old ideas about good and evil, to revive a sense of the sacred which is being lost and to devise a more balanced relationship between North and South, and East and West. This would be in a new world order where the necessary rules of commerce, tempered by a new sense of meaning and new ideals, could express a fresh balance between nature and history. To advance further without risking disaster, the spirit of the market should now be endowed with certain ethical features, such as meaning, laws of citizenship and an art of living together based on mutual respect and sympathy between the world's peoples and societies.

Jasmina Sopova. *UNESCO Courier* (December 1997), pp. 47–49

BIBLIOGRAPHY

*Sparks (Etincelles*, 1945); Spurting Blood (*Gerbe de sang*, 1946); Vegetations of Light (*Végétations de clarté*, 1951); Translated from the High Seas (*Traduit du grand large*, 1952); Black Ore (*Minerai noir*, 1956); Journal of a Sea Creature (*Journal d'un animal marin*, 1965); A Rainbow for the Christian West (*Un Arc-en-ciel pour l'occident chrétien*, 1967): *A Rainbow for the Christian West*, 1972; Hallelujah for a Woman-Garden (*Alléluia pour une femme-jardin*, 1973); For the Revolution: For Poetry (*Pour la révolution: pour la poésie*, 1974); Poet in Cuba (*Poète à Cuba*, 1976); The Pole of Plenty (*Le Mât de cocagne*, 1979): *The Festival of the Greasy Pole*, 1990; Hello and Goodbye to Négritude (*Bonjour et adieu à la négritude*, 1980); Hadriana in All My Dreams (*Hadriana dans tous mes rêves*, 1988); *Ainsi parle le fleuve noir*, 1998; *Le metier a metisser*, 1998

# DIALLO, Nafissatou Niang (1941–1982)
Senegal

One can consider [Nafissatou Niang Diallo's *Le Fort maudit*] from a dual perspective. It can be considered as a novel of destiny, of fatality—a sort of tragic drama whose vicissitudes lead to the fall of the individual. It can also be read as a social testimony, because, through the narration of real and fictitious events of the past—the action takes place in Senegal in the nineteenth century—a certain number of African customs and traditions are evoked.

A tragedy in five acts, it is like the works from the classical period. The first act, the longest, which coincides with the entire first part, is situated in the kingdom of Cayor. . . . This first act is written in great detail. It appears as if the author did not wish to make an impressive evocation of plenitude but desired rather to narrate in detail that which ordinarily remains in the shadows. This she does in order to show the indelible mark of these happy years on the heroine. For this reason, the rhythm of the first part is slow and melodious, an expression of a peaceful existence, a tranquil reflection of a well-balanced life.

In contrast, the second part of the novel presents a rocky and quicker-paced rhythm: although much shorter, it corresponds to the last four acts of the novelistic tragedy that is *Le Fort maudit*—that is to say, the drama reaches a climax. . . .

*Le Fort maudit* is indeed a tragedy in that a total confrontation takes place and in that Fariba Naël Ndiaye can be considered as the maleficent agent (physically, he is cold and hard, and morally, he is egoistic, cruel, and sly, truly a "diabolical" being) of an inescapable fatality, who has come to destroy the happy destiny of Thiane, changing it into misfortune. All the psychological traumas of the latter (the rape of her mother, the death of all her near ones) are themselves at the origin of the metamorphosis of the heroine. They inaugurate a new phase in her life as evidenced by her physical and moral evolution: beauty and irony disappear completely, whereas certain harder traits become accentuated. Traits that become a headstrong and stubborn child grumbling against inaction are changed thereafter by an inextinguishable thirst for vengeance and by a hatred which triumphs over her to the point of illness. . . .

The very construction of the novel confirms this circularity of the heroine's destiny, because *Le Fort maudit* begins with a kind of prologue, by the evocation of the death of Thiane, the narration of which is repeated at the end of the work. Posed as a hypothesis, this death is also the conclusion of the novel—the image of the cycle, of the spiral whirlwind of this human adventure.

The story of a destiny, *Le Fort maudit* also stands as a testimony to a certain number of telling traits of Negro-African civilization. Without necessarily having an ethnographic design, Diallo has admirably portrayed traditional life on whose behalf she makes an apology through her praise of the kingdom of Cayor.

Undoubtedly, the writer's pen is somewhat critical with regard to polygamous life. . . .

Other than this custom, traditional life seems to have only virtues and positive aspects. . . .

Such is the purity of traditional civilization that it seems to engender only good. If Baol is the opposite of Cayor, a kingdom without morality and harmony, it is because it has abandoned all its traditions. Its degeneracy, as attested by its bloodthirsty delirium and its disregard for the community spirit, is in some manner corroborated by its fascination "for the marvels of Western technique."

We then understand that the crushing defeat of Cayor by Baol could symbolize total dispossession—of life, of the nation and traditions. . . .

Thus Diallo's novel is inscribed in a certain thematic lineage of African literature. Through the detour of history and by recourse to a story, the novelist embarks on the discovery of Africanity. One is aware that this search for identity remains one of the most fecund themes in the writings of once colonized people. This inexhaustible theme is marvelously personified here and makes *Le Fort maudit* more than a pleasing fiction to read. It makes it the spiritual biography of a tree in search of its roots.

André-Patrick Sahel. *L'Afrique Litteraire*. 63–64 (1982), pp. 83–85

A witness of the reactions of the postindependence generation to the strictures of the caste system is Nafissatou Diallo who, in her autobiography, *De Tilène au plateau [une enfance dakaroise]*, tells how she is determined to marry the handsome stranger with whom she has fallen in love with no knowledge of his family's origins: "Even if he was a sorcerer, a griot, a jeweller," she insists, "you wouldn't make me respect your darned traditions!" Fortunately, these young victims of love at first sight are of equal noble birth and there are no obstacles to their union. . . .

Diallo's *De Tilène au plateau* offers a very different chronicle of Dakar society of the same period as that covered by [Amar] Samb. The title of this autobiography, translated as *A Dakar Childhood*, refers to the district of the Dakar Medina where the author was born in 1941, and the Plateau, the smart residential part of the capital. The details that Safi gives of her home and childhood are probably typical of life in a high-caste family at that time, with the protocol of an Islamic home and day-to-day domestic activities. The story begins with the account of the little Safi playing truant from the Koranic school and her eventual admission to the French primary school. She graduates from the Lycée to enter the Training School for Midwives in Dakar, and the book ends with the death of her beloved father, her marriage, and subsequent departure for France. However, this bald outline gives little indication of the story's charm and universal appeal. Safi reveals herself as a mischievous, rebellious child, turning into a coquettish, petulant, somewhat arrogant adolescent, always in hot water at home and at school, always the ringleader in all manner of pranks which she recounts with simple, honest recall. The chapter describing her father's final illness, her grief at his death, and eventual resignation to this loss is a sincere and moving expression of a personal emotion and universal experience.

Nafissatou Diallo's style is simple and straightforward, eschewing literary effects and giving the impression of spontaneity and honesty of composition. She recounts her childhood pranks with lively humor and describes the storms of rebellious adolescence with insight and no self-indulgence. The reader who wishes to know about urban Islamic life in the 1940s and 1950s will find much of great informative interest. But the essence of the book's appeal, which to my mind will make it a minor classic, is the universality of Safi's story with which girls of all cultures and backgrounds can identify. And without setting out to moralize, it tells how a normal, high-spirited girl develops into a mature, responsible career woman, wife, mother, and talented writer.

> Dorothy S. Blair. *Senegalese Literature: A Critical History* (Boston: Twayne, 1984), pp. 12–13, 120

Diallo's second novel, *Awa, la petite marchande*, is . . . for young people. Juvenile literature is of particular importance in Africa, where it often replaces traditional stories and legends as a source of moral instruction. This work is written in the first person and is what Bede Ssensalo calls a "pseudo-autobiography," for if one did not know it was fiction, one would take it to be autobiography. As a result, the reader identifies closely with the heroine, Awa. She is nine years old at the beginning of the novel and is the second of six children in a poor fisher family. After his father and brothers were drowned, however, her father, Salif, left fishing and now works as the cook of a Lebanese shopkeeper, for which he is despised by the rest of the extended family. To supplement the limited family income, Awa's mother, Yacine, sells fish. When the father loses his job through illness, Awa is forced to leave school, which she loves, and become a fish seller too. Nobody in the extended family helps them and their situation becomes desperate. Finally, a friend has Salif hospitalized and when he is cured, finds a job for him and Awa with the ex-governor who is returning home. The last third of the novel takes place in France, which is presented as the land of opportunity. Salif and Awa both make good: Salif learns to read and write and obtains a diploma in mechanics; Awa completes her primary education. After three years, during which they have been sending money home, they return to Senegal to a new villa and bright prospects for the future.

Despite its fairy-tale character, this novel is interesting for its didactic intent and its social criticism. Diallo presents Awa as a role model for young people, particularly girls, to show that hard work at home and at school brings its reward. Related to this is her desire to arouse sympathy for poverty, to demonstrate that it is not necessarily the fault of those concerned, and to advocate education as a way of escaping it. (It would have been difficult, perhaps impossible, however, for Awa and Salif to succeed without leaving for France.) Her depiction of Senegalese society is not a flattering one. Money is the most powerful force, corruption is widespread, and there is a general contempt for the poor. One cannot even rely on one's family for help. Friendship though does exist, and without it Awa's family would have sunk into penury and her father would probably have died. Diallo comes out clearly in this novel against polygamy: in fact, the only shadow which hangs over the ending is the possibility, because of the improved status of the family, that Awa's mother will have to accept a co-wife or wives: "Allait-elle connaître la vie infernale de la polygamie?" Awa asks herself. Diallo also criticizes the forced marriage of young girls to old men. Thus through *Awa, la petite marchande* Diallo hopes to contribute

to a change in attitudes which will lead to an improvement in the status of women and to a more egalitarian society.

When we look at Nafissatou Diallo's literary production as a whole, we can see that she became acutely aware of her responsibility as a woman writer. Although her works are different in form, they are not fundamentally different in intent, for each presents as a role model a young woman who has to make basic choices about her life. On an artistic level, there is a remarkable similarity between her energetic and determined heroines, who, if one compares them to Safi [in *De Tilène au plateau*], all appear to be projections of Diallo herself. The author's relationships with her father and grandmother also reappear in a thinly disguised form in her novels. With each book, however, her didiactic purpose and feminist consciousness seem to evolve. It is significant that her final work is for young people, perhaps because they are the most open to change. It may be that she had come to see her didactic role as more important than her artistic vocation. Some critics would call this a degeneration. And yet in the African context, where literature is expected to be *engagée*, this evolution could be interpreted as a full acceptance of one's social duty. Nafissatou Diallo was only forty when she died, however. Who knows what else she would have written, had she lived?

> Susan Stringer. In Ginette Adamson and Eunice Myers, eds. *Continental, Latin-American and Francophone Women Writers* (Lanham, Maryland: University Press of America, 1987), Vol. II, pp. 169–70

In African and Caribbean literature, the 1980s have brought forth new writings, not only by new writers in first novels, but new themes. A new motif of girlhood is emerging and proving to be significant enough to warrant extended fictional treatment.

Nafissatou Diallo's *De Tilène au plateau: une enfance dakaroise* is a forerunner of this new genre, even though the author denigrates her effort. . . .

Translated as *A Dakar Childhood*, [it] is a barely fictionalized autobiography. Diallo calls the work a tribute to her progressive but severe and patriarchal father. She recognizes that her father was ahead of his time in urging her education and in causing his untraditional views to prevail in the family: "I was the first girl in the family that Grandpa in his old age had finally allowed to go to school." It was a French school. Nonetheless, she underwent a strict Muslim upbringing at home. When she met the son of a Koranic schoolteacher, danced with him, and kissed him goodnight, she suffered such a severe beating from her father afterward that she could not leave her room for a week. She continued her education, however, finished high school, and went on to study mid-wifery. She married at twenty and finished her career preparation.

A few years later, mourning her father's death, she recalled her childhood sentiments: "Father dominating everything—And so I thought that one day I would write about him. He had been neither a politician nor a caliph, only a man of honor. . . . I would tell this to his children, to his grandchildren; why should I not tell it to the world? Why should I not say to the world . . . that it is the unimportant modest folk who support and carry the weight of the great?" Her tribute is straightforward. The chronology of her childhood is specific in remembered detail. She does not pretend to criticize her cultural milieu or to interpret the events of her own life as significant beyond personal narrative. But she treats themes which subsequent writers will amplify: the need for motherly understanding, the importance of education for women, the imprint of puppy love on adolescence, the quickly changing mores for women living today. Her goal is modest: "I am not the heroine of a novel but an ordinary woman of this country, Senegal. . . . So here are my memories of my childhood and adolescence. Senegal has changed in a generation. Perhaps it is worth reminding today's youngsters what we were like when we were their age."

Charlotte H. Bruner. *CLA Journal.* 31, 3 (March 1988), pp. 324–26

In recollecting the vanished world of pre-independence Dakar, *De Tilène au Plateau* foregrounds social practices that keep girls on the margin of social and textual space, including her childhood self, named Safi be Diallo. While her struggle to acquire agency is often thwarted in the childhood experiences Diallo narrates, *De Tilène au Plateau* maps the coming to voice of a tentative subject who is poised discursively between the competing genres of autobiography and ethnographic memoir. It is, then, an early and important marker for the emergence of African autobiographical subjectivity precisely because of its dilemma in posing a coherent autobiographical subject. What I call the subject-in-process of Diallo's narrative exceeds the discursive boundaries of ethnographic representation and gestures toward a freer discursive space in which "des tabous de silence" "the taboos of silence," that constrain her representation of growing up female will be lifted for future autobiographers.

Diallo's dilemma is, in a sense, which "lifeline" to write: that of the dutiful daughter of the family and the new nation who embodies traditional values; that of the reliable ethnographic guide to Dakar's vanished pre-independence past; or that of an autobiographical subject voicing a resistant impulse to re-member female self-assertion for which no adequate literary space as yet exists. This third discourse, at odds with the requirements of both filial duty and public memory, is unstable and overwritten by the two normative discourses. Yet Diallo's covert voicing of a female writing subject comprises one of the earliest and most enduring instances of women's autobiographical subjectivity in African literature.

One of two "first" and groundbreaking women's autobiographies published in Senegal in 1975, *De Tilène au Plateau* has remained available and widely read, though it is not used in university curricula. The other autobiography, Malian Aoua Kéita's *Femme d'Afrique: La vie d'Aoua Kéita racontée par elle-même*, a memoir of the Malian independence struggle written during her years in Senegal, is long out of print. Diallo and Kéita, then, are among the first generation of women autobiographers in Africa, though women's lyrical self-presentations in poetry began a decade earlier. As they both worked in Senegal as midwives, they have been seen as performing midwifery for the autobiographical fiction to come by African women (Aminata Sow Fall, Mariama Bâ, and Ken Bugul in Senegal, as well as Buchi Emecheta, Bessie Head, and many others). But in this view Diallo and Kéita are "naturalized" as non- or "preliterary" documentary recorders of culture, and hence outside the texts that have inflected written African subjectivity. Rather, I would argue, Diallo's (and, to a lesser extent, Kéita's) texts made a literary intervention in the articulation of specific gendered, ethnic African subjectivities, above all by trying to negotiate the hybrid genre of autoethnography.

Autoethnography can be defined as an ethnographic presentation of oneself by a subject usually considered the "object" of the ethnographer's interview. As such it is a hybrid form of autobiography being deployed by postcolonial writers to renegotiate their own subject positions in writing.

The geographic locations of *De Tilène au Plateau* are specific, from the Guards' Camp in the Tiléne district where her large family lived until it was razed for the current Iba Mar Diop Stadium; to the Plateau area behind the current city center, the Place de l'Indépendence, with its schools, markets, hospitals, and locales known to inhabitants as familiar sites of everyday life. Independence in 1960 and subsequent modernization erased these sites of her childhood, but they are memorialized in the text, as *De Tilène au Plateau's* double narrative of Diallo and Dakar entwines her personal story with the city's narrative of coming of age in an era of dramatic urbanization.

*De Tilène au Plateau* also employs a kind of literary hybridity as heteroglossic text of multilingual, as well as multivoiced, writing. Like many other narratives of francophone Africa and the Caribbean, Diallo's text is linguistic métissage or braiding that lets a native African language, her Wolof, permeate the French language in which it was written, to create kind of polyvocality. Diallo in a sense "initiates" non-Wolof speakers to Dakarois heteroglossia by employing Wolof words without translation for familiar objects, practices, and relationships. (The words are translated and a glossary supplied only in the English edition.) Her use of Wolof words, proverbs, and syntax, in a text written predominantly in the alien French language, like that of Mariama Bâ in *Scarlet Song*, suggests (while inverting) the linguistic métissage of contemporary Dakar, where French words may be mixed with the dominant Wolof of its urban patois. Diallo also innovates upon autobiographical form by frequently and extensively using dialogue as well as conventions of characterization and setting, to dramatize her narrative with the vividness of oral storytelling. While readers of traditional autobiography might consider this practice a "lying" fictionalization, it is so widespread in modern autobiographical writing—for example, in Harrie Jacobs's *Incidents in the Life of a Slave Girl, Written by Herself* (1863), Richard Wright's *Black Boy* (1945), or Buchi Emecheta's autobiographical fiction *In the Ditch* (1972)—as to be a staple of the genre. Like many autobiographers, too, Diallo employs a kind of temporal métissage by blending past and present narrative times in a form of prosopopoeia. That is, the narrator Diallo often switches from the past time of her childhood self, the narratee Safi, when a memory so powerfully overtakes her that she "sees" it as present; this occurs notably when she remembers her grandmother: "je la revois" / "I can still see her." One of the most compelling tropes of autobiography, this "present-ification" demonstrates the narrator's continuing engagement in a story that is apparently "past," and insists on the transformative power of memory to link temporal moments across a gap of unspoken years, in this case of her adult married life. In these ways Diallo adapts Western autobiographical practice to the linguistic diversity and storytelling expectations of her West African audience, providing familiar contexts for her tentative performance of subjectivity.

Diallo's text, then, traces a more complex agenda than an ethnographic reading might suggest. She constructs a heteroglossic text that performs education for its readership in the complexities of growing up female in Senegalese society. This complexity can be discovered by observing the text's literary multidiscursivity, above all, the tension between the explicit discourses of filial devotion and collective memory that the adult narrator professes and her representation of bodies, particularly that of the narratee Safi, as "unruly." While Diallo's narrative avoids articulating the subversive implications of these scenes of bodies, the embedded subjective "I" enacts them and thus fractures the coherence of a dutiful ethnographic subject.

Julia Watson. *Research in African Literatures*. 28, 2 (Summer 1997), pp. 34–52

BIBLIOGRAPHY

*Of Tilène on the Plateau: A Dakar Childhood* (*De Tilène au plateau: une enfance dakaroise*, 1975); *The Cursed Fort* (*Le Fort maudit*, 1980); *Awa, the Little Merchant* (*Awa, la petite marchande*, 1981); *A Dakar Childhood*, 1982

# DIOP, Birago (1906–1989)

## Senegal

Birago Diop is indeed an enchanter, because he is a storyteller, a real one, a member of the race that is on the road to extinction in European countries, one of those people who grab hold of you, whether you like it or not, to make you see miracles through their eyes and listen to secrets through their ears. . . .

On some evenings—"for in the black country, tales are not to be told until nightfall"—the old storyteller Amadou Koumba told Diop tales he had already heard as a child; but Amadou also taught him others and embellished them with maxims and proverbs. Diop absorbed them, around the fire, while the tom-tom rolled, and the crowd beat on inverted calabashes in time to the chants. And the stories and legends bore fruit [in *Tales of Amadou Koumba*].

That is how we—the deaf, blind, busy, and gloomy—get to know Fari the She-Ass, Golo the Monkey, Kakatar the Chameleon, Koupou-Kala the Crab, Bouki the Hyena, Leuk the Hare. . . .

There is a whole universe in which human beings play an almost exclusively subordinate role. It is a whole world—a world that is very young and very old. It is old because it has wisdom and humor, but young because of its new ways of looking at things, and that extra-keen, dazzling faculty of perception which you only have at the dawn of life but which you retain if you are a poet.

Magdeleine Paz. *Presence Africaine*. No. 5, 1948, pp. 890–91†

The first virtue of the Negro-African storyteller, as of any true artist, is to cling to reality, to *make things live* . . . Birago Diop, following the model of Amadou Koumba, depicts the men and animals of Africa such as we perceive them. Not only men and animals, but also the "bush" with its poor villages and immense sandy spaces. . . . But, beyond the silhouettes of the living, the storyteller reveals their *essences*, those inner realities that are their miseries and their dreams, their work and their worries, their passions. He shows us the role played by food in these villages that are periodically threatened by drought and famine.

Because nothing that *exists* is foreign to him, the Negro-African storyteller integrates into the traditional subjects those of today,

especially those of "colonial" life: the Commandant de Cercle, the School, the Hospital, the Machine, the Marabout and the Missionary, trading and money. . . .

As a faithful disciple of Amadou Koumba, Diop renews his links with tradition and revives ancient fables and stories—in the original spirit and the original style. He renews them, however, by translating them into French, with an art that, while respectful of the genius of the French language—this "language of graciousness and courtesy"—at the same time preserves all the qualities of the Negro-African languages.

Léopold Sédar Senghor. Preface to Birago Diop, *Les nouveaux contes d'Amadou Koumba* (Paris, Présence Africaine, 1958), pp. 14–15, 22†

There is as much cunning and malice in [Diop's stories] as there is in Aesop and La Fontaine. One must hardly ever allow oneself to deviate from Nature and realism in order to please Man, even when confronting him with hard truths. With Diop's latest book [*New Tales of Amadou Koumba*] we have to deal with a three-fold moral criticism.

This is proved by his story called "The Bone." The central character is Mor Lame; his gluttony is not explained but is *dissected and exposed* with a skill which the reader should be allowed to unravel for himself. But will one say that the author does not mean to do the same for Moussa? Moussa is "the more-than-brother," the "Bok-m' bar" and incarnates parasitism which is the cancer of African families. . . .

The third complex criticism concerns the authority of Serigne-le-Marabout (a witch-doctor), against which nobody seems to have the right to rebel. This authority incarnates a shocking tradition which, alas, still exists. . . . Serigne is a cad, an evil-doer whose many negligences are castigated in the story "The Excuse." . . .

Must it be repeated for the benefit of those who have not yet understood, that the significance of Negro-African literature lies in the disinterment of abolished Negro cultural values? Birago Diop, certainly as wise as his master, Amadou Koumba, sets into his stories more than one jewel of Negro-African speech. . . . The author is equally a poet, and he proves that in his latest work he has mastered the secret of writing, which is perhaps the most difficult of all diagnoses.

Olympe Bhêly-Quénum. *Presence Africaine* (English ed.). 8, 1, 1961, pp. 160–61

The *griot's* [storyteller's] function in the community was as much to instruct as to entertain, and many of [the *Tales of Amadou Koumba*] are fables, pointing a clear moral, particularly those in which the characters are humans. This moral is often as direct as in traditional folk-tales. . . . In "The Inheritance," we have the most elaborate allegory of all the tales—a sort of multiple fable, with several layers of meaning. All man's existence and its many possible vicissitudes are illustrated symbolically by the fantastic adventures of the three sons in their pilgrimage. At the same time their father's mysterious bequests contain a message about community living, just sharing and a wise assessment of the value of worldly goods.

Sometimes Birago Diop's tales seem to have a more doubtful moral. Are we to believe that loyalty and diligence in a lifetime of service are always repaid by neglect and cruelty in old age? Is a good turn always repaid by evil? Is it so that we should rely on False-hood if we are to get on in this life, as obviously Truth is a bad guide? And what of the more tragic element of ''Little-Husband,'' where we see a love that dare not declare itself hound its object to death? In these tales, and particularly in those where conventional ethics are cynically reversed, Birago Diop adds the more sophisticated element of irony to the straightforward morality of the traditional fable, and proves himself more than the mere mouthpiece of his household *griot*. Just as he showed up many of the foibles of human nature in his portraits of man and animals, so here too there is satire, sometimes more subtle and deep-seated, of human and social weaknesses.

> Dorothy S. Blair. Foreword to Birago Diop, *Tales of Amadou Koumba* (London: Oxford University Press, 1966), pp. xiii–xiv

Birago Diop, Master Griot, was born in 1906 at Ouakam, a suburb of Dakar. After completing his education at Toulouse and writing most of the poetry published later as *Lures and Lights*, he was a qualified veterinary doctor and, returning to Africa, he met Amadou Koumba N'Gom, the old griot, whose stories became the inspiration for almost all Diop's future work. . . .

His work as a veterinary officer, requiring an objective approach to men and animals, tempers the passion which he might feel through his involvement in the movement for African freedom. It also gives him the sense of dispassionate commitment to the problems, needs and weaknesses of men and animals which is expressed in his stories. In return, his involvement and feeling for animals and men must surely temper the clinical attitude of the practician. This, too, is seen in his stories; everything, good or evil, is approached with the same equable humility and humour.

Like La Fontaine, Diop has spent his life in close contact with men and animals, and in observing them. The ''tales,'' so he tells us in the introduction to *Tales of Amadou Koumba*, were written to fulfil his own need to re-establish contact with his own country while he was in exile in France and then, later, when he was traveling through the Sudan, Upper Volta and Mauretania as veterinary officer and in Tunis as ambassador. Apart from the similarity of the vagabond life, there are many other comparisons to be made between the seventeenth century fabulist and Diop. In the first place, they share the same interest in popular, traditional tales. They have, too, the same capacity for objective but charitable assessment of human behaviour. Finally, and the point at which they meet as artists, both have a profound understanding and feeling for the rhythm and vocabulary of the French language; Diop, too, introduces African dialects and onomatopoeia into the stories to give greater effect, using them to establish links with the popular, oral tradition which is the source of his inspiration.

> A. C. Brench. *The Novelists' Inheritance in French Africa* (London: Oxford University Press, 1967), pp. 14–15

[In *Tales of Amadou Koumba*] the woman is placed under guardianship, first that of her father, then that of her husband. Many tales illustrate the unlimited powers of the father. The father disposes of his daughter as he pleases; he can marry her off to anyone he likes. He does not have to answer to anyone. He does not take the trouble, in any of the tales in the book, to consult his daughter on the choice of her future husband. Tradition makes it the daughter's duty to bow to her father's will, as she later will have to submit to her husband's wishes when he gets the notion to take other wives. In ''An Errand'' Mor, Penda's father, decides to find an intelligent husband for his daughter; yet he does not choose the best way to reach this goal. Nowhere is Penda's consent to this marriage ever brought up. She seems rather like a kind of trophy, since she will belong to the man who will send Mor dried beef in return, by means of Bouki the Hyena, the intermediary. . . .

The marriage guardianship is maintained with equal strictness; but the clever wife can turn things to her advantage. Generally, she is not recognized as having any particular rights in marriage. She has only duties; at least, she can only assert her rights insofar as she carries out her duties perfectly, duties that exceed her rights to the point of practically canceling them out. This situation comes from a combination of traditional African and Islamic attitudes toward women. . . .

In Birago Diop's tales, humor and satire triumph; he leaves no room for sentimentality. . . . Since he does not have any intention of producing an ethnological document, Diop does not make the effort to define precisely woman's place in society. His indictment of women should not be taken literally. . . . These delightfully sketched portraits of women are too suffused with the author's humor to have originated from any motive other than the desire for healthy amusement.

> Mohamadou Kane. *Les contes d'Amadou Coumba* (Dakar: Université de Dakar, 1968), pp. 75–76, 78–79†

Africans believe that although man's body decomposes after death to mingle eventually with the earth, the spirits of the dead continue to live an intense life, especially if the descendants strive to maintain the invisible existence of their ancestors through offerings, prayers, and sacrifices. After establishing this fact, specialists in African civilizations debated it at such lengths that they finally exhausted the topic. Nobody, however, aside from these experts, has described this concept better than Birago Diop, and he has succeeded by enhancing his descriptions with all the charms of poetry.

Diop accomplished this remarkable feat in ''Breaths,'' his most beautiful poem, which is a living synthesis. ''Breaths,'' contains at least three concepts: the superiority of objects over living beings; the presence of the dead in nature; and the idea of a vital universal force. . . .

Between the African storyteller and the poet of Negritude, between *Tales of Amadou Koumba* and *Lures and Lights*, there is a definite relationship, one combining profane and religious wisdom within the framework of a traditional Africa. . . . *Lures and Lights* shows reality in general and African reality in particular, through a double perspective that justifies its title.

> René Piquion. *Ébène* (Port-au-Prince: Imprimerie Henri Deschamps, 1976), pp. 179–81†

BIBLIOGRAPHY
*Les Contes d'Amadou Koumba*, 1947; *Sarzan*, 1955; *Les Nouveaux Contes d'Amadou Koumba*, 1958; *Leurres et lueurs*, 1960; *Contes et lavanes*, 1963; *Birago Diop, ecrivain senegalais*, 1964; *Contes*

*choisis*, 1967; *L'Os de Mor Lam*, 1967; *Contes d'Awa*, 1977; *Memoires* (Autobiography), Volume 1: *La Plume raboutee* (1978), Volume 2: *A Rebrousse-temps* (1982), Volume 3: *A Rebrousse-gens: Epissures, entrelacs, et reliefs* (1985), Volume 4: *Senegal du temps de L'Harmattan* (1989), Volume 5, *Et les yeux pour me dire, L'Harmattan* (1989); *Mother Crocodile: Maman-Caiman*, 1981

# DIOP, David (1927–1960)
## Senegal

The works of this twenty-nine-year-old Senegalese writer display a lyricism directed toward practical goals. The poems he writes are militant, but . . . he bears essentially poetic arms. David Diop celebrates our African riches with humor and sensuality. His voice is always sober and concise. Yet his concern for exactness never stifles the final object of the poem. A spirit of healthy rebellion— sometimes underlying the poem, sometimes right on the surface— dominates his lyricism. His poems are a "hymn to the taut muscles," in which the lyrical vitality is never locked in a "coffin of words.". . .

In *Hammer Blows* "the heart and the brain are joined in the straight line of battle," and their union is a lesson in morality that we should remember as we see around us so many intellects who discredit the power of the heart in the name of a colorless and frozen intelligence. Through the culture of his people the poet finds the universal meaning of humanity. It is therefore not surprising that he brings us hope. . . .

Diop also knows how to write about the dizziness of physical love. To his eyes, the act of love is not a biological or recreational act but one of the most dazzling forms of participation in the world, in life. Love is a glorious dance in the sun by the senses, a dance during which the partners, who become equals through the incandescent virtues of blood, discover the riches they have in common. . . .

> René Depestre. *Presence Africaine*. December 1956, pp. 110–11†

*Hammer Blows* is a thin booklet, but there is more in this short work which is disturbing in its compactness than in many modern *complete works*. Before qualifying this poetry—which is always a means of curtailing it or justifying what is foreign to it—let us recognise its fundamental merit, which is of being *poetry* above everything else. The closer a work comes to the *intrinsic poetic phenomenon*, the more it defies analysis. . . . This is true of David Diop's poetry. It is difficult to analyse by reason of its singular poetic compactness and its high content of poetry. The work is complete in itself and perfectly impervious. It is like those works of art whose beauty is beyond question but defies explanation.

On reflection, it may perhaps be suggested that this verbal achievement cannot be accounted for solely by talent and that unexplainable spontaneity causes a poet to write poems in the same manner as appletrees yield apples. Indeed, on closer examination, one finds that the great impulse that underlies, illuminates and sanctifies David Diop's lyricism is beautiful as the daylight and life itself—Love. Love with a capital "L," in all its forms with all its subtleties and climes. Filial love . . . passionate love with that

irresistible breath which comes from deeper than the heart . . . the love of the fighter who exorcises the subtle devils and unmystifies . . . the man who claims the penalty and assumes the crimes of others . . . and lastly outright love: love of life, rhythm, and grace. . . .

*Hammer Blows* is a work of profound faith in Man. The poet's African temperament breathes through these verses which are written in a generous, fiery vein.

> *Presence Africaine* (English ed.). June—September 1960, pp. 244–45

In September 1960 the young poet David Diop died in a plane crash off Dakar. With him went his wife and all his manuscripts. At the age of thirty-three the most promising of West Africa's younger French poets was thus snatched from the scene, leaving only a single pamphlet of seventeen short poems behind him. That little pamphlet, *Hammer Blows*, was enough to establish David Diop as the most interesting and talented African poet of the fifties. Its appearance in 1956 aroused hopes of a career which never happened, but the unifying passion and fire of these few poems earn Diop a place here as the spokesman of a new age, the age for whom Senghor must appear a figure too deeply committed to the idea of a French Community uniting many peoples under the umbrella of a single civilization; the age, in short, of the Guinean Revolution.

David Diop was born in Bordeaux in 1927, the son of a Senegalese father and a Camerounian mother. His youth was spent partly in France, partly in West Africa. This background might superficially suggest the "cultural mulatto" far more strongly than Senghor's. In fact, we are now in a new political atmosphere. Diop uses his French culture, not to seek a reconciliation, a synthesis, or even a polarity of tensions, but to unleash an unrelenting hatred of Europe and all that it stands for. Across centuries of bitterness and hate, he proclaims the dawn. It is a dawn to which Europe has contributed nothing but the prelude of darkness. But if the extremity of his position may repel in cold prose, the urgency and fervour of his verse give it the quality of a "Marseillaise." . . .

> Gerald Moore. *Seven African Writers* (London: Oxford University Press, 1962), p. 18

David Diop's literary career began while he was still a student at the Lycée Marcelin Berthelot near Paris, in the late 1940's. His teacher, Léopold Sédar Senghor, was impressed with the youngster's "original inner life" and selected several early poems for inclusion in the history-making *Anthology of New Negro and Malagasy Poetry* (1948), which Jean-Paul Sartre prefaced with the famous essay "Black Orpheus." Later, David Diop contributed to *Présence africaine*, the cultural review of the Negro world edited in Paris, and participated in the Negro Writers and Artists Conference in Paris (1956) and Rome (1960). . . .

Until his untimely death, David Diop was emerging as a leader of the younger generation of "negritude" writers, those who reached their twenties in the postwar years. Many of his poems take up images, themes and accents already introduced by such older French-speaking West Indians in the negritude school as Jacques Roumain and Léon Damas. The influence of Aimé Césaire on David Diop's work is especially strong. While the younger poet's gifts cannot be compared with Césaire's, his work has a distinct personal stamp that stems from its directness, simplicity, and raw emotional power. The impact of every line, every word, is intentional. The angry young man meant his poems to "burst the eardrums of those who do not wish to hear them." . . .

The incident that inspired the poem ["To a Black Child"] is the 1955 lynching in Mississippi of a Chicago youngster named Emmet Till. David Diop had not been to America, but like nearly all Africans and West Indians in the negritude movement, he identified closely with the American Negro. He was deeply shocked by the Till affair, and by the fact that the murderers, though known, were acquitted in a trial that made a mockery of justice. . . .

Léopold Sédar Senghor had hoped to see his young countryman's talent mature, his bitterness and anger soften with understanding and compassion. It was President Senghor who pronounced the funeral oration in Dakar, recalling David's courage during the "long calvary" of his youth, the months and years of sickness [in sanatoriums with a recurrent illness that plagued him from childhood]. These, and the more purely psychic anguishes, David Diop has recorded in a series of lucid images: "ragged days with a narcotic taste," "anxious hangings on the edge of cliffs," and "sleep inhabited by alcohol," together with a love that brought "necklaces of laughter," his second marriage. "Through your long hospital nights," said President Senghor, "you identified with your crucified people. Your sufferings became their sufferings; your anguish, their anguish; your hope, their hope." Senghor's words were a generous tribute to a voice he found "hard and black as basalt," a voice destined never to reach maturity, but which sang ardently and unforgettably of "Africa my Africa."

Paulette J. Trout and Ellen Conroy Kennedy. *Journal of the New African Literature and the Arts.* Spring–Fall 1968, pp. 76–78

According to Gerald Moore, David Diop "uses his French culture . . . to unleash an unrelenting hatred of Europe and all that it stands for." Considering the poet from another viewpoint, the editors of *Présence africaine* interpret Diop's "fundamental drive" as "Love." A more comprehensive description of Diop's inspiration might define him as a poet of passion. *Passion*, derived from the Latin *patior, pati, passus sum*, which means *suffer*, is not limited to erotic experience. Rather, it is violent and intense emotion which may run the gamut of feelings from hatred to love, and from the limits of pain to those of pleasure. . . .

"Negro Tramp" reveals several of the fundamental elements of Diop's passion: abomination of the whites ("their big mouths full of principles"); compassion for others who suffer; a belief in the fertility of revolt ("I excite the hurricane for future fields"); and an almost paradisiacal dream of what will come. In this way, Diop's fury against the oppressor provides the ferment for his dreams of revolution. . . .

But Diop's poetry goes beyond his hate. Often his poems fall into two-part structures. After his tirade against what oppresses him, he soars upward to hope. . . . Mediating between his hatred and his vision are the poet's compassion and faith in creative revolt. . . . As Diop treats it, rebellion is not an act of hatred; rather, it is a process of creative violence which includes notions of fertility, hope and even love. Through revolt he seeks to overcome his suffering and his subjection. Storms, symbolic of the forces of destruction, are for him images of reconstruction. He calls them "virile tempests." Often erotic imagery describes the passion of his re-creation since he regards revolt as fertile when nourished by

love. In "The Vultures," for example, his hands, "profound like revolt," will "impregnate the belly of the earth." Hope, in the figure of spring, will be born in the flesh beneath his steps imbued with light. . . . Revolt merges with the erotic impulse in the passion of Diop's re-creation.

Enid H. Rhodes. *Essays in Criticism.* Fall 1970, pp. 234–35, 237

While Senghor can be described as a literary liberal in terms of his philosophy of life and his aesthetic credo, David Diop's work epitomizes agitation and radicalism in its entirety. Diop's only single volume of poetry, *Coups de pilon*, published during his lifetime, voices cynicism and bitterness against an age threatened by racism, colonialism, exploitation and war.

Born in Bordeaux, France, in 1927 to a Senegalese father and a Cameroonian mother, David Diop spent most of his life in France but because he was often ill, he visited Africa frequently in order to improve his failing health. Unfortunately he died in 1960 in an air crash off Dakar at the age of 33.

During his lifetime, David recorded bitter memories connected with racism and World War II. He was also nostalgic about Africa which features prominently in his poetry. Whereas one finds in Senghor an abiding faith in the positive values of both European and African cultures, David Diop's work symbolizes outright and total denunciation and rejection of colonialism and Western civilization. . . .

Three major themes recur in David Diop's poetry, namely, his criticism of Western civilization and its attendant colonialism; his nostalgia for and glorification of Africa; and his strong belief in a future Africa which is prosperous, united and strong.

Of the above themes, perhaps the one which dominates much of David's verse is his attack of Western civilization. In his treatment of this theme, his attitude recalls on the one hand that of McKay's—assertive, militant and defiant; on the other hand that of Kofi Awoonor's—bitter, mocking and sarcastic.

David's uncompromising indictment of Western civilization arises from the fact that it is the source of many human woes: slavery, alienation and exploitation. . . .

The poet's criticism of Western civilization can be found in the poems "Africa," "The Vultures," and "Listen Comrades." In "Africa" he not only projects the future state of Africa but recounts the vicissitudes of the continent right from its heydays until the period of colonialism. The poet notes, for example, that during its heydays Africa was noted for its brave and heroic leaders, its fertile lands, and for its great agricultural potentials. With the onset of Western colonialism, however, the continent was not only looted, its citizens were brutalized and subjugated beyond recognition. He laments:

Africa tell me Africa Is this you this back that is bent This back that breaks under the weight of humiliation This back trembling with red scars?

In "Listen Comrades" the poet, with restrained emotion, discusses the way and manner death dogged the path of the indigenous population during the era of the slave trade. In their mad rush to exploit the African continent and enslave its people, the colonial powers killed the local citizenry in great numbers. Not even the aged ones were spared. "Mamba with his white hairs" was also killed; for the poet, he symbolizes all those who suffered death and persecution in the hands of the colonialists. But rather than give in to despair and cynicism, the poet stoically exhorts the local people to look forward to a future filled with hope and freedom attainable through their own spirited struggle.

Of all David's poems, "The Vultures" represents his most sarcastic and satirical work in terms of delineating the evil and ugliness of Western colonialism. It is also probably his most famous single poem. The poem is significant in the sense that it is one of the few African lyrics in which animal or bird imagery is employed to dramatize human behavior.

In this piece the poet draws a character sketch of the colonialist symbolized as the vulture, a predatory, sinister bird. Unlike Kofi Awoonor's "The Weaverbird" where the poem continually draws the reader's attention to the character of the weaverbird in its ingratitude, here in "The Vultures" the poet does not allude to the bird in the body of the poem but leaves the reader to draw his own conclusions by comparing the poem's title with what is discussed in the entire piece. The interesting thing here is that David allows the narrative to develop unobtrusively while relying on the imaginative ability of the reader to appreciate the poem's moral import.

The poem is couched in irony: the colonialist is the architect of Christianity, yet he "did not know love." He preaches civilization, still he breaks all moral codes through "exhorted kisses/of promises broken at the point of a gun." In this poem, colonialism is vigorously assailed because it is the embodiment of human oppression, religious hypocrisy, and economic domination.

As a satiric allegory the piece dramatizes the negative aspect of human nature. The Vulture, for example, surreptitiously preys on its victims which it kills for food. By implication the colonialist comes to Africa, not as a friend, but as an enemy. The employment of the images "killed," "slapped," and "bloodstained monument of tutelage" help to underscore the wickedness and brutality of the colonialist in his worst elements.

David's sense of nostalgia, his second theme, arises from his often long absence from the African continent. Also fueling this theme was his proneness to illness, which inspired his yearning to return home in order to improve his health, or more realistically, to reflect on those times when he lived and enjoyed the comfort and beauty of his boyhood days in Africa. . . .

David also captures the mood of the Negress and Negro who, like him, are exiled in foreign lands. This is especially demonstrated in the poems "To a Black Dancer" and "Nigger Tramp," pieces which depict the pitiful condition of these exiles and of their hopeful wish to return to their fatherland.

In "To a Black Dancer" the poet extols the beauty of the Negress and the wonderful effect this beauty has on him. For example, her "breasts and sacred powers," her "naked . . . smile," her "magic . . . loins," her "myths"—all "burn around me." . . .

When we come to David's final theme—that is, his belief in a future Africa that is united, progressive, and strong—it is important to emphasize the fact that virtually all of his poems end on an optimistic note couched in a simple resolution, as in "Africa":

In splendid loneliness amidst white
and faded flowers
That is Africa your Africa
That grows again patiently obstinately
And its fruit gradually acquire
The bitter taste of liberty.

"Listen Comrades":

It is the sign of the dawn
The sign of brotherhood which comes
to nourish the dreams of men.

and "The Vultures":

In spite of the desolate villages
of torn Africa
Hope was preserved in us as in
a fortress
And from the mines of Swaziland to
the factories of Europe
Spring will be reborn under our bright steps.

Two interesting things stand out strongly from the above passages. Firstly, is David's strong awareness of the ephemeral nature of Western colonialism which strengthens his resolve and hope for the future. Secondly, by projecting a note of optimism against a general background of injustice, the poet portrays himself as a far more sensitive and mature individual than the colonialists.

> Isaac Irabor Elimimian. *Theme and Style in African Poetry* (Lampeter, Wales: The Edwin Meller Press, Ltd. 1991), pp. 36–43

BIBLIOGRAPHY
*Coups de pilon*, 1956; *Hammer Blows, and Other Writings*, 1973

# DOVE, Rita (1952–)
## United States

[With] the consistently accomplished work of thirty-three-year-old Rita Dove, there is at least one clear sign if not of a coming renaissance of poetry, then at least of the emergence of an unusually strong new figure who might provide leadership by brilliant example. Thus far, Rita Dove has produced a remarkable record of publications in a wide range of respected poetry and other literary journals. Two books in verse, *The Yellow House on the Corner* and *Museum*, have appeared from Carnegie-Mellon University Press. A third book-length manuscript of poetry, "Thomas and Beulah," is scheduled to be published early in 1986 by the same house. Clearly Rita Dove has both the energy and the sense of professionalism required to lead other writers. Most importantly—even a first reading of her two books makes it clear that she also possesses the talent to do so. Dove is surely one of the three or four most gifted young black American poets to appear since [Amiri Baraka] ambled with deceptive nonchalance onto the scene in the late 1950s, and perhaps the most disciplined and technically accomplished black poet to arrive since Gwendolyn Brooks began her remarkable career in the 1940s. . . .

In many ways, her poems are exactly the opposite of those that have come to be considered black verse in recent years. Instead of looseness of structure, one finds in her poems remarkably tight control; instead of a reliance on reckless inspiration, one recognizes discipline and practice, and long, taxing hours in competitive university poetry workshops and in her study; instead of a range of reference limited to personal confession, one finds personal reference disciplined by a measuring of distance and objectivity; instead of an obsession with the theme of race, one finds an eagerness, perhaps even an anxiety, to transcend—if not actually to repudiate—black cultural nationalism in the name of a more inclusive sensibility. Hers is a brilliant mind, reinforced by what appears to be very wide reading, that seeks for itself the widest possible play, an ever expanding range of reference, the most acute distinctions, and the most subtle shadings of meaning. . . .

As a poet, Dove is well aware of black history. One of the five sections of *The Yellow House* is devoted entirely to poems on the theme of slavery and freedom. These pieces are inspired by nameless but strongly representative victims of the "peculiar institution," as well as by more famous heroic figures (who may be seen as fellow black writers, most of them) such as Solomon Northrup, abducted out of Northern freedom on a visit to Washington . . . and the revolutionary David Walker. . . . In these works and others such as "Banneker" in the later volume, *Museum*, Dove shows both a willingness and a fine ability to evoke, through deft vignettes, the psychological terror of slavery. She is certainly adept at recreating graphically the starched idioms of the eighteenth and early nineteenth centuries, at breathing life into the monumental or sometimes only arthritic rhythms of that vanished and yet still echoing age. Her poems in this style and area are hardly less moving than those of Robert Hayden, who made the period poem (the period being slavery) virtually his own invention among black poets. Dove's special empathy as a historical poet seems to be with the most sensitive, most eloquent blacks, individuals of ductile intelligence made neurotic by pain, especially the pain of not being understood and of not being able to express themselves.

Arnold Rampersad. *Callaloo*. 9, 1 (Winter 1986), pp. 52–54

Rita Dove has always possessed a storyteller's instinct. In *The Yellow House on the Corner*, *Museum*, and the forthcoming *Thomas and Beulah*, this instinct has found expression in a synthesis of striking imagery, myth, magic, fable, wit, humor, political comment, and a sure knowledge of history. Many contemporaries share Dove's mastery of some of these, but few succeed in bringing them together to create a point of view that, by its breadth and force, stands apart. She has not worked her way into this enviable position among poets without fierce commitment. . . .

*Museum* begins with travelogues, which prepare the reader for travel poems that eclipse the personal by introducing overlooked historical detail. "Nestor's Bathtub," a pivotal poem in this respect, begins with the lines "As usual, legend got it all wrong." This announces a dissatisfaction with the conventional ordering of events and an intention to rejuvenate history by coming up with new ways of telling it. In successive poems ("Tou Wan Speaks to Her Husband, Liu Sheng," "Catherine of Alexandria," "Catherine of Siena," "Boccaccio: The Plague Years," and its companion piece, "Fiammetta Breaks Her Peace"), Dove adopts a variety of personae that bear witness to the struggles of victimized women in societies in which men are dubiously perceived as gods.

This strategy continues into the book's second section, though the subjects and personae are primarily male ("Shakespeare Say," "Banneker," "Ike"). . . . As in *The Yellow House*, in *Museum* Dove focuses on characters, and chooses characters to speak through, from the historical rosters of those whose lives have been the stuff of fable. Toward the end of this section, her identification with historical and mysterious male-female consciousness is most complete in "Agosta the Winged Man and Rasha the Black

Dove." In this poem she tells the story of a pair of German circus performers, an inscrutable deformed man and an equally inscrutable black woman who dances with snakes. These characters are performers, who like the poet, look at the world in unique ways. . . .

The poem that follows, "At the German Writers Conference in Munich," examines and exploits this preoccupation from another angle. In the poem another art—another way of performing—is described. The calm, stiff characters of a tapestry are not outwardly grotesque as are the characters in the preceding poem. Nevertheless, they appear to be out of step with their woven environment, existing as they do in a world of flowers. The two poems, together, illustrate a brilliant shifting of focus, a looking out of the eyes of characters, then a merciless looking into them.

The third section of *Museum* contains a focusing down of this strategy in a tight group of family poems in which the father is the dominant character. He is perceived by the innocent narrator as the teacher, the bearer of all that is magical in the world. . . . Whether he is making palpable an impalpable taste or miraculously rescuing roses from beetles ("Roses"), or deftly retrieving what is magical from a mistake ("My Father's Telescope"), he is clearly the narrator's mentor, inspiring a different way of meeting the world. . . .

But even in this tender, celebratory section, Dove includes one poem, "Anti-Father," which satisfies her self-imposed demand that she tell all sides of the story. . . . The innocent narrator, not a knowledgeable woman, reverses roles here, contradicting the father but offering magical insight in doing so.

The closing section of Rita Dove's second volume summarizes all that has preceded it, and in two remarkable poems, anticipates *Thomas and Beulah*.

Robert E. McDowell. *Callaloo*. 9, 1 (Winter 1986), pp. 61, 64–66

[*Thomas and Beulah*] engages history, in this case, personal history . . . and refers obliquely to twentieth-century American history, but from the family album snapshot on the cover through the appended "Chronology" (first item: "1900: Thomas born in Wartrace, Tennessee"), we read this book as a family chronicle. However, the poems themselves are not about an individual's *relationship* to her history, nor about the weight of history. They are, more, history allowed to speak for itself. The title page tells us that the "poems tell two sides of a story and are meant to be read in sequence." The history contained in *Thomas and Beulah*, indeed, is found in the unfolding story—or juxtaposed stories—told of the youth, marriage, lives, and deaths of two people. We even forget that the poems are historical, in part because they mix past and present tense, in part because of the frequent use of the past and present progressive, and in part because of the vividness of the characters revealed. . . .

It is worth adding that most of the language in *Thomas and Beulah* could have been spoken by the people whose story is told, which is to say that the poems do not seem to impose on their subjects. Rather, they slowly build a context for the objects, images, and scraps of reported speech and song that appear and keep reappearing. This is an impressive achievement, although it also means that the poems have more power taken together than individually. To give one . . . example: when Thomas watches the "shy angle of his daughter's head," sees his son-in-law swallow, and feels for the first time "like / calling him *Son*" ("Variations on Gaining a Son"), attentive readers confronted only with this poem will recognize the oblique reference to fishing and to the common-place, "hooking a man." But it is only in the context of the other poems about Thomas, about his own marriage, about his more literal fishing trips (in "Lightnin' Blues" and "One Volume Missing"), and his desire for a son that these lines have their full impact. This is, of course, an appropriate way to reimagine and represent the lives traced in the book, since they are lives not fully examined by those who live them. The marriage of Thomas and Beulah, in particular, is clearly one where communication is tacit, contained precisely in repeated phrases and motions that have gained meaning over the years. The poems recreate both the accretion of meaning and the taciturnity, perfectly right for this subject, although, given other subjects, one might want more.

> Lisa M. Steinman. *Michigan Quarterly Review.* 26, 2 (Spring 1987), pp. 433, 435

Rita Dove's *Thomas and Beulah*, winner of the 1987 Pulitzer Prize, has a distinctive, ambitiously unified design. It traces the history of two blacks who separately move north, to Ohio, meet and get married in the 1920s, and go on to raise four girls, enduring many vicissitudes before their deaths in the 1960s. Arranged serially and accompanied by an almost essential chronology, the poems, we are told in a note beforehand, are meant to be read in order. Much as Michael Ondaatje has done in his poemlike novel, *Coming through Slaughter*, Dove reconstructs the past through a series of discontinuous vignettes which enter freely into the psyches of the two main characters.

It is important that the poems are arranged chronologically because we often need all the help we can get in clarifying many of the references. Even with the chronology as a guide, the poems sometimes seem unnecessarily obscure and cryptic. More often, however, the difficulty of the work is justifiable because the insights are exactly as subtle as they are oblique. In exploiting the virtues of ellipsis, Dove evidently has faith we will have gumption enough to stare a hole in the page until our minds leap with hers across the gaps. . . .

One of the great strengths of this book is the depth of Dove's sympathetic understanding not only of Beulah but also of Thomas; she manages to convey the inner savor both of Thomas's early ebullience and of his later frustration and despair at not being allowed a part in the world equal to his considerable sensitivity. The mandolin provides him with a creative outlet, but it becomes the bittersweet outlet of the blues. . . .

In her forays into the black vernacular, Dove chooses not to be phonetic; instead, she concentrates on diction and speech rhythm and does so with dialectical pizzazz, as in the conclusion to "Jiving." . . . Here, the juxtaposition of two voices and styles highlights the virtues of both. It's difficult to make such switches in the level of diction while still maintaining a plausible narrative voice; yet Dove most often succeeds. Because she has thoroughly imagined her characters, Dove can handle her vernacular material convincingly from a decided stylistic remove.

> Peter Harris. *Virginia Quarterly Review.* 64, 2 (Spring 1988), pp. 270–72

The events in *Thomas and Beulah* are narrated in strict chronological order, which is detailed in the appended chronology. The subjection of story time to historical time, unusual in modern narratives, gives Dove's sequence a tragic linearity, a growing sense that what is done cannot be undone and that what is not done but only regretted or deferred cannot be redeemed in the telling. The narrative runs from Thomas's riverboat life to his arrival in Akron and marriage to Beulah, to their children's births, his jobs at Goodyear, his stroke and death. Then the narrative begins again with Beulah: her father's flirtations, Thomas's flirtations and courtship, their marriage, a pregnancy, her millinery work, a family reunion, and her death. In the background, the Depression and the March on Washington mark respectively the trials of the couple's and their children's generations.

The sequence of *Thomas and Beulah* resembles fiction more than it does a poetic sequence—[William] Faulkner's family chronicles in particular. Dove's modernist narrator stands back paring her fingernails like an unobtrusive master or God. The cover shows a snapshot, of Thomas and Beulah presumably, and the volume may be considered as a photo album, or two albums, with only the date and place printed underneath each picture. Thomas and Beulah are probably Rita Dove's grandparents; the book is dedicated to her mother, Elvira Elizabeth, and the third child born to Thomas and Beulah is identified in the chronology as Liza. But whether the couple is actually Rita Dove's grandparents is less important than the fact that all evidence of their relation has been removed. Any choice of genre involves an economy of gains and losses. Objective, dramatic narration—showing rather than telling—has the advantage of letting the events speak for themselves and the disadvantage of dispensing with the problematics of narrative distortion and a camera-eye or God's-eye view. *Thomas and Beulah* tells it like it is and assumes it is like it tells us.

> John Shoptaw. In Henry Louis Gates, Jr., ed. *Reading Black, Reading Feminist* (New York: Meridian, 1990), pp. 374–75

As a black person living in the predominantly white societies of the Old and New Worlds, having entered an interracial and intercultural marriage (her husband is a German writer), and trying to forge an autonomous poetic voice against the background of a male dominated Euro- and Afro-American literary tradition, Dove has often crossed social and literary boundaries, violated taboos, and experienced displacement, e.g., living "in two different worlds, seeing things with double vision," wherever she has stayed (the United States, Germany, Israel). Talking to Judith Kitchen and Stan Sanvel Rubin about her European experiences which inspired her second book, *Museum*, Dove admits that she had a sense of displacement while she was in Europe, and that she expressed this sense through various characters and situations in *Museum*. She remarks, however, that her stay in Europe broadened her world view and contributed to her growth as a person and an artist. . . . Dove's complex experiences in the United States and abroad (Europe, North Africa, Israel) have affected both her vision and her poetic method. Although she deals with the problems of racism and sexism, she does not adopt the polemical voice of either a black nationalist or a feminist poet, and therefore she does not let indignation, anger, and protest control her verse. Although she focuses on the black experience in many of her works she goes beyond the definition of black literature which reflected the black ideal that prevailed since the late 1960s: "Black literature By blacks, About blacks, directed To blacks. Essential black literature is the distillation of black life." Her poem "Upon Meeting Don L.

Lee, in a Dream,'' included in her first book, *The Yellow House on the Corner*, expresses her reaction to the black nationalist aesthetic. The poet Don Lee, one of its major representatives, is described as ''always moving in the yellow half-shadows,'' as a man with ''lashless eyes,'' surrounded by a chorus of chanting women dressed in robes and stretching ''beaded arms to him.'' After setting the stage and introducing the black male poet in a kind of priestly role, Dove creates a dialogue between him and the first-person speaker who is obviously her mouthpiece; and then, through a cluster of surrealistic images, she suggests the decay of the ideology that Don Lee embodies. . . .

By combining fact and fiction, biographical and autobiographical with historical events over a period of sixty years, as well as characters and values from different races and classes (low-class American blacks, middle-class white Americans, French aristocrats, etc.), by identifying with both male (Thomas) and female (Beulah) consciousness, by creating a background of black music, and by describing Southern Thomas's journey north and the wanderings of unemployed men during the Depression, Dove balances opposites, bridges conventional divisions (private-public, white-black, high-folk culture, male-female, rural South-industrial North, low-high class, America-Europe, past-present, etc.), and she transcends boundaries of space and time in *Thomas and Beulah*. Her international characters and settings in *The Yellow House on the Corner*, *Museum*, and *Grace Notes*, the journey motif that runs through them, her references to artists and artifacts since the ancient times, her individual portraits of real or mythical men and women from the United States and other countries, as well as the instances of love, struggle for freedom and dignity, and sensitivity to beauty, but also of violence, disease, decay, and death that she observes everywhere—all of them enable Dove to expand her range of reference even more. She appropriates, defies, subverts, and reconstructs the traditional male-centered poetic discourse to convey her own complex vision. She speaks with the voice of a world citizen who places her personal, racial, and national experience within the context of the human experience as a whole, and celebrates its richness and continuity. She also speaks with the authority of an artist who claims the world's civilizations as her rightful heritage.

Ekaterini Georgoudaki. *Callaloo*. 14, 2 (Spring 1991), pp. 419–20, 429–30

The discipline of writing *Thomas and Beulah*, a family epic in lyric form, required Rita Dove to focus, as never before, her talent for compression. How to get years of her grandparents' joy and anguish into spare lines without presuming to sum up for them; how to telescope distances of place, background, dreams, without narrating—these were some of the problems she solved so brilliantly in that book. The past shed its patina as bits of voice and image shone through to bespeak whole epochs and regions. The book moved us by its under-statement, the major ally of compression, and by its sympathetic imagination, that refused to make Thomas and Beulah stereotypes, the mere objects of our pity or nostalgia.

In *Grace Notes* Dove returns to the range of subjects and settings that characterized her first two books (she is remarkably broad in the scope of her references without ever being showy). All the features we have grown to appreciate in this poet arise here in their finest form: descriptive precision, tonal control, metaphoric reach within uncompromising realism. Moreover, she has brought these talents to bear upon a new intimacy and moral depth, served by memory and imagination working together. . . .

The poems of [the second section] deal with being not in its social and autobiographical dimension but in its ontological dimension of origin and destiny, first things and last things, though as always in terms of the local, the familiar. In ''Ozone'' the poet returns to the dual idea of wound and flight, the hole in the ozone a kind of cosmic wound out of which we yearn to escape, to pursue a star to its vanishing point. Yet we ''wire the sky so it won't fall down,'' comforting ourselves and protecting ourselves from self-annihilating dreams. Section three comes down from this height to explore the poet's present life and her ties to others, especially her young daughter. But the poems of this section are informed by the ultimate questions asked in the section before: what unites us, where does our identity begin and end, what is the meaning we derive from our bodies? . . .

Many of [the poems in the fourth section] take the implicit form of dialogue as they attempt to define a stance toward the world. In ''Ars Poetica'' she considers one writer's desire to merge with the elemental, another's desire to master it. Her own way of putting herself on the map is to be ''a hawk,'' a traveling ''x-marks-the-spot.'' This attitude reemerges in ''Dialectical Romance'' where, in arguing against a definition of God she imagines ''a program so large there could be no answer except in working it through.'' In ''Stitches,'' about an accidental gash sewn up in the emergency room, the difference is emotional and within herself—the part that feels pain, experiences alarm and watches the seamstress Fate ''pedaling the needle right through,'' and the part that stands outside and laughs ''in stitches'' over the ironies of her life. One part of the poet finds the laughter distasteful in the midst of pain . . . it is answered by the part that finds in wit a choice of resistance. . . . The ways we find to rise above our vulnerability, above the wounds we suffer, is Dove's constant theme. How to cope, especially, with prejudice, is the theme of ''Arrow,'' about the poet's response, and that of her students, to the racial stereotyping by an ''eminent scholar'' in a lecture, and the sexism of the poet he discusses. The arch poet-teacher assures her students ''we can learn from this,'' though she herself is burning from the poison of the scholar's ''arrow.'' . . .

It is to the castoff, the ''truly lost,'' the ''lint'' of the world that Dove turns in the final section of *Grace Notes*. What vitality is left for Genie, ''born too late for *Aint-that-a-shame*?'' Quite a lot, it seems, dream of ''a breezeway and real nice wicker on some astroturf.'' For Billie Holliday and women like her, caged canaries, the bitter message is: ''If you can't be free, be a mystery.'' There are grace notes even for the castaways and their cool view from the edge wields a strange kind of power over us, though hardly a power one envies. Zebulun, the wretched Jewish dyer, purifier of purple pigment from juice of snail, cries out to God: ''You gave my brother countries; / me you gave the snail! / God answers: / After all / I made them dependent on you / for the snail.'' This is ambiguous comfort, as is the unwanted, homely (despite the glorious press) revelation of the Roman on the road to Damascus.

In a volume of poems full of resistance, offering ways of coping with and transcending wounds, these last poems have the eerie placidity of surrender; they remind us that our vulnerabilities are real and often untranscendable. The volume which began with black American adolescence, its fears and aspirations, ends in an Old Folks Home in Jerusalem, ancient, mythical desert place where the pangs of difference, worldly hope, even survival are no longer in question. "So you wrote a few poems" almost cuts the wing, coming as it does from the scene of Jews enduring their final suffering. But the last words of the volume are not simply bleak: "Everyone waiting here was once in love." The invisible wings of the human spirit continue to flutter.

Bonnie Costello. *Callaloo*. 14, 2 (Spring 1991), pp. 434–38

[The] strength of [Dove's] first novel, *Through the Ivory Gate*, is her prose, her ability to describe and suggest. The novel's heroine, Virginia King, is a gifted musician and actress. She takes up a temporary post in an elementary school in her hometown of Akron, Ohio, a home coming that provokes a flood of memories. As Virginia helps the schoolchildren to develop a puppet show, she remembers her own childhood—the early days in Akron, her family's move to Arizona, her university studies, her love for a fellow student called Clayton.

The story is gentle and the style plain, at its best describing the sky over Lake Erie, a neighbor's homemade pastries, the décor of a restaurant or the face of a long-lost aunt. It is a happy book, about the pleasures of living. The author has a talent for sanguine observation.

The novel moves, as does memory, through association. One chapter starts in Akron, with Virginia playing the cello. She remembers events in class that morning, and is reminded of her own childhood. She remembers lying on a bed and listening to the Arizona rain. She thinks about the children's puppet show, with its magic football and drum majorettes. This cues different memories of becoming the only black drum majorette in her high school. We get flashbacks within flashbacks. . . .

The book deals sparingly but effectively with the issue of race. Virginia becomes a mime artist and puppeteer partly because there are few parts for black actresses. When she gets her first straight-A report card, a white school friend pushes her over and calls her a nigger. The book begins powerfully with the young Virginia's first encounter with a Sambo doll and the confusions this causes her. . . .

These themes of fantasy, childhood, and oppression are brought together, perhaps a touch too explicitly, in a scene toward the end. Virginia dreams she is lecturing on the subject of Sambo to an audience of adult heads screwed onto children's bodies. "The first thing to bear in mind about Sambo," she begins, "is that Sambo is all of us. We all want to make merry, to wear bright colors and sing in the sun all day." The oppression of a race is seen in the context of the oppression of children and of joy.

Geoff Ryman. *New York Times Book Review*. October 11, 1992, pp. 11–12

When Rita Dove wrote the first of the forty-four poems appearing in her Pulitzer Prize-winning collection *Thomas and Beulah*, she did not anticipate that others would follow. Rather, the writing of each of the collection's poems seemed to necessitate another, until Dove developed a sequence which she molded into a distinctive, unified narrative. Among the many remarkable traits of Dove's

chronicle is its conveyance of feeling, experience, and attitude in a seemingly static form, while simultaneously maintaining a narrative thread recounting events that span over four decades. Dove's concentration on protagonists Thomas and Beulah's distinctive, gendered perspectives plays a central role in establishing this flowing yet constant feel. The importance of gendered experience is evident in every facet of the collection from its organization to its thematic substance. To reinforce her gendered theme Dove moves freely into the psyche of her characters. . . .

From the outset Dove establishes Thomas and Beulah's different perspectives by dividing her book into distinctly masculine and feminine sections prefaced by individualized epigraphs. Still, by this structure, Dove does not deny the oneness of the couple's experiences, linking them together with the overall preface of [t]hese poems tell two sides of a story. . . . Thomas' section, entitled Mandolin, bears a masculine, aggressive, demanding feel, borne out in the titles of the poems. Titles such as "The Event," "Satisfaction Coal Company," and "Thomas at the Wheel" provide the reader with an early and clear sense of Thomas' dominance and responsibility. Beulah's section, conversely, appears second in the collection, is shorter than Thomas', and exudes a sense of confinement, dependency, and denied aspirations. The epigraph to Beulah's section bears out the point. [Once], but, by implication, no more, her fire-lit heart . . . felt furies / [b]eating, beating, Dove tells the reader. . . .

With her carefully planned framework in place Dove moves to more firmly establish Thomas's and Beulah's gendered perspectives in the first poem of each of their respective sections. In these initial poems Dove connects both Thomas and Beulah's opinions, attitudes, and decisions to formative experiences from their childhoods or adolescences. In both Thomas' and Beulah's cases causal incidents related directly to gender provided them with senses of self that embodied prescribed gender roles. For Thomas, a manly, and ultimately fatal, challenge to best friend and fellow river boat dandy, Lem, imprinted him with a lifelong sense of lost male companionship. This loss, directly connected to Thomas' masculine daring, informed Thomas with a confused and frustrated understanding of masculine aggression that, in the face of uncontrollable circumstances, often proved grievously destructive. Dove dutifully and skillfully returns to this dual theme of Thomas as both aggressor and victim throughout the story. . . .

With the importance of formative gender experiences firmly established, Dove next describes the development of the couple's relationship. The connection Dove makes between her character's early life experiences and their courtship, marriage, and intimate life is clear, as each immediately adopts traditional passive or aggressive marital roles which, as with their earlier experiences, ultimately prove frustrating and unsatisfactory. Nowhere is this more true than in the couple's sexual relationship. From the outset, Thomas is the dominant figure. He, like Beulah's father, is the approacher, the questioner, the proposer. Thomas is King of the Crawfish in a flashy yellow scarf wooing Beulah by any means he can, including the slight deception of tears made possible by a gnat flying in his eye. . . .

Thomas assumes sexual domination to be a natural part of his masculinity while Beulah, in contrast, cringes at his sexual forcefulness, either repelling or silently enduring his advances. During courtship, the mores of the time allowed, if not demanded, a certain prudishness on Beulah's part. Here Dove's extensive historical research into Thomas and Beulah's era pays off, as she manipulates her understanding of mid-twentieth-century social standards to convey a striking image of Beulah's gentle rejection of Thomas' advances. Beulah would not set a foot / in [Thomas'] turtledove Nash, Dove writes, because such behavior in the 1930s and 1940s would have suggested a type of promiscuity that wasn't proper. In those days, a single woman riding alone in a car with a man suggested impropriety, but a wife who refused sexual relations with her husband all but defied her marriage vow. . . .

Although Dove depicts sexual relations as particularly frightening and unpleasant to Beulah, the author stops short of denying Beulah's ability to enjoy intimacy. In fact, as Dove constructs the story, the sexual acquiescence demanded in Beulah's marital relationship is a central factor rendering intimacy unpleasant and belittling to her. When mentally travelling outside those constrictive marital bonds, Dove suggests, Beulah is able to muse about the pleasure of sexual experimentation. To make her point Dove includes a brief scene in which Beulah thinks back to an intimacy shared with an adolescent sweetheart. Beulah's remembrance of this encounter indicates a denied desire for loving contact in which emotional freedom, not gender role restriction, is the defining factor.

In addition to the intimate roles Dove portrays as directly related to gender, marriage contained financial responsibilities also linked to gender expectations. Here again, Thomas' role as of head of the household placed him in a dominant position, designating him as the financial provider for the family. Nowhere is the importance of male economic provision more clearly borne out than in the poems describing Thomas and Beulah's early relationship. Before winning Beulah as a bride, Thomas had to demonstrate his financial stability to both his prospective mate and her father. . . .

While Thomas' role of economic dominance may at times be gratifying, it also carries responsibilities that can be frustrating and debilitating. With gender roles tied to financial stability, Thomas' masculinity is at the mercy of his employer and the economy. Dove's depiction of lean economic times, such as the Great Depression, bears out the relationship between Thomas' masculine self-perception and his ability to provide for his family. Thomas' frustration during long periods of unemployment or dependence on unsatisfactory jobs forces him to question his family commitment. Here again, the symbol of the mandolin reinforces Dove's point. Just as with his frustrated sexuality, economic hardship pins Thomas' mandolin to the wall, only this time the luxurious silk scarf, symbol of Thomas' lost financial stability, hangs in faded . . . rivulets around the instrument. . . .

Although Dove emphasizes Thomas and Beulah's individuality when exploring economic and sexual roles, she never allows the reader to forget that together their experiences tell a single story that is neither masculine nor feminine. Throughout the frustration of separate gender statuses, Thomas and Beulah maintain a nurturing relationship, supporting each other in difficult times and deeply grieving when death causes a final separation. Even Thomas' forceful masculinity cannot hide the emotion that he feels for Beulah as he steals slivers of watermelon to satisfy her cravings during pregnancy, and he feels his heart slowly opening upon receiving consent to marry. . . .

Thomas and Beulah did not devise the gender roles they played; they inherited them. Under such preestablished constraints they had no choice but to struggle toward a unified perspective of the world, constructed from two convention-laden, ready-made gender perspectives. Dove's narrative is, consequently, not the story of angry, frustrated, and bitter individuals, but rather, quite simply, the story of average black Americans struggling under the weight of what society tells them to be. In the end, the couple's loving relationship testifies that Thomas and Beulah were good at unifying the separate selves which society had prescribed for them, even though, as Beulah acknowledges, [they would] never [have] believed it.

Emily Walker Cook. *CLA Journal*. 38 (March, 1995), pp. 322–30

Visiting a Greek island, Rita Dove remarks that everything there "is either old / or scathingly young with whippet thighs clamped over a souped-up Vespa." That moment is characteristic, both in its fascination with travel and history and in its polarity of the old and the new. For at least a decade Dove has been extending the boundaries of her art, while also endeavoring to recover the past, be it that of European literary tradition or African-American history and culture. In *Thomas and Beulah* (1986) Dove invented an experimental form—a sequential diptych comprised of narratives and monologues—as a vehicle for reconstructing her family history. Now, in her two most recent books [*Mother Love* and *The Darker Face of the Earth*], she has created fresh configurations of the traditional and the experimental, the historical and the contemporary. In *Mother Love*, a collection consisting mainly of modified sonnets, Dove enlists the myth of Persephone to explore the dynamics of mother-daughter relationships. . . .

In her preface to *Mother Love*, Dove defines the sonnet as "a *heile Welt*, an intact world where everything is in sync, from the stars down to the tiniest mite on a blade of grass." Entertaining the argument that "any variation from the strictly Petrarchan or Shakespearean forms represents a world gone awry," Dove suggests that form can be a "talisman against disintegration," and that the strict form of the sonnet, "violated" by modem practice, suits the story of Demeter and Persephone, "a tale of a violated world." In theory, at least, the sonnet's structure creates a "beautiful bubble," a defense against the "vicissitudes of fortune."

In practice, Dove's way with the sonnet is anything but strict. Although she usually adheres to the rules, she interprets them very liberally. Line-lengths vary widely. Rhymes are distant and approximate. Strong enjambment is frequent, and caesurae appear in unconventional places, most often after the first metrical foot:

> She is gone again and I will not bear it,
> I will drag my grief through a winter
> of my own making and refuse
> any meadow that recycles itself into hope.
> "Demeter Waiting"

Here the rhymes (winter/into; bear/meteor) are nearly inaudible, and the meter is so irregular as to sacrifice the play of the speaking voice against the metrical beat. What is gained is a sense of freedom and a tenor of colloquial vigor. What is lost is the music of traditional form—the balance of the expected and the unexpected, the consonant and the dissonant. The sonnet becomes a little speech rather than a little song.

Dove's rendering of the Persephone story is likewise problematical, though also respectful of the myth's original context. Unlike many postwar poets, Dove does not merely appropriate the myth for personal use. In her preface she acknowledges its impersonal context and its significance as a metaphor for fertility and regeneration. At the same time, she offers an interpretation of the myth as a representation of a ''modern dilemma,'' namely that of the daughter ''who must go her own way into womanhood,'' shedding maternal protection. In the central poems of the collection, the daughter is an aspiring artist, a venturesome American who exchanges the safety of her home for the louche attractions of the Parisian demimonde. . . .

To view this anxious ingenue as Persephone, and to recognize that the narcissi signal her impending fall, is to enhance the poem with interesting resonances. But for this reader the pleasures of the text lie less in those resonances than in the poem's momentum, its suspenseful syntax, its deft deployment of assonance and rhyme, its musicality and expressive concision. If not an encumbrance, the myth seems somewhat superfluous.

The same might be said of *Mother Love* as a whole, where the mythological framework, however suggestive, matters less than what Louis MacNeice called the brushstrokes—the local felicities that strike the eye and please the ear. ''I am the footfall that hovers,'' says Dove in ''Missing.'' ''[W]e've earned the navels sunk in grief,'' says the speaker in ''Used,'' referring to those who have given birth. ''But it was more difficult,'' recalls the speaker of ''Lost Brilliance,'' ''each evening to descend: all that marble / flayed with the red plush of privilege / I traveled on, slow nautilus / unwinding in terrified splendor. . . . At such moments Dove's lyric gifts rightfully assume the foreground, and her ambitious program recedes into the middle distance.

In *The Darker Face of the Earth*, Dove undertakes another ambitious project, made all the more so by the archaic nature of her chosen genre. To elect to write a classical tragedy in the late twentieth century is to posit continuities between the classical tradition and the pluralistic, fragmented character of contemporary American culture. And to elect dramatic verse as one's medium is to assume that the same audience which values serious drama will also be receptive to verse spoken on stage. Those are risky assumptions, though if T. S. Eliot's argument in ''Poetry and Drama'' (1951) is sound, Dove is coming to the task from the right direction. ''It seems to me,'' writes Eliot, ''that if we are to have a poetic drama, it is more likely to come from poets learning how to write plays, than from skillful prose dramatists learning to write poetry.''

In a statement of her own, Dove speaks of her interest in the ''unfolding'' of character and fate. ''[T]here's a fascination with seeing the layers of personality stripped away to reveal, finally, the essential man (or woman).'' She also likens the Greek world view to that of slaves in the antebellum South. ''There was so little chance of changing the course of one's life if one were a slave. Rarely in our history has there been a system that fostered such a sense of futility—a futility that is analogous, in many ways, to the Greek concept of fate.''

Enabling though it is, Dove's argument is also vulnerable, insofar as it conflates the world view of Greek tragedy with that of Protestant Christianity, as practiced in the antebellum South. Nor is it entirely persuasive to liken a general sense of futility—the curse of subject peoples everywhere—with a specific belief in fate. In the play itself, what is most inveigling is not, in fact, the unfolding of the plot, which seems no more inevitable than that of *Schindler's*

*List* or *Stalag 17*, but the unfolding of character, particularly the character of Dove's tragic hero, Augustus Newcastle, who is the offspring of a slave and the lady of the manor. An amalgam of high ideals and earthy desires, Augustus believes that ''[t]rust and patience / are diseases of the soul.'' After years at sea, he finds himself a slave on the plantation where he was born. A charismatic orator, he becomes the leader of a rebellion—and an unwitting partner in incestuous relations. In the process, his hubris and blindness drop away. . . .

That a character who, by turns, resembles Oedipus and Othello should speak in verse is not implausible, and in their context Augustus's speeches are both opulent and apt:

> One fine soft night in April
> when the pear blossoms
> cast their pale faces on
> the darker face of the earth,
> my mother was sleeping in her cabin. . . .

Addressed to the pretty mistress Amalia, these lines possess what Eliot called dramatic inevitablity. Eloquent in themselves, they also support action and character.

In the play as a whole, however, it is not always so. At points, the poetic conceits seem more decorative than functional, as when a leader of the rebellion urges his followers to go to their people and ''gird them for battle / with ideas, so when the fires lick / the skies of Charleston, they will / rise up of one accord. . . .'' Elsewhere, the verse serves mainly to inform:

> One of our members has procured
> a metal mold, and is in the process of
> producing cannon balls, which are stored
> under water near the dock.

Serviceable but undistinguished, these lines might have been cast more effectively as prose. Yet, whatever the consistency of its verse, Dove's play is clearly the work of a lyric poet. Taut, compressed, and richly imagined, it moves swiftly to its end. Its cast includes a voodoo prophet named Scylla, a father named Hector, and other slaves with emblematic names (Psyche, Phebe, Diana). Recurrent images of snakes, stars, and a curse that is ''still not complete'' create a mood of dread and bind the fourteen scenes together. And with the deaths of Amalia and Augustus, the play ends abruptly, leaving the audience to construe the meaning of the events. In all of these ways, as in its vivid language, the play resembles a modern lyric poem.

Whether one also regards it as a tragedy will depend on one's definition of tragic drama. Certainly the events depicted in the play reflect a tragic flaw in American history and culture. But insofar as the definition of tragedy includes the collision of two noble ideals, the play is a less-than-perfect fit. And insofar as tragedy requires a hero whose freedom of choice and power of action surpass the ordinary, Augustus Newcastle is not entirely suited to his role. Its use of tragic conventions notwithstanding, *The Darker Face of the Earth* might better be viewed as a modern morality play, or as an existential parable, resonant with history and redolent of evil.

Ben Howard. *Poetry*. 167, 6 (March 1996), pp. 349–53

Clear-eyed and coolly unhurried, Rita Dove in her previous collections has always refused to be confined by category; her poems wander into unexpected metaphor and subject matter—which could range from the black migration to the Han Dynasty. At first glance then, *On the Bus With Rosa Parks* might seem a departure: in such publicized territory, what could she add? And here and there in this new volume, her writing becomes depressingly easy to follow: "Don't lower your eyes," Dove chides tourists confronted with poverty in "Lady Freedom Among Us," "don't think you can ever forget her." These slips into sermonizing might be the aftereffects of the author's term a few years ago as poet laureate of the United States. Fortunately, the rest of the book was written by the old, fearlessly curious Rita Dove, whose meditations on Rosa Parks and other civil rights veterans deepen a dialogue over what might be described as public history versus private. The poet's eye and voice, trained for the nearly invisible detail, rescue characters from obscurity by illuminating their ordinariness. This suits Rosa Parks—who made history by "sitting there, / waiting for the moment to take her"—as it does the family sketched in "Cameos," the sequence set before World War II that opens the book. Most winningly, Dove casts an appraising eye on her own privileges, comparing those historic bus rides with a cruise she takes on the QE2, and elsewhere, with simply the view from her front porch: "I vowed I'd get off / somewhere grand," she notes at the end of this collection. "Who am I kidding? Here I am."

Matthew Flamm. *New York Times Book Review* (April 11, 1999), p. 24

BIBLIOGRAPHY
*Ten Poems*, 1977; *The Only Dark Spot in the Sky*, 1980; *The Yellow House on the Corner*, 1980; *Mandolin*, 1983; *Museum*, 1983; *Fifth Sunday*, 1985; *Thomas and Beulah*, 1986; *The Other Side of the House*, 1988; *Grace Notes*, 1989; *Through the Ivory Gate*, 1992; *Selected Poems*, 1993; *The Darker Face of the Earth: A Verse Play in Fourteen Scenes*, 1994; *A Handful of Inwardness: The World in the Poet*, 1994; *Stepping Out: The Poet in the World*, 1994; *Mother Love: Poems*, 1995; *On the Bus with Rosa Parks*, 1999

# DUNBAR, Paul Laurence (1872–1906)
## United States

*Folks from Dixie* consists of distinct and brilliant little sketches of the various negro types of the South, most of them extremely amusing, a few of them pathetic, all of them cheerfully impersonal, as if written from the standpoint of an interested but not deeply sympathetic observer, with an eye for all picturesque accidents and an intuitive knowledge of the temperaments he has to portray. Of the imagination and profound sentiment pervading Mr. Chesnutt's writing, making itself most felt where least stress is laid upon it, there is barely a hint. . . .

Mr. Dunbar's other books of prose are novels in which the negro race plays no part. They have neither conspicuous merits nor conspicuous defects. Like Mr. Chesnutt's novels, both [*The Uncalled* and *The Love of Landry*] are free from any elaboration or complexity of plot, following a single thread of interest from the beginning to the end. Mr. Chesnutt and Mr. Dunbar have, indeed,

despite their unlikeness, what we may call a marked family resemblance in this extreme simplicity, and in a certain homeliness of metaphor relieved at times by the quaintness of phraseology characteristic of the race that gives them their great distinction among writers. We feel that much of what they have written could not have been written in just the same way by anyone less than kin to the people whose individuality they bring before us with such remarkable truth. They have added to our complex literature an element entirely new and greatly to be prized.

Elisabeth L. Cary. *The Book Buyer*. August 1901, p. 28

[Dunbar] was a child of the city, a small city, true, where Nature was not so ruthlessly crushed away from the lives of men. There were trees and flowers near home, and a never-to-be-forgotten mill-race, which swirled through all his dreams of boyhood and manhood. Like the true poet that he was, he reached out and groped for the bigness of out-of-doors, divining all that he was afterwards to see, and in his earlier verse expressing his intuitions, rather than his observations.

Love of nature was there, but the power to express this love was not. Instead, he harked back to the feeling of the race, and intuitively put their aspirations into song. Tennyson and Lowell meant much to him, because they had expressed his yearnings for the natural world, and his soul yearned toward their verse. . . . The poet loved Tennyson, he walked with him in his earlier years, he confessed his indebtedness to him in his later days; he always praised him, and defended him hotly against the accusation of too much mere academic phrasing.

In the poem "Preparation" we see more of this groping toward the light; the urban child trying to throw off the meretriciousness of city life. Say what you will, or what Mr. Howells wills, about the "feeling the Negro life esthetically, and expressing it lyrically," it was in the pure English poems that the poet expressed *himself*. He may have expressed his race in the dialect poems; they were to him the side issues of his work, the overflowing of a life apart from his dearest dreams.

Mrs. Paul Laurence Dunbar. In Mrs. Paul Laurence Dunbar, Prof. W. S. Scarborough, and Reverdy C. Ransom, *Paul Laurence Dunbar* (Philadelphia: Reverdy C. Ransom, 1914), pp. 6–7

As a man, Dunbar was kind and tender. In conversation he was brilliant and polished. His voice was his chief charm, and was a great element in his success as a reader of his own works. In his actions he was impulsive as a child, sometimes even erratic; indeed, his intimate friends almost looked upon him as a spoiled boy. He was always delicate in health. Temperamentally, he belonged to that class of poets who Taine says are vessels too weak to contain the spirit of poetry, the poets whom poetry kills, the Byrons, the Burnses, the De Mussets, the Poes.

To whom may he be compared, this boy who scribbled his early verses while he ran an elevator, whose youth was a battle against poverty, and who, in spite of almost insurmountable obstacles, rose to success? A comparison between him and Burns is not unfitting. The similarity between many phases of their lives is remarkable, and their works are not incommensurable. Burns took the strong dialect of his people and made it classic; Dunbar took the humble speech of his people and in it wrought music.

> James Weldon Johnson. Preface to James Weldon Johnson, ed., *The Book of American Negro Poetry* (New York: Harcourt, Brace, 1922), p. xxxv

Among the American writers who have been unable to judge what they could and could not do Dunbar is conspicuous. In 1898, the year of *Folks from Dixie*, he published his first novel, *The Uncalled*. It was to a certain extent autobiographical, an exposition of Dunbar's own ordeal in deciding whether he ought to enter the ministry. Since he was really writing about a personal experience, one cannot help wondering why he did not put himself into the story as a colored man. The action deals with the conflict in the mind of a white youth living in a small Ohio town who feels that he should not become a preacher but who is forced by circumstances into a seminary and then into the pulpit. There is not a single Negro character in the book.

As a story about whites written by a Negro it introduces us to the second type of fiction which the Negro of the period attempted. Such a type Dunbar should have painstakingly avoided. All of the bubbling spontaneity which he showed in his tales on blacks is replaced in *The Uncalled* by cheap conventional story-telling, with echoes of Dickens and the popular magazine, and with an English which is often downright faulty.

The book came as a great disappointment to Dunbar's admirers. Despite its weakness, it seems to have had some commercial success, and in 1900 Dunbar published a second novel in which all of the characters are whites, *The Love of Landry*. It is a story of Easterners, all treacly sentimentalists, who think that they find the sublime beauty of reality on a Colorado ranch. It was, if that is possible, even a poorer performance than *The Uncalled*.

> Vernon Loggins. *The Negro Author* (New York: Columbia University Press, 1931), pp. 316–17

Dunbar's conception of his art was based on his theory of life. He felt that he was first of all a man, then an American, and incidentally a Negro. To a world that looked upon him primarily as a Negro and wanted to hear from him simply in his capacity as a Negro, he was thus a little difficult to understand. He never regarded the dialect poems as his best work, and, as he said in the eight lines entitled "The Poet," when one tried to sing of the greatest themes in life, it was hard to have the world praise only "a jingle in a broken tongue." His position was debatable, of course, but that was the way he felt. . . .

To a later school of Negro writers, one more definitely conscious of race, Dunbar thus appears as somewhat artificial. The difference is that wrought by the World War. About the close of that conflict Marcus Garvey, by a positively radical program, made black a fashionable color. It was something not to be apologized for, but exploited. Thenceforth one heard much about "the new Negro," and for a while Harlem was a literary capital. In Dunbar's time, however, black was not fashionable. The burden still rested upon the Negro to prove that he could do what any other man could

do, and in America that meant to use the white man's technique and meet the white man's standard of excellence. It was to this task that Dunbar addressed himself. This was the test that he felt he had to satisfy, and not many will doubt that he met it admirably.

> Benjamin Brawley. *Paul Laurence Dunbar* (Chapel Hill: University of North Carolina Press, 1936), pp. 76–77

When propaganda enters into prose fiction it acquires necessarily some of the broad solidity of the prosaic medium, and this firm quality immediately puts the reader on the defensive. The reader's reaction is as of one being gulled, being shown a thing for the good of his soul. These are the things one comes to feel in too many of the stories of Dunbar. Like a leaden ghost, Purpose treads the print of "Silas Jackson," "The Ingrate," "One Man's Fortunes," and "At Shaft 11." Not only is the technique of the stories faulty, but plausible, character-derived motivation and convincing situation are lacking. The story that brushes aside esthetic ends must be faultless in construction and style in order to succeed. It must captivate by sheer perfection of form. Dunbar was not aware of this. He brought to this difficult art only a zest in the message of his serious tales, and an instinctive sense of the humor inherent in certain situations in his burlesque stories. The latter are saved from failure; but a story representative of the former, "The Strength of Gideon," with its powerful theme and well-defined plot, boils off in the end to a watery pottage.

The gem of Dunbar's stories is "Trustfulness of Polly." In it Dunbar did not seek to express the Negro, but to re-create him. It was written in 1899, five years before his writing career ended, but he never again found such perfect focus of characterization, motivation, theme, plot, and style. It is a story of the low-life school, a type that was not to become popular until twenty years after Dunbar's death. It deals with that insidious evil (then as now) in the life of the New York Negro, the policy game. "The Trustfulness of Polly" is the first story of Negro low-life in New York written by a Negro. Not only is it significant as the forerunner of the long list of low-life stories from [Claude McKay's] *Home to Harlem* to [George Washington Lee's] *Beale Street*, but it presaged the courageous, if misled, objectivity with which the post-war Negro artist was to see the life of his people.

> J. Saunders Redding. *To Make a Poet Black* (Chapel Hill: University of North Carolina Press, 1939), pp. 60–61

It appeared to me [when I first read *Majors and Minors*], and it appears to me now, that there is a precious difference of temperament between the races which it would be a great pity ever to lose, and that this is best preserved and most charmingly suggested by Mr. Dunbar in those pieces of his where he studies the moods and traits of his race in its own accent of our English. We call such pieces dialect pieces for want of some closer phrase, but they are really not dialect so much as delightful personal attempts and failures for the written and spoken language. In nothing is his essentially refined and delicate art so well shown as in these pieces, which, as I ventured to say, described the range between appetite and emotion, with certain lifts far beyond and above it, which is the range of the race. He reveals in these a finely ironical perception of the negro's limitations, with a tenderness for them which I think so very rare as to be almost quite new. I should say, perhaps, that it was this humorous quality which Mr. Dunbar had added to our literature, and it would be this which would most distinguish him, now and hereafter. [1896]

W. D. Howells. Introduction to *The Complete Poems of Paul Laurence Dunbar* (New York: Dodd, Mead, 1948), pp. ix-x

Catering to the demands of publishers and readers of his time, Dunbar generally evaded themes such as those presented in Chesnutt's novels and usually specialized either in the treatment of white American life or in the perpetuation of the plantation tradition. Three of his novels—*The Uncalled, The Love of Landry*, and *The Fanatics*—deal almost entirely with white characters; and the fourth, *The Sport of the Gods*, though a promising naturalistic study, illustrates the plantation-school concept that the Negro becomes homesick and demoralized in the urban North. . . .

Though amateurish in execution, *The Sport of the Gods* is Dunbar's worthiest effort in fiction and suggests abilities which possibly did not achieve fruition because of the author's early death. Written under the influence of naturalism, which [Vernon L.] Parrington defines as "pessimistic realism," *The Sport of the Gods* follows Émile Zola's *Nana* (1880), Stephen Crane's *Maggie: A Girl of the Streets* (1893), Frank Norris' *McTeague* (1899), and other novels in which man is conceived as a powerless figure in an amoral and careless world. Showing race prejudice as an all-destructive virus, the book reveals social corruption in the South as well as in the North. In the Southern small town, interracial distrust is exposed, and the vaunted chivalry of Dixie gentlemen is debunked through the characterization of Francis and Maurice Oakley. In the New York setting, inexperienced Negro youth are pictured in a treacherous environment which deterministically produces degeneration and disaster. By treating the challenging and comparatively unworked Harlem low-life scene, Dunbar analyzed a background that was later to intrigue Claude McKay, Carl Van Vechten, and other writers of the 1920s.

Hugh Gloster. *Negro Voices in American Fiction* (Chapel Hill: University of North Carolina Press, 1948), pp. 46, 50–51

Dunbar is probably still the best-known Negro poet among Negroes. For many years he was a race hero in the company of Joe Louis and Booker T. Washington, and his disfavor (like theirs) among the intelligentsia may take a while to spread to the lower orders. He was a successful magazine poet of the turn of the century (he died at thirty-four), sponsored by William Dean Howells; a master sentimentalist who wrung the heart of a simpler America. Today, reading his collected poems—three hundred pages of Golden Book moralism, purple poesy, and dialect pastorals in the James Whitcomb Riley vein, of hometown nostalgia and barbershop wisdom ("Keep a-Pluggin' Away") is like eating jars of peanut butter. He was lionized for his "plantation nigger" narratives ("When de Co'n Pone's Hot," "When Malindy Sings"), which even uncritical Negroes might find hard to take today. Only two or three poems—"We Wear the Mask," "Sympathy"—appear to hide genuine, adult, and still honorable emotions. . . .

Dunbar wrote a number of his harmless "plantation nigger" folk stories in a manner less aggressively sentimental than that of his poems, stories told half in dialect, half in an orotund, authorial-declamatory voice. Two or three make what is, for Dunbar, strong anti-slavery or anti-lynching protests; but they are outbalanced by a far greater number of reactionary pieces or worse, depicting plantation darkies as jolly children all, whose best friend—even after Emancipation—was always Ol' White Massa.

David Littlejohn. *Black on White* (New York: Grossman, 1966), pp. 23–25

During the years between the Civil War and World War I, Negro poetry produced no personality that can be set beside Dunbar's. His inadequacies may be deplored, yet one must admit that none of his contemporaries had the same delicate sensibility, the variety of inspiration, or the extraordinary feeling for rhythm and musicality that served him equally well in his English verses and in his dialect poetry. Nor did anyone else suffer as he did from the sense of his own weaknesses. In short, throughout this long period he remained the only genuine lyric poet. . . .

Dunbar's death marked the end of an era. Although he survived by a few years the century of his birth, the attitude he embodied to the very end was that of a bygone age. It was the ambivalent attitude of the Negro during Reconstruction—uncertain of himself, subservient, and still a quasi-prisoner within the mentality that two hundred and fifty years of slavery had transformed into second nature. In addition to that, the flaccid, falsely distinguished poetry of the late nineteenth century, which constitutes so large a part of Dunbar's work, was also headed for extinction as a result of the renewal which, beginning in 1912, would so significantly alter the appearance of American poetry. Thus the first prominent poet of the black race was at the same time the last representative of a world doomed to disappear. [1963]

Jean Wagner. *Black Poets of the United States* (Urbana: University of Illinois Press, 1973), pp. 127, 149

A month or two ago, while in Dayton, O., I attended a meeting of the Western authors. About half way down the informal programme the presiding officer announced the reading of a poem by Paul Dunbar. Just the name for a poet, thought I. Great was the surprise of the audience to see stepping lightly down the aisle between the rows of fluttering fans and the assembled beauty and wit of Dayton, a slender Negro lad, as black as the core of Cheops's pyramid. He ascended the rostrum with the coolness and dignity of a cultured entertainer and delivered a poem in a tone "as musical as is Apollo's lute." He was applauded to the echo between the stanzas, and heartily encored at the conclusion. He then disappeared from the hall as suddenly as he had entered it, and many were the whispered conjectures as to the personality of the man, and the originality of his verses, none believing it possible that one of his age and color could produce a thing of such evident merit.

After repeated inquiries I succeeded in locating the rising laureate of the colored race, and called upon him. He was an elevator boy in one of the down-town business blocks. I found him seated in a chair on the lower landing, hastily glancing at the July *Century*, and jotting down notes on a handy pencil tablet. . . .

Poor Dunbar! He deserves a better fate. Dayton, the terminus of the old underground railway, should be proud of him, and yet, with all his natural brilliancy and capability for better things, he is chained like a galley slave to the ropes of a dingy elevator at starvation wages. [Summer, 1892]

James Newton Matthews. Quoted in Jay Martin, ed., *A Singer in the Dawn: Reinterpretations of Paul Laurence Dunbar* (New York: Dodd, Mead, 1975), pp. 14–15

Paul Laurence Dunbar is a natural resource of our people. He, like all our old prophets and preachers, has been preserved by our little people. Those who could command words and images, those whose pens thundered across the pages, those whose voices boomed from lecterns, those who set policy for our great publications then, as now, were quite silent. Not ever quite knowing what to do about one of America's most famous poets, when they spoke his name it was generally to condemn his dialect poetry—as if black people aren't supposed to laugh, or more as if Dunbar's poems were not the best examples of our plantation speech. One gets recitation after explanation of Dunbar's poetry, his love of his ''white poems,'' his hatred of his need to please the white critics, but something rings quite hollow to me. I refuse to believe Paul Dunbar was ashamed of ''Little Brown Baby.'' The poem has brought too much happiness to me. I categorically reject a standard that says ''A Negro Love Song'' should not make me feel warm inside. . . .

Dunbar preserved a part of our history. And accurately. It would be as foolish to say all blacks struggled against slavery as it would to say all acquiesced to it. The truth lies somewhere in the blending.

Perhaps Dunbar's greatest triumph is that he has survived all those who would use his gift for their own dead-end purposes.

Nikki Giovanni. Afterword to Jay Martin, ed., *A Singer in the Dawn: Reinterpretations of Paul Laurence Dunbar* (New York: Dodd, Mead, 1975), pp. 243–44

BIBLIOGRAPHY

''*Keep a-Pluggin' Away*,'' 1893; *Oak and Ivy*, 1893; *Majors and Minors*, 1895; ''A Negro Love Song,'' 1895; ''Preparation,'' 1895; ''When de Co'n Pone's Hot,'' 1895; ''When Malindy Sings,'' 1895; *Lyrics of Lowly Life*, 1896; *Folks from Dixie*, 1898; *The Uncalled*, 1898; *Lyrics of the Hearthside*, 1899; *Poems of Cabin and Field*, 1899; ''The Strength of Gideon,'' 1899; ''Sympathy,'' 1899; *The Love of Landry*, 1900; ''One Man's Fortunes,'' 1900; *Candle-lightin' Time*, 1901; *The Fanatics*, 1901; ''The Poet,'' 1902; *The Sport of the Gods*, 1902; *In Old Plantation Days*, 1903; *Lyrics of Love and Laughter*, 1903; *When Malindy Sings*, 1903; *The Heart of the Happy Hollow*, 1904; *Li'l Gal*, 1904; *Chris'mus Is a Comin', and Other Poems*, 1905; *Howdy, Howdy, Howdy*, 1905; *Lyrics of Sunshine and Shadow*, 1905; *A Plantation Portrait*, 1905; *Joggin' Erlong*, 1906; *The Complete Poems of Paul Laurence Dunbar*, 1913; *Speakin' o' Christmas, and Other Christmas and Special Poems*, 1914; *The Best Stories of Paul Laurence Dunbar*, 1938; *Little Brown Baby: Poems for Young People*, 1940; *The Letters of Paul and Alice Dunbar: A Private History*, 1974; *The Paul Laurence Dunbar Reader*, 1975; *I Greet the Dawn: Poems*, 1978; *The Collected Poetry of Paul Laurence Dunbar*, 1993; *Selected Poems*, 1997

# E

## EDGELL, Zee (1941– )
### Belize

[Zee Edgell's novel] *Beka Lamb* is a competently written work which in no way reflects the magical realism of its Latin American neighbors. If anything, it is a solid specimen of the traditional novel, employing flashback to recount the sad ending of a likable seventeen-year-old who finds herself pregnant out of wedlock. The villain of the piece is a rather self-satisfied young member of Belize's Hispanic population; the novel's weight is thrown heavily in favor of the black Creoles. Beka's own triumph over her tendency to lie—the declared main action of the novel—does not engage the reader to the same degree as does Toycie's story.

The story of Toycie's fall from virtue is really a frame from which to hang a considerable amount of information about the everyday life of Belize's newly emergent urban middle class, a population still too close to poverty to have developed a set of bourgeois assumptions. Despite Edgell's understandable desire to explain contemporary Belizean events, despite the highly tradition-al form of the novel, and despite the material of yet another West Indian novel of childhood, *Beka Lamb* could signal a significant change of pace in the West Indian novel because it bypasses what have become the pieties of the times. Beka's engrossment in her milieu calls to mind the novels of Michael Anthony, novels singularly devoid of a sense of estrangement. Anthony's characters are totally integrated West Indians, so absorbed in life's little moments that they bring to West Indian fiction a quality of sweetness rare in the literature of commitment. While Edgell's conservative style may somehow be a function of Belize's position outside the mainstream of West Indian affairs, she cannot be accused of naivete as she has lived in Jamaica, Britain, Nigeria, Afghanistan, Bangladesh, and the United States.

> Elaine Campbell. *Journal of Commonwealth Literature.* 22, 1 (1987), pp. 142–43

Set within the framework of a colonial society, a society aspiring to independence, *Beka Lamb* examines the dialectical relationship between that society and the individual. The personal stories of the girls Beka and Toycie are used as ways of examining the colonial society. The relationship between Toycie and Emilio in particular suggests the exploitative colonial one. And Beka's journey to self-assurance compares with her country's move to independence. In addition, the traditional ways are shown in conflict with the values promoted by the Church and educational institutions. The result is dramatic change whose impact, emphasized by the constant refer-ences to "befo' time" and "tings bruk down," is seen in the disintegrating society, its former wholeness and stability eroded by the colonial experience. But disintegration is only part of the life cycle. Edgell's heroine learns this truth, and by implication inde-pendence is therefore a real possibility for her country. . . .

Central to this novel is the close relationship between Beka and Toycie, which not only points up the support that women provide for each other but also reveals the experiences of the adolescent female. Edgell presents both Beka and Toycie as adolescents in the quest for identity. Through them she explores different facets of female adolescent experience—their awakening sexuality, rela-tionships, fantasies, and fears. The friendship between Toycie and Beka defines and charts both girls' growth into and beyond their specifically adolescent crises. Toycie also functions as Beka's alter ego. She lives out things that remain mere possibilities for Beka, showing quite clearly how Beka, like so many things in her country, "could bruk down." Toycie and Beka also seem initially to represent a body-mind dichotomy, but Beka is shown as resolv-ing this split as she moves toward unity. . . .

In *Beka Lamb*, Edgell portrays the importance of adolescent girls' private relationships. And while she admits to the tension that society creates she demonstrates that finally it is the girls' person-alities and their means of resolving conflicts that determine their growth. The mother-daughter relationship in its various forms also provides central support for the adolescent. There is a direct relation between its presence and the adolescent's definition of self. In addition, Edgell examines stereotypical female means of coping—emotional and passive. Such ways are shown as negative: heroines who practice them fail to attain wholeness. In contrast, there are strong and independent women who through an active creativity impose their will on the world. Edgell has affirmed that emotionality and passivity are not the only feminine ways of coping.

*Beka Lamb* offers us a more complex picture of the female adolescent. Through Toycie and Beka, Edgell examines the con-flicts she faces with her awakening sexuality and society's increas-ing expectations. Such expectations are often ambiguous. They acknowledge her visible growth and supposed maturity but not her sexuality. Beka and Toycie are thus most vulnerable in that area. Miss Flo makes oblique references to Beka's sexuality and Miss Ivy's confession helps her. But generally, the adult women remain silent about their daughters' sexuality. And while Edgell does not claim that biology controls a girl's perception of self and the choices she makes (that is, that biology is destiny), she does take into account the pressure society exerts on a woman to conform to its image of femininity, especially during adolescence. Like other women, Beka must confront and surmount these pressures to achieve selfhood.

> Lorna Down. *Ariel.* 18, 4 (October 1987), pp. 39–40, 50

Toycie in Zee Edgell's *Beka Lamb* is . . . driven to madness. Toycie, a vibrant, brilliant, ambitious seventeen-year-old is Beka Lamb's best friend. Through Beka's recollection we learn of the childhood pastimes and ambitions of Toycie, a student at St. Cecelia Catholic Academy—a sophisticated high school for girls. From Beka's grandmother, Ivy, we learn that the academy previ-ously accepted only girls from the higher social strata of Belize; thus it is a singular achievement for Creole girls like Beka and Toycie to attend this bastion of educational grandeur controlled by the expatriate Sisters of Charity. In Caribbean life, earning a secondary school certificate is an honor, and earning one from a prestigious secondary school is an immediate passport to a better standard of living. For this reason, relatives, friends, and neighbors take exceptional pride in the Creole girls who attend the academy. In fact, they see this gesture as a step toward the end of the history of discrimination that is associated with the school. Toycie had seen many girls terminate their education at the elementary level; hence, her primary obsession is to graduate from high school and repay her aunt who had reared her since she was three years old. Her other obsession is to promenade along Fort George, admiring the beautiful homes of the wealthy. Toycie has another reason for wanting to stroll by Fort George: her boyfriend, Emilio Villanueva, who attends St. Anthony Jesuit College, works at [a] Fort George hotel. Emilio is a pania; that is, he has a mixture of Maya Indian blood and Spanish blood. Beka dislikes their liaison and warns Toycie about being ''involved'' with a pania, since panias scarcely ever marry Creoles, but Toycie continues the friendship believing that Emilio loves her and will marry her as he claims. . . . [Regardless] of Beka's disapproval, she continues to be Toycie's steadfast confidante, not once reporting the secret meetings between Toycie and Emilio, especially the nocturnal ones at the cay during the summer vacation.

When Toycie returns to school after the summer vacation, she has lost the gaiety and enthusiasm that seniors display at the beginning of their final year. She seems despondent and distracted. Often she ''stares into space in a trance as if waiting for some signal that would restore her to normalcy.'' She tries to compose herself, but when unable to stifle a vomit while at worship, she is sent home by Sister Virgil.

Later Toycie confides in Beka but refuses to tell her aunt, Miss Eila, that she is pregnant. Yet Miss Eila seems to have surmised the problem for she matter-of-factly remarks about Toycie's illness. . . . Having no one else to turn to, Toycie decides to inform Emilio, thinking that he would marry her. . . . Emilio does not marry Toycie; in fact, he claims that he wouldn't and he couldn't because he could not be sure that after marriage she would be faithful to him—although he had no reason for doubting her fidelity. The pregnant Toycie was expelled from school despite pleas for another chance from her aunt and Beka's father. . . .

Toycie's expulsion triggers the second phase of her decline. The girl who was ''so brave, so encouraging to others, whose eyes were usually lively with anticipation of tomorrow's promise'' now looks at her friend with dull resignation, too nauseated, too disoriented to recognize or appreciate anyone's concern or sympathy. The girl who formerly spent hours to ''titivate'' before going on her stroll now sits disconsolately with her hair in disarray. Her blazing spirit now gives way to rocking back and forth in her aunt's chair. . . .

Everyone is saddened by Toycie's condition and departure [to the country]. The effect on Beka is twofold: she is inspired to work harder and she no longer depends on her family's praise as her motivation. Beka wages a personal one-girl vendetta for her friend and when the news arrives that Toycie, after wandering off in a storm, is killed, Beka realizes that now more than ever, she must excel not only for herself, but also for Toycie.

> Enid Bogle. *Zora Neale Hurston Forum.* 4, 1 (Fall 1989), pp. 11–13

[In *Beka Lamb*], published shortly after Belize's independence, the devalorization of colonial modernism and its authority is achieved through an appeal to figures and tropes of difference and ambivalence. As they are represented in language and ideology, such figures express the kind of diversity which according to [Edouard]

Glissant allows Caribbean peoples to repossess their historical spaces. In Glissant's words, ''Diversity, which is neither chaos nor sterility, means the human spirit's striving for a cross-cultural relationship, without universalist transcendence. Diversity needs the presence of peoples, no longer as objects to be swallowed up, but with the intention of creating a new relationship. Sameness requires fixed Being, Diversity establishes becoming.'' The colonial power fixes the colonized as objects of labor and/or appendages of the colonizing culture. Rewriting the Caribbean national allegory thus demands a narrative strategy that confronts the objects and historical forces blocking the desire for that diversity that establishes becoming. As a strategy of individual and national identity, ambivalence disperses the fixed sites of colonial cultural production; in semiotic terms, as Julia Kristeva says, it ''implies the insertion of history (society) into a text and of this text into history.''. . .

[A] novel that begins with its ending often promotes a moment of interpretation which is definite and conclusive; the reader is supposed to follow the incidents related in the flashback from the vantage point and certain knowledge denoted by narrative closure. But this is not the case in *Beka Lamb* we are not certain that Beka, by winning the coveted essay contest, has initiated the decisive transformation of moral character and social class which her family and community expect. On the contrary, Beka's ostensible transformation is presented by the narrator as if it were merely the subjective (and possibly erroneous) assumption of her family—''It seemed to her family . . .''—a mode of representation clearly intended to create doubts about the given significance of the essay contest and the colonial economy of meaning with which it is associated.

The very notion of a radical shift in Beka's character and position in the community is further undermined by the problematic expression of temporality in the novel. We are told, on one hand, that ''before time'' (that is, in the past), Beka had no hope of winning the essay contest because ''the prizes would go to bakras [whites], panias [mestizos], or expatriates.'' A new consciousness is hence dawning on Belize, and the Creole majority is now being recognized as a powerful force. On the other hand, however, this ''new'' consciousness cannot be apprehended except in relation to the past. In fact, as we read the novel and retrace Beka's struggle to establish her identity within the social order of colonialism (represented by the school) and the as yet unrealized dream of national culture (expressed by her grandmother and other nationalists), we begin to realize that the essay contest is loaded with ironic implications. Initially represented as the sign of historical transition—from past to present, Creole to bakra, colony to nation—the essay instead draws our attention to the difficulties of forging new identities and expropriating colonial modernism and its discourse. The essay marks the gap between an unrealized identity and the realities of colonial domination and repression; it becomes a synecdoche of what is referred to euphemistically as ''these hard times.''. . .

[If] writing after colonialism is posited as a means of mastering the linguistic codes of colonial modernism, it is because the alternative to writing, as Edgell suggests in *Beka Lamb*, is madness or social death. Indeed, in this novel, both Beka and her friend Toycie provide contrasting forms of dealing with displacement: Toycie engages life at its most fundamental and spontaneous level—that of eros and sexuality—and thus triggers the process that leads to the mental institution and her eventual death; Beka strives to master writing, leading to the award that restores her self-esteem. But mastery of writing is not, of course, presented as a simple and singular process of liberation; on the contrary, it is cast as the result of a painful reflection on how the self (and its cultural community) are constituted in, and constitute, language. For even where the facts have been collected, there is still the problem of organizing them into a coherent narrative; it is only when all the disparate parts of the essay have been organized that the self has mastered the appropriated forms of representation. Thus the essay Beka writes is an allegory of her own struggle to rewrite herself in a world dominated by often hostile signifiers. Ironically, once she has won the essay contest she has moved closer to the colonial orb, and hence aggravated her self-alienation in the process that was supposed to pull her out of the prisonhouse of colonialism.

> Simon Gikandi. *Writing in Limbo: Modernism and Caribbean Literature* (Ithaca, New York: Cornell University Press, 1992), pp. 218–20, 230

San Joaquin is a small mestizo community seventy-two miles from Belize City where residents believe in spirits, ghosts, Catholicism, evangelism, and the sanctity of the home. In this community, lives a powerful landowning family whose son takes the daughter of a descendant of a poor Indian family as a common-law wife. After three children and years of abuse in one form or another, the wife kills the husband and faces perilous consequences. It is into this milieu that Zee Edgell lures her reader with her fourth novel, *The Festival of San Joaquin*.

Told in five parts, Edgell's efforts are to be lauded for their sheer force and imaginative quality. The story is at once simple and deceptively complex. Luz Marina Figueroa, the central character, is released from prison at the start of the story, having served fifteen months for the murder of her husband. In an act of sheer will, she decides to return to San Joaquin, where her three children are being raised by the mother of her deceased husband, the powerful Dona Catalina Casal. It is Luz Marina's hope to make herself worthy of regaining her children while finding security in the proximity of their presence. This story shows the possibility of womanhood, of ways of being in the world as mother, daughter, and wife, and its commentary is haunting.

Told from the first-person point of view, that of Luz Marina, the novel is something of a departure from Edgell's first two works. Here the plight of the uneducated mestizo woman is central to the plot. The story is told in sober and uncertain voice and manages throughout to capture both the interest and the imagination of the reader. The psychological and the sociological significance of the act committed is deftly explored. According to Luz Marina, ''I never wanted to raise my hand against Salvador Joaquin. I never wanted to lose my children, or to stand exposed like this to the public gaze. Having to do these things killed something inside me, and now I am someone I don't want to be.'' In effect, Luz Marina fights back in a community where women are expected to endure passively the whims of their men, and the result is a woman as disoriented as the community to which she returns. As her mother explains, ''Here in San Joaquin we are always to blame . . . whether we do or we don't. It must be our fate, a part of the good and the bad of our lives as daughters and mothers.''

Of interest too is the use and merging of religious thoughts. San Joaquin is the patron saint of the community, and the Festival of San Joaquin ''is a prayerful week of solemn processions, church services, candles and incense.'' Additionally, the same residents who observe the festival also believe in life after death in a world of spirits, the H'men who knows the prayers and medicines that would keep them safe, and an evangelical church which accepts sinners ''into the fold.'' Mama Sofia embraces it all in her one statement ''It's the same God,'' in her avid belief in prayer, and in her fidelity to the idea that ''life is large.''

As with Edgell's other works on Belize, *The Festival of San Joaquin* considers the political realities of the time—in the land-grabbing deals executed to sell to foreign investors for sizable profits, and in the personal dramas of the residents of San Joaquin (the sexual corruption of Salvador as well as the maiming of Luz's father during the festival). The multiethnic society that is Belize is unobtrusively accounted for in the presence of the Creole attorney, the Mexican fortune hunter, and the Indian descendants. In short, the work has enough intrigue, twists, and depth to qualify it as a fine achievement.

> Adele S. Newson. *World Literature Today*. 72, 1 (Winter 1998), p 184

BIBLIOGRAPHY
*Beka Lamb*, 1982; *In Times Like These*, 1991; *The Festival of San Joaquin*

# EKWENSI, Cyprian (1921–)
## Nigeria

The hero of *People of the City* is Amusa Sango, crime reporter for the *West African Sensation* by day and dance-band leader by night. He has only recently arrived in the big city (Lagos, I imagine) and finds the mixture of new experiences a bit too rich and indigestible. So do most of the younger generation, among them Miss Dupeh Martins, aged sixteen, who is content to ''hang about the city hotels and ice-cream bars with not a penny in her handbag, rather than marry a farmer with a thousand pounds a year.'' She, and her boy friends in their 25s. ties, and the petty racketeers who peddle penicillin injections, seem almost indistinguishable from European or American delinquents, but primitive Bush influences, though less strong than you might have expected, are plainly felt.

There is not much story but plenty of action. Sango witnesses a mining riot and a *crime passionnel*, has some love-affairs, and leaves for the Gold Coast (reputed land of freedom and enterprise) with a lost girl named Beatrice. The picture may be incomplete but you feel it is true so far as it goes. Mr. Ekwensi writes with a curiously impressive artlessness. Some of his dialogue is excellent.

> Maurice Richardson. *New Statesman and Nation*. November 27, 1954, p. 718

[*People of the City*] is a simple tale, and yet a genuine one, for . . . Ekwensi is a journalist, and he notices and records accurately and honestly, the result being that this novel probably portrays Lagos life more accurately than any other piece of serious writing in Nigeria. It is a sympathic portrayal, and one that captures the charm, humor and pathos that is at the heart of this section of Lagos society. Therefore, while Ekwensi does not create he does record. But his language is journalese, and the influence of America is found equally in his vocabulary and his female characters. Nevertheless even here he is probably reflecting the pseudo-American behaviour of the Lagos younger set today, striving to be part of the modern world with all its relaxations and moral sophistications, and breaking away from any suggestion of association with the strict rules of tribal behaviour.

*Jagua Nana*, Ekwensi's second major novel, is an amusing and well-written story about a Lagos prostitute, who, fearing her advancing years (though confident of her charm and beauty), tries to marry a man "on the way up." Her great desire is respectability, which she interprets to mean "class." Her pursuit of the young school-teacher, Freddy, and eventual disillusionment form the basis of the novel. Again Ekwensi's journalistic outlook has given this book an authenticity that is appealing and there is also a developing sympathy for the simpler and less fortunate members of society. As a satire of certain aspects of Lagos life, political campaigns, the secret habits of "big men," life in crowded tenements, and even the activities of the British Council, *Jagua Nana* has considerable merit, though it tends towards sentimentality in the closing stages.

> Martin Banham. *Review of English Literature.* April 1962, pp. 91–92

Those who know Ekwensi's *When Love Whispers* and the reasons for its popularity when it appeared several years ago will not be surprised at either *People of the City* or *Jagua Nana*. Ekwensi began his writing career as a pamphleteer. Writing, it is true, was to him then, as now, a way of expressing himself. But he wrote to a formula (it would be interesting to know how he inherited it) for a public that could neither endure the full-length novel nor appreciate the taut and delicate balance of the short story. Because he was the greater artist than the other pamphleteers of the time, and also because perhaps he sought recognition of a greater order than he could have realised from these publications, Ekwensi turned away from pamphleteering, as such, to write the first modern Nigerian novel.

Even so, the background out of which Ekwensi's *People of the City* emerged is not difficult to trace. The episodic nature of the plot, its lack of organic development, its very "innocence" can be traced to the formula of the pamphlet. The story itself may be engaging, but the incidents, as they pile up, appear to have no further motivation than the good fortune that some principal characters are involved. Hence, too, though several episodes are powerfully narrated, the total performance is somewhere short of being impressive. This failure some have seen as a "masterly blend of ingenuousness and sophistication"! Of course it is no such thing. The fact is that Ekwensi has not grown clear of the world of the newspapers and of pamphleteering. . . .

The peculiar favour which *People of the City* received was in no small measure connected with the fact that Ekwensi was tackling rather seriously the problem of the African city. Indeed the image of Ekwensi now current is that of the sophisticated and blunt man of the 20th century, not of the folklorist and the primitivist. I am therefore inclined to see the publication of *Burning Grass* as an important event, and in a way, a happy one. It represents, in germ, an awareness (I hope) on the part of Ekwensi that fiction is not always the story of prostitutes and bandleaders.

> M. J. C. Echeruo. *Nigeria Magazine.* December 1962, pp. 63, 65

Ekwensi's *People of the City* is a novel of urban manners in what one might call the analytic, as opposed to the synthetic, sense. Like Balzac or Dickens, Ekwensi is intrigued by the relentless potential honesty of "the facts." But he does not at the same time weave a coherent veil of illusion, he does not organize the appearances into a coherent expression of current social values beneath which the realities starkly lie. *People of the City*, in its form, is a novel of bad manners, a rogue's tale, really, despite its superimposed plot which is designed to show to a susceptible popular audience the moral evolution of the hero, "exemplary" in the Onitsha market sense. . . .

*People of the City* gives a tantalizing sense of the extraordinary possibilities of hybrid city life in West Africa as material for fabrication and scrutiny in the novel. Those two basic and complementary drives, the hectic pursuit of pleasure and the equally hectic flight from poverty and fear, which lie right at the social foundations of all modern city life, are here and there disclosed and in all of the complexity of their new-old African setting. But Ekwensi cannot sustain and develop these insights, and it is too bad that, so far, his first is also his most exciting book.

> Judith Illsley Gleason. *This Africa* (Evanston: Northwestern University Press, 1965), pp. 126, 130

Ekwensi's writing may be described as superior yellow journalism. It was no less than this twenty years ago and is no more than this today. Ekwensi has always had an eye for the lurid, an ear for the strident, a taste for the spicy, and a stomach for everything. As a consequence, his novels have been racy, action-packed melodramas, full of sound and fury but empty of substance and significance. His latest novel, *Iska*, is no exception.

*Iska* records the ups and downs of a beautiful Ibo girl, Filia Enu, who secretly marries a Hausa civil servant in Kaduna, capital of Northern Nigeria. When he is killed in an Ibo-Hausa barroom brawl, she moves to Lagos, capital of Western Nigeria, and begins to associate with prostitutes, politicians, and pot-smoking neer-do-wells. . . .

Filia Enu is a Nigerian Moll Flanders but Ekwensi, alas, is not a Nigerian Defoe. He lacks not only the genius which enabled Defoe to build a lasting monument out of the rubble of his heroine's life, but also the art and craft which a novelist needs to cement such fragments into a coherent, harmonious structure. Filia herself cannot pose as a model of neat construction. Her fall into sin and later regeneration are entirely unconvincing because Ekwensi seems unable to decide whether to blame her or Lagos for her plight. She is allowed to waver too freely between good and bad. Above all, she lacks the flesh, blood, sweat and perfume that make Jagua Nana, the happy harlot heroine of one of Ekwensi's earlier novels, so appealing.

But even with these defects, *Iska* is not an entirely unsatisfactory reading experience. Ekwensi's writing, though flecked with clichés, always has some bounce and sparkle. *Iska* has the merit of being topical as well.

Bernth Lindfors. *Africa Today.* June 1966, p. 29

Each of Ekwensi's books forms a complete unit in itself, and they are all different; only perhaps *Jagua Nana* and *People of the City* resemble each other. Ekwensi applies his versatile mind to any type of topic. The range is from politics, as in *Beautiful Feathers*, to a book of purely anthropological interest like *Burning Grass*; and the author adopts a style appropriate to his subject. He is sometimes criticised for writing in styles that are too sophisticated for West Africa and that seem to have been adopted primarily for the foreign market. It is also said that the style and content of his books are such that they could equally well have been written by a foreigner who knew Nigeria well. This is only partly true. It is true that Ekwensi adopts a more catholic approach to writing than most West African writers. Present events seem more important to him than the obscure glories of the past. What he holds dear is literary efficiency and the ability of the creative artist to reflect the lives and aspirations of his society; and indicate the way the future may go. . . .

Cyprian Ekwensi's realism is deliberate. His aim is not to make city life look more romantic or attractive than it is, but to present it as he knows and sees it. It is no secret that his attitude has offended many in high places. Man at times lives in ignorance of himself and does not always like to be told his failings. Ekwensi deserves our applause for having the courage to open the eyes of city dwellers to the evils which they are perpetrating and to bring to their notice the possible undesirable effects of a social life which is morally lax and decadent.

Odalele Taiwo. *An Introduction to West African Literature* (London: Thomas Nelson, 1967), pp. 61, 162

The political question posed [in *Beautiful Feathers*] is this: how should an African nation-state attempt to implement the concept of continental unity? Achebe had failed to portray fully the vast political forces in motion in a nation-state; in *Beautiful Feathers* Ekwensi is no more successful in presenting the complex subject of Pan-Africanism with all its multilayered possibilities. . . .

But *Beautiful Feathers* is concerned with more than Pan-Africanism. Ekwensi emphasizes the social immorality at work in society not only by presenting many scenes of infidelity but by making the wife of a young, idealistic, and highly respected Pan-African leader, Wilson Iyari, unfaithful to him. Thus, the second problem posed in the novel is this: how is it possible that a man who is working for and stands as a symbol of African solidarity cannot achieve the same solidarity in a much smaller unit, that of his family?. . .

*Beautiful Feathers* is a slight novel where minor incidents are related in language more suited to a weightier, denser treatment of the subject of Pan-Africanism.

Wilfred Cartey. *Whispers from a Continent: The Literature of Contemporary Black Africa* (New York: Random House, 1969), pp. 193, 195

Ekwensi's limitations as a novelist are many and it is as well to mention them at the outset. He has often declared that he considers himself a writer of popular fiction, and if we define popular fiction to be that which pleases or is read by a class of reader commonly indifferent to literature, we understand that Ekwensi directs his work to a wider audience than, say, Achebe, Clark or Soyinka, and suggests, as well, the limitations that work may possess. His novels do not possess the unique qualities which are inherent in works of literature—a formal beauty of design and execution which lead the reader on to a new awareness of the greater potentialities of self. Rather, Ekwensi's work is concerned with the external features of modern Nigerian life, especially the life in and of the city. His heroes seek for but never make profound discoveries about themselves. Perhaps this accounts for the fact that in each of the full-length novels we find the same kind of hero—almost a stereotype—who, progressively lacking energy, becomes unconvincing as a character.

His plots suffer in the same way: just as we find the same kind of hero in each of the novels, so we find him (or her) in more or less the same circumstances. Moreover, Ekwensi pays little attention to his plots and his novels are full of inconsistencies and contradictions. . . .

Yet despite these limitations—which are considerable—Ekwensi is a serious novelist whose writing reflects his serious concern with some of the most pressing problems facing modern Nigeria. Ekwensi's fiction represents, almost exclusively, an attempt to come to terms with the chaotic formlessness and persistent flux of the modern Nigerian city—that is, with Lagos.

Douglas Killam. In Bruce King, ed., *Introduction to Nigerian Literature* (London: Evans Brothers, 1971), pp. 79–80

BIBLIOGRAPHY

*Ikolo the Wrestler and Other Ibo Tales*, 1947; *When Love Whispers*, 1947; *The Leopard's Claw*, 1950; *People of the City*, 1954; *The Drummer Boy*, 1960; *The Passport of Mallam Ilia*, 1960; *Jagua Nana*, 1961; *An African Night's Entertainment*, 1962; *Burning Grass*, 1962; *Yoba Roundabout Murder*, 1962; *Beautiful Feathers*, 1963; *The Great Elephant–Bird*, 1965; *The Rainmaker and Other Short Stories*, 1965; *The Boa Suitor*, 1966; *Iska*, 1966; *Juju Rock*, 1966; *Lokotown and Other Stories*, 1966; *Trouble in Form Six*, 1966; *Coal Camp Boy*, 1971; *Samankwe in the Strange Forest*, 1973; *The Rainbow Tinted Scarf and Other Stories*, 1975; *The Restless City and Christmas Gold*, 1975; *Survive the Peace*, 1976; *Divided We Stand*, 1980; *Motherless Baby*, 1980; *Behind the Convent Wall*, 1987; *For a Roll of Parchment*, 1987; *Jagua Nana's Daughter*, 1987; *Gone to Mecca*, 1991; *King Forever!*, 1992; *Masquerade Time*, 1992

# ELLISON, Ralph (1914–)
## United States

Fleeing toward Hell, Dante beheld a man whose voice seemed weak from a long silence, and he cried to him, saying, "Have pity on me, whoever thou art, shade or real man!" Shade or real man?

Visible or invisible? The Invisible Man [in *Invisible Man*] would have smiled in recognition if hailed like that. He lives, he tells us, in an underground hole. To fill this dark hole with light, he burns 1,369 bulbs. He burns them free. A fine Dostoevskyan touch. In his ''Notes from the Underground'' Dostoevsky says: ''We are discussing things seriously: but if you won't deign to give me your attention, I will drop your acquaintance. I can retreat into my underground hole.''

The Invisible Man is also discussing things seriously. His report in this novel might be subtitled, ''Notes from Underground America,'' or ''The Invisible Black Man in the Visible White Man's World.'' That is part of his story, but the deeper layer, revealed, perhaps, in spite of himself, is the invisible man becoming visible. The word, against all of the odds, becoming the flesh. Neither black nor white flesh, however, for where the color line is drawn with profundity, as it is here, it also vanishes. There is not much to choose, under the skin, between being black and invisible, and being white, currently fashionable and opaque. . . .

Perhaps it is the nature of the pilgrim in hell to see the visible world and its inhabitants in allegorical terms. They do not exist, so much as they represent. They appear to be forces, figures of good and evil, in a large symbolical frame, which makes for order, but diminishes our interest in their predicament as people. This may well be the price of living underground. We are deprived of uniqueness, no light illuminates our individuality.

The reader who is familiar with the traumatic phase of the black man's rage in America, will find something more in Mr. Ellison's report. He will find the long anguished step toward its mastery. The author sells no phony forgiveness. He asks none himself. It is a resolutely honest, tormented, profoundly American book.

Wright Morris. *New York Times Book Review*. April 13, 1952, p. 5

It is commonly felt that there is no strength to match the strength of those powers which attack and cripple modern mankind. And this feeling is, for the reader of modern fiction, all too often confirmed when he approaches a new book. . . . But what a great thing it is when a brilliant individual victory occurs, like Mr. Ellison's [in *Invisible Man*] proving that a truly heroic quality can exist among our contemporaries. People too thoroughly determined—and our institutions by their size and force too thoroughly determine—can't approach this quality. That can only be done by those who resist the heavy influences and make their own synthesis out of the vast mass of phenomena, the seething, swarming body of appearances, facts, and details. From this harassment and threatened dissolution by details, a writer tries to rescue what is important. Even when he is most bitter, he makes by his tone a declaration of values and he says, in effect: ''There is something nevertheless that a man may hope to be.'' This tone, in the best pages of *Invisible Man*, those pages, for instance, in which an incestuous Negro farmer tells his tale to a white New England philanthropist, comes through very powerfully; it is tragicomic, poetic, the tone of the very strongest sort of creative intelligence. . . .

In our society Man—Himself—is idolized and publicly worshipped, but the single individual must hide himself underground and try to save his desires, his thoughts, his soul, in invisibility. He must return to himself, learning self-acceptance and rejecting all that threatens to deprive him of his manhood.

This is what I make of *Invisible Man*. It is not by any means faultless; I don't think the hero's experiences in the Communist party are as original in conception as other parts of the book, and his love affair with a white woman is all too brief, but it is an immensely moving novel and it has greatness.

Saul Bellow. *Commentary*. June 1952, pp. 608–9

In the thirty years' span of my active reviewing experience, there have been in my judgment three points of peak development in Negro fiction by Negro writers. In 1923 from a relatively low plateau of previous problem fiction, Jean Toomer's *Cane* rose to unprecedented artistic heights. . . . In 1940, Richard Wright's skillful sociological realism [in *Native Son*] turned a hard but brilliant searchlight on Negro urban life in Chicago and outlined the somber tragedy of Bigger Thomas in a well-studied setting of Northside wealth and Southside poverty. . . .

But 1952 is the significant year of Ellison's *Invisible Man*, a great novel, although also not without its artistic flaws, sad to say. Ralph Ellison is a protege of Wright, who predicted for him a bright literary future. Written in a style of great force and originality, although its talent is literally smothered with verbosity and hyperbole, *Invisible Man* is both in style and conception a new height of literary achievement. . . . Stylistically [it] unrolls in a volcanic flow of vivid, sometimes livid imagery, a tour de force of psychological realism. A double symbolic meaning piled on top of this realism gives the book its distinctive and most original tone and flavor: *Invisible Man* is actually a surrealistic novel because of this, and but for its lack of restraint would rank among the very best of the genre. But the unrestrained bravado of treatment, riding loose rein at full gallop most of the time and the overprecious bravura of phrase and diction weight it down where otherwise it would soar in well-controlled virtuosity. Many readers will be shocked at Ellison's daring franknesses and dazed by his emotional intensity but these are an integral part of the book's great merit. For once, too, here is a Negro writer capable of real and sustained irony. *Invisible Man*, evidently years in the making, must not be Ralph Ellison's last novel.

Alain Locke. *Phylon*. 14, 1, 1953, pp. 34–35

[In *Invisible Man*] elements of farce, tragedy, pity, hatred, and love are mixed with a vivid exhilaration for which I really cannot find a parallel. An American critic quoted on the wrapper compares Ellison to ''Kafka or Joyce,'' and there are certainly pages of writing here which justify the mention of such names. All the same, Ellison's strength lies in his being the opposite of writers who through a limited contemporary experience have created an intellectual picture of modern civilisation. He has had an immense experience of what it is like to be an *object* acted upon by modern conditions, which have had the result of beating him into a white-hot rage of sensibility and thought. His great achievement is that he is not content to be a ''social realist'' learning the lesson of oppression and building up a solid case against social evil. He becomes a humanist who sees the farcical side of the most tragically cruel social situations, who caricatures suffering until it becomes a warmly rich part of the human comedy, and who realises that rebels are as mean and power-seeking and greedy as the people or forces they are rebelling against. . . .

Mr. Ellison is as much a born American writer as, say, Thomas Wolfe; and perhaps he has Wolfe's weaknesses of a certain disorderliness and lack of control, and of being too attracted by violence. But the vivid ease with which his large scenes of movement are handled is truly remarkable.

Stephen Spender. *Listener*. January 15, 1953, p. 115

Ellison's protagonist [in *Invisible Man*] is invisible not through his own desire but through the force of circumstances; not because he passes by unnoticed but because nobody manages to understand his true spiritual identity.

This incomprehension arises from the fact that everyone sees the protagonist through a screen whose existence they are unaware of, just as they are unaware of the attempts they make to make the protagonist fit into the pattern on that screen (actually, a preconceived psychological pattern), which the character in his humanity does not fit into at all. . . .

The protagonist does not have a name. In this way, I believe Ellison suggests that he is viewed by the many other characters with whom he comes into contact, not as a distinct individual but as an anonymous (because undifferentiated) member of a certain race, in this case, the black race. This undifferentiated anonymity is complemented by the vastness of the panorama presented in the novel. Unlike the majority of contemporary American novelists, who tend to concentrate on a limited number of characters or on a particular class of society and to condense into a few events the writer's feelings and conception of life (in this tendency Hemingway's influence can be recognized), Ellison uses a technique that seems closer to the nineteenth century: he creates a vast tableau in which the protagonist moves through incidents too numerous to be summarized. [Oct. 27, 1953]

Salvatore Rosati. *L'ombra dei padri* (Rome, Edizioni di Storia e Letteratura, 1958), pp. 136–38

That Ralph Ellison is very good is dull to say. He is essentially a hateful writer: when the line of his satire is pure, he writes so perfectly that one can never forget the experience of reading him—it is like holding a live electric wire in one's hand. But Ellison's mind, fine and icy, tuned to the pitch of a major novelist's madness, is not always adequate to mastering the forms of rage, horror, and disgust which his eyes have presented to his experience, and so he is forever tumbling from the heights of pure satire into the nets of a murderously depressed clown, and *Invisible Man* insists on a thesis which could not be more absurd, for the Negro is the least invisible of all people in America. (That the white does not see each Negro as an individual is not so significant as Ellison makes it—most whites can no longer see each other at all. Their experience is not as real as the experience of the Negro, and their faces have been deadened in the torture chamber of the overburdened American conscience. They have lost all quick sense of the difficulty of life and its danger, and so they do not have faces the way Negroes have faces—it is rare for a Negro who lives it out to reach the age of twenty without having a face which is a work of art.)

Where Ellison can go, I have no idea. His talent is too exceptional to allow for casual predictions, and if one says that the way

for Ellison may be to adventure out into the white world he knows so well by now, and create the more difficult and conceivably more awful invisibility of the white man—well, it is a mistake to write prescriptions for a novelist as gifted as Ellison.

Norman Mailer. *Advertisements for Myself* (New York: G. P. Putnam's Sons, 1959), p. 471

*Invisible Man* is a novel of salvation, a salvation won with difficulty through a series of ordeals. The hero is at first docile, allowing himself to be soothed by the double illusion of submissiveness and "social responsibility." Then the harsh lesson of reality shows him the need for struggle and rebellion. But the rebel may be deceived by illusory utopias. It is only when he has rejected yet another of mankind's deceptions or distortions—political action—that he acquires a kind of clear-sightedness. This clarity of vision could lead to crime (the character of Rinehart, the nocturnal charlatan of Harlem, tempts him at one point), but the narrator comes out of his cellar with an identity and a philosophy which have been paid for dearly but which are truly his own and not imposed from the outside. . . .

*Invisible Man* is a very powerful book, one that gives the reader the feeling of having been thrown up in the air by a bulldozer. It is also a work of art, admirably written and constructed, a work which, a dozen years after its publication, remains profoundly contemporary. Closer to us than Richard Wright, a better novelist than James Baldwin, Ellison occupies a unique place in contemporary American literature.

Pierre Brodin. *Présences contemporaines: Écrivains américains d'aujourd'hui* (Paris: Nouvelles Éditions Debresse, 1964), pp. 55–57

Even if Ralph Ellison were not the author of *Invisible Man*, his recent collection of essays, *Shadow and Act*, would be a very significant work. There are astute commentaries on literature, music, and society, and the commentaries are enriched and validated by an underlying sense of a life being lived with energy, sympathy, and joy. But Ralph Ellison is the author of *Invisible Man* and of an impending novel which, if we are to judge from excerpts, promises to illustrate new powers and to extend his fame; and this fact inevitably imputes a further significance to the essays. Here we can see how, over more than a score of years, in another dimension, the mind and sensibility of Ellison have been working, and we can hope to see some enlightening relations between that dimension and the dimension of his fiction. . . .

*The basic unity of human experience*—that is what Ellison asserts; and he sets the richness of his own experience and that of many Negroes he has known, and his own early capacity to absorb the general values of Western culture, over against what Wright called "the essential bleakness of black life in America." What he is saying here is not that "bleakness" does not exist, and exist for many, but that it has not been the key fact of his own experience, and that his own experience is part of the story. It must be reckoned with, too. . . .

To be an artist partakes, in its special way, of the moral force of being a man. And with this we come again, in a new perspective, to

Ellison's view of the "basic unity of experience." If there is anguish, there is also the possibility of the transmutation of anguish, "the occasional joy of a complex double vision."

Robert Penn Warren. *Commentary*. May 1965, pp. 91, 94–95

My hat is off to the author [of *Invisible Man*], his overall skill and—with some reservations—to his most original conception, as also to his guts and integrity. But alas, did I say it was interesting after, say, page 245. I wouldn't quarrel with its necessary complexity, but in my opinion the book itself—with a few miraculous cloudbursts of recovery—begins to fail and become arider and arider, even fall to pieces (pardon my mixed metaphors) approximately from this point on. I more or less dissent too from the opinions expressed by certain reviewers of the book in this regard. However noble the multiple intention, the book itself begins to fail as a work of art, in my opinion, though fragmentarily still it can still show itself a hell of a sight better than many or most novels. Possibly this is because the beginning, likewise the enclosing theme, is so good. Either that or he leads you to expect too much of himself. But the irony utterly ceases to be out of the top drawer, becomes somewhat derivative finally. The reporting of the communist brotherhood is as boring very often as their dialectics probably were in real life. One has been invited so often to these cocktail parties of well-heeled communists before and the essential and important points are too often clouded as a result of the technical out-of-touchness of the writing. . . .

The race riot, so highly praised by others, strikes me as at worse resembling one of those very early Soviet futuristic films such as *Arsenal*, where symbol and the thing symbolized, man and meaning and photographic virtuosity are so confused that it is only your respect for the ingenuity of the director and the hope of what he may do at the next moment that keeps you from leaving the theatre out of exasperation with the sheer inertia and muddle he imposes: but above all this I had the feeling that here Ellison was not writing what he wanted to and knew it. My final feeling is, though, that his final remark is universally justified and that in the main he does, like Kafka, strike at the soul of man himself. At least he strikes at mine, and I shall certainly prize the book as the work of someone I feel may be important indeed. [May, 1952]

Malcolm Lowry. In Harvey Breit and Margerie Bonner Lowry, eds., *Selected Letters of Malcolm Lowry* (Philadelphia: J. B. Lippincott, 1965), pp. 316–18

If the most damaging criticism one can make of *Invisible Man* is that its characters and situations are too abstractly conceived and executed, it is also true that perhaps its greatest strength is its capacity to show in action the power that ideas and ideologies can exert. One of the ways this is done is through bravura set-pieces of rhetoric, which Mr. Ellison uses brilliantly for his dramatic and ironic purposes. So it comes as a disappointment, in reading this collection of essays [*Shadow and Act*] to find Mr. Ellison occasionally serving up his rhetoric straight, with little apparent awareness of its dangers. . . .

The most moving passages in the book I found to be those of direct autobiography: the glimpses we are offered of the author's parents, of his boyhood in Oklahoma City (where he and a group of

his friends formulated the ambition to become "Renaissance Men"), of his adventures riding freight trains during the Depression, of the period when he earned his living by hunting birds, of his entanglement with the Communist Party. It is a tribute to his agility of mind that all these unexpected, convincing details should be used to illustrate his literary and cultural arguments; but they also make me rather sorry we don't have more of them simply for their own sake.

Dan Jacobson. *New Statesman*. January 20, 1967, p. 82

Both Baldwin and Wright seem to have overlooked the rich possibilities available to them in the blues tradition. Both profess great pride in Negroes, but in practice seem to rate the theories and abstract formulations of French existentialism over the infinitely richer wisdom of the blues. Both, like most other intellectuals (and/or most of the social scientists), seem to have missed what should be one of the most obvious implications of the blues tradition: *It is the product of the most complicated culture, and therefore the most complicated sensibility in the modern world.* . . .

Somehow or other James Baldwin and Richard Wright seem to have missed the literary possibilities suggested by this. Ralph Ellison has not. . . .

*Invisible Man* was *par excellence* the literary extension of the blues. It was as if Ellison had taken an everyday twelve bar blues tune (by a man from down South sitting in a manhole up North in New York singing and signifying about how he got there) and scored it for full orchestra. This was indeed something different and something more than run of the mill U.S. fiction. It had new dimensions of rhetorical resonance (based on lying and signifying). It employed a startlingly effective fusion of narrative realism and surrealism; and it achieved a unique but compelling combination of the naturalistic, the ridiculous, and the downright hallucinatory. . . .

And like the blues, and echoing the irrepressibility of America itself, it ended on a note of promise, ironic and ambiguous perhaps, but a note of promise still. The blues with no aid from existentialism have always known that there were no clear-cut solutions for the human situation.

Albert Murray. *The Omni-Americans* (New York: Outerbridge & Dienstfrey, 1970), pp. 166–67

It is now 1970—which means that 23 years have passed since Ellison has given us his first and so far, only novel [parts of it were first published in 1947]. This is a matter of great discussion among writers younger than he. Just why have 23 years been allowed to pass with just one other book (but several articles), *Shadow and Act*, nonfiction, left to stand as the slim wedge between Ellison and oblivion? (Writing is a craft or profession or rite of stupidity that can bring oblivion swifter than anything else I know about.)

I wish I could answer that. It is known that on his lecture swings Ellison does read parts of his new novel. I draw the comparison between him and Katherine Anne Porter, whose *Ship of Fools*, dealing with the mentality from which sprang German fascism, was 20 years in coming and turned out to be a dud, despite all the fanfare and the inept film of the novel.

I do not wish this for Ellison. I don't wish it for anyone. But many things transpire during the course of a couple of decades; one can lose touch with them, and it is suspected that this may be the case with Ellison. I do not know this for a fact. I *do* know that his contacts with the young writers I know have been absent, or very unsatisfying. . . .

We urgently need older writers to help mold anew the tradition of Black communication, whether it be written or oral. And we are running out of senior Black writers. Wright talked to people; so did Langston Hughes; Himes is eager to talk to people, should they make the long trek to Spain. And John O. Killens, who must rank near the top in this endeavor, is still running writing workshops. We need Ellison and Baldwin to give us a hand. We've got a Black wave of writing and writers sweeping over the land who would be so much more enriched through contacts with them.

John A. Williams. *Black World.* December 1970, pp. 10–11

The task of that ironic picaresque, the nameless hero of *Invisible Man*, is exactly this: to move from invisibility to vision. Through the dangers, corruptions, and temptations awaiting him, he recapitulates the history of his own race, conducting a ceaseless ''psychological scrimmage'' with everyone, himself included. Exploited by all—white Communists and African nationalists, Southern bigots and Northern liberals, women and men alike—he proceeds, less in the manner of an arrow than a boomerang, from innocence to disillusionment to the edge of a new wisdom, a dialectic sense of himself. In the surreal cool cellar lit by 1,369 light bulbs where he ends, he perceives the essential chaos of the mind, and finds freedom in a form that can ''condemn and affirm, say no and say yes, say yes and say no.''

*Invisible Man* is a profound and brilliant work, which engages issues of History, Soul, and Art still alive in our midst. It may be criticized for being too prolix, too diffuse, in specific parts; yet the novel is resourceful in its syncopation of reality, musical in its organization of themes, its screams and grotesque laughter issuing from a heroic consciousness willing to surrender nothing to its own ease. Ellison's novel is more than an example of Black fiction; it stands as an early landmark in all of postwar literature.

Ihab Hassan. *Contemporary American Literature* (New York: Frederick Ungar, 1973), pp. 74–75

*Invisible Man* invades the comfortable universe of detached literary analysis with a reading experience which, in the tradition of all authentic art, could involve us in profound personal change (''things as they are/Are changed upon the blue guitar''). As everyone knows, the reader is asked to come to terms with overwhelming sets of contraries—black and whiteness as interdependent aspects of each other, racism and American democracy, responsibility within anarchy, the one and the many, naturalism and fairy tale, sociology and myth, chaos and order. This is paradox of a vastly different order from the arid device we learn to cherish and chatter about in discussing modernist literature; we cannot cope with it meaningfully without the *agon* of remaking ourselves so as to accommodate its way of responding to the world.

Hence a basic irony in the career of this very successful book, a ''classic'' to educated readers in America and Europe, almost smothered in commentary, and yet largely ignored on its most demanding and meaningful levels. Since its 1952 publication in America, one or another dimension of its readers' makeup has

consistently interposed itself to short-circuit the book's total vision: first it was the white self-image, later the black; most recently it is the renewed assault of sociology upon art which sets the balance askew. To be sure, any book, especially one like *Invisible Man*, must assert its worth within the context of our chaotic everyday lives. But the pressure of social and racial upheavals has created so much uncertainty that the tolerance for broad reflection and inner change has all but disappeared in the frenzied search of all parties for immediate, tangible panaceas. One misreads a novel if one seeks to extract from it short-range social panaceas, and *Invisible Man* has certainly been a dramatic casualty of such misreading.

Jacqueline Covo. *The Blinking Eye: Ralph Waldo Ellison and His American, French, German and Italian Critics, 1952–1971* (Metuchen: New Jersey, Scarecrow, 1974), pp. 124–25

Scholars and teachers have eagerly awaited the publication of a book of this kind [*Flying Home and Other*] for many years. For a variety of reasons which are still difficult to understand fully, Ralph Ellison's short stories have never been collected until now, making many of them all but impossible to use in the classroom and extremely difficult to use for scholarly purposes, since many of his stories were published in obscure journals which have been defunct for quite some time. The Buster/Riley stories, despite their intrinsically high quality and the considerable light they shed on Ellison's development, are virtually unknown to all but a small group of Ellison specialists. ''Flying Home'' and ''King of the Bingo,'' two extraordinary stories which rank with the very best American short fiction published since 1945, have appeared in a variety of anthologies, but most are now out of print and some have become too expensive or too specialized for many courses. Ellison's unpublished stories, like his much-awaited second novel, have been rumored for years to be very high in quality, but could only tantalize several generations of critics, scholars, and teachers, who have hoped for their eventual publication.

*Flying Home and Other Stories*, superbly edited by John F. Callahan, is therefore an important event in American and African American literary life, since it collects for the first time what Callahan considers to be ''Ellison's best published and unpublished freestanding fiction.'' Designed as ''a reader's edition'' and not intended to be a ''variorum or scholarly edition,'' the book contains thirteen stories, six of which were unpublished in Ellison's lifetime. (Two were published in 1996 issues of *The New Yorker*.) These stories are of enormous value, since they now make possible a careful study of Ellison's considerable achievements as a short story writer and also enable us to see in a much clearer way Ellison's development as an artist in the crucial period when he emerged as a writer in the late 1930s and early 1940s. Moreover, this book finally makes it possible to bring Ellison's short fiction productively into the classroom, where it can be studied for its own merits and for the ways in which it illuminates his great novel *Invisible Man*.

Certainly the most eye-opening part of this book is its cluster of six new stories, which Callahan aptly describes as ''stories that had never been published, never-mentioned, stories no one knew about.'' Most of them are initiation stories of one kind or another in which young protagonists are abruptly awakened into a painful awareness of the harsh realities of adult experience. ''A Party

Down at the Square,'' for example, is narrated by a nameless white boy who describes a lynching which he is forced to watch while making a summer visit to his uncle in Alabama. ''Boy on a Train'' focuses on a young black protagonist who is suddenly thrust into the early stages of adulthood after the death of his father as he, his mother, and brother are forced to take a train to a strange new place where they hope to begin a new life. ''Hymie's Bull'' and ''I Did Not Learn Their Names'' deal with anonymous black picaros riding the rails during the darkest years of the Great Depression, all the while encountering shocking moments of violence and surprising experiences of human tenderness and solidarity. ''The Black Ball,'' which Callahan describes as ''perhaps the most subtly crafted of the unpublished stories,'' brilliantly dramatizes the psychic wounds of a single father and his son as they try to establish a decent life for themselves in a racist society intent on ''blackballing'' them. The only bit of comic relief in this group of previously unpublished fiction appears in ''A Hard Time Keeping Up,'' which culminates in an amusing episode of mock-violence.

Of these six stories, only ''Hymie's Bull'' can be precisely dated, since it was scheduled to appear in a 1937 issue of New Challenge, but the journal folded before the story could be published. ''A Hard Time Keeping Up'' and ''The Black Ball,'' judging from convincing external evidence, were completed during the period from late 1937, when Ellison was in Dayton, Ohio, following his mother's death there, until April 1938, when he returned to New York to work for the New York Writers Project of the WPA. Callahan speculates that the other three stories were completed before 1940, since they were found in an envelope labeled by Ellison as ''Early Stories'' and containing his 1940 address of 25. All six stories, therefore, are a rich source of information about Ellison's early development as a writer when he was strongly influenced by leftist politics in general and Richard Wright's example in particular. (The lynching described in the collection's opening story, for example, clearly reflects Wright's commitment to depicting racial violence in an uncompromisingly frank and graphic manner, and the proletarian sympathies implicit in ''I Did Not Learn Their Names'' and ''The Black Ball'' demonstrate with equal clarity that Ellison was strongly influenced by leftist thought, even though he never became a member of the Communist Party.)

Those who have unfairly charged Ellison throughout his career of lacking sufficient anger and militance will find very little evidence in these six unpublished stories to support their claims. Most of the stories smoulder with anger and repulsion which often match that found in typical Wright stories of the period. Just as the white boy in ''A Party'' is finally sickened by the lynching which he wants to run away from but is forced to watch, the young protagonist in ''Boy on a Train'' is so outraged by the sudden loss of his father and the segregated conditions which he and his family must endure that he finds himself ''smouldering inside'' and finally acknowledges a fierce, nearly Ahabian desire ''to kill God and not be sorry.'' The nameless central character in ''Hymie's Bull'' takes a perverse pleasure in observing a fellow hobo coldly slit the throat of a railroad ''dick.'' And his counterpart in ''I Did Not Learn Their Names'' perhaps speaks for most of the central characters in these stories when he frankly reveals, ''I was having a hard time not to hate in those days.''

One crucially important thematic pattern which informs these six unpublished stories, and which becomes even more pronounced in Ellison's later fiction, is Ellison's unwillingness merely to express this rage; throughout the stories he searches for ways to enable his characters to transcend raw anger and resentment which will either paralyze or destroy them and to develop human resources which enable them to deal productively with such feelings. As Callahan has arranged the stories, one can see the outlines of an overall narrative portraying the central character's growth from an alienated and impotent observer to a more mature person who can master his feelings and deal with the world in existentially productive ways. Although the first two stories end with characters emotionally and psychologically blocked by traumatic experiences, later stories describe ways of overcoming this condition. The narrator of ''I Did Not Learn Their Names'' thus balances his suspicion of people and his resentment over his marginalized position in American society with the fact that a crippled white man has saved his life and an elderly white couple not only share their food with him but also reveal to him some of the intimate details of their lives. He is finally able to go beyond his own suffering by identifying with the pain of others and sensing a common bond between them, realizing that on the most fundamental levels ''you were all the same.'' In a similar way, the single father in ''The Black Ball'' is able to contain and transcend his frustrations with a racist society by identifying with and joining the cause of a white union organizer who has also been wounded by a society which ostracizes him for defending a black man who was wrongfully accused of rape. In each case, Ellison's protagonists are able to repair the damage done to the self by moving beyond their personal grief to a larger vision of solidarity with others. In this way, they are able to overcome ''a smouldering sense of self-hate and ineffectiveness.''

The four Buster / Riley stories in this collection provide Ellison with another resource for mastering and transcending pain, a comic tradition rooted in American and African American folklore. The humor which sparkles throughout these pieces is closely tied to the blues which Ellison has described in Shadow and Act as ''a near-tragic, near-comic lyricism'' that enables one to triumph over pain by developing a ''sheer toughness of spirit'' characterized by deepened consciousness and emotional resilience. The three stories which bring the collection to such a brilliant conclusion (''King of the Bingo Game,'' ''In a Strange Country,'' and ''Flying Home'') likewise dramatize a process of self-actualization in which the central characters overcome a numbing alienation by a comic reintegration with the world which is triggered by deepened and expanded consciousness.

What these thirteen stories emphatically demonstrate is that Ellison's Invisible Man did not spring like Topsy out of nowhere but were the product of a long period of artistic and philosophical growth dating back to 1937, when he emerged as a writer. For all of his career Ellison was fascinated by stories of initiation and was able to endow these narratives with richer, more nuanced meanings as he was able to conceive of more complicated central characters and bring them to life with techniques which became increasingly more expressive, and subtle. His existential heroes can finally turn the ''black eye'' of pain into a very different ''black eye'' of deepened consciousness and broadened sympathies. As Ellison developed this remarkable blues vision, he was forced to experiment with and master a great variety of styles. Starting with a very disciplined and understated realism which he learned from Hemingway, he learned to see the small details of real life in fresh ways. He combined this with a lucid naturalism which he picked up from Wright and which gave him a deepened understanding of how the social environment impacts upon the lives of individuals. He then developed an ability to alternate these styles with a finely textured, many-layered symbolism which he learned from Joyce and Malraux. Going one step further, he was able to judiciously blend these styles with comic techniques from American and African American folk tradition, developing a distinctive voice which can only be called "Ellisonian." *Flying Home and Other Stories* is an important book because it documents more fully than any other primary source this remarkable literary development, in addition to adding six stories of high quality to the Ellison canon.

> Robert J. Butler. *African American Review*. 32, 1 (Spring 1998), pp. 164–67

BIBLIOGRAPHY
*Invisible Man*, 1952; *Shadow and Act*, 1964; *Going to the Territory*, 1986; *The Collected Essays of Ralph Ellison*, 1995; *Conversations with Ralph Ellison*, 1995; *Flying Home and Other Stories*, 1996; *Juneteenth*, 1999; *The Letters of Ralph Emerson*, 1999

# EMECHETA, Buchi (1944–)
## Nigeria

Buchi Emecheta, an Igbo woman living in London with her five children, has joined the vanguard of contemporary women writers such as Flora Nwapa, [Ama Ata] Aidoo, Grace Ogot, and Bessie Head with the publication of her five novels: *In the Ditch, Second Class Citizen, The Bride Price, The Slave Girl,* and *The Joys of Motherhood*. Currently, she is in the process of writing her sixth novel, *Destination Biafra*, which chronicles the happenings of the Nigerian Civil War. More so than her female predecessors, Emecheta documents the experiences of the modern African woman in her novels. She chronicles their struggle for equality in a male-dominated world.

Formerly, images of African women were drawn exclusively by African men who idealized them in their writings. Their one-dimensional, romanticized images of the African woman, primarily as mother, is contrary to that illustrated by Emecheta in her novels. Rather than simply portraying the African woman symbolically as part of the warm and secure African past, she offers faithful portrayals, patterns of self-analysis and general insights into the female psyche, ignored by, or inaccessible to, African male writers. Emecheta's perspective on African women in Nigerian society is therefore a welcome occurrence. Male writers lack the empathy, sympathy, and consciousness of their female characters' psyche. They do not know what it means to be an African woman in an African society. This explains why the multidimensional role of African women is not accurately reflected in modern African literature. In any event, the importance of Emecheta's works does not lie in her attempt to address a group or fill a gap. Her writings introduce new themes in African literary history: the emergence of self-conscious feminism—women's liberation and the celebration of the black woman. She is an advocate of women's liberation and is of the opinion that male writers make African women their housemaids or prostitutes in their books. Therefore, "all women suffer oppression and need to be liberated." Emecheta's female characters epitomize the difficulty of being a black woman in a

changing Nigerian society, particularly in the early twentieth century. Her novels center around the extraordinary courage and resourcefulness of Nigerian women which often prevent black families from disintegrating. She reports the problems and pleasures of the black female and not only does she include her personal experiences but also those of other women in her home town of Ibuza, Nigeria. It is in this way that the young author writes to raise the images of Nigerian women to a level commensurate with historical truths.

> Marie Linton Umeh. *Presence Africaine*. 116 (1980), pp. 190–91

The story of *The Bride Price* is a study of the relationship between the collective traditions of the communal will and Aku-nna's own strength of will (and in this regard she is the fictional counterpart of the autobiographical Adah Obi). This is the central theme on which Emecheta focuses her novel. The result is a tightly organized structure which is a decided improvement over the episodic fitfulness of *In the Ditch* and which fulfills the promise of *Second Class Citizen* where the development, decline, and last-minute salvaging of Adah's individuality provides the narrative with a definite coherence and an element of suspense. In *The Bride Price* the concern with narrative suspense and development occasionally lends itself to the rather melodramatic scenes of Aku-nna's abduction and subsequent elopement. But on the whole, it works to Emecheta's advantage, delineating Aku-nna's growth from an inexperienced and naive childhood into a knowing and rebellious womanhood. The narrative development is heightened by the pervasive sense of a malevolent and increasingly menacing destiny, from the sudden death of Aku-nna's father to her own deathbed terror of an avenging deity. Emecheta's central theme also benefits from the manner in which the tightly controlled narrative flows for the most part through Aku-nna's consciousness and at regular but limited intervals through external viewpoints (of mother, uncle, cousins, and future husband) which focus directly on Aku-nna herself (as daughter, bride-price bait, age-group member, and wife respectively). Within this subjective context Emecheta's narrative presents both the communal will and Aku-nna's personality simultaneously by emphasizing the manner in which Aku-nna grows up into womanhood. Her growth is, simultaneously, the development of her own personality and will, and her perception of the rituals, the values, and the institutions through which her community celebrates its traditions and exercises its will. In turn, these rituals and their attendant sense of proper form permeate Emecheta's narrative form with a definite sense of proportion. Her fictive structure is beginning to become a direct symptom of her thematic concerns.

> Lloyd W. Brown. *Women Writers in Black Africa* (Westport, Connecticut: Greenwood Press, 1981), pp. 49–50

Now that Emecheta has won acclaim, she has determined to make London her home base and writing her main endeavor. She faces, therefore, the constant problem for the expatriate and exiled writer. What authentic background can she draw from her fiction? What audience shall she address? Her personal experience in contemporary Nigeria becomes increasingly remote. In 1980 she accepted a fellowship at Calabar, which she uses as a locale for *Double Yoke*, a brief college novel in which the male protagonist, Ete Kamba, cannot overcome his traditional, adverse reaction to the knowledge that his girl has given herself before marriage, even to him. Emecheta met some absurd criticism for centering her novel on a male protagonist.

In her latest novel, *The Rape of Shavi*, Emecheta undertakes a futuristic science-fiction type of narrative. A planeload of British scientists seeking escape from an ''inevitable'' nuclear holocaust is grounded in a traditional African country. The technological and economic changes they provoke leave the African nation much worse off than before. A return to past traditionalism for either group, however, is not satisfactory either.

In 1982 Emecheta published her major work to date, *Destination Biafra*. Different from any of her others, it is larger and more substantive. Here she presents neither the life story of a single character nor the delineation of one facet of a culture, but the whole perplexing canvas of people from diverse ethnic groups, belief systems, levels of society—all caught in a disastrous civil war. Though she herself at the time was a student in London, out of the fray, she has compiled family histories, eyewitness accounts, and political documents to tell this story. Her personal anguish at the loss of many relatives and friends—particularly of an aunt and uncle who died trying to escape the bombing of Ibuza, and an eight-year-old namesake who, with a tiny sister, died of starvation—is apparent. Her outrage at the greed, corruption, and sadism of many of the antagonists on all sides fitly demonstrates the illogicality of seeking to explain the war. She felt the book ''had to be written.'' In relief, she wrote: ''I am glad this work is at last published. It is different from my other books, the subject is, as they say, 'masculine,' but I feel a great sense of achievement in having completed it.''

Charlotte and David Bruner. *World Literature Today*. 59, 1 (Winter 1985), p. 11

*Double Yoke* is a love story told in the blues mode. The story laments a loss; yet it sings a love song. Its theme of the perilous journey of love, is a major preoccupation in author Buchi Emecheta's dramatic work. On an equally fundamental level, *Double Yoke* describes the tragic limitations of Nigerian women in pursuit of academic excellence and the anxiety of assimilation. Similar to her early novels, *Double Yoke* assesses the predicament of women in Africa. By describing the sexual and cultural politics in Nigerian society, Emecheta again campaigns against female subjugation and champions her case for female emancipation. Nko, the author's intellectually oriented heroine, provides some insight into the psyche of modern African women who are encumbered by traditional African misconceptions attached to the university-educated female.

Firstly, *Double Yoke* is a love story but with tragic implications. Buchi Emecheta is at her best in describing the anxiety lovers often experience because of mutual distrust at one time or another and the inability to reconcile their difficulties. According to the author, love, if betrayed, is directly responsible for the misery that afflicts the human soul. The tale of the terrifying journey of the possibilities and failures of love is then at the dramatic center of *Double Yoke*. . . .

There is satire too in *Double Yoke*. As well as the clash between the old and the new, there is a clash between the genuine and the false. In the character of Reverend Professor Ikot, pretentious and immoral university professors in Nigeria are attacked. Ikot, like the true trickster figure, is shrewd, cunning, and loquacious. Posing as a religious leader and educator, he dupes others but is rarely duped himself. His strong archetypal appeal, ability to outwit others and articulate his ideas enable him to exercise power and control over people. Even when caught in the act, he exploits the situation and emerges a winner. Note how he handles his confrontation with Ete Kamba in one of the most dramatic scenes in the book. Playing on the intelligence of his people, he fabricates a story knowing full well what the policemen want to hear. Emecheta, pointing to the exploitation of students on university campuses and the abuse of Christian teachings, protests against the corrupt, opportunistic nature of contemporary Nigerians. Rather than working towards the acquisition of souls or imparting knowledge to students, Ikot preoccupies himself with ''getting a piece of the cake.'' Almost risking his chances of being the next vice chancellor at Unical, he shamelessly destroys the lives of both Nko and Ete Kamba.

Finally, Ete Kamba exemplifies primacy of the group ethic over individual self-interests, which is so embedded in traditional African society, by sympathizing with Nko upon hearing of her father's death. Ete Kamba begins to realize that despite their inexperience they have to resolve their problems for no other reason than because they love each other. Ete Kamba and Nko choose to grow from their blunders and bear their double burden together. Ete Kamba's deep feeling of affection for Nko, despite a certain myopia which blinds him to manifest ambiguities within himself, helps him to understand that no one knows very much about the life of another. This ignorance becomes vivid, if you love another.

This ending is not altogether convincing even in these modern times. It then becomes obvious that author Emecheta is ascribing her personal modes of thought even though they may be way ahead of her audience. Most of us are still very conservative. In the fusing of the old and the new traditional African society's intolerance of one's right to choose one's destiny rather than consider the common good seems to be strengthened. In spite of this, *Double Yoke* is quite entertaining while it explores several political and social issues common in African literature. Emecheta's simplicity of style covers her exploration of these important issues in strikingly new and provocative twists.

Marie Linton Umeh. In Carole Boyce Davies and Anne Adams Graves, eds. *Ngambika: Studies of Women in African Literature* (Trenton, New Jersey: Africa World Press, 1986), pp. 173, 178–79

In 1980, Emecheta put out her second children's book, *Nowhere to Play*. The plot is based on a story by her twelve-year-old daughter Christy and involves the same family that appears in *Titch the Cat*. However, this story takes place five years earlier in the London public housing estate, near Regent's Park in Rothay's Albany Street. Like the wife Emecheta portrayed in her second novel, *Second Class Citizen*, the children of the housing project are second-class juveniles with no place to play. In each of the five chapters, the little neighborhood gang, made up of Irish Catholic, East Indian, and Nigerian children, seeks an open area nearby in which to play. Each time they are refused or ejected. Their mothers have forbidden them to cross the busy streets to go to the park after a car accident to Dan and a near miss for June occurred the year previous. So the summer holidays find the group ''Chased from the Green'' in chapter two, ''Expelled from the Crown Bushes'' in chapter three, ''Knocking Dollies Out of Bed'' in chapter four (after they ran through the flats knocking on all the doors), and finally "Frightened from the Church" in chapter five.

The incidents are commonplace. The adults' rejection of the children is neither unkind nor malicious. The youngsters are an irresponsible group, naturally needing space and freedom to express their high spirits. They care for and tease each other. Little Irish Moya lags behind the others, hampered by her skirt, worn because her father doesn't believe women should wear trousers. She shrieks at a bee, and the others have to go back to cajole her to follow the group again. "Were you trying the Tarzan call?" they tease.

Emecheta's easy style and natural dialogue are well suited to these stories. The children portrayed are loving, caring, and uninhibited. Emecheta is neither sentimental nor poignant. The children do need a place to play; the adults do need their own privacy as well. But there is not the threat of crime, sadism, drugs, or pornography. The children are healthy, lively, and lovable. Their adventures bring a chuckle not a grimace.

Charlotte Bruner. *African Studies Review.* 29, 3 (September 1986), p. 135

The novels of Buchi Emecheta, an Igbo woman writer, explore the varying definitions of womanhood and motherhood as experienced by her women protagonists in Nigerian society. A fundamental purpose of womanhood, [that is] to flower into motherhood, is rooted in the paradoxical relationships of both the traditional structures of patriarchy and the modern structures of urbanization. Emecheta is concerned equally with the dual issue of the biological control of women whereby sexuality and the ability to bear children are the sole criteria which define womanhood; and the economic control of women within the colonially imposed capitalist system whereby women are placed at a disadvantage graver than they had faced in precolonial economic structures. Capitalism which brought the mixed blessings of urban development and modern ways of life, did not change traditionally accepted modes of oppression, such as bride-price and polygamy, and, in fact, often reinforced them. . . .

Emecheta's women protagonists are depicted as belonging at every stage of their lives to some male figure—as a female child grows from girlhood to womanhood to motherhood, she is controlled and owned by her father, her husband, then her sons. Her biology defines her womanhood; only as a mother is she culturally believed to be a complete human being. Mothering as a concept, involving such invisible tasks as household chores, is inculcated throughout the period of her socialization. She learns to make sacrifices for her brothers and to look after the younger children. In Igbo society it is the father and not the mother who is believed to be one's "life, shelter" remarks the narrator in Emecheta's novel *The Bride Price.* . . .

In Emecheta's next and finest novel, *The Joys of Motherhood,* womanhood is defined exclusively as motherhood. The chapter headings interestingly trace the ups and downs of the protagonist Nnu Ego's fate, all revolving around her success and failure as a mother: "The Mother," "The Mother's Mother," "The Mother's Early Life," "First Shocks of Motherhood," "A Failed Woman" and so on to the last chapter, "The Canonized Mother." Emecheta vividly charts Nnu Ego's history as mother starting from Nnu Ego's mother, developing into Nnu Ego's present life consumed by demands of constant childbearing, culminating in her death at forty. By the conclusion of the novel one recognizes the irony of the title—the joys of motherhood are experienced by Nnu Ego as the sorrows of motherhood. Emecheta seems to find no escape for women from the bonds of biology.

Ketu H. Katrak. *Journal of Commonwealth Literature.* 22, 1 (1987), pp. 159, 163, 166–67

[In] *The Joys of Motherhood,* more than in any of her other novels so far, Buchi Emecheta achieves success in her handling of her theme and language both of which are characterized in the tradition of African narrative art, by precision, subtlety, and a sense of inviolable mission. *The Joys of Motherhood* is not only an ironic commentary on the destinies of African womanhood, it is also a parable on the misplaced values of life in general in Africa as elsewhere. The irony becomes more biting as the story progresses. Nnu Ego has placed all her hope for joy and success in her children, yet she is continually disappointed. The final irony in the novel is devastating. Directly contrasting with what society and Nnu Ego's own beliefs have promised her, she finds no joy in her grown children. The spoiled boys have become selfish, egotistical men, due in large part to Nnu Ego's own attitudes toward her male children. Nnu Ego is given a fancy funeral, but it is too late. While dying, as in her life, she did not have the support or comfort of her children. . . .

Through an examination of imagery, figurative language, omniscient commentary and irony it is possible to understand the growth of Emecheta as a writer in her three novels: *The Bride Price, The Slave Girl,* and *The Joys of Motherhood.* Buchi Emecheta presents the plight of the African woman in a culture involved in a clash between traditional society and Western influence. In spite of the author's pessimism as an artist, and despite the stereotyped male characters, these novels exhibit strong artistry which makes Buchi Emecheta one of the best storytellers in modern Africa.

Ernest N. Emenyonu. *Journal of Commonwealth Literature.* 23, 1 (1988), pp. 140–41

Emecheta's interest in the story of the slave woman dates at least from the time she was writing *The Bride Price,* as passing reference is made to a similar incident. However, it was not until *The Joys of Motherhood* that Emecheta discovered the possibility of fully integrating the story into the larger narrative, for although the story is told in detail in *The Slave Girl,* the incident itself is only a minor character's recollection of a brutal event that she witnessed in her youth. Nonetheless, the slave woman's story is not extraneous to the meaning of *The Slave Girl.* The image of woman as slave pervades the novel, and it is the struggle of its heroine, Ojebeta, to come to terms with her bondage, to accommodate herself to the fact that "all her life a woman always belonged to some male," that provides much of the biting irony that is so characteristic of all of Emecheta's work. In addition, as will be shown, the slave woman's story does serve as a paradigm for much of the female experience in the novel, although this seems to occur at the level of subconscious artistry.

This practice of experimenting with an idea before fully developing it appears to be one that Emecheta has adopted as part of her creative strategy. In *The Bride Price,* with the same kind of casualness with which she inserts the slave woman's story into *The Slave Girl,* she introduces the *ogbanje* myth of the Igbo into her text. This she seizes on in *The Slave Girl*, making it the novel's single most important source of energy. However, even with *The Bride Price* a careful consideration of the function of this myth in its creative adaptation is essential to an understanding and appreciation of the work. The heroines of both novels are identified as *ogbanje*, the Igbo term for spirit-children, children believed to be destined to die and be reborn repeatedly to the same mother unless a means can be found to break the cycle. In its cultural form the *ogbanje* myth is a "myth of infant mortality" common to many West African societies. In *The Bride Price* Emecheta translates *ogbanje* to mean "a 'living dead,'" and in both novels she uses the ambiguous status of such children to represent the state of her sex in a society that denies the female any measure of self-determination.

In *The Slave Girl*, with evident conscious intent, Emecheta employs this image as her archetype of female experience. In addition, the *ogbanje* myth determines the form of the novel, the subgenre to which it belongs. *The Slave Girl* is a *bildungsroman*, but one of a peculiarly female type: a story of entrapment. Ojebeta's journey through life is a journey from autonomy and self-assertion into dependency and abnegation, from the freedom and fullness of girlhood into the slavery and self-denial of womanhood. On the figurative level of meaning, it is an *ogbanje*, "a 'living dead,'" that Ojebeta is to become.

> Florence Stratton. *Research in African Literatures*. 19, 2 (Summer 1988), pp. 147–48

Emecheta has been rightly identified as having perpetuated and reinforced certain negative stereotypes about Igbo culture and Africans in her writing. This is perhaps the symbolic equivalent of the false self, an attitude which both revenges hurt feelings about the mother through attacking her culture and makes peace with the new and alien environment. In *The Slave Girl* Ojebeta asks, after her mother's death, "Why did she leave me behind with no one to look after me?" She is sold into domestic servitude by her brother (a story which Emecheta identifies as her own mother's in *Head above Water*), and there follows the story of her growth to maturity in the household of "Ma" Palagada. There are many times when the mother role becomes a crucial element in relations between Ojebeta and the world: from the opening question of Okoline at Ma Palagada's market stall, "Where is your mother?," to the promise of Ojebeta's husband-to-be, to be father to her as she will be mother to him. As a result of the shift from one home to another, because of her mother's death and the selling, Ojebeta must "learn to be somebody else." The false self is created for the false mother, to hide the real self which can no longer grow in harmonious relation to the real mother.

> Elaine Savory Fido. In Susheila Nasta, ed. *Motherlands* (New Brunswick: Rutgers University Press, 1992), p. 340

[In *The Family*] Emecheta returns to the London black immigrant milieu that she knows so well, but for the first time the main character is not a Nigerian but a West Indian. The theme is incest, and although this is new in Emecheta's work, it lends itself to the well-known scenario of girls and women oppressed by men and fighting for self-respect. The book starts off in Jamaica. Gwendolen is left behind with Granny, as first her father and later her mother leave for the "Moder Kontry" and settle in London. While in

Granny's care, Gwendolen is sexually assaulted by Uncle Johnny, who misuses his position as old family friend. The village blames Gwendolen, but luckily her family sends for her, and she goes to London. Her arrival in London gives Emecheta the opportunity to describe immigrant slum conditions through eyes that are innocent of the social meaning of such observations. Gwendolen's family is at the bottom of the social scale, illiterate and unable to cope with the complexities of British society, but they are surviving and gaining pleasure and support from a primitive church community. Granny dies and the mother goes back to Jamaica; during her absence the father starts an incestuous relationship with Gwendolen, who is sixteen. She becomes pregnant, but she also meets a white boy and starts a sexual relationship with him. The outcome of all this is optimistic if slightly confusing. The father commits suicide; the mother is partially reconciled with her daughter. Gwendolen lives with the baby in a council flat and is happy, and the boyfriend remains a friend, despite the shame of the paternity of the baby. This modern ending rests on a new set of relationships formed on the basis of personal choice rather than on blind acceptance of the established pattern of race and family relationships. There seems to be an implicit suggestion that this alternative mode of social organization might avoid a repeat of the experiences of the main character.

Despite variations and contradictions in Emecheta's work, critics—both approving and disapproving—tend to be drawn to her novels for their ideological content. Her criticism of aspects of African cultural tradition invites the charge of being a traitor to her culture, and her feminism, though mild in Western eyes (she refuses to be called a feminist), has enraged some male African critics to a vitriolic attack on her books, which they claim misrepresent Igbo society.... As a role model for other women she is important, and, despite certain stylistic limitations, she represents a new and vigorous departure in fiction about women in and from Africa.

> Kirsten Holst Petersen. In Bernth Lindfors and Reinhard Sander, eds. *Dictionary of Literary Biography*. Vol. 117 (Detroit: Gale Research, 1992), pp. 164–65

Ritual is not only a literal aspect of African women's literature, it is a textual strategy as well. Consider how the events in Buchi Emecheta's *The Bride Price* collect into its carefully reticulated, dense patterns. Because of the density of language, event, and detail, the mythologies of this work ritualistically share this distinctively gendered strategy with its African-American counterparts.

In *The Bride Price*, the metaphorical (re)membrances (as fracturing as they may be for Aku-nna and her mother) are significant to the novel's textual events and Emecheta's telling. When Aku-nna's mother goes to the village home "to placate their Oboshi river goddess into giving her some babies" there is no break in Emecheta's attentive, detailed prose. Whereas Flora Nwapa's work is characterized by a preponderance of speech, Emecheta's is characterized by a gradual but inevitably thickening linguistic ritual between circumstance and event that propels the work toward the destiny promised in the cultural mythologies.

There are no stunning moments of revelation, no especially gleaming sections of prose and no words of such distinction that they draw individual attention to themselves in Emecheta's work. Instead, her novels are characterized by the finest of balances—a careful, evenly weighted prose that weaves through the pages of her texts and collects figural energy as it proceeds. The result of such stylistic evenhandedness is a novel like *The Bride Price* that is luminous precisely because of its finely wrought crafting.

Ritual within this text is layered into ceremonies of death, marriage, fertility, and birth, and draws attention to the cultural patterns that frame the ways of telling these stories. Storytelling itself is important to Emecheta's characterization of Aku-nna, who recognizes in her Auntie Uzo's stories the parallels between her life and the lives of her ancestors. Emecheta writes that of all the storytelling Aku-nna heard in her village, her aunt's stories "attracted her most." The reader discovers that this is a fatal attraction because it foreshadows Aku-nna's inability to separate herself from the tradition that these stories represent. She is bound to their texts because of her attraction to the cultural (re)membrances in her aunt's words. The "call" of her aunt's instructive stories, "intensely charged with philosophical lessons," was psychic bait for Aku-nna's spirit. Eventually, the conflict between Aku-nna's willing participation and enjoyment of ritual, and her efforts to extricate herself from its control, push the gathering elements of this novel toward its dramatic conclusion. Aku-nna's death at the end of *The Bride Price* represents a metaphorical response to her intimate connection to the village myth—a story that promises tragedy will overcome any girl for whom no bride price is paid.

In a discussion of another of Emecheta's works, *The Joys of Motherhood*, Cynthia Ward notes the author's interest in "telling the story of Nnu-Ego from many different angles, *as her mothers told her hers*" (emphasis added). The exchange between the author, her characters, and their ancestral mentors complicates voice and underscores the multiple generations (both literal and figural) who are counted on to pattern (re)memory and who weave the ritual complex of voices in Emecheta's work. The collection of images recalls what I have labeled earlier in this text as an "absent/presence," and predicts the consistency of the spiritual presence of both deities and ancestors in this work.

The collected presences can be linked to the importance Emecheta's culture places on storytelling. In this regard, there are cultural parallels that Emecheta and Ama Ata Aidoo share. Aidoo also calls attention to the relationship between the stories she heard as a child from her grandmother and her development as a writer. In addition, her school training encouraged her to create oral performances as an accompaniment to all her written work. Both experiences heightened the creative skills she would eventually exploit between spoken and written texts.

> Karla F. C. Holloway. *Moorings and Metaphors: Figures of Culture and Gender in Black Women's Literature* (New Brunswick, New Jersey: Rutgers University Press, 1992)

In *The Rape of Shavi* Emecheta takes her fiction for the first time into the speculative arena, imagining a fabulous African country that is visited by a group of whites who are fleeing what they think is imminent nuclear war. Though the novel is set in 1983, the world the whites discover in Shavi is that of a traditional, timeless culture, a world that has apparently escaped the influences of European civilization and modernization. Because of Shavi's isolation, the effect of the whites' sudden arrival is tantamount to colonization—even though the Europeans' only intent had been the guileless one of seeking refuge from a nuclear holocaust. The result is a study in cultural conflict, as the Shavians try to decide whether to adopt new

ways of thinking the Europeans have introduced—and, to a lesser degree, the Europeans reconsider the putative superiority of their own culture. Since the Africans have their entire way of life destroyed, this exchange is a perfect illustration of what can go wrong in a so-called symmetrical discussion between peoples of different cultures, in which we try to understand them, and *they* try to understand us. It functions, in other words, as a warning to Western readers, reminding us of what can go wrong if we do not approach an alien text with the proper critical tools and the proper cultural humility.

Like Emecheta's other fiction, this novel also thematizes the heterosexual couple, using, in this case, the rape of an African woman by a white European man to symbolize the worst possible consequences of colonization. But the exchange between the West and Africa in this novel is not marked only by such obvious violence. It is also marked by the other Europeans' genuine attempt to engage in symmetrical conversation with their African hosts. Moreover, as Ali Mazrui might argue (1983), the African culture does seem perfectly capable, in the end, of throwing off the mantle of colonization. Before Shavi can reach this point, however, it suffers grievous harm as a direct consequence of the conversation it has had with the West. In contrast to the rebellious characters in Emecheta's earlier fiction, the person in Shavi most interested in engaging the West in conversation and thus challenging the voice of tradition is not a woman but a man—the crown prince himself who, one might think, had a vested interest in maintaining tradition rather than subverting it. Complicating his unexpected rebellion is the fact that the Voice of the Fathers is authenticated in the voice of a goddess who speaks through a corrupt priest. . . .

Because *The Rape of Shavi* has both flat characters and a simple plot, I think it likely the novel is intended to be a political parable or fable. . . .

[Even] as Emecheta portrays the process of what is, after all, an inadvertent colonization, she also defends the value of what the Africans have lost. Implicit in her narrative, therefore, is a critique of Western discourse and a celebration of traditional African thought. Though her mythical kingdom has been inspired by the African past, Emecheta has thrust it into the future, where it functions as a model of society contrary to many Western principles of organization. The new African-inspired world Emecheta envisions here is based on an ethics of communal life where people really do care for and about one another. But the alternative world she imagines is no utopia; it is marked by corruption, a falling away from traditional values, and an astonishing disregard for human beings who are born disabled. By focusing on the weaknesses in their own culture that make the Shavians vulnerable to colonization, Emecheta's fable folds back upon itself, reminding us that perfection in the body politic is a worthy but ultimately unattainable goal. Because the characters are not fully individualized, the dialogic heteroglossia in this novel is not as densely complex as it is in her earlier fiction. But as minimal as the heteroglossia may be, Emecheta does raise some interesting issues to contemplate as the competing voices of tradition and modernism jockey for supremacy in the novel. . . .

Emecheta sets up a situation in Shavi similar to the one in Achebe's *Arrow of God*, where the weakness in the African culture make it vulnerable to the language games of British colonialism. In *The Rape of Shavi* the people and their gods also exist in a delicate equilibrium that has already been disturbed when the strangers arrive—a disturbance evident in the fact that the king and queen have begun to publicly humiliate each other. In failing to inform the queen of his intentions, the king, for example, has broken a crucial link with the past, which leaves his country vulnerable to Western influence. At the same time, Anoku, who serves as the chief priest of Ogene, has secretly begun to put his own self-interest before that of his people by attributing to the goddess a prophecy he himself has concocted in order to betroth his daughter to the crown prince. Just as Anoku ensures his power by claiming Ogene's authority for something he himself has spoken, the whites colonize Shavi through the language they speak, the worldview they represent. The whites make virtually no effort to learn their hosts' language though the crown prince quickly learns English—and he introduces European technology and warfare into his peace-loving country. I want to argue, therefore, that the social upheaval in Shavi is mainly caused by the fact that the language (worldview) of the white interlopers is able to supplant the language of African tradition. . . .

Unacquainted with Enlightenment thought, the Shavians have not divided the life-world into discrete spheres and thus fail to distinguish between what we in the West would call rationality and irrationality. . . . When the Europeans begin to interrogate the Shavians, therefore, the very act of answering the foreigners' questions forces the Shavians to think differently about themselves. Because the Europeans construct their questions based on their own intellectual divisions, for the Shavians to reply, they, too,

must begin to think in these genres—even though they may not be at all suitable to their way of life. . . .

Another way to describe the events that ruin Shavi, therefore, is to say that Emecheta illustrates what happens when the pragmatics of narrative knowledge do battle with the pragmatics of (Western) scientific knowledge. Before the arrival of the Europeans, the Shavians affirmed their identity and organized themselves into a cohesive group through myths and the prophecies of their goddess. . . .

> Katherine Fishburn. *Reading Buchi Emecheta: Cross-Cultural Conversations.* (Westport, Connecticut: Greenwood Press), 1995

BIBLIOGRAPHY

*In the Ditch*, 1972; *Second–Class Citizen*, 1974; *The Bride Price: A Novel*, 1976; *The Slave Girl: A Novel*, 1977; *The Joys of Motherhood: A Novel*, 1979; *Titch the Cat*, 1979; *Nowhere to Play*, 1980; *The Moonlight Bride*, 1981; *The Wrestling Match*, 1981; *Destination Biafra: A Novel*, 1982; *Double Yoke*, 1982; *Naira Power*, 1982; *Adah's Story: A Novel*, 1983; *The Rape of Shavi*, 1983; *Head above Water*, 1986; *Family Bargain*, 1987; *A Kind of Marriage*, 1987; *The Family*, 1989; *Gwendolen*, 1990; *Kehinde*, 1994

# F

## FARAH, Nuruddin (1945–)
### Somalia

The title [of Nuruddin Farah's first novel, *From a Crooked Rib*] is taken from a Somali traditional proverb: "God created Woman from a crooked rib; and anyone who trieth to straighten it, breaketh it." The proverb is well known to Ebla, and the novel traces her progress as experiences teach her its implications and, finally, its limitations (no doubt a man coined it). Even before the novel begins, she has made her first steps towards thinking and deciding for herself, and has run away from her grandfather, despite her sense of duty and perhaps love, or pity, for him—something unheard of in the nomadic, pastoral society in which she has grown up. . . . Like a Jane Austen heroine, and many others too, she is endowed with qualities of mind and disposition which distinguish her from everyone around her and for which no explanation is given. She is just innately exceptional: "She thought of many things a woman of her background would never think of." She wants her actions to correspond to the meaning of her name, Ebla: graceful. . . .

In transferring from the crude but time-honored selfishness of her ignorant grandfather to the knowing, modern selfishness of the city, Ebla unwittingly tests her ambition to be "graceful" to the uttermost. Against a (by now) familiar background of squalor, corruption, double-crossing, and crass greed, she succeeds in mating innocence with experience, and constructs a scheme of self-reliance under which both she and others benefit (not profit) from her goodness of nature. She may have made little headway in the writing of her name, but she has learned to articulate her principles, if only to herself. . . .

It has become something of a cliché to praise Farah's ability to portray female sensibility "from the inside," and certainly the plight of women in an anachronistic society is one of his chief preoccupations, but the remarkable achievement in his account of Ebla is the access it gives us into that particular kind of mind, irrespective of sex: a mind in the process of self-formation. It is in the later novels, set in the postrevolution era, that the portraits of individuals are juxtaposed with the portraits of a society in the process of self-deformation.

D. R. Ewen. In G. D. Killam, ed. *The Writing of East and Central Africa* (London: Heinemann, 1984), pp. 194–96

The African writer who has done the greatest justice to female existence in his writing, in the number of female characters he projects and the variety of roles accorded them as well as in the diversified attitudes toward life represented, is the Somali author Nuruddin Farah. The perspective from which Farah projects his women is almost unique within the context of African creative writing. With the possible exception of [Sembène] Ousmane and [Ayi Kwei] Armah, whose women possess some vision on which they base their actions, Farah seems virtually alone among African writers in depicting the progress which women have made within the constricting African social landscape. Problems there may be,

and for some they are insurmountable. Nevertheless, a good many women are succeeding in scaling the hurdles; and Farah exhibits them, together with their achievements and the challenges with which they are confronted. So pervasive and consistent is his espousal of the female cause that he has been described [by Kirsten Holst Peterson] as "the first feminist writer to come out of Africa in the sense that he describes and analyzes women as victims of male subjugation."

Farah's championing of the cause of women is part of his crusade against tyranny and victimization not just of women, but of all who are denied their legitimate rights—social and political, private and public. . . . With his novels *From a Crooked Rib*, *A Naked Needle*, *Sweet and Sour Milk*, and *Sardines*, we are introduced to yet a new trend in the large corpus of modern African creative writing, particularly the novel. The central feature of this new trend is the demythification of the traditional and communal concept of African life, the generally glorified African past, which overidealized the beauty, dignity, and excellence of African culture. Farah, like [Cyprian] Ekwensi and [Wole] Soyinka (in his novels), is completely immersed in the present. His novels offer an incisive picture of contemporary African realities compounded with vestiges of tradition and elements of modernism. He sees his function as the molding of opinion (through authentic information) against social and political oppression. He champions the cause of individual freedom and exposes such aberrations as nepotism, misused tribal allegiances, female suppression, and stifling materialism, which are responsible for the debasement of humanity and the standard values of the modern African. . . . *From a Crooked Rib* discusses the feminine plight and the general odds which weigh against the female in a traditional Islamic cultural environment. The first two books of his proposed trilogy, *Sweet and Sour Milk* and *Sardines*, give prominent places to women and highlight the repressive and horrifying aspects of the Somali military regime. . . .

The realistic feature of Farah's portrayal of women is that they are seen to take active part in various forms of life around them. Even when they are cast in the traditional mold, like Qumman [in *Sweet and Sour Milk*] or Idil [in *Sardines*], they are active in those areas where they are permitted to operate. Qumman's solicitousness over her dying son and her decision about drugs and medication clearly indicate that she is a vital element in the Keynaan household and in Somali society. She organizes the religious rituals involved with Soyaan's funeral rites, arranging for the presence of the sheikhs and watching over the corpse. More than this, Farah illuminates the changing role of women in a changing society. He even shows some of the men discussing the plight of women. Both Soyaan and Loyaan [in *Sweet and Sour Milk*] advocate a new relationship between men and women which will recognize woman's essential humanity. For such a commitment to the cause of women, Nuruddin Farah is unique among African creative writers.

Juliet I. Okonkwo. *World Literature Today*. 58, 2 (Spring 1984), pp. 217, 221

Farah's political novels have great relevance for the growing reaction against the debilitating developments in most postindependence African societies. Thematically, they are significant not only in their Somali or African context, but also in all societies where oppressive regimes have become entrenched. In an age in which people have become more politically conscious, national politics have progressively assumed more complex dimensions in the African continent, and Farah's novels present an incisive picture of contemporary politics and politicians. He leaves one in no doubt about his attitude to the maneuverings of the Jomo Kenyattas, the Idi Amins, the Bokassas, and the Siyaad Barres of Africa. Although his novels manipulate a deep political consciousness, he is careful not to adopt an ideological stance as Ngugi [wa Thiong's], [Ayi Kwei] Armah, [Wole] Soyinka, or Sembène Ousmane have done. He seems committed to the mirroring of the foibles, cruelties, and imperfections of men in society; and this has contributed to his success. . . .

*Sweet and Sour Milk* and *Sardines* present the terror and inhumanity which are the hallmarks of a tyrannical and dictatorial fascist state. The novels register with suffocating intimacy the brutality, suspicion, [and] mental and physical degradation which are consequent upon unstable totalitarian governments operated by megalomaniacs with a lust for unbridled power. In *Sweet and Sour Milk*, the General, who is also the head of state, had declared that he is the country's constitution, and possesses the right to pass laws and sign decrees at will. The General employs all the resources he can muster to keep the people in abject subjection and a state of humiliation. There is no longer the tragicomedy of revolutionary rhetoric in the midst of gross underdevelopment, as found in Farah's previous novel, *A Naked Needle*. *A Naked Needle* had quietly registered the revolution ushered in by a bloodless coup.

Juliet I. Okonkwo. *Africa Today*. 32, 3 (1985), pp. 57–58

In *Sweet and Sour Milk*, the opening novel of his trilogy, Farah shows the "fine ear of the people" put to sinister use. When the novel opens, Loyaan realizes that the recent death of his twin brother was not a natural one. Soyaan had written and kept in safe keeping a secret memorandum entitled "Dionysius's Ear." In it Soyaan seeks to discredit the military dictator, known as the General, who rules the Somalia of Farah's novels. The General's despotic methods are compared to those of Dionysius the Elder who controlled Syracuse in the fourth century B.C. Dionysius had a cave dug in the shape of the human ear where he kept those who resisted him. When they whispered their secrets to each other, their words were carried along underground passages to the ears of chosen listeners. Soyaan argues that the General "has had an ear service of tyranny constructed" and that he has selected illiterates as "ear servants." . . .

In *Sardines*, the middle novel of the trilogy, Dulman, who as singer and actress is an exponent of the oral, admits that she has been caught (her name implies that she is a victim) between oral and written forces. Her early success was the result, she believes, of the Somali attachment to their oral traditions. "One can communicate," she says, "with the hearts of Somalis only through their hearing faculties." Dulman distrusts the written word which she associates with the General's era. He "made his people read and write" and she becomes his victim when her name is written on a wall.

Farah explores different responses to the spoken and written word throughout his trilogy but never more so than in *Close Sesame*. Here the transition from an oral to a written society defines

the historical background for his central character. Deeriye, the sixty-nine-year old protagonist of *Close Sesame*, has been a freedom fighter all his life. Born and raised [a] devout Muslim in the Ogaden, he was imprisoned when young and newly married for defying the Italian colonial power. In 1972, the year Somalia became officially literate, Deeriye was imprisoned again, but this time for defying the enemy within, for openly criticizing the first public executions ordered by the General.

Fiona Sparrow. *Journal of Commonwealth Literatrure*. 24, 1 (1989), pp. 165–66

*Close Sesame* is the third book in the trilogy *Variations on the Theme of an African Dictatorship*. The connecting theme in the novels is arbitrary power, that of the president, the police state, or the patriarchal family, as seen by some of the oppressed, young intellectuals, or women. In the third book, the approach is paradoxically centered on an old man, a traditional and pious character, and from this unexpected angle, the debate on the legitimacy of rebellion against an unjust ruler will take a new dimension. Through him, time and history will be the main subjects of *Close Sesame*, as well as giving shape and texture to a complex narrative technique.

*Close Sesame* being part of a trilogy, this in itself gives a temporal dimension to the experience of reading, as we meet again characters who have matured or changed from *Sweet and Sour Milk*, *Sardines*, and even *From a Crooked Rib*. The other novels, set in the contemporary world and in a recognizable political system revolved around fictitious events. This time, fictitious elements are secondary to the urgent choices to be made in a context anchored in reality with dates and known facts. By examining how fiction and historical facts are organized and balanced in the book, we can see how the scope and crafts of Farah as a novelist are evolving and also how the text can function as fiction *and* comment on Somalia's history, past and present, for its various readers. . . .

In its treatment of history, *Close Sesame* is committed, but not didactic. The novel gives us too much a sense of the complexity of human interaction for that. Farah in his exile of thirteen years writes to his people, clearly stressing the need for reflection and action. Yet the book, with its direct historical references, far from being a pamphlet, is more a meditation on time and history. The subject is Somalia, but the scope of the book can be extended to the whole of postcolonial Africa. It can be read also, more generally, as a dramatization of the human consciousness of the past and of time fleeing. The subject is very ambitious, but in presenting a protagonist who was a national hero and is a mystic, the book presents us both with a sense of eternity as felt in repeated moments of prayers, and of the sequences of human conflicts and achievements. Some of the best passages, blending the awareness of the minutiae of daily life and the feel that there is an overall meaning to human endeavor . . . are passages of poetry, close to the poetical vision and rhythm of the great oral intertexts.

Jacqueline Bardolph. *Journal of Commonwealth Literature*. 24, 1 (1989), pp. 193, 205–6

With this sweeping gesture of irreverence ["Living begins when you start doubting everything that came before you."] Nuruddin

Farah announces his break with the past in the epigraph to his novel, *Maps*. Farah focuses the cryptic iconoclasm of Socrates's ''everything'' on the ambiguity surrounding the gender assignation of his novel's protagonist, Askar, and the uncertainties about the integrity of the boundaries that define the nation state, Somalia. These unstable categories of gender and nationality are situated in a contrapuntal relationship, so that each term, in the course of the novel's development, comes to subvert or complicate the meaning of the other. . . .

[The] transformation of the anti-imperialist struggle in Africa into a nationalist movement exacerbated a crisis of individual and collective identity that is staged in the African novel. Critics have seen these two levels of trauma in terms of an allegorical correspondence between the psychic crisis of the (usually educated) individual and the sociopolitical crisis of the modern nation state. However, I think we can also read the crisis of individual identity as a crisis of gender and sexual identities that parallels and intersects with the sociopolitical manifestations of disorder, and it is this process of destabilization that Farah's *Maps* enacts. Farah's refusal to accept the categories of gender and nation as sacrosanct or independent of each other is not without precedent in modern African literature. Novelists writing as early as Camara Laye and from ideological perspectives as divergent as Ngugi [wa Thiong'o] and [Chinua] Achebe, [Wole] Soyinka and [Ayi Kwei] Armah, can be seen as contributors to a debate about the efficacy of an identity built around contested ''natural'' categories when read from the vantage point of Farah's text. Conversely, the ways in which these writers have approached the question of identity elucidates Farah's method and the context for his concern in *Maps*. . . .

Farah is unremitting in his insistence that there can be no easy certainties or identities in the Somali situation or about the historical events that have produced it. At every turn in the narrative we are challenged to call our assumptions into question: about imperialism (the ''imperial'' powers in the Somali conflict today are other African countries); about our sense of the ''natural'' justice of the nationalist cause, even where a nation state like Somalia can boast a specific rather than generic identity. Ultimately Farah calls into question the most cherished myths of modern African identity—from the ''natural'' moral superiority of oral pre-technological cultures over literate cultures (Ethiopia has had a written tradition for centuries, the Somali language had no orthography until 1972); to the unquestionable nature of ethnic or nationalist loyalties, and the inevitability of certain gender distinctions. . . .

Farah's destabilization of national and sexual boundaries forces a remapping of the terrain that would take more fully into account the complexity of the modern nation state in Africa. In the process, the evocation of ''traditional'' truths as the paradoxically static yet organic point of departure for the nation state is replaced by a sense of the dynamic interaction and internal contradictions of both the traditional and the modern in today's African nation. Such a strategy could in [Mikhail] Bakhtin's terms truly challenge a Western paradigm of linearity and consolidation; not merely by endlessly pulling out the deconstructionist's rug from under the feet of the dominant/imperial culture, but by confronting and accepting the way in which any act of identity within human culture situates itself in relation to the fluctuating social forces that constitute its specific historical moment.

Farah's text offers no answers, but it challenges us to resist the reflexive urge to pin down a single version of the African reality as ''true'' without first attempting to take seriously the conflicts, tensions, and absences inherent in any narrative of the past or present. His stance makes it possible to reread many of the earlier narratives of the nationalist era in ways that escape the paternalism inherent in Western notions of ''otherness,'' as well as the uncritical assertion of essence that underlies much of the discourse around nationalism and sexualities in modern African fiction.

Rhonda Cobham. *Research in African Literatures.* 22, 2 (Summer 1991), pp. 83–84, 94–96

Nuruddin Farah announced the imminent arrival of his novel *Gifts* in 1986, shortly after the publication of his extraordinary novel of the Ogaden War, *Maps*. However, readers then had to wait (surprisingly, for this prolific novelist who had published six novels in fifteen years) until 1992 for the book's African publication, by a Zimbabwean press, and until 1993 for its European distribution. . . .

Farah's new novel is, first and foremost, a love story. Duniya, a twice-married thirty-five-year-old single parent, slowly succumbs to the loving gift offerings of the once-married Bosaaso, recently returned from America. Duniya is that familiar figure in Farah's fiction: the Somali woman imprisoned by patriarchal Islamic tradition, her position negotiated by men. At the outset of her marital career she is herself a ''gifted'' property, given by her father in a customary marriage to a man three times her age, and one of the subsequent ''givens'' of her destiny is to be controlled by the uncles, half-brothers, and husbands whose charge she is in and in whose houses she is temporarily accommodated. Woman, as she says, is a ''homeless person.'' Duniya moves from her father's house into her aging husband's and from there into a tenancy to the journalist-landlord Taariq, who makes her his live-in companion and then his wife, and who turns out to be a drunken and demanding husband. After the divorce from Taariq, she takes a tenancy to her petulant half-brother Shiriye, but she quarrels with his wife and moves out to live with Bosaaso. Even the alternative pied-à-terre provided by her expatriated brother Abshir at the end of the book to help her preserve her independence is but another male gift; and as gifts have conditions and built-in dependencies, Duniya has grown wary and distrustful of them and has cultivated a habit of looking them in the mouth.

The personal story is foregrounded, however, against a larger social and political canvas and opens out into the wider perspective of international gifts from First to Third World countries, each chapter ending with a newspaper snippet about American and United Nations aid to famine-stricken nations in the Horn and others parts of Africa. Political gifts to nations, like personal gifts to people, bind together donor and recipient in ways which change their relationship. Either may be given with the best or worst of motives and results. They may express affection, compassion, loyalty, or penance; meet contractual obligations; assert superiority and dominance or create dependency; or angle to get something in return, in the hope (though hardly in the case of Africa) that yesterday's recipients will become tomorrow's donors. And since shortages both of food at the national level and of love at the domestic one are man-made (famine, the result of maladministration, ''is a trick up the powerful man's sleeve''), one effect of outside aid to remedy them may be to bolster corrupt power and influence, whether of an Ethiopian emperor or a domestic patriarch. . . .

[Death] notwithstanding, *Gifts* is a sunny and radiant novel, its gentle, teasing humor a welcome relief after the dark menace and shrill psychological agonies of the *Dictatorship* trilogy, and its disciplined clarity of style refreshing after the somewhat mannered esoterics of *Maps*. This is Farah's first African-published book, and it is clearly aimed at a broader and more African-based readership; thus the learned epigraphic allusions to Western literature which open the chapters in the earlier books have been replaced by captions briefly summarizing the events that follow. This is a new, different Farah, interspersing his narrative with the familiar poetic dream literature and oral folklore of Somali tradition but in a much more accessible form than before. *Gifts* is a poetically evocative as well as (politically) a mildly provocative work, and is full of unexpected echoes, startling insights, and subtle quirks of characterization that will continue to delight Farah's readers.

Derek Wright. *World Literature Today*. 68, 1 (Winter 1994), pp. 195–96

It would be perverse to claim Farah as a thoroughgoing postmodernist or to try to limit him to any one school of writing, because his writing is as richly diverse in its origins as his personal background. Farah was born in 1945 in Baidoa, in what was then Italian Somaliland, and was educated in the Ethiopian-ruled Ogaden and Mogadiscio and then at the British universities of Essex and London and the Punjab University of Chandigarh. English, his chosen medium of expression, is his fourth language, existing alongside Somali, Arabic, Amharic, and Italian. He comes, originally, from a nomadic tradition, and his travels, studies, and employments have been nomadic on a global scale: he has lived or held academic appointments in Italy, Germany, the United States, Nigeria, Gambia, Uganda, and the Sudan. He is thus one of Africa's most multicultural and multilingual writers, and his highly eclectic body of fiction draws freely on many cultural and religious sources and on readings in many of the world's literatures. It is a living testament to the process of cultural hybridization that is a standard feature of the postcolonial world. I propose in this article, however, to limit myself to some of the postmodernist tendencies at play in Farah's work, focusing on the points where postmodernism and postcolonialism appear to converge and paying special attention to the literary and cultural rezoning habit that has become a distinctive mark of the Western postmodernist imagination.

Farah's somber, nightmarish trilogy of novels, *Variations on the Theme of an African Dictatorship,* reveals many of the standard features of the postmodernist fiction: for example, the collapsing of ontological boundaries by multiple, superimposed orders of reality; the conspicuous and ingenious play of analogic motif and parallelism; the "transworld" identities of characters who reappear in novel after novel (and, as with the respectively adolescent and mature Eblas of *From a Crooked Rib* and *Sardines*, do not always correspond with their intertextual signifiers); and the favoring of fragmented, composite characters—spaces inhabited by multiple presences—over unitary personalities. The latter tendency is particularly marked in *Sweet and Sour Milk*, where confusions of identity amid a malaise of political misinformation cause Loyaan, during his investigation of his brother's death, to fear that he may not be an autonomous being, but perhaps really part of a composite fabrication put together from the literature of twins, a Siamese-soul called Soyaan-Loyaan, with interchangeable parts. In *Sardines* Farah provides not a collection of individuals but a syncretic portrait of Somali womanhood in which all the women, packed into the same suffocating social sardine tin, become aspects of one another, their characters interpenetrative and complementary. In *Maps* a number of boundaries—sexual, national and ontological—are straddled by the protagonist Askar, a child of the disputed territory of the Ogaden, and there is in this multilayered fiction a puzzling indeterminacy about where metaphor ends and literal reality starts; where mindscape passes into landscape, the personal into the public body, physiological into topographical space. In *Maps* the reductive elements in Askar's behavior, which are privileged by conventional psychological—realist readings (for example, his obsessed idea that his dead Somali mother still lives inside him), are countered by more expansive, postmodernist tendencies. Askar aspires to be, at once, male and female. . . "half-man, half-child," ethnocentric Somali and culturally hybrid Ogadenese. He also fancies himself to be both a real child and the epic miracle-child of his adoptive mother's oral tales, who was present at his own birth and born out of his mother's death (one who has "met death when not quite a being"). He claims to hold "simultaneously multiple citizenships of different kingdoms: that of the living and the dead; not to mention that of being an infant and an adult at the same time". Like his prototypes, Grass's Oskar (= Askar) and Rushdie's Saleem, he is a liminal creature, an occupant of the between-worlds space of the zone. Like them, he is a composite construct assembled from diverse sources and finally, as he struggles on the last page of the novel to free himself of blame for his adoptive mother's death, fragmenting back into his constituent parts: defendant, plaintiff, juror, witness, judge, and audience. The dreamscape of the novel is the improbable space where alone these incongruous elements can coexist.

In these novels Farah also shares concerns expressed by more conventional African authors who owe little or nothing to postmodernist writing. Like them, he is troubled by the imperial powers' zonal expropriation of Africa's political, ethnic, and cultural space in both the colonial and independence periods and, moreover, by the continuation and reinforcement of these territorializing habits by postcolonial African regimes. But it is in his treatment of that very process, and of those regimes' tyrannical imposition of arbitrary, quasi-fictional identities upon their nations, that Farah's work comes closest to postmodernist fiction. Such features are especially marked in *Sweet and Sour Milk* and *Maps*.

In *Sweet and Sour Milk* the General's dictatorship is built around a security corps of illiterate spies and informers working entirely in the oral medium (thus there are no arrest warrants, death certificates, or lists of detainees), and after a while, as I have demonstrated at length elsewhere (Wright 1989), the public oral code of discourse privileged by the regime begins to infiltrate Farah's own written text. The latter takes on, insidiously, the oral narrative's reconstructive and reinventive capacities, its talent for improvising alternative versions in the retelling of tales; its subsequently unstable order of meaning, susceptible to variation, omission, and shifts of emphasis; and, most dangerously in the present political context, the fluid indeterminacy and interpretative openness that follow inevitably from a form of discourse that is audience-oriented rather than performer-centered. In the next novel *Sardines*, the oralist Idil, who is the General's matriarchal representative on the domestic front, is fully at home in this many-versioned reality:

> And by the time you were ready to ask her a question, you would discover that she had already moved on . . . she had changed residence and had nomaded away, impermanent. . . .

Idil's ball of thread rolled away. . . . She began to thread-draw in her mind a past with patterns different from the one she had the intention of re-narrating. . . . Idil counted the number of holes she had to jump in order to form a pattern. (78)

Derek Wright. *Critique: Studies in Contemporary Fiction.* 38, 3 (Spring 1997), pp. 193–205

BIBLIOGRAPHY

*A Dagger in Vacuum,* 1970; *From a Crooked Rib,* 1970; *The Offering,* 1975; *A Naked Needle,* 1976; *A Spread of Butter,* 1978; *Sweet and Sour Milk,* 1979; *Tartar Delight,* 1980; *Sardines,* 1981; *Yussuf and His Brothers,* 1982; *Close Sesame,* 1983; *Maps,* 1986; *Gavor,* 1990; *Gifts,* 1992; *Secrets,* 1998

# FAUSET, Jessie (1882–1961)
## United States

Without polemicizing, [Jessie] Fauset examines [the] antagonism [of social conventions], criticizing the American society which has institutionalized prejudice, safeguarded it by law and public attitude, and in general, denied the freedom of development, the right to well-being, and the pursuit of happiness to the black woman. In short, Fauset explores the black woman's struggle for democratic ideals in a society whose sexist conventions assiduously work to thwart that struggle. Critics have usually ignored this important theme which even a cursory reading of her novels reveals. This concern with exploring female consciousness and exposing the unduly limited possibilities for female development is, in a loose sense, feminist in impulse, placing Fauset squarely among the early black feminists in Afro-American literary history. It is this neglected dimension of Fauset's work—her examination of the myriad shadings of sexism and how they impinge upon female development—that is the focus of this discussion. A curious problem in Fauset's treatment of feminist issues, however, is her patent ambivalence. She is alternately forthright and cagey, alternately "radical" and conservative on the "woman question." On the one hand, she appeals for women's right to challenge socially sanctioned modes of feminine behavior, but on the other, she frequently retreats to the safety of traditional attitudes about women in traditional roles. At best, then, we can grant that Fauset was a quiet rebel, a pioneer black literary feminist, and that her characters were harbingers of the movement for women's liberation from the constriction of cultural conditioning. . . .

Fauset's oblique and ambivalent treatment of women's roles in "The Sleeper Wakes" and in *There Is Confusion,* respectively, is less apparent in her next three novels, *Plum Bun, The Chinaberry Tree,* and *Comedy: American Style.* She continues her exploration of women's roles, their lives' possibilities, and her criticism of social conventions that work to restrict those possibilities by keeping women's sights riveted on men, marriage, and motherhood. These domestic and biological facets, Fauset suggests, while important, are just one dimension of a woman's total being, one aspect of her boundless capacities and possibilities. Seen in this light, then, fairy-tale illusions about life give way to mature realities, and women, instead of waiting for their imaginary princes, aggressively take charge of their lives and move toward achieving authentic selfhood.

The idea of Fauset, a black woman, daring to write—even timidly so—about women taking charge of their own lives and declaring themselves independent of social conventions, was far more progressive than critics have either observed or admitted. Although what Fauset attempted in her depictions of black women was not uniformly commensurate with what she achieved, she has to be credited with both presenting an alternative view of womanhood and a facet of black life which publishers, critics, and audiences stubbornly discouraged if not vehemently opposed. Despite that discouragement and opposition, Fauset persisted in her attempt to correct the distorted but established images of black life and culture and to portray women and blacks with more complexity and authenticity than was popular at the time. In so doing, she was simultaneously challenging established assumptions about the nature and function of Afro-American literature. Those who persist, then, in regarding her as a prim and proper Victorian writer, an eddy in a revolutionary literary current, would do well to read Fauset's work more carefully, to give it a more fair and complete appraisal, one that takes into account the important and complex relationship between circumstances and artistic creation. Then her fiction might finally be accorded the recognition and attention that it deserves and Fauset, her rightful place in the Afro-American literary tradition.

Deborah E. McDowell. In Marjorie Pryse and Hortense J. Spillers, eds. *Conjuring: Black Women, Fiction, and Literary Tradition* (Bloomington: Indiana University Press, 1985), pp. 87–88, 100

Jessie Fauset, whose fiction falls to some extent within the romance genre, makes greater use of the Cinderella Line as narrative strategy than does either Alice Walker or Toni Morrison. Olivia Cary, the unpleasant central character of *Comedy: American Style,* resembles the "typical mother" in marriage novels—Mrs. Bennett in [Jane Austen's] *Pride and Prejudice,* for example. The subtext of Fauset's novel follows the Cinderella Line: Olivia dreams her light-skinned daughter Teresa marries a princely (white, rich) husband. The achievement of Olivia's dream, however, is thwarted by the larger, racial issue which informs the novel, the issue of "passing." Jessie Fauset, whose novels espouse essentially middle-class values, nevertheless offers, particularly in *Comedy: American Style,* a critical perspective of these very values. This ambivalence results in a subversion of the Cinderella Line. Teresa, who has passed at her mother's insistence, marries not a prince but a pauper. At the end of the novel both mother and daughter, defeated in the marriage quest, are left without a culture and without a language, in the threadbare clothing which signifies an unhappy ending. . . .

As a woman writer writing *as* a woman, if not *for* women, Fauset was likely to notice the aesthetic relationship between skin and clothing. This kind of thing is important in the daily lives of most middle-class women and, I would guess, of many middle-class men. By including chestnut hair and puff sleeves in her fictional world, Fauset is only being true to the tradition of American realism. But these concerns are not merely gratuitous. . . . Fauset uses clothing as a way to articulate not only the racial differences between mother and daughter but also the hierarchy of class/race which she then addresses throughout the novel: the desperate, white-identified mother; the middle-class daughter caught between her mother's notion of "a cruder race" and her own desire to be like her peers; the black-identified Marise in her "glowing, gay colors"; the naturally gifted, light-skinned Phebe, who is already accumulating capital.

Fauset also captures here the excitement of adolescent anticipation, the thrill of choosing for oneself what one is to wear and not to wear. Thus Teresa is transformed, through clothing, from "mouse" to warm, young black woman. As she puts her "nice narrow feet" into "bronze slippers," she becomes reminiscent of Cinderella on her way to the ball—in this case a neighborhood party. It is in fact Teresa's crowning moment. For later she meets a young black man, falls in love, and is humiliated by her mother, who forces her into a disastrous marriage. The Cinderella Line has reversed itself irrevocably.

Mary Jane Lupton. *Black American Literature Forum*. 20, 4 (Winter 1986), pp. 410–12

Fauset's four novels, *There Is Confusion, Plum Bun, The Chinaberry Tree*, and *Comedy: American Style*, contain numerous shared perspectives with [Edith] Wharton, especially on issues confronting women. Fauset's critique of the economics of marriage for women, of fairy-tale illusions of love and salvation, of mother-daughter conflict and alienation, of the tension between class and gender for privileged women (a theme only partially plumbed in both authors), and of the deep rivalries and divisions that sever bonds between women, all bring to mind Wharton. Further, although no one to my knowledge has explored the similarities and contrasts between the two authors, quite specific echoes and parallels exist. The marriage of Fauset's Teresa Cary in *Comedy: American Style* to a conservative, economically straitened Frenchman, complete with tyrannical mother—a marriage which entombs the young American heroine in a suffocating Old World contract which she totally misjudged—has a strong parallel in Undine Spragg's disastrous French marriage in [Wharton's] *The Custom of the Country*. Likewise the suicide in this bitterly satiric Fauset novel of a kind, gentle young man who puts a revolver to his head because of the heroine's rejection of him recalls Ralph Marvell's death in Wharton's equally scathing novel. Fauset's portrait of the casual, careless sexual predation of a privileged educated young white man in *Plum Bun* bears very interesting comparison, it seems to me, with Wharton's portrait of Lucius Harney in *Summer*. Indeed, the whole issue of marriage for profit in *Plum Bun* evokes several Wharton novels—*The House of Mirth, Summer, The Custom of the Country*. . . .

A major theme in both authors is the agonizing break between mothers and daughters experienced by women at the turn of the century, the drama specifically of a daughter leaving her mother's world, even renouncing it, and the bitter split that consequently exists between the two worlds, one of the daughter, the other of the mother. In Wharton, think of the distance between Lily Bart [in *The House of Mirth*] and her mother, Undine Spragg and hers, Charity Royall [in *Summer*] and hers. Likewise in Fauset, Joanna Marshall [in *There Is Confusion*] strikes out on her own, Angela Murray [in *Plum Bun*] radically cuts herself off from her mother's world, and Olivia Blanchard does the same. Similarities abound; the younger generation in the work of both authors seeks freedom and self-determination, especially economic and sexual, in ways their

mothers never dreamed of. But there are also basic differences. In Wharton the mothers of her most interesting rebellious young women—Lily, Undine, Charity—represent a world that should be left behind, a past that is confining and suffocating. They represent an impoverished past for women—whether it is the spiritual poverty of Lily's mother or the literal misery of Charity's. They evoke a negative past from which the daughters rightly rebel.

In Fauset, in contrast, the rejected mothers represent a positive world: one of purpose and group pride born of struggle. They are a strong confident group whose lost, confused daughters have much to gain from coming back home to them. Unlike Edith Wharton, that is, for Jessie Redmon Fauset the generation of mothers whose daughters came to maturity in the two or three decades before 1920 do have an important life-giving vision to offer. It is based on the corporate value of community action and rootedness, female friendship, solidarity with men in the race struggle, membership in a church, and commitment to the bonds of family. This dramatic contrast between the impoverished inherited maternal world in Wharton and the rich one in Fauset leads inexorably to the conclusion that it is not just class or personal history or gender but also and perhaps most important race which leads Edith Wharton to her bleak, hopeless endings. Had she been a black American writer of comparable generation, education, and class, she would have had behind her, as Fauset did, a generation of strong inspiring mothers to offer support and wisdom—even if their daughters, as we see in Fauset, were too foolish to listen to them.

Elizabeth Ammons. *College Literature*. 14, 3 (Fall 1987), pp. 211–12, 214–15

Fauset responded to an emerging black urban working class by a mediation of her authorial position as a class perspective. She represented in her fiction a middle-class code of morality and behavior that structured the existence of her characters and worked as a code of appropriate social behavior for her readers. Fauset's intellectual contribution was the development of an ideology for an emerging black middle class which would establish it as being acceptably urbane and civilized and which would distinguish it from the rural influx. Unlike earlier women novelists, Fauset did not consider the aftermath of slavery and the failure of Reconstruction as a sufficient source of echoes and foreshadowings for her new relation to history. Fauset represented this new history through a generational difference, a difference figured as a recognition of the need for the protagonists to revise the irrelevant history of their parents, a history tied to the consequences of slavery.

Hazel V. Carby. *Reconstructing Womanhood: The Emergence of the Afro-American Woman Novelist* (New York: Oxford University Press, 1987), pp. 166–67

Like Jane Austen, Jessie Fauset is concerned with the commonplace details of domestic life, and at her best, as . . . critic Sterling A. Brown has observed, "succeeds in a realism of the sort sponsored by William Dean Howells."

In the foreword to *The Chinaberry Tree*, Fauset reveals her social and artistic preference for depicting "something of the homelife of the colored American who is not being pressed too hard by the Furies of Prejudice, Ignorance, and Economic Injustice," and who as ". . . naturally as his white compatriots . . . speaks of his 'old' Boston families, 'old Philadelphians,' 'old Charlestonians.' And he has a wholesome respect for family and education and labor and the fruits of labor. He is still sufficiently conservative to lay a slightly greater stress on the first two of these four.'' By stressing the genteel tradition and everyday rituals of the urban black elite, Fauset limits her presentation of truth and reality to the class of people she knew best. . . .

The moral of her novels is that the respectable, genteel black American ''is not so vastly different from any other American, just distinctive.'' In *There Is Confusion* dark-skinned Joanna Marshall and light-skinned Peter Bye overcome color prejudice and achieve success by confronting the truth of their family backgrounds and committing themselves to education, hard work, respectability, and each other. Even so, neither the characters nor the author-narrator has much sympathy for commonplace minds or people. In *The Chinaberry Tree* adultery and illegitimacy overshadow the lives of three black women in a small New Jersey town. Fauset is more concerned with the realistic details of Aunt Sal and Laurentine's daily routine and their ability to rise above the ostracism of their community than she is the narrowness of small-town notions of respectability. As the central unifying metaphor, the chinaberry tree is a sentimentally contrived symbol of the illicit love of Aunt Sal and Colonel Holloway and of the shadowy past that unites Sal with her illegitimate daughter, Laurentine, and illegitimate niece, Melissa. Unlike Howells, Fauset does not shrink from the unpleasant aspects of the black bourgeoisie as she approvingly reveals that their morals and manners are not appreciably different in kind from those of the white bourgeoisie.

Bernard W. Bell. *The Afro-American Novel and Its Tradition* (Amherst: University of Massachusetts Press, 1987), pp. 107–8

Though the emphasis in Harlem Renaissance writings was professedly on things ''Negro,'' Fauset's poetry, with few exceptions, was both conventional in form and curiously silent on questions of race. Except for two or three experimental pieces, her roughly two dozen published poems are unremarkable imitations of Western poetic conventions in spirit, form, and theme. Her two predominant themes are nature and unrequited love, both timeworn, ''universal'' poetic subjects, which she treats with a casual matter-of-factness. Seldom is there a concrete reference to race, gender, or any of the controversial political and social issues of her day that readers might take as evidence of a ''black woman's'' signature.

If readers look for such a signature merely in the presence and number of references identified narrowly with race and gender, then Fauset's poems will disappoint. In an era when many black writers were celebrating their racial origins and distinctiveness and calling for representation of those origins in the arts, Fauset was writing poetry whose indebtedness to the Western literary tradition is everywhere apparent. . . .

Critics have been severe in their assessments of Fauset's poetry, especially of its ''Western'' predilections, impugning in the process her consciousness of and commitment to her race. Viewed from a different perspective, however, her ''universal'' (read ''Western'') lyrics of love and nature can be said to make problematic the very idea and category of ''Western'' seen in opposition to ''black.'' Behind all of Fauset's work, both as editor and as writer, is a sensibility, catholic and global in its reach, that complicates simplistic orthodoxies. For her, ''blackness'' was not synonymous

with ''African-American'' but included black people the world over. Hence, the French references in her poetry are not necessarily evidence of a flight from blackness but, rather, of her awareness of ''the French connection'' to a number of French-speaking blacks in other parts of the world. As Fauset herself had noted in her translation of Haitian poets, ''Both France and the classics are the property of the world.''

Deborah E. McDowell. In Lea Baechler and A. Walton Litz, eds. *Modern American Women Writers* (New York: Scribners, 1991), pp. 126–27

To no modern race do its women mean so much as to the Negro, nor come so near to the fulfillment of its meaning. (Du Bois, *Darkwater*)

[The] cultural promise and imperatives characterizing the Harlem Renaissance foregrounded the bourgeois African American woman as the icon of racial achievement—despite (or, perhaps, because of) the fact that her very existence as a bourgeois black woman ran counter to mainstream racial prejudice. For the woman herself, this situation produced an obligation to perpetually ''perform'' her identity to a public for whom, it seemed, she vanished without a trace the moment she was ''offstage''—out of sight and in repose.

[Jessie Redmon Fauset's 1924 novel *There Is Confusion* takes on] the problem of performance explicitly and with extraordinary comprehensiveness. Fauset sends her bourgeois heroine out into dangerous public territory—but never quite beyond the protective reach of that heroine's working-class double. In the feminine economy which underwrites this novel, the working-class Maggie Ellersley acts as a lightning rod for the destabilizing publicity set off in the text by the bourgeois Joanna Marshall's necessary pursuit of a theatrical career. . . .

Immediately upon its publication in 1924, *There Is Confusion* was recognized for its salience to the public relations project at the heart of Renaissance concerns. Reviews of the book focused on its function for the black bourgeois class generally: Writing for *Opportunity*, Montgomery Gregory asserted that ''the great value of this novel [lies] in interpreting the better elements of our life to those who know us only as domestic servants, 'uncles,' or criminals.'' Alain Locke announced that ''the novel that the Negro intelligentsia have been clamoring for has arrived with Jessie Fauset's first novel, *There Is Confusion*,'' enthusiastically declaring that it ''throbs with some of the latest reactions of the race situation in this country upon the psychology and relations of the colored and white American of the more intelligent classes.'' He furthermore reflected that ''we scarcely realize how by reaction to social prejudice we have closed our better circles physically and psychologically.''

*There Is Confusion* is most obviously a romantic novel, and though the text clearly exceeds this generic classification, it is through romance that Fauset finally resolves the problem of performance for genteel Negro womanhood. Ambitious in scope, the novel spins out a saga of generations driven by urgent questions of racial responsibility, feminine destiny, and the challenge of life in public. Fauset works her novel to elaborate the metanarrative of a race—and finally, a nation—in pursuit of its own progress. Though there is an overt determinism attached to the lineage of the characters, there is equally a sense of contemporary historical crisis about the generation whose story is the narrative focus. The implication is that this group of young people stands at the threshold of a new era for the race, an era whose racial triumphs and failures will be triumphs and failures of publicity. The characters are clearly divided (with some crossover, in the course of events) into those who hearken to the racial call and those who fail to see the larger racial meaning of their own lives; yet the presence or absence of a sense of mission and strategy is finally irrelevant to a character's implication in publicity. The two women protagonists bear this out: The working-class Maggie thinks only of her private concerns, while the bourgeois Joanna is possessed of visionary racial consciousness. And yet, in her capacity as (in essence) a ''girl of the streets,'' Maggie is a magnet for the distress and volatility of life in public and, hence, the structurally enabling condition for Joanna's own pursuit of a stage career that is sanctified and safely bourgeois.

Nina Miller. *African American Review*. 30, 2 (Summer 1996), pp. 205–20

BIBLIOGRAPHY
''*The Sleeper Wakes*,'' 1920; *Plum Bun*, 1929; *The Chinaberry Tree*, 1931; *There is Confusion*, 1932; *Comedy, American Style*, 1933

# G

## GAINES, Ernest J. (1933–)
### United States

Ernest J. Gaines' novel, *Catherine Carmier*, was not reviewed in any of the popular national book reviewing media. Yet, it is a well-written story about a young man's return to his rural hometown community in Louisiana. Jackson Guerin returns home armed with a college degree to find that things have not changed too much among the Creole, black and Cajun families, most of whom are farmers. One exception is that during the previous summer a few outsiders from the big cities had tried to get Negroes to vote. . . .

Catherine, the heroine, is of a Creole family and is a sensitive and intelligent young woman who is controlled by and unbelievably dependent on her father, Raoul. There is a touching and warm love affair between Catherine and Jackson that carries the story. The Carmier family traditionally looks down on their black brethren, as is historically true of many families in many sections of Louisiana. Raoul, the proud patriarch with only a drop of Negro blood, clings tenaciously to the silly notions of skin color. He hates the Cajuns because they are white and control the best land, and the Negroes because they represent to him everything inferior. Catherine, torn between a desire to please Raoul and her feelings for Jackson, never reconciles the ambivalence of her life. Although she professes her love for Jackson, Catherine cannot leave her father. Therein lies the essence of the book. On the surface this might not seem to be much meat for a plot, yet the conflicts of values and of family traditions are, in the main, well presented.

The striking part of this work is that there is no bitterness nor clarion call for racial equality in it. While there are divisions among people because of differences in skin color and education, *Catherine Carmier* is outstanding for its simplicity and the universality of its people.

Miles M. Jackson. *Phylon*. Fall 1965, pp. 216–17

As a subjective, emotive and often-treated theme, the colour problem bristles with traps. No one could be detached in either writing or reading about this subject. For the author there are the dangers of hysteria and over simplification. Worst of all, he may, with the best motives in the world, produce a book that is first-rate pleading, second-rate art.

*Of Love and Dust* avoids these traps. The theme—that a white man may love a negro woman but a southern negro may not love a white woman and live to tell the tale—is ominously familiar. But treated by Ernest Gaines with objective quietness, a familiar situation has made, if not a major novel, an impressive one. The Louisiana plantation talk, which can make this kind of novel almost unreadable, is never obtrusive. It is a steady, dense, unshowy book in which passion is cumulative rather than explosive, but no less powerful for being so. The drama, between Marcus, the young, rebellious negro, and the baby-doll wife of his overseer, is worked out with a steady, almost balletic certainty of step before the watchers, paralysed by heat, weariness and fear. We are drawn in,

forced to observe, by the narrator, the negro tractor-driver Jim Kelly. He is a good, intelligent man, torn in his attitude to Marcus between anxiety and admiration. The anxiety is touching and understandable, but I could not share his ultimate respect for a character whose mindless rebellion seems petty and petulant beside Jim's wiser, more experienced grief.

This is my only reservation. Otherwise, Mr. Gaines's ear and eye cannot be faulted. He neither pleads nor passes judgment. There is no black and white moralising about the colour problem. The effect is all the stronger for this restraint.

Janice Elliot. *New Statesman*. June 7, 1968, p. 769

Gaines somehow manages to show that there is more even to a redneck than his racism. Racists are dangerous, unstable, vicious individuals, but never that alone. They are people, fully realized in Gaines's fiction, and have a haggard futility, a pale and shrieking dullness, a pained unsatisfiedness that makes them appear wounded and deficient and far less complete than the blacks they attempt to intimidate.

Gaines's people are never completely wiped out by whites, even when they are killed by them. They are too large and the whites around them too small. His heroes would fight to walk upright through a hurricane. They do no less when confronted with a white world intent on grinding them down. They fight to maintain small human pleasures and large human principles in a hostile and morally degenerate world. They have seen the level to which humankind can sink and have managed to remain standing all these many years.

Gaines is much closer to Charles Dickens, W. E. B. DuBois, Jean Toomer and Langston Hughes than he is to Richard Wright or Ralph Ellison. There is nothing in Gaines that is not open—to love or to interpretation. He also claims and revels in the rich heritage of Southern black people and their customs; the community he feels with them is unmistakable and goes deeper even than pride. Like the beautifully vivid, sturdy and serviceable language of the black, white and Creole people of Louisiana, Gaines is mellow with historical reflection, supple with wit, relaxed and expansive because he does not equate his people with failure.

Alice Walker. *New York Times Book Review*. May 23, 1971, p. 12

Ernest Gaines' *The Autobiography of Miss Jane Pittman* covers a period of struggle for life and dignity extending beyond the Civil War to the 1950's. Miss Jane Pittman, the novel's chief character, reveals the tough spirit within herself and others and provides an interpretation of people and events that accord with the more forceful slave narratives found in such a work as B. A. Botkin's *Lay My Burden Down*. It provides an insight lacking in Faulkner, who naturally inclined to a concern with the Southern past which explained more about whites than blacks. Gaines' stark tones are more like those of Margaret Walker's *Jubilee*, although it differs

269

from *Jubilee* in being told as first person narrative and does not repeat *Jubilee*'s concerns. *The Autobiography of Miss Jane Pittman* also has something of the folk spirit of the little noticed novel *All God's Children* by Alston Anderson (1965), but surpasses it in sweep and density.

Through the novel, the reader gets a sense of the continuity of a black spiritual assertion both in everyday life and in its struggles against oppression. The most interesting section of the novel deals directly with Miss Jane's experiences during Reconstruction, her marriage, and the hopes she directly pursues. There is a loss of intensity where she is not directly the center of the action, but *The Autobiography of Miss Jane Pittman* is a fine remaking and regrasping of the dense past deriving from secure grasp of black culture and its mixtures.

George E. Kent. *Phylon*. Winter 1972, pp. 307–8

Gaines uses the rural Louisiana countryside as the setting for most of his stories. The countryside and most particularly the quarters, those ancient structures which have served as homes for generations of Black people back to the times of slavery, are captured in a purposely ill-defined time between the Second World War and the present, a time not quite yesterday, not quite today. The struggle for ascendency in the small Southern backwater Gaines has created is not between white and Black. The racial order, with the Blacks who are on the bottom, rich white people who are on the top and the Cajuns (the descendents of the white Arcadians who were resettled in Louisiana by the British after the close of the French and Indian Wars in the late eighteenth century), who, no matter how high their income, are not quite as good, at least in the eyes of Blacks, as the Anglican whites, but no matter how poor, are at least one step above the Blacks, is slowly changing. But change, in an overtly racial manner, seldom moves beyond the periphery of Gaines's attention. His concern is for the ways in which people attempt to hold on to or break from the past, adjust to the present or influence the future. Thus, his major theme, in its broadest sense, is the clash between the old and the new, the past and the future. The old is violated by the new, not out of wanton destruction; rather it is attacked in an attempt to wrench new definitions, new images of manhood and dignity, new realities out of the old.

Sherley Anne Williams. *Give Birth to Brightness* (New York: Dial, 1972), pp. 170–71

Pessimism does indeed seem to be foreign to Gaines's interpretation of his world, and this is indicated by a piece of external evidence involving the composition of *Of Love and Dust*. It is plausible that Marcus dies at the hands of Sidney Bonbon. The system depicted in the novel encourages such an outcome. But it is not the ending Gaines originally chose. In the first version he sent to the publisher, Marcus and Louise escape the plantation and, like two errant and fun-loving children, go off to the city on a spree, thumbing their noses at the code. Gaines's publisher asked for another conclusion; Gaines supplied it, and did no irreparable damage to the integrity of the novel. But the great difference between conclusions is instructive. Gaines's first inclination was not toward making Marcus a martyred revolutionary. It was toward

creating a joyful and ironic triumph over a stifling system, which would have harmonized perfectly well with Marcus as a swaggerer and a dandy.

Gaines's best work roughly follows the course of that first version of *Of Love and Dust*. It has a general tone of comic irony and it shows inertia being overcome by new and more vital forces, though not without pain and some sense of loss. It is the tone and the theme we get in the short story collection *Bloodline*, and his third novel, *The Autobiography of Miss Jane Pittman*. In them, Gaines still writes about his fictional city of Bayonne and the area around Baton Rouge, about the old resisting the young, the whites murdering and cheating. But the time and the power have shifted to the side of rebirth and virility, the energy now flows toward illumination and successful change, not darkness and failure. They contain no political or psychological rationalizations because their content and form grow out of convictions and observations with which Gaines is more consistently comfortable. And we are burdened with no gratuitous assertions about an optimistic future because the stories themselves embody that optimism.

Jerry H. Bryant. *Southern Review*. Autumn 1974, pp. 855–56

The greatest difference between the historian and the novelist is this: The historian simply demands a recognition of history; seldom does he encourage men to alter it; the novelist demands recognition of history only as a prelude toward changing it. The Jane Pittmans, Ned Douglasses, and Jimmy Arrons are able to assault the patterns of the past, only when they understand the matrix of the society in which they live; only through such understanding can they move to alter reality. Gaines demands such understanding from his people as evidenced in his novels from *Catherine Carmier* to *The Autobiography of Miss Jane Pittman*, and the formula for his historical novels is easy to discern: Realization precedes action; recognition of the truth of history is a prelude for rebellion and revolution.

This is the final theme, arrived at by the author, after three novels. If *Catherine Carmier* suffered from an intricate, not well-developed plot structure, and if *Of Love and Dust* loses strength and power through flaws in the makeup of the major protagonist, *The Autobiography of Miss Jane Pittman* reaches near perfection because of the unity of form and content, because the themes are interwoven into the fabric of the novel in such a way as to complement the form. The autobiographical novel which takes history as its material must be so well structured that events proceed in chronological order—if not on the printed page, then in the eyes of the reader. If clarity is to prevail, smooth transition from episode to episode is demanded. Through limiting the use of flashbacks and stream of consciousness, and depending upon the central narrator to move the story along, Gaines avoids a chaotic novel.

The result is a people's novel, one revealing unwritten history and depicting the examples of those who, in refusing to accept reality without question, rebelled against it.

Addison Gayle, Jr. *The Way of the New World* (Garden City: New York, Doubleday, 1975), pp. 364–65

Ernest J. Gaines's most recent novel, *In My Father's House*, published in 1978, was not widely reviewed. The notices that did appear were respectful but a bit gingerly and unenthusiastic in tone, as if the reviewers did not quite know how to respond to the book. The relative neglect of the work, in comparison to the more compelling *The Autobiography of Miss Jane Pittman*, is understandable. But it is unfortunate in view of the fact that *In My Father's House* is an important work, showing significant development in Gaines's art and thought, especially in light of his depiction of and reaction to the 1970s.

One reason for the lukewarm response to *In My Father's House* is the voice Gaines uses. In fact, according to his own testimony, he had trouble completing the novel because it employs an omniscient narrator, while he wrote most of his earlier works in the first person. His use of omniscient narration led to a phenomenon much noted by reviewers—a severe detachment, a distance between story and narrator. The reader does not get as personally involved with Philip Martin as he does with Miss Jane or Jim Kelly or the narrators of the stories in *Bloodline*. Yet are not detachment and the consequent irony precisely what Gaines aimed to create in *In My Father's House*? He does not intend for the reader to become intimately involved either with the characters or with the story.

Gaines's distancing of his readers—and himself—from this novel may not indicate a change in his philosophy, but it does, I think, reflect a change in his attitude toward his characters' potential development. Considered in sequence, Gaines's first three novels show a gradual development in his characters' ability to grow, change, and prevail. All the characters in *Catherine Carmier*, his first novel, are victims of social or environmental forces, while in *Of Love and Dust* Jim Kelly and Marcus Payne achieve growth through fighting the inertia of Southern black life and, within limits at least, gain the capacity to shape their lives. Gaines's sense of this power on the part of his characters culminates in the depiction of Jane Pittman, who prevails over seriously adverse circumstances. The *Autobiography* reconciles the dichotomies of the earlier novels: Past and present, young and old, man and woman. In *In My Father's House* the reconciliation falls apart. Discussing the novel while he was still writing it, Gaines contended that it does not reflect a change in his views: "I cannot write only about Miss Jane and man surviving. And I cannot write only about man failing. I write about both." Certainly his works do portray both survival and failure, but I think *In My Father's House* questions the emphasis on black progress reflected in the *Autobiography*, and . . . suggests that Gaines feels that a modification of the positive conclusion of the *Autobiography* is in order.

Frank W. Shelton. *Southern Review*. 17, 2 (April 1981), pp. 340–41

The prime characteristic of the pseudo-autobiographical novel . . . is the author's deliberate attempt to convince the reader that the events described actually occurred. The pseudo-autobiographical novel employs all the elements of the autobiography. It reads as an autobiography and is often presented as such. In Ernest Gaines's [*The Autobiography of Miss Jane Pittman*], for example, the word "autobiography" even occurs in the title. Indeed, unless the reader knows facts to the contrary, there is very little to indicate that such a work is not a verifiable autobiography. . . .

As in all autobiographies, *The Autobiography of Miss Jane Pittman* has one main character. Miss Jane, the narrator, is the central figure around which the story evolves. All the other characters are minor and are seen through her eyes. They are important to the story only to the extent that they illuminate Miss Jane's character. As a consequence, the facts or historical events of the story are related through the context of her experience. . . .

The book is written in the form of a series of tape-recorded interviews of a black woman who was once a slave. In his attempt to simulate the autobiographical form, Ernest Gaines went out of his way to demonstrate Miss Jane's dependence upon what William Howarth calls an "essential control" in autobiography, memory. Due to her age, however, many times her memory fails her. . . . In fact, in the introduction to the book, the schoolteacher who "conducted" the interviews talks about the difficulties caused by the lapses in Miss Jane's memory; at some points she was said to forget everything.

Another strategy Ernest Gaines employed to make his book look like a real autobiography was to model it after a major subgenre of the Afro-American autobiography, the slave narrative. In the tradition of this mode, the ex-slave would risk recounting his life only after he was safely out of the slave states. Similarly, the fictional Miss Jane tells her story from a position of relative impunity. When she agrees to talk to the schoolteacher, she is already over a hundred years old. Her life has run its course and is only a few months from its glorious end. The incidents she narrates, including the bold and militant act of drinking from a fountain marked FOR WHITES ONLY, are of no consequence to her future life.

Bede M. Ssensalo. In Eldred Durosimi Jones, ed. *African Literature Today*. 14 (1984), pp. 94–95

The interaction between the community and the individual, along with its role in the shaping of human personality, is a primary concern of Ernest J. Gaines in much of his fiction. It is in probing the underlying community attitudes, values, and beliefs to discover the way in which they determine what an individual will or has become that Gaines gives poignancy to the pieces in his short-story collection *Bloodline*. Because his fiction focuses on the peculiar plight of black Americans in the South, Gaines must consider an additional level of significance—the strong communal bonds characteristic of Southern black folk culture. In these stories, black folk culture, with its emphasis on community-defined values and behaviors, shows signs of deterioration, while Western individualism and the development of more personally-defined values appear as catalysts in the demise of the black folk world-view. In such a cultural climate, the spiritual and emotional well-being of both the community and the individual is threatened. Faced with the necessity to act and finding traditional solutions no longer viable, the characters in Gaines's stories struggle desperately to restore some semblance of normalcy to their worlds. The dramatic conflict endemic to the stories in *Bloodline* arises out of the efforts of various characters to reconcile their individual needs with community prerequisites. Two of the stories in *Bloodline*, "A Long Day in November" and "The Sky Is Gray," are particularly illustrative of the conflict between community perspective and individual needs. The conflict in these two stories further illustrates the importance of the changes taking place within Southern black culture to the development of the social consciousness of children. While the action of the stories revolves around two young boys, the resolution of the conflict resides with their parents.

John W. Roberts. *Black American Literature Forum.* 18, 3 (Fall 1984), p. 110

The fictions of Ernest J. Gaines reflect and refract the place, history, traditions, folklore and folkways, situations, and people of his native South. . . .

His first published major work, *Catherine Carmier*, has two principal characters, Catherine and Jackson, who in order to confirm and demonstrate their feelings for each other, must break away. Catherine must break from an emotionally incestuous relationship with her father, Raoul, and the intraracial discrimination that he represents; and Jackson, from the expectations of his elders, personified by his Aunt Charlotte, that he remain there to be "the one," their Moses. The time of the novel is set during the stirrings of what would develop into the Civil Rights Movement. Gaines followed this novel with *Of Love and Dust*, an exploration of the protocols of interracial sex and love in a time of rigid taboos, before the social revolution in the South in the 1950s and 1960s. The novel's tensions develop as the protocols are violated or prove ineffective as lust becomes love. The result is that the delicate equilibrium that makes for overtly peaceful coexistence among the ethnic groups—black, white, and Cajun—is upset. His next book, *Bloodline*, is a collection of shorter fictions, each about a black male in a conscious or subconscious movement toward identity, self-esteem, maturity, dignity. . . .

Gaines's fictional people are generally well-realized and unfailingly human characters capable of humor and high seriousness, of foolishness and wisdom, of indifference and compassion, of jealousy and uncompromising, sustaining love. His central characters are usually Negroes. In depicting them and their conflicts and struggles, Gaines is not a hostile, combative writer; his fictions, at least on the surface, do not have as a major purpose indictment and condemnation of whites and racism. Rather, with great warmth, he celebrates the indomitable strength and resilience and moral reserve of black people. Trapped in circumstances of place and history and custom, his protagonists do not capitulate; they adapt to or deflect adversity as they bide their time or revolt. Most importantly, they endure. . . .

The fiction of Ernest J. Gaines demonstrates his thorough factual and experiential knowledge of his native, regional South. More importantly, his fiction demonstrates his penetrating understanding of the complexities and subtleties of universal human nature that affect and are affected by these regional realities.

Theodore R. Hudson. In Louis D. Rubin, Jr., ed. *The History of Southern Literature* (Baton Rouge: Louisiana State University Press, 1985), pp. 513–15

In *A Gathering of Old Men*, Gaines returns to the territory and narrative techniques of his earlier works. He tells the story of a group of old black men who, though denied dignity all their lives, have a final opportunity to assert their manhood. The chance comes when a Cajun field boss, Beau Boutan, is killed in front of the shack of Mathu, the only man in the community to have consistently stood up to both the Cajuns and the whites. As soon as word spreads of Boutan's death, the black men begin arriving on the scene, each

carrying a recently fired shotgun that could have been the murder weapon. Much of the novel is devoted to the "confessions" of these men, each of whom tells the sheriff why he had sufficient motive for the crime. These voices, plus a few others, are, as in "Just like a Tree," the bearers of the narrative. In effect, Gaines again creates a communal history of black life in rural Louisiana.

That history is violent, oppressive, and dehumanizing. The story told by Uncle Billy, the oldest of the men, is typical. . . . Though the beating that caused [his son's strange] behavior occurred years earlier, the pain clearly remains just as acute as when the violence took place. A perpetual present has been created, because the anguish is lived with daily. Billy does not simply relive that original violence; he lives the history generated out of that act. In this sense, the assault continues every moment of his life. . . . [Each] trip to Jackson is another act of violence, another assault on the humanity of Billy and his wife. To kill Beau Boutan is not to seek revenge on his father for the treatment of Billy's son; it is to exact justice for continuing criminal behavior. Killing Beau does not balance the books, according to some talionic code; such a principle would implicitly suggest that Billy's suffering could be canceled. The murder neutralizes nothing; it is simply a refusal to allow the crimes of the racists to be erased. Each story told by the old men serves a similar purpose: to expose the marks that have been made on them throughout their lives and to attempt, for the only time in their lives, to get recognitions of their own definitions of reality. The "ink" for their self-marking is the blood of Beau Boutan; the script written by each is, like Uncle Billy's, the story of his own bleeding.

Keith E. Byerman. *Fingering the Jagged Grain: Tradition and Form in Recent Black Fiction* (Athens: University of Georgia Press, 1985), pp. 98–99

The action in Gaines's fiction takes place in the quarters, homes, jails, saloons, stores, yards, and fields; in the city of New Roads (named Bayonne and St. Adrienne for Gaines's mother, Adrienne Gaines Colar) and on False River (St. Charles River, for his brother Charles); at gates and public gatherings; and on the roads and in other places. In its infinite details, the world of the fiction of Ernest Gaines encompasses the countryside, the villages, and the town of New Roads in Pointe Coupée Parish. . . .

Gaines concentrates on Pointe Coupée/St. Raphael Parish as a center of meaning in order to "record" the lives of the people he knew as he saw them, and to use their experiences to construct a myth that articulates the struggles of a static world fiercely resistant to change. St. Raphael Parish is like William Faulkner's Yoknapatawpha and James Joyce's Dublin: it equals the modern world. To understand the Gaines canon, we must explore its symbolic geography. We can begin with the quarters, the focal place and central metaphor of his parish. To examine the quarters community as a phenomenon in Southern history, and as a physical, social, and political entity in Gaines's work is to tell much about the symbolic, temporal reality of his fictional world. . . .

As a symbolic space, the quarters, in the hands of Ernest Gaines, takes on epic dimension; like William Faulkner's Yoknapatawpha, it is a microcosm in which humankind, undaunted in its Sisyphus-like struggle, wills to prevail. Through the quarters as a center of meaning, Gaines, on the one hand, explores facets of a particular

Southern experience which, on the other hand, becomes symbolic of modern human experience in its questions about the individual, the family, the community, and the past. Gaines's quarters and the rest of his St. Raphael Parish are also unlike Faulkner's north Mississippi county; Gaines's quarters . . . is not fixed geography with characters who appear in more than one narrative. Instead, Gaines's quarters, like the rest of his St. Raphael Parish, is a fluid concept which he shapes and reshapes as he creates each narrative. Together the narratives do not recount the doings of a single community; rather they record the spiritual, social, economic, political strivings of a people in the act of becoming. Although it is a dying physical entity in historical reality, the quarters in Gaines's fiction is a ritual ground of communion and community to which Gaines, the man and the artist, returns again and again for perception and sustenance.

Charles H. Rowell. *Southern Review*. 21, 3 (Summer 1985), pp. 734–35, 749–50

Historians, like many nonhistorians, tend to be interested in causes as well as effects. Gaines, the novelist-historian, in [*The Autobiography of Miss Jane Pittman*] is not satisfied merely to attempt the re-vocation of a past essentially as it was. . . . [He] seeks a meaning in that past, an indication of how and why it assumed the form it has today. He broods, indeed, over what may be gained from his didactic scrutiny of history with much of the intensity and fervor with which [William] Faulkner peers into the southern past in [his] Yoknapatawpha novels. This brooding, this peering, in *Pittman* appears hardly to be an exercise in futility. Quite to the contrary, the results from it may well be, in *Pittman*, the crowning achievement of a major piece of fiction. . . .

In the final analysis Gaines wrote *Pittman* to insist to his readers that a credo common among American whites and the injustices that credo has occasioned American whites to perpetrate upon American blacks has accounted almost as unequivocally for the major problems of black America as, according to St. Augustine, the Good Lord accounts for the City of God. Why does a woman of Jane's human stature, a woman who has so much to give, who, though barren, can play so well the surrogate mother of two remarkable men, whose sense of humor is matched in its abundance, its acuteness, and its lack of sour self-defensiveness, only by her propensity for compassion, who is respected by all who get to know her well, be they black or white, or magnates or nonentities, and who has lived so long that her age alone has made her a fondly beloved figure truly admired in her community—why does such a person find herself calumniated as she is in America? How has her life been so unnecessarily (as well as, sometimes, so venomously) circumscribed? And why is she, even at her advanced age, treated by whites as if she were still a child? Is she responsible for the indignities heaped upon her? If she is not, who is? And has a system, a prescribed routine, rather than individuals reacting to their own observations and following their own leads, been her bane, and if a system, what is its nature and what, principally, the thing that makes it work? Jane's problem, and the one she shares with all black Americans, Gaines does say in *Pittman*, is indeed with a system. That system works, along with other reasons, Gaines does also say, because of its simplicity. And it has worked so well that not only whites contribute to its success. So do blacks. And if

that system is to end, whites must free themselves of their willingness to maintain its vitality, but so, also, must blacks.

Blyden Jackson. In J. Gerald Kennedy and Daniel Mark Fogel, eds. *American Letters and the Historical Consciousness* (Baton Rouge: Louisiana State University Press, 1987), pp. 268–69

In the Louisiana Bayou area that he calls Bayonne, Gaines reveals the actions, impulses, and provocations that produce the body of ideals of the culture. Most criticism of his works acknowledges the keen ear, the sensitivity in rendering dialect, and the superb handling of voice in his fiction. Another acknowledgement which should be made is Gaines's mastery of the ethical precepts in the culture of his area in western Louisiana—precepts derived from plantation tradition and from reactionary elements that bring about changes. When these changes have occurred in his work, they have occurred at great sacrifice by men who may be called *deliverers* by virtue of the trials they undergo and the far-reaching implications of the results.

The courage of characters who accept responsibility for change creates the dynamic flow of Gaines's fiction and this courage is often of a sacrificial quality. Social changes won by those willing to take risks are the vehicles through which Gaines reveals his high regard for sacrifices made in social activism. The gains per se are given little attention, while their motivation and implementation are the points of focus. It can be demonstrated that the experiences of certain characters in Gaines's stories propel them to an activism that most often leads to a sacrificial death. These characters can not accept the ''safer'' rules of the system and in resisting conformity endanger themselves. . . .

Through his heroic deliverers Gaines demonstrates the ethical precepts of their milieu. In the stratified Bayonne community these precepts occasionally clash. The principles of conduct which through tradition seem good and morally obligatory for the planters are not good for Cajuns and blacks. Gaines's heroes are those blacks who perceive their duty to their community and attempt to bring about change. In each instance they build upon heroic actions of the past. Phillip Martin follows Martin Luther King's example, and the old men in *A Gathering of Old Men* follow the fallen ones who preceded them. Combined with this is a respect for the wisdom of the elderly and an instinctive hope for the future. Gaines's heroes learn that the bonds of continuity that link generation to generation and father to son are good and hence worth any sacrifice that will retain or atone for that relationship. The sense of duty is the force which is constantly evolving while linking the past with the present. Gaines has succeeded in defining it through several characters who exemplify responsible action in their environment. In instances in which their adventures end in death, they leave their wisdom, from which others can draw strength. When they survive and return to society, they are stronger in the mythic sense of the indestructible being. They are all purveyors of duty in the community and their actions set in motion changes which benefit the society. This duty, transmitted at great cost, is the life-line to which Gaines's characters cling as a necessity for surviving in the world with dignity.

Audrey L. Vinson. *Obsidian II*. 2, 1 (Spring 1987), pp. 35–36, 46–47

Near the end of Ernest J. Gaines's novel *A Lesson Before Dying*, set in the fictional town of Bayonne, Louisiana, in 1948, a white sheriff tells a condemned black man to write in his diary that he has been fairly treated. Although the prisoner assents, nothing could be farther from the truth in that squalid segregated jail, which is an extension of the oppressive Jim Crow world outside.

A black primary schoolteacher, Grant Wiggins, narrates the story of Jefferson, the prisoner, whose resignation to his execution lends credence to the lesson of Grant's own teacher, Matthew Antoine: the system of Jim Crow will break down educated men like Grant and prisoners like Jefferson to "the nigger you were born to be."

Grant struggles, at first without success, to restore a sense of human dignity to Jefferson, a semiliterate, cynical and bitter twenty-one-year-old man, who accepts his own lawyer's depiction of him as "a hog" not worthy of the court's expense. The social distance between the college-educated Grant and Jefferson appears as great as that between the races, and class differences often frustrate their ability to communicate. It does not help that Grant has intervened only reluctantly, prompted by his aunt, a moralizing scold and a nag, and by Jefferson's godmother, Miss Emma. . . .

Despite the novel's gallows humor and an atmosphere of pervasively harsh racism, the characters, black and white, are humanly complex and have some redeeming quality. At the end, Jefferson's white jailer, in a moving epiphany, is so changed that he suggests the white-black alliance that will emerge a generation later to smash Jim Crow to bits.

> Carl Senna. *New York Times Book Review.* August 9, 1993, p. 21

The connection between racism and humor in Gaines's fiction matches what he observed while growing up in the region about which he writes. On the plantation in Pointe Coupee Parish, people responded to their deepest troubles with humor, and his own brother, so Gaines says, was particularly good at telling jokes about blacks and whites that fit the situation there: "A story can be tragic, and he [my brother] can make it very funny. You see, where I came from, my people were sharecroppers. . . . Their competitors were the Cajuns, the white people there. The people you make fun of more are the people who are closer to you. So when my people had to make fun of something, when they had to laugh, they made fun of the whites. You always make fun of your competitors. They are the people very close to you. And we had this relationship all the time."

Despite the laughter directed at Cajuns in the oral traditions that have influenced Gaines's storytelling style, his own fiction relies primarily on African Americans, not whites, as comic figures. Many are universal humorous stereotypes. Others are modeled on stock depictions of blacks in popular humor dating back to antebellum blackface minstrelsy, images associated with a tradition of racist humor in America. One of the consequences of stage minstrelsy, as Eric Lott notes, was "the dispossession and control by whites of black forms that would not be recovered for a long time." Gaines is among those contemporary African-American writers employing some of the stock humorous stereotypes and situations of this tradition. Yet his work is not racist. He uses these emotionally charged character types intentionally as part of the social critique in his fiction. They always appear alongside fully developed black characters and are never the sole representatives of African-American culture in a text. Furthermore, over the course of his career, Gaines's comic figures have become increasingly complex reinventions of stereotypes and their conventional, demeaning connotations. His humorous stance subverts racist attitudes by conveying the full humanity and reality of African Americans and their experience. Gaines's movement away from simplistic duplication of humorous black stereotypes is related to significant changes in his treatment of comic white figures. These laughing-stocks, who in early stories retaliate against blacks when humiliated by them, in later works must endure public scorn when seemingly impotent blacks subvert their accustomed authority and ability to punish. This difference is a measure of the comic vision that Gaines has come to develop more thoroughly in his fiction, a vision in which humor holds the promise of both humanizing and harmonizing the ethnic groups whose conflicts he chronicles.

> David Estes. In David Estes, editor. *Critical Reflections on the Fiction of Ernest J. Gaines.* (Athens: University of Georgia Press, 1994), pp. 228–48

From Ernest Gaines's earliest published works of the late 1950s and '60s to his most recent novel, *A Lesson Before Dying*, Gaines consistently writes about black men who face the problems of being denied the dignity and self-worth found in the status of "manhood." In *A Lesson Before Dying* Gaines again picks up this theme as the narrator of the story, Grant Wiggins, a black college-educated school teacher, takes on the responsibility of convincing Jefferson, a non-educated black laborer who has been sentenced to death for a murder he didn't commit, that Jefferson is indeed a "man," and not a "hog" as his white attorney declared as part of his defense strategy:

> Do you see a modicum of intelligence? Do you see anyone here could plan a murder. . . . a cornered animal to strike quickly out of fear, but to plan? . . . . I would as soon put a hog in the electric chair as this.

While much of Gaines's work addresses the issue of establishing manhood, *A Lesson Before Dying* is distinct in that it focuses on this issue in a most direct way: the problem Grant and Jefferson are faced with is a problem of redefining Jefferson, from his identity given to him by the white dominant culture, hog, to a new identity, man.

Within the scope of this problem, *A Lesson Before Dying* explores the roles of social institutions such as education, law, and especially religion as they all have a part in producing human dignity and self-worth. It is in the mythologies and ideologies these social institutions produce that the foundations for definition and identity are created. Jefferson does feel that he has experienced a change in identity by the novel's end, and that change is made possible through his and the black community's appropriation of social institutions and of myths and ideologies themselves. Gaines recognizes that for a change in Jefferson's identity to have any lasting "substance," language itself, the complete make-up of discursive formations surrounding Jefferson, must change also. More specifically, Jefferson's becoming a man at the novel's end is an act based on the reinscription of (among other things) a most essential foundation for discourse, the Bible. In doing so, Jefferson is understood as a man because his life first takes on Christ-like significance.

It is important to remember that although Jefferson's symbolic importance in the novel is central, this is Grant's story. Grant is the novel's narrative voice, and he is the person given the primary responsibility of transforming Jefferson's status to that of "man." Obviously, Grant's own situation is somewhat similar to Jefferson's in that both he and Jefferson are undergoing a profound change in their own self-perceptions. Grant doesn't want the responsibility for initiating this transformation mostly because he feels any effort made toward this end would be futile. Grant makes it clear that even he, a black man who has become college educated, cannot express himself in the way he wishes in his community. He finds his own freedom extremely limited, if it indeed exists at all, and he sees the future of his students to be lacking in any promise of advancement. . . .

Grant realizes that the powerlessness of Jefferson is, in fact, not so different from the powerlessness he himself feels. While Jefferson is imprisoned in a literally confining structure of white law, Grant is also imprisoned within the structures of white discourse. The most obvious example of such discursive confinement is that of the educational system itself. The schoolhouse is a detention camp of sorts in which Grant is allowed to teach only the ideology that will keep himself and his black community powerless. And Dr. Joseph, the school superintendent, is, in effect, a type of warden whose role is to make sure Grant and the students stay powerless. . . .

In order to subvert a discursive formation that defines Jefferson as a hog, Grant comes to learn that simply recognizing the problems that cause such injustices is not enough; nor is it enough to "put one's faith" in institutionalized religion which seems to promote passivity and patience more than any active approach to change. The change that is needed is one in which the foundations for definition, for identity, are subverted. And although Grant isn't necessarily aware of the changes he is helping to bring about, Gaines presents the solution to changing identity as nothing short of a revolutionary

In Jefferson's resistance to the white patriarchal labeling of him as a hog, Ernest Gaines shows that such resistance makes Jefferson similar in god-like stature to Louis. In fact, Gaines again overtly establishes the Christ-like significance of Jefferson. Besides the obvious connection of this innocent man being put to death for a less than just cause, Jefferson's death is timed by the town's officials so as not to conflict with a religious holiday, as Christ's death is timed by Roman and Jewish authorities so as not to coincide with the Jewish Passover. . . .

Jefferson's Christ-figure significance establishes an allegorical dimension to *A Lesson Before Dying* that reinforces the role of myth in the re-creation of Jefferson. With Jefferson as the Christ, Miss Emma, Jefferson's *god*mother, takes on the role usually reserved for God the father: she is the initiator of the discursive movement; from her ultimately springs a new identity for Jefferson and his "followers." In this sense she has the creative potential associated with God. Her role as god*mother* is also significant in that it establishes the new mythology being created as matriarchal. This may be Gaines's way of expressing the fullness of this discursive shift away from both whiteness and patriarchy, and it may be a statement by Gaines about an absence of father figures from such impoverished black communities of the Deep South. But it is important to note that although Gaines presents her as the initiator of this discursive shift, her power diminishes after this effort. Her principal role from that point is as a provider of physical nourishment in the form of the food she makes for Jefferson; the *meta*physical nourishment he needs as a symbolic and mythical

figure is taken over by the other "god-figures," mainly Grant and Reverend Ambrose.

The significance of Grant and Reverend Ambrose in this regard is important in the appropriative scheme Gaines sets up. In appropriating the white patriarchal order, a complete shift to matriarchy would not be necessary (or believable). The educational and religious significance of Grant and Reverend Ambrose is that they represent a discursive order reinscribed with black faces, but not necessarily with matriarchy. In appropriating the Christian mythos, Gaines must maintain a patriarchal order with its symbolically central "God become man." In this respect, Jefferson's "manliness," as a gendered entity, bears its greatest importance. In order to re-create Jefferson as a powerful source of identity within a patriarchal order (white or black), Gaines must insure that Jefferson's iconographic value increases in direct proportion to his ability to "reflect patriarchy."

Moreover, the allegorical resonance of Jefferson as Christ figure is again compounded with Gaines's inclusion of Jefferson's journal. In it Jefferson relates all of the simple expressions of love he encounters in the days before his death. . . .

Along with the allegorical impact Jefferson's writing has as a Biblical text, one must not overlook the symbolic and revolutionary impact to be found simply in the act of Jefferson's writing. In "Writing 'Race' and the Difference it Makes" Henry Louis Gates puts this idea in perspective as he discusses the symbolic importance of writing in Western culture in the eighteenth century:

> Writing, especially after the printing press became so widespread, was taken to be the visible sign of reason. Blacks were "reasonable" and hence "men," if—and only if— they demonstrated mastery over "the arts and sciences," the eighteenth century's formula for writing.

Although the plot of Gaines's novel is, of course, set well after the eighteenth century, a similar argument is used by Jefferson's attorney in declaring Jefferson's lack of manhood; he notes Jefferson's illiteracy as proof of this lack:

> "Oh sure, he has reached the age of twenty-one, when we, civilized men, consider the male species has reached manhood, but would you call this—this—this a man? No, not I. . . . Mention the names of Keats, Byron, Scott, and see whether his eyes will show one moment of recognition. Ask him to describe a rose, to quote from one passage of the Constitution or the Bill of Rights."

Set against this white patriarchal prescription for manhood, Jefferson's writing must be recognized as a radical act in itself. Of course, Grant's college education is seen as a threat to Pichot and his fellow patriarchs. But Jefferson's writing isn't simply a cry for legitimacy in white culture. Perhaps his writing "across the lines instead of above them," as well as his already noted concentration on the issue of mutual giving, is indication enough that Jefferson's discourse is "going in a different direction," truly a "new testament" of how legitimacy and manhood can be obtained.

Into this unfolding, biblically allegorical scheme that *A Lesson Before Dying* takes on, the significance of Paul, the guard who befriends Grant and Jefferson, seems to fit almost too neatly. Like his namesake of the New Testament, Paul is the converted soldier struck by a "bolt of lightning" to ultimately preach "the word" of the Christ:. . . .

"I heard the two jolts, but I wouldn't look up. I'll never forget the sound of the generator as long as I live on this earth.... Allow me to be your friend Grant Wiggins. I don't ever want to forget this day. I don't ever want to forget him."

Paul's eagerness to read the journal after Grant is finished and to help Grant spread "the word" to Grant's students that Jefferson was the "bravest man" at the execution adds to his parallels with the biblical St. Paul.... most significant connection to his biblical namesake rests in the importance St. Paul places in justification by faith above the law....

[The] transformation of Paul confirms that some "substantial" change can be effected. Although Paul is acknowledged from the beginning as being "from good stock," he is also a representative of white patriarchal law. His change has its greatest value in its symbolic importance: it shows that white patriarchy has not contained this new discourse; instead, white patriarchy is now being changed, not just penetrated. While "practical," "substantial" change still seems remote, the symbolic power in the transformations of the black community and especially of Paul show that the potential for such change is great.

And perhaps that potential is the most significant New Testament connection of all. Christ's presence in the New Testament signifies the promise of eternal life—not its fulfillment. As with Christ, Jefferson's symbolic value has only begun in his death. The point here is that *A Lesson Before Dying*, like the New Testament, resists closure. It is the novel itself that confirms the promise of the "projective" power within the "appropriation of the word." The transformative power that Jefferson's word has on Grant and on Paul is projected to readers in Grant's (gospel) narration. The novel itself becomes the promise renewed and extended.

Ultimately, the *Lesson Before Dying* that Ernest Gaines provides is a lesson about manhood. Gaines makes it clear that "being a man," especially for a black man in the white-supremacist South, has more to do with appropriating discursive power than with being male. For Jefferson, as for the white patriarchs of his community, the power to define oneself and to define others is confirmed in the ideologies produced by the social structures of culture. With this in mind, Gaines shows how becoming a man is truly an act of mythical and even biblical proportions.

Philip Auger. *Southern Literary Journal*. XXVII, 2 (Spring 1995), pp. 74–85

Gaines's fiction offers us numerous instances to observe the articulate witness and hence his/her relationship to Ellison's hero. Gaines's "witnesses," particularly in the novels rendered in the first person, tell the tale of their break from convention. This requires them to find a balance between the communal voice and their individual voice. Thus, Jim Kelly relates events in *Of Love and Dust* which other narrators relate to him in order to fill out his narrative. Miss Jane defers to other members of the community when her memory fails. Felix, in the story "Bloodline," allows us to hear all the voices in the story. These narrators combine aspects of Stepto's narratives of ascent and immersion. They carve out a free space where they can tell their tales, but this movement is enabled through an engagement of community. In other words, they cannot relate the particulars of their "ascent" without a simultaneous "immersion" in the community. Furthermore, these narrators remain in the South. Thus, their ascent is figurative, not

geographical. They are credible commentators on change in the South because they have witnessed the substance of that change—either directly or vicariously—and by choosing to endure it move from Faulkner's "enduring saint," to participating sinner.

The last scene in *Of Love and Dust* offers an example. The last image Jim sees is Aunt Margaret walking back to the plantation. The growing distance between Jim and the old woman dramatizes her retreat into silence, as his departure signals his movement toward narration, whereby he can fuse remembrance and utterance. This act of "remembering" anticipates his reconstruction of the past. In a moment that recalls and then revises Lena Burch at the beginning of Faulkner's *Light in August*, Jim has indeed "come a far piece." He chooses to break from the plantation's illusion of order to enter a space where he recovers his integrity. Integrity symbolizes the need to unify history and place and leaves him no choice but to leave the Hebert plantation. Gaines's use of gothic convention is oriented toward the liberation of his characters. They emerge from the "ruined house" to articulate a new ordering of materials that form a more cohesive unity. This unity rests on a new set of narrative conventions where the articulate witness breaks the silence that accompanies being "buried alive" in the symbolic crypt of Jim Crow and engages in acts of disclosure that finally "speak for" a habitable South.

We can also see the progression from the incoherence of exclusion toward the coherence of the communal voice, where Gaines's characters loose themselves from the horrific silence Jim Crow imposes and discover their potential as agents of change. Gaines's fiction works out the creative tension existing between the spoken and the written word. Characters like Ned Douglass, Jimmy Aaron, Miss Jane, Charlie, Aunt Fe, Jefferson, and Grant suggest that the boundary between these two forms of discourse is permeable. In this sense, it reflects the African American notion of the boundary which exists between the living and the dead. The dead live on in the voices of the folk and in the succeeding generations who listen to these voices. In valorizing the communal voice, Gaines and his characters engage in the search for a voice that leads to a new sense of personal worth and integrity and thus reverse the South's social exhaustion. It is this revitalized story that becomes a crucible in which we confront all the things we are and do not turn away.

Herman Beavers. *Wrestling Angels into Song: The Fictions of Ernest J. Gaines and James Allan McPherson* (Philadelphia: University of Pennsylvania Press, 1995), pp. 173–80

BIBLIOGRAPHY
*Catherine Carmier*, 1964; *Of Love and Dust*, 1967; *Bloodline*, 1968; *The Autobiography of Miss Jane Pittman*, 1971; *In My Father's House*, 1978; *A Gathering of Old Men*, 1983; *A Lesson Before Dying*, 1993

# GILROY, Beryl (1924–)
## Guyana

I enjoyed and learned much from *Frangipani House*, an elegantly written and heartening novel by one of our distinguished women novelists (Sylvia Wynter, Merle Hodge, Marion Glean, Erna

Brodber, Joan Cambridge, and Michelle Cliff are some of the others who readily come to mind). Beryl Gilroy's Mrs. Mabel Alexandrina King (affectionately called Mama King by friend and frightened foe), old, ill, but splendidly her own woman, is put away by her family in Frangipani House, a Dickensian rest home on the outskirts of Georgetown. It's the kind of place that the city folks point to and say, ''Over yonder—Frangipani House! People dies-out dere! They pays plenty to die-out inside dere! Death comes to the lodgers in Frangipani House!''. . .

Beryl Gilroy's aptly, understatedly honed, symbolic inference, together with her driving social conscience, makes of all Guyana an allegorical Frangipani House, and certainly one either to escape from or be changed radically.

Andrew Salkey. *World Literature Today.* 61, 4 (Autumn 1987), p. 670

In Georgetown, British Guyana, during the late 1940s there was a retirement home for upper middle-class ladies called ''The Gentle-woman's Home.'' It was a chintzy, exclusive place, set aside for elderly whites, and near-whites, of ''good'' background but impe-cunious circumstances. Beryl Gilroy's *Frangipani House* with its ''sleepy-headed windows dressed in frill bonnets of lace . . . sleek and comfortable on the town's edge'' recalls that genteel establish-ment. But hers is a fictional home for working-class black women in colonial Georgetown, and sets out to give dignity to the lives of those forgotten ''relics of work-filled by gone days,'' consigned to Frangipani House by relatives glad to be directly rid of them. The story revolves around Mrs. Mabel Alexandrina (''Mama'') King, an ailing grandmother in her seventies who shows remarkable energy and resourcefulness. The author, in attempting to give Mama King dramatic stature, makes her a kind of picaresque, poor black Caribbean Queen Lear. Discarded by her ''pelican'' off-spring, she begins to fear madness, fantasizing about her past and brooding on the ingratitude of her family. She escapes from the home in the company of a group of itinerant Hindu beggars . . . is attacked by ''choke-and-robbers'' and falls into a coma from which she awakes in [a] hospital. Surrounded by her now con-cerned offspring, all wanting to take care of her, she chooses to go with her granddaughter, Cindy, who is pregnant. The novel ends with the birth of Cindy's twins (Mama King having taken over from the starchy midwife) and the reestablishment of the old woman as loved matriarch.

The novel's intention—to protest against the institutionalizing and isolating of the elderly—is admirable, but badly served by a hyperbolical, self-conscious style: ''Every step to hospital was like an orchestral instrument contributing its part to a symphony of pain . . . pain tailored by fate to fit her frail body.'' When the women in the home decide to sing a hymn, one of them says: ''I'll call the others. Let us blend our voices in a thick, heavenly sound.'' The brown, middle-class ''matron'' is a kind of dragon lady . . . and while the beggars' natural goodness is contrasted with uncaring middle-class attitudes, ''the unstirring contentedness of their lives'' to which Mama King is admitted, comes across as pseudo-pastoral nostalgia. The novel is effective, however, in its rendering—through a dialect voice—of Mama King's inner life, her memories of the past. Through the unwinding of the reel of memory, ''my whole life pass before me—like a film at a picture show.'' The

picture of colonial Guyana that emerges (of the hard but vital life of the black working class and of the color-based, hierarchical society in general) is imaginatively and powerfully evoked.

Michael Gilkes. *Third World Quarterly.* 9, 4 (October 1987), pp. 1371–72

Most West Indian fictions about migration have been concerned with an individual's adjustment to a new social environment and have been written in the autobiographical mode. *Boy-Sandwich*, however, expands the range of this type of writing by considering the experiences, aspirations, and reactions of three generations of [a Guyanese] family long settled in Britain, though it retains the form of an autobiographical narrative embellished with astute social observations and penetrating analyses of interracial and interpersonal behavior.

The narrator is an eighteen-year-old boy . . . burdened with the responsibility of caring for his institutionalized grandparents, who have lived in Britain longer than most of their neighbors and who are Empire loyalists who have worked hard, paid their taxes, been frugal, and raised a family that includes a grandson now ready to go up to Cambridge. As the protagonist Tyrone Grainger comments, ''I was the filling and they were the slices of bread.'' Such figurative language abounds in the novel; in fact, the texture of the style is a delight in a time when language is not always valued and crafted in fiction. The bananas in an old people's home are described as ''like fingers covered with large neglected sores,'' and an elderly inmate is said to be ''tucking pain away in his body like a coin in his purse.'' Fear is ''a solid rock inside people's hearts.'' Dialect, not always handled convincingly, is here used with great skill as an elucidation of character and role; it is neither an entertainment nor a decoration. Language, perhaps more than any other element, differentiates the three generations of the family and the family from others.

A. L. McLeod. *World Literature Today.* 64, 1 (Spring 1990), p. 348

Mama King, the heroine of *Frangipani House*, is a sixty-nine-year-old black Guyanese peasant, who after many years of hard work, her faculties still intact, finds herself discarded by her loved ones. She . . . is unique in West Indian fiction, embodying that indomita-ble urge—so often stifled by male conditioning and female self-effacement—the Caribbean woman has for self-realization and freedom of expression. . . .

In Gilroy's novel, Mama King, who has worked so very hard and has unstintingly provided for her children and grandchildren, is installed in a tiny room in Frangipani House to spend the remainder of her days, with forty-two other black women, ''waiting, waiting, waiting for 'the call from heaven.''' The ambivalence of the institution is strongly imaged at the outset. . . .

The ''iron gate'' that encloses and incarcerates is ''finely wrought''; the windows are dressed to resemble the inmates of the house; the hibiscus flowers, always beautiful, are of course ephem-eral; and the mammee apple tree is as sterile as the matron and as the life that obtains within the institution. Frangipani House provided, on the one hand, ''constipated self-seeking care,'' and, on the other hand, an "answer to a prayer from children who prospered abroad and who wanted superior care for their parents." The irony of the images above is reinforced in "prayer," "prospered," and, most of all, in "superior."

Although Mama King had been ailing for a considerable time with malaria, then quinsy, then pleurisy, she . . . is still remarkably alert and strong. The well-publicized philanthropy of her youth, her emphasis on her personal independence, her sense of pride in self, and five hundred dollars a month, provided by her solicitous daughters, earn her the dubious privilege of "the room by the garden," which has a fair-sized glass window on one side. At first Mama King, nursed by the strangeness of the routine, by the ordered rhythm of institutional life, and the cleanliness of everything around her, regains her health. With the return of health comes the desire to be free, as she . . . begins to be overwhelmed by a feeling of being trapped. The urge to be vital, mobile and free reasserts itself powerfully, and she spends the rest of her sojourn thinking of ways of escaping Frangipani House. . . .

Mama King chooses to flee the sterile security of Frangipani House for the warm fellowship of a group of beggars led by Pandit Prem. Although one cannot be absolutely sure about the racial composition of the group of mendicants, one can reasonably assume that they are Indo-Guyanese. And it is quite significant that Mama King, an Afro-Guyanese can confess, "I free and happy with Pandit them." Gilroy, consciously, it seems, has set up what appears to be an ethnic hierarchy, in which groups are judged according to the way they treat their old folk. Token and Cyclette pay for "white people care" for Mama King in Frangipani House. This care is "ordered," and clean, but cold, sterile, and expensive. Opposed to this is the African tradition in which the old have a place and function.

Roydon Salick. *Commonwealth Essays & Studies.* 14, 2 (Spring 1992), pp. 98, 100, 104

*Stedman and Joanna* is a well-written and, above all, convincing account of an interracial love affair set in eighteenth-century Surinam (and in fact received an award in Gilroy's native Guyana for historical fiction). Divided into three parts—"Before Joanna," "Joanna, My Love, My Life," and "The Sea Change"—the novel chronicles John Gabriel Stedman's life from his gaming and womanizing youth, through his adventures and coming of age in Surinam, to his decline in Europe. . . .

Among other themes and motifs, the novel examines the debilitating effects of slavery: the sexually abused slave woman, the failure of Christianity, the cruel mistress, the horror of the black codes, and the maroons who fought against colonial powers for independence. Running throughout the novel is the suggestion that death—of one sort or another—accompanies the institution of slavery. . . .

What remains the crowning achievement of the novel, however, is the depiction of the love between Joanna and Stedman. It is a love that transcends color and class. Even though Joanna is never fully able to discard her "coat of deception" (the multifaceted personas she must adopt as a black slave woman), she enjoys with Stedman an enviable love. One is tempted to compare the work with Barbara Chase-Riboud's *Sally Hemmings*, whose story opens in 1787, ten years before the death of Stedman. Although both novels offer

fictionalized accounts of historical personages, Gilroy is more convincing in the ethics that inform the individual lovers.

A. S. Newson. *World Literature Today.* 67, 1 (Winter 1993), p. 219

Like *Stedman and Joanna, Inkle & Yarico* is a historical romance. Set in Barbados, it is a historical romance in the true sense of the genre—historical in that the characters actually existed, and a romance in the elements of adventure contained within. It is a genre much used by the contemporary writer for various ends. Doris Lessing's *Love, Again*, for example, employs the genre within a contemporary story about the realities of aging. Gilroy seems to use it to illuminate the heart of the class struggle in Britain.

The story is told in the first person by Tommy Inkle, the youngest of three sons of an upper-class British family, who describes himself as "the tallest, the strongest, the Adonis of the family, greatly petted by my mother and spoilt by my father." His adventures begin when he is dispatched to Barbados to investigate the affairs of a plantation owned by the family. He leaves behind a fiancée, Alice Sawyer, with the promise of returning to marry her one year from his departure date. His plans are thwarted as the ship encounters inclement weather, and the remaining crew is forced to take shelter on an island inhabited by Black Caribs. The crew is promptly clubbed while Inkle takes shelter in a cave with the help of the chief's daughter Yarico. When he is discovered by the rest of the tribe, his life is spared as Yarico declares him her lover. . . .

Gilroy's work is at once simple and complex. It is travel literature communicated through an unreliable narrator. Inkle's way of being in the world is informed by cultural miscalculations and fear. From his initial or learned observations on civilization to his assessment of female enterprise among the Black Caribs, he resists transculturation or change. His father, a wheeler and dealer in London society, tells him in his last letter before his departure to Barbados: "There are six classes of mankind. The rich who live plentifully; the middle sort who live well; the working trades who labour hard but feel no want; the country folk who fare indifferently; the poor that toil hard, but who do not suffer want; and the miserable who suffer want. Remember: you are of the first class." His father's words reinforce and firmly ground Inkle's cultural arrogance and prevent meaningful interaction with the host of characters he encounters in his adventures. At one point, Chief Tomo admonishes him to think less with his head and more with his heart—something Inkle is unable to do for his fear of "losing civilization." Even during the trial of his initiation, Inkle muses, "If I died in my attempt to become a man . . . the implications for my 'tribe' would be severe."

The work is also something of a parody on European expansion, where Inkle might be viewed as the forthright explorer, chief Tomo as the betrayed other (African and Indian), Alice Sawyer as the symbol of yearning, the ideal for whom the explorer labors, and Yarico as the simple native or "nature's child." The reality, however, is that each character is more complex than his or her respective descriptions and actions suggest. Gilroy offers no simple answers or explanation; rather, hers is an exploration in the nature of human contact and deportment. And in the end, the doubts linger. Inkle's last words are: "As for Yarico, what is she now in my scheme of things? I cannot tell! I cannot tell!"

The novel is based on a historical narrative originating in the late seventeenth century which appeared in a number of seventeenth-and eighteenth-century versions. Gilroy's afterword contains the version written by Richard Steele in 1711. Steele's account features the couple's affair, Inkle's rescue, and the subsequent sale of Yarico to a Barbadian merchant. Gilroy's account expands upon the implications of race, class, and culture in a most satisfying way.

Adele S. Newson. *World Literature Today.* 71, 2 (Spring 1997), pp. 435–37

BIBLIOGRAPHY

*Green and Blue Water* (series of three titles), 1955–62; *Green and Gold* (series of four titles), 1963–65; *Nippers and Little Nippers* (series of 13 titles), 1970–75; *Arthur Small*, 1972; *Bubu's Street*, 1972; *In Bed*, 1972; *My Dad*, 1972; *New Shoes*, 1972; *No More Pets*, 1973; *Outings for All*, 1973; *The Present*, 1973; *Rice and Peas*, 1973; *Carnival of Dreams*, 1974; *Knock at Mrs. Herbs*, 1974; *New People at 24*, 1974; *The Paper Bag*, 1974; *Visitor from Home*, 1974; *Black Teacher*, 1976; *In for a Penny*, 1978; *Frangipani House*, 1986; *Boy–Sandwich*, 1989; *Echoes and Voice* (poetry), 1991; *Stedman and Joanna, a Love in Bondage; Dedicated Love in the Eighteenth Century*, 1991; *Sunlight and Sweet Water*, 1993; *Yarico*, 1996

# GIOVANNI, Nikki (1943–)

## United States

Nikki Giovanni is a product of the thunderous and explosive 1960s, endowed with a powerful and inquiring mind absorbed with the black America of that decade—our vision of ourselves. And, like a painter's brush, her life depicts what black America can see and feel. . . .

[Giovanni] has absorbed her atmosphere—she knows her world from chief to thief. In "Nikki-Rosa" she wrote five words that stated to the world a new commitment, "Black love is Black wealth," and made one quixotic judgment: "[They'll] probably talk about my hard childhood and never understand that all the while I was quite happy." The world of Nikki Giovanni is very real, sometimes too real for comfort, too naked for delight. A person who enters that cavern of poetic adventures can never be the same again. But she asks no more of her readers than of herself. In *Gemini* she raked her emotions bare to write of the death of her grandmother—moved from her home of eighteen years for a cutoff of a cutoff, knowing that neither she nor her mother would ever be able to read that essay without crying, without wondering if more could have been done.

Ida Lewis. Foreword to Nikki Giovanni. *My House* (New York: William Morrow, 1972), pp. x–xii

A poet may be musician, preacher, articulator of a culture, but she or he is also a dreamer. In a series of poems about herself as dreamer, Giovanni explores the conflicting and confusing relations between her roles as poet, woman, and black.

In "Dreams," she describes her younger years—"before i learned / black people aren't / supposed to dream.". . .

A few years later, in "The Wonder Woman," she must deal with the fact of having become that sweet inspiration. "Dreams have a way / of tossing and turning themselves / around," she observes; also that "the times / make requirements that we dream / real dreams.". . . The wonder woman is a totally public personage who cannot—must not—integrate her personal needs and experiences into that role if they do not coincide. Giovanni makes this clear in poems about female stars, like Aretha Franklin, and in poems about herself, such as "Categories.". . .

"Categories" goes on to question even black/white divisions (political and public), if they can—and they do—at times violate personal reality, describing in its second stanza an old white woman "who maybe you'd really care about" except that, being a young black woman, one's "job" is to "kill maim or seriously / make her question / the validity of her existence."

The poem ends by questioning the fact and function of categories themselves . . . but, in doing so, it is raising the more profound matter of the relations between society and self. The earlier "Poem for Aretha" . . . begins with a clear sense of the separation between public and private selves. . . . Again Giovanni explains the significance of the musician/artist to society: "she is undoubtedly the one person who puts everyone on / notice," but about Aretha she also says, "she's more important than her music—if they must be / separated." (It is significant that the form of both these poems is closer to thought than speech. No answers here, only questions, problems.)

One means of bridging the gap between public and private is suggested in "Revolutionary Dreams." . . . "Militant" and "radical" are poised against "natural" here, as they were in "Categories." But this poem makes the connection to gender: the "natural dreams," of a "natural woman" who does what a woman does "when she's natural." The result of this juxtaposition is "true revolution." Somehow the black woman must be true to herself as she *is* to be both a poet and a revolutionary, for the nature of the revolution itself is in question. . . . In the poems of *Black Feeling, Black Talk/Black Judgement* and of *Re: Creation*, the doubts are present, and possibilities for solution occur and disappear. However, *My House* as a book, not only the individual poems in it, makes a new statement about the revolution, about the very nature of political poetry, when the poet is a black woman. . . .

*My House* is divided into two sections, "The Rooms Inside" and "The Rooms Outside." The inside rooms hold personal poems about grandmothers, mothers, friends, lovers—all in their own way love poems. "Legacies," in which the poet describes the relationship between grandmother and granddaughter, is a very political poem. . . . Black heritage is explained in personal terms. The little girl in the poem recognizes an impulse to be independent, but the speaker recognizes as well the importance of the old woman, of her love, to the grandchild in achieving her own adulthood. Although the poem ends by observing that "neither of them ever / said what they meant / and i guess nobody ever does," it is the poem itself that provides that meaning through its understanding. . . .

It is fitting to the purpose of *My House* that its final poem, which is in "The Rooms Outside," is "My House.". . .

The first stanza follows Giovanni's familiar oral structure. Phrases stand against one another without the imaginative extensions of figurative language: word against word, repeating, altering, pointing. A love poem, to one particular lover. It starts in a tone reminiscent of both "Beautiful Black Men" and "All I Gotta Do"—the woman is there to adore her man: "i only want to / be there to kiss you"; "as you want"; "as you need." But although the gentle tone persists, an extraordinary change is rung with a firm emphasis on the personal and the possessive in the last three lines: "where i want to kiss you," "my house," "i plan." She is suiting his needs to hers as well as vice versa. . . .

In bringing together her private and public roles and thereby validating her sense of self as a black woman poet, Giovanni is on her way towards achieving in art that for which she was trained: emotionally, to love; intellectually and spiritually, to be in power; "to learn and act upon necessary emotions which will grant me control over my life," as she writes in *Gemini*. Through interrelating love and power, to achieve a revolution—to be free.

Suzanne Juhasz. *Naked and Fiery Forms: Modern American Poetry by Women. A New Tradition* (New York: Octagon, 1978), pp. 165–71, 174

Nikki Giovanni has . . . been called the "Princess" of black poetry because of her regal attitude toward her race in championing its right for real equality for every individual: she was a strong advocate of individualism during a period when the trend in the black community was away from individualism toward the mass. At the same time, she realizes the necessity for universal recognition of the talent that lies in her race for achievement in the artistic, scientific, and political worlds—for the wealth of love to be found in the individuals who compose it. If there appears to be a dichotomy in her thinking it is because the poet is as realistic as she is idealistic: she understands that changes are won by both individual pragmatism and functional unity. . . .

Like Gwendolyn Brooks, Nikki Giovanni has happy memories of her childhood. Her parents, like Brooks's, had a struggle to make ends meet, but they always managed to celebrate Christmas and the birthdays of their two children, Nikki and her sister Gary, with secret preparations and surprise presents, so that those days became events to look forward to, and happy memories. If her parents quarreled—again like Brooks's—it was over finances; but in the Giovanni household, the arguments were complicated by the fact that "Gus," Nikki's father, who held down three jobs at one point, was always trying to increase their income further by various investments that failed, or he would have to sell treasured stock to make the mortgage payments; then he would be depressed, and turn to drink. But it didn't matter so much because everybody was together; they were a family, and though there might be differences of opinion and disapproval, there was always love, a strong feeling that gave richness to the poorest home. A key phrase in "Nikki-Rosa" contains words that became famous in connection with Giovanni: "Black love is Black wealth," and from a number of poems in [*Black Feeling, Black Talk/Black Judgement*] . . . this poet is concerned with love, family love and relationships, as much as she is concerned with the oncoming "Black Power through Revolution." Poems like "Nikki-Rosa" and "Woman Poem," and "Knoxville, Tennessee," all contain recollections of happy moments in her childhood in contrast to polemic poems like "The True Impact of Present Dialogue, Black vs. Negro," which begins, "Nigger / can you kill / can you kill / can a nigger kill a honkie?" an idiomatic chant presenting a call to action, action against acceptance of white supremacy; or, "Our Detroit Conference—for Don

L. Lee," another chantlike poem, employing a play on the words "bitter" and "black" to display the deep resentment felt by the people of her race in regard to the injustices of the past.

Jean Gould. *Modern American Women Poets* (New York: Dodd, Mead, 1984), pp. 330–31, 333–34

Giovanni's books after [*Black Feeling, Black Talk/Black Judgement*] did more than repudiate violence. As critic Eugene Redmond pointed out, they offered her views from a new perspective: that of the rite of passage toward womanhood. The growing-up motif is a common one in literature, especially among women writers. It has provided some of their most memorable work and, in Giovanni's case, a unifying theme in her work.

In *Gemini*, she is the feisty woman child who, to the consternation of her mother, defies middle-class convention and gets suspended from Fisk [University]. She traces her relationship with her older sister, that evolves from shameless idolatry to the realization that love "requires a safe distance." In these essays we are introduced to other members of her family, including a wise and warm grandmother and a newly born son, who reappear in later books.

As the title suggests, *My House* continues this theme, and Giovanni explores the legacies passed from generation to generation; and the lighthearted pleasures of love and mischief. Sex sans politics does allow more playfulness. . . .

The evolvement away from the political poems had a significant impact on her career. Her work became distinguished from that of others in her generation at a time when it was propitious to stand out from the rest. By the early 1970s, the black movement was in disarray, factionalized, and largely reduced to internecine bickering. Giovanni, however, could still maintain an appeal across ideological lines. . . .

If there is a median in [her] career, it came in 1975 with the publication of *The Women and the Men*. Pursuing the rite-of-passage theme eventually leads to becoming a woman; an adult, graced or burdened with the responsibilities of maturity. *The Women and the Men* recognized a coming of age. For the first time, the figure of the woman-child is virtually absent. In "The Woman" section, the dominant theme is the search for identity, for place, in the community of black women. In the poem "The Life I Led," whose title is already suggestive, the poet even envisions her physical aging process: "i know my arms will grow flabby / it's true / of all the women in my family." The free-spirited love poems are grounded in the concern that "my shoulder finds a head that needs nestling." . . .

In each of Giovanni's books, there is a poem or two which signals the direction of a subsequent book. In *The Women and the Men*, "Something to Be Said for Silence" contains the lines "somewhere something is missing / . . . may be i'm just tired"; and in "The December of My Springs," another poem, Giovanni looks forward to being "free from children and dinners / and people i have grown stale with."

The next book, *Cotton Candy on a Rainy Day*, recognizes the completion of a cycle. "Now I don't fit beneath the rose bushes anymore," she writes, "anyway they're gone." The lines are indicative of the mood of this book, which talks about a sense of emotional dislocation of trying "to put a three-dimensional picture on a one-dimensional frame," as she wrote in the title poem. She has evolved to be that creature which often finds itself estranged from the history which created it: a bright black female in a white mediocre world, she notes in ''Forced Retirement.'' The consequences are an emotional compromise to a bleak reality, for compromise is necessary to forestall inevitable abandonment. Although the men in her life ''refused to / be a man,'' Giovanni writes in ''Woman,'' she decided it was ''all / right.'' The book is immersed in world-weary cynicism, as the lines, ''she had lived long and completely enough / not to be chained to the truth'' suggest.

Paula Giddings. In Mari Evans, ed. *Black Women Writers (1950–1980): A Critical Evaluation* (New York: Doubleday, 1984), pp. 212–15

The most significant development in Giovanni's career has been her evolution from a strongly committed political consciousness prior to 1969 to a more inclusive consciousness which does not repudiate political concern and commitment, but which regards a revolutionary ethos as only one aspect of the totality of black experience. Her earlier political associates and favorable reviewers of the late 1960s often regarded her development after 1970 with consternation, as representing a repudiation of her racial roots and of political commitment, without perhaps fully understanding the basis for her widened concerns and interests. Giovanni's shift in interest from revolutionary politics and race as a collective matter towards love and race as they affect personal development and relationships brought strong reviewer reaction. . . . The problems involved in studying the relationship between this shift in her poetry and the somewhat delayed shift from favorable to less favorable criticism, as her artistry grew, are complex. And they are further complicated by the fact that, at the very time the negative reviews of her poetry markedly increased, her popularity with readers surged dramatically ahead. . . .

Studying the relationships between the positive and negative reviews and between the opinions of reviewers and popular audiences is made more difficult by an anomaly presented by Giovanni's *Black Feeling, Black Talk/Black Judgement*: two thirds of the poems in this 1970 volume are brief, introspective lyrics which are political only in the most peripheral sense—that they mention a lover as someone the speaker met at a conference, for instance. The remaining third, poems which are strongly political and often militant, received practically all the attention of reviewers. Critics ignored almost completely the poems that foreshadow nearly all the poetry Giovanni was to write in the next thirteen years. In short, the wave of literary reviews that established Giovanni's national reputation as a poet also established her image as a radical. Yet, by the summer of 1970, when these reviews began to appear, Giovanni had been writing solely nonpolitical, lyric poetry for a year. The label ''the poet of the black revolution'' which characterized her in the popular media was already a misnomer in 1970, when it began to be popularly used. . . .

It is my contention that Giovanni's rejection of the pressure to write primarily a didactic, ''useful'' political poetry was not only a sign of her integrity but an inevitable sign of her development. A truly comprehensive criticism of her work must be willing to recognize both her continuing commitment to the attainment by black people of power in America and a commitment to personal freedom for herself as a woman and an artist. Critics need not only to see the importance of politics in her life but to perceive also that a commitment to politics, pursued with ideological rigor, inevitably

becomes constricting to an artist. That Giovanni still writes political poetry can be understood by attending to the anger which she expresses in each volume at the oppression of blacks, women, and the elderly; she continually deplores also the violence which oppression spawns. She illustrates the conflict between ideological commitment, exacted by political beliefs, and the demands of the artistic sensibility which tend to find such commitment confining and stultifying. She illustrates in her own work and career the same arc that the poets of the [W. H.] Auden generation in England illustrated: the passing beyond a doctrinal basis for one's poetry to a work responsive to an illuminating of the whole of the individual's experience. Giovanni's case is both complicated and made clearer by her connections with the Black Liberation Movement, which has not yet won all its objectives, particularly her affinities to the work of those closely tied to Marxist-Leninist ideology and Pan-African goals. . . .

In her poetry Giovanni has chosen to communicate with the common reader, as well as with artists and critics; consequently, she has used graphic images from everyday Afro-American life and stressed the ''orality'' of her usually short poems, often by assimilating into them the rhythms of black conversation and the heritage from jazz, blues, and the spirituals—reflecting these origins both in rhythmic patterns and borrowed phrases. She has tended to focus on a single individual, situation, or idea, often with a brief narrative thread present in the poem. Her choice of such simple forms has meant that academic critics might well be less interested in her work than in that of the more complex and intellectualized poets most often associated with modernism, such as T. S. Eliot, Ezra Pound, and W. H. Auden. She avoids the allusions to classical literature and mythology, the relatively obscure symbolism, the involved syntax, the densely-packed idiom, and the elliptical diction often characteristic of such poets. If the verbal and structural forthrightness of Giovanni's poetry in some measure accounts for the paucity of academic criticism of it, this elemental quality accounts also for her popular acclaim by thousands who come to hear her read her work. Like a folksinger, she senses the close relationship of poetry with music, since her poetry, like music, depends on sound and rhythm and is incomplete without oral performance and without an audience.

Margaret B. McDowell. In Joe Weixlmann and Chester J. Fontenot, eds. *Studies in Black American Literature* (Greenwood, Florida: Penkevill, 1986), Vol. II, pp. 143–44, 151–53

Nikki Giovanni has, with special force, made the case for the relation of autobiographies to changing political conditions. She attacks the assumption ''that the self is not part of the body politic,'' insisting, ''there's no separation.'' Giovanni believes that literature, to be worthy of its claims, must reflect and seek to change reality. And the reality black people have known has left much to be desired: ''It's very difficult to gauge what we have done as a people when we have been systematically subjected to the whims of other people.'' According to Giovanni, this collective subjection to the whims of others has resulted in the alienation of black Americans from other Americans. For as black Americans ''living in a foreign nation we are, as the wandering Jew, both myth and reality.'' Giovanni believes that black Americans will always be ''strangers. But our alienation is our greatest strength.'' She does not believe that the alienation, or the collective history that produced it, makes black experience or writing incomprehensible to others. "I have not created a totally unique, incomprehensible feat. I can understand Milton and T. S. Eliot, so the critic can understand me. That's the critic's job."

Personal experience must be understood in social context. Its representation is susceptible to the critic's reading, regardless of whether he or she shares the personal experience. Giovanni rejects the claim that black writing should be the exclusive preserve of black critics—that it is qualitatively different from white writing, immune to any common principles of analysis, and thus severed from any common discourse. There is no argument about the ways in which the common discourse has treated black writing, especially the writing of black women: shamefully, outrageously, contemptuously, and silently. The argument concerns who can read black texts and the principles of the reading. For, as [Wole] Soyinka said, if the denial of bourgeois culture ends in the destruction of discourse, the refusal of critical distance ends in the acceptance of an exceptionalism that portends extreme political danger. Giovanni explicitly and implicitly makes the main points: the identity of the self remains hostage to the history of the collectivity; the representation of the self in prose or verse invites the critical scrutiny of the culture. Both points undercut the myth of the unique individual and force a fresh look at the autobiographies of black women.

Elizabeth Fox-Genovese. In Henry Louis Gates, Jr., ed. *Reading Black, Reading Feminist* (New York: Meridian, 1990), pp. 183–84

BIBLIOGRAPHY
*Black Feeling, Black Talk*, 1968; *Black Judgement*, 1968; *Black Feeling, Black Talk/Black Judgement*, 1970; *Poem of Angela Yvonne Davis*, 1970; *Re: Creation*, 1970; *Gemini: An Extended Autobiographical Statement on My First Twenty–five Years of Being a Black Poet*, 1971; *Spin a Soft Black Song: Poems for Children*, 1971; *My House*, 1972; *Ego Tripping and Other Poems for Young People*, 1973; *The Women and the Men*, 1975; *Cotton Candy on a Rainy Day*, 1978; *Vacation Time: Poems for Children*, 1980; *Those Who Ride the Night Winds*, 1983; *Sacred Cows. . .and Other Edibles*, 1988; *Grand Mothers: Poems, Reminiscences, and Short Stories about the Keepers of Our Traditions*, 1994; *Knoxville, Tennessee*, 1994; *Racism 101*, 1994; *Shimmy Shimmy Shimmy Like My Sister Kate: Looking at the Harlem Renaissance through Poems*, 1995; *The Genie in the Jar*, 1996; *The Selected Poems of Nikki Giovanni (1968–1995)*, 1996; *The Sun Is So Quiet*, 1996; *Love Poems*, 1997; *Blues For All the Changes*, 1999

# GLISSANT, Edouard (1928–)
## Martinique

[Edouard] Glissant's continuous inquiry into the meaning of the Caribbean past constitutes one of the salient features of his literary work and philosophic thought. Rejecting the main thrusts of Négritude, its nostalgia for Africa and its overreaction to white racism, as inadequate for the situation of the Afro-Caribbean, Glissant proffers the concept of Antillanité. Among other things, Antillanité encompasses a lucid apprehension of the Caribbean past experience and a projection of a future course toward the shaping of a distinct regional collective consciousness and destiny. The function of the Afro-Caribbean writer is to commit himself to the "decisive act, which, in the domain of literature, means to build a nation." Nation-building exacts a vision that can "perceive of the consciousness, the one and only operative, of our being." Furthermore, Glissant maintains that "for those whose allotted share of history is only darkness and despair, recovery of the near and distant past is imperative. To renew acquaintance with one's past is to relish fully the present." A conscious collectivity is bound together by the heritage of a common past. . . .

In one of Glissant's early works, the play *Monsieur Toussaint*, the celebrated Haitian Maroon, Mackandal, is among the six dead who surround Toussaint and signify a temptation, a potential, a conflicting loyalty Toussaint is faced with. Mackandal expects Toussaint to avenge him for his violent death with massacres of whites and destruction of their property. But Toussaint, the nation-builder who wants the new order in Haiti to be based on peace, justice, and prosperity, refuses to yield to the temptation of requiting violence with violence. For the lawgiver, administrator, and proprietor Toussaint, Mackandal's insistence on equal retribution can lead only to the impasse of self-perpetuating violence. On the other hand, Toussaint, imbued with the ideas of the Enlightenment and the French Revolution, remains estranged from the ethos of his people, and the Haitian Revolution, propelled by its own revolutionary dynamics, bypasses him and abandons him to his tragic solitude. The confrontation between the Maroon and the builder or the intellectual is further amplified in Glissant's novels.

The first novel, *La Lézarde*, deals with the postwar scene in Martinique at the time of the first elections, when the island became a French overseas department. The plot of the novel revolves around a group of young radicals who plan the assassination of a turncoat in order to prevent the betrayal of Martinican aspirations to the metropolitan interests. To execute the plan and cover their tracks, the radicals inveigle a young shepherd, Thaël, who has been living up in the mountains like a latter-day Maroon, into drowning the traitor. In the course of their political pursuits the young activists visit Papa Longoué, a *quimboiseur* of Maroon lineage, who has refused to compromise with the modern times. He leads an isolated life on the mountain slopes, gathering his herbs, cultivating ancient African mysteries and wisdom. He is the last link with Africa, reliving in his memories passed from generation to generation the Middle Passage, the arrival of Africans in the New World, the days of *marronnage*. As a final gesture of adamant refusal, on his deathbed Papa Longoué forbids his friends to take his corpse down to the cemetery for burial.

Papa Longoué embodies negation in its ultimate form. Thaël, however, signifies an evolution of the Maroon prototype. Like Papa Longoué, Thaël leads a solitary life up in the mountains surrounded by legends and prophecies. But unlike Papa Longoué, he accedes to the request of his friends from the plain to descend from the heights and commit himself to political action in solidarity with the people. When Thaël returns to his mountain abode with his new bride, Valérie, following the elections won by the people's candidate, he assesses his adventure: "We left the mountains, we drank from the Source." But the ultimate significance of his incursion into the life of the plains people remains ambiguous. Valérie is killed by his dogs, who had grown hungry and furious during his absence—in a way, a reminder of the punishment that slave owners inflicted upon runaway slaves. The final scene of the novel offers no resolution to the ambiguity of Thaël's adventure. As his faithful dogs are licking his hands, Thaël can only think of the ways he would kill them to avenge Valérie's death. The meeting of the mountain Maroon and the plainsman, the past and the present, the old traditions and modern mentalities signals the need for further rapprochement, but at the same time a kind of atavistic curse hangs over those who commit themselves to incautious action. Glissant's second novel, *Le Quatrième Siècle*, projects much further the trajectory of the Maroon's evolution in the face of the choices between the sterility of negation and the uncertainties of compromise.

Juris Silenieks. In William Luis, ed. *Voices from Under: Black Narrative in Latin America and the Caribbean* (Westport, Connectcut: Greenwood Press, 1984), pp. 119–21

Edouard Glissant's most recent volume of poetry, *Boises*, is dedicated "to every country which is diverted from its course and suffers the failing of its waters." The dedication, the book's subtitle (*Natural History of an Aridity*), and the concluding words of the final poem—"So we must retrace the dried watercourse and descend into many absences, to wind along to the place of our rebirth, black in the rock"—all refer us to the major themes of Glissant's work: the need to recapture, but also to transcend, a vanished, unrecorded history; and the struggle to preserve a sense of cultural identity in the face of metropolitan French policies that discourage and inhibit the onward flow of a specifically Caribbean tradition in Martinique and Guadeloupe. . . .

Along with the image of the parched and devastated land, that of the dried watercourse, with its suggestions of drought and sterility, has come to haunt Glissant's latest works. Its meaning is twofold: as the river is a traditional symbol of the passage of time, its ceasing to flow denotes the absence of a sense of history and continuity in the French Caribbean islands today; and the failing of the water also represents the inroads of modern industrialization, a destruction of the landscape that is itself symbolic, in the author's eyes, of the destruction wrought upon his race first by slavery and then by economic and cultural imposition. Slavery, with its enforced separation from African roots, began a long process of physical deprivation and emotional impoverishment. . . . This historic loss of identity is paralleled by a divorce between man and the land today which is, for Glissant, symptomatic of the state of alienation that characterizes his country: the feeling of dispossession, the moral disarray. The situation has been aggravated by the policy of assimilation to France which has sundered, for French West Indians, the connection with a meaningful African past and has disregarded the folkways of their slave ancestors. Glissant's second novel, *Le Quatrième Siècle*, is an imaginative reconstruction of the Caribbean past as it would have appeared to all those living through it, with major emphasis upon the viewpoints of two interwoven families whose African ancestors arrived on the same ship: one, Longoué, to escape immediately and take refuge in the Maroon forests; the other, Béluse, to accept his fate as a plantation slave. Members of these families appear in his other novels: *La Lézarde* [translated as *The Ripening*], *Malemort*, and *La Case du commandeur*. . . .

*The Ripening* records a moment in the history of Martinique when it seemed that the breach between the land and its inhabitants could be healed, that with the assumption of departmental status the island could hope for real progress and fruitfulness; in the novel the river is depicted as curving around the town as if "to enfold a portion of humanity, to reassure its people and help them." On the contrary, in *Malemort*, the title of which is a medieval word meaning cruel and tragic death, the predominant mood is a compound of grief, cynicism, and disillusionment. The author sardonically exposes the contradiction between the lip service officially paid to the notion of fostering a sense of Caribbean cultural identity, and the true attitude of metropolitan France towards the islands: "Of course there are problems here but a Frenchman's a Frenchman, whether he's a Breton, an Alsatian or a West Indian." The crushing of independent private initiative and self-development is rendered in microcosm by the failure of a modest local attempt to create a commune which would have brought a few families back to the land. The area is requisitioned by a metropolitan company whose giant tractor charges noisily backward and forward, ripping the earth apart, fouling the freshwater pools and "ravaging all this dream of land reform." The tractor's blind attempt to uproot three tall ebony trees echoes an earlier moment in *Le Quatrième Siècle* when Saint-Yves Béluse (a descendant of the African who accepted slavery), desiring, like his former masters, to exploit the land, plans to uproot and sell the wood of three ebony trees, seeing only their commercial value and not the fact that they have looked down upon the lives of his ancestors and are a precious link with the past. Such indifference to the landscape is indifference to the meaning and importance of history. On the other hand, care for the landscape and attachment to it are, for Glissant, essential means whereby a community cut off from its original roots and ties may slowly come to know its new country and take root in it, regaining through the landscape a lost sense of historical continuity and nationhood, "*suffering* the land and becoming worthy of it." . . .

[Glissant's] deft intertwining of poetic fiction and political thesis is in keeping with [his] conviction that the function of his art is not merely to reflect the Caribbean environment, but to support and illuminate the stages of its growth, to testify to the slow formation of a nation whose existence is not yet recognized even by its own nationals, and still less by those who contest its right to independence.

Beverley Ormerod. *An Introduction to the French Caribbean Novel* (London: Heinemann, 1985), pp. 36–39

*Le Discours [antillais]* frightens as much as it fascinates. Western intellectuals, especially the French, have a need to organize, classify, and order the world. Glissant's multiplicity of themes, at times dealt with in a systematic fashion, at other times in a fragmentary fashion, his series of blank spaces, his theoretical texts, his poetic texts, his accounts of experiences, and his other texts, give the reader the sensation of being dragged over a precipice.

*Le Discours* reveals another facet of this poet, critic, novelist, and playwright: an unflagging researcher with an admirable production of theoretical writings, engaged in blazing new trails (or in following old ones from a new perspective) in search of clues that may better explain the reality of his country. The importance of *Le Discours* (and the difficulty in its reading) lies also in its great diversity. By discussing a whole variety of topics in the most diverse manners in a sequence not always clear to the reader, Glissant demonstrates that the study of a situation as original and complex as that of Martinique demands an entirely new approach. He is aware of the fact that "no method is ever innocent," and one of his main concerns is to escape the pitfalls of Cartesian logic and academic formalism, the great danger for Antillean intellectuals. . . .

It seems to me that one of the key concepts of Glissant's analyses is that of *dispossession* (the subtitle to book one of *Le Discours*). This concept also appears under the names of "lack," "absence," and "privation" and forms part of an economic and political but also philosophical consideration. On the other hand, considering that Glissant's literary project is fundamentally concerned with the land, the history, and the language of his people, as became apparent in 1969 with *L'Intention poétique* . . . one may say that Martinique, according to Glissant's criteria, is the locus of threefold dispossession: of place, of history, of language.

> Diva Barbaro Damato. *World Literature Today*. 63, 4 (Autumn 1989), p. 606

Glissant's last novel, *Mahogany*, establishes itself not only as the confirmation of an ancient and exemplary coherence—the rigorous coherence revealed by the continuity of the project in Glissant's poetry, novels, and theoretical works—but also as *détour*, humorous and playful recollection, and threefold *marronnage*: once again, *marronnage* of language, *marronnage* of structures and laws governing the narrative (since the character becomes creator), and lastly, *marronnage* by the chronicler, regarding the official Text of History, and, as such, a *marronnage* of Time. This enlightening and necessary reflection of the novel's discourse upon itself is also a well-reasoned and playful duplicity of the narrative, since, as we are told: "Whether sung or chanted, the depth of time comes back up to the surface. The rigidity in elucidating History yields to the pleasure of telling stories."

This game involving the author and the narrator and the character's autonomy toward his creator demonstrate the necessary complexity of a relationship that would not only be from self to the Other but from self to self. In the same way that *Mahogany* shows the reflection of the literary discourse upon itself, it also seems to indicate the possible reflection of the community upon itself, this reflection being the only guarantee of true progress, despite uncertainty, chaos, and misery. . . .

[It] often seems that Glissant's words, already so far ahead of us, await us like the words of someone who divined there in the depths that which we have yet been unable to see. These patient, obstinate, rigorous, brilliant, and burning words also affirm, as we are told in *Mahogany*, that "in this country of Martinique, those who search pass on to those who speak, who named them but did not recognize them. Thus we move forward to the edge of the world."

> Priska Degras. *World Literature Today*. 63, 4 (Autumn 1989), pp. 618–19

It seems fitting to discuss the Antilleanity of Edouard Glissant, as this appears to be the most obvious aspect of his personality and his entire work. Born and raised in Martinique, the French Antilles, Glissant has devoted all his life and creative activity to the quest for the Antillean identity. . . .

Glissant's impassioned attachment to the Antillean land could only lead him to use his talent as a writer to describe its landscape, which is always related to the people. . . . This means that different parts of the island of Martinique correspond to different historical events or activities of the people, as illustrated in *La Lézarde* or *Le Discours antillais*. In both cases Glissant gives the reader a guided tour from the top of the mountain—which happens to be in the North—to the sea, which is in the South, and along the way he comments upon every pertinent face of the landscape. The mountain, with its thick forest and intricate fern trees that stop sunlight, was the privileged refuge of the Maroons. It is the symbol of the past, of faithfulness to Africa and refusal of servitude. The center, called the *plaine*, with its sugar cane fields, its decaying sugar and rum factories, was once entirely occupied by the plantations and the slaves, who would first land at the Dubuc mansion, now in ruin, before distribution to their masters. The junction of the mountain and the *plaine* is made by the Lézarde River, whose winding brings us next to the city and the people who use it for their laundry and their bath. In recent years its delta has been used for airport traffic and various enterprises, which has caused the crabs to disappear. Finally, comes the southern part bordering the coast, with its coconut trees, whose trunks were used to cross the sea by those slaves who unsuccessfully tried to join Toussaint L'Ouverture in his revolt. The beaches and other parts of the island are now put at the disposal of tourist companies and their customers, a modern substitute for the plantations. In *Mahogany* Glissant parabolically compares Martinique to a colonial museum, a showcase not only for the everyday visitors but also for researchers such as sociologists and psychiatrists, who may be inquisitive about the possibility of such a human phenomenon. . . .

In a systematic and didactic way, Glissant will undertake to rewrite the history of the Antilles in his autobiographical novel *Le Quatrième Siècle*, published in 1964 and honored with the Charles Veillon International Award. Under the pretext of writing the first official history of his island, Mathieu, a young activist who may represent Glissant himself, asks an elderly *quimboiseur*—a witch-soothsayer and griot—to tell him what he knows about the topic. He expects that the old man, Papa Longoué, who can encompass the past, the present, and the future, will also provide information for his own political activities and will help him at the same time discover his own identity along with public truth. This historical novel turns out to be the chronicle of several families, including two black, two white, and one mulatto. The two black families stand for Africans like the Longoués, who refused slavery and started a community of Maroons, and others like the Béluses, who were assigned to plantations by their acceptance of enslavement. Eventually these two lines will converge as components making up the Caribbean people. Similarly, the white families, the La Roches and the Senglises, will serve as types. In between, the development of the Targin family illustrates the mulatto class that usually derives from miscegenation between white masters or overseers and female slaves. It is recorded that this new group grew away from the others and remained a floating element within society. This explains the development of the divisions of class and color which were to persist within the Antillean population even after emancipation.

> Daniel L. Racine. *World Literature Today*. 63, 4 (Autumn 1989), pp. 620–22

Among Glissant's earliest published works, *Les Indes*, a six-part epic poem that relates Caribbean history from Columbus's voyage to the European conquest and slave trade, illustrates the poet's relationship to collective memory and the Antillean landscape. *Les Indes* begins as an epic, promising praise for European adventure and discovery. . . . Despite the joy and optimism, accentuated in the poem by alliteration and the inversion of syllables (*lyre d'airain / l'air lyrique*), sailors who embark on Columbus's ships experience fear of the unknown, boredom at sea, and risk death from disease, all trials the Africans will face in turn. The opening of new space for Europeans (''Sur Gênes va s'ouvrir . . .'') will result in closed space, confinement for the Africans who, unlike the European sailors working freely on deck, are shackled and brutalized in the ship's hull. Glissant's epic becomes an ''anti-epic'' even before the poet depicts the horrors of the slave trade, for Columbus's discovery of the Caribbean islands opens the way for exploitation as conquistadores, seeking riches, arrive to plunder. . . .

Glissant's most recent collection of poetry, *Pays rêvé, pays réel*, attests to his continued commitment to unearth the past in its complexity, contradictions, and opacity. A long poem divided [into] eight sections, it bears traces of the legacy of Columbus's voyage; annihilation of the Caribs, Middle Passage, slavery, marronage, all inform the poet's view of the past and the present. However, Glissant now rejects chronological organization, discarding the linear narration of the epic poem. Instead, he posits two time-frames, a *pays rêvé*, the atemporal oneiric landscape of a mythic Africa, and a *pays réel*, the Martinican landscape of his fiction. Each evokes a cast of characters: *pays rêvé* depicts mythical Africans that include Ichneumon, the storyteller, Milos, the blacksmith, and Laoka, an African goddess; *pays réel* presents protagonists of his earlier novels, Mathieu, Thaël, and Mycéa, political radicals intent on transforming Martinique's social and political structure. Thus, Glissant moves toward dissolving two boundaries, one between dream and reality, the other between poetry and prose.

An important distinction between poetry and prose lies in the special relationship each has to memory. In his study of Glissant's work, Daniel Radford explains that . . . Glissant's poetry probes inner consciousness in a way that his prose, constrained by time, geography, and grounded in realism (albeit poetic realism), cannot. Transmitting the historical reality of conquest and slavery in the Caribbean, *Les Indes* does not lend itself to the evocation of an oneiric landscape of mythic ancestors. *Pays rêvé, pays réel* moves beyond the epic to explore cultural identity as a concept embracing both the unconscious and the conscious—myth, dream, and reality in all their contradictions and opacity. Furthermore, unlike *Les Indes*, it does not deal with historical incidents but rather allows historical images to emerge from the collective unconscious. . . .

Written three decades after the epic, *Pays rêvé, pays réel* is far more pessimistic than *Les Indes*, which pays tribute to rebels who used their creative energy to combat the destructive powers of European conquerors. The more recent poetry is haunted by the fear that this energy has been depleted, that Martinican creativity is drying up just as the Lézarde River has become an insignificant stream. . . .

In the process of recovering a lost past marked by the earlier choice between dependency and flight (the slave either submitting to the colonial plantation order or fleeing to the *mornes*), Glissant finds a reflection of yesterday's dilemma in French Caribbean reality today, as Martinicans decide between dependency (social security handouts at home), or flight (emigration to France). Ironically, flight, which as *marronnage* once preserved identity,

now often leads to further alienation. Sustained by the collective memory of indigenous resistance to colonial conquest and domination, the poet, despite his pessimism, remains firmly committed to using his own creative energies to articulate the collective voice of his people. Clearly, Glissant has not abandoned the hope that the energy which sparked former resistance will continue to flow.

Mildred [P.] Mortimer. *L'espirit createur.* 32, 2 (Summer 1992), pp. 67–68, 72–75

Edouard Glissant's eminence not only in French Caribbean literature but in Caribbean literature as a whole is undisputed. There is also evidence of his emerging status as a theorist whose concepts and terminology have gained widespread acceptance. The use of such terms as *opacité, détour* and relation is increasing as these notions have become the investigative tools of literary critics as well as of those whose concerns are anthropological, sociological and linguistic. Since one of the distinctive features of Glissant's work is the fusion of the imaginative and the theoretical, it comes as no surprise that his influence should transcend the narrowly literary. This is especially so given the present theoretical context of postmodernism and the general interest in cultural diversity that Glissant's ideas seem to have anticipated.

No one initially seemed to know quite what to make of Glissant and his work. He offered a bewildering range of ideas at a time when surrealism, negritude and *francophonie* were the dominant movements. He was neither exclusively poet, novelist, dramatist nor essayist but creatively combined all categories, often simultaneously. This at least partly accounts for the early difficulty in assessing Glissant's significance and in establishing his literary and ideological credentials.

Some of the difficulties presented by Glissant's work were, perhaps, unique at the time. What does one make of a writer whose literary ancestors do not appear to come from his own cultural past? In particular, what does one do with a black francophone writer who invokes neither Marx, Breton, Sartre nor Césaire? Glissant professed an attachment to writers as diverse and puzzling as the novelist from the American South, William Faulkner; Saint–John Perse, born in Guadeloupe but destined to be a poet wandering across cultures; and the little–known French travel writer Victor Segalen, whose meditations on cultural displacement and diversity have deeply influenced Glissant. It was not until the 1970s that the nature of Glissant's literary enterprise was understood, and it was no coincidence that an accurate grasp of Glissant's ideas would emerge within the context of Caribbean writing as distinct from negritude or francophonie.

In the 1980s, Martinique's literary politics notwithstanding, appreciation of Glissant's impressive undertakings by French Caribbean critics has been increasingly insightful. In *Caraïbales* (1981) Jacques André uses a Freudian methodology to analyse Glissant's work. In 1982 Daniel Radford devoted one book in the series 'Poètes d'aujourd'hui' to Glissant. The power of Glissant's ideas in the French West Indies has, perhaps, been most dramatically apparent in the essay *Eloge de la Créolité* by Jean Bernabé, Raphael Confiant and Patrick Chamoiseau published in 1989. Both Confiant and Chamoiseau represent a new literary generation, steeped in Glissant's language and ideas. As Glissant's reputation as a major Caribbean writer becomes more recognised, special issues of journals such as *CARE, World Literature Today* and *Carbet* have been devoted to him.

With an oeuvre comprising six novels, seven books of poetry and four books of essays by 1993, Glissant is now thé major writer and theorist from the French West Indies. This is no small achievement since the francophone Caribbean has produced such influential literary figures as Jean Price–Mars, Jacques Stephen Alexis, Jacques Roumain, Aimé Césaire and Frantz Fanon. Perhaps, more than any of his predecessors, Glissant's ideas and his writing are centred on the Caribbean and the socio–cultural dynamism of the archipelago. In a region characterised by impermanence, instability and hybrid forms, Glissant undertakes the daunting task of tracing each 'fold' of Caribbean reality, of establishing hidden continuities and creating a 'neo–baroque' form of expression in his works. Most importantly, the major thrust of his ideas is the conceptualising of a Caribbean identity within the Americas. It is precisely this impulse that informs the strength and originality of Glissant's all–encompassing literary endeavour.

> J. Michael Dash. *Eduoard Glissant* (Cambridge: Cambridge University Press, 1995), pp. 1–3

Because of the nonhistory of the Caribbean, time and space are not and cannot be expressed in the same way as in Western literatures. For Glissant, the sea and land/landscape are inseparable from Caribbean history. Man's relationship to the land becomes so important in his discourse that landscape becomes a "character" in this story or history:

> Décrire le paysage ne suffira pas. L'individu, la communauté, le pays sont indissociables dans l'épisode constitutif de leur histoire. Le paysage est un personnage de cette histoire.

In order to understand the depth and importance of the land/landscape, one must "passionately live the landscape" as Glissant explains in his earlier work *L'Intention Poétique*: "Passionnément vivre le paysage. Le dégager de l'indistinct, le fouiller, l'allumer parmi nous. Savoir ce qu'en nous il signifie. Porter à la terre ce clair savoir." For Glissant, it is a question of bringing back to the community a consciousness of its history through an understanding and knowledge of that land.

The role of the writer or intellectual is paramount in bringing a consciousness to the people. Glissant's role in leading Martinican writers down the difficult path to a conscience exprimée is evident in the works of the Martinican intellectuals and writers Jean Bernabé, Patrick Chamoiseau and Raphaël Confiant. . . .

Glissant's project of Antillanité—embedded in the lived experience, the creole language, and the hidden history of the Caribbean—is the process of giving a voice to the Caribbean people by awakening them to their unique position in the planetary scheme of "histories." It represents as Diva Damato states, "an opportunity for his people to come before the world, to participate in the relations between peoples" ("Poetics of the Dispossessed").

Edouard Glissant's concept of antillanité is inseparably tied to Caribbean culture, landscape and most importantly, history. His work is permeated with his anguish and his obsession with history, or rather, the "non–history" of the Antilles and Martinique. The relationship between literature and history is not an impossible one for Glissant. In what Blanchot would call the "disaster" of Caribbean and New World histories, Glissant sees the birth of a new civilization in which diversity reigns. However, Glissant does not consider the writer's engagement as either immediate or transparent as does Sartre. Glissant's literary engagement reveals itself neither as transparent—"Nous réclamons le droit à l'opacité"–nor immediate. His engagement involves the arduous task of "forging a voice" for a diffracted collectivity and community by foraging the obscurity of Martinican realities and pasts in order to bring to the community the voice (parole) rightfully theirs. . . . The search for origins is a recurring theme in Glissant's novels and his literary return to these "uncertain sources" by bringing to light the history/histories of the Caribbean people is one of the slow paths to health. . . .

Glissant's writing of this nonhistory—not only a quest for the past, present and future histories of Martinique, but also the search for a literary expression—does not reveal itself transparent. Could this be the reason for the lack of a positive reception in his native Martinique? Two novelists profoundly influenced by his work, Patrick Chamoiseau and Raphaël Confiant reproach Glissant with being too involved with his own literary projects to help them in their efforts to continue his quest of a Caribbean identity. Or is it, as Henry Louis Gates ascertains, that literature by black writers has always been expected, for all kinds of complicated historical and political reasons, to be committed? Literature by Black writers is not expected to be merely committed or engagée: it must manifest an engagement transparent. It would appear that perhaps the expectations of criticism (Sartre is a prime example) are different for black writers than for white writers.

Glissant's prose style is not transparent. His novels do not unfold themselves to the reader in a balzacian fashion and discourage the reader in search of exposition, description, and linear development. He gives the reader some help in deciphering the complexities of his novels by providing glossaries of creole words or expressions, chronologies, genealogies, as well as names of plants and animals native to Martinique and unfamiliar to the reader. Because of this "distance" between the reader and text, Glissant's works have a deeply disturbing effect on the reader. Even the *Discours antillais*, which locates the Caribbean discourse for the reader "frightens as much as it fascinates," as Diva Barbaro Damato explains:

> Western intellectuals, especially the French, have a need to organize, classify, and order the world. Glissant's multiplicity of themes, at times dealt with in a systematic fashion; at other times in a fragmentary fashion, his series of blank spaces, his theoretical texts, his poetic texts, his accounts of experiences; and his other texts, give the reader the sensation of being dragged over a precipice.

It is interesting to note that in the English translation of the *Discours antillais, Caribbean Discourse*, many of the original textual devices that "give the reader the sensation of being dragged over a precipice" have been omitted. The reader in English is spared the precipice: gone are the empty spaces in the text; the introductory pages to each "book"—pages left deliberately blank except for the titles, subtitles and repères (landmarks, points of reference) all of which serve as guides to the reader—have been collapsed into one page. The repères are omitted more often than not. The changes may be deemed minor cosmetic changes or judgements on the part of the translator and editor. Nonetheless these changes detract from the reader's reaction to the text. These blank or empty spaces weigh heavy with meaning, as Glissant points out at the beginning of Livre IV—Un Discours Eclaté: the subtitle page is entitled "inconscient, identité, méthodes" and the following page contains only the word and footnote "repères". The footnote reads: "Seule une page blanche en peut ici tenir lieu." Other indications or "landmarks" Glissant gives the reader such as the chronological numbering of the topics discussed—the deliberate creation of a sort of order—have been omitted because the English translation has left out certain sections of the *Discours*. The few landmarks given the reader to locate the discours antillais have been taken away. The blank pages indicative of the blank pages of Caribbean history have been effaced. These omissions function in the same way as the use of sound in the editing of films to detract the viewers attention from a change in scene in order to create a false sense of narrative continuity. The omitted landmarks ultimately undermine Glissant's desire to communicate to the readr the sense of discontinuity and chaos that is part of the Caribbean experience.

Glissant not only conveys this sense of discontinuity and chaos in the *Discours*, he also indicates and locates the complexities of Martinican history, society and identity for the reader and critic, but it is a difficult location. Glissant demands that his reader delve into the complexities of the Caribbean universe along with him; he challenges the reader to join him in this journey—these wanderings—into the uncertain. What does Glissant expect of his reader? The reader of Glissant's works must follow a procedure similar to that of the writer: he must "dig deep" into the text to find its order.

In the novels of Edouard Glissant, the reader is witness to how his critical discourse articulates itself in his fiction—how as a writer, he explores the hidden history and the historical memory of his country in order to re-establish a chronology and more importantly a continuity between the past, present and future.

Debra L. Anderson. *Decolonizing the Text: Glissantian Readings in Caribbean and African American Literatures.* 1995, pp. 37–36

*Introduction a une poetique du divers* is the right point of departure for the reader who may be picking up Glissant for the first time. A connected series of four public lectures Glissant gave in Quebec, *Introduction* is clear and straightforward in its exposition of such issues as creolization throughout the Americas and on a global scale, relation and its connection to Glissant's rhizomatous theory of culture, the choice of a literary language in a postcolonial climate, and the possible application of chaos theory to poetics. The edited debates that followed the lectures add a useful dimension; they clarify Glissant's significance for the intelligentsia of Quebec.

*Traite du Tout–Monde* should ideally be read after assimilation of the subjects treated in *Introduction*. Coming as it does after *Le discours antillais* (1981) and *Poetique de la relation* (1990), *Traite* makes greater demands upon the reader. It assumes familiarity with *Le quatrieme siecle* and the saga of the Longoue and Beluse families of which that novel is a part, as well. The subtitle of *Traite*, Poetique IV, situates *Soleil de la conscience* (1956) on the threshold of this series that now spans four decades.

It is quite clear from the combined intellectual and creative weight of these three volumes why Glissant has emerged in the 1990s as one of the foremost theoreticians of postcolonial literature, after having long been one of its great practitioners. Neither

his poetry nor his contribution to theater will be mentioned in this review, as they would have to be for a complete survey of Glissant's work. But fragmentary as this sample must be, it nonetheless permits a representative glimpse of the author's range.

*Le quatrieme siecle*, better than *La Lezarde*, which preceded it in 1958, situates the principal themes and motifs and many of the stylistic traits that were to characterize Glissant over the next thirty years. He imagined in this novel two Africans, Longoue and Beluse, who became respectively the ancestor of a Maroon community and the ancestor of Creole slaves in the 1780s. The time of narration is set in the twentieth century, however, as Papa Longue, descendant of the original Maroon, recounts the dual ancestral chronicle to Mathieu Beluse. Some readings of the novel have privileged the position of the Maroon, Longoue, to the detriment of the Creole slaves who descend from Beluse. This is notably the case of Richard D. E. Burton in his book *Le roman matron* (1997). Glissant's later essays on the culture of creolization, however, have clarified the situation. The creolization process on an island like Martinique required the contribution of both the Maroon who refused the servile condition on the plantation and the slave whose provision ground on the margin of the plantation modified those very conditions. Whereas in Le discours antillais Glissant continued to deplore the absence of a positive myth of the Maroon ancestor in Martinique, his later work has rendered his position both more complex and ambiguous. . . .

Glissant's extraordinary breadth is quite apparent in these titles. If *Le quatrieme siecle* takes place entirely in prerevolutionary Martinique, both *Introduction* and *Traite* are global in scope. *Traite du Tout–Monde* further recalls the title of Glissant's most recent novel, *Tout–Monde*. Like the novel, this latest volume of essays is more postmodern in perspective. The reader of the novel could sense how chaos theory had, in recent years, enlarged Glissant's concept of relation and made it more fluid. *Traite* ranges from the French poet Yves Bonnefoy to Nelson Mandela without skipping a beat. What are we to make, however, of the section entitled "Le Traite du Tout–Monde de Mathieu Beluse"? This Beluse is, of course, Glissant's fictional creation, as I noted above, and one of the major figures in his multivolume family saga. But a literary theoretician to boot? A later section of Traite is entitled "Objections a ce dit Traite de Mathieu Beluse, et Reponse." By now the mind boggles. The author has imagined objections to his character's theoretical positions and responses to those objections. Glissant has entered into dialogue with himself, of course, and the style of these passages falls somewhere between fiction and essay.

A. James Arnold. *World Literature Today*. 72, 3 (Summer 1998), pp. 670–1

BIBLIOGRAPHY
*Un champ d'iles*, 1953; *La terre inquiete, Editions de Seuil*, 1954; *Les Indes: Poemes de l'une et l'autre terre*, 1955; *Soleil de la conscience*, 1956; *La Lezarde*, 1958; *Le sel noir*, 1959; *Le sang rive*, 1960; *Monsieur Toussaint*, 1961 *Le quatrieme siecle*, 1964; *L'intention poetique*, 1969; *Malemort*, 1975; *Boises*, 1977; *Le discours antillais*, 1981; *La case du commandeur*, 1981; *Pays reve, pays reel*, 1985; *Mahagony*, 1987; *Poetique de la relation*, 1990; *Fastes*, 1991; *Tout-Monde*, 1993; *Poemes complets*, 1994; *Introduction a une poetique du duvers*, 1997; *Traite du tout-monde*, 1997

# GOODISON, Lorna (1947–)
Jamaica

We need to remember, as we discuss Lorna Goodison's work, that she is an artist as well as a poet. The keenness of her observation, her certain demarcation of shapes, her canny sense of physical and sociological textures are undoubtedly related to that other cousin sensibility. Poems like "Guyana Lovesong," which carefully vignettes that country, object of a visit by hurt persona; "On Houses," where the houses image the need for the soul to repose in relationship, in a loved and familiar Other person; "Port Henderson 6 AM," which celebrates dawn—"the horse of the morning / spectacular"—as seen from that place; "Wedding in Hanover," which describes the ritual of the country bride bathing with her young woman friends (the "elected virgins") at the river . . . are all imbued with this clearness, brightness, nice perpetual acuity. Even the romantic "Moonlongings" in which the poet fantasizes about traveling on the moon to her sleeping lover, paints a vivid picture, muted though the tones may be.

It is this painterly self that gives us the surrealist "Sketches of Spain," "Xercise for Tony Mc," "The Day She Died," "Saggitarius," and "Whose Is That Woman?" The first of these in particular not only combines objects to make a picture of the orderly derangement of another world, but creates in addition a mood with the haunting quality of the music of Miles Davis, to whom it is dedicated. . . .

Lorna Goodison's use of language is exciting in its versatility; it is married to the range of content of the poetry and deployed with the confidence which perhaps resides only in the supposed "matriarchs" who (our men tell us) make these societies. The poetry rejoices in this place and the myriad facets of life experience which it offers. The exhilaration of beating the would-be robber and rapist in "For R & R in the Rain" is the excitement of overcoming the impulse to violence in these societies. For the present, at least, it is truly a woman's triumph.

> Pamela Mordecai. *Jamaica Journal.* 45 (1981), pp. 39–40

Sooner or later, as the work of a poet assumes volume and personality, a few key images are likely to emerge, which serve as distinguishing marks, signatures of a sensibility. So we notice, for example, in Goodison's work, developing from *Tamarind Season*, a fascination with imagery of water and wetness—rain, river, sea. This water imagery signifies variously fertility, creativity, the erotic, succor, freedom, blessing, redemption, divine grace, cleansing, purification, and metamorphosis. In "On Becoming a Mermaid," for example, the woman imagines herself undergoing, through the agency of the buoyant element, "a sea change into something rich and strange" and self-possessed, liberated from the tyranny and ache of sexuality. "Jah Music bubble[s] up through a cistern"; Keith Jarrett, the pianist, is a "rainmaker," slaking the soul-drought of the poet far from home; and she cries, after the example of Gerard Manley Hopkins, "In this noon of my orchard / send me deep rain."

Then there is the continuous extending of linguistic possibility, which has been one of Goodison's most distinctive features. She has been steadily refining her skills at sliding seamlessly between English and Creole, at interweaving erudite literary allusion with the earthiness of traditional Jamaican speech, images from modern technology with the idiom of local pop culture. This process is the perfecting of a voice at once personal and anonymous, private and public. It may reach a kind of maturity in *Heartease* and will be an important factor in the increasing "largeness" of her work, as that work fuses private and communal pain and resolution. . . .

The deepening of the pain, and a corresponding discovery of new resources of resilience and a redemptive joy of life, are features of Goodison's development as a poet. Combined with the widening and subtilizing of her resources of form and expression, they have ensured that her work has indeed been getting "larger," and that her voice, personal and unmistakable as it is, is increasingly, and whether she knows it or not, the voice of a people.

> Edward Baugh. *Journal of West Indian Literature.* 1, 1 (October 1986), pp. 20–21

[Lorna Goodison's] two volumes of poetry to date, *Tamarind Season* and *I Am Becoming My Mother*, show a progression towards harmony. Less polemical than [Christine] Phillips (although some poems, like "Judges" in *Tamarind Season* are very strong), Goodison is a very skilled craftswoman of sounds. In "Judges" the point is partly the rhythm, which beautifully mirrors the Jamaican voice. . . .

[Some] of Goodison's poems find the crossroads between gender and race, and are neither strongly polemical nor primarily sensuous and resolving of issues. In "England Seen," for example, there is a very good sense of humor about Icylyn "chief presser hair," who goes "afro" in the summer, and the poem plays with the anxieties of women about looks (particularly here of black women in a white society). Middle-class aspirations are comically treated. . . .

Goodison occasionally treats class as a theme (as also do Phillips, [Olive] Senior and [Esther] Craig). In Goodison, voice of the dialect or Creole speaker is much more often interwoven into the texture of the line than it is in the other writers who tend to write either in one linguistic mode or the other in different poems. Goodison's humor is a medium for dealing with potential confrontation. . . . But for the most part, she is a poet of sensuous language, who is, to judge from her newest work, like *Heartease*, both technically confident and moving towards harmony and healing.

> Elaine Savory Fido. In Carole Boyce Davies and Elaine Savory Fido, eds. *Out of the Kumbla: Caribbean Women and Literature* (Trenton, New Jersey: Africa World Press, 1990), pp. 37–38

With two books of poems to her name, *Tamarind Season* and *I Am Becoming My Mother*, Lorna Goodison has already been the subject of an article by Caribbean poet and critic [Edward] Baugh which indicates that she is working upon a long sequence poem called *Heartease*. Her first book indicated some affiliations with the experimental jazz-oriented writing which characterized the work of one of the most interesting young male poets, Anthony McNeill's *Credences at the Altar of Cloud*. *Tamarind Season* contains one piece called "Xcercise for Tony Mc," while both volumes have a number of poems about jazz musicians. Her second volume, though, has allowed Goodison to evolve more of her own voice and concerns, particularly in relation to the experience of being a woman. Here she has made an affiliation with the great Russian poet Anna Akhmatova as a model of that activity so many of the Caribbean women poets see as central: acting "as a person who could speak for everybody, for people, for ordinary people, for people suffering." . . . Baugh sees this as an identification of the communal with the personal. Again, part of this process involves a reclamation of history. Like Jean Breeze in her "Soun de abeng fi Nanny," Goodison has a poem celebrating Maroon resistance leader Nanny, heroine of Jamaican national culture. She is, as . . . Baugh points out, one of a lineage of powerful female figures, public and private, in Goodison's work, including Rosa Parks of the Alabama bus boycott, Winnie Mandela, and Goodison's own mother, as in the powerful "For My Mother (May I Inherit Half Her Strength)." . . . The historical continuity of this female experience is central to Goodison's stated commitment to "write about women more than anything else, the condition of women," and she does so with a continual insinuation of hope and promise. "We Are the Women" ends with a familiar image from Afro-Caribbean ancestry, the buried navel string of the newborn child, the guarantor of future safety. . . . "Bedspread" presents an imaginary monologue by Winnie Mandela addressed to her imprisoned husband from the bright Azanian colors of the quilt woven in the past by "woman with slender / capable hands / accustomed to binding wounds" and ingrained with "ancient blessings / older than any white man's coming." It is a process of weaving the future which continues, the poem argues, despite the long confinement of [Nelson] Mandela and offers the certainty of change.

Goodison also has a number of poems about children and child care, a crucial area of concern for Caribbean women. . . . Goodison has a sharp awareness of the emotional complexities of such issues. She manages to present the ambiguities of hope during the present time while keeping faith with the progressive potential of the future and particularly the role of women in that transformatory process. It is this commitment that allows the woman speaker of her title poem to see herself as giving birth to herself, and becoming her mother in a double sense. In this awareness, Lorna Goodison is representative of much of the freshness and vigor to be found in Caribbean women's poetry. Given the recent emergence of these writers and the fact that most of them are at the very beginnings of their poetic developments, they promise a very bright future and new directions for Caribbean literature itself.

Bruce Woodcock. In Gina Wisker, ed. *Black Women's Writing* (New York: St. Martin's Press, 1993), pp. 73–75

The evocative power of Lorna Goodison's poetry derives its urgency and appeal from the heart-and-mind concerns she has for language, history, racial identity, and gender (and these are not as separate and consecutive as I have listed them, but rather as alternating and interwoven as they usually occur in the hurly-burly of human existence).

In the exceptionally engaging and indeed enticing selection of the poet's work recently issued by the University of Michigan Press [*Selected Poems*], which includes spiritual, humanistic, and political themes ranging from the southern Caribbean to North America, there are poems that depict the inconsolable condition of women struggling against the aridities of "love misplaced" and the resulting social inequities and enforced loneliness ("We Are the Women," "Mulatta Song," "Mulatta Song II," "Jamaica 1980,"

"Garden of the Women Once Fallen"). There are also the lyric narratives, in part expressed in the demotic, in part in the Creole standard, that extol, commemorate, and offer us lasting metaphorical strophes and images of human excellence and achievement ("To Us, All Flowers Are Roses," "Guyana Lovesong," "For Don Drummond," "Jah Music," "Lullaby for Jean Rhys," "For Rosa Parks," "On Becoming a Tiger"). And by the way, I consider "Heartease I," "Heartease II," and "Heartease III" to be among the most thematically important and sensitively written lyric demotic compositions in the collection (and surely among the finest of their kind in Caribbean poetry in English).

Then there are Goodison's mother poems, contemporary elegies, odes, and praise songs, substantially contemplative and emotional *yet* unsentimental, and which at once instruct and delight heart and mind and are some of the most memorably tender statements in the book ("I Am Becoming My Mother," "Guinea Woman," "The Woman Speaks to the Man Who Has Employed Her Son," "Mother the Great Stones Got to Move"). Altogether, these are the poems I like best, the ones that reveal the poet's regional and at the same time her universal sense of compassion. Of course, my all-time favorite Goodison poem is "For My Mother (May I Inherit Half Her Strength)," a resonant *cri de coeur* in support of the primacy of motherhood and family unity.

Andrew Salkey. *World Literature Today.* 67, 4 (Autumn 1993), pp. 876–77

Goodison's is first of all a woman's voice, grounded not just in sorrow, but in resolution and independence; the voice of a woman who in her own litany is daughter, sister, mistress, friend, warrior, wife, and mother; the voice of a woman for whom home is a place where simple things are central, a place located here and now with pigeons roosting over the door and tomatoes growing in the garden, a place that nourishes the spirit and imagination. . . .

Goodison's poetic imagination includes both men and women, in Jamaica and elsewhere, with whom she shares a life of struggle and of freedom. But she grounds her imagination at home. In the poem "We Are the Women," she confirms her special bond with other West Indian women, past and present, notable and unknown. Silver coins and cloves of garlic, the precious and the commonplace, come together here in a ritual witnessing whose apocryphal character represents a collective wisdom outside the canon, unauthorized but true, the shared secrets of resistance and restoration. . . . The complementary images of rooting and burying, and of the land and the sea (the anchor to our navel strings), bring together here the whole history of slavery: the drowning at sea and the death on land and the harrowing legacy of sexual exploitation; the hiding away of secrets and the determination of those entrusted with them to give voice to new hope and to give birth to a new generation of . . . conquerors who will finally set their people free. . . .

Goodison's inspiration comes from a deep understanding of her experience as a West Indian woman. Images of that inspiration are drawn from the traditions of European literature, but they are transformed by Goodison not only into distinctly West Indian terms but also into her own. Literary tradition has given us the image of a female muse as the source of poetic inspiration. Goodison's muse is not some woman of shadowy power and intermittent presence, as a tradition dominated by men would have it, but is instead the figure of a man, overwhelming and unreliable at times (as muses tend to be), and created as a woman's image of inspiration. She writes about her muse in all the ways that are familiar to readers of European literature . . . except that her muse is different, inspiring her desires and dreams—and occasionally prompting her dismay—as a woman as well as a poet. She finds his image in the peace of God, and His wrath; in the preciousness of her son to her, and the fears she holds for him; in the power of love, her sometime destiny and her despair. Her muse is an image of otherness, a power beyond and within herself, both of her own devising and determined by her literary heritage. . . .

Through all the divisions and deceptions, there is a deep reserve of hopefulness in Goodison's work, sustained by the links she has forged between the poetic and the personal. There are risks here, mainly of self-conscious ingenuity and sentimental indulgence. But she takes them openly, with almost cavalier disregard for the different conventions of life and literature, in order to challenge our customary distinctions between reality and the imagination, and to bring a spirit of reconciliation back into poetry. In "My Last Poem (Again)," written several years later, she negotiates between images of love to which she has in a sense become hostage, and between the men who are figures of fear and hope to her—as a woman and as a poet. . . .

At the heart of Goodison's poetry is a profoundly religious sensibility, embracing a purpose that both transcends human understanding and is part of everyday life. There is much pain in her poetry, beginning with a recognition of the sorrow and suffering that are part of the heritage of all West Indians. But out of this heritage comes the dignity of a "Survivor," representing all those whom grace has touched . . . which in some measure should be all of us. . . .

Goodison, like [Edward Kamau] Brathwaite and [Derek] Walcott, writes poems of possibility—the possibility of understanding the past and present experience of West Indians, the possibility of sharing their heritage of pain, and the possibility of peace and light and love. Their poetic testaments are simply and unmistakably their own, bringing together the Old World of European and African inheritances with the New Land and literature of the West Indies.

> J. Edward Chamberlin. *Come Back to Me My Language: Poetry and the West Indies* (Urbana: University of Illinois Press, 1993), pp. 196, 203–4, 207, 209–10, 212, 216

[In *Baby Mother and the King of Swords* (1990), all] but one of the fourteen stories, "The Dolly Funeral," are about the condition of women in heterosexual relationships, and the majority of these examine the characteristic situation in which male egotism and insensitivity exploit and abuse female love, romanticism, and generosity of self, or seek to do so.

The main concerns of the collection are indicated by the title and the two terms "Baby Mother" and the "King of Swords." The King of Swords, from the tarot pack, is a resplendent, enticing figure, depicted with one hand beckoning the onlooker toward him. The other hand, holding an upright sword, is hidden behind his

back. "Baby Mother," a popular Jamaicanism used mostly among the lower classes, identifies a woman who has had a child out of wedlock, though it is sometimes used to indicate a victim of incest. While the woman may refer to the man as her "baby father," "baby mother" is the primary term and often carries overtones of pathos, for often the man runs away from the responsibility of fatherhood.

Dottie, the protagonist of "By Love Possessed," is the archetypal woman-as-loser. Like all of her sister-victims in the book, but more so than most she suffers from the capacity to be possessed by "bad love" or "misplaced love," to use terms from Heartease. These women, desperate for love, are beguiled by the promises of "The King of Swords." Dottie's tragedy would have been more harrowing, however, if Goodison had made her a little less "blind" and vulnerable, and her great love, Frenchie, not such an absolute two-dimensional no-good.

Still, there is appreciable variety in the treatment of the basic scenario. There are stories—"The King of Swords," "I Come Through," "From the Clearing of Possibility"—in which the woman comes through the darkness and extremity of her "anxiety valley" into the calm and light of Heartease. As "The King of Swords" makes clear, the turning point is reached when the protagonist can name the enemy for what he/it is.

The story "The King of Swords" adopts the persuasive tactic of having the protagonist remark a basic similarity between the man who is psychologically victimizing her (the last in the series of such men) and the aunt with whom she had had to live after her parents had gone to live in England. Indeed, most of the story is taken up in describing the humiliation inflicted on the girl by "Aunt." This tactic broadens the meaning of the story by showing how, as the companion poem says, "The King of Swords is a master of disguise (sometimes he is a woman)." But the King of Swords remains essentially "he," a masculine principle, and the tactic of pointing the similarity between Aunt and the man helps, interestingly enough, to confirm this point. The misfortune of women like the aunt is that they have been socialized and psychologically warped by the traditionally accepted "doctrine" about woman's place and woman's sexuality which derives from a patriarchal system.

Two particularly refreshing stories are "I Don't Want to Go Home in the Dark" and "Moon." Their female protagonists, while being no less sensitive, idealistic and giving-their-all-in-love, and no less susceptible to the wounds of misplaced love, have managed to achieve a sophisticated capacity for objectivity, which saves them from being "destroyed" by the handsome, no-nonsense, macho, and, in one case at least, utterly egotistic men to whom they have been attracted.

Perhaps the saddest of the stories and one that deepens in a special way the perspective in which we see women's anguish in the business of the heart is "Shilling." It tells of a sixteen-year-old schoolgirl, full of naive adolescent romanticism and ripe with innocent sexuality, who is tarnished for life when she is taken advantage of and humiliated among her peers by the boy whom she idolizes when he turns to her momentarily after he has been embarrassed and frustrated by his conceited girlfriend.

"Bella Makes Life" is unique in being the one story in which the conventional gender roles are reversed. Here Goodison is showing the vulnerability and "psychic wounds" of men she discussed in her 1991 interview. But the reversal—the exception that proves the rule—is not of itself the most telling feature of the story. The story is engaging in the way in which it seems to resist the clear-cut moral judgment it ostensibly invites. Despite her selfish, devil-take-the-hindmost dash into a bizarre display of self-confidence and success, despite her ''loudness'' and her unreflecting conversion to the more materialistic tenets of the American Dream (all of which add to the humor of the story), one cannot help feeling a sneaking admiration for Bella, if only for her sheer energy of personality. She is probably the most unforgettable ''character'' in the collection.

Edward Baugh. *Dictionary of Literary Biography, Vol. 157:*
*Twentieth-Century Caribbean and Black African Writers* (Detroit: Gale Research, 1996)

BIBLIOGRAPHY
*Tamarind Season*, 1980; *I Am Becoming My Mother*, 1986; *Heartease*, 1989; *Baby Mother and the King of Swords*, 1990; *Selected Poems*, 1992; *To Us, All Flowers Are Roses*, 1995; *Turn Thanks*, 1999

# H

## HANSBERRY, Lorraine (1930–1965)
### United States

If *A Raisin in the Sun* had been written by a white instead of a colored woman and if it had been written about a white family, it would have done well to recover its investment. As it is, it has received praises from all sides and the public is flocking to see it. As a piece of dramatic writing it is old-fashioned. As something near to the conscience of a nation troubled by injustice to Negroes, it is emotionally powerful. Much of its success is due to our sentimentality over the ''Negro question.''

Miss Hansberry has had the good sense to write about a Negro family with vices as well as virtues, and has spared us one of those well-scrubbed, light-skinned families who often appear in propaganda pieces about discrimination. If she avoids the over-worked formulas of the ''Negro'' play, however, she does not avoid those of the ''domestic'' play. . . .

It may have been Miss Hansberry's objective to show that the stage stereotypes will fit Negroes as well as white people, to which my own reply must be that I never doubted it. They will fit anybody. Rather, anybody can be made to fit them. The play is moving as a theatrical experience, but the emotions it engenders are not relevant to the social and political realities.

Tom F. Driver. *New Republic.* April 13, 1959, p. 21

Although *A Raisin in the Sun* occasionally slips over into triteness, it makes an extraordinarily compelling evening's theatre—which shows once again, I suppose, the degree to which drama is an extra-literary activity. As a play it may be patchy, but as a vehicle for the actors it is superb. One reason is that a powerful rhetoric comes naturally to Miss Hansberry. This puts her in a rather small club of writers, most of the other members of which are Celts. But with a difference: the rhetoric of a talented Negro writer always gives you the impression that it is about something, which is certainly not true of the Irish or the Welsh.

Miss Hansberry has more than a gift of the gab; she also has a great deal to say on questions that deeply concern her. So her rhetoric is not just colourful; it has a natural dignity, which presumably has something to do with the fact that the rhythms and diction of passionate Negro speech come straight from the Bible. The language is felt and meant to a degree where it can afford to be simple. Finally, Miss Hansberry's characters continually talk about the subjects which concern all Negroes: the jobs they can get, the areas they can live in, the strategies by which their pride is preserved or undermined, the problem of assimilation and racial independence. This means that the otherwise nice, rather sentimental family life, with its humdrum quarrels, ambitions and pieties, is continually strengthened by outside loyalties and outside hatreds.

A. Alvarez. *New Statesman.* August 15, 1959, p. 190

There is a sort of inverted miracle in the way Miss Hansberry [in *The Sign in Sidney Brustein's Window*] manages to distort so many things—taste, intelligence, craft—and be simultaneously perverse as dramatist, social commentator, political oracle, and moral visionary. A further miracle is her union of bitchiness with sentimentality. But it is borrowed bitchery, for in her incredibly awkward drama, in which scene stolidly follows scene like a row of packing cases and character talks to character like droning telephone poles, Miss Hansberry plunders from every playwright around, most thoroughly, Edward Albee.

The play can be said to be about the editor of a weekly New York newspaper who joins a local political crusade, is disillusioned, then revived by the knowledge that ''love is sweet, flowers smell good, and people want to be better.'' But Miss Hansberry is a master of changing the subject, so that there is a plethora of entirely separate plots: a domestic drama; an interracial one; the tragedies, respectively, of a good-hearted whore, a fainthearted queer, and a lily-livered liberal; the melodrama of a blackhearted dope pusher, and the tragi-comedy of a cheated-on wife.

Yet none of this suggests the uses to which Miss Hansberry puts her dragooned themes. They serve exclusively as containers for her venomous anger: she hates homosexuals, liberals, abstract artists, non-realistic playwrights, white people unwilling to commit suicide, Albert Camus, Jean-Paul Sartre, Samuel Beckett, William Golding, and, especially, poor, plundered Edward Albee. Miss Hansberry ostensibly wants to attack sham and hypocrisy, but her lack of charity chokes the play and becomes itself an intellectual vice which, ironically, stings her with its backlash. Her attack on ''success'' name-drops furiously, and her savage assault on intellectuality brandishes every intellectual catchword that can be snatched from the *Zeitgeist*.

Richard Gilman. *Newsweek.* October 26, 1964, p. 101

One of the biggest selling points about *A Raisin in the Sun*—filling the grapevine, riding the word-of-mouth, laying the foundation for its wide, wide acceptance—was how much the Younger family was just like any other American family. Some people were ecstatic to find that ''it didn't really have to be about Negroes at all!'' It was, rather, a walking, talking, living demonstration of our mythic conviction that, underneath, all of us Americans, *color-ain't-got-nothing-to-do-with-it*, are pretty much alike. People are just people whoever they are; and all they want is a chance to be like other people. This uncritical assumption, sentimentally held by the audience, powerfully fixed in the character of the powerful mother with whom everybody could identify immediately and completely, made any other questions about the Youngers, and what living in the slums of Southside Chicago had done to them, not only irrelevant and impertinent, but also disloyal: *A Raisin in the Sun* was a great American play, and Lorraine was a great American playwright because everybody who walked into the theatre saw in Lena Younger—especially as she was portrayed by Claudia McNeil, his own great American Mama. And that was decisive. . . .

It was good that people of all color, strata, faiths and persuasions could identify so completely with Lena Younger, and her family, and their desire to better themselves in the American way. But that's not what the play was about! The play was about Walter

Lee, Lena's son, and what happened to him as a result of having his dream, his life's ambition, endlessly frustrated by poverty, and its attendant social and personal degradation. Walter Lee's dreams of ''being somebody,'' of ''making it,'' like everybody else, were not respectable to Mama, and not very important to us. He wanted a liquor store which would enable him to exploit the misery of his fellow slum dwellers like they were exploited by everybody else. Walter Lee is corrupted by the materialistic aspirations at the heart of Western civilization, and his corruption is bodied forth in his petty, little dream. But it was his dream, *and it was all he had*! And that made it a matter of life or death to him, revolutionary, dangerous in its implications. For it could explode if frustrated; it could destroy people, it could kill, if frustrated! That's what Lorraine was warning us about. But we would only listen to Mama, and Mama did not ever fully understand Walter Lee!

Ossie Davis. *Freedomways.* Summer 1965, pp. 399–400

*The Sign in Sidney Brustein's Window* is a good play. It just misses being great. Miss Hansberry tried to sum up in the personality structure and the private conflicts of a single character all the social anxieties, the cultural confusion and the emotional debris that litter and torment our days. The remarkable thing is that Miss Hansberry nearly succeeded.

Sidney Brustein is modern man in confrontation with a world he never made and which he must remake to conform to the definition of himself. But this definition of himself is buried under layers of casual, cynical collaboration with expediency and the code of the disengaged, the uncommitted, and it begins to come clear to him only as these layers are stripped away by successive encounters with aspects of stone-hard truth. His wife, Iris, represents one aspect of it, her sister, Mavis, another, and her sister, Gloria, a third. Then there are the men: Alton, the Negro; David, the homosexual playwright; and Wally, the negotiator, who strips away the last layer, and Sidney discovers himself to be one ''. . . who believes that death is waste and love is sweet and that the earth turns and men change every day and that rivers run and that people wanna be better than they are and that . . . tomorrow, we shall make something strong of this sorrow.'' Given all the characters and all the situations, and given especially the character of Sidney Brustein, this hymn of affirmation is the right ending for the play.

Saunders Redding. *Crisis.* March, 1966, p. 175

When *A Raisin in the Sun* burst on the scene with a Negro star, a Negro director plus a young Negro woman playwright everybody on Broadway was startled and very apprehensive about what this play might say. What obviously elated the drama critics was the very relieving discovery that, what the publicity buildup actually heralded was not the arrival of belligerent forces from across the color line to settle some long-standing racial accounts on stage, but a good old-fashioned, home-spun saga of some good working-class folk in pursuit of the American Dream—in their fashion. And what could possibly be thematically objectionable about that? And very well written also. We shall give it an award (A for effort), and so they did, amidst a patronizing critical exuberance I would have thought impossible in the crassly commercial institution of Broadway. Not a dissenting critical note was to be heard from Broadway critics, and thus the Negro made theater history with the most

cleverly written piece of glorified soap opera I, personally, have ever seen on a stage. Only because it was about *Negroes* was this play acceptable, and this is the sobering fact that the aspiring Negro playwright *must* live with. If this play—which is so ''American'' that many whites did *not* consider it a ''Negro play''—had ever been staged by *white actors* it would be judged second-rate—which was what the British called it, and what the French said of the film version.

Harold Cruse. *The Crisis of the Negro Intellectual* (New York: William Morrow, 1967), p. 278

Black people ignored the theatre because the theatre had always ignored them. But, in *A Raisin in the Sun*, black people recognized that house and all the people in it—the mother, the son, the daughter and the daughter-in-law—and supplied the play with an interpretative element which could not be present in the minds of white people: a kind of claustrophobic terror, created not only by their knowledge of the house but by their knowledge of the streets. And when the curtain came down [after one of the early performances], Lorraine and I found ourselves in the backstage alley, where she was immediately mobbed. I produced a pen and Lorraine handed me her handbag and began signing autographs. ''It only happens once,'' she said. I stood there and watched. I watched the people, who loved Lorraine for what she had brought to them; and watched Lorraine, who loved the people for what they brought to *her*. It was not, for her, a matter of being admired. She was being corroborated and confirmed. . . .

She was a very young woman, with an overpowering vision, and fame had come to her early—she must certainly have wished, often enough, that fame had seen fit to drag its feet a little. For fame and recognition are not synonyms, especially not here, and her fame was to cause her to be criticized very harshly, very loudly, and very often by both black and white people who were unable to believe, apparently, that a really serious intention could be contained in so glamorous a frame. She took it all with a kind of astringent good humor, refusing, for example, even to consider defending herself when she was being accused of being a ''slum lord'' because of her family's real-estate holdings in Chicago. I called her during that time, and all she said—with a wry laugh— was, ''My God, Jimmy, do you realize you're only the second person who's called me today? And you know how my phone kept ringing *before*!'' She was not surprised. She was devoted to the human race, but she was not romantic about it.

James Baldwin. Preface to Lorraine Hansberry, *To Be Young, Gifted and Black* (Englewood Cliffs, New Jersey: Prentice-Hall, 1969), pp. x–xi

Structurally, Lorraine Hansberry remains essentially within the bounds of the conventional realistic well-made play, something almost anachronistic amidst the styles of the 1960s. The term ''well-made'' can be misleading because of its unfortunate connotations with the emptiness of nineteenth century tradition, but we need only look at the plays of a modern dramatist such as Lillian Hellman to recognize that orderly development of plot and a neatly planned series of expository scenes, complications, and climaxes can greatly assist in thematic and character development of a superior nature. Plot in Miss Hansberry's plays is of secondary importance, for it is not her main dramatic purpose. Nonetheless, because the audience has considerable interest in *what* is happening as well as *to whom*, both *A Raisin in the Sun* and *The Sign in Sidney Brustein's Window* are thoroughly enhanced by well-ordered revelation of the events which are so important in the lives of the characters. The straightforward telling of a story remains a thoroughly honorable literary accomplishment, and Miss Hansberry has practiced this ancient dramatic art with eminent respectability. Moreover, the scene, incident, and dialogue are almost Ibsenesque, avoiding overt stylization for its own sake and performed within the standard ''box'' set that progressively becomes more rare.

Jordan Y. Miller. In C. W. E. Bigsby, ed., *The Black American Writer* (De Land, Florida: Everett/Edwards, 1969), Vol. II, p. 161

Despite [Lorraine Hansberry's] need to *say* something, to make a social point, she did not want to sacrifice art to argument, to go agitprop as a few of the young black playwrights have recently done. She was forced, then, to embrace the traditional American realism, to do as serious American playwrights from James A. Herne to Arthur Miller have done, to use plot to make her points and character to express her sense that it is all more complicated than it seems. There are traps in the form, the temptation of easy devices (the lost insurance money in *A Raisin in the Sun*) and pat character reversals (Mavis's revelations in Act II of *The Sign in Sidney Brustein's Window*). There are virtues, however—characters, like Sidney Brustein and Walter Lee in *A Raisin in the Sun*, which transcend stereotype, become so rich and suggestive that the message itself is always about to be swallowed in human complexity. In *The Sign in Sidney Brustein's Window*, Miss Hansberry attempted to go beyond the simplicity of *A Raisin in the Sun*, to introduce non-realistic elements, but they were systematically cut away in the Broadway production.

It is impossible to guess how she might have grown as a writer, but her two plays indicate that she had wit and intelligence, a strong sense of social and political possibility and a respect for the contradictions in all men; that she could create a milieu (the family in *A Raisin in the Sun*, the Greenwich Village circle in *The Sign in Sidney Brustein's Window*) with both bite and affection; that she was a playwright—like Odets, like Miller—with easily definable flaws but an inescapable talent that one cannot help admiring.

Gerald Weales. *Commonweal*. September 5, 1969, pp. 542–43

I commend *Les Blancs* to your immediate attention, not so much as a great piece of theater (which it may or may not be) but, more significantly, as an incredibly moving experience. Or, perhaps, as an extended moment in one's life not easily forgotten or regularly discovered in a commercial theater that takes such pains to protect us from knowing who and what and where we are in 20th-century America. . . .

The play divides people into sectors inhabited on the one hand by those who recognize clearly that a struggle exists in the world today that is about the liberation of oppressed peoples, a struggle to be supported at all costs. In the other camp live those who still accept as real the soothing mythology that oppression can be dealt with reasonably—particularly by Black people—if Blacks will just

bear in mind the value of polite, calm and continuing use of the democratic process. . . .

The play is flawed—what play not completed by its original author would not be? Yet, beyond the imperfection of its ragged perimeters, or its frequently awkward transitional sections and fitfully episodic construction, there is a persistent glow, an illumination. Somewhere, past performance, staging and written speech, resides that brilliant, anguished consciousness of Lorraine Hansberry, at work in the long nights of troubled times, struggling to make sense out of an insane situation, aware—way ahead of the rest of us—that there is no compromise with evil, there is only the fight for decency. If even Uncle Sam must die toward that end, *Les Blancs* implies, then send *him* to the wall.

Clayton Riley. *New York Times*. November 19, 1970, p. 3

*The Drinking Gourd*, a three-act drama well suited for television presentation, is what may be called in television jargon a documentary of American plantation slavery. It is a compact yet comprehensive, authentic, and vivid portrayal of the ''peculiar institution,'' correctly called the sum of all villainies, as it was especially in the cotton kingdom on the eve of the Civil War. The action in the drama is framed between a long prologue and a brief epilogue both of which are spoken by a soldier ''perhaps Lincolnesque'' in appearance. The prologue kaleidoscopically reviews the history of American slavery from its beginning to the middle of the nineteenth century. The epilogue avows that by that time the Civil War had become necessary to keep slavery from destroying the United States. . . .

Imaginative, unified, easily documentable, and intensely interesting story that it is, and being good theater as well as good dramatic literature, *The Drinking Gourd* is in the best tradition of historical dramas—much more so than *Les Blancs*, which is also an historical drama. In both of these works, nevertheless, as in the drama which first won her acclaim as a playwright, Miss Hansberry skillfully used original and vivid dialogue to reveal character and develop action. In *Les Blancs* she wrote all of the dialogue in standard informal spoken English, having no reason to use any other kind. In *The Drinking Gourd* she used the same kind of English to represent the speech of semiliterate and illiterate people. This she did convincingly without resorting to mutilated English, which has so often been perpetrated as ''dialect,'' whereas it represents nobody's actual speech.

W. Edward Farrison. *CLA Journal*. December 1972, pp. 193, 196

The untimely death in 1965 of Lorraine Hansberry, one of the most poetic voices in the American theatre today, deprived us of one of our most gifted dramatists and of one of our best authors, but she left a legacy for the newer Black dramatists in that she pointed the way to a new direction, a newness in content and attitude, and a purpose for Black theatre. ''Positive and unflinching, deadly serious'' [Loften Mitchell], she won the 1959 New York Drama Critics Circle Award for her first play, *A Raisin in the Sun*, which was monumental in commitment.

The anger of the play is somewhat tempered when compared with the anger of later, more notably ''Black'' dramatists, such as Baraka and Baldwin. But her play is a well-crafted one, reflecting the world of Blacks on two levels of awareness. One is the daily struggle for existence shown in Mama's relentless desire to endure in the face of her son's and daughter's "modern" objections to their lot in life, and the other is the illusionary world of dreams. The dreams center on the money Mama is to receive from her husband's life insurance, which creates new hopes in a family almost without hope. . . .

The play indeed strikes an awareness of the changing attitudes of the Black man. As the play ends, Mama's world seems to be a thing of the past, while the family, it is hoped, is on its way. They all agree to move into a house in a white neighborhood, against the whites' judgment, and we notice how Mama's dormant fear of equality has been replaced with a new-found optimism and self reliance. . . .

Miss Hansberry's *A Raisin in the Sun* brought something new and honest to the New York stage, but it also brought with it a warning. The Chicago of the Negro, with all its frustrations, anger, and small hope of the late 40's and early 50's, was recreated for New York and the American theater. The Black theater of protest had its inception. Others would take up, with more anger and less sentimentality, what Lorraine Hansberry had begun.

Robert J. Willis. *Negro American Literature Forum.* Summer 1974, pp. 213–14

[*Raisin in the Sun*] typifies American society in a way that reflects more accurately the real lives of the black U.S. majority than any work that ever received commercial exposure before it, and few if any since. It has the life that only classics can maintain. Any useful re-appreciation of it cannot be limited, therefore, to the passages restored or the new values discovered, important though these are: it is the play itself, as a dramatic (and sociopolitical) whole, that demands our confirmation of its grandeur.

When *Raisin* first appeared in 1959, the Civil Rights Movement was in its earlier stages. And as a document reflecting the essence of those struggles, the play is unexcelled. For many of us it was—and remains—the quintessential civil rights drama. But any attempt to confine the play to an era, a mind-set, an issue ("Housing"—) or set of topical concerns was, as we now see, a mistake. The truth is that Hansberry's dramatic skills have yet to be properly appreciated—and not just by those guardians of the status quo who pass themselves off as dramatic critics. For black theater artists and would-be theorists especially, this is ironic because the play is probably the most widely appreciated—particularly by African Americans—black drama that we have.

*Raisin* lives in large measure because black people have kept it alive. And because Hansberry has done more than document, which is the most limited form of realism. She is a critical realist, in a way that Langston Hughes, Richard Wright, and Margaret Walker are. That is, she analyzes and assesses reality and shapes her statement as an aesthetically powerful and politically advanced work of art. Her statement cannot be separated from the characters she creates to embody, in their totality, the life she observes: it becomes, in short, the living material of the work, part of its breathing body, integral and alive.

George Thompson in *Poetry and Marxism* points out that drama is the most expressive artistic form to emerge out of great social transformation. Shakespeare is the artist of the destruction of feudalism and the emergence of capitalism. The mad Macbeths,

bestial Richard III's, and other feudal worthies are actually shown, like the whole class, as degenerate and degenerating.

Hansberry's play, too, was political agitation. It dealt with the very same issues of democratic rights and equality that were being aired in the streets. It dealt with them with an unabating dramatic force, vision, political concreteness and clarity that, in retrospect, are awesome. But it dealt with them not as abstractions, fit only for infantile-left pamphlets, but as they are lived. In reality.

All of *Raisin's* characters speak to the text and are critical to its dramatic tensions and understanding. They are necessarily larger than life—in impact—but crafted meticulously from living social material.

*A Raisin in the Sun* is about dreams, ironically enough. And how those psychological projections of human life can come into conflict like any other product of that life. For Lena, a new house, the stability and happiness of her children, are her principal dream. And as such this is the completion of a dream she and her late husband—who has literally, like the slaves, been worked to death—conceived together.

Ruth's dream, as mother and wife, is somewhat similar. A room for her son, an inside toilet. She dreams as one of those triply oppressed by society—as worker, as African American, and as woman. But her dream, and her mother-in-law's, conflicts with Walter Lee's. He is the chauffeur to a rich white man and dreams of owning all and doing all the things he sees "Mr. Arnold" do and own. On one level Walter Lee is merely aspiring to full and acknowledged humanity; on another level he yearns to strut his "manhood," a predictable mix of machismo and fantasy. But Hansberry takes it even further to show us that on still another level Walter Lee, worker though he be, has the "realizable" dream of the black petty bourgeoisie. "There he is! Monsieur le petit bourgeois noir "himself!," cries Beneatha, the other of Lena Younger's children. "There he is—Symbol of a Rising Class! Entrepreneur! Titan of the system!" The deepness of this is that Hansberry can see that the conflict of dreams is not just that of individuals but, more importantly, of classes. Not since Theodore Ward's *Big White Fog* (1938) has there been a play so thoroughly and expertly reflective of class struggle within a black family.

Beneatha dreams of medical school. She is already socially mobile, finding a place, as her family cannot, among other petty bourgeois aspirants on the rungs of "education," where their hard work has put her. Her aspiration is less caustic, more attainable than Walter's. But she yearns for something more. Her name Beneatha (as who ain't?) should instruct us. She is, on the one hand, secure in the collegiate world of "ideas" and elitism, above the mass; on the other, undeceived by the myths and symbols of class and status. Part militant, part dilletante, "liberated" woman, little girl, she questions everything and dreams of service to humanity, an identity beyond self and family in the liberation struggles of her people. Ah, but will she have the strength to stay the course?

Hansberry has Beneatha grappling with key controversies of the period, but also some that had yet to clearly surface. And she grapples with some that will remain with us until society itself is changed: The relationship of the intellectual to the masses. The relationship of African Americans to Africans. The liberation movement itself and the gnawing necessity of black self-respect in its many guises (e.g., "straightened" hair vs. "the natural"). Written in 1956 and first seen by audiences in the new revivals, the part of the text in which Beneatha unveils her hair—the "perm" cut off and she glowing with her original woolly crown precedes the ''Afro'' by a decade. Dialogue between Beneatha and her mother, brother, Asagai and George Murchison digs into all these still-burning concerns.

When *Raisin* appeared the movement itself was in transition, which is why Hansberry could sum up its throbbing profile with such clarity. The baton was ready to pass from ''George's father'' as leader of the ''Freedom Movement'' (when its real muscle was always the Lena Youngers and their husbands) to the Walter Lees and Beneathas and Asagais and even the Georges.

In February 1960, black students at North Carolina A & T began to ''sit in'' at Woolworth's in a more forceful attack on segregated public facilities. By the end of 1960, some 96,000 students across the country had gotten involved in these sit-ins. In 1961, Patrice Lumumba was assassinated, and black intellectuals and activists in New York stormed the United Nations gallery. While Ralph Bunche (George's spiritual father) shrank back ''embarrassed''—probably more so than by slavery and colonialism! But the Pan African thrust had definitely returned.

And by this time, too, Malcolm X, ''the fire prophet,'' had emerged as the truest reflector of black mass feelings. It was of someone like Malcolm that Walter Lee spoke as in a trance in prophecy while he mounts the table to deliver his liquor-fired call to arms. (Nation of Islam headquarters was Chicago where the play is set!) Walter Lee embodies the explosion to be—what happens when the dream is deferred past even the patience of the Lena Youngers.

Young militants like myself were taken with Malcolm's coming, with the immanence of explosion.

We thought Hansberry's play was part of the ''passive resistance'' phase of the movement, which was over the minute Malcolm's penetrating eyes and words began to charge through the media with deadly force. We thought her play ''middle class'' in that its focus seemed to be on ''moving into white folks' neighborhoods,'' when most blacks were just trying to pay their rent in ghetto shacks.

We missed the essence of the work—that Hansberry had created a family on the cutting edge of the same class and ideological struggles as existed in the movement itself and among the people. What is most telling about our ignorance is that Hansberry's play still remains overwhelmingly popular and evocative of black and white reality, and the masses of black people dug it true.

The next two explosions in black drama, Baldwin's *Blues for Mr. Charlie* and my own *Dutchman* (both 1964) raise up the militance and self-defense clamor of the movement as it came fully into the Malcolm era. . . . But neither of these plays is as much a statement from the African American majority as is *Raisin*. For one thing, they are both (regardless of their ''power'') too concerned with white people.

It is Lorraine Hansberry's play which, though it seems ''conservative'' in form and content to the radical petty bourgeoisie (as opposed to revolutionaries), is the accurate telling and stunning vision of the real struggle. . . . The Younger family is part of the black majority, and the concerns I once dismissed as ''middle class''—buying a house and moving into ''white folks' neighborhoods''—are actually reflective of the essence of black people's striving and the will to defeat segregation, discrimination, and national oppression. There is no such thing as a ''white folks' neighborhood'' except to racists and to those submitting to racism.

The Younger family is the incarnation—before they burst from the bloody Southern backroads and the burning streets of Watts and Newark onto TV screens and the world stage—of our common ghetto-variey Fanny Lou Hamers, Malcolm X's, and Angela Davises. And their burden surely will be lifted, or one day it certainly will ''explode.''

Amiri Baraka. Robert Nemiroff, ed. *A Raisin in the Sun and The Sign in Sidney Brustein's Window* (New York: New American Library, 1987), pp. 9–20

BIBLIOGRAPHY
*A Raisin in the Sun*, 1959; *The Sign in Sidney Brustein's Window*, 1964; *Les Blancs*, 1970; *Les Blancs: The Collected Last Plays of Lorraine Hansberry*, 1972

# HARPER, Michael S. (1938–)
## United States

[Naively] I set out to write an omnibus essay-review, insufficiently aware of how many laminations and concentricities inform Michael S. Harper's complex and coherent oeuvre. . . . This is very likely the finest poetry now being written in a woebegotten and woebegone country—perhaps the best since John Berryman—and the serious reader had better buy or at least read all of it at once. . . . First, a clarification and an admonition. Clarification—Harper is a black poet; Harper is an American poet. Asked if he saw any contradiction in terms, he replied: ''None at all. They are two aspects of the same story.'' In the same interview he spoke of his responsibility (calling, vocation) to connect ''black idioms and black traditional motifs'' with ''American institutions, the American lexicon, the American landscape.'' Beyond that, Harper writes toward ''a totally new aesthetic, a totally new world-view'' not yet existing, and a place never before conceived. In other words, ''a poet has a responsibility to his people. And when I say people, I mean all people.'' To start with, Harper wants to re-create America, substituting for the Declaration of Independence (''a document written for a handful of men to protect their interests and commodities'') what he calls ''the democratic Promise.'' Like John Coltrane, Harper makes his way by ''extension and overextension.''. . .

Admonition—Harper's aesthetics are not easy, either for himself or for his reader. His key verbs are *to do* (action) and *to go* (process). But he must always move against the resistances of American history, which stand in nearly total contradiction to his poetics and politics. It is not only a matter of breaking cages (Harper's metaphor for preconceptions), nor of overt racial oppression.

Edwin Fussell. *Parnassus*. 4, 1 (Fall/Winter 1975), pp. 5–6

With the publication of his sixth book of poems, *Nightmare Begins Responsibility*, Michael S. Harper has begun to receive the kind of thoughtful, critical attention he has always deserved. Reviews of *Nightmare* and ''reconsiderations'' of his entire canon have poured forth, not just in newspaper book columns, but also in journals like the *New Republic, Parnassus,* and *New Letters*. Rarely content simply to quote a powerful line, reviewers like Laurence Lieberman are writing extraordinary praises such as "Michael Harper is uniquely creating in his poetic art an indispensable . . . segment of the American moral conscience." We need to hear this; we need to be assured (or informed) that, despite occasional evidence to the contrary, poets still mine the human predicament, especially in its American contortion, not to relish it but instead to retrieve and to present artfully its moral and spiritual teachings. What interests me, and is the concern of this essay, is how Harper's studies of his kin figure fit into this; how kinship is for him a recurring metaphor for poetic process, the artist's obligations to traditions, and for living a life morally and well.

In pursuing these questions, I find myself less concerned with portraits, even though they are often considerable efforts like "Reuben, Reuben," and more attentive to poetic sequences or series. My search is for evidence of kinship-in-process, and sequences of poems, possibly because they *are* sequences, seem to yield up what I'm after. In *Dear John, Dear Coltrane*, for example, "We Assume: On the Death of Our Son, Reuben Masai Harper," "Deathwatch," and the aforementioned "Reuben, Reuben" are three extraordinary portraits of Reuben and Michael, the sons "torn away." Taken by themselves, they are powerful statements of horror fused to love. . . . But to receive the fuller, more variegated expression of kinship suggested by these portraits we must return them to their surroundings, to the landscape Harper has meticulously seeded with other poems. There are no "labeled" sections to *Dear John*; it is the only Harper volume not predivided by numbers or titles. But moving backward from the Reuben/ Michael portraits to "American History," and forwards to "After the Operations," we discover that the poems grouped therein have a certain unity. As they sustain each other we gain a context, present and historic, in which to receive the dead sons and their grieving kin.

> Robert B. Stepto. *Massachusetts Review*. 17, 3 (Autumn 1976), pp. 477–78

For Michael Harper the mission of poetry is bound up with eloquence and the magic of the spoken word, the oral tradition. Harper is a poet whose vision of personal and national experience is worked out in the Afro-American grain—the tradition of pain and rejuvenation expressed in the sorrow songs, the blues, and folktales, the whole range of Afro-American oral tradition, a tradition, it is important to remember, which also touches formal American/ Afro-American rhetorical patterns, from Abraham Lincoln and Frederick Douglass in the nineteenth century to Martin Luther King in the 1950s and 1960s. Harper is alert to the possibilities of rhetoric and the complexities of that ancient and American rhetorical tradition whose purpose was to challenge, vex, please, persuade, and, at last, illuminate the audience. He is a poet not of paradox but of the paradoxical, of simplicity in the midst of complexities, affirmation in the midst of tragedy—but affirmations so aware of the incongruities of eloquence that his voice intensifies the sense of tragedy and devastation. . . .

At forty, Harper has written a dozen or more extraordinary poems, poems long-lived and stunningly original, poems that transform his stance as an American/Afro-American poet into a reality with the power of illumination. *Images of Kin* is a collection of Harper's best and most representative work. Beginning with *Healing Song [for the Inner Ear]*, a selection of recent, previously uncollected poems, and "Uplift from a Dark Tower," Harper's important poem stalking Booker T. Washington's connection with the Trask family and its Yaddo estate, *Images of Kin* reverses chronological lines and travels back through Harper's prolific earlier volumes: *Nightmare Begins Responsibility; Debridement; Song: I Want a Witness; History Is Your Own Heartbeat*; and *Dear John, Dear Coltrane*.

Arranging and organizing one's poems can be a difficult and perplexing task, particularly this early when the writer's trajectory may not yet be clear. In the case of *Images of Kin*, Harper seems to have been governed by an urge to see, feel, and make known the past in the present moment—understandably, given his emphasis on healing and transformation. Nevertheless, in my view the cutting edge of the current work is somewhat diluted by its being presented first. In the sense that [William Butler] Yeats called poetry a quarrel with ourselves it may be that some of the current poems need the dramatic declaration and details of the early work, particularly *Dear John, Dear Coltrane* and *History Is Your Own Heartbeat*. Not that Harper's early poetry is always simple and direct. It is not, and neither is the later work inaccessible or uncompelling, but I think that even the best of the current poems ("Tongue-Tied in Black and White," "Bristol: Bicentenary Remembrances of Trade," and "Smoke," for instance) are richer for the contexts worked out and made familiar in earlier poems. The moments of controlled eloquence in the current poems might have a greater impact if the collection were arranged chronologically.

> John F. Callahan. *Black American Literature Forum*. 13, 3 (Fall 1979), p. 89

Certainly a commitment to kinship gives Harper a scope and freedom of position, as well as a substance and fineness of relationship, that [James Weldon] Johnson does not imagine, nor [Richard] Wright and [Ralph] Ellison, for all the sweep of their works, approach. Kinship and, with it, a fuller range of psychopolitical complexity may have come into [Ellison's] *Invisible Man* through Mary, who embodies patience, compassion, and practicality. But the inflated and drifting ambition of the invisible man will not let him operate on Mary's level. He is with his oratory what Ras is with his weaponry, a believer in grand and instant solutions. Only on this level does Ras, the creator of the riot, prevent the invisible man from going back to Mary. To go back is *physically* within his compass, but psychologically he is blocked by his persistent grandiosity. With Wright the case is even more problematical. Wright offers overpowering accumulation, without overpowering range.

But there are signs that Harper's scope and his orientation to kinship may come largely from the will. A note of harshness, an air of impatience not tempered by humor, a kind of vulnerability pitched near dark resentment and rage: these belie the grace and strength kinship would seem to connote. The metamorphosis of "The Families Album" is forced and problematical: "this old house which was hers / made her crooked back a shingle, / her covered eye this fireplace oven." "Sambo's Mistakes: An Essay," which is evidently inspired by A. J. Langguth's *Jesus Christs*, does not reflect the elastic irony of its source, but falls into a dehumanized, rigid violence. One is only arrested for the moment when, after a detailed account of Sambo's difficulties and disabilities, the poem comes up with its one-word litany of Sambo's "Strengths:

guns.'' Uncomplicated by strength of principle and of heart, the strength of guns is tantamount to anarchy.

> Michael G. Cooke. *Afro-American Literature in the Twentieth Century: The Achievement of Intimacy* (New Haven: Yale University Press, 1984), pp. 121–22

In *Nightmare Begins Responsibility*, Harper presents, as an introduction, a set of aphorisms entitled, ''Kin.'' The sentences are set forth as a basic chord structure of the songs he will perform throughout the book. As such, they are useful to the reader, enabling one to keep in mind just what themes are important to the writer, and they are useful in determining whether the writer fulfills his self-imposed intentions. Several of these aphorisms are especially pertinent as descriptions of the vocation of the *Poet* as Harper sees himself. . . .

As a human being, Harper believes that ''life's terms'' must be met; and as a poet, Harper argues that the existing techniques and traditions of poetry must be confronted. It is enough to master the forms, because in mastery the artist demonstrates power. But something must be added to nature, to life, to the ''available realistic or legendary material.'' The world in which Michael Harper lives is not significantly different from the world of Paul Laurence Dunbar or John Coltrane. That world is the real and legendary *America*, a world where the souls of black folk are continually threatened with dreams which turn into nightmares. For Harper, technique is natural, the easy part of poetry. What he wrestles with in his poetry is what he sets out for himself in his declaration of intentions: understanding and conscience. Harper's methodology derives from the music of his maturity. If the dream becomes a nightmare, if the legend is a lie, say so; confront the wall head-on, swallow the fire straight, with no soothing ''chaser.''

> Joseph A. Brown, SJ. *Callaloo.* 9, 1 (Winter 1986), pp. 210–11

The poems [of *Debridement*] are about a black soldier who won the Congressional Medal of Honor for heroism in Vietnam but then, when he returned to civilian life in Detroit, was unable to cope with a paradoxical combination of fame and poverty and was eventually shot to death while trying to rob a suburban grocery store. The sequence is not, as it might appear at first reading, just an attempt to rewrite Vietnam according to a different myth—i.e., the myth of America as oppressor, which stems, of course, from slavery, the central fact of black American history. Such an approach would be just as reductive, just as false to the particulars of human experience, as the myth of the liberator. Instead, the sequence attempts to heal the mythological wound of Vietnam by replacing the possible closed myths with what Harper calls an ''open-ended myth,'' a myth that takes into account the contingencies of human experience and tries not to distort the particulars of that experience. Thus, the sequence is in part critical: It analyzes the collision of mythmaking discursive strategies through which our understanding of Vietnam has been generated, and it dramatizes the mythological machinery through which cultural and historical ''truths'' are systematically maintained by a sort of cultural blindness and historical amnesia. But the sequence is also creative: By remaining always conscious of the poem's status as a mediating and therefore potentially reductive or distorting mythical discourse and by constantly exposing the reductiveness and distortions of the established myths

which infiltrate the sequence, Harper offers in *Debridement* a new sort of history, a new sort of mythology—a language of ''open-ended myth'' capable of articulating between the brutal human reality of warfare and the broader cultural meanings of that violence.

> Kyle Grimes. *Black American Literature Forum.* 24, 3 (Fall 1990), p. 419

''Uplift from a Dark Tower'' offers the simultaneous compressing and magnifying of personal and historical experience, a sense of the paradox and modal possibilities of jazz and blues. ''Uplift'' is complex in its narrative texture and pluralistic visions. Clearly in the jazz tradition, the poem is defined by its metaphoric variations, its sense of the poet as articulator or articulate hero, its simultaneity and multiple thought contexts as it breaks out of the traditional confinements of landscape, personality, and history; the poet, like the jazz musician, ''seizes . . . the territory.''. . .

In Harper's poetry, jazz is not a metaphor for battles and dilemmas of self but for the resolution in journeys of the spirit. The African-American's own music has a unifying effect, which brings a sense of wholeness to the individual, not in solitude as Hermann Hesse's *Steppenwolf* or James Joyce's [*A Portrait of the Artist as a Young Man*], but in communion (or if solitude, then communing solitude). One also sees the potential of the jazz perspective for reintegrating the whole of American experience in a ''rainbowed'' text. For the African-American artists the music is universal, complex, and multileveled in its identities. They claim for their music the ''thousands and thousands'' of possibilities that the Steppenwolf would claim for his own. It is music that renders visible the ''spirit of a people'' and can also have cosmic dimensions, music that ''strengthens and confirms.''

The poet's vision from the dark tower, then, like the jazz musician's, ''conjures being,'' reclaims the whole. It is a modal perception. As defined by Harper, ''The African Continuum is a *modal* concept which views the cosmos as a totally integrated environment where all spiritual forces interact . . . the music that provides images strong enough to give back that power that renews.'' His own ''Uplift from the Dark Tower'' is such music.

> Gayl Jones. *Liberating Voices: Oral Tradition in African American Literature* (Cambridge: Harvard University Press, 1991), pp. 44, 53–54

Black man:
I'm a black man;
I'm black; I am—
A black man; black—
I'm a black man;
I'm a black man;
I'm a man; black—
I am—

This is the opening stanza of ''Brother John,'' the first poem in Michael Harper's first book, *Dear John, Dear Coltrane*, published in 1970. A first poem necessarily informs all others, but Harper has actually used fragments from this poem that act as a refrain in subsequent books. So the poet himself has highlighted this lyric, expecting the reader to know how—and why—it reverberates.

Beginning with a blatant statement of condition, the stanza then pulls the statement apart, emphasizing and deemphasizing in turn ''black,'' ''man,'' and the combination of the two, ending on an assertion of identity—the affirmative iamb of ''I am.'' From there, the poem continues to celebrate both jazz and the jazzman in a series of riffs on Charlie Parker, Miles Davis, and John Coltrane, each time reiterating part of the first stanza as a refrain. Then comes a harmonic progression to Brother John, who is simultaneously singular and universal—''he's a black man; black''—before the variation on the opening that ends the poem:

I'm a black man; I am;
black; I am: I'm a black
man; I am; I am;
I'm a black man;
I'm a black man;
I am; I'm a black man;
I am:

Each punctuation mark dictates a timed pause, creates a rhythm that approximates jazz, allows Harper to create a syncopation of his own—a celebration of being that includes blackness as part of its meaning. . . .

From ''Brother John'' forward, Harper has explored what it is to be black in our society and, in so doing, has opened up to all readers the wealth of black contributions to our history and our art. His work has never flinched as it faces the hard questions of racism and race relations. In a dense, staccato style, Harper has taken another look at American history, collapsing time and condensing fact so that the juxtapositions often startle us. At the same time, he has offered up personal experience in conjunction with national events. In making us most aware of our differences, he has made us most aware of similarity. ''Tranetime'' is for anyone who can listen and respond.

*Honorable Amendments* is Harper's first book in ten years, and its appearance makes us suddenly aware of the too-long absence of this strong, energetic teller of truth. Harper's style has been one of syntactical compression, of declarative statement, of fact superimposed on fact building layers of ambiguity until they make demands on the reader just at or beyond the breaking point. The effect is discomfiture. We do not know what we need to know to read these poems, and somehow our not knowing is a part of the way they open up the world. First, we are asked to realize how little we know of what has shaped this country; second, we are treated to what we do know from another perspective; third, we are asked—no, required—to alter our own perceptions to encompass those of the poems.

In *Honorable Amendments*, the range of epigraphs, historical notes, and dedications covers Ralph Waldo Emerson to Ralph Waldo Ellison, Eugene McCarthy to Martin Luther King Jr., the dictionary to traditional oral formulations. Harper's subject matter is eclectic, moving from Grant's autobiography to Lincoln's second inaugural address to the poet's own trip to South Africa to the plight of the Cherokee to the art of Romare Bearden to Langston Hughes's boyhood to Frederick Douglass to Coleman ''Hawk'' Hawkins (for whites) and Coleman ''Bean'' Hawkins (for blacks), and right down to Jackie O—which is to say that the book is about (if books can be said to be about) a refiguration of American history in order to expand, adjust, redress, inspire. Amendment is necessary if we are to understand each other, and this book presents some alternative aesthetics through which we may also make amends. . . .

One believes that Harper has looked it up—has looked up everything—and found it wanting. One also believes that he is offering up his version, his unique slant on American literature. The challenging ''quilt that!'' takes on more of the tone of imperative: turn this, too, into art.

The years since 1970 have been stormy, and they've seen myriad changes. But ''I'm a black man'' still haunts me, forces its rhythms on me, its insistence and its assertion, its triumphant otherness. So I turn, now, to ''Laureate Notes'' from *Honorable Amendments* to see what, if anything, has changed. Written to the Providence *Journal*, it raises all the old questions. . . .

Possibly the most accessible poem in the collection, ''Laureate Notes'' could be said to ''stand for the whole'' as it makes its simple claim on our humanity. The police (their brown uniforms have connotations of fascism) stand for the whole of society. Twenty-five years later, ''Laureate Notes'' does not end with the strong identity of ''I am'' but with a series of impersonal acronyms and the scary prediction of what ''will be.'' Yet here ''will be'' equals ''is'': Harper lets us know that time has run out. ''Justice will take us millions of intricate moves,'' said William Stafford; in this poem, the perfect angle to view justice is from above—and it's clear that most of those intricate moves have yet to be taken.

''Laureate Notes'' is another assertion of identity: a personal editorial made public, a pronouncement. And it predicts future assertions. Fact: there is more than one ''slant.'' Fact: the newspaper was built on the backs of the boys in the dark ''folding the news, / in the hot, in the cold.'' Fact: the police can be seen to use excessive force. Fact: a boy has been hassled. Fact: from now on, it will be difficult to talk to him about justice, about law. Fact: the rhythms make a jazz of the experience, the music of a future that, if we don't heed its warnings, will spell more misunderstanding. As time present is torn between time past and time future, so the language is torn, charged with pun and double meanings (e.g., newspaper / toilet paper; film negative / negative stereotype), like the double vision of history / today Harper makes us see.

If ''Brother John'' was celebratory, in some ways ''Laureate Notes'' is one of Harper's most pessimistic poems, its ending definitive. The poems of *Honorable Amendments* are difficult to read—even in ''Laureate Notes,'' the third stanza fuses pronouns to the point of confusion. The poems can be daunting, at times condensed to inaccessibility, yet the book does not exclude me from its experience. It invites me to learn more, to learn the limits of my knowledge. And this is probably because I sense that Michael Harper stands with Ralph Ellison in refusing to play what has come to be called the ''race card'': ''and who knows but that on the lower frequencies, I speak for you.''

Harper's voice—honest, penetrating, combative, censorious, exultant—is to be welcomed back. His is a voice of reason, I think, but impassioned reason, impatient reason. The ending of ''Late September Refrain,'' yet another praise for Coltrane, could almost be called the poet's self-portrait:

A mouthpiece is different from a reed,
which flanges into the spaces of the mouth
where even spit evaporates to the song.
The mouthpiece is the tunnel,
viaduct, headband of the sun;
it is the fields, and the call of the fields.
It is shining in your example:
I say your name; John William Coltrane.

I say the refrain: a love supreme!

Michael Harper just might be the mouthpiece through which American history and American literature can find a way to reconciliation.

> Judith Kitchen. *Georgia Review*. 50, 2 (Summer 1996), pp. 398–402

BIBLIOGRAPHY
*Dear John, Dear Coltrane*, 1970; *History Is Your Own Heartbeat*, 1971; *Photographs: Negatives: History as Apple Tree*, 1972; *Song: I Want a Witness*, 1972; *Debridement*, 1973; *Nightmare Begins Responsibility*, 1975; *Images of Kin: New and Selected Poems*, 1977; *Rhode Island: Eight Poems*, 1981; *Healing Song for the Inner Ear*, 1985; *Honorable Amendments: Poems*, 1995

# HARRIS, Wilson (1921–)

## Guyana

If Mittelholzer the novelist uses the trees and the jungle to produce the goons and goblins of his fantasy, Wilson Harris, the poet, takes a more serious view of it. His metaphors [in *Eternity to Season*] are based and nourished on the plurality of the forest. For him, the jungle is "the world creating jungle." . . . Wilson Harris' world is in a unique sense created by the jungle, and his metaphors of the "world-creating jungle" which travels "eternity to season," touch and explore and express limits of experience and perception on a dimension reflected elsewhere perhaps only by Rainer Maria Rilke. . . . These images are valuable realizations, arising as they do out of Harris' profound imaginative experience of the forests of British Guiana. His statement and projection of this world is one of the significant achievements of West Indian writing, and it is more than unfortunate that his poetry should be considered by many to be so "difficult." . . .

The same sense of the restriction of the individual to external pressures and conditions can also be found in the work of the Nigerian "forest" writer, Amos Tutuola. But whereas in the work of Mittelholzer and Tutuola, despite all the fantasy, the attention and concern is fixed on the individual and on his position within the context of human society; in Harris', human society (*domesticity and lights*) is itself an aberration; something to be abhorred. Human society is *artificial*. . . .

> Edward Brathwaite. *Bim*. January–June 1960, pp. 105–6, 110

I admire Wilson Harris's novels greatly; he is one of the very few living novelists whose works are too brief for my taste. On the other hand, think of him as an author picking away at a theme from different angles in book after book, as Eliot picked away in *Four Quartets*, and he turns into a writer creating, in instalments, one of the major fictional statements of our time.

*The Eye of the Scarecrow* is a novel about confrontations and tensions in a Guyanese setting. The narrator's childhood past meets the present and generates current; the jungle has one voice and

civilisation another. Mr. Harris's fine tetralogy had this potent theme—the modern man's thrust against the wild, the wild's counterthrust—as well as a poetry not usually associated with the novel-form. *The Eye of the Scarecrow* has, if anything, a deeper poetry. It also has a power like the blow of the Guyanese heat.

> Anthony Burgess. *Spectator* December 3, 1965, p. 745

It is from Yeats's great phrase about "the unity from a mythology that marries us to rock and hill" that we may, justifiably, begin an examination of Wilson Harris's singular exploration of his corner of the West Indian experience. To Harris, this sacramental union of man and landscape remains the lost, or never established, factor in our lives. We enjoy, we exploit, we are coarsely nourished by our respective Caribbean territories—but illegitimately. We have yet to put our signatures to that great contract of the imagination by which a people and a place enter into a domestic relationship rather than drift into the uncertainties of liaison. No other British Caribbean novelist has made quite such an explicit and conscious effort as Harris to reduce the material reckonings of everyday life to the significance of myth. . . .

It is important to remember this element of the dream, and of the dream's sister, death, if we are to come to any understanding of these four Wilson Harris novels—*Palace of the Peacock, The Far Journey of Oudin, The Whole Armour* and *The Secret Ladder*. For the quartet opens with one dream of death, and closes with another dream of creation. Between these two dreams lies an evocation of being not accessible to any reviewer's summary. If we are to share the writer's experience, we must accept possession of the living by the dead; we must accept the resurrected man and the fact that "the end precedes the beginning" and that "the end and beginning were always there." Harris's world is not only one of prosaic action, but one of rite and mythical formation. "The first condition for understanding the Greek myth," said [André] Gide, "is to believe in it." And it is not improper that Harris makes belief the condition for entry into his Guyanese world.

> John Hearne. In Louis James, ed., *The Islands in Between* (London: Oxford University Press, 1968), pp. 140–41, 145

Anyone interested in gaining insight into the nature and potentialities of imagination should look deeply into Wilson Harris's *Tumatumari*. This eighth of Harris's extraordinary novels reveals his unusually original imagination at its present high state of development—a height to which it has evolved in the practice of the creative process he describes theoretically in his lectures and essays.

It is a process in which the imagination plays a role that is "passive" as well as active, not imposing itself upon the material under scrutiny but immersing itself in it, freeing itself as completely as possible from its own preconceptions and limitations, and being itself continuously transformed in the experiment. The imagination is encouraged to respond readily to all that the material suggests, to engage in the freest association of ideas, words and images, until the underlying relationships and processes (and the necessary ways to express them) emerge to be more actively observed and organized. . . .

In spite of the almost indescribable difficulty of *Tumatumari* as a whole, large sections of it read along smoothly enough, and many passages can be enjoyed for their sheer sensuous beauty (while others read like the output of a computer). The novel can be read simply as "experience"; in fact this novel, like all of Harris's novels, should be read for the first time in just this way and not primarily for the intellectual pleasure of it. What will happen with this kind of relaxed approach to it is that some of the underlying philosophical significance will gradually come through to provide illumination for subsequent readings in which intellectual perceptions and sense perceptions will be united. . . .

But even if this point is valid, that an additional view of history is needed to supplement Harris's view in which mankind is assumed to have a representative consciousness and experience before the unity of man, in this sense, is achieved, yet the question is of minor importance in relation to *Tumatumari* with its stimulating wealth of ideas and the contact it makes possible with Harris's rare mind and imagination and his commitment to Man.

> Joyce Adler. *Journal of Commonwealth Literature.* July 1969, pp. 20, 30–31

Wilson Harris's long sojourn in the Guyanese interior has made him an equal participant in the worlds of forest and savannah, the first expressing eternity and the perpetual flux of life, while the second speaks of season and the limited mortality of individual plant or tree. His poetry shows how long he has brooded upon the power of this contrast, which embraces the dual fate of man, who must die in season and seek freedom in eternity. The great uniting river of time flows through all things, stemming from eternal sources and seeking an oceanic repose, it rolls the bodies of the dead over and over till they are rounded like pebbles. This is the imaginative geography of Harris's *Palace of the Peacock*, as it is of Africa. Indeed, the African parallels to much of Harris's thought and imagery are remarkable. The River Congo plays in the poetry of Tchicaya U Tam'si the very role allotted to the Mazaruni or the Canje in the work of this Guyanese novelist whose veins mingle the blood of many races. . . .

In the years since it appeared Harris's novel has gradually made its way to a commanding place in the sensibility of the modern Caribbean. Artists, poets, historians and novelists have alike been haunted by its imagery. Despite obscurities of language that are occasionally impenetrable, despite the overworking of words like "musing" and "dreaming" in the interests of casting the reader adrift, *Palace of the Peacock* abounds in those insights and unifying flashes of illumination which Wilson Harris uniquely offers to the persevering reader. Every fresh reading of the book is a pilgrimage in which we relive Harris's vision of Guyana's history, his intimate interpretation of landscape and his longing to liberate man from the dialectics of hatred imposed on him by time and circumstance. Savannah and forest, mountain and waterfall, have interacted with a profoundly reflective temperament and a passion for spiritual truth to produce a masterpiece. [1969]

> Gerald Moore. *The Chosen Tongue* (New York: Harper & Row, 1970), pp. 75–76, 82

In *The Waiting Room*, a blind woman, convalescing after a series of operations, sits like a statue in a room full of antiques and relics of her past. There is little authorial direction, the language is dense and involuted, and the narrative yields itself fragmentarily. But it is apparent that through a process of memory of which she is not in full control, Susan Forrestal is reliving her unfinished affair with a rapacious lover she had dismissed in the past. As the disjointed memories of her absent lover float into the woman's consciousness, the reader becomes aware that the statuesque person, the inanimate relics in the room and the absent lover are bound together in the waiting room, in the way that the enthralled Ulysses was bound to the saving mast while his crew moved free on the deck below, their ears, however, deafened to the Sirens. Such a distribution of strengths and weaknesses between animate and inanimate objects in the room allows for a relayed digestion of the whole catastrophe while offering mutual protection from its annihilating powers.

So the ground of loss or deprivation with which most West Indian writers and historians engage is not for Harris simply a ground for protest, recrimination and satire; it is visualized through the agents in his works as an ambivalent condition of helplessness and self-discovery, the starting-point for new social structures. By the time that *The Waiting Room* comes to be written, Harris's exploration of this condition in the person has gone so far that the personal relationship—violent rape, irresponsible lover, involuntarily responsive mistress learning to digest catastrophe—absorbs the burden of an equally rapacious imperial relationship. Susan Forrestal, blind, helpless, and deprived, involved in the waiting room in the development of new resources and capacities for relationships with people and things, becomes the exciting ambivalent emblem of a so-called "hopeless," "historyless" West Indian condition.

> Kenneth Ramchand. *The West Indian Novel and Its Background* (New York: Barnes & Noble, 1970), pp. 11–12

As one ventures deeper into the novel [*Ascent to Omai*] images proliferate in an astonishing way to produce reverberations of meaning. Victor is an everyman figure who, early in the novel, comes to represent the people of an "Old" as well as "New" world: post-as well as pre-Columbian Man. Like Prudence of *Tumatumari*, he seems to be the soul of Man seeking in the "well of the past" the means of a new birth. "Omai" is an American rootword with multiple meaning used to suggest the "peak experience" of the mystics—the unpredictable flash of spiritual illumination. "Omai" is also the mythical El Dorado, the "lost worlds" of Roraima and Atlantis: a place which exists and does not exist—a "hill of cloud." Victor's ascent of the hill has an archetypal significance: one thinks of Moses' ascent of Sinai, the "eight-fold path" of the mystics, Dante's hill of purgatory. There are echoes of a symbolic retracing of the Middle Passage. . . . Victor's quest is symbolic not only of Caribbean Man's search for ancestral origins, but also of Mankind's longing for a pre-lapsarian world, and there are deeper echoes, such as the suggestion, in the appearance of the spectral pork-knocker as a "tabula rasa," a doppelganger with a "faceless face," of a "regressus ad uterum"—a return to formlessness—from which, as in mythology, the hero is reborn. The use of memory as a means of acquiring the necessary self-knowledge for this painful regeneration (here one thinks of the section in *Palace of the Peacock* called "The Straits of Memory" where the characters all gain self-knowledge in extremity) is a vital process of the inner alchemy which helps Victor to come to a new understanding of himself. By going beyond History and its "crass realities," by achieving a ''new dimension'' of *feeling*, Victor gains insight and so breaks out of the prison of History. A new direction is now possible.

Michael Gilkes. *Literary Half-Yearly*. January 1974, pp. 124–25

The novels of Wilson Harris ([*Companions of the Day and Night*] is his thirteenth) form one ongoing whole. Each work is individual; yet the whole sequence can be seen as a continuous, ever-widening exploration of civilization and creative art. *Ascent to Omai*, for instance, took subjective consciousness to a point beyond which further communication seemed impossible. This was answered, after two excursions into the realm of folklore, with *Black Marsden*, in which the creative imagination is Marsden, a trickster/illusionist whom the artist hero finally throws into the street. In *Companions of the Day and Night* the hero of *Black Marsden* is sent manuscripts by Marsden himself which he orders into an assertion of the creative interpenetration of history and imagination.

At a recent conference at Stirling [Scotland], Wilson Harris explained his present preoccupation with moments in which a suppressed cultural pattern erupts through a decaying later one. In *Black Marsden*, it was Scottish history in Edinburgh. In this novel, it is Mexico City, where Christian and Western patterns overlie traditional cultures going back to pre-Conquest Toltec times. Recurrent archetypes are the focus for conflicting cultural strata; and the naked, creative, suffering human spirit is embodied in the Fool, Nameless, or Christ, with his answering image of spiritual love, Mary or Beatrice. In the ancient Mexican religion he was a human sacrifice; in the Catholic conquest, the figure of Christ; in the modern world, a political martyr. . . .

*Companions of the Day and Night* is not Wilson Harris's finest novel. It does not have the architectonic strength of *Tumatumari* or the better known *Palace of the Peacock*. The surrealist fantasy weakens the texture of the sacrificial drama. But never has the wily magician Black Marsden created more startling effects, or Mr. Harris's extraordinary use of language been more assured.

Louis James. *Times Literary Supplement*. October 10, 1975, p. 1217

Its constantly evolving character notwithstanding, a remarkable unity of thought conveys this considerable opus [*Palace of the Peacock*]. Two major elements seem to have shaped [Wilson] Harris's approach to art and his philosophy of existence: the impressive contrasts of the Guyanese landscapes, with which his survey expeditions made him familiar, and the successive waves of conquest which gave Guyana its heterogeneous population polarized for centuries into oppressors and their victims. The two, landscape and history, merge in his work into single metaphors symbolizing man's inner space saturated with the effects of historical—that is, temporal—experiences. The jungle, for example, is for Harris both outer and inner unreclaimed territory, the actual ''landscape of history'' for those who only survived by disappearing into it and a metaphor for that inner psychological recess to which his characters relegate both their forgotten ancestors and the living whom they dominate. It contrasts with the savannahs and is itself full of contrasts. Though teeming with life, much of it is invisible to the ordinary ''material'' eye, just as those who,

willingly or not, lead an underground existence and remain unseen save to the ''spiritual'' (imaginative) eye. The jungle's extra human dimensions suggest timelessness and offer a glimpse of eternity, while the constant renewal of the vegetation confirms its existence within a cyclical time pattern. In Harris's words the jungle ''travels eternity to season''; and the Amerindians, who move to and fro between that secret primeval world and the modern areas where they can find work, subsist, as he writes in *Tumatumari*, ''on a dislocated scale of time.'' They are an essential link between the modern Guyanese and the lost world of their undigested past, and must be retrieved from their buried existence in both real and symbolical *terra incognita* if Guyana (and the individual soul) is to absorb all its components into a harmonious community. . . .

Harris's fiction began to appear at a crucial time for both the nascent West Indian fiction and the novel in English since, in the 1950s and early 1960s, the trends in English and American fiction indicated that many inheritors of established traditions had ceased to believe in them. The dissolution of values and forms due to the combined action of history and science had left artists in a void similar in kind to that experienced with more tragic intensity by West Indians throughout their history. With a few notable exceptions, English and American novelists reacted to this loss of certainty by either seeking refuge and renewing their faith in realism, or turning experimental fiction into an art of the absurd, technically brilliant and [innovative] but often undermining the very purpose of art. Wilson Harris is among the very few West Indian writers who pointed out the irrelevance of both trends to a ''native'' art of fiction. While insisting that the disorientation of the ''diminished man'' in formerly strong societies had been experienced for centuries by the conquered populations in the Caribbean and the Americas, he warned particularly against the influence on West Indian writers of the postwar European art of despair. His own ''art of compassion'' does not involve, as has sometimes been suggested, a withdrawal from history in order to transcend it. It is, on the contrary, intensely concerned with the impact of history on the ordinary ''obscure human person'' and expresses a passionate denial of what has been termed the ''historylessness'' of the Caribbean; it shows that people exist by virtue of their silent suffering as much as by celebrated deeds or a materially recognizable civilization, of which incidentally obscure men are the unacknowledged executors.

Hena Maes-Jelinek. In Bruce King, ed. *West Indian Literature* (Hamden, Connecticut: Archon Books, 1979), pp. 179–82

If Wilson Harris has any direct forebear, it is T. S. Eliot with his meditations on time and tradition, and his fragmentation of narrative into a mosaic of dissociated images and symbols expressive of the chaos of modern culture and the individual mind attempting to piece together an encompassing vision out of personal disorder. While the allusions, techniques, symbols, and even occasional phrases are similar, Harris differs from Eliot in trying to create a new world myth of process whereas the American poet sought to lose himself in an impersonal tradition, salvaged from the ruins of the Old World. Harris refers to fossils not as records but as gateways to an imaginative participation in the culture and events of the past. It is only through such an extension of the imagination that rigidly fixed cultural and racial boundaries, with their social superiorities and animosities, can be destroyed, and the many peoples of the New World can renew their contact with each other, recognizing that their shared history involves more basic experiences than are accepted by such stereotypes as colonizer, slave, or exterminated Indian. . . .

The four novels in the *Guiana Quartet* roughly form a chronological sequence from the days of conquest (*Palace of the Peacock*), the period of slavery and Indian indenture (*The Far Journey of Oudin*), the establishment of a frontier society and law (*The Whole Armour*), and the imposition of a modern state on the land (*The Secret Ladder*). As the setting approaches modern times and notions of reality, with linked cause and effect, it becomes more necessary to show the primitive truths of experience that are hidden to the compartmentalized mind. The attack on what we might call scientific thought is also a freeing of the imagination from the boundaries imposed by colonization and Europe on the New World. Thus the role of Cristo in *The Whole Armour* both has analogies to the role of Christ in the Christian scheme of redemption and is different as is fitting to a New World context. Underlying the novel is an awareness of basic myths of death and renewal: Abram is killed by a tiger; Cristo is made by Magda to disguise himself in Abram's garment, then he kills the tiger and wears his skin. In his tiger skin he returns to the village and initiates a chain of events that changes the lives of important characters within the story. Sharon, formerly a frigid "snow-maiden," becomes Cristo's lover in the jungle. Cristo is hunted by the tiger and by the law as a murderer. His death or sacrifice is part of the tragedy of renewal in a world of process. Such sacrifice is necessary: "Cristo would be free in the end, it seemed to state, in an armor superior to the elements of self-division and coercion. Magda fell on her knees and prayed. There was nothing else to do."

> Bruce King. *The New English Literatures: Cultural Nationalism in a Changing World* (New York: St. Martin's Press, 1980), pp. 109–10, 112–13

For Wilson Harris, "exile," deliberately sought and accepted, becomes the necessary first step in the development and growth of the creative imagination. And it is the sense of exploration, of self-discovery (as part of a dynamic "drama of consciousness") that marks his work. His early novels, from *Palace of the Peacock* to *Heartland*, deal with this main theme of the spiritual journey of the hero who has to discover, by trial and error, an "authentic" existence. In *Palace of the Peacock*, Donne, the leader of a boat crew on a journey up river in the Guyana interior, is on a quest that has many significances, the chief of which is the search for illumination or true selfhood. All the characters die, yet experience a rebirth or reawakening in the process. Theirs is also a circular journey, like Sir Gawain's, from outer, encrusted personality to naked, inner self. . . .

In the later novels, this theme of the journey toward selfhood is extended to include and emphasize the idea of the imprisoning quality of personality and the positive value of "*identitylessness*" of a "liminal" state, as a means toward a genuine resensing of the world. The need for a rejection of preconceptions and biases about social and political freedom, about history and tradition, becomes paramount.

In *Tumatumari*, Prudence, as the prevailing consciousness in the novel—the figure of Mnemosyne, the Greek Muse of Memory (as well as the embodiment of the rootless, historyless, identityless condition of West Indian society)—makes an imaginative journey back through history through the labyrinth of memory. It is an "adventure into the hinterland of ancestors." . . .

In *Black Marsden* the hero, Clive Goodrich, sees the landscape of Scotland as inextricably interwoven with that of his native South America: tropical and Mediterranean civilizations merge in spite of contrasts because he himself has gained freedom from his own, imprisoning "I" which tends to "fix" other people, other cultures in static frames like the eye of a camera.

Later still, in *Companions of the Day and Night* the hero, "Idiot Nameless," is literally without identity, the nameless, archetypal fool. The book is a sequel to *Black Marsden*. Clive Goodrich receives from Marsden a confused collection of manuscripts, sculptures, and paintings—"the Idiot Nameless collection"—the work of an unknown man, a tourist, whose dead body has been found at the base of the Pyramid of the Sun in Teotihuacan in Mexico. The novel is a flashback as Goodrich edits the writings which begin to reveal "door-ways through which the Idiot Nameless moved." He gradually enters the Nameless collection and becomes aware of "the mystery of companionship . . . and . . . frightening wisdom" they embody. . . .

[*Da Silva da Silva's Cultivated Wilderness; and, Genesis of the Clowns*] carries forward this theme of the "interior journey" with great technical skill and imaginative power. The hero of *Da Silva* is married and lives in a Holland Park flat in Kensington. He is a composite man. Born in Brazil of Spanish, Portuguese, and African stock, orphaned early, he survives cyclone and flood to be adopted by the British Ambassador. Growing up in England with access to his rich benefactor's library, he gradually becomes convinced that his "parent-less" condition obliges him to create, to "paint" himself and his world anew. Seeing everything in terms of his art, he discovers new "illuminations" and "unpredictable destinies" within the most apparently solid and uniform people and events. As his "canvases" multiply, the range of his awareness widens. Relationships with Jen, with Manya (the model with "a reputation for chaos"), with schoolmistress Kate Robinson, with Legba Cuffey (composite rebel slave leader/West Indian barman/Haitian folk god), gain in complexity. The bare framework of his life becomes a crowded canvas of interlocking past and present lives as he "cultivates" the apparently static wilderness of identity, historical fact, and urban existence.

> Michael Gilkes. *The West Indian Novel* (Boston: Twayne, 1981), pp. 145–46, 149

*The Eye of the Scarecrow* occupies a privileged place in Wilson Harris's fiction: chronologically, in the sequence of the author's novels, it opens a "second phase" after the Guyanese cycle. Stylistically, it explores new modes of expression and presents some difficulty for a reader who has not yet become acquainted with Harris's work on language. More so than previous works, *The Eye of the Scarecrow* is rooted in history and based on recognizable places: the East Street house in Georgetown where the narrator spends his youth was built on the site of a plantation which was in turn owned by nationals of the main successive colonizing powers. In the background of the plot we find evocations of the great strike of 1948, which was a decisive step towards political awareness and a prelude of independence for Guyana. Here dates relate the story to actual events. Yet, as always with Wilson Harris, history and time are used unconventionally. . . .

Memory is so important for the writer not because it merely enables one to relive forgotten moments but also because of its creative potential. The narrator of *The Eye of the Scarecrow* sees himself as if he "were a ghost returning to the same place (which was always different), shoring up different ruins (which were always the same)." In this interplay between difference and identity lies the center of the artist's quest when he realizes that well-known and commonplace objects have unexpected aspects, whereas the most unrelated elements can be put into mysterious dialogue and resonance. Reflection is the first stage of recognition in the same way as surprise and disorientation are preliminary to more profound knowledge. To see the world—and oneself—in reverse is a necessary step to genuine awareness in Harris's world. The creator discovers—and helps the reader to accept—that radically different facts, people, or ideas can echo one another and pertain to a common logic. For him, deconstruction reconstructs, the distinction between the two processes being that the first applies to static structures whereas the second helps to elaborate transformational and more fruitful patterns. . . .

In *The Eye of the Scarecrow*, paradox is more than ever an instrument of discovery. The movement which Harris sees at the heart of resonance and meaning becomes "the flight of stillness." In a novel mingling plot and self-reflexivity, the author progresses in cyclic fashion. Events, characters, and ideas echo one another; but the importance does not lie in the static repetition of self-contained elements. In each mirror-pattern, the image evokes the model without reproducing it exactly. Thus the creator shows the necessity for both relationship and "exile." . . . The artist considers that genuine identity does not lie in traditional harmony. On the contrary it opens onto difference of a radical kind. Behind every shape lurks a shadow; behind consonance one may perceive dissonance. The artist, demonlike, lifts the veil on new perspectives. He dons the raiment of the scarecrow to open our eyes and become our own vicarious gauge of experience, our engineer of depth.

Jean-Pierre Durix. *World Literature Written in English*. 22, 1 (Spring 1983), pp. 55, 68–71

In his recent fiction Harris becomes more and more interested in the novel as a form of art akin to painting. In *Da Silva [da Silva's Cultivated Wilderness]* and *The Tree of the Sun* much of the plot arises out of a picture which Da Silva, the protagonist, is painting in his studio. The artist is created by his work as much as he creates it. The novel brings to light a subtle sort of mutuality which enables the characters to reach unsuspected dimensions and discover hidden layers of history. This passion for visual effects also leads Harris to experiment with graphic representations inserted in his texts. This starts in *The Waiting Room* but becomes even more noticeable in *Ascent to Omai* with a series of eight concentric circles around a point called "Stone/Epitaph One." Each circle is given the name of one of the major metaphors of the novel (Madonna, Baboon, Raven, Parrot, Iron Mask, Rose, Whale, Petticoat). The graph illustrates Harris's particular use of language. All-important but separate images are brought into forced contact, thus engendering new forms and meanings, which symbolically exemplifies Harris's general theory of art as an attempt to overcome fixed polarities. The work of the writer causes a shock similar to the fall of a stone in a pool. The energy fans outward and then inward again when it has rebounded on the edges. The elements—here the different ripples—are animated by a current which causes them to react to each other and to be transformed by the different collisions. Harris suggests that images can be given one-sided equivalents only on a superficial level. With his bold couplings of apparently disparate units he suggests that one can reactivate seemingly sterile representations.

Jean-Pierre Durix. *World Literature Today*. 58, 1 (Winter 1984), p. 21

Among the novels of Guyanese author Wilson Harris, *The Secret Ladder* is generally considered different from the others because of its relative clearness and straightforward narrative. . . . However, despite its apparent simplicity, *The Secret Ladder* already poses the problem of the functioning of the imagination in a subtle way which has frequently been overlooked.

The novel unfolds along a seven-day period, an echo of the creation of the world in Genesis. Art is thus equated with the essential activity which consists in giving shape and meaning to chaos. The title certainly contains an allusion to Jacob's dream in the Bible. Writing for Wilson Harris means the abolition of the barriers between the material world and what, for want of a better world, I will call "otherness." The novel is a dreamlike experience in which the reader, like Jacob, is promised some kind of revelation, the annunciation of visionary possibilities. . . .

The narrative structure of *The Secret Ladder* follows a relatively straight-forward line, both in the succession of events and in its temporal organization. The plot unfolds in a linear way and is conveyed to the reader through an alteration of dialogues and narrative interventions. The third-person narrator describes settings, suggests moods and frequently interprets the characters' thoughts. . . . The voice which speaks through this third person might appear omniscient. Yet the only certainties which it provides concern the impossibility to *know* anything for sure, to distinguish appearances from the hidden life which binds the elements in creation. Its comments are never definite except in unmasking prejudices. They provide paradoxical representations which, far from closing the plot, question any possibility of exhaustive meaning. Wilson Harris leaves few opportunities for the reader to "translate" images into one-sided equivalents. Metaphors become significant only through the networks of ever-changing relations which they form. Even if the world of *The Secret Ladder* is less puzzling than that in *Palace of the Peacock*, the reader can rely only on the narrator's intervention to guide him through a maze of complex evocations. The latter becomes a guide who lets the former into a less and less recognizable land where certainties vanish one after the other. The reader is like Dante following a sort of Virgil whose words become more and more mysterious. Through the device of "omniscience," the narrator of *The Secret Ladder* proves that omniscience does not exist.

Jean-Pierre Durix. *Ariel*. 15, 2 (April 1984), pp. 27, 35–36

In his two previous collections of critical essays, *Tradition, the Writer and Society* and *Explorations*, [Harris] presents the reader with a vision of a new society which underlies his aesthetic concepts, and with his notions about the function of the writer. His latest critical work, *The Womb of Space: The Cross-Cultural*

*Imagination*, will again serve as "an indispensable guide to Harris's understanding of his own novels," but it is much more than that. It is an attack on the traditional critical establishment, for which "literature is still constrained by regional and other conventional but suffocating categories."

Utilizing a genuinely comparative approach, Harris juxtaposes and analyzes the work of two dozen writers from Europe, Africa, the Americas, Asia, and Australia and finds that on a cross-cultural level "each work complexly and peculiarly revises another and is inwardly revised in turn in profound context." The writers he discusses include William Faulkner, Edgar Allan Poe, Ralph Ellison, Jean Toomer, Juan Rulfo, Jay Wright, Jean Rhys, Paule Marshall, Djuna Barnes, Patrick White, Aimé Césaire, Derek Walcott, Christopher Okigbo, Edward Brathwaite, Mervyn Peake, Emma Tennant, Claude Simon, Raja Rao, and Zulfikar Ghose. Each of these writers, Harris contends, has unknowingly (intuitively) been attempting to free himself or herself from the shackles of cultural homogeneity, since homogeneity "as a cultural model, exercised by a ruling ethnic group, tends to become an organ of conquest and division because of *imposed* unity that actually subsists on the suppression of others."

> Reinhard Sander. *World Literature Today.* 59, 3 (Summer 1985), p. 477

The action of *Carnival* centers around the psychic journey of the narrator Jonathan Weyl, who, under the guidance of his "interior-guide" Everyman Masters, travels back in time from his present-day domicile in the imperial center, London, into the "Inferno" of Guyanese history of the 1920s. He there witnesses a series of actions, each of which portrays emblematically one way in which the colonial encounter can be allegorized, but each of which, in itself, provides an inadequate "reading" of colonial history and the investments of power within it. To use the language of the novel itself, each separate action constitutes a "frame" within which at least two kinds of meaning operate. In the first instance, there is an absolutist and blinding meaning that "conscripts the imagination" and binds the characters to some kind of overwhelming pattern of perception—fear, desire, anger, and so on—that seems imposed from an outside source. But behind this, there is a second kind of meaning that teases itself into the interstices of the narrative and that can be "glimpsed through barred gate and segmented mask"—the kind of meaning the text associates with the concept of "Carnival evolution." Here, "sovereign" forms of perception that inhere in the hierarchical structures of tradition are shown to contain decentering or fissuring impulses that can erupt into consciousness and thus liberate vision from its material restraints into the imaginative reaches of what Harris calls "a kind of far viewing." The two kinds of meaning are in dialectical relation to one another, each exerting pressure on the kinds of meanings Weyl, Masters, and the characters within the tableaulike episodes will derive; and because the two levels of meaning can never come together, there always remains a slippage of signification which engenders new characters, new episodes, and new meanings as the narrative proceeds. The pattern of the novel is thus incremental, each frame in the narrative generating new patterns of association that qualify the meanings of the preceding frames, and each in turn being modified and disrupted by the frames that develop out of it. . . .

Much of what takes place in Harris's writing, or in his speech for that matter, seems baldly modernist: its gnomic obscurity, its search for "new" forms, its Romantic highbrowism, its syncretic drive, its apparent subjectivism—all of them elements which modernism's detractors see as contributing to "a tyranny of the creative imagination over the public." Where such a profoundly unsocial characterization falls short in regard to Harris's work is in the kind of cultural *work* his fictions, as *postcolonial* documents, seek to perform. The canonical center, if nothing else, is *textual*, and as a site for the operations of a dominant discourse it has consistently worked to textualize or "prefigure" colonial space as a projection of its own metaphysical, social, and cognitive systems—that is, as a term within a European cultural thematics, unmarked by any measure of difference save that constituted by the concept of "lack." But by rewriting signs of the canon into fictive structures of *difference*, Harris's text functions discursively as what Homi Bhabha identifies as a "hybrid object": that is, as a peculiar agent of replication within which the authoritative symbol is both retained and resisted. . . . *Carnival*—like the true and false shaman figures within it, whose immeasurable blows on the mudshore flats initiate the novel's dialectical action—both *dis*figures and *re*figures the discursive space of power upon which tradition actuates. It reoccupies the theater of textuality and replaces its authoritative signs with dialogic fictions whose narratives, at even the minutest level of representation, are always double. And it subjects the absolutist monuments of history to the gaze of an excentric and non-complicit reading practice which seeks not only to transform inherited codes of recognition into new ways of "reading" tradition but also to deconstruct those monuments through the discursive reoccupation of the ground upon which their shadows fall.

> Stephen Slemon. *Ariel.* 19, 3 (July 1988), pp. 59–60, 69–70

Though *Carnival* seemed like a climax in [Harris's] opus, *The Infinite Rehearsal* probes even deeper into the labyrinths of self and nature to present as facets of the same allegorical quest the survival of modern civilization and the creative process of fiction writing. Significantly, it is a "rewriting" of the ever-modern myth of Faust, who longed to reach heights accessible to God only and thereby pierce the mysteries of creation but paradoxically attempted to do so through a pact with the devil. There can be no such pact in Harris's novel because good and evil are not separate moral categories. Like Harris's earlier fictions, this novel reads as a dialogue between the living and the dead, close and distant voices, or sovereign and lost traditions. The first-person narrator, Robin Redbreast Glass, is dead but speaks through W. H., his "adversary," with whom he nevertheless shares "an approach to the ruling concepts of civilization . . . from the ruled or apparently eclipsed side of humanity." Since his Da Silva novels, Harris has entered his own fiction as a character "in search of a species of fiction" as if the fiction preexisted, a "living text" brought to the fore through a polyphonic narrative in which both he and the existences or "agents of personality" he creates are vessels rather than the omnipotent author and sovereign characters of realistic fiction. Tenuous, even uncertain facts underlie Glass's narrative. He introduces himself as a "gravedigger in a library of dreams and a port-knocker [a gold and diamond prospector] in the sacred wood [echoes of Dante and [T. S.] Eliot]." He drowned in 1961 at the age of sixteen with his Aunt Miriam, his mother Alice, and a small party of children, actors in Aunt Miriam's childhood theater in which she staged plays "revising the histories of the world," in order to revise also the deprivations she called *"illiteracies of the heart and mind."* Only Peter and Emma were saved. Glass and W. H. are each a fictionalized character in the other's narrative, and each claims to have been in bed feverish with flu when the accident occurred, after which W. H. occupied Aunt Miriam's little theater while Glass set out for the "sacred wood" "in the multitextual regions of space." Actually, the shipwreck in which Aunt Miriam, the female creator, and her young actors drowned can be read as the shipwreck of civilization. Both Third- and First-World catastrophes are evoked as the Guyana strike and riots of 1948 (also the hub of the historical reconstruction in *The Eye*), the destruction of earlier Western civilizations, the two World Wars, Hiroshima and Nagasaki, the civil war in Lebanon, and the Chernobyl disaster.

> Hena Maes-Jelinek. In János Riesz and Alain Richard, eds. *Semper Aliquid Novi: Littérature Comparée et Littératures d'Afrique* (Tübingen: Gunter Narr, 1990), pp. 159–60

Wilson Harris, the Guyanese-born, English-settled dreamer of South American mythologies, has continued his cycle of poetic novels with *Resurrection at Sorrow Hill*. Like the other novels of this long series, begun with *The Guyana Quartet*—which comprised the novels *Palace of the Peacock*, *The Far Journey of Qudin*, *The Whole Amour*, and *The Secret Ladder* (1960–63)—this latest text hangs its intensely complex fabric of poetic legendizing and abstract discourse upon a simple, quasi-realistic skeletal frame story. Imagine an insane asylum located in the remote Camaria region of Guyana where the patients and the psychiatric director articulate fantasies of their "real" and imagined lives to one another over a period of years, as recorded in the asylum "dreambook" written by one of their members, named Hope. A pivotal idea, the notion of dual personalities, allows Harris's characters to create mythical doubles of themselves, who in turn interact among one another in a kind of hallucinatory, epic theater in which the mythic resonances and opportunities for thought become far more important than any tracings back into realistic social behavior. Such a simple, open-ended frame story allows Harris almost totally free rein to pursue his poetic confluence of universal myths within this remote Guyanese location.

Populating the novel are Monty, a Venezuelan murderer who thinks he is Montezuma, the last king of the Aztecs; Len, a former physics and chemistry professor who went berserk and masterminded an ostentatious bank robbery and who then came to the Sorrow Hill asylum as Leonardo da Vinci; Mark, an arsonist who claims he is Karl Marx; Nameless, who masquerades as Socrates and proposes the creation of a theater of Second Comings; Archie, a disturbed polymath who thinks he is an archangel; and the central characters Hope the mad diarist, his rival Christopher D'eath, the jailer and husband of Hope's beautiful beloved Butterfly, and the sorrowful widowed director of the asylum Dr. Daemon. Beyond the identification of these mad characters with their historical or legendary doubles, Harris expends little effort in trying to document any reasons, in real psychological terms, for their assumed identities. After his abrupt introduction of each succeeding character, the author moves almost immediately into his characteristically turgid prose, which lacks nearly all temporal, spatial, or real-life demarcations. The characters are fictional figments of Harris's own legend-making mind who operate in a grand, fluid matrix of mingled myths and abstract concepts.

The central constellation of characters form the most obsessive, repetitive fragments in Harris's novel. Hope has an adulterous affair with D'eath's wife Butterfly; the lovers are shot by D'eath and later commiserate with Dr. Daemon, who lost his own young bride, Ruth, through drowning. Yet this central story is far richer on an allegorical plane; only there does it begin to assume its true significance in the context of Harris's mythic purpose. We can read them as Hope's (everyman's) desire for love (Butterfly), under the threat of death (in a Christian, redeemable world), all within the precinct of the human spirit (Dr. Daemon) afflicted by sorrow (Ruth). Later, when Mark (Karl Marx) burns down the church of Father Robson, who himself fell in love with June (Mark's beloved), we encounter a further extension of Harris's essentially Christian allegory: the historic attack on Christianity by Marxist ideology. The acts and proclamations of the archangel (Archie) cap the novel and, in fittingly Christian terms, form an inspired, apocalyptic denouement.

Such a transparent, one-to-one allegorical reading of Harris's novel ignores what is perhaps the most important aspect of his prose, however—the language itself. It could be said of Harris's novels what has been said of James Joyce's, that the most important "character" in the work is the prose itself. It is the discursive and poetic interaction among Harris's mythic figures that carries the most compelling messages of the entire novel: the unfolding of innovative interpretations of uniquely combined myths and archetypes within the context of an indeterminate New World, where all the world's accumulated cultural fragments may creatively mingle to form new visions and concepts. Harris's greatest creative gift is for the construction of a consummately freewheeling discourse in which the innovative juxtaposition of widely disparate ideas and myths forms a quasi-surrealistic poetic reverie, constantly reaching for the never-before-spoken. His is a mind split open and spewing its contents like the maddest of lunatics and the greatest of innovative geniuses. Like Joyce's, Harris's prose is difficult reading yet tremendously stimulating to the pertinacious reader who can cast aside all desire for realism and can take the time to savor many rich new conceptual flavors exuded phrase by phrase, sentence by sentence, stirred by the hand of a master poetic chef.

> Stephen Breslow. *World Literature Today*. 69, 1 (Winter 1995), pp 203–04

Reading Wilson Harris is like staring into the luminous, fluid palaces at the heart of a log fire. Those addicted to pushbutton heating don't know what they're missing. But, like a log fire, you may need patience to get it going. Harris, a Guyanese novelist who was writing magic realism before the term was invented, puts it down to the influence of the rainforest on him as a young surveyor: "There was this peculiar density, depth, and transparency in the rainforest . . . One thing would correspond with another in startling ways."

After that, for the writer in him, "language began to bend, to shape itself." He deplores realism as blind to the "parallel universes of the Imagination", and postmodernism as having "denied depth" and "ruled out the unconscious". A great original, he is both poet and mythmaker.

The historical record of Jonestown, the theme of his 20th novel, speaks of a charismatic religious leader who founded a cult in California and led his followers to a utopian settlement in the

Guyanese rainforest. In 1978 the murder of outside investigators was followed by mass suicide. Among the 913 who died were 276 children. Jim Jones, the messianic leader, was killed by a shot to the head—a wound, says *Britannica*, ''probably not self-inflicted''. In that ''probably'' a gulf opens. What do we know of Jonestown who only these things know?

Harris transforms the banner headline of Jonestown into something rich and strange, weaving a new pattern from ancient and contemporary threads. The catastrophic end is set against another unexplained collapse of a people in Central America: the Maya, whose mathematics and myths, in particular their book of origins, the *Popol Vuh*, enable Harris to find the seeds of regeneration.

[Jonestown] is a dream-book, a visionary narrative set down by a Jonestown survivor. History relates that two men escaped at the height of the killing. Harris creates Francisco Bone, but this narrator is twinned with a skeleton death-figure and antagonist, Deacon. Deacon is Jones' right-hand man, but becomes the avenger who kills him. Bone is the left-hand man and the dreamer, who goes on to enact a redemptive odyssey.

Harris entwines these two paths, of nemesis and imaginative insight. Thought and action, life and death, are turned inside out like a sleeve. He calls Jones ''Jonah'', making him an inverted Christ (the whale was traditionally read as death or hell, defeated by resurrection) and a tragic figure like *Moby Dick's* hero.

Bone is told by his guide to entitle his dream-book *Imagination Dead Imagine*, a rich signifier (taken from Beckett) of language's power to transcend the closures of time and space. The narrative reaches back through the Jonestown Day of the Dead, to a last supper, to Bone's Guyanese childhood, and to the archetypal myths of the world which met in the Americas. For Bone and Deacon can also be seen as the heroic twins of the Mayan *Popol Vuh* whose task is to defeat death. . . .

The Maya believed in cyclical time in which history repeats itself whenever the divine influences coincide. They also thought that the world would come to a sudden end and had sophisticated numerologies for prophecy. Harris likewise loops the lasso of time; he unmasks the past in the present and looks to the future. Epochs can get out of kilter, tripping on phallic violence. Influenced by Jung, Harris seeks the archetypal feminine to restore the balance.

One of three Virgins in his story sits by a cradle, empty ''save for a beautiful toy, a wheeled chariot . . . within which lay a minute cherry from a flake of bloodwood in a Christmas tree''. Although the pre-Columbian Maya did not use the wheel, they did have wheeled toys. And, in the *Popol Vuh*, the divine twins' mother-to-be defeats death by offering the clotted bloodlike sap of a tree. In Harris's evolving discourse nothing is lost. The ''unfinished genesis of the imagination'' has been his motto, and where better to seek it than in a cross-cultural cradle?

Although the dialectics of Harris's novel are not simple, his imagery is compulsive if you let go of preconceptions. Readers interested in mind-altering substances, without a rainforest to hand, could find a session with *Jonestown* a truly consciousness-raising experience.

Paula Burnett. *New Statesman*. 125, 4292 (July 12, 1996), p. 48

Wilson Harris is usually described as a Caribbean writer. He should also be thought of as a South American writer. His early years leading government surveys in the interior of Guyana and his contact with the Amerindians—their culture, myths, and condition of being forgotten by the dominant culture—deepened his imagination and concern about all those nameless people in South America who, since the period of the conquistadores, have remained lost in written history. But, above all, Harris has to be thought of as a universal writer, not only because of his concern for all women and men of all times and places but because his imagination plunges into the depths of the earth and also out into the universe. His implied question is: Why must we build bridges between cultures, times, places, earth, and space? Our day is filled with potentialities for a totally destructive human future or a truly creative one. His Christ figures may be of pre-Christian times or non-Christian cultures of any time or land. He speaks of the pagan past from which we all have come. His novels may be set in places other than Guyana, but wherever they are set, Harris has all of us in mind. He has hope that humanity will begin to change and re-create itself. Humanity in his fiction is ''at the crossroads.''

Although Harris's work gives evidence of enormous reading of the work of others, it is fundamentally unlike that of anyone else. Awakening the imagination of his readers beyond its usual limits, he challenges us to think in entirely new ways. His style—if we can consider anything so honest a ''style''—is sometimes breathtaking, uniting all the arts and senses, sometimes bare or scientific. At times there are abrupt and, for a while, puzzling narrative switches. . . .

Harris conceives of his novels as epics, a form he believes need not be lost in a remote past. Some critics have divided Harris's work into periods. To me it has always seemed to be one continuing and growing work, never possible to complete. Other critics today think so as well, although Harris's style has changed and his philosophy has become more probing. The reader of Harris's work cannot drift tranquilly along with the narrative. Every word is necessary, almost all are resonant in their suggestiveness. Symbols, charged with new or enriched meanings, reappear. Since each character represents the potentialities of humanity, we who read are participants in the narrative and the thought/feeling of the work.

So Harris's novels need to be read with utter attention. His is an integrated imagery of the arts and sciences. The appeal is to the whole person—inner, outer, mind, heart, ''soul''—and to aspects of ourselves of which we are unaware. That is why the novels take the form of dreams, dreams being freer than conventional thinking and feeling. Harris's sense of time—of the past alive in the present and of the seeds of the future in both—is central. Most of his characters have names from the past or are symbolic—e.g., Penelope, Amaryllis, Poseidon, Faust, Bone, Hope, Abram—but their nature has changed to show the negative and positive potentialities of humanity. The implied question is: Which of these will we develop for a changed future? The creative or the destructive? Harris calls his opus a comedy. Although he does have an irrepressible sense of humor, his use of comedy resembles Dante's in *The Divine Comedy*. All the characters, representing humanity, are dead. When they are ''resurrected,'' how will they (we) think, feel, act? None of the characters represents a static extreme of good or evil. In the unforeseeable future things may be different. For example, a representative character, the female Emma, may become archbishop. If there are no true changes, the human race will end—all possibility of resurrection gone. But Harris retains his hope that we will fundamentally change in time, that the ''soul,'' by which he means the hidden unity of humanity, will prevail. . . .

Wilson Harris, like Melville, can be viewed from apparently endlessly different angles. The essays here are different and yet enrich each other. They are part of the ongoing project of opening up the work of this most universal and most human of authors.

Joyce Sparer Adler. *The Review of Contemporary Fiction.* 17, 2 (Summer 1997), pp. 8–11

It is the mark of the new that we never know what it will be until it arrives. Of one thing only we can be sure, that it is unpredictable and is never the outcome of existing "trends." The wind that bloweth where it listeth is unconstrained, blows round corners. Current ideologies determined by mechanistic and "evolutionary" premises are likely to see the future as the product of the past, whereas perhaps that past is the product of the future in a living— and therefore purposeful—universe. Teleology, rejected by Darwinian evolutionism returns. In Wilson Harris's world it is premises which are in question, the unknowable determinants. Thus the figure of Virgil and the meaning of his epic are changed by Dante, and Dante in turn resituated by what he becomes for Wilson Harris. The past is living and continually changing because of the future which changes it. Or perhaps there is only one time, one place, one total being in which every human life, every creature and every particle, has its eternal presence within a whole participated by all. Throw away our preconceptions and all becomes very simple—but it is precisely our preconceptions of which we are least aware.

If Harris's work and his world are difficult to come to terms with (as I have gradually discovered), it is not because they are more complex but because they are simpler, closer to the reality of actual experience, than the way of seeing that our highly complex Western civilization has imposed on us, as if it were an unquestionable norm. In reality that "norm" is fragmented and incoherent. We live, for example, as if our waking and our sleeping selves were different persons; our past and our present were separate worlds, as if our dead are no longer with us when they no longer share our present. More and more we have come to live in the immediately sensibly perceptible space circumscribed by our bodily senses at a given moment. Wilson Harris, by contrast, sees clearly that there are really no such boundaries and frontiers to the universe we inhabit. The final imaginative realization to which he leads us is an unbounded unity, of which every part has access to the whole, and that living whole includes every part. He gives us access to ourselves in a way that does not destroy but restores an original simplicity, the simplicity of our original Edenic state, which we have lost and to which we are forever seeking to return—and which in reality we have never left, otherwise than by thinking ourselves into the unnoticed complexity of the modern world.

We find ourselves in a simpler, but also a very much larger world than the restricted universe of Western materialism. Wilson Harris restores us to the world of soul, as it rightly belongs to us; however we may have struggled to accommodate ourselves to the lifeless universe of a materialist ideology for which not consciousness, but "matter" is the ground of what we have chosen to call reality. In that lifeless world we ourselves are mortal, and meanings and values have all but vanished into an ultimate nihil. In Harris's world our "carnival masks" are worn by the ever-living; they are at once our human guises, which we present to the world, and the "windows" through which the ever-living may look into world's carnival—as Lear imagined "God's spies." The masks change, come and go, sometimes we do not know if the guiser is the same or

another, whether the mask is the same or another, for the law of this old-new world Harris opens for us is metamorphosis, continuous and subtle and liberating. Indeed, liberation is the final meaning, the shedding and assuming of selves in an open universe. It is, as it seems, a Christian universe, whose work and end is redemptive— indeed, Harris uses the word resurrection in his title *Resurrection at Sorrow Hill. The Cross and the Two Thieves*—the two Brothers enacting the parts of Good and Evil—move through the great Epic of Redemption—Christo is the name of another epic masquer.

The impression of characters who come and go, disappear only to reappear elsewhere, is at first reading bewildering but we come to accept the truth of this interweaving of unbroken continuities flowing like water mingling in the one river. No one and nothing can be pinned down—Wilson Harris's intent is at the opposite extreme from the depiction of clear-cut and unique identity of "characters" in a nineteenth-century novel, created by their authors, participants in a world where individuation seemed more significant (and in a certain tradition of the novel this is still so) than epic universality. Harris writes of a quantum world—by quantum so applied to persons I take him to mean the property of a particle which is at the same time a wave, simultaneously located and unlocated. We are all increasingly aware of such a world, as measurable matter converges with immeasurable mind, aware of the space-time universe itself continually traversed by waves and particles, coming and going on their invisible trajectories to which we are continually but for the most part unconsciously exposed—if indeed these quanta are not ourselves. This is a most modern paradigm and also most ancient, the world soul traversed by angelic and elemental spirits, its aspect at once novel and deeply familiar. To read his novels is to experience a new strangeness that yet comes to us like a memory of something already and forever known. "Originality," in the sense of something never previously thought of and quite different from the already known, is incomprehensibly nowadays deemed an academic virtue and encouraged even among students of philosophy. Yet what is can only be itself, and its recognition leads not into outer space but is always a homecoming—"so it is true after all"—a building, not a dismantling, of what we term reality.

This recognition and assent belong not to reason but to the Imagination, which is a totality, is, according to William Blake, "the human existence itself," perhaps the Self of Vedant with its triple aspect, being-consciousness-bliss (sat-ohitananda). Reason, so far as I know, has no means of making a value judgment of a work of imagination. But this unscholarly account of a personal response to the world of a new great writer's vision would be incomplete without making reference to the power of Imagination, which for Harris himself is central. The first is too simple for the professional critics of today, though well known to the writers of the Jewish Bible: the response of the body, when the hairs of the head rise up in response to the presence of the Spirit. My gray hairs stir red in response to a quality in the writings of Wilson Harris that I would venture to call beauty—a word which has lost all meaning, one might be tempted to believe, for modern secular criticism and for a great deal of the work criticized also. Beauty has come to be deemed a falsification of reality, whose presently accepted image is closer to that powerful nihilist painter Francis Bacon's rotting yet protesting corpses than to Dante's "perfect human body." Yet for Plato, as for all traditional thought, beauty is the very aspect of the real, announces its presence in a numinous manner (the body's response of the hair stirring at the roots), the sense of deep recognition of what we are and what our universe, that we know also as the Good and the True. Of which indeed we have no knowledge other than this instantaneous assent of the Imagination.

In the novels of Wilson Harris a new and fresh beauty announces the sacred presence. Amazingly beautiful descriptions of the natural world, river and waterfall, tropical forests, tropical flowers, human participation in something cosmic, in a great mystery, the Great Battle, in resurrection and metamorphosis. And we know ourselves back on familiar-unfamiliar ground, the lost country, back where we belong. Yet all is simple, the people who wear the carnival masks are almost anonymous, and for all the marvelous exotic scenery of *The Guyana Trilogy* and elsewhere, the author deals with simple central human issues of the one human story in which we are all involved. No other writer known to me at this time writes from the imaginative depth and truth communicated by Wilson Harris.

> Kathleen Raine. *The Review of Contemporary Fiction.* 17, 2 (Summer 1997), pp. 42–45

BIBLIOGRAPHY

*Fetish*, 1951; *Eternity to Season*, 1960; *Palace of the Peacock*, 1960; *The Far Journey of Oudin*, 1961; *The Whole Armour*, 1962; *The Secret Ladder*, 1963; *Heartland*, 1964; *The Eye of the Scarecrow*, 1965; *Tradition, the Writer and Society*, 1967; *The Waiting Room*, 1967; *Tumatumari*, 1968; *Ascent to Omai*, 1970; *The Sleepers of Roraima: A Carib Trilogy*, 1970; *The Age of the Rainmakers*, 1971; *Black Marsden*, 1972; *Fossil and Psyche*, 1974; *Companions of the Day and Night*, 1975; *Da Silva da Silva's Cultivated Wilderness; and, Genesis of the Clowns*, 1977; *The Tree of the Sun*, 1978; *Explorations*, 1981; *The Angel at the Gate*, 1982; *The Womb of Space: The Cross-Cultural Imagination*, 1983; *Carnival*, 1985; *The Infinite Rehearsal*, 1987; *The Four Books of the River of Space*, 1990; *Resurrection at Sorrow Hill*, 1993; *Jonestown*, 1996; *Selected Essays of Wilson Harris: The Unfinished Genesis of the Imagination*, 1999

# HAYDEN, Robert (1913–1980)

**United States**

This first volume of poetry [*Heart-Shape in the Dust*] represents the emergence of a new and vigorous talent in American letters, with an obviously encouraging prospect of attaining an even higher level of achievement in the future. The reason for this promise—"promising" is often a patronizing term on the lips of a critic, a Pharisaic "assent with civil leer"—is that Mr. Hayden has something to say, and he knows how to say it. There is a true marriage of form and content, a happy fusion of mastery of technique with the rough and raw material of life-experience. Among Negro American poets only two challengers to Mr. Hayden come readily to mind: Sterling Brown and Langston Hughes. . . .

It is always invidious to quote poetry in truncated form, and some of Mr. Hayden's best poems are longish; "These Are My People," a mass chant, is a case in point. Varied are his moods and language. Like Sterling Brown, he has the exceptional faculty of investing a poem in dialect with tragic dignity, as, for example, "Ole Jim Crow." He has a spontaneity and an originality of

expression which impart to his verses an accent all their own. Whatever he has learned from British or American literary tradition he has succeeded in integrating in his style, and so while the reader may discover faint echoes of past and contemporary masters, he will find it difficult to identify them with the accuracy which imitation always guarantees.

> William Harrison. *Opportunity.* March 1941, p. 91

yes really [*the lion and the archer*] is like that and like this so you can see it is original and l'art and worth a dollar because whenever something is printed in 12 point without capitals you know because it has been known for forty years that it is original and full of dazzleclustered trees and jokes of nacre and ormolu and poltergeists in imperials and of course worth a dollar for a swooney evening on the leopard skin exploring the navel with candybar joy

indeed all for a dollar you can join robert hayden's heart when it escapes from the mended ferris wheel and the clawfoot sarabande in its dance. . .

Yes really it is like that and more like that than like this and maybe just maybe someday somewhen mr hayden will get right into selden rodman's anthology instead of *the negro caravan* (dear mr editor dont worry because you can minuscule the word when it's art) which will prove the oneness of mankind and the vision of being "violently opposed" to the wickedness of thinking that while there is sociology and politics the poet is the first sociologist and the vanguard politician

> Cedric Dover. *Crisis.* August 1948, p. 252

Seriously dedicated to his work, Hayden is a conscious artist rather than a spontaneous one, a deliberate worker, a careful polisher. While he does not scorn Negro themes and has used them in his most successful poems to date, he would like his work to stand or fall by objective poetic standards. As was the case with Countee Cullen, one gets the impression that Hayden is bothered by this Negro thing. He would like to be considered simply as a poet.

> Arna Bontemps. *Phylon.* 11, 4, 1950, pp. 356–57

If war presents a growing problem for poetry, being an American Negro presents a worse one. The subject matter is inescapable—and if one is a Negro, he will not wish to escape it. The subject matter is explosive and elemental; hard stuff for poets, it provides a discouraging paradox: the more you face it, the more you are driven to one of two extremes—sentimentality or hyper-erudition. Hughes or McKay would illustrate the former; Tolson, the latter. [In *Selected Poems*] Hayden is saddled with both. He oscillates from semi-dialect blues and corrupted ballads to Poundian notation; predictably, he resorts to the former for portraits of his childhood, family, and friends, and to the latter for "historical evidence" poems describing the white man's burden. Predictably, too, with a subject so fearfully basic and seemingly insoluble, Hayden is capable of high eclecticism when dealing with salvation (on the theological plane); witness his poems concerned with the Baha'i faith, a prominent nineteenth-century Persian sect whose leader was martyred. Might not the example of Jesus have sufficed? For the white man, probably.

Hayden is as gifted a poet as most we have; his problem is not one of talent but frame of reference. It is fascinating, moving, and finally devastating that the finest verse in this book [a speech in "Middle Passage"] is spoken by a Spanish sailor, a witness of the *Amistad* mutiny, who describes the slaughter of their captors by "murderous Africans.". . . Hayden is a superb ironist in this passage. The crime of it is he has not chosen his forte; it has chosen him.

David Galler. *Poetry*. July 1967, pp. 268–69

The section of [Stephen Vincent Benét's] *John Brown's Body* which is closest to Hayden's "Middle Passage" is the one that appears immediately after the "invocation," "Prelude—the Slaver." Benét presents here the captain of a slave ship who is moved to comment on a profession in which he is skilled, while actually transporting a cargo of black ivory from Africa to America. The impulse toward self-revelation is aroused by the questions, often not stated but implied, posed by a young mate, who is inexperienced and innocent. . . .

Hayden takes over the problem of reconciling Christianity and slavetrading in "Middle Passage," though the machinery of his narrative is much more complicated. The first of three parts offers the log entries, the prayers, and the ruminations of a pious member of the crew of a slaver. The conflict, however, is internal rather than external. The spur toward self-revelation is not an innocent youth on a maiden voyage, but the consciousness of the speaker, as he feels the threat to body and soul in the hazards and the emotional excesses that come from participation in the slave trade. . . .

His narration is not simple because it is made complex by the fact of his piety. On the one hand, there is the sailor's prosaic voice, instructing us in entries in ship's logs and, finally, in a legal deposition, of the hazards of a rebellious cargo, disease, and lust. On the other hand, there is the voice praying for "safe passage" to bring "heathen souls" to God's "chastening." What the sailor tells has so much cruelty and depravity that it seems finally to overwhelm the teller of the tale. The secure sense of accomplishing God's design departs, and there is only the cry, despairing now, rather than confident: "Pilot Oh Pilot Me."

Charles T. Davis. In Donald B. Gibson, ed., *Modern Black Poets* (Englewood Cliffs, New Jersey: Prentice-Hall, 1973), pp. 99–101

In "We Wear the Mask," probably the most widely reprinted of all Afro-American poems, Dunbar defines a tactical masquerade consciously assumed as a pragmatic defense in a hostile world. . . .

For Hayden's diver [in "The Diver"] the temptation to "fling aside the mask" is overcome in his ambiguously motivated ascent. What he rises towards, however, remains as vague as the reasons for his rising; he faces, in fact, much the same kind of indeterminate, existential future as Ralph Ellison's invisible man who resolves to emerge from the cave of his self-imposed meditation and seek a "socially responsible" form of salvation on the streets of America. Like the invisible man, the diver must return to a world which he cannot control from a temptation which he has, if not defeated, at least neutralized, although a temptation, it must be noted, which differs from that of Ellison's protagonist in springing from the emotions rather than the intellect, in residing in the wet

and ill-defined phantasms of the unconscious rather than the dry and well-illuminated categories of the understanding, and in luring him to eternal activity rather than eternal memory or contemplation; unlike the invisible man, his ascent is not the result of a conscious act of the will and he has for protection not a private cloak of invisibility but a life-supporting mask of cultural awareness developed through generations of introspection. Hayden offers a modern audience the period Dunbar had implicitly promised, a time when the grinning, lying, laughing mask of anguish and forbearance has metamorphosed into the tactically expressionless mask of the emerging diver.

Maurice J. O'Sullivan, Jr. *CLA Journal*. September 1973, pp. 91–92

Hayden's poetic career spans the years from the period of the late-Harlem Renaissance down to the current Black Arts Revolution. His first publication shows the influence of the Renaissance, but as that influence diminished, Hayden, unlike Gwendolyn Brooks and others of his generation, did not adopt the militant, nationalist, anti-Western-tradition stance of contemporary Black Arts writers. On the contrary, he has tried in every way to make even his so-called Negro poetry conform to and measure up to the best that Western civilization has produced. A superb craftsman, and a perfectionist, Hayden has consistently written for a "fit audience, though few.". . .

Always a skillful craftsman in verse, Hayden has grown and improved with the years. When he decided to abandon the kind of racial protest verse that he wrote in his first work, he seemingly decided to give up most of the conventional verse forms used in the early volume. In *Heart-Shape in the Dust*, for example, one finds quatrains (with varying line-lengths and rhyme-schemes), Shakespearian sonnets, mass chants, and other conventional forms. In his *Selected Poems*, one finds practically no rhyme (even his sonnet, "Frederick Douglass" is not rhymed). In this later volume, he employs a number of varied, unshackled, free-flowing verse forms, and he handles them effectively and on occasion brilliantly. . . . Perhaps Hayden's most impressive poetic techniques are those found in "Middle Passage." In this long poem, Hayden subtly and musically blends several kinds of writing—prose statement, refrains, excerpts from other poems, and lines from an old hymn—to produce a symphonic whole. To achieve his effects, the poet depends on the well-chosen, suggestive word *and* a cadence that reflects the varying moods of the poem.

Arthur P. Davis. *From the Dark Tower* (Washington, D.C.: Howard University Press, 1974), pp. 175, 179–80

Too much fame too soon has been the ruin of many poets. Until recently, black poets have not had to suffer this dubious blessing. Poets like Robert Hayden won recognition abroad but were ignored by our own literary king-makers. Hayden's collection of new and selected poems [*Angle of Ascent*] in a climate that is more openly aware should bring him the fame his talent deserves, and, luckily, it comes too late to harm that gift. . . .

Hayden keeps his eyes and ears open to the magic of the moment, to the moose in the wood ("tall ungainly creatures/in their battle crowns") to the "Creole babies,/Dixie odalisques,/speeding through cutglass/dark." A window washer, a religious confidence man, hunters or country dancers play their momentary part in his parody of freak and minstrel shows. Anger and love move these images into being, and, as in all true poetry, language gives them life. Robert Hayden will survive in his poems, long after current fashions of literature fade.

James Finn Cotter. *America*. February 7, 1976, p. 103

Although *Angle of Ascent* is not a complete representation of Hayden's canon, it is his most comprehensive collection. It includes all of the poems that the poet wished, in 1975, to preserve. Yet, there is a problem in that Hayden was constantly revising his poetry, and the "final" version often presents a more mature and experienced statement in the guise of an earlier poem. This is especially true of "Crispus Attucks" and of all of the poems selected from *A Ballad of Remembrance* that first appeared in *The Lion and the Archer* (1948) and *Figure of Time* (1955). Also it is true of certain poems included in the "Words in the Mourning Time" section of *Angle*. Therefore, although *Angle* is beautifully organic in arrangement, it does not demonstrate the total development of the poet.

*Angle of Ascent* makes available to the reader the best of the out-of-print poems, all of *A Ballad of Remembrance*, six of the eight poems in *The Night-blooming Cereus*, and all but one of the poems in the difficult to obtain *Words in the Mourning Time*. Since *Angle* includes poems Hayden first published in 1948 and the emended version of a 1942 poem, it does present a perspective, if limited, of the poet's canon. . . .

To an appreciable extent, *Angle* is biographical. However, of greater importance than the use of personal information is Hayden's use of the material as a metaphor, as a set of images for his poetry. The importance of *Angle of Ascent* lies in its timeliness and relevance to modern life. It profoundly conveys the Afro-American experience; it is an expression of a modern man's search for God; and ultimately it is a testimony to Hayden's long trek to mastery of his art.

By turning the dials of his television set, which is now possibly equipped with world-wide satellite coverage, the reader of *Angle* can see the centers of the world—Vietnam, Africa, South America, Europe. What he sees and hears will be news of the agony of oppression and famine, civil strife and war, man's fight for freedom. Both the agony and the breadth of this experience are vivid examples of *Angle's* direct relationship to the twentieth century. The full dimension of human misery and hope in these struggles is exhibited in this volume; the suffering and the indomitable will to transcend are very clear to any man who does not wish to deceive himself with systematic lies.

*Angle* is concerned not only with Hayden's attitude toward man and society, but also, we noted, with his attitude toward God. The book reveals his deepening attraction to the Bahá'i religion. It went far beyond its initial attraction to him of the vision of world brotherhood in which black, white, red, yellow would enjoy the millennium. To opt for Baháism was not only to reject a social hierarchy, an economic system, and a political government, but to revolt against a moral order that was content to treat the black man, the red man, and the yellow man each as but half a man; and it meant to subordinate, if not to spurn, the theology in which the moral order claimed to be based. Accordingly, the key note in the title poem of *Words in the Mourning Time* praises Bahá'u'lláh: "logos, poet, cosmic-hero, surgeon, architect / of our hope of peace" (part 10, lines 17–18). By 1975, our poet pointed his reader

to "The Nine-Pointed Star." This paramount Bahá'i religious symbol is the source in the poem that "signals future light" for man.

Moreover, Hayden's commitment gained for him not only temporal sanction and support for his art but also a valued place in the Bahá'i spiritual hierarchy alluded to in "For a Young Artist" and "Stars." In his personal faith and in his poetry Hayden demonstrated this precept: "To love God means to love everything and everybody, for all are of God . . . love everyone with a pure heart, fervently . . . hate no one . . . despise no one . . . love will know no limit of sect, nation, class or race." To the end, it was this rock that succored him during the mental and physical anguish of his terminal illness.

*Angle* demonstrates the level of mastery Hayden had attained. Although his subject matter remained generally the same, as did his interests, by 1975 his style had evolved from heavily symbolic to spare: instead of a profuse symbolic effect, a specific lucid one; instead of many images, the precise observation and the precise word convey a specific emotion. The poet's initial gift for versifying, abundantly clear in his apprentice work, had become the power to examine verbal behavior, to effectively utilize diction and syntax, colloquial speech and rhythm, and to explore nuances of emotion.

*Angle* also demonstrates the extent of Hayden's mastery of "the tradition"—that is, both the Afro-American and the Euro-American traditions. It is a mastery that exploits his use of what T. S. Eliot called a "historical sense" and a "sense of its presence." In this view he had a historical sense that compelled him to write not merely with intimate knowledge of his own generation but with a feeling that the literature of Europe from Homer to Rilke and Yeats, the literature of Africa including Senghor, the literature of South America, including Márquez and Donosco, and the whole literature of his own country all have a simultaneous existence and comprise a simultaneous order.

Accordingly, *Angle* reveals Hayden's demonstration that his complete meaning is not to be seen alone. He makes clear in tributes and in allusions to his fellow artists that his significance, his appreciation, is the appreciation of his relation to poets and other artists both dead and alive. The result is a group of poems that will last as long as the English language lasts.

Pontheolla T. Williams. *A Critical Analysis of the Poetry & Robert Hayden, 1940–78.* (Urbana: University of Illinois Press, 1987)

BIBLIOGRAPHY
*Heart-Shape in the Dust*, 1940; *The Lion and the Archer*, 1948; *Figure of Time: Poems*, 1955; *A Ballad of Remembrance*, 1962; *Selected Poems*, 1966; *Words in the Mourning Time*, 1970; *The Night-Blooming Cereus*, 1972; *Angle of Ascent: New and Selected Poems*, 1975; *American Journal*, 1978; *Collected Prose*, 1984; *Robert Hayden: Collected Poems*, 1985

# HEAD, Bessie (1937–1986)
## South Africa

Like many other black South African writers, Bessie Head lives in exile from South Africa. Her chosen place of exile is neighboring Botswana, where she has lived since 1964, in her words, "as a stateless person,'' who is required to register with the local police. Her three novels are set in Botswana, and her themes reflect the exile's prevailing sense of homelessness. But in its most profound sense, Head's fiction draws significantly upon the experience of being a nonwhite in South Africa, for the denial of civil rights to the South African nonwhite encourages Head's sense of homelessness in much the same way that the system of apartheid fragments the individual's sense of personal integrity. Physical exile and the permanent status as a refugee in Botswana are not distinguished, in Head's fiction, from the stateless condition which South Africa represents for nonwhites living in that country. Indeed, Head's personal background confirms this symbolism. She was born in an asylum for the insane to a white woman who had been placed in the institution for having dared to become pregnant by Bessie's black father, and her enforced condition as orphan is an intrinsic part of a continuing experience which has denied her a national identity in southern Africa, especially in Botswana and South Africa.

Head's racial experience as a South African ''colored'' (to borrow the quaint South African designation for racially mixed persons) has encouraged a profound alienation from prevailing ethical traditions and from many existing social institutions. This rebelliousness goes hand in hand with a certain skepticism about what she sees as the special disadvantages of women. This skepticism inspires a search, in her novels, for humane sexual roles and political values within a harmonious social order. In her fiction, the limitations of the woman's role and self-image, and the historical dispossession of the nonwhite are the very essence of a pervasive social malaise. In Head's view, that malaise assumes the proportions of a far-ranging moral crisis: racism, sexism, poverty, and entrenched social inequities are both the special ills of her world in southern Africa and the symptoms of a universal moral disorder. This revulsion at the moral wasteland of her world has also inspired an intensely moral idealism, one that assumes the force of a crusade in her fiction, sparking the quest for a more creative and less power-hungry sense of self. Head's work as a writer is closely integrated with her personal life in Botswana, for she has chosen to live in a rural village, working in a farming cooperative in which political refugees of all kinds and colors attempt to develop a thriving community out of Botswana's unpromising terrain—creating, in Head's words, ''new worlds out of nothing.''

Lloyd W. Brown. *Women Writers in Black Africa* (Westport, Connecticut: Greenwood Press, 1981), pp. 158–59

[Head's] three novels all deal with the reorientation of the exile to a new, somewhat hostile society. The autobiographical basis evident in the experience of her lead characters gives credence to her fictionalized and hence, generalized, exile-portraits. The progression from the position of affirmation of *When Rain Clouds Gather*, her first novel, to the uncertain, thin hope of survival through individual inner strength of her latest, *A Question of Power*, mirrors Bessie Head's own unrewarded struggle for acceptance in her new community.

It is significant that her first exile figure, Makhaya, in *When Rain Clouds Gather*, is a male. He achieves satisfaction in meaningful work with Gilbert, the English engineer, as they initiate land reclamation in Botswana. He achieves marital satisfaction and intellectual companionship with Paulina, a passionate and vigorous woman who leads the village women in making agricultural experiments. His success is paralleled for the village, Golema

Mmidi, itself. This tiny community triumphs over its evil overload through group action. The villagers, in common concern, defeat the chief's persecution of Paulina. Makhaya shares in this fulfillment. So, despite the poverty, the unremitting labor, the tragedy of a child shepherd's death, Makhaya—and the reader—achieve affirmation. This affirmation has its basis in shared human concern. . . .

In her second novel, *Maru*, her personal identification with the fictionalized woman's position, suggested earlier in her characters of Maria and Paulina in *Rain Clouds*, is clear. In *Maru* the first central female character, Margaret Cadmore, is an Englishwoman teaching in Africa. She adopts and educates an abandoned Bushman child and gives the child her name. The second Margaret Cadmore becomes the main protagonist of the novel. This Margaret is light-skinned—a suspicious color—just as Bessie Head in South Africa is identified as ''colored.'' Neither character nor creator is a member of the black majority—of South Africa, of Botswana, or of the African continent itself. . . .

*A Question of Power* reflects a variety of emotional crises resulting from stress upon this sensitive writer. Even the name of the lead character, like the nursery rhyme refrain—Elizabeth, Betty, Betsy and Bess—evidences the self-identification of the writer with her lead character. Head takes the reader through Elizabeth's emotional breakdowns which immediately follow her exile and then recur later and provoke her dismissal from her teaching assignment. ''Something was going drastically wrong with her own life. Just the other day she had broken down and cried . . . 'I'm not sure I'm quite normal any more.''' Shortly thereafter, Elizabeth receives the school board report: ''We have received a report that you have been shouting and swearing at people in public. Such behavior is unbecoming to a teacher. We are doubtful of your sanity, and request that you submit to us a certificate of sanity within fourteen days of receipt of this notice.'' The hospital suggested is too far away, the situation humiliating, the other teachers hostile. The conditions of conforming to accepted social patterns in what is basically still a conservative man's world in a black African society almost defeat her. ''She fell into a deep hole of such excruciating torture that, briefly, she went stark, raving mad.'' Her hallucinations deny her sexuality and her Africanness.

Charlotte H. Bruner. In Carolyn A. Parker and Stephen H. Arnold, eds. *When the Drumbeat Changes* (Washington, D. C.: Three Continents Press, 1981), pp. 263–64, 268–69

Bessie Head, in a volume of short stories entitled *The Collector of Treasures [and Other Botswana Village Tales]*, is concerned with ideas similar to those in her novels. This time she makes use of incidents that have been related to her, and of Botswana history, legend, and myth, as the basis for her fiction. She explores the meaning and values of traditional life and as usual goes right to the heart of everything that she examines. What is it for instance, she wants to know, that prevents a city-reared girl, significantly named ''Life'' in the story that takes its name from the character, from finding her niche in the village community? Or rather, why is it that the rest of the people do not find the everyday round of village life deadly dull—''one big, gaping yawn''—in its unbroken monotony? The answer lies in contact between people. . . .

The help people give each other . . . brings meaning to a hard life. When in the title story, Dikeledi, who has killed her husband, is befriended by another inmate in prison and thanks her for all her kindness, the woman replies, with ''her amused, cynical smile'':

"We must help each other . . . This is a terrible world. There is only misery here." The treasures that are collected by Dikeledi in this story—one towards which the other stories lead, as the author tells us, "in a carefully developed sequence"—are "deep loves that had joined her heart to the heart of others."

Ursula A. Barnett. *A Vision of Order* (London: Sinclair Browne, 1983), pp. 198–99

Bessie Head's reputation as a writer rests on three novels, a collection of stories, and a book on Serowe village. The three novels . . . form something like a trilogy. In each of them the novelist exhibits strong disapproval for the misuse of power by any individual or group. This dislike is evident in the way she dramatizes the process of the abdication of power which gets more complex from the first novel to the last. By the time the reader gets to the end of the third novel the novelist's message is clear: the naked display of power by the racists in South Africa or any other bigots elsewhere can lead only to disaster. There is no way of avoiding the rewards of oppression, whether it is of blacks by whites, whites by blacks, whites by fellow whites, or blacks by fellow blacks. The wise thing to do is to conceive of power in a progressive evolutionary manner. But, given man's insatiable lust for power, this is hardly possible. The novelist considers at length the psychological basis for power and finds that this has been largely eroded in a world dominated by conflict and the desire for political ascendancy. It is because of this stated position that Bessie Head is, for example, said to express "an indiscriminate repugnance for *all* political aspirations in *all* races."

The collection of stories, *The Collector of Treasures*, affords the author a chance to display her mastery of the art of storytelling. She understandably concentrates on the position of women and takes every opportunity to project a feminist point of view. She needs all the artistic talent displayed in her previous works to succeed with *Serowe: Village of the Rain Wind*. Here she combines imaginative writing with the fruits of a year's research study to produce work of great distinction. She succeeds magnificently in her reconstruction of the village life of Serowe. The daily occupations, hopes, and fears of the ordinary people of the village come alive in the reader's mind mainly because of the opportunity given the inhabitants to tell their own stories. The conception of history here is edifying—history is made out of the preoccupations of the common man, not out of the lofty ideals, cruelty, or benevolence of the wealthy and powerful. This reflects the concern for the underprivileged and oppressed masses of the people which is easily discernible in Bessie Head's writings.

Oladele Taiwo. *Female Novelists of Modern Africa* (New York: St. Martin's Press, 1984), pp. 185–86

Bessie Head is a crusader for sexual and social justice for all men and women. Her favorite theme is the drama of interpersonal relationships and their possibility for individual growth and regeneration. She explores not only social harmony but also what is unique in each individual who contributes to it. In the realization of this task she employs an imaginative power and an original grasp of style which match her forceful moral vision. In all this, the woman's identity is fundamental; for it is still easy to encapsulate the central issues of all Head's novels into the vital issues of power

and identity. . . . She truly approaches her characters as individuals and, with her usual sensitivity and thoroughness, journeys through the innermost recesses of their lives. The product of this exploration is the emergence of that uniqueness which makes each of them special. To Bessie Head, South Africa typifies power in its ugliest form, and the revulsion with which she views such a moral wasteland has aroused in her a special reverence for human life and dignity.

Head's characters are refugees, exiles, victims, all of whom are involved in a very personal and private odyssey of the soul from which they finally emerge regenerated, as well as spiritually and psychologically enriched. These characters inhabit the harmonious new worlds which operate in her novels; but like Ngugi [wa Thiong'o], she seems to imply that it is only from the interaction of both men and women in relationships of mutual love and respect that such a society can be created. Like Ngugi also she has a number of solid, resilient, and resourceful women in her novels. Through them she explores the limitations of women's roles, their disadvantages and their bruised self-image, and celebrates their occasional successes. . . .

Head's three novels can be seen as a systematic study of women's roles and handicaps in society, especially an unjust one like South Africa. She has also x-rayed their emotional, psychological, and spiritual endowments in the context of a human society, sane and accommodating. Her women are invariably thrust into a hostile landscape from which they must grow and realize their identity. There are passionate women like Dikeledi and Paulina; reserved women like Maria and Margaret; wise old women like Mma-Millipede; silent but self-confident women like Brigitte; loud and pushy women like Camilla; and frightened and mentally tormented women like Elizabeth. Even weird Thoko has a special value in this landscape. Head assesses the Botswana woman's worth by the degree of inner strength, individuality, and drive with which she is able to rise above the brutalizing and restrictive roles assigned her by an unimaginative society. The degree of humility and sincerity with which she adapts herself to a strange people and society contributes to the harmonious coexistence of all in her environment. In exploring their day-to-day activities Head does not fail to point out that quite often these women perpetuate their own problems through mental conditioning and their acceptance of social norms and taboos and also because of unfounded interpersonal jealousies. For all, their lives are a constant struggle and movement towards self-discovery.

Virginia U. Ola. *Ariel*. 17, 4 (October 1986), pp. 39–40, 46–47

Bessie Head's novel *A Question of Power* raises the problem of how one can write about inner chaos without the work itself becoming chaotic. . . . Bessie Head writes of the human "capacity to endure the excruciating." Appropriately, the novel is set in a village called Motabeng, "the place of sand." Motabeng suggests a lack of certainty and firmness. Like life and the world, all is loose, shifting and changing. Yet we search for little rocks and patches of firm ground in the sand; for permanence within the wider impermanence; for value within the ultimate valuelessness. . . .

The central character in *A Question of Power* is Elizabeth, and the novel covers a little more than a year in her life (around 1970) a time when she experienced a nervous breakdown and was committed to an asylum. The hallucinatory is real to Elizabeth and therefore presented as factual. The reader is placed within her world, and experiences something of Elizabeth's bewilderment and strain. Such a subject was foreshadowed in *Maru* where the characters, while being individuals, also represent forces. That novel confronts the mystery and power of man, the extraordinariness within the apparently ordinary. People were "horrible" to Maru because he could see into their thoughts and feelings, see their very bloodstreams and hear the beating of their hearts. The novel goes beyond psychology and dreams to the psychic and the supernatural. Not only are Maru and Moleka aspects of one person, but within the half of Maru there are further divisions such as between his compassion and idealism on the one hand, and his cruelty and cunning on the other. The interest in psychic states, Margaret's nightmares, her awareness of something within her "more powerful than her body could endure" all prepare us for the fracture which is the subject of *A Question of Power.* . . . To say that *A Question of Power* is about one "fall" or breakdown is to oversimplify the novel. The work describes a series of defeats and successes and, in this way, more truthfully represents the pattern of human life. "The dawn came. The soft shifts and changes of light stirred with a slow wonder over the vast expanse of the African sky." But dawn and night alternate, and in the experience of some the nights are more frequent and longer.

> Charles Ponnuthurai Sarvan. In Eldred Durosimi Jones, ed. *Women in African Literature Today* (Trenton, New Jersey: Africa World Press, 1987), pp. 82–84

African literary criticism . . . often denies that Head's work can be understood as expressing any kind of Western-influenced feminism. But few can dispute that, if feminism is broadly defined as the insistence that women have suffered systematic social injustice because of their sex, Head's work, particularly *The Collector of Treasures*, has a discernible feminist content. She clearly delineates the oppressiveness of tribal life for women, compounded by urbanization. But Head herself refuses to be labelled as a feminist, and close reading of her work indicates that her attitudes about women are ambivalent. A consistent pattern in her fiction is for the female hero to endure trials only surmountable through the intervention of a godlike man. Most of Head's presentation of *good* relations between the sexes (which has been diminishing in her work) embodies a sentimental ideology of romance. A woman like Life, who acts "with the bold, free joy of a woman who had broken all the social taboos," gets murdered in the end. And Head's presentation of sexuality, especially in *A Question of Power*, betrays such anxiety and distaste that one suspects she has displaced racial and ethnic self-doubts and dilemmas on to sexuality as well. Just as the greatest insult a colored can receive, in her work, is to be taunted as a half-caste, the most disgusting epithet for women who transgress norms is a "he-man": ". . . it was meant to imply that something was not quite right in her genitals, they were mixed up, a combination of male and female." This dread concerning one's sexual make-up and capacity for a healthy sexual relationship pervades *A Question of Power*, which attempts to exorcise Elizabeth's fear that, like [Doris] Lessing's Mary Turner, she suffers from "something not quite right . . . something missing somewhere."

In Head's work, moreover, a distaste for homosexuality also conveys a considerable malaise about sexual identity and capacity.

It would seem that the reconciliation of opposites, whether psychologically or in social relationship with another, is something she envisages with difficulty. Such a conflation of writer and implied author is, of course, risky, more often than not mistaken, and perhaps intrusive. But Head has repeatedly stressed that *A Question of Power* is autobiographical: "A private philosophical journey to the sources of evil"; "my only truly autobiographical work." Enlightened feminism neither fears nor hates men, but elements of these attitudes frequently occur in Head's work. Lloyd Brown is one of only two critics to have noticed that "the imaginative power with which [Head] can describe hatred, death, and poverty . . . fails her when the subject is largely one of love or sexual passion"; the other being the ever-perceptive [Lewis] Nkosi.

> Susan Gardiner. In Cherry Clayton, ed. *Women and Writing in South Africa: A Critical Anthology* (London: Heinemann, 1989), pp. 231–32

The present anthology [*Tales of Tenderness and Power*] represents the second collection of Bessie Head's shorter writings. They cannot all be classified as short stories in the usual use of that designation: some are fictional or semifictional, some historical stories. But most of them have one thing in common. They are closely rooted in actual events. The only purely fictional story is "The General." Even in "Chief Sekoto Holds Court," the incident described is probably based on fact, though Head has shaped the events to her own purpose. All the others are stories clearly related to or identifiable with personal, national or historical events, or we have her word for it that the story is based on fact. . . .

Often choosing a mundane event as her starting point . . . Bessie Head proceeds to give her story a subtle lift, even universal significance as she, the teller of tales, intrudes with humorous comments or her own view of things. Often she introduces an element of tenderness to the original event. She was easily moved by a generous action and responded quickly to real goodness, which she continued to believe does exist, especially in the lives of ordinary people. Yet she had, as well, a sharp nose for the power people, whom she exposed at every opportunity. . . .

Bessie Head always retained her individualism. Though feeling strongly about racism and sexual discrimination—and having gained by the bitterest experience a considerable knowledge of both problems—she would never allow herself to be totally identified with either African nationalism or feminism. Her vision included whites and blacks, men and women. What she feared was the misuse of power, what she strove towards was human goodness and love. The idea of the basic goodness and decency of the ordinary person never left her. Though she became increasingly susceptible to the evil around her as she grew older, including the constant misuse of power at local, national and international levels, she clung bravely to her ideals.

> Gillian Stead Eilersen. Introduction to Bessie Head, *Tales of Tenderness and Power* (London: Heinemann, 1989), pp. 10, 14–15

The publication of [Head's] eulogistic social history *Serowe: Village of the Rain Wind* in 1981 and her "major obsession, the Khama novel" *A Bewitched Crossroad* in 1984 (research for both of which had begun in the early 1970s), was the culmination of a long, hard battle for acceptance. Her death in 1986 was premature, a foreshortening of what could otherwise have been a long and rewarding relationship as a citizen with her adoptive country Botswana. . . .

The generic classification of the pieces in [*A Woman Alone: Autobiographical Writings*] poses a challenge to the literary critic. They span a number of overlapping genres: letters, journalism, autobiography, fictional sketches, essays, forewords, explanatory notes on novels. Were one to assume these generic markers to denote discrete and insular categories, it would appear possible to label the pieces in the present volume accordingly. At the end of this exercise, however, one would be left with a number of alarming and messy anomalies: how could "Snowball: A Story" be classified a fictional sketch when three quarters of the piece is devoted to the author's reflections on her day-to-day life in District Six? And why does the piece "An African Story" (so misleadingly titled) fall into neither of the categories "fictional sketches" or "journalism," or even wholly into "autobiography" for that matter? Its title promises fictional narrative, and indeed it begins like a story, but then quickly becomes autobiographical, even anecdotal, and ends with a philosophical reflection on the future of South Africa. And this indeterminacy characterizes almost every piece included in the present volume.

The truth is that the majority of the pieces assembled here defy classification. At their two extremes they represent autobiography and (very nearly) pure fiction. Most of them are however strung somewhere between these two extremes, and each (with a few exceptions) represents an amalgam of self-reflection, semifictional narrative, journalistic reportage, and cultural comment. The significance of each piece (and the justification for its inclusion in the present volume) is that it reveals something about the extraordinary life of the author Bessie Head.

Craig MacKenzie. Introduction to Bessie Head, *A Woman Alone: Autobiographical Writings* (London: Heinemann, 1990), pp. xii–xiii

Parameters are required for appreciating *A Gesture of Belonging*. It contains only letters to [Randolph] Vigne: [Vigne] compensates for this with an introduction and commentaries. We see that Head needed Vigne as a father. She is a quivering being: her insights are in terms of dreams, the soul, etc. At moments she seems to receive messages like a radio. Her notion of God is eccentric, profound. "I think I can say, with authority, that God in the end, is not an old man in the sky or invisible, but certain living individuals whom I adore," she states. The most valuable letters give insights into her novels. "*A Question of Power* is stark, bleak tragedy from beginning to end," she says. "It is written at two levels. The everyday level involves a development project. The people I work with come in and keep moving steadily and sanely through the book, just as beautiful as they are in real life. The second level is a journey inwards into the soul, with three soul characters, who are really disembodied persons, the concentration is on arguments of power, good and evil and it is really in the form of dream sequences which had a thread of logic, the sort of logic of war."

Bessie Head was all "right brain," it seems. No wonder she liked Tayeb Salih's *Wedding of Zein*. Her imagination gives her trouble where ordinary, logical people do fine: she goes through sheer terror when she has to open a bank account and issue checks.

She is blind where others see. "Friends come and go for strange reasons," she says. After she left Iowa, she wrote to Paul Engle that when most people looked back on their trail, they saw achievement and order; she saw only chaos. I was astounded she did not accept that much of the chaos was of her own making. So it is not surprising that, seeking balance, she identifies with her male protagonists, noting that they also have the female element in them.

Peter Nazareth. *World Literature Today*. 66, 2 (Spring 1992), p. 391

Given Bessie Head's vehement feminist claim in *The Collector of Treasurers* (1977) that in Botswanan society women are of no account or are treated like 'dogs', her story 'Snapshots of a Wedding' seems surprisingly muted. Its subject is the marriage between a young man and a school-educated woman, called Neo for 'new'. After an idyllic opening—the wedding takes place at the 'haunting, magical hour of early dawn' (p. 76)—the story begins to establish the specific voices which make up the community. 'This is going to be a modern wedding' (p. 76), says one of the relatives of the groom. One of the bride's relatives responds: 'Oh, we all have our own ways. . . . If the times are changing, we keep up with them'. Uneasy about the marriage, the female members of the community instruct Neo in her duties: 'Daughter, you must carry water for your husband. Beware, that at all times, he is the owner of the house and must be obeyed. Do not mind if he stops now and then and talks to other ladies. Let him feel free to come and go as he likes' (p. 79).

At such a point, the story may seem to be less about the community's desire to 'keep up with' women like Neo than about forms of control. Even though she will be keeping her job as a secretary, rather than being 'the kind of wife who went to the lands to plough', Neo adjusts in other ways to community demands, becoming less aloof and more engaged in the life of the village. The community despises Neo for her 'conceit and pride' and appreciates the 'natural' Mathata, who is 'smiling and happy' despite her impregnation and abandonment by the man whom Neo is going to marry. This opposition—whereby the educated woman is conceited and the uneducated woman content—is one of the givens of the story.

There are suggestions of an ironic stance being taken in the text towards this rural community's construction of a dutiful wife: the phrase 'we all have our ways' may seem sinister to some readers, and so may the manner in which the relatives 'nod their heads in that fatal way, with predictions that one day life would bring [Neo] down'. The reference to the sacrificial ox—'unaware of his sudden and impending end as meat for the wedding feast'—offers itself as a veiled allusion to the bride about to be sacrificed, and the fact that the marriage takes place at the police camp adds to the coercive undertones.

But these hints of the sinister or coercive can in the end only be part of the repressed of the text. The community of women exhort Neo to obedience in terms of the idyllic, which is in itself a marker of authorial sympathy—even yearning—in Head's writing: 'The hoe, the mat, the shawl, the kerchief, the beautiful flute-like ululating of the women seemed in itself a blessing on the marriage'. Moreover, the final command 'Be a good wife! Be a good wife!', given by the aunt, is placed in the context of ritual and habitual gesture which form so important a part of Head's presented world.

The aunt pounds the ground in a gesture symbolic of the act of pounding the newly-laid floor of the young couple's dwelling and, just before this, an old woman dashes towards Neo and chops at the ground with a hoe, symbolising the agricultural work which traditionally falls to women. Such acts—pounding floors, smearing walls, thatching roofs—contribute throughout Head's collection of stories to a harmonious village atmosphere, for they belong to a life made up of group activities and the sharing of tasks. The very congruence in this story between the aunt's gestures of pounding, the old woman's gestures of hoeing and the words themselves might add to the atmosphere of coercion lurking in the story's subtext. However, in the story's smooth return to the opening atmosphere of idyll, the village women deny the possibility of the existence of 'new' women who are other than 'good' wives.

The 'new' woman appears in expanded form under the name Life, in the short story of that name. The way she is depicted will help clarify Head's relation to modern women and the community, as well as to feminism. Life, who returns to her village from Johannesburg after an absence of many years, represents the world of urban capitalism, its commercial ethic particularly evident in the contamination of sex by money. In the rural world, sex flows freely ('People's attitude to sex was broad and generous'); in the world introduced by Life, money flows freely and sex becomes unfree - paid for by the men, and then paid for, in a different way, by Life. When she marries Lesego, he demands fidelity, and kills her when she disobeys.

This might have been a story about a 'new' woman coming into a world which is characterised by male ownership of the female body, and trying to insist—within a tradition of feminism—that her body is her own. But this is not, quite, the story Head writes, although in one important respect a feminist judgement is being made: the brief prison sentence Lesego is given for killing an unfaithful wife stands in obvious and sharp contrast to the death sentence delivered on Dikeledi in 'The Collector of Treasures' for killing the husband who abuses her and leaves her to feed, clothe and rear their children alone. Life is associated with the beer-brewers, 'a gay and lovable crowd who had emancipated themselves sometime ago'. The term 'emancipated' puts them in their place: it is offered with as much sharp disfavour as the term 'hysterical', used in relation to Life's behaviour. Life exhibits 'the bold, free joy of a woman who had broken all the social taboos'; the gaiety of the beer-brewing women is similarly out of bounds. They may have emancipated themselves from the commands. 'Do this! Do that!' (which echo the commands under which Neo has been told to live) but this leaves them with 'a language all their own' (p. 39), divorced from the codes, gestures and rituals by which a culture knows itself.

Thus 'Life', like 'Snapshots', seems to become a vehicle for the rejection of all that Head takes women's emancipation to be. Yet both stories are more complex than this, for in their refusal of contemporary models of emancipation (as Head chooses to represent them) another possibility is opened up.

In 'Snapshots of a Wedding' the 'new' woman is drawn back into a community by means of a series of gestures which make up the community's way of constructing a world. The exhortation to hoeing is 'only a formality' (the women know that Neo already has a secretarial job, and do not expect her to hoe). This reference to 'formality' suggests that the words 'Be a good wife! Be a good wife!' themselves be placed in the context of what Head called, elsewhere, the 'courtesies' of community life.''

In 'Life' the direction of Head's thinking in this regard becomes clearer. The villagers recall a world of communality—the tasksharing marks a barter economy—but they are also caught in a world of barely flourishing peripheral capitalism, whose figure is the set of anaemic calves owned by Lesego. Even before Life's arrival 'the men hung around, lived on the resources of the women'. The farmers and housewives, a group of women set apart from the beer-brewers, and called 'the intensely conservative hard-core of village life', admire Life's independence, for they live in a world where only men 'built up their own, individual reputations'. But they turn away from her when she becomes a prostitute, in a moment important in the story as a whole, not least because it prefigures one of the story's closing moments. This is a comment made to Lesego by Sianana: 'Why did you kill that fuck-about? You had legs to walk away'. Like Sianana, the 'conservative' women are marginal to the plot, whose focus falls on a drama enacted between the 'new' woman and characters not fully representative of rural society, as Head sees it—Life as against Lesego, not Sianana; in accord with the beer-brewers, not the farmers and housewives. But their response, as we shall see, is crucial.

The final word on the drama between Life and Lesego takes the form of a drunken song sung by the beer-brewing women about two worlds colliding. The worlds they refer to are the worlds we have seen in conflict: contemporary South Africa (Life) and contemporary Botswana (Lesego). The words they sing come from a song sung by Jim Reeves, a cowboy-type, like Lesego, as well as a voice from a corrupt world. There is no consolation to be drawn from either world; neither can offer the writer the future she wants. Her solution is to go the world represented by the marginal characters, which functions as a sign of the past. It becomes the writer's business to reconstruct this past, and to depict it more fully, in subsequent stories. 'Snapshots of a Wedding' also alludes to this project, pointing to the way the 'past' tries to contain the educated woman. The complexity of the concept of containment, suggesting incorporation and expansion as well as limitation and control, precisely reflects the precariousness of Head's literary-political project.

Dorothy Driver. Gira Wisker, ed. *Black Women's Writing* (New York: St. Martin's Press, 1993), pp. 160–64

The taboo against interracial sex—officially expressed in the Immorality Act of 1927 and its amendment in 1950(1)—has roused the fictional imagination of a range of South African writers. In *God's Stepchildren* (1924) Sarah Gertrude Millin explores interracial unions to prophesy against ''miscegenation'' while affirming the ideal of racial purity. Novels like William Plomer's *Turbott Wolfe* (1926) and Alan Paton's *Too Late the Phalarope* (1953) deal with aborted relationships between white and black South Africans, their protest against race laws revolving around the deviant acts of individuals and deriving from a South African liberal tradition. Two years after the repeal of the infamous Act, the theme is revisited in Lewis Nkosi's *Mating Birds* (1987) and explores the enduring pathology of racism.

Among the many responses to interracial sex and the Immorality Act, Bessie Head contributes a singular voice by disavowing realism and protest, fusing autobiography with fiction, and exploiting circuitous narrative strategies. Revealing her ongoing concern with liberating identities for marginalized subjects, these strategies are illustrated in lesser-known fictions: her letters and her posthumously published novella *The Cardinals*.

First issued together with previously unpublished meditations and stories in 1993, *The Cardinals* was given to Patrick Cullinan shortly before Head left South Africa for Botswana in 1964. It is not surprising that the manuscript was rejected by several publishers and was retained for a long time by Cullinan, a publisher and prominent literary figure in South Africa. With its abrupt shifts in emphasis, its meandering plot, and its uncertain use of point of view, *The Cardinals* is not what is conventionally thought of as a ''well-wrought'' novel. And because the sixties were a time when few publishers or readers of South African fiction were interested in ''open-ended meanings'' or ''writerly texts,'' the fact that Head's first novel was published posthumously is as revealing about transforming interests in South African literature as it is about her recently elevated status in literary studies.

In both her fiction and the autobiographical accounts within her letters, Head returns again and again to a narrative about the illicit union between a socially superior mother and a subordinate father, the mother's trauma after being made to relinquish her child, and the daughter's rejection by her mother's family and stigmatization by society. Usually, as in her autobiographical stories and *A Question of Power*, the child of a union between an upper-class white woman and a black stablehand is placed in foster care while her mother is incarcerated in a mental institution. The mother commits suicide after spending several years there, her family disowns the child, and the child bears the scars of being an outcast, an orphan, and an heir to her mother's ''insanity.''

Usually, too, the father is given little direct reference. Head has alluded to her own father to speculate that he was probably killed after the discovery that he was a white woman's lover and to claim about her mother: ''I feel more for her than for my father because she died a terrible death, in a loony bin while he is most probably still alive somewhere.'' Dismissing the father, Head forges a determined orientation toward a mother figure silenced by master narratives of apartheid, psychiatric reports, and the prejudice of her family: ''I still say she belongs to me in a special way and that there is no world as yet for what she has done. She has left me to figure it out''. Rejecting official versions of her mother's identity, the daughter inscribes her subjectivity and policed desires. . . .

By turning to the mother as the point of origin, Head identifies her own cultural inscription and that of Elizabeth, the central character of *A Question of Power*, locating parallel processes of subjugation in mothers and daughters. The principal of the mission school which Elizabeth attends as a child warns her of the dangers of this affiliation when she says: ''We have a full docket on you. You must be very careful. Your mother was insane. If you're not careful you'll get insane just like your mother''. Head's autobiographical story in her letters registers a similar affiliation and redefines the mother's legacy of madness: ''A birth such as I had links me to her in a very deep way and makes her belong to that unending wail of the human heart. . . . She must have been as mad and impulsive as I.''. . .

What immediately distinguishes *The Cardinals* from Head's other narratives is a preoccupation with the father, who initiates and constantly supervises the writing of his daughter Mouse. The child of a union between a woman of the upper social strata and a poor fisherman, Mouse is handed over to a woman living in one of Cape Town's slums. After spurning her fisherman lover and giving up her child, her real mother commits suicide, and Mouse's father never learns of her birth. Mouse prefigures the later character Elizabeth, as well as the autobiographically represented Head, by being black, female, and, as her successive renaming in the novel illustrates, constantly spoken for or about—denied the authority to speak her own identity.

As ''Charlotte,'' Mouse finds work with the tabloid *African Beat*, where she meets up with her father Johnny, by then a cynical journalist who eventually persuades her to share his home and oversees her development as a writer. The characters never discover that Johnny is really Mouse's father, and the novella ends at a point when ''the cardinals'' are about to make love. Informing us in her epigraph that the cardinals ''are those who serve as the base or foundation of change,'' Head signals the triumphant meanings of her novella. *The Cardinals,* however, fitfully unravels its surface optimism and constantly hints at qualified and contesting meanings.

The novella repeatedly suggests that Mouse's desire to write will lead to the ultimate discovery of an unknown self and the power to write her own identity. As ''Miriam,'' her first encounter with the written word occurs at the age of ten, when an old man enters the slum as a letter-writer with his manual ''The Art of Letter Writing.'' Miriam is captivated by his activity and intuitively identifies the potential for her deliverance through writing. . . .

Mouse's induction into the gendered textual space over which Johnny presides occurs in the context of strongly connoted gendered meanings. The masculine world is normative and superior, the exemplar of sovereign masculinity being Johnny: cynical and perceptive, although often abrasive and violent, he proves to be the character whose views about his society and other characters are most reliable.

Another authoritative male character is the nameless man who helps Mouse find a wheelchair for her story about an old woman who needs one. Although commissioned by the editor, the story promises to be one independently constructed and told by Mouse. When she sets out to create this narrative, the nameless hero intervenes. In an appropriative process echoing Johnny's control over her writing, this character ultimately authors her story by assuming a pivotal role in shaping it.

The world marked as ''feminine'' is contrastively. emotional, hollow, and inferior. Johnny frequently reminds us of the binary gender system, while his girlfriends are stereotyped as fickle, conniving, and superficial. Mouse's mother Ruby appears to defy stereotypes of womanhood when she pursues a passionate relationship with Johnny by defying social taboos, yet she treacherously capitulates when she publicly rebuffs her lover and gives up her baby daughter.

With her reconstruction of an autobiographical story in *The Cardinals,* then, Head has the mother choose to reject her lover and child. Despite her eventual grief and suicide, Ruby's guilt is established at the start of the novella, where an omniscient narrator denies the reader access to her subjectivity. Relinquishing her baby together with five shillings, Ruby is seen to leave the slum with guilty haste. Condemned by the narrator in the opening pages, she is introduced as a subject who bears the marks of weakness and deceit, which are connoted as feminine.

*The Cardinals* repeatedly affirms a masculine world whose authority is persuasively inscribed in the texts that Mouse confronts and imbibed through the act of writing. Accepting the fictions of female inferiority and of masculinity as a desired model, the central woman character will therefore acquire an identity that silences her unknown self. But the text also hints at the limited path of Mouse's entry into writing with its insistent delineation of the power hierarchies of her world, covertly warning of her ongoing entrapment at the same time that it seems to celebrate her progress: while Johnny will allow Mouse to escape culturally ascribed silence for a public domain of self-defining authority, her freedom will be achieved at the cost of discovering an independent textual space and identity that cannot be discovered in dominant narratives. She will have to continue the word of her father at the same time that he "engenders" her and penetrates her sexually. With the anticipation of this ambiguous birth in chapter 4, Mouse becomes the author of Johnny's paternal story; after he gives her a brief autobiographical outline, she writes his story and submits it for his approval. . . .

At the end of *The Cardinals* the central woman character does seem poised to break out of her socially designated condition of silence. But she will transcend her silence only by being elevated to the symbolic status of her father and accepting his fiction of selfhood which denies her authority to construct her own. At the same time that the text celebrates Mouse's anticipated entry into writing through the inadvertently incestuous cardinals, it seems unable to ignore that her progress toward writing is embedded in power relations and narratives that inhibit the discovery of an independent desire.

*The Cardinals* discloses the covert and contradictory paths which Head pursued in her representation of marginalized subjects and her celebration of creativity. While much of her fiction explores her characters' circuitous defiance of the identities imposed on them, *The Cardinals* ambiguously confronts the dominant texts that speak for and about a central female character.

Head has claimed that the central male character of her first long piece of fiction offered a prototype of the mythical man she exalted in her later fiction: "He gets better with each story." That her subsequent writing shows a continuing fixation with powerful father figures and authoritative masculine codes is not because she was unaware of their relation to hegemonic narratives. *The Cardinals* illuminates her alertness to the way master narratives shape the public domain of writing and the fictions available to marginal subjects. It also reveals the way she both subverts and reproduces dominant meanings and codes, struggling with a vision which available codes are not able to sustain. The recuperation of paternal meanings in the novella identifies one direction in her writing as the quest for discursive empowerment through the instrumentality of available languages, strategies, and forms. While her search for meanings beyond dominant narratives develops into the construction of a maternal narrative, this narrative was but one inconsistent strand within a much broader and ambivalent process of writing. Head's restless struggles both against and with available narratives, forms, and discourses were rarely univocal, linear, or intentional ones. Her lesser-known fiction encodes traces of her complex battle to construct identifies beyond dominant fictions and to discover the conditions for her own creativity.

Desiree Lewis. *South African Literature in Transition.* Fall 1996

Head's narratives are important precisely because they use Third World women's experience to create a feminist aesthetic. Bessie Head's interest in exploring the complexities of women's inherently subversive identities within the context of the various ways that women are exiled by patriarchal structures is clear from the beginning of her writing career.

However, an enduring picture that emerges from *Maru*, after the rejection of nostalgia begun in *When Rain Clouds Gather*, is the artist's identity. Margaret Cadmore's role as an artist is the one that emerges as the strongest icon in Head's second novel. Her resistance lies at the level of her artistry. Even though Dikeledi takes away her paintings soon after she has painted them, Margaret is no longer tied to them. Her woman artist's identity is the one that engages Head most and that identity is subversive in that it refuses dialogue but rather turns inward to examine and create. Even though her marriage to a paramount chief coerces her status as a woman, it is finally her pictures that communicate and not her. The part that draws the pictures, unlike any other part, belongs to herself alone not to the Masarwa and certainly not to Maru.

It is the artist's identity in *Maru* that renders any other struggle, either with gender or with race, secondary to that exploration. Perhaps this is the reason why Head wants to escape after just teasing into existence the subjects of race, gender, and oppression. Her primary concern remains with the role of an outcast, exiled artist. As an artist, Margaret does survive even as she is unable to survive as a woman and Masarwa. She survives, in that she enters the domain of the "soul" to create, which perhaps is the only value of her marriage to Maru. It removes her from Dilepe where her "enormous vitality" would be wasted on another sort of struggle, and not the one she would choose. Therein lies the only choice she is interested in making. For the rest, she does remain a passive woman and a Masarwa. However, in that she resists as an artist. Head is making a very strong statement about her own priorities and the importance of a woman's artistry. Margaret gives up everything, society, power, economic viability, and independence, but never the inalienable artist in her, which Maru recognizes but cannot curb for she continues to "totally love Moleka," in the "other" room.

What is most crucial to the development of a Third World feminist aesthetic is Head's creation of uncompromising women characters. They marry, they bear children, they struggle to survive as single mothers, but they never give in to their victimhood—indeed they celebrate life through their work. For Margaret Cadmore, it is her paintings. For Dikeledi in "The Collector of Treasures" the joy comes from her children and her working hands, which like Margaret's are artist's hands and can craft whatever is placed in them. In jail, she is able to knit and create beautiful things as she was able to sew and earn her living before she killed her husband. Her jouissance comes from her relationship with her close woman friend, which becomes the treasure she finds, like an artist, amid the ashes.

In *The Collector of Treasures*, one of the most enduring images that Head negotiates is a space for what I have called "women talk." This sphere allows Head to create a theory of women's dialogue by expressing the desire and experience of women in her short stories. Postcolonial feminist discourse is rooted in the experience and desire of women as they struggle and resist enormous odds. Since their identities are tied to that resistance, it takes as many forms as one perceives in Head's narratives.

In *A Question of Power* "the gesture of belonging," after the artist, woman, and exile's horrendous "workout," constitutes the postcolonial woman's aesthetic domain. In her narratives, Head creates that domain, functions in that domain, and presents it to a postcolonial feminist audience. The whole question of power as it relates to individual/societal good and evil is not just appropriated by Head, but, rather, it is "feminized" by her. The "journeys into the soul,'' an aesthetic that had primarily belonged to the patriar-chal persuasion, is unhinged from its old foundation and placed in the center of a woman artist's dialogue with herself and other women. . . .

[In] the histories *Serowe: Village of the Rain Wind* and *A Bewitched Crossroad*, Head's purpose is a little more general, even though she pays special attention to comparing Mackenzie and Hepburn's missionary accounts with those of local Black historians who were still alive when she was doing research for these books. However, she brings to these histories not only a Southern Afri-can's outrage at the recorded accounts of her history but through ''rememory'' and envisioning she is able to create a model for other postcolonial historians. She sees the coincidence between the individual and collective identity creating a model for dialogue in postcolonial nations. In her shorter historical pieces, she is much more specific about challenging local traditional authority over the roles women played in the migratory patterns of several branches of the Bamangwato tribe. In ''The Deep River: A Story of Ancient Tribal Migration,'' Rankwana refuses to take the blame for step-ping outside tradition because as the youngest wife of a very old chief she fell in love with his son and had a child with him. I believe that these stories and other historical data are informed by Head's feminist commitments even though she always hesitated in adopt-ing that title.

What emerges from Head's narratives is a dialogue on several aspects of women's identities. In *A Question of Power*, the text challenges into focus women's sexuality, and even though Head ultimately halts Elizabeth's understanding of her own sexuality by making her reject it altogether, she has carved out a space for women's dialogue with their sexual-political identities.

In the last analysis, Bessie Head, woman writer exiled from South Africa and never allowed to really ''belong'' in Botswana, through her narratives did far more in terms of contributing to postcolonial feminist discourse than anyone has recognized thus far. She is and will remain a pioneer of feminist dialogue and historiography. She began what became a way of talking about postcolonial feminist aesthetic concerns.

Huma Ibrahim. *Bessie Head: Subversive Identities in Exile* (Charleston: University Press of Virginia, 1996), pp. 238–40

BIBLIOGRAPHY

*When Rain Clouds Gather*, 1968; *Maru*, 1971; *A Question of Power*, 1973; *The Collector of Treasures, and Other Botswana Village Tales*, 1977; *Serowe: Village of the Rain Wind*, 1981; *A Bewitched Crossroad*, 1984; *Tales of Tenderness and Power*, 1989; *A Woman Alone: Autobiographical Writings*, 1990; *A Ges-ture of Belonging*, 1991

# HEARNE, John (1926–)

## Jamaica

From the outset John Hearne established himself as a writer of considerable technical competence. *Voices under the Window*, an intensely dramatic story of political intrigue and revolution, is written with the disciplined craftsmanship and skill one seldom

looks for or finds in a writer's first novel. It seemed to augur well for his future and his second novel, *Stranger at the Gate*, more than fulfilled earlier promise and consolidated Hearne's reputation. It was here, in this second book, that he contrived the stage that was to be the setting for all his later novels. Like [George] Lamming, he mapped out an imaginary island in the Caribbean. This he called Cayuna. But it was not a mere sketchy or fanciful province of the imagination. It was a re-creation and extension of his own Jamaica and to the evocation of life on this stage, the life not only of its humans, but of its beasts and birds, its landscape and its legends, Hearne brought to bear a care and skill that seems to be the stamp on everything he has written. . . .

Hearne's characters spring from every level of Cayunan socie-ty, a society which like every society in the Caribbean is a dynamic mixture of the light and dark races and bloods. They are boldly and convincingly drawn. And the technique of unfolding these charac-ters is cinematic. They move before you like on a swiftly spooling reel of action film. They move, too, towards the same dark end and defeat: Roy McKenzie, the dedicated communist leader in *Strang-er at the Gate*; Jojo Rygin, the violent but big-hearted animal in *[The] Faces of Love*; Eleanor Stacey, the young lover in *The Autumn Equinox*—they storm through the pages with hope that bitters into futility through some kind of treachery and betrayal.

Ivan Van Sertima. *Caribbean Writers* (London: New Bea-con Books, 1968), pp. 14–15

From [Hearne's first novel], *Voices Under the Window*, the reader is aware that the writing is not typical of the main current of West Indian literature. [George] Lamming has said that the West Indian novel is peasant; Hearne's are uncompromisingly middle class, and concerned with an intellectual's moral dilemma. Mark Lattimer in this first work is a ''white'' middle-class Jamaican lawyer. Like Roy McKenzie in *Stranger at the Gate*, or Jim Diver in *Autumn Equinox*, Mark has devoted himself to ''the common people.'' . . .

The neat structure of this fable is held within a fast-moving, accomplished piece of storytelling that largely compensates for the somewhat wooden characterization. And if the moral design seems over-neat, it is interesting to note the questions it raises and leaves unanswered. Lattimer becomes politically involved, and all the overt implications are that such involvement is good. But do Lattimer's politics have any real significance, as politics? Speaking of his work to Brysie, his colored mistress, he declares ''the slogans were taking me over . . . after a while (the people) aren't souls any more. They're the New Jamaica or some crap like that.'' And again, ''To do anything worthwhile you have got to do it *alone*.'' His death occurs when he happens to be in Coronation Lane on political business, but Hearne makes it quite clear that he was not killed because he was on political work; his death is a chance, meaningless tragedy that might have occurred if he had never joined the People's Party, and had been in Kingston for some other reason. The hero's conscience impels him to the ''committed'' life, but how far has this any objective meaning? . . .

Behind the meticulous observation we find in Hearne's novels lies his intense nervous energy. The eye hungers for detail after detail. When description gives way to narrative, one has the sense of a brake being let off a high-powered car under full throttle. The scene of the hurricane in *The Faces of Love* is one of the most powerful scenes in Caribbean fiction. The same nervous energy can be seen in his characterization. Like his seeing eye, his characters, too, exist in a heightened state of self-awareness and intensity. Even laughter is said to "spurt," shyness to be "fierce," and people are "deliberately casual." Their humor is muscular, their stalwart wit indomitable. In bed with a dark barmaid, the hero of *Land of the Living* makes bright remarks about a French play. Their intense entities are formalized and made larger than life by their moral purpose in the story. This can be a major limitation. Until *Land of the Living*, their actions are predicted by Hearne's direction; there is little sense of spontaneous human action, the discovery of new and unexpected moral perspectives. At its best, however, Hearne's method gives his characters a sense of heightened significance, the moral drama they play out gains power and meaning from its definition.

> Barrie Davies. In Louis James, ed. *The Islands in Between: Essays on West Indian Literature* (London: Oxford University Press, 1968), pp. 109–11, 114–15

Hearne always remains frankly a middle-class "campus" novelist of a type familiar in America. Indeed, modern American fiction and short-story writing in the *New Yorker* or *Atlantic Monthly* tradition are the dominant influences in Hearne's narrative style, plot-making, and dialogue. He also displays an American relish for the material impedimenta of middle-class living; cars, long drinks, and cigarette lighters gleam and sparkle from his pages. The setting is not so much urban as suburban; for few prosperous Jamaicans, and Hearne's main characters are always prosperous, choose to live in central Kingston. Even in *Land of the Living* his Central European refugee hero, a professor at the university, is consciously making a sortie into another world in his affair with the black bar-keeper, Bernice. It is almost with a sigh of relief that he abandons this secret liaison and turns to a public, socially accepted involvement with the drunken Joan Culpepper, who at least has the merit of being a member of his own set. Thus in Hearne's work the values and social habits of the professional middle class and the masses coexist in the same island but are held consciously apart; any fuller contact between them is conducted deliberately, is never free from tension, and can be broken off at any time as a release from this tension.... The impulse towards democratization which Elsa Goveia has detected in West Indian literature appears to be absent from Hearne's carefully shaped novels. Rather, he is intent on reporting West Indian experience, from a certain viewpoint, to an international English-speaking bourgeois readership. For such a readership his books hold no difficulties of form or style such as [George] Lamming, [Roger] Mais, or [Wilson] Harris may present; they are essentially familiar, and their generally favorable critical reception in the West belongs with this quality. Whereas many exiled West Indian writers create out of their memories of folk experience, Hearne, who lives mainly in Jamaica, reports with more immediacy in time and place but from an angle which somewhat detaches him from the mainstream of popular life.

> Gerald Moore. *The Chosen Tongue* (New York: Harper and Row, 1969), pp. 93–94

The West Indian who comes near to being an exception to the peasant feel is John Hearne. His key obsession is with an agricultural middle class in Jamaica. I don't want to suggest that this group

of people are not a proper subject for fiction; but I've often wondered whether Hearne's theme, with the loaded concern he shows for a mythological, colonial squirearchy, is not responsible for the fact that his work is, at present, less energetic than the West Indian novels at their best. Hearne is a first-class technician, almost perfect within the limitation of conventional storytelling; but the work is weakened, for the language is not being *used*, and the novel as a form is not really being *utilized*. His novels suggest that he has a dread of being identified with the land at peasant level. What he puts into books is always less interesting than the *omissions* which a careful reader will notice he has forced himself to make. He is not an example of the instinct and root impulse which return the better West Indian writers back to the soil. For soil is a large part of what the West Indian novel has brought back to reading; lumps of earth: unrefined, perhaps, but good, warm, fertile earth.

> George Lamming. In Edward Baugh, ed. *Critics on Caribbean Literature* (New York: St. Martin's Press, 1978), p. 26

In *The Autumn Equinox*, John Hearne frames his fictional state of Cayuna with different stages of revolution in Haiti and Cuba. Cayuna harbors the deluded remnant of the reactionary government in Haiti, but the actual state of the new revolutionary government there is not set forth. With Cuba, the Castro revolution is in progress, and Cayuna becomes an innocent base for revolutionary propaganda. Since the government and politics of Cayuna receive no substantial attention, we are thrown out of the novel in two directions: first, we ask what makes Cayuna (née Jamaica) so innocent of revolutionary impulses, and so immune to the ferment all around; and, second, we wonder how to place the historical Haiti and Cuba in the interpretative scheme of *The Autumn Equinox*....

The rational despair of *The Autumn Equinox* is embodied in Nicholas Stacey, the man who refrains from resenting or resisting his lot, as bastard, as abused stepchild, as betrayed brother, as neglected heir. His one chance to see and occupy an unconventional world, that is, one not defined by an authority seated in his disfavor, all but paralyzes him. Old Nick, who has so little of the devil in him, does not so much share as submit to a boundary-shattering engagement with Teresa Galdez, his first wife's sister (intimations of incest partly explain the inaction of the characters, as action is taboo and implicitly directed against the self). He tries to compensate by "adopting" Teresa's daughter, Eleanor, but he is comfortable only as long as she is docile, or in other words a child. He is baffled by her emergence as an independent young woman, and accordingly seeks to send her away or to co-opt her into his business. Her tacit revolution is stymied by her gratitude, her love for him; she finds it easier to let Jim Diver go than to go away from Nick. The unspoken law of familiarity thus yields another version of the ubiquitous indecisiveness of West Indian literature in the revolutionary situation.

> Michael G. Cooke. *Yale Review*. 71, 1 (Autumn 1981), pp. 32–34

John Hearne's *The Faces of Love* and *Land of the Living* are good examples of novels which reveal the state of racial complacency and the sense of community in the West Indian psychological makeup. In both novels Hearne depicts a multiracial society and illustrates that the nature of love has little or nothing to do with racial origins. In both novels love affects the lives of people who pay, at best, only superficial attention to their racial makeup. The characters are aware of themselves and each other as persons, without having to undergo the process of racial identity (or even the search for it). Still, their sense of community is strong, and in their interactions they confront complex social and political issues without calling attention to the possible connections between these issues and race.

In *The Faces of Love* Rachel Ascom, the black daughter of a German woman, treats material values as the only mirror which can reflect her essence and thereby validate her existence. The possibility of pride in either aspect of her racial makeup never pierces her consciousness. ''I am nothing, you see,'' she tells Fabricus, who is one of her many past lovers and the narrator of the novel. ''I come from nothing and none of you people will ever forget that when I make a mistake. Everything I become I've got to show. That's why I buy such good clothes. Every time I spend ten times what I should on clothes it's like a standard I set myself.''

Because of her deep-seated insecurity, Rachel ''uses love as a compensatory exercise of power.'' While her black lover, Jojo Rygin, is in prison, Rachel initiates a romantic relationship with a white Englishman, Michael Lovelace. Soon after, Jojo is released and Rachel begins to manipulate the love triangle. The forceful and ebullient Jojo feels sure that his coming wealth will be sufficient grounds for Rachel's choosing to marry him. Meanwhile, Michael, a newcomer to the West Indian scene, undergoes no psychological changes as a result of his participation in the activities of this West Indian community—he is the editor of the island's leading newspaper, *Newsletter*. He is affected only by his love for Rachel, which seems, like himself, unconnected to any particular cultural reality (his or Rachel's). In fact, Hearne intentionally contrives an interracial and intercultural love triangle and then proceeds, presumably just as intentionally, to avoid confrontation with the possible implications of such a situation. Indeed, such implications are irrelevant to Hearne's thematic concerns.

> Melvin B. Rahming. *The Evolution of the West Indian's Image in the Afro-American Novel* (Millwood, New York: Associated Faculty Press, 1986), pp. 78–79

Hearne's first five novels end with the affirmation that integration is possible for his educated, middle-class characters, and this integration is based upon the strength of one's immediate relationships with others; the uneasy guilt of Mark Lattimer has been replaced with the intimate world of Stefan and Joan. Yet the peace seems an uneasy one, since basic questions, such as whether the social structure of Cayuna will survive the disparities within it, are left unanswered. Moreover, the underlying tension that exists is presented by Hearne himself: the texture of his novels allows for the darker sides of West Indian society to be presented by such characters as Johnson in *Stranger at the Gate*, by Heneky in *Land of the Living*, and by the riot in *Voices under the Window*, for example. Overall, however, the vision is positive: after *Voices*, the resolution of the novels is consistently toward the comic. . . .

It is with this in mind that one turns to examine the world of *The Sure Salvation*, published twenty years after *Land of the Living*. There are several departures from the patterns established in Hearne's earlier novels: the context is no longer contemporary West Indian society; the setting carries symbolic and allegorical overtones; and Hearne has altered the narrative style to allow himself to wander through an unprecedented number of intimately presented characters. In viewing the work from the aspect of integration, one is struck by the reversal of the positive note established by the earlier works. Isolation and fragmentation are paramount; each character, as Edward Baugh writes, revolves on his own ''particular, obsessive, flawed center of self.'' This point is more importantly illustrated by the relationship between the two most powerful men on board, Hogarth and Alex, since a personal betrayal is the result of five years of working together in what Hogarth thought was mutual trust. Yet it is not only the individual failure of each that work against the type of friendship Hearne has described in positive terms in earlier works. At the central point of betrayal, Hogarth launches into a denunciation that goes beyond the immediate and personal to a racial and social statement with a hint that the breakdown is predestined, a fact of their difference in race. . . . Hogarth and Alex both exit unreconciled and separate, Hogarth to trial and prison, Alex very much alive on the very mainland on which he has planned to establish his kingdom. There are no real heroes in this novel, though it is Hogarth who comes closest to the protagonists of earlier novels. It is a significant break in the pattern that this time it is the protagonist who is left on the outside with nothing achieved: the darker side has finally triumphed.

> David Ingledew. In Daryl Cumber Dance, ed. *Fifty Caribbean Writers* (Westport, Connecticut.: Greenwood Press, 1986), pp. 202–3

John Hearne's novel, *The Sure Salvation*, focuses upon the traumatic historical events which have given birth to what is now the West Indies. The action occurs on a barque ironically named the *Sure Salvation* which is being used to take an illegal shipment of slaves from Africa to Brazil in 1860. Hearne's depiction of the bewildered sensibility and horrific condition of the slaves is remarkably unsentimental; he captures both their plight and their peculiar dignity in a fashion so objective as to render their abominable physical condition and spiritual malaise as distanced. A peculiar mist or opaque glass seems to stand between them and our perceiving eye. Hearne realizes that the cruel fact of slavery is a grotesquerie that the human consciousness can only approach or conceive in vague shadows or tearful glimpses if we are not to despair of humanity's future by succumbing to the cruel legacies of the past. This rendition, strangely enough, simultaneously heightens and diminishes the suffocation and immobilization which the slaves are made to suffer. . . .

In *The Sure Salvation*, John Hearne shows that the erosion of self—the reality of individuality in the process of becoming the void of self—is itself an illusion if it is seen in terms of immediate and total loss. Rather, there is a *metamorphosis* of self, an evolution of consciousness which is necessitated and compelled by human endurance even in the furnace of apocalyptic occurrence.

> Daizal R. Samad. *World Literature Written in English*. 30, 1 (Spring 1990), pp. 11–12

## BIBLIOGRAPHY

*Voices under the Window*, 1955; *Stranger at the Gate*, 1956; *The Faces of Love*, 1957; *The Autumn Equinox*, 1959; *Land of the Living*, 1961; *The Sure Salvation*, 1981

# HEATH, Roy A. K. (1926–)
## Guyana

The fiction of Roy A. K. Heath includes, so far, several short stories and four novels: *A Man Come Home, The Murderer, From the Heat of the Day*, and *One Generation*. The readers of these works tend to be struck immediately by certain aspects of the author's style. Reviewers are quick to home in on Heath's extremely realistic portrayal of his fictional world: the city of Georgetown, Guyana and outlying towns and villages, and the language, activities, and concerns of the characters. . . .

Apart from the ironic, there are hints of a tragic mode in the novels as well. In all four novels the main protagonists are relentlessly thwarted in their plans and modest aspirations, and they are eventually destroyed—three of them end up dead and the other insane. These characters can command, on occasion, the tragic gesture, but for the most part we watch them flailing helplessly in their domestic webs and we do not really see in them the stature or self-knowledge of the tragic protagonist—they are more victims than heroes and it appears as though their ironic presentation diminishes or qualifies the sense of tragedy. . . .

*From the Heat of the Day* is the first [novel] of a projected trilogy, of which the second, *One Generation*, has also appeared. The trilogy is about the events and fortunes of the Armstrong family and the first novel takes us back to the 1920s, to the point where Armstrong is courting Gladys. He is from a village and of a status socially inferior to that of his wife, whose family lives in the desirable Queenstown section of Georgetown. . . .

[*One Generation*] is divided into two quite distinct parts; the first part completes the business of *From the Heat of the Day*, in that it is concerned with the decline and death of Armstrong and the rising to full maturity of his two children—especially Rohan. The second part concerns the brief and tragic life of Rohan after his father dies.

Armstrong's decline is almost baroque in its horror, and is an ironic reversal of his earlier life. Here we find him bullied by his children, forced to appear in rags because his children seek to prevent him from spending all his pension on drink by insisting that he buy his own clothes, contracting filaria which causes his feet to swell, developing a horrible personal odor which can't be obliterated, and, finally, falling into the clutches of a stern woman of some dubious religion who ministers to his illness and to what is left of his soul. All the fates he strove to avoid befall him in the end, emphasized by the force of Heath's irony and in turn emphasizing the extent to which any control he may have exerted over his life in the past was transient and illusory. He dies the victim he always was; we are not even spared such final details of his degradation as the fact that the horse that drew the hearse "defecated copiously" as Armstrong's coffin was removed from it. Nevertheless, to emphasize that even at the point of death there is a simultaneity of the ridiculous and the grandiose, in a flourish of "atmospherics" reminiscent of [Edgar] Mittelholzer, there's a terrible storm on the night of Armstrong's death.

Mark A. McWatt. In Erika Sollish Smilowitz and Roberta Quarles Knowles, eds. *Critical Issues in West Indian Literature* (Parkersburg, Iowa: Caribbean Books, 1984), pp. 54–56, 58, 62–63

Through seven novels in ten years, Roy Heath has laid claim to being *the* chronicler of urban life in Guyana. In *Orealla*, his latest work, set in 1927, the sights and sounds and smells and gossipy surface of life in Georgetown are convincingly rendered by Heath: the gorgeous tropical flora, the tones of the Stabroek tower clock, the stench of the open sewage in trenches dissecting the city, the "Creolese" spoken by Heath's lower-class characters. Along with these things he effectively exposes the inhumane aspects of caste and color conventions in Guyana.

In addition, Heath often writes beautifully; there is, for instance, the long dreamy paragraph . . . about Ben, his central character, recollecting his childhood at Skeldon and thinking of freedom and "that calm the aboriginal Indians had always known, that had never ceased to elude him." This elusive contentment is embodied in his friend Carl, the detached, independent, nonmaterialistic Amerindian who eventually forsakes Ben and drifts back to his home settlement of Orealla.

Robert E. McDowell. *World Literature Today.* 59, 2 (Spring 1985), p. 310

Roy Heath's first published novel, *A Man Come Home*, is an unusual work of West Indian fiction in that it does not have any large historical or sociological view or argument to present; rather, it encloses the reader within a very powerfully evoked world of the range yards and the poorer housing areas of Georgetown, Guyana, and it concentrates on the actual processes of life and experience within this context.

The "man" referred to in the book's title is Bird Foster, but neither he nor any other character in the novel achieves the status of hero or even main protagonist. Heath presents instead members of the Foster family—and their yard-dwelling friends and neighbors—and concentrates upon portraying their relationships and experiences in a thoroughly convincing way. As one critic has remarked, the novel "projects a sharp sense of time lived, giving the texture of experience so subtly that the reader is enchanted into accepting the world of the novel as his own.". . .

It is perhaps appropriate that *A Man Come Home* should be the first novel published, for in this book Heath displays most of the major themes and concerns that dominate the later works. Already in this novel one has the sense of the family or household and its domestic concerns as somehow central to the work's design and the locus of curiously powerful emotions and conflicts. It is the context of actions that are frequently tragic in their consequences. Heath exposes the accumulated animosities and frustrations within the domestic situation as well as the sudden explosions of violence that they ultimately precipitate. In this novel, for example, we see the gathering mistrust and animosity between Foster's mistress Christine and their daughter Melda as the girl (the last child) grows older and more independent. When Melda announces that she is pregnant and refuses to discuss it with Christine, Heath portrays, in his powerful, understated technique, how the mother's anger and anxiety over flow into violence. . . .

In *The Murderer* the novelist's focus is somewhat narrower, the psychological portrait of Galton Flood more intense and relentless. There is no doubt here that Galton is the central figure of the work, and while the reader still finds himself firmly in touch with the urban landscape of Georgetown, he also finds himself inside the mind of Galton. Heath probes far more insistently into the shaping influences and motivation of his main character than he did in *A Man Come Home*. What we find, as this relentless exploration proceeds in the novel, is something that we would have suspected from the earlier work: that the domestic household and the interweave of relationships therein can be sinister and frightening and their effects destructive in the extreme.

Mark A. McWatt. In Daryl Cumber Dance, ed. *Fifty Caribbean Writers* (Westport, Connecticut: Greenwood Press, 1986), pp. 209–11

Roy Heath is a contemporary West Indian novelist whose work commands serious attention. It provokes interesting speculation about where he fits in the tradition of the West Indian novel developed in the 1950s by writers such as Edgar Mittelholzer, George Lamming, Samuel Selvon, V. S. Naipaul, and Wilson Harris. Since 1974 when his first novel, *A Man Come Home*, was published, he has produced six other novels, three of which, *From the Heat of the Day, One Generation*, and *Genetha*, make up his ambitious Guyana trilogy. . . .

Heath's fiction is not overtly concerned with the theme of nationalism, or of the search for a West Indian identity, or of the heritage of colonialism, or of independence and its aftermath. He is not especially interested in history, at least not in the manner of Mittelholzer. He does not see history as a simple series of cause and effect because characters are often not sure why they have acted in a certain way. For Heath, human motives are usually complicated and often contradictory. His people have to struggle to survive in society because they are poor, and because they are separated from each other by considerations of class and sex. They have difficulty understanding their own natures and the urges that both drive and inhibit them.

On the one hand, this tendency to ignore so many of the themes that are central to West Indian writing might suggest that Heath is out of touch with the important issues in the life of the area, possibly because he is an expatriate. On the other hand, it might indicate that he is so self-consciously Guyanese and West Indian that he can see the struggle to survive in the Caribbean as not simply a regional problem but as a form of anguish shared in differing degrees by people everywhere in all periods of history. Heath deals with the materially poor and the dispossessed, but one senses from his fiction that the state of dispossession is not peculiar to the poor and is the inevitable condition of life in general. . . . Freedomlessness is an affliction of all his people. Genetha, the central character of the last novel of Heath's trilogy, speaks for them thus: "For me that's the problem. Freedom and the secret of a settled mind."

In this trilogy, Heath uses a structure that is episodic—indeed this is true of all his novels—and in *From the Heat of the Day*, the narrative often switches abruptly from the relationship of the husband and the wife, to examine relationships Armstrong has with his men friends with whom he goes drinking and whoring, and with the whores whose company he seeks out. Sometimes the relationships of Gladys and her servants, Esther and Marion, are focused on. This method of short, jerky chapters emphasizes the fragmented, paranoid states of the people in Heath's world. The general impact of this method, however, is one of concentration rather than diffusion because the episodes with Armstrong and his friends, and

Gladys with the servants repeat with variations what is going on between husband and wife.

Anthony Boxill. *World Literature Written in English*. 29, 1 (Spring 1989), pp. 103–5, 108

Roy Heath's latest work [*Shadows Round the Moon*] is described as "the first volume of his autobiography": it ends (like V. S. Naipaul's *Miguel Street*) with his departure for England at about age twenty.

The initial half has . . . reminiscences of colonial life and Caribbean culture, with occasional reproductions of Guyanese dialect conversation; but the observations seldom transcend the superficial, and the reconstruction of personal experiences does not take on a dimension exceeding the purely individual. Nevertheless, there are some insights into the social life of the sole anglophone country of South America. . . .

The second half of the volume makes amends for the shortcomings of the first: there are several perspicacious observations on religion, family relationships, and colonial administrators, and postcolonial manners and aspirations are occasionally alluded to. Here too are to be found examples of the author's skill at inventing impressive similes: "The first pleasure at being chosen for a post in the Treasury wore off like a woman's make-up in a persistent downpour" is one: another is "The psyche, like an ancient book whose pages rustle at night and disturb our sleep." Equally interesting, however, are the dicta on Guyanese society, where the "town, the graveyard of all cultures" is subjected to as much criticism as "the civil service," which "represented the ambition of a class, which saw in it a guarantee of material security." Some of these views are supported; unfortunately, no support is offered for the view that the 1832 abolition of slavery "was absurdly attributed to the efforts of the antislavery societies."

A. L. McLeod. *World Literature Today*. 64, 4 (Autumn 1991), pp. 753–54

[In *Shadows Round the Moon*] Heath suggests that his fascination with the hidden and the grotesque arose as a reaction against the prohibitions of a Creole society riddled with "secrets and secret places." His protagonists characteristically pursue restless dreams of freedom and independence, but their quest leads them in an ironic cycle, into themselves and the patterns of their past. Heath's employment of a constantly shifting viewpoint suggests the impossibility of an individual seeing himself clearly or comprehending his relation to others. The greatest strength of Heath as a writer, perhaps, is his ability to convey the complexity of the individual, through a loose, episodic narrative strategy that conceals as much as it reveals. His style, occasionally florid and artificial in the earlier novels, has grown increasingly controlled and ironic: it is a style, comments another contemporary Guyanese writer, Wilson Harris, "that truncates emotion." . . .

The Guyana of Heath's sixth novel, *Kwaku; or, The Man Who Could Not Keep His Mouth Shut*, is a country in a state of collapse, with rampant "chokean'-rob," a tottering rural economy, and the omnipresent governing party. For Kwaku Cholmondley, a shoemaker in the village of "C," the only defense is an air of idiocy, though Kwaku is privately convinced of his special mission in life, "a journey to be undertaken." Pursuing respectability, he marries

Miss Gwendoline, who bears him eight children, yet Kwaku gains no reputation until—forced to leave the village after a plague of locusts destroys its one cash crop—he attains success as a healer in New Amsterdam.

There Kwaku has little more going for him than a few garlic concoctions, a sense of ritual, and the common touch. He is convinced of his worthlessness, though to the villagers in "C" he has become a man of reputation. His insecure need to command respect leads to his downfall: he fails to fulfill a rash promise made to a fisherman, who retaliates by blinding Miss Gwendoline with an obeah curse. Back in New Amsterdam, Kwaku's herbal practice languishes, he is beaten up by his own sons, and he ends up touring the rum shops, capering for dollar bills. The narrative tone of *Kwaku* passes skillfully, almost imperceptibly, from comic to tragic, yet Kwaku is, finally, a heroic character, loyal to his family to the end and able to cope with misfortune by accepting it, even as his country "seemed to be sinking under its weight of debt and ambitions."...

The bride in Heath's *The Shadow Bride* is Mrs. Singh, who has come to Guyana from South India as bride to a wealthy, if disreputable, Guyanese. Once free of her husband—gossip has it she poisoned him—she becomes an authoritarian figure in her household, determined to control her son, Betta, and the assortment of servants and "hangers-on." Like many of Heath's characters, Mrs. Singh is trapped in images of the past: her nostalgia for her Indian home is so strong she raises Betta apart from other children, until he complains that he knows more of Kerala than Guyana....

Betta's journal, which he has begun in order to record his medical studies, becomes a means of self-exploration, through which he understands the way he is intricately bound not only to the East Indian community at its point of crisis, as thousands of East Indians desert the estates for the city with the end of indenture, but to his mother, whose crisis he had failed to recognize: "he had seen fit to ignore his mother's plea for help, he, who did not hesitate to speak of ideals." If mother and son are both confined by their past, Betta, fortified by a disintegrating but still powerful communal tradition, is able to recognize and accept the irony of his motivations without submitting to despair: "He could not," the novel concludes, "have acted otherwise."...

Heath's eight novels have added a new dimension to the literary map of Guyana, complementing Wilson Harris's fantastic journeys into the Guyanese hinterland. Heath has become a novelist of international stature by remaining in compassionate contact with the world he knows best.... His work may be "indelibly Guyanese," but it belongs also to "the small group of works that make the reader understand more about the nature of human suffering and violence."

Ian H. Munro. In Bernth Lindfors and Reinhard Sander, eds. *Dictionary of Literary Biography,* Vol. 117 (Detroit: Gale Research, 1992), pp. 199, 201–3

Through all his adventures, Kwaku keeps up his cheerful spirit of independence. The contrast between his voice and the narrator's complex moral musings lends *The Ministry of Hope* a darker, more sardonic flavor than its predecessor. "A high proportion of Kwaku's consultations were sought by tourists who, having heard of his reputation while on holiday in the islands, came to him complaining of sham illnesses with portable tape recorders and requests for interviews," the author informs us. "They loved everyone and everything they set eyes on and would have elevated Kwaku to the rank of saint had he not insisted on being paid. They came nonetheless, insisting that nothing was more picturesque than images of poverty."

Kwaku comes from a long line of literary buffoons who manage to triumph over the "intelligent" people around them. The language Mr. Heath employs to describe this process is luxurious and densely baroque in places, sweetly comic in others. The hero's clowning conceals an essential wisdom and goodness. In the end, he is unable to become as hardened and corrupt as the people he tries so desperately to emulate, and in this lies his greatest success.

*New York Times Book Review,* May 11, 1997, p. 33.

BIBLIOGRAPHY
*A Man Come Home,* 1974; *The Murderer,* 1978; *From the Heat of the Day,* 1979; *Genetha,* 1981; *One Generation,* 1981; *Kwaku: or, The Man Who Could Not Keep His Mouth Shut,* 1982; *Art and Experience,* 1983; *Orealla,* 1984; *The Shadow Bride,* 1988; *Shadows Round the Moon,* 1990; *The Armstrong Trilogy,* 1994; *The Ministry of Hope, or, The Metamorphosis of Kwaku: A Novel,* 1996

# HIMES, Chester (1909–1984)
## United States

[In *If He Hollers Let Him Go*] Himes pits an educated, Northern Negro against poor Southern whites in a West Coast shipyard, and the results are violent and shocking. The author's stripped and functional prose style, developed in the slick magazines, takes on a new quality when it describes, in psychological terms, the contrast between a Negro believing in democracy and the brutal realities of our industrial system. In the end, Robert Jones, the hero, is crucified on a cross of chromium and steel....

Jerky in pace, *If He Hollers Let Him Go* has been compared with the novels of James M. Cain, but there is more honest passion in 20 pages of Himes than in the whole of Cain. Tough-minded Himes has no illusions: I doubt if he has ever had any. He sees too clearly to be fooled by the symbolic guises in which Negro behavior tries to hide, and he traces the transformations by which sex is expressed in equations of race pride, murder in the language of personal redemption and love in terms of hate.

To read Himes conventionally is to miss the significance of the (to coin a phrase) bio-social level of his writing. Bob Jones is so charged with elementary passion that he ceases to be a personality and becomes a man reacting only with nerves, blood and motor responses.

Ironically, the several dreams that head each chapter do not really come off. Indeed, Himes's brutal prose is more authentically dreamlike than his consciously contrived dreams. And that is as it should be.

In this, his first, novel, Himes establishes himself not as what has been quaintly called a New Negro, but as a new kind of writing man.

Richard Wright. *PM.* November 25, 1945, pp. m7–m8

In *If He Hollers Let Him Go*, published in 1945, Chester Himes studied, with rage and sometimes with disturbing perception, the struggle and defeat of one Negro war-worker on the West Coast, our native tensions intensified by war and the protagonist's relationships with his upper-class mulatto girl and the sexual tensions between himself and a female white war-worker. It was one of those books for which it is difficult to find any satisfactory classification: not a good novel but more than a tract, relentlessly honest, and carried by the fury and the pain of the man who wrote it. It seemed to me then one of the few books written by either whites or Negroes about Negroes which considered the enormous role which white guilt and tension play in what has been most accurately called the American dilemma.

*Lonely Crusade* can almost be considered an expansion of the earlier novel. Much of the rage is gone and with it the impact, and the book is written in what is probably the most uninteresting and awkward prose I have read in recent years. Yet the book is not entirely without an effect and is likely to have an importance out of all proportion to its intrinsic merit. For, just as the earlier book was carried by rage, this book is carried by what seems to be a desperate, implacable determination to find out the truth, please God, or die.

In less than four hundred pages Mr. Himes undertakes to consider the ever-present subjective and subconscious terror of a Negro, a dislocation which borders on paranoia; the political morality of American Communists; the psychology of union politics; Uncle Tomism; Jews and Negroes; the vast sexual implications of our racial heritage; the difficulty faced by any Negro in his relationships with both light people and dark; and the position of the American white female in the whole unlovely structure. This is a tall order and if we give Mr. Himes an A for ambition—and a rather awe-stricken gasp for effort—we are forced also to realize that the book's considerable burden never really gets shoulder high. It is written almost as though the author were determined within one book, regardless of style or ultimate effect, to say all of the things he wanted to say about the American republic and the position of the Negro in it. Part of the failure of the book certainly lies in this fact, that far too much is attempted. . . .

The value of his book lies in its earnest effort to understand the psychology of oppressed and oppressor and their relationship to each other.

James Baldwin. *New Leader*. October 25, 1947, p. 11

This reviewer was impressed by the controlled force of Mr. Himes' earlier novel, *Cast the First Stone*. Now *The Third Generation* has been published, a far less skillfully modulated work which yet seizes the reader with a strong, if incoherent impact of its own. Much obviously autobiographical truth and a great deal of agonized sincerity has gone into the writing of it. . . .

Mr. Himes' difficulty stems from the fact that his novel is not one but two. *The Third Generation* starts as a basically robust saga of a family's search for a place in the sun. Its view point is collective; it projects an acquisitive, restless and dynamic psyche. But suddenly the author changes focus. The narrative acquires an abrupt Oedipal undercurrent. Mr. Himes' camera focuses exclusively on Charles and his relationship to his mother. Thus the excesses at the end sometimes read like gratuitous melodrama.

Chalk it up to Mr. Himes' narrative talent, then, that his novel always lives and sometimes fascinates despite the bifurcation and

despite a rather rough-hewn style. Count it as Mr. Himes' even greater merit that he has not written merely a protest novel. In this novel the suffering of the Negro is not for a propaganda end. It is rather a means of dramatizing all human fear and hatred of which prejudice is only a particularly shameful expression. It is this attitude on the author's part that lends his story much of its homely power.

Frederic Morton. *New York Herald Tribune Books*. January 10, 1954, p. 6

Chester Himes' *If He Hollers Let Him Go* is an impressive failure—with accent on the adjective. It takes the novel of pure race consciousness to its utmost limit, where it strangles to death in its own contradictions. The novel is Wrightian to the core, which is hardly surprising in view of the author's background and experience. . . .

In its denouement the novel reveals a fatal structural flaw. Here is a black nationalist, hypersensitive, neurotic, unable to mobilize his energies for anything but the race war, driven by his obsession to the brink of murder. The whole novel moves inexorably toward the opposing view that some kind of accommodation is the price of sanity. The protagonist chooses; he is born again; but suddenly we are confronted with a chain of events whose logic seems to justify his former view of reality.

Earlier in the novel, Himes has argued convincingly that in every human being there is an inner world which lies within his power to control. Is it now his thesis that in all crucial matters concerning a Negro's fate, the will of society is decisive? If so, we feel put upon, for we have been following Jones' inner conflict as if it mattered. Suddenly it is revealed as meaningless—no matter what Jones decides, society will dispose of his future. Such a thesis requires that the tensions of the novel be resolved on a sociological plane; the very basis of a psychological novel is destroyed.

At bottom the trouble is ideological: neither revenge nor accommodation is acceptable to Himes, and as a result, the novel flounders to an inconclusive finish.

Robert A. Bone. *The Negro Novel in America* (New Haven: Yale University Press, 1958), pp. 173, 175–76

Himes's earlier novels were partly autobiographical, or at least based on the author's experiences. Using the methods of traditional novelistic psychology combined with the instantaneous imagery that has been the rule in American literature since Dos Passos, Himes has no trouble creating verisimilitude, and sometimes the sincerity of these novels is moving. Their shortcoming, as I have said, is that they support or illustrate a *thesis*, which is correct but which we think we already knew (our mistake). We quickly grow weary—or perhaps it is our guilty conscience, as when someone speaks to us about the Algerian war. The truth is, nevertheless, that an unhappy destiny, a destiny that contains nothing but misfortune, engages our interest only when it is enhanced by genius . . . . On the other hand, Himes's detective novels, or rather picaresque novels, aim at entertainment—and through the narrative alone. . . .

Himes submits to a genre, the mystery novel, and he observes its conventions. Novel after novel, we follow the incessant struggle of cops against crooks and crooks against one another. His plots owe little to mathematics, to the logic of a detective story; much to light opera and to shifts in point of view; he is closer to James Hadley Chase than to Agatha Christie. . . .

[In his mystery novels] Himes does not burden himself with a moral. He tells stories. It is up to us to laugh and, if we like, to think.

René Micha. *Les temps moderne.* February 1965, pp. 1512–13, 1522–23

Chester Himes has mellowed, in the direction of humour, since his earlier effort, *If He Hollers Let Him Go*, a book violently black-versus-white, full of hot-tempered fistfights, bitterness, tragedy, and above all hatred. *Cotton Comes to Harlem* is a rollicking, funny book that begins with a Back-to-Africa movement launched in New York's Harlem. . . .

Chester Himes is an American Negro, born in Jefferson City, Missouri, and now living in France. One can understand why he chooses to live in France. Mr. Himes may be a funny writer, but he is also a novelist, and even in a book like this—with a laugh on nearly every page—it is evident he is concerned with the Negro's plight in Harlem, aware of every corruption from whores and dope-addiction to mere urine-stained walls, aware of the unkillable hope in the minds of many of these people and of the hopelessness of their situation as it is now. He can poke fun at white and black alike—as when a white policeman is slowly seduced by an undressing Negro beauty whom he's supposed to guard. It is his value as a writer, and it makes this book a novel, that he can jest at all of it, make stiletto social comments, and keep his story running at the speed of one of his Buick ''Roadmasters'' in the days of yore.

*Times Literary Supplement.* January 20, 1966, p. 37

Chester Himes is one of the most prolific of all Negro novelists. At this writing, he is the author of six major novels and a number of lively potboilers about a couple of Harlem detectives. Although he enjoys a good reputation in France, where he now lives, for the most part the American critics have dismissed him as being of the Wright school of naturalism, whose ''protest'' is no longer fashionable. Such criticism is not altogether fair. Himes's interests are considerably different from Wright's, and his firsthand knowledge of certain areas of American life is more developed. His protagonists are generally middle-class, fairly well-educated, somewhat sophisticated in the ways of the world, and often intellectually oriented. They are concerned with ideas and the application of ideas to their experience; they are constantly searching out rational explanations for the irrationalities of their lives. They move with considerable aplomb among white liberals and radicals of both sexes, and engage them in dialectics on their own terms. Himes is also a more deliberate prose stylist than Wright. He seldom intrudes, moralizes, or explains. His characters are usually sufficiently articulate to say what they mean—and what they mean issues often enough from their character and intelligence. Himes does parallel Wright in his bitterness, fury, and frustration. He has given up on America, and rarely returns now on visits. . . .

[*The Primitive*] is Himes's most pessimistic work. He has lost faith in the human capacity to reason its way out of its dilemmas. Jesse and Kriss, two intelligent human beings, are as muddled and distressed about their own identities as the worst racists. But here lies the trouble. Himes has, in a curious way, written two books—one about Jesse and Kriss, and one about racist America—and the two do not quite mesh, because Jesse and Kriss are too atypical and too idiosyncratic. Himes's ideas require a novel with a wider scope than one shabby Harlem tenement, one Gramercy Park apartment, and a few decadent intellectuals. Whether or not he will succeed in writing such a novel remains to be seen.

Edward Margolies. *Native Sons* (Philadelphia: J. B. Lippincott, 1968), pp. 87–88, 99

Himes is perhaps the single greatest naturalistic American writer living today. Of course, no one in the literary establishment is going to admit that; they haven't and they won't. Reviews of his books generally wind up in the last half of the Sunday *New York Times Book Review*, if they are reviewed at all. Himes will tell you that he doesn't care; that all his career he has been shuffled under the table. Perhaps this is, after all, the smallest of hurts he has suffered. . . .

It gave me the greatest pleasure to be able to see Himes again, to see him at a time when a kind of physical comfort was coming his way at last; to see him still producing long, articulate and sensitive works. He let me read the first volume of his autobiography, *The Quality of Hurt* (394 pages, ending in 1955). It is a fantastic, masculine work whose pages are haunted by vistas of France and Spain, of family life in the United States, of his first marriage, of Richard Wright and Robert Graves and others. American male writers don't produce manly books. Himes' autobiography is that of a man.

John A. Williams. *Flashbacks* (Garden City, New York: Doubleday, 1973), pp. 294–95, 297

Himes chose his title, *The Quality of Hurt*, from Shakespeare's, ''The quality of mercy is not strain'd/It droppeth as the gentle rain from heaven,'' and the chapters and Books are connected to each other by ''hurts'' Himes endured in a long History of Hurts. He was hurt by his mother, a strong-willed, highly-intelligent woman who could handle a pistol so well, she ''beat anybody to the draw.'' She taught Himes and his brothers so expertly that when they entered school they were ahead of their classes, but she also ''squeezed the bridges of our noses to keep them from becoming flat.''

He was hurt by the reception to his writing, especially *Lonely Crusade*, the adverse criticism of which was one of the major factors leading to his exile. He was hurt by accidents so unbelievable as to lead one to compare the plight of the Himes family to the fictional Gothic ones, laboring under a curse. A chemistry accident almost totally blinded his brother, Joseph; the tormented relationship between his mother and father led to their divorce. He was hurt by a judge who sentenced him to 20-to-25 years for armed robbery, and he was hurt by his inability to support his Black wife, Jean. . . .

One of the remarkable things about *The Quality of Hurt* [is] the absence of rancor and self-pity. . . .

As for his capacity to calmly narrate these Hurts without cloying, Himes writes, ''I hate exhibiting my wounds.''. . .

Chester Himes is a great writer and a brave man. His life has shown that Black writers are as heroic as the athletes, entertainers, scientists, cowboys, pimps, gangsters, and politicians they might write about. Many Blacks have given Himes a bad time but his belief in the excellence and uniqueness of American Blacks continued unmitigated. . . .

The achievement of volume I is even more staggering when you realize that another volume is on the way. Surely, that will be an additional monster destined to mind slam the reader.

Ishmael Reed. *Black World.* March 1972, pp. 25, 35, 86

The five novels Himes wrote between 1958 and 1961 [*For Love of Imabelle, The Crazy Kill, The Real Cool Killers, All Shot Up*, and *The Big Gold Dream*] are classic detective stories. Each poses a problem, or a series of problems, usually expressed in hideous physical violence, which extends its corruption into personal and communal life, and threatens the always precarious balance by which individuals survive in Harlem. Each network of dangerous mysteries is explained by a single discovery of guilt, which restores that balance and redefines the worth of those characters with whom we sympathize. The discovery, of course, is made by Grave Digger and Coffin Ed, the heroic figures who embody all the attributes of the traditional literary detective. Opposed by violence and unreason, they struggle courageously to uncover truth; trapped in a hopelessly venal institution, they remain incorruptibly honest; burdened with a body of law ludicrously inappropriate to the conditions of Harlem life, they are lonely dispensers of justice. They implement most of their solutions outside the law; many of their methods defy it. The responsibilities and dangers involved in the search for decency rest upon them personally rather than upon the institutional apparatus which supposedly protects them.

But Grave Digger and Coffin Ed are more than familiar literary heroes; their cultural antecedents ultimately give them the moral authority they exercise. Simply enough, they are the ''bad niggers'' of Black Folklore . . . . Like all ''bad niggers'' they may seem at first glance improbable (or undesirable) models for humanity. But the ''bad nigger'' is an emotionally projected rather than a socially functional figure; he is valuable as a symbol of defiance, strength, and masculinity to a community that has been forced to learn, or at least to sham, weakness and compliance. As ''bad niggers'' Coffin Ed and Grave Digger are part of the continuing evolution of a black hero, and are thus studies in cultural lore rather than examples of individual character. In the Harlem series they lay all of their traditional qualifications on the line in a desperate fight against the crimes that endanger the integrity, even the collective sanity, of the black community.

Raymond Nelson. *Virginia Quarterly Review.* Spring 1972, pp. 265–67

I know that Chester, whose friendship I value highly, is puzzled and annoyed by the comparative indifference of the American public to his books. At World and at Putnam's we paid him modest advances. We recovered our investment, not from hardback sales, but from the paper-back reprints. But the reprints, in turn, did not fare well. It is very hard to find any of Himes' paperbacks in the bookshops of America, although most of them are in print. Luckily, this is not true in Europe, especially France. The French readers love him. Gallimard, the foremost publishing house in France, publishes Himes' books with profit. Chester Himes is a VIP in Paris as anyone can see who visits the French bookshops. This is also true in Barcelona.

Himes has talent to burn: he has wit, a fine comic sense, an understanding of scenic values; he's an inventive plotter; his characters are alive and easy to become involved with: his stories have action, animal heat, tension. He also usually has something vital to say. Added up, he should be popular in America. But he isn't. . . .

As an author his reward must come soon—I mean his American reward. Meanwhile, his *critical* reception continues good; the critics and the aficionados love and understand him and his worth. When his autobiography is completed and published (possibly in 1976) some dramatic changes may occur for him—for the better.

William Targ. *Indecent Pleasures* (New York: Macmillan, 1975), pp. 291–92

To mention humor at all in discussing a novel that ends with a drunken murder scene seems macabre, but *The Primitive*, while tragic in outline, is filled with incidents and conversations that are handled with ironic Rabelaisian gusto. Gargantuan drinking and eating scenes are described in a style that effectively blends the high and the low, and the literary allusion and street language are combined in a manner that makes *The Primitive*, despite its gruesomeness, more engaging than any of Himes's earlier novels. It is also a work in which Himes pushes to conclusion, in a psychologically satisfying way, two themes of frustration that had haunted him since *If He Hollers Let Him Go*: his anger at being rejected as a writer, and the black man's obsession with the white woman and what she represents. For Himes, *The Primitive* represents a stopping point, an end to his confessional phase, and a settling of scores. . . .

It is the last of his confessional novels and ends the autobiographical emphasis that occasionally interferes with the structure of his work. The novel was finished in Europe and coincides with Himes's rejection of the United States and his desire for a different kind of life in a different culture free from American ''alchemy'' and the pressures that drove Jesse Robinson to destroy himself in the process of becoming ''equal.''

James Lundquist. *Chester Himes* (New York: Frederick Ungar, 1976), pp. 93, 105

As a writer of detective stories, Himes does not get high marks when he is measured against the narrow parameters against which such fiction is usually judged. He does not dwell on deep, mysterious secrets, international conspiracies, or dilettante sleuths. In many of his stories, the mystery is rather superficial, and the detectives have very little part in the solution.

Himes's criminal Harlem should not be judged along with traditional mystery fiction. To consider him thus would be to devalue his work. Perhaps unknowingly, Himes was following in the footsteps of a select few writers who actually had some knowledge of the world that they sought to fictionalize. It comes as no surprise that the work of old timers like Hammett or Donald Goines and even newer writers like James Colbert and O'Neil De Noux is so realistic when you realize that they have experienced real life in the dangerous netherworld of urban America.

Himes' writing is particularly effective because he was able to combine realistic depictions of ghetto life and ghetto dwellers with symbolic elements that emphasize Black culture and heritage. His ability to ennoble otherwise comical characters and to create the aura of hope in an atmosphere of failure and degradation is in the highest traditions of the fiction writer's art.

At the same time, Himes created in Grave Digger and Coffin Ed two protagonists who could stand side-by-side with other romantic American heroes. It is worthy of note that the hard-boiled detective is as much a myth figure to 20th century Americans as Arthur and Roland are to Britain and France. Because America became urbanized so quickly, this mythical detective has replaced the cowboy as the definitive American hero archetype.

He is a loner with high ideals and a man who sacrifices material comfort and risks his own life and happiness to protect the innocent and the helpless. Perhaps because they are Black men upholding white laws, Digger and Ed fit this mold better than many of the white detective characters who have preceded them. Himes has told their story in a saga in which we watch them through ten years of danger. They meet death head-on more than once, inadvertently cause damage to their families because of their devotion to duty, and risk the hatred of their superiors because of their deep belief in justice. At the end of their history, we see them older, more tired, and perhaps less effective than at their beginning. In spite of that, we cannot escape the fact that they have ennobled themselves through their sacrifices.

Himes created something truly unique in this series. Unlike many practitioners who have written about the same character through twenty or thirty adventures, we never tire of Coffin Ed and Digger. Because they grow and change, Himes made them new each time we met them and charged them with a dynamism that is not evident in Travis McGee, Spenser, and other detective characters. When Digger and Ed's adventures come to a close, the reader inevitably faces it with a feeling of regret rather than one of relief.

Himes was an unusual and talented man. He was also angry and embittered, but these emotions tended to enhance his talent rather than reduce it. His entry in the field of crime writing was an auspicious one and from an historical point of view an important one. He infused a tired genre with new life and undoubtedly provided the impetus for many future writers to approach the hard-boiled story from a fresh and bold perspective.

There are two reasons why Himes's *Série Noire* stories are viewed as the first black detective fiction. First, their two detectives are indeed black policemen. Second, all the novels are set within the boundaries of black Harlem during the late nineteen fifties and sixties, where "anything can happen." They explore social relations of blacks and offer a vivid portrayal of racial conflict and shocking violence of power at play. Himes's Harlem, a space inhabited primarily by blacks, represents an extreme form of a society gone crazy because of racial madness: "This is Harlem. . . . Ain't no other place like it in the world. You've got to start from scratch here, because these folks in Harlem do things for reasons nobody else in the world would think of." Particularly striking in this special place is its "otherness" of language as well as the subversion of gender and race identity by transvestites, transsexuals, albino blacks, and people who play on various gradations of "blackness" which determine social and cultural status.

To this "crazy" world, Himes brings his two hard-boiled black detectives, Coffin Ed and Gravedigger Jones (Ed Cercueil and Fossoyeur), and that insertion creates the basic structural tension in all the novels. Because of their profession, Jones and Ed are forced to mediate between the white world of law and the black world of the streets. While at the police precincts, their language is generally conventional and nonviolent, conforming to the rules of social discourse necessary for their acceptance by the white society; but once on the streets, their language and code of conduct follow a diversity of other rules prevailing in mad Harlem. Eventually, their participation in the two worlds leads to their rejection by both blacks and whites. As Coffin Ed puts it at the end of *The Heat's On*:

> What hurts me most about this business is the attitude of the public toward cops like me and Digger. Folks just don't want to believe that what we're trying to do is make a decent peaceful city for people to live in, and we're going about it the best way we know how.

But that ultimate failure only caps a dramatic evolution of their mediating function and the various strategies they adopt to fulfil it.

Initially two main strategies appear to be at their disposal for their constant move across the racial (and social) border: they can adjust their language in order to deal effectively with each group, and they can disguise their appearance in order to blend with the group or to manipulate it. But neither Coffin Ed nor Gravedigger Jones is given to disguise. Their blending ability rather stems from their indistinguishable appearance: except for Ed's scarred face (from an acid burn which melted it), they appear alike both to whites and blacks: "tall, loose-jointed, sloppily dressed, ordinary-looking dark-brown colored men." They do not play any role beyond their functional role, that of black cops. By the same token, however, they set a contrast with the other inhabitants of Harlem, who seem obsessed by disguises. *A Rage in Harlem* was originally titled *The Five Cornered Square* after a particularly gullible character who is conned by everyone and hence so square that he seems to have five corners. This Jackson is also a failure at disguises; when he tries to disguise his voice over the phone when calling his landlady, she has no trouble hearing right through his muffled voice: "I know who you is Jackson. You ain't fooling me." In contrast, Jackson's identical twin brother, Goldy, is a master at disguises and fools everybody. Goldy spends his days dressed as Sister Gabriel, much to the indignation of Jackson: "There's a law against impersonating a female." Goldy's costume allows him to move about freely and to carry out his secret activities without arousing suspicion. He lives by his "wits" not only in the world of the streets but also in the world of the cops. For Goldy, like Ed and Jones, also straddles two worlds: a criminal among Harlem blacks, he is an informer for the police. His disguise works for both roles, but, in his dealings with the detectives, he also has recourse to the second strategy: a special language adjusted to that of his interlocutors. When Jones greets him with "What's the word, Sister?" he responds with "And I saw three unclean spirits like frogs come out of the mouth of the dragon," that the black detective understands readily. In a later passage, he uses this same biblical talk to evade a white policeman for "he knew the best way to confuse a white cop in Harlem was to quote foolishly from the Bible." Eventually, it is Goldy's language that kills him and restores the social order: he "Talked himself into the grave."

No such dangers are faced by the two detectives. While indifferent to disguises, they are masters at language strategy. Though they do not yet play as central a role as they will in later novels Ed and Jones demonstrate from the start their linguistic versatility. Jones has no problems understanding Sister Gabriel, and he controls a potentially explosive situation with a simple voice imitation trick: "'Straighten up,' he shouted in a big loud voice. And then, as if echoing his own voice, he mimicked Coffin Ed, 'Count off.'" Rather than highlighting rational deductive power as the essential function of the detective, Himes shows that rationality is itself a function of language and that it is language which determines the exercise of authority and power. As James Baldwin writes, "A language comes into existence by means of brutal necessity, and the rules of the language are dictated by what the language must convey." The power of the two detectives derives from their mastery of communication rather than from a display of brutal force. In fact, Ed and Jones are not very violent in *A Rage in Harlem*: they put their trust in words, when dealing with blacks or with whites.

To that extent, and despite its title, this first novel written in France is rather optimistic. Perhaps Himes identified his second career (a black American writer's mediation between a French white audience and a black Harlem) with the mission of his two black detectives who must similarly mediate between a white American society as represented by the police and the same black Harlem. Himes's earlier "serious" novels failed to communicate the urgency of the black problem in his own society; he might have now entertained the hope that, in France, his skills at a different form of communication, adjusted to the norms of the *Série Noire's* readers, would succeed to bridge the racial and social gap. For Himes, as for many others, writing fiction and detecting may have seemed to be a similar verbal attempt to bring out a believable truth; a hopeful double undertaking.

But violence and frustration return in *The Real Cool Killers*. . . .

This turn toward increasing violence has however a more specific reason. It is not Harlem that is changing, but Himes's vision of Harlem. And this evolution cannot be explained by the influence of changes in the detective genre. True, other contributors to the *Série Noire*, such as Chandler and Hammett, featured strong and hard-boiled detectives. But Marlowe and Sam Spade, however coarse, solve their problems through intellect and deductive reasoning. I rather believe that, on the level of the plot, the violence of Coffin Ed and Grave Digger Jones is a direct consequence of their difficult role as black detectives maintaining a white law in the black world of Harlem. As Digger explains, "colored hoodlums had no respect for colored cops unless you beat it into them or blew them away." In contrast to *A Rage in Harlem*, where they still commanded respect, in the last novel of the series, *Blind Man with a Pistol*, Jones and Ed will almost completely lose their authority among the blacks. In fact, they are threatened and attacked by a group of teenagers with a racial agenda: "'We're the law,' Coffin Ed said. . . . 'Then you're on whitey's side.'" The two detectives justify their violence against blacks—men and women—by a paradoxical double argument: their brutality is necessary to curb crime, but it is also excusable because they belong themselves to the very people they brutalize. They think that it is the only way for them to gain respect because their official title no longer holds any weight and the traditional means of questioning are no longer effective. For them, violence is an "innocent" feature of their profession as detectives in contrast to "the white men on the force who commit the pointless brutality." Yet, by the end of the series, they fail not only the citizens of Harlem who reject them, but also the white world of the police precincts which also rejects them:

> Now after twelve years as first-grade detectives they hadn't been promoted. Their raises in salaries hadn't kept up with the cost of living . . . when they weren't taking lumps from the thugs, they were taking lumps from the commissioners.

The direct cause of their failure seems to be a double alienation, from both blacks and whites. Which means that they experience a growing double gap in communication or, more generally, a double collapse of their mediating function between the two worlds.

The question is: what motivated Himes, from novel to novel, to undermine and finally negate his early trust in mediation? Was it because his own mediating function as a novelist was also progressively collapsing? A distinction must be made here between the process of mediation and its content. On the one hand, over the twelve years, Himes's novels remained successful, and the faithful French readers continued to enrich their image of Harlem. On the other hand, however, it is quite likely that Himes himself was increasingly moving away from his earlier light vision of Harlem, and his somewhat hopeful perspective on the solution of the problems of blacks in America. In other terms, I think that Himes was coming to doubt any possibility of navigating between the two incompatible worlds of white and black. The solution to divisive racism could not be found in mediating the white man's law. The strained atmosphere culminating in *Blind Man with a Pistol* testifies in that sense to Himes's growing impatience with the mounting racial tension in America and its echoes in Europe. His novels illustrate, one after another, the progression of that tension among the characters of his fictional Harlem.

Nora M. Alter. *Alteratives* (New York: French Forum Publishers, 1993), pp. 11–24

In the penultimate chapter of Chester Himes's 1969 crime novel *Blind Man With A Pistol*—the last in his series of stories set in Harlem—the eponymous character makes his first appearance [and initiates a series of events that leads to violence and chaos]. . . .

With this incredible scene—simultaneously violent, disordered, grotesque and humorous—Himes draws his series of Harlem crime novels to its logical conclusion, as the barely controlled chaos which had permeated his world view explodes into a maelstrom of racial apocalypse. Coming in 1969, the scene contained numerous symbolic references to specific recent events as well as to more general racial tensions. A year after the assassination of Martin Luther King, Jr., Himes portrays an ineffectual, intellectual black minister pleading nonviolence and reconciliation who, ironically, is the gunman's accidental first victim. At a time when both political parties sought to outdo the other in calling for "law and order"—a racially-charged code term for cracking down on urban violence—Himes shows a white bystander scornfully declaring "what these niggers need is discipline." Fat Sam, a handyman for a white family, embittered by his low pay, demeaning work, and degrading contacts with his white employers, pathetically seeks to exert what power he can by forcing the other passengers to listen to his tirade. Outside the subway, Himes depicts the impotent anger of Harlem's black population confronting a distant, bureaucratic city government which cavalierly destroys its homes. Meanwhile, tensions with white police, the only immediate and tangible targets of the imperious city government, have reached the breaking point. Finally, the title character symbolizes the blind rage of African Americans who lash out in violence, with other blacks usually being their first victims. As Himes writes in the preface, the novel's central metaphor derived from a true incident a friend told him about, "and I thought, damn right, sounds like today's news, riots in the ghettos, war in Vietnam, masochistic doings in the Middle East. And then I thought of some of our loudmouthed leaders urging our vulnerable soul brothers on to getting themselves killed, and thought further that all unorganized violence is like a blind man with a pistol.''

In the interactions between the blind man and the people he meets on the street and subway and between the residents of Harlem and the police, Himes conveys what Mikhail Bakhtin termed heteroglossia. With this concept, Bakhtin referred to the way in which discourse is entangled, shot through with shared thoughts, points of view, alien value judgments and accents. The word, directed toward its object, enters a dialogically agitated and tension-filled environment of alien words, value judgments and accents, weaves in and out of complex interrelationships, merges with some, recoils from others, intersects with yet a third group: and all this may crucially shape discourse, may leave a trace in all its semantic layers, may complicate its expression and influence its entire stylistic profile.

Some recent scholars of postmodern theory give a largely benign view of this concept, seeing in this heteroglossia a mélange of discourses of various racial, ethnic and other subcultures in which everyone can find his own niche. According to Jim Collins, the chorus of competing voices is so complex that the issue of power becomes problematic and the source of power, ultimately, unlocatable. But Himes's vision is much more sinister, as he sees in this cacophony of voices what Strother Martin would call "a failure to communicate'' and the implications of this failure, Himes predicts, will be catastrophic. And unlike Collins, Himes firmly situates power in the distant, undemocratic, and white city government and portrays the competing discourses in Harlem as being a dialogic of the powerless. . . .

Himes viewed absurdity as a concept central to an understanding of race. As an expatriate living in Europe during the height of the civil rights struggle, Himes gained enough distance from the American situation to formulate a concept of race relations that contrasted sharply with most African Americans' understanding of the issue. Himes viewed race as a dialectical relationship which progressed toward increasing absurdity. As he wrote in the second volume of his autobiography:

Racism introduces absurdity into the human condition. Not only does racism express the absurdity of the racists, but it generates absurdity in the victims. And the absurdity of the victims intensifies the absurdity of the racists, ad infinitum. If one lives in a country where racism is held valid and practiced in all ways of life, eventually, no matter whether one is a racist or a victim, one comes to feel the absurdity of life.

Racism generating from whites is first of all absurd. Racism creates absurdity among blacks as a defense mechanism. Absurdity to combat absurdity.

Himes's adoption of the hard-boiled crime genre allowed him to escape the standard categorization of black writers, which fit all writing by blacks under the heading "protest.'' Like Ralph Ellison's *Invisible Man*, African American authors in the post-war period were invisible because of the dominant white culture's determination to force them into a predetermined, stereotyped mold of protest writer, a problem Himes had faced repeatedly. In the shadow of Richard Wright, black writers were expected to portray, with naturalistic despair, the effects of racism. But at the same time blacks were given only this one creative outlet, the public was

growing weary of black protest novels. Himes too was dissatisfied with the form. In his autobiography he wrote:

I had the creative urge, but the old, used forms for the black American writer did not fit my creations. I wanted to break through the barrier that labeled me as a "protest writer.'' I knew the life of an American black needed another image than just the victim of racism. We were more than just victims. We did not suffer, we were extroverts. We were unique individuals, funny but not clowns, solemn but not serious, hurt but not suffering, sexualists but not whores in the usual sense of the word; we had a tremendous love of life, a love of sex, a love of ourselves. We were absurd.

Ironically, only by allowing himself to be typecast as a writer within another fictional genre—one relegated to second-class citizenship in the field of literature—could Himes escape the confines of being a black writer.

The universe of Himes's Harlem crime stories is marked by chaos, ambiguity, absurdity and violence while his description of it is filled with "that bitter self-corroding irony which white people call 'Negro humor.''' Harlem's residents are so accustomed to the disorder of their surroundings that they feel comfortable in it. As Grave Digger says at one point, "so much nonsense must make sense.'' Even the elements themselves contribute to this sense of chaos and violence, as all of Himes's stories take place either in the oppressive heat of summer or the bitter cold of winter. In the Harlem of his crime stories, Himes found a perfect metaphor for his worldview, which he described in his autobiography.

Some time before, I didn't know when, my mind had rejected all reality as I had known it and I had begun to see the world as a cesspool of buffoonery. Even the violence was funny. A man gets his throat cut. He shakes his head to say you missed me and it falls off. Damn reality, I thought. All of reality was absurd, contradictory, violent and hurting, It was funny, really, if I could just get the joke. And I got the handle, by some miracle.

David Cochran. *Midwest Quarterly*. XXXVIII, 1 (Autumn 1996), pp. 11–30

BIBLIOGRAPHY
*If He Hollers Let Him Go*, 1945; *Lonely Crusade*, 1947; *Cast the First Stone*, 1952; *The Third Generation*, 1954; *The Primitive*, 1955; *For Love of Imabelle*, 1957; *The Real Cool Killers*, 1958; *The Crazy Kill*, 1959; *Run Man, Run*, 1959; *All Shot Up*, 1960; *The Big Gold Dream*, 1960; *The Heat's On*, 1961; *Pinktoes*, 1961; *Cotton Comes to Harlem*, 1964; *Blind Man with a Pistol*, 1969; *The Quality of Hurt*, 1972; *Black on Black: Baby Sister and Selected Writings* 1973; *My Life of Absurdity*, 1976; *Plan B*, 1983; *The Collected Stories of Chester Himes*, 1990

# HODGE, Merle (1944–)
## Trinidad

*Crick Crack, Monkey*, which was first published in 1970, belongs to a group of West Indian novels, such as [Michael Anthony's] *The*

*Year in San Fernando* and [Geoffrey Drayton's] *Christopher* which deal with the theme of childhood. The central character, Tee, moves in two worlds—the world of Tantie and the world of Aunt Beatrice—and those two worlds are bound together in a coherent and unified way by the response of the central character, who is also narrator, to the experiences of both worlds. The child, Tee, moves in a context in which there is strong opposition between certain social and cultural values, and, as narrator, she recounts the intensely personal dilemmas of her life in that context. This she does with a remarkable depth of insight and with a vivid evocation of childhood memories. The reader is made to share in the diversity and richness of Tee's experiences without being able to discern at times where the child's voice with a child's perception of things slides into the adult voice and vision of the omniscient author. Child vision and adult vision are made to coalesce at several points in the novel.

The two worlds of childhood which Tee inhabits result from the nature of her domestic circumstances. Her father, who has emigrated to England, is the brother of Tantie, and her deceased mother is sister to Aunt Beatrice. Tee oscillates between these two spheres of existence and emerges as a deeply disturbed being—a plight derived from the essential conflict of Creole middle class and Tantie's world. The conflict externalized in these two classes of society generates acute feelings of ambivalence within Tee. Both in form and content the novel is indeed a response to the inner pressures of a profoundly felt and complex experience. The vivid exploration of the child's inner world confers on the novel its essential strength. The child's feelings, thoughts, and actions, as she responds to the social and cultural environment in which the novel is set, reflect the authenticity of remembered experience.

> Roy Narinesingh. Introduction to Merle Hodge, *Crick Crack, Monkey* (London: Heinemann, 1981), p. vii

Merle Hodge's *Crick Crack, Monkey* was the first major novel by a postcolonial West Indian woman writer to problematize and foreground questions of difference and the quest for a voice in a social context that denied social expression to the colonized self and hence cut it off from the liberating forms of self-expression which define the Caribbean narrative. For Hodge, this emphasis on voice as a precondition for black subjectivity in a colonial situation was necessitated by both ideological and technical reasons. First of all, in the plantation societies of the Caribbean, the voices of the oppressed and dominated slaves and indentured laborers survived against the modes of silence engendered by the master class. For these slaves and laborers, then, the preservation and inscription of a distinctive voice would signify the site of their own cultural difference and identity. Second, the voice was, in radically contrasting ways, an instrument of struggle and a depository of African values in a world in which the slaves' traditions were denigrated and their selfhoods repressed ([Edward Kamau] Brathwaite; [Edouard] Glissant). In terms of narrative, the recovery of voice becomes one way through which unspoken and repressed experiences can be represented.

In Merle Hodge's novel, then, the voice is a synecdoche of the unwritten culture of the colonized, the culture of . . . Tantie and Ma, and its privileging in text signifies an epistemological shift from the hegemony of the written forms; alternatively, the negation of the spoken utterance through education and assimilation is a mark of deep alienation. When Tee opens her retrospective view of her childhood at the beginning of *Crick Crack*, she discovers that the past cannot be narrated without a cognizance of the voices that defined it. The voice is shown to be both central to the subject's conception of her past and as a paradigm that defines the context in which her multiple selves were produced. At the opening of the novel, a moment in which the birth of a new baby is superseded by the death of the mother, the world appears to Tee merely as a relationship of voices: "a voice like high heels and stocking," "an old voice . . . wailing," "some quavery voices," "a grumble of men's voices." Tee's subsequent alienation in the colonial world is prefigured by her inability to identify with these fetishized voices as easily as she identifies with the voice of Tantie and Ma.

> Simon Gikandi. *Ariel.* 20, 4 (October 1989), pp. 20–21

Merle Hodge . . . explores the tension between the African-Caribbean and metropolitan cultures. Unlike the majority of other novels addressing this question, *Crick Crack, Monkey* examines the African-Caribbean woman's cultural identification. In Hodge's novel, Cynthia, or Tee, must choose between Aunt Beatrice's attempts to imitate British upper-class society and language and Tantie's more honest acceptance of Creole manners and dialect.

Living in a society colonized by Europeans, Beatrice has become what O.R. Dathorne calls an "expatriate of the mind," denying the worth of locally evolved culture to identify with a foreign tradition. Tee, whose mother has died, is the object of a long custody battle between her Aunt Beatrice, who attempts to identify with the metropolitan culture, and Tantie, who accepts the indigenous black culture. Her acceptance of the black Creole cultural tradition is based on the recognition that imported cultural values evolved in a different environment and historical experience.

Although Tee feels more comfortable with Tantie, the young woman's later contact with Beatrice's values makes it impossible for her ever again to identify completely with the black Creole culture. When the potentially positive bonding between Tantie and Tee is disrupted and Beatrice wins custody of Tee, the girl suffers a gradual cultural displacement. At the novel's end, when Tee goes to her father's house in London, she has already internalized the racist values of the white colonials. Although Hodge does not offer a convincing alternative to the ambivalent balancing of two cultures, she does offer in Tantie a positive model of strength and endurance. She and the other women characters survive, physically and psychologically, because they have formed strong ties with other women in their families or communities. The potentially healthy relationship of Tee and Tantie is unfortunately interrupted by Beatrice's intrusion of values from the dominant culture.

> Laura Niesen de Abruna. In Selwyn R. Cudjoe, ed. *Caribbean Women Writers* (Wellesley, Massachusetts: Calaloux, 1990), pp.92–93

Tee's journey in *Crick Crack, Monkey* is not one of personal development but rather of psychological disintegration. The breakdown of her character begins imperceptibly in Tantie's home. Although Tantie's household provides an anchor for the sensitive infant, it is terribly flawed. The presence of a tantie marks the absence of a mother. Tee's first handicap is orphanhood.

Chapter one ends with Tee's awareness of the absence of her mother and father, the former by death, the latter by exile: "Then Papa went to sea. I concluded that what he had gone to see was whether he could find Mammy and the baby."

The orphaned child has only her adopted home to serve as her moral exemplar and formal education at school to be her teacher. Both fail her. Tantie's world is a morally broken environment full of indecencies and obscenities. There is first the problem of Tantie's many lovers who offend Aunt Beatrice's sense of uprightness: "And then what about all those men, did we like all those men coming," Aunt Beatrice questions Tee and Toddan; and second there is the problem of physical and verbal violence that Tee has to endure.

On one hand, Tantie's world gives Tee negative moral values, and on the other the education system alienates her from herself and her culture. By the end of primary school, Tee has developed a schizophrenic personality characterized by self-hate and an admiration for all things foreign thanks to colonized teachers like Mr. Hinds and a British-oriented curriculum that symbolically starts with "A for apple." It is at this time that she creates her double, Helen, the epitome of the British child she would like to become: "Helen wasn't even my double. No, she couldn't be called my double. She was the Proper Me. And me, I was her shadow, hovering about in incompleteness."

Tee's journey through life, like the picaroon's, is marked by loss of innocence, by petty theft, and finally by self-contempt. Having rejected self and family, she has no alternative but to flee her country.

Ena V. Thomas. In Selwyn R. Cudjoe, ed. *Caribbean Women Writers* (Wellesley, Massachusetts: Calaloux, 1990), pp. 212–13

*Crick Crack, Monkey* shares with the nationalist novels of the late 1960s and early 1970s a sense of postcolonial angst, even despair. Both in its construction of female roles and in the way in which its structure revises the terrain upon which quest narratives like [George] Lamming's [*In the Castle of My Skin*] inscribe themselves, Hodge's novel transforms the narrative conventions by which it is contained. . . .

"Crick-crack monkey" is part of a call and response chanted at the end of folk tales in the southern Caribbean. . . . The "crick-crack" probably imitates the breaking of a branch as the self-opinionated monkey falls out of the tree and slips on the skin of a pomerac fruit. But the literal meaning of the phrase is less important than its symbolic function as a marker separating the fantasy world of the story from the "real" world of the storyteller and her audience. The child protagonist, Tee, shouts this response to end the Anancy stories her grandmother tells during holidays in the countryside where, she imagines, the magic of an earlier world not yet deformed by the demands of growing up survives. But the tag is also used in the novel by city youths as a means of challenging the stories told by Manhattan, a member of their circle who claims to be an expert on the American way of life. . . .

Hodge utilizes the deflationary technique associated with the tag implicitly in other contexts to emphasize the hiatus between

fantasy and reality in the options open to Tee. Thus, the fantasy world of respectability and pseudowhiteness associated with Tee's prim Aunt Beatrice is undermined when Tee's younger brother, Toddan, shatters the teatime idyll with his earthy insistence that he must make "ca-ca." Tee's raucous, big-hearted Tantie, is undermined by similar devices, in spite of the positive, caring values which distinguish her from Aunt Beatrice. Sexual independence in Tantie's life has degenerated into sexual promiscuity; freedom from social taboos has degenerated into alcoholism. This is why the decision of one of her older wards, Mikey, to fight for her honor on the street touches Tantie so profoundly. Mikey's intervention on her behalf is the answer to the "crick-crack" challenge of the boys on the bridge to the myth of Tantie's respectability. However, his heroic stance does not change the fact that Tantie's lifestyle is in many respects as inauthentic as that of Aunt Beatrice and that it offers Tee no viable alternative in her search for a role model. . . .

*Crick Crack* resembles the novels of many male Caribbean writers in that it offers us no way of resolving this contradiction between sterile middle-class fantasy and sordid lower-class reality. But the fact that Hodge sets up the problem by recourse to an oral form suggests that its resolution may be achieved through the folklore associated with Tee's grandmother. . . . [It] is important to note that Hodge uses the crick-crack tag self-reflexively, to provide the deep structure of the text and to critique the narrative to which it gives shape.

Rhonda Cobham. *Callaloo*. 16, 1 (Winter 1993), pp. 46–48

The *marasa* principle, drawn from traditional Hajtian lore, suggests at once a pairing of texts for consideration and a commitment to a creative critical process which illuminates a third or wider field of expression beyond binaries. Following the nature-oriented and mystical philosophies from Asia, Africa and the Caribbean, this particular theory when applied to comparative literature is based on the notion that $1 + 1 = 3$.

The *marasa* sign clarifies the dynamics of social change, the transformation of cultural oppositions within plantation societies. Movement beyond double consciousness or the binary nightmare of a psyche divided by memory between Africa and Europe occurred particularly in the development of indigenous religious practices (Vodoun, Santería, Shango, Candombloa, Creole languages and mixed-race identities drawn together rather than apart. Coming to marasa consciousness in the late twentieth century means that the structure of analysis is triadic: African/Asian, European, and "New World." This third position looks back at the contradictions of racial definitions of the mixed-blood self as fundamentally black, oppositional stances within colonial educational systems and new letters and liberation movements by commenting on these phenomena in an environment of continuous change. . . .

Hodge's *Crick Crack, Monkey* is oppositional in theme, characterizations, structure, narrative technique, and language. Essentially, Hodge represents opposed class differences, defined as "ordinaryness" and respectability through the protagonist's aunts, Tantie and Aunt Beatrice. In the opening pages of the narrative, the protagonist, Tee, and her brother are orphaned. When their widowed father departs abruptly from Trinidad for England after his wife's funeral, the children are left in a working-class family with a single head of household, riotous Tantie, whose vulgar speech in Creole, working-class wit, and determination dominate the first twelve chapters of the narrative.

Most criticism of the novel focuses on the opposition between the two worlds of Tantie and Beatrice—the bourgeois city dweller and relative to whom Tee is sent for continued education beyond the local primary schools. Using the Caribbean culture's symbolic landscapes—house/yard as sites of expression suggesting women's domains and respectability, as opposed to the road/bridge areas of unbridled male behavior—we examined how these paradigms existed in the narrative, discovering how Hodge expands the landscape of affiliations described in Roger Abrahams's *Man-of-Worlds in the West Indies* (1983) by including the bush or the mountain refuges of former maroons as part of Tee's legacy. This is the place to which Tee returns for the summer months, to her grandmother Ma, to traditions of storytelling (thus the title of the novel), and to a fading memory, what Zee Edgell's characters refer to as ''befo' time.'' Deliberately devoting brief space to memories of Tee's summer home Pointe d'Espoir, in chapter 4, Hodge suggests that there is no possible return to communal identity for Tee, even though she resembles her great-great grandmother, called Euphemia by the countryfolk. . . . The nickname has replaced Euphemia's ''true-true'' name, which Ma has trouble remembering: ''[Ma] couldn't remember her grandmother's true-true name. But Tee was growing into her grandmother again, her spirit was in me. They'd never bent down her spirit and she would come back and come back: if only she could live to see Tee grow into her tall proud straight grandmother.'' Nonetheless, references to Pointe d'Espoir, and to the world of Tantie's adopted son Mikey, where unemployed men signify on one another at the bridge, open the narrative to levels of expressive behavior not confined to the glorious and rowdy Creole speech of Tantie or to the repressed anglophile domesticity surrounding Aunt Beatrice. Marasa consciousness encourages readers to appreciate a wider range of expression beyond the obvious binary oppositions in the narrative.

> VèVè A. Clark. In Margaret R. Higonnet, ed. *Borderwork: Feminist Engagements with Comparative Literature* (Ithaca: Cornell University Press, 1994), pp. 267–76

BIBLIOGRAPHY
*Crick Crack, Monkey*, 1970; *For the Life of Laetitia*, 1993

# HUGHES, Langston (1902–1967)
## United States

[Hughes] represents a transcendently emancipated spirit among a class of young writers whose particular battle-cry is freedom. With the enthusiasm of a zealot, he pursues his way [in *The Weary Blues*], scornful, in subject matter, in photography, and rhythmical treatment, of whatever obstructions time and tradition have placed before him. To him it is essential that he be himself. Essential and commendable surely; yet the thought persists that some of these poems would have been better had Mr. Hughes held himself a bit in check. In his admirable introduction to the book, Carl Van Vechten

says the poems have a ''highly deceptive air of spontaneous improvisation.'' I do not feel that the air is deceptive.

If I have the least powers of prediction, the first section of this book, ''The Weary Blues,'' will be most admired, even if less from intrinsic poetical worth than because of its dissociation from the traditionally poetic. Never having been one to think all subjects and forms proper for poetic consideration, I regard these jazz poems as interlopers in the company of the truly beautiful poems in other sections of the book. They move along with the frenzy and electric heat of a Methodist or Baptist revival meeting, and affect me in much the same manner. The revival meeting excites me, cooling and flushing me with alternate chills and fevers of emotion; so do these poems. But when the storm is over, I wonder if the quiet way of communing is not more spiritual for the God-seeking heart; and in the light of reflection I wonder if jazz poems really belong to that dignified company, that select and austere circle of high literary expression which we call poetry. . . .

Taken as a group the selections in this book seem one-sided to me. They tend to hurl this poet into the gaping pit that lies before all Negro writers, in the confines of which they become racial artists instead of artists pure and simple. There is too much emphasis here on strictly Negro themes; and this is probably an added reason for my coldness toward the jazz poems—they seem to set a too definite limit upon an already limited field.

Dull books cause no schisms, raise no dissensions, create no parties. Much will be said of *The Weary Blues* because it is a definite achievement, and because Mr. Hughes, in his own way, with a first book that cannot be dismissed as merely promising, has arrived.

> Countee Cullen. *Opportunity*. February 1926, pp. 73–74

Fine clothes may not make either the poet or the gentleman, but they certainly help; and it is a rare genius that can strip life to the buff and still poetize it. This, however, Langston Hughes has done, in a volume [*Fine Clothes to the Jew*] that is even more starkly realistic and colloquial than his first—*The Weary Blues*. It is a current ambition in American poetry to take the common clay of life and fashion it to living beauty, but very few have succeeded, even [Edgar Lee] Masters and [Carl] Sandburg not invariably. They get their effects, but often at the expense of poetry. Here, on the contrary, there is scarcely a prosaic note or a spiritual sag in spite of the fact that never has cruder colloquialism or more sordid life been put into the substance of poetry. The book is, therefore, notable as an achievement in poetic realism in addition to its particular value as a folk study in verse of Negro life.

The success of these poems owes much to the clever and apt device of taking folk-song forms and idioms as the mold into which the life of the plain people is descriptively poured. This gives not only an authentic background and the impression that it is the people themselves speaking, but the sordidness of common life is caught up in the lilt of its own poetry and without any sentimental propping attains something of the necessary elevation of art. Many of the poems are modelled in the exact metrical form of the Negro ''Blues,'' now so suddenly popular, and in thought and style of expression are so close as scarcely to be distinguishable from the popular variety. But these poems are not transcriptions, every now and then one catches sight of the deft poetic touch that unostentatiously transforms them into folk portraits. In the rambling improvised stanzas of folk-song, there is invariably much that is inconsistent with the dominant mood; and seldom any dramatic coherence. Here we have these necessary art ingredients ingenuously added to material of real folk flavor and origin. . . .

After so much dead anatomy of a people's superstition and so much sentimental balladizing on dialect chromatics, such vivid, pulsing, creative, portraits of Negro folk foibles and moods are most welcome. The author apparently loves the plain people in every aspect of their lives, their gin-drinking carousals, their street brawls, their tenement publicity, and their slum matings and partings, and reveals this segment of Negro life as it has never been shown before. Its open frankness will be a shock and a snare for the critic and moralist who cannot distinguish clay from mire.

Alain Locke. *Saturday Review.* April 9, 1927, p. 712

Langston Hughes has often been compared to Dunbar. At first this comparison seems far-fetched and foolish, but on closer examination one finds that the two have much in common, only that where Dunbar failed, Langston Hughes succeeds. Both set out to interpret ''the soul of his race''; one failed, the other, just at the beginning of his career, has in some measure already succeeded.

The younger man has not been content to assemble a supply of stock types who give expression to stock emotions which may be either slightly amusing or slightly tragic but which are never either movingly tragic or convincingly comic. When Langston Hughes writes of specific Negro types he manages to make them more than just ordinary Negro types. They are actually dark-skinned symbols of universal characters. One never feels this way about the people in Dunbar's poetry. For he never heightens them above their own particular sphere. There is never anything of the universal element in his poems that motivates Mr. Hughes's.

Moreover, Langston Hughes has gone much farther in another direction than any other Negro poet, much farther even than James Weldon Johnson went along the same road in *God's Trombones*. He has appropriated certain dialects and rhythms characteristically Negroid as his poetic properties. He has borrowed the lingo and locutions of migratory workers, chamber-maids, porters, bootblacks, and others, and woven them into rhythmic schemes borrowed from the blues songs, spirituals and jazz and with them created a poetic diction and a poetic form all his own. . . .

But Mr. Hughes has also written some of the most banal poetry of the age, which has not, as in the case of Mr. Cullen, even sounded beautiful.

Wallace Thurman. *Bookman.* July 1928, pp. 560–61

In *Not without Laughter* Langston Hughes has outlined almost every aspect of the racial problem in the United States. Poverty dominates everything else. Almost all the characters in *Not without Laughter* are engaged in a constant struggle against it, although their endurance and their good will cannot be questioned. In hotels, middle-class homes, or construction yards wages are ridiculously low. If a member of the black community manages by chance to acquire the outer signs of affluence, he immediately arouses the hostility of the whites. If, when provoked for one reason or another,

he reacts, it will not take long before he and his innocent brothers experience the terrors of burning or lynching. . . .

*Not without Laughter* is unquestionably the result of the young novelist's personal experience. While traveling throughout the United States, Hughes gathered a great many facts. With his very personal art and his plain style, free from all vain literary contrivances, he has created a masterpiece which has been read with interest and excitement in the United States and which has been published in England, France, and Moscow.

René Piquion. *Langston Hughes: Un chant nouveau* (Port-au-Prince: Imprimerie de l'État, 1940), pp. 145–47†

The double role that Langston Hughes has played in the rise of a realistic literature among the Negro people resembles in one phase the role that Theodore Dreiser played in freeing American literary expression from the restrictions of Puritanism. Not that Negro literature was ever Puritanical, but it was timid and vaguely lyrical and folkish. Hughes's early [collections of] poems, *The Weary Blues* and *Fine Clothes to the Jew*, full of irony and urban imagery, were greeted by a large section of the Negro reading public with suspicion and shock when they first appeared in the middle twenties. Since then the realistic position assumed by Hughes has become the dominant outlook of all those Negro writers who have something to say.

The other phase of Hughes's role has been, for the lack of a better term, that of a cultural ambassador. Performing his task quietly and almost casually, he has represented the Negroes' case, in his poems, plays, short stories and novels, at the court of world opinion. On the other hand he has brought the experiences of other nations within the orbit of the Negro writer by his translations from the French, Russian and Spanish.

How Hughes became this forerunner and ambassador can best be understood in the cameo sequences of his own life that he gives us in his sixth and latest book, *The Big Sea*. Out of his experiences as a seaman, cook, laundry worker, farm helper, bus boy, doorman, unemployed worker, have come his writings dealing with black gals who wore red stockings and black men who sang the blues all night and slept like rocks all day.

Unlike the sons and daughters of Negro ''society,'' Hughes was not ashamed of those of his race who had to scuffle for their bread. The jerky transitions of his own life did not admit of his remaining in one place long enough to become a slave of prevailing Negro middle-class prejudices. So beneficial does this ceaseless movement seem to Hughes that he has made it one of his life principles: six months in one place, he says, is long enough to make one's life complicated. The result has been a range of artistic interest and expression possessed by no other Negro writer of his time. . . .

Hughes is tough; he bends but he never breaks, and he has carried on a manly tradition in literary expression when many of his fellow writers have gone to sleep at their posts.

Richard Wright. *New Republic.* October 28, 1940, pp. 600–601

Langston Hughes's poetry is what, in terms of the art of the motion picture, would be called documentary. His concern is to document the moods and problems of the American Negro, to set side by side in simple and lively form pictures and impressions which will add up to a presentation of the American Negro's present situation. This kind of writing is worlds apart from the subtle distillation of meaning aimed at by other contemporary poets. For Mr. Hughes, the idiom of poetry is valuable only to the degree that it pins down a situation and draws it to the attention of his readers. The ultimate meaning, the subtler vision of reality, the oblique insight into man's personality and man's fate are not for him; he has a more urgent and immediate problem, to project the living American Negro onto the page. And he does so, on the whole, with success.

David Daiches. *New York Herald Tribune Books.* January 9, 1949, p. 4

Few people have enjoyed being Negro as much as Langston Hughes. Despite the bitterness with which he has occasionally indicted those who mistreat him because of his color (and in this collection of sketches and stories [*Laughing to Keep from Crying*] he certainly does not let up), there has never been any question in this reader's mind about his basic attitude. He would not have missed the experience of being what he is for the world. . . .

Langston Hughes has practised the craft of the short story no more than he has practised the forms of poetry. His is a spontaneous art which stands or falls by the sureness of his intuition, his mother wit. His stories, like his poems, are for readers who will judge them with their hearts as well as their heads. By that standard he has always measured well. He still does.

Arna Bontemps. *Saturday Review.* April 5, 1952, p. 17

Unfortunately, Sandy disrupts the symbolic unity of [*Not without Laughter.*] Presumably torn by the conflicting forces which divide the family, his inner struggle fails to materialize. There is no laughter in his life, but only an altogether commendable determination to be a credit to the race. At this point, the novel bogs down in hopeless ideological confusion. . . .

Hughes tried to reject the Protestant ethic (joy is wrong), while retaining the success drive on which it is based. It is an untenable halfway house, which Claude McKay and Jessie Fauset would equally scorn to occupy. In any event, Hughes' ideological ambivalence has disastrous aesthetic consequences. The novel and its main character simply part company. Instead of supporting the defense-of-laughter theme, Sandy emerges as a symbol of racial advancement, which is hardly a laughing matter. Given his main theme of suffering and self-expression, Hughes might better have written the novel around Harriet, who emerges from a life of prostitution to become "Princess of the Blues."

*Not without Laughter* has been compared in some quarters to the first book of [James T. Farrell's] *Studs Lonigan* trilogy. No service is rendered either to American literature or to Hughes by this exaggerated claim. A mediocre novel, *Not without Laughter* was undertaken before its author was prepared to meet the rigorous requirements of the genre. Ideologically confused and structurally defective, the novel gives a final impression of sprawling formlessness. The author, to his credit, is fully aware of these shortcomings, if some of his friendly critics are not. In his autobiography, *The Big Sea*, Hughes makes a courageous apology to the characters of his early novel: "I went to Far Rockaway that summer and felt bad, because I had wanted their novel to be better than the published one I had given them. I hated to let them down."

Robert A. Bone. *The Negro Novel in America* (New Haven, Connecticut: Yale University Press, 1958), pp. 76–77

Hughes, in his sermons, blues and prayers, has working for him the power and the beat of Negro speech and Negro music. Negro speech is vivid largely because it is private. It is a kind of emotional shorthand—or sleight-of-hand—by means of which Negroes express, not only their relationship to each other, but their judgment of the white world. And, as the white world takes over this vocabulary—without the faintest notion of what it really means—the vocabulary is forced to change. The same thing is true of Negro music, which has had to become more and more complex in order to continue to express any of the private or collective experience.

Hughes knows the bitter truth behind these hieroglyphics: what they are designed to protect, what they are designed to convey. But he has not forced them into the realm of art where their meaning would become clear and overwhelming. "Hey, pop!/Re-bop!/ Mop!" conveys much more on Lenox Avenue than it does in [Hughes's *Selected Poems*], which is not the way it ought to be.

Hughes is an American Negro poet and has no choice but to be acutely aware of it. He is not the first American Negro to find the war between his social and artistic responsibilities all but irreconcilable.

James Baldwin. *New York Times Book Review.* March 29, 1959, p. 6

The conception of *Soul Gone Home* is that of fantasy, and it contains some ironically comic moments, but its impulse is far removed from comedy. In a vignette-like episode, Hughes creates with great economy the kind of play Zola called for in his preface to *Thérèse Raquin*. Although a fantasy in concept and structure, its atmosphere and effects are those of naturalism. Like one of Hughes' poems, *Soul Gone Home* bristles with implications and reverberates with connotations. That which is unsaid becomes almost more important than what is put into the dialogue. The repressive dominance of the white culture is suggested only by the arrival of ambulance attendants, who are white as the mother knew they would be. The tragedy is that of a people so repressed that they can no longer love, and the ironic implications build to a shocking climax. Its impact is stark and uncomplicated, and it is a difficult play to forget.

Hughes does not always write in a serious vein, as readers of his stories and poems well know. His folk plays of urban Negro life, at once humorous and revealing, are a true contribution to American folk drama. The three included [in the collection *Five Plays*]— *Little Ham, Simply Heavenly*, and *Tambourines to Glory*—are, if one must define them, comedies. But the triple specters of poverty, ignorance, and repression can be seen not far beneath the surface of the comedy. The "numbers racket," "dream books," and the "hot goods man" in *Little Ham*, Simple's wistful sadness that no Negro has seen a flying saucer, and Laura's attitude toward the "religion business" in *Tambourines to Glory*, all indicate the near poverty, the ignorance, and the superstition that prevail in the world of which Hughes writes. Nevertheless, it is a colorful, wonderful world he presents to us, and we cannot but admire the spirit and vigor of his characters. He gives us a dynamic view of a segment of life most of us will never know and can discover nowhere else. At times he may sacrifice dramatic action for the sake of portraying nothing more than the people of Harlem absorbed in living out their lives from day to day, but if the humor of the scene and Hughes' infectious interest in his characters carry us along with him, what more can we ask?

> Webster Smalley. Introduction to *Five Plays by Langston Hughes* (Bloomington: Indiana University Press, 1963), pp. xi-xii

For many years Hughes, often hailed as "the poet laureate of the Negro people," has been recognized by white critics as an author-poet of the protest genre. Others, more conservative and denunciatory, have assailed Hughes as radical and leftist, to mention the more polite language. In both instances the critics referred to Hughes's treatment of imperfections in the American Dream that we, as a nation, hold so dear. . . .

Probably the greatest portion of Hughes's poetry does not refer specifically to the American Dream, despite the habit of many critics' labeling him a protest writer primarily. But in *Ask Your Mama: 12 Moods for Jazz* he returns to the Dream, in jazz tempo with barbs appropriate for a dream too long deferred. With an impish introduction of the melody "Dixie" in the background, the poet combines dreams and nightmares to produce a mural of black power in the South. . . .

But the grandiose dream sequence, itself reflecting how one-sided the American Dream has been in the South, is short-lived. The poet returns to the pessimistic here and now. The Negro can't keep from losing, even when he's winning, he moans in blues tempo. *Ask Your Mama* relates to the vest spectrum of the American Dream, as it affects Negroes. There are the hardships of blockbusting, or integrating a white residential area, the bitterness of Negro artists, the stereotyped attitudes of whites toward Negroes, the hope of a better material world for ambitious Negroes, and the eternal suspicions cast upon any Negro who does anything worthwhile or, often, anything that is ordinary for white folks to do.

> James Presley. *Southwest Review.* Autumn 1963, pp. 380, 383–84

*Ask Your Mama* strikes me as something like the synthesis and the culmination of Langston Hughes's work. . . .

In this collection Hughes tries to attain his old dream of being a complete poet-musician. He has at least succeeded in breaking away from the approach of his early collections, which are primarily gatherings of poems at times quite incongruous, with the exception of *Montage of a Dream Deferred*, which anticipates *Ask Your Mama* in its elaborate structure and deliberate counterpoint. In short, *Ask Your Mama* does not simply contain poetry that is more or less sung; rather, it resembles a film's sound track improvised with great freedom by the imaginary or real musician, in the best tradition of jazz.

Despite the new form of *Ask Your Mama*, Hughes has in no way given up his favorite themes. Nor does he seek innovation in the manner of Joyce and the T. S. Eliot of *The Waste Land*, who were concerned mainly with form. As the jacket of the collection says, the poetry is "full of allusions to current events," and "current events" for Langston Hughes can only be those that concern the economic and social conditions of the black man—primarily those of the black American, but also those of blacks throughout the world.

> François Dodat. *Langston Hughes* (Paris: Pierre Seghers, 1964), pp. 65–67†

*Not without Laughter*, the novel Hughes wrote in 1930, and *Tambourines to Glory*, written in 1958, contain the strong points of his best poetry, vigor, simplicity, and a sure sense of human relationships, but they lack a certain depth of characterization and unity. *Not without Laughter* is certainly the better work of the two, transcribing as it does a warmly human picture of Negro life. This novel is also important for its emphasis on life within the Negro group. Jimboy, Annjee, and Aunt Hager are certainly aware of racial discrimination, but they live their own lives not without laughter.

In the 1930's Hughes wrote a series of short stories on racial misunderstanding which appeared in leading literary magazines and afterwards received favorable attention in compiled form as *The Ways of White Folks*. They are dramatic and show penetrating insight, making the reader realize, as [Sterling Brown] put it, "that there is a greater depth in Negro-white relationships of the most casual sort than other writers have suggested." More recently Hughes has written stories on a variety of themes, race being but one. The collection entitled *Laughing to Keep from Crying*, published in 1952, shows Hughes's broadening interest in minority groups of all kinds, timid Negro leadership, and the curious workings of love and hate. Although both collections have strong and weak stories, *The Ways of White Folks*, with its subtle emphasis on Negro-white behavior, seems the superior book. [1967]

> Donald C. Dickinson. *A Bio-Bibliography of Langston Hughes*, 2nd ed. (Hamden, Connecticut: Shoe String, 1972), p. 114

Langston Hughes loved literature. He loved it not fearfully, not with awe. His respect for it was never stiff nor cold. His respect for it was gaily deferential. He considered literature not his private inch, but great acreage. The plantings of others he not only welcomed but busily enriched.

He had an affectionate interest in the young. He was intent, he was careful. The young manuscript-bearing applicant never felt himself an intruder, never went away with Oak turned ashes in the hand.

Mightily did he use the street. He found its multiple heart, its tastes, smells, alarms, formulas, flowers, garbage and convulsions. He brought them all to his table-top. He crushed them to a writing-paste. The pen that was himself went in.

> Gwendolyn Brooks. *Nation.* July 3, 1967, p. 7

From his first book, *The Weary Blues*, published in 1926, through today—or rather, through yesterday, when he died—the entire oeuvre of this great poet has been marked by the tireless struggle for the freedom of black men in those "free" United States of America. Drama, biography, the novel, history, the short story, the humorous sketch, autobiography—Langston Hughes has used his talent in all these genres to reach this goal. . . .

He has been criticized—and he is not the only one—for treating the racial issue exclusively, and for ignoring everything else. Why should we forget, say such critics, that this is also the century of Proust and Joyce? Why should the black artist not take his place within the context of American and world culture, abandoning or reducing his dependence upon ethnic and folk art? I am not in disagreement with this line of reasoning. But it would have been very difficult—not only when Hughes began to write but even now—for a black artist to have written something like *Ulysses* or *In Search of Lost Time*, masterpieces of world literature that they are, at the same time that blacks were being burned alive in the South. I do not know whether they were immolated by readers of Proust and Joyce, but without a doubt their persecutors were savages of the worst kind that there were—that there are—savages who should have been—who should be—exterminated with bullets or with poetry.

Nicolás Guillén. *Presence Africaine* No. 64, 1967, pp. 36–37

Langston Hughes's new poems [in *The Panther and the Lash*], written shortly before his death last summer, catch fire from the Negro American's changing face. To a degree I would never have expected from his earlier work, his sensibility has kept pace with the times, and the intensity of his new concerns—helping him to shake loose old crippling mannerisms, the trade marks of his art—comes to fruition in many of the best poems of his career: ''Northern Liberal,'' ''Dinner Guest: Me,'' ''Crowns and Garlands,'' to name a few.

Regrettably, in different poems, he is fatally prone to sympathize with starkly antithetical politics of race. A reader can appreciate his catholicity, his tolerance of all the rival—and mutually hostile—views of his outspoken compatriots, from Martin Luther King to Stokely Carmichael, but we are tempted to ask, what are Hughes's politics? And if he has none, why not? The age demands intellectual commitment from its spokesmen. A poetry whose chief claim on our attention is moral, rather than aesthetic, must take sides politically. . . .

''Justice,'' an early poem that teaches the aesthetic value of rage, exhibits Hughes's knack for investing metaphor with a fierce potency that is as satisfying poetically as it is politically tumultuous. . . . But this skill is all but asphyxiated in many of the new poems by an ungovernable weakness for essayistic polemicizing that distracts the poet from the more serious demands of his art, and frequently undermines his poetics. Another technique that Hughes often employs successfully in the new poems is the chanting of names of key figures in the Negro Revolution. This primitive device has often been employed as a staple ingredient in good political poetry, as in Yeats's ''Easter 1920.'' But when the poem relies too exclusively on this heroic cataloguing—whether of persons or events—for its structural mainstay, as in ''Final Call,'' it sinks under the freight of self-conscious historicity.

Laurence Lieberman. *Poetry.* August 1968, p. 339–40

Langston Hughes had a view of art and the role of poetry different from both Countee Cullen and Claude McKay. The poets who influenced him were Carl Sandburg and, in a limited way, Vachel Lindsay. He, along with Sterling Brown, shared the American poetic vision that ran from Walt Whitman through Sandburg—its belief in the validity of the intuitive sense and the spontaneity of art. Hughes not only believed that art should be the immediate expression of the self, but he also shared with Whitman, Sandburg, and Lindsay a deep, open, optimistic faith in the common man. Hughes and Brown were democrats, accepting, without question, the rightness of the unadorned and unpretentious expression of ordinary people. . . .

In truth, Hughes was not writing to be approved as a literary poet (Brown sometimes did). While his poems appealed to an audience which included whites, Hughes created for himself a black audience, especially school children. And he expected his poems to be taken on the simple and unpretentious level on which they were written. One would be right in saying that Langston Hughes backed out of the Negro-artist dilemma by choosing not to deal with art as serious ''high culture.'' His casual and almost anti-intellectual attitude about art permitted him a wide freedom of subject and a personal honesty. It allowed him to make the very important point that the people's language, and voice, and rhythms were legitimate stuff of poetry. But this same freedom deprived him of the control and mastery that might make each (or indeed any) of his poems really singular. Langston Hughes avoided the Scylla of formalism only to founder in the Charybdis of folk art.

Nathan Irvin Huggins. *Harlem Renaissance* (New York: Oxford University Press, 1971), pp. 221, 226–27

Everyone can see that [Hughes's Simple] stories are humorous because of the main character's posture and attitude about the truths of life presented in them. Few readers, however, recognize that Simple is completely a creation of his own words, his own rhetoric, and that all of the reader's impressions of what Simple is like—his moral nature, his hopes, dreams, and fears—are derived not with reference to an external universe but only with reference to the structured context in which Simple lives and moves and has his being. In the stories, there are few descriptions and few references to actions. As it works out in the context, the narrator, Boyd, sees Simple in a bar or on a street corner or sitting on the stoop in front of the place where Simple lives, and all of these encounters give rise to speeches by Simple. The reader hears and believes, laughs at, sympathizes with and trusts the things which Simple says. These effects are produced through Hughes's presentation of his character and by the series of rhetorical devices and types of embellishment that Hughes employs. . . .

Simple himself is a past master of language, as a rhetorician should be, and he can make words do anything he wants them to do. Yet in almost every instance in the stories where speech is structured to yield a comic effect, Boyd is involved. Part of this is due to the nature of rhetorical speech as addressed. Boyd serves in one respect as Simple's immediate audience, although in actuality he is consubstantial with Simple, that is, Simple and Boyd share the same value scheme, attitudes, hopes, and aspirations for the justice, truth, honesty, and racial equity which Simple promulgates over and over again. Boyd is the more moderate, less militant, Simple. In a larger sense, however, Boyd is representative of Simple's wider audience, and he reflects Hughes's assumptions that people of the United States and of the world subscribe to Simple's ideas about peace, freedom, and brotherhood; in a word, that the world constitutes an audience which is consubstantial with Simple, a world which is, therefore, able to appreciate Simple's essential humanity.

Harry L. Jones. In Therman B. O'Daniel, ed., *Langston Hughes: Black Genius* (New York: William Morrow, 1971), pp. 134, 138–39

Called the poet laureate of Harlem, Hughes retained all his life a deep love for that colorful city within a city, and he never tired of delineating the changing moods of that ghetto. Except for one, there are specific poems on Harlem in every major poetical work. To Hughes, Harlem was place, symbol, and on occasion protagonist. It is a city of rapid transformation: the Harlem of the first two works is a gay, joyous city of cabaret life, the Harlem that jaded downtown whites seeking the exotic and the primitive flocked uptown to see. This Harlem of "Jazzonia" was never the *real* Harlem; that begins to appear in *One Way Ticket* after a riot and a depression have made the ghetto into an "edge of hell" for its discouraged and frustrated inhabitants, though still a refuge from the white man's world.

The fullest and best treatment of Harlem (and Hughes's best volume of poetry) is found in *Montage of a Dream Deferred*. Actually one long poem of 75 pages, it employs a "jam-session technique" to give every possible shade and nuance of Harlem life. Very few cities have received such a swinging and comprehensive coverage.

Arthur P. Davis. *From the Dark Tower* (Washington, D.C.: Howard University Press, 1974), p. 64

Perhaps it should be said, though not in scorn, that [Hughes] was limited. As he poetized at the beginning of his life, he poetized at its end, and vice versa. He never wrote an epic, large or small. Gravity of any kind was not his style. Nor was tediousness his bane. All of his poems, except a very few, are brief; and none are very long or ponderous from attempts at grandeur or sublimity. . . .

Hughes's touch may have been (for he was, of course, not perfect) in his art too much of precisely that, a touch. As he can be related to the ballad, he can also be related to Impressionism. Indeed, it is hardly too much to say that all his poetry ever does is collect impressions. It is highly probable that, in all of Negro literature, he must be accorded the title of the Great Impressionist. Thereto, of course, attaches a limitation. Impressions tend to lack depth, if not also concentrated power. Hughes's impressions do come from the right places. They are taken by an artist who does not stand in his own light. And they do witness to the reality of a group experience of American life. Yet they are still impressions. Hughes was not a genius at synthesizing big things. He could, and yet he could not, quite see the whole forest as some writers do. It may have been his greatest lack and probably the reason he has never seemed as "serious" as writers like Ellison and Wright, or Tolson at his best. Even so he saw enough of Negro America, whether in the particular or the general, to be the best of the triad of McKay, Cullen, and Hughes. Through many years he saw enough

to be a leading interpreter of the Negro in twentieth-century America and twentieth-century literature.

Blyden Jackson. In Blyden Jackson and Louis D. Rubin, Jr., *Black Poetry in America* (Baton Rouge: Louisiana State University Press, 1974), pp. 54, 57–58

The finest black poet of the decade, Langston Hughes, rejected metaphysics and superstition altogether; loyal to perhaps the essential modernist criterion, Hughes for the most part looked not before and after, but at what is. Hughes went in the only direction a black poet could go and still be great in the 1920s: he had to lead blacks, in at least one corner of their lives—in his case, through poetry—into the modern world. His genius lay in his uncanny ability to lead by following (one is tempted to invoke Eliot's image of the poet's mind as a platinum filament), to identify the black modern, recognize that it was not the same as the white modern, and to structure his art (not completely, to be sure, but to a sufficient extent for it to be historic) along the lines of that black modernism.

Modernism began for Hughes on January 1919, a month short of his seventeenth birthday, when the Cleveland Central High School Monthly, in which he had been publishing undistinguished verse for more than a year, announced a long poem "in free verse"—apparently the first in the history of the magazine. "A Song of the Soul of Central" ("Children of all people and all creeds/Come to you and you make them welcome") indicates that Hughes had made his individual pact with Walt Whitman. With Whitman's influence came a break with the genteel tyranny of rhyme and the pieties of the Fireside poets and the majority of black versifiers. Already conscious of himself as a black, however, Hughes could not accept, much less internalize, a vision of the modern defined largely by the fate of Europe after the war. Sharing little or nothing of J. Alfred Prufrock's sense of an incurably diseased world, Hughes looked with indifference on the ruined splendors of the waste land. In practice, modernism for him would mean not Pound, Eliot, or Stevens, but Whitman, Vachel Lindsay, and, above all, Sandburg. The last became "my guiding star." Hughes, however, did not remain star-struck for long; within a year or so he had emancipated himself from direct influence. In one instance, where the well-meaning Sandburg had written: "I am the nigger / Singer of Songs, / Dancer," Hughes had responded with the more dignified (though not superior) "Negro": "I am the Negro: / Black as the night is black, / Black like the depths of my Africa."

The key to his release as a poet was his discovery of the significance of race, as well as other psychological factors (beyond our scope here) that amount to a final admission of his aloneness in the world, with both factors combining to make Hughes dependent on the regard of his race as practically no other black poet has been. He responded by consciously accepting the challenge of Whitman and Sandburg but also by accepting as his own special task, within the exploration of modern democratic vistas in the United States, the search for a genuinely Afro-American poetic form. At the center of his poetic consciousness stood the black masses,

Dream-singers all,
Story-tellers,
Dancers,
Loud laughers in the hands of Fate—
My people.

Or, as he soon more calmly, and yet more passionately, would express his admiration and love:

> The night is beautiful,
> So the faces of my people.
> The stars are beautiful,
> So the eyes of my people.
> Beautiful, also, is the sun
> Beautiful, also, are the souls of my people.

Before he was nineteen, Hughes had written at least three of the poems on which his revered position among black readers would rest. The most important was "The Negro Speaks of Rivers" ("I've known rivers:/I've known rivers ancient as the world and older than the flow of human blood in human veins. / My soul has grown deep like the rivers.") "When Sue Wears Red" drew on the ecstatic cries of the black church to express a tribute to black woman unprecedented in the literature of the race.

> When Susanna Jones wears red
> Her face is like an ancient cameo
> Turned brown by the ages.
> Come with a blast of trumpets,
> Jesus!. . .

The third major poem of this first phase of Hughes's adult creativity was "Mother to Son," a dramatic monologue that reclaimed dialect (Dunbar's "jingle in a broken tongue") for the black poet ("Well, son, I'll tell you: / Life for me ain't been no crystal stair. / It's had tacks in it, / And splinters"). With this poem and the resuscitation of dialect, Hughes came closer than any of the poets before him to what I have identified as the great hurdle facing the committed black poet—how to allow the race to infuse and inspire the very form of a poem, and not merely its surface contentions. Until this step could be taken, black poetry would remain antiquarian, anti-modern.

To a degree greater than that of any other young black poet, however, Hughes trained himself to be a modern poet—I am conscious here of Pound's words on the general subject, and on Eliot in particular. His high school, dominated by the children of east European immigrants, and where he was class poet and editor of the yearbook, was a training ground in cosmopolitanism. Mainly from Jewish classmates, "who were mostly interested in more than basketball and the glee club," he was introduced to basic texts of radical socialism. Although at 21 he began his first ocean voyage by dumping overboard a box of his books, the detritus of his year at Columbia (he saved only one book—*Leaves of Grass*: "That one I could not throw away"), it was not out of ignorance of what they might contain. "Have you read or tried to read," he wrote in 1923 to a friend, "Joyce's much discussed 'Ulysses'?" By the age of 23 he could speak both French and Spanish. In 1923 he was writing poems about Pierrot (a black Pierrot, to be sure), after Jules Laforgue, like Edna St. Vincent Millay in *Aria da Capo*, and another young man who would soon concede that he was a poet manqué and turn to fiction to confront the gap between lowly provincialism and modernism—William Faulkner. If Hughes went to Paris and Italy without finding the Lost Generation, at least he was able in 1932 to assure Ezra Pound (who had written to him from Rappallo to complain about the lack of instruction in African culture in America) that "Many of your poems insist on remaining in my head, not the words, but the mood and the meaning, which, after all, is the heart of a poem."

Hughes also shared with white modernists, to a degree far greater than might be inferred from his most popular poems, an instinct toward existentialism in its more pessimistic form. One poem, written just before his first book of poems appeared in 1926, suggests the relative case with which he could have taken to "raceless" modernist idioms. From "A House in Taos":

> Thunder of the Rain God
> And we three
> Smitten by beauty.
> Thunder of the Rain God:
> And we three
> Weary, weary.
> Thunder of the Rain God
> And you, she and I
> Waiting for the nothingness. . . .

Hughes, however, had already committed himself to a very different vision of poetry and the modern world, a vision rooted in the modern black experience and expressed most powerfully and definitively in the music called blues. What is the blues? Although W.C. Handy was the first musician to popularize it, notably with St. Louis Blues, the form is so deeply based in the chants of Afro-American slave labor, field hollers, and sorrow songs as to be ancient and comprises perhaps the greatest art of Africans in North America. Oral and improvisational by definition, the blues nevertheless has a classical regimen. Its most consistent form finds a three-line stanza, in which the second line restates the first, and the third provides a contrasting response to both. "The blues speak to us simultaneously of the tragic and the comic aspects of the human condition," Ralph Ellison has written; they must be seen "first as poetry and as ritual," and thus as "a transcendence of those conditions created within the Negro community by the denial of social justice." "It was a language," Samuel Charters asserts in *The Legacy of the Blues*, "a rich, vital, expressive language that stripped away the misconception that the black society in the United States was simply a poor, discouraged version of the white. It was impossible not to hear the differences. No one could listen to the blues without realizing that there were two Americas."

A long brooding on the psychology of his people, and a Whitmanesque predisposition to make the native languages of America guide his art, led Hughes early in 1923 to begin his greatest single literary endeavor: his attempt to resuscitate the dead art of an American poetry and culture by invoking the blues (exactly as George Gershwin, the following year, would try to elevate American music in his Rhapsody in Blue). If Pound had looked in a similar way, at one point, to the authority of the Provincial lyric of the middle ages, Hughes could still hear the blues in night clubs and on street corners, as blacks responded in art to the modern world. At the very least, Pound and Hughes (and Whitman) shared a sense that poetry and music were intimately related. To Hughes, black music at its best was the infallible metronome of racial grace: "Like the waves of the sea coming one after another, always one after another, like the earth moving around the sun, night, day—night, day—night, day—forever, so is the undertow of black music with its rhythm that never betrays you, its rooted power." In the blues, in its mixture of pain and laughter, its lean affirmation of humanity in the face of circumstance, all in a secular mode (no "shantih, shantih" here; no brand plucked from the "burning!"), he found the tone, the texture, the basic language of true black modernism. A line from the epigraphic note to the volume says it all: "The mood of the Blues is almost always despondency, but when they are sung people laugh."

Over a period of five years, starting some time around 1922, he slowly engaged the blues as a literary poet, first describing the blues from a distance, then enclosing the blues within a traditional poem, as he did in the prizewinning "The Weary Blues" ("Droning a drowsy syncopated tune, /Rocking back and forth to a mellow croon, / I heard a Negro play"), until, at last, in his most important collection, *Fine Clothes to the Jew* (1927), he proposed the blues exclusively on its own terms by writing in the form itself, alone. Thus he acknowledged at last the full dignity of the people who had invented it.

Savagely attacked in black newspapers as "about 100 pages of trash [reeking] of the gutter and sewer," containing "poems that are insanitary, insipid, and repulsing," this book nevertheless was Hughes's greatest achievement in poetry, and remarkable by almost any American standard, as the literary historian Howard Mumford Jones recognized in a 1927 review. "In a sense," Jones wrote of Hughes, "he has contributed a really new verse form to the English language."

More important, blues offered, in a real sense, a new mode of feeling to the world (Eudora Welty has reminded us that literature teaches us how to feel) and a new life to art. To probe this point we would have to make a fresh reading of art and culture in the 1920s, for which I do not have the time or, truly, the skills. But instead of dismissively talking about the jazz age we would have to see that 1920, when the first commercial recording of a black singer, Mamie Smith's *Crazy Blues*, appeared, was perhaps as important a year for some people (certainly the millions of blacks who bought blues records in the decade, and the millions of whites down to our day who would thereafter sing and dance to the blues and its kindred forms) as was 1922, the year of Eliot's The Waste Land, for other people. We would see Gershwin's *Rhapsody in Blue*, premiered at Paul Whiteman's concert "An Experiment in Modern Music" in New York in 1924, as a modern American landmark that is in fact an alternative to the spirit of European modernism. We might go further, not simply to the work of other musicians such as Stravinsky and Bartok and Aaron Copeland but also to the work of writers like Faulkner, whose genius was emancipated in *The Sound and the Fury*, I would suggest, by a balance between the modernism of Joyce, which dominates the first section of the novel, and the counter-modernism of the blues, which dominates the last in spite of the religious overtones there, and in spite of Faulkner's ultimate unwillingness to take on the consciousness of a black character whose life is informed by the blues. To me, it is instructive that Joycean technique facilitates the utterance of the idiot, Benjy, but that the blues temper informs the most affirmative section of the book, that dominated by black Dilsey Gibson and her people ("they endured").

Far from suggesting that only Langston Hughes in the Harlem Renaissance discovered the black modern, I see the whole Harlem movement as struggling toward its uncovering. Why? Because it was inescapable; it was what the masses lived. In one sense, reductive no doubt, the Harlem Renaissance was simply an attempt by the artists to understand blues values and to communicate them to the wider modern world.

Finally, I would suggest that this question of modernism, and Hughes's place in it, needs to be seen in the context not merely of Harlem but of international cultural change in the twentieth century. By the age of twenty-one, he belonged already to an advanced guard of writers, largely from the yet unspoken world outside Europe and North America, that would eventually include Neruda of Chile, the young Borges of Argentina (who translated "The Negro Speaks of Rivers" in 1931), Garcia Lorca of Spain (see his "El Rey de Harlem"), Jacques Roumain of Haiti (see his poem "Langston Hughes"), Senghor of Senegal (who would hail Hughes in 1966 as the greatest poetic influence on the Negritude movement), Césaire of Martinique, Damas of French Guyana, and Guillen of Cuba (who freely asserted in 1930 that his first authentically Cuban or "Negro" poems, the eight pieces of Molivos de Son, were inspired by Hughes's visit to Havana that year). To these names should be added painters such as Diego Rivera, following his return from Paris in 1923, and his friends Orozco and Siquieros.

The collective aim of these writers and artists was to develop, even as they composed in the languages and styles of Europe and faced the challenge of European modernism, an aesthetic tied to a sense of myth, geography, history, and culture that was truly indigenous to their countries, rather than merely reflective of European trends, whether conservative or avant-garde. Finally, let me suggest that Hughes's virtual precedence of place among them has less to do with his date of birth or his individual talent than with the fact that he was the poetic fruition of the Afro-American intellectual tradition, where these questions of race and culture and this challenge to civilization had long been debated, and under the harshest social conditions. In 1910, after all, when DuBois founded *Crisis* magazine, he gave it a challenging subtitle—but one he had already used for an even earlier publication. He called it "A Record of the Darker Races."

Arnold Rampersad. *The Harlem Renaissance: Revaluations* (New York: Garland Publishing, 1989), pp. 49–72

BIBLIOGRAPHY
*The Weary Blues*, 1926; *Fine Clothes to the Jew*, 1927; *Not Without Laughter, Knopf*, 1930; *The Negro Mother and Other Dramatic Recitations*, 1931; *Dear Lovely Death*, 1931; *The Dream Keeper and Other Poems*, 1932; *Scottsboro Limited: Four Poems and a Play*, 1932; *The Ways of White Folks*, 1934; *A New Song*, 1938; *The Big Sea: An Autobiography*, 1940; *Shakespeare in Harlem*, 1942; *Jim Crow's Last Stand*, 1943; *Freedom's Plow*, 1943. *Lament for Dark Peoples and Other Poems*, 1944; *Fields of Wonder*, 1947; *One-Way Ticket*, 1949; *Simple Speaks His Mind*, 1950; *Montage of a Dream Deferred*, 1951; *Laughing to Keep from Crying*, 1952; *Simple Takes a Wife*, 1953; *I Wonder as I Wander: An Autobiographical Journey*, 1956; *Simple Stakes a Claim*, 1957; *Tambourines to Glory*, 1958; *Ask Your Mama: 12 Moods for Jazz*, 1961. *Something in Common and Other Stories*, 1963; *Simple's Uncle Sam*, 1965; *The Panther and the Lash: Poems of Our Times*, 1967; *The Collected Poems of Langston Hughes*, 1994; *The Return of Simple*, 1994; *The Block: Poems*, 1995; *Carol of the Brown King: Poems*, 1997; *The Pasteboard Bandit*, 1997

# HURSTON, Zora Neale (1903–1960)
## United States

One can readily see why Miss Hurston's first novel, *Jonah's Gourd Vine*, was received with small enthusiasm from certain quarters of the Negro race. With a grasp of her material that has seldom been equaled by a writer of her race, she had every opportunity of creating a masterpiece of the age. But she failed. She failed not from lack of skill but from lack of vision.

The hero, John Buddy, who rose from an outcast bastard of an Alabama tenant farm to a man of wealth and influence, could have been another Ben Hur, bursting the unjust shackles that had bound him to a rotten social order and winning the applause even of his enemies. But unfortunately, his rise to religious prominence and financial ease is but a millstone about his neck. He is held back by some unseen cord which seems to be tethered to his racial heritage. Life crushes him almost to death, but he comes out of the mills with no greater insight into the deep mysteries which surround him. Such a phenomenon, although not intended by Miss Hurston as a type of all Negro manhood, is seized upon by thoughtless readers of other races as a happy confirmation of what they already faintly believe: namely, that the Negro is incapable of profiting by experience or of understanding the deeper mysteries of life.

Nick Aaron Ford. *The Contemporary Negro Novel* (Boston: Meador, 1936), pp. 99–100

Filling out Janie's story [in *Their Eyes Were Watching God*] are sketches of Eatonville and farming down "on the muck" in the Everglades. On the porch of the mayor's store "big old lies" and comic-serious debates, with the tallest of metaphors, while away the evenings. The dedication of the town's first lamp and the community burial of an old mule are rich in humor but they are not cartoons. Many incidents are unusual, and there are narrative gaps in need of building up. Miss Hurston's forte is the recording and the creation of folk-speech. Her devotion to these people has rewarded her; *Their Eyes Were Watching God* is chock-full of earthy and touching poetry. . . .

Though inclined to violence and not strictly conventional, her people are not naïve primitives. About human needs and frailties they have the unabashed shrewdness of the Blues. . . . Living in an all-colored town, these people escape the worst pressures of class and caste. There is little harshness; there is enough money and work to go around. The author does not dwell upon the "people ugly from ignorance and broken from being poor" who swarm upon the "muck" for short-time jobs. But there is bitterness, sometimes oblique, in the enforced folk manner, and sometimes forthright.

Sterling A. Brown. *Nation*. October 16, 1937, pp. 409–10

Only to reach a wider audience, need [Zora Neale Hurston] ever write books—because she is a perfect book of entertainment in herself. In her youth she was always getting scholarships and things from wealthy white people, some of whom simply paid her just to sit around and represent the Negro race for them, she did it in such a racy fashion. She was full of side-splitting anecdotes, humorous tales, and tragicomic stories, remembered out of her life in the South as a daughter of a travelling minister of God. She could make you laugh one minute and cry the next. To many of her white friends, no doubt, she was a perfect "darkie," in the nice meaning they give the term—that is a naïve, childlike, sweet, humorous, and highly colored Negro.

But Miss Hurston was clever, too—a student who didn't let college give her a broad *a* and who had great scorn for all pretensions, academic or otherwise. That is why she was such a fine folk-lore collector, able to go among the people and never act as if she had been to school at all. Almost nobody else could stop the average Harlemite on Lenox Avenue and measure his head with a strange-looking, anthropological device and not get bawled out for the attempt, except Zora, who used to stop anyone whose head looked interesting, and measure it.

Langston Hughes. *The Big Sea* (New York: Alfred A. Knopf, 1940), pp. 238–39

Out of her abundant stores of vitality Zora Hurston fashions an autobiography [*Dust Tracks on a Road*] which shoots off bright sparks of personality. . . . A woman of courage and action, she would scorn any academic retreat from the touch and feel of ordinary life. Not only is there nothing of the recluse in her nature, but there is, to state it positively, a preference for the jostling of the crowd. She feels a challenge to elbow her way along her traffic-jammed road with a roving eye for adventure. Tracks she leaves behind her in the dust, witnesses of her presence which only she among all those people can make. Mixing with others only enhances her individuality. . . .

Free of many routine moral obligations, Zora Hurston busies herself with unwrapping the happiness contained in each moment. She engenders an atmosphere of surprises both for herself and others who know her. Shrinking from the dullness of dogmatism, she blossoms out with an originality of thought and conduct. Although the author can hardly inform us that this originality is the secret of her charm, we can quickly detect it on each page of her autobiography. Even her literary style shows an out-of-the-ordinary quality, a concrete and earthy imagery, an uneven rhythm which reflect imagination, warmth, and impulsiveness. It is a safe guess that few people were bored in her presence. Angered sometimes, amused often, at least they must have responded positively to the unexpected course of her behavior. Sustained by her unflagging spirit, Zora Hurston is enabled to present a strong case for the doctrine of individuality in her own person.

Rebecca Chalmers Barton. *Witnesses for Freedom* (New York: Harper, 1948), pp. 101, 114

The style of [*Jonah's Gourd Vine*] is impressive enough. Zora Neale Hurston, whom Langston Hughes has described as a rare *raconteuse*, draws freely on the verbal ingenuity of the folk. Her vivid, metaphorical style is based primarily on the Negro preacher's graphic ability to present abstractions to his flock. . . .

The genesis of a work of art may be of no moment to literary criticism but it is sometimes crucial in literary history. It may, for example, account for the rare occasion when an author outclasses himself. *Their Eyes Were Watching God* is a case in point. The novel was written in Haiti in just seven weeks, under the emotional pressure of a recent love affair. "The plot was far from the circumstances," Miss Hurston writes in her autobiography, "but I tried to embalm all the tenderness of my passion for him in *Their Eyes Were Watching God*." Ordinarily the prognosis for such a novel would be dismal enough. One might expect immediacy and intensity, but not distance, or control, or universality. Yet oddly, or perhaps not so oddly, it is Miss Hurston's best novel, and possibly the best novel of the period, excepting [Richard Wright's] *Native Son*.

Robert A. Bone. *The Negro Novel in America* (New Haven: Yale University Press, 1958), pp. 127–28

An effervescent companion of no great profundities but dancing perceptions, [Zora] possessed humor, sense of humor, and what a fund of folklore! Although she seemed to have very little indignation for the imposed status of her race, she knew her people. Probably this insensibility was due to the fact that her awakening powers and subsequent recognition tended to act as a soporific to her early sufferings and neglect. . . .

Her book of folk tales, *Moses, Man of the Mountain*, was written out of race memory, if such a thing there be; her autobiography, *Dust Tracks on a Road*, was the result of experiences conditioned by race. But she herself was a gift both to her race and the human race. That she died in poverty and obscurity was because for a decade at least she had deliberately removed herself from the large group of us who felt puzzlement and still do. Where lurked her ultimate defeat, ending in retreat? Why and how?

Despite her bright accomplishments, her books, including *Tell My Horse* (the result of her explorations into Haiti), *Their Eyes Were Watching God, Dust Tracks on a Road*, are Negro Americana, to the smell of fried chitterlings, which by the way she loved.

Yet the inescapable conclusion persists that Zora remains a figure in bas relief, only partially emerging from her potential into the whole woman.

Fannie Hurst. *Yale University Library Gazette*. July 1960, pp. 18–19

Miss Hurston's most accomplished achievement in fiction is *Moses, Man of the Mountain*, which provided a format in which she could best utilize her talents for writing satire, irony, and dialect. . . . If she had written nothing else, Miss Hurston would deserve recognition for this book. For once, her material and her talent fused perfectly. Her narrative deficiencies are insignificant, for the reader knows the story. Her ridicule, caricature, and farce are appropriate. The monstrous Hattie of *Jonah's Gourd Vine* and Mrs. Turner of *Their Eyes Were Watching God* reappear aptly in the jealous, accursed Miriam, who actually becomes a sympathetic figure after she has been cursed with leprosy. Finally, attuned to folk psychology, Miss Hurston gave the Hebrew slaves an authenticity that they lack in the solemn Biblical story. . . .

In her final novel, *Seraph on the Suwanee*, Miss Hurston for the first time focused upon white protagonists, in a work so stylistically different from her earlier efforts that it reveals her conscious adjustment to the tastes of a new generation of readers. Although *Seraph on the Suwanee* is Hurston's most ambitious novel and her most artistically competent, its prolonged somberness causes many readers to yearn for the alleviating farce and carefree gaiety of the earlier works.

Darwin T. Turner. *In a Minor Chord: Three Afro-American Writers and Their Search for Identity* (Carbondale: Southern Illinois University Press, 1971), pp. 109–111

Miss Hurston's first, and perhaps best, novel, *Jonah's Gourd Vine*, is based loosely on the lives of her parents. Her intimate knowledge of the material gives the work an immediacy that the other works lack. Moreover, her skillful use of folk customs, folk superstitions, and above all else, folk speech helps make *Jonah's Gourd Vine* an unusual and fascinating work. Both Dunbar and Chesnutt had used folk material in their fiction, but neither had the knowledge of folk tales that Miss Hurston had (she was a trained anthropologist); and though both knew folk speech, neither gave it the poetic quality that Zora Neale Hurston gives it in this work; neither fused it as thoroughly as she does. . . .

The author's two folklore collections, *Mules and Men* and *Tell My Horse*, are fascinating works. Miss Hurston had a natural flair for collecting material from the folk. She had no difficulty in becoming one with the people from whom she sought songs or stories or customs, whether in the Deep South or in Haiti. She also had a great and natural gift as a raconteur of the stories she collected. Although the two works she published are impressive, one likes to think that with her undoubted ability as a collector and interpreter of folklore she would have made a far richer contribution to the field if she had continued to work in it.

Zora Neale Hurston has probably never received from Negro critics the credit she deserves, whereas white critics have occasionally over-praised her work. The reason for this, or at least part of it, is that she wrote counter to the prevailing attitude of protest and militancy which most Negro writers since 1925 have taken. Repelled by Zora Neale Hurston's unrealistic good-will stance, Negro critics have tended to dismiss her. This is unfortunate because, whatever one may think of her racial attitude, she had a real if uneven talent as a fiction writer and superb gifts as a collector and interpreter of folk materials.

Arthur P. Davis. *From the Dark Tower* (Washington, D.C.: Howard University Press, 1974), pp. 115, 119–20

Despite structural and formal defects, *Jonah's Gourd Vine* is most important for its depiction of the character of the black woman. Lucy is far from being completely developed as a character. She does, however, contain elements seldom seen in fiction by men which feature black women. Moreover, Miss Hurston, in her portrayal of Lucy, has begun early to deal with the conflict between black men and women, which receives fuller explication in Chester Himes's *Lonely Crusade* and John Williams' *Sissie* later in the century. The conflict centers around two victims of the same oppressive society. Take John and Lucy as metaphors of black men and women. . . .

John, the metaphor of black men, remains, for Miss Hurston, essentially a creature of appetite, insatiable even though offered such a delectable morsel as Lucy Pearson. Her loyalty, perseverance, and love border upon the messianic. What her husband lacks in courage, strength, and initiative, she more than compensates for. The conflicts, therefore, given such personalities, can be resolved only when black men correct the defects in character. That this was the author's implicit commentary upon black men might be attributable to her distorted conception of them. The chances are, however, that she was less interested in John Pearson than in Lucy, less interested in the men of her novels than in the women, who receive more multidimensional treatment.

In *Jonah's Gourd Vine* and *Their Eyes Were Watching God*, she views them as modern women, patterned upon paradigms of the past, those of the courage and strength of Harriet Tubman and Sojourner Truth. Far from being the images of old, the willing copartners of white men in the castration of black men, her women are, instead, the foundations of a new order, the leavening rods of change, from whose loins will eventually come the new man. Past stereotypes aside, therefore, her women need only search for greater liberation, move even beyond the stoiclike devotion of a Lucy Pearson, move toward greater independence and freedom. Put another way, black liberation meant burying the old images and symbols that had circumscribed black women along with black men. What is needed, McKay had argued in *Banjo*, is "Women that can understand us as human beings and not as wild over-sexed savages." In the context of *Jonah's Gourd Vine* and *Their Eyes Were Watching God*, this meant that both sexes must move collectively outside of American history and definitions.

Addison Gayle, Jr. *The Way of the New World* (Garden City, New York: Doubleday, 1975), pp. 143–44

Alice Walker, in introducing a collection of Zora Neale Hurston's writings, asserts that the fundamental thesis that Hurston embodied and exhibited as an ethical resource was that one "must struggle every minute of life to affirm black people's right to a healthy existence." The work of Hurston is quite diverse. Some of her writings are purely satirical and entertaining. Other pieces are colloquial in style and avowedly persuasive. All reveal a fundamental truth: self-fulfillment in a situation of oppression requires hitting a straight lick with a crooked stick. In other words, all of Hurston's work is a type of ambiguous featherbed resistance.

Zora Hurston understood the elaborate facade of myths, traditions, and rituals erected to couch systems of injustice in America. Thus, the complexity of being a Black woman artist writing for the *Saturday Evening Post*, the *American Mercury*, and the *American Legion Magazine* caused Hurston to combine her private experiences with various linguistic modes, so that her writing at times appears fairly oblique and nonthreatening. Hurston used irony, wit, and humor to entertain White readers as she reported the Black community's understanding and manifestations of courageous living. In different ways of saying much the same thing, Hurston's writings are sometimes very belligerent. She took for granted the inseparability of words and actions. Her work is imbued with a conscious hope that language can expose "the weight that racism lays on the whole world."

All in all, Zora Neale Hurston's life and work relate to the struggle for racial justice. Identifying resources for a constructive ethic was not her explicit goal but can be frequently explicated from the stance she took on various issues. Testifying to a vision of a just society, Hurston made particular claims on the moral agency of her audiences. She encouraged protest against the dehumanization of Black personhood. Across the boundaries of her own experience, Hurston wrote about the oppressive and unbearable, about those things that rub Black women raw. Her richness and chaos, her merits and faults witnessed to an ethic that can be lived out only in community.

Katie G. Cannon. *Katie's Cannon: Womanism and the Soul of the Black Community* (New York: The Continuum Publishing Company, 1995), pp. 89–90

BIBLIOGRAPHY

*Fast and Furious* (with Clinton Fletcher and Time Moore), 1931; *Mule Bone: A Comedy of Negro Life in Three Acts*, (with Langston Hughes), 1931; *Jonah's Gourd Vine*, 1934; *Mules and Men*, 1935; *Their Eyes Were Watching God*, 1937; *Tell My Horse*, 1938; *Moses, Man of the Mountain*, 1939; *Dust Tracks on a Road*, 1942; *Seraph on the Suwanee*, 1948; *Spunk: The Selected Stories of Zora Neale Hurston*, 1985; *The Complete Stories*, 1994; *Folklore, Memoirs, and Other Writings*, 1995; *Novels and Stories*, 1995; *Collected Essays*, 1998

# I

## IYAYI, Festus (1947– )
### Nigeria

Festus Iyayi's *Violence* provides us with an alternative view of man in society as well as a new formal option in the Nigerian novel. Its sustaining ideological premise, which also provides it with a title, is the materialistic contention that in a society where relationships among men are governed by the laws of capitalist production and its attendant jungle ethics (eat or be eaten!), the various injustices which the oppressed masses have to suffer amount to variations on a grand theme of violence. . . .

Iyayi depicts a world in which man's philosophical options and moral choices are determined by the objective forces of economic relations in society. Consequently, the view of man and society that prevails in *Violence* derives from the Aristotelian axiom that man is *Zoon politikon*, a sociopolitical animal, who, in being a product of social determinism, is nevertheless an active product and, to that extent, is also the principal agency of change and progress in society. This conviction would seem to unite Aristotelian political philosophy with traditional African social philosophy with its emphasis on communalism.

Accordingly, the immediate social setting of the novel is played up to a position of prominence. The sociohistorical context is unmistakably real, nearly anarchic, and can be easily located in postwar petro-dollar Nigeria. The characteristic features of this milieu are carefully presented as atavism, aggressive individualism, limitless acquisitiveness, and conspicuous consumption. In the immediate locale of the action which is thinly disguised as Benin, the capital of Nigeria's Bendel State, the most noticeable fact of social existence is the coexistence of abject penury with scandalous affluence. More importantly, Iyayi is at pains to capture the prosaic reality and the raw immediacy of the material conditions under which the exploited classes live. The situation is such that the poor even have to sell pints of their own blood to those of the sick who can afford the giveaway price . . . in order to ensure the next meal for their family. Medical facilities, jobs, decent shelter, and food are luxuries which only the rich can afford.

It is against this horrifying social spectacle that the different characters derive their identity as either exploiters or victims of exploitation. The principal contrast, in terms of material conditions, is between Obofun and his wife, Queen, on one hand and the Idemudias on the other. The former are wealthy hoteliers and government sponsored contractors while the latter are a poor couple driven by poverty and unemployment to the periphery of society, a situation in which they can hardly afford the next meal and have to live on pittances and handouts from benevolent neighbors.

However, the implications of Iyayi's ideological standpoint for characterization in this novel are not exhausted by this simple positing of two couples living in contrasting material conditions. Far from simplifying the problematic of the novel in a polarization of characters, Iyayi weaves into them certain psychological attributes which add up to a negation and indictment of the capitalist ethos which is a central theme. Thus, although materially rich, Obofun and his wife fail to achieve mutual fulfillment in their "marriage of convenience." The emotional content of their marriage has been corroded by their pursuit of money and business opportunities. Consequently, they both degenerate morally to a point where Obofun resorts to lechery and womanizing while his wife, in her endless quest for easy profit, becomes more of a glorified prostitute. . . .

The tragic essence of *Violence* lies more [in] the anarchic social setting and blood-curdling experiences which it constitutes as its central problematics. But its formal integrity lies in the peculiar kind of resolution which it forges for its tragic dialectic. Here again, Idemudia as the hero of this "tragedy" is also the carrier of its peculiar aesthetic proposition. In spite of his poverty and marginalized condition, he does not acquiesce or succumb to oppression. At different moments in the novel, he revolts against the indignities meted out to him by society on account of his material limitations. At the height of his humiliation in the hospital because of his inability to pay the exorbitant bills, he resolutely declares: "I am going to escape somehow from this so-called hospital in which I am being held as a prisoner . . . I am going to continue to struggle, to fight."

> Chidi Amuta. *Commonwealth Essays & Studies*. 7, 1 (Autumn 1984), pp. 99–101, 104

[In *Violence*] the working people, represented by Idemudia and others who gather at Iyaso Motor Park, are constantly looking for work. Here again, people are forced to sell their labor power to the local bourgeoisie in order to survive. In most cases they are employed merely on a daily basis, so there is no job security. Since the surplus value created is to be shared between the local and the foreign masters, Idemudia and his comrades are grossly exploited as manual laborers in off-loading cement bags and as workers with building contractors. . . .

[The] working people are presented as individuals who believe in struggling for their liberation—as fully conscious human beings who are prepared to face their problems with courage. At the same time, they are not presented as infallible heroes but also have their human weaknesses. Idemudia, for example, is tempted to propose sex to Queen even though he realizes that this might adversely affect the ongoing struggle between Queen, the contractor, and Idemudia's own labor union. . . .

In Festus Iyayi's novel a balanced picture is given, both of the working people and of the exploiters. Neither social class is infallible. They both show a degree of human failing and human strength, although it is abundantly clear that Iyayi is on the side of the working people. As a radical writer he is not complacent towards the plight of those who have only their labor to sell. But he does not legitimize Idemudia's attempt at beating his wife; neither does he approve of the (understandable) "sexual methods" of Adisa, who searches for money to pay off Idemudia's hospital bill. . . .

Iyayi's concept of art tallies with that of [Frantz] Fanon. In his novel, he sees working people as people always in the process of asserting their existence through struggle. They face the future with determination. At the same time, a balanced view is given of the members of the neocolonial comprador class. They are also portrayed as human beings, but as human beings debasing themselves and others in their efforts to appropriate the surplus value created by the working people. On the whole, Iyayi's concept of art is progressive and Fanonist.

Tunde Fatunde. In Georg M. Gugelberger, ed. *Marxism and African Literature* (Trenton, New Jersey: Africa World Press, 1986), pp. 111–14, 116

[*Heroes*] is one of those artistic texts which carries within it a clue as to how its author intends it to be read. A key to understanding the novel lies in the words of one of its characters, Sergeant Audu, a Federal soldier fighting on the Asaba front during the Nigerian Civil War. Several of Audu's men die heroically in an ambush, abandoned by their officer, who had arranged to be driven away to safety. At this point, Audu remarks bitterly: ''After the war, many generals will write their accounts in which they will attempt to show that they were the heroes. . . . They will tell the world that they singlehandedly fought and won the war. The names of soldiers like Otun, Emmanuel, Ikeshi and Yemi will never be mentioned. . . . The soldiers pay for the unity of this country with their lives and yet, what happens? . . . Always the generals get the praise. Always they are the heroes.''. . .

Iyayi's attack on bourgeois historiography in *Heroes* is incisive and convincing. His main character, the young journalist Osime Iyere, is initially a firm supporter of the Federal cause. He accepts the Federal government's contention that the war must be fought and won in order to protect Nigerians from the tribalistic attitude and greed of the Igbos. As the novel progresses, however, the contradictions in this argument begin to appear. When the Federal army arrives in Benin to ''liberate'' the town from the Biafrans, Osime observes that, far from protecting the inhabitants, they slaughter civilians just as indiscriminately as the Biafrans had done earlier. At the Asaba front, the Federal officers indulge in endless rounds of parties as the rank and file are sent into battle to die. In Lagos, far from the battlefront, the head of state and commander in chief of the armed forces, General Gowon, remains oblivious to the carnage in Asaba as he celebrates his wedding with the vulgar insensitivity typical of his class.

These contradictions provide dramatic evidence of Iyayi's thesis that the war originated less in tribal sentiment than in class interests: indeed, he succeeds in reducing the war to a greedy squabble between factions within the ruling class. As Osime reflects, ordinary Igbos, as opposed to those of the ruling class, ''never had any quarrel with the Hausas or the Yorubas until the politicians and generals allowed their lust for power and greed for profit to run riot.'' Osime insists that the real basis for solidarity is not tribe but class. He points out to a fellow journalist: ''The fact is that the ordinary Igbo man has a great deal more in common with the ordinary Hausa and the ordinary Yoruba than he has in common with the Igbo businessman and general and politicians.'' Similarly, members of the ruling class, irrespective of tribal origin, are, in the final analysis, bound together by mutual interest.

What is needed in order to change this situation, Iyayi tells us, is a ''third army,'' an army whose role would be ideological in that it would fight ruling class propaganda and enable ordinary Nigerians, be they Igbo, Yoruba, or Hausa, to recognize their common interests and reject the divisions that their respective ruling classes

seek to promote between them. The combined forces of the Nigerian people would then take up arms to destroy the entire ruling class, irrespective of tribal considerations. Iyayi sums up his message in a striking image of Gowon and Ojukwu, seeming enemies but in reality fellow members of the ruling class, fleeing together from the Nigerian people, because, in the war to end all wars, ''they would be on the same side, where they actually do belong.''

Fírinne Ni Chréacháin. *Research in African Literatures.* 22, 1 (Spring 1991), pp. 43–45

The relationship between the historical event and its fictional representation, situated as it is in the vast mine-pitted terrain of ''realism,'' is an extremely complex one, and this study of *Heroes* will focus on just one dimension: the selection and handling of particular historical events by the artist as a means of intervening in the making of history. . . .

The task which Iyayi explicitly sets himself in *Heroes* obviously has much in common with that of the radical historian: to expose the ideological bias of bourgeois historiography and, by adopting the perspective of the exploited majority, by rewriting history ''from below,'' to reveal the class interests that are the motive force of history. This project is expressed with remarkable economy in the novel's title: in a single word, Iyayi signifies his determination to substitute one set of actors for another, to replace the generals, the ''heroes'' of bourgeois historiography, with the ''unknown soldiers'' who represent the masses and are the heroes of radical history. Iyayi is equally explicit in stating the purpose of radical history and radical art. The exposure of ruling-class self-interest is a step towards liberating the exploited from the dominant ideology, and ultimately towards mobilizing them against the ruling class. As Osime tells the soldiers, ''I want you to know the truth, and knowing the truth helps until there are so many who know the truth that you can do something about it.''. . .

Central to his art is the judicious use of the *typical*, of what people will recognize as characteristic of the society, in terms of events and the agents shaping them. For Iyayi, the Asaba-Onitsha crossing, in which hundreds of ordinary Nigerians from all over the country lost their lives but which brought no benefit to the Nigerian masses, is clearly such an event. Similarly typical is Gowon's wedding, which came to symbolize all the callousness of a corrupt regime. Iyayi knows that any reference to Gowon's wedding is capable of stirring the memories of Nigerians of his own generation, of reawakening old resentments against the ruling class and the upper echelons of the military which are part of it. For those too young to remember the war, the artistic combination of the Asaba tragedy and the wedding provides a paradigm which exposes the contradictions, not just of a war they did not experience, but of the cruel realities of their own lives today.

Fírinne Ni Chréacháin. *Journal of Commonwealth Literature.* 27, 1 (1992), pp. 48–50, 56–57

*The Contract* opens with the return to Nigeria of Ogie Obala, the son of a wealthy businessman, from his studies overseas. Iyayi takes full advantage of his protagonist's initial shock of arrival, the frenzy he sees all around him, to introduce his theme. In the taxi bearing him home, Ogie is subjected to a diatribe by the driver on the importance of money in the society to which he has returned. . . . Arrived home, his father is quick to confirm the driver's outburst, though without the former's bitterness and outrage. . . . When [Ogie] visits [his girlfriend Rose Idebale] a week after his arrival, he tells her that he will be joining his father's firm. His job will be to award government contracts. The whole issue of contracts is at the heart of large-scale corruption, if only because of the amounts involved. The commonly accepted practice is for the awarding firm to automatically demand ten percent commission of the value of the contract as a matter of course, and for the interested parties to bid against each other on that basis. Rose is only too well aware of the damage this is doing to the country. . . .

[The] theme of *The Contract* is corruption and its corrosive effect on one man's soul: "I have eaten the apple," Ogie says, and so he has. In this context, Ogie's death is merely a diversion because it absolves the writer from the necessity of examining the full implications of the moral depths he has plumbed. But this is precisely what the novel demands. Physical death is by no means the worst thing that can happen to a person; far worse is the death of the soul that comes with eating the fruit of sin. This is what Rose meant, after all, when she declared, "How could you fight it alone and hope to come out of it alive." She meant that he was heading for a spiritual annihilation that she·has daily witnessed in those around her, but which she firmly rejects as a possible option for herself.

Rose, like Idemudia in *Violence*, is the person who will not be corrupted; who will hold herself aloof from the prevailing squalor and follow only the dictates of her conscience. It is for this reason that she rejects Ogie's proposal of marriage. . . . This is not bravado for its own sake. Even when she discovers that she is pregnant by him, and that her pregnancy could easily be her passport out of the rathole to which her poverty condemns her, she remains faithful to her beliefs.

Adewale Maja-Pearce. *A Mask Dancing: Nigerian Novelists of the Eighties* (London: Hans Zell, 1992), pp. 79–80, 84–85

The most significant narrative and plotting strategies commonly used by African Marxist novelists suggest that they form a creative community united by ideologically coherent attitudes toward history and culture. First, combinations of labor strikes and massive protest rallies are their main methods of fomenting plot conflicts and managing causation and duration: Ngugi's *Devil on the Cross* peaks during an angry march on the banquet of a local Chamber of Commerce, and a peasant protest march on Nairobi marks the climax of *Petals of Blood*; the strike in [Ousmane Sembere's] *God's Bits of Wood* culminates in a massive public rally in Dakar Iyayi's *Violence* closes on the eve of a strike. The volatile emotions normally invested in planning, executing, and resolving strikes and political rallies provide ideologically appropriate and historically realistic dramatic vehicles for the novelists' themes. (Because the state is often the largest employer in most African countries, a well-executed national strike, can make the entire political economy nervous.) By exploring the thoughts of the workers and marchers, the novelists demonstrate the instructive effects of the mass agitations; those demonstrations thus become expositions on the psychic cultivation of class consciousness and class antagonism. The novelists convert ordinarily reformist actions into metaphors of

subversion by dwelling on the catalytic effects of those actions on the cultivation of heightened social awareness among the poor and the disenfranchised.

Second, all elements of characterization in the novels—class, motivation, place—are described as factors of economic relations. Material wealth (or lack thereof) becomes a metonym of property and social relations; even physique is a metaphor for class affiliation, and consumer preferences reflect class sympathy, if not outright membership. The novels do not flirt with utopian alternative societies, not even with the very attractive models of pre-Gorbachev eastern Europe. They derive their attraction-and abhorrence, of course-from their "impolite" non-nationalistic descriptions of social inequities. They describe the postindependence instabilities in Africa as indicators of structural faults that cannot be fixed with "correct" political appointments, the formulation of the right ethnic equation, or the cultivation of individual patriotism. . . .

At the paradigmatic level, the novels predicate their materialist explanations of reality with allegorical characterization, iconic consumer choices, and symbolic living arrangements. In the typical African Marxist novel, members of the bourgeois class are almost always ugly, portly, and ghoulish. Conversely, peasants and working-class characters are careworn and famished. The distended stomachs and the rosy cheeks of the politicians, industrialists, and bureaucrats attest to the glaring expropriation of the haggard poor. The grotesque portraiture also demystifies the widespread cultural belief that rotund physique signifies divine favor. The most remarkable examples of the caricatures include Chui in *Petals of Blood*, Queen in *Violence*, and Gitutu in *Devil on the Cross*. Chui has a miserably "huge stomach"; Queen, the major industrial tycoon in Iyayi's novel, has a euphemistic "pair of neat legs". Gitutu's exorbitant paunch illustrates this strategy best: a belly that protrudes so far that it would have touched the ground had it not been supported by the braces that held up his trousers. It seemed as if his belly had absorbed all his limbs and all the other organs of his body. Gitutu had no neck—at least his neck was not visible. His arms and legs were short stumps. His head had shrunk to the size of fist. . . .

In the typical African Marxist novel, topos reflects the socioeconomic affiliations of the inhabitants. Those who enjoy bounteous wealth, good health, and corpulent build also have palatial homes They are members of parliament, company directors, top bureaucrats, and police officers. The writers use one cunning method to represent comfortable living spaces as excessive appropriations traceable to the repression of the underclass: the Occupants of the big houses are usually involved, in one official capacity or another, in the active (sometimes deadly) suppression of the little agitations of honest people who seek a slight improvement in their own living conditions. The inhabitants of the oases of comfort either own the industrial plants or give direct orders for the arrest of "trouble makers.". . .

Post-Ousmane stories about an epoch that has produced an indigenous petty bourgeoisie depict conspicuous consumption as another marker of inequitable social appropriation. Automobiles, clothing, eating habits, and other ordinarily idiosyncratic behaviors assume symbolic meaning in the radical novel. Affluent choices, especially in the context of the lack of basic needs suffered by the laboring communities, indicate the skewed allocation of economic surplus. Ngugi's characterization of the indigenous industrial class as the "mercedes tribe" names iconically the emergence of a social, economic, political, and cultural group wealthy enough to be identified by its vehicle of choice. Ngugi's characterization for the bourgeoisie—the tribe—contrasts with the more progressive transethnic identities that the working people forge in the heat of their political and economic protests.

In Iyayi's *Violence*, character identification by consumer preference is even more portentous. The only car that splashes mud on pedestrians on Owode Street soon after a rain shower is a Mercedes. To mark how the employers spend the profits garnered from the laborers' exploitation, Iyayi places either a Volvo or a Mercedes at every scene of personnel decision. Also, wherever adultery is committed or a bribe is exchanged one will find these symbols of irresponsible pleasure. The cleverest use of automobile as an index of social and class relations occurs in an episode in which the protagonist reminisces on a job search at a petrol station. He remembers, among other things, the pity on the face of a young man who, mistaken for a prospective employer, was overwhelmed by a mob of job seekers. Idemudia recollects vividly that when the crowd drew back from the Lada truck, ''he saw the man shaking his head and then all of a sudden, he understood why . . . anger had been in the man's eyes but he had not given himself time to reason why the man should have felt concerned''. Both the young man's physical gestures and the make of his vehicle signify ideological empathy. Lada is a low-cost, Italian-made, Russi an-assembled utility vehicle.

African Marxist novels are too often accused of lacking subtlety in their single-minded pursuit of political relevance. They are frequently faulted for concocting ''unhistorical'' plots, characters, and resolutions. . . . These criticisms, I suggest, are inherent in all self-consciously ''cognitive'' arts. Writings that try to combine the politicians' propensity for transparent signification with the artists' cultivated opacity cannot escape excessive enthusiasm. In African radical fiction, the politician usually meets the artist in the portrayal of the protagonist. The leader of a strike or protest combines the politicians' realism (most manifest during negotiations) and the artists' idealism (in articulating the demands). In stating the workers' grievances, the radical hero consolidates the provocative ''sociological'' facts embedded in plot, characterization, and setting into a revolutionary outrage. The successful radical protagonist therefore must balance the demagoguery of realistic politicking and the imagination of a restorative future. The protagonist, in other words, translates the exchanges between the defenders of capitalist present and the questioning protesters.

Adeleke Adeeko. *Critique: Studies in Contemporary Fiction.* 38, 3 (Spring 1997), pp. 177–91

Festus Iyayi, the prizewinning author of *Heroes*, affirms with his more recent collection of fifteen short stories [*Awaiting Court Martial*] that his creative mill is still full of grist. No thinking and sensitive Nigerian reader can drop this text without some pang of shame or guilt; and indeed, no reader can go through *Awaiting Court Martial* without wondering and despairing, as America's Mark Twain once did, about us all as this ''damned human race.'' Iyayi's stories probe our irrationalities, our bestialities, our inscrutable motives, and even the sources of our occasional tenderness. No matter how innocuous or safely guarded, they are all bared. In the end, it becomes easy to see that the system and environment which make us what we are might be culpable, but then we are doubly culpable for allowing ourselves to bow to all those ugly impulses which aggregate into the character of our societies. In the relentless morphology of Iyayi's thought, each story is a veritable whorl, indispensable in the total intensity of the collection.

There are stories of the decrepitude of the Nigerian polity; playing out its telltale dictatorial high-handedness, brutality, and insensitivity without showing us the faces of the dictators except by remotest obliquity and tangential reportage. In most cases when we see or hear those contiguous to power, through malfeasance and arrogance of class, we understand the nature of those bigger forces they serve. In the volume's title story, the narrator, a professional executioner, is awaiting court martial for refusing to execute his convicted brother Alubiya. The narrator is willing to submit to death rather than succumb to the dictates of a mindless power game, having been privileged to know his convicted brother as a most tender and humane soul. Of course, no one understands or will understand, but the protagonist is exemplary and adamant in his moral steadfastness: ''Let them go ahead and shoot me . . . they would indeed have simply been spitting at the sun.'' That rare posture is what the polity needs for rejuvenation.

Thus, we find in another short story, ''Saira,'' that the eminent could kill and kill again and get away with it, because few have the courage or will to protest the damnable. Moral action is always stymied by fear of death or fear of incarceration. In ''Saira,'' when the impotent multimillionaire Alhaji Bako Bello murders his wife Fatima, he needs less than ruses and the reckless bonhomie of the moneyed class to cover up both his wife's death and that of his maid Saira, who ''hangs herself'' in jail. This decadent society is not in want of seeing eyes, but the brutal dictatorships know how to distort both its acts and the visions of the morally sensitive. This is also clear in ''Extracts from the Testimony,'' where the modus operandi of the regime is reflected in its recurrent strategy of defame and destroy, or in ''When They Came for Akika Lamidi,'' in which the system demonstrates how brazen it can be or how far it can go to snuffle media-related campaigns which dare expose its activities.

The author of *Awaiting Court Martial* is not satisfied in simply blaming the system. The people get a generous share of the blame too, as we find in the story of the kind of senseless killing which marked the civil war in Nigeria. It was a war in which one no longer knew who the enemy was, and Iyayi is careful in ''No Hard Feelings'' to demonstrate that the issue of tribalism is not as troubling as is our well-distributed congenital callousness. This is so much so that one who endeavors to rise above such muck is considered almost weird or abnormal by the rest of us, There is cause for the good ones among us to wonder whether it is even worth it to raise a finger in the morass. The powerful opening story, ''Jegede's Madness,'' walks us back to the past of the leading characters to suggest that we are probably all victims of the atavistic and the circumstantial, and that we should therefore accept our lot stoically. The equally powerful closing story, ''Sunflowers,'' exhorts us to hold on to our tender cores and believe in the beauty of our dreams.

Iyayi's collection is a sad, almost existential world of blurred beauty and blighted hopes and dreams. In all this drama of futile struggles and embattled accomplishments, there is somewhere, however unreachable, a grail of secret hopes. And there is something consistently cathartic about the way each story unfolds or the manner in which some characters live out their multifarious crises. Without any visible or annoying ideological placards, Iyayi's vicarious labor is heightened by an evocative vision which misses nothing in the concrete and natural or ethereal environments. . . .

> Chimalum Nwankwo. *World Literature Today.* 72, 1 (Winter 1998), pp. 189–90

BIBLIOGRAPHY

*Violence,* 1979; *The Contract,* 1982; *Heroes,* 1986; *Awaiting Court Martial,* 1996

# J

## JAMES, C. L. R. (1901–1989)
### Trinidad

[C. L. R.] James said that he wrote *Minty Alley* "purely to amuse myself one summer." For some time he had been interested in the literary possibilities of "yard" life, and had published a short story, "Triumph," which dealt with the picturesque life in a Port-of-Spain "barrack-yard." James had actually decided to live in such a yard in order to experience the life of its inhabitants at first hand: "I went to live there, the people fascinated me, and I wrote about them from the point of view of an educated youthful member of the black middle class." In *Minty Alley*, James drew on this experience to illustrate not only what he saw as the natural joie de vivre of the slumdwellers, their ability to transcend repressive surroundings, but also the possibilities for mutual enrichment which might come from a middle-class involvement with, and understanding of, the "yard" folk. Mr. Haynes, a young, middle-class Negro orphaned by the death of his mother, decides to look for cheap lodgings in a slum yard to escape both loneliness and the expense of living in his parents' large, mortgaged home. His faithful servant, Ella, tries to dissuade him, but he persists, and takes a room in No. 2 Minty Alley, where he becomes involved in the life of the yard community. The others respect his higher social status as an educated man, a householder, and a white-collar worker and he uses his position as "father-confessor" and ombudsman to the residents to keep the unstable yard relationships from becoming too explosive. He enjoys this new life, gaining a measure of maturity during the process (thanks partly to an affair with young Maisie, the fiery-tempered beauty of the yard), and is very unhappy when, owing to the death of Benoit, one of the yard's most vital characters, and the insoluble conflict between Maisie and her aunt, Mrs. Rouse, the bereaved landlady of the yard, the community disbands and the property is sold. Haynes goes back to his dull, middle-class life, which had been temporarily heightened by the experience of No. 2 Minty Alley, which itself, inevitably, undergoes change, becoming a respectable, residential area.

As this summary of the plot suggests, *Minty Alley* . . . is intended by its author to be a sympathetic study of slum life from a middle-class viewpoint. . . . James's stance is one of subjective involvement. He attempts this through his black character, Mr. Haynes, who functions as an extension of his author's voice and sympathies. From the outset James is clearly an advocate for lower-class vitality as opposed to the dullness and snobbery of middle-class life.

> Michael Gilkes. *The West Indian Novel* (Boston: Twayne, 1981), pp. 28–29

In *Beyond a Boundary*, James describes his departure for England in 1932 as a necessary step in what was to be a literary career: "I had a completed novel with me. But that was only my 'prentice hand. Contrary to accepted experience, the real *magnum opus* was to be my second novel." James was to distinguish himself internationally as an imaginative political theorist, and as a sensitive commentator on the West Indian social and cultural scene, but no second novel ever came to be written. The first was *Minty Alley*. . . .

*Minty Alley* is more than just a novel of the yard narrated from an unusual point of view. And Haynes is not simply a narrative device. The novel is really about the mutually impoverishing alienation of the educated West Indian from the people. James allows Haynes's economic necessity to coincide with the character's "need to make a break" from the protecting world of middle-class mother and faithful family servant. The young man's growing involvement with, and appreciation of, the inhabitants of the yard are made to correspond with the degrees by which he comes to have his first sexual affair with Maisie, the yard's young firebrand. It is a function of the author's lack of sentimentality, that Maisie should leave for the United States by the end, rather than hang about in the hope of leading the affair with Haynes to a conventional conclusion. But Haynes has had his awakening. His returns to the respectable house that has replaced the old Minty Alley are as much an ironic comment on the rising West Indian bourgeoisie as a wistful backward glance at what is being lost.

> Kenneth Ramchand. *The West Indian Novel and Its Background* (London: Heinemann, 1983), pp. 69–71

James wrote his fiction well before he was thirty. He had always been a voracious reader, feeding his insatiable curiosity with a wide variety of material. In his twenties, he was intellectually stimulated by the young artists and thinkers who were changing the direction of West Indian culture. "La Divina Pastora," brief and complete as a miniature portrait, was his first success. Then came "Triumph," which he still considers one of his finest works, and finally the novel *Minty Alley*. All concern the grassroots people, whom James considered the lifeblood of the culture.

"La Divina Pastora" is the story of Anita Perez, whose shy but affluent lover Sebastian Montagnio visits nightly but cannot break through his inhibitions. He smokes while Anita knits or sews and her mother sits on the ground just outside chatting away in patois. Marriage to Sebastian (or somebody) is Anita's only chance to escape her daily labor in the cocoa fields, and that hope is fading with Anita's fading beauty. The routine is broken when Anita visits her aunt in Siparia and presents her case at the alter of the renowned saint La Divina Pastora. Anita leaves as a sacrifice her only ornament, a little gold chain. Upon her return, Sebastian, jarred by her unprecedented absence, becomes more demonstrative and even asks to take Anita to the cocoa-house dance. Discounting the influence of La Divina Pastora, Anita wishes she had her gold chain back to wear to the dance. By the end of the dance, a coolness has arisen between the lovers. Later, undressing for bed and telling her mother about the dance, Anita suddenly falls silent, then faints—for on her table, in its accustomed place, is the little chain.

Brief though it is, the story is perfectly crafted. It is an interesting balance of realism and mysticism. The objective narrator neither denies nor affirms the powers of La Divina Pastora but merely tells concisely what happens. The ending leaves many questions unanswered—which is, of course, the way of our lives and of good fiction. The basic *fact* of the story, the dominant thought with which the reader is left, is the impact of generations-long poverty.

"Triumph" portrays life in the urban barrack yards. Again the story focuses on the plight of impoverished women, whose only resource ultimately is their sexuality. In "Triumph" Mamitz has lost her lover and is therefore destitute since, like the other women in the yard, her survival depends upon her ability to maintain a relationship with a man. Her friend Celestine, suspecting that their enemy Irene has put a curse on Mamitz, performs Obeah rites, after which Mamitz attracts not one but two lovers. Popo is a flashy playboy who soon moves on. Nicholas the butcher is a steady type who pays Mamitz's rent and supports her well. When Popo returns for a brief but impressive fling, Irene hastens to tell Nicholas, who rushes to the scene. Fortunately, Popo has left. The ensuing quarrel is classic, but Mamitz convinces Nicholas of her fidelity. Her triumph is the dramatic display of the money Nicholas has given her, nailed in small denominations to the double doors of her house, proclaiming to the yard-world the defeat of the enemy Irene.

> Eugenia Collier. In Daryl Cumber Dance, ed. *Fifty Caribbean Writers* (Westport, Connecticut: Greenwood Press, 1986), pp. 232–33

Although C. L. R. James's *Beyond a Boundary* is not autobiography in the traditional sense, it is more than a cricket memoir by a major West Indian writer. It is a complex narrative, rich in personal insight, seasoned with cricket history, cultural mythography, and Marxist polemics. In answer to the perennial question *what do men live by?* James, theorist, historian, Pan-Africanist, and pamphleteer, spins an intriguing, idiosyncratic tale of West Indian cultural emergence within the context of a national sport. He employs cricket as a metaphor for a nascent West Indian community from which, as an expatriate and "British intellectual," he is estranged. The center of interest is the self and its relationship to the surrounding world; as autobiographer, sentimentally tied to both [William Makepeace] Thackeray and [William] Hazlitt, James self-consciously reshapes the past into a pattern of stages where he mediates a battle between the "old world" of tradition and the "new" one of revolt. . . .

*Beyond a Boundary* is a carefully crafted account of the author's past as seen through the veil of exile. It is a journey into a childhood marked by Victorian sensibility, an errant view of early adulthood spent at the heels of cricketers and at the shrine of ancient learning, a journey that led to the seat of empire where sports and politics became integral pawns on the playing fields of a class war.

> Consuelo Lopez Springfield. *Carolina Quarterly*. 35, 4 (December 1989), p. 73

James's speeches, like the brilliant orations of [Edmund] Burke and [Benjamin] Disraeli, abound in messianic images. As a Marxist Milton or modern Moses, he embraces a romanticized past. His historical vision portrays the world's proletariat as a legion of saints struggling against the monstrous forces of capitalist evil to achieve a new society. Images of rebirth contrasted with those of decay suggest a choice: redemption through a baptism of fire—socialist revolution—or spiritual death. If James were to travel through time to a distant past, in nineteenth-century England he would feel at home. In the House of Commons, before the leading speakers of the day, he would oppose the rights of privilege and property. In speeches noted for their ardor and keen sense of the sweep of history, he would juxtapose the dominant image of the masses as mindless barbarians to show that their conscious activity is democracy in motion. Popular struggle, James tells audiences, will destroy the corruption and disillusionment of our age. "The world now lives in a state of despair such as it has never known before," James warned Trinidadian union delegates. To change the destructive course of events, he urged them to "take over the destiny of this country, your own destiny, and shape the society along the lines that you desire, making possible what has been denied to you all these years.". . .

In his speeches before audiences in four main geographical areas of the globe, James's pride in his own accomplishments as a scholar and as a political figure underlines ethical appeals. But his humility, his acknowledgement that contact with ordinary people enables him to understand history, attests his firm belief in creative interaction. Discussing *[The] Black Jacobins* with an audience of West Indians in 1966, James declared, "It is only of late years with my acquaintance with the West Indian people and actual contact with them, political and in some degree sociological, that I have learned to understand what I wrote in this book." His words recall a younger James reporting on cricket matches, interacting with the "common folk" of his native land, and learning, from them, of social ties and obligations. In turn, James assured them that their rebellious history, pregnant with democratic zeal, insures their continued efforts to resist oppression. "If we want to know what the ordinary population can do, let us know what they have done in the past," he told them. "The Negro people in the Caribbean are of the same stock as the men who played such a role in the history of their time," he argued; "we shall be able to do whatever we have to do." On the pages of history, ordinary people have left an indelible mark, James reminds us; human emancipation lies within the struggle towards democracy in our own daily events. His efforts to reveal the conflicts inherent in our times through the portholes of our pasts help to persuade us that our boldest aspirations can be forcefully enacted. Our common history is his rhetorical tool; and, on the basis of his trust in humanity, he wields persuasive power.

> Consuelo Lopez Springfield. *Carolina Quarterly*. 36, 1–2 (June 1990), pp. 89, 94–95

Now, the reader of *Beyond a Boundary* will already sense modernist strategies of subversion and defamiliarization in the mixed generic conception at the heart of James's discursive strategy. Indeed, a reader encountering James's text for the first time can be forgiven for wondering how a history of cricket in the West Indies provides one of the central paradigms in my study—the notion that the Caribbean self must of necessity move from a position of silence and blankness to a cognizance of its own marginal status in the colonial economy of representation as a precondition for the recentering of the colonial subject in history. James must have pondered the same question when he wrote this book because he initiates his discourse with an epigraph that, rather than assuring the reader that he or she is in the familiar territory of the Caribbean *bildung*, goes out of its way to confuse the terms by which we read this text. In this succinct and carefully crafted epigraph, James is emphatic that his text is "neither cricket reminiscences nor autobiography"; rather, he offers us a document in which generic boundaries are collapsed and the distinction between facts and fiction, discourse and narrative, is rejected. The autobiographical form James adopts in the book is not a means toward writing a coherent history of self, but a structure for framing displacement in a temporal sequence "in relation to the events, the facts and the personalities which prompted them."

Simon Gikandi. *Writing in Limbo: Modernism and Caribbean Literature* (Ithaca: Cornell University Press, 1992), p. 44

Perhaps the most impressive aspect of James's life was his purposeful creativity as an essayist, historian, literary critic, and pamphleteer. Major works include: *Minty Alley*, a novel; *The Black Jacobins: Toussaint L'Ouverture and the San Domingo Revolution*, a justly famous historical study; "The Revolutionary Answer to the Negro Problem in the USA," a subtle Marxist polemic; *American Civilization*, an investigation of the connection between popular culture and democratic politics in American history; *Mariners, Renegades and Castaways*, a work of literary criticism; and *Beyond a Boundary*, an evocative study of the impact of cricket on Caribbean society. Diverse in subject matter and tone, these books and essays share in common a beautiful appreciation of the English language as well as a learned and articulate populism.

These writings also constitute only a small portion of a largely unexplored canvas. James wrote on dialectics, modern art, the slave trade, the city-state, the rise and fall of the Communist International, Shakespeare's stagecraft, Aristotle's poetics, existentialism and alienation, contemporary African politics, the Rastafari, the West Indian nation, the history of Pan-Africanism, the future of the novel, and a host of other topics. As this list makes clear, James was a prolific, eclectic writer whose work was driven by an innate curiosity and a rare sense of political determination. His entire corpus betrays the mark of a singular intellect, one that was concerned above all with the power of reason and especially with the inventive potential of the masses engaged in social movement.

Moreover, and in large measure through his writings as well as through speeches and other activities, James made a special contribution to the construction of a postcolonial West Indian identity. An early critic of colonialism, James argued strenuously in favor of a political and economic federation of the West Indies, and also actively promoted indigenous cultural forms-such as calypso and other types of popular music-as expressions of a West Indian nation in the process of formation. His forays into fiction, which largely date from the 1920s and which were produced in the context of a flourishing, politically engaged literary subculture, mark him as a major figure in the development of Caribbean literature and letters.

Thus, while only a handful of organizations or publications in the region can meaningfully claim to be "Jamesian" in inspiration, his broad legacy continues to shape the work of intellectuals, writers, and others in the Anglophone Caribbean. By combining a concern for the autonomy of culture with an active pursuit of the social revolution, James helped carve out a bold identity for Caribbean artists and intellectuals, one that draws on European ideals even as it condemns the imperial project. His legacy also signals a willingness to move beyond conventional conceptions of

liberal democracy and to try and open up the political process in countries like Trinidad and Tobago to new kinds of institutions and new forms of civic participation.

James was able to play an important role in the deepening of the anticolonial project not only in the Caribbean but across the entire African diaspora. This can be seen in his work with the International African Service Bureau, a London-based organization formed in the mid-1930s that agitated on behalf of African national independence and exerted a tremendous influence on postwar movements for decolonialization. His dispensation was also manifest in his work in the 1940s in rethinking the political significance of African-American struggles for social equality. During what might be termed the "third wave" of black-diasporic mobilization, in the 1960s and early 1970s, James defined himself primarily as a teacher. His calls for new forms of pan-regionalism and participatory socialism in the Third World went largely unheeded, however. Yet through his friendships with such notable figures as George Padmore, Kwame Nkrumah, Jomo Kenyatta, Richard Wright, and others, James was able to forge a space for his idiosyncratic brand of radical and democratic politics within the context of Pan-African and black nationalist movements.

James's politics were forged in the crucible of classical Marxism, and in many respects his life and work can only be understood with reference to his lifelong attachment to Marxist principles. Raised in a disorderly political culture that seemingly attached equal value to the incompatible ideals of late Victorian romanticism, Marcus Garvey, and trade union activism, James underwent an ideological conversion in the early 1930s, when he embraced Trotsky's Left Opposition and declared himself an anti-Stalinist and a revolutionary socialist. It was as a Trotskyist that he penned some of his best-known writings, addressing fundamental questions facing the international revolutionary movement. These included the nature of revolutionary leadership, the degeneration of the Russian Revolution, and the linkage between movements in the Third World in general, and the African diaspora in particular, to struggles in the advanced industrial world. And it was as a disaffected post-Trotskyist that he began working with a small circle of friends and comrades to develop an alternative Marxism suited to the postwar era.

Kent Worcester. *C.L.R. James: A Political Biography* (Albany: State University of New York Press, 1996), pp. xii–xiv

BIBLIOGRAPHY

*La Divina Pastora, 1927; Triumph, 1929; The Life of Captain Cipriani: An Account of British Government in the West Indies*, 1932; *Minty Alley*, 1936; *World Revolution, 1917-1936: The Rise and Fall of the Communist International*, 1937; *The Black Jacobins*, 1938; *A History of Negro Revolt*, 1938; *Mariners, Renegades and Castaways: The Story of Herman Melville and the World We Live In*, 1953; *Modern Politics*, 1960; *Party Politics in the West Indies*, 1962; *Beyond a Boundary*, 1963; *State Capitalism and World Revolution*, 1969; *Notes on Dialectics: Hegel, Marx, Lenin*, 1971; *The Future in the Present*, 1977; *Nkrumah and the Ghana Revolution*, 1977; *Spheres of Existence*, 1980; *All the Rendezvous of Victory*, 1984; *C. L. R. James's 80th Birthday Lectures*, 1984; *Cricket*, 1986; *The C. L. R. James Reader*, 1992; *American Civilization*, 1993

# JOHNSON, Charles (1948–)

## United States

Perhaps closest to [Ralph] Ellison's novel [*Invisible Man*] in overall mythic design is Charles Johnson's *Faith and the Good Thing*. Faith, cautioned by her dying mother to get herself a "Good Thing," begins a Platonic search in the cave of life for Truth, an Arthurian quest for the Grail, or, like the African Kujichagulia, a climb toward the peak of Mount Kilimanjaro and the source of knowledge. Traveling from rural Georgia to urban Chicago, she embraces numerous roles and ideologies—her mother's fundamentalist Christianity, middle-class materialism and opportunism, a streetwalker's self-sacrifice, an artist's solipsism. As she passes from one ideology to another—ever hopeful—she also finds herself involved with a variety of people, most of whom exploit her for their own ends, few of whom see her according to her own needs and complexity. Burned by an apocalyptic fire at the novel's conclusion, she becomes a wraith: seen and not seen, a visual symbol of her former existence and an obvious analogy to Ellison's Invisible Man. Faith's invisibility differs, however, from that of Ellison's protagonist, for throughout her travels she has been in touch with the unseen world—not the unseen world of Plato's perfect forms, Kujichagulia's absolute answers, or the nightmares of Ellison's protagonist, which are no alternative to his waking world; she is in touch with memories, or more accurately, the spiritual presences of three human beings who persist in haunting her; they keep alive the faith in her, the faith which gives her her name and identity, the faith that believes that the search itself is its own end. These familiar presences are "the living dead," and only when Faith stops searching, momentarily convinced she has found the "Good Thing" in a materialistic middle-class life, and joins "the dead living," do they cease to appear before her. Following [a] fire and a hospital internment—events which also force Ellison's protagonist to new perspectives on himself—they are restored to her, however, as she herself becomes one of them.

Indeed, as Faith, the wraith, returns to the swamp from which she had started her journey, she is reincarnated as the Swamp Woman. In his cellar Ellison's hero gains perspective on his personal agonies by reviewing in a dream sequence the ambiguities of his own life and of black Americans from the days of slavery; similarly, Faith's sufferings seem to give her access to the werewitch's esoteric and folk wisdom, her knowledge of Western and African philosophical and cabalistic systems as well as her consciousness of the terrible history of oppression. Like Ellison's protagonist's, Faith's journey has also been cyclical, returning her to her own past—the swamp and the Briar Patch of her own mind—as well as to the historical past, represented by the conflation of her experiences with the Swamp Woman's lore. By Faith's return to the swamp as well as by the old crone's marvelous subsequent assumption of Faith's guise and her return to the world to continue Faith's search, Johnson demonstrates his commitment, however, to myth rather than history, for he seeks to guarantee its truth by suggesting its endless repetition. Finally, Faith, like Ellison's protagonist, contemplates the possibilities of the mind to conceive a pattern for living; she, living in a state of faith rather than of paralysis, imagines both progress and responsibility beyond the control of history. . . . Finally, then, unlike Ellison's protagonist, she envisions a way to reconcile the many with the one.

In the conclusion of his novel, Johnson informs us that Faith's way will not be a solitary one. Not only do we learn that she is preparing to relate Aristotle's Illusion and "Stagolee's great battle with Lucifer in West Hell" to two children who seek her out in the swamp as she herself had once sought the werewitch, but we are also reminded that we ourselves have been children throughout the novel, listening to Johnson relate Faith's own tale. Ellison, too, somewhat perfunctorily, reminds us in the last sentence of his novel that we have also been an audience for his protagonist's story when he queries, "Who knows but that, on the lower frequencies, I speak for you?" Johnson's repeated imperative reference to his readers as "Children" and Faith's preparations for her young visitors suggest, however, a more than rhetorical involvement with others; the "Good Thing" is not only the search itself but also the fact that the search is everyone's, and that we are on it together. For other black writers following in Ellison's footsteps, the "Good Thing" is even more emphatically the involvement with others as well as one's personal search.

Elizabeth A. Schultz. *CLA Journal.* 22, 2 (December 1978), pp. 106–8

Since most contemporary novels involving race are scandals of contrivance, unwheeled wagons hitched to cardboard horses, it's a particular pleasure to read Charles Johnson's *Oxherding Tale*. This is his second novel and . . . it separates him even further from conventional sensibilities. In [*Faith and the Good Thing*], Johnson told the tall tale of a black girl's search for meaning—What is the good life? What is good?—and soaked it through with skills he had developed as a cartoonist, television writer, journalist, and student of philosophy. This time out, he has written a novel made important by his artful use of the slave narrative's structure to examine the narrator's developing consciousness, a consciousness that must painfully evaluate both the master and slave cultures.

The primary theme is freedom and the responsibility that comes with it. Given the time of the novel, 1838 to 1860, one would expect such a theme, but Johnson makes it clear in the most human—and often hilarious—terms that the question of freedom in a democratic society is essentially moral, and that social revolution pivots on an expanding redefinition of citizenry and its relationship to law. The adventure of escape only partially prepares Andrew Hawkins, the narrator, for the courage and commitment that come with moral comprehension. Andrew's growth is thrilling because Johnson skillfully avoids melodramatic platitudes while creating suspense and comedy, pathos and nostalgia. In the process, he invents a fresh set of variations on questions about race, sex, and freedom.

Stanley Crouch. *Village Voice.* July 19, 1983, p. 30

Charles Johnson's *Oxherding Tale* . . . extends convention by showing an interracial romance that is not doomed to failure or fraught with unhappiness, and in doing so signals a new direction for a vexed issue in American fiction. *Oxherding Tale* shows an interracial relationship that quietly and matter-of-factly succeeds. Set in the antebellum South, *Oxherding Tale* conflates and juxtaposes past and present in Andrew Hawkins, the contemporary narrator. His origins are comic: one night, after sustained drinking, plantation-owner Jonathan Polkinghorne and his slave, George

Hawkins, swap wives and the outraged Anna Polkinghorne becomes pregnant with Andrew. After a series of bizarre adventures and philosophical explorations—the novel is an entertaining mixture of picaresque and slave narrative forms (what Johnson calls "genre crossing")—Andrew decides to pass for white to escape to freedom. . . .

The plot of *Oxherding Tale*, though it is complex and entertaining, is, as Andrew points out in the opening sentences, "mere parable" for deeper concerns of individual identity and spiritual development. Passing for white gives Andrew the opportunity to begin again, to "reconstruct his life from scratch." As he admits later, he "milked the Self's polymorphy to elude, like Trickster John in the folk tales my father told." Throughout the narrative, Andrew is many things: slave, student, lover, teacher, husband, nineteenth- and twentieth-century man combined, philosopher, and writer. Andrew the narrator comments on the literary conventions as he experiments with them. He is hardly a "character" in the traditional sense of the term since he serves for Johnson more as a palimpsest: a fluid repository for metaphysical musings and literary echoes and experimentation. In one of his essayist asides (another metafictional defamiliarizing device), Johnson clarifies this strategy: "The Self, this perceiving subject who puffs on and on, is, for all purposes, a palimpsest, interwoven with everything—literally everything—that can be thought or felt." Thus Andrew's decision to pass for white resonates at more than just the level of physical survival and expands into phenomenological issues of freedom and identity.

Jonathan Little. *Studies in American Fiction*. 19, 2 (Autumn 1991), pp. 143–44

*Oxherding Tale* acknowledges the marginalization not only of black men but of women, black and white. Johnson explores questions of race and gender by locating them within a complex, experimental network of slave narrative conventions, Afro-American tropes, eighteenth-century narrative strategies, literary constructs of the first-person narrator, and philosophical constructs of the Self and of freedom—all of which are subsumed in Johnson's version of Zen Buddhism. Johnson has described his book as "a modern, comic, philosophical slave narrative—a kind of dramatization of the famous 'Ten Oxherding Pictures' of Zen artist Kakuan-Shien" that represent a young herdsman's search for his rebellious ox, which symbolizes his self. . . .

Johnson's attitude towards women tends towards a glorification of the Eternal Feminine, an attitude which can (and, in this book, several times does) flip over into the concomitant terror of women as all-encompassing and all-powerful. The fact nevertheless remains that Johnson makes a strong attempt to understand feminist issues and to inscribe them in his book. And his technical innovations—particularly the shifts in narrative and temporal perspective—help break the bounds of canonical (Western androcentric) literature.

Jennifer Hayward. *Black American Literature Forum*. 25, 4 (Winter 1991), pp. 689–90

Since the 1974 publication of his first novel, *Faith and the Good Thing*, Charles Johnson has repeatedly called for a revitalized Afro-American literary aesthetic. Decrying what he terms black

fiction's largely "splintered" perspective, Johnson suggests that Afro-American writers concentrate on the new goal of achieving "whole sight," a broadened literary outlook that embraces (to quote Clayton Riley) the "entire world—not just the fractured world of American racism and psychic social disorder." We know more, Johnson claims, than oppression and discrimination. Contemporary black writers not only need to project a new vision into the preexisting tradition of literature, but must at the same time invent the very fictions that will embody it. Johnson's project thus requires first a rebirth and then a rebuilding of Afro-American literature. . . . [*Oxherding Tale*] is an explicit response to his own call. *Oxherding Tale* is necessarily informed by, while at the same time re-(or even de) forming, several precursive literary strategies, including the slave narrative and the Eastern parable. Through its self-consciously postmodern, cross-cultural blend of (principally) Afro-American tradition and the philosophy of Zen, *Oxherding Tale* attempts what Buddhists call opening the "third eye," or what Johnson sees as the final aim of serious fiction: namely, the liberation of perception.

William Gleason. *Black American Literature Forum*. 25, 4 (Winter 1991), p. 705

A freed slave, a roguish fellow, stows away on a ship in New Orleans to avoid creditors and a forced marriage, not realizing the clipper is bound for Africa to capture slaves. Put to work as a cook, he encounters a crew of misfits, a cruel and brilliant captain, legendary tribesmen, storms, and rebellions, and is transformed by the journey.

So goes the tale of *Middle Passage*, which won the National Book Award for fiction . . . and brought a flurry of attention to [Johnson]. . . .

In *Middle Passage* and his two other published novels . . . he sought to develop "an Afro-American philosophical fiction," he said, adding, "I feel we don't have enough of that in black American literature." He then cited important exceptions: works by Jean Toomer, Richard Wright, and Ralph Ellison, "Those were the writers I was most inspired by," he said.

The ex-slave and lyrical narrator of *Middle Passage*, Rutherford Calhoun, has been well educated by his former master, and can speak of, say, someone's "Sisyphean" love and of an "Icarian, causa sui impulse."

But the real philosopher on board, said Mr. Johnson, is the captain, Ebenezer Falcon. He is based loosely on Sir Richard Francis Burton, whose contradictions fascinated the author. "He was an explorer, an imperialist, a translator, a quasi-genius," he said, "and also the biggest bigot in the world."

As for the slaves, captured members of a tribe called the Allmuseri, "They live and *breathe* philosophy," Mr. Johnson said. "I wanted to make them the most spiritual tribe ever. What I admire about them is their profound connectedness to everything around them. They are biologically related, but what truly unites them is their shared vision, their values."

Eleanor Blau. *New York Times*. January 2, 1991, p. C9

Rutherford Calhoun, the narrator of *Middle Passage*, begins his career as a thief. Stealing, for Rutherford, is more than just an occupation; it is a philosophy, indeed a phenomenology. He treats the world as a mine of property from which to hoard "experiences"—as "if *life* was a commodity, a *thing* we could cram into ourselves." Rutherford then meets the Allmuseri, who are themselves being stolen from Africa in the summer of 1830, and finds that his life and his philosophy are indigent. As he learns about their philosophy, their history, their language, he finds himself, for the first time in his life, in a position of wanting to possess something that, by definition, could only be *had* if it is not possessed. "As I live, they so shamed me I wanted their ageless culture to be my own. . . ." During the course of the Middle Passage, Rutherford discovers several things. First, he learns that a culture cannot be possessed because it is an unstable entity. The Allmuseri, he learns, "were process and Heraclitean change . . . not fixed but evolving." He also learns, though, that bonds and connections are a matter of surrendering to another order of being, and are not simply determined by racial or biological destiny. . . .

Eventually, and after a course of adventures rivaling the plots of [Herman Melville's] *Moby-Dick* and "Benito Cereno," Rutherford surrenders to that order and discovers that "experience" is not a property belonging to a "subject" but rather an intersubjective process by which subjects are formed and transformed. . . . In the end, the exposure to the Allmuseri . . . leaves [Rutherford] and his world altered. "The voyage had irreversibly changed my seeing, made of me a cultural mongrel, and transformed the world into a fleeting shadow play I felt no need to possess or dominate, only appreciate in the ever extended present." This is, essentially, the phenomenology of the Allmuseri. . . .

In his meditations on artistic creativity, Charles Johnson has noted that there is a "curious, social, intersubjective side of art [which] is, as the best aestheticians report, central to the artistic personality and the creative process." Part of Johnson's achievement is to promote this intersubjective aspect of art and describe the immense benefits obtaining for us if we act on this desire to inhabit fictional worlds which challenge our parochialism. But the greater part of Johnson's achievement is to enact intersubjective relations in the making and to discover in the phenomenology of the Allmuseri a theory and a symbol for the postmodern condition discernible in much of the fiction written by those Johnson calls "Americans who happen to be black." The discovery of the Allmuseri has been, one suspects, at least one of the reasons that his most recent novels have not only enjoyed a fate different from his first six, but have broken new and very fertile ground in the field of African-American letters.

Ashraf H.A. Rushdy. *African American Review*. 26, 3 (Fall 1992), pp. 376–77, 393

It is the summer of 1966. More to the point, it is one of those long, hot summers that leave a trail of smoldering ashes, shattered nerves and broken lives in cities throughout the decade. A sad but dauntless Martin Luther King Jr. is marooned in Chicago, struggling to forge strategy for social transcendence as all around him sirens roar, windows explode, contradictions surface, hope dies. Had King listened to Dylan in those years, he might have found communion with the penultimate line of "Stuck Inside of Mobile With the Memphis Blues Again": "And here I sit so patiently/Waiting to find out what price/You have to pay to get out of/Going through all these things twice."

As street rage spills blood and irony all over King's ideals, he is roused from fitful slumber by a lapsed philosophy major named Matthew Bishop, who tells the Reverend Doctor there is "something . . . pretty strange outside" waiting to meet him. King is so shaken by what he encounters that he takes Christ's name in vain. It is his double—or at least a frayed-at-the-edges duplicate named Chaym Smith, who even shares the 1/15/29 birthday with the great man. Smith, a walking blues shout with tattered clothes, dreadful luck and corrosive wit ("Sometimes," he tells King, "I figured God fucked up and missed with me, but he had you for backup"), is offering his services as a professional Doppelgänger who can draw some of the fire, literal and figurative, directed at King. He's been doing some of that already:

> I been catching hell since you come to Chicago. Last week a couple of boys pushed me off the El platform. . . . I was 'bout that far from landin' on the third rail. Lots of people know where you're stayin' in town, but some don't. They see me and come to my place. Some of 'em tore up my room. Scared my landlady so much she's askin' me to leave. But where am I gonna go? Hell, I can't walk down the street or go to the store without somebody stoppin' me. Some of 'em spit in my face. That's colored as well as white. That's why I come here. I figure if I'm catchin 'hell' cause of you, I might's well catch it for you instead.

King is almost stricken by this desperate offer. But he tells Bishop—who also serves as the book's narrator—to drive Smith to a secluded house on the outskirts of Carbondale, six hours from Chicago. He instructs Bishop and another volunteer, Amy, to "get [Smith] back on his feet. Help him understand what the Movement's about." He has no idea what he's asking.

One doesn't have to travel very far through *Dreamer*'s volatile passages to know that Charles Johnson is taking a devil of a chance. It's not the first time. *Oxherding Tale* (1982), an antebellum slave novel, cakewalked with epistemology, performing some fancy spins and dips with conventional expectations for slave melodramas and black literature. It even brought Karl Marx onstage for high-stepping intellectual vaudeville. Part of the book's legend is that it was a tough sell to publishers. And it still has trouble finding the wide audience it deserves. After writing several TV scripts; a masterly short-story collection, *The Sorcerer's Apprentice* (1986); and a provocative book of criticism, *Being and Race: Black Writing Since 1970* (1988), Johnson returned to pre-Civil War America in *Middle Passage* (1990), in which an 1830s mutiny on a slave ship is an occasion for exploring the various ways one can be. Not just be black or white or even American. Just be.

Johnson is an opportunist in staking a claim on imaginative territory where issues of identity can be explored. One question for further study: Is identity an open window to the soul or a locked room where potential is often found murdered with no signs of forced entry? That Johnson could make "race novels" work on such problems has dazzled his admirers and bewildered almost everyone else.

In engaging King's ghost, Johnson sets himself up for more ferocious versions of the tut-tuts he caught in some quarters for his antic spins on slave narratives. He raises the stakes in *Dreamer* not only by presuming to enter the mind and heart of a martyred icon but by imposing a Prince-and-the-Pauper thriller motif to explore what it meant—still means—to lead, to follow, to seek a path to freedom.

Does it work? Not if you expect tidy, satisfying conclusions, which are what many readers expect from yarns like this. Johnson takes for granted that, as many African-Americans have resigned themselves to believing, the Movement was both an episode in U.S. sociopolitical history and a continuing process—except that few bothered to call it a "Movement" after King's assassination. (Three decades later, the word "struggle" is used more often.) Johnson deliberately leaves many issues, even a central narrative thread, unresolved by the book's end. No doubt he anticipates loud, unpleasant noises to ensue because of this. But that's nothing compared with the contentiousness the rest of the novel will arouse.

The source for such anger will be the astringent outbursts of Chaym Smith. It's bad enough that this Korean War vet, discharged psychiatric patient, artist manqué and lapsed Buddhist is a hapless ruin, a living rebuttal to America's promise as embodied in the dreams of his physical double. His is the brightly burning misanthropy of someone who has been marginalized within the margins. From such isolation, he has extracted his own sense of worth, though it's not likely to be shared by others. "Truth is," Smith tells Bishop on the car ride from Chicago,

> being on the outside is a blessing. Naw, it's a necessity, if you got any creative spark at all. . . . the way I see it, the problem with all the fuckin' anointed and somebody like Abel . . . is that they're sheep. That's right, part of the obedient, tamed, psalm-singing herd. They make me sick, every one of 'em. See, I ain't never been good at group-think. . . . Call 'em what you want, Christians or Communists or Cultural Nationalists, but I call 'em sheep. Or zombies—that's what Malcolm X called the Nation of Islam, you know, after he broke away from Elijah, his surrogate daddy. There's not a real individual in the bunch. . . . Nobody who thinks the unthinkable, or is cursed (or blessed) with bearing the cross of a unique, singular identity . . . except for him.

Bishop, alternately fascinated and repelled by such tirades, is certain that by "him," Smith refers to King. And it isn't until he recalls a speech by King himself, railing against the "'mass mind,' the cowardice of the herd," that Bishop begins to wonder whether these guys aren't twin brothers.

What makes Bishop more receptive than he wishes to be to Smith's iconoclasm is that he too feels marginalized by his private dreams—dreams that, he senses, he has no right to own, given the imperatives of history. Earlier in the book, he tells King that Nietzsche was one of the philosophers he'd been reading in college. King urges him to "get the Nietzsche out of your system. He's seductive for children—all that lust for power—but he's really the one we're fighting against." But among the many questions Johnson poses with Smith's disturbing presence is this: Do public dreams of justice and equality consume private dreams of individual fulfillment? Or glory? Or even (as Bishop thinks he hears Smith say) immortality?

History tends to put such inquiries in the deep freeze. Yet what makes Johnson's book so daring is its suggestion that such musings were never far from King's psyche. The mid-sixties found King risking and finding failure in Chicago, where nonviolence hit a brick wall of corruption and institutional polarity. He was at odds with younger, impatient Movement soldiers making revolutionary noises. He found himself shut out from a once-hospitable Johnson Administration, which thought he should keep his damn dovish opinions on the Vietnam War to himself.

So King had reason, in the two years before his death, to feel as marginalized as Chaym Smith. This convergence of dual selves comes when Smith, now fully prepped, polished and ready to do his job, is assigned to pick up an award for King at a suburban Chicago church. In the all-but-inevitable chaos greeting the Reverend, Bishop sees who he first assumes is Smith delivering a serrated riff on the nature of reality and truth and love. "I have no choice but to love others, because I am the others." At one point he even says, "Every man and woman is a speculum, our mirror. Our twin." A frightened Bishop believes Smith may be giving up the game. Later, Bishop finds Smith among the crowd clamoring for King's autograph. So it was King after all, saying what a despondent Smith says was "my stuff. Not things I've ever said, but stuff I've felt. . . . How does he do that?"

Which is what I'm tempted to ask of Johnson when he offers, as counterpoint to Bishop's narrative, some journeys into King's own mental processes during these last years of struggle and doubt. How does Johnson do it? How does he handle, with insight and sympathy, the Reverend Doctor's torment over the value of the risks he takes for the Movement's sake? Or the cost in time missed with his wife and children? The novelist's empathy is always viewed with more suspicion than the historian's facts, even though both impose shape on reality and should be tagged as potential liars. But Johnson, in his daring presumptions, is one extraordinary liar.

Sooner or later, you know the Feds are going to get mixed up in this. When they do, it opens up still more ambiguities, more trapdoors, more dilemmas. When the "Wise Guys" come for Smith, there's an ominous sense of events big-footing their way to Memphis for an unnamed and unspeakable act they want Smith to carry out. "They got me over a barrel," he tells Bishop before he disappears. "What they want me to do to embarrass him . . . the shit they're up to in Memphis. . . . I'd die before I'd let anybody lock me up again, but I don't know if I want to live if I do what they're asking."

Bishop never finds out what they are asking, and neither do we. The last view we get of King in *Dreamer* is in his Memphis hotel room, feeling trapped and uncertain, wondering in talks with Ralph Abernathy just where he can go from this point.

As for Smith, he remains as lost in history's swirling maw as *Gravity's Rainbow's* Tyrone Slothrop was at another critical point in the twentieth century. All Bishop knows for certain is that he has prospered internally from being exposed to both sides of the same anxious drive for transcendence personified by two brown men— both 5 foot 7 and weighing 180 pounds—who came a long way and sustained many hard blows before discovering that it's possible to see oneself in every face you encounter, to see the resemblances in each other. In its fierce and heedlessly inventive way, *Dreamer* challenges its readers to wake up to that painful, unavoidable fact.

Gene Seymour. *The Nation*. April 27, 1998, pp. 27–29

BIBLIOGRAPHY
*Black Humor*, 1970; *Faith and the Good Thing*, 1974; *Oxherding Tale*, 1982; *The Sorcerer's Apprentice*, 1986; *Olly Olly Oxen Free: A Farce in Three Acts*, 1988; *Middle Passage*, 1990; *Dreamer*, 1998

# JOHNSON, James Weldon
# (1871–1938)
## United States

[*The Autobiography of an Ex-Colored Man*] is indeed an epitome of the race situation in the United States told in the form of an autobiography. The varied incidents, the numerous localities brought in, the setting forth in all its ramifications of our great and perplexing race problem, suggests a work of fiction founded on hard fact. The hero, a natural son of a Southerner of high station, begins his real life in a New England town to which his mother had migrated, runs the whole gamut of colorline experiences, and ends by going over on the other side.

The work gives a view of the race situation in New England, in New York City, in the far South, in city and country, in high and low society, with glimpses, too, of England, France and Germany. Practically every phase and complexity of the race question is presented at one time or another. The work is, as might be expected, anonymous.

> Jessie Fauset. *Crisis*. November 1912, p. 38

In [*Fifty Years, and Other Poems*] Mr. James Weldon Johnson . . . gathers together a group of lyrics, delicate in workmanship, fragrant with sentiment, and phrased in pure and unexceptionable English. Then he has another group of dialect verses, racy of the soil, pungent in flavor, swinging in rhythm and adroit in rhyme. But where he shows himself a pioneer is the half-dozen larger and bolder poems, of a loftier strain, in which he has been nobly successful in expressing the higher aspirations of his own people. It is in uttering this cry for recognition, for sympathy, for understanding, and above all, for justice, that Mr. Johnson is most original and most powerful.

In the superb and soaring stanzas of "Fifty Years" (published exactly half-a-century after the signing of the Emancipation Proclamation) he has gives us one of the noblest commemorative poems yet written by any American—a poem sonorous in its diction, vigorous in its workmanship, elevated in its imagination and sincere in its emotion. In it speaks the voice of his race; and the race is fortunate in its spokesman. In it a fine theme has been finely treated. In it we are made to see something of the soul of the people who are our fellow citizens now and forever—even if we do not always so regard them. In it we are glad to acclaim a poem which any living poet might be proud to call his own.

> Brander Matthews. Introduction to James Weldon Johnson, *Fifty Years, and Other Poems* (Boston: Cornhill, 1917), pp. xiii–xiv

*The Autobiography of an Ex-Coloured Man*, of course, in the matter of specific incident, has little enough to do with Mr. Johnson's own life, but it is imbued with his own personality and feeling, his *views* of the subjects discussed, so that to a person who has no previous knowledge of the author's own history, it reads like *real* autobiography. It would be truer, perhaps, to say that it reads like a composite autobiography of the Negro race in the United States in modern times. . . .

Mr. Johnson . . . chose an all-embracing scheme. His young hero, the ostensible author, either discusses (or lives) pretty nearly every phase of Negro life, North and South and even in Europe, available to him at that period. That he "passes" the title indicates. Miscegenation in its slave and also its more modern aspects, both casual and marital, is competently treated. The ability of the Negro to mask his real feelings with a joke or a laugh in the presence of the inimical white man is here noted, for the first time in print, I should imagine. Negro adaptability, touchiness, and jealousy are referred to in an unself-conscious manner, totally novel in Negro writing at the time this book originally appeared [1912]. . . . Jim Crow cars, crap-shooting, and the cake-walk are inimitably described. Colour snobbery within the race is freely spoken of, together with the economic pressure from without which creates this false condition. There is a fine passage devoted to the celebration of the Negro Spirituals and there is an excellent account of a Southern campmeeting, together with a transcript of a typical oldtime Negro sermon. There is even a lynching. But it is chiefly remarkable to find James Weldon Johnson in 1912, five or six years before the rest of us began to shout about it, singing hosannas to rag-time (jazz was unknown then).

> Carl Van Vechten. Introduction to James Weldon Johnson, *The Autobiography of an Ex-Coloured Man* (New York: Alfred A. Knopf, 1927), pp. v–ix

An experiment and an intention lie behind these poems [in *God's Trombones*]. It will be remembered that in *The Book of American Negro Poetry* Mr. Johnson spoke of the limitations of dialect, which he compared to an organ having but two stops, one of humor and one of pathos. He felt that the Negro poet needed to discover some medium of expression with a latitude capable of embracing the Negro experience. These poems were written with that purpose in view, as well as to guarantee a measure of permanence in man's most forgetful mind to that highly romantic and fast disappearing character, the old time Negro preacher.

The poet here has admirably risen to his intentions and his needs; entombed in this bright mausoleum the Negro preacher of an older day can never pass entirely deathward. Dialect could never have been synthesized into the rich mortar necessary for these sturdy unrhymed exhortations. Mr. Johnson has captured that peculiar flavor of speech by which the black sons of Zebedee, lacking academic education, but grounded through their religious intensity in the purest marshalling of the English language (the King James version of the Bible) must have astounded men more obviously letter-trained. This verse is simple and awful at once, the grand diapason of a musician playing on an organ with far more than two keys.

> Countee Cullen. *Bookman*. October 1927, pp. 221

In the familiar shaping of an epigrammatic idea, God makes James Weldon Johnson a creative artist, but he made himself a race-agitator. He had an intellectual motivation for the cause into which he threw the energies and devotions of his manhood's prime; and while the heat of debate, the tactics and strategies were pursued with ardour and often with consummate skill, there was none of the passion nor exalted moods of rationalization, which forged the spirit of [Frederick] Douglass or [Booker T.] Washington or [W. E.

B.] Du Bois on the anvil of a diabolical oppression. If these race champions, Douglass, Washington, and Du Bois, flame across the pages of race and American history with a greater glory for stirring the hearts of their people with higher hopes and clearer visions, and a more determined effort to realize them, than James Johnson, that same history will record in its footnotes and appendices, that with Booker T. Washington he stands forth as one of the two best organizers of a racial program. . . .

James Weldon Johnson has lived a crowded life and he has recorded it minutely in this autobiography [*Along This Way*], which is incontestably the first work of its kind in American literature. Unlike any other autobiography, that of Frederick Douglass, Booker T. Washington, or even Dr. [Robert R.] Moton, it escapes from that category of racial recitals in the narrower sense, and remains the narrative of a man who for sixty years of his life has passed through an amazing series of social and intellectual adventures and events which lifted him steadily to a foremost place as an American citizen.

> William Stanley Braithwaite. *Opportunity.* December 1933, pp. 376–78

A few of us tried to bring the Negro writers together in an organization with the late James Weldon Johnson as President. There are about twelve creative writers of some distinction in Harlem and an equal number of journalists. No one could accuse James Weldon Johnson of believing in any kind of Segregation. He was a member of numerous white cultural and artistic organizations, and his prestige then meant much in setting up a group, especially as he was a lecturer on Negro culture at New York University. He was the perfect person around whom we could organize—well balanced, a meliorist in his attitude toward race relations. . . .

However, Negro intellectuals among themselves, even more than the masses, are hard to organize. The Harlem Renaissance movement of the antic nineteen twenties was really inspired and kept alive by the interest and presence of white bohemians. It faded out when they became tried of the new plaything. And so even the prestige of James Weldon Johnson was of no avail. . . .

Suddenly, tragically, James Weldon Johnson was killed in the spring of 1938. And the group of Negro writers came together for the last time at his funeral.

> Claude McKay. *Harlem: Negro Metropolis* (New York, E. P. Dutton, 1940), pp. 247–49

Published anonymously in 1912 with a preface by Brander Matthews and reissued under the author's name in 1927 with an introduction by Carl Van Vechten, *The Autobiography of an Ex-Coloured Man* is noteworthy because of its restraint, its comprehensiveness, and its adumbration of the Negro Renascence of the 1920's. At a time when most Negro fictionists were giving blow for blow and painting extravagantly favorable pictures of members of the race, Johnson set out neither to glorify Negroes nor to malign whites but to interpret men and conditions as he knew them. . . .

Besides being more detached than any preceding novel of American Negro life, *The Autobiography of an Ex-Coloured Man* is groundbreaking in its introduction of a well-realized cosmopolitan milieu. Unlike most earlier Negro fiction, it is not localized in the South but moves out into the broader field of European and Northern urban life. . . .

In addition to being more impartial and more comprehensive than any earlier novel of American Negro life, *The Autobiography of an Ex-Coloured Man* is a milestone because of its forthright presentation of racial thought. Admitting the dual personality which some Negroes assume—one role among their own group and the other in the presence of whites—Johnson is himself not guilty of such a two-sided character. Not attempting to ''wear the mask,'' he gives a calm, dispassionate treatment of people and situations as he sees them.

> Hugh M. Gloster. *Negro Voices in American Fiction* (Chapel Hill: University of North Carolina Press, 1948), pp. 79–80

In the language of *God's Trombones* Johnson found a much more flexible medium than Dunbar dialect for the interpretation of folk material. Traditional dialect attempts (sometimes unsuccessfully) a strict fidelity in metre and in rhyme scheme; Johnson adapted to an artistic form the rhythms of an actual sermon, the accents of actual speech and intonation. He freed himself from the necessity to rhyme, thus subordinating strict poetic form to the artistic interpretation of his subject matter. In *God's Trombones* Johnson approximated the vivid imagery of the folk, an imagery far superior to any he attained in the *Fifty Years* dialect poems and certainly an imagery which rivaled the best of Dunbar's. Johnson used all the tricks of the folk preacher's trade—hyperbole, repetition, juxtaposition, personal appeal to his listeners, the knack of making Biblical happenings have an intense meaning to current life. Johnson even used punctuation and capitalization to achieve his effect—dashes to indicate the frequent and dramatic pauses, capitalization to emphasize important words, such as ''Old Earth'' and ''Great White Throne.'' The sensitive reader cannot fail to hear the ranting of the fire-and-brimstone preacher; the extremely sensitive reader may even hear the unwritten ''Amens'' of the congregation.

> Eugenia W. Collier. *Phylon.* Winter 1960, pp. 358–59

If allowance is made for his borrowings from the Bible, from the spirituals, and from the Negro sermons he had heard, what then is the poet's share in *God's Trombones*? Johnson was certainly not the creator of these sermons but, as Synge remarked of his own indebtedness to the Irish people, every work of art results from a collaboration. In *God's Trombones*, the artist is clearly present on every page, and he gives even while he receives. The simplicity and clarity, so striking in these poems, are the fruits of his efforts. His musical sense is manifested in the choice of sonorities for the free-verse line which, in his hands, becomes docile and supple, and adjusts to the preacher's rhythm as well as to the rise and fall of his voice. Taking what were, after all, the heterogeneous elements of his raw materials, the poet has marked them with the unity and the stamp of his own genius, so that these sermons, as they come from his hands, have undeniably become his own to some degree.

If he deserves any reproach, it might be for his excessive zeal in idealizing and refining—or, in other words, for having thought it necessary to impose too much respectability on essentially popular material whose crudity is one of its charms, as it is also a voucher for its authenticity. His sermons are still folklore, perhaps, but stylized folklore. . . .

This work, furthermore, was the offspring of an outdated mentality. Like its author, the work set out to have a Negro soul, but one garbed in the distinction and respectability of whiteness. Despite appearances, its tendency was at odds with that total coming to awareness marked by the Negro Renaissance, and no more is needed to explain why *God's Trombones* remained an isolated venture. [1963]

> Jean Wagner. *Black Poets of the United States* (Urbana: University of Illinois Press, 1973), pp. 383–84

For a reference point in Johnson's literary career, we must look to the year 1918. The year before he had published a respectable volume of poetry [*Fifty Years*], which, though it summed up his poetic efforts over the previous several decades, did not lay out a clear path to follow. In 1918 Johnson established that path with his poem "The Creation," published two years later. . . .

In "The Creation," as in the bulk of his literary activity in the 1920s, Johnson used a soft-sell tactic. He wished to impress both the black and the white middle-class with the overall contribution of black Americans to American culture. He came to feel during this period that the most effective way to do this, as well as to expose the basic nature of race prejudice, was indirectly through works of art. . . .

"The Creation" makes no mention of prejudice, discrimination, or the grinding poverty to be found in black communities of both rural and urban American. Nor did Johnson point out that the spontaneity of black poetic rhetoric often grew out of a desperate effort to survive in a social situation which seemed to breed endless oppression. He, of course, knew the situation, and he communicated it to the American public in his role as an official of the NAACP. In "The Creation," however, Johnson followed the path he had laid out in his song writing twenty years earlier. He chose not to emphasize the expressly tragic nature of the black experience, as he had done in "O Black and Unknown Bards"; rather he took a much ridiculed aspect of that experience and turned it into a work of art readily appreciated by his readers, both black and white.

> Eugene Levy. *James Weldon Johnson: Black Leader, Black Voice* (Chicago: University of Chicago Press, 1973), pp. 298, 301

Johnson had read and been greatly impressed by [W. E. B.] Du Bois's [*The Souls of Black Folk*], and it is not surprising that the mulatto status and the varying musical inclinations of his narrator [in *The Autobiography of an Ex-Colored Man*] act as symbolic projections of a double consciousness. The narrator modulates between the black world and the white (often with less than equanimity) and seems torn between the early melodies of his mother and the Chopinesque style that wins his white beloved. In a sense, *The Autobiography of an Ex-Colored Man* is a fictional rendering of *The Souls of Black Folk*, for Johnson's narrator not only stresses his bifurcated vision, but also his intellectual genius. He maintains an open, critical attitude toward the many sides of black American culture, condemns in unequivocal terms the limitations of the black situation, and assiduously records his movement from a naïve provincialism toward a broad cosmopolitanism. The narrator, in short, is a black man of culture recording the situations

and attitudes that have succeeded in driving him underground, to a position the larger society might define as criminal. . . .

*The Autobiography of an Ex-Colored Man* is both the history and the confession of one of the "talented tenth" (that class of college-bred black Americans in whom Du Bois placed so much faith); it offers the rehearsal of a "soul on ice" who draws substance from a world that could not recognize his true character nor sympathize with his longings. Each of its episodes is an effort at personal definition and a partial summing up of the black American past.

> Houston A. Baker, Jr. *Virginia Quarterly Review.* Summer, 1973, pp. 438–39

BIBLIOGRAPHY
*The Autobiography of an Ex-Colored Man*, 1912 (reprinted 1927); *Fifty Years, and Other Poems*, 1917; *The Book of American Negro Poetry*, 1922 (editor); *God's Trombones: Seven Negro Sermons in Verse*, 1927; *Along This Way: The Autobiography of James Weldon Johnson*, 1933

# JONES, Gayl (1949–)
## United States

[Gayl Jones's first novel] *Corregidora* is a bizarre romantic story that exposes the intimate life of the main character, Ursa Corregidora, with such candor and immediacy that its narrative texture seems like a screen onto which her unique psychological history is projected. The novel is a carefully controlled creation of storytelling in which the process of communication develops from the author's determination to relay the story entirely in terms of the mental processes of this character, and thus without any authorial intrusion. The narrative itself is composed of two stories that are so closely related that they are inextricably intertwined. One concerns the course of ordinary external events in a small town in Kentucky, while the other evolves from Ursa's personal recollections. Together they create the illusion of an actual record of a living person.

Ursa Corregidora is black and obviously female. These characteristics neither typecast the novel into a racial or feminist category, nor do they detract from the universality of the protagonist's plight. Rather, they enhance the psychological intensity of Ursa's evolving portrait as well as serve to enrich the novel's narrative texture by relying on symbols and allusions that naturally arise from her racial and mythic histories. In this manner the story achieves subtle psychological form and universal meaning. Without the historical references and allusions, Ursa would lack important interpretative potential beyond the fictional world which she inhabits. She would be merely an unusual aberration of human character rather than a distinct personality encountering situations imbued with human paradox.

The external drama of *Corregidora* involves Ursa's estrangement from her husband, Mutt Thomas, who in a jealous rage pushes her down a flight of stairs in the spring of 1948. Her injuries result in her having to have a hysterectomy. She is extremely bitter about her condition, especially since she has a family obligation to bear children, an imperative first impressed on her by her great-grandmother in order to preserve the details of her slave heritage. She divorces Mutt and, as a result, seems to be left with no alternative but to live out her life alone like all the Corregidora women before her. Perhaps she would have remained content to have done so were she not frightened by a lesbian encounter while convalescing at the home of a friend, Cat Lawson. This experience makes her worry whether men will still find her desirable, or whether she will eventually succumb to homosexual embrace. In order to quell her fear, she marries the first man who shows an interest in her—Tadpole McCormick, the owner of the club where she sings. Their marriage is short-lived, and Ursa soon finds that she is again alone with her fear. After twenty-two years of uneventful living and singing the blues in another club just across town, Mutt returns, and they are reunited.

Claudia C. Tate. *Black American Literature Forum.* 13, 4 (Winter 1979), p. 139

*Corregidora* provides a clear account of the ambiguities of childbirth under slavery and provides as well a vision in which the traditional African celebration of childbirth is joined to a New World rebellion against history. Ursa Corregidora, the singer whose life the novel portrays, is the fourth-generation descendant of a Brazilian slave and a Portuguese plantation owner. She has grown up in the American South in a household shared with her mother, her grandmother, and her great-grandmother. They pass on to Ursa their common fund of memories, extending back to the sexual abuse suffered by her great-grandmother and grandmother under slavery in Brazil. Corregidora, the great-grandmother's owner, had fathered Ursa's grandmother and later hired both women out as prostitutes (to white men only). Ursa's mother was the product of incest between Corregidora and his own daughter. Corregidora's sexual abuse of his female slaves makes a mockery of the traditional African point of view in which sexuality and childbirth were seen as inseparable and sacred. Yet in the great-grandmother's vision "making generations" is nevertheless celebrated because, as in traditional Africa, descendants ensure a continuity of time. Ursa's great-grandmother wants this continuity so that the white slaveowner may not repudiate his own past. She tells Ursa, "When they did away with slavery down there [Brazil] they burned all the slavery papers so it would be like they never had it." "Making generations" is part of her plan to make this burning of records futile. . . . In Ursa's great-grandmother's vision, one's children and one's children's children thus counter the fragmentation of time that is fostered by the white repudiation of the past.

Bonnie J. Barthold. *Black Time: Fiction of Africa, the Caribbean and the United States* (New Haven: Yale University Press, 1981), p. 125

*Corregidora* espouses action, but remains a book of delay and avoidance and denial. It is at bottom a book about meaning, or attempted understanding. It continually rings changes on the idea of "pretending not to know what's meant," or not knowing and yet not asking, or being "afraid to ask more." As a result its exploitative sexual action remains strangely verbal; that is, it comes across as something that violates speech taboos more than human bodies or standards of personal integrity or moral principles. Intimacy is not at issue, though intimate things are at work. The meaning of these actions accordingly remains obscure, and the actors thwarted

in two spheres. In like manner the engagement with the past proves less a matter of reimmersion than of arrest and obsession. (There is an immersion scene of sorts, but it involves the literal drowning of the runaway adolescent slave, with the cruel notation that after three days his body rose; we find no redemption here.) . . .

Ursa Corregidora herself illustrates the basic quandary of the text, that movement seems impossible until meanings are known, and meaning seems available only through movement. The emphasis on sex results from the fact that it so readily stands as a synecdoche for movement. But sex itself is a movement toward a larger goal than the "generation" that is specified. We need to see generation as merely instrumental, the real objective being *propagation*, that is, the spreading of the word, not just the multiplication of seed.

The past, as Wilburn Williams, Jr. notes, offers "possibilities of inspiration and renewal," but it also "can exert a malignant influence on the present." The Corregidora legacy is supposed to inspire a verdict but it only perpetuates itself inertially, with a faintly malignant influence. The only "verdict" that actually appears in the novel is tainted by its prevailing and reductive sexuality. . . .

In only one aspect of *Corregidora* does its obsessive and somewhat cryptic activity evolve into a measure of understanding, a measure of available meaning. That aspect is the blues. Ursa Corregidora is a blues singer whose experience of losing her baby (and her womb) at her husband's hands leads to a new style and voice for her, and to a new level of success. The blues can be taken as a subtheme of the novel. The meaning and work of the blues become all but a formal topic, receiving explicit discussion and analysis. The amplifying presence of the blues seems to give historic depth, validity, dignity, and power to Ursa's experience and to her being. And yet it is important to recognize that the same temporal alteration or denaturing that besets the Corregidora issue also infects the blues subtheme in the novel. Though at one point Ursa sings to Mutt before they make love, the blues cannot be said to break out of the condition of an isolated phenomenon of a nightclub. The novel may abound in blues-worthy incidents or situations, but its action rather deploys than absorbs the blues.

Michael G. Cooke. *Afro-American Literature in the Twentieth Century: The Achievement of Intimacy* (New Haven: Yale University Press, 1984), pp. 218–19

The action in *Eva's Man* begins where [*Corregidora*] left off and envelops us in the despair of one woman's failure to achieve redemption. In fact, the unrelenting violence, emotional silence, and passive disharmony in *Eva's Man* are the undersides of the blues reconciliation and active lovemaking in *Corregidora*. Eva Medina Canada poisons her lover Davis Carter and castrates him with her teeth once he is dead. Important to our brief study here is that Eva never gains control over her voice, her past, or her identity. Instead of wielding language as useful evidence for justice and regeneration as Ursa has done, Eva is defeated by words and brandishes first a pocket knife against Moses Tripp, then uses arsenic and teeth against Davis. Eva never comes to terms with her past; she chooses to embrace received images of women as femmes fatales. Ursa and Eva are further separated by their vastly different capacities for love.

In relation to Jones's concern with opening avenues for reconciliation between the sexes and breaking down barriers erected against it from both self and society, it is important to see *Eva's Man* and *Corregidora* as companion texts. Primarily through their attitude toward language and fluency with idioms necessary for personal deliverance, we encounter one woman's fall and another's rise. The clear contrast between them makes Ursa appear as Eva's alter ego and reveals Jones to be a gifted ironist: Eva, surnamed Canada, the promised land for fugitive slaves, contrasts with Corregidora, Brazilian slavemaster. Yet it is Ursa who actually frees herself from bondage and Eva who succumbs to it. Eva has imprisoned herself in the debilitating stereotypes of Queen Bee, Medusa, and Eve long before she is locked away for her crime. And Eva remains only dimly aware of her own responsibility in being there. . . .

Eva remains imprisoned literally and figuratively by her silence that simply increases her passivity and her acceptance of the words and definitions of others. Elvira, more like Tadpole and Mutt in *Corregidora* than the rejected lesbian Cat Lawson, tries to get Eva to talk and, by talking, to assume full responsibility for her acts. Eva's silence is more abusive than protective and inhibits her from developing her own "song" or voice about self and ancestry. Silence also blurs more truth than it reveals and Eva, unlike Ursa with her foremothers, is unable to gain the larger historical consciousness necessary to end individual alienation. Moreover, Eva's guilty silence, her inability to use language, makes her unable to hear others. Eva fails to grasp Miss Billie's important advice about the past and being true "to those people who came before you and those people who came after you." Miss Billie, angered and exasperated by her own daughter's lack of interest in marriage (in making generations), tries to elicit some response from Eva: "You got to be true to your ancestors and you got to be true to those that come after you. How can you be true to those that come after you if there ain't none coming after you?" Eva's deafness to this historical responsibility renders her even more deaf and inarticulate about her own redemption. The prison psychiatrist warns: "You're going to have to open up sometime, woman, to somebody." . . . When she finally talks, Eva confuses fantasy and reality, no longer able to distinguish between them. Ironically, language fails Eva; it has atrophied from disuse. And Eva's sexual coupling with Elvira happens in prison. Eva has failed to free herself or to speak anything more significant than the chilling "Now" at the novel's close which announces her solo orgasm.

Melvin Dixon. In Mari Evans, ed. *Black Women Writers (1950–1980): A Critical Evaluation* (New York: Doubleday, 1984), pp. 245–47

[Gayl Jones] creates . . . radical worlds. Not only are the societies depicted . . . thoroughly and directly oppressive, but she also denies readers a "sane" narrative center through which to judge world and narrator. Most frequently, her narrators have already been judged insane by the society; and this assessment, given the teller's actions and obsessions, seems reasonable. But we cannot therefore assume that we have entered a Poesque world of confessors of personal guilt or madness, for it is equally apparent that society has its own obsessions and that its labeling of the narrators as mad facilitates evasion of the implications of those obsessions.

Given the irrationality of both narrator and world, the reader must rely on the text itself to provide whatever sense is to be made of the story. Jones's stories and novels work because they effectively give voice to those who have suffered. By structuring the

experiences, the texts become blues performances, rendering as they do stories of the convolutions and complications of desire. Patterns of repetition, identification of sufferer and solo performer, and use of the audience as confidant—all characteristics of the blues—suggest that the worlds of [her protagonists], no matter how disordered, are worlds of human experience.

Keith E. Byerman. *Fingering the Jagged Grain: Tradition and Form in Recent Black Fiction* (Athens: University of Georgia Press, 1985), pp. 171–72

It is no simple task to summarize the stories and sketches that Gayl Jones's *White Rat* comprises. They enact moments and mindscapes that resist not only the narrator's moralization of experience, but the reader's quest for "hidden meaning." In part, the difficulty resides in the characteristic absence in her fiction of authorial intrusion and judgment. Jones prefers to write in the first person, giving the impression that "it's just the character who's there." In constructing the interiority—the psychology—of her characters, Jones, in effect, allows them to speak for themselves. Yet, at the very heart of her stories are silences, silences that speak eloquently to the pleasure of her text. In a Pinteresque fashion, Jones's work resonates with both the plentitude and paucity of language in human relationships in the modern world. Her stories both thematize and formalize silence as a stratagem that reveals the discontinuities and breaks in the connections and bonds between individuals. Sometimes these silences are expressed by a recalcitrant refusal to speak, and, at other times, by an eruption of speech that displaces that which is left unsaid.

Mae G. Henderson. Introduction to Gayl Jones. *White Rat* (Boston: Northeastern University Press, 1991), pp. x–xi

Jones is keenly aware of her responsibilities as an African-American writer, of how her work may participate in a retrograde politics. Further, she suggests that the contemporary predilection for postmodernist forms, "technical innovation," cannot be assessed in purely aesthetic terms but must be held morally and socially accountable. Yet the vocabulary and rhetoric in these statements are an index to the ambivalence and anguish she feels about how these ideological formulations can be artistically constricting. She perceives "conflict" and "dilemmas." She observes how a preoccupation with oppression may interfere with artistic achievement. Revealing her anxiety most poignantly, perhaps, is the shift in pronoun in "I used to think one could be." Gayl Jones seems torn between political accountability and artistic freedom, but she believes that the two may be fused in a "technical innovation [that] isn't devoid of its human implications."

In spite of her awareness that technical innovation can be infused with moral and political responsibility, Jones' comment (made after the publication and initial reception of her first two novels) that she "used to think" that she could escape certain constraints on the representation of sexuality and gender suggests that she has retreated in her position. This sort of withdrawal is unfortunate in that it demonstrates the censorial pressure that the critical community can bring to bear on writers. Criticism of *Eva's Man* indicates that the representation of sexuality and gender is, in fact, perceived as politically problematic. More recent criticism, which offers alternative readings of the text, is, then, put in the awkward position of ''rescuing'' the text not only from some of its critics but also from some pronouncements of its author.

Much criticism of *Eva's Man* simply does not do justice to the complexity of the text. . . .

Despite Gayl Jones' consistent preoccupation not only with language and representation but also with sexuality and reproduction, most of the criticism of *Eva's Man* does not adequately address these issues. The novel needs a larger conceptual framework, one that addresses, for example, the privilege of heterosexual and genital sexuality, the reproductive imperative, and the phallus as ''privileged signifier.''. . .

The text of *Eva's Man* is, in fact, everywhere concerned with language. It engages a variety of public discourses which, because of their position of dominance and privilege, are instrumental in the construction of black womanhood. The novel opens with the representation of Eva's crime in the media and its popular reception. Elvira informs Eva that ''they's people that go there just so they can sleep in the same place where it happened, bring their whores up there and all. Sleep in the same bed where you killed him at''. In a repetition of the Trueblood episode in Ellison's *Invisible Man*, the site of violent and aberrant sexuality becomes a space for occult ritual. The crime undergoes a bizarre reenactment, or retelling. It is as if by retelling, and having it be retold, the media and other authorities hope to contain it. As if, by explaining it, by fixing it in certain authoritative discourses, an otherwise intractable and outlawed trajectory of desire may be brought within the bounds of the law. As if sheer repetition, acting like a narcotic, may make the experience manageable: ''They want me to tell it over and over again.''

As if in response to the current academic preoccupation with ''being silenced'' or of ''finding a voice,'' Jones suggests that silence itself may be empowering. Eva is not silenced; in fact, hegemonic institutions invite and encourage her loquacity. Her participation would only provide ''data'' which would allow her subject position to be gathered or recuperated into the different forms of institutional discourse. What we have in the text is a literary representation of institutional discourse and its deployment of various categories of containment. . . .

The psychiatrist does provide incitement, represented as benevolent incitement: ''His voice was soft. It was like cotton candy. He said he wanted to know how it felt, what I did, how did it make me feel.'' This is followed by his assurance, '''I want to help you, Eva''' and '''Talk to me'''. Further, the juxtaposition of the statements ''My knees were open. I closed my knees'' and '''You're going to have to open up sometime, woman, to somebody. I want to help you''' indicates that this sort of interrogation is tantamount to a form of sexual violation that Eva has experienced all her life and that the psychiatrist ironically reenacts. Language must, in fact, penetrate the field in which the object of knowledge is constituted in order to recuperate it in an ordered textuality and epistemological coherence. We have, then, an ostensibly and insistently benevolent motivation. His voice is ''soft . . . like cotton candy,'' and he is explicitly and obsessively repetitive: ''I want to help you.'' In the same breath, however, his language is violent.

It is this urge to circumscribe a nomadic meaning within manageable territory that motivates the internal logic and consistency of public discourses. These are represented in the text by law enforcement officers who arrest and interrogate her, the lawyers who try her, and the psychiatrists who attempt to treat her. The officers, with whom Eva admittedly has minimal contact, begin the process through which various institutions will try to explain her crime. . . .

Eva, then, has to answer to certain institutional forces for her crime, forces represented by a set of public discourses. Her silence or the unmanageability of her responses provokes a desire for ''easy answers,'' for ''explanation,'' for closure. Similarly, in her engagement with private discourse, impassivity and impenetrability drive Davis to rely on categories that have been disseminated by institutional discourses and made available to private individuals. Davis has at his disposal the category of madness, of the unnatural, in which his desire for closure can contain recalcitrant elements. We witness here another moment of collusion between public and private discourses in their representation of the other.

*Eva's Man* is not a pleasant novel but an extremely disturbing one. Gayl Jones, in fact, calls it a ''horror story'' (*Harper*). As a response to oppression, murder and mutilation may not be justifiable, may not even be the most effective strategy. The text, however, does not endorse murder and genital mutilation. Instead, it asks us to speculate on the ''imagined possibility'' of dismemberment. Given the preponderance of dominant structures, the text speculates on how the oppressed subject might negotiate these structures of violence, what the dismantling of a phallogocentric structure might entail, so that, if the violence is disturbing, it serves to underline the violence of the discursive formations which circulate around and circumscribe the subject. Attention to the language of the text, analysis of language and representation, far from being apolitical, unmasks the politics of language and the ideology of representation which are some of the most powerful instruments for the construction of the subject.

Biman Basu. *Callaloo*. 19, 1 (Winter 1996), pp. 193–208

When Gayl Jones published *The Healing* last year—her first novel in 22 years—reviewers celebrated its departure from the shocking and horrifying subjects of her early work: rape, incest, sadomasochism, the psychosexual legacies of slavery, the terrible pleasures of heterosexual attachments, the bruising face of love. While *Corregidora* (1975) and *Eva's Man* (1976), both novels, and *White Rat* (1977), a collection of short stories, all garnered their share of critical acclaim, readers invariably found them chilling and frightful, none more so than *Eva's Man*, named for the title character, who poisons her lover, bites off his penis, then wraps it in a silk handkerchief. Critics who have habitually pondered the connection between Jones' fiction and her life couldn't resist the speculation that, with *The Healing*, Jones had broken the spell, had ''healed'' herself, turned back from what Valerie Sayers termed the ''pain of old-fashioned, aching bluesy love'' and headed toward a more affirmative vision.

Her latest novel, *Mosquito*, which chronicles the adventures of Sojourner Nadine Jane Johnson (a.k.a. Mosquito), truckdriver and member of the Perfectability Baptist Church, seems to follow in the more hopeful directions charted by *The Healing*. Set in a south Texas border town, *Mosquito*, unlike Jones' taut and economical early work, is sprawling and unruly, spilling over into territory too broad and meandering to map or summarize easily. Reminiscent of Ishmael Reed's seriocomic *Mumbo Jumbo*, *Mosquito* is the novel as parody and pastiche. A composite layering of multiform texts, dense with allusions to myth and folklore, popular culture and literature, it offers an especially witty take on the fate of narrative (and of reading narrative), and on the making and marketing of literature in the Electronic Age. . . .

[The] first chapter introduces the novel's controlling concerns with shifting identities, with literal and metaphorical border-crossings, with communicating across the barriers of language, race, region, religion and cosmology. True to her acknowledged Spanish and Latin American influences in the novel—Cervantes, Carlos Fuentes and Gabriel Garcia Márquez—Jones populates a world in which no border walls off the "real" from the "fantastic," nor "true lies" from "fabricated truths." Animals, spirits, plants and humans trade shapes and places and consort with ease. Scenes, characters and genres blur together, as the narrative and guideposts jut out at almost every corner, they double all too often as roadblocks forbidding easy and straightforward passage along this novel's meandering paths.

According to the publisher's blurb, enlisting Jones herself, the novel is about "the need everyone has to define themselves . . . to tell his or her own stories." And it does appear that everybody gets a turn at the narrative wheel. Almost everyone Mosquito encounters is a writer wannabe equipped with copious scribblings and opinions on the craft: her friend, Delgadina, a Chicana bartender; Monkey Bread, her childhood friend and assistant to a Grade-B Hollywood movie actress. Employing plain, vernacular speech, Mosquito herself "tells peoples stories," according to Monkey Bread. "Cept sometimes she tells peoples everything but the story."

*The* story, at least primarily, concerns Mosquito's involvement in the sanctuary movement and her developing romance with Ray, the former immigration agent turned priest, who is also an agent in this new underground railroad movement. But it soon becomes apparent that *Mosquito*, like all good postmodernist texts, is less concerned with Telling a Story than with telling how stories get told (or not). Of course, readers are now fully schooled in novels that tell about telling, and the jaded ones among them may bristle at the prospect of yet another novel on the subject—and one over six hundred pages at that. Have no fear. *Mosquito* will reward the most patient readers, even if it drives them to distraction's brink along the way.

While Jones' first novels featured characters who often refused to speak, Mosquito refuses to shut up. Never at a loss for words, she furnishes running disquisitions on everything from the love interests of black male filmstars (seldom black women, she observes), to "whiteness," to the "Nazi aesthetic" of Madonna and Barbie, to ethnic food, to romance novels, to the problems of African American literature historically. She rattles on about the "girlie pop psychology books" featured on *Oprah* and *Sally*, warning women against men who are "mad, bad, and dangerous to know." She has no truck with such books or their counterparts in fiction. Following a reading by an African American woman novelist, she buttonholes the writer: "Why the man in that story got to be such a son-of-a-bitch?. . . Is you a feminist?" to which the writer replies: "This is a blues novel and it uses the subject matter of the blues?. . . [T]his is what she'd sing about . . . if you're going to write a blues "that ain't the whole repertoire," then shifts into overdrive on the heterogeneous lyrics of the blues. . . .

If *Mosquito*'s "border story" seems to elevate opinion over story, then television can partly take the rap. It is television, of course, that has seamed the borders formerly separating the culture of the book from the culture of electronic communication. But now, thanks to Oprah's Book Club, all that has changed. "A lot of [people] ain't gonna read a book unless they's heard about it in the

mass media," Mosquito observes. That particular form of border-crossing takes its share of hits, as does the much-maligned publishing industry in the era of media conglomerates.

A devotee of television, Mosquito constantly carries a pocket television and haunts trade shows that showcase state-of-the-art technology. Her insistent references to sitcoms, the Learning Channel, soap operas, music videos and talk shows betray television's stamp on her associative imagination. And if the tales she weaves have much the feel of notebook scribblings, half-thoughts and partial phrasings jotted on the run, these very features find analogies in the electronic realm, especially the talk shows that generate ever more talk and "opinion," matched only perhaps by the "chat groups" that jam the "Information Highway.". . .

Whatever Dislocation Readers of *Mosquito* might experience at the level of story will be matched by confusion about the storyteller. If the novel tweaks and trifles with conventional expectations of narrative, it leaves questions of authorship suspended in ambiguity. The prefatory note announces:

> This Book is from the Daughters of Nzingha Archives Mosquito is the "spiritual descendant" of Kate Hickman, a New World African character invented by Lucille Jones and the strength of one of her novels, Stop Dat Moda (excerpts published in Obsidian, BOP, and Callaloo). Electra Lucilla Martin Wilson Jones (Lucille Jones, the Good Spirit) is the Spiritual Mother of Mosquito. However, Ray's Aunt Electra is fictional.

This prefatory note is signed by Nzingha, a spirit creature of no specific place or time. Appearing to Mosquito in a dream, Nzingha says of herself, "I am who you imagine me to be." At the end of the novel, Mosquito adds "Nzingha" to the list of her "entitles," signing herself "Sojourner Nadine Jane Nzingha Johnson." Who writes here—Gayl Jones? Her late mother Lucille Jones? Kate Hickman? Electra? Delgadina? Monkey Bread? They all come together to tell a polyphonic story, but it's impossible to tell them all apart.

Readers will surely close the novel with the nagging suspicion that this truck-driving frustrated storyteller has clearly taken them for a ride. And why not? It's been done before. In another implausible literary allusion, Mosquito mockingly reminds the reader that in *The Life and Opinions of Tristram Shandy, Gentleman* Laurence Sterne also had his jibe at readers. You will recall his suggestion at novel's end that readers have passed their time on an equally voluminous cock-and-bull story.

Is *Mosquito* a cock-and-bull story? Let the reader decide (and beware). In a letter to Monkey Bread, Mosquito describes Delgadina's "border novel," explaining tautologically that those who read it must "cross a border to get into the novel. I tells her that they's a lot of people that ain't going to want to cross that border to get into her novel." Jones could be said to anticipate her own readers' response, knowing that some just won't "cross that border," but if they don't they'll miss a wildly satirical, if unwieldy, novel that crosses the border from the taut, lyrical, almost elliptical style of Jones' early work into the prolixity that often characterizes writing in the computer age.

Full of spirit and adventure, burlesque and caricature, *Mosquito* eludes the literary border guards and fingers the new commissars of culture. But in the end, this book on books may well get caught in the maw of its own devices, may well drive readers to take Monkey Bread at her word: "I wants all my listeners to keep listening," she writes, ''but I don't require that they listen to the whole story, just what they thinks is worth hearing.'' The story is worth hearing, even if it can't be swallowed whole.

Deborah McDowell. *Women's Review of Books*. XVI, 6 (March 1999), pp. 9–10

BIBLIOGRAPHY
*Chile Woman*, 1974; *Corregidora*, 1975; *Eva's Man*, 1976; *White Rat* , 1977; *Song for Anninho*, 1981; *The Hermit-Woman*, 1983; *Xarque and Other Poems* , 1985; *Liberating Voices: Oral Tradition in African American Literature*, 1991; *The Healing*, 1998; *Mosquito*, 1998

# JORDAN, A.C. (1906–1968)
## South Africa

[*The Wrath of the Ancestors*] is a grim tragedy of a young, educated but inexperienced chief of the Pondomise [a Xhosa tribe], who (along with his wife) sets out fully determined to educate his people—to lift them out of the pale of darkness, ignorance and superstition. Alas! the chief and his wife understand the customs and religious feelings of the people but imperfectly. In his zeal to eradicate superstition the chief cuts across the feelings of the Reds,'' his educated wife does not *hlonipha* [follow traditional ways] and she kills the *inkwaklhwa*—a snake regarded by the Reds as the ''guardian'' of the tribe. By this thoughtless act she has incurred the wrath of the ancestral spirits and brought a curse upon the ''Royal House.'' Things are brought to a point and the tribe is split into two camps—Reds versus the educated. The result is a delirious succession of treacheries, crimes, mental tortures and other atrocities, ending in a general funeral. The chief and his wife commit suicide by drowning themselves and their only child. The whole action becomes a nightmare. A tribal tragedy!

To justify such a tragic end reference must be made to the difference in religious outlook of the Red and the educated man. To an educated Christian man such a tragic end is a perversion of the accepted moral standards, that is, a triumph of evil over good. But to a Pondomise whose religious outlook is different the tragedy is the inevitable retribution of the *iminyanya* [ancestral spirits], whose wrath has been kindled by a wanton non-observance of the tribal customs on the part of the chief and his wife. Whatever the moral outlook, the author has deliberately chosen to make the end such as it is, strictly consistent with the title *The Wrath of the Ancestors*. Is not the way of freedom and salvation from the overwhelming evil and superstition of this world littered with the bones of martyrs?

I. Oldjohn. *South Atlantic Quarterly*. April 1940, p. 77

No review of the vernacular novel can fail to mention the work of the African author, A. C. Jordan, who set a new standard by his *The Wrath of the Ancestors*. It was on a larger scale than former novels and was an attempt to reveal the workings of the African soul as it awakened to the claims of a higher type of life, while yet set in a primitive environment and fighting a grim fight with conservative and reactionary forces. . . .

The author did more than tell an enthralling story. He showed himself to have a conception of artistic values that was praiseworthy. At the close of the book . . . the forces of paganism and reaction win and there is a veritable blood-bath. Some who read the book in manuscript begged the author to give it a different and more happy ending. But he turned a deaf ear to their pleadings. ''This is how it came to me,'' he declared, and declined to do violence to his own artistic conceptions.

R.H.W. Shepherd. *Standpunte*. June 1953, p. 46

Jordan comes to grips with real life, his feet firmly set on the ground. In [*The Wrath of the Ancestors*] he makes a penetrating study of the central problems of a nation emerging from a tribal way of life. His mind, keen and sharp as an assegai, penetrates the turmoil of change and discerns two groups, those who advocate progress and those who cling to the past. He sees in their clash the central conflict and challenge of his people. Here is no facile evasion of the troublesome facts of life, but a very real effort to meet these challenges. This clash of the old and the new is ever with us, it is universal and eternal. It may and does assume various forms, having in each country an individual existence demanding an individual solution. But fundamentally it remains the same. The reader feels, no matter what his nationality, that here is a situation from real life, one in which he could easily be involved. Thus the novel assumes a universal interest and like a true work of art it transcends locality and age. . . .

The novel has proved to be equally popular with urbanized and tribal Africans. It is not difficult to see why. The book is steeped in tribal atmosphere so that even the urban African is caught up in that current. This, I think, is because he still feels in his bones the influence of the old tribal life. He instinctively loves it and respects it. His feeling must be akin to that which inspires the cry of an exile longing to see again his motherland. Even though the African be a Christian, his outlook is still largely coloured by the old tribal civilization. Generations of town life have not broken the links with a past which is instilled by song and story. Deep within the African, chords of sympathy with a golden age gone by are touched to music. Vilakazi exploits this sympathy to an extreme degree. The imagined glories of the past become an obsession and his cry a nostalgic utterance. Much the same is true of W.B. Yeats in his early poetry, when he dreamed his way through a world of mythological creation, divorced from real life and so largely valueless. But Jordan gives these Africans aspirations, and the beauty and dignity of the tribal way of life, due recognition, without losing his balance or perspective.

John Riordan. *African Studies*. 20, 1, 1961, pp. 53–54

The final crisis in [*The Wrath of the Ancestors*] . . . focuses on Thembeka. From the beginning of her reign, the young queen antagonizes the tribe because she goes about in short dresses and bareheaded. One day, she finds a serpent coiled near her child and kills it. Now, as anthropologists know, among the Pondos, ''different clans regard a particular species of snake as being a manifestation of their *ithongo* (ancestral spirits), and treat it with respect, not killing it or driving it away when it comes to the *umzi* (compound, kraal), for it is *umninimizi* (the owner of the *umzi*). Whether the snake is poisonous or not makes no difference. Clearly, this is one of the points on which modern and traditional attitudes cannot be reconciled. It is perhaps the most important of such points, since devotion to the ancestral spirits is the cornerstone of many traditional societies, with the consequent belief—skillfully described by Jordan at the beginning of the book—that the ancestors inevitably take revenge on those who harm snakes.

To the Western mind, in killing the snake, the queen has courageously done her duty to save her child's life; in the traditional African view, she has committed the most grievous offense that can be conceived. This antinomy is the real core of the tragedy, and it is the source of further dilemmas and calamities. For the tribe is so outraged that Zwelinzima, in order to keep the throne, is compelled to renounce the queen to take another, more acceptable wife. Thembeka, in her turn, is frenzied by the wreck of her love and marriage; she drowns herself and her son, upon which the chief himself commits suicide. The whole process is of course a case of self-fulfilling prophecy: it is the tribe's belief in the wrath of the ancestors which is responsible for those catastrophic events, which in turn confirm and strengthen that very belief. This, however, is not how Jordan's tribesmen view it. . . .

The paradox defined by Oldjohn, or the response of Shepherd in *Bantu Literature and Life*—"At the close of the book, the forces of evil, of paganism, and reaction, win"—[is] enough to show that *The Wrath of the Ancestors* is a deeply disturbing novel, where the interplay of character and circumstance cannot be described in simple terms.

Albert S. Gérard. *Four African Literatures* (Berkeley: University of California Press, 1971), pp. 85–87

[*Tales from Southern Africa*] is a companion to Jordan's *Towards an African Literature*, though each volume is an independent work relating to the larger whole of African literature. Jordan's view, that of an Africanist born, bred and steeped in African culture and mores, is that concentration must be paid to the earlier, and oral, tradition before real awareness of African identity through the modern literature can be achieved. In this work he translates and "retells" *ntsomi* tales—Xhosa stories narrated, and performed, by a storyteller and passed traditionally down the generations by word of mouth. The difficulties of keeping the tone of the *ntsomi* are enormous, for they are an oral and dramatic and collective art (listeners contribute their reactions, comments and additions, and often these are incorporated into the next rendition). The narrator in the original tales described each character by *becoming* that character in dramatic performance. Consequently, these tales, even in the spare modern descriptive devices added by Jordan, are not really *ntsomi* but an approximation of the folk art.

The stories are frightening, funny, exciting, homey, exotic at turns—and always socially oriented. They are moral guides as well as entertainment. This book will interest specialized and general readers of all ages. The stories can be read easily for pleasure and insight. The two introductions [by Jordan], one on the political-social deprivations of the Xhosa artist and the other on the *ntsomi* tradition, are rewarding, stimulating studies.

*Choice*. December, 1973, p. 1557

BIBLIOGRAPHY
*Ingqumbo yeminyanya* (The Wrath of the Ancestors), 1940; *A Practical Course in Xhosa*, 1966; *Tales from Southern Africa*, 1973; *Towards an African Literature*, 1973; *Kwezo Mpindo ZeTsitsa*, 1975

# JUMINER, Bertène (1927– )
## French Guiana

In addition to more than one-hundred scientific publications, [Bertène] Juminer has written three novels [*Les Bâtards, Au seuil d'un nouveau cri*, and *La Revanche de Bozambo*]. He has also written a play, adapted from the latter novel, entitled *Archiduc sort de l'ombre*. . . .

With the exception of Léon-Gontran Damas, Juminer is the best known—and his works the most accessible—of the contemporary French Guyanese authors. . . .

Juminer's first novel *Les Bâtards* [translated as *The Bastards*] is to a great extent autobiographical, being inspired by the author's two-year assignment at a hospital in the town of Saint-Laurent in his native [French Guiana]. During this period, Juminer was particularly struck by the almost total alienation of the educated, black elite from the great majority and their "local" culture—and by the quality, or the lack of it more precisely, of many of the French administrators. Juminer found that these individuals were nothing like the Frenchmen he had known and usually respected in France. Accordingly, his novel centers around the intertwined stories of the two main characters, Robert Chambord and Alain Cambier, as well as a subordinate, but very interesting character, Turenne Berjémi (an anagram of the author's name), all of whom are educated and to a high degree assimilated into French culture. They are, needless to say, aware of, and responsive to, their own culture which is first and foremost black. Their consequent intermediate position between these two cultures is indicated by the title *The Bastards* and their predicament as unusual beings emphasized by such an opprobrious term.

*Au seuil d'un nouveau cri* is an intriguing, didactic novel, which is skillfully structured into complementary parts, "Le Cri" [translated as "The Cry"] and "L'Echo" [translated as "The Echo"] dealing, respectively, with the black man's past and his present, vis-à-vis oppression. "Le Cri" recounts an epic myth in which slaves revolt against the tyranny of their masters and gain their freedom. "L'Echo" is a contemporary portrait of the problems of the black man, with an exhortation to him to rise, as did his ancestors, to wrest freedom from the clutches of the oppressors.

In terms of mood, structure and style, [*La Revanche de Bozambo*, translated as *Bozambo's Revenge*] is a radical departure from Juminer's two previous novels. Here the mood is satirical. An absurd world is created in which there is a reversal of roles between Europe and Africa (a reversal brought about ironically by Europe's continuing ability to maintain a genuine peaceful coexistence between its two dominant political ideologies: capitalism and communism). The situations brought about by the reversed role create a great deal of comic relief, for it is Juminer's contention that laughter—be it ever so bitter—is beneficial, for it offers the black man a temporary release from the ever present tension created by his oppression and, at the same time, it puts the oppressor into a perspective which blows away the cant and mystification of Western colonial claims.

Paul L. Thompson. Introduction to Bertène Juminer. *Bozambo's Revenge* (Washington, D. C.: Three Continents Press, 1976), pp. ix–x, xii–xiv

It is in [*Au seuil d'un nouveau cri*] that Juminer deals with the phenomenon of a special mutual attraction, and presents a black man-white woman couple in a society that rejects such a combination violently. The situation is presented through fiction, and it is through the thoughts of Juminer's principal character that he analyzes it, building a theory to explain it. . . .

In the second part of the work, "The Echo," Juminer proposes his world view and his explanation of the special black man-white woman mutual attraction only suggested in "The Cry." The narrator, still addressing the hero as *"tu,"* reflects on the problem of the omniscient, omnipotent colonists, who specifically prevent the hero's being a man. They depend for their power source on a world they themselves have created, a world in which everyone and everything is devoted to them. However, it seems that in the white man's organization of the world the white woman has finally rebelled and upset things. For a long time, she was a slave, "whose only compensation was derived from a well-organized mythology, in which one saw a knight risk his life for a beauty, a prince marry a shepherdess. Reality remained no less bitter and unacceptable." The white man had allowed no meaningful place in his society for the white woman, and now, militant, she demanded it. The more like the white master she became, the more he feared her. Unwilling to abandon his former privileges altogether, the white man threw himself into colonialism as compensation. Meanwhile the colonized man, assumed here to be black, became increasingly depersonalized as the result of the white man's educational system. In the course of time he realized the need to rebuild society from the bottom up, and it is in the struggle toward a common humanity that the educated black man encountered the white woman: "One need not look elsewhere than to this comradeship in misfortune for that affinity, conscious or unrecognized, existing between the militant white woman and the colored intellectual."

Elinor S. Miller. *Black American Literature Forum.* 11, 1 (Spring 1977), pp. 25, 29

The novels of Juminer are important because of his use of the ideology of revolutionary struggle and the influence of Frantz Fanon that can be seen in his works. Frantz Fanon's influence upon Juminer is best manifest in the latter's second novel, *Au seuil d'un nouveau cri*, in which Juminer goes back into the history of the Caribbean and draws upon the revolutionary struggle of the maroons in "The Cry" . . . and the contemporary communist cell which is set in Paris in the second part of the work, "The Echo." The work is also significant because Juminer fuses Fanon's theory of the cathartic nature of revolutionary violence into the portrayal of his characters in a technique which this author has called sociopsychological realism.

On the other hand, *Bozambo's Revenge* is written from the perspective of revolutionary struggle conducted at the level of guerrilla warfare as the central theme. Juminer calls this work a novel, but it can best be described as an allegory, i.e., a figurative

treatment of colonialism by the transformation of symbols (white is black and black becomes white; Europe becomes the colonial backwater and Africa the metropole), a system of "cultural reversals" as one critic has called it. *Bozambo's Revenge*, therefore, operates as a symbolic narrative which imparts to us some information about the colonial situation without giving us a sense of the multidimensional nature of the colonial experience, or the peculiar psychological conditions which this experience creates and the implications of the colonial situation on the ever evolving nature of . . . contemporary life. Indeed, in trying to turn "colonialism inside out" as the subtitle suggests, he pares away all of the rich complexity of the colonial experience.

Selwyn R. Cudjoe. *Caribbean Quarterly*. 25, 4 (December 1979), p. 2

Dakar [Senegal] and its surroundings, a few years after independence, is the scene of [*Les Héritiers de la presqu'île*]. Bob Yves Bacon (whose real name is Mamadou Lamine N'Diaye), a young Senegalese, has established his profession of "détective privé, diplômé de l'Académie de Paris et du New Jersey" [private detective, graduate of the Academy of Paris and of New Jersey], and is attempting to assert his rather exotic practice. . . .

Cases are rare, but Alassane Ibou N'Diaye solicits his services in order to untangle a conjugal imbroglio that is embarrassing him greatly. We don't learn much about the resolution of this matter, the story having been pushed to the background in order to make room for the development and analysis of the character of Bob Yves Bacon. . . .

If [the plot] surprises by lack of intensity, it is because it is appropriate to go beyond it to find in the novel an investigation of the interior, based on the suggestion of an imaginary and aesthetic universe rather than a totalizing and definitive vision. . . .

This space is a two-faced Africa, where Bob Yves Bacon evolves. His pseudonym is a reminder of the West: of Europe and America simultaneously. The country, the city, the man, and the places become indistinguishable and only symbolize the path of a people and a man in search of themselves. Bob Yves Bacon, in rejecting his given birth name and in choosing a profession that is nonexistent and useless in Senegal, has resolutely chosen the West and refused the traditional reality of his country. . . .

The characters who surround Bob Yves Bacon also represent one or another facet of Senegalese city life. Ibou, the keeper, Nafissatou, who knows the value of money, and Mado, who is trying to express himself as a woman—each one . . . shows a possible way and allows the ambiguity of the detective to emerge. With this little fresco, Juminer gives us sociological observations rather than psychological comments. . . . In fact, each protagonist appears as an element of the symbolic quest of Bob Yves Bacon, a stage of the initiatory course, until the affirmation of his authenticity, when he exclaims at the end "Je suis Sénégalais, je m'appelle Mamadou Lamine N'Diaye!" [I am Senegalese, my name is Mamadou Lamine N'Diaye]. . . .

The novel, a simple stylistic effort, does not innovate much on the level of composition. The two levels of the narration—the immediate and the profound— are blended closely. Nevertheless, one deplores, on several occasions, the rather obvious desire to present clichés of characters, places, and society. . . .

Thus, the heirs take possession of their patrimony, i.e., of their buried self. They are heirs twice over—of ancestral Africa as well as Europe—and they have appropriated, in an equitable manner, the wealth of their double inheritance. . . . In reality, *Les Héritiers de la presqu'île* describes to us a different experience, but isn't the important thing the fact that it speaks to all who are exposed to it?

Isabelle Gratiant. *Presence africaine*. 121–22 (1982), pp. 430–31†

During the past twenty-five years the Caribbean-French and the Afro-French worlds have witnessed some extraordinary political, economic, and social changes which have motivated concerned black writers of French expression to look at old themes from a new perspective. Even though the familiar message and the themes remain in *La Revanche de Bozambo*, Juminer deviates somewhat in this third novel from his grave and austere tone in the previous novels and produces a diverting work which is a combination of fantasy and morality. Less complex perhaps and shorter than its two predecessors, *La Revanche de Bozambo* allows Juminer greater freedom to call attention to controversial discussions on racial imperialism and the timeless evils of colonialism.

*La Revanche de Bozambo* is written in the third person, and its plan of action is heightened by the proficiency of an omniscient narrator who sees all, hears all, and anticipates all. In addition to allowing the reader to share the privilege of seeing what is contained in the minds of each of the characters, the narrator intrudes into the action at intervals and supplies a good measure of wit and wisdom, thus augmenting the entertaining power of those aspects of the tale which he is obliged to relate or explain. On one level we are placed in contact with a world saturated with political and social satire where the relationships between blacks and whites are exploited. In this particular fantasy of the author, Africa becomes the colonizer and Europe the colonized; the whites are the natives and the blacks are the imperialists in this novel of reverse colonialism. . . . There is no sentimentality in this situation, for the blacks are not what one would call "forgiving" masters. In exchanging conditions, morals, style of living, prejudices, and racism with the whites, they are equally merciless in their treatment of them. In this farce of reversed functions, the blacks usurp the roles of *adorables créatures* or villains, roles historically enjoyed by the whites. Thus, present-day Europeans are forced to hear the raw truth about themselves and, in the novel, to submit to all the traditional and imaginable humiliations inflicted upon them by a racist society dominated now by Africans. Contemporary black society is satirized in its turn by the author's use of components based on white or European norms. Through the role-playing of the black colonizers, both whites and blacks are mocked to a degree when Africans are made to assume the odious mentality of European imperialists. Consequently, we discover the employment of satire as an offensive and a defensive weapon when, through personal intervention, the narrator's subjective attitude is exposed creating a contrast with his objectivity.

Robert P. Smith, Jr. *CLA Journal*. 26, 1 (September 1982), pp. 25–26

[A] forceful treatment of satire and caricature is found in Juminer's novel, *Bozambo's Revenge*. . . . [The] situation presented is a skillful sleight-of-hand, a fantastic farce which draws on all the registers of a successful comedy, but whose often ferocious humor serves a twofold purpose: to remind the reader of colonial rule and to point out the many humiliating experiences the native traveler from Africa or from the Caribbean countries was—and still might be—subjected to upon arrival and during his stay in Paris.

Juminer presents a hypothetical situation: after having colonized the Light Continent, blacks are now the ruling class. The novel takes place in a big city called Bantouville (once called Paris), which African genius has created from swamps bordering the banks of the Sekuana River, which the natives still call the Seine. The protagonist is Anatole Dupont, a young Provençal, who arrives in Bantouville for the first time. He has come to further his education. . . .

Juminer leaves no stone unturned. He introduces well-known characters and events, transformed to suit his purpose, in order to captivate the reader with his fantasy. Thus we learn that thirty years ago university students had formed a "White-is-beautiful" movement, and that Colonel Bozambo's secretary, while looking for the file of Anatole's uncle (a known agitator), came across the file of a certain D'Egoulles (de Gaulle). Even literature becomes a part of the satirical network: The narrator mentions the "thrilling book" *Uncle Jules' Hovel* by Koumba Couli-Cagou, Vivi Oumarou's account of the white hero Laclôture, and quotes from Lamine Zamba's *Record of a Return to the Land of My Ancestors*—"My whiteness is neither a bombax nor a baobab." . . .

The novel's principal plot, laid out in a scenario familiar to countries ruled by a military government, is the preparation of a coup d'etat; Colonel Bozambo's revenge is directed against his own people, fellow government officials whose conduct—both public and private—had been a great embarrassment to the state. Juminer's biting satire is directed against both blacks and whites. His perspective of Paris is not necessarily "darker" in the sense that it expresses more bitterness, or a greater resentment; he sees the city as a conglomerate of power and its abuses, irrespective of the color of the people who find themselves in command. Though his approach is quite different from that of many other francophone writers, he shares with them the experience of a French colonial education, as well as years of study in France. More important still is that for him . . . Paris has been a magnet.

Ingeborg Kohn. In Jonathan A. Peters, Mildred P. Mortimer, and Russell V. Linnemann, eds. *Literature of Africa and the African Continuum* (Washington, D. C.: Three Continents Press, 1989), pp. 107–9

BIBLIOGRAPHY

*Les Bâtards* (The Bastards), 1961; *Au seuil d'un nouveau cri* (On the Threshold of a New Cry), 1963; *La Revanche de Bozambo* (Bozambo's Revenge), 1968; *Archiduc sort de l'ombre* (The Archduke Emerges from the Shadow), 1970; *Les Héritiers de la presqu'île* (Heirs to the Peninsular), 1981; *La Fraction de Seconde*, 1990

# K

## KANE, Cheikh Hamidou (1928–)
### Senegal

It is . . . as a philosopher of the absolute that Cheikh Hamidou Kane debates his own problem in *Ambiguous Adventure*. He writes about a problem connected to the history of our times, and more precisely to the dramas of African decolonization, for his novel concerns the moral crisis of a Senegalese intellectual torn between the spiritual traditions of his race and Western culture. . . .

[Samba Diallo, the protagonist] regards his Islamic blackness as a mystic wisdom that delivers to man the "interior heart of things," creating in him the happiness of contemplation, the fullness of life in which death itself ceases to be a trial since God's presence envelops everything. As for Western culture, Samba Diallo sees it as an objective philosophy that looks at the surface of the world in order to grasp it physically and to act upon it. Therefore, Africa will never conquer the West without becoming unfaithful to its soul, for it is not in the nature of things that the man who contemplates God should be powerful in history. But will not the victorious West lose the world? For it is not in the nature of things that the world, separated from God, should continue to exist. Samba Diallo's tragic death—he is killed by a fanatic from his country who considers him a traitor—undoubtedly means that the author does not perceive any solution.

Pierre-Henri Simon. *Le monde.* July 26, 1961, p. 9†

Strongly molded by a traditional Moslem education, Kane came to France to continue his studies in philosophy and colonial administration. Out of the rift between these two very different experiences, he created a novel, *Ambiguous Adventure*, which immediately won him a place among the best writers in Africa as well as among the most committed.

The "ambiguous adventure" in this "ambiguous Africa" is that of a society whose system of values is being attacked and eaten away by a foreign system of values. What attitude should the African adopt toward the European civilization that has already taken a foothold in his continent by force, troubled people's minds, and created new needs? Should he go to the white men's schools "to learn how to conquer without being right" and in this way acquire technical and scientific power, "because the hand is what defends the spirit"? But if one enters the whites' schools, he also courts disaster, for in addition to technology the European school also teaches its morality, religion, and philosophy, and separates one from his African civilization. It creates rootless people—the elite, yes, but unable to think for themselves, as Césaire would say.

This problem is set forth by Kane with an art and a depth that have not been achieved before now in world literature. The real problem of modern Negritude has finally been approached, and race no longer has anything to do with it; it is really a matter of cultural differences—irreducible differences. Kane's diagnosis does not leave any doubt about his position: either the African will succeed in synthesizing these two antagonistic cultures, or he will perish. This is the meaning of the death of the hero, Samba Diallo,

at the end of the novel. According to the author's own interpretation, it is the "proof through absurdity that African civilization exists, and exists to such an extent that if an individual yields to the temptation to eradicate it or to abandon it, he inevitably destroys his soul and his personality."

Lilyan Kesteloot. In Lilyan Kesteloot, ed., *Anthologie négro-africaine* (Verviers, Belgium: Gérard, 1967), p. 277†

The harmonious balance of form, the nobility of the characters and their sentiments, the predominance of reason over the emotions and yet the perpetual presence of the deep, mystical forces which lie behind men's actions, the sober language, simple but majestic images, all place *Ambiguous Adventure* in the classical tradition of French literature. In many ways it recalls Racine and Pascal. At the same time it must not be forgotten that the same clarity and mystery are to be found in the religious works of Islam. It is, possibly, because Kane has found this conjunction in form, style and thought between Islam and Europe that *Ambiguous Adventure* is able to stand between the two cultures and present the problem of assimilation with complete objectivity.

The language is, throughout, clear and simple. In the dialogue the sentences are short and straightforward. . . .

White and violet, together with red, silver, purple, the colours of nobility, of suffering, those of the sky and the desert, are the most frequent in the descriptions both of characters such as the Knight, the Chief, and "la Grande Royale" and of the settings of Samba's homeland. In contrast, the settings in Paris are dull, colourless, uninspiring. It is as if the contrast between European materialism and Islam exists even in their surrounding.

There is no excess in *Ambiguous Adventure*. Each word, each phrase has its meaning and adds to the whole meaning. The climax, in the final chapter, in which the ambiguity is resolved, recalls [Paul] Valéry's "The Graveyard by the Sea." Life and death, man and the universe, the finite and the infinite become one in the blinding, perpetual instant of complete understanding.

A.C. Brench. *The Novelists' Inheritance in French Africa* (London: Oxford University Press, 1967), pp. 107, 109

The importance of Cheikh Hamidou Kane, a great West African writer, comes from the fact that, in his novel *Ambiguous Adventure*, he treats two convergent problems: the European movement toward awareness and the African movement toward awareness. He treats these two problems as an existentialist philosopher and above all as a humanist of the absolute, and therein resides the profoundly universal interest of his work. . . .

The hero's conflict is that of an individual torn between the traditional view represented by Master Thierno and the reformist tendency represented by la Grande Royale. Samba Diallo incarnates the contradiction between the conservative values of Islam and progressive or reformist forces. . . .

In the center of each system, traditional or modern, African or Western, there lies a subtle negation of the individual as an absolute truth or autonomous liberty. . . . According to the Westerner [Lacroix, the spokesman for technological civilization], nature must be mastered so that the demands and needs of man will be better served; whereas the African [the Knight who is the hero's father] asserts that man should submit to the grandeur of nature—that is, seek the profound meaning of the world by contemplating the slightest movement in nature. . . . The tale simply presents two forms of tyranny or alienation of which man is the victim, namely, metaphysical tyranny or the tyranny of the absolute, and technological tyranny.

> Sunday O. Anozie. *Sociologie du roman africain* (Paris: Éditions Aubier-Montaigne, 1970), pp. 148–49, 152–55†

There are at least two senses in which *L'Aventure ambiguë*, Cheikh Hamidou Kane's only novel to date, can be said to have attained the status of a classic. First, in the way in which it brings a distinctive treatment and a 'high seriousness' to a problem that is central to contemporary African writing and to modern African awareness, namely the problem of cultural conflict, the novel stands out as an exemplary work, a prototype as it were of African expression in our times. Secondly, the art that informs and shapes this work proceeds from an imaginative spirit that is essentially classical. The severe restraint and austerity of the style, the soberness that marks the presentation of the human problems and the moral and spiritual issues with which the novel is concerned; the conscious architecture of characters and situations employed in the novel to translate ideas for which the narrative scheme serves largely as a framework of development: all these features of the novel reflect an intention behind the work, directing its meaning towards a large statement upon the African condition and in a more general way, upon human fate. *L'Aventure ambiguë* is palpably an allegory derived from a meditation upon the African situation, a work in which the balance is finely held between the contemplative function of imaginative inspiration and the reflective significance of a conscious and deliberate art.

The key to the allegorical character of the novel is furnished by the central character. In Samba Diallo, we have, like in the novels of Andre Malraux, an 'articulate hero', that is, a character who expresses the ideas that he stands for and who at every moment is engaged in taking a measure of the forces involved in his individual fate. Samba Diallo combines an intense self-consciousness with a lucid introspection. Like Malraux again, Kane calls his work a 'récit', that is, not a novel in the ordinary sense, a story issuing largely from the play of fancy, but rather, a narrative that is barely removed from a direct reporting from fact. Whether or not the novel is a transposition in imaginative terms of the author's life, as suggested by Vincent Monteil, there seems little doubt that a large measure of direct involvement by the author with his principal character supplies to the work much of its moving power. In Kane's designation of his novel as a recit, as indeed in the whole manner of Kane's writing, one discerns at all events an insistence on his part on the representative value of Diallo's adventure; *L'Aventure ambiguë* can be said to present itself as a casestudy and its hero as a model.

But if, in this view, Samba Diallo appears to us somewhat of an abstraction, he is nonetheless a credible creation, the radical representation of a recognizable type of individual temperament and destiny. Indeed, the emphasis on individual consciousness in this work is unusual in the general run of African novels. In other words, Samba Diallo is far from being a stock figure, a disincarnated

symbol. We respond to him as to an individual who is implicated in an intense personal drama, and our interest in him is commanded by what we understand immediately as the character's peculiar form of response to the burden of existence. And it is through the intensity of this response that the character acquires his representative value and that we are drawn into an involvement with the author's exploration of the alienated condition and sensibility. Thus it is the intimate correlation between the hero and the situation which he symbolizes that brings alive for us the total significance of the novel.

> Abiola Irele. *The African Experience in Literature and Idedogy* London: Heneman Educational Book, Ltd., 1981, pp 167–68

BIBLIOGRAPHY
*L'aventure ambiguë* (Ambiguous Adventure), 1961

# KELLEY, William Melvin (1937–)
## United States

*A Different Drummer*, a first novel by twenty-five-year-old William Melvin Kelley, born in New York and educated at Harvard, is in some ways a better book than [James Baldwin's] *Another Country*. For one thing, the major characters are more respectable and wholesome; and despite their weaknesses and failures, they never lose sight of the dignity and decency that might reasonably be expected of civilized human beings. For another thing, the experiences of the characters and the language by which they communicate their experiences are more acceptable to readers of normal sensibilities. Furthermore, racial overtones which are basic to both books are more subdued and indirectly expressed in *A Different Drummer*, really as if they are incidental explanations rather than central arguments. . . .

There are several weaknesses in this novel. First, the author fails to provide meaningful and convincing motivation for the major incidents in the story. The lynching of the Reverend Bradshaw, which is intended to be an emotionally charged climax, falls flat. It is a meaningless, unconvincing, ludicrous ending to a plot that is in other respects highly imaginative, largely original, and absorbing. In fact, the Negro cult leader is entirely extraneous to the basic development of the plot. Second, Tucker's motivation is obscure and far from compelling in terms of cause and effect. A writer who accepts the challenge of analyzing the hidden motives of his characters is obligated to produce reasonably believable results.

But, despite its shortcomings, this book is tremendously encouraging. It reveals a Negro novelist with unusual talents who can tell without bitterness a moving story with strong racial overtones.

> Nick Aaron Ford. *Phylon*. Summer 1963, pp. 128–30

For all the random virtues of the [stories constituting] the Bedlow cycle, the heart of *Dancers on the Shore* is in the linked stories about the Dunford family—the doctor father, the mother, elder son Chig, sister Connie and brother Peter. The milieu alone is arresting: they are well-to-do Negroes whose children attend private schools and Ivy League colleges, and the ambiguities of race touch them only obliquely. Their public existence as Negroes is only occasionally in evidence. . . .

Not one of these stories is unsatisfying; indeed, such is the consistent interest of the Dunfords that one reader, at least, looks forward to a fuller representation in a novel. Certainly the material is there.

As is customary with story collections, the quality of Kelley's work is variable, but the range of his imagination, combined with the evidence of his best work, offers impressive evidence of the continuing development of the talent that was also visible in his first novel, *A Different Drummer*.

Michele Murray. *Comonweal*. July 3, 1964, p. 459

As a writer, Kelley is a long-distance runner. He intends to earn a living from his books, and at 30 has already published four. Moreover, the books are unified in over-all design. Each volume is part of a larger saga, so that what lies in store for his readers is a sort of [Faulknerian] Yoknapatawpha legend in reverse: an epic treatment of American history from a Negro point of view.

Kelley's novels are marked by a progressive mood of disaffiliation from the dominant values of his culture. The hero of *A Different Drummer*, for example, represents the earlier, nonviolent phase of the Negro revolution. Under the astonished gaze of his white neighbors he sows his fields with salt, slaughters his livestock and burns his home, thereby inspiring a vast migration from the rural South.

The hero of *A Drop of Patience* is a blind jazz musician. His blindness is an emblem of the Negro's vulnerability, so long as he accepts the values of the white middle class. Abandoned by his white mistress, he cracks up, spending several years in and out of mental institutions. Gradually he recovers, finding a sustaining vision in the folk values implicit in his craft.

Now, in *dem* (''lemme tellya how dem folks live''), Kelley turns to an overt satire of the ways of white people. His present mood is bitter, disillusioned, alienated to the point of secession from American society. The expatriate impulse, however, has found in satire a controlling form. Kelley's images are able to encompass his negative emotions. The result is a sharp increase in perception for the victims of his satire.

Robert A. Bone. *New York Times Book Review*. September 24, 1967, p. 5

The title of W. M. Kelley's second novel, *A Drop of Patience*, is taken, significantly enough, from Shakespeare's *Othello* (IV, II). It is the story of Ludlow Washington, a Negro jazz musician. The irony in this book springs from the fact that the hero, forced to live in a coloured social pattern, does not and cannot recognize the difference between black and white, as he was born blind. . . .

He escapes to New York, where he meets Ragan, a white girl as lonely as he is; the two fall passionately in love, and this affair is a crucial point in Ludlow's life, in his career, and in the novel. It is an ordeal in the course of which his racial education is examined and the gaps in it filled in for him to ''see'' through his blindness. It is as if the Negro community, wiser now, wanted to remind the ''blind'' man of his wilful deafness to their warning, one stressed particularly by Norman Spencer, never to ''depend on no white man for

nothing,'' for ''he ain't strong enough to keep his promises.'' If the message is not understood, Kelley clearly indicates, the knowledge can only come through suffering. . . .

In the preface to *Dancers on the Shore*, a collection of his short stories published in 1965, Kelley claimed that ''a writer should ask questions'' about man's life and the important topical issues of his day. The answers should come from ''a sociologist or a politician or a spokesman.'' But in *A Drop of Patience* it looks as though he had lost ''patience'' with asking questions only and had decided to answer them himself. Not that an artist cannot assume the role of spokesman; James Baldwin is a good example of the ability of the two to coincide. But, as Norman Mailer puts it, Baldwin's ''affirmations are always full of little denials, his denials full of little reservations,'' while W.M. Kelley's statements and ''answers'' in his second novel possess a tone of finality from which the book suffers considerably. . . .

Of W. M. Kelley's two attempts at fictional actualization of the American Negro's search for his identity, the first one [*A Different Drummer*], executed in social, historical and political terms and in the form of a fantasy, was a brilliant success. . . . His second novel, dealing with the Negro's identity in terms of culture, can be accepted with reservations only.

Josef Jařab. *Philogica Pragensia*. No. 12, 1969, pp. 167–70

William Melvin Kelley's ivy league tutelage along with his unassuming demeanor (for he is unperturbably cool), are totally disarming. He comes into town with no guns showing, with no loud booming agonies of black rage. His style is a quiet, easily readable, point by point, well-tempered, traditional form of writing. There is nothing about him to put one on guard. Before you know it though, even at the very instance when you are about to say, ''Hey, man, com'ere and tell us what you learnt in that white school,'' he has stuffed your mouth full of cyanide.

Kelley's first novel, *A Different Drummer*, tells the story of what happens when all the black people vacate the South, as well as what has gone on during the years before. This book is not a ''parable,'' no more than Howard Fast's *Freedom Road* is a parable. Kelley depicts the very incidents, the acts and thoughts of brutality and inhumanity that whites have historically inflicted upon blacks in the South. He depicts the rage set off in the whites when the blacks, whom the whites have repeatedly deemed unwanted, decide once and for all to leave. He depicts the very *atmosphere* in and by which blacks are victimized, but which has been created and enforced by whites alone. Kelley depicts reality. In fact, Kelley is often closer to reality as a novelist than was Howard Fast who, it would seem, was incapable of writing anything but masterpieces. But Kelley is often closer to reality because, unlike Fast who was a communist, Kelley's works are free of the restrictions of any kind of ideological feedback—Marxist, anti-Marxist, or otherwise. [1969]

Calvin C. Hernton. In John A. Williams and Charles F. Harris, eds., *Amistad 1* (New York: Random House, 1970), pp. 219–20

*Dunfords Travels Everywheres* picks up the motto of *Finnegans Wake* in its title, points to Joyce in an epigraph, and even bravely attempts the late idiom, making a rumbling, punning amalgam of minstrel paper, journalese, advertising copy, and radio serial into a new language, an escape from "languish," from the "Langleash language," a descent into a racial collectivity of blacks, the tongue of New Afriquerque cropping up suddenly in the ordinary prose of the novel. . . .

There is an affinity with Joyce. Kelley, too, as a black American and a writer, is caught in the language and culture of an enemy country, and his use of *Finnegans Wake* reflects a legitimate distress: it is a mockery both of "good English" and of black manglings of it. The trouble is that the effort looks in the wrong direction. The experimental idiom is ingenious, but it is, also, thin and obscure. . . .

Kelley's real gift is for evoking an uncomplicated tenderness—there are remarkably drawn old men and children in his short stories—and for grand, improbable, epic exaggeration: the sudden sight of slaves in this book, or in his first novel, *A Different Drummer*, the exodus of the entire black population from a Southern state. From a man who can do these things, *Dunfords Travels Everywheres* seems gratuitous, an attempt to be new at all costs. Homage to Joyce? A book more clearly Kelley's own would have been better.

Michael Wood. *New York Review of Books.* March 11, 1971, p. 43

[*Dunfords Travels Everywheres*] has three parallel story lines. One line is the story of Chig Dunford, a confused, impotent black male who seems to prefer the company of whites and who also seems incapable of offering a challenge to anybody. It is also the story, or rather a few episodes in the life of Carlyle Bedlow who secures grounds for divorce for a Harlem dentist and saves a buddy from a very sophisticated congame. The third line, narrated in the distorted but highly symbolic language of the subconscious or the dream seems to contain another main character (called at times Mr. Charcarl, Mr. Chigyle, Mr. Chuggle and other names) whose adventures are similar to those of Chig Dunford but grounded on a different plane of reality. These sequences are alternated in ways that seem arbitrary but which may contain some pattern of meaning. . . .

Admittedly, *Dunfords Travels Everywheres* is a difficult novel. Its weakness, however, is not so much one of technique as of a certain confusion of meaning. If Kelley means to say that whole hearted and uncritical acceptance of the white world on the part of blacks is dangerous and castrating, he fails to provide us with much that is really positive and useful in Carlyle Bedlow's black world. The image of the con-man is one of the oldest and most honored of the black tradition. Bedlow's finesse in rescuing his buddy Hondo is certainly commendable and well executed. It is a decided contrast to Dunford's failure to do anything about the captive Africans. But Bedlow's approach bears no relation in the novel to issues outside the range of the Harlem under-world which is its setting and certainly cannot stand as the solution to the problems Kelley raises. The experiments in form and style in *Dunfords Travels Everywheres* are valuable in themselves as experiments but the ultimate message of the novel hardly justifies the difficulty of reading it.

Cynthia J. Smith. *Freedomways.* No. 2, 1971, pp. 205–6

Cultural plurality is the key phrase necessary in any attempt to understand the over-all meaning of *Dunfords Travels Everywheres.* . . . For Dunford, salvation is possible because he has not forgotten elements of a language system which speaks to the question of diversity and non-conformity, is capable of retaining contact with his cultural past. Thus his travels, which take him through the cultural capitals of the Western world, lead inevitably back to Harlem, where cultural democracy, not cultural hegemony, is the prevailing factor.

In *A Different Drummer* and in *Dunfords Travels Everywheres*, Kelley is cognizant of a black cultural history which his characters either know or must discover. Caliban, intuitively, has always known that the cultural system which defined him was not that of the Euro-American imagists. Dunford, on the other hand, must discover his cultural heritage anew, and in so doing undertake the journey to a black identity. Eventually the journey will lead outside the definition of the West, away from images and symbols that represent Western man, and toward those, rich and enduring, in the African/Black heritage. At the end of the novel he has come to partial awareness, has made his break, tenuous though it may be, with the paraphernalia of imagistic language handed down from the West and gained a new perception of himself.

Addison Gayle, Jr. *The Way of the New World* (Garden City, New York, Doubleday, 1975), pp. 374–75

[Kelley] turns the usual stereotypes on their heads by contending that the black race, traditionally associated with dark jungle evil, seems, from his experience and observation, to be the more passive and gentle of the two races. The white race, thinking itself just and fair, need not be so complacent in this belief, because Kelley constructs a credible argument that the white race is very aggressive and violent. The stereotypes of black sexuality and easy living are shown to have some validity and to be positive rather than negative traits.

Paradoxically, Kelley's fiction is both idealistic and pessimistic at the same time. In *A Different Drummer* and *A Drop of Patience*, he idealistically envisions deep wells of strength in black people, strength which they will need to deal with white man's violence, to carry them forward to a time when humanity will once again feel its common roots. However, the last two novels, *dem* and *Dunfords Travels Everywheres*, are quite cynical, depicting the black man trying to deal with whites, but being betrayed time and again by a white man he thought he could trust. The developing message seems to be that right now, no black person can trust any white person. But Kelley is not so idealistic as to think that the black people can win any open confrontation with whites, so each black man must use his imagination to wage his own figurative guerrilla war for recognition of his humanity.

Jill Weyant. *CLA Journal.* December, 1975, pp. 219–20

BIBLIOGRAPHY

*A Different Drummer*, 1962; *Dancers on the Shore*, 1964; *A Drop of Patience*, 1965; *dem*, 1967; *Dunfords Travels Everywheres*, 1970

# KENNEDY, Adrienne (1931–)

**United States**

With *People Who Led to My Plays*, Adrienne Kennedy has invented a new form of autobiography. Presented to the reader as a "scrapbook" of words, pictures and memories, this slim volume is more accurately an odyssey which poetically documents the coming to artistic maturity of one of the most daring voices in American theatre. Like her lyrical, surrealistic plays, in which the psyche is alternately masked and laid bare, this memoir reveals a disturbing confusion/convergence/juxtaposition of cultures, histories, mythologies, symbols, landscapes, dreams and personal experience.

Covering a period of 25 years, the book is divided into five sections, from "Elementary School" and "High School" through "College," "Marriage and Motherhood" and "A Voyage." Within each time-frame, Kennedy identifies recurring themes, images and experiences that both obsessed and shaped her. In the first section, the seemingly enchanted and safe world of childhood is revealed in all its terror and uncertainty. At sea in a racist and violent wartime society in which watchtowers are erected in schoolyards to ward off Hitler and his armies (who may at any moment invade Cleveland), Kennedy was anchored and nurtured by her social-worker father who urged her to become a "great woman" like "Marian Anderson, Eleanor Roosevelt, Mary Bethune and Helen Keller," by her beautiful, imaginative and mystical mother, and by an extended family which included aunts, uncles, "distant" cousins, grandparents, neighbors and even a specter, Kennedy's Great Aunt Ella.

An endless source of fascination, Kennedy's mother is perhaps the most frequent entry in the book. Kennedy recalls how her mother's dreams were as exciting to her as movies of Frankenstein and Dracula:

> When my mother was making oatmeal on winter mornings as I sat waiting with my bowl at the kitchen table, I secretly yearned that my mother would talk more about the people she had dreamed about. There is no doubt that a person talking about the people in his or her dreams became an archetype for people in my monologues, plays and stories.

In the "College" section (1949–1953), we bear witness to how the virulent racism of American Society affected the developing artist. Kennedy coped with this brutal reality by conjuring the image of Jesse Owens, which "helped and sustained" her through the "dark rainy winters" and the dehumanizing, "often open racial hatred of the girls in the dorm." Again and again, we watch the artist imagining her way out of isolation by creating a psychic community.

In the final time-frame, "A Voyage," Kennedy comes to artistic maturity. In the fall of 1960, she traveled to Africa with her husband. During this voyage—via London, Paris and Madrid to Casablanca—image, memory, feeling and impression began to collect and intensify. Directly upon her arrival in Ghana, Patrice Lumumba, the Congo's young and heroic Prime Minister, was murdered. . . .

As Kennedy told me, "I couldn't cling to what I had been writing—it changed me so. I didn't realize it was going to have such a big impact on me . . . the main thing was that I discovered a strength in being a black person and a connection to West Africa." During this period, she began to work in a surrealistic mode. In Rome, she made an artistic breakthrough—her characters began to

have other personas. All of the historical people who fascinated her became an extension of her heroine, Sarah, in *Funnyhouse*.

"My plays are meant to be states of mind," wrote Kennedy. *People Who Led to My Plays* is as dramatic, as personal, as disturbing and as radical as the rest of her oeuvre. Now through her generous work, more young writers may come to understand how the artist selects material from a myriad sources and transforms it into a vision.

> Rachel Koenig. *The Women's Review of Books*. V, 1 (October 1987), pp. 14–15

Negro-Sarah of *Funnyhouse*, She Who Is in *The Owl Answers*, Clara in *A Movie Star*, and to some extent, the brother and sister protagonists of *A Rat's Mass* invite the reader to "subject" them— that is, to attempt to construct and read their subjectivity, only to prove, ultimately, that it is an unfinishable task. Indeed, this appears to be their function. As an example, She who is Clara Passmore who is the Virgin Mary who is the Bastard who is the Owl encompasses and suggests multiple personae within a single figure, defying the construction of a "personality" that might be read psychoanalytically. Their indecipherability as whole characters, combined with their "content" (again, an inadequate term) as figures, moves the reader/viewer to a consideration of historical parameters, in a fashion as unlike Brecht as it is unlike realism.

A major trope in this operation pivots around body imagery, particularly in terms of skin color. The "pallid" color of Kennedy's undeniably mulatta heroines, sometimes called "yellow" or "high yellow" or "Yellowish alabaster," specifies the ambivalent history of the neither/nor. During the days of slavery, the mulatto (male) was often considered desirable chattel because of his supposed combination of strength and intelligence, the infusion of white "blood" supposedly serving to create a superior laborer. The derivation of the term, most likely from the Spanish for mule, even designates a creature bred for one purpose, to do hard work, and also implies sterility. This parameter of the term, although patently false when applied to humans, required active maintenance in both attitude and law; any transgression meant harsh penalty, usually death. In stunning contrast, the mulatta (female) was frequently praised for her beauty (by white standards), but also embodied the wild, exotic sexuality attributed to African women, posing a threat to white home life by her mere presence. . . .

It is [the] condition of "mixed blood" that cannot be resolved which frustrates Kennedy's heroines in their desire for a place, or perhaps a "race," of their own. As Negro-Sarah says, "I long to become even a more pallid Negro than I am now." Negro-Sarah also accurately describes her particular condition of "homelessness": "I know no places. That is, I cannot believe in places. To believe in places is to know hope and to know the emotion of hope is to know beauty. It links us across a horizon and connects us to the world" (*Funnyhouse*, 7). The mulatta's search for origins and insistence on claiming her white heritage destabilizes the terms of the sexual economy that birthed her, inducing white anxiety for threatened structures of family (tied indubitably to capitalistic enterprise) and patrilineal dominance. It is key that "blood," in racist geneology, follows the *maternal* condition, a fact that is not lost on Kennedy's heroines. They persist in challenging this genealogy by searching for fathers, fathers who would presumably grant them a different heritage, although this, too, proves futile. . . .

At one point in *The Owl Answers*, She Who Is reveals a blacker body in contrast with her pallid face. While this might be a reference to the earlier practice among some black women of tinting their facial skin "to make themselves more acceptably white for black men," it also makes visible (literally) the impossible lie of "passing"—that no matter how pale the face, the body (the entire figure) must read black in a racist culture Blackness, as constructed by the dominant group, is literally determined, one might say "figured," in the blood. Claiming whiteness is impossible with even one "drop" of black blood. Yet the *maternal* heritage, referring back to blackness and African origins, is bankrupt in these plays. Not peopled by strong, self-sacrificing matriarchs, freedom fighters, or escapees from slavery, this "black" heritage is no more accommodating than the white one is remote. Africa itself sometimes emerges in the plays as a romanticized land of both dreams and strength, a beautiful land both desired and feared; but the various mothers of Kennedy's plays are weak, passive figures, unable to escape either white or black abuse, unable to give positive guidance to their offspring, usually recommending suicide (as with the mother of *The Owl Answers*, who kills herself, saying it is the "way out of Owldom," the way "to St. Paul's Chapel." Africa, in *Funnyhouse*, is "where my mother fell out of love with my father", where the mother's hair begins falling out—the dream of saving the race dies hard in this Africa, and spells the end of the parents' marriage. Kennedy here resists the early rhetoric of the 1960s black community, in its passionate return to African roots, through the vivid portrayal of the mulatta's neither/nor status—outsider to both the black and white communities, as well as the emblem of the black community's tendency to be "colorstruck." In this, she prefigures the black women's novels of the early 1970s, such as Morrison's *The Bluest Eye* and Walker's *Grange Copeland*, in which the black community itself comes under critique for its own racism and sexism.

The mulatta body politics of Kennedy's plays also includes sexual politics. These figures are objects of desire for both black and white men, not by virtue of some individual attraction, but because of the sexuality imputed to their skin color. In *The Owl Answers*, She Who Is is pursued nearly to the point of rape by a nameless Negro Man for whom she too is apparently nameless, since they seem to meet anonymously on the subway. In *Funnyhouse*, Negro-Sarah lives with Raymond, a white Jewish man who "is very interested in Negroes" and who accuses her of cruelty when she refuses to accept her black heritage. ("Hide me from the jungle" [*Funnyhouse*,1].) They variously appeal to their fathers for a rape-free heritage, which, again black or white, is depicted as an impossibility. . . .

If "history is what hurts," Kennedy's figures are the walking wounded—these bodies bleed so freely, so often, that one must suspect irony; like slasher films, the gore can become routine. But unlike Sweeney Todd or Freddy's nightmares, there is no reference in these texts to a "real" person/character (bleeder or bleeding) for whom we are to feel shock or sorrow. Instead, the reference is to history—that which hurts—and our shock and horror are reserved for hard looks at the violence underpinning a culture dependent upon racial domination, hard looks at one's own position within that culture. In the case of the mulatta, the mensurable properties of "blood" (as in the blood that "taints," Faulkner's "outcast blood," the "mixed blood," the demarcation of one-half, one-fourth "black blood," etc.) are literally laid waste by the visible leakage of red, that is, "human," blood from black bodies. The racist preoccupation with blood, the mystification of its properties, foregrounds the ideological construction of "community," here determined (as always?) by the manipulation of "knowledge" by the dominant group. In *A Movie Star*, the ambivalence and pain of childbearing for black women, noted earlier, is made literal through Jean Peter's repeated bleeding through her skirts and the changing of bloodied sheets related to dialogue about Clara's miscarriage and failed marriage. Perhaps one of the most compelling stagings of blood occurs as the focusing image of *A Lesson in Dead Language*, when all the female pupils stand to reveal bloodied skirts. An obvious reference to menstruation and its fearful properties for young girls, the larger context is historical—Caesar, Pompeii, Christianity—grounding their experience of their bleeding in Western culture (which, it should be noted, appears as a "dead language") and rooted in the ideological state apparatus of education: the girls are literally taught to menstruate ("Lesson I bleed"), learning the requisite social stigma/stigmata of being female. Once again, Kennedy makes gender visible as a process of culture in relation to the female body; like the mulatta's skin color, the evidence of menstruation, over which they have no control, entraps females in a particular cultural condition, situates them in history. . . . as emblem of complex power relations across racial lines. As a strategy of resistance, Kennedy's "body politic" bleeds, but is not broken.

In Paul K. Bryant-Jackson and Luis More Overbeck, editors. *Intersecting Boundanes. The Theatre of Adrienne Kennedy*. (Minneapolis: University of Minnesota Press, 1992), pp. 157–67

*Funnyhouse of a Negro* indicts the avant-grade consciousness it reflects. Focusing on the "is-ness" of a woman whose life has been shaped largely by her immersion in Euro-American culture, Kennedy implies that the cost of such immersion has been the destruction of both her sense of "somebody-ness" and her connection with the Afro-American tradition that makes "as-if-ness" possible. The distortion of historical relationships—expressed through the relationship between the protagonist and her parents—lies at the root of Sarah's losses, which involve both her racial and her sexual heritage. She is as isolated from other women, particularly her mother, as she is from other blacks. Devoid of contact with any reality outside her own consciousness, Sarah cannot tap the psychological and communal resources needed for surviving, much less transcending, the nightmarish funhouse world in which it may ultimately prove impossible to distinguish between a Beckett play and the latest newsreels from Vietnam, El Salvador, South Africa, Rwanda, or Bosnia. . . . *Funnyhouse of a Negro* reinforces its basic implications. Only by maintaining or recovering the sense of connection embodied in the folk tradition will it be possible to recover the psychological and communal resources needed to resist the nightmare.

From this perspective, Kennedy's play can be seen as a direct, if peculiarly postmodern, manifestation of one of the basic elements of the Afro-American folk tradition: call and response. Grounded in the traditions of the folk preacher and the blues singer, the call and response dynamic in many ways stands directly opposed to the (post)-modernist aesthetic, which focuses on alienated, isolated individuals such as the protagonist of *Funnyhouse of a Negro*. Writers such as Beckett, Thomas Pynchon, and John Ashbery, while they differ in many ways, have developed techniques designed to explore the linguistic, psychological, or philosophical richness of the isolated consciousness. Frequently, they view the "audience" as a problematic abstraction that may amount to nothing more than a fleeting idea in the isolated psyche. In contrast, the call-and-response form derives its power primarily from the artist's ability to establish contact with a real audience that actively contributes to the creation and impact of the artistic work. Without an "amen" from the congregation, the sermon—or the song, novel, poem, or play—is reduced to so much sound and fury. If the audience affirms the validity of the call, however, the leader can then draw on the combined energies of self and community. In relation to *Funnyhouse of a Negro*, call and response offers a way of overcoming individual isolation since the communal response to a cry of alienation in effect denies that the alienation is entirely an individual experience. Shared pain becomes a source of strength. As [George] Kent wrote in his essay on Langston Hughes, reaching out to the black community allows the folk-based artist to share the hope embodied in the principle of as-if-ness: "Choosing the life of the black folk was also a way of choosing himself, a way of possessing himself through the rhythms and traditions of black people. His choice enabled him to allow for prevailing ideologies without being smothered by them".

The dramatic effectiveness of *Funnyhouse of a Negro*, derives primarily from the ability of its picture of Sarah's fragmented is-ness to elicit an "amen" from the theatrical congregation. The success of Kennedy's call can be explained in relation to Kent's discussion of the principle of is-ness. Kent argues that the successful presentation of is-ness involves three basic elements: the need to present the conflicting and contradictory poles of a single situation, character, or theme; the need to give each pole of the contradiction truthful representation; and the need to present the contradictions in a way that leads the viewer to accept both, saying, "It be's that way." The strange postmodern quality of Kennedy's call—not all that different from the surrealistic quality of Robert Johnson's "Crossroads" or Howlin' Wolf's "Killing Floor"—should not obscure the fact that it does almost exactly what Kent suggests. *Funnyhouse of a Negro* presents a highly convincing representation of the contradictions faced by the Afro-American community that, since the midsixties, has experienced the psychological impact of Euro-American attitudes with increasing intensity.

Craig Hansen Werner. *Playing the Changes: From Afro-Modernism to the Jazz Impulse*, (Urbara: University of Illinois Press, 1994), pp. 109–115

Adrienne Kennedy's characters speak obsessively of their own births as well as the births—which are so often the deaths—of their children. Their monologues focus on rape and incest, miscarriage and child murders. Such preoccupations psychologically paralyze the characters, fixing them at—and regressing them to—a primitive stage in development which Melanie Klein, a psychologist of the British object relations school, calls [see Introduction to *The Work of Melanie Klein*, rev. ed., 1974), the "paranoid-schizoid position," an infant stage which normally precedes integration. According to Klein, the life instinct and the death instinct, which are both present in the infant from birth, create a polarity of anxieties that the infant deals with through splitting and projective identification; that is, the infant learns to split external objects into

representations of good and evil, projecting hopes and fears away from the subject and onto the object. In later phases, the infant learns to unify such splits and to deal with whole objects. Kennedy's characters, however, rarely reach this point of integration: they never progress beyond the paranoid-schizoid position. These characters remain prisoners of object relations, their worlds disordered by irrational, irrevocable splits. . . .

*Funnyhouse of a Negro*, Kennedy's first-published and most famous play, vividly reflects Klein's theories of object relations. The cast of characters includes "Negro-Sarah" and the four "selves" she creates through projective identification: the Duchess of Hapsburg, Queen Victoria Regina, Jesus, and Patrice Lumumba. Other characters include Sarah's Jewish-poet-boyfriend, Raymond, and her landlady, Mrs. Conrad. Sarah's mother appears as an apparition crossing the stage. An author's note at the beginning of the text suggests: "Funnyhouse of a Negro is perhaps clearest and most explicit when the play is placed in the girl Sarah's room. The center of the stage works well as her room, allowing the rest of the stage as the place for herselves. . . . When she is placed in her room with her belongings, then the director is free to let the rest of the play happen around her." Sarah, thus, has split into four majestic selves who occupy the space around her and seemingly take over her world.

When Sarah first appears in the play, she is "a faceless, dark character with a hangman's rope about her neck and red blood on the part that would be her face". In the final scene, "we see her hanging in [her] room." Rosemary K. Curb [*Theatre Journal*, 32:2 (1980)] suggests that this play, "set in the central character's mind, portray[s] the elusive, almost timeless moment just before death, when horrifying images and past events replete with monotonous conversations kaleidoscopically flash through the memory and imagination of the protagonist." Funnyhouse of a Negro is a surrealistic vision of death and oppression, operating on the level of morbid fantasy to depict the mind of a young woman who cannot distinguish the persecutory object from the ideal.

The "action" of the play consists of a series of monologues spoken by Sarah's selves. Even when two appear together, they fail to engage in dialogue; instead, one continues a haunted monotone at the point at which another leaves off. Queen Victoria and the Duchess of Hapsburg meet in the Queen's chamber, but their identities seem questionable: they seem not to know who they are. They speak the lines of Sarah's selves, of British royalty appropriated by a schizoid African-American woman who both represses and projects. They speak of themselves as Duchess and Queen but they speak too of their father in the jungle and the harm he has done their (Sarah's) mother. In subsequent scenes, the selves appear in various combinations, contradicting and corroborating one another's narratives. Sarah's inner world is unstable; the characters who exist outside it, however, are reductive and unresponsive. Mrs. Conrad reduces Sarah's projections to a mundane insanity, offering rational explanations for Sarah's seemingly irrational behavior. Like Mrs. Conrad, Raymond exists both within and outside of Sarah's hallucinations. The "funnyman of the funnyhouse," he tortures Sarah's selves with coldness. His clinical distance borders on sadism and characterizes his attitude throughout the play. In the last scene he discovers Sarah's body and tersely comments: "She was a funny little Liar"—leaving the audience to wonder whether or not she was a liar at all. Raymond fully embodies the persecutory object, but the four internalized selves present more equivocal positions: they cannot be neatly categorized. . . .

"The counterpoint between stage and text," writes Paul Lawley of Beckett's *Not I* [*Modern Drama*, 26:4 (1983)], "enacts the play's fundamental conflict: between the need to deny the imperfect self and to maintain, even in agony, a fictional other, and the wish for oblivion which would come with the acknowledgment of the fragmented self." This sentence could apply equally well to *Funnyhouse of a Negro*, in which Sarah's denial of herself (of her past, of her guilt) conflicts with her creation of herselves. Lawley argues that the striking stage image of Beckett's play contradicts the Mouth's desire not to be: there she is. She is, however, much reduced. Sarah, on the contrary, has been multiplied. While trying to erase herself, she has instead created four repetitions. Sarah's hallucinations are of a grand scale while Mouth's are minuscule. Yet they share a common goal of self-obliteration, and they share a common sadness that they were not aborted before birth. In his essay "The Fragmented Self, the Reproduction of the Self, and Reproduction in Beckett and in the Theatre of the Absurd," [Bennett] Simon focuses on such processes of splitting and fragmentation as peculiar aspects of modernism: "[I]n the twentieth century . . . the self is disintegrated, deconstructed, shadowed, fragmented, submerged, unstable, and scarcely able to tell a coherent story." He correlates these self-destructive processes with modern and postmodern concerns about reproduction: "The modern problematic of the self goes hand in glove with a set of modern concerns and anxieties about conception and contraception." Such anxieties, which clearly dominate the writing of both Kennedy and Beckett, link together playwrights of absurdist drama: "The theatre of the absurd is a dramatic culture that has been marked from its beginning with a preoccupation with birth and reproduction."

"*Funnyhouse of a Negro* . . . grows out of the absurdist and expressionist traditions yet forges a style of its own" [David Willinger, *Theatre Journal*, 48:2 (1996)]. Kennedy's writing is ultimately original, incorporating absurdist elements yet creating something very different. Her play lacks the humor and the sense of the ludicrous which characterize the absurd; her characters' detachment is not ironical but imposed. Their world is not fundamentally without meaning, but such meaning is deliberately withheld. Here, feelings of detachment are not philosophical but physical, resulting from mortal violence. "An important part of the absurd," according to [Bennett Simon, in *The World of Samuel Beckett*, 1991)] "is the sense of being cut off from the roots and, as a usually unstated corollary, of having no branches, no offshoots, no descendants." Kennedy's characters, to the contrary, feel very much attached to their roots—roots which shackle and suffocate them. They have too many roots, knotted, tangled roots which pull them in opposing directions, like the life and death instincts which divide them. These women are bound by their roots; and their bond reflects not only love, but hate. For in the world of these plays, blood is a sign of guilt and birth is a result of rape. Sarah wishes to extricate herself from her roots, but she simultaneously enmeshes herself in their web. The past—like every aspect of her life—embodies both persecutory and ideal.

Sarah transforms her world into a house of mirrors where she watches herselves in the glass; she becomes an outsider observing her life. She speaks objectively and emotionlessly about herself and seems detached from her past even as she recreates it, never mentioning the noose on her neck or her imminent death. She speaks in the present tense of what was and gives her past to her four historical projections in hopes of self-eradication. Instead, her voice is multiplied by four, her image refracted by funnyhouse mirrors which trap her amidst their reflections.

Claudia Barnett. *Modern Drama*. 40, 3 (Fall 1997), pp. 374–84

BIBLIOGRAPHY
*Funnyhouse of a Negro*, 1962; *The Owl Answers*, 1963; *A Lesson in a Dead Language*, 1964; *A Rat's Mass*, 1966; *A Beast Story*, 1966; *Sun: A Poem for Malcolm X Inspired by His Murder*, 1968; *Cities in Bezique* (contains *The Owl Answers* and *A Beast Story*), 1969; *Boats*, 1969; *An Evening With Dead Essex*, 1973; *A Movie Star Has to Star in Black and White*, 1976; *A Lancashire Lad*, 1980; *Orestes and Electra*, 1980; *Black Children's Day*, 1980; *Diary of Lights*, 1987; *People Who Led to My Plays*, 1987; *Deadly Triplets: A Theatre Mystery and Journal*, 1990; *The Alexander Plays* (contains *She Talks to Beethoven, The Ohio State Murders, The Film Club*, and *The Dramatic Circle*), 1992; *Sleep Deprivation Chamber* (with son, Adam Patrice Kennedy), 1996

# KILLENS, John Oliver (1916– )
## United States

Early in [*Youngblood*], Joe Youngblood sums up the theme: "How do you live in a white man's world? Do you live on your knees—do you live with your shoulders bent and your hat in your hand? Or do you live like a man is supposed to live—with your head straight up?" This thematic question pervades the thinking, controls the action, dominates the conversation of all the characters—whether they be black or white.

The Youngbloods decided to live with their heads straight up. They paid dearly for the decision. Joe, the father, finally paid with his life. As a family, they were flogged, defrauded, victimized. Yet they found allies in unexpected places. One of them, Oscar Jefferson, was white. He allied himself with the Youngbloods, at first reluctantly, timidly, and finally forthrightly. Part of the richness and authenticity of *Youngblood* stems from the inclusion of the story of Oscar Jefferson.

This is a fine novel, vivid, readable. Even its minor characters, yellow haired Betty Jane Cross, Dr. Jamison, Reverend Ledbetter, Richard Myles, George Cross, Jr. are as arresting as its major ones.

*Youngblood* has one serious shortcoming. In order to dramatize the fear, the hate, the terror that accompanies what Hodding Carter called "this tragic predicament of race," Mr. Killens has used many scenes of hate-inspired violence, some of them worthy of the Grand Guignol. The repetition of these scenes tends to deaden the sensibilities of the reader.

Ann Petry. *New York Herald Tribune Books*. July 11, 1954, p. 8

Among the contemporary American critics who attribute greatness to William Faulkner's depiction of Southern life, one—Irving Howe—has claimed that "No other American novelist has watched the Negroes so carefully and patiently" and that "none other has listened with such fidelity to the nuances of their speech and recorded them with such skill." John O. Killens' first novel,

*Youngblood*, should be a revelation to both Faulkner and Howe, for here is a graphic portrait *of* people, not merely *about* them. It is of people because its characters are realized primarily in terms of natural, human inclinations. And what Mr. Killens measures out in bitter, dramatic doses—frequently interspersed with rollicking humor—is the cruel impact of the way of life in the South on a Negro family and community. . . .

It is Jefferson, however, who stands as the most memorable of Mr. Killen's characters, for through him Mr. Killens has illuminated one of the most misunderstood personalities in modern America: the tragic cracker. From his father, young Jefferson has learned to expect brutal thrashings; from his mother, a mixture of love and deception; from his friend Jim, the facts of life in race relations. The result is a serious minded personality pondering the grave issues of right and wrong and finally realizing, in his slow, hesitant manner, that nearly all life as it is lived in the South is one huge, complicated lie.

> Henry F. Winslow. *Crisis.* October 1954, pp. 511–12, 515

In this big, polyphonic, violent novel about Negro soldiers in World War II [*And Then We Heard the Thunder*] John Oliver Killens drags the reader into the fullness of the Negro's desolating experience. The author, formerly a member of the National Labor Relations Board in Washington and now a movie and television writer, served in the Amphibian Forces in the South Pacific. His novel, therefore, has the depth and complexity of lived experience. It calls James Jones to mind, though Killens writes with less technical control and more poetically. But his battle scenes have the same hallucinatory power; his characters live and speak the raw language of the streets and the barracks.

This non-Negro reader who served in the Pacific alongside Negro troops recognizes the events and characters of this novel; but he sees them with a sort of brain-twisting transformation of insights. He never gave much thought, for example, to the hideous irony of asking the Negro to fight (in segregated units) and die in order to preserve the very freedoms which he could not enjoy at home. Few non-Negroes knew the Negro soldiers' common motto, the Double V for Victory: victory against Fascism overseas and victory against Fascism at home. Nor did it ruffle us to hear the band play "God Bless America" while we boarded troopships and then switch to "Darktown Strutters' Ball" when the Negro troops' turn came. But here, living it through the Negro's reaction, we cannot believe our ears. . . .

The reader, living all the indignities of the Negro soldier, sees clearly how it looked from the other side of the color line. Discrimination in the armed forces has been eliminated. But the deep wounds of Negro soldiers have not. This novel magnificently illumines the reasons why. Their second victory—against Fascism at home—is slow in coming.

> John Howard Griffin. *Saturday Review.* January 26, 1963, pp. 46–47

John Oliver Killens has written two long, detailed, humorless, artless, almost documentary race novels, *Youngblood* and *And Then We Heard the Thunder*. The first is a sort of Negro family epic, the expected tale of two generations of long-suffering blacks and their sadistic white masters in a Georgia town. The second tells the interminable story of Negroes (and whites) in wartime, where the ordeal of World War II seems less harrowing, in the long run, than the race war inside it. It runs through pages of somber "graphic realism," i.e., pages of vapidly obscene barracks chatter and hard-boiled crudeness of description: that's the way it was.

Both books are sincerely well intended, and packed to bursting with details of Negro (Southern, army) life, episode after episode, as retailed by a careful, intelligent, unimaginative Negro with absolutely no sense of the art of fiction. They represent the kind of novel most Americans with great stocks of experience would probably write, if they had the will and were Negroes. The books are useful, and, to readers who make no great demands on their novelists, mildly moving and exciting.

> David Littlejohn. *Black on White* (New York: Grossman, 1966), pp. 143–44

Killens is not a cerebral novelist, but his intellect works well in his art. It does not betray him into pretentiousness and into a pseudo-sophisticated fooling around with ideas that might better be left to moral philosophers. His theme—so far there is only one, with variations—is simple, clear: the price of submission to unreasonable authority, economic or cultural, civil or military, social or sexual, intellectual or emotional. His treatment of this theme is as diverse as it is direct. No beating about the bush for Killens. No setting of "snares to catch woodcocks." And above all, none of the intellectual equivocations that some of his more "arty" and self-conscious contemporaries are inveigled into. His philosophy is plainly ethical: man has Man's soul to save. Sometimes the odds against man's saving his soul are terrific. It is the odds that make Killens's stories, that supply the dramatic action. The theme is pursued in the context of the American race situation.

And why not? It has always been *the* situation, and honesty demands, of the Negro artist especially, a frank acceptance of the fact. For the Negro writer to deny it, or even to gloss it, is to betray himself, and to lose the soul that he must save. And since both black men and (increasingly) white are caught up in the race situation, the creative writer is provided with a scope—in characterization, in incident, in setting, in atmosphere and mood—as broad as the scope of America itself (and as valid to his work as his imagination, his sensibilities, and his artistic genius can make it). Broader, indeed. *And Then We Heard the Thunder* ends in Australia, and the concluding episode in the book is just as right, true, and credible as the opening episode in Harlem.

Killens's art is naturally vivacious and robust. His style is not notable for its grace. His language is the earthy, literal, idiomatic language of his characters. His comedy—for he has a comic gift—is likely to be broad, meant only to evoke laughter; but he also uses it to other purposes. His sense of the comic flows from an ironic perception of the difference between appearance and reality, and from the equally ironic knowledge that neither appearance nor reality is always the same for black men and white. Killens uses comedy as an escape into pride and dignity and into a sense of that human equality the substance of which he strives for both as writer and man.

> Saunders Redding. *African Forum.* Spring 1966, pp. 25–26

Whenever Ronnie Gilbert, a Southern Negro college student in 'Sippi, is deeply moved by someone or something he exclaims, "Baby I'm shook to my natural chittlins!" And that is just what this great novel will do to all who read it.

Beyond doubt we in the U.S. live in an age of tempestuous and twisting emotions, of brutal violence, of intrigue, of massive and mass produced ignorance and miniscule understanding, of heroism and cowardice. These are the ingredients used as Killens unfolds his story of how the Negroes in Wakefield County, Mississippi reacted after the Supreme Court outlawed school segregation in 1954. . . .

Killens is a master delineator of the deep meanings in the earthy ungrammatical language of the rural Negroes. For like them, he has used it not only as a medium of communication but as a weapon of struggle. The sermon on freedom by Rev. Purdy is a consummate exercise in word imagery, each pulsing with power, alive with motion and igniting the next sentence with an electric energy of its own.

Thus we have a poetic tapestry, richly woven with folkways, speech, movement, ideas, colors, smells, sounds and emotions. It is a fusing of the non-contemporary events like Malcolm X's death, persons like Martin Luther King, Lorraine Hansberry and others, into the living, breathing amalgam of black-white relations in the U.S. today.

John Henry Jones. Freedomways. Fall 1967, pp. 373–74

John Oliver Killens' satire The Cotillion brings humor and fun into both the hangups of black middleclassness and the often solemnly treated idea of moving into blackness. The easier of the two targets, of course, is the satire of the middle-class aspirations represented by Lady Daphne, etc., since the aspirations and aberrations of middleclassness have so often been outlined. His achievement with Daphne, mother of the heroine, is that she remains human and loveable, although narrow. The more difficult job is to deal with the main impulse of the story—to bring the beautiful Yoruba Eveylyn through a mad universe into real fulfillment—in popular terms, her blackness.

The book is good fun, although its humor is rather broad and seems to have excessive coping power as evidenced in the relations between mother and daughter. But the novel seems a refreshing change for a literature that so often seems to ignore the things boasted of in real life traditions: the humor, signifying, etc. What one would like to see is Killens' resources used for still more subtle analyses and in complex equations.

George E. Kent. Phylon. Winter 1972, p. 308

In the works of John Oliver Killens, John Williams, Ernest Gaines, and William Melvin Kelley, a new tradition is begun, one which depends for its viability upon black perceptions based upon black definitions of reality. John Oliver Killens is the spiritual father of the new novelists. It is his direction—more so than that of Ellison—that the young writers have followed. He is the first of the modern period to begin anew, with conscious determination, the quest for new definitions, to attempt to give new meanings to old cultural artifacts. . . .

Differences in setting and plot are apparent in [And Then We Heard the Thunder and The Cotillion]; yet, on one level, the novels share similar themes and situations, deal with the same conflict—the attempt at self-education by each of its protagonists. Both Solly Saunders and Yoruba must move from a preoccupation with the self to embrace black people everywhere; from concern with their individual status as victims of the American society to an awareness of their own strengths and egos. Each must begin the study of history, must find there the artifacts which sustained their forefathers, and, having done so, manifest a love toward black people at home and abroad. More so than any novelist in black literary history, Killens is the novelist of love.

Addison Gayle, Jr. The Way of the New World (Garden City, NewYork: Doubleday, 1975), p. 317

BIBLIOGRAPHY
Youngblood, 1954; And Then We Heard the Thunder, 1963; Black Man's Burden, 1965; 'Sippi, 1967; Slaves, 1969; The Cotillion, 1971; Great Gittin' Up Morning: A Biography of Denmark Vesey, 1972; A Man Ain't Nothin' But a Man: The Adventures of John Henry, 1975; Great Black Russian : A Novel on the Life and Times of Alexander Pushkin, 1989

# KINCAID, Jamaica (1949–)
## Antigua

The magic of [Jamaica Kincaid's] At the Bottom of the River comes from its language. It is as rhythmic and riddlesome as poetry. Lovely though the words are, they often read like a coded message or a foreign language. Throughout At the Bottom of the River the reader is left wondering how to decipher this writing. The decoder comes in the form of Jamaica Kincaid's novel Annie John. Annie John was published in 1985, two years after At the Bottom of the River. Its chapters had all appeared as individual stories in the New Yorker. Annie John tells the same story as At the Bottom of the River, that of a girl coming of age in Antigua, but uses straightforward novel talk and presents few comprehension barriers to the reader. Annie John is a kind of personification of At the Bottom of the River. It fleshes out the fantasy and philosophy of At the Bottom of the River's poetry, and between the two books there exists a dialogue of questions and answers. They ultimately read as companion pieces or sister texts. . . .

Since Annie John tells the same story as At the Bottom of the River, it is instrumental in illuminating the difficult text of the latter. It fills in the spaces. It replaces the fuzziness of At the Bottom of the River with facts. For example, Annie is an exceptional student and at fifteen is accelerated to a class with girls who are two or three years older than herself. Once this specialness is clearly defined in Annie John, the intense imagination and inventiveness of At the Bottom of the River is easier to understand. Then a strange thing happens, however. Annie, at fifteen, has a nervous breakdown. The same breakdown occurs in At the Bottom of the River in the story "Blackness," but the language in "Blackness" is so clouded and intentionally sparse that the point is almost completely missed. The story reads as a mere mood piece, with passages like,

''In the blackness, then, I have been erased. I can no longer say my own name. I can no longer point to myself and say 'I.''' . . .

Compared to *At the Bottom of the River, Annie John* reads like a photo album. Though it is immensely helpful in translating *At the Bottom of the River, Annie John* looks at the surface of things and lacks rationale, explanation, motivation. *At the Bottom of the River* acts as the cerebral text for the pictures in *Annie John*. Together the two books allow the reader to develop one cohesive story.

Wendy Dutton. *World Literature Today.* 63, 3 (Summer 1989), pp. 406–7

Some of the finest fiction from the West Indies has been written by Jamaica Kincaid. Her collection of short stories, *At the Bottom of the River*, makes interesting use of dream visions and metaphor as the imaginative projections of family life and social structure in her West Indian society. In these stories Kincaid explores the strong identification and rupture in the daughter-mother relationship between the narrator and her mother. The process is mediated through metaphor and, when it is threatening, through surrealistic dream visions.

Each of these stories demonstrates tensions in the daughter-narrator resulting from a prolonged period of symbiosis between mother and child, especially because the mother views her daughter as a narcissistic extension of herself. In ''Wingless,'' the narrator dreams the story as a mirror of her own situation and then imagines herself as a wingless pupa waiting for growth. The narrator uses a dream vision to mediate her sense of helplessness as a child dependent on her mother's care and attention.

In this dream, the mother is perceived as powerful, even more potent than the male who attempts to intimidate and humiliate her. Thus an incident of potential sexual violence becomes an easy victory for the mother. . . . The strong mother threatens death to those who confront her. But there is also a wonderful parable here of the integrity of the woman who shields herself from assault by refusing to listen to the tree-satyr who is trying to assert his power over her.

The story that best demonstrates the daughter's ambivalent relationship with her mother is ''Girl.'' The voice is the girl's repeating a series of the mother's admonitions. . . . The first of the mother's many rules concerns housekeeping. Unlike the girl's father, who can lounge at the circus eating blood sausage and drinking ginger beer, the woman is restricted to household duties. The many rules are experienced by the narrator as unnecessarily restrictive and hostile. The mother's aggression is clear in the warnings of the price a girl will pay for ignoring her mother's advice. The penalty is ostracism—one must become a slut, a fate for which the mother is ironically preparing the daughter. The mother's obsessive refrain indicates hostility toward her adolescent daughter, activated when the girl is no longer an extension of herself but a young woman who engenders in the older woman feelings of competition and anger at losing control of her child. Her anger may also result from the pressures felt by every woman in the community to fulfill the restrictive roles created for women. Of the ten stories in the collection, ''Girl'' is the only one that is told as interior monologue rather than dream and thus seems to be the least distorted vision. The ambivalence of the mother-daughter relationship is presented here in its most direct form. The reasons for their

mutual distrust are very clearly stated: resentment, envy, anger, and love.

Laura Niesen de Abruna. In Selwyn R. Cudjoe, ed. *Caribbean Women Writers* (Wellesley, Massachusetts: Calaloux, 1990), pp. 93–94

The works of Jamaica Kincaid, with their forthright acceptance of Caribbean identity (and of course the fact that she has legally renamed herself ''Jamaica'') present an explicit identification. . . . Having already accepted Caribbean identity, she can then pursue the meaning of her woman self as she does in ''Girl''; her inner personal self as she does in ''Wingless'' and ''Blackness,'' which is a clear redefinition of the concept of ''racial'' blackness; her relationship to the landscape and folklore, as she does in ''In the Night'' and ''Holidays''; and all of these in the title story ''At the Bottom of the River.'' Both *At the Bottom of the River* and *Annie John* explore the female self in the context of landscape and Caribbean folk culture. Central to both books also is perhaps the best presentation in literature so far of the conflicted mother-daughter relationship.

Heritage and identity are intrinsic to the narrative and have as much significance as the gender issues with which she begins *At the Bottom of the River*. ''Girl'' begins with a catalogue of rules of conduct for the growing Caribbean supernatural girl/woman. These merge into surrealistic images of the Caribbean supernatural world but conclude with the woman-to-woman motif which recurs throughout both texts. In *Annie John*, a similar landscape is created. Here, the maternal grandmother, Ma Jolie, clearly an ancestral presence, is characterized as a mysterious healer who appears on the scene at a time when her granddaughter is experiencing a terrible psychological dislocation which is manifesting itself in physical illness and disorientation. Much of this dislocation is located in Annie's attempts to understand and define herself against her mother. *Annie John* differs from *At the Bottom of the River* in that it is an autobiographical narrative which . . . functions as a decoder of much that is unexplainable in the mysterious world of the first work. But in both, the necessity to identify with, yet separate oneself from, the mother is a central issue. ''My Mother'' in *River* pursues this maternal identification/separation fully. There is a need for bonding as there is for separate space. The ability of each to separate and thus grow ensures harmony.

Carole Boyce Davies. In Carole Boyce Davies and Elaine Savory Fido, eds. *Out of the Kumbla: Caribbean Women and Literature* (Trenton, New Jersey: Africa World Press, 1990), pp. 64–65

[Jacques] Derrida in *Positions* speaks of the necessity of ridding oneself of a metaphysical concept of history, that is linear and systematic. His claim is for a new logic of repetition and *trace*, for a monumental, contradictory, multileveled history in which the *différance* that produces many differences is not effaced. Jamaica Kincaid's *At the Bottom of the River* and *Annie John* represent examples of writing that break through the objective, metaphysical linearity of the tradition. At the same time, her voice manages to speak up for her specificity without—in so doing—reproducing in the negative the modes of classical white patriarchal tradition.

Kincaid's voice is that of a woman and an Afro-Caribbean/American and a postmodern at the same time. This combination is therefore not only disruptive of the institutional order, but also revolutionary in its continuous self-criticism and its rejection of all labels. Perhaps we could say that it is a voice coming *after* the struggles of the women's movement first for recognition and then for separation; the voice of the third "new generation of women" as [Julia] Kristeva defines it: an effort to keep a polyphonic movement in process in the attempt to be always already questioning and dismantling a fixed metaphysical order, together with a determination to enter history. Her narrative, in fact, is a continuous attempt to turn away from any definitive statement and to utter radical statements. . . .

The main theme of her writings is the inquiry into the feminine role and racial difference. Kincaid criticizes the very existence of sexual and racial difference, rather than the modes of their existence: there's no place left for reform; the change that is invoked is not one of guards, but of structure.

> Giovanna Covi. In Carole Boyce Davies and Elaine Savory Fido, eds. *Out of the Kumbla: Caribbean Women and Literature* (Trenton, New Jersey: Africa World Press, 1990), pp. 345–47

We have known for some time that Jamaica Kincaid writes with a double vision. From one point of view, her early fiction and sketches in *The New Yorker*, her collection of dream visions, *At the Bottom of the River*, and her novel *Annie John* all concern the coming-of-age narrative of a young woman in Antigua. Much of Kincaid's fiction, especially the intensely lyrical prose poetry of *At the Bottom of the River* and the autobiographical novel *Annie John*, focuses on the relationship between mother and daughter and the painful separation that occurs between them. Careful examination of the psychoanalytical implications of these relationships will surely open up the meanings of these texts. A psychoanalytic analysis from a feminist perspective, one examining mother-daughter bonding, would point out that the narrators in Kincaid's fiction resist separation from the mother as a way of denying their intense fear of death. The fear of separation is further complicated in *Annie John* because the narrator leaves the island for Britain with the clear intention of making a break with her environment. Both she and her mother, who is also named Annie, have left their respective mothers and their own homes to seek a more comfortable life elsewhere. The process of Annie's leaving her mother is mirrored in the process of leaving the island. Displacement from an initial intimacy with her mother's realm is reflected in a growing away from the environment until, at the end of the novel, Annie can only dream of leaving her own home for England.

> Laura Niesen de Abruna. In Susheila Nasta, ed. *Motherlands* (New Brunswick: Rutgers University Press, 1992), pp. 273–74

With *Lucy* Jamaica Kincaid continues a story of West Indian female development. Whereas the earlier *bildungsroman* style works *At the Bottom of the River* and *Annie John* dealt with the adolescent years of a girl in the Caribbean, the new book presents a single learning year—the nineteenth—in the life of a character called Lucy, in the new setting of the United States. Lucy is an immigrant engaged to work as an au pair for a wealthy white couple

and their four young daughters. Her year is complexly lived with its attendant difficult times, but it provides Lucy with learning experiences that enable her to manage the cultural change and her passage. By the end of the year she can appreciate the commitment of sisterhood (with her employer, for instance), has negotiated a social world of friends and lovers, and has embarked on an independent life provided for by a job as a photographer's helper. She has, moreover, survived the separation from her West Indian mother and upbringing, tasting an independence she has craved for many years. However, the persistence of unreconciled ambivalence toward her mother, guilt about her recently deceased father, and fears concerning her uncharted future becloud this newly gained freedom. The end of the work thus suggests a problematic future, though the fact that Lucy identifies herself as a writer—the act of inscribing her name, Lucy Josephine Potter, across the top of a journal notebook signifies this—indicates a self-authenticating, defining, and authorizing gesture of significance.

> Evelyn J. Hawthorne. *World Literature Today*. 66, 1 (Winter 1992), p. 185

*Lucy* is a novel which interrogates and refuses Euro-American theories of many kinds, from those old "fairy tales" of history, fiction, anthropology, to more contemporary notions of psychology and ecology. Lewis's and Mariah's interpretation of the world around them is constantly contrasted with that of Lucy, and their "axioms" are constantly relativized by her different views. The yellow of the daffodils (those flowers which "looked simple, as if made to erase a complicated and unnecessary idea") is associated throughout with the yellow of Mariah's hair and that of her clonelike children. It is a yellow substance "like cornmeal" which forms the ground on which Lewis chases her in her dream. The yellow of cornmeal conjures slave provisions and slavery and is associated with the colonialist "daffodil complex" Lucy strives to articulate to Mariah. But to Lewis and Mariah the significant aspect of the dream is the pit with the snakes. "Dr. Freud for Visitor," Mariah archly remarks to Lewis, and both the stress on this particular aspect of the dream and the naturalization of a particular European interpretation of dreams exposed as culturally grounded *theories* which Lewis and Mariah regard as fact. Like the earlier "fixtures of fantasy" historically instilled in colonial subjects, these new "fixtures" are interrogated in *Lucy* by the different and often more complex interpretations offered by Lucy herself.

This "alternative" reading of a "classically Freudian" dream, emphasizing racial oppression over sexual psychology, does not of course deny the importance of gender oppression or the complex sexualities complicit in race oppression. But in *Lucy*, Lucy uses her sexuality against these oppressions, just as she uses the body to reclaim self-identity from the capture and abuse of the black female body within the European "book." If Lucy could not openly rebel against the recitation of [William] Wordsworth in Antigua, in New York she increasingly rejects new European theories about her sexuality and her body offered by Mariah. She interrogates contemporary Euro-American feminism against the background of her own experience, wondering why Mariah relies on books to explain her life. . . .

Mariah's simplicity and "innocence," her reliance on books, is contrasted early in the novel with another kind of body/script interaction. Relying on "the ories" to explain her life, Mariah has little grasp of the way words enter and mark colonized bodies, and this is part of her "simplicity." Lucy understands the interpellative and body-marking (and body-erasing) power of text, but contrasts and counteracts its potential power with that of the body itself. Mariah's faith in her books is equated with her "yellow" simplicity, and her apparently perfect body is contrasted with that of Sylvie, Lucy's mother's friend who has been in jail. Sylvie has a mark like a rose on her face, a scar from a bite she received in a fight with another woman. This mark "bound her to something much deeper than its reality, something she could not put into words."

Helen Tiffin. *Callaloo*. 16, 4 (Fall 1993), pp. 919–20

Shortly after its publication in 1983, Jamaica Kincaid's *Annie John* received high praise from critics who welcomed the verve and strength of this new, black female voice. Even though reviewers differed in regard to the novel's political, cultural, and ideological themes, a clear majority of them agreed on the central importance of Kincaid's conflictual presentation of the mother-daughter relationship. And for good reason. Kincaid's involved descriptions of familial alliances generate provocative psychological interpretations. . . .

Much of this fascination comes from the intensity, range, and paradoxical quality of Kincaid's mother-daughter bond. In particular, the psychoanalytical essays attempt to understand how Annie John, the lead character, could at the same moment both love and hate her mother with equal intensity. And yet, such a singular approach fails to address other pertinent issues. Even though mother-child concerns do seem to call for developmental readings, the novel's concern with self-identity also brings it into a second arena: the *Bildungsroman*.

Of course, this "coming of age" literary convention differs significantly among nationalities and periods, but some broad characteristics do seem to cross cultural lines. A sensitive child-hero begins his life in a provincial area where he quickly perceives constraints on his "natural" development. He grows frustrated with his family, school, and friends. Finally, at a fairly early age, he leaves the repression of home for the "real" education that occurs in a sophisticated, worldly, and often urban setting. *Annie John* more or less follows this "romantic" scheme. I invoke the metaphor of romanticism here because the hero takes his youthful innocent unity, his "naturalness," on a quest of maturation that leads him to question and yearn for the inevitable "lost innocence" of family and intimate society.

Notice, however, the above masculine pronouns. Such a male-gendered summary is not my invention, but the traditional interpretation of the *Bildungsroman*: white, male, and European. . . .

My call for a gender-integrated romantic-quest critique begins at the threshold of the novel, through the very terms of a woman story-teller recollecting a psychological journey within a masculine culture. As Adlai Murdock states, "There should be no question as to the general validity of describing the West Indies as a male dominated culture" [*Callaloo* 13, Spring 1990]. However, like most heroes, the lead character accomplishes this quest by relying on a composite of gender-blended information sources: she often experiences the male dominated outside world through the interpretations of females, primarily her mother, grandmother, and other women friends. Rather than explore this mixture of voices as a version of the Bildungsroman, critics have tended to address only the female personality development of Annie John. In so doing,

they have only briefly referred to the romantic elements inherent in the quest, which tie a masculine narrative structure to those more gender specific emotional and developmental concerns.

When the romanticism in Kincaid's contemporary Bildungsroman is not identified, the traditional masculine quest structure appears to thwart female psychological growth; in fact, however, the quest and the bonding plot suggest an affiliation, not an antagonism. The fusion of romantic quest and psychological union underscores Kincaid's complexity. . . .

Although Kincaid's interest in the mother-daughter dyad of dependence seems incompatible with the Bildungsroman hero of independence, their combined presence belies that notion and holds itself open for just such a cooperative approach. A careful look at Kincaid's romantic use of concepts like paradox, sympathy, and organicity suggests that, rather than canceling each other out, theories of maturation and the quest hinge on each other.

This effort to intermix female psychology and the mostly male Bildungsroman matches the integrative unfolding of Annie John herself. The dramatic and unpredictable evolution of Annie's sense of "self" resembles the oftentimes tumultuous uncertainty of any female/male relationship. Moreover, Annie's frequent displays of paradoxical behavior remind the reader that many romantic concepts also rely on such oppositions. And finally, much like a critic identifying the presence of paradox in a character's life, Annie must recognize her femininity by comparing and distinguishing it from the island's examples of masculinity. Considering these similarities between the novel's presentation of oppositional forces and my reinstituting them into a quest paradigm, a reading emphasizing the structural interaction of influences from both genders seems appropriate. Indeed, a romantic perspective which strives for integration might best articulate how these two apparently contrary movements operate in concert.

At a certain level of interpretation, many confrontations and incidents in Annie John appear to be in keeping with typical mother-daughter bonding conceptions. Another look, however, at the scenes which supposedly give credence to only a psychological appreciation also introduces romantic elements; these include references to mythical events and evocations of a natural world displaying unity and harmony. Kincaid's subtle arranging of these and similarly romantic themes advocates for more than bonding interpretations; her presentation argues for a romantic psychological-quest reading.

Annie's descriptions of her childhood support a mythical and romantic understanding of personality development. For example, Annie relates a childhood memory about swimming on her mother's back and compares their activity to "the pictures of sea mammals." In an act symbolic of an amniotic baptismal ceremony, Annie and her mother merge into one being, reliving the birth experience. In a related scene, Annie and her mother bathe together; filling the tub with articles of the natural world, they create "a special bath in which the barks and flowers of many different trees, together with all sorts of oils, were boiled in the same large caldron." Such imagery suggests a unity of world and person, a romantic link between nature and humanity. Moira Ferguson reads the passage in a similar fashion, citing the water's "vitality" and "awakening" powers [*Jamaica Kincaid*, 1994]. Even the mother's odors connect Annie to nature: "She smelled sometimes of lemons, sometimes of sage, sometimes of roses, sometimes of bay leaf." Kincaid creates an atmosphere of wholeness and innocence reminiscent of the prelapsarian garden of Eden. In fact, Annie uses the garden metaphor as a description of her childhood maternal connection: "It was in such a paradise that I lived." At another point Annie describes this relationship as a "perfect harmony" (27). Ferguson calls this romantic moment "a return to primal, undifferentiated harmony." All of these depictions suggest ways in which the earlier mentioned theories of personality are expressed through the romantic symbolism of natural and mythical allusions.

Perhaps Kincaid's most telling romantic metaphor is this notion of "paradise"; the evocation here of a prelapsarian organic unity implies that the mother-daughter bond arises in a naturally perfect prelinguistic, pre-oedipal state. In Kincaid's collection of short stories, At the Bottom of the River, she describes her life with her mother in these same romantic terms; mother and daughter live timelessly, in "a bower made from flowers whose petals are imperishable." The sensual quality of these alliances even pre-empts the rationality of language. At a crucial bonding moment in the novel, Annie communicates with her mother without using the cultural system of language: "At times I would no longer hear what it was she was saying." The experience of being "one" with her mother surpasses the content of discursive meaning: "I just liked to look at her mouth as it opened and closed over words, or as she laughed."

With either story, the psychological or the mythical quest, mother and daughter must eventually accept separation. The nature of the mother-daughter bond is that, at some point, it must transform and divide itself into a recognition of separate identities. However, even here, in the depiction of division and loss, Kincaid gives more evidence for a link between romantic and psychological concepts. . . .

Although the literary history of the quest appears not to sustain or emphasize this fusing of a hero with a parent, I suggest that Kincaid's narrative refashions the quest; it transforms this bonding into an ongoing force of the questing paradigm. The hero for Kincaid gains our attention with her proficiency at attaching and relating, rather than emphasizing the conventionally understood Bildungsroman and monomyth hero's quality of independence and setting out alone.

By contrast [Joseph] Campbell's hero must risk it all as he journeys alone to battle the tyrants and monsters. This traditional hero hears the call, refuses it, and then overcomes the fear and "cross[es] the threshold" (82). Kincaid's child-hero infuses herself with a collection of maternal dynamics which are not found in Campbell's overall description of the journey. Instead, the monomyth hero begins with division and only later moves into a sense of unity. Campbell cites "separation" as the beginning trope of the quest, "separation-initiation-return: which might be named the nuclear unit of the monomyth" (30) Campbell, in opposition to Kincaid, defines the hero as someone who doesn't take with him the unifying quality of the child's family; the monomyth focuses on the initial relinquishment of the home, the known, and moves quickly to the desire to push out into the darkness of the unknown.

Of course, that moment of renunciation, the opportunity to declare oneself in an unknown land, occurs with all heroes at one time or another. Kincaid's hero, though, defers the psychological splitting off from family and opens up the possibility for a different paradigm, one that resists such early singularity. In fact, she subverts Campbell and elements of the Bildungsroman by suggesting that mother-daughter bonding continues throughout the quest as it redefines that tradition. According to Kincaid, then, the quest pattern can be rewritten to include this emotional bonding without

sacrificing the hero's eventual separation from it. Thus Kincaid's story, in its broader contours, supports the monomyth's conflictual connection between unity and separation as it redefines the role of the hero. And yet, instead of focusing on Campbell's independent hero venturing out, Kincaid stresses the paradoxical, frightening, and mysterious early connection with the mother.

Even at the end of the novel, Annie cannot understand why she is terrified at accepting and showing love to her mother. She only understands that the commitment between a daughter and a parent seems to transcend all. When her mother says ". . .I'll always be your mother and this will always be your home" (147), Annie is temporarily shaken as she privately admits feeling distant from her mother. She must wake herself out of this hypnotic "stupor." Her "stupor" represents a paradoxical collision: the forces of a modern male identity quest colliding with a female bonding experience.

These two interpretations of the quest are not essentially opposed; Campbell's hero eventually returns to the community and generates a unity similar to the pervasive return of the child to the parent. Both writers see their heroes' journeys as at least twofold. Each journey provokes confrontations with political and mythical identities, the first grounded in the historical moment and the second timeless and metaphysical.

Louis F. Caton. MELUS. 21, 3 (Fall 1996), pp. 125–42

To convey a world unhinged by conquistadorian greed and its aftermath, Jamaica Kincaid writes about growing up on an island in the Caribbean and leaving it, all the while exploring the formation of personal and political identity.

A narrator in multiple guises and in generically diverse texts travels back through historical epochs to the beginning of known communities in Antigua and Hispaniola, and then lands in contemporary New York and indeterminate regions. A composite character, she is first a black Antiguan nine-year-old, then an adolescent, and later an adult. She is also an Amerindian. Semiautobiographical, sometimes inchoate accounts of life, death, and contestation in At the Bottom of the River, Annie John, and Lucy play off in Annie, Gwen, Lilly, Pam and Tulip, "Ovando," and A Small Place against a wider context of past, present, and future struggles in precolonial and Amerindian communities and black and white Antiguan communities.

Jamaica Kincaid's texts constitute a continuous and evolving narrative—what I have loosely called a bildungsroman—of a plural, multivocal, precolonial, colonial, and postcolonial female subjectivity by a postcolonial writer. These texts, that is, constitute an ongoing, checkered saga about colonial origins, the construction and interrogation of personal-political identity, and the conditions of possibility in psychic and material life. Together, the fictional and nonfictional narratives represent the formation of colonial and postcolonial subjectivities. In Trinh T. Minh-Ha's words, "Auto-biographical strategies offer another example of ways of breaking with the chain of invisibility." Narrative itself, furthermore, tells the history as well as marking the connections among narrative, history, and the writer's distant though resistant stance throughout. Diverse protagonists eventually claim marginality as a badge of honor. More specifically, in At the Bottom of the River the narrator probes her relation to externality, trying to fathom her ontological status. In Annie, Gwen, Lilly, Pam and Tulip, she tries to recuperate a sense of life before and on the brink of intervention. Moreover, if

*At the Bottom* introduces the first section of a personal-political bildungsroman, then *Annie John* constitutes its adolescent dimension. Annie John tries to work through her adolescent feelings, how relationships coexist, how they falter, disappear, and reappear in a refashioned form. She learns and teaches herself to cope.

Coterminous with her investigation of how gender is implicated in the formation of the female subject are Kincaid's formulations of motherhood and colonialism—a doubled negotiation. In *Annie John*, Jamaica Kincaid parallels the fictional daughter's ire at her mother with her anger at Christopher Columbus; she inflects daughterly domestic rage with fury at metropolitan expropriation. Biological motherhood is a *mise en abyme* that conveys the diatribe against colonialism. Muted yet subtly present in *At the Bottom*—more so in *Annie, Gwen, Lilly, Pam and Tulip*—anticolonial resistance provides Annie John with inner security and a public identity, not dissimilar to her mother's identity (we later learn in *A Small Place*) as a historical troublemaker.

For Jamaica Kincaid this choice of a semiautobiographical mode, at both personal and political levels, amounts to an act of self-exorcism, an avowal of what signs her cultural integrity. Jamaica Kincaid puts it this way: "I'm clearly the kind of writer interested in the autobiographical for [use in] fiction and nonfiction," and she further adds: "I would say that everything in *Annie John* happened—every feeling in it happened—but not necessarily in the order they appear. But it very much expresses the life I had. There isn't anything in it that is a lie, I would say. [I choose to write fiction over autobiography] because autobiography is the truth and fiction is, well, fiction." Put another way, Jamaica Kincaid is, in her own words, "really interested in breaking the form." In several texts, she presents discursive alternatives to a Western linear modality, a decolonizing style that is attuned to realpolitik.

In *A Small Place*, which doubles as an anticolonial, postcolonial polemic, Kincaid temporarily abandons the facade of fiction while at the same time recognizing that polemic can rarely be unmediated chronicle. In that polemic, the concentration on mother-daughter relationships that characterized sections of *At the Bottom* and *Annie John* has shifted to explicit assault on a colonial mother or motherhood. *A Small Place* attacks a dual foe—false friend of the majority—British colonialism and the present Antiguan government that ushered the island into a partially independent existence in 1967 and then full independence in 1981. An incensed daughter-speaker draws these two "motherhoods" together to explicate the consequences of colonialism on people's past and present lives. One of Kincaid's own statements underscores this nuanced use of maternal linkages: "I identified [maternal] restrictiveness with the restrictiveness of my surroundings." *A Small Place* is part three of this ongoing story that now plays itself out against a broader historical and more explicitly political canvas.

The movement from *A Small Place* to *Lucy* is circumlocuitous. In a poetic, though seemingly conventional novel, Kincaid traces the next segment in the life of a young African-Caribbean woman. *Lucy* narrates the tale of self-imposed exile mediated through Lucy's growing awareness of her configuration as the other in the professional and artistic postcolonial milieus she frequents. The voice and sensibility of earlier narrators resonate in Lucy herself while the dialectic of conquest and contestation of *A Small Place* manifests itself. Additionally, the slippage of mother from one potent referent to another is particularly striking in *Lucy*, where the effects of postcolonial attitudes and Lucy's sense of retribution are at their most diaphanous. Hence Lucy's use of the camera, her

stalwart decision to reverse the colonial (coded as maternal) gaze. She wants her turn at framing life.

Even in *Lucy*, too, the text that most closely resembles a mainstream novel, blanks in the chronicle resonate. The author, Kincaid intimates, is a questionable author-ity. Abandoning orthodox mimetic claims, Kincaid fictionally speculates on how events might have gone, how lives might have been diversely experienced, why people ambiguously reacted, how temporary solutions were reached.

This reading of multiple mothers clarifies what has never quite added up in Kincaid's texts as a whole: her love for her mother and brothers (*At the Bottom of the River* and *A Small Place* are dedicated to them) compared to the fury she collectively vents over these family members—indirectly as well as frontally. The love-hate ambiguity permeates the texts because Kincaid uses mother and brother as crucial discursive markers in a sometimes veiled, often overt anticolonial discourse.

By mapping *At the Bottom of the River, Annie John*, and *A Small Place* onto the terrain of Lucy, thereby concretizing cultural differences between Antigua and the United States, *Lucy*, furthermore, functions as a limit text. It establishes certain boundaries yet allows earlier texts to expand within them.

Memories enter largely into Kincaid's elaborations of a worldwide, centuries-long scenario. By relying on memory that can always be rewritten and hence can also be faulty, she underscores the existence of a host of perspectives, questioning notions of absolute meaning or epistemological certainty; collectively the texts refuse a Cartesian, hegemonic modality, relying on nuance, inner resonance, reverie, self-reflection, and heterogeneous utterance to convey meaning. There is no normative archimedean point for political critique. Unitary thinking is stillborn in these texts that acknowledge, too, some personal harmony, a healthy embrace of life. Thus Kincaid draws back from definitive closures, preferring not to conclude. Since all events have already happened—she argues—they are always in the process of being rescripted. Ends and beginnings continually merge and overlap but always with a sense that the imperial project constantly induces discontinuity and change.

Jamaica Kincaid's texts—as central trajectory—represent the articulation by a postcolonial artist of popular struggle, with Kincaid's voice as an Antiguan "organic" intellectual sounding the cultural void. Collectively, her texts are part of the discourse—in Ranajit Guha's phrase—of opposition and counterknowledge; they project a transformed vision that privileges the former outsider. Only through time and by dint of collective political acts—Kincaid's texts suggest—will popular victories erupt. The days of marauding tourists—metonymic for hostile external-internal forces—are numbered. Through multiple interventions in fiction and semiautobiography that document public lives and events in Antigua, Kincaid chronicles a minisaga of that island in all its unfolding complexity. She puts a new fast spin on social critique, reminding us that received patterns of events do not tell the whole story.

Moira Ferguson. In *Jamaica Kincaid: Where the Lard Meets the Body.* (University of Virginia Press, 1994)

But what I see is the millions of people, of whom I am just one, made orphans: no motherland, no fatherland, no gods, no mounds of earth for holy ground, no excess of love which might lead to the things that an excess of love sometimes brings, and worst and most painful of all, no tongue.

The above quote, taken from the Antiguan writer Jamaica Kincaid's polemical work on the history and effects of the British colonial rule of her native island, thematizes what I see to be the central concerns of many Caribbean authors whose protagonists are exiles. In describing the violence of colonial conquest, Kincaid emphasizes a fundamental loss of security and belonging, using the word "orphan" to describe the colonial condition of existential rootlessness. The seizure of land, the disruption of sexual and familial relationships, the erasure of culture—all these make up the legacy of colonialism, but none matches the force of the loss of the tongue, the linguistic power to define oneself and one's world. To lose one's tongue is to experience a permanent exile. While Kincaid acknowledges the missing tongue as a trope of cultural alienation, she extends this trope's signifying potential in her 1990 novel, *Lucy*, which traces the story of a young woman who has emigrated from Antigua to the United States. By focusing on the tongue in her description of Lucy's awareness of her body as a source of resistance and of sexual pleasure and by figuring the tongue as creating both connection and separation, Kincaid carves out what I would term the space of the female exile, a space that is shaped by the complex interaction between the female body and masculinist cultural imperatives. . . .

While Kincaid joins the chorus of Caribbean writers who have written extensively of exile, her novel *Lucy* serves as a counterpoint to . . . exhortations of the "pleasures of exile," as her heroine complicates notions of exile as existential freedom. Kincaid instead offers her own alternative to the "blank page" of Lamming and Depêstre.

The immediate urge to erase can be seen as the simplest and most unproblematic impetus for exile. To leave a place is to erase it from one's daily experiences, and Kincaid's heroine Lucy embarks on her self-imposed exile at age nineteen with this idea in mind: to escape from the stifling restrictions of her island home. Described as "a very small island, twelve miles long and eight miles wide," Antigua limits Lucy's aspirations, while the vastness of North America takes on the power of a "lifeboat to save [Lucy's] small, drowning soul." Lucy here expresses the feelings of many Caribbean authors, who speak of escaping the parochial atmosphere of their small countries. Hoping to escape the strictures of this "small place," Lucy makes, in "one swift act" the move from Antigua to New York City to take on the role of an au pair for a wealthy family, but this crossing of the ocean does not provide the exhilarating sense of release and freedom Lucy had anticipated in leaving Antigua. Lucy experiences exile not as a means for the kind of universal selfhood of which Lamming and Depêstre speak, but as a bewildering confrontation with the alien, remarking on "how uncomfortable the new can make you feel." From the first pages of the book, Kincaid calls into question masculinist notions of exile as release, as an erasure of or an escape from one's past history and past self.

Lucy first attempts to define her exile by likening herself to someone who is perhaps the most famous of the modern-day European exiles, the painter Paul Gaugin. Gaugin, a French-born artist who never felt at home in his native land and traveled to "the opposite part of the world" to find happiness, provides a compelling model for Lucy's inarticulate longings. . . .

But no sooner does Lucy posit an affinity with Gaugin than she recognizes the irony of her choice. Lucy recognizes that Gaugin's

rebellion and exile give him "the perfume of a hero," while her own exile elicits no such heroic script: "I was not a man; I was a young woman from the fringes of the world, and when I left my home I had wrapped around my shoulders the mantle of a servant."

As a model for exile, Gaugin evokes images of the disaffected European searching out the primitive and exotic in the South Sea islands. . . .

Lucy's words show her awareness that Gaugin's narrative would have cast her in the role of the "exotic other" through which Gaugin found creative inspiration and artistic self-definition. Lucy cannot serve as "other" to herself, and the "liberation" that Gaugin's exile emblematizes eludes Lucy. Coming to the metropolitan center in the posture of a servant, Lucy does not escape so much as recreate the history of servitude imposed on the so-called fringes by the culturally and economically dominant center of Western Europe.

While the vestiges of colonial servitude pose one complication to the narrative of exile exemplified by Gaugin, Lucy also singles out her gender as crucial to the disjunction between her story and Gaugin's. In order to understand the gender specificity of exile, it is crucial to look at Lucy's relationship with her mother, for it is through Lucy's troubled relationship with her mother that her most profound ambivalence about home emerges. Just as Lucy views her island home alternately as a place of beauty and as a place of unbearable suffocation, so does she see her mother both as the one great love of her life and as the figure she must separate herself from if she is to have any sense of self. Indeed, mother love threatens Lucy with annihilation, as she claims in the following passage: "I had come to feel that my mother's love for me was designed solely to make me into an echo of her; and I didn't know why, but I felt that I would rather be dead than become just an echo of someone." Yet while physical separation severs one tie, it remains helpless in severing the profound tie between Lucy and her past. Says Lucy, "I used to think that just a change in venue would banish forever from my life the things I most despised. But that was not to be so. As each day unfolded before me, I could see the sameness in everything; I could see the present take a shape—the shape of the past."

The image of the present taking on the shape of the past, coupled with Lucy's contention that "my past was my mother" reveal perhaps the strongest barrier to her potential for rebirth through exile. Lucy is keenly aware that lying beneath the problem of having "no tongue" (except that which is taught by the colonizers in school) is her inescapable bond with her mother. That her mother is not other but an extension of self is Lucy's repeated claim, as well as her most persistent fear. . . .

The "whole story," then, is the story of wholeness, that is, the original bond between mother and child in which self and other merge into an indivisible whole.

To this narrative of wholeness Lucy adds the accompanying story of maternal betrayal, a rupture of the mother-daughter bond that occurred swiftly and definitively in Lucy's childhood with the birth, in quick succession, of three male siblings. An only child until her ninth year, Lucy has her Edenic world shattered by the birth of these brothers, each of whom both father and mother imagine occupying an important and influential position in society. Not only does Lucy's mother not imagine greatness for her daughter, she educates her for the position of nurse, essentially what Lucy's mother has become for Lucy's aging father. Such low expectations for a girl Lucy expected from her father, as his sons were "his own kind", but for her mother to imagine greatness for her sons and servitude for her daughter marks a betrayal at once intensely personal and emblematic of the gender hierarchy to which Lucy's mother ascribes. . . .

In training Lucy to wear the "mantle of a servant," Lucy's mother acts as an agent of colonial discipline, expecting Lucy to fulfill the role of good wife and good colonial subject; and this education in servitude strikes Lucy as the ultimate betrayal by the figure she identifies as "perhaps the only true love in my life I would ever know."

Both of these descriptions of Lucy's mother capture the all-encompassing presence and power of the pre-oedipal mother, leading the reader to wonder why Lucy, as an adult, still sees her mother wielding such power. The answer to this question lies in the intersection between Lucy's mother's roles as a mother and as an agent of colonial discipline. Lucy sees her mother's numerous prohibitions and attempts to guide her daughter's behavior as an extension of the power that colonizers exercise over the colonized, and Lucy instinctively resists the silencing power of these authorities, refusing to "become an echo," whether of her own mother or of the "mother country" Britain. . . .

Exile for Lucy, then, is the act of planned separation from her disloyal mother, who would consign her "identical offspring" to essential dependence and powerlessness. Lucy explains her desire to leave her homeland in the same terms she uses to resist the suffocation of mother love. . . .

Yet Lucy's experience of existence as a continuum, in which the present takes on the shape of the past and the daughter takes on the shape of the mother, undermines the possibility of rebirth through exile. Physical separation in itself is not enough; what Lucy needs is the tongue—the sharpness of language—to articulate a connection that creates distance, which is Lucy's response to the (m)other who betrays her "identical offspring" by assuming the role of agent for colonial discipline.

Kristen Mahlis. *Modern Fiction Studies.* 44, 1 (Spring 1998)

BIBLIOGRAPHY
*At the Bottom of the River*, 1983; *Annie John*, 1985; *A Small Place*, 1988; *Annie, Gwen, Lilly, Pam and Tulip*, 1989; *Lucy*, 1990; *The Autobiography of My Mother*, 1995; *My Brother*, 1997; *My Garden*, 1999

# KOMUNYAKAA, Yusef (1947–)
## United States

At the core of Komunyakaa's pursuit of a unified vision and literary canonization is his stern resistance, textualized formalistically as well as thematically in his poems, to those forces in the hegemonous counterculture aimed at excluding him as an African American from the ranks of humanity. Indeed, in the singularity of his perseverance and in both the high quality and quantity of his poetic output, Komunyakaa approaches the intensity of no less a figure than prototypical canonization quester Ralph Ellison in his bid for mainstream American literary status. Komunyakaa, however, lacks the irritability Ellison sometimes displays in his attitude toward

other African American writers, in particular the young black writers of the culturally insurrectionary 1970s.

The unified vision Komunyakaa seeks involves the integration and aesthetic instillation in his poetry of cultural material from both his African American and his European American sources. A useful sampling of Komunyakaa's artistry at work—including his quest for a unified vision, his bid for literary canonization, and his push for the completion of his humanity—can be found in two poems from his ironically titled fourth collection, *I Apologize for the Eyes in My Head* (1986): "When in Rome—Apologia," the last two lines of which supply the title of the book, and "I Apologize.". . .

A particularly illustrative passage appears in "I Apologize," a dramatic monologue that intertextualizes Robert Browning's prototypical dramatic monologue "My Last Duchess": "I'm just like the rest of the world: / No comment; no way, Jose." After staking his claim for unqualified status in the human race and issuing his somewhat tongue-in-cheek declaration of no comment (ironically noting the extent to which further comment might implicate him in the negatives as well as the positives of the humanity he holds in common with his white auditor), the persona comments anyway. . . .

Like most of Komunyakaa's poems, "I Apologize" is markedly obscure. On first reading, the persona might be the typical, racially or ethnically unspecified, Peeping Tom, but we soon realize that he is the archetypal reckless eyeballer, the fated African American male in the U.S. South of not too many years ago who is accused of looking too long, and by implication with sexual intent, at some white woman, a tabooistic infringement for which he is likely to be lynched. The accused's only defense, his only recourse in such a predicament, is a desperate and futile excuse. This is typified in the poem's opening lines, which also encapsulate the kind of redemptive humor black people engage in among themselves: "My mind wasn't even there. / Mirage, sir. I didn't see / what I though I saw. / . . .I was miles away, I saw nothing!". Then there is the sheer desperation of the poem's concluding line and a half—"This morning / I can't even remember who I am"—an apparent plea of insanity.

"When in Rome—Apologia" aptly intertextualizes Browning's monologue as well. Both of Komunyakaa's poems allude to the fate of the wife of Browning's jealous persona, the Duke who had his spouse killed for smiling excessively at other men. In Komunyakaa's poems, however, an ironic readjustment of roles takes place, for it is the would-be suitor whose life is at stake, prompting his desperate plea:

> Please forgive me, sir,
> for getting involved
> in the music—
> it's my innate weakness
> for the cello: so human.
> Please forgive me
> for the attention
> I've given your wife
> tonight, sir.

We note the gap posited by the interstanzaic enjambment between "involved" and its complement "in the music," suggesting a deliberate, playful withholding of the right information from the "sir" of the poem—the sense being I won't say it but it's not music I'm talking about, it's life: Excuse me, just a dumb nigger, for insisting on being involved on an equal basis with you in life.

Ironically, the speaker's "innate weakness" is the humanity he has in common with his auditor, as expressed in the phrase "so human." And the use of a highly prized wife to epitomize the cultural exclusion that diminishes the persona's human status is an appropriate choice in view of the idea that enjoys considerable currency among African American artists and intellectuals that, not only are women co-creators with men of culture, they are singularly carriers and dispensers of it as well. Furthermore, the irony informing the speaker's plea borders on sarcasm, thus implying that irony may be too exalted a sentiment to spend on the insensitive "sirs" of this world.

The petitioner's final, desperate plea evidences a loss of control which is due to intoxication: "I don't know / what came over me, sir. / After three Jack Daniel's / you must overlook / my candor, my lack of / sequitur." In a statement that engenders the title of the book, the poem concludes: "I apologize for / the eyes in my head" (24), an ambiguously metonymical reference to the outer (physical) and inner (intuitive) facilities of sight that interact in the process of creating poems. Forgive me, the implication goes, not only for insisting on seeing all that there is humanly possible to see in the world but also for being so presumptuous in my reputed inhumanity as a person of African descent to aspire to write poetry of a quality and comprehensiveness equal to your own.

Who is the forbidden woman in these poems? Is she the same as the "white wife" of the surrealistic poem "The Music That Hurts," personified there as "Silence"? Although Komunyakaa's poems incline toward non-referentiality, they are not characterized by the non-figurativeness non-referential poetry reputedly strives for. Thus, viewed in the context of Komunyakaa's work as a whole, music in these three poems is metaphorical of life; its opposite, "Silence," signifies outsiderness, comprehending an absence of humanity. Add to this the act of seeing as literally and figuratively a means for fulfilling one's humanity, and Komunyakaa's ironic apology may be stated as Sorry, but have I not eyes to see all that there is to be seen in the world, which accords with my right as an American citizen and, preeminently, as a human being? In the very act of laying claim to and pursuing canonical status in his poems, Komunyakaa demonstrates his "qualification" for it in rhetorical and aesthetic maneuvers that include a repudiation of racial or ethnically based limitations or boundaries. He comes across as a person who is well-versed in the poetic traditions of Anglo-Europe and Anglo-America, and who is also aware of the abundant technical and material properties that are available for the advancement of the art of poetry in America, especially the rich resources that abound in African American life and culture.

Not all of Komunyakaa's poems contain African American cultural material, and in some of those that do, the material is not always easily recognizable, possibly identifying these poems as exemplary achievements of Komunyakaa's unified vision. These are among the numerous poems by Komunyakaa that occupy the right end of an accessibility continuum that ranges from obscure on the right to clear on the left, and they provide a unique glimpse into Komunyakaa's artistry, especially in the extraordinary challenge the poems present to the reader who must work to discover, process, and integrate the works' African American cultural material into the fabric of meaning of the poems. The poem "I Apologize" is a case in point, with its subtle inscription of the persona's African Americanness in a poem not easily identifiable as the work of an African American author. Clues to the persona's identity appear in one of a sequence of desperate alibis he concocts in his apologetic response to the person he addresses as "sir," who implicitly has accused him of reckless eyeballing. "I was in my woman's bedroom / removing her red shoes & dress", he pleads, adding in cadences reminiscent of Browning's poem and in mildly contradictory terms as he attempts to extricate himself, that he could not have committed the "crime" because

I was miles away, I saw nothing!
Did I say their diamond rings
blinded me & I nearly lost my head?
I think it was how the North
Star fell through plate glass.
I don't remember what they wore.

The "sir," as indicated earlier, is a white man; the "they" of the last line quoted above are white women, the reputed objects of the defensively comedic African American male persona's reckless eyeballing. The white women, whom he denies having seen at all, yet whose attire he contradictorily indicates he cannot "remember," are identified with diamonds and refined attire, in contrast with the "red shoes & dress" worn by the person whom we justifiably assume to be the persona's African American woman, with whom he was supposedly, and perhaps actually, too preoccupied in her bedroom to be paying attention to anyone else. The red shoes and dress allude ironically to the reputed fondness of black women for the color red and to the disparagement to which they were subjected in white society's stereotyping of them as sexually promiscuous, as scarlet women.

Another, possibly less obscure, allusion is to the North Star, a symbol of freedom derived from its use as a guide by fugitive slaves on their journeys out of slavery. The persona claims he was more concerned with the star than the white women's diamond rings. Throughout the poem the persona is portrayed as a ludicrously bumbling trickster figure, offering one lame excuse after another in his effort to escape the lynching he is likely to receive for his reckless eyeballing. For all its comedic trappings, however, "I Apologize" is a serious dramatization of the obstacles confronting the African American poet who wants his humanity acknowledged—and a rightful place in the American literary canon.

Alvin Aubert. *African American Review*. 27, 1 (Spring 1993), pp. 119–23

Most of Yusef Komunyakaa's poems rise to a crescendo, like that moment in songs one or two beats before the bridge, when everything is hooked-up, full-blown. Over the course of Komunyakaa's seven books, much has been made of the recurring themes in his work: autobiography, African American experience in the South and in Vietnam. Much has also been said about the music in his poetry, the song lyrics and musicians' names. . . .

While many critics have remarked on the musical names (Coltrane, Billie Holiday, Leadbelly) that crop up in Komunyakaa's work and the work of other African American poets such as Cornelius Eady, they often regard these ghostly appearances as emblems or elegies, an African American musicians' museum. But while building such a gallery might be worthwhile, there's more to these ghosts than that. In Komunyakaa's poems, they're clanking the very chains of language.

Pinetop's boogiewoogie keys stack against each other like syllables in tongue-tripped elegies for Lady Day & Duke.

Don't try to make any sense out of this; just let it take you
like Pres's tenor & keep you human.

Komunyakaa is an innovator; his language plays on the infinite
nature of vocabulary. In scads of borrowed lyrics, from the upbeat
"Ta-ra-ra-boom-de-ay" down the druggy slope of "Purple Haze,"
the lexicons of jazz and blues supply him with a raw, articulate alter
ego: "The tongue labors, / a victrola in the mad African-American
mouthhole / of 3 A.M. sorrow." Like a brother less self-conscious
than the poet, music as Komunyakaa hears it is not merely a
celebration or even a culmination of heritage and culture, but an
entire alternate linguistic anatomy.

Music appears when and where traditional vocabulary falters.
When, for example, a hot day triggers a black man's lust for a white
woman, the poet segues to Johnny Mathis's "Beside Her Like a
Whisper"; when a black farmer works his stubborn land and turns
up nothing but rocks, he hums "Amazing Grace." Each song
comes with scores of connotations. The light-skinned Mathis and
the prayer "Amazing Grace" become evocative synonyms for
more familiar and flatter words like impossibility, forbidden,
coaxing, and even goddammit.

Komunyakaa speaks out of more than one side of his mouth—
there's the narrator, his musical partner, the language we're used
to, and the edges of something newer. Neon Vernacular,
Komunyakaa's eighth collection, pushes the layered dialogue
further. It contains about 30 pages of new poems, followed by
generous selections from previous books. One of the longer new
poems is "Songs for My Father," a piece in minute-long, verselike
sections caused by sounds the poet hears—a hyenalike laugh, a
meditative quiet, the noises of lovemaking—each of which remind
him of his father.

The 170 long-playing pages amplify Komunyakaa's tonal range.
He says, "The beast & the burden lock-step & waltz," and they do.
Neon Vernacular gives rise to the hope that Coltrane, Duke, and
Gordon will materialize as synonyms for sinewy or lugubrious,
dimensional or heard in the turn-of-the-century thesaurus.

Robyn Selman. Voice Literary Supplement. (June 1993),
pp. 6–7

Reading the Vietnam poems of Yusef Komunyakaa, one is reminded that culture is made as often on battlefields as it is in the thinker's
notebook, or in the schoolroom; that heroes, those bloody-handed
fellows, are the originals of our great men. There are days when the
sun seems to rise for no other purpose than to illuminate some killer
of genius: to make his uniform glow like a nation's stained glass
windows on Sunday. True, Michelangelo is the equal of Napoleon
in fame, but it is Napoleon's example that is most often followed:
More men aspire to populate tombs than to carve them.

Komunyakaa is more the Michelangelesque carver than the
populator of tombs. Yet though his Neon Vernacular: New and
Selected Poems ranges far and wide in its subject matter, it turns
willy-nilly round his battlefield epiphanies and traumas, round the
question of survival when that question is, in Emily Dickinson's
phrase, "at the white heat." "At the Screen Door," for instance, one of the "new" poems in Neon Vernacular, chronicles
Komunyakaa's return after many years to his Louisiana home
town; yet its true subject is the question of survival and survival's
cost in coins of madness. In this poem, Komunyakaa, at what

appears to be his mother's door—at the fountainhead of his life—
wonders, as any bemused prodigal son would, "Is it her?" But in
the next clause war rears its head: "will she know / What I've seen
& done, / How my boots leave little grave-stone / Shapes in the wet
dirt. . .?" At that door he recalls a buddy who ended up in "a
padded cell . . . After all the men he'd killed in Korea / & on his first
tour in Vietnam, / Someone tracked him down. / That Spec 4 he
ordered / Into a tunnel in Cu Chi / Now waited for him behind / The
screen door, a sunset / in his eyes, / a dead man / Wearing his
teenage son's face. . . ." In the poem "Please," Komunyakaa
reports an occasion when he gave a similar order—an order that so
haunts him that in the midst of lovemaking he cries out, "Hit
the dirt!" This arduous journey into the self recalls the climbs
in the Tour de France that, too difficult to rate, are called
"beyond category."

As both "Please" and "At the Screen Door" demonstrate,
Komunyakaa often chooses as his subject experiences painful
enough to destroy the personality, not so much to exorcise them as
to connect them to insights that, like certain icons and kings of the
old religions, might heal the halt and the sick. The bridges he strives
to build between pain and insight are those of the jazz musician—
that improviser's leaping among epiphanies on which, Komunyakaa
has said, his consciousness, was nurtured: "I think we internalize a
kind of life rhythm," he told an interviewer [Vince F. Gotera]:
"The music I was listening to when I was seven or eight years old
and the music I listen to today are not that different. . . . I listen to a
lot of classical jazz, as well as European classical music. I think you
do all those things side by side" [Callaloo, 1990]. Discovering
rhythms that tie two moments or two traditions of music together,
Komunyakaa pulls the one thread of pleasure in the valley of death
and unravels, one poem at a time, that dour place woven from
suffering. This unraveling can disorient and blind those grown
accustomed to the Valley of the Shadow, and it is something like
the disorientation and still earthly rage that salvation brings that
one finds in the last image of "At the Screen Door," where
Komunyakaa writes of "Watching a new day stumble / Through a
whiplash of grass / Like a man drunk on the rage / Of being alive.". . .

[The best poetry of] Yusef Komunyakaa—the poetry in which
he directly describes his Vietnam experiences, and the poetry for
which that experience acts as a kind of antimatter power source—
[is] an invaluable resource. It gives even some of Komunyakaa's
lesser work and apprentice efforts the patina of the man of action's
recollections of his formative kneescrapes and triumphs. For
Komunyakaa is the real deal twice over—a brilliant poet in his best
work and a hero who came back from Vietnam not only with a
Bronze Star like a piece of the firmament on his chest, but with a
knowledge of what it is to live without vanity, without any tradition
but the Darwinian one that says: first survive, then return to history
and its haze of manners and names.

Michael Collins. Parnassus. 18, 2 (1993–94), pp. 126–50

Yusef Komynyakaa's Neon Vernacular presents about twenty
years worth of poetry: poetry that shudders with desire, past and
present, frustrated and fulfilled. Remembrance is the motive force
behind much of this work, but the past is rarely presented as a
scene, neither a background for a current emotional state nor a
canvas on which the poet can show off his descriptive powers.
Rather, in Komunyakaa's strongest poems, time is the medium for
a complex dialogue, which is intensified by the poet's mordant wit

and flashy but carefully modulated language. Komunyakaa's sense of personal time is infected by the disease of history. When memory and anecdote constitute the poem's body, it's best not to seek a cure.

Thus, much of Komunyakaa's best poetry emerges from his experiences in the Vietnam War. This work, which dates from the mid-eighties, has an immediacy that goes well beyond typical poetry of remembrance while preserving all of its powers of reflection.... [These] poems depend on the interplay of searing images and a sad, knowing, cautious voice which enunciates them over a temporal distance both too long and too short for words....

An able lyricist, Komunyakaa knows that it's always best to add a touch of vinegar to even his most insidiously sweet lines, as in this passage on body painting in "Passions," from *Lost in the Bonewheel Factory* (1979):

> To step into the golden lute
> & paint one's soul
> on the body. Bird
> goddess & slow snake
> in the flowered tree. Circle,
> lineage, womb, mouth, leaf-footed
> godanimal on a man's chest
> who leaps into the moon
> on a woman's belly.

"The Way the Cards Fall," from *Copacetic* (1984) has a kind of grace comparable to that of Williams's "Widow's Lament in Springtime"....

Komunyakaa doesn't always hit the mark like this; sometimes the lyric memories come a little too easily, as in new poems such as "A Good Memory" and "Songs for My Father." Nor am I completely convinced by his vernacular, which can sometimes sound contrived....

But like the jazz musicians he celebrates and elegizes, Komunyakaa never takes his instrument for granted. Twisting, searching, and almost always resisting the easy harmonies, Komunyakaa's poetry reminds us that form is a vexation, a summons, a responsibility, "Like an unknown voice rising/out of flesh." This is work that chastens more often than it solaces. Yet its urgency is not to be denied.

Norman Finkelstein. *Ohio Review.* 52 (1994), pp. 136–39

Yusef Komunyakaa speaks in a gravelly Southern baritone, tinged with a Cajun flavor that reflects his childhood years in Louisiana. He is a man who chooses his words carefully, splicing his speech with long silences, until his conversation resembles something close to a jazz riff—very fitting for this acclaimed poet who says "oral language is our first music, and the body is an amplifier."

Music, more specifically radio music, playing from a waist-high, wooden radio in his mother's living room, was Komunyakaa's first link to the world outside his hometown of Bogalusa, Louisiana. Born in 1947, Komunyakaa grew to revere the radio, and it became a shrine for him: he would listen to Louis Armstrong, Dinah Washington, and Mahalia Jackson and feel a connection to something larger than the rituals of sports and hunting in his own rural town. The jazz and blues Komunyakaa heard as a child have gone on to inform much of his nine published books of poetry. Not

afraid to confront complex moral issues, much of Komunyakaa's work embraces the duality of despair and hope, and music often provides the panacea. All kinds of musicians show up to play: Otis Redding, John Coltrane, Ray Charles, Charles Mingus, and Thelonius Monk, to name a few. The result is a celebration of African American heritage and culture.

In 1994 Komunyakaa received the Pulitzer Prize, the Kingsley Tufts Award, and the William Faulkner Prize from Université de Rennes for *Neon Vernacular: New and Selected Poems*, a collection that prompted many to deem him the progenitor of a wholly new poetic vernacular. Fiercely autobiographical, the spare poems in the book deftly interweave surrealistic imagery, montage, and folk idiom. They offer detailed glimpses of Komunyakaa's rural upbringing, his identity as an African American, as well as his experience in the jungles of Vietnam. Komunyakaa's lines are consistently short and unrhymed, strung together with consonance to arrive at a unique syncopation. The compression and jazz-inspired enjambment create a music-like tension....

*Dien Cai Dau*, which means "crazy" in Vietnamese, stands as a watershed. Fourteen years after returning from Vietnam, instead of merely "writing around the war," Komunyakaa finally "uncapped a hidden place" inside himself. "I tend to tell people that we are walking reservoirs of images. We take in everything, even what we're not overly conscious of, it's still there, pulsating in the psyche." Komunyakaa was standing on a ladder, renovating his house in New Orleans, when poems about Vietnam started spilling out. *The Village Voice* wrote that *Dien Cai Dau* "drove a shaft of light into the inarticulate spectacle of the Vietnam War." The poems grapple with the numbing violence of the war and with the frustrations of black soldiers in predominantly white platoons. Empathy with the enemy is also explored, as in "Starlight Scope Myopia," where the speaker of the poem looks to the other side: "Caught in the infrared/what are they saying?//Are they talking about women/or calling the Americans//beaucoup dien cai dau?/One of them is laughing./You want to place a finger//to his lips & say 'Shhhh.'"...

In *Magic City*, published in 1992 Komunyakaa turned back to his youth, revisiting it with an unflinching eye. The result is poetry that refuses to offer a simple reprieve for our history of racism, poetry that insists we pay witness to life in all its contradictions. At times, these poems are achingly personal, as in "My Father's Love Letters," where the speaker must transcribe letters to his mother for his illiterate father: "On Fridays he'd open a can of Jax/After coming home from the mill,/& ask me to write a letter to my mother/Who sends postcards of desert flowers/Taller than men. He would beg,/Promising to never beat her/Again."....

Susan Coaley. http://www.emerson.edu/ploughshares/Spring 1997/Yusef_Profile.html

Perhaps more consistently than any other poet of the [Vietnam War], Komunyakaa embraces literal dark spaces in his search for truths that transcend wilful "clear images." Everywhere in his Vietnam poems [of *Dien Cai Dau*] we find images "disappearing," "blurred," "splintered," "blinded," "dissolved," and "shattered" in "shadows," "darkness," "mist," "dust," "dusk," and "smoke." His poems are about seeing and not seeing. In fact, a great many of them contain the very words "see" and/or "eye."

Some of the poems' titles indicate Komunyakaa's preoccupation: "Camouflaging the Chimera," "Starlight Scope Myopia," "Seeing in the Dark," and "Eyeball Television.". . .

Mistrusting the "clear images," Komunyakaa insists instead upon seeking adventure "under our eyelids". A poet of insight rather than sight, he says "I close my eyes & I can see". As a poet of insight, he gains the freedom to explore subterranean, pre-rational landscapes. This result in a poetry of rich, surrealistic, disturbing associations: in "'You and I are Disappearing,'" he rushes freneticaly through ten similes (as if to say no one simile, or five, or even ten will adequately express the searing memory), likening a napalmed girl to "a sack of dry ice," "the fat tip/of a banker's cigar," and "a shot glass of vodka"; he visualizes a burning Buddhist monk as turning blue pages; "Booby-trapped pages" float through dust; a voice is "shiney as a knife/against bamboo shoots"; the odor of perfume is described in terms of color; a "moon cuts through/night trees like a circular saw/white hot"; a woman holds "the sun/in her icy glass". This is but a small sampling of Komunyakaa's efforts to penetrate into the deep interior life lurking beneath "sweet geometry." It gives his poetry a strangely vital and nightmarish quality. Never coming to resolution ("yes, no, yes"), his poetry, at its best, strikes an uneasy balance between irretrievable loss and a glimmer of hope, as when standing in front of the Vietnam Veterans Memorial, he sees "In the black mirror/a woman's trying to erase names:/No, she's brushing a boy's hair."

The Spanish would say Komunyakaa's poetry has "*duende*," for which we have no one-word translation. Roughly, it refers to the pre-rational wild spirit of death, darkness, and blood. Keeping company with it results in a profound form of misbehavior. . . .

Many of his poems "fuse themselves in a longing greater than their visible expressions." Among them are "A Greenness Taller Than Gods," "You and I Are Disappearing," "Re-creating the Scene," "2527th Birthday of the Buddha," "Missing in Action," and "Nude Pictures." But in what I think is his greatest poem, "Eyeball Television," Komunyakaa fuses *duende* with a cultural critique and a repudiation of the motifs of sight, vision, eyes, and darkness. And again, although the poet *might* opt for "clear images" if he could, he can't. Because he can't, he sees instead behind the eyes, thereby offering a complicated critique of the way the war is perceived and written about.

The persona of the poem is a POW limited to a "pinhole of light" as he "sits crouched in a hole/covered by slats of bamboo." While there, he recalls television shows, ". . .hundreds of faces/ from *I Love Lucy, Dragnet,/ I Spy,* & *The Ed Sullivan Show*," plus ". . .*Roadrunner* on channel 6." He tries to maintain the "sweet geometry" of a reassuring TV world. But his *inner* "focus" shows a world that is epistemologicaly and ontologically crumbling. What he sees is reminiscent of the wild sequences in Dali's and Buñuel's *Un Chien Andalou:*

> Holding the world in focus in his solitary cell, he sees Spike Jones' one-man band explode. Two minutes later Marilyn Monroe is nude on a round white sofa that dissolves into a cloud. Shaking his head to get her pose right again, he finds himself pushing vertical & horizontal hold buttons, but only Liberace's piano eases into the disconnected landscape.

"Pushing vertical & horizontal hold buttons" describes not only the soldier's efforts to make sense of a surreal experience, but

worse, the efforts of the military, political, and media establishments to mediate the war in tidy packages of "clear images." In this poem, Komunyakaa deconstructs all packages. Eventually, even the senses melt like Dali's clocks:

> He hears deliberate heavy footsteps of the guards coming for him. The picture fades into the sound of urine dripping on his forehead, as he tries to read the lips of Walter Cronkite.

The poem's final line is supremely ironic, for it implicitly attacks America's ultimate "He"—Walter Cronkite, a man, who surrounded by epidemic madness, could nevertheless confidently say during the entire course of the war, and without laughing, "That's the way it is." On CBS, yes, but never in Komunyakaa's *dien cai dau, duende* poetry.

> Dan Ringnalda. *Journal of American Culture.* 16,3 (Fall 1998), pp. 21–27

BIBLIOGRAPHY

*Dedications and Other Darkhorses*, 1977; *Lost in the Bonewheel Factory*, 1979; *Copacetic*, 1984; *I Apologise for the Eyes in My Head*, 1986; *Toys in a Field*, 1986; *Dien Cai Dau*, 1988; *February in Sydney*, 1989; *Magic City*, 1992; *Neon Vernacular: New and Selected Poems*, 1993; *Thieves of Paradise*, 1998

# KOUROUMA, Ahmadou (1940–)
## Cote D'ivoire

Ahmadou Kourouma's *Les Soleils des indépendances* has not yet been evaluated at its true worth, although the review *Études Françaises* of Montreal recognized its quality and awarded it their annual literary prize. It is a novel that is profoundly African in style and subject, inspiration and expression. It could be considered the first real African novel, in which the fact that it is written in French seems almost incidental. It might almost be deemed to manifest those values that Jean-Marie Abanda Ndengue calls *Négrisme*, which he defines as the result of a fruitful marriage between the culture of the Negro-African world (Négritude) and those values introduced by the values of Western colonization—whether military, economic, political, or cultural. In the case of Ahmadou Kourouma, we find a Malinké who has adopted the most popular literary form of the modern Western world—the novel, and mastered the literary language of the former colonists; but he writes a French which seems the spontaneous, indigenous tongue of Africa, such as only Birago Diop had used before for his *Contes d'Amadou Koumba*, and [Léopold Sédar] Senghor for his poems, and composes a novel which owes little to traditional Western European models. His language is neither the labored high-school exercise of African novelists of mediocre talent or inadequate literacy, nor the polished, flexible medium of the best of his compatriots. Like Senghor and Diop he has—probably unconsciously—emancipated himself from the attitude of awed respect for the French vocabulary and syntax bearing the seal of the Académie Française. He has evolved a rich, spontaneous expressiveness that seems the natural idiom of his Musulman, Malinké hero, Fama Doumbouya, expostulating, vociferating, vituperating, or merely meditating in his own vernacular. . . .

Superficially, the theme of *Les Soleils des indépendances* seems to be . . . that of a childless marriage, which is not only a personal tragedy but also a source of social inferiority in an African society. But Fama's barren union is only one aspect of his tragedy; moreover, it is treated with . . . profundity, originality, psychological insight, and elaboration of dramatic and episodic detail. . . . The true subject, of which Fama's sterility is only the individual symbol, is the collapse, with no hope of regeneration, of the only society into which he was fully integrated. This is an extension of the "Things-Fall-Apart" theme, originally illustrating the catastrophic impact of colonization on African rural society, now applied ironically to the disillusionment and eventual tragedy that independence brings to those for whom the colonial era was a time of prosperity and privilege.

*Les Soleils des indépendances* is a novel symmetrically structured in the shape of a parabola. The first of the three parts presents Fama at the nadir of his social humiliations and personal despair at the impossibility of his twenty-year-old monogamous marriage to Salimata ever bearing fruit. In part two, his fortunes rise to a summit, with the possibility of his reintegration as the honored chief of his native village and the promise of a nubile young bride who seems capable of being "as fertile as a mouse." Part three tells of Fama's decline and death after vicissitudes worse than he had ever anticipated in the miseries of his earlier existence. The tragic equilibrium of the novel is likewise assured by the presentation of Fama as the victim of circumstance and of his own character. Irascible and arrogant, susceptible and superstitious, intractable and uncompromising, born to riches, honor, autocracy, and ostentation, ambitious but politically naïve, he is incapable of accommodating himself to poverty, compounding with sycophancy, or quite simply of understanding the realities of his present existence. For Fama Doumbouya, last legitimate descendant of the princes of Horodougou, a region of the fictitious "Ebony Coast," the colonial era had been a time of prosperity, in that it favored the free-trading enterprise in which he was engaged. Independence has brought Fama nothing but an identity card, a membership ticket of the single party in power, poverty, and the humiliation of a life of quasi-beggary. Too old to return to the land, the last prince of Horodougou is unfortunately completely illiterate, so [he] could hope for none of the perquisites of power in the new regime. The man whose totem was the royal panther is reduced to earning his living as a "hyena," a "vulture," that is a professional assistant at Musulman funeral rites, which even with independence are long and complicated. . . .

*Les Soleils des indépendances* is not a novel that can be neatly tagged and docketed like many earlier French-African works of fiction. It is not simply a political, sociological, psychological, or anthropological study. Fama Doumbouya is manifestly the victim of a changing world to which his inculcated principles, lack of formal education and inflexible temperament prevent him from adapting. But his story is not simply that of a society in transition, the novel of metamorphosis. Similarly, while the author throws light on social custom, details of the female excision, consultation of sorcerers, these passages are not included for their exotic interest and to enrich the local color, but are closely integrated into the psychological study of Salimata's predicament. Like many creative black writers of the last decade, no longer committed to the

anticolonial cause, nor to any partisan issues, Ahmadou Kourouma can permit himself ironic comment on contemporary African politics and politicians, without passing final judgement on the situation. He merely suggests, with objective and lucid intelligence, that all is not a utopia in the territories illuminated by the suns of independence. The conclusion to be drawn is consistent with the Muslim African inspiration and texture of the novel: no political change can bring Paradise on earth to mortal existence plagued by: "Colonization, District Commandants, Epidemics, droughts, Independence, the single party and revolution . . . all kinds of curses invented by the devil."

Dorothy S. Blair. *African Literature in French* (London: Cambridge University Press, 1976), pp. 300–4

Even a cursory reading of *Les Soleils* [*des indépendances*] would identify the society in the text as distinctly Malinké. Thus the novel may be said to be about the Malinkés. But, like every novel, it mediates that referential society through the obliquities of language and narrative. While the social reality that appears in the novel is most meaningful when related to the Malinké society outside the text, this verbalized society is both the result of representing and a way of seeing the outer social world. Ahmadou Kourouma is himself a Malinké, steeped in the traditions of his people. But he is also a well-educated Ivoirian with a modernist outlook; he is an actuary by profession. Kourouma chooses to express his observations about his people through a created self (often the narrator), or sometimes more subtly through a fictional character like Fama. He maintains a critical distance between his people and himself, by adopting a satirical tone. . . .

Clearly, the novel's main focus is the capitalist Ebony Coast, although the novel is not more ideologically biased against capitalism than it is in favor of socialism. In highlighting the plight of Fama, an impoverished *dioula* living in a slum in the Ebony Coast's capital, Kourouma is not primarily interested in the class of northern *dioulas* living in the capital. It is revealing that Fama is no longer a prosperous *dioula*, but a jobless Malinké. True, he likes to think of himself as set apart by birth and profession from the beggars, the blind, the maimed who can hardly conceal their misery, but the novelist shows him as belonging very much to the pariahs of society. In fact, Fama's condition provides Kourouma with the opportunity to raise one of the central issues in the novel: what has independence really brought to the ordinary man? In a powerful authorial interpolation, Kourouma himself provides an answer. . . . Fama is one of these pariahs who crowd the little slum markets in search of alms. The one thing that they are sure of getting in plentiful supply is "lagoon water . . . rotten and salty as well as the sky, either dazzling with fierce sunshine or loaded with rains which fall on the jobless who have neither shelter nor beds." They have nothing else to do except "roam about, stink, pray and listen to the rumbling of their empty stomachs." Nobody seems to care for them, certainly not the affluent corrupt elite "who could afford to have cloths made out of bank notes." It is the novel's unrelenting focus on the lot of the "wretched" which adds ideological substance to its criticism of the postindependence era. . . .

*Les Soleils* is a complex novel which calls for "plural" readings, the kind of novel which frequently frustrates the critic's imperialistic attempts to domesticate or "naturalize" it with his reading strategy. However, from whatever angle one reads it, one cannot miss two of the novel's axes: its critical celebration of traditional African culture and its criticism of postindependence African politics. It is one of the most authentically African novels, and possesses a remarkably original perspective. Without being uncritical of tradition, *Les Soleils* views independent Africa mainly through the critical lens of a traditional African nurtured on the culture and worldview of his people. It speaks about Africans, not without affection, but without excessive indulgence. Above all, it speaks to Africans with an African voice.

> Kwabena Britwum. In Kolawole Ogungbesan, ed. *New West African Literature* (London: Heinemann, 1979), pp. 80–81, 87–89

[*Les Soleils des indépendances*] reveals many aspects of the engaging artistry of the griot—master storyteller, trustee of the lore, the genealogy, and the wisdom of traditional African societies. It is by virtue of its flawlessly oral quality that here, more than in any other African novel, the reader encounters the shape and sound of oral performance. As [Martha] Cobb found in her study of the literature of the slave diaspora, ''the verbal techniques of oral art are embodied in a *concrete* speaker-audience relationship.'' The textual voice that emanates from Kourouma's work relies upon two devices highly reminiscent of the *call and response* format of oral performance—alternance between first and second person, and a special fondness for the exclamatory and interrogative mood. The surprising effect that these produce in Kourouma's novel is to elicit the readers's *response*. They help to sustain a dynamic and flexible relationship between the narrator and the audience.

Kourouma achieves almost immediately that ambiance of ease, of relaxed familiarity, indeed of intimacy so readily identifiable with the storytelling setting, so indispensable a factor in the relationship between storyteller and audience. From the first sentence, the narrator transforms the isolated reader into an ''audience'' and then proceeds to enlist his sympathetic cooperation. Although the narrator is occasionally reminded that there are non-Malinké present . . . the general tenor of the narrative, strengthened by asides like ''Que voulez-vous?,'' ''Dites-moi,'' and ''Mais attention,'' reveals a close bond, indeed almost a kinship between the Malinké narrator and the listeners gathered around. The narrator who says *je* plays no role in the events of the story yet is decidedly well informed, as only an insider could be, concerning the particular Malinké milieu depicted. He is equally knowledgeable about the protagonists Fama and Salimata, although the perspective he enjoys is not solely that of an omniscient narrator, nor does he identify exclusively with any single character. Rather, the point of view indicated by textual voice qualities—the inflections, the intonations, the idiom—is at once that of a distinct narrative *je*, Fama, Salimata, and the social group to which they belong. . . .

Kourouma brings new dynamism and energy to the traditional role of the narrator. By the same token, he alters the role traditionally reserved for the readers, by making them sense that they are directly and physically present in the narration. In *Les Soleils des indépendances* it is the narrative voice that so beguiles the listener. No technique or device in the oral performer's arsenal is absent. Their skillful manipulation, in conjunction with the poignant and tragic story of one man's fate, ensures Kourouma's novel a place of distinction in recent African fiction.

> Rosemary G. Schikora. *French Review.* 55, 6 (May 1980), pp. 812–13, 817

By focusing upon Fama, the disinherited Malinké prince, Kourouma breaks the pattern of writers who portray cultural hybrids in African literature. Indeed, by presenting an illiterate protagonist in a society where literacy is a prerequisite to joining the ruling elite, Kourouma explores the psychological and sociological effects of marginality in a context that differs from the earlier works of writers like Camara Laye and Cheikh Hamidou Kane. Whereas their protagonists struggle to integrate newly acquired European language and technology with traditional African social and spiritual values, Kourouma portrays the plight of the individual who has been left behind. Unskilled in modern technology as well as illiterate in French . . . Fama cannot join the ruling elite in the new era of the ''suns of independence.'' He represents the disgruntled displaced masses lured from the village to the city by promises of opportunity only to encounter an ever-deepening poverty.

Fama lives in a topsy-turvy world. In fact, ''le monde renversé'' becomes a metaphor for the protagonist's condition. In Fama's mind, independence is the root of all evil, responsible for his misfortunes and those of his society as a whole. With the coming of independence to his country, the hereditary Malinké prince of Horodougou has been deprived of all his former privileges. The reader initially encounters Fama in the capital city, far from his village of origin; here the prince without a kingdom is reduced to accepting handouts as praise-singer at Malinké funerals. In addition, he is plagued by sterility, believing incorrectly that his wife, Salimata, is responsible for the couple's lack of an heir.

In *Les Soleils des indépendances*, Kourouma uses elements of oral tradition to alter the relationship between the narrator and the reading public, and to stretch the limits of conventional French syntax. . . . Kourouma thus assumes the narrative voice of the griot, and although limited by the written word on the printed page, he attempts to re-create both the spontaneity of oral performance and the characteristic interchange between performer and audience.

> Mildred Mortimer. *Research in African Literatures.* 21, 2 (Summer 1990), pp. 36–37

[*Monnè, outrages et défis*] is the story of Djigui Keita, King of the Soba nation in the Mandinka region. When Samory invited him to raze his own city to the ground and to join with Samory in fighting against the French intruders, Djigui decides to confront the ''Nazarenes'' (i.e., Christians) because he assumes that the magic he inherited from his ancestors, the protection of Allah, and a hastily built wall will be sufficient to repel them. In contrast to his expectations, he was defeated by the French troops and obliged to swear allegiance to the new rulers of the territory. Thus begins the long life of *monnè* that destiny imposed upon him—a life that he lived, helpless and bitter, until the eve of independence.

Deprived of the reality of power, Djigui Keita, king of a conquered people, witnesses, along with his griot and his court, the ''pacification'' of the territory and the establishment of a colonial administration in which civil servants eventually replace the military. Naturally, the king's collaboration is required to assure the smooth functioning of the *indigénat*, forced labor, and the recruitment of soldiers after the outbreak of World War I, but the colonial regime actually plunges the people of Soba into a state of misery and despair. Torn between the suffering of his people and the endless demands of the white administrators, Djigui ignores the true meaning of the projects with which he is being associated. . . .

Kourouma's novel dramatizes the incommunicability that emerges in the numerous misperceptions and misunderstandings that characterize relationships between the colonial administration and the "natives." This incommunicability is linked to a cultural incompatibility, to a conflict between divergent ambitions and dreams, but also to the impossibility of mutually comprehensible linguistic communication. Just as Malinké means nothing to the French, French means nothing to the Malinké. Under these circumstances, the interpreter can allow each party to understand whatever seems suitable to him.

Through the act of writing, Kourouma reacts against this impossibility of mutual understanding. This is what justifies his project, begun in [*Les*] *Soleils* and continued in *Monné*, of Africanizing the French language. In his second novel, Kourouma seems less daring than in the first, but his desire to imprint French with the mark of African culture through the use of words (as in the title) remains dominant. His technique includes syntactic nonconformity; a wit that enlivens the narrative and manifests itself in rustic humor, imagery, and metaphors (often with sexual connotations); proverbs; fantasy; and, above all, the joy of storytelling that is so characteristic of oral cultures and so aptly illustrated in the pompously sententious chapter headings in *Monné*.

Guy Ossito Midiohouan. *Research in African Literatures*. 22, 2 (Summer 1991), pp. 232, 234

Going beyond the justly acclaimed brilliant demonstration of the use of African voice and point of view in his first published novel, *Les Soleils des indépendances*, Ahmadou Kourouma achieves, with *Monné, outrages et défis*, a master-piece of literary creation in the French language. Kourouma confirms his position in contemporary international literature, while offering an injection of sorely needed vitality to the French novel.

*Monné* is admirable in all its dimensions: for the depth of its underlying ideas and the breadth of its historical vision; for virtuosity in style, sense of humor, and razor sharp sense of reality; for a heart of gold beating in a warm, upright body; for comprehension without complacency; for that heady mixture of humor and wisdom laced with just a soupçon of healthy vulgarity that makes Africa so exasperating. Ahmadou Kourouma speaks out, speaks straight, speaks true as only a man who has earned his voice by the sweat of his mind, body, and soul, and at the risk of his life can speak.

Kourouma's brilliant transformations of French linguistic usage and literary methods are part of an audacious project which should be appreciated in the context of the stubborn persistence of academic constraints on literature published in France, where the taboo against "writing what is spoken" is maintained against all good sense, and the written form must be elaborated within a closed system of *canons d'écriture* which discourage convincing experiments in raising voice to literary heights.

At the same time, Kourouma transgresses the taboo against the liberal use of foreign words, integrating an extensive Malinké vocabulary into the body of his text. These Malinké words, accents, and rhythms are not props to convince readers—African or other—that they are in the presence of an African novel; on the contrary, they are essential to the structure of the work, to its philosophical, sociological, and historical ambitions. In the same way, the African music of Kourouma's syntax is determined by the necessity to communicate a particular mental structure which is not French. As a result, Kourouma succeeds in creating a literary version of recent African history as seen and experienced from a Malinké point of view.

Nidra Poller. *Research in African Literatures*. 22, 2 (Summer 1991), pp. 235–36

In [*Monné, outrages et défis*], Kourouma attempts to re-create the ample universe of an epic past. Like *Sarraounia* (by Abdoulayi Mamani), *Tchaka le Zoulou* (by Thomas Mofolo), *Soundjata ou l'épopée mandingue* (by Djibril Tamsir Niane), his epic echoes the foreign presence in Africa, the indigenous resistance and the shattering conquest of the continent. The story, narrated in the style of a griot, evolves around Djigui Keita, the affable king of Soba and the ally of Samory, *mandingue* emperor. Djigui decides to turn a deaf ear to the retreat order given by the emperor, whose army has massacred a French battalion, and to face alone the troops marching under the command of Faidherbe. As defense strategies against the advance of the "Nazarenes," this king turns to his ancestors and to Allah, while fortifying the town of Soba with a wall, the *tata*. But the French army, without striking a blow, capture it. Thus follows the submission of the *mandingue* empire, the implantation of the colonial regime and the clash of cultures. The king, Djigui, wishing to ensure the perpetuity of his dynasty, begins to corroborate with the occupant, resulting in the eruption of murderous violence in the *mandingue* kingdom, orchestrated by social and political powers. Throughout the narration, the peasants appear in hostile and sordid spaces: the south, lice-infested swamps, abandoned and deserted villages. One also finds them in social institutions like mosques, forced labor yards, and battlefields. The population, subjected to taxation and exploitation, travels henceforth through an *unnamable* time punctuated by "monnew" and anxiety.

This critical period of African history allows Kourouma to demonstrate the ancient values incarnated by marabouts, prophets, griots, and fetishists, all of whom are partisans of traditional power. But the presence of foreigners in the *mandingue* space establishes a new (spoken) word and a new power, because in traditional Africa, saying word means saying power. Thus the structures of a new society impose themselves through protagonists like the governor, the general, the captain, the commander, the marksmen. To this list is added the interpreter who has henceforth become a buffer, an agent of peace instead of an "established crook." The Cote d'Ivoire writer rehabilitates the interpreter throughout his novel. As for the Nazarenes, they start the disorganization and the destruction of all the operating forces in the ancient space.

The work gives an important place to the religious dimension. The spiritual experience of Fama, the fallen prince of *Les Soleils des indépendances*, is matched by that of Djigui, the dispossessed king. Incessant Islamic prayer, the immolation of victims to the spirits of ancestors are, for the latter, rites for the protection against the invading Nazarenes. All this is evidence of religious syncretism and of the permanent alliance between Islam and animism on which Christianity is grafted. In this perspective, the work can be viewed as a quest for God.

And there is no lack of mystical resonances. Djigui, for having disowned and rejected the alliance of Samory and then having collaborated with the foreigner, is forced to assume the tragic consequence of his choices. He resorts to lies and deception with his Nazarene collaborators; the construction work of the railway lines initiated by his new allies remains incomplete. Later, Béma, his own son born of a wife unworthy of the king allies himself with the Nazarenes, falsifies his father's signature and dethrones him. The fallen king is outraged by this treason. . . . He falls and dies on the way to Toukoro. . . . The dead are metamorphosed into phantoms who haunt the activities of the collaborators. The entirety of events marks the fantastic in the novel and is inscribed in the disintegration of traditions and the ruin of the ancient world. The downfall of the king, Djigui, seems to correspond to that of his people who are abandoned to slavery, forced labor, and colonization.

Kourouma has not done away with the crude language that characterized *Les Soleils des indépendances*. The traditional African aesthetic—proverbs, local talk, chants, poetry and music, words and dialogue—dominate the attentive gaze that he poses on the *Crépuscule des temps anciens*, on *mandingue* history, and on African history. *Monné, outrages et défis* remains a magnificent celebration of life, of the 125-year period that would have been the reign of Djigui. The novelist knew how to marry the real and the imaginary and to bring to light the experience of the African people in their encounter with the outside, in their national and international politics, in their conflicts, in their corruption, in their suffering, in their oppression, in their religiosity, and in their disorder. The historian, the sociologue, the ethnologue, the linguist, and the fan of African studies will each find a great source in *Monné, outrages et défis*.

Eronini E. C. Egbujor. *Canadian Journal of African Studies*. 26, 3 (1992), pp. 544–555

[L and R (Rene Lefort and Mauro Rosi]: Your first novel, *The Suns of Independence*, published in 1970, has won acclaim as a masterpiece and has sold 100,000 copies. But you had a hard time finding a publisher for it. Why?

[A.K. (Ahmadou Kourouma)]: The book was rejected for two reasons. First, my style had a certain originality stemming from the particular way in which I used the French language. Some readers found this disconcerting. Second, many people disliked the conception of the novel. I had structured it in the kind of way used by the American writer John Dos Passos earlier this century. I ended the fictional part of the book with a section I would describe as documentary. After telling the story of the protagonist, Fama, I described situations and events that took place in Cote d'Ivoire at the time of the Cold War. I talked about things that might be called sensitive. Some African publishers even sent the manuscript back to me with scathing, almost insulting comments. . . .

[L and R]: How would you describe the Malinke language?

[A.K.]: Some people may disagree, but it seems to me that African languages are on the whole far richer than European languages. They have a wide range of words to denote one and the same thing and a multitude of expressions to describe one and the same feeling, as well as many mechanisms for creating neologisms. Malinke alone has around ten of these. African languages are rich in proverbs and sayings which people constantly refer to. So it's not surprising that sometimes we get bogged down when we use French to describe our lives and our psychological universe. The French language, on the other hand, is the product of a Catholic, rationalist civilization. That's obvious from its structure, its way of analysing and describing reality. Our language is influenced by fetishist spirituality and is closer to nature.

[L and R]: Western authors often speak of writing as a physical, vital, organic need. For you, it is more a way of getting a hearing.

[A.K.]: For us African writers, writing is also a matter of survival. When I wrote *The Suns of Independence*, I wanted to campaign against abuses of social and economic power. That was a vital and absolute necessity! All contemporary French and other European writers have devoted some of their work to the four years of occupation and oppression that their countries endured during the second world war. But in Africa we had 100 years of occupation, and it's vitally important for us to talk about this and analyse its consequences and effects. We had as many massacres as Europeans did during the last war and under authoritarian Stalinist regimes. In my second novel, *Monnew*, which was published in 1990, I wanted to get across the message that we too have endured great suffering. That suffering is also the subject of the novel I recently finished. Its title is *En attendant le vote des bites sauvages* ("Waiting for the wild animals to vote"), and it's based on the tragedy of the Cold War in Africa.

[L and R]: The sufferings you describe are intense and extreme. But in this novel you express gratitude to a dictator for his "courage" in telling his compatriots that they were "thieving, lazy savages."

[A.K.]: That remark does not refer to the people "down below", as we say, but to those "on top", the dictators' buddies. Resignation was the only option for the people down below, whom I describe as "coarsened by their beliefs and their poverty, patient and dumb". The Cold War prevented African countries from finding a way out of their predicament. It kept a millstone around their necks. Foreign powers gave the orders and pulled the strings, picked the dictators that suited them and sent in their military whenever there was any resistance. . . .

[L and R]: One criticism that has been made of your most recent novel is that in Africa reality and magic seem to be inseparable. Your anti-hero, the dictator Koyaga, defeats all his adversaries largely because of the strength of his magical powers.

[A.K.]: I don't believe in magic. And when Africans ask me why I don't, I say that if magic really existed, we wouldn't have allowed the abduction of 100 million people, of whom perhaps 40 million reached the Americas and 60 million died on the way. If magic really worked, the slaves would have turned into birds, say, and would have flown back home. I don't believe in magic because when I was a boy, I saw forced labour. If magic existed, the victims of forced labour would have been able to escape. But in a novel you have to describe your characters' mentality and ideas. Power and magic are inseparable in the minds of most Africans. The dictator not only has power and money, he also has the best fetishists and sorcerers. Because they are the best, the dictator is invulnerable and his power is limitless. For the dictator's entourage and for the people at large, power and magic are one.

[L and R]: So how can Africa be successful in a world where science and technology are increasingly important?

[A.K.]: Rationality will gain ground at the same time as democracy, which is still far off but is slowly coming in. It won't solve every problem, but we already have its foundation stone-the spoken word. Everywhere, we say what we want, and that's quite an achievement. And one important thing we can say - and see - is that the chief's almighty power is on the way out. The press can now expose corruption and abuses of power; a leader has to campaign against his opponents in elections; it's possible to get rich without being a stooge of the government. The leader is no longer a superman. He no longer has everything going for him. He has to shoulder duties and responsibilities. He is becoming like everyone else. And consequently the magical part of his power is disappearing.

[L and R]: And yet at the end of your latest novel the dictator is forced to hold elections, but "if people refuse to vote for him, the animals will come out of the bush, get hold of ballot papers and elect him with a landslide majority."

[A.K.]: Odd as it may seem, many people think that kind of thing is possible. They're even sure presidents get elected that way. But we're making some headway. Before, either there weren't any elections at all, or if an election was held, the dictator only had to ask for 99 per cent of the vote for his wish to be granted. Now he is forced to cheat. Votes from wild animals are the last refuge of dictators in distress.

> Rene Lefort and Mauro Rosi. *UNESCO Courier* (March 1999), pp. 46–49

BIBLIOGRAPHY

*Les Soleils des indépendances* (*The Suns of the Independences*), 1968; *Monné, outrages et défis* (*Monné, Outrages and Defiances*), 1990; *Le diseur de verite: piece en 4 actes*, 1998; *En attendant le vote des betes sauvages*, 1998

# KUNENE, Mazisi (1930–)

## South Africa

Upon reading Mr. Kunene's poems, one immediately discovers that there is a poet, the secret of whose charming and touching verse is its simplicity, clarity and originality. To those who know him, the poet in question has never failed to win admiration because of his simplicity. He is not, like so many of us, mentally castrated in the Western tradition, a caricature of European culture. This is clearly demonstrated by the idiom and cadence of his poems which are steeped in the traditional Zulu oral poetry: apt lyrical associations interspersed with images from the sonorous world of the Zulu heroic epic. . . .

He invokes the familiar landscape of the land of Shaka, with word-pictures that are not mere structures superimposed over the overall piece of exotica. Rather they are associated with the deepest thoughts of the poet's people, with the sentiments of the land to which he is first and foremost addressing himself. They may be concrete place-names and proper names of historical significance;

or some other phenomena that have come to be accepted as expressive of the best in human nature or the worst in life. But all these do undergo a complicated process in the creative mind of the poet, when they finally come out on paper they are closely and fittingly knit into the mosaic of words that transport ideas and aspirations and force a corresponding reaction on the part of the reader. . . .

Mr. Kunene has firmly established himself in the realist tradition. In doing so, he has not sacrificed the lively Zulu imagery at the altar of a fastidious demi-god of intellectualism.

> Mofolo Bulane. *New African*. June 1966, pp. 111–12

Mazisi Kunene's *Zulu Poems* are all rich, rhetorical, full of emotional and intellectual over- and undertones that reverberate through all the musical variety of the chanting, singing, philosophising voice which he derives from an ancient and rich tradition. . . .

Away from home, out of his land—unfortunately, even unhappily, but of necessity—it is the pity of this that is crystallised in the simple, succinct expression of "Exile.". . . There are fullness and expressivity in this poem which speak not only in the rich metaphors of home but also of the loss entailed by conditions at home, expressing at the same time a condemnation of those conditions, and a resolution, bitter, present and active, to change, to improve, to revolutionise that situation in the place from which exile has driven one and in the places to which exile has forced one, may still send one. This awareness of the brutality and/or decadence of the world that chose "the bridegroom of steel" ("Europe"), this awareness of a trauma and an agony which needs revolutionary ardour, a revolutionary awareness of decadence and, more than anything, a revolutionary perception of goals to be attained, is another of the strands that this memorable volume weaves into the South African cultural pattern.

> Langa Mokwena. *African Communist*. No. 2, 1971, pp. 119–21

Mazisi Kunene is a poet who speaks through a muted instrument. Very strange for a poet who is also full time in South African resistance politics based in London. There is no uptight posturing at all in his diction, which has a flow and beat peculiarly reminiscent of Kofi Awoonor. He writes his verse in Zulu and has rendered a translation of a significant portion of it, and he is head and shoulders above his predecessors in the area of Zulu poetry. What he says about Zulu poetry being a communal voice is true of all Bantu poetry in Southern Africa, indeed true of most African poetry we know of in indigenous languages. There is a fascinating interplay in Kunene's [*Zulu Poems*] between the intense motivation peculiar to the political mood of today and the motivation that underlies oral poetry on the lips of an elder. This latter motivation is prophecy. Here is very little exploration.

Kunene speaks through a lyric that makes bold forthright statements which, taken together, have the effect of having taken the reader through some exploration of a kind. He admonishes the proud, the tyrants, those who worship steel and so on. In general he warns against self-deceit. As a prophet, the persona waxes more and more apocalyptic. The "widowed leopard," says the prophet, who is referring to the predatory white man, will retreat howling into the hill. She will walk about destitute, giving way to the young triumphant bulls of the earth who must take our place. The white people's guilt will pursue them, "driving them from wall to wall." Today's children must "burst forth with our tomorrows." No matter what the white man does, the one who is forever felling trees, the African is abundance itself. Always there will come a season of new fruit. Kunene sees the function of a poem as that of taking from people the "yearnings of their souls" and turning them into a huge fountain that will multiply into oceans.

Ezekiel Mphahlele. *The African Image*, rev. ed. (New York: Praeger, 1974), pp. 239–40

Kunene's most ambitious poem, "Anthem of Decades," utilizes the style of the long Zulu epic poem which at times runs to five hundred or more lines. What appears in his collection *Zulu Poems* is only an extract of 186 lines. . . .

The epic characterizes the victory of one force over another; the victor, representing a higher morality and will, triumphs not because he is good and the other is evil; in his victory will be shown his humility dramatized in the act of cleaning the vanquished combatant's wounds. As Kunene points out, the characters are not gods, but personalized ideas, representing anthropomorphic conceptions of the universe as embedded in Zulu philosophy and thinking. Imprecise, the Zulu concept of the deity or Supreme Creator shares a pantheistic nature that is clouded in vagueness and mystery. . . .

It seems that in this poem Kunene attempts to unite the principles of creation and of the struggle between forces as contained in Zulu thought. The material is completely derived from Zulu cosmology. It is obvious also that the poem is suggested by *Paradise Lost*, even though its denouement presents a vision totally different from that of the Christian epic. Its predilection for abstractions seems obviously to be based upon an attempt to achieve for it a preciseness. But the language and style are based in Zulu imagery. The principles that inhabit the landscape of the poem share of the Zulu conception of the world and express its creation myths.

Kofi Awoonor. *The Breast of the Earth* (Garden City, New York: Doubleday, 1975), pp. 199–201

Many of [Mazisi] Kunene's shorter poems seem like chips from the creation epic. They take up some of the same concerns and use the same cosmic imagery. "From the Ravages of Life We Create," for instance, focuses on the emergence of creation from destruction, the renewing process of life, the inter-relationship of grief with joy. Each of the images says almost the same thing, but each defines the concept in some particular way. Suns are "torn from the cord of the skies," to mingle in shame with fallen leaves, but the cord itself remains and the combination of winter suns and leaves offers a hint of the process of natural decay that feeds the next generation of life. The "wedding party" image of fecundity is mingled with "the moon disintegrating," a suggestion of renewal only through decay, whether the decay is in inanimate nature or a woman's monthly cycle. The power of man as it is found in the searching intellectuality that can never rest is again asserted, and the poem ends in a

splendidly original image combining the notion of man's power and his limitations, the good and the evil that he is capable of: even a plague of locusts "with broken wings" can shelter the earth from the intense heat of the sun. . . .

Kunene draws on Zulu oral traditions not only in these poems on epic subjects but also in his elegies, which, as he points out in the Introduction to *Zulu Poems*, use the traditional device of understatement. Understatement of the grief felt by the poet is achieved by adopting an almost lighthearted sense of grievance against the dead person. The magnitude of death may be scaled down to seem equivalent to the embarrassing absence of the guest of honor from a feast, for which the poet reproves the dead one. "Elegy for My Friend E. Galo" chides the friend for dying "without my knowing" while the poet was out collecting firewood, buying expensive cattle, and preparing stories for the celebration. At the end, however, there is a bitterer tone, as the poet turns from the imagery of the feast to that of predatory locusts and "the discordant symphony of naked stars": what had been made to seem casual absence from a celebratory occasion is now recognized as part of the universal mortality of man and nature. "An Elegy to the Unknown Man Nicknamed Donda" is addressed not to the dead man but to the poet himself, as he muses on what he should do in his grief. He decides to take the elephant's advice to follow Donda into death, "the place of the setting sun." Death is again understated: here it seems to be just an everyday journey where one might meet an uncomprehending traveler. The ending this time recognizes not the universality of death, but its personal quality: one man's grief is another man's idle curiosity. In both these poems, the feeling is personal. In "Elegy for Msizi," however, the voice is largely a communal one, representing the grief of the Bhele clan. Msizi's fame and achievement are matched by the magnitude of grief felt for him, and the poet ends with a prophecy of the clan's future greatness. . . .

To compose a national epic demands both historical skills and literary courage of high order. Kunene's *Emperor Shaka the Great: A Zulu Epic* was a long time in gestation, not only in the sense that some of the materials used are over two centuries old but also in so far as Kunene's own composition spanned many years. In [a] 1966 interview with Alex La Guma . . . he said that he was writing this work, in Zulu, partly because he considered Shaka "a great political and military genius" and partly because he hoped, through a national epic, to "express the general experience of mankind," emphasizing "the oneness and the unity of man." This second reason is, in fact, a belief that he attributes to Shaka himself many times in the epic, for he presents Shaka as wishing neighboring peoples to live in peace (though under a strong unified leadership) and as respecting the customs (though not the acquisitiveness and ill manners) of white traders. A third reason lying behind Kunene's demanding and ambitious work is the respect he has for Shaka's court poet, Magolwane, "one of the greatest of African poets, indeed I would say one of the greatest world poets." To Magolwane he ascribes a revolution in Zulu poetry, including the introduction of political and social analysis, penetration of character, philosophical ideas, and abundant imagery (notably of ferocious animals). A great deal of Magolwane's "epic" or "poem of excellence" about Shaka (other writers call it a "praise-poem" or "praise-song") is in fact incorporated in Kunene's work. . . .

Kunene's shorter poems of the 1970s, many of them collected in his *The Ancestors & the Sacred Mountain*, concentrate on three main subjects. One large group is concerned with the liberation by bloodshed of South Africa, another looks forward millennially to the time after liberation (and sometimes looks beyond South Africa to the world and, indeed, the universe), and a third concerns the ecstatic nature of poetry. In these poems and the smaller groupings (such as the poems about individuals, the laments, the poems on motherhood, and the personal poems) the sense of the ancestors, observing and encouraging, is always present. In addition, some poems are directly about the ancestors or forefathers. They represent for Kunene the whole company of those ''who have made their contribution to human welfare and progress,'' as he says in the introduction to *The Ancestors*. It is to them and not to inventors of material improvements that the Zulus look for standards, guidance, and inspiration in continuing social life, and they treat them as a collective repository of wisdom rather than as a group of individual heroes. . . .

For Kunene, then, the social and cultural history of the Zulus as incorporated in the cult of the ancestors, can provide guidance, inspiration, and vision on every moral and political matter. Personal grief, insecurity, and even rage are swallowed up in a communal experience capable of producing the most intense ecstasy. The poet is possessed by a sexual and religious frenzy that authenticates and gives certitude to his message. Yet unlike the possession of, say, the Romantic poets, this is possession of a spokesman who has a social duty to announce truth to the clan. In this respect, it is like the traditional possession of the singer of an epic who ascribes the glory of the tale of the tribe to divine inspiration.

> K. L. Goodwin. *Understanding African Poetry* (London: Heinemann, 1982), pp. 175–78, 196–97, 200

The poems for Kunene's first volume in English, *Zulu Poems*, were taken from a larger selection he had originally written in Zulu, and were translated by the poet himself. His subsequent work in epic poetry was also first written in Zulu, though there is little chance of its being published in South Africa today. Kunene's allegiance as a poet, however, is to an African world-view rather than a particular African language. His purpose in translating, and therefore promulgating these poems among a larger audience, is to encourage a return to oral tradition in literature. . . .

Kunene's second epic, *Emperor Shaka the Great*, was published in 1979, again written first in Zulu and then translated by the poet himself. Running to more than 17,000 lines, it is a monumental work. It is the story of the great warrior king who united several Nguni tribes to form the Zulu nation. Again this is not an academic or chauvinistic attempt at historical or heroic preservation, but an imaginative interpretation of African philosophy. Kunene tries to replace what black South Africa lost under conquest: the feeling for the continuity of history, not as an object lesson for modern times, not as stimulus for nostalgia and pride, but as part of one's own life. He demonstrates how we live in the past and present, and thus shape our future. Through the knowledge of Shaka's vision, Kunene tells us in the introduction, many may understand the dreams and realities that have shaped the destinies of the peoples of Africa. In this respect it may possibly stand beside some of the world's great epics. This is something time will decide and it is impossible to make decisive comments so soon after publication of a work of this kind. Many rereadings will be required, together with a thorough study of the historical, linguistic, and philosophic background. Also a reading in the original language is probably

essential, even though Kunene's translation into English, is, as always, impeccable.

> Ursula A. Barnett. *A Vision of Order* (London: Sinclair Browne, 1983), pp. 104, 108

[*Zulu Poems*] was in no sense an urban poetry like that which was written in the townships from the middle of the 1960s: it did not reflect the African's confrontation with the white city and its restrictions; it contained no descriptions of the black ghettos or of humiliating contact with the whites. Several of the poems have a pastoral setting; they are concerned with nature, love, and friendship, with the cycle of seasons and the generations. Yet Kunene is not at all indifferent to what is going on in the world, especially in his own country, or to the clash of cultures. How could he be when for so long he traveled the world to bear witness against apartheid and concerned himself with the problems of the Third World?

But, by temperament and because . . . he has other platforms from which to express his political views, his poetry has no trace of the language of protest. He avoids the purely anecdotal and the abstract and seeks within his own culture the images, symbols, and metaphors which through their concreteness attain the universal. A quite definite elevation of thought runs through his poems and gives them their life, a combination of dignity and lyricism—a lyricism which is at times contained but which at others expresses itself with force and passion. Indeed, his criticism can be sharp. . . .

Committed Kunene certainly is, but in the best sense of the word. Beyond the ''situation'' itself, it is in the values of his own culture, through recourse in the first instance to his own language, that his commitment and resistance are expressed. Evidence of this is to be found in the lengthy introduction to *Zulu Poems*, which is a fascinating guide to his own civilization and an invitation to attempt a deeper understanding of his poetry. In spite of the geographical separation, the poet has remained in complete communion with his people. It is with the firm conviction that those who follow him will take up the torch that he writes ''To the Killer.'' . . .

Through his attachment to his mother tongue and to his African values, Kunene foreshadows the tendencies that will emerge fully into the open with black consciousness. He is not concerned with a love for the past or a return to a parochial view of culture harmful to the political battle of the present but with the urge to regain his dignity and force the white man to acknowledge the African, the ''other,'' he has so long ignored and humiliated.

> Jacques Alvarez-Pereyre. *The Poetry of Commitment in South Africa* (London: Heinemann, 1984), pp. 126–28

To Kunene, man is a multifaceted being with an expandable psychological universe which reaches out to various directions: the Earth, the Sun, the Moon, the Pleiades, the gods, and the Supreme Creator. The Earth is his focal point of operation, having within its folds the interrelated worlds of man (with its tangled historical experiences), water, plants, animals, and inanimate objects. Man relates harmoniously to these various elements because of the symmetry holding the components of the cosmos together. In other words, he forms part of the rhythm generated by the interaction of the forces of society and the cosmic system, which move cyclically in an ever-expanding process of life-death-rebirth. He is free when he operates in harmony with the forces and in chains when he is alienated from them. There is thus an interrelationship between human freedom and the cosmological canvas of man's existence.

This world-view permeates the creative consciousness of the African artist who generally stresses realism since man is basically earthbound, inextricably tied up to the destiny of society. Subjective effusions of emotions give way to more or less intellectualized expressions of group values. Literature therefore deals with "concrete events, concrete situations, and is firmly rooted in traceable social events. As in Chinese literature, the abstract is incidental."

This vision of African cosmology informs the metaphorical universe of *Zulu Poems*, which can be studied in three parts: the nature of the power structure of the apartheid regime, the African resistance to it, and Kunene's call for a universal brotherhood of man. . . .

Kunene . . . draws heavily from the African oral tradition in defending African civilization against the ravages of colonialism. And in doing so, he deploys the resources of Zulu cosmology in fighting against apartheid which he portrays as a horrendous system run by individuals who have dehumanized themselves by cutting themselves off from the fold of mankind through their subjugation of a segment of the South African population which, by cosmological design, forms an integral part of the South African society.

Kunene writes with a buoyant spirit and shows that life has glamor despite the determination of the Afrikaner settler regime to make it perpetually unbearable for the African. A nonconformist who is spiritually uncowed, he holds in contempt the self-proclaimed mission of the white racists to ensure the psychological enslavement of the African. He knows quite well that racism "is a dangerous superstition which has been used to define economic privilege and maintain exploitation." Accordingly, through his embodiment of the spirit of resistance of his people, he suggests in *Zulu Poems* that the apartheid regime will eventually succumb to the pressures of opposition mounted against it.

Chidi Maduka. *The Griot.* 4, 1–2 (1985), pp. 60–61, 70–71

[The] trend of Kunene's embellishment of Shaka [in *Emperor Shaka the Great*] is towards the exculpation of the public figure, and towards the "understanding" of the individual. The poet writes from the perspective of the ruling family, stressing Zulu— and by extension, African—values and continuities, and, as ruling families are apt to do, emphasizes nationalism. The pedagogical implication of the poem, looked at in Kunene's terms, is that it may broaden and deepen the understanding of the "children" it is addressed to. It does not aim at philosophically simplistic comprehensibility such as [the Nigerian critic] Chinweizu advocates, nor proletarian immediacy such as we find in Ngugi [wa Thiong'o]'s recent work. Yet events in South Africa as I write do *render* the themes of *Emperor Shaka the Great* relevant to the immediate experience of its readers, especially the actual children who are stoning the police and being shot in the townships. The poem is in Zulu (originally) and deals with a Zulu hero, but Shaka can no longer be seen as only Zulu since to a large extent he is now an African figure who transcends ethnic boundaries, and Zulu is a

language many non-Zulus speak. The poem has an obvious relation to the modern quest for black unity in South Africa, for organization and martial courage at a time when the conflict is becoming more violent, when anti-apartheid parties are still not united, and when a significant number of blacks man the armed forces and the police. . . .

We learn from this poem to see Shaka from a particular point of view, one possibly very close to his own view of himself; but we do not passively "swallow" this, as Kunene the propagandist would perhaps wish. Kunene the *poet* goes deeper and is more compelling. He does affect his readers, but how this relates to their everyday political and personal lives remains very obscure. The ancient question (which we find also in Shakespeare, whose ideology is not so far from Kunene's) about the difference between poetic and other kinds of communication comes back to us again. . . . [Although] African poets, and other literary artists and critics, have emphasized the pedagogical role of the writer, they have not yet sorted out what this role consists in, what kinds of communication are possible, what literary discourses are like and how they mesh with educational systems, political movements, and so on. There is always a difference between what you may wish to teach me and what I may wish to learn from your trying to do that.

John Haynes. *Ariel.* 18, 1 (January 1987), pp. 48–50

Mazisi Kunene's poetry is ultimately hopeful, but he admits in "Journey into the Morning" that "the vision of a new era is born of the nightmare". That nightmare will, he tells us—albeit briefly— in other poems, entail violence. "First Day after the War," "To a Friend Whose Family Was Killed," and "Brave People" all allude to the fighting that will be necessary; "The Rise of the Angry Generation" refers to the blood "red feathers" (7) of the "great eagle" (1) that is emblematic throughout Kunene's poetry of the new black nation. "Victim" is more explicit, speaking about "[t]he child [who] has chosen to avenge his parent" (18); both that poem and "252 or' At the End of a Volume" refer to the violent explosions that will accompany the emergence of the new black nation. Still more explicit is "The Torturer," in which Kunene declares:

> You will die early at dawn
> When the sun is red and the children are walking
> And people are shouting to the morning.
> You will die at dawn
> When the crowds are running to the festival. (1–5)

Late in [*The Ancestors & the Sacred Mountain*], Kunene seems to take inspiration from the children of Soweto. "From them," the poet says in "Vision of Peace," "we must learn to create the unending movement". To do so, his fellow black South Africans must listen to the "curse" that the dying children uttered:

> "Those who have killed without mercy,
> Those who are without fear of the victim's eyes,
> Those who laugh at the tumbling skulls,
> Shall walk the chameleon's path into the holocaust"

Kunene, however, devotes relatively little time to discussing these violent prospects; similarly, he devotes relatively little to indicting either the white oppressor or blacks who have "sold out" to

Western ways. Most of *The Ancestors & the Sacred Mountain* is devoted to presenting a rich, elaborate vision of the emergence of a glorious African nation in what is presently South Africa. . . .

Kunene suggests that, for a time, the African spirit has been asleep. Now, however, that spirit is awakening. The spirit seems to find its origin in the earth and, more particularly, in the grand mountains that thrust the earth upward into the skies and toward the sun. The spirit is that of the ancestors, and they, although dead, reside in these mountains. The mountains are, thus, sacred, and, from them, descend the waters that are also sacred. Kunene's poetry speaks often of ''morning'' and ''birth'' and he associates the new generation of black South Africans with these beginnings. The present generation—*his* generation—has lost the African spirit of the ancestors; the new generation, however, has rediscovered this spirit. That rediscovery is the occasion for celebrating, feasting. Kunene figures this rebirth, early in the collection, by talking about the eagle's triumphant flight. Later in the collection, Kunene re-figures the rebirth in cosmic terms: the rebirth of the African spirit is akin to the birth of a new planet. . . .

''A Heritage of Liberation'' leads off the collection. The poem is addressed to Kunene's contemporaries, telling them that they must ''Take these weapons for our children's children''. The ''weapons'' are not, however, guns but, rather, the legends from the ancestors. As Kunene and his brethren retell these stories of freedom fighting from the past, they will ''let our children live with our voices''. Kunene goes further. So that ''generations hereafter / May inherit our dream of the festival'', Kunene's generation ''must follow the trail of the killer-bird'' into revolutionary action. If not, both they and their children will ''sleep the sleep of terror''. Kunene and his fellows may well die in the fighting; if they do, he tells the new generation to ''bury us in the mountain'', which is sacred. Through their fighting and perhaps their death, they will ''bequeath to you [the new generation] the rays of the morning''.

''A Heritage of Liberation'' refers to the eagle; ''The Rise of the Angry Generation'' uses that fierce but beautiful bird as its central image. The eagle, symbolic of the black African people, will build ''its nest with old leaves'' (suggesting the lore of the African past), inspired by ''the dream'' and focused on the glorious ''morning'' that is to come. From this nest will emerge ''the mysterious young bird'' (10). At this birth, ''The once proud planet shrieks in terror'', for the planet knows that ''the merciless talons of the new generation'' will ''not [be] deterred by false tears'' and will *act* exhibiting ''the wrath of the volcanic mountains'' and ''the abiding anger of the Ancestral Forefathers''.

Both of these early poems in Kunene's collection present his vision with a violent edge. More pacific is ''Journey to the Sacred Mountains''. In this poem, the persona narrates an imagined journey into the mountains where the ancestors ''walk eternally on earth''. Among them are ''The Holy Ones'', and they speak. Notice how the images of mountains and water are used:

Their voices broke through the waterfalls
Anthems echoed from the mountains
They eddied to the horizon like a great wave.

''The whole earth was [then] enveloped in their dream'', the persona tells us. . . .

Another poem, ''Phakeni's Farewell,'' a ''Tribute to Robert Rasha, one of South Africa's greatest political leaders,'' is neither as violent as the first two poems we considered nor as peaceful as

''Journey to the Sacred Mountains.'' Reading ''Phakeni's Farewell,'' we find ourselves in the chaos before ''a gathering storm''. In this chaos, the poet notes, ''the ancestral song is heard'', the eagle can be seen soaring above. However, *this* generation seems trapped in chaos; hope is to be found in ''the new generations.''. . .

The philosopher-poet will, as Kunene sees matters, play a crucial role in the development of this future. He speaks of this role in ''The Maturation of a Philosopher-Poet.'' His ''day of greatness has come''. Like a bird, he will sing. ''The children of the earth have assembled'', Kunene tells us, to hear the song. . . .

The new generation will restore what *once* was; Kunene's generation will serve as midwives or prophets or heralds or the martyred initial wave of troops.

''My Swazi Boy or Song of the Frogs'' seems to look at the role Kunene's generation will play from the perspective of the new generation. The persona seems to be that of a young boy, who has been affected by the ''eyes'' and the ''lightning'' of a stranger. This stranger offers ''fingers [that] heal the pain'' and a ''face'' that refreshes ''like a spring''. This stranger's ''body glistened at the first sign of the morning''. This stranger's mission seems to be to carry the young boy across ''the river of dreams'' and then to give him ''an eternity of light burning from the mountain'' of the ancestors. In other words, the stranger is the philosopher-poet of Kunene's generation who connects the ancestors and their noble dreams with the new generation of Africans who will renew those dreams.

The time when ancestors and the new generation connect is referred to as ''Communion'' in Kunene's poem by that title. The poem features three voices. The first, that of the intermediate generation, narrates. The second, that of the ancestors, prophesies an ''Ancestral festival'' when the symbolic rains will come, the voice of ''the mountain-singer'' will be recalled, and ''You shall regain the power of the dream''. The third voice, a child's, delivers the poem's closing lines, although her words and the those of the Ancestors are ambiguously merged at the very end. . . .

The ancestors and the new generations have found communion here, even in the way their words join in announcing the destruction of white South Africa and the emergence of something momentously new afterwards.

Kunene's vision of ''a new earth,'' expressed in this poem and others, suggests that his vision extends beyond South Africa. And it does. Not surprisingly, given that he settled in the United States after departing South Africa, some of his poems deal with the oppressive actions of the United States government. He talks about U.S. involvement in Vietnam in neo-imperialistic terms; in ''To a Navaho Boy Playing a Flute,'' he uses the same terms that he uses in poem after poem about South Africa to deal with the relations between the American government and its native people. A young boy leads the persona to the mountain and ''the feast of the Forefathers'', who reside there. If the persona can ''learn the poems of the Dead'', then there is rain, there is dreaming, there is singing, there is a new morning, and there is even a sense of the planet—maybe even the universe—renewing itself. Kunene's vision then is quite transferable, quite global. . . .

The last two poems we will discuss, ''The Return of Inspiration'' and ''In Praise of the Ancestors,'' present that search as ultimately successful. In the first poem, ''a great singer'' from the past leads the persona to the sacred mountain. There, ''my powers broke open'' from ''the wombs of the earth''. These powers are depicted as ''travelling up and down my body, / . . . like a clan of ants lost in a forest''. So empowered, the persona ''hurried to the ancestral place / Where all fears are banished through courage''. There, he seizes his ''grandfather's great ugubhu'', a stringed instrument, and is ''seized by the ecstasy of the song''. Through this song, he is led to ''the ancestral shrines'', where his ''heart was opened'' and he saw the ancestral spirit incarnate and ''glowing dream''. . . .

The ancestral spirit informs the inspiring dream of a new African nation. This spirit emanates from the earth, if not from the primal dust out of which the universe was formed. The spirit, once it informs a nation, will provide shelter. Led by visionaries of Kunene's generation, the new generation will recover the greatness of the ancestors in this new land.

Theodore F. Sheckels. *The Lion on the Freeway: A Thematic Introduction to Contemporary South African Literature in English* (New York: Peter Lary Publishing, Inc., 1996), pp. 222–31

BIBLIOGRAPHY
*Zulu Poems*, 1970; *Emperor Shaka the Great: A Zulu Epic*, 1979; *Anthem of the Decades: A Zulu Epic*, 1981; *The Ancestors & the Sacred Mountain*, 1982; *Isibusiso Sikamhawu*, 1994; *Umzwilili Wama-Afrika*, 1996

# L

## LABOU TANSI, Sony (1947– )
### Congo

[Sony Labou Tansi's] *Je Soussignée Cardiaque* presents the drama of a school-teacher, Mallot, who refuses to submit to the master of the place where he has just been appointed. . . .

Refusing to submit to the whims of this ridiculous despot, just as he had earlier refused to submit to other insupportable powers, Mallot is obliged to leave the village with his pregnant wife and daughter.

Fighting against destiny—his destiny—even though he does not wish to be a hero, Mallot revolts. He asks for a certificate of incapacity, obtains it, and, thus hoping to escape the trap of the net, goes to the ministry in order to meet the Director General of Education. There, too, he meets with defeat.

Thus, from refusal to revolt, he, who three times and in different ways declared his independence and his desire to be free, finds himself in prison. This is how he appears in the first scene, which introduces the narration of his revolt seen in the form of a dream. It is in his cell that we find him in the last scene. "Mon papa a ratée sa Nelly" [My father failed his Nelly], he says to his daughter before the soldiers in charge of his execution come to fetch him.

> Bernard Magnier. *Presence Africaine*. 120 (1981), p. 98†

Sony Labou Tansi's novel [*La Vie et demie*] opens with a scene of such intensity as is rarely achieved in literature: The tyrant of an African kingdom has just seized his most active opponent.

From the first pages of the novel, we enter into the style and language particular to this young author: a violent, stormy style scattered by lightning flashes of serene poetry, and a language dramatically altered by his triumphant Africanness.

We penetrate into the universe of this novel, midway . . . between the cruelest of political realities and its universal and mythic transposition. Martial, the symbol of immortal liberty, is sadistically massacred by the tyrant who cannot overcome his indestructible refusal. Along with the rest of her family, Chaïdana, Martial's daughter, has to feed on the corpse of the assassinated father.

The cruelty of the tyrant rebounds on him. Chaïdana, endowed with "a corpse and a half," is henceforth her father. She takes up the battle using other, less political means of which Martial, the hero, disapproves. He reproaches her throughout the novel by means of symbolic and memorable slaps. As for the tyrant, who is marked by the seal of "the black of Martial," the indelible color that reveals his crime, he slowly loses his reason, subjected to the terrifying appearances of the hacked-up corpse of his enemy. Martial, after his death, has definitively opted for a charismatic and quasi-messianic personality, appropriate for galvanizing the oppressed masses. His prophetic phrase: "I don't want to die this death," becomes the symbol of active revolt, whereas the "black of Martial" becomes the forbidden color.

Using her incomparable, "formal" beauty, Chaïdana assassinates all the members of the government and becomes the tyrant's own wife, wife of her father's assassin. Slowly, her vengeance grows, and the hatred of this overfull, almost double body invades the heroine, and she feels raped by the incestuous phantom.

Following a monstrous pregnancy, Chaïdana gives birth to triplets, two boys and a girl, also called Chaïdana.

Sony Labou Tansi's novel abandons the tone of sarcastic criticism that is found in the first part and henceforth moves to a rhythm of an African "shamanist" mystique. . . .

The entire last part of the novel is almost impossible to summarize. It is a bloody, disorderly chronicle, marked by the seal of the tragic insanity of the leaders of total derisive power. "Martial's People," the opponents, tortured, mutilated, and decimated, continue to resist. . . .

The author succeeds, with a single sentence, in situating his narration in the antediluvian past. "Thus was born the Nile." However, he does not succeed (does he wish to?) in making us forget that the fable and the tale offer, in colonized countries with oral traditions, symbolic and sarcastic reflections of social reality.

Nevertheless, he takes care in warning us that the tale is not a tract: "The day that I will be given the opportunity to speak of a somebody today, I will not take a thousand paths, especially a path as torturous as the Fable."

In any case, as an African, he chooses African images that deal with the universal contradiction between opposition and revolt, tyranny and battle, in his culture.

Inventor of language, of myths, and a caustic contemporary griot, Sony Labou Tansi undertakes, in this novel overflowing with a healthy and corrosive humor, an astonishing dialogue with the human.

> Ina Césaire. *Presence Africaine*. 129 (1984), pp. 163–65†

Labou Tansi lacks the stature of his Nigerian counterpart [Wole Soyinka] but has nevertheless produced an impressive body of plays and novels. With subtlety and grace of style, his latest novel, *L'Anté-peuple*, eases us into a world of deceptive assurances. Dadou, a director of a girls' training school, finds himself the object of a student's infatuation. Gradually and inexorably, with that same sense of obsession which characterizes the more heavily allegorical novels *The Voice* [by Gabriel Okara] and *La Plaie* [by Malick Fall], Dadou falls into patterns of self-destructive behavior and, equally passively, falls victim to a sequence of disasters which spring as much from the failings of men as from the workings of a malevolent society. The hint of a fallen universe that lies behind this social decadence is repeatedly echoed: realism yields to satire, defined by the image of a world far worse than that of our experience.

At times, and not always with complete success, we leave the flow of mimetic narration for a heightened, poeticized series of reflections whose effect is to break the sense of a chain of experienced events and to install in its place a symbol for experience. There is, as a consequence, the haunting feeling of unreality, an unreality disturbingly echoed in many strains of Congolese or Zairoese literature—notably in the works of [V.Y.] Mudimbe, but also in Henry Lopes and Tchicaya U Tam'si. What this recent body of works has constructed is the image of an upended society, often electric and dangerous, as in the most modern mechanism of power and its dynamics in contemporary Zaire, of life flickering in the muscled rhythms of the crowded streets, bars, and nightclubs—but especially in the wrenching malaise of despair. The course of events which complete Dadou's decline are eventually cast into the mold of a prehistory in which the *anté-peuple* are left awaiting some divine intervention to put an end to a desperate state of affairs apparently beyond the powers of human beings to repair.

> Kenneth Harrow. *World Literature Today.* 58, 2 (Spring 1984), p. 316

Sony Labou Tansi burst on the literary scene in 1979 with the astonishing novel *La Vie et demie* and continues, with each succeeding work, to confirm his prodigious talent. Set in an indeterminate African country sometime after independence from its colonial occupiers, his fourth novel [*Les Sept Solitudes de Lorsa Lopez*] pursues (albeit somewhat more diffusely) the theme of profound disenchantment with the new indigenous regimes which have replaced the former European ones. Rather than depict a bloodthirsty and grotesque tyrant opposed to the forces of decency, as he did in *La Vie et demie* or in *L'État honteux*, the novelist here establishes a moral dichotomy in the opposition between the high-principled coast and the brutal and venal interior of his nameless and troubled land.

Even here, however, the people of the coastal city and former capital Valancia have undergone a kind of degradation since the transfer of the capital inland to Nsanga-Norda. A series of murders, beginning with the unspeakable, atrocious crime committed by the eponymous Lorsa Lopez, are met with silence born of fear by a population that once prided itself on its integrity and love of truth. In the end, it is above all the women of Valancia, led by the remarkable Estina Bronzario (the name describes the woman), who possess the strength to stand up to the despotic authorities of Nsanga-Norda. Though the latter ultimately have Bronzario assassinated because, as she explains, ''of the privileged relations we have with the truth,'' the ruthless forces of guns and money receive their just deserts as the sea completely inundates Nsanga-Norda. . . .

[No] summary of events can possibly capture the extravagant nature of the author's fertile imagination or his inspired verbal inventiveness. Infused with vigorous and colorful dialogue, neologisms and enumerations, startling images, humor, and trenchant satire (a parrot is tried for murder), the whole takes on mythological dimensions in a larger-than-life Estina Bronzario or in cliffs that cry out their anguish before man's inhumanity to man. Like those cliffs, Sony Labou Tansi shouts (''mon écriture sera plutôt crié'') his distress but also his abiding hope (he sees despair as an ''absurdity'') in this parable of cowardice and courage.

> Fredric Michelman. *World Literature Today.*, 61, 1, (Winter 1987), p. 142

In undertaking the reading of Sony Labou Tansi's novel *L'Anté-peuple*, we propose two essential objectives: firstly, to respect the work keeping in view our position of an observer unfamiliar to African, albeit francophone, literature, and [secondly] to establish a significant rapport between the work studied and us.

It is in this manner that we will attempt to express all that we derive from this novel and to learn of the degradation of a social system which plunges an individual into the absurdity of an existence ruled by impulses that emerge onto a chaos that is uncontrollable. Nevertheless, the same individual fights against disorder in order to establish the triumph of the supreme values emanating from him and which is the quest of the truth governing the entire work. . . .

All social life is regulated by a series of laws and tacit and non-tacit rules. Its occurrence is harmonious if the rights and social duties are a means to better maintain peace and security. . . .

It is easy to establish the transgression of these elementary laws. The rationale is supplanted by emotion, truth by lies; in short, the protection of the individual loses its consistency without the ability to master the law fundamental to existence.

Let us follow the path of the characters who are victims of this diversion of the law. By order of entry into the narration, it is Dadou, Yealdara, Maître Malvoisi, and the prison director. . . . Whether it is the director of a school, a sociologist, or a lawyer, each of these characters finds himself confronting a system rendered absurd and ridiculous due to its inconsequence. Dadou, for example, fights against emotion by forbidding himself from succumbing to the advances of Yavelde. Yealdara, revolted by the injustice that has befallen Dadou, renounces the privileges offered to her by her family and leaves them. Maître Malvoisi has no apparent reason to defend his client except the concern to see justice done. . . . As for the prison director, because he is suspected of sympathy for Dadou, he is accused of a completely imaginary conspiracy and when given the alternatives of imprisonment or escape, he can only choose the latter. . . .

Facing these characters who act in good faith are those individuals who, thanks to their power, adapt the laws to suit their fancy, thereby bringing about the downfall of certain others.

Characters whose behavior is dictated by impulsive and tyrannical personal interest are, among others, Yavelde, Nioka Musanar, and the berets. Yavelde, for example, cannot understand how her director can refuse her advances. Incapable of understanding his point of view, she seeks to avenge herself by abusing her social privileges, which are considerable if one recalls that her uncle is the commissioner of the zone. In Machiavellian fashion, she commits suicide after having accused Dadou of forcing her to have an abortion. . . . As for Nioka Musanar, he plays a direct role in the future of the defendants, who are equally condemned to their destruction. . . .

Dadou, Yealdara, the director, and the others whose lives are deeply compromised, are not beings limited by their actions. On the contrary, they serve as the arm of the lever of a movement which will reestablish justice and truth in general. This victory over the irrational is purely imaginary since it is the result of a dream, but it is a dream filled with hope. . . .

Sony Labou Tansi is above all a novelist; it is with a stormy imagination in the service of self-respect that he takes us into his domain, which is that of language. The language is that of an embittered man who denounces in all forms hypocrisy, mediocrity, and impulsiveness. However, we could not understand the message of the novelist if he did not make reference to a reality that flows from experience. Henceforth his work is the privileged moment where experience passes through the aesthetic of language. In the same way, the narration returns to life through us, the readers, who capture it as narrated time. It is from this point that we pass from fiction to reality. This leads us to believe that Sony Labou Tansi, by the madness of his words and situations, leads us to put an end to a degraded and corrupted reality in order to reinvent a new world.

Nadine Fettweis. *Zaire Afrique.* May 1989. pp. 247, 249–51, 260†

The form and language of *La Vie et demie* are . . . indicative of contemporary trends in African fiction that [takes] neocolonialism as its focus. With regard to narrative form, we note that Sony Labou Tansi refers to his narrative in the *avertissement* as a fable, a form both didactic and ''ideal.'' That is to say, the narrative manifests no conventional sense of what is realistic. Following the example of [Gabriel] García Márquez and of many tales of the oral tradition, *La Vie et demie* ''dwells in possibility,'' a fertile ground for that very imagination so beset by Katamalanasia. Thus Sony Labou Tansi proposes tyrants who, in their crassness, are of the same ilk as Ubu Roi and who, in their enormity, are of the same size as Gargantua. The narrative abandons the canons of realism that governed fiction in the 1950s and 1960s. . . .

As for the language of *La Vie et demie*, its subversive character resides, first of all, in its abundant irony. . . . [It] is obvious that the regime's language, in view of itself and of Katamalanasia, self-destructs for the reader (as for the citizens) when it is held up to ''ce qui existe.'' The novel plays on the incongruency between Katamalanasian reality and terms and phrases such as ''le Guide Providentiel'' or ''on interdit la douleur sur toute l'étendue du pays.'' The narrator's pervasive neologism, *excellentiel*, is equally trenchant.

Yet there is a still more sophisticated arsenal of verbal and narrative procedures that convey the bankruptcy of Katamalanasia. *La Vie et demie* juxtaposes logic and illogic, measure and the immeasurable, seriousness and folly. This alternation is manifested verbally in the text's absolute precision, on the one hand, and its repetition *ad nauseum*, on the other. The text obeys both these apparently opposing impulses, and yet, for the purpose of Sony Labou Tansi's fable, they are complementary, for the first suggests a matter-of-fact, ordinary reality, while the second gives the narrative its dimension of the fantastic. Indeed, the presence of both impulses suggests the tension between narrative as (empirical) chronicle and as (ideal) fable and thereby recalls the problematic of contemporary African fiction to which Ngugi [wa Thiong'o] refers. The tension between verbal empiricism and extravagance is sublimely comic and absurd. . . .

*La Vie et demie* is thus discourse about the betrayal of discourse. But the untrustworthiness of language does not become a source of profound disillusionment and doubt as it does in the theater of the absurd and poststructuralism. Because language disorder is contextualized in Sony Labou Tansi's novel, verbal *délire* suggests neither that language is ontologically empty nor that life is metaphysically problematic. Indeed, many texts by African and diaspora writers caution against blind faith in discourse that serves power: the racist, colonial discourse ([Ferdinand] Oyono, [Aimé] Césaire), a capitalist or religious discourse (Sémbène [Ousmane]), the male discourse ([Buchi] Emecheta). Yet for all these writers, there is faith in language and discourse: texts, like *La Vie et demie*, that demonstrate the unbelievability and violence of colonial and

neocolonial discourses, are texts which also believe in their own words, the power of their words to portray truth, to be heard or read, to make a difference.

Eileen Julien. *Research in African Literatures.* 20, 3 (Fall 1989), pp. 379, 382

Labou Tansi's creative voice is one of the most vital of this decade in African letters. A playwright and theater director in Brazzaville, his literary production also includes four novels, all written since 1979: *La Vie et demie, L'État honteux, L'Anté-peuple* and *Les Sept Solitudes de Lorsa Lopez.* With the English translation of *L'Anté-peuple* in 1988, his fiction is reaching an even broader public. In each of the novels, Labou Tansi continues to expand the conventions of the postmodern novel. . . .

In *Les Sept Solitudes*, the heroine and her community must now confront a postcolonial bureaucracy with its residue of dishonor, corruption, and political abuses. In this fictional world, male discourse—the discourse of authority and power—destroys both history and women. Not only is the wife of Lorsa Lopez brutally killed; the collective history of the people is also destroyed. The capital city and all its monuments and historic artifacts are moved, ''decapitalized'' for the seventh time, to a new seat of government in another city. Countering this dissolution is the mediating voice of the heroine, Estina Bronzario. She creates history, rather than destroys it, and binds it to stability, continuity, and social cohesion—the values prized by traditional societies. . . .

Labou Tansi sets *Les Sept Solitudes de Lorsa Lopez* in a generic mode appropriate to a politics of resistance, to the mode of exuberant satire. Yet he also draws on the conventions of several other literary traditions, especially the fable, fantastic literature, and oral literature, with their repetitions, cycles, incantations, and Rabelaisian accumulations. When compared with *L'Anté-peuple*, the severe linearity of male discourse that shaped the latter work appears to give way at the level of structure and narrative voice to a resistant, feminine discourse. The latter discursive mode allows Sony Labou Tansi to achieve what he sets out to do. . . .

Thus, Labou Tansi opts for a position familiar to the critics of contemporary aesthetic discourse. He rejects a neocolonial paradigm of centrality that ''takes the rest of the world as its body, extension and periphery.'' He prefers instead a new center, one peopled by those who can ''name'' and ''breathe,'' for they are the ones who also know liberation. Yealdara of *L'Anté-peuple* gives us an intimation of what it means to be able to name and breathe in new ways. With *Les Sept Solitudes de Lorsa Lopez*, the centrality of Estina Bronzario and her capacity to rename is beyond question. The two novels demonstrate in quite distinctive ways how the structure and resolution of the narratives have been informed by women, in one instance through the prism of male discourse, in the other through women's liberating discourse of resistance.

Louise Fiber Luce. *French Review.* 64, 5 (April 1991), pp. 739, 745–46

BIBLIOGRAPHY
*Conscience de Tracteur*, 1979; *La Vie et demie* (Life and a Half), 1979; *Je Soussigné Cardiaque* (I the Undersigned Cardiac), 1981; *L'État honteux* (The State of Shame ), 1981; *L'Anté-peuple* (The Antipeople), 1983; *Parentheses of Blood*, 1985; *Les Sept Solitudes*

*de Lorsa Lopez* (The Seven Solitudes of Lorsa Lopez), 1985 *Les Yeux du Volcan*, 1988; *Le Commencement des Douleurs*, 1995

# LA GUMA, Alex (1925–1985)

## South Africa

The landscape of [Alex La Guma's early fiction] is invariably urban and unrelentingly sordid. Not for him is there any escape to the white suburbs or to the noble landscapes where one can momentarily forget the South African tragedy. And for his characters too, there is often only the escape of death. Their poverty and abandonment have no other end. *A Walk in the Night* begins as the story of Michael Adonis's aimless journey through District Six, but in the course of the narrative we have a sense of all its characters locked in similarly random and wasting motion. Willieboy's own journey ends in the back of a police truck and Doughty's at the end of a bottle. Adonis is clearly destined to drift into violent crime and towards a violent end. Foxy and his depraved gang move through the plot like a sinister chorus, looking vainly for Sockies. Only the orphaned Joe, the most destitute of all, has any sense of dimension extending beyond Hanover Street, with its filthy alleys and the illusory promise of its neon signs. But he is unable to convey his sense of this to the damned spirits who walk the dark labyrinth of these streets. His sense of wonder is as lost upon them as his sense of nature. . . .

Whereas many of [La Guma's] short stories exhibit an ironic humor, *A Walk in the Night* is a somber work, as dark as the streets through which its action is threaded. Those exhibiting random acts of charity, like Adonis, are also capable of random acts of violence. Constable Raalt is capable of little else but brutality, through which he channels all his rage at his inadequacies as a husband. The young police driver will, we are sure, soon pick up the brutal attitudes and corrupt practices of his senior. The only glimpses of a fuller humanity are in the marginal characters of Frankie Lorenzo and his wife (who play no part in the action) and Joe. . . .

Unlike the ironic commentary which characterizes the early stories the increased scope of the novel brings from the author a greater degree of commitment. If *A Walk in the Night* shows us characters caught up in an inexorable fate, *And a Threefold Cord* indicates more possibilities of choice and development, even though its actors are sunk lower still in poverty and abandonment than those of the earlier book.

Structurally, the new novel also differs considerably from its predecessor. *A Walk in the Night*, as befits its title, is confined to the events of a single night as well as those of a single district. But, although it starts by following the footsteps of Michael Adonis, it soon broadens out to show us other actors who are likewise "doomed to fast in fires," so that the center of the narrative's attention is continually shifting. *And a Threefold Cord* offers the same concentration of venue and concerns the events of a few days only, but it is more exclusively centered upon the consciousness of Charlie Pauls. In this sense, it may be said to have a "hero." All the other figures who appear in the book, from the Pauls family through their African and colored neighbors to Susie Meyer, the poor-white wreck George Mostert and the white policeman felled by Charlie's heavy fist, are connected with his movements around the shantytown in the brief time span of the plot. . . .

As already suggested, each of La Guma's novels establishes a distinctive, closed world and confines its actions entirely within it. This confinement reaches its logical conclusion in his third novel, *The Stone Country*. The panorama of fiction can be internal as well as external, and we need not traverse the steppes of Russia or the battlefields of Napoleonic Europe to encounter examples of every sort of human personality in action. It is a true if sad comment on twentieth-century literature, that many of its finest novels have accepted the walls of a prison, a labor camp, or a hospital as the limits of a sufficient world; for the prisoner or patient at least knows precisely what he longs for, which is often more than the free man can boast of. . . .

In 1979, after a silence of seven years, La Guma published a short novel which marks, in some respects, a return to the manner of his short stories and of *A Walk in the Night*. Whereas *In the Fog of the Seasons' End* traces a developing situation which begins with the arrest of Elias and ends with his death and the safe departure of the young guerrillas, *Time of the Butcherbird* centers upon a single episode. That episode is the murder—or perhaps the execution—of the nationalist politician Hannes Meulen. We sense its approach from almost the first page; thereafter we merely follow the gradually converging movements of Meulen and his assassin until their explosive encounter. . . .

*Time of the Butcherbird* is remarkable not only for the density with which it recalls rural South Africa after thirteen years of exile and for the sureness of its touch with all the inhabitants of the wretched little *dorp*, but for the poetic interpretation of landscape and action. This is particularly evident on the first page and the last, and in all those intervening sequences which involve Murile with the old shepherd Madolena. The story ends with these two setting out across the scorched *veld*.

Gerald Moore. *Twelve African Writers* (Bloomington: Indiana University Press, 1980), pp. 108–11, 113, 118, 120

La Guma's writing career began in 1956 when he joined the staff of a progressive newspaper, *New Age*, for which he wrote striking vignettes about life in Cape Town. However, when he was forced to abandon journalism in 1962 because shortage of funds forced the newspaper to reduce drastically its staff, La Guma became completely isolated from his community; his house arrest precluded any re-employment and participation in the social and political life of his country, and because he was a banned person, all his novels were published outside South Africa. *A Walk in the Night* was published in Nigeria, *And a Threefold Cord* and *The Stone Country* in Berlin, *In the Fog of the Seasons' End* in New York, and *Time of the Butcherbird* in London.

His novels graphically depict various facets of South Africa's disfranchised population: his first novel draws a portrait of the precarious and alienated life in the slums of Cape Town; his second records the dignified attempt of shantytown dwellers to survive amidst hunger, apartheid, and the winter; *The Stone Country* depicts life in a South African jail; his fourth and best novel [*In the Fog of the Seasons' End*] . . . describes a few days in the life of a man working in the political underground; and the latest novel [*Time of the Butcherbird*] depicts the poverty to which rural black South Africans are consigned and their powerful desire to seek revenge for their oppression. In spite of their diversity, all these novels have one fundamental factor in common: the marginality of life for the nonwhite in South Africa. Although not all his novels take up the theme of marginality, they inevitably end up commenting on and indirectly depicting the material, social, political, and spiritual poverty to which apartheid relegates the darker, "inferior" people. Thus La Guma's novels constitute a transformed, fictive version of his own marginality, which initially consists in his social and political disfranchisement and then is followed by his enforced internal isolation and later "voluntary" external exile. His personal experience of exclusion from a full and free life is only a more dramatic version of the exclusion experienced by all nonwhite South Africans. His novels, then, represent the effects of the manichean bifurcation imposed by apartheid. . . .

[*In the Fog of the Seasons' End*] extends and clarifies the different preoccupations of his earlier novels. What had previously been an opposition between the assumption that individuals have a right of access to certain basic forms of self-fulfillment and the *deprivation* of this right, with the major stress falling on the latter, now becomes an overt and explicit struggle between the colonized nonwhite and the colonizing white sections of the South African population: the initial overt statement of the issues involved in this fight, in the form of a brief debate between a political prisoner, Elias, and a major in the secret police, is followed by the story of a sustained struggle between the police and one cell of an underground revolutionary movement which is attempting to depose the South African government. Yet since the depiction of this struggle necessarily involves some cloak-and-dagger scenes, La Guma cautiously avoids sensationalism by understating the drama, by making his characters weary rather than elated, and by ironically equating the precarious conditions of the fight to the unreality of "gangster" and "western" films, which will restore one to the normal world of complex reality at the end. He is perfectly able to eschew a romantic view of revolution, for by the end of the novel one is left with a feeling of an arduous and political struggle that will probably kill all the protagonists and continue into the next generation.

Abdul R. JanMohamed. *Boundary 2*. 11, 1–2 (1982–1983), pp. 273–74, 279–80

La Guma's *In the Fog of the Seasons' End* does not trace the whole evolution of the black man on the continent but, through Beukes (the main character of the novel), La Guma strives to show every African's effort to overthrow the invaders' rule. Beukes and his companions are not just fighting for the liberation of South Africa: they embody the courage and determination of freedom fighters all over the continent. Various battlefields such as Namibia, Angola, Mozambique and so on are still lingering in our minds. La Guma, in focusing on Baukes's urban guerrilla warfare does not intend to put the first stages of African history (slavery and colonization) into brackets but to underscore . . . that the question of the total liberation of Africa is no longer vested in supermen or heroes but in the common people. . . .

[In *In the Fog of the Seasons' End*] the characters . . . show [a] high sense of solidarity in their fight against the apartheid system which indistinctively casts individuals of different social strata—doctors, dentists, teachers, factory workers, messengers, taxi drivers—in the same mold only because they are black. They all contribute to some extent (and according to their particular skills) to the success of the underground movement: most of them for political reasons and some for sentimental ones. The patent illustration of the second category of fighters is revealed through the

portraits of Henry April, the van driver who serves as a link between the nationalists "inside" and "outside" the country, and of Tommy, the dancer, who nevertheless takes part, in his own way, in the fight. . . .

Christophe Dailly. *Presence Africaine*. 130 (1984), pp. 124–25, 128

Since La Guma's novels are written about a society which has made racial divisions mandatory, it is to be expected that they will contain references to race-based ideologies which create different perspectives of the same experience. In both *In the Fog of the Seasons' End* and *Time of the Butcherbird*, English-speaking whites regard the countryside as something entirely apart from them. For Edgar Stopes it is *bundu* inhabited by "bloody Dutchmen . . . not like us, modern, up-to-date." In the earlier novel when Beukes sits wounded outside a suburban garden in a white suburb, he listens to the conversation of young white English speakers inside. One characterizes Frikkie as a farmer who smells of sheep all the time; another defends him: "Don't be silly, he doesn't go near the farm." That brief spat operates within a single ideological framework. Frikkie is condemned because he is rural; he is defended because he keeps as far away from his farm as he possibly can. It is implied in the context that Frikkie is rich and he is defended precisely because his money does not come from his own labor. He is acceptable because it is only money which links him with the land. Far from turning to the land for some saving perspective, the rejection of the land by Edgar and these young whites is total. If we are going to look in the novels for conventional expressions of pastoral it will certainly not be among La Guma's English-speaking characters. In the novels they are represented as being entirely urban. . . .

The conventional location of pastoral art—the countryside—is more obviously present in *Time of the Butcherbird* than in [*In the Fog of the Seasons' End*]. . . . Although some of the novel is set in Johannesburg, its principal setting is a drought-stricken rural area where both the Afrikaner community and Hlangeni's people (as the whites call them) respond in their different ways to the drought. For the blacks the ordinary problem of survival in the few hectares which have been left them becomes even more acute. For the Afrikaners, the drought provides an opportunity to assert their sense of community in their prayers for rain and allows the dominee to claim the drought as a manifestation of God's anger and to pronounce judgement on the evils of the cities. "There is corruption in our cities," he says and goes on to assert that for the Afrikaners the land itself is Jerusalem, the source of values to a chosen people. The New Jerusalem, together with Arcadia and Eden, are conventional alternatives to the corrupt city of Western pastoral. As the novel demonstrates, however, in the random racist brutality of the countryside there is a far greater corruption than anything the dominee could dream of in the cities. For both communities, invocations of the past are central to their communal lives. The ubiquitous pictures of the Great Trek and the Boer War, memories of fighting the British or massacring a group of San serve to recall the Afrikaners to a past which is heroic in their mythology, and can provide the decadent present with a new sense of purpose. For Hlangeni the past is recalled with simple nostalgia. He has submitted to orders that he and his people should move from the land and now confronted by his powerlessness, stripped of his traditional authority, "He tried to force his mind back to another time, a far-off youth, when he had dreamed of warriors.'' Hlangeni through dream and then again through dream lives at two removes from his warrior inheritance. But as he steps from his dilapidated house, it seems for a moment that he will draw from the past an informing inspiration for the present. The absence of a praise-song which once would have announced his presence provokes in him ''a twinge of pride'' at the heritage which should be his and he speaks with an uncharacteristic authority.

> Anthony Chennells. In Emmanuel Ngara and Andrew Morrison, eds. *Literature, Language and the Nation* (Harare: Baobab Books, 1989), pp. 42, 45–46

Alex La Guma, writing as a committed, active (rather than former) communist, out of the experience of a political activist inside his own country and outside it in exile, goes some way to detach himself from . . . ideological conventions. In his novel, *In the Fog of the Seasons' End*, there is a genuine attempt to eradicate the personality cult and the notion of the heroic leader figure. The revolution he depicts is not a heroic epic of platforms and seething masses, romantic imprisonments, and popular deliriums, but a silent back-street affair of secret assignments, dreary trudging about with leaflets, and a constant haunting fear of detection, betrayal, and the repulsive and shameful realism of the torture cells. His main characters, Beukes, Tekwane, and Isaac, are drained of much of their individuality in the interests of their functions as revolutionary units. La Guma is much too skillful a writer to present them as cardboard stereotypes, mouthpieces for didacticism and propaganda. The reader is always in full possession of their humanity, of their placement in a network of relationships— Beukes with his wife and child, Tekwane with his widowed mother, Isaac, more superficially, with his workmates—but this is all background detail. . . . Background in terms of the subject matter, in that these networks are only mentioned fairly briefly, but background also in terms of characterization, for all these men have deliberately cut themselves off from connections in order to dedicate themselves entirely to their political activities, free from the distraction of domestic demands. (The impossibility of reconciling the two is emphasized in the presentation of Bennett, distracted from the simplest obligations by a demanding wife and his own fear for the safety of his family.)

Yet for all their single-minded dedication, none of these figures emerges as the romantic hero of the revolution: theirs is a drab and unexciting struggle, with little prospect of early success and no possibility of individual glory or power. La Guma underlines this subordination of the individual to a cause most emphatically in his account of the day of the strike, where he picks out various symbolic figures and charts their normal activity—the Washerwoman, the Bicycle Messenger, the Outlaw, the Child—to emphasize the outrageous cruelty at the hands of the police, among the crowd gathered outside the police station. La Guma not merely makes no effort to conceal the artificiality of his literary device here, but actually stresses it typographically by his use of capital letters. For these four are more significant as representatives of their people, oppressed to the point of senseless obliteration, than they could ever be as individuals.

This combination of diverse stylistic devices reveals the extent of La Guma's literary skills enabling him to present the social and objective historical significance of events without divorcing his main characters from everyday reality or humanity. If he had attempted to individualize the victims of police brutality on the day of the strike it would have confused the reader and blurred the dialectical message: but if he had attempted to subordinate the characterization of his main figures to his dialectics it would have emptied his message of all power to evoke a response from the reader. Beukes, Tekwane, and Isaac are cogs in the machine of the movement, but they are sentient cogs, feeling not only in their capacities as functionaries, but also in their individual consciousness, the bruises suffered by the movement as a result of organized repression. And their attempts to try to heal the breaches, to put things together again so that the party can function, are attempts to heal their own psyches and find mechanisms to deal with their own hurts and fears. They work like moles in the dark, groping blindly, but testing each move, each contact first.

> Jane Watts. *Black Writers from South Africa* (New York: St. Martin's Press, 1989), pp. 214–15

The writings of Alex La Guma establish him as an important literary figure who, throughout his career spanning three decades, consistently portrayed South African society in a trans-ethnic perspective. The nature of trans-ethnicity articulated in his writings is a reflection of his opinions and activities that characterised his journalism and politics, two other areas in which he made a mark. The 'threefold cord' of his creative writings, journalism and politics has established his credentials as one of the foremost integrationists who saw trans-ethnicity as the way forward for the ethnically-fragmented society of South Africa.

La Guma's technique of arguing his case for a trans-ethnic society rests on destroying the notions of ethnic 'separateness' and 'superiority' that underpin social attitudes and legislative edifice built over the last three centuries in South Africa. He highlights some of the problems common to all ethnic groups, and criticises both individual characters and institutions that nurture and sustain divisions along ethnic origins. Among the problems that La Guma finds common to all the ethnic groups are sexual jealousy and a sense of revenge. Raalt (an Afrikaner), Stopes (an English-Speaking White), Sam (a Coloured) suspect their wives to be carrying on extra-marital affairs. All three are impatient for vengeance. More importantly, La Guma denies the Cartesian logic of a 'rational' European and an 'emotional' or 'superstitious' African by pointing out the case of Philipa who seeks 'non-rational' cures for her diseases. The comparisons of such practices amongst the different ethnic groups is done through the use of irony.

La Guma's articulation of trans-ethnicity has been consistent throughout his literary career. He maintained the stand from the 1950s, when such notions were popular, to the late 1970s, when the claims made by and for the Africans for a dominant share of power became more fashionable. La Guma's writings provide a historical link between the liberal, the radical and the Black Consciousness phases of South African literature which had the high tides of popularity in the 1950s, 1960s and the 1970s respectively. La Guma's faith in trans-ethnicity found expression in all the three phases with each phase leaving its mark on La Guma's oeuvre. He shared the notions of the phase but stuck to his belief that the best way forward for South Africa was to affirm that South Africa belongs to all those who live in it, an idea that buttresses the Freedom Charter.

The most vivid expression of La Guma's trans-ethnicity is to be found in the words of Joe, the archetypal representative of the

Strandlopers, whose humanity makes him question 'Isn't we all people?'. The characters who carry forward, symbolically, the trans-ethnic notions in the later works of La Guma include Charlie, a Coloured; Mpolo, an African; and Harris, a White. Embedded in Joe's question is another notion of egalitarianism that cuts across divisions based on economic status. Thus, the plight of the poor, to which social class most of La Guma's characters belong, is also covered in La Guma's concern with trans-ethnicity. The displacements and the dispossessions of the Coloured community from the Sea Point, of the Africans in the symbolic Karoo, and of the 'poor white' from their landholdings, are all portrayed with an empathy for the affected.

Trans-ethnicity provides a thematic continuity between La Guma's pre- and post-exile writings. The vision of a South Africa in which political power and economic justice would be based on grounds other than ethnicity illuminates his entire career in writing. Exile, since 1966, has added to the problem of transcending the racial and regional barriers that pin down South African writers to their ethno-geographic origins. While the idea of trans-ethnicity persists, the medium of felt experience of actual life in South Africa dried up as time passed by. Consequently, in his fiction based on life in South Africa, the near-naturalism of his early works gave way to to overt symbolism in his later works. The problem of articulating political sympathy while lacking actual lived experience, even a distant one, becomes acute in dealing with Africans in the rural areas. Exile has also resulted in La Guma's choice of non-South African settings for two of his stories. Trans-ethnicity, however, remained the most significant concern of La Guma's fiction linking different phases of both his own career and South African literature in English.

> Balasubramanyam Chandramohan. *A Study in Trans-Ethnicity in Modern South Africa. The Writings of Alex la Guma, 1925–1985* (Lampeter, Wales: Mellen Research University Press, 1992)

BIBLIOGRAPHY
*A Walk in the Night*, 1962; *And a Threefold Cord*, 1964; *The Stone Country*, 1967; *In the Fog of the Seasons' End*, 1972; *A Soviet Journey*, 1978; *Time of the Butcherbird*, 1979

# LAING, Kojo (1946– )
## Ghana

In a general way, the proportions in which Ghanaian words from various sources are represented in [*Search Sweet Country*] reflect what is known about the relative frequency of the source languages as second languages in Accra, at least among people of southern origin. Although Laing's purpose is not to make a sociolinguistic statement, he in effect does just that: his Accra is polygot and multiethnic almost to the point of being non-ethnic. Its language is the mixed language of a nation-in-the-making, not the language of any single group, traditional or otherwise.

The names of the characters are even more revealing. A few, mainly peripheral characters have Muslim or Frafra names. Several have English nicknames (e.g., Ebo the Food, Baby Yaa, Manager Agyeman). The majority of names are Akan, especially although not exclusively from the Fante dialect, but few of the major characters have names that are entirely Akan, especially if titles and nicknames are taken into account. It might be significant that most of those who do are women: Adwoa Adde, Yaaba Boadi, and all the members of a household that is a major element in the structure of the novel: Araba Fynn, Ewurofua, and Nana Esi. Ahomka, the name of Kofi Loww's child, is an Akan word meaning "gladness"—a word that is used as a personal name in the Fante dialect. Loww's father's name, Erzuah, is Nzema, a language closely related to Akan but quite distinct.

Sackey is a Ga name, derived from the Akan equivalent Sakyi but preserving an older pronunciation. Since his first name, a common day name, is spelled Kwesi, instead of Kwashi (as it would be in Ga), Professor Sackey's "tribal" identity is uncertain, as is appropriate for this character. Indeed, the names in the Sackey family embody a linguistic division that reflects the divided nature of that household. The given names of Sackey and his son are the day-names Kwesi and Kwame (of Akan origin but used throughout southern Ghana), whereas his wife and daughter use the English names Sofi (the usual Ghanaian pronunciation of Sophia) and Katie. The distribution of names in the Sackey household reflects emotional disunity and a lack of communication, with allegiances divided according to sex.

The mixed nature of the names of the key characters Kofi Loww and Kojo Okay Pol is more problematic. Kofi (another day name) is used in every southern Ghanaian language. "Loww" is the author's orthographic invention and can be regarded as English, like Soon and Pinn (all three are also puns). This character above all is of Accra, in the new, non-traditional sense, and his name reflects this. The name "Kojo Okay Pol" is more ambivalent. Like the other day-names, "Kojo" is English, probably a slangy nickname such as those commonly affected by young men. "Pol" can presumably be attributed to the character's northern father, but the name does not exist in any language of northern Ghana. It is obviously a sexual pun. This name thus consists of a non-committal southern name and a comic pseudo-northern name, linked by a half-digested, superficial word in English, the language that joins the country into a single entity, albeit rather unsatisfactorily. This character's name, as well as the character himself, thus encapsulates the country's problem of forging an inner integrity from diverse sources.

Place names are significant in the same way. Many are Ga: Bukom, Odorkor, Chorkor, Kaneshie, Labone, Osu, Legon. But just as many, including names of traditionally Ga areas, are English: Ussher Fort, Jamestown, High Street, Asylum Down, Castle. A relatively small number are Akan in origin (e.g., Maamobi and Mamprobi), and several are from other languages (e.g., Adabraka and Madina from Arbic via Hausa, Makola probably from Yoruba, Nima from Fulani).

In *Search Sweet Country*, Accra is multifaceted and multivoiced, like the country that it represents. This quality of the city is reflected and displayed in names and local vocabulary; however, in a novel that is preoccupied with using the past to get beyond the past, "traditional Ga" cannot be displaced or ignored. Although none of the characters actually live in Jamestown or behind the Central Post Office, Kofi Loww spends much time contemplating and walking through this area, Adwoa Adde hovers over it, and K. O. Pol rides around it on his motorbike. One aspect of it is represented by ½-Allotey as he wrestles with his ancestral spirits, although he is not specifically Ga, despite his name. In any case, he is the one major character who is essentially non-urban, by both upbringing and inclination. The special presence of the Ga is explicitly acknowledged, and dismissed, in the linguistic psychology used to describe Araba Fynn; as her grandmother Nana Esi says, "And I'm worried about your Fante, Araba, the Ga is pushing it out of the way. . ." (note that the language is treated as a solid, pushable object). Towards the end of the book the author in his own voice observes:

> You would not want to divide this morally sakola city into tribal groups, SIR, for it had devoured all the different tribes long ago. . .and the Gas, the land being theirs, were spat back out, only to be reswallowed the more.

The national language, the unifying idiom for which the people of the novel are searching, will not be Ga or Akan, or any other currently spoken language; it will have to assimilate and transcend all these languages, figuratively as well as literally. The configuration of names of people and places begins to accomplish this goal: it accurately reflects ordinary usage, while pointing towards what the language of the future must be.

Like Kojo Laing's long poems, his novel conducts its search by means of an intense language of imagery. It also employs a remarkable innovation: a poetic syntax that is typical (with variations) of both poetry and oratory in Akan and Ga, but more or less foreign to writing in "standard" English. This new syntax is almost totally absent from Laing's poetry.

Patterning based on alliteration is a prominent feature of Akan poetic style, and it can be found in both Laing's poetry and his novel. It is obviously a feature of personal names in the novel: Beni Baidoo, Adwoa Adde, Osofo Ocrar., Sally Soon; but it can also be found in the counterpoint of "b" and "cr" sounds, stretched out by the echoing in "ful"/"fowl" that occurs in the opening sentence: "In the bush just beyond Accra, the bush that handfuls of wild guinea fowl raised with their cries, sat Beni Baidoo." Two sentences later, there is an urgent interplay of "s" and "sh" sounds: "When this cigarette smoke got too much, he would rush to the sea and steal some of the freshness of the breeze. The language of the sea spoke in shells that he could understand. . ." The rush and whisper of the sea are thus evoked, heightening the desperation that Beni Baidoo represents.

Similar examples can be found on every page, in every context, saved from triteness by the wide variety of patterns created. In the following sentence, for example, the alliterating words occur in a series of pairs, not in one interwoven sequence, but the "c," "f" and "g" pairs are bracketed by "h," so that resolution of the present situation by the future healing is projected by sound as well as by meaning. . . .

Phonetically-based patterning is common enough in poetry; it is also of course entirely consistent with the concrete style, but it is less common in prose. In Laing's work, it pervades all forms. The value placed on language as physical substance, whether acoustic or graphic, does not alter with the shift in genre. This fact is one of the sources of the novel's special texture. A description of Accra at night, for example, is marked by an interplay of strident "s" and staccato "k" sounds, against a quieter chorus of "t's," that crowd in and then recede again as the reader, accompanying Kofi Loww and the taxis, moves into and through them, so that the sound of the description reflects the sound of the night city itself:

> Back in the streets Accra had one eye shut: at one o'clock, the taxis were driving towards sleep; and with the open eye,

with the one bright head-light, they moved to the cines, the wake-keepings, the spiritual churches, the still-talking compounds, the society meetings, the discos, the night-classes, the late journeys, the night kenkeys, the kelewele, and the evening profits.

The spiritual Town of the poetry is made physical presence in the novel by projecting it onto an actual city. Alliteration is one of Laing's ways of representing as directly as possible the physical substance of the city through the physical substance of the writer's medium, language.

M. E. Kropp Dakubu. *Research in African Literatures.* 24, 1 (Spring 1993), pp. 19–35

While a student in Glasgow in 1967 and 1968, Laing published poems in various Scottish poetry magazines. Some of this early work won the BBC's University Notebook Award for Poetry in 1967. Laing cites "Funeral in Accra," a poem he wrote in 1965 to commemorate his father's death, as his break with juvenilia. In it he was able to shake off the inhibiting influences of the European authors of his schoolboy reading and began to use a poetic language that, while following the norms of standard English in grammar and syntax and even vocabulary, was uncompromisingly his own and also distinctively African in image and idiom. "Funeral in Accra" was first published in 1968 in Lines Review along with "African Storm" and "Jaw," the last a long poem (265 lines) in the dense, wholly original diction that is the hallmark of Laing's writing.

"Jaw" reflects Laing's reaction to his experience as a student and the strength afforded him by his marriage. The first of a trilogy of poems central to Laing's oeuvre, it was followed by "Resurrection" (600 lines), written mainly after his return to Ghana and published in 1972, and "Christcrowd" (more than 1,200 lines), which was completed in 1973 when he was working in the Ashanti region but remains unpublished. These poems contain the seeds of all Laing's subsequent work; he considers his shorter poems and even his novels to be footnotes to the long poems. Each poem is cyclical in its internal structure. As a trilogy they are also a cycle, moving back and forth between the worlds of inner and outer reality as the poet struggles to forge a unity of the social and the psychic, the physical and the spiritual.

The starting point of "Jaw" is adolescent anger and psychological dislocation arising from the shock of a different culture, the experience of racism in a strange land, and especially the determination to fight back. Life is seen as a struggle for self-realization, and literature is a principal weapon in the struggle. Most of the images that inform all Laing's work are present here, at least in embryo: language as physical substance; the sea; the concrete imagery of hands, animals, plants, and food as opposed to automobiles, airplanes, and guns. Laing also deliberately mixes images from different continents, thus insisting on the falseness of racial barriers. Since the physical jaw is the symbolic meeting place of body and spirit, the poem's last line, addressed to a silent, perhaps beloved, companion of the speaker, is an assertion of faith in the value of personal relationships and the possibility of wholeness: "You are the inner jaw and the resurrection."

The last word leads directly into the second poem of the trilogy, for which Laing shared a VALCO Literary Award in 1977. If "Jaw" represents the author's assertion of defiant existence and the inner integrity of his being, "Resurrection" represents an aggressive movement outward to face the threat and challenge of society with its false and destructive categories, primary among which is race. The image of the Town that is at the core of Laing's novels makes its first appearance in "Jaw," but it is much more extensively developed in "Resurrection." It represents the multiplicity of social presences that must be faced if the individual is to maintain inner wholeness. The imagery of the physical as the foundation of the spiritual is emphasized, as are the themes of social lies, false priests, and language that fragments instead of conjoining. At the end of the poem the poet is still angry, but he has gathered strength and courage to approach the Town on his own terms. In "Christcrowd" Laing creates a spiritual world that integrates the physical and social.

An important intellectual source for these works is existentialism, including the works of Jean-Paul Sartre and Søren Kierkegaard but particularly the existential phenomenology of the Scottish psychiatrist R. D. Laing, whose writings were popular at the time Kojo Laing was a student. Kojo Laing responded particularly to R. D. Laing's main theme of psychological alienation, the idea that the central problem of modern life is the conflict between the inner and the outer modes of the individual's experience, of himself and his surroundings, which results in ontological insecurity and fragmentation of the personality. The goal of human life—and the goal of the long poems—is wholeness of being and experience, the "concrete."

An important aspect of Laing's literary approach to the struggle for wholeness and authenticity is the role he gives to language as both symbol and instrument, meanings that underlie the title "Jaw." As the last line of that poem indicates, the jaw makes both expression of the inner self and communication, or participation in the Town, possible. But language is also a weapon, both in the struggle for self and in the hostile outer world's inauthentic speech, and so the jaw in these lines from "Resurrection" is also the ground for battle between the inner and the outer:

I see a crowd of people on the corner of my mouth.
They talk there, they wipe their feet there.
They exchange their lies there.

Laing's treatment of language as a physical substance, a concrete object, is seen above and in a quotation from "Jaw":

For only a few kept insults burn,
angered and impotent on my jaw,
in the hospital of the poem.

Laing seems to have been influenced by the French Concrete poets and by the Scottish Concrete Poetry movement, whose members also published in Lines Review. The fascination with language as object, especially as graphic object, is particularly important in "Resurrection," with its numerous linguistic metaphors, even puns, in lines such as "And I hold hard onto the two Rs of inner presences" and "He sticks his thumb through the E of HEAL." He even combines puns with graphic devices, in a line such as "I will listen quietly to your woes in the next four blank lines"—followed by four blank lines. Ironically, language is also an obstacle to be overcome. This idea is already present in "Jaw"—"I am the letter T joined onto an H while E looks on / unwillingly."—and "Resurrection"—"I make war on the ten letters of Past Tenses!"—although it is more fully developed in later work. While the writing in "Resurrection" (as in much of Laing's work) sometimes

teeters on the brink of the ridiculous, it is usually saved by the poet's manifest passion. . . .

Laing's only published collection of poems, Godhorse (1989), is a selection of work covering twenty years, from "Funeral in Accra" of 1965 to "Twenty years flying," written in Accra in 1984. The book and the poems chosen for The Heinemann Book of African Poetry in English (1990) were written before his novels even though they were published later than the first two novels. Although many of Laing's poems remain uncollected and unpublished, the selection in Godhorse is reasonably representative. Many of the poems work out the themes of his long poems in relation to personal events and concerns; most are ultimately related to the concern with existential authenticity and psychic wholeness.

While Laing's fundamental themes do not change, a shift in emphasis and tone is detectable in his poems written after 1979. Thematic continuity is illustrated by "Funeral in Accra," "Soon father" (1976), and "Zoom sail the graves!" (1984), which are all meditations on the death of Laing's father. The impressionism of "Wall," the lightness of "Three Songs," and the youthful enthusiasm of "If you dare to swim"—all written before 1975—give way to the implied experience of "The rain slants" (written 1981), the angry poem "Tatale Swine" (written 1983), and the passionate parable of "Godhorse," which presages the battles with the natural world in the first novel. Laing reworks the early influences of the Concrete Poetry movement and existentialism into a concrete existentialism of his own.

Some themes gain greater prominence in the later poems. "Zoom sail the graves!" and "No needle in the sky" (1984) are both concerned with language and the poet's task. "I just can't sit on chairs" and "Courage" (1979) are also concerned with the poet's burden, but the focus is on his relationship to the social world. The difficulties attending authenticity in personal relations, which undoubtedly touch on his own marriage, are explored in "The Huge Car with the Sad Voice," written in 1970 but revised in 1980, and "The rain slants." The title poem, "Godhorse" (written in 1984), represents the human striving for spiritual wholeness, which includes the social: the failures of the man and woman reflect the failure of their society, the nation that is "half a country."

Laing's existential concern with the authentic relationship between inner and outer experience does not lessen. In the poems he wrote beginning around 1979 the poet's outer world appears oppressively impersonal and morally neutral. The disjunction between the inner and the outer is particularly apparent in "Godhorse," indicating Laing's more somber approach to the problem of the social individual in the world and his deeper realization of the magnitude of the struggle for personal and national wholeness. The old man's struggle in the poem to stay on the horse and to make contact with Mansa represents the struggle for complete and meaningful life. He fails to create a world in which such a life is possible, but his failure does not suggest it is impossible to do so.

The obsession with Christian imagery and with inadequate and racist priests that informs "Christcrowd" and appears in "Godsdoor" (1972) and several other shorter poems, such as "Grasscutters in the West" (1984), begins to include the non-Christian in "Godhorse" and other poems. This does not, however, mean that Laing thinks the non-Christian priests are necessarily better than the Christian, for the "bishops and fetish priests" of "Godhorse" are equally unable to make what has been fragmented into a whole: "the religious men wanted to bless the impudent hooves"—they accept the horse's uncontrolled speed without relating it to their lives.

A prosodic shift complements Laing's mature approach. In the later poems the lines are still fast moving and forceful, but they are also more regular in length, uniformly long. There are no more short poems such as the "Three Songs" or "Dog." The result is a solidity of form that expresses a consolidation of inner resources in the battle to make the outer a part of the inner self. The aggressive imperatives and declaratives characteristic of "Jaw" and "Resurrection" and present in many of the shorter poems have for the most part disappeared.

M. E. Kropp Dakubu. In Bernth Lindfors and Reinhard Sander, editors. *Dictionary of Literary Biography, Volume 157: Twentieth-Century Caribbean and Black African Writers* (Detroit: Gale Research, 1996), pp. 140–149

[*Search Sweet Country* is, a] book of wonders in which everything—animate and inanimate, natural and supernatural—is endowed with sentient power and energy. "In his [Kofi Loww's] head the buildings, the markets, the streets became alive, became almost passionate with existence." In Laing's universe all things have the power of agency. Buildings dance to the rhythm of human heartbeats, trees exchange roots and hurl down squirrels while their leaves "chatter with profound nonchalance"—"the forests were jealous of sound and were able to create and destroy echoes"—and the blue-soiled earth dresses itself in hats, churches, and people. One remarkable feature of this sur-real undifferentiated flux is the novelist's metaphoric displacement and reallocation of qualities and functions to things to which they are not usually thought to belong. The effect of this is to suspend normal sense-relations and perceptual processes and to produce a kind of behavioral synesthesia in which beards "disagree," smiles detach themselves from their owners and move according to their own momentum, and people "eat" thoughts, gather laughter in cups, and "wear" each other's features: "his eyes . . . contained so much that . . . there had to be more than one human being wearing them." In one such whimsy the flying witch Adwoa Adde, before embarking upon the "aerial history of Ghana" in which she gathers the complaints and confessions of Accra's downtrodden citizens, borrows a body constituted from dismembered, repositioned human limbs supplied by her spirit mentor. In another scene the same ancestral spirits, by a reverse process, borrow ½-Allotey's mouth and nose, leaving him partly disembodied, with a hungry stomach and a squint, as he enters the mystic trance that releases healing energies from his farm.

Much of this, admittedly, is comic invention for its own sake, as in the quirky cameos of the cemetery spirits who borrow the State House and the football stadium for their numinous assemblies, and of Aboagye Hi-speed who devises the first do-it-yourself "automatic one-man funeral" and disappears when he stands sideways. But Laing's bizarre figures and conceits cannot simply be dismissed as idle gimmickry. Beneath the rhetoric of fragmentation and disintegration, of borrowed parts and fractured wholes, there is the deeper underlying metaphysic of an animist universe in which, since everything is holistically an aspect of everything else, then nothing is ever wholly either one thing or another. In this hybridic cosmos everything is constituted of halves. As ½-Allotey's name indicates, to be allotted only part of everything and to be given

everything in parts is what it is to be fully alive. As Professor Sackey tells him, "you either live fragmented and half yourself, half your heart, or you keep slow and whole and die."

The Ghanaian world of the novel is constituted of antithetical halves that must somehow be reconciled, though they can never be unified into wholes. Hence Sackey, when he contemplates the mind of the contemporary Ghanaian intellectual, is distressed at the absence of a "territory between the supernatural and the purely factual" because most of his nation's people live in the half-and-half, in-between territory where the numinous and the material liminally coexist. Indeed, most of the novel's action takes place in what Kofi Loww calls "perfect African time—time that existed in any dimension," where the ancestors bring their 50-year-old groundnuts to market alongside the living vendors and where flying witches are still visible "even when . . . vision was blocked by goats, Mercedes Benzes, semi-prostitutes, harmattan or plantain cake." Thus the Professor warms to ½-Allotey's experimental farm venture, with its problematic mixture of subsistence and spirituality, commerce and metaphysics, and applauds his attempts to blend modern therapy with traditional herbal medicines and to infuse new ideas into ancient libation rituals (which outrages the reactionary elders of Allotey's village). Ghanaian Christianity and political morality are represented in the book by similarly complementary but irreconcilable halves—the pragmatic Bishop Budu and his unworldly priest Osofo, the high-principled Kofi Loww and the expediency-serving Okay Pol—and the academic world by Sackey's own quirky mélange of rarefied intellectualism and irrepressible ordinariness.

The "search" of Laing's "sweet country" is therefore the pursuit of wholes by halves, and it is an endeavor that causes the characters' careers to cross in ways that emphasize their interpenetrativeness and simultaneity. This collective search for a more meaningful identity and a more authentic mode of existence during a period of inauthentic political values is symbolized, albeit in partly parodic fashion, by the ancient Beni Baidoo and his quixotic obsession with founding his own village, a dream that he confides to everyone. . . .

Baidoo plays many roles: prophet and clairvoyant, psychologist and political commentator, trickster and fool. Similarly, Kofi Loww, who lends the hue of his eyes to buildings and the sky, feels that "each time [he] took a step he lifted a whole country," and the witch Adwoa Adde discovers on her communal aerial patrols that she is "forced into relationship with everything, and her pulse was the movements of thousands in sleep." Moreover, although she projects her own spiritual vitality outward onto the urban environment, she is herself a projection of the people's collective imaginings and of popular belief about witches; the relationship between her intrinsic and imparted identities is at times a problematic one. . . .

[Yet], if Laing fabulates predominantly imagined worlds, proclaimed through self-regarding images, then these are worlds that themselves toy in unexpectedly serious ways with the very idea of imagined worlds. Societies and nations, like Baidoo and the witch Adwoa, exist both in actuality and notionally in people's minds, as themselves and as they are imagined to be. If the novel's characters are largely unaware of the surreal poetic fiction in which the author has enclosed them, then this is partly because they are themselves deeply immersed in fictions about national values, culture, and language in the country they inhabit. "I only want a little authenticity," the acolyte Osofo protests to his bishop, but Ghanaian public life appears to offer none at all. Instead there are only the

National Redemption Council's pompous official fictions of "revolution and self-reliance" and slogans such as "If Ghanaians help the government, the government will help Ghanaians," which mask corrupt collusion and bribery with a facade of moral reciprocity. Equally inauthentic is the belief that materialistic imperatives hold supreme sway in the nation's life; that most Ghanaians, as Sackey puts it, would choose a Mercedes-Benz in preference to a soul and are perfectly content with the gifts of beer and food that in the novel purchase their acquiescence, respectively, in the airport debacle and on the antigovernment march. The truth is that, although they behave as if they are satisfied, they obviously are not: Kofi Loww disdains the free beer; the official who provides it later dissociates himself from the whole affair; and the marchers disperse disgruntled and disillusioned. More fantastically, during the horse stampede, the crowd is asked by the panic-stricken Okay Pol to disbelieve the evidence of its own eyes: "I must warn you all that what you are seeing here is not true . . . you must be interrogated to confirm this . . . the government needs your support . . . these are agricultural horses, to push on Operation Feed Yourself, and they will pull the plough." Under police pressure, the spectators are persuaded to subscribe to the triple fiction that farm horses are used in Ghana (which they are not); that such horses are imported (again untrue); and that these thoroughbred racehorses are those same drays. The point of such episodes is that what is inauthentic in the popular imagination is not so much the fictions themselves as the cynical belief that charades like these are an accepted, understood part of Ghanaian life. In other words, Ghanaians have come to behave according to an idea of themselves and of how much they are willing, uncritically, to swallow; they have to be reminded that beneath these public falsehoods there are deeper and more genuine human needs and a longing for more authentic values. In the case of Okay Pol, release from the impossible contradiction between fact and official fiction is achieved only by a preposterous piece of bad faith and some disingenuous comic hyperbole: "Pol believed there was some merit in having horses for agriculture . . . and that if a few were racehorses, then you would obviously have faster farms." By such devices Laing demonstrates that the idea that the populace has to subscribe to fictions is itself a fiction.

Derek Wright. *New Directions in African Fiction* (New York: Twayne Publishers, 1997), pp. 140–55

BIBLIOGRAPHY
*Search Sweet Country*, 1986; *Woman of the Aeroplanes*, 1988; *Godhorse*, 1989; *Major Gentl and the Achimota Wars*, 1992

# LAMMING, George (1927–)
**Barbados**

The act of ripping the sensitive human personality from one culture and the planting of that personality in another culture is a tortured, convoluted process that must, before it can appeal to people's hearts, be projected either in terms of vivid drama or highly sensual poetry.

It has been through the medium of the latter—a charged and poetic prose—that George Lamming, a young West Indian Negro of Barbados, has presented his autobiographical summation of a tropical island childhood that, though steeped in the luminous images of sea, earth, sky, and wind, drifts slowly towards the edge of the realms of political and industrial strife. Notwithstanding the fact that Lamming's story, as such, is his own, it is, at the same time, a symbolic repetition of the story of millions of simple folk who, sprawled over half of the world's surface and involving more than half of the human race, are today being catapulted out of their peaceful, indigenously earthy lives and into the turbulence and anxiety of the twentieth century.

I, too, have been long crying these stern tidings; and, when I catch the echo of yet another voice declaiming in alien accents a description of this same reality, I react with pride and excitement, and I want to urge others to listen to that voice. One feels not so much alone when, from a distant witness, supporting evidence comes to buttress one's own testimony. And the voice that I now bid you hear is sounding in Lamming's *In the Castle of My Skin*.

Richard Wright. Introduction to George Lamming, *In the Castle of My Skin* (New York: McGraw-Hill, 1953), pp. ix–x

It is easy to understand the incomprehension which has greeted Mr. George Lamming's third book. Mr. Lamming is a Barbadian Negro, and unless one understands the West Indian's search for identity, *Of Age and Innocence* is almost meaningless. It is not fully realised how completely the West Indian Negro identifies himself with England. Africa has been forgotten; films about African tribesmen excite derisive West Indian laughter. For the West Indian intellectual, speaking no language but English, educated in an English way, the experience of England is really traumatic. The foundations of his life are removed. He has to look for new loyalties. . . .

I thought this a better novel than *The Emigrants* [his second novel]. But Mr. Lamming creates difficulties for the reader. He has devised a story which is fundamentally as well-knit and exciting as one by Graham Greene. But you have to look hard for it. Mr. Lamming suppresses and mystifies; he shies away from the concrete, and grows garrulous over the insignificant. He is not a realistic writer. He deals in symbols and allegory. Experience has not been the basis of this novel. Every character, every incident is no more than a constituent idea in Mr. Lamming's thesis: the reader's sympathies are never touched. San Cristobal, the imaginary island which is the setting of Mr. Lamming's novel, could never exist.

I can understand Mr. Lamming's need for fantasy. His conception of the search for identity is highly personal; it has arisen from a deep emotion which he has chosen to suppress, turning it instead into an intellectual thing which is fine in its way, but would be made absurd by the comic realities of West Indian political life. Here is one West Indian writer who feels hindered rather than inspired by the West Indian scene.

Mr. Lamming is only thirty. He is one of the finest prose-writers of his generation. Purely as a work of fantasy *Of Age and Innocence* is really quite remarkable. It fails through its sheer unreadability. Mr. Lamming should be warned by this that his best subject, as in *In the Castle of My Skin* and the first 50 pages of this novel, is himself.

V.S. Naipaul. *New Statesman*. December 6, 1958, p. 827

[*Season of Adventure*] is about freedom—political freedom—in the West Indies; about the fact that if you were to release a diseased cat from a sack, it would still be diseased, although free; even more it is about the etiology of the disease, or diseases, as discerned in West Indians above the line of poverty or below it, falsified by an education or uneducated, with the echoes of respectability in their ears or the direct sound of the steel drum. It is about the ways in which a neglected, disconnected drift of humans does not "work," though its individuals live, think, feel, posture, whore, lie, cheat, murder and delude themselves, like everyone else. It is even about a universal revolution.

So much for abouts. It is, *per contra*, as a novel, extra-politically, extra-sociologically, a hot fuddle of sententious and sensational verbosity, unremitting, frequently ridiculous, which boils and boils and keeps moving a number of approximate dolls attached to names and explicatory functions. "Her sister had died of tetanus thirteen days after a wasp stung her on the left nipple of her tumoured breast." Dawn winds always break, drums have a "dark refrain." Peculiarities yes; but not that imaginative idiosyncratic extra "realness" one expects in novels above the average—a level this book does not reach.

Others think otherwise, I know, about the peculiarity of Mr. Lamming's fiction. I think they are being had in a dislike of drabness, much as one might be had by a mixture of grimacing and erotic sculpture in coloured plasticine slapped to a building which, after all, was only town councillors's asbestos. In *Season of Adventure* the peculiarity is upheld by very ordinary novel-making.

Geoffrey Grigson. *Spectator*. October 28, 1960, p. 663

One of the most interesting novelists out of the West Indies is George Lamming. Lamming was—and still is—regarded as a writer of considerable promise. What is the nature of his promise? Let us look at his novel *Of Age and Innocence*. This is a novel which somehow fails, I feel, but its failure tells us a great deal. The novel would have been remarkable if a certain tendency—a genuine tendency—for a tragic feeling of dispossession in reality had been achieved. This tendency is frustrated by a diffusion of energies within the entire work. The book seems to speak with a public voice, the voice of a peculiar orator, and the compulsions which inform the work appear to spring from a verbal sophistication rather than a visual, plastic and conceptual imagery. Lamming's verbal sophistication is conversational, highly wrought and spirited sometimes: at other times it lapses into merely clever utterance, rhetorical, as when he says of one of his characters: "He had been made Governor of an important colony which was then at war with England."

It takes some effort—not the effort of imaginative concentration which is always worthwhile but an effort to combat the author's self-indulgence. And this would not arise if the work could be kept true to its inherent design. There is no necessary difficulty or complexity in Lamming's novels—the necessary difficulty or complexity belonging to strange symbolisms—and I feel if the author concentrated on the sheer essentials of his experience a tragic disposition of feeling would gain a true ascendancy. This concentration is essential if the work is not to succumb to a uniform tone which gives each individual character the same public-speaking resonance of voice. . . .

In terms of the ruling framework he accepts, the individuality of character, the distinctions of status and privilege which mark one individual from another, must be maintained. This is the kind of realism, the realism of classes and classifications—however limited it may be in terms of a profound, poetic and scientific scale of values—the novel, in its orthodox mould, demands. Lamming may be restless within this framework (there are signs and shadows of this in his work) but mere extravagance of pattern and an inclination to frequent intellectual raids beyond his territory are not a genuine breakthrough and will only weaken the position of the central character in his work. [1964]

Wilson Harris. *Tradition, the Writer and Society* (London: New Beacon, 1967), pp. 37–38

The problem facing George Lamming's work (and this is the burden of all true experiment and exploration) is one of form. His insights require poetry, and Lamming has been remarkably successful in deploying this within his novels' structure. But as he has moved from the childhood world of *In the Castle of My Skin*, he has become more and more concerned with the political and psychological ramifications of social living and consciousness (*The Emigrants, Of Age and Innocence, Season of Adventure*), and he has had to rely more and more on "prose" while still trying to retain the poetry. This tug of war has affected the shape of his work; preventing it from achieving a clear, coherent, overall whole. Yet such is his power of realization, that any given section of his work reveals a hard, unwinking gleam that marks its authenticity. . . .

But the "shape" of Lamming's work is also conditioned by the kind of tradition he is working towards. He seems to be moving away from the European tradition of the "house" towards a different and more "Caribbean" form altogether. *Season of Adventure* opens with the experience of a voodoo ceremony and its effect, particularly, on a West Indian girl who, until she is faced with the Gods of the *tonelle* [voodoo ceremonial canopy], thinks that her sophistication renders her immune from the language of the drums. Within this alternative tradition, Lamming appears to be saying, lie the hidden and half-forgotten forces through which Caribbean society can be forged. . . .

Edward Brathwaite. *Bim.* July-December 1968, pp. 162–63

In a sense, *Season of Adventure* is a celebration (the first literary one) of the steel band. Not only does the sound of the steel drums hang in the air throughout the novel: at the climax is a glorious parade of all the bands marching on to Freedom Square celebrating the coming of a new government . . . . But Lamming's nationalism is not the local-culture-waving [V. S.] Naipaul goes out of his way to snipe at. *Season of Adventure* is an analysis of the failure of nationalism in the newly independent San Cristobal. . . .

In the novel *Season of Adventure*, Lamming explores the problematic relation to Africa in terms proper to works of fiction. The middle-class West Indian's denial of the masses, and his shame of Africa are seen as obstacles to the fulfilment of the person, and the inauthentic existence of the unfulfilled person is a kind of death. Fola is imagined as such a dead person, and the creative task of the novel is to probe this condition and to feel for the problems and possibilities of re-birth. . . .

*Season of Adventure* is the most significant of the West Indian novels invoking Africa, and a major achievement, for several reasons: because it does not replace a denigrating excess by a romanticizing one; because it embodies a corrective view without making this the novel's *raison d'être*; because it is so emphatically a West Indian novel—invoking the African heritage not to make statements about Africa but to explore the troubled components of West Indian culture and nationhood; and because it can do all this without preventing us from seeing that Fola's special circumstances, and by implication those of the West Indian, are only a manifestation, although a pressing one in the islands today, of every man's need to take the past into account with humility, fearlessness and receptivity if the future is to be free and alive.

> Kenneth Ramchand. *The West Indian Novel and Its Background* (New York: Barnes & Noble, 1970), pp. 136, 143, 149

[Lamming's] first novel, *In the Castle of My Skin*, written in prose that was dazzlingly original, described a journey from childhood to adolescence; his second, *The Emigrants*, was the work of a brilliant but detached narrator accompanying a shipload of nomadic West Indians to Britain. *Of Age and Innocence* and *Season of Adventure*, his third and fourth books, almost defeat the reader with the sheer density of their prose, but they were occasionally seeded with ideas and illuminating insights that finally made the labor of reading them worthwhile. They took one back from Britain to the Caribbean, and it was as though Lamming was attempting to rediscover a history of himself by himself. His single nonfiction work, *The Pleasures of Exile*, was a neo-Gothic piece with ideas arching like flying buttresses; along with these ideas were varied and disparate existentialist happenings.

In all of Lamming's previous works he seemed to be balanced in an uneasy equipoise between the white colonizer and the black or brown colonized. But his most recent novel, *Natives of My Person*, the glittering product of 10 years of writing and rewriting, has finally released his spirit from its restive thralldom; he sheds the fear and the guilt of the colonized and makes an uninhibited journey to the heart of the colonizer. In order to accomplish this feat he abandons the slave—that ancestral archetype forever looming large in the West Indian psyche—to a limbo on the Guinea Coast. The slave ancestor in *Natives of My Person* is neither native nor person but a gigantic shadow forever lurking in troubled regions of the white imagination. The author gives us deliberately distorted glimpses of the slave coast where master and slave become phantoms moving in and out of primordial silences and where everything that lives is threatened with a sudden death. . . .

*Natives of My Person* is undoubtedly George Lamming's finest novel. It succeeds in illuminating new areas of darkness in the colonial past that the colonizer has so far not dealt with, and in this sense it is a profoundly revolutionary and original work.

> Jan Carew. *New York Times Book Review.* February 27, 1972, pp. 4, 30

It will be our argument that although it is set in a village in a period well before any of the West Indian islands had achieved independence, *In the Castle of My Skin* is a study of a colonial revolt; that it shows the motive forces behind it and its development through three main stages: a static phase, then a phase of rebellion, ending in a phase of achievement and disillusionment with society poised on the edge of a new struggle; that it sharply delineates the opposition between the aspirations of the peasantry and those of the emergent native élite, an opposition which, masked in the second phase, becomes clear during the stage of apparent achievement.

The novel itself is built on a three-tier time structure corresponding broadly to our three stages: the first three chapters describe stable life, a village community whose social consciousness is limited to a struggle with immediate nature; the next six chapters deal with a village whose consciousness is awakened into a wider vision, involving challenge of and struggle against the accepted order of things; while the last chapters show the ironic denouement; a new class of native lawyers, merchants, teachers has further displaced the peasantry from the land. But underlying the story's progress in time is a general conception of human history as a movement from the state of nature to a "higher" consciousness; it is a movement from relative stability in a rural culture to a state of alienation, strife and uncertainty in the modern world. . . .

In light of what has happened to the peasant masses in Africa, the West Indies, and all over the former colonial world, *In the Castle of My Skin* acquires symbolic dimensions and new prophetic importance: it is one of the great political novels in modern "colonial" literature. [1972]

> Ngugi wa Thiong'o. *Homecoming* (New York: Lawrence Hill, 1973), pp. 110, 126

To help put across his points about disintegration of personality [in *Water with Berries*], especially in people who are products of a colonial past, Lamming makes elaborate use of a pattern with which by now his readers should be quite familiar. I refer to the Prospero-Miranda-Caliban triangular relationship of Shakespeare's *The Tempest*. Lamming is especially interested in the attitudes of the black man-Caliban toward the white woman-Miranda, and he explores a number of these relationships from various angles. Sometimes his use of this pattern is decidedly ironic. The frequent references in the novel to another of Shakespeare's plays, *Othello*, emphasizes this irony.

However, the *Tempest* pattern which might have been the strength of this novel proves its undoing. Lamming's persistent use of it comes to seem contrived. Even some of the names he has chosen—Myra for his Miranda figure and Fernando for his Ferdinand figure—seem too obvious. In his unrelenting faithfulness to this *Tempest* pattern Lamming loses touch with the characters he is creating; they cease to be credible, and the reader fails to be moved by their final catastrophe. The last impression that this novel leaves, unfortunately, is that the only real thing in it is its reliance on the *Tempest* theme, and that it has been severely overwritten.

By contrast, Lamming's style is admirably suited to the circumstances of his next novel, *Natives of My Person*. Its formality suggests the prose of the sixteenth-century travel account. Its richness, which is frequently Conradian, evokes well the complexity of the relationships between the characters on shipboard. The ship is used here, much as in a Conrad novel, to isolate a group of characters and to suggest a world in microcosm with its own social structure and system of order. . . .

By contrast to the pretentious complexity of the symbolical pattern of *Water with Berries*, the superficially simple allegory of *Natives of My Person* provides richly complex insights into human personality and the history of colonialism.

Both these novels deserve to be read carefully: *Natives of My Person* because it is a remarkable success, and *Water with Berries* because, despite its failure, it is a serious attempt to follow up on ideas which Lamming has raised in earlier books.

Anthony Boxill. *World Literature Written in English.* April 1973, pp. 112–13, 115–16

George Lamming is the most outspoken nationalist of the generation of West Indian novelists who grew to maturity in the turbulent 1930s and 1940s. His six novels chronicle the sweep of West Indian history, from the colonial setting of *In the Castle of My Skin* through the achievement of independence in *Season of Adventure* to a postindependence uprising in *Water with Berries*. His most recent novel, *Natives of My Person*, is the culmination of his work, reaching back to the beginnings of colonialism and, through allegory, suggesting the underlying, recurrent patterns of Caribbean history. Each of his novels is both complete in itself and part of a continually developing vision linked to the changing political scene in the Caribbean, with its urgent problems of political and psychological decolonization, and to Lamming's evolving understanding of the human condition.

His earliest writing, the poetry and short prose he wrote before emigrating to England in 1950, expresses primarily a rejection of West Indian society and politics. From 1946 to 1950, while living in Trinidad, he devoted himself to the creation of an "artistic personality" through poetry. Romantic and ethereal in the earliest poems, the persona soon came into conflict with West Indian colonial society. In 1948, Lamming describes a Trinidadian "Dutch party," with the poet on one side, brooding on the "permanent disease of society," and the "glittering chatter" of the party on the other. The West Indies in Lamming's poetry is a spiritually sterile prison for the creative spirit: "islands cramped with disease no economy can cure." In the short story "Birds of a Feather," his young protagonist dreams of a "way of escape." The colonial politics of the time are seen as an exercise in futility. . . . Lamming speaks of retreating from "the multitude's monotonous cry / For freedom and politics at the price of blood," to an aesthetic world where the spirit can "Live every moment in the soul's devouring flame."

Emigration to England marked a turning point in his attitude towards the West Indies. A black West Indian in an unfriendly city, he discovered not creative freedom, but alienation. . . .

His experience in England showed Lamming the need to define himself not only as an artist but as a West Indian. The poems he wrote before beginning work on *In the Castle of My Skin* return to the society he had earlier rejected. "The Boy and the Sea" celebrates the freedom of boyhood, and "The Illumined Graves" introduces a central motif of his later work: the living seeking communion and reconciliation with the dead on All Souls' Day.

Ian Munro. In Bruce King, ed. *West Indian Literature* (Hamden, Connecticut: Archon Books, 1979), pp. 126–27

In George Lamming's partly autobiographical *In the Castle of My Skin*, young G feels himself to be part of the communal village experience; he and his friends are close to the land and the "folk." But as the boy grows up he discovers himself to be more and more an individual, a stranger in his own society. His gradual alienation from friends, from the village, and finally from the island environment is more than a case of "growing up," of leaving the world of childhood behind. And it is not finally a question of class nor even of education, but of sensibility. For G has the questing, sensitive awareness of the creative artist. And in his development the natural, undifferentiated world of the village and the world of literature and art inevitably draw apart. The gulf looms, even where . . . there is no irresistible cultural pull toward Europe. G's overriding concern becomes the need to *preserve* this new identity, his integrity as a private individual, "the you that's hidden somewhere in the castle of your skin." It is a selfprotective measure in a society that apparently can no longer contain or nourish the individual mind. Near the end of the book, G, a high-school product by now, cannot find acceptance with the villagers, nor can he relate meaningfully to his new status. . . . Yet G, at the end of the book, recognizes that the reason for his sense of alienation is not simply the high school. . . . Emigration, exile, is the obvious next step. But in the next novel, *The Emigrants*, there is another disillusionment and the inevitable return, the subject of *Of Age and Innocence*, which embodies an act of repossession of the native landscape, a reorientation of feeling through the experience of Fola in the *tonelle* during the ceremony of souls. But San Cristobal is an imaginary island, where the Haitian voodoo ceremony can effect a "return to roots" alongside the music of the steel band as a message of the society's indigenous cultural health. Even if one accepts, through Fola's "conversion," the cultural return to the "folk," one is left with that other dilemma: that of the artist, Chiki, who feels that his creative talent is drying up. Caught between his peasant origins—the world of the *tonelle*—and his European-oriented Christian education, he cries because he is afraid that his creative growth is stunted. . . . This is a persistent symptom of a psychological and cultural division which still needs to be exorcised. Indeed, in *The Pleasures of Exile* Lamming explicitly sought exile to *confront* that other culture, the world of Prospero, in an attempt at self-definition. This was a head-on, articulate tackling of that deeper, cultural schizophrenia. For Lamming it is important that Caliban and Prospero should meet again within a new horizon. . . .

*In the Castle of My Skin* is generally regarded, like V. S. Reid's *New Day*, as a "classic" of West Indian fiction. It is one of the earliest novels of any substance to convey, with real assurance, the life of ordinary village folk within a genuinely realized, native landscape: a "peasant novel" (it is Lamming's term) written with deep insight and considerable technical skill. *Castle* is also a partly autobiographical novel of childhood, and, like *New Day*, celebrates the particular feeling of a particular community through the author's ability to re-create the sights, sounds, and even odors of his native Barbados. The assertion of a rooted, indigenous life merges with the theme of a lost, rural innocence to suggest comparison with other, more famous "childhood" novels: with James Joyce's *A Portrait of the Artist as a Young Man*, for example, where Stephen Dedalus's love/hate relationship with his native Ireland ends in voluntary exile; or with Mark Twain's *Adventures of Huckleberry Finn*, that early assertion of American literary independence, native wit, and lost innocence.

*New Day, Huckleberry Finn*, and *A Portrait of the Artist* all celebrate, in different ways, "the prototype of the national experience"; but in Lamming's novel there is no such celebration. No sense of a national consciousness emerges. To Lamming's young hero, G, Stephen Dedalus's vow "to forge in the smithy of my soul the uncreated conscience of my race'' would have sounded remarkably like arrogance; and Huck Finn's confident, existential *Americanness* would have seemed impossibly precocious. Nor could he have seen himself, like Reid's Johnny Campbell, as a member of an illustrious, proud family. G's ninth birthday, with which the book opens, is a sad reminder of his own shaky sense of identity. . . .

The consciousness which develops is that of the private individual within the framework of his own little village community. Even *other* village communities remain largely outside the young G's focus. His is a gradual, often painful growth toward a personal view of the immediate community: it is a much narrower stage than Reid provides for his drama of the events of the great 1865 Morant Bay rebellion (there is, by contrast, only a timid riot in *Castle*), yet the ''inner'' action is equally urgent. For Lamming's villagers are acquiescent colonials whose acceptance of their island as a ''Little England'' is uncritical; and it is an acceptance that leaves them without authentic identity whether they know it or not. When Trumper (recently returned from America) speaks of ''his people,'' G (whose name we never discover) thinks he means the villagers. ''You ain't a thing till you know it,'' snorts Trumper, ''and that's why you and none o' you on this island is a Negro yet.'' But Trumper's return and his conversation with G occur during the last few pages. The idea of national or racial consciousness as a goal remains peripheral, outside the range of G's experience.

Michael Gilkes. *The West Indian Novel* (Boston: Twayne, 1981), pp. 86–87, 123–24

In the six novels he has published since 1953, George Lamming identifies colonialism as the political institution that has shaped the structure and direction of West Indian society. He has striven consistently as a writer to portray the development of this society in its totality. He describes the complex motivations and interrelationships of the West Indian community within the framework of its political history. Each novel explores a stage in, or an aspect of, the colonial experience, so that the novels are finally the ''unfolding of a single work.'' Each individual novel is originally related to Lamming's political concern with how the structure of power reflects colonial history and how this in turn affects the intimate details of private and public life in a representative community.

There are two distinct movements in this body of work that mark a clear progression in thematic and artistic method. There is a well-coordinated continuity in the first four novels, from *In the Castle of My Skin* to *Season of Adventure*, that gives these volumes epic stature. Together they describe the struggle of the West Indian people to be free of the political, economic, and cultural domination that characterized their history. Lamming describes the breakdown of colonial rule and the emergence of an independent republic in the Caribbean, followed by the fall of this republic and the emergence of the second republic in a continuing struggle to break free of the psychological and political thrall of colonialism. He begins with the initial promise and failure of the emerging labor movement of the 1930s in *In the Castle of My Skin*. This is the prelude to *The Emigrants* in which Lamming describes, with deep sympathy and understanding, the attitudes and the motivations of thousands of West Indians who emigrated to the ''Mother Country'' after World War II. In *Of Age and Innocence* he describes the

return of the emigrant to the Caribbean and the sudden growth of independence movements in the 1950s. *Season of Adventure* is Lamming's last direct fictional statement on the now largely independent, self-governing Caribbean. It marks a high point in Lamming's fiction with the unqualified promise of Gort and Fola, the folk artist and the middle-class revolutionary who ties her educational advantages to the African and peasant values of Gort's drum. In Gort and Fola, the masculine and feminine principles in the society are identified in productive harmony with each other, as an oppressed working class struggles for freedom from the inherited bias and injustices of the postcolonial regime. This is Lamming's concluding and most optimistic statement about the future of an independent Caribbean. Revolution is seen as a continuing process with certain guarantees of success in the Gort/Fola alliance. . . .

*Season of Adventure* marks the end of one movement in Lamming's work. He explains that ''there was at that moment no further point for me to go without in a sense going beyond what has actually happened in the society.'' For twelve years Lamming published no further novels. Then in 1972, his last two novels were published simultaneously: *Water with Berries* was released in London in October, and *Natives of My Person* was released in New York in the same month. The shift in focus and artistic method immediately set these novels apart from his earlier efforts.

In *Water with Berries* Lamming turns his attention to those West Indians, artists in particular, who never re-entered the mainstream of life in the Caribbean. He examines the continuing drama of conflict and rejection that attends West Indians domiciled in Great Britain. Interestingly enough, this is the shortest of Lamming's novels. It offers a much reduced canvas of characters and makes them carry the burden of the book's comment on the immigrant experience. The relative compactness of the novel is clearly tied to its allegorical design and marks a new development in the writer's artistic method. The allegorical structure of *Of Age and Innocence* had been heavily underscored with a wealth of descriptive detail about his characters and their fictional setting. It would seem that working with Great Britain as a known setting in *Water with Berries*, as opposed to San Cristobal, Lamming no longer felt he had to chart the history and structure of the society in the convolutions of an elaborate plot. In *Water with Berries*, as few as eight characters, and the interrelationships among them, sustain the multiple levels of allegory that comprise the novel's statement about the conflict between immigrant and native Briton.

*Natives of My Person*, with its very different setting and European cast, confirms Lamming's continuing concern to define the scope of the colonial experience. In this instance, he explores the crises of late sixteenth-century and early seventeenth-century Europe which inspired Europe's annexation of the New World. . . . In *Natives of My Person* Lamming goes back in history to describe the genesis of colonialism. He describes a sixteenth-century voyage that was the beginning of plantation society in the West Indies. But while the historical fiction is complete within itself, the novel is also a sustained allegory of the structure of power in postcolonial countries. In this novel, Lamming returns to the elaborate architecture of the first four novels as he once again attempts to chart a whole society in the full complexity of the historical moment. But he considerably limits the multiple demands of setting and custom that weight his earlier fiction by structuring this novel around a real and symbolic ship's journey. This is by far the most finely executed of his novels, and especially impressive in that it penetrates the consciousness of another race, another culture, and a distant moment in history.

> Sandra Pouchet Paquet. *The Novels of George Lamming*
> (London: Heinemann, 1982), pp. 116–18

*Season of Adventure* is, in a way, an imaginative projection of the "true meaning of Africa for the West Indian people and their intellectual classes." The novel opens with echoes of two distinctly folk idioms—the steel drum and the religious Ceremony of the Souls—both of which recall continental African practices. The steel drums and their music recall the African drums whose music is used as the "intensive language of transition and its communicant means, the catalyst and solvent of its regenerative hoard." The Ceremony of the Souls on which the novel is based is a voodoo religious ceremony practiced in Haiti by "peasants who have retained a racial, a historic, desire to worship their original gods." The Haitian peasants regard this ceremony as a solemn communication in the process of which they hear the secrets of the dead at first hand. During the ceremony, the dead return to offer, through the medium of the priest, a full and honest report on their relation to the living. The African antecedent of the Ceremony of the Souls is the Masquerade Cult (the Cult of the Ancestors) which manifests in concrete and imagistic terms the African rendezvous with the past.

In San Cristobal, the recently independent fictional West Indian island on which *Season of Adventure* is set, all signs of the past and the living links with aboriginal civilizations are denigrated by the small ruling middle-class elite, who perpetuate an educational system which displays a fear of any affirmation of ancestral heritage as a tool for shaping a revolutionary future. Members of this elite group are enthralled by foreign values and systems; they shy away from their African and slave pasts and the need to use these for creating a viable alternative to their inherited colonial power structure. The only survivors of their systematic denigration of the past in this island are the Ceremony of the Souls and the steel drums. Fola, the middle-class mulatto heroine of the novel, is taken by Charlot, her European teacher of History to the *tonelle* to witness a Ceremony of the Souls. As Fola watches the women dance feverishly, she, in a moment of inspiration/possession, recognizes the ancestral link between her and the worshippers, between her West Indian island and Africa. She is shaken out of her middle-class entombment and becomes aware of the need to take the all-important backward glance into her and her society's past in order to possess the future.

> Funso Aiyejina. In Eldred Durosimi Jones, ed. *African Literature Today*. 14 (1984), pp. 119–20

[George Lamming] has become a successful literary figure in the English-speaking Caribbean. Although he achieved early success in England, Lamming has opted not to remain an exile like his contemporary, [V. S.] Naipaul. He lives and works in the West Indies, where he is now as famous as a vigorous and influential polemicist as he is as a creator of fiction. Lamming was among the first prominent anglophone Caribbean writers to espouse the cause of black consciousness in the 1960s, and he has argued eloquently for a regional identity. He has been a vocal and scornful critic of Naipaul and others who have remained in permanent exile; his objections have rested less on their physical removal from the

Caribbean than on their unwillingness to deal directly with West Indian subject matter.

And yet Lamming himself has been caught up in the typical West Indian need to escape to an ideal, although his evocation of that ideal is quite different from that of either Naipaul or [Aimé] Césaire. Like so many West Indian writers, Lamming returns to childhood, and his very first novel, *In the Castle of My Skin*, still stands as the classic of the quite numerous genre of West Indian childhood narratives.

Lamming's view of childhood, and the uses for which he mobilizes his image of youth, are, however, quite different from the common run. His distinctive tone is part of the source of his power as an opinion leader. Other famous Caribbean childhood novels, such as the Barbadian Geoffrey Drayton's *Christopher* or the Trinidadian Michael Anthony's *The Year in San Fernando*, take what might be the expected approach of dwelling on the innocence of childhood and the creation of a kind of magical, special world sheltered from adult fears and responsibilities. These novels are written in the first person, and preserve the point of view of the young boys who narrate them. Lamming, on the other hand, infuses his first-person narrative with the voice of the wise adult. The little village that is the setting of *In the Castle of My Skin* is not a place of refuge; the changes that were to happen in the course of time are already reflected in Lamming's descriptions of it as it was when he was a child.

Lamming is explicitly political in a different way from the other childhood escapists. Lamming has affirmed his belief that as an artist his responsibility is to his own consciousness, to his society, and to the "community of man," not necessarily in that order. Lamming expresses a particular disdain for the West Indian bourgeoisie, because in his view only the "peasants" (including, in his later formulations, the urban proletariat) are the true bearers of pure folk culture. It should be noted that Lamming's reference to "the folk" extends beyond those people who live in the West Indies. His use of the term is global, symbolic, inclusive, as was Césaire's use of "black." By the same token, the middle class is an artifact of colonial exploitation. He does not, therefore, depict the "coming of age" of his four young heroes as a psychological process. Rather, he sees the maturation of his protagonists essentially as a microcosm that symbolizes the evolution of rural, peasant society and the growth of consciousness among the formerly oppressed and ignorant peasantry. The village in *Castle* is "growing painfully . . . into political self-awareness," and Lamming's political aims generally serve to push his account of the boys' adventures to the background, so that he can concentrate on detailing "the complex shiftings in the community at large."

The common problem is the confusion of West Indian identity. The solution again is to clear the heads of people so that they can start fresh. Naipaul did so by first setting up the romantic allure of the sophisticated world of the metropole, and then debunking even that myth; Césaire did it by exalting the race that transcends the locality and its specific sufferings. Lamming does it by equating the clear-headed, straightforward approach of childhood with the earthbound good sense of the immemorial peasant. The "folk" could be seen as "the ground of psychic wholeness and source of new community." He was not one to mourn the passing of the old order. Rather, he wished the people to greet the coming of the new order with the unabashed, can't-put-nothin'-over-on-us common sense of the common people. The peasants were no less confused than the intellectuals about their identity, but, Lamming suggests, they did not let their confusion hold them back. His was therefore a plea for the unashamed acceptance of local history and culture. His was among the first strong voices to suggest that the West Indies themselves had something valuable to contribute to the identity of its people.

Michael V. Angrosino. In Philip A. Dennis and Wendell Aycock, eds. *Literature and Anthropology* (Lubbock: Texas Tech University Press, 1989), pp. 125–27

In *The Pleasures of Exile*, the reconsideration of the relationship between the margin and the center takes textual form; in many ways, the experience of exile is about reading and rereading the colonial narrative of history and the canonical text. In such texts, especially in the gaps his reading exposes, Lamming seeks his space of representation and identity. In reflecting on the meaning and ideological implications of rewriting the colonial experience, Lamming also questions certain doctrines of European modernity: the historical beginnings it is supposed to engender, the gift of language it is supposed to proffer, and indeed the assumption that in the modern world (the colonial world) a common identity is shared by the colonizer and the colonized. As a state of limbo, exile becomes Lamming's carnivalesque space of representation. According to Joyce Jonas, in this space where he is no longer bound by old laws concerning representation or interpretation, Lamming functions as a trickster. . . .

The need to counter the Apollonian fiction of empire seems to explain Lamming's desire to valorize the disruptive and diachronic functions of narrative. As he notes in regard to *In the Castle of My Skin*, he uses methods of narration in which things are never as tidy as critics would like: ''There is often no discernible plot, no coherent line of events with a clear, causal connection.'' Indeed, rather than appeal to a holistic world that might counter . . . loss and displacement . . . Lamming develops narrative strategies that underscore the converse process: his novels are primarily about a destabilized world of childhood and adolescence (*In the Castle*), of emigrants displaced in the place they hoped to claim through language and tradition (*The Emigrants*), and of the failure of the nationalist dream of a national culture that transcends race and class (*Of Age and Innocence*). Such persistent themes suggest that Lamming has accepted displacement as a strategic narrative possibility that allows the writer to deconstruct the colonial vision and to introduce the narrative of Caribbean history into the text. So although Lamming's early works are intended to evoke a narrative of decolonization and liberation, as several critics have argued, such a narrative is not possible until the writer has overcome the obstacles that block the realization of a national community of language and culture and of nationalism as a state of belonging. As a result, there is explicit tension between the author's desire for a grand narrative that will restore coherence to the Caribbean social body and the mechanisms of psychological blockage generated by colonialism. If Lamming's early novels are motivated by the desire to ''return a society to itself''—as he told graduating students at the University of the West Indies in 1980—then these narratives have had to seek a detour around the ''hidden forms of censorship'' in the dominant culture.

Simon Gikandi. *Writing in Limbo: Modernism and Caribbean Literature* (Ithaca: Cornell University Press, 1992), pp. 57–58, 72–73

*The Emigrants* is a novel about Caliban in exile in more ways than the obvious physical exile of the characters themselves. The tragic sense of life is seen in its theme. A shipload of West Indians goes to England. They are filled with the excitement of travel and the anticipation of finally seeing the country that has for centuries dominated their islands. Instead of feeling at home, however, they are shocked to discover that they are considered outsiders in England. Torn between nostalgia for what they have left behind and the necessity to cope with what confronts them, they suffer the anguish of exile.

There is first of all the sheer physical suffering caused by a climate that is bitterly different from that of the Caribbean. Second, it is confusing to confront a white majority who are employed in a wide variety of jobs that the newcomers have traditionally associated with menial labor at home. Did white people actually do manual work? They had seen only white landlords who were served, not who served. This demands a refocusing of ideas. Third, while each of the immigrants is ambitious to prove himself, theory is easier than practice. It is difficult to keep any sense of identity. Terror stalks the exile, filling him with a sense of disintegration and disillusionment. . . .

*Water with Berries* was published more than fifteen years after *The Emigrants*, but again the theme is exile fraught with the terror of utter alienation. In the earlier novel, the reader interprets the situation of the uprooted West Indian from the viewpoint of Prospero and Caliban. In the later book, the author himself draws an explicit parallel, making it a kind of reverse allegory of *The Tempest*.

Lamming acknowledges in *The Pleasures of Exile* that he may be accused of blasphemy because he deliberately uses Caliban as a symbol of the West Indies. This is an accusation that can be refuted: for symbols, after all, can be plucked from thin blue air. However, matters become complicated when he goes further and chooses *The Tempest* as the symbolic *structure* for *Water with Berries*. Even the names of his characters echo those of Shakespeare's play. One woman is called Myra; another is Randa; a third is compared to Ariel. It is now that we are faced with the problem that confronts him. For if Shakespeare has become such an important frame of reference, it suggests the problematic nature of cultural entrapment. And does this not dramatize the tragic sense? Lamming tries to escape the influence of the ''mother country'' but cannot liberate himself from its stranglehold.

Margaret Paul Joseph. *Caliban in Exile: The Outsider in Caribbean Fiction* (New York: Greenwood Press, 1992), pp. 59, 65–66

Lamming speaks of exile in many voices in *The Pleasures of Exile*. He is at once embittered, resigned, militant, critical, and angry. Exile becomes a precondition for the West Indian writer, out of place in ''a society which is just not colonial by the actual circumstances of politics, but colonial in its very conception of its destiny.'' Exile is also a mixed blessing for the writer who leaves the Caribbean, especially if the final destination is London, which provides distance from the frustrations of home space without quite severing its roots. But the ambiguous privilege of exile rapidly dissolves with the realization of irrelevance in England and increasing estrangement from the struggles at home. As in *Water With Berries*, Lamming posits such a moment of recognition as a timely one for return to the island in *Of Age and Innocence*. In fact, going to England helps accelerate the return by exploding the myth of England and the infallibility of the English. Paravecino's tirade to Crabbe says as much: "You can't pride yourself on liberty and deny them the experiment too. Nor can you go on enjoying the privileges of a lie at the expense of people who have discovered the lie." Following the trajectory of the fleeing intellectual from *In the Castle of My Skin*, *Of Age*, written between *The Emigrants and Water With Berries*, returns the intellectual to the independence movement in San Cristobal. The connections between novels are often specific, as in Mark's recollections of the pebble and the crab that recall G.'s encounters with them in *In the Castle*. But while G. is directed by a sense of expectation regarding his impending departure for Trinidad, Mark's dominant feelings on the airplane to San Cristobal are of pessimistic and fearful gloom.

Mark unearths long-buried childhood memories on the island and regains some sense of belonging, but he continues to remain a largely negative character, with only a muted sense of expectation upon his return home after some twenty years away. Briefly energized by the struggle to take over the colonial state, he feels a momentary sense of direction when thrust into the midst of the daily political meetings. Lamming's notion of the purpose behind return after exile is made abundantly clear when Mark burns his biography of an eighteenth-century pirate and turns his attention to the task of rallying for Shephard, Singh, and Lee. Mark has no regrets: "each account can only be a fresh corpse which we assemble in order to dissect again. Nothing was lost when I burnt the last pages of the pirate's biography. I had only burnt a little corpse whose original I could never know." If the emphasis in *Season* is on reviving the dead, Mark's determination to put the dead to rest does not contradict the writer's agenda in the former novel. The difference lies in the choice Lamming makes regarding resurrection for some and incineration for others. In reconstructing the nation's history, Lamming reverses the moment of forgetting and the moment of remembering. In Mark's gesture, the colonial focus "from the dreary pile of history" is burned in a replay of the burning of the canefields. In Fola's witnessing of a Vodoun ceremony, however, those that have been forgotten, her black ancestors, resurface to direct the season of her adventure.

But for Mark, there is no such adventure in store upon his return, which completes itself literally, but fails metaphorically. The locked-in interiority and the rather bemused reflections of G.'s diary are repeated in Mark's diary, the only form of writing he now maintains. Characterized by a taciturn unwillingness to communicate openly, either to his lover, Marcia, or to his English friends, Bill and Penelope, who accompany them to San Cristobal, Mark's almost total sense of isolation imprisons him in a silence broken only by his observations in his diary. Even these notes are not entirely successful and actually lead to Marcia's madness when she realizes, upon reading Mark's diary, how little he values her. While language has potentially liberating capacities, it can also wound. And while it may clarify and stimulate, especially in the oral tales of San Cristobal, the language of Mark's diary has little productive potential. As in Penelope's case, the revelations in Mark's diary are structured through a solipsistic, claustrophobic stream of consciousness.

Similar to Roger's reaction to his white wife in Water With Berries, Mark's increasing sense of commitment to the national struggle creates a distance from his white lover and friends, who are all perceived to be an embarrassment in the tense racial politics of the island. Although Bill, Penelope, Marcia, and Flagstead are,

in spite of some qualms, largely sympathetic to universal franchise, they are all outsiders from England, isolated from the native white community that is largely reluctant to give up power and from the colored population that feels whites have for too long held the reins of government. Mark's increasing diffidence comes from a sense not that his memory has failed him, but rather that, like his friends, he too is an outsider, "out of touch" with San Cristobal after so many years of absence. As a result, he tries to distance himself from the English visitors, uneasily conscious of belonging neither with them nor with the residents of San Cristobal.

Supriya Nair. *Caliban's Curse: George Lamming and the Revisioning of History* (Ann Arbor: University of Michigan Press, 1996), pp. 125–27

BIBLIOGRAPHY
*In the Castle of My Skin*, 1953; *The Emigrants*, 1954; *Of Age and Innocence*, 1958; *The Pleasures of Exile*, 1960; *Season of Adventure*, 1960; *Water with Berries*, 1971; *Natives of My Person*, 1972; *Conversations: Essays, Addresses and Interviews 1953-1990*, 1998

# LIKING, Werewere (1950–)
## Cameroon

A relatively recent appearance in African theater is the Cameroonian writer Werewere Liking. She was conscious of how rich in possibilities African theater itself was and was amazed that, despite this, French-language theater in African remained so strongly oriented to the old-style European theater where classical dramaturgy sets the tone. . . .

The myth on which one of her plays, *Une Nouvelle Terre*, is based answers the question of the origin of the Bassa in the Cameroon: what were the beginnings of this people, how did they establish themselves in the Cameroon? Bassa tradition sings of two brothers, Koba and Kwan, their courage and tenacity and their arduous, testing journey. Leaving their original home territory, they cross, miraculously, the mythical *White River* (the Nile?) on a "Likogui leaf." Eventually, they arrive at the "Stone with the Hole," Ngok Lituba, in the central southern area of the Cameroon. Here was the birthplace of the Bassa, in the impenetrable cave. Here "une nouvelle terre" ("a new land") began. They developed into a powerful and prosperous people. With the passage of time things did not go well for them. Because of this a ritual was needed through which they could rediscover the purity of the myth, the uncorrupted mythical setting in which the original powers acted positively on the society. That purity can only be re-created through catharsis. The cause of the destruction of good in the society had first to be found. That must happen through group activity, and for that an old Bassa ritual is used in *Une Nouvelle Terre*. . . . [The] original myth, which was meant to explain the origin and bond of the Bassa with their tribal lands, is linked by the author with the complex problems of modern society. She achieves this by means of an entirely different element of Bassa tradition, namely the initiation rite of the Ngué masked figure, which works as a theatrical process. . . .

In the dramatic works of Werewere Liking, written in French, rituals and other old customs occur which are clearly the product of thorough preliminary research. Researched material has thus been used in different and new ways in the theater. In . . . *Une Nouvelle Terre* a ritual based on one of the three existing initiation rites of the Bassa is used. Here an important role is played by the masked Ngué figure. . . . [The] artist, the "Ndinga," initiates the restoration of harmony, along with the child, carried by the masked Ngué figure and in whose name he speaks. The accompanying rhythm is always recognizable because it returns each time the Ngué speaks. Finally, thanks to the ritual, harmony is restored. The village receives new hope, a new ideal, new energy, a new future. Symbols play an important role in the play. . . . Thus, contact with the other world is re-established; the initiation ritual constitutes the most essential element, enriched with the positive achievements of the present. A new village comes into being, thanks to the creative word of the Ndinga. The oral "text" of the myth and the use of the traditional Ngué initiation ceremony both contribute to the thematic coherence of this modern French-language play, about which there is much more to say than is possible here.

Mineke Schipper. *Theatre Research International*. 9, 3 (1983–1984), pp. 219–21, 225–26

[*Spectacles rituels*] contains two ritual dramas by the Cameroonian writer Werewere Liking, together with commentaries on these by Marie-José Hourantier, who staged their first productions, in Abidjian, in the early [1980s]. In her introductory essay Hourantier refers to traditional ritual as a model "one may examine endlessly" in order to regain contact with "certain primordial ideas." The theater derived from this is intended to question contemporary social rules and codes, to examine a world which most people find no longer responds to their needs. The plays expose wounds, dramatize states of unease and self-blame, and above all, seek to accuse: to find the proper targets to blame for social injustice and to exorcise these.

[In *Les Mains veulent dire*] a mentally ill woman is interrogated as to the cause of her sickness. She, and a child who doubles her responses, act as truthtellers: they are special and valuable because they are so open in revealing their distress. The woman's husband can understand no reason for her illness. . . . Women's experience is central to the play, but the accusations are also aimed at a society which is ordered, in any case, to serve only a few. Some of the speeches which specify social injustice have a scorching impact; the play might benefit from more of these, from more direct reference to the base, since it's here it takes off in full air-breaking flight. . . .

The second play, *La Rougeole-arc-en-ciel*, is shorter but more ambitious, using a disturbingly dense and fragmented language to present deliberate caricatures of alienation. . . .[As] Hourantier explains it, the plays are intended to have a healing effect, drawing their audience through a process of interrogation, accusation, and exorcism, and so providing a renewed sense of viability and wholeness. The idea of therapeutic drama might need to be approached carefully; there is a danger, for example, of patronizing men and women who can identify pretty confidently the political initiatives which would heal their lives, but are denied the power to effect these. All the same, these plays mark an interesting and provocative experiment.

Chris Dunton. *West Africa*. November 13–19, 1989, pp. 1894–95

[In] less than fifteen years Werewere Liking has become a significant dramatist in Cameroon because her innovative ritual aesthetics steers clear of the prevailing extroversion of contemporary drama. Her experimental plays represent a major breakaway from the mainstream of current dramatic expression. From the beginning she asserted her presence with a vision and artistry that recoiled from Eurocenteredness. Evincing a taste that was completely antipodal to the prevailing cosmopolitan trend, she set out to probe the deeper layers of her specific cultural experience. While concentrating on the exploration of her people's traditional modes of thought, she has still been able to tackle the most pressing problems of her time, thanks to the extreme flexibility of her ritual matrix. And although the uniqueness of her vision is yet to gain recognition, it could help establish a dramatic tradition of longterm goals if it were to command followership. Indeed, the distinctively traditional canons that underlie her dramatic style are pointing the way to the future development of a theater of national significance, since they are more relevant to the country's insistent preoccupation with cultural identity. . . .

When Werewere Liking came to the fore in 1978, she was bent on showing more loyalty and reverence to the aesthetic tradition of her ancestors, by reorganizing the past not in terms of "modern" perspectives, but according to its own laws. This did not, however, mean that she was going to uncritically extol her Bassa cultural past, but simply that she was setting out to explore its well-tried formulae and techniques to see what originality they could lend her work. Although in her particular case . . . the traditional self dominates the alienated one, she does not reject her duality which finds expression in the way she harmoniously integrates into her drama some elements inherited from Western theatrical forms and thought so as to reflect more faithfully, through her own experience, the cultural situation of all contemporary Africans. The paramount difference here is that, for the first time on Cameroon's stage, the society is seen as evolving from a traditional vantage point: there lies the profoundly innovative nature of Liking's ritual drama. . . .

*La Puissance de Um* concerns the death of Ntep Iliga, a leader of a Bassa clan. Responsible members of the community are convened by Ngond Libii, the widow, to proceed to the ritual burial. Instead of letting the ceremony follow its normal course, the widow surprisingly refuses to act the role prescribed by tradition. She first claims responsibility for her husband's death and shows impatience to get rid of his corpse. From the burial ritual that was going to take place, what we now see developing is a trial ritual. Then, suddenly, she shifts the accusation from herself to the whole society which she holds responsible for producing mediocre males [like] her late husband who was notoriously callous, improvident, profligate, alcoholic, and lazy, yet passed for a successful descendant of the clan in his lifetime! . . .

*Une Nouvelle Terre* . . . starts with a deceptive conflict involving a man, Nguimbus, and his wife, Soo. It opens in an apocalyptic world where institutions and people (apart from a handful of miraculous survivors) have been wiped out. Man and wife are faced with the alternative of escaping or accepting to leave with the general chaos: where the former favors a timid policy based on inaction and silence, the latter rejects mediocrity and compromise. But a smooth transition is made from the couple's divergence to the scrutiny of the powers that be. It is the existing political system, headed by a self-seeking, ruthless, and grabbing Chief whose authority on the people passes through a gun-wielding Cop, which has generated tyranny, oppression, misery, that ultimately lead to chaos in the society. . . .

The third play, *Les Mains veulent dire*, dramatizes a therapeutic ritual organized to cure an insane woman. Kadia, the high priestess called to preside over the ceremony, discovers that the woman suffers from self-guilt originating from ill-digested Christian teachings and from marital infidelity. But it is mostly her option for mundane, shallow appearances (under the husband's instigation) which has led to failure in her marriage, sterility in her life, and finally to madness. In the subsequent search for a scapegoat, the husband is found guilty of exploiting his wife's financial generosity and psychological immaturity; but he tries to cover up his own failure as a husband by having her publicly certified. What appears as madness is in fact the woman's escape into self in order to avoid further victimization. This play re-enacts the ritual quest for personal identity, independence and wisdom. . . .

The flexible medium of Liking's drama is not only firmly rooted in African soil, but it also reflects contemporary situations. Her whole technique is not to restrict the reader, but to make his/her mind function on a wider environment in which moments of intense poetic expression—provided by chorus-figures who comment [on] the action—constantly alternate with ordinary speech. The overall impression is that of a forceful and vital idiom which makes all characters—and more so the rural people, who are neither naive nor gullible like the majority of their counterparts in African drama—very much alive before us with the issues that concern them. Even political jargon is dragged in without the author indulging in didacticism, for she uses parody as an element of her style to torture ''empty'' words. . . . By doing so she stresses ''modern'' verbal insignificance. Through her controlled rendering in which seriousness and humor appear in shifting perspectives, Liking distances herself from the void of political sloganizing and journalese, a thing which her contemporaries, bent on imitating reality, can hardly achieve. Yet her ritual method is not argumentative, nothing is demonstrated, no judgments are passed. What seems to count more is the manner rather than the meaning. The semiotics of the theater expectedly plays a role equal in importance to that of verbal expression in the drama. More than ever, the reader is forced to enter into a permanent dialogue with a variety of objects, symbols, gestures, bodily marks, and costuming whose ''words'' though needing no arguments, are central to the understanding of the author's complete meaning.

Jeanne N. Dingome. In János Riesz and Alain Ricard, eds. *Semper Aliquid Novi: Littérature Comparée et Littératures d'Afrique* (Tübingen: Narr, 1990), pp. 317–21, 324

In plays such as *La Queue du diable, Du Sommeil d'injuste*, and *La Puissance de Um*, Liking assumes that a re-enactment of repressed fears and hostilities will enable actors and spectators to coalesce into a community that emotionally repudiates the false values behind such feelings. For example, the mimed flash-backs in *La Queue du diable* reveal the truth about a man's incest with his daughters and the hatred that inspires his wife with a desire to kill them. The death of her son impresses upon her the horror of the situation she has helped create. A chorus of wailing women comments on the fate of women in their society, and actors planted in the audience cite proverbs in judgment of the events being enacted in front of them.

In *Du sommeil d'injuste*, an ailing chief is portrayed by two actors—one playing the actual individual lying on the sickbed, the other portraying the persona he presents to the public. Throughout the play, the public persona refuses to recognize that he is terminally ill and continues to believe that he can control the world through an exercise of will. Although his ''nation-building'' policies have brought the people to the verge of starvation, he insists that everyone pretend to be happy. In the end, the figure on the bed arises, gazes into the mirror, and collapses dead on the floor. By participating in the process by which the truth emerges in spite of people's attempts to repress it, the spectators of both plays presumably open themselves to the cosmic force that can endow their lives with purpose, meaning, and joy. In this state of mind, they become capable of recognizing and repudiating the false consciousness that has been foisted upon them by petty dictators like the terminally ill chief.

A similar movement toward heightened awareness characterizes *La Puissance de Um*, in which a woman initially refuses to mourn her dead husband because he never created anything with his own hands during a life governed by outmoded customs and the obsessive pursuit of wealth and pleasure. As she begins to reflect, however, she and the rest of the community realize they are all responsible for the man's death. Living at the crossroads of modern and traditional cultures, they now understand that his assimilation of corrupt norms was merely a symptom of what was happening to the entire village, for it too is menaced with fragmentation and purposelessness. By acquiescing in his false constructions of reality, the other villagers helped obscure the truth that could have liberated them from this malaise.

Richard Bjornson. *The African Quest for Freedom and Identity: Cameroonian Writing and the National Experience* (Bloomington: Indiana University Press, 1991), pp. 450–51

Writing primarily as a dramatist, Werewere Liking incorporates both initiation and collective healing in her works of ritual theater, such as *Une Nouvelle Terre*. Indeed, this is the basis for [Pierre] Medehouegnon's acknowledgement of her as a pioneer of ritual theater as a subgenre. However, as the following discussion intends to demonstrate, Liking, in her two novels, *Orphée-dafric* and *Elle sera de jaspe et de corail*, provides a rebuttal to Medehouegnon's opinion of the unsuitability of other, nontraditionally African genres for the adaptation of traditional ritual in literature. As we have said, for Liking the imperative facing African societies and African people in contemporary times is for a renascence stimulated by first purging themselves of the destructive behaviors inherited from traditional society or sown by the colonial experience. Replacing these with behaviors and attitudes based in an Afrocentric discourse relevant to contemporary reality, the purged organism can grow healthy. As the two novels under consideration demonstrate, Liking makes a case for the urgency of a cultural/philosophical self-reassessment and regeneration to rescue ''Africa strangled, endangered, betrayed.''

In the two novels under consideration, ritual is the basis of both structure and content. *Orphée-dafric* not only incorporates initiation but is also based on a myth. As is obvious from the title, Liking has adapted the Greco-Roman Orpheus myth to a contemporary story of an African's quest for enlightenment. Acknowledging the frequent occurrence of the Orpheus quest also in the lore of African societies, Liking finds a symbolic descent into hell necessary for

Africa to extract itself from the infernal state into which it has fallen. So, referring to a Bassa ordeal by fire, Liking unites the universal myth with the particular ritual, ''tropicalizing'' the myth in the process by incorporating very specific Bassa/ Cameroon cultural material, for example, retaining the name of Orpheus for her (peasant-class) hero while giving the Bassa name ''Nyango'' to her (middle-class) Eurydice counterpart. At the other end of the mythology-reality continuum from *Orphée-dafric* is Liking's second novel *Elle sera de jaspe et de corail.* . . . Its genre label of ''chant-novel'' suggests its ritual nature, proposed for the healing of a socially and morally diseased African village, and, by extension, of Africa in general. . . .

Liking's Orpheus story takes the form of a double-frame narrative: a nuptial-night dream within the external story of a marriage celebration, with its ritual nuptial kayak ride, [and] wedding night consummation of the marriage. The initiation is effected through the structure as well as the content of the narrative. Following the same initiation schema described by Medehouegnon for [Amadou Hampaté] Bâ's novel *Kaydara* and Liking's play *Une Nouvelle Terre*, Orpheus is taken through the three stages of novitiate, disciple, initiate. Since Orpheus's initiation is executed entirely in the course of a dream, its duration of nine years is artistically telescoped into the twenty-four-hour wedding night slumber, which is punctuated by sessions of ecstatic lovemaking. Orpheus, dreaming that Nyango drowned during the nuptial kayak ride on the White River, is compelled to go to search for her in the unknown land of the ancestors. Thus, Nyango's love is the driving force that propels him on the odyssey toward the ultimate understanding. . . .

The ''chant-novel'' *Elle sera de jaspe et de corail* illustrates the healing ritual through its polymorphous form. This ritual character of the work is signalled by the author's own genre designations ''(*journal d'une misovire*),'' as well as in the publisher's ''*chant-roman*.'' Structurally, the work flows between first-and third-person narrative befitting the style of a diary, generously interspersed with poetry, theatrical dialogue, theoretical commentary, dream-state action—within the framework of the text's ''action,'' which is the writing of a journal. The journal-writer, or diarist, is performing a function analogous to that of the *historian* described by Liking in the healing ritual: ''For it is he who, through his *chant* and his music, *will narrate and move the event forward*, even mythify it. Relative to the total event, *he is the 'script.'* He notes everything: the incongruity of the most meaningful and most dissociated objects brought together in a ritual, the most absurd and contradictory audience attitudes, the most deep-seated conflicts, the most imperceptible and unperceived suggestions of the crowd'' (emphasis mine). In addition to the participation in the ritual by the diarist as ''historian,'' we hear the voice of the community in the form of two of its intellectuals, and the intermittent voice of the unseen spirit, *La nuit noire*. Thus, Liking's text is the ritual cast in a literary form. Not simply a matter of the ritual as content of the novel, the ritual becomes, here, the genre fitted to the content.

Anne Adams [Graves]. *Callaloo*. 16, 1 (Winter 1993), pp. 155–56, 158–59

The figure of Pan escapes definition. Should one even attempt to ascribe a gender? Try to seize him (or her) as the forest god and Pan will turn up as the spirit of fertile fields. Imagine Pan as an impish charmer and Pan transforms into a wily adversary. Pan is multiple

and everywhere, englobing but also electrifying. Used as prefix, 'pan' imparts to political movements and aesthetic projects a utopian vision, the progressive notion of broad-based co-operation and community. Yet 'pan' can also evoke a potentially discordant assembly.

Motor, guide, inspiration, and founder of the KiYi M'bock theatre company, Werewere Liking evinces a modern-day Pan, replete with all the qualities of the mythic archetype and associated prefix. At once creative artist and arts promoter, reclusive writer and sociable mistress of ceremonies, Liking is multifaceted and multidimensional. One of the few internationally known African women artists of her generation, she, alone, has the moxie and stamina to run a major theatre company which tours throughout the world.

Any reading of Werewere Liking's pieces would have to locate their greatest impact in her sweeping use of music and dance. Spectators are especially moved, emotionally soldered, even 'rescued', through their senses. Dancing, particularly, conveys the feeling of an undifferentiated social body and a link with what has been called the 'rythme cosmique'. Becoming one with the drums, dancers celebrate the possibility of liberating the conscious will, of releasing and channelling energies, and of defeating alienation, both from person to person and space to space. *Singuè Mura* and *Un Touareg s'est marié à une Pygmée* connect through rhythmic contagion to the bodies of their publics, joining members of the performance group to each other and fusing the group on stage with the audience. In Werewere Liking's work, kinaesthetics, or the public's physical adhesion to performance, provides an important means of absorbing her Pan-African aesthetic, for in Africa identification with a symbolic body through rhythmic contagion carries both political and traditional authority.

*Singuè Mura: considérant que la femme.* . . and *Un Touareg s'est marié à une Pygmée*, while both healing rituals of sorts, are far more pointedly politicized and engaged than Liking's ritual theatre repertory. Both are rife with scenes, such as the confrontation of The Wicked Little Sorcerers and Singuè Mura's nurse friend Hannah, in which the damages of certain overriding structures are made comically clear. The patriarchal Sorcerers, for example, are transformed on stage into a seething multi-masked rapist and categorized by the Ngangans, or village healers, as 'éternels adolescents destructeurs, une armée juste bonne pour le viol et le crime'.

*Un Touareg s'est marié à une Pygmée* includes, among other social commentaries, satirical takes on self-inflated, self-aggrandizing national and local leaders, angry rebuttals of constraining border definitions, and a furious appraisal of the historically true mass burial of the living wives of the Benin Royal Court. Hitting hard, Liking opposes Nkrumah's great Pan-African dream to 'les Politicards [qui] ont voulu rêver petit / Et . . . ont engendré des nations comme des crottes/ Jaillies de leurs querelles intestines.' Her attacks on women's subjugation, on tribalism, on nationalism are further indications of her particular brand of Pan-Africanism, for she assaults those traditions which, now vitiated, no longer make sense in the African world.

One might, in conclusion, query the success of Liking's theatrical Pan-Africanism. From the relatively simple perspective of the quality of the dramatic experience, there is no doubt that her work is entirely convincing. Critics throughout Africa, Europe, and North America have acclaimed her acute sense of spectacle and visual imagination. The power of her actors, their superior dancing and musical skills, their ability to make several dimensions of life coexist on stage are undeniable. As Kathryn Wright has remarked in a discussion of the KiYi's percussion piece *Perçues Percus*, the variety of movement and density in drum passages allow spectators to assimilate different emotional intensities. *Perçues Percus*, like all of Liking's work, elicits the range of response which is always a sign of sound aesthetics.

Determining Liking's achievements from the perspective of reaching a broad-based African public evokes, however, the inevitable spectre of inadequate contact with 'average Africans'. Those people who go to the dinner-spectacles at the KiYi Village are mainly tourists or relatively well-healed Abidjanians, more often European than African. The goal of reinvigorating Africans with proof of their own creativity is unobtainable if what the KiYi does goes inexperienced. In this light, it is heartening to know that several million television viewers watched the impressive 200-person, four-hour fresco Liking directed on the occasion of the state funeral of President Houphouët Boigny (7 February 1994). The KiYi Village achieved overnight recognition throughout the Ivory Coast. What this means in terms of more spectators going to the KiYi's performances or more money available for taking theatre to a non-elite is still to be determined.

Certain African critics have also been concerned that because she has so often been co-produced in Europe, Liking's work has begun to anticipate the expectations of European audiences. Perhaps a kind of intraculturalism is inevitable in any theatre work which tours as much as the KiYi's does. Nonetheless, the KiYi continues to hold out against a hegemonic notion of culture. Like the best of world music, the company combines tradition and high-tech without losing its rootedness in the former.

There is, in any case, more than one African audience these days. Not all Africans are initiates. Not all are going to receive the KiYi's symbols in the same way or adhere completely to the work's spiritual vision. With those who are open to her work, Liking does succeed in the consciousness raising and myth building fundamental to her Pan-African project. If she refuses to attack directly leadership issues, as do many of her men contemporaries, she does go after patriarchy and the especially complex issue of maternity in ways male writers do not. Bringing women's issues to the fore may well be the most important Pan-African contribution she makes. And while she slashes at malfunctions in African society, as well as at neo-colonial and imperialistic cabals, she also celebrates a strength of spirit and vital set of artistic traditions which potentially unite her audience. Liking's theatre imparts a sense of the dignity and wonder possible in a life in which deep cultural connections are still viable.

Judith G. Miller. *Theatre Research International*. 21, 3 (Fall 1996), pp. 229–38

BIBLIOGRAPHY

*On ne Raisonne pas le Venin*, 1977; *La Queue du diable* (The Devil's Tail), 1979; *La Puissance de Um* (The Power of Um), 1979; *Une Nouvelle Terre* (A New Earth), 1980; *Du sommeil d'injuste* (The Unjust Sleep, 1980; *Orphée-dafric* (African Orpheus), 1981; *Les Mains veulent dire* (The Hands Wish to Speak), 1981; *La Rougeole-arc-enciel* (Rainbow Measles), 1983; (*Elle sera de jaspe et de corail* (She Will Be Made of Jasper and Coral), 1983; *Une Vision de Kaydara d'Hamadou; –Hampaté–Bâ*, 1984; *Marionnettes du Mali*, 1987; *Spectacles rituels* (Ritual Spectacles), 1987; *Statues Colons*, 1987; *Singuè Mura*, 1993

# LOPES, Henri (1937–)
## Congo

*La Nouvelle Romance* by Congo-Brazzaville's Henri Lopes is a cacophony of sound, the song of modern Africa with all its discordant notes and jarring rhythms. It is a vignette of marriage that is used by the author as a foil to portray the clashes which occur every day in the life of the young African. Lopes presents life as a whirl of dualisms: man and woman, husband and wife, married and unmarried, white and black, colonial and independent, East and West, Europe and Africa, communist and noncommunist, Mercedes and any old car, café-crème and café-au-lait. Underscoring the theme of disharmony, he shifts the action in each chapter from one character to another and from one place to another. To heighten contrass, he uses language—formal French, casual French, translations of traditional expressions, slang, street jargon, and popular terms borrowed from English. He makes frequent use of flashbacks, and once, to emphasize the heroine's dilemma, he uses an extended flashback within a flashback. . . .

*La Nouvelle Romance* is the first novel to come out of francophone Africa that addresses the challenge posed by women's liberation to young Africa; but while affirming the need for change, the author leaves unanswered the question whether the result will be harmony or heightened discord. The work also directly attacks abuses and corruption in government and debates political philosophies, a fact that is of particular interest, since the author himself has been minister of education and prime minister of his own country. Although its conclusion tends toward the didactic, *La Nouvelle Romance* is an excellent literary work which provides a poignant picture of the universal dilemma of the young educated wife of the twentieth century.

Philip A. Noss. *World Literature Today*. 52, 2 (Spring 1978), p. 329

The novelistic work of the writer and Congolese statesman Henri Lopes, like that of Sembène Ousmane and earlier the poetry of Aimé Césaire, constitutes a veritable mirror in which contemporary African society is reflected. This society is described and analyzed with a merciless lucidity: its principal characters are the African elite who have taken the place of the white colonizers. Students, politicians, officials, revolutionary militants, educated women, etc.—all can see their images there, recognizing themselves and either shaking with anger or laughing secretly. It matters little. This is involved (*engagée*) literature that wishes to be both soul-searching and conscience-awakening.

Henri Lopes does not take pleasure in the role of an impartial observer, who from above the clouds contemplates with a critical eye "this hideous spectacle" (Césaire's words) of an Africa simultaneously young and old, entangled in its own contradictions, whose intellectual elite is not only its sole responsible party but also its only hope. On the condition that Africa becomes aware of its responsibilities and accepts its role fully, the author also recognizes himself as part of this intellectual elite, simultaneously as actor and accomplice of the African drama whose spectacle he unravels from his first collection of short stories, *Tribaliques*, to his recent epistolary novel, *Sans tam-tam*, and including the captivating *La Nouvelle Romance*.

Yumba wa Kioni. *Zaire Afrique*. 132 (1979), p. 77

Henri Lopes is one of Congo-Brazzaville's most recognized prose writers. What has become his literary signature is a single-minded attention to—almost a preoccupation with—the ideological parameters of the problems that affect the social, economic, and political progress of contemporary African society. His short-story collection, titled *Tribaliques*, recipient, one year after its publication, of the Grand Prix Litteraire de l'Afrique Noire, includes stories such as ''L'Honnête Homme,'' ''La Fuite de la main habile,'' and ''Monsieur le député,'' whose very titles imply an exposition of some of the self-acknowledged nemeses of African nations today. By effecting a tone of familial frankness Lopes engages the conscience of the members of his African family, warning, exhorting, nagging the family members to do some housecleaning.

In addition to the above-mentioned *Tribaliques*, consisting of eight short stories, published in 1971, Lopes's oeuvre includes three novels, *La Nouvelle Romance*, *Sans tam-tam*, and *Le Pleurer-rire*. Depicting commonly found situations from all strata of contemporary African life, Lopes's works evoke such subjects as the pressures of tribal differences on individuals' lives in a now highly mobile society; the questions of management of a state's industrial resources; the means and ends of popular education; or the sociology and psychology of the changing relations between men and women. In a significant portion of his work—seven out of ten total pieces—women and/or women-focused issues take a central place in the narrative. . . .

The presentation of the experience of the African woman is one of the qualities that makes Henri Lopes's work important in the literature of contemporary Africa. Factors such as the high frequency of women as narrators or focal characters, and topical content covering the broad spectrum of issues of the African woman's experience make the novels and short stories of this unfortunately little-discussed writer a literary forum for African women's consciousness. By virtue of the quantity of attention Lopes devotes to women, the urgency for integration of women's issues into the African social process is made unequivocal. Lopes's women characters articulate their own self-consciousness. Even the fact that some of them are not able to articulate their self-consciousness is a part of their statement through the author as spokesperson. This situation is, however, representative of the contradictions surrounding women's relationships with all the other agents affecting their lives.

While the context of Lopes's creative practice is the family of African people, the context within which his works is set is quite frequently specifically Congolese but with situations drawn along broader African lines. The use of the homebased setting enables Lopes to be self-critical of Africa in general, with the attention directed at his own country. The problems, issues, contradictions which Lopes points to are presented unmistakably as African, not Congolese particularly. Thus from his own ideological stance Henri Lopes presents, in his work, the issues of social change in African society. The issues of women's status have a high place on his agenda for social change in Africa.

Anne Adams Graves. In Carole Boyce Davies and Anne Adams Graves, eds. *Ngambika: Studies of Women in African Literature* (Trenton, New Jersey: Africa World Press, 1986), pp. 131–32, 137–38

This novel [*La Nouvelle Romance*] is at the same time the story of a football player who accedes to diplomatic functions and, in parallel, that of the maturation and liberation of his wife.

A modest employee in a bank, Bienvenu Nkama, known especially under the nickname of Delarumba, is a notorious football virtuoso. Married, he has no children with his legitimate wife, but has gathered and brought under his conjugal roof those children that he has had with his different mistresses. At this level, in fact, Delarumba leads such a dissolute life that his profession feels its effects: one fine day, he loses his job for the third time due to his repeated latecomings. . . .

Learning the very same day of his firing that the diplomatic work pays better than any other career, and that there is a vacancy in his country's embassy in Bonn, Delarumba puts all his efforts into soliciting and obtaining this post. . . . But his behavior does not improve much; he continues to sleep out, shows himself to be capable of embezzlement, impregnates a young Belgian whom he refuses to marry, and finally is caught redhanded while trafficking drugs. For the last two reasons, Belgium declares him persona non grata and expels him from its territory. But immediately on his return to his country, the president of the republic receives him and names him cultural consular to Washington.

Parallel to the lapses of conduct of Delarumba and his capricious posts, we witness the sad and progressive maturation of Wali, his spouse. The most obvious proofs of this maturation are her decision to study and that of leaving her husband in order to continue in Paris the studies undertaken at Brussels. Oriented at first toward personal liberation, her studies become at the end of the novel the *sine qua non* condition of the revolution. This consists of destroying the monolithic and phallocentric society in order to replace it with another, more just, welcoming, and dynamic. It is this renewal that is suggested by the title of the novel.

Makolo Muswaswa. *Zaire Afrique*. 30 (1990), pp. 230–31

Throughout his short stories and four previous novels . . . Henri Lopes has dealt extensively with the role of women in contemporary Africa. With his latest novel, *Sur l'autre rive*, he goes one step farther: his first-person narrator and protagonist is a woman. It is her voice which takes us back in time on a painful inner journey, constituting the central portion of the narration.

Living at present under a fictitious identity on the island of Guadeloupe, Marie-Eve has a chance meeting with a shadowy figure from the past. This encounter releases a torrent of memories of another life (recalled in an extensive flashback) that she had attempted to erase forever. Well over a decade earlier, Madeleine (the narrator's true name), a talented and apparently happily married Congolese painter, suddenly vanishes from her home in Brazzaville, leaving behind a pile of charred canvases. She is assumed, to the astonishment of her family and friends, to have drowned herself in the Congo River. She had in fact been trapped in a sexually dysfunctional relationship with her insensitive husband, and, more serious from a traditional African point of view, she is childless. Prior to her disappearance, during a short vacation in Gabon which was ironically to have been a kind of second honeymoon for the hapless couple, she inadvertently meets a Nigerian chief with whom she had a torrid affair some years before. This event impels Madeleine to relive—in what amounts to a flashback within a flashback—their passionate but ultimately ill-fated liaison. She had, on more than one occasion, yearned to be delivered from her unhappy existence, but this stirring of the embers of her one true encounter with love sweeps away any remaining vestiges of restraint.

Soon after her return from Gabon, Madeleine flees, dissolving into another identity a continent away. Her motivation for so drastic an act (she could have chosen divorce) continues to elude her to the end. Her unhappy marriage and the constant intervention of her husband's extended family in their personal affairs are certainly provocation enough for her need to escape. (Lopes reminds us here that the struggle between tradition and modernism is still often unavoidable, even in an urban African setting at the close of the twentieth century.) But, try as she may, she cannot explain why she chose a solution so desperate as to be tantamount to a kind of suicide. She can only speak vaguely of an "irresistible [inner] force" and is haunted by the question, "Was this an act of courage or cowardice?" What *is* clear is that she can never completely "drown the landscapes of her memory," and a certain melancholy pervades the existence of this fugitive from the past, ostensibly fulfilled by her art and the love of the man with whom she now shares her life.

Although the novel does not contain the daring linguistic and structural innovations of the author's remarkable *Le Pleurer-rire*, it is illuminated by moments of pure poetry and is nonetheless audacious for the challenge it raises: can a man pour himself into the psyche of a woman and speak authentically in her voice? The sensitivity with which Lopes has allowed his narrator to weave her memories and feelings into a touching tapestry of the heart leads this reviewer at least to answer in the affirmative.

Fredric Michelman. *World Literature Today*. 68, 1 (Winter 1994), pp. 187–88

Black revisionist authors have put the historical spectrum from slavery to racism under a fresh microscope. To some—Fred d'Aguiar in particular—the first begat the second and so slavery, like racism, is unavoidable for a black writer. The Tanzanian novelist Abdulrazak Gurnah has explored Arab and African slave-trading, while the Guyanese David Dabydeen has reversed a familiar fall-from-Eden model by describing the India from which "coolies" were transported as an impoverished, brutal land.

None of these recent works is written by a professional historian, but all address the stuff of history with the liberty of literature. Especially in the Caribbean, apex of the triangular trade, writers from C. L. R. James to Earl Lovelace have treated history as an active stimulus.

Following a succession of award-winning works, the Trinidadian Lovelace [in *Salt*] traces the links between a mythologised past and the present. His novel *Salt* takes its title from a latter-day Creation fable. Ever since the insurrectionary Guinea John had "put two corn cobs under his armpits and flew away to Africa, taking with him the mysteries of levitation and flight", his descendants had

committed the error of eating salt and made themselves "too heavy to fly". The weight is that of history, and of the need to return and recover it—whether in Africa's past or contemporary Europe.

The weight also belongs to the "new strange burden" of education. Guinea John's descendant, Alford George, becomes a schoolteacher, his mission to correct "copybooks filled with misspelt words". He gives pupils the means to jump through hoops until, just possibly, a College Exhibition will launch the longer leap to England. After 19 years Alford confronts his contribution "to a system that gave all its rewards, put all its prestige, towards training a few students to escape. To fail to escape was defeat; defeat even before you began."

Not to escape, but to stay, involves a change of consciousness. In Alford's case it is to accept the other burden of office. Ever since his classmates denied him a place in the cricket team but appointed him umpire, he has been offered posts of responsibility that suit him but which he has never chosen.

George enters politics and accepts the proffered party leadership. He feels himself fulfilling the destiny that comes laden with the salty burden of a seafaring history. Yet he is hemmed in by the portraits that now look down at his desk. From Antonio Sedeno's invasion of Trinidad in 1530 through Walter Raleigh's piratical adventurism, Trinidad has been subjected to a foreign history. "'And where was ours?' he thought."

George devises the campaign slogan "Seeing Ourselves Afresh". He tries to make his homeland less a springboard for escape to a mythic past (Africa) or a mythic future (Europe) than a place that can realise its own destiny for the people from those regions—and from Asia—who once crossed the briny to reach it.

Earl Lovelace employs a vocabulary that reconciles through diversity. Alford's critique of the "misspelt words" not found in the *Oxford English Dictionary* gives way before the vibrant hybridity of a book whose language tells an ancient tale in a wholly original voice. To take just one example of its poetry, a "stick fight" ditty crosses three cultures with its chant of "Aye ah yaye a yae, Joe Prengay, lend me your bois to play." A calypso replies that "Yankees gone/And Sparrow take over now. . .". Even in England we can look out of our windows and see that sparrows are not migratory birds.

Amanda Hopkinson. *New Statesman*. 125, 4302 (September 27, 1996), p. 60

*Le Lys et le Flamboyant* is presented as the work of Victor-Augagneur Houang, of mixed African, European, and Chinese parentage; it purports to be a first-person account of the life of a beautiful and talented singer whom Victor knew as a child and with whom he later had a brief love affair in Paris. This woman, whose stage name is Kolele, became an almost mythic symbol of the African artist who played a part in revolutionary movements, especially encouraging the participation of African women in building a new society. Victor, however, as the reader learns in the final pages, cannot publish the book we have just read. It was rejected by the Editions du Seuil, which accepted another version of the story, written by "Henri Lopes" twenty years ago, a version much improved, according to Victor, by the labors of its American translator. Victor refers frequently to how his account differs from that of "Lopes," a childhood friend of Victor's, who appears in the story, usually as a figure of some ridicule, even when he is part of the government of Congo-Brazzaville. (The real Henri Lopes was for a time prime minister of Congo-Brazzaville and is now associate director of UNESCO.)

The major difference between Victor's account and that attributed to "Lopes" is in the importance Victor places on the fact that Kolele was a mulattress. Kolele is not so much a symbol of Africa as a symbol of all those of mixed parentage, or simply of mixed allegiances, who do not belong to any one country, who have no fixed home, no fixed address, whose fidelity is to the human race. Victor is rejected by the parents of white children with whom he wants to play and is told by his mother not to play with African children. Where does he fit? As an adult he shows more sympathy for African victims of racial injustice than for any other group, but he is cynical toward all political groups. He describes the pretensions and hypocrisy of modern African rulers, and the lack of liberty in Maoist China, as well as the evils of the colonial and neocolonial era.

The situation of the mulatto has been a recurring theme in Lopes's work. *Le chercheur d'Afriques* (1990) tells of a young man who goes to France to find his father, who had abandoned his African family. (Lopes has often referred to his own family, in which both grandmothers were African and not married to his European grandfathers.) Another recurring theme is the need to "disappear" in order to remake one's life in a new environment. Kolele frequently abandons family and friends, as did the heroine of *Sur l'autre rive*.

Victor usually relies on his own memories, but recognizes their limitations; as he is a filmmaker, he is happiest with photographs as a means of recalling the past. His recollections of a revolt in the Central African Republic, when he was a schoolboy, are, he realizes, colored by the reactions of the adults of mixed race with whom he lived. "Lopes's" version of the revolt, however, is said to be a mere copy of events of the 1848 revolution in Paris. How does one escape from literature? How does one find any truth?

Adele King. *World Literature Today.* 72, 1 (Winter 1998), p. 185

BIBLIOGRAPHY
*Tribaliques*, 1971; *La Nouvelle Romance*, 1976; *Sans tam-tam*, 1977; *Le Pleurer-Rire*, 1982; *Le Chercheur d'Afriques*, 1990; *Sur l'autre rive*, 1992; *Le lys et le flambouant*, 1997

# LORDE, Audre (1934–1992)
**United States**

[Audre Lorde's] *The Black Unicorn*, is a big, rich book of some sixty-seven poems. . . . Perhaps a full dozen—an incredibly high percentage—of these poems are searingly strong and unforgettable. Those readers who recall the clear light and promise of early Lorde poems such as "The Woman Thing" and "Bloodbirth," and recall as well the great shape and energy of certain mid-1970s poems including "To My Daughter the Junkie on a Train," "Cables to Rage," and "Blackstudies," will find in *The Black Unicorn* new poems which reconfirm Lorde's talents while reseeding gardens and fields traversed before. There are other poems which do not so much reseed as repeople, and these new persons, names, ghosts, lovers, voices—these new I's, we's, real and imagined

kin—give us something fresh, beyond the cycle of Lorde's previously recorded seasons and solstices.

While *The Black Unicorn* is unquestionably a personal triumph for Lorde in terms of the development of her canon, it is also an event in contemporary letters. This is a bold claim but one worth making precisely because as we see in the first nine poems, Lorde appears to be the only North American poet other than Jay Wright who is sufficiently immersed in West African religion, culture, and art (and blessed with poetic talent!) to reach beyond a kind of middling poem that merely quantifies "blackness" through offhand reference to African gods and traditions. What Lorde and Wright share, beyond their abilities to create a fresh, New World art out of ancient Old World lore, is a voice or an *idea* of a voice that is essentially African in that it is communal, historiographical, archival, and prophetic *as well as* personal in ways that we commonly associate with the African griots, *dyeli*, and tellers of *nganos* and other oral tales. However, while Wright's voice may be said to embody what is masculine in various West African cultures and cosmologies, Lorde's voice is decidedly and magnificently feminine. The goal of *The Black Unicorn* is then to present this fresh and powerful voice, and to explore the modulations within that voice between feminine and feminist timbres. As the volume unfolds, this exploration charts history and geography as well as voice, and with the confluence of these patterns the volume takes shape and Lorde's particular envisioning of a black transatlantic tradition is accessible.

Robert B. Stepto. *Parnassus.* (Fall/Winter 1979), pp. 315–16

For Lorde, as for many women of color, [the] celebration and assertion of female identity has been a key survival technique, a way of combatting a subtle but potent enemy: silence. As Lorde tells us in *Zami [A New Spelling of My Name]*, she did not speak until she was five years old, and when she finally found a voice, she talked in poetry—first by reciting verses she had memorized, then "when I couldn't find the poems to express the things I was feeling, that's when I started writing poetry." To Lorde, poetry represents a refusal of "dishonesty by silence"; her foremost goal as a black woman poet then becomes "the transformation of silence into language and action"—a transformation essential if women are to overcome what Adrienne Rich has called "the terrible negative power of the lie" among them. Silence is a destructive quality, Lorde asserts, because "it's the nameless. As Adrienne has said, 'what remains nameless eventually becomes unspeakable, what remains unspoken becomes unspeakable.'" To speak the unspeakable is thus a key task for Lorde as for Rich, to revision herself and other women. . . .

Another primary aspect of the "poet warrior's" task is paying tribute to the women from whom she gleans her power, "recreating in words the women who helped give me substance." In Lorde's writing of the last twenty-five years, we find four main sources of creative inspiration, all female. First, she celebrates as muses the women who make up her own family: her mother, her mother's West Indian female relatives, and her sisters, literal or figurative. Second, she pays homage to the women lovers who have "helped sustain" her, and to her own erotic power, which she considers a vital creative force. Third, she seeks sustenance from African goddesses, mythological women whose names and legends survive in black cultures as tributes to a strong matriarchal legacy: Yemanja, Mawulisa, Seboulisa, the "Women of Dan," her

African warrior sisters. Finally, Lorde names as muses and acts as a mouthpiece for those women who have been victims of a racist, sexist, homophobic society—her ''sisters in pain.'' Many such women have been violated, murdered, silenced, yet it is for and by them that the poet-warrior is empowered to speak. If women, black or white, are to survive, Lorde insists in ''Meet,'' they must bring to bear on behalf of one another their passionate convictions, their powerful eroticism, their terrible anguish, their fluid and mutual identities.

> Mary K. DeShazer. *Inspiring Women: Reimagining the Muse* (New York: Pergamon, 1986), pp. 170–71, 173

Lorde began her published work in 1968 . . . with *The First Cities.* When she arrived via five volumes of verse and a growing reputation at *Between Our Selves* and *The Black Unicorn*, she had gone from merely writing poetry to casting wise and incantatory magic. . . . *The Black Unicorn* is a majestic voicing of statements and propositions whose applications are further worked out in her later book, *Our Dead Behind Us*. Much of the struggle of defining and instating herself was done in the earlier volume, so that now she can simply put herself in motion, acting and being who she is. And because we know—and she knows that we know—where she is coming from, there is no need for her to repeat herself. At this hard-earned point, we can read Audre Lorde in her own light. . . .

Lorde's seemingly essentialist definitions of herself as black/lesbian/mother/woman are not simple, fixed terms. Rather, they represent her ceaseless negotiations of a positionality from which she can speak. Almost as soon as she achieves a place of connection, she becomes uneasy at the comfortableness (which is, to her, a signal that something critical is being glossed over) and proceeds to rub athwart the smooth grain to find the roughness and the slant she needs to maintain her difference-defined, complexly constructed self. *Our Dead Behind Us* is constant motion, with poem after poem enacting a series of displacements. The geographical shifts are paralleled by temporal shifting in a ''time-tension'' which Mary J. Carruthers sees as characteristic of lesbian poetry. . . . The ubiquitous leave takings [in the poems] are not surprising—''Out to the Hard Road'' (''I never told you how much it hurt/leaving''), ''Every Traveler Has One Vermont Poem'' (''Spikes of lavender aster under Route 91/ . . . I am a stranger / making a living choice''), ''Diaspora'' (''grenades held dry in a calabash/leaving''). . . .

Lorde's tricky positionality—as exemplified by her relationship to home and poetic lines—also extends to community, which she likewise desires, but problematizes and finds problematic. An early poem, ''And What about the Children,'' alludes to the ''dire predictions'' and ''grim speculations'' that accompanied her interracial marriage and mixed-race offspring. . . .

However uneasy her identity may be, it is imperative for Lorde that she read the world as a meaningful text and not as a series of interesting and elusive propositions. For her, to ''read'' is to decipher . . . the signs of the times, to decode—as the lesbian/gay community does—the submerged signification of the visible signs, and to sound out clearly and ''to your face'' uncompromising truth as she sees it, in that foot-up, hands-on-hip loudness that is self-authorized black female jeremiad, sermon, and song. From the beginning, her vatic voice has defined her moral and didactic arena—in the same way that her presence claims its territory on the

stage or in a photographic frame. She and Adrienne Rich, especially, have been criticized for their heavy seriousness. However, with so many dead behind her, Lorde is too busy pulling the bodies from bars and doorways, jungle tracks and trenches to find time for unrestricted poetic laughter. Her task is to foreground the carnage in a valiant effort to make such senseless dying truly a thing of the past.

> Akasha Gloria T. Hull. In Cheryl A. Wall, ed. *Changing Our Own Words* (New Brunswick, New Jersey: Rutgers University Press, 1989), pp. 153–56, 159–62

Audre Lorde's *Zami* . . . explores the struggle to define a self amid the over-whelming Caribbean culture of the household. The conventions of autobiography allow for the centering of a self caught in the conflicts of a Caribbean/American household which eschews any thought of private individual space: ''a closed door is considered an insult.'' Nevertheless, there is an engagement with Caribbean folk culture through the recalling of folk healing, songmaking, the notion of ''home.'' Above all, she is able to make an explicit connection between her lesbianism and the fact that Carriacou women have a tradition of ''work[ing] together as friends and lovers.'' By accepting ''Zami,'' a word still identified negatively in the Caribbean, she is like Michelle Cliff, ''claiming an identity'' she was taught to despise. The definition of ''Zami'' is a bold epigraph to the work. And the tension in accepting identity seems to be finally resolved here. Her essay ''Grenada Revisited,'' for example, is one of the best evaluations of the Grenada invasion and, as I see it, a fitting conclusion to *Zami*. Buttressed by concrete images of Grenada, pre-and postrevolution, she concludes with a tribute to the strength and resilience of the Grenadian people. . . .

The heritage/identity question is definitely established in the Grenada essay as is the woman-identification in the acceptance of the term ''Zami.'' But Lorde's expressed connectedness has its impetus from revolutionary Grenada and the sense of possibility which it held. Clearly then, for Lorde, cultural identification has to be addressed along with an overtly, antihegemonic discourse. She therefore moves the discussion, beyond a singular Pan-African identification to a fuller acceptance of a gender-identified relationship with history and an ideological consciousness of the meaning of Grenada's thwarted revolution within the context of power, powerlessness, and empowerment.

> Carole Boyce Davies. In Carole Boyce Davies and Elaine Savory Fido, eds. *Out of the Kumbla: Caribbean Women and Literature* (Trenton, New Jersey: Africa World Press, 1990), pp. 62–63

*Zami* is a Carriacou word ''for women who work together as friends and lovers.'' Just as the title implies, *Zami* is woman-identified from the outset and thoroughly suffused with an eroticism focusing on women. Lorde connects her lesbianism to the model her mother, Linda, provided—her pervasive, often intimidating, strength; her fleeting sensuality when her harsh veneer was lifted—and also to her place of origin, the Grenadian island of Carriacou, where a word already existed to describe who Linda's daughter would become. . . . [In] *Zami* relationships between women are at the center of the work. Here they are complex, turbulent, painful, passionate, and essential to the author's survival.

Although Lorde continuously explores the implications of being a black lesbian and she has an overt consciousness about her lesbianism . . . she does not define lesbianism as a problem in and of itself. Despite homophobia, particularly in the left of the McCarthy era; despite isolation from other black women because she is gay; and despite primal loneliness because of her many levels of difference, Lorde assumes that her lesbianism, like her blackness, is a given, a fact of life which she has neither to justify nor explain. This is an extremely strong and open-ended stance from which to write about black lesbian experience, since it enables the writer to deal with the complexity of lesbianism and what being a black lesbian means in a specific time and place. Lorde's position allows black lesbian experience to be revealed from the inside out. The absence of agonized doubts about her sexual orientation and the revelation of the actual joys of being a lesbian, including lush and recognizable descriptions of physical passion between women, make *Zami* seem consciously written for a lesbian reader. This is a significant point because so little is ever written with us in mind, and also because who an author considers her audience to be definitely affects her voice and the levels of authenticity she may be able to achieve. Writing from an avowedly black lesbian perspective with black lesbian readers in mind does not mean that a work will be inaccessible or inapplicable to non-black and nonlesbian readers. Works like *Zami*, which are based in the experiences of writers outside the "mainstream," provide a vitally different perspective on human experience and may even reveal new ways of thinking about supposedly settled questions.

Barbara Smith. In Joanne M. Braxton and Andrée Nicola McLaughlin, eds. *Wild Women in the Whirlwind: Afra-American Culture and the Contemporary Literary Renaissance* (New Brunswick, New Jersey: Rutgers University Press, 1990), pp. 238–39

The struggle to claim her racial, sexual, feminist, and warrior identities forms the core of Audre Lorde's poetics and politics. . . .

Many of Lorde's early poems contain images of women as warriors: "warrior queens" ("Harriet"); "like a warrior woman" ("Chorus"); "like my warrior sisters" ("125th Street and Abomey"); "Assata my sister warrior" ("For Assata"). At times the epithet *warrior* becomes an emblem of hope for future generations: "I bless your child with the mother she has / with a future of warriors and growing fire" ("Dear Toni Instead of a Letter"). For Lorde, the term *warrior* evokes centuries of history of African women's resistance to white authorities and other forces of suppression. Foremost among such warrior women were the legendary Amazons of Dahomey, about whom Lorde writes in "The Women of Dan." Here she enacts a strong revisionist impulse, for she insists that women's warring be not stealthy but open, visible. . . .

Dangerous to others but not to herself, the poet names her new weapons, erotic heat and poetic words, a combination vital for continued growth and vision. . . . Like Mawulisa, a peace-loving Dahomean goddess about whom she often writes, Lorde resists war as a deceptive, vindictive enterprise. She refuses to be silenced or to destroy unnecessarily. Instead, she openly warns contemporary oppressors of her watchful presence and embraces her warrior identity through a passionate, ritualistic celebration with her sisters of Dan. . . .

"Sisters in Arms" illustrates the complexity of Lorde's most recent use of the warrior construct; in fact, it interweaves related images of the poet-warrior, the war correspondent, and the warrior muse. Sexuality and political struggle intersect, as Lorde describes sharing her bed and her arms (in both senses of the word) with a South African woman who learns that her fifteen-year-old daughter has just been brutally murdered near Durban, her body "hanging / gutsprung on police wheels." The poet feels agony and helplessness. . . . So Lorde does what she can—buys her lover a ticket to Durban (ironically, on her American Express card) and comforts her physically before her departure.

Written retrospectively, the poem reveals Lorde's fury at both the South African government's continuing atrocities against its black people and the *New York Times's* scant coverage of what it euphemistically deems the "unrest" there. As a war correspondent, she reports graphically the horrors the *Times* chooses to hide: "Black children massacred at Sebokeng, / six-year olds imprisoned for threatening the state . . . / Thabo Sibeko, first grader, in his own blood / on his grandmother's parlor floor." The newspaper's evasions and these terrible truths haunt Lorde as she gardens haphazardly and recalls moments of intimacy and pain with her South African sisters. . . . Lorde knows that the sisters who lay in one another's arms may also bear arms together one day, stronger for having shared erotic experience: "someday you will come to my country / and we will fight side by side?" Since she cannot go to South Africa, Lorde invokes in her stead the African warrior queen Mmanthatisi, who led the Sotho people during the *mfecane*, an earlier black South African uprising. As this warrior muse "dresses again for battle, / knowing the men will follow," the poet chronicles her preparations, dreaming of Durban and the possibility of revolutionary change.

Mary K. DeShazer. In Suzanne W. Jones, ed. *Writing the Woman Artist: Essays on Poetics, Politics, and Portraiture* (Philadelphia: University of Pennsylvania Press, 1991), pp. 266–68

In her essays collected in *Sister Outsider*, Audre Lorde performs a complex act of cultural revisioning wherein she reappropriates the ground of creativity for women of all kinds. She does so by envisioning a figure of "the black mother who is the poet . . . in every one of us," and linking her with an "erotic" lifeforce that she finds necessary to creative work. The figure revises well-known Greek myths that represent the erotic either in terms of the male god Eros, whose passions are sexual, or Aphrodite whose activities are seductive. It also revises the Jungian tendency to associate women with Eros, understood as psychological relatedness in opposition to Logos, the principle of abstract thought supposedly embodied by men. Neither exclusively physical in orientation nor wholly concerned with relationship, Lorde's female figure of the erotic potential that lies within both women and men is a deep-seated capacity for joy and excellence that she hopes women will realize in order to effect social change. . . .

Lorde's figure of an erotic wellspring provides the basis for belief in female authority because it removes the necessity for certification of one's ideas by the dominant group. The creative impetus is in all of us in our capacity for feeling. Lorde speaks of creative process as a matter of tapping or honoring the "deep place" from which perception comes; rationality, she says, serves feeling and knowledge by building roads from one place to another, but "Perceptions precede analysis just as visions precede action or accomplishments.'' The figure of the black mother within allows us to stop questioning our perceptions before they have a chance to become poems.

Lorde's figure of the black mother poet, then, symbolizes the belief in one's own authority to create, and her association of it with the erotic, with Eros in female form, is a potentially useful strategy for rethinking women's relationship with love, a concept that has often worked in Western culture to prevent women from realizing creative as opposed to procreative potential. Lorde's figure addresses the root problem of women's motivation for creative activity. If a woman believes that the source of creativity lies within her, perhaps she can more readily marshal her resources to combat the external conditions of her life. With the help of figures such as Lorde's . . . figures that refuse to freeze and ration creative energies—perhaps women can not only survive as artists but also re-envision survival itself as a matter of reclaiming what has been repressed and nourishing the capacity to change.

Estella Lauter. In Suzanne W. Jones, ed. *Writing the Woman Artist: Essays on Poetics, Politics, and Portraiture* (Philadelphia: University of Pennsylvania Press, 1991), pp. 398, 415–16

Audre Lorde terms *Zami: A New Spelling of My Name* a ''biomythography,'' a combination of autobiography, history, and myth. I have chosen to discuss it here because it is the one extended prose work of which I am aware that approaches black lesbian experience with *both* verisimilitude and authenticity. *Zami* is an essentially autobiographical work, but the poet's eye, ear, and tongue give the work stylistic richness often associated with well-crafted fiction. . . . Because *Zami* spans genres and carves out a unique place in African-American literature as the first full-length autobiographical work by an established black lesbian writer, it will undoubtedly continue to be grouped with other creative prose about black lesbians.

The fact that *Zami* is autobiographical might be assumed to guarantee its realism. But even when writing autobiographically, an author can pick and choose details, can create a persona which has little or nothing to do with her own particular reality, or she might fabricate an artificial persona with whom the reader cannot possibly identify. A blatant example of this kind of deceptive strategy might be an autobiographical work by a lesbian which fails to mention that this is indeed who she is; of course, there are other, less extreme omissions and distortions. Undoubtedly, Lorde selected the material she included in the work, and the selectivity of memory is also operative. Yet the work is honest, fully rounded, and authentic. . . . The candor and specificity with which Lorde approaches her life are qualities that would enhance black lesbian writing in the future.

Barbara Smith. In Chandra Talpade Mohanty, Ann Russo, and Lourdes Torres, eds. *Third World Women and the Politics of Feminism* (Bloomington: Indiana University Press, 1991), p. 122

For feminist academia Lorde is particularly effective as a token: since she is black, lesbian, and a mother, her work compactly represents that generally repressed matter towards which white feminists wish to make a gesture of inclusion—but since Lorde conveniently represents so much at once, she can be included without her presence threatening the overall balance of the white majority vision. As a token of particular identities, moreover, Lorde is included as one who speaks for the marginal, not for the mainstream. Paradoxically, in other words, Lorde occupies diametrically opposed positions in two literatures: in one her words are consumed for the light they can shed on the mainstream of black female possibility; in the other her work stands alongside, but is not read as directly bearing upon the mainstream, white feminist consciousness. It is my project here to challenge both these ways of reading Lorde, to suggest that *Zami* produces a way of seeing that has significance as a commentary on how the black community as a whole both lives and theorizes itself, and that Lorde's textual practice also has the power to address not merely the problems of identity politics but also the issues of lesbian aesthetics. . . .

Lorde's biomythography *Zami* initially constructs a lesbian existence that has needs and features in common with the lesbian myth produced by white Anglo-American novelists. Her sexual coming out is described within a series of metaphors for recognition familiar from that tradition: making love is ''like coming home to a joy I was meant for''; the act of lesbian sex is naturalized through being presented as a return to an original knowledge that the protagonist has temporarily forgotten: ''wherever I touched, felt right and completing, as if I had been born to make love to this woman, and was remembering her body rather than learning it deeply for the first time.'' This is a country of the body rather than of a people. Audre's community as a young lesbian in New York is defined by sexuality, and it is a community that attempts the utopian separation and newness of a lesbian nation: ''We were reinventing the world together''; ''we had no patterns to follow, except our own needs and our own unthought-out dreams.'' Yet membership in such a community is purchased at the price of nonrecognition of blackness; Lorde repeatedly describes Audre's ''invisibility'' to the white lesbian community as black; she is admitted only under the assumption of sameness. The lesbian community believes in itself as obliterating difference, ''that as lesbians, we were all outsiders and all equal in our outsiderhood. 'We're all niggers,' [Muriel, Audre's white lover] used to say.'' Yet in Lorde's analysis the lesbian community is not elsewhere but is rather a microcosm of the world outside, as her description of the lesbian bar the Bagatelle shows. . . . In the white model, the real world recedes before the lesbian community's power to redefine: one reclothed oneself in a new identity and a new way of relating. It is one of Orlando's freedoms in Virginia Woolf's imaginary biography that s/he is able effortlessly to switch between costumes; her sexual fluidity is signaled by this flexibility, and in the same moment it indicates a crucial aspiration: the capacity both to switch between costumes and to cross-dress stands for freedom from gender imprisonment. George Sand said of her experience of cross-dressing, ''My clothes knew no fear.'' But for Audre a rigidly stratified dress code, each item signifying a particular class or role position, expresses not freedom of play but her imprisonment within a system of hierarchized differences. The ''uncharted territory'' that she finds in trying to discover new ways of relating in ''a new world of women'' is not just uncharted but inaccessible: there is no pathway for the black lesbian that leads from the actual lesbian community, where class distinctions are precisely observed and race is unmentionable, to lesbian nation. It is from this experience that Lorde constructs the ''house of difference'' that she finally articulates as ''our place''; it is a refusal of the aspiration to unity that lesbian nation encodes. The "house of difference," then, is a movement away from otherworldliness. It accepts the inevitability of a material world where class, race, gender all continue to exist. It is, therefore, a step back towards acknowledging the necessity of reasserting ties of identity with the black community. . . .

Lorde's challenge to current aesthetic inquiry lies in her assertion of an abiding connection between individual and social identity. This is how she is able to maintain a connection between political subversion and textual subversion, a link that in contemporary discussions of a lesbian aesthetic seems to have become an abyss. Unlike that of the postmodern lesbian subject, Audre's identity is never established only by the transgressions of the bedroom: it is from the bedroom that Audre and Kitty emerge, and it is from this "lesbian narrative space" that Audre goes out to refigure the black family of Harlem as including her; but the reconstruction that happens in the street is as crucial as that conducted in the mythic bed.

Anna Wilson. In Sally Munt, ed. *New Lesbian Criticism: Literary and Cultural Readings* (New York: Columbia University Press, 1992), pp. 77–78, 81–82, 89–90

[The] title poem [of *The Black Unicorn*] uses its controlling trope to construct a poetics of identity; the black essence of coal is deployed in a new guise in the feminized figure of the black unicorn. . . . As an allegory for Lorde and for the black woman poet, the unicorn is at once angry and erotic, regendered and recolored, reaching the site of deepest female power. Insofar as the political agendas in the poem generate spaces for identities made doubly absent in dominant cultural and literary discourse, they also reflect the dangers of their re-empowerment. *The Black Unicorn*, although reclaiming an alternative mythos for black women poets, is cognizant of the problems attending its mythmaking. . . .

Even as *The Black Unicorn* examines the complexities of political agency in poetry, the history of Lorde's publications maps the socioeconomic boundaries of literary institutionalization. As her volume of poetry wrestles in the interstices between speaking local resistance and grand narratives for change, Audre Lorde's identity as poet enacts its histories between literary academia and grass-roots audiences. Her various speeches and essays became available in the late 1970s and through the 1980s mainly through small press broadsides and alternative journals for an otherwise marginalized readership. Dominant literary discourse perpetuates and legitimates the absences. Lorde's poems appear in none of the better known feminist anthologies, edited, as Jan Clausen points out, for a feminist but also primarily heterosexist and white community of readers. . . .

The hierarchy operating among presses publishing Lorde's work and the chronology of early and late publications significantly charts the "growth" of [an] unknown poet to a name increasingly better known. Although her poetry is still noticeably "unread" within English departments, Lorde has become a feminist and lesbian name to be cited as her activist prose engages women's studies and African American studies programs. The presses publishing her poetry bear ironic witness to her double status in literary and mainstream feminist discourse. Her first two volumes of poetry, *The First Cities* and *Cables to Rage*, were published by Diane di Prima's Poets' Press and Paul Breman, small presses

catering to the needs of relatively unknown writers. As the black community took up her work, her publishers changed. The Broadside Press in Detroit, a small press oriented to a black readership, published her next two volumes, *From a Land Where Other People Live*—nominated for a National Book Award for Poetry—and *New York Headshop and Museum*. As her name came to be recognized in select literary and activist audiences, Eidolon Editions published *Between Our Selves* in a special edition of eleven hundred copies. This pattern of small presses, however, changed as Norton published Lorde's next three volumes of poetry, *Coal*, *The Black Unicorn*, and *Our Dead Behind Us*, as well as a volume of her selected poems, *Chosen Poems, Old and New*. Norton, of course, is the same press that underwrites the literary canon in the United States with its Norton editions and anthologies, basic texts for students in English literature. Publication of her poetry by Norton indicates that Lorde is now available in academic bookstores. Lorde's work is not usually found in the poetry sections, but is probably available in black studies or women's studies sections—another ironic gloss on Lorde's literary status as activist writer.

Sagri Dhairyam. *Feminist Studies*. 18, 2 (Summer 1992), pp. 237, 239–40

[In *The Cancer Journals* Lorde's writing of self is both the account of a transformation of her body through cancer surgery and the reconstruction, textually, of her sense of self. . . .]

In contrast to the rigorously shaped chronology and narrative coherence of *Zami* (even when autobiography is disturbed by "biomythographic" elements), the dynamics of process evident in *The Cancer Journals* suggests some aspects of the distinction I wish to draw between autobiography and autography. This reading of *The Cancer Journals* examines who and how Audre Lorde means when she says "I."

In 1978, Audre Lorde had her right breast removed, having discovered it contained a malignant tumor. That cancer metastasized and caused her death in November 1992. *The Cancer Journals*, published in 1980, is her writing of the experience of breast cancer and her understanding of it in its social context. It is a slim volume composed of personal exposition, a speech, essays, and a selection of dated journal entries, embedded in and set off from the main text in italics. The writing of this text exemplifies [Alicia] Ostriker's view that "when defining a personal identity women tend to begin with their bodies". The site of self-as-object, to be seen, as well as subject, experiencing and experienced, the body becomes the locus of tension about identity: "I have a body" struggles with "I am a body." Lorde's surgery left her with the realization that, in her words, "I am who the world and I have never seen before." In this assertion, Lorde is allied with "the world" as specularizer gazing at the unfamiliar external self, and is simultaneously reconstructing a self who is a recipient of the gaze. The doubly mirroring "I" is ontologically changed as her body is changed, and the "I am who" requires an internal and external revision of knowledge. . . .

In the period of decision before surgery Lorde describes the "concert of voices" inside herself. She understands the discordant "voices" as "those myriad pieces of myself and my background and experience and definitions of myself I had fought so long and hard to nourish and maintain." These "pieces of self" do not have to function as a unified, coherent whole, perhaps because of the presence of the "I" who fights for their right to be heard. The multitude is full of contradictions: one "thin high voice was screaming that none of this was true"; another detached itself and provided a cool commentary; yet another demanded sleep. Lorde does not distinguish how she identifies an "I" who listens to the many voices of her selves, but certain entries from the journal of the time reveal that no central "I," separate from the other parts of self, maintained a consistent presence, a transcendent control. The deep subjectivity functions as an "ear" to the voices, and as an arbiter counting costs. Of her decision to have a mastectomy, for example, Lorde says, "I would have paid more than even my beloved breast . . . to preserve that self that was not merely physically defined." Yet the surgery, as the journal entry at the time shows, is modifying that undefined but "real" self: "*I want to write of the pain I am feeling right now, of the lukewarm tears that will not stop coming into my eyes—for what? For my lost breast? For the lost me? And which me was that again anyway?. . . I want to be the person I used to be, the real me*" (October 10, 1978). Physical pain, and the desire to make that immediate in the writing, is diverted into the psychic pain of loss. Longing for the familiar and the known, speaking from the position of the estranged, and consequently (in this moment) the less "real," Lorde struggles to accept all the "me's"—even the ones that contradict her belief that one self is as "real" as another.

Lorde encourages a multiplicity of selves, and the spirals of selves (Black, lesbian, feminist, mother, poet) that touch, meet, cross, and blur according to context must all be given voice. These "selves" could be considered "discourses"; that is, they could be the complex of what one says about one's Blackness, for example—how it means, how it is interpreted/understood/experienced. But, when seen as "discourse," the self loses its link to the body, to the self indicated but not (or not yet) written. To think of self as merely discourse seems arid, and to choose "discourse" as the dominant trope for discussing this I, this writing, is to disfigure the passion with which Lorde allies her written self to her physical self.

Audre Lorde in her various manifestations appearing here makes for a writing that lives close to the vulnerable and uncertain flesh, and yet enjoys rhetorical authority, sureness, and even righteousness. *The Cancer Journals* is the transformation of all that into a powerful text of feminist subjectivity.

Lorde depicts identity as an ongoing process where perceptions of similarity and difference serve as points of redeparture leading to further change. In *Zami*, for example, 'self'-transformation occurs only in the context of others, thus indicating an intersubjective construction of personal identity and an interactional self-naming process. Throughout her biomythography, Lorde equates other women's words with her growing sense of agency and ability to define herself. She implies that through both language and silence the women in her life—her mother, friends, and lovers—have shaped her and so enabled her to rename herself. By choosing the name "Zami," which she translates as "*women who work together as friends and lovers*", Lorde redefines herself as the others and underscores the transformational, communal nature of self-definition and subject formation. . . .

Silence—the absence of language and the refusal to name—plays a significant role in Lorde's interactional self-naming. From her mother, who used silence to protect herself and her daughters from a racialist reality she was powerless to control, Lorde first learned the importance of speech. More precisely, her mother's strategic silences demonstrated language's double-edged power, both its restrictive and its liberating potential. . . . However, by

focusing entirely on the special nature of her mother's language—on her euphemisms for unmentionable bodyparts and the puzzling phrases reminiscent of her island home—it becomes easy to overlook the ambivalent effects of her secrecy. . . .

[An] analysis of the distinctions Lorde makes between herself and her mother—especially as they influence the personal and collective ethnic identities she invents—yields important insights concerning the ways maternal secretiveness shaped the daughter's theory of transformational language, as well as her creation of a racialist "blackness."

Throughout the early sections of *Zami* Lorde associates her mother's silence both with the linguistic distortions surrounding U.S. racial discourse and with the Eurocentric, masculinist standards that structure racialist divisions. During her childhood, her father and mother spoke as "one unfragmentable and unappealable voice." Together, they chose to withhold "vital pieces of information" concerning the realities of racism in everyday life. Perhaps most importantly, it was "from the white man's tongue, from out of the mouth of her father" that her mother learned to use language defensively, to ignore or misname the racism and discrimination she was unable to change. In order to deny the prejudice that threatened her family, she would not openly acknowledge her own "blackness"; nor would she discuss the differences in skin tone between herself, her husband, and her three daughters.

These strategic silences served an important but highly ambivalent purpose. Lorde writes that by refusing to name those aspects of racist U.S. culture she was powerless to alter, her mother attempted to deny their existence. For instance, she did not tell her young daughter that the "nasty glob of grey spittle" that often landed on her coat or her shoe was motivated by irrational racialist hatred; she attributed it instead to the lack of manners in ignorant "low-class people" who spit into the wind. Similarly, young Audre's desire to become class president of the predominantly "white" sixth grade was met with maternal scorn—not because the "white" children would never vote for a "black" girl, but because it was "'foolishness'" and "'nonsense'" to run.

This selective use of language restricted her ability to define herself and prevented her from understanding how her skin color and ethnicity positioned her in the racialist structure of twentieth-century U.S. social systems. Because she "had no words for racism," she was unable to comprehend its implications or its effects in her life. She didn't know why the children in grade school called her names. Nor could she understand why her "white" high school friends didn't invite her to their parties, houses, or summer homes. She blamed herself rather than other people's racist beliefs for the "invisible barrier" isolating her from the rest of the world. Because racism went unacknowledged in her family, Audre's feelings—her sense of injustice when she lost the grade school election, her anger when her family was refused service at a drugstore in the nation's capitol—were either ignored or condemned. Not surprisingly, then, Lorde writes that as a child she was unaware of what it meant to be "Colored".

The personal and cultural confusion Lorde describes in *Zami* illustrates an important component of her theory of transformational language, as well as a recurring pattern in her work: The erasure of differences—even when motivated by the desire to establish bonds among differently situated subjects—inadvertently widens the gap between disparate groups. By exploring the inadequacy of her mother's silence, Lorde exposes the limitations in well-meaning attempts to establish generic, pseudo-universal definitions of identity. In *Zami*, the absence of a racialized discourse leads to an assumed commonality that, paradoxically, creates further divisions.

> AnaLouise Keating. *Women Reading Women Writing: Self-Invention in Paula Gunn Allen, Gloria Anzaldúa and Audre Lorde* (Philadelphia: Temple University Press, 1996), 146–49

BIBLIOGRAPHY
*The First Cities*, 1968; *Cables to Rage*, 1970; *From a Land Where Other People Live*, 1973; *The New York Head Shop and Museum*, 1974; *Coal*, 1976; *Between Our Selves*, 1976; *The Black Unicorn*, 1978; *The Cancer Journals*, 1980; *Zami: A New Spelling of My Name*, 1982; *Chosen Poems Old and New*, 1982; *Sister Outsider*, 1984; *Our Dead Behind Us*, 1986; *Burst of Light*, 1988; *Need: A Chorale for Black Women Voices*, 1990; *Undersong: Chosen Poems Old and New*, 1992; *The Marvelous Arithmetics of Distance*, 1993; *The Audre Lorde Compendium: Essays, Speeches, and Journals*, 1996; *The Collected Poems of Audre Lorde*, 1997

# LOVELACE, Earl (1935–)
## Trinidad

[In *The Schoolmaster* Earl Lovelace] catches so surely the essence and color of the region in northeast Trinidad where the real Kumaca and Valencia are to be found, and renders us so susceptible to his fictional landscape (and, incidentally to its source—a visit seems a logical extension of the literary experience), that we might think nothing is wrong with Kumaca. The fictional village, however, has its human derelicts: the old man Miguel Paponette living on memories of those days only he can remember when he owned the king of all gamecocks; Francis Assivero who has lost his lands and his standing, now works as a cocoa picker on another man's estate, and, according to his son "dies daily inside himself, because Mama is looking at him and does not complain, and because he knows the man he was, and remembers, and goes again and again to the shop of Dardain." Then there is the boy Robert languishing in a dark hut with the poliomyelitis there is no one to diagnose or relieve, for Kumaca has no doctor and the track that leads to the nearest medical attention is sure to be too uncomfortable for the patient to be carried out. Finally, there is Ignacio Dardain, the economic serpent in the village, slowly undermining the old ways while exploiting them.

> Kenneth Ramchand. Introduction to Earl Lovelace, *The Schoolmaster* (London: Heinemann, 1979), pp. vi–vii

In Lovelace's *The Schoolmaster*, Pauline Dandrade makes this pithy remark: "Kumaca not even in the world." The smallness of Lovelace's Kumaca matches the impotent smallness of the West Indies, and Pauline's remark, we may say, is a metaphor for the West Indian's search for identity and a significant place in the world. Of course the search for these things has always been important to all human beings; but given the nature of the West Indian past, this search has been a matter of chronic anxiety for the people living in the tiny, impoverished islands. This search is at the heart of *The Schoolmaster*. It is also the central theme of Lovelace's

*While Gods Are Falling*, his first novel, and *The Dragon Can't Dance*, his latest work. Walter Castle, hero of the first novel, faces a daily struggle to extricate himself from the squalor and crime of a Port-of-Spain slum where "life has no significance beyond the primary struggles for a bed to sleep in, something to quiet the intestines, and moments of sexual gratification." One thinks of Calvary Hill, the dunghill setting of *The Dragon Can't Dance*. Here the pervasive nihilism can only be alleviated by the sensual excesses of Carnival, furtive sex and occasional violence. To a man, the residents of Calvary Hill are desperately searching for "the tune that will sing their person and their pose, that will soar over the hill, ring over the valley of shacks, and laugh the hard tears of their living.". . .

The need for selfhood is given special emphasis in *The Schoolmaster*. Benn's confrontation with Captain Grant, his rich, white employer, underscores this need rather effectively. Benn's wizened foal, which he buys from Grant and then nurses to vibrant health, [is] an emblem of his self-worth. Grant knows this, and he blackmails Benn: he can sell the animal back to the Captain or lose his job. Benn can defy Grant and lose his job, or he can grovel "like a little field nigger." Instead, he gives Grant the beautiful animal ("just like am a white man myself"), against the Captain's vigorous protests. It is too much for the utterly abashed Grant. The next day he shoots the animal, symbolically, of course, killing Benn. Like Francis Assivero, another villager, Benn is trapped by the severity of the . . . existential situation. His donkeys are Father Vincent's only transportation between Zanilla and Kumaca, and this gives him a temporary importance. Once the road is built, however, this fragile importance will end, and he will have to scratch out a living planting and selling yams. From time to time this brings him close to despair; but his spirit, like Walter's, cannot be cowed. Benn's determination to be somebody in the face of humiliation and degrading poverty ennobles him. [In *The Dragon Can't Dance*] Aldrick, too, does not give in. After serving stiff jail terms for their abortive rebellion against poverty and the nothingness of their existence, the rebels, Aldrick excepted, return to Calvary Hill thoroughly chastened. For them Calvary Hill has become "the Hill of accommodation." Not so for the recalcitrant Aldrick whose brooding rebelliousness is too implacable to be quelled by forces who "want us to surrender because we can't win." Lovelace rather ironically sets Aldrick's unappeased restlessness against Philo's final, tawdry victory—the bedding of Cleothilda, sometime beauty queen, but now a dried-up, old prune.

> Harold Barratt. *ACLALS Bulletin*. 5, 3 (December 1980), pp. 63, 66

In his fourth published novel, *The Wine of Astonishment*, Earl Lovelace charts the history of a Spiritual Baptist community from the passing of the Prohibition Ordinance in 1917 until the lifting of the ban in 1951. The choice of subject matter reflects Lovelace's continuing awareness of the vital role of the artist in the decolonization process. Beginning with the publication of his first novel, *While Gods Are Falling* in 1965, one can discern in Lovelace's fiction an ongoing commitment to "the task of re-education and regeneration" which, Chinua Achebe has suggested, is one of the first duties of the writer in a postcolonial society. It is a commitment that has consistently influenced the direction of Lovelace's creative energy, encouraging him to explore in his works those experiences which have shaped the social and psychological development of the black West Indian community. . . . As a syncretistic religion, born out of Africa's encounter with Europe in the New World, Lovelace sees in the Spiritual Baptist system of faith and worship, in their ''Africanization of Christianity,'' a living example of the creative and regenerative impulses inherent in the black Creole cultural tradition. The conflict between the Bonasse Spiritual Baptists and the established authorities is therefore conceived as only one other episode in the centuries-old struggle between Prospero and Caliban; and it is this which accounts for the symbolic significance of the church in the world of the novel. In tracing the history of this particular community, Lovelace is reflecting on the more general experience of the black man in the Caribbean. The novel therefore returns us to the now familiar black West Indian world of deprivation and oppression, but with the important distinction that, here, the image of the black West Indian as courageous victim is superseded by the image of the black West Indian as authentic hero-figure.

In *The Wine of Astonishment* Lovelace moves away from the third-person narration of his earlier novels, electing instead to relate the events from the point of view of a middle-aged peasant woman who is, herself, a member of the Baptist church. The change has certain obvious advantages. Lovelace's Eva is cast in the tradition of those clear-thinking, resolute, and spiritually resilient mother-figures who have always peopled the world of Caribbean fiction. Thus, although her sympathetic ''inside'' view of the Shouter Movement conflicts sharply with the recorded perceptions of the wider society, the associations which she provokes dispose the reader to prefer her authority to that of the establishment's colonial regime. And this authority is further enhanced by Lovelace's linguistic skill which, from the outset, encourages the reader to believe that he is in fact listening to the artless, unstructured narrative of a simple peasant woman.

Marjorie Thorpe. Introduction to Earl Lovelace, *The Wine of Astonishment* (London: Heinemann, 1982), pp. viii–ix

The search for a hero-figure constitutes the basis of Earl Lovelace's four published novels. At a time when major writers throughout the Western world appear to be convinced that the age of heroes has long passed, this may seem a somewhat romantic undertaking; and particularly so in the West Indies where, some have argued, there has never been an age of heroes. ''What have we to celebrate?'' is the question that has been asked. To urge our capacity for survival and endurance does not always seem enough. Our literature is full of those who have suffered and endured. But what of the man who attempts to move beyond endurance? the man who stands up against his fate and battles it, and whose defeat only serves to counterpoint that greatness of spirit, that dignity and wholesomeness which we associate with the hero-figure? The need to explore the experience of such a man carries Lovelace from crowded city slums to remote country districts, takes him as far back as the prewar years and ultimately brings him into contact with every aspect of Trinidad society. More important, however, it leads him to re-examine the values which form the foundation of his Creole world, and to attempt in his novels a definition of heroism within the context of the modern West Indian society.

An important aspect of these novels is the distinction which is made between those false heroes whom the society esteems, and the true hero-figures whom the novelist seeks to celebrate. Lovelace's false heroes all enjoy some measure of authority within their particular communities, although the sources of this authority are varied. It may be based on a character's economic success, or it may be a consequence of his superior social status; it may be associated with political eminence, or it may even be the authority of force. But whatever its foundation, two features always emerge: first, that authority carries with it no moral responsibility; and secondly, that it is authority which finds its most usual expression in vulgar display and egocentric action.

Marjorie Thorpe. In Erika Sollish Smilowitz and Roberta Quarles Knowles, eds. *Critical Issues in West Indian Literature* (Parkersburg, Iowa: Caribbean Books, 1984), pp. 90–91

Earl Lovelace is as engaging a polemical ironist in his novels . . . as he is in his new and very impressive collection of three plays. Apart from nothing Lovelace's accuracy for confronting social-political inequities and inconsistencies with durable irony and Selvonian satire, I must mention the playwright's extraordinary lyrical gift, his splendid rendering of Trinidadian demotic speech, and his well-honed crafting of nicely differentiated dialogue passages.

*Jestina's Calypso* [in *Jestina's Calypso, and Other Plays*] is the story of an affectionate deception, in which Jestina uses the photograph of her beautiful hairdresser friend Laura to impress a pen pal in the United States. A deeply acrimonious comedy, its central meaning moves easily from personal pathos to metaphorical neocolonial suggestion.

*The New Hardware Store* is the portrait of a petit-bourgeois ''realist,'' who is tyrannical with his staff and whose black conservative credo can be summed up in his own words: ''This is just an island. We only part of some thing that they directing from another region. You could change that?'' The political *picong* barbs against the store owner are the most deadly in the volume, and in all three plays picong abounds.

*My Name Is Village* is a musical based on a lighthearted didactic narrative. An aging carnival stickman and his son are surrounded by a welter of contradictions: the drama derived from their differing generational points of view; the tug of their village and the pull of the city; recognition versus anonymity; style and fancy up against mediocrity and dullness.

Andrew Salkey. *World Literature Today*. 59, 3 (Summer 1985), p. 480

The main preoccupation in Earl Lovelace's fiction is liberation: he thinks that it is dangerous to move ahead without a proper understanding of its true meaning. Liberation is not merely winning political independence or discarding the yoke of imperialism; it involves true transformation. Decolonization of the mind is a preliminary step towards liberation. As Frantz Fanon says, ''decolonization cannot be successful without any period of transition. It is a nonviolent phenomenon.'' Lovelace thinks that reclamation of the self is an important step in achieving liberation that needs to be qualified by vision, and that vision is something that does not burst out from a vacuum but needs to be informed by contemporary awareness. He is also of the opinion that the greatest responsibility of the people is in electing good leaders, and that they should see that power is not concentrated in the hands of a few. Therefore, he says, the greatest task of the artist lies in educating the masses—not only at the political level but also at the social and cultural levels. The artist believes that the people should first be made to feel proud of themselves and be made to realize, to discover, their mission on earth. These are the principal concerns of Earl Lovelace, and they are to be discerned most clearly in *The Schoolmaster, The Wine of Astonishment,* and *The Dragon Can't Dance.* . . .

A powerful and moving novel like *The Wine of Astonishment* also raises philosophical questions about the meaning of life. It chronicles the different ways in which the members of a small community adhere to their identity as they find themselves caught up in the corrupt machinery of political life. Bee, a major character, is disappointed after meeting Ivan Morton, who is elected to the village council by a small congregation of Baptists in the Trinidad village of Bonasse to fight for their cause. But they soon realize their mistake, for Ivan is seen to follow the same route as the authorities. The changed Ivan admonishes Bee not to worship the spirit; he associates spiritual religion with primitive backwardness and barbarism. Bee, after the embarrassing confrontation with Ivan, decides not to send his elder son to high school because the school promotes colonial values. The narrator of the book does not share Bee's disappointment, for he is clearly more optimistic; he persuades Bee to have patience with the world and not to quarrel with it: "The world is not a market place where you quarrel over the price you have to pay. God fix the price already, and if we could pay ours, we have to be thankful. Things have meaning."

The last sentence of this statement, "Things have meaning," seems to be the thesis of the novel, besides illuminating the importance of the need to reconcile and compromise with the world.

Lovelace's persistent preoccupation with the discovery of the meaning of life is continued in his brilliant novel *The Dragon Can't Dance.* Carnival, the novel's theme and organizing principle, is a grand occasion for communal fantasy. The poverty of men and women alike is gloriously overcome for two days in the year when Carnival gives them identity and stature. But such an identity, according to Lovelace, is a dubious one, and the author engages himself in the task of articulating the values that his society should uphold. Aldrick, an important character in the novel, in the process of growth and self-education sees clearly the conflict between his role as the dragon in the Carnival and his essential manhood. He discovers that "He had been cheating himself of the pain, of love, of his living" and that two days of dancing as the dragon is but a poor substitute. In a gradual process of growth he outgrows the pleasure, joy, and zeal of participating in Carnival.

K.T. Sunitha. In A. L. McLeod, ed. *Subjects Worthy Fame* (New Delhi: Sterling Publishers, 1989), pp. 124–25

Earl Lovelace's works begin with the Trinidadian folk . . . but considered outside of their setting, they reflect the drama of any people emerging from colonialism and facing the subtler temptations of international enterprise that seeks to recolonize them. But having said that, one must still affirm that Lovelace's characters are rooted in a landscape to which they have a spiritual and linguistic affinity. So complete is the synthesis that one is tempted to refer to it as pantheistic. . . .

All four of Lovelace's novels deal explicitly or implicitly with the community's role in conferring dignity on the individual. The reader is invited to think of community as a mirror in which the individual sees his/her values and beliefs reflected and as ramparts within which the individual feels secure. In all four novels, Lovelace presents us with threatened communities and agglomerations of people adrift, frantically in search of salvation, but he explores this theme most profoundly in *The Wine of Astonishment.* Here the forces, both colonial and indigenous, that conspire to destroy the community are pictured as they shave away with each onslaught a little more of the communal resolve. . . .

Lovelace's other novels (and even his plays) treat this theme in various ways. In *The Schoolmaster,* Dardain calmly introduces the capitalist values and quietly robs the villagers of their land. When the schoolmaster, Mr. Warrick, arrives, he adds to the rapine. Before the community gets around to killing Mr. Warrick he has already done irreparable damage to its most sacred values, has already destroyed its pristine way of life.

*While Gods Are Falling* and *The Dragon Can't Dance* present us with the victims of progress totally alienated from one another in a world where wealth is accorded primacy. In the first of these novels . . . we witness the characters in a community setting where wealth has no other value than to foster drinking and gambling rituals. According to Lovelace, such characters do not value money because they do not have it. But we also meet them in the slums of Port-of-Spain deeply suspicious of one another, long after the forces of progress had caused them to be uprooted from their rural traditional communities. The novel concludes with the vision that community is possible among the uprooted. In *The Dragon Can't Dance,* Lovelace returns to the theme of community among urban dwellers. This time he reveals in great detail the origins of the principal characters and shows that their deepest longing is for a community to which they can contribute and in which they can feel comfortable. As Angelita Reyes notes, Lovelace shows that the ritual of Carnival, for as long as it lasts, generates that communal feeling; when it ceases the games of economic and class power resume. But Carnival too ceases to have that bonding effect when it becomes appropriated by capitalist concerns to glorify business and sell products. The final vision, which belongs to Philo the calypsonian, is that a Babbitry, a formulaic material quest, infects Trinidad.

H. Nigel Thomas. *World Literature Written in English.* 3, 1 (Spring 1991), pp. 1, 6

One of Lovelace's major themes is the idea of "personhood." In order to be free, man must first discover himself and his place in relation to his world. It is only through such awareness that he can then relate to the larger world of which he is a part. By affirming that every man belongs to the community of mankind, Lovelace refutes the notion of a First and Third World. Like his fellow West Indian writers, he shows the danger of imposing Western standards on Caribbean societies, which robs them of their heritage and their identity. Lovelace also dispels the myth which portrays the slave as a victim, without the strength to survive. He warns his fellow West Indians against such customs as Carnival, which confer illusory power to men while luring them away from their fundamental duties and responsibilities to each other.

*Jestina's Calypso* is the poignant story of a homely black woman, who believes that her Trinidadian pen pal, now living in New York, is going to marry her. As she prepares herself for his arrival, she becomes the laughingstock of the village. The young man arrives, sees Jestina's face, and immediately takes a flight back to New York. Fundamentally, there is nothing wrong with

Jestina's aspirations ''to want to be, to be a whole person, some-body with a journey in front of [her],'' but her stubborn belief is at once tragic and noble. Lovelace speaks of it as that complex ''courage, and guts and wickedness,'' the kind that makes ''Little Man, the stickfighter,'' fight to his death.... But unlike her Trinidadian pen pal, who went to America to fulfill his dreams at the price of losing his own identity and values, Jestina stayed. ''You are here,'' Laura tells her, ''swayed, unbroken, you have survived, Jestina.'' Unlike those who parade their emptiness, playing illusory kings and queens, Jestina drops her pretense and dares to face her own ugliness. In this act lies her beauty. Redemption, Lovelace teaches, lies in the courage to seek oneself by breaking away ''from all the lies heaped on your life.'' This advice comes from Prettypig, who is enacting Jestina's response to her disappointed pen pal, from a woman whose name symbolizes Jestina's beautiful ugliness.

In *The New Hardware Store* Lovelace shows the tragic empti-ness of people who have not been able to break from the lies luring them away from basic human decency. Survival, to some, means material success, a lesson Mr. Ablack, the new owner of the hardware store, has learned well. In his vocabulary are the words, ''hustle,'' ''scheme,'' ''bribe,'' ''smile,'' ''bow,'' all having to do with his ultimate goal, ''Now is the time to produce production. Productivity.'' To others, it implies playing roles: Rooso, the nightwatchman and advertiser for Ablack's hardware store, is also a clown, entertaining people by making them laugh at him and giving them a chance to feel superior. Like the masquerader, who is no more than the mask he wears, Rooso will be remembered as the calypsonian but not as the man: ''and you wouldn't even remember my name was Rooso.'' Yet, like Aldrick of *The Dragon Can't Dance*, he becomes the hero of Lovelace's play because he

changes, and in the process *becomes*. He realizes that his roles, as perfect as they may be, are only illusions: ''I had to dance the stickman dance, I had to ... kick my feet in a Bongo ... I play slave, guerrilla. I follow the crowd, play marcher, play servant, savage, skylarker.'' At the end of the play, his undressing before leaving Ablack is symbolic of the stripping of his roles in order to face the naked self. It is only then that he becomes a man ready to fulfill his responsibility to himself and to others.

This is also the lesson Cyril Village gives his son, Roy Village, in *My Name Is Village*. Roy Village wants to be ''a big man'' with the power of a Jab Malassie in a world of progress, the features of which the Town Tester enumerates to the Yes Men: ''speed,'' ''Color Television,'' ''tall building.'' For this, he rejects his father's identity of ''old stickman'' who doesn't want to ''get dirty'' and is ''meek and mild.'' But by the end of this short play, Roy has learned from his father that true greatness cannot be imported; it is right at home in the world his people have made for themselves: ''This is we world because is we who love it and with we hands make things grow out of it.''

Pierrette M. Frickey. In Bruce King, ed. *Post-Colonial English Drama: Commonwealth Drama since 1960* (New York: St. Martin's Press, 1992), pp. 230–32

BIBLIOGRAPHY
*While Gods Are Falling*, 1965; *The Schoolmaster*, 1968; *The Dragon Can't Dance*, 1979; *The Wine of Astonishment*, 1982; *Jestina's Calypso, and Other Plays*, 1984; *A Brief Conversation and Other Stories*, 1988; *Salt*, 1996

# M

## MAILLU, David (1939–)
### Kenya

Capitalizing on the song school, [David] Maillu has produced a . . . series of works using the dramatic monologue technique, be it in the form of a letter, as in *Dear Daughter*, or verse, as in his three-decker *The Kommon Man*. . . .

Totally disregarding form, he talks to the reader directly; matter becomes all-important. The values he portrays are common to most of these novels. Their market is largely urban and so, too, is their setting, with all the attendant social attitudes brought about by rapid urbanization along a Western pattern—rootlessness, cynicism, materialism, and escapism. The parallels with nineteenth-century Britain are striking. Of the general process Louis James has written that "the essentially rural lower-class culture which expressed itself in ballads, broadsheets, and chapbooks, was fragmented when the worker moved into the towns." While Maillu's works can in no way be termed traditional they do contain fragments of that tradition in his fondness for aphorisms like "the chameleon can change its colors but it cannot change its behavior" and "when two bulls fight, it is the grass that suffers most." Edward Hinga still recalls the traditional fine for sleeping with an unmarried woman but is embarrassed by elders judging his affairs. . . .

There are gratuitous, graphic descriptions of sexual intercourse in Maillu's work as when Maiko has sex with his secretary, Ema, to ensure her promotion, but this is followed by a short poem decrying the practice. Again the Kommon Man vividly imagines his wife's affair with Makoka but the whole trilogy is a condemnation of her materialist-inspired actions. The sexual content in these novels is certainly ambiguous. Maillu, for example, has many serious points to make about the state of society and, in part, *The Kommon Man* is intellectually demanding. Is the sexual content then the carrot to entice the ordinary reader to serious thought on the problems of urban life or is the philosophy a rather lengthy afterthought and conscience salver? Maillu's stand is not unequivocal. . . .

[If] the ordinary reader turns to . . . Maillu's *The Kommon Man*, combing through the trivia, soft porn, trite moralizing, and cynicism, he may find the hymn of the common man which speaks as clearly of social injustice as does Okot p'Bitek's *Song of Lawino*, but with less anger and more cynicism.

> Elizabeth Knight. In Eldred Durosimi Jones, ed. *African Literature Today*. 10 (1979), pp. 178, 182, 184, 188

In the 1970s David Maillu emerged as the most significant popular writer in Kenya. This he accomplished not by writing school books for local branches of international publishing houses nor by soliciting the patronage of government-subsidized Kenyan publishers but by establishing his own firm, Comb Books, and inundating the market with novelettes and volumes of verse he himself had written, published, and then energetically promoted. His first "mini-novel," *Unfit for Human Consumption*, the costs of which had been underwritten partly by a loan from a friend and partly by a trade agreement with a distributor, had sold so well that he had been

able to invest the proceeds in a second book, *My Dear Bottle*, a poetic apostrophe to the consolation of inebriation. This too had been swallowed up quickly by a pop-thirsty reading public, and Maillu had plowed the profits back into the firm just as quickly, bringing out in the next year another mini-novel, *Troubles*, and another humorous soliloquy in verse, *After 4:30*, as well as reissuing the first two sold-out titles. By repeating this kind of pyramiding procedure, Maillu in four years was able to publish twelve books he himself had written (including a Swahili translation of *My Dear Bottle*), reprint the best-selling works several times, and publish four books by other Kenyan authors who had similar stories to tell. . . .

When Maillu first appeared on the East African literary scene, he introduced an innovation that no other writer in his part of the world had exploited so fully: he talked dirty. True, Charles Mangua had done this a little earlier in Kenya in two extremely popular novels, *Son of Woman* and *A Tail in the Mouth*, but Mangua wrote humorous picaresque tales in which a streetwise hero talked tough and dirty. Maillu may have learned something from Mangua, but his own civil-servant heroes were not roughshod rogues but middle-class victims of biological urges that ultimately destroyed their careers; they talked weak and dirty. . . .

If we compare Maillu's latest works with those he wrote and published during Comb Books' brief heyday, one change becomes apparent immediately: the dirty talk is gone. His heroes may be sexually active but they are not sexually obsessed, and their physical interactions with members of the opposite sex tend to be described with restraint, even reticence. This is true not only in the two novels he has published in the Macmillan Pacesetter Series, *For Mbatha and Rabeka* and *The Equatorial Assignment*, but also in *Kadosa*, the first novel brought out by David Maillu Publishers Ltd., and in *Tears at Sunset*, the yet unpublished novel written for the Koola Town Self-Help and Community Development Scheme. Moreover, carnal love has no place in *Jese Kristo*, a morality play performed at the Kenya National Theater in October and November of 1979 and published in the program prepared for that production, or in *Hit of Love*, a one-hundred-page poem issued by David Maillu Publishers Ltd. in a bilingual (English-Kikamba) format. . . .

Maillu's success in adapting to new popular formulas is evident in the first two Pacesetters he has written. *For Mbatha and Rabeka* is built on a classic love triangle. Mbatha, an idealistic primary-school teacher, is planning to marry Rabeka, his beautiful childhood sweetheart who teachers at the same village school, but while she is in Nairobi recovering from a liver ailment, she meets Honeycomb Mawa, a panel beater foreman with Bodyliners Limited, who shows her the town in his Saab sportscar, wining and dining her at all the top establishments in the Rift Valley and escorting her to high-class international parties. Rabeka, dazzled by the urban glitter and impressed by Mawa's sophistication and wealth, begins to long for life in the fast lane. . . .

Maillu second Pacesetter, *The Equatorial Assignment*, was an African adaptation of the James Hadley Chase type of thriller. Benni Kamba, Secret Agent 009 working for the National Integrity Service of Africa, is pitted against beautiful Konolulu, known professionally as Colonel Swipta, an agent for a multinational

European organization intent on destabilizing Africa for the benefit of the Big Powers. NISA has its headquarters at a Saharan desert outpost run by the brainy Dr. Triplo, and Colonel Swipta works at a mountain station called Chengolama Base run by the unscrupulous and equally brilliant Dr. Thunder. Benni Kamba's mission is to infiltrate Chengolama Base and destroy it before Dr. Thunder can launch his secret weapon, a missile called Thundercrust that would obliterate NISA. Agent 009 accomplishes this by making romantic overtures to Colonel Swipta, killing her after gaining her trust, and then detonating the Thundercrust on its launching pad, thereby destroying Chengolama Base. The good guys win; the bad guys die. . . .

This is light fiction written with a light touch. Unlike *For Mbatha and Rabeka, The Equatorial Assignment* does not deal with semiserious social issues or with real people in recognizable situations. It is escape literature pure and simple, an indigenous variant of an extremely popular foreign genre. Benni Kamba is an African James Bond. . . .

Literary critics have not been very generous in their assessments of Maillu's work. No one has lavished praise on him, and few have admitted finding any redeeming value in what or how he writes. The general feeling among serious academics appears to be that such literature is beneath criticism for it is wholly frivolous, the assumption being that a scholar should not waste his time on art that aims to be truly popular. Yet Maillu cannot be ignored in any systematic effort to understand the evolution of an East African literature, for he has extended the frontiers of that literature farther than any other single writer. One may regard his writing as undisciplined, unrefined, uncouth, and outrageously excessive, but it is precisely because he has been spectacularly audacious and unmannerly that he is important. He has broken most of the rules of good writing and has gotten away with it, thereby releasing an embryonic literary culture from the confining sac of conformity to established conventions of taste and judgment. Maillu, a primitive pioneer and intrepid trailblazer, has liberated fenced-off aesthetic territory. Now that he has pushed the boundaries of decorum back, others can stake out their own claims in the same untamed wilderness.

Moreover, Maillu is important because he possesses tenacity and resourcefulness. He has learned to survive by adjusting to new circumstances and imposing his will on the world about him. He has taken risks that the prudent would have eschewed and has discovered through trial and error, as well as trial and success, just how far he can carry others with him. One has to admire his courage both as a publisher and as an author. Perhaps no one else would have persisted so long in the struggle when buffeted continually by the criticism that everything he produced was unfit for human consumption.

Bernth Lindfors. *Kunapipi*. 4, 1 (1981), pp. 130, 132–34, 136–37, 141–42

Maillu's works could be easily dismissed as being too pornographic and formless. The author may not be given any credit for the few creative devices that sympathetic critics glean out of these works because such devices are purely accidental and the currency and importance of the themes in contemporary society are vitiated by low artistic taste. That Maillu's writing is amateurish is a truism; that within his fictive world there are the two opposed camps of art and action is apparent. These two camps are opposed because

Maillu appears to have sacrificed intellectual and scholarly obligations in order to bear the self-imposed sociopolitical burden of the writer as a teacher, which the limits of his literary education do not permit. A criticism of these works implies examining how far Maillu succeeds in marrying morality and aesthetics, content and form—an exercise which raises aesthetic questions. . . .

He refuses to be bound by conventional forms. He adopts the poetry format in writing *After 4:30, My Dear Bottle*, and *The Kommon Man* . . . but his style is essentially a prose style. It is hard to classify his writings as poetry or prose; rather, it is safer to use the looser and noncommitting term, works. This is because, apart from the two letters, *Dear Monika* and *Dear Daughter*, and the mini-novels, his works . . . could be classified as books of poems or short stories. Whether or not they qualify as any of these classes is another matter. Their format disqualifies them as short stories; and when pitted against some other poetry written in East Africa, they may not pass as good poetry. The ones arranged in verse are essentially disjointed items of colloquial utterances. They lack the terseness, texture and complexity of language which create the images, metaphors and symbolic meaning which characterize good poetry. . . .

His works, for what they are worth, cannot be appreciated more than those of a writer pandering to popular taste by portraying Nairobi as a city of self-destructive sex. They could be enjoyed as a change made in East African literature, which, until the emergence of Okot p'Bitek, was primarily concerned with hackneyed culture conflict and colonialism. But if Maillu refuses to tow the lines of writers like Ngugi [wa Thiong'o] and others who stuck to the conventional forms they learned from British and American literatures, his refusal should have prompted him to create new and mature fictional techniques and style that would challenge the ones the older and established East African writers adopt. His themes may be topically relevant to East African society, to the social problems facing Africa as a whole. The books serve as his contribution to the social reform. Maillu's success in publishing these works, in spite of his not-too-high literary education, might be considered a promise of his greater future achievements. But since he adopts the same style, point of view, and discusses the same redundant theme in all ten works—a fictional mode which eventuates in amateurish, unliterary, and monotonously repetitious works—we question his seriousness and commitment as a social reformer. The contemporary African societies are too educated to accept *any* and *every* writing as literature. Genuine experiments in language and form will continue to be conducted in African literature, but certainly the age of "Onitsha market literature" is fast becoming an anachronism.

Kalu Ogbaa. *Ufahumu*. 10, 3 (spring 1981), pp. 57, 59, 66

If nothing much has been heard about Maillu in West Africa, it is because writing of the type he does and publishes is regarded with a certain amount of disdain by academic critics. For the man in the (East African) street, however, Maillu's name is a household word. He is by far the most popular writer in East Africa, even though Ngugi was Thiong'o is the Kenyan writer best known to the outside world. These two Kenyan writers address two largely disparate audiences and their work may indeed be regarded as complementary. . . .

Maillu is a fairly careful craftsman when it comes to vocabulary and characterization. But he has a penchant for repetition not only of themes but also of incidents and reflections. His reputation has so far been based on his exploration of sexual relations between men and women, and yet in private life he is neither frivolous nor a libertine. On the contrary, he is ascetic and prefers the peace and quiet of his suburban Langata residence west of Nairobi to the hurly-burly of city life. The serious strain in Maillu is clearly portrayed in a supernatural novel *Kadosa* which is due to appear soon. While he traces the origin of the ideas of *Kadosa* to [Mikhail] Bulgakov's *The Master and Margarita*, there is much in Maillu's forthcoming work to indicate originality in plot and characterization.

To date, however, his reputation has rested on works dealing with the lives of city prostitutes and layabouts. He has been criticized . . . for displaying a limited and unidimensional view of human character, especially female character. In his defense, he has argued that whatever vulgarity one can point to in his work can also be found in real life.

E. O. Apronti. *Pacific Moana Quarterly*. 6, 3–4 (July–October 1981), pp. 162–63

David Maillu is a writer who deserves greater attention from serious critics than he currently enjoys. His lighthearted style and his ''vulgar'' language probably account for the . . . [critical] neglect of his writing, nevertheless his social vision is much more profound than readers may realize, for he addresses himself to some of the most serious problems facing independent Africa today. . . . *After 4:30* can be summarized as a book on women's liberation. The protagonist of the novel, the typist, is a highly conscientized proletarian woman who is bitterly critical of male ideology on the question of the place of women in society. . . .

In this male-dominated society, women find themselves oppressed and exploited at work, at home, everywhere. Male executives make use of their positions as bosses to demand sex from their typists. Unless she submits to her boss's sexual desires, a typist has no hope for promotion. And junior men, subjected to such treatment by the same women, lord it over their wives at home. In a male-dominated bourgeois society, wives are at the beck and call of their husbands. Those women who marry wealthy men pay for the luxury of their homes with misery and tears. . . .

In *My Dear Bottle* the protagonist is not a militant feminist, but a male drunkard. The drunkard is a member of the working class and is a failure in life. His world is a world of wishful thinking, but try as he may, he cannot emulate his boss who is himself a member of the wealthy bourgeoisie and enjoys all the advantages that accrue to those who belong to that class, including the use of big cars like the Mercedes Benz. In many ways, the drunkard is the male equivalent of the typist in *After 4:30*. Like the typist, he is a spokesman for the less privileged section of the population, and he is similarly far from idealized. He makes it clear that if he were in power he would indulge in corrupt practices. Nevertheless, what he says about what he would get up to were he a minister is meant to be a reflection of the corruption of those in the upper echelons of society. Thus Maillu takes a drunkard, who himself has faults, and criticizes the injustices of society through him. . . .

In the final analysis, however, Maillu's novels cannot be described as ''socialist art.'' His final word on socialism is pronounced by the drunkard's learned friend who is critical of both capitalism and socialism. The major criticism against communism, or what he calls ''another form of capitalism where a chosen élite must control the entire population,'' is that its rulers exercise their power through fear. Though he is a radical writer who sides with the workers and the less privileged sections of society, his position is no more than that of a social critic; he does not examine the possibility of collective bargaining for the workers, or define the problem in terms of the class struggle. However, the point must be made that Maillu's writings draw their strength from proletarian culture and should find a place among the works of those who are committed to the cause of the less privileged classes of bourgeois society. He may with some justification be condemned as a ''pornographic jester,'' but his style should not obscure the fact that he raises questions capable of pricking the consciences of those in positions of power and authority.

Emmanuel Ngara. *Art and Ideology in the African Novel* (London: Heinemann, 1985), pp. 55–58

David Maillu makes a handy target because of his status as *primus inter pares* on that long list of Kenyan popular writers who have produced the racy romances and titillating thrillers that have dominated the region's literary output since the early 1970's. He did not originate the popular genre in Kenya, but he has been its most famous, or at least infamous, practitioner; in the volume of his output and the nature of his subject matter, Maillu is Kenya's answer to Nigeria's Cyprian Ekwensi. Shortly after Charles Mangua's surprise bestseller *Son of Woman* demonstrated the potential local market for such writing, Maillu did a little market research of his own, discovering in an informal survey that readers were interested in half a dozen rather fundamental topics: sex, politics, human relations, religion, death and money. He tailored his writing accordingly, quickly producing bestsellers with titles that speak for themselves: *Unfit for Human Consumption, My Dear Bottle, After 4:30* (about what happens between bosses and secretaries at the end of the workday), *The Kommon Man*, and the like. These works, all from the 1970's, put Maillu on the literary map, but in the stigmatized category of ''popular'' writer. Stories of Kenyan schoolgirls reading his scandalous *After 4:30* under their desks abounded, and for a time his books were banned in Tanzania.

These days Maillu's reputation appears to be on the mend, for three main reasons. In the first place his sheer tenacity, the unmatched volume of his production and his willingness to innovate have earned him the grudging respect of his erstwhile detractors as well as a significant place in Kenyan literary history. Someone who has published as much as Maillu has (almost fifty titles over twenty-five years) simply cannot be ignored. The second reason for Maillu's rehabilitation, in academic circles at least, is the relatively recent respect accorded to popular culture as an acceptable object of study in addition to elite culture and folk culture. Popular literature is being taken seriously, in part because it is perceived to offer insight into ''the reality experienced by a majority of East Africans,'' presenting a ''true mirror of the hidden reality of the region's social experiences''. Finally, Maillu's reputation is slowly changing since much that he has written since the 1970's has surpassed his initial repertoire of popular themes. As Francis Imbuga notes in his retrospective review of East African literature in the 1980's, ''there is reason to believe that Maillu will gradually settle down to address more serious themes of East African experience''.

In attempting the daunting task of categorizing Maillu's works, one might divide them into two broad groups: his popular pieces, most of which are set in Nairobi and feature urban conflicts; and his moralistic or didactic works, which tend to centre on rural values and settings. Most of the works Maillu produced under his Comb Books label before it folded would fall in the former category, as would the Benni Kamba adventures. The later, didactic works have been more readily taken up by mainstream publishing houses, and include moralistic lessons about growing up (as in *The Ayah* or *For Mbatha and Rabeka*) as well as treatises on African tradition (such as *Our Kind of Polygamy* or *The Black Adam and Eye*).

It is within this context that we wish to discuss Maillu's little-known linguistic innovation, the macaronic novella *Without Kiinua Mgongo*, which he composed entirely in a mixture of Swahili and English. If nothing else, *Without Kiinua Mgongo* is remarkable as an historic artifact in Kenya's literary history, and it offers credence to the claims that Maillu deserves credit for testing the boundaries of literary expression in East Africa. The language of the novella is unprecedented in the region's literature, featuring what we are defining as a version of linguistic code-mixing in a manner that is reminiscent of (although it does not precisely match) the code-mixing and code-switching of Nairobi speech. But *Without Kiinua Mgongo* is also a fascinating sociological artifact because of the way that the linguistic form that Maillu has selected matches the work's ideological subtext—a decidedly conservative and hegemonic subtext—in particularly close ways. Linguistic form and ideological content forge a remarkably harmonic marriage in *Without Kiinua Mgongo.* . . .

[What] makes the work a delight to read, is the macaronic language that Maillu employs. Throughout the novella he joins English vocabulary to Swahili syntax in a manner reminiscent of common Nairobi speech. Here, for example, is the description of Katherine's overweight mother, who contrasts with her scrawny husband:

> Lakini what Bwana Mbuta had lost in weight, alicompensatiwa na bibiye, Hilda. Hilda, extravagantly fleshy, alikuwa mnene, mwili wote macurve matupu, commonly referred to hapa nyumbani as Mummy; mwenye silaha matiti na behind kubwa. Hivi iwe akikuangukia, you're finished.

Although Maillu has previously published in his mother tongue Kamba and in English (at one point even providing a side-by-side version of each in the didactic epistolary work, *My Dear Mariana/ Kumya Ivu*), his *Without Kiinua Mgongo* represents a unique linguistic experiment in East African literary history, since it is written entirely in this macaronic combination of English and Swahili. . . .

We conclude with three general observations regarding the congruence of ideology and linguistic form in *Without Kiinua Mgongo*. First, it should be noted that the model of authentic indigenous culture on which Maillu's works rely is based on a very specific interpretation of African traditional culture whose accuracy is open to question. Certainly, the literature shows, not all Kenyan writers would concur either with Maillu's account of how traditional society functions or with his prescription for the way a culturally mixed society should be; the depictions of rural society in Grace Ogot's *The Promised Land* or Nagugi's *The River Between*, to name only two important works from Kenya, offer radically different perspectives. Maillu's vision of an idyllic (and static) African tradition seems highly debatable.

Secondly, even though ideology and linguistic form complement each other so readily in *Without Kiinua Mgongo*, there seems no necessary or inevitable correlation between the two. The use of a particular linguistic form does not necessarily lead to a specific

ideology, and neither is the inverse true—a writer's ideology need not necessarily lead to the use of a particular form, such as code-mixing. While covert, emotive structures may indeed help to shape a work's overt ideological discourse, as JanMohamed would argue, linguistic patterns like code-mixing are surely separable from those structures. In another salient example from Kenya, Ngugi's use of Gikuyu and oral forms in his recent novels is certainly ideologically motivated, but there are significant differences between the perspectives of Maillu's work and, say, *Devil on the Cross*, particularly in relation to gender issues. While it is logically and intuitively satisfying that Maillu's version of code-mixing should reflect his ideology, that connection is not due to any organic relationship between ideology and linguistic form.

Finally, it seems surprising that the type of linguistic experiment represented by this novella has not caught on more in East Africa. To our knowledge, this is the only such published prose work from Kenya, apart from a second title by Maillu that is currently out of print. It is hard to imagine that any stigma associated with reading non-standard language would be any more significant than the stigma attached to reading popular writing in general. Code-mixing is, after all, a common phenomenon in East African speech. As we have suggested, however, one result of code-mixing is to limit one's audience, so this may account for the general reluctance to emulate Maillu's example. *Without Kiinua Mgongo* was a Maillu Publishing House production, which suggests that other publishers were reluctant to gamble on this experiment, which would have a limited readership outside of East Africa. That the book has not been reprinted since 1989 implies that those publishers may have been prudent from a financial point of view. A final reason might again relate to form. *Sheng* and other types of code-mixing are often seen as part of an oral cultural tradition, appearing frequently in drama as well as in some poetry, rather than in prose. But while this association of code-mixing with oral forms seems logical, it is not necessarily inevitable, and there should be no reason why more works featuring code-mixing of various types should not be forthcoming in East African writing.

J. Roger Kurtz and Robert M. Kurtz. *Journal of Commonwealth Literature*. 63, 1 (spring 1998), pp. 63–73

BIBLIOGRAPHY

*Ki Kyambonie: Kikamba Nthimo/Muandiki*, 1972; *Kisalu and His Fruit Garden and Other Stories*, 1972; *My Dear Bottle*, 1973; *Unfit for Human Consumption*, 1973; *After 4:30*, 1974; *Troubles*, 1974; *The Kommon Man*, 1975–1976; *Dear Daughter*, 1976; *Dear Monika*, 1976; *Kujenga na Kubomoa*, 1976; *English Punctuation*, 1978; *English Spelling and Words Frequently Confused*, 1978; *Jese Kristo*, 1979; *Kadosa*, 1979; *Benni Kamba 009 in the Equatorial Assignment*, 1980; *For Mbatha and Rabeka*, 1980; *Hit of Love*, 1980; *Looking for Mother*, 1981; *Kaana Ngy'a*, 1983; *The Ayah*, 1986; *Benni Kamba 009 in Operation DXT*, 1986; *Untouchable*, 1987; *Our Kind of Polygamy*, 1988; *The Poor Child*, 1988; *Pragmatic Leadership: Evaluation of Kenya's Cultural and Political Development, Featuring Daniel arap Moi, President of Republic of Kenya*, 1988; *The Thorns of Life*, 1988; *The Black Adam and Eve*, 1989; *How to Look for the Right Boyfriend*, 1989; *Kusoma na Kuandika*, 1989; *Mbengo and the Princess*, 1989; *My Dear Mariana: Kumya Ivu*, 1989; *P. O. Box I Love You Via My Heart*, 1989; *The Principles of Nyayo Philosophy*, 1989; *Without Kiinua Mgongo*, 1989; *Anayekukeep*, 1990; *Broken Drum*, 1991; *Journey into*

*Fairyland*, 1992; *The Last Hunter*, 1992; *The Lion and the Hare*, 1992; *The Orphan and His Goat Friend*, 1993; *The Priceless Gift*, 1993; *Princess Kalala and the Ugly Bird*, 1993; *Dancing Zebra*, 1995; *The Lost Brother*, 1995; *Sasa and Sisi*, 1995; *African Indigenous Political Ideology: Africa's Cultural Interpretation of Democracy*, 1997; *Zwadi*, 1998

# MAIS, Roger (1905–1955)
## Jamaica

By his life, even more than by his work, Roger Mais grew into something of a legend. He was a man of violent sympathies, passionately dedicated to the vision of a new Jamaica, and when in 1944 he was sent to prison for his writings, a part of all protesting Jamaicans served the term with him. The political ferment of the 1940s—its early enthusiasm, its ultimate phase of treachery and disillusionment—was to leave a graver mark on him than on any other of the island's writers. His novels, paradoxically enough, are completely free of the political issues that dominate the work of Vic Reid, yet it was his fierce participation in the national struggle that sparked his creative personality; it was from this he drew the inspiration for works of a raw but vivid and moving power.

Poet, painter, and playwright, one of Jamaica's most fertile and talented short-story writers, Mais came to the novel rather late, and in his first book, *The Hills Were Joyful Together*, he crystallized all the indignation and sympathy of a remarkably intense life. Unlike the shapely and rounded short stories of this period his novel is a jagged creation, but what is lost in form on the bigger canvas Mais compensates for by the release of dramatic energy. In this first book he gives us a portrait of the Jamaican lower-class life, a tenement yard embracing the lives of twenty-five people. The result is something vital, eloquent, and disturbing.

His second book, *Brother Man*, is a more finished, mature, if less powerful, work. The rhetoric and the turbulent spirit of *The Hills* is here again but Mais is more restrained and the drama now is touched with pathos. It is the story of Brother Man, a messianic but convincingly human figure, who holds up the ideal of the Christian life against the challenge of a brutal environment. The people tolerate him as long as they can trade on his eccentricities. But in the end the rival power and influence of the obeah man, Brother Ambo, asserts itself and Brother Man is framed and disgraced, stoned by his followers and abandoned. Mais attempts here to create a character of almost Christlike proportions. The lines of Brother Man's life parallel those of his model in many significant details—the years of wandering and preparation before his mission among the people, the healings and fastings, the going up into the hills for meditation and prayer, the eventual betrayal by one of his own followers, and mortification at the hands of the very people he had sought to save. What emerges, however, is a crude, though compassionate, portrayal. It is not informed by the difficult spirit of tragedy that would have lifted it out of the sentimental context in which it moves and remains.

*Black Lightning*, his last novel, is a complete departure from the first two in setting, mood and intention. The portraits of vigor which had redeemed the limitations of these earlier books are less in evidence. It is a work of subdued tone, at best femininely tender.

Mais had actually begun to collapse, both as man and artist. When the advance copy of his last novel was sent out to him from London he lay in bed, dying. He had sought, as he said in his own words, "to write the story of man, the eternal protagonist amid eternal process—man whom I met at the top of a hill in St. Andrew, Jamaica, dirty, hungry, and in rags." One would like to think, in tribute to his memory, that, in some modest but memorable way, he succeeded.

Ivan Van Sertima. *Caribbean Writers* (London: New Beacon Books, 1968), pp. 20–21

Mais drew the mystical element in his writing from the rhythmical, figurative style of both [the] Bible and Jamaican patois. He used words to reach behind the symbols of language and objects to the nameless reality beyond symbols, the timeless Word of St. John's Gospel. So that when in Mais, words fail, the reader is usually left not with a sense of emptiness, but of vision outreaching vocabulary.

This is true of both the language and main character of *Brother Man*. Here, Mais is again exploring the microcosm of the slums. But he is concerned with a wider concept and the enclosed yard gives place to a Kingston slum street. Surjue [in *The Hills Were Joyful Together*] was destroyed against both tenement and prison wall. Is there any way for human values to survive in the modern human predicament? His answer is one of the utmost daring. He developed Ras, the figure of the gentle Good Samaritan and observer in *The Hills*, and created Brother Man, John Power. John Power has human features. He is the focal point of the community, the healer of mind and body, the religious leader, and the helpful undemanding neighbor. He strengthens, through his own understanding and stability, the mentally unstable Cordy.... Mais insists on Brother Man's basic humanity when he shows Power finally taking [the prostitute] Minette in total, unashamed love. Yet Mais uses his portrait of a Rastafarian cultist—the Rastafarian greeting, "Peace and Love, Brother Man," comes at once to mind—only as a fulcrum between the human and the ideal. We learn something of John Power's thoughts, but very little of his motivation, because as his name implies, he unites in himself Everyman—hence the common name, John—with the ultimate motivation, Power. In him the humanity that gleams fitfully, fragmented, in the various characters of *The Hills*, comes together. And his significance moves beyond that of John Power the Healer and Leader, to that he assumes in the final confrontation with the hysterical, violent mob that cannot endure his goodness. He is Mais's vision of the reincarnate Christ. This is no escape into sentimental mysticism from the political realities. Mais's conviction of spiritual values was too absolute.

As with *The Hills*, sociological or ethical values are inadequate for a criticism of *Brother Man*, because physical conditions are interpreted under the eye of the artist. Human and artistic values, for Mais, meet, each illuminating the other. In a sense, the personality of Brother Man is a work of art beyond the levels of normal literature, exploring the artistic pattern of life itself. And so the artistic faults in the book also imply a limitation of the vision. At times the physical, human presence of Brother Man loses its definition. The Word is no longer incarnate. The plot, too, is uneven and episodic, diverted by a multiplicity of subsidiary characters. When moving on a plane of such heightened symbolism, any deviation into mechanical narration or portraiture jars heavily. But at its key points the novel is usually successful, as in [its] biblically simple hint of resurrection after virtual crucifixion.

Jean Creary. In Louis James, ed. *The Islands in Between: Essays on West Indian Literature* (London: Oxford University Press, 1968), pp. 56–58

Mais was a poor dramatist, but the dramatic elements in his first novel, *The Hills Were Joyful Together*, do not consist only in the stagelike use of its yard setting, with glimpses of a more "private" life through the doors and windows opening upon it, but also in the long exchanges of dialogue between a constantly varied selection of its inhabitants. Mais even begins his book with a cast list and follows this with a description of the yard which amounts to a stage direction. The choice of a cast which embraces whores, cardsharpers, thieves, layabouts, and drunkards is not without its twin dangers of patronage and sentimentality. . . . With Mais's characters, however, we have said nothing when we have said "whore" or "cardsharper." In this sense they are the very opposite of stagey. And because they all retain the capacity to surprise, because they retain through all their suffering and degradation something of their autonomy as human beings, Mais manages to remain completely inside his story. A setting of this kind may be chosen by writers in search of folk authenticity or of a sanction for their political radicalism. In such cases they can hardly avoid calling attention to their astonishing knowledge of low life, or wagging an invisible finger at their comfortable readers. Because the characters in Mais are so abundantly alive he avoids these perils also.

The inhabitants of the yard in *The Hills Were Joyful Together* may be divided into those who accept their lot with a certain amount of philosophy and those who seek to escape it through drink, sex, evangelical religion, or crime. Prominent among the first group is Ras, the angular, bearded Rastafarian barrow-pusher who is the yard's only peacemaker. The others either seek or avoid trouble, but seldom attempt to quell it. Ras makes his presence and his values felt gradually as the plot advances, as acts of folly or violence involve more and more of the yard-dwellers in tragedy. The group of active escapists is dominated by Surjue, a man whose sense of right and wrong may not accord with that of the law but who possesses nonetheless a particular kind of personal integrity and valor. Surjue and his woman Rema are deeply in love, but he is restless and looking for a break. His gambling crony Flitters finally induces him to go on a "job" and, when the police catch them on the roof, runs off leaving Surjue to take the rap. Angry though Surjue is with Flitters, he refuses to tell the police the names of any of his accomplices. To do so would be to violate his own curious sense of honor, but he has no qualms about arranging for Flitters to be hunted down and murdered by his underworld acquaintances. The same unyielding defiance brings terrible treatment to Surjue after his conviction, making him the favorite victim of the more sadistic warders. Hearing that Rema is going mad in her loneliness, Surjue resolves to escape and see her. Again he is unlucky; just as he is about to haul himself to the top of the wall he is shot and killed by the guards. . . . Surjue's death ends a novel whose small cast has already been ravaged by similar tragedies, many of them resulting from heedlessness or from the violence which continually wells up in their random relationships. Surjue never knows that Rema has died before him, burned helplessly in a fire she herself has started in a crazy effort to drive off her delusions. Surjue's own escape plan

had involved the deliberate starting of a fire to panic the warders and set them running in the wrong direction. Despite this sardonic coincidence, Mais does not appear to invoke a Hardyesque fate to account for such things. They simply happen, especially to those who court disaster like Surjue by trying to make their own rules.

Gerald Moore. *The Chosen Tongue* (New York: Harper & Row, 1969), pp. 86–88

[*Brother Man*] is Mais's "best" published work because it brings together in one minor classic, all the aspects of his instincts and talents. . . . The problems of urbanization . . . in *The Hills Were Joyful Together*—growth of slums, increase of crime, alienation, cul-de-sac sense—were now much more evident. But the city had also started to absorb this sense, making it part of its survival style. Bedward, the August Town pentecostal preacher, had already laid the basis for a millennial mythology with his attempt to ascend into heaven. More quietly, and more significantly, he had also given his flock a sense of their own unique cultural identity. His ideas spread through the city, giving strength to the countless "revival" Afro-Jamaican churches thumping at the crossroads and backstreets of the corporate area. Among these were the Rastafari, a remarkable, bearded "Israelite" group who date their foundation from the coronation of the Emperor Haile Selassie I of Ethiopia, the former Ras (Prince) Tafari, and a statement attributed to Marcus Garvey prophesying this. The shoemaker, Brother Man (John Power), hero of this novel, is a member of this sect. "Brother" and "Man" are appellations characteristic of them: "I-re, brother," "Hail the man," "I-man," etc. . . .

Brother Man is perhaps too Christlike to be always "true"; unlike the ideal of the Rastas, he is not fully enough grounded in reality. But this is a tendency Mais shows in all his novels. What he does achieve in *Brother Man*, however, is the depolarization of his rural and urban norms into a single equator, and the condensation of his moralizing tendency into a single mask. The novel is in this sense a "humanist" triumph, if by this term we understand an emphasis on humane elements within an alienating environment. Had Mais not limited so severely his characterization and thematic variations, we might have had a major novel by any standard. . . .

Yet in writing this novel, Mais moved towards certain important formal and stylistic interventions which make it far more important than its limitations would suggest. In fact, as we begin to examine *Brother Man*, the first thing that strikes us is the remarkable coincidence of "style" and "formal structure"; a coincidence, indeed, which we associate more with poetry than with prose fiction. By "style" I mean the way—action flow—the book is written; its use and movement of language. By "from," I refer to how the work is built: its "architructure." Both these are unusually clear in *Brother Man*.

Edward Brathwaite. Introduction to Roger Mais. *Brother Man* (London: Heinemann, 1974), pp. x-xii

Mais's technical achievement in his novels seems to me to have been underrated by most critics who have ignored or criticized his style and concentrated on his passion and social anger. Although he has been justly criticized for lapses into sentimentality and prolixity . . . the accuracy and directness of his descriptive writing has rarely been matched in the West Indian novel to date. But the heart of Mais's achievement is not technical. What he did was to present a view of Jamaican life from inside, an uncompromising and complete picture of the suffering and misery of day to day existence in the Kingston slums. His novels celebrate the strength and spirit of the Jamaicans who inhabit [the] slums, and show the impoverished existence of those who, ironically, ought to be heirs to the most beautiful island in the West Indies. In this Jamaica there are no tourist pictures of gleaming beaches and blue, forest-clad mountains. These novels reflect a world whose unremitting demands shut out everything but the immediate daily grind. Poverty, crime and dirt are ever-present realities; race and color the sources of conflict and petty snobbery; while sexual passions alternatively assuage and irritate his characters' restricted feelings. In his first novel, *The Hills Were Joyful Together*, Mais details the lives of the inhabitants of a Jamaican yard. In a manner reminiscent of the tenement plays of Sean O'Casey he abjures narrative and plot in favor of a fragmentary, imagistic series of scenes in which each character is introduced as an aspect of the life of the yard. In a sense the yard itself is the subject of the novel, a setting which so permeates and governs the actions of its inhabitants that their lives are inseparable from the conditions it imposes on them. Gradually a series of patterns emerge defining conditions which are the springs of individual lives. Zephyr, the warm-hearted whore; Euphemia, the seductive wife of Shag who awakens to sexuality through an unwanted bur irresistible physical passion for the no-good Bajun Man; Shag himself, a dying man, whose pent-up violence is released viciously and pointlessly by circumstances which he can barely comprehend; all these and others interact in a story whose motivation is in the physical and economic conditions they must all endure.

Gareth Griffiths. *A Double Exile: African and West Indian Writing between Two Cultures* (London: Marion Boyars, 1978), pp. 116–17

[In *Black Lightning*] Jake, the blacksmith of a tiny, rural village by day and a sculptor by night, is both a society-oriented artisan as well as a private artist. He stubbornly refuses the advice of the village elders, who feel that, as an educated man, he ought to look for a more suitable job. . . . His commitment to a social role, however, leaves only the nighttime for his woodcarving, an artistic urge that he clearly cannot ignore, and about which he feels some anxiety. Jake, working on his Samson-figure by the light of a lamp held by young Miriam, has a sudden sense of panic. . . . But the moment passes, and he is able to resume his work. . . . Indeed, Jake's nocturnal carving has an obsessional note, for he identifies with the Samson-figure, seeing himself as a strong man threatened by weakness, the need to depend on others. The community-minded Jake is really a lonely and proud individual at heart, and his jealously guarded carving represents this private, artistic self. As the work proceeds, Jake comes to be more and more dependent on others. His wife, Estella, deserts him (a "betrayal," one feels, that is intended to remind us of Delilah's treatment of Samson), and his friendship with the accordion-playing hunchback, Amos, becomes more complex. . . .

Jake's carving represents a Promethean *hubris* which creates within him a sense of secret guilt. Jake knows that it was not merely Samson's betrayal by Delilah that brought humiliation, blindness, and death, "but what must have lain secretly underneath . . . that

the Bible never gave any clue of at all." In the climactic scene in the book when, during a thunderstorm, he takes an apprehensive Amos to see the carving in the loft, the link between the Samson-figure and Jake is clear. The figure has become that of the blind Samson, leaning on the shoulder of a boy. Worse, it has begun to resemble Jake. . . . Like Milton's tragic hero in *Samson Agonistes*, Jake, convinced that he has been blinded for his sin of pride, broods inwardly. Estella returns to the village, but it is too late. Jake destroys his carving and, finally, himself. Unable to reconcile the demands of social awareness—his blacksmith's job—with the more urgent demands of his art, he chooses self-destruction as a means of escape from an insoluble crisis of loyalties.

Mais, like his character Jake, began his career with a sense of social duty: the need to champion the cause of the despised and neglected black urban poor. As the development of his work suggests, however, the split between his role as spokesman for a community and his concern as an individual artist continued to grow.

Michael Gilkes. *The West Indian Novel* (Boston: Twayne, 1981), pp. 37–40

It is possible that if Mais had lived he may have written stranger and more complex fictions that may have revisioned the trauma of violence that afflicts his work. In some degree his work was crudely influenced by Hollywood cinema as Kenneth Ramchand, I think, makes clear. Nevertheless . . . there is a seed of forces in his narrative that carries the thrust of potential revisualizations of violence in *The Hills Were Joyful Together* and his last novel *Black Lightning*.

*The Hills Were Joyful Together* is shot through by great violence, tight and hideous lives, slums and prisons: emotional claustrophobia. And yet the violence is overshadowed by an elusive sensation that the characters wrestle with fate, with a sky god, who overshadows them and sculpts or carves them out of the hills. Such a view is justified, I think, in *Black Lightning* where parallel forces, violence and creativity, loom unmistakably. The sculptor Jake carves a compulsive Samsonian figure who strikes back from the sky with black lightning. Jake is smitten and blinded. Jake's coming death by his own hand is a parody of the sky god, the parody of creation that succumbs to despair, save that Jake's fall is threaded into a miraculous therapy that heals the inner or psychical malaise that afflicts Amos, Jake's half-crippled friend who "lives" the activity of the stricken yet striking sculpture. Amos can do nothing to save his blind master and friend but in absorbing into himself the blow that the wood receives under Jake's hand, and in coming "alive" as if he is Jake's carving, he brings an element of differentiation into the parody of the sky god—to which Jake succumbs—in the renewal of his own life, a renewed inner dimension, or psychical body.

Wilson Harris. In Robert Sellick, ed. *Myth and Metaphor* (Adelaide: Center for Research in the New Literatures in English, 1982), pp. 6–7

We cannot come to *Black Lightning* with the same expectations we bring to [Mais's] two earlier novels. . . . This work does not follow in the tradition of social realism found in those works. If we look for a crowning achievement to mark the end of Mais's life, then we may be disappointed and puzzled by this novel. Mais would have been untroubled. He was by all accounts not an easy man; his business was asking questions, not answering them. He was obsessed with the question and cared little for the audience's attitude. We know many of the social concerns and questions which preoccupied him, for his writing is devoted to these issues. Yet he constantly goes beyond the predictable boundaries; at the end of his life he was more involved with painting—a more enigmatic, less didactic art than writing. John Hearne, a close friend of Mais's, felt that this was the direction which Mais would have taken, had he lived. Certainly there is much in *Black Lightning* to show us that it was created by a consciousness keenly aware of shape, outline, lighting, color, and texture. It is the product of a painter's eye. It has something of the frozen energy of pictorial art which conveys emotion directly; it strives to appeal to us in ways beyond the reach of words. . . .

The direction taken in *Black Lightning* is inward, but it is not a study of character. The protagonists are simply sketched; we know very little about them beyond the immediate role played by each. This is one of the problems of the novel. We do not know what any of them looks like, save for the broadest generalizations: Amos is a hunchback with a monkey face; Bess is middle-aged and fat; Jake is "tall, powerfully built"; Glen and Miriam are young. The plot, too, is simple and deals baldly with a tragedy in a small village. We know nothing of the antecedents of the main actors in this tragedy, and the tragic act itself—Jake's suicide—is handled with explicit explanations from Jake's wife, Estella, that only deepen the mystery. What we have in this novel is the story of a respected, able man, talented and sensitive, who loses his wife, his talent, and his health, who is then struck blind by lightning and, filled with a despair which no one can dispel, takes his own life. We must ask ourselves whether this chain of events is credible as presented: is a wife's desertion enough to set off such a tragic decline? Is Jake a conventional tragic hero brought down in prideful despair? These are the views that the plot insists upon, but in the end we hesitate. At a deeper level than that of plot, we are moved by a tension and terror not openly explored in plot or characters. At the end of the novel we find ourselves shaken, yet we can hardly say why. The effect of *Black Lightning* is to point us inwards to levels of our being where language hardly works but where the raw energy of consciousness exists. This is the level of forgotten nightmares and unspoken dreams; of the unconscious reaction, the sudden anger, fear, or joy; it is where memory lives, not in sharp detail but in wordless, unimaged feelings. It is the level of myth, symbol, and pure emotion. . . .

Lightning is the symbol of divine energy, creativity, and justice. Black lightning suggests a diabolic opposite. Lightning maims or kills the body; black lightning maims or kills body and soul. Jake, artist-blacksmith, servant of his people, greatest of his kind, destroys his humanity because he finds it intolerable. His only ostensible sin is that of being stronger, better, and wiser than his peers. For this he exacts a terrible revenge on himself. His self-hatred is uncomfortably close to the self-destructiveness which is one part of the Jamaican consciousness, and his heroic stature drives this home to us. His self-hatred being what it is, small wonder that Amos and Estella never consider following him into the woods. They are as much victims and objects of that passion as Jake himself is.

Mais is plainly fascinated with the opposition of creativity and destruction, and of the creator as destroyer. This can be seen in the imagery and symbolism of his two other novels, but in neither does

he go so far as to speculate on how the creator might be brought to destroy himself.

Jean D'Costa. Introduction to Roger Mais. *Black Lightning* (London: Heinemann, 1983), pp. 7–8, 21–22

A God-conscious island, Jamaica could not consider nationalism without giving attention to its religious traditions. Mais's works incorporate this essential religious background, though the views he proffers could not have populist appeal, nor could they be agreeable within nationalist discourse.

Christianity and obeah form the core of the belief systems that Roger Mais inherited from his Caribbean (Jamaican) culture; of the two, Christianity plays the major role. This twofold heritage, pointing to the European and African components of the culture, is evidenced in Mais's subject matter and themes, and especially with respect to Christianity, in the archetypes and language that he uses. Of these two belief systems, Christianity is the most pervasive, presence in his three published novels—*The Hills Were Joyful Together*, *Brother Man*, and *Black Lightning*. The majority of the novels' characters, for instance, overtly express a Christian faith. The role of reformer and social critic in *The Hills* is given to a prison chaplain; *Brother Man* and *Black Lightning* have protagonists who are fashioned according to biblical archetypes. In contrast, the folk belief of the Jamaican masses, obeah, seems to be treated with skepticism by this writer of middle-class origins.

Evelyn J. Hawthorne. *The Writer in Transition: Roger Mais and the Decolonization of Caribbean Culture* (New York: Peter Lang, 1989), p. 87

Mais's lasting contribution to Caribbean literature lies in and, from an aesthetic point of view, in some of the large quantity of unpublished material that now forms the Roger Mais Special Collection at the University of the West Indies Library at Mona, Jamaica.

*The Hills Were Joyful Together* is the first Jamaican "yard" novel: several families and individuals rent rooms in a collection of ramshackle houses (shacks) enclosed in a characteristic African compoundlike space, the houses forming a square with a yard in the middle, a kind of theater where the public life of the tenement takes place. The Trinidadian writers C. L. R. James and Alfred Mendes had already written about such yards a generation before but not with Mais's sense of duality and drama.

In *Brother Man* Mais makes a dramatic change from his earlier style of narrative reportage with chorus effects into a remarkably structured "jazz novel" (as Edward Kamau Brathwaite calls it in his introduction to the 1974 Heinemann edition of *Brother Man*), where words are "notes" that develop into riffs, themes, and "choruses," themselves part of a call/response design based on the aesthetic principle of solo/duo/trio improvisations, with a return, at the end of each "chorus," to the basic group/ensemble/community.

In addition Mais was the first Jamaican writer to bring into the novel the powerful subterranean influence of Rastafarianism, the Jamaican religious and cultural phenomenon that first appeared in the 1930s, part of the anticolonial push for a new Jamaica—a new African Jamaica. The Rastas claimed descent from the "Lion of Judah" and marked their "birth" as being simultaneous with Prince Ras Tafari's ascension to the Ethiopian throne, when he was renamed Emperor Haile Selassie I. *Brother Man*, the protagonist of the novel, is not the "dread" figure that some Rastafarians would soon become (as in Orlando Patterson's *The Children of Sisyphus*, 1964) but rather a benign Christ figure, in keeping with Mais's own aesthetic iconography—the quest for transcendent "mythopoets" in whom individualism would be eventually subsumed.

In Mais's last published novel, *Black Lightning*, the mythopoetic idea is larger than ever, represented by Jake, the blacksmith and secret sculptor, and even more so by the "Samson" he is carving out of a huge block of mahogany. But the Gnostic nature of his enterprise is signaled by the relative lack of detail about the act of carving and its inevitable collapse; he chops it up for firewood.

Most critics and commentators believe Mais was interested in symbols stemming almost exclusively from the stories about biblical characters (Samson, David and Bathsheba, Joshua, Judas, and Lazarus) and from Greek mythology (Zeus, Apollo, and Aulis). But the reinterpretation of the iconography of *Brother Man* as "jazz" and Rastafarian—involving the search for a New World aesthetic and form of expression—is fruitful. It has in turn led to a reinterpretation of *Black Lightning* as a search for ancestral (African) symbolism, which (because of his class and education) Mais might not have know much about but which (because of his nativity commitment) he felt he ought to explore. And this exploration, surely, must have been influenced by the long tradition of Jamaican black consciousness, mediated through the Bible and Greek mythology and the affinity of these with African/ancestral beliefs.

In *Black Lightning* the title term, though widely used among contemporary Rastas to mean "black transcendence," is not used by Mais in the Rastafarian sense but in the traditional African sense of the "negative—or visual imprint—of the (blinding face of god." The god in this case is Shango, orisha (god) of thunder and lightning, who, in Yoruba tradition, is a blacksmith and brother of Ogun (also a blacksmith and sculptor). According to legend, sometimes Shango is mistaken for Jakuta, the stone thrower.

Mais's choice of a blacksmith and carver deeply involved with thunder and lightning and called Jake thus seems meaningful. One can add to this matrix the continuing Shango legend that his wife, Oya, goddess of the Niger, was said to have had such an influence over him that he could do nothing without her—which is apparently the case with Jake's wife, Estella, or so she says. Shango was a mortal king who dared to become a god. Like Jake and the legendary Prometheus, Shango wanted the "lightning," in other words to see God's face, this desire being evidence of what Wole Soyinka has called Shango's "destructive egotism." Who in *Black Lightning* is more destructively egotistical than Jake?

The novel fails, though, because Mais, like Jake, abandoned an enterprise (Africanism) that he was not fundamentally happy with, that he did not or could not at that time properly understand. But the attempt helps readers recognize that, though it failed, it was part of a theme, judging from the Mais archives, with which he was deeply involved (the combination of biblical, Greek, Gnostic, agnostic, and African symbols in Jamaican culture).

All Mais's published novels had been written before he left Jamaica for Europe, and they represent the mature and optimistic phase of his career. He began his ancestral research with the European roots of Jamaican culture but developed an increasing awareness that Africa had to be included to make sense of his country's plural society. *Black Lightning* was the result.

As well as the ancestral, he was interested in the creole, the political reconstructionism of the 1930s, and the sociocultural problems of the "yards." There was a need for a nativist aesthetic. Many at that time were asking and writing about West Indian culture, and by 1948 there was the University of the West Indies; there was also renewed talk of self-government and the new, exciting prospect of a West Indian federation; and writers, artists, and intellectuals from the region were beginning to reflect this optimistic future and to search for forms to give it a local face. *The Hills Were Joyful Together* and *Brother Man* are Mais's contribution to this movement. *Brother Man*, certainly, is a major contribution to a nativist aesthetic.

When he left for London, Roger Mais was probably hoping to consolidate his achievements. Like the other West Indian novelists then gathering in London, he must have been hoping to extend his concerns into the cosmopolitan and the international. His untimely death from cancer (in Jamaica in 1955) ended those aspirations.

Edward Kamau Brathwaite. *Dictionary of Literary Biography*, Volume 125: *Twentieth-Century Caribbean and Black African Writers* (Detroit: Gale Research, 1993), pp. 78–81

BIBLIOGRAPHY
*And Most of All Man*, 1939; *Face and Other Stories*, 1942; *Atalanta at Calydon*, 1950; *Come Love, Come Death*, 1951; *The Hills Were Joyful Together*, 1953; *Brother Man*, 1954; *Black Lightning*, 1955; *The Three Novels of Roger Mais* (contains *The Hills Were Joyful Together*, *Brother Man*, and *Black Lightning*), 1966; *Listen, The Wind, and Other Stories*, 1986

# MAPANJE, Jack (1944–)
## Malawi

Among African poets writing in English, [Wole] Soyinka stands out as having created a "human voice" for his poetry. But that voice (and the trait is not always endearing), tends always towards magniloquent self-dramatization, towards bardic posturing. [Mongane] Wally Serote ranges conversationally, and with quite frequent success, across the Johannesburg scene, but his idiom is not wholly self-made—it is that of someone who has listened to a lot of jazz talk, read a good deal of "black protest" verse. Stressing . . . that other kinds of achievement in verse than this may be equally, sometimes more, valuable, I am still convinced that Jack Mapanje offers something good which one finds nowhere else on the continent.

Mapanje, in his early thirties, teaches in the Department of English at Chancellor College, Zomba, Malawi. Some ten years of adult writing have produced enough for one slimmish volume. This doesn't mean that he is a sluggish person. His teaching is mostly in linguistics and in "oral literature"; he defends the claims of the latter to serious attention with great energy and erudition. He writes poetry not only in English but also in Chichewa, Malawi's other official language. . . . Mapanje is fully aware of the actual and potential status of African languages as an alternative medium. He does not think that he is going to solve Africa's problems by writing verse in English. Almost uniquely, he accepts his actual small audience—other staff and students at Chancellor, a few poetry lovers elsewhere in Malawi, and any enthusiast (like myself) from outside who may happen to drop in on the conversation. He does not attempt to shout across the Zaire river and the Sahara, nor direct a megaphone at the slums of South Africa. He writes for people whose faces he sees or remembers, and a high proportion of his poems carry dedications to his friends.

Angus Calder. *ACLALS Bulletin.* 5, 3 (December 1980), pp. 137–38

Only a small proportion of the contributors to the Heinemann African series are poets, and a single new volume of poetry is therefore a publishing event of some importance. With this volume [*Of Chameleons and Gods*] the Malawian poet Jack Mapanje deservedly joins the ranks of such distinguished poets as Okot p'Bitek, [Dennis] Brutus, [Christopher] Okigbo and [Léopold Sédar] Senghor.

We are warned in the poet's introduction that not all the poems will be easily accessible. Mapanje explains that "where voices are too easily muffled" it is difficult to "find a voice (or voices) as a way of hanging on to some sanity," and as a result the poems sometimes "seem to be too cryptic to be decoded." Notes and a glossary help explain specific objects, places, and legends, but a knowledge of political affairs is also sometimes required. This presents less difficulty when Mapanje writes of events in the neighboring states in the south and east—Steve Biko, Soweto, and Wiriyamu are household words in Africa—but recent events in Malawi are not as well known. Nevertheless, the intention is clear. As a poet who is deeply versed both in oral tradition and in his English academic background, Mapanje successfully uses African and contemporary myth and imagery to comment on the state of affairs in Malawi. The tone is somber or ironical, and hope for the future dims in the face of events. In the final poem of the volume Mapanje speaks of the futility of "occasional verse" when, in the "year of the child," "Skeletal Kampuchea children staring, cold / Stubborn Irish children throwing grenades" are "objects too serious for verse."...

Mapanje's deep love for his own country is demonstrated not only by his bitterness and despair over shattered dreams and "bloated images," but also by the setting and imagery of the poems. The rich landscape of Malawi sets the emotional atmosphere of the poems: "the soft beaches" of the "golden lake," the arid Namizimu Mountains, the gliding Shire River which "mystifies our golden lives," the luscious fruit of the land. The terms used to describe the beauty of the land stand in contrast to the metaphors for man: cockroaches, "toxic frogs," "green hounds." Mapanje's voice is original yet free of artifice. Quietly but strongly it emerges from the turbulent center of Africa.

Ursula A. Barnett. *World Literature Today.* 56, 4 (autumn 1982), pp. 737–38

"We Wondered about the Mellow Peaches," which is included in Jack Mapanje's collection of verses entitled *Of Chameleons and Gods*, excites curiosity and arouses interest. But, at first reading and out of context, it does not reveal much in the way of coherent meaning.

Who is the "generous" Alberto referred to in the second line? Why does the opening sequence bring together a selection of attractive sounding fruit desserts with a reference to "township / Lambs brutally chopped"? What is the significance of the allusion to Chilobwe? Why does the poet return to Alberto in the seventh line? How could "whiskers" map moves and pay bills? For a few lines after these enigmas, the reader seems to be on firmer ground when the poet speaks of wasting his "melodious song," which is, presumably a reference to Mapanje's feelings about his earlier poetry. But when he moves on to indicate *what* he has wasted his song *on*, then the clouds of obscurity settle once more—and, in Malawian terms, there is a regular *chiperoni*. Who or what are "parochial squirrels / And hammerheads"? What are they doing "running messages / Up and down bowing peach trees"? How can the Range Rovers to which they bring "Flashy girls with mellow peaches and vermilion / Strawberries" be "lascivious"? What does the poet mean by regretting not having "erected an edifice," not having set up "votive slabs" and not chalking "the rude walls"? What does he imply by the reference to the chameleon having "lost grip of his own colors"? Which years are referred to as "the restive decade"? Why do the last two lines of the poem make important sounding observations about "conspiracies and goats" and at the same time dismiss the observations as "fuss"? Finally, what on earth does the poet mean by tugging at our sleeves and, in a chuckling whisper, recalling—quite groundlessly—that "we all wondered about the mellow peaches"?...

Mapanje writes as a mature student of the oral tradition and of the English language. He writes, under the suspicious eyes of security officers and the censorship board, for his friends and fellow countrymen about events which have affected him and his people. Circumstances have introduced a degree of obscurity into his work, but he communicates with an alert, attentive, "home" audience by employing the conventions of riddling and by using a consistent, resonant system of codes.

James Gibbs. *Journal of Commonwealth Literature.* 22, 1 (1987), pp. 31–32, 43–44

When Jack Mapanje . . . entitled his collection *Of Chameleons and Gods*, he confessed that he was being advisedly "cryptic" in his poetry since he was writing about situations which forced him to adopt such a style. The choice of title and style are significant in that Mapanje's poetry can be claimed to be as illusive as the animal that is their trademark. The poet himself reveals in the introduction that the identification is a conscious metaphor: "one is tempted like the chameleon . . . to bask in one's brilliant camouflage." The illusiveness of the verse is also deliberate and one way of approaching its underlying meaning is, of necessity, to go through the mythological background of the chameleon informing the poet's inspiration. . . .

The need for taking such a mythological excursion is felt not only in the title but also because the volume's central, most profound, and one of its longest pieces, "If Chiuta Were Man," borrows heavily from Malawi's creation myths featuring the animal itself. The argument posited . . . is that the ambiguities revealed by the chameleon in lore and life are similar to those observed in Mapanje's poetry. . . .

In "If Chiuta Were Man," Mapanje borrows extensively from the cluster of creation myths centered on the chameleon. The earliest published version has the chameleon and the salamander as the two messengers. The second published version from an unidentified ethnic group has the chameleon and the lizard carry the two messages: that men would never die at all, and that even if men died they would rise again thereafter. The effect on man is the same. The third version gives a partial reason why conflicting messages were given from the same sender(s). It was two old men who, entrusted with holding the sun up high lest it fall and bring death to living things, sent the chameleon and the lizard separately and independently of each other.

The three versions above place the chameleon and the lizard as central to the message of life and death. Once the messages are delivered, the narratives end with an explanation of why men hate the chameleon and/or the lizard. Two other published versions . . . however, extend the narrative to explain what happened to man, animal, and god to bring about a separation, or such punishment as death. In the fourth version, the chameleon reports to God (Mulungu) the discovery of a pair of human beings in his fish trap. God advises the chameleon to watch what the human pair do next. This narrative then describes the invention of fire and the driving out of God and animals from the place of creation. The animals flee into the forest while God climbs to the sky on the spider's web. Mapanje uses the second part of this narrative in his poem. The fifth version was also useful to Mapanje since it contains more details not only of the fire making but also the actual coming down together of man, animal, and god to live together on earth and the subsequent cataclysm.

Steve Chimombo. *Journal of Commonwealth Literature.* 23, 1 (1988), pp. 102, 105–6

[Mapanje] appeals first for a return to "traditional literature and modes of thought as the source of metaphor and inspiration." In suggesting this, Mapanje is not, as it may appear, advocating a nostalgic or neotraditional literature of drums and masks and flywhisks and rain-shrines. He means that he wishes the new generation of young Malawian artists to have available, even when writing in English, something of the range of devices and density of metaphor the oral poet shares with his audience. At the center of his argument is a long section on the art of riddling, a subject that has long fascinated him. Riddling, he argues, is at the heart of all new metaphors. The "rebellious nature of the riddle" lies in the fact that it surprises the audience into realizing the things that are not "patterned as they appear." . . .

Mapanje firmly rejects the notion, still current in some discussions of writing from East and Central Africa, that oral modes are simple and unsophisticated or that wit and polish and complexity in a writer are signs of Western influence. To Mapanje, the language of the oral poet is sophisticated and mischievous, dense with history refined to metaphor, yet capable of dynamic effects of communication precisely because those metaphors are understood and have achieved currency. To re-create in Malawian English a language of such local resonance, recapturing the toughness and complexity of oral poetry and especially its capacity for intellectual rebellion, has become his literary program. From this perspective, the coded metaphors of his poems contributed to meetings of the Writer's Group in the early 1970s were not primarily the product of circumstances in which the Group came together. They were the offspring of a marriage of the English language with a Malawian oral aesthetic. . . .

The profoundly oral nature of Mapanje's style needs little demonstration. The poems are dominated by the speaking voice, usually in the first person and the present tense. They shift line by line both in tone and syntax, from bald statement to quiet reflection to satiric jibe to open interrogation. They are intensely dramatic with strong beginnings and forceful endings and incorporate a good deal of direct speech. These effects are, of course, an achievement of artifice. Mapanje is not in practice an oral poet with his audience present before him. He writes his poems in several drafts, working through as many as a dozen versions before hitting on the form and the images appropriate for what he wishes to say. But the direction of these revisions is always toward greater immediacy of impact and variety of tone, the illusion of orality. Equally demonstrable is the extent to which Mapanje has adopted the oral poet's stance of public spokesman. Poem after poem uses the first person plural "we" in a manner not available to post-Romantic European poets. Of the forty-seven poems in *Of Chameleons and Gods*, no fewer than eighteen end with questions and [a] further eleven with exclamations. It is the stance of the praise poet, telling the chief what no one else will say and licensed by the medium of which he is master.

To his audience in Malawi the poems are packed with references to the people, places, and events of the country's recent history. A reading of the landscapes of Malawi is also a reading of ethnic tensions and political rivalries. Mapanje's poems represent not history as code but history as drama, evaluation, and judgment. They address the agenda which has been set by President Banda since the events of the cabinet crisis of 1964 and they seize back President Banda's own appropriation of the past by offering an alternative account of history, custom, and tradition. In the process, they become the best guide available within Malawi to events over the past generation. In a country where intellectual and moral enquiry have been savagely repressed, Mapanje's satire challenges like a conscience.

Leroy Vail and Landeg White. *Review of African Political Economy.* 48 (1990), pp. 30–31, 38

A key point about Mapanje is his village background with which he has maintained strong links. Thus, rural life and the lakeshore area of Mangochi often feature in the poetry. This happens in "Messages," "Requiem to a Fallen Son," "The Sweet Brew at Chitakale," "The Palm Trees of Chigawe," "These Too Are Our Elders," "Visiting Zomba Plateau," "Epitaph for a Mad Friend," "In Memory of Matthew, 1976," and "An Elegy for Mangochi Fishermen." By and large, however, these poems reflect rural life as a backcloth to some other theme: they do not regularly foreground that life for its own sake, though it is clearly valued. But the poet's overseas experience stamps the verse too, as happens in a series of expatriate poems which often present not just an African view of Britain but also a springboard for contrast and comparison of British life with the African home scene.

There is a reliable freshness in Mapanje's work, an air of spontaneity and a feeling that each venture elicits new technical responses. And a tertiary training in education and language rather than literature perhaps explains why the poet, though familiar with the canon of English literature, shows no firm allegiance to any outside tradition of which he sees himself a part. Rarely does he consciously echo British and world literature and in this differs from his local colleagues or from other African poets such as [Dennis] Brutus, [Wole] Soyinka, [Christopher] Okigbo, [Michael] Echeruo or [Jared] Angira. One cannot imagine his quoting an entire [John] Donne sonnet within a personal poem, as [Felix] Mnthali does to great effect; nor see him, as we are asked to see Angira in *Juices*, appearing among glittering company at a party given by Chaucer! But then it is worth noting that, while writing mainly in English, Mapanje has also written a good deal in the vernacular and that he is deeply conversant with local oral tradition. . . .

Though a lively mind and open sensibility draw him to many subjects, certain issues predominate. Fundamental . . . is emotional and psychological survival and the therapeutic role that writing plays in this as it does for [Frank] Chipasula, [Steve] Chimombo, [Edison] Mpina, and Mnthali. A prolific use of questions and exclamations reflects a mind striving by turns to probe, jest, and assert, and to create space for free movement. One topic receiving repeated treatment is the modern response to tradition which he feels lacks proper respect. Too often what happens is mere debasement; of, for example, dancing styles, music, carving, and indeed of all the various ways in which the dead are remembered. Another concern, widely shared, is the demoralizing effects of urban life on former villagers. And like all his local contemporaries he worries about a blighted promise and wasted talent, frets about a censorship which must stifle artistic effort, and deplores injustice meted out to humble people endlessly beset by fear of drought and sickness. He is concerned about family and friends, about those who suffer in neighboring states such as Mozambique and South Africa.

Adrian Roscoe and Mpalive-Hangson Msiska. *The Quiet Chameleon: Modern Poetry from Central Africa* (London: Hans Zell, 1992), pp. 47–48

Each section of *The Chattering Wagtails of Mikuyu Prison* concerns a phase in Jack Mapanje's life, and each has a particular tone. A characteristic mood is struck for the opening section by "Kadango Village, Even Milimbo Lagoon Is Dry," in which the poet, on returning to his family home in Malawi, is confronted by evidence of hunger. In a series of lightning sketches Mapanje conveys telling impressions, and by loading the language he makes words work for him, nudging the reader toward inescapable conclusions. The repressive government has, it seems, added misinformation to misery by smothering all news of this suffering: "Our fat-necked custodians despatch another tale."

The poem which gives the second section its title is built around a reaction to scenes on a maternity ward and is characteristically angry. On the ward the poet sees "Sixty inmates of spasming women top & tail / On thirty beds." He describes the "inmates" as "atoning for the ghost / Revolution twenty years ago." As if these scenes, and the inability to talk openly about them, were not enough, there is the prospect of a visit from the man who has been called "a black tin god." In that part of the world where Father Christmas wears a homburg to "visit the sick at Christmas, some caesareans will," the poet writes, "be / Prematurely discharged." Others will be "jostled into / Neat lines, clapping their praises" so that, as far as Hastings Banda is concerned, there will be "one patient per bed.". . .

Jack Mapanje's virtues are his clarity of vision, his accessibility, his honesty, and his stubbornness. He has written thoughtful and thought-provoking poems, which are undoubtedly the work of a word artist able to sketch relevant images and of a wordsmith quick to hammer out telling phrases. The country's "ghost revolution" is now history, and Mapanje was among the gravediggers. The "fat-necked custodians" have used up all their credit, and Mapanje is

among the chattering wagtails who now speak of what went on in Banda's Malawi.

James Gibbs. *World Literature Today*. 68, 2 (spring 1994), pp. 411–12

All of Jack Mapanje's poetry grows in stature when placed in the Malawian context from which most of it springs, but the best of it is so emotionally charged that it can be appreciated with a minimal understanding of the circumstances in which it was produced. Through his verse he pushes back the frontiers of oral poetry; he speaks and ask questions in a country where unquestioning silence was, until recently, demanded. For years Mapanje walked a perilous path, trying out different voices, testing his vocation, neither courting danger for its own sake nor allowing himself to make disreputable compromises.

In 1987 he fell afoul of the repressive government and was imprisoned without charge or trial in one of the prisons in which Malawian "rebels" were expected to "rot." After more than three years of detention, Mapanje was released and allowed to leave the country of his birth. The poetry he has written since his release draws on his prison experience and continues to function as his side of a dialogue with Malawi, which since May 1994 has been freed from the shadow of repression.

Mapanje's poetry holds its own as verse, meticulously crafted, compressed, resonant, individual, deeply felt, and profoundly moving. But since many of his poems are densely allusive and rooted in his country's culture and politics, they are best appreciated if their Malawian context is taken into account. The reader benefits by knowing, for example, about the nation's machinery of repression and about the terms and idioms in which the one-party state proclaimed itself. The former Malawian head of state, the Life President Ngwazi Dr. H. Kamuzu Banda, constantly spoke about the importance of "peace and calm, law and order," and no public address was complete without reference to the four "cornerstones" of the Malawi Congress Party: loyalty, obedience, unity, and discipline. The reader, though, should realize, too, Mapanje's underlying love for his country, sold in tourist brochures as "the warm heart of Africa," and its saving graces, which include families, flowers, colleagues, and schools.

Mapanje writes mostly in English, but this does not mean that he fails to communicate with his fellow Malawians. Through his use of existing oral forms; his adoption in poem after poem of a conversational manner, tone, and register; and his publications in ChiChewa, a language second only to English in Malawi, he builds many bridges to readers and listeners. While it is notoriously difficult to estimate the impact of a poet, and while one is initially skeptical that a Malawian poet writing mostly in English could make much of an impression, the attention he has received from the repressive authorities suggests that Mapanje has reached his audience. In a country where all communication channels are rigidly controlled, the people listen attentively. . . .

Mapanje's second collection of poems, *The Chattering Wagtails of Mikuyu Prison*, contains the two Mikuyu Prison poems . . . as well as forty-three others, separated into four sections. The first two sections, titled "Another Fools' Day Homes In" and "Out of Bounds," are made up of poems from the early and mid-1980s into 1987. The third section begins with "The Streak-Tease" and the date 25 September 1987; it contains ten prison poems. It is followed by "The Release and Other Curious Sights," a section of a dozen poems, including "In Memoriam" and "Tethered Border Fugitives upon Release," over which the experience of prison hangs and from which further insights into Mapanje's prison experience can be obtained. Comparison between the 1993 versions and those poems which had appeared earlier indicates that the poet revised his poems for book publication. Words are occasionally changed; lineation is sometimes altered. In the book Mapanje tends to break his lines unexpectedly and so gives his poems a sharper, more challenging edge.

Every aspect of the collection gains significance from the reader's knowledge of Mapanje's imprisonment. The volume is poignantly dedicated to the memory of the mother who "gave up waiting," to his wife and children, and to "the good humour of" his fellow inmates. The dedication is followed by two quotations from the Bible which are resonant and indicate, among much else, the importance of the Bible to the prisoners: the prison's three copies fed some of the spiritual needs of a community under great pressure, many of whom seemed to have been shut away because a country had gone mad, because reason, justice, sense, human feeling, even God himself had fled.

Some of the poems written in prison touch on aspects of Mapanje's life which concerned observers might have hoped to have heard about. Of the many letters and cards written to Mapanje and in support of his case one at least reached its destination. "To the Unknown Dutch Postcard Sender (1988)" is a moving poem prompted by the delivery of a card addressed to him "Near Zomba, Malawi." The postcard provided Mapanje with an outside contact, someone new to talk to, and he makes the point that the card with its signature comes most opportunely just after he has signed his detention order. . . . The poem celebrates a positive moment, an event to be savored when it must have been easy to think that friends had forgotten and the international community had proved impotent. It is clear that it is a moment that will be shared, for the poet refers to the fellow prisoners of his section when he offers "many thanks on behalf of these D4s too!"

The poem reveals the extent of his deprivation. The postcard, which he would "probably have spurned outside," is scrutinized carefully and described in detail. As in other poems, Mapanje slips in indictments of the system through his references to the circumstances in which he and his fellow inmates are forced to live. And he uses telling descriptions: a "shattered spirit" is impossible to visualize, but the words "mottled bare feet squelching / On this sodden life-sucking rough cement" make an impact on several senses. In the final section of the poem Mapanje appears to stress the positive, while taking advantage of every opportunity to draw attention to the harsh realities of existence: he suggests that the genuine pleasure taken in the "Groeten uit Holland" will eliminate the "fetid walls," "cold cells," "midnight centipedes," "rats nibbling at / the rotting corns of our toes," "midnight piss from those blotched lizards," and "scorpion stings."

In "You Caught Me Slipping Off Your Shoulders Once," included in the final section of the collection, Mapanje speaks to a fellow inmate, Tukula Sizala Sikweya, celebrating the news of his release with "all those D4 / Wagtails." Celebrating, too, Sikweya's endurance, his robust individually, and, quite literally, his support, there is a reference to the "lion shoulders" on which Mapanje climbed to glimpse the wife and children he had not seen for twenty-two months and also "Pat O'Malley in white collar." Eased into the poem through an account of a resilient detainee, the reader is drawn into sharing a moment of heartrending intimacy. In

diction and reference the poem offers few difficulties, and close attention to other poems removes most of these. There is just enough complexity to make the reader appreciate Sikweya's remarkable qualities, enough detail—"green acacias dancing to Lake Chilwa breeze / The chickens pecking under the guard's granary"—to establish the setting, and then the wave of feeling crashes through. Mapanje writes that his "heart / Started" and his "feet began to sweat." The pace of the poem, and the juxtaposition of those two sensations, one of heart, the other of feet, indicate the art which conceals art, the craft by which Mapanje makes a complex, moving work appear to have simply rolled off the tongue. As in other poems, the details of the appalling conditions in prison are given almost as asides.

Mapanje's imprisonment was clearly filled with terrible experiences. Inmates were tortured, sometimes to death. For many months his friend Blaise Machila was kept naked and in chains in a nearby cell. In reading Mapanje's poems the presence of the pain caused by these experiences should not be disregarded, and it should never be forgotten that the celebrations he writes about took place against this background of suffering. As a poet who wants to share his experience and tell the truth without posturing, Mapanje writes his poems as part of his way of coming to terms with the "horror" of what he has seen. He knows that man cannot stand much reality, and he shares with his readers as much as he can within the limits of art.

Mapanje's status as a prisoner is the subject of the first poem in the final section of the collection. It is prefaced by a question presumably addressed to Mapanje by someone in the security forces: "(We've detained more distinguished people than you in this country, but we've never had the same amount of trouble as we've had over your case. WHO ARE YOU?)"

In the title of the poem, "The Release: Who Are You, Imbongi?," the word Imbongi may be translated as "praise singer," but it is clear that Mapanje, true to the functions of praise singers as described in *Oral Poetry from Africa,* tempered praise with criticism. The question posed, of course, can be answered in various ways. Physically, Mapanje was a slight, bespectacled figure with a limp. He might have been seen as only "a middle-aged academic with a wife, and three children." Clearly the security officer knew that there was more, much more, than these descriptions implied. He knew that, to him and what he represented, Mapanje was trouble.

In the poem Mapanje is reminded even as he departs Mikuyu that he has "left behind fellow inmates." He is assured that "Mikuyu will gladly welcome / You back" and told that distinguished inmates had been released only to be "accidentalized." But, in his answer to the question "who are you," Mapanje as imbongi suggests that he's a maccah, a burr, "the persistent / Brown ant that crept into the elephant's / Ear" and drove him to destruction.

To the elephant Mapanje may be a brown ant, but he clearly plays other roles as well. After the chameleon, the Cheshire cat, and the riddler, the role of the brown ant is a new one. What Mapanje would be too modest to say is that he is a poet of international stature, with a sure command of the skills required for his profession, acutely sensitive, and courageous in defense of the highest principles.

James Gibbs. In Bernth Lindfors and Reinhard Sander, eds. *Dictionary of Literary Biography,* Volume 157: *Twentieth-Century Caribbean and Black African Writers* (Detroit: Gale Research, 1996), pp. 170–80

BIBLIOGRAPHY
*Of Chameleons and Gods*, 1981; *The Chattering Wagtails of Mikuyu Prison*, 1993; *Skipping without Ropes*, 1998

# MARAN, René (1887–1960)

## Martinique

*Batouala*, which has won the Prix Goncourt, is a rather weak book. . . .

Maran might respond that, as a novelist, he is exempt from presenting an overall view and that he has the right to choose the facts he describes. But he has given up his right to make this response by the tone of his preface, which is entirely political. He has given himself a mission and is trying to rally all French writers to his side. He may often be right. But he must submit to the rule of all criticism, without which there can be no honesty: to provide a complete account. Descartes established this rule at a time when Maran's ancestors were busy hunting wild animals. But Maran must get to know it. . . .

The antithesis between the noble savage and the conquering barbarian is a literary device that is not very new: Voltaire used it in *Alzire*. Civilization, to be sure, does not bring only benefits; it brought us Maran's book. Nevertheless, while Batouala laments the passing of the good old days, he is irritated because the railroad is not being built quickly enough. And he does not mention the hospitals, which, I believe, are of some service. I have seen regions in Guinea in which yellow fever and malaria were eliminated by the administration so denounced by Maran, who writes, "They are killing us slowly."

I have stressed the fundamental ideas of this book because they coincide, in what is most routinely literary about them, with the tendencies of the realist school of around 1880, which are still in part those of the Académie Goncourt. For them, literature was a shooting gallery, and the figures to be shot at were the judge, the bourgeois, the soldier, and the colonist. . . . This is probably one of the reasons why the Académie Goncourt chose to give its prize to this novel. I have trouble imagining any other reason. For the other elements of the novel are ordinary. The descriptions of customs are often entertaining but do not have any more merit than those found in so many accounts by travelers who never claimed to be men of letters. And as for the structure, it is worthless.

Henry Bidou. *La revue de Paris.* January 15, 1922, pp. 400, 402–4†

*Batouala*, the novel by René Maran, a negro, winner of the Académie Goncourt prize of 5,000 francs for the best novel of the year by a young writer, is still the centre of a swirl of condemnation, indignation and praise.

Maran, who was born in Martinique and educated in France, was bitterly attacked in the chamber of deputies the other day as a defamer of France, and biter of the hand that fed him. He has been much censured by certain Frenchmen for his indictment of French imperialism in its effect on the natives of the French colonies. Others have rallied to him and asked the politicians to take the novel as a work of art, which it is; great art, except for the preface, which is the only bit of propaganda in the book. . . .

Launched into the novel itself, the reader gets a picture of African life in a native village seen by the big-whited eyes, felt by the pink palms, and the broad, flat, naked feet of the African native himself. You smell the smells of the village, you eat its food, you see the white man as the black man sees him, and after you have lived in the village you die there. That is all there is to the story, but when you have read it, you have been Batouala, and that means that it is a great novel.

Ernest M. Hemingway. *Toronto Star Weekly.* March 25, 1922, p. 3

From the beginning [Maran's] literary career has been a succession of unexpected bombshells. The first of these came in 1921, when *Batouala* received the Goncourt award. A storm of protests greeted this decision. How could the Académie Goncourt have selected a book the preface of which bitterly denounced the French colonial system? And the story itself, did it not exaggerate the seamy side of life in French Equatorial Africa? Besides, who was René Maran? Gradually it became known that the author of *Batouala* was a thirty-four-year-old Negro born in Martinique in 1887. Natives of French Guiana, his parents were then stationed in Fort-de-France, where the father was an underclerk in the colonial service. In 1894, after the father had been transferred to a post in Gabon, it was decided to place the boy in a Bordeaux boarding school, where he developed mentally, physically—he became captain of the football team—and spiritually. . . .

In a reminiscent mood one Friday afternoon, M. Maran told me that when the news of the Goncourt award reached him in Africa, he was even more astonished than the French reading public. Hardly daring to believe the telegrams, he left his beloved bush for Paris where he was to encounter additional surprises. Despite his novel's success in France and elsewhere, publishing houses were refusing to handle his works. According to Maran, this refusal was dictated by politicians who feared his outspoken pronouncements on colonial matters. . . .

One should not infer, however, that Maran is merely a radical or a rabid racialist. In most of his books it is almost impossible to detect the author's racial identity. Nor has Maran played the political game; he prides himself on the fact that he has never voted. He loves France, which even in the preface to *Batouala*, he calls the "country that gave me everything," and he loves his art.

Mercer Cook. *French Review.* January 1944, pp. 157–59

Maran's vocabulary embraces the entire French-speaking world, in time and in space. His historical works, in particular, show him as a lover of the spicy, dense French language of the late Middle Ages. He takes pleasure in reviving archaic words, dialect, and technical terms. . . . Maran's writing embodies the very best qualities of French prose. As Charles Kunstler notes, his prose is "clear, firm, highly colored, and harmoniously rhythmical."

In these last two qualities, one perceives the black man, more precisely the *black writer*, who, when writing in French, can define himself only through his style. For the black writer, the French language is, as Brunetto Latini said, the "most delightful." And Maran is captivated by the "delights of good style." But what essentially characterizes Maran's style is the power of his images and the power of his rhythm—above all, the power of the images, which command attention: supple images in his poems, dynamic images in his ''African'' novels. In this way, Maran was the forerunner of the Negritude movement in the French-speaking world. One has only to reread *Batouala*. . . .

However, the black French writer is not merely a stylist. When he becomes a novelist, he is also a psychologist. All the black novels in French derive from Maran, whether their author is Ferdinand Oyono or André Demaison. After *Batouala*, one could no longer portray Negroes living, working, loving, crying, laughing, or speaking like whites. Nor would it do to have them speak pidgin French; rather, they would speak Wolof, Malinké, or Ewondo in French. For Maran was the first to express the ''black soul,'' with a Negro style, in French.

Léopold Sédar Senghor. In *Hommage à René Maran* (Paris: Présence Africaine, 1965), pp. 12–13†

Today's reader is less responsive to the [social criticism] in *Batouala* than to the realism in its depiction of collective life, to the skill with which ethnographic detail is joined to the plot. The main episode in *Batouala* is the great festival of circumcision. A clever progression has us move from the calm, serious religious ceremony to the explosion of the people's frenzy, provoked by the ritual dance in which two women simulate the sexual act. Couples are then formed at random, including Batouala's wife and her lover. [Batouala], the chief, catches them, but he is prevented from taking his revenge by the unexpected arrival of the *commandant de cercle* [regional military administrator], who drives everybody away. The scene, far from being a digression, really contributes to the action of the novel and prepares the ending.

*The Book of the Bush*, Maran's masterpiece, does not contain any scenes that are as well developed as the central scene in *Batouala*, but it lets us enter intimately into African life, showing us the daily activities of the Bandas [a small river tribe of the Ubangi], the clearing of new land, the hunt, and races in the forest. It also depicts the animals of the bush, each with its own physiognomy. Therein lies Maran's true originality—his perception of life in equatorial nature: the sun, a source of health and joy; water, which sometimes brings fertility and sometimes devastation; and the vegetation, which is like a great cry of liberation rising from the earth toward heaven. The human actors [in the novel] merely participate in [nature's] drama of life and death; and the tragic story of Kossi and Yassi, happy at first and then pursued by fate and men's hatred, blends into the adventure of their people, torn by rivalries and victimized by the vengeance of the gods, who engulf all the land's riches under a flood.

Roger Mercier. *Tendances*. October 1965, pp. 419†

When René Maran encountered French Equatorial Africa, he wanted to dip deep into his ancestral roots. He learned the Banda language and . . . his book *Batouala* was to challenge the colonial literature that made the Negro a caricature and denied him any culture. . . .

In his novels, especially *Batouala*, Maran shows the true face of Africa. He reveals the existence of Negro civilization, defends that civilization, and, in so doing, denounces those who try to undermine the Negro's humanity. In this novel we have our first defense and illustration of Negro culture, of the Negro ''nation.''. . .

Sometimes the author informs us about old Africa and its customs; sometimes he presents this land, formerly virgin and peaceful, now in conflict with the conqueror who is trying to destroy it by every means of exploitation. . . .

Thus, Maran's work introduces us to the authentic Africa of our brothers. It laid the foundations for Negro-African literature, especially the literature that came to be called Negritude.

But René Maran the individual is somewhat disconcerting. Although he was a Negro, the writer remained primarily French in spirit and thought. Did he himself not admit, ''I am a European with black skin''? This man, who was no better than anyone else, refused to accept his race totally. [As Frantz Fanon wrote,] he ''is neither more nor less than a black deserter. He is a neurotic who needs to be freed from his infantile fantasies.'' His return to the roots therefore remained superficial. The struggle that he led for the rehabilitation of Negro values was like Montaigne's humanism. Like Montaigne, Maran could write that ''every custom has its reason.'' It was, moreover, in the name of this humanism that Maran refused to be any forerunner of present-day Negritude.

Barthélemy Kotchy. *Presence Africaine*. 76 (1970), pp. 147–49†

Before Maran, literary expression [in Martinique] conformed in its themes and formal patterns to the French norm. Its tone was dictated exclusively by the prevailing fashion in Paris, its sentiments largely determined by the attitudes of the average Frenchman towards the Antilles. The Caribbean scene features in this literature, particularly in the poetry, as a decorative element, never as a human scene. The French West Indian writer contributed mainly to the Parnassian taste for the exotic, without ever feeling the need to assert any form of individuality. In the years between the end of the nineteenth century and the First World War, Martinique experienced something of a literary renaissance, but produced nothing more than a literature of acquiescence and of what one might call the exterior regard.

René Maran brought a new development into the outlook of Martinican writing, in an indirect but decisive way. It is worth remarking that Maran began his literary career as a symbolist poet, albeit at the decadent stage. Born in 1887 in Martinique of Guyanese parents, Maran did not really get to know his native land and his experience of the colonial situation was to be made in Africa itself. He was taken to France at the age of four and apart from occasional journeys to Central Africa where his father was a colonial officer, spent all his youth in France. He attended College at Bordeaux, and grew up in his education, in his attitudes and in his tastes a Frenchman. His French beginnings in literature were therefore, despite the colour of his skin, perfectly natural. He published two volumes of poetry in his early years in the intimate vein of the later symbolists, and came to be considered a promising regionalist poet, who blended a feeling for landscape with a rare psychological insight. These are qualities which were later to be given forceful expression in his African novels. When it is considered, however, that his second volume of poems, entitled *La Vie intérieure* (1912) was composed almost entirely in Central Africa, where by 1910 Maran had taken up a post in the French colonial administration, the cleavage between the subtle and evanescent inner life to which he gave he was later to document in *Batouala*, cannot but strike one as being in every way absolute.

Maran's direct experience of Africa was to change the course of his literary preoccupations and to transform to a considerable extent his own social and human awareness. His correspondence during this period conveys the changes that this experience began to effect in his outlook, and which were to wrench him away from the immaterial vision of his symbolist verse and impel him towards the mindful confrontation with human beings and with events which produced *Batouala*.

The sensitive nature which his lonely youth in France had bred in him did not prepare him for the shock of life in colonial Africa, and it was perhaps because of this that it made such a profound impression upon him. But apart from the immediate psychological impact which his experience had upon him, the fact of his blackness came to have a special significance for him in Africa. Maran does not seem to have been oblivious of this fact even in France, for in a letter to one of his friends, written in connection with an obscure love affair, he leaves us in no doubt as to what the fact of his blackness meant to him:

> And then I am Negro. These five words carry with them all the maledictions, because whatever I do, I remain, secretly, infinitely sensitive.

He may have, as a result, felt a distance separating him from his French colleagues and thereby acquired that measure of detachment necessary to cast an objective and critical eye upon the colonial system. Moreover, the irony of his own position as a black man administering other black men does not seem to have escaped him, and in one of his letters the inevitable feeling of his racial identity that this ironical situation inspired in him is given clear expression. He writes:

> Here, with a French heart, I sense that I am on the soil of my ancestors, ancestors that I reject because I do not share either their primitive mentality or their tastes, but who are nevertheless my ancestors.

Maran's ambivalent attitude towards his African origins implied however a minimum of identification and indicates that his situation was that of a marginal man, placed at the sensitive centre of a conflictual situation. At any rate Maran had precise ideas about what he wanted his novel to do, for it is clear from his correspondence that he conceived it with a critical intent. He spent seven years of careful labour upon it and though he was preoccupied with the problem of style in its elaboration, this preoccupation was in fact largely motivated by his concern to render his expression adequate for the purpose which he attached to the work. Without a doubt, this purpose was to give 'O' testimony of the colonial situation.

In an obvious sense and from the purely documentary point of view, the novel presents an overall picture of African life which is negative. Yet a close examination of the work, of its levels of meaning, of its narrative technique and of its symbolic structure reveals the profound identification which Maran had achieved within his own sensibility with Africa, an organic sympathy with African life and people which belies the conscious detachment of Maran's realism.

The first quality that strikes one in this respect is the poetic intensity of Maran's descriptive passages. The whole work itself can be taken as one long prose poem in which the African scene is invested with an unaccustomed symbolic power. . . .

What is more, the very structure and movement of Maran's prose capture for us those elements in the oral tradition of Africa which give it its distinctive flavour. It is a style full of those insistent repetitions of words and sonal values weaving a pattern of refrains and of alliterations through his narrative, and which we can now recognize as deriving from those elements which compose the essence of the oral tradition of Africa.

Maran could not have achieved these effects unless he had listened with an unusually attentive ear to African speech. In one remarkable passage which indicates how well and closely Maran had observed his Africans to the point of identification, he brings together these distinctive features to recreate the distinctive rhetorical manner of the African countryside and to lend dramatic tension to his narrative. . . .

We have then, in *Batouala*, something far in advance of exotism, something more than a mere outside representation of a foreign atmosphere, but an evocation that goes a long way towards restituting the inner quality of life in a specific human universe. Maran not only portrayed Africa in his novel, but by integrating into the whole design of the work such elements as would break through the confines of an externally contrived representation, takes his readers further into the intimate recesses of African experience.

This, more than the explicit anti-colonial passages, makes Maran an innovator in modern African literature, and indeed, the creator of the modern African novel. He pointed the way by this single work, by its demonstrative value, to those African writers in French who came after him, by achieving a reconversion of the European language to render immediate the atmosphere of Africa. Furthermore, within this scheme of his novel, Maran also created an African, for the first time in French literary history, as a true tragic figure, endowed with an authentic imaginative life. Maran impresses his hero upon our feelings and, indeed, upon our intelligence. The African thus comes alive as a hero, that is, as a man with feeling, with his passions, and above all, with his own manner of apprehending the world.

*Batouala* also establishes a direct relationship between the lives of his African characters and the colonial situation, between the external framework of African life at a precise historical moment and the destiny of individuals involved in it. It is from this perspective that the novel performs the social function which its author claimed for it in the preface he added to the second edition, published after the work had obtained the Prix Goncourt in 1921. We know that Maran, after the storm provoked by his novel, was dismissed from the colonial service and withdrew into stoic retirement. His writings afterwards indicate that he was agitated by a personal conflict of loyalties. On the one hand, he continued to express his attachment to France and its culture by cultivating a delicate prose, with a dedication reminiscent of Flaubert, and to the French empire by writing four volumes on its heroes and builders. On the other hand, he also cultivated his African vein in a stream of animal and symbolic novels, the most remarkable of which is *Le Livre de la brousse* (1934). In particular, he poured his personal conflicts into an autobiographical novel, *Un Homme pareil aux autres* (1947).

Maran never 'committed' himself politically, but the true import of his career, especially when viewed against his background, resided in the fact that a West Indian, utterly assimilated to French culture, had been confronted with the contradiction of his position and had begun to move towards a view of things outside and beyond the French scheme of values. The critical intelligence which underlies *Batouala*, as well as the imaginative sympathy which he achieved in his novels with the African continent—and which implied a positive valorization of the continent—indicate a reflective consciousness which was bound to affect the vision of the West Indian in his double relation to Europe and to Africa. For Maran had written out of a frame of mind which was not simply moral or liberal, but denoted a sense of concern and involvement, limited perhaps in scope and intensity, but nonetheless real.

> Abiola Irele. The *African Experience in Literature and Ideology* (London: Heinemann Educational Books, 1981), pp. 128–33

BIBLIOGRAPHY
*Le Visage calme*, 1922; *Djouma, chien de brousse*, 1927; *Le Coeur Serre*, 1931; *Le Livre de la brousse*, 1934; *Les Belles Images*, 1935; *Betes de la brousse*, 1941; *Un Homme pareil aux autres*, 1947; *Bacouya, le cynocephale*, 1953; *Le Livre du souvenir*, 1958

# MARECHERA, Dambudzo (1952–1987)
## Zimbabwe

*The House of Hunger*—a novella, poems, and short stories—is an unrelenting depiction of the stunning effects of poverty and its concomitants of cruelty and pain. As significant as its Rhodesian locale is the novella's adumbration of a species of poverty which can only be known in those countries where racial oppression is a way of life. . . .

*The House of Hunger* . . . is a controlled explosion of passions. [Dambudzo] Marechera is wonderfully aware of the direction of his work as he leads the reader through new and terrible realms of human suffering. The newness derives from his adamant refusal to imitate the structure and narrative method of the traditional English fictional forms, and, instead, to thrust his reader into a world of distorted experience for which most will have no frame of reference. The distortions are of time and place, the normally consoling solidity in the ''backgrounds'' of most fiction. Here the dislocation of both dimensions is skillfully contrived to suggest the continuous disconnectedness of the protagonist from the very tactile and earthbound world—of which he is a part and yet not part. Living as he does a fragmented life, the protagonist of this tale, a boy in a Rhodesian township, charts his crazy existence by reference to violence, pain, and revenge. He is exposed from the beginning to brutality as a way of life—a father and brother whose mode of life is physical assault against women; a mother so desperate with her own physical and mental pain as virtually to ignore this urgently needful son; a world beyond the family that offers more vice and cruelty in the form of bullying the weak and being beaten by the strong—a world which is secure only for the traitor and the whore who have grasped its terms. The white world, in larger terms responsible for the chaos, is regarded for much of the time as a kind of disgusting irrelevance. Yet the novella is redolent with a deep black rage against the whites who have confined the African spirit into these houses of hunger where the only release is intestinal violence. . . .

*The House of Hunger* defies the traditional reduction into story and neatly plotted parts. While these elements are present they are so subtly intermixed into the brittle mosaic that any attempt to extricate them leaves scars on the surface of the work. The misery and madness, pain and want are present in every line simultaneously. The story is only one hard subterraneous vein in this flinty landscape of despair. The novella describes the growth into awareness, madness, and maturity of the protagonist. What lends it its power is the imagistic precision with which it is told, the rhapsody of violence and rage with which it is woven together. Its images, the stuff of real poetry, take their form from the elemental world, and by the poetic force with which they are yoked to the life here described, they crowd the mind with a tangible reality.

> Derek Cohen. *Canadian Journal of African Studies.* 15, 2 (1981), pp. 337–39

Though Marechera's work is written against the background of preindependence Zimbabwe, it represents a considerable development in African literature. His work is not pure anticolonial protest, as one might have expected from preindependence Zimbabwe. He writes in a deeply introspective vein and shows a keen interest in unveiling the psychic responses of his protagonists. There is an almost total absence of celebration, romanticizing the African past or glorifying the African personality, such as one finds in the literature of the Négritude movement; none of the exclusive preoccupation with the iniquities, as such, of the white racist minority regime or the guerrilla struggle, as in South African literature or in the early fiction of East Africa. Marechera's work also differs in tone from the gentle prodding irony and satire (largely corrective or reconstructive in intention) of the postindependence novel, especially in West Africa. His expression of disillusionment in his work is deeper even than [Ngugi wa Thiong'o's] or [Ayi Kwei] Armah's; its cynicism more complete than anything [Wole] Soyinka has ever been accused of. There is an element of resignation and a devil-may-care type of attitude in his work. But on closer examination this apparent resignation and the frivolity and recklessness of his characters mask their extreme sensitivity and vulnerability. Their perverse behavior also manifests a kind of assertiveness that can be seen as some form of defensive mechanism against life's utter senselessness and brutality, against all the chaos in their families and the disarray in the nation, which threaten Marechera's characters and infect their whole personalities. . . .

The title story of *The House of Hunger* . . . is written against the background of discontent. It is an expression of disillusionment with both the past and the present, and is written without any illusions about the future. The novella deals with the misery and the sordidness of life in his home and in Rhodesia in general, which is dubbed ''the House of Hunger'' and from which the central character of the story seeks to escape, as Marechera himself was to do.

> Mbulelo Vizikhungo Mzamane. In Eldred Durosimi Jones, ed. *African Literature Today*. 13 (1983), pp. 203–5

[Marechera] is so preoccupied with violence that the social dimension of his stories fragments into a kaleidoscope of personal protestations. There is virtually no social framework into which his narrative settles. His attempt at psychological realism is a break from both sociopolitical realism and the more conventional stance of the narrator in other Zimbabwean fiction. *The House of Hunger* is not about the processes of alienation or the dynamics of opposing cultures and traditions. The stories allude to an image of a house. The village house, home, and center of cultural consciousness, is metamorphosed into the African mind in Zimbabwe. It is beset by spiritual drought. "Capitalists," "imperialists," and "the bloody whites" are for Peter what have "held the House of Hunger in a stinking grip." Rather than validate this as [Stanlake] Samkange's *The Mourned One* did, Marechera writes a fiction in which the assertion of feelings becomes the substance of the narrative. Hence the varied modes of his fiction are more obtrusive and telling than those found in other Zimbabwean writers. The political dimensions of experience in Zimbabwe are taken for granted in a way that the narrator's violent response to his place in that society is less interesting for its causes than its startling manner of protest. In the title story the narrator, emerging from an abrasive domestic background, goes for a drink with an acquaintance, Harry. They meet his friend Julia in the bar. On the surface that is the story. But beneath this thin series of events are several layers of consciousness which constitute the inner imaginative life of the narrator. By various techniques—stories within stories, patterns of imagery (stitches, stains, blood, breaking)—the fiction establishes the territory of the narrator's mind. Weariness and disillusion with life, protest at missionaries, black informers, whites, education, repeated physical violence, sexual perversion, are markers on a drought-stricken landscape. . . .

Marechera breaks away from most trends in Zimbabwean fiction by accenting the intensity of the inner world of his narrators. The sociohistorical and political context that so concerns other Zimbabwean writers is there as a world with which the narrator has difficulty making contact. His starting point is the opposite to that of other writers. "The silent but desperate voices inside me" have a problem not with understanding that external world but in putting words to it. At one level *The House of Hunger* illustrates the devastating effects of growing up in colonial Rhodesia, but the vision of that devastation is not presented in social realist terms. Here the black narrator is left almost speechless while in the internal world of his consciousness there is a hyperactive verbal iconoclasm that leaves nothing standing but its fictions about itself. Marechera's verbal dexterity outstrips that of most African writers but, as his recent book *Black Sunlight* indicates, his serious concerns with the metaphysics of creativity, and with language itself as a violent instrument, take his fiction beyond the accepted bounds of "African" literature. The writing is sometimes obscure, and his identity crisis as a black Zimbabwean living in exile has thrown him into the searing problems that surround a writer's relation to reality.

T.O. McLoughlin. In G. D. Killam, ed. *The Writing of East and Central Africa* (London: Heinemann, 1984), pp. 110–11

Marechera's first book, *The House of Hunger*, won the *Guardian* Fiction Award in 1981. It is a collection of stories about a brutalized personal life and a society ground by the white penal system of then Rhodesia. And, if he treats he white with complete cynicism, it is no more nor less than how he treats all experience. Nothing gets special treatment; it is informed by a consistent vision, which puts the book into the class of one that had to be written. . . .

Marechera is by no means the complete artist yet. In his second book, *Black Sunlight*, he perversely exaggerates all the qualities praised in his first book and renders up a concoction. Nonetheless, he is the first black Zimbabwean writer to enjoy freedom, not freedom, of course, in a purely political sense, but freedom of experience and access to his material, without the obstructions and shibboleths of the past. His handling of the theme of the white is my touchstone to this judgment. It is the climate in which *the* great Zimbabwean writer will emerge (who might be the matured Marechera himself). And, it is one which the whites were not able to achieve for themselves, for all their privileges. After all, excepting the single figure of Doris Lessing, they were not able to produce a writer of international stature in ninety years.

Colin Style. *Ariel.* 16, 3 (July 1985), pp. 62–63

Marechera's philosophy derives from his extreme individualism, rejecting any kind of rules and constraints. While he strongly disapproved of colonial rule, he is equally critical of the government of independent Zimbabwe. This creates a lot of enemies for him. He, in turn, feels like a misunderstood lone campaigner. . . .

Behind his vacillating face—his "black mask," as he so often refers to it in his stories—is a permanent storm, a battle of contradictions which threaten to blast his mind. *Mindblast [or the Definitive Buddy]* illustrates this explosion of mind, soul, senses, concepts, and reason. . . .

He remains between the two worlds of Africa and Europe, between the experience of physical poverty and cultural wealth, between colonialism and racism and the rebellion against them. . . .

The world for Marechera is split up, shattered into many pieces which he cannot put together. He himself is split. This motif one finds frequently in his work, especially in *The House of Hunger*. His own distorted mirror image stares back at him like a jeering monkey, or the actual split of the personality into twin brothers where the one does and says things which the other finds embarrassing and beyond his control. His writing is full of contradictions and paradoxes. It disturbs the mind, it disrupts realities and patterns of thought so far taken for granted. At the same time, it creates pictures of striking beauty and lucidity, opening new horizons and dimensions of feeling, of grasping, of sensing life. This distinguishes him from all other African writers and gives him a special significance in modern African literature.

Flora Veit-Wild. *New African.* 223 (April 1986), p. 52

Metaphor in Marechera attempts to artistically contain chaos. In the absence of significance, of correspondence, of relationships, which means the death of culture, we have "sharp howling winds scattering grit." The drought is psychological and spiritual sweeping away normal referential language. The narrator typifies the collapse of inner and outer coherence. Metaphor in *The House of Hunger* is singular in anglophone African literature not for any yearning after authentic culture but as a protest at its absence. . . .

The metaphoric narrative of Marechera—"the drought had raised its great red hand"—exemplifies the argument that metaphor operates by a radical departure from the normal functions and relations within language, and between language and the world referred to. Metaphor is a Janus figure that makes nonsense if you look from one point of view and remarkable vision from another. It shatters literal sense. To start with the relation between the metaphor ''hand'' and the object which that term designates in normal usage is destroyed. . . .

Metonymy is rejected by Marechera because the conditions for the accepted or authentic manner of vision within his culture—semantic homogeneity, metonymy—have disappeared. The incoherence in life calls for a radical departure from the normal linguistic manner to a mode that attacks and distorts language itself.

In this light *The House of Hunger* and *Black Sunlight*, his second novel, are unique cultural statements within Shona society, no less authentic for being in English or for their verbal pyrotechnics. Such writing could continue in Zimbabwe, it might be argued, if the liberation war had not ended, or if the writer had profound ideological differences with the governing mores of independent Zimbabwe. History has ruled out the first possibility, but the second, if Marechera's latest book, *Mindblast*, is a fair indication, is still open to dispute.

T.O. McLoughlin. *Nouvelles du Sud.* 4 (1986), pp. 85–86

Dambudzo Marechera's death left a gap in Zimbabwean society: nobody else was as outspoken. People soon realized that life would now definitely be a lot more boring.

> Dambudzo Marechera is dead. . . . With his death, Zimbabwe has lost one of its most prolific and ingenious writers, an international wizard of the written word.
>
> Hate him or love him, hate his lifestyle or his ideas even, but he was a fact of life that couldn't be ignored. His books are now part of the country's literary treasure.
>
> Literature has lost a star. And the Zimbabwe International Book Fair will never be the same without a Dambudzo Marechera. Fearless, outspoken and blunt, he never minced his words and epitomised the independent figure that every writer strives to be. He was free and he practised that freedom. He may have done things that were not ''morally acceptable'' to convention, but he cared little that people looked askance at him; he was there and he made things different.

Ray Mawerera, ''In Memory of Dambudzo Marechera,'' *Parade* (Harare). October 1987, p. 6

Dambudzo Marechera is an outsider. He cannot be included in any of the categories into which modern African literature is currently divided: his writings have nothing in common with the various forms of anticolonial or antineocolonial protest literature, nor can they be interpreted as being an expression of the identity-crisis suffered by an African exiled in Europe.

Marechera refuses to identify himself with any particular race, culture, or nation; he is an extreme individualist, an anarchistic thinker. He rejects social and state regimentation—be it in colonial Rhodesia, in England, or in independent Zimbabwe; the freedom of the individual is of the utmost importance. In this he is uncompromising, and this is how he tries to live. . . .

In *Black Sunlight* Marechera fuses the diverse forms of self-expression and lifestyle of London's ''alternative'' scene: when he wrote the book, in 1979, he was living in a huge commune of artists, drug addicts, meditators, and individualists of all kinds. In a process of philosophical and poetic self-discovery, the book explores the relationship between Marechera's concept of the total freedom of the spirit as it can be manifested in art, and the political action which aims at gaining this freedom—anarchism. Marechera discusses in many different ways questions of reality, of man's capacity to perceive reality, of illusion and delusion, and of the task of the artist in relation to all these. . . .

At the same time, *Black Sunlight* is a poeticized confrontation with the theories of the futurists . . . and the surrealists, whom it quotes and itself tries to emulate in their *écriture automatique*. Like them, Marechera seeks the liberation of language from the fetters of syntax, a free ''stream-of-consciousness'' similar to that of James Joyce. In *Black Sunlight*, different planes of consciousness, recognizable stories and dreamlike visions, memories, and reflections continually blend, flowing into images which are no longer recognizable to the intellect, but which the reader must feel and imagine.

This novel also presents Marechera's dichotomous view of women. On the one hand, the various female characters—from the anthropologist rescuer to the individual woman terrorists—are depicted as being very positive, self-assured, independent, having a positive attitude toward life, and are strong, stronger even than the men. Blind Marie, the photographer's wife, as the symbol of sensibility, is wild and unspoiled, rooted in her own ''black sunlight.''. . .

*Mindblast [; or the Definitive Buddy]* is a miscellany of three plays, a prose narrative, a collection of poems, and a park-bench diary. In a more accessible style than in his first two books, Marechera describes with wit, intelligence, and vivid imagery his view of the newly independent state of Zimbabwe: the materialism, the political intolerance, the stupidity and corruption, the socialist slogans, how a few become rich while the masses become poorer. At the same time, the author's own existence as an artist preys on his mind, full of hate, self-pitying, or ironic; he is out of place, made to feel an outsider, misunderstood, despised, taken for a madman. . . .

For Zimbabwe, with its lack of public criticism, *Mindblast* represents an important contribution. However, overall, the book suffers from a viewpoint which is too abstruse for the ordinary reader to identify with: the egocentric existence of the poet acted out in the bar and saloon. The most powerful literary statement is to be found in the poems. Unfortunately, Marechera's poems—apart from those in *Mindblast*—have never been published in a single collection, only sporadically in anthologies and journals. Strongly influenced by T. S. Eliot, they illustrate in a concentrated form the extraordinary creative power of Marechera's writing. With a highly unusual choice of words and their contextual associations, through the juxtaposition of opposites to the point of paradox, through the combination of the contradictory, he creates unexpected, inspired, shocking images of great intensity.

Flora Veit-Wild. *Zambezia.* 14, 2 (1987), pp. 113, 117–19

*The House of Hunger* is . . . a depiction of not only social deviances but also spiritual and physical exhaustion of the individual in a callous society. Marechera sees even sex as an instrument of domination and also as a function of white domination. *The House of Hunger* which serves as a metaphor for these stories epitomizes the prison nature of township life. There is so much hatred, violence, and horror that one wonders at the impossibility of sane minds retaining their sanity. The characters stumble from one absurdity to another, from one hopeless situation to another and most times they disintegrate in a blaze of horrifying activities.

Frustration is also another aspect of Dambudzo Marechera's writings that is significant. The characters who are nonconformists are seen by a majority of the people as eccentric iconoclasts. In the short story entitled ''The Writer's Grain,'' he tells the story of a writer whose works are found wanting and whose personal life is about breaking up. This frustration makes the writer become almost mad with bitterness. Furthermore, in *Black Sunlight* . . . the author uses a principal character known as Christian, a press photographer who moves through the society to depict the frustrations of the people. It is through the personal frustration of Christian that Marechera records glimpses of the prevalent chaos and social disorder. The novel is also suffused with incidents of sex and violence. The result of this aimless destruction reflects the general aimless direction of the people. Marechera writes: ''In our wake, smashed institutions, smashed minds. Smashed traffic signs. Smashed courtrooms. Smashed armories.''. . . The author presents these signs of destruction as imaginative photographs of a society doomed to violence.

The third novel, *Mindblast [; or the Definitive Buddy]*, which does not rise up to the standards set by *The House of Hunger*, is equally concerned with a society in disarray. Most of the characters are also replicas of the numerous deranged, embattled, bitter characters that people the stories of Dambudzo Marechera. However, it is in the use of language that the author succeeds in drawing the greatest attention to his work. The South African writer Mbulelo Mzamane feels that his narrative technique incorporates an interesting avant-garde experiment. In confirmation, Juliet Okonkwo presents the most interesting assessment of Marechera's style when she states: ''Marechera displays genius in the manipulation of words and ideas. He communicates mostly in images and makes language do new things through the application of words and expressions to actions and thoughts which are normally strangers to each other. His usual comparisons come from the habit of seeing the relatedness of many things.'' It is this ability that makes his loss to the literary world very painful.

Ezenwa-Ohaeto. *ALA Bulletin*. 14, 1 (winter 1988), pp. 7–8

All of Marechera's narratives, including *The House of Hunger*, the novel *Black Sunlight*, and his text collection, *Mindblast; or the Definitive Buddy*, demand much from the reader. The main reasons are the writer's mixing of narrative modes or genres, and what I would like to call his technique of fragmentation. None of his prose, not even the very short ''The Slow Sound of His Feet'' . . . is either pure fiction or pure autobiography, but both. None of his stories are told in a realistic or nonrealistic manner throughout but move back and forth constantly between different modes. Finally, the author attacks the concept of linear time that we ascribe traditionally to narrated fiction. As a result, past, present, and future experience, reflection, and nightmarish dreams merge in Marechera's work and can hardly be distinguished. Such narrative strategy naturally questions the unity of the mind and the progress of time, two fundamental presuppositions of most postcolonial writing, whose intention it is to overcome the experience of dispossession and not to confirm its lasting continuity after independence. Marechera challenges these assumptions, and by breaking away from conventional ways of storytelling, he does not merely dabble in formal experimentation—as some of his critics maintain—but

radically questions the view held by many postcolonial writers that it is not only possible, but morally obligatory, to reinstate a sort of status quo that is considered to represent one's identity.

Marechera's persona, his first-person narrator in ''The Slow Sound of His Feet,'' is unable to restore a life that is both meaningful and worth living. His experience is one of loss and, toward the end, perhaps one of temporary escape. The young student tells us how he loses first his father, then his speech, and finally his mother. Even his sister, appearing in one of his nightmares, seems dead.

These events are presented so that we cannot be sure whether the student dreams them or actually experiences them. Though he repeatedly uses phrases like ''mother woke me up,'' ''I woke up,'' or ''when I woke up,'' or ''when I opened my eyes,'' the borderline between waking and sleeping-dreaming, between the outer and inner world, is crossed and recrossed so subtly that we feel the whole episode is one long moment of reminiscing in which memories, dreams, and momentary thoughts and feelings coalesce into a state of profound loss and alienation. . . .

Marechera paints a harrowing picture of individual suffering and of a totally isolated and alienated young man, a person who bears much resemblance to the author himself: his father, too, was killed in a car accident, the author suffered from a stutter, had lost his teeth, and had been brutally beaten up as a student. . . . [The] loss of speech and language symbolizes the destruction of man as a human and a social being; it is a loss that counts more than that of one's parents. . . . Marechera's student is reduced to someone who is merely able to record sense impressions: ''The hot flush of it shook us in each other's arms. Outside, the night was making a muffled gibberish upon the roof and the wind had tightened its hold upon the windows. We could hear, in the distance, the brass and strings of a distant military band.'' The loss of one's language stands for the destruction of the mind, and if the unity of the mind is destroyed, the world can neither be re-created nor can a vision of it be projected into the future. Marechera's narrative technique symbolizes his view of a world fallen apart and torn asunder.

Dieter Riemenschneider. *Research in African Literatures*. 20, 3 (fall 1989), pp. 405–7

The posthumously published volume *The Black Insider* . . . consists of the title text, three short stories, and two poems, preceded by editor Flora Veit-Wild's introduction, wherefrom we learn that a number of unpublished manuscripts—six novels, five plays, over a hundred poems, and several essays—were left behind by the late author. . . .

''The Black Insider,'' written in 1978, is ''an important and unique literary contribution to the question of what exile has meant for a whole generation of Zimbabweans,'' states the editor. The story is autobiographical. In the shadow of war a variegated group of people is encapsuled in a dilapidated old building, where they pass their days in squalor and poverty and utter degradation, alienated, color-aware, uprooted from their culture. . . . Throughout, Marechera shrewdly and thoughtfully depicts the poverty, disillusionment, failure, alienation, squalor, and, above all, loneliness of a black intellectual highly disappointed by society: ''I am the rape / marked on the map / the unpredictable savage / set down on the page / the obsequious laborer / who will never be emperor.'' He consciously plunges into intoxication, finding there a temporary relief: ''It had been hell, the whole week. Alone in his flat eating semolina and soya beans. Trying to write his weekly poem. Feeling suffocated by the stale gasfire air in the room. Trying to think out the pattern behind the deeds (or lack of them) in his own life.''

Nadezda Obradović. *World Literature Today.* 65, 3 (summer 1991), p. 538

Published posthumously, *Cemetery of Mind* easily brings to mind Christopher Okigbo's *Labyrinths* (1971) in many ways. With Dambudzo Marechera's death, African literature lost a young star whose meteoric appearance has left an illuminating trail. Though better known for his collection of short stories *The House of Hunger* (1978), Marechera in fact deserves far more praise as a poet. He is highly imagistic, fresh, shocking, and delightful despite the pervading angry and sad mood in his poems. His life and writing remind me of Cesar Vallejo and Osip Mandelstam in some ways.

Compiled by Flora Veit-Wild, who has done an excellent job of assembling the poems, *Cemetery of Mind* is divided into twelve sections—a quasi-epic form to reflect the struggles of the poet at home and abroad. The poetic voice grows more agonized, darker, grimmer, and more intensely passionate as the poet becomes increasingly defiant at finding neither Britain nor Zimbabwe hospitable. The growing morbidity is accentuated by hunger, homelessness, drink, sex, and disease. Marechera writes on political and social issues, but as he becomes more personal, love and death become major preoccupations before the ''darkling complexion of the horizon.''

The poet's words are finely honed, the lines elegantly crafted. It is most satisfying that the free spirit and wandering mind of the poet are disciplined in his craft. This tension is never lost on the careful reader. In Marechera, opposites meet, not just the black-white love relationship but also in flowers and metal, beauty and ugliness. It is the conflict within, reinforced by these images of opposites, that gives enduring strength to *Cemetery of Mind*. Marechera has very strong opening and concluding lines, which not only make the poems memorable but impress the experiences themselves indelibly on the reader. For instance, he closes ''Landscape Gardening'' with the line ''They win whose silence is a grenade blast.''

The initial section, ''Liberty,'' is very Okigboesque, especially in ''Fragments,'' in the use of symbolism, characters, and foreign references (e.g., to Michelangelo, Ezra Pound, and the Bible). The ''Emptied Hearts'' section, written in London in 1979–80, uses rhyme and uninhibited language to express the poet's experience. The third and fourth sections, ''Throne of Bayonets'' and ''Buddy's Selected Poems,'' again exhibit a variety of experienced techniques: the poet uses catalogue and juxtaposition for sarcastic effects in the former and talks of social and political contradictions in Zimbabwe in the latter. In ''Oracle of the Povo'' he reflects both on the corruption he finds all around and on the irony of those who fought for Zimbabwean independence going unrewarded. He then pays tribute to the liberation fighters who died.

From ''The Kamikaze Pilot Returns'' through ''A Writer's Diary in Harare'' onward, the poet becomes more shocking, personal, and morbid, as he foresees his imminent death. There is much about love and death, which are related in his personal experience. In ''The Declaration'' he reveals that he has contracted AIDS: ''And with loathsome cry I resort to the memory of one long ago / I loved—and condemned me to this slow, long lingering

disease.'' He tries the sonnet form in the Amelia poems, some of the most moving and best-crafted in the collection. . . .

To read *Cemetery of Mind* is to be cast under a spell, to be transported from the physical into the realm of the soul. Marechera's unconventional life immensely enriched his poetry. By the time one has read the poems, one can only exhale and wonder about the poetic genius of such a young man. The consolation is that the poetic charmer will live forever in our minds.

Tanure Ojaide. *World Literature Today.* 68, 2 (spring 1994), p. 417

Toward the end of Dambudzo Marechera's *House of Hunger* an old man wanders into the narrative, where, surrounded by flies, he sits telling ''stories that were oblique, rambling, and fragmentary.'' The story he narrates comprises a jumble of dislocated ''folktale'' images of chameleons, dwarves, and fantastic happenings—in short, an already-disillusioned 1970s anticipation of 1980s ''magical realism.''

With his characteristic chutzpah, Marechera uses the episode to upend a series of deeply ingrained stereotypes regarding oral literature. Unlike the archetypal African oral storyteller who normally inaugurates a novel, this one concludes it. The interlude also provides subversive rereadings of oral narrative, a form often assumed to be traditional in theme, premodern in literary style, and order-affirming in its ethical orientation. The type of narrative we see here is in fact postmodern, grotesque, and subversive. In terms of style, it is decentred, open-ended, and has no narrative closure. As regards ethics and theme, it subverts all forms of authority. Marechera also slices through the stereotype of oral literature as discrete from literacy and other media, existing in some mythical ''traditional'' sphere removed from international space and literate time. The storyteller is, after all, perfectly capable of subverting literacy to oral ends: he shreds a newspaper for rolling cigarettes. He also refers in passing to the novel as a minor and dangerous genre: ''A writer drew a circle in the sand and stepping into it said 'This is my novel,' but the circle, leaping, cut him clean through.''

Marechera raises provocative questions regarding oral literature and globalisation, a pair of issues which are seldom put alongside each other, since oral literature is generally confined to the airless space of local tradition. Yet Marechera is a writer who consistently asks us to stitch together those things that we normally keep apart, and in this instance he takes the most perversely original instance to instantiate the problem. In effect, the concluding section of the novel asks us to consider what the globalisation of Shona oral forms might look like. We are all familiar with the globalisation of written metropolitan forms. A bold reversal of this pattern does much to throw light on the hidden imperial assumptions of much globalisation theory, which can tell us about the impact of metropolitan forms on ''peripheral'' areas but little about the reverse.

In the final paragraph of the story, Marechera, through the vagrant storyteller, pulls off another inversion, a fablesque trick through which the biter ends up being bitten. The biter is Harry, a township character and police informant. The old storyteller encounters Harry and directs him to a brothel used by Rhodesian soldiers, who beat him to a pulp. The old man discovers a packet of photographs that Harry has dropped. These are all of the protagonist and his friends and include notes clearly intended for the police. The old man returns the packet to the Marechera-type protagonist. Since much of the book has comprised annotated "portraits" of the protagonist and his friends, the storyteller in effect gives back the story, but in another medium, and so asks us to reimagine all that we have read. Marechera simultaneously raises questions about his novel—and indeed all other novels—as a form of surveillance. What this final paragraph does is to cross-hatch a range of media and genres: "oral" fable, written novel, and photograph. This interleaving in turn points to Marechera's subversion of simple binary oppositions of oral and written, text and picture.

> Isabel Hofmeyr. *World Literature Today*. 70, 1 (winter 1996), pp. 88–92

BIBLIOGRAPHY

*The House of Hunger*, 1978; *Black Sunlight*, 1980; *Mindblast; or the Definitive Buddy*, 1984; *The Black Insider*, 1990; *Cemetery of Mind*, 1992; *Scrapiron Blues*, 1994

# MARSHALL, Paule (1929–)
## Barbados

As a first-generation West Indian-American and the author of three novels and a collection of short stories, Paule Marshall gives evidence in her work of a marginal duality similar to that felt by immigrants. While not herself an immigrant, Marshall grew up in an immigrant community whose legacy to her and her work is a share of its alienation. Marshall's first novel, *Brown Girl, Brownstones*, may explain the source of that marginality. The basic conflict of this novel, between the protagonist's mother and father, overshadows the protagonist's coming of age and her search for identity. The mother has accepted the crass values of the upwardly mobile Barbadian immigrant community in which the family lives, while the father maintains a dreamer's futile pride in the cruel face of American racism and disappointment. Their daughter, Selina, vacillates between these two extremes, neither a Barbadian nor an American, but a permanent and unhappy outsider. The novel ends with her escape to Barbados, where, we presume, her alienation will continue—if not deepen.

In her second book, the collection entitled *Soul Clap Hands and Sing*, Marshall explores the alienated marginality seen in Selina through different characters. The four stories comprising the collection are set all over the Americas: in Barbados, Brooklyn, British Guiana, and Brazil. Each story focuses on an elderly, marginal man, and the point at which he realizes the extent of his alienation. Despite the implication of the volume's title, a line borrowed and modified slightly from [W. B.] Yeats's "Sailing to Byzantium" ("An aged man is but a paltry thing, / A tattered coat upon a stick, unless / Soul clap its hands and sing, and louder sing / For every tatter in its mortal dress"), the concern of the stories is not with the age of the men who are their protagonists, but with their souls. Each of the protagonists has lost, as he has gained partial admission into the dominant culture or the ruling class, his soul—his faith in God, in his fellows, and in himself. . . .

Each of these stories is a story of marginality, a story of the pain of the immigrant, the returned immigrant, the upwardly mobile individual who has forfeited his place in a society which is rapidly changing. Each is critical of, yet at the same time sympathetic to,

the plight of these old men for whom Soul has long since ceased to sing. Paule Marshall has not, as many of her readers seem to think, merely set up straw men like coats on sticks to be knocked down by the force of her political argument. There is no character in these stories who is without blame, who is completely human and responsible. This fact, and the fact that her sympathies are divided between the old men and the characters through whom they receive their visions, indicate that she understands and shares something of their marginality.

> Marilyn Nelson Waniek. *Callaloo*. 6, 2 (spring-summer 1983), pp. 46, 55

At first thought, *The Chosen Place, the Timeless People* seems the least typical of Paule Marshall's novels. Each of the other novels is focused upon the experience of single individuals; however far-reaching the implications, Marshall's vision in these works moves outward from the situation of a woman in a problematic family situation. *Brown Girl, Brownstones* and *Praisesong for the Widow* are fictions of the private life, while *The Chosen Place, the Timeless People* seems, in contrast, to be primarily a fiction of the public life. The novel's length, its range of psychological themes, the international and interracial cast of characters, and—most distinctively—its economic and political dimensions make it seem a very different kind of novel indeed.

But second thoughts, as they often do, complicate all these seemings. For one thing, there is a social, even a political, dimension to both *Brown Girl, Brownstones* and *Praisesong for the Widow*. In each of these novels, a woman explores her connection to the world—the *umbilicus* is the family, that most personal of social institutions. Both Selina and Avey achieve a new relationship to their families that is more fulfilling to them as human beings in a larger social world. Further, it seems to me, all novels by significant writers share thematic concerns that are constants—concerns, if not obsessions—which along with other qualities of craft and vision lift an author's work above the level of the commercially viable. *The Chosen Place, the Timeless People* does not lie outside the continuing concerns of Paule Marshall. Quite to the contrary, this second novel develops very similar concerns to those which are more readily seen in the earlier and later novels.

The vehicle of the author's most charged concerns in each of these works is the female protagonist. The size and complexity of *The Chosen Place, the Timeless People* has obscured, for many readers, the similarities between Selina Boyce in *Brown Girl, Brownstones*, Merle Kinbona in this novel, and Avey Johnson in *Praisesong for the Widow*. These three protagonists comprise, in fact, a history of human psychological development. Marshall's gallery of portraits carries our attention from childhood to old age. Selina Boyce is the image of woman experiencing the "identity crisis" of youth; Avey Johnson is the figure of the mature woman dealing with the "crisis of integrity" which accompanies the final stages of development. In these same Eriksonian terms, Merle Kinbona, the vexed and difficult protagonist of *The Chosen Place, the Timeless People*, is an image of the crisis of the middle years, the "crisis of generativity." Paule Marshall's longest and most complicated work of fiction has at its center a figure of human consciousness coming to grips with the need to be a cause, the need to make things happen, but in a world where such efforts are all but impossible to achieve. Like the portrait of Selina which began the set, and the portrait of Avey which seems to complete it, Marshall's portrait of Merle is both richly psychological and richly social. But in *The Chosen Place, the Timeless People* the relationships between the psychological and social dimensions of the character are developed within a denser context of ideas, actions and ideologies which are particular to the middle years of persons—and societies.

Joseph T. Skerrett Jr. *Callaloo*. 6, 2 (spring-summer 1983), pp. 68–69

In two of her three novels to date, Paule Marshall undertakes an in-depth study of the West Indian society at home (in *The Chosen Place, the Timeless People*) and abroad (in *Brown Girl, Brownstones*). Being the daughter of West Indians and having spent a part of her adult life in the West Indies, Marshall is undoubtedly better acquainted with the nature of West Indian life than any other Afro-American novelist. This more than superficial acquaintance serves her in good stead as a novelist, for it is the basis of her ability to create credible West Indian characters and to affect a peculiarly West Indian atmosphere, as that atmosphere is created by West Indians in Harlem and as it shapes island life in the West Indies. . . . [For] the first time, we have an Afro-American author who demonstrates, without caricature, how racial complacency affects the West Indian lifestyle. It is because of her grasp of the West Indians' sense of community and racial complacency that Marshall is able to exploit a wide range of West Indian sensibilities, especially in *Brown Girl, Brownstones*. She is not apt to be swept away by idealism . . . when she follows a character along the road to racial identity and cultural relevance. Nor is she apt to distort by easy symbolism . . . the subtle but trenchant tensions which attend the stable but struggling personality or the personality in the state of metamorphosis. To discuss the characters and themes of her novels is to reveal the essential ''West-Indianness'' of the author.

*Brown Girl, Brownstones* traces the development of Selina Boyce, daughter of a Barbadian couple living in Brooklyn. Through Selina's observation and participation in the lives of the West Indians who board at her parents' Brownstone home, Marshall is able to synthesize her interest in individual characters with her interest in the dynamics of this Barbadian community. As Selina matures, so does her and the reader's understanding of the individual and domestic forces which shape her life and the lives of her parents. . . . Selina is caught in the middle of a temperamental and ideological clash between her mother (Silla) and her father (Deighton). She gradually understands that a life of hard work and unfulfilled dreams has transformed Silla into a self-centered, scheming, possessive, and vindictive woman whose tenderness is buried somewhere under the debris of her Barbadian past. . . .

In the characterizations of Silla and Deighton, Marshall demonstrates a battle of wills that is universal in its implication. In terms of sheer survival Silla wins, but only because she replaces love of self and love of family with love of the values of white middle-class society. Deighton loses because he has to fight in an environment where his personal armor (love, tenderness, and casualness) is turned against him in a world where aggressive and materialistic competition is glorified. But Silla and Deighton are both losers in the sense that the essential humanity of each is eventually destroyed.

Melvin B. Rahming. *The Evolution of the West Indian's Image in the Afro-American Novel* (Millwood, New York: Associated Faculty Press, 1986), pp. 110–12

[In *Praisesong for the Widow*], Marshall continues to explore the dynamics of the West Indian cultural landscape, and its African heritage. The very title of the novel attempts to celebrate cultural transition and African continuity.

In traditional Africa, the praise-song is a chant or poem-song which dramatizes the achievements of an individual or community within the realm of history and extended family. Performed by the griot or griotte, the oral historian, genealogist, and musician, the praise-song is a highly developed ''genre'' in African oral literature. It is both a sacred and profane modality. In Marshall's invocation of praise-singing we see how the sacred overlaps with the profane reality. Avey Johnson's praise-song fulfills a vital function: it allows her to create a new opportunity for spiritual empowerment as she learns a new understanding of social propriety. . . .

A summary of *Praisesong* shows that Avey Avatara Johnson is a comfortably middle-class, self-conscious, elderly widow, who during a Caribbean cruise with two friends abruptly decides to leave the ship. When the ship docks for a few hours on the Caribbean island of Grenada, she disembarks and plans to fly back to her home, New York City. Significantly, her trip has been jolted by dreams of her long dead Great-Aunt Cuney of Tatem, South Carolina. Destiny intervenes, and she misses the plane to New York only to get involved in the annual festival of the ''out-island'' people—people of the smaller island, Carriacou—who live and work in Grenada. The excursion back to their native land (Carriacou and by way of myth/ritual, Africa) is in fact their annual rite of rejuvenation, their rite of the eternal return, their transhuman communication with the African past and its sacred forces. The Big Drum ceremony is the enactment of their African past, their native land. The dance creates temporal space between reality and the spirit world. By going to Carriacou and experiencing the intensity of neo-African ritual dancing and music, Avey Johnson rediscovers her own sense of place as an American of African ancestry. She rediscovers what it means to bond with people and with the spirit, and not with *things*. As she leaves Carriacou, she resolves to renew her ties with her own ancestral and spiritual home, Tatem, South Carolina.

Avey Johnson's classical journey occurs on two levels: she is, in essence, the heroine embarking on a quest for spiritual enlightenment and renewed strength to deal with the human world. The journey becomes a validation of Avey's American social consciousness. By the middle age of life, Avey has settled for the illusion of El Dorado; that is to say, she has given in to the complacency of upper-middle-class living and values. However, the spiritual void in her life began even before the death of her husband. By dividing the novel into four sections, with the ritual-implied titles of ''Runagate,'' ''Sleeper's Wake,'' ''Lavé Tete,'' and ''The Beg Pardon,'' Marshall demonstrates how the journey motif is inherent to Avey's spiritual and social awakening. Through transhuman communication, Avey reestablishes order out of her own chaos.

Angelita Reyes. In Adam J. Sorkin, ed. *Politics and the Muse: Studies in the Politics of Recent American Literature* (Bowling Green, Ohio: Bowling Green State University Popular Press, 1989), pp. 185–87

Paule Marshall's project in this deceptively simple novel [*Praisesong for the Widow*] is a bold one. This novel becomes a journey not only for Avey, but for her readers, for to appreciate the widow's experience's fully, the reader must journey with her in the same active process of recognizing and reassembling cultural signs. . . .

Marshall's concern is to take us through a journey of self-recognition and healing. Her text requires of us that we have a knowledge of ''diaspora literacy,'' an ability to read a variety of cultural signs of the lives of Africa's children at home and in the New World. Marshall articulates the scattering of the African peoples as a trauma—a trauma that is constantly repeated anew in the lives of her lost children. The life of the modern world and the conditions under which Afro-Americans have to live, the sacrifices they must make to succeed on the terms of American society, invariably mean a severing from their cultural roots. As Avey learns to her cost, this is tantamount to a repetition, in her private life, of that original historical separation. This is a sacrifice too high. To understand the nature of the journey and the magnitude of the sacrifice, it is necessary not simply to mark the passage of Avey's journey, but to become fellow travelers with her. It is not only Marshall's heroine, but Marshall's readers as well, who need to acquire ''diaspora literacy.'' For to do so is to be able to see again the fragments that make up the whole, not as isolated individual and even redundant fragments, but as part of a creative and sustaining whole.

Thus the first task for the reader is to learn, like the widow whose journey we experience, to recognize the cultural signs of a past left littered along our roads of doubtful progress. The crucial factor about *Praisesong* is that it is a novel about the dispossession of the scattered African peoples from their past and their original homeland and, in the present, from their communities and each other. The boldness of Marshall's project here is to take us through a private history of material acquisition and cultural dispossession, which becomes a metaphor for the history of the group, the history of the African in the New World. The challenge therefore is not to look at literacy or cultural artifact as abstraction, but as a concrete aspect of our lives, where our meaning—our story—becomes what we can read and what we can no longer, or never could, read about ourselves and our lives. The act of reading becomes an exercise in identifications—to recognize life experiences and historic transformations that point the way toward a celebration, a coming together attainable only through an understanding and acceptance of the demands of the past. . . .

*Praisesong for the Widow* is a tribute in praise of the homecoming of a woman who succeeds in making an awesome physical and spiritual odyssey. Avey's epiphany is presented to us as an arduous progress through a partially familiar landscape littered with cultural artifacts as clues. The widow's narrative becomes a map, with music, song, dance, dress, and ritual as the cultural registers we need to decode to follow her across the terrain to journey's end. But journey's end is Africa. By the end of her journey, Avey has symbolically reversed the diasporic journey and that wrenching Middle Passage. Through Avey's life, Africa is once more reinvented with worth, the continent is no longer fractured from human history but restored to consciousness with valid meaning. Through the healing of one of Africa's lost daughters, a scattered people are made whole again, and the question ''What is your nation?'' is no longer a bewildering and devastating mystery.

Abena P.A. Busia. In Cheryl A. Wall, ed. *Changing Our Own Words* (New Brunswick: Rutgers University Press, 1989), pp. 196–99

Marshall is one of the few Afro-American women writers who focuses on the relationship between black people in the United States and the West Indies in her literary work. . . . In *Brown Girl, Brownstones*, Marshall portrays a girl growing up within the West Indian community in New York. Her second novel is set on an imaginary island in the Caribbean. In *Praisesong for the Widow*, Marshall describes a journey through the West Indies.

Important themes in Marshall's work are the relationship between the individual and the community, relations between women and men, ritual, dance and the influence of the past on the present, often symbolized by older characters such as Miss Thompson in *Brown Girl, Brownstones*, Leesy Walkes in *The Chosen Place, the Timeless People*, and both Great-Aunt Cuney and Lebert Joseph in *Praisesong for the Widow*. . . .

Analyzing the objects in *Praisesong for the Widow*, one can trace one of the most important lines of the story as follows: as a child, Avey hears the story of the landing of the slaves, the Igbos, in Tatem, from her great-aunt Cuney who had learned it from her grandmother. By narrating this story again and again, great-aunt Cuney entrusts Avey with the mission to keep the memory of the past alive. . . . We can explain in Greimasian terms that Avey is the subject, Great-Aunt Cuney the destinator, and the object is to carry out a mission. Although the precise meaning of this mission still escapes her, little Avey feels that she has been given a task. . . .

In the course of the story, the subject Avey neglects this particular object—the mission—and tries to acquire other objects, like social ascension and material wealth. The destinator here is society, not a personified sender. The norms and values in this society are determined by white people. . . .

In their struggle for social ascension, Avey and Jay have to accept the norms and values of the dominant group in society. They neglect their own cultural heritage. They become successful members of the black middle class, but underneath the surface, Avey always has the feeling that they have given up some essential part of themselves. At the end of the story, the subject reaches the initial object, that is, fulfillment of the mission. Avey sets out to make the history of the African in the United States known.

Lucia Nankoe and Essa Reijmers. In Geoffrey V. Davis and Hena Maes-Jelinek, eds. *Crisis and Creativity in the New Literatures in English* (Amsterdam: Rodopi, 1990), pp. 492–94

Paule Marshall's three novels—*Brown Girl, Brownstones*; *The Chosen Place, the Timeless People*; and *Praisesong for the Widow*—successively illustrate stages of the historically grounded female quest . . . the decision to investigate the historical past, difficulties in assimilating it, and a purposeful incorporation of historical past into the present self. . . . Selina is exasperated by her family's expectations of her, including both her probable occupation and her relationship with the tribe. Initially rejecting the heritage embodied in her mother . . . [she] eventually brings both her mother's and another older woman's knowledge to the task to of self-construction. . . . Selina, at the end of *Brown Girl, Brownstones*, embarks for the Caribbean islands of her progenitors. In *Chosen Place*, Merle Kinbona . . . [experiences] pain and confusion at the overwhelming historical oppression that has constructed the present. Lacking [the] ability to escape to another context, she is forced to find the materials for reinterpretation of self and history in her immediate surroundings. Like *Brown Girl*, this novel ends with the beginning of a journey. Merle's departure for Africa, unlike her earlier voyage to England, takes her to a site that may invigorate while it discloses its mixed histories; it incorporates the origins of free black cultures, the historical past of slavers, the personal past of an unforgiving husband, and the future in the form of Merle's daughter. . . . [The] form of Merle's life has not yet coalesced, but reinterpretation of history . . . can construct a fuller version of the self. Completing the cycle, *Praisesong* links the acceptance of tribal history to the full experience of one's personal history. When Avatara almost simultaneously rediscovers both, she emerges as an avatar of her ancestral women griots. . . . Avatara knows both form and content of her historical message for the present. Unlike the earlier novels, *Praisesong* ends with the female quester's return home.

In her depictions of female quests, Marshall follows [Zora Neale] Hurston in making storytelling central. Listening to stories motivates some questers. Telling stories helps to heal others. Above all, the sense of community involved in the participatory interchange of teller and audience strengthens the questers' identities. In *Brown Girl*, with its adolescent quester, older characters generally tell stories to younger ones. In *Chosen Place*, the middle-aged exchange stories. Selina must absorb the narratives of her parents and their generation, and Merle must draw out and contribute to the flow of personal stories in her mostly middle-aged circle. Merle's search for her daughter, however, implies subsequent participation in the intergenerational pattern: questers do not choose one pattern or the other, but participate in each at different stages in their lives or in different roles during the same stage. *Praisesong* exalts the intergenerational narrative by making it Avatara's vocation. Both her process in claiming it and her conception of storytelling purposes, however, diverge from those of Marshall's earlier novels and from a large portion of other African-American fiction. All three of Marshall's novels emphasize the integral relationship of storytelling and the female quest. Collaboratively constructing stories, both tribal and individual, furthers the development of both community and individual. The quester must find an empowering, participatory audience to help her articulate her own destiny within its larger destiny.

Missy Dehn Kubitschek. *Claiming the Heritage: African-American Women Novelists and History* (Jackson: University Press of Mississippi, 1991), pp. 69–72

Paule Marshall's new novel, *Daughters*, is the story of Ursa Mackenzie, a woman born in the West Indies, educated at an Ivy League college in the 1960s, and active in the Civil Rights Movement until joining the white corporate world as vice president of the National Consumer Research Corporation. She has a boyfriend she doesn't like and a best friend who feeds and scolds her. She calls herself young, restless, and upwardly mobile. . . .

While *Daughters* is primarily Ursa's story, it's also the history of a group of other women who are in direct or remote ways connected to her. Attempting to trace how, exactly, Ursa came to be in such a dazed, silent state, Marshall explores the lives of the women who surround her: her father's mistress, Astral Forde; and Celestine, her father's maid. She also moves far back in history, to a time before Ursa was born, reviving the voices of her real and spiritual grandmothers. Like Ursa, some of these women have made one compromise too many; they have seen too much personal

and political disappointment. In many ways, *Daughters* is a feminist novel, not so much about empowerment as about inertia, exhaustion, and the struggle to recover will. . . .

*Daughters* is structured as a series of uncanny parallels between New York and the West Indies, between past and present women. We're asked to see Ursa as an incarnation of Astral Forde, whom we also see going in for an abortion, or of Congo Jane, an ancient revolutionary who also "loved pretty things." After a while this method seems simplistic; the plot grows heavy with forced echoes. By making her women mirror one another, Marshall seems to hope they will be seen as descendants of one vast, overarching spirit-of-women, an unbroken daughter-chain.

Emily White. *Voice Literary Supplement*. November 1991, pp. 6–7

For Paule Marshall, the transformation of the instruments of Western culture under the power and influence of the folk is a primary condition for the production of black culture in the New World. In her principal works, the folk return not only to disturb the dominant version of history and culture, but also to promote an Afro-American modernism that, by sustaining the tension between the persistent ancestral voice in black cultures and imposed European forms, seeks to affirm an indigenous language of history and self in the space of the other while unraveling the ideological and political necessity that justifies a Caribbean narrative. . . .

Moreover, the question of how to represent and understand colonial modernism and its narrative of history is of the utmost importance to Marshall; it provides the ideological and theoretical underpinning for most of her major works. If her texts seem to keep on returning to the terms by which the colonized can articulate the past, it is because she believes that the present order of oppression and reification can only be reversed if its material conditions—and what she might consider to be the necessity of history—are fully comprehended. But Marshall's novels are unique in another sense: they probe the rules by which the black experience in the New World can be interpreted and represented. These novels struggle with the linguistic and psychological blockage that hampers the hermeneutical act, the rules of overdetermination that often make it impossible for the reader to gain access to those original meanings that have been repressed in the Middle Passage of the black experience. Marshall's major works thus strive to provide a metacommentary on the painful coexistence of European modernist institutions and the dynamic survivals of the African experience in the islands. In addition, Marshall's subjects often make narrative turns toward the Caribbean landscape in an attempt to capture what she aptly calls "thoughts and feelings about the Middle Passage," and to elaborate "the psychological damage brought on by history."

Although Marshall perceives history in terms of its effects, rather than as what Fredric Jameson . . . calls "a reified force," her novels—like those of her contemporary, George Lamming—also strive to unmask the necessity of alienating history and even to provide a theoretical justification for an alternative episteme. Indeed, underlying Marshall's well-known concern for the nightmare of history and its alienating necessities is the desire for an ideal (and hence modern) version of the black experience which both transforms African culture and transcends the colonial tradition. . . . The roots of Caribbean modernism can actually be traced to the paradoxes and contradictions [Sylvia] Wynter recognizes in the Africans' attempt to adapt themselves to the Caribbean landscape while transforming its nature. . . .

In effect, folklore and popular culture played a central role in the transplanted Africans' quest for an indigenous language that could help them transcend reified history. According to Wynter, ''Folklore was the cultural guerrilla resistance against the market economy.'' This resistance constitutes a key subtext in Marshall's novels: it is represented by the stories told by Barbadian immigrants in *Brown Girl, Brownstones*, the indigenous Carnival sustained by the peasants of Bournehill in *The Chosen Place, the Timeless People*, and the national dances of Carriacou replayed by the displaced descendants of African slaves in *Praisesong for the Widow*. Whereas colonial history is represented as painful and alienating, a servant of the plantation system and the market economy, the voices of the subaltern affirm the history of the Africans, and the forms that history takes, as the ''absent cause'' that is shaping a Caribbean national culture.

> Simon Gikandi. *Writing in Limbo: Modernism and Caribbean Literature* (Ithaca: Cornell University Press, 1992), pp. 169–71

Without cohesive impulses shaping black women's writing in the fifties and sixties, comparative relationships between Marshall's fiction and that of her contemporaries are important for what they reveal about the vision that unifies Marshall's work. *Brown Girl [, Brownstones]* signals its discreteness in several ways—through depicting the assimilation efforts of immigrant Afro-Caribbeans and their tentative failures and successes with materialism in the American capitalist system; through balanced characterizations of black males and females; through the complex rendering of Silla Boyce as wife, mother, and materialist; and finally through its simultaneous attention to a girl's coming-of-age and her recognition of cultural displacement.

What sets Marshall's vision apart is her perception of the consequences of cultural displacement for people of African descent, consequences that may significantly exacerbate the oppressions of gender, race, and class. Other writers' imaginations in general embrace survival and chronicle defeat in a racist society. Marshall adds considerations of gender and class to what happens to her characters. Moreover, she contrasts physical and material survival in Eurocentric spaces with spiritual affirmation that can be acquired through cultural embrace and connection. She links problems such as identity, insecurity, and spiritual malaise to psychic fragmentation and moves toward acquiring wholeness through identification with African origins. Thus, a consistent strand in Marshall's fiction up to *Daughters* (1991)—*Brown Girl, Brownstones, Soul Clap Hands and Sing* (1961), *The Chosen Place, the Timeless People* (1969), *Praisesong for the Widow* (1983), *Reena and Other Stories* (1983)—is the exploration and systematic exposure of the fractured psyche of people of African descent.

Marshall's fiction offers a cogent conception of people of African descent. The unity of her writing distinguishes it from that of other writers. She writes with grace and perception and with recognition of the special history that has continued to exercise a vital role in the lives of African Americans. In re-creating experiences of the African diaspora population, Marshall's corpus constitutes an artful, original, and sustained presentation of the causes

and effects of a fractured psyche. As important, her fiction demonstrates how self healing may be generated within the black cultural matrix. . . .

*Fractured* means broken, splintered, or ruptured; in the traditional literary sense, *psyche* refers to the invisible soul that complements the physical body, a presence rooted in myth but validated through psychology. Thus, a fractured psyche affects identity and threatens psychic survival unless it is repaired. Joseph A. Baldwin's research emphasizes the necessity of understanding an ''African psyche . . . to explain the obvious aberration in it to account for the current self-destructive predicament of African American mental health'' (''African Self Consciousness,'' 179). He investigates the disparity between the American black psyche and its African component using the negative influence of Western reality and demonstrates the need for a racial-cultural consciousness with African origins. This position meshes with the ideas of Marshall's fiction.

Marshall's fiction derives its contours from the history of coerced Africans in the West. Her male characters endure the oppressiveness of race and class, while her female characters contend with the triple jeopardy of gender, race, and class. As characters face a tenuous future, they constantly live with the numbling knowledge of the past as a part of their present. For people of African ancestry, memory decrees that the lessons of history forecast an unstable future. History serves as a powerful record that justifies uncertainty, fear, and outrage, resonating with the trauma of the Middle Passage, of terrible displacement from the familiar, of powerlessness over family, of the violence and displacement of Reconstruction, and of subsequent governmental legitimization of discrimination. The intangible scars of these acts have become the legacy of subsequent generations of African-Americans in spite of the ideology of democratic equality. The conflicts of Marshall's characters—their search for an identity, for fulfilling relationships, and for spiritual wholeness—originate in the perpetuation of oppression. Without writing overt historical fiction frozen in the specificity of an epoch, Marshall has written fiction that is historical because it both recognizes and addresses the influence of the past upon the lives of the present.

> Joyce Owens Pettis. *Toward Wholeness in Paule Marshall's Fiction* (Charlottesville: University of Virginia Press), 1995

BIBLIOGRAPHY
*Brown Girl, Brownstones*, 1959; *Soul Clap Hands and Sing*, 1961; *The Chosen Place, the Timeless People*, 1969; *Praisesong for the Widow*, 1983; *Reena and Other Stories*, 1983; *Merle: A Novella and Other Stories*, 1985; *Daughters*, 1991

# MAXIMIN, Daniel (1947–)
## Guadeloupe

*L'Isolé Soleil* is primarily a history book in which Daniel Maximin retraces or reconstitutes, with great precision, the evolution of the West Indies, especially Guadeloupe, from the period of slavery till the current time. It begins with the statute of departmentalization in 1946 . . .

The precision of information on which Daniel Maximin relies, the depth of the painting he traces, and the multitude of the aspects he evokes make *L'Isolé Soleil* a veritable historical account and, in addition, confer on this book an obvious epic dimension. . . .

This reference to history is insistently accompanied by a questioning of the nature of history and its effect: in short, the significance that it is capable of assuming.

At the very heart of the text, a chasm opens up—like a sort of challenge—that constantly troubles the comprehension of the reader.

This effect is derived primarily from the manner in which Maximin inextricably links the particular destinies of some heroes—historic and novelistic—with that of an entire people. . . .

The chasm is due equally to the difficulty that we experience in grasping the truly significant events of Caribbean history. Events that involve the characters are relentlessly alternated with those of diverse cataclysms—volcanic eruptions, earthquakes, cyclones—which mark the narration, including the aerial catastrophes which seem to echo back to the gods, and in one of which Louis-Gabriel, the father of Marie-Gabriel, dies. . . . There is in this elaboration of human events and geological accidents, a certain expression of the revitalization of history and the efforts deployed by man in order to master it. Pessimism? Not necessarily. Rather, it is a fascination in the face of that which, seen from a certain spatio-temporal level, is based on both the tragic and the ridiculous.

To this is finally added a number of developments in which the author, through the dialogue lent to his protagonists, proceeds to evaluate this history, searching in particular to define its specific effects. On this level, one is aware of the manner in which Maximin does not limit his approach of the past to positive information habitually represented by objective facts, events, chronology, and biography of the actors involved. He shows that history exists beyond the familiar terrain of historians. It also exists at another level, in the conscience—and more still without doubt, in the unconscious—of the West Indians of today. He underlines its symbolic dimension. . . .

The men and women that Maximin places on the scene are torn between two contradictory demands. On the one hand, they wish to bear witness to the violence that played in the theater of their country and to describe fully the rich culture of their people; on the other hand, they wish to affirm and live out their own individualities, even at times to extremes. They believe that nobody, under whatever pretext, however noble it might be, has the right to deprive them of this individuality.

How to be oneself? What to do so that life, thought, and action are not confined within a system of preestablished categories that are as frustrating as they are fascinating, especially those of race and sex? Such is the problem that each one of them finds himself confronting. . . .

The realization of such a project is evidently not without agony. In particular, it supposes that the dual image of father and mother ceases to occupy definitively, in the conscious and the unconscious of the subject, its former abusive place.

Oral and written literature are testimony to the fact that the heroism of the fathers and the fecundity of the mothers constituted an anchor which allowed the Caribbean people to conserve their integrity in the face of the formidable force of destruction that was slavery. . . .

In reading these texts, one must have noted a preoccupation that constantly animates the two young people: *life*. Life, which in order to develop, with all its concealed potential, has to escape definitively the stifling shade of parental authority and of the heroes of Caribbean history.

With regard to this plan, one is aware of the manner in which Maximin alternates, throughout his novel, two distinct images of birth which clearly contradict one another. On the one hand is the "Negro" birth, linked to the canonical theme of African fecundity. . . . On the other hand is the painful but exalting birth of the individual who attempts to give shape to his existence, outside of any preexisting category. . . .

The biological and institutional link, which is strongly coded on the cultural level, is thus substituted by a relation in which liberty occupies a crucial space. . . .

It is obviously in relation to this theme of birth and life that one must situate the totality of reflection of the different protagonists, throughout *L'Isolé Soleil*, on the power of art and literature.

In this respect, one cannot avoid being struck by another opposition, no less fundamental, that is articulated in the novel: literature and music. Both are dreaded and desired because of what one can call their power of life and their capacity to allow the birth of life.

Bernard Mouralis. *Presence Africaine*. 121, 22 (1982), pp. 418–20, 423–26†

*Lone Sun* is the first novel published by Daniel Maximin, a high school teacher and radio journalist born in Guadeloupe, who has lived most of his life in Paris. *L'Isolé Soleil*, the title of the French edition published by Le Seuil, is both typical of a first work of fiction—it is a novel about the writing of a novel—and an unusual achievement in the familiar genre of the *Kunstlerroman*. Its highly allusive style, and its delight in associative wordplay mixed with elusive autobiographical details, show the strong influence of modern poetry. The novel's vast scope aims at the recuperation of the lost history of an entire people, the black diaspora of the Caribbean. A complex narrative texture invites the reader to participate in an elusive puzzle composed of fragments of narratives, dreams, diaries, legends, folktales, and oral history. Its main characters, who are trying to become writers, often exchange pieces of work in progress, along with technical advice.

Read exclusively on an aesthetic level, it is as though the youthful exuberance and overflowing talent of the author did not know when to stop, to impose limits. The richness of the language presents a challenge to the uninitiated reader and, more importantly perhaps, to translators faced with puns in French, English—and sometimes a curious private mixture of Italo-Spanish—and the rhythmic and thematic influence of black music, in particular, Afro-American and Afro-Cuban jazz. Fragments of Antillean folktales, folk characters, and bits and pieces of Creole aphorisms and proverbs are woven into the plot. But the patient reader is amply rewarded, for Maximin has been careful to provide textual clues. Privately encoded images answer each other. Often, one character will take the trouble to explain them to [another]. For example, the twelve proverbs that punctuate the narrative are elucidated very early on in Jonathan's notebook and serve as a guiding thread. In a narrative governed by clusters of images that bind the present to the past, the surface playfulness is an introduction to more serious political considerations. . . .

When reading Maximin, it is often hard to determine where life ends and fiction begins. Often, his most serious and far-reaching passages start with a small detail from real life. For example, he has claimed that the novel's title comes from a memory of his adolescent years. Playing with words, he discovered that the French language could simultaneously pun upon the words for *lone* and *sun*, turning *soleil* into *isolé*, a fact he makes clear at the end of the passage by the same title, ''Lone Sun.''. . .

*Lone Sun* develops a dual plot line, presenting itself as a dialogue between history and literature; thus, it continues the inquiry started by C. L. R. James. But it is also a cautionary tale that situates Maximin fully within his own generation. Marie-Gabriel, whose father has just died, searches among the great men of the past for a hero to write about and finds one unmentioned in the history books, Louis Delgrès. Adrien warns Marie-Gabriel against the paralyzing effect of hero-worship, whether of her real father or her putative one, cautioning her against ''those who have left us nothing but their death as a stunning memory.''. . .

This multivoiced narrative strategy carries over into the linguistic registers in order further to decenter the exploded writing self. The full impact of the original depends a good deal on what I would call a systematic ''surprise effect''—grammatical as well as semantic—the better to remind its French readers that Creole, too, is a foreign language not entirely assimilable to French cultural codes. This makes translating Maximin a nearly impossible task, and demands of his editors a higher than usual amount of tolerance. *Lone Sun* refuses a unifying narrative voice because such a voice would in turn imply a unified, homogeneous audience.

> Clarisse Zimra. Introduction to Daniel Maximin. *Lone Sun* (Charlottesville: Caraf Books, 1989), pp. xi-xii, xxxiii, 1, lvii-lviii

In *L'Isolé Soleil*, Maximin tells us that the individual on his or her own path must look inside as deeply as possible to find his or her own voice if he or she wants real freedom: ''Brise ce premier miroir et écoute been le silence de ton double devant ta main qui saigne et ton regard aveugle'' [Break this first mirror and listen carefully to the silence of your double standing before your bleeding hand and blind gaze]. Valorizing the inner voice and creating the framework for journeys—journeys by both ''le même'' and ''l'autre'' [the one who is the same and the one who is similar]—are among [Simone] Schwarz-Bart and Maximin's most meaningful contributions. The inner journey is essential to a literature of liberation, because only through such an exploration can the individual, and the collectivity, become free. . . .

If Creoleness is to succeed, the ''acceptation de soi'' must characterize the group's attitude toward itself as well. *L'Isolé Soleil* exemplifies this vision more fully than [Joseph Zobel's] *La Rue cases-nègres* and [Schwarz-Bart's] *Pluie et vent sur Télumée Miracle*, because it affirms French Caribbean historical and literary figures, showing how extensive this heritage is. Maximin's second novel, *Soufrières*, affirms the group more completely, because it focuses on the group experience of enduring the eruption of Guadeloupe's volcano, La Soufrière. . . .

The relationship of *La Rue cases-nègres, Pluie et vent sur Télumée Miracle*, and *L'Isolé Soleil* to history, presents another shift in emphasis. José tells the story of his own life and his grandmother's *prise de conscience*, anchoring his text in realistic details. Schwarz-Bart depicts Télumée's quest for internal harmony, showing how she eventually exemplifies the wisdom of her community as she achieves individuation or self-understanding.

Clearly, Zobel, Schwarz-Bart, and Maximin all use real history to present the negative experience of colonial life. However, [Maximin] explores the resonance between the past and the present much more fully.

Maximin's protagonists journey to self-understanding and rebirth, but they engage as well in a quest to find the historical roots of the collectivity. The history of the collectivity is merged with Marie-Gabriel's personal story, because she recreates herself in telling [her mother] Siméa's story, and Siméa's story recreates part of the collectivity's story. Making a double point about truth, Maximin shows that although a full-blown history written by Caribbean people cannot exist because those who would write it died long ago, the truth of the people's resistance to oppression can be affirmed by reading between the lines of colonial history books. This revisioning of French Caribbean history, which reflects the polyvalent dimension of contemporary life, fulfills the impetus of Caribbeanness and Creoleness, because it repairs gaping holes and redefines part of the fabric of Caribbean reality.

> Ann Armstrong Scarboro. *Callaloo*. 15, 1 (winter 1992), pp. 15–16, 19–21

The project at the heart of Daniel Maximin's *L'Isolé Soleil* . . . is the rewriting of Antillean history—the reinscription of the other America seen through the tormented mind and soul of the educated savage, Caliban, inheritor of his master's tongue. . . .

Maximin's *L'Isolé Soleil*, like the narratives of his compatriots Maryse Condé and Edouard Glissant, takes as its subject the rewriting of a history of his home islands; it seeks to wrest from the occupier the history of Guadeloupe—from the reconquest of the islands by the French under General Richepanse in 1802, and the reimposition of slavery, to the present-day clashes between the French occupiers and the Antilleans, who persist in demanding independence. . . .

Siméa, the mother of Marie-Gabriel (the principal character/ narrator), makes annotations in the margins of the copies of *Tropiques* sent to her from Fort-de-France. In the April 1942 number, Suzanne Césaire has contributed an article entitled ''What Is a Martinican,'' followed by a nine-page extract from Léo Frobéniu's *History of African Civilization*. Siméa remonstrates with Suzanne Césaire for seeking their ''black essence'' in the writings of a white ethnologist, just as her comrades have called on white psychoanalysts, political thinkers, and poets to help to define them. ''Will we always need *them* and their *reasons*? What's the use of rejecting their reason only to adopt their science? It's up to us to invent a future, without expecting much from the African past and the European present.'' She adds that ''identification [of the Antillean with the European] is the enemy of identity,'' and that Suzanne Césaire should speak of all the Antilleans, not solely the Martinicans.

These very principles—the invention by the Antilleans of their own future and the cultivation of a sense of Antillean community— guide the project of Maximin's/Marie-Gabriel's narrative. The epigraph of that narrative speaks of the nightly eruption of cries of ''joy and misery, chants, poems of love and rebellion choked in the throats of men and women undressed of their anguish, writing to each other from island to island, a story in the shape of an archipelago traced by our four races, seven languages and dozens of bloods.'' The refrain of silenced cries reverberates throughout postcolonial literature—in the motives of muteness, of aphasia, of the unarticulated words of the Other's history/story that, "hidden in the depths of silence," under the words of the oppressor's history/story, seek to enunciate themselves. This other history, this other story, is the "intractable" (*intraitable*), as Jean-François Lyotard terms it, the repressed, the stifled, the unsaid, existing below the level of words. *L'Isolé Soleil* takes on the task of expressing the inexpressible.

The narrative proper opens with a narrator whose identity initially remains unrevealed, and who describes events on the birthday of the seventeen-year-old Marie-Gabriel. As she climbs a mango tree, she discovers in a cavity a ring engraved with the name "Angela," put there, we are told, two centuries earlier by Jonathan (later, we'll be told, a ring belonging to a young girl under the care of Marie-Gabriel's mother, Siméa, during World War II). Marie-Gabriel awaits her father who, returning after several years' absence in Paris, will die that same day as the plane explodes over Guadeloupe. . . .

A journal entitled "Désirades" that [Marie-Gabriel's] father was carrying with him on his return to the island, and which he intended to give to her, perishes with him in the explosion. Absent father, absent journal, absent cries—the life of the Guadeloupeans is marked by absence, like the Martinican crowd in Fort-de-France, described by Aimé Césaire as: "this noisy crowd, so astonishingly passing by its cry . . . passing by its cry of hunger, of poverty, of revolt, of hate, this crowd so strangely chattering and mute . . . this strange crowd that does not crowd. . . ." Such is the state of mutism inflicted upon the Antillean whose story has been appropriated by the Other, but it all the more describes women's voices muted in male history.

On the one hand, we find in *L'Isolé Soleil* a cluster of metaphors built around the notion of absence; on the other, a lexicon rife with metaphors of solarity, explosion, fire, detonation, and eruption. Over everything rises Soufrière, the active volcano that holds over the island the omnipresent threat of a fiery cataclysm. While Western novelists paint the Antilleans as children falling off to sleep, their heads filled with childhood memories and magical tales, while record jackets of calypso recordings sold in Parisian shops speak of "the gay, carefree temperament of the Caribbean islanders," Marie-Gabriel equates her people with "sleeping volcanoes" that need to be awakened. It is they who will explode.

John D. Erickson. *Callaloo*. 15, 1 (winter 1992), pp. 119–21, 128

The quest to understand the past in order to know oneself and one's culture is at the heart of both novels by the contemporary Guadeloupean novelist Daniel Maximin, *L'Isolé Soleil*, and *Soufrières* (*Sulphur Mines*, or in the singular, *La Soufrière*, the name of the volcano that dominates the island of Guadeloupe). In these two novels, he reserves a prominent place for references to literature as well as to other forms of art, such as painting and music, which often seem to be the key to developing that understanding. Beyond being simply gratuitous allusions to other works of art, these references constitute an essential part of the framework of the two novels. They also speak to the nature of the human experience and to the role of art forms in that experience. Specifically, the use of art forms in *L'Isolé Soleil* and *Soufrières* reflects the freedom of the human spirit and the desire to communicate the relationship of the past to the present, and to give tentative and renewable form to the life of individuals in the Caribbean. . . .

*Soufrières* is the story of five different days over the span of five months, leading up to the eruption of the volcano La Soufrière on the islands of Guadeloupe in 1976. However, the title, a plural noun, shows that the novel is more than simply the story of one specific volcano's eruption. It is also the record of the essential background of Caribbean life brought to the surface by the narrative, the story of the hopes and desires of various individuals, including Adrien and Marie-Gabriel from *L'Isolé Soleil*, each with his or her own personal "bubbling volcano," each needing to come to an understanding of the past before being free to face the future with confidence.

Though the subjects of the two novels seem at first glance different, they are in fact very complementary, and we can see the second as a continuation of the first in several ways. First of all, both have as their point of departure a specific and real historical event. Secondly, the major characters in *Soufrières* were already present in *L'Isolé Soleil* as those who reflected on the historical events of the preceding centuries. And thirdly, apparent in both novels is these characters' preoccupation with writing, with the interplay of literature and history, and with the goal of using that interplay to help them understand themselves and their place in the twentieth century. . . .

The infusion of hope helps one understand the past, and Maximin suggests that the hope which helps understand the past can also help modify the future. The three lines that end the novel are presented as a poem, and juxtaposed as they are with the old Creole round that the tape recorder sings sweetly to Elisa, who finally feels that she has found her place in the world ("nicely positioned between sky and earth"), they can be taken as representing an old Creole song, suggesting hope and healing just as the old traditional songs instilled identity and understanding: "When the thread of the days/follows the needle of hope, / it patches up destiny."

As Siméa expresses in her journal: "A page of poetry . . . will always be able to express . . . the essence hidden in a passing moment, an eternity of dreams, an instant of true life." Writing, along with other art forms, is able to capture eternity, linking meaningfully for individuals and for countries the events of the past, the experiences of the present, and the hopes of the future.

Understanding the contemporary culture of the Caribbean and developing an awareness of the Antillean identity depends on the interplay between history and writing about that history. Writing, the act of placing words on paper in the various forms we see in these two novels, encourages not only reflection, but also action. But most of all, writing by the characters in Maximin's novels is an affirmation of their self, of their community, and of their culture.

Lauren W. Yoder. In Helen Ryan-Ranson, ed. *Imagination, Emblems, and Expressions* (Bowling Green, Ohio: Bowling Green State University Press, 1993), pp. 109–11, 124–25

[In *L'Ile et une nuit* the third in a series of novels interrelated through their narrator/protagonist, Marie-Gabriel, the Guadeloupean novelist, poet and essayist Daniel Maximin seems eager to reiterate through literary expression Edouard Glissant's famous demand, "Nous réclamons le droit à l'opacilé" (*Discours antillais*). While Maximin's first novel, *L'Isolé Soleil* (1981), is complex and full of obscure allusions for readers inexperienced in Antillean history and literature, it works nonetheless to convey its double project consisting of a selective description of the long and painful history of colonization and slavery in Guadeloupe, as well as a contemporary tale of three youths and their search for self-identification in 1960s postcolonial Guadeloupe. His second novel, *Soufrières* (1987), recounts the struggle surrounding the eruption of the remaining active volcano on Basse-Terre, Guadeloupe, la Soufrière, and the continuing story of the principal characters of *L'Isolé Soleil*, Marie-Gabriel, Adrien and Antoine.

This third novel takes Maximin's literary experiment to the extreme, however, in presenting a hybrid work that claims to be a novel on the cover, yet reads like a prose poem. Devoid of dialogue and character development, this text describes the inner thoughts of one woman during her seven-hour struggle one night to survive a vengeful hurricane beating down on her family's generations-old residence, Les Flamboyants. Varying the narrative address in every chapter, each named for an hour of the night, Maximin crates a *mélange* of voices all emanating from Marie-Gabriel. The title, an obvious reference to the *Mille et une nuits* and Sheherazade's heroic storytelling act of survival, aids the reader somewhat in deciphering the narrative meandering of the text. A reading of Maximin's first two novels also seems obligatory for providing what little character development might be possible for the narrator of this tale, named on few occasions, Marie-Gabriel. Assuming this is the same character, and there are numerous distinct references to *L'Isolé Soleil* to confirm the assumption, the reader can piece together tidbits of a storyline that might explain some of the interior monologue that Marie-Gabriel voices to battle mentally and physically against the onslaught of winds and rain destroying her home in Guadeloupe.

As he does in his first two novels, Maximin sprinkles allusions of Antillean literary figures, American jazz musicians, and others into the text. Yet these allusions are so completely detached from a broader storyline in this work as to make them float in the text with little meaning. The work is frustrating in the sense that it offers minuscule moments of exciting poetic expression in an opaque text that seems self-indulgent and disjointed. That Marie-Gabriel uses words to survive against the ravages of the natural disaster of the hurricane is wholly consistent with Maximin's writing project as presented in his other novels. Yet this seems to be the extent of the message of this particular manifestation of Marie-Gabriel's character.

We are told in the end that this will be the last installment of the story of her life. It would have been much more satisfying to learn more of the details of her activities, relationships and dialogues, all of which might help to understand the numerous poetic gestures that Maximin uses to explore Guadeloupe's past and present and their relationship, both literary and historical, with the rest of the world. *L'Isolé Soleil* is an exciting work because it combines literary experimentation in the form of varying narrative expression, bilingualism (Creole is used significantly in the text), and intricate plot and character development. Its difficulty gives the work an aura of obscurity, and yet also entices the reader to unravel its secrets. Unfortunately, *L'Ile et une nuit* has taken the demand for obscurity to the extreme and works to exclude the reader from the hidden meanings of the text.

Cynthia Mesh-Ferguson. *French Review*. 70, 6 (May 1997), pp. 953–54

BIBLIOGRAPHY
*L'Isolé Soleil* (Lone Sun), 1981; *Soufrières* (Sulphur Mines), 1987; *L'Ile et une Nuit*, 1995

# MCKAY, Claude (1889–1948)

## Jamaica

Claude McKay, although still quite a young man, has already demonstrated his power, breadth and skill as a poet. Mr. McKay's breadth is as essential a part of his equipment as his power and skill. He demonstrates mastery of the three when as a Negro poet he pours out the bitterness and rebellion in his heart in those two sonnet-tragedies, "If We Must Die" and "To the White Fiends," in a manner that strikes terror; and when as a comic poet he creates the atmosphere and mood of poetic beauty in the absolute, as he does in "Spring in New Hampshire" and "The Harlem Dancer." Mr. McKay gives evidence that he has passed beyond the danger which threatens many of the new Negro poets—the danger of allowing the purely polemical phases of the race problem to choke their sense of artistry.

Mr. McKay's earliest work is unknown in this country. It consists of poems written and published in his native Jamaica. I was fortunate enough to run across this first volume. . . . However greater work McKay may do he can never do anything more touching and charming than these poems in the Jamaica dialect.

James Weldon Johnson. Preface to James Weldon Johnson, ed. *The Book of American Negro Poetry* (New York: Harcourt, Brace, 1922), pp. xliii-xliv

Claude McKay's [novel] *Home to Harlem* . . . for the most part nauseates me, and after the dirtier parts of its filth I feel distinctly like taking a bath. This does not mean that the book is wholly bad. McKay is too great a poet to make any complete failure in writing. There are bits of *Home to Harlem*, beautiful and fascinating: the continued changes upon the theme of the beauty of colored skins; the portrayal of the fascination of their new yearnings for each other which Negroes are developing. The chief character, Jake, has something appealing, and the glimpses of the Haitian, Ray, have all the materials of a great piece of fiction.

But it looks as though, despite this, McKay has set out to cater for that prurient demand on the part of white folk for a portrayal in Negroes of that utter licentiousness which conventional civilization holds white folk back from enjoying—if enjoyment it can be called. That which a certain decadent section of the white American world, centered particularly in New York, longs for with fierce and unrestrained passions, it wants to see written out in black and white, and saddled on black Harlem. This demand, as voiced by a number of New York publishers, McKay has certainly satisfied, and added much for good measure. He has used every art and emphasis to paint drunkenness, fighting, lascivious sexual promiscuity and utter absence of restraint in as bold and as bright colors as he can.

If this had been done in the course of a well-conceived plot or with any artistic unity, it might have been understood if not excused. But *Home to Harlem* is padded. Whole chapters here and there are inserted with no connection to the main plot, except that they are on the same dirty subject. As a picture of Harlem life or of Negro life anywhere, it is, of course, nonsense. Untrue, not so much as on account of its facts, but on account of its emphasis and glaring colors. I am sorry that the author of *Harlem Shadows* stooped to this. I sincerely hope that he will some day rise above it and give us in fiction the strong, well-knit as well as beautiful theme, that it seems to me he might do.

> W. E. B. Du Bois. *Crisis.* June 1928, p. 202

*Home to Harlem* is a book that has been a pleasure to the author to write. It is hard otherwise to explain the easy charm and assurance that glow upon every chapter. The author is coloured and describes a negro coming home to Harlem, the coloured quarter of New York, after the war. Once there, he has various adventures, and the book is a series of incidents strung together without much relation to each other. As a novel it is rather inadequate, as a study of coloured people it is fascinating and delightful, radiating enjoyment of life, and frank and promiscuous passion. One feels that the coloured people are a flabby crowd, but this moral reflection is entirely obscured by the simplicity of their relationships, the sweet distress of their hedonism and their equable view of life. So much art is created out of discontent with the world as it is, and is a minority report upon life, that it is a joy to come on all this frank glorification of existence in the rich dialect and naïve enthusiasm of this unpretentious story.

> Cyril Connolly. *New Statesman.* August 18, 1928, pp. 591–92

In *Gingertown*, a book of short stories published last year, the sketches of Mr. McKay's native island were, to one reader at least, the most richly rewarding of the volume. Now Mr. McKay returns to Jamaican subject matter in his third and most successful novel. A quiet story, quietly told, *Banana Bottom* really approaches originality more than his Harlem fiction did. Mr. McKay seems really at home in this province; it is hardly likely that any novelist would be more so. . . .

This plot exists more as a framework for the characterization of many interesting folk figures than in its own right. . . . All of these are ably sketched. Mr. McKay insists that all of them are imaginary, but they all have the ring of real life.

The picture of the folkways of the people is similarly convincing. Life on this island seems a quiet pastoral. Occasionally sensational incidents break the easy tenor of life in *Banana Bottom*—Tack Tally's suicide, the obeah-man, and the fall from grace of Herald Newton being examples—but, for the most part, things seem to flow easily. Mr. McKay describes, with what seems remarkable memory since, according to reports, he has been away from Jamaica a long time, the dances, revivals, the marketing, the small town gossip, the school affairs, the color complications, the folkways such as the hawking of ballads, the ordinary life of the villagers and farmers. The dialect sounds true; in places it is rich in humor and shrewd wisdom. The flowers, fruits, and garden produce of the rich bottom-land are described frequently and with a great deal of charm.

But against this idyllic background, Mr. McKay does impose one problem: how far should the "missionary" attitude toward Negroes be allowed to go.

> Sterling A. Brown. *Opportunity.* July 1933, pp. 217, 222

To turn from the poems of Claude McKay to the novels he has written is to be aware of something very close to a tragedy. For

years he had been writing exquisite or dynamic verse, and the favor of the public, judged at least by commercial standards, was but luke-warm. Now there was a change of tone and emphasis. It is impossible for him to write incompetently; on everything he puts the stamp of virility. After the success of [Carl] Van Vechten's *Nigger Heaven*, however, he and some other authors seemed to realize that it was not the poem or story of fine touch that the public desired, but metal of a baser hue; and he decided to give what was wanted. The result was a novel, *Home to Harlem*, that sold thousands of copies but that with its emphasis on certain degraded aspects of life hardly did justice to the gifts of the writer. . . .

*Gingertown* is a collection of twelve stories, six of which are set in Harlem and the others in the West Indies. The author shows that he is best when he is on his native hearth, but all of the stories are marked by robustness, though again and again the characters are wanton or gross. *Banana Bottom* goes back to Jamaica and in telling of the career of Bita Plant gives a fine satire on the ways of benevolent folk. An exceptional character is Squire Gensir, an Englishman interested in studying folk-ways but without any semblance of patronage. This book like the others has elements of strength, but one can not help thinking what Mr. McKay might do if he would take a little vacation from slums and water-fronts, see life somewhat more as a whole, and conceive the really great novel of which he is undoubtedly capable.

> Benjamin Brawley. *The Negro Genius* (New York: Dodd, Mead, 1937), pp. 244–46

*Harlem Shadows* [is McKay's] best known collection of poems. This book spoke the passionate language of a persecuted race, and its author did not make the least attempt to disguise his feelings. He did not attempt to please his white readers; his voice is a direct blast at them for their policy of discrimination. Many of the poems are saturated with protest. For example, in the octet of "Enslaved," McKay traces the ills and suffering of the race during its sojourn in various lands; then in the sestet he calls for the complete destruction of "the white man's world." One can easily find here the philosophy of a race expressed in the few lines of a poem. This is not the poetry of submission or acquiescence; this is not the voice of a gradualist; nor is this the naïve dialect of the jackass driver. It is one of scorching flame, a voice conscious of persecution, that dares to strike back with vehemence. . . .

In the title poem, "Harlem Shadows," one finds various shades of this protest, yet there is also some semblance of beautiful lyricism. There are some good interpretations of life in Harlem, the Negro section in upper Manhattan. The poem is mediocre, but reveals the author's bitterness toward the conditions which produce the Negro prostitutes of Harlem. I question the poet's choice of such as a title poem for his book. Certainly this is a sordid aspect of the race to thrust forward. In addition, it is not the best poem in the collection. The greatest justification that can be found for it is that it is realistic, and accurately describes a phase of existing life.

One must admit that the author's most powerful dudgeon lay in this protest poetry. Whether he wrote an epigram, a sonnet, or a longer poem, his thought is sustained. He expressed the deepest resentment, but even when doing so his feelings were lucid. He did not stumble as he attempted to express himself. This dynamic force within his poetry caused him to be constantly read and re-read by his admirers and critics. They realized that here was a man of deepest emotions, as well as one who was a skilled craftsman.

Robert A. Smith. *Phylon*. 9, 3 (1948), pp. 271–72

Every now and then someone said he had heard that Claude had once been married, but he seemed bitter whenever any discussion of love or courtship arose and there was nobody who dared to ask about his past. In self-defense I had to acquaint myself with Claude's likes and dislikes of people and things. High up on the list of his many peeves were: "yellow Negroes," "people who spout religiosity," and "the Reds." He could say "you Catholics" with so much contempt it was useless to do anything but utter a silent prayer for him. That all of these prayers were answered is part of a later story. . . .

[A] member of the Negro Writers' Guild who had known Claude in Jamaica told me how the young poet acquired his dislike for fair complexions. According to his friend, Claude had once been a policeman. His immediate superior, a stern, uncompromising, sometimes unreasonable taskmaster, was a mulatto. The indignities—real and imaginary—which Claude suffered at this man's hands left their mark. I can also imagine that Claude, dressed up in a policeman's uniform, was not an obedient subordinate.

Ellen Tarry. *The Third Door* (New York: David McKay, 1955), pp. 129, 131

McKay's position, so different from that of Countee Cullen and most other Harlem Renaissance writers, stemmed not only from his personality, but also from his various social situations. To whatever groups he allied himself, McKay remained always something of an outsider without deep and lasting commitments. Though he worked with the Negro lower classes in America and France, his interests and hopes extended beyond the next job, drink, or woman, for his writing provided a means of detachment from proletarian life. While on *The Liberator*, as the only Negro on the staff, McKay felt a special duty to represent the feelings of his race to his fellow staff members. Floyd Dell discoursed on art, and Michael Gold explored whatever socio-economic iniquities came to his attention, but McKay's *Liberator* work was almost wholly concerned with race. Furthermore, McKay felt apart from most Negro intellectuals because of his social radicalism and because of Negro intellectuals' criticisms of his own work. Finally McKay was a Jamaican. From personal experience he knew, as did returning Negro veterans, that American-style racial prejudice was not world-wide. Moreover, though most Negro veterans felt themselves to be Americans, McKay felt free both to praise and criticize America without a sense of identification with and commitment to America. . . .

Because McKay was not fully a member of any one group, and because of his radical education and outspoken personality, he set the outer limits of the Harlem Renaissance. No other important Negro writer in the 'twenties protested so fiercely and single-mindedly against prejudice as did McKay in his sonnets of 1919. And no other important Renaissance figure disregarded possible effects on the Negro public image so fearlessly as did McKay in his prose fiction. From his Jamaican days to his strange conversion to Catholicism, McKay forever spoke his mind, sometimes brilliantly, sometimes clumsily, but always forthrightly. In so doing he did

much to make the Harlem Renaissance more than a polite attempt to show whites that Negroes, too, could be cultured.

Stephen H. Bronz. *Roots of Negro Racial Consciousness* (New York: Libra, 1964), pp. 85–86, 89

*Home to Harlem* and *Banjo* had ended with the departures of exiles. *Banana Bottom* begins with the return of a native. The characters of the first two novels extracted a living on the edges of society, the characters of the third are rooted in a landscape. The violent debates of the earlier works, in which there is only a thin line between author and character, are now succeeded by the controlled idyllic tone of a distanced narrator. The central character is not a figure of *malaise* like Ray of the preceding novels, nor does McKay find it necessary to externalize *malaise* in the form of a complementary but separated pair such as Jake and Ray or Banjo and Ray.

The polarized pair of heroes of the first two novels are replaced by a single heroine. Bita Plant, the daughter of a Jamaican peasant, is brought up by the Reverend Malcolm Craig and his wife Priscilla. After seven years abroad at an English University and on the Continent, Bita returns to her native land. *Banana Bottom* tells the story of how she gradually strips away what is irrelevant in her English upbringing, and how she marries Jubban the strong silent drayman in her father's employ. To put it in this way is to make it clear at once that McKay's theme is still cultural dualism. The differences between *Banana Bottom* and the other novels are differences in art. Bita Plant is the first achieved West Indian heroine and *Banana Bottom* is the first classic of West Indian prose.

Kenneth Ramchand. *The West Indian Novel and Its Background* (New York: Barnes & Noble, 1970), p. 259

[Harlem Shadows] not only swung the debate between the Black Ancients and the Black Moderns decisively in favor of the Moderns; but even more so, it served as the forerunner for the three most important literary movements among Black Writers: the Harlem Renaissance, Negritude, and the Cultural Nationalism of the present time. A poem such as "Outcast" bears more than accidental relationship to statements later made by Léopold Senghor and Aimé Césaire regarding Negritude. . . .

The theme of "Outcast" is the disharmony between body and spirit occasioned by the imprisonment of the body and the cultural plunder of the spirit. Slavery, in imprisoning the body, forced the spirit to dwell in a house of bondage where words were felt but never heard; and jungle songs which might have been sung were too soon forgotten in the face of cultural genocide. Thus, a silence was imposed upon the spirit, old cultural artifacts were destroyed, cultural ties were ripped asunder and truth and creativity distorted and stifled. . . .

Returning, then, with McKay to other times, when Western images and symbols were not so well solidified in the Black psyche, when Black men did not believe that their manifest destiny was to be changed into white men, when a people—from the jungles of Timbuctu to the streets of Harlem—were conscious of their beauty and self-worth—returning to such times, Black poets have sought to make their impact throughout the world. The function of such poetry is, beyond a doubt, revolutionary, and it is in this sense that *Harlem Shadows* is a revolutionary document and Claude McKay is a revolutionary poet. He is the militant poet, the angry poet, the poet who calls for revolutionary action.

Addison Gayle Jr. *Claude McKay: The Black Poet at War* (Detroit: Broadside, 1972), pp. 37–39

By and large, [*A Long Way from Home*] is a pleasantly unpretentious account of [McKay's] experiences in New York, London, Russia, Europe, and North Africa. It contains interesting descriptions of the many individuals he had met during his travels, including such famous personalities as Frank Harris, Charlie Chaplin, George Bernard Shaw, H. G. Wells, Paul Robeson, and Henri Cartier-Bresson. Those chapters devoted to his work on *The Liberator* and his travels in England and Russia are detailed and especially valuable from a historical point of view.

McKay could not refrain, however, from occasionally bitter attacks upon his critics. These included several black journalists who had condemned his fiction, as well as those American Communists who considered his political independence a form of degenerate bourgeois adventurism. McKay also questions in *A Long Way from Home* the motives of many blacks whom he felt had merely used the Negro Renaissance to advance their social status among whites. In his final chapter McKay offers a general criticism of America's established Negro leaders. He maintains that their single-minded opposition to segregation was detrimental to any effective black community organization and to the development of a positive group spirit among blacks. . . .

McKay's criticisms in *A Long Way from Home* were only partially indicative of how completely involved he had become in the social and political controversies that dominated the American literature scene in the 1930s. By 1937 his best efforts were going into the occasional articles he managed to sell to such journals and newspapers as *The Nation, The New Leader*, and the New York *Amsterdam News*. In these articles he set forth more fully his position regarding the future of social change, both within and without the black community. Broadly speaking, McKay tried to maintain throughout the 1930s and 1940s the independent, left-wing stance he had first adopted as a *Liberator* editor after World War I. In this regard his position was similar to George Orwell's in England. Unlike the younger Orwell, however, his days as a creative writer were drawing to a close. The energy he had previously devoted to poetry and fiction went instead into his polemical articles.

Wayne F. Cooper. Introduction to Wayne F. Cooper, ed. *The Passion of Claude McKay* (New York: Schocken, 1973), pp. 36–37

McKay depends upon atmosphere to carry [*Home to Harlem*]. The style is appropriately impressionistic, full of hyphenated adjectives aimed at vivid impressions of Harlem life. The beginnings of a dramatic structure may be seen, however, in the characters of Jake and Ray. Jake represents pure instinct. . . . Ray embodies the dilemma of the inhibited, overcivilized intellectual. . . . His is that profound disgust which modern life sometimes evokes in men of artistic sensibilities.

Through a faulty denouement, the symbolic import of Jake and Ray is imperfectly conveyed. Ray, disgusted with all that is sordid and ugly in the lives of the dining-car waiters, ships out on a freighter bound for Europe. Jake, in the closing pages of the novel, finds his lost Felice, whose name signifies joy. By contrasting Jake's happiness with Ray's restless wandering, McKay attempts to convey the superiority of instinct over reason. But at bottom, Jake and Ray represent different ways of rebelling against Western civilization. Jake rebels instinctively, while Ray's rebellion occurs on an intellectual plane. Both characters acquire a broader significance only through their negative relationship to contemporary society. McKay's failure to develop this relationship is the failure of the novel.

Jake is the typical McKay protagonist—the primitive Negro, untouched by the decay of Occidental civilization. The validity of this symbol, however, depends upon McKay's view of contemporary life. Since the author cannot take this view for granted, he introduces himself into the novel as Ray, in order to expound it. But Ray hardly helps matters; in *Home to Harlem* he does little more than state his prejudices. As a result, the novel is left without a suitable antagonist. Jake and Ray are vivid enough, but what they would deny is not always clear. The novel, unable to develop its primary conflict, bogs down in the secondary contrast between Jake and Ray.

Robert A. Bone. *The Negro Novel in America* (New Haven: Yale University Press, 1958), pp. 68–69

[McKay's] religious poetry is the expression of an inner growth, and his discovery of God the result of his individual search for truth. From a more general vantage-point, his poetic opus may be considered as the account of a vast attempt at a synthesis between the antagonistic elements of the black world and the Western world warring within him. There can be no denying that McKay, like every black exiled in a white milieu, was for a long time a divided man, so that it is possible to speak of his cultural dualism. But he never acquiesced in being torn apart by this dichotomy. His whole being urged him to find unity. The critique to which he subjected the antinomies deprived them, little by little, of their contingencies and laid bare their authentic values.

In Jamaica, he affirmed the primacy of the soil and contrasted it with the inanity of the dream, cherished by the mulattoes, of a heightened social status. He rejected the mirage of Africa as a source of racial pride, looking on it as merely pathetic. He shunned the nationalism of a [Marcus] Garvey, whom he regarded as a charlatan, and while he defended Negro folklore against whites, who would have denatured it, he nevertheless could not find spiritual sustenance in it. On the other hand, it was his natural instinct to evaluate the possibilities of spiritual advancement offered by Western, Christian culture, but there too he perceived the corroding evil that sowed hatred between men. In his dialogue with the West, conducted through the medium of his hatred, this emotion was slowly filtered of its dross as he came to grasp the necessity of raising himself above it. Unless the individual is engaged in a ceaseless effort to transcend himself, no victory over hatred will ever be possible. Neither rationalism nor Communism could provide the higher principle capable of reconciling the conflicting theses of his cultural eclecticism. At long last he discovered this principle within himself, and at the same time he discovered God. Thus his spiritual itinerary is an account of the internalization of his racial feeling. [1963]

Jean Wagner. *Black Poets of the United States* (Urbana: University of Illinois Press, 1973), pp. 248–49

The poetry of Claude McKay is classic expression—clear, sculptured, restrained. Much of his early and best work is written in sonnet form. He seems to like the limitation which the sonnet placed on him, and he used those limitations superbly. Very few writers surpass him in economy of phrasing. It should be noted that his restraint in the use of racial tags and terms makes his poems more than Negro affirmations of defiance and protest. His poems—that is, his best poems—are, as Max Eastman has said, "characteristic of what is deep and universal in mankind."

Although he was much more prolific as a fiction writer than as a poet, McKay in all probability will be remembered for his verse far longer than for his prose. He seems to be a curiously ambivalent figure: though rigidly classic in his poetry, he was convinced that the primitive side of Negro life was more honest and more significant than the sophisticated side, the side that had adopted Western culture. . . .

Seen in perspective, McKay is not as impressive as he looked in the twenties and thirties. In all probability, very little of his fiction will survive, with the possible exception of *Banana Bottom*; it is too loosely constructed and too topical. His major thesis, the superiority of the primitive black to the middle-class Negro and to the white, was not tenable when he wrote it, and in spite of many foolish things now being said in the name of *blackness*, is not tenable now. The works of McKay which seem most likely to survive are those few poems of the "Flame-Heart" type and that group of racial sonnets of the "If We Must Die" attitude. McKay never bettered these early sonnets and lyrics. Excellent poetry in any language, they will survive their century.

Arthur P. Davis. *From the Dark Tower* (Washington, D.C.: Howard University Press, 1974), pp. 39, 44

If McKay's conflicting views were an enigma to his friends, the ambiguities of his work are a bafflement to his critics. Naturally, the variant readings of the man and his fiction today constitute the central problem of McKay scholarship. Wayne Cooper, McKay's biographer [who wrote *Claude McKay: Rebel Sojourner in the Harlem Renaissance*], trying to find an acceptable solution, locates the source of all ideological paradoxes in the personal pathology of a personality "characterized always by a deep-seated ambivalence" that was caused mainly by "dependence upon a succession of father figures."

There is another way, however, to explain the presence of incongruous elements in McKay's work. It is more than likely that his work seems paradoxical because it has been read in an inappropriate context. Beginning with James Weldon Johnson's *Black Manhattan* (1930), critics have concluded, certainly to their satisfaction, that McKay was "of the Harlem group," indeed that he was "one of the movement's ornaments" [according to George E. Kent in his article "Patterns of the Harlem Renaissance"]. In the latest study of the Harlem School, *The Harlem Renaissance: Revaluations* (1989), Geta LeSeur affirms that "Claude McKay

remains today part of the acknowledged literary triumvirate of the Harlem Renaissance. He shares this prestigious position with Langston Hughes and Jean Toomer." Her view is typical of the current scholarship's understanding of McKay's affiliations.

One fruitful close reading of McKay's work—a reading heretofore denied him—however, forces us to the conclusion that to anchor his consciousness in Harlem is to dislocate his true emotional geography; it is, indeed, to misread the map of his political awareness. If we would account for all the elements of his thought, we might have to take McKay for what he really was in life: a colonial writer who happened to stop over in Harlem on his lifelong quest for a spiritual home, on a quest, incidentally, that no colonial writer has ever effectively escaped. His association with Harlem, it can be affirmed, was no more than what Harlem itself has been to Afro-American letters: "a moment in renaissancism" [according to Houston A. Baker Jr. in his *Modernism and the Harlem Renaissance*]. Such being the case, by continuing to identify his work exclusively with Harlem's ethos, we have not only robbed it of its uniqueness but also denied it the central place it deserves in the global discourse of black writers that McKay so ably initiated. Arbitrary points of reference have led us only to skewed inferences.

Unable, or unwilling, to read McKay as a writer from Jamaica, then a British colony, and hence as one with a mind-set entirely different from that of the Harlemite, many critics have landed themselves in a puzzle. James Weldon Johnson, a person whom McKay in the dedicatory note to *Harlem: Negro Metropolis* (1940) calls a "friend and wise counselor," finds McKay's lifelong nostalgia for Jamaica intriguing. "Reading McKay's poetry of rebellion," says Johnson, "it is difficult to conceive of him dreaming of his native Jamaica and singing," Such perplexity results, obviously, from an ignorance of, or from ignoring, a basic fact about the colonial sensibility: that it straddles two worlds—the one of its origin, the other of its adoption. Politically, its values and attitudes derive from, and swing between, the two sets. It sides, at once, with each of the two antagonists: the victim and the victimizer.

That McKay should have been assimilated into the Harlem Renaissance looks rather natural in retrospect. For one thing, noticed when literary history understood artistic works in terms of schools or movements, Claude McKay was bound to be read as part of the Harlem Renaissance, especially since to be black and to have a powerful literary voice was considered nothing less than miraculous. . . . But to credit McKay with the boom and bloom of black art and literature, or with the general growth of interest in Harlem, is to be guilty of the *post hoc, ergo propter hoc* fallacy. That the birth of the Renaissance followed McKay's departure from Harlem need not argue for his paternity of the movement. . . .

New Yorkers had discovered the existence of a fashionable clique, and an artistic and literary set in Harlem. The big racket which crepitated from this discovery resulted in an enormously abnormal advertisement of bohemian.

The truth is that McKay was even less responsible for the Harlem Renaissance than Pound had been for the Chicago School of Poetry. He was for the Harlem Renaissance, but certainly not of it.

Yet to stress McKay's colonial heritage is by no means to minimize his value to the movement or the overall worth of his work. To the contrary, his work did, indeed, carve out a path which black writers all over the world, not only the Harlemite, could, if they would, follow. Some of them . . . dared not follow McKay's lead. But a few others did. Aimé Césaire, according to the interview published in *Discourse on Colonialism* (1955), was inspired by McKay's novel *Banjo* (1930), which for him was "really one of the first works in which an author spoke of the Negro and gave him a certain literary dignity." That McKay's self-assurance, like his passionate devotion to the cause of the black race, did a yeoman's service to the advancement of African American literature is a fact widely, and correctly, accepted.

What is little suspected, however, is the pervasive presence of the colonial sensibility in his work. This essay seeks to identify only a few of the traits distinguishing the colonial strain. . . .

Linguistically, his work bears the mark all too common to the writing done in colonies. It is pulled by two gravitational forces: the one of his native tongue, the other of the language of the colonizer. In his first book of poems published in the United States, *Harlem Shadows* (1922), McKay confesses to the linguistic tension that had been part of his upbringing. "The speech of my childhood and early youth," he writes, "was the Jamaica dialect . . . which still preserves a few words of African origin, and which is more difficult of understanding than the American Negro dialect. But the language we wrote and read in school was England's English." The dual versions of the language, like those of the island culture, internalized during the period of his cognitive development, haunt McKay's work to the very end and affect its tone and texture in various ways. . . .

The argument of McKay's later poetry, like the diction of his earlier poems, is disposed around two poles: the vernacular and the metropolitan. The progression of his well-known poems readily reveals the bipolar tensions that underlie the conceptual design of his verses. Whether it be "To One Coming North," "North and South," or "The Tropics in New York," the absent landscape of Jamaica is so powerfully present in the poems as to displace the New York scene, the immediate locale and the subject of the poem. . . .

One reason why McKay's attitude towards black characters is less than respectful is that, unlike Harlem writers—Jean Toomer, Zora Neale Hurston, and Rudolph Fisher, who went to their folk roots—McKay went for literary inspiration to Anglo-Saxon masters, to Dickens, Shaw, Whitman, and Lawrence. As a person raised in a colony, it was impossible for him totally to divest his mind of the literature and the attitudes of the colonizer and to adopt the literary genealogy of the African-American peers of his generation.

Nothing in McKay's writing so powerfuly registers his ambivalence towards the interest of the Harlem community as his shifting attitude towards the Harlem prostitute. If the narrator of the poem "Harlem Shadows" is the rueful patriarch bemoaning the corruption of the "little dark girls who in slippered feet / Go prowling through the night from street to street," that of the novel Home to Harlem gloats in the depredations of Jake and his associates who, like predators, go stalking through the night, always "hungry foh a li'l brown honey." The poem and the novel, read together, suggest an author running with the hare and hunting with the hound. . . .

The only character of McKay's who ever finds a home is Bita (*Banana Bottom*, 1933), but such arrival for a fictional character becomes possible only when the writer's fancy returns to settle in his native land, as, for once, it did. The home for McKay was never Harlem, but Jamaica, where alone his characters could regain their integrity.

It can well be argued that McKay's vacillation between alternating preferences for the native culture and the metropolitan, like his pull between the pastoral and the urban, between an allegiance to Marxism and a desire for free peasantry, can be satisfactorily explained only in terms of the colonial's attachment to the simple rhythms of his native world and to a fascination for the metropolitan systems of the West, whose cruelty and inequity would constantly drive his thoughts back to the security of a remembered community. A creature of colonial experience, McKay was condemned to dwell in the limbo of the imagination of the colonized, unable forever to state a clear-cut preference. That is the primary reason why his work seems so paradoxical, why it bears the print of the journeys between the polarities of a divided mind.

To comprehend him satisfactorily, therefore, one must approach McKay not from one direction alone, but from two. One must read McKay, indeed one must re-read McKay, in a context different from that of the Harlem Renaissance, the context he has long been relegated to. In order to appreciate the nature of his ambiguities, one must recognize the intellectual baggage he brought with him to Harlem—the English attitudes, a European sensibility, and the general impedimenta of a colonial mind, congnitive elements altogether unknown to most Harlemites.

P. S. Chauhan. *CLA Journal.* 34, 1 (September, 1990), pp. 68–80

BIBLIOGRAPHY

*Songs of Jamaica*, 1912; *Constab Ballads*, 1912; *Spring in New Hampshire, and Other Poems*, 1920; *Harlem Shadows: The Poems of Claude McKay*, 1922; *Home to Harlem*, 1928; *Banjo: A Story without a Plot*, 1929; *Gingertown*, 1932; *Banana Bottom*, 1933; *A Long Way from Home*, 1937; *Harlem: Negro Metropolis*, 1940; *Selected Poems*, 1953; *The Dialectic Poetry of Claude McKay*, 1972; *The Passion of Claude McKay: Selected Poetry and Prose, 1912-1948*, 1973; *My Green Hills of Jamaica, and Five Jamaican Short Stories*, 1975

# McMILLAN, Terry (1952–)
## United States

Terry McMillan's first novel, *Mama*, opens with the elaborate plans of its memorable title character, Mildred Peacock, to defend herself against an attack from her alcoholic husband Crook. Mildred's self-protective scheme, almost militaristic in its multiple options and tactical flexibility, serves as an accurate reflection of the survivalist mentality that compels her subsequent adventures and misadventures. . . . *Mama* delineates Mildred's ultimate rejection of a fearful existence as victim of an abusive man, her resilience in the face of much—perhaps too much—adversity, her ability to fend for herself and her five children in both the urban wasteland of Point Haven, Michigan, and in a materially seductive Los Angeles, and her general resolve to gather her rosebuds whenever the opportunity presents itself.

If viewed in a cursory way, McMillan's novel seems, in its figuration of an unquestionably resourceful black female protagonist, consistent with the impulses of the emerging black women's literary tradition. However, *Mama* is, in the final analysis, more accurately read as what Hortense Spillers's essay "Cross-Currents,

Discontinuities: Black Women's Fiction'' calls a moment of ''discontinuity'' in the tradition, one in which the author ''reaches behind her most immediate writing predecessor[s]'' and embraces not the lyrical mode of contemporary Afro-American women writers such as Paule Marshall, Toni Morrison, and Alice Walker, but the clearly realistic models of black female precursors such as Ann Petry. In its rather self-conscious rejection of the examples of these immensely influential writers, McMillan appears intent on protecting herself from unjustified considerations of indebtedness to these contemporaries.

In its purposely stark, unlyrical delineation of an unredeemed and unrepentant female character (whose most significant psychological transformation is her ability to tell her oldest child Freda that she loves her), *Mama* stands boldly outside of the mainstream of contemporary black women's fiction. Unlike the tradition's most representative texts, *Mama* offers no journeys back to blackness, no empowering black female communities, no sustained condemnation of American materialism or male hegemony. What it does provide, in its largely episodic depictions of the travails of Mildred and her family, is a moving, often hilarious and insightful exploration of a slice of black urban life that is rarely seen in contemporary black women's fiction.

Michael Awkward. *Callaloo*. 11, 3 (summer 1988), pp. 649–50

Terry McMillan's new novel is a love story waiting to explode. The lovers of *Disappearing Acts* are both intelligent and good-looking, both possessed of dreams—but Zora Banks is an educated black woman, and Franklin Swift is an unschooled black man. It's Brooklyn, it's 1982, and it's clear from page one that the two of them are sitting in a minefield and something's going to blow.

McMillan's first novel, *Mama*, was original in concept and style, a run-away narrative pulling a crowded cast of funny, earthy characters. *Disappearing Acts* is also full of momentum, and it's a pleasurable, often moving novel. In this intricate look at a love affair . . . McMillan strikes out in a whole new direction and changes her narrative footing with ease. But *Disappearing Acts* is also a far more conventional popular novel than *Mama* was. Despite its raunchy language and its narrative construction (Franklin's voice and Zora's alternate), its descriptions, its situations, even its generic minor characters are often predictable. I say this with some surprise, because it seems to me that Terry McMillan has the power to be an important contemporary novelist.

Much of the predictable feel of the story has to do with Zora Banks's narrative. Zora, who reaches her thirtieth birthday in the book, has come to New York from Ohio; she is a musician who makes her living teaching in a junior high school but feeds her soul by writing songs. She dreams of landing a recording contract, and seems on her way to that goal when she falls hard for Franklin Swift, separated and the father of two, who is working on the renovation of her apartment building. The progress of their love affair is punctuated by construction layoffs for Franklin: as his resentment escalates, so does Zora's frustration. She becomes pregnant, and by the time their son is born they are both enraged and near desperation. . . .

I have my doubts about the ending of *Disappearing Acts*, but I'm a hard-hearted reader; I leave you to your own conclusions. Nevertheless, I admire the risks Terry McMillan has taken in making Franklin Swift come to such intense life. I imagine she'll make a long and challenging career of taking such chances.

Valerie Sayers. *New York Times Book Review*. August 6, 1989, p. 8

Even though Zora and Franklin are last-week contemporary, they are also like classic folklore characters come to life in Brooklyn. She's the wily black woman of yore, the smart-talking Eve who's always got a little something on the rail for the lizard, as we used to say. She's also a sophisticated shopper who likes fancy cheeses and bottled water, and she says ''shit'' all the time. Zora has all the tugs of feminism versus the feminine that a modern black woman who's read [Alice] Walker and [Ntozake] Shange is supposed to have. She's not unlike Zora Neale Hurston's sassy folk women—characters *Cosmo* would never dare to pop-psychoanalyze.

Complicated as Franklin is supposed to be, he is a savvy urban John Henry—he don't take no tea of' the fever. An intellectual Tina Turner meets a hardhat Ike. They are both bricks, and though they may chip each other, they ain't never gonna blend. They live and work in New York City, but are in a very insulated world; their problems are completely personal. Their relationship is doomed by mutual expectations and ended by an outburst of gratuitous male violence. Let's just say it wasn't needed for the love affair to fall apart.

These two are as they are; like other folk-heroes, they don't change much or drag skeletons out of the closet, and they learn their lessons the hard way. They've been created by years of past mythologizing, drawn their images from popular culture, black and white. They are black, sho' nuff—the last thing I would say about McMillan's people is that they ain't black—but they're black in big, bold strokes. And that means her work will continue to raise questions among African-Americans about the fuzzy line between realism and popular misconception. And at the same time, McMillan is, as she said, less race-conscious. She confines herself to the day-to-day life struggle, as told from behind the mask Claude McKay so poignantly described. McMillan uses, almost exclusively, the performance side of black character, emphasizing the most public, most familiar aspects of us. If you smell a little song-and-dance in the self-sufficient ribaldry, it's there.

Thulani Davis. *Voice Literary Supplement*. May 1990, p. 29

The four women in *Waiting to Exhale* are black, but aside from that distinction (and the fact that the author brings a wicked wit to this often sentimental form of fiction), no new literary ground is broken. But going over the old ground is still great fun with . . . McMillan's characters for company. Savannah Jackson, a public-relations executive, is, like the others, in her mid-thirties. She is cool, competent, and shrewd, the strongest of the group. But her private relations with men are singularly unsatisfying. ''What I want to know is this,'' she asks. ''How do you tell a man—in a nice way—that he makes you sick?''

Savannah decides she's had it with cold Denver. Her college roommate, Bernadine Harris, who is living the ideal black urban professional life, complete with an entrepreneur husband, two children, pastel-perfect interior decor, and a BMW, urges her to come to Phoenix. It's warm. It's beautiful. It's the good life. But by the time Savannah arrives, Bernadine's marriage is in ashes and her husband has flown off—with his beautiful, young, and exceedingly blonde bookkeeper.

As Gloria, hairdresser to them all, notes: "I don't know which is worse, trying to raise a teen-age son or dealing with a husband who leaves you for a white woman." Gloria is worried about her sixteen-year-old son, Tarik, a smart, talented kid who, overnight, has turned sullen, secretive, and stunningly hostile.

She should relax. Gloria is a great mother, a straight-talker. ("I never really expected you to come up to me one day and say, 'Yo, Ma, I'm doing the wild thing now,' but my Lord, Tarik. This is just one reason why I've always wanted you to have a father. Let me ask you something. And don't lie to me. Are you using condoms?'") She is also a shrewd businesswoman and a loving friend: a super woman. But Savannah, Robin, and Bernadine are distressed that she is hiding behind a wall of fat, endangering her health as she protects herself from men, from love—from the possibility of pain.

Pain? Robin, the eternal optimist, is the expert. She looks for love in all the wrong places and, naturally, never finds it. . . .

Terry McMillan's heroines are so well drawn that by the end of the novel, the reader is completely at home with the four of them. They observe men—and contemporary America—with bawdy humor, occasional melancholy, and great affection. But the novel is about more than four lives; the bonds among the women are so alive and so appealing they almost seem a character in their own right. Reading *Waiting to Exhale* is like being in the company of a great friend. It is thought-provoking, thoroughly entertaining, and very, very comforting.

Susan Isaacs. *New York Times Book Review.* May 31, 1992, p. 11

McMillan frequently draws from her own life for her fiction. Critics often object to her simple characters and dialogue-driven plots. Nonetheless, they regard her as an important chronicler of 1990s black life. The four central women in *Waiting to Exhale* are all members of Black Women on the Move, a networking organization in Phoenix. Besides Robin, there are Bernadine, Savannah, and Gloria—respectively the wife of a successful entrepreneur, a TV public relations executive, and a hair salon owner. The novel's emphasis on brand names—BMW, Coach leather, Calvin Klein, and Perrier—has earned the author the title of "the black Judith Krantz," but this is indicative more of how unfamiliar whites are with successful blacks than of the novel's content. Except for Bernadine, who is truly affluent, these women are only solidly middle class—it is their delight in their success that makes them seem richer.

Daniel Max. *New York Times Magazine.* August 9, 1992, p. 22

Written for and about educated black women, *Waiting to Exhale* reflects the growing numbers of successful African-Americans who have fled the drugs and violence of the ghettoes for fashionable neighborhoods, while trying to preserve a uniquely black cultural heritage. McMillan's characters believe in black solidarity. To act like a white is an act of betrayal. "White folks" hover disconcertingly on the novel's margins.

*Waiting to Exhale's* four protagonists live in Phoenix, Arizona. Apart from being black, female and thirty something, they have one thing in common: "None of us have a man." And they're holding their breath until they get one. Savannah wants to feel "important to somebody," though she's not yet desperate: she's just "thirsty," not "dehydrated." Bernadine has been betrayed by her acquisitive husband, who traded her in for a new trophy-wife, his twenty-four-year-old (blonde) bookkeeper. Gloria has given up waiting for a man who can make her toes curl and takes comfort in God, her hair salon, a promiscuous adolescent son, and much too much food. Robin's toes curl for "pretty men with big dicks," but she's hung up on an unscrupulous cad and doesn't know a good man when she sleeps with one. *Waiting to Exhale* chronicles these women's bedroom capers in their exhaustive—and exhausting—searches for Mr. Right.

He's hard to come by. Black men prove to be "'Stupid.' 'In prison.' 'Unemployed.' 'Crackheads.' 'Short.' 'Liars.' 'Unreliable.'" And worse. McMillan's generalized male-bashing has understandably alienated some black men. Her portrayal of women may be more sympathetic, but it is equally shallow. Her characters' preoccupation with deodorants, douches, and dates soon grows wearisome. And the attention McMillan draws to male-female rifts within the African-American community seems at odds with the black solidarity she otherwise implicitly approves.

But whether her views are politically correct or not, McMillan has hit a nerve. Many African-American women identify with her heroines. Using the vibrant street-talk McMillan grew up speaking, her protagonists tackle sexual issues that most women can relate to.

It may in part be concern to avoid accusations of racism that has prevented some critics from putting this book firmly where it belongs—among the glitzy, commercial women's novels. Its one true importance is that it appeals to a market that American publishers have previously overlooked—the new black middle class.

Frances Stead Sellers. *Times Literary Supplement.* November 6, 1992, p. 20

Popular novels ask complicity from the reader in the name of genre: we all know reality isn't like this. But *Waiting to Exhale* never winks at the reader. It comes at you with a completely straight face, with such intensity about its own convictions that the sincerity is irresistible. If the women characters are sentimental about love, then they are fierce about being sentimental; if they are conventional in their expectations, then they are defiantly prepared to be identified as such. The novel is at the same time hilarious, to the verge of camp, but the thoughts and feelings it captures are too much like life for it not to make a striking impression. There's nothing self-aggrandizing or moralizing about it.

It's a book that knows to whom it is addressed. For sheer topicality, McMillan doesn't miss a base on the wide playing field of issues, and her characters touch them in the most self-aware manner. Caring for one's elderly parents, condoms for teen-agers, day care, feeding the homeless on Thanksgiving, diet, high blood pressure, nail care, AIDS, anti-drugs, including Xanax dependence—anything that could be on the professional black women's list of concerns is there, woven into the conversations of supermoms, much like the false braids in the hairstyles McMillan's women disdain at the beauty salon that functions as their club away from the networking parties haunted by black men.

Very with-it and dialogue-driven, *Waiting to Exhale* is the story of four friends in their mid-thirties, each at a critical point in her life. Savannah and Robin are unmarried, childless, and speak in the first person. The two who do have children, Gloria, a single parent, and Bernadine, on the eve of a nasty divorce, are written about in a very internal third person. Though each chapter is from the viewpoint of one of them, laying out her case history, taking up threads of developing situations, the woman share a common voice and are moving toward the same pole-position in the self-realization sweepstakes: dreaming of opening a catering service, doing something creative in production work at that cable channel, becoming a mother, or busting the estranged husband who is trying to hide his considerable financial assets. They recognize that black men have treated them the way they have because they, black women, have let them get away with it all these years. The love of a black woman isn't a black man's right.

McMillan's black women read *Essence*. They know that glossies targeted for their white middle-class sisters are just as full of hints, tips, and desperately cheerful features about sex and finding Mr. Right. They know it's a cynical, self-perpetuating market that goes after those gullible, hopeful bucks, which perhaps makes it all right that they continue to flip through it to check out the latest fashions. They may be fools for love, and fools for "bad" dresses they can wear the hell out of, but they are not victims. They make choices. In fact, out there in Phoenix, Arizona, these women act out, act up, and talk about big dick in a way that makes their white female thirtysomething (by now) counterparts in recent fiction of downtown scenes seem tame by comparison.

It used to be said, maybe still is, that blacks talk differently among themselves from the way they do among whites, and *Waiting to Exhale* is an extension of that, showing how differently black women talk among themselves from the way they do in the company of black men. When they are down, they pop their hymns, Paula Abdul or Anita Baker tapes, into the car tape deck. They say "Fuck you" to one another with affection, get drunk, and tell a friend some home truths for her own good. They call each other up and give advice: that they ought to use black men the way black men have been using them. "Get some," they say. Or "get some for me" and "get some to tide you over." And yet for all their rueful independence, cruising, salaries, and responsibilities, the musketeer-like code of "getting some" is apt to be forgotten the morning after. The man is never a trick. He's the one who "got some" and didn't call back.

Savannah, Bernadine, Robin, and Gloria belong to an organization called Black Women on the Move, which is as safe as NOW. McMillan's women have the same relation to affirmative action and the "glass ceiling" as any middle-class white woman. There is nothing overtly feminist in *Waiting to Exhale*, but if the men can make the women doubt their own worth, the women have the last laugh. McMillan makes full, vivacious use of the tactic that makes Kate Millett's attack on Henry Miller in *Sexual Politics* so devastating: ridicule of masculine fantasies of sexual prowess. . . .

Terry McMillan's women wouldn't date a white man, though they have nothing against black women who do. But when Bernadine's husband leaves her for his young, blonde bookkeeper, she recovers, burns his clothes and BMW, cuts her hair, drops by the software company she sweated to help him build, and slaps the shit out of the red-faced girl. Sometimes they don't know or don't want to believe that the black men they go out with who are afraid of commitment are already married, but sometimes they do know.

Their lives are full of topics that are covered every week on the *Oprah Winfrey Show*, but these black women never have to ask

themselves the very Oprah-like question of why they're attracted in the first place to Scuzzes Who Lie, because, conveniently, for most of the novel's four hundred pages the black men are all No Good or Losers. But they keep the faith in the one black man who won't be like that, who is "sensitive," not threatened, and yet has a dick hard enough to make them quit smoking—it's either that or acupuncture—and when two Mr. Rights do come along, one is an inspired retired handyman, happy to fix everything around the house, and the other vows to use his law practice to get the state of Arizona to stop putting liquor stores in black neighborhoods. . . .

Part of the appeal of McMillan's work lies in the forceful way it reflects the history of black women as also that of a labor force. *Mama* (1987), *Disappearing Acts* (1989), and now *Waiting to Exhale*—each successive novel takes place on a higher level of prosperity as McMillan charts the fortunes of black women rescued or created by higher education. In Ann Petry's grim novel *The Street* (1946), the heroine's job as a maid causes her to lose her marriage and home. She longs to get her son away from the bad influences of the tenement and becomes a bookkeeper. White men look upon her as a whore and she kills the black man who assaults her, an illustration, perhaps, of James Baldwin's contention that in black fiction the place where sex ought to have been was filled by violence. The most convincing way black writers of his day could make something happen to make their point was to have a catastrophe. The times and taboos have changed for McMillan's determined women. You can have a catastrophe and move on. . . .

In *Mama* the girl raped at age fourteen in a depressed Michigan town of the 1960s can throw away her hot comb and find sexual fulfillment, Malcolm X, and a community-college education in Los Angeles. She can get away from her mother's life of welfare checks, scrubbing floors, the husband with the brown leather belt, the casual prostitution when there are no jobs or substitute husbands. Even *Mama* can try to get away from her platinum wig to make a life like her daughter's.

In *Disappearing Acts*, Zora—her daddy liked to read—is a school teacher who wants to make a career as a singer. She gets an apartment in a Brooklyn brownstone with enough space for a practice room and, fortunately or unfortunately, the builder taking a break on the steps looks like "a black Marlboro man." This novel is largely a dress rehearsal for *Waiting to Exhale*, with a similar circle of catty but supportive, slightly differentiated black women friends, except in this case the alternating voices are unequal, male and female. The edge is in the female voice and McMillan struggles to keep up the man's side of the story, to fill out his inner life with sports, beer, bitterness, shame, horniness.

In *Waiting to Exhale*, the black women are professionals whose children are not likely to fall out of the middle class. They are the grandchildren of the insecure migrants that Dorothy West wrote about in *The Living Is Easy* (1947), a novel of black middle-class life in pre-World War I Boston. McMillan's women repay student loans, send cash back home by Federal Express so widowed mothers can keep the gas on, and tolerate for as long as they can the strain of love for sexy but insolvent black men. They are far from the black neighborhoods of fiction that depended on messages of social consciousness. In Phoenix, they choose white suburbs and schools. The extended black family is contained in long-distance phone calls, and political consciousness consists of being annoyed that Arizona has no Martin Luther King Day.

These women have arrived, are just as Keynesian as any white in recent fiction, and tend to spend their way out of crises. They do not question material reward, because it's all been earned. Doubts about having sold out when they get promotions belong to a pre-Anita Hill era. A condo or a Cherokee is no obstacle to having soul—unless it belongs to a black man. Bernadine despises her husband's Porsche and investments because he's competing with the whites he reads about in *Money* magazine. She never wanted a Rolex. When an absent but well-off father turns up to explain that he doesn't want to get back together with the family because he's gay, the wife senses immediately that something is wrong, closes her eyes, and discovers the problem: ''He sounds white.''. . .

Darryl Pinckney. *New York Review of Books.* November 4, 1993, pp. 33–37

Is a happy woman in charge of her own fate de facto an unsympathetic character—someone people don't want to read about and cannot empathize with? If so, the defenders of serious literature will no doubt join in unison to eject Terry McMillan's rip-roaring new book, *How Stella Got Her Groove Back*, from the Eden of politically and academically correct approval. Because, in *How Stella Got Her Groove Back*, no women weep; and Stella, in fact, revels. She revels and even gloats at being a woman, revels in being in solitary possession of her mind, her body, her child, her house, her finances, her beauty, her creativity and finally, of her sexy, strapping young dream lover, whom she finds and triumphantly lashes to her side. If this is unserious literature, it is unserious literature of the most serious kind, perhaps even, in its own way, revolutionary.

Terry McMillan is the only novelist I have ever read, apart from writers of children's books, who makes me glad to be a woman. . . .

Fans of McMillan's previous novels, the hugely popular *Waiting to Exhale* and the more critically esteemed *Disappearing Acts* and *Mama*, will recognize McMillan's authentic, unpretentious voice in every page of *How Stella Got Her Groove Back*. It is the voice of the kind of woman all of us know and all of us need: the warm, strong, bossy mother/sister/best friend. Fans and enemies alike will also get their share of the brand names that McMillan uses to signify arrival into this country's upper-middle class: BMW and Calvin Klein, Nordstrom's and Macy's. Having just spent an evening with a friend who crowed ecstatically all night over a new pair of Gucci loafers, which did in fact seem to lend her some special glow, I don't find the product emphasis fatuous or crass. Even Emerson recognized that for a woman, which McMillan indubitably is, ''the sense of being perfectly well-dressed gives a feeling of inward tranquillity which religion is powerless to bestow.'' But readers of this book will find more than wise words. . . .

At the outset of the book, we learn that Stella, 42, an affluent single mom in San Francisco, has gone a little stale, like champagne that's been uncorked and not tasted for too long. She's content, but she spends more time taking care of business and conducting lengthy Molly Bloom-like internal harangues with herself and external harangues with her sisters than trying to find happiness for herself. So, defying her stagnation, she packs herself off to a luxury resort in Jamaica, where from get-go, every young stud's eyes swing appreciatively in her direction. Sure enough, Stella soon finds the ''real thing'' in the form of a noble, gentle, fine 20-year-old man, Winston Shakespeare. When McMillan describes Stella's first vision of the boy wonder, you want to howl with laughter at her audacity, and shout, ''Go, girl!'':

When I look at him I almost have a stroke. He is wearing baggy brown shorts and has to be at least six three or four and he is lean but his shoulders are wide broad and as he walks toward my table all I can think is Lord Lord Lord some young girl is gonna get lucky as I don't know what if she can snag you. . . . when he smiles he shows off a beautiful set of straight white teeth that've been hiding behind and under those succulent young lips.

Name another time you've read a man objectified by a woman in this way, if you can. Stella, of course, turns out to be the lucky girl, and soon finds that she's hooked. Back in California, her sister Vanessa encourages her, while her sister Angela moans in despair at the folly of a May-December romance in which her sister is not May. Vanessa boldly comes to Stella's defense: ''Men have been dating younger women for [expletive] centuries and does anybody say anything to them?'' she sputters. Women may talk like this to each other, but few of us write like this.

To those who say this could never happen in real life, I offer the evidence of the young dive-master I met last summer in Belize under an apricot moon, whose gallantry and openhearted effusiveness restored my own faith in romance, even if he was no Winston Shakespeare. McMillan's book may be the stuff of fantasies, not reality; but if fantasies could be bought whole, every woman in the country would be lining up to buy them from Terry McMillan. And maybe then other writers would dare to write them, too. And, maybe this is happening right now—and fiction at last is about to understand that women are ready to read about themselves not only as schemers or sufferers, but as the adventurous heroes of their own lives.

Liesl Schillinger. *Washington Post Book World.* May 5, 1996, pp. 1, 8

In presenting Mildred Peacock, a welfare-dependent mother of five who marries three times, works numerous odd jobs, is incarcerated for writing bad checks, and even prostitutes herself in order to provide for her children, McMillan creates another rift on the literary landscape of African-American fiction. The fundamental purpose of motherhood as presented in *Mama*, I believe, is to enable McMillan to expose the problematic assumptions associated with the Eurocentric motherhood myth and to protest the effects of the myth's historical victimization of black women in an era of rising black consciousness, the 1960s.

The motherhood myth is anchored in Judeo-Christian belief in the words of God: ''Be fruitful and multiply.''. . .

Packaged with the motherhood myth is the Eurocentric ''cult of true womanhood,'' which confines a woman's activities to the care of her home, children, and husband. . . .

*Mama* invalidates the assumptions implicit in the cult of true womanhood and challenges the gender symbolism which white Americans have traditionally attributed to mothers. But before proceeding with McMillan's attack on the myth and its attendant assumptions, it is important to reveal her protagonist's ambivalent celebration of motherhood in an unchristian-like environment and her unalterable oppression as a poor black mother of five in a racialized history that has glorified white motherhood while denigrating black mothers. These factors add support to the argument debunking the motherhood myth and the problematic assumptions associated with it.

Mildred Peacock's ambivalence toward motherhood occurs when she allows the fascination of maternity to consume her at seventeen years old even though she later questions God's relevance to her life as a mother.

The magic of Mildred's pregnancy involves the simple operation of nature, but the church ritualizes childbirth in order to propagate the Judeo-Christian myth of motherhood. The celebration of motherhood at Shiloh Baptist on Easter, Mother's Day, and Christmas—the days most associated with the regeneration process and the only days Mildred attends church—reaffirms the sacredness and tranquility of maternity and perpetuates the myth. Mildred's going to church with a negative opinion of God suggests her celebration of motherhood without patriarchal dictum. She regards God as an unreliable, double-dealing figure who caused her mother's early death and prevented Mildred from picking up her paycheck to feed her children during a heavy snowstorm.

Mildred's ritual celebration of motherhood seems more Afrocentric than Eurocentric. As Barbara Christian notes, "motherhood is for most African peoples symbolic of creativity and continuity." It is spontaneous rather than imposed, immediate rather than planned for. From an Afrocentric perspective, maternity associates itself with religious worship, but generational connectedness is its mainstay. Mildred even ignores the biblical imposition of compulsory pregnancy and says, "Having babies was routine to a lot of women, but for [me] it was unique every time". After giving birth to Freda, her first child, she spontaneously "let her body blow up and flatten for the next fifty-five months" with four more children. . . .

A disenfranchised African-American mother, Mildred has neither a private nuclear household nor communal support to help her rear her children. One after the other, each child takes to the streets and becomes delinquent. Freda snorts cocaine, Money is jailed for stealing, Doll becomes pregnant before marriage, Angel lives with a white man before marrying him, and Bootsey steals. This fractured family enables McMillan to point significantly at the injustice of a society that holds up the motherhood myth for the black woman to follow but offers no positive social outlets to assist her in rearing her children. In fact, Mildred refuses to be called "mother." She tells her grown daughter Angel, who calls her Caucasian mother-in-law "Mom": "You ain't been calling me no damn mother, and don't start now. And besides, if you look over here at me, you'll notice that I ain't white" Mildred's response clearly acknowledges the distinction between her life as mama and that of the white woman's as mom. . . .

Terry McMillan makes clear in *Mama* that any attempt to have Mildred Peacock emulating the "saved" mother proposed by the Eurocentric myth is an impossible feat shaped by a history of social and economic deprivation. For McMillan, poverty, teenage pregnancy, unstable work outside the home, and marriage to the nonsupportive, errant father of her children, all play a role in structuring a view of mamahood which deflates the motherhood myth and the assumption inherent in the cult of true womanhood. By externalizing Mildred's struggles with a gender myth in a racialized history, McMillan expands the parameters of black womanhood and brings a new voice to black fiction. Mildred Peacock's need-to-be-told story makes necessary and relevant the rift *Mama* creates on the literary landscape of African-American women's fiction.

Rita B. Dandridge. *CLA Journal*. 41, 4 (June 1998), pp. 405–16.

BIBLIOGRAPHY
*Disappearing Acts*, 1989; *Mama*, 1987; *Waiting to Exhale*, 1992; *How Stella Got Her Groove Back*, 1996

# MÉTELLUS, Jean (1937–)
## Haiti

Like [Émile] Zola, the poet and novelist Jean Métellus . . . has chosen to depict [in *La Famille Vortex*] a slice of life from his native country through a single family. For narrative economy, he condenses the transcription of an extraordinary, wide, and complex reality. A well-to-do family with seven legitimate children, the Vortexes are presented with their ups and downs amidst the Haitian struggle for power. Their social actions and democratic aspirations are drowned in the miasma of military and police brutality. Left alone in their comfortable countryside villa, Solon and Olga Vortex live only for their reunions with their grown children, particularly at Christmastime. Except for the absence of their daughter Astrid, a musician whose career has exiled her to the United States, they are shown enjoying this opportunity for the last time in 1949 before the "hemorrhage of exile."

The oldest son Edward, a military officer who shares his father's poetical talent and his mother's honesty and Indian features, has to follow his patron President Estimé to New York after a coup d'état. And because Edward's brother Louis (an English teacher) has also been a supporter of the deposed president, he is rushed to France by another brother, Bishop Joseph, after being beaten up and incarcerated by the officers of General Férére, now in power. A sister, Sylvie, who teaches at the school of hotel management, will soon follow her brothers into exile. Socially committed, she is shocked by the poverty of the slum areas she visits in Port-au-Prince and raises questions about the insultingly luxurious parlor of a neighboring prostitute that is frequently visited by high-ranking officials of the military government. Accused and threatened for "social provocation," she is forced to flee to France. Her twin brother Sylvain, a physician, is also a leader of a labor union and the Popular Democratic Party. Thanks to his popularity, he manages to survive through Estimé and Férére until his followers raise him to power. But before he can implement his democratic program, he is ousted by a violent military coup and compelled to embark to New York. This does not prevent his brother Joseph from becoming cabinet counselor to the new president. A fighter for Haitian priests' promotion to the church hierarchy, he is also a champion of unity between the clergy and the government. But for voting against a law to dissolve existing organizations, including Christian ones, he is irrevocably destituted and forced, in his turn, to leave for France. Ludovic Vortex is then the only child remaining, but one wonders for how long, as he is harassed by military police searching his house for some pretext on which to arrest him. . . .

Rather than elaborating on characterization, *La Famille Vortex*, which exemplifies a society offering itself to history, focuses on the interactions of a human aggregate indissociable in its eddies and frictions. The behavior of its characters is briefly described more to indicate the weave of history in the making than to provide psychological analysis. Most of Haiti's conflicting world is skillfully presented in physical, social, political, ethical, and spiritual terms. The contrasts between different strata of Haitian life are enhanced by the author's alternation of realistic and poetic descriptions in stylistic levels more akin to classical or colloquial Hexagone French than to a francophone dialect (with some rare exceptions).

Daniel L. Racine. *World Literature Today.* 57, 3 (summer 1983), p. 502

Beyond the central theme of injustice or racism, and beyond the very Haitian references, the diverse parts of [*Hommes de plein vent*] are linked by the extraordinary poetic power of expression, a grounding in body images that permits the author to write: ''j'arrache de mes entrailles un chant illimité'' [I tear out from my entrails a limitless song]. . . .

At the beginning of [this] collection, as in our modern history, we encounter the figure of Christopher Columbus, a man of thought who wished to encounter ''vies épaisses de promesses'' [lives full of promise]. His greed to conquer is the manifestation of a poetic attempt: a refusal of limits, and of lands bogged down by conventions. His is then the figure of the poet itself. . . .

Writing poetry that is *engagée* [committed], where good or bad ''ideas,'' which take the place of poetic value, are affirmed, is common practice. But being able, in a flamboyant affirmation of a vision of historical reality, to accede to a poetic expression that seizes with an unequaled density, is quite rare. The author, however, is successful at this.

When he evokes the Ku Klux Klan, the brutal madness of the fanatics of hatred appears before our eyes in all its horror. . . .

In the entire work, the coherence, the force, and the splendor of images organized in waves and in glowing rhythms attest to the reality of a poetry in which the usual analytical dichotomies are no longer pertinent. . . .

In *Hommes de plein vent*, we find words whose arresting vehemence, enriched with images, provokes us to think of the writings of the prophets. The text restores an essential and sacred function to language, a song of power, pain, and hope that revives the hearts of men and immerses us in the acute consciousness of a world tormented and ravaged by history.

This is a poetry for living, but for living tall and grand. Aesthetes and critics armed with the scalpels of analysis will find their share in it, but the value of Métellus's work lies elsewhere. It is not the obvious literary quality of the work that is essential, but all that this quality demands and makes possible, because poetry draws from, and inscribes in its violence, the truth about man and life. . . .

The poetry of Jean Métellus is not a poetry of self but of the world. If language is essential to it, it is not so much as language, but as a living force that must communicate itself. The founding images are those of a vital movement. Words become the medium of a natural impulse. . . .

Here then is a poetry which, far from being separated from the body, seems on the contrary to be its emanation and its very sign. The importance of the physical world and of the senses is an adequate indication. It is, in fact, in his astonishing images of carnal vitality that Jean Métellus demonstrates his superiority.

Alain Deschamps. *Nouvelles du sud.* 1 (1985), pp. 87–89†

Having established himself as one of Haiti's foremost new writers, with four novels and three volumes of poetry, Jean Métellus has now turned to the theater with a four-act play narrating the fall of the Indian kingdoms to the gold-hungry Spaniards in the 1490s. *Anacaona* . . . is a rather odd mixture of old and new, verse and prose, epic and tragedy, history and fable, and black and Indian cultures. Métellus has found an obviously interesting historical figure, the poet-queen from a peace-loving culture, given power by her older brother seemingly paralyzed by an intuition of looming disaster, married to a somewhat opportunistic warrior from an inimical group. She must make the final decision: to fight or bargain.

Having already seen the massacres produced by the superior arms of the Spanish, and also the results of the Spaniards' treachery, Anacaona hesitates; her indecision in the long debate with her advisor Yaquimex reflects classical notions of tragedy. The tension between the roles of poet and queen dramatizes the struggle between individual and historical forces. Ultimately, however, the play seems neither tragedy nor epic, but more of a poetic reverie, an attempt to realize the impossible, to make this Indian queen accessible to the twentieth century.

Hal Wylie. *World Literature Today.* 61, 3 (summer 1987), p. 480

*Les Cacos* . . . shows us once again how history can be enlivened and made fertile by the art of an author. Perhaps one must be more precise and say that the author reveals to us, in all the diverse meanings of the word, that which certain dictionaries and historical essays tell us with far too much discretion. . . .

The novel adds to history to the extent that it shows us, in a setting alive with authentic events and precise facts, human beings in their everyday reality. We see these *cacos*, i.e., these revolutionaries, not as perfect heroes of an intrepid and pompous guerrilla, but as the inhabitants of this country, attached to their land, their customs, their beliefs, their language also, and with their faults, their courage, their weakness, their certitudes, and their hesitations. . . .

One of the great originalities of this work lies in this, the detailed, lively, and flavorful painting of psychologies and attitudes. The novelist helps us to capture the historic truth of an epoch in the hearts and in the spirit of the protagonists, in the subtle detail of their reflections and their reactions. References to current life are numerous, in measure with novelistic necessity and avoiding the falsity of exoticism or local color. . . .

Religion and beliefs, in their expression and popular practices, play a very important role in thoughts as well as social and political attitudes. Here we touch upon a sort of poetic or even magic realism—either in the emotion or in the irony that allows us to better understand Haiti and Haitians. The language of the narration also helps us, either by the rather developed quotations of the Creole language, with its French translation, or by the very French of the writer, subtly impregnated with this essential linguistic reality.

One then understands that the life and tragic destiny of the few principal heroes, *les cacos* Alexandre and Thémistocle whom we follow in their daily life, to the maquis and to combat, are not the only elements of the novelistic plot. It is true that their characters are numerous, but, in truth, it is an entire people in the diversity of their pain and their combat, that Jean Métellus is describing to us.

Pierre Gamarra. *Europe.* 67, 722–23 (June 1989), pp. 174–76†

In *Charles Honoré Bonnefoy*, the title, like a nameplate or a door or a desk, introduces an exemplary man of science who has "la passion d'enquêter, de comprendre, d'expliquer." Faithful to his name, he truly is a man of good will, dedicating his whole life to the pursuit of truth, observing, and probing, in a constant dialogue with the human body.

The first ninety pages of the novel cover a single day in June, the day when, after thirty years as head of neurology at La Salpêtrière Hospital in Paris, Bonnefoy, at seventy, is supposedly retiring and holds his last public consultation, lionized by students and colleagues. It is far from being the end for Bonnefoy (or the novel), however. The septuagenarian regards his retirement as the beginning of a new life, continuing with renewed vigor to pursue his lifetime interests. . . . Bonnefoy is in love with life, in all its aspects, including intellectual stimulation, and is ready (the very next day) to embrace new responsibilities at a public assistance hospital near Paris, always "au service de la vérité," even if it means for him, at the end, a broken nose!

The novel is written mostly in dignified classic French (using *vous* and the preterit), as befits a well-bred man always wearing a three-piece suit. He has refined tastes (fine cuisine and fine books), and is fond of quoting to himself, as he goes on his walks, such authors as Dante, [Agrippa] d'Aubigné, [Jacques Benigne] Bossuet, [Louis] Bourdaloue, Saint-Simon, and Mme. de Sévigné. Bonnefoy is not an isolated case, one of the characters remarks, but rather "une sorte de quintessence de ce milieu." Specialized terms deriving from cases studied by the neurologist naturally abound in the novel. . . . There is a long monologue in the form of a professor's farewell speech, and large chunks of doctor-patient dialogues interspersing description/narration. The book is a serious one, written by a moralist and expressing his philosophy, particularly about aging and the public image of old age, which he fights to change through his own example.

*Charles Honoré Bonnefoy*, like its protagonist, exudes an appetite for life, "une grande joie de vivre." Like Métellus, Bonnefoy is an artist and a poet in his appreciation of nature, as seen in flowers, fruit trees in bloom, gardens. He has an impressionist's love of light and "tastes" colors like a Haitian primitive painter. He too likes to paint, as he likes to cook or to caress the books he collects, celebrating "the motionless poetry of the printed page." A man of the intellect, he is also a man of the senses.

Danielle Chavy Cooper. *World Literature Today*. 65, 4 (autumn 1991), p. 754

Jean Métellus is probably Haiti's most active author at present. Trained as a linguist but currently working as a neurologist in France, Métellus published several novels—including *Jacmel au crépuscule*, *La Famille Vortex*, *Une Eau-forte*, and *L'Année Dessalines*—as well as several volumes of poetry and one play in the 1980s. These works have made a name for him even though little scholarship has yet been devoted to them.

Readers have already encountered members of the Vortex family in other novels. [In *Louis Vortex*] Louis recapitulates, in many ways, the story of his father, but brings us up to the 1950s; it seems likely that he also reflects the existence of the author, for the theme, clearly delineated here, is exile. Indeed, this work is more an essay, or meditation, upon the problem of being obliged to live far from one's childhood roots, than it is a real novel. The fictional

character of Louis Vortex serves to allow a certain detachment necessary for analysis of the particular patterns of stress and alienation experienced in exile.

Like Vortex, Haitian literature has a bifurcated existence today; there are almost two separate literatures, one inside and one outside the country. In *Louis Vortex* Métellus suggests that Haiti itself has come to have the same double existence: within/without. . . . Many writers live in exile, and studies have been written on the way this reality influences their writings; but few care to discuss their feelings about exile. Métellus shows in Vortex why the exiled person finds himself in a double bind which becomes almost a kind of bad faith. When Louis starts to develop new roots in France, he is accused by his friends of betraying his family and homeland. Métellus is original in analyzing the dialectics between the two countries, old and new, and the resulting psychological complexities.

Exile involves several kinds of alienation, each dramatized in certain episodes of *Vortex*. Louis is first seen as numb, but he is eventually drawn into three involvements that remake him. His friendship with Nadine becomes a love affair, a substitute for his wife and family left behind in Haiti. His fervent Catholicism lands him a teaching job at a Catholic school; religion and vocation become one. Later, he turns from religion to political faith, resigning his job in order to devote himself completely to the overthrow of the oppressive regime.

Louis's authentic self, however, is hard to find. We know he is a Don Juan, a lover of fine food, and a smooth talker. Eventually his penetrating analysis distances him from his activist friends as he sees their opportunism, personal agendas, and illusions. Here Métellus seems to be using the 1950s as an allegory for the confused political situation of 1992; the events of the return of Louis's friend Regis to Haiti are more plausible in the post-Duvalier context; the "collective fury" reflects the *déchoucage* (retribution) and "necklacing" of the last five years.

Louis finally decides to abandon the hope of return and to accept exile, sending for his wife and children. The rhetorical bent of the novel leads to the justification of integrating oneself in the host society. Many will find this a painful message, but the logic of Métellus's essay-novel is quite forceful.

Hal Wylie. *World Literature Today*. 66, 4 (autumn 1992), p. 759

In his dramatization of the genocide of Haiti's indigenous Indian population, Jean Métellus sets himself the task of reading the island's future in the archives of Haiti's graveyards. Without being didactic, Métellus's *Anacaona* and *Colomb* do have a teaching purpose. They retrace the history of the Indians who lived in Haiti (Ayti) before the arrival of the Conquistadors and their African slaves. In this retracing of history we have a political theatre which calls into question that which and those who allowed this atrocious massacre to take place, and which echoes the dilemmas facing post-Duvalier Haiti. . . .

*Anacoana* and *Colomb* come to us within this historical and theatrical context where retracing a country's history acts as both a looking forward and a looking backwards, a search for brighter tomorrows and an understanding of a more sombre past. Like many Haitian exiles, Métellus views his work as a bridge-building between life in his adopted home (for Métellus, Paris) and his native land. Turning from novel and poetry in the mid 1980s,

Métellus seized on the character of Anacoana, the famous poet-queen of Xaragua (southern Haiti) who married Caonabo, the ruler of Maguana (south-central region of the island), in order to bring about peace. In *Anacaona*, Métellus plunges his audience into the kingdom of rich Indians massacred by the Spanish for Ayti's gold. By invoking Anacaona's memory, Métellus aims to inspire his people to stand up tall in the aftermath of the Duvalier nightmare and build a new realm of justice and freedom, just as Anacaona had bravely faced the Conquistadors centuries ago.

In constructing Anacaona's past, Métellus has us relive on stage the poet-queen's dance and verse. Her lyrical strength and beauty rivet our attention on that which was lost when the conquering Columbus and Cortes enlarged the Old World by crushing the New. Furthermore, though it retraces Anacaona's history and political commitment, the play gives pride of place to 'la parole haïtienne'. The Queen's poetry has the power of the samba to communicate her legacy. The beautiful poetry orchestrates the clash between Indian and Spaniard. Her strong dramatic, lyrical voice puts fear in the conquistadors. And her poetry thus precipitates the drama as the invaders kill the queen in order better to 'pacify' the country. Though Anacoana has forged peace on the island by charming Caonabo, her poetry strikes fear in the hearts of the Spaniards. She offers to negotiate but they imprison Caonabo after the defeat of his army and hang Anacaona. In the aftermath of bloodshed, Yaquimex, a resistor, communicates with the African slaves and they plan to escape and establish rebel communities in the mountains. By reinvigorating the poetess's voice, Métellus weaves and binds together the two parts of his literary and theatrical work: he recounts Haiti's tragic past and gives a leading role to poetry.

In *Colomb*, Métellus again allies history and poetry. This time, however, he focuses on the Spanish side of affairs choosing Columbus as his central character. In this five-act tragedy, Métellus searches for a way of understanding and explaining that Columbus's fault was not the discovery of the Americas but his failure to stop the plundering of their new discovery.

Métellus thus places his theatre firmly in the context and tradition of Antillean drama epitomized by Aimé Césaire. This tradition is full of Caribbean history with a very African and diasporic side with the creation of a dynamic and powerful poetic abounding in African imagery. Métellus's political commitment offers a slightly different perspective on Caribbean history. Whereas Césaire, Édouard Glissant, or Derek Walcott focus on the Haitian slave revolt of the late 1790s and early 1800s, Métellus goes further into the past to evoke the Ayti's history prior to slavery. Capturing the Indians' struggle against invasion, Métellus's classical style does not take away from his commitment since he raises the spectator to new artistic heights which allow him/her to complete the false or incomplete vision of Haitian history offered by television and newspaper reporters, and biased history.

By celebrating *Anacoana* and by re-visiting Columbus through Haitian poetry and imagery, Métellus brings to the stage the first genocide in Ayti, and he reminds us of the destruction and loss, but also invokes the immense capacity of the Haitian people to rebuild. As the Haitian people broach a new era, the work of Jean Métellus accompanies René Préval, the newly elected President, in the struggle to bring justice and freedom to the Caribbean's oldest independent state.

Guette Adanser. *Theatre Research International.* 21, 3 (fall 1996), pp. 245–55.

BIBLIOGRAPHY

*Au Pipirite Chantant*, 1978; *Jacmel au crépuscule* (Jacmel at Dusk), 1981; *Hommes de plein vent* (The Men of Full Wind ), 1981; *La Famille Vortex* (The Vortex Family), 1982; *Une Eau-forte* (An Etching), 1983; *Voyance*, 1985; *Anacaona*, 1986; *L'année Dessalines*, 1986; *La Parole Prisonnière*, 1986; *Haiti: Une Nation Pathétique*, 1987; *Les Cacos* (The Revolutionaries), 1989; *Charles Honoré Bonnefoy*, 1990; *Le Pont Rouge*, 1991; *Colomb*, 1992; *Louis Vortex*, 1992; *Voix Nègres*, 1992; *Prénoms; de Femmes*, 1996; *Voyage à Travers le Langage*, 1996; *Les Dieux Pèlerins*, 1997

# MITTELHOLZER, Edgar (1909–1965)
## Guyana

There is always a certain fascination in reading of primitive peoples, of their ways and customs and what seem to be their curiously restricted lives, but such accounts are usually to be met with in biographies or books of travel; it is seldom that the novelist succeeds in presenting these people in such a way as to hold the interest of the reader of fiction, who does not easily identify himself with the lives and thoughts of primitive society, but that is what Mr. Edgar Mittelholzer has, with this novel [*Corentyne Thunder*], succeeded in doing. He shows us an old East Indian commander living with his two daughters on the savannah in British Guiana. Their home was a one- roomed mud hut, their food rice and salt fish, with a curry feed once a month when the moon was full, and their relaxation when the day's work was done, singing to the beating of a goatskin tom-tom. . . .

There is an odd beauty in this book and a haunting pathos. The scenes, painted vividly and yet with an admirable restraint, live on in the mind, and the differing personalities that emerge, almost painfully, through the clouded mentalities of the principal characters, are instinct with life.

*Times Literary Supplement.* May 24, 1941, p. 249

[*A Morning at the Office*] is a story well worth a place on the bookshelf. The language flows with ease and grace, and the form of the novel is surprising and entertaining. The author maintains a clear unity by relating his frequent digressions to a particular morning in a Trinidad office. Though lightly held together, the threads of the story firmly weave the pattern of fourteen lives into an artistic tapestry depicting an authentic moment in West Indian life.

The authenticity never falters, and therein lies the power of the book. The writer is benignly objective and uses the morning as a convincing opportunity to describe the people of the West Indies whom he loves with fine understanding of human strength and weakness, and whom he knows in all their enchanting variety of race. . . .

Within the poetic licence of a theory of "Telescopic Objectivity," the author tells certain incidents in the past of a key, a desk, and a door in the office. These incidents influence the present and future of people in the office. I found this device intriguing and extremely well handled by the writer.

This novel is admittedly limited in scope, but within the limits that he has set himself the author shows that he is a serious craftsman of vivid imagination from whom, I hope, will come much, and more profound, writing. *A Morning at the Office* is a distinct indication of his ability.

Margery Foster-Davis. *Carolina Quarterly*. 1, 4, 1951. pp. 43–44

I felt a great admiration for Mittelholzer for the simple reason that he refused to take any permanent employment in Trinidad. There was a reverse of the division of labour in the family. His wife went to an office; and he did the housework, shopping and the lot, leaving himself some seven or eight hours a day for writing. In Trinidad at the time (it's as late as 1946) a man who made Mittelholzer's commitment, and for the same reason, was regarded in much the same way I imagine that the French peasants came to regard Joan of Arc. They didn't call him a witch; but they said he wasn't altogether right in the head. This is always a way in the West Indies of warning that no-one will take you seriously. . . .

Why Mittelholzer is important is that he represents a different generation from [Samuel] Selvon and myself. He had suffered the active discouragement of his own community, and he had had their verdict sanctioned by the consistent rejection of his novels by publishers abroad. And in spite of this he made the decision, before anyone else, to get out. That is the phrase which we must remember in considering this question of why the writers are living in England. They simply wanted to get out of the place where they were born. They couldn't argue, you will see, pointing to similar examples of dejection in West Indian writers who were now regarded as great figures, because there were no such West Indians. They had to get out, and in the hope that a change of climate might bring a change of luck. One thing alone kept them going; and that was the literary review. *Bim*, which was published in Barbados by Frank Collymore, was a kind of oasis in that lonely desert of mass indifference and educated middle-class treachery.

George Lamming. *Tamarack Review*. Winter 1960, pp. 48–49

[Mittelholzer's] novels abound in examples of the need for strength on the individual level, and he was consistent in the application of this philosophy even as regards himself, because we know that when he could no longer master the forces acting on his own life, he applied the principle so often expressed in his novels of victory or death, and with fortitude, sought a flaming end. This death-wish by fire was foreshadowed in his last novel, published posthumously, and looking back over the last books, we think we can discern the narrowing of horizons, the withering of faith and the crisis in belief in which he passionately identified himself with the deepening gloom on the international scene. . . .

The body of his work has a remarkable consistency and unity about it. There is a considerable complexity of elements and parts involved which he organized successfully into his stories. These stories, as a general rule, exhibit the inherent plausibility of poetic truth. We get the impression that in his stories we are kept above the humdrum of everyday living at a pitch of intense wakefulness, filling our imagination and stirring our emotion. Each novel, with its drums of suspense and magic compulsion creates a new world into which we are drawn and in which we seem to live with the illusion that we are seeing life steadily and whole.

I feel that this body of work represents a most remarkable achievement for any writer and I know that it has brought entertainment and enlightenment in many languages to thousands in many parts of the world, and bearing in mind the limitations of the society which produced him, and the pioneer nature of his tremendous single-mindedness and discipline, I feel Edgar Mittelholzer must take a high place indeed in the history of our young literature of Guyana and the Caribbean.

A. J. Seymour. *Edgar Mittelholzer: The Man and His Work* (Georgetown, Guyana: Ministry of Education, 1968), pp. 43, 53

[Mittelholzer's] work is interesting in many ways, especially for its pioneering quality; for it was his second novel, *A Morning at the Office*, which first won wide recognition for British Caribbean writing, stimulated critical interest in the region, and paved the way for the remarkable march of English-speaking Caribbean novelists who followed. Mittelholzer himself has received less critical acclaim than some of these later novelists, for example, Vidia Naipaul; but the popularity of his work has not been seriously rivalled by any other Caribbean novelist. Mittelholzer is too idiosyncratic a writer to be closely compared with any of his contemporaries, and if a parallel literary career is to be found, the closest is that of another pioneer, the early nineteenth-century American novelist Charles Brockden Brown. . . .

Since his moral aims are unfulfilled, Mittelholzer cannot be correctly called a moralist; nor can he be described as a pornographer in spite of his accounts of "the manifold perversions and vagaries of the sexual instinct," for these do not constitute his main theme or reflect his prevailing intention. He is, like the Marquis de Sade, a moralist manqué, and because he fails to achieve his moral aims, the purely artistic value of his work is inconsiderable. . . .

Only three of Mittelholzer's novels, those dealing with West Indian nationalism and colour-consciousness, fall into this category of the novel of manners; the remaining twenty-two deal mainly with psychological themes that are of both local and universal significance. Thus his greatest contribution to Caribbean literature in English is the treatment of themes not wholly limited by application to local conditions. And, in spite of the outrageous eroticism and trivial fantasy of his work, as Caribbean writing develops more universal themes, Mittelholzer will gradually come to be regarded as the true innovator of a literature that is finally free from parochialism.

Frank Birbalsingh. *Journal of Commonwealth Literature*. July 1969, pp. 88, 98, 103

In the Kaywana trilogy [*Children of Kaywana*, *The Harrowing of Hubertus*, *Kaywana Blood*], the master's lashes on the body of the slave, the throbbing sexual energy temporarily sweeping away barriers of race and even those between a mother and son, and the fearful possibilities of in-breeding and heredity, are all played out against what [O. R.] Dathorne has called the "brooding landscape" of the Guyana jungle. The trilogy goes back to the seventeenth century; through the fortunes of one family, Mittelholzer recreates the violent history of Guyana to the dawn of the twentieth century. The Von Groenwegels believe in the preservation of the strong blood. Their motto is never to surrender even if the whole world is pitted against them, a doctrine which is passed from parents to children: their mission in life is to nurture the strong streak in the family even at the expense of inbreeding. Hendriekje, a second-generation Groenwegel, perfects this outlook into a Nazi-like obsession with the power and purity of a master race of which she is the great grandmother. She argues that the stronger always survive and the weaker get crushed. Life is brutal. This is not pleasant, but a Von Groenwegel must face it as the truth. With such an obsession, a clash across the colour-line (which is also the dividing line between the slave and the master) is inevitable. And when it comes, it is full of relentless cruelty as the slaves, temporarily free, attempt to assuage a century of terror by punishing the white oppressor. . . .

The subterranean corrosive effects of . . . what yet another West Indian writer [Elliot Boshen] has called "tint discrimination" are well examined and exposed in Mittelholzer's early novel, *A Morning at the Office*. With their different shades of colour and racial origins, people working for Essential Products Ltd. superficially make a harmonious cosmopolitan picture. But they are all trapped in their skins. . . .

In this novel, Mittelholzer has portrayed the secret, psychic forces that govern people's inner thoughts in a society which has made minute differences of the skin the basis of morality and human relationship. Such a society alienates its human individuals and makes them live as exiles from themselves and from a country to which they rightly belong. [1972]

Ngugi wa Thiong'o. *Homecoming* (New York: Lawrence Hill, 1973), pp. 102, 105, 107

BIBLIOGRAPHY
*Creole Chips*, 1937; *Corentyne Thunder*, 1941; *A Morning at the Office*, 1950; *Shadows Move among Them*, 1951; *Children of Kaywana*, 1952; *The Weather in Middenshot*, 1952; *The Life and Death of Sylvia*, 1953; *The Adding Machine*, 1954; *The Harrowing of Hubertus*, 1954; *My Bones and My Flute: A Ghost Story in the Old-Fashioned Manner*, 1955; *Of Trees and the Sea*, 1956; *A Tale of Three Places*, 1957; *Kaywana Blood*, 1958; *The Weather Family*, 1958; *With a Carib Eye*, 1958; *The Mad MacMullochs*, 1959; *A Tinkling in the Twilight*, 1959; *Eltonsbrody*, 1960; *Latticed Echoes*, 1960; *The Piling of Clouds*, 1961; *Thunder Returning*, 1961; *The Wounded and the Worried*, 1962; *A Swarthy Boy: A Childhood in British Guiana*, 1963; *Uncle Paul*, 1963; *The Aloneness of Mrs. Chatham*, 1965; *The Jilkington Drama*, 1965

# MOFOLO, Thomas (1877–1948)
Lesotho

Those who believe that the negro races are incapable of great achievements should read *Chaka* . . . which paints a partly accurate and partly imaginary picture of the rise of the Zulu power in old South Africa, and combines it with a realistic study of a noble character consciously ruining itself by deliberately cultivating the quality of ferocity. . . .

The development and ruin of the central character are traced in a way that recalls the Nemesis of the Greeks. We watch with growing sympathy the cruel trails and extraordinary prowess of Chaka's boyhood, his first dealings with witch-doctors and his first romance. We watch his successive temptations by the supreme witch-doctor with alarm and soon with horror; for a trail of death and cruelty is the price of each advance towards Chaka's ultimate ambition—the lordship of all South Africa. When indeed the tempter offers him "such a chieftainship that if a man were to leave the place where thou now art, in his youth, on foot, and go to the bounds of thy territory, he would be an old man before he returned," at the price of murdering "the one thou dost love more than any other on earth," we first catch a real glimpse of the terrible path on which Chaka has entered. Gradually, as he grasps after greater and greater chieftainships and the terror of the Zulu arms penetrates across mountain and desert to the remote tribes of the North, Chaka paying each time the witch-doctor's price of greater and greater cruelty, murdering his own mother, whole tribes and peoples, whole regiments of his own armies, all our sympathy flies; but we read on, fascinated, until the final scene of Chaka's own murder by his brothers comes with a feeling almost of relief. It is a grim story, but it is not mere realism. Again and again the reader feels that he is obtaining, even amid the greatest horrors, a genuine insight into the mind and traditions of the African peoples as they were before the coming of the white man.

*Times Literary Supplement.* July 30, 1931, p. 596

Fekisi, the hero of [*The Traveller of the East*], a Mosuto herd boy, by courage and force of character becomes a leader among his fellows. Life among the cattle, on the pastures, at the drinking-places, at milking-time, and in the kraal at night raises questions in the mind of the boy. He gropes after the origins and meanings of things. . . . Dreams and visions impel him to seek the answers he craves. He resolves to leave the village secretly and travel to the East. His cattle alone discern his growing purpose and crowd closely round him, lowing in grief. The nightscene in which he takes leave of them, praising them in a great cattlesong, is equal in dramatic quality to the finest parts of *Chaka*. . . .

The story, though enriched by imagination, is obviously autobiographical in part. Fekisi's quest is so broadly human that the Western reader recognizes a familiar pilgrim way, yet the whole setting is so distinctive that every step is a discovery of the African mentality. Books such as this are the literary hope of Africa: they show us the African mind at its best and should be read by those who want to see the African in his true light.

G. A. Gollock. *Africa.* October 1934, pp. 510–11

The brazen foolishness of the average European (and American) is equaled only by his self-importance since he lost contact with the great primal myths of humanity. These ostentatious blind men could not be advised too strongly to read a book like *Chaka* by Thomas Mofolo, whose publication in France in 1940, if I am not mistaken, went practically unnoticed. This amazing book, written by a black from southern Africa, is a mixture of several literary genres. A folk tale by its subject as well as by its precise depiction of familiar details, an epic in its structure and style, this book also aims at edification, like a moral or philosophical tale, like a cosmogony. It is a masterful challenge to those who hold the theory of the inequality of the races.

Some people will retort that the author is an educated black, taught by white colonists and therefore stamped by European culture. One need only read this book, however, to realize that its beauty and power are derived essentially from its local material and its author's heritage. In *Chaka* Mofolo uses legends and (if I can believe my friend the poet Senghor) historical facts to develop one of the fundamental themes in world literature—the will to power. . . .

Chaka is Faust, a young Faust thirsty for power, to whom Issanoussi-Mephistopheles, the supreme Tempter, proposes a bargain whose price is Chaka's damnation. Yet how gentle and childlike Doctor Faust seems compared to Chaka! Faust's only crime, after all, is wanting to escape from the laws of nature and to enjoy for eternity the most precious possession—youth. Chaka, on the other hand, agrees to become a *monster* in order to rule. A renegade, a traitor, a perjuror, the murderer of his brothers, his mother, and his wife, he takes on the symbolic role as enemy of humanity. Because *Chaka* makes us see the numerous crimes through which all personal power is purchased, Mofolo's work is healthy and necessary. Reading it, one is reminded of the monstrous cult that still surrounds a soldier of fortune like Napoleon in France, especially in our schools.

Luc Decaunes. *Presence Africaine.* No. 5, 1948, pp. 883–84†

Thomas Mofolo, having schooled himself in the traditions of his own people, as well as in the mission literature of the English (of which Bunyan was probably the most notable example), as a writer was able to synthesize the customary notion of ''doctoring'' the chieftain with the folk-Christian idea of a pact with the devil. This fusion gives a strong spinal column of credibility to his Chaka story. The double necessity of a periodic magical renewal (Zulu) and of a final reckoning (Christian) ensures an accumulation rather than a mere concatenation of horrors, a regular teleology of the evil will. Each time Chaka is doctored, he becomes further involved with the diabolical sources of his strength. More and more ambitious deeds of violence are actually required of him until Chaka, sickened with visions of horror, is finally murdered by those who are nearest to him in blood. . . .

In what way is Chaka an assertion of [Mofolo's] Negritude? Perhaps in the same way that Milton's Satan is an assertion of the poet's proud, rebellious will. Senghor, like the English romantics who later made Satan the hero of the piece, has temporarily abrogated the moral framework in which Mofolo wrote. The highest tribute Mofolo's imagination could pay to the bloody hero whom his mission teachers condemned was to put him in league with the Christian devil. The horror and atrocities of his career put the great Zulu forever on the map of Africa, and any honest person who had not been exposed to modern theories of the great Immoralist, of the romantic Scourge, would have left him to the vultures in the end. That the vultures would not have him is proof of his magical invulnerability in legend, of Mofolo's deepest desire to leave him so.

Judith Illsley Gleason. *This Africa* (Evanston: Northwestern University Press, 1965), pp. 56, 65

Mofolo's skill in enlivening a situation is amply illustrated in many parts of [*Chaka*]. A good example is the scene at the river pool where Chaka is bathing at dawn, when he is visited by the King of the Deep Waters. In the calm and tranquility which reigns all around, things begin to happen suddenly, vigorously, briefly—e.g., the sudden quivering of the tuft of hair on his head and the throbbing of the skin under it; the sudden chilly wind that agitates the reeds and makes them sway madly to and fro; the sudden vigorous billowing of the water, etc.—all these things, happening one after another, begin suddenly, proceed vigorously but only briefly, and everything is normal again just as suddenly. Mofolo very skillfully uses the doubled verb and the ideophone to dramatize these happenings. He doubles his adverbs and some of his adjectives for emphasis; occasionally he draws out a vowel to achieve emphasis through syllable length.

Mofolo is a master in the creation of an atmosphere. The piece about the last days of Chaka is quite a masterpiece in itself, when Chaka is *alone*, and all his greatness and renown have turned sour in his mouth. He is alone in many senses: He is outside of the village with only a few regiments; it is night; the warriors for their part are sleeping, yet *he* is kept from sleep by his horrible dreams; the stillness of the night is pierced by the howl of a dog left alone as its owners either perished at the spear of Chaka's warriors, or ran for their lives—he is now no better than that dog; he is alone, like the orphans and the widows and widowers of those whose corpses have been devoured by the wolves, of which he is reminded by the shriek of a wolf in the tranquil night; but worst of all, he is alone in the knowledge of his guilt and its magnitude, and his gnawing conscience, striking violently at him in his state of subconsciousness, i.e., in his sleep *via* his dreams (for consciously he has suppressed any trace of conscience), reminds *him*, and *him* alone, that he has destroyed himself.

Daniel P. Kunene. *The Works of Thomas Mofolo* (Los Angeles: University of California, African Studies Center, 1967), p. 28

While the central idea of *Chaka* is coherently and impressively Christian, it would be an oversimplification to suggest that any other types of outlook were altogether foreign to Mofolo. . . .

It is difficult to escape the impression that at [the novel's] final stage the Christian and the Sotho in Mofolo have made room for the African, who renounces, for a brief while, his tribal rancors and his new definitions of good and evil to ponder on the past greatness of his race and on its present subjugation, finding some undivulged hope, perhaps, in the notion that the white man's empire, too, will wane some day.

It may have been this final impression that, in later times, was to enable Senegal's Léopold Sédar Senghor and Mali's Seydou Badian to extol Chaka, in poetry and on the stage, as the heroic, self-denying ruler, who does not hesitate to sacrifice the tenderest passion of the heart in order to ensure the greatness and to defend the freedom of his people. Mofolo's conception of Chaka is entirely different and, as far as can be ascertained, much closer to historical fact. The Sotho author is by no means blind to his hero's inherent greatness, but he judges him and indicts him in the name of an essentially ethical view of life. Besides the technical skill and the depth of outlook which it evinces, Mofolo's novel is unique in its successful combination of traditional African and modern Christian elements.

Albert S. Gérard. *Four African Literatures* (Berkeley: University of California Press, 1971), pp. 125–27

[In *The Traveller of the East*] Mofolo alters the hero-quest tale in an important way; not only is there little link with nature but . . . there is an abomination of man. In addition the whole, allegorical interpretation is centered on the protagonist; it is *his* search, for *his* needs, for *his* boon. Nothing like this had existed in traditional oral literature, and perhaps Mofolo is really visualizing this as the only possibility for the new emerging individual consciousness; it should bear the consequences of egocentricity. The burden of the responsibility of the tribe could be carried by one man in the oral tales, because behind him and ahead of him there was the *wholeness* of the tribe. He had come from the tribe, and to the tribe he would return. His adventures only made him more loyal, more readily able to appreciate what he had left behind; they confirmed the superiority of the tribe. But Mofolo's hero is alienated because he has lost the ability to connect with the consciousness of the tribe, which is itself disintegrating. His death confirms his pointless vacillations and the illogicality of alienation.

By contrast Mofolo's *Pitseng* is a disappointment. All his life Mofolo had to choose between the amiable offerings of Christian camaraderie and the set diet of an uncompromising art. The difficulties of the situation were made even more emphatic, especially since he was an employee of [the mission at] Morija. Only by taking this into consideration can one accept the second novel at all; it was an attempt to pacify his teachers, employers, and publishers. . . .

To say that Mofolo's two great novels [*The Traveller of the East* and *Chaka*] belong to the genre of *Pitseng* and are mere exercises in the complacency of missionary teaching is to misunderstand them and Mofolo. They are above all the quests of befuddled individuals, catapulted from the security of tribal consciousness into the personal uncertainty of metaphysical speculation. What should concern the reader of today is not the individual inquiry but the tragic necessity for it.

> O. R. Dathorne. *The Black Mind* (Minneapolis: University of Minnesota Press, 1974), pp. 125–26, 128

Thomas Mopoku Mofolo's *Chaka* has been considered the initiator of what amounts to a literary subversion of the collective black image of Shaka, the Zulus, and, in general, traditional Africa and its legendary heroes. The detailed investigation of selected black texts reveals that the current dominant black representation of Africa and its legendary heroes constitutes a black counter image that challenges the Eurocentric portrayals that malign traditional Africa and peoples of black African descent. In fact, it is this black image of pre-European Africa and its legendary heroes that Mofolo's *Chaka* seriously questions. A truism from Arthur Schopenhauer's *Essays and Aphorisms*—a truism declaring that the nations of the world are perpetually plagued by ''wars and tumults''—situates Chaka's revolutionary wars within the larger universal military context. The location of the Zulu King's warrior-oriented reign within the universal martial tradition appears to challenge the views that perceive his career as just another incidence of savagery and bloodletting in ''Dark Africa.''

Such a critique needs to begin by identifying the elements of oral epic traditions Mofolo has incorporated into *Chaka* and taking a critical look at how he has manipulated these in order to achieve his creative purpose. Some of the major oral epic elements assimilated by the novel are the noble ancestry of the hero, the mysteriousness of his birth and early youth, his supernatural and magical endowments, his pre-eminence as hero, his ability to invoke supernatural agents to aid him in his destiny, and his heroic martial ferocity. Besides the above heroic attributes, Mofolo's *Chaka* also manipulates two major epic narrative techniques: epic horror and praise singing. These African epic elements all work together to provide the structuring framework of the novel. . . .

Though Mofolo assumes the guise of the traditional African bard in his text, his preoccupation with portraying Chaka as a villain demands a massive revision of the African oral epic traditions. The most fundamental feature of the epic tradition of the Africa oral arts is the *izibongo*, which Mofolo has completely inverted in order to effect his subversion of the collective image of Chaka. African oral epics are often structured around two antithetical discourses. The discourse of glorification is devoted to exalting the image of the epic hero, while that of vilification is attuned to denigrating the villains, who are always the epic hero's archenemies. At the end of the tale, the villains are normally defeated by the epic hero. Praise songs play a major role in elevating the hero and vilifying the villains.

Mofolo has revised the *izibongo*, which informs and shapes African oral epics and heroic poetry, in order to effect his fictional subversion of the cumulative representation of Chaka and pre-European Africa. The stylistic and thematic importance of the *izibongo* in African epics is highlighted by Harold Scheub in his ''A Review of African Oral Traditions and Literature,'' where he declares that the African epic is developed within a network of praise songs: ''Weaving through the entirety of the actions of the epic is a panegyric pattern, providing the work's primary structure.'' Mofolo achieves his objective by exploiting—with a devastating effect—his ability to repeatedly negate Chaka's prodigious acts of valor, which would traditionally merit praise singing and celebration in African oral epics. The glorified version of Chaka presented by the traditional narrator—the account which lists Chaka's feats of bravery—is subverted by the neotraditional voice, similar to that of the *histor*, which comments on Chaka's acts of valor by generalizing, moralizing, and telling the reader what to think: to envision Chaka as an evil despot. Mofolo's stylistic virtuosity in thus inverting praise singing to vilification accounts for his phenomenal success in portraying Chaka as an epic villain.

> Kwame Ayivor. *Research in African Literatures*. Spring 1997; pp. 49–77

BIBLIOGRAPHY
*Moeti oa bochabela* (*The Traveller of the East*), 1907; *Pitseng*, 1910; *Chaka*, 1925

# MORRISON, Toni (1931–)
## United States

I've just finished reading Toni Morrison's book, *The Bluest Eye*, and my heart hurts. It's all I can do not to lie down and cry myself into some kind of relief from the life-pain of Pecola, the central character. She is a girl born black, poor and, by majority standard, ugly. It is also an account of the people that surround her, especially Pauline, her mother, and Cholly, her father. They are the kind of people that all black people know of—or are—to varying degrees. . . .

Toni Morrison has not written a story really, but a series of painfully accurate impressions. How all of the people she talks about arrive where we meet them is what she is about with such great precision. She gives us a sense of some of the social elements of some of the people, black and white, that contribute to the erosion of innocence and beauty. To read the book, however, is to ache for remedy.

In *The Bluest Eye* she has split open the person and made us watch the heart beat. We feel faint, helpless and afraid—not knowing what to do to cover it up and keep it beating. We think of remedies past and remedies in progress to apply somehow while the thrashing heart still beats. We must think faster and work harder and hope that maybe a new breed of people, tight with God, in some dark privacy, has a plan ready to set it all—alright.

Ruby Dee. *Freedomways.* No. 3, 1971, pp. 319–20

*The Bluest Eye* was set among unforgiving provincial black people in a small Ohio town and charted the experience of two little sisters as they watched a friend first become a pariah and then sink into madness. The book's general outline—how witnessing and understanding tragedy forces the surrender of innocence and topples wide-eyed, precocious kids into unwilling maturity—is a familiar one in American, especially Southern, fiction; but its language was unique, powerful, precise and absolutely convincing, both spare and rich at once.

Now comes *Sula*, which features another pariah, spans the years 1921 to 1965, and seems to take place in the same setting. . . . While the setting and the characters continually convince and intrigue, the novel seems somehow frozen, stylized. A more precise yet somehow icy version of *The Bluest Eye*, it refuses to invade our present in the way we want it to and stays, instead, confined to its time and place. . . .

Reading it, in spite of its richness and its thorough originality, one continually feels its narrowness, its refusal to brim over into the world outside its provincial setting.

Sara Blackburn. *New York Times Book Review.* December 30, 1973, p. 3

[In *Sula*] Morrison at first seems to combine the aims of the Black Freedom Movement and women's liberation. Sula and Nel discover when they are 11 years old "that they were neither white nor male, and that all freedom and triumph was forbidden to them." When they grow up, Nel slips on the collar of convention. She marries, has two children, becomes tied to her "nest," a slave to racism and sexism. Sula goes to the big city, gets herself an education, and returns a "liberated" woman with a strange mixture of cynicism and innocence. . . .

But the perspective Morrison gives us upon these two black women is not pure black freedom or pure women's liberation. We may wish that Nel had absorbed some of Sula's independence of mind and willingness to take risks, and had not plunged so completely into the humdrum atmosphere of conventional family life, with all its sexist and racial overtones. Yet we cannot approve the freedom that licenses Sula casually to steal Nel's husband and condemn her childhood friend to a ruined life, while she just as

casually abandons him. That is not freedom but selfishness, and it is immoral, however contemptuous we may be of the pitifully conventional virtues of married life, or however much we may feel that marriage oppresses women. Besides, the freedom that Sula achieves is as much a prison as it is liberation. Totally free, she becomes obsessed with herself, unable to love, uncontained by the normal rules and boundaries we have come to associate with human beings.

Morrison does not accept—nor does she expect us to accept—the unqualified tenets of either of the two current freedom movements. There is more to both society and the individual, and she subjects each of these to a merciless analysis.

Jerry H. Bryant. *Nation.* July 6, 1974, p. 24

The ordinary spars with the extraordinary in Morrison's books. What would be a classically tragic sensibility, with its implacable move toward crisis and the extremes of pity and horror, is altered and illuminated by a thousand smaller, natural occurrences and circumstances. There is death, and violence and hubris; but young girls bicker about menstruation and complain when their mothers insist that they apply clothespins to their noses as a beauty tactic. Spring brings ants and peach pits and scratched knees; fall, cod-liver oil and brown stockings. The very ordinary restlessness of two girls on a summer day suddenly gives way to tragedy; death joins the stock of adolescent secrets they share. But teenage boys continue to strut on street corners; and errands must be run for parents. Morrison has a musician's sense of tone, texture, and emotional balance. Her themes are the stark and painful plots; her improvisations are the sounds, smells, tastes, habits, idiosyncrasies that surround them. . . .

Toni Morrison's books are filled with loss—lost friendship, lost love, lost customs, lost possibilities. And yet there is so much life in the smallest acts and gestures—Sula and Nel giggle over an old joke, the whores gossip in front of Pecola—that they are as much celebrations as elegies.

Margo Jefferson. *Ms.* December 1974, pp. 34–35, 39

*Sula* is more fully dominated by the title character [than *The Bluest Eye*], and Sula's characterization is the more complex; in both novels, however, the protagonist is forced into premature adulthood by the *donnée* of her life. Pecola's comprehension of her world is never articulated for either the other characters or the reader; Sula, too, remains a partial enigma both in and out of her narrative. But the pain that each experiences is made vivid and plain. Taken together, the two novels can—and I think must—be read as offering different answers to a single question: What is to become of a finely attuned child who is offered no healthy outlet for her aspirations and yearnings? Pecola escapes in madness; Sula rejects society for amoral self-reliance. For both, sensitivity is a curse rather than a blessing. Morrison's second novel, though richer in many ways, is essentially a reworking of the material of the first with an alternative ending. Though her characters' problems are conditioned by the black milieu of which she writes, her concerns are broader, universal ones. Her fiction is a study of thwarted sensitivity.

Joan Bischoff. *Studies in Black Literature.* Fall 1975, p. 21

If metaphor, and much of [Toni] Morrison's writing in general, represents a return to origins, it is not rooted in a nostalgia for the past. Rather, it represents a process for coming to grips with historical transition. Migration to the North signifies more than a confrontation with (and contagion of) the white world. It implies a transition in social class. Throughout Morrison's writing, the white world is equated with the bourgeois class—its ideology and lifestyle. This is true of *Song of Solomon*, where Macon Dead's attitudes toward rents and property make him more "white" than "black." It is true of *Tar Baby*, where notions of bourgeois morality and attitudes concerning the proper education and role of women have created a contemporary "tar baby": a black woman in cultural limbo. And it is made dramatically clear in *The Bluest Eye*, whose epigrammatic introduction and subsequent chapter headings are drawn from a white middle-class "Dick and Jane" reader. In giving voice to the experience of growing up black in a society dominated by white, middle-class ideology, Morrison is writing against the privatized world of suburban house and nuclear family, whose social and psychological fragmentation does not need her authorial intervention but is aptly portrayed in the language of the reader: "Here is the family. Mother, Father, Dick, and Jane live in the green-and-white house. They are very happy."...

In Morrison, everything is historical. Objects, too, are embedded in history and are the bearers of the past. For those characters closest to the white bourgeois world, objects contain the residues of repressed and unrealized desires. For Ruth Foster in *Song of Solomon*, the daughter of the town's first black doctor and wife of the slumlord, Macon Dead, a water mark on a table is the stubborn and ever-present reminder of her husband's remorseless rejection. The bowl of flowers around which their hatred crystallized is no longer present; only its sign remains, an opaque residue indelibly written into the table. If, for the bourgeois world, experience is capable of being abstracted to the level of sign, this is not the case for the world of the marginal characters. To cite an example from the same novel, Pilate, Ruth Foster's sister-in-law and in every way her antithesis, enjoys a special relationship to all levels of natural experience—including a specific shade of blue sky. Now, color does not function as a sign in the way that the water mark on the table does. While it bears a concrete relationship to a real object (the blue ribbons on Pilate's mother's hat), it is not an abstract relationship in the way that the water mark stands for the bowl of flowers. For Ruth Foster, the water mark is an "anchor" to the mental and sexual anguish imprisoned in the sign. In contrast, when Pilate points to a patch of sky and remarks that it is the same color as her mother's bonnet ribbons, she enables her nephew, Milkman (Ruth Foster's overly sheltered son), to experience a unique moment of sensual perception. The experience is liberational because Pilate is not referring to a specific bonnet—or even to a specific mother; rather, the color blue triggers the whole range of emotions associated with maternal love, which Pilate offers to anyone who will share the experience of color with her.

In contrast to the liberational aspect of *Song of Solomon*, Morrison's ... novel *Tar Baby*, registers a deep sense of pessimism. Here, cultural exiles—both white and black—come together on a Caribbean island where they live out their lives in neatly compartmentalized bourgeois fashion: the candy magnate, Valerian Street, in his stereophonic-equipped greenhouse; his wife, cloistered in her bedroom; and the servants, Ondine and Sydney, ensconced in their comfortable quarters. Daily life precludes the "eruption of funk," a lesson poignantly taught when Margaret Lenore discovers the bedraggled wild man, Son, in her closet. While Son's appearance suggests Rastafarianism and outlawry, any shock value stirred by his discovery is canceled when he, too, proves to be just another exile. Except for one brief incident, when Ondine kills a chicken and in plucking it recalls a moment from her distant past when she worked for a poultry butcher, there are no smells, tastes, or tactile experiences to summon up the past. Rather, there is a surfeit of foods whose only quality is the calories they contain.

In contrast with Morrison's earlier novels, the past in *Tar Baby* is never brought to metaphoric juxtaposition with the present. Rather, it is held separate and bracketed by dream. When Valerian Street, sipping a brandy in his greenhouse, lapses into daydream, his recollection of the past, which in essence contrasts entrepreneurial capitalism to modern corporate capitalism, does not intrude upon his present retirement. The past is past, and the significant historical transition evoked is perceived as inaccessible and natural. ...

As Morrison sees it, the most serious threat to black culture is the obliterating influence of social change. The opening line from *Sula* might well have been the novel's conclusion, so complete is the destruction it records: "In that place, where they tore the nightshade and blackberry patches from their roots to make room for the Medallion City Golf Course, there was once a neighborhood." This is the community Morrison is writing to reclaim. Its history, terminated and dramatically obliterated, is condensed in a single sentence whose content spans from rural South to urban redevelopment. As throughout Morrison's writing, natural imagery refers to the past, the rural South, the reservoir of culture which has been uprooted—like the blackberry bushes—to make way for modernization. In contrast, the future is perceived as an amorphous, institutionalized power embodied in the notion of "Medallion City," which suggests neither nature nor a people. Joining the past to the future is the neighborhood, which occupies a very different temporal moment (which history has shown to be transitional), and defines a very different social mode, as distinct from its rural origins as it is from the amorphous urban future.

Susan Willis. In Henry Louis Gates Jr., ed. *Black Literature and Literary Theory* (New York: Methuen, 1984), pp. 264, 268–71

*Sula* is the story of black women.... The story begins with a description of the Bottom, a black slum of the Southern town Medallion; and with the story of a World War I soldier who is released from an army hospital while still having problems with hallucinations, is arrested for his peculiar behavior, and is finally sent home to the Bottom, which he had not seen since going into the army. He seems to be crazy, and doesn't know what has happened to him. He establishes an annual holiday in the Bottom called National Suicide Day: on this day every year people can let out their anger and their violence acceptably. He lives alone, and generally celebrates the holiday alone. He supports himself by catching fish twice a week and selling them. This is how the book begins. It begins this way to register that the people in it, and the work they do, and the life they lead, are not normal. But this is the life of the vast majority in the South; from 1971, when the book was published, until this very day.

We are introduced to two girls: Sula and Nel. They are very good friends. The level of their lives is very low, and they go through much together. There is something harmonious between them. They are not separated even by the accidental death of a small boy who drowns while playing with them; even by the bizarre incinerations of two of the people Sula lives with. They grow up around, and in spite of, the daily poverty and tragedy. Nel gets married to a man named Jude. Sula sees that he is a handsome, hard-working, well-meaning young man. She helps with the wedding and reception, and then leaves town.

Ten years pass between the wedding and the beginning of the next chapter: 1927–37. Nel is still with Jude; they are living well, and have two or three children. Sula returns well-dressed, sophisticated, and college-educated. She and Nel seek to rediscover that friendship which they had before, but Sula is unable to accommodate herself to the old society. One day, Nel comes home to find Sula and Jude together in the bedroom, and Jude leaves her that day. Sula does not particularly want Jude; she begins sleeping with men in the town and is further distanced from the other townspeople. She becomes, at one point, really attached to a man; but it is, of course, at that point that he leaves her. . . .

Now, this black woman has gone to all of these most important towns and places of social life in the United States, found them no good, and has gone back to Medallion. That is a very bold thing to write about. [Morrison] tells us why Sula returns—because everywhere she goes the men and the problems and emptiness with them are always the same. The important thing about that is that it could, and would, be said by women on every level of society in the world today, from the highest to the lowest. This woman could not find a man who would treat her as another human being, and she got tired of it and went back to her hometown. So on the one hand, the friendship between women, that is so often ignored, is really of great importance; and on the other hand, no matter how hard she tries, she just learns that friendship with a man is impossible.

Toni Morrison is saying that in this society, with the lives they lead, this is what happens to men and women; this becomes characteristic of the love relationship. I find it astonishing and revealing that Morrison should insist that this tremendous insight come from a poor black woman, on the lowest level of American society. She is also saying that the real fundamental human difference is not between white and black, it is between man and woman.

C.L.R. James. *At the Rendezvous of Victory: Selected Writings* (London: Allison & Busby, 1984), pp. 264–66

There is nothing in the history of the belletristic relationship between the West Indian and the Afro-American to prepare the reader for the portrait of Elihue Whitcomb in Toni Morrison's *The Bluest Eye*. And although his is undoubtedly a negative portrait (perhaps the most insidious of all the West Indian portraits in the Afro-American novel—the most insidious because through a process of intellection he refines his profound emotional and spiritual illnesses almost beyond recognition), the reader cannot justly resign him to the status of a stereotype. Like his illnesses, he is multidimensional and, unlike the West Indian stereotypes, there is nothing in his make-up or in the tone of the narration to suggest that the portrait is meant as an attack on that small group of inbred West Indian mulattoes on whose idiosyncrasies and vagaries the portrait is based. To find possible prototypes to the deracinated but highly stylized consciousness of Elihue, the reader must look outside the parameters of Afro-American literature, perhaps to the narrator of

Orlando Patterson's West Indian novel, *An Absence of Ruins*, or even to the narrator of Dostoevsky's *Notes from Underground*. But unlike Dostoevsky or Patterson, Morrison allows the reader to approach her character through the limited omniscience of a narrator. It is because of the emotional, moral, and aesthetic detachment of the narrative voice that the reader is able to see Elihue in all his transcendent corruption without calling judgments into play, without, that is, making an attempt to label Elihue.

Melvin B. Rahming. *The Evolution of the West Indian's Image in the Afro-American Novel* (Millwood, New York: Associated Faculty Press, 1986), pp. 54–55

In theme and style Toni Morrison's novels are a fine example of vintage wine in new bottles. Her exploration of the impact of sexism and racism on the lives of black women in her gothic fables provides a more complex and, perhaps, controversial vision of the personalities and bonding of fiercely alive modern black women than the idealized images of most writers of the 1960s. Particularly in *The Bluest Eye* and *Sula*, she distills history and fact with the poetic freedom and gothic vision of modernist and postmodernist writers. Her sharp eye for the concrete details and telltale gestures that evoke a sense of place and character in the fables and *Song of Solomon* are complemented by a wonderful gift for metaphor and metonymy that are as penetrating in their insightfulness as they are arresting in their freshness and suggestiveness. Her characters are eccentric and maimed as a result of their experience as black men and women in an environment that rigidly defines their humanity by economic, sexual, and racial myths, but still they persevere in their efforts to cope with or triumph over the obstacles in their path to self-esteem, freedom, and wholeness. Thus Pecola is destroyed psychologically, Sula dies an outcast among her own, and Milkman follows the path of his African ancestor, but both Claudia and Nel survive the terror and tragedy of their friends' lives, achieving in the process a precarious adjustment to the worlds of Shirley Temple and the Bottom. Pilate's moral victory is even more Pyrrhic. Because Morrison probes the awesome will to live of her characters in order to suggest the truth of their psychic experience and the complexity of their humanity, her gothic fables . . . are a quintessential blend of realism and poetry, bizarreness and beauty, revelation and lyricism.

Bernard W. Bell. *The Afro-American Novel and Its Tradition* (Amherst: University of Massachusetts Press, 1987), pp. 276–77

Morrison transforms myths of American materialistic culture with the earned wisdom of a people grown wise through suffering. At once polemical and mythic, her novels juxtapose unrelenting realism and the transcendent authority of mythic truth. A source of the mythic substructure of her fiction is most certainly the Bible, if not the conventional interpretation of its meaning. Acknowledging her upbringing in a highly religious family whose "resources were Biblical," Morrison has noted that her family combined the Bible with other sources. "They did not limit themselves to understanding the word only through Christian theology." Her novels similarly reflect an amalgamation of mythic matter, depicting a world couched at times in seemingly contradictory truths: rebels becoming heroes, good creating evil, gardens that oppress, sins that redeem. They preserve the essential truth of myth by ironically modifying or reversing more orthodox assumptions of meaning. . . .

Though by no means imitating the Romantic poets, Morrison creates a parallel view of a fortunate Fall: the necessary and potentially redemptive passage from a garden state of debilitating innocence to painful self-knowledge and its consequences. But whereas Romantic writers tended to see the Fall more essentially as personal experience than the embodiment of communal myth, Morrison sees the fortunate Fall as a return to the true community or ''village'' consciousness. The victorious end for her involves not only the escape from the white man's Eden, but the discovery of the black consciousness muted in a white society. Certainly Morrison understands well what the Romantics learned long ago, that in a society operated by an oppressive order, not to sin in the conventional sense perpetuates an immoral justice. In such a world, innocence is itself a sign of guilt, because it signals a degenerate acquiescence. Not to fall becomes more destructive than to fall. Those of her characters who accept the debunked values of the dominant white culture construct or escape to spurious Edens: the quintessential white middle-class ''Dick-and-Jane'' house, as well as Geraldine's imitation of it, and the pretentious Fisher estate where Pauline Breedlove evades her blackness in *The Bluest Eye*; the proper if sterile Wright house in *Sula*; the Deads' house and the ''nigger heaven'' Honoré Island in *Song of Solomon*; the white man's paradise Isle de Chevalier in *Tar Baby*; the deceptive Sweet Home in *Beloved*.

And those who disrupt these Edenic worlds play the ambiguous role of serpent in a specious paradise. Morrison's novels often present us with conventionally evil characters, outsiders in a decadent, white-dominated culture, Cains and Liliths in the guise of Cholly Breedlove or Sula Peace or Guitar Bains or Son Green or Sethe Suggs. On the one hand, characters of potential violence or cruelty and, on the other hand, rebels against a morally deficient system, each one tells us in unequivocal terms that evil can be redemptive and that goodness can be enslaving. In the language of existential theology, those who sin against the flawed order become the agents of experience and so run the risk of freedom. Those who do not are often doomed to spiritual stasis and moral entropy. For Morrison herself has stated, ''Evil is as useful as good,'' and ''Sometimes good looks like evil; and sometimes evil looks like good.''. . .

In Toni Morrison's fiction, characters one way or another enact the historical plight of blacks in American society. She offers no apology for her black female perspective. Though the black experience frames and informs her fictional narratives, it in no way reduces their universality. For all their complexity and diversity, the novels are woven together by common themes: the passage from innocence to experience, the quest for identity, the ambiguity of good and evil, the nature of the divided self, and especially, the concept of a fortunate fall. Morrison works the gray areas, avoiding simple-minded absolutes. Guitar tells Milkman at one point that ''there are no innocent white people,'' but Milkman knows that there are no innocent blacks either, least of all himself. Blacks as frequently as whites inflict extreme physical and psychological violence on blacks: the Breedloves torment each other, and Cholly rapes his daughter; Eva Peace burns her son, and Nel and Sula betray the other self; Milkman callously rejects Hagar, and Guitar kills Pilate; Son takes revenge on the child-like Cheyenne, and

Jadine abandons Son; Sethe murders her daughter, and Beloved demands uncompromising payment—and of course much more. There is no doubt, though, that underlying all these manifestations of cruelty is the pernicious racism of American culture which wields its power to pervert and distort the moral center. Clearly, Morrison wants us to see the most insidious form of evil in the malevolent ability of racism to misshape the human spirit.

Terry Otten. *The Crime of Innocence in the Fiction of Toni Morrison* (Columbia: University of Missouri Press, 1989), pp. 2–5, 95

In *The Bluest Eye* and *Sula*, two of Morrison's early works, the apparent dominance of an ''ideology of the aesthetic'' directly conflicts with subtextual eruptions of feminine and feminist issues. Through complex strategies of representation, shifts in perspectives, and fragmented stories of feminine or feminist desire, the Morrison narrative, in spite of its apparent single voice, is marked by ideological ruptures and dissonance. . . .

*The Bluest Eye* depicts the struggle between two warring factions. The Dick-and-Jane frame has as its referent not only the primer but the cultural values of the dominant society. It is read and deconstructed by the lived experiences of the Breedloves. Juxtapositions of the two narratives not only reinforce the dominant theme of the novel but illuminate the novel's textual processes. Contrasts between the Dick-and-Jane world and the ''real'' world of the Breedloves are structured around several sets of binary oppositions: white/black, affluence/poverty, desirability/undesirability, order/chaos, valued/devalued. The ''truth'' of the authoritative discourse is challenged by the internally persuasive discourse. The comfortable home of the Dick-and-Jane myth is contrasted with the squalid living conditions of the Breedloves; the Dick-and-Jane family has its counterpart in the misery and violence that seem normal among the Breedlove clan; the Dick-and-Jane myth celebrates familial love, while rape and incest are rife in the Breedlove household.

The conflict is transparent, but the focus on the aesthetic and the struggles between the discourses suppress other issues in the text. The resulting text is marked by ideological dissonance and rupture. . . .

Critical readings of *Sula* have focused on the novel's extensive treatment of the relationship between Sula and Nel, a relationship generally assumed to reveal the work's specific feminist dimension. Yet closer readings show that the Sula-Nel relationship, although one of the novel's dominant themes, is contained within a larger textual enterprise. Moreover, that larger enterprise determines the relationship and is the dominant focus of the novel.

Central to *Sula* is the construction of myth, and through its strategies of narration, the form of the novel becomes dominant. The attention to minor details to effect the real, the graphic descriptions of individual acts, the detailed incorporation of folklore—all constitute the larger theme in which the Sula-Nel narrative is enclosed. . . .

*The Bluest Eye* and *Sula*, then, are narratives marked by tensions and dissonances generated by contending discourses. The primary focuses—the production of ''literariness'' and the semiotic and mythological construction of a black ''village'' or community—are disrupted by the insertion of feminine desire, which takes the form of embedded narratives that relate stories of the oppression of women, ambivalent, and ironic characterizations and representations of males, and shifts in narrative perspective that allow specific mediations by the external narrator.

Elliott Butler-Evans. *Race, Gender, and Desire* (Philadelphia: Temple University Press, 1989), pp. 63, 68, 81, 89

A decade before Michael Jordan made black synonymous with a brand name, Toni Morrison used [one] of her novels to demonstrate the futility of affirming blackness with a white label. In *Song of Solomon*, Morrison depicts the anguish of Hagar, who wakes one morning to the realization that the reason for her boyfriend's lack of interest is her looks. . . .

Morrison reveals her sensitive understanding of how commodity consumption mutilates black personhood when she has Hagar appear before her mother and grandmother, newly decked out in the clothes and cosmetics she hauled home through a driving rainstorm: her "wet ripped hose, the soiled white dress, the sticky, lumpy face powder, the streaked rouge, and the wild wet shoals of hair." If Hagar had indeed achieved the "look" she so desperately sought, she would only have been a black mimicry of a white cultural model. Instead, as the sodden, pitiful child who finally sees how grotesque she has made herself look, Hagar is the sublime manifestation of the contradiction between the ideology of consumer society that would have everyone believe we all trade equally in commodities, and the reality of all marginalized people for whom translation into the dominant white model is impossible.

Morrison's condemnation of commodity consumption as a hollow solution to the problems of race, class, and gender is as final and absolute as are Hagar's subsequent delirium and death. Unable to find let alone affirm herself, unable to bridge the contradiction in her life by way of a shopping spree and a Cinderella transformation, Hagar falls into a fever and eventually perishes.

Susan Willis. In Cheryl A. Wall, ed. *Changing Our Own Words* (New Brunswick, New Jersey: Rutgers University Press, 1989), pp. 178–79

*Sula* is too complex to be classified because Toni Morrison writes from an African point of view—an African aesthetic. Names are a vital connection to life in traditional African culture, and Sula is an African name. In the Babangi language, it means any one or a combination of the following: to be afraid, to run away, to poke, to alter from a proper condition to a worse one, to be blighted, to fail in spirit, to be overcome, to be paralyzed with fear, to be stunned. In the Kongo language Sula means electric seal—a meaning which is highly applicable to the critical thrust of this analysis. Knowing the Africanness of the major character's name adds a dimension that clarifies much of the mystery of the novel for the reader and places a demand on the critic to search for a blueprint for the novel based upon an African world-view—a blueprint that is sorely needed for African-American fiction as people of African descent wrestle with problems of identity, as we move into the twenty-first century. . . .

*Sula* is Morrison's most complex work in reference to traditional African culture. This is true because the African presence and cultural rootedness is woven into black American culture without contrivance and with such extraordinary subtlety that neither the characters nor the reader are immediately aware of it; just as most

of us are oblivious to the fact that after some three hundred plus years in America, African tradition continues to manifest itself in our lives. Black people in the Bottom of Medallion, Ohio, consider Sula and Shadrack pariahs of their community, and do not recognize their African presence.

Vashti Crutcher Lewis. In Joanne M. Braxton and Andrée Nicola McLaughlin, eds. *Wild Women in the Whirlwind: Afra-American Culture and the Contemporary Literary Renaissance* (New Brunswick, New Jersey: Rutgers University Press, 1990), pp. 316–17

In Toni Morrison's *Beloved*, a constraining definition of motherhood is a major component of the overwhelming historical past in which Sethe is mired. An extremely rich book, *Beloved* contains myriad themes—relationships between black men and women, the differing oppressions of more-brutal and less-brutal slave masters, the effects of printed materials on African-Americans of the nineteenth century, the characters and motivations of white abolitionists, and the nature of black spiritualities. This argument does not seek to explicate the entirety of the novel but, instead, to highlight a central theme. Morrison shows black women's construction of motherhood under slavery; then Sethe's paralysis because she is hampered by the limitations of this idea in the very different conditions of freedom; and finally, *Beloved* shows the joining of the past and the future to mother Sethe and offers a liberating vision of motherhood.

*Beloved* delineates African-American women under slavery who refuse to mother children not conceived in mutual desire and who fiercely defend those who are. Sethe's mother, for instance, "threw away," without naming them, all her children resulting from rape on the Middle Passage and the plantation. Similarly, when Ella bears a child fathered by one of a father-son pair who confine and rape her for years, she refuses to nurse it, and it dies soundlessly after five days. As Nan, Shipmate and friend to Sethe's mother, informs her, Sethe lives because she results from a union in which her mother "put her arms around" a black man, because the possibility of a child is chosen rather than imposed. After Sethe kills her daughter rather than allowing her to be reenslaved, she puts only "Beloved" on the tombstone, not the child's given name. In this novel, then, the very existence of any African-American person testifies to mother love and acceptance.

Missy Dehn Kubitschek. *Claiming the Heritage: African-American Women Novelists and History* (Jackson: University Press of Mississippi, 1991), pp. 165–66

The black community in *Beloved* thinks of the erratic behavior of white people as "a far cry from what real humans did," neatly inverting the stereotype Morrison chooses to pursue in *Playing in the Dark*, in which whiteness, in North American literature, is what is human, and blackness is a deviance, exciting, regrettable, or unmentionable. "Until very recently," Morrison says, "and regardless of the race of the author, the readers of virtually all of American fiction have been positioned as white." We known a character in [Ernest Hemingway's] *To Have and Have Not* is white, for instance, "because nobody says so." We would, if we were in any doubt, know he is a man for the same reason, and we may not have progressed as far as we think since 1937. . . .

Morrison's case in these lectures is not angry and partial, as some have thought, but global and rather wishful. "Africanism is inextricable from the definition of Americanness," she says. It probably should be, on the grounds that a fudged acceptance of historical responsibility is better than a blank refusal. But is it? The proposition assumes that the guilt of whites with respect to slavery is as large as it ought to be, and that the secret power of blacks bears a relation to their suffering. This is a noble story, but it isn't a story Morrison tells in any of her novels.

The story she does tell in *Jazz* has a similar generosity, but it has a nuance and a complication the lectures lack. This is not only because good fiction says more than even the most intelligent discursive prose. The story itself is different. It concerns not the black haunting of white minds, but the slow and difficult liberation of black minds from black and white oppression, from complicity with the all-knowing master of ugliness.

Morrison's chief metaphor for this movement is in her title. This is not a novel about jazz, or based on jazz, and I think reviewers' comments about the improvisatory quality of the writing underestimate what feels like the careful premeditation of the work. Each chapter after the first, for example, picks up an image or other cue from the preceding one, and takes it into new territories: caged birds, hot weather, a hat, spring in the city, the phrase "state of mind," a looks, a person, the words "heart" or "pain." This is musical and elegant, as if a tune were to be shifted into a new arrangement, but what it borrows from jazz is a sense of flight and variation, not a method of composition.

Michael Wood. *New York Review of Books.* November 19, 1992, p. 10

At the heart of Toni Morrison's novel *Beloved*, Sethe, at a critical moment, is unable to tell her lover, Paul D, the story of her dead child. "Sethe knew that the circle she was making around the room, him, the subject would remain one. That she could never close in, pin it down for anybody who had to ask. If they didn't get it right off—she could never explain." Paul D, at this point, has already seen the newspaper article featuring Sethe's picture and a story about a runaway slave who kills one of her children when the owner catches up with her. Desperate, he confronts Sethe, wanting an explanation. But she realizes that it is not a question of filling in or countering this "official version" with her own version: "Sethe could recognize only seventy-five printed words (half of which appeared in the newspaper clipping), but she knew that the words she did not understand hadn't anymore power than she had to gain." For Sethe, language cannot contain the event. . . .

How do we write or remember a history without documents, but "any songs or dances or tales"? How do we read the story "unaccounted for"? Morrison's novel is a testament to this unrelatable loss, a loss that is embodied in Beloved, and that is, in part, why Sethe cannot tell her story. Beloved, the one through which the murmurings of these millions who were killed, who lost their names, languages, families, traditions, are transmitted, is herself an impossible figure to represent. Everybody knew what she was called, but nobody anywhere knew her name. Disremembered and unaccounted for, she cannot be lost because no one is looking for her, and even if they were, how could they call her if they don't know her name?"

In this novel, the past, whether recorded or unrecorded, is one that cannot be kept at bay. It lives alongside the present,

seeking revenge, haunting the living: Stamp Paid thinks about "the mumbling of the black and angry dead" that surround 124, and Baby Suggs realizes that "'[n]ot a house in the country ain't packed to its rafters with some dead Negro's grief.'" These ghosts, like Beloved, are a reminder that the past can never really be past, that it cannot be escaped or ignored, because it is always already living alongside the present, dismantling the authority of the word, interfering with the linear narrative of history:

"Someday you be walking down the road and you hear something or see something going on. So clear. And you think it's you thinking it up. A thought picture. But no. It's when you bump into a rememory that belongs to somebody else. Where I was before here, that place is real. It's never going away."

"Rememory" impedes the logic of symbolic language, which cannot master loss but is only a mechanism that allows for a documentation of history that leaves much of the past suppressed, repressed, buried in the name of order and outside of the order of the name. Whether the past is crushed or forgotten, the novel suggests, it never really goes away because the present does not rule it, just as the symbolic does not rule loss.

Beloved, who returns from the dead to disrupt Sethe's household and the community, refuses to allow the present to feel "at home"—comfortable and reconciled with the past. She refuses to participate in the museum of history, to be part of a past that is exchanged, or sacrificed, for a future ideal. This ghost/woman is a reminder of lost futures, of futures that have failed to be, and thus she counters the dreams of a future to come that reconciles itself to the past. While, at the end of the novel, Beloved disappears without a trace, she "disappears," paradoxically, pregnant, carrying a future, like her own, that will not have been.

*Beloved* foregrounds what Rebecca Comay refers to as "countermemory which calls all accounting memory into question." Accounting-memory seeks redemption from and reconciliation with the past. Countermemory "memorializes itself as the will-have-been of what was-not-to-be: a future whose only moment inscribes the missed moment of betrayed and relinquished hope. Its presence is thus its forgone absence, its possibility just its impossibility: its self-disclosure just the gap left by its prior failure to appear." This understanding of loss, which destabilizes historical accounts, is not a rejection of history, but rather an acknowledgement that loss is a condition of history. . . .

Beloved's return disrupts the order of the symbolic, which in its insistence on the separation of self and other, white and black, male and female, past and future, orders both the racist and patriarchal paradigms in the novel. This approach to documentation has made a mockery, a hopelessly inadequate representation, of her story. Even her name, Beloved, which is inscribed on her tombstone, is borrowed from the preacher's funeral sermon, seven letters exchanged for the ten minutes of sex Sethe has with the engraver. Hence, she in turn mocks the desire to represent, to categorize, and to name. She is both adult and child, woman and ghost; at the same time that she is the unspeakable and the unknown, she is culturally and historically situated. . . .

But even as Beloved remains the "unspeakable," she offers the possibility of imagining another origin to the world. Beloved is a call from elsewhere. As the sister of Beloved, the daughter of Sethe, and the granddaughter of Baby Suggs, Denver calls into question representability and permanence and accepts in language both the possibility and impossibility of meaning. Denver as the transitional figure, born in a river that separates the free from the non-free, born with the help of a white woman and bearing her name, operating in both an oral and literate culture, also encounters a schoolteacher, but one who, instead of confining names, opens up the possibilities of language, "the beauty of the letters in her name." Denver's sense of the beauty of words seems to be inspired precisely by her ingestion of Beloved (she drinks her blood along with Sethe's breast milk), who topples symbolic logic, a logic which has forced the other to bow to the self, the world to kneel to the word. . . .

In "The Site of Memory," Morrison writes of the Mississippi River, which was straightened out to make room for homes and farms. When the River overflows, Morrison suggests, it is not flooding but "remembering where it used to be." She imagines the act of writing as an effort to return, like the River, to a place of origin. The origin, the lost place, is as much a part of history as the documents and facts that testify to the "here's and now's." Even as she works within the genre of existing slave autobiographies, which she wants to "fill in and complement," Morrison wants to hold onto the memory of where she was before she "straightened out"; working with what is there, she holds onto the force that has been lost to the order of the symbolic, the futures that have not been.

Teresa Hefferman. *Studies in the Novel*. 30, 4 (winter 1998), pp. 558–71

In Morrison's novels fruit pies and other sweet foods have a special significance. A particularly potent symbol for black women because of its association with stereotypes of femininity—"What are little girls made of? Sugar and spice and all that is nice"—and the history of slavery, sugar (and spice) being two of the main products of slave plantations, sugar acts as a signifier of race and gender power structures in her texts. For the hungry, sugar has a seductive appeal, but sugar satisfies desire only temporarily, without providing sustenance, and it can also cause disease. I will argue that Morrison's novels expose the devastating effects of hunger wrought by dispossession and warn of the dangers for black women of assimilating American "apple pie" ideology, but that they also simultaneously highlight the nourishing values of a black cultural heritage.

Morrison's novels demonstrate that, in a context of oppression and exploitation, black experience is epitomized by hunger. Morrison has said, "I think about what black writers do as having a quality of hunger and disturbance that never ends," and her novels express that hunger. The opening pages of *The Bluest Eye* (1970), a text that explores the disabling effects of dominant bourgeois values on black women and the destructive results of the internalization of white definitions of beauty on black female identity, make it clear that racial discrimination and inequality are indexed by who eats what. Claudia, the narrator, notes how social exclusion is accompanied by a lack of access to food, and Rosemary's bread and butter foregrounds the relationship between dispossession and desire:

> Rosemary Villanucci, our next-door friend who lives above her father's cafe, sits in a 1939 Buick eating bread and butter. She rolls down the window to tell my sister Frieda and me that we can't come in. We stare at her, wanting her bread, but more than that wanting to poke the arrogance out

of her eyes and smash the pride of ownership that curls her chewing mouth.

This incident reflects the experience, of the whole community. Claudia remarks that the threat of homelessness "bred in us a hunger for property, for ownership," and the threat of want ensures that the women "canned, jellied, and preserved all summer to fill the cupboards and shelves." Through Pecola, the central character, Morrison highlights the potentially self-destructive dangers that such a ravenous appetite can breed, although Pecola is characterized not by hunger but by thirst. Pecola is taught by her community and her society that because she is poor, black, and ugly, she is worthless. Consequently, seeking acceptance and a positive sense of self she wishes to be white, and every night she prays for a pair of blue eyes in the belief that they will make her beautiful and happy. While staying with the MacTeer family, Pecola becomes besotted with a picture of Shirley Temple on a cup. Pecola worships the white ideal of beauty and virtue represented by Shirley Temple and the milk. Her sense of worthlessness is metaphorically represented as emptiness, as thirst, and she attempts to find meaning in her life, to fill herself, by imbibing white cultural values. The danger in this is first intimated when her love of the cup induces her to greedily drink most of the milk, thus depriving other members of the household, and ultimately culminates in Pecola's descent into insanity.

Like Pecola, Beloved is also greedy. In *Beloved* (1987), Morrison's revisionary account of slavery which explores the consequences of a mother's attempt to save her daughter from slavery by killing her, the hunger of Beloved, the murdered daughter who returns to live with her family, outstrips that of all Morrison's other characters. When Sethe, Beloved's mother, and Denver, her sister, and Paul D, her mother's partner, first encounter her, Sethe thinks that the young girl looks poorly fed, and, ironically, when she decides to let Beloved stay, she explains to Paul D that "Feeding her is no trouble." However, as the nove' progresses, Beloved's insatiable appetite and her desire for repar tion threaten to destroy them all.

While Beloved is characterized by hunger, her hunger is or extreme manifestation of the hunger, both literal and metaph that all the characters in the book experience as part of the slavery. Moreover, given that 1987, the year of the novel' tion, marked 124 years since the abolition of slavery, th the house to which Beloved returns—124—suggests hunger that African Americans are still coming to te late twentieth century. The only difference betw those around her is that she is more voracious: ' of everything—first. The best chair, the bigges plate, the brightest ribbon for her hair." Wher daughter, in a desperate attempt to prove gives Beloved everything she has: "lul bottom of the cake bowl, the top of the m eggs, she got both." While Beloved hungers for forgiveness, all three v when their food and money run ou on food and fancy goods in an eff insatiable because nothing can r

As well as exposing the de by dispossession, Morrison k dominant (white, male, bo "apple pie" ideology, an sentation of sugar. . . .

Fruit pies play an important part in *The Bluest Eye, Song of Solomon* (1977), and *Tar Baby* (1981). In one scene in *The Bluest Eye*, Pecola, visiting her mother at work in the "beautiful" white house of the "beautiful" white family who employs her, accidentally knocks over a freshly made pie. Her mother, who unconsciously equates whiteness and economic power with beauty and thus loves the Fisher family because they are beautiful and rich and hates her own family because they are ugly and poor, scolds Pecola furiously, ignoring her bums. However, she gently reassures the daughter of the family, promising to make another pie. While she has sugary words of comfort for the white girl, she "spits out words . . . like rotten pieces of apple" to the three black girls present. Pauline happily reproduces the very values that subjugate her.

In *Song of Solomon*, which traces Milkman Dead's transition from an adherence to dominant American values to a recognition of the value of ancestry, the image of the pie is again important. Milkman's father, Macon Dead, is a property developer, and his desire for a slice of metaphoric pie—the American Dream—reveals how entrenched he is in white bourgeois American values. Macon attempts to protect his family through wealth which he acquires via property deals with white businessmen:

> He knew as a Negro he wasn't going to get a big slice of the pie. But there were properties that nobody wanted yet, or little edges of property somebody didn't want Jews to have, or Catholics to have, or properties nobody knew were of any value yet. There was quite a bit of pie filling oozing around the edge of the crust in 1945.

Macon's pursuit of the American Dream creates a "bottomless greed" that makes him obsessively materialistic, selfish, ruthless, and heartless. The unhealthiness of the values by which he lives is expressed by the image of the pie, which "spilled over into his very lap, had stickied his hands and weighed his stomach down into a sagging paunch." The destructive nature of such values is illustrated by the way in which Macon's materialism divides him from his sister, Pilate, a woman who, as her illegitimate production of alcohol suggests, lives outside the dominant rules of society. Macon forbids his family to associate with Pilate because, as a bootlegger, she might harm his reputation with white bankers. His greed is such that he is even prepared to steal from her. When Milkman tells his father about the green sack he has seen hanging from the ceiling in Pilate's home, Macon is convinced that it is full of gold. His interest is such that he is diverted from his dinner to the conversation: "As suddenly as an old dog drops a shoe when he smells raw meat, Macon Dead dropped his pleading look and flared his nostrils with some new interest."

Like Macon Dead, Jadine in *Tar Baby* represents the dangers of the American Dream for the black community. Jadine possesses unusual class status because she is the niece of Sydney and Ondine, a butler and cook employed by Valerian, a wealthy white sweet manufacturer who has retired to the Caribbean, but she has also been adopted as Valerian's protegee. Valerian has paid for her education, and since graduating from the Sorbonne, she has established a successful modeling career and has won a place at law school. So although she was born into a working-class black family, Jadine moves in the affluent circles of white privilege. Her major concern is "making it," and Jade envisages her success in terms of the quality of food she eats:

> The dinner party was memorable and nowhere had anything begun to spoil. Like the arugula leaf, life was green and

nicely curved. Nothing was limp. There were no tears or brown spots. The items on her shipping list were always there.

*Tar Baby* still makes it clear that, for Morrison, the apple pie functions as an evocative symbol of American ideological values when apples become the center of a power struggle between Valerian and Son, the working-class black man who breaks into his home and falls in love with Jadine. Margaret is adamant that she wants a traditional American Christmas dinner of turkey and apple pie, despite the fact that turkey is unavailable and apples are contraband on this Caribbean island. Margaret wants these foods in particular because Michael, her estranged son, has promised to come home for Christmas. As the novel progresses, it emerges that Margaret abused Michael as a child, and her desire for apple pie becomes symbolic of her attempt to be a good mother and create the facade of a happy family. Margaret and Ondine end up fighting, and in her fury Ondine accuses Margaret of child abuse: "You white freak! You baby killer! I saw you! I saw you! You think I don't know what that apple pie shit is for?" When Valerian fires two employees who have stolen some of the apples intended for the pie, apples that he has made them break the law and row eighteen miles to collect, Son defends them and in doing so makes the connection between the apple pie and black oppression explicit: "Two people are going to starve so your wife can play American mama and fool around in the kitchen."

Valerian epitomizes the equation of sugar with exploitative, white, male power in Morrison's fiction. The novel's setting, an unspecified Caribbean island, is a reminder that the United States' economic, political, and cultural imperialism in places like Cuba was closely tied to sugar production. Known as the Candy King, Valerian even had one of the sweets he once produced named after him, but the fact that "Valerians" are a commercial disaster creates a subtle sense of foreboding and points to the dangers implicit in his patriarchal, imperialistic power. As Son points out when Valerian fires Gideon and Therese, his wealth is based on the exploitation of Caribbean islanders and Caribbean produce, namely, sugar and cocoa. . . . Whereas Jadine "buys into" the culture that sanctions this exploitation, Son—dubbed "the chocolate eater"—desires to steal back that which the dominant culture has appropriated, as his theft of Valerian's chocolate when he is hiding in his house indicates.

Emma Parker. *Contemporary Literature*. 39, 4 (winter 1998), pp. 614–21

Morrison's novels allow us to examine the quality of human relationships under the constraints of historical processes and social relations, in the context of a collective. The emphasis on the interiority of her characters, the acknowledgment and enactment of desire in all its unruly forms, becomes a way of countering the diminishing of the subordinated, alienated self. Morrison remarked in a television interview that people often say her characters appear larger than life; she countered that they are "as large as life, not larger. Life is large." That individuals' large desires remain unfulfilled or thwarted creates the ambience of loss—a loss that adds powerful affect to the critique of history.

Through the evocation of specific, historicized landscapes of loss and erosion, the reader is made to see in individual loss—usually incurred by exceeding social limits—the limitations of the socius. It is thus that emotions of loss become charged with the intelligence of a critique. By endowing pain—itself mute and inchoate and all too personal—with a narrative that is as intelligible as it is social, Morrison makes room for recovery that is at once cognitive and emotional, therapeutic and political. Loss is both historicized and mourned so that it acquires a collective force and a political understanding. Morrison's fictive circles of sorrow invite readers to become conscious of the terrain of their lives, to recognize the terrain as not simply individual or personal but as thoroughly social, traversed by the claims of the past, occupied by conflicting ideologies of identity (class, gender, race, nationhood) that give rise to the boundaries of the self. In the novels, the place of the individual is de-isolated, the boundaries of the self shown to be permeated by the collective struggle of historical agents who live the long sentence of history by succumbing to (repeating), contesting, and remaking it.

Each novel charts a destruction recalled through the mnemonic prisms of multiple characters; the story of destruction and loss becomes a historical and political testimony that we as readers participate in as belated witnesses. As the story of loss is transferred to us, we become its interpreters, collaborating in the work of understanding. Each novel draws us into its circles of sorrow with the imperative to make sense; we do so by yielding our own knowledge of destruction and loss, by struggling alongside the characters. Unlike the healing transference between client and analyst in the consulting room—where the healing is private and concealed—the literary therapeutic narrative is social and collective, opening out into the politics of the world. The strategy of Morrison's novels is always to make sense of the individual psyche and memory in wider social and political terms. As a chronicler of African American experience, Morrison's contribution has been to create, in the face of public dissociation of a painful past, a space where the traumatic material may find a coherent articulation and a collective dimension. Her novels create a ''public space of trauma,'' a space Laurence Kirmayer defined as ''provid[ing] a consensual reality and collective memory through which the fragments of personal memory can be assembled, reconstructed, and displayed with a tacit assumption of validity.'' The construction of such a space is all the more urgent given ''the failure of the world to bear witness.'' ''The social world fails to bear witness for many reasons. Even reparative accounts of the terrible things that happen to people (violations, traumas, losses) are warded off because of their capacity to create vicarious fear and pain and because they constitute a threat to social and political arrangements.''

> Gurleen Grewal. *Circles of Sorrow, Lines of Struggle* (Baton Rouge: Louisiana State University Press, 1998), pp. 13–15

BIBLIOGRAPHY
*The Bluest Eye*, 1970; *Sula*, 1973; *Song of Solomon*, 1977; *Tar Baby*, 1981; *Dreaming Emmett*, 1986; *Beloved*, 1987; *Jazz*, 1992; *Playing in the Dark*, 1992; *The Dancing Mind*, 1997; *Paradise*, 1998

# MOSLEY, Walter (1952–)

What makes Walter Mosley's mysteries so compelling isn't his man Easy Rawlins's powers of ratiocination but the black dick's racial metaphysics. Race politics foreshadow the action in these books the way decadence foreshadowed everything that happened in Raymond Chandler's. Mosley doesn't just raise the race card to thicken the plot. He beats you down with spades, then rubs your nose in ethnic stool. Says Easy Rawlins:

> I had played the game of ''cops and niggers'' before. The cops pick you up, take your name and fingerprints, then they throw you into a holding tank with other ''suspects'' and drunks. After you were sick from the vomit and foul language they'd take you to another room and ask why you robbed that liquor store or what did you do with the money? [*Devil in a Blue Dress*]

The spotlight Mosley throws on race as power game and psychoanalytic tool makes him matter more than his being a black guy writing detective fiction straight outta 1950s Compton. Mosley is a savvy observer—philosopher first, and a mystery writer second.

His black literary forebears are everywhere in evidence. Baldwin broke the Foucauldian ground Mosley likes to work, interrogating white supremacy everywhere, from the corridors of power to the souls of black folk; race is not so much Mosley's ''theme'' as the grid set on top of his American characters. Ellison's influence shows as Mosley works the paradox of how black folks' retarded social position provides certain intellectual and moral advantages Rawlins tells the story:

> Mr. Todd Carter was so rich that he didn't even consider me in human terms. He could tell me anything. I could have been a prized dog that he knelt to and hugged when he felt low.
>
> It was the worst kind of racism. The fact that he didn't even recognize our difference showed that he didn't care one damn about me. But I didn't have the time to worry about it. I just watched him move his lips about lost love until, finally, I began to see him as some strange being. Like a baby who, grows to mansize and terrorizes his poor parents with his strength and his stupidity. [*Devil in a Blue Dress*]

In all of American fiction, only Richard Wright treats America's race problem more savagely as the shaper and breaker of men, women, and children. The black mystery's avant-garde—Chester Himes and his hoodoo stepchild, Ishmael Reed—would smile with recognition at every cartoonish plot turn, and at Mosley's wealth of exaggerated working-class character types. But Mosley's work is more psychologically insightful, empathetic, and pathos-ridden than that of Reed or Himes, and merely a hair less crazed with invention. In bridging the gap between naturalism and Negro-ism, Mosley creates queasily poignant moments that bring to mind his fellow Los Angelenophile, filmmaker Charles Burnett. . . .

Mosley writes in a page-turning style filled with tough, terse, sucker-punch sentences. *White Butterfly*, his third book in the Easy Rawlins series, lacks *Devil in a Blue Dress*'s big surprises, and *A Red Death*'s Herculean kitchen-sink subplotting. (Book two had tangents sprung loose from such fact-totems as the Holocaust, Garveyism, McCarthyism, black-Jewish relations, and black-church soap-operatic skullduggery all woven into a demented plot of domestic violence, madness, and murder.) However, for all the riches that preceded it, *White Butterfly* is the Easy Rawlins book with the heaviest heart, the deepest soul, the most boiling-over racial brain matter. Rawlins is so color-sensitive in this book that not even his librarian is spared the African-centric ire:

To her Shakespeare was a god. I didn't mind that, but what did she know about the folk tales and riddles and stories colored folks had been telling for centuries? What did she know about the language we spoke?

I always heard her correcting children's speech. "Not 'I is,'" she'd say. "It's 'I am.'"

And, of course, she was right. It's just that little colored children listening to that proper white woman would never hear their own cadence in her words. They'd come to believe that they would have to abandon their own language and stories to become a part of her educated world. They would have to forfeit Waller for Mozart and Remus for Puck. They would enter a world where only white people spoke.

Easy Rawlins was born emotionally complex, ethically confusing, intellectually enraged, and engaged. In *A Red Death*, Rawlins is revealed as a property owner who pretends he's a handyman to throw black and white folks off his well-endowed hide. He is a college-educated war veteran who speaks mushmouth black English to stay down with the folk and to divert white anxieties about smart niggas.

As Rawlins matures in the first two books, his deceits seem less strategic than eccentric, unanalyzed, maybe even counter-productive. *White Butterfly* pushes at Rawlins's existential doubt by way of the blues strains that turn up in his relationship with his younger, apprehensive wife. Even in the wake of raising an infant with her, Rawlins has told his hardworking spouse—a nurses' aide at the local hospital—nothing of his hidden wealth or his secret life as the 'hood's resident private eye. But she knows he's hiding something, denying her access to his life. The serial murders of prostitutes that are ostensibly the mystery element in *White Butterfly* are really just props for Mosley's handling of the Rawlinses' misshapen marriage. . . .

What emerges within Mosley's fluent mystery is a subtle essay on black male anxiety about openness, intimacy, and vulnerability. Mosley deftly meshes Rawlins's domestic troubles with the standard pulp fare: brutal cops, homicidal patriarchs, wicked sirens, surrealist nightmares. His crisp and writerly sleight-of-hand won't let you be distracted from the pulp by Rawlins's failure as a husband—but you know that is where Mosley's heart lies. In fact, the contrast between the profane and the profound dimensions of the story makes you wonder if Mosley will opt next to further deepen the genre with these sorts of interpersonal issues, as Chandler did around male-bonding in *The Long Goodbye*—or whether he'll move outside the genre altogether.

Greg Tate. *Voice Literary Supplement.* 109 (October 1992), p. 41

In 1961, John F. Kennedy was president of the United States, Martin Luther King was leading civil rights demonstrators in Alabama and Georgia, and Easy Rawlins was searching for Black Betty out of South Central Los Angeles.

*Black Betty* is Walter Mosley's latest novel, and Easy Rawlins is his private eye, just as Philip Marlowe was alter ego for Raymond Chandler in that same city, and Sam Spade served that purpose for Dashiell Hammett 400 and some miles farther north in San Francisco. I mention Chandler and Hammett and their private detectives, Marlowe and Spade, because I think Mosley and Rawlins fit that mold. The writer and his private eye are tough, shrewd, and knowledgeable about their cities, and they know the things, the good and the bad, that makes those cities move.

Easy Rawlins is raising two adopted children—Jesus, a little Mexican boy he rescued from a brother, and Feather, a little girl of mixed black and white parentage, and Easy is doing all he can as a single parent to bring them up well. Easy is originally from the South and he cooks his children scrambled eggs, grits and bacon for breakfast, and hamburgers at night—when he is at home. When he is in the streets searching for Black Betty, an assignment offered him by Saul Lynx, a white private detective of suspicious honesty (who thinks Rawlins can get more information than he in black South-Central L.A.), then Easy Rawlins can be as tough with the bad guys as he is tender with his children who are always on his mind. He keeps reminding himself that he ought to give up this line of work and get a regular job to support himself and his two children—but at present he needs the money that Saul Lynx is paying him to find Black Betty.

There are two or three stories going on in the novel, and it can become a little annoying, especially when you can't make the connection. But the writing is so good, and the characters that Mosley is constantly introducing are so interesting that you can't put the book down. Mosley describes people and things very well, and he has a tremendous ear for dialogue. His description of the homes of the haves and have-nots of Los Angeles, and his description of that hot Santa Ana wind, and of the desert (of a *single flower* in the desert) is as good as you would find in Chandler at his best. And his dialogue is just as good, whether he is dealing with the hoods in the street, or the police, or children, or matrons in their grand Beverly Hills mansions.

In his search for Black Betty, Easy Rawlins comes up against more bad people than anyone should have to meet. Saul Lynx is a shadowy figure himself, but he is only a shadow compared to some of the others who are real, evil and brutal. The little men all have guns, and the big ones use their muscles. Mouse is small and he is just out of jail. He is looking for someone to kill, and Easy Rawlins is on his short list. Easy has to prove to Mouse that he was not responsible for sending him to jail. Mouse only half believes him, so Easy has to find the real culprit. Another bad guy is "Commander" Stiles of the Los Angeles Police Department, who likes getting information with his fist when you are not expecting it, and, even if you are, you are surprised at his sudden move. Then there is Calvin Hodge, the Texas lawyer who represents the people who are trying to find Black Betty. Hodge likes to call the 41-year-old black detective "boy," and he has the size and build to back up his words. There are others, just as cruel, and they leave enough dead bodies to prove it.

After all this, I was mildly disappointed when I first met Black Betty. Maybe I expected too much, too many drums and trumpets. She does not sing an aria, nor does she give us a soliloquy. But what she does is wrap up things. There are a couple of other little murders on the side after she comes on stage, but she gives us the answers to the main story, which is why she had to leave the mansion after a sudden death in the family.

But Mosley is not quite satisfied that Black Betty has given us all the answers. He feels that we need to know more about the remaining characters, and I think he did this hurriedly. He felt that he needed to tell us more about Mouse and some of the others when I don't think it was necessary.

This novel can be read as a simple detective story, and it can be seen as a comment on a people, place and time, as any good piece of fiction should be. Though the civil rights movement in the South is hardly ever mentioned—and certainly no character speaks to prophesy the Watts Riots—Easy Rawlins and other blacks in South Central suffer many of the same indignities that their/our brothers were suffering in the Southern part of the United States at that same time. Maybe this is what Mosley was doing, using the search for Black Betty as a means to let Easy Rawlins show us the L.A. of 1961—while predicting what could happen 30 years later. I wouldn't go so far as to say that that is the meaning of the book, but all the undercurrents are there. Blacks play subordinate roles in all cases, unless they are in their own neighborhood. There are lines that separate the poor from the well-off, and there are cops to enforce that rule. The explosion happened in '65, but the pot had been simmering 30 years earlier and more.

Easy Rawlins is 41 now after this fourth book, and he is tired. He wishes to spend more time with his two adopted children, and less time beating up, and being beaten up by, the bad people. But I along with thousands of others hope he doesn't give up the private eye business altogether. Marlowe was good, but he gave us information from one point of view, the white point of view. Easy Rawlins has access to places Marlowe would not dare tread. I like Marlowe and I like Spade—but we need Easy out there. Look after your children, Easy—but don't forget us.

Ernest J. Gaines. *Los Angeles Times Book Review.* June 5, 1994, pp. 3, 12

The "RL" of Walter Mosley's new novel, *RL's Dream*, is Robert Johnson, the Delta blues singer who died young and violently in 1938. (No one knows why Johnson called himself RL, and Mr. Mosley doesn't attempt an explanation.) Admired by blues connoisseurs in life, he was rediscovered by the largely white, middle-class folk and blues revival of the 1960's, and reborn in a big way 25 years later to a pop audience that acknowledged him as a dark-of-night backwoods conjurer who prefigured everything from Chicago blues to hard rock—a tormented visionary who bartered his soul to the Devil. And what did he get in return—genius? women? recognition? It is difficult to speak concretely of Robert Johnson, as it is of many artists who lived lives so short, messy and contrary that if not for their work they would seem like figures in mythology.

Although Mr. Mosley brings him to ground in a tangled vignette that arrives about midway in the book, allowing him to breathe hotly on the page, it is ultimately the mythic Robert Johnson who haunts this often startling, emphatic modern-day fable. Mr. Mosley's RL is at once a blues virtuoso who makes dancers go wild, whose "blues would rip the skin right off yo' back," and a gloomy apparition of futility. One disciple who can't shake the dread is Atwater (Soupspoon) Wise, a black Mississippi orphan who briefly traveled with Johnson. Now dying in New York, he is obsessed with recounting and defining their association. Mr. Mosley zooms in on him on the Lower East Side, hobbling in blind terror and befouled agony, with a busted hip and advanced cancer, hallucinating "a young man with short nappy hair and one dead eye." When he arrives at his apartment, he is expelled for nonpayment of rent and left to die on the street.

Enter Kiki Waters, in pain herself after being stabbed that day by a 10-year-old black boy. One of the most unlikely saviors to enter American fiction in some years, Kiki was born in Arkansas, where she was the victim of unspeakably savage sexual attacks from her father. She is a white woman in her early 30's—alcoholic, fiercely independent, unpredictable, scary and smart. A tenant in Soupspoon's building, though they have never met, she throws a tantrum over his eviction and insists that he move in with her. She quickly dispatches her sometime boyfriend (a Negro convinced by his mother that he isn't), the landlord and others who stand in her way. Undeterred by Soupspoon's stench, she undresses him, carries him—despite the pull on her stitches—to the tub and bathes him. Soup thinks, in concert with the reader: "Maybe she was crazy. Drunk maybe, or insane." Yet she shakes loose "the loneliness that had been his life for years."

*RL's Dream* is about Soup's last stand as a musician and how he and Kiki alternate roles of nurturer and invalid. It is a story of the Deep South but set in another country, up north. They live in New York but dream of the piney woods. "While Soupspoon was counting dead bodies in his sleep, Kiki called out, 'No, daddy.' Her dream was Southern too." Yet their obsessive recollections have entirely different tenors. Atwater's are elegiac—even his litanies of violence, murder, racism. "For all that it was barren, the Delta was a beautiful land too. It was a hard land but true. It had the whippoorwill and the hoot owl and crickets for music, It had pale dead trees that stood out in the moonlight like the hands of dead men reaching out of the ground." Kiki's are horrific—she drinks herself into a stupor for fear of remembering.

It may be useful, at this point, to assure his many admirers that this is indeed the work of the Walter Mosley who has written four justly celebrated detective novels set in Los Angeles during the 15 years following World War II, and starring the serenely cool and competent Easy Rawlins. In *RL's Dream*, Mr. Mosley has risked a lyrical and original—if imperfect—leap beyond genre fiction, working for the first time in the third person and substituting an omniscient probing of damaged lives for the modulated fastidiousness of Rawlins. His superb reportorial eye is fully focused on New York's street life as well as the tar-paper bucket-of-blood juke joints of the Delta. Several episodes are as well tuned as anything he has written including the violent conclusion, and especially a tense and comic tour de force in which Kiki embezzles a million-dollar insurance policy from her company to pay for Soupspoon's chemotherapy. More impressive still is the cast—excepting a few stock roles (villain, milquetoast), it is mostly original and often credible.

Still, episodes do congeal into misguided sentimentality, underscored by gnomic utterances designed to render Soupspoon a kind of cosmic bluesman. Sitting in the park, Soup meditates on ants and worms. As he begins his observation ("Everybody's doin' their business"), you suddenly recall that his name is Wise and wish it weren't. Wise sayings mount up all too quickly. On music: "It's all about getting' so close to pain that it's like a friend, like somebody you love." On blues: "Blues is the Devil's music an' we his chirren. RL was Satan's favorite son." Yet when he considers RL's remark "They ain't no getting' away from you stank, Soup," he concludes, "The words just didn't make sense." Oh? Unhappily, they make a lot more sense than the examples of Soup's lyrics, most of which are self-consciously arty and even foolish, confirming the reader's suspicion that Mr. Mosley knows very little about the blues or the lives of bluesmen. Incidentally, it is inconceivable that those listening to Soupspoon use the names Robert Johnson and RL interchangeably wouldn't ask why or register confusion.

Such moments of unreality, including an episode in which an 18-year-old beauty seduces Soupspoon, are jarring because Mr.

Mosley's intonation is usually dead on. By the story's almost too perfect conclusion, you know Kiki—"this redheaded white girl, drunk and jagged, who thought slaps were kisses and whisky was milk"—well enough to recognize her on the street. The author's pleasure in her is confirmed in the crazily ripe future he gives her. Nor does Mr. Mosley miss a beat with Randy, her black boyfriend who thinks he's Egyptian; or Mavis, Soup's former wife and once RL's lover, who inhabits an apartment decorated entirely in white and is still mourning her 5-year-old son. The boy's accidental death half a century ago was indirectly related to the rowdy night Mavis spent dancing to RL and Soupspoon in a juke joint.

> Gary Giddins. *New York Times Book Review.* August 13, 1995, pp. 11–12

In *White Butterfly*, the third of Walter Mosley's four detective novels, there is a reference to bluesmen "Sonny Terry, Brownie McGee, Lightnin' Hopkins, Soupspoon Wise." The first three are historical. Soupspoon Wise is not, and Mosley makes him the central figure of *RL's Dream*, his first novel outside the detective genre. . . .

By choosing a black Southern bluesman and a white Southern woman as his primary characters, Mosley sets the stage for an exploration of the complex domain of black male-white female relationships and the history and suffering that binds black and white Southerners in an almost incestuous intimacy. Having set the stage, however, he forgets to put on the play.

*RL's Dream* has the same weakness as Mosley's detective fiction, namely, a story line that is manufactured, rather than proceeding logically from the lives of its characters. Toward the end of this novel, for example, there is the abrupt appearance of a black teenage girl. As readers, we are not given enough time to establish a sympathetic relationship with her, so that when she sleeps with Soupspoon we are left more puzzled than edified.

Another weakness of the detective novels is also found here—a permeating tone of racial anger and self-pity. In Mosley's fiction there is very little, if any, joy in black life. Also absent is any sense of the dignity that comes when one endures with his humanity intact.

Mosley's fictional detective, Easy Rawlins, is an anti-hero who seldom attains dignity but knows what it is. The principal characters of *RL's Dream* seem to lack even that knowledge. Kiki is an alcoholic who goes into violent rages when she is drunk and Soupspoon is simply a dying old man whose claim to fame was that he knew Robert "RL" Johnson. However, even the title character is an ill-defined and unsympathetic figure. One gets no sense that the author loves his characters, and if he does not, why should the reader?

In the mid-'60s I collected country blues in Mississippi and Alabama from unknown and unrecorded bluesmen much like Soupspoon. I also interviewed many of the legendary bluesmen including Son House, one of Robert Johnson's teachers. What remains with me even now is the dignity and self-possession with which those men carried themselves. There was no self-pity in their voices, their posture or their music. In their hands the blues was a weapon that defended their humanity from forces that would deny it. The blues were also a catharsis, cleansing the spirit of despair and enabling singer and listener to remember that despite it all black people were more akin to angels than apes.

For a novel to be true, the voice in which it is written must be true to our humanity, so that when we read we recognize ourselves,

for better and worse. As bluesman J. D. Short once told music critic Sam Charters: "Sometime the people that's listening at you have actual [sic] been through some of the same things that I have been through and automatically that takes effect on them and that causes their attention to come."

*RL's Dream* does not cause our attention to come.

> Julius Lester. *Book World—The Washington Post.* August 20, 1995, p. 7

Black narrative writing in America often employs a detective-like protagonist struggling against an evil society—as Theodore O. Mason, Jr., points out [*Kenyon Review*, 1992]—yet, curiously, detective fiction itself is a genre that has attracted few black writers (most notably, in decades past, Rudolph Fisher and Chester Himes). In Walter Mosley's four L.A. detective novels, he joins the small cohort of black detective fiction writers, apparently as part of a radical project to enter the mostly white, male, and conservative populist terrain of American detective fiction. At the same time, however, Mosley's often uncritical use of the traditional hardboiled detective formula seems to work against this project by employing a black detective narrator in a previously invisible textual location—black Los Angeles. Indeed, there is a tension between Mosley's subject and his method, and this tension prompts my basic question about Mosley's L. A. novels: Are they—with their use of a black narrator, black characters, and black locations—authentically transgressive texts, or are they discursively subsumed under the detective story formula (and especially the L.A. detective fiction paradigm, as constructed by Chandler) and do they come, thus, to represent at best nostalgic traces of the hardboiled tradition? In other words, are the novels merely exotic versions of the American detective story, as opposed to subversive texts? My answer to these questions is an Ellisonian yes and no. In terms of their use of black characters and locations—and also in terms of their generic "violations" of the hardboiled detective story—Mosley's novels indeed function as texts of difference. Yet when they deploy the Chandlerian hardboiled detective and ultimately embrace the essentially conservative thematics of the L.A. detective story, Mosley's novels mute their subversiveness and reinforce the reassuring quality of formulaic detective fiction. In this light, I will read Mosley's novels as metacritical allegories that reflect a fundamental ambivalence about his own intervention into white (detective) discourse. . . .

Ironically, the tough-guy detective narrative would seem to resemble (or at least be useful to) the black narrative of resistance or opposition, yet the traditional detective never operates on behalf of blacks, and African Americans have almost no discursive presence in these novels (except as part of the textual landscape—in Chandler, for example, occasionally as "comically" terrified hotel porters). Above all, it would seem virtually impossible to reconcile the black narrative of liberation with the conservative politics and poetics of the detective genre, a politics that ultimately reflects a larger American moral code from which whites have generally had few difficulties excluding the Africanist Other.

Mosley's task is thus a difficult one. It is not simply a matter of appropriating a genre for one's own use, because one also has to negotiate with all of the ideological baggage that accompanies it.

Let me start by comparing two opening scenes, the first from Raymond Chandler's *Farewell, My Lovely* (1942) and the second from Walter Mosley's *Devil in a Blue Dress* (1990). *Farewell, My Lovely* begins—as Philip Marlowe, Chandler's harboiled detective narrator, tells us—on "one of the mixed blocks over on Central Avenue, the blocks that are not yet all Negro." Marlowe is on a missing person's case and notices "a big man . . . not more than six feet five inches tall and not wider than a beer truck" staring up at a sign above a bar. The other people on the street, "slim quient negroes," pass "up and down the street and stare at him with darting side glances." Almost immediately, we might say, racial difference is marked in terms of demographics and racial identity: The person Marlowe and everyone else notices is described as a "man," while the blacks are identified in racial terms. . . .

This is a somewhat similar scene [in *Devil in a Blue Dress*]—a white man enters a black bar during the 1940s (here, in 1948 as opposed to 1942)—but, of course, we are seeing the scene from the opposite point of view. The white man—a gangster, significantly named Albright—gets the attention of Mosley's black detective narrator, Easy Rawlins. But Rawlins is not immediately hostile to Albright. Nor, as we soon discover, does anyone else stop chattering and chanting. Rawlins even notices Albright's eyes, but they are marked by their lack of color, a whiteness that matches the rest of his exessively white costume. Ultimately, Rawlins admits to feeling fear, but this momentary reaction dissipates, because his experience as a soldier in World War II, in which he fought and killed white German soldiers, has changed his attitude toward whites in general.

Clearly, if we can use these two scenes are representative, Walter Mosley's L.A. detective novels seem to rewrite the hardboiled tradition, especially the novels of Raymond Chandler. For Mosley, South Central L.A. is not merely an exotic location— or, worse, a plot device to begin a novel. Rather, it is the community where Mosley's novels are set. In a sense, Mosley elevates black L.A. in his novels into a significant location. If L.A. embodies, as Gerald Clarke suggests, an "enigmatic otherness . . . a city of dramatic extremes which remains untouchable and insubstantial," then black L.A. is—to borrow a phrase from Christopher Miller—the other's other, a photographic negative of a photographic negative, a hidden supplement of what already seems superfluous. One can hardly imagine New York without Harlem, or Chicago without its black South Side, but in L.A. (at least until the Rodney King incident, and perhaps not even after that) the black section has seemed barely to register in the American cultural imagintion. . . .

Mosley's four L.A. detective novels—*Devil in a Blue Dress* (1990), *A Red Death* (1991), *White Butterfly* (1992), and *Black Betty* (1994)—all present essentially the same story, and each reinforces Mosley's own ambivalent sense of the genre. In each novel, Easy Rawlins is asked (or commanded) to locate someone in the black community or to solve a series of deaths or murders. In each novel, Rawlins successfully carries out his assigned task, although in doing so he triggers some kind of violence, often a murder, which he must then attempt to solve.

His third novel, *White Butterfly*, finds a now married and even wealthier Rawlins—at the request of the L.A. police department—investigating the separate, brutal murders of four women (three black and one white), all of whom have apparently been killed by the same person. As in the other novels, Rawlins is asked to look into the matter because the authorities have no access to the black community. The police tell him, "You know all kinds of people in the community. You can go where the police can't go. You can ask questions of people who aren't willing to talk to the

law." The three black women, Rawlins finds out, were murdered by a psychotic black murderer whom the white police in Oakland incompetently failed to arrest. (They also try to cover up their incompetence.). . .

In a sense, of course, these novels do break with the hardboiled tradition in that race plays a major role in each. In *Devil in a Blue Dress*, Rawlins's unwillingness to tolerate the racist actions of his supervisor gets him fired. . . .

But Rawlins is also capable of performing for whites, when he wants—in trickster fashion—to fool them. In *White Butterfly*, at a meeting with white investors who want to buy property from Rawlins, he comments that, after being introduced to the whites, "I nodded shyly and ducked my head in reverence. It was the way I used to grease white men in the south." At other times, Rawlins overtly confronts racist authorities. . . .

Rawlins, in this sense, is clearly of—or at least from—the black community in L.A. Like many others in the community, he migrated from the South after World War II. . . .

And Rawlins, despite his growing wealth, can sympathize with the poor blacks in Los Angeles. Having been "raised on a share-cropper's farm" (*Devil*) himself Rawlins, in a scene from *White Butterfly*, clearly empathizes with a profoundly injured man he must interrogate. . . .

Mosley also seems to deviate from the traditional detective story formula through his use of sex and sexuality in his novels. Detective fiction, as many commentators have suggested, is often marked by a lack of overt sexual activity, especially on the part of the detective himself. . . . But Rawlins spends a great deal of time in and out of beds, and at times his descriptions of his sexual conquests are both graphic and brutal. In Mosley's third novel, *White Butterfly*, Rawlins drunkenly returns home late at night and rapes his wife—something that has no small effect on her decision, at the end of the story, to leave him. Indeed, in all of his novels, Mosley includes so much black male sexual activity that he seems to invoke the stereotype of the black male's voracious sexual appetite, a stereotype that pervades contemporary scholarship on race. . . .

Mosley in essence defends his use of a brutalized black male sexuality by claiming that "poverty is tattooed on black and brown skins. Ignorance and violence, sex and criminality are deeply etched in Hispanic and African hues"; and, indeed, there is even a sense in which Mosley criticizes Rawlins's relentless heterosexuality, for at the end of each novel we find a chastened and psychologically shattered Rawlins almost completely alone. Yet Rawlins's overactive libido clearly presents problems in any argument that attempts to "heroize" him, and Mosley's representation of black male sexuality (and "criminality") as "deeply etched in . . . African hues" indeed exemplifies rather than subverts hooks's description of the discursive criminalization of the black-male subject. What is more, Mosley's redeployment of sexuality ironically repositions him under the rubric of white-male detective fiction, because Chandler's apparent de-emphasis of sexuality actually represents a kind of disguised sexuality, a homosocial violence that binds men together. Mosley, in his novels, makes manifest (much like Mickey Spillane) what is latent in Chandler, a relentless misogyny coupled with an inability or unwillingness to question the underlying "law" of white patriarchal society. As bell hooks points out, "Black men who embrace patriarchal masculinity, phallocentrism, and sexism . . . do not threaten or challenge white domination . . . but reinscribe it." It is also important to note that Mosley's version of an essentialized black-male sexuality is complemented by a kind of insatiable black-female sexuality. Women in Mosley's detective novels are often either femme fatales or sexual objects who exude sexual attraction and desire. . . .

All that remains possible is some kind of allegiance to a masculine-warrior moral code. Even if unjustly assaulted by the police—and Rawlins is often called upon to demonstrate his extraordinary physical courage and endurance, because in each novel he is arrested and brutally beaten by the police—he must uphold this code. In the end of each novel, he uncovers the murderer, no matter what the personal cost. In fact, this devotion to an abstract sense of duty contributes to the destruction of his marriage in *White Butterfly*.

Rawlins's acceptance of a hardboiled detective moral code may also be seen in his adoption of what might be termed an individualist philosophy, one in which his own experience, rather than larger historical patterns, takes precedence and gives meaning to his life.

Ultimately, in his L.A. detective fiction, Mosley addresses, but doesn't fully answer, larger questions about the uneasy relationship between African-American literature and American literature as a whole. African-American authors, of course, are free to intervene in any discursive landscape, but Mosley's entry into hardboiled detective fiction, a (white-male) genre rather inimical to a progressive struggle for racial equality, justice, and freedom, carries with it a heavy price; and Mosley cannot fully disentangle himself from the reactionary politics that are embedded in the genre. At the same time, however, one might say that, just as there has always already been an Africanist presence in American literature, so there has also always already been a black presence in American hardboiled detective fiction, and Mosley is actually making manifest what has previously been latent. Indeed, it is Toni Morrison who insightfully asks "whether the major and championed characteristics of our national literature—individualism, masculinity, social engagement versus historical isolation; acute and ambiguous moral problematics; a thematics of innocence coupled with an obsession with figurations of death and hell—are not in fact responses to a dark, abiding, signifying Africanist presence." In this sense, the mean streets a detective must go down are indeed "dark with something more than night," as Raymond Chandler memorably notes. But Chandler, like so many other white writers, didn't necessarily know what he really meant.

Roger A. Berger. *African American Review*. 31, 2 (summer 1997), pp. 281–94

Mosley's recurring characters, Ezekiel "Easy" Rawlins and Raymond "Mouse Navrochet, are down directly from African-American folklore and they are not black-faced copies of the hard-boiled tradition. . . .

Although Mosley places Easy in this hard-boiled tradition, he adds an extra dimension. The primary difference is that Mosley situates his protagonist squarely within traditional Black culture by using aspects of the oral tradition and the slave narrative. From the folklore identified with these traditions arise two heroic characters: the bad Black man and the trickster.

These Black heroes are different from their hard-boiled counterparts. The trickster as Black hero is not on a quest. He does not want to rescue a damsel in distress nor does he desire to accomplish a noble deed. His one goal, according to Dary Dance in *Shuckin'*

*and Jivin': Folklore from Contemporary Black Americans*, is to outsmart the man, to humiliate him, to out perform him mentally, verbally, physically . . . or to force him to recognize him and to respect him.

Mosley uses these two heroic figures as he reconstructs post-World War II Los Angeles from an African-American perspective. He guides readers through a tangle of after-hours juke joints, corrupt politicians and violence, all filtered through the eyes of "Easy" Rawlins, who comes from the same oral tradition as Zora Neale Hurston. Rawlins says at one point, "He told me a few stories, the kind of tales that we called 'lies' back home in Texas" (*Devil*). The use of traditional culture is easily understood since Mosley considers Emancipation a joke and he describes 1940s and 1950s Los Angeles as a gigantic, transformed plantation. Even the factory system is equated with the plantation system. . . .

The novels include allusions to slave passes, those notes given to enslaved Africans that provided them with freedom of movement. Late one night, "Easy" goes to an office building. The security guard asks him, "Did he give you a note saying you're to come in here after hours?" (*Devil*). Consequently, Mosley's hero and antihero adapt their activities and behavior to this southern plantation-like environment. . . .

But Mosley's adaptation of traditional Black culture in his U.S.A. trilogy can most clearly be recognized in his depiction of his heroes: "Easy" Rawlins as the trickster and "Mouse" Navrochet as the bad Black man.

According to Lawrence Levine in *Black Culture and Black Consciousness*, heroes, including the trickster and the bad man, symbolized the strength, dignity, and courage many African-Americans were able to manifest in spite of their confined situation. However, though the post-bellum trickster is different from the slave trickster, they share one important characteristic: they, too, are circumscribed by the limits of reality. . . .

Both trickster figures, those before and after the Civil War, have some attributes in common. Both stress the tactics of deception and misdirection. Unlike Easy's counterpart in the hard-boiled tradition, by the third novel, *White Butterfly*, "Easy" is no longer solitary. He is a husband and father and he has taken his military separation pay and bought a small house. Sensing that property values in southern California will increase, he continues to invest secretly in real estate. . . .

Thus begins "Easy's" trickery and misdirection. Although he functions in the novels as a private investigator, his alter ego is as a janitor in the buildings that he owns. He is different from other African-Americans in his community who have also migrated from the rural south. He has graduated from high school, he has taken college courses and he uses the library frequently. "Easy" tells one friend who is complaining about his lack of knowledge about Africa that "Liberty got its do' open man. Ain't nobody tellin' you not to go" (*Red*). But he "masks" his knowledge from others, Black or white, superiors, peers or subordinates. . . .

[A] careful reading of the texts reveals that his use of language is determined by the situation in which he finds himself or the person with whom he is speaking. If he does not wish to give information, if he wishes to appear less intelligent or if he simply wishes to "put a person on," he lapses into the Black vernacular. For example, dressed in his best brown suit with a "cream colored shirt, real gold cufflinks, brown . . . shoes and argyle socks," Easy went to the police station. Easy adds, "I had on a hand-painted silk tie, double-knotted to perfection. And this woman had called everybody but me. I had been there . . . for over an hour'' (*Butterfly*). When the receptionist finally called him, she asked his name and the spelling. Easy replied, ''I don't know.'' ''What?'' ''I ain't never been to school an' my momma us'ly signs all my papers. Ain't nobody evah axed me t'spell it at all really. You the first one.'' Easy knows that his dress does not change the certainty that a particular speech code is expected of him. He is Black. On the other hand, he can and does speak standard English if he feels the situation warrants it.

Both trickster figures, traditional and contemporary, gain the same satisfaction in seeing the powerless outsmart and discredit the powerful. In all three novels, the guilty persons are Euro-American men of power and influence who are eventually outmaneuvered and humiliated by Easy. In Mosley's first novel, *Devil in a Blue Dress* (1990), Easy is hired by Dewitt Albright, a Euro-American man who wears a thin facade of civility. Easy must locate the fair-haired, blue-eyed mistress, Daphne (the devil of the title), of Albright's powerful employer. Since Daphne is known to frequent Black jazz clubs, Easy is the man for the job. Because he is Black, because he is familiar with the Watts community, because he is a lover of jazz and because he ''is in the business of favors,'' Easy provides the white establishment with entrance into the black community. Daphne, the missing mistress, is one of the few tragic mulatta characters found in African-American fiction. The tragic mulatta is usually a creation of Euro-American writers who conclude that not being accepted as white is the tragedy. Mouse interprets her situation:

> She wanna be white. All of them years people tellin' her how she light-skinned and beautiful but all the time she knows that she can't have what white people have. So she pretend and then she lose it all. She can love a white man but all he can love is the white girl he think she is. . . . She look like she white and you think like you white. But brother you don't know that you both poor niggers. And a nigger ain't never gonna be happy 'less he accept what he is. (*Devil*)

Nonetheless, Easy not only outmaneuvers the powerful Euro-American but he cuckolds him by becoming Daphne's lover.

In *A Red Death* (1991), Easy uses stolen money to purchase several real estate properties. To maintain a low profile, he employs a cold, hard, unemotional man, Mofass, to act as landlord while Easy assumes the role of the janitor. When an Internal Revenue Service agent becomes determined to jeopardize Easy's comfortable lifestyle by conducting an audit of his finances, Mofass tells Easy how to reinforce his ''mask,'' ''Act po', that what you do. Them white people love t'think that you ain't shit'' (*Red*). But Easy caves in to I.R.S. Agent Craxton's demands and slips on his double-agent mask. For all his power and influence, Agent Craxton falls prey to Easy's trickery.

Additionally, both trickster characters display the same lack of idealism. Neither the slave trickster nor Easy are romantic characters as in the hard-boiled tradition, nor do they try to be. Though Easy struggles with the concept of honor, he rarely succeeds. He has an affair with the wife of his best friend, Mouse; he cheats on his wife with a prostitute. He uses stolen money to expand his real estate holdings. There are times when he perhaps could have influenced Mouse, but he makes deliberate choices not to.

However, in making moral decisions, Easy only listens to an inner voice that ''is hard. It never cares if I'm scared or in danger. It just looks at all the facts and tells me what I need to do'' (*Devil*).

Mouse, too, is as pragmatic as Easy. Mouse recognizes that African-Americans cannot succeed playing by the white man's rules. African-Americans have to develop a different game with different rules. Mouse tells Easy, ''you gotta have somebody at yo' back. . . . That's just a lie them white man give 'bout makin' it on they own. They always got they backs covered'' (*Devil*).

Like the slave trickster, Easy represses his true feelings whether about his work, his money or his wife. The only emotions he allows himself to express are those concerning his baby daughter, Edna, or his adopted son, Jesus. But somehow this repression of feeling and lack of idealism allowed him to survive. . . .

Mosley does more than create protagonists in the hard-boiled tradition. Through exploration of his cultural identity, he has created a unique hero from an African-American perspective. By using aspects of traditional Black culture, Mosley has taken the two heroic characters, the trickster and the bad Black man, and updated them while retaining many of their historic attributes of deception, misdirection and violence. Therefore, it is difficult not to conclude that Mosley has not only adapted and reconceived the genre of the detective novel into a vehicle for the continuation of African-American cultural traditions but he has also reshaped the genre by exploring and extending it into African-American literary traditions.

Mary Young. *Journal of Popular Culture*. 32, 1 (summer 1998), pp. 141–50

BIBLIOGRAPHY
*Devil in a Blue Dress*, 1990; *A Red Death*, 1991; *White Butterfly*, 1992; *Black Betty*, 1994; *R. L.'s Dream*, 1995; *Gone Fishin'*, 1996; *Always Outnumbered, Always Outgunned: The Socrates Fortlow Stories*, 1997; *Blue Light*, 1998

# MPHAHLELE, Ezekiel (1919–1983)
## South Africa

This collection of five short stories [*Man Must Live, and Other Stories*], written by an African teacher of Johannesburg, reflects a dangerous tendency on the part of the African intelligentsia to become isolated from their people. Those who are charged with the education of the African people must inevitably superimpose upon the aboriginal raw culture in which the average pupil was nurtured, the more complex pattern of European culture and ethics. The resultant conflict between two modes of thought and life can lead either to the extinction of the weaker culture or to a fusion of cultures drawing strength equally from both sources.

Unfortunately the author of these stories has had the gods of his fathers exorcised by the missionaries. He has forgotten that he is an African. If you changed the names of the characters in his stories, they might be creatures of any race or clime. They believe in ideal love, heavenly justice, patience and the other delectable virtues; they have to struggle both with their own inherent weakness of the flesh and spirit and with the selfishness and callousness of others, just like the heroes of Victorian novels. But never once do they complain about the pass laws, the pick-up vans or the insolence of the white man, though they all live in urban locations where beer raids are the order of the day. They do not share the sufferings and the problems of the majority of their people. They are not genuine characters. . . .

The author of these stories is evidently sensitive and observant, if introspective, and he writes with great facility and precision. But the sharpest intellect cannot function in a vacuum. Art, of course, cannot be made to measure. Nor are we complaining because Mr. Mphahlele is non-political. All we do say is that he should return to his people for inspiration, otherwise his muse will wither and die.

B. P. B. *Guardian*. January 9, 1947, p. 3

"I'm the personification of the African paradox," writes Ezekiel Mphahlele in the current issue of *The Twentieth Century*, "detribalised, Westernised, but still African—minus the conflicts." His autobiography [*Down Second Avenue*] explains how he reached this point. It is valuable for several reasons. It rings true; it is the work of a new kind of self-emancipated South African; it lights up both the conditions in which he struggled to make the best of his powers, and the self that has evolved. Because the struggle was bitter and because this man of forty is truthful, his book has a partly bitter flavour: it is not the bitterness of despair or fanaticism, but the taste of the life he has known. . . .

Although he found, through white and Christian institutions and individuals, scope for his abilities, he also won it by his own brains and guts. In doing so he has come to find that formal Christianity is no longer for him, but he is able to enjoy, say, Chekhov and Vivaldi, he values his white friends too much to want to shoo them out of Africa, and he has gained, among other things, the use of the English language. If he wishes to use it, he has the talent, as this book shows, to interest and enlarge the understandings of readers whose brains are more important to them than their pigmentation. Respect for himself as a man and a writer he has already won. He is a participant in the great, non-racial effort of winning the durable from the transient.

William Plomer. *New Statesman*. April 25, 1959, pp. 582–83

To read Ezekiel Mphahlele after a diet of West and Central African writers is like twiddling the focusing knob on a pair of glasses. His whole dilemma is so utterly different from theirs that his books help to clarify their position as much as his own. For the Negro in urban South Africa has in truth more in common with the American Negro than with his neighbours in tropical Africa. He inhabits a society which is dominated by Whites in a far grimmer and more universal sense than any tropical colony (except perhaps Angola) has ever been. And this domination is expressed, not merely in colonial ritual and pantomime, but in every department of life. His residence, his movements, his place and grade of work, his education, his sexual life are all subject to regulation, all governed by an alien mythology about the black man's place in the scheme of things. He cannot even walk down a street at certain hours or drink a glass of beer without breaking the law. An outcast in his own country, he has to scrutinize every doorway, every bench, every counter, to make sure that he has segregated himself correctly. He is on the run. . . .

[Mphahlele's] whole life has been an unrelenting struggle to achieve the way of life for which his urban upbringing and liberal education had prepared him. But to achieve that life he has had finally to become an exile. . . .

There is nothing [in *Down Second Avenue*] of Camara's poetic nostalgia, his elegy for a life full of its own dignity and significance. Mphahlele's writing is more like the taste of blood on the tongue. Yet the two men are contemporaries and perhaps not fundamentally different in temperament. What divides them is three thousand miles of Africa.

Gerald Moore. *Seven African Writers* (London: Oxford University Press, 1962), pp. 92–94

In the past what had always put me off Ezekiel Mphahlele's writing was a certain dullness of tone, much like the ponderous speech of a dull-witted person so that it was often difficult to pursue the story to its ending. The gems were often embedded in a thick mud of cliché and lustreless writing: a succession of simple clauses, for instance, linked together by semicolons. The texture of the prose had the feel and look of sweaty labour much like the stains of honest sweat on the cloth-cap of the toiling proletariat. . . .

The danger with this kind of writing is that it can often become a substitute for action in the story, or a substitute for a more ingenious solution to the problem of flashbacks. At his slowest it contributed to a considerable amount of dullness in Mphahlele's writing. Yet some of these problems of style were clearly attributable to external causes: the strain of maintaining an equilibrium in a dangerously melodramatic situation. If one went too far the other way in an effort to match with language the violence of the streets, the prose became strained, brittle and frayed; so that the flatness in Mphahlele's writing was sometimes due to an honourable attempt to remain "cool under fire."

It seems to me that in the latest work Mphahlele's writing has become tighter, more solid and assured as he acquires a more properly synthesised vocabulary to deal with the stresses of South African life. He has achieved greater authority and a better grip on his own particular idiom: the result is a happier fluency of tone.

Lewis Nkosi. *Black Orpheus*. March 1966, pp. 51–52

Ezekiel Mphahlele has become a spokesman for many Africans who live in South Africa. He is a gifted writer and a humane and compassionate man. His first major work was the autobiographical tale of his early life in the slums of Pretoria's Second Avenue district, *Down Second Avenue*. It has been reprinted several times, for it is a work of impressive sensitivity, with the anger and the compassion beautifully held in balance. It asks the inevitable angry question as to the injustice of such poverty—in this case rendered the sharper by the bitterness derived from colour prejudice. . . .

Exile has not been easy, as the very title of this new prize-winning novel makes clear, *The Wanderers*, with its suggestively generalized subtitle, *A Novel of Africa*. In this book with an almost painful accuracy the author describes his experiences as a wanderer with his family, as he moved across the continent seeking for those essential roots which a writer must have. The story of the novel overlaps the incidents in the brief concluding section of *Down Second Avenue* and then carries on to the writer's determination to leave East Africa for London. Yet the book is not a simple autobiography, it is a novel constructed with skill and art. Perhaps it shares something of the attitude of Arthur Miller when he wrote that powerful play *After the Fall*. You felt that you were being allowed to see more deeply than before that last deep intimacy in the sensibility of a man and an artist. If this is often painful it is because human truth is painful, and such human truth is the stuff from which derives all significant art.

John Povey. *African Arts.* Winter 1969. p. 12

Unlike *Down Second Avenue*, with its emotional tension, its cumulative structure, and its overwhelming sense of inevitability, *The Wanderers* might very well go any number of different ways, to any number of different conclusions. His life, Mphahlele implies in "Exile to Nigeria," had become adjusted in South Africa to the ever-present enemy, had adapted itself to a continual defensiveness, had structured itself around the negative response; in Nigeria that structure, negative as it was, exists no longer because the oppressor is no longer in his life. Mphahlele is thrown off balance by thrusting at something and expecting resistance but finding nothing there. This accounts for what he calls the "void" and also for the notable lack of tension and of energy-directing vitality, and for the virtual absence of subject in *The Wanderers*.

Another reason that *Down Second Avenue* is the better of the two books is that, paradoxically, life, as described in the earlier book, presented a necessary pattern that art, in *The Wanderers*, never comes up with. Or perhaps it would be fairer to say that Mphahlele is a finer artist as an autobiographer than he is as a novelist. Everything in *Down Second Avenue* is drawn up behind the author to show the way inevitably to exile; it is an account of the calculus of exile and as such the book achieves meaning for itself and for the life it describes. *The Wanderers*, on the other hand, is aimless, disjointed, an account of a simple, inert, mass wandering. The people are wandering into further exile, but now the exile has no goal and no meaning; it is the conclusion of nothing and a part of no pattern; it is merely moving on with neither desire nor regret—both of which were strong on departure from South Africa. . . . Deprived by exile of his natural subject, Mphahlele fails to come up with another.

James Olney. *Tell Me Africa* (Princeton: Princeton University Press, 1973), pp. 280–81

The language [in *The Wanderers*] adequately moves its freight—an ambitious panoramic story of wandering exiles, black and white, from South Africa. The South African episodes are the most vivid and affectionate; the polychrome peculiarities of this deplorable state, with its "colored" and Indian minorities as well as blacks, are rendered in a sharp sequence of vignettes and accents. Mr. Mphahlele, whose black characters talk a little like stage Englishmen, hears peculiar speech everywhere. . . .

When Timi Tabana, a black schoolteacher exiled for writing newspaper articles about a slave system of penal labor, travels to London, the colony of exiled South Africans there seems to him pathetic; the "South African English accent the white spoke . . . irritated him as it had never done in his home country." And in Nigeria, after his initial exhilaration at being freed from South Africa's tyranny of passbooks and police, he is irritated by the effeminate way Nigerians slap at each other, and urges them to hit with fists, in good South African style. Prostitution and idleness are also new to him. One of the friends he makes there, in a small circle of intellectuals and mixed marriages, is named Awoonor (another is "an American historian, John Galbraith"), and, whether or not

this means Kofi Awoonor, *The Wanderers* moves into the dispirited terrain of *This Earth, My Brother* . . . Timi's problems become those of the free: a sense of futility, elusive responsibilities, a meagre security. . . .

*The Wanderers* shows the English-speaking whites (but not the Afrikaners) as people who, like the blacks, are unequally matched against the vast, murderous inertia that is Africa. [Nov. 13, 1971]

John Updike. *Picked-up Pieces* (New York: Alfred A. Knopf, 1975), pp. 323–24, 326

Mphahlele's collection of short stories *The Living and the Dead, and Other Stories* marked the beginning of a new period in his creative career. The evil faced by his heroes is more concrete than in his preceding works of fiction. Simultaneously, the author's conviction is strengthened that weak human force is incapable of overcoming it. This pessimism, resulting from cruel personal experiences, is reflected in this collection, as it is in the works of the prose writers emerging at the beginning of the Sixties. It is further emphasized by Mphahlele's crudeness of expression. . . .

In his collection of short stories *In Corner B*, Mphahlele is well aware of the relationship between form and content, the necessary balance between descriptive passages and dialogue, etc. This collection shows not only the author's increasing interest in the technical aspects of fiction writing, but also his keen sense of linguistic experimentation and modern expression. Yet unlike some of his colleagues, he has never abandoned a realistic, true-to-life portrayal of reality. His latest novel *The Wanderers* is partly autobiographical. Moreover, Mphahlele is an adviser of young African authors who are about to set out into the sphere of creative writing. Mphahlele, who does not believe in magically inspired talent and who tries to be as practical as possible, feels that a writer should listen closely to his people's speech and should capture the mood, atmosphere and verbal pictures or images evoked by what a character says or does, in the character's own language.

Vladimír Klíma. In Vladimír Klíma, Karel František Růžička, and Petr Zima, *Black Africa: Literature and Language* (Dordrecht, Netherlands: D. Reidel, 1976), pp. 254–55

[Es'kia] Mphahlele's fierce prose evokes all the strain of . . . [his] adolescence. Both structure and style in *Down Second Avenue* show the attempt to enlarge the normal limits of autobiography, so that the book will be both a record of events, more or less chronological, in the author's life, *and* an immediate, impressionistic evocation of certain typical moods and moments which don't belong at any special place within it, but must be allowed to spill their fear and anguish over the book as a whole. These are evoked in the sections called Interludes, which contain some of Mphahlele's most angry and electric writing in the book. The search for immediacy has muted the common tendency for the writer (especially the exile) to see even the painful events of youth and childhood through a certain softening haze. In the Interludes, we actually hear the steely clang of police boots in the yard, the thunder of hard knuckles on the door at dawn, the sirens, the cries, and the sickening blows which authority rains upon the unprotected. . . .

It was during . . . [his] years in Nigeria that Mphahlele achieved his greatest period of fertility as a writer. *Down Second Avenue,* presumably completed by 1958, was published in the following year. In 1961 the newly established Mbari Publishing House in Nigeria brought out a volume of his short stories entitled *The Living and Dead [and Other Stories]*. All of these stories, except the rather weakly melodramatic ''We'll Have Dinner at Eight,'' had already appeared in such South African magazines as *Drum, Student, Standpunte, Purple Renoster*, and *Africa South*. But, although they are thus the harvest of his last four years in the republic, the opportunity to publish them in book form was peculiarly the kind of opportunity brought to Mphahlele by his departure. The following year, 1962, brought the appearance of his book of critical essays, *The African Image*. The years since 1962 have seen no comparable burst of creativity, surely the fruit of that ''sense of release'' of which Mphahlele wrote. His second collection of stories, *In Corner B*, published in East African in 1967, also contained hitherto uncollected stories from his South African days, as well as reprinting three of the stories already used in *The Living and Dead*. Mphahlele's main production since 1962, apart from various critical introductions, has been his largely autobiographical novel *The Wanderers* in 1971, a revision of *The African Image*, and one further volume of essays, *Voices in the Whirlwind [and Other Essays]*, in 1972. . . .

Mphahlele . . . is the most important black South African writer of the present age, by virtue of his all-around achievement and his lifelong commitment to literature. Others may have equaled or excelled him in autobiography, or in criticism, or in the short story. But Mphahlele's contributions in all three of these fields add up to a career of major distinction. If he cannot give us the great black South African novel which has been so long awaited, it seems probable that no one at present can. The fragmentation of creative achievement into the poems and short stories in which black South Africa has been so prolific must be seen as the obverse of those conditions which make major fiction so difficult of achievement there. The corpus of Mphahlele's work remains rich enough, however, in qualities of insight, compassion, and intelligence.

Gerald Moore. *Twelve African Writers* (Bloomington: Indiana University Press, 1980), pp. 46, 52, 65–66

*Chirundu* was completed some three years after *The Wanderers* but was not published until five years later. . . . This was the first work since [Mphahlele's] very first volume, *Man Must Live [and Other Stories]*, to be published in South Africa. The banning order, imposed on him in 1966, had recently been lifted, and the publishers immediately availed themselves of the opportunity to add the doyen of black South African literature to their list of authors. . . .

*Chirundu* concerns the trial of cabinet minister Chimba Chirundu, whose wife accuses him of bigamy. Chirundu contends that Bemba marriage laws, according to which he married Tirenje, look upon a marriage as having ended if a wife leaves her husband, and her family takes no steps to bring her back. Tirenje counters that the traditional marriage was subsequently registered under old colonial ordinance, the divorce rules of which supersede the traditional ones. Since no divorce proceedings took place, Tirenje claims, her marriage still holds and Chirundu's marriage to Monde is bigamous. Chirundu does not expect to win the case but is ''out to fight a system.'' He says that the ordinance should recognize traditional marriage as something that cannot be superseded. He tells his advocate that he does not want to plead guilty, he wants to ''speak

up so that when the government gets around to marriage laws this inanity will not be repeated.'' Mphahlele sees the confrontation not as a clash between tradition and Western values as would at first appear. Rather, he is investigating the effect of a foreign culture on an African one and how one should deal with the resulting conflicts. Should all Western culture be discarded, he asks. Chirundu tries to discuss polygamy with Tirenje before their marriage, but Tirenje is too young and inexperienced to get her point across. . . .

Mphahlele's ideal modern Africa, which he presents in much of his writing, both fiction and nonfiction, is a synthesis of tradition and the best of what Europe has brought it. In the novel, Tirenje and Chirundu's nephew Moyo represent this ideal. In her school days, Tirenje falls under the influence of a young woman teacher, the first woman in her country to have obtained a B.A. degree, who tells her women students to wake up and fend for themselves.

Tirenje, described as firmly built, walking like a woman who knows where she is going, with an earthy tone to her voice and a steady look in her eyes, is contrasted with Monde, who is modern in a superficial way. She has gained her veneer of Western sophistication by mimicry.

Ursula A. Barnett. *A Vision of Order* (London: Sinclair Browne, 1983), pp. 145–47

In *Chirundu*, Mphahlele is primarily concerned with the nature of political power in ex-colonial Africa and the problem of adapting traditional cultures to modern social structures. The personal relationships of the main characters represent situations and relationships which exist between various groups in the society. Mphahlele examines the choices for the individual and the society as a whole, operating as they do between African and Western institutions. Social relationships, in this context, Mphahlele shows, become ''largely incoherent, pulling against and contradicting each other.'' The situation which Mphahlele describes for a particular Central African territory may be regarded as a paradigm for all ex-colonial African societies which show social structures that are inconsistent in themselves because of social and political pressures which operate in contrary directions. . . .

The main characters in the novel, Chimba Chirundu, his wife, Tirenje, and his nephew, Moyo, belong to the Bemba ethnic group. The two important relationships depicted are Chimba's relationship with Tirenje, whom he marries both under Bemba customary law and British ordinance, and his relationship with Moyo, his sister's son. In *Chirundu*, the circumstances of the breakup of the marriage between Chimba and Tirenje symbolize the breakdown of relationships between previously allied groups in the society. It also indicates the loss of certain guidelines of conduct in the society, for in the context of which Mphahlele writes, the marriage relationship or kinship affiliation, as represented in that of Chimba and Moyo, provides stable guidelines of conduct for the individual. The metaphor of marriage or kinship to describe other types of alliances is thus, in this instance, culturally derived.

The conflict in the novel arises from the circumstances under which Chimba takes a second wife. By marrying his second wife, Monde, under British ordinance, Chimba becomes guilty of bigamy which does not exist under Bemba customary law. The conflict of interests arising from Chimba's bigamous contract supplies the background for dealing with the theme of power and the conflict between the politicians and their grassroots supporters, who, like

Tirenje, are abandoned by the politician who is busy consolidating his power.

Joyce Johnson. *Kunapipi*. 6, 2 (1984), pp. 109–10

In *Chirundu* there are obvious parallels with ''mainstream'' African fiction. At one level *Chirundu* is concerned, as are many postindependence African writers, with the dynamics of the emerging state, the impact of power on leadership, the attempt to reconcile technical and traditional modes, and the complexities of inherited economic structures. . . .

Yet the relationship between ''African'' and ''South African'' occurs at a deeper level. Mphahlele's attempt to relate African and South African themes arises partly out of the peculiar circumstances of Zambia in the late 1960s and his choice of Zambia as setting. Independent since 1964, Zambia has been hailed as Africa's second chance after Ghana. Yet such independence was belied by Zambia's insidious relationships with its southern neighbor, South Africa. In choosing Zambia as setting, Mphahlele recognizes the interaction between Zambia and South Africa, their close geographic proximity and interconnected histories. . . .

*Chirundu* is not, as one critic suggests, ''part of established Pan African literature,'' but a novel that reveals a dialogue between South Africa and independent Africa immediately to the north and identifies concerns common to both societies. The ambiguities of Zambia at the end of the 1960s render it an intriguing setting for such a venture.

Dorian Haarhoff. *English in Africa*. 13, 2 (October 1986), pp. 39–40, 44

There is one writer in whose work it is possible to trace, over a period of forty years, both the problems of literary production experienced by South African writers and the stages in the development of an appropriate critical approach: for Ezekiel Mphahlele functioned as artist and critic throughout that period, encountering in his creative and confronting in his critical work the alienation of consciousness and the appropriation of discourse, while his later criticism records the efforts of black writers towards reappropriation.

While it would distort the corpus of his writing to divide it, whether critical or creative, into stages, there are nevertheless certain identifiable features appearing progressively within it, which sometimes correspond to, and sometimes seem to be partially responsible for, precipitating changes in the attitudes of black writers. In his earliest years, his writing is white-oriented: he addresses a predominantly white readership, in the forms and language of white culture, to record his protests on behalf of his black brothers. The events and pressures leading to his exile, together with the distancing effect of that experience, produce a raised consciousness that eventually resolves itself into an identification with the general ideas and aims of the black consciousness movement, despite his removal from the scene of its inception and growth. Lastly, with his return to South Africa, he was compelled to confront the whole issue of the liberation struggle, which had finally and reluctantly moved beyond the long years of patient nonviolence. . . .

Mphahlele wrote his critical works during periods when he felt too barren and infertile to attempt creative writing. They became, I would argue, far more than his fiction or poetry, seminal forces in the development of South African literature. He used both versions of *The African Image* and *Voices in the Whirlwind* as a search for personal, intellectual, and cultural identity, and they helped the establishment of a communal cultural identity in his country. The resonances of his work can be traced throughout the black consciousness movement in South Africa and beyond it, into the 1980s, providing young writers with aspirations and goals, and helping them to develop the means—the literary skills, styles, and genres—with which to attain them. He is the grand old man of South African letters, to which he has contributed, inside and outside South Africa, for forty years. His criticism helped to launch a self-propagating cultural theory—feeding into the work of younger writers, then, years later, taking up what they produced and analyzing their contributions in such a way as to prepare the ground for further cultivation. . . .

Throughout his writing, creative as well as critical, the impact of Europe on himself and his community provides a leitmotif—a leitmotif which is given different emphases at different periods, at times being overshadowed almost completely by contemporary preoccupations, but repeatedly surfacing and always, after such a period of dormancy, having suffered a sea-change. His attitude to the effects of European culture and education were equivocal from the outset. He was always aware of the conflicts set up by its introduction into an African context even when he was most receptive to the potential benefits it brought with it. However, throughout his life the balance shifts consistently, to the point where he is acutely aware of the damage it has inflicted, though even then he recognizes that there is much to be salvaged from the wreckage.

Through the course of his three major critical works, we can chart a growing awareness of his own emergence from a Western-style education. At the beginning when he embarked on English literature courses he was too involved, too subordinated to the structure, too much an agent of the power that had produced him, to be conscious of the implications of its operations upon himself as an individual and upon the African community as a societal network. With his incursions into Négritude and black American literature, he gained the necessary distance from his own educational background to achieve his consciousness.

Jane Watts. *Black Writers from South Africa* (New York: St. Martin's Press, 1989), pp. 57–58, 63

Mphahlele's commitment to the liberation of his fatherland is well articulated in his literature, culture and politics. His creative and critical works show that his response to the politics of apartheid and of independent Africa has passed through three distinct phases. The first phase, discernible in the early short stories, is characterized by a non-violent form of protest that demonstrates his struggle for better race relationships and the end of apartheid. The survivalist posture maintained by Mphahlele in this early phase provides him with the psychological energy he needs for the battle he wages to remain human in a dehumanizing set-up. Survival is a concept that predates Mphahlele's writing. The emphasis Mphahlele gives it in his writing is as a result of the unusually pronounced threat to the Black man's existence in South Africa.

The second phase of Mphahlele's response to apartheid is marked by a modest form of protest of which liberal humanism is an essential part. *Down Second Avenue* covers this stage of Mphahlele's writing. Liberal humanism is not the terminal point in

Mphahlele's protest as some critics imply. Our reveals that there is a third phase in Mphahlele's works that responds to apartheid and the politics in Africa. In this later phase, Mphahlele abandons the non-violent, apolitical stance of the early phase and the liberal humanism of the second phase and advocates outright revolt. *The Wanderers, Chirundu* and *The African Image* in its revised 1974 edition mark this stage. It is a stage that contemplates revolutionary violence as a viable approach to the eradication of apartheid and the reconstruction of independent Africa. The revolutionary approach is what Mphahlele refers to as the second revolution or the real one. The first and 'false' revolution is the struggle for, and attainment of, independence.

Mphahlele returned to South Africa in 1977 after 20 years of self-exile. The return was, in the first place, prompted by his inability to live under the dehumanizing and crippling conditions created by apartheid. He went back to the same socio-political reality. The return to South Africa is thus a major contradiction in Mphahlele's creative and political life. Facts emerge from this decision which prevent a condoning or condemnation of this prolific writer. There is the fact that the writer is first and foremost committed to his art. In Mphahlele's case, this means commitment to the cause of the Black South Africans. Mphahlele's commitment also demands continuous writing against inhumanity, violence and segregation. His return to his homeland shows also that the writer will always find it more spiritually rewarding to live and write amongst his people. When he distances himself from his society, he is not likely to live a self-fulfilling, creative life. Hence, until he returned to South Africa, Mphahlele's consistent focus was still South Africa. This tyranny of place compels him to examine the problems of the African continent and the world outside in relation to South Africa. This is manifested in *The Wanderers, Chirundu* and *Voices in the Whirlwind and Other Essays*. The problems of the world outside South Africa, especially independent Africa, are responsible for Mphahlele's conclusion that it is more meaningful to go back and teach in South Africa and live in solidarity with his fellow Black people. To go back and teach in South Africa when the Bantu Education he fought so hard against in the early '50s still existed shows some amount of frustration and defeat, but on another level, it shows a commitment which only the courageous writer is capable of. It also shows a determination to fight against human injustice with the most readily available weapons. For Mphahlele, these are teaching and writing.

Tyohdzuah Akosu. *The Writing of Ezekiel (Es'kia) Mphahlele, South African Writer: Literature, Culture, and Politics.* (Lewiston, New York: Edward Mellen Press, 1995), pp. 300–03

*Afrika My Music* takes up [Mphahlele's] life story where *Down Second Avenue* left off, and the greater part covers the years of exile. He tells of literary matters in African countries in which he played a role, all seen from the viewpoint of a newcomer to these regions. The word portraits of writers such as Camara Laye, Ngugi was Thiong'o, [Wole] Soyinka, [J. P.] Clark, [Christopher] Okigbo, [Kofi] Awoonor, and others are too brief to be revealing, but they give thoughtful glimpses of the people he met. The South African section takes readers only as far as his work in Lebowa. Mphahlele calls the first chapter "The Sounds Begin Again," but the sounds

are not the "sirens in the night," the "thunder at the door," or the "wordless endless wail / only the unfree know," to which Dennis Brutus refers in his well-known poem "Sirens, Knuckles, Boots" . . . the first line of which Mphahlele chose as the title of this second autobiography. Neither are the sounds the earthy, vibrant ones he records in *Down Second Avenue*. They are the thinner, plaintive noises of a man whose homecoming was not a triumphant return to his roots. The picture he draws of modern South Africa is an impersonal one, which is available to readers in greater detail in many social documents. . . .

There is one more book-length work of fiction Mphahlele has written and published. *Father Come Home* is a historical novel for children that takes place in the early 1920s after the Native Land Act had been passed, driving Africans from large, fertile areas into small, arid reserves. As a consequence, men were forced to leave their families and work in mines. The story concerns the growth to independence of fourteen-year-old Maredi Tulamo, whose father has left the family and returns only many years later. Adventures occur when the boy goes off in search of his father, but he gets only as far as a farm where he remains to work. The white farmer is not an important character in the novel. White life has become peripheral again, as it was in Mphahlele's earliest fiction. The man is neither unkind nor cruel: "he was simply in charge of [the laborers'] fate. . . ." It is with life in the village that Mphahlele is primarily concerned, the suffering of the wives and mothers left behind, and the hardships and values of the community. The narration is filled with folklore and includes epics about warriors, sung by the stranger Mashabela, a musician, poet, and healer, who moves into the village.

Mphahlele draws on his own life as a herd boy in the northern Transvaal, where he suffered the pain of growing up without a father. There is psychological insight in the story of the boy whose life is ruled by a longing for his father, but when at last the father comes home, there is no fairy-tale ending. Maredi finds it difficult to relate to the man and has to learn to adjust. The story is told in simple language for children, but the touching plot and the vividly depicted geographical and historical background appeal equally to adults. The work fills part of a great need in South Africa for a children's literature that is meaningful for black children. . . .

Es'kia Mphahlele's vision of an African culture, with a creative energy strong enough to survive and renew itself perpetually, is responsible for his involvement in every phase of black life, literature, and education in South Africa. Because his vision is essentially a Pan-Africanist one, his legacy will survive the present regime in South Africa and will benefit future generations in his own country and beyond.

Ursula A. Barnett. In Bernth Lindfors and Reinhard Sander, eds. *Dictionary of Literary Biography*, Volume 125: *Twentieth-Century Caribbean and Black African Writers, Second Series*, (1993), pp. 104–7

BIBLIOGRAPHY

*Man Must Live and Other Stories*, 1946; *Down Second Avenue*, 1959; *The Living and Dead and Other Stories*, 1961; *The African Image*, 1962; *In Corner B*, 1967; *The Wanderers*, 1971; *Voices in the Whirlwind and Other Essays*, 1972; *Chirundu*, 1979; *Afrika My Music*, 1984; *Father Come Home*, 1984

# MQHAYI, S. E. K. (1875–1945)

## South Africa

*Reward* is the title of the seventh volume recently issued in the Bantu Treasury Series edited by Professor C. M. Doke. The author, S. E. K. Mqhayi, from whose numerous Xhosa productions the present poems have been chosen, explains that the title is designed to indicate "things rare and profitable." This claim is justified by the contents because the author is without a peer among writers of Xhosa poetry, living or dead, when judged by the quantity and calibre of his output, much of which has not yet been published in book form.

The arrangement of the poems in this book is in five sections: 1. Didactic poems on subjects like Truth, Hope, Love, and so forth. 2. The passing of the old years and advents of new ones. 3. Obituary eulogia. 4. Praises of Africans who have travelled overseas. 5. Miscellaneous poems.

It is rare indeed to find other good poetry written in Xhosa on some of the subjects named, but with Mqhayi it is characteristic and it has deservedly earned him the popular appellation of *"Imbongi yesizwe"* (equivalent to Bantu Poet Laureate). Many of the poems are informative, and indeed "profitable" because informative, e.g., [a poem] in appreciation of the bi-monthly agricultural journal published at Umtata by the Bunga. The topic of the expiration of one year and the incoming of a new one is almost Mqhayi's annual exercise and monopoly, and he does it with gusto. The variety of stanza forms in this selection inevitably invites comparison with *Zulu Songs* by B. W. Vilakazi (Volume 1 in the same series) but in the Zulu language. Both authors employ forms definitely imitative of English rhymes such as the long and short metres, the sonnet and the heroic couplet. Both excel in their infinite variety of rhymes and rhythmic movement such as is also to be found in *The Orchard* by J. J. R. Jolobe (Volume 2 in the same series).

With regard to diction, Vilakazi frequently uses archaic and extraneous words imported from the neighbouring South African tongues. But Mqhayi in the pieces included in this book employs archaic words with a moderation that just obviates their getting in between the reader and the subject matter as an obstacle, and he makes very few excursions into non-Xhosa words. This moderation, however, is absent in many of Mqhayi's poems outside of this volume.

D. D. T. Jabavu. *African Studies.* 2, 3 (1943), pp. 174–75

A lover of the human race, [Mqhayi] associated himself with several progressive movements and institutions. He understood alike the illiterate and educated, and as a result, his social influence was very wide. Because of his active interest in his people, his knowledge of their history, traditional and modern, was amazing. Through the press, by public orations, and in private letters, he had a message of encouragement to give to the social leaders of his people. . . . His contribution to Southern Bantu Literature is easily the largest and most valuable that has hitherto been made by any single writer. . . .

*The Case of the Twins* includes fiction, history and poetry. The book owes its title to the novelette that covers its first half—the lawsuit of the twins. the plot of this novelette is suggested by Verses 28–29 of the 38th Chapter of the book of Genesis. As the author states in the preface, the purpose of the story is to give a picture of legal procedure among the Xhosa people, and to show the democratic spirit in which it is carried out. . . .

If we turn to his poetry, we find that Mqhayi, though perhaps possessing more talent, is nevertheless more limited in scope than some of the younger Nguni poets. Essentially a poet of the traditional type, for theme he is almost wholly confined to concrete subjects, usually human beings. He is confined to lyrical verse, chiefly odes and elegies. Even historical themes he was never able to put into narrative verse. . . . A sense of effort and strain is always with us when we read his rhymed verse, and very often we feel that in order to observe rhyme, the poet has sacrificed sense, virility and easy flow of language. His favourite rhyme scheme is the heroic couplet, and because he invariably writes end-stopped lines, his rhymed verse makes dull and monotonous reading.

But if we judge Mqhayi by what he has achieved instead of judging him by what he has failed to achieve, then there is no doubt that his best poetry is of a high order. . . .

Mqhayi takes the highest place in Xhosa literature. He has done more than any other writer to enrich Xhosa. In his hands it receives a fresh impress, and he has revealed all its possibilities as a powerful medium of expression of human emotion. His prose as well as his poetry contains expressions that became proverbial long before his death.

A. C. Jordan. *South African Outlook.* September 1945, pp. 135–38

[Mqhayi] eliminates all real conflict from the world created by his fancy. In *Don Jadu*, the hero passes from town to town, solving all problems overnight, and leading raw tribesmen from a primitive state to an advanced civilization in a matter of weeks. Everywhere he is acclaimed and glorified and rejoices inwardly all the while. Thus does Mqhayi allow his imagination, fostered by a repulsive hunger for self-glorification, to run riot and escape into a world of pure fancy, where probability is grossly violated and logical development of incident unknown. True, Mqhayi's imagination is colourful and productive, but it is not disciplined. His mastery of language is undoubted, but he blatantly tries to impress by playing with big words and archaisms. His glittering façade of words is unsupported and so we go away unsatisfied.

John Riordan. *African Studies.* 20, 1 (1961), p. 53

As cattle was the foundation of Xhosa economy, and therefore of Xhosa society, this was a problem of life and death for the Xhosa nation as a whole. *Don Jadu* grew out of these experiences and this realization. It was not meant as a realistic description of a situation that everyone knew anyway. It was designed as a blueprint for the future coexistence of both races in South Africa. And it was conceived in a spirit of compromise and syncretism. There are only three things that Mqhayi forcefully rejects: the South Africa government, the prison system, and imported hard liquor as opposed to the native home-brewed beer. His ideal state is not a preliminary study in Bandustan. It is a multi-racial society that places a high premium on education and progress, and it is a Christian society that has incorporated many of the beliefs and customs dear to African hearts. In the elaboration of this Bantu utopia, Mqhayi exhibits uncommonly powerful intellectual imagination. . . .

It was perhaps as a poet that Mqhayi was chiefly valued by the Xhosa audience, not least because he had completely mastered the form and the spirit of the traditional praise poem (*izibongo*) while adapting it

*The Wanderers* shows the English-speaking whites (but not the (''Poet Laureate''), and Vilakazi calls him ''the Father of Xhosa poetry,'' because ''he is responsible for a transition from the primitive bards who sang the *izibongo*.'' The main function of the tribal bard (*imbongi*) was to strengthen the cohesion of the group, usually by celebrating the glorious figures of the past and extolling the authority of the reigning chief. Mqhayi's volume on Hintza is an example of this, as are the obituary eulogies of local figures in *Reward*. But since the central preoccupation of the *izibongo* in its purest form is to promote the prosperity and the greatness of the group, it does not deal solely with the chiefs, but also with any public events that may be significant in that respect. . . .

If we were to believe Vilakazi, Mqhayi's attempts at innovation were not always successful. His poems dealing with nature, the Zulu critic says, are ''dull,'' and those on religious subjects are ''mere oratorical exercises'' when compared with those of his successor [J. R.] Jolobe. Mqhayi ''excelled in heroic poetry of the traditional type, and showed great skill in weaving his people's customs, legends, and myths into his poems.''

Albert S. Gérard. *Four African Literatures* (Berkeley: University of California Press, 1971), pp. 58–60

Although from the onset Mqhayi tried to get away from mission-school writing, he did not involve himself with recreating the oral literature. Instead he worked fairly closely with oral sources (in addition to indigenous idioms, his work is full of the precision of one directed but not hamstrung by a tradition) and his story [''The Case of the Twins''] emerges as another exercise in the attempt to establish individuality. Mqhayi makes the ''case'' even more difficult by presenting the contestants as twins. Who could claim to be different? His story, ostensibly about the right to rule, concerns the dubious assertion of individuality. The mere fact that they are twins not only heightens their similarity, but makes their case for separate recognition futile and ridiculous. The author asserts the predominance of the tribe, since it is an old tribal member who finally helps the court to decide. . . .

What Mqhayi did was to establish the artist's independence from the patronage of religious bodies. This does not mean that he was ahead of his time, for as late as 1942 when he published *Reward*, a collection of verse, the sections into which he divided the poems were along fairly conventional lines. For instance, the selection includes poems on ''truth,'' ''hope,'' and ''love,'' on the ''passing of years,'' on death, and perhaps, nearest to the tradition, poems of praise for Africans who had gone overseas. He imitated English rhyme as well as the sonnet and heroic couplet. But his poetic gifts were not entirely dissipated in producing conventional laudations. He expressed the new individual consciousness through satire and in the manner of the Sotho writer Azariel Sekese he even attacked royalty.

O. R. Dathorne. *The Black Mind* (Minneapolis, University of Minnesota Press, 1974), pp. 132–33

BIBLIOGRAPHY

*U-Samson*, 1907;''Ityala lama-wele'' (The Case of the Twins), 1914; *Ama gora e Mendi* (The Heroes of the Mendi), 1920; *U-Sogqumahashe: Ishikhumbuzo sika Ntsikana*, 1921; *I-Bandla la Bantu* (The Church of the People), 1923; *U-bomi bom-fundisi John Knox Bokwe* (The Life of the Reverend J. K. Bokwe), 1925; *Isikumbuzo zomPolofiti u-Ntsikana*, 1926; *U-Don Jadu*, 1929; *U-Mhlekazi u-Hintsa: um-bongo ewasiya izibongo zamadoda ngomnyaka we* (Hintsa the Great, 1937; *U-Mqhayi wase-Ntab'ozuko* (Mqhayi from the Mountain of Glory, 1939; *I-nzuzo* (Reward), 1942; Mqhayi in Translation, 1976

# MTSHALI, Oswald (1940–)
## South Africa

Many people write poetry, but there are few poets in any generation, in any country. There is a new poet in Africa, and his name is Oswald Mbuyiseni Mtshali. . . .

Mtshali's relationship with his immediate world—his philosophical approach, if you prefer—is married successfully with his style. The most striking poems are often those where the verbal magic—in this case the creation of mood or sense of place—contains a sting that finally shrivels the verbal magic away, leaving a question or statement burning in the mind. . . .

The world you will enter through [his] poems is a black man's world made by white men. It finds its epitome in the ghastly vision of township dogs fighting over the corpse of an abandoned baby—surely one of the most shocking poems ever written, and yet a triumph, since it could have been achieved only by forging from bitterness a steely compassion, by plunging into horror deep enough to bring forth tenderness. If, in this world, the poet Mtshali belongs automatically to an elite, it is the dead-end elite into which black artists and intellectuals are thrust by any color-bar society. The daily circumstances of his life remain those of the majority population of South Africa. The image of bread recurs again and again in his work: even snow suggests the labor for bread—''Trees sagged and grunted under the back-breaking flour bags of snow.'' The fact that man cannot live by bread alone is seen as a need for the ''rare bread, solitude'' which he seeks to ''feed my hunger to read / to dream, and to write.''

This is the imagery of survival. Oswald Mtshali, ironist, knows all that threatens man, abroad as well as at home: the Berlin walls of distrust, and the ''moats of fright around his heart.'' He knows, finally, that even man's apparent virtues threaten him, in some times and places.

Nadine Gordimer. Foreword to Oswald Mbuyiseni Mtshali. *Sounds of a Cowhide Drum* (New York: The Third Press, 1972) pp. xi–xii, xv

The themes of Mtshali's poetry derive inevitably from the deepest and bitterest personal experience of his life as a messenger in Johannesburg. But the events provoke not the anticipated rage of immediate resentment, they are absorbed into poetry, distilled in his lines into moods of wry irony, and a curiously sustained tender awareness that persists through the anger. . . . Perhaps it would not be fanciful to note in passing a partially equivalent agony to be found in the work of Wilfred Owen during [World War I]. He too had to find a mechanism in his writing to distill the brute blood experience of the gangrene of war into poetry suffused with the realization that pity and compassion are moods that allow the best response to such a confrontation with unimaginable horror. . . .

Mtshali's voice can of course be strident and declamatory "for that is the sound of a cowhide drum / the Voice of Mother Africa." Yet, he accepts equally the implications of his role as a poet, his obligation to strike that cowhide drum so that its reverberations are true and valid, and therefore as complex and varied in its tones as the human feelings it lauds. He recognizes that distaste does not preclude humor, that power may flicker in moments of delight, that a saint is a beast, and the noble are also fools. Mtshali is a poet and sees himself specifically as an artist. . . . [His] lines indicate a significant degree of introspection, of a personal vision of poetry that is different from debate about the public efficacy and function of his verse. Quite openly he declares that neither "curses" nor "praises" can deflect him from his dedication to his art. Mtshali sees the poet as "a mole burrowing," drawing not only upon outward experience but also upon his deep private spirit. There is an acceptance of his role, of the function of words, rather than the anxious concern for their validity. Poetry, in a sense, is taken for granted as a pure discipline that allows the inspection of circumstance. It is for this reason that in Mtshali's work, the violence is controlled by a poetic sensibility that utilizes the devices of poetic expression for the recognition of experience. Both tone and technique are at the service of art; and just because his verse is, in the entirely nonderogatory sense, "artistic," it is the more effective and passionate. For above all, Mtshali as a poet, is a worker in words that are rich, daring, suggestive, catching mood and scene into the concentrated explosion of work and experience that makes the imagery of poetry.

John Povey. *Ufahumu*. 4, 1 (spring 1973), pp. 151–52

Mtshali is essentially the urban poet; his importance lies in having brought Africa in literature to the townships, thus making black literature once again an important medium in South Africa. . . .

Few people doubt . . . that the publication of *Sounds of a Cowhide Drum* had begun a new era in black South African poetry. Asked why he chose the title of the collection from the last poem, Mtshali explained that the cowhide drum is a symbol which can be used to express many moods and different occasions of his life. "When war is declared, drums are beaten in a particular way; and when a baby is born, another tune is played on the drum."

He succeeded because of his genius in putting . . . [the experience of black township life] into words. White readers found his poetry fascinating because it gave them a window into black life, and black readers identified with his projection of their thoughts. . . . Mtshali makes his impact by his astounding capacity for absorbing and reflecting impressions and reproducing these, not instinctively—the simplicity is deceptive—but with the deliberate awareness of the craftsman. . . .

Mtshali's greatest asset . . . was his ability to communicate, at a time when blacks were eager to find a spokesman and still willing to communicate with whites who were prepared to listen. By looking upon poetry as a form of communication rather than as the intellectual pursuit of crystallizing individual thought, Mtshali became an exponent of African culture. Moreover, Mtshali's

writing moves with the rhythm of feeling to provide a particular emotional atmosphere which [H.I.E.] Dhlomo saw as essentially African.

Ursula A. Barnett. *A Vision of Order* (London: Sinclair Browne, 1983), pp. 33, 35, 51, 53

Oswald Mtshali, the distinguished South African poet, has also spent his time in exile in the United States. . . . In 1971, when he published his first collection of poems, *Sounds of a Cowhide Drum*, Mtshali exploded upon the South African literary scene—a distinct new voice marked by delicate lyricism. Since that time his fame has steadily increased.

Mtshali states in a note at the beginning of his new collection of poems that *Fireflames* . . . "had a long gestation period," and that each poem for him is "like a long-overdue baby." The analogy is an apt one, given the content of this new volume—especially the opening poems, which painfully describe family relations. In the midst of human tragedy, Mtshali believes that a sense of hope and faith will prevail, especially in the infant's cosmos: "A child is the angel of the world . . . a picture of righteousness."

The tone changes in many of the subsequent poems, where history is referred to as "spring cleaning," and Mtshali describes his sense of uprootedness twelve thousand miles away from his homeland. There are vivid poetic evocations of a number of martyred South African black leaders, a commemoration in Harlem of the Soweto uprising and, finally, bittersweet images of the author's experiences in New York City, made bearable by Harlem. . . .

*Fireflames* has been handsomely illustrated with woodcuts by eight South African artists. I wouldn't say that the poems within the volume are particularly radical or inflammatory, yet the volume was banned in South Africa after its publication in 1980—simply another example of the rampant censorship within the country. All this, of course, to Mtshali's country's detriment.

Charles R. Larson. *World Literature Today*. 58, 3 (summer 1984), pp. 383–84

Mtshali's poems are intended, in the first instance, for the fringe of the English-speaking white population that reads poetry. But, although this public may well be educated, it is no less ignorant of the real conditions of the African with whom it rubs shoulders without seeing.

When Mtshali demands the right to speak, when he reveals to the whites the "hidden face" of South African society, he is undertaking a political act of which only the black prose writers of the late 1950s and early 1960s who are now banned in South Africa were capable. Although he never presents the communities in a position of conflict, although he always adopts a restrained albeit firm tone, although he plays at being naive the better to attack, he nonetheless fulfills his role as the revealer of the truth, in other words, as a man of protest.

Rather than restrict himself to the more usual portraits, Mtshali prefers to sketch characteristic little scenes which enable him to reveal some fundamental features of the African's situation. Thus, he constantly switches from the swarming crowds of the township, where the African lives at night and [on] weekends, to the white city, where he works during the day: from the one to the other and vice versa, in the constant back-and-forth movement of the pendulum that is the underlying pulse beat of the urban life of South African blacks.

The dominant impressions conveyed by the township are all confirmed by the sociological surveys: hunger, poverty, fear, for the majority; a relative prosperity and violence for the rest. . . .

At the heart of the poems directed especially at the black community, Mtshali returns constantly, and in several cases fairly explicitly, to the same crucial idea: the chief enemy of the oppressed is not the white man but the black man himself—because of his passivity and his lack of courage and aggressiveness. He allows himself, in fact, to be exploited, to be reduced to the state of an animal, to accept the imposition of the fatality of color distinction in which white is the symbol of domination and monopoly, and all without the slightest protest. All he does is turn to prayer, drink, or drugs, which are of little effect against the weapons of the white man. In this way, he wastes his vitality and sweeps aside the heritage of his ancestors. In other words, Mtshali invites the Africans to radically change their thinking.

This is something that would have difficulty in getting past the censor if the message were clearly stated: even in a country where the potential audience for poetry is minimal, there are limits the regime would not allow to be exceeded. Mtshali was well aware of this, so out of necessity, as well as from personal preference, it seems, he veiled his thoughts and used ''the language of the slaves''—a network of allusions, references and hints which are clear only to those who share his culture.

Jacques Alvarez-Pereyre. *The Poetry of Commitment in South Africa* (London: Heinemann, 1984), pp. 172–73, 179

[The] ''new'' wave of committed poetry was first made prominent by Oswald Mtshali. When his first collection of poetry, *Sounds of a Cowhide Drum,* was published, Mtshali was working as a motorscooter messenger in Johannesburg. The poetry, which was generally well received at its publication by both blacks and whites, deals with the familiar concerns of race and politics similar to those examined by older poets such as Dennis Brutus. But it is the manner in which these concerns are expressed that has made *Sounds of a Cowhide Drum* so successful. Mtshali's cynical and sarcastic attitude, his oblique and ironic use of vivid, suggestive similes and images, and the profound meaning that lies beneath the apparent simplicity of his poetry, all contribute towards their total effect. This technique, however, is said to have disgruntled younger, radical writers like Mbulelo Mzamane, who wanted to see ''revolutionary fire'' in Mtshali's poetry. . . .

While critics like Mbulelo Mzamane have attacked what they consider to be an overemphasis on this Blakelike innocence and simplicity, they have overlooked the fact that what at first appears to be a poem celebrating innocence and the rapport between the shepherd and his environment, becomes a biting critique of the system's inequality; this is entirely compatible with the indirect approach Mtshali sets out to adopt.

Mtshali's manner of protest is reiterated in another poem that also focuses on a child character, and the technique of rhetorical questioning is again effectively employed. Like the shepherd in ''The Shepherd and His Flock,'' the boy in ''Boy on a Swing'' is a type character representing the suffering majority of blacks. Nadine Gordimer has perceptively described this singular representation that characterizes the ''new'' poetry saying, '''I' is the pronoun

that prevails, rather than 'we,' but the 'I' is the Whitmanesque unit of multimillions rather than the exclusive first person singular.''

Piniel Viriri Shava. *A People's Voice: Black South African Writing in the Twentieth Century* (London: Zed Books, 1989), pp. 71–73

It was in 1948 that the policy of racial discrimination was consolidated in South Africa and since then the legislation of the South African government has been geared towards a total repression of all categories of nonwhites. Among the several laws promulgated towards this end are the laws against franchise, laws against interracial marriages, laws for residential segregation based on color, pass laws, detention laws, and several other acts which have generated unabating violence. That these laws are designed to make various racial groups live mutually exclusive lives, to protect the whites, and to further exploit the nonwhites, especially the blacks, is graphically depicted by Oswald Mtshali. His portrayal in his collection of poems, *Sounds of a Cowhide Drum,* demonstrates that the legislation engenders restriction of movement and association, repression of thought and speech, and denial of educational opportunities to the blacks. . . .

Mtshali evokes and ridicules some of the laws which engender restriction of movement and association. They include: the separate Amenities Act for separate social facilities such as hotels, lavatories, parks, and post offices; the Immorality Act, for the prevention of sexual or marital relations among the different races; and the Pass Laws, which require the African to carry a document on him at all times for effective control of his movement and easy distribution of his labor.

In a colloquial style, Oswald Mtshali, in ''Pigeons at the Oppenheimer Park,'' makes a sarcastic and concentrated evocation of the typical slogans and usual tactics of the evidently prejudiced law enforcement agent, and dares the white policeman to apply the laws to the contravening birds. . . . We are told that ''these insolent birds . . . not only sit on White Only benches . . . the hallowed benches,'' but ''they also mess them up with birdshit.'' The persona then sarcastically asks, ''Don't they know of the Separate Amenities Act?'' . . .

Mtshali's use of the bird imagery evokes the borderlessness of the sky, the birds' region, where they fly freely and this suggests the poet's longing for the spirit of such [an] environment which contrasts sharply with his own real world riddled with restrictions. . . .

Mtshali's diction is very effective in its evocation of the sacredness with which the blacks are expected to regard the things of the white man and [their] attendant restrictions. Words such as ''hallowed,'' ''chant,'' ''holy,'' and ''congregation'' used to describe the park, its bench, its fountain, and its water are words usually associated with the worship of God. Their use in this context heightens the effect of his depiction of the disparity in the apartheid system. . . .

It is evident that Mtshali's poetry is evocative of the denial of the right of the blacks to express their thoughts freely and develop intellectual powers; it is also evocative of the censorship of the press, and the banning of committed literary works.

''Handcuffs'' is suffused with images of somatic pain and repression of thought and speech. It is a concentrated evocation of the agony of a people in bondage. Ordinarily, handcuffs are instruments of restriction and repression; the poem's title is symbolic in that here they serve to evoke the effects on the blacks. . . .

Mtshali depicts that the repression is so total and overwhelming that it encompasses not only the physical but also the intellectual and the spiritual creates certain urgent needs whose fulfillment it, at the same time, makes impossible. It is like beating a man and asking him not to cry. . . .

Mtshali in his ''This Kid Is No Goat'' evokes the irrelevance of the schools' syllabus to the needs of the blacks. He views the education given as misguided, with a strong inhibitory religious influence. The protagonist laments his brother's incapacitating education metaphorically, depicted in the latter's ''clutching a rosary as an amulet against'' discrimination and oppression. . . .

Consequent upon their inability to go to school, most black children spend their lives in the streets and rely only on raw life experience for their learning. This leads to their acquisition of bad habits such as drunkenness, stealing, and other forms of violence which eventually drag them to jail. This feature is portrayed by Mtshali in ''This Kid Is No Goat'' where the protagonist's brother, denied the opportunity to go to school, has to enroll at ''Life University'' which connotes his complete reliance on the everyday raw experience of life for his learning, and the consequences of this are unfortunate. . . .

It can . . . be concluded that Oswald Mtshali's depiction of the horror of social discrimination in South Africa is vivid, effective, and comprehensive. Its comprehensiveness shocks the reader into awareness of the extent to which apartheid has brutalized the black populace and this constitutes a subtle indictment urging a revulsion against apartheid. Mtshali's colloquial style is gentle and refreshing, and his skillful wielding of metaphors and irony earns his portrayal the seal of poetry.

David Olusegun Agbaje. *Literary Half-Yearly.* 32, 2 (July 1991), pp. 17–20, 27–28, 33–35

BIBLIOGRAPHY
*Sounds of a Cowhide Drum*, 1971; *Fireflames*, 1980

# MUDIMBE, V. Y. (1941–)
## Zaire

To read Mudimbe is to be brought into a discourse whose archeological field is broad and deep: breadth arising from the extensive reading in many schools of thought, indeed in many disciplines, varying chiefly over the hard and soft sciences, including also history and literature, and with certain ''réflecteurs'' prevailing— notably [Michel] Foucault, and to a lesser extent [Jacques] Lacan, [Louis] Althusser, and [Jean-Paul] Sartre . . . depth arising from the sense of an historical consciousness in which can be traced the evolution of a diachronic phenomenon that has been occurring ever since the first Portuguese missionary-explorer ever set foot in the Kingdom of the Bakongo in 1483, and maybe, in terms of a typology of the encounter, for a much longer time.

The point of entry into this discourse for us is not, however, in the continuation of contemporary European thought, or of one of its branches abroad, but in the formation of a text of the encounter between Europe and Africa whose meaning is elaborated largely in the language of the above-mentioned thinkers. Mudimbe acquaints us with the issue at hand at the outset of his two major works of

critical enterprise, *L'Autre Face du royaume* and *L'Odeur du père,* by stating that he intends to raise the question of whether and under what conditions one can practice the social sciences in Africa. . . . As a social scientist, Mudimbe is particularly interested in raising the issues of political, existential freedom, and greater individual and social fulfillment in terms of the practices of the social scientists, and as the source of meaning for those practices, in their discourses. At the end of *L'Autre Face du royaume* we see that this problem is the pretext for examining the larger issue of the relationship between European and African discourses. The problematic element in this relationship is easily stated: How are the social scientists, the thinkers, the researchers in Africa, to produce today a discourse that will be productive in terms of Africa's needs and special conditions when the norms of the sciences, indeed of virtually all the disciplines being practiced in Africa are shaped by the Western tradition; and, indeed, it goes deeper than norms to encompass the entire discourse: its codes, its values, its assumptions on what constitutes truth, acceptability, worth in terms of information and research—all the unstated presuppositions.

Kenneth Harrow. In Stephen Arnold, ed. *African Literature Studies: The Present State/L'État présent* (Washington, D.C.: Three Continents Press, 1985), pp. 91–92

The plot of [V. Y. Mudimbe's] *L'Écart* revolves around Ahmed Nara, a young and very brilliant historian who is working on a thesis on the Koubas. Throughout the novel, this character is a neurotic affected by emotional troubles. He is aware of this state of affairs but is incapable of getting rid of these problems. . . .

In this situation of existential anguish, Ahmed Nara, like the majority of contemporary African intellectuals, is a person with a self-analyzing consciousness. This role is played here by Dr. Sano, who is the double of Nara. He is also the expression of a secret split, a hidden disarticulation. He is living in the gap or in between, because he does not wish to conform to the norms accepted by all, and because of this, wishes to create a new path for himself.

Indeed, from the beginning of the novel, Nara is bored by the ''dullness'' of life, by the feeling of a vague, indefinable, and unnamable dissatisfaction. . . .

Apparently spineless, unwilling, and in addition obsessed, Nara lives for Aminata alone. The attachment to this woman is a consolation, a liberation. It is even a deliberate act. . . .

Although intensely in love with each other, Nara and Aminata discover a difference in race. . . .

Opposing Aminata and her friends, Soum in particular, is Nara, who declares his black identity, his Négritude. But, in opposition to this notion of race firmly established in Nara, Soum presents the notion of social classes going so far as to reject even Négritude, which he describes as ''merde.'' He also has the firm conviction that one must lead the fight against social structures. He suggests to Nara adherence to the Communist party. . . .

Neither the thesis work, nor the domestication by Aminata, nor the appeal of his leftist friends to participate in their revolution can eliminate Nara's anguish. . . .

Finally, the gap or distance is in effect the distanciation with the community of men and the desire to change oneself first and then one's surroundings.

*L'Écart* does not limit itself to the analysis of the unhappy and stifled consciousness of an African intellectual, but reveals at the same time the difficulty experienced by this intellectual in living in a topsy-turvy world. A sociological reading of the novel shows us that Mudimbe talks in halftones of his own world. He sends back its own image to Africa. This is to say that *L'Écart* is not divorced from reality. Beyond the capture of the tortured consciousness of this African intellectual, there is a complete lucid political reflection on the situation of the continent.

Among the ills evoked are general unemployment, the quantitative and qualitative deterioration of teaching, the merciless exploitation of the weak by the strong, the exaggerated military parade, famine, the irresponsibility of political leaders, the silencing of the only political party, etc. . . .

At the level of writing, we gather that there is a search for a new language that is reflected by the practice of broken-up style, often incomplete, and marked by frequent points of suspension. . . .

Almost nothing of the substance of the traditional novel remains: the classical well-punctuated style has disappeared.

The theme of *L'Écart* enriches the francophone, novelistic production of Zaire in particular, and of the Negro-African world in general, through a novel interrogation: the neurosis of an African intellectual who lucidly examines Africa eroded by corrosive ills. It is, then, a "committed literature that desires to give birth to souls that are awakened to their consciousness."

> Mbuyamba Kankolongo. *Zaire Afrique*. 144 (1988), pp. 227–29, 232†

V. Y. Mudimbe's second novel, [*Le Bel Immonde*, translated as *Before the Birth of the Moon*], is a very rich, very disturbing story about individual pain and loss in a young society's struggle for independence and nationhood. It is set in Zaire in the mid-1960s, a period which was arguably the country's most perilous and chaotic. Fourteen million people drawn from some two hundred ethnic groups struggled to bind themselves into a nation after generations of alternately brutal and paternalistic Belgian colonial rule. During those years betrayal, assassination, greed, deceit, and confusion were as common as equatorial rain. But Mudimbe spends little time discussing these crises on the macrocosmic scale. Instead he skillfully extracts from the historical panorama two very complex and troubled people—a government minister and a prostitute—who, through their protean love affair, tell us more about the pains of the young nation than could any history book. In the first of his four novels to be translated into English, Mudimbe shows what sociopolitical upheaval does rather than what it is.

> Reginald McKnight. *New York Times Book Review*. April 30, 1989, p. 43

Mudimbe's novel, *Le Bel Immonde*, has a unique style in which the action stagnates a little, then rushes forward, and then returns to the original point. The crux of the plot is an affair between a powerful minister and a young prostitute. An affair that is transformed with the passage of time, from a simple fancy to a kind of romance, especially for the official who is married and father of a family. The attachment of the woman is all the more surprising, because one learns soon that she prefers Sappho's taboo to male warmth.

The destiny of the two characters is further linked by a political factor: the combat that the country is leading against the woman's ethnicity. Her father having died recently at the hands of the legal forces, the prostitute is recruited by the insurgents to serve as a spy

against the minister. In the meantime, the latter, wishing to protect himself against the enemies, makes a sacrifice of his mistress's friend to the spirits of his ancestors. But he is suspected no less by his colleagues and, therefore, in order to demonstrate his good faith, he undertakes a mission in the region of the insurgency. Soon after the departure of her lover, the prostitute is arrested and questioned at length. In desperation, and in order to get out of this problem, she ends up betraying the minister, of whose death in a car accident one finally condescends to tell her. Free and quite relieved, she starts her life over as if nothing has happened. The novel returns to the starting point: a nightclub where the prostitute devotes her time to soliciting, all the while scouting for an eventual homosexual partner.

That's it as far as the plot of *Le Bel Immonde* is concerned. As for the rest, this novel with the ambiguous title is marked by an uncommon heterogeneity, which is translated on several levels. Firstly, the themes treated or evoked go from adultery to betrayal, while passing through lesbianism, transvestitism, love, death, human sacrifice, anthropology, and themes of a sociopolitical nature such as prostitution, malpractice, and rebellion. Furthermore, the entire ambience of the work seems to have the same bizarre nature: the night-club scenes reappear constantly, whereas many other episodes seem to be experienced in a dreamlike state or in a state of semiconsciousness.

But it is especially at the level of structure that this heterogeneity is best represented. In fact, the composition of the novel shows different genres: about ten pages are devoted to the epistolary genre. One also finds a radiophonic discourse, a journal article, as well as numerous passages from the novel in the from of memoirs. Finally, the entire novel is punctuated by transitional poems that announce, the majority of times, the nightclub scenes. . . .

In conclusion, we can say that, in *Le Bel Immonde*, Mudimbe seems to participate in the inclinations of the new Western novelistic form. He distances himself from the traditional norms of the genre in treating heterogeneous themes, in creating anonymous characters with hazy and fleeting personalities, and through the blend of narrative modes.

> Victor O. Aire. In Jonathan A. Peters, Mildred P. Mortimer, and Russell V. Linnemann, eds. *Literature of Africa and the African Continuum* (Washington, D.C.: Three Continents Press, 1989), pp. 153–54, 156†

[In *Entre les eaux*] Mudimbe presents Pierre Landu as one who embodies the extreme poles of an impossible purity. Pierre is a priest whose need to be true to his vocation leads him to join the revolution in his homeland, ostensibly Zaire. His narrative-confession is all the more appropriate given his dual identity as priest-revolutionary. He is a devout Christian from early youth, and completes his training for the priesthood in Rome in the Jesuitical seminary, the Angelicum. There, with his young, Italian friend, Fabrizio, he is seduced by the beauties of Italian culture, especially Medieval and Renaissance art, and Baroque music, while at the same time learning about the latest trends in Marxist thought; he is led to conclude that the true calling of Christ's ministry is best embodied, in our times, in Marx himself.

Despite his initiation as a youth in the religion of his ancestors, Pierre accepts Christianity. Yet he fails to find a way to harmonize his new religion with his traditional past. He remains torn, despite his early alienation from that past, because the new culture and religion which attract him are manifestly not his own, and because he cannot fulfill the expectations of his priesthood without denying his African priesthood and family. He is "entre les eaux," unable to be true to either path, aware of his failure to live up to either the imported ideals of Marxism or Christianity, or to fall back on the traditional way of life.

> Kenneth W. Harrow. In Jonathan A. Peters, Mildred P. Mortimer, and Russell V. Linnemann, eds. *Literature of Africa and the African Continuum* (Washington, D.C.: Three Continents Press, 1989), pp. 164–65

Mudimbe's theoretical books, *L'Autre Face du royaume* and *L'Odeur du père*, and his novels, *Entre les eaux* and *L'Écart*, engage as their subject the enabling as well as the regressive elements in Western discourse, thereby liberating spaces in Africa from which more empowered discourses can be uttered. . . .

[Mudimbe] calls for a reformulation of discourse in Africa. He argues that "we Africans must invest in the sciences, beginning with the human and social sciences. We must reanalyze the claims of these sciences for our own benefit, evaluate the risks they contain, and their discursive spaces. We must reanalyze for our benefit the contingent supports and the areas of enunciation in order to know what new meaning and what road to propose for our quest so that our discourse can justify us as singular beings engaged in a history that is itself special." For Mudimbe, Africans must rid themselves of the smell of an abusive father, of the presence of an order which belongs to a particular culture but which defines itself as a fundamental part of all discourse. In order to produce differently, they must practice a major discursive insurrection against the West.

For Mudimbe, the most radical break with the West can be obtained only through a linguistic revolution in which European languages are replaced by African languages. Just as the originators of Greek thought set into motion a reorganization of knowledge and life through their transformation of ancient Egypt's use of science and methodologies, the West dominates the rest of the world today because it has appropriated Greek thought in its languages. In like fashion, for Mudimbe, at least "a change in the linguistic apparatus of science and production would provoke an epistemological break and open the door for new scientific adventures in Africa."

Mudimbe further argues that the other insurrectionist practice against the abusive father is obtained through the excommunication of Western *ratio* from African discursive practices that take place in European languages. In other words, Mudimbe calls for a reformulation of discourses inherited from the West and a subtle discursive technique aimed at deconstructing Western control over the rules that govern scientific statements. While working within Western languages, the new practice nevertheless departs from the traditional duplications of the Western canon in Africa and moves toward the construction of an African regime of truth and socially appropriated sciences. The new and cannibalizing discourse swells, disfigures, and transforms the bodies of Western texts, and establishes its order outside the traditional binary oppositions such as primitive/civilized, (neo) colonized/colonizer, slave/master, receiver/donor.

> Manthia Diawara. *October.* 55 (winter 1990), pp. 79, 88–89

*Entre les eaux* by V. Y. Mudimbe analyzes the inner conflict of an African priest whose theological training, including years of study in Rome, has made it impossible for him to relate to those to whom he is intended to minister. Seduced by Western culture—and by the relative comfort accompanying his status—he nevertheless sympathizes with the plight of the people and leaves his order to join a Marxist revolutionary leader in the forest. In spite of the action stemming from rebel forays, the real subject of the novel is the internal dilemma of the priest, Pierre Landu, as he tries to decide between his duty to his people and the obligation he feels to the church, between conscience and comfort, between Marxism and Christianity. Key to the novel's effectiveness and to the portrait of the alienated intellectual is the attitude of the revolutionary group toward the priest. Rarely trusted, constantly spied upon, Landu is regarded as the symbol of the social injustice and unwarranted privilege upon which the revolution is based.

> Janice Spleth. *Studies in Twentieth-Century Literature.* 15, 1 (winter 1991), pp. 126–27

On the prefatory page of his first book of poetry, entitled *Déchirures*, Mudimbe exclaims: "J'aimerais crier contre les poèmes pour que surgisse l'indiscrète insistance de l'extase" ["I would like to cry against poems so that the indiscreet insistence of ecstasy may surge!"]. . .

Irony is not the least pregnant figure in *Déchirures*. In the fifteen stations, or tableaus, offered to the reader's contemplation through the poet's own mind's eye, multiple elements could be regarded as the climax of despair, horror, and alienation. The first three sections unroll like a nightmarish film or dream whose sequences lead the dreamer from night to midday through dawn and morning. In its turn, at the microcosmic level, each subsection mirrors the larger dream in which the apotheosis of a redemption and a resurrection bathed in warmth, light, and joy is evoked, or even announced, as the eventual outcome of the whole drama. . . . Constantly, however, in all three sections, the intensity of the pain felt by the speaking subject at the obsessive sight of the omnipresent wounds, lacerations, or sterile landscapes is prevalent. In section two, the first-person narrator, whose presence has been discreetly announced in [section one], steps into the drama as a full-time contemplator, but also as an actor. Not unexpectedly, following the heroic path traveled by many prophetic figures, this narrator speaks both from outside and within the drama. As the text develops, the speaker's status as both savior and victim asserts itself more and more strongly. . . . Remarkable in these sections are the associations between the lofty red cannas, evoked as a burgeoning forest of loved idols, and the red dancing Africa present in the speaker's blood (". . .l'Afrique en danse rouge de mon sang"). Here, with authority, the speaker announces the resurrection of a blossoming land where he, again, will be able to love. Such a resurrection, however, remains encompassed within the humble vision afforded by writing. In fact, it is not easy to interpret such a line as "dans les brouillons maladroits de l'écriture" ["in the clumsy drafts of writing"]. Is the reader to assume that dream will never meet reality, that beauty, fecundity, and love will for ever remain a clumsy and tentative figure of speech? Or, on the contrary, is the reader to believe that the speaker is imparting to the word, if not the power to change the world, at least the power to plant the seeds of a new season?

The third section offers no relief to the reader's questioning. In this section, the speaker retreats to the contemplation of horror while seeking complete union with the sufferers. In [the first three subsections], various outside images, paintings, places, [and] milieus pass by the traveler's side like inconsequential mirages opposed to the "fertile eyes" of dream, a dream depicted through an interplay of alliterations and assonances in such a way as to suggest the sharpness of a blade and the torture of numerous lacerations: "Dans la rêve, le rêve effilé, si long et si lent des estafilades, des taillades" ["In the dream, the sharpedged dream, so long and lingering with slashes and gashes"]. The fifteen remaining subsections bring the reader close to the infinite misery of the Kisangani tragedy. The desire to be one with the African brothers and sisters' suffering is translated in a striking and uncompromising figure of speech: "Pouvoir être cette meurtrissure, cette gangrène éternelle . . ." ["I wish I were that bruise, that eternal gangrene . . ."]. Towards the end of section three, the speaker recalls the responsibility incurred by the Christian Church in the various stages of the African holocaust. The reader is left with a burning figure/tableau: numbed with indifference, the guilty ones slumber before the "split veil," following the death of so many cross-bearers. . . .

*Déchirures* was written by a young man who, as stated on the prefatory page, worked on an obsessive thought (*idée fixe*) for ten years, in fact from 1961 to 1971, a thought expressed through "variations" and "repetitions." If, for this reader, the "idea" of a state of ecstasy—in which the split between body and "soul," self and other, secular and sacred, grief and bliss, art and life might become transcended through acts of love—is indeed provocatively powerful in the texts, the various exchanges evoked in the poems do not, however, culminate into the vision of one triumphant climax. Individual sections or poems do (such as the beautiful, heartlifting "Gloria" poems, section thirteen). If, on the other hand, one tried to assess the poems from another angle in which the writing and reading processes would also be placed within the context of an ecstatic journey, there again, the overall experience might not measure up to the ambition. Yet, going through these poetic pages one more time, this reader knows that many fragments from *Déchirures* have forever become part sof her knowledge of human history, part, also, of her grief and part of her bliss. . . . The next step should be to situate *Déchirures* in relation to the other two collections of poems. Obviously, a comprehensive and detailed study of Mudimbe's poetry and fiction is still needed. As years go by, it seems to me that Mudimbe has been increasingly purging his style of all unessential ornaments. To use a quick analogy, I would say that reading his latest work is like contemplating a face whose beauty would rely exclusively on its bone structure. If many of us have good reason to believe that Mudimbe will be remembered as one of the leading African theoreticians and scholars of his generation. I, for one, fervently hope that his rare gift as a creative writer, his rare style and dream, will elicit even more interest among future readers and critics.

Bernadette Cailler. *Research in African Literatures.* 24, 4 (winter 1993), pp. 15, 18–19, 26

Irony is not the least pregnant figure in *Déchirures*. In the fifteen stations or tableaus offered to the reader's contemplation through the poet's own mind's eye, multiple elements could be regarded as the climax of despair, horror, and alienation. The first three sections unroll like a nightmarish film or dream whose sequences lead the dreamer from night to midday through dawn and morning. In its turn, at the microcosmic level, each subsection mirrors the larger dream in which the apotheosis of a redemption and a resurrection bathed in warmth, light, and joy is evoked, or even announced, as the eventual outcome of the whole drama. Thus, in I.1, the prophetic tone hails a "future black summer" through the use of the invocatory subjunctive: "qu'une pente renouvelle. . ." ["may a slope renew. . ."]; as early as in I.2, the tone is more confident (and perhaps reminiscent of Césaire's "Grand Midi"); the "form" to come is said to be already "spying upon the blind people we are," and finally appears to be present in a core of "light." Constantly, however, in all three sections, the intensity of the pain felt by the speaking subject at the obsessive sight of the omnipresent wounds, lacerations, or sterile landscapes is prevalent. In section II, the first-person narrator, whose presence had been discreetly announced in I.2, steps into the drama as a full-time contemplator, but also as an actor. Not unexpectedly, following the heroic path traveled by many prophetic figures, this narrator speaks both from outside and within the drama. As the text develops, the speaker's status as both savior and victim asserts itself more and more strongly. Thus, the allusion to the "calvary" (II.3) precedes the self-assured—although torn with grief—anaphoric declarations: "Je jure. . . / Je crie. . . / Je hurle. . ." —declarations culminating in the lines: "Je sais / que je redonnerai à mes cannas. . . / les idoles de mon coeur haute futaie" (II.7,8) ["I swear. . . / I scream. . . / I roar. . ."—"I know / that again I will give my cannas. . . / the idols of my heart high forest"]. Remarkable in these sections are the associations between the lofty red cannas, evoked as a burgeoning forest of loved idols, and the red dancing Africa present in the speaker's blood (". . . l'Afrique en danse rouge de mon sang," I.9). Here, with authority, the speaker announces the resurrection of a blossoming land where he, again, will be able to love. Such a resurrection, however, remains encompassed within the humble vision afforded by writing. In fact, it is not easy to interpret such a line as "dans les brouillons maladroits de l'écriture" (II.8) ["in the clumsy drafts of writing"]. Is the reader to assume that dream will never meet reality, that beauty, fecundity, and love will for ever remain a clumsy and tentative figure of speech? Or, on the contrary, is the reader to believe that the speaker is imparting to the word, if not the power to change the world, at least the power to plant the seeds of a new season?

The third section offers no relief to the reader's questioning. In this section, he speaker retreats to the contemplation of horror while seeking complete union with the sufferers. In III.1, 2, and 3, various outside images, paintings, places, milieus pass by the traveler's side like inconsequential mirages opposed to the "fertile eyes" of dream, a dream depicted through an interplay of alliterations and assonances in such a way as to suggest the sharpness of a blade and the torture of numerous lacerations: "Dans le rêve, le rêve effilé, si long et si lent des estafilades, des taillades" ["In the dream, the sharp-edged dream, so long and lingering with slashes and gashes"]. The fifteen remaining subsections bring the reader close to the infinite misery of the Kisangani tragedy. The desire to be one with the African brothers and sisters' suffering is translated in a striking and uncompromising figure of speech: "Pouvoir être cette meurtrissure, cette gangrène éternelle. . ." (III.4) ["I wish I were that bruise, that eternal gangrene. . ."]. Towards the end of section III, the speaker recalls the responsibility incurred by the Christian Church in the various stages of the African holocaust. The reader is left with a burning figure / tableau: numbed with indifference, the guilty ones slumber before the "split veil," following the death of so many cross-bearers.

It seems to me that section IV, while echoing the rebellious and prophetic section II (especially II.7, 8), obliterates, at least momentarily, the distance between the text, as futile dream, as "brouillon" ("rough draft"), and the text, as seminal vision, as "creative work." Throughout the three subsections, the vision oscillates between two types of anaphoric statements: "Elle finira par revivre" and "elle revivra" ("Sooner or later it will live again" and "it will live again"), the series of "elle revivra" appearing in the second subsection, as if the speaking subject were trying to temper his enthusiasm by returning to the less triumphant statement in the last piece, a piece in which, incidentally, once again, as he had done in II.8, the subject resorts to the authoritative "Je sais" ("I know"). Typical of a Rimbaldian kind of desultory discourse, several lines force the reader to fill in blanks, a technique which makes such portions of the text even richer semantically (see the first two stanzas). Remarkable is the fact that the identity of that which "will live again" is subtly caught in a net of lines linked to one another without punctuation and through various enjambments. Little by little, such a technique builds a vast tableau of the world to come, a tableau culminating in a stanza rich in syntactic and semantic ambiguities:

Elle finira par revivre
dans la transparence étranglée les sourires amers des partisans
l'allégresse du peuple qui sait et qui ne sait pas
le poids d'un mythe Liberté. (IV.3)
[Sooner or later it will live again in the strangulated transparency the bitter smiles of partisans
the cheerfulness of the people who know
and do not know the weight of a myth Liberty]

On the one hand, the reader should remember that "Elle" refers to a number of realities alluded to in several of the preceding stanzas (such as "the harmony of the scattered stones. . ." or the "frantic dream of the uncompleted tasks. . ."); on the other hand, the final word, "Liberté," can be read either as an opposition to "mythe" or as the delayed subject of "finira par revivre" and therefore as the sum total of all the realities evoked in previous sections of the poem. But in the first reading, "Liberté" will have to be equated with "le poids d'un mythe" and will be read as the direct object of the two clauses ". . . qui sait / et qui ne sait pas." In such a reading, the self-assured "Je sais" becomes confronted and counterbalanced with the less assured—in fact more "open"—dream of the people. If this reader is not mistaken in her approach to the text, it would appear that the ways and vision of the people stand out here as being more "poetic" than the self-reliant posture and oratorical delivery of the speaking subject: s(h)e who knows and does not know will always be a better poet than s(h)e who knows.

Bernadette Callier. *Research in African Literatures*. 24, 4 (winter 1993), pp. 17–28

V. Y. Mudimbe's third novel, *The Rift* (*L'Écart* in the original), appeared initially in 1979, six years after his first novel, *Entre les eaux* (1973; *Eng. Between Tides*). With his first three novels, Mudimbe had made an important impact on African fiction writing; he had created impressive studies of introspection, of the

mental anguish generated by the exigencies of political life and moral choice in contemporary Zaire. He had updated the crises of political commitment as we had known them in the 1950s, when the language of engagement, of existential good faith and bad faith, seemed to provide us with the correct way to formulate the critical issues of our times. Even the question of the "correctness" of writing fiction was posed in existential terms.

*The Rift* brings us to the end of that trajectory, and much as it seemed in the avant-garde in 1979, it now appears a period piece— an important period piece whose place in African literature is assured, but also one whose time has already passed. Such are the ironies of translation that works with an immediacy and pertinence for their times can only become available to those in need of a translated version when the market conditions permit.

The importance of *The Rift* lies in the way that Mudimbe represents the psyche of Ahmed Nana, an anthropological-historical researcher into Kuba history and customs. Nana is apparently undergoing a nervous breakdown—or at least his ratiocinations are sufficiently fractured so as to suggest a mental *écart,* a gap or fissure or rift (as it is translated). The gap is expressed in Nana's writing, which is usually fragmentary, at times frenetic, and above all telegraphic, signaling pieces of information with which we, or Nana's analyst, must reconstruct the sense, reconnecting signifiers and signifieds.

The novel echoes the by now familiar Mudimbe topoi: concern with faith, set against political corruption and postindependent failures; the need for and impossibility of forming love relationships; the need to understand the present and past realities of African societies, and the impossibility to do so using the indispensable tools provided by Western epistemology—the crisis of the anthropologist posed by the colonized space of the Africanist discourse. Finally, the novel provides us with a bridge between the intellectual "interpreters" of the 1960s, as seen in Soyinka's novel of that name, who represent the encounter between the intellectuals' modernism and the realities of contemporary African life, and their latter-day counterparts, as portrayed most compellingly in the fiction of such writers of the 1970s and 1980s as Henri Lopes, Sony Labou Tansi, and Ben Okri.

Kenneth Harrow. *World Literature Today*. 68, 3 (summer 1994), p. 626

BIBLIOGRAPHY

*Déchirures*, 1971; *Initiation au Francais*, 1971; *Autour de la nation*, 1972; *Francais: Les Structure Fondamentales I*, 1972; *Francais: Les Structures Fondamentales II*, 1972; *Reflexions sur la vie quotidienne*, 1972; *Entre les eaux*, 1973; *Entretailles et Fulgurances d'une lezarde*, 1973; *L'Autre Face du royaume: Une introduction a la critique des languages en folie*, 1973; *Les Fuseaux parfois*, 1974; *Carnets d'Amerique*, 1976; *Contributions a l'etude des variations du genre grammatical des Mots francais d'Origine latine: I. Mots a initiale vocalique*, 1976; *Le Bel Immonde*, 1976; *Air: etude semantique*, 1979; *L'Écart*, 1979; *La Culture et la science au Zaire 1960-1975: Essai sur les sciences sociales et humaines*, 1980; *Visage de la philosophie et de la theologie comtemporaines au Zaire*, 1981; *L'Odeur du pere*, 1982; *The Invention of Africa*, 1988; *Shaba Deux*, 1989; *Fables and Parables*, 1991; *The Idea of Africa*, 1993; *Les corps glorieux des mots et des etres*, 1994; *Tales of Faith: Religion as Political Performance in Central Africa*, 1997; *Nations, Identities, Cultures*, 1997

# MUGO, Micere Githae (1942– )
## Kenya

Dedan Kimathi fought for the total liberation of the Kenyan people from foreign domination and oppression. He did not achieve this in his lifetime: the struggle continues, and Kimathi is the legitimate hero of the revolution. Ngugi [wa Thiong'o] and his colleague Micere Githae Mugo have collaborated in writing a play with a number of specific purposes. It is a "song of praise" for the feasts of leadership and resistance of the most brilliant of the generals of the independence struggle who . . . are neglected, often repudiated heroes, their deeds for the most part not known by the present generation of young Kenyans. . . . The play [*The Trial of Dedan Kimathi*] is an attempt to restore the character of Kimathi to his legitimate place in the history of Kenya.

Secondly, the play establishes the connection with the masses in the present struggle by reasserting Kimathi's values. More than this the play is a self-conscious assertion of the part that literature should play in the revolution. . . .

The authors present a play in which time past and time present are made to merge in a continuous present where Kimathi on trial in Nyeri and the mythic Kimathi, who stands on the dock in the present-tense, debate the causes and prosecution of the continuing revolutionary struggle. Ngugi and [Mugo] state in their notes that "the action should on the whole be seen as breaking the barrier between formal and infinite time, so that past and future and present flow into one another.". . .

The authors achieve their purpose by employing a number of theatrical techniques and characteristics of the non-naturalistic theater. The play, which has an opening, three movements, and fourteen scenes, makes use of mime, dancing, drumming, singing, music, sudden blackouts, and artful changes in lighting. The authors further enhance the suggestion of a time continuum by creating characters whose conduct in time past is coincident with their current values and motives. Moreover, the characters are typed. There is nothing introspective about them. Positions have been adopted, and in the play they are debated and put on trial. Further, the authors employ language in such a way [as] to bridge the gap in time. Kimathi, for example, speaks a revolutionary language appropriate to his role in both past and present, but the vocabulary in scenes devoted to past time often uses a language inappropriate to the past time period, drawn from contemporary revolutionary rhetoric—but this is nevertheless effective in suggesting the coincidence of the struggle.

> G. D. Killam. *An Introduction to the Writings of Ngugi* (London: Heinemann, 1980), pp. 86–87

The playwrights use Kimathi's "trial" at Nyeri as a starting point. The core of the action of the play, the story element, concerns a peasant woman who separates a ragged urban youth from fighting a similarly impoverished girl, and then co-opts him in her efforts to get a gun to Kimathi in jail. The youth is not initially aware of the nature of the mission, but his and the girl's eventual understanding of the struggle and commitment to it lead to the climax of the play—the firing of a shot in the courtroom after Kimathi has had the sentence of death passed on him. The shot symbolizes the continuation of the struggle through the young boy and the girl.

The core of the play—a core of meaning as well as a storyline—has woven around it a cumulative portrait of Dedan Kimathi, developed through four symbolic trials, which are not to be confused with the "trial" staged by the colonialists in the Nyeri courthouse. These four symbolic trials take place in the cell in the jail, which itself is symbolic of a state of mind, or of a "wilderness." The play is in three movements, which we are advised to imagine as one single movement, with actions, events, incidents—all the parts of the play, in fact—moving along with great urgency. The four trials of Kimathi occur in the second movement.

Other elements of stylization in *The Trial of Dedan Kimathi* tend to reinforce this determination of the playwrights to explain the reasons why things happen in a certain way, and how they can be changed. Thus, the four trials which Kimathi undergoes are symbolic because they represent "temptations" to end the struggle; their apparent reasonableness has to be answered by a deeper analysis. . . .

There are other symbolic groupings on the stage. The courtroom scene occurs three times. It is the same event on the first two occasions, namely Kimathi's appearance before the white judge, which results in an adjournment. The third court scene—the climax of the play—is Kimathi's reappearance in court and the pronouncement of the death sentence upon him. Whites and Africans are symbolically divided in the courtroom. . . .; In the final courthouse scene, the whites' side now contains, symbolically, the blacks whom we earlier saw as some of Kimathi's "tempters." The blacks' side, made up of people in very ragged clothes, consistently supports Kimathi whenever he speaks. The whites are settlers, and they react towards Kimathi with frenzied hate. With Kimathi in chains in the dock, challenging the white judge's right to try him, the scene visually shows how Kimathi brings the oppressors into confrontation with the oppressed.

> Michael Etherton. *The Development of African Drama* (London: Hutchinson University Library for Africa, 1982), pp. 168–69, 172–74

In Ngugi wa Thiong'o's and Micere Mugo's *The Trial of Dedan Kimathi*, time and space coalesce in a symbolic drama of growth and development. Past and present events surrounding the Mau Mau revolt are re-created on stage to provide an historical perspective to and continuity of the anticolonial movement in Kenya. Spatial shifts from distant guerrilla encampments in the Nyandarua forest to local prisons and courtroom installations in Nairobi emphasize the breadth and depth of the Mau Mau rebellion. The rapid montage design of the play overrides the accustomed cause-effect rational processes of the audience and consequently prohibits simplistic and limiting interpretations of staged events. In this structure, the characters are similarly transformed from their spatial and temporal individuality to symbolic, collective proportions.

*The Trial of Dedan Kimathi* is composed of two narrative plot movements: the first focuses on the capture, imprisonment, and subsequent trial of [Dedan Kimathi]; the second features the transformation of two young Kenyans from childhood to adulthood in a symbolic "rite of passage." Both of these plot movements utilize the character of Kimathi . . . as a symbol of the Mau Mau movement. . . .

Ngugi wa Thiong'o [and Micere Mugo use] the image of Dedan Kimathi as a model against which the activities of the boy and girl are measured. Under close scrutiny, they discover that their own attitudes and behaviors fall short of the mark set by this standard bearer. Vowing to forsake their fallen world, they pursue the path blazed for them by Kimathi. . . .; Their imitation of his heroic deeds identifies them as newly initiated freedom fighters. As such they themselves become metaphors of the continued spirit of anticolonial resistance and rebellion in Kenya.

In this analysis, metaphor differs from symbol in that it represents a unique creation of the artist within the given work itself. It comes to life as a result of the insight of the artist and does not depend on the external culture or literary background for its existence and emotive power. The artist is free to manipulate it according to her/his own thematic designs. A symbol, however, depends on and utilizes outside influences for much of its efficacy although the artist can highlight particular details or associations to conform to her/his purposes. Every symbol, from its inception, is a metaphor. But it is a metaphor that has been socially accepted and repeatedly used by others. The creative insight and new associative meaning that sparked the first use of the metaphor is conventionally accepted as the meaning of the symbol. . . . Accordingly, in *The Trial of Dedan Kimathi*, the unnamed boy and girl are metaphors for all the lost youth of Kenya. Their transformation in the play becomes the model for others to follow.

E. A. Magel. *Canadian Journal of African Studies*. 17, 2 (1983), pp. 239–40

As with [Ola] Rotimi's play [*Ovonramwen Nogbaisi*], the emotional appeal of *Dedan Kimathi* consists in the spectacle of the sufferings of a blameless protagonist with whom the audience is invited to identify. Like Oba Ovonramwen, Dedan Kimathi is the victim of an imperialism which he struggles heroically to counteract but which finally destroys him: his only weakness is in any other context a virtue—love and mercifulness to those closest to him, who nevertheless betray him. On trial for his life before a hostile court, Kimathi is like Ovonramwen in his stoicism, which in no way, however, implies resigned submission. He refuses to be influenced by the attempts to seduce him away from the cause he leads: like Ovonramwen, albeit in far more vehement terms, he addresses his captors and accusers, indicting them for their crimes and exhorting the masses to continue the struggle.

[Mugo and Ngugi wa Thiong'o], like Rotimi, reinforce empathy with their heroic protagonist through their portrayal of his enemies. The imperialists are much more full-bloodedly villainous than in *Ovonramwen Nogbaisi*: they are portrayed as hysterically racist, for example in the outburst of the white settler, whom the stage direction describes as "foaming with rage like a madman," in the court. Though Moor and his compatriots are depicted as callous in their humiliation of Ovonramwen, they are far from being the brutal torturers of *Dedan Kimathi*. The audience is invited to feel nothing but disgust and contempt for the whites and their black and Indian stooges, whose various attempts to "tempt" Kimathi are shown as obviously determined by economic considerations. Most emotive of all, perhaps, considering the Kenyan

audience for which the play was originally written, is Kimathi's betrayal by his brother and close associates, despite his initially merciful attitude towards him. Kimathi's torture by the white colonialists and their allies doubtless stirs a black audience; but the spectacle of his betrayal and martyrdom by those who should be his cohorts in the struggle is likely to arouse the strongest emotions and establish an especially powerful empathy. . . .

The struggle for national liberation is thus invested by the Kenyan dramatists with specifically religious connotations, including a martyred redeemer. The affective power of the Christian myth, and of the sacrificial Christ-figure, is exploited to lend emotional and ethical force to the authors' call for a continuation, inspired by the memory of Kimathi, of the anti-imperialist struggle in Kenya. This struggle, and the values that it and its leading martyr embody, are shown as being ultimately successful.

Brian Crow. *Ariel*. 14, 3 (July 1983), pp. 25–27

[Mugo] and Ngugi [wa Thiong'o] were inspired by a woman they met when they visited Karumaini, Kimathi's birthplace. The defiant pride of the woman, who had been Kimathi's pupil at Karumaini Independent School, her continuing love of her former teacher and leader, and her insistence to the visitors that "Kimathi will never die" challenged Mugo to create the Woman of the play, a multifaceted individual presented as of almost equal importance to Kimathi himself. [Mugo], an actress, as well as a writer, educator, administrator, and political activist, played this central role of the Woman during the play's premier run.

We know from history that many Kenyan women supported, even fought alongside, the men during their struggle for national liberation. . . .

So, in one sense, [Mugo's] emphasis on the Woman can be seen as evidence of her commitment to socialist realism, an implicit assertion that classes and their historical conflicts, not gender, is the authors' main concern. The Woman functions historically in the play, as Kimathi does, carrying out acts of subversion; she operates politically by analyzing the exploitive colonial economic situation and eloquently announcing the Freedom Fighters' plans for recovery from imperialism. Linked to Wanjiru, a guerrilla "who fought like a tiger," she is a "mother, a fighter all in one." She becomes symbolic, moreover, of all the women of her class, not only those who actually helped the guerrillas; the authors state explicitly, "the Woman now represents all the working mothers."

Arlene A. Elder. *Matatu*. 3, 6 (1989), pp. 81–82

*Micere Githae* Mugo's collection *My Mother's Poem and Other Songs* is a welcome female addition to contemporary African poetry that is considerably male-written. The poet's acknowledgment note and preface raise expectations of fireworks with the promise not only of "raw, unpalatable, or indigestible . . . dishes" in her "creative menus," but also of "exploding silences." . . .

Even before one starts to read the poems themselves, there are strong suggestions of the poet's leftist/Marxist and feminist orientation in references to Amilcar Cabral, the African nationalist fighter, and Audre Lorde, the late African American/Caribbean lesbian/feminist. One is not therefore surprised to find the poems cluttered by many isms such as imperialism, capitalism, and neocolonialism and by an abundance of such feminist diction as "matriots" and "herstory."

Mugo is a poet with a mission in her society, which embraces the black race, the underprivileged class, and her specific female gender. She appears to speak for Africans and blacks, women, and the downtrodden. "Mother Afrika's Matriots" highlights the achievements of African, African American, and Afro-Caribbean women, as the poet attempts to rewrite history into "herstory." Poems such as "To Be a Feminist Is" and "The Woman's Poem" are very passionate in the poet's assertion of her womanhood. To her, to be a feminist is "to denounce patriarchy / and the caging of women." However, these feminist poems (like the Marxist ones), though moving, tend to be ideologically too one-dimensional and thus dissipate all possibilities of fine poetry. Mugo's unabashed feminist posture in her poetry suffers from inconsistency as she uses "herstory" instead of "history" but "historical" instead of "herstorical."

Mugo also comes out strongly here as a Marxist and pan-Africanist. In "The Isle of Youth" she writes about Cuba, where she absorbs "the sunshine / of revolutionary visions." She expresses solidarity with blacks worldwide in "On This Tenth Milestone," proclaiming, "we shall fight / till we stand / on both feet." The poet's language appears to be poetically weakened by the direct political and feminist ideologies and the embracing of abstractions such as "liberating knowledge," "probing dialogue," "neocolonial treachery," and "imperialist history." The Marxist tone reminds one of African writing of the 1970s and early 1980s, and the poems would have been better placed in their historical perspective if they had been dated.

The poems are generally too talkative, without description, narration, or strong images. "My Mother's Poem," for all the attention it is meant to draw as a title poem, conveys the poet's mother's role upon her father's death but exhibits little or no orature apart from the staggered verse form. The refrain in "Mother Afrika's Matriots" is refreshing, but the poem contains prosaic feminist outpourings. The closing prose poem of the collection carries the same prosaic and ideological qualities of earlier poems.

In conclusion, the high expectations raised in the preface and introduction are not met by the poems themselves. Instead of expressing her experience in concrete and sensuous images, Mugo mouths ideas. For instance, Jared Angira, who is Kenyan and Marxist like Mugo, succeeds (as in Cascades) in better expressing socialist ideas poetically through vignettes and specific experiences rather than through abstractions. It appears that the medium of fiction as used by Ngugi wa Thiong'o may be more apt in expressing the ideas that Mugo brings to poetry. Whatever orature exists in My Mother's Poem and Other Songs is minimal and not put to poetic advantage. Feminism and Marxism take control of the voice, and one hears ideas which are not adequately fleshed out into poetry.

Tanure Ojaide. *World Literature Today*. 69, 3 (summer 1995), pp. 631–32

BIBLIOGRAPHY

*Daughter of My People, Sing!*, 1976; *The Long Illness of Ex-Chief Kiti*, 1976; *The Trial of Dedan Kimathi* (with Ngugi wa Thiong'o), 1976; *Visions of Africa: The Fiction of Chinua Achebe, Margaret Laurence, Elspeth Huxley, and Ngugi wa Thiong'o*, 1978; *African Orature and Human Rights*, 1991; *My Mother's Poem and Other Songs: Songs and Poems*, 1994

# MUNONYE, John (1929–)
## Nigeria

[John Munonye's] novels are mainly domestic, centered around the family and its problems for the man, woman, and even the children. He . . . has quite often evoked the typical marital situation which normally results in polygamy, especially childlessness, but has in addition rejected polygamy as the solution for such a problem. In *Obi*, Munonye successfully dramatizes the pressures on a childless couple from family members and friends, especially the mother-in-law and in particular the *umuada*, a group which has heretofore not been treated in such detail. These are the married daughters of a family. Their place within the community or in any marriage contracted by one of their "sons" forms one of the sources of tension in *Obi* and *The Only Son*.

In *Obi*, the *umuada* are presented as the greatest single source of challenge to the fatherless hero of the novel, Joe. A further topic of the book is the clash between traditional religion and Christianity to which Joe and his wife, Anna, belong. Joe believes in total allegiance to his religion, while certain members of the society believe that when the issue of childlessness arises in a marriage, religion should be forgotten and a man should be free to take a second wife, especially if there is no male child to succeed to the ruling of the "Obi," the family house. . . . His immediate family, with their belief in the traditional religion and their hopes for him as their specially gifted son, also had their own ideas of what they expected Joe to be and do for the family. His allegiance and love for his wife contribute an added problem since he has the responsibility to shield her in a society where she is regarded as a stranger and a useless wife. . . .

In his third novel [*Oil Man of Obange*] Munonye examines the tragedy of a man who sacrifices everything, including his own life for the welfare of his children. The tragedy is intense because it is much more personal and domestic. The very little happiness in the hero's life comes from seeing his children healthy, happy, and successful at school. At his death a friend comments: "His life was a whole planting season. It is a pity he died so early, before the fruits of his labor began to appear." During his life, Jeri derives most of his courage from his daughter and receives most of his jeers from his only sister. Although Jeri is married, his wife is done away with early to make way for his only daughter Celia, whose development from a little child to a responsible young lady is easily traceable. This technique is a departure from the theme of *Obi*, which treats in depth the marital problems of a childless couple. Marcellina features simply as the typical quiet, hard-working, and understanding Christian wife of a Godfearing man. She encourages Jeri at his work, worries over his safety, and rejoices at his successes. These, in addition to serving as the focal point of a well-organized and happy family, are her functions. From Onugo we also hear that she is the only one whose advice her husband takes. As a good mother, she settles the little bickerings among her children and serves as a worthy representative of a husband whose unusual job of an oil man compels him to spend most of his time outside the home. But when Marcellina dies of a tetanus infection, her duties in the family are shifted to her only daughter, Celia. . . .

Although Munonye's novels contain a recognizable number of female characters, he exhibits the same unwillingness or inability of most West African writers to enter the minds of their female characters—the inability to create characters with conviction or surprises, not so easily predictable, and always shielded from the realities of a changing society. Hardly do these women characters show any awareness of their societies in the sense of projecting their talents or abilities beyond the borders of their homes or the market towards the betterment of the society as a whole. From the emotional point of view, they are also splendidly and consistently mediocre, always reacting with superhuman endurance to their problems. Anna is a good example of such a flat character. Only once does she break down weeping under the pressure of such a central and grievous problem heightened by a host of unsympathetic in-laws.

Marcellina is equally flat and weak in portrayal. Blessed by a happy Christian home, a devoted husband, and healthy children, she makes her brief sojourn in the book, dies, and is mourned by almost everyone in the village. Even in the case of Celia, the author fails to develop her in any recognizable psychological way. Her little growth is more from accident than design and even her own form of adolescent rebellion does not last longer than a week. She soon falls back into being the prim and proper young girl she has always been.

U. Ola. *Okike*. 21 (July 1982), pp. 78, 81–82, 85–86

Undoubtedly one of the most prolific novelists in Nigeria, with six full-length novels to his credit, Munonye is in danger of remaining in critical limbo for far too long. For a writer of his training and ambition to be totally ignored by the critics is disheartening. . . .

*Oil Man of Obange* is in a class by itself among Munonye's works; it is the one novel that deserves a second reading. Here, most of the flaws that encumber his other books are surprisingly absent. It has the high seriousness that is lacking in his other novels. The story it tells is timeless. There is skillful composition, a miniature canvas painted with intensity of feeling. In *The Only Son*, Munonye was playing the proverbial sedulous ape to [Chinua] Achebe's *Things Fall Apart*. *The Only Son* was a first novel with the usual flaws—formlessness, authorial intrusions into purely narrative passages, boring digressions that lead nowhere other than the privileged glimpses they give of the Igbo cultural milieu, and a lack of thematic depth. His second novel, *Obi*, was scarcely an improvement. His initial faults persisted, while new ones disturbingly intruded—no innuendo, no mystery, no foreshadowing, nothing left to puzzle the mind and tantalize the imagination—in other words a poor concept of plot. The conclusion one is forced to draw after reading *Obi* is that even though Munonye succeeds quite often in evoking almost the same situational scenes as Achebe, he falls far short of the latter in his handling of plot, in creating characters with the complexity and dignified stature of Ezeulu, and in his narrative technique. *A Wreath for the Maidens* reads almost exactly like [Cyprian] Ekwensi's *Survive the Peace*. Both are topical novels about the Nigerian Civil War—shallow, reportorial, and doomed to die a natural death once the issues that keep them current fade into the limbo of memory. *A Dancer of Fortune* borders on farce, unrelieved by its great narrative skill or the

profundity of its thematic concerns; while the latest novel, *Bridge to a Wedding*, which continues the odyssey of Joe and Anna in *Obi*, contains no exciting new developments worth noting.

But *Oil Man of Obange*, Munonye's third novel, has the makings of a classic, if we understand a classic as a work of art that is among the best of its kind. A classic, one must also add, starts with what is traditional in its genre but goes further, since ultimately it advances the whole tradition, dealing with eternal truths presented in such a way that it pleases generation after generation. *Oil Man of Obange* is such a work. . . .

[One] must observe that in *Oil Man of Obange*, Munonye has written a novel that might survive him. The canvas is small and compact, the style is lucid, even engaging; the action is emotionally charged and often gnaws at our hearts: the plot reveals proper foreshadowing and motivation. These are qualities which have eluded Munonye in most of his other novels. *Oil Man of Obange* marks a turning point for the better, in Munonye's novelistic technique.

Charles E. Nnolim. In Eldred Durosimi Jones, ed. *African Literature Today*. 12 (1982), pp. 163–65, 173

There seems to be a consistent attempt by John Munonye to view and treat the heroes of his novels as individuals who break out beyond the framework and limitations of their community. These individuals feel no longer constrained by the conventions of their milieu. They are invariably individuals with problems, but who seem to be up against society in their attempts to find solutions to these problems. The various methods and ways of solving these problems constitute the distinguishing marks of these heroes. Whether we deal with Nnanna in *The Only Son*, who has to attend school against the wishes of his relatives and thus becomes isolated from his immediate community; or with Joe in *Obi*, who finds himself in conflict with the traditional group in his village on the issue of his marriage; or with Jeri in *Oil Man of Obange*, who leaves the traditional economics to embrace the Western one and becomes an oilman suffering alienation and isolation by so doing; or even with Ayasco in *A Dancer of Fortune*, who is forced by the circumstances of his trade to resort to intrigue, blackmail, and exploitation in order to survive and look after his family, we are all the time dealing with different manifestations of the individual trying to be himself, and to survive in an often hostile society determined to thwart the individual's efforts at self-realization.

Munonye's heroes generally are presented in isolation, facing their fate as they make their choices, often guided by certain moral sense which ultimately brings them to disaster. They and their problems present us with a series of faltering uneasy attempts to match the desires of the individual with the desires of the community. Most often, this delicate balance act falls apart as the tension flares up leading to the destruction of the isolated individual. . . .

Munonye is one of the African novelists concerned primarily with the traumas in the African society caused by Western cultures, and with their influence on the individual's psyche. He depicts the frustrations, the disappointments, the anger, the cynicism over unfulfilled hopes, and the inability of the individual working alone to reverse these situations. The central question which the three novels . . . attempt to answer is, what is the best attitude to take towards Western cultures? The dialectic of these novels is that salvation and survival may well lie in an integration of the old and the new. . . . Accordingly, the novels are not tracts of antitraditional pose or pro-Western stance. They are the author's blueprint for the

African's survival in the face of conflicting values. He is convinced that the African situation demands and deserves serious and delicate consideration. To survive, the African cannot afford to close his eyes to the new ways, or to refuse to draw inspiration from the solidarity of the past based on communalism. Mere individualism exercised outside the communal interest is bound to falter because it is antithetical to the African way of life. Stated differently, the question Munonye raises is not whether the principles of the new religion and Western education are valid for Africa, but of finding out whether the Africans are capable of overcoming the enormous obstacles of a changing universe.

Julius N. Ogu. *International Fiction Review*. 11, 2 (summer 1984), pp. 90, 92–93

*Bridge to a Wedding* may lay no claim to being—artistically speaking—Munonye's profoundest [work], but as a forthright document of his viewpoint on the cultural/ideological implications of colonization for subject peoples, it is his most significant. The terminal novel in a trilogy [including *The Only Son* and *Obi*], it resolves the various dimensions of crisis, conflict, and alienation generated and compounded in the anteceding novels by the defection of a native son to the alien institutions introduced by colonialism. Of course, in a panoramic sense, it detracts from the completeness and autonomy of each of these novels, forcing them to become the exposition and complication of a strange and torturous drama of which it is, itself, the denouement. More important for our purposes here, *Bridge to a Wedding* reiterates far more forcefully the idea (first broached in *The Only Son* and amplified in *Obi* and even in *Oil Man of Obange*) of apostasy as the key to the treasures of a brave new world of opportunity and redefined social eminence, of the material and psychological accretions of colonialism as unfailing indications of commitment to progress. The fact that this is Munonye's latest (and possibly last) novel, and that he felt compelled in it to return to the theme of conflict of cultures, after moving in an Achebean trajectory from the ethnographical novel to satire, would seem to suggest that it might be Munonye's defining position novel on the contact of Europe with Africa. . . .

The bridge, when built in *Bridge to a Wedding*, is more like one needed by an offensive army to ensure the rapid success of a campaign than one necessary to facilitate a peaceful interpenetration of the sensibilities of the village and the city, the past and the present, the young and the old. The march over it toward "civilization" is attended by no ambivalence, no self-doubt, no complications, indeed no contemplation of the ideological meaning of colonialism for subject cultures. This is, perhaps, part of what [Charles] Nnolim means when he observes that in John Munonye's novels, there is "no casting around of a great soul athwart the mighty purposes of existence in a world full of insoluble tensions where the problem of 'how to be' becomes a burning question." Neither in this novel nor in *The Only Son*, *Obi*, and *Oil Man of Obange* does Munonye grapple with much apprehension regarding the "bounty" that is the advent of colonialism. In these novels Africa's subjugation by Europe seems simply to mark the dawn of a blessed new morning of glorious opportunity and civilization, rousing us with the bright promise of liberation from the inadequacies and injustices of ourselves and our past.

Azubike F. Iloeje. *Research in African Literatures*. 16, 4 (winter 1985), pp. 526–27, 538–39

Munonye has an excellent ear for human dialogue. He is able to capture the various verbal nuances which not only identify personalities, but also announce relationships existing between persons, whether cordial or hostile, distant or intimate. The characters establish their humanity through this ever-present infectious sense of humor, the exchange of repartee or abuse, and the use of proverbs fashioned out of their intimacy with forest and earth. This aspect is also underscored by his language, woven with a deceptive simplicity, with hardly any sustained "poetic" flights or complex metaphorical structures. Thus, language itself becomes a mirror of the social organization present in the world of the author's fiction, a reflection of tribal ethos and of the stream of traditional life in its uncomplicated flow.

[*Oil Man of Obange*,] to my mind, is his most powerful novel. . . . Jeri, the hero, is the first truly modern hero in African literature: the picture of the simple, diligent common man struggling courageously to adapt himself without dishonor to the exigencies of the modern world, refusing to yield to poverty, traditional narrowmindedness, or the corrupting ethos of the new capitalist world. For a man alone, the problems Jeri faces are simply overwhelming: there is his polluted past composed of crises, feuds, and a costly vendetta; there is his poor, infertile land and the unpredictable antics of seasons: then comes the sudden death of his wife, leaving him alone with the burden of the children; then his accident and long convalescence and, finally, his robbery by thieves at a moment when, at the cost of heavy debts, he starts the process of retrieving himself again. Through all these misfortunes, until the end, he bears his cross with courage, resilience, and exemplary fortitude, making no long speeches or grand gestures, only loving his children, bearing his pain in silence; his old bicycle becomes the symbol of a larger plight, that of the oppressed but indomitable wretched of the earth, a symbol of their pathos and of their heroic destiny.

Femi Osofisan. *Presence Africaine*. 139 (1986), pp. 175–76

To date, six novels by Munonye have been published. . . . In most, if not all, of these works, the average man locked in a grim, existential combat with the invariably hostile forces of society is a recurring motif. Indeed if [Chinua] Achebe can be described as the novelist of epic personages, the uncanny explorer of extraordinary souls, Munonye must be seen as the novelist of the common man par excellence. And it is precisely this immersion in the predicament of the ordinary folk and a faithful and sensitive rendering of their whims and follies which give Munonye's works their compelling realism and often faintly "naturalistic" quality. For example, few are the like of Okonkwo, the hero of Achebe's *Things Fall Apart*, and Ezeulu, the protagonist of his *Arrow of God*, but the Igbo society, and in fact the whole world, is teeming with only sons like Nnanna, sullen exiles like Kafe, and tragic speculators like Jeri. As a matter of fact, Ayasko, the protagonist of *A Dancer of Fortune*, derives his name from the traditional appellation given to that breed of itinerant dancers. . . .

Munonye's works teem with such characters: outcasts, lonely exiles, eccentric martyrs; and in his narratives, threatened abortion, secondary infertility, and outright barrenness cast a forlorn shadow. These in themselves serve as a powerfully symbolic projection of the human condition and they give Munonye's vision its bleak and pessimistic hue. What cannot be denied, however, is the fact that despite his often tragic view of the human condition, Munonye's sympathy is always with the underdog and the downtrodden.

It is only in *A Dancer of Fortune* that this sympathy for the oppressed is transformed from a passive and acquiescing element to an active and rebellious one. Here, the embattled individual rises to the occasion to beat the society at its own game of treachery and fraud. In this haunting work, fraught with social tension and unease, Ayasko, the hero, bides his time until he is strong and powerful enough to turn the tables against his tormentors. Munonye has very harsh words for those who may feel uneasy at this rather inelegant resolution of social conflict.

'Bayo Williams. *Obsidian II*. 2, 1 (spring 1987), pp. 76–77

Perhaps, because of Munonye's acknowledged indebtedness to [Chinua] Achebe, and because major parts of his novels deal with plot and conflict situations reminiscent of Achebe's novels, critics of Munonye have tended to miss the point that Munonye's fiction offers a social vision almost antithetical to Achebe's. As I have stated elsewhere: there is "a distinctly un-Achebean optimism regarding colonialism and its implications that seems to inform Munonye's novels" of culture conflict. . . . I believe that there is a consistent pattern in Munonye's ethnographical novels, of either actual and ultimate (*The Only Son, Obi, Bridge to a Wedding*) or transcendental (*Oil Man of Obange*) vindication of the aberrancy and apostasy of the hero. When Charles Nnolim can say nothing more about the social perspective projected in Munonye's first novel than that in it the writer has been "playing the proverbial sedulous ape to Achebe's *Things Fall Apart*," I am convinced that it has escaped Nnolim's attention that, in many ways, *The Only Son* rewrites *Things Fall Apart*; its conclusions differ from, and at the same time, complement those of Achebe's first novel. In his ethnographical novels, Achebe primarily portrays the resistance of older Igbos to colonially induced change; Munonye, on the other hand, chronicles the receptivity of younger Igbos to change. Whereas the psychology of the stubborn resister is at the center of Achebe's novels, the psychology of the resolute defector is both fundamental and ascendant in Munonye's. . . .

The problem quite early in *The Only Son* is how to bring up Nnanna Okafo in a manner required and demanded by the existing precolonial Igbo society, a patrilineal, male-dominated, agrarian society organized on dependent femininity. The problem also concerns proffering him an effective program of education necessary for his proper integration within the social structure. The untimely death of his father has jeopardized the prospects of Nnanna's growing up in the prescribed manner. The novel opens in the 1920s, about thirteen years after the death of Okafo; both his widow and her only son are left, according to custom, in the custody of Amanze, Okafo's younger brother. The expected program of surrogacy, however, collapses as distrust, conflict, and suspicion descend on the extended family. Not only, Chiaku feels, has Amanze repudiated his responsibilities, he has also expropriated his late brother's estate, the rightful inheritance of Nnanna. . . . Here we have a kinship crisis centering on Chiaku's perceived sense of wrong and inequity in the allocation of patrimonial inheritance. We might suspect, at this early point, that a morality drama is in the offing, with good confronting evil, right deployed against avarice and theft. This predictable path towards the resolution of the conflict never develops in the novel; the factor of

colonialism effectively nullifies . . . any hope of recovering the lost birthright in its precolonial form.

Azubike F. Iloeje. *World Literature Written in English*. 29, 1 (spring 1989), pp. 8–9

[Since] generally, John Munonye's fiction is not preoccupied with a gloomy view of the universe, the essential goodness of man is his delight: his protagonists are not surrounded with the powers of darkness, nor are the depicted as fallen creatures in a fallen world without God and without hope where man is lost. There are no betrayers and the betrayed in Munonye's canon, no catalogue of defeated men and women in a defeating and malevolent or chaotic universe; no anarchic men and women or nihilists seeking destruction of the system. Where in Achebe, the incurable pessimist, the mythic pattern which informs his tragic vision is the myth of the triumph of error over reason; of the victory of conflict and disintegration over peace and unity; of the triumph of despair over hope; of the defeat of the culture hero by the demon within.

In Munonye, the incurable optimist, the mythic pattern which informs his comic vision is that of the triumph of reason over error, of the victory of the culture hero through strict adherence to Christian ways over the demon within.

Again the folkloric formula of exile and return which is part of the journey motif in Achebe's major novels end, inevitable, in defeat and humiliation for the protagonist, in adherence to Achebe's tragic vision. But in Munonye, the incurable optimist, the journey motif or the exile and return end in a triumphant homecoming, especially at the end of the triology involving *The Only Son, Obi*, and *Bridge to a Wedding*, following Munonye's comic vision. In Achebe, an Okonkwo, and Ezeulu, and Obi Okonkwo comes home after the initial separation from their people, to an ignoble end in suicide, to a demented and insane old age, to life in jail, respectively. But in Munonye Joseph Kafo's Odyssey ends in triumphant homecoming for he, like the hero of myth returns at a more enhanced status than when he left, bringing home a boon (completes his obi, builds Obieke's home for him in a gesture of brotherly love, and effects a reconciliation between himself and Obieke, and between himself and Akueze's family through the intervention of Ebeneto). And just to stretch the comparison with Achebe a little further, while in Achebe there are no happy marriages (only functional ones), no soft and romantic moments between husbands and their wives, no intimate family counsels involving a father, his wife and their children, Munonye is the novelist of the home and the hearth, the novelist of happy marriages and happy family life. Even Ayasko, that king of evasion and self-deceit, finds warmth and affection in an understanding wife (Bessie) and their happy children; while *Bridge to a Wedding* is in itself, a paean to happy life. Achebe's concerns, largely tragic, end in death of the individual and disintegration of traditional societies. Munonye's concerns, largely comic, end in happier options which promise life and progress for individuals and betterment and progress for societies. While Achebe lookson with dismay at the tragedy that befalls individuals and societies under the impact of colonialism, Munonye looks forward with gusto to the challenges posed by the colonial intrusion, as old towns are renamed and modern conveniences and a network of roads replace Achebe's "the evil forest".

In Munonye, there are no unhappy marriages, no barrenness, no absence of love between husband and wife, no family conflicts that are not easily resolved through discussion or even a humorous teasing. And children in Munonye's cannon never came to an evil end, never fall into the hands of evil men, never disappoint their parents in school (in fact, in *Oil Man of Obange* it is the unusual blessing of having a set of unusually brilliant children that drove Jeri to his death trying to maintain all of them in school).

Munonye's nature is energized by the myth of the rising sun, the vision of summer and fruition, the fruitful garden, the lush grove replete with pastoral images of bleating sheep and the song of birds. And where in Achebe, the masked spirit is imbued with the respect and awe accorded our elders and is referred to as an "ancestral" spirit one of which was called Evil Forest who had "transfixed to the spot for two days" a fellow Egugwu that "had dared to stand his ground before him, Munonye's comic spirit debunks the magic and the terror with which Achebe invests the masked spirit. In *The Only Son* the classroom teacher and his pupils take time out to debate the secret of the "masquerade leaf" as the teacher makes the profane statement that "those things which you see are bad men, pagans in dirty masks and crests". With that, Achebe's ancestral spirits ("ancestors of the clan who had been committed to Mother Earth") had degenerated in Munonye to a matter for frivolous debate in classrooms.

To sum up, a bird's eye view of Munonye's major novels (with the exception of *Oil Man of Obango* and *A Wreath for the Maidens*) points to a novelist whose over-all tone and attitude are on the warm side of the spectrum of human relationships. For him, life is an April day that laughs and weeps in one breath where the tears are, to paraphrase Shakespeare, like "burrs thrown at you in holiday fashion." He makes the best of a seemingly bad situation because, as far as he is concerned "hope springs eternal, so that in The Only Son," a bildungsroman, the vulnerable little protagonist, Nnanna, survives the insecurity of life occasioned by his father's death when he was but six months old, outgrows the effeminizing influence of a doting, anxious and possessive mother and, as he grows into a young adult he takes his destiny in his hands by embracing christianity and charting his own course in life.

That life he embarks on became a forty-year odyssey in which he and his seemingly barren wife, Anna, overcame overwhelming temptations that would have overcome a less resolute pair (he: not to succumb to societal pressures to marry another wife; she: not to succumb to temptations to advert to pagan practices, like wearing charms and amulets, in order to achieve pregnancy).

In the very end, though their doubly unshakable faith in the christian religion and the efficacy of "christian" medicine, Anna achieves pregnancy and by the end of the trilogy their steadfastness is rewarded with the birth of six children—Rose, Benedict, Nnanna, Chika, Ikeme, Clara—all of whom when home were the source of their mother's keenest enjoyment in *Bridge to a Wedding* "Mrs. Kafo was full of joy, studying them with her eyes and mind and counting her blessings."

Charles E. Nnolim. *Commonwealth Novel in English*. 7 and 8 (1997–98), pp. 203–10

BIBLIOGRAPHY
*The Only Son*, 1966; *Obi*, 1969; *Oil Man of Obange*, 1971; *A Wreath for the Maidens*, 1973; *A Dancer of Fortune*, 1974; *Bridge to a Wedding*, 1978

# MURRAY, Albert (1916–)
## United States

Mr. Murray is not primarily a political person. He commands no cadres, no followers. He speaks for himself, and he speaks as a literary critic, an essayist, and a short-story writer. But he also speaks as a man who is proud of his people and their considerable achievements. In *The Omni-Americans* his purpose is to set forth those achievements and to warn against America's "experts," especially what he calls "social-science survey technicians"—people who ask a lot of questions and tabulate the responses and proclaim without modesty or qualification lots of conclusions and prescriptions. They do not, says Mr. Murray, see the richness, the complexity of the black man's experience in America (or, for that matter, anyone's experience); they merely contribute to the caricatures that so many of us cannot get out of our heads. Mr. Murray says that social scientists are most comfortable seeing the problems people have, not the people: the fears, the tensions and hates they feel compelled to reveal, the hesitations and infirmities, the exhaustion and despair. He does not deny that millions of blacks have had the worst possible life. He was born near Mobile, he has taught literature at Tuskegee Institute and lived in Chicago and New York as well as the rural South, so he has seen how political discrimination and economic hardship produce the mean lives that some men and women live—and hand on as an awful inheritance to their children. Nevertheless, he insists that black people have never been as used up and shattered as some of their more hysterical observers have maintained. He sees and hears in Alabama and in Harlem things quite different from what most of us are accustomed to read in newspapers and magazines and books. He sees people who have shrewdness and toughness and style and a liveliness that three centuries of American history have been unable to destroy. He sees children who can run and sing and dance and laugh. He sees youths who are thoroughly in tune with concrete realities. He sees men and women who have "soul," who do indeed have rhythm, who swing, who throb with a vitality, a responsiveness, a spirituality that will not be denied. He hears jazz and the blues and work songs and spirituals and gospel songs. He hears people who have no trouble testifying and signifying, who have no "communication block," who have long known "dialogue" and "group support" and "emotional crisis" and "interpersonal relationships." And from all he has seen and heard he has decided that his people demonstrate an elegance of taste, can live intense, lives, can have a gusto that certain observers and scientists naturally would miss—given their limited, outlook, their pretensions, their insistence upon suiting everything to a "theory" or a "conceptual sys" Mr. Murray simply wants to balance things out.

This book contests "the systematic oversimplification black tribulations" to be found in the press and in the journals and books social scientists fill up with their specific prose—a prose that certainly lacks the direct, strong, lucid words "disadvantaged" children use every day. In the eagerness to examine black parents, black youths, black families, the serious problems and flaws of white people are nearly ignored. To Albert Murray, it is as if white hypocrisy, duplicity, boredom, crime, and family instability were off-limits for those interested in "pathology" and "deprivation." Sometimes Mr. Murray states his complaint against social scientists so sweepingly and angrily that he undermines his own important argument. . . .

Though everybody acknowledges Duke Ellington's abilities, many of us are less willing to give him and Ralph Ellison and Langston Hughes and Alain Locke and Arna Bontemps and W. E. B. Du Bois and James Weldon Johnson and John Hope Franklin their place in a particular culture, which is black and yet which draws widely upon this nation's traditions and customs, its folklore, its idiosyncrasies and ceremonies and values—thus the title of the book. Albert Murray thinks that we should be mindful of that culture: built up and tested and strengthened in the rural South, then brought into the cities, where "Walkin' the Ground Hog" and "Fishing in the Dark" and "See That My Grave Is Kept Clean" gave way to "Harlem Air Shaft" and "Concerto for Cootie" and "Sepia Panorama." Himself a Southerner, Mr. Murray knows his people's muscles and nerves, knows how attentively they can listen, how closely they can look, how artfully they go about their business, how keenly they judge their blustery "betters"—who are so sure of themselves and of everything around them and yet so unaware of a whole world of sharp eyes and ears and intelligent minds and hearts, torn and saddened but capable of generosity and hope and devotion. "Scenery is fine, but human nature is finer," wrote young John Keats to a friend. Albert Murray, whose love for the poet's language, the novelist's sensibility, the essayist's clarity, the jazzman's imagination, the gospel singer's depth of feeling is so apparent, would no doubt agree with that nineteenth-century white man's strange suggestion that no matter what distracts us from each other or about each other, we are what really matters—each of us and all of us.

Robert Coles. *New Yorker*. XLVI, 35 (October 17, 1970), pp. 185–86, 189

I must admit to a bias in favor of Albert Murray's novel [*Train Whistle Guitar*], partly because it is located in the South, the ancestral home of most black Americans, but more specifically because it endeavors to re-create a community of black people who have a clear perspective on themselves and the world about them. Murray's is a vision of human beings who feel good about themselves. *Train Whistle Guitar* is the story of one boy's exploration of the possibilities offered by his community. Scooter, the narrator, is a preadolescent who springs directly from the Negro American briarpatch. He is an embodiment of tradition. And while Scooter's voice is not that of a preadolescent, one can overlook this in view of Murray's inventiveness. The rhythms of the blues idiom inform his prose. The book is thin because of its condensation, and because of the limitations imposed by its innovative structure. The music of a guitar re-creating a train whistle provides the framework; the book's episodes are calculated to intrude into the reader's consciousness like the image-provoking sound of a train whistle, imposing rhythmic order on the poetry inherent in Scooter's memory.

Scooter prides himself on the extent of his involvement in his community. The point of observation in his world is the chinaberry tree in his front yard. Up in its branches the preadolescent surveys his community, north, south, east, and west, in order to get his bearings and to begin to perfect a design for living in terms of the entire world. His is a town rich in mythic possibilities. Its name is Gasoline Point, Alabama; but, the narrator cautions, the town is also the briarpatch, and "more a location in time than an intersection on a map." The black citizens of Gasoline Point refuse to see themselves as victims, refuse to allow their imaginations to become

limited by color; and most important of all, they refuse to concede that human style and conscious extension of the imagination are not the most important matters in life. Scooter learns from them. In his imagination, he is also Jack the Rabbit and Jack the Bear and Railroad Bill and Jack Johnson. His chinaberry tree is also a beanstalk and a spyglass tree. Nestled high in its branches, Jack the Rabbit studies the life lessons, provided by a neighborhood of self-defining people, which when mastered will allow him to graduate from the briarpatch.

Scooter's favorite hero is Luzana Cholly, who, at least from the perspective of a boy, is a freight-train-blues-seeming, tobacco-smoking, guitar-strumming maker of myths and a blues extension soloist par excellence. The boy resolves to grab a freight, like his hero, and thunder off to adventures in New York. World-wise from his own experience of freight trains and chain gangs, Luzana Cholly is obliged to instruct Scooter in the skills and wisdom which must be acquired before any would-be hero can confront the city. One must first learn discipline and transcendence and craft. For instruction in these, Luzana Cholly is inadequate, and Scooter must seek other mentors.

But mentors and learning situations abound in Gasoline Point. What emerges most vividly from this novel is Murray's evocation of the richness of Scooter's community and its dramatic sense of human experience. Scooter finds within the experience of his community all the styles, ambiguities and affirmations necessary to initiate him into the responsibilities of manhood. He discovers the randomness of death, the limitless magic of the human imagination, the delights of sexual experience, and the proper measurements of manhood and heroism. He also acquires an appreciation of irony, which should be the essential instruction of a community immersed in the vitality of the blues idiom. . . .

Much of Albert Murray's nonfiction has been devoted to the clarification of those areas of black American experience which, in recent years, have been drawn into the categories of the social science technicians. But unlike many other black writers, especially some who began writing during the sixties, Murray has refused to make his counterstatements in the terminology of social science. In *The Omni-Americans* (1970), he emphasized this refusal by challenging those black writers who depicted their own experiences, or the experience of the group, in terms of conformity to or deviance from white middle-class norms. While well-intentioned writers as diverse as Richard Wright, Kenneth Clark, Claude Brown, James Baldwin, and Gordon Parks paid homage to the norms and definitions of the social science technicians, Murray maintained that social science methodology was insufficient to deal with the richness and complexity of human experience in general and black American experience specifically. Far from being the pathological victims of white oppression, he argued, in their music, speech, styles, and attitudes, black Americans exhibited a resilience, a self-esteem, and an orientation to continuity in the face of adversity that are downright enviable.

In *The Hero and the Blues* (1973), Murray takes to task those writers who abandon to the social sciences the story-teller's role as mythmaker and value-maker. "If the story-teller subordinates his own legitimate esthetic preoccupations to those of the social and political technicians," he warned, "he only downgrades the responsibility which he alone has inherited."

Far from extending the implications of the traditional literary categories, according to Murray, contemporary American social science very often corresponds to an over-simplification of the melodramatic success story by its insistence that "the essential problems of humanity can either be solved or reduced to insignificance by a hero or man of good will who can apply adequate scientific insights to Public Administration and medicine." As a result, those black writers who view their experience from the perspective of the social technician avoid confronting those problems inherent in the human condition. If they project a hero at all, Murray argues, he is a social science hero, "a cripple among cripples," whose only function is to indict the system by displaying his wretchedness. Murray rejects this finger-pointing victim, whether in the fiction of Richard Wright, James Baldwin, or black polemicists, because for him the function of any storybook hero is not to address himself to the humanity of the dragon, but to forge a sword with which the dragon can be conquered. His conception of heroism, and his knowledge of the circumstances which produce heroic action, will not concede validity to such a dimensionless protagonist.

Instead, Murray reminds his readers of Ernest Hemingway's remarks that writers are forged in injustice, poverty, and war; that perhaps the best early training for a writer is an unhappy childhood. To Albert Murray, these observations have particular implications for those who would regard the black American experience as a rich source for fiction. In his view, the image of the sword being forged is inseparable from what he terms "the dynamics of antagonistic cooperation"—a concept as indispensable to any fundamental definition of heroic action as it is to an understanding of the tradition of confrontation and improvisation which finds expression in the blues idiom of black Americans. "All good storytellers," he says, "have always known that irony and absurdity are not only thorns in the briarpatch in which they themselves are born and bred but are also precisely what literary statement is forever trying to provide adequate terms for." Heroes are not produced by predictable circumstances. Rather, it is the extraordinary individual who gains heroic stature in proportion to the number of obstacles he overcomes in his effort to confront the dragon with a well-forged sword in hand. And for Albert Murray, the hero most compatible with the existential absurdity of contemporary American life is the master craftsman, one for whom knowledge and technique, or style, have become that with which he not only performs, but also plays, "as the hero in combat and the blues musician in a jam session can maintain the dancer's grace under the pressure of all tempos."

*Train Whistle Guitar*, then, represents Murray's fictional statement of the blues idiom definition of heroic action. Scooter becomes an imaginative extension of Luzana Cholly, Soldier Boy Crawford, and all the other residents of Gasoline Point. These people confront, acknowledge, and proceed, in spite of as well as in terms of, "the ugliness and meanness inherent in the human condition." What is more, they do it with style, sustaining their integrity and human dignity even while experiencing personal tragedy. They are a community of people who exhibit the dancer's grace under pressure.

[The work of Albert Murray] should prove instructive to those writers attempting to find literary solutions to the problem of achieving an adequate perspective on a broad area of American life. The incorporation of blues idiom techniques into prose may well provide a means of reducing part of the rapid change we see about us to manageable form. For those who seek an uncluttered understanding of the quality of life among black Americans, *Train Whistle Guitar* offers valuable insights. It is to be hoped that more such imaginative re-creations of folk experience will emerge from those black writers who are now exploring the blues territory in the South.

James Alan McPherson. *Atlantic Monthly.* 234, 6 (December 1974), pp. 118, 120–23

The lavish illustrations, the artful arrangement and choice of pictures in *Stomping the Blues* are part of the ritual celebrating and evocating black music.

The incantatory qualities of Murray's prose work just as effectively as the pictures to bring the musicians and music to life. Like Pater on Renaissance painters or Hemingway on bull fighting, the art of Murray's prose style becomes as interesting, absorbing as the subject matter. A subtle reciprocity occurs: as the writer unravels the mysteries, the formal aesthetic core of the activity being investigated (blues, painting, bull fighting), its rules and rituals become a guide, a standard of conduct informing the way the subject is written about. Without minimizing Murray's insights on the blues. . . . I would like to leave for experts on blues music an evaluation of what Murray has said and how his comments relate to other major statements about the blues, and focus this essay on two other issues: do the structure and technique of Murray's essay parallel devices employed by blues musicians, and if Murray's prose can be seen as an extension, refinement, modification of the same tradition nourishing blues music, what are the implications of this relationship between music and writing for a definition of Afro-American culture. . . .

Murray's central metaphor in *Stomping the Blues* is language. In a good poem or a convincing essay objects linked, compared and contrasted by simile or metaphor go beyond the stage of having a logical, analogous relationship to one another and assume a temporary, magical equivalency. The reader feels that he or she is understanding something basic about the intrinsic nature of the objects compared, not simply the inevitable circularity and overlap of the meaning of words. When Murray talks repeatedly about vernacular, idiom, accent, voice, voicing, speech, phrase and fluency he is not only extending the metaphoric relationship between language and music but establishing a continuity along which "language" and "music" are two rather arbitrary signposts.

The power of words to clarify, order and arrange is the tip of an iceberg, the foundation of the power is out of sight, below the surface. It has to do with preconscious recognition of order, design, necessity, the cycles and rhythms of nature. Incantatory language, magic formulas attempt to give form to this level of sound, relating directly rather than referentially to the meaning and force of things. Music plunges downward for its force, words are the force distilled, lightened, tamed and domesticated for convenience. But words can plunge downward, can seek revitalizations. When they do this they lose their hard, brittle outlines, they bend, merge, glow as the arbitrary sheath containing them disintegrates and their auras of force are released. . . .

This is the fundamental ritual of Afro-American speech: evocative, incantatory, transforming. The word seeking to return to its origin in song, approaching song (as the work, play movements of a dance-beat-oriented people approach dance movements) to validate the truth of the experience the word seeks to celebrate. *Stomping the Blues* is an important book in a variety of ways, but nothing it accomplishes is more effective than its enactment of this primal ritual. . . .

The same point that Murray makes about the blues, that they are essentially the embodiment of a ritual and that Afro-American musical tradition maintains its force and coherency thru a recapitulation of these ritualistic elements in various forms and combinations—from field cries to avant garde Jazz—can be made about the narrative voice of *Stomping the Blues*. . . .

The structure of *Stomping the Blues* preserves the ritualistic qualities of black speech and sustains the parallels between the playing of Afro-American music and writing. Each section of the book (''The Blues as Such,'' ''Singing the Blues,'' ''The Blues as Statement,'' etc.) is an interlude, a rap, a seeming improvisation on some aspect of the blues. The method inside each section is associative: a general concept or insight is stated then changes are rung in a theme and variations fashion. Murray's evocation of the blues is neither linear nor exhaustive. A single word, ''play,'' or concept—instruments played in a drumlike fashion, or pattern of imagery—trains and railroading—becomes a point of departure and the reader is treated to a series of factual, metaphoric, provocative, evocative excursions into the territory these ideas suggest to Murray's imagination. The manner in which Murray's text and the photos reinforce one another is significant. There is no predictable, hierarchical arrangement of words and pictures. Rather, the blocks of prose meander through the photos. Or vice versa. The reader may be initially disconcerted by the seemingly haphazard arrangement, but once he relaxes and stops treating the pictures as interruptions, once he realizes he is on his own time, that the repetitive, compulsive left to right eye scanning across lines of print has been purposely short-circuited, and that the reader is being encouraged to turn pages slowly to get into and round the pictures, that the captions beneath the pictures are another worthwhile digression, a different mode of word painting within and around the continuous (?) narrative, he is ready to enjoy the music. Pictures are a commentary on words and words comment on the pictures but together they point to another dimension, the space created by Visual Poetry where media converge and evolve a new experience. The reader is being invited to share the pictures, to discover and reminisce simultaneously, to order the expressive media of the book and proceed at his own pace. . . .

John Edgar Wideman. *The American Poetry Review*. July-August 1978, pp. 42–5

[In *The Spyglass Tree*], the writer and music scholar Albert Murray takes up the story of Scooter, the youthful hero whom he first portrayed in his critically acclaimed novel *Train Whistle Guitar*. Whereas that earlier volume seemed to draw inspiration from *Tom Sawyer* and *Huckleberry Finn* to delineate Scooter's boyhood in a small Southern town, *The Spyglass Tree* performs a kind of jazz improvisation on Goethe's *Wilhelm Meister* and Joyce's *Portrait of the Artist as a Young Man* to create a picture of Scooter's emergence into manhood during the 1930's. . . .

There's an autobiographical mood to this novel, and Mr. Murray's own narrative has a decidedly musical feel to it. Words, phrases and motifs echo throughout Scooter's story, like an insistent melody; and his looping reminiscences have a way of turning into jazz riffs worked on a handful of themes. The Faulknerian prose moves back and forth in time, encompassing Scooter's memories, dreams and observations within single sentences, illuminating the pull this young man constantly feels between his hicktown roots and the lofty realm of academia, between the modest world of his family and the bright glittering world of intellect and books.

Although portions of *The Spyglass Tree* are mannered and forced—an extended sequence about Scooter's involvement in a violent dispute between a white moneylender and a black restaurant owner seems especially melodramatic and contrived—the book, as a whole, works beautifully to conjure up a vanished place and time. Like all good *Bildungsromane*, it leaves the reader with a vivid portrait of a young man, and his struggles to come to terms with his receding past and his beckoning future.

Michiko Kakutani. *New York Times*, November 22, 1991, p. C29

With *Train Whistle Guitar*, Murray shifts from the nonfictional mode to the semi-fictional account of his coming of age. Perhaps the work can best be described as a psychological autobiography, for while many of the people, places, and things appear to be creations of the author, the attendant emotions are no doubt, grounded in Murray's personal experience. The time is the 1920s; the place is Gasoline Point, Alabama; the person is Scooter, the structure is episodic; the impact is impressionistic. Together, these elements combine to yield perhaps the most phenomenal African American Bildungsroman written to date.

*Train Whistle Guitar* echoes many of the themes set forth in *South to a Very Old Place* and treats most of the concerns in a far more elaborate fashion than Murray was able to accomplish in the earlier work. At the core of the novel is Murray's insistence that the legacy of the black Southern experience is a positive, wholesome one. Moreover, Murray portrays the black community as one that nurtures and cares for its young. To illustrate this point, he populates *Train Whistle Guitar* with a number of characters who, despite whatever physical or moral weaknesses they may possess, always manage to find something positive and edifying to pass on to the Scooters of the black community.

One such character is Luzana Cholly. The vernacular form of Louisiana Charlie, Luzana Cholly is a sharp-dressing, guitar-playing, card-gambling, sporty-limp-walking, tobacco-chewing, ass-kicking, no-shit-taking, lady-loving, prison-serving, train-hopping, rail-riding legend who represents ''the Man [Scooter] wanted to be like.'' Scooter and his partner Little Buddy Marshall, both approximately twelve years old, set out to imitate Luzana Cholly in everything he does, from the walk, to the talk, to hopping a boxcar to follow their idol on one of his many excursions. . . .

The example set by Luzana Cholly is anything but rare and isolated, according to Murray. Numerous other examples of elders' taking charge of youth are offered in *Train Whistle Guitar*. There are Mr. Baker and Miss Lexine Metcalf, principal and teacher at the Mobile County Training School, both of whom are committed to teaching all students, but especially and particularly dedicated to preparing the best young minds for greater educational challenges after high school. Both Baker and Metcalf are examples of the legendary black teachers of the segregated South who understood that it was their responsibility to develop the whole student and send him or her forth from the black community as an example of all that was good and wholesome and positive. These teachers never lost interest in their students, even after they had become ambassadors of black pride and integrity to the larger society. Such teachers, Murray implies, are perhaps a dying breed, but he pays homage to their vigilance and endurance throughout *Train Whistle Guitar.*

Yet another role model is Soldier Boy Crawford, a World War I veteran who is the pinnacle of African American racial pride. Along with the local barbershop owner, Murray points out that although Papa Willie owns the shop, he is not a barber. Papa Gumbo Willie McWorthy, Soldier Boy Crawford sets in motion a strong offensive against those who would condescend to African Americans as a race of people. . . .

From Soldier Boy and Papa Gumbo Willie, then, Scooter and Little Buddy learn pride in their African American heritage, however mixed it may be; furthermore, they learn that where one comes from is considerably less important than how well one learns to treat his fellow human beings. This lesson is one that guides Scooter throughout the course of his growing up and on into adulthood.

People are only one part of Murray's literary reconstruction of Gasoline Point. There are also the places—the geography that is peculiar to the locale. In establishing the importance of place in *Train Whistle Guitar,* Murray moves beyond mere local color to a far deeper significance associated with place. In this regard, Murray joins fellow Southern writers—Faulkner and Welty, in particular—in expressing the theory that place is at least as important as people—or, more specifically, that the South is at least as important as Southerners. So not only does Murray take his readers on a tour of Mobile and its outskirts, including the railroad crossings and yards, the rivers and swamps, the homes and businesses, but he also makes the reader feel how much the emotions of "home" are tied into the physicalities. . . .

*Train Whistle Guitar* is a novel rich and dense in its myriad celebrations of the black Southern experience. Every episode, nearly every page, is chock full of reminders for many who experienced similar comings of age, or introductions to those ignorant of the same. The celebratory remembrances range from the music, secular and sacred, that underscores, indeed permeates, all aspects of black Southern life, to the stories and the storytellers that inevitably find their place in whatever is going on at the moment. Or Murray may celebrate the language, whether it be the dozens, the "cussing," the codes, or the metaphors peculiar to black folk speech; or he may relish the memory of food, so central to all occurrences in the black community, from "eating fried mullet with hot sauce and bakery bread and drinking Nehi Orange Crush" in a local cookshop, to the Sunday morning breakfasts which may feature as entrees "porkchops or fried chicken [and] batter-fried oysters with grits and butter." In any event, each of these facets is an integral and important ingredient of what Murray calls "the also and also of all that was also the also plus also" of the Southern black experience. . . .

*Train Whistle Guitar* is a phenomenal account of growing up black in the segregated South. Not only are the subject and theme refreshing, but they are rendered with a literary artistry that is indeed rare in semi-autobiographical works. In addition, Murray very ably refutes claims of degradation and pathology by presenting a view that does not disclaim or ignore the negative, even painful aspects of black life, but, rather, shows how such negative experiences are not at all overwhelming when compared to the positive aspects.

Warren Carlson. *African American Review.* 27, 2 (summer 1993), pp. 287–95

In *The Blue Devils of Nada,* using artistic, literary, and critical cultural forms from ancient Greek tragedy, to modernism, to sports, to philosophy, to visual art, to music, Murray examines the work of Duke Ellington, Count Basie, Louis Armstrong, Romare Bearden, and Ernest Hemingway. His improvisation writes a new song: a song on American "character, outlook, attitude, native value system, and lifestyle."

America, Murray has argued, is a mulatto, composite culture, shaped by the conjunctions of influences from the Yankee to the Native to the Black. This fact is, he maintains, the essence of our national creativity, but also the source of our greatest tensions. Murray's work articulates a notion of culture that can acknowledge the existence and interdependence of this multiplicity of voices that makes up "the American" and that can create a form of expression through which free and mutual selves can interact and respect, if not either resolve or transcend, the tensions in our culture. He argues that this form already exists, that it is an indigenous form, and he calls it the blues idiom.

The blues idiom, enacted by the blues hero, emerges from Southern roots that teach one to function in terms of rootlessness and to face squarely an historical reality of pain and suffering: "*To protest the existence of dragons (or even hooded or unhooded Grand Dragons for that matter) is not only sentimental but naive.*" The blues idiom also includes connecting the knowledge gained in one's personal experience to history and to the canon of the West. The blues musician, through the play which is interplay between the individual and the tradition as well as between persons and groups, is able to move beyond the binaries that are the dragon's, the dominant ideological stance, to slay the dragon and, thereby, to gain "the ultimate boon to which the dragon denies you access.". . .

While the social sciences disregard play, imagination, and creativity, Murray, emphasizing them, argues for the importance of metaphor. The poetic metaphor, because its "net" is more loosely woven, can trap and stylize large areas of experience. Style is essential for Murray; it is form individualized and made elegant. Individual experience and regional particularities can be stylized into universal significance. The blues idiom is the most powerful metaphorical structure, offering a way to make a response to the human condition that is meaningful, significant, and individually stylized. As a performative construction of identity and community, blues improvisation also creates the capacity to function in situations of confrontation. The blues idiom offers a creative, disruptive counterstatement to the ideology of the dragon in the terms of the common culture. It offers "not attempts to go beyond the form, but rather . . . efforts to take [the form] as far as it would go." This extension, which is improvisation, is to riff from the tradition the method that can make the solution fit the indigenous style; it is to make the tradition your own. The fully orchestrated blues statement offers a model for life that, for Murray, can deal with tragedy, comedy, melodrama, and farce naturally and simultaneously. The blues statement "expresses a sense of life that is affirmative." To improvise is to establish one's style: "the dancing of an attitude."

This dancing of an attitude is what each artist Murray discusses is able to do. Each is able to improvise on the cultural forms and influences around him. . . .

*The Blue Devils of Nada* is brilliant and beautiful. It demonstrates its thesis: that the blues hero can stylize a variety of influences into his own voice. Murray riffs biography, history, art history, and criticism, along with film and literary criticism and philosophy, into his own masterpiece. This work is Murray at his most elegant—and elegance, style, is the point. The arts, for Murray, are *"the vernacular imperative to process (which is to say to stylize) the raw native materials, experiences, and the idiomatic particulars of everyday life into aesthetic (which is to say elegant) statements of universal relevance and appeal."* The folk is stylized into the fine; each individual plays the instrument of self in his or her own way; and nothing is lost. That elegance, however, is tough. The book's juxtapositions and deep examinations challenge the reader to move beyond his or her established conceptions and interpretations. Murray's voice carries an urgency and an edge. He insists on commitment, on the reader's becoming part of the second line, both in the "high spirits and earthy cavorting" of the New Orleans street parade and in the seriousness of the dedication of the young musician, admiring a style, who apprentices himself to a master, mentor, and "true father." From serious play comes functional mythology in aesthetic form—like the blues.

Art, Murray insists, is a vital response to our common dilemma as Americans. It creates possibilities, expressive and applicable forms. It is one of the ways that we create human values and define what is good and what is not. To take on this task is the responsibility of the artist and the way to engage, creatively and transgressively, as well as responsibly, the realities of life. "You cannot," Murray said once, "slay the dragon with a formula." For nada, for nothing, except the sheer joy of exercising your creative powers at the moment of dire challenge to and deepest need of yourself and your world, improvise: Dance your attitude, defeat the dragon, and take the boon home. Albert Murray does.

Carolyn M. Jones. *African American Review.* 31, 1 (spring 1999), pp. 168–70

BIBLIOGRAPHY

*The Omni-Americans: New Perspectives on Black Experience and American Culture,* 1970; *South to a Very Old Place,* 1972; *The Hero and the Blues,* 1973; *Train Whistle Guitar,* 1974; *Stomping the Blues,* 1976; *Reflections on Logic, Politics, and Reality: A Challenge to the Sacred Consensus of Contemporary American Thinking,* 1989; *The Spyglass Tree,* 1991; *The Seven League Books,* 1996; *The Blue Devils of Nada,* 1996; *Conversations with Albert Murray*

# MWANGI, Meja (1948– )
## Kenya

*Kill Me Quick* was published in 1973 and was quickly given the President Kenyatta Award for Literature. Since then, Meja Mwangi has published two more novels and several short stories. His fourth novel is about to be published.

Like Ngugi wa Thiong'o, East Africa's first novelist, Meja Mwangi is a Kikuyu; as with Ngugi, Mwangi's second novel was published first; and like Ngugi, Mwangi has published two novels about the Mau Mau, *Taste of Death* and *Carcase for Hounds.* Thus comparison between Mwangi and Ngugi is inescapable. However, Mwangi is very different from Ngugi. . . .

Although Ngugi has set the pace for other East African writers, Mwangi confesses he finds Ngugi very difficult to read, if not unreadable. Questioned further, Mwangi says that he feels Ngugi is best able to write about the life and problems of people in or from the village, while he likes to write about the urban dispossessed, of which he himself is one. Ngugi's style reflects his concerns, just as Mwangi's style is swift-moving because it reflects the urgency of life in the city. . . .

Meja Mwangi makes no claims to being a political writer, or to understanding why things in newly independent Africa have gone wrong, let alone providing solutions. In this respect, too, he appears to differ from Ngugi, who understands the forces at work, analyzes them, and suggests solutions. Mwangi makes statements that sound cynical. He says that there could not be another Mau Mau movement, since so many of the people involved in the first one see that they gained nothing while others benefited. The end of *Carcase for Hounds* implies that the kind of brotherhood and justice General Haraka fought for can only be achieved in the life beyond. The death of the Mau Mau leader in *Taste of Death* leads finally to confusion, while the death of Kihika in Ngugi's *Grain of Wheat* does not diminish the continuing validity of his example and message for the people. However, we cannot leave the matter there and say that Ngugi believes in the future while Mwangi does not. The reverse side of Ngugi's "messianism" is, as he says at the beginning of *Secret Lives,* that he experiences moments of despair. It is hard to imagine Mwangi making such a statement.

Peter Nazareth. *Afriscope.* 6 (April 1976), pp. 25, 27

Meja Mwangi is certainly one of the most exciting . . . East African writers. He is already the author of two successful novels, *Kill Me Quick* and *Carcase for Hounds,* in which he amply demonstrated his characteristic qualities—a touching compassion for the social or political underdog, a quietness of tone which emphasizes rather than obscures the very serious problems being analyzed, and a remarkably controlled though unpretentious prose style.

Mwangi's latest novel, *Going Down River Road,* displays all these characteristics. Set in Nairobi's seething brothel, pub, and cheap nightclub area, the novel presents with commendable power and detailed demonstration the fortunes of the hero, Ben, against the background of all those social forces which we have now come to associate with the growth of modern African cities. Mwangi hits on the clever device of using the framework of the construction of the luxurious twenty-four-story Development Building as a means of presenting the experiences of the ordinary workers, whose lifestyles are in such stark contrast with all that the Development Building represents, but who must look forward to the completion of the building with apprehension since it would mean the loss of their jobs. Mwangi's exploration of urban problems is if anything, more detailed, more sensitive, and ultimately more convincing than anything that [Cyprian] Ekwensi has ever written. The squalor, degradation, and misery are tellingly presented through case histories such as that of Wini, Ben's girlfriend, who had a child at the age of fourteen and was forced into prostitution to keep herself and the fatherless child, but still possessed enough moral courage to see her through a secretarial course. She eventually gets a decent job, but is forced to abandon her baby and elope with her boss as a way out of the urban impasse. There is the sixteen-year-old prostitute who fornicates with Ben in the same room in which her friend is simultaneously having fun with another man, while her month-old baby screams in the corner. Such scenes give convincing social motivations of conduct while generating tremendous sympathy for the unfortunates who are trapped in the situation. Far from being titillating, the sexual details stamp unforgettably on the reader's mind the hopelessness of the masses in the struggle to survive. The prostitutes are dogged by a basic insecurity and the fear of hunger; the fun-loving teenage girls who are hired out by their boyfriends are so vulnerable to the sadistic whims of drunkards, thugs, and drug-addicts. Indeed, violence is never far from the surface. It degenerates quite often into motiveless hatred and even murder. The inhabitants of the River Road area occasionally demonstrate a certain comradeship in adversity and the reader is made to experience the warmth of populist amusement spots such as Eden or the Karara center, but he still senses the absence of real friendship which is ultimately attributable to the dehumanizing effect of the impersonal city where everyone is involved in the scramble to survive. Mwangi does not flinch from presenting the grim realities of the housing racket, the corruption of the politicians, the high cost of living and its consequences, and organized as well as petty crime.

Mwangi's preoccupation with the social realities of the city does not prevent him from creating some interesting characters and exploring some significant relationships. The hero, Ben, is the most fascinating of them all. A central consciousness through whose eyes almost all the events and the other characters are viewed, he survives in the mind of the reader as a kind of antihero whose huge bulk and physical strength go oddly with his lack of resolution and real guts. There is even a slight hint of some kind of emasculation in this young man who, in spite of his sexual prowess, seems unable to father his own child or have a lasting relationship with a woman and at the end adopts a child who everyone knows to have been fathered by another man.

> Eustace Palmer. In Eldred Durosimi Jones, ed. *African Literature Today*. 9 (1978), pp. 105–6

[During the Mau Mau conflict] the whites . . . insisted that the Mau Mau were nothing more than a group of destructive terrorist elements; the blacks argued back with naked emotion that they were freedom fighters. But recently, whether it be because the ''freedom fighter'' image has taken firm hold among the Kenyan people, or because a new generation which did not experience the war has grown to adulthood, the Kenyan ''Mau Mau complex'' seems to have disappeared. This can be clearly seen, for example, by looking at the cold objectivism of Meja Mwangi's creative technique as he treats the Mau Mau liberation struggle in his novel *Carcase for Hounds*. Mwangi's work deals from the inside with the indomitable fighting spirit of the Mau Mau soldiers, who, although pushed into the Aberdares Range by government troops, maintain rigid discipline and finally, ablaze with love for their comrades and their sense of mission, give their lives in a battle. The pursued and the pursuers (puppets of the whites) are former comrades who had once shared food and friendship; as we read we are reminded of Che Guevara, and the conflict of Vietnam flickers through our minds. The tragedy of such conflict between brothers is pathetically distressing. But in Mwangi's novel there is no longer a trace of the meanness and sense of humiliation seen in Ngugi [wa Thiong'o]'s *Grain of Wheat*. What one finds here is simply a refreshing, mechanical light dryness which amounts to one kind of sublimation. In this sense the title of the book (from Shakespeare's *Julius Caesar*) can also be read as biting satire aimed at the insensibility and unashamed egotism of humans who fabricate a grand and glorious cause. . . .

Mwangi's approach in his works, of trying to describe the mechanism of the internal contradictions of contemporary Kenyan society in the process of modernization, clearly sets him apart from the older generation of writers in two ways. The first is that while Ngugi's main interest is in the fate of individual human beings, Mwangi has pinpointed his interest on social mechanisms. Secondly—and this is a phenomenon common to West and South Africa as well—such writers as Ngugi and [Chinua] Achebe turned their attention to the outside by focusing on the struggle against Western white culture at the time of independence. Now, in the 1970s, it is on interior questions that they are fixing their glance. . . . This tendency to portray the internal contradictions peculiar to African society is also proof positive that the inner-directed younger generation has grown up soundly. While talking with Mwangi, I got the feeling from the grandness of his conceptions, the broad range of his interests, and his flexibility, that he is a man of great latent talent. In order to understand his promise more fully, one should examine his novel *Kill Me Quick*. . . .

In the prizewinning story two young men, Meja and Maina, manage to graduate from middle school through the sacrifices of their families. Shouldering the expectations of their relatives, they dream of wreathing their homes in glory, and with hearts full of hope for success, they set out for Nairobi in search of good jobs. But with the high unemployment rate in Kenya it proves to be impossible to find work, and they are forced into living as drifting back-alley beggars. Finally they find employment on a white man's plantation with half-pay—that is, one man's wages for the two of them. Then one day suspected of thievery, they are given the sack. After finding their way once again to the back streets of Nairobi, they commit theft at a supermarket and in the resulting chase get separated. Maina then joins a gang which, with the slums on the outskirts of the city as its headquarters, plagues the busy sectors of Nairobi with pickpocketing and thievery. He thus commits one crime after another on the main streets, and in the meantime he falls in love with a beautiful but impoverished girl of the slums; this love, however, comes to nothing. Finally he is caught by the police and thrown into a solitary confinement cell. It is in prison that he again meets Meja. Maina is accused of murder, but Meja, knowing him, tries desperately to convince the other inmates of Maina's innocence. In the mutual trust and friendship of comrades, even in such wretched circumstances, there is evidence of human warmth.

What Mwangi wanted to write of in this novel was the social mechanism which twists the lives of innocent young men who want to live honestly, which drives them into ill-doing, and which can produce only tares and no good wheat. Here the internal contradictions of Kenyan modernization are exposed, and at the same time certain characteristics peculiar to East Africa are revealed. . . . What kind of society can it be that forces a life without hope on a good people, that drives them into crime? We see here the figure of Africa laboring over modernization.

> Satoru Tsuchiya. *World Literature Today*. 52, 3 (summer 1978), pp. 570–71

Meja Mwangi is certainly one of the most exciting of the new East African writers who have made social comment and analysis the dominant trend in the contemporary African novel. *Going Down River Road* must surely rank as his most important work so far, but in the two earlier novels—*Kill Me Quick* and *Carcase for Hounds*—he had already shown his characteristic qualities: a touching compassion for the social or political underdog, a quietness of tone which emphasizes rather than obscures the very serious social problems being analyzed, and a remarkably controlled though unpretentious prose style.

*Kill Me Quick* presents with great pathos and commendable realism the fortunes of two adolescents in modern urban Kenya whose hopes and aspirations, buttressed by a successful secondary education, are eventually dashed by the nature of the Kenyan political, social, and economic system. *Kill Me Quick* and *Going Down River Road* give a very detailed and convincing analysis of the causes of juvenile delinquency, prostitution, and big-time as well as petty crime. In doing so, Mwangi has staked his claim to a territory hitherto dominated by [Cyprian] Ekwensi, and he carries out his analysis with greater depth of presentation, strength of characterization, psychological understanding, and awareness of the implications of the issues he raises. . . .

*Carcase for Hounds* is about the activities of the Mau Mau during their struggle for the liberation of Kenya. Inevitably the novel has to concentrate on the presentation of life in the jungle. And Mwangi proves himself as much at home in the uncanny mysteriousness of the jungle as in the hustle and bustle of the city. Indeed, the powerful evocation of setting must surely rank among this novel's claims to attention. The jungle is unmistakably there—its power, its darkness, its mystery, its terror, its discomfort, and its luxuriance; and this evocation of setting is done not just to provide local color, but meaningfully to reflect the characters' moods and circumstances. . . .

These two novels are a fitting prelude to the Mwangi who is revealed in *Going Down River Road* . . . [which] explores the harsh realities of city life to a much greater depth than *Kill Me Quick*, and with a greater realism than Ekwensi's *Jagua Nana*. It is a novel which is also preoccupied with human relationships; indeed it presents with commendable power and detailed demonstration the fortunes of the hero, Ben, against the background of all those social evils which we have now come to associate with the growth of modern African cities. Mwangi does not flinch from details which would most tellingly present the squalor, degradation, and misery that characterize the lives of most of his characters.

Eustace Palmer. *The Growth of the African Novel* (London: Heinemann, 1979), pp. 307–8, 311–12, 314

Meja Mwangi exorcized his particular Mau Mau ghost with the two novels *Carcase for Hounds* and *Taste of Death*. The latter traces the history of Kariuki, a soldier who fought in World War II, and who joined the freedom fighters because of the bullying tactics of the homeguard in his village. He takes part in the daring rescue from prison of the leader, several ambushes, is captured by the British, tortured, sentenced to death, then escapes to remain in the forest with two companions until independence. His story is interlaced with details of British attempts to destroy the freedom fighters by psychological and military means. Inspector Cowdrey plays a leading role in the former activities. He is the chief interrogator of Mau Mau suspects and is fanatical in his search for the leader whose capture he sees as crucial in defeating the Mau Mau. The demented Cowdrey leaves Kenya at independence, his wife having been brutally murdered, and his career and dreams shattered. *Carcase for Hounds* is more confined in both time and space covered. It concentrates on a few days in the lives of General Haraka and his gang, and D. C. Kingsley and his men who are out to

capture them. Caught between the two are the frightened and confused villagers of Pinewood and Acacia Ranch.

In both novels, Meja Mwangi concentrates attention on the freedom fighters, or "forest fighters," as he consistently and with studied neutrality calls them. Unlike previous novels, his work also depicts in some detail the whites and civilians, giving a more complete picture of the struggle than, say, Ngugi [wa Thiong'o] and [Lennard] Kibera, who concentrate more on the civilians, or [Godwin] Wachira, who is concerned almost exclusively with the leading freedom fighter. Part of Meja Mwangi's uniqueness lies in this wholeness of vision, a characteristic that can be seen developing from the earlier *Taste of Death* to *Carcase for Hounds*. The former covers a long period of time—from the early 1950s to independence in 1963—and has a large cast of characters, but there is little depth of characterization or subtlety of plot. In part, this can be explained by the audience. The book is a secondary-school reader and, naturally, keeping the readers excited and involved overrides other artistic considerations. Characters tend to fall into stereotyped modes of behavior. Kariuki is the stock freedom-fighter hero. He leads daring rescues, is a crack short, and does not break down despite terrible torture. Lieutenant Davis is the disciplined army officer who maintains a stiff upper lip throughout and gets through a Mau Mau ambush alive because of his reliance on strict military discipline. Cowdrey is the inherently racist white, caught up in the emergency in an attempt to preserve his privileged lifestyle.

While this tendency to stereotype may be expected of a young writer, there is some evidence of the more mature style that is to burgeon in *Carcase for Hounds*. There are little touches that add some life to the characterization. Lieutenant Davis's driver is an interesting example. British soldiers, if they are portrayed at all in fiction of this period, are either the leading officers masterminding operations and interrogations, or young privates raping and murdering villagers. Meja Mwangi adds some individuality and credibility to his portrayals. In contrast to the calm Lieutenant Davis, the anonymous driver is scared stiff at the nearness of death, intent only on escape and contemptuous of his superior's orders: "To hell with your orders. I am not going to sit here and be blown to hell because of your lunatic orders." Similar details of personality and social relationships appear, sparingly, in other portraits.

Elizabeth Knight. In Eldred Durosimi Jones, ed. *African Literature Today*. 13 (1983), pp. 147–48

It is easy to see how the novels of Meja Mwangi, as they appeared through the years, were related in their tone and subject matter to the literary production of his country. The first two novels, in order of writing—*Taste of Death*, appearing in 1975, and *Kill Me Quick*—are in the same vein of angry realism and are both documents and pamphlets. *Kill Me Quick* follows two uprooted adolescents, school-leavers, barely surviving in the slum jungle of Nairobi. . . . *Taste of Death* is a Mau Mau novel which . . . shows both sides of the conflict as doomed to suffer and lose. Taking up the same subject, *Carcase for Hounds* moves further from fictionalized history; the narrative concentrates on the character of a rebel general, truly tragic in his mad pride, doomed to fail in his growing isolation in front of greater technological power. Although it owes a debt to the legend and the historical reports on people like [Dedan] Kimathi and Mathenge, this chief dying in his cave, insane and stoical, has the grandeur of romantic figures of fiction. *The*

*Trial of Dedan Kimathi* by Ngugi [wa Thiong'o] and Micere Mugo will portray the dead general with a special effort to blend history and legend, facts and a political message for the present. Mwangi creates a lonely figure, a hero for our time with no message but chilly despair in an absurd world.

*Going Down River Road*, Mwangi's second urban novel, is also a great move forward from *Kill Me Quick*. There is less of the journalist's eye for striking facts, less lingering on the sensational and the exceptional. The thieving gangs of Mathare Valley have been replaced by a group of laborers who are building the new Nairobi. The unrelieved gloom of the first book is far less effective than the humorous tone in which the hero's sad journey through the city is related in the [second] book. The allegory in the building of the hotel (which stands for the New Kenya), the elements of burlesque and the sad scenes at the brothel, the nightmare visits to the bars—all merge into a strongly constructed whole, drawing in one's imagination the map of a city truer and more vivid than any single, African city, or any big city, with all its lonely aimless lives.

This freedom to re-create, to transcend documentary appeal, this very personal narrative voice, with as good an ear for sharp dialogue, for handling of all minor characters, a feeling of pity which is never condescending, mark Mwangi as a writer of great stature with the promise of much good work to come.

Jacqueline Bardolph. In G.D. Killam, ed. *The Writing of East and Central Africa* (London: Heinemann, 1984), p. 46

Mwangi's *The Bushtrackers* . . . is the "novelization" of a screen-play by one Gary Strieker. Though the story is set in Kenya it involves the Mafia, it has a black American villain and a white co-hero, and it presents a string of situations familiar from American thrillers in the less familiar setting of Tsavo Game Park. It is not mere hackwork. The story, however shallow, is told in a fast, extremely exciting way, and Mwangi excels himself in the evocation of the Kenyan bush. . . .

Mwangi's narratives are not perfect. Leaving aside the technical flaws in *Taste of Death* and *Kill Me Quick* on the grounds that such a young writer was bound to make mistakes . . . one must still acknowledge lapses in his more masterful later books. They are generally in what filmmakers call "continuity." *Carcase for Hounds*, on the whole a complete tour de force of gripping narrative, begins with two Mau Mau moving through the forest. They come to a river. The big one, General Haraka, tells his lieutenant, Kimamo, to cross first. The smaller refuses—"'No. You go first. I will cover you.'" The big one shrugs and goes first. Yet sixteen pages later we have a paragraph beginning "Haraka sighed. Kimamo, so reliable . . ."—and a couple of pages further on, "Kimamo was the man. Hard, brave . . ." How do we reconcile these thoughts with the apparent cowardice on Kimamo's part which we saw earlier? In *Going Down River Road*, Mwangi's fourth novel, there's a still more abrupt jump. Ben Wachira's girl has just left him to run off with her white employer. Ben gets violently drunk in the Karara Center, hits a prostitute with a beer bottle, then passes out on the floor. "Typical of Karara Center, no one gives a thought to the lonely drunk." The next chapter opens immediately, and at its beginning we see Ben entering the Karara Center again. "A tired drunken smile breaks over his rough bearded face. Good old Karara Center, stuffy as hell, warm as home. Here at least are people. People he understands, people who are people, human beings." . . .

[If] others, like myself, feel jolted on first, even on second reading of both those passages, then Mwangi's irony is not working properly. . . . But the point I want to make now . . . is that one feels such jolts with special severity because one is traveling so fast. Like a car splendidly driven at top speed, Mwangi's narratives make the road seem so easy that the odd pothole (over or round which a slower vehicle could be gently maneuvred) strikes the passengers, though so briefly, with surprise.

Angus Calder. In G. D. Killam, ed. *The Writings of East and Central Africa* (London: Heinemann, 1984), pp. 178–80

The reader who is interested in a good, well-told story with a linear sense of time will find a ready-hearted accommodation in [*Striving for the Wind*]. It is an old-fashioned fabulation in the popular vein. It does not displace a good narrative with any of the off-putting cleverness that goes with postmodernist story-telling. As in his earlier novels, *Going Down River Road* and *Kill Me Quick*, Meja Mwangi is a self-conscious folk-performer who laces the wisdom of the village square with barroom banter; it's the narrative style of the city slick and the village wag rubbing shoulders on the page. As such, it has the normal accompaniment of stock characters: the good on one side, the evil on the other, and the fight to a finish drawn out between them. Except that Meja Mwangi does not allow the kind of easy resolution that transports the simple-minded.

Baba Pesa, the "Father of Money" in *Striving for the Wind*, is as much of a stock character as you can find, one of the lucky few who bought the farms abandoned by white farmers in the wake of the Mau Mau struggle. He has "hundreds of acres of land, woodlands, and grazing fields down in the valley, forests up in the hills where only the elephants and buffalos roam . . . cows and cars, goats and tractors and all the money in the world"; what more did he want? He is obviously not satisfied with the lot that he has acquired through further armtwisting of the poorer neighbors; he wishes to take over all the farms on the next hill and the next and the next. His greed is fastened, almost as we first come across him, upon the land of his immediate, near-destitute neighbor, Baru. His reason is that he cannot bear to see Baru's hovels each time he looks over his fence from his veranda. But Baru will not let himself be intimidated into selling. He is the typical rural dweller, poor, uneducated, and at a moral distance from the moneyed ethic which sees neighbors as tools to be used rather than as fellow human beings to share snuff and wine with. Baru is as stubborn as the ox that drives his plough: he may not have a tractor or a Mercedes Benz car like Baba Pesa; he may be scratching a living, never having enough to pay fees for his son in the village polytechnic, but he is not going to give away his land and slouch landless into the desolation of city life like many with whom Baba Pesa has dealt. He bears abuse and ridicule like all the big and small people of Kambi village upon whom the Father of Money has trampled capriciously. . . .

The story barely manages to avoid being judgmental. Not that the author did not try. The measure of his success however is that he presents the rural poor without romanticizing their lives. Having drawn a line between the good and bad, he makes quite a visible effort to be evenhanded. Yet, it is clear where his hammer falls. This gives *Striving for the Wind* its point, making it one of those novels which manage, whatever their literary quality, to remove indifference to a social malaise. It does not relieve it of a certain wearisome familiarity; for one may well ask when the Baba Pesas of this world will stop getting away with so much? Surely, until there is an answer to the question every novel out of Kenya, no matter how apolitical, would continue to make one wonder about the difference between ''permitted'' literature and the literature which says the unsayable.

Odia Ofeimun. *West Africa.* 7–13 September 1992, pp. 1547–48

In *Striving for the Wind* . . . Mwangi tries to return to his roots as they were so powerfully displayed in *Kill Me Quick* and *Going Down River Road.* . . . Mwangi's attention is focused on a world of rural poverty and greed, a world he knows firsthand, in which the future of Kenya is continuously being debated between Baba Pesa (meaning ''Father of Money'') and his university dropout son Judas (Judas, the betrayer). Mwangi rejects the shifting spaces of his thrillers, focusing instead on a static, weary, and worn-out landscape; he rejects the idiom of the movies, seeking instead to capture the language of rural despair and the tyranny of the nouveau riche; the alienated authorial tone of the thrillers gives way to a profound voice that sustains the pessimism and angst of the rural poor.

So in *Striving for the Wind* readers see Mwangi at his most serious. But this novel is as dull as the land and people it represents, and by the time readers finish it, and as they reflect on the labor and pain Mwangi has put into it, they begin to realize that his real talents are not in this kind of ''tractor'' fiction, but in the phantasmal world of the thrillers and movies he loves so much. One cannot help but wonder what Mwangi has inherited from the movies tradition. On the one hand, the movies have endowed him with the palpable wealth of Americana—in habits and idiom—that is largely responsible for his artistic fluency and his engagement with his African popular audience, which lives and thrives on such material. On the other hand, however, this appropriation of Americana has impoverished him as a novelist in the areas in which he was strongest—his sense of the African landscape and its people, the language of the urban poor, and the discourse of contemporary politics. Mwangi's real talent is manifested in the novels in which he marries the techniques of the thriller with a profound exposition of the African scene.

Simon Gikandi. In Bernth Lindfors and Reinhard Sander, eds. *Dictionary of Literary Biography,* Volume 125: *Twentieth-Century Caribbean and Black African Writers* (Detroit: Gale Research. 1993), p. 119

BIBLIOGRAPHY
*Kill Me Quick*, 1973; *Carcase for Hounds*, 1974; *Taste of Death*, 1975; *Going Down River Road*, 1976; *The Bushtrackers*, 1979; *Bread of Sorrow*, 1987; *The Return of Shaka*, 1989; *Weapon of hunger*, 1989; *Striving for the Wind*, 1990

# N

## NAYLOR, Gloria (1950–)
### United States

Gloria Naylor's *The Women of Brewster Place* is set in one of those vintage urban-housing developments that black people (who are, in truth, "nutmeg," "ebony," "saffron," "cinnamon-red," or "gold") have inherited from a succession of other ethnic groups. The difference is that while the Irish and Italians used it as a jumping-off place for the suburbs, for most of its "colored daughters," Brewster Place is "the end of the line": "They came because they had no choice and would remain for the same reason." But the end of the line is not the end of life. With their backs literally to the wall—a brick barrier that has turned Brewster Place into a dead end—the women make their stand together, fighting a hostile world with love and humor.

There's Mattie Michael, dark as "rich, double cocoa," who defied her over-protective father to take a man who was pure temptation, almost a force of nature—a Pan. Pregnant and disowned, she made the instinctive matriarchal decision (I mean that word in the mythic, not the sociological, sense) to live without a man and invest all her love back into her child. Left in the lurch by the grown, spoiled son who results, she becomes the anchor for the other women of Brewster Place.

There's Etta Mae Johnson, survivor and good-time woman, who comes home to Mattie when her dream of redemption by marrying a "respectable" preacher is sordidly ended. There's Ciel Turner, whose husband, Eugene, ominously resents her fertility: "With two kids and you on my back, I ain't never gonna have nothin' . . . nothin'!" There's Kiswana (formerly Melanie) Browne, idealistic daughter of middle-class parents, who has moved to Brewster Place to be near "my people." Cora Lee, a welfare mother, likes men only because they provide babies, but she can't cope with children once they are older. She is *almost* lifted out of the inertia of her life by the power of art when Kiswana takes her to see a black production of Shakespeare in the park. And finally, there are Theresa and Lorraine, lovers who embody the ultimate commitment of woman to woman and yet arouse unease or loathing in most of the other women of Brewster Place.

Despite Gloria Naylor's shrewd and lyrical portrayal of many of the realities of black life . . . *The Women of Brewster Place* isn't realistic fiction—it is mythic. Nothing supernatural happens in it, yet its vivid, earthy characters (especially Mattie) seem constantly on the verge of breaking out into magical powers. The book has two climaxes: one of healing and rebirth, one of destruction. In the first, Mattie magnificently wrestles Ciel, dying of grief, back to life. In the second, Lorraine, rejected by the others, is gang raped, a blood sacrifice brutally proving the sisterhood of all women. Naylor bravely risks sentimentality and melodrama to write her compassion and outrage large, and she pulls it off triumphantly.

Annie Gottlieb. *New York Times Book Review.* August 22, 1982, pp. 11, 25

Gloria Naylor's second novel, *Linden Hills*, is a modern version of Dante's *Inferno* in which souls are damned not because they have offended God or have violated a religious system, but because they have offended themselves. In their single-minded pursuit of up-ward mobility, the inhabitants of Linden Hills, a black, middle-class suburb, have turned away from their past and from their deepest sense of who they are. Naylor feels that the subject of who-we-are and what we are willing to give up of who-we-are to get where-we-want-to-go is a question of the highest seriousness—as serious as a Christian's concern over his salvation. . . .

Naylor's tale is an allegory based on the physical and moral topography of Dante's *Inferno.* It covers four days in the life of a twenty-year-old black poet, Willie Mason, who lives in a poor neighborhood called Putney Wayne that lies above Linden Hills. Working temporarily as a handyman to earn money to buy Christmas presents, Willie passes through Linden Hills and, like Dante, analyzes the moral failures of the lost souls he encounters. By the time Willie escapes from the frozen lake at the bottom of Linden Hills and crosses to the safety of a nearby apple orchard, he has experienced a spiritual awakening. The "new" Willie has decided to give up his aimless drifting and to take charge of his life. He becomes, as his name implies, a decisive builder. He accepts responsibility for his life, he refuses to blame his problems on others or on fate, and he realizes that he can choose a middle way between the poverty of the ghetto and the depravity of Linden Hills. . . .

*Linden Hills* is an uncomfortable and dangerous book which pricks the conscience. It takes the reader on a perilous pilgrimage and forces him to consider the hidden cost of his choices. It strips him of the ease of innocence. Naylor has risked much by writing such a disturbing tale. Her readers may view her subject too narrowly. If they do, she could lose a black audience that feels unjustly challenged and a white audience that thinks the novel's hard questions are not meant for them. Naylor also risks offending modern sensibilities that regard an allegory about moral accountability too medieval for their tastes. But because Naylor knows who she is, where she has been, and where she wants to go, she dares to tell her tale and dares the reader to reckon with it.

Catherine C. Ward. *Contemporary Literature.* 28, 1 (1987), pp. 67, 69, 80–81

[What] happens if we resist the temptation to subsume into a narrative of sexual binarism the dispersed array of subject positions that *Linden Hills* frames—what happens, that is, if we respect another (nonmonistic) feminist injunction and refuse to impose a hierarchy of political signification? The question arises here because part of what distinguishes black women's fiction in the contemporary scene is a sense of a historical community and its peculiarities, sometimes antic, sometimes grim, but never quite reducible to a masterplot of victim and victimizer. At their best, these texts are porous to history and propose and articulation of power that is more decentered and nuanced than most of us are accustomed to. Attention must be paid: master narratives of sexual oppression, crucial as they are, can so easily render the sociopolitical subtext opaque.

And that is especially important in *Linden Hills*, which depicts the irruption of class politics into the terrain of race politics. . . . For any reading that subsumes the whole issue of class politics into a purely racial (or sexual) binarism will miss the novel's sedimented ambivalence. Linden Hills (in contrast to Putney Wayne, say) is indeed modeled after mainstream "white" affluence and appropriates its symbolics. But even in these resemblance effects it presents the confusing phenomenon of the black bourgeois, a socioeconomic disruption of an overdetermined alliance of color and poverty. To situate the narrative in the social real, we would want to ask whether black poverty remains a viable means of retaining difference in an age of mass culture. And we need also to ask about the politics of difference as such.

Henry Louis Gates Jr. *Contemporary Literature*. 29, 4 (1988), pp. 617–18

Gloria Naylor's *The Women of Brewster Place* is a novel composed of seven connecting stories. In beautifully resonant language, Naylor makes strong sexual political statements about the lives of working poor and working-class black women and does not hesitate to explore the often problematic nature of their relationships with black men—lovers, husbands, fathers, sons. Loving and supportive bonds between black women are central to her characters' survival. However, Naylor's protrayal of a lesbian relationship in the sixth story, "The Two," runs counter to the positive framework of women bonding she has previously established. In the context of this novel a lesbian relationship might well embody the culmination of women's capacity to love and be committed to each other. Yet both lesbian characters are ultimately victims. Although Naylor portrays the community's homophobia toward the lovers as unacceptable, the fate that she designs for the two women is the most brutal and negative of any in the book. . . .

Many a lesbian relationship has been threatened or destroyed because of how very differently lovers may view their lesbianism, for example, how out or closeted one or the other is willing to be. Naylor's discussion of difference represents a pressing lesbian concern. . . .

In "The Two," however, Naylor sets up the women's response to their identity as an either/or dichotomy. Lorraine's desire for acceptance, although completely comprehensible, is based upon assimilation and denial, while Naylor depicts Theresa's healthier defiance as an individual stance. In the clearest statement of resistance in the story, Theresa thinks: "If they practiced that way with each other, then they could turn back to back and beat hell out of the world for trying to invade their territory. But she had found no such sparring partner in Lorraine, and the strain of fighting alone was beginning to show on her." . . .

In considering the overall impact of "The Two," I realized that because it is critical of homophobia, it is perhaps an effective story for a heterosexual audience. But because its portrayal of lesbianism is so negative, its message even to heterosexuals is ambiguous. A semisympathetic straight reader's response might well be: "It's a shame something like that had to happen, but I guess that's what you get for being queer." The general public does not want to know that it is possible to be a lesbian of whatever color and not merely survive, but thrive. And neither does a heterosexual publishing industry want to provide them with this information.

The impact of the story upon lesbian readers is quite another matter. I imagine what might happen if a black woman who is grappling with defining her sexuality and who has never had the opportunity to read anything else about lesbians, particularly black ones, were to read "The Two" as a severely cautionary tale. Justifiably, she might go no further in her exploration, forever denying her feelings. She might eventually have sexual relationships with other women, but remain extremely closeted. Or she might commit suicide. As a black lesbian reader, I find Naylor's dire pessimism about our possibilities to be the crux of my problems with "The Two."

Barbara Smith. In Joanne M. Braxton and Andrée Nicola McLaughlin, eds. *Wild Women in the Whirlwind: Afra-American Culture and the Contemporary Literary Renaissance* (New Brunswick, New Jersey: Rutgers University Press, 1990), pp. 225–27, 231

The setting of *Linden Hills*, Naylor's second novel, makes it clear that she is creating a geographical fictional world similar to or in the manner of [William] Faulkner's Yoknapatawpha county. Her first novel is set in Brewster Place, her second in Linden Hills. Brewster Place and Linden Hills are geographically in the same area; both are inhabited by blacks, and in both novels, characters refer to each of these places as proximated neighborhoods, though quite different in their orientation. Linden Hills is a posh upper-middle-class settlement, Brewster Place the last stop on the road to the bottom in American society; where you live when you can't live anywhere else. The outside world perceives Linden Hills as a symbol of black achievement, while Brewster Place is seen as a manifestation of failure. Ironically, through her two novels' respective characters and structure, Naylor portrays Brewster Place as a black community (though flawed and vulnerable) held together primarily by women, while Linden Hills is characterized as a group of houses that never becomes a community, a showplace precariously kept in place by the machinations of one wealthy black patriarchal family. . . .

*The Women of Brewster Place* begins with an introduction about the history of that street, which is followed by a series of stories, each about a particular woman who lives there. The novel concludes with Mattie Michaels's dream-story about a block party in which all the women appear, as well as a coda which announces the death of the street. Created by city officials, it is destroyed by them. Although each of their narratives could be called a short story, the novel consists of the interrelationship of the stories, as a pattern evolves, not only because the characters all live in Brewster Place but also because they are connected to one another. With the exception of the lesbians in "The Two" . . . Naylor emphasizes the distinctiveness of each story by naming it after the specific woman on whom she is focusing, even as she might include that woman in another's story. By using this form, one that heightens the individuality of her characters so that they are not merely seen as faceless "female heads of households," while stressing their interrelationships, Naylor establishes Brewster Place as a community in spite of its history of transients—a community with its own mores, strengths, and weaknesses. Even when that specific Brewster Place is destroyed, its characteristics remain, for most of its inhabitants must move to a similar street. Brewster Place, then, stands for both itself and other places like it. . . .

In *The Women of Brewster Place* and *Linden Hills*, Gloria Naylor's portrayal of her two neighborhoods demonstrates the effects of class distinctions on the African-American community and how these distinctions are gender oriented. As well, when read together, her two novels present "solutions" idealized during the last decade by important powerless American groups, solutions which are characterized by Naylor, finally, as ineffectual routes to empowerment.

By creating a tapestry of nurturing women in her first novel, Naylor emphasizes how female values derived from mothering—nurturing, communality, concern with human feeling—are central to Brewster Place's survival.... *The Women of Brewster Place* was preceded by a decade of American feminist writing that responded to patriarchal society's devaluation of women by revalorizing female principles. In reaction to the Western patriarchal emphasis on the individual; on the splitting of human beings into mind and body; and on competition, conquest, and power, these writers saw the necessity of honoring female values. If women were to become empowered, it was necessary for them to perceive their own primacy, their centrality to their society, as well as to analyze how dangerous patriarchal values were to a harmonious social order.

> Barbara Christian. In Henry Louis Gates Jr., ed. *Reading Black, Reading Feminist* (New York: Meridian, 1990) pp. 348–49, 353, 363–64

Naylor's desire to write the experience of black American women was born from an impatience with the critical establishment's assumptions that black writers should provide "definitive" reflections of black experience. The emphasis on the definitive, she argues, denies the vast complexity of Afro-American experience. In a conversation with Toni Morrison, she speaks of her struggle to realize the dream of writing the lives of black women without falsification and sentimentality, making visible those whom society keeps invisible. She dedicates the novel [*The Women of Brewster Place*] to those who "gave me the dream, believed in it . . . nurtured it . . . applauded it.".

Although *Brewster Place* is a novel about women and concentrates on exploring the experiences of women, it does not enlist a dogmatic feminist ideology. There is little of [Alice Walker's] *The Color Purple's* celebration and rejoicing in the discovery of self, sexuality, and creativity in the face of male abuse and repression. Celie [in *The Color Purple*] is encouraged to trade her razor—she wants to slit Albert's throat—for a needle, the implement of her autonomy and creativity. If *The Color Purple* mediates a feminist solution to the problems of the oppressed Celie, Naylor's novel is far more tentative about celebrating the efficacy of female friendship and supportive connection, but there are no radical transformations; Naylor does not, as Walker does, draw on feminist ideology as an agent of transcendence. Naylor calls attention to the particular problems of black women without suggesting that such problems are gender issues alone. When she says that she hopes the novel does not make a bitter statement about the men, she is, I think, voicing a concern that the problems she addresses will be oversimplified if they are seen only in terms of male-female relationships....

Naylor's novel does not offer itself as a definitive treatment of black women or community, but it reflects a reality that a great

many black women share; it is at the same time an indictment of oppressive social forces and a celebration of courage and persistence. By considering the nature of personal and collective dreams within a context of specific social, political, and economic determinants, Naylor inscribes an ideology that affirms deferral; the capacity to defer and to dream is endorsed as life-availing. Like Martin Luther King, Naylor resists a history that seeks to impose closure on black American dreams, recording also in her deferred ending a reluctance to see "community" as a static or finished work. There are countless slum streets like Brewster; streets will continue to be condemned and to die, but there will be other streets to whose decay the women of Brewster will cling. The image of the ebony phoenix developed in the introduction to the novel is instructive: The women rise, as from the ashes, and continue to live.

> Jill L. Matus. *Black American Literature Forum*. 24, 1 (spring 1990), pp. 50–51, 62–63

The rape scene in *The Women of Brewster Place* occurs in "The Two," one of the seven short stories that make up the novel. This story explores the relationship between Theresa and Lorraine, two lesbians who move into the rundown complex of apartments that make up "Brewster Place." Lorraine's decision to return home through the shortcut of an alley late one night leads her into an ambush in which the anger of seven teenage boys erupts into violence....

In Naylor's representation of rape, the victim ceases to be an erotic object subjected to the control of the reader's gaze. Instead, that gaze, like Lorraine's is directed outward; it is the violator upon whom the reader focuses, the violator's body that becomes detached and objectified before the reader's eyes as it is reduced to "a pair of suede sneakers," a "face" with "decomposing food in its teeth." As the look of the audience ceases to perpetuate the victimizing stance of the rapists, the subject/object locations of violator and victim are reversed. Although the reader's gaze is directed at a body that is, in Mulvey's terms, "stylized and fragmented by close-ups," the body that is dissected by that gaze is the body of the violator and not his victim.

> Laura E. Tanner. *American Literature*. 62, 4 (December 1990), pp. 574–75

The legend of Sapphira Wade, "a true conjure woman," forms the opening event of Gloria Naylor's *Mama Day*. In a story fraught with overwhelming psychic and physical intensity, Sapphira's (absent) presence is the single most powerful image in the book. The ramifications of her necromancy in 1823 are still being played out in the contemporary lives of her children's children's children on the island of Willow Springs. They are left to inherit the shimmering spirit of her memory and the unavoidable stature commanded by her mythic presence....

A narrative voice uses "we," "ours," and "us" to retell the story of Willow Springs and involve the reader in its simultaneous recall of historical, spiritual, and physical events. The reader's voice is invited to join its community of tellers: "Think about it: ain't nobody really talking to you.... Really listen this time: the only voice is your own.... You done heard it the way we know it.... You done heard it without a single living soul really saying a word.'' This voice—ancient, aware, and able to bridge the subjective and objective worlds and to match imagination with magic—connects the story's disparate events and maintains its presence over all of them. In addition, the ancestral and narrative voices of the island's past and present generations as well as the personified island itself—its dust and purple flowers, the gardens and cemeteries, its abandoned houses and (re)membered rituals—gather to tell Naylor's story.

The ancestral voices in this story are primarily the voices of the island's generations. All of them mediate the text, bridging the events of Naylor's contemporary story of the lovers Cocoa and George with the haunting presence of Sapphira Wade, Cocoa's grandmother of five generations past, whose propensity for conjuring leaks into the present-day world. George is destined never to leave the island of Willow Springs, and Mama Day readies him for the paradise for which Cocoa, perhaps because she has been geographically disengaged from her place in the island's history, could not prepare him.

Naylor's novel emphasizes how a collective revision of an ancient community substantively inserts a metaphorical language into the text. This language carries a symbol system more weighty than the individual word. For example, at one point in the story, Miranda tries to remember her ancestor's name. But her failure to do so is a ''loss she can't describe.'' Although she tries to use her psychic gift to discern the print on a damaged slip of paper where Sapphira's name is illegible, she can not read it. In her frustration, she falls asleep murmuring the names of women. It is the murmuring of the spoken text (rather than the effort to read) that enables Miranda finally to meet Sapphira Wade in her dreams. The importance of this oracular event is acknowledged at the point when Miranda is able to sense the being, the presence in this word: ''Daughter.'' It is described as a ''word [that] comes to cradle what has gone past weariness,'' and is the word that Miranda senses as the relational word of the oracular text. It also acknowledges the contradiction and paradox within the textures of this novel. There is enough metaphorical dislocation in *Mama Day* to contain the ambiguous histories of the spirit as well as the body. The text is implicated in this revision because the collection of tellers and listeners who organize its body and who include (in black women writers' texts) the reader as well, loses its alterity—its separation—at this juncture. In the same way that Miranda is cradled by the word that acknowledges her spiritual ancestor, the words of the text are incorporated into the generative spiritual body of Sapphira's linguistic acknowledgment.

Karla F. C. Holloway. *Moorings & Metaphors: Figures of Culture and Gender in Black Women's Literature* (New Brunswick, New Jersey: Rutgers University Press, 1992), pp. 86, 126–27

Gloria Naylor, in *Bailey's Cafe*, addresses female circumcision in Africa (in this case, Ethiopia) as part of a larger examination of the sexual mutilations inflicted on women in contemporary society. . . . Naylor's characters are based on archetypes—mostly from the Bible—but . . . they are not universalized. The novel takes place in a blues cafe down a dead-end street at the tip of New York City. On this city block are Bailey's cafe, Eve's garden and boarding house, and Gabe's pawnshop. The novel's fluid time sequence culminates [on] New Year's Eve, 1949. As in her other novels, Naylor infuses day-to-day living with an alternate, magical reality. . . .

The stories of these characters vividly illustrate the range of bodily and psychic mutilation African-American women have experienced. The focal point of the novel is the introduction of ''Mary (Take Two),'' a fourteen-year-old, circumcised Ethiopian Jew named Mariam. Her story serves both to expose genital mutilation and to highlight relations between blacks and Jews. Young and slow-witted, Mariam has undergone infibulation and, though no man has touched her, is pregnant. She has magically traveled from Addis Ababa to New York after being expelled from her village for refusing to reveal the identity of her unborn child's father. Gabe, the Jewish pawnshop owner, announces her arrival to the rest of the street. He brings her to Eve to figure out how to help her. Eve learns her story and later repeats it in Bailey's cafe. The story of Mariam's circumcision is so gruesome that Bailey and the other men have to leave. Eve, in telling the tale, metaphorically describes it by cutting open a succulent plum.

Although she has been abused, Mariam, carrying new life, brings life and hope to the dead-end street. Naylor ends *Bailey's Cafe* as she did her first novel, *The Women of Brewster Place*, with a kind of miracle; readers familiar with her most recent novel, *Mama Day*, will find a special surprise.

*Bailey's Cafe* is Naylor's finest novel to date. Her rendering of life in a New York alley reflects the city's magic, its jazz, its violent stories, its street-lamp sparks of hope. It examines a broad spectrum of black women's lives while dealing with the complexities of a multi-ethnic American society still caught up in restrictive notions of color, gender and culture. It is more literary than polemical, bridging ancient stories and modern problems to create a context for the mutilations women have suffered and a space for curing their (our) souls.

Gay Wilentz. *Women's Review of Books*. 10, 5 (February 1993), pp. 15–16

The works of Gloria Naylor offer a peculiarly interesting challenge; because, rooted as they are in a decidedly African-American tradition, the distance between them and their African literary cousins may seem wider than the temporal and geographical separation of the Atlantic and the postpartum trauma of the Middle Passage. Yet, it is precisely this historical and cultural gap that must be reviewed if Naylor's ''Authorial Dreams of Wholeness'' [as Michael Awkward stated in his *Inspiring Influences*, 1989] are to be appreciated in terms of a ''parentage'' that presupposes an extended family, rather than a nuclear one. . . .

Just as the post-independence writers in Africa recognized that their historical moment made it rather problematic to continue writing literature about the colonial legacy and the clash of cultures in the pre-independence mode; so too, African-American writers, like Naylor, began to focus their attention on the more immediate problems faced by African Americans in the post-Civil Rights and Women's Rights era. Both on the continent and in the diaspora, this period has been one of reassessment, of a long, hard look at the cold reality of African and African-American life prefaced by the title question of Langston Hughes' poem, ''What happens to a dream deferred?,'' which Naylor uses as the epigraph to *The Women of Brewster Place*.

Naylor's first novel focuses on the lives of those African Americans who fell through the cracks of the promised ''Great Society.'' Ironically, the ''Dawn,'' which is the title of the novel's prologue, describes the corruption that has marked the birth of Brewster Place and briefly chronicles the various waves of immigrants and wanderers who have tried to make this "bastard child of several clandestine meetings" a home. The prologue ends with a description of the present inhabitants of the now walled-in street, "these multi-colored 'Afric' children of its old age" who have little hope of escape, "because they had no choice." However, they, especially the women, worked as hard and were as passionate as any of the former inhabitants of Brewster Place. Despite the enormity of this knowledge, this seemingly premature termination of hope, the women were not completely beaten into the gloom and anonymity of the gray winter landscape, which signals the arrival of Mattie Michael to Brewster Place. . . .

Mattie Michael is forced to begin "her long, winding journey to Brewster" because, like her modern-day sisters in the poverty-stricken inner cities, she had not learned how to defend herself against the seductive talk of the world's Butch Fullers. Furthermore, the limited horizons of an impoverished South were not the best environment for creating lasting and supportive family units, especially for the Michaels. Samuel Michael, Mattie's father, was a man of very few words and so did not know how to respond to the knowledge of his daughter's pregnancy, except in a blind rage. Naylor expertly sketches the contours of the assumptions that have molded this man. His possessiveness was not only restrictive of his daughter's maturation, but contributed in no small measure to her subsequent fall.

Samuel Michael's words echo throughout the novel with ironic intensity, insinuating themselves not only into Mattie's relationship with her son, Basil, but also other relationships, in which one partner's sense of what is "fit" for the other results in disaster. Samuel Michael's desire to see no fault in his daughter releases a similar desire in Mattie. She becomes overprotective of Basil, constantly making excuses for his immaturity, until his recklessness lands him in jail. Ultimately, Mattie loses her suburban home when Basil jumps bail, and she finds herself back on that "long, winding journey to Brewster." In the midst of all this, the wisdom of Miss Eva (Eve), "a yellow, blue-eyed spirit who had foreseen this day and had tried to warn her," like that of Brewster Place itself, goes unheeded. Yet Brewster Place is not the same as Miss Eva's house in the suburbs, and Mattie's journey, like those of her sisters, is a flight from her individual and their collective pasts, which are seen as our long, wasted existence.

The novel's apparent end, "The Block Party," is, as Michael Awkward notes, a totalizing gesture. But the novel does not end with the suggestions of a mystical unity grounded on a shared dream, baptized in the rainstorm and riot of women breaking down a wall. Rather, the novel ends in the return of the omniscient narrator's ode to "Brewster Place [which] still waits to die" because "the colored daughters of Brewster, spread over the canvas of time, still wake up with their dreams misted on the edge of a yawn." Naylor's bracketing of the "Seven Stories" by the opening prologue, "Dawn," and the epilogue, "Dusk," mimics the closure of the socioeconomic and natural environment depicted in the stories themselves. . . .

If we have been distanced by the narrative strategies of *The Women of Brewster Place* and its characters' socioeconomic status, then Naylor resolutely attacks any sense of consolation that we might have felt, because of that distance, by exposing the truth, as she sees it, beneath the middle-class hell of *Linden Hills*. Naylor has stated, in an interview, that *Linden Hills* is "a microcosm of the Black middle class experience, the hyphenated American experience in its worst possible scenario." This fiction is prefaced by an epigraph that records a conversation between Lester Tilson (although here unnamed) and Grandma Tilson, recalling the "multicolored 'Afric' children" and the ancestral wisdom of "Miss Eva" in *The Women of Brewster Place*. . . .

The epigraph poses the problem which troubles the child, Lester, and, one suspects, many who have grown up in the Judeo-Christian tradition: What is the nature of hell? Is it to be experienced after death, or in this life? And, who or what is the devil? Grandma Tilson's answer, "the highest bidder," leaves us in no doubt. Naylor's novel is concerned with the here and now; but, this interest is intertwined with a certain uneasiness for the souls of people who have relinquished their ties with family and community, with religious and spiritual values, and, finally, with "their own ethnocentric sense of self" [*Gloria Naylor Interview with Kay Bonetti*, 1985], in order to realize the American Dream, or rather, Luther Nedeed's spiteful version of it. . . .

In *Linden Hills* there are many characters who are on the verge of nervous breakdowns, are insane and/or commit suicide because they find themselves in impossible situations. Unlike Armah's protagonist, whose residency in the asylum is temporary, Naylor's "ghosts" have bought themselves a more permanent "zip code" in the Linden Hills twilight area. One which "is also an area of knowledge, twisted knowledge perhaps, but knowledge resulting from real information." As Willie and Lester begin their journey, they encounter Norman Anderson and his wife, Ruth, who once lived in Linden Hills; Norman suggests that the two young men do odd jobs in the Hills. We learn that Norman suffers from his own personal affliction, "the pinks." This malady seems to be an *epidermalization* of his soul's fear of insignificance, of a dissolution into the American nightmare. Norman's sickness is, in the words of Amiri Baraka, "[t]he flame of social dichotomy. Split down the center, which is the early legacy of the black man unfocused on blackness." Although the Andersons live outside of Linden Hills, they are not immunized against the diseases of a world that has been able to manufacture a Linden Hills.

Similarly, the adolescent sexual chauvinism and nervous homophobia of Naylor's major characters begin to surface during this section. Such behavior should be seen in terms of the general ideology of a homophobic and patriarchal society. Against such ideological dominance, Willie and Lester have their poetry and memory as a means of resistance. Since Willie, unlike his fellow poet, Lester, refuses to write down his poetry, he has opted for the more customary role as oral poet; yet, traditionally, he cannot perform in public as a legitimate poet. He needs to find and establish a rapport with his *hadzivodu*, god of songs, as Kofi Awoonor notes in *The Breast of the Earth*.

In this light, Willie and Lester's passage through Linden Hills gains a consequence that incorporates and transforms the notion that Naylor's authorial project only emulates a classical European tale and ignores the rich resources of African orature. Even though Lester writes his poetry, both young men are on a voyage of discovery, working their way toward maturity and understanding as both poets and human beings. Each encounter with, and each task for, the residents of the Hills brings each young man closer to the recognition of his personal hadzivodu. The "diviners," or intermediaries in this case, are the "dead" and "half-dead" of Linden Hills—those who have sold "that silver mirror . . . to the highest bidder'' (see frontispiece of *Linden Hills*) and for whom they work. . . .

I would suggest that Naylor's first two novels are the beginning of a project of atonement, which comes to a ritual end in the third, *Mama Day*. Naylor's second novel describes what happens in the affluent suburb of Linden Hills during the course of six days; it ends at the start of the seventh, Christmas Day. However, Naylor's narrator chooses to close the work with the following words: ''Each with his own thoughts, they approached the chain fence. . . . Hand anchored to hand, one helped the other to scale the open links. *Then, they walked out of Tupelo Drive into the last days of the year.*'' From this perspective, it is especially significant that Naylor's third novel, which is so unlike either of the previous works, should be concerned with the Day family and ''the legend of Sapphira Wade. A true conjure woman'' (*Mama Day*). . . .

We are taken to an island between ''two distinct worlds,'' ideologically and culturally speaking: one is on the ''Mainside'' (late twentieth-century America), and the other is the world of Sapphira Wade and ''the Other Place'' (a place of legend, magic, and the connection to a common African past). Mama Day's niece, Coca, is able to ''go Mainside'' and return each year in a ceremony of affirmation and renewal because her familial ties remain unbroken. The view that Willow Springs is a world completely apart from the modern world (Western bourgeois society) is only partially true. Although Willow Springs does not ''belong'' to Georgia or North Carolina, its geographical proximity to those two southern states evidences both a ''historical'' and a more mundane relationship. However, this connection only confirms the nature of Naylor's artistic choices, which give her fictional island a greater sense of *being there* in a sense that Shakespeare's island, in the *Tempest*, is not.

The first narrative voice we hear speaks with a power derived from a tradition in which life and death exist as a continuum. This is why Sapphira Wade's presence is felt throughout the novel. Ultimately, we hear the voices of Africa and its countless daughters and sons, who endured the Middle Passage, in the voice of the hurricane, which ''will come, rest, and leave screaming . . . while prayers go up in Willow Springs to be spared from what could only be the workings of Woman. And She has no name.'' The last sentence echoes the first line of Willie Mason's six hundred and sixty-sixth poem, which was forming in his mind in the early morning hours of Christmas Day in Linden Hills. . . .

Willow Springs is not a piece of real estate, like Linden Hills, to be exploited by developers. It is a living community, with a vibrant complex of cultural traditions and practices, such as The Candle Walk. The island of Willow Springs is home, a spiritual focus, the geopsychic space that usually keeps the Dantean vision, refigured by Baraka and Naylor, safely across the bridge on Mainside. But, as Baraka reminds us, ''Hell is actual. . . . One thinks of home, or the other ''homes'' we have had. . . . The struggles away or towards this peace is Hell's function'' (*The System of Dante's Hell*). Similarly, the collective ancestral voice of Willow Springs echoes Grandma Tilson's warning in its positive form. But this fictional island is not without its problems and ''dammed souls,'' like Junior Lee and his envious ''wife,'' Miss Ruby, who puts a hex on Cocoa. Naylor, however, reminds us that there are other islands that have more than their share of problems.

Just over half of the first section of *Mama Day* takes place Mainside, on those other islands, Manhattan and Long Island, New York. We are introduced to Cocoa and George, whose meeting, courtship, and eventual marriage, Naylor describes through their individual voices, so that we get a layered, richly textured, polylectical view of the whole romance. . . .

George is a man literally driven by a faulty heart, an inordinate desire for order, control, and a narrow empiricism. After a protracted and often humorous courtship and a few years of marriage ''Mainside,'' George finally agrees to go to Willow Springs. This visit, which ends in his death, is necessary because it becomes the occasion for George's reeducation, his return to the source and immersion into his un-remembered history, as well as his confrontation with ''the other place'' and liberation. A crucial moment in his reeducation comes during the poker game with Dr. Buzzard. George, in his narrative segment, comments on the funeral dirge Dr. Buzzard and the other men sing: ''I didn't understand the rhythm and I refused to spoil it by attempting to join in. *Perhaps if I had known that I only had to listen to the pulse of my blood . . .*'' (emphasis added). The narrative, spoken in the past tense, shows that the speaker has learnt to trust what was inside of him as much as, if not more than, what he could empirically prove. Willow Springs, or more specifically, Mama Day, becomes the catalyst that leads him to recognize his god-image, to understand that life is shaped by history and experiences that go beyond simple demonstration. Ultimately, George's ability to learn, in spite of himself, allows him to accept ''the Other place.'' As part of the choral narrative voice, he reveals that, as he lay on Cocoa's bed, after staggering from the chicken coop, bloodied and dying, he felt only ''total peace.''

Cocoa's sickness to near death, like ''the pinks'' that afflict Norman Anderson in *Linden Hills*, is also necessary to purge her of certain habits of thought, which are injurious to her calling as the heir to the legacy of Sapphira Wade and Mama Day, the new medium between the two worlds that influence Willow Springs. She realizes that the world and its repetition in song is a complex polyrhythmic endeavor and that ''there are just too many sides to the whole story.'' To exist harmoniously with one's household and public gods cannot be achieved by a vision that insists on there being one, and only one truth. The admission of multiple ''truths'' should not be taken as the condoning of an extreme relativism, as that leads to an insulated monologue. Rather, we acknowledge these ''other'' truths, which have a coherence and validity in their specific context(s), because they enrich and help us to hear the multiple voices and counter-rhythms of ''the whole story.'' George's peace is possible, because he is finally able to admit ''the Other place'' into his self. He can bring his self ''home'' to ''the Other place'' and the true Conjure Woman's Africa.

We may, therefore, see Naylor's three works as bearing a family resemblance that has been overlooked, for the most part. Chinua Achebe, in a short essay, ''Named for Victoria,'' discloses that, ''Although I did not set about it consciously in that solemn way I now know that my first book, *Things Fall Apart*, was an act of atonement with my past, the ritual return and homage of a prodigal son.'' Like her literary cousin's declaration about his first work, this critic has attempted to show the evidence of a more extended atonement by another of Africa's unwilling prodigal daughters. Naylor's three works constitute a series of rituals that successfully establish her personal *hadzivodu*.

Vincent O. Odantten. In Femi Ojo-Ade, ed. *Of Dreams Deferred, Dead or Alive: African Perspectives on African-American Writers* (Westport: Greenwood Press, 1996), pp. 115–27

Gloria Naylor's *The Men of Brewster Place* is a profound work that explores the other side of the gender issue. It is a continuation of Naylor's *The Women of Brewster Place* and depicts the men who played only minor roles in that book.

The men of Brewster Place are presented as rational Black men who are able to think for themselves and who realize that they have problems they must solve. Naylor's positive depiction shows them as men struggling to correct their faults, or as individuals trying to make sense of their lives.

The book is divided into 10 chapters that start with "Dusk" and end with "Dawn." It discusses the lives of seven characters known as the sons of Brewster Place—Ben, Brother Jerome, Basil, Eugene, Moreland T. Woods, C.C. Baker, and Abshu.

Naylor's methodology is quite clever. Although Ben died in *The Women of Brewster Place*, the "Author's Notes" in this sequel states that Naylor "takes her poetic license to resurrect [Ben's] spirit and voice to narrate major portions of [the] novel." Ben tells the story of how he ended up in the place called Brewster. It is the story of a caring father and a loving husband who had a wonderful daughter but was plagued with a domineering wife. It is the story of a man who is unable to cope and becomes a drunkard.

All of these men have unique situations that tie them to Brewster Place. The gifted piano player, Brother Jerome, captures the plight of all Black men of Brewster Place through his playing of the blues. Although he is labeled a "retarded child," he is the silent, brilliant force that is able to put things together through his music.

Basil tries to recapture all that he has missed in life by attempting to be a father to two boys whom he adopts. However, he is left in a state of confusion when things do not turn out the way that he had wished. . . .

[The] barbershop is the central metaphor that serves as a house of refuge, a place where debate and understanding take place. The barbershop is the place where all of the Black men come to be themselves and to discuss their lives and society. It is at the barbershop that they sing "the Black man's blues." They discuss their present conditions, vent their frustrations, and dream about more promising futures.

The barbershop is also the place where the character Greasy ends his life. . . .

It is through Greasy's death that the Black men notice that, they are all the same, that their problems are also the same ones that Greasy once fought on a daily basis. They are all men who are hurting, struggling, coping, and trying to make the best out of what is left of their lives. Naylor uses these characters as an attempt to touch upon all issues that Black men face.

It is refreshing to see someone address the Black male character and explore him realistically. Certainly, this work should be an inspiration to all who read it, and it should also encourage other writers to explore Black male characters from similar vantage points.

Jackie Thomas. *Black Issues in Higher Education*. 15, 21 (December 10, 1998), p. 31.

BIBLIOGRAPHY

*The Women of Brewster Place: A Novel in Seven Stories*, 1982; *Linden Hills*, 1985; *Mama Day*, 1988; *Bailey's Cafe*, 1992; *The Men of Brewster Place*, 1998

# NDAO, Cheik Aliou (1933–)
## Senegal

[In *L'Exil d'Albouri*, Cheik Aliou Ndao] takes his inspiration from real characters and an authentic episode in the nineteenth-century history of the Empire of Mali. The author, an English teacher at the William Ponty Normal School, has succeeded in composing an epic drama, free of any contemporary political inferences, somewhat in the [Pierre] Corneille tradition, with realistic elements. The language is elevated, the characters well opposed, the king's moral dilemma clearly and convincingly stated, and the action economically conducted to its inevitable historical climax.

Albouri, differing from the ruthless historical Shaka, and without the proselytizing mysticism of El Hadj Omar, is caught in a conflict between his sense of responsibility to his people and the concept of honor and courage. The situation is rapidly presented of the Djoloff Empire of Mali—which included present-day Senegal—on the dawn of invasion by the Spahi troops, armed by the French general, Faidherbe. Albouri decides on a strategic withdrawal to Ségou, the home of a friendly prince. The basic moral dilemma is then revealed in the confrontation between Albouri and the queen mother. To the challenge that retreat signifies lack of courage, he argues prudence, the superior arms of the enemy, and the necessity to save his people from slavery. . . .

Samba, a griot, in traditional fashion, speaks the epilogue, telling of the king's death from a poisoned arrow, his son's capture by the Mauritanians during the retreat before the Spahis, the final dispersal in the face of the colonial invasion of all the people who had accompanied Albouri into exile. The final words are a feeble afterthought—an attempt to infuse a committed message into a play that is rich with tragic conflicts and elements of fatality. Without them, *L'Exild'Albouri* has all the essential criteria for good theater: by probing into the hidden motives of the king's actions, by not clearing him of the charges of human error, Ndao has achieved a work of tragic dimensions and psychological authenticity.

In 1973, when Cheik Ndao published *Le Fils de l'Almamy*, his second historical tragedy which he had written about 1967, he took up the promise of Samba's reincarnation, making the griot Maliba speak a short prologue, in which he repeats Samba's final words in the epilogue to *Albouri*: "The Word does not die." But this device adds nothing to the force of his new tragedy, for the message of the destiny of Karamoko, son of the Almamy Samory, and of Samory himself, is not a message of hope, but the conflict of two intransigent characters at the beginning of the twilight of the Samorian Empire.

*Le Fils de l'Almamy* more than confirms that Ndao is a tragic writer of impressive stature and originality, whose works have universal, moving appeal. This second work is even richer in characterization, more consistent in action, and economical in structure than the earlier play. It has a classic concision, a disturbing complexity of personalities caught in a critical moment of history, which makes them victims of circumstances, of interested ill-wishers, and of the clash of their own inflexible characters, in which one is doomed to destroy that which he loves, and at the same time shatter his own existence. It is the tragedy of the honor of a son pitted against the honor of a father.

The Almamy Samory Souré, the last warrior king of the Sudan to be subjugated by Faidherbe's armies, is painted as proud, uncompromising, intolerant, somber, and suspicious, but at the same time a great and courageous patriot, with his own concept of honor, synonymous with the glorification of his country and his people. Neither his limited experience nor his unlimited arrogance can allow him to conceive of his country's defeat by any but mysterious, supernatural forces. He is, by his very nature, receptive to the plots woven at court for the destruction of his son, Karamoko.

The play, as the title suggests, is the tragedy of Karamoko, a man born before his time, the only one to understand that Africa had not the means to confront the powerful war machine of Europe and to believe sincerely in the possibility of peace with Europe, when the tradition was one of uncompromising belligerency. He is the victim of his own vision as well as of the plots and machinations that his unconciliatory nature inspires at the court. It is also the tragedy of Sendi, his devoted wife who goes mad with grief at his terrible fate. Samory, persuaded that his son is a traitor, has his hut walled up for him to die Antigone's death. But it is first and foremost the tragedy of Samory himself, shown here not as the legendary conqueror, nor as the defeated emperor, but like his son, the victim of his own times and his own intractable, proud, and suspicious character. After carrying out the cruel judgment on his son, on whom he has laid such hopes for the continuance of his own glory and that of his dynasty, Samory gives orders to raise camp for the attack on the French and to quit the place of accursed associations: it is with the sense that his personal greatness, like that of his empire, is irrevocably doomed. . . .

In [his] first novel [*Buur Tilleen, roi de la Médina*], Cheik Ndao paints the portrait of the respected elder of an earlier society, who cannot adapt to changing customs and standards. . . . Gorgui Mbodj, a man of honor and principle, preferring personal humiliation rather than not uphold the proud traditions of his race and caste, makes himself and his family the victims of his stiff-necked intolerance. . . . Ndao makes only one indirect reference to the end of the colonial era, his story illustrating more specifically a sempiternal generation gap than a contemporary social evolution. Gorgui, the proud descendant of princes, had some years previously been banished from his region for affronting a district commandant who had humiliated him before his own subjects. Since then he has lived in poverty in the Medina, his only link with his proud past is his stallion Sindax, from whom he has refused to be separated; his only consolation for his wretched condition is to ride through the streets of the Medina in the afternoon, reliving the glory of the court of Walo. He has refused to sanction his daughter's marriage with a man of inferior caste and prefers to turn her out on the streets, in time-honored melodramatic fashion when she becomes pregnant.

There are clearly many predictable ingredients in the plot of *Buur Tilleen*, which culminates in Raki's death in childbirth together with that of her infant. On the other hand, the portrayal of the complex character of "Buur Tilleen" is authentic and moving. The conflict between his sense of honor and his real affection for his wife and child is presented with economy and understanding. In the end, when he reverts to animist practices to try and conjure the threat of death to Raki, we realize how irrevocably the pattern of his life has been rent, even before the final tragedy, and how real will be his remorse. Cheik Aliou Ndao has succeeded in portraying the tragedy—albeit on a small canvas—that ensues when noble aspirations go hand in hand with human weakness. He has attempted to make us enter more deeply into the emotions and dilemmas of Gorgui and his wife Maram by adopting the technique of the inner monologue for the opening passages which present the immediate crisis in their lives and the background of their past history. It is a

pity that he is not consistent in using this narrative technique throughout, as it might have infused a little more life into the other protagonists, in particular Raki and Bougouma, the two lovers and representatives of the younger generation.

Dorothy S. Blair. *African Literature in French* (Cambridge: Cambridge University Press, 1976), pp. 111–14, 311–12

Ndao's play *L'Exil d'Albouri* won the first prize at the Algiers Festival in 1969, and is perhaps the most striking of the historical plays dealing with the first contacts between African rulers and the white colonizer. Ndao has a good sense of dramatic economy and relevance, so that he is able to create scenes which are dramatically effective, and his dialogue moves the action forward rather than keeping it static, as so often happens in plays of this group. Another common difficulty is that of adequately portraying the psychology and particularly the motivation of the characters; in this respect Ndao is less successful. In *L'Exil d'Albouri*, Ndao puts forward a very interesting dramatic situation. Realizing that he cannot hope to defeat the French in battle, Albouri, contrary to what is expected of a warrior, decides to go into exile rather than be captured by the enemy, believing that this will preserve the honor and integrity of his country more effectively than subjection. The historical situation is relatively simple to portray, and at this level the play works well. The use of the griot as a commentator who will always be there and can project the significance of events beyond the immediate present effectively links the audience with the historical situation. The drama itself, however, is meant to spring from the conflict between Albouri and his brother on the one hand, and between Albouri's mother and sister (who agree with his decision) and his young wife (who is afraid of exile) on the other. There is also tension between Albouri and his wife, who complains she never sees her husband. These conflicts are sketched in rather than developed, and are therefore not as effective as they could have been in showing Albouri's dilemma. We are given the skeleton with far too little of the flesh. Motivation is at times lacking or even contradictory, as when Albouri, after expressing complete confidence in his brother in the opening scenes of the play, suddenly reacts to his brother's opposition to the exile proposition. . . . One could make the same criticism of a subsequent play by Ndao, *Le Fils de l'Almamy*. It deals with the conflict between the great Samory and his son, who has spent a year in France and returned convinced of the uselessness of resisting the white man's arms. One feels the need for a fuller treatment of the relationship between the father and the son and, once again, motivation is at times badly handled, as when Samory believes without hesitation a malicious story told him by one of his wives whom the king knows to be jealous of the favorite son. There is some question of a potion intended to create strife between father and son, but it is not clear how or even whether it is administered.

Martin Banham and Clive Wake. *African Theatre Today* (London: Pitman, 1976), pp. 66–68

One of the most successfully staged plays presenting a Resistance hero of the late nineteenth century is Cheik Ndao's *L'Exil d'Albouri* which was awarded the Gold Medal for drama at the Algiers

Festival of African Arts in 1969. Albouri Ndiaye ruled the Djoloff kingdom between 1875 and 1890 when, rather than live under foreign domination, he went into exile shortly before Colonel Dodds invaded his capital, Yang Yang. Albouri was the last free Djoloff king because his successor, Samba Laobé Penda, was dethroned and deported to Gabon and replaced by Albouri's son, Bouna, who was reduced to the rank of a chief in 1900. One of Cheik Ndao's purposes in this play is the rehabilitation of African history which had been distorted by the colonial notion of "pacification" that was transparent in the historical plays of the early Ponty repertoire. Ndao uses the technique of reversal to achieve his purpose. The sowers of discord are the Spahis led by their European officers who "have burnt thousands of villages; they wreak havoc and destroy the granaries. Worse than the year of the plague! They come with machines which spit fire and demolish our fortifications." Conquest, not peace, is the goal of the foreigners who by a combination of troops, treaties, and treachery seek to wrest control from the local rulers. In the face of this threat, Albouri is portrayed as an upright and lucid ruler, bold and proud but not foolhardy, a patriot who has the best interests of his people at heart. As a foil to the notion of the "precolonial night" Ndao underlines the fact that Albouri's lineage stretches back to Ndiadiane Ndiaye who founded the Djoloff kingdom in the fourteenth century. Thus the myth of pacification is destroyed as the focus shifts to Albouri's noble attempt to resist the invader and to preserve the independence of his people.

Although Cheik Ndao warns us in his prologue that historical fact and fiction are intermingled, his aim being to compose a work of art not a historical treatise, he is concerned with presenting a faithful picture of the social reality of the time. Contrary to the mistaken notion that the kings ruled as absolute despots, he depicts Albouri as governing in concert with his council of representatives of different social groups. A special role is reserved for Samba who opens and closes the play. Samba functions as a griot and as a depository of the traditional wisdom, albeit a stylized griot. Costumes, decor, instruments, and accessories are carefully noted with a view to expressing authenticity and are used functionally. Ndao eschews the folkloric tendencies of Ponty theater.

*L'Exil d'Albouri* is not, however, an uncritical panegyric of the past. In the conflict that opposes Albouri and Samba Laobé Penda, the latter represents the blind reproduction of traditional thought patterns and gestures of the past whereas Albouri incarnates the spirit of innovation. Samba Laobé Penda is obsessed with the symbol of the throne whereas Albouri is more concerned with effective independence. In creating the role of the Diaraf of the Slaves and in exposing Samba Laobé Penda, the Diaraf of Thingue, and their associates as people who under the guise of patriotism promote their own ambitions and class or caste privileges, Ndao seeks to project the values of social equality which should form the basis of contemporary society. He explicitly states in the prologue that his aim is "to assist in the creation of myths which galvanize the people and which lead to the future." His vision of a just and democratic society, faithful to the spirit of the best elements of tradition but open to new solutions in order to meet the challenges of the present, is subtly harmonized with his evocation of authentic Djoloff society in the late nineteenth century. The other historical plays that fall into this group generally develop in their own way the same three themes of authenticity, exemplary values embodied in the hero, and rehabilitation of the historical record.

Gary Warner. *Triquarterly*. 9, 3 (1983–84), pp. 188–89

If [Bernard] Dadié and [Guillaume] Oyônô-Mbia are the doyens of the satirical vein in black French theater, Cheik Ndao is the doyen of tragedy, or, rather, of dramatized history-with-a-lesson. The former want to change men by showing them their foibles, while Ndao exhorts men to realize the greatness within themselves through the example of the past. So it is, especially in his *Du sang pour un trône ou Gouye Ndiouli un dimanche*. The scene is the kingdom of Kawoon in the Saloum region of Senegal in the early 1860s. Lawbé Fall is king, seconded by the Queen Mother Linguère. The king's father, Macodou Fall, had long ago deserted his kingdom for the conquest of other lands and has lost his throne as a result. The whites however, are near, and Macodou has returned to the Saloum with the idea of uniting all its kingdoms into one. Macodou places himself at the head of the black brotherhood resistance composed of both animists and the Muslim Foutanké people. Lawbé and his counsellors learn of Macodou's return and of his intentions; they also discover that he has a marabout (i.e., a Muslim) in his retinue. Lawbé is mistrusted by his own advisers because of the blood connection, but he himself fears the threat to his own leadership represented by his father; he also condemns his alliance with the Muslim Foutanké. His opposition to his father reassures the Royal Council, which had been prepared to kill him, and there is battle on one Sunday at Gouye Ndiouli, hence the second title. Lawbé wins decisively though after that he plans to wage war on the Foutanké. In this manner the play ends, under the sad cloud of fratricidal war among black Africans, weakening the area for the onslaughts of the whites which are being prepared in the wings.

The most striking feature of the play is that it has no villains. If the village that harbored Macodou should have received permission from Kawoon before so doing, it acted so out of respect for him. If the council plots to kill Lawbé, it is for *la chose publique*, as too are Lawbé's wars on his own father and the Muslim Foutanké. His father is not at all villainous either, since he thinks that the whites are the menace. The role of griots in the play is most important and impressive. They are narrators, genealogists, moderators, counselors, entertainers, funambulists. Ndao is the first black [francophone] dramatist to humanize thoroughly the griot caste, which has over it a curse that derives from incestuous cannibalism in the past, reminiscent of the curse over the House of Atreus. Principally this is done via the wise "Maître de la Parole" . . . Niambali who, with his two wives, truly comes to life in these pages. One is impressed by the feeling of authenticity in this and just about every other detail of the play. *Du sang pour un trône* as written is perhaps more a dialogued novel than a stageable play; what is in effect a genre in itself, the dialogued novel is especially exemplified by Benjamin Matip's *Laisse-nous bâtir une Afrique debout*. The fact that Ndao reused a theme should not surprise. On the one hand there are such continental figures as Shaka, treated often, and on the other there are the more regional ones: Abraha Pokou (four plays), Lat Dior (three plays), and Lawbé-cum-Macodou.

Harold A. Waters. *Triquarterly*. 9, 3 (1983–84), pp. 201–2

Ndao stands apart from his contemporaries, David Diop and Lamine Diakhaté, by virtue of the strongly personal note that imbues his lyric poetry. Although his commitment to Africa's cause is irreproachable and the themes of liberty and country are evident in his first verses, he is primarily a sincere and sentient poet who weds the expression of his private sensibility to that of public issues. He writes . . . that his ambition has always been to remain faithful to himself, "to marry the idea to the form. I believe," he continues, "that the poet has the right and indeed the duty to rise up against injustice, but *artistically*, otherwise you are dealing with slogans. I also believe that sincerity must be the basis for the poem, and that we must not cheat. That is why I have not hesitated to sing of all the white women who have inspired me, in a period of exacerbated black nationalism.

Some of the poems included in *Kaïrée*, Cheik Ndao's first published collection, for which he was awarded the Prix des Poètes de Langue Française, date back to 1955. The rest were written between 1958 and 1961, a period of intense loneliness and nostalgia for Africa. Like [Léopold Sédar] Senghor in *Chants d'ombre*, he expresses the languor induced by the long European winters with "the endless silent rain of white locusts" eroding his insomniac nights. In "Paysages," he expresses his nostalgia in an evocative series of images, seeking to banish the autumn melancholy by clothing the European scene in the sights of Africa, with "hills reddened by the sun's wounds . . . furrowed by termites . . . baobabs tearing up the heavens." . . . Even in poems inspired by contemporary political situations, the remarkable play of images maintains the lyric harmonies and sensual qualities of the verse. This can be found in the song of the three mourners from "Larmes de flammes pour Lumumba," or the love song, "Poem for Laora," in which the artist's eye for color combines with the musician's ear for dancing rhythms to express the upsurge of his emotion. Elsewhere, in "Guinté" (the name of a Senegalese dance), the relentless stamp of feet, the singers' incantations, and the tom-tom's furious beat combine to conjure up monsters and jinni, as well as an irresistible erotic force. . . .

In 1970 he published a second book of poetry, *Mogariennes*, which owes its title to a pleasing conceit: it is formed from the prefix and suffix respectively of the names of two important towns which the poet visited in his travels to Mali in 1963: *Mopti* and *Bandiagara*. So the poems of *Mogariennes* trace a personal itinerary and also pay homage to the women of Mali. We find similar personal themes to those of the earlier *Kaïrée*, but treated with more maturity and sureness of touch. The first poem, "Un Cygne sur la mer," dates from the school year 1962–1963 which Ndao spent in Wales as French teacher at Bishop Gore Grammar School in Swansea, where the "Child of the Savanna" finds empathy with a "Daughter of the Celts" and literary kinship with Dylan Thomas, while not forgetting the women of the Joliba River.

The untitled verses of the long poem, which gives its name to the collection, follow his pilgrimage from Europe back to Africa, from Dakar to Mali. The poet weaves a spell of proper names to conjure up the precolonial past of the great West African empires, and evokes the color and texture of places whose *genus loci* presides over his present travels as over his childhood experience. Although there are verses in this volume inspired by white women which are the pure expression of personal emotion, Ndao never forgets his identity as a black man committed to his African origins. The theme of his homeland is always present, even when he acknowledges the charm of Europe; like Senghor, he expresses the seduction that the landscape of France exerts over "The son / Of the sands of the russet grass / On the plains of Salum," who sends his greetings to the mountains of France.

Ndao returns to political themes in "Afrique II," which alludes to the illusory freedom that "independent" Africa enjoys under a neocolonial hegemony and to the continual struggle for even this incomplete freedom still being waged in Angola and Southern Africa. Finally, in "Hello Joe," he proves a master of Swiftian polemic. The pseudobonhomie of the title introduces the bitterly ironic note that infuses this attack on "G. I. Joe," the representative of all that is hateful in America's power-wielding throughout the world and repression of black and red men at home. He recalls a childhood terrorized by American soldiers in Senegal throwing beer bottles from jeeps, fracturing black skulls, raping girls on beaches, and shooting at women "to kill time." There follows violent invective against American intervention in Korea, Cambodia, and Vietnam, against the insidious support Wall Street gives to repressive regimes for the sake of multinational business interests, all expressed in a vitriolic parody of the Lord's Prayer.

The corrosive passion of "Hello Joe" is unique in Cheik Ndao's poetry, as if he had accumulated all his anger at injustice and repression throughout the world and vented it in this one long virulent outburst. Generally his lyricism is more suited to an elegiac mode, whereby themes of country, national heritage, African identity, and African history are refracted through the prism of personal experience to assume a more universal dimension.

> Dorothy S. Blair. *Senegalese Literature: A Critical History* (Boston: Twayne, 1984), pp. 90–91, 101–2

[In *Excellence, vos épouses!* the] opening crisis could have been lifted straight from the contemporary political diary of any African country. The Leader, in the latest surprise reshuffle, drops a faithful old Minister. It's one of those graceless jerk dances in which the Minister only happens to hear of his dismissal through the media.

The man sent on this express trip from grace to grass is a figure of touchingly familiar mediocrity. He's not burdened with excess intelligence, innate or acquired. His major claim to fame is that he was a founding member of the Party, one of the first riders on the independence wave. For that sole achievement our Minister expects a lifetime of lucrative posts and sugared privileges, financed by a grateful, if beggared, nation.

The country has grown poorer since independence, but the elite has grown rich. Our friend the Minister, for instance, has children in Western universities, taking courses available in Dakar. He has enough money to maintain four wives, the last a Dakar University Pharmacy student about the age of his own oldest child. This pseudo-progressive girl, the ambitious first child of a large slum family, has a secret dream: she plans to use the amorous Minister as an economic cushion just for the time it takes to grab her degree, then cut him loose. That is merely one of the innumerable betrayals that give this novel its thematic substance. . . .

Rottenness . . . has been and remains the common denominator of the country's public life. Quite accidentally, though, our Minister has come to be perceived as the one Party big shot uninvolved in the elite's determined plunder of the nation. The reputation results from no surfeit of integrity. It's just that this Minister, from his modest background as an agricultural extension officer, has been slow to discover the golden road of international contracts and coded bank accounts. Temperamentally careful, he has a habit of covering up his dirt. A grateful Muslim, he deals with his sexual weaknesses by marrying the women who infatuate him. Sure, he tups the occasional female militant accompanying ministerial delegations on tours of European capitals and hotels. But after such slips he always feels a respectable amount of remorse, later.

Unfortunately for our Minister, though, the Leader, like the head of every irretrievably moldy government, needs a green symbol to cover up the general decay. The Leader has fixed on our unsophisticated Minister to play the oxymoronic part: paragon of Party purity.

Trouble arises in the form of a lean and hungry generation, clawing its way up the Party pyramid. Ambitious young activists dig up buried dirty secrets, using them to knock down old Party faithfuls blocking their path to power.

The Leader is thus informed of a buried scandal: while serving as public works minister, our fig leaf of a minister once cashed a bribe from a Scandinavian bidder for a national highway contract. What the Leader discovers, in effect, is that his beloved fig leaf is just as lousy as the general body politic. In righteous anger he tears it off and throws it away. That's how His Excellency the Minister is precipitated into the warm, hospitable ranks of the unemployed. . . .

Here is a threat of tragic outcomes, but the novel ends softly, on a comic note. Capricious as always, the Leader rehabilitates the fallen Minister. It was, after all, a round trip: from grace to grass to an awkward kind of grace again.

The Leader, dipping generously into the nation's empty coffers, has established diplomatic relations with a faraway country just to create an ambassadorial sinecure for our friend. The new ambassador, weak in geography as in all intellectual matters, has not the slightest idea what or where the new country is. No matter, the pressing issue is not to find out where in the world the embassy is, but to settle a matter of national importance: which of wives one, two, three, or four is to accompany His Polygamous Excellency?

Cheik Aliou Ndao starts his book as if he's getting ready to bite into his social subject. But when he opens his authorial mouth, we see he has taken care to remove his dentures. His intention is: to caress the subject with his gums, not to draw blood. A prudent, limited goal, well achieved.

Ayi Kwei Armah. *West Africa.* October 29, 1984. pp. 2171–72

BIBLIOGRAPHY

*Kaïrée,* 1962; *L'Exil d'Albouri* (Albouri's Exile), 1967; *Mogariennes,* 1970; *Buur Tilleen, roi de la Médina* (Buur Tilleen, King of Medina), 1972; *Le Fils de l'Almamy* (Almamy's Son), 1973; *L'île de Bahila,* 1975; *Le Marabout de la Secheresse,* 1979; *Du sang pour un trône ou Gouye Ndiouli un dimanche* (Blood for a Throne, or Gouye Ndiouli on Sunday), 1983; *Excellence, vos épouses!* (Excellency, Your Wives!), 1983; *Un Bouquet d'épines Pour Elle,* 1988

# NDEBELE, Njabulo (1948–)
## South Africa

Njabulo Ndebele argues that to be intellectually engaging, contemporary black writing must go beyond mere description: "It seems to me that a large part of the African resistance to the evil of apartheid has, until recently, consisted of a largely descriptive documentation of suffering. And the bulk of the fiction, through an almost total concern with the political theme, has in following this tradition, largely documented rather than explained." . . . The

method that Ndebele advocates is what "literature" needs, but as long as blacks continue to expect literature to play a role in their struggle there will be controversy over what form writers should use.

Ndebele seems to have made his choice. His recent collection of stories, *Fools and Other Stories,* combines both explicit and implicit comment. The content of the stories, particularly that of "Fools," is similar to that of the short stories of the 1950s. Social, economic, and political concerns are revealed through various forms of township experience. . . .

Ndebele's subtle protest against the system appears towards the end of the story where the two protagonists, Zani and Zamani, attempt to "break up a picnic on the Day of the Covenant, Commemorating December 16, 1838, the day the Boers killed thousands of Black South Africans and dethroned their ruler, King Dingane." As blacks enter the picnic grounds, a Boer appears and picks a quarrel with Zani. An ugly situation ensues in which the angry Boer lashes at any black person in his way with a whip. The symbolic significance of the episode is revealed when Zamani, the schoolteacher, shows typically heroic, unflinching endurance as the Boer madly lashes at him. . . . Ndebele's calm portrayal of heroic and passive resistance in this episode is probably one of the most effective in black writing. Yet there is a built-in problem regarding his characters' level of political consciousness and the kind of resistance they embody. Zani, who, of all Ndebele's "fools," is the most "politically aware," comes across as an incautious idealist. His attempts at politicizing Zamani's young primary school pupils sound naive and politically immature. Although his idea of breaking up the picnic is seen as noble, the act itself is ill-planned. Zamani, who hesitantly supports the idea, is a blind fellow-traveler. Despite the fact that he is the central character in the symbolic episode cited above, Zamani's politics are riddled with indecision and sometimes utter confusion. His decision to take part in breaking up the picnic is a result of compassion for Zani and not political commitment. The principal of Zamani's school (who has organized the picnic) . . . [cares] only about his own importance. The picnickers themselves are portrayed as a group of hedonists whose sole concerns are drinking, dancing, and lovemaking rather than the political boycott Zani is advocating.

Since Ndebele is aware of the flaws of his characters, one can only conclude that, like his poem, "The Revolution of the Aged," "Fools" is a story that deliberately sets out to celebrate passive, antirevolutionary resistance. "The veiled symbolism of this episode . . . is clear: apartheid will wear itself out in the end." . . . The society Ndebele depicts is in desperate need not only of political awakening, but also of a more effective form of resistance.

Piniel Viriri Shava. *A People's Voice: Black South African Writing in the Twentieth Century* (London: Zed Books, 1989), pp. 152–54

Njabulo Ndebele approaches politics indirectly by exploring subjective experience in *Fools and Other Stories.* Having articulated the need for black writers to move beyond the documentation of oppression, Ndebele avoids explicit discussion of apartheid until the end of the book [in "Fools"]. . . . The other, earlier stories are all told from the point of view of preadolescent boys in Chaterton township, but although his protagonists are often children, their problems prefigure the dilemmas of the student, the artist, and the intellectual in confronting conflicts of race and class. The time of Ndebele's narratives is unspecified until the last story, when we learn that it is 1966, ten years before the explosion of the Soweto youth. The choice of childhood and adolescence as a subject—culminating in the teenager Zani's groping toward revolutionary activity in the story "Fools"—is clearly related to the 1976 rebellion, and to the tragedy of youths' having to sacrifice themselves to political struggle.

Ndebele's stories do not project a unified black experience. They are stories of self-division, intellectual yearnings, and class division. The characteristic protagonist is a black child who is somewhat better off economically than the average township child. Thus in the first story, "The Test," Thoba feels challenged to prove himself physically by imitating the dominant boys in his group, boys from poorer families. Reproducing the hierarchies of the playground and the street, apartheid is almost nonexistent in "The Test," present only in the Dutch Reformed Church that marks the limit of Thoba's run in the freezing rain and in the persistent cough of Nana, a sickly boy whom the others protect. In "The Music of the Violin," a similar conflict is presented in sharper terms, as Vukani resists being forced to play the violin because of the humiliation that carrying the instrument brings him from classmates and the adolescent gangs on the streets. The class pretensions of Vukani's mother are underlined by her daughter, Teboho, a university student who accuses her mother of becoming a "white black woman." The intervention of Teboho saves Vukani from the agonizing personal isolation in which he experiences his need to reject the violin, alone in his room "as good as any white boy's." At the end of the story, Vukani's father stands up for him against Vukani's mother, who has also resisted allowing the father's relatives to visit, violating traditional African attitudes toward the extended family.

It is in the third story, "Uncle," that the problem of the relation of the individual—especially the artist and the intellectual—and the group is most fully examined. The uncle who comes to visit, although a jazz musician and somewhat suspect in his family, is the only positive adult role among the major characters in *Fools and Other Stories*. The uncle tries to give his nephew a sense of African pride, telling him to travel and know the places in his country so that "it will be your country. And then you must ask yourself: what can I give to all those places?" Stressing social responsibility, he tells the boy to develop goals, claiming that the ancestors "say that you do not really know what you want, and that is very dangerous for someone who is going to be a man." However, the uncle also indicates the value of isolation and apparent selfishness, sometimes ordering his own friends and the bewildered boy from the room when practicing. He explains: "The best way to avoid endless struggle . . . is to struggle very hard for a short period of time." In music, he tells the nephew, knowledge is a prerequisite for improvisation; without knowledge, "you'll soon tire of playing anything, because your playing will have no direction. Unlearned freedom frustrates; nothing elevating and lasting ever comes of it." Teaching his nephew about African history, Arabic culture, and the hope of regaining that history for Africans, the uncle is as at home on the street as in the library; he defeats the local bully whose girlfriend he has seduced, and his music is popular. . . . [The] uncle relates his skill and knowledge to the needs of the class he represents, but he is also an embodiment of Ndebele's demand for some distance between art and politics if art is to have relevance to either politics or itself.

Raymond A. Mazurek. *Studies in Short Fiction.* 26, 1 (winter 1989), pp. 75–77

Njabulo Ndebele's collection of stories *Fools [and Other Stories]* is a celebration of life in the black townships. The stories are set entirely within the world of the townships and white people remain a distant, almost irrelevant presence for the black characters. Within the collection there is a great diversity of characters, drawn from virtually every class and sector of the black township population. This is part of Ndebele's vision of a diverse, yet united black community. For all the violence in the township (the student activist Zani in the story "Fools" is stabbed, for example, and a young boy is viciously kicked by church elders in "Uncle"), Ndebele offers a view of this world which revels in its communalism and vibrancy.

The collection's best story, "Uncle," for example, ends with a scene of triumph in which people from all corners of the township gather together in an informal way to enjoy the music of a variety of performers. The work ends with the young narrator's delighted cry: "Oh, Uncle, everybody is here." Here one has an affirmation central to Ndebele's thinking about society (and one might add, to that of many black writers): namely the need to include and incorporate everybody within one's sense of community. And, obviously following from this, the necessity for socialist transformations within society that take into account the broad spectrum of needs of that society.

Interestingly, as in many works of black fiction since the students' uprising of 1976, the central characters or narrators in the majority of Ndebele's stories are young children or teenagers. Ndebele is clearly addressing himself, in the first place to a new generation of young black South Africans, the people for whom his vision of a unified community is of greatest relevance.

One senses throughout *Fools* that the small triumphs of the characters over a range of hardships in their everyday lives stand for the confidence of black people in their struggle against oppression. Again, it is in the story "Uncle" that Ndebele establishes most explicitly a connection between the actions and sayings of his characters and the broader context of black people's lives. Uncle's statements, in particular, have a resonance for the entire community. . . . This quiet, unobtrusive, often humorous form of guidance and illumination, indicating the future role for the black community in South African history and its celebration of communalism, are the most distinctive features of Ndebele's volume of stories.

Martin Trump. *Rendering Things Visible: Essays on South African Literary Culture* (Athens: Ohio University Press, 1990), pp. 168–70

In the article ["*Turkish Tales*, and Some Thoughts on South African Fiction"], Ndebele develops a thesis about storytelling, and the relationship between storytelling and fiction writing. He takes his admiration for the stories of the Turkish writer, Yashar Kemal, as the basis for a diagnosis of what is wrong with fiction by African writers in South Africa. Kemal's strength lies in his understanding of the conventions of storytelling, and in his ability to draw on the oral storytelling traditions of Turkey in the composition of his own written stories. Kemal's stories are critical stories, exploring the predicament of an impoverished rural population dominated by a ruthless, if paternalistic, land-owning class of Aghas. Because Kemal understands the conventions of storytelling narrative so well, and because of his familiarity with local storytelling traditions, he can draw his reader into an ''imaginative'' yet critical reflection upon the social processes of rural Turkey.

What of local African writers? They are not like Kemal, says Ndebele. They also want to write critical stories. The apartheid laws, by which a minority white population holds a majority black population down in impoverished subjection, offer as pressing an occasion for critical reflection as the predicament of rural Turkey. Unlike Kemal, though, local writers show little regard for the conventions of storytelling, and little interest in the oral storytelling art that is so popular among the wider African population. Instead, in order to provide their stories with the desired critical character, they resort to sloganizing, and to a journalistic, rather than a storytelling, mode of narrative, presenting the reader with ''evidence'' of the cruelty of apartheid rather than composing a thought-provoking story. . . .

In this context, an inadequate conception of political commitment is prevalent among writers. Political commitment comes to mean, broadly, condemning apartheid and its agents, especially African ''sell-outs,'' and sympathizing with the plight of the majority of the African population, who are the victims of this policy. It does not involve a serious analysis of the *culture* of this ''victimized'' population, of the themes that resonate in the daily lives of the people. It fails largely to connect with these resonances, to engage with them imaginatively or analytically.

Political commitment has overlooked culture; it has confined itself to a comparatively narrow range of attitudes and slogans, shared or debated among the intelligentsia. This is where Ndebele's conception of ''storytelling'' comes in as an antidote. Storytelling requires precisely the cultural insight or capacity for imaginative analysis—analysis which engages seriously with the resonances of popular experience—that has been wanting in the literature of African writers.

Storytelling is the antidote suggested by Ndebele for the ailing condition, as he sees it, of African fiction writing. This antidote arises out of a profoundly critical reflection on prevailing conceptions of how to express political commitment in literature. . . .

What characterizes each of Ndebele's stories is its prominent and sensitive treatment of the ''inner life''—the intellectual and emotional processes—of the protagonist. This concern with the inner life, focused upon a strategic theme or incident, provides the principle of coherence of each story. It also differentiates Ndebele's stories from those which he criticizes for their sloganistic and journalistic ambience. Little of the fiction published by African writers in South Africa shows the same degree of concern with the exploration of the inner life that Ndebele exhibits. Clearly, it takes a lot of skill and insight into the craft of fictional narrative to compose the fascinating accounts of personal experience that distinguish the stories in *Fools*. Furthermore, the skill involved in composing these accounts is inseparable from the practice of cultural analysis.

Michael Vaughan. In Martin Trump, ed. *Rendering Things Visible: Essays on South African Literary Culture* (Athens: Ohio University Press, 1990), pp. 186–88

Writing under literary censorship after the Sharpeville crisis in 1960, Ndebele belonged to a group of poets whose ''indirect approach'' in condemning the government enabled them to publish their works. Despite their cautiousness, however, they were eventually forced into exile. Ndebele now teaches at the University College of Roma, Lesotho, a nominally independent country surrounded by South Africa. Although Ndebele relies on multiple meanings, he does so not to evade an issue, but to make his criticism even more effective, and only the most obtuse censor could fail to see his devastating indictment of apartheid in *Fools*. As much as his carefully nuanced descriptions generate a dizzying multiplicity of meaning, the political implications are definite, and to praise such a work for its ''indeterminacy'' is to engage in another form of repression. . . .

Ndebele daringly chooses to have *Fools* narrated by a black South African who, like [Feodor] Dostoyevsky's Underground Man, scarcely qualifies as heroic or even likable. Teacher Zamani, known as Tee, grovels, abases himself, hurts his wife, Nosipho, punishes himself, and rapes a student named Mimi, who bears his child. A few years after the rape, at the time of the story (1966), Tee meets Mimi's now eighteen-year-old brother Zani. Although Zani agrees with his mother that ''When you look at [Tee] you see disgrace,'' they both seem to pity more than hate him. . . .

The two men . . . still have, as Zani would insist, a responsibility to bolster their respect for themselves and their fellow blacks as a prelude to taking back their government. By the end of the story, Tee has moved slightly toward reclaiming respect. When a stone hurled at Zani by a toadying black principal accidentally hits a passing car, a furious Boer emerges; to the Afrikaner, ''The possibility of resistance to his power seemed as unthinkable . . . as the revolt of chickens.'' Yet Tee—chicken-hearted, oppressed, humiliated, further self-humiliating, and hurtful—does manage a revolt. He refuses to run, though the Boer whips him. He laughs, until, finally, the Boer weeps, taking on the frustrated, sadomasochistic powerlessness that has always been Tee's lot. . . .

Ndebele is well aware of this seeming dilatoriness of the literary sign, expanding and dawdling, but he is also careful to prod it to finally yield up its meaning. He grants that ''The language of art is by definition a language that demands to be interpreted.'' In a sardonic and self-reflexive line in *Fools*, Ndebele further indicates his awareness that metaphor is a method that encourages ages thought but also produces dangers of evasiveness or delay. When the school board rehires Tee after only a three-month dismissal for rape, the delegation is too ashamed, of him and of themselves, to broach the subject directly. . . .

Zani sometimes resembles the despicable Tee because the younger man has to recognize humbly that his bookishness gives him ''the obscenity of high seriousness.'' The sympathetic Zani also resembles Tee because the latter deserves some sympathy as a victim. The opposition between Tee and Zani is ''deconstructed'' occasionally not because signs somehow inherently contradict themselves but because Zani must recognize his limitations and Tee, his potential. Similarly, the polar opposition of Tee and the Boer is undone to show the parallel limitation of the men, since both have wept in sadomasochistic excess. This resemblance, however, does not dissolve all differences. The government is not excused and the system of apartheid represented by the Boer must be defeated. Yet the brief, shocking similarity of the Boer to Tee may prepare for a future healing, after blacks have taken majority rule, if a slight basis of kinship could be recognized between the races.

K. J. Phillips. *Mosaic*. 23, 4 (fall 1990), pp. 88, 94–97, 99

Ndebele daringly chooses to have *Fools* narrated by a black South African who, like Dostoevsky's Underground Man, scarcely qualifies as heroic or even likeable. Teacher Zamani, known as Tee, grovels, abases himself, hurts his wife, Nosipho, punishes himself, and rapes a student named Mimi, who bears his child. A few years after the rape, at the time of the story (1966), Tee meets Mimi's now eighteen-year-old brother Zani. Although Zani agrees with his mother that "When you look at [Tee] you see disgrace," they both seem to pity more than hate him. The idealistic Zani wants Tee to grant him access to pupils so that he can lecture the uncomprehending ten-year-olds to "STAY HOME AND THINK!" on the holiday which he calls Dingane's Day and which the Boers, or white Afrikaners, call the Day of the Covenant. This holiday commemorates the Battle of Blood River in 1838, when, as the Boers gloss the event, God covenanted with them so they could kill King Dingane and thousands of Zulus.

Focusing the political issues at the heart of the novel are two "signs," both of which generate multiple meanings but both of which are not so totally infinite in range that meaning can be "deferred." The first of these is central to the rape scene, which Ndebele describes in a powerfully written flashback where metaphoric language and the literal detailing of the whereabouts, movements, and sounds of a chicken predominate. Mimi arrives at Tee's house with a chicken sent by her mother to thank him for fine teaching. Instead of taking the proffered gift, Tee rapes the girl. When she finally escapes, he tears the head off the chicken. The familiar domestic animal, presented as a gift, can serve as a sign of appreciation: in this case, soon made ironic, since Tee loses all claim to respect. By the time Tee kills the animal, and in the context of several other references to chickens throughout the book, the word "chicken" has generated other meanings. Like Kant's peacock, this chicken refuses to stay in the barnyard as it "occasions much thought.". . .

In addition to serving as a sign for attacking Mimi, decapitating the chicken becomes a sign for Tee's self-destructiveness. Because Ndebele describes Tee's first motion toward Mimi in the unromantic sentence "I bump into the head of the chicken with my tummy," its head might suggest his own genitals between him and her, so that beheading becomes a kind of castration. Tee deliberately wallows in actions that will debase him in his own eyes and in the eyes of others. Ndebele leaves no doubt that although this display of potency might make Tee seem more of a "man" in the sense of "male," Tee simultaneously disqualifies himself as "man" in the sense of "human" and "humane." For when Tee later goes to his mistress Candu only to remain impotent, the failure resembles the rape in that both are self-serving attempts to punish himself as he humiliates others, to a greater or lesser degree.

Another set of connotations accompanies the decapitation of the chicken. Tee desires to punish himself *by* raping (since he knows that he will no longer respect himself) and *for* raping. After Mimi has run outside, he hears the chicken squawking "like a voice of atonement." Because he both wants atonement and denies that he needs it, he furiously pursues the sound to stifle it, to forestall repentance and thus any comfort to someone as unworthy as himself.

The decapitation of the animal further expresses Tee's frustration and rage, his dissatisfaction with himself and his political situation. Tee might really like to "tear the head off" the white South African government, but he remains incapable of acting. Tee can turn destruction only against the innocent. Nevertheless, an

after-image of explosive violence potentially affecting the country remains from the much simpler death of the chicken.

While the cynical Tee can destroy only at home, Zani in his idealism announces future "hatchings," introducing further connotations of the word "chicken." Tee's wife, Nosipho, tells Zani that listening to him and his dreams is like "waiting for eggs to hatch, until you hear the first cries of a chick." The line occurs far enough from the rape scene that the use of "chicken" to contrast the two men—Tee as killing and Zani as nurturing—is not obtrusive.

Yet if Zani mainly contrasts with Tee, they are also equated in interesting ways, also through imagery of chickens (which reads much less pervasively than I make it seem here). . . .

Sometimes the characters make metaphors with the word chicken, but literal descriptions of chickens come to seem metaphoric too. Because of this expansive power of language, the innocuous barnyard label can reconcile Zani and Tee, and then go on to consolidate them as well with all South African blacks, in their herded domesticity imposed by whites. The man who cuts Zani's arm in a fight tries to justify himself for resisting Zani's political efforts: "'Can you let someone tell you that you have the mind of a chicken?' asked the knife wielder, heaving wildly to free himself from the tight grip of the men. He heaved hard and repeatedly, like someone trying to push a car that is in gear. The fury of it made some onlookers laugh." Although this scene precedes the flashback of Tee's rape, in retrospect this man's "heaving" resembles Tee's. The similarity makes it clear that both frustrated rages, of the knifer and the rapist, are politically caused.

The two men are, though, not entirely exonerated by this determinism. They still have, as Zani would insist, a responsibility to bolster their respect for themselves and their fellow blacks as a prelude to taking back their government. By the end of the story, Tee has moved slightly toward reclaiming respect. When a stone hurled at Zani by a toadying black principal accidentally hits a passing car, a furious Boer emerges; to the Afrikaner, "The possibility of resistance to his power seemed as unthinkable . . . as the revolt of chickens." Yet Tee—chicken-hearted, oppressed, humiliated, further self-humiliating, and hurtful—does manage a revolt. He refuses to run, though the Boer whips him. He laughs, until, finally, the Boer weeps, taking on the frustrated, sadomasochistic powerlessness that has always been Tee's lot.

K. J. Phillips. *Mosaic*. 23, 4 (fall 1990), pp. 87–107

BIBLIOGRAPHY
*Fools and Other Stories*, 1983; *Rediscovery of the Ordinary: Essays on South African Literature and Culture*, 1991; *Bonolo and the Peach Tree*, 1992; *The Prophetess*, 1992; *Sarah, Rings, and I*, 1993

# NETO, Agostinho (1922–1979)
## Angola

Agostinho Neto is one of the few lusophone African writers with an international reputation. He has spent much of his life in the struggle of his people to win independence. Whereas some Angolan intellectuals chose to live in Europe during the thirteen years of guerrilla warfare, Neto remained in his homeland organizing resistance to Portuguese domination. Moreover, Neto did not isolate himself from the great masses of Angolans living outside urban centers. He personally visited interior sections, eating with the people and frequently sleeping in their mosquito-infested huts. For Agostinho Neto his own life has taken on meaning only in conjunction with the lives of the oppressed people of Angola. . . .

In 1961 Casa dos Estudantes do Império in the Colecçao Autores Ultramarinos published a small volume of Neto's poetry under the title *Poemas*. A much larger selection appeared first in Italy in 1963 under the title *Con occhi asciutti*. This book was later published in Yugoslavia, Russia, and China. The first complete Portuguese edition came out in 1974 as *Sagrada esperança*, the title Neto preferred. It was awarded the Poetry of Combat Prize by the University of Ibadan in 1975. The forty-eight poems in this collection constitute nearly all of Neto's poetic work and cover a period from 1945 through 1960. . . .

Neto presents a gallery of victims in his early poems. Forced labor, hunger, loss of dignity, loss of hope, humiliation, even death, assault the body and spirit of the African living under colonialist domination. Life in the musseques is *ansiedade* (anguish). There is "saudade dos dias nao vividos" (nostalgia of days never lived) in "Sábado nos musseques." But Neto does not despair. In the very first poem of *Sagrada esperança*, "Adeus a hora da largada," he asserts his faith in himself and the people to create a new destiny.

Agostinho Neto does not often write of an individual love—that is a luxury; he writes about his love of his people, of his land and of liberty. And he writes primarily for his people. Unlike the francophone Négritude poets whose voices were heard more in Europe than in Africa, men like Neto, Costa Andrade, and António Jacinto brought their words to their own marketplace where the Angolan people came to know them. Many of Neto's poems have been put to music by soldiers who would sing these hymns of Africa. Poems such as "Havemos de voltar" and "Criar" are particularly well known. Ruy Mingas, among others, put out a record of Neto's poems and his songs can be heard in the streets of Luanda today, for in Neto's words the dreams of Angola are expressed.

Donald Burness. *Fire: Six Writers from Angola, Mozambique, and Cape Verde* (Washington, D.C.: Three Continents Press, 1977), pp. 19–20, 24, 33

Neto's poetry is seen by Donald Burness as one of combat. Militancy in Neto's poems, as in those of many other African writers of Portuguese expression . . . is a determining factor. Most lusophone African intellectuals, committed in the liberation struggle, would easily subscribe to Amilcar Cabral's view that the struggle itself was an act of culture. Their militancy, however, did not imply, as Neto's case so well illustrates, that they put aside the specific demands of the means employed. It is difficult to accuse Agostinho Neto of carelessness in his approach to poetry. Images and metaphors are judiciously set in the organic unity of the poem, so that the implicit message may be conveyed more effectively. All stylistic devices—anaphora, alliteration, enumeration, parallelism—contribute to intensify the rhythmic quality of poetry (seen as a counterpart of some black musical forms) and not to overcharge or smother the contents of the text. . . .

The theme of *identification* is present in one of Neto's most famous poems, "Mussunda amigo." The text is at the same time a melancholy recollection of a childhood and adolescence in common (the narrator remembers the time when he and his friend Mussunda used to buy mangos, or lamented "the destiny / of the women from Funda" with "clouds" in their eyes) and the expression of a deep confidence in the permanence of a sense of communion that nothing can destroy. The final statement, "We are," avoiding as it does the rhetoric of any exclamatory emphasis, echoes nonetheless a determined militancy, the idea that in spite of everything, of the ditch that colonialism put between the intellectual and the masses ("Here I am / Mussunda my friend / writing poems you can't understand"), they persist, they *are*, they affirm their existence simultaneously as an ontological and a historical barrier against which colonialist violence can do nothing. The African intellectual is fully aware of the contradiction implicit in his literary endeavors inaccessible to his illiterate countrymen; he knows, however, that there is always a point of convergence that makes them, after all, "inseparable."

Fernando Martinho. *World Literature Today*. 53, 1 (winter 1979), pp. 47–48

Neto's poetry is a perfect synthesis of history and art. ["Sábado nos musseques," translated as "Saturday in the Musseques"], for instance, tells of the deplorable condition of living in the slums. It begins with a straightforward statement: "Musseques are poor neighborhoods of poor people"—an expression most critics would consider too prosaic. But this manner of expression has worked and is consistent with Neto's objective, which is to educate his people and define their struggle in clear and precise terms. In this way, obscurantism, silence, and extinction are challenged. In "Saturday in the Musseques," Neto analyzes social life in a slum, showing that violence, oppression, brutality, alcoholism, sexuality, and other related social ills, are all symptoms of the anxiety in which the oppressed wallow. . . .

Neto's poetry is noted for its simplicity and directness. Its figurative expression is spare and unobtrusive, for Neto uses metaphor and symbols, not for ornamentation or deliberately as a poet seeking an effect would do, but as a man would use them in conversation or in silent musing. Everything comes naturally, as for example, his metaphors drawn from the medical profession: "no penetration of the germ of exploitation" [in "A Voz Iqual," translated as "With Equal Voice"], and "Injustice inoculated into the living system in which we revolve" [in "A reconquista," translated as "Reconquest"]. Neto's thoughts and feelings are communicated with ease and certainty, and so achieve maximum effects. . . .

Neto's poetry is for the people from whom it draws many of its virtues. Basil Davidson has noted that [*Sagrada esperança*, translated as *Sacred Hope*] . . . shows the poet's "vision of himself as not alone, but peopled with his own humanity, as having no personal 'career' outside the meaning of his people's life, as enjoying no worthwhile privilege save that of sharing in a necessary struggle for the future, shaking off the past, transforming the present." In many poems, Neto expresses his conviction that an individual cannot make a revolution without uniting with his people. This is a call to all people who need to change their condition. . . . Neto's use of poetry to propel revolutionary action and change, his clarity of expression that has made it possible for him to communicate with most of his people, regardless of their social class, and his sober confidence, are virtues, which other African poets will do well to emulate.

Ossie Onuora Enekwe. *Okike*. 18 (June 1981), pp. 3–6


The poetry of Agostinho Neto is often perceived as one of combat, revolutionary verse whose primary objective is to awaken the poet's compatriots, to help them become aware of their unenviable plight as a colonized people. This revolutionary element is dominant throughout Neto's opera. It is prevalent in the later poems in which the author already envisages an independent Angola, as one can easily deduce from such titles as: ["Havemos de voltar," translated as] "We Shall Return," "With Equal Voice," and ["O içar da bandeira," translated as] "The Hoisting of the Flag," as well as in the poems he started to write around 1945. Unlike the later verse, written in the advent of the eruption of the armed struggle and thus after Neto had been imprisoned for his poetry and political militancy, the earlier poems are works of social protest rather than of rebellion. . . .

["Adeus à hora da largada," translated as] "Farewell at the Hour of Parting" . . . is an outright and unqualified denunciation of Portugal's unwelcome presence in Angolan territory. Although the colonial power is never directly identified, it becomes emphatically clear that the poet deems it responsible for most of his society's ills, the most conspicuous of which is probably forced labor. Contract workers may well be the only people who are "burning" their lives in the coffee plantations of Angola and Sao Tomé, but Neto does not consider their ordeal more degrading than anybody else's and there are, as he shows in the poem, many other individuals getting burned by the fires of colonialism. Large segments of the populace feel alienated from life and attempt to get from alcohol, parties, and dancing what they are otherwise unable to acquire. Communication has broken down to such a degree that dialogue is almost impossible between parent and child. The whole nation seems to have fallen victim to a situation it obviously did not create and over which it has little or no control. The chaotic state of human relations, perhaps more than anything else, appears to be a vivid reflection of the extent to which society has disintegrated.

"Farewell," however, is not a pessimistic work. In fact, like most of Neto's poetry, it is infused with a dominant element of hope. The author does use "Farewell" as a means of exposing Portugal's policies in his native land, of showing how the people and resources of Angola are being exploited by a country that claims to be in a fraternal crusade to "civilize" Africa. As he does so, he evidently cannot avoid emphasizing the atrocities being committed in the name of religion or civilization. But he also utilizes the poem as a means to alert his compatriots to the realities under which they live as well as to rally them in an attempt to reacquire the autonomy they lost to Portugal or, rather, the sovereignty the Portuguese usurped from them.

A. R. Brás. *Ufahumu*. 11, 2 (fall 1981–winter 1982), pp. 82, 87


The poems collected in *Sacred Hope* span several years in Neto's career as well as various stages in the struggle for national liberation. Consequently, the themes range from [the] need to use valuable elements from the past to shape the future to reflections on the deprivations and sufferings of the people under colonial rule. . . .

For Neto, the historical experience of the people is the first condition of art, hence he writes from a position of absolute immersion in their plight. His voice is their voice and it reveals the various dimensions of their plight under colonial tutelage. In this respect, there is, in the poems, a strong sense of realism which is able to capture the subtle nuances of life among the common folk while constantly relating this to the relations of dominance and subordination which define the colonial equation. . . .

Much as he is engaged with the realities of the colonial "present," Neto's verse is also a means of positing a cultural antithesis to the hegemony of colonial values. Thus, the landscape of his verse is furnished by prominent landmarks in Angola in particular and Africa in general. The River Congo, the Kalahari Desert, and the Maiombe Forest become means of authenticating experience and reinforcing the poet's identification with his people and their roots. In this respect, Neto's verse shares with Négritude poetry a certain nostalgic re-creation of Africa and its vital rhythms. But for Neto, affirmation of racial cultural identity is a complement to liberation action, not a substitute for it. . . .

The poet cherishes freedom, not for its own sake and at all costs but in the context of his people's struggle to regain their dignity after the years of humiliation and denigration. Consequently, even in prison, the poet's attitude is one of stoic defiance and pride towards his persecutors. . . .

Yet in spite of the repression of armed tyranny, hope emerges as the dominant theme in most of Neto's poems. The constant reaffirmation of optimism and faith in the future is not just an anodyne to drown the pangs of present adversity but a way of imbuing the sacrifices implicit in the struggle for freedom with a sense of purpose. The struggle becomes a painful process of building for future success; looking forward to a time when the poet/combatant shall lose his anonymity and emerge distinguished in a new "catalogue of human glory."

Neto's poetry is characterized by a general contemplative tone which is unhurried, painstaking, and shrewd in its attempt not to compromise the organic proximity between the poet and his people. Consequently, the emotions which permeate and exude from his verse are those of patriotic heroism and sympathetic identification with those who bear the burden of oppression.

Chidi Amuta. *The Theory of African Literature* (London: Zed Books, 1989), pp. 186–89


A space where the dark is tempered by the light, despair by hope, the past by the future, the individual's ambitions by the collectivity's determinations: this is the essential provision of Agostinho Neto's poetry. Combat poetry? This would be a reductive, even condescending characterization, and would tend to minimize the stature of one of the twentieth century's most important African poets. It is a perilous term for a perilous genre—a term, among others, we *might* apply, but one that seems in any case ineluctably associated with Neto's name . . . and one that therefore provokes us to see in him a nucleus around which critics have gathered other poets of this modern genre we call militant or guerrilla poetry. Neto's importance in relationship to this genre, and his poetic gifts apart from it, therefore call for a mainstreaming of his literary contributions. "Protest poetry" might, however, more aptly describe his ouevre; the term is certainly a somewhat better representation of his content than "guerrilla poetry" or "poetry of combat" would allow. But whatever the word used to sum up that content, it is best to see contextually how this talented poet fuses his ideologies with his structures, and intertextually, how he avoids the diatribes, the invectives, and the stereotypically strident rhetoric of most guerrilla poetry in a way scarcely imitated by his poetic "counterparts."

In his earliest poems . . . Neto establishes the juxtapositions of dark versus light, of despair versus hope, of individual versus collectivity; and these oppositions, especially that of the self versus the group, will be the leitmotif of his life's work, collected under the general title of *Sagrada esperança*, or *Sacred Hope*. And however Marxist his readers find the theme of confraternity inherent in such poems as "Farewell at the Hour of Parting" to be, the oversoul, the spareness, the structural as well as the grammatical and syntactic fusions, all subvert any tendency toward the doctrinaire that are potentially inherent in a bare ideological approach; and these traits consequently guarantee the poem's aesthetic success.

> Janis L. Pallister. *Studies in Twentieth-Century Literature.*
> 15, 1 (winter 1991), pp. 137–38

BIBLIOGRAPHY
*Poemas*, 1961; *Sagrada esperança* (Sacred Hope), 1974; *Poemas de Anggola*

# NGUGI WA THIONG'O (1938– )
## Kenya

Mr. James Ngugi is, in East African terms, a prolific worker. Already he has written a full-length play [*The Black Hermit*], two novels (of which [*Weep Not, Child*] is the first published) as well as a number of articles in the *Sunday Nation* in Nairobi. Indeed, since he left Makerere, this latter work has been his means of livelihood, so that his articles have increased in quantity and expertise, as well as in the area they cover.

Of *Weep Not, Child*, the first thing to be remarked is what an important place it has, and is going to have, in the history of novel-making in East Africa. Now, after all the waiting, the first novel in English has been written here by an indigenous East African. Immediately I am reminded of Dr. [Roger] Bannister and the Magic Mile, and I feel grateful to Mr. Ngugi in knowing that, where he has broken the barrier, the rest of us will quickly follow. This is excellent. And yet this should not be allowed to blind us into empty hero-worship, to undeserved praise when the novel itself is discussed. . . .

True enough it talks about things of the greatest potential importance, but it does so unconvincingly. (I am reminded here of that old one about a house being built of bricks but a collection of bricks not necessarily being a house). Mr. Ngugi narrates the misfortunes in which people are caught, in a reporting, almost cataloguing manner which strangely enough for all its blood and thunder lacks any breath of real life. Part of the trouble lies in his characterization. I feel that all his characters are a continuation of his beliefs and desires and that he manipulates them at the end of a string throughout. It is as if his thoughts and words took human shape and became now a Ngotho, now a Njoroge and so on. And the

result is a sterile and unmoving reproduction of many James Ngugis. And the result of this is that we feel not a flicker of spontaneous sympathy for his characters, whatever their misfortunes. Now this is a tragedy for the whole work, because Mr. Ngugi has staked all on his characters. . . .

Mr. Ngugi can rest assured that his first published novel is a historical landmark. And when the spark comes, what he will write after it may well be a great deal more.

> John Nagenda. *Makerere Journal.* November 1964, pp. 69–71

In [*The River Between*] the hero and heroine are caught between warring factions of traditional and Christianised Kikuyus, and though the hero makes an admirable attempt to reconcile the two cultures, both within himself and in the dismally divided community, he fails because as an educated African he has begun to set great store by his own personal aspirations; also he shows the same ambiguities and equivocations of modern heroes everywhere who have submitted to the cult of self-doubt and scepticism.

This seems to me a very worthy successor to Ngugi's first novel, *Weep Not, Child*, which dealt with the Mau Mau conflict. Ngugi's main achievement is a series of evocative passages which are distinguished by their lack of contrivance or any striving after effect for its own sake. There is no reason to doubt that Ngugi owes a special debt to the Nigerian, Chinua Achebe, whose *Things Fall Apart* seems to have greatly influenced him. The main failure of Ngugi's writing so far has been his inability to allow for easy transition from one scene to another in a way that would suggest a clear progress of the novel. The action tends to jump and most of the scenes are not allowed to develop sufficiently to give the novel its accumulative power. Ngugi's advantage over [recent South African writers] stems from the fact that he has situated his characters in a community where choice can be seen to be real so that personal failure or success can be assessed in universal, human terms. Such an assessment to be possible requires certain minimum conditions of freedom.

> Lewis Nkosi. *New Africa.* May 1965, p. 70

*The River Between* uses the same style and achieves the same kind of effect [as *Weep Not, Child*]. But in this novel there is a need for more definition and sharpness. For this is a full historical novel—a novel, that is, about contemporary society which examines certain features of that society by exploring their origin and development in the past. The obvious comparison is with Achebe's two novels about the early contacts between Africans and Europeans in his own part of Eastern Nigeria, *Things Fall Apart* and *Arrow of God*. The comparison, I think, is fair and the reason why it is unfavourable to Ngugi is that the impressionistic and personal approach used in *Weep Not, Child* is insufficient in a novel attempting to explore the roots of a particular problem. Such a novel must show the characters acting in a social context and under social pressures and therefore must demonstrate to us convincingly that nature of their society. Achebe's novels do this. The tribal societies he shows us are completely articulated and comprehensible and his characters act out their destinies under social pressures that are made clear to us. In *The River Between* this is not so. Although like Achebe, Ngugi has set up certain connections between his two novels—for example the school at Siriana occurs in both of them—the exact historical period of the events in *The River Between* is never revealed, at least to the reader unversed in the details of European penetration into the various regions of Kenya. The social structure of the tribe and its political organization, although the plot turns on these matters, is never demonstrated to us in such a way that we can understand their operation in the action of the novel. Hence the characters are seen in relationships only sketchily defined except in terms of emotion, and the real content of the social and political ends which they set themselves remains unspecified.

> John Reed. *Journal of Commonwealth Literature.* September 1965, p. 119

The first novel to come out of East Africa was James Ngugi's *Weep Not, Child*, written three years ago while the young Kenyan was reading English Honours at Makerere. . . . *Weep Not, Child* is a story of Kenya during the Mau Mau Emergency period. Those bloody years are recreated through the experiences of three families. . . . If we consider the story on the anagogical level . . . there is a deeper message. Ngugi is a disciple of Walt Whitman (from whose poem, ''On the Beach at Night,'' comes the title of the novel). Ngugi believes in Whitman's concept of the brotherhood of man and remains optimistic that man can be improved. . . .

The first few pages of *Weep Not, Child*, and some latter passages are reminiscent of Alan Paton's *Cry the Beloved Country*. When Njoroge identifies himself with David and the Kikuyu with the children of Israel, it is a poor imitation of Flaubert. Ngugi commits many technical sins, probably because he is more engrossed in espousing his ideas and ideals than in adhering to artistic precepts. The novel consists of too many unrelated essays and stories; things just do not dovetail. Then, too, Ngugi explains and summarizes situations which would lend themselves to easy dramatization.

> Taban lo Liyong. *Africa Report.* December 1965. pp. 42–43

The non-Christian black African's view of his world, as it is presented in *The River Between*, is especially antithetical to the Calvinistic view of nature. If, at the beginning of time, God separated, forever, the good souls from the bad, then it must follow that a man's surroundings have little effect on his fixed fate. (''That's the way those people are; you can't change them.'')

All this, which may seem a digression, is actually at the center of any discussion of the novel as it evolved in Middle-class Christian Europe (and later in America). If nature, environment, is of no real importance in the life of man, then neither can its role in the novel be important. And generally this is the case. Nature, in most European and American novels, is used as a backdrop, a stage-set. It is passive—just there.

But the African writer, with a different set of traditions and values, a different attitude toward his surroundings and his place in them may use those surroundings in a different way. James Ngugi does. Time and again, in *The River Between*, nature is at center stage, playing an active role, influencing a character's feelings and thoughts in a way only human beings do in most European and American novels: ''He was angry with the rain. The rain carried away the soil, not only here but everywhere. That was why the land, in some parts, was becoming poor. For a time, he felt like fighting with the rain.'' Or: ''And sometimes she would run to Honia (river)

and just stay there watching the flow of the water. Then she would go home feeling at peace. So the river, especially on Sundays, was her companion.'' These are not simply turnings of literary phrases. They bespeak new ways of feeling and seeing.

All this is very exciting to me as a writer, because it suggests new ways of telling a story, new relationships of character and setting. More importantly, it is entirely possible that the black African writer will accomplish for the black American what his own writers have been unable to accomplish—that is, to suggest to him standards other than those of his oppressors, by which he may judge himself, his world, and his place in it.

> William Melvin Kelley. *African Forum.* Winter 1966, p. 114

Hope does exist in Ngugi's work, but it is a hope that gives little comfort. Just as men are apparently fated to fight each other—at least the empirical evidence seems to support such a view—so are they fated to desire peace. It is indeed the pattern of Ngugi's three novels that a hero who seeks to avoid conflict and violence is thrown into contact with a man who desires them. The antagonist justifies his belief in violence because of the injustices done to him and his people in the past; his solutions to these problems of injustice are an armed conflict with the oppressor and a retaliation in kind and of equal severity to the opposition. It is instructive to look at Ngugi's three published novels (he is, of course, a young writer who may take different paths in the future), because they show that no man can deny or hide his conflicts. Only the brave ones resolve them, and in this resolution lies the hope of the future for mankind. But first this hope must be shorn of its illusions.

Ngugi seems to be saying that only when people accept the present reality can they change their tomorrows. . . . It is the dream of tomorrow that makes a new day possible, but it is the illusions about tomorrow that keep it from appearing. . . .

In his ability to dramatize such insights and to provide perspective on the land about which he has chosen to devote his literary life, Ngugi is a writer who combines movement with pacifism, tradition with inventiveness. He too is trying to reconcile, to create a unity of art—a pattern to which most great writers in the world have been drawn.

> Martin Tucker. Introduction to James Ngugi, *Weep Not, Child* (New York: Macmillan, 1969), pp. 10–11, 17

*A Grain of Wheat*, James Ngugi's latest novel, is an extremely interesting piece of work because it brings a new theme to African literature—the effects on a people of the changes brought about in themselves by the demands of a bloody and bitter struggle for independence. How fit is one for peace, when one has made revolution one's life? Set in the immediate post-Mau-Mau period the novel looks back to the personal tragedies of a number of people who were active in Mau-Mau, and examines how the experience now shapes their lives. In the uneasy peace, they have to come to terms with one another, but their relationships are determined by the experience that has put all human relationships through the test of fire—the guerilla revolution itself.

Here are the wild-looking bearded men who lived in the Aberdares for years, emerging after the revolution with almost all their instincts for normal life lost; brave men half-broken by the experience; and men accepted as brave men who must live the rest of their lives with the secret knowledge that they were traitors. Mugo, a local small farmer, is such a man. He has betrayed a fellow Gikuyu to the British; as a result of various events which enmesh him in the sense of his own guilt, he brings his own world crashing down around his head by confession, and the words of one of the Mau-Mau veterans who are his judges at a private trial sum up the light in which Ngugi presents him: "Your deeds alone will condemn you. No one will ever escape from his own actions."

It is the measure of James Ngugi's development as a writer that none of the protagonists in this novel is marred by the pseudo-nobility of some of the characters in his earlier work, and yet he succeeds in placing the so-called Mau-Mau movement in the historical, political, and sociological context of the African continental revolution. What the white world perhaps still thinks of as a reversion to primitive savagery (as opposed, no doubt, to civilized savagery in Nazi Germany) is shown to be a guerilla war in which freedom was won, and which brought with its accomplishment a high price for the people who waged it.

> Nadine Gordimer. *Michigan Quarterly Review.* Fall, 1970, p. 226

*A Grain of Wheat* is Ngugi's most ambitious and successful novel to date. In the depth of its psychological penetration and the power of its characterization, in the subtlety of its narrative technique, in the density of its texture, and in the sophistication of its language, it exceeds all expectations raised by the two earlier novels, promising though they were. Its complexity of form recalls the involutions of Conrad's *Lord Jim*, on which it seems consciously to have been modelled.

Most novels, including African ones, present experience chronologically, with the story moving logically from the beginning, through various complications and problems to the resolution and conclusion. Others ignore this convention, and present experience through a series of impressions, digressions, casual anecdotes, and incidents which are not necessarily presented in chronological order. This is the method of *A Grain of Wheat*, which opens on the eve of Kenya's Independence and ends four days later. But very little in the novel actually happens during those four days; instead the reader is taken back by numerous "witnesses" to a whole series of events in the past. This is Ngugi at his most baffling and exasperating, withholding information, supplying it belatedly when he chooses, employing flashback within flashback, "reflector within reflector, point of view within point of view, cross-chronological juxtaposition of events, and impressions" [as Dorothy Van Ghent wrote of *Lord Jim*]. In no other novel of Ngugi, and possibly in no other African novel, is the reader asked to be more alert and to participate more fully. . . .

*A Grain of Wheat* is a profoundly satisfying work of art. Ngugi has clearly attained maturity and produced a novel which can stand unashamedly with some of the more lasting English works of fiction.

> Eustace Palmer. *An Introduction to the African Novel* (New York: Africana, 1972), pp. 24–25, 47

A few weeks ago (as I write these words in December 1972), Heinemann published a book of essays in London called *Homecoming* by a writer named Ngugi wa Thiong'o, and from this simple event in the publishing world, which in itself was not very

important, can be drawn some implications of considerable significance for a book about African literature. The writer of *Homecoming* is not, of course, someone new on the scene but the same Gikuyu novelist whom we have encountered as James Ngugi, now writing under a name that, while different, is less new than it is old: a reversion to a traditional, as it were pre-colonial and pre-Christian, African name—Ngugi-son-of-Thiong'o. This little event, though unremarkable in itself, requires us to see, for one thing, that in African literature we are dealing with a living and changing literature and with writers who are very much alive. . . .

Besides providing this kind of salutary warning for impatient critics, Ngugi's name-change indicates that he personally intends henceforth to refuse the Western identity that is implied by a baptismal name and will choose instead to refer himself, by way of a more traditionally African identity, to his father, his family, and his ancestors. Likewise, the Marxism that Ngugi proclaims throughout his book, carrying African Socialism one step further in logical rigor to African Marxism, points to the same tendency and desire to merge individual achievement and identity with communal effort and existence. With his name-change and his Marxism, Ngugi raises a question that inevitably recurs in any discussion of African literature and that can be taken to be the basic issue, so far at least as the African writer himself is concerned, of African literature: that is, the twofold yet single question of the writer's relation to his past and to his community, which involves a definition both of his own and his community's identity.

This is not to say that Ngugi's notions are typical and that other African writers are doing or thinking the same. On the contrary, most other novelists would, to one extent or another, disagree with him in his paradoxical politics of reactionary revolution. Ngugi seems to want to make his past his future: he would revive social and cultural structures of the past as a reality of the future, and what he calls for to accomplish this is a present revolution not to achieve something new but to restore an ideal pre-colonial state that he, at least, takes to have been one of original peace, harmony, justice, and goodness.

> James Olney. *Tell Me Africa* (Princeton: Princeton University Press, 1973), pp. 283–84

[Ngugi wa Thiong'o's] strength as a novelist proceeds from the way in which he encrusts his political vision with material derived from his own Kenyan background—the peasant values which are the real values as opposed to those new First World values which are taken on by the blacks who become the leaders in the postindependence circumstance. These are contemptible people so far as Ngugi is concerned because of the way they exploit their own kind and, secondly, for their repudiation of the heroes of the revolution who brought about those circumstances in which they are able to act as they do. Thus, Dedan Kimathi is Ngugi's legitimate hero: his vision was straightforward, unflinching, uncompromising, ultimately successful. But now he has been repudiated. . . .

*Weep Not, Child*, the first published novel but the second written, brings Ngugi to his central theme which is the struggle for Kenyan independence and the effect of the struggle on the lives of individuals within the Kenyan context. *Weep Not, Child* is less complex in its form than *A Grain of Wheat*, and less complex still than *Petals of Blood*. But the theme is the same where we find reference to various historical revolutionary activities before the

Mau Mau independence movement got under way in the 1950s. In both *Weep Not, Child* and *A Grain of Wheat*, the causes and the prosecution of Mau Mau aspirations are dramatized. . . .

The materials of *Petals of Blood*, Ngugi's fourth novel, are related to those of the earlier novels but are more abundantly conveyed. In a novel almost double the size of *A Grain of Wheat*, he widens and deepens his treatment of themes which he has narrated and dramatized before—themes related to education, both formal and informal; religion, both Christian and customary; the alienation of the land viewed from the historical point of view and as a process which continues in the present; the struggle for independence and the price paid to achieve it. And to these themes he has added artistic representation of the betrayal of the independence movement and its authors, the nature and cost of modernity as this coincides with the emergence of a Kenyan middle class, and of the need for the creation of a cultural liberation struggle fostered by the peasants and workers. This is a political novel in the widest sense. . . .

Concern over the land is a central theme in the novel as it has been in the earlier ones. Ngugi is concerned about what has happened to the land: how the African has been alienated from the land first by the imperial colonialists who helped themselves to the land, paying into the pockets of a few whatever worth they consigned to it, and subsequently by a class of African landlords who, because of their connections with the forces of world capitalism, are able to manage the purchase price. And it is the question of how to reachieve the land that links the Kenyan people with the struggles of other movements in the Third World. The struggle has an historic as well as contemporary dimension and more than once in the book the unity of experience and purpose is conveyed in references to "Chaka . . . Toussaint . . . Samori . . . Nat Turner . . . Arap Manyei . . . Mondlane . . . Cabral . . . Kimathi . . . Nkrumah" and others.

> G. D. Killam. *An Introduction to the Writings of Ngugi* (London: Heinemann, 1980), pp. 14–15, 19, 96, 102

*A Grain of Wheat* is a . . . complex novel, both in style and language. The simple narrative technique has gone; we have moved very far from the structure of traditional stories; and though the texture of the language is in some cases thin, the simplicity of the earlier novels is frequently replaced by a complexity which surpasses what many other writers have written. . . .

*A Grain of Wheat* is above all a book which deals with the effects of great events of the external world on individual people. The events portrayed take place in the context of the Mau Mau war and the coming of Uhuru, but the writer focuses our attention not on the events as abstractions, but on their effects on the individual soul and the individual mind, and on person-to-person relationships. . . .

In terms of varieties of language, the novel is limited. In choosing Standard English, Ngugi has deliberately shunned the linguistic experiments of [Chinua] Achebe and [Gabriel] Okara, who both try to reflect African modes of thinking. In consequence, linguistic differentiation as a method of depicting characters is minimal in *A Grain of Wheat*. There is no noticeable difference between the language of Gikonyo and that of Mugo, Mumbi, or even Karanja. The question of their educational or social background is irrelevant. Whether educated or uneducated, Ngugi's characters speak meticulous English, the language of the author. Whether the writer is translating or quoting his speakers verbatim are not questions that cross our minds as we read through the book. . . .

If any African novel has a claim to complexity, it is *A Grain of Wheat*. . . . Though the language itself is not labored and complicated, Ngugi's narrative technique is sufficiently complex to make the book one of the most sophisticated in the African literature so far published. If the narrative structure is complex, the response it calls forth in the reader is equally complex. The reader's attitude to characters and his impressions about the thread of events keep on shifting as the narrative shifts from one person to another, from one event to another, from one focus to another. He may dislike a character in one part of the novel; but in the next he may like him better, or at least learn to understand or accept the character's faults. The characters themselves get a better understanding of themselves and others, of their own motives and other people's motives, as the story progresses to its end.

> Emmanuel Ngara. *Stylistic Criticism and the African Novel* (London: Heinemann, 1982), pp. 81, 86, 97–98

Ngugi was arrested on New Year's Eve, 1978. The precise reasons for the imprisonment have never been revealed since no charges were laid.

*Detained: A Writer's Prison Diary* is Ngugi's "prison memoir," the record of his incarceration. The importance of *Detained* to an understanding of Ngugi's career, both in the direction it has taken since his release from prison and in accounting for the intellectual process which leads him to his present position, cannot be overemphasized. It described the purposes of the detainers and the effect of detention on the sensibility of the detained person. Committed to the struggle of alleviating the suffering of the generality of people, recognizing the connection between himself and his fellow detainees and, as well, other advocates in other cultures, the detained person must find the spiritual and psychological resources to withstand the punitive methods of his jailers. . . .

The political theme in the novel [*A Grain of Wheat*] is a leitmotif to the human interchanges the novel explores. *A Grain of Wheat* is Ngugi's most finished piece of writing in conventional fictional terms. Here his concern for individual sensibilities, shaped by but in important ways isolated from social issues larger than the individual, is conveyed. Figures in these novels are participants in the events which shape the destiny of the country by accident rather than choice, through ignorance rather than apprehension. Ngugi's compassion for their bewilderment is profound, the more so, perhaps, because of their ignorance.

And, as with the other novels, the ending forecasts the beginning of the next book. . . .

*A Grain of Wheat* . . . forecasts at its close the development of the political context in which Kenyan will be ranged against Kenyan, and in his recent writing, produced from 1977 to 1982, Ngugi evokes a wholly contemporary setting, theme, and treatment. The setting is the Kenya created out of [Jomo] Kenyatta's repudiation of his revolutionary sensibility and his collusion with former political rivals and international finance capitalists. The analysis [Ngugi] offers is presented in *Detained [A Writer's Prison Diary]*, the diary he kept in prison, in which he records the experience of being incarcerated for almost a year following the publication of *Petals of Blood* and the production of *Ngaanhika Ndeenda [Ithaako ria Ngerekano*, translated as *I Will Marry When I Want]*. . . .

*Petals of Blood* is a pivotal work in the Ngugi canon, since it marks his last major piece of writing in English before he took the decision to turn to Kikuyu as his medium of expression. The novel is cast in the form of a crime thriller and opens with the murder of three industrial and economic leaders of the new Kenya—Chui, Mzigo, and Kimeria—and the arrest of the four principal suspects—Munira, Abdulla, Karega, and Wanja. . . . The narrative of the novel shifts backwards and forwards in time, adopting a variety of narrative and temporal perspectives—thus the present-time action of the novel takes place over about ten days; the lives of the principal characters are revealed over a span of twelve years; and, as an expanded canvas, moving backwards and forwards in time, the history of Kenya is conveyed from precolonial times (where Ngugi records the mythic basis of Kenyan society in ways with which we are familiar from the earlier novels) and especially from the beginnings of European exploitation of Kenya which began in the 1890s. . . .

*Petals of Blood* is a novel about faith and the possibilities of the workers and peasants reasserting their traditional role as producers of the national wealth which they will have to create for their own use. The rhetoric of the novel is subsumed by Ngugi's harmonizing of the characters in the exemplary roles they are given. Rejecting a number of possible abstract solutions to the depressed state of the people, Ngugi places his faith in the militant unity of peasants and workers—whose collective voice is heard off camera at the close of the novel but who thunder into the fray in *Devil on the Cross* [first published in Kikuyu as *Caitaani Mutharaba-ni*].

> G. D. Killam. *The Writing of East and Central Africa* (London: Heinemann, 1984), pp. 124, 133–36

In *A Grain of Wheat*, Ngugi shows his socialist inclinations by focusing his attention on the common people and their predicament. The novel depicts the events leading to the coming of Uhuru, but the focus is not on the major events that are recorded in history books. [Jomo] Kenyatta is mentioned, but only as part of the history of the people of Kenya—Ngugi does not project the interests and views of outstanding figures like Kenyatta and other people in the upper echelons of society. The book talks about independence celebrations, but we are not shown the celebrations which took place in Nairobi, the capital city of Kenya. Rather, we are taken to an insignificant place out in the country—Thabai. Similarly, the characters we deal with are small village people and members of the peasant class—Gikonyo, Gitogo, Mumbi, Karanja, and, of course, their British overlords.

We witness here colonial Kenya giving way to the independent Republic of Kenya which is the result of the sacrifices of the people of Kenya who suffered and died for freedom's sake. As the Bible quotation prefixed to the beginning of chapter 14 suggests, there was in Kenya "a new heaven and a new earth; for the first heaven and the first earth were passed away." But the crucial question is whether Uhuru has brought forth much fruit as a result of the people who died. In other words, has independence brought about a change of system for the better?

> Emmanuel Ngara. *Art and Ideology in the African Novel* (London: Heinemann, 1985), pp. 59–60

The only fictional work I have found which elevates female circumcision to a position of thematic central importance, *The River Between*, has the issue serve as battleground in the clash between conservative tribal elements and the patriarchal Christian church. . . .

Ngugi's novel, in any case, deals with female circumcision not from a feminist, but from a humanist and progressive standpoint, leading its readers gently and ironically to understand that male insistence on female "rites" is displaced impotence and is ultimately deconstructive. He shows, for example, how the brothers are mistaken in viewing circumcision as a still unsullied source of cultural integrity from which strength can be drawn in preparation for the battles ahead, to repossess the land. Ngugi further links this futile hope to renewal of the martial image, in turn tied to the vehement insistence on female mutilation. For without removal of the clitoris, without "purity," it is assumed that female sexual energy would threaten the tribe with destruction.

> Tobe Levin. In Carole Boyce Davies and Anne Adams Graves, eds. *Ngambika: Studies of Women in African Literature* (Trenton, New Jersey: Africa World Press, Inc., 1986), pp. 209, 211

*Devil on the Cross* is the story of Jacinta Wariinga, ostensibly narrated by the "Giccandi Player" or "Prophet of Justice" at the request of Jacinta's mother, "so that each may pass judgement only when he knows the whole truth." In many respects the pattern of Wariinga's life resembles that of Wanja in *Petals of Blood*. Both approximate to the exemplary tale of Kareendi, told by Wariinga as the story of "a girl like me . . . or . . . any other girl in Nairobi." Sexual exploitation and discrimination are dominant factors in Kareendi's life. She is given few opportunities to develop her potential and is constantly at the mercy of men for her livelihood. She is very often reduced to the cursed "cunt" Wanja protests about in *Petals of Blood*. . . .

Ngugi portrays sexual confrontation between men and women as part of the destructive rivalry on which contemporary Kenyan capitalism thrives, and through which injustices and inequalities are perpetuated.

The ending of *Devil on the Cross* is optimistic insofar as it offers possibilities of new social orders in the future, but it is not conclusively "happy." Both Wariinga and Gaturia go through enlightenment and liberation in the process of finding themselves and each other but, like the ill-fated lovers of Ngugi's earlier novels, they are to find that the larger social forces impinge on their personal relationship. The fact that there is no simple "happy" ending reinforces the point, made in *Petals of Blood*, that "La Luta Continua!" As Ngugi has said: "The problem of men and women cannot be satisfactorily solved under the present system. Sexual relations are the reflection of an unequal economic system." Wariinga refuses to settle down to marriage with Gaturia, because she discovers that her prospective father-in-law is her seducer, "the Rich Old Man from Ngorika." When Wangari delivers her condemnation of the thieves at the Devil's Feast, "her voice carried the power and authority of a people's judge." Wariinga also speaks with the voice of "a people's judge" when she condemns the Rich Old Man to die. Wariinga's execution of her oppressor, like Wanja's execution of Kimeria in *Petals of Blood*, is more than personal revenge. It carries the force of communal retribution and justice.

Both Wariinga and Wanja rise above the tale of Kareendi because they do not finally accept defeat and humiliation. Having come to the realization that there are more than the "two worlds" of "the eater" and "the eaten," Wariinga commits herself to the "third world": "the world of the revolutionary overthrow of the system of eating and being eaten."

Ngugi has tailored the content, form, and style of *Devil on the Cross* for his intended Kikuyu-speaking worker and peasant audience. His only concession to his foreign readers is to have made an English translation. Properly the work should be read aloud and communally in its original Kikuyu. An individual private reading of the English version can obviously not do justice to a work whose principal significance lies in its use of the Kikuyu language. But, in a novel which is so intimately concerned with Ngugi's individual and communal identity, it is also significant that images of women are such a prominent feature. Wariinga the female protagonist of *Devil on the Cross*, is the successor to a line of heroines who have become increasingly central to the structure and meaning of Ngugi's novels.

> Jennifer Evans. In Eldred Durosimi Jones, ed. *Women in African Literature Today* (Trenton, New Jersey: Africa World Press, 1987), pp. 131–32, 136–37

*A Grain of Wheat* is situated on the border between a messianic and intellectualist field of vision, by the late 1960s representing decolonization as a failure, and a more concretely committed socialism, casting the decolonizing process in similarly radical but more soberly material and historical terms. The novel leaves the reader with an image of hope, embodied in Gikonyo's carving of a stool in the shape of a pregnant woman, but also with the fear that, as represented, the victory of British colonialism will prove to have been a Pyrrhic one. It would only be in his fourth novel, *Petals of Blood*—a novel that it would take him seven full years to write—that Ngugi would be able to find a less intellectualist register for his new political sensibility. And even here, in the formulaic quality of the final pages, in which the specter of proletarian internationalism is rather implausibly seen to be arising in the collective political imagination of Kenyan workers and peasants, there is the suggestion of a residual intellectualism.

Nevertheless, in several respects, *Petals of Blood* is definitive of the new politically committed writing that has emerged in Africa since 1970. Set mostly in the countryside, it portrays a community struggling against an environment that a combination of factors have contrived to render sterile and harsh: drought and desertification, colonial neglect and despoliation, postcolonial mismanagement and venality. To the members of this community, independence is only a word: its substantive impact on their lives has been virtually nonexistent. Between these villagers and an authentic independence there stand daunting obstacles—economic, historical, political, psychological. Yet through the whole novel there is Ngugi's insistence upon the transformability of existing conditions. Meaningful social change will come, he suggests: perhaps not tomorrow nor the next day, nor even the day after that, but still it will come, for "the peasants, aided by the workers, small traders and small landowners ... [have] mapped out the path" for themselves to follow.

> Neil Lazarus. *Resistance in Postcolonial African Fiction* (New Haven: Yale University Press, 1990), p. 213

*Matigari ma Njiruungi*, literally meaning "the patriots who survived the bullets," is the name of the protagonist in Ngugi wa Thiong'o's latest novel [*Matigari ma Njiruungi*, published in English as *Matigari*]. . . .

*Matigari ma Njiruungi*, who was Settler Howard Williams's servant during the colonial days, decides to end his exploitation by shooting Williams, who happens to be speaking on the telephone when Matigari reaches out for the settler's gun. It is John Boy, another servant, who saves his colonial master. Suddenly both Williams and John Boy wrestle with Matigari, but he escapes through the window. Thereafter the struggle between the two opponents continues in the forest, and after many years of hunting each other, Matigari, armed with an AK-47, eliminates his two enemies. Following his victory, he hides his weapons near a *mugumo* (fig) tree and is determined to occupy Williams's house, which he claims as his own. Upon arrival, however, he finds John Boy Jr. in occupancy, with the blessing of Williams Jr., from whom he has bought the house.

Throughout the novel Matigari is depicted as a disillusioned and frustrated revolutionary who, after killing his two enemies and thus contributing to the liberation of his country, finds himself grappling with the problems of postindependence neocolonialism. In his effort to understand his postcolonial country, he approaches many people, seeking to know how and where he can find truth and justice. . . . Before embarking on his search for those qualities, he endeavors to reestablish links with his family, whom he has not seen for many years while engaged in his country's fight for liberation from colonialism. Among the people he comes across as he searches for his family members are the young boy Muriuki, the trade-union worker Ngaruro wa Kiriro, the young woman Guthera, and the young man Macharia; it is with these people from different backgrounds that he discusses the socioeconomic and political problems plaguing his supposedly independent and free country. These individuals accompany and support Matigari as he seeks to regain what he regards as his rightful property: namely, Settler Williams's house. In his exertions to secure the house, Matigari is arrested and jailed; he later escapes with help of Guthera and is subsequently committed to a mental hospital, assumed by the authorities to be a lunatic. Nonetheless, he succeeds in escaping from the hospital as well, and rumor begins to circulate in the country about his greatness and superhuman (even divine) qualities; there are people who elevate his image to that of Christ and predict his return to save their country from exploitation and oppression. Thus, as the moment of Matigari's long-awaited return to Settler Williams's (now John Boy Jr.'s) house becomes imminent, throngs of people, including members of the security forces, surge toward the house. To facilitate his trip, Matigari seizes a Mercedes-Benz belonging to the adulterous wife of the Minister of Truth and Justice. He evades the dragnet of security forces who are in pursuit of this mysterious and elusive "criminal." The climax of the satire is reached when Matigari's pursuers at long last trap him and are certain of his impending capture.

Matigari's nonviolent approach to finding truth and justice for himself and his people proves increasingly futile, given the state's widespread violent repression of dissent and workers' strikes. He therefore resolves to resume armed resistance in order to establish justice based on truth, which he believes to be an essential cornerstone for the true liberation of his people. Toward the end he seeks to retrieve his AK-47, which he had hidden. However, he is unable to do so due to a trap by the security forces. He manages to elude his pursuers when he drives the car into Williams's house, from which he eventually escapes in the prevailing confusion caused by the car crash and the subsequent explosion and fire. In the ensuing manhunt Guthera is shot and severely wounded, but Matigari carries her as he slips through the security dragnet yet again. The novel concludes with Matigari still intent on resuming his struggle, especially after Macaria has retrieved the AK-47 for Matigari's use.

In sum, the novel is a powerful satire, couched in strong language intended to question the meaning and validity of postcolonial African claims to socialism in the midst of capital accumulations by the few, to democracy under a one-party system, to maintenance of law and order under political repression, to democratic institutions under authoritarian rule. In the Kikuyu . . . version of the novel, for instance, the author questions the democratic nature of the KKK, which is supposed to stand for Kiama Kiria Kirathana (meaning "the ruling party"). In the English translation Wangui wa Goro offers an excellent rendition of the Kikuyu original. Ideally, of course, the novel should be read in both languages for a full appreciation of the richness of Ngugi's latest important contribution to African literature.

Jidlaph Kamoche. *World Literature Today.* 64, 2 (spring 1990), pp. 348–49

Together, *Decolonising the Mind* and *Devil on the Cross* propose different approaches to the novel. First of all, Ngugi insists that a literary invention like "the novel" can be used, regardless of its origins, either to promote and reinforce repressive ideologies or to undo them. Second, he insists that novels can be produced and consumed in elitist or populist ways. Furthermore, Ngugi's essay and narrative suggest that orality can be an idiom out of which writers write and through which they target a specific audience rather than a set of traits or an atmosphere represented by writers to suggest an African identity. These two texts thus challenge the notion of the novel and of orality as essences. . . .

Ngugi depicts language, not surprisingly, as dynamic, differentiated, determined by one's class and one's gender; it is one of several registers of wealth and class. Levels of power in current society can be surmised by the foreign languages one knows and particularly by one's attitude toward them. Thus Wangari, the least powerful of the travelers in *Devil*, speaks only Kikuyu during the story—we guess that she does not speak English or speaks little of it. On the other hand, Mwireri was Mukiraai knows English quite well; he has studied at foreign universities and is schooled in money-making schemes. Gatuiria, the young composer and student intellectual, also mixes English and Kikuyu but wishes, the narrator tells us, that his speech were rid of the foreign tongue. . . . The so-called modern thieves in the forum of the competition—attended by foreigners and for the benefit of these international visitors—speak English, of course. Language, like the number of women, cars, and guns a man owns, is a sign of status. Thus while choice of language and mode of language do not necessarily measure honesty, they are predictors of the dimensions of crime (when crime exists), since they correlate to one's class and access to international institutions: the names of buildings, banks, moneymaking enterprises are all in English. . . .

Now, "oral" language in any written text is obviously neither oral nor—were such a thing possible—a transcript of standard speech, characterized by rhythms, pauses, tones, and unconventional sounds. What is usually meant by the "orality" of . . . Ngugi [is] the proverbs, analogies, and the cadences of phrasing, which literary convention holds to be oral. In the case of *Devil on the Cross*, as Ngugi describes it, the intended audience and the probable means of distribution and consumption of the novel in Kenya seemed to require "oral" language. . . . *Devil* was written to be read aloud for people schooled in oral stories. Here, orality is not "preyed upon," a resource *for* the narrative, inside its frame, "possessed" by it. Oral language is thus not the object of representation that can be read as quaint and *passéiste* [of the past]. Orality here means the language and tradition in which the narrative is articulated, the medium in which Ngugi's audience will hear this story. Intended for telling or reading aloud, *Devil* does not showcase a neat orality. Proverbs, repetitions, riddles, "songs," and so on reveal the addressee and are not uniquely referential. . . .

*Decolonising the Mind* and *Devil on the Cross* suggest . . . that "oral tradition" is not the sign of a coveted set of values; it is rather a set of aesthetic conventions with which Ngugi's audience is conversant and from which he chooses several elements. Just as he chose multivoiced narration in preceding novels, here he chooses proverbs, parables, and the motif of the journey. *Devil* thus gains a particular currency and comprehensibility by associating itself with traditional storytelling, but it does not muster authority from traditional high genres. It cannot in any case rely on the questionable authority outside the protagonist (and, we infer, outside the narratives themselves), for Ngugi's novels proposes a caricature of power. As I read it, *Devil* does not conceive of orality as a source either of authority or of precious authenticity to be held and treasured. It does not use the "oral tradition" as a bulwark to inspire confidence or action by association with a people's past grandeur or wisdom and virtue. It is neither the "source of truth" nor an exemplary quality of African culture to be retreated into or represented textually; rather, it offers verbal means and procedures for constructing and analyzing an issue. *Devil* treats the same issues that are at the heart of other Ngugi texts, but it does so in parables. In so doing, it demonstrates that oral traditions are not synonymous with static codes and principles.

*Devil* is deconstructive and reconstructive in other ways as well. Not only does it take orality out of the past, but . . . it focuses on the constructedness of the order of things, their inner workings and tensions. Ngugi's exposition of the relationship between the Kenyan thieves and international capital is masterful, as is the revelation of their vulnerability in the jealous dispute about belly size and in the thieves' anger at being duped by one of their own who has stolen their unsatisfied wives and offered them counterfeit English schooling for their children. These cleavages in their ranks are analogous to the "appeals to tribe and religion," which the thieves themselves use to divide peasants and workers.

Eileen Julien. *African Novels and the Question of Orality* (Bloomington: Indiana University Press, 1992), pp. 142, 144–46

Like the journey to the city in *Petals of Blood* and the matatu trip in *Devil on the Cross*, the prison in *Matigari* provides a chance for the prisoners to share ideas about the neo-colonial situation in their country. In his drunken stupor, the man arrested for drunkenness lightheartedly comments on the moral barrenness and the hardheartedness of the leaders. The other prisoners include a peasant farmer arrested for selling a bottle of milk without a permit, a man jailed for stealing food, and a third one detained on a vagrancy charge.

Ngugi has endeavored to demonstrate in every possible way that people who get convicted are mainly peasants and workers who commit crimes out of desperation and the need to survive. Through this kind of portrayal Ngugi questions the morality of arresting people who steal because they are hungry while national thieves go unpunished even though their theft has condemned the majority of a whole country to a life of destitution. As in *Devil on the Cross* he also questions the validity of the vagrancy law. As far as Ngugi is concerned this law was instituted by the colonial government so that they could regulate the movement of people from the rural areas to the city. Ngugi objects to the enforcement of a law that was meant to protect the interests of the settler community in an independent country. . . .

Common purpose and circumstances bind the prisoners together and makes them open up to one another. In the spirit of sharing Matigari puts the food he had bought early in the day at the disposal of all the other prisoners. The manner in which Matigari gives out the food and the lighthearted enactment of the Christian ritual of the Last Supper by the drunken prisoner seem to suggest not only the spirit of sharing but the sealing of a covenant that the prison inmates entered into for the liberation of their country from neo-colonial oppression, just as people had done by taking the oath to fight against colonialism:

> And he took the bread and after breaking it he said: This is my body, which I give to you. . . He then took up the cup, and after blessing it he said: And this cup is a testament of the covenant we entered with one another with our blood. Do this to one another until our kingdom comes, through the will of the people (Ngugi, Matigari, 57).

In this novel, Ngugi seems to be viewing religion not just as a tool of oppression or an ideology that has been misused by the elite for their own benefit. In fact, as in his earlier works, he seems to have been able to identify more of those aspects of religion that have some relevance to the struggles of the masses. For example, Guthera's religious attachments helped her resist sexual manipulation by the superintendent. Also, through the enactment of the Last Supper the prisoners were able to renew their determination to fight against neo-colonialism. In both cases we find a strong identification with Ngugi's earlier public statements on religion, especially his speech to members of the East African Presbyterian church in 1972 where he called for a return to the communal values exemplified by St. Peter and other founders of Christianity.

The life story of each prisoner shows the magnitude of the injustice perpetuated by those who have political and economic power as well as their conspiracy to exploit the labor of the poor for the benefit of international capitalism and for their own enrichment. It also illustrates how justice in the land has been distorted by forces of law and order controlled by the same people who are guilty of committing injustice against the poor. . . .

*Matigari* is a novel based on a Gikuyu folktale about a man who went in search of a cure for a certain disease. This man went from one place to another, meeting different people to whom he posed one and the same question. Ngugi has used the same technique in the novel. The plot consists of a quest, first for a house and then for justice and truth. It is through this technique that Ngugi is able to dramatize the betrayed hopes and the continued exploitation of the masses by multinational capitalism. But unlike the man in the folk

story, Matigari never found what he looked for. Ngugi has relied mainly on dialogue and the question and answer method in this novel. The views of the different characters become manifest as they interact. As in *Petals of Blood*, he has employed parables to let characters tell their life stories to one another, to let us know more about their past, and to explain the present and their general world view. The role of the omniscient narrator and the authorial voice is quite minimal in this novel. This makes *Matigari* an open novel because our judgment is not influenced by these elements. We draw meaning from incidents as they are acted out by the characters. Also this novel is not set in any particular country. The reader is presented with events from which he has to find meaning and choose his own setting, which may be anywhere in the African continent or wherever neo-colonialism prevails.

The author has incorporated a variety of songs to indicate both the desire of the masses to subvert the prevailing social order and the attempts of the powers that be and their supporters to sabotage the struggle. For example, the use of circumcision and Mau Mau songs as well as those that convey militancy demonstrates the masses' desire to continue with the struggle until they prevail. There are also songs that call for conformity. Through the songs sung by the professor of parrotology and the editor Ngugi demonstrates some of the repressive techniques used by the neo-colonial government. The radio broadcasts are an important stylistic device. These serve as commentaries on current events in the country and elsewhere. They also highlight some of the repressive and subversive activities going on in Kenya and other parts of the world such as the student revolt in Kenya, the protests and destruction of government property in South Africa, and El Salvador. This technique places the struggle of the Kenyan masses in a global context.

In all the three novels, Ngugi deals with the impact of political independence on African nations, especially on the people of Kenya. His view is that this independence has been usurped by the elite who took over power from the former colonial officials but did not attempt to change the socio-economic and political structures of the colonial era. According to him this class has only used its position to enrich itself at the expense of the masses. Ngugi argues that the retaining of the capitalist economy by those who took over the leadership when his country became independent has left it open to exploitation by both Western nations and the local elite. He shows that this economic system supports theft and sectionalism which is responsible for social disintegration. He illustrates the way cultural values are corrupted and put to the service of those in power and how politics becomes a means to material gain under neo-colonial conditions. Ngugi believes that this helps to perpetuate an economic system that is based on the exploitation of the country's material and human resources. However, he strongly suggests that this exploitative environment can be changed through a joint effort of all the oppressed groups in the community.

Clara Tsabedze. *African Independence from Francophone and Anglophone Voices: A Comparative Study of the Post-Independence Novels by Ngugi and Sembène* (New York: Peter Lang Publishing, 1994), pp. 78–87

The term postcolonial literature is inherently problematic. A useful and generally acceptable definition of this nebulous and diffuse genre appears in the 1989 book, *The Empire Writes Back*.

What each of these [various postcolonial countries'] literatures has in common . . . is that they emerged in their present form out of the experience of colonization and asserted themselves by foregrounding the tension with the imperial power, and by emphasizing their differences from the assumptions (if the imperial culture.

According to this definition, Ngugi wa Thiong'o's book *Matigari* can be considered a definitive postcolonial novel, as it sets a traditional Gikuyu folktale in the context of an unnamed contemporary African country. Ngugi liberally blends his re-telling of that tale with Western cultural and religious ideas. Most notably, he integrates many stories from the Bible, particularly those dealing with the life of Christ, into his version of this traditional African narrative. Additionally, his critique of the postcolonial world relies in large part upon Western Marxist thought and, as postcolonial critic Kwame Appiah notes, places Ngugi both politically and artistically squarely in the camp of "Left modernism." Throughout *Matigari*, Ngugi employs a Marxist, yet distinctly African, perspective, to critique and expose both the overt and subtextual sociopolitical structures that exist in many postcolonial African states. As he meticulously and ironically exposes the true nature of these structures, as well as the intuitions and realms of discourse that perpetuate them, he chips away at their psychosocial power over African society. The Western reader stands accused in his or her own silent complicity with Western (post) imperial activities and attitudes.

In analyzing *Matigari*, it is tempting to try to locate the novel's autobiographical, nonfictional strains and to conclude that Ngugi's mythical country is a thinly disguised rendition of the author's homeland, Kenya. This assumption is only natural, considering the author-activist's own experiences, which have included imprisonment at the hands of a repressive Kenyan regime. However, such reductive historicizing encourages the reader to underestimate Ngugi's project in writing Matigari. He is purposely vague in establishing both the temporal and spatial settings of his novel; he refuses to define where and when his story takes place, insisting in a prefatory song:

This story is imaginary.
The actions are imaginary.
The characters are imaginary.
The country is imaginary—it has no name even.
Reader/listener: may the story take place in the country of
your choice!

If readers disregard that advice, then they may underestimate and, consequently, miss the book's broader political implications. *Matigari* is not the story of one isolated country but a schematized documentation of the entire postcolonial experience. In his novel, Ngugi recounts the way in which Western institutions and codes supplant those that are native to Africa in the service of both the continent's former colonizers and their newly arisen African imitators. In that regard, *Matigari* can be viewed as an abstract philosophical work with both descriptive and prescriptive elements.

The final line of Ngugi's preface, "may the story take place in the country of Your choice," establishes the novelist's narrative double-consciousness. On its surface, the statement appears merely to serve as a framing device to identify and establish the novel's romantic, quasi-allegorical nature. Although the song fulfills that function, it also demonstrates Ngugi's self-consciousness about the divided nature of his audience. That awareness results in the bivocal narrative stance that Ngugi adopts throughout *Matigari*. From the perspective of his Western readership, Ngugi's apparent blessing functions as an oblique accusation. It unhappily recognizes that a sociopolitical apparatus like the one portrayed in *Matigari* may be installed in any third world nation that is targeted by the power brokers of the West. Conversely, from an African perspective the line represents a genuine blessing. Not only does it anticipate the novel's revolutionary conclusion, but it stands as a rallying cry for the "wretched of the earth" to follow Matigari's lead in rebelling—both politically and psychologically—against postcolonial domination.

In *Matigari*, Ngugi explores the various ways in which a postcolonial oligarchy may control and exploit a formerly colonized people. In fact, the book reads like a veritable how-to manual for the installation and maintenance of a postcolonial military dictatorship. The book begins as Ngugi's hero, Matigari ma Njiruungi, returns from what has apparently been an extended guerilla war. After many years of fighting, he has vanquished his longtime foes, Settler Howard Williams and his retainer, John Boy Sr. It quickly becomes obvious that Matigari is an allegorical figure who is meant to embody the spirit of all African freedom fighters. That metonymy is reinforced by many of the character's statements about his personal history, which has been defined entirely by opposition to colonial rule. . . .

Matigari naively assumes that because his former oppressors are dead, all will be right in his homeland. He sees all African driving a luxury car and enjoying Western-style products; and not yet become acquainted with the ways of the postcolonial world, he interprets that scene positively. Soon he comes to understand that many of his countrymen have adopted attitudes and allegiances that are as European as the cars they are driving.

Matigari's initial naivete is not surprising. In fact, it is typical of the way that many Africans, especially African intellectuals, reacted to independence. . . . how a substantial number of African writers perceived and subsequently represented the transition process:

The transfer of power at independence seemed to constitute an event like the storming of the Winter Palace. In common with other progressive intellectuals in the postcolonial era, radical African writers tended to drastically over-value the emancipatory significance of independence.

Matigari sadly learns that although the apparent social order of his country may have changed with political independence, many of the ills of colonialism are still in effect. Through the education of his protagonist, Ngugi hints at his own development both as a postcolonial writer and as a political activist. His artistic and political development is strikingly evident when one compares his early works such as *Weep Not, Child* with his later novels such as *Devil on the Cross* and *Matigari*. The later novels are not only more characteristically postmodern but exhibit a more ironic and, perhaps justifiable cynicism.

[Ngugi critiques] such aspects and mechanisms of the postcolonial state to discredit them and make any future applications less effective. Ngugi's appropriation of Western modes of discourse to further his own political agenda might seem problematic at best, and at worst, directly counterproductive to his task. Moreover, it might seem particularly surprising to encounter well-known Western stories and political strategies in a novel written by the author of the essay "On the abolition of the English department," who has often expressed his opinion that "colonization is only a passing historical feature which can be left behind entirely when 'full Independence' of culture and political organization is achieved.'' However, it would be a mistake to conclude that Ngugi's use of Western subject matter and ideas—particularly Marxism and Christianity—is counterproductive to his revolutionary. Afrocentric aim. In fact, his careful blending of Western and African ideas seems to indicate that in writing Matigari, Ngugi is attempting to create an objective space from which to better consider both cultures. The creation of such a space is an important step for (post) colonial subjects to overcome their ''peripeteia of values.'' Ngugi's development of such a space reflects his own psychological and artistic development. It has been suggested that this evolution may help account for the stylistic and thematic difference between the author's early novels and his more recent works. The earlier works, such as Weep Not, Child, Petals of Blood, and A Grain of Wheat, were penned when the author still used his baptismal name, James. He composed the later novels, such as Matigari and Devil on the Cross, after reverting to his Gikuyu name. Unquestionably, names play an important part in how people both define and express their social identities and their conceptions of themselves.

Despite Ngugi's use of Western stories and ideas, his decision to write Matigari in Gikuyu defines his primary audience as an African one. Although Ngugi uses the Christian story, he does so without foregrounding or endorsing the Eurocentric traditions and practices that are often associated with Christianity. Because the New Testament would be quite familiar to many of his African readers, they would easily engage with Matigari's themes of redemption and rebirth. In addition, Ngugi's Gikuyu audience would relate especially to, and appreciate, the novel because the culture has had a strong messianic tradition that has played an important part in recent Kenyan history. . . .

As a result, the life of Christ becomes a convenient intercultural device and subtext which Ngugi uses wisely in furthering his primarily African agenda. It also allows him to produce a novel that is readily accessibly to Western audiences.

Although Ngugi portrays Matigari as a Christlike savior, ultimately, both writer and hero conclude that Africans must do for themselves rather than relying solely or even primarily on Western religious values and ideals. They reach that conclusion because the Western institutions that espouse Christian values and ideals have traditionally served to propagate colonialism: many of Africa's first and most committed colonizers were Western missionaries. As a result, Matigari renounces his belt of peace and his Christlike role and re-arms himself for a new struggle: to achieve real economic and cultural determinacy for Africans in the postcolonial era. Quite significantly, it is an African parable that leads Matigari to his decision to fight: ''When the worker in metals returned from where he practiced his skill far away from home, and found an ogre starving his expectant wife, did he send the ogre a peace greetings? Did he not first sharpen his spear?.'' Just as Matigari renounces the belt of peace once it has lost its social relevance, Ngugi employs Christianity only so far as it meshes with and furthers his African agenda.

If it seems that Ngugi is either subverting or supplanting many of the Christian ideals and Biblical stories that he appropriates for use in Matigari, he may be doing so to challenge and shock his Eurocentric readers. Ngugi announces that in future relations with their former colonizers, Africans will be happy to appropriate useful elements from Western culture but will reject those elements that prove either nonessential or oppressive. In doing so, Ngugi

cannot help tossing stones at those who would claim Christianity as a white, guiltless, and exclusively Western religion. He taunts such readers by claiming that the Second Coming will have a decidedly African flavor, a possibility that is beyond the scope of many Western imaginations. ''Where is the oldest church in the world? In Ethiopia, Africa. When he [Jesus] was a baby, where did he flee to? Egypt, Africa. What has happened before can happen again.'' Furthermore, Ngugi chastises his Western readers by suggesting that when Christ returns, it will be for the express purpose of liberating the people of Africa from their postcolonial oppressors. Such rhetoric is a powerful weapon as it uses some of the West's most sacred religious criteria to establish Western guilt stemming from a history of colonial and postcolonial practices. In this regard, Ngugi's novel can be read as a warning to those people who would continue to exploit the continent and its people. Matigari suggests that such attempts will not be tolerated and, if necessary, will be met with appropriate and legitimate violence.

However, the novel stands primarily as a powerful call for Africans to reject the role of a people enthralled by either overt colonialism or any of its newer and more oblique guises. Ngugi encourages his African readers to strive for real independence. He does so partly by actively challenging any form of discourse that foregrounds while, Western cultural codes and seeks to label black African culture as atypical or aberrant. Only through such a self-conscious and politically savvy examination of the (post) colonial condition may subjects reverse ''peripeteia.''

Steven Tobias. Critique: Studies in Contemporary Fiction. 38, 3 (spring 1997), pp. 163–76

BIBLIOGRAPHY

The Black Hermit, 1962; Weep Not, Child, 1964; The River Between, 1965; This Time Tomorrow, 1966; A Grain of Wheat, 1967; Homecoming: Essays on African and Caribbean Literature, Culture, and Politics, 1972; Secret Lives, and Other Stories, 1974; Petals of Blood, 1977; The Trial of Dedan Kimathi (with Micere Githae Mugo), 1977; Mtawa Mweusi, 1978; Caitaani mutharaba-ini (Devil on the Cross) 1980; Writers in Politics: Essays, 1981; Detained: A Writer's Prison Diary, 1981; Njamba Nene na mbaathi i mathagu, 1982; I Will Marry When I Want (with Ngugi wa Mirii), 1982; Barrel of a Pen: Resistance to Repression in Neo-Colonial Kenya, 1983; Decolonising the Mind: The Politics of Language in African Literature, 1986; Writing against Neocolonialism, 1986; Matigari ma Njiruungi, 1986; Njambas Nene no Chiubu King'ang'i, 1986; Njamba Nene and the Flying Bus, 1989; Njamba Nene's Pistol, 1989; Moving the Center: The Struggle for Cultural Freedoms, 1992; Writers in Politics: A Re-engagement with Issues of Literature and Society, 1997; Penpoints, Gunpoints, and Dreams: Toward a Critical Theory of the Arts and the State of Africa, 1998

# NTIRU, Richard (1946–)
## Uganda

[Richard] Ntiru is a very society-conscious poet, and is always exploring and exposing something of the dichotomy that exists in the human situation, something of the shadow between the idea and the reality—in our attitudes and intentions and wishes and performance. On the whole he is much more in control of his material and expression in the shorter poem; in the longer poem he has a tendency to disappear into imprecision.

Ntiru's indebtedness to other literatures is a conscious one. There is undisguised borrowing from other poets: significantly from T. S. Eliot, but also from [William] Blake, Claude McKay, and others. Sometimes it is for the sake of parody, with very refreshing effect when it works, as in ''Ojukwu's Prayer'' (compared with Claude McKay's ''If We Must Die''). In ''Chorus of Public Men,'' which is modeled on T. S. Eliot's ''The Hollow Men,'' Ntiru presents us with dissatisfied, worn-out men who are much more concrete than Eliot's shadowy personages. The social setting is much more immediate, and for the East African reader the poem may easily have more appeal than its prototype.

> Timothy Wangusa. In Eldred Durosimi Jones, ed. *African Literature Today*. 6 (1973), p. 50

[In *Tensions*, the] content, the themes, are African, but it is exceptional to find a particular atmosphere or sense of locale. Where in [J. P.] Clark and [Gabriel] Okara we have the rivers of Ijawland, where in Kofi Awoonor the Atlantic visibly washes the coasts of Ghana, where [Jared] Angira and [Onyango] Ogutu constantly reflect the shape and feel of Western Kenya and where Okot [p'Bitek], [Okello] Oculi, and [Joseph] Buruga reflect the rolling grasslands of Uganda, in the early Ntiru all this is lacking. The home landscape has either made no impression on him (which is unthinkable) or it represents an area of his memory drowned for the moment in a flood of academic and philosophic matter.

Nor does the humorous find much room in Ntiru's work. The mirth of a [Wole] Soyinka in his comic mode or the bitter laughter of an Okot or Angira are not heard. For Ntiru life seems a gloomy, rather joyless passage through time. There are serious flaws in man's vision and it would be immoral to laugh and let them pass. If modern man can wallow in wealth while his brother starves, he must be told about it; and this is how Ntiru's art is defined, for its basis is moral rather than sensual, its urge is to censure rather than to celebrate. Modern man is discarding a joyful response to the mystery of birth and cultivating the murderous practice of ripping children from the womb. He must therefore be upbraided for it. The world failed to understand the justice of the Biafran cause and must therefore be scolded.

Yet according to Ntiru's ''Portrait of the Little Self,'' neither the poet nor his censure can change much, for this piece gives us a picture of frustrated ambition, cancelled initiative, useless speculation, and a web of those tensions implied in the volume's title. The poet can neither laugh nor cry to any effect. He can neither address society with profit nor usefully stay silent. What remains, according to the poem, is for the artist to lie in a narrow bed and contemplate the ''silence beyond silence'' of the grave. . . .

Ntiru is better elsewhere and it would be unfair to suggest that this poem is typical of *Tensions* as a whole. The more tangibly human, earthy subjects suit him better, even if he believes that his strengths run towards a more abstract style of verse. One example is ''The Happiness of a Mother,'' written ''for aborters and abortionists who take Malthus seriously.'' The joy of birth is described as something at once intensely private and personal, yet social too, and the point is made that life, even crippled life, is always better than the tomb. . . .

The image of poverty amidst luxury is apt to spark a strong response in Ntiru. The language of ''The Pauper'' is concrete and visual, and the whole portrait is edged with a coloring of human sympathy. The poor man leans ''on a leafless tree / Nursing the jiggers that shrivel'' his bottom. He trudges on ''horny pads'' ''Gullied like the soles of modern shoes,'' all under the eye of an inscrutable God. . . .

''Morning Arrows,'' dedicated to Okello Oculi, upbraids the sun for unveiling each day a world filled with pain and frustration, shining a fierce light on every what that scars mankind's face. This is a good imitation of the hectoring Oculian style, but gaining from its control under the reins of Ntiru's discipline. The rough and tumble energy is here, the bold phrasing and repetition; yet the poem enjoys a restraint, a submission to discipline and decorum that makes this essentially an Ntiru poem.

> Adrian Roscoe. *Uhuru's Fire: African Literature East to South* (Cambridge: Cambridge University Press, 1977), pp. 108, 110–11

The poetry of Richard Ntiru ranges over satire of situation, invective and raillery, ironic praise, direct moral exhortation, elegies and laments, disquisitions on love (rather than love lyrics), and mystical, symbolic, and prophetic scenes. Like Taban lo Liyong, Ntiru has a wide-ranging acquaintance with world literature, both imaginative and didactic. Like Okello Oculi, he expresses disgust for institutions and people as he lampoons them. Like Christopher Okigbo he aspires to a mystic communion with a symbolic virgin. . . .

The objects of his satire and castigation are both social and metaphysical. He rails against the venality of politicians, civil servants, large corporations, and all those who seek to control and oppress the human spirit. But he also expresses dissatisfaction with the gods for their indifference to suffering and injustice. The best of his poems are probably those that present a single scene of suffering or oppression and those that employ an anaphoric rhetoric to execrate abuses—that is, the poems that come closest to [David] Rubadiri models. The weakest are the Oculian diatribes that wander in focus and oscillate in tone.

''Introduction'' is a good example of the narrative vignette. Its satiric object is the person who emphasizes status and appearance rather than worth and performance. Like many of Ntiru's works it is cast in the form of a dramatic monologue, spoken in a rather irritable, exasperated tone of voice. ''The Latest Defector'' is another vignette in monologue, this time more abstract in its diction and less sharp in its visual details. Its satiric target is the hypocrisy of sexual relations, with perhaps also the hint of a political application. ''The Pauper'' is addressed to a representative pauper, but more as a literary fiction than as a mimetic re-creation of an actual encounter. The satiric target is multiple: the godhead, society, tourists, politicians, and the author himself, for all are guilty of knowledge and even inquisitiveness unmatched by practical reform. . . .

''Ojukwu's Prayer,'' dating from the time of the Biafran War, is one of the best of the ''literary fiction'' type of dramatic monologues. . . . The structure is filled in with images of pseudo-philanthropic gestures, increasing in intensity from throwing a bare bone to a dog to being slaughtered by Russian bombs. One of the charitable gestures is the supply of high-protein manufactured food by Western relief agencies. This ill-informed policy is savagely ridiculed in ''''Formula Two,'''' a vivid descriptive account of the operation of relief agencies in Biafra. . . . The infilling images are of bones and skeletons as the poem builds up a scene of men, women, and children—or, rather, women with children in the front, sullen men resentful of their ignominy behind—lining up for "their rationed taste / of the wholesome high-protein relief meal." . . .

Ntiru's longer, more ambitious poems are less successful. They employ the high-pitched, strained tones of Okello Oculi combined sometimes with the surrealistic allegory of Bahadur Tejani. The allegory is fitful, being conveyed largely in isolated patches such as—to take examples from "The Secret of the Skeleton"—"the last hurdle / which is also the first hurdle / in the circular race" or "The Watchman of Dark Cave between Light and Darkness / lifted his Rod of Seven Eyes" or "Who would dally at the River of Continuity." Ntiru's characteristic intensity and his horror of sexual violence emerge strongly from this poem. But his imagemaking power is insufficient to sustain the kind of allegory of life and death that he aspires to. On its smaller scale, the failure is akin to that of Gabriel Okara in "The Fisherman's Invocation." But it is an honorable failure insofar as Ntiru is constantly pushing beyond the limits of what he knows he can accomplish.

> K. L. Goodwin. In G. D. Killam, ed. *The Writing of East and Central Africa* (London: Heinemann, 1984), pp. 219–21

Richard Ntiru's intense poetic career provides the reader of modern East African poetry written in English with a very good example of the versatility of this tradition. He, like most of his contemporaries of this region, handles a rich variety of themes which range from the personal and descriptive to the near-abstract which, in his hands, find expression through fitting pseudo-existentialist linguistic structures. But most importantly, Ntiru is a poet who seems to be irresistibly attracted to the extra-personal public events which impinge on the lives of both his contemporaries and society at large. Thus, basically, in spite of the wide and varied thematic territory within which his imagination operates, the unmistakable poetic forte of Ntiru is the sympathetic appraisal of the social and political realities of his society. This focus is always directed toward the manner in which the new sociopolitical order ushered in by *uhuru* or political freedom from colonialism has affected or failed to affect the fortunes of the generality of the people in the society. . . .

The beauty of Ntiru's poetry lies mainly in some specific areas. In the first place, he is able to explore with a protean turn of mind each new topic he decides to focus his attention on in each new poem. This versatility he is able to achieve through a constant correlation of imagery, music, and thought, the three chief means by which, in the words of Ezra Pound, the language of poetry could be charged "with meaning to the utmost possible degree." In addition, his poetry displays both a keen ear for rhythm and a mature sense of the musical potential of words. All these qualities give the reader of the poet's work a pleasurable sense of a harmonious blend of euphony and sense.

> A. Rasheed Yesufu. *Commonwealth Essays and Studies.* 8, 2 (spring 1986), pp. 94–95

Ntiru's dominant vision of human nature is that of futility, loneliness, insecurity, and ultimate meaninglessness. This view of human life in society is definitely influenced by his knowledge of modern European literary attitudes. This fact creates an initial problem for one who comes to his work with the singleminded expectation of finding the more popular perception of man held by his contemporaries in East Africa. The question an uninformed reader of modern African literature is bound to ask is, "Is it actually compatible to the African psyche and social nature to feel a sense of futility, loneliness, and insecurity in the midst of the much-avowed communalistic spirit of Africa?" The answer to this question is yes, because the society about which Ntiru writes is not the pristine type which thrived on a communalistic ethos. Rather, it is a world similar to those portrayed by Ayi Kwei Armah in *The Beautyful Ones Are Not Yet Born*, by Kofi Awoonor in *This Earth My Brother*, and by other writers who mirror the modern soul in its perennial confrontation with the disillusionment of its time. It is also a society which, according to [critic Rosette] Francis, has undergone "an accelerated degree of change that produces profound alterations and tensions." These changes in society, the way man reacts to them, and how he now behaves toward his fellow men account for his sense of futility, loneliness, and insecurity. Since, as [Alexander] Pope remarked in *An Essay on Man*, the proper study of mankind is man, Ntiru studies man in his society to investigate the actual nature of the human mind.

In order to give man a local dimension compatible with his reflection of his society, Ntiru often operates along a line similar to that of his contemporary Jared Angira. However, in place of Angira's bellicose Marxist dichotomy, Ntiru sees men in his society as divided into two economic classes. These classes are not exclusive, since one could easily move from the lower to the higher one, as in "Flashback." But it is always clear that he sympathizes with the "paupers" of his society. Hence, in spite of the absence of the revolutionary zeal of Angira's language, the tone of Ntiru's work is never mistaken in its purely moral concern. He is concerned not with revolution but with the exposition of human failure and the need to reverse its trend, possibly through a spiritual retreat. . . .

Ntiru . . . sees man's ultimate state as loneliness, since man's basic motivation in his interactions is neither love of others nor selflessness. The ultimate expression of this innate quality of man is made in "To a Late Rich Miser." In this poem we see that even the man of wealth will experience loneliness in his final hours on earth and eventually leave the world alone. The loneliness of the "late rich miser" here is symbolic of that of all men. He is someone who has enjoyed the gregarious pomp that high society can offer; but the time comes when all that becomes immaterial. At this time everyone—from the family to "the poor folk that has wealthed [him]"—has to withdraw physically. The miser, however, has a way of alleviating the pangs of loneliness. He thinks about his wealth, but eventually everything (including this) will slip away and leave him alone. . . .

It is this loneliness of man that Ntiru further captures in his image, in "The Pauper," of the pauper who, even though he is in the city center where beautiful cars reflect him and which is filled up with "beautiful people" and tourists, is still lonely. He sits, "alone on hairless goatskins" as the busy world hurries by oblivious of his plight. Ntiru seems to say that he is also the quintessential man.

Ntiru expresses the futility of human life by focusing on the inexorability of fate. He sees man as continuously progressing toward his predetermined fate; there is virtually nothing he can do to change the course of events already in motion as well as those which are bound to come to pass. These are the points which the poet makes in "The Prophecy." By the title he seems to suggest that human life is something of a vindication of a divine prophecy for man; that what constitutes one's fate is already part of a plan known to the gods. Hence he sees it as futile for man to attempt to control, in any way, his own or his fellow human beings' fate. . . .

Ntiru's poetry is that of the human condition; and in his moral sympathy with the seemingly hopeless situation of man in his world, the poet's vision is ultimately a bright one. However, one needs to trudge through a verbal terrain of disillusioning details in order to arrive at the thrill of a hopeful future which will be achieved through the sacrifice made by man. It is with regard to this dominant view that his work, in spite of the uncomfortable current of skepticism which runs through it, should be seen as that of a man who is in love with men and his society. In this perspective, his vignettes of degeneracy on the personal and societal levels becomes his own way of recommending an opposite way of life for a man; and his Heraclitian vision, predicated upon a fire of strife and tension, leads man to a vista of a New Jerusalem.

> A. Rasheed Yesufu. *Ariel.* 18, 3 (July 1987), pp. 32–33, 37–39, 45

BIBLIOGRAPHY
*Tensions*, 1971

# NWAPA, Flora (1931–1993)
## Nigeria

In 1966, Flora Nwapa wrote *Efuru*, the first novel to be published by a woman writer in Nigeria, followed shortly afterwards by *Idu* and more recently by a collection of short stories. The first novel is set in rural Igboland. Efuru is a beautiful, wealthy and respected woman who, however, cannot bear children successfully or be happy in marriage. Her only child dies in infancy while her first husband deserts her and she feels forced to leave her second one. The reason for this unhappiness is that she has been chosen by a river goddess to be her companion and, as far as earthly companions are concerned, she must remain alone. . . .

Efuru is portrayed as a very independent character. Unconcerned with her parents' opinions, she chooses her own husband, a young man who has not even enough money for her dowry, and runs away to live with him. "Efuru and I have agreed to be husband and wife and that is all that matters." Having married the man of her choice, Efuru does not stop there and is no picture of meek obedience. She refuses to go to the farm and, instead, decides to trade. In contrast with her, Adizua, her husband, is almost a failure. He is so unsuccessful at farming that he joins his wife in trading but, once again, he is no good and Efuru is the brain behind the business. In every detail of her life, Efuru shows surprising determination and independence of character. She does not think twice about being seen everywhere with her husband, thus refusing the traditional pattern whereby the husband walks in front while the wife walks behind. In order to go trading, she decides to employ a maid to look after her baby daughter who is only eight months old. . . .

With Eneberi, her second husband, Efuru acts as an adviser. When he contemplates building a house of his own, she refuses,

explaining that a canoe would be better at that stage. Later, she is so broad-minded that she accepts Eneberi's child from another woman under her roof, and she does not even blame him when she discovers that he has spent a few months in jail. It is not only in her marital relationship that Efuru shows surprising independence. She so believes in science and technique that she takes Nwosu, her maid's father, to a doctor-friend to have an operation on his male organ. Here again, Flora Nwapa carefully describes Nwabata, Nwosu's traditional wife, all in tears, refusing to allow her husband to go to [a] hospital where he will most certainly be poisoned by white witchcraft.

The complexity of Efuru lies in the fact that, although she shows such determination, she still remains strongly attached to traditions. She never questions polygamy ("only a bad woman would like to be married alone by her husband") and goes out of her way to find a second and third wife for Eneberi. But is it really logical that she should be more upset by her husband's absence at her father's funeral (i.e., an offense against tradition) than by the discovery of the reason for his absence (his imprisonment on a charge of theft)? If she is so levelheaded about taking a man to have an operation on his male organ, should she really be so upset at having bad dreams that she runs to her father who in turn takes her to see a *dibia*? This contradiction can only be accepted as representative of the dichotomy in Efuru's (and Flora Nwapa's) mind. As far as the physical world is concerned, she can accept Western techniques and progress; but as for the spiritual one, she does not get rid of her traditional habits and beliefs. Flora Nwapa makes it very clear, however, that she does not fully accept these powers of the *dibias*, since one of them is obviously mistaken in pronouncing Efuru guilty of adultery, which brings about the catastrophe and destroys her life. But the biggest contradiction is that Efuru, for all her qualities and gifts, considers her life as valueless since she fails to have a child. She can deliberately and willfully decide to leave her husband and therefore live by herself, but she cannot follow the logical consequences. She cannot find in herself enough resources to counterbalance her sterility and never thinks of devoting her energies to something else. To ask her to do so would be asking too much. If a woman rejects the view that the "birth of a child is a crowning glory," is she still an African? Flora Nwapa categorically refuses the cliché of the weak and obedient female slave, mere appendix to her husband's life; but she cannot go to the end of her analysis. The main objection, however, is that by making her heroine unique among her fellow villagers and by reporting the unanimously hostile and adverse comments of the other women on every one of Efuru's decisions and actions, Flora Nwapa gives, in fact, a disturbing picture of narrow-mindedness, superstition, malevolence, greed and fear in traditional Africa—a picture which might be contrary to what she has thought to defend.

> Maryse Condé. *Presence Africaine.* 82 (1972), pp. 133–36

Flora Nwapa's *Idu*, like her previous novel [*Efuru*], deals with the culture and life-ways of the Igbo and more specifically the fishing and farming residents of Oguta, who find occupation and pleasure in the Oguta Lake, and to whom the "fantasies" of the "woman of the lake" are a reality. These are the people about whom Flora Nwapa writes in these novels, but this is not enough to make her an authentic Igbo novelist. An Igbo novel (or Igbo literature as a whole) emanates from Igbo life and language. It embraces the social, political, economic, and emotional forms under which Igbo life is manifest. The evaluation of an Igbo work of art is essentially an appreciation of the validity of content as well as the appropriateness of technique. What the writer says about the Igbo is as important as how he says it. Neither alone can constitute his success, but the failure in both could mean his failure as an artist. Flora Nwapa's *Idu* is a successful Igbo novel by both standards. . . .

The realism of her themes and her ever-increasing sensitive use of language are two of Flora Nwapa's most enduring qualities as a novelist. Of the former, one might tend to say she is overpreoccupied with the concern for children in marriage in an age when the fear of overpopulation is acute and some ecologists are talking about "zero population growth"; but then among the Igbo (and I fear most Africans) "What we are all praying for is children. What else do we want if we have children?" One might tend to find Flora Nwapa's characters too talkative and gossipy, and her Ajanupas and Onyemurus too boring by virtue of the same organ that gives them distinction—their tongue—but these novels are mostly about women by a woman, and one should not take lightly the line in which Nwapa says, "You know women's conversation never ends."

> Ernest N. Emenyonu. In Eldred Durosimi Jones, ed. *African Literature Today.* 7 (1975), pp. 28, 32

Whereas [Ama Ata] Aidoo's short stories are based on the skillful manipulation of diverse narrative forms, Flora Nwapa's technique as short-story writer is more uniform. This uniformity is not really a shortcoming in the work of this Nigerian writer. *This Is Lagos, and Other Stories* actually owes much of its undeniable power to a consistently spare and taut style skillfully adapted to the writer's intense irony and to a brooding sense of tragedy throughout the collection. . . .

On the whole it appears that Nwapa's very choice of genre, as well as her choice of techniques within the selected genre, are interwoven with her most fundamental perspectives. Her perception of contemporary life in urban Nigeria demands a short-story format, one that does not depend to any significant degree on the kind of oral modes that are so integral to much of Aidoo's short fiction. It is a format which reflects the largely literate, Western middle-class world within which her women move (as in the case of Bisi or Amedi). That literate world's dominance in the lives of older, rural-oriented women like Mama Eze is emphasized by the uniformly literate method which describes *their* experiences. In Nwapa's hands the short story seems especially appropriate for brief, even deliberately unfinished glimpses of urban life. Thus many of the stories leave their protagonists in the middle of seemingly insoluble crises or, at best, in the face of disturbing and unanswerable questions. Taken together, these suggestively abbreviated vignettes suggest the fragmentary nature of the social experiences out of which they arise. In addition, the spare language which Nwapa sustains throughout suggests that thinness of spirit and that limited humaneness which the stories themselves attribute to the society as a whole.

The rural and largely traditional world of the older Nigeria, as it is envisaged by Nwapa, seems to require a different style—an expansive use of language reflecting the formal richness and ornate modes of traditional oral cultures. It seems to demand the detailed duplication of those social conventions intrinsic to everyday relationships in that milieu of elaborately defined roles. When Nwapa turns to that milieu, she selects the genre that most easily accommodates an expansive language and elaborate design, for these features reflect the complexities of a society that is always more ambiguous (fulfilling in some respects, while limiting in others) than the general meagerness of urban life.

> Lloyd W. Brown. *Women Writers in Black Africa* (Westport, Connecticut: Greenwood Press, 1981), pp. 122, 134–35

Flora Nwapa . . . arrived on the [Nigerian] literary scene at a time when it was almost completely dominated by men. She was at first received with mixed feelings. Some received her works with admiration while others considered them as an unwarranted imitation of what the men were doing. It took some time for the works to be considered on their own merit. When finally this was done, it was discovered that she was writing in depth, at least initially, on topics which were better handled by a woman, even if her methods and approaches were not significantly different from those employed by other writers. Flora Nwapa's topics have been to some extent unique to her. Her reputation as a writer rests solidly on her achievements in *Efuru* and *Idu*. In these works she concentrates on marriage, mother care, home and family life, the status of women in traditional society, the hierarchical structure of Igbo society, and the place of the gods in the maintenance of peace and order in tribal communities. She creates a self-contained world in which her villagers live a full life based on their own customs and beliefs, with only minimum influence from outside sources.

She has since written two shorter novels—*Never Again* and *One Is Enough*, and also has to her credit two collections of short stories—*This Is Lagos [and Other Stories]* and *Wives at War [and Other Stories]*. These latter works have benefited from her personal experiences of the Nigerian Civil War, especially as they concern her hometown, Ugwuta. She writes with insight on the ravages of war—the loss of men and property, the psychological effect on the human environment and the abrupt large-scale disruption of a way of life. She also takes a great deal of interest in the moral laxity, social decadence, and the craze for wealth which result from the mass movement of people from their secure homebase to the comparative insecurity of the city. The point at issue is usually so well dramatized that the social risks being taken by groups and individuals become obvious for all to see. So effectively has the novelist diversified her literary interests in recent years that her versatility as a creative artist is no longer in doubt. . . .

*Never Again* is devoted to the ravages of war, especially its effect on human beings. In particular Flora Nwapa concentrates on the capture of Ugwuta by the federal troops during the Nigerian Civil War and its recapture by the Biafran soldiers. The work owes its dramatic impact to the way the author uses incidents at Ugwuta to highlight the nature and extent of the conflict between the two sides. Ugwuta is important because of its nearness to the Uli is airstrip through which Biafra gets its supply of ammunition and other materials. Uli is the only reliable line of communication with the outside world. Once Ugwuta is captured, it will require only a little more effort on the part of federal troops to take Uli, which is so essential for the resistance. Given this importance, it is not surprising that the author devotes so much attention to the people's resolve not to see Ugwuta fall. . . .

Flora Nwapa successfully dramatizes the human dimensions of the war. The painful experiences of Kate, her husband Chudi, and members of their family are typical of the hardship which the war brings upon the citizens. They have fled Enugu, Onitsha, Port Harcourt, and Elele, and are thoroughly tired of moving from place to place. Now they are required without much notice to flee from Ugwuta. Kate and Chudi necessarily become skeptical about the ability of the secessionist army to contain the onslaught of the federal troops. For this they are called saboteurs by their friend Kal, who threatens to hand them over to the army. The situation is so confused that it is difficult to know when it is safe to talk or whom it is safe to talk to. . . .

The author leaves no one in any doubt that she regards the war as a mad pursuit by both sides. She takes a balanced view of the whole affair. War brings untold hardship to people and ought to be avoided at all costs. The leaders on both sides should have adopted a rational approach to a peaceful settlement. In her view secession hardly solves a political problem because "there was already oppression even before the young nation was able to stand on her feet." On the other hand, Nigerian soldiers should not have attacked Biafra with such brutal force. That only makes matters worse. Consideration ought to have been given to the close affinity between the two sides. . . .

In *One Is Enough* the novelist continues to show interest in home and family life. The emphasis here, as elsewhere, is on the disastrous effect on the woman of childlessness in marriage in a traditional society. Amaka gets into trouble not because she is a failure as a wife but because, after six years of marriage, she has not been able to produce a child. She obviously possesses the sterling qualities which should ordinarily endear a woman to a man. She is well domesticated and works hard to please Obiora and his people. She is successful in business and is willing to use her wealth to make her household comfortable. Furthermore, she is a good family woman and regards married life as honorable and sacred. . . . Unfortunately these qualities are not enough in the circumstances. Without a child, Amaka cannot command the respect of the villagers. Nor does she have their sympathy or consideration. She is, in fact, rated lower in their esteem than the woman who has two children for Obiora but who "did not know her right from her left" and who "behaved atrociously and embarrassed Obiora." This other woman is clearly idiotic and a total misfit. Even so, she is brought to the house to displace Amaka. When Obiora eventually realizes his folly and wants Amaka back, he is prevented by force of tradition from carrying out his legitimate wishes. So little importance is attached to the element of love in marriage. The marriage between Obiora and Amaka might have succeeded if the villagers had not held a childless woman to such merciless ridicule.

Oladele Taiwo. *Female Novelists of Modern Africa* (New York: St. Martin's Press, 1984), pp. 47–48, 61–65

[In *One Is Enough*] Amaka . . . is apparently unable to have children after six years of marriage. One day, she discovers that her husband has been keeping a mistress who has already borne him two sons. . . . [She] decides to leave him and make a new life for herself; but Amaka . . . is sufficiently her own woman to realize a fully independent existence. In this she is supported by her mother and her aunt, both of whom inculcate in her a sense of her own worth as a woman. Even before Amaka gets married, her aunt puts her off an unsuitable prospect by reminding her that, "'What is

important is not marriage as such, but children, being able to have children, being a mother. Have your children, be able to look after them, and you will be respected,'" and then proceeds to illustrate the truth of her claim by reference to her own experience. . . . And after Amaka leaves her husband, her mother recounts the good sense of her sister when she found herself in a similar predicament. . . . So Amaka travels to Lagos, sets herself up as a contractor, and makes a fortune. Eventually she meets a man she desires. It happens that he is a priest, but they consummate their relationship anyway and she becomes pregnant. He begs her to marry him but at first she refuses. He leaves the priesthood for her sake and mobilizes her family to plead on his behalf. She eventually yields; but before they can go through with the marriage, he rediscovers his vocation after he miraculously escapes death in a motor accident.

The convolutions of the plot in the second half of the novel are an unnecessary complication. There is no intrinsic reason why her lover should be a priest; there is even less reason why he should then go through fire in order to understand, at last, that he cannot marry the mother of his child. But the point about the affair is to make Amaka pregnant. We have it on the testimony of both Amaka's mother and her aunt that this is all that men are good for, a sentiment which Amaka herself, following her own disastrous marriage, takes sufficiently to heart to act in the way that she subsequently does. Almost any man would have sufficed, provided only that he met certain basic requirements. Why she should choose a priest for her purposes is itself a mystery; why she should then encourage his feelings towards her to the extent that he endures purgatory on her behalf is a betrayal of the moral universe the author has herself generated through the testimonies of the mother and the aunt.

"In her position, what does she want from a man?," Amaka's mother asks her rhetorically in respect to Ayo, the only one of her daughters with enough sense to take what she needs and then "gracefully" go her own way. Indeed, what did Amaka want from a man whose life was already complicated by the rigorous demands of a vocation which in any case precluded his assigned role in the scheme of things? In a word, nothing; and yet the author complicates what should have been a relatively straightforward story that achieves the same end towards which it was already moving. That said, however, *One Is Enough* . . . is among the few Nigerian novels which subvert the otherwise male-dominated view of the Nigerian society, at least as far as the majority of the novelists— male *and* female—are concerned.

Adewale Maja-Pearce. *A Mask Dancing: Nigerian Novelists of the Eighties* (London: Hans Zell, 1992), pp. 153–55

Flora Nwapa in *Women Are Different* dramatizes [the] notion of fulfillment as four female characters are portrayed through the presentation of their individual attitudes towards achieving self-satisfaction. The novel also enhances Nwapa's reputation, which . . . critic [Oladele Taiwo] points out when he says that "she has moved from the discussion of weighty traditional matters to topics relating to the social complications of modern life." This adherence to complications of modern life is not derogatory, for the society has evolved from the traditional to the modern and "the women we now meet in novels by women are often educated and have sophisticated expectations of life both in the town and country." The four major characters in *Women Are Different* are educated, and they possess sophisticated expectations. However, they occasionally contrast and even contradict themselves through their decisions, aims, and aspirations; but these contrasts coalesce to present those vital issues that militate against the mental and social development of women. . . .

Flora Nwapa has clearly worked out for herself a theory of life which explains the tribulations confronting women in the society. It may be too early [to expect] from her a consistently rational theory, since it may take time to evolve a theory of life, but it is clear that she has through this notion of fulfillment explained many of her convictions. The society may be unprincipled, but she is not prepared to accept a view which has been widely accepted if it contradicts the essence of womanhood. Moreover, Nwapa has shown that fulfillment can only be derived through the trust and honesty in human affairs which men have invariably lacked. The women who people the novel *Women Are Different* are thus portrayed as an exploited, group of people whose ideals are often shattered by insensitive partners. The novelist thus insists that for the society to progress all instances of exploitation, even in emotional affairs, must be eliminated in order to douse the flash points of conflicts.

Ezenwa-Ohaeto. *Neohelicon*. 19, 1 (1992), pp. 323–24, 332

[Nwapa's] writing is situated outside of conventional male narrative history; she chooses to engage neither with the manly adventures and public displays of patriarchal authority described by male writers from her community nor with the narrative conventions of their accounts. Instead she concentrates, and at length, on what was incidental or simply contextual to male action—domestic matters, politics of intimacy.

In both *Efuru* and *Idu*, Nwapa's interest is in the routines and rituals of everyday life specifically within women's compounds. Women press into Nwapa's narrative as speakers, actors, decision-makers, brokers of opinion and market prices, and unofficial jurors in their communities. But Nwapa's specific intervention as a writer goes beyond her interest in women subjects. What also distinguishes her writing from others in the ''Igbo school'' are the ways in which she has used choric language to enable and to empower her representation, creating the effect of a women's verbal presence within her text, while bringing home her subject matter by evoking the vocality of women's everyday existence.

Though it may have attracted a certain amount of negative comment, the apparent lack of conventional novelistic complexity in *Efuru* and *Idu*, I would argue, far from being a deficiency, instead clears the space for the elaboration of another kind of narrative entirely—a highly verbalized collective women's biography—''transsubjective, anonymous,'' transgressive, a narrative method which bears comparison with Zora Neale Hurston's re-creation of porchside comment and of gossip on the road. . . .

Nwapa thus extends the boundaries of the African novel to include the women's side of the compound, a domain of village life which writers like [Elechi] Amadi have neglected for reasons not only of patriarchal lack of interest but also perhaps (a fact not given sufficient attention) of ignorance. Nwapa refracts a women's presence into her text through creating the conceit of women representing themselves in voice. Dialogue dominates in both novels, especially in *Idu*, as numbers of partly curious, partly phatic, and frequently anonymous women's voices meet, interact with, and interpellate one another. This vocality, rambling and

seemingly unstoppable, pulls against the confinements of the women's lives—their market rivalries, their anxieties about husbands, families, and children. Therefore, if, as Nwapa portrays it, though not always overtly, male values in the society remain normative, women's talk can be interpreted not only as a way of life but as a mode of self-making. The impression of the fullness and autonomy of women's lives which Nwapa creates must remain partially qualified by their acquiescence in patriarchal views and values. Yet, at the same time, in their discourse, even as they speak, not only do the village women share their woes and confirm female bonds, they also transpose their lives into a medium which they control. The reader is made privy to the women representing and so, in effect, re-creating their lives in speech.

Elleke Boehmer. In Susheila Nasta, ed. *Motherlands* (New Brunswick: Rutgers University Press, 1992), pp. 11–12, 14–15

Nwapa's reflections on the role of women in both precolonial and modern Nigerian society place women at ''the heart of the turmoil of their continent,'' as Maryse Condé notes. From rural women such as Efuru and Idu to the new urbanites Soha and Amaku, these women make choices about their lives, taking what they can from both the traditional and modern cultures to try to forge a life for themselves and their communities.

Of the early writers in anglophone African literature, Flora Nwapa has been perhaps the least acknowledged; probably this lack of attention has a simple explanation: Nwapa is a woman writing about the lives of women, a situation that makes her even further removed from the attention of the literary mainstream than the already marginalized male African writers. With new approaches to African literature and with more women critics, Nwapa's works—particularly her first two novels, *Efuru* and *Idu*—are receiving more of the recognition they deserve. She is continuing to work with her publishing house, Tana Press/Flora Nwapa and Company; and her novel *Women Are Different*, which further explores the place of women in Nigerian society, was published in 1986. She has also published *Cassava Song and Rice Song* and is working on a collection of short stories. For most contemporary critics of African literature, Nwapa's position as a foremother of modern African women's writings is secure, for through the voices of her classic novel *Efuru* and her other works, the previously undocumented women storytellers in African villages are heard.

Gay Wilentz. In Bernth Lindfors and Reinhard Sander, eds. *Dictionary of Literary Biography*. Volume 125: *Twentieth-Century Caribbean and Black African Writers, Second Series,* (Detroit: Gale Research, 1993), pp. 182–83

Complexity, multiple presences, and cyclic rather than linear principles are definitive aspects of the works of black women writers. In this sense, telling as a complication of history is also a (re)membrance and a revision of history both in its mythic and its gender-specific dimensions. For example, telling in the form of a goddess's prophecy is an important feature of Flora Nwapa's *Efuru*. Nwapa's title character becomes a priestess of the goddess of the lake, a ''symbolic acceptance of self,'' writes Carol Davies, who claims that such acceptance is a positive note because it includes the realization that her ''existence was not totally defined by her motherhood.'' However, her existence does become enmeshed with a creatrix, and the imagery of the goddess she worships is woven into Efuru's own imagery and the narrative structures of the text. The pronominal reference (marked here with an [*]) in a passage Davies also cites, is, I think, deliberately obscured. Because the fertility of both the goddess and Efuru are lamented here, creativity is mythically extended past the physical to metaphysical spirituality—the realm of true creative possibility: ''Efuru slept soundly that night. She dreamt of the woman of the lake, her beauty, her long hair, and her riches. She had lived for ages at the bottom of the lake. She was as old as the lake itself. . . . She gave women beauty and wealth but she had no child. She[*] had never experienced the joy of motherhood.'' The recursive nature of the ambiguous ''she,'' that points both to the goddess and Efuru, is an example of the figurative depths of black women's written language. Even if the characters' generative powers fluctuate, are abandoned, raped, or redefined, the language sustains its generative powers.

In Nwapa's *Idu*, there is a reflection on the issue of motherhood and birth. Idu suspects that ''when a woman is good, God, our ancestors, and the Woman of the Lake all look at her stomach, not at her head, but at her stomach''. Consider the psychic fracture this separation underscores. Idu feels that her entire cultural community dissects her. Wholeness is the sacrifice of motherhood.

This sense of fracture informs Nwapa's creative revisioning of motherhood. The contradictory, layered, and plurisignant tones of her first novel (*Efuru*) lead to the literary climax of *Idu*, her second novel. Even though Nwapa's struggle to assert the vitality of the truly engaged feminine principle of creativity is the essence of *Efuru*, Idu's reflection and resolution testify to the overwhelming significance of biological motherhood in all aspects of African traditional life. The important deities, the ancestors, and the supreme god all look at a woman's stomach as a means of rewarding goodness. Idu's lament, that they ignore her knowledge (her head), articulates her frustration over the consequences of childbirth and motherhood in her community. The ambivalence is clear in the themes of *Idu* and *Efuru*; but *Idu* speaks directly to the dire consequences of womanspirit denied. The novel's conclusion specifies the pathos of its thesis. It is also an illustration of a recursive text. Idu tragically summons her spiritual energy, wills herself dead and follows the husband to whom she had devoted her life to the spirit realm. Only her child Ijoma is left. She decides that the child she is carrying will not be born, which is a declaration of control over the childbirth issue. Finally in control of her spiritual life, Idu chooses death and relinquishes motherhood in a pitiful claim of self-determination.

> Karla F.C. Holloway. *Moorings and Metaphors: Figures of Culture and Gender in Black Women's Literature* (New Brunswick, New Jersey: Rutgers University Press, 1992), pp. 33–4, 179

BIBLIOGRAPHY

*Efuru*, 1966; *Idu*, 1970; *This Is Lagos, and Other Stories*, 1971; *Emeka—Driver's Guard*, 1972; *Never Again*, 1975; *Mammy Water*, 1979; *The Adventures of Deke*, 1980; *Journey to Space*, 1980; *Wives at War, and Other Stories*, 1980; *The Miracle Kittens*, 1981; *One Is Enough*, 1981; *Cassava Song and Rice Song*, 1986; *Women Are Different*, 1986

# NZEKWU, Onuora (1928–)
## Nigeria

*Wand of Noble Wood* begins with Pete, a Lagos journalist, approaching the stage of his life when traditionally he should be thinking of marriage. He finds it hard to reconcile the marriage ideals that have grown on him during his city career with the ideals of his birthplace; and his dilemma is complicated by a pregnant mistress who as a stranger to his home town would be unacceptable there as his wife. . . .

A major criticism of this novel is the excessive amount of straight explanation of the characters' social environment and its effects on their behaviour. Nzekwu must learn to limit the filling-in of broad social background to what is strictly required for understanding the plot. He must also learn to suggest this background in the course of unravelling the plot, rather than interrupt the action with larger chunks of anthropological analysis. On the positive side, the pure though austere style is a delight to read. The conflict of ideals is vividly evoked—for instance in a brilliant passage in Chapter Four where Pete and a friend are arguing about the principles of marriage, and where both veer wildly back and forth between traditional and modern arguments. Finally, this is a powerful tragedy. The suggestion of a situation somehow too perfect to last, the succession of incidents sounding small but sinister notes through the haze of bliss, and the final disaster which seems as inevitable as it is startling—all these are beautifully managed. Nzekwu is a newcomer to novels. His faults, albeit aggravating, are those natural to a newcomer. His talents promise an exciting future.

> Robin Horton. *Nigeria Magazine*. September 1961, pp. 219, 221

Before Nigerian independence it used to be a saying in the Secretariat in Lagos that, if the Africans were to leave, tribal warfare would break out among the British administrators. The publication of Mr. Onuora Nzekwu's second novel [*Blade among the Boys*] must bring a resurgence of that partisan feeling to many a modest home in Budleigh Salterton or Torquay where retired officials from Eastern Nigeria look back with pleasure on their days among the cheerful, hardworking Ibos. The West may be richer, and the North haughtier, but in literature the East has wiped the eye of the lot of them, and the rest of West Africa as well. Cyprian Ekwensi, Chinua Achebe and Onuora Nzekwu make an unbeatable Treble Choice.

*Blade among the Boys* has a typically Ibo theme, a young man's education. In Iboland school-children are punished not by being given extra work but by being sent home for a day. Mr. Nzekwu's hero is desperately studious and determined to get on. His tragedy is that his (European) teachers are all tyrants, seeking unfairly for any excuse to ruin his career and succeeding at the last in expelling him for absurdly inadequate reasons. After a period in which he prospers as a railwayman he takes up again his vocation as a priest, only to be expelled once more after two years at the seminary. This time, however, the fault is with the girl his family have chosen him for a wife, who seduces him by the aid of a love potion bought from a ''herbalist''.

The other theme is the irresistible one of the conflict of cultures. It is sharpened by making Patrick a Roman Catholic, educated at a mission school. Mr. Nzekwu tries to hold the balance fair, but he cannot help presenting the traditional Ibo religion and culture in the more attractive light. It is this that will be the main attraction to the European reader: the masquerades, the prayers, the charms and the tribal social structure are described from within and with a luminous comprehension.

*Times Literary Supplement.* August 10, 1962, p. 571

Onuora Nzekwu was born in Northern Nigeria, but his secondary schooling and teachers training took place in Onitsha (Eastern Region). He has taught both in Onitsha and in Lagos. His researches into the history of Onitsha gained him his present position as editor on *Nigeria,* a ''middle-brow'' (as opposed to *Black Orpheus*) magazine primarily devoted to arts, crafts, and historical and cultural affairs. Nzekwu might be taken as a kind of mean between the extremes of Ekwensi and Achebe. As an essentially popular writer, he lacks Ekwensi's ear for speech or eye for detail. This is not his interest; his is a pedagogical approach. Nor does he make use of the Western-cultural tradition, in a formative way, within the texture of his books, in the depiction of ''ancestral'' behavior, as Achebe does. Nzekwu's appetite for sensation can be irritating if considered as calculated to sell his books abroad, but fascinating if taken to be the genuine expression of a modern mind obsessed by the more violent aspects of immemorial practices and lore.

Nzekwu's books may be taken as illustrative of the effects of the ambiguities of British colonial practice upon a bright, highly strung, and somewhat disorganized personality. The hidden theme common to both Nzekwu's books, *Wand of Noble Wood* and *Blade among the Boys,* is that of the supernatural revenge taken by the old dispensation upon the new. The traditional society's ways have been disturbed, violated by new patterns from the West which have been planted first by Europeans and then cultivated by ''emancipated'' Africans themselves. The spiritual forces behind the old community manage to break through, using *their* elected human agents in retaliation. It is important to note that in Nzekwu's books these retaliatory occurrences are presented as being really supernatural in origin—another example of his uniqueness. There is absolutely *no* evidence of irony with regard to these occurrences in the books. In addition, as atavisms they have a personal rather than a communal intent and effect, which is to say that they have an emotional impact on and affect the destinies of isolated individuals only. This is why, unlike similar mysterious and violent manifestations with a broader scope, those described by Nzekwu seem to the skeptical Western reader to be obsessional, a tumultuous inner life turned inside out.

Judith Illsley Gleason. *This Africa* (Evanston: Northwestern University Press, 1965), pp. 168–69

*Blade among the Boys* tells the story of an Ibo boy, born in Northern Nigeria, moving to the coast because of the death of his father, determined to go into the Church and finally failing to do so because of an involvement with a girl.

The standards which Nzekwu applies in this novel seem to be those of a generation ago. The boy, Patrick, fails to become a priest when he gets a girl pregnant. She is presented as a warm and intelligent person who loves Patrick. Yet their act—and it becomes

this, their ACT—is seen as a grim sin. Patrick is dismissed from the seminary, and the authorities wish him ''God's forgiveness and blessings.'' The novel finally becomes a fairly confused lecture in mission morality, a bending to what must appear to those on the outside as an unjust and totally uncomprehending authority.

The traditional Ibo way of life is generally treated patronizingly. There are exceptions, however, in the form of one or two lively scenes, such as the one in which the ancestral masks have assembled in the village square, and all women have prudently gone indoors, when suddenly an English missionary lady heaves into sight, surrounded by a lot of little schoolgirls. The lady will not budge from her course and neither will the masqueraders. They feel insulted that she will not go away, and she feels insulted that they will not. Finally, in desperation, they pursue her. The little girls flee in all directions, shrieking, and the lady drops her dignity and sprints like a gazelle. It is regrettable that Nzekwu does not more often allow his characters simply to be, as he does in this scene.

Nzekwu's third novel, *Highlife for Lizards,* concerns a woman of great spirit and independence, Agom, and it is the most successful of Nzekwu's writing. His picture of Agom is more fully drawn than anything else he has done, and local beliefs and rituals are handled with greater insight and sympathy than is shown in his previous novels.

Margaret Laurence. *Long Drums and Cannons* (London: Macmillan, 1968), p. 192

Nzekwu's style can be terse and exact, which is in the tradition of realistic writing, and is capable of evoking a sense of place and event which gives the reader all he needs to know of the scenes and actions before him. Yet too often the narrative is marred by solid interpolations of anthropological and sociological data. It is for the most part a prose of explication rather than implication. In the third novel, *Highlife for Lizards,* he dramatises materials which he merely expounds in the earlier two novels and the result is more compelling and convincing than with the earlier books.

Within these limits, Nzekwu is a serious writer. He is concerned with issues of social, cultural, political and religious consequence at the individual and the societal levels. His novels display their concerns and conclusions through stories of personal relationships which reflect problems of belief, choice, and action, central to a generality of contemporary Nigerians. If there is none of the variety of devices which characterise, say, Achebe's or Soyinka's work— the irony, the fierce and abrasive satire, the gift for caricature, the cold assault on the failures of individuals and society—neither are there any false consolations offered. Nzekwu is a less finished artist than some of his peers; yet he is serious in exploiting the social role of the writer. Perhaps it is fair to say that Nzekwu is essentially a novelist of manners, by which we mean that he is concerned almost exclusively with the variety of problems which confront his own generation, the group of people in transition between the traditional and the modern, who are in an important sense unique since they sum up the ambiguities created by the impact of colonialism on traditional culture and make discoveries about their own natures, values and beliefs, which preclude the generation which follows them from being like them. It is not so much a difference from other cultures that distinguishes the men and women who appear in Nzekwu's novels—since the histories of all peoples comprise a continuous process of growth and modification—but rather a matter of the intensity of this difference.

G. D. Killam. *African Literature Today.* 5 (1971), pp. 22–23

BIBLIOGRAPHY

*Wand of Noble Wood*, 1961; *Blade among the Boys*, 1962; *Ezra Goes to School* (with Michael Crowder), 1963; *Highlife for Lizards*, 1965

# OGOT, Grace (1930– )

**Kenya**

[Grace] Ogot's writing deals mostly with aspects of traditional African society. Her novel *The Promised Land* . . . tells the story of the Western Kenyan Luo pioneer family, which seeks a more satisfactory life in Tanzania where conditions are better. The family is defeated when a curse is placed upon Nyapol, the hero of the novel, by an envious and vindictive neighbor. The novel is subtitled *A True Fantasy* not so much because the events of the novel are offered as historically accurate, but because the physical manifestations which result from the curse placed on Nyapol (his flesh breaks out in festering, painful, thornlike growths which drive him mad) are meant to show the force, the truth of the belief in indigenous religion. The novel fails to convince because there is too sharp a break between its two halves. The realistic and matter-of-fact evocation of domestic conditions of the first part gives way to passages describing Nyapol's hallucinations in his pain. There is as well a rather contrived eighth chapter interpolated into the text to show the utter inability of Western medicine (as practiced in a mission hospital) to cope with African medicine used by a pagan practitioner for nefarious purposes. The reader's credibility is too much strained. . . .

The stories in her *Land Without Thunder*, which offer themes dealing with traditional village occasions, events in mission hospitals in colonial days, the tragedy of young girls in contemporary Nairobi, and the problems of sophisticated Africans at an Egyptian airport, have an authenticity which is quite convincing and reveal a fine command and inventive use of the short-story form.

> Douglas Killam. In Bruce King, ed. *Literatures of the World in English* (London: Routledge & Kegan Paul, 1974), pp. 126–27

The nine stories contained in *The Other Woman: Selected Short Stories* are studies in common human problems and experiences, though their settings and almost all their characters are Kenyan. The same theme is explored in all but three of the other stories, but there are differences in the nature of action and in the predominance of various narrative devices. Thus "Pay Day" and "The Middle Door" deal with the theme of courage in the face of man's inhumanity to fellow man; "The Other Woman" and "The Honourable Minister" satirize marital infidelity and show it visited with nemesis; and "The Fisherman" and "The Ivory Trinket" depict the disastrous consequences of evil words addressed by husbands to their wives. Two of the three remaining stories, though they differ widely from these six in terms of experiential details, handle themes which are generally similar to two of those already indicated: "The Family Doctor" is about the need for perseverance in the face of a malignant illness; and "Fishing Village" deals with a despicable rogue who baptizes his thievery and duplicity *in nomine diaboli*, calling them "intelligence," and who justly falls victim to nemesis. Only the ninth and last story, "The Professor," deals with an entirely different theme: the shocking, inevitable capitulation of professional (academic) idealism before the forces of sociopolitical reality.

The success of most of the stories as works of art consists of Ogot's effective narrative skill, imagination, and language. Her masterly combination of the techniques of flashback, foreshadowing, and discovery makes for reading with breathless attention and sustained interest. The stories themselves are such terrific inventions with several layers of suggestiveness as can be the result only of a rare imaginative activity, and the language is lucid and fresh.

> R. N. Egudu. *World Literature Today*. 52, 1 (winter 1978), p. 165

Grace Ogot is one of Africa's outstanding storytellers. She went into the lead early and has worked hard ever since to remain there. She has written several collections of short stories and full-length novels in English and Luo. *The Promised Land, Land Without Thunder, The Other Woman, Island of Tears,* and *The Graduate* are established and well received. The writings in Luo—*Ber Wat, Miaha, Aloo Kod Apul Apul, Simbi Nyaima*—may be new to many outside Kenya, but they have proved extremely popular at home. For example, a recent dramatization of *Miaha* in Luo-speaking areas of Kenya excited the people and showed to what extent drama could be used as a medium of transmitting indigenous culture. The drama version of two stories from *Land Without Thunder*—"The Rain Came" and "The White Veil"—staged by the Albert Wandago Production at the Cultural Center, Nairobi, was also well received and had almost twenty runs. So, not only has Grace Ogot been writing stories and novels, she has also been promoting creativity in other directions. A few of her books have been translated into several international languages, and some have been adopted for use as school texts . . . in Kenya.

In an interview she talked about her new books in the press, her motivation for writing, her craftsmanship, and the recognition that writing has brought her so far. She has three completed novels in the pipeline; two of them she has worked on for ten years. These two are historical novels. *In the Beginning* deals with the history of the Luo people from about 97 A.D. to about 1300 A.D. when the people make a Wi-nam settlement, and what compels them to leave this settlement. For greater effectiveness the story . . . concentrates on three generations of one family. It hinges on a family spear, an inheritance of great cultural worth, which has to pass from one generation to another. At one stage a member of the family makes a mistake and an elephant walks away with the spear. The owner of the spear refuses compensation. So the man at fault goes in search of the spear. This action eventually leads to the separation of two brothers who later found two nations. The second novel, *Princess Nyilaak*, virtually continues the historical fiction where the first has left off. Nyilaak was born around 1517 A.D., and her story takes us up to about 1750 A.D. She is the daughter of the ruler of the Luo people. In the absence of a male child she is designated to succeed her father. For this reason the oracles decree that she should not marry. Her mother does not like this decision and does everything in her power to oppose it. Nyilaak has an encounter with Ochak, a prince from another part of the land, marries him secretly, and becomes pregnant by him. Ochak is hunted down by Nyilaak's father, and is killed and cremated. Nyilaak is banished from the land, and her twin sons are to be killed. However, through the intervention of the elders, she is reprieved with her two sons and she later becomes a ruler. Nyilaak later founds the Alur society in Uganda, and one of her sons succeeds her as ruler.

The third novel, *A Call at Midnight* is different in texture and orientation from the first two. . . . It is a social comment on family life, especially the responsibility of the father to his wife and children. A father deserts his family, and ten years after he has left home there is a telephone call to his wife that her husband is critically ill in [a] hospital. The wife says she has no husband. The [nurse] . . . replies that dying men don't just call on any women in the city. All the time the man has been away from home he has maintained an illegal contact with another woman in a smuggling business. This woman dupes him of a large sum of money, dopes him, and leaves him unconscious by the roadside. This is why he goes to [the] hospital in the first place. He recovers from his illness, paralyzed, and returns to his matrimonial home. The wife is rather unhappy about his return, but the children feel it is much better to have a crippled father than not have any at all. When these three novels are published, they will confirm Grace Ogot's position as an outstanding female novelist in modern Africa. . . .

By her writing Grace Ogot has not only brought pleasure and satisfaction to many readers, she has also set a high standard of artistic performance from which young female writers can benefit. They will find her preoccupation with the African woman and family edifying, and her style lucid and attractive. She is particularly proficient in the use of verbal art. She integrates oral tradition into the living situations of her stories, especially in those scenes set in the rural areas. This gives her works the necessary authenticity. . . . Furthermore, her works are capable of reawakening in readers, especially female readers, the memory of the life they lived in infancy, and make them examine how firm their grasp of cultural matters is. Such an assessment is made easy by the fact that most of her heroines are ordinary people, sometimes gifted, but not fighters or revolutionaries. On city life she shows the experience of an observant woman. She puts her finger on items which make city life inferior in quality to rural life—avarice, greed, corruption, sexual laxity. Once she takes a fault she dramatizes it in such a way that the danger in that attitude of mind or approach to life becomes obvious. She combines realism with frankness in pointing out the foibles in society. In *The Graduate*, for example, all the difficulties put in the way of Jakoyo by Europeans and fellow Africans are realistic in the context and point to an unpardonable weakness in human nature. By consistently calling attention to these faults, she is directly advocating reform.

Oladele Taiwo. *Female Novelists of Modern Africa* (New York: St. Martin's Press, 1984) pp. 128–29, 161

Questions of social morality and the quest for nationhood have preoccupied African writers dealing with postcolonial society. Novelists like Kofi Awoonor, Ayi Kwei Armah, Chinua Achebe, Wole Soyinka, Ngugi wa Thiong'o, and Meja Mwangi have all examined these two dimensions of Africa's postcolonial reality. So has Grace Ogot. . . .

A study of Grace Ogot's fiction reveals that whereas problems of nationhood loom large in her short novel, *The Graduate*,

problems of morality are more central in her short stories, especially such short stories as "The Middle Door," "The Honourable Minister," "Elizabeth," "The Professor," and "Pay Day." Nevertheless, her treatment of moral problems also suggests that postcolonial society's moral problems pose a deadly threat to its quest for national authenticity. . . .

[In *The Graduate*] Jakoyo encounters no ethnic obstacles on his way to answering the nation's call. Similarly, other potential sources of frustration are either glanced over or rendered as comedy. Thus, as his plane prepared to land [at] Nairobi's airport, "Jakoyo's heartbeat rose, as joy, fear, even pain settled upon him, shooting numerous questions in his mind." His misgivings are soon proved unfounded. His wife proves faithful and loving as ever. Though his daughter, Awino, who was born shortly after his departure for America, at first dislikes him, a lovely present soon wins her over. Even the clear evidence of culture shock and Jakoyo's alienation (he speaks Swahili with a Yankee accent) is underplayed. His dominant feeling is one of "a new life . . . a new beginning, a new era that would turn him into a new man." The break with the past is symbolized in his stuffing into his "air-sick bag" the dirty toilet tissue he had used in the plane, and dumping the bag "where it belonged."

Even nature smiles a warm welcome to Jakoyo. And the customs and immigration officials are all friendly, courteous, dutiful, and efficient. No one insults him. No one attempts to extort a bribe from him, as happens to his Nigerian counterpart in Achebe's *No Longer at Ease*, in which a corrupt customs official offers to let the hero Obi Okonkwo bring in his radiogram duty-free if Obu would give him a two-pound bribe. . . . An ideological issue (the opposition between Eastern bloc socialism and the Western-dependent capitalism of most African countries) which provides the grit to Marxist writers like Ngugi wa Thiong'o and Sembène Ousmane is laughingly raised and dismissed. An official asks Jakoyo: "Any prohibited Marxist literature?" and accepts his crisp assurance that there is none.

Grace Ogot's short novel *The Graduate* has raised a number of problems facing African states in their quest for an authentic nationhood. This paper discusses only one of such problems, with specific reference to postcolonial Kenya. The paper shows that because most of Ogot's themes center on women, women's issues have also formed the matrix within which sociohistorical or sociopolitical phenomena are discussed. This applies naturally to her exploration of Kenya's quest for authentic nationhood.

Ify Achufusi. *Journal of Commonwealth Literature*. 26, 1 (1991), pp. 179–80, 186–87

Ogot is devoted to relating native Luo folktales to the younger generation of Kenyans. Many of her writings are also based on the day-to-day life of people she has known or read about. As a nurse she has been intrigued by the continuing use of traditional medical cures in Kenya. As Ogot explained to Bernth Lindfors, "Stories of African traditional medicine and of the medicine man against the background of modern science and medicine fascinated me." This fascination led to the writing of *The Promised Land*; the short stories "The Old White Witch," "The Hero," and "Night Sister," in *Land Without Thunder*, and "The Family Doctor" and "The Professor" in *The Other Woman*. . . .

Ogot is well aware of the social, political, and economic changes taking place around her and continues to retain a respect and a close understanding of the traditional thought of her people. An understanding and appreciation of Luo traditional ways, customs, superstitions, and history are the strengths of Ogot's writing. Her close attention to an accurate recalling of details was exhibited when she changed the title of her story "Ayiembo's Ghost" to "The Ivory Trinket" . . . as soon as she learned that ghosts are not dead in Luo traditions. Another example is the recitation of the Nyamgondho legend in "The Fisherman." . . .

The tragic aspects of history and life fascinate Ogot: six stories in *Land Without Thunder*, three stories in *The Other Woman*, and two stories in *The Island of Tears* have an element of sadness in them. Ogot's belief is that "There are more tragic incidents in life than there are comic ones." To support her statement, Ogot has written about Tom Mboya's funeral in the title story of *The Island of Tears*; the death of Dr. Sserwadda from poliomyelitis in "The Hero"; the mother's desperate attempt to find a doctor to save her child's life in "The Family Doctor"; and the sacrifice of the life of Oganda, a king's daughter, for the survival of the village in "The Rain Came." In short, tragedy cuts across class lines and touches a cross-section of Kenyan rural and urban society.

> Brenda F. Berrian. In Bernth Lindfors and Reinhard Sander, eds. *Dictionary of Literary Biography.*, Volume 125: *Twentieth-Century Caribbean and Black African Writers, Second Series,* (Detroit: Gale Research, 1993), pp. 184–86

[*The Promised Land* is a] cautionary folk tale in its warning against the loss of traditional African social mores and customs in postcolonial times, with an emphasis on the effects on a central female character. Ogot in an interview has pointed out the importance of tradition in modern African culture, arguing, "Western education should only add new ideas to the old, blending with what makes a man what he is. A person's background is extremely important" (in Bernth Lindfors, *Mazungumzo: Interviews with East African Writers, Publishers, Editors and Scholars*). She has also remarked on the connection between a colonial regime's discouragement of writing traditional tales and its fear that these might encourage nationalist feelings, saying, "quite a few potential writers received no encouragement from colonial publishers who were perhaps afraid of turning out radical writers critical of the colonial regime". Like many African folk tales, in which Ogot has professed an early and abiding interest (Lindfors), the novel describes a human encounter between the known or logical realm and the less explicable spirit world. The lesson concerns the negative effects of British colonialism on traditional African society, in particular on women. This "True Fantasy" tells the story of the newly-married Nyapol, whose husband Ochola decides he wants to leave their ancestral home and seek his fortune in Tanganyika. Nyapol dislikes the idea, saying that they have enough material goods and that deserting their families is wrong. Once in Tanganyika, they are financially successful, but a local male witch becomes jealous and puts a spell on Ochola that gives him warts all over his body, turning him into a "half-man-half-animal". Many African medicine men try to cure Ochola and fail, as does a British doctor practicing western medicine. An African medicine man finally cures him, telling Ochola that he and his family must leave right away for their original home, which they do, leaving all their wealth behind.

The trip from Nyapol and Ochola's home to Tanganyika is made on a Western ship which associates the ill-fated journey with the negative aspects of colonialism. Like Ochola in Tanganyika, people become animals when boarding the ship: a man steps on a child and the narrator notes, "There was something inhuman about his eyes—he did not look back at the child". The pregnant Nyapol thinks,

> The white man was so clever to be able to make such a big thing, and to enable it to keep afloat on the broad waters. . . . Why could he not stand at the gate and say that only a few people at a time should walk up the gangway? That is what Ondijo did with his small boat. . . . Perhaps the white man was not so wise after all.

Other unfavorable associations with Europeans occur to Nyapol on the boat trip away from her home. Nyapol is sickened by the smell of a European woman, which reminds her of the European priest who sexually molested her younger sister. And to pass the time on the boat, African musicians sing a song, the last line of which is "Sleep, sleep, sleep, sleep in the land of the white man." The narrator then explains that "Hundreds of Luo men, who went to Burma to help the white man fight his enemy, never came home. . . . Neither did the white man keep his word to divide the spoils with the families of the men who died fighting for him".

Just as colonialism results in the unrenumerated hardships of the Luo people in the British army, it continues its effect in postcolonial times on gender relations, specifically marriage in this novel. When Nyapol's husband insists they go to Tanganyika, she "wished she had not married. Marriage was a form of imprisonment in which the master could lead you where he wished". Abiodun Goke-Pariola has pointed out that, contrary to many critics who believe the Christianity and Westernization that came with colonialism to be liberating forces for African women, instead, "even societies . . . that were matrilineal were virtually turned around as a Europe that was at the high point of Victorian sexism pillaged the African continent". One can speculate that Elspeth Huxley, while promoting gender equality, erred in not seeing the involvement of colonialism in such sexism.

Goke-Pariola asserts that many female protagonists in African novels "see traditional society as an ally against what, for many, is a new phenomenon of sexism with a vengeance". A revulsion against the Western European colonialism that marginalized African women not only because of their race, but their gender, can be seen in Ogot's character Nyapol, who clings to tradition, while her husband embraces the new opportunities presented by colonialism and Western technology. Even after many attempts have failed to cure Ochola (to make him human again), he still does not heed Nyapol when she pleads,

> You've a father! You've enough land! Why don't we face reality and return? Perhaps the air of our motherland would cure you. Let's sell everything here. Let's go back home. I'm prepared to nurse you forever, Ochola, if I can only be amongst our people.

Nor does he pay any attention to his brother, who wonders, "Why could Ochola not see that their ancestors were not pleased with them?". Written at an historical juncture where Kenya has just gained its independence and is no longer a colony, Ogot's story reflects concern over the after-effects of colonialism—in particular the loss of traditions which precipitate the greater marginalization of women (Nyapol is literally forced from the center of her universe). Thus the entire novel becomes a cautionary tale that disrupts the "logical" world created by Western European discourse and conventions.

Ogot herself refuses to make a distinction between a "myth" and a true story: "When we tell such stories to fellow Luos or to fellow Kenyans, we don't call them myths. We just say that they are true stories of events that occurred in other generations in the distant past, at the beginning of our society" (Lindfors). In so doing she refuses to condone the socially-accepted practices of patriarchy and colonialism as the only logical vision of reality. She also stresses the importance of folk tales as a mode of enculturation: "I feel that children's imaginations are developed by the stories connected with myths and legends. It helps their creativity, and gives them a background, a traditional setting that many of us today feel they should know. It also gives them a future to look forward to" (Lindfors). When asked about future tendencies in East African literature, she replied "the desire to dig into the past and resuscitate our treasured oral literatures and folktales is strong" and connected this interest to socio-economic issues in a country's political life. The folk tale, for Ogot, performs the function of commenting indirectly on the aftereffects of colonialism, particularly on male/female relations.

Written slightly later than Huxley's memoirs, Ogot's novel/folk tale presents a view of the effects of colonialism that, unlike Huxley in her political writing, refuses to separate the institutions of patriarchy and colonialism. Like the folk tales in Huxley's memoirs, however, Ogot's novel as a whole proposes an alternative view of reality to that which promotes colonialism and patriarchy as logical, rational institutions of society.

The use of the folk tale as narrative disruption in Huxley's autobiography, and folk tale conventions in Ogot's novel, are similar in that both function as examinations of gender relationships under colonialism. Ogot's novel is obviously conscious comment on the negative aspects of both gender and racial marginalization under the modernizations resulting from colonialism.

Kathleen Flanagan. *Women's Studies*. 25, 4 (June 1996), pp 371–84

BIBLIOGRAPHY
*The Promised Land*, 1966; *Land without Thunder*, 1968; *The Other Woman: Selected Short Stories*, 1976; *The Graduate*, 1980; *The Island of Tears*, 1980; *Aloo Kod Apul Apul*, 1981; *Ber Wat*, 1981; *Miaha*, 1983

# OKARA, Gabriel (1921–)

## Nigeria

*The Voice* is a serious and pessimistic story which reflects the post-independence mood of disillusionment which is becoming increasingly articulate among the African intellectuals. The atmosphere of the story is dense with evil, with corruption and with all sorts of manipulation among politicians and their beneficiaries. Okara as a poet-novelist steeps his story in symbolism and imagery but the most persistent symbol and the one which permeates the entire atmosphere of the story is darkness, a palpable darkness within which people grope about frantically in search of vulgar material satisfaction. It is to this darkness therefore that Okolo is attempting

to introduce a spark of light that will show the people the way to a more purposeful life. His fate, grim and terrible as it appears, could overtake any would-be reformer in a social situation in which the collective traditional outlook has been surplanted by unmitigated individualism and the attendant callousness and greed which inspires those with power to make themselves ruthlessly unassailable.

Okara's characters are not fully individuated. They stand for good or evil, virtue or vice, and are therefore ideal for exploring a moral theme. His experiment with language is even more interesting for whereas Achebe and other West African novelists are content to translate oral tradition into English by keeping as close as possible to the original meaning, Okara is the only writer who actually goes so far as to transliterate, even to the extent of reproducing syntactical forms. This gives the action of his story a peculiarly heavy-footed and tortuous movement which again seems to fit the serious moral tone and pessimistic mood of the story.

Emmanuel Obiechina. *Nigeria Magazine*. March 1965, p. 62

[Okara's] is an inward concern, the "mystic inside," to use his own words. This concern with the self, the soul, runs through all his work, and it is realized by the poet in terms and images of objects and phenomena that most impinge upon his conscious. Snowflakes, a piano, drums, social airs, an *aladura* or beachside prophet, a river, a stork, a girl too distant to possess, these are what make Okara spark. . . .

Were Okara not an undisputed artist, he could easily fall among the "pioneer" and "pilot" poets. . . . The tall palm trees, the jungle drums, the innocent virgins, the mystic rhythms, the dark flesh, and the old wish not to lose face in a double sense within the alien crows and clash of so many colours washing in from outside are all well-worn wares of that otherwise respectable house. But in the gifted hands of Okara they become articles of original style and lasting worth.

John Pepper Clark. *Transition*. 18, 1965, p. 25

In 1964 the poet G. Okara, who is very well-known in Africa, published the novel *The Voice*, in which he portrayed the drama of a man, whose morals and principles contradict the morals of certain politicians. The bad characters representing the nascent bourgeoisie, corrupt politicians and officials have already been painted by Achebe and Ekwensi. The hero of Okara's novel, who is a seeker of truth and justice, fights such morals and behaviour. The novel is pessimistic, the hero dying in the clash with the powers that be without having found the truth he sought.

*The Voice* shows the development of contradictions within Nigerian society, the interests and policy of certain strata of society which come into contradiction with the interests of other social groups. The novel does not show Okara's own stand in the matter. The hero is rather conventional and nowhere does he state his position in society. Evidently, the author expressed the sentiments of a certain recently born section of the intelligentsia. He has chosen as his subject the political life in Nigeria, which he generalised in a conventional way and even presented almost as a caricature. Although the author does not display any class sympathy the conflict in the novel brings out the widely different opinions and sentiments in Nigerian society. The social import of the novel lies in the fact that it describes the morals of various social strata.

V. Vavilov. In M. A. Korostovtsev, ed., *Essays on African Culture* (Moscow: Nauka, 1966), p. 161

[The] self-conscious language [of the "questing" hero of Gabriel Okara's *The Voice*] is the device of the narcissist, a subterfuge within which the hero can contemplate his creator's navel while remaining himself impenetrable in the barrier of contrived language. *It*, the object of our hero's search, may not exist, and the hero does not himself appear to believe in it. Certainly, there is no communication of the psychic drive which sets a man on a course of single-minded enquiry into the heart of the matter or existence; it is only an occasion for the hero's narcissistic passivity. His will to motion can hardly be calculated in terms of his effect on the community. Okolo is too set a set-piece; the catalytic effect of his quest on the external world is more expected than fulfilled. Okolo has lost himself in an animism of nothingness, the ultimate self-delusion of the narcissist.

Wole Soyinka. *African Forum.* Spring 1966, p. 62

Anne Tibble, in *African/English Literature*, compares the theme of *The Voice* to that of Dostoevski's *The Idiot*. Okolo and Myshkin do have much in common. Both need to speak the heart's truth; both are rejected by the establishment in society; both possess qualities which could be called saintly. Gabriel Okara's character has a more limited range, for Okolo is shown only in one aspect, as truth-seeker and questioner, whereas the subtly terrifying thing about Myshkin is that he really is partially idiot as well as saint, and his character fluctuates before the reader's eyes. Okolo remains constant, with no suggestion that there may be another side to his personality.

Another comparison would be with Eman in Wole Soyinka's *The Strong Breed*. Both are men of compassion and perception who are martyred by communities who fail to understand them and who therefore fear them. But Eman is a more complex character than Okolo, for in some ways he seeks his own martyrdom and his death has implications of saviourhood in it—he offers himself in order to redeem all. In terms of Christian parallels, Eman is a Christ figure, whereas Okolo could be called a Jesus figure, the difference being one of emphasis. In the case of Okolo, the emphasis is upon his teacherhood, the fact that his "spoken words" may plant some seed of truth and desire for truth. There is nothing messianic about him, nor is there any suggestion that his death will, in itself, achieve anything. It is the survival of his words and his faith which is important. He does not seek his martyrdom as Eman does, for although Okolo is drawn back to his village, it is because he feels some sense of mission there, the need to make his "teaching words" heard among his own people, rather than any need to die.

Margaret Laurence. *Long Drums and Cannons* (London: Macmillan, 1968), p. 196

The superior quality of Okara's work seems to lie partly in its overall intensity of mood. Here is a committed poet, utterly sincere in all he brings to the poet's task and clearly anxious to persist in the cultivation of his poetic sensibility. His fellow poets are perhaps more prolific, at times more technically adventurous; but for the most part they lack the fine richness of soul, the pervading sense of an inner life and a constant preoccupation with the basic themes of life and death, which are the dominant features of Okara's work. A withdrawn melancholy figure, Okara has something of the Celtic colour of soul, with its sensitivity and large resources of sadness, yet without the Celtic sense of humour. The lyrical "I" means the collective "we" for Okara and his private experience is felt to be one that is shared by his compatriots. He is Nigeria's best example of the poet singing in solitude yet singing for his fellow men. . . .

But it is hard to be authentically African while using the poetic voice of a Welshman, and Okara had to strike out on a more independent path. A basic problem was linguistic in nature. Despite the English language's history in Africa, despite its having been "transplanted" into African societies, poets choosing to use it face a situation in which the poetic diction and imagery provided for the home tradition are at odds with the features of their own inner landscapes which have been shaped by an entirely different culture and environment. One way of bridging this gap, which means in effect the creation of a new, Africanised English idiom, is to use a device which, for want of a more accurate term, we will call transliteration. Okara decided that he would write his verse in his native Ijaw and then translate it literally into English, the second version being considered the primary work of art. . . .

[The basic aspects of Ijaw thinking] emerge by way of a device which allows the poet adequately to render authentic indigenous experience, "to put into the whirlpool of literature the African point of view, to put across how the African thinks." Through transliteration Okara has created a new idiom and found his own voice.

Adrian A. Roscoe. *Mother Is Gold* (Cambridge: Cambridge University Press, 1971), pp. 28–29, 31

The most concerted attempt to preserve the mother tongue through translation is Gabriel Okara's attempt in *The Voice* to transfer Ijaw syntax and lexical rules into English. The closeness with which Okara does so can be determined by comparison with Ijaw sources, and, as one would expect, he is unable to remain consistent in his method. But the failure does not lie in this inconsistency, which would not wholly invalidate the method, or even simply in "an annoying literary squint" [Sunday O. Anozie], but in a fundamental misconception about the nature of language—that anything as complex as total meaning can be conveyed by preservation of very few of its parts. Syntax alone is not the vehicle of meaning, nor are a language's rules of collocation.

It has been remarked [by G. D. Killam] that Okara is a much better poet than novelist and that *The Voice* is most successful in short lyrical passages. Without wishing to beg the question of the incompatibility of "the language of poetry" and "the language of prose," I think it quite possible that the fundamental weaknesses of meaning in *The Voice* are less apparent when subject to the firmer organization and control demanded by a verse-form. Indeed, there is a sense in which they are more acceptable, or at least accepted, there. However, the importance of Okara's work depends not on his success or failure but in the clearly conveyed realization that the artistic liberty of the African writer in English lies in the integration of expression and experience. By revealing one route to that end to be a cul-de-sac, *The Voice* remains a positive force in the development of the West African novel in English.

Peter Young. In Edgar Wright, ed., *The Critical Evaluation of African Literature* (London: Heinemann, 1973), p. 42

One of the oldest of the contemporary writers is Gabriel Okara. He was born in 1921 and so far as chronology is concerned he belongs to the generation of dedicated versifiers. But his mind is closer to the contemporary ethos. Nevertheless, he is the link between the two generations of poets, for some of his dicta sound surprisingly like Negritude. . . .

Yet his first poems do show an individual concern, although the action (and it is very correct to speak of action in an Okara poem, since the situation is intensely dramatized) tends to be converted into weak posturings. At the center of every poem is a protagonist, and the poem charts the history of his attitudes by subtly juxtaposing dissimilar images that help to emphasize his quandary. . . .

Okara achieved success not only by using symbols to illustrate certain attitudes, but by reorganizing the trite language of the public poem. ''Piano and Drums'' introduces technical terms at appropriate points to emphasize the cerebral nature of western culture, and it is a measure of stylistic exactitude that the harsh images associated with the piano culminate in the word ''counterpoint'' which later on the poet, almost naïvely, associates with ''daggerpoint.'' Okara also reorganizes language by rendering it lyrical, and it is the ease of a songster that makes him such a satisfying poet. He adopts the techniques of song-writing by repeating whole phrases, each time with a slightly different emphasis, by beginning with dependent clauses, and by making the poem grow into a long main statement which gathers momentum as it develops.

O. R. Dathorne. *The Black Mind* (Minneapolis: University of Minnesota Press, 1974), pp. 263–65

BIBLIOGRAPHY
*The Voice*, 1964; *The Fisherman's Invocation,* 1978

# OKIGBO, Christopher (1932–1967)
## Nigeria

Okigbo is chiefly a poet for the ear and not for the eye. We cannot see much of his poetry. The images change quickly and he hardly ever gives us time to build up a consistent and lasting vision in our mind's eye. But we can *hear* his verse, it fills our mind like a half forgotten tune returning to memory. Everything he touches vibrates and swings and we are compelled to read on and to follow the tune of his chant, hardly worried about the fact that we understand little of what he has to say. The obscurity of Okigbo's poetry is of course deliberate. . . .

Yet, unlike some modern poets, Okigbo is not simply enjoying a private joke. One feels, on the contrary, that the mysterious names help him to throw a veil over the immediate meaning of the poem, that he is carefully creating a kind of code which he never wants us

to solve completely. Because any literal allusions would detract from the song and the music, would make us pause in the middle to reflect, and this is exactly what the poet wants to avoid. He wants to carry us away on his chant—or rather on his *incantation*. For incantation is, I think, the best word one can find for Okigbo's poetry. The moment you start to read you feel you have intruded into the sacred enclosure of a secret cult. You have no right to be there, but you are too fascinated to leave. The chanting can be understood by the initiates alone, but you are receptive to its beauty. You cannot decode the meaning, but you feel it affects you physically, the incantation causes a rush of ill defined but exalted feelings in your mind. . . .

To say that in reading Okigbo's poems we are terribly conscious of the man's intellect at work does not mean at all that the poem is without feeling. Its effect on the reader is in fact *physical*, and though the language is ritualistic the effect is orgastic.

Ulli Beier. *Black Orpheus.* 12, 1963, pp. 46–47

[Okigbo] himself says his one theme has been a combination of the processes of creation and self-purification. . . .

[The poems in *Heavensgate*] are each carefully scored out like a musical piece. Some sections in fact require playing to the flute, although to what tune the poet, like Senghor with his kora, does not say. Together, they confirm to my mind the possession by the poet of a rare gift of literary imagination. This operates by a process I will not call predatory as that employed by vampires and parasites. Rather it seizes upon what attracts it and distils therefrom, without destroying the original, a fresh artifact.

A later work, ''Silences,'' slight as it is, presents a remarkable mosaic of world literature, music and painting. It is a stimulating game detecting within it the originals and borrowed bits. It becomes even more exciting since this is a game the poet delights playing against himself.

John Pepper Clark. *Transition.* 18, 1965, p. 25

Okigbo takes pride in acknowledging his indebtedness to the literature of Europe. The first of his ''Four Canzones'' he himself identifies with Virgil's First Eclogue, for example. The interesting fact is that, as it is, this particular ''canzone'' loses nothing as a Nigerian poem for deriving from Virgil. It is evident, of course, that the inclination to adapt and translate from other poets is something Okigbo ''copied'' from Ezra Pound. Yet, we can say in this case that the Virgilian experience—the experience of that eclogue of exile—is not alien to the Nigerian environment. . . .

The poetry of Okigbo is almost the poetry of echoes. . . .

In the face of [the] very obvious echoes from nontraditional poetry, what can we say of Okigbo's poetry? The first point is that Okigbo takes pride in this indebtedness. For him this is not ''plagiarism,'' not even parasitism. When, earlier, I referred to Okigbo's ''literary'' imagination, I was trying, actually to find the terms of praise or censure appropriate to Okigbo's sense of his poetry. Okigbo's poetry is a poetry of the responses to pattern and organization. His poetry is also the poetry of an African, a native. Its significance derives from these two elements. On the one hand, a very strong traditional feeling (which we will come to presently), a feeling for the subject of Africa; on the other, an ''individual'' poet who loves to write, not as an African, but as a ''prodigal''—a poet who wants to feel that his poetry belongs to the literature of the "literate generation."

M. J. C. Echeruo. *Nigeria Magazine.* June 1966, pp. 151–53

The "difficulty" of Okigbo is such as to demand a real familiarity with his poetry, which handles a common body of symbols and turns continually upon a central pre-occupation. It is not such as to prevent his being the outstanding poet of English-speaking Africa. The familiarity he demands is no greater than that required by Eliot, by the later Yeats, by Rilke or Valéry; required, in fact, by any modern poet whose poetry rises above the occasional or the descriptive and seeks to record a whole cycle of spiritual and historical exploration.

Just how much does he owe to Eliot as a precursor in this type of poetic quest for reality? More, I believe, than is usually owed by a poet of his original talent to a single mentor. But then Eliot himself found it necessary to quote and echo other poets to an extent unprecedented in European literature. What Okigbo learnt from Eliot, and thus brought into the tradition of African poetry in English, was the art of handling complex ideas in simple language, by the constant re-arrangement of a selected group of words and symbols. Okigbo rehandles such words as laughter, dream, light, presence, voice, blood, exactly as Eliot teases out all the possible meanings of beginning, middle and end in "East Coker." Both poets use fragments of Catholic liturgy mixed with others from the classical world, paganism and magic; but where Eliot depends upon his reading of [Sir James] Frazer and Jessie Weston, Okigbo is able to draw upon a living knowledge of his forest village. It is above all the constant presence of this landscape which makes it such nonsense to dismiss Okigbo as "non-African." Obscurity itself has, in any case, a most respectable African ancestry in the poetry of oracle priests and diviners, whose concern lies close to Okigbo's own. Finally, nothing could be less like Eliot's dry world-weary tone than the lyrical, passionate voice of Okigbo with his rich, darting imagery and abundant youth. His apprenticeship was long, but the completion of his visionary sequence from *Heavensgate* to "Distances" in only three years (1961–64) is an achievement that African poetry will not easily surpass. [1969]

Gerald Moore. *The Chosen Tongue* (New York: Harper & Row, 1970), pp. 175–76

Okigbo's last poems, written from December 1965 to January 1966, are entitled "Path of Thunder." They were hailed as "poems prophesying war" but they are more than this; they are poems announcing Okigbo's involvement in the war as well, and all through them the ravages of war and death are described. It is clear from them which side Okigbo had chosen to support, but these are anything but partisan poems. They are an attempt to link all the earlier poems to the events in Nigeria in 1965–66. In all the poems that precede these it is sometimes hard to tell where they are set; they are certainly set in the open, in jungles or holy forests, but the symbols are universal, with the exception of some small obscure details that must be Nigerian. But "Path of Thunder" is different. The concern is Nigerian; the voice is definitely Okigbo's (these are the only poems in which he used his own name) and they are about politics and war. . . .

The cycle of poems heads towards an untimely end. Okigbo died in battle in 1967, near Nsukka. It seems clear that he was trying to control his material, all the factors that influenced his loyalties, trying to make these images fit the larger structure of his imagined poem, *Labyrinths.* And I think all of it does fit, for he conceived the poem so that it would embody all experience, and however unpoetic war is, he managed to combine this as well.

Paul Theroux. In Bruce King, ed. *Introduction to Nigerian Literature* (London: Evans Brothers, 1971), pp. 135–36

By its theme and craft "Path of Thunder" differs from the poetry written by Christopher Okigbo up to and including the first half of December 1965. This is so because in it Okigbo makes, for the first time ever, a forthright and direct political statement which itself undisguisedly defines the poet's own revolutionary option. But genetically speaking, "Path of Thunder" cannot be separated from the earlier poetry written by Okigbo, since it directly springs from the same parent stock or source of inspiration. Its very title, "Path of Thunder," is sufficiently indicative of the point from which it has taken its off-shoot and consequently branched off into what, given life, could have become a new tree. . . .

[It has been implied] that in Okigbo's poetic sensibility there seemed to exist a genetic struggle between a romantic pursuit of art for its own sake and a constantly intrusive awareness of the social relevance of art—its function, that is, as a means of embodying significant social comments. This tendency may then explain why in the Chorus [of "Lament of the Silent Sisters"] part of the poet's central theme—the atmosphere of political and social insecurity in the country, and indeed all over Africa—should be expressed within, and as though secondary to, an overriding artistic imperative.

Another possible, and much more likely, explanation is that Okigbo in 1962 was afraid of the possible consequences of committing to his poetry statements that would have direct political connotations in the Nigerian scene. This may mean also that he had not at that time fully resolved within himself the problem of whether art should be separated from politics or a poet be free from ideological commitments. At that time, too, the conclusion he came to with himself was obviously "Yes": refuge for the creative writer should be sought only in art and silence.

Sunday O. Anozie. *Christopher Okigbo: Creative Rhetoric* (London: Evans Brothers, 1972), pp. 174–75

[Okigbo] brought into his poetry all the heirlooms of his multiple heritage; he ranged with ease through Rome and Greece and Babylon, through the rites of Judaism and Catholicism, through European and Bengali literatures, through modern music and painting. But at least one perceptive Nigerian critic has argued that Okigbo's true voice only came to him in his last sequence of poems, "Path of Thunder," when he had finally and decisively opted for an African inspiration. This opinion may be contested, though I think it has substantial merit. The trouble is that Okigbo is such a bewitching poet, able to cast such a powerful spell that, whatever he cares to say or sing, we stand breathless at the sheer beauty and grace of his sound and imagery. Yet there is that undeniable fire in his last poems which was something new. It was as though the goddess he sought in his poetic journey through so many alien landscapes, and ultimately found at home, had given him this new thunder. Unfortunately, when he was killed in 1967 he left us only that little, tantalizing hint of the new self he had found. But perhaps he will be reincarnated in other poets and sing for us again like his sunbird whose imperishable song survived the ravages of the eagles. [1973]

Chinua Achebe. *Morning Yet on Creation Day* (Garden City, New York: Doubleday, 1975), pp. 44–45

All types of influences are to be found in Okigbo's verse. . . . Such imitation does not mean that Okigbo is at worst a derivative poet or at best a welder of two poetic traditions. He is much more complex than this and part of his success derives from his distinctive and private voice.

It is a voice that is not always clear; a hotchpotch of trivia makes it at times inarticulate—a solemn reference to yam tubers is based on a lewd Ibo song about the testicles of a ram—and titles of books like [Camara's] *The Gaze of the King* or of films like *Island in the Sun* are numerous in his poetry. Then there are snatches of the Bible as well as a poker-faced pidgin version of Little Bo Peep meant to look as "classical" as possible: *"etru bo pi alo a she e anando we aquandem . . . /ebili malo, ebili com com, ebili te que liquandem."* Words and allusions to a private mythological world abound— allusions to Enki, to someone named Flannagan who "preached the Pope's message," to Yunice "at the passageway." All this can be terribly misleading and can be stumbling blocks not only for eager non-African postgraduates bent on finding the "Africanness" of the work, but even for Nigerian Ibo speakers like Okigbo himself. . . .

Okigbo has himself helped to obscure the real issues relevant to an appreciation of his poetry by asserting that he does not strive toward meaning in his poetry, in the acceptable sense of the word. He has described himself to me as a "composer of sounds." . . .

Yet there is meaning in Okigbo's poetry even though it might be obscured by his anxious desire to pun or to exploit the more obvious devices of language for its tonal rather than its semantic effects. From this viewpoint "Distances" is the most pretentious and least successful of his poems. Besides the emblematic writing (which not only is out of place here but also does not succeed) there is a tendency to write nonsense; only sometimes is this redeemed by lines of beauty and meaning.

O. R. Dathorne. *The Black Mind* (Minneapolis: University of Minnesota Press, 1974), pp. 272–73, 276–77

Christopher Okigbo, the Nigerian poet killed in the 1967 civil war, was perhaps the most eclectic African poet of our time who wrote in English. A graduate of the University of Ibadan, he was part of the new community of African writers who did not study abroad and therefore escaped, to a large extent, the alienation and frustration of the earlier generation. Educated entirely in Africa, even though within the rigid framework of the colonial pattern, he was exposed to the best in colonial education in English and American letters. Thus the literary influences on him were varied and numerous. A few of these new writers, as illustrated earlier, also took their literary direction from the oral traditions which, given the half-hearted cultural intentions of the British, still had great

influence on some of them. The important thing is that the writers were free to choose their models. . . .

The words that sum up Okigbo's poetry are ordeal, agony, and cleansing. His poetic growth came through a unified consciousness and awareness of other cultures. External sounds and internal music coalesce into bursts of poetic brilliance. He was in essence a restless, tormented soul whose poetry assumed high-pitched, prophetic resonance and clarity. In his work he combines the choral voice of Greek classical verse, the litanic cadence of the mass, and the ritualistic pattern of traditional poetry.

Kofi Awoonor. *The Breast of the Earth* (Garden City, New York: Doubleday, 1975), pp. 217–18

Okigbo's earliest poems, dated 1957 (a year after he left Ibadan University) ranging from 1957–61, are entitled *Four Canzones*, and they show the influence of his classical education. The first canzone "Song of the Forest" is modelled on the first verse of Virgil's First Eclogue, *Tityrus*. . . .

Okigbo's short exercise is nothing of the scope of Virgil's Eclogue which is a long interchange between the shepards. Tityrus and Meliboeus in which Virgil brings together Rome's imperial destiny, the young Augustus who is to fulfill it and the misery of rural Italy into a single poetic vision. Okigbo does not develop his eclogue; nor does he expatiate on public themes. He brings into the poem rather the personal subjectivity of the poet in the twentieth century, in this way imitating Virgil innovatively, therefore achieving a new approach to the pastoral in material and tone. Might not Okigbo's imitativeness, which is to be permanent in his work, owe something to his knowledge that in the Roman tradition of verse, imitation, even plagiarism was systematized and honorable? As Virgil took from Theocritus, (among others), so did Okigbo from Virgil, making something new of the pastoral.

In fact, Okigbo's second canzone seems to be a variation of the pastoral device. Instead of two shepards in a dialogue, there are two characters A and B who is solo and unison poetize about the misery of life, deciding to "rest with wrinkled faces/watching the wall clock strike each hour/in a dry cellar" until they choke and die rather "than face the blasts and buffets" of "the mad generation" presumably in the cities. Despite the imitation of Virgilian pastoral poetry and the echoes of Pound however, these early canzones also show some African traits. Firstly, three of them are written to be read or sung to musical instruments after the style of Senghor and in the tradition of the indigenous presentation of African oral poetry. Secondly, like Achebe in his novels, Okigbo reveals a partiality to the "goose pimpling" ogene. Thirdly, the poems voice neo-African themes, such as the contrast between the old and the new after colonialism; the traditional and rural in Africa contrasted with the urbanized and the Westernized; the alienation of the Westernized African; the Hobson's choice he faces between joining "the mad generation" in the filthy Westernized cities or remaining with the alienated and restless poor in the hinterland; the challenge posed by Western intellectual activity to African thought, in particular African religion—the last a very close subject to Okigbo's heart because he was of the priest's family in his native village.

The fourth canzone "The Lament of the Lavender Mist" carries forward the theme of memory as an important experiential dimension to our poet's imaginative vision. This theme is now more symbolically expressed than previously. In style, the canzone is more broken in rhythm than the earlier pieces. It is evocative of meaning cumulatively through phrase juxtapositions; repetitions and rephrasings; freely collocating images from Christianity and African religion. . . .

On one level, "Lament of the Lavender Mist" can be read as the history of a love relationship; on another as an account of the poet's love for his art and his evolution as poet. It is the mythopoeic form employed in this Lament which is to energize Okigbo in the following long poems: *Silences* (*Transition*, 1962), *Heavensgate* (Mbari, 1962) and *Limits* (Mbari, 1962).

The first part of Silences, subtitled "The Lament of the Silent Sisters" was inspired according to Okigbo in his introduction to *Labyrinths*, (New York, 1971) by the events of the day which were the Western Nigeria crisis and the death of Patrice Lumumba. This Lament shows the poet borrowing from all and sundry, taking poetic flight from any image which touched his imagination. He has admitted in an interview in *Transition* to have been influenced in this period by "everything and everybody". Not only does this lament reveal the rewards of predatory and eclectic reading, it indicates yet another new poetic direction, (more evident in the Black Orpheus version) towards the conscious and experimental use of the resources of the song form such as choruses, refrains, and repetitions; the conveyance of meaning through a contrapuntal use of assonance, dissonance and even pure sound itself. The poet corroborates this intention in his introduction to *Labyrinths* where he says that *Silences* is "an attempt to elicit the music to which all imperishable cries must aspire . . . and the motif itself is developed by a series of related airs from sources as diverse as Malcom Cowley, Raja Ratnam, Stephane Mallarme, Tagore and Lorca" among others.

Most striking in the "Lament of the Silent Sisters" is the symbolist influence of transfering the modality of one sense to another. . . .

The second part of "The Silent Sisters" entitled "The Lament of the Drums" is an agitated poem about deprivation and loss; unavoidable pain and mourning expressed through analogues of unanswered praise songs and unconsummated feasts, uncommencable journeys, and unanswered letters; unstemmable tears of waling populations; and the lament of Ishtar for Tammuz. The emotions of this poem were aroused according to the poet in *Labyrinths* in the introduction, by the imprisonment of Chief Awolowo and the death of his eldest son, both Yorubas—which should interest expositors of the ethnic nature of the Nigerian civil war. Like *Distances* (*Transition*, 16, 1964) which is to follow, *Silences* foreshadows orgies of violence and carnage on the national landscape. *Distances* is a unified apocalyptic vision of consummation, rendered as a ritual of sacrifice involving the poet, who as victim and votive personage, walks the experiential stations of his cross, beyond "Death, herself . . . paring her fingernails" to his homecoming which he is sole witness".

Okigbo's last poems from "The Lament of the Masks" (1965), to "Path of Thunder" (*Black Orpheus* 21 [Feb. 1968], pp. 5–11) exploit, more than his earlier writing the attributes of African traditional poetry. Not only are popular proverbs and sayings, epigram and innuendo used, dramatic and situational African images abound such as the ritual of circumcision in "Elegy of the Wind", animal allegory used in the manner of the folktale in "Hurrah for Thunder" in a mode Clark later employs in *Casualties* in a more sustained manner.

Okigbo's poetry will have to be evaluated in two sets since the published forms of his poems under the title Labyrinths are so dissimilar to their earlier published forms and so reworked as to be completely new poems. His introduction to the volume sheds light on the artists who have influenced him. No mention, however, is made of Senghor, to whom one finds similarities in poetic modes and in formal presentation; situational and verbal—the main difference being the stance of the poet protagonist.

Okigbo is significant because he did what most of the West African writers in English were doing in the 60's—a very personal poetry in a personal idiom—and he brought this mode to a virtuoso point. He represents their initially "art for art's sake" attitude which changed over time. His development therefore traces a West African pattern of artistic evolution from private anguish to public commitment. In addition, Okigbo exemplifies a neo-African wedding of the African to the Western poetic traditions to the rejuvenation of the effeteness and world weariness of the latter. He is, to my mind, one of the finest African poets in English, to be valued for the sheer beauty of his finely honed verse, his most delicate sensibility and the artistic discipline which informs the structure and the lyrical simplicity of his verse, a simplicity which conveys a false impression of facility.

Omolara Leslie. Donatus Ibe Nwoga, ed. *Critical Perspectives on Christopher Okigbo* (Washington, D.C.: Three Continents Press, 1984), pp. 288–98

Christopher Okigbo is obviously the most significant poet of [1960s Nigeria] not only because of his national relevance but also because of his artistic excellence. He can rightly be described as the poet of Nigerian history, for there is a movement in his work which parallels that of the history of Nigeria from her contact with the white man to the early stages of the civil war, when Okigbo died. *Heavensgate* and *Limits* are a re-enactment of the cultural (especially religious) alienation which the country experienced during the colonial era; "Distances" is a conclusion to *Heavensgate* and *Limits* and a final reversion to indigenous traditional religion; "Silences: Lament of the Silent Sisters" and "Lament of the Drums" are a study in Nigeria's post-colonial politics with its confusion and lack of any sense of direction which led to the disillusionment of the masses; and "Path of Thunder" is an assessment of the coup d'état of January 1966 and a verdict that is also a prophecy of war.

If Okigbo's poetry is "one long elaborate poem" as one critic remarked, [O. R. Dathorne, *Journal of Commonwealth Literature*, No. 5, 1968], or if it has "organic relatedness" as another observed [S. O. Anozie, *Christopher Okigbo*, 1972], and as the poet himself stated the binding link must be sought in the story of the country from the colonial period to the beginning of the civil war rather than in any other source. In spite of Anozie's argument that what makes all of Okigbo's poems one long poem is verbal linkage, the fact remains that each sequence of poems except perhaps "Four Canzones" crystallizes around a chapter in Nigeria's historical experience. If Okigbo is the hero of most of his poems, he is so only in the sense that he carries the burden of his people's cultural and historical evolution. The sufferings of a nation can also be seen as those of any one man in the country.

Okigbo's poetry is therefore much less personal than many people think. The religious conflict which is dealt with extensively in Heavensgate and Limits, for example, is grounded in firm historical reality. . . .

It is significant that these examples of historical relevance and factual links are found in Okigbo's early poetry, for it is often with reference to his early work that critics have asserted that Okigbo was pursuing "art for its own sake" [Christopher Okigbo, 1972], or that "meaning" was not his concern [Studies in Black Literature 1, 1976]. Okigbo himself gave this impression that he did not care for meaning: "Personally I don't think that I have ever set out to communicate a meaning. It is enough that I try to communicate experience which I consider significant". In spite of this statement, however, there is meaning in his poetry—meaning that is historical, not just personal, though it is coloured by personal experience. Indeed even "Four Canzones," Okigbo's earliest poem which has no overt historical links still has much social relevance. The first and third canzones compare and contrast the city and the village and find that the latter possesses all the blessings which the former lacks. The second canzone is a social comment, while the fourth deals with a private love experience. In this way "Four Canzones" constitutes a logical introduction to Okigbo's later poetry, giving an early hint of the three major areas of experience which were to be developed in his poetry: namely, cultural atavism (nostalgia), socio-political problems, and the nature of carnal love. Thus of all Nigerian poets, Okigbo can be said to be the most Nigerian from the point of view of not just nationality alone but, most importantly, of comprehensive national consciousness. Hence his central position in the growth of Nigerian poetry.

This consciousness is not limited to the content of Okigbo's poetry: it is also present in the form of his verse. More than any other Nigerian poet writing in English, Okigbo has explored and exploited the art of his indigenous (Igbo) traditional oral literature and the vernacular rhetoric of his people. The incantatory quality of his poems derives from the musical nature of Nigerian oral poetry, at times adopting its very form. Okigbo has also drawn some of his images from Nigerian folk tales and from the local environment. For example, the image of a bird standing "on one leg" in the second section of "The Passage" recalls the story of a fowl that went to a strange land and stood on one leg because it did not understand the customs of the people of that place. The experience re-enacted in the poem is that of solitude in spiritual (religious) exile, when, though the protagonist had been initiated into Christianity, he was ignorant of the customs of the new religion, and had therefore to stand apart, at a loss, like a bird on one leg. Examples of imagery based on the local environment are rife in Okigbo's poetry. Many of his poems are set against the background of shrines in groves which are customarily the scene of traditional religious worship and sacrifice. He can also fashion a specific image out of a particular feature of his rural surroundings: "Faces of black like long black columns of ants" ["The Passage"]. Furthermore, Okigbo enhances the form of some of his poems by working into them vernacular expressions which have been translated literally. In "Lament of the Lavender Mist" for example, he equates the lady of the poem with "Kernels of the waters of the sky"; this is a word-for-word translation of the Igbo term for hailstone, itself an object considered by the Igbo people to be a symbol of purity and delicate beauty. Also the expression "shadow of rain" in "Eyes watch the stones" is a direct translation of the Igbo term for the nimbus cloud which is the harbinger of rain.

By means of these and other artistic devices, Okigbo gave his poetry the imprint of Africanity, and subsequent poets have seen this as a major factor in making Nigerian poetry truly Nigerian in spite of its being written in English.

> Romanus N. Egudu. In Albert S. Gerard, ed. *European-Language Writing in Sub-Saharan Africa,* Volume 2 (Akademiai Kiado, 1986), pp. 750–54

BIBLIOGRAPHY
*Heavensgate*, 1962; *Limits*, 1964; Labyrinths, with *Path of Thunder,* 1971; *Collected Poems*, 1986

# OKRI, Ben (1959–)
## Nigeria

With the possible exception of "What the Tapster Saw," which is more allegorical than the rest, [Ben] Okri's six stories [in *Stars of the New Curfew*] are all "true" reflections on life in Nigeria. The first goes back to the Biafran War; the rest are set in the present; all are vivid and frightening. The love story, "When the Lights Return," is like a guilt-ridden dream in which the heroine, white-clad Maria, is presented with Okri's consummate skill as the archetypal mistress of moral blackmail. In the background: the Lagos ghetto of Munshin, peopled with loathsome soldiers and a dead man who rises from a rubbish heap to preach revolt.

Okri's writing is suffused with helpless anger at the alienation of Nigerian society, the corruption not only of the rulers but also of the ruled who seem to connive at their own oppression. "The strongest fear in this town," one of his characters says, "is to be defenseless, to be without a powerful godfather, and therefore at the mercy of the drums. New starts are growing every day. They grow from the same powers, the same rituals . . ."The trouble with most people is that they cannot *see* the nature of the evil surrounding them. In "Worlds that Flourish," the hero, a clerk who is sacked without apparent reason, leaves his job without bitterness and tells his neighbor he feels "fine." This is "because you go around as if you don't have any eyes," the neighbor says. But even vision does not protect you in Okri's Nigeria. When the exclerk begins to see, he flees the city in horror, to end up in the village of the dead. There he rediscovers his neighbor who has been killed by a soldier who now displays *three* eyes.

> Suzanne Cronje. *New Statesman & Society.* 1, 8 (July 29, 1988), pp. 43–44

In a short story the hero ought to discover some truth about himself, his fellow men, or society that has universal significance. Through him the reader achieves enlightenment, if not moral upliftment. For example, suffering makes us noble, we are our brother's keepers, labor makes us free, and so on.

The heroes in Ben Okri's collection of short stories [*Stars of the New Curfew*] do not have these simple consolations; they cannot find relief, much less salvation, in homilies. One hero hates suffering because it does not improve or ennoble, but sobers and hardens. The nightmares that they experience in life make them see life itself as nightmare. When it is discovered that reality is hallucination, the need for hardness and sobriety becomes obvious, and the experience of meaningless suffering becomes an epistemology of pain and illusion. . . .

Readers unfamiliar with the reality about which Okri writes will praise his fantastic imagination and wealth of invention. While not detracting from Okri's artistic powers, it is only fair to point out that what he writes about may appear hallucinatory and nightmarish but is nonetheless real. There is more description here—very accurate description—than invention. Okri holds up a mirror to actors in a neocolonial society who are incapable of distinguishing between tragedy and comedy. . . .

The style of these stories is lean, economical, almost claustrophobic. Floral embellishment would have destroyed the effects [it aims] to produce. The skeletal language—like clean-picked bones— allows us to see men, women, and children struggling viciously or gracefully for survival, then wondering if there is any purpose to it all, or whether survival is an end in itself.

P. F. Wilmot. *West Africa.* August 1, 1988, p. 1396

*The Landscapes Within* deals with the process of maturation of a young, bright, sensitive, and lonely artist as he tries to survive the general philistinism, corruption, and inhumanity that characterize big city life in Lagos. As a child, Omovo had moved with his parents from Igboland after the Nigeria-Biafra Civil War and had progressed quite well at school until he was prevented from taking the all-important school certificate examinations because of his father's failure to pay the necessary fees on time. Life becomes increasingly miserable for the young man when, not long after the death of his mother, his father remarries and, as a result of domestic tension, Omovo's elder brothers—Okur and Umeh—are kicked out of the family fold by their father.

After the struggle that usually accompanies a novel dealing with personal development, Omovo is finally able to find a job; and though he does have some friends (such as a painter called Dr. Okocha, Keme, the journalist, and Okoro, a veteran of the Nigerian Civil War), he becomes a lonely and sad person who finds solace only in painting and in the company of his lover-cum-friend Ifeyinwa, a married neighbor. Omovo and Ifeyinwa become attracted to each other because of some similar qualities (they are both sensitive, introverted, impressionable, intelligent, and great lovers of both literature and the visual arts), and also because they both feel trapped in a morally corrupt and physically degrading environment. Ifeyinwa has been forced into a life of misery because she was pushed into a loveless marriage after her father's suicide.

In scenes that clearly echo Ayi Kwei Armah's *The Beautyful Ones Are Not Yet Born* (on both the literal and symbolic levels), Okri shows how Omovo becomes more and more aware of the extensive malaise that pervades his society. But, unlike Armah's anonymous protagonist, who merely drifts aimlessly and helplessly in a sea of corruption, Omovo thinks that not only can he see through the wholly materialistic nature of the society, but that he can even depict the dirty quality of the corrupt society on canvas. He increasingly learns, however, that for his actions to be more meaningful he has to do more than merely express a symbolic disgust with corruption. Thus, by the end of *The Landscapes*

*Within*, Omovo, who is often depicted as passive, nearly always given to reverie, has become capable of making down-to-earth assessments of events around him and able to act accordingly. After a series of terrible, even tragic, events (for example, he is forced to resign from his job because he dares display some modicum of integrity; Ifeyinwa, while trying to escape from her brutal husband, is senselessly killed in an insane war between her village and a neighboring village), the protagonist finally sees the need to forge a new vision of reality. Inspired by a poem written by his brother, Okur, Omovo suggests (albeit implicitly) that it is not enough for him as an artist to be merely cognizant of the filth around him; he should be ready to act.

Abioseh Michael Porter. *World Literature Written in English.* 28, 2 (autumn 1988), pp. 203–4

"Little flowers in the shadows that's what we all are. Nobody knows what the larger shadows will do to the flowers; nobody knows what the flowers will become," says the mother to Jeffia, the protagonist of Ben Okri's novel *Flowers and Shadows*. The titular leitmotif iterates through the entire book, in variants spoken by different characters, as an omnipresent scorching sun beats down upon them all and surveys their actions.

Jeffia, an eighteen-year-old boy, suddenly starts noticing things about himself, as if the hushed, smooth life of his big home with its well-kept gardens, nicely furnished and air-conditioned rooms, servants, three cars, and other luxuries of well-to-do Nigerian society had ceased to exist. He is faced with the squalor of his surroundings, the filthy roads full of beggars and hungry people, the corrupt police, and suspicions about his father's integrity. The death of his best friend aggravates the situation even further and deepens his insight. . . .

Ben Okri was nineteen when he wrote *Flowers and Shadows*, and the acclaim it received was confirmed by the success of his second, *The Landscapes Within*. The short-story collections *Incidents at the Shrine* and *Stars of the New Curfew* offered further proof of his gifts. Okri has served as poetry editor of *West Africa* and in 1987 received the Commonwealth Writers Prize for Africa and the Aga Khan Prize for Fiction, sponsored by the *Paris Review*.

Nadezda Obradović. *World Literature Today.* 64, 4 (autumn 1990), p. 687

With *The Landscapes Within*, Ben Okri extends the line of novels (most notably by [Chinua] Achebe, Ngugi [wa Thiong'o], [Wole] Soyinka and [Ayi Kwei] Armah) which have sought to capture the disappointment and disillusion in postindependence Africa. And as the work of a stylist, the novel traces its line from works by Soyinka and Armah—whose writings it also recalls as a literary work in which the effort to imply, demonstrate, or posit aspects of the theory or practice of art is central or considerable. The novel paints the decline and decay, the materialism and corruption of a nation and the sense of loss and futility among the people; but it does all this so as to make conspicuous the sensitive character of its protagonist, Omovo, a young man aspiring to become a distinguished artist. In pursuing this primary interest, *The Landscapes Within* throws its spotlight on the turbulent, clustered mind of Omovo in order to make clear the lines of a mind's growth. . . .

*The Landscapes Within* is, above all else, a portrait of Omovo as a young man and artist, with special attention paid to his growing mind. He is shown picking his difficult way emotionally through the welter of life's experiences and intellectually through a clutter of ideas and concepts. His efforts to interfuse life and art, and to reach or grasp views and take attitudes on the aesthetics of art are also revealed. In these efforts, his ideals and models, as well as his preferences and affinities, underline the eclecticism of his mind. Out of the quarried pieces and fragments, however, Omovo is yet to build a coherent theory of art; but then, as he himself says: "I am still learning." It is to stress the education of his mind, to emphasize the point that the young man is still learning that, again and again, the author draws attention to the rather vast cultural background (African and European) from which Omovo seeks his inspiration in painting, literature, and music.

Ayo Mamudu. *Commonwealth Essays & Studies.* 13, 2 (Spring 1991), pp. 85, 91

Ben Okri has been successful as a sensitive and careful [short-story] writer and poet. His short stories evoke the materially empty but mentally throbbing lives of people reduced to poverty in the ghettos of Lagos and other cities of Nigeria. His colorful characters fight themselves and their neighbors in a space that is forever narrowing physically; but they call forth another space, somewhere beyond the hand of poverty, and lay claim to it.

*The Famished Road,* his latest novel . . . teems with these dual spaces, these poor characters, these aspiring human beings who are forever defending their humanity against all forms of authority beginning with that of the slum landlord. Right from the beginning, the central character, Azaro, is captured in his duality, a being conscious of the world of his unborn companions who are forever wanting him back in their world and his poor parents, Mum and Dad, who tell him frankly that they have nothing to offer him except love and a promise of a good life. When those offerings are placed against the enticing images of the unborn, it is not always clear in the mind of Azaro which of the two worlds he should lean towards. The world of the living he enjoys through wandering in towns and in the forest, seeing double all the time and frightening his poor parents who sometimes react, not with the love they promise him, but with anger and frustration. In crossing a busy street, should Azaro allow himself to be knocked down by a car, thus permitting him to join the world of his unborn companion spirits who are anxiously awaiting his return [or] should he cross the road to the other side successfully and make his parents happy. . . .

This is not one story, but many stories. More than that, this is the story of the transition of many families from poverty through the ghettos of the cities to the posh areas of the town. It is the portrait of a world that stubbornly, perhaps because of the poverty of the people, clings to the superstitions and traditional healing devices of ancient Africa. It is also a narration of the failure of the modern state to effect for the better the lives of the majority of its citizens. It is also a successful portrait of the physical and mental world of the wretched of the earth.

The presentation of that spiritual world is not a gimmick of literary style borrowed from Latin America as a few writers from Africa are being deceived into practicing. Here, the mental image of the world of the traditional African is laid bare, side by side with

the modern world brought into being as a result of the encounter with Europe. In this Ben Okri is being true to the world he depicts.

Kole Omotoso. *West Africa.* April 1–7, 1991, pp. 474–75

Ben Okri is the novelist of portents and of wonders. His last book, *The Famished Road,* had the Abiku-child Azaro wandering in from the world of the spirits, nosing the everyday world with his curiosity, exploring a terrain which, it gradually became clear, had more than a little in common with Nigeria on the brink of independence. In this environment Azaro the spirit-child existed as witness, interpreter, and victim: never quite in charge, never quite *savant.* Wonders took place before his astonished eyes, and we, the readers, participated in his astonishment.

In *Songs of Enchantment,* Azaro reappears, and so do the other members of the cast: the stalwart mother, energetic and wayward father, Madam Koto, bar owner and source both of mayhem and of strength. But this is very far from being a sequel. It is arguably a better novel since, riding on the back of its brother, it has no need to use its strength. Despite its relative shortness, the pace of this new book is leisurely, masterful. It takes its time and achieves its effects slowly. . . .

Okri shows us a society in the throes of convulsions familiar to those who contemplate the dilemmas facing Africa and the Third World. He is less concerned about the causes of these convulsions, or indeed the ways of ending them than the potential for transfiguration that lies inside the events. Okri shows us revolutions in the making, and the way that these evidences of instability hold within themselves the energy which may redeem them. It is why so many of his characters seem occupied in telling stories, since each story—a novel within a novel—is a paradigm of that sublime unpredictability of the phenomenal world which, seen through eyes alert to its magic, can mend the wounds of society even as it seems to rend them. Such novelists are needed because they teach us that, if we wish to progress and revive our forces, the very material for that revival may lie within the conditions of seeming defeat.

Robert Fraser. *West Africa.* April 12–18, 1993, p. 616

In my view *The Famished Road* is an example of decolonized fiction. It asks us, as critics, to look beyond the postcolonial and to recognize a new direction in African literature, one which, while recognizing historic situations, is not limited to a historic perspective. The meaning of the road in *The Famished Road* and its "abiku" traveller. . . , Okri presents the regenerative forces of replacement, rather than the debilitating colonial legacy of displacement, and therefore moves beyond the historical catalepsy which has marked so much postcolonial writing.

It is apparent from the novel's opening sentences that Okri's symbolism embraces more than historical concerns: "In the beginning there was a river. The river became a road and the road branched out to the whole world. And because the road was once a river it was always hungry." The rotation of definite and indefinite articles (a river becomes the river which becomes a road which then becomes the road, harking back to that time when there was once a river), is language which subtly chooses the cyclical transformations of myth over the chronological sequence of history. The biblical overtone of "[i]n the beginning" also suggests the mythic possibilities of the narrative. The opening lines immediately place us in "illo tempore", beyond ordinary time. The transformation that Okri describes is self-transformation. The road has not been built by anyone in particular; it simply "becomes". That the transformation is not a satisfactory one (which is implied by the road's insatiable hunger) suggests that an error of cosmic proportion has taken place, cosmic because neither human being nor historical event is to blame. It is the nature of this road to be hungry, "hungry for great transformations." It demands of itself and others imaginative acts of self-renewal. . . . The origin of the "famished road" lies in myth, not history. And so the fate of colonialism in *The Famished Road* is that, not only is it disqualified in its claim to be a devouring force, colonialism itself becomes devoured, as mythopoeia overwrites history.

Azaro, the narrator, is an "abiku", a child who keeps dying and returning to the same mother, and who moves constantly between the world of spirits and the world of the living. The "abiku" has appeared before in Nigerian literature. In Chinua Achebe's *Things Fall Apart*, for instance, the protagonist's daughter is an "ogbanje", the Igbo word for abiku. In making Azaro the narrator, Okri presents the "abiku" as a distinctly African archetype, one who in his liminal state would appear to be an ideal example of postcolonial duality. However, on close reading, we come to realize that Azaro's duality is not simply a symptom of his postcolonial milieu.

The sense of duality which dominates postcolonial writing has its origin partly in early colonialist writings where it is expressed in the colonialist's problematic response to the alien surroundings. Like the narrator-explores of these writings, Azaro is presented as an outsider embarking on a journey of discovery. He explores the "world of the living" and more specifically, the meaning and nature of the "famished road". Like Conrad's Marlow, he witnesses a number of nightmarish and bewildering spectacles. Yet for all their similarities, there are notable differences between Azaro and the narrator-explores of colonialist writings. Conrad writes that Marlow feels "bewitched and cut off from everything [he] had known once" as he travels up the Congo. Okri, on the other hand, deliberately obscures the difference between Azaro's former and present worlds; both are characterized by timelessness, cyclical recurrence and transfiguration. . . .

The unique self-transforming nature of Okri's "road" also breaks the historic catalepsy and moves the narrative beyond postcolonial concerns. Throughout the novel, Azaro notices people leaving "sacrifices" for the road. He learns that they do this to appease the "famished road" so that it will not devour them. Azaro's father tells his son how the road came to be "famished". It is a story that draws upon the Yoruba myth of Ogun who is, among other things, the Guardian of the Road. Azaro's father tells him that there was once a King of the Road, an insatiable giant, who ran out of food in the forest where he lived, so he turned to "the roads that men travel". As long as people fed him, he would allow them to pass freely, but when they stopped feeding him due to a famine, he went on a rampage eating everything and everyone in sight, even corpses. Delegations were sent "to reason with him", and they too were eaten. Finally the people gathered all the poisons of the world and fed it to the King of the Road. . . .

Repetition is a predominant theme in both the myth and the story. Although the people manage to poison the King of the Road, he does not die; he merely changes form. They are unable to break the cycle of his ravenous hunger, and they have to continue

appeasing him. Their misfortune is expressed as a continuing cycle rather than as a succession of events. The story also emphasizes the dualistic nature of the road. It has both god-like and human qualities. Azaro's own duality, as a spirit child, is thus reflected in the story of the road and in the myths of his people. The presence of this story within the larger narrative suggests that the "doom of repetition" which is the fate of the "abiku", and which generally pervades the novel, is understood by the narrator and the other characters not in historical but mythical and endogenous terms.

Margaret Cezair-Thompson. *Journal of Commonwealth Literature*. 31, 2 (fall 1996), pp. 33–44

"There is a story", Azaro's father tells Azaro, "of an African emperor who ordered all the frogs in his realm to be exterminated because they disturbed his sleep. The frogs were killed and he slept serenely till the mosquitoes, whose larvae the frogs fed on, came and spread disease. His people fled and what was once a proud land became a desert waste".

*Infinite Riches* is a version of that story. It is set, as were the two earlier volumes of the *Famished Road* sequence, in the African ghetto which is home to Ben Okri's narrator, the spirit-child Azaro. We have never known much about the location of this ghetto (mapping is not Azaro's business), except that it borders a city and a forest. The city is where Azaro's father carries loads and where his mother hawks goods. The forest, home of the community's myths and stories, is where Azaro makes contact with the spirit world; where his imagination takes flight and where his narrative is nourished. The first sign that the ghetto's ecology is being disrupted, that the mosquitoes are taking the place of the frogs, is the sound of electric saws in the forest.

There are political and economic explanations for the devastation of the forest. Colonial government is coming to an end. What follows is internal division, a politics of violence, and, as Volume Three of the novel cycle seems to look forward to Volume Four, the possibility of an apocalyptic civil war. With the end of colonialism, the shaky economic structure it had given rise to, the mildly corrupt entrepreneurialism of Madame Koto, is also breaking down. In its place, and unchecked amid the political chaos, corporate imperialism cuts down the forests, stripping the place of its resources.

Broadly speaking, this sequence of events is the plot of *Infinite Riches*. The novel opens with the wrongful arrest of Azaro's father and with his brutalization at the hands of the police. The event has local consequences: chiefly that this previously combative man is rendered quiescent, while his wife is made powerful by the campaign for his release. Primarily, though, the purpose of this opening episode is to thread the life of the ghetto into the transition from colonial to post-colonial existence which, Okri's geographical vagueness suggests, could be read as the generic plot of postwar African history. The question for this, and, one suspects, for later volumes in the series, is whether Azaro's community can resist being taken over by forces and stories not of its own making.

This is a hard enough question for any writer, but it is particularly hard for Okri, because in asking it he risks losing the readers he won with the first book of the cycle, *The Famished Road*. Through its daring reconception of the relation of imagination to politics, the earlier novel aimed to touch what is left of the human spirit. It succeeded, and the effect was transformative. What this third volume allows one to see, however, is that *The Famished Road* could achieve such a sublime impact, in part because the ghetto community it presented was self-contained. Outside forces were at work, but, desperate politicians and new motor cars aside, they tended to stay outside. Azaro's narrative, as a consequence, was free to take its own shape, to move between the extreme limitations of his material environment, and the fabulous possibilities of the spirit world. What emerged was a mentality just about in balance. Azaro, and his father, returned from the world of visions just sufficiently inspired to meet the struggles of their daily existence.

In *Infinite Riches*, this precarious ecology is severely threatened; the destruction of the forest by half-seen forces marks the arrival of alien stories, of new, domineering ways of thinking. As a consequence, Azaro's narrative is no longer his own. He is still the guiding presence in the book, and his wanderings still produce surging, intoxicating catalogues, whether they are of the grotesque minglings of political rallies or the impossible metamorphoses of imaginary space, but now he has to take account of those who would write the history of Africa differently. Okri's concern, in other words, as he contemplates the post-colonial moment, is with the "battle of rewritten histories". Azaro, accordingly, is obliged to listen, and as he does so, other narrative centres emerge. The last Governor-General is writing a confused history of the emergent nation, which glorifies the civilizing effect of the British and celebrates the natural beauty of the place. Madame Koto raves against her people; against their refusal to embrace her mercantilist image of progress and their insistence on honouring "too many gods". The corporation men develop her discourse, the shallow realism of "superstitious Africans" leading inexorably to the all too eloquent language of violence. . . .

This multiplicity of narrative voices leads to an angry self-consciousness in Okri's writing here, which, in certain respects, is knowingly and unavoidably diminishing. His ear for the competing voices is acute; the Governor General's reflections, for instance, provide a brilliantly clear essay on the contradictions of the colonial mind. But, as a wised-up Azaro weighs the strengths and weaknesses of alternative narratives, his own story cannot avoid taking on a studied quality.

This, however, is all part of the larger story Okri's cycle is determined to tell. *Infinite Riches* does not have the transforming impact of *The Famished Road*, but it has its own kind of power. Throughout the novel, Okri resists the temptation to reach too quickly for the uplifting possibilities of Azaro's way of thinking and writing. This is precisely because he is dealing with a moment when such spiritual lyricism must take stock of other ways of thinking if it is to continue to claim explanatory and inspirational force. Okri persists in his self-restraint to the end; the novel culminates with the aftermath of an appallingly violent political rally. It is a moment, as Azaro registers, not for inspiration but for reckoning.

David Herd. *Times Literary Supplement*. 4980 (September 11, 1998), p. 23

BIBLIOGRAPHY
*Flowers and Shadows*, 1980; *The Landscapes Within*, 1981; *Incidents at the Shrine*, 1986; *Stars of the New Curfew*, 1988; *The Famished Road*, 1991; *An African Elegy*, 1992; *Songs of Enchantment*, 1993; *Astonishing the Gods*, 1995; *Birds of Heaven*, 1996; *Dangerous Love*, 1996; *A Way of Being Free*, 1997; *Infinite Riches*, 1998

# ONWUEME, Tess
## Nigeria

Tess Onwueme's victory at the Association of Nigerian Authors (ANA) drama contest in 1985 called attention to the artistic potential of her dramaturgy. Until then she had had only two published plays, *A Hen Too Soon* (1983) and *The Broken Calabash* (1984). Like most artistic debuts, *A Hen* was an amateurish work. The play revealed two basic problems: the conception of artistic verisimilitude was poor, and the linguistic facets fell short of the level for which accomplished African dramas are now recognized. In a short critique of Onwueme's first play entitled "A Writer Too Soon," Afam Ebeogu, despite awarding the work an overall passing grade, finds weak points in its "hackneyed" theme and in the nonsustenance of the feminist undertone.

*A Hen Too Soon* is conceived on the beaten track of modernism versus traditionalism. An educated girl, Gladys, is to be given away in marriage to a man as old as her father. She objects, but because tradition is stronger than iconoclastic gestures, she marries Oboli, the father of the affluent Amuzia. The marriage is a failure because Oboli is unable to give Gladys a child. Amuzia, who later marries Gladys for his father, undertakes to accomplish what his father has been unable to do to the girl's satisfaction. The child Gladys bears as soon as Oboli dies is "neither boy nor girl" but instead a monster. The play ends on a melodramatic note, as kinsmen gathered in the new obi under the chairmanship of Ogbe argue as to the rightness of Gladys's course of action following her husband's failure to "perform." The eventual verdict is an appeal that the audience should "go now and think about these." There is little to think about, because the poetic verisimilitude of the play is unlikely, and therefore there can be little willing suspension of disbelief on the part of the audience; there is simply no real girl with Gladys's qualifications and character traits living in Nigeria in the penultimate decade of the twentieth century. Altogether, *A Hen Too Soon* was a fair price for a debut and a signal of the bounty that was to come.

*The Desert Encroaches* (1985), described by Olu Obatemi as "positively ambitious," is a clarion call for change in a world dominated by the arms race, by the covetous lust for others' resources, by oppression and repression, by ideological rigidity and similar lethal maladies. The work is Onwueme's "large" play because of its scope and the range of its concerns. As the world faces a possible nuclear war, the playwright calls for peace, for a new attitude which will supplant the present struggle of "shooting the stars, scuffling for ascendancy, daring each other, while we burn below." Her tangent is largely African and Third World because, according to Donkey, "we are the earth's surplus." The characters are animals, which establishes the allegorical purity of the play. These animals are grouped according to the three main divisions of today's world: the North/West, the Eastern Commune, and the South. The Parrot (Okilii) and the Dove are said to have no fixed address and are respectively given the functions of social commentator and peacemaker. . . .

The Dove, the holder of the olive branch, urges "animals of the four winds" to "twist the parallel poles" so that they will no longer read "a sharp North and a sharp South" but "a circle . . . a circle with equal radii. Where the North is equidistant from the South. Where the East is equidistant from the West." These are optimistic but naïve voices, because the differences are deep-seated. The specter of oppression looms large in a world dominated by Lion (USA) and Bear (USSR). Donkey's remarks—for example, "The earth I mine, the seeds I man, but at harvest I am 'manned',"—encapsulate the source of the fear and suspicion between Third World countries and the big powers.

In movement 4 the big animals of the West meet to consider their strategy for perpetuating their preeminence. Lion tells Hyena and Wolf: "We must plan as one in our sector to agree as a common front. We cannot be taken in with all that nonsense and the peaceful jazz at the assembly." Hyena's comment to the effect that "there is the master and there is the servant" represents both the view of the big countries and the motivation of oppressive individuals and multinational firms. The play ends on a positive note when the Director (Okilii/Parrot) speaks in this vein:

> Yes I can see a new dawn coming. . . . A new sun rises . . . we must not only ask for peace but force it to be accepted. . . . Will you join hands with the other forces in making the world a better place for us to live in?

*Ban Empty Barn* (1986) is another of Onwueme's experimental plays in which animals are characters. The scope here is less global; the focus of interest is Nigeria with her deep-rooted hierarchical structure of oppression. The "central" characters are two hungry chicks, Bene and Bede. With their mother Nene, they scratch the earth without earning much from the effort. As the play opens, they are engrossed in a discussion on the quality of the lives of animals in general. Their human master's barn is without food, and he himself is experiencing difficult times. The truth is that he is a victim of the gluttony of middlemen and the country's unevenly applied austerity measures. His wife is quarrelsome, more so when he is unable to supply enough money for the baby's food.

The play is a study both of power and of its various means of perpetuation. Dede boasts, "The rule of governance is nothing but imposition." While Dede is preening himself, proud of the crown he carries on his head, Keke, a rival cock, "with a startling speed knocks off Dede's crown [and] pushes him into the pool of water" in what is clearly a coup d'état. Keke describes his action as possessing "military precision" and remarks, "Kingship, wealth, money, name / opportunity / just opportunity / Grab it at the right time! / Precision . . . precision . . . / I AM KING NOW" (57). However, there is soon a collective coup d'état when all the chickens "pounce on Keke, seize him, toss him up and down. They make a mockery of him. Smash his crown. Plume him to size and sit him on the ground." *Ban Empty Barn* ends here, and one can surmise that the collective putsch is Onwueme's preference, not the seizure of the separate components of state machinery.

In *The Broken Calabash* (1984) the world of the play is no longer fabular. The work seems to be an attempt to return to the thesis of *A Hen Too Soon*, which the dramatist might have realized was poorly handled in the earlier play. Here both the theme and the language are better implemented. The play is not a feminist work in the vulgar sense of the term; it is instead an effort to assert the individual self and, in that way, earn some self-actualization. . . .

Tess Onwueme has also published *The Artist's Homecoming* (1986), *Cattle Egret Versus Nama* (1986), *Mirror for Campus* (1987), and *The Reign of Wazobia* (1988). In each of these plays she attacks the forces of backwardness and in that way calls for new social forms and values in order to create and forge a new personal and social understanding. In *The Artist's Homecoming* Rufina's father is as domineering as was Courtuma in *The Broken Calabash*.

Chief Fatoba is class conscious and will not allow his daughter to be friends with Dupe, whose mother "sells fish in the market" and whose family "live down the gutter" (87). This is unacceptable to Rufina, who forthrightly says, "I do not see anything improper in her [Dupe].". . .

Tess Onwueme's feminist play is *The Reign of Wazobia*. Although the struggle by women who want to earn personal satisfaction in life is central to most of her stage work, it is in this play that the dramatist sets out to place conscious emphasis on what women can do to force society to reckon with them. Her suggested solution, it seems, is rebellion. The king of Ilaaa in Anioma Kingdom has just died. Tradition demands that there be selected a female king-surrogate, who will reign for three seasons before another king emerges. Wazobia, an educated female, is the new regent. However, at the expiration of three seasons Wazobia refuses to quit the throne. This is the drama's central conflict. . . .

Each of Tess Onwueme's published plays so far, it would seem, is a clarion call for social change, the cultivation of new attitudes and new hopes. The society she targets in her works for the stage is both national and international, and at each level her position seems to be that the old order of traditional, social, and economic oppression must give way to a new and more healthful one. Her quest for social change goes beyond the raising of feminist consciousness in society to include a swipe at the diminishing status of supposedly independent African countries as a result of the powerful gains of neocolonialism. In her plays there is the consistent vision that, at both the social and the personal level, a clear disparity exists in the quality of people's lives, a situation which has been promoted by the oppressive tendencies immanent in our kind of polity. In the end we observe in Onwueme's dramatic corpus an artistic desire to change the status quo through the ridiculing of the obnoxious in our tradition as well as by exposing the political and economic conditions in the society depicted in her drama.

J. O. J. Nwachukwu—Agbada. *World Literature Today*. 66, 3 (summer 1992), pp. 464–67

An "operatic drama" in seven movements, *The Desert Encroaches* is an unusual blend of African fable and polemic. Familiar animals such as the tortoise and the lion are joined by a strange bear. Then at times humans take over: a director, a one-legged solider. Dominant in most movements are the lion with a cowboy hat (Reagan?) and the bear from the North (Russia?). With their "nuclear germ" these two threaten the future of "the rest of us." It is Onwueme's rage that powers the drama. Why should "the animals from the North and West" be able to threaten the rest of us with universal annihilation? Though vociferous in their demands for peace, the "animals of the South" have not yet acted in unison, yet they know that they and others must act or die.

R. F. Bauerle, *World Literature Today*. 61, 1 (winter 1997), p. 147

In my 1993 review of *Go Tell It to Women* (sic) by Tess Akaeke Onwueme (sic) for *World Literature Today*, I said that perhaps Movement Five "Should be worked over by the author," and, mirabile dictu, this has come to pass for the whole opus. Curiously, nowhere in *Tell It to Women* is there any allusion at all to the earlier version of this "epic drama for women."

The theme remains the same. Onwueme defends rural African women—those in *Tell It to Women*, with Yemoja as their centerpiece, are from the Idu Kingdom—against their city counterparts, here embodied by the lesbian lovers Daisy, Director of Women's Affairs, and Ruth, "a feminist scholar."...

Having reread *Go Tell It to Women* and now having read *Tell It to Women*, I cannot help but compare the two in the light of my first review. Early on in it, I cited the repetitious natter. That is still the case, though less so, since the text proper has been reduced from 404 to 211 pages....

Onwueme has neatly telescoped the action down to five Movements, from the previous version's Prologue and six Movements. In version one, the Prologue presents the argument, Movement One has the heroine Yemoja still in the Idu Kingdom, and Movement Two has the spiritually blind Ruth and Daisy mistreating her in the city. In the new version, the argument is integrated into the whole text, and, save for a minimal passage concerning Yemoja's village, the action commences in the city.

In my earlier review, I saw *Go Tell It to Women* as a dialogue-novel. While *Tell It to Women* is less so, the work remains proselike. I don't envisage the whole opus performed, at least on a Western stage, a stage where, so to speak, Zeit ist Geld, and in an ambience where even standup comedians and professors are limited by convention to saying the same thing three times only. On the other hand—pray God this isn't condescending—in a venue where the West doesn't rule the roost I can see the whole work performed before an audience who, far from needing to pop a couple of No Doz, might even join in and add a number of repetitions of its own.

> Harold A. Waters. *World Literature Today*. 72, 3 (summer 1998), pp. 672–73

BIBLIOGRAPHY
*A Hen Too Soon*, 1983; *The Broken Calabash*, 1984; *The Desert Encroaches*, 1985; *Ban Empty Barn and Other Plays*, 1986; *The Artist's Homecoming*, 1986; *Cattle Egret versus Nama*, 1986; *Mirror for Campus*, 1987; *The Reign of Wazobia*, 1988; *Legacies*, 1989; *Go Tell It to Women*, 1992; *Three Plays* (*The Broken Calabash*, *Parables for a Season*, and *The Reign of Wazobia*), 1993; *Riot in Heaven*, 1996; *The Missing Face*, 1997; *Tell It to Women*, 1997

# OSOFISAN, Femi (1946–)
## Nigeria

[*The Chattering and the Song* and *Once upon Four Robbers*] depict [Femi] Osofisan's radical approach to historical and social realities and the urgent need for a social revolution that will give birth to a socialist state in Nigeria. *The Chattering and the Song* deals with a revolt led by a group of enlightened radical youths challenging the forces of rot, corruption, and dictatorship, ending in the offer of a model for a new society that will replace autocracy in all its forms. This theme comes out positively in the central dramatic scene of the play, which is also a play-within-a-play. Here, Osofisan re-creates—even rewrites—the history of Oyo during the chaotic period

of the rebellious Bashorun Gaha who overthrew the reigning Alafin and set up a reign of terror, killing all the princes of Oyo except Abiodun, who was crippled in one leg. Abiodun grew up to challenge and overthrow this despot, reestablishing law and order. But as ... [Gerald] Moore rightly observes, Osofisan is against all forms of autocracy, however benevolent: for him, "heroism is a collective, not a kingly virtue." Osofisan throws his sympathy with Latoye, the rebel, to demonstrate the essence of a social revolution that will liberate society from the yoke of oppression. Latoye defies the Alafin by summoning his creative powers to raise the consciousness of the oppressed, represented in the play by the king's bodyguards (acted by the musicians). Instead of portraying the aspect of history where the old—the authoritative Alafin—uses his magical powers to subdue the young rebel, Osofisan depicts the successful challenge to traditional tyranny....

But if Osofisan appropriates the historical past for his social vision in *The Chattering and the Song*, he confronts contemporary reality in *Once upon Four Robbers*, which is a metaphorical treatment of the phenomenon of armed robbery. His dialectic treatment of history ... in the first play is continued in this new play, where he looks at the Nigerian condition from a purely Marxist viewpoint. He regards the armed robbers—Alhaja, Hassan, Angola, and Major—as products of an unjust social system.... In the program notes for the premiere of *Once upon Four Robbers*, Osofisan describes the robbers as a tiny part of the Nigerian masses who have been brutalized by social stratification—the existence of two extremely distinct social classes—in Nigeria. He attributes the violence of armed robbery to this social structure....

The two plays ... show Osofisan's employment of the revolutionary potential of theater to embody the political and ideological character of his work. Like his contemporaries, he aims to propose a socialist ethical perspective for Nigeria by first reawakening the people's consciousness to a reality beyond the decadence of the present. There are dangers inherent in such a commitment. As these young playwrights are aware, one of the grave dangers is that artistic depth might be sacrificed for political content; that the writers might resort to sheer propaganda as in the Farmers' Anthem in *The Chattering and the Song*. A more serious fault is Osofisan's inability, occasionally, to carry through a theatrical device set in motion in certain episodes. An example is the way Mokan's emotion gets in the way of his successful completion of his role as Aresa, the Alafin's chief bodyguard. His vindictiveness makes him reveal himself, for the first time, as a secret policeman. This sudden revelation of identity and his arrest of Sontri and Yajin, puzzlingly blurs the device and changes the mood of the play. A macabre dimension is thus attained from the position of a wedding entertainment play. But such faults are very few, as Osofisan appreciably succeeds in employing theatrical mechanics to harmonize the related arts of music, dance, mime, and verbal arts, achieving an impressive aesthetic quality which gives authenticity to his strong political bent. This must be the trend of a theater like Nigeria's, which is growing more and more revolutionary.

> Olu Obafemi. In Eldred Durosimi Jones, ed. *African Literature Today*. 12 (1982), pp. 121–24, 133–34

In *Morountodun*, Osofisan ... uses the Agbekoya Farmers' Rebellion of 1968–1969 as the background for the portrayal of the individual's response to social change. Yet because he was commissioned to write a play celebrating the International Year of the

Woman, he manipulates this event to examine the role of women in political activism. Additionally, he questions the function of myth in a contemporary setting. In accord with his aim to create a theater that encourages audiences to think, Osofisan begins with a group of actors onstage preparing for a performance, thereby calling attention at the outset to the role-playing, illusory nature of theater. But before these actors can even begin their production, the theater hall is invaded by a group of women traders demanding that the performance be cancelled. Hence, the audience is confronted almost immediately with community people altering theatrical production for attention to social issues. . . .

Osofisan incorporates traditional techniques into his drama: songs (sung in Yoruba), riddles, proverbs, and enacted parables. At other instances, also in accordance with traditional practices which call attention to the artificial, nonrealistic quality inherent in performance, Osofisan has Titubi stop the forward movement of the action to relate, by re-creating an event, the process by which she was won over to the farmers' perspective. Because all these devices represent familiar performance modes for the audience, they have the potential to lessen audience resistance to the political positions espoused. . . .

By exploiting traditional aesthetic structures while affirming and challenging his audience's abilities to exert positive control over their society, Femi Osofisan creates a theater with great potential to articulate his countrymen's aspirations and capture universal dreams of a just, sane world. How that potential is realized in the actual modes of production is another crucial consideration, which an extended discussion of his work would have to engage.

Sandra L. Richards. *Theatre Journal*. 39, 2 (1987), pp. 225–27

*The Chattering and the Song* and *Morountodun* both manifest Osofisan's concern with reinterpreting history in favor of the oppressed. The subject is history together with myth, and the issue, a reappraisal of the relevance of these to contemporary concrete reality.

In *The Chattering*, a casual celebration of a wedding eve ends up as a complex spectacle of re-enacted history merged with contemporary reality, and a proposition for the utilization of men and women's natural assets to surmount present and future social woes. For Sontri and Yajin's wedding eve, a play presumably written by Sontri is to be acted. Sontri is an angry young man through whom Osofisan denounces society's injustices. Sontri's play has its material in the so-called heroic deeds of an Alafin of Oyo, Abiodun. This play-within-[a]-play is actually a re-creation of history, not from the side of the so-called victors (the kings and the lords as is usually the case), but from that of the victims. Alafin Abiodun, like the present-day ruling class, feeds on the blood and sweat of others, yet his is the race of the "heroes." The "rebel" (played by Leje), arraigned before Abiodun (played by Sontri), rises to challenge, and succeeds in breaking the nerve center of Alafin's tyranny: the myth of a god-abetted subjugation of one human being by another. Herein lies Osofisan's point of departure. By reversing Latoye's and Abiodun's roles, Osofisan sides with the oppressed. Latoye becomes the true hero through his emancipation of the guards, while Abiodun becomes the villain because he has used his position to oppress and exploit.

The play-within-a-play does not end, but is arrested at a strategic point: when the people's awareness has been aroused and

the people have been, like Brechtian spectators, inspired to take action for the improvement of their condition. Latoye has commanded that Abiodun be seized, but Mokan (playing Aresa, Abiodun's head of bodyguards) reveals his identity as a secret policeman on Sontri's trail. Sontri is arrested as an agitator—an action which gratifies Mokan, who has been out to avenge Yajin's rejection of him. Sontri's arrest is to prove the point (to Nigeria's "angry young men"?) that the revolution needs not just anger but good organization and tact—a channeling of anger for results. Using masks, Leje who is Osongongon, the farmers' leader, is able to get close to the ruling class, know their plans and lay counter strategies to their oppressive measures against the progressive movement. . . .

*Who's Afraid of Solarin*? is parabolic mainly at a generalized, metaphorical level. This play, adapted from [Nikolai] Gogol's *The Inspector General*, shows a motley of social types. Ineptitude, indolence, indiscipline, gross misconduct—name the vice: the characters in the play depict a society at the nadir of depravity.

In the play, rumors of an impending visit of the Public Complaints Commissioner, Solarin, give everybody the jitters. The councillors and their chairman have shirked their various duties and have misappropriated public funds. The pastor of a church has also stolen the contributions of his congregation. As they all live in fear of the commissioner's wrath, they decide to seek the protection of Baba Fawomi, an Ifa priest. But Baba Fawomi is a mere charlatan, who merely plays on the gullibility of his clientele to enrich himself. Where the true Ifa priest divines without any mind to profit-making, Baba Fawomi taxes his clientele very heavily for services he is incapable of rendering. A rascal, Isola Oriebora, cashes in on the officials' ignorance and impersonates the commissioner. He swindles everyone: he seduces the pastor's daughter, extracts bribes from the officials, and then absconds. The arrival of the true commissioner is announced.

Osofisan's "revolutionary aesthetics" flag in *Who's Afraid*? This is partly because he merely throws the jabs at a decadent society without suggesting an alternative. He ridicules the vices and fails to show a way out. By arresting reality at an unsavory moment and failing to propel it forward, Osofisan's satire acquires a tinge of cynicism. The cynicism figures also in the characterization of Isola Oriebora. Like Efua Sutherland's Ananse [in *The Marriage of Anansewa*] and the trickster hero of the so-called moral fable, Oriebora gets away with his tricks. Oriebora's progress becomes a promotion of a negative ethic.

Modupe O. Olaogun. *Okike*. 27–28 (March 1988), pp. 46, 54–55

From the late 1970s, in such plays as *The Chattering and the Song* and *Morountodun and Other Plays*, as well as in his critical essays and interviews, Osofisan has consistently espoused the cause of a socialist revolution. To this end, he dedicated himself to the systematic destruction of all forms of social myths, whether religious as in *No More the Wasted Breed* in *Morountodun and Other Plays*, or the mystification of history in *The Chattering and the Song* or the mythification of "government power" in *Morountodun*. . . .

Osofisan's poetry in *Minted Coins* makes radical departures from views established in his earlier works—his view of the nature or philosophy of history and existence in general, as well as his view of traditional myths, legends, and history. There is an apparent shift from the basic materialist philosophy that informs his mature plays; [from] the materialist philosophy that "unmasks" all myths, to an idealist philosophy of life and history, which not only accepts the belief-contents of myths but accepts a philosophy of life (new in his artistic career) that is strongly underlined by traditional myths, the philosophy of the cyclical nature of existence. . . . "Minted coins" symbolize desires—for love, wealth or power—which are basically good but can be corrupted. Because of their passing from hand to hand, coins stand for "the meeting, parting and returning," that is the essence of all life. Moreover their roundness evokes the cyclical nature of time.

Aderemi Bamikunle. *Commonwealth Essays & Studies*. 11, 1 (autumn 1989), pp. 109–10

Femi Osofisan's reputation rests on a series of plays which have marked him as a leading figure among the younger generation of dramatists in Nigeria. Osofisan's first published work was not, however, a play, but a novel. This work, *Kolera Kolej*, appeared in 1975. It remains something of a maverick. . . . Yet there is more to *Kolera Kolej* than its neglect would suggest. In its manipulation of form and language, for instance, it is fairly adventurous. Further, an analysis of its structure reveals a way of thinking—a preoccupation with formal matters—that is dominant in those of Osofisan's works that are highly regarded. . . .

*Kolera Kolej* is an audacious piece of work. Its internal disjunctions are constantly stimulating: the narrative voice is one that can tease, lacerate, or turn blunt and earnest, within the space of a few lines. Clearly Osofisan's imagination is taken here with the possibility of creating novel form through the combination of dissimilar materials. In the plays that followed *Kolera Kolej*, this tendency emerges repeatedly: in the use of contrasting voices and language forms, in the notion of the play-within-[a]-play. The technique relates, of course, to the process of dialectic: argument progresses through the radical juxtaposition of unlike elements. In *Kolera Kolej*, however, Osofisan's technique has produced a dialectic that is not altogether coherent. . . .

To date, more than a dozen of Osofisan's plays have appeared on stage. The two discussed below [*Morountodun* and *Once upon Four Robbers*] both demonstrate Osofisan's predilection for structuring contrasts: for those disjunctions in register and dramatic style which enable him to build his argument by a process of contradictions and which lead his audience towards a conclusion only by way of a series of revisions in the judgment-forming process.

The bulk of *Morountodun* is written in a clear, idiomatic English. Occasionally, however, the language shifts into a more intense, heightened register, to express especially forceful emotions, as in the heroine Titubi's comments on the historical figure Moremi; while, for a "Moremi play" inserted into the main action, Osofisan devises a more decorous and formal style. . . .

By contrast with the multistranded complexity of *Morountodun*, *Once upon Four Robbers* focuses with fierce concentration on a single idea, establishing armed robbery as an "apt metaphor" for life in contemporary Nigeria and the armed robber as both product of and moralizing commentator on an "unjust society." The public execution of these robbers may mean death and disgrace, "but so also does hunger, so does unemployment"; Osofisan reverses the orthodox morality (that armed robbers are vile) in an attempt to

provoke a sharper awareness of those injustices that the establishment prefers to ignore. The play exposes a scandalous disjunction between the public recognition of a symptomatic evil and the systematic neglect of evils that are fundamental.

Osofisan's robbers pour scorn on the mentality of the rich and castigate a system in which menial labor is equated to "respectability." The self-seeking individualist is condemned, whether in the person of the army sergeant who embezzles money recaptured after a theft, or in the case of Major—one of the robbers, who betrays the others and is then immediately identified with the absurd, ten-Mercedes-owning rich.

Major's betrayal places a moral gulf between him and his fellow robbers. He is shown as having betrayed an ideal—the ideal of solidarity practiced by the militantly antisocial. Osofisan succeeds in convincingly rendering the principle of solidarity; it is, however, a weakness in the play that he never achieves a *categorical* distinction between Major's solitary acquisitiveness and the group acquisitiveness of the robbers; he never really establishes what the robbers mean by "justice" or how, except in a sophistic sense, they can claim to be fighting for it. . . .

Osofisan's imagination is charged with the notion of conflict, with the actual but often unspoken state of war existing between different social classes. His work attempts to articulate this conflict and, in particular, to establish disjunctions—tangible contradictions—through which the *real* relationship between opposing ideologies can be assessed.

The frequency with which Osofisan's work sets up these disjunctions indicates the extent of his imaginative involvement in the dialectical process. The technical expertise he has at his disposal is considerable; hence the variety of means he is able to devise to provoke us into new recognitions: ranging from shifts in language mode to songs that are, superrealistically, self-exposing, to the creation of model, or the play-within-the-play. . . .

Osofisan's work very rarely dramatizes the life of the masses; it is the dilemma of the leaders, their psychological development, that seems to preoccupy Osofisan rather than the lives of the people they lead. *The Chattering and the Song*, for example, succeeds as an exciting and inventive play partly because it is a play about exceptionally exciting and inventive people. Further . . . in most cases Osofisan is engaged in a process of special validation: the man in *Kolera Kolej*, Titubi, and, to some extent, Sontri in *The Chattering and the Song* are very nearly redundant, or even counterrevolutionary: each has to be shown to have a useful role to play—a large part of the tension in Osofisan's work lies in the process by which the apparent reactionary is revealed finally as a functioning revolutionary. The one piece discussed above that does focus in some sense on the average man is *Once upon Four Robbers*, in which the masses are approached only very obliquely, as their condition is dramatized through the metaphor of armed robbery. This preoccupation with the leadership role may not be a weakness, but in the work of an avowedly radical writer like Osofisan, it is a distinct peculiarity.

Chris Dunton. In Eldred Durosimi Jones, ed. *The Question of Language in African Literature Today* (Trenton, New Jersey: Africa World Press, 1991), pp. 81–82, 85, 88–89

The title play in Femi Osofisan's latest collection [*Birthdays Are Not for Dying, and Other Plays*] is an ambivalent melodrama of corruption, strained moral rectitude, and calamity. Kunle Aremo is obsessed with carrying out his late father's wish that, at the age of thirty, he take sole control of the company his father built up. He stages a board meeting on his birthday at which his father's corrupt business associates are exposed and dismissed. These include his father-in-law, whose daughter Kunle condemns both as unfaithful and as the mere tool of a marriage of convenience. His own son, whose paternity he disclaims, falls ill and is left to be rushed to the hospital by his distraught wife. In his moment of triumph Kunle is rebuked for his righteous action by the only uncorrupted member of the board for humiliating his elderly associates. With a mysterious threatening gesture, concealed from the audience, Councillor Lekan Bamgbade reawakens in Kunle an old childhood trauma, which leads, with the crazed connivance of a wife just bereaved of her son, to a climax reminiscent of Greek tragedy. What promised to become a simple morality play shows righteous justice dashed on the rock of human passions and confounded by the confusing claims of compassion.

The second drama, *Fires Burn and Die Hard*, again focuses upon an entanglement of material and intangible moral values. A new market to replace one destroyed by fire is about to be opened, the marketwomen rejoicing at the prospect of regaining ''a veritable home . . . a hive of comfort and companionship, for all who were born female, in a land where men are raised to be tyrants.'' Then the diviners foresee fresh disaster: one of the market women herself had set the fire; and, if no cleansing sacrifice is performed, the tragedy will recur. The incendiary, herself president of the Market Women's Association, confesses, learning ''Profit is a demanding creed,'' for her son's righteous determination to report his discovery that she sold contraband goods had caused her to burn the evidence. Ironically, her illicit wealth had only been for him.

The short work *The Inspector and the Hero* is comparatively simplistic, a morality play whose message Nigeria doubtless needs, but it makes for weak drama. The plot is simply stated: a wealthy politician, on the brink of becoming state governor, is tracked down and exposed by a police inspector who resists all attempts to threaten or bribe him into silence. Whereas the politician makes his childhood poverty an alibi for his ruthless acquisition of ''money and power,'' the inspector, of equally humble origins, lives by another ''dream,'' that of a cleansed society.

Michael Thorpe. *World Literature Today.* 65, 4 (autumn 1991), pp. 754–55

Femi Osofisan occupies an eminent position among contemporary Nigerian playwrights because his plays are the most frequently performed within the country today though they are less well known outside. . . .

Like other contemporary African dramatists—Ngūgī wa Thiong'o, Efua Sutherland, Wole Soyinka, Ama Ata Aidoo, J.P. Clark, Ola Rotimi—Osofisan is engaged in the quest for suitable forms with which the African experience can be transmuted into drama. In Nigeria, Soyinka has perfected the satiric art as a medium of interpreting human experience in the theatre. But Osofisan differs greatly from Wole Soyinka or any other African playwrights in his conception of form, stylistic innovations and manner of organizing his plays. The uniqueness of Osofisan as a dramatist lies in the enormous range of his theatrically viable forms and his ability to fuse social themes and ideological commitment with appropriate dramatic forms without sacrificing one for the other. It

is a measure of the playwright's skill that this structure never appears boring or overdone. . . .

Osofisan's work is consistently impressive because of its technical accomplishment. He does not only fashion a dramaturgy that is adequately equipped to express contemporary reality, but constructs plays that offer questions rather than prescriptions. The plays not only promote his political ideology which is a commitment to societal change for the better, but also constitute a populist thrust for the English language theatre in Nigeria. The message of art may be universal but form is an individual matter. What marks out the efforts of the artist is his ability to stylize his forms. . . .

More than its revolutionary ideology, it is the aesthetics of Osofisan's drama that bewitches at first encounter. And at the heart of this aesthetics is a dramaturgy that uses all the known elements of Yoruba or African playmaking processes. The dramaturgy has a hybrid brilliance, grafting different forms of comedy, realism, compressionism, absurdism, epic and traditional African theatres, and making them his own. Rather than being bound to a particular form, he creates comprehensive, wideranging structures that are eclectic in form but suitable for transmitting African dramatic enactments on all types of stages be they thrust, proscenium or arena.

Finally, his exploration of form and deployment of techniques certainly make him one of the most exciting African dramatists writing at the moment. His works to date represent extraordinary diversities in style, technique and form. But whatever the divergencies in approach, the thematic preoccupation of the works remains the same: a vision of a better society that is free from the shackles of oppression, injustice and corruption.

Thus the overall effect of the appropriation of the familiar traditional performance modes and conventional devices in the plays of Osofisan is the creation of a popular African theatre form through which he makes critical social commentaries about the state of the nation and through which opinions and ideas in the society are capable of being influenced. Consequently has drama represents contemporary Nigerian literature of protest that manifests the struggles of a people whose country is undergoing a painful process of transformation from colonial through noncolonial to a wholly self-determining nation.

Eldred. D. Jones. *New Trends and Generations in African Literature* (Trenton: Africa World Press, Inc., 1996), pp. 102–18

Femi Osofisan's prolific career, experimentation with form, ideological commitment, and profundity of themes, plus the sheer poetry of his drama, have distinguished him as without doubt the leading dramatist of the generation of African writers following Wole Soyinka and Chinua Achebe. The publication of *The Oriki of a Grasshopper and Other Plays* will expose to the wider world a highly talented African dramatist influenced by both traditional Yoruba culture and Western—particularly French—dramaturgy. The four plays in the book reflect not only Osofisan's individual development and talent but also the general mood and direction of contemporary African drama.

I reread the title play one day after watching a production of Athol Fugard's two-character play *The Island*. The similarity of the two works with their ''pre-texts'' is very striking, Osofisan's play informed by Beckett's *Waiting for Godot* and Fugard's by Sophocles' *Antigone*. Osofisan's work also brings to mind Camus's play *Les Justes* as well as (according to Abiola Irele) Sartre's *Huis Clos* in its focus on a moral dilemma. Thus, while *The Oriki of a Grasshopper* deals with familiar Nigerian university experiences of the 1970s and early 1980s with their riots, police brutality, and ivory-tower revoluntionaries, it also shows Osofisan's exposure to the traditions of literary drama, especially the modern French theater, which he has studied and teaches.

Both Claudius and Imaro, two supposedly contrasting characters of bourgeois and proletarian tendencies respectively, belong to the same generation but make different choices. Here Osofisan tackles the practical problems of being a revolutionary on an African university campus. The futility of utopian idealism and the impracticality of most revolutionaries are humorously depicted; as students, for example, Claudius and Imaro once farcically raised "sticks"—actually the tattered remains of posters left out in the rain—at the prime minister as he rode by ensconced in his car; he waved back at them, thinking he was being cheered.

One of my favorite Osofisan plays is *Esu and the Vagabond Minstrels* (1991). Here the dramatist immerses himself in Yoruba folklore, exploring the symbolism of Esu—the god of chance, who mediates between the gods and humankind—and weaving a parable about compassion and greed. Of the five minstrels depicted, only Omele heeds the priest's exhortation for every individual to use his or her power to reduce suffering. In the end, however, Osofisan complicates what looks to be simply didactic material with a dramatic twist and surprise. . . .

*Birthdays Are Not for Dying* lacks the dramatic profundity and intensity of *Esu and the Vagabond Minstrels* but nevertheless displays Osofisan's facility with proverbs and praise-name epithets. . . .

*Morountodun* is perhaps the author's best-known play, a work that is studied in most Nigerian universities. Here Osofisan brings together in one play ideas and techniques he has tried elsewhere and now intensifies. He turns around the Ife legend of Moremi and has Titubi, a privileged young lady, co-opted (like Patty Hearst, as Irele rightly observes [in her introduction to the back]) and converted to the cause of those she is supposed to fight, in the process being transformed from Moremi to Morountodun. Of course, the very fact that this young woman is capable of such a revolutionary endeavor could be Osofisan's praise of women. The play articulates the plight of the common people—here the agbekoyas—and affirms the necessity of struggle to cast off oppression and exploitation.

Osofisan's plays are not "brainy" in the sense of such Soyinka works as *The Road* or *A Dance of the Forests* but rather relate immediately to contemporary society in a secular way. Where the metaphysical or supernatural is brought in, as in the figure of Esu, it is humanized. In addition to Yoruba folklore, in many of the plays there is an abundance of irony, surprise, suspense, humor, spectacle, and song that will keep the audiences intellectually entertained. *The Oriki of* a *Grasshopper and Other Plays* attests to Femi Osofisan's development and preeminence in the new drama of Africa, which embodies both indigenous African and European literary-theatrical influences. The plays are not only committed literature making a statement on the Nigerian—or larger African—situation but also constitute a questioning of the human condition in all its ramifications. They are a great pleasure to peruse or to watch

and will equally engage both African and European readers and audiences.

> Tanure Ojaide. *World Literature Today*. 71, 1 (winter 1997), pp. 207–08

BIBLIOGRAPHY
*Kolera Kolej*, 1975; *A Restless Run of Locusts*, 1975; *The Chattering and the Song*, 1977; *Who's Afraid of Solarin?*, 1978; *Once upon Four Robbers*, 1980; *Morountodun and Other Plays*, 1982; *Beyond Translation: A Comparitist Look at Tragic Paradigms and the Dramaturgy of Old Rotimi and Wole Soyinka*, 1986; *Farewell to a Cannibal Rage*, 1986; *Midnight Hotel*, 1986; *Two One-Act Plays*, 1986; *Wonderland and Orality of Prose: A Comparitive Study of Rabelais, Joyce and Tutuola*, 1986; *Minted Coins*, 1987; *Another Raft*, 1988; *Cordelia*, 1989; *Birthdays Are Not for Dying, and Other Plays*, 1990; *Aringindin and the Night Watchmen*, 1991; *Esu and the Vagabond Minstrels*, 1991; *Yungba-Yungba and the Dance Contest: A Parable for Our Times*, 1993; *The Album of the Midnight Blackout*, 1994; *The Engagement*, 1995; *Twingle-Twangle: A Twynining Tayle*, 1995; *The Oriki of a Grasshopper, and Other Plays*, 1995; *Midnight Hotel*, 1998

# OSUNDARE, Niyi (1947– )

## Nigeria

Niyi Osundare's volume *Village Voices* reveals him as a rural lyricist, one who plucks poetic images from the fields of his youth, but without sentimentality or nostalgia. . . . He recalls how satirical songs were composed and used to shame wrongdoers; public humiliation was an effective social sanction. "This kind of creativity is a source of great inspiration. It has also sensitized me into the realization that poetry can never be divided from the society in which it has grown."

What Osundare calls "the poetry of abuse" arises directly from Ekiti tradition. . . . Osundare, whose first volume is entitled *Songs of the Marketplace*, says when he can't write, he takes a bus to market and returns to "mediate, not manipulate the experience, make it even more beautiful and give it back to society.". . .

*Songs of the Marketplace* opens with a definition: "Poetry is / the hawker's ditty / the eloquence of the gong / the lyric of the marketplace . . . man / meaning to / man." Such a definition is fundamentally communal, far from what Osundare called "the formalist and reified mentality of the European age of decadence." He says that "right from the beginning, I have been brought up to see the whole artistic enterprise as essentially socialized." For him . . . art is explicitly political. "I believe very strongly in socialist humanism. I believe that capitalism has not only failed us but ruined us, that we must share what we have. This is what the farmers are saying in *Village Voices*." In their words, then, "Let me be / an active grip / in a hand of equal fingers," and again, "Let no-one tell us again / that fingers are not equal / for we know / how the thumb grew fatter / than all the others."

> Jane Bryce. *West Africa*. July 21, 1986, pp. 1524–25

[Osundare's] poetry has shown considerable development resulting in contrasting poetic practices in both [*Songs of the Marketplace* and *Village Voices*]. The contrast is clear at the level of form and content. Though many of the poems of *Songs of the Marketplace* are about Nigeria, a good proportion are about events in the Third World and on Third World personalities: the situations in Nicaragua ("The Fall of the Beast") and South Africa in "Soweto" and "Namibia Talks.". . . . In *Village Voices* the focus shows complete concentration on the situation of the underprivileged in Nigeria. In *Songs of the Marketplace*, the poetic voice is still very much the voice of the poet as an individual as he roams the national and international political systems, satirically exposing the social contradictions, pretensions, oppression, and exploitations in the systems. In *Village Voices* the poetic voice has become the communal voice of the rural population of exploited peasants in their stand against their exploiters. Osundare's attitude towards this social group has undergone considerable change. In "Ignorance" in *Songs of the Marketplace*, the poet regards the oppressed as an ignorant lot, whose ignorance makes possible the rule of the oppressors. They are like the "sheep" that have "all agreed / to give their crown to a wolf." The result of a shift to a socialist perspective in *Village Voices* has led to a new confidence in the mass of underprivileged Nigerians and in their world-view and the art traditions that express that world-view. It is the explorations of the traditional world-view and relevant art tradition that is the special [quality] of Osundare's poetry.

There is quite a variety of themes in Osundare's poetry. Apart from the concern with international politics as it affects Third World nations in *Songs of the Marketplace*, there are the fascinating poems of "Songs of dawn and seasons," based on a close observation of the seasons of the year, climatic phenomena, and how they affect the cycles of human existence. These poems are very striking in their vivid images of nature that tickle the visual and aural senses. But they are more fascinating because of their subtle suggestion that the movement of the seasons is an analogy for the cycles of life moving from dryness and decay, with its discomforts and expectations, into the promise and fulfillment of hopes in the "Dawn." "Inchoate hour / soothtime / For straightening twisted word / for the ears of a waking day / Dawn / is time recall the future / foretell the past."

The most important preoccupation in both volumes of poetry is the politics of Nigeria, especially the marginalization of the peasantry and low-income workers in Nigerian society. . . .

If there is a general socialist/Marxist tendency in recent Nigerian literature, Osundare's poetry represents the most refined expression of the perspective's interpretation of contemporary politics. We are used to the elite addressing the system on behalf of the underprivileged. What we are not quite used to is the underprivileged's analyses of the social system they build but which they do not benefit from. This is what we see in poem after poem in *Village Voices*. Particularly in "The Land of Unease," "A Villager's Protest," "The New Farmer's Bank," "A Farmer on Seeing Cocoa House, Ibadan," and "Listen, Book Wizard" among others, the peasant, armed with the world-view of traditional life assesses [the] urban-based system run by the classes of politicians and their intellectuals and finds it wanting. In contrast with the inequitable distribution of the nation's resources, the peasantry

shows its preference for egalitarianism that is the basis of [the] traditional social system.

Aderemi Bamikunle. *Literary Criterion*. 23, 1–2 (1988), pp. 81–84

As a critic, Osundare has not been prolific or, perhaps to be more accurate, he has not published many articles that can be found in North American university libraries. What is most remarkable about Osundare's very fine scholarship is its preoccupation with artistic quality. The Marxist is always in view, but he avoids the sociological rehashing of plot and the belabored paraphrasing of content and political arguments that are so common among Marxist critical writings. Implicit in all of Osundare's analyses is his conviction that a writer's first responsibility is to his/her craft. For example, the title of his article "'As Grasshoppers to Wanton Boys': The Role of the Gods in the Novels of Elechi Amadi" would lead one who knew that a Marxist had written it to expect an antireligion, antimysticism tract, ridiculing an author (not characters) for belief in the supernatural. Instead, we are treated to an erudite piece of scholarship which argues with other critics in an elegant, unstrident manner, and which demonstrates through comparison with a wide range of writers from many periods and places why Amadi is a third-rate writer; Amadi's deficiencies as a political thinker are subordinate to the point of being subliminal to this argument. . . .

Osundare is amazingly prolific as a poet. To date he has published two volumes, *Songs of the Marketplace* and *Village Voices*. A third volume is in press with Heinemann: *The Eye of the Earth*. A fourth, *A Nib in the Pond* is searching for a publisher, and two more volumes are near completion: *Requiem for the Second Republic* and *Daughter of the Rain* (love poems). All of the poems in these collections are produced separately from the average of two poems he writes each week "as a matter of policy and challenge" . . . for his extremely popular weekly Sunday column "Songs of the Season" in the national *Nigerian Tribune*. For about three years now he has been experimenting in this column with "verse journalism."

Stephen H. Arnold. *World Literature Written in English*. 29, 1 (spring 1989), pp. 1–3

[Niyi Osundare is] a poet who mastered the technique of fusing oral traditions and modern poetic trends quite early in his career. In *Village Voices*, Osundare explores both the elasticity of poetic language and the intricate web of life in his society with a penetration unmatched by even the most notable poets. The personae in the poetry are varied and the thematic concerns multiple. If Chinweizu is the poet for the ordinary man, Osundare is the poet for the suffering man. His poetry confirms James Reeves's observation that "what poetry does to the mass of ordinary experience is to make permanent and memorable whatever in it is vital and significant." There are the parallelisms, adept use of vivid allusions, stark imagery, and pointillism of committed poetry. . . . With this mission Osundare commences a poetic exploration of the Nigerian social climate. The vision is that of a sensitive artist reluctant to allow his voice to become muzzled by rampant injustice. The division of the collection of poems illustrates the poet's sense of organization.

Metaphor is the idiom of this poetry. It is a technique that enables the poet to adopt abundant materials such as witty aphorisms and phrases from the Yoruba oral traditions. In addition, his poetry is highly political and social. It is not an attempt to beat the newspaper headline news of the day but a matter of effective generation of ideas related to stark realities. ''A Dialogue of Drums'' cautions reason as two drummers engage in dialogue to discover the effectiveness of their practice. Osundare uses dramatic language in this poem to capture humanity's weakness and predilection for sycophancy.... The voices who raise the songs are numerous. They include the street fighters, caricatured members of the ruling classes, farmers, politicians, and marketwomen. Osundare matches language with characters, and this technique necessitates the creation of appropriate patterns of linguistic behavior. In ''Not in My Season of Songs'' the language is that of a mature adult; in ''Eating with All the Fingers'' it is that of a troubled elder; and in ''Feigning a Rebel'' it is the language of a poor villager. Language is made a component part of his poetic art and illustrates his ability to mold the chosen character to suit the artistic creation.

In the highly lyrical poem ''Akintunde Come Home,'' the poet creates a persona whose language indicates that he is a father. The frequency of proverbs and witty aphorisms are the marks of a wise father; and Osundare exploits these linguistic devices in this poem, which appeals to Akintunde to return home from the land where money is god, and since all men cannot be Irokos, stresses that, though the home may be full of meatless meals, it could still harbor amiable souls.

Ezenwa-Ohaeto. In Eldred Durosimi Jones, ed. *The Question of Language in African Literature Today* (Trenton, New Jersey: Africa World Press, 1991), pp. 160–61

In Osundare's ideal, ''Poetry'' is ''man / meaning to / man.'' With this introduction, *Songs of the Marketplace* is meant to be popular poetry rendered in [a] ''popular'' art form shared by the community. His poetry is best appreciated as developing towards achieving this ideal.

The central preoccupation of his poetry is thus established in this first collection: the concern he feels for the suffering and deprivations of the masses; the disgust he feels for their exploiters and oppressors, the politicians; and the hope he harbors of the oppressed overturning the system to their own advantage. The subject matter of this collection is common enough, as the poet or his poetic persona quests through his society exposing one social malaise after another: the social suffering and deprivation of the masses (''Excursions''), large scale maladministration and mismanagement (''Sule Chase''), political fraud (''Rithmetic Ruse,'' ''Siren''). Everywhere the poet goes, the university (''Publish or Perish''), the Railway Corporation (''The Nigerian Railway''), the civil service (''Excursions''), the story is the same: fraud on a pervasive large scale, inefficiency and mismanagement in high places with the masses bearing the burden of the fraudulent mismanagement of the leaders....

In many respects it is in *Village Voices* that Osundare realizes his ideals in poetry. Here his social vision based on the sociopolitical values of the traditional village life (a vision which he juxtaposes with the urban-based ''dog eat dog'' contemporary socio-political system) finds perfect expression in the artistic forms of oral tradition. The organizing impulse for the poems is the revolutionary confrontation between rural man with his

(somewhat idealized) vision of life and the oppressive, exploitative neocolonialist national political administration. By this confrontational juxtapositioning the poet uses tradition to assess the value of modern civilization and governance in order to condemn it. In order to allow the voice of tradition full scope to do this, Osundare adopts a poetic posture that modernists will call the posture of impersonality. His poetic voice is subsumed under the communal voice as he prefers to speak through various personae from the rural areas who adapt various forms of traditional art to denounce the national capitalist system....

Osundare continues the celebration of traditional culture in *The Eye of the Earth*, but in a different mode from *Village Voices*. The most obvious difference is that in *The Eye of the Earth* he assumes his own poetic voice. He speaks as the prodigal, the alienated man, once ''jilted from the farmstead'' returning to the traditional society of his youth, to a stage of the traditional culture which was before the ''Cancerous god called MONEY'' from the West ''smashed old customs.'' The organizing impulse of *The Eye of the Earth* is the journey motif. The substance of the collection is the ''journey into these times [youth of the poet] and beyond,'' a journey ''into the house of memory.'' The central preoccupation is to contrast what life meant in those times when ''Earth was ours and we earth's,'' with what life means in contemporary times when after the destruction of the ''Core of [their] ancient humanistic ethos,'' commercialism and ''the god of money'' have forced a desecration of the earth, the bedrock of ancient customs and culture....

Osundare uses the oral traditions far more than many other writers. Not only has he used the many forms of art from the oral traditions as core elements in his poetic technique in *Village Voices* and to some extent, *The Eye of the Earth*, but he has also proved in the two books of poetry that the oral traditions can ''provide for a meaningful critique of the contemporary problems.'' In his hands traditional social wisdom has become a weapon for very incisive criticism of contemporary political economy. Also his judicious use of elements of the African oral tradition has produced poetry that is distinctively African. There are definitely problems and limitations to attempts at transposing elements from the oral traditions to the written traditions in a non-African language. But the example of Osundare and the Ghanaian poetic experiments by Atukwei Okai and Kofi Anyidoho have proved that African poetry can gain in strength and distinctiveness by appropriating techniques and qualities from African performance poetry and dramatic ritual.

Aderemi Bamikunle. In Eldred Durosimi Jones, ed. *Orature in African Literature Today* (Trenton, New Jersey: Africa World Press, 1992), pp. 51–54, 58, 60–61

Divided into four sections, *Waiting Laughters* uses the multiple situations of waiting in harsh times and places to explore poetically the ''gloom and despair which seem to have gripped contemporary African society.'' Despite the current gloom, the poet looks forward to relief in ''laughters.'' The formally organized and well-crafted volume gives a lie to the view, associated with Ken Goodwin and other critics of African literature, that the new generation of African poets tend to sacrifice form and craft for ideological commitment.

Two characteristic qualities of Osundare are intensified in the poems here: the linguist and the folklorist. A trained linguist, the poet plays with words, makes music with alliterations, assonances, and other forms of repetition, and creates startling images and figures, especially similes, metaphors, and personifications. In Osundare's poetry all things are personified, and they *live* actively. Sometimes the alliterations seem overused and contrived, but this is made up for by the variety of form, which assumes an Okigboesque quality in some parts of the book.

Osundare's use of Yoruba folklore enhances the vitality of the poems. The various segments of each section are chants to be accompanied by different African musical instruments. In the third section, where Osundare is at his best, his written orature combines traditional wisdom and form with sophisticated use of English to evoke instances of waiting. This results in exhilarating and memorable images. He turns experiences into fables for lasting impressions and uses apparently known folktales to express the contemporary African predicament of waiting painfully for succor from socioeconomic doom.

Thematically and stylistically, *Waiting Laughters* combines the strengths of two earlier works, *The Eye of the Earth* and *Moonsongs*. The poem ends with hope, not merely for relief as "A boil, time-tempered, / about to burst," but for action that will bring about positive change. Occasionally the lines seem overloaded with similes and metaphors, and the poet barely allows the reader time to reflect on one series of images before deluging the lines with more. Sometimes, as in the second section, the formal experiment, though visually impressive on the page, does not seem to be effective when two distantly spaced words are set per line in order to reflect vocal emphasis.

Tanure Ojaide. *World Literature Today.* 66, 1 (winter 1992), p. 192

*Selected Poems* brings together samples of [Osundare's] verse issued by different publishers over almost a decade. The selection begins with poems from *A Nib in the Pond* . . . and ends with the Malthouse-produced *Waiting Laughters*, which earned the poet the Noma Prize. The volume easily accomplishes a major aim of a selected edition of a poet in his prime: it lets the reader follow the development of the poet from his first collection to the latest.

In *A Nib in the Pond*, as will be expected of a first work, the poetic rhythm is not as sure and smooth as in the later poems. At this point the poet is an activist, one who wants to "wake a slumbering world." The message appears more important than the form here. The poet is a spokesperson for the oppressed, as in "Promise Land" and "I Am the Common Man." These poems set the thematic and stylistic features that will characterize the later poetry. Osundare ranges on the side of the common people and uses cosmic images of the sun and moon to register his commitment. . . .

*The Eye of the Earth* and *Waiting Laughters* stand out as the most impressive collections represented in the selection. In these two works Osundare is at his best, celebrating, singing, and playing with words. He so fuses his message with the form that one goes through the poems marveling at the amazing lyricism in the poet's repertoire. *The Eye of the Earth* celebrates the earth but also warns that human beings should take care of the environment if they care about their future. . . .

*Selected Poems* confirms Osundare's place as a major African poet who uses the resources of the folklore of his people, his study of the English language, and his concern for the underprivileged

and the destiny of Africa to bring passionate intensity, wit, musicality, and sensitivity to his writing.

Tanure Ojaide. *World Literature Today.* 67, 4 (autumn 1993), pp. 878–79

The twin issue of *waiting* and *laughter* as the major aspects in the collection *Waiting Laughters* provide a thematic focus on hope in the midst of despair as the poet utilizes various devices informed by his oral traditions. This collection, significantly subtitled "a long song in many voices," immediately calls to mind many of those elements associated with music that are usually exploited by the oral performer. The collection is in four sections, and the first section immediately sets the scene through the poet's pervasive use of images. These images are structured in parallels and they engineer responses that are related to the poet's satiric purposes. The poetic scene is set thus:

I pluck these words from the lips of the wind;
Ripe like a pendulous pledge
I pluck these murmurs
From the laughter of the wind
The shrub's tangled tale
Plaited tree tops
And palms which drop their nuts.

This statement of purpose is clearly related not only to the poetic objective to pursue a dedicated creative enterprise in either asking for accounts of "pledges" or insisting on appropriate redemption of those pledges but also to the conscious use of local imagery like "plaited tree tops" and "palms which drop their nuts." These images foreshadow the subsequent condemnation of the injustices associated with inequitable distribution of resources related to the "dropped palm nuts."

It is, however, interesting that the poet refers to a "tangled tale," which could be a metaphor for the impediments to the equitable distribution of wealth in the economy of "dropped palmnuts." Furthermore, this image emphasizes the issue of hope because "palms which drop their nuts" symbolize abundant wealth and the remedy to the "tangled tale," which the poet implies is the possibility for the "shrub" to benefit from the tall palmtree; in other words, the deprived people in the society could benefit from the privileged group.

This social concern is illustrated further in the same poem when the poet uses the element of cumulative repetition which blends technique with subject matter: Thus the poet like an oral poet-performer intones:

And laughing heals so fugitive
In the dust of fleeing truths
Truth of the valley
Truth of the mountain
Truth of the boulder
Truth of the river.

The poet continues in this kind of association of opposites by further linking the truth of the flame with the truth of the ash, the sun with the moon, the liar with the lair, the castle with the caste, and the desert with the rain. All these objects or behavior or status possess their own truths, but the poet implies that those truths cannot subvert the inviolable truth of life, which is the primary focus of *Waiting Laughters*. In depicting these truths with objects that are in opposition but placed in apposition, the poet clearly seeks to establish the omnipresence of truth, especially in a society that is prone to manipulations of truth. He insists that the truth, for instance, could be in the valley as well as on the mountain and in the flame as well as in the ash, but it still remains the truth.

As the poem progresses through other voices, since the poet conceives his work as a long poem in many voices, the poet's orality becomes part of the poetic movement. His cumulative repetition, which is heavily dependent on the Yoruba oral poetics, becomes clear, for part of that poetics includes the creative use of imagery associated with the environment; an apt deployment of refrains and chants; the exploitation of proverbial structures, aphorisms, and even idiomatic expressions; and the deliberate repetition of phrases in order to emphasize or evaluate observations. . . .

The cumulative repetition of what should be taught the persona is portrayed to generate success, which is the expected purpose of patience. The images of rain that "eats rocks" and "the branch that counts the seasons" stress the optimism of the poet that the trope of *laughter* in the title indicates. In addition, the manner in which these images are deployed and the repetition of the phrase "Teach us the patience" produce the semblance of a poet-cantor addressing an audience and clearly involving them in the incantation with the use of the pronoun "us." Thus the envisaged dividend of the education implied in the incantation is the act of obtaining strength like the sand, the branch, and rain for decisive action. In addition, the fact that the poet insists that there is the need to learn wisdom from some of these inanimate objects shows that there is also the need to reexamine the environment and derive from it the kind of knowledge that will enable the people develop and progress.

Repetitions of phrases, whole lines, and even stanzas are regular features of Osundare's poetry. He also uses certain proverbs with regularity. There is a proverb that appears twice in *Waiting Laughters*. The poem "The Feet I See Are Waiting for Shoes," where the poet criticizes the injustice of social deprivation of stomachs "waiting for coming harvests," water pots waiting in famished homesteads, and the eyes "waiting for rallying visions," ends with the following proverb:

> Time it may take
> The stammerer will one day call his
> Fa -Fa - fa - ther - ther's na - na - na - me!

The written orality in that last line, which is aimed at reproducing oral speech, lends credence to Osundare's conscious exploitation of orality. Nevertheless, this same proverb also appears in the poem "Waiting like the Crusty verb of a borrowed tongue," where the poet interrogates the issue of historical experience, the limitations of borrowed languages, and the appropriate utilization of talent for general benefits through an apt medium, as he questions:

> History's stammerer
> When will your memory master
> the vowels of your father's name?
> Time ambles in diverse paces

Just as the poet states that time "ambles in diverse paces," so his use of the proverbial lore is subjected to diverse paces. In this second use of the proverb it is no longer starkly embedded because its intrinsic idea has been worked into the texture of the poem. It is no longer the issue of a child desiring to pronounce the father's name but a fundamental issue where one who is "history's

stammerer" or history's destroyer must memorize "the vowels of the father's name," and create positive history in the interest of the society. In effect, Osundare's use of Yoruba proverbial lore has undergone changes as he refines and weaves the associated ideas into the poem rather than leaving them bare as we find in his early collections of poetry. This use of proverbs is much more interestingly presented through a chain of proverbs in the poem "Waiting like Yam for the Knife—," which questions the weakness of the oppressed in subduing the oppressor in whatever form. The persona justifies the dedication of the poet to the social use of poetry when he praises himself:

> My tongue has not stumbled
> I have not told a bulbous tale
> In the presence of asopa,
> I have not shouted "Nine!"
> In the backyard of the one with a missing finger

These instances of what the persona has not done are part of the Yoruba proverbial lore which states, for instance, that one does not talk about bulbous objects in the presence of an asopa, who is a man with swollen scrotum. Nevertheless, these instances of injunctions inserted through the proverbs are used ironically and satirically because the persona has mentioned all the instances of abnormalities in the society through indirect references as well as ridiculing the perpetrators of those abnormalities. This is in the tradition of Yoruba oral poetics, which makes great use of insinuations, and the orality of Osundare's poetic craft derives its energy from such exploitations.

> Ezenwa-Ohaeto. *Research in African Literatures*. 27, 2 (summer 1994), pp. 70–80

The best way to view the poetic developments of Osundare is to view his poetry against the stated ideals of revolutionary poetry as found in *Songs of the Marketplace* and *A Nib in the Pond*. His poetry is to be socially committed on the side of the underprivileged. As such it is to avoid all forms of elitism in language use by being accessible. As a corollary, his subjects will be down-to-earth as he avoids such metaphysical flights of the imagination of the elitist poetry of his predecessors.

Thematically Osundare kept these ideals up to *Village Voices* by writing some of the most politically explicit poetry in Africa on the situation of the underprivileged that are alienated from the sociopolitical processes of their nations. The climax of his revolutionary concerns and views is found in *Village Voices* where his peasants show they have the understanding of the system and the strength or power and the zeal and readiness to turn the system around to their advantage. One wonders whether this is not the wishful thinking of the poet. There have been instances of "successful" rebellion by peasants against corrupt governments in the area where Osundare comes from, but these have not changed the nature of maladministration, exploitation, oppression, and alienation of this class. Perhaps that is why Osundare's point of view changed from *The Eye of the Earth*. His confidence in the revolutionary powers of the masses has waned with every subsequent collection. He still consistently says that the masses have the power to alter History, but increasingly in the face of a view that History and its processes are subject to the revolutions of Time, his boasts about the power of the masses sound hollow. True, there will be changes, as he still says at the end of *Waiting Laughters*; but changes are not likely to be permanently positive and, what is worse, man does not fully control changes and thus cannot predict when they will come. ''Waiting'' and ''waiting'' in hope for the ''laughter'' is the only assured prediction of mankind in the face of the revolutions of History and Time. Increasingly from *The Eye of the Earth*, poetic technique and diction have consistently been foregrounded and politics has played second fiddle.

Development in poetic technique, too, is not unrelated to changes in the tempo of the writer's convictions about social revolutions. In *Songs of the Marketplace* and *A Nib in the Pond*, Osundare is mainly concerned with vivid exposition of the various forms of social malaise. Explicit description of instances of corruption, exploitation, and maladministration is the major technique, with sarcastic and ironic comments buttressing his criticism of society. By the time he has written *Village Voices*, Osundare's political views apparently have taken a ''socialist'' turn. It is not doctrinaire and not riddled with revolutionary jargon, but the point of view reflects familiar revolutionary views of the powers of the peasantry as the most revolutionary class in the society. It is probably because of this belief that Osundare has faced off in *Village Voices* in a technique of poetic impersonality to allow the peasants to speak for themselves instead of speaking for them. One would way that the peasants overidealized their power. But be that as it may, Osundare's distinct voice as poet began to merge with his revolutionary use of the oral traditions. In speaking for themselves, his peasants adapted the various traditional art forms that have always expressed the somewhat egalitarian peasant culture to assess contemporary political and social system. They use these forms to assert their importance as props for the national government, reminding that they can bring governments down that do not do their will. Osundare achieves his ideals of revolutionary poetry in the explicitly political poems in *Village Voices* in accessible language modelled on the poetic idiom and prosody of traditional African art forms.

Thereafter Osundare assumes his voice again in *The Eye of the Earth* and subsequent books of poetry. Although he has not completely abandoned the politics of revolutionizing society, the political message has apparently become subservient to poetic technique and formal experimentation. The poet has abandoned the style of individual lyrics for a form of poetry in which a whole body of poems is organized around one or two motifs, the poems evolving as stages of a single poem. This form has dominated the poems of *Moonsongs* and his latest work *Waiting Laughters*. The advantage of this form is mainly that its expansive nature, similar to the form of ritual poetry, allows the writer to do many things artistically. The poem is usually thus a pastiche of narratives, descriptions, dramatization of incidents, songs, incantations, eulogy (rarely) and satires. His subject has become more abstract, relating to ''unrevolutionary'' views of History and Time. His language has also become rather abstract and elitist, modelled on a complex system of symbolism, personifications, and highly structured images. The strength of his language depends on the recurrence of these images with their pile-up effects. Perhaps politics is still important to him, but at this stage one has a feeling that the poet enjoys, and indulges in, the playing with words, and his poetry is more fascinating for his mastery of the word and rhythm than for the worth of his politics.

Aderemi Bamikunte. *Research in African Literatures*. 26, 4 (winter 1995), pp. 121–37

BIBLIOGRAPHY
*'As Grasshoppers to Wanton Boys': The Role of the Gods in the Novels of Elechi Amadi, 1980; Songs of the Marketplace*, 1983; *Village Voices*, 1984; *The Eye of the Earth*, 1986; *A Nib in the Pond*, 1986; *The Writer as Righter*, 1986; *Moonsongs*, 1988; *Songs of the Season*, 1990; *Waiting Laughters*, 1990; *Selected Poems*, 1992; *Midlife*, 1993

# OUOLOGUEM, Yambo (1940–)
## Mali

The most striking feature of the novel [*Le Devoir de violence*] is its style, the originality of which can only be compared with that of Amos Tutuola or perhaps Okot p'Bitek, both writing in English. While preserving the spontaneity of the oral tradition, [Yambo] Ouologuem's chronicle of oppression and debasement, of horror and violence, is told in a truly epic yet also sarcastic manner: his many parentheses, full of exclamations and Koranic formulas, give the sentences a broken, sinuous syntax which does not mar the novel's unity of tone. Unfortunately, those qualities are practically absent from the last part of the book, where the narrative rhythm becomes slow and heavy, and the tone pedantic.

The unique significance of *Le Devoir de violence* for the history of French African writing lies in the image it offers of the ''Black Continent,'' an image as far removed from the romanticism of Négritude as from the anticolonial realism of the novelists. The work is clearly intended to offer the Western reader an alternative picture, less complacent, less imbued with anti-European rancor, presented as more faithful to the reality of Africa. . . .

By deliberately selecting from the African past only those elements which may debase it, Ouologuem created a myth different from, but as dangerous as, the one he was seeking to destroy. . . . It is worth noting that such ethical values as motherly love or the sense of solidarity and the social harmony inherent in the clan system, as well as such cultural values as dance and music, are all absent from Ouologuem's Africa. The legendary modesty of Muslim society is completely ignored. Ouologuem's image of black Africa is one of total permissiveness and generalized promiscuity. Do we have here ''the true image of Africa''? The African reader does not hesitate to answer in the negative: Ouologuem's Africa is a myth born of what he himself called in his *Lettre à la France nègre*, ''la gymnastique opératoire de l'écriture.''. . .

This inverted interpretation of history seems to have been dictated by Ouologuem's wish to create an authentic African literature, for he considers that the works written before independence could not have been genuinely African. . . .

The literary influences that have entered into the service of Ouologuem's aesthetic purpose do not of themselves explain his approach to his subject. Political motives, namely, the bitter disappointment experienced by many African intellectuals since the end of colonial domination, must also be taken into account. During the struggle for independence, enthusiasm was at its highest; everyone aspired to a better world with plentiful opportunities for individual development. But those great expectations were ill-founded: the greater part of independent black Africa has since swayed between anarchy and dictatorship; its history is already ridden by civil wars and military coups, while its politics is too often the product of clan nepotism and shameful corruption.

J. Mbelolo Ya Mpiku. *Review of National Literatures.* 2, 2 (fall 1971), pp. 140–45

There are reports that Ouologuem has written at least one other novel under a pseudonym, but it was, as a matter of fact, the wished-for next book published under Ouologuem's own name which began to cause many critics to have some nagging doubts, not because of the contents per se but because of its flimsiness of diction and weakness of structure. One critic, not yet aware of the full importance of foreign sources in the composition of *Le Devoir de violence,* put it bluntly but accurately when he exclaimed that "Disappointment came, however, when Ouologuem published his second book, *Lettre à la France nègre,* a pamphlet in every way inferior to his novel." The only way, in fact, that it is superior to *Le Devoir de violence* is in its authenticity, for there is no reason to think that this work is not fully the product of Ouologuem's own talents and abilities! Critics found it difficult to reconcile the novel and the book of essays. The discrepancy was disappointing, and it was so great that it could not simply be attributed to the "sophomore jinx" which has temporarily blighted many a career. A year or so after the publication of Ouologuem's first novel, disquieting charges of borrowings, extensive imitation, and outright plagiarism began to circulate as rumors and then in a series of articles which in turn drew two reactions: on the one hand, a number of people wrote to the authors and editors of these articles supplying further examples of stylistic indebtedness; and, on the other, some critics sought to minimize the significance of plagiarism in general and to defend Ouologuem in particular. . . .

The fact that *Le Devoir de violence* is largely a paste-up of unoriginal material which has been appropriately adapted to fit the book's general *structure d'accueil* does not mean that it is without significance. . . . If it is not deeply African in its contents, it may be that one or more major African impulses were nevertheless present in the attitude of the author with regard to the notion of plagiarism—even, perhaps, unbeknownst to him—as well as in the general characteristics emerging within the larger structure of his work. In other words, I contend that while the basic contents and method of composition are not spontaneously African, Ouologuem has—in opting for an episodic structure, contrived though it might be—remained faithful to at least one fundamental African impulse found expressed in the majority of Franco-African literary works from [Camara] Laye's *L'Enfant noir* to [Ahmadou] Kourouma's *Les Soleils des indépendances.* The African writer tends, by virtue of age-old traditions of the *khawaré or veillée poétique* and the oral folktale, to prefer to channel his creativity into short, self-contained episodes without undue attention to logical or smooth transitions. Within the larger *structure d'accueil* of the *khawaré* we have a variety of songs, dances, poetic chants, and musical renditions; and it was inevitable that African novels should either adopt compatible European forms like the diary, the collection of tales, and the series of salient memories neatly encapsulated in chapters, or else twist prose into an episodic structure.

Eric Sellin. *Yale French Studies.* 53 (1974–76), pp. 142–43, 158–59

[Few literary works out of Africa have] attracted so much attention or aroused so much controversy as Yambo Ouologuem's first novel. The last word has yet to be said in this matter and the final judgment [is] still to be made. When *Le Devoir de violence* appeared in 1968, to be awarded the Prix Renaudot . . . it caused a sensation in France such as no other black writer's work—even including [René Maran's] *Batouala*—has ever known. The acclaim from France was followed by enthusiasm from the Anglo-Saxon world, particularly from America, on the publication of the English translation, under the title *Bound to Violence.* Glowing American reviews followed glowing French reviews. *Le Monde* greeted the work as "perhaps the first African novel worthy of the name.". . . One dissenting voice from the chorus of praise came from that usually percipient Nigerian critic, Abiola Irele, who denounced Ouologuem's novel as "a meandering succession of sordid happenings, excesses and extravagances, presented as a historical narrative of a fictitious but 'typical' African empire" and condemned the work for indicating that "the past has only bequeathed to the present generation of Africans a legacy of crime and violence.". . .

The storm, which brought red faces to the firm of Le Seuil and eventually to Heinemann, who were bringing out the English version in England, broke in 1971, when Eric Sellin . . . first challenged Ouologuem with plagiarism, proving by clear illustrations that the resemblances between the African novel and [André] Schwarz-Bart's *Le Dernier des justes* . . . was not simply one of categories, but were also textual. . . . But the echoes spread wider and the controversy became more bitter when the *Times Literary Supplement* of May 5, 1972, printed an article submitting the striking resemblance between two pages of Ouologuem's work and an extract from an early novel by Graham Greene—*It's a Battlefield,* published in 1934. . . . Schwarz-Bart expressed himself completely unconcerned by the use that the black writer had made of his work, in fact maintaining that he was "deeply touched, overwhelmed even" and "happy that his apples should be . . . taken and planted in different soil." Mr. Greene was somewhat less enchanted about the indirect flattery of [Ouologuem's] unacknowledged debt.

Dorothy S. Blair. *African Literature in French* (Cambridge: Cambridge University Press, 1976), pp. 305–6

When [*Le Devoir de violence*] was first published in 1968, it was highly praised in Europe and America. However, it was received with mixed feelings in Africa. Ouologuem was hailed by non-Africans as the first African intellectual of international standing since [Léopold Sédar] Senghor. Speaking to journalists in France, he claimed that his book spoke of leaders who posed as "bawling revolutionaries while opening their tattered purses to capitalism." He concluded: "My aim is to do violence to the misconceptions of Africans so that we can realize what the real problems are. This is 'our duty of violence.'" This duty is necessitated by the need to reformulate the philosophies on which the African society is based, in view of centuries of brutalization through a three-pronged act of violence—slave-trading activities from the North and South, internecine wars and razzias, and colonization—which has created a new breed of humiliated Africans whom Ouologuem refers to in his novel as "the niggertrash." His duty of violence is based not on physical violence, for Africans have surfeited themselves with that, but on intellectual violence, a sort of brainstorming aimed at making the people aware of the necessity for revolutionary change. . . .

The sheer beauty of Ouologuem's art deepens our perception of the history of the blacks from about 1200 A.D. to the present day. His message is that violence, in all its ramifications, is a necessary evil, if true and lasting political freedom is to be achieved. . . . The reader is inevitably drawn into a vortex of words full of mystery, meaning and communication, right from the first paragraph of the novel. . . . Like the griot or chronicler retelling for the umpteenth time the tribe's history and explaining the more salient points of that history, Ouologuem sets off with lightning speed and draws us straight into a world of blood and tears in which, from century to century, we see the Saifs, rulers of Nakem, striving to aggrandize their empire or enrich themselves. Legends of the good and bad Saifs are used to describe events in those centuries when the written tradition had not yet superseded the oral.

Yusufu Maiangwa. In Kolawole Ogunbesan, ed. *New West African Literature* (London: Heinemann, 1979), pp. 73, 76

One of the distinctive marks of Ouologuem's art . . . is his brilliant use of language. There can be no doubt of his mastery of his French medium which one suspects is even reflected in the excellent English translation [of *Le Devoir de violence*]. At times his prose exudes [a] tough intellectual quality. . . . It can [also] be lyrical, as in the description of the Tambira-Kassoumi love affair, and it can exude a poetic grandeur as in Sankolo's account of his experiences. Ouologuem also makes occasional attempts to modify the language and give it an African flavor, as in "May your path be straight" or "May God hear you and reward you." His superb descriptive power is partly due to his use of images. They are drawn largely from the world of traditional life as in "the members of that society who had no more courage than a wet hen" and "his face in anger turned as yellow as pepper." Appropriately, in a novel concerned with violence, most of the images are taken from the more repellent aspects of the animal kingdom as in "The crown forced men to swallow life as a boa swallows a stinking antelope," "That same night, at the hour when the jackals fill the bush with their howling, the emperor gathered together his whole court . . ." and "the Arab conquest . . . settled over the land like a she-dog baring her white fangs in raucous laughter."

Ouologuem's realization of his characters is also faultless. So many of them stand out in this motley throng because the author presents them in detail through thought and action. Apart from the superb portraits of the Saif, Raymond, Tambira, and Kassoumi, the reader is not likely to forget Sankolo, Bouremi, Chevalier, Awa, Wampoulo, Kratonga, Shrobenius, and even Kadidia. Ouologuem relies not so much on a complex plot and structure as on a full and detailed presentation of the experiences of his characters, thus achieving a novel of remarkable solidity and significance. His achievement is rare in the whole history of the African novel.

Eustace Palmer. *The Growth of the African Novel* (London: Heinemann, 1979), pp. 218–20

The implications of Ouologuem's work are different as one moves from the world within the novel to the role of the novel in the world, but on each level the force of an *injunction* is evident. Within the fictive world which the novel projects, the Nakem empire is in

subservient bondage to its rulers, held on a short leash: "Dans l'attente de ce grand jour de la proche éclosion du monde où le serf est l'égal du roi, la négraille—*court lien à méchant chien!*—accepta tout." [In his hope for that great day, the forthcoming blossoming of the world, when the serf will be equal to the king, the *négraille*—short leash for a bad dog!—accepts everything.] The "petit trait horizontal" [little horizontal leash] between Saif and *négraille* is the symbolic and real joint of a generalized injunction: political power. The populace is enjoined to efface itself before both the African notables and the incoming French. But if a false identity is forced on the *négraille* (through public education, Christianity, etc.), the Saifs are equally false in their manner of adopting whatever identity suits their needs: the former thus become nothing, the latter everything. The bonds of power within the Nakem are bonds of violence by which bodies and identities are both made and broken—Ouologuem makes it amount to the same thing. . . . Violence is the language by which connections are made and therefore broken, no more apt to make sense than any other language. . . .

The "injunctive" nature of an author's work to which I first referred—that of binding an object and bringing it into the light—is radically disturbed by Ouologuem's negativism. What is brought to light is the fact that nothing can be brought to light; that which is bound is "bound to violence," torn apart like the two birds bound together. This may explain the impression shared by more than one reader of *Le Devoir de violence*, that they are reading strictly *n'importe quoi*, a brilliant mish-mash.

But it is on the outermost level, that of the politics of Ouologuem's literary practice, that his novel is at its most significant. As within the novel, there is a refusal of identity, but here it is the identity of the text, the author, and the genre which is negated. Ouologuem subverts the authoritative role of creator by pillaging European literature to compose "his" text. The whole notion of "text"— important not only to the legalities of copyright but also to modern criticism—is undermined, as if by sleight of hand. But most importantly, Ouologuem's act violates the national and continental boundaries by which integral bodies of literature are perceived. A "corpus," whole unto itself and distinct from all others, is generally assumed in the face-off between Europe, Africa, etc. It is here where dangerous metaphors get their foot in the door, metaphors which Ouologuem explodes: for if one body is distinct from another, one can or must be different, perhaps older and therefore better. This is the root of theories such as [Georg] Lukács's, which projects a hierarchy according to age, between "childlikeness" and "virile maturity," between epic and novel. But *Le Devoir de violence* is written in the excrescences, the orifices, and the intrusions between European and African literature, by an author without authority. Ouologuem's response to the condition of the African novel (if we can interpret his actions on such a plane) defies the rules of identity and injunction by which his work could be placed in a position of "childlikeness." Depicting all ties as destructive, Ouologuem strikes an uncompromising stance of pure negativity.

Christopher L. Miller. *L'espirit createur*. 23, 4 (winter 1983), pp. 72–73

It is now possible to say that Dogon myths, West African traditions, form the core of *Le Devoir de violence*; but in Ouologuem's written transformation of the myths, they are generalized, spread out. In the narrative, the Dogon myths are interlaced with a variety and multiplicity of other texts. Without commenting on the ethical questions relevant to the patchwork of quotations that Ouologuem took from a wide variety of English, French, and African sources, and which he then stitched together to make up the fabric of the text, suffice it to say that this literary composite—what some critics have chosen to call an anthology—substantially contributes to the generalization of the narrative. The collection of fragments from oral literature, the Bible, Arab histories, [François] Villon, [Gustave] Flaubert, Graham Greene, André Schwarz-Bart, and on, and on; these fragments together, transformed, make up Ouologuem's picture of life. . . .

Ouologuem—along with many other African writers—is concerned with the problems of reconciling the past with a difficult present in an Africa going through an uncomfortable, often violent, period of transition. In *Le Devoir de violence* he explicitly rejects the romanticized histories of the Négritude writers and of the Europeans like [Leo] Frobenius—who appears in the text as Schrobenius—those histories which lead to complacency. In an attempt to deal with the realities of the present, and the possibilities of the future; instead of writing a chronological history, Ouologuem has united scattered fragments of the past and set them down, piecemeal, in the present. By combining fragments from different times, places, and cultures, Ouologuem places violence and evil in Africa in a larger perspective, which enables us to see it and understand it . . . and possibly deal with it.

Sandra Barkan. In Kofi Anyidoho, Abioseh M. Porter, Daniel Racine, and Janice Spleth, eds. *Interdisciplinary Dimensions of African Literature* (Washington, D.C.: Three Continents Press, 1985), pp. 110–11

Immediately hailed as "the first truly African novel," [*Le Devoir de violence*] was awarded institutional acclaim in France as the winner of the Prix Renaudot. The novel tells the epic history of a fictional African people from its precolonial origins to the contemporary present. Much of Ouologuem's success apparently came from the explicitly indigenous—that is, "original" as both primitive and new—nature of the text. It is written largely in the oral storytelling style of the traditional griots; it borrows heavily from traditional tales and folklore, is luridly savage in its depiction of violence and perverse sex, and responds in this way to the occidental taste for the exotic—the "real" Africa.

The problems start subsequent to the text's publication in English, whereupon a scandal erupted in the pages of the *Times Literary Supplement* when it was reported by an "anonymous critic" that the text included extensive "plagiarism" of Graham Greene's novel *It's a Battlefield*. Critic Eric Sellin had already discovered another instance of plagiarism in this "authentic" African text: it read like a rewrite of André Schwarz-Bart's novel *Les Dernier des justes*. These discoveries, as well as instigating a virulent polemic in and out of the *Times Literary Supplement*, jeopardized for a time the text's and the author's reputations, as Greene filed suit for plagiarism and the text was re-edited with the offending passages expurgated. The "anonymous critic" asks sarcastically if Ouologuem has discovered "a style of literary imperialism intended as a revenge for the much chronicled sins of territorial imperialists." Defenders claim, of course, that the accusations of plagiarism are no more than a thinly disguised racism, for

the "authentic African novel" which borrows heavily from European sources is exposed as somehow neither authentic nor African. Ouologuem himself had maintained that the novel is "not traditional," is written with "references to international examples," and is "not just an African novel." In the same vein, its defenders maintain that the insistence on Africanness in its folkloric mode denies the essential reality of a contemporary Africa created by the assimilation of Western traditions imposed by those very colonial forces which continue to ghettoize the African by valorizing only traditional folklore. The irony, of course, is that the *real* Africa is precisely the one that the West rejects in the form of accusations of plagiarism. Formed by Western values and culture (Ouologuem was preparing a thesis in Paris at the time), modern African writers are as literate and as steeped in Western literature and cultural knowledge as are their Western counterparts. . . .

In the same year, 1968, Ouologuem published *Lettre à la France nègre*, a series of open letters to various sectors of French society. In one letter, addressed to "les pisse-copie Nègres d'écrivains célèbres" (to hack nigger-writers of famous authors), he ironically advises black writers to stick to the mystery or detective novel. . . . Ouologuem proposes a formula for producing an infinite number of assembly-line type novels by juggling in any order a number of passages stolen from major mystery writers. For demonstration purposes, he provides a number of these passages, rated according to their quotient of humor, suspense, violence, eroticism, and so on. Explicitly advocating a kind of wholesale plagiarism, Ouologuem points out the infinite possibilities available to the hack writer of second-rate fiction, the fate that he imputes to the black African writer. It is not coincidental that Ouologuem practices a form of this very strategy in his own "literary" novel. What appears as a rhetorical joke in the context of the political essay becomes a crime in the literary text.

Marilyn Randall. *New Literary History.* 22 (1991), pp. 536–37

Yambo Ouologuem, the Malian author of *Le devoir de violence* and other literary works, has not been interviewed in nearly three decades. In fact, his doings have been shrouded in mystery ever since he "disappeared" from the West, in effect turning his back on literature. Like Arthur Rimbaud, J. D. Salinger, and others, Ouologuem has become an enigma for many, a mysterious figure as well as a highly respected author. The reasons for Ouologuem's silence are complex and will perhaps never be fully known. It is certain, however, that Ouologuem has blamed the publishers of *Le devoir de violence* for plagiarism controversies that followed the novel's appearance in 1968. In the early seventies, Ouologuem claimed that numerous unauthorized deletions had been made in his manuscript, specifically references to Graham Greene's *It's a Battlefield*, Andre Schwartz-Bart's *Le dernier des justes*, and other sources. Rather than acknowledging these revisions, the novel's publishers simply disavowed all responsibility and placed the onus entirely upon Ouologuem. Nevertheless, Ouologuem's refusal to write cannot be easily attributed to any ancient grudges he might bear towards the French literary establishment. What complicates matters is Ouologuem's wholehearted return to Islam, the faith of his childhood. In the mid-1970s, Ouologuem returned to Mali, where he is now widely known as a devout marabout, or Muslim holy man. However, as I have argued elsewhere ("Qur'anic Hermeneutics"), even the writings of Ouologuem's "apostate" period cannot be fully understood without reference to Islam, specifically Tidjaniya Sufism as it has historically been practiced throughout West Africa.

During a year's residence at the Universite de Ouagadougou in Burkina Faso, I sought to find Ouologuem and conduct an interview with him, for I hoped to better understand the reasons for his ''conversion'' to Islam and his rejection of literature. . . .

I had learned enough about Ouologuem from my colleagues at the University of Ouagadougou to make me cautious. More than once, I had heard it said that Ouologuem had gone mad. One night, on a bus trip to the village of Titinga Pacere, the renowned Mosse poet and ''bendrologist,'' the mere mention of Ouologuem's name generated passionate argument and controversy among my African colleagues. Some claimed that Ouologuem was a ''great genius''—even the ''African Joyce''—while others insisted that he was a ''shameful plagiarist'' and ''madman.'' That same week, I had a dream about Ouologuem in which he consented to be interviewed, but he was not happy about it. In fact, he was contemptuous of the whole affair. When I awoke, I told my wife about my dream, but I did little else, for it seemed somehow inevitable that the interview would take place. Rationally, I could not have explained why this was so, but I felt certain something would happen very soon. . . .

Ouologuem never saw our approach because his back faced us, and he was deeply engrossed in conversation with Tall and Timbely [his uncle]. He wore a sky blue boubou with a white scarf, white slippers, and a white prayer cap. His arms dramatically flayed about as he spoke, the packet of letters clutched in one hand. He immediately noted our presence, but did not break off his speech. When Timbely introduced us, he irritably shook our hands but did not allow interruption of the flow of his lecture, an energetic clarification of the different orders of Muslim religious leaders. However, his speech became faster and angrier, his eyes glaringly fastened upon his uncle. As he spoke, I became transfixed by his face, which seemed to me profoundly ugly, not unlike a bust I'd once seen of Socrates, the dog-faced philosopher, or perhaps Danton. His cheeks were round and enormous, and they were set in an intense if not bellicose grimace. I lost his train of thought, and only caught up again when he made a heated reference to Judas Iscariot, all the while glowering at his uncle.

Timbely only smiled serenely, and soon we all sat upon metal chairs, brought out by the judge and his secretaries, as as ''primitives,'' the local Dogon (as well as Peul, Malinke, and others) ridiculed the Senegalese as French ''boot-lickers'' and self-hating blacks. In any event, almost everyone present seemed to share Ouologuem's sentiments about Senghor, or they were at least amused by his rapid-fire monologue. When I asked him his views on the Rushdie affair, Ouologuem refused to comment (as he did with any of my direct questions), but it was clear he had given the matter a great deal of thought. His friend, the judge, seemed particularly upset that Ouologuem would not respond to my question, and he informed us that they had been discussing Salman Rushdie only a day ago. However, Ouologuem steadfastly refused to comment, except to say that his remarks would probably be misunderstood and used against him. In fact, Ouologuem returned to his invective against Senghor and, to the amusement of all, he began to ridicule negritude, especially its reception in the United States. At this point, it dawned on me that Ouologuem believed I was myself an African American in some remote way, a suspicion that was later confirmed when he confided that he had foreseen this visit in a dream.

It was evident that the situation of the African American, especially in the United States, incessantly occupied his attention, and even formed a private obsession with him. He spoke at length of his time in the United States, his appreciation of Malcolm X, his meetings with Cassius Clay, and his participation in the formation of Black Studies programs at several American universities. When Robert asked him which states he visited, Ouologuem again refused to answer directly, but he finally laughed and said, ''In any case, I was not in any pious state.'' Unexpectedly, he blurted out, ''You know, we Africans cannot be held accountable for the actions of our brothers over there. This is a fallacy. Many would disagree with me, of course, and I have heard it said that if your goat destroys your neighbor's garden, you are responsible for the damage. Still, these Africans who are causing so much trouble are not Muslims.'' Like Senghor and all advocates of negritude, he said, blacks in the United States are too obsessed with skin color. ''They have been infected by too many poisonous ideas. In Islam, however, there is no color.'' Here, Ouologuem cited two or three hadith wherein it is said that people of all colors are equal in God's eyes.

''Blacks in America must repent,'' he insisted. ''Until they do so, they will continue to live in their own private hell, and this has nothing to do with us in Africa.'' Here, Ouologuem claimed that his own problem, as well as that of his fellow Malians, was hardly a question of skin color but rather imperialism. With the arrival of the French in Mali, the plight of his fellow Dogon was more closely akin to that of the American Indian, ''a new spaghetti Western'' in Africa. Above all, he feared that an extraordinarily rich culture, and its many ancient customs, could be destroyed in favor of the most vulgar technological innovations—all in the name of modernization and ''progress.'' Later, I was to learn how serious he was about this when I discovered that, much to the frustration of his wife and mother, Ouologuem refused to allow electricity to be installed at his house in Sevare. Ouologuem also refused to have his photograph taken by me, citing the biblical injunction against graven images. Timbely, Tall, and everyone present expressed their outrage at Ouologuem's refusal, and even pleaded with him to change his mind. I also reminded him that I had seen a movie theater across from the Mosquee Rimeibe, but he would not budge. The Qur'an tolerated no equivocation on this issue, he said. In fact, this was one of the most defining features of Islam, as opposed to more infidel variants of Ibrahimic religion. As for the movie theater, this was a fault of the local Muslim community, much to be regretted. . . .

''I will speak with you tonight at your insistence,'' he said, [a few days later], ''but it would be better if I said nothing.'' He spoke in English now, and James had been right about his mastery of the language, which was total. ''You must know that you are in grave danger,'' he said. ''You and the Liberian are in grave danger here. There are people who would like to kill you. I refused to speak with you because I wanted to protect you. For now, I shall pray for you.'' From where I sat on a short-legged metal chair, Ouologuem seemed larger than he actually was, his face, scarf, and prayer cap illuminated by moonlight. ''It has been four years now since I saw you in a dream,'' he said, rubbing his eyes. ''I dreamed that a Jew would bring a Liberian and an African American.'' Here, he stopped and looked me over: the fact that I did not seem to be black disturbed him, but only slightly. ''These things that I know are hard for you to understand, I realize this. I have the authority to speak the way I want to speak, but if I decide to talk to people like you, I must put things in simpler terms. Still, it would be better if I said nothing at all.''

"Silence is always better, you see. This is why I refuse to answer your questions. We speak too much, myself included. Jesus was a silent man. Muhammad was a silent man, too. We forget this with all our books and radios. We drown ourselves in meaningless noise. But if you are able to be silent, you will see that it is much better than speaking.'' He paused for a moment and placed both hands on his knees. He seemed tired now, as if indeed the effort to speak exhausted him. "I have seen Jesus more than fifty times,'' he said. "I have spoken with him and with the Prophet. The angels, too, including Gabriel, and they're mostly silent. You must be very careful with people who speak a lot. They think that they know a lot, but they really know nothing.'' Ouologuem himself fell into silence at this point, as if listening for the sound of the wind blowing through the trees.

It was James who finally spoke. "You are truly a blessed man,'' he said softly. "God has truly blessed you.''

"I am not a blessed man,'' Yambo insisted. "Far from it. I am simply a man who is seeking God's blessing.''

"But you have knowledge,'' James said, "and knowledge is power.''

"No, knowledge is not power. When you are blessed by God, then you acquire wisdom. And when you acquire wisdom, then you have power. Knowledge in itself is not power. You see, God has allowed me to Journey to the very frontiers of the human mind. I have seen them unfold before my eyes.'' With this, Ouologuem swept his hand over his head, urging us to look up at the stars. "The world we live in is truly magnificent,'' he said. "In Allah, all things are possible if we are only open to them.''

There was another long moment of silence, until Ouologuem's mother cleared her throat, signaling for him to dismiss us. "If there's just one message you have,'' I said quickly, "if there was just one thing you'd like to say to black people in America, what is it?'' I am not sure why I asked such a question, but I said the first thing that came to mind.

"Go back to America and tell my black brothers that I've been fasting for the last ten years on their behalf. I've been fasting so that they'll come back to Africa. Tell them to come back to help ease our suffering, and Allah will be merciful. That is the first thing you must say. Then you may tell them that I am now preparing to take over the leadership of the educational system in Mauritania, where blacks suffer more than anywhere on earth. I hope to help establish there a truly Islamic government that will administer to the total affairs of Mauritanians, including Arabs. The worst enemies for blacks right now are racist Arabs, Arabs who have been satanically blessed with oil and who are now funding the Jews and apartheid-type governments everywhere. It is the Arabs who are sponsoring all these organizations that are against blacks, and who invest their money in Switzerland, America, and South Africa. Many have tried to stop me in this, but I am not so easily defeated. The French have tried to stop me. Even the CIA has offered me a few million dollars. The CIA has already done what it could to me, and they think they have defeated me, but they are mistaken. That is all I have to say.''

Ouologuem arose from where he sat, preparing to dismiss us. He again apologized for not shaking our hands and told us that it was time for his evening prayers, that we had detained him long enough. He disappeared into the darkness of his courtyard, and we were led to the gate by his mother. The interview had reached its conclusion. . . .

My search for Yambo Ouologuem had ended. Back in Ouagadougou, I met several more times with Sekou Tall and Mountaga, who both insisted that Ouologuem was no madman. Tall promised to write me a piece for my book, offering his own perspective on Ouologuem's current doings. Mountaga only nodded serenely and said that Yambo was "dur'' (or "hard in his faith''), and that was all. He was one of the "hard ones,'' not unlike his own father. As for the books Yambo had written some years ago, Mountaga said, these were all literary questions, and so they had of course ceased to interest him.

Christopher Wise. *Research in African Literatures* 29, 2 (summer 1998), pp. 159–82

BIBLIOGRAPHY
*Le Devoir de violence* (The Wages of Violence), 1968; *Lettre à la France nègre* (Letter to Black France), 1969

# OYONO, Ferdinand (1929–)
## Cameroon

"Cameroon has been a country over which a curtain of phantasmagoria was drawn. The Cameroonian writer therefore must try to lift this curtain before he does anything else,'' asserted Ferdinand Oyono during a recent debate on black literature. He has applied himself to this effort of demythologizing, this "restoration of the truth,'' in his two novels: *The Life of a Houseboy* and *The Old Negro and the Medal*. . . .

Toundi the adolescent [houseboy] and Meka the old Negro initially share the same illusions about their white masters. . . . We witness the slow movement toward self-awareness on the part of two Africans facing the colonial situation. Before their bitter experiences, neither Meka nor Toundi had grasped the true, private nature of the whites. They saw the whites through a curtain of prohibitions and taboos, and they spoke with a mixture of admiration and fear about the whites' power, about their ability to shape men and objects according to their needs. Then one fine day the commanding officer asks Toundi [in *The Life of a Houseboy*] to bring him a bottle in the bathroom. The leader of the whites is "naked in his shower.'' And he is not even circumcised! "I feel that the commanding officer no longer frightens me,'' notes the houseboy. This is the first crack in the wall of white respectability. It widens decisively when Toundi discovers with amazement that his master's wife has been shamelessly sleeping with another white man in the neighborhood. There is a lot of naïveté in the adolescent's gradual discovery of the adultery of the white woman, whom he had previously seen as practically a goddess of virtue. This episode gives rise to pages full of humor and truculent descriptions that, however, avoid turning into caricature.

This same comic spirit, supported by an intense realism, is again present in *The Old Negro and the Medal*. Oyono casts harsh, ruthless light on the contradictions between the whites' sugary words and their behavior. . . .

At no time does either of these novels take on the tone of an indictment. Oyono feels no compulsion to wink at the reader in order to show him the path to take through the long commentaries. He lets the facts speak for themselves and direct the dramatic movement of the narrative. The facts themselves condemn a system in which noble sentiments exist only on the surface.

David Diop. *Presence Africaine.* December 1956, pp. 125–26†

In Ferdinand Oyono's *The Old Negro and the Medal*, the old Negro Meka who has lost two sons in the war and who has given his lands to the Catholic Mission is to be presented with a medal by the High Commissioner on a ceremonial visit. . . .

Meka's place between the two worlds is not an assumption of the novelist's. It is Meka's own self-dramatization as he stands there between the platform of the whites and the African crowd behind him. At the moment when he experiences his isolation, Meka is not a tragic but a comic figure. His attempts to draw strength from the thought of his ancestors looking on, and from prayer to the Christian God, are comic because of the incongruities. His shoes are hurting and he needs to relieve his bladder. Oyono's vision is a comic vision of a world where everything is taken so seriously. This does not exclude indignation—indignation at the thoughtlessness, even barbarity, of the whites in leaving an old man to wait so long under the sun, indignation at the grievousness of Meka's sacrifices. . . .

The Europeans are comic because of the shameless insincerity of their gesture of friendship, and Meka is comic because he accepts it until events have taught him better. He has made himself a fool and suffered by trying to fit himself to their ways. But he has also made the whole white administration appear fools by making his own speech at the reception and inviting the High Commissioner to dinner at his village. At the end of the novel when Meka, sadder and wiser, is back at his house with all the friends and relatives who have descended on him to celebrate and share in the great honour bestowed upon him, we have the final joke. One of the guests suggests the way Meka should have shown his contempt for their medal. He should have appeared at the ceremony wearing only a traditional *bila*, or brief slip. Then the High Commissioner would have had to bend down and pin the medal onto the slip. Oyono's reaction, like the reaction of his characters, is laughter, an ancient classical laughter at the lords of the earth caught in undignified postures and the humble trying to ape the lords.

John Reed. *Makerere Journal.* 7, 1963, pp. 1, 7–8

Ferdinand Oyono's novels celebrate the disillusionment of the African with the white man's world. His heroes set out in a state of innocent enthusiasm; then comes the moment of truth, opening the door into a new world of bitterness or corrosive resignation. Despite the brilliance of his comic writing, this fatal *consequence* gives a kind of tragic intensity to his plots as a whole, particularly in *The Life of a Houseboy*, his first novel. He is probably the greatest master of construction among African novelists now writing. . . .

His latest novel [*The Road to Europe*] is more ambitious [than his first two works], for it depicts a situation which is in itself diffuse and hard to grasp, the situation of the young man educated beyond his fellows, but still not sufficiently so to assure him a career. Barnabas, the hero of *The Road to Europe*, has been expelled from a seminary for a supposed homosexual attachment. In his native town he finds himself at once despised and exploited;

despised as a layabout who thinks himself "too good" for ordinary work; exploited as being able to write French and keep accounts. He writes to the colonial authorities for permission to study in France, and the action of the novel covers the year or so during which he waits in vain for a reply. . . .

At last Barnabas decides to act. He travels to the capital and confronts the authorities who have kept him for so long in the doldrums of frustration and idleness. But in vain. The road to Europe is still closed and the bureaucratic clown whom he confronts in the vast halls of officialdom gives him every kind of advice except to persevere in his ambition. The realist Oyono achieves a brilliant flight of fantastic comedy when Barnabas and his travelling-companion, Bendjanga-Boy, stand stupefied before the huge silent barracks of the administration buildings.

Gerald Moore. *Presence Africaine* (English ed.). 18, 2 (1963), pp. 61, 70–72

All the old values [Oyono] depicts still survive in spite of the new [postcolonial] era. The Houseboy always exists, even if the relations between boss and servant are governed by the social laws now in force in Africa as in Europe. The Old Negro is on the road to extinction, for he cannot be "recycled" into another sector. Nevertheless, he is a respected electoral agent. This fossillike character, although quite likable, no longer has his place in today's Africa. He suffers from being a product of colonialism; herein lies his anachronistic role. The "intellectual" [in *The Road to Europe*] is still a malignant presence, and the myth of a gracious Europe remains. The universities of Africa are not absolutely without Africans, but one might wish that they were better attended by the holders of baccalauréat [secondary school] degrees, who still prefer to live as expatriates, as in the time of Aki Barnabas. . . .

Ferdinand Oyono's originality lies not so much in having depicted the morals of an historical moment in Africa, before 1958, but in having described a situation in which mutual incomprehension is more obvious, more often operative, than unilateral rebellion.

Roger Mercier and M. and S. Battestini. *Ferdinand Oyono* (Paris: Fernand Nathan, 1964), pp. 57–58†

The economy seen in Oyono's use and presentation of material is also evident in his language. Events and actions are described through the eyes of the characters; so, for much of [*The Old Negro and the Medal*], as with Toundi's diary [in *The Life of a Houseboy*], there is a conscious effort to avoid "literary" French and to use language common to everyone. The language is, therefore, simple and direct. Oyono has also reduced the dialogue and description to a minimum. Each word is chosen to give maximum effect; not only to create a precise image but to evoke associations which suggest unexpressed thoughts and details. . . .

While, in [*The Life of a Houseboy*], Oyono tries deliberately to present stereotypes to heighten the comic effect, in *The Old Negro and the Medal*, the lack of physical detail is due more to the characters' long familiarity with each other. . . . This lack of physical description is compensated by the detailed analysis of the characters' thoughts and background. In this way Oyono introduces the reader into the characters' world, not as an observer but as a participant. . . .

There is little that either [the Europeans or the Africans] can be proud of in this society. Both are corrupted and sterile. Both live behind façades which hide the insufficiency of their lives. The social criticism is cruel but Oyono shows the Africans' growing understanding of the fact that they can mock Europeans, can reject them and their social order. As yet there is no sign of a positive alternative but at least the Africans can reassert their dignity through laughter.

A. C. Brench. *The Novelists' Inheritance in French Africa* (London: Oxford University Press, 1967), pp. 59–60, 63

Oyono's education meant more struggle, more isolation, more frustration than Beti's. And this has, without a doubt, contributed to the greater sadness of Oyono's satire. His irony is harsher, his laughter more nervous than Beti's. His criticism is, however, more with reference to circumstances of the colonial situation than against the system as a whole. He deals with individual personalities within the colonial setup—the new administrator, the Catholic priest, the prison director, the schoolmaster's wife—unveiling their shortcomings and their cruelty, more than he questions the colonial set-up as a whole. Neither does he, like Beti, ever refer to the implicit complicity between those who say they came to Africa "to save heathens' souls" and those whose proclaimed motive was "to civilize savages."

His satire can be said to be more destructive, more demoralizing. It does not leave the mind with much hope of a better understanding or amelioration of human relationships. At the end of Toundi's diary [in *The Life of a Houseboy*] there is no comment either by Toundi himself or by the . . . [diary's] supposed translator. The debate is closed definitively; indeed, there has not been much of a debate throughout the novel. The same thing would be said of Oyono's *The Old Negro and the Medal*, but not of Mongo Beti's novels.

Edris Makward. Introduction to Ferdinand Oyono, *Boy!* (New York: Macmillan, 1970), pp. xv–xvi

[Oyono's *The Old Man and the Medal*] is an important text because it is part of the anticolonial literature created by such black writers as Aimé Césaire in his poem "Femme noire" (1945) and his novel *Return to My Native Land* (1947), and by Ousmane Sembène in *Les bouts de bois de Dieu* (1960), both of whom appropriated physical and psychological stereotypes of Africans created by Europeans and used them to assert the difference and identity of black culture and to denounce colonialism and the physical and psychological situations which it fostered in the colonies. Among such negative images were those of the African as (physical) body, a psychologically deprived, deficient, handicapped, or unstable individual. From Aphra Behn's *Oroonoko* (1688) and Daniel Defoe's *Robinson Crusoe* (1719) to Pierre Loti's *Roman d'un Spahi* (1881) to Joseph Conrad's *Heart of Darkness* (1902) to the racist, pseudo-scientific writings and theories of the nineteenth and early twentieth centuries (such as Arthur de Gobineau's theory on race amalgamation as the cause of the fall of "great" European races)—in all

of these the African/colonized body was already a terrain of imperial gaze. These texts are built around negative physical and psychological representations of the colonized or of Africans.

Oyono's representation of the "conflicts" between Europeans and Africans is significant, however, not because it complies with the nature of African literature as a literature of conflicts—African literature has evolved from the encounter between Africa and Europe, as Achebe reminds—but because it differs from that of a great deal of African writings by authors such as Cheik Hamidou Kane, Ousmane Sembène, Ayi Kwei Armah; and Bessie Head, among many others who situate the conflicts of this encounter at psychological and/or political levels. Oyono builds his entire story around stereotypes in which he approaches characters physically, psychologically, and politically, emphasizing their inner and outer lives. Unlike Conrad, for example, whose representation of the African is emphatically negative, Oyono uses what Bakhtin refers to as "double-bodied" imagery, i.e., an imagery that combines positive and negative poles, to capture and reflect on the experiences of the Africans with the representatives of the colonial administration. His grotesque African characters are a satire of the colonial situation. The novel is like an example of Oyono's reaction against the predominant stock images of the time because he presents a more realistic and balanced view of the African characters. His characters are believable; they are decent beings who also have weaknesses: they can be self-indulgent and/or duped, for example.

In Oyono's text (set in post-World War II Cameroon under French occupation), the body is a medium of representation and reflection on the colonial system and its effects on the Africans and their responses to it. It is a metaphor for a contested terrain, a battleground for colonial conflicts and dislocations. In the text, Oyono draws a map of conflicts in terms of creating a cartography of the human body as the terrain of pain and colonial struggle, a metaphor of abuse, and alienation. Most characters in the novel have deformed, badly scarred, oversized, or protruding bodies, and a close examination of the way the narrative presents these deformities, along with the characters' interpretations of the colonial situation, reveals a peculiar meaning attached to these deformities: they are associated with futile attempts of the Africans to fit into the colonial situation (through a tolerance and an emulation of its ways) and with the colonizer's methods of duping the natives into believing and trusting.

Opportune Zengo. *CLA Journal*. 41, 1 (September 1997), pp. 24–43

BIBLIOGRAPHY
*The Life of a Houseboy* (*Une vie de boy*, 1956); The Road to Europe (*Chemin d'Europe*, 1960); The Old Negro and the Medal (*Le vieux nègre et la médaille*, 1956): *The Old Man and the Medal*, 1967

# P

## P'BITEK, OKOT (1931–)
Uganda

*Song of Lawino* is transposed from p'Bitek's own original version in Acoli: the author accepts the term "translated," but even though in recreating the poem in English he must, as he deprecatingly admits, have "clipped a bit of the eagle's wings and rendered the sharp edge of the warrior's sword rusty and blunt, and has also murdered rhythm and rhyme," nevertheless I think "transposed" is a juster description, since he has given us a work which stands in its own right in its new medium; we might even for once guardedly accept from the publisher's blurb the claim that the author has "almost incidentally evolved a new African form of English literature." This new "form" is a collection of thirteen related songs of some one to five hundred short, irregular lines, grouped in compact paragraphs, capturing a sinewy, fluent rhythm, with the compactness emphasized by the catching up of key words, and the telling repetition of certain lines and ideas (difficult to illustrate briefly), like an unpredictable refrain. . . .

Lawino lovingly, defiantly, intimately celebrates the way of life and the way of being in her village, in order to win back her husband [Ocol], who has become brashly alienated from his own background and in all matters emulates the ways of the foreigner, above all in marrying a second, sophisticated wife. Each song concerns a different aspect of life: in the third the relationship between men and women is epitomized in the dance. . . . In each song Lawino pinpoints with sharply humorous accuracy the incongruity of the European conventions, assumptions and attitudes being adopted in an Acoli village, which lives according to a meaningful pattern of its own, rooted in reality. . . .

David Cook. *Journal of Commonwealth Literature.* December 1967, pp. 12–13

I don't know what [the critic] Ali Mazrui finds in *Song of Lawino* to call it an important event. *Song of Lawino*, all considered, is an event but not the East African event. A popular event, yes. A great event? Yes. Since there is literary drought. Translation: the meaning is lost—the meaning of deep Acoli proverbs are made very, very light by their rendition into English *word for word*, rather than *sense for sense*, or *proverb for proverb*. . . .

Too much space and energy (the little there is in this light literature) is taken up with pointing out the foibles in the Western ways of life—these foibles that are easily seen by the eyes of the simple, *unedu*, uneducated Lawino. . . .

The trouble with his method is that his discussion is conducted in a low key: it is the simple that he deals with (the girl is limited both in vocabulary and knowledge of complex things), and he leaves the discussion of basic Christianity, basic Acoli religion (and basic many other complex things) aside—we are treated to "tribes" of "dungs" on latrine walls (Ministry of Works, please check), "red" lips—things to be seen with the eyes, things to be heard with the ears, or felt with the skin—but little to be felt with the intellect. (Lawino had lost out on intellectual development long

ago.) So, Okot also suffers from the Negritudist impediment of rhythm above sense.

I had expected an epic; I got a ballad.

Taban lo Liyong. *The Last Word* (Nairobi: East African Publishing House, 1969), pp. 140–42

A few critics have reacted against what they see as [Lawino's] jealousy-motivated defence of every aspect of tradition [in *Song of Lawino*]. They thus turn the fundamental opposition between two value-systems into a mere personal quarrel between Lawino and her husband. We must in fact see the class basis of her attack: Lawino is the voice of the peasantry and her ridicule and scorn is aimed at the class basis of Ocol's behaviour. The poem is an incisive critique of bourgeois mannerisms and colonial education and values. For it is Ocol's education, with the values it inculcates in him, that drives him away from the community.

With its critical realism the poem qualifies as a major contribution to African literature. Like [Frantz] Fanon on the subject of the pitfalls of national consciousness in *The Wretched of the Earth*, Lawino is asking Ocol to consciously negate and repudiate the social calling that the colonial legacy has bequeathed to the African intelligentsia. The significance of *Song of Lawino* in East Africa's literary consciousness lies not only in this ruthless exposure of the hollowness and lack of originality of a colonial middle class but also in its form. The author has borrowed from the song in the oral tradition. The African song gets its effect from an accumulation of details, statements and imagery, and in the variation of the tone and attitude of the poet-reciter to the object of praise. Lawino employs all these tactics in her disprise of Ocol.

*Song of Lawino* is the one poem that has mapped out new areas and new directions in East African poetry. It belongs to the soil. It is authentically East African in its tone and in its appeal. This can be seen in its reception: it is read everywhere, arousing heated debates. Some critics have even attempted a psychoanalysis of the creator of Lawino. It is the first time that a book of modern poetry has received such popular widespread acclaim. The effect on the young poets has been no less stunning, though a trifle dangerous. Many want to write like Okot p'Bitek. Unfortunately some have been taken in by its deceptive simplicity. [Sept., 1969]

Ngugi wa Thiong'o. *Homecoming* (New York: Lawrence Hill, 1973), p. 75

*Song of Ocol*, the sequel and reply to *Song of Lawino* by the same author, is a book which has been written in the minds of many people from bus passengers to University teachers, from stalwarts of traditional African cultural values to cultural iconoclasts and schizophrenics.

This short, characteristically readable poem is a surprise not only because it has been written by p'Bitek, but also because of the way he has written it. It is a negative reply, sometimes with Socratic irony, sometimes with nostalgic sham mockery, and when the author relieves Ocol of his mock-heroic, mock-epic tone and stance, we see self-questioning, uncertainty, and even insecurity and lack of conviction.

Thematically and poetically, *Song of Ocol* is weaker than *Song of Lawino*. The artistic corollary follows that Ocol's stature is less than that of Lawino with her fire of attack, vigour of challenge, conviction of assertion and freshness of genuine self-praise abundantly lacking in Ocol. At some point one shudders at the poetic truth in Lawino's nasty remark about the effect of books on Ocol's manhood. . . .

Where Lawino convincingly and vigorously asserts the positive value of her Acoli ways, Ocol just dismisses them to defend his wounded ego without a realistically, logically or poetically sustained opposing argument. To maintain the false identity which has been imposed on him, he pathetically succumbs to self-alienation from the realities of his past and kicks against the cultural gravitation of his roots in vain. . . .

*Song of Ocol*, in its expansive sweep from Masailand to Ancient Mali, from the Kingdom of the Bakongo to Sudan, aspires to the status of an epic, but *Song of Lawino* in its positively intensive assertiveness remains a more accomplished work. Ocol maintains his mock-heroic stance only falteringly and in the end the author deposes him to subject the cultural foundations and socio-political values of his fellow modern men to devastating inquiry. It is evident that both poetically and thematically, p'Bitek identifies with Lawino. He denies Ocol the articulation to champion his adopted values and makes him beg Lawino's question, which detracts from the artistic finish of the poem.

R. C. Ntiru. *Mawazo*. June 1970, pp. 60–62

As I see it, p'Bitek's power as a poet is of the kind that perpetually raises his work above the particular emotions and experiences— necessarily very tangled in any poet, and in him probably most severely tangled—from which it sprang. This is to be a really good poet. I don't believe anyone could seriously think about modern Africa without trying to weigh the meaning of *Song of Lawino* and *Song of a Prisoner*. I believe *Song of Lawino* has an importance far beyond the boundaries of Uganda; it is, when generalized, a poem about the situation in which we all find ourselves, being dragged away from all our roots at an ever-quickening rate. I believe, as I have said, that beyond the note of alarm and anguish that it strikes as to the condition of some newly independent African countries, *Song of a Prisoner* is full of the despair and anger, fiercely expressed, of anyone anywhere who is politically in chains.

But having said all this, one is left with a last—and perhaps, in the end, even more important—thing to say. And that is that Okot p'Bitek is a marvellous poet. I wish I could read him in his own language. But in English he has found a tone, a pattern of verse, a rhythm, that are highly original and inventive. It would not be easy to mistake p'Bitek, in English, for anyone else. Though—and perhaps my friend Taban lo Liyong will note this—his matter is never light, his manner often is, in a sense that any writer must envy. I count him among the few masters I have read of literary mischievousness. He can modulate from one mood to another with a skill that, though startling in its effect, rarely draws attention to itself. He is a master of writing for the human voice—and sometimes, I suspect, for the animal or insect voice, too. Much in his style might be made the basis of an argument for drumming, as a musical accomplishment for a poet, in much the way that one might have said experience of the lute was a formative influence on

Elizabethan verse. And finally, Okot p'Bitek, as man and poet, is one of those valuable souls who add manifestly to the gaiety of the nations, at the same time that much of what he expresses is closely concerned with their agony.

Edward Blishen. Introduction to Okot p'Bitek. *Song of a Prisoner* (New York: Third Press, 1971), pp. 39–40

I think perhaps the main weakness in *Song of a Prisoner*, if we compare it to *Song of Lawino*, is the lack of individual characteristics in the prisoner and the lack of clarification of the situation. Lawino's success springs from the fact that she is both a credible individual and a spokesman of betrayed Africa. Her individuality springs from p'Bitek's exploitation of the dramatic possibilities of the Lawino-Ocol-Clementine eternal triangle. The prisoner has individual characteristics and the reader can work out a particular situation, if he is prepared to expend the effort. But p'Bitek makes this very difficult. From a casual reading the prisoner appears to be a composite of prisoners: vagrant, murderer, dismissed bodyguard, and even disgraced minister.

Part of the explanation for this is doubtless the fact that p'Bitek wished to comment on as many areas of life as he could. But a more charitable and dramatically credible explanation is that the prisoner is suffering from hallucinations. At least once during the song the prisoner is actually tortured. Throughout the song he is suffering the ill effects of torture. His reactions obviously contain a degree of lucidity, varying from rage at his tormentors to a universalisation of his suffering, or dreams of triumphant release or peaceful escape. . . .

The prisoner is a villager in the town, whose traditional accomplishments qualify him only as bodyguard or murderer. As the leader's bodyguard he has seen the paraphernalia of wealth that the politicians enjoy, and he resents his exclusion from it. He has been denied a place ''in the lift to progress,'' but, more fundamentally, modern Africa denies him the opportunity of expressing his own manhood. Though he is much further removed from his Acoli tradition than Lawino, the prisoner, like Lawino, is bewildered by modern African politicians who have no respect for the things which he has learnt to respect.

G. A. Heron. *East Africa Journal*. August 1971, pp. 5–6

In his preface to *The Horn of My Love*, a collection of Acoli traditional songs, Okot p'Bitek argues the case for African poetry as poetry, as an art to be enjoyed, rather than as ethnographic material to be eviscerated. The latter approach has too often predominated, even among those scholars who have actually troubled to make collections. This book, with Ulli Beier's valuable anthologies, can help to build up the stock of African poetry for enjoyment.

The Acoli (pronounced ''Acholi'') are a grassland people of the Uganda-Sudan borders whose songs and ceremonial dances are still remarkably alive. Not preserved, with all that this word implies of mustiness and artificiality, but continually changing; continually acquiring new words, new tunes, and in the case of the dances, new steps or instruments. Okot p'Bitek himself describes the many changes of style and title undergone by the Acoli *Orak* (Love Dance) over the past seventy years. Dances do not change in this way unless they are still in the mainstream of the people's cultural experience. . . .

[This] is a book of poetry to be handled and enjoyed, rather than a ponderous headstone placed on the living body of a popular art. It can be read with equal enjoyment, in these facing texts, by Acolis relishing the felicities of the original languages and by English readers relishing the muscularity of Okot p'Bitek's translations. Those familiar with his own poetry, especially *Song of Lawino*, will recognize here the indigenous poetic tradition in which that fine work is embedded. The bitterness of Lawino's sense of betrayal is not a personal but a cultural bitterness. And it takes on additional depth and meaning for those who understand, from these songs, why a husband who cannot show his body in the dance arena is an insult to his whole clan, not just to his deserted wife.

Gerald Moore. *Times Literary Supplement*. February 21, 1975, p. 204

Acoli traditional culture is a living culture in which folklore contributes to the governing of society. Regularly performed before responsive audiences, Acoli folklore genres are as old as Acoli society itself, but they are also individual creations by means of which people fulfill their psychological needs. Over a period of time, these genres become imprinted on the society's collective consciousness, but each performance is unique in the sense that it takes place at a specific time and place. Highly specialized genres like oral songs are performed by adult professional singers who often accompany themselves on a musical instrument. The proverb is another specialized genre, and it is used by Acoli elders to give weight and authority to arguments, teachings or other forms of discourse.

The Acoli word for proverb is *carolok*, meaning that which alludes to the real thing or to a fact. The allusive character of proverbs is of course not uniquely Acoli. Ruth Finnegan records similar findings and notes [in *Oral Literature in Africa*, 1970] that "the figurative quality of proverbs is especially striking: one of their most noticeable characteristics is their allusive wording, usually in metaphorical form. This also emerges in many of the native words translated as 'proverb'." As for other peoples, the allusive metaphor is a storehouse of wisdom and philosophy for the Acoli. The form of the proverb and its relative brevity help endow it with the poetic quality of rhythm. . . .

Similes are frequently used by poets who, as [Clive Scott, in *A Dictionary of Modern Critical Terms*,] points out, do not wish, for one reason or another, to use metaphors. For them, similes serve as "the repository for their inventive boldness" and play an "alleviatory role, letting air and whimsy into involved narrative or analysis. . . ." Okot adopts similes for this reason in his *Song of Lawino*. For example, Lawino's clinical and somewhat repugnant description of Tina is achieved through the use of similes. Her intention is clear: she wants to discredit Tina and to prevent her from competing for Ocol's love. Okot also uses similes to describe the sordid night-club atmosphere which he is contrasting with the beauty of the Acoli Orak dance. If proverbs convey the social and moral norms that govern society, similes communicate the wit, irony, and humor that enliven social intercourse. Unlike proverbs, similes can be used by anyone who desires to employ a comparison to express succinctly what might otherwise require a long narrative description. . . .

Besides his creative borrowing of literary features from Acoli traditional culture, Okot has blended the different modes of Acoli oral songs in the *Song of Lawino*. Satire dominates the early

sections of the poem, which ends on a note of lament reminiscent of Acoli dirges. In the rest of the poem, Okot adopts the openly critical mode of the Bwola, Otole and Apiti dance songs in which singers discard their satirical masks and directly confront the people they are satirizing. This approach is particularly appropriate for his criticism of politicians and Catholic missionaries. Although Lawino sometimes sings her own praises, she returns to the lament at the end of her Song. She laments the "death" of Ocol on two levels: the loss of a husband who can no longer consummate their marriage and the loss of a "Son of the Chief" who can longer uphold his people's culture because he has assimilated Western values.

Okot's creative use of satire derives from his knowledge of Acoli satirical songs, which he classified in his [B. Litt thesis of Oxford] as songs of justice. These songs contain open criticisms of those who do not conform to social norms. Okot himself recognizes the wide range of subjects that can be satirized by the oral poet when he says, "Any act, behaviour or spoken, so long as it is a breach of, a divergence from the straight and narrow path of customs, is seized upon as a subject for these poems." In *Song of Lawino*, the traditional social norms provide a standard, and Lawino uses the poetic licence accorded to her by Okot to criticize anyone who departs from this standard. Ocol and Clementine are the principal targets of her satire but she herself does not escape completely unscathed, for she is the member of a community whose social norms she accepts and whose demands "she perceives as her own," but "she is also a Subject who has to conform to the society's norms without choice or perish" [Annemarie Heywood, "Modes of Freedom," *Journal of Commonwealth Literature* (1980)]. Ocol chose to perish rather than be a "Subject" of the traditional society, thereby subjecting himself to the alienation and cultural death that Lawino laments.

Lawino's attack on Ocol is two-pronged: she criticizes him as the husband who deserted her for another woman and as the nonconformist who refused to respect the social and cultural norms of her society. According to Lawino, Ocol deserted her because she was an uneducated traditionalist who was inappropriate for his new social status as a university graduate. Thus, she claims, "he has fallen in love" with Clementine, a modern girl whose "apemanship" equals his own; however, Lawino does not maintain this line of argument for long. She soon draws other members of her clán into the affair by telling them that Ocol's insults are directed against them:

He says Black People are primitive
And their ways are utterly harmful,
Their dances are mortal sins
They are ignorant, poor and diseased. . . .

Lo Liyong erroneously agrees with Ocol and dismisses Lawino as an uneducated village woman who cannot comprehend what Ocol says. In reality, Lawino's selective accounts of Ocol's abuses of her clansmen reflect back on the missionary teachings and prejudices that he absorbed from them. Whereas Lawino admits her limitations with regard to Western culture and technology, Ocol's exaggerated allegiance to the new culture leads him to dismiss traditional culture as irrelevant to modern society. But because he cannot gain full access to this modern society, he remains an alien in both cultures.

In the twelfth section of the *Song of Lawino*, Lawino destroys Ocol's pride by contemptuously describing his newly acquired house and life-style. The section is appropriately titled "My Husband's House Is a Dark Forest of Books." Lawino argues that these books have destroyed the Africanness of the educated class and transformed them into mouthpieces for the colonizers' propaganda against Africans. She concludes:

> For all our young men
> Were finished in the forest
> Their manhood was finished
> In the classroom
> Their testicles
> Were smashed
> With large books. . . .

Okot himself describes the university graduate in the following terms: "At the end of the third year he dons his black gown and flat-topped cap. In his hand he carries the piece of paper they give him at graduation—the key to power, money and a big car. Over dressed in his dark suit he walks out of the University gate, out into the world materially comfortable, but culturally castrated, dead" [*Africa's Cultural Revolution*].

In Acoli society, the oral composer-singer wears many masks, just as he plays many different roles. The transition from satirical composition to open critism, reminiscent of the Bwola and Otole dance songs, is a subtle one in the *Song of Lawino*. like the composer-singer, the writer discards his mask and plays the role of an angry member of society who has been wronged by another individual or by those in power. His poetic outburst is direct, and it is intended to correct the wrong that has been done, as Okot himself points out: "I really hold that an artist should tease people, should prick needles into everybody so that they do not go to sleep and think everything is fine . . ." [Lee Nicholas, "Conversation with Okot p'Bitek." *Conversation with African Writers*, 1981]. In *Song of Lawino*, Lawino's needles are directed at middle-class, educated Africans who inherited the multi-party system introduced by their colonial masters as a way of sowing discord among Africans. Okot criticizes the politicians primarily because they are more concerned about their own stomachs than about the need to work together to eliminate the three encourges: poverty, disease, and ignorance. The masses never benefited from flag independence and whenever they confront the looters to demand their share of the national wealth, the Ocols of African society have a ready solution:

> Trespassers must be jailed
> For life
> Thieves and robbers
> Must be hanged.

In reality, the opposite is true: the politicians and their collaborators should be hanged for having wronged the masses.

The form of Okot's poetry is clearly derived from Acoli oral songs, which in many cases are inseparable from the dances during which they are performed. Viewed from this perspective, *Song of Lawino* falls into three overlapping parts. The satirical criticism in the first nine sections is directly related to the Orak dance songs that Okot classified in his B.Lit. thesis as songs of "poetic justice." In Section Eleven, the mode is that of the political and topical songs that accompany the Bwola, Otole, and Apiti dances. The composer-singers of these songs do not wear the satirical masks of the Orak composer-singers, for their criticisms are collectively expressed by the participants in the dances; therefore, the lead singer cannot be held responsible for criticisms embedded in collectively performed songs. Sections Twelve and Thirteen are characterized by a mixture of modes, but the dominant one is that of lament. Lawino's

attempt to dissuade Ocol has failed, and he has therefore died a cultural death. Their marriage has also ended, and her lament echoes the form and themes of an Acoli dirge.

Okot's poetic style is essentially vocal rather than visual; in fact, it is less concerned with the formal pattern on the written page than with breath. The mixture of humor, satire, and lament in *Song of Lawino* reflect Acoli oral poetic forms, which are interwoven with proverbs, similes, metaphors, symbols, and other figures of speech to constitute a powerful personal commentary on the social, political, religious, and economic situation in post-independence Uganda and by extension, in the entire Third World.

> Charles Okumu. *Research in African Literatures*. 23, 3 (fall 1992), pp. 53–66

BIBLIOGRAPHY
*Song of Lawino*, 1966; *Song of Ocol*, 1970; *Song of a Prisoner*, 1971; *Africa's Cultural Revolution*, 1973; *The Horn of My Love*, 1974; *Artist, the Ruler: Essays on Art, Culture, and Values*, 1986; *Lak tar* (White Teeth), 1989

# PETERS, Lenrie (1932–)
## Gambia

Lenrie Peters was born in Bathurst, Gambia, of parents who came from Sierra Leone. Educated at Trinity College, Cambridge, and University College Hospital, London, he is a poet-physician, as was the American William Carlos Williams. Peters's knowledge of medicine, like Williams's, enters his work by indirection—through empathy. But Peters's bias for opera and lieder is evident in the rhythms of his apparently "free" verse.

Peters is good at vignettes, like head- or tailpieces in a book, which shade off gradually into the background. . . . Despite certain technical uncertainties, *Poems*, by Lenrie Peters, is a unique first volume. Its author is one who will bear watching.

> Melvin B. Tolson. *African Forum*. Winter 1966, pp. 122–23

From Lenrie Peters, a Gambian doctor, comes one of the real disasters in African fiction brought to print by Heinemann in the last two years [*The Second Round*]. In the present scramble for African titles, it is the kind of disaster which is bound to be repeated until a well-developed cynicism by importuned readers succeeds in stemming all this chaff.

The plot of the novel—if we might call it that—is a trite one. A Sierra Leonean doctor who has been training in Britain on a government scholarship returns to Freetown already slightly changed by his sojourn in the West, truly the "man of two cultures" rendered shop-soiled by African fiction. In his fictional progress through the novel, Dr. Kawa is surrounded by a gallery of afflicted zany characters who would dance with the best cats on a hot tin roof. An important man driven out of his mind by a nymphomaniac wife, a lover dying from cancer, a raped girl who doesn't know what to feel after this brutal violation because "I have not been raped before!"—all make their ghastly melodramatic appearances before the sorely tried Dr. Kawa, perhaps already fatally softened by Western training, takes flight up-country. One wishes him well, though naturally one worries about how the doctor will make out.

I am even more worried about Dr. Lenrie Peters' future as a novelist.

Lewis Nkosi. *Africa Review.* December 1966, p. 8

*Satellites* establishes Lenrie Peters as a major African poet writing in English. He had previously published twenty-one of these poems with Mbari [*Poems*]; this volume expands his range and solidifies his work. Born in Gambia, educated in Sierra Leone and at Cambridge, Peters is also a novelist, playwright, physician and surgeon. He speaks as a citizen of the world. Though his imagery and outlook are often African (Poem #10 on Freetown evokes the city more vividly than does all of Graham Greene's *The Heart of the Matter*), he rejects the slogans of propagandists, even in poems dealing with race, religion, and emergent African nationalism. His is an intensely personal voice expressing the "triumphant/irony of loneliness," where each individual is a satellite in his separate orbit. Engaged in "the cold war of the soul," "I will go alone darkly until I have done." There is considerable disillusionment with "love making without/transit of love," Christianity without Christ, politicians without integrity, doctors without dedication; but there remains hope for "harmony with nature/and strength in goodwill." Because of war, hypocrisy, conformity, "the path lies steeply forward," but the poet believes in passionate life, and "Life makes living true."

His verses have remarkable range in both language and content; subjects include sex, war, homecoming, surgery, the death of Churchill, the OAU, the Chinese bomb, parachute jumps, autumn, the passing of youth, the elusiveness of God, the nature of creativity, and the role of the artist. The style varies from elliptical obscurity to lucid lyricism and slashing satire; witty, learned, allusive but not pedantic, it is metaphysical verse made modern, a fusion of wit and passion, "circuitously direct like the heart" and kept at "the cutting chaotic edge of things."

Robert E. Morsberger. *Books Abroad.* Winter 1969, pp. 151–52

Peters in his presentation of lyrical passion, his depiction of human emotions, is atypical, unlike any other African novelist—his use of the poetic to describe his characters' feelings and the episodes in his story [*The Second Round*] makes him a writer standing alone. Frequently his dialogue sounds British instead of African—an influence it was probably impossible to eradicate completely, since Peters lived in England for such a long time. Because of this, there are aspects of the writing which must surely confuse the African reader. . . .

Must we reject a novel such as this for being unaccountable to the current African situation? Is Lenrie Peters really being unfaithful to Africa by writing a story which may not appeal to the average African reader? Because he fails to incorporate oral literary materials or anthropological background into his writing should Peters' novel be excluded from the category "African writing" and placed, instead, with, say, British fiction? In failing to deal with the usual African themes is Peters rejecting his African heritage and adopting that of the West? I fail to see how the attitudes that prompted these questions can have any true bearing on the significance of Peters' *The Second Round.* Certainly the history of literature is full of examples of writers who have been misunderstood or ignored by their own countrymen, and later rediscovered after having been appreciated by peoples from totally different cultures; for the history of art is, in many ways, a history of man ahead of his time, outside of his time, away from his time. I am not saying that Peters' novel will eventually be appreciated by the African reader. Rather, I am saying that the history of creative artists and writers is a history of exceptional men, and I rather suspect that African writers will in the future show a much more detailed concern with the individual in African society, as African society itself changes, for better or for worse, from a concern with the communal to a concern with the individual.

Peters' novel is not so much ahead of its time as his main character is a prophetic indication of things to come: a man (much like Clarence in Camara's *The Gaze of the King*) deeply alienated from life on all sides of him. In his depiction of the alienated African, Lenrie Peters has created a haunting story of one man's attempt to hide from the demands of the culture and the people around him, to ignore the basic foundations on which all society is based. It is a fine novel—and the fact that its appeal at the moment seems to be limited to a non-African audience certainly does not weaken its power.

Charles R. Larson. *The Emergence of African Fiction* (Bloomington: Indiana University Press, 1972), pp. 240–41

Much of *Satellites* is informed by a seriousness of purpose derived from a belief that poetry has a function, one made especially urgent by the compulsions of modern society, the "life with Figures/or chanting laws." Peters sees the intuitive life—upon which the growth of the individual largely depends—as increasingly assailed by "statistics, graphs and charts." In the face of an over-assertive intellect man suffers, *inter alia*, a retreat of the body's thinking. This weakening of links between emotion and intellect is a major theme of twentieth-century literature, one which Léopold Senghor exploited by giving prominence to claims regarding the unique nature of the African personality when he worked out the foundations of Negritude. To some extent the position Peters takes is in the tradition of Senghor's well-known stand except that he is mainly concerned with the dissociated sensibility as a contemporary problem. . . .

In *Satellites* the poems on broad African themes are underwritten. They are not undertaken with Peters's characteristic utterance and merely confirm that the subject had little power to move him. Perhaps Africa as a subject proves too large unless personalized by and engaged through elements of the kind offered by Negritude. Senghor delivers a new humanism out of the African virtues, Peters sees them as elements feeding his power as a poet. Senghor's view is perilously close to propaganda, though Senghor himself was too skilful a poet to be guilty of that. Peters, on the other hand, was never exposed in quite the same way. By making them part of his stylistic equipment, the thrusts of the African inheritance, the habit of seeing things as representational and so forth, were means to an end, rather than ends in themselves.

Edwin Thumboo. *African Literature Today.* 6, 1973, pp. 93, 98

BIBLIOGRAPHY
*Poems*, 1964; *The Second Round*, 1965; *Satellites*, 1967; *Katchikali*, 1971; *Selected Poetry*, 1981

# PETRY, Ann (1911–)
## United States

[Ann Petry's Country Place is] one of the finest novels of . . . [its] period. *Country Place*, moreover, is a manifestation not so much of assimilationism as of versatility. Mrs. Petry's early work, which includes both short stories and a novella, is strongly racial in emphasis. Her first novel, *The Street*. . . ., attracted considerable attention both here and abroad as an eloquent successor to *Native Son*. . . . Of an environmentalist who chooses to focus on society we can demand more than a superficial social analysis. The trouble with *The Street* is that it tries to make racial discrimination responsible for slums. It is an attempt to interpret slum life in terms of Negro experience, when a larger frame of reference is required. . . .

*Country Place* is a novel of another magnitude, large enough to justify a better acquaintance with its author. . . . It is from the theme of lost illusion that the narrative structure of the novel flows. *Country Place* develops a strong narrative drive, paced by a storm whose intensity is reminiscent of the New England hurricane of 1938. The action of the novel takes place in a single week (one cycle of weather), reaching a climax along with the storm. Through a kind of [King] Lear motif the storm reduces each character to moral (or literal) nakedness. Faced with the death of their dreams, they are forced to re-evaluate the past, balancing achievement with desire. The storm thus becomes considerably more than a narrative device; it suggests first of all the widespread uprootedness caused by the war. Ultimately it emerges as a symbol of time and flux, relentless killers of the dream.

Mrs. Petry's style, like her narrative strategy, supports her main intent. . . . Concrete, poetic, her style persistently seeks an "objective correlative" to human emotion.

> Robert A. Bone. *The Negro Novel in America*. (New Haven: Yale University Press, 1965), pp. 180–84

Petry has penetrated the bias of black and white, even of male and female, to reveal a world in which the individual with the most integrity is not only destroyed but is often forced to become an expression of the very society against which he is rebelling. She shows that the weak, regardless of race, are misled by illusions and stifled by poverty.

Particularly for Lutie Johnson in *The Street*, the struggle for survival alone is so demanding that even her attempt to struggle also for some status as a human being "despite poverty, racial and sexual stereotypes, and loneliness" gives her more stature in her failure than most people earn in victory.

Lutie can scarcely be said to be attracted to the stereotypes which would define her as a black woman. Her tension grows out of the seeming inevitability of her conforming to the stereotypes despite all efforts she may make to break free.

[Again, in *Country Place*,] Petry shows . . . that the sordidness of reality, the inequities and false illusions of society, and the

inadequacies of the possibilities for women rob strong and weak alike of a chance for personal development and a sense of security. . . .

In Link Williams, the young black hero of [*The Narrows*], Petry has succeeded in creating in depth a man of integrity and stature, no mean feat for a woman writer. But Link, too, is driven to violence and eventually destroyed despite "or because of" his integrity.

Camilo [in *The Narrows*] conforms to female stereotypes some of the most negative, in fact just as all of Petry's other women do eventually, whether or not they struggle against such conformity.

Ann Petry does not ignore the particular problems of blacks; her portrayals, especially of Link Williams and Lutie Johnson, in both their individual triumphs and their socially-caused failures, display potentiality enough for admiration and oppression enough for anger to satisfy any black militant. Her first concern, however, is for acceptance and realization of individual possibilities black and white, male and female. Her novels protest against the entire society which would contrive to make any individual less than human, or even less than he can be.

> Thelma J. Shinn. *Critique: Studies in Modern Fiction*. XVI, 1 (winter 1974), pp. 110–20

While something of an anachronism in the 1990s, the African-American protest novel of the 1940s and 1950s maintained a symbiotic relationship with the mythic American Dream: It decried a history of American racism which made achieving the Dream as chimera for blacks. While Richard Wright is considered the "father" of the genre, and *Native Son* (1940) its quintessential document, Ann Petry emerged as another strident voice—a progenitor or native daughter. While her novel *The Narrows* (1953) deviated somewhat, it nevertheless continued the Wrightian tradition. Link Williams, the protagonist, differs superficially from Bigger in that he has attained a Dartmouth education and enjoys relative freedom from economic hardships; it would *appear* that he has the means to acquire the bootstraps over which Bigger can only ruminate. However, Link's "success" cannot shield him in an America which insists upon his inhumanity. When he breaks the taboos of class and race by having an affair with a white New England heiress, his violent murder becomes ritual—an inexorable response to a black stepping out of his "place." While Petry's "New England" novel echoes *Native Son* thematically, more ostensibly it also foregrounds the black *male* as the victim of an America which denies African-Americans their very personhood. But in *The Street* (1946), Petry recasts the Herculean quest for the American Dream in an unequivocally female context. Indeed, the novel represents the "distaff" side of the African-American literary tradition, emerging as a groundbreaking work in its examination of the black woman's pursuit of happiness. Not only does Petry depict how women pursue the Dream in traditionally "American" terms, but, more deftly, she illustrates how black women suvert the quest for the American Dream and fulfill their own version of it. . . .

Lutie Johnson, the protagonist in *The Street*, embodies the female version of the archetypal quest. Patterning her life after Benjamin Franklin's, Lutie embarks on an expedition she hopes will bestow the trappings of success upon herself and Bub, her eight-year-old son. However, Lutie's odyssey from Jamaica, New York, to Lyme, Connecticut, to Harlem bestows upon her little more than disillusionment. Ultimately, what Calvin

Hernton calls the "three isms"—racism, capitalism, and sexism—launch an implacable assault on Lutie, precipitating the novel's tragic conclusion.

While it would be tempting to view the novel as a treatise on how men, black and white, collude to destroy the All-American black girl, Petry's text discourages this sort of naturalistic preoccupation with character as subject and object. Instead, one might view this seminal examination of the black woman's search for the Dream as a mosaic—much like Alice Walker's tropological quilt—that includes other women, other stories, and other voices. In addition to presenting Lutie and her blind adherence to American values, Petry depicts two black female characters who circumvent the quest: Mrs. Hedges, who operates a bordello in the apartment building where Lutie lives and who also oversees the day-to-day events on "the street," and Min, the downtrodden and subservient companion of William Jones, the building superintendent.

Far from being minor characters, Mrs. Hedges and Min embody what I see as a history of black women *subverting* the vacuous Dream myth through an almost innate ability to secure their own space despite the twin scourges of racism and sexism. Existing in a milieu where the Dream's core assumptions belie their lived realities, these black women *undermine* the myth, altering it to ensure both economic survival and varying degrees of emotional stability. And because "traditional" principles have been the bane of black people since America's inception, questions involving the "morality" of how these women survive become ancillary ones given their predatory, hostile environment.

Superficially, Mrs. Hedges and Min adhere to the ideals of "hard work" and "ingenuity" in a country where "anything is possible." However, these women more accurately replicate techniques used by such archetypal African-American trickster figures as Charles Chesnutt's Uncle Julius or black folklore's Peetie Wheatstraw in (re)inventing lives independent of the white American Dream. While denied opulent lifestyles and material objects, Petry's "minor" women attain life's basic necessities, and, given their tenuous existences, they (re)construct their own "dream" by tapping into a tradition of what Peter Wheatstraw in *Invisible Man* calls "'shit, grit and mother-wit'." Thus, *The Street* transcends the boundaries of the "*roman-à-thèse*," the thesis presumably being that white racism extinguishes all black hope. The denizens of Petry's Harlem face a world more Darwinian than Franklinian, and they act according to their individual circumstances.

Keith Clark. *African American Review.* 26, 3 (fall 1992), pp. 495–505

In *Miss Muriel and Other Stories* (1971), Ann Petry reveals her continuing fascination with the way people are shaped by the company they keep. Although these stories were originally published over a long period of time (from the 1940s to 1971) they cohere geographically and thematically. All of the works take place in New York or New England, and, while taking up a multiplicity of perspectives, they share a preoccupation with race, gender, and class, among other characteristics that often incite prejudice. But Petry's stories, like her novels (*The Street*, 1946; *Country Place*, 1947; and *The Narrows*, 1953), refuse to settle for easy truths. They do not moralize, and they do not avoid showing minority characters who inflict pain as well as suffer from it. For Petry, prejudice in all

its permutations is finally a creative as well as destructive force. In *Miss Muriel*, individuals, their relationships with others, and their communities are clearly formed by human bias, not just harmed by it.

Three of the collection's 13 stories are set in and around a drugstore in the fictional village of Wheeling, New York. The Wheeling drugstore stories—"Miss Muriel," "The New Mirror," and "Has Anybody Seen Miss Dora Dean?"—draw on Petry's experience as an African American growing up in the small resort town of Old Saybrook, Connecticut. There is a great deal of realistic description of Wheeling's shops, streets, and geographic location, and the family that appears in these stories has much in common with Petry's own. The stories, like the town they portray, are multifaceted and defy easy categorization.

The 57-page title story is the collection's longest, and it introduces the volume's wide-angle focus on prejudice. First published in 1963, "Miss Muriel" concerns prejudice in a small community, but it is not limited to one particular strand of human bias. Instead, the story illustrates how numerous prejudices—of race, gender, sexual orientation, and age, to name a few—coexist and paradoxically create the very community that they threaten to destroy.

For the narrator of this complicated tale, Petry makes a seemingly ingenuous selection: a 12-year-old girl. Like Petry (born in 1908), the narrator grows up in the early twentieth century, the daughter of middle-class African American parents who run the local pharmacy. There, the girl overhears conversations that fuel her imagination and influence her notions of adulthood. Also like Petry, whose novels make frequent use of multiple perspectives, this character is acutely aware of people's shifting attitudes toward each other. Petry does more than draw on her own background and personality, however. Through the persona of a 12-year-old, she succeeds in defamiliarizing adult biases and assumptions. In "Miss Muriel," the grownups appear enigmatic, comical, evasive, defensive, and flawed. We begin to see that their (or, more precisely, our) assumptions about each other do not have fixed boundaries; prejudice is rarely a clear-cut matter of sexism, racism, or any other "ism."

Although "Miss Muriel" is never explicitly identified as a diary, the story takes that form in its loosely episodic, ostensibly artless progression. Like a diarist, the narrator records events shortly after they happen. This format creates a compelling immediacy and accommodates the speaker's struggle to understand the nuances of her own story. When her young, beautiful aunt, who lives with the family, becomes the object of male attention, the narrator can neither forestall nor fully comprehend the conflicts at work within her community, her family, and herself. She can almost (but not quite) see the convoluted interactions among her family members and acquaintances as a forewarning of what her own future holds.

On the verge of adolescence, the narrator is understandably fascinated by her aunt's love life. She takes an active interest in Sophronia's three suitors, Mr. Bemish, Chink Johnson, and Dottic Smith. Her detailed descriptions reveal that each man believes that he has the right to invade the family's pharmacy/home and pursue Sophronia on her home turf. Although the three are very different from each other, they share the assumption that Sophronia is a pretty object rather than a person in her own right. Their rivalry shows how courtship can devolve into a conflict in which the pursued woman has little voice or power.

The suitors are themselves objects of prejudice, however. We learn from the narrator that the white shoemaker, Mr. Bemish, has at least two obvious strikes against him: his age and his race. His glass eye makes her feel "squeamish", and the rhyme with Bemish sets the stage for an unsetting portrait of a distinctly undignified old man. The second suitor, Chink Johnson, is a tall, swaggering black man whose raffish appearance and undocumented past call his integrity into question. The opposite of the simpering Bemish, Chink is a blues pianist who has recently found work at the Wheeling Inn. The name "Chink" sounds hard and tough (far from the soft, yielding sound of "Bemish"), reflecting his aggressive demeanor. The name "Chink" is also an ethnic slur, possibly an indication that Chink Johnson is considered an outsider even among fellow blacks. Although the name is never explained, it is one more suggestion, among many in the story, that prejudice simultaneously creates and obfuscates individual identity. Sophronia's third suitor, Dottle Smith, appears to be parodying the other men's behavior rather than truly courting Sophronia. With his gender-neutral name, Dottle has characteristics stereotypically associated with gay men: He is an effusive, highly dramatic man with a penchant for reciting poetry, and his buttocks sway from side to side when he walks. More to the point, he has brought along young male companions on past visits, and the narrator knows that her father considers him unacceptably effeminate.

The narrator pays close attention to her father's reactions to all three men. Rather than merely report his objections to the suitors, she struggles to understand his views and to distinguish them from her own feelings. She knows that her father is prejudiced against Bemish's race and age, Chink's sexually suggestive music and lower-class status, and Dottle's mannerisms. The range and vehemence of his objections imply that he might well censure anyone interested in his sister-in-law. Although Sophronia is an adult capable of making her own choices, he is extremely protective of her. . . .

Like the suitors, the father believes that he has the right to control Sophronia's destiny. He in effect enters into the rivalry with them. Moreover, his patriarchal interest in Sophronia's love life casts his sister-in-law in the role of a child, not much different from the narrator. Sophronia herself does not assert her right to run her own life. Although she does not reject the suitors outright merely because her brother-in-law wants her to, she does not tell her would-be protector to mind his own business, either. The object of everybody's scrutiny, she is a poignantly passive figure whose private liaisons become the stuff of public spectacle.

As the chronicler of Sophronia's courtship, the narrator is no less subjective than her father is. Her father's angry reactions and her own emerging prejudices inevitably influence her views of Bemish, Chink, and Dottle. Even as she proclaims her affection for them, her contact with the three men reveals strong feelings of ambivalence. In regard to Mr. Bemish, for example, she must confront both her own and his prejudices about age. Convinced that he is condescending to her because she is a child, she chastises the old man for calling her "girlie" instead of addressing her by name. Then, when Bemish claims he is too old to remember all the neighborhood children's names, she responds, deadpan: "Does the past seem more real to you than the present?" Although she is many years his junior, the narrator treats Mr. Bemish as her equal or sometimes even as her inferior. She is too young to know—or perhaps too self-confident to care that her behavior is impudent.

Bemish's behavior, however, does not exactly inspire respect from anyone. His undignified pursuit of Sophronia contains a distinct element of slapstick. . . .

The narrator's relationship with Chink is equally complex. His presence is far more powerful than Bemish's, so she cannot pull rank on him. Her relationship with him raises the issues of sexuality and male dominance. Chink's strong sexual presence is as intimidating as it is intriguing. At 12, the narrator cannot ignore either his virility or his disturbingly sensual music. His overt masculinity provides a bracing contrast to Bemish's asexual foolishness and Dottle Smith's effeminate mannerisms. The narrator seems to take a voyeuristic pleasure in Chink's increasingly successful courtship of Sophronia. . . .

Yet the narrator does not trust Chink. She decides that he "is not a gentleman", and Chink's behavior seems to bear out this class distinction. As she and Sophronia watch in dismay one afternoon, Chink drives a wagon full of giddy young women into the woods, with one woman perched flirtatiously on his lap. To make matters worse, he is "singing a ribald song". The virility that has beguiled both aunt and niece evidently has just as powerful an effect on other women, and Chink plays it for all it is worth. Although his race and class may have prevented him from achieving a high social status, his sex enables him to wield power over others. He does not hesitate to assert that power, regardless of how his behavior may be interpreted by Sophronia, the main object of his desire.

The narrator's view of Dottle Smith is influenced by her conviction that he is not romantically interested in her aunt. She considers his behavior a charade, a matter of going "through the motions". In his self-appointed role as comically attentive beau, Dottle mocks both Chink and Mr. Bemish. Although the narrator does not come to such an explicit conclusion, she is able to distance herself sufficiently from Dottle to describe his maneuvers in detail:

He always calls her Miss Sophronia. If we are outdoors and she comes out to sit in the yard, he leaps to his feet, and bows and says, "Wait, wait. Befo' you sit on that bench, let me wipe it off," and he pulls out an enormous linen handkerchief and wipes off the bench. He is always bowing and kissing her hand.

Dottle's attentions to Sophronia seem too lavish, too theatrical, to be genuine. He may be making fun of the other men, but in doing so, he is also making fun of Sophronia. She is a pawn in his game, a means by which he parodies the courtship ritual.

Dottle's racial militance creates a further complication. The narrator observes that Dottle and her Uncle Johno are "what my father calls race-conscious". Although both Dottle and Johno are light enough to pass as whites, they adamantly insist on their minority racial status. Dottle's stories and jokes reveal his preoccupation with race, and the narrator, struggling to understand her objections to Mr. Bemish's color, admits, "I believe that my attitude towards Mr. Bemish stems from Dottle Smith". She is not convinced, however, that race alone is a sound basis for determining allies and enemies. The story's opening scene, in which she cheerfully describes her best friend, a white girl with whom she has much in common, indicates her relative freedom from racial prejudice. But from her observations of Dottle and Chink, she learns that race is of vast importance to adults—and that race relations are hopelessly entangled with relations between the sexes.

The narrator's own race consciousness receives a jolt when she gets caught in the middle of the adults' ever-smoldering, if never fully articulated, dialogue about race and sexuality. The trouble starts when she parrots one of Dottle's race-related jokes to Chink. Chink is not amused by the narrator's temerity or the joke's punch line—a white clerk insisting that a black customer ask for ''Miss'' Muriel cigars. Refusing to accept humor at a black man's expense, Chink brusquely tells the narrator, ''It ought to be the other way around. A black man should be tellin' a white man, 'White man, you see this picture of this beautiful black woman? White man, you say Miss Muriel!'''. Regardless of the race of the man delivering the inane put-down, the joke has a sexually charged subtext. ''Muriel'' is portrayed as an object, not a person, whose ownership will be decided by men. The bickering over courtesy titles—the crux of the joke—alludes to large issues of race relations and sexual politics. These are public issues that nevertheless determine the quality of personal relationships. . . .

The very tensions that polarize the community also paradoxically keep the townspeople engaged in an endless debate with each other. ''Miss Muriel'' illustrates the ways in which prejudice, though often seen as a purely destructive force, also creates the social environment in which people live and die.

Hilary Holladay. *Studies in Short Fiction.* 31, 4 (fall 1994), pp. 667–74

BIBLIOGRAPHY

*The Street*, 1946; *Country Place*, 1947; *The Drugstore Cat*, 1949; *The Narrows*, 1953; *Harriet Tubman, Conductor on the Underground Railroad*, 1955; *The Common Ground*, 1964; *Tituba of Salem Village*, 1964; *Legends of the Saints*, 1970; *Miss Muriel and Other Stories*, 1971

# PHELPS, Anthony (1928–)
## Haiti

Like brotherhood, the consciousness of the poet's mission (a long-standing tradition in French poetry) is a strong theme in [Anthony] Phelps's work. In his first novel [*Moins l'infini*], he fictionalizes the artist group who communicated in a kind of code through weekly broadcasts of poetry readings. There Phelps shows realistically the power of the word, the commitment of the engagement. . . .

For Phelps, words have power, strength, even physical form. . . . For words, lines, even the visual appearance of punctuation are all art-images for this poet. In an early love poem parentheses marks are two lovers inclining toward each other. Elsewhere parentheses form barriers against the outer world, protecting the lovers' union. He notices that tiny Haiti, a mere footnote in world power, nonetheless is marked by an asterisk star. Crossword puzzles are patterns of squares and spaces. The phrase ''Points Cardinaux,'' both a volume title and the password for the revolutionaries in his novel, is graphically a cross or a plus. Algebra involves equation—equal signs, parallel lines—roads in the ''algèbre des grandes villes.'' Phelps often signs with a flower sketched as part of his signature, an image more enduring than reality.

Besides form and shape, he finds that words have power of their own. They resist, they slip from grasp, they melt, they telescope, they subdue. . . .

In his word-joust with [René] Depestre over cross-words, Phelps shows himself reluctant but eager to believe in a better future. Despite the difficulties of his past, imprisonment, [and] exile, he is a poet of affirmation, even of happiness. And he finds strength in personal human relationships. He frequently affirms these ties in dedications or allusions. . . .

He also finds affirmation in a new country, with its new vocabulary, in new ideas of political organization, in solidarity with others of the Third World—faith for a future based on socialistic structure and love. . . . The title of his first novel, *Moins l'infini*, a phrase taken from the poetic theme song of the resistance poets, limits Haiti's tyranny as less than infinite, and looks beyond for a better future.

Charlotte Bruner. *The Gar.* 33 (February 1979), pp. 23–24

Anthony Phelps, poet, storyteller, novelist, is always a child of his island Haiti, even in exile in his adopted country Canada with his Canadian wife. He early wrote a poetic epic of his island's history, *Mon pays que voici*. His novels concern the Haiti of the 1960s, the period of his own activism and exile. His later stories and poems reflect his deep nostalgia for the island landscape and people. Only recently was he able to return to find again his identity, to rediscover his heritage (not African but Caribbean), to exorcise the hate and anguish of the past, to share with his wife the long-dreamed-of beloved's return, to bask today in the ''unknown sun'' of tomorrow's new hopes.

*La Bélière caraïbe* in its seven parts and brief epilogue symbolically leads the reader; the bellwether poet shows the way: ''je nomme ma route / dans le vent veuf / Poète / Païen / en toute saison'' [I choose my path / according to the widower-wind / Poet / Pagan / in all seasons]. He recasts past memories: ''je corrige le brouillon de ma vie / au jardin extravagant de la mémoire'' [I correct the rough draft of my life / in the wild garden of memory]. He has been a wanderer: ''Nomade je fus'' [I was a nomad]; now, returning, he has direction. After his ''Vacances de paupières'' [pun on ''pauper's vacation'' and ''eyelids holiday'' (sleep)], when he imagined a dreamlike return, he will now experience the real ''lente et savante caresse du recommencement'' [slow and knowing embrace of beginning again]. It takes only a Proustian odor of sapotilla to roll back the years, to expose the child within the man: ''Jamais l'homme en moi ne trahira l'enfant que j'étais'' [the man in me will never betray the child that I was]. But he is no longer crippled by the past: ''Béquilles sur l'épaule'' [shouldering his crutches], he comes forth in ''L'automme de l'oeil'' [the autumn of the eye]. He has wandered (''j'ai honoré mon quota d'errance / et j'ai bien voyagé'' [I have fulfilled my quota of wandering / and I have traveled well]), always with the shadow of the Caribbean at his back, ever reminded of its people, its foliage, its voices. He recognizes that the homeland has always mastered his thoughts, his sadness, been ''Capitaine de mes douleurs'' [captain of my griefs]. Now the wanderer must find again his roots and his identity from all his history: ''Celui qui m'a acheté / et celui que je suis / l'acheteur et le vendeur en moi mêlés'' [Who bought me and what I am / buyer and seller mixed into one]. Self-cognizant, he can discover ''Non point le règne de cannibales / mais tendresse'' [Not in the least the cannibal kingdom / but tenderness], and derive the present: ''Père Caraïbe / Passé Piégé / Présent gagné'' [Father Caribe / the past trapped / the present gained]. Though as a *retourné* he must observe the "Protocole du Midi," his heart can speak when words may not, and those who follow his meaning walk also in his path.

Anthony Phelps obliquely traces his struggle for self-knowledge—looking beneath his "patchwork" sin, through a maze of memories, to reveal the mature poet, strong in adversity, ever the islander, tender yet resolute.

> Charlotte H. Bruner. *World Literature Today*. 55, 2 (spring 1981), pp. 363–64

Phelps is a master of psychological nuances. Unlike others, he does not give in to the temptation to turn his novels into a forum of exhibitionism for professional heroes who win every battle, regardless of how desperate the situation may be, because right and justice are supposed to triumph under all circumstances. Indeed, both *Moins l'infini* and *Mémoire en Colin-Maillard* end with the failure of the protagonists. The revolutionary project remains viable and valuable, though; despite themselves, Marco and Claude moved farther away from that project. No, this "Negro of capacity who will perform the indispensable deeds," whom they felt vibrate in themselves, no, it will be another, not they. In the course of the action they realize that the road to revolution is staked out with labyrinthine passages and that they, too, "not [as] a piece of wood" but like "other men" are subject to the same existential ambivalence. As Claude's mother said, "It is not like mathematics, where one and one are always two."

The structural organization of the narration also follows political uncertainty. Phelps does not mind using some writing devices from the *nouveau roman*: The linear discourse is rejected and the narrative time dislocated; the hero evolves inside a complex, multidimensional world where past, present, and future, dream and reality are superimposed, are juxtaposed and penetrate each other depending on the narrative situation. As in [Gérard] Etienne's *Le Nègre crucifié*, there exists an equalization between the substance and form of the discourse, which itself is in the image of the desperately ruined nation: "And the Building is fissured, crisscrossed with cracks, dislocated." There is the further image of the hero's impenetrable fate as it appears to Monsieur X in its almost Dedalean entanglement.

> Juris Silenieks. In William Luis, ed. *Voices from Under: Black Narrative in Latin America and the Caribbean* (Westport, Connecticut: Greenwood Press, 1984), pp. 141–42

[Phelps] is a poet representative of that which is dying and which is being born in contemporary Haitian literature and society, someone who does his best to see the decline of certain aspects of traditional society and the difficult formation of new social traits. His poetry presents a sample of the ideology of a fraction of the Haitian diaspora of his time, an ideology marked by a tragic vision of the popular emigration. . . .

The poetry of Anthony Phelps includes a major theme, that of waiting. In Phelps's work, waiting is not only the title of a poem in the collection *Motifs pour le temps saisonnier*, it is very appropriately one of the key factors of the work. . . .

The theme of waiting is found in *Éclats de silence* and also in *Motifs pour le temps saisonnier*, but with an incomparably greater resonance.

*Motifs pour le temps saisonnier*, the most well-constructed and the most structured of the poetic books of Phelps, orders, arranges, and structures the poems in three categories: poems of completed time, poems of fragmented time, and poems of woven time. The leitmotif of time is correlated to the theme of waiting. In migrating from one collection to another and from one period to another, the theme of waiting moves from a personal dimension to a collective dimension. It becomes a political waiting.

That is because, in the meantime, Anthony Phelps became, from May 1964, a political exile, a refugee in Montreal, nurturing the nostalgia of return to his native country. While anticipating this return, he lives in waiting . . . in the living, active and impatient waiting for the end of the time of oppression that he believes rules his country. . . .

The dialectic of exile and the kingdom, along with the attendant exodus and nostalgia, plays from one end to the other in this poetry of waiting. . . .

Phelps's waiting is the hope for this "kingdom," this "city," symbols of his liberated country. . . .

Only, the time of liberation takes long to come and the light of hope surrenders to the dark night.

In the eyes of Phelps, the abomination of desolation is this exodus, this flight from hunger that pushes his people into so many foreign countries. . . .

Anthony Phelps is a poet from the left, but he is a complete stranger to the Négritude movement. His counter-Négritude is even the common denominator of the group Haiti-littéraire of which he is chief. . . .

Phelps's repudiation of Négritude is not without consequence on the level of social practice. If the blacks of the New World do not feel themselves to be sons of Africa, and if, as already asserted by Franklyn Frazier against Melville Herskovits, the blacks of the Americas do not maintain any ties with the blacks of Africa, then the umbilical cord which linked them to the alma mater is broken. Africa and its battles for liberation are strangers to them. . . .

The poetry of Anthony Phelps has an analogous social function in the Haitian migratory adventure of the second half of the twentieth century. His tragic vision of the phenomenon speaks of his social background, the interaction of social groups, and the economic stake of their conflict of interest.

> Claude Souffrant. *Presence Africaine*. 135 (1985), pp. 74–77, 82, 84, 89†

The [Haitian] poet who has emerged as the major voice among those who went into exile from the generation of the 1960s is Anthony Phelps. This is so because Phelps's poetry avoids the paralyzing self-pity and longing of the exile and explores, in the manner of a [Jacques] Roumain or a [René] Depestre, a poetics of "errance." . . . Feeling is structured in Phelps's poetry through a poetics of remoteness and restlessness. His early renunciations of indigenism and political engagement echo through his later writing in exile. Phelps reserves his political statements and overt references to Haiti for his novels. His poetry is one of absence, remoteness, wandering, of the suppressed referent. A poetic language emerges which is not the language of the tribe but a discourse whose symbolic values are "spread" to include a range of experiences. For instance, instead of using the Creole "poto-mitan," Phelps uses the expression "arbre milieu" to produce a special cluster of associations. In describing himself as "Poète / Païen / en toute saison" [Poet / Pagan / for all seasons], Phelps immerses himself in an elemental world of sun, salt, summer, dawn, wind, and earth. . . .

Phelps seems to have always privileged in his poetry moments and sites of intense feeling and of equilibrium. Words like *été, Midi, seuil*, and *milieu* have a special significance for Phelps. In order to attain these moments of vision, the poet must shed illusory identities: "une peau sans couture lisse et d'unique trame" [a skin seamless smooth and of unique texture]. Phelps's poetic strategy is to expose self ("la marche de l'écorché") and to expose text ("le texte nu") in order to discover self in relation to world. Indeed, he pushes the state of exile to extremes in *La Bélière caraïbe* in order to explore his rootlessness. . . . It is in such an exploration that the Caribbean emerges as the "Midi" for Phelps—a zone of intense encounter, of multiple unstable possibilities. It is not a land of nostalgia, trapped in memory but rather the "Lieu de mon métissage" where future possibilities become evident. . . . Through Phelps's poetic universe Haiti is reinserted in a process which is Caribbean and American, in the widest sense of the word.

J. Michael Dash. Callaloo. 15, 3 (summer 1992), pp. 758–60

BIBLIOGRAPHY
*Éclats de silence*, 1962; *Mon pays que voici*, 1968; *Le Conditionnel*, 1970; *Moins l'infini*, 1973; *Et moit, je suis une île*, 1973; *Mémoire en Colin-Maillard*, 1976; *Motifs pour le temps saisonnier*, 1976; *La Bélière caraïbe*, 1980; *Mê me le soleil est nu*, 1983; *Orchidée nègre*, 1987; *Les doubles quatrains mauves*, 1995

# PHILIP, M. Nourbese (1947–)

**Jamaica**

In working on the poems that comprise the manuscript *She Tries Her Tongue*, I came up hard—to use a Jamaican expression, I "buck up" against the weight of Eurocentric traditions and became aware that even poetry and the way it was brought to, and taught in, the Caribbean was a way of management. I was, in fact, working in a language which traditionally had been yet another tool of oppression, a language that has at best omitted the reality and experience of the managed—the African in the New World—and at worst discoursed on her nonbeing. The challenge for me was to use that language, albeit the language of my oppression, but the only one I had, to subvert the inner and hidden discourse—the discourse of my non-being.

How does a writer who belongs to one of those traditionally managed groups begin to write from her place in a language that is not her own? How does she discover or uncover a place and language of empowerment? These were some of the questions that faced me. The power I sought was not the same power the white European male/father has used to manage, control, and destroy the other, but a power directed at controlling our words, our reality, and our experience.

"You better know your place." In the Caribbean this expression was often used to remind children of their essentially inferior position in society or to chastise someone who had been perceived to have stepped out of his or her social position. In *She Tries . . .* I set out to be unmanageable. I refused to "know my place," the place set apart for the managed peoples of the world. I intended to define my own place and space and in so doing I would come up against the role of language and the issues relating to that. I was also to discover that I could not challenge the language without challenging the canon that surrounded the poetic genre. . . .

*She Tries . . .* was the result of my refusal to "know my place." Since completing that manuscript I have become aware of certain shifts. As a writer, I had been aware for some time of a reader over my right shoulder: white, Oxford-educated, and male. Over my left shoulder—in the shadows—was an old wizened and "wisened" black woman. *She Tries . . .* succeeded in pushing the reader to the right further into the shadows, and the reader over my left shoulder has emerged more clearly from the shadows into the light. *She Tries . . .* has also taught me my place.

One of the unexpected results of being unmanageable in my writing life has been that many of the poems in *She Tries . . .* have become unreadable in the traditional sense; in my being unmanageable, the poems themselves have also become unmanageable. One aspect of allowing the poetry to become unmanageable arises from my giving in to the urge to interrupt the text. One can hazard many reasons for this urge. It may arise from a need to reflect a historical reality: the African in the New World represented a massive interruption of both the European text of the Old World and the African text of a more ancient world that had continued uninterrupted for millennia, as well as the text of the aboriginal world of the Americas and the Caribbean.

A friend with whom I raised this issue of interruption of text suggested that the urge was probably the result of Caliban/Prospero relations: wanting both to be in the space of power long dominated by the white European father and to return to our lost paradise.

Whatever the reason, the urge to interrupt the text is there and I have acted upon it time and again in both poetry and fiction. The result is that the poem no longer reads as it ought to; it becomes unreadable both because of the interruptions and because so many things happen on the page or pages, as the notes from the working journal reveal. However, in making the poem unreadable, it becomes a more accurate description and expression of what our experience as managed peoples in the Caribbean has been. The African's encounter with the New World was catastrophic and chaotic: how does one and how ought one to manage such an experience in poetry or in writing? How does one make readable what has been an unreadable experience?

The form of the poem becomes not only a more true reflection of the experience out of which it came, but also as important as the content. The poem as a whole, therefore, becomes a more accurate mirror of the circumstances that underpin it.

Another unexpected result of the attempt to allow oneself to be unmanageable within and without the text was the eruption of the body into the text—tongue, lips, brain, penis—the body insisted on being present throughout *She Tries. . . .*

When the African came to the New World she brought with her nothing but her body and all the memory and history which body could contain. The text of her history and memory was inscribed upon and within the body which would become the repository of all the tools necessary for spiritual and cultural survival. At her most unmanageable, the slave removed her body from control of the white master, either by suicide or by maroonage—running away, where the terrain allowed, to highlands, there to survive with others as whole people and not as chattels. Body, text, history, and memory—the body with its remembered and forgotten texts is of supreme importance in both the larger History and the little histories of the Caribbean. I believe this to be one of the reasons why the body erupted so forcibly and with such violence in the text of *She Tries.* . . .

There is a second reason, which has to do with the fact that for the black woman a double managing is at work. Historically for her there was the management of the overseer's whip or gun, but there was the penis, symbol of potential or real management in male-female relations. Today the overseer's whip has been replaced in some instances by more subtle practices of racism; the penis continues, however, to be the symbol of control and management, used to cow or control. The ultimate weapon of management and control for the female is rape; this knowledge and the consequential fear is, I believe, latent in all female bodies.

In the poem "Universal Grammar," I appended an excerpt from *Mother's Recipes on How to Make a Language Yours*, or *How Not to Get Raped*: "Slip mouth over the syllable; moisten with tongue the word. / Suck Slide Play Caress Blow—Love it, but if the word / gags, does not nourish, bite it off—at its source— / Spit it out. / Start again" I was suggesting in this excerpt from the imaginary Mother's Recipes the link between linguistic rape and physical rape, but more than that the potential for unmanageability even when faced, as a woman, with that ultimate weapon of control—rape. *Mother's Recipes* was an attempt to place woman's body center stage again as actor and not as the acted upon.

Working through the poems contained in *She Tries* . . . resulted in an epistemological break for me; my relationship with Western European traditions, particularly as they relate to literature, and systems of knowledge has been irrevocably ruptured. The understanding of how the underpinning of knowledge is often nothing but power—power of the white European male to define his knowledge as absolute—was a painful but liberating experience. An excellent example of this exercise of power may be seen in how the roots of classical Greek civilization, which are embedded in Afro-Asiatic civilizations, have been erased over the centuries. Where this erasure was not possible, the African source of Greek civilization, most notably Egypt, was Europeanized and Egyptians make to appear light-skinned and a part of Mediterranean rather than African culture. The rupture to which I have referred has resulted in my becoming an epistemological orphan; how to construct a replacement for the old epistemological order is a task which is both challenging and difficult but which is essential.

Marlene Nourbese Philip. In Selwyn R. Cudjue, ed., *Caribbean Women Writers: Essays from the First Literary Conference* (Wellesley: Calaloux Publications, 1990), pp. 295–300

The notion of nation language and its literature as a violent but recreative and redemptive act has received extensive attention in the scholarly literature (Baugh; Brathwaite; Kubayanda; Saakana). A particularly significant contribution to the discussion is Marlene Nourbese Philip's *She Tries Her Tongue: Her Silence Softly Breaks*, which won the prestigious Casa de las Americas

prize in 1988. Her "Introduction" identifies several dimensions of the centrality of language to the experience of the New World African. . . .

At least half the poetry in Philip's volume participates in her profound meta-critique of issues involved in a redefinition of the experience of enslavement and colonization, issues such as self-negation, identity, survival, and development in the African diaspora. Philip's poem "Discourse on the Logic of Language" is the ultimate creative expression of that experience. . . .

The terms *discourse* and *logic* in the title of Philip's poem are crucial to our appreciation of the issues at state. In particular, they invoke all the problematics of a typical situation of the "colonial discourse" and its antithesis the "discourse of decolonization." The poem provides for us a linguistic map of "the mechanisms which a center uses to deny its periphery any voice, the means which the self employs to interpret its needs, and the processes utilized by the other to appropriate its own being in the world" (Kubayanda, *On Colonial/Imperial Discourse*). What we have in Philip's poem is not simply a discourse, but a plurality of discourses, each asserting an ideological space within which the colonial/imperial subject's consciousness must grapple with notions of self and other, notions of power and marginality, notions of birth and biology, and above all, notions of rationality as a subjective (re)interpretation of historical experience carefully measured against primal laws of being and becoming in a world too often threatened by silence and nothingness.

At the center of "Discourse on the Logic of Language" is what we may identify as the poetic text proper. It opens with the statement "English/is my mother tongue" and closes with the counterstatement "english/is a foreign anguish." Between these two assertions is located the language of paradox as a controlling/totalizing figure of speech. But such paradox is an invention of history, not a logic of birth or biology. To fully understand the invention of this paradox and to estimate the full consequences of this historical invention, we must turn to the omnipresence of the tongue as a physical, metaphysical, and symbolic reality. The complex manifestations and significations of the tongue are captured in three separate discourses that constitute subtexts to Philip's central poetic text.

The final one of these subtexts is a scientific/pseudo-scientific discourse on the tongue as a physical, metaphysical, and symbolic reality. It is significant that even within a scientific mode of apprehension, the tongue transcends the normal boundaries of human physiology; it traverses historical space and insinuates considerations of ideological and power contestations. The first part of this pseudo-scientific discourse establishes the connection between the brain, the tongue, and human speech. Embedded in the purely scientific discourse is a second-level subtext on the authority of one of the two "learned" nineteenth century doctors after whom those parts of the brain chiefly responsible for speech are named:

Dr. Broca believed the size of the brain determined intelligence; he devoted much of his time to 'proving' that white males of the Caucasian race had larger brains, and where [sic] therefore superior to women, Blacks and other peoples of colour.

The second part of this subtext of "scientific" discourse is made up of a set of four multiple-choice questions, questions that compel us to admit the multiplicity of facts and issues relevant to our understanding of the tongue as the principal organ of human language, and the defining organ of ideological space. The second question with its multiple answers underscores the multifunctionality of the tongue: ''In man the tongue is (a) the principal organ of taste. (b) the principal organ of articulate speech. (c) the principal organ of oppression and exploitation. (d) all of the above.''

The second of the subtexts is a cryptic but highly volatile historical discourse which gives full meaning to the alternative answer (c) above. It is framed in the all-consuming language of power that admits of no possibility of dissent, power that claims absolute monopoly and ownership of the other as slave. . . .

As absolute as this logic of exploitation may sound, we observe that the severity of the intended domination is held in check by certain conditionalities that testify to a deeper and even more unyielding logic, the logic of inevitable rebellion. Rebellion against the ''quieting of the tongue'' is inevitable because it is instinctive; it is instinctive because there are few things deeper than the tongue as the bond that binds individuals to their human essence, the bond that binds a people to their ancestral space and time. To capture this deeper logic in all its power and complexity, we need the densely symbolic discourse of myth. This is precisely what we find in Philip's principal subtext. I refer to it as the principal subtext because in it we find the ultimate realization of an idealized/primal meaning of mother tongue; the poet herself underscores the significance of this subtext by giving it a graphic prominence that is suggestive of the premordial essence of the experiences captured by the discourse:

WHEN IT WAS BORN, THE MOTHER HELD HER NEWBORN CHILD CLOSE: SHE BEGAN THEN TO LICK IT ALL OVER . . . UNTIL SHE HAD TONGUED IT CLEAN. . . ./ THE MOTHER THEN PUT HER FINGERS INTO HER CHILD'S MOUTH—GENTLY FORCING IT OPEN; SHE TOUCHES HER TONGUE TO THE CHILD'S TONGUE, AND HOLDING THE TINY MOUTH OPEN, SHE BLOWS INTO IT—HARD. SHE WAS BLOWING WORDS, HER MOTHER'S WORDS, THOSE OF HER MOTHER'S MOTHER, AND ALL THE MOTHERS BEFORE—INTO HER DAUGHTER'S MOUTH.

As we read Philip's main poetic text against this subtext, we experience an acute sense of the trauma that must have followed the attempted ''quieting of the [mother] tongue.'' We feel the anguish and also the determined quest for wholeness and for restoration of the articulate self. The poet repudiates her violator's language, labelling it as ''a father tongue . . . a foreign language /not a mother tongue.'' But in the absence of any retrievable mother tongue, such repudiation can only lead to further isolation and total silence, forcing the poet into a fervent prayer for rebirth and deliverance from her historical anguish. . . .

In the title poem of her collection, the poet moves us through her entire history of rebellion against silence, capturing her struggles in the ragged rhythms of a poetic sequence that is a series of disruptions continually overcome by violent and even lyrical erruptions into self-affirmation. ''When silence is /Abdication of word tongue and lip'' the quest for ''pure utterance'' must break ''the culture of silence/in the ordeal of testimony,'' take us beyond ''The grief sealed in memory'':

each word creates a centre

circumscribed by memory . . . and history
waits at rest always
still at the centre.

Kofi Anyidoho. *Research in African Literatures*. 23, 1 (spring 1992), pp. 55–62

[In *Frontiers: Essays and Writings in Racism and Culture*, Philip] has much to say about some of the major cultural controversies of the day: the ROM exhibit, the dispute at The Women's Press, the demonstration at the PEN Conference in Toronto, which led to her notorious altercation with June Callwood. Philip is a polemicist, passionate in debate, often strident, always controversial, an inveterate writer of letters of protest, a campaigner prepared to go out onto the streets to demonstrate for what she believes in, and sometimes vehement in her criticism of other writers (her review of Neil Bissoondath's *A Casual Brutality* is a case in point). June Callwood will certainly not have been alone in feeling provoked by her activities. It is necessary, therefore, to be quite clear about Philip's intentions.

In ''exile'' in Canada, Philip writes interestingly of what she regards as the formative influence on her, namely the experience of decolonisation. Displaying a proud awareness of her African and Caribbean heritage and of the centuries of struggle preceding independence, she is entirely convinced ''that, if only one were to struggle long and hard enough, one could and would make meaningful and radical change for the better.'' Her conviction that ''one can change the odds'' is certainly at the base of the laudable commitment to struggle for what she believes to be right which informs all her activities and her writing. She has adopted the activist position of James Baldwin, whom she admiringly quotes on the necessity for the writer to ''disturb the peace of those invested in maintaining the status quo.'' This she has certainly achieved.

Nourbese Philip's political and cultural stance is determined not least by her concern at the ''erasure'' of African culture under colonialism. Much of her work is characterised by the will to reassert that African cultural identity within the Western—here, Canadian—context. This consciousness informs her priorities, which she defines as: ''to defy a culture that wishes to forget; to rewrite a history that at best forgot and omitted, at worst lied . . . to honour those who went before, to grieve for that which was irrevocably lost (language, religion, culture).'' Philip finds little sympathy for such a project in Canada, however. What she encounters is a lack of acceptance, which prompts her to assert—repeatedly—the dignity and worth of African culture. The main aim of her writing she sees as ''the need on the part of what has traditionally been seen as Canadian culture as represented by arts councils and organisations to respect those cultures—African, Asian and Native—that had long established circuits of culture, which Europeans interrupted.'' As a black Canadian writer she sees herself contributing to the creation of a distinctive black culture unlike that of Britain or the US. In much of her writing, she complains about the lack of support this literary project is receiving from the literary establishment—a fact she puts down to racism. About racism in Canada she is frequently scathing: the country is ''steeped in racism,'' it is ''racist in its well-springs.'' Indeed, Canadian racism is, we are told with some exaggeration, "as deeply embedded in this country as in the US," it is "as virulent as any found in the US." Since she observes "a general reluctance in Canadian society to tackle this issue," Philip makes it her purpose to put racism firmly on the agenda. . . .

Philip is throughout concerned to demonstrate that racism "permeates" the institutions of Canada, most particularly those in the sphere of the arts. Arts organisations, such as the Ontario Arts Council, the Toronto Arts Council and Metro Cultural Affairs, thus come in for much criticism. She berates them for their "failure to represent the ethnic composition of Toronto and Ontario on their boards, councils, panels and juries"—a factor which, she believes, negatively affects the funding of black artists, with whose aesthetics such organisations are, she maintains, unsympathetic. Alleging that "mainstream culture receives by far the lion's share of funding and government support," she postulates "a causal relationship between the composition of the various boards and committees of these funding agencies and the underfunding of Black artists and groups." Nor is she convinced that the appointment of black artists by several arts organisations indicates any genuine commitment; she regards them as tokenist co-optations, as "hair-line fractures in the at times overwhelming and oppressive structures standing guard over 'Canadian culture'." . . .

Marlene Nourbese Philip's commitment to a non-racist Canada is beyond doubt. It ill behooves a reviewer to doubt the sincerity of her case when she writes out of personal experience, much of which, to judge from this volume, must have been bitter. Her campaign against what she regards as racism in Canadian arts institutions has, however, encountered a good deal of opposition and one may suppose that her vituperative attacks have forfeited her some support in the arts community, while her allegations of systemic discrimination may be regarded by some as not wholly credible. Certainly, to the foreign observer surveying Canadian publishing, it does not seem as though minority voices are being silenced; rather the opposite seems the case. Nor does it help her case, when, on occasion, she indulges in polemical exaggeration, as when she argues that Callwood's famous expletive is "tantamount to declaring open season on individuals like myself" or alleges that "this sort of irrational response to legitimate protest comes close to being the verbal equivalent of actions of governments such as the Chinese government toward its dissenters." One wonders, too, what publishers might think of her suggestion that they be required to give account of "the number of manuscripts from African, Asian and Native Canadians they have seriously considered over the last fiscal year."

Geoffrey V. Davis. *Canadian Literature*. 151 (winter 1996), pp. 129–33

M. Nourbese Philip's suite of poems [*She Tries Her Tongue, Her Silence Softly Breaks*] is contextualized by her superb introductory essay on the centrality of language to any movement for self-determination in the Afro-Caribbean. She argues persuasively that English has historically been expressive of the "non-being" of the displaced African, while the various forms of the Caribbean demotic or vernacular "language of the people" seek to "heal the word wounded by the dislocation of the word/image equation." Poems such as "Universal Grammar" and "The Question of

Language Is the Answer to Power" enact an alternative grammar and phonetics lesson, using what Philip calls "unmanageable form" to signify the diasporic African subject's refusal to be managed. Through juxtaposition and fragment, she raises important questions around the interrelation of language, history, and social power.

Most moving for me is her elegiac tone, the "ordeal of testimony" that gives witness to the "anguish that is English" in the history of Empire and its aftermath. The speaker's last prayer is that "body might become tongue." Philip's emphasis on body, voice, "polyphony and rhythm" returns poetry to its physical roots, as it returns the speaker to her cultural roots where the pulse of African drums is never far from the page. This book, rich in craft and questions, will reward readers interested in questions of postcoloniality and poetic form alike.

Brenda Carr. *Canadian Literature*. 154 (fall 1997), pp. 136–37

BIBLIOGRAPHY
*Thorns*, 1980; *Salmon Courage*, 1983; *Harriet's Daughter*, 1988; *She Tries Her Tongue, Her Silence Softly Breaks*, 1989; *Looking for Livingstone: An Odyssey of Silence*, 1991; *Showing Grit: Showboating North of the 44th Parallel*, 1993; *Frontiers: Essays and Writings in Racism and Culture*, 1993; *Coups and Calypsos*, 1994; *A Genealogy of Resistance, and Other Essays*, 1997

# PHILLIPS, Caryl (1958– )
## St. Kitts

[In Caryl Phillips's *A State of Independence*] Bertram Francis, a nineteen-year-old Island Scholarship winner (the island, maybe St. Kitts, maybe not, but certainly a symbolic social composite of all the anglophone Caribbean islands), leaves to study law in England, abandons his bursary after two years, works at odd jobs, saves wisely, and returns home a would-be businessman twenty years afterward, on the eve of independence. During his absence, Dominic, his only brother, whom he loved and who loved and doted on him, is killed by a hit-and-run motorist; Jackson Clayton, his best friend and a gifted schoolboy cricketer, has become deputy prime minister; Father Daniels, the teacher who had prepared him for the coveted scholarship, has died; and his mother has become seriously ill, embittered, and withdrawn. Bertram, who hadn't bothered to write his family or friends while he was away, is coldly rejected by his mother and by the deputy prime minister, who considers him a cheeky interloper, but not by Patsy Archibald, his former girlfriend, whom he gave up as soon as he had won his scholarship.

A very, *very* bleak novel indeed, allegorizing . . . accurately, a densely bleak Caribbean, socially and politically, where states of independence are, for the most part, neocolonial, dispiriting, and hopeless, and where true individual independence for the ignored, the poor, and the dispossessed continues to be beg-borrow-or-steal emigration to Britain or Canada or America. Caryl Phillips has written a well-modulated and sensitively focused novel of inconsolable Caribbean anguish. . . . His first book, *The Final Passage*, the story of a young Caribbean wife abandoned by her husband in

London, left me creased by anger and wholehearted pity; this one, harrowed by personal recognition and near panic. I welcome this new, young miniaturist-realist, already the finest of his kind among Caribbean novelists.

Andrew Salkey. *World Literature Today.* 61, 1 (winter 1987), p. 145

In 1987, [Phillips] turned away from the Caribbean in order to explore his other nominal "home": Britain and, by extension, the rest of Europe. This time, he found fiction less suitable for his aims, explaining that "the tension between myself and my environment is so urgently felt that the fictional mold seems too delicate a vessel to hold it." Accordingly, *The European Tribe* documents a year of the author's wanderings, from Belfast to Gibraltar, Auschwitz to Moscow. Certainly it constitutes a kind of travel book, although one unlikely to appear with Arthur Frommer's signature on the cover: *Europe on Ten Dollars and Twenty Slurs a Day.*

No innocent abroad, Phillips quickly discovers the appalling extent of racism in Europe's most progressive nations. The French despise the Arabs, the Germans despise the Turks, and the British despise the Spanish and Moroccans (in Gibraltar) and just about everyone else (at home). Even Norway, with a nonwhite population of .35 percent, displays a toxic reaction to the handful of black people who have snuck, like trace elements, into the national bloodstream.

Taken strictly as a Baedeker, *The European Tribe* is a trifle thin. The countries flash by too quickly; there's a severe shortage of actual encounters with other people; and Phillips's prose, usually nimble and endowed with a winning, modest lyricism, falls here and there into chamber-of-commerce staleness (the black and red of a Spanish duenna's garb, for example, "seems to characterize Spain's proud and regal spirit"). But Phillips has more in mind than a verbal slide show. He wants to argue. And the arguments that gradually emerge from this grand tour are mostly corollaries of [Derek] Walcott's "homeless satellites."

One, which joins a fine portrait of James Baldwin to a discussion of Othello—two very different examples of "black European successes"—is the tricky notion of accommodation. Must a black man always pay for his integration into white society with the destruction of his identity? Is any success worth such a terrible price of admission? On his ten acres at St. Paul de Vence, a lily-white hill-village north of Nice, Baldwin retained his identity to the end; but there's a suggestion, in Phillips's portrait, that his isolation was lonely, even debilitating. Othello, on the other hand, adapted himself absolutely into "the mainstream of the European nightmare," going so far as to marry into the family, and earned nothing for his pains but a "European death—suicide."

Othello also points Phillips in another key direction: toward the Venetian ghetto and, a few chapters later, Auschwitz. Phillips admits his early sympathy for Jews: "As a child, in what seemed to me a hostile country, the Jews were the only minority group discussed with reference to exploitation and [racism], and for that reason, I naturally identified with them." The Jews, of course, are not only a despised minority but history's homeless people par excellence, and as such they're natural inhabitants of Phillips's universe of noncitizenship. At the same time, he can't move cogently beyond this initial sympathy. He deplores the cozy

rapport between Israel and South Africa; he makes a dogged, inconclusive attempt to understand the sour relationship between Americans blacks and Jews. In fact, these issues—and Phillips's argument that the economies of Western Europe have been largely rebuilt on the backs of migrant labor pools—are simply too sprawling to fit comfortably into the wafer-thin chapters of *The European Tribe.* They nonetheless add to Phillips's composite of a black-and-white Europe, a continent that has by now incubated an entire, oxymoronic generation of native-born "foreigners."

James Marcus. *Village Voice.* October 24, 1989, p. 57

The winner of Britain's Malcolm X Award . . . [Phillips's *The Final Passage*] concerns a young West Indian couple whose dissatisfactions with life on their small island eventually lead them to emigrate to London. Leila and Michael, unhappily matched, are shakily held together by custom, mutual lack of communication, and their infant son. A mulatto sometimes referred to on her island as "the white girl," Leila yearns in vain for a closer relationship with the taciturn mother who raised her alone. Michael, darker skinned and sullen, spends more time with cronies at the Day to Dawn Bar and with another woman (with whom he also has a child) than he does with his official family. When Leila's mother abruptly departs for England to seek medical treatment, Leila's desire to be near her coincides with Michael's vague ambitions and results in their leaving the island as well. Caryl Phillips . . . reveals his characters' muted existence in a narrative that shifts backward and forward in time. *The Final Passage* is at its best in long, carefully observed sequences like Leila and Michael's wedding, in which experience and emotion are made almost tangible through detailed descriptions of sights, speech and behavior. Less successful are passages in which the author spells out his principals' thoughts and feelings in an expository manner that clashes with the approach taken in the rest of the book. Finally, as husband and wife adapt individually to the dreary reality of life in London in the 1950s, the novel assumes a nearly unrelenting bleakness of scene and spirit. Michael and Leila's passage from the brightly colored foreground of a rural landscape to the cluttered background of a drab cityscape is depressingly complete.

Tom Nolan. *New York Times Book Review.* April 29, 1990, p. 38

*Higher Ground,* a "novel in three parts," consists of three stories. "Heartland" . . . set on the African coast, is told by a slave acting as translator, brutally treated by his masters and rejected by his own. Beyond cruelty and degradation lie continuum and death—or the attempt to recover some self-respect and inner peace. The "profit" of a marginally privileged position proves finally unacceptable when set against the "loss" it entails, and the narrator himself is transported to the United States: his loss is now his profit. A brutal memoir, heightened by detail and dispassion: readers will understand, sympathize to a degree, and fight a recoil from the narrator.

"The Cargo Rap" . . . is made up of fifty letters written by "Rudy" Williams between January 1967 and August 1968 to his parents, sister, and two female lawyers who take an interest in his ''case.'' At the age of nineteen, the armed Rudy tried (in his words) to persuade a shopkeeper to pay back a small portion of the collective historical debt owed by American whites to their black countrymen dating from the slave trade onward. Rudy's sentence is one to twenty years, depending on good (servile) behavior, and he spends most of his time in brightly lit solitary confinement. The parallels with the life and *The Prison Letters* of George Jackson are evident. Jackson died in a prison riot; Rudy's sanity flickers out, and his last letters are to generalized ''Brothers and Sisters'' and, poignantly, his mother, who had died a month earlier. The story is remarkable for the power with which it depicts the psychological and physical damage sustained by black Americans and for its character portrayal, bearing in mind its epistolary nature. Awareness comes too late to Rudy, and the reader, both involved and detached, notes the increasing disequilibrium.

''Higher Ground'' . . . is about a Jewish girl hustled out of Poland by her parents to escape the Holocaust. The trauma of her experiences and the cold incomprehension she encounters in England drive her first inward to bleak loneliness, then to numb sexual experience and a loveless marriage, and finally to a breakdown and attempted suicide. The novel's epigraph is the traditional prayer, ''Lord set my feet on higher ground,'' safe from the floodwaters of life; and the stories, though dealing with very different centuries, continents, and characters, are unified by this theme of individual lives damaged, if not destroyed, by cruel, man-made waters. Images of being marooned, of shipwrecked lives, of the impossibility of escape across the sea to another land, recur. It is not possible to deal adequately with Phillips's work within the space of a brief review; all I can do here is urge that it be read, for *Higher Ground* is a moving and disturbing book.

Charles Ponnuthurai Sarvan. *World Literature Today.* 64, 3 (summer 1990), p. 518

The journey behind his first novel, *The Final Passage*, was the one [Phillips] himself took part in, albeit unwittingly—the emigration [in] the postwar years from the Caribbean to this country. The journey that lies behind both [Phillips's] last novel, *Higher Ground*, and his new novel, *Cambridge*, is a more historic, more primal, and more terrible journey, the journey of the slave trade westwards from Africa.

[Phillips] has maintained, however, a keen interest in Europe or, to be more precise, in Europe's pretensions and delusions about the place of European civilization in the world. His book of essays, *The European Tribe*, was devoted to the subject. In *Higher Ground*, a novel in three parts, we travel from Africa in the slave trade days to North America at the time of the Black Power Movement, only to end up in a Europe still nursing its wounds from the last war. In *Cambridge*, [Phillips] has reversed the direction of this journey to bring a European consciousness face to face with Europe's global perpetrations. He does this through the person of Emily, a woman of the early nineteenth century who escapes an arranged marriage by traveling to her father's estate in the West Indies (her father being an absentee landlord), where she is exposed to and, indeed, exposed by the effects of slavery and colonialization.

Like its predecessor, *Cambridge* is a novel in three distinct parts, the first and longest of which is Emily's own account of her journey and her observations when she arrives. From what seems at first to be an inquisitive, self-consoling travelogue, there emerges a drama revolving around a handful of characters: Emily herself; Brown, an Englishman whom we understand has somehow ousted the previous manager of the estate; the Cambridge of the title, a Negro slave who has suffered the singular and equivocal fate of having lived in England and having been converted to Christianity; and another slave, Christiania, who, despite her name, indulges in decidedly un-Christian rites and appears to be on the verge of madness.

The second part of the book is Cambridge's own account of how he came to be Anglicized and Christianized. The third, written in the form of a report (which we guess to be far from reliable), describes how Cambridge comes to be executed for the murder of Brown. And the brief epilogue of the novel tells us the effect of all this on Emily. These last few pages are particularly astonishing. Coming at the end of a novel of enormous accumulative power, they pack a tremendous punch and, written in a prose of tense intimacy, they show how facile it is to assess either [Phillips's] work as a whole, or his heroine, by any crude cultural or racial analysis. [Phillips] is interested in human beings. Emily's plight at the end of the novel plainly has its cultural and racial dimension, but it's essentially one of personal trauma—psychological, sexual, moral, and . . . existential.

Graham Swift. *Kunapipi.* 13, 3 (1991), pp. 96–97

*The European Tribe* is, as Phillips describes it in his preface, a ''narrative in the form of a notebook in which I have jotted various thoughts about a Europe I feel both of and not of,'' written on the occasion of his travels, over the span of nearly a year's time, ''from Europe's closest neighbor, Morocco, to her furthest flung capital, Moscow.''. . .

As I read it, *The European Tribe* performs a strategic (I am almost tempted to say ''satirical'') reversal of the traditional perspective and mode of operation of the (European) travel narrative: it ''tribalizes'' the European, decentering him/her from the self-ascribed position of ''Universal Subject of Knowledge,'' and turning him/her into an object of study; in doing so, it ''defamiliarizes'' the European, and begins to supply a ''mental framework and a set of practical directions for confronting the [as of now] unknown and different'' (in a way, it begins to *break through* the established, ''stereotypical'' *self*-conceptions of Europe and its native people); this framework is built around a reconstituted knowledge of the history of complicity/culpability of different countries in colonial enterprises and the enslavement of others; this involves bringing to visibility the personal (hi)stories, subjectivities, and voices which ''official history'' had attempted to render invisible.

Phillips sets out across Europe to try and ''understand'' the Europeans, and thus himself (as, in part, a ''product'' of their culture—in which he has been raised—but also, importantly, of their history of colonization, expropriation and slave trading). In doing so, he is quite consciously setting out to reconstruct and recount the ''other side'' of the story that is normally told, by Europeans, about Europe, weaving historical information about the countries he visits, anecdotes, and personal reflections and meditations into the story of his own travels.

Hank Okazaki. *Literary Criterion.* 26, 3 (1991), pp. 38–41

Can Phillips be described as a British (or a black British) writer? In the bulk of [Joseph] Conrad's work, Poland—in terms of setting—is not significant, yet his Polish life shaped a part of his basic awareness. So too with Phillips, and even if little of his work thus far is set in England, his British years, from infancy to manhood, have given him great advantages. The term *advantages* may surprise, given the degree of racism—covert or overt, suave or crude—that pervades contemporary Britain. Still, I would argue that having grown up in Britain has heightened Phillips's awareness and fine (in the two meanings of *sharp* and *excellent*) sensitivity. This is not to suggest that Phillips is some bruised plant trembling delicately in unkind winds. His difference and exile have positively defined him; they make up his essential being, and, if often a source of hurt or anger, of alienation and loneliness, they also constitute his awareness and strength. It is the turning of what a hostile society and a denigrating culture would impose as misfortune and limitation into advantage and a wonderful broadening out of understanding and sympathy, a turning of prisons into castles (with acknowledgment to George Lamming and his novel *In the Castle of My Skin*), a moving from pain to knowledge and beyond to joy and pride, and thence to celebration.

To return to the question: Can Phillips be labeled "British" despite his "return" to the Caribbean? Not to do so would leave our taxonomic lust unsatisfied. If anything, his latest work, *Higher Ground*, shifting from the days of slavery somewhere on the coast of black Africa to a contemporary maximum-security prison cell in the United States and then to a Polish-Jewish woman suffering incomprehension, loneliness, and a breakdown in Britain during World War II, shows a liberated Phillips, a writer who can penetrate the inner being of people vastly different from himself in time, place, and gender, yet people very much like us all in the common and eternal human inheritance of pain and suffering. In a recent essay ["Living and Writing in the Caribbean: An Experiment"], Phillips writes that his "branches have developed, and to some extent continue to develop and grow, in Britain" but that his "roots are in Caribbean soil." Eluding labels that will seize and fix him, he finally remains Caryl Phillips.

Charles Sarvan and Hasan Marhama. *World Literature Today*. 65, 1 (winter 1991), p. 40

Set firmly and with a sustained and vivid sensuous immediacy in the nineteenth century, and taking place mostly in the exotic world of the British West Indies though some scenes are set in London and the English countryside, *Cambridge* tells two stories that are closely related, indeed inextricably joined in time and place.

These two stories ought to be one (and are united in the novel), but prove to be more separate than the central characters are able to imagine, because of a multitude of assumptions, prejudices, and fundamental misapprehensions that isolate individuals not so much from one another as from the possibility of any clear and present understanding of others' motives, actions, or points of view. These personal and social misunderstandings lead inexorably to tragedy. At the center of the human tragedy is the institution of slavery, by then unlawful in Britain but still practiced legally in the West Indies.

Among many credible, well-realized characters, black and white, the two major figures are Emily Cartwright, a sensitive and thoughtful Englishwoman, unmarried and "almost thirty," and a proud and powerful slave called Cambridge, who lives on her father's plantation and whom Emily dubs Hercules in the privacy of her diary. In a story with layers of irony, it is ironic that Cambridge never knows about Emily's nickname for him. Nor can she ever know the names that he has had—his "true Guinea name, Olumide"; his first slave name, Thomas; his Christian name, under which he preached as a missionary in England, David Henderson. She, in fact, knows next to nothing of his personal history and she figures less in his life and thoughts than she imagines. Though both the central characters reveal themselves to be complex, ambiguous, and conflicted, they also come across (a triumph of Caryl Phillips's craft and art) as fundamentally good and decent people who try to be honest with themselves and who mean to do well, but who fail because of personal limitations and huge social forces beyond their control.

George Garrett. *New York Times Book Review*. February 16, 1992, pp. 1, 24

The main body of Phillips's novel [*Crossing the River*] consists of four taut narratives—two white voices, two black; two male, two female. But its structure is poetic, built on a single refrain: "Why have you forsaken me?" The voices are richly counterpointed, and the forsakings are as various as the author's extraordinary imagination can make them.

In the prologue, a nameless African father, his crops having failed, sells his children to the master of a slave ship. Haunted for 250 years by "the chorus of a common memory," he discovers "among the sundry restless voices" those of his lost children: "My Nash. My Martha. My Travis." Gradually, as the stories in the main text unfold, we realize that this father has taken on the mythic proportions of the continent of Africa, that his abandonment represents the irreversible history of entire peoples. . . .

In the most spectacular accomplishment of the novel, Phillips produces the journal and letters home of one James Hamilton, captain of the slave ship Duke of York on its voyage from Liverpool to "the Windward Coast of Africa" and thence across "the river" that is the Atlantic.

Like Edward Williams, the twenty-six-year-old Hamilton has reason to go searching in Africa: his father died there, and the death is shrouded in mystery. The elder Hamilton was without religion, perceiving that his profession of slave ship captain was incompatible with a profession of faith. There are hints that he "traded not wisely" and that he "cultivated a passionate hatred, instead of a commercial detachment," toward his slaves. . . .

Throughout, Hamilton is perplexed by the mood of his cargo, who "appeared gloomy and sullen, their heads full of mischief." Just before departing from Africa, he is "approached by a quiet fellow" from whom he buys the "two strong man boys, and a proud girl," of the prologue. . . .

Identity, in both individuals and peoples, is composed of the story we tell ourselves of the past. That story is necessarily partial and selective, but if it deliberately omits significant events the resultant self is inauthentic. One of the values of fiction is that it can tell the story anew, can go back and include a neglected truth. *Crossing the River* does this and is therefore a book with an agenda. Phillips proposes that the diaspora is permanent, and that blacks throughout the world who look to Africa as a benevolent fatherland tell themselves a stunted story. They need not to trace but to put down roots.

The message, however, is neither simply nor stridently conveyed. Phillips's prologue strikes it as a stately note, and its resonance continues to deepen; only in the epilogue does it become uncomfortably literal. Phillips's theme sounds throughout, perhaps most poignantly in the laconic notation of Captain Hamilton:

"We have lost sight of Africa."

Janet Burroway. *New York Times Book Review.* January 30, 1994, p. 10

The European slave trade of the eighteenth century is one of the metaphors of postmodern, postcolonial discourse, having to do with a past and ever-present condition at once specific and universal: examples such as Toni Morrison's *Beloved,* Charles Johnson's *Middle Passage,* Marina Warner's *Indigo,* and Barry Unsworth's *Sacred Hunger* come to mind. Caryl Phillips himself uses the metaphor both in his 1989 triptych *Higher Ground* and in his 1991 novel *Cambridge,* and he returns to it in *Crossing the River,* a four-part novel dedicated to "those who crossed the river."

Realism here is framed by fantasy, and a voice speaks from a distance of 250 years, beginning with a summation both simple and terrible: "The crops failed. I sold my children." (African complicity is not glossed over.) The first mythical expulsion was from Eden, and the slave trade marks yet another uprooting and forced homelessness, sets in motion yet another journeying down metaphoric "weary paths," without signposts, without a returning. The "river" is also ocean, is the Missouri and the biblical Jordan. The ancestral voice confessing with guilt and pain and love to selling three children (Nash, Martha, and Travis) functions as the foreword.

In Part 1, "The Pagan Coast," William Nash is liberated by his master and comes to Liberia under the repatriation scheme established by the American Colonization Society: to apply Derek Walcott's words, it is a homecoming without a home. The slaves were exploited (William by his homosexual master), then "returned" to a totally alien, inhospitable region, there to be abandoned and forgotten rather than assisted and encouraged in their new life. It is a second betrayal of the slaves, and the settlers live in squalor and die of disease, their hopeful roots withering in difficult soil. As with Rudy in *Higher Ground,* William's letters betray his increasing desperation and imbalance. Christ on the Cross cried out, "Why have you forsaken me?" Crucified by History, William addresses the same words to his absent, slave-owning, earthly "father."

In Part 2, "West," Martha, her husband, and their daughter are sold to different owners and never see one another again. Old before her time, she joins a wagon train of "colored folk" who are "prospecting"—not for gold but for a new life in California. Unable to work or even walk, her body swollen, Martha is abandoned. As she is dying alone in a strange place, her life presents itself in a series of scenes and incidents, described by a voice which is sometimes the narrator's, sometimes Martha's often the two merge marvelously and movingly in free indirect discourse. So much misery in one's life, perhaps greater than that endured by Christ? Her cry and question is the same as her brother's: "Father, why hast thou forsaken me?"

The third part, "Crossing the River," provides a Western perspective through the diary of a fictional ship's captain, James Hamilton, engaged in the slave trade: in Lacanian terms, the same signifier has very different signifieds. The author acknowledges that the fictional entries are based on John Newton's *Journal of a Slave Trader, 1750–1754....*

In the third part of *Higher Ground* the focus shifts to Polish-Jewish Rachel, and through her we discern but vaguely the African American to whom she is attracted. Similarly, in the long fourth part of *Crossing the River,* "Somewhere in England," we see Travis only through the perspective of English Joyce. Travis, an African American soldier stationed in England during World War II, marries Joyce but soon after is killed in action in Italy. Joyce hands over their baby son for adoption, and abandonment repeats itself, becoming one of the novel's motifs. Joyce's dislocation and disturbance are evident in her memoir, which is presented at random, as if the pages had come loose, without proper sequence or respect for chronology. Lapse of memory even leads to the same entry's being made twice. Twenty years later (1963), the son of Travis and Joyce journeys, searching for and finding his mother, now remarried (presumably to an Englishman) and with children.

In an afterword, the ancestral voice, compelled to spectate human history, speaks of all those who have suffered deprivation and pain. There is compassion but also admiration for resilience, and an optimism that they will arrive "on the far bank of the river." In the words of T. S. Eliot ("Ash Wednesday"), "the lost heart stiffens and rejoices." Crossing the River is a strange work, mixing memoir and letters, diary entries and third-person narrative, detailed realism and fantasy (Travis, sold in the eighteenth century, turns up in the twentieth). It is ironic, bald and factual, personal and moving. There are anger and compassion, condemnation and love, courage and hope in a novel which consolidates Caryl Phillips's reputation as an outstanding contemporary writer.

Charles Sarvan and Abdul Aziz Bulaila. *World Literature Today.* 68, 3 (summer 1994), pp. 624–25

Caryl Phillips's fiction is about historical transit, about people traveling from birthplace to homeland, or from to homeland places unknown. His subjects flee persecution or search for a sense of belonging, bringing identity and culture with them as they go, or re-creating it—an act of imagination....

A typical Phillips protagonist has led a life marked by discontinuity and the trauma of what the author calls "broken history."...

Eva Stern, the young narrator of *The Nature of Blood,* tells a fractured and retrospective life story that gradually reveals a grim tale of internment in a World War II German concentration camp. But Phillips situates Eva's narrative in a much larger context of European racism. *The Nature of Blood* audaciously cross-cuts her voice with the story of Shakespeare's Othello, the Moor who marries a Venetian nobleman's daughter, as well as with the history of the persecution of the Jews of the Italian town of Portbuffole in the 15th century. The slim novel offers up a bewildering array of voices. Even Othello's tale is interrupted—by what seems to be the voice of a modern African-American black nationalist, warning the general of Venetian racism and urging, "brother, fly away home." Like members of the black African diaspora, Phillips implies, European Jewry are a people for whom a "home" to which one might fly cannot be taken for granted.

Phillips has written before, in an autobiographical context, of the links between African and Jewish identity. In his award-winning 1987 travel book, *The European Tribe,* he discusses visiting Anne Frank's house in Amsterdam and remembering his thoughts as a child in England when he first read her diary: ''If white people could do that to white people, then what the hell would they do to me?'' Learning about the Holocaust, he says, ''made me realize that the definition of belonging or not belonging in a society was something that went well beyond my own personal preoccupations as a black kid in Britain.''. . .

Opening up any one of his novels, the reader immediately confronts a voice—sometimes a voice without a clear context, or a context that is shifting uncontrollably. Phillips's novels to date have focused on both modern Caribbean emigres, and on the 18th- and 19th-century slave trade (sometimes within the same novel). *Cambridge* tells a story of violence and cruelty on an early 19th-century slave plantation from two points of view: that of a prim English spinster who has traveled to visit the plantation, owned by her father, and of the educated slave named Cambridge, with whose execution the novel ends. *Crossing the River*, short-listed for a Booker Prize, yokes together four different narratives, spanning two centuries, to tell a disturbing and moving tale of slavery and its aftermath.

Phillips creates fiction out of fragmented narratives, out of alternating viewpoints that don't necessarily reduce to one coherent vision. But the strategies of literary, post-modernism—fractured narratives, shifting points of view, the representation of unstable identities—are something other than formal experimentation for him.

''The structure of the novels, with the different voices, is partly a response to the subject matter,'' Phillips explains. ''The subject of my books tends to be the whole question of broken or diasporan history, of interpretation of personal history and how that relates to the larger official history that's been given. In other words, it's an attempt to reinterpret, and put together, through different voices, a different kind of view of the world, a different history. One of the things I've tried to do with fiction is to try to suggest that there's a great virtue in having roots that come from more than one place. You can make something new out of diverse pieces.''

At a formal level, *The Nature of Blood* is Phillips's most disjointed novel. Phillips explains that he hopes he has been able to prepare readers for the challenges of this book with his earlier work. . . .

Phillips wants his readers to understand what it feels like to experience identity, history and narrative as discontinuous—and then, perhaps, to turn those discontinuous pieces into a new whole. *The Nature of Blood* ultimately insists on a redemptive power in the recognizable identity of a human voice, in the distinctiveness that marks one persons life narrative as uniquely her own. Phillips explains, ''I've always thought that you can do anything with fiction as long as you do it boldly, as long as you're not tentative about it, if you don't pussyfoot about. And that's what I wanted to do with *The Nature of Blood*. I just thought, if the voices are strong enough, arresting enough, then people will work with it, they will understand within a couple of sentences where they are and will remember where they were.'' He laughs and adds, with fingers crossed, ''That was my hope, anyway.''

Ivan Kreilkamp. *Publishers Weekly*. 244, 17 (April 28, 1997), p. 44.

[Caryl Phillips's two novels, *Cambridge* and *Crossing the River*,] form an imaginative [illustration that] formations of imperialism,

racism, and slavery cannot be dismissed as a premodern or atavistic aberration in the rise of Western humankind. *Cambridge* in particular, explores contradictions in the white world of masters and mistresses where beauty, taste, and civilization lay hand in glove with the savage exploitation of others, and the blindness by which cruelty is inflicted. Set in an unspecified small island in the Caribbean during the period between the abolition of slave trade and the emancipation of slaves, *Cambridge's* world of masters, mistresses, and slaves is a world that lurches uncertainly towards its own demise. Despite its bleakness, the novel offers the possibility of change in its central protagonist—the mistress of the plantation. Emily Cartwright's decision to stay on the island after the fall of the Great House reflects a growing awareness of her own part in the history of the plantation; her relationship with her black housekeeper at the end of the novel shows a hesitant realization of their entwined fates; *Cambridge's* portrait of a lady is of one irretrievably marked by the institution of slavery. *Crossing the River* is the more optimistic of the two novels and takes as its theme a diasporan and ''affirmative connection'' based on the survival of the descendants of slaves. Its extended meditation on the question of kinship, its exploration of loss and yearning in the connections between (substitute) fathers and sons, mothers and daughters, husbands and wives, lovers and partners within and across racial lines, offers a poetics of the diaspora and an alternative narrative of freedom and belonging. *Crossing the River* offers a chorus of voices from acrss the generations; its character portraits are individual and yet also representative. These portraits are part of a diaspora, presided over by an imaginary father who listens to the ''many-tongued chorus'' of his children. The movement from *Cambridge* to *Crossing the River* is precisely one where history is conceived of as a redemptive act: the past is seen as our partners in future.

*Cambridge's* exploration of slavery comprises the juxtaposition of three main narratives framed by an epilogue and prologue. The first two of the three narratives are written in first-person voice: those of Emily Cartwright, the mistress of the plantation, and Cambridge, a slave on the same plantation. The third narrative seems to be a reproduction of an unsigned report in a contemporary newspaper sympathetic to slave owners detailing the events leading up to Cambridge's death. These three narratives can also be characterized by their generic affiliations—that of the Englishwoman's diary or journal of travel, the slave narrative, and that of a colonial newspaper concerned with defending the rights of settlers. The juxtaposition of these narratives forces the reader to mediate between the self-contained realities of their different worlds, and provides rich opportunities for the ironic exposure of the willful self-delusion of the slave-owning communities. . . .

*Crossing the River* is like a chorus of voices with their separate histories linked together by virtue of their permutations on the patterns of love, desire, loss, yearning that accompany the separation between parent and child, husband and wives, lovers and partners. They repeat, mutate, and transform the motif of exile from kinsfolk in the originary rupture of families under slavery; and in doing so achieve the vital task of connecting lives across time and space. In his exploration of black Atlantic expressive cultures, [Paul] Gilroy privileges music as the quintessential embodiment of the restless migrations and transmigration of culture across national frontiers and racial barriers. Phillip's invocation of stories and voices offers a similar poetics of performance that looks towards the ways in which suffering and survival can offer new routes to the future.

Gail Low. *Research in African Literatures*. 29, 4 (winter 1998), pp. 122–41

BIBLIOGRAPHY
*Strange Fruit*, 1981; *Where There Is Darkness*, 1982; *The Shelter*, 1984; *The Final Passage*, 1985; *A State of Independence*, 1986; *The European Tribe*, 1987; *Playing Away*, 1987; *Higher Ground*, 1989; *Cambridge*, 1992; *Crossing the River*, 1993; *The Nature of Blood*, 1997

# PLAATJE, Sol T. (1877–1932)
## South Africa

[*Mhudi*], as the sub-title states, is an epic of South African Native life a hundred years ago, and deals principally with the Barolong tribe, the hero and heroine of the tale belonging to that people.

The story opens with a most vivid description of the big massacre of the Barolong by the warlike hordes of the Matebele. For many years afterwards descendants of the clan so butchered were taught ''almost from childhood, to fear the Matebele—a fierce nation—so unreasoning in its ferocity that it will attack any individual or tribe, at sight, without the slightest provocation. Their destruction of our people, we are told, had no justification in fact or in reason; they were actuated by sheer lust for human blood.''

It was by the merest accident, the writer adds, that he discovered the cause of the hatred of the Matebele. Two emissaries of King Mzilikazi of the Matebele had been sent to collect tribute from the subject Barolong tribe, but their Chief, tired of the Matebele supremacy, ordered their death. And so began the terrible massacre, for as one of the emissaries cried while manacled and waiting the carrying out of the sentence, ''A Matebele's blood never mingled with the earth without portending death and destruction.''

While the opening chapters tell of the scattering of the Barolong, subsequent ones relate their re-uniting and their co-operation with a few Boers in the overthrow of Mzilikazi. Throughout the book the delightful romance of Mhudi and her husband runs like a shaft of light and relieves many a sombre page. Glimpses are given of obsolete Native customs, superstition in its absurdities and tragedies finds faithful portrayal, and the changes wrought by the advent of the Boers are full of interest. . . .

As a writer of English, Mr. Plaatje seems to hold the premier place among Bantu authors.

M. S. S. *South African Outlook*. December 1930, p. 255

Plaatje's women [in *Mhudi*] are more impressive than his men. Next to Mhudi is the stately Nandi, Mzilikazi's best loved and chief wife. For a number of years she chooses the path of an exile in order to escape the wrath of her husband who has been influenced by a jealous junior wife to kill Nandi, on the strength of some false story about the queen's unfaithfulness. When her husband has been reduced to the status of a monarch without an empire, she follows

him in order to console him, knowing that he must need her. Just as the Chaka-figure excites images of heroism and fighting grit in the South African Negro, the Nandi-figure, whether in Chaka's mother or Mzilikazi's wife, is a symbol of beauty, long-suffering motherhood, gentleness and dignity. . . .

Perhaps Plaatje was too much of a historian, journalist and politician to visualize character independently of the historical events in which people were involved. But he had compassion, and this balanced the historian's detachment in him; his love for human beings was profound, and for this reason Mhudi comes alive even in the midst of epoch-making clashes, even if we consider her dialogue stilted. Somehow he sees his pathetic villain's (Mzilikazi's) fate as poetic justice, but he never gloats over it. This kind of poetic justice, the dream-like quality of the narrative, the use of the pathetic fallacy, and the weaving in of songs, are in the tradition of Bantu oral literature.

Ezekiel Mphahlele. *The African Image* (New York: Praeger, 1962), pp. 175–76

Plaatje's novel, *Mhudi: An Epic of South African Native Life a Hundred Years Ago*, written at least ten years before its publication by Lovedale Press in South Africa in 1930, is an attempt at blending African folk material with individually realized characters in the Western novelistic tradition; the result has been both admired and denigrated by commentators.

Plaatje's story of the two Bechuana natives who survive a raid by a warring Zulu tribe, fall in love (one episode describes the admiration which the hero inspires in his female companion when he subdues a lion by wrenching its tail), and triumph over the mistreatment they endure from the Boers whom they have aided, is leavened by humor and a sense of proportion. Although the novel contains idyllic scenes of native life, the hero Ra-Thaga, and Mhudi, who becomes his wife, are not sentimental Noble Savages but peaceful citizens forced to accept the harshness of the invading white world. The political theme of Boer cruelty is present but not overwhelming; the speech by the dying, defeated Matabele warrior Mzilikazi is dramatically prophetic as he describes the coming Boer ingratitude for the aid of the Bechuana tribe. Yet Plaatje's comments on the Boer attitude are not obtrusive even when they are bitter, and they reflect a wit that bites deeper than surface humaniarianism.

Martin Tucker. *Africa in Modern Literature* (New York: Frederick Ungar, 1967), p. 257

To the student of literature the interest of [*The Boer War Diary*] is two-fold. In terms of the development of a corpus of African literature, it must be one of the earliest works (and possibly the only diary by) a black South African. Perhaps it is the first in the English language. Plaatje, as we know, was to become a leading figure in the development of black South African literature, both in English and in the vernacular. The diary, unlike his later work, is not carefully edited by its author; it was not intended for publication and he has not attempted the literary perfection aspired to in *Native Life in South Africa, Mhudi* and his other published volumes. In this sense the personality of the author is displayed with far greater clarity here than in any of these later works. In the diary we see the humour and compassion, the determination and the faith that underlie his subsequent writing; but here it is not masked by any of the inhibitions contingent upon Plaatje's rigid perception of the rules of style, manifested so clearly later on.

The second aspect of literary significance relates to the actual use of language. Here again there arises an interdisciplinary interest—this time between literature and linguistics. Perhaps because he had no need for careful correction, Plaatje indulged freely in the use of words and phrases from Dutch, Sotho, Tswana, Xhosa and Zulu. But, as will become evident, this usage is not random. It tends to correspond, in the sociological sense, to the structure of the relationships and situations described by the author.

John L. Comaroff. Introduction to *The Boer War Diary of Sol T. Plaatje* (London: Macmillan, 1973), p. xxvii

It seems appropriate and necessary to discuss Plaatje's style. Some critics who have looked at it have rapidly dismissed it. Janheinz Jahn (in *Neo-African Literature*), for instance, derides Plaatje's ''padded 'Victorian' style.'' And no doubt many readers have quickly rejected it for its imitative or derivative nature. This is a very superficial judgment. . . . Two examples may here suffice to show that his language use is at least interesting and not totally random and unintentional.

In his use of Biblical and epic language Plaatje does indicate he is sensitive to register. . . . He is, in other words, at an early stage, encountering the same problems which many later African writers in English have confronted: the tension between what they want to say and a language which has ''foreign'' and often oppressive connotations, how to translate the registers of one language into those of another language. . . . Secondly, and even more interestingly, there is Plaatje's introduction of proverbs and the fable into the novel form. This has been a frequent device of later African writers—a typical example of the fusion of African and European elements within the modern African novel. . . .

In all Plaatje's writings, the two elements of prophecy and rebuke are ever-present. And, in spite of any faults it may have, *Mhudi* must clearly be seen as one of the most interesting and significant landmarks in South African literary history.

Tim Couzens. Introduction to Sol. T. Plaatje, *Mhudi* (Johannesburg: Quagga, 1975), pp. 10–11, 15

In many ways [*Mhudi's*] actual sequence of events, the development of the individual characters and the interaction of their relationships, is not of primary importance. For Plaatje did not conceive of *Mhudi* as anything approaching a realistic novel in the western literary tradition. He himself gave his book the sub-title 'An epic of native life a hundred years ago', and it is as an epic that *Mhudi* is best defined. Just as in Shakespeare, clearly an important influence upon Plaatje in writing *Mhudi*, he expected his readers to suspend a sense of realism to allow for the delivery of long set-piece monologues and dialogues; to allow him to bring historical events backwards and forwards in time as it suited him in the construction of the narrative, and exploit for dramatic purposes an assumed historical knowledge on the part of his readers; and he

composed his characters not so much to reflect the way they might realistically have behaved, as to provide a vehicle for the expression of a variety of human qualities and ideas which Plaatje wished to explore.

*Mhudi* was the outcome of a quite conscious and deliberate attempt on Plaatje's part to marry together two different cultural traditions: African oral forms and traditions, particularly those of the Barolong, on the one hand; and the written traditions and forms of the English language and literature on the other. The full extent to which these African oral traditions have found their way into *Mhudi* may never be fully known, although if Plaatje's own collection of Tswana folk-tales had survived we would probably have been in a much better position to make some sort of assessment. But some of the ways at least in which Plaatje incorporated these traditions and cultural forms can be identified. The slaying of Bhoya, as Plaatje explained in his foreword, was one obvious example of the way in which he incorporated into his story what he had heard from old Barolong people he had talked to. His use of proverbs and African idiom was similarly a quite deliberate attempt to try and convey something of the richness of the cultural reservoir upon which he was drawing. Often the technique of literal translation was strikingly successful. 'I would rather be a Bushman and eat scorpions than that Matabele could be hunted and killed as freely as rockrabbits,' said Dambuza, one of Mzilikazi's warriors, at the Matabele court; and later he observes: 'Gubuza, my chief, your speech was the one fly in the milk. Your unworthy words stung like needles in my ears.'

Plaatje was struck particularly by the way in which Tswana oral tradition and the written traditions of English literature—above all, Shakespeare, which he knew best—shared a common fund of literary and cultural symbols. In *Mhudi* he was concerned to explore the possibilities that this perception presented, above all in relation to omen and prophecy, and their association with planetary movements—characteristic both of Shakespeare and the oral traditions of his own people. It was something that had always fascinated him. 'In common with other Bantu tribes,' Plaatje had written in his newspaper at the time of the reappearance of Halley's Comet in 1910, 'the Bechuana attach many ominous traditions to steller movements and cometary visitations in particular', and he had added: 'space will not permit of one going as far back as the 30s and 50s to record momentous events, in Sechuana history, which occurred synchronically with the movements of heavenly bodies'. Ten years later Plaatje did find time to do exactly this in writing *Mhudi*, even if he had then to wait a further ten years before the results of this literary exploration were published.

Plaatje's awareness of the literary possibilities that lay in the manipulation of symbols that had meaning in both Tswana and English cultures also found expression in the humorous lion stories that appear in the early part of the book. These serve as a means of testing the courage of both Mhudi and Ra-Thaga, and are contrasted later on with the cowardly reaction of Lepane, a traveller, faced with a similar dilemma. That lion stories of this kind were a familiar motif in Tswana tradition emerges from the story that Plaatje himself reproduced in his *Sechuana Reader*: like the lion story that appears in Chapter 5 of *Mhudi*, its central point is the way in which the protagonist proves his bravery by holding on to the lion's tail. At the same time, lion stories of this kind, serving a similar function of demonstrating bravery and cowardice, are a familiar motif in English literature as well—in Bunyan's *Pilgrim's Progress*, and Shakespeare's *Love's Labour Lost, Julius Caesar,* and *A Midsummer Night's Dream*, all of which Plaatje knew well.

In 1916, in his contribution to the *Book of Homage to Shakespeare*, Plaatje had expressed the view that he thought it likely that 'some of the stories on which his [Shakespeare's] dramas are based find equivalents in African folk-lore'. When he had looked into this question more closely he had found this prediction to be correct: the lion stories in *Mhudi* were one of the more humorous outcomes, and so too—in a more general sense—was Plaatje's exploration of the symbolism and meaning of planetary omens and prophecies. It was the kind of cultural borderland that Plaatje delighted in exploring. The tragedy was that so few people were in any kind of position to appreciate to the full just what it was that he was doing.

Brian Willan. *Sol Plaatje: South African Nationalist, 1876–1932* (New York: Heueman, 1984), pp. 349–71

BIBLIOGRAPHY
*Native Life in South Africa,* 1916; *A Sechuana Reader,* in *International Phonetic Orthography* (with Daniel Jones), 1916; *Mhudi: An Epic of Native Life a Hundred Years Ago,* 1930; *The Boer War Diary of Sol T. Plaatje,* 1973

# R

## RABÉARIVELO, Jean-Joseph
## (1901–1937)
### Madagascar

One of the greatest French-speaking African poets is undoubtedly the Malagasy Jean-Joseph Rabéarivelo. His work has been much less boosted than that of some other French-speaking poets (he has been almost ignored by translators, so far), presumably because his writing does not seem to fit into the now fashionable Négritude movement.

Rabéarivelo died in 1937, which is two years before [Aimé] Césaire published his famous *Cahier d'un retour au pays natal*. The poet died tragically by taking his own life. His death came as a complete surprise to most of his friends, and the mystery that surrounded it has never really been solved. . . .

Nothing could be further removed from the themes and images of current French African poetry than the writing of Rabéarivelo. Colonialism and the African personality do not figure in it. There are no tom-toms, palm trees, and black nude women. There is no oppression and no revolution. In fact Rabéarivelo is not concerned with the everyday issues of here and now. . . .

The world Rabéarivelo describes is a strangely unreal world. There is an extremely tantalizing quality about these poems, because on the one hand he can make us see his visions so clearly— and on the other he destroys them again by removing them right out of our sphere of knowledge and experience. Thus he speaks of ''blind light'' or ''insipid salt''; these are images that destroy themselves and produce a sudden shock in the reader. On the whole Rabéarivelo is careful to remove his poems from the sphere of everyday existence. Occasionally he mentions his native land, ''Imerina,'' but more often he locates his action near the ''frontiers of sleep.'' Nearly all of his images suggest that we move in strange, unexplored zones: ''all seasons have been abolished in those unexplored zones that occupy half of the world,'' or ''soil which is neither hot nor cold, like the skin of those who rest far from life and death.'' Rabéarivelo speaks of ''leaves which no wind can shake'' or ''unidentified trees'' or ''unknown flowers of no climate.''. . .

Rabéarivelo's poems are clear and precise visions of a strange and personal world. Like [Charles] Baudelaire, his favorite French poet, Rabéarivelo had a disgust of reality. In his poetry he has destroyed and dismembered reality. And out of the fragments he has built a new mythical world; it is a world of death and frustration, but also transcended by a sad beauty of its own.

> Ulli Beier. *Introduction to African Literature* (Evanston: Northwestern University Press, 1967), pp. 99–101

There is a distinct difference, both in quality and texture, between Rabéarivelo's early poetry and his mature poetry. The early poetry is technically competent, but it is based on the imitation of techniques and emotions reminiscent of late nineteenth-century French poetry. Nevertheless, the theme of departure—the poet's longing to break out of his prison—is present already in these early poems. His ''Paroles de l'hiver,'' typical of this period, evokes

''the distant mountains that speak my agony,'' the mountains that hold him prisoner on his island. Other early poems anticipate [Léopold Sédar] Senghor's lament that he is torn between his love for France and for Africa and finds himself unable to choose. On the one hand, Rabéarivelo wants to identify himself with French culture. . . . On the other, he regrets his loss of contact with traditional Malagasy culture. . . .

Although the personal themes of loneliness and despair are already present in Rabéarivelo's early poems, had he written nothing else they would have become merely literary curiosities. They still possess the impersonality of the borrowed language, so that the emotions are intellectual and therefore rhetorical.

The mature poems are dramatically different. They are written in a poetic language which is the poet's own, in spite of its antecedents, and they fully express the poet's experience of colonialism. His new language derives in part from [Jules] Supervielle, but he has assimilated the peculiar quality of the traditional Malagasy *hain-teny*. This new poetry is a direct product of the poet's despair, but instead of lamenting his despair, he uses it to create an imaginary paradise beyond it. His poetry becomes his escape from his prison, a substitute for the mental and physical freedom he will never know.

His paradise is a world remote from reality, but it is created out of the elements of nature which are at one and the same time typical of Madagascar and universal—the night sky, the stars, the sun, the moon, the prairies and the desert, birds and cattle, the wind and the rain. All these are transformed and molded by the poet's fantasy into a vision of joy and beauty. His poems invariably tell of the journey to this paradise, which is at the heart of the night, the opposite of the glaring light of day, representing reality. Inevitably there is a return to reality, but this return is not always, or even generally, seen as a loss so much as a triumph, for the poet returns with the poem. The paradise his imagination creates is synonymous with poetry. The experience is disguised in the image.

> Clive Wake. *Review of National Literatures*. 2, 2 (fall 1971), pp. 108–10

Rabéarivelo's first three books, *La Coupe de cendres*, *Sylves*, and *Volumes*, were published locally in Madagascar in very small editions. These collections of short poems are still imitative of the melancholy [Charles] Baudelaire and later minor French poets, the ''Fantaisistes.'' One of these poets was a French colonial official, Pierre Camo, much older than Rabéarivelo, who became his great friend and literary mentor. Camo lived ten years in Madagascar, and his influence as a cultural leader extended to the French community on Mauritius as well. It was Camo's encouragement that gradually weaned Rabéarivelo from the ''maudlin self-centeredness'' of his early poetry to a mature style more strongly expressing his own inner world. The later volumes, *Presque-songes*, *Traduit de la nuit*, and *Chants pour Abéone*, are considered by critics to contain the Malagasy poet's finest work. Here, abandoning imitative rhymes and meter in favor of free verse, Rabéarivelo has mastered a sense of form and created dreamlike poems of strange and compelling imagery, drawn from his own fantasies as well as from a Malagasy culture foreign to Western readers. Rabéarivelo's originality lies in the skillful blending of these elements. . . .

*Vieilles chansons des pays d'Imerina*, published in 1939 after the poet's death, is quite different in form and language from Rabéarivelo's other work. These are French renderings of traditional Malagasy *hain-teny*, formal love poems which are sometimes dialogues, sometimes monologues. Rabéarivelo also wrote poems directly in *hova*, and he sometimes translated into the musical Malagasy tongue poems he had originally written in French. . . .

Rabéarivelo was certainly a victim of the colonial situation as much as a beneficiary of it. The paradox was that the Western culture he had acquired with such effort and assimilated with such brilliance dazzled him with the riches of the wider world and at the same time continually denied him real access to its bounties, leaving him imprisoned on his island. He was a solitary, tormented person whose struggles with the real world were as much internal as external. In the end, they became overwhelming. The spectacular gesture of his suicide became both the poet's only way out and his most violent form of protest against endless poverty and humiliation.

> Ellen Conroy Kennedy. *The Négritude Poets* (New York: Thunder's Mouth Press, 1975), pp. 224–26

Rabéarivelo's early poetry is fairly obvious; there is little depth of feeling in it, and what feeling there is is mainly rhetorical. Neither the texture of the poetry nor its themes are particularly subtle or complex. The poet uses a borrowed literary language and style to express an experience of which he is not yet himself deeply conscious. However, between the publication of *Volumes* in 1928 and *Presque-songes* in 1934, Rabéarivelo's poetic sensibility underwent a profound transformation, and with it the quality and style of his poetry. During this period he abandoned the conventional meters, fixed-form poems, and borrowed language of his early poetry, substituting for them a masterly use of free verse and a totally new approach to imagery. Most significant of all, he was, suddenly (or so it seems), in possession of a subtly complex, rich, and vital personal poetic world, completely coherent and sure of itself. The explicitly stated tensions of his cultural exile gave way to the more complex insights of the poet's intuitive perception of himself and of his place in the world. . . .

In his mature poetry, Rabéarivelo uses his imagery in a way reminiscent of the contemporary surrealists, especially [Paul] Eluard, another poet fascinated by the *paysage intérieur*. Like Rabéarivelo, Eluard had a great predilection for nature imagery or, more specifically, for the image of the landscape. The image is always, or nearly always, the center of the poem. The object which provides the first element in the metaphor, the reality, is not mentioned. Only the image survives. The result is that the poem, through its imagery, is at one extra remove from the poet himself, since the element directly linking it with the poet is omitted. This creates a strangely remote, altogether independent world. Rabéarivelo draws nearly all his imagery from nature but, although his outlook is largely that of the romantic—self-centered, introspective—they are not affective images but nearer to objective symbols. The important thing about his nature imagery is that it is drawn entirely from his native Malagasy landscape, and it is therefore thoroughly

real to his imagination. Indeed, on the visual level alone, his imagery gives the reader a remarkably vivid impression of the Malagasy countryside. . . .

Rabéarivelo was an individualist in the way the poets of [Léopold Sédar] Senghor's generation were not. Rabéarivelo's experience of colonialism produced a reaction of turning inward, since the poet could not break out of his prison in any other way. Senghor's generation were aware of themselves as the spokesmen of all black men, and their poetry was therefore outward-turning. The evolution of Senghor's poetry is totally different from Rabéarivelo's. The early Senghor was inclined towards introspection, driven to it by his initial sense of exile and loneliness in Paris, but very soon it turned outwards as his sense of responsibility towards other men increased. His poetry is self-centered, but he wants it this way, because he has chosen to be the ambassador of his people, who must keep their gaze turned on him. Rabéarivelo's early poetry shows signs of an objective concern with the cultural tensions created by colonialism, but he found it impossible within the narrow confines of his prison world to see beyond his own predicament and, in his mature poetry, had to create a freedom within himself. This could only exacerbate the tensions, with the final tragic result of suicide.

But Rabéarivelo's positive contribution to modern African poetry in French is nevertheless considerable. Before the doctrine of Négritude sought, by conscious practice, to create a specifically African poetry, Rabéarivelo had, unconsciously, welded together trends in modern French poetry and the traditional Malagasy *hain-teny*, and built his edifice on the solid ground of the Malagasy countryside, to produce poetry of striking originality.

> Clive Wake. In Edgar Wright, ed. *The Critical Evaluation of African Literature* (Washington, D.C.: Inscape, 1976), p. 157, 163, 172

Rabéarivelo's appearance alongside his fellow Malagasy, Flavien Ranaivo, in an anthology largely devoted to verse from West Africa and the French West Indies is not difficult to understand. In [Léopold Sédar] Senghor's eyes Rabéarivelo was significant both as precursor and as emblem, since, though from the other side of the continent and exempt from the more drastic excesses of the French educational system, his life bore witness to two essential elements in the black francophone predicament: a liege-bond to French literature and a countervailing desire to assert his local uniqueness through an imitation of indigenous forms. Like so many of the writers of French expression who were to follow in his stead, Rabéarivelo had been torn between two impulses. He wrote some early verse in *hova* and later, in his last published collection, followed the structures of the local Madagascan *hain-teny* or proverb poem. But at its most delicate and evocative his poetry reminds us most strongly of [Charles] Baudelaire, of his beloved [Arthur] Rimbaud, of the voluptuary lusciousness of [Stéphane] Mallarmé.

It has become customary to bewail Rabéarivelo's physical and cultural isolation, and also his lack of any clear commitment to a truly national identity. In practice both forms of commiseration are misplaced. When compared with . . . anglophone poets . . . Rabéarivelo enjoyed two supreme advantages. In the first place, though he never reached Paris, his acceptance among a small group of expatriate French writers resident in Madagascar had exposed him to recent developments in French literature. In the second, he possessed immediate access to an indigenous tradition which in his later French verse he learned to reproduce with a certain fidelity. All that he lacked compared with a later generation of more committed francophone writers was a cause, something which before the ideologically inflamed years of the late 1930s was not so mandatory a requirement for a self-respecting *indigène* as might now perhaps appear. When in the 1940s the banner of Négritude was raised aloft, Rabéarivelo was dead and the poetry of French-speaking Africa had changed decisively.

Robert Fraser. *West African Poetry* (Cambridge: Cambridge University Press, 1986), pp. 43–44

It is very difficult for all men and especially a poet to avoid thinking about death. Rabéarivelo has left us, in his poems, in his journal, and by his suicide, irrefutable traces of this obsession. . . .

*Presque-songes*: The title of the collection of poems promises that we will remain on the threshold of dreams and the night and the threshold of death. . . .

The words of a living being in the world of the living, *Presque-songes* is rooted in the real world. Imerina, the native land which appeared in the poet's work with *Sylves*, became, in *Volumes*, one of the principal themes of inspiration, as the spectacle of hidden splendors and a pretext for expressing the uprooting of a colonized land. In *Presque-songes*, on the contrary, it emerges free, in the description of the twilight sceneries, in the scenes of the unpretentious picturesque genre, such as the hills of Iarivo, the zebus of the red lands, the women's clothing, *valiha* and dances, and the *makis* of the tropical forest. The thirst of the living is expressed here in the efforts of the inventor. . . . Thus, too, is the treatment of death transformed.

Faced with the dichotomy that the immediate experience of man has inscribed in language and which makes of life and death two contradictory realities in which the affirmation of one equals the negation of the other, the poet establishes in his refusal of the tragic, and by diverse strategies, a connection between that which was presented as absolutely incompatible. And this act favors life, because he summons the dead into our land of the living so that although dead, they are at the same time alive.

There are two kinds of dead in *Presque-songes*: the recently dead of the three parts of "Thrènes," whom he personally knew, even loved and whom he names or could name, and the anonymous collectivity of the ancestors whose evocation few poems ignore. The conscience of a radical rupture and of a tragic distance, which the poet tries to resolve, is associated with the former alone. The dead ancestors are presented from the start as being immanent to our world. . . .

One then understands that among all the poems, "Thrènes" offers to our senses the most crude material presentation of death. It is the scandal of the decomposition of the bodies and of their destruction. . . .

In the shock of the close encounter of a living being with death, the latter is experienced as discontinuity. It is the reverse, the inverse of life: the dead are "under the ground," in the night, in silence, in nothingness. . . .

Concretizing this schism between the living and the dead, with "Thrènes" and "Reconnaissance à Paul Gauguin," Rabéarivelo has demarcated, at the end of the work, a kind of enclosure reserved for the dead. Nevertheless, the choice of the appropriate poems already gives death a social character. . . .

The dialectic continues with socialized death becoming death salvaged and brought into the world of the living. This is predicted by the dedication, "A tous mes amis, morts et vivants" . . . the reduction of the opposition is accomplished through the jolts of the poem.

Marie-Christine Rochmann. *Presence Africaine.* 145 (1988), pp. 165–67†

BIBLIOGRAPHY
*La Coupe de cendres Sylves* (Woods), 1927; Volumes, 1928; *Presque-songes* (Near-Dreams), 1934; *Traduit de la nuit* (Translated from the Night), 1935: 24 Poems, 1962; *Chants pour Abéone* (Songs for Abéone), 1937; *Vieilles chansons des pays d'Imerina* (Old Songs of Imerina), 1939; *L'interférence*, 1987; *Poèmes*, 1990

# REED, Ishmael (1938–)
## United States

In *The Free-Lance Pallbearers* . . . the idea was to satirise Negro and white attitudes; Mr. Reed gives us an imaginary futuristic America, but with some clearly recognisable men and institutions. Such plot as exists is part of the satire. Mr. Reed depends on language exclusively. He is a witty with-it writer and his wisecracks are frequent and good. Yet having dispensed with the conventions of form and narrative, his novel has no means of obtaining variety and pace. The pages are all alike and although few in number, they drag with the efforts to keep up the jokiness.

David Pryce-Jones. *Punch.* January 29, 1969, p. 179

[Reed] writes "movie books" irresistibly recalling humor columns in high-school papers. *The Free-Lance Pallbearers* features a young gentleman named Bukka Doopeyduck who wanders through a constipated country called Harry Sam; *Yellow Back Radio Broke-Down*, set in the Wild Old West, stars the Loop Garoo Kid, a black cowboy, and Drag Gibson, a bad cattleman. Testimonials from weighty sources declare Mr. Reed a comic master; he himself announces his style to be "literary neo-hoodooism"; and I can only crustily say that I read him without a guffaw, without a laugh, without a chuckle, without the shade of a smile. Packed with *Mad* Magazine silliness though his work is, Mr. Reed has one saving virtue: he is hopelessly good-natured. He may intend his books as a black variation of Jonathan Swift, but they emerge closer to the commercial cooings of Captain Kangaroo.

Irving Howe. *Harper.* December 1969, p. 141

*Yellow Back Radio Broke-Down* . . . is not merely a satire on the Old West, with a black cowboy as the hero; it is not merely a parable about the contemporary black struggle vis-à-vis the white establishment; it is not merely a parody on the annexation fight between the Union and the territory of Texas; it is not merely a realistic account of the slime, genocide, corruption, degeneracy and hypocrisy that infest American history and every institution and motive in our national fibre; *Yellow Back Radio Broke-Down* is ALL of these things, and more!

Ishmael Reed is a poet. Like LeRoi Jones, he has taken the American language out on a limb and whipped it to within an inch of its life. In so doing he has revitalized the American language with the nitty-gritty idioms of black people's conceptualization of what it means to live in dese new-nited states of merica. As a poet and a novelist, Reed has the imagination of a psychopath who is God, or who is Satan Himself—ghosts, voo-doo, rattlesnakes, weird rites, hoo-doo, superstitions, multiple schizophrenia, beasts, metempsychosis, demons, charms, visions, hallucinations. In fact, the novel is Reed's voo-doo doll. He once said that the novel is the worst literary form God ever visited upon mankind. Reed has risen the novel from a dead doll with pins in it into a living breathing walking talking animal. This is a thing more authentic, more difficult, more dangerous, more human than science can ever achieve. By this I mean Ishmael Reed employs the mumbo-jumbo witch-doctor experiential epistemology of the Afro-American folk heritage in combination with the psychotic semantic categories of the West to achieve a highly original, secular and existential portrait of what is going on, and has gone on, in our daily lives. Reed is not mad, he is supersane; it is America that is mad and, like the other secular existential black writers Reed depicts—no, Reed *explodes*—this madness before our very eyes.

> Calvin C. Hernton. In John A. Williams and Charles F. Harris, eds. *Amistad 1* (New York: Random House, 1970), pp. 221–22

[''Jes Grew''] is a phrase coined by James Weldon Johnson to refer to the songs that ''jes' grew'' up among black people, belonging to no one and everyone. Reed sees a historical significance in the phrase. It stands for the quality of natural spontaneity and joy and rhythm innate in the black spirit. . . .

*Mumbo Jumbo* is about the *near* success of [the] transformation from old to new in the 1920s, an ''explanation'' of why Jes Grew didn't reach pandemic proportions and change the face of America at that time. The reason Reed advances is as imaginative as his dissection of the Christian myth in *Yellow Back Radio Broke-Down*, and as important to the conception of black art as the work of Amiri Baraka. Jes Grew, says Reed, is an energy in search of a form, by means of which it can survive and flourish: ''It must find its Speaking or strangle on its own ineloquence.'' The artist must provide that Speaking, the ''liturgy'' that is to become the voice of the ancient but heretofore mute consciousness. It is only through such a form that the sacred energy can be preserved and by which it can mutate into more forms as a testament of its inexhaustible variety. The failure of Jes Grew in the 1920s didn't result from [Woodrow] Wilson's sending the Marines to Haiti or from anything else the whites did. It failed because blacks didn't provide a Speaking equal to the power of Jes Grew. It's impossible not to see in this a reference to the Harlem Renaissance, and to read in it a suggestion that the literary art of that movement didn't provide forms that came up to those emerging from the Jes Grew musicians in New Orleans and Chicago. The total potential of black energy was not tapped.

This is an inference from the novel. We may carry it further. The trouble with the writers of the Harlem Renaissance was that they mistakenly sought to embody their energy in the liturgical forms of the white tradition, dooming their efforts from the start. The ending of *Mumbo Jumbo* suggests that the current upsurge of artistic activity among black artists is guided by an impulse more favorable to Jes Grew, the determination to reject white forms and recall black. What failed in the 1920s seems to be succeeding in the 1960s and 1970s.

> Jerry H. Bryant. *Nation*. September 25, 1972, pp. 245–46

*Mumbo Jumbo* isn't at all concerned with the traditional province of fiction, the registration of individual consciousness. Rather, as in his earlier books *The Free-Lance Pallbears* and *Yellow Back Radio Broke-Down*, Reed opens fictional art to the forms and mythic possibilities of popular culture, pursuing not psychological description but a perspective on history. . . .

He develops a wild and funny fantasia upon historical themes, part critique of the ''Harlem Renaissance'' of the 1920s, part farcical thriller about international conspiracy, part satire on blacks who yearn for ''serious'' (i.e., white-inspired) culture instead of trusting their own traditions and qualities, part philosophical disquisition on the destructive intentions of Faustian man. The result is something like a successful crossing of [Thomas] Pynchon, Sax Rohmer, Madame Blavatsky, and the Negritude writers of French Africa. . . .

Reed's is a quick and mocking mind, and I'm not finally sure how seriously he means his historical myth. But I'm content to read it, as I read the ''systematic'' works of Blake and Yeats, not primarily as analysis but as an act of continuous and powerful invention, a demonstration that the imagination, black or white, when released from conventional forms and the idea of a monolithic history, can be wonderfully entertaining and instructive, moment by moment, about the sorry narrowness of our self-understanding and our expectations about art.

> Thomas R. Edwards. *New York Review of Books*. October 5, 1972, p. 23

The satirical-grotesque distortion of American reality is the basis of Ishmael Reed's book, *The Free-Lance Pallbearers*, a potpourri of picaresque elements in its structure, and of slang in its linguistic fabric. . . .

The technique of concentrated distortion, which serves as the basis for the exaggeration or minimization of the particular, and is derived from the exploitation of slang, is the most important aspect of Reed's novel, just as it is a primary component of Ellison's novel: the similarity between the two is, however, limited to this, and to the particular way of playing with names at which the author of *Invisible Man* is a master.

Reed also produces surnames and first names that are full of allusions and irony, like Eclair Porkchop, Elijah Raven, U2 Polyglot, Nosetrouble, Rutherford Hayes, and so forth, but these names lack the symbolic density to which the entire narrative constantly contributes in *Invisible Man*; the more frequent impression is that playing with slang, for example, may too often be an end in itself. *The Free-Lance Pallbearers* is therefore a promising novel, but not quite a successful one, just as [Baraka's] *The System of Dante's*

*Hell* is an experimental attempt worthy of attention but certainly not a complete work.

Piero Boitani. *Prosatori Negri Americani del Novecento* (Rome: Edizioni di Storia e Letteratura, 1973), pp. 268, 271–72†

Ishmael Reed is a prolific writer who . . . works in more than one medium. His novels . . . have already consolidated his reputation as one of those black writers who refuse to be categorized according to the relevance of his theme. He asks no favors of any orthodoxy, but lets his imagination make its bid for the creation of new forms. Yet one cannot fail to notice the craft and discipline with which he controls the natural swing and bounce of his verse.

In his latest collection [of poems], *Conjure*, Reed's tone and rhythm derive from the militant tradition of the black underground. But his is an unusual brand of militancy; it is much concerned with the politics of language. He argues for a clean, free struggle between the liberating anarchism of the black tongue and the frozen esthetic of a conventional White Power. "May the best church win/ shake hands now and come out conjuring." His verse is distinguished by a fine critical intelligence, and his stance before the wide variety of American life is supremely confident. He can evoke with poetic realism the savagery which shaped the pioneering spirit as well as crystallize the fraudulence at the heart of the "civilizing" mission.

George Lamming. *New York Times Book Review*. May 6, 1973, p. 37

In his collection of poetry, *Conjure*, Reed unequivocally asserts that Neo-HooDoo, this new direction in Afro-American literature, constitutes "Our Turn," a radical severance of his destiny as a writer from the fate of his White contemporaries. . . . [Reed makes] the considerable claim that he has found a way of writing fiction unlike those decreative and self-reflexive fictive modes in which his White contemporaries seem imprisoned. Reed is careful, of course, not to establish Neo-HooDoo as a school. It is rather a characteristic stance, a mythological provenance, a behavior, a complex of attitudes, the retrieval of an idiom, but however broadly defined, Neo-HooDoo does manifest one constant and unifying refrain: Reed's fiercely professed alienation from Anglo-American literature. Ultimately, then, Neo-HooDoo is political art, as responsible as Richard Wright's *Native Son*, but without Wright's grim realism or the polemical separatism that characterizes Imamu Baraka's work. For Reed the problem is to get outside the "Euro-Am meaning world" (Baraka's term) without getting caught as an artist in a contraposed system. . . .

But where are the "original folk tales" and native idioms in Reed's fiction? How far indeed does Neo-HooDoo (both as myth and mode) take him from established literary canons? His discourse in *Yellow Back Radio Broke-Down* and *Mumbo Jumbo* curves in and around colloquial Black English, which serves him as a stylistic device, not as a language. It is withal a learned and allusive discourse as mixed in its diction as Mark Twain's. His forms are not narrative legends taken from an oral tradition, but rather the popular forms of the Western and the Gangster Novel. . . . *Yellow Back Radio Broke-Down* is a Black version of the Western [William] Burroughs has been writing in fragments and promising in full since the fifties. Not only is the content of the fiction eclectic in its composition, but Loop's performance as a *houngan* in it has a good deal of Burroughs' "Honest Bill." For the core of his narrative, Reed borrows almost intact the sociological drama Norman Mailer describes in *The White Negro*—that migration of White middle-class youth in revolt against the values of their own culture toward the counter-culture of Black America— and then weaves into this phenomenon a barely disguised account of the student uprisings at Berkeley and other campuses. . . .

*Yellow Back Radio Broke-Down* . . . turns into a book about Neo-HooDooism. And every explanation, every concealed footnote, betrays the artifice of the myth. Reed's mythopoeic lore is as arcane as the cryptic references strewn about in Burroughs' fiction. And his art, it would seem, bears as much relation to James Brown doing the "Popcorn" or Jimi Hendrix stroking his guitar as does T. S. Eliot's, whom Reed consigns in his manifesto to the graveyard of Christian culture.

Neil Schmitz. *Twentieth-Century Literature*. April 1974, pp. 127, 132–33, 135

The plot of *The Last Days of Louisiana Red* is impossible to recount. Like Reed's last novel, *Mumbo Jumbo*, it takes the form of a hoodoo detective thriller, features the master practitioner Papa LaBas, and generally focuses upon the struggle between the upright Gumbo Workers and the dangerous advocates of "Louisiana Red." For so many story lines and themes, however, a concept as linear as "plot" seems inadequate.

Consider, for example, that one of the characters is named Chorus, a performer supposedly in his 30s who has been out of work since people started writing plays like *Antigone*. Or that Reed draws constant parallels between the Antigone myth and his own tale. Or that contemporary versions of Kingfish, Amos and Andy appear. Or that a white teacher of Afro-American literature is undone by his study of Richard Wright's *Native Son* and is captured roaming the Berkeley Hills in a chauffeur's uniform, raving in black Mississippi-Chicago dialect of the 1940s. All of this is peculiar and improbable but somehow in the context Reed creates it fits together logically and even makes sense. . . .

Reed appears deeply concerned with the relationship between the sexes, but on this topic his perspective is frighteningly distorted. Throughout *The Last Days of Louisiana Red* there is joking contempt toward women, particularly black women. When he satirizes the women's movement his originality disappears and he falls back on the tired stereotype of feminists as man-hating dykes. The method for subduing these "fierce, rough-looking women" is attack and rape.

Reed's most astounding statements occur in a confrontation between Papa LaBas and Minnie, a Moocher leader. LaBas accuses Minnie and all black women as co-conspirators with white men in keeping black men in submission. LaBas intones: "Women use our children as hostages against us. . . . The original blood-sucking vampire was a woman . . . I can't understand why you want to be liberated. Hell . . . you already liberated."

The violence and humorlessness of this diatribe, delivered by a character whom Reed respects, indicate that he wants his opinions to be taken straight. Reed's views on a difficult problem are antediluvian and for this reader they cloud the entire impact of his work. If he is so insensitive in this area, how can he be so incisive in others? (Can I laugh with a man who seems so hostile toward me?) As a critic I found *The Last Days of Louisiana Red* brilliant. As a black woman I am not nearly so enthusiastic.

Barbara Smith. *New Republic.* November 23, 1974, pp. 53–54

Ishmael Reed's *The Last Days of Louisiana Red* satirically attacks the forces he feels make life difficult for blacks, and for Americans in general. The unifying metaphor is "Louisiana Red," a pungent sauce symbolizing the rage causing internal fighting and dissension. Within the satirical fire the targets are numerous: the false motions of America, adversary and treacherous offerings of women, a persisting slave mentality among blacks, "moocherism" (hustling others) under various guises, the psyche of the white "liberal," criminality masked by black revolutionary pretensions, black simple-minded violence and sexual obsession, hypocrisy of an African leader, etc.

By discussions of the stories of the Greeks, involving the role of the chorus, and the plays and mythic backgrounds of *Antigone* and *The Seven against Thebes*, Reed creates a flexible frame in which disorder parallels and mirrors for the disorder in black life, and life in general. Thus Antigone's defiance of the male authority of Creon in Sophocles's play *Antigone* (and in myth) and her presumed unbounded ambitions are emblematic of the out-of-bounds modern black women. Into this disordered situation comes the conjurer or psychic detective LaBas and his assistants, who must set things aright. And there is also disorder in the world of conjurers, bearing upon the disorder in the day-to-day world. . . .

Reed's satire, as implied by statements in different parts of the book, wishes to act as a corrective. It would rescue blacks from sociological determinism and defeatism, and release energy for an individualistic march to freedom. The old virtues of self-reliance, hard work and struggle, and imagination and intuitive powers, are called into play. There would be then the correction of negative and parasitic types who "have their own boot on their own necks." . . .

Among novelists writing today, Reed ranks in the top of those commanding a brilliant set of resources and techniques. The prose is flexible, easy in its shift of gears and capacity to move on a variety of levels. The techniques of the cartoon, the caricature, the vaudevillean burlesque, the straight narrative, the detective story, are summoned at will. But his management of his resources in *The Last Days of Louisiana Red* fails to create a lasting or deep impression.

George E. Kent. *Phylon.* June 1975, pp. 190–92

Ishmael Reed's fifth compact novel [*Flight to Canada*] should add to his reputation as one of America's most freshly—and bizarrely—imaginative satirists. He was having pointed fun with historical figures in fictional situations before E. L. Doctorow's *Ragtime* brought best-seller attention to the technique. Now he introduces an Abraham Lincoln who is neither the sainted leader of legend nor the villain pictured by political cartoonists of the time—but a kind of good-natured illiterate who gets a little tangled up in trying to explain Lincoln's actual dubious ideas for "compensatory emancipation" or sending away the slaves to colonize far parts. . . .

But it is not only white people, including one as sympathetic as Lincoln, who are shown to be victims of racial attitudes in this novel about a would-be poet fleeing a fantastic emperor of the Southland. Mr. Reed's targets include members of all races, not omitting his own black race, which his books repeatedly present as needing to resist being divided and conquered through such means as accepting others' images of blackness. In this book the slaves put down each other, if in less obvious ways than their masters do, and one of the fugitives finally discloses that he ran away not only from the slavemaster but from the slaves too.

Yet this free man has become another kind of slave, to the profits from pornography. Mr. Reed ranges from intellectual subtlety to the depths of degradation in symbolically linking self-enslavement to the impulse to enslave others. Sometimes he uses obscenities and erotic passages that raise the question whether he himself has been caught in the trap of literary fashion. Most of the time, a satirist's reforming intentions seem clear beneath prose that combines highbrow and lowbrow to provide a series of snaps, crackles, and pops commenting on our times. Yes, our times as well as Lincoln's. For in this book the assassination at Ford's Theater is callously covered by TV, for example, and Mr. Reed has blended the periods as if history existed all at once instead of in the fetters of time.

Roderick Nordell. *Christian Science Monitor.* October 20, 1976, p. 25

A close reading of [Ishmael] Reed's works strongly suggests his concerns with the received form of the novel, with the precise rhetorical shape of the Afro-American literary tradition, and with the relation that the Afro-American tradition bears to the Western tradition. Reed's concerns, as exemplified in his narrative forms, seem to be twofold: the relation his own art bears to his black literary precursors, including [Zora Neale] Hurston, [Richard] Wright, [Ralph] Ellison, and James Baldwin; and the process of willing-into-being a rhetorical structure, a literary language, replete with its own figures and tropes, but one that allows the black writer to posit a structure of feeling that simultaneously critiques both the metaphysical presuppositions inherent in Western ideas and forms of writing and the metaphorical system in which the "blackness" of the writer and his experience have been valorized as a "natural" absence. In six demanding novels, Reed has criticized, through signifying, what he perceives to be the conventional structures of feeling that he has received from the Afro-American tradition. He has proceeded almost as if the sheer process of the analysis can clear a narrative space for the next generation of writers as decidedly as Ellison's narrative response to Wright and naturalism cleared a space for Leon Forrest, Toni Morrison, Alice Walker, James Alan McPherson, and especially for Reed himself.

By undertaking the difficult and subtle art of pastiche, Reed criticizes the Afro-American idealism of a transcendent black subject, integral and whole, self-sufficient and plentiful, the "always already" black signified, available for literary representation in received Western forms as would be the water dipped from a deep dark well. Water can be poured into glasses or cups or canisters, but it remains water just the same. Put simply, Reed's fictions argue that the so-called black experience cannot be thought of as a fluid content to be poured into received and static containers.

For Reed, it is the signifier that both shapes and defines any discrete signified—and it is the signifiers of the Afro-American tradition with whom Reed is concerned.

Reed's first novel lends credence to this sort of reading and also serves to create a set of generic expectations for reading the rest of his works. *The Free-Lance Pallbearers* is, above all else, a parody of the confessional mode which is the fundamental, undergirding convention of Afro-American narrative, received, elaborated upon and transmitted in a chartable heritage from Briton Hammon's captivity narrative of 1760, through the antebellum slave narratives, to black autobiography, and into black fiction, especially the fictions of Hurston, Wright, Baldwin, and Ellison. The narrative of Reed's Bukka Doopeyduk is a pastiche of the classic black narrative of the questing protagonist's "journey into the heart of whiteness"; but it parodies that narrative form by turning it inside out, exposing the character of the originals and thereby defining their formulaic closures and disclosures. Doopeyduk's tale ends with his own crucifixion; as the narrator of his own story, therefore, Doopeyduk articulates, literally, from among the dead, an irony implicit in all confessional and autobiographical modes, in which any author is forced by definition to imagine him- or herself to be dead. More specifically, Reed signifies upon [Wright's] *Black Boy* and [Baldwin's] *Go Tell It on the Mountain* in a foregrounded critique which can be read as an epigraph to the novel: "read growing up in soulsville first of three installments—or what it means to be a backstage darky." Reed foregrounds the "scat-singing voice" that introduces the novel against the "other" voice of Doopeyduk, whose "second" voice narrates the novel's plot. Here, Reed parodies both Hurston's use of free indirect discourse in *Their Eyes Were Watching God* and Ellison's use in *Invisible Man* of the foregrounded voice in their prologue and epilogue that frame his nameless protagonist's picaresque account of his own narrative. In his second novel, *Yellow Back Radio Broke-Down*, Reed more fully, and successfully, critiques both realism and modernism. . . .

Reed's third novel, *Mumbo Jumbo*, is a novel about writing itself—not only in the figurative sense of the postmodern, self-reflexive text but also in a literal sense. . . . *Mumbo Jumbo* is both a book about texts and a book of texts, a composite narrative composed of sub-texts, pre-texts, post-texts and narratives-within-narratives. It is both a definition of Afro-American culture and its deflation. . . .

The text of *Mumbo Jumbo* is framed by devices characteristic of film narration. The prologue, situated in New Orleans, functions as a "false start" of the action: five pages of narration are followed by a second title page, a second copyright and acknowledgment page, and a second set of epigraphs, the first of which concludes the prologue. This prologue functions like the prologue of a film, with the title and credits appearing next, before the action continues. The novel's final words are "Freeze frame." The relative fluidity of the narrative structure of film, compared with that of conventional prose narrative, announces here an emphasis upon figural multiplicity rather than singular referential correspondence, an emphasis that Reed recapitulates throughout the text by an imaginative play of doubles. The play of doubles extends from the title and the double-Erzulie image of [Josephine] Baker on the novel's cover ("Erzulie" means "love of mirrors") to the double beginning implicit in every prologue, through all sorts of double images scattered in the text (such as the "two heads" of PaPa LaBas) and

the frequently repeated arabic numerals 4 and 22), all the way to the double ending of the novel implied by its epilogue and "Partial Bibliography." The double beginning and double ending frame the text of *Mumbo Jumbo*, a book of doubles, from its title on. . . .

It is indeterminacy, the sheer plurality of meaning, the very play of the signifier itself, which *Mumbo Jumbo* celebrates. *Mumbo Jumbo* addresses the *play* of the black literary tradition and, as a parody, is a *play* upon that same tradition.

Henry Louis Gates Jr. *Black Literature and Literary Theory* (New York: Methuen, 1984), pp. 297–99, 305, 313

In a fundamental way it is pointless to evaluate Reed by conventional literary standards, since the cultural assumptions on which these standards are based are themselves his primary target. The pertinent question is whether he in fact creates and practices a new aesthetic or whether, like the black nationalist writers and critics he so often attacks, he turns literature into polemic. Like his opponents, he castigates, satirizes, and vilifies white cultural values; like them he views the dominant society as excremental, repressive, and death-driven. Both implicitly and explicitly, he sees blacks as allies of the life force and whites as death seekers. Unlike the nationalists, however, who emphasize present oppression, Reed seeks nothing less than the demystification and deconstruction of cultural history. He works backward to Egyptian myth to locate the source of the black-white conflict, which he sees as coinciding with the Osiris-Set conflict. From this primal struggle, apparently won by the forces of death, has come the underlying pattern of human experience, which is the effort of life, fertility, and creativity to assert themselves against the control of death, sterility, and repression. Through systemization and violence, the dominant culture has not only maintained its power, but has made itself appear as the true, beautiful, and natural. It presumes to be the only valid voice, the only Word. But because creativity is anarchic, individualistic, and irrepressible, it continually intrudes itself upon the controlling patterns. It is this intrusion, this breaking of the pattern, that Reed designates Neo-HooDoo. His fiction consistently operates dialectically: it exposes and denigrates the oppressive nature of Western culture so as to free the non-Western voices which express life and creativity. And this very act of exposure is the saying of the words which in voodoo practice give one access to the spirits. Thus, Reed serves the function not only of *Guedé*, but also of the *houngan* (priest) whose litany opens the way to an alternative world.

His six novels—*The Free-Lance Pallbearers*, *Yellow Back Radio Broke-Down*, *Mumbo Jumbo*, *The Last Days of Louisiana Red*, *Flight to Canada*, and *The Terrible Twos*—are variations on the theme of cultural conflict. Each presents some aspect of human history and makes clear the continuous character of the struggle by collapsing conventional literary time structures. In such simultaneity, as in the use of the forms of popular literature such as the western and the detective novel, Reed calls into question the dominant society's control of both history and language. His play with time and genre is a way of denaturalizing assumptions about these aspects of culture and revealing the underlying manipulative functions of both. In this, he resembles postmodernist white writers like John Barth and Donald Barthelme. However, his fictions differ from theirs in that his undercutting of literary and cultural values is premised on an alternative value system, Neo-HooDoo. The similarity to metafictional practice is clearest in the early nihilistic works, but, beginning with *Mumbo Jumbo*, he lays claim to a different mythology and aesthetic.

Keith E. Byerman. *Fingering the Jagged Grain: Tradition and Form in Recent Black Fiction* (Athens: University of Georgia Press, 1985), pp. 218–19

Uppity, pretentious, pompous, sexist, and sophomoric are the most frequent if not the kindest names hurled by unsympathetic critics at Reed for the Neo-HooDoo aesthetic he develops between 1967 and 1983 in his four books of verse, five anthologies, and six novels.

At the heart of Reed's Neo-HooDoo aesthetic, which is largely constructed from residual elements of syncretistic African religions (Voodoo, Pocomania, Candomblé, Macumba, and Hoo-Doo) in the Caribbean and the Americas, especially Haiti, Brazil, and the United States, is a belief in the power of the unknown, particularly as expressed in artistic freedom and originality. In the prose poem ''Neo-HooDoo Manifesto'' he tells us that ''Neo-HooDoo is a 'Lost American Church' updated'', that ''Neo-HooDoo borrows from Haiti Africa and South America. Neo-HooDoo comes in all styles and moods,'' and that ''Neo-HooDoo believes that every man is an artist and every artist a priest''. An incredibly eclectic mixture of ancient and contemporary techniques and forms of non-Western and Western cultures, Reed's six novels . . . challenge the reader to be as culturally egalitarian and imaginatively bold as the author.

Bernard W. Bell. *The Afro-American Novel and Its Tradition* (Amherst: University of Massachusetts Press, 1987), pp. 330–31

Ishmael Reed's *Flight to Canada* presents the reader with many conundrums, all asking the rhetorical question, ''Who is to say what is fact and what is fiction?'' Through Uncle Robins's narrative, the amanuensis-cum-reflector . . . Raven Quickskill, demonstrates that the Afro-American, Ur-slave, is necessarily entrapped in slavehood concepts that contradict his experience. His experience tells him that he can choose either the slavehood concepts disseminated by his master or adopt the personal attitudes of those slaves who reject traditional slavehood values and attitudes. Whichever choice he makes leads to emotional conflict. Some of the slaves, however, use their knowledge of the slave community and the plantation society to grapple with and overcome the slavehood images of Southern society. Reed, through the pseudo slave narrative, elicits and evokes an image of the infernality of life in the South for Afro-Americans by re-creating the images that were so well-known to the slave community, the black freeman, and the whites who read slave narratives and heard blacks tell their tales. . . .

In spite of the rhetorical structure of *Flight to Canada*, the narrator-agent gives the reader several exposures from which to develop a composite picture of the major black characters. He does not, however, make the compositing process easy, for each exposure is influenced by the ''witchery [which he puts] on the word,'' an influence which raises several questions: What effect does his necromancy have on the narrative, if any? (He admits he could not stand Uncle Robin when they were in slavery.) Does he manipulate the slavehood experiences and images of the slaves in the narrative? What are his relations with the other slaves really like? What

do they actually think of him? Do the house slaves see themselves as the field slaves see them, and vice versa? How do the field slaves see each other? How do the house slaves see each other? These and many other questions about interpersonal relations among slaves, as well as their images of each other, are raised by this book.

Charles De Arman. *CLA Journal*. 33, 2 (December 1989), pp. 157–59

Ishmael Reed extends the notion of syncretism into the level and texture he uses in his novels, thus creating a kind of contemporary bathetic language, whose principal rules of discourse are taken from the streets, popular music, and television. In Reed's novels, it is not uncommon to find the formal blend of language mixed with the colloquial, as it is Reed's contention that such an occurrence in the narrative is more in keeping with the ways contemporary people influenced by popular culture really speak. By purposely mixing the myriad aspects of language from different sources in popular culture, Reed pulls into individual *cardinal functions* (one closed set of narrative actions: [Roland] Barthes) words and expressions which create the fictive illusion of real speech. Though the emotive effect is bathetic, evoking interest and humor because of seeming incongruencies, the language Reed uses comes from concrete paroles (selected, individual utterances from the field of all available language usage [langúe]: [Ferdinand de] Saussure) of the present day. The involved reader in the text knows that contemporary language is not static, is in fact in tremendous flux, and that actual people mix levels of diction constantly to achieve the desired communicative effect; and the proof of the validity of Reed's artistic method is the ease with which his characters display bathetic discourse. . . .

All of Reed's books exhibit *dystaxy*, i.e., the disruption of linear narrative, but certainly the book which gives the best example of Reed's use of dystaxic, synchronic development in its various forms is *Flight to Canada*. The ''time'' of the novel is the antebellum period. But that time period overlaps with the present (1976) through the use of contemporary indices such as language lexicon, cardinal references, and the situational responses of the characters. For example, the characters make long-distance phone calls when in distress; Raven Quickskill, the crafty slave who escapes, joins the lecture circuit and uses a jet to travel through Canada, where he delivers his abolitionist speeches, reads his poetry, and collects his honoraria; Josiah Henson's spirit appears to lambast Harriet Beecher Stowe for stealing from Henson's slave narrative the plot for *Uncle Tom's Cabin*. Leechfield, another escaped slave, is making a fortune selling photographs of himself with women through an antebellum pornography magazine: ''I'll be your slave for the night,'' one pictorial caption might read, not unlike the ''personal'' ads in the *Village Voice*. . . .

This narrative self-referentiality is not always so simple to decipher, as all of Reed's novels are readerly texts; he expects the reader to be familiar with past fiction and nonfictional events external to the particular novel at issue. Reed also expects the reader to ''make'' the text and its implications by way of understanding the narrative games being played. The fact that the 1976 publication of *Flight to Canada* is a direct response and a counterblast to the publishing of Alex Haley's *Roots*, and that both books can be appreciated much better with this knowledge, is something of which Reed expects the interested reader to be aware. Moreover, without a readerly knowledge of historical and contemporary personages, much of the satirical effect of any Reed novel is lost. A part of the cause of oppression, in Reed's scheme of things, is ignorance, and he will not accept ignorance from his readers; thus, an aspect of any Reed novel is didactic. Again, the point of syncretism as a literary method for Reed is that it pulls together from all existing language-level and discourse possibilities those utterances which he feels are most effective in illuminating the fictional situation he has created.

> Reginald Martin. *Modern Language Studies.* 20, 2 (spring 1990), pp. 3, 7–9

In three novels, *The Free-Lance Pallbearers, The Terrible Twos,* and *The Terrible Threes,* Reed launches grotesque attacks on American social, economic, and political avatars of control. . . .

In *The Terrible Twos* and *The Terrible Threes,* Reed traces the tangled skeins of interconnection in American power centers, showing how broadcasters buy legislators, how advisers close to the president answer to backroom industrial interests, how the military can be influenced or bought, and how fake Hollywood glamour creates the illusion of reality. The reader learns how a tiny group of fanatics not answerable to any legal power could bring about the nuclear destruction of an African nation. Blackmail, drugs, the sale of information, secret societies, the manipulation of images: these are what *The Terrible Twos* and *The Terrible Threes* are about. Reed seems to fear that this degree of interconnectedness may make the system impervious to legal improvements. . . .

Control is also a helpful tool for understanding Reed's other novels. *Reckless Eyeballing* has confounded and revolted reviewers but makes some sense as a demonstration of how an alert and reasonably sophisticated individual persuades himself to submit to the forces of control. The results are nightmarish, though members of mainstream culture will not at first find them noteworthy: Ian Ball does not know his real self anymore. An island hex is the ostensible cause of his cloven personality, but magic only reinforces what his attempts to "make it" in New York have already effected: a split self with the inauthentic half dominant. . . .

Reed's works have often been treated as scattershot endeavors—*Reckless Eyeballing* as an attack on feminists; *Yellow Back Radio Broke-Down* as a western; *Mumbo Jumbo* as a HooDoo detective story; and *The Terrible Twos, The Terrible Threes,* and *The Free-Lance Pallbearers* as political satire. Most critics have found no stable core of concerns aside from a satiric attitude toward the world. I argue that Reed has an ongoing project in his explorations of control and that his grotesque vision of America resembles the visions of other artists sensitive to the workings of control. Reed and these other artists feel cheated of some lost element of the American dream and protest this betrayal with images of filth and violent perversion. The critique of America is flashy and is even compelling to readers disturbed by inequities in the country's treatment of its citizens. Reed's contribution to this strain in American thought becomes evident only when one looks at all his novels together. Examined individually, they are disparate and variably successful; however, the limitations of any one signify little in the series of hallucinatory portraits of America's soul. Each might be likened to a seance in which Reed depicts America as seen from the HooDoo spirit world. . . . The evils Reed attacks are not just African-American problems; his focus on control demonstrates that he belongs to a group of bitter satirists—female and male, black and white—whose experience with cultural lies appalls them. Their artistic violence aims at breaking through to vantages beyond those of ordinary social and literary consciousness. Such perspectives, they imply, reveal truths normally ignored by privileged members of society. Those ugly truths, not the bourgeois self-image that the contented have cultivated to protect their own comfort, are the reality.

> Kathryn Hume. *PMLA.* 108, 3 (May 1993), pp. 508, 515–16

With his ninth novel, Ishmael Reed proves again that he is not afraid to plunge into the maelstrom. *Japanese by Spring* is full of contemporary issues plaguing the American consciousness: Rodney King, Anita Hill/Clarence Thomas, the United States attack on Iraq, and so on. As he moves through his fifties, has Reed lost his fictional abilities? No. For Reed, the novel is supreme. If you want to understand anything, put it into a novel and let the novel decide. And so Reed himself is also a character in the work: "He sometimes went around with a tacky beard in order to appear to be a man of the people. He sometimes wore clothes so long that they became ragged and his family would have to go to Macy's to buy him new clothes."

The protagonist is Benjamin Puttbutt, a black junior professor at white Jack London College. He is being nice to the English and Women's Studies departments and attacks black men for not shaping up—one of his heroes being Thomas Sowell—because he wants to get tenure. He even turns a blind eye to the outrageous racist actions against him by a student, Robert Bass, whose father is a rich contributor to the college. A radical in the 1960s, he will do anything that goes over: "Now that the writer was considered as obsolete as a 1960s computer, he could share in some of the profits of the growth industry of the 1980s and 1990s. Criticism. All you had to do was string together some quotes from [Walter] Benjamin, [Roland] Barthes, [Michel] Foucault and [Jacques] Lacan and you were in business. Even a New Critic like himself could make some cash." However, he is double-crossed and denied tenure.

Puttbutt has been studying Japanese because he sees it as the wave of the future. Suddenly, the college is bought by a Japanese group, and his Japanese teacher becomes acting president and makes him his right-hand man. While the Japanese do to the Eurocentrics what the latter have done to others, Puttbutt makes Crabtree, an English professor, teach Freshman Yoruba. Crabtree changes. "I have learned a language that transports me to a culture that's two thousand years old," he says. "Have they ever produced a Tolstoy? They have produced Tolstoys. Have they produced a Homer. They have hundreds of Homers. We were just too lazy and arrogant to find out."

> Peter Nazareth. *World Literature Today.* 67, 3 (summer 1993), p. 610

In *Japanese by Spring* (the title comes from a short-course text used by our hero), Reed updates his ongoing quarrel with the world created by politicians and maintained by the denizens of Madison Avenue; he takes on, this time, the "groves of academe," especially the archaic silliness of tenure and all of its attendant quirkiness—teaching assistants, publish or perish departments, political infighting, assemblyline techniques. In his main character, "Chappie" Puttbutt, a schmoolike black, untenured professor at Jack London

University and member of a long line of military officers (father a general, mother in military intelligence), Reed has created an alter ego who represents everything he objects to in academic life. Puttbutt, author of *Blacks, America's Misfortune* (his dissertation subject, an obscure 1920s poet, Nathan Brown), studies Japanese so as to be ready for the inevitable "invasion" of the West Coast. But plot is almost never as important as Reed's satiric intent; his great skill is to create topical scenes and characters to represent his favorite subjects of ridicule. He is most successful when he devastates them by revealing their true characters: academic hustlers, feminists, antifeminists, black supremacists, white supremacists, chiseling administrators, power brokers who use students for their own ends—in short, all that's wrong with higher education that could go so much higher but probably never will. Reed's very personal brand of satire is humor as classical as [François] Rabelais and [Johnathan] Swift, and as meaningful.

Jack Byrne. *Review of Contemporary Fiction*. 13, 3 (fall 1993), pp. 210–11

Ishmael Reed maintains a complicated relationship with African-American experience, clearly visible in his 1976 novel, *Flight to Canada*. Relying upon the conventions of antebellum slave narratives for its structure and style, *Flight to Canada* forges a concrete link with the earliest form of African-American letters. Despite this novel's ostensible origins in the slave narrative, Reed "refuses to be a slave to his narrative" (Richard Walsh, *Journal of American Studies*, April 1993). This is apparent not only from Reed's conscious and deliberate use of anachronisms within his text—slaves fleeing on jumbo jets, slave quarters furnished with telephones and cable television, and carriages equipped with "climate control air conditioning, vinyl top, AM/FM stereo radio, full leather interior, power-lock doors, six-way power seat, power windows, white-wall wheels, door-edge guards, bumper impact strips, rear defroster and soft-ray glass"—but also from his reluctance to resolve various other conflicts within the text: he never reconciles Lincoln as either a player or a fool, never fully distinguishes between Raven's narrative and that of Robin, and never explains why Quaw Quaw and Pirate Jack are together at the beginning of the novel, when, chronologically, she has already discovered that he uses her father's head for an ashtray and that Jack has buried her brother in the museum of natural history. While these inconsistencies have sent critics off in search of new ways to characterize Reed's aesthetic—anachronistic, Neo-HooDoo, necromancy, or others—I find a plausible explanation for Reed's particular deployment of history and his use of anachronism within the writings of William Wells Brown, a man important not only as the first African-American playwright and novelist, but also as a character within Reed's novel. While characterizations of Reed's work as anachronistic or as an example of his Neo-HooDoo aesthetic are useful starting places for an examination of Reed's relationship with history, they fail to account fully for Reed's particular deployment of history. Although the historical figures of William Wells Brown and Frederick Douglass are both available to Reed, *Flight to Canada* relies upon themes, stylistic devices, and characters introduced and developed in the works of William Wells Brown, revealing an affiliation between Reed and Brown in their individual belief in HooDoo, their use of anachronism, their particular political and social views, and, importantly, their styles.

Reed's tricky and unstable relationship with history is apparent throughout the novel. Not only are we bombarded with historical speculation and inaccuracies, but Reed also consistently references history as strange and bizarre—as in the quotation in the title of this essay, which comes from a longer quotation: "Strange, history. Complicated, too. It will always be a mystery, history. New disclosures are as bizarre as the most bizarre fantasy." Furthering this conception of history as flexible, mutable, and, perhaps more importantly, incomprehensible, Reed intersperses his text with questions such as "Where does fact begin and fiction leave off?" and statements such as "slavery was an anachronism." Later, as Reed's protagonist rails against revisionary history, the difficulty of pinning down Reed's particular relationship with history becomes clear.

One compelling way to theorize Reed's work is to label it anachronistic and then discuss how anachronism inflects his text. According to Barbara Foley ("History, Fiction, and the Ground Between: The Uses of the Documentary Mode in Black Literature," *PMLA*, 95, 1980), African-American writers are constantly in need of living up to the legacy of truthfulness in their writings. This legacy emerges from the earliest African-American writing—the slave narrative—and the need to authenticate the narrative with letters vouching for the slave's veracity and for the true authorship of the work. *Flight to Canada* challenges this legacy by using Reed's own blend of anachronistic history to make whatever he wants out of it, to include "the politics and prejudices of the writer, rather than any meaning inherent in the 'facts' themselves" and to "mold the interpretations that we commonly accept as truth." Like Robin's in *Flight to Canada*, Reed's conception of history has the ability to revise "the 'authorized' versions of things." Reed's "revisionary" move is necessary in the creation of a historical perspective which invites comparison between the past and the present, heightening our understanding of both the historical and social dynamics of the novel. This use of overlapping time periods recalls the African-American oral tradition by creating a synchronic effect. This move also roots the book in a more contemporary reality, imitating the types of discourse available through mass-media communications. *Flight to Canada* includes aphorisms to achieve this synchronic, anachronistic effect: "There are more types of slavery than merely material slavery. There's cultural slavery" and "slavery was a state of mind." Reed's yoking of distinct and somehat incompatible time periods serves not only to inform our understanding of each period specifically but also to substantiate Reed's argument that slavery exists long after Lincoln's emancipation proclamation.

Matthew R. Davis. *Mississippi Quarterly*. 49, 4 (fall 1996), pp. 743–83

BIBLIOGRAPHY
*The Free-Lance Pallbearers*, 1967; *Yellow Back Radio Broke-Down*, 1969; *Conjure: Selected Poems, 1963-70*, 1972; *Mumbo Jumbo*, 1972; *The Last Days of Louisiana Red*, 1974; *Flight to Canada*, 1976; *Shrovetide in Old New Orleans*, 1978; *A Secretary to the Spirits*, 1978; *The Terrible Twos*, 1982; *God Made Alaska for the Indians: Selected Essays*, 1982; *Reckless Eyeballing*, 1986; *New and Collected Poems*, 1988; *The Terrible Threes*, 1989; *Japanese by Spring*, 1993; *Airing Dirty Laundry*, 1993

# REID, V. S. (1913–1987)

## Jamaica

[V. S. Reid's *New Day*] belongs to literary history in the Caribbean. When it appeared in 1949, it was a pioneering claim that a West Indian island could have its own national history and culture. By focusing on the life of the common people and on their popular idiom several years before Creole became "acceptable" in Jamaica, Reid foreshadowed important elements in the literary movement that was to follow. . . .

In this book Reid offers his own considered answers as to what constitutes "a people," as to what in terms of the human spirit was the justification for independence. His answers involve race, history, geography, sensations of touch, taste and sight, religion and politics. . . .

Reid also developed from the native Jamaican use of imagery. Popular imagery in the Caribbean . . . is concrete, down-to-earth, often witty. Reid goes further and makes it anthropomorphic: "green water walks fast past the prow" of a boat, and a flagpost "points empty finger at the sky." It is unlikely that any Jamaican countryman would use images just like this. But Reid has a justification, one that becomes even more fulfilled in his second novel, *The Leopard*. Reid creates a world that is personalized, dramatic, active. If wind and waves have human qualities, natural forces fuse with the lives of people: "gale wind was staring in his countenance," or "thunderhead opens in my Father's eyes." . . . Reid's imagery gives his action a heightened drama, and interpenetrates character and history with the natural life of his island. It must be pointed out that Reid does not claim this insight for all his characters.

> Louis James. *The Islands in Between: Essays on West Indian Literature* (London: Oxford University Press, 1968), pp. 64, 67

[*New Day*] rests upon a single proposition; that Jamaica has a history. This history is distinct from that of its various racial groups separately viewed. No group of people, however polyglot, can inhabit an island through 450 years of turbulence and change without forming a history and culture uniquely their own. It follows that there is such a creature as a Jamaican, and that we can only get to know him by looking at his island and following its story.

This central proposition is built into the structure of Reid's novel, for the life of a single man, his narrator, bridges the bloody Morant Bay Rebellion of 1865 and the new constitution of 1944. The first event signaled the abolition of representative government after more than two hundred years; the second announced its return. As the old man compares these events in his mind, relating them to one another and to the larger history of the island, the lineaments of Jamaica begin to emerge. . . .

Reid's book, written so soon after the latter event, is not concerned to ask whether that promise has been fulfilled. It announces by its very title a hope only, but a hope which had not been there before at any time in the island's history.

Yet the importance of *New Day* does not rest only on its central concern with Jamaica and its people. The same new confidence that dictated its theme extends into the style itself, for the whole book is couched in the form of a long monologue by the aged narrator as the crowds celebrating their new measure of freedom surge under his

window. Hence it is written throughout in a style approximating Jamaican country dialect of the mid-nineteenth century. To use this style of speech even for dialogue, except to produce comical "quashi" (country bumpkin) effect, was effrontery enough to the delicate colonial sensibility which rotated around wistful connections with "Home" and garden parties at King's House. To write an entire book in this despised dialect, albeit spoken habitually by nine tenths of the population, and in off-moments by the rest, was radical indeed.

> Gerald Moore. *The Chosen Tongue* (New York: Harper & Row, 1969), pp. 3–4

Reid the novelist [in *New Day*] constructs his story not by going directly back to an earlier event like Emancipation, but by making use of possibilities of characterization and evocation of place, possibilities traditionally open to the novelist, to create for the reader a sense of the specific human and geographical context in which the riots took place. The parched soil of the parish of St. Thomas, which Reid makes us feel clutching at our throat, and white against our vision, is both a symbol of the condition of the people and a literal factor driving the black poor to despair. And Reid's use of historical document (quotation of part of the Queen's reply to the petition of the poor people of St. Ann's parish) is made acceptably novelistic by a choruslike presentation of the parishioners' different responses to it, thus partly suggesting the chronic nature of the discontent and enacting in dramatic language the different attitudes of the several economic and ethnic groups involved. . . .

Cutting across the differing class interests of the characters is the tension which Reid suggests between Pa John Campbell and his son, Davie. The psychological complexities inherent in the clash between generations—father and son, old and young—lend themselves naturally to Reid's presentation. Reid's success here lies in the way he makes use of this and at the same time consolidates our sense of the historical peculiarity of his individuals by relating the tension between them to the socio-economic situation. John Campbell bides his time, believing in justice and in the wrath of the Lord (behavior generally in keeping with the policy of the colored group which, however uneasily, accommodated itself to the wishes and intentions of the legally white plantocracy); his son Davie breaks from this pattern to associate himself with the revolutionary cause of the blacks led by Deacon Bogle. The relationship Reid builds out of this is one of the triumphs of the novel, and it is a novelist's triumph of characterization. The author interests us in father and son as unique contending individuals even while allowing their conflict to contain within it the essence of the broader socioeconomic class struggle. Finally, Reid's intuition allows us to understand not that Davie is "thinking black" whatever that means, but that to conceive of the historical conflict as basically socioeconomic is to absorb the black versus white formula in a more socially integrative, realistic, and humane theoretical framework.

> Kenneth Ramchand. *An Introduction to the Study of West Indian Literature* (Sunbury-on-Thames: Thomas Nelson, 1976), pp. 34–36

[*The Leopard*] is a black Jamaican's imaginative rejection of anti-Mau Mau propaganda. In this novel the blacks are far from perfect, but they are fully human beings; they have a culture, history, morality, religion; they experience a wide range of human emotion. . . .

The emotional heart of the novel is the relationship between Nebu and Toto. Toto is not only physically deformed; psychologically and morally he is a cripple. He has never known a mother, and his father has been incredibly malicious. Toto's physical deformity has set him apart from other children, and he reveals his insecurity in overreaction: "'It is I who will not play with them, you black fool!' he shrieked at Nebu." A potential killer, he is deceitful, willing to feign piety or love according to the moment's need; like the cat's paw he is "the killer" that can seem "sheathed and innocuous." "The toto is false as a worm's skull." He is malignant, hateful at the core, unredeemed by the fact that he too can be made to suffer. In the American version of *The Leopard*, Nebu sums him up explicitly: "He hated so deeply that he would rather see his true father die than live himself." Toto is a sadist. He has enjoyed watching the house cat break the back of a mouse: "The boy shivered deliciously remembering. . . ."(But the memory prefigures his own death, struck down by a larger cat.) Toto enjoys the sight of pain. He is disappointed that Nebu is so impassive: "Suffering unmoved just like the dog long ago. And he was furious at Nebu for not exposing the pain., What thrill was there if it was not exposed?" He was happier with the stout Somali woman who used to lift him up and down stairs. "'We got along famously,'" he tells Nebu. "'She never reported me to my father but she often cried. Her face was not cut from lumber, as was the dog's and yours.'". . .

Many readers have felt an allegorical dimension in the novel and particularly in the Nebu-Toto relationship. "It would not be fanciful to see the half-Bwana as a West Indian, having two fathers, the dead European . . . and the dying African." "*The Leopard* is in its finest aspect a parable on the relationship between alienated West Indian and embarrassing African ancestry." "Toto is symbolic of all cultures produced by a meeting of civilizations, whether in the Caribbean, or in Africa or India." Each of these judgments can be supported in detail. But Reid is anxious that readers also retain an awareness of the novel in its broadest significance, as it examines the ebb and flow of love and hate, between groups, between individuals and within a single person. In exploring a specific situation, Reid wishes to make us feel some human truths not limited by space and time.

> Mervyn Morris. Introduction to V. S. Reid. *The Leopard* (London: Heinemann, 1980), pp. vii, xiii–xiv

*New Day*, beginning with Paul Bogle and the rebellion at Morant Bay in 1865 and ending with Garth Campbell and the promise of internal self-government in 1944, is a largely imaginative reconstruction of the social and historical realities which shaped the identity of modern Jamaica. And if there are disparities between Reid's account of the Morant Bay rebellion (and its repercussions) and the accounts of historians, then such differences are explicable in terms of the different demands of history and fiction, and of Reid's view of what it means to be a Jamaican. For the novel is above all a powerful assertion of a genuinely felt experience: it powerfully reflects a landscape of real feeling, and therefore is an important landmark in the development of the Caribbean sensibility. It is the first West Indian novel written entirely in dialect form and, appropriately enough, is experienced by the reader directly through the eyes of a young boy, Johnny Campbell. The entire

novel is concerned with the recollection of the aging John Campbell (on the eve of the New Constitution of 1944) of his childhood as the youngest member of the middle-class, near-white planter family out of which (as in the case of the Manley family) Jamaica's most famous leaders have come. But *New Day* is not mere "emotion recollected in tranquility": all the senses are evoked to present Johnny's childhood world as a *lived* experience. The use of natural imagery and metaphor, of a dialect-construction of strong, actively physical verbs, a vernacular syntax, contribute to the reality of the world of the novel.

> Michael Gilkes. *The West Indian Novel* (Boston: Twayne, 1981), pp. 117–18

*The Leopard* may be seen in two lights. In the first place it is the West Indian novel of imaginary Africa and the African personality *par excellence*. . . .

By opting to narrate much of the novel through a series of flashbacks seen from Nebu's point of view, Reid commits himself to projecting his central character's personality from the inside. In doing so he utilizes stock ideas of romanticism and primitivism. Like [Léopold Sédar] Senghor, and like people who do not come from any of the countries of Africa, Reid refers to Nebu as an "African," and he uses this term in free variation with the word "Negro." Although we learn in chapter twenty-three that Nebu is "an effigy . . . fixed forever in gray stones," and in chapter thirteen that he is "a blue black god squatting quiet beyond comprehension," he is saved for humanity (and as we shall see below, for the *msabu* Gibson) by the "rich warm blood [that] was pumping along the African's veins." Indeed, even when asleep he is in rhythmic communion with the earth-force: "His eyes were closed and only the gentle heaving of the blanket showed that life was thereabout. His sleep was in rhythm with the land, and if the rain had ceased or the wind had died, he would have instantly waked." Little wonder that when, armed at last with a rifle, he runs to the bush, "the bush was waiting and drew him in with a hundred green arms in heat for him." Our response to one whole side of Reid is a response to a highly sensuous prose in the service of decadence.

> Kenneth Ramchand. *The West Indian Novel and Its Background* (London: Heinemann, 1983), p. 154

Throughout his career, Vic Reid has continued to write with the goal of helping Jamaicans, particularly young Jamaicans, to know themselves through an awareness of their rich and heroic history. In keeping with this goal, he wrote three novels especially for young readers: *Sixty-Five*, which treats the Morant Bay uprising; *The Young Warriors*, which focuses upon the Maroons; and *Peter of Mount Ephraim*, which is based on the Daddy Samuel Sharpe slave rebellion of 1831. *The Jamaicans*, which treats the valiant struggles of the seventeenth-century Jamaican guerrilla Juan de Bolas to preserve the freedom and dignity of his people, was motivated by the novelist's recognition that Jamaicans needed to know this aspect of their history. . . .

*The Jamaicans* focuses upon a band of escaped slaves who, under the leadership of de Bolas, establish a mountain stronghold above Guanaboa Vale and reach a truce with the Spaniards, who in return for not attempting to dislodge them are spared raids upon their haciendas. These guerrillas, who derive their sustenance and protection from the land, are well-nigh invincible when fighting in the jungles. . . . The alien Europeans (the occupying Spanish and the imperialistic British) have no such relationship with the land, and thus, despite their advantage in terms of weapons and men, they find themselves at the mercy of the blacks whenever they venture into the jungles. When the black warriors enter battle, they are also inspired and emboldened by their glorious history. Old Miguel often reminds his countrymen of the valiant deeds of five generations of mountain soldiers who had been "from the earliest landings of their African ancestors, fighting their way from the coast into the high country, linking up with and leading the few remaining Arawak Indians [in battle against the colonizers]." . . .

[De] Bolas, recognizing that the English are winning the war, determines that the guerrillas' goal should be to win the respect of whichever European power prevails. Thus, to force the conquering English to recognize the desirability of negotiating with them, de Bolas and his men audaciously attack and destroy the powerful English stronghold at St. Jago (Spanish Town). They win an easy victory over the English, who are consequently forced to deal with them on their own terms. Pablo regards Juan de Bolas's new alliance with the English as traitorous, however, and thus the two brave warriors are thrust into mortal combat, thereby effecting what no European ever could—the destruction of the two bravest and most indestructible of the guerrilla heroes. Reid suggests that their deaths are symbolic for the future of Jamaica, for in their final embrace they become one: as Old Miguel observes, "if they see now, they will know they are one . . . they know they are neither African, nor Spanish, nor English, but of the Jamaican earth." . . .

Reid has recently completed two works: *Nanny-Town*, a novel based on Nanny, a priestess-warrior who led the Blue Mountain Maroons against the English and forced them into signing a treaty which gave her people autonomy, and *The Horses of the Morning*, a biography of [Norman Washington] Manley, who was clearly the prototype for Garth of *New Day*. He is presently working on a novel, *The Naked Buck*, which will be more contemporary in its setting and will focus on ordinary Jamaicans, including the Rastafarians, who though they may not be "necessarily heroic in the accepted term . . . [are] people who are determined to use their folk intellect, and their folk understanding, and their own historical precedence to find a place for them[selves] in this world."

Daryl Cumber Dance. *Fifty Caribbean Writers* (Westport, Connecticut: Greenwood Press, 1986), pp. 383–86

*Nanny-Town*, Reid's last published novel, celebrates the priestess-warrior, Jamaica's aboriginal queen mother, who marshaled the Blue Mountain Maroons and led them to political and material independence from the English. If this work breaks new ground, it is in the depiction of a woman as hero. (Reid's admiring portrait of Edna Manley in [*The Horses of the Morning*] is notable as well.)

In *Nanny-Town* there is a marked tension between the conviction that youth must learn to pull together as a group and that they should have the imagination and vigor to go their own ways, for the sake of progress. Even generically a conflict appears in Reid's work, since he writes historicized rather than historical fiction and writes fiction about a past time not for its own character nor even for its analogues with the present, but essentially for its argumentative, directive, developmental bearing on the future.

The teaching relationship that is pervasive in Reid's work expresses that aim, but it also clashes with his sense of the cyclic character of human time, embodied in his preoccupation with morning and evening. He was taken, he said, with "the commitment of the morning, and then the thinking-back of the evening," and his love of the countryside stemmed in part from his steady, palpable experience of the natural cycle. He felt that he enjoyed morning and evening, in the spirit of that cycle, "far more than most," and appropriately he expected to die "in the evening rather than morning." Yet he saw, throughout his work, how many things failed to square with one another. The untidy dynamism of events coming into conflict with the considered and desired ritual order of interpretation poured out of Reid's own perceptions and washed through the work he wrote about, and for, his country. Perhaps it is that split vision and split sympathy, caught in a nutshell in Nebu's existence as "half Kikuyu, half Masai," as well as half penitent and half avenger, that gives Reid's work its greatest interest and impact.

Michael G. Cooke. In Bernth Lindfors and Reinhard Sander, eds. *Dictionary of Literary Biography.* Volume 125: *Twentieth-Century Caribbean and Black African Writers, Second Series* (Detroit: Gale Research, 1993), pp. 259–60

The West Indian perspective and the sense of history that emerge in [*New Day*] can be traced to the emergence of a national consciousness during this period. For without doubt, the nationalist political agitation for change in the West Indies also facilitated an important historical awareness that became part of a growing sense of a West Indian people distinct from other groups. The idea was not really new in West Indian thought. As far back as the eighteenth century, Edward Long, Bryan Edwards, and other Jamaicans thought in these terms and vigorously argued the distinctiveness and separateness of a Jamaican society. But their idea of a free and separate Jamaica did not really envisage the freedom of slaves or even of ex-slaves as free and component members of a developing society. Reid's conception of a West Indian people was thus a radical advance over the view of the early Jamaicans and over the vision of Mittelholzer, whose [Kaywana] trilogy had affirmed the dominance and continuity of the planter class even though his novels had dealt with miscegenation and the mixing of bloods as a significant phenomenon in the history of the Caribbean.

Reid's historical perspective in *New Day* claims and dramatizes a solid place for the ex-slave as a component member of a developing society, and it is such a vision of West Indian development that informs his historical attitudes throughout the novel. It explains his major decision to link the Morant Bay rebellion with earlier slave rebellions and with the granting of a new Jamaican constitution, and the sense of continuity that these links imply also affirms his view of the ex-slave's progress and development in the West Indies. He had already taken for granted the facts of migration and displacement and was instead seeking to give the ex-slave roots in his new landscape. Thus the novel does not celebrate loss but rather dramatizes the emergence of a people. Its meticulously created world affirms the ex-slave's rootedness and identification with his new world and presents this world as important evidence of the adjustment of vision and consciousness which slaves had to make in a new landscape.

Reid focuses on postemancipation Jamaican society as the background for this development and proceeds to create the social and physical geography of that world. Because of the underlying sense of Jamaican identity, his picture of the economic barriers, social stratification, and color divisions is balanced with a pervading sense of a distinctly peasant sensibility borne out of an involvement with the soil and symbolized by a powerfully evoked landscape linked to the consciousness of the people. Soil, sea, rock, forest, scents and sea smells, plant and animal life—the world that physically surrounds Jamaica—make up the imagery and rhythms of Reid's created world, coloring the very idioms and modulations of people's speech. Such distinctive speech patterns are so central to the novel's historical perspective that they operate consistently throughout the work. . . .

This is the organic world that encloses, interacts with, and determines the nature and quality of people's lives in Reid's world. It is thus naturally the authentic background of the Morant Bay rebellion. For Reid perceived it not just as physical rage and violence but as an aspect of the self-awareness and sense of identity of the people. Throughout the excitement and agitation, the conch shells blow to signify the movement and modulations of people's feelings: the pain and helplessness, the wildness and anger that characterize the depth and confusion of feelings generated by economic and social frustration and underlying the entire process of Negro emergence in this region. Reid appears to accept at this time that the ex-slave has found a place in the existing order; that having become a Jamaican, he has also acquired a distinct sensibility and evolved a particular language, and his rebellion, rather than overthrow this order, should become a form of creative resistance within it.

From an uncomplicated relationship in *New Day* we move towards a deeper probing of the conscious and subconscious ramifications of the ancestor complex in *The Leopard*. The various nuances in the tortuous relationship between the half-white Toto and his African father, Nebu, explore both the stresses and possibilities of this relationship. The historical perspective and the mythical framework provide leeway for making inferences that cut across the immediate context of rebellion and violent confrontation which form the subject matter of his novel. The landscape of the novel is thus both the particularized landscape of Kenya and the imagined landscape of the New World. Its quality of beyondness and timelessness creates a context for those generalized truths explored in relation to the Mau Mau struggle and their repercussions in the birth of the mulatto.

The major characters in *The Leopard* are also equally subsumed in this myth: Nebu is at once *kikuyu* man, archetypal African, and West Indian slave ancestor, coping with both the paradoxes of rebellion and the burdens of fathering a mulatto. Toto becomes in the same context the archetypal mulatto: half white and half bwana, showing the peculiar psychic complexes that are part of the heritage of West Indian man. Placed in such a thematic relationship to the exploration of rebellion, freedom, and identity, the relationship between Nebu and Toto becomes one aspect of the human factor, the paradox which qualifies the clear-cut polarities of the violent racial confrontation. On one hand, hatred and violence may be justified, may even be natural and cleansing in a situation of oppression. Yet on the other, they may be qualified by considerations that put other meanings on the confrontation between oppressor and oppressed. When Nebu trails the unknown white man in the

bush, he believes he is pursuing an enemy, a murderer, a dangerous man-animal whom he would be justified in killing. Yet the white man he trails turns out to be no other than Bwana Gibson, the man he has wronged and whom his morality forbids him to harm, a man who also brings him face to face with "Toto," the human product and factor in the confrontation of violence with violence. . . .

In this treatment of the feelings involved in violent confrontations between oppressor and oppressed, Reid not only moves some way but actually deepens the complex forces and impulses inherent in what may appear as a straightforward opposition. In *New Day* such deeper nuances are subsumed in the demands of a specific time and space of history and in Reid's own anxiety to create an optimistic sense of progress by consolidating the span of a particular family. Within this consolidation the dilemmas of mulatto identities in an ex-slave and racially stratified society may be suggested in the ironical presentation of the older Campbell, but this presentation does not involve as deep a probing of their inner conflicts and subconscious ramifications as is possible in *The Leopard*. For though the general contexts of the meeting of races in a situation of conquest may be similar in the two novels; *New Day* is in a representational sense a "history," while *The Leopard* is essentially a dialectic that brings out the nuances and contradictory impulses inherent in the dual identities of Caribbean people and attempts to reconcile them. As a representation it invests more in imagination, inner dialogue, and psychic ramifications than in the classification and consolidation of things and people. The Kenyan landscape and the dilemmas of the novel are thus more archetypal than real, and characterization more a visualization of what could be possible than a consolidation of what is.

With such a framework Reid is able to suggest more possibilities than he could with the historical medium in *New Day*. He can present contrasting interpretations of the place of violence in the confrontation between oppression and liberation and can grapple more deeply with the moral and psychological challenges of the West Indian's relation to the white ancestor instead of accepting the mulatto condition as an unproblematic situation. The contrasting modes of representation in the two novels differentiate the varying possibilities not only of history and fiction but also within fiction itself, of fiction that consolidates and that which invests in dialectics and imaginative possibilities. In the West Indian context of redefinition, where perceptions of self, society, and history require revolutionary reassessments, fiction that mediates a given reality to produce other possible meanings can transcend fixed conceptions of Caribbean history. Both of Reid's novels attempt this transcendence by endowing given events with figurative meanings. But the different forms of their representations interestingly reveal the limits of the "historical" form and the expansive scope of the imaginary and the dialogic.

Nara Wilson-Tagoe. *Historical Thought and Literary Representation in West Indian Literature*. (Gainesville: University of Florida Press, 1998), pp. 39–51

BIBLIOGRAPHY

*New Day*, 1949; *The Leopard*, 1958; *Sixty-Five*, 1960; *The Young Warriors*, 1967; *Buildings in Jamaica*, 1970; *Peter of Mount Ephraim*, 1971; *The Jamaicans*, 1976; *Nanny-Town*, 1983; *The Horses of the Morning*, 1985

# RIVE, Richard (1931–1989)

## South Africa

[Richard Rive's play] *Make like Slaves* is one fortunate example of a credible creative expression of the longing for humane resolution along the lines of reconciliation. But Richard Rive's resolution demands a reciprocal, intelligent understanding among the embattled parties. The play offers a mordant dissection of a specialized category of the . . . racial situation and reveals . . . some thread of hope for the breakdown of racial barriers. He does this by the paradox of confronting reality; indeed at the end it is possible to surmise that he suggests the impossibility of resolution. But the integrity of his treatment is revealed by the fact that he inscribes over this failure the fact of individual shortcomings. We are left to feel that, given a more sensitive white woman or a less abrasive (and guilt-ridden) colored man, given indeed time for the continuation of a process which has begun in the play—the process of self-examination and the recovery of the ability to see individuals as opposed to groups—a small part of the battle would be won. The strength of Richard Rive's writing is that he does not exaggerate the pace of this process, nor does he anywhere suggest that, if a negative, external event were interjected into this evolutionary process it would not, at least for the duration of that event, halt or distort the tempo of the positive development. And even that awareness, hovering in the background, its pity, gives more value to the gains that have been made.

> Wole Soyinka. *Myth, Literature, and the African World* (Cambridge: Cambridge University Press, 1976), pp. 73–74

Much of Rive's work is strong stuff—the novel *Emergency* is a story of miscegenation set against the background of the Sharpeville episode—but his specialty, as in the stories in the present volume [*Selected Writings: Stories, Essays, Plays*], is the ironies inherent in racial relationships. In a Christmas story, for example, an Afrikaner hotelkeeper frets because his attempts to be broad-minded about the intellectual ability of "kaffirs" are costing him the business of white customers; meanwhile he gives refuge in his stable to an African couple and their infant and looks up for a "bright star" which is not there. Another story features an unresolved argument among "Coloreds" who cannot agree whether they should let a very dark friend into their soccer club. "Yes," says one, "but there are Coloreds and Coloreds." One of the essays describes a funny episode when Rive discovered that the waitress in an Oxford restaurant was giving him bad service not because of his race but because she thought he was an "Oxford snob." . . .

Rive knows that "liberal condescension" which overrates some black writers because they are black and the bigotry of holding a white writer "responsible for the wrongs of a regime he may very well oppose" are the two enemies of a true understanding of South African literature and experience. Though the stories and plays in this selection are probably of minor importance, the essays make the book a valuable South African document.

> Robert L. Berner. *World Literature Today*. 52, 2 (spring 1978), p. 331

The main factual history of South Africa which forms the background of Rive's *Emergency* is the Sharpeville shootings of Monday, March 21, 1960. . . .

The main action of the novel takes place in Cape Town and focuses on the days March 28 to March 30, 1960. Structurally, the novel is divided into three parts. Each part is headed by a day of that three-day period, and each section describes roughly the events of that day in Andrew Dreyer's life. Thus, the narrative moves in a linear progression over a three-day period. But the novel is not completely chronological. There are a series of flashbacks which reconstruct Dreyer's early life.

*Emergency* is not, of course, history: it is fiction. Rive's problem is therefore how to reconcile history with fiction in a work of fiction and yet retain historical credibility. The method he adopts is to treat each day in a separate section, narrate historical events, mention names of historical places and organizations. But he also treats the events imaginatively, introduces fictional characters, and goes beyond the mere narration of the historical events into the hearts and feelings of both the blacks and whites who live in South Africa.

> Okpure O. Obuke. In Eldred Durosimi Jones, ed. *African Literature Today*. 10 (1979), pp. 192–93

*Writing Black*, an "essentially selective autobiography," is a stream of countless little episodes spiced with brief, often devastating sketches of unforgettable characters. Rive's design rarely abandons us to the singular beauty or horror of the individual episode or sketch. Beyond the significance of each episode, each finely-wrought character sketch, we find the larger patterns of converging significance. What Rive says of his memory of Paris is true of the book as a whole: a kaleidoscope of impressions.

There is a principle of recurrence at work in the structure of this book. Through this principle we experience a gradual accumulation of knowledge often culminating in important revelations. We move from slum to slum, from District Six in Cape Town through "the grimy heart of old Naples" and London and Paris, to the "ugly, sprawling ghetto in East Austin," Texas. . . . These slums lie smoldering in the shadow of the elegant sections of town. Perhaps it is true, as one artist-critic says, that "all civilization is built on a series of thefts." . . .

Racism and prejudice loom large in the background of Rive's narrative, yet he gives us delightful humor where one would expect bitterness and anger. In the end, however, *Writing Black* succeeds as more than an entertaining account of one black artist's growth into stardom. It is a thoughtful and efficiently organized recollection of how one talented, determined and singularly fortunate creator achieves maturity in a world where so many other potential creators must die so young.

> Kofi Anyidoho. *World Literature Today*. 56, 3 (summer 1982), pp. 562–63

[Richard Rive's] first volume of stories, *African Songs*, appeared in 1963. Then, in the same year, came *Quartet*, his collection of stories by four writers, including himself. More recently he published his *Selected Writings*, which included seven short stories.

Although Rive says that he is a short-story writer rather than a novelist, he does bring some of the faults of the novel to his short fiction. There is a certain naiveté about his work which assumes that people will act in a certain way, and always do. The childlike character in "African Song," for example, comes to the city from the country without a pass and, as the police draw nearer to him at a meeting, has visions of love and joy while the people sing the Xhosa anthem. In "The Bench," Karlie is another innocent from the country who is so affected by hearing his first political speech about black being as good as white that he refuses to get up from a bench marked "whites only" and looks at the policeman who arrests him "with the arrogance of one who dared to sit on a 'European' bench." Rive's early promise of realism shown in "Willieboy" did not come to fruition.

We often know what the outcome of a story will be, which leads to lack of tension and makes the story appear contrived. One knows, for instance, that "No Room at Solitaire" will be an illustration of a South African version of the biblical tale. The story concerns a hotelkeeper, Fanie van der Merwe, who discusses Christianity with a customer and they wonder how one would "know Him when He comes again." A colored couple arrive at the back door and ask for shelter because the woman is about to give birth and is ill. The hotelkeeper refuses but the servant puts them up in the stable. When Fanie and his customer hear of this, the story inevitably ends.

> Ursula A. Barnett. *A Vision of Order* (London: Sinclair Browne, 1983), pp. 194–95

Richard Rive's *Emergency* is the only novel to fictionalize political events in Cape Town in 1960. . . . His novel moves back and forth in time and encompasses the childhood years of the main protagonist, Andrew Dreyer, in District Six. These childhood sections are the liveliest parts of the book and recall [Es'kia] Mphahlele's *Down Second Avenue* and Peter Abrahams's *Tell Freedom*. This section of the novel brings District Six to life in the best tradition of Alex La Guma, although Rive does not display La Guma's aptitude for reproducing dialect. There are autobiographical elements in the portrayal of Andrew Dreyer, who is darker than the rest of his family. As a result he is discriminated against. He distinguishes himself at school, proceeds to the University of Cape Town, where he graduates with a Bachelor of Arts degree, before taking up teaching. By following events in Andrew Dreyer's life, Rive takes the reader through some of the great [African National Congress] campaigns of the past such as the Defiance of Unjust Laws Campaign of 1952–1953, culminating in Sharpeville and Langa. The novel in its adult section contains lengthy political tracts, which are interesting in themselves but slow down action in the novel. . . .

*Emergency* remains Rive's major work in fiction. He stayed on in South Africa, after most of his contemporaries had left, and took more to literary criticism, after *Emergency* and his earlier collection of short stories, *African Songs*, had been banned.

> Mbulelo Vizikhungo Mzamane. *Ariel.* 16, 2 (April 1985), pp. 35–36

The novel ["*Buckingham Palace*," *District Six: A Novel of Cape Town*] is in three sections, dated 1955, 1960, and 1970, each of them introduced by an apparently autobiographical preface which relates Rive's own life as a resident of "Buckingham Palace" to

that of the people whose lives he describes. His method resembles the romantic realism of [John] Steinbeck's *Tortilla Flat*: episodic, funny, unafraid of sentiment, but always able to balance it with a sometimes harsh vision of the social reality in which the stories take place. Considering that no character is seen for sustained periods in the novel, many of them are remarkably vivid: Zoot September, whose real name is Milton because his aunt studied poetry for her teaching certificate and "never recovered from the experience"; the Jungle-Boys, violent Muslim rugby players who enforce moral behavior in the neighborhood; Pretty-Boy, who judges a beauty contest in terms of the contestants' "sweetmelons"; and Katzen, the Jewish landlord who will not obey the official order to evict his tenants because he was himself a victim of persecution in Nazi Germany.

Rive shows us that when a ruthless bureaucracy makes war on human values, its greatest ally is usually a perverted public opinion. When Katzen dies, his son Dieter (named after a friend murdered by the Nazis) sells his father's property to the local housing board—and thus helps evict the residents of District Six—with no apparent understanding of why his father believed that apartheid resembled the anti-Semitism from which he had suffered in Hitler's Germany.

> Robert L. Berner. *World Literature Today.* 61, 4 (autumn 1987), p. 673

Richard Rive, in *Emergency*, takes the South African struggle itself for his subject matter, and adopts a straightforward news report-type narrative framework for his presentation of the events of 1960 in Langa and Cape Town during the campaign against the pass laws (the "Sharpeville" of the south). Though Rive avoids the romanticizing mythmaking pitfalls of [Peter] Abrahams's fictional subject matter, nevertheless he carries over his predecessor's concentration on the psychological development of the individual hero. The historical and social context of the novel—the march on Cape Town on March 28, the strike on March 29, the protest march against the arrests on March 30, the declaration of the state of emergency, and the resumé of the history of the liberation struggle—all function as a back-cloth against which Andrew Dreyer can work back over his childhood and youth, search out his political orientation and identify his priorities.

Consequently there is no conflict between the traditional novel framework Rive adopts and the work's thematic significance. Where the problem (that is the *literary* problem) does arise is in the long didactic passages where Abe, Braam, and Andrew hold long discussions on the issues at stake. Not only does Rive fail to evolve a sufficiently realistic dialogue—his characters speaking like university essays rather than heated human beings—but the discussions are intrusive and insufficiently related to the action of the novel to be accepted naturally by the reader. Hence they impede rather than push forward the functioning of the text as an instrument of the struggle, focusing the reader's attention on one character and his ethical dilemma rather than on the progress of the struggle. The literary conventions [Rive] adopts, though they may inhibit the novel's contribution to the struggle, nevertheless nicely convey the liberal education of the writer and his own hesitations concerning total commitment.

> Jane Watts. *Black Writers from South Africa* (New York: St. Martin's Press, 1989), pp. 213–14

The novel *Buckingham Palace; District Six* travels back into the past in order to recall the defeats and the triumphs of a community that was broken up by the forces of apartheid in Cape Town. It is arguably Rive's best individual work. In it he manages, by means of chapters that focus closely on individual characters or small groups, to utilize one of his greatest talents: his ability as a short-story writer. The unity of the novel is achieved by means of the common destiny that faces all of his District Six characters. Rive later adapted the novel into a play, which was performed in Cape Town shortly after his death.

There is a great deal of potency in dealing with the destruction of a community such as District Six in the way that Rive does. He celebrates qualities in the district that are being ravaged by the policies of apartheid, such as trust between people of different backgrounds and the spirit of cooperation that exists among residents of a close-knit community. But there is no doubt whatsoever that the forces of violence ultimately have their way. District Six is finally destroyed by the authorities, and its residents are scattered. Yet out of this defeat a spirit of resistance has arisen, clearly illustrated in *Buckingham Palace; District Six*, which brings to fruition many of his earlier treatments of the subject. . . .

Rive is not the only author to have dealt with the destruction of a vibrant South African community. Fellow writers of his from the Cape, such as [James] Matthews and [Alex] La Guma, have also paid homage to the community that was District Six. Further afield, Can Themba, Bloke Modisane, and Miriam Tlali have written about the similar destruction of Sophiatown in Johannesburg. Rive's stories and novels about District Six share much with the work of these authors. In this respect his works form part of a central stream of South African writing that deals with communal responses to the institutionalized violence of the state. Rive, like many of his fellow writers, finds an answer to this violence in the communal strength of the people in places such as District Six.

Rive's works of the 1980s indicate that there was little falling off in his powers as a writer. Indeed, after the long gap since his first works of fiction in the 1950s and early 1960s, there had been a renewal of creative energy in his more recent work. His death deprives South Africa of one of its most urbane writers.

Martin Trump. In Bernth Lindfors and Reinhard Sander, eds. *Dictionary of Literary Biography*. Volume 125: *Twentieth-Century Caribbean and Black African Writers, Second Series* (Detroit: Gale Research, 1993), p. 263

Rive's brief radio play [*Make like Slaves*, 1971] features two voices, referred to in the script as "He" and "She." They had met en route to Cape Town from London. Now, months later, she comes to his apartment to ask for help. She has been trying to help the black people of South Africa by organizing a group of them into a theatrical troupe and having them perform a play that depicts, in three acts, the African's story. . . .

The black players she has assembled, however, are not cooperating with her. They are always late; they seem to resent either her or the script or both.

She turns to He because, as a colored South African, he might be able to serve as an intermediary between white and black. Being "brown," he might—she naively assumes—be able to understand the two other colors:

You're in the middle so to speak. Being brown you can speak to them and to me. They'll understand. I'll understand. They'll listen to you.

As the play progresses, however, we learn that the colored man she has turned to knows very little about the black South African people. . . .

He tries to blame his isolation on the system, but the audience realizes that it is more a reflection of his personal decision not to get involved. However, one cannot help but interpret Rive's "he" as a commentary on the many South African coloreds who have not found common cause with their black brethren. This comment on South Africa's colored population, however, is secondary in the play to its portrayal of white ignorance.

"She" comes across as sincere: she wants to help the oppressed black people. She cannot, however, come to terms with cultural differences. She is obsessed with punctuality. Again and again, she brings up the fact that the blacks do not arrive for practice on time. "Eight o'clock is eight o'clock in anybody's language," she says. She is blindly unaware that different cultures have different attitudes toward time and that her insistence that the blacks be punctual is her imposition of her European culture (a neurotic version of it) on them.

She also cannot understand why the blacks in her theatre company might dislike the play—and her. Rather than allowing the players to develop the script, she imposes it on them. Not only has she denied them freedom, but she has interpreted their history for them, repeating the mistakes of many colonial and post-colonial historians of Africa. Her doing this for them reflects condescension on her part. These players, unlike *real* actors and actresses, she tells us, cannot do just anything, but this play is "the type of thing they can do" because it's "the type of thing they can feel." Slavery is, she tells us, "part of their experience, a part out of their past." When "He" suggests that the players might resent the reenactment "being done at the whim of some foreigners," she misses his point entirely and says, "They might or might not enjoy it, but they can certainly do it . . . and with conviction". . . .

"She" starts talking about "sides"; "She" uses the loaded phrase "You people." The racism that is within her, despite her good intentions in coming to South Africa, surfaces. But "She" learns little from her outburst, for when "She" and "He" arrive at the troupe's practice, she refers to the lack of punctuality of most of its members sarcastically and she tells the players to practice the third act and "to make like slaves." Early in the play she hears the *Missa Luba* in the colored man's apartment. Impressed by the music but ignorant of what it is, she appropriates it as the accompaniment to the third act's portrayal of work on the plantations in the New World. In so doing, she creates an incongruous, ironic picture to conclude the play with. The irony, of course, rebounds on her and reveals the extent to which she doesn't "get it." She doesn't "get" the *Missa Luba* or his brief discussion of Countee Cullen or his explosion of her reliance on racial or national stereotypes: she remains naively oblivious to much of what the play reveals. Most importantly, she doesn't "get" that she is, not very far beneath her superficial liberalism, quite racist.

Theodore F. Sheckels. *The Lion on the Freeway: A Thematic Introduction to Contemporary South African Literature in English* (New York: Peter Long, 1996), pp. 145–48

BIBLIOGRAPHY
*African Songs*, 1963; *Emergency*, 1964; *Make like Slaves*, 1973; *Selected Writings: Stories, Essays, Plays*, 1977; *Writing Black*, 1981; *Advance, Retreat*, 1983; *Buckingham Palace, District Six*; *Emergency Continued*, 1990

# ROBERT, Shaaban (1909–1962)

## Tanzania

[Shaaban Robert] was the first assimilated Swahili African writer to write in a variety of genres, some from English models, in order that he should be read and not sung. He wrote to be published by English publishers. He was a master of traditional techniques. Like the earlier Swahili writers, he was very conservative, highly respected, and a guardian of conventional Islamic values, all factors that some might consider tend to mitigate against good creative writing. He was naturally averse to innovation in the conduct of society in general and of individuals in particular. Like so many other African writers in the vernacular, he liked to preach or sermonize. In the Koran the meaning of the Arabic word used for ''heresy'' is ''innovation.'' Yet in a tentative way Shaaban Robert was a literary innovator.

His lifestyle and experience, most of all his religion, made him less of an innovator than the short story writers of the mid-1960s who wrote in vernacular papers, such as *Mwafrika* and *Tazama*, and who dealt only with the realistic seamier side of life in which religion is rejected or ignored. Shaaban Robert is the Swahili John Bunyan, whose characters often have names indicative of their moral character. At times the motives of his heroes are too good to be true, like the young clerk, Mr. Best Human Nature (Bw. Utubora), who is motivated to sacrifice a salary of unbelievable proportions in Zanzibar to go ''back on the land'' as a hired gardener on the mainland. In modern Tanzania, where the vast majority have never been off the land, ''the simple life'' is more often equated with a well-paid office job. But the cultivation of the soil is encouraged not only by the government but in Swahili literature, by other Muslim Africans, as the duty of the good citizen. The important thing for Shaaban Robert was to give his hero a motive that was not only relevant to the country's needs but also morally irreproachable. . . .

It can be said that the function of the writer in any society is to bring the contemporary mind to a new elevation of ideas and spirit, but the contemporary mind of Shaaban Robert's Africa was conditioned almost entirely by its African experience of comparative deep poverty in things material and intellectual. This is no criticism of the African way of life, but only a reminder that even Shaaban Robert shared the experience of his contemporaries. . . .

Shaaban Robert's writings are realistic only in the sense that they reflect a real situation in which the writer is not so far ahead of his readers as to lose them altogether. He was writing not for the educated elite but for people like himself who had received no higher education. This is one of the reasons for his great popularity in Tanzania, a country committed to the principles of *Ujamaa* or— for want of a better term in English—African socialism, by which any kind of intellectual capitalism unrelated to the life of the people is regarded as a hindrance to national development. Shaaban's desire to serve his people is in line not only with the political ideals

of his country but also with the public preference for a writer who stays close to what in general people can understand.

> Lyndon Harries. *Review of National Literatures*. 2, 2 (fall 1971), pp. 45–46, 48

[Robert] is incomparable in the sense that there is no other Swahili writer with whom he can be compared for the range of his literary performance. His poetry can be compared with that of his contemporaries like Amri Abedi or [Mathias E.] Mnyampala, and his stories stand comparison with other Swahili stories, but he is alone in having also experimented in essay writing, allegory, prose-paraphrase of his own poetry, and autobiography. Comparison in a particular genre with works from another culture in some other language would no doubt place Shaaban at a disadvantage, but such a comparison would have to allow for the disadvantages Shaaban suffered from the literary poverty of his own environment.

He was an innovator who used the limited materials at his disposal in order to develop Swahili literature on a wider scale. His own limited education, which he freely acknowledged, kept him more firmly rooted in tradition than an innovator can afford to be. But he made a start in the direction that Swahili literature could be expected to go. The remarkable fact is that, in spite of the enhanced status of Swahili as the national language of Tanzania since independence, there has been practically no further advance in the literary situation from what it was when Shaaban left it. In spite of the high regard in which he is held, no Swahili writers have appeared to continue from where he left off. His ideal of a national literature representing the life and thought of the whole country, and not only of the Swahili coast, is still only a dream.

> Lyndon Harries. *Presence Africaine*. 93 (1975), pp. 198–99

Shaaban Robert's first wife, whose name was Amina, certainly inspired the poet with profound love which he expressed in a poem, ''Amina,'' after she died. In Swahili literature most elegies were written for great men such as Mbaraka Ali Hinway . . . and Shaaban Robert himself. . . . Amina was perhaps the first woman to be so honored in Swahili literature. The poem was written presumably in the late 1940s. Although students of Western literature will find the poem an expression of restrained conventional poetic feelings, yet it is, by the standards of Swahili poetry and its tradition, an innovation in creative emotion, stronger than any others, less rigid and almost daring in its expressiveness. But Swahili poetry is never purely personal. Invariably the author has to extend his feelings to include those of his fellow townsmen, indeed of all the Swahili people. He speaks for the community and so he has to generalize his ideas. Thus the poem becomes a praise-song on marriage in general, rather than a personal lament on the end of his marriage. We should not see this as a loss of personal contact between the poet and his readers, who—if Western—would be interested in the unique expression of his individual agony, to find in it the reflection of their own sorrows. On the contrary, the Swahili poets elevate their own grief by lifting it above their narrow personal anxieties and raising it to the status of a mourning shared by all their fellow men, then making it into a lesson for all men. ''In spite of this grief, marriage is still more than worth all the troubles I have seen.'' In this way, with religious devotion, grief is overcome and sublimated into a blessing for all members of the community. The traditional phrases and proverbs are already the shared property of the community, who expect to reap spiritual benefit from such proverbs, old and new, which are often repeated long after the poet, who is remembered as the author, has died. The audience of a Swahili poet still expects these variations on traditional themes. . . .

Shaaban Robert was the last poet—and one of the most famous—to write quatrains in Swahili. He translated the quatrains of Omar Khayyam into Swahili verse, but not directly. He used as intermediary the famous version by Edward Fitzgerald in English verse. In many respects, however, Shaaban has rendered the flavor of Omar Khayyam's oriental moods better than Fitzgerald; not because he knew Persian, but because he was a Muslim himself, and understood Omar better than Fitzgerald, the nineteenth-century Romanticist, ever could have. . . .

Shaaban Robert wrote several prose works, the finest of which [is] his autobiography *Maisha Yanga*. . . . His other prose works are mainly of an allegorical character, strongly oriental in setting and in flavor, like *Kufikirika (The Conceivable World)*. They contain so many profound—if not moralistic—thoughts, that we might prefer to call them perhaps "philosophical tales." Two of his works, *Insha na Mashairi (Compositions and Poems)*, and *Masomo yenye Adili (Noble Lessons* or perhaps *Righteous Readings)*, contain a majority of poems interspersed with fables. He writes a moral lesson (*adili*) at the end of each of these prose as well as poetry passages. Here are some examples. "Our joys and misfortunes are mysteries in this world." "All our prosperity is attained by our actions." "Character is everything; a fine character is needed for scholarship, upbringing, independence and good manners." "A multitude of little people is better than the greatness of one."

> Jan Knappert. *Four Centuries of Swahili Verse: A Literary History and Anthology* (London: Heinemann, 1979), pp. 267–68, 270, 274

The decisive figure in the modernizing process that affected Swahili literature was Shaaban Robert from the Tanga area in Northern Tanganyika. Though he started writing poetry in the 1930s, his first volume, *Pambo la lugha*, did not appear until 1948, when it was issued in the "Bantu Treasury" series published in Johannesburg. This was the first of many works in prose and verse which made him, in the words of Wilfred Whiteley, "the most notable literary figure to have appeared on the Swahili scene in this century." Because of his exceptional position as a professional man of letters, because of the abundance and diversity of his literary output, and because of his deep knowledge and subtle handling of the Swahili language, he enjoys an exalted reputation among Tanzanian literates and Swahili scholars. He has even been called "the Shakespeare of Africa."

[Robert's] parents both belonged to the Yao tribe of present-day Malawi, but he himself was born on the northern coast of Tanganyika, and was obviously an intellectual product of Swahili culture. Because of this dual situation, he was very conscious of the desirability of striving for the cultural unification of the whole of East Africa through the spreading of the Swahili language, instead of limiting his concern, as classical Swahili writers had done, to the Swahili community in a narrow sense. . . .

The most important contribution of Shaaban to the modernization of Swahili literature is no doubt his addiction to prose writing.

His first composition in this respect was probably the first part of his autobiography, *Maisha Yangu* . . . which won first prize in the 1936 East African Literary Competition, but did not reach print until 1949. The second part, entitled *Baada ya Miaka Hamsini* . . . was completed in 1960 and published in 1966. . . .

One of [Robert's] earliest prose stories *Kufikirika* (completed by 1946, printed 1967), is probably the first Swahili work that attempts to face the question raised by the intrusion of foreign innovation in a highly conservative state. The title is the name of an imaginary kingdom, whose rulers have to decide whether to follow their ancestral customs or to call upon the help of modern science, in this case medicine. The action is dominated by a mysterious character who appears in the guise of a soothsayer, a progressive teacher, and a wise peasant. Shaaban's attitude is that the law exists only for man's welfare: it should not be observed to the point of endangering his very survival.

*Kusadikika, chi iliyo angani* narrates the trial of a young man who is indicted for advocating the introduction of legal studies in the imaginary country of Kusadikika. In order to defend his views against the impressive public prosecutor, a die-hard reactionary bent on preserving the vested interests of the ruling hierarchy, he tells a parable about ministers of state sent to various foreign countries, whose reports, on their return, were completely ignored by the rulers. The very title shows that this is a companion piece to the earlier story. Shaaban has now enlarged his perspective: where modern medicine was the only paradigm of modernity, he now takes in wider problems of intellectual, social, and economic advance. As the accused is described as a commoner, and as the public prosecutor makes the point that the greatness of the kingdom has been due to people of nobler origins, there is an element of social criticism which may well refer, albeit ambiguously, to the aristocratic structure of Swahili society or to the inequality in colonial society.

> Albert S. Gérard. *African Language Literatures: An Introduction to the Literary History of Sub-Saharan Africa* (Washington, D.C.: Three Continents Press, 1981), pp. 137, 139–40

*Kusadikika* is a story set in colonial Tanganyika disguised as a country floating somewhere in the sky. With this fantastic setting, Shaaban Robert managed so successfully to fool Her Royal Majesty's representatives in the then Tanganyika Territory that they allowed the novel to be circulated in the country.

*Kusadikika* tells the story of a people who have been turned into robots. They believe whatever their rulers tell them. Several Kusadikikans visit other planets, and when they come back to Kusadikika with the knowledge that could help change people's lives, they are suppressed and jailed by the oppressive aristocratic government in Kusadikika. Karama (Spiritual Talent) is one of the *Wajumbe* who have visited those other planets and who have witnessed so much development in those other countries—development which he would like to see taking place in Kusadikika. He decides to lead his people's struggle by defending his case in court. His major opponent is the Prime Minister of Kusadikika—Majivuno (Pride) who opposes everything that Karama says. Finally, however, Karama manages—through a long lecture in court—to convince the King about the truth behind the *Wajumbe's* demands. Consequently all the imprisoned *Wajumbe*—Buruhani (A Gift of God),

Fadhili (Mercy), Kabuli (Acceptance), Auni (Help), Ridhaa (Gracious Thanksgiving), and Amini (Trust)—are set free; and the development plans are carried out by the *Wajumbe*. . . .

[One] must take into account the fact that *Kusadikika* belongs to the protest tradition in Swahili literature. It is, basically, about liberation struggle. Shaaban Robert lived and wrote at a time when contradictions between colonial governments and the colonized people in Africa were rapidly sharpening. These struggles were not without leaders, and the leaders are represented in the novel by Karama and the other political detainees—the *Wajumbe*.

> F.E.M.K. Senkoro. In David F. Dorsey, Phanuel A. Egejuru, and Stephen H. Arnold, eds. *Design and Intent in African Literature* (Washington, D.C.: Three Continents Press, 1982), p. 65

Even though the writer completed it in 1946, [*Kufikirika*] did not appear until 1967, five years after [Shaaban Robert's] death, thanks to the cultural leadership of Tanzania that had by then won its independence. It can be assumed though that in the fifteen to sixteen years of his life between then and his death he must have reworked it more than once, polishing, improving, altering, and perfecting it. This can be seen from the exceptionally smooth flow of the writing, the almost unbroken line of the action as well as from a few features that could only have been introduced into the text under the influence of the ideals in the year following liberation.

*Kufikirika* (like *Kusadikika*) is also an imaginary land. In it, the idealized model of the traditional Swahili society (in some cases the East African society in the broader sense) is confronted with a confused, transitional path of development or one that appears from the outset to lead nowhere. Its figures in many respects recall the heroes of folk tales: their characteristics are unchanging, striking, and almost extreme. His heroes wrestle with (moral) black and white, good and bad, sober certainty and unthinking confusion. In the text itself the influence of the classic Swahili epic can be felt almost palpably in the linguistic means repeatedly used by the writer. . . .

Its origin can be placed in the period when the writer gradually moved away from poetry—although he never gave up poetry-writing completely—and rather chose prose forms to express his increasingly more complex thoughts that could no longer be contained within the framework of the traditional lyric and epic.

However, as a result the static picture of society formulated in the work and regarded as ideal, in the final analysis is made up of local semifeudal and partly free trading elements that cannot be linked to a concrete period of time, idealizing a newer and humanized combination of these elements. The essence of this is concern for people, in cases even in spite of their demands or even their will. As regards its extreme solutions, all this could even be described as the "gentle terror of wisdom and goodness." In certain respects this social ideal overlaps the Tanzanian social reality of one and a half to two decades later. Having acquired greater practical, political, and tactical experiences, these ideas can also be found in the social and political superstructure of *ujamaa socialism* that is sometimes also colored by naive aspirations and ideas. . . .

In his later works his notions of the workings of the social mechanisms acquire a more concrete and sounder form. . . .

[*Utobora mkulima* and *Siku ya watenzi wote*] are his last major works on an epic scale, written at the height of his creative powers. The literary policy background to the fate of these works has not yet been fully clarified, but it is certainly worth reflecting on the fact that they could not appear until six and seven years respectively after the death of Shaaban Robert. . . .

The novel *Siku ya watenzi wote* . . . contains perhaps the most pure essence of the author's idealized theory of society. In it, educated and simple people, lost and floundering in the dead end of a foreign civilization imposed on the local population from outside, work out and find for themselves a way out of their wretched situation holding out little hope. Ayabu, the hero of the novel, who quite clearly appears as the author's alter ego, is the well-intentioned and wise teacher of the people who also enjoys a certain prestige. It is he who, relying on the active assistance, or at least the passive goodwill of those who are weaker and less able to act than he is, organizes material and moral assistance for the unfortunates who have fallen victim to the colorful and tempting environment which holds many dangerous traps for them and is actually cruelly alienated. Sparing neither his material resources nor his material property, he goes almost to the limit of self-sacrifice to provide bread and work for the misfortunate with the help of his organization based on charity.

In the meantime dangerous pitfalls and promising possibilities alternate rhapsodically in his own life. The hero has to struggle with the hundred-headed hydra of alienating and harsh social reality in the field of his own chosen profession, while at the same time the fearful traps of the despised external world increasingly force their way into his private life too. He comes to the realization that the possibility for the individual's well-being cannot float in some kind of ethereal heights above the traps and mires of the surrounding world. He must free himself of all trace of the selfishness that inevitably lurks inside him before he can finally win his love and human happiness. This time the final outcome in Shaaban Robert's novel is idyllic; the good man earns his well-deserved reward, but the path to improvement and prosperity is not closed irrevocably to the bad.

> Géza Füssy Nagy. *Neohelicon*. 16, 2 (1989), pp. 51–55

BIBLIOGRAPHY
*Pambo la lugha* (Beauty of the Language), 1948; *Maisha Yangu* (My Life), 1949; *Kusadikika, chi iliyo angani* (Kusadikika, a Country of Believers), 1951; *Insha na Mashairi* (Compositions and Poems), 1959; *Masomo yenye Adili* (Noble Lessons), 1959; *Baada ya Miaka Hamsini* (After Fifty Years), 1966; *Kufikirika*, 1967; *Siku ya watenzi wote* (The Day of All Workers), 1968; *Utobora mkulima* (Utubora the Farmer), 1968

# ROTIMI, Ola (1938– )
## Nigeria

[*The Gods Are Not to Blame*] is a reworking of *Oedipus Rex* in Yoruba terms, but it assumes an identity of its own, and is a remarkable piece of theater. The classic tale is given vivid life by its transposition to Africa, and some new dimensions. It is noticeable, for instance, that [Ola] Rotimi's play contains much humor—but it is not humor that detracts from the awfulness of the theme. Rather, in the tragicomic method of [Sean] O'Casey, Rotimi is able to maintain the integrity of the subject while exploring a wide range of human emotions and reactions. Rotimi's Oedipus is King Odewale, and Queen Ojuola his mother/wife. At the start of the play the Narrator introduces the Priest of Ifa to divine the future of the newborn son of Queen Ojuola and King Adetusa. . . . The priest gives the dreadful message of the gods: "This boy, he will kill his own father and then marry his own mother!". . . . From the mimed and ritualized opening, the play develops into immediate action with the inexorable working out of fate seen in ironic contrast to the strutting self-confidence of mortals. One of the most successful creations of this play is the character of Alaka, the old man who brings the supposedly good news of the death of Odewale's "parents" to him, and unwittingly reveals the horrific truth. Alaka is half clown, half philosopher, a man of rural wisdom, who reveals the true nature of the King's parenthood through a performance that is tantalizingly slow, warm with his goodness and innocence, enlivened by his country wit and manners, and finally exploded by his words. African theater accommodates this kind of character with particular understanding and response. Dramatically his presence is extraordinary, and his creation a triumph of theatrical craftsmanship and instinct.

> Martin Banham and Clive Wake. *African Theatre Today* (London: Pitman, 1976), pp. 43–44

In *Kurunmi* Rotimi achieves the twin objectives that he aims at in his first play [*The Gods Are Not to Blame*]. The career of Kurunmi (even as sketched in the historical note that accompanies the play) provides very suitable material for a tragic hero along the lines Rotimi subscribes to. Kurunmi is a man fighting a cause which he believes is just; he fails because he makes a fatal error of judgment but also because he is pitched against forces that he alone cannot withstand. Also, the historical background of a constitutional deadlock, unsuccessful peace moves, and eventual war is easily recognizable as a parallel to the Nigerian Civil War, and so the sociopolitical objective he intends in his first play comes out more clearly here. Altogether, Rotimi has been careful not to divert attention from the main concern of the play. The series of battles that take place in act three are all important as aspects of the historical event, but the playwright's intention is not to recount the facts of history. Rather, he is interested in the study of man caught up in a particular situation. The battles are important because they help to focus attention on Kurunmi's changing fortunes before the final blow that spells his doom. Rotimi therefore avoids needless details. Each scene in which there is an encounter between the armies of Ijaiye and Ibadan carries the action of the play a step forward. Great economy is effected through the diary records of the Manns (scenes five and nine), and the defeat of the combined army of Egba and Ijaiye marks the climax of the action and the downfall of Kurunmi.

Just as he has been careful in the selection of his material, Rotimi also pays greater attention to the appropriateness of language to the action which he depicts. There are still instances when the language provokes laughter, but these are moments calculated to effect comic interludes. Besides, such humor only serves to accentuate the tragic action, especially as most of the scorn comes ironically from Kurunmi himself and is directed at his enemies. . . . But quite apart from such instances Rotimi now takes greater pains to preserve the profundity of the traditional literary types he renders in English.

> Akanji Nasiru. In Kolawole Ogunbesan, ed. *New West African Literature* (London: Heinemann, 1979), pp. 26–27

Rotimi's reputation was established by *The Gods Are Not to Blame*, a successful adaptation of the Oedipus legend which is innovative both on the level of the medium and in the development of the African theatre. It is his commitment to his audience which decided the distinctive character of the medium in this play. His intention was to reach a very wide, many-layered audience, hence his attempt to create a new idiom, a kind of language close to the rhythms and speech patterns of his native language but not deviating too radically from standard English and adequate to carry the weight of his themes. It is in these two areas—language and the African theater—as much as in the themes themselves that his significance as a new talent depends. . . .

In *Our Husband Has Gone Mad Again*, Rotimi has written a delightful, lighthearted satirical comedy which is more hilarious and farcical than satirical. The ingredients in this comedy are: an extravagant political figure rather than politics itself; the comic and absurd situations in a polygamous marriage with an attendant cultural conflict; the crucial but disruptive influence of women in politics; and well-known and accepted attitudes to politics, power, social prestige and society.

> Alex C. Johnson. In Eldred Durosimi Jones, ed. *African Literature Today*. 12 (1982), pp. 137–38

*Ovonramwen [Nogbaisi]* is another play which is based on nineteenth-century events in Nigeria. It portrays the tragic consequences of the clash between the powerful Oba of Benin, Ovonramwen Nogbaisi, and the British colonialists who were scheming to control the source of trade. In theatrical terms Rotimi is doing what modern Nigerian historians such as Onwuka Dike and Obaro Ikime are doing: reconstructing African history, correcting false views of the clash between African nations and the colonists. In *Ovonramwen* Rotimi shows the fall of Benin as an effect of the British scheme to control African nations for economic reasons, not just of the Benin monarch's tyrannical rule. Phillips, the representative of the queen of England, affirms that they must disregard Benin tradition and enter Benin during the Ague festival, because "the conduct of trade in the colonies demands direct contact with the interior that produces the goods." Although the British intrusion into Benin plays an important role in directing the dramatic action toward its catastrophic end, the contradictions within the Benin kingdom aid the foreign element. . . .

*If . . . : A Tragedy of the Ruled* also reveals Rotimi's personality and interest in contemporary history. His concern for the oppressed receives theatrical attention here, as the play exposes the exploitation of the people by the rich and powerful men of society. His concern for the masses and his insight into a possible means of solving that problem show in his recognition of group cohesion and franchise as viable tools that can be used for the liberation of the oppressed. However, the people fail to use this power to effect good leadership, and this leads to the tragic conclusion of the play. Thus, *If* is sociopolitical and ends on a pessimistic note, but through a powerful instrument of mass communication (theater) Rotimi succeeds in sensitizing the consciousness of the people. The fact that the dramatic personages fail to utilize their power properly served as a warning to the original audience, which was preparing for general elections at the time the play was first produced. The play therefore seemed to foreshadow the political reality of contemporary elections and politics in Nigeria and sounded a warning to the electorate.

In *If*, Rotimi once again shows his love for music, since songs and chants are dynamically integral to the action. For example, the contemporary music of Sunny Okosun, ''Fire in Soweto,'' is not just a melodious element used for entertainment. The message of the music underlines Rotimi's intention of using the South African example to sensitize the audience to their own plight in Nigeria. In addition, the music is used as a basis for awakening the consciousness of the audience through the poignant dialogue between the then-ignorant Betty and the politically conscious Hamidu. Similarly, the children's song, which follows the rhythm of a religious catechism chanted by rote, contains a message which is directly relevant to them as future leaders of the nation. . . . In this way music becomes a dramatic technique that not only entertains but also serves a political purpose, for it rouses the political consciousness of the people at various levels.

It is in Rotimi's unpublished play, *Hopes of the Living Dead*, that the oppressed get what they failed to achieve in *If*, and it shows a new angle to Rotimi's historical plays. The issue of political struggle resurfaces here in the plight of the lepers and their struggle for redemption from their oppressors. As with *Kurunmi* and *Ovonramwen*, the source of *Hopes* is historical, in this case the experience of lepers in Port Harcourt in the late 1920s and early 1930s. Rotimi's treatment of the subject is serious; even though the play uses a good deal of music and humor, these do not diffuse the pathos of the action. The work does deviate, however, from the usual tragic denouement of Rotimi's plays, as the oppressed lepers triumph and the play concludes on a merely pessimistic note. . . .

Another work that uses the comic mode is *Holding Talks*, an absurdist play which employs humorous and absurd situations to explore the weariness and dissatisfaction resulting from inaction. Rotimi shows his impatience with the contemporary attitude toward events, demanding instant action. He admits that the play is a ''reaction to a growing preference of our Age for talking even in the face of situations demanding action and obvious solutions.'' A barber is hungry. Nothing is done. He collapses and still nothing is done. Instead, his appalling situation becomes the subject of discussions and press photographs, at the end of which nothing has changed for him, as he continues to lie there naked. The plot consists of many strange incidents which appear unreal, illogical, and funny, yet on close appraisal we realize that they parody our very existence. For example, the policewoman engages in an argument with Man over the procedure for investigative interrogation instead of taking the dying or dead man to the hospital. Man and Apprentice also waste a lot of time arguing about whether the barber just collapsed or is actually dead. The illogicality of the situation and the triviality of the arguments evoke bitter laughter. It

is in this seeming illogicality that the play's historical perspective can be gleaned, for the actions parody contemporary life's penchant for discourse and the application of bureaucratic red tape even when situations demand instant action.

Chinyere G. Okafor. *World Literature Today.* 64, 1 (winter 1990), pp. 26–27

*Hopes of the Living Dead* returns to one feature of the earlier plays in that it takes a historical incident as its inspiration, but with a firm allegorical intent, and with a sophistication of the dramaturgical experiments we have [seen] in *If*. The play is based on the life of Ikoli Harcourt Whyte. Harcourt Whyte has an enduring reputation as a composer of choral music, but the play is about Harcourt Whyte the leper. Together with forty other lepers Harcourt Whyte was, in 1924, being treated in Port Harcourt General Hospital in an experimental program initiated by a Scottish doctor, Dr. Fergusson. On his departure the experiment was discontinued and the colonial authorities attempted to disperse the lepers without any hope of continuing treatment. The lepers were led in their resistance to this move by Harcourt Whyte, despite attempts to bribe him away from their struggle by the offer of special privileges. He demanded from his fellow patients self-reliance and self-help; and the triumphant finale of the play is the establishment of the Uzuakoli Leper Settlement where the people could live in security, work for themselves, and receive appropriate treatment. The vulnerability amongst the patients that the authorities hoped to exploit was the diversity in their backgrounds and languages. The unity that Harcourt Whyte demanded meant surmounting the ignorance and prejudice created by these divisions. The parallel with the political unity of present-day Nigeria is clear.

There are many striking features about the play. The story is a genuinely exciting and moving one, made all the more effective by the fact that it is essentially true. Its pertinence in terms of today's ''sick'' society makes it constantly immediate and relevant, and its underlying message is instantly clear to its audience. Theatrically the play is energized by the cliffhanging action and by the skill of Rotimi's character-drawing, and is enriched not only by splendid moments of physical farce and verbal comedy but also by Harcourt Whyte's songs and music. A cast of about thirty performers plus singers indicates the scale of the production, and another scale of significance is that of the languages used. Rotimi observes that over fifteen languages are employed in the play. . . .

Niyi Osundare, reviewing the production of the play at Ibadan University (and importantly drawing our attention to the fact that in *Hopes of the Living Dead* we have for the first time in a Rotimi play a woman in a dominant position of community leadership in the character of Harcourt Whyte's co-leader Hannah), describes the language as ''a vehicle for [the play's] thematic thrust. So many times the stage turns into a cacophony of tribes as each character shouts his desperation in his own language. At such moments, tension takes possession and communal unity receives a savage punch. It is part of the abiding optimism of the play, however, that 'though tribe and tongue may differ,' a common problem steers the people towards a unified goal.''. . .

The play is a lesson in resourcefulness, accepting no obstacle as too great to be overcome. Typical of this is a scene where one inmate, an ex-army corporal, repulses efforts by the police to eject the patients from their ward. Frustrated at not being able to pick up a police rifle that he has knocked from its owner's grasp because he has no fingers on his hands to grip it with, he sees his leprous mutilation as his weapon and advances upon the police with his arms extended, causing them to flee in panic. The scene is moving, triumphant, and farcical, all at the same time.

> Martin Banham. *Modern Drama.* 33, 1 (March 1990), pp. 74–76, 79

BIBLIOGRAPHY

*The Gods Are Not to Blame*, 1971; *Kurunmi*, 1971; *Ovonramwen Nogbaisi*, 1974; *Our Husband Has Gone Mad Again*, 1977; *Holding Talks*, 1979; *If . . . : A Tragedy of the Ruled*, 1983; *Statements toward August 83*, 1983; *Hopes of the Living Dead*, 1988; *African Dramatic Literature: To Be or to Become?*, 1991

# ROUMAIN, Jacques (1907–1944)
## Haiti

Jacques Roumain is an excellent writer of prose. Although a descendant of aristocrats, he takes great pleasure in listening to the common man and proclaiming his adherence to Communism. He is interested in taking notice of the psychological difficulties that overwhelm our generation. Having been acquainted on two occasions with the "damp straw of prison cells," he nevertheless has found success with stories like *The Prey and the Darkness*.

> Max Rose. *La littérature haïtienne* (Brussels: Éditions de "Conférences et Théâtres," 1938), p. 25

Haitian-, European-, American-trained Jacques Roumain, poet, ethnologist, archeologist, and journalist, had won an enviable reputation as the militant and uncontested leader of the younger Haitian intellectuals long before his death at the age of thirty-seven. Some of his verse had been translated by Langston Hughes and others in this country, and by Nicolás Guillén in Cuba. Moreover, in Haiti he had published various prose works: *The Prey and the Darkness*, *The Enchanted Mountain*, and *Puppets*, all of which helped to develop the mastery that is so evident in *Masters of the Dew*. . . .

*Masters of the Dew* tells of one Manuel who returns after fifteen years in Cuba to find his village suffering from drought, and divided by a family feud. He discovers water, devises a means of bringing it to the village and of reconciling the two opposing groups of peasants, only to be killed by a jealous rival. As he dies, he pleads with his mother not to reveal the name of the murderer, so that the feud will not be renewed. . . .

Jacques Roumain's hero . . . realizes that injustice is by no means a purely Haitian phenomenon. . . . He describes the exploitation of the workers in the Cuban sugar fields: "They have nothing but the courage of their arms, not a handful of land, not a drop of water, except their own sweat.". . .

The style of Jacques Roumain's *Masters of the Dew* is particularly striking. He writes in French, but often obtains a Creole flavor by the mere addition of a syllable, a word, or a phrase. . . .

Sometimes he employs an old French word that has been retained in the patois. . . . The result . . . is often a poetic prose, capable of being read and admired by men of good will the world over. . . .

Like Manuel, Jacques Roumain died prematurely. But he left a great Haitian novel to convince his compatriots that "Union makes strength"; to teach his fellow-authors that a novel can be at once Haitian and universal; and to enrich contemporary French literature.

> Mercer Cook. *French Review.* May 1946, pp. 408–11

The son of wealthy parents . . . Jacques Roumain lived for a number of years in Zurich, where he became familiar with German culture and grew accustomed to the free expression of ideas. When he returned to Haiti, he formed a literary movement together with other writers his age, a movement sparked by the irreverence that youth so often shows toward its elders. Dismissing past achievements too lightly, the young iconoclasts, vigorously ridiculing the Haitian literature that had been produced until then, emphatically decreed the need to create an art based on national pride and a real knowledge of the Haitian milieu. . . .

Roumain's second novel, *Puppets*, is the urban counterpart of [his first,] *The Enchanted Mountain*, its sociological complement; *Puppets* is a study of the upper middle class of Port-au-Prince. Because the bourgeoisie is defenseless against the attacks of the proletariat as well as those of the aristocracy (and Roumain by conviction and temperament belonged to both groups), if *Puppets* were nothing more than a list of grievances against the unfortunate Haitian ruling class, it would have little merit. Fortunately, while the brief novel ironically criticizes the prejudices and sometimes pathetic triviality of the local elite, it poses a problem of major interest: that of the new generation that refuses to accept the comfort and respect it was born into, to submit to "hypocritical conventions" in exchange for betraying its revolutionary ideals.

> Rémy Bastien. *Cuadernos americannos.* July-August 1954, pp. 244–46

The fathers of the Haitian novel . . . left us a formula for narrative art that does not seem to have influenced Roumain: precise, detailed, truculent, caustic description of the customs and daily activities in Haiti—in short, Haitian critical realism. In Roumain we find a kind of symbolic realism. For him, the novel is a great popular poem with classical outlines and almost symbolic characters. Without underestimating the immense artistic value of Roumain's form, we must bear in mind that he did not develop or continue Haitian critical realism.

Another unusual aspect of his work deserves to be emphasized. In this country in which tribal hatreds and jealousies and tribal customs have not been completely eradicated, in this country in which living conditions are so harsh and man's chances to succeed are so unfavorable, it is very rare to see a man take love for his fellow man as far as Roumain does. He is the champion of a love that is so powerful, so generous, that it surprises us in Haiti. The character of Manuel in *Masters of the Dew* is unique in our milieu and our fiction. His patriotism and his basic attachments are tinged with love for his village, love for the land, love for life, exemplary filial love, unequaled love for his Annaïse, a cult of perfect friendship, and even total forgiveness toward his enemies and his murderers. Could this be the book that contains Roumain's basic message, a message that life did not permit him to carry out in person? [1957]

> Jacques-Stéphen Alexis. Preface to Jacques Roumain, *La montagne ensorcelée* (Paris: Éditeurs Français Réunis, 1972), pp. 24–25

In [*The Enchanted Mountain*], written at the age of twenty-three, Jacques Roumain already seems in full possession of his artistic abilities. What strikes one first in this tale is its extraordinary precision: a simple story, related without digressions, with a deliberate intention to be brief; a clear, spare language that only approaches lyricism by accident; the avoidance of any complicity with the negative characters in the story or of any pity for the victims. Let me say the word that comes to my mind as a description of his novel—classical. Classical because of the clarity of its construction; classical because of the inflexible detachment that the author imposes upon himself; classical because of the moderation of its style. . . .

This somber story of love and death is related with an inexorable sobriety. Events move quickly and collide, following an implacable logic: the logic of unleashed passions; the logic of ignorance and madness; the logic of mysticism. . . .

One can justly speak of [Jean] Giono's influence on Roumain, but only of the influence of *Hill*, a novel published in 1929, one year before Roumain had begun writing his novel. . . . Comparisons can be pursued in their similar mystical conception of the world. . . . Mysticism is, after all, an irrational atmosphere of misfortune. . . .

Let us not forget, however, the original, vivid contribution to Roumain's works made by our voodoo. Everything considered, Giono's influence on Roumain can only be regarded as catalytic. Haitian cultural material extends in all directions from Roumain's book and assures his literary autonomy.

> Roger Gaillard. *L'univers romanesque de Jacques Roumain* (Port-au-Prince: Henri Deschamps, 1965), pp. 9–12

A writer, a diplomat, and a militant Communist, Jacques Roumain was also a great traveler. He lived, among other places, in Germany and in Belgium. But all his works are deeply rooted in his native land. His novel *Masters of the Dew* remains the most beautiful novel to come from the Caribbean. But it was even more through a few poems, the most aggressive ever written by a black poet, that he strongly influenced Césaire, Damas, and David Diop, not to mention his compatriots. . . . Even the gentle Senghor, on the rare occasions when he gets angry, spontaneously seizes Roumain's accents, rhythms, and images. Nothing is at once more violent and more humanist than the three poems in *Ebony Wood*. All the major themes of Negro revolt are condensed in a few pages: slavery, exile, forced labor, lynching, segregation, colonial oppression, nostalgia for Africa, and a gathering of the Negro diaspora under the revolutionary banner: "We shall no longer sing sad spirituals of despair."

But Roumain is not satisfied with making demands on behalf of his race. He insists on justice for all the "prisoners of hunger" and broadens his scope to include the "oppressed of all countries" beyond differences of color. What constitutes Roumain's greatness and what excuses the brutality of his language is precisely the fact that he was able to give breadth to his humanism. And his rough poetry, full of prosaic expressions drawn from political slogans, is nevertheless charged with such force and such intense emotion that it might be said that his pen brings us the very voice, the great cry, of the "wretched of the earth."

> Lilyan Kesteloot. In Lilyan Kesteloot, ed. *Anthologie négro-africaine* (Verviers, Belgium: Gérard, 1967), p. 50†

Jacques Roumain . . . was a very knowledgeable ethnologist and archeologist. The love he bore for his country was tempered by a profound political understanding. The poet in him was able to communicate this knowledge and this love to us. Thus, the black peasants in *Masters of the Dew* are brothers of all the peasants in the world who seek life-giving water and fruitful land.

In this book, as in the best fiction, one can find both reality and symbolism. First, there is the problem of water (one of the major problems of farmers in many countries) linked with the problem of the monopolization of plots of land by speculators who take advantage of bankrupt peasants. Then, more generally, we find the problem of liberation and of the harvest. . . .

This theme of harvest and planting is found both in the struggle to find water and to unify the peasants and in the love between Manuel and Annaïse. Thus, the lyrical song is sustained by a powerful dramatic pulse that maintains the reader's profound interest from the first page to the last. Roumain's style should be discussed at length. He has reshaped the French language so that we can hear all the music of his people and his land.

> Pierre Gamarra. *Europe*. January 1971, pp. 194–95

BIBLIOGRAPHY

*La proie et l'ombre* (The Prey and the Darkness), 1930; *Les fantoches* (Puppets), 1931; *Gouverneurs de la rosée* (Masters of the Dew), 1944; *Bois-d'ébène* (Ebony Wood), 1945

# RUBADIRI, David (1930–)
## Malawi

[David Rubadiri] is the first novelist in East Africa to present a sympathetic, though critical, portrait of Indians in East Africa. The most damning comment [in *No Bride Price*] on Indians comes from an Indian, Sandra, the idealistic daughter of the Indian High Commissioner in East Africa. She criticizes them for not mixing more with Africans, for not taking out citizenship quickly, and for sending their money to India. . . .

By putting the criticism of Indians in the mouth of an Indian and discussing the problem as tragic, Rubadiri both criticizes Indians and reveals that Indians are not the stereotype "Asians" of the popular press. Of course, the ubiquitous Indian businessman is there in the novel, exploiting [the protagonist] Lombe's financial helplessness; but when Minister Chozo makes a speech about the "cancer of inward exploitation by a certain minority group . . . inwardly eating the nation and making it impotent," he is really thinking about Mr. Patel's frightening but legitimate bills!

In fact, Chozo and the other Ministers are revealed as the real cancer of the nation. Chozo is greedy, crude and lecherous. He wants to sleep with Sandra and he wants Lombe to ''make a fixture,'' promising to make him his private secretary as a reward. When Lombe does not do this, the Minister suspends him for corruption, for taking bribes from an Indian businessman and for using his high office to sell confidential information to certain embassies.

Rubadiri contrasts the hollow, corrupting life of the city with the healing, communal power of life in the village. The village people are simple and everyone's problem is their problem. When Lombe first returns to the village, he is drawn inevitably into the communal dancing. . . .

Rubadiri satirically contrasts this communal life with the hollow ''African socialism'' preached by the big people in the big new government in the big city. . . .

Miria is a child of the village who has been spoiled by the city but [who still retains] her innocence and femininity. She loved Lombe and she had expressed this love by the way she had looked after him. Lombe did not realize how deep this love was until Miria left him. The novel becomes a search, Lombe's search for Miria. He discovers during the search that Sandra reminds him of Miria for Sandra too represents the subtle, mysterious, feminine element in life. (In contrast, the European woman who seduces Lombe is a predator, like a praying mantis, although we are made to feel a tinge of sympathy for her). But Miria dies in childbirth after Lombe's child has been brought out piece by piece.

Peter Nazareth. *Literature and Society in Modern Africa* (Nairobi: East African Literature Bureau, 1972), pp. 176–79

[In *No Bride Price*] Lombe never rises to the top of the civil service because foreigners are preferred by the insecure politicians at the top. The Minister finally destroys Lombe because the latter refuses to yield a girlfriend. . . .

*No Bride Price* . . . contains several key ideas. First there is a civilian organization that works to bring the government to power. This organization embraces the alienated educated who are debarred from work and who live the bar-cocktail-party route along with the seamier side of the top echelon of business and diplomacy. The implication here is that the educated who cannot get into the system will ally with the army to throw out uneducated bureaucrats and politicians from public life. More interesting is the idea Rubadiri puts forward when he argues that Gombe, the ''father of independence'' in this particular country and the one who had played the dominant political role in the ending of the colonial situation, is the head of the underground organization which allies itself with the army to bring about the coup. Rubadiri argues that the ''father of the nation'' had quit the government because it had become corrupt and his interest in the new order is to achieve good government. This suggests that the only way to get ''good,'' that is to say noncorrupt, government is to use the young educated and the military. . . . The ideas expressed here are important because they point to the army as the savior of the nation from corruption and to the rejection of the domination of the politicians. It should be noted that Lombe, the civil servant, is rehabilitated into the new order. Perhaps the future may see more and more of this kind of alliance between the political bureaucracy, the intellectuals looking to the

African past for the major values of society, and the military who by their very definition are professionals.

G-C. M. Mutiso. *Socio-political Thought in African Literature* (New York: Barnes & Noble, 1974), pp. 35–38

The most exciting aspect of *No Bride Price* is to be found in the correlation between the images and the structure of the book. If it is true that the title of the book refers to the greedy new African elites who fail to pay voluntarily the very dear dowry of total sacrifice and to marry the best possibilities of a modern African country after independence, it is even more true that many African writers have failed to marry the viewing of their experience simultaneously from two opposing world-views. A number of African writers have joined Western writers in carefully delineating the existential pains of isolated individuals who succumb to the worst aspects of the materialistic West within the framework of Christian guilt. Only a few have taken the risk of embracing a usable African past in the midst of an African experience that will increasingly have to come to terms with a technological revolution growing geometrically and eventually touching every corner of the planet. Rubadiri is one of these.

A Western literary historian or critic dealing with the relationships and ideas of the main characters in *No Bride Price* would have to face the fact that life in Africa, traditionally, has been strikingly different from life in Western civilization. . . .

These differences in the mindset of Africans and Westerners become clearer and yet more complex as Lombe discusses them with his platonic Indian girlfriend, Sandra. She has witnessed and been moved by the power of the physical, social, and religious needs of Lombe's village answered in song, dance, and music without fully understanding the implications of that power. . . .

Rubadiri clearly uses a sympathetic non-African (Sandra) to demonstrate Lombe's total involvement in the communal African experience of dance, music, and song. . . . Forcing the English language to describe differences between an African and a Western world-view through the voices of Lombe and Sandra, the impersonal author introduces a continuum of viewpoints in which African and Western ways of thinking serve as the extremes. . . .

If anarchy is frightening for the West, it is much more terrifying for an African life revolving around closely knit communities. Like the falcon unable to hear the falconer, the African leaders of Lombe's country have forgotten the African tradition of concern for community and are like birds turning in the widening gyre of exploitation. Inevitably, then, as Chinua Achebe has realized in his first novel, ''things fall apart.'' Lombe has left a village life and the ''ceremony of innocence'' to become that ''urban African hung in the middle desperately trying to avoid the chasm below'' with ''the center no longer able to hold.''

While the ''worst are full of passionate intensity'' in the novel, it is not entirely true that ''the best lack all conviction.'' However, since conviction must be inspired by a firm rejection of neocolonial exploitation based upon a positive attraction to the best aspects of African traditions, Rubadiri directs the reader toward an appreciation of African traditions without harming the sense of ''surface realism''. . . . This he does subtly by embodying these African traditions in the structure and imagery of his novel.

Mark Shadle. *Pacific Moana Quarterly.* 6, 3–4 (July-October 1981), pp. 123–25

The tumultuous disturbance of a thunderstorm is used in "An African Thunder-storm" to symbolize the effect on Africa of Western conquest and colonization. It is a symbolic poem, the implied meaning being hinted at only in the first line—"From the west," the direction where the storm originates. The western clouds are described in a series of suggestive, uniformly uncomplimentary images; they are "Like a plague of locusts," "Like a madman chasing nothing," and "Like dark sinister wings." The rhetorical figure of anaphora (in the repeated "Likes") is one that would become very familiar in later East and Central African poetry. Here it draws together the various similes used to describe the storm clouds. In the last verse-paragraph of the poem, the pace and confusion become more and more intense as the storm strikes. Now there is no time for the leisureliness of simile; the description has become literal and metaphorical: "the smell of fired smoke / In the rumbling belly of the storm." "Rumbling belly" is another uncomplimentary description of the West, suggestive perhaps of dyspepsia caused by the greedy ingestion of colonies. "Fired smoke" describes not just the smoke from undergrowth or stubble at harvest time but, more importantly, the smoke of firearms and of crops burnt deliberately by the invaders. The end of the poem, then, contains a last glance at the symbolic meaning.

A later poem, "The Tide That from the West Washes Africa to the Bone," discusses the same subject and once again uses a single overriding image. This time, however, the West is presented as a blood-red tide washing over Africa; Rubadiri is writing a more personal poem, for he admits that the tide of Western civilization and attitude has swept through him, dissolving the indigenous "bone and sinew." Where a more sanguine or ingenuous poet might have sought a vision of reintegration beyond this desolation, Rubadiri contents himself with a final riddling statement, beginning for the fourth time with his anaphoric formula: "The tide from the west / With blood washes Africa / Once washed a wooden cross." The primary meaning seems to be that it was the spirit of Western acquisitiveness and conquest that in an earlier age condemned a great spiritual leader to death on the cross. But the meaning may go beyond this to express a hope—rare in Rubadiri's poetry—that just as Christianity triumphed over the bloody death of its leader, so Africa will triumph over the Western tide of blood. Rubadiri avoids overt sentiment and hope. On the whole, however, his is poetry of vehement statement of what has happened and is happening; it is not a prophetic call for action. . . .

The contrast between old and new, hope and disappointed reality, runs through many of Rubadiri's poems. "Saaka Crested Cranes"—one of his few optimistic poems—contrasts the age-old crater lake with the eternal life symbolized by the crested cranes. "The Witch Tree at Mubende" has camera lenses "prying the old and the new." "Paraa Lodge" contrasts the elephants and hippos with noisy American tourists.

"Christmas 1967" represents a somewhat different style from most of Rubadiri's works. Instead of a single scene it presents a collage of incidents and memories joined together at an incongruous Western celebration of Christmas. It includes mercenaries in the Biafran War, famine and the dubious methods of Western relief agencies, a *coup d'état*, the queen's insensitive Christmas message ("all in the oral tradition"), Vietnam, a reminiscence of mercenaries in the Congo (Major Schramme), the Pope's Christmas message and legation to Nigeria and Biafra, death and birth, and a brief glance at "Journey of the Magi" again. But despite the jaggedness with which the fragmentary images are placed together, Rubadiri's

control has not deserted him. The theme of Western mercenaries and power brokers interfering in former colonies and the theme of birth (initially the birth of Jesus) and death join the fragments together. Rubadiri has perhaps the most consistent control of any East [or] Central African poet. In this poem he has simply bent towards the darting, conversational fragmentariness that is a characteristic of much East African poetry.

[K. L.] Goodwin. In G. D. Killam, ed. *The Writing of East and Central Africa* (London: Heinemann, 1984), pp. 215–16

*No Bride Price* is a novel about the platonic relationship between an Indian woman and an African man. Their love is almost ethereal, to stress which the writer has employed the technique of contrasting it with other love episodes that the hero gets entangled into. But the Indian girl Sandra and the spiritual affinity between Lombe and herself remain central to the narration in the framework of the plot which deals with the problem of urbanization, the resulting alienation and their effects on the young people in a newly independent African country.

J. Lombe is more a type than an individual who represents those unfortunate ones who are caught in the predicament of changing values and changing circumstances in a newly independent African country.

The problem of survival has forced him to take up a job in the city and like many other young men of his generation, Lombe is suffering from the effects of alienation. His own village is like a haven for him but he has no place there as he has received university education and has lost his contact with the rural rhythm; his fate is to work in the city and live there whether he likes it or not. Lombe's mind finds a striking similarity between Miria, his housemaid and beloved (later discovered to be his step-sister) and Sandra, his Indian girlfriend whose father is the ambassador. Tensions of his job and the evils of city life lead him to have many sexual encounters with different city girls, but his soul is comforted by only these two. Chaudry, Sandra's brother is a friend of Lombe and it is in a party given by their father that Sandra and Lombe meet. Sandra's easy manners, spontaneity and her openmindedness draw Lombe towards her in no time. The author has been faithful to the reality in depicting the relationship between an African male and an Indian female, and so the maximum closeness Sandra and Lombe experience of one another is in their third meeting on the evening at Sandra's house in a veranda where they sit holding each other's hands and chat[ting], while Sandra is trying to understand Lombe's troubles and offer him comfort and help. Sandra is depicted as a liberated woman for whom race or caste barriers do not exist, and she is aware of Lombe's attraction towards her; and yet, to have shown anything more than this would have been unrealistic and to this effect there is comment in the novel.

Yashoda Ramamoorthy. *African Quarterly*. 24, 3–4 (1987), p. 76

BIBLIOGRAPHY
*No Bride Price*, 1967; "Paraa Lodge," 1967

# S

## SALKEY, Andrew (1928–1995)
### Jamaica

Andrew Salkey's origins are urban middle class, which is unusual among West Indian writers. Perhaps it isn't surprising that his public comment on his first book should be in the nature of a cynical aside—that it was written to catch the market for "peasant" novels. For although the country is a tangible presence in any Jamaican town, including Kingston, the differences between townsman and countryman are self-consciously observed. They are for instance reflected in the emotional attitudes of the two parties that dominate the island's politics; and the term "bugguyaga" (bumpkin is as near as you can get to it in standard English) is capable of expressing a stringency of contemptuous reference. Therefore Salkey set his first novel, *A Quality of Violence*, in a rural setting not in contemporary Jamaica, but at the turn of the century. There is another possible reason why this precise period should be chosen. The Morant Bay uprising, which cost nearly five hundred Jamaican lives, took place in 1865, and the earthquake which razed Kingston occurred in 1907. Salkey has carefully chosen a period about which not a great deal is known and which is sufficiently free from the possessive clutch of modern Jamaican intellectuals to enable him to establish his drama on his own terms. He wants his readers to sense for themselves the presence of a defining history. . . .

*A Quality of Violence* emerges as a shapely, patterned fable on the conflicting possibilities—Mother Johnson or Brother Parkin—that ultimately make up the Jamaican consciousness. Salkey does not seek to provide confident "answers"—his concern is with the inherent possibilities of the real "question." The form of the book goes beyond reflecting the disordered violence that lies at its center. The action is choreographed, and the formal presentation of the book is intentionally reminiscent of the movement of dance, for the meaningful ordering of emotion is the true activity of the novelist.

Salkey's second novel, *Escape to an Autumn Pavement*, appeared in 1960. This time the setting is London and the theme is the by now conventional one of the experience of the West Indian migrant. But the central character is not the wittily resilient working-class or peasant migrant we associate with Samuel Selvon. Johnny Sobert is a middle-class Jamaican and to that extent is only a colored man in London. In Jamaica itself he is clearly defined as apart from the Negro mass of the population. I do not remember this being noticed when the book was reviewed in England. Most reviewers suggested that it was smart, or slick, or that it handled problems of sexuality and migrant bitterness in, finally, trivial and conventional ways. When I first read the book, this was in fact my own impression but, as with *A Quality of Violence*, experience of Jamaica obliges a positive shift in perspective. An essential difference between Johnny Sobert and a Selvon migrant is that the Selvon migrant is at the bottom, even in his own country. A man like Sobert, on the other hand, though he may feel a furtive guilt at the economic and social injustices which prevail in Jamaica itself, does not have any doubt that he really belongs in the respectable middle class. But London imposes an inferiority. The protective dikes of status and comparative affluence are eroded away. And it is, in significant measure, as a result of this that Sobert takes refuge in the consistently defensive sarcasm that reviewers in the main objected to.

Bill Carr. In Louis James, ed. *The Islands in Between: Essays on West Indian Literature* (London: Oxford University Press, 1968), pp. 101, 104–5

[*Escape to an Autumn Pavement*] is a fast-moving tale told with a slightly self-conscious toughness, the word "crap" being used with obsessive frequency. Sobert lives in a rooming house where he happens to be the only black resident, though there is an Indian girl whom he satirizes with pitiless intensity. He also works in a nightclub which is run by two English girls, and caters mainly [to] American servicemen. With all these people Johnnie has to achieve a more or less direct, individual relationship, since there is no warm, uncritical group into which he can retire whenever he gets hurt or confused. At first he moves through the days with a certain jazzy but cool insouciance, but soon he gets drawn into an affair with the insatiable Fiona, the wife of his landlord, who lives on the floor below. For a while he is flattered and sensually delighted by this involvement, but gradually Fiona begins to appear in the guise of a succubus, not merely available but inevitable and demanding. Johnnie has already felt himself attracted to Dick, a white chauffeur and fellow tenant whose apparent detachment makes him seem like an escape from the morass of female sexuality into which he feels himself sinking. The suspicion that Dick is a homosexual is one that Johnnie does not allow to rise very far in his mind; when Dick proposes that they move out and share a flat, he eagerly falls in with the arrangement, telling himself that it implies just that and no more. He breaks with Fiona and luxuriates for a while in the sense of relief this brings him. Resolutely averting his attention from the mounting strain in their relationship, he continues to treat Dick as a friend, confidant, and flatmate, while Dick patiently waits for a sign which never comes. For Dick believes that Johnnie is an unavowed homosexual who needs time to come to terms with himself and must not be hurried. His very agreement to share the flat was, in Dick's eyes, an admission of his real nature. But when Johnnie takes up with Fiona again and begins making assignations with her, Dick's patience finally snaps. He quits the flat and leaves a note telling Johnnie that he must now make a decision between them. The reader is left with the suspicion that neither Fiona nor Dick is really as important to Johnnie as they suppose, and that he will probably choose neither. He ends the book as he began it, alone. . . .

What is liberating about Johnnie Sobert is his relative self-sufficiency as a West Indian in London. He neither depends upon membership of an immigrant group which experiences and reacts to London collectively, nor does he play unduly the part of a professional black man. The last is a particular hazard for those with genuine personality and bounce, since the audience is always waiting and will soon clarify the limits within which the role is licensed to be played. Johnnie's sexual ambiguity and stillborn rebelliousness are problems he must encounter as a man, an individual alone in a big city, but not specifically as a black immigrant. Too much dwelling upon the last can bring out something disturbingly like a Christ-complex, or a self-congratulatory mystique of Negro potency.

Gerald Moore. *The Chosen Tongue* (New York: Harper & Row, 1969), pp. 105–7

The significance of [*In the Hills Where Her Dreams Live: Poems for Chile* 1973–1978] is its very existence: the Salkey-Cuba connection, which perhaps represents an important point of departure. It comes at a time of crisis in the Caribbean, where Jamaica, Cuba, and Haiti are all undergoing political transformations which have repercussions in Miami. The hurly-burly in the Third World seems to confuse the Western press, which gives only minimal coverage. But the revolt against imperialism is taking on new forms and spreading; new connections are being established. The ideas of [Salvador] Allende, [Frantz] Fanon and [Fidel] Castro are being used to give shape and force to this movement.

Andrew Salkey knows a good part of the world from his travels and studies. Currently teaching at a college in Massachusetts, he has written novels, poetry, short stories, radio plays, and travel journals in the new journalism tradition, has edited several volumes of Caribbean writing, and does interviews for the BBC. Much of his work shows a penetrating interest in the politics of the Caribbean and a dedication to the development of the Left. However, the specific nature of this commitment remains somewhat vague, even when dealing with Cuba. He seems to find it easier to attack the poverty, ignorance, and oppression associated with imperialism than to suggest new alternatives, though trade union organizing is shown as important in his novel *Riot*. . . .

Cuba has become perhaps the most controversial country in the world; the revolutionary regimes in Cuba and Chile are being intently studied by Third World peoples everywhere, to see how they happened, what went wrong, and what went right. Salkey expresses sympathy for both regimes but hesitates in making critical evaluations. Judgment is, however, necessary in order to reveal their meaning and relevance for other countries. Cannot a poem be lyrical, analytical, and dramatic at the same time? Mythic and historical? Salkey is to be commended for having made such great strides in doing political poetry and other writing; few have tried the way, and many of them have stumbled. In a world where literature is defined by bourgeois academies and journals which tend to frown at mixing politics and poetry, such a writer must struggle upstream. But in the day of decolonization, he may be moving with the mainstream of history.

Hal Wylie. *World Literature Today*. 54, 4 (fall 1980), pp. 686–87

The theme of Andrew Salkey's fourth volume of poetry is contained in the title *Away*. The poet has left home, Jamaica, in flight from colonial devastation, physical (''home was a dry river bed'') and spiritual (''a flood man myself''). . . .

The protagonist has moved to the metropolis, living out an unending history (''his ill-chosen country of shopkeepers,'' a Napoleonic reference) which is a continuing conspiracy against the colonized. All roads lead to Rome—and all lead from Rome: in the centers the poet finds some of the pieces of the jigsaw puzzle: Haiti, Cuba, Vietnam, Martinique, Mexico, Brazil, Uganda, Guyana,

Ethiopia, South Africa, and America (of the Indian and black American). Why didn't even radical Caribbean thinkers like [Marcus] Garvey, [George] Padmore and [Frantz] Fanon return? Because nothing fundamental has changed under ''our kind of quick-sell independence / and brand-new, advertised nationhood.'' The man who returned found ''the villagers clawed at him / and what little he'd brought back,'' so he had to leave again; the postcard from Uganda shows wildlife, but the real hunted are people, the hunters using modern tanks and equipment. So, as the last section says, ''Only Change Will Do.'' . . .

Despite the pessimism of some poems, and the suspicion that change is frequently cosmetic, Salkey believes that real change can come about, that history can be made to boomerang, that Davids can defeat Goliaths because they have the raw materials to make the slingshots. And he celebrates the few Davids he remembers, like the barmaid who finds a way to keep the bar filled during the strike, so that the owner does not see ''how far the ownership of the bar had changed; / it was now a repossessed *public* house.'' Here is Salkey's lyricism, in hints of the return home.

Peter Nazareth. *World Literature Today*. 55, 2 (spring 1981), p. 364

In Andrew Salkey's *Anancy's Score* he re-enters the *literary* folktale as the trickster hero of twenty stories with ancient and contemporary settings, all of which comment on present-day politics and society in the New World. . . . But in individual stories in the volume as well, traditional West African Anancy is placed at the center of contemporary events and incidents, and the implication throughout is that after the ''fall,'' this tragic meeting of the two old worlds, New World man is forced to reenact in the present the brutalities and futilities engendered in him by his genesis and history. Like Barbadian novelist George Lamming, Salkey sees the perpetuation of this fall in the politics of imperialism in the contemporary world. Stories like ''Vietnam Anancy and the Black Tulip'' or ''Soot, the Land of Billboards'' make the implications of Caribbean history more generally applicable. . . .

The last tale in *Anancy's Score*, ''New Man Anancy,'' points towards the reestablishment of community integrity through a rejection of the colonial obsession with other and better worlds (especially that of the European colonizing power), and with a concomitant forging of links between Caribbean man and his new land. In a postlapsarian world this is a slow and self-conscious choice and process; but it can be achieved, Salkey seems to suggest, by the next generation. . . . [It] is not Anancy alone who will effect this change, but a sort of Jeun Payee character helped by an old man (the Caribbean past) and a new love of the earth itself. . . .

While the two stories that enclose the other eighteen do seem to provide a structural and thematic framework that encompasses Old World fall and New World redemption, the overall effect of the volume is that of stasis. Insofar as Anancy stands for Caribbean man in *Anancy's Score*, he seems unable to move beyond an imprisoned present which, for all the forms in which he appears, denies his inherently transformative character and the apparent philosophical structure of the volume. It is in the work of Edward Brathwaite and Wilson Harris, where Anancy's protean character can simultaneously express negative past, static present, future possibility, and the mechanism by which these become the creative future, that he is a volatile metaphor and archetype rather than arbitrary equation in a series of set-piece satires.

Nevertheless, Anancy in Salkey's stories . . . is associated with Caribbean history, politics, and the attempt to transcend or reform the destructive contemporary political destiny that is the product of this history.

Helen Tiffin. In Robert Sellick, ed. *Myth and Metaphor* (Adelaide, Australia: Center for Research in the New Literatures in English, 1982), pp. 26–29

Salkey's protagonists' aspiring, snobbish, middle-class backgrounds apparently . . . make it impossible for them to achieve any kind of meaningful relationship with people from the lower classes. Jerry Stover [in *The Late Emancipation of Jerry Stover*], for example, frequently makes love to his family's maid Miriam, but only when he is drunk—obviously when he is sober, he prefers to retain class distinctions. When she informs him that she is pregnant, he stifles a desire to laugh and gives her some money for an abortion. Further, even though Jerry seems sympathetic toward the lower-class Rastas, he regards them as inferiors and never comprehends their plans for revolution, nor does he have any faith in their envisioned revolutionary society.

Thus, unable to relate to people in any meaningful way, unable to find any avenue through which they can satisfactorily express themselves, unable to determine who they are, Salkey's lost middle-class seekers inevitably settle for seeking and asserting themselves through desperate, meaningless, uninhibited, often violent and perverted sexual acrobatics. Their lives, marked by incessant sexual activity, often described explicitly and titillatingly, might best be characterized through a phrase from [*The Adventures of Catallus Kelly*] as "a riot of fornication." Sex inevitably seems the only conscious option for action of which they are capable— even when they are "involved" in other apparent options such as Black Power Movements, political involvement, Rastafarian activity, and the like. Inevitably the field for action ends up the bed (or the car seat, the floor, whatever—the setting for copulation is often not a consideration among Salkey's characters).

Given the meaningless ritual of self-discovery that we witness with Salkey's protagonists, the emptiness of their beings, the inanities of their world, we are not surprised that there is nothing to discover and no meaningful world in which to discover it. We are neither surprised nor disappointed then in the outcomes of their quests: Catallus Kelly returns to Jamaica and is committed to an insane asylum; Johnny Sobert, still unable at the end of [*Escape to an Autumn Pavement*] to acknowledge his love for Dick or to end his brutalizing relationship with Fiona, is last seen agonizing over the fact that both of them are waiting for him to come to them. At the conclusion of *The Late Emancipation of Jerry Stover*, most of Jerry's cohorts (they are called the Termites) have been killed by a landslide, and we last view Jerry aimlessly wandering through the streets of Lower Kingston. Finally [in *Come Home, Malcolm Heartland*], Malcolm Heartland (who, though weak, is notable among Salkey's characteristically passive characters in these novels for taking *some* action on his own—he at least makes a decision to return to Jamaica and appears to be making some efforts to work toward it) meets his death as a result of his involvement with the black revolutionaries.

Unlike the lost, weak, undirected sons in Salkey's novels, the mothers are strong, determined women who know what they want, consistently strive for it, and attempt to give some direction to the lives of their sons. In these novels and in a few other instances in Salkey's works, there is, however, the implication that the power, strength, and domination of the women contribute to the ambivalence and emasculation of the men and are thus destructive.

Daryl Cumber Dance. *Fifty Caribbean Writers* (Westport, Connecticut: Greenwood Press, 1986), pp. 422–23

[From 1960 to 1967] Salkey devoted his energy to writing novels for children. He produced a quartet of books about Jamaica— *Hurricane*, *Earthquake*, *Drought*, and *Riot*. In 1966 he published *The Shark Hunters*, a reader for schools. The years after 1960 also saw the development of Salkey's work as an anthologist. *West Indian Stories*, *Stories from the Caribbean*, and *Caribbean Prose: An Anthology for Secondary Schools*, all edited by Salkey, bring together the works of a variety of West Indian writers. The anthologies are aimed at school children and no doubt were inspired by intentions similar to those that provoked his fiction for children: to provide West Indian youths with the opportunity to read about themselves, their landscape, and their societies so that they could develop a strong sense of who they were and so that they would not grow up to be like the lost heroes of Salkey's adult novels.

*Hurricane*, *Earthquake*, *Drought*, and *Riot*, all set in Jamaica, deal with children who have come to terms with disasters, both natural and man-made, which affect their societies. The incidents of the stories are from Jamaican history, and their settings are all specifically Jamaican. The language of the characters, however, does not always sound authentic. The children who are the central characters are lively and inquisitive but remarkably mature and understanding. They are helped at times of crisis in their lives by strong, loving relatives. Although some critics have accused these novels of being too nostalgic and sentimental, and although the books were not considered suitable for Jamaican children by the Jamaican Ministry of Education, Salkey's reputation as a children's novelist was established by this quartet. . . .

In 1969 Salkey published another novel for young people, *Jonah Simpson*. It is an attempt to familiarize the young Jamaican with the exotic past of the country while suggesting that the violent history of the town of Port Royal still has an effect on the present. . . .

*Joey Tyson*, the most explicitly political of Salkey's novels for children, deals with the turmoil caused in Jamaica by the government's decision to revoke the work permit of Walter Rodney, a lecturer at the University of the West Indies, because the government disapproved of his involvement with the poor. A boy, Joey Tyson, has his eyes opened to the reality of Jamaican politics.

With *Come Home, Malcolm Heartland*, Salkey returned to the adult novel. The central character decides to leave his career as a lawyer in London to return to his home in Jamaica, where he wishes to make a contribution, but he is murdered because he disagrees with the attitudes of the black revolutionaries with whom he is associating. This novel, like those before it, expresses Salkey's growing disillusionment with the typical West Indian's ability to find himself.

Anthony Boxill. In Bernth Lindfors and Reinhard Sander, eds. *Dictionary of Literary Biography*, Volume 125: *Twentieth-Century Caribbean and Black African Writers, Second Series* (Detroit: Gale Research, 1993), pp. 272, 74

Andrew Salkey's *Anancy's Score* was published two decades ago. The new volume [*Anancy, Traveller*] also consists of twenty stories that know the score, but in a much more complex world in which a near-invisible neocolonialism has tightened its tentacles. To help us catch on, and keep from being caught, Anancy is now traveling through space and time, on land, through the air, inside the oceans, and inside the mind. "For all we know," Anancy tells Brother Tacuma and Caribbea, "we might have to invent a brand new substance for the world, something that it never have before the happening of the thunderstorm of direct loss." Using the trickster form, and a Caribbean demotic, Salkey brings up everything: past/present history of exploitation; buried heroes such as Paul Bogle, Malcolm X, Marcus Garvey, and Nanny; and villains masquerading as heroes, including Columbus and Bartolomé de las Casas. Anancy tells us what is happening, using disguises which the agents of the mightiest imperialist power on earth will not be able to penetrate.

When colonialism put on the mask of freedom, it was an opportunity for many writers of the Caribbean and the Third World to be very creative to pull off the mask. However, when the mask has been removed only to reveal a series of masks, just the way each curtain parts on the new "Tonight Show" to reveal yet another curtain, Salkey's Anancy form shows itself to be endlessly inventive, for it has a goal: to help the people find real freedom. *Anancy, Traveller* is a complex and wise work, one to dip into constantly in order to strengthen one's nerve.

> Peter Nazareth. *World Literature Today.* 67, 2 (spring 1993), p. 429

In 1962 Jamaica was granted independent status as a member of the British commonwealth, and the island immediately experienced both a surge in feelings of nationalism and a cultural renaissance. Beginning in 1966, the Institute of Jamaica funded archaeological teams to excavate local sites of historical import, including Port Royal and some Indian burial grounds at White Maul. In 1968 British honors were replaced with Jamaican or National honors, the British honor of knighthood, for example, making way for the Order of Jamaica. The year 1968 also marked the creation of the new rank National Hero, awarded posthumously that year to Marcus Garvey, Paul Bogle, and George William Gordon. Rastafarianism, a Jamaican-born religion fast gaining worldwide attention and followers, was celebrated in the 1972 film *The Harder They Come*. The island contributed to the musical world with developments in reggae, ska, and calypso, and reggae in particular helped to make available to the Jamaican population an Afro-Caribbean identity. . . .

Addressed to and emerging from this culture, Andrew Salkey's epic poem *Jamaica*, published in London in 1973 by Hutchinson and reissued with the subtitle *An Epic Poem Exploring the Historical Foundations of Jamaican Society* in 1983 by Bogle-L'Ouverture, signals the beginning of Jamaican national literature. . . .

*Jamaica* fulfills one of the primary functions of a traditional epic poem: teaching its audience members about their own national history as part of their "training in citizenship," as Eric Havelock declares. But though traditional in his desire to teach his readers to recognize, value, and embrace Jamaican history, Salkey shuns one of the most deeply embedded characteristics of epics with Jamaica: he avoids acknowledgement of its generic predecessors, or what Joan Malory Webber calls his "hostile but loving responsibility to

its [the genre's] rejected past." His 107-page epic makes no reference to any other epic, or to any other literature from the Western tradition, for that matter; but he crafts this omission as part of the "training in citizenship" and historical instruction his poem offers his Jamaican readers. Salkey self-consciously signals a Jamaican national literature as his poem addresses his own people in language that, although English, heralds its distinction as an island language. Salkey uses this language to tell his people how to escape the distorted picture of their past foisted on them by their colonizers. Salkey believes Jamaicans can lay claim to a national culture by studying and knowing the island itself, thereby undoing the devaluation of Jamaican culture which was part and parcel of the colonial process. In learning the island's history as it is imprinted on the land and reinforced in the islanders' relationship with the land, Jamaicans will realize that the violence Jamaica has endured—both natural and human—actually contributes to its survival. Salkey's epic presents this reconfigured notion of violence in the appropriate Caribbean metaphor of the hurricane.

Salkey's poem is divided into four parts of unequal length, framed by introductory and concluding poems that express a desire to participate in history by obtaining land. Part 1, Caribbea, consists of only one poem, "Xaymaca," a tribute to the resilience of the island and its surrounding sea. The longest section, part 2, Slavery to Liberation, offers a tour of two hundred years of Jamaican history, dedicating poems to the Port Royal earthquake of 1692, the Maroon uprising of 1796, the emancipation of slaves set into motion in 1833, the Morant Bay Rebellion of 1865, and the Kingston earthquake of 1907. Part 3, Mento Time, follows a poet-wanderer as he records the musical and vocal sounds of Kingston. Jamaican history provides the focus again for part 4, Caribbean Petchary, covering the popular unrest of 1938, the granting of universal adult suffrage in 1944, and the hurricane of 1951. This part closes with another tribute to a Jamaican entity with "Caribbean Petchary," a tribute to a local bird. To read *Jamaica* is to immerse oneself in the history and the language of Jamaica.

Ironically, Jamaicans themselves have had little access to this epic. Never published in Jamaica, the poem nevertheless qualifies as national literature, which critics are careful to define by content rather than relative popularity. (Indeed, low literacy rates combined with high poverty rates limit readership of any literature in the Caribbean.) C. L. Innes identifies national literature as that "addressed not just to the colonizing power, nor even primarily to it, but to the people of the emerging nation, and [which] seeks to engage them in their own project of self-definition." If that project defines the self solely in opposition to the definitions and descriptions employed by the colonizing power, it risks the label nativist rather than national, the former a kind of writing Kwame Anthony Appiah criticizes for "the topology that it presupposes." Focusing primarily on Africa, Appiah criticizes literature that leaves unquestioned the "ideology of universalism" which is usually "eurocentric hegemony posing as universalism," especially when that literature "inhabit[s] a Western architecture."

Though we may consider the epic the quintessential Western genre, the pillars of Homer and Virgil laying the foundation for the tradition, the truth is that the epic is not a uniquely Western or European genre. Guida M. Jackson's recent *Encyclopedia of Traditional Epics* identifies precolonial epics from areas as diverse as Africa, Australia, the Caribbean, and Southeast Asia. Jackson's introduction identifies several conventions common to most epics, suggesting that even the definition employed by critics steeped in the Western tradition is not derived from European epics on-ly. It is within this non-Western epic tradition that Salkey's poem participates.

Even though the language in which Salkey pens *Jamaica* is English, he ensures that his readers will notice that his is not the English of England: In the introductory poem, ''I into history, now,'' all the reader need do is observe the punctuation, the pronouns, and the simile to realize that Salkey is not ''charming . . . or denouncing'' his oppressor but ''addressing his own people'':

> I sittin' down,
> scratchin' me 'ead
> an' watchin' the scene,
> an' I ol' as Anancy
> but wit'out f'him brain-box[.]
> All o' we losin' out,
> 'cause we won't own up to weself[.]

Addressed to the ''we'' of Jamaica, the language that Salkey uses here is explained later, when two elderly Jamaican men, Joshua and Emmanuel, converse in a particularly metapoetic portion of the poem. Emmanuel suggests that they look at problems in Jamaica:

> Take the language t'ing, now,
> as f'instance!
> It not even f'we own
> proper yet.
> Look how we force
> f'fingle wit' it
> when we want
> f'write as we talk;
> look how much mark an' stop
> we got f'drop
> 'pon top o'it
> when we write it down!

The written form of Emmanuel's lament perfectly matches its meaning. No reader can navigate that passage without recognizing the finagling both Emmanuel and Salkey must perform in order to communicate. This is not Received Standard English, a language Salkey rejects because it is not the language of the title island, but an English with which his Jamaican readers are entirely comfortable.

> Michelle DeRose. *Contemporary Literature*. 39, 2 (summer 1998), pp. 212–37

BIBLIOGRAPHY
*A Quality of Violence*, 1959; *Escape to an Autumn Pavement*, 1960; *West Indian Stories*, 1960; *Earthquake*, 1965; *Drought*, 1966; *The Shark Hunters*, 1966; *Riot*, 1967; *The Late Emancipation of Jerry Stover*, 1968; *The Adventures of Catallus Kelly*, 1969; *Jonah Simpson*, 1969; *Havana Journal*, 1971; *Georgetown Journal: A Caribbean Writer's Journey from London via Port of Spain to Georgetown, Guyana, 1970*, 1972; *Anancy's Score*, 1973; *Jamaica*, 1973; *Joey Tyson*, 1974; *Come Home, Malcolm Heartland*, 1976; *Hurricane*, 1977; *In the Hills Where Her Dreams Live: Poems for Chile 1973–1978*, 1979; *Away*, 1980; *Danny Jones*, 1980; *The River That Disappeared*, 1980; *The One: The Story of How the People of Guyana Avenge the Murder of Their Pasero with Help from Brother Anancy and Sister Buxton*, 1985; *Anancy, Traveller*, 1988; *Anancy and Other Stories*, 1993; *In the Border Country and Other Stories*, 1998

# SANCHEZ, Sonia (1934–)
## United States

There are few writers alive who have created a body of work that both teaches and celebrates life, even at its darkest moments. Sonia Sanchez does this and more throughout her many volumes of poetry, short stories, plays, and children's books. She is prolific and sharp-eyed. Her telescopic view of the world is seldom light, frivolous, or fraudulent. She is serious—serious to the point of pain and redemption. Her bottom line is this: she wants black people to grow and develop so that we can move toward determining our own destiny. She wants us not only to be responsible for our actions but to take responsible actions. This is the task she has set for herself, and indeed she believes that what she can do others can do. . . .

Sanchez writes poetry that is forever questioning black people's commitment to struggle. Much of her work intimately surveys the struggles between black people and black people, between blacks and whites, between men and women, between self and self, and between cultures. She is always demanding answers, questioning motives and manners, looking for the complete story and not the easy surface that most of us settle for. Her poetry cuts to the main arteries of her people, sometimes drawing blood, but always looking for a way to increase the heartbeat and lower the blood pressure. Her poetry, for the most part, is therapeutic and cleansing. Much of her work is autobiographical, but not in the limiting sense that it is only about Sonia Sanchez. She is beyond the problem of a consuming ego; and with her, unlike many autobiographical writers, we are not always aware of the protagonist's actual identity. Black experiences in America are so similar and the normal distinctions that set black people apart are not always obvious to outsiders. This is to note that, for the most part, her experiences are ours and vice versa. She is an optimistic realist searching the alleys for beauty and substance. . . .

All of Sanchez's books are significant: *Homecoming* for its pace-setting language, *We a BaddDDD People* for its scope and maturity. She [displays] an uncommon ability for combining words and music, content and approach. The longer poems are work songs, and she continues to be devastating in the shorter works. *Love Poems*, a book of laughter and hurt, smiles and missed moments, contains poems that expose the inner sides of Sanchez during the years 1964–73, in which she produces several masterworks. *A Blues Book for Blue Black Magical Women*, her black woman book, is a volume of sad songs and majestic histories. Her work becomes longer and balladlike. This book highlights black women as mothers, sisters, lovers, wives, workers, and warriors, an uncompromising commitment to the black family, and the black woman's role in building a better world. *I've Been a Woman: New and Selected Poems* contains more than a decade of important work; it is truly an earth-cracking contribution. This book not only displays the staying power of Sonia Sanchez but also confirms her place among the giants of world literature. Throughout the entire body of her work, never apologizing, she affirms and builds a magnificent case for the reality of being black and female, lashing out at all forms of racism, sexism, classism, just plain ignorance, and stupidity. It must be noted that she was taking these positions before it was popular and profitable.

> Haki Madhubuti. In Mari Evans, ed. *Black Women Writers (1950–1980): A Critical Evaluation* (New York: Doubleday, 1984), pp. 419–20, 422–23

The title of Sonia Sanchez's first collection, *Homecoming*, marks with delicate irony the departure point of a journey whose direction and destination can now be considered. *I've Been a Woman*, her most recent book, invites such an appraisal, including as it does a retrospective of her earlier work as well as an articulation of a newly won sense of peace: "shedding my years and / earthbound now, midnite trees are / more to my liking." These lines contain an explicit reworking of images that dominate "Poem at Thirty," one of the most personal statements in *Homecoming*. That early poem pulses with a terror rooted in a consciousness of age as debilitating. Midnight and traveling, images of perpetual transition, bracket the poem's fear. . . . In the new poems of *I've Been a Woman*, Sanchez re-evokes these images in order to establish her new sense of assurance. Midnight no longer terrifies; rootedness has succeeded sleepwalking as an emblematic image.

Correlating these poems in this way allows a useful perspective on the work of a poet whose development has been as much a matter of craft as it has been a widening and deepening of concerns. *Homecoming* largely satisfies [Amiri] Baraka's demand in *Black Art* for "assassin poems, Poems that shoot / guns" but there is from the beginning an ironic vision in Sanchez's work that ensures that she differentiate between activist poetry and what she herself has labeled, in *We a BaddDDD People*, "black rhetoric." The difference is that between substance and shadow, between "straight / revolutionary / lines" and "catch / phrases." And it is clear from Sanchez's work in *Homecoming* that she believes that the ideal poetry demands the practice of a stringent discipline. The poems in that collection are characterized by an economy of utterance that is essentially dramatic, like language subordinated to the rhythms of action. The verse of *Homecoming* is speech heightened by a consciousness of the ironies implicit in every aspect of black existence. The poems read like terse statements intended to interrupt the silence that lies between perception and action. . . .

The new poems in *I've Been a Woman* benefit from the sense of continuity and evolution conferred by the earlier work. The impact of the section entitled "Haikus/Tankas & Other Love Syllables" is immeasurably enhanced by *Love Poems*, for instance; the new poems, drawing on a relatively limited stock of images (water in various forms, trees, morning, sun, different smells) are an accumulation of moments that define love, age, sorrow, and pride in terms of action. Particular configurations recur: the rhythms of sex, the bent silhouettes of old age, the stillness of intense emotion. But taken together, these poems are like the spontaneous eruptions that punctuate, geyserlike, the flow of experience.

The other new poems in *I've Been a Woman* consist of a series of eulogies, collectively titled "Generations," in which Sanchez explicitly claims her place among those who speak of and for black people. There is a schematic balance operating here: the individual poems respectively eulogize Sterling Brown (age), Gerald Penny (youth), Sanchez's father, and the idea and reality of mothers. The synthesis implied in this design is enacted in the poetry itself; the imagery and rhythms of the verse in this section convey an overwhelming sense of resolution and serenity.

> David Williams. In Mari Evans, ed. *Black Women Writers (1950–1980): A Critical Evaluation* (New York: Doubleday, 1984), pp. 433–34, 446

Sonia Sanchez started writing plays because the longer dramatic form was useful when a poem could not contain her political message. The first published play by Sanchez appeared in *The Drama Review* special issue on black theater, edited by Ed Bullins. The short play *The Bronx Is Next* is set in Harlem in the midst of a racial revolution. Revolutionaries are burning all the buildings in a poor section to force the construction of livable housing units. A character called Old Sister, who is judged by the male leaders to be too attached to her oppressive past in Birmingham, is sent back to her apartment to go up in smoke with her possessions.

The play's other female character, called Black Bitch, projects the strident Sapphire stereotype so despised by male leaders of the movement as a threat to male superiority. The woman is devalued as both promiscuous, if not actually a professional prostitute, and nonseparatist. Not only is she caught in a compromising intimacy with a white policeman, but she spews forth condemnation of black men's abuse of black women, to which the male leader responds, "Oh shit. Another black matriarch on our hands." The leader immediately punishes and humiliates her with a brutal sexual assault and then sends her back to her apartment to burn in the holocaust. Although the Black Bitch character criticizes abusive men, she is portrayed as an enemy of the revolution who must be sacrificed for the future purity of the black nation. In the context of the dramatic piece, her complaints sound trivial and irrelevant if not downright black-hating.

Sanchez created her second play *Sister Son/ji* for *New Plays from the Black Theatre*, also edited by Ed Bullins. This dramatic monologue presents in flashbacks five periods in the life of a black revolutionary woman. Although the single speaking character does not present herself as a feminist, she acknowledges woman's frequent devaluation by abusive men intoxicated with self-importance. As Son/ji grows from her first act of resisting racism to a sense of betrayal by male revolutionaries who seduce and abandon women to maturity borne of loss and survival, the reader/ audience watches the character grow into solitary strength. . . .

The third revolutionary play published by Sanchez in the 1960s, *Uh, Huh; But How Do It Free Us*? presents three scenes which have no narrative connection but which illustrate the oppression created by power imbalance implicit in sexual polarity. The oppressed women in each scene suffer as a direct result of male selfishness and vanity. The male antagonists in the first and third scenes are portrayed as less pernicious than the female competitors for male attention.

The absurdist middle scene throws light on the power struggles in relationships dramatized more realistically in the framing first and third scenes. In the absurdist scene four (black) brothers and one white man ride rocking horses as a theatrical metaphor for their narcotic addictions. A black woman and a white woman, both called whores and costumed appropriately, cater to the sadomasochistic fantasies of the men by whipping them and bringing them cocaine upon demand. The scene concludes with a bizarre "queen contest" between the black whore and the character now called "white dude" prancing around the stage in drag and shouting, "See, I'm the real queen. I am the universe." Finally the white dude punches his opponent to the floor declaring, "Don't look at her. She's black. I'm white. The rightful queen." The scene suggests that all women are servants and caretakers for all men, regardless of race, but that only black men possess the true macho qualities inherent in the American masculine stereotype. White men easily degenerate into women.

The first and third scenes both centrally portray black revolutionary leaders whose vanity requires the sexual and nurturing attention of several women. Malik's two wives, both pregnant, are not sufficient to feed his insecurity. The reassurance of conquest is luring him on to pursue other women. The conservative homebody Waleesha contrasts with younger revolutionary activist wife Nefertia. Despite his past attentions, Malik has apparently tired of both of them by the time the play opens. Michele Wallace notes that the inordinate value placed on black masculinity tended to devalue black women's humanity to such an extent that young black women were dropping out of school because their boyfriends had convinced them that doing anything other than having babies and performing domestic chores was "counterrevolutionary."

> Rosemary K. Curb. In Karelisa V. Hartigan, ed. *The Many Forms of Drama* (Lanham, Maryland: University Press of America, 1985), pp. 20–21, 24–25

Sanchez's finest poetry, perhaps her strongest artistic achievement until *homegirls & handgrenades*, is represented by *A Blues Book for Blue Black Magical Women*. . . . Dedicated to the poet's father and to Elijah Muhammad "who has labored forty-two years to deliver us up from this Western Babylon," the book carries an epigraph from the Koran. In five parts, it begins with "Introduction (Queens of the Universe)," addressed to black women, urging them to "embrace / Blackness as a religion / husband," and to turn away from acquired, false Western values. The voice is that of the poet as teacher, a guide at one with her audience yet standing a little apart in order to gain and share perspective.

The longest section, part two, "Past," details the poet's physical and spiritual growth, beginning with an address to the "earth mother," whose voice responds. . . .

Part three, "Present," lyrically affirms her position. She accepts the Nation of Islam as her faith. In part four, "Rebirth," the poet returns to an ancestral home, one imaginatively inspired by Sanchez's travels in the Caribbean (Bermuda, Jamaica, Guyana). She also traveled to the People's Republic of China before finishing the book. In "Rebirth," her plane trip becomes a metaphor for her spiritual odyssey, "roaming the cold climate of my mind where / winter and summer hold the same temperature of need." The poet states that she has destroyed her imperfection, has "become like a temple," made her form from the form of Allah, and is "trying to be worthy."

> D. H. Melhem. *MELUS*. 12, 3 (fall 1985), pp. 90–91

It is appropriate when analyzing a work such as *homegirls & handgrenades* to wonder about what might have been the motivation for its subject matter and form. It might be declared by some that this is just another in a long line of Sonia Sanchez's books of poems. . . . Part of Sanchez's early effort was to experiment with words in verse to create a new perspective on how blacks should perceive themselves within the context of a nation struggling to admit them into the fold of social equality. Although that task remains incomplete, one can nevertheless sense a development on the part of the poet as she advances her work to include the mystical *A Blues Book for Blue Black Magical Women* as well as *Love Poems* where there can be seen an attempt to reconcile all the various aspects of black culture for the benefit of progress. *I've Been a Woman* and *Under a Soprano Sky* are further examples of how the author has examined, in particular, the plight of black

women as they strive toward freedom in a world not always conducive to that undertaking.

Nonetheless, it is in *homegirls* where Sanchez delivers what Henry Louis Gates [Jr.] has characterized as "the revising text . . . written in the language of the tradition, employing its tropes, its rhetorical strategies, and its ostensible subject matter, the so-called black Experience.". . . . This tradition of signifying on what other writers have done is a deep-rooted feature of black writing that has as its origin the culture of blacks as a whole. It is, interestingly enough, the mark of black culture in its most creative posture, that of being able to play upon what is available, in terms of form and substance, and convert it into something new and unique.

Such is the achievement of Sanchez, who, in *homegirls*, has rendered a marvelous collage of thirty-two short stories, poems, letters, and sketches that often ring loudly with the truth of an autobiographical fervor.

> James Robert Saunders. *MELUS*. 15, 1 (spring 1988), pp. 73–74

The newest book by Sanchez, *Under a Soprano Sky*, is dedicated to her father and to her late brother, Wilson Driver, Jr. The new poetry carries forward the poet's lyricism, her political commitment, her confessional/moral declensions, and what may be called her transcendental imagery: sensory images infused with spiritual awareness. Three elegies set the tone. "A poem for my brother (reflections on his death from AIDS)" is a brave poem that identifies the poet's life journey with her brother's journey into death. Its nature imagery and transcendence of death take it into the grand precincts of pastoral elegy. . . .

The second of the three, "elegy (for MOVE and Philadelphia)," a strong, ambitious work in eight parts, treats of the "philadelphia [sic] based back to nature group" (as MOVE is described in a footnote) whose headquarters were bombed by the police, with the mayor's approval, on May 13, 1985, killing men, women, and children, and destroying a block of houses in the ensuing fire. The tragedy gained national notoriety. The poet relates the events with heavy irony, through which she weaves biblical lamentation: "who anointeth this city with napalm? / who giveth this city in holy infanticide?" She concludes, however, with traces of hope: since "there are people / navigating the breath of hurricanes," there may be "honor and peace. / one day." In the related third elegy, "Philadelphia: Spring, 1985," a Philadelphia fireman reflects on the carnage after seeing a decapitated body in the MOVE ruins, when "the city, lit by a single fire, / followed the air into disorder."

> D. H. Melhem. *Heroism in the New Black Poetry* (Lexington: University Press of Kentucky, 1990), pp. 144–45

BIBLIOGRAPHY

*Homecoming*, 1969; *We a BaddDDD People*, 1970; *The Bronx Is Next*, 1970; *It's a New Day: Poems for Young Brothas and Sistuhs*, 1971; *Ima Talken' bout the Nation of Islam*, 1972; *Sister Son/ji*, 1972; *Dirty Hearts*, 1973; *Love Poems*, 1973; *A Blues Book for Blue Black Magical Women*, 1973; *The Adventures of Fat Head, Small Head, and Square Head*, 1973; *Uh Huh; But How Do It Free Us?*, 1975; *I've Been a Woman: New and Selected Poems*, 1978; *Malcolm Man/Don't Live Here No More*, 1979; *I'm Black When*

*I'm Singing, I'm Blue When I Ain't*, 1982; *A Sound Investment and Other Stories*, 1979; *homegirls & handgrenades*, 1984; *Under a Soprano Sky*, 1987; *Wounded in the House of a Friend*, 1995; *Does Your House Have Lions?*, 1995; *Black Cats Back and Uneasy Landings*, 1995; *Like the Singing Coming off the Drums: Love Poems*, 1998

# SARO-WIWA, Ken (1941–1995)
## Nigeria

In this modest contribution to Nigerian poetry in English [*Songs in a Time of War*], Ken Saro-Wiwa writes chiefly about the political manipulation and human waste of warfare. The war references are to the Biafran war, during which Saro-Wiwa served as a Federal administrator. Though these poems lack the immediacy and vivid particularity of J. P. Clark's war poems, they do convey a constant longing for silence and for the soft-breathing life of peaceful nighttime, as well as a sense of open landscape with a slightly menacing quality.

"The Escape" is a poem detailing the author's flight from the Delta region to Lagos as the Biafran troops advanced westward in September 1967. Among its images of fear and apprehension are one of the day hung out in front like a curtain, "A drawn-out horizon taut with uncertainty." During the river voyage he comes upon a scene in which

> White birds stood on stumps in mid-stream
> Silent and watchful . . .

In the same poem, the slightly archaic (Edwardian or First-World-War) diction that Saro-Wiwa uses can be sensed in "Naval guns boom as of yore." His point here is that, though his repetition of colonial experience might encourage a sense of déjà vu, in a civil war within an independent country "the issues are far greater."

Despite Saro-Wiwa's abhorrence of war and his concentration on the sorrow and pity of it all, he cannot resist some condemnation of Biafra's leaders, particularly in "Epitaph for Biafra":

> Didn't they test the hardness of the egg
> On the skin of their teeth
> Before dashing it against the rocks?

It is in such images that he manages to rise above the prosaic and declaratory quality of much of the verse. His best poems have a sensory quality that vivifies them, whether it is the "white balls of fire" that "Ascend the sky at dusk" in a war poem or the witty image of the "Tired and breathless spaceman" who, remembering an encounter with a courtesan, is able to "Toil on for the pleasures / Of the final splashdown."

The last poem in this small volume is a long satire in pidgin. In it the words "Nigeria" and "confusion" appear as a refrain, as Saro-Wiwa expresses both lament for and condemnation of Nigeria's openness to exploitation, corruption, and the temptation to borrow (both fiscally and culturally). Addressing the country, he says

> Nigeria, you too like borrow borrow
> You borrow money, cloth you dey borrow
> You borrow motor, you borrow aeroplane
> You dey borrow chop, you borrow drink
> Sotey you borrow anoder man language. . . .

It is a poem written in sorrow, not in resignation or hopelessness, for he has faith in the natural resources of the country and he does not despair of all the people, for

> Oh yes, som Nigerian pickin get sense
> And better go follow dem all.

> Ken Goodwin. *World Literature Written in English*. 27, 2 (autumn 1987), pp. 232–33

*Prisoners of Jebs* is a collection of 53 sketches, first published as a weekly column between January 1986 and January 1987 in the Nigerian *Vanguard* newspaper. In the "Author's Note," Ken Saro-Wiwa tells us that he wanted his column to "examine weekly events in Nigeria," and to the extent that a knowledge of Nigerian politics of this period is helpful for an appreciation of many of the references, it is unlikely that the book will have much appeal to non-Nigerians.

The scene is set in the first sketch, "The Building of the Prison," in which we are told that the Organisation of African Unity, celebrating its 25th anniversary, decide that "prisoners drawn from member-nations, locked up in a pollution-free environment and forced to think day and night about the problems of the continent . . . would certainly usher in progress." Nigeria is unanimously chosen as the site, and an off-shore prison, courtesy of the Dutch and the Bulgarians, is duly constructed.

This leaves the way for the kind of satire of Nigerian life that has now become the stock-in-trade of a number of inventive Nigerian journalists. Nigerians have never been slow to criticise their society; on the other hand, Nigerian society affords plenty of material: "The Nigerians had voted millions for the running of Jebs. The Nigerians always vote millions for the running of their institutions. And as is usual in Nigeria, Jebs' millions disappeared in no time. It was quite astounding, the ability of Nigeria's millions to perform the disappearing trick."

Or again: "In keeping with its reputation as Africa's most populous state, Nigeria had the most prisoners. And they were the loudest inmates. They showed off, broke all queues, played loud music, shouted at the top of their voices, refused to do manual labour, and ate and drank most."

Almost every Nigerian newspaper, of which there are an estimated 23 dailies and 29 weeklies, delights in this kind of social comment. This probably represents the nation's greatest hope: nobody can accuse Nigerians of being unable to laugh at themselves, a pre-requisite for fundamental social change.

Social satire of this kind also serves a useful function if you happen to be stuck in a car in Lagos during one of the legendary "go-slows"—the experience of anybody who has to go to work every day. Unfortunately, journalism rarely survives longer than the date on the newspaper. After the first half-dozen sketches in *Prisoners of Jebs* I found myself growing just a little weary, partly because the joke had worn a little thin, partly because the form itself precludes any development of character.

> Adewale Maja-Pearce. *New Statesman and Society*. 1, 7 (July 22, 1988), p. 44

Saro-Wiwa's first novel *Sozaboy* is also probably his most challenging work in critical terms. It is a record of the war experiences (the Nigerian civil war) of a naive youth, Mene. . . .

In *Sozaboy* Saro-Wiwa boldly confronts three critical areas of fiction writing: language, point of view and plotting. The area of language has attracted the most critical interest, and the reason is clear: Saro-Wiwa breaks with precedence and writes in what he calls 'rotten English'. . . .

One of the more striking and positive aspects of Saro-Wiwa's linguistic experimentation is that he possesses enough artistic control to sustain the tone and idiom for the entire length of the book. An additional achievement is that the author manages somehow not to lose the seriousness of import of certain scenes and incidents to what might initially appear to be a linguistic parody. For instance, Mene's brutal experiences still strike the reader with deep horror, even in this level of expression. It is also this linguistic level or medium which stamps a distinctive personality on Mene, the narrator, and also exposes the naive quality with which the author endows him. The author therefore remains faithful to his definition of his 'rotten English' and largely succeeds in making it work as a narrative medium. At no time, indeed, does the reader lose a consciousness of the grimness of the war situation that is being described. . . .

In a novel with a first-person narrative point of view, such as *Sozaboy*, the crucial challenge for the author is to convince the reader that the opinions and perceptions which are expressed or implied by the naive or unreliable narrator are credibly his, and not those of an intrusive author hiding behind the mask of a naive character.

In *Sozaboy* Saro-Wiwa battles with this technical challenge by determinedly sustaining the naive image of his protagonist. Mene is remarkably, even incredibly naive. He perceives events and incidents at a surface or literal level. He is easily carried away, and when notions get into his head he acts on them as though they were reality. Agnes is the first girl in his life and he is quickly overwhelmed by her relatively sophisticated romantic adventurousness. In no time at all he marries her. His joining the army in war time and putting his life at obvious risk is precipitated by nothing more serious than his wife's wish for a 'soza husband who can defend her when trouble come', and a childish notion that he will rise fast in the ranks and return to protect his Dukana kinsmen from the harassments of war-time soldiers. In training at the military camp, what impress him most are the parades, road marches and the singing. The possibility of danger and death do not even come into his consciousness. . . .

Ultimately, *Sozaboy* will survive as a work of art mainly on the success of its bold experiment with language. This, I think, is a considerable achievement for a first novel.

In *Prisoners of Jebs* (1990) Saro-Wiwa returns to conventional satire and language. As a satirist he scores excellent marks, employing with adroitness the literary devices of ridicule, humour, deliberate exaggeration, and so on. His knowledge of the Nigerian, even African, environment is all-encompassing, and this makes it possible for him to people his satirical world with characters from all tiers of Nigerian and African society—politicians, military top brass, contractors, sycophants, tribalists, journalists, members of the judiciary, drug traffickers and more.

Having created his allegorical setting, his Lilliput, Saro-Wiwa proceeds. Swiftian fashion, to excoriate Nigerian society. The dominant tone is one of acerbic humour: the reader is encouraged to laugh, but not to overlook the serious issues of ethnic domination, corrupt judiciary and governments, armed robbery, ill-educated journalists (symbolized by Peter Dumbrok), wastage and stealing of public funds (the Prison Director), the toleration of filthy environments (the Prison itself) and the irrelevance of much of the African military set-up (the 'snoozing generals' arrive at Jebs and promptly fall asleep).

Fate and events on the Nigerian scene, and the African continent generally, stock Saro-Wiwa's satirical arsenal. An exaggerated celebration of a minor football cup victory, wasteful overspending on a continental meeting, the suspicious escape from custody of a drug-pusher or an armed robbery suspect, the loss of his money bags to foreign thieves by an African president, the unguarded utterances of prominent politicians, the geo-political ambitions of Gaddafi, an unfavourable review of his book—all these are turned to satirical advantage by the author. This trait also makes the story appear too topical in content: but most successful satires reflect the contemporary events of their times—so long as the satire is anchored to the basic or enduring foibles of the particular society that generates it, and the satirist is able to maintain a certain allegorical distance. . . .

What Saro-Wiwa's satire refuses to do is to pretend that the ills of Nigerian society are merely skin-deep and transient: it refuses to promote a false optimism about a future that will correct itself without a reformed, penitent populace. Acute to the percent lapses of his society accounts for the frequent harshness of tone. What Saro-Wiwa said of the social goals of his television series 'Basi and Company' could well apply to *Prisoners of Jebs* and its sequel, *Pita I ambroh's Prison* (1991): 'We were creating an awareness of predicament. This was the most important thing. We are in trouble as a nation. And unless people realise this, they would not be able to change their habits'. To create the necessary awareness. Saro-Wiwa through his satire makes himself society's gadfly, an last with little respect for corrupt sacred cows.

N. F. Inyama. In Eldred D. Jones, ed. *New Trends and Generations* (Trenton: Africa World Press, Inc., 1996), pp. 35–49

Ken Saro-Wiwa's published plays are one-acters, mostly collected in the two volumes *Four Farcical Plays* (1989) and *Basi and Company: Four Television Plays* (1990). Common to both volumes is Saro-Wiwa's best-known play, *The Transistor Radio*, which began life as a review sketch performed at the University of Ibadan in 1964 and was later fleshed out and adapted into, successively, a 600-line stage play, a radio play (published in a Heinemann anthology in 1973), and then the television play that formed the kernel of the hugely successful *Basi and Company* comedy series. Comparison of the three versions throws light on Saro-Wiwa's intentions as a dramatist, on his working methods as a professional writer, and, more generally, on questions having to do with the ideology of the text. Points of interest are the gradual abandonment of Pidgin from stage to radio to television scripts; the softening of dialogue and the gradual removal of didactic elements; the building-up of dramatic elements useful for generating fresh situations in a sit-com (such as the consolidation of ''closed'' characteristics, such as Basi's wit, and recurrent dynamics, for example Dandy and Josco's plotting against Basi). Other Basi scripts gathered in *Basi and Company* include *Comrades All*, which is basically a direct spin-off from the plot of *The Transistor Radio*, and *The Mattress*: consistently in these plays plot is generated from intrigue and counter-intrigue, from the comic motif of ''the swindler swindled.'' This is one of the most familiar—and most appreciated—motifs in Nigerian English-language theater. . . .

Apart from the stage version of *The Transistor Radio*, the *Four Farcical Plays* volume contains *Bride by Return, The Wheel*, and *Madam No Go Quench Again*. *Bride by Return* is a slight piece (thematically, at least; here, as in *The Transistor Radio* and *The Wheel*, the dialogue is expertly written for effective comedy). The central dynamic depends on the audience's recognition of businessman Nubari's pretentiousness and its appreciation of his ludicrous back of self-awareness. In performance it would be fascinating to try to gauge an audience's reaction to—and, in their own comments, interaction with—Nubari's constant enthusing about English culture and the English language. Interestingly, in the context of Saro-Wiwa's other work, although he dialogue touches on the fact that Nubari has made his fortune from winning a contract, the potential theme of corruption is not developed. The play's audience is left to construct a morally significant personal (and typifying) history for Nubari and to read him in that light, or to enjoy what is simply given, the comic mechanism that distances them from him at a less significant level, that of his patent ridiculousness. As with many satirical plays in the Nigerian English-language theater, one wants to know how exactly does an audience respond to the characterization of the (at one level or another) unlovely rich, undeservedly powerful.

This question arises again with *The Wheel*, a play whose plot deals explicitly with corruption and the way this is entrenched within an institution as—in chain reaction—successive applicants for preferment or employment succumb to the need to bribe to achieve their goal. This is perhaps the most theatrically effective of the short plays, and one that with adaptation from the Nigerian context travels successfully (excerpts were performed to enthusiastic audiences in Lesotho and in Pietermaritzburg, South Africa, in November 1995). Saro-Wiwa's comic invention here is well-nigh irresistible, as he sustains the play's essential repetitive structure through ingenious parallelism, not only avoiding monotony but pointing the humor as each fresh change is rung, as each successive applicant bribes his way into power and (now an employer) compels the next applicant to bribe him in turn. The dialogue is expertly designed to show how each successive patron, each successive supplicant, strategizes corruption, to show their shifting emotional states of anxiety, expectation, and gratification. For its two actors the play is a gift, allowing them to establish its basic ground-plan and then to highlight variation: for example, by suggesting—as they swap, turn, and turn around, from role as patron to role as supplicant—different species of arrogance, intelligence, voracity.

Again, though, some doubts arise about the nature of the impact of the play's satire: whether the verve with which the bribery is carried out, the comedy drawn from variation as the chain reaction proceeds, and the dramatic technique of self-exposure used as each applicant enthuses about his skill in corruption, do not seriously compromise the effectiveness of the play's exposé. . . .

The last two scenes of *The Wheel*, admittedly, add a slightly different dimension to the play. The final supplicant is, unlike the others, impoverished, illiterate, a Pidgin speaker whose explicit references to his poverty and whose anger at having to bribe his way into a job appear to impact on the audience through a slightly different compound of empathy and alienation from that provoked in the earlier scenes of the play. Even so, the character's pleas of

poverty are part-comic, his succumbing to corruption comic-empathetic. Questioning the affective function of satire in performance is, I suppose, something of a critical cliché. It is, though, an unavoidable question, in a situation in which satire is such a prominent medium, one which attracts such audience loyalty.

It is in the unpublished plays that one finds Saro-Wiwa working both on a more ambitious scale and with more searching, more disturbing subject matter. Below I describe three plays: *The Supreme Commander*, staged by Paul Okpokam in Calabar shortly after the Civil War; *Dream of Sologa*, an adaptation of Gabriel Okara's *The Voice*, written in 1966 and, as far as I know, not performed to date; and *Eneka*, which was acted in Port Harcourt in 1971 (?), with a cast that included Elechi Amadi and Okogbule Wonodi. *Eneka* was sufficiently provocative to lead the then military governor of Rivers State, A. P. Diete-Spiff, to disband the troupe who performed it, after attending the play as guest of honor (pers. comm. 21 Jan. 1991).

*The Supreme Commander*—Saro-Wiwa's adaptation of Gogol's *The Government Inspector*—comes in the form of a long one-acter (though the photocopied typescript from which I am working indicates a break in performance about half-way through, as the comedy of intrigue and exposure moves into its second stage). As in the Gogol and in Osofisan's adaptation, *Who's Afraid of Solarin?*, which was first staged six to seven years after the Saro-Wiwa, The Supreme Commander combines different species of comedy: a notable difference between the Saro-Wiwa and the Osofisan is that the latter, while incorporating much caustic satire aimed at Nigeria's governing elite, contains many more extended elements of pure (and brilliantly executed) farce. Taken together, the Gogol, Saro-Wiwa, and Osofisan plays provide a case study in the construction of satire, its impact on its audience, and its relationship to other comic modes. . . .

*Dream of Sologo*—Saro-Wiwa's dramatization of Okara's *The Voice* is in three short acts, corresponding to the novel's setting: village, city, return to village. With a total running time of about 70 minutes, the play comprises highly succinct dramatization of the key scenes of the novel, the most substantial omission being the boat journey that takes the hero, Okolo, from his village to Sologa.

Saro-Wiwa makes no attempt to repeat Okara's experiment in translingualism, yet generally sticks closely to the substance of the novel's dialogue.

Two points stand out . . . sharply, and with obvious and poignant resonance vis-à-vis Saro-Wiwa's work as political and human rights activist. First, here is a strong emphasis from the very opening lines on the role of the complacent, the collaborators with a dictatorial regime, who warn each other, ''Don't think,'' who ''dance as the drum dictates.'' This, of course, as a major theme of the novel, but more than any other motif it is this one that is foregrounded in Saro-Wiwa's severe condensation of the original. Second, there is Saro-Wiwa's reworking of the novel's ending. While, like Okara, Saro-Wiwa has Okolo and Tuere die, in a move that draws the material closer to Soyinka's *The Strong Breed*—and then beyond—he emphasizes the posthumous effectiveness of the outcasts' message, having (in Ukule's account) Chief Izongo lose his authority over the village, calling meetings and wandering from market to market, trying to convince a now-alienated population to speak to him, finally committing suicide in Tuere's hut. . . .

The opening and expository scene of *Eneka* has elderly villagers discussing their deepening poverty under the corrupt and exploitative rule of the provincial chief, Ezomo. In a phrase that recalls Brecht—and that anticipates recognitions such as those on which Osofisan's *Once upon Four Robbers* is built—they complain that "the man whose goat is stolen becomes the thief, the man who stole the goat the judge." As the play develops there is an emphasis on the leadership's wastage of the land's resources. . . .

Thematically, much of the interest the play offers derives from the same kind of triple conflict found in *Dream of Sologa*: here, between Ezomo and his court; the progressive forces led by Eneka; those complacent villagers (at first in the majority) who recognize Ezomo's corruption but find it safer and easiest not to resist this. Throughout the play's first half (roughly fifty minutes) there are two basic dramatic foci: the interlinked plotting for power and advantage at Ezomo's court and at the court of the Oba of Benin (under whose jurisdiction Uzebu falls); the campaign by Eneka to persuade Uzebu to rise against Ezomo.

> Chris Dunton. *Research in African Literatures*. 29, 1 (spring 1998), pp. 153–62

BIBLIOGRAPHY

*The Transistor Radio*, 1972; *Tabari*, 1973; *Tambari in Dukana*, 1973; *Songs in a Time of War*, 1985; *Sozaboy: A Novel in Rotten English*, 1985; *A Forest of Flowers*, 1986; *Basi and Company: A Modern African Folktale*, 1987; *Prisoners of Jebs*, 1988; *Adaku, and Other Stories*, 1989; *Four Farcical Plays*, 1989; *On a Darkling Plain: An Account of the Nigerian Civil War*, 1989; *Nigeria: The Brink of Disaster*, 1991; *Pita Dumbrok's Prison*, 1991; *Similia: Essays on Anomic Nigeria*, 1991; *The Singing Anthill: Ogoni Folk Tales*, 1991; *Genocide in Nigeria: The Ogoni Tragedy*, 1992; *Mr. B's Mattress*, 1992; *Second Letter to Ogoni Youth*, 1993; *Ogoni: Moment of Truth*, 1994; *A Month and a Day: A Detention Diary*, 1995

# SCHWARZ-BART, Simone (1938–)
Guadeloupe

The problems of alienation and troubled consciousness; the awareness of past victimization, present disarray, and future uncertainty; and the urgency of the quest for self and group identity are themes that have been consistently explored by Simone Schwarz-Bart in her first two novels, *Un Plat de porc aux bananes vertes* and *Pluie et vent sur Télumée Miracle*. Her latest novel *Ti Jean l'horizon* mirrors her continuing concern with the cultural and psychic legacy accumulated in the history of her native Guadeloupe in particular, in the French Antilles in general and, by extension, in all the former European colonies of the Caribbean. But whereas *Un Plat de porc aux bananes vertes* and even more so *Pluie et vent sur Télumée Miracle* limit their perspective in space and time, *Ti Jean l'horizon*, beginning from a specific locus, explores the outer limits of the primordial. Taking its inspiration from the magical world of the Antillean stories, the novel, divided into nine books, follows the fabulous adventures of the mythical hero in his quest for lost identity and lost love.

The novel opens in Fond-Zombi, Guadeloupe. The inhabitants are polarized into two distinct groups, those living in the forested plateau (the "gens d'En-haut") and those on the neighboring lowlands (the "gens d'En-bas"). The forest dwellers, retaining

almost intact their ancestral African culture and their tradition of revolt against plantation life, lead a rude, uncultured existence under the domination of Wademba, the last of the Maroons. The more "civilized" plains dwellers are despised by the mountain folk, who believe that they have lost their original identity as they continue a precarious existence as serfs of the plantation owners. However, the easy existence of the villagers proves attractive to some of the forest dwellers. Thus the companion of Wademba and later his daughter Awa leave the mountain hideout to settle on the lowlands. Ti Jean L'horizon, born of the union of Awa and a lowland dweller, represents a synthesis of the two polarized cultures.

> Wilbert J. Roget. *World Literature Today*. 55, 1 (winter 1981), p. 163

In Schwarz-Bart's [*Ti Jean l'horizon*], the hero is at once an orphan (his mother's husband dies before he is born) and a divine son to Wademba (also known as "The Immortal"), the island's cultural protector. Wademba has overseen Guadeloupe's generations since the slave-trade crossing, and upon his death he entrusts the protection of their cultural legacy to Ti Jean. Furthermore, he confers upon him a mission to return to Africa and to restore the links to the cultural homeland. In taking on this spiritual and cultural enterprise, Ti Jean "orphans himself." As Jesus renounced his worldly parents in order to embrace his spiritual family, Ti Jean leaves his home and his wife-girlfriend in order to regain the larger family ties between his Caribbean people and their African homeland. . . .

In Schwarz-Bart's [*Pluie et vent sur Télumée Miracle*], the motif of flight is associated with the same spirit of strength and freedom as in *Ti Jean* and [Toni Morrison's *Song of Solomon*]. When misfortune sets in, Télumée feels "Le maré-cage était sous mes pieds, c'était l'heure de me faire légère, adroite, ailée. . . .'' [The swamp was beneath my feet, it was time to become light, quick, winged.] Flight in this novel, as in the others, does not always necessarily have positive value, however, as when Lange Medard flies off with Télumée's adopted daughter, Sonore. In [Morrison's] *Tar Baby*, the negative aspect of flight is evidenced in Jadine's final flight from the island, from the daisy-tree women and from Ondine who would envelop her in her arms. It is also a flight from Son who might have been her passport on a flight similar to Milkman's or Ti Jean's, had she been willing.

The most complex and perhaps the most fascinating flight to be found in these novels is that of Ti Jean. His journey, like the others, is both internal and external, both self-discovery and discovery of the outer world. But Ti Jean's journey is internal and external in another way as well. When Wademba dies, his ghost soul slips through Ti Jean's lips and enters his body. Ti Jean's journey to Africa, with which he has been charged, occurs inside the belly of the bird-beast—or Wademba himself. Thus his journey is a cosmic voyage of a doubly internal sort—both within himself (an existential self-searching) and within his "father's" belly (an adventure backwards into Wademba's African legacy). The paradox of the doubly inner voyage is that it leads to the outside world of present time and to the discovery of the cultural legacy that each African descendant embodies. . . .

In *Pluie* [*et vent*], Télumée, who triumphs over affliction (the "rain" and "wind" of the title), helps others in the community to endure and to overcome their own painful struggles. She also has "witch powers" in the art of healing learned from her grandmother. Her healing powers, as well as her personal integrity, lead her to be regarded in her old age as the grandmother of the entire community: "Maman Miracle, tu es l'arbre contre lequel s'appuie notre hameau, et que deviendra le morne sans toi, le sais-tu?" [Mother Miracle, you are the tree against which we prop up our hamlet, and what would become of this little knoll without you, do you know?] Ti Jean's life, perhaps more than Son's, resembles a black version of the Christ story. He is born of a mysterious conception, fathered by the bird-god Wademba. He goes on to make sense of the cosmos, indeed to regenerate it, and to trace the history of his people. When he returns to Guadeloupe, the magic ring, the perfect circle of the cosmos, given him by Wademba, comes to his aid, "telling him the sign, and the path, and the way." From out of the belly of the beast, he restores the sun to his people. . . . Ti Jean's return to his community inaugurates a transformation, a new era of hope and strength; and his marriage to Égee—who is likened to the damp, the sands, to the brilliance of flame itself—signifies a hierogamous union, a wedding between Guadeloupe and the cosmos itself.

> Josie P. Campbell. *Comparative Literature Studies*. 22, 3 (fall 1985), pp. 397, 401–3

[*Pluie et vent sur Télumée Miracle*] opens and closes upon the same scene: an old woman standing in her garden, dreaming of the past and waiting tranquilly for death. The figure is that of the narrator, Télumée, who has received, late in life, the admiring nickname "Télumée Miracle." Her upright posture suggests dignity, strength, and a resolute will to resist adversity; these are the qualities to which the narrative continually reverts, and which serve to create its prevailing moral climate. Behind Télumée's vertical stance there is a second, latent image, that of a tree. Unexpressed at the start of the novel, this image becomes explicit as the story advances and she is successively compared to a bamboo, a poinciana or *flamboyant*, a coconut palm, and an acomat. The tree, with its stable roots and promise of upward growth, is a familiar presence in the work of [Aime] Césaire and [Jacques] Roumain: a symbol of constancy and harmonious integration, of triumphant recovery from the uprooting and alienation consequent on the fall of slavery. . . . In Simone Schwarz-Bart's [*Pluie et vent sur Télumée Miracle*] the tree . . . is above all associated with courage and tenacity. At the end of the novel, which tells the story of Télumée's life in early twentieth-century Guadeloupe, the image is specifically linked to the theme of her indomitable spirit by the tribute which her neighbors pay to her: "Mama Miracle, you are the tree our hamlet leans against." . . .

Critical discussions of this novel have stressed the way in which the narrator's life, like that of her female ancestors, falls into a recurrent pattern of ascent, ruin, and subsequent renaissance, in seeming obedience to a cyclical view of man's progression through time. The pattern is only lightly delineated in the case of Télumée's great-grandmother Minerva, the first of the Lougandor women: she is freed from a cruel master by the abolition of slavery in 1848, then is abandoned in a state of pregnancy by a transient lover, but is rescued by a tender and steadfast man who loves Minerva's child as if she were his own. It is more firmly sketched in when the narrator recounts the life of her mother, Victory, an unmarried girl struggling to bring up her first child, Regina, when she is abandoned by a faithless new lover from a neighboring island. She is rescued from months of alcoholic despair and degeneration by the gentle, compassionate Angebert, the future father of Télumée. Then Angebert's

sudden, violent death casts her back into solitude; but two years later she meets the great love of her life, and soon sets sail with him for the island of Dominica. Briefly though they appear in the narrative, both Minerva and Victory have essential virtues in common with their respective daughters, Toussine (Télumée's grandmother) and Télumée herself. Minerva, the founder of the Lougandor line, who bears the name of the goddess of wisdom, is a woman who walks with her "head high" and has "an unshakable faith in life." Victory, whose slight body perhaps reflects her moral status as the most lightweight of the Lougandor women, is nonetheless a valiant fighter who also "carrie[s] her head high on a slender neck" and is moved by a "determination to stay serene however harshly the winds might blow." Forever singing at her work, keeping her griefs and disappointments to herself, she survives poverty, a miscarriage, the loss of her lovers, and the sole responsibility of two young children, without losing an innate knack of resilience and optimism; "not a fallen woman," she goes through life "with the same expectation, the same lightness she had when no man's hand had yet touched her." At some of the lowest moments of Télumée's life, Victory's example helps to sustain her: singing about her domestic tasks so as to distance herself from a faultfinding white employer, or mentally thanking her laundress mother for the "steel wrists" she has inherited, which enable her to endure the heavy labor of cutting cane.

> Beverley Ormerod. *An Introduction to the French Caribbean Novel* (London: Heinemann, 1985), pp. 108, 110

[The plot of *Ti Jean l'horizon*] follows the traditional thematic schema for quest literature, even down to the formal division of the story into seven episodes, each with a title announcing the adventure to come. The biological child of his good-natured Antillean father and the spiritual child of his African grandfather Wademba, Ti Jean moves in three spheres that make up the topography of his Guadeloupe: the hilly retreat of the Old Ancestors who remember and celebrate the heroism of runaway slaves; the village below inhabited by Guadeloupeans who discard the old in favor of the new and the modern; and the mysterious domain of spirits who roam the woods—the dead and the souls partially transformed into animals. The call to adventure comes when a huge cowlike beast appears on the island and swallows scores of inhabitants as well as the sun itself. When the Beast swallows Ti Jean's fiancée Egée, the young hunter returns to the Old Ancestors for counsel and his grandfather's magical arms: a belt of strength, a ring of wisdom, and an old musket from the times of the slave revolts. Once inside the Beast in search of Egée, Ti Jean journeys to other worlds: first to Wademba's homeland in Africa, then to the Kingdom of the Dead, then around the polar seas to France, and finally back to Guadeloupe. Ti Jean returns with a full measure of *connaissance*, a deep understanding of all three domains. Having learned the secret of the Beast, Ti Jean uses the musket to kill it and restore both his people and the sun to their proper place. Ti Jean himself undergoes a final transformation from an old man back into a youth who finds his lost love waiting for him and assumes the wisdom and the destiny of his island.

Ti Jean's journey is fascinating in that it leads the reader to the farthest possible limits in what is not just a quest but also a questioning of the Antillean search for identity. The young hero's passage to the inside of the Beast triggers an ironic, otherworldly look at ideas and cultural experience normally accepted as a matter of fact. In this case, that look, like the laser gaze of the Beast itself, deconstructs four myths traditionally associated with Antillean quest: the return to Africa, the power of the spirit world, the Promised Land of France, and the heroic, linear dimensions of machismo.

Kitzie McKinney. *French Review*. 62, 4 (March 1989), pp. 654–55

Some works in Caribbean feminine expression can be viewed as breaking the chain of alienation. They propose images of women who find a voice to claim a parcel of power over reality and destiny. These works provoke interesting questions and uncover uncharted domains for women and the Caribbean as a whole. Such is the project of Simone Schwarz-Bart in *Pluie et vent sur Télumée Miracle*, strangely translated under the title *The Bridge of Beyond*. Schwarz-Bart affirms the forces of life against those of death and destruction. She articulates a poetry of presence and plenitude against absence and fragmentation. With her, the notions of Caribbean self and Caribbean history become thinkable. Télumée, her heroine, like the other women of the Lougandor family to which she belongs, expresses all that is possible to express in spite of the adverse conditions threatening her resolve to live. A system of liberating myths is elaborated in this novel, which celebrates the regenerating power of love and the possibility of conquering what in the brutal logic of realism seems impossible: freedom. To the reality of the plantation, of conditions of the Antilles, Schwarz-Bart opposes the indomitable spirit of women who refuse to be subjugated. Télumée draws her energy from the language and culture of the island, which mediates her entrance into the world of identity, presence, and continuity. Télumée is not extradited outside of her body, whose beauty she offers to her lover, Elie. She feels ''right in her place where she is,'' that is, in the island. The island in Schwarz-Bart's fiction is not a place to be fled nor a prison in which one slowly dies; it is the locus of self-discovery and human realization. One can speak of Schwarz-Bart's aesthetic practice as a veritable ''poetic of space.'' There is a certain solemnity in this novel, which celebrates the reappropriation by the islanders of their territory. Schwarz-Bart introduces her own Creolized language to take possession of the landscape. She selects a precise vocabulary to name familiar sites, trees, flowers, and plants of the island. It is as if the legitimate occupation of the Caribbean soil by its inhabitants depended on the act of naming. Time is reconquered as the Caribbean existence is replaced in its historical continuum. The quest for the African source is central in Schwarz-Bart's reconstruction of reality. Other dimensions are conquered as the author undertakes a bold exploration of the magical realm that lies beyond empirical reality. In this perilous enterprise, Schwarz-Bart never succumbs to sterile and factitious imagery. The point of departure and the point of arrival of her narrative is always the human experience.

In *Ti Jean l'horizon* . . . Schwarz-Bart executes one of the most accomplished Caribbean literary compositions. In this daring epic, history converges with the marvelous, playful notes alternating with grave tones, and vivacious spirit blends with an introspective mood. It is a polyphonic construct in which the author harmonizes different voices to tell a tale of indestructible love, the love of Ti Jean for Egée, a ''négresse sans fard ni pose'' [negress with neither makeup nor attitude], whom he calls his ''Little Guadeloupe.'' It is

also the fantastic tale of the hero's search for the sun, symbol of freedom, which has disappeared, swallowed by a monstrous Beast from ''elsewhere.'' At the end of his long journey through the present and the past, the realms of reality and surreality, Ti Jean, the hero, feels ''old as the mountains'' but convinced that ''everything is intact.'' The end, for him, is only the beginning because ''already, life was being reinvented, passionately, in light of torches simply painted in the soil.'' Schwarz-Bart in her fiction brings to an apotheosis the creative force already illustrated in the remarkable works of Jacques Roumain, Jacques S. Alexis, and Edouard Glissant. Like these writers, she concretizes through a conscious aesthetic practice a *Weltanschauung* that recognizes the urgency of collective liberation. Her recently published play *Ton beau capitaine* also deserves mention here. In this piece, Schwarz-Bart, with an economy of words and brilliant insight, succeeds in relating the struggle of man and woman to forge a language to communicate over the waters that separate them. It is the story of a Haitian migrant worker in Guadeloupe and his wife, who remains in Haiti. It is a story of dreams shattered but unceasingly reformed, of truth emerging from lies, of desire indefinitely postponed, of two people searching for unknown words to formulate their love. A masterpiece of conciseness and vision, this play is significant not only because of the themes it explores but also because it suggests the development of a dialogue between the Caribbean societies. It signifies that Guadeloupe is aware of Haiti in an eminently urgent manner. It implies that a cross-discursive space has been created where a new debate on the destiny of the Caribbean is taking place.

Marie-Denise Shelton. In Selwyn R. Cudjoe, ed. *Caribbean Women Writers* (Wellesley, Massachusetts: Calaloux Publications, 1990), pp. 354–56

Simone Schwarz-Bart's novels . . . attempt to treat the predicament of the woman and West Indian society at the level of the individual enduring life: self-esteem and self-worth are restored through a process of revalorizing of images and a heritage seen in negative terms by most *Antillais*. Schwarz-Bart reverses the connotations of the closed space and emphasizes only its positive, nurturing aspects. Her heroines' voyages are symbolic interior journeys. Coupled with the defeated, fettered figure is the other face of the islander, that of the hardy intrepid adventurer, braving the elements in order to survive, of the Maroon who lives by wits and is a figure of revolt and resourcefulness. This is the image evoked by the Guadeloupean novelist Simone Schwarz-Bart in the original title of her novel *The Bridge of Beyond* which, in the original French (*Pluie et vent sur Télumée Miracle*) means ''Rain and Wind on Télumée, the Miracle woman.'' Télumée, indeed, is called ''*marron sans bois*''—a testimony to her qualities of survival, self-sufficiency, and independence. Here the woman is a figure of strength and resistance and the island, hamlet, boat, or room becomes not a negative space but a positive one, not a restrictive enclosure, but a solid base from which to venture out to brave the waters of life, the open sea, that sea which at once protects and threatens, isolates and frees, gives and takes life.

Schwarz-Bart's vision does not deny either history or the realities of island life. Guadeloupe, Télumée's island, is described as ''cette île à volcans, à cyclones et moustiques, àmauvaise mentalité'': battered by hurricanes, infected with mosquitos and with her share of people who as we say in Creole ''have bad min'' (are bad minded). It is a tiny speck on the map, but for Schwarz-Bart's heroines it is not a land with no past and no history. Schwarz-Bart makes explicit in her work that her concept of the island is at variance with the view of those who consider it unimportant or insignificant. Moreover, it is not necessary to look overseas to Europe or to Africa to find a sense of worth. Schwarz-Bart's heroines struggle resolutely to resist and reject the negative attitudes of the people around them and assert their power to remain afloat and upright in the waters of life. The Lougandor women journey not to France or to Guinea, but deep within themselves.

Télumée, an old lady, standing in her tiny garden, transcends the limitations of her island and her history and affirms her desire to relive her life, to suffer and to die in exactly the same circumstances. But one must come to terms with the reality in order to transcend it. Whatever hand life deals, one must play it. The Lougandor women, Télumée's clan, accept their destiny but refuse to be bowed by it. Télumée's life is rooted in positive values and in a belief in herself acquired at her grandmother's knee. It is a security conferred by a belief in an alternative vision of reality to which many *Antillais* do not subscribe or have access. Télumée has never "suffered from the exiguity" of her homeland, for, according to Télumée, "the country depends on the size of one's heart." One's reality is conditioned by one's point of view.

> Elizabeth Wilson. In Carole Boyce Davies and Elaine Savory Fido, eds. *Out of the Kumbla: Caribbean Women and Literature* (Trenton, New Jersey: Africa World Press, 1990), pp. 53–54

Simone Schwarz-Bart's novel *The Bridge of Beyond* is a celebration of life, manifest through a story told. The heroine. Télumée, has puzzled out a meaning for her life, and she shares it with us. It is the essential feature of Télumée's story that she tells it. In doing so she integrates the entire fabric of her life, by naming herself and each person in her life, and situating them all in time and place, on her island home of Guadeloupe. Throughout the text, and the life that the text embodies, words are a charged and living force, for good or ill, and silence can be tantamount to destruction or annihilation. Thus Télumée's story is a triumph simply because it exists as an ordered narrative. As a story told, it is a gift of life. . . .

Télumée learns to harness her words through an essential and insoluble spiritual union which reveals itself in the story through song and storytelling. The principal bonding relationship in this story is that between grandmother and grandchild, a tie reflected by the fact that, in the telling, Télumée's autobiography becomes at one and the same time her grandmother's biography. The fact that Télumée is situated in the text principally as storyteller serves to emphasize the grandmother's crucial role in her life, for within Télumée's own narrative, it is her grandmother who is presented as the storyteller. Thus it is Toussine who, by giving Télumée the comfort of words and the wisdom they contain, makes of Télumée a storyteller, and bequeaths to her the wisdom she finally transmits to us through autobiography. In a text wondrously conscious of the giving and receiving of words, Télumée's narrative teaches us to accept that there are words that separate, and words that bind. She passes on, as her legacy to us, that gift of metaphor which she herself received from her grandmother, and which served to liberate her own life. . . .

*The Bridge of Beyond* opens with the words "A man's country may be cramped or vast according to the size of his heart. I've never found my country too small." Two hundred pages later, the last sentences are "Sun risen, sun set, the days slip past and the sand blown by the wind will engulf my boat. But I shall die here, where I am, standing in my little garden. What happiness." Yet in between these two statements we have had a record of a great deal of suffering, a great deal of pain, a lot of betrayal. What matters to Télumée in the story of herself and her people, is that by the end she is sure of who she is, and where she is; and it is the grandmother who has helped her learn both, *and taught her how to tell us this*. The miraculous Télumée does manage to make sense of her world, and she tells us, and her narrative is a testimony to the bond between women for the articulation of liberty. Throughout the narrative, the guiding principle remains the same: to find the balance between alienation and annihilation. Both internal and external enslavement must be combatted. We must not be controlled either by our dreams, or by those of others. Life is beleaguered, but in the end, both its pains and its joys must be weathered, and it is this triumph which is manifest through narrative. Télumée has withstood the "rain and wind" upon her, and knows she is "not a statue of salt to be dissolved." She therefore leaves us, although unable to comfort the forlorn Elie, with a sense of joy in herself, and in her world.

> Abena P. A. Busia. In Carole Boyce Davies and Elaine Savory Fido, eds. *Out of the Kumbla: Caribbean Women and Literature* (Trenton, New Jersey: Africa World Press, 1990), pp. 289, 291–92, 299

Simone Schwarz-Bart's play *Ton beau capitaine* was inspired by the real-life circumstance of Haitian men who leave their native land in search of work. Set in 1985, it presents agricultural worker Wilnor Baptiste, who lives in Guadeloupe while his wife Marie-Ange remains behind in Haiti. During their years of separation they communicate by way of audiocassette. Wilnor's simultaneous absence from Haiti and presence in Guadeloupe are the subjects of this 1987 play. Consequently, patterns of isolation, separation, displacement, and exile are found throughout the text.

Even before the play opens, Schwarz-Bart underlines the poverty and isolation of Wilnor. All the action takes place in Wilnor's one-room shack, creating a claustrophobic atmosphere. Furnished with only a stool, an old crate, a stove, and a floor mattress, it resembles a prison cell. Far away from his family, he is indeed condemned to a life of loneliness. His clothes—one suit, one shirt, one tie, one pair of shoes—a few dishes, a plastic mirror, and a borrowed radio/cassette player complete the setting.

There are only two characters listed. Wilnor, described as a tall and thin thirty-year-old, and the tape player. Marie-Ange never appears onstage; her voice is heard only on the tape. That Wilnor is onstage alone throughout the play accentuates his isolation. He even dances two communal dances—the quadrille and the *lérose*—alone. Traditionally the quadrille is performed with a partner and three other couples. Here it functions paradoxically to reinforce his solitude and provide some consolation during his nostalgic moments. . . .

As a closing to his taped response, Wilnor repeats five times, "Ton beau capitaine," each time with a different intonation. The first time, while looking in the mirror, he says, "Ton beau capitaine. Wilnor." Dissatisfied with that sign-off, he removes his shirt and tie and repeats a second time, "Ton beau capitaine," but "sur un ton moins assuré" [in a less-confident tone of voice]. The "points de suspension" reflect his hesitancy. Still uncertain, he covers his mouth with his hand and hunches his shoulders in resignation as the third "Ton beau capitaine" audio signature is posed as a question. Then the music begins as Wilnor does a desperation dance. He stops and says, "Ton beau capitaine?" Then he dances to a drumbeat. Hands over his head, he reaches for the sky as if to fly away. This final gesture reflects Wilnor's desire to escape his prisonlike existence and rejoin his wife in Haiti. Then, in the darkness, one last ironic "Ton beau capitaine?" is heard. There is no happy ending here. The couple remain separated.

> Renée Larrier. *World Literature Today.* 64, 1 (winter 1990), pp. 57–58

Although one might interpret Schwarz-Bart's *Ton beau capitaine* as the psychological disintegration of her principal and only fleshed-out character, Wilnor, too much else inflects his transformation to see it as purely negative. A short synopsis of this transformation might read as follows: Wilnor, an exiled Haitian agricultural worker, living in a shack in Guadeloupe, responds in a staged conversation to the news in the cassette sent by his wife, Marie-Ange, still dwelling in Haiti. Her slow and slippery confession of adultery and of the illegitimate child on the way, challenges the very foundations of Wilnor's ego. His sense of self as head of household and aspiring capitalist, his future as prodigal husband returning home with pots of money are all jeopardized by Marie-Ange's revelations. He wonders just what kind of a captain he is, if a captain at all.

Seemingly alone on stage, Wilnor, in the context of the virtual or realized production, is not, however, alone. Present through her recorded voice, Marie-Ange lives also in Wilnor's guts, her song sometimes emerging from his mind rather than the cassette player. At the play's end, the destabilized Wilnor, unsure of who he is, is also liberated because he knows that he is more than himself. He consequently advises his wife:

> Encore un mot, juste une petite recommandation. Repose-toi maintenant au long des jours que Dieu nous donne. Ne te mets pas l'ame en peine, si tu veux que l'enfant rentre dans la vie du bon pied. Mastique bien tes aliments, gardetoi un coeur joyeux et ecarte de ta vue toute laideur. . . . Souviens-toi bien de ca: je veux voir cet enfant beau comme un ange.

Wilnor evolves from an 'I' into a 'we', which includes the baby on the way. Flying through dancing—the metaphor is explicit in the stage directions and dialogue—thereby joined to the lilting song of 'Marie, the Angel', Wilnor comes to the brink of acceptance of a differently configured family and a sense of fatherhood which precludes possessiveness. While Schwarz-Bart does not give us closure, she does present a last vision of Wilnor as a winged creature, who is going somewhere—but surely not to the suicide of Duras's character Anne-Marie Stretter in *India Song* (1976). Nor are Wilnor and Marie-Ange mired in the unbearable paradigm of separation/non-separation which paralyses Agatha and her brother throughout Duras's play *Agatha* (1981). A dense composite, Wilnor is like the host in voodoo ritual, privileged to invite inside an other, the ghostly guest, thus connecting both his and Marie-Ange's mental and spiritual worlds, reanimating the spaces between them. . . .

In most of Marguerite Duras's plays, as in Cixous's *Portrait de Dora* (1976), memory is the stuff of action. The characters remember, or voices remember for them, looping back, obsessively exploring, recounting a character or characters who are absent to themselves, frequently yearning for a plenitude which has become pure pain. There is perpetual disjunction between what is remembered and the act of remembering, the process of recall is hesitant.

Memory, while also hesitant, is not the stuff of Schwarz-Bart's *Ton beau capitaine*, although Wilnor and Marie-Ange both recollect the happy times together in Haiti before he left. But Wilnor, as has been suggested, is suspended in a nowhere time, which is not even the nostalgic space of memory. He is not sustained by his past, and indeed is almost done in by his fantasized future.

There is, however, another, deeper, geographical memory, an historical one which permeates and undergirds the play, encompasses the characters, and inscribes *Ton beau capitaine* in something wider than Wilnor and Marie-Ange's personal drama. This is the memory of the Middle Passage, the disastrous and killing sea voyage, the tearing away from the Motherland of some 15,000,000 people of African descent. Irony of ironies, the Haitians (represented by Wilnor in Schwarz-Bart's play), those who were the first to free themselves from European colonization, are on the move again and again dying in the waters of the Caribbean. Marie-Ange would like to be 'le bateau', which would take Wilnor, her captain, away to 'un pays loin, loin, tres loin . . . ou les gens vous regardent pas comme des moins que rien, des cocos secs.' She would abolish the embedded memory of the ocean holocaust with a sea flight to an egalitarian world. Wilnor, however, is caught in the community's fate: neocolonialism holds him in economic bondage. . . .

In Schwarz-Bart's plays, as in [Ina] Césaire's, women characters speak, see, hear, or direct—even through a kind of remote control. Men's subject positions are interfered with and troubled. Europe is displaced, while Africa, the lost mother, is reconfigured, celebrated, and made present through dance, trance, and song. Both playwrights create the sense of a people and a history in process. They show a culture whose vibrant spirituality has allowed women and men to work through and conquer a multitude of psychic horrors.

> Judith Miller. *Theatre Research International.* 23, 3 (autumn 1998), pp. 25–31

BIBLIOGRAPHY
*Un Plat de porc aux bananes vertes* (with André Schwarz-Bart), 1967; *La mulatresse solitude* (with André Schwarz-Bart), *A Woman Named Solitude*, 1967; *Pluie et vent sur Télumée Miracle*, 1972 (Rain and Wind on Télumée, the Miracle Woman): *The Bridge of Beyond*, 1981; *Ti Jean l'horizon*, 1979; *Ton beau capitaine*, 1987 (*Your Handsome Captain*), 1988

# SEMBÈNE, Ousmane (1923–)
## Senegal

The black quarter of Marseille is rather solidly depicted [in *The Black Docker*]. . . . What is odd is not, as some have said, that a black docker has written a novel but that the message, which was promised and expected, is not expressed.

A minority lives in France in conditions that are often atrocious. This minority has its problems. It is struggling in an atmosphere that comes close to creating despair. Its only support is pride; its only arms, work; its only morality, strictness. This minority of Negro workers in France spares no pains. It struggles in order to triumph over the guilty conscience of the propertied classes, supervisors, and torturers. Its message in its stammerings is one of brotherhood. This minority begs for neither pity nor favors. It proclaims its right to live. All its ideas, virtues, and ''tribulations'' deserve our respect if not our sympathy.

What the world was expecting from Sembène was the exact expression of this message. Therefore, this novelist would have done better if he hadn't ''drowned'' such a subject in additional material ranging from sexual obsessions to inferiority complexes.

A world like that of the Negro dockers in France—strange in its dignity, striking in its strictness, and eager for brotherhood—deserved a better presentation to a public that is unaware of its very existence.

Sembène did not succeed this time. Nevertheless, this novelist has something to say. Without any doubt the message that he did not know how to express in his first book will become stronger in his following works.

Lamine Diakhaté. *Presence Africaine.* April—May 1957, p. 154†

The novel in French West Africa has often been used as an instrument against colonialism. The great Cameroonian writers Oyono and Beti have tried to explode the myth of ''France Outre Mère'' in their books, but none has shown as violent hatred of the white man as Ousmane Sembène. [*Oh Country, My Beautiful People*] is about an African who has served in the French army during the great war and returns to his home in Senegal with a white wife. The book sets out to describe the difficulties the hero encounters with his own people, who object to his European wife and look with suspicion on the new way of life he is trying to introduce. It also attempts to show the conflict between the hero Faye, and the white rulers of the country, who think that he is undermining their position of prestige by living with a white woman. Faye himself is described as a rather Europeanised character. . . .

The author resolves the conflict between the progressive African and the Europeans who try to keep him down into a Wild West type of violence. In the very opening scene of the novel super-man Faye punches a white man into submission and on the next occasion he successfully fights the entire crew of a ship single handed! His sense of justice is so strong that he uses his fists whenever he sees injustice or exploitation, and needless to say, he always floors his opponent. The white victims of his fury try to retaliate at first by attempting to violate his wife. Finally they manage to hire some Africans who attack Faye in the night and kill him.

The improbability of all these scenes makes it impossible for us to accept Faye as a martyr. The author thinks of Faye as a tragic hero. Although he is killed in the end, his spirit lingers on and the work he began is continued by his people. Unfortunately this ending falls rather flat. One feels that the conflict between Faye and the colonialists would have taken a rather more subtle form—which does mean that it would have been less dangerous.

U. Beier. *Black Orpheus.* November 1959, pp. 56–57

Ousmane Sembène, a fervent African socialist, attempts, in *God's Bits of Wood*, to show how Africans can act independently and responsibly to achieve their freedom. This novel, set among the strikers who, in 1947, paralysed the Dakar-Niger railway, describes how the men, women and children even, come to realize their strength and dignity. The novel is the story of the way in which they are forced to face famine and poverty, to take upon themselves the responsibility for their situation and refuse to change it except on their terms. . . .

Sembène attempts to demonstrate the various ways in which [the Africans] suddenly become aware of their imposed inferiority and how they oppose their pride and will to the brute force being used against them. They begin to see their situation objectively, to analyze it dispassionately, to oppose rational, passive resistance to violence.

Their passive resistance contrasts with the violence found in [André] Malraux's *The Human Condition* which, in several respects, this novel resembles. This method of non-violent resistance, used both in Africa and India in the struggle for independence, as well as by coloured people in America and elsewhere in the fight for civil rights, is essential for Sembène. Violence is degrading, brutish. Whenever it is used by the strikers it fails to achieve anything. It can only lead to more violence, as is shown in the efforts of the employers and administration to break the strike. . . .

Sembène has introduced entirely new concepts into the African novel in French. The characters are almost free of colonialist influence, confrontation with Europeans and European civilisation is no longer a major theme and, because of this, the presentation of African values, as in the works of Birago Diop and Laye Camara, is not an implied or explicit comparison with those of Europe.

A. C. Brench. *The Novelists' Inheritance in French Africa* (London: Oxford University Press, 1967), pp. 110, 112–13, 119

*Emitaï* deals not so much with characters as with a collective entity, the people—a Marxist conception of the hero. . . . The author shows Africa caught in the trap created when traditions and beliefs are confronted by Western materialism. The objective realities embodied by the soldiers and their guns are pitted against the objectivized realities of the gods. The result, Sembène shows, is the massacre of the peasants. The spiritual world is conquered by the brutal force of the weapons. The helplessness of the peasants is pathetic, ''but how much time they wasted by calling upon the gods,'' the author seems to say. . . .

We are far from the Western world's frantic search for adulterated exoticism. There are no tom-toms, no dances, none of the authentic ''primitive life'' that merchandisers consider absolutely indispensable in selling Africa. In *Emitaï* folklore has been used in the English sense of the word—the collection of traditions, legends, songs, and popular customs of a country; in this case, folklore determines the very content of the film.

''Real African films will be made by Africans.'' All African film-makers say so, and everyone who knows Africa's specific nature thinks so. But many others are not yet convinced. Sembène confirms the point of view of the former and will prove to the latter that they are wrong. And it will have taken him only six films to do so.

Africans feel at home with Sembène's films; they find in them their own customary reactions, reactions so habitual as to be no longer noticed. How many Europeans living in Senegal came into real contact with that country only by seeing *The Money-Order*! Thanks to Sembène, Black Africa has an identity; Africa is presented to the world not only physically but also psychologically. Sembène's films are accomplishing with the European masses the same work that Black African literature has done and is continuing to do with the elite. . . .

> Paulin Soumanou Vieyra. *Ousmane Sembène, cinéaste* (Paris: Présence Africaine, 1972), pp. 136–37, 158–59†

Sembène's new film [*Emitaï*] has been marred by censorship but what we can see of it is a masterpiece—a new style of film, unlike the "Museum of Natural History" documentary quality that hinders *The Money-Order* stylistically, and totally different from all western manners of story-telling on film. Few films cannot be related to other films in their story or in their style; Sembène's *Emitaï* can be related to Sophocles's *Antigone* in its story, but not to any film in its style. This is true in its manner of photography—almost entirely long shots, never extracting its characters from the environment, but making the environment an integral part of the story—and in its pace. There are no flash or quick shots, the editing is never manipulated to gain speed on events, everything is made ultra-clear, as if the length of the action and the objectivity of the photography were enough to clarify not only the story but Sembène's thought processes behind the story. . . .

Here he breaks away from all the [D. W.] Griffith-inspired devices—subjective angles, cross-cutting, the speeding up of reality by progressively shorter shots, the devices of emotional story-telling—that have plagued film-makers ever since Griffith. Who has bothered to get away from the bourgeois syndrome besides [Jean-Luc] Godard (and possibly Rainer Werner Fassbinder) previously in commercial story-telling film?

> Lyle Pearson. *Film Quarterly*. Spring 1973, pp. 46–47

*Xala*, Ousmane Sembène's new novel, will probably not elicit the same emotional response as *The Money-Order*. A completely different aspect of life in Senegal and in Dakar is presented in this satirical tale, which sometimes borders on comedy or farce. But the farce, it must be stressed, is not gratuitous; it is based on the observation (which one feels is very careful) of daily life, customs, language, and social relationships.

The storyteller presents a "new greedy native bourgeoisie." El Hadji Abdou Kader Beye, the pompous, ridiculous hero of *Xala*, is a corrupt businessman, a rich tradesman. On the night of his wedding to his third wife, he discovers he is impotent: he has the *xala*. The story is about curing the *xala*. Also, and more important, it is about discovering who tied the noose on this unfortunate fifty-year-old man, who cast this particularly treacherous spell, who sought to destroy his power, in every sense of the word? Suddenly, this up-to-date bourgeois, this modern import-export businessman, whose comfortable daily life is full of the benefits of all of today's technical devices, finds himself horribly helpless. Another device, ancient and subtle [that of the *Xala*], has just cracked the beautiful façade and threatens to destroy it completely. But, as the reader will see, this apparent return to the past finally uncovers the road to progress, to the future. But progress, like the story itself, sometimes skirts the straight line. . . .

The richness of social observation in this brief novel is all the more striking because it is a tale, a fable. It seems to me that in depicting contemporary customs in today's Dakar, in which the aftereffects of colonialism are still noticeable, Sembène has rediscovered the precision and the zest of the old art of storytelling. It is an African art, but also a universal art.

> Pierre Gamarra. *Europe*. March 1974, pp. 295–96

The central theme of *Xala* is the downfall of the arrogant and insatiable new bourgeoisie of independent Africa, people "with long teeth" biting hard to control the national economy and subjugate the common man. Sembène is less worried by their existence than by the immoral way in which they make their wealth and spend it. Whether it concerns Mbaye of *The Money-Order* who robs Dieng of his money or El Hadji who goes about expropriating the poor and imprisoning them if they talk, buying cars for young girls and living a scandalously luxurious life, the story is the same: these men constitute a danger to the people and society. This is the important point that Sembène is making: wealth can only be meaningful when it is used to the advantage of society; the moment it becomes too personal and almost a cult, it corrodes man and gradually eats away the fabric of society by creating an unhealthy social life for the "have-nots." There is an Ibo proverb which says "the big tree stands because man wants it to stand," but the moment its existence is no longer in the interest of man, it is felled. This seems to be the lesson the author is trying to give in *Xala*. In fact, when the poor, the beggars and even the bankers find that El Hadji is more of a danger than an asset, they decide to pull him down. . . .

In both novels, Sembène's language is so simple that most African readers will find no difficulty in understanding what the author is saying about them. Most of the time, he translates his thoughts and those of his characters from their local dialect into French, thereby cutting down the latter to the level of the common man. His creation of images is very African and original and his satire much to the taste of the villager who would like you to say things as they are.

One might of course accuse the author of taking joy in painting a universe of misfortune and the downfall of man: Dieng is a perpetual victim; El Hadji, a one-time victimizer, is now victimized. The fact remains that, in traditional Africa, the most effective way of keeping traditional morality intact and correcting the society was to punish evildoers severely and leave good behaviour to propagate itself, since it was believed to be self-evident and self-inspiring. This seems to dictate Sembène's literary aesthetics in *The Money-Order, Xala* and even in *White Genesis*. He takes his cue from the people to create literature for the people.

> A. U. Ohaegbu. *Presence africaine*. 91 (1974), pp. 130–31

Sembène's masterpiece is perhaps his collection of short stories *Man from Volta*. In these stories, the style of which often resembles the folk tale as told by a *griot* (teller of folk tales), Sembène avoids the dangers he had encountered in more complex narratives; each tale is a gem of concision and lyrical beauty. In his collection, Sembène is a champion of women's rights and shows a keen penetration of female psychology. In "Her Three Days," for example, he gives a touching portrayal of the suffering experienced by a neglected third wife whose husband now prefers his younger fourth wife. There could be no stronger indictment of the evils of polygamy. The story "Letters from France" is written from the point of view of a young wife, who had been forced to marry an older man. To her girlfriend she confesses the bitter unhappiness of her daily life. The young wife's disillusion and depression, when she finds that France is nothing like the country she had fantasized, are similar to the emotions experienced by Diouana, the tragic protagonist of the story "The Black Girl of . . . ," which Sembène later adapted for the screen.

> Debra Popkin. In *Encyclopedia of World Literature in the 20th Century* (New York: Frederick Ungar, 1975), Vol. IV, p. 342

Sembène Ousmane is an exception in French-speaking West Africa. He is almost the only writer who started publishing novels during the colonial period, and still does, denouncing the evils of the postindependence era as he did for preindependence. He is the only one who, realizing the limitations of literature, especially literature written in French in largely illiterate societies, turned to another medium and made several films, thus becoming a pioneer in the field of African cinema. More important even, in our countries where the prestige of the socalled intellectual is so great, he constantly refused to be more than a man of the people close to his roots. . . .

*Xala* is set in Dakar, since the Senegalese society is what Sembène Ousmane seems to know best. The hero, El Hadji Abdou Kader Beye, belongs to the new class born after independence. He is a businessman just nominated as the Head of the Chamber of Commerce and Industry, the first Senegalese to occupy this seat. As the crowning of his happiness, he decides to marry a third wife, the young N'Gone. The story opens with the description of the wedding party, complete with male and female griots, champagne, and expensive gifts. As well as a car, El Hadji has promised 2,500 gallons of petrol to the new bride. The two other wives are also present at the ceremony and portrayed with great skill by Sembène Ousmane, who makes us aware of their different personalities through their behavior in the circumstances. But on his wedding night, El Hadji up to now so fortunate, discovers he has the *xala*—which means that he is suddenly impotent. This impotency is the writing on the wall. It is not only his physical manhood which is at stake, but his dignity and even his wealth. In his desperate attempts to cure his disease, he neglects his business which goes from bad to worse since in fact El Hadji was just a pretense of a businessman, living on credit and with no real financial power. This is, in my point of view, the most striking aspect of Sembène Ousmane's novel: the constant criticism, the constant demythification of the characters and aspects of society.

> Maryse Condé. In Eldred Durosimi Jones, ed. *African Literature Today*. 9 (1978), pp. 97–98

Sembène's work in both fiction and film, starting with the publication of his first novel, *Le Docker noir* . . . charts a steady progression away from a type of romantic individualism towards the communal struggle and communal consciousness celebrated in his later work. It is not that his work ever lacked an ideological content, of a generally radical tendency, but that the artistic means of expressing this content demanded many years and many experiments for their discovery.

The immaturity of *Le Docker noir* as a novel may also be attributed to what finally proved one of Sembène's strengths—his very lack of that sophistication in education and experience which severed many of his contemporary writers from the lot of their fellows. . . . One of the chief concerns of Diaw Falla, the novel's hero, is to help [the black dockworkers] break out of [their] isolation, which is not only that of their blackness but that of the poverty they share with their white fellow workers. Instead of holding aloof from unionism and political action as "white men's business," they must throw themselves into both if they are to change their lot.

Here already is that insistence on the primacy of change which runs all through Sembène's work. But to some extent it runs counter to another tendency in *Le Docker noir*: Diaw's concern to change his own condition by the use of the pen. This brings him up against the perpetual dilemma of the artist; the need for isolation and withdrawal in order to create seems at times a betrayal of that very comradeship in suffering which he seeks to celebrate. Most dockers do not read novels and cannot hence feel liberated by them. . . .

Since the early 1960s, Sembène has been increasingly absorbed by his work as a filmmaker, and the fiction he has written since then (notably *Le Mandat* and *Xala*) has shown the signs of this absorption. Unlike many filmmakers of literary leanings, he has always recognized that the short novel provides the ideal basis for a film script, because the film can then develop and celebrate visually what is offered by the text, instead of having to cut and brutally condense a full-length novel. Hence he has not attempted to film any of his major novels. His major films to date, *Emitaï*, *The Money Order*, and *Xala*, all show this strong sense of visual and dramatic situation and all produce a result which is probably in many ways richer than the literary text (in the case of *Emitaï*, this is a speculation, as the original text has never been published). . . .

*Xala* is the closest of Sembène's novels to film form, and was clearly written with one eye already on the script. There is an abundance of dialogue and a relative absence of the sort of commentary or reflection which cannot be rendered visually. The plot concentrates solely upon the brief career of Abdou Kader Beye's third marriage, his immediate relapse into *xala* (impotence), and his eventual or supposed cure at the hands of the beggars.

> Gerald Moore. *Twelve African Writers* (Bloomington: Indiana University Press, 1980), pp. 70, 79–80

[Sembène Ousmane] evolved from fumbling beginnings as an autodidact to the full mastery of his art, producing five full-length novels, a collection of short stories, and two longish novellas in sixteen years. For nine years, he devoted himself to filmmaking, hoping by this medium . . . to reach people in the heartlands of Africa who are not yet—or are insufficiently—literate to be reached by the printed page, especially in French. . . .

Some of the facts of his life are reflected in his first novels, all written during the colonial era. He was born in a little Casamance fishing village, like the heroes of *Le Docker noir* and *O pays, mon beau peuple*! He earned a precarious living as a stevedore in Marseilles, where, like the hero of *Le Docker noir*, he supplemented his lack of formal education by wide reading and wrote his first novel as a passionate outcry against the hardships suffered by the black minorities in France, deploring in particular the conditions of the black dockworkers. His theses, more appropriate to a polemical tract than a novel, presented difficulties that the inexperienced Sembène proved, not surprisingly, unable to deal with satisfactorily. . . . Nevertheless, it is of great interest to trace his evolution as a novelist from this hesitant beginning where as an apprentice he tries out the tools of his trade.

Dorothy S. Blair. *Senegalese Literature: A Critical History* (Boston: Twayne, 1984), p. 80

Two important observations may be made about the theme of growing consciousness in [*Les Bouts de bois de Dieu*, translated as *God's Bits of Wood*]. First, Sembène Ousmane has prophetically expressed in the art form of the novel what has since actually taken place in some liberation struggles in Africa. In Zimbabwe, women in the now-ruling ZANU-PF party became more and more outspoken about the oppression of women, not only in colonial and capitalist Rhodesia, but also in traditional Shona society, which was feudalistic and characterized by the subordination of woman to man. . . .

Secondly, the novel shows clearly that the workers and their women are not simply automatons acting under the spell of history. Theirs is "conscious activity of conscious men." The workers need the organizational skill of Lahbib and Bakayoko. To be successful they need the energy and intellectual acumen of Bakayoko. For the march of the women to succeed, the leadership qualities and untiring dedication of Penda are required. The exploited masses of French West Africa have indeed become conscious of their existence as a result of the relations of production, but they are not driven blindly to their success by the inexorable march of history. Individuals react to the situation differently according to their own being, talent, and level of political consciousness. Thus, while the majority of workers join in the strike, Sounkare, the watchman, chooses the opposite course; and privileged individuals like El Hadji Mabigué are used by the company and the state apparatus to frustrate the efforts of the strikers. These men and women are therefore not driven like robots by history. They also act upon and create history. . . .

[It] is important to emphasize that Sembène Ousmane is not only concerned with socio-political issues, that he is not only projecting socialist ideology, but is also alive to the need to project his social vision in a genuinely artistic form. . . .

On the sociological level, [Sembène Ousmane] successfully demonstrates that the strike has generated a new social psychology, marking a new level of sociopolitical awareness and a tendency towards democracy, justice, and progress. The workers have positively rejected the exploitation of man by man. The women have broken the chains of their psychological and social domination by men, and their men—Bakayoko included—have come to accept this. The masses of French West Africa have also come to the realization that their language and culture are not inferior to French language and culture—hence the emphasis on Ouolof and the return to old ceremonies and customs long forgotten. Indeed, the new awareness is an expression of the fact that "the masses do not want to go on living in the old way, that the existing conditions have become intolerable and should be changed."

Emmanuel Ngara. *Art and Ideology in the African Novel* (London: Heinemann, 1985), pp. 65–66, 73

In ["Souleyman," translated as] "The Bilal's Fourth Wife" [collected in *Voltaïque*, translated as *Tribal Scars and Other Stories*], Sembène, with great humor, pokes fun at Senegalese attitudes toward divorce. He attacks the practice of double moral standards, which place women at a disadvantage. Sembène uses the character of Yacine to question and to disagree with the patriarchal Moslem marriage rules drawn up by males centuries ago. In spite of the rumors and intense external pressures, Yacine reveals a tremendous self-confidence. First, she refuses to be coerced by Suliman and her family into a divorce. Second, she is adamant about being treated on equal footing as a woman by the Cadi (special council of male elders called to review her case). Third, she questions why the woman is not free to take a lover when a man in a Moslem society can have four wives with the approval of the Koran and legal laws. These unyielding stances force the male elders to accept, with reluctance, the fact that there are two sides to every marital disagreement, and the woman's position is just as important as the man's. . . .

Sembène's short story, ["La Mère," translated as] "The Mother" is another example of the application of double moral standards in a Moslem society in Africa. This point is presented through the personage of the tyrannical king. The king, who has no intentions of cultivating the love and respect of his constituents, alienates himself and evokes the hatred and fear of his subjects to the point that they dream about seeing him burned alive. Meanwhile, these same subjects are passive and obey the king's orders to murder men over fifty years old. Thus, the king thinks that he owes no allegiance to anyone. He proceeds to pass a law that he will deflower every virgin before she is married. Over the years, only a few brave mothers succeed in saving their daughters from such a fate. When it is time for the king's daughter to marry, he repeals the law—separate rules for the poor and rich. . . .

Mores of another kind are explored in the short story, ["Ses trois jours," translated as] "Her Three Days," where one meets Noumbé, the third wife of Mustapha. When the story opens, Noumbé is preparing for her husband's visit during her allotted three days as dictated by the Koran. Drawing upon his film-making skills, Sembène zooms in on Noumbé to show her haggard face, her weakened body after the bearing of five children in rapid succession, her anxieties and fears of being replaced by the fourth wife, and her fight to handle a heart condition. Although Noumbé is still young, she looks older because of her full financial duties of providing for her children. . . .

Like Noumbé, Nafi in ["Letters de France," translated as] "Letters from France" has been raised in a patriarchal society where man rules over woman, and one class over another. Viewed as a second-class citizen by her society and father, she is tricked into marrying a seventy-three-year-old man, who lives in Marseilles, France. The topic of love is not entertained, for marriage is based on loneliness, a wish to live in France, and an old man's desire to retain his lost youth. Nafi, the young wife, will serve Demba, her husband, be an instrument for his pleasure, bear his children, greet his friends, and care for him in his old age. By selecting a young wife, like Suliman in "The Bilal's Fourth Wife," Demba hopes that she will be easier to control and that he thereby will gain much from the unbalanced relationship. Unfortunately, the carefully laid plan backfires when Demba succumbs to cancer. . . .

Sembène's female characters are not losers. In the four short stories each woman triumphs no matter how small the victory. By presenting such women, Sembène opens up opportunities for

African women to develop a more positive self-awareness and to draw upon capacities that have lain dormant within themselves. In order for Senegalese women to move forward, they must cast off outdated ideas and modes of behavior and view their plight realistically. In short, they must place themselves on the outside in order to look in. By doing so, they may begin to take steps to eliminate ignorance and mass illiteracy and improve their status in the twentieth century. All four women—Yacine, the mother, Noumbé, and Nafi—challenge the traditional order, which condemned them to a secondary role. They, as mothers, are believable as characters. They, as mothers and women, through the prism of social and political contexts, will turn their faces to the future with hope for the future generation, their children.

> Brenda F. Berrian. In Carole Boyce Davies and Anne Adams Graves, eds. *Ngambika: Studies of Women in African Literature* (Trenton, New Jersey: Africa World Press, 1986), pp. 196–98, 200, 202–4

Senegalese writer and filmmaker [Sembène Ousmane] is one African artist who, far from being reluctant to depict African traditions and scenes in his works, is pleased to point out, time and again, that many of the plots for his creative works come from real life. An analysis of his works also shows that African traditional beliefs and practices have a profound thematic, structural, or symbolic function in novels that are as far removed from each other in design and purpose as *O pays, mon beau peuple!*, *L'Harmattan*, and *Xala*. This same pattern applies to films like *Xala* and *Emitaï*. . . .

Sembène had several political aims in making *Emitaï*. One of these was to show that in black Africa there was no total passivity to colonialism but, instead, varying levels of resistance (just as there were in the United States, for example, slave uprisings and revolts, the news of which was often suppressed for fear of engendering others). The Jola resistance refuted a number of propagandist views like those of Dominique O. Mannoni, who suggested that Africans (including Senegalese sharpshooters) were looking for authority figures to whom they could attach themselves and found such models among European whites. Sembène shows in *Emitaï* a people, with a political will of their own tied to their religious beliefs, who achieve a moral victory at the very moment when they are defeated by a technologically greater adversary who uses their own young men as mercenaries. At the same time, the film eloquently shows the lack of political consciousness among the black soldiers who followed the orders of French officers unquestioningly and never once thought of rebelling against the whites.

> Jonathan A. Peters. In Eileen Julien, Mildred Mortimer, and Curtis Schade, eds. *African Literature in Its Social and Political Dimensions* (Washington, D. C.: Three Continents, 1986), pp. 69, 71

In the search, during the late 1960s and early 1970s, for a more concretely committed, less elitist, more accessible African literature, the work of [Sembène Ousmane] of Senegal proved to be of path breaking significance. The real importance of Sembène's work lay in the daring simplicity of its overall conception. Even in his early work, dating back to the 1950s, Sembène had broken radically with the urban, intellectual biases prevailing in African literature. His most celebrated novel, *God's Bits of Wood*, had

taken as its central focus a major railroad strike that had occurred in French West Africa in the late 1940s. Scrupulously avoiding abstraction or grand theorizing, it had devoted itself to a very close and concrete exploration of the material effect of the strike on the lives of a number of people—men, women, and children, strikers and strikebreakers, beggars and small traders, and proletarian activists—living and working in various communities along the thousand-mile rail line between Bamako and Dakar. Through this means, Sembène had been able to convey immediately and compellingly a sense of the movement of ideas in time, and of the intersection between thought and action in political events. Where other African writers might have spoken *about* the politicization of the laboring classes, Sembène, a self-proclaimed Marxist, had made this process the very subject of his novel, addressing it not simply as series of external events but phenomenologically . . . with an eye to its human and conceptual implications. . . .

In his subsequent work (he is also one of Africa's most acclaimed film directors), Sembène has continued to give prominence to the dispossessed strata of modern African society. His novels, stories, and films represent landless peasants, slum dwellers without work, beggars, and aged people for whom nothing is assured, not even their own survival. By drawing attention to the daily struggles of this "invisible" multitude—invisible, that is, to the architects of African "modernization"—Sembène is able not only to show that they are casualties of the existing order, but also, subtly but unmistakably, to hint at their potential revolutionary impact on society, latent in the first instance, in their sheer numbers.

> Neil Lazarus. *Resistance in Postcolonial African Fiction* (New Haven: Yale University Press, 1990), pp. 207–9

The two novellas "Niiwam" and "Taaw" were originally published in French in a single volume by Présence Africaine in 1987. The preface to the new English edition, "Sembène Ousmane, Voice of the Voiceless," retraces the author's life and work through 1988, noting that "Taaw" was made into a film in 1970 (after *Le Mandat* made Sembène's international reputation). The "Commentary on the Translation" examines several problems: the audience aimed at by the Senegalese writer when he writes in French; the differences between standard French and that used in Senegal; Sembène's personal departures from standard French; the polyglossic quality of speech in Senegal; and the idiom of students and the young unemployed. Conclusion: it would be pointless to have the latter speaking like their counterparts in Cape Flats or Harlem. The English text serves its purpose if the reader gets the sense that English "can open and welcome other voices and other tongues."

"Niiwam" is very simply constructed. In Dakar, Thierno, an old and very poor man from the interior, leaves the morgue to go bury the corpse of his son Niiwam. Having no money, he and his wife have not eaten since the previous day. He leaves her weeping by the entrance (women do not go to the burial). An old ragman who washes corpses and buys their clothing tells Thierno that the cemetery is in the village of Yoff and pays his way on the bus. The remainder of the story details the actions and words of the driver, the conductor, and passengers as the bus crosses and exits the city. A fashionably-dressed, haughty Senegalese woman sitting by Thierno excites hysteria among the passengers on discovering that it is a corpse he is holding on his lap. However, an Islamic holy man takes up Thierno's defense, reminding the passengers of the respect due the dead. The two men descend from the bus and walk toward the burial ground amid the sand dunes. Meanwhile, the woman is now screaming because she has been robbed: a young man lifted her purse and passed it to an accomplice, now outside the bus. During the trip Thierno has been a mere spectator—guilty, nervous, unobtrusively swatting flies away from his son's corpse.

Taaw, the eldest son of Baye Tine and first wife Yaye Dabo, was once a good student. However, on [traveling] eleven kilometers four times a day to and from the secondary school and later being mistreated by an uncle's envious cowives, he twice failed his classes and was forced to drop out. He has no job and his girlfriend is pregnant. As in ''Niiwam,'' however, the title character does not undergo the greatest transformation. All her life Yaye Dabo has been quietly obedient to the men of her immediate family and her husband. She tries to make ends meet on the little money he gives her and to allay his violence against herself and her sons. When Taaw wins scholarship money, Baye Tine uses it to move the family to a *bidonville* near Dakar and buy a young second wife. He is particularly enraged at the insolent scorn of Taaw, who once stopped him from beating Yaye Dabo and broke one of his teeth while knocking him to the ground. For this Taaw received a six-month prison sentence from the council of old men. Back at home, he and his father do not speak to each other. Yaye Dabo grows in strength and independence, thinking about her husband, social customs, relatives, and cowives. When Baye Tine, angered and frustrated by forced retirement, threatens to repudiate her, she shocks him by repudiating him in front of the neighborhood wives. She pushes him to the ground and steps over him, ''an act violently condemned in Wolof society, particularly when done by a woman.'' Never again will Yaye Dabo be a woman of the past, seeing the world through other people's eyes.

Melvin B. Tolson Jr. *World Literature Today*. 67, 2 (spring 1993), pp. 432–33

*Guelwaar*, is a simple story, which, like many folk tales, discloses much more than its narrative. The time is today. The chief settings are a Catholic village and a Muslim village. A prominent Catholic dies in a hospital at the same time as a prominent Muslim. When the Muslim family come for their relative's corpse, the morgue attendant mistakenly gives them the Catholic's remains (the face stays wrapped), which they bury in a Muslim cemetery. When the Catholics come for their relative, the mistake is discovered. Much of the film is about the Catholics' efforts to disinter the Catholics from the Muslim cemetery and bury him where he belongs. (No attention is paid to the Muslim corpse waiting patiently in the morgue for burial.)

Obviously, from one angle, this is a farcical story, which Sembene doesn't overlook. But the film soon deepens into the social seriousness entailed in religious dispute, brewing up the threat of violence. One unexpected development arises through flashbacks of the deceased Catholic, Guelwaar. (This is a sobriquet that means Noble One.) He had been strongly opposed to Senegal's dependence on foreign aid, and at one point it's suspected that his body's disappearance is connected to his political views. His hatred of economic dependence was so strong that, though he deplored his daughter's working as a prostitute in Dakar in order to send money home, he preferred it to her begging or to the begging his family would have needed to do otherwise. This patriarchal view of the

matter is never questioned. At the finish Guelwaar's opposition to foreign aid is put into practice by young men of the village.

The film is spoken in French and Wolof: French, which is still the official language of Senegal, is apparently something of a social marker. However, more impressive than the language used by anyone is the manner of speaking. In ordinary domestic conversation, one person addresses another with his or her full name, followed by a slight pause before proceeding, as if beginning a letter. This gives the ordinary chat of a village something of the arch of formal discourse.

Another very taking element at Sembene's disposal is Senegalese textile design. The women's gowns, for every-day use, are full in fold and gorgeous in pattern. The contrast between the skimpiness of the way of life, the cane huts and the dirt floors, and the richness of those materials is inescapable. The most extraordinary aspect of this design bonanza is that no one ever mentions it: it's taken for granted.

But the most important component of the film is Sembene's directorial simplicity—simplicity crystallized, heightened, by skill. One small instance. The village priest is talking to the prostitute, returned for her father's funeral, urging her to reconsider her life. She stands not quite facing us while he walks a short distance back and forth behind her. This compact design makes his remarks, gentle and empathic, seem to be wearing away at her while simultaneously we can see their effect on her. A quiet touch of directing deftness.

There's a risk, when discussing directors who deal simply with people they know and love, of shoveling them all into the same basket. Sembene is not Idrissa Ouedraogo, and not just because Ouedraogo is from Burkina Faso instead of Senegal. But Sembene and Ouedraogo share a belief in film as a modern medium that can take over ancient work, that of the bard—using film as a treasury, free of the printed page, of what each man holds dear.

Stanley Kauffmann. *New Republic*. 209, 10 (September 6, 1993), pp. 30–31

[In *Les bouts de bois de Dieu*] that we witness the mastery of semantic and linguistic devices that has produced a distinctive cultural vision in Ousmane Sembène's work. For many of us this great novel remains his masterpiece, and we look forward to the day when he will produce a film version of this great African epic. . . .

Penda is the main protagonist of this novel. During the march from Thies to Dakar, the wives and daughters of the striking railroad men reach a crisis situation. Penda is leading the march, but the seriously alienated Awa, who defines herself as the ''wife of the foreman Sène Massène,'' attempts to gather some of the women around her in revolt. In the three pages that it takes Sembène to describe this particular incident we have three distinct semantic registers. Firstly, we have the standard international French of the protagonist Penda and the women who are ideologically close to her. This standard international French represents, in the text, the use of standard Wolof as a means of communication. This is a discourse that is firm but persuasive. It is a semanticism of positive cooperation but which, in an unambiguous manner, establishes Penda as leader.

Secondly, we have the orders addressed to the men. This is a significant sociolinguistic phenomenon since in the long march between the industrial town and the capital city Penda gives only commands to the men she encounters. . . .

Four imperatives, four orders in three short sentences addressed to a group of men under her direct command. The rapid succession of verbs in the imperative form and the rapid succession of pronouns underline the superior/inferior relationship. Symbolically, Penda wears a military belt around her waist and this item of clothing emphasizes her position of authority. This is a new female discourse that announces the birth of a new gender relationship. This is not the voice of pleading but the assurance and security of a woman who is aware of her importance, her duties, and her responsibilities in her society. The men are forced to accept her command and some of the women find it difficult to adjust to this new situation.

Thirdly, in Penda's words to Awa and the other women in revolt, the semantic elements of the discourse are characterized by a refusal to respond directly to Awa's cruel taunts. Awa's mixture of Wolof and French bears only a surface meaning that is destructive and unsettling in its intention to manipulate. This very unstructured and individualistic language register, which is neither Wolof nor French nor a recognizable pidgin based on the two languages, aptly reflects the social and cultural alienation of this character who is used as a foil to Penda's characterization. Finally, Penda uses a method of rallying the women that seems, on the surface, to have nothing at all to do with the circumstances. By counting the women she uses a deeply held fear of enumeration to stir them all. The belief system of the women goes far beyond Islam to a realm of consciousness in which indigenous religion and culture reign. Without replying to their protests she continues relentlessly counting—using the deep connotations of this enunciation which transforms a seemingly innocent exercise in the French language into a very threatening discourse in Wolof that is evocative of witchcraft. But this discourse is destined to achieve a particular social aim which is crystallized in the paragraph that closes this incident:

La colère et la crainte se partageant leur coeur, les femmes rassemblèrent leurs pagnes, ajustèrent leurs mouchoirs de tête, rejoignirent la route et reprirent la marche. A quelque distance les hommes suivaient, menés par Boubacar.
[Anger and fear tearing at their hearts the women took up their pagnes, adjusted their head scarves, went back on to the road and began to march again. A little distance away the men followed, led by Boubacar.]

The intensive usage of the passé simple in French emphasizes the rapid succession of actions as they continue on the march with the men following them. It is as though Sembène is telling us that it is only women who can organize themselves to undertake their own struggle against oppression. Sympathetic men will have no alternative but to follow and serve.

We learn in this same novel that one of the men had molested Penda while she was in the union building. She slapped him publicly, thereby asserting herself and demanding respect from all of the men. To their sexual violence she replied immediately with violence, humiliating her assailant and asserting her right to appear anywhere without being molested.

Sembène uses the male characters of his novels and short stories primarily to convey certain symbolic messages through their clothing, their gestures or the social context. The characterization of Bakayoko, the male protagonist of *Les bouts de bois de Dieu,* is a brilliant illustration of this depiction of a male character who despite his positive attributes is intellectually and socially incapable of undertaking the struggle on behalf of the women. He is the leader of the men who, through their atavism, have to have a clearly identifiable single male voice to galvanize them to action. Herd-like creatures through their socialization, men appear to be incapable of meaningful social and economic revolt. The railroad workers who follow Bakayoko win a few concessions from the company but nothing has changed in their relationship with one another and with their bosses. On the other hand, after Penda's death and the return of the women to Thies, the mothers, wives, and daughters of the railroad workers have significantly altered their relationships with one another, with their men folk and even with the company. This, surely, is the final test of meaningful change in society that women are capable of the positive transformation of gender relationships through the consciousness-raising process of revolt.

Throughout his prose fiction it is very clear that it is primarily through the discourse on and of his female characters that Sembène's ideological messages are conveyed. The narrative discourse of the text gives us a very clear indication of Sembène's perspectives on the condition of women. From the descriptions of the comfortable, wealthy old woman Djia Umbrel (*Le dernier de l'Empire,*) reading a book on African women written by an African woman, to the three wives of El Hadji Abdou Kader Bèye in *Xala* and the poor women of *Les bouts de bois de Dieu* and "Taaw," we obtain a consistent vision of oppression and of a growing revolt against subjugation.

Ousmane Sembène's use of the French language, which he has forced to its semantic limits by producing a new polysemy that is primarily Wolof; his acknowledgement of the primacy of indigenous culture and Islam as the motivating forces of the modes of thought of a people; his commitment to change and his consistent ideological discourse are the textual, literary evidence of a determined revolutionary purpose. . . .

[The] exercise of writing in French, that is, the process of concretizing in written form a number of social concepts and realities observed and experienced in an entirely different semantic, syntactic and symbolic framework, leads to a most intimate knowledge of the aesthetic demands placed on an author who seeks to articulate the aspirations of a people. This explains why the films made on the basis of the published works are even more powerful social statements than the written texts. It is not simply that the visual qualities of the cinema are used to impress us. I would like to suggest that in the particular case of Ousmane Sembène, the aesthetic quality of the film, its psychological and social impact, its lucid ideological discourse are the direct result of the struggle with questions of articulation and the need to bring to the written text a degree of limpidity that permits the intricacies of a multiplicity of contradictions to be expressed.

This is the genius of Ousmane Sembène, that his vision and his work are the expression of his ideology; that his films in Wolof or other African languages are presented in a semantic and symbolic language that conveys several aspects of the same message at one and the same time.

In the field of discourse analysis a distinction is made between the énoncé (that which is enunciated) and the énonciation (the process of enunciation). Ousmane Sembène has mastered the art of manipulating the process of enunciation in order to convey his message succinctly but in detail. He has mastered the intellectual feat of expressing Wolof concepts and semantic patterns in a language that appears at first to be ill-suited to such cultural enrichment. His serious themes and particular linguistic devices are the negation of the exoticism that a certain audience seeks in

African works. His writing is a most careful, studied, and determined enterprise in which his stylistic versatility has been a consistent element.

Ousmane Sembène has achieved his literary success not in order to win prestigious literary prizes but to provide a social and political service to African peoples wherever they may be found. Though his prose fiction is in French he has provided us with a monument to African cultural expression and has demonstrated that, without compromise, and without adhering to some mystical ethos of the French language, this language can be transformed to serve the needs of African peoples as is true of even the most banal means of communication.

I cannot conclude these remarks without reiterating the most important lesson of Sembène's work: It is only through the positive transformation of gender relations, the acknowledgement and respect of the human rights of women, their affirmation and seizing of their economic and social rights, that meaningful, revolutionary change will be engendered in society. When the history of African feminist thought of the late twentieth century is written, a significant chapter should be devoted to the work of Ousmane Sembène.

> Frederick Ivor Case. Samba Gadjigo, et al., eds. *Ousmane Sembène: Dialogues with Critics and Writers* (Amherst, Massachusetts: Five Colleges, Inc., 1993), pp. 6–13

BIBLIOGRAPHY

*Le Docker noir*, 1956; *Oh Pays, mon beau peuple!*, 1957; *Les Bouts de bois de Dieu* (God's Bits of Wood), 1960; *Voltaieque* (Tribal Scars, and Other Stories), 1962; *Vehi-Ciosane; ou, Blanche-genese, suivi du Mandat* (The Money Order, With White Genesis), 1965; *Le Noire de. . .* (Black Girl) (film), 1966; *Mandabi* (film), 1968; *Emitai* (film), 1971; *Xala*, 1973; *Xala* (film), 1974; *Ceddo* (film), 1978; *Dernier de l'empire* (The Last of the Empire), 1981; *Niiwam; suivi de Taaw: nouvelles*, 1992; *Ousmane Sembene: Dialogues with Critics and Writers*, 1993; *Guelwaar*, 1996

# SENGHOR, Léopold Sédar (1906–)
## Senegal

Some lines [in *Songs of Darkness*] . . . seem to have been borrowed from the enumerative language dear to [Saint-John Perse]. It is possible that Senghor knows Saint-John Perse's work, and that Saint-John Perse's vast solemnity and the primitive strength of his declamation have moved the poet of *Songs of Darkness*. Nothing can evoke the dark continent better than great elemental images coupled with constant reminders of the symbols that still remain from a very ancient civilization. . . . Senghor's fondness for inversions . . . ritual images, and noble and sacred language, and the care he takes almost to anchor his poetry in an incantatory tone—all these things, as beautifully arranged as they are, do not offer anything new or really creative.

The fact remains, nevertheless, that this poetry not only is very readable but also charms and sometimes overwhelms the reader. The images are those of a real poet, although their rhythmic garb seems borrowed. . . . The pacing of the poems is flawless, sustained by an inspiration with happy variations. A religious theory, in the form of a fresco or a frieze, unfolds in many places. An incurable

nostalgia for an ancient and beloved land often overflows the somewhat stiff harmony of the lines. We see Senghor's men live and suffer—men of the African soil, of a thousand years of slavery, but men whose pride is never crushed. There is anger in these lines, a sung anger that takes the form of incantation. There is also, as in the poem "Snow over Paris," a sense of universal human suffering.

> Pierre Emmanuel. *Temps present*. August 3, 1945, p. 3

Under the influence of their French masters, but even more under that of the black elite of the United States, French-speaking black intellectuals have been totally devoting themselves for the past few years to what they rightly consider their primary obligation—the rehabilitation and glorification of their race. Following the example of the black Americans, to whom nothing specifically Negro remains foreign for long, and who therefore prompt them to persevere on the path they have committed themselves to, they eagerly study the past of their race, which seems to have been destined for misfortune from the beginning of time; and in essays that are often authoritative they record their discoveries, discoveries that have led their brothers in the United States to the most erudite exegeses and at times the most unexpected commentaries.

Léopold Sédar Senghor would certainly never dream of minimizing the importance of the contributions made—on the one hand to Europe as a whole, on the other to colored Frenchmen—by the creative genius of those whom the Yankees attack with the insulting and scornful nickname of Jim Crow. Senghor is moreover aware of all he owes to France and to himself, in other words, to the race of his ancestors. Thus, he has served both France and his race with his heart and his mind: his mind disciplining the reasons of his heart, reasons of which reason itself is unaware; and his heart burning his mind with the fine flame that ignites it. His earliest writings, "What the Black Man Brings" and the admirable poems in *Songs of Darkness*, marked by a very pure musicality, are totally suffused by this double, demanding passion. . . .

Some of his teachings may seem subversive to the European, who is ordinarily sensitive only to what touches him from close by or from a great distance. Senghor, however, does not say anything that should displease Europeans. A black man, he sees himself as part of Black Africa, and feels one with the civilization of the land that witnessed his birth. Why would he behave otherwise? Did not Clemenceau accept the French Revolution and its excesses in the same way? But Senghor is carrying out a noble plan. The white race has its defects and the black race has its own. Both also have their own good points and virtues. To reconcile these differing virtues and good points, to help them form a synthesis, is this not a task worthy of a great heart? Senghor has dedicated his life to the achievement of this harmony, this reconciliation, this synthesis.

> René Maran. *Les lettres francaises*. September 10, 1947, p. 4†

M. Senghor was the delegate from Senegal-Mauretania to the Assemblée Constituante which framed the Constitution for the Fourth Republic in 1946, and he served on the committee of the Assemblée Constituante entrusted with the job of seeing to it that the new Constitution was drawn up in impeccable French. This important political role placed M. Senghor in an excellent position to translate his ideas into action. . . .

His principle and slogan for the "new Africa" of French West Africa is: "Assimilate, don't be assimilated." He thus counsels African natives to assimilate French culture without losing their native character. . . . as for France, if the poet harbors any resentment towards the oppressors and exploiters of his Fathers, through whom he addresses France, he tactfully subdues it; and his appeal to his ancestors is clothed in characteristic Christian tolerance and patience as regards "the lord of gold and of the suburbs." He sees the hand of God in the defeat of France in 1940, and he asserts that his own participation in the war was the occasion of a "replanting of fidelity" to France. Obviously, like the Fathers whom he addresses . . . the poet has not allowed his heart to become hardened by hate, and his dream of human brotherhood fills his heart with hope. . . .

Edward Allen Jones. *French Review*. May 1948, pp. 447–48

Most notable among . . . French Africans is Senghor . . . now President of the Senegal Republic. . . . From the age of seven Senghor began an intensive study of the French language. His outstanding promise soon took him to Dakar, and at the age of twenty-two he sailed for France to continue his studies at the École Normale Supérieure in Paris. Here he was soon joined by Aimé Césaire, seven years his junior, and the two men began the long series of conversations and experiments which prepared them for the task of "giving a tongue to the black races." Another acquaintance of this period was Léon Damas of French Guiana.

None of these three men began to publish until the late thirties; they had first to master the strange status of the "assimilated" man living in a society to which he does not belong. We discover from Senghor, as later from Laye Camara, that the overwhelming impression of the star pupil from French Africa who won his way to Paris was one of isolation. Only in this new context did he discover the fallacy that had underlain his whole education. He was not and could never be a Frenchman. He had therefore to settle down and rediscover what it was to be an African. . . . The supreme irony, and perhaps the ultimate justification, of "assimilation," is that it has contributed more than anything else to this process—the rediscovery of Africa.

This search for an identity can take a form as simple as Senghor's poem "Totem." . . . It can also assume the length and complexity of Césaire's *Notebook on a Return to My Native Land* or Damas' *Black Label*. The style which Senghor made for himself actually owes little to the scornful whiplash of Césaire's poetry, or to the staccato lines and typographical tricks of Damas. But [Césaire] undoubtedly exercised a powerful influence on Senghor through his intellect and personality, an influence which Senghor has generously acknowledged in his memorable "Letter to a Poet." . . .

From Césaire [Senghor] caught something of the new literary attitude of Négritude, which demanded of its poets a strong verbal rhythm, a wealth of African allusions and a general exaltation of "the African personality." The true past of the Negro must be rediscovered beneath the layers of colonial history, his culture vindicated, and his future prepared.

Gerald Moore. *Seven African Writers* (London: Oxford University Press, 1962), pp. 2–4, 6

As a policy, cultural assimilation was only applied effectively in the Dakar region of Senegal, to the almost complete exclusion of the rest of French West Africa. Senghor is a product of this system, and Negritude and the form it takes in his poetry and thought are a reaction against it.

Senghor has completely assimilated French culture, and this has given him a great love for France, even though in politics he has so often been in opposition. His French education has given him a preference for systematized thought, of a sort particularly reminiscent of the France between the two World Wars. Many of his major political speeches, two of which can be read in his recent book, *Nationhood and the African Road to Socialism*, resemble philosophical treatises in the grand French manner. While it has provoked on one level a profound reaction against the arrogance of French culture and the way it has taken him almost by force, Senghor's education has led to his oddly ambiguous attitude to it.

One can trace the development of his drama through the various phases of his poetical works much more easily than in his essays, from the early poems of almost diffident self-discovery—*Songs of Darkness* and *Black Hosts*—to the splendid self-assertion of *Ethiopics* and the Odes of *Nocturnes*. If one only reads the prose, or if one reads the poetry superficially, one's impression will be that Senghor is making an extreme and unrealistic assertion of the supremacy, let alone the equality, of African values over those of Europe. In this context, one cannot help being puzzled by a completely unrelated and apparently illogical love of France ("Lord, among the white nations, set France at the right hand of the Father"), and one assumes it is the classic, love-hate relationship. This is to miss the point of Senghor's vision. Senghor, in actual fact, refuses to choose between Africa and Europe. After an initial hesitation, his poetry moves towards a symbiosis of the two. What he is aiming at, and what his cultural background makes him so ardently long for, is not a cultural racialism, which his philosophy of Negritude seems at times to imply, but what he has been calling recently the "Culture of the Universal," the vision of a united universe to which every culture of mankind will make its contribution, and he calls on Africa to stir itself so as not to be late at the rendez-vous of the nations.

C. H. Wake. *Books Abroad*. Spring 1963, p. 156

The hymnic rhetoric of Léopold Sédar Senghor, unbroken by apologies, confessions, second thoughts, is the expression of a personality so firmly possessed of his Serer inheritance that he is able to evoke its atmosphere without the aid of names and phrases that are to alert the listener that he must attune himself to Africa. The names and events to which Senghor allusively refers are required by his hymnic narration like the names of the gods in Homer or Pindar or rather like the names and events the *griots* [storytellers] of Senegal were wont to weave into their songs of praise. Senghor's songs, often (ostensibly?) written for accompaniment by one or the other native instrument, are on occasion marred by a touch of preachiness and an enjoyment of verbal virtuosity for its own sake. Yet it is, as far as I can judge, Senghor and Senghor alone who has been able from his sympathetic identification with both cultures, Sérère and French, to lift an inherited art form without distorting or sugaring it, to the level of complexity which a Western audience of today requires. Like the word of the Hebrew Prophets and the word in the universe of magic, Senghor's is more than word—it is creative power which conjures up and moulds realities. . . .

Senghor does not, and cannot, have a successor. He stands on the crest of the ridge between two cultures equally alive. Africa, to him, "is connected through the navel" with Europe, he responds equally to Seine and Sine, to the roofs of Paris in the fog and the roofs which guard his dead in Senegal.

G. E. von Grunebaum. *French African Literature: Some Cultural Implications* (The Hague, Mouton, 1964), pp. 31–32

*Black Hosts*, most of the poems of which date from 1942 to 1944, has the appearance of a series of exercises in good citizenship, interspersed with memories. These memories are perhaps more the result of conscious choice than an irresistible impulse; they are brought in as if to justify poems that are politically committed. Looking back today, we can see that the 1940's were not the best years for this excessively didactic poetry. Nevertheless, one may grant that these poems offer a rather faithful psychological portrait of an increasingly influential person, who has chosen poetry as his field of action. It would be useless for the reader to look for any expression of personal suffering, intimate music, or excessive rage: all the poems in this collection are useful, direct, and cold, like a testimony without embellishment. . . .

Eight years elapsed between *Black Hosts* and *Ethiopics*. As a statesman, Senghor grew in stature and power, while the poet in him took the time that was needed to write texts that would have more than immediate goals. Above all, the idea of Négritude became subtler and more complex. Paying homage to Ethiopia also meant addressing a subject that excluded the relationships between the colonized and the colonizer: this work deals with permanence and duration. A sense of wisdom comes to light, as well as an ease, as if mystery were finally allowed to creep in among Senghor's excessively bare facts. The poems sometimes take on the mystique of legends; Senghor is concerned with the essence of things, profane or sacred; he is grateful to the ministrations of time, whether or not they have been understood; he catches himself dreaming of a language that might be an end in itself or might at least leave some invisible nourishment for the imagination; he plays at being difficult, and sometimes the results are fortunate. . . .

The return to obscure sources and ancestral trances is certainly a very important achievement for Senghor. For the first time, the reader feels he has been carried away by a delightful, pure delirium, something that disorients him and simultaneously plunges him into a labyrinth of noble and baffling truths, which appeal neither to his reason nor to his analytical faculties. The reader is charmed, and asks only to be charmed some more.

Alain Bosquet. *La nouvelle revue français.* November 1964, pp. 882–83

Senghor's reactions [to New York] are surprise, wonder, suspicion, and disappointment. . . .

In New York Senghor saw himself as the child of the bush, of nature, who, it seems, was uprooted from his communion with the trees, rivers, flocks, gods, and the dead; it seems that he felt ill at ease. The external beauty of this American metropolis masks an immense emptiness. Man is dehumanized. Only material life counts. The man of flesh and blood disappears in this "desert" inhabited by anguished men. It is a "desert" because it lacks the sap of human life—love. . . . How much more human, thought Senghor, was Paris, the city in which he had studied! . . .

[In Senghor's poems about New York] the influence of Arthur de Gobineau on his thought is apparent. . . . The black man, even in this overpopulated "desert," keeps his rhythm, the rhythm of life and of dancing. The consolation found in Senghor's stay in New York is the rhythmic gift of the Negro to American culture . . . The poet prefers his nights in Harlem to his days downtown. . . . The contrast between the two areas of the city is striking: the rigidity of white Manhattan and the flexibility of Harlem; the reification of the former and the feminization of the latter. Harlem is alive. . . . It seems that the black man in Harlem, despite the loss of Africa, has conserved his black heritage.

Sebastien Okechukwu Mezu. *Léopold Sédar Senghor et la défense et illustration de la civilisation noire* (Paris: Didier, 1968), pp. 124–27

Quite apart from the lustre which attaches to his name as a statesman, and also quite apart from the halo of Négritude which hovers over his poetry, Senghor was (assuming he will not produce any more poetry) a good poet. He introduced into French poetry a shot of African images which were as original and genuine as they were interesting and profound. His was a voice with a message; a message of humanity and a concern for human values. This message could, in the socio-political climate of the post-War period, not fail to impress. He spoke in the name of a continent—presumptuous and arrogant as it might seem—which was seeking its role in the destiny of mankind, in the "Civilisation of the Universal." It was a voice which was filled with the emotions and tensions and inconsistencies and hopes and fears and frustrations of a continent seething with new ideas, and it was this voice which endeavored to induce the peoples of our [African] continent towards making an original contribution to mankind's common civilisation. . . .

Even though the narrow cult of Negritude has in fact already died a natural death its message as seen by Senghor—viz. to contribute something of lasting beauty to the world—will yet remain the guiding star of generations of African poets to come. As poet, Senghor's image will survive many a generation. . . . Quite apart from his very original poetical note, Senghor has contributed more than any other poet or writer to integrate French Africa culturally into Metropolitan France. At Strasbourg, it will be remembered, he once spoke about the emergence of a Eurafrican political community; through his poetry he has materially contributed towards the formation of a genuine cultural Eurafrican community. In so many ways a product of two continents, Senghor represents a living link between Europe and black Africa. . . .

A statesman who can write poetry with the warmth and abandon of Senghor is a phenomenon which has no peer anywhere else in the world today. No African has brought greater credit to Africa in the last two decades; long after the eccentricities and the fulminations of the Nkrumahs, the Tourés, the Kenyattas will have been relegated to oblivion, will people the world over still revel in the verse of this poet whose very name is a verse of music and whose verse is one of the closest approximations to music the spoken world has ever reached in any language at any time.

Barend van Dyk Van Niekerk. *The African Image in the Work of Léopold Sédar Senghor* (Cape Town: A. A. Balkema, 1970), pp. 111–12

The collection *Nocturnes* is a synthesis of Senghor's work. All of his themes appear in it: the evocation of African scenery, the role of ancestors, the bonds of blood, the relation between the visible and invisible universe. The keyword "night," found in the title of the book, binds its parts together. Daylight has always been idealized by French poets; and its apex, noon, when the sun reaches its highest point, is often invoked: "Noon the just," says Paul Valéry. "Horror was its zenith," answers Léopold Senghor and gives new meaning to black and white. The daylight is angular, cruel, the color of snow and ice. Night is plentitude, delivery from the "reasoning of the *salons*, sophistry, pirouettes and pretexts." It is black, fluid, womb-like, full of anguish yet full of hope, a mixture of possibilities. It is serene, peopled by familiar spirits of one's ancestors, yet lurking with hidden dangers. Night is delivery from the slavery of reason. Night is also the collective hour when people of the village can be reunited in rhythmic harmony to listen to the songs of the *griots*, or village story-tellers and minstrels. Night is thus Negritude. . . .

Beyond the expression of strife, differences, and new found pride, one finds in Senghor's poetry the self-examination of the individual to the sources of his inspiration, the spiritual itinerary of a poet searching for the lost "Kingdom of childhood," his haunting powers of evocation, and his luminescent images which are enduring. His is a poetry of harmony, where in fact white is not the opposite of black, but where both worlds are reconciled by a man who, at the crossroads of two cultures, is in search of awareness.

Paulette J. Trout. Introduction to Léopold Sédar Senghor. *Nocturnes* (New York: Third Press, 1971), pp. xv–xvii

[Senghor's] use of language—typically a formal, almost Biblical tone—is quite unlike the trenchant, ironic Damas's, or the incendiary Césaire's. Unlike Damas or Césaire, Senghor has produced no single work of poetry with the far-reaching impact of *Pigments* or *Notebook on a Return to My Native Land*, which so miraculously encompass the passion and revolt of the black man in the Western world.

Senghor is essentially a poet of meditation, of nostalgia, a weaver of songs about what is closest to his heart. Stylistically, he blends a highly cultivated sensitivity to the French language and its literature with an esteem for the age-old traditions of his Serer kinfolk and their Wolof neighbors. Western critics with a background in the written literatures of Europe and America quickly see Senghor's resemblance to such French poets as Paul Claudel and Saint-John Perse—with their preference for long, flowing elegiac lines of verse—or to Walt Whitman. But anyone who has seen African poets and praise-singers perform—with all their variations of gesture, rhythm, and tone—to the accompaniment of drums and varied musical instruments—stringed ones like the kôras and khalams, or the wooden, xylophone-like balafongs—can imagine a whole other side to Senghor's poetry, derived from local traditions. This African aspect is oral. It can only be experienced in actual

performance and is only suggested to the uninitiated who merely read from the printed page.

Senghor's best lyric poems are pure enchantment. Like his "Night of Sine," they operate insidiously on the reader, slowly enfolding him into a world rich with unfamiliar sights, scents, tastes, feelings. To fully appreciate much of Senghor's poetry, one has to acquire a whole new vocabulary of Senegalese allusions, to become acquainted with palaces, persons, customs, the natural and supernatural, the past and present, of another world, another culture.

Ellen Conroy Kennedy. In Ellen Conroy Kennedy, ed. *The Negritude Poets* (New York: Viking, 1975), pp. 124–25

Senghor speaks often of African thought as a humanism. This word embraces a prophet's vision of a renewed humankind, and it is from this vision that Senghor tells us the message he has for his fellowman, which must be carried through the continents, to those who wait to hear the words that will bring enlightenment to the soul. Speaking of African philosophy, Senghor reminds us that "man is the active center of the cosmos. His essential human function is to capture all the scattered forces which lie at the ground of matter, all the aspects, the forms and colors, odors and movements, sounds, noises, tremblings, and silences of the universe. He must reinforce their life by enhancing their force. The undefinable word Life, in essence, explains African philosophy, its art and religion. Man helps God's force and becomes similar to Him. He animates, through art, the visible and invisible universe, singing about it, giving it rhythms. It is for this reason that the Africans say, 'God needs man,' that is, he needs men and humankind."

Senghor speaks the memories of the African man. His books are written before he writes them. History has already left him its accounts. He struggles to give them form, to allow the French language to make these accounts communicable to humankind. Senghor found his companions among the great figures of French literature; in the philosophers, the poets, the painters, and above all, in the startling figure of Teilhard de Chardin. France was not a limit, he wandered in the lands of the English, the Spanish. Neither Asia nor the Middle East were beyond his purview. He was present wherever man formed cultures, and his presence caused him to see and hear how the inflow and outflow of cultures create the civilization of the universal. We have little to conclude, but much to awaken. There is much that needs to be said about humankind, so much that belongs to us physically and spiritually, and so much which we need to acquire. We cannot allow ourselves to be trapped by preformed fixities. We learn from Senghor, as we learn from our ongoing conversations that we are always at a distance from what we are going to say; we need to catch up and find a relationship between what we have said and the reality we believe we have spoken about. In some way, there is always a gap, an unbridgeable one, that never seems to be filled in. This is not our despair; it is our journey to the reality of our being. Senghor knows how to read his companions. He fought with them for a prize, and like Jacob he received one. He gained the power to write well.

What fascinates the reader about Senghor is the realization that what he is being told seems to have already been revealed to the poet. Senghor speaks the poetic-religious traditions of the African, but with it he tells the story of another great literature. He, like a master juggler, balances the two, not wanting one to yield to the other. Between them stands the poet, the master player who knows that both are necessary for his survival. The story of the juggling is the marvel and mystery of this great poet-politician. Few of us would want to imitate him, few of us could. We are sensitive to the voices which come from many lands and find a dwelling within him. We observe how he listens to the past, how his listening guides his pen, and how writing and hearing become one. Senghor shows us how to read by showing us the art of writing, the drawing together of rhythm, sounds and images, song and dance, life and thought.

William Kluback. *Léopold Sédar Senghor: From Politics to Poetry* (New York: Peter Lang, 1997), pp. 115–17

BIBLIOGRAPHY

*Chants d'ombre*, 1945; *Communaute imperiale francaise* (with Robert Lemaignen and Prince Sisowath Youteyong, 1945; *Commemoration du centenaire de l'abolition de l'esclavage* (with Gaston Monnerville and Aimé Césaire), 1948; *Hosties noires*, 1948; *Chants pour Naeett*, 1949; *Ethiopiques*, 1956; *La report sur la doctrine et le programme du parti* (Report on the Principles and Programme of the Party), 1959; *Rapport sur la politique generale*, 1960; *Nation et voie africaine du socialisme*, 1961; *Nocturnes*, 1961; *Rapport sur la doctrine et la politique generale; ou, Socialisme, unite africaine*, 1962; *Theorie et pratique du socialisme senegalais*, 1964; *Liberte 1: Négritude et humanisme* (Freedom 1: Negritude and Humanism), 1964; *Négritude, arabisme, et francite: Reflexions sur le probleme de la culture*, 1967; *Politique, nation, et developpement moderne: Rapport de politique generale*, 1968; *Elegie des Alizes*, 1969; *Le Plan du decollage economique; ou, La Participation responsable comme moteur de developpement*, 1970; *Pourquoi une ideologie negro-africaine?*, 1971; *La Parole chez Paul Claudel et chez les Negro-Africains*, 1973; *Lettres d'hivernage*, 1973; *Paroles*, 1975; *Pour une relecture africaine de Marx et d'Engels*, 1976; *Pour une societe senegalaise socialiste et democratique: Rapport sur la politique generale*, 1976; *Liberte 3: Negritude et civilisation de l'universel*, 1977; *Ce que je crois: Negritude, francite, et la civilisation de l'universel*, 1988; *Oeuvre Poetique* (The Collected Poetry), 1990

# SENIOR, Olive (1941–)
## Jamaica

The majority of tales [in *Summer Lightning and Other Stories*] feature a female character, but the dominant perspective is that of the child, and it is evocation of the child's world, an often mysterious jumble of magic and horror, that is [Olive] Senior's main achievement. The stories deal with threats from the external world, whether physical or emotional, and the half-understood and painful conflicts within.

Each story is fitted with a narrative language integrated into the dominant point of view; often, narrative language is the speaker's language and spans the Jamaican Creole continuum, stretching its resources to the full. . . .

Senior subtly exposes the repressiveness and self-sacrifice at the core of conventional morality as it has been applied to women, and the spiritual and emotional deformities which result. Only Bekkah, in "Do Angles Wear Brassieres?," has the inner resources

to challenge the stultifying restrictions imposed by authority on the girl-child; Ma Bell, in "Country of the One Eye God," representing the final phase of life, emerges as a victim whose complicity in her oppression is largely the result of a false value system inculcated by traditional religion.

Most of the stories, then, at once portray an almost idyllic community organically connected to the Jamaican landscape and reveal the frightening inadequacies in the society for the nurturing of the maturing individual.

Evelyn O' Callaghan. *Journal of Caribbean Studies*. 6, 2 (spring 1988), pp. 143–44

Senior's short stories and poetry are the work of a creative talent of great sensitivity which expresses tremendous understanding of the human condition, particularly that of poor people, both rural and urban. The attempt to categorize her writing into a particular genre immediately gives one an uncomfortable feeling. For the work is knit together by a common landscape and a recurring concern for humanity. Both poetry and prose bring the country paths of her childhood and the urban experiences of her young womanhood into focus. The themes of both concern the experiences of people in these environments who represent different points along a scale of social and financial privilege.

The point of view preferred, particularly in the prose published so far, is the child's eye view. . . .

The child's eye view is not childlike. It is a clear vision through which the irrationalities of adults, the inequities in society and, from time to time, the redeeming features in the environment, are expressed. The exploitation of the child's vision allows Senior space for the imaginative forays her readers find most engaging, and for the dramatic presentation of human foibles seen from the point of view of the little person looking and feeling from under. . . .

The narrative voice in fact records children's reaction to phenomena, to their own condition, and perhaps more critically, to the adults with whom they interact. "Bright Thursdays" for example describes a small girl's discomfort as she adjusts to the strange and demanding formality in the upper-class home of a newly acquired guardian (an unacknowledged grandmother), after the easy casualness of life with a working-class mother who had been a servant to a member of the family. In "Ballad" the child eulogizes her favorite adult, Miss Rilla, a woman of whose lifestyle her step-mother heartily disapproves and on whom she expects God to exact punishment. In "Confirmation Day" the young candidate is perplexed by the symbolism of the Anglican communion into which she is being inducted, is no less perplexed by the memory of another, more dramatic initiation (by water in the village river) into a less sophisticated flock, and finally rejects what both have to offer in the supreme indictment of the Christian religion: "I'd rather be a child of someone else, being a child of god is too frightening.". . .

Other thematic interests in Senior's work include historical matters reflecting Senior's personal research into the history of the Jamaican people at home and in countries to which they have migrated, especially Panama. . . . "Nansi 'Tory" is concerned with the Afro-Jamaican, the man who did not return to Africa; "Searching for My Grandfather" is about the Jamaican who did not return from Panama. "Arrival of the Snake-Woman" explores the Jamaican situation in which ex-African and ex-Asian strive to find a place in the postcolonial society.

The village is a microcosm of Jamaica. Senior gives a believable description of the integeration of a postemancipation immigrant into a rural village. Through the child's eye, the author reveals early attitudes of the races to each other, the garbled versions of history available to the unlettered poor, and the interplay of Afro-Caribbean religion and American evangelism. Without implying any evaluation, the author allows the haphazard pattern of Jamaican family life and of community living to become part of the reader's consciousness.

Velma Pollard. *Callaloo*. 11, 3 (summer 1988), pp. 540–41, 543

Olive Senior writes out of a clear awareness of a conflicted life which is only by effort brought into any kind of control and clarity. She spoke recently of her childhood lived between two homes, a village, "darkskin" one and a "lightskin," middleclass environment, where she was alone and being groomed for status and advancement. In her recent volume, *Talking of Trees*, she uses as a superscription to a section of the book [Bertolt] Brecht's statement, "What kind of period is it / when to talk of trees / is almost a crime / because it implies silence / about so many horrors?" and of course this is the source of the book's title as well. Similarly, she quotes Martin Carter, "But what the leaves hear / is not what the roots ask." Her vision is often one of solitude: "Alone I will walk through the glass." In "Cockpit Country Dreams," she speaks of father and mother saying different things as "Portents of a split future.". . . Poetry becomes the balancing point, the crossroads at which all directions have to meet. . . . Senior determines life through an awareness of many directions and contradictions facing the individual, and her poetry becomes the place where at least distances and schisms can be spoken of and accepted. . . . Part of the solution to these tensions is the control which poetry gives. In "To the Madwoman in My Yard," the poet speaks with an exasperated understanding and sisterhood but in the end they are divided by the certainty in the poet that "Life Equals Control.". . . [She] draws a good deal on a sense of African culture, of ancestors who are still present and of rituals, of the African past and its relation to the contemporary experience through family stretching back to slavery; and this provides an emotional base for much of her painful poetry of isolation and displacement.

Elaine Savory Fido. In Carole Boyce Davies and Elaine Savory Fido, eds. *Out of the Kumbla: Caribbean Women and Literature* (Trenton, New Jersey: Africa World Press, 1990), pp. 33–35

Contemporary West Indian poetry includes both singers and storytellers, with no tidy distinction between the ways in which they bear witness to their experience as West Indians and to the past and future of the West Indies. The range of these experiences is very wide, as are their perspectives, and the languages and forms in which they write. Diversity is one of the most significant features of contemporary West Indian poetry, in fact, and has helped ensure that these experiences become part of the present heritage of West Indians and (almost as importantly) are not appropriated by somebody else.

This heritage, the heritage of slavery, is founded in loss—or what Edward Baugh once described as "the one grief of the

world." For Baugh, West Indians are connected by the difficult grace that brought them together, and by the persistent, patient love that holds them together. At the heart of his own work is a love of language, and of his land and its people; and a conviction that literature can be both its most powerful expression and what Michael Smith called "a vehicle of giving hope.". . .

Olive Senior [writes] from the center of [her] people's lives, with a sure sense of the struggle that has shaped them. Senior grew up in rural Jamaica near the Cockpit Country, the refuge of the Maroons. She is best known as a writer of short stories, including *Summer Lightning [and Other Stories]* and *Arrival of the Snake-Woman*, though she has also written social and historical studies. For several years she was editor of the magazine, *Jamaica Journal*, in which capacity she drew from her own heritage to bring lively attention to all aspects of Jamaican life, landscape, and language. "Ancestral Poem," from her book *Talking of Trees*, tells of this heritage, the poet's hard-won freedom from its rituals and rigors, and its continuing hold on her imagination. This is a complex poem, its juxtapositions at first relatively untroubled, but quickly becoming very disturbing, as thoughts and emotions are intersected by the menace of ingrained ritual and encased memory, and then by the violence and betrayal that are their legacy. The second stanza, in parentheses, portrays one of those moments outside any frame of resolution—a moment of fierce and indelible irrationality, represented by the confusing of her father on earth with the Father in heaven, a confusion that intensifies the disabling bewilderment of the moment and of her memory. The irony of the final line of this whole passage, where the deeply ambivalent ritual of religious confirmation provides a gesture of freedom in a language that accumulates betrayal and abstraction, is hauntingly reminiscent of one of the themes of this book, for the ambiguous syntax is generated by the local use of the word "me" in a literary context. And the final word "freedom," with its rhetorical flourish, is as much a gesture of ill-fated definance of her heritage as a description of any new liberation. . . .

The voices in "The Mother," another of Senior's poems, speak of the life of the West Indian poor, for whom the legacy of slavery has produced new forms of disgust and despair, and whose only hope may be in bearing witness to their own lives in their own words—words full of suffering and self-hatred and the sad ironies of self-conscious pretense and pathos.

J. Edward Chamberlin. *Come Back to Me My Language: Poetry and the West Indies* (Urbana: University of Illinois Press, 1993), pp. 248–51

The stories of *Summer Lightning*, [Senior] says, focus on the Jamaica of her childhood and emphasize the problems and perspectives of poor rural children, while those in *Arrival of the Snake-Woman* are more expansive, involving characters "of different races and classes," rich and poor, in both rural and urban settings. But both collections are explorations of Jamaican experience and identity within a larger network of competing cultures. . . . An awareness of that enveloping, sometimes corrosive larger culture is never very far in the background of Senior's stories precisely because the problematic relationship between the isolated, enclosed societies of the West Indies and the wider world is such a pervasive fact of Caribbean life. . . .

The major themes of *Summer Lightning*—the search for personal and cultural identities, the nurturing role of the West Indian mother in Creole society, the problematic and complex relationships between traditional ways and the wider world—are continued and expanded in *Arrival of the Snake-Woman*. "The View from the Terrace" takes up the question of identity most directly, focusing as it does on the lifelong struggle of its protagonist, Mr. Barton, to associate himself with what Senior has called "the colonial superstructure" that "determined everything." From early childhood, Barton has longed for "a world that somehow seemed rooted on its axis" and finds it in the literature of "daffodils and the downs and snow and damsels in distress"—the imagined world of England. Cultivated by teachers and "a succession of English bosses . . . who appreciated . . . his liking for things 'civilized,' i.e. English," he develops a distaste for black people (although he is himself darker than his first wife) and a deep-seated discomfort for his native country. But trips to Europe make him aware that he is not really English, either, and his second marriage, to an "incredibly vulgar" white Englishwoman, ends in divorce. . . .

The idea of home—where it is, what it is—is never very far from the center of Senior's attention. Barton's "European" house in "The View from the Terrace" is divided from Miss Vie's "Jamaican" hut by a deep ravine; in "The Tenantry of Birds," Senior attempts to bridge that gulf, bringing the two kinds of homes, with all their iconic associations, together. The "tenantry" of the title is a "rather bedraggled," somewhat wild-looking bird tree growing in an otherwise very formal, English garden belonging to a wealthy Kingston couple. For the wife, the tree represents a small part of the countryside where she spent many pleasant summers as a child. For her husband Philip, a university professor and political activist, the tree is an "un sightly" excrescence which he would like to cut down. Nolene, the wife, is particularly fond of watching "the star boarders . . . the pecharies" drive out the "rough, uncouth, chattering and uncaring" kling-kings-klings when they attempt to take over. This detail provides the story with its governing metaphor and Nolene with the example she later needs to take similar action of her own. As Philip becomes more involved in politics (and acquires a black mistress), the marriage disintegrates. He sends Nolene to Miami with their children "for safety's sake," as he puts it. One of the most delicate points Senior makes is that Philip, who, like his wife, is a light-skinned Jamaican of the privileged social class, does not immerse himself in island politics because of any innate sensitivity to island culture. His political activity is motivated more by ambition and ego than by sympathetic understanding; and his behaviour toward his wife is closely akin to that of master to servant—or of colonial power to colony.

Richard F. Patteson. *Ariel.* 24, 1 (January 1993), pp. 16, 23–25

The nine stories in Olive Senior's collection *Discerner of Hearts* are set in Jamaica, from the colonial period to the present day. Unfortunately, they are not chronologically arranged, so that "Zig Zag," which clearly, like the opening title story, is pre-Independence, comes at the end, after "The Cho Choo Vine," which glances at Rastafarianism. In most, black is not yet beautiful and white is the index of social advantage. Taken together, the collection, regardless of chronology, reflects a constricted society whose relationships are overdetermined by class and color; caste-power, or the lack of it, is constantly felt.

The viewpoint, with one exception, is female, in first or third person. At the center are two monologues which subtly blend Jamaican patois with Standard English. In "You Think I Mad, Miss?" Francina Mytella Jones goes from car to car in the street, begging to the accompaniment of a fractured litany of her betrayed life, while in "Swimming in the Ba'Ma Grass" Miss Lyn utters a poignant elegy for a husband murdered by a trigger-happy policeman, who is the law. . . .

Most of the stories use a standard narrative, mainly in the third person, except for the child's subjective viewpoint of "The Case against the Queen," carefully differentiating the patois of servants and the less-educated—those whom the servant Cissy, in the title story, realizes "needed to be so careful, to live good in the world, for there was nothing else between them and the night." In this story, although the daughter of the house, Theresa, belongs to that class whom "nothing seemed to threaten," she desires to reach out and empathize with her family's fearfully superstitious servant. In "Zig Zag" Sadie, the daughter of a shabby genteel white family, also reaches out to the servant Desrine and her numerous progeny in the bush, but she can do little; her equivocal status is pointed up when her mother deplores her "looking so black" from staying out in the sun. However, being white or light-skinned is a depreciating asset, an outmoded recipe for success in the world.

Old colonial caste gives way before the new materialism. The black servant's son, newly returned with "his Panama strut, his American accent," can aspire to Brid, his mother's poor white employer's daughter, and she in her innermost heart desires him. This story, and others, ends with a defining moment of self-realization; the inner life, often suppressed, emerges uppermost. The reader ponders this and what it implies or promises. With "The Lizardy Man and His Lady" we witness from the traumatized standpoint of children and servants the deadly, contemporary "big big" world of "coke and the crack and all them sinting."

Michael Thorpe. *World Literature Today.* 70, 2 (spring 1996), p. 455

BIBLIOGRAPHY
*The Message Is Change: A Perspective on the 1972 General Elections*, 1972; *One upon a Time in Jamaica*, 1977; *A-Z of Jamaican Heritage*, 1983; *Talking of Trees*, 1985; *Summer Lightning and Other Stories*, 1986; *Arrival of the Snake-Woman*, 1989; *Working Miracles: Women's Lives in the English-speaking Caribbean*, 1991; *Gardening in the Tropics*, 1994; *Discerner of Hearts*, 1995

# SEPAMLA, Sipho (1932–)
## South Africa

Over the past few years, there has been an upsurge in the publication of English poetry in South Africa . . . and a very important contribution has been by black poets, such as [Mongane] Serote, [Oswald] Mtshali, and others, to whom English is a second language. A new and already mature poetic voice, that of [Sipho] Sepamla, now rings out with an enviable sureness of diction [in the collection *Hurry up to It*!] Publication within South Africa probably obviates the shrillness that sometimes mars the poems of political exiles such as [Keorapetse] Kgositsile, but has not prevented Sepamla from mercilessly exposing the injustices of the white regime. . . .

The very first poem ("To Whom It May Concern") sets the tone. It is an ironical and Brechtian statement on the tragic situation of the black in South Africa—so tragic that it verges on the ridiculous; to keep his sanity he has to cultivate humor, black in both senses. . . . He has learned to accept the insults and indignities, but only for now, for the anger is always there, and the smoldering revolt: "God! where can the end lie / If not in me / I want you to trample the world once more / And I shall make it in your image." In an adaptation of a poem by the Colored Afrikaans poet Adam Small ("Feeling Small"), Sepamla exults over the white man for acting out of fear.

What is apparent is the directness and simplicity of the language, lit up with poetic insights, and the vividness of the very sparingly used images: "[his head] sways to the left and to the right / To allow only truths to pass." There are also a number of tender love poems, including one especially fine one in an e. e. cummings manner, expressing the awe and wonder of love in a stutter: "I am / None them they others / For I am / I know / Feel when I feel / Yours" ("In love").

Barend J. Toerien. *Books Abroad.* Summer 1976, pp. 707–8

Sipho Sepamla's collection [of poems], *The Soweto I Love*, is particularly interesting because his is an inside . . . view of the black struggle, suffering, and hopes for the future. It is no accident that a simple tabulation of the words used in his poems and their meanings would invariably have to do with fear, anger, stench, and humiliation. Thus I counted the following words and phrases which all link up, one way or the other, with the concept of fear: *terror, fleeing, cowed, scared, alarm, frantic, scare, cowardly, hounded, panic, scurry and scuttle, tremble.* . . .

Upon first reading his poetry, one tends to think of it as simple and naive. . . . A second and more thorough scrutiny teaches that the simplicity is singularly deceptive and hides a deeper, more profound meaning. The terror of his South African landscape is poignantly portrayed precisely through this simplicity of language: the at times inverted sentence structure further creates the impression of an awkwardness with the English language. Only when he abandons his special style, however, does he really sound awkward, as for example in the poem "I Saw This Morning" where the very direct "he was crippled by" and "he was wheeling round his teacher" jar. This simplicity, coupled with a staccato English and fairyesque quality—the Big Bad Wolf image—is hauntingly portrayed in "A Child Dies." His poem "Like a Hippo" must at first glance appear to the Western reader like the work of a child, an impression which quickly gives way to an understanding of the greater symbolism in the poem—again deceptively simple, like some of the oral stories with a tremendous sting in the tail. . . . The Hippo becomes the state = Afrikanerdom = apartheid.

Sepamla has hitherto successfully avoided writing "poetry conscripted for the victims." Like the Afro-American artist, the poet in South Africa can, to a large extent, function as a "guerrilla fighter who can talk Black English and ignore accepted aesthetics." There is after all the fundamental realization that while the language of the black artist in South Africa is Western, his idiom is definitely non-Western (black, if one wishes).

The poet's anger is contained with poise and does not spill over into a bitterness. . . . He seldom allows himself a comic ironic stance, yet when he does exploit humor as a device, the effect is clear, as for example in "Shop Assistant" which evokes images of another South African poet, Adam Small, who writes in Afrikaans, and his lampooning of white women in the poem "Oppie Parara.". . . Sepamla's "Civilization Aha" falls short of the reference to "Western Syphilization" by the Afro-American poet Jon Eckels. Although oral in tone at times, his poetry draws its strength from the urban proletariat environment which spawned him, the poet.

Vernon February. In Eldred Durosimi Jones, ed. *African Literature Today.* 10 (1979), pp. 256–57

[*The Soweto I Love*] was written immediately after the harrowing events in Soweto in 1976 and these events still have Sepamla in their grip. In some of the poems, such as "I Saw This Morning," he describes and articulates the terror which the riots brought in their wake. In others, for instance "At the Dawn of Another Day" he gives an account of the actual uprising, and, with emphasis in printed pattern, explains the causes and aims. . . .

Besides the Soweto uprisings, he writes of suicide, murder, and rape in prison; and Robben Island is the metaphor for the authorities' attempts to break the black man's spirit. He has nothing but contempt for the white way of life, and he expresses pride in the action of the youth of today. The careful poet of the telling phrase, the subtle and witty lines, and well-constructed verse has given way to a writer standing too close to events, sick with abhorrence, and giving way to a need to let the words pour out of him. . . .

[Sepamla's novel] *The Root Is One* takes place during a six-day period in Johnstown, a black township whose citizens are about to be forcibly removed, and its adjacent white town, Bergersdorp. Berger is a phonetic spelling of *burger*, Afrikaans for citizen. The story concerns Juda, a young man who is involved first in organizing a strike and then in attempts to stop the removal. He is the son of a man known to be a "sell-out" (someone who plays along with the authorities), and who, in the course of a story, is killed by a mob when he advises them not to fight against the removal. Juda is terrified of arrest and through the six days we watch his moral disintegration, ending in a betrayal of his friend Spiwo to the authorities and his own suicide.

*The Root Is One* is a novel of unrelieved gloom and pain. It opens with the "dim, dull dawning" of the first day and a dream of "a terrible thing which is going to happen soon." It ends on the sixth day in a night of faint light cast by a horn-shaped moon which looked like a septic wound. The deepening night swallows up "the whole act and the people of Johnstown," and as they go away "unburdened their hearts of one's deeds; as they gesticulated in their talking, they hurled away the root of their agony."

This is not the work of the confident, witty, and satiric Sepamla who celebrated the purpose of living in his early poems. It is instead the poet of the 1977 volume *The Soweto I Love*, whose mood is one of total pessimism. Life is a nightmare. The brave who act against oppression, like the young man Spiwo, are arrested, tortured and perhaps killed, and those who succumb to fear and betray, like Juda, experience the same fate in their dreams. A crowd collects around the house in which Juda has hanged himself. . . . Sepamla provides no answer to the question which he poses in the novel. For the moment endurance is all. The pain which the people must endure must be "carried in the hearts of the living for days on end.

The pain of suffering is like mist: it settles on every home,'' as one of the crowd puts it.

*The Root Is One* makes painful reading. Sepamla provides no relief, not in the theme, not in the story he wishes to tell, nor in the literary handling of the material. It is the work of a man in chains who has suffered so long that his vision of escape and freedom is dead.

> Ursula A. Barnett. *A Vision of Order* (London: Sinclair Browne, 1983), pp. 63–65, 156–57

Sipho Sepamla is a writer whose poetry makes the reader see and think: he has a gift for the precise, incisive stroke, and he knows how to find the words best suited to the description of his aspirations and those of his fellow blacks. As a satirical poet, he has a solid sense of irony and humor. As a lyric poet, he can be both fiery and tender; and he can rise above the demands of the ''situation'' to express the most universal human emotions.

Sepamla's activities are many and various. In his early forties, he is a man of the theater, a critic, and a poet. He also edits two literary reviews, *New Classic* and *Sketsh*. In the former he publishes both poets and short-story writers, white and black; in the second, more popular in appearance and content, he provides his readers with a review of the main theatrical events as well as extensive extracts from new plays. His editorials are inspired essentially by the daily life of the South African black, and it would be true to say that after the departure of [Oswald] Mtshali and [Mongane] Serote, along with [James] Matthews, he became one of the principal driving forces in his community. . . .

It can be seen that Sepamla's deep sense of commitment in no way interferes with his qualities as a poet. But this commitment, as unambiguous as it may be, extends well beyond the frontiers of his own community. For here is a man who is convinced that the South Africa of tomorrow will be built with the help of all its inhabitants. His poems constantly place the emphasis, not only on the common biological identity shared by all the people of his country, but also on the common destiny that binds all South Africans.

> Jacques Alvarez-Pereyre. *The Poetry of Commitment in South Africa* (London: Heinemann, 1984), pp. 215–16, 223

The images of black consciousness in Sepamla are not abstractions. The mere fact that a South African writer is against apartheid implies that he is against racial discrimination. If he happens to be a black writer then the motive becomes more pronounced because the black man in South Africa is on the lowest rung of the ladder of political acceptance. Moreover, Sepamla adds another dimension to this general aim when he concentrates on the tragic events that took place in the black township of Soweto. . . .

The wordiness in this poetry . . . is ameliorated by the subtle irony that is the foundation in Sepamla's art. He applies it to link history with [recent] events. There are no rough edges although it may be expected that such adherence to reality is prone to exhibit unpolished, scraggly, raw materials derived from memorable incidents. He definitely illustrates that ''every poet is molded by his age, by the great events of Great Event that took place during his impressionable years.'' It is the intricate web of life that exploded in Soweto in 1976 which is the great event that informs this collection. . . .

Black consciousness is therefore illustrated as both a way of life and an attitude of mind in the poetry of Sepamla. The attitude of mind is reflected in the evocation of rioting men, women, and children who wish to assert their dignity and value systems. This evocation is typical of the eloquence of Soweto poetry which uses the imagery of the streets to incorporate its theme. . . .

When children become bold enough to show signs of rejecting the value systems that seek to make them strangers in their own country, it is an optimistic sign. The description of this incident justifies Sepamla as an eloquent poet who uses the eloquence of the streets to codify his poetic diction.

> Ezenwa-Ohaeto. *Presence Africaine.* 140 (1986), pp. 18, 20

*A Ride on the Whirlwind* downplays . . . sociological and historical concerns . . . without losing sight of them entirely. The action begins two days after the uprising with the arrival at Park Station of the guerrilla Mzi, sent by the Resistance Movement in Dar es Salaam to kill a brutal black policeman, Andries Batata. He meets with Uncle Ribs Mbambo, his contact man, and through him the student leader Mandla, who with a small group of followers is directing resistance in Soweto from the house of Sisi Ida. Mandla and Mzi form an alliance and together blow up a police station: Mzi subsequently assassinates Batata. Several of Mandla's followers, as well as Sisi Ida, are arrested after an accident with explosives at the house. Descriptions of their torture follow. The novel ends with Mandla fleeing into exile and Mzi attempting to persuade a white helper to drive him to Swaziland. . . .

[In the novel] a closeness to and identification with the action on the part of [Sepamla] can sometimes be noticed. The difference of views expressed by the characters does not, finally, constitute any basic challenge to the ideological thrust with which the reader is left. In *A Ride on the Whirlwind*, there is one incident of a far-ranging criticism being made of the organized resistance to the Sophiatown removals in the 1950s; but the person who makes them, the she-been owner Noah Witbaatjie . . . very quickly turns out to be a police spy. The [novel], therefore, [explicates and naturalizes] the inevitability and correctness of black political aspirations. While readers will identify with these aspirations, the manner in which liberation is supposed to happen and the way South African society is imagined are still worthy of attention.

> Kelwyn Sole. *Research in African Literatures.* 19, 1 (spring 1988), pp. 67–70

Sipho Sepamla has been quietly building a reputation as one of the most perceptive, ironic, and sensitive South African poets. He may lack the verbal outrage of Mongane Wally Serote or the violence of Mafika Paschal Gwala, but he certainly exhibits a poetic quality undebased by his experiences in South Africa. *From Goré to Soweto* captures his peculiar reality with telling accuracy. . . .

Sepamla's observations on South Africa and other parts of the world serve as pedestals for an incisive condemnation of the dehumanization he has felt. The poetic portrayal of reality is achieved through the use of an ironic vision which enables him to imbue his poetry with succinct imagery and to engineer a reaction appropriate to the events described, as in the collection's very first poem. . . . A similar alienation or oppression of spirit emerges in ''Wattville,'' with its implication of life as a prison for black South

Africans: "we would be village / if only we were not crammed / into a crooked square mile / drawn by men drunk with power." Familiar thematic issues in South African verse are made fresh via subjection to his poetic furnace, as in "I love Soweto."...

The poet regards all natural human emotions as debased due to the debasement of life itself. An enormous bitterness forms his poems but is admirably controlled, as in "Moment Beyond Now."... Still, the reality of death is the reality of South Africa, with its constant riots. In "May Day," dedicated to the memory of dying youths, Sepamla warns "What we are saying so often / Some comfort can be gained from the trigger / But the real shit lies beyond / On the count of tomorrow's yield." That ominous warning also contains a hope that injustice will be eliminated in the poet's homeland, but this hope does not cause him to ignore the violence in real life.... A society which consumes its young, the poet implies, is making preparations for doom; but his special sorrow is that the extermination is directed only toward black babies, a primitive and savage practice for a society which prides itself on its civilized nature. The uncertainty of life effected by such savagery is illustrated in "28 July," where the speaker's loss of his home becomes a metaphor for his society's loss of the land: "I stand frozen in my house / Occupied territory / Taken over like the land yesteryears / No one tells me anything / but to keep my hands above my head." It is thus not surprising that in "A Man for the Land" the poet confirms that, despite the tragedy of their existence, the people will survive.

> Ezenwa-Ohaeto. *World Literature Today.* 64, 1 (winter 1990), p. 184

BIBLIOGRAPHY
*Hurry up to It!*, 1975; *The Blues Is You in Me*, 1976; *The Soweto I Love*, 1977; *The Root Is One*, 1979; *Children of the Earth*, 1983; *A Ride on the Whirlwind*, 1984; *Selected Poems*, 1984; *Third Generation*, 1986; *From Goré to Soweto*, 1988; *A Scattered Survival*, 1989

# SEROTE, Mongane (Wally) (1944–)
## South Africa

[With *Tsetlo*, Mongane Serote] emerges clearly as the most gifted, original, and intense of the black [South African] poets, and he penetrates the South African situation (and, indeed, the universal situation of the oppressed in ferment) in a way which I think is quite new in our literature.

His emotional burden is neither guilt nor anger—though these feelings are material to his vision—but a profoundly humane grief....

It is necessary to make this bald affirmation because I want to guard against seeming to make the wrong emphasis when I claim that Serote's poetic sensibilities and passions have carried his political vision forward to a point morally in advance of anyone else's—in the South African context at least.

It takes boldness to invoke a vision of nemesis, yet many have done so—most whites reacting in a blur of fear or masochistic relish, most blacks in a red haze of revenge-lust. In either case the actors in the prophecy are dehumanized. Serote is exceptional in

holding to a vision as direly purposive as any, but which sheds no shading of human complexity: on either side, people are both dangerous and desperately vulnerable—and retain an almost unbearable claim on that heart of his.... He shows, by a piling up of significant details from publicized events and from his own ranging observations of black lives misshapen by deprivation, humiliation and violence, what it is in our situation that could—perhaps must—eventually erupt in actions he starkly symbolizes by Lod Airport. But he does not gloss over the fact that such actions would be atrocities, as destructive of the doers' spirit as of the victims' flesh. At the end of "Introit," a poem on the bloody mission of emancipation, he says with apocalyptic despair: "I wonder where I'll cleanse my hands."

I know of no one else whose grief extends in this way and not only over the oppressed (he grieves for their violence and depravity as well as their sufferings in these "civilized times"), but also over those who have to be overthrown and over their blood-corrupted executioners.

> Lionel Abrahams. *Rand Daily Mail.* June 17, 1974. Repub. in Michael Chapman, ed. *Soweto Poetry* (Johannesburg: McGraw-Hill, 1982), pp. 74–75

[*No Baby Must Weep*] concerns the trajectory of the personal development of the subject/narrator of the poem. Starting from the earliest experiences that shape his subject's life, Serote is determined to show that none of the influences is random or chance, but rather that they embody all the contradictions of the circumstances and times in which the narrator is living. Further, the poem is inseparable from the current moment of the narrator's mental and emotional state, which is itself laden down with layer upon layer of turmoil inherited from the past.

The poetry itself seems to stem from the endless striving of the narrator for an understanding of the burden bequeathed to the current moment by the past. Serote tirelessly traces the connection between his subject's current anguish, the suffering of the past, and what there may be to hope for in the future.

Serote is not primarily concerned with writing about the over political repression of the black man in South Africa. Instead he assumes this level, and leaves it behind in his search for some essential *meaning and significance* in the experience of dispossession and oppression. Serote journeys through the images and representations of the shared cultural experience of oppression of the black man in South Africa. It is in this sense that Serote's statement is a political work, an affirmation that there is meaning and significance behind the seemingly repetitive patterns of denigration that black South Africans have endured. Serote is determined to plumb the depths which hide in everyday realities, the greater realities that consume the past and embody the future....

Serote's poem involves the reader in personally experiencing something of the pain inherent in traversing [the] distance between masses, history, and the personal realities of an individual subject. The irony and the pain in traversing this distance lies in the extraordinary loneliness that the subject, alone, has to endure once he has perceived the extent of the distance to be covered before liberation and the resolution of some of the contradictions of existence.

In this work Serote has isolated the essential political and psychological reality of Africa today, the double bind that in one breath separates the individual from the masses through the culture of oppression/exploitation and at the same time renders the individual's future in separation from the masses inconceivable.

Alex Levumo. *Staffrider*. 2, 1 (March 1979). Repub. in Michael Chapman, ed. *Soweto Poetry* (Johannesburg: McGraw-Hill, 1982), pp. 76–77

Serote's poems, like [Oswald] Mtshali's, were first published in the literary journals *Purple Renoster, Bolt, New Coin,* and *Contrast,* during 1971 and 1972. Again it was *Purple Renoster* which introduced him, with what was in fact the first poem by a black contributor in these journals. It made its impact immediately, with its title "What's in this Black 'Shit'" and its graphically outspoken condemnation of white inhumanity to black. It is included in Serote's first collection, *Yakhal'inkomo,* also published by Renoster Books, in 1972. . . .

Critics naturally compared his work with that of Mtshali and generally found him the more accomplished poet, through it was felt that the work was very uneven. The title of the collection represents the cry of cattle at the slaughter-house, as Serote explains in the preface and again in the August 1973 issue of *Bolt.* It is based on a story told him by a sculptor friend who saw people kill a cow near a kraal, and in the kraal were cattle looking on and he heard them cry. . . . Serote compares the sound with the music of a tenor saxophone player, expressing the same cry of fear and rage. . . .

*Tsetlo,* his second collection, was published by Ad. Donker in Johannesburg in 1974. Whereas *Yakhal'inkomo* was the agonizing cry of the cattle watching their kind being slaughtered, *Tsetlo,* more subtly, is the tiny bird with the "weird sweet whistle which it plays while it flies from branch to branch in the bush, luring people to follow it. . . . And then it stops. It may lead you to sweet honey, to a very dangerous snake or to something very unusual." Serote's concept of the world has widened and the mood has deepened. Sadness is still predominant, but it has become firmer. He no longer speaks of returning to the bosom of Alexandra and lying amid the rubble, but mourns its passing and remembers it, in "Amen Alexandra," like ". . . a thunder clap / that froze in our hearts." There is less talk of tears and desolation. . . .

His probing continues in his subsequent two volumes, *No Baby Must Weep* and *Behold Mama, Flowers.* . . .

Serote's quest for truth and meaning takes on a new impetus in exile. He has walked far, and hopes that the road will lead him somewhere other than into nightmare, that it "can whisper wisdom" to him. . . . *No Baby Must Weep* is a single long poem on a theme of contrast between the darkness of life and the bright hope of birth. . . . The poem is strongly autobiographical. The first pages tell of his childhood in the township; this theme recurs, but later events take place within the poet himself. The world is real only insofar as he experiences it, and he expresses his experience symbolically. The mother becomes Africa; and the poet, if he can succeed in throwing off all physical trappings, even that of fear, will become one with the earth, with Africa. Black life is represented by a river, deep and dark, where the horrors of life and death form only little ripples on the surface. The sea represents a free Africa into which the poet longs to emerge. . . .

Neither this poem, nor the long title poem in the collection *Behold Mama, Flowers,* is entirely successful. . . . [There] are . . . too many banal passages and repetitions of phrases and moods that become monotonous. In *Behold Mama, Flowers,* Serote loses sight of the theme introduced in the foreword, of a child seeing pieces of human flesh and bones floating down a river and saying "behold mama, flowers," though he picks it up again at the end where the agony is tinged with hope. . . . The remaining poems in this collection are dedicated to various writers and friends. Most of the poems in this collection were written in the United States, but some were written in Botswana, where he was living at the time of [this] writing.

Ursula A. Barnett. *A Vision of Order* (London: Sinclair Browne, 1983), pp. 55–60

The most obvious problem that faces the reader in *To Every Birth Its Blood* is the relation between the two parts of the novel. The second part's sudden shift from first-person narration to third-person narration, the time shift, and the shift of focus to a set of characters referred to but never central in the first part, are initially disconcerting and bewildering. But gradually, on closer examination, significant patterns begin to emerge.

In relation to the second part, the first part of the novel reveals itself as the story of defeat and despair. This section is seen through the eyes of ex-journalist and unsuccessful actor, Tsi Molope. Personally defeated, Tsi registers the world as defeated too. For example, the members of his immediate family (the Molopes), are broken or damaged: one brother, Fix, has been detained; another brother, Ndo, is irrationally violent and constantly abuses his wife, his parents are old, empty and silenced, having fought to make a future for their children, and failed; and his sister Mary, initially bewildered by a frightening world and misguided by trashy escape fantasies, falls pregnant and is rejected by her parents.

More generally, the bitter realities of black experience in an apartheid society are felt with painful intensity. His home, Alexandra, is itself seen as a symbol of the defeat of the black man: it is the "Dark City," the polar opposite of the "Golden City" which is the symbol of the white man's success; and the two are understood as integrally related. There are the degrading incidents, too, which spell defeat: the permit raid, the humiliating visit to the police station to obtain a new permit, the insults of the liftman in Tsi's newspaper building—all the "shit" the black man resents, but has to put up with.

In the same way . . . the first section is pervaded by the uncertainties and fears surrounding Fix's detention, as well as the activity-in-exile of Tsi's friends, Anka, Boykie, Themba, and Tuki. Furthermore, the arbitrariness with which state power is employed is underlined by the central incident which dominates the first half of the novel. Responding to the news of further detentions, and reflecting on the way he could no longer bring himself to observe the "tumor" and "rot" of apartheid society as a reporter, Tsi thinks back to the experience of naked police intimidation and brutality that has fundamentally changed his life. This incident is related as a flashback, a point which tends to be missed in the complex inter-weavings of Tsi's thought processes. He recalls how, on the way back from a newspaper assignment in the Transkei, he and his photographer friend Boykie were stopped by police, physically assaulted, and held in solitary confinement for a week. According to Boykie, who had been driving, the ostensible reason for this police action was that there had been a dead body lying in the road. This incident galvanizes Boykie into furious hatred and opposition to the system, but Tsi's response is to feel undermined and emasculated: for him the incident serves to focus the black person's vulnerability and impotence. This is underscored by the response of Tsi's white-run newspaper. The incident is immediately made into a "story"—an insignificant story, moreover, "in some corner, on page two" in which Tsi is also racially categorized as a "black reporter." This is the point from which it becomes impossible for Tsi to report the "terrible township images," and from which his sense of defeat and despair takes over. It is thus inaccurate to respond to Tsi as simply a "feckless drunkard," as reviewers have tended to do. Rather, one should see that this series of traumatic events has wrenched him out of a relatively comfortable and stable position of social adjustment, and precipitated a severe state of psychological weariness and *anomie*.

Part one of the novel presents, through Tsi, an anatomy of a people's defeat. This defeat involves a world of experience which separates people from each other in their individual suffering, and is thus accurately portrayed through an isolated individual consciousness. From an epistemological viewpoint, what is captured here is the psychological response to a battering external world: it is an exploration of the way in which the environment acts upon and damages individuals. And it is precisely this subject-object relationship which is to be reversed in the second part of the novel.

> Dorian Barboure. In M. J. Daymond, J. U. Jacobs, and Margaret Lenta, eds. *Momentum: On Recent South African Writing* (Pietermaritzburg, South Africa: University of Natal Press, 1984), pp. 172–74

In Serote's poetry traditional motifs do not occur, as in much of West African literature, as vestiges of a largely bygone culture, standing in contradistinction to and now being superseded by and wrestling with Western culture, but as examples of a living tradition, which the African growing up in the city takes in as completely as he absorbs Western culture. Serote's poetry, despite its urban setting, blends Western influences and traditional elements.

"Hell, Well, Heaven" is Serote's definitive statement in the "Who am I, Where did I come from, Where am I going" idiom. This poem sets the tone for the rest of his early poems, which have been collected in *Yakhal'inkomo* and *Tsetlo*. It describes the reawakening of the black people following the suppression of black cultural and political expression after the Sharpeville massacre of 1960. The poem celebrates the renaissance of the late 1960s, when a new generation of black artists, sculptors, musicians, dramatists, and poets blossomed throughout the country, against the tide of the most repressive legislation ever enacted by the South African racist regime. . . .

In "Alexandra," which first appeared in the last issue of *Classic*, the township is personified and presented in the guise of an unloving, uncaring mother. The mother image has reference to origin, to roots. Serote traces his roots to Alexandra township: "And Alexandra, / My beginning was knotted to you, / Just like you knot my destiny." The statement is intended to counteract government efforts to remove every African from the cities to resettle them in some impoverished "Homeland" or Bantustan. He is not renouncing his traditions, as such. He is simply asserting his right to live where he was born and became what he has become. . . .

At this stage in his development Serote was searching for an adequate vehicle to convey his African personality, for a poetic form that was consistent with black consciousness. This quest yielded its results in "Ofaywatcher-Blackwoman-Eternity," which appeared in 1974 in James Mathews's *Black Voices Shout*.

"Ofaywatcher-Blackwoman-Eternity" is a tribute to black womanhood, after the manner of [Léopold Sédar] Senghor's "Black Woman." This poem represents an advance in Serote's technique. Where before his use of traditional oral motifs had been almost unconscious, he now handles them with conscious and consummate skill. The poem opens with a note of applause for black women: "Silent like a leaf falls to earth." His gestures manifest veneration, as when he describes his actions: "I bend, I bow my head." As in the opening line of "City Johannesburg," Serote's mode of address, which this time, he sustains to the end, is in the manner of *izibongo*. . . .

Towards the end of "Ofaywatcher-Blackwoman-Eternity," Serote strikes a note of celebration through his reference to dance and music: "You who dances to drums / Who dances to horns." The instruments used are traditional. They are in tune with the traditional form of the poem and attune the reader's mind to those virtues which are traditionally associated with women: their sympathy, patience, understanding, and endurance. "Ofaywatcher," a figure which appears in several of Serote's other early poems, derives from black American culture and refers to a black person who has set himself or herself up as the watchdog of the community, a role Serote has taken upon himself through his poetry.

> Mbulelo Vizikhungo Mzamane. In Landeg White and Tim Couzens, eds. *Literature and Society in South Africa* (New York: Longman, 1984), pp. 152–55

In spite of the disappointments recorded in *Tsetlo*, there is enough to justify the hope of a change, the responsibility for which lies in the hands of the younger generation, the children and the young men and women of the 1970s. They will not be afraid to address the white man on equal terms; they will not fear to hate the authors of their centuries-old suffering. They will regain the courage of their ancestors and hear from across the seas the message of liberation addressed to them by their brothers who have gone into exile in Europe and the United States. There would be nothing new here that was not already spoken of by [Oswald] Mtshali, except that Serote says directly, in his own voice, and *clearly*, what Mtshali hinted at or expressed by means of a fable. Serote—and this is the chief characteristic of black consciousness—dares to look the white man in the eye and, especially, to speak to him plainly.

He is, however, less anxious to speak to the white man or to reveal to him the "hidden face" of South African society than to speak to his fellow Africans, not in the language of the political militant, like Stokely Carmichael for instance, but by trying to bring about the cultural and psychological transformation that must necessarily precede political action proper. If we add that his work also shows his rejection of the white liberals, the prophecy of a retributive violence, and a stress on what is and is not to be done, we can say that Serote is the voice of the black consciousness movement, minus its didacticism but with the lyrical power of the poet. . . .

[If] we seek a poem to serve as a banner for black consciousness, a poem which bears the mark of the new relationship between the young generation of Africans and the whites, we must turn to "What's in this Black 'Shit.'" This poem is an expression of self-assertion and courage, in the metaphorical form suggested by the title: Serote implicitly returns to the dialogue idea only to leap immediately from servile or forced submission to the orders of the white man to categorical refusal. In both cases, there is denial of the other man's words; but in the second the roles are reversed, the only way, say the followers of black consciousness, for the African to regain his dignity and make an impression on the white man.

Jacques Alvarez-Pereyre. *The Poetry of Commitment in South Africa* (London: Heinemann, 1984), pp. 190–91

What is Mongane Serote telling us? There are words and images that he uses and frequently returns to. Again, he does this relentlessly, compulsively, as if to extract the last drop of meaning from them. He returns to them like someone who repeats a call so that he may hear it echo in the hills, several times, to measure its quality and reach. . . .

In a sense they weave themselves into a refrain: a sad one, that sums up for us the anguish, the fear, the monstrous wound, that is this life, this odyssey. ''Eyes are broken''; ''mothers stare their babies in the eye''; ''street lights look like wet eyes''; ''the horrors of my stomach throb to my eyes''; ''my heart bleeds through my eyes''; ''droplets of tears as big as eyes''; ''Thick footsteps pulsate on black shadows''; ''the dark shadow wraps my heart''; ''a bloody (Saturday) night whose shadows fall like blinking eyes''; ''waste of resettlements screaming, forming ridged shadows over his body'' (i.e. of a murdered man); ''her eyes fell a cold shadow on my heart.''. . . .

These repeated images are turned around and inside out in a manner that quite clearly portrays a poet searching for meaning, up and down the vertical and horizontal planes. A man who has, since he was a child, been groping instinctively for a father figure, a mother's warmth and the intimacy of her body odor, for her hand, for a brother's reassurance. Even as a man, he seeks to reconnect with the mother. But, as in so much poetry of the black world, the mother figure does not stay at the physical level of femininity for long. Soon she takes on a symbolic meaning: she is by turn the biological mother, the protective maternal principle, love, Alexandra, Africa. This is particularly reminiscent of Léopold Sédar Senghor's poetry in its Négritude essence, of African-American poetry going as far back as the Langston Hughes of the 1920s.

Mongane Serote lives in exile in Botswana. But he will always return to his Alexandra in spirit, his beginnings. In *Yakhal'inkomo*, the township comes across raw, dusty, with its furrows alive with maggots. Later, in *Tsetlo*, Alexandra is still enveloped by the dust kicked up by traffic and bulldozers, but it is now refined in the memory, by an act of poetry. It is a ''cruel memory,'' the memory of teardrops ''as big as eyes.''

Es'kia Mphahlele. *English Academy Review*. 3 (1985), pp. 67–68

Mongane Wally Serote is . . . one of South Africa's leading poets of the post-Sharpeville generation, at a time when the rest of Africa has for the most part achieved independence, while South Africa's black population continues to bear the brunt of the apartheid policies of the white minority. Such has been the effect of these policies that the older generation of black writers had been virtually erased from the cultural memory of their people, through bannings and exile, when Serote began writing. Serote himself has described this: ''When I started writing, it was as if there had never been writers before in my country. By the time I learned to write, many people—[Es'kia Mphahlele, Keorapetse] Kgositsile, Mazisi Kunene, Dennis Brutus—had left the country and were living in exile. We

could not read what they had written, so it was as if we were starting right from the beginning.'' It was during this period that black consciousness came into being as the black South Africans' response to, and rejection of, white political and cultural domination. Like Négritude, with which it has close affinities in many respects, black consciousness sought to foster pride among black South Africans in their own cultural heritage and creativity and to establish an independent and free identity. Serote's own work is an expression of this movement.

Writing nearly forty years later than [Léopold Sédar] Senghor, in a situation in which colonizer and colonized have none of the closeness that Senghor felt bound him so closely to France in spite of their disagreement over the question of colonialism, their whole attitude to culture is worlds apart. Where Senghor sees the relationship between African and European culture in the form of equivalent and equal parallels, Serote sees it in the form of ironic contrast. The result for Serote is an emphasis on realism and the comment it makes on the relations between black and white in South Africa, while Senghor functions in the realm of idealism.

Clive Wake. *Research in African Literatures*. 16, 1 (spring 1985), p. 15

Mongane Serote, in his first novel, *To Every Birth Its Blood*, hurls himself literally into the pool of blood which envelops revolutionary South Africa. The novel is inspired in the first place by the Soweto student uprisings of 1976. Building on this revolutionary climate, Serote extends the battle to a people's war which must finally overthrow the apartheid system. Like [Alex] La Guma, Serote chooses his own suburb in Johannesburg, Alexandra Township, to depict the destruction of the minority regime. By choosing a place he knows well, the writer familiarizes the reader with the oppression of South Africa in a firsthand way. . . .

Mongane Serote's achievement in his first novel is remarkable. Themes related to the apartheid system are often difficult to present in an interesting, non-dogmatic, and imaginative manner. The context of South African literature demands highly skilled writers, and Serote demonstrates in *To Every Birth Its Blood* that he is a bona fide member of such a group. His intimate and authentic understanding of the sociopolitical environment of black and white South Africa makes his story believable. He has the uncanny ability to extend South African writing beyond the mere reportage of current injustices to a realm in which many progressive South Africans are engaged in revolutionary struggle. He demonstrates that he is both an observer and participant in this ongoing human drama. We are not simply assaulted by the cruel, bare facts of South African life; these facts are interwoven beautifully with the authentic dialogue and realistic setting. The characters, both black and white, are real; and their demands are carved clearly on the reader's mind. We feel that we know the dilemma of Tsi Molope and David Horowitz, the white liberal journalist, and that we can fully understand the reasons for the revolutionary action that will bring the required change. Through Serote's observant eye and behind-the-scenes knowledge, we are given a magnificent tour of how meticulous revolutionaries plan their actions. As a poet first, the novelist provides us with stark, concrete imagery and metaphor, and he succeeds to orchestrate a flowing, rhythmic tale of woe and triumph. In the use of plaintive and defiant music by Miriam Makeba, John Coltrane, Hugh Masekela, and Dollar Brand, Serote not only melds artistic forms, but also pursues his historical theme of enslavement and defiance of the black man in Africa and America.

Cecil Abrahams. *Matatu*. 2, 3–4 (1988), pp. 34–35, 39–40

*To Every Birth Its Blood* "delves into the heart and soul of a nation heading for disaster and creates and awareness of why it is inevitable." Like his predecessors of the 1950s, Serote extensively examines the issues of economic deprivation and political oppression to illustrate this impending disaster. . . .

What distinguishes *To Every Birth Its Blood* . . . is the novel's uniquely dispassionate portrayal of underground political activity and the harassment of blacks by the police. The revolution that Serote anticipates in the title poem of *Behold Mama, Flowers*, is realized in the second part of the novel. The suffering, frustration, desperation, and despair that dominate the first part of the novel give way to the ever-growing influence of a political organization simply referred to as the Movement. Although the role of the collective is emphasized in relation to the activities of the Movement, Serote's method, unlike that of [Alex] La Guma's [*In the Fog of the Seasons' End*], is conventional. . . . In other sections of the book, the extensive influence of the Movement is compared to the wind and the sea. This all-embracing imagery and symbolism have much to do with Serote's background as a poet. In [Peter] Abrahams's *Night of Their Own* and La Guma's *In the Fog*, language is deceptive rather than poetic.

Serote does not romanticize revolution. Death in the struggle is portrayed in a calm and humane manner. Two of the outstanding members of the movement, Oupa (the protagonist's nephew) and Mandla, are captured and killed. The protagonist's attitude to their deaths, particularly to that of Oupa, is credible, moving, and unsensationalized. . . . Towards the end of the novel, the protagonist leaves South Africa for Botswana. He has hope for the future of blacks inside South Africa although the movement has been partly fragmented. The novel ends with the birth of a child, which—as in La Guma's *In the Fog*—symbolizes an optimistic future. Whereas La Guma's novel closes with an overt proclamation of impending, full-scale armed struggle, Serote's *To Every Birth Its Blood* ends with implied endorsement of the struggle.

Piniel Viriri Shava. *A People's Voice: Black South African Writing in the Twentieth Century* (London: Zed Books, 1989), pp. 84, 150–51

Like Serote's earlier works, *No Baby Must Weep* is ultimately an optimistic poem. It begins, however, with a very pessimistic definition of "men." The love that ought to be within men is dead, Serote's autobiographical persona tells us. As a result, men are

> huge
> tall
> fat
> things
> outsmarted by cats in gentleness
> shamed by tigers in agility

Men "know nothing about songs," "are more petty than birds," and cannot "be moved / by the sight of machine-gunned children." They are often drunk, and they are always burning something be it cigarettes, dagga, or petrol. They either can't make love, or scare off the "cats when they make love in the dark." They are greedy and likely to die of heart attacks inspired by their crazed chasing after wealth.

Serote's definition of "men" is interesting for at least two reasons. First, Serote keeps his definition a-racial: at times, he seems to be glancing at white men; at times, black men; at times, both. Serote's point then seems to be that all men have lost the love that ought to be within them. Second, Serote keeps returning to men's inability to hear songs. For a writer—for a poet, this inability is particularly troubling and frustrating. . . .

The discouraged, sometimes distracted poet finally abandons his condemnation of "men" and declares, numerous times, that "i am the man you will never defeat". . . .

He will sing, and those who join him in song will also not be defeated by loveless men. His song takes him to the source of love—the highly symbolic mother. "[W]eary from running," "bruised" by the wind, "burnt" by the sun, he tries to renew himself through the mother's smile, passion, and rhythm. The mother comes to symbolize Africa. The return to the mother is a return to the womb; the poem then transforms the sea-like womb into the sea, and the sea becomes a second symbol for Africa. As the second symbol is born from the within the first, there is a sense of renewal—available to the persona and to the reader.

But the sea is still distant. The persona must follow the river to reach the sea. A reader who has seen the townships that comprise Soweto can visualize the persona's problem: the river, which Barnett has suggested represents African (as opposed to Western) life, is only a near-dry creek or a ditch there. What dominates the scene, as the poem presents it, are the streets, which the poem describes repeatedly as dirty, dusty, "bloody muddy," and leading nowhere.

Serote's persona becomes trapped in this urban scene, these "squeaking blood-stained hungry-rat battlegrounds.". The scene is populated by whores, murderers, and "cops [who] shoot first and think after.". And victims! Serote chooses to emphasize how the children are victimized, how they suffer. The symbolic streets have "woven the children of this town into their dust" and have "made the children of this town gasp in their dongas."

The "grannies," who comprise the oldest generation to be found there, remember the African past, and they embody that African past in their songs. Based on these songs and rooted in the slum-and-township suffering, Serote's persona will find the river and follow it to the sea. There, he will immerse himself in the water and sing and celebrate. But even at the point in *No Baby Must Weep* where he "say hallelujah / and claps hands / and do dance / and ring laughter," he recalls the suffering of slum-and-township life. He especially recalls "shit like that / getting my children killed." *Only if* people pursue the course that the persona has charted back to Africa will violence in general, violence against children, and the weeping of babies stop.

Theodore F. Sheckels. *The Lion on the Freeway: A Thematic Introduction to Contemporary South African Literature in English* (New York: Peter Lang, 1996), pp. 90–92

BIBLIOGRAPHY

*Yakhal'inkomo*, 1972; *Tsetlo*, 1974; *No Baby Must Weep*, 1975; *Behold Mama, Flowers*, 1978; *To Every Birth Its Blood*, 1981; *The Night Keeps Winking*, 1982; *Selected Poems*, 1982; *A Tough Tale*,

1987; *On the Horizon*, 1990; *Third World Express*, 1992; *Come and Hope with Me*, 1994; *Freedom Lament and Song*, 1997

# SERUMAGA, Robert (1939–1980)
## Uganda

*Return to the Shadows*, [Robert Serumaga's] first novel, deals with a military coup in an African country. To know who has grabbed power and from whom is irrelevant; even the new political leaders are no more than an impersonal voice on the radio, "the voice of the people of Adnagu." The country is in a state of complete chaos, which is not untypical; there have been enough coups in the past for Joe, the main character, to have his "drill." Whenever power changes hands, he runs to his country home, returning to the city only when he knows he can make a little profit on the confusion. But this time it is different. The novel opens with Joe and his ex-servant walking on a country road toward his mother's home. On the way a mysterious struggle is going on in Joe's mind; a hazy recollection of strange events the night before mixes with repressed feelings of guilt, resentment, and recurrent memories of certain "shadows" which went away without giving him answers. As the story goes on, flashbacks into Joe's past provide a clearer account of recent events and allow some insight into his slightly illegal transactions and political activities in the past. He had once tried to work toward getting his country out of the mess, but he had run into corruption everywhere. Now again it was chaos, the intellectuals were indifferent, and the population terrorized by soldiers and thugs.

The novel has a double theme: it goes back over the process by which this society has degraded itself, following a few minor characters in their decadence. But mostly it deals with the intellectual in a sick country, who tries first to escape by returning to the "shadows" beyond life, but gradually comes to forget his resentment and guilt, and slowly regains faith in action. It is a hard story, which places little confidence in idealism and efficiency; but it yields an interesting close-up view of the human effects of political unrest in Africa.

> Marie-Claire Bue. *Books Abroad*. 44, 2 (spring 1970), pp. 364–65

[Robert Serumaga] seems to be convinced that modern Africa has done so much to destroy itself that it is beyond redemption. In *Return to the Shadows*, he pictures an African society in a chronic state of political instability, with one military coup rapidly following another. His hero, a wealthy lawyer, economist, and businessman, has developed the habit of retreating to his home village whenever there are battles in the capital; but this time he arrives to find his mother raped and his nieces and cousins killed. He goes back to the city, witnesses more senseless brutality, recognizes the criminal greed and corruption of his closest friends, and debates frequently with an alter ego about the proper role of a moral man in an immoral society. "But what does a man do against the evil powers of the world? Fight? This way he is drawn into using the same means against which his soul is campaigning. He is pulled down to the level of the beasts who have made his blood boil in the first place. Evil drives out the good until the devil inhabits every corner of the world. What can one do?" After much agonizing, he

decides that the only useful thing he can do is return to his village and bury his dead. He gives up all hope of reforming his society.

> Bernth Lindfors. *Review of National Literatures*. 2, 2 (fall 1971), pp. 33–34

Serumaga, in addition to being a playwright, created the professional theater company, Theatre Limited, in Kampala; and under that name or that of the Abafumu Company, they have toured Serumaga's own drama *Renga Moi*. *Renga Moi* draws upon song, music, and dance to present its story of [a] chief's defense of his village and the tragedy that surrounds him. Serumaga, like other African playwrights, draws increasingly upon the visual, and on dance and movement, to replace (or reinforce) the verbal. As we have noted in respect of some West African work, [Serumaga] . . . is increasingly aware of the strengths of indigenous theater forms and materials and increasingly confident in his use of them in his own work. Serumaga's plays in English are *A Play*, *Majangwa*, and *The Elephants*.

The last of these plays is a powerful study of a small group of people in an East African university who find themselves fighting for possession of each other—and for their sanity. David, a research fellow, has lost his parents in violent and horrifying circumstances as a child, as a result of which he went through—and still remains close to—a kind of madness. He takes into his home the artist Maurice, a refugee from a neighboring territory that has been attacked by mercenaries. He protects Maurice from the truth of the massacre of his own parents by deviously controlling the letters that Maurice sends home to produce apparently authentic replies. Maurice flourishes as an artist, increasingly drawing attention to himself; and in his growing assurance and confidence, David apparently finds a strength that enables him to keep his own horrors at bay. This precarious relationship is shattered by a young American Peace Corps girl whom Maurice has fallen in love with and wishes to marry. She discovers David's subterfuge, and the play comes to a powerful climax as David and the girl Jenny struggle over Maurice. Although such a plot outline suggests simply a lively and intriguing—perhaps melodramatic—drama of human relationships, in fact the play offers more. Maurice's status as a refugee is one that all the main characters share in one way or another: David fleeing from the traumas of his youth, and Jenny from the suffocatingly materialistic upbringing which she had in the United States. . . .

Certainly all the characters in this play have the feeling of being consumed from within; and though some of Robert Serumaga's prose is a little forced, the overall impact of this play is very successful. In dramatic construction it illustrates both an eye and ear for theatrical rhythms, and a particular device used in this play—punctuating the action with the brief appearances of a bewildered old man looking for a hospital—is well conceived. The intrusion of this poor man's real sense of being outmaneuvered by events points the action of the play to a wider world than that presented on stage.

> Martin Banham and Clive Wake. *African Theatre Today* (London: Pitman, 1976), pp. 87–88

[The] impulse towards experiment is best seen in Robert Serumaga, who now dominates not just Uganda but the East African scene as a whole, in much the way that [Wole] Soyinka has come to dominate West Africa. When Serumaga's *A Play* appeared in 1968, the signs of a strongly individual talent were unmistakable. The nightmare of a guilty man on the anniversary of his wife's death, *A Play*, superficially, seemed highly derivative, with echoes of [Bertolt] Brecht, [Samuel] Beckett, Soyinka, and even [Christopher] Okigbo ghosting forth. Lines such as "this is a death cell not a theater," and "we must pass the time, somehow, before we die tomorrow," or "We are all just different kinds of germs. Different kinds of death," strike the authentic note of absurdist theater, not the note of *The Exodus* or any other kind of traditional piece. Yet despite derivative elements and occasional linguistic ineptness when a wrong register is used (see, for example, the Old Man's "undeniable cardiac contortions"), elemental forces are at work; and there is a sense of familiar viewpoints being expressed with originality and force. Serumaga's work now is far more maturely independent. As actor, producer, playwright, director of Theatre Limited and the Abafumi Company, he delights in unchained experimentation. *Majangwa* explores the life of an entertainer and his wife. Having failed to impress audiences with the traditional arts of dancing and drumming, these two turn to obscenity as a desperate throw for success—rather as British cinemas in decline turned to pornography and wrestling. James Gibbs describes these obscenities as "startling salaciousness," carrying the disturbing suggestion that "they constitute a symbol for the plight of the creative artist in a sick society." *Renga Moi*, Serumaga's most recent piece using music, ritual, dance, and four Ugandan vernaculars, is now in the repertoire of a company that has played to enthusiastic houses as far apart as Manila and Chicago. *Renga Moi* was particularly welcomed at the Belgrade International Festival; and a lengthy review in the newspaper *Politika* included the following comment: "a peculiar mixture of originality, the ancient and exotic, traditional and experimental, national and international." . . . Serumaga is boldly saying that language does not matter at all, and away with all those vexing problems of linguistic register and cultural transference. Four vernaculars are fine, and silence even better. Yet this is probably as much personal weakness as preferred philosophy. The texts of Serumaga's plays often suggest a slight discomfort with English, and his strengths are more technically theatrical than linguistic. *The Elephants* is a useful example of a play with a measure of psychological power, but which, stylistically, is rather vapid. Except in isolated cases, and despite Serumaga's claim in the introduction that "every word matters," there is neither rhythmic energy nor pungency of statement. Though stylistically it is a more even performance than *A Play*, the intensity of the author's account of city alienation is reduced by the nagging feeling that the rural world alternative is available only yards away beyond the city gate. But *The Elephants'* warm reception in Nairobi and elsewhere suggests how skillfully Serumaga has exploited those areas of his craft where he knows his strengths lie.

Adrian Roscoe. *Uhuru's Fire: African Literature East to South* (Cambridge: Cambridge University Press, 1977), pp. 262–64

After several well-received international tours of his plays by his own Theatre Limited-Abafumu Company, Robert Serumaga has probably become the East African dramatist best known to audiences outside the region. This is a result not only of his dedication

to theater but of his extraordinary entrepreneurial ability, a commercial and publicity sense at least comparable to his acting and writing talents. . . .

Serumaga's most recent Abafumu Theatre Company production, *Renga Moi*, is an attempt to broaden the ethnic base of *Majangwa* and to reach into the nonverbal expressionism of African ritual, as perhaps sifted through the techniques of [Jerzy] Grotowski and Julian Beck. It is based on an Acholi myth from northern Uganda, in which the warrior chief of the village of the Seven Hills must choose between defending his people from an armed attack and completing the ceremony which will preserve the lives of his newly born twins. He leads his villagers into battle and sees his children sacrificed to propitiate demonic spirits, only to find that on returning home after successfully staying off the attackers, the villagers decline all responsibility for the deaths of the twins.

The story of Renga Moi and his village is dramatized through gestural acting, music, and the interweaving of four Ugandan languages, all directed by an English-speaking narrator-diviner on stage (played by Serumaga).

Andrew Horn. *Literary Half-Yearly*. 19, 1 (January 1978), pp. 27, 33–34

Serumaga is concerned with both the agony of self-discovery and the tragic collapse of the gifted deceiver. But it is never the character's failure alone. Society is always shown to have betrayed him and forced him into compromise, deceit, and degradation; it is, therefore, civil community and its directive polities which Serumaga most condemns. It is this particular attack, not on specific social structures but on human community itself, which goes so abrasively against the grain of East African writing and theater. . . .

*Renga Moi* is based on an Acoli legend from northern Uganda, in which the warrior chief of the Village of the Seven Hills must choose between defending his people from armed attack and completing the ceremonies which will preserve the lives of his newly born twins, during which ritual he is expressly prohibited from shedding blood. Selflessly he decides for the common weal and leads the villagers into battle. But during his absence, grave privation strikes the village and, to propitiate the misfortune-bearing spirits, the powerful priest-diviner (who frames the action with an English commentary and was played by Serumaga), decrees that Renga Moi's twins will be sacrificially impaled. Upon returning home after successfully staving off the attackers, Renga Moi finds that the villagers decline all responsibility for the deaths of his twins. The warrior turns on the diviner and kills him; but this resolves nothing as the infants are already dead and their twin spirits will surely seek revenge on the father who abandoned them.

*Renga Moi* is Serumaga's clearest statement of the problem which has been his central concern from the beginning of his writing career. As he said in an interview during the play's London run, "we are posing a universal question about the choices an individual has to make, between himself and his social commitment." Renga Moi's choice is to act for the community; but, like Majangwa [in the play of that name], he discovers that the community not only undervalues his giving of himself, it ravenously demands more. Like the mob which drained Majangwa's life force and then burned his drum, the villagers of the Seven Hills accepted the warrior's self-abnegatory heroism and then destroyed his very flesh. Social commitment, Serumaga seems to be arguing, is an illusory ideal. The self-sacrificer is betrayed; the brave warrior, like the intellectual and the artist, is savaged by society and remains always an *isolato*—a man alone. . . .

Although the play's array of tongues, use of total theater and open staging techniques, inclusion of spectacular dances like *larakaraka* and *otole*, and adaptation of wrenching communal rituals elicits a greater visceral than intellectual response, it is wrong to conclude, as have some, that it lacks either design or programmatic purpose. Serumaga seems to be working towards the development of a nonverbal, theatrical objective correlative. . . .

In Serumaga's most recent work, he has continued to move away from the intellectualism of his earlier plays towards extraverbal expressive forms. A Kenyan review of the 1978 Abafumi production *Amanyakiriti* comments that the "cast became living sculptures" and that the play "appealed to the deepest emotions through mime, dance, and song, leaving the audience awestruck and in some cases in tears."

Although he is often clearly derivative and prone at times to neglect both idea and form for style, and his polished and startling surfaces may sometimes conceal confused or pedestrian thought, Serumaga does remain unique in East African theater: a man whose achievement is, admirably, more theatrical than literary and whose work shows a clear and logical development. He is, above all, sensitive to the gallops, lurches, and hiatuses of human speech, to the thrusts and hesitations of human action. The rhythms of his plays are always meticulously calibrated.

But, like his protagonists, Serumaga remains an *isolato* both professionally and ideologically. While so much of contemporary East African writing has been concerned with both a perception of community and a community of perception, Serumaga has persistently argued that community can only be destructive of the individual. Each of his embattled individualists—intellectual, politician, scholar, theatrical performer, and heroic warrior—is crushed by society, turning inwards in an implosive, nihilistic solipsism. Each becomes a strafed consciousness scrutinizing itself, its thoughts centripetal and distorted.

> Andrew Horn. In Eldred Durosimi Jones, ed. *African Literature Today*. 12 (1982), pp. 23, 36–39

Serumaga's concern is to dramatize the deterioration of society rather than to analyze why this has happened. A comparison with [Harold] Pinter is valid: Serumaga is creating a closed world in which society can be seen as absurd. In *Majangwa*, the traditional artistry of Majangwa and his wife, street entertainers, had degenerated into pornographic, live sex shows. His wife hates this, but he says that they have to survive and, after all, they still perform a social function: they give people some excitement and make it possible for them to continue living. But for Majangwa himself, death is as meaningless as an accident: "Death comes out of it [the road] in search of a victim or two. He comes out at night, but sometimes in the daytime. And each time the crack is repaired somebody dies. Killed by a passing car or a falling tree."

Serumaga's "writing of the absurd" is seen to best effect in his novel, *Return to the Shadows*. Serumaga, as Taban lo Liyong says, always was a royalist, and it might seem that his novel was a thinly-veiled attack on the Obote government for the crisis precipitated in 1966, particularly as the country in the novel is named Adnagu. Actually, this is not the case: the novel is about the nature of

political violence and the involvement of the people themselves in creating the conditions of violence.

> Peter Nazareth. In G. D. Killam, ed. *The Writing of East and Central Africa* (London: Heinemann, 1984), p. 17

BIBLIOGRAPHY
*A Play*, 1968; *Return to the Shadows*, 1969; *The Elephants*, 1971; *Majangwa*, 1972; *Renga Moi*, 1973; *Amanyakiriti*, 1978

# SHANGE, Ntozake (1948–)
## United States

Ntozake Shange gives voice to the ordinary experiences of black women in frank, simple, vivid language, telling the colored girl's story in her own speech patterns. Shange's gift is an uncanny ability to bring to life the experience of being black and a woman. Those who hear or read her choreopoem *for colored girls who have considered suicide/when the rainbow is enuf* may feel overwhelmed by so much reality, so much pain, so much resiliency, so much life force. They may even feel they have actually lived through the stories they have heard.

Like Adrienne Rich, Shange is acutely aware of the nothingness experienced by women in a society defined by men. But Shange is also aware of a double burden of pain and negation suffered by women who are black in a society defined by *white* men—where black women are not even granted the ambivalent recognition some white women receive for youth and beauty or for being wives and mothers of white men. Shange's poem also reflects the double strength black women have had to muster to survive in a world where neither being black nor being a woman is valued.

Though Shange's forte is the vivid recreation of experience, *for colored girls* is more than the simple telling of the black girl's story. It is also a search for the meaning of the nothingness experienced and a quest for new being. In Shange's poems, the experience of nothingness is born of the double burden of being black and a woman, but the stories she tells bring a shock of recognition to every woman who has given too much of herself to a man. The heart of the experience of nothingness in *for colored girls* is a woman's loss and debasement of self for love of a man. But what makes Shange's poems more than just another version of *Lady Sings the Blues*—a theme of sorrow and survival too familiar to black women (and white women)—is Shange's refusal to accept the black woman's sorrow as a simple and ultimate fact of life. She probes for a new image of the black woman that will make the old images of the colored girl obsolete. Shange envisions black women "born again" on the far side of nothingness with a new image of black womanhood that will enable them to acknowledge their history while moving beyond it to "the ends of their own rainbows."

*[For] colored girls* began as a series of separate poems, but as it developed Shange came to view "these twenty-odd poems as a single statement, a choreopoem." In the stage production, six actresses dressed in the colors of the rainbow—yellow, red, green, purple, blue, orange—and one dressed in the brown of earth and warm-toned skin alternately speak the twenty-odd poems, each a story. While one speaks, the others listen attentively or mime the

story, their interest creating a sense of sisterhood and sharing. Often a story told by one woman evokes sympathetic ''yeahs,'' or the telling of a related story, or even dancing from the other women. In a sense the dialogical form of Shange's play recreates the consciousness-raising group of the women's movement, wherein, sharing experiences and stories, women learn to value themselves, to recognize stagnant and destructive patterns in their lives, to name their strengths, and to begin to take responsibility for their lives. The sense of dialogue in Shange's choreopoem is an invitation to the women in the audience to tell their stories. What emerges is a tapestry of experiences, interwoven with a sense of plurality and commonality.

Carol P. Christ. *Diving Deep and Surfacing: Women Writers on Spiritual Quest* (Boston: Beacon Press, 1980), pp. 97–98

There are as many ways of looking at Ntozake Shange's *for colored girls who have considered suicide/when the rainbow is enuf* as there are hues in a rainbow. One can take it as an initiation piece, for instance, particularly with its heavily symbolic ''Graduation Nite'' and the girlhood perspectives of the mama's little baby/Sally Walker segment and in the voice of the eight-year-old narrator of ''Toussaint.'' *[For] colored girls* also might be seen as a black feminist statement in that it offers a black woman's perspective on issues made prominent by the women's movement. Still another approach is to view it as a literary coming-of-age of black womanhood in the form of a series of testimonies which, in Shange's words, ''explore the realities of seven different kinds of women.'' Indeed, the choreopoem is so rich that it lends itself to multiple interpretations which vary according to one's perspective and experiences. . . .

*[For] colored girls* is certainly woman's art, but it is also black art, or Third-World art, as Shange probably would prefer to have it designated. Its language and dialect, its geography, its music, and the numerous allusions to Third-World personalities make it an intensely cultural work. Much of these characteristics, however, are peculiar to Shange's upbringing, education, and experiences, with the result that the piece loses universality at points, as in the poem ''Now I Love Somebody More Than.'' But even here, black audiences are sure to know which lady loved gardenias; they will know the Flamingoes and Archie Shepp and Imamu. Then there is the poem ''Sechita,'' in which the dancer is linked to Nefertiti, hence to Africa and Olduvai Gorge, the ''cradle of civilization''— all of which puts into perspective the cheapening of Sechita by the carnival audience. While ''Sechita'' speaks to the degradation of black womanhood, ''Toussaint'' speaks of the black woman's discovery of black pride. It also speaks, with subtle irony, of the black woman's awakening to the black man.

Sandra Hollin Flowers. *Black American Literature Forum.* 15, 2 (summer 1981), pp. 51–52

That [*for colored girls who have considered suicide/when the rainbow is enuf*] is autobiographical is nowhere more evident than in the kind of women Shange wrote about and in the play's splendid isolation from the power poles of black culture: the extended family and the black church—and from salient aspects of black literary and political history as well. During the performance one does not notice what a narrow range of black women Shange

portrays because, in part, Shange has converted her study of Afro-American dance, which taught her to accept ''the ethnicity of my thighs and backside,'' into the body language of her choreopoem with dazzling effectiveness. Shange says, ''dance as explicated by Raymond Sawyer and Ed Mock insisted that everything African, everything halfway colloquial, a grimace, a strut, an arched back over a yawn, waz mine. . . . I moved what waz my unconscious knowledge of being in a colored woman's body to my known everydayness.'' In *for colored girls*, we not only hear lines that real black women speak, delivered with acutely accurate inflections, but we also see familiar strides and shrugs and sweeps and recognize the grammar of black women's bodies. . . .

Shange speaks directly from and to the experience of a growing (but still small) section of African-American women who are born into the middle or upper middle class (or attain it through education or marriage), and are able to secure some college education and travel outside their neighborhoods in New York, Chicago, Atlanta, or Philadelphia to California, Europe, or the Caribbean. Though the black women in the audience may not have ''considered suicide,'' they are familiar with the rootlessness, alienation, and isolation Shange portrays and are, to some extent, either as distanced as the ladies of the rainbow from the sustaining bedrock of black culture or as unable to work out a synthesis between traditional black culture and technocratic, impersonal, individualized, hectic, mobile, modern America. They have experienced . . . despair, loneliness, low self-esteem, and negative self-image . . . and this theater event offers them ways to understand, manage, and transcend that pain. A dimension of the play's appeal to white audiences also becomes clear. Alienation and despair are keystones of modernism. The individual angst of *for colored girls* (and Shange's resolutely apolitical solution) touches modernist themes familiar to educated whites since the beginning of the twentieth century, though its ending on a defiantly hopeful note is, like the vivid colors of the women's dresses, part of *African-American* spirit. The unanswerable question is how Shange fastened on troubles with black men as *the* roots of black women's pain. To do so, she had to ignore a range of other causes, including value conflicts between black parents and children, which provided so much of the fodder for black drama of the 1960s; the impact of the new sexual freedom on black women; the frustrations . . . come in the wake of expectations raised by the women's movement and the continued rejection of black women by the larger system; and the oppressive fist of white America keeping black men and black women on the bottom rung— together. If fastening on black men as the cause of black women's blues is inaccurate and unfair, it is also effective (because of the very real tensions between black women and black men), and safely apolitical.

Andrea Benton Rushing. *Massachusetts Review.* 22, 3 (autumn 1981), pp. 544–45, 547–48

In *spell #7*, subtitled a ''quik magic trance manual for technologically stressed third world people,'' Shange tackles the iconography of ''the nigger.'' Underneath a huge blackface minstrel mask, a master of ceremonies promises to perform a different kind of magic designed to reveal aspects of black life authentically. The minstrel performers move through the pain of dance steps and memories associated with black entertainment for white America on to the release of more private, improvisational party styles. In doing so, they banish the hideous mask along with their stage personae, thereby creating a safe space in which to expose secret hopes, fears, or dreams. But two confessions, coming at the end of each act, puncture the whimsical or contained quality of most of the fantasies to reveal an almost overwhelming anguish. . . .

Despite the public, political implications of contrariness, one may wonder how these pictures of wounded, stagnating women are an indication of Shange's combat breath. For an answer, one must examine the thrust which Shange's playwriting assumes, for most often she is not writing tidy plays in which a crisis is resolved within the structure of the play. Nowhere is the thrust beyond the theater clearer than in *spell #7*, for the play attempts to create a liberated stage space supportive of black self-expression. Because Sue-Jean's and Maxine's confessions threaten to reveal a pain almost beyond cure, the magician/master of ceremonies must halt the action in order to reassure his audience that it will indeed love his black magic. Under his spell, the cast takes up the refrain "bein colored & love it" and tries to manipulate it in order to conjure forth the joyous celebration of church. With the magician's defiant reaffirmation of the right of blacks to exist as they choose to define themselves, the minstrel mask returns, and the audience leaves.

To a certain extent, Shange, like her fictional magician, performs a sleight-of-hand which theoretically allows the drama to end on a positive note, provided that the communion between actors and audiences, brought into being by the refrain, becomes a sufficiently strong countervailing force against all the negativity represented by the minstrel mask. But given the earlier image of Sue-Jean and the final picture of a bejeweled Maxine, it is hard to imagine the actors ultimately being able to create a space for themselves and audiences. In a sense, in performance the play has two possible endings: It can culminate in hard-won triumph or in painful defeat, depending on the interaction of the energies of all those who have experienced the event.

Sandra L. Richards. *Black American Literature Forum.* 17, 2 (summer 1983), pp. 74–75

In *Sassafrass, Cypress & Indigo*, Ntozake Shange, drawing from the personal realm of women's everyday experience and from the ancient or folk traditions of women's spirituality, incorporates a number of these "trivial" images, activities, and modes of expression—dolls, flowers, stones, feathers, apples, the moon, trees, the ocean, menstruation, dreams, spells, recipes, rituals for trance journeys, letters, journals, weaving, dancing, psychic healing—to depict the individual and the archetypal personalities of three sisters—Sassafrass, a weaver; Cypress, a dancer; and Indigo, a healer—and to evoke their world. . . .

Structurally, *Sassafrass, Cypress & Indigo* may be viewed as a circle of concentric rings, as Shange introduces Indigo first, then Sassafrass, then Cypress, then returns to Sassafrass, and finally to Indigo again. This structure suggests the circular *temenos* (sacred space) in practices of women's spirituality and so emphasizes the depth of the connection between the sisters, as well as their interrelatedness. This structure also reflects the extent to which each woman is connected to the transpersonal realm, with Indigo at the center as most psychic, then Sassafrass, and then Cypress as most worldly of the three at the outermost edge. In this sense, the circular structure suggests gradations in the similarities they share, as well as clarifying their unique and different personalities. The circle motif suggested by the overall structure of the novel appears, too, at the conclusion of the novel when Cypress and Indigo return

home to celebrate the birth of Sassafrass's first child as the two women and their mother, Hilda Effania, circle around Sassafrass to be with her in support and encouragement. Here, the circle of women can be connected with themes of interconnection, healing, and empowerment.

While the structure of *Sassafrass, Cypress & Indigo* may very well be viewed as a circle of concentric rings, it can also be viewed as a textured weaving with various recurring strands/motifs—letters from Hilda Effania to her daughters, recipes for special occasions, images and rituals of transformation, manifestations of aspects of the immanent, archetypal Goddess. Personal and transpersonal, warp and woof, weaving together, creating new patterns, reclaiming the past, transforming the present. That the structure of the novel is suggestive of a weaving complements the facts that Hilda Effania is a weaver, as is her oldest daughter, Sassafrass; that the relationship of the three sisters evokes an allusion to the Greek Moerae, the Triple Goddess, the weavers of destiny; and that the archetypal Goddess is sometimes viewed in a global, contextual way as "the interwoven fabric of being . . . the web of connection . . . the pattern."

Jean Strandness. *Journal of American Culture.* 10, 3 (fall 1987), p. 11

In her plays, especially *for colored girls* and *spell #7*, Shange develops her narration primarily through monologues because monologic speech inevitably places the narrative weight of a play upon its spoken language and upon the performances of the individual actors. But she does not use this device to develop "character" in the same fashion as Maria Irene Fornes and other Method-inspired playwrights who turn toward monologic language in order more expressively to define and "embody" their characters both as woman and as individuals. Rather, Shange draws upon the uniquely "performative" qualities of monologue to allow her actors to take on *multiple* roles and therefore to emphasize the centrality of *storytelling* to her work. This emphasis is crucial to Shange's articulation of a black feminist aesthetic (and to the call to humanity to accept that "black women are inherently valuable") on two counts. First, the incorporation of role-playing reflects the ways that blacks (as "minstrels," "servants," "athletes," etc.) and women (as "maids," "whores," "mothers," etc.) are expected to fulfill such roles on a constant basis in Western society. Second, the space between our enjoyment of the "spectacle" of Shange's theater pieces (through the recitation of the monologues and through the dancing and singing which often accompany them), and our awareness of the urgency of her call for blacks/women to be allowed "selves" free of stereotypes, serves as a "rupturing" of the performance movement; it is the uncomfortableness of that space, that rupture, which moves and disturbs us. . . .

All of Shange's theater pieces, even *a photograph: lovers in motion* and *boogie woogie landscapes*, unfold before the audience as collections of stories rather than as traditionally linear narratives; the events are generated less from actual interactions as they unfold in the "present" of the play (except perhaps in *a photograph*) than from the internal storytellers' *recreations* of individual dramas. The implied privilege of the storyteller to create alternate worlds, as well as the fluidity of the stories themselves and the characters in them, relies heavily upon the immense power that African and Afro-American tradition have assigned to the spoken word. . . . Shange takes the notion of exchange and collectivity among storytellers even further in her use of the space in which her pieces are performed. Monologue creates "narrative space"; Shange depends upon the power and magic of the stories within her plays to create the scenes without the use of backdrops and other "theatrical" effects. [For] colored girls is the most "open" of the plays in this sense, as it calls for no stage set, only lights of different colors and specific places for the characters to enter and exit. [B]oogie woogie landscapes conjures up the mental images of the title within the confines of Layla's bedroom: "there is what furniture a bedroom might accommodate, though not too much of it. [The] most important thing is that a bedroom is suggested." Although the sets of both spell #7 and a photograph are fairly specific (a huge minstrel mask as a backdrop and, later, a bar in lower Manhattan for the former; a photographer's apartment for the latter), they still call for this space to be reborn in different imaginary ways as the characters come forth and tell their stories. . . .

Unlike for colored girls, spell #7 makes use of a central storyteller figure, Lou, who "directs" the monologues which are performed in the course of the play. It is appropriate that Lou is a magician, for even the title of spell #7 (the subtitle of which is "geechee jibara quik magic trance manual for technologically stressed third world people") refers to magic-making. In his opening speech, though, Lou warns of the power (and danger) of "colored" magic. . . . The image of the narrator as "magician" implies that the storytellers themselves will be under the control of a certain "author"; yet as the actors perform their pieces, the stories seem at times to slip away from a guiding narratorial force and to become deeply personal. In a sense, the performers threaten to overpower the narrator in the same way that the third grader's request to be made white is beyond the power of Lou's magician father: the stories take on a kind of magic which is independent of their "director," and yet to enter this realm may be painful and perilous. Lou, then, is like a surrogate author who is responsible for the content of the play, but who also cannot fully control what happens to it once the performers begin to take part.

Deborah R. Geis. In Enoch Brater, ed. Feminine Focus: The New Women Playwrights (New York: Oxford University Press, 1989), pp. 211–13, 219–20

Shange's dramatic work, especially [for colored girls], represents a moment of crucial importance in black and American history. . . . Writers with whom she is often compared, such as Imamu Amiri Baraka and Nikki Giovanni, seem to speak of a different, earlier moment. Where these and other writers attacked the obstacles to black self-realization, Shange's dramas represent the tortured moment of becoming itself, the moment of emergence and discovery. Ambivalence and paradox mark this moment; a dynamic world full of potential inhabits the same sphere as an old dead world in which nothing can change. The future for Shange's characters fluctuates between a positive, realizable potential, such as [Karl] Marx envisioned, and a negative emptiness, such as [Walter] Benjamin envisioned, which must be filled by individual effort and suffering. The process of becoming is Shange's subject, "our struggle to become all that is forbidden by our environment, all that is forfeited by our gender, all that we have forgotten."

In spell #7, boogie woogie landscapes, and colored girls, there is no one outcome to the process of becoming, no one unifying end—but there is the process itself, in which all are engaged. What

is more, communal expression may well be the only outlet for a certain range of feelings, according to Shange: "in addition to the obvious stress of racism in poverty / afro-american culture . . . has minimized its 'emotional' vocabulary to the extent that admitting feelings of rage, defeat, frustration is virtually impossible outside a collective voice." Again and again, Shange's dramas wander through a maze of personal and collective experience, only to coalesce in a chant that unites the subjective and the inter-subjective. . . .

There is, however, a paradox about Shange's work. . . . [Her] works are inscribed with the tensions of a very specific time and place. Further, these pieces announce themselves as being "for" a particular audience, such as colored girls or technologically stressed Third-World people. Those pieces contain a great deal of aggression toward an oppressive white culture, an aggression that begins with an attack on white English: "i cant count the number of time i have viscerally wanted to attack deform n maim the language that i waz taught to hate myself in." "The mess of my fortune to be born black & English-speaking" has motivated her to cultivate non-white orthography, syntax, and what she has called verbal "distortions." Yet despite all this effort at exclusion, her works remain remarkably "open" texts—that is, they anticipate and welcome the indeterminacy of any dramatic text and the unavoidable variation of performance. As a result, these texts that are addressed to, dedicated to, and written for a particular audience nevertheless throw themselves open to a multiplicity of audiences and performances.

John Timpane. Studies in American Drama, 1945–Present. 4 (1989). Repub. in June Schlueter, ed. Modern American Drama: The Female Canon (Rutherford, New Jersey: Fairleigh Dickinson University Press, 1990), pp. 198–200

Shange's a photograph: lovers in motion . . . contradicts her image as a feminist black-man-hater. Sean David, like Beau Willie Brown [in for colored girls], is Shange's effort to denounce what Erskine Peters calls Shange's portrayal of black man "basically as pasteboards or beasts.". . . Just as Beau Willie is presented with compassion, so too is Sean David. . . . And while Sean David exhibits the abusive behavior of some men, he is never close to being a "pasteboard." Instead, he dominates the action and wrestles continually with the complexities of success as a black artist, the complexities of real manhood, and the complexities of his relationship with his father.

Sean David is the first male character who takes center stage in a published play by Shange, and he is one of her most confused characters. We witness his complex social, physical, and psychological realms, particularly through his treatment of three confused female lovers. At a glance, Sean might seem the stereotypical male whose self-image is determined by his sexual prowess. And he boasts of his ability to juggle several female lovers while retaining complete control over each. Yet Shange undercuts his empty confidence by showing that Sean cannot keep his women apart any more than he can separate the suffering depicted in his Vietnam photographs. . . .

Sean's hostility subsides when he admits his need for real love, not just sex—which is precisely what Shange's colored girls discover and long for. Like Beau Willie, Sean David is not an abusive black man without redeeming qualities; he is confused. . . . What moves Sean away from the stereotypical black man is his ability to admit to himself that he is in pain and has been misguided in his move toward knowing who and what he is. . . .

Shange has described *From Okra to Greens/A Different Kind of Love Story: A Play/with Music & Dance* as a "feminist poem in motion," set within the framework of a variant of the boy-meets-girl love story. In the play, Okra (the black female) gives Greens (the black male) a gift—her sociopolitical views on the black women's existence within the local, national, and international arenas. In one sense, Greens represents Shange's ideal black male, though his coming to know the complex realities of female existence is a gradual process. Unlike Sean David, there is no question that Greens is what Shange argues every black woman needs and seeks in a black male companion. . . .

Significantly different from other black males in Shange's dramas, Greens acknowledges and celebrates the irresistible power of love that is both physical and spiritual. And unlike any other man in Shange's presentations, Greens recognizes the power play between male and female partners that manifests itself even in the intimacy of the bedroom. In "some men," one of the most poignant poem sequences in the play, Shange offers a feminist editorial on male behavior. Careful not to stereotype all men as insensitive and abusive, Shange signifies on the behavior of "some" men, like Sean David, who possess twisted definitions of manhood. In both the poetry collection *A Daughter's Geography* and the published booklet *Some Men*, in collaboration with Wopo Holup, Shange allows a single female persona to address males' behavior. As a participant in the exchange in this dramatic version, Greens offers an alternative male perspective to the one being condemned in the sequence. Greens represents those men who do not behave and think as *these* men.

Neal A. Lester. *African American Review* 26, 2 (summer 1992), pp. 322–25

it's ours, alla ours, don't nobody own history
cant nobody make ours but us
my photographs are the contours of life unnoticed unrealized
    & suspect
no buckwheat here no farina & topsy
here we have the heat of our lives in our ordinariness we are
    most bizarre
prone to eccentricity
even in our language. . . .

Shange's artistic practice shares with that of many African-American women the daring identification of what Cheryl A. Wall calls an "unwritten space" in African-American literary discourse, and the bold inscription in that space of an "Afro-American female self." I borrow the preceding epigraph from the dramatist's characters Michael and Sean, in *photograph*, as a remarkably close reading of the *phenomenon* of this literature: the bold rupture of the imprisoning walls of a dominated margin in which black women's lives have long been confined—"don't nobody own history"; the unapologetic assertion of difference—"most bizarre/ prone to eccentricity"; and the epistemic challenge of its representations, because they are of life previously "unnoticed/ unrealized and suspect," to conventional modes of seeing. "[H]ere we have the heat of our lives," Sean affirms, in a tone that recalls Hortense Spiller's when she writes of "the palpable and continuing urgency of black women writing themselves into history."

Shange's drama decisively participates in the urgency. Her practice simultaneously critiques and democratizes the conjunctural space in which I locate Soyinka, Baraka, and Walcott. It is, at the same time, unrelenting in the common quest for an anti-imperialist identity. Shange's practice is able to "speak" simultaneously in so many "tongues" because of what Mac G. Henderson defines as "at once characteristic and suggestive about black women's writing": its "interlocutory, or dialogic character," borne out of an engagement with a profoundly heterogeneous space. Thus it is that a task which appears insurmountable in the three dramatists—constructing a gender-informed cultural identity—is the point of departure for Shange's practice. . . .

Shange, borrowing from Frantz Fanon on French colonialism in Algeria, "Algeria Unveiled," in his *A Dying Colonialism.* describes the character of her intervention in the discourse of black cultural difference as "combat breathing". . . .

"Combat breathing" is agonistic breathing. Harassed, pursued, and intimidated but nevertheless confounding all attempts to unravel the secrets of its resilience, combat breath is characteristically tactical. Neither are its contours carved in stone nor are its modulations predictable. A veritable weapon in the hands of the dominated against, in Shange's words, "the involuntary constrictions in amputations of their humanity," combat breath resists recuperation by the dominant by being a "hazard to definitions." It confronts the oppressor as a "problem," "incomprehensible," utterly ambivalent and inaccessible.

Shange recalls in an interview a poetry reading session at which a man asked her why she never wrote about men. "It irked me," Shange reflects, "that someone would think that women were not an adequate subject. I really got much more involved with writing about women for that reason. I was determined that we were going to be viable and legitimate literary figures." This is the determination Shange pitted against the blindness of the insights of the nationalist discourse of black self-refashioning. For while this discourse "exorcised a lot of demons" and "was a rite of passage" which "told us we could do anything we wanted," it is nevertheless regrettable "the flaw in the nationalists' dream": "they didn't treat women right."

Trying to "treat women right" or make women "legitimate literary figures" obviously complicates the terms of the debate on black cultural identity, but it also specifically constitutes a great formal challenge to the black female dramatist. This is not because there is no recognizable tradition of African-American female dramatists to fall back upon for inspiration, but because the demands of the moment are radically new horizons and previously unexplored and unconsidered domains. Besides, there is an additional burden for the female playwright committed to the dramaturgic appropriation of black performance forms. Cheryl Wall argues that women were "historically denied participation" in many of these forms, citing the example of speechifying, which, "whether in the pulpit or on the block, has been a mainly male prerogative." And, of course, the usual and the biggest challenge of all: the overwhelming, unrelenting subjection of black America to the hegemonic Eurocentric theatrical norms, to the lure and reward of "artificial aesthetics":

for too long now afro-americans in theater have been duped
by the same artificial aesthetics that plague our white
counterparts/ "the perfect play," as we know it to be/ a truly
european framework for european psychology/ cannot function efficiently for those of us from this hemisphere.

"... those of us from this hemisphere"? Shange soon discovers that this phrase needs rephrasing. She does this in her essay "How I Moved Anna Fierling to the Southwest Territories, or, my personal victory over the armies of western civilization." The essay was prompted by what she sees as the negative reactions of a white audience to the production of a Shakespeare play, *Coriolanus*, by a black and Latin troupe. . . .

Shange as "black and English-speaking" is simultaneously African and American, and with a legitimate claim to the English literary and dramatic tradition. Her unspoken challenge in the quotation is how to recognize all her traditions without blurring their differences and the character of the relations between and among them, not unlike Alice Walker's move in her well-known essay "In Search of Our Mother's Gardens." Shange can claim Shakespeare, but as her essay shows, the challenge is to know when subjectivity is obviously subjection. The white audience in Shange's narrative ignores the complex performative articulation involved in such negotiations in their amazement that blacks could understand Shakespeare.

Central to Shange's combat aesthetics is an affirmation of the very elements for which America has historically constructed the black as a minstrel and natural entertainer: music and dance. Shange's thrust is a reevaluation of this "peculiar" difference, appropriating it as a source of strength against the grain of its dominant reading as a sign of intellectual efficiency. The accent of this strength is unmistakably individual and collective. Shange, who studied dance with Raymond Sawyer, Ed Mock, and Halifu, writes that it is only with dance that "I discovered my body more intimately than I had imagined possible. With the acceptance of the ethnicity of my things & backside, came a clearer understanding of my voice was a woman & a poet." Music and dance, as forms in perpetual motion—"pure solution"—have the potential to transgress institutionalized permits and open up zones of possibilities which, even if not realized or realizable, are capable of luring the dominated into the subversive realm of dream. "The freedom to move in space, to demand of my own sweat perfection that could continually be approached, though never known, poem to me, my body & mind ellipsing, probably for the first time in my life."

In Shange's theater, music and dance are not conceived as ornamental elements added on to enrich the drama but as the very constitutive fabric of the performance, setting and upsetting the pace, underscoring and contradicting the mood, creating and destroying moods, showing the form (the way it is) and the formlessness (the way it is is contingent, alterable) of history.

What Shange, who regularly collaborates with musicians and dancers, writes of her *spell #7* is applicable to most of her other pieces: that "music functions as another character." "[w]e are an interdisciplinary culture," she says, and "we must use everything we've got." . . .

Tejumola Cilaniyan. *Scars of Conquest/Masks of Resistance: The Invertia of Cultural Identities in African, African-American, and Caribbean Drama.* (New York: Oxford University Press, 1995), pp. 120–26

The poignancy in Shange's writing derives from her successful mingling of languages. Poetry and music exist in the same spaces as dialogue and dreams. The extreme sensitivity of her writing to extending women's creative spheres past the biological and into the spiritual realms testifies to her commitment to explore extensive dimensions of generation. Women's sharing of their most intimate and creative language is a significant feature of Shange's method. Part of this sharing is clearly evident in the recipes and letters from the sisters' mother, but it is also an important dimension of the lesbian relationships in this novel. Some of the most generative and thickest language surrounds Shange's descriptions of the women's dance collective, the Azure Bosum. Dense in color and texture, and full and round in shapes and forms, this imagery represents the deepest levels of this novel's stylistic effort. Here, the language is as full-bodied as the women's gender dance—"a dance of women discovering themselves in the universe." In the house Cypress shared with the dancers from the Azure Bosum, she "saw herself everywhere . . . nothing different from her in essence; nothing not woman."

Shange attributes the textures of her story to a woman-centered ideology. Her opening lines—"Where there is a woman, there is magic [and] a woman with a moon falling from her mouth . . . is a consort of the spirits" immediately insist upon a relationship to the air and its spirits—a hallmark of the translucent text. In addition it specifies the way that the cultural tradition is gendered. Women are connected to necromancy and spirituality—the dimensions of text that center the black woman writer's tradition. In many ways, *Sassafrass, Cypress & Indigo* is a modern story that traces three sisters' coming-of-age outside of their mother's house. However, the internal irony is that none of them can spiritually leave their mother's presence (and the implicit symbolic presence of the more ancient cultural Mothers). This dimension of the text places Shange's work in the shared traditions of the African-American woman writer's canon.

The first glimmer of the plurisignance in this text occurs in an opening narrative that introduces the reader to the character Indigo as a child "of the south.". . . This lyrical explanation of her persona dissolves and is replaced by the first of several variations of recipes and instructions that appear in the narrative. The first, an italicized passage that details how to manage a "Moon Journey," quickly returns to the regular type of the original text. The italics serve as the visual collocation for the series of instructions, recipes, dream sequences, and memories that flow into the pages of Shange's novel. Since the distinctiveness of the italic type collects these bits and pieces, some of the interpretive work is accomplished for the reader. Their visual appearance makes it clear that these dreamings are to be gathered together. Their sound makes it evident that these gathered words add their own voice to the story of the sisters and their mother.

Shange's layering of women's knowledge affirms a context for black women's experience in *Sassafrass*. Through these layers she assures that at least some of this information will be accessible to the community of women who are responsible for spiritual as well as physical generation. The text encourages the reader's perception of Cypress's newly discovered ability to "lay waste to the tunnels, caverns, and shadows of the other world" (the West) and to "draw upon memories of her own blood." Male things, Western things, and material distractions are released in Shange's novel. What remains affirms womanspirit, an African imagination, and the ability of the spoken text to metaphorically assure these as the fertile grounds of a (re)membered generation.

Karla F. C. Halloway. *Moorings and Metaphors: Figures of Culture and Gender in Black Women's Literature.* (New Brunswick, New Jersey: Rutgers University Press, 1992).

BIBLIOGRAPHY
*for colored girls who have considered suicide/when the rainbow is enuf*, 1975; *Sassafrass*, 1976; *Melissa & Smith*, 1976; *A Photograph: A Study of Cruelty*, 1977; *Natural Disasters and Other Festive Occasions*, 1977; *Nappy Edges*, 1978; *From Okra to Greens: A Different Kinda Love Story; A Play with Music and Dance*, 1978; *Boogie Woogie Landscapes*, 1979; *spell #7: a Geechee Quick Magic Trance Manual*, 1979; *Black and White Two Dimensional Planes*, 1979; *A Photograph: Lovers in Motion*, 1981; *Sassafrass, Cypress & Indigo*, 1982; *Three for a Full Moon*, 1982; *A Daughter's Geography*, 1983; *See No Evil: Prefaces, Essays and Accounts, 1976-1983*, 1984; *From Okra to Greens: Poems*, 1984; *Betsey Brown*, 1985; *Three Views of Mt. Fuji*, 1987; *Ridin' the Moon in Texas: Word Paintings*, 1987; *The Love Space Demands: A Continuing Saga*, 1991; *Liliane: Resurrection of the Daughter*, 1994; *I Live in Music*, 1994; *Whitewash*, 1997; *If I Can Cook, You Know God Can*, 1998

*Twentieth-Century Caribbean and Black African Writers* (Detroit: Gale Research, 1996), pp. 371–80

BIBLIOGRAPHY
*Unjust Regalia*, 1969; *The Master and the Fraud*, 1971; *The Night Before*, 1972; *Lamps in the Night*, 1973; *Bar Beach Prelude*, 1976; *A Sanctus for Women* (also performed as *The Angry Bridegroom*), 1976; *Afamako—the Workhorse*, 1978; *Farewell to Babylon*, 1978; *The Master and the Frauds*, 1979; *Kalakutah Crosscurrents*, 1979; *Barabas and the Master Jesus*, 1979; *Farewell to Babylon and Other Plays*, 1979; *Our Man the President*, 1981; *Without a Home*, 1982; *Flamingo*, 1982; *Circus of Freedom Square*, 1985; *Flamingo and Other Plays*, 1986; *The Missing Bridesmaid*, 1988; *Tornadoes Full of Dreams*, 1989; *Arede owo*, 1990; *My Life in the Bush of Ghosts*, 1990; *Mammy-Water's Wedding*, 1991; *Ajantala-Pinocchio*, 1992

# SOWANDE, Bode (1948–)
**Nigeria**

Among the Nigerian playwrights who came to prominence during the 1970s and have continued to be productive, Bode Sowande is a major figure. He works mostly in English and has written almost exclusively for theater buildings equipped with modern technology, but he draws extensively on Yoruba sources, makes use of Yoruba songs, and in his recent work has moved toward Yoruba-language theater and flexible staging. His writing shows his preoccupation with the dilemma facing a man of integrity trying to maintain humane values and moral qualities in a corrupt world. He has used his often highly theatrical dramas to call for change and repeatedly asks for his plays to be produced without an intermission, clearly hoping to make as great an impact on his audience as possible. In addition to writing plays, Sowande is a director and the founder of a high-profile drama company, Odu Themes, which has completed many television contracts. These activities have combined to establish him as a significant presence in the Nigerian theater and to lift him to prominence on an international stage.

From early in his career Sowande has taken an individual line within Nigerian university theater and more recently in the Nigerian theater that exists beyond the limits of the campuses. He has been sniped at by the leftist critics of the Nigerian press who see him as too much of an academic to take the struggle to the people in revolutionary forms. He has also crossed swords in the press about and with the dominant figure in the local theater in English, Wole Soyinka. Shared Egba ancestry and a common commitment to emphasizing the role of the individual in the process of social change have, if anything, increased rather than lowered the temperature generated by his disagreements with Soyinka. However, controversy has not prevented him from following his own path. His belief that the privileged must join the struggle in order for revolutionary change to occur provides his writing with a particular emphasis, and the background against which he works—Nigeria during the last two and a half decades—inevitably gives it urgency.

James Gibbs. In Bernth Lindfors and Reinhard Sander, editors. *Dictionary of Literary Biography*, Volume 157:

# SOW FALL, Aminata (1941–)
**Senegal**

Aminata Sow Fall's first novel, *Le Revenant*, is less a character study than a comedy of manners. The urban Senegal that she depicts, like that of Ousmane Socé's *Karim* forty years before, is still dominated by the need for ostentatious display. Status is gained by external signs of wealth and unregarding generosity. A bride is won and a wife retained only by extravagant expenditure on gifts lavished on in-laws, friends, retainers, and opportunistic hangers-on. The hero, like Karim, is an amiable but weak young man who cannot withstand the pressures of this exacting society and, yielding to temptation, misappropriates large sums and lands in prison. He loses his wife and child, his family and friends reject him, and he sinks into degradation and despair until the very taste for ostentation which has been his undoing provides the means for his revenge. The author does not condemn her hero for embezzling millions of francs nor his wife for abandoning him when he has fallen on evil days. She attacks only the society that saps all moral integrity, those who exploit questionable customs and perpetuate wrong values, who are superficial, hypocritical, and lacking in human warmth. Her characters are divided into victims and exploiters. The wife is presented as the typical "investment" expected to give lifelong returns to her family who manipulates her and denies her the freedom to act on her love and loyalty to her husband. Bakar becomes a criminal because he has not the strength of character to withstand his in-laws' rapacity. His mother is oppressed by an autocratic, egoistic husband, confident that male superiority cannot be questioned. Even Bakar's loyal and admirable friend imposes on his wife and children by the extravagant hospitality he offers to a host of parasitical card players.

Dorothy S. Blair. *Senegalese Literature: A Critical History* (Boston: Twayne, 1984), pp. 132–33

With this her third novel [*L'Appel des arènes*], Aminata Sow Fall provides yet another view of what is developing into a multifaceted portrait of contemporary Senegalese society. It constitutes, at the same time, a continuation of her acerbic criticism of that society and especially of its urbanized and privileged upper and middle bourgeoisie. While her first two books, *Le Revenant* and *La Grève des Bàttu*, depicted respectively the ruinous penchant of the Senegalese for ostentatious public generosity and the world of urban beggars harassed by self-important and hypocritical government officials, *L'Appel des arènes* is set against the backdrop of the milieu of traditional wrestling, an ancient national sport. The plot revolves around the conflict between the adolescent Nalla and his parents over Nalla's neglect of his studies in favor of an almost obsessive fascination with the world of wrestling and his adoring devotion to his newfound friend Malaw, champion of the arena. . . .

As if to underline the value of tradition, the author often assumes a distinctly oral tone: use of the present tense in descriptions, repetitions, conversations spiced with words in the original Wolof and traditional praise-songs interspersed throughout.Used with more consistency and smoother integration into the whole, these and other such techniques could put Sow Fall into the forefront of those writers who are forging European words and genres into an authentically modern African art form.

> Fredric Michelman. *World Literature Today.* 58, 1 (winter 1984), pp. 153–54

Aminata Sow Fall's novelistic work consists of three texts, *Le Revenant*, *La Grève des Bàttu*, and *L'Appel des arènes*. As in the novels of Mariama Bâ, Islam is present in these novels except in the last one, but the manner in which it is presented is more general and social. . . .

[*Le Revenant*] depicts a certain Dakaran society, which under the pretext of respecting the customs and religion, leads a flashy and ostentatious lifestyle on which fortunes are spent. Throughout her text, Aminata Sow Fall denounces even more violently than does Mariama Bâ the ravages caused by this "pseudo-Islam," devoid of all humanity and spirituality. . . .

The novelist systematically presents great socioreligious moments which give rise to "folles depenses" each time.

During a baptism, the two families face each other like adversaries on a battlefield. The richness of the make-up and the jewelry foretells the generosity of the gifts. During the ceremony, the guests never think about the actual reason for their reunion. . . .

In the second novel of Aminata Sow Fall, *La Grève des Bàttu*, hardheartedness is placed at the center of the novel and serves as the criterion for distinguishing between the true and the false believer. The novelist indirectly poses the problem of the absence of charity through the collective confrontation of the beggar and the almsgivers.

In this novel, the false believer is no longer denounced by an individual, but by a whole class of penniless people. These people take action collectively when charity is put into question by the inhuman modernism of the administrators who nevertheless need to use the virtues of charity for their own personal ends.

Popular Islam presented in a human point of view, often malicious and always deeply rooted in traditional life, triumphs over unscrupulous egoism, camouflaged under the guise of modern progress.

> A. C. Jaccard. *Nouvelles du Sud.* 6 (1986–87), pp. 177–80†

*Le Revenant* is social satire, attacking the evils of today's inhumane, materialist society without reference to whites. The African nature of the work is limited almost exclusively to the social custom which demands the distribution of large sums of money at ritual baptisms. In [Sow Fall's] second novel, *La Grève des Bàttu*, three "patrons" are mentioned, only one of whom was white; and it is the vicious nature of a boss, not of a white, which is attacked. Selected for this study because of its ironic satire, this work is typical of current trends in the absence of racial issues. . . .

To recognize the satire of the work, the reader must share with the author the opinion that the system is bad. As it is theoretically possible that some readers might feel that breeding human children for food is a good solution for the problem of starvation, so there might be readers who feel that dumping beggars hundreds of kilometers outside the city, beating and killing them, is a good solution for their cluttering up the public streets. However, few among the African audience would fail to catch that the satirical intent is to demonstrate the grave faults in a system which, however humanely designed originally, has deteriorated in practice.

> Elinor S. Miller. *French Literature Series* (Columbia: University of South Carolina Press, 1987), pp. 144–46

Through a first appraisal of Sow Fall's novels, readers are provided with a fairylike enchantment which seeks its essence from universal as well as specific patterns. In such a process, the readers may be led to follow a silver thread which carries them beyond Senegalese reality into a realm of dreams and fantasies. This enchantment enraptures from without and may even work as an escapist element. . . .

Although Fall's works are written, they bear the mark of Africa's oral literature. Since the novel is a genre imported to Africa, it is of necessity influenced by the original literary form of Africa: the oral tradition. Besides the many Wolof expressions which she uses, Sow Fall seems to take special interest in quoting such Wolof proverbs as the one reflected in Serigne Birama's answer concerning the beggars: "Ligééy de Mooy degg" (It is every man's duty to work). In *Le Revenant* a peddler tells Bakar: "Lu jongoma begg yal nay jamm . . ." (Woman's desire is . . . God's wish). Bakar also remembers: "Bañ Gatia nangoo dee" (Rather death than shame). This proverb is a line from a song his mother used to sing. This leads us to the musical element included by the griots to accompany their narration. Aminata Sow Fall includes a griot in *Le Revenant*, and she even gives us a translated Wolof rendition of the praises he addresses to Yama at the ball to chant her beauty. . . .

A modern griot, Aminata Sow Fall is a genuine voice of Africa. Her style emanates humor, and the content of her novels expresses wisdom, popular beliefs, and social criticism. Her narratives, based on fictitious events, provide useful universal truths and at the same time entertain and arouse curiosity. In the true tradition, her artistry and *divertissement* are functional. Her stories contain the moral element present in all African tales. Sow Fall discloses that those events that "go wrong" in life are mainly due to the very nature of man. The reader has to discover those truths as they occur in most tales, as opposed to fables, where the message is emphasized. *Le Revenant* indicates that selfishness and corruption are finally punished. *La Grève des Bàttu* shows that one cannot solely rely on magic forces to achieve success and that it is the fairness of one's previous actions which leads to a successful future. Both Bakar and Mour have ''sinned'' and are punished.

Françoise Pfaff. *CLA Journal*. 31, 3 (March 1988), pp. 347, 357–58

Published in 1976, *Le Revenant* sets the stage for what could be called a vast *comédie humaine*. Here [Sow] Fall defines the milieu in which her characters evolve: the urban area of Dakar, capital of Senegal. It is a society at a cross-roads, caught in a process of rapid social change: ''Tradition has been pierced to the heart, and what Bakar resented the most in that situation was the corruption of morals.'' Indeed, the old value system based on *ngor* (nobility), *jom* (dignity), and communal values has been replaced by only one criterion: money or material wealth. Under the impulse of that new divinity, all relationships have become a game, and society itself a stage ruled by money. The negative effect of money over collective and individual life is embodied in the corruption of social life and the drama of Bakar, the main character. . . .

On the surface, [*La Grève des Bàttu*, translated as *The Beggars' Strike*] appears as mere reportage on a Senegalese society faced with the dilemmas and traumas of economic development or ''modernization.'' Confronting a severe cycle of drought that endangered their agriculturally based economics, public officials sought economic survival through the development of tourist industries. At the same time, hard-hit rural areas saw their population flee and invade the cities in a search for subsistence. With no formal education or skills, this displaced rural populace became beggars in the streets and public places, including those visited by the tourists. In order to maintain the flow of tourists from all over the world, public officials had to rid the city of its beggars. Therefore a campaign was launched to drive ''the dregs of society'' to a relocation area on the outskirts of the city.

[Sow] Fall's social vision goes beyond the issue of modernization to explore its implications for humans and their conduct. To reach such a depth of insight, she draws from an imagination fed by a strong knowledge of her countrymen and [countrywomen]. What would happen if, as a protest, the beggars decided to go on strike, thus depriving the entire population of the possibility of giving alms? In her fictional world [Sow] Fall brings to life a well-organized group of beggars—Salla Niang, Gorgui Diop, and Nugiraine Sarr—who decide to go on strike against the brutalities perpetrated by public officials, represented by the Director of Health and Hygiene, Mour Ndiaye, and his assistant, Keba Dabo. Exploring the consequences of this strike, [Sow] Fall highlights the collective and individual dramas generated by the contradictory demands of a changing society. . . .

Aminata Sow Fall was first a teacher and a specialist in education who participated in a committee for the reform of French programs in public schools. Education and the issues it raises in a changing society lie at the very heart of her third novel, *L'Appel des arènes*. Through the simple story of a schoolboy and his family in a small Senegalese town, [Sow] Fall stresses the disarray of a humanity confused by the content of an imposed educational system that does not correspond to its realities. Ndiogou and his wife Diattou are both professionally successful, Western-educated individuals of a type often referred to as ''been-tos,'' people who have sojourned in Europe for their education. He has returned home with a degree in veterinary medicine, she with a degree in nursing.

Despite their professional success, however, both Ndiogou and Diattou have been victimized by their education abroad. Fascinated by the Western values of progress and civilization, and alienated from Africa, they reject the cultural realities of their country. Desiring to distance herself from everything that reminds her of her past, Diattou seeks a complete personal transformation: ''Diattou concentrated on changing herself. She worked hard to domesticate her vocal cords and polish them. She learned to regulate her walk and gestures on the pace of the West. She became Toutou.'' What she draws from her Western experience is the intense desire to create an African aristocracy marked by progress and materialism. For her, progress comes to mean a total rejection of all that has belonged to her country's social values as well as to her own past values and cultural identity. . . .

*L'Ex-père de la nation*, deals with the hot topic of political life in an imaginary African country easily identifiable as Senegal. This reflection on political behavior is presented as the memoirs of Madiama Niang, former head of state, jailed after his dismissal from office. Through this flashback on his own past reign and personal tragedy, Madiama introduces the reader into the daily intrigues and vices of political life. . . .

Progressively, Madiama discovers himself to be a man trapped in a tragic situation, isolated from his relatives and stifled by power. The irony here is that he cannot even resign from the presidency that is killing his ideals of democracy and justice. He finds himself a hostage. Here [Sow] Fall goes beyond the sphere of domestic politics. The president, those around him, and the entire country are taken hostage by foreign powers through capital investment. As Madiama discovers later, dependence on foreign capital denies his nation its very foundation: the freedom to make choices and preside over its own destiny. This realization of his failure coincides with the last stage in Madiama's rule. The same hidden threads that brought him to power work to overthrow him. His very decision to find an honorable exit through resignation proves to be self-destructive. After an arranged public disturbance, a shadowy coup d'état topples him and he is thrown into jail, to be replaced by a more willing player.

*L'Ex-père de la nation* goes beyond the personal drama of an imaginary head of state to explore the tragedy of African political life. The nation Madiama presided over is like a confiscated ship in which, like worms, public officials greedily thrive on the sweat of the people. In this atmosphere of tension and competitiveness, freedom, humanity, and justice are replaced by hypocrisy as a way of life.

Samba Gadjigo. *World Literature Today*. 63, 3 (summer 1989), pp. 411–14

BIBLIOGRAPHY

*Le Revenant*, 1976; *La Grève des Bàttu*, 1979; *L'Appel des arènes*, 1982; *L'Ex-père de la nation*, 1987; *Le Jujubier du Patriarche*, 1993

# SOYINKA, Wole (1934–)
## Nigeria

Some of the praise lavished recently on the tentative beginnings of a Nigerian literature in English is going to sound rather foolish twenty or even ten years from now. Wole Soyinka's *The Swamp Dwellers*, is, I like to think, his *Titus Andronicus*; indeed it is very like that play in its blend of literary allusiveness with melodrama, and also in its occasional *longueurs*. . . .

*The Swamp Dwellers* is not, I would submit, a play about the Niger delta; but about disappointment, frustration. . . . Now this despair may be a reprehensible state of mind; it is also a tragically common experience and thus a fit subject for tragic treatment by the dramatist who does not judge or exhort but says only: "life is like that."

For us wholly to accept that life is like that, and so be the better reconciled to it, it is necessary that the symbols of the play should have an archetypal force and that its language should carry the overtones of past usage. Wole Soyinka's play fulfils both these conditions. . . . The biblical language in which the blind beggar describes his people's struggle with the soil is . . . not used out of literary pretentiousness; it serves to link their fate with that of all who have tried to sow the desert. It is particularly effective with a Nigerian audience which may not respond so readily to the play's other overtones of language. And this may be the major shortcoming of *The Swamp Dwellers*: it has an African setting, but it is written for an audience reared on Yeats and Synge. The Ibadan audience's reaction to its February performance often suggested a failure in communication, as if Mr. Soyinka, after some years out of the country, had forgotten what does and what does not move Nigerian playgoers. It may well be that there is more future for him here as a playwright in the development of the indigenous dance drama, on the lines indicated by his gay and sardonic curtain-raiser, *The Lion and the Jewel*. Or perhaps he will be able to combine the popular and indigenous with the literary and derivative, as the Elizabethans learnt to do.

M. M. Mahood. *Ibadan*. June 1959, pp. 28–29

The first Soyinka play I encountered was *A Dance of the Forests*. I confess I found this impenetrable. After coming to know *The Lion and the Jewel*, and even more *Three Plays*, it seems probable to me that I shall one day return to *A Dance of the Forests* and gain more from it. But I have learnt that a number of my friends have allowed the difficulty of this play to deter them from reading more, so I must try to persuade such people to investigate the rest of Soyinka's published drama. . . .

I find myself anxious to investigate why I *enjoy* these plays so much. For me Soyinka's writings are linked to those of Brecht, Miller, Pinter, N. F. Simpson and sometimes Ionesco among modern play-wrights by a particular kind of enjoyment that makes me want to stop immediately and read the same page more than once. The words constantly catch the rhythm of a human existence, so that one becomes aware of a character as a complete consciousness, and therefore of the complex relationship between different beings. . . .

Soyinka lets us enter into each character's private awareness, and also keeps us conscious how they appear to the outside observer: we are at once subjective and objective. We see how human beings are. We feel a spark of that outflowing towards humanity which any God worthy of man's awe must feel infinitely. A man matters to us in this context not simply because he is good, or because he does this or that, but in himself because he is himself. I think the kind of enjoyment I alluded to is related to this sense of being close to comprehending human activity at its source. A

dramatist who starts at this point does not need a "plot" to keep us absorbed. He can now unfold a pattern of the way human beings sometimes behave.

Because of this approach Soyinka can, incidentally, draw us very closely into his Nigerian world; and any dramatist must bring his setting to life. The scenes are essentially Nigerian—so much so that in a lesser playwright (or for me in *A Dance of the Forests*) they might obscure the whole drama for the uninitiated. However he is never writing *about* the Nigerian background as such, but about human beings who happen to exist very fully in this particular time and place. So we see how the familiar human passions, failures, achievements, greatness or littleness of spirit, are manifested in a previously unfamiliar environment. We make contact with this society in the only meaningful way, from the inside, via what we already share in common with it.

David Cook. *Transition*. March-April 1964, pp. 38–39

If J. P. Clark is clearly inspired by a classical ideal of austere archetypal characters and events, Wole Soyinka is of a far more romantic turn of mind: he revels in variety and diversity, alternating between farce (*The Trials of Brother Jero*), tragedy (*The Strong Breed*) and romantic mythology (*A Dance of the Forests*), changing from prose to verse within one play and employing the full panoply of the great African tradition of dance and mine. And whereas J. P. Clark's verse removes his plays into an almost timeless sphere, Soyinka's are firmly set in the present—a very recognisable independent Nigeria with its corrupting town life set against superstition and backwardness in the countryside (for example in *The Swamp Dwellers, The Lion and the Jewel*) and ambitious members of Parliament falling for the career prospects held out to them by fraudulent sectarian cultists (*The Trials of Brother Jero*). . . .

Wole Soyinka is a highly accomplished playwright. My only criticism of his dramatic technique concerns his somewhat overfree, and somewhat confusing, use of flash-back scenes. In practice the flash-back (which is largely a cinematic technique) does not work very effectively on the stage which does not possess the subtle fade-outs of the screen; so that flash-backs as a rule involve clumsy sceneshifting in the dark, loss of continuity and easy flow of the action. This is not to say that the flash-back should not be used; merely that it should be used with caution and be introduced with the utmost degree of clarity. . . . But this is a minor technical criticism of Soyinka's work. I have no doubt whatever that he is a master-craftsman of the theatre and a major dramatic poet.

Martin Esslin. *Black Orpheus*. March 1966, pp. 37, 39

Wole Soyinka's play *The Lion and the Jewel* has had various favourable reviews but one wonders why. This is a bad play. It is neither profound nor skilled technically. Soyinka has fallen into the trap of many present day African writers who dress up poor skill with exotica. . . .

Technically the play is a failure. We are given long soliloquies which are far from enhancing the dramatic quality of the play and these lines bore us with their weak prose-poetry. They lack wit, the only quality which sustains any soliloquy.

The numerous dances are thinly linked with the main action. It is difficult to understand how modern African writers fail to grasp the symbolic meaning of African dances. More often than not they depict them as sensual material, exotic entertainment but devoid of intellectual content. Scarcely do they realise that this "village exotica" contains profound intellectual experience.

The result is that, in Soyinka's play, in one episode there are several different dances, some of them quite irrelevant to the drama. This arises, one would suspect, out of a failure to understand the meaning of communal drama. By its very nature communal drama must use dramatic, symbolic expressions. The symbolic expressions are effected through bodily movement, masks, music and dance. Dance itself in the traditional drama is closely linked with the meaning and development of the story. One can understand of course how writers reared in the European form of "conversational drama" would find it difficult to infuse the techniques used in the communal symbolic drama.

Soyinka's attempt or rather his use of dancing to heighten the effect is unsuccessful precisely because all the dances are illustrative and therefore parallel to the action rather than are expressive of it. Indeed they are too many to make a successful unified image. They start and peter out before any meaning can be adduced from them. Why should dances have any meaning? Because that is the nature of drama which this play purports to convey.

The play is disappointing since Mr. Soyinka is himself a good writer. The vultures who eat up everything African will eat even a carcase but the African writer must learn to detect these birds. They are bound to be his death in the end.

Mazisi Kunene. *New Africa.* March 1967, p. 9

[In Soyinka's work] the theme of sacrifice leads into the theme of martyrdom, which for Soyinka means the *chosen* death. It can be seen in *A Dance of the Forests,* in Demoke's death wish, the one aspect of himself which he is unable fully to face, and which is symbolically expressed by the Half Child, the *abiku,* the child born with death in its soul. The same theme can be seen in *The Road,* with Professor's desire to know his own death without dying, and his inevitable death caused by his determination to know beyond the limits of human knowledge. Again, in *The Strong Breed,* Eman not only fulfills his destiny and duty, but also is drawn to a death which he himself has chosen and yielded to. Noah, in *The Interpreters,* is a man nudged falsely into the role of saintly martyr by his master Lazarus, who has messianic tendencies himself but who is compelled to fulfil them through his manipulation of someone else's life. What comes out, again and again, in all these works, is the concept of a man *giving* his own death—giving his death in order to learn its nature, in order to defeat it and in order to prove stronger than the finality.

Surrounding this central desire to control death, there are other important characteristics exhibited by Soyinka's people in their dramatic ballet-like encounters with death, encounters which are as delicately precise and as ritualistic as a bull-fight. They wish not only to conquer death by somehow anticipating it and learning it. They also desire to impose a meaning on it, a meaning which may not intrinsically be there at all. The murderer and the martyred messiah interest Soyinka for exactly the same reason—both are drawn magnetically towards death, both are fascinated with its nature, both may desire their own deaths more than anything else, even though one appears only to want to kill and the other appears only to want to save.

The murderer, the scapegoat, the messiah—none of these, in Soyinka's writing, are seen as *them.* They are, undeniably, ourselves. If there is a core to his work, it is certainly this.

Margaret Laurence. *Long Drums and Cannons* (London: Macmillan, 1968), pp. 75–76

At the time of the writing of this review, Christopher Okigbo has already been killed fighting [in the Nigerian civil war], and Soyinka is undergoing some kind of political persecution. And these two have poetic genius. Yet to be able to admit this about them, one has to go through a series of painful admissions, as one would have to do, in order to understand the events which have so terribly eliminated Christopher and are daily grinding out Wole.

Of the published African poets in English, the only one whom Soyinka reminds us of is Christopher Okigbo himself, as much in his profundity and the frightening adroitness of his handling of English, as his obscurity to any but the few initiates or experts. However, whether Soyinka intends it or not, "Idanre" has to be understood. Because, as he has implied in the foreword to the poem and in the poem itself, it is a creation myth with nightmarish parallels to the living world. . . .

The poems [in *Idanre, and Other Poems*] are . . . interesting for the way in which together they describe another side of Soyinka himself, hitherto only glimpsed in the plays. Here, the fun-provoking satirist disappears, leaving us with only the serious and often gloomy visionary. Soaked in Yoruba mythology and obviously possessed by the grim Ogun, the poet gives us nothing for laughs now. . . .

Like [Okigbo's] *Heavensgate* and *Limits, Idanre, and Other Poems* is something good and difficult. We may have to knock our heads against it for a little while. But it should be worth it, somehow.

Ama Ata Aidoo. *West Africa.* January 13, 1968, pp. 40–41

People who saw *Kongi's Harvest* presented at the Dakar Festival in 1966 complained of its obscurity. Since that performance and its earlier production in Nigeria (I have seen neither), the play has undergone what I understand has been major re-writing, attesting in some measure to the validity of the early criticism. In its revised form the play is still obscure, or at least somewhat unsatisfying, especially in its ending. Although I think *Kongi's Harvest* is quite a good play, in part for the kind of pomp and fanfare also found in [John Pepper Clark's] *Ozidi,* it is obviously not Soyinka's best drama to date. (That choice would be a toss-up between *The Lion and the Jewel* and *A Dance of the Forests.*) There is much of the bawdy humor Soyinka is famous for and the usual cleverly planned pieces of stage business, but reading the play two years after its earliest productions I am led to believe there are still sections that could be improved with more re-writing. . . .

I would prefer to forget the parallel with Nkrumah and Ghana which *Kongi's Harvest* is supposed to conjure up in the reader's mind, for the play is larger than that. The hunger pangs of new, unproved governments and the blind quest for power are symbolized in Kongi's and Danlola's coveting of the sacred yam. Soyinka has composed a more universal satire on power and corruption, political image-building, and at least one branch of political theory ("If the square of XQY (2bc) equals QA into the square root of X, then the progressive forces must prevail over the reactionary in the span of .32 of a single generation''—a reference to Nkrumah's *Consciencism*).

Charles R. Larson. *Africa Report.* May 1968, pp. 56–57

Soyinka's novel, *The Interpreters*, contains some guidance about the Yoruba gods, but will be best remembered for its Joycean scatology and dashing language: the first sentence—''Metal on concrete jars my drinklobes''—stands in my head alongside ''Stately, plump Buck Mulligan.'' Easier to follow than [*Idanre, and Other Poems*], the novel will be of special interest to black Americans. Easier still, best of all are Soyinka's plays. I doubt if there is a better dramatic poet in English. . . .

He has written a mock-learned essay, ''Salutations to the Gut,'' in which he argues that the god Obatala's name is a corruption of ''Opapala'' (hunger, I think). Anyway, he claims that ''Hunger, not Sex, is the First Principle'': he solemnly quotes absurd remarks in praise of food, by Dr. Johnson and John Gay. He discusses cannibalism—giving examples only from European history—while the noble and mockheroic passages are all from Yoruba verse, some of it left untranslated. This is the taunting aspect of his tribalism. I saw him once on television, persuading a British interviewer that Nigerian babalawos, ''native herbalists,'' can deal with mental illness at least as skillfully as European psychiatrists. The perturbed interviewer asked Soyinka if he would consider consulting a babalawo for his own mental health. He replied that he would not trust the quacks of Lagos, but might consider a good babalawo in his grandmother's village—but he seemed amazed, as if the likelihood of his going mad was too remote to be considered. He did not know then that he would be shut in a North Nigerian jail-house. . . .

This modern poet seems to belong to another century, to a world like that of Marlowe and Jonson, with great lords and private armies, high deeds and monstrous treacheries, gods, witches, and old wives' tales—poets in prison. This is the country where people are concerned, still, to make a good death.

D. A. N. Jones. *New York Review of Books.* July 31, 1969, p. 8

Writing his first novel [*The Interpreters*] Soyinka broke drastically with the unilinear plots and lone heroes which have hitherto prevailed in African fiction, whether Anglophone or Francophone. To find any work organized with comparable complexity we shall have to look back to Ousmane Sembène's great novel of the Dakar-Niger railway strike, *God's Bits of Wood*. Although the latter is a naturalistic political novel, where Soyinka's is symbolic and mystical, both writers contrive to advance the action through a number of separate figures of more or less equal importance, whose paths only cross or converge occasionally. In Sembène's work it is the purpose and situation of the strike which links all his characters and forms the real subject of the novel; in Soyinka's it is the common concern of ''the interpreters'' with discovering their own real natures within the total scheme of the great canvas which Kola, one of their number, is painting.

His relative inexperience in the art of fiction is revealed in the manner of Soyinka's opening, which requires the reader to assess and relate a number of widely different personalities who are all introduced, without history, in the first few pages of the novel. This

helps to explain why a number of readers of this rich and fascinating work have ''given up'' after the first fifty pages or so. At this point the mind is congested with partial hints and obscure clues as to what is going forward, but has almost nothing tangible to work upon, either in the form of a discernible plot situated in time or in that of identifiable central characters. It is only the persevering reader who gradually discerns the pattern of self-discovery which discriminates and yet unites the little group of friends as their affairs begin to move towards crisis in the later pages of the novel.

Gerald Moore. *Wole Soyinka* (New York: Africana, 1971), pp. 78–79

The artist in Soyinka's world . . . is seen as the conscience of the nation. In *A Dance of the Forests* the Court poet is one of the few people who dares raise his voice whenever the king and his whorish queen overreach themselves. And Eman, the Christ-like figure in *The Strong Breed*, has an artist's sensitivity. He remains a stranger to the people: those who have much to give, he says, fulfil themselves in total loneliness. Certainly this is the lot of Sekoni, the civil engineer in *The Interpreters*. After completing a power station to which he has devoted much of his energy, thought, and vision, he is told by the Council that the station is not good enough, that it is not going to be used. It is not even going to be tested. We later discover that the Councillors had made an agreement with the contractors to break the contract, as this meant more money for them all. They were going to share out the loot from public funds. The shock breaks Sekoni. He turns to carving.

Confronted with the impotence of the élite, the corruption of those steering the ship of State and those looking after its organs of justice. Wole Soyinka does not know where to turn. Often the characters held up for our admiration are (apart from the artists) cynics, or sheer tribal reactionaries like Baroka [in *The Lion and the Jewel*]. The cynicism is hidden in the language (the author seems to revel in his own linguistic mastery) and in occasional flights into metaphysics. Soyinka's good man is the uncorrupted individual: his liberal humanism leads him to admire an individual's lone act of courage, and thus often he ignores the creative struggle of the masses. The ordinary people, workers and peasants, in his plays remain passive watchers on the shore or pitiful comedians on the road. [1966]

Ngugi wa Thiong'o. *Homecoming* (New York: Lawrence Hill, 1973), p. 65

Wole Soyinka, the Nigerian patriot, poet, and political activist, was arrested on orders of the Nigerian federal government at the beginning of the Nigerian civil war. He is a Yoruba from Western Nigeria, and his offense was that of having been in touch with Biafra and with the leader of the secession, Odumegwu Ojukwu, in an effort to bring about an end to the war. . . .

*The Man Died* is in the main an account of Wole Soyinka's prison experience, but it is interspersed with ''flash backs'' about the politics of the two years leading to the Nigerian civil war. The section dealing with his actual prison experience is based partly on memory and partly on notes and jottings that he managed to make in prison on toilet paper. During his hunger strikes he was often lightheaded and near delirium, and there are long passages based on these experiences. Generally these do not work. Soyinka at his best can write very well indeed, but his weakness is still a tendency to the grandiloquent—a tendency that proves fatal to his attempt to convey the inner reality of his experience. Mostly these parts of his book come out in just a whirl of words, most of them too large and fancy to be of much service for his purpose. There are, however, moments when he seems to strike precise reality: not just what it feels like to be a prisoner but what it felt like for *him* to be a prisoner. . . .

I find *The Man Died* on the whole a rather bad book, though bad in interesting ways. But I think Soyinka has it in him to write a great book of which *The Man Died* should have been a rejected sketch. He is potentially a notable writer, but only potentially; and those who have praised him as already a mature writer, because it sounds nice to praise African writers, have done him no service by this particular version of racism. He has lived an extraordinary, interesting life at the center of events in a crucially important period in African and world history. If he would write about this straight and plain, with no prose poetry and with his indignation there but firmly under control, he would be giving us a testimony of world importance.

Conor Cruise O'Brien. *World*. February 13, 1973, pp. 46, 48

It is not at all surprising that much of the creative literature which has come out of Nigeria in the past few years has been a literature fostered by the three-year Nigerian Civil War. J. P. Clark's *Casualties*, Chinua Achebe's *Girls at War* and Wole Soyinka's *Madmen and Specialists* are all powerful literary records of the devastating effects of that conflict on the country and the survivors. Soyinka's new collection of poetry, *A Shuttle in the Crypt*, is the most intensely personal of these books, though he never lapses into any self-centered sentiment about his two years of solitary confinement in a military prison. As he himself says in the Preface, "It is a map of the course trodden by the mind, not a record of the actual struggle against a vegetable existence—that belongs in another place."

Most of the poems were written in jail and in a sense can be seen as radial expansions of the two poems in the leaflet *Poems from Prison* which came out in 1969. . . .

In places Soyinka achieves the effective liturgical rhythms of T. S. Eliot ("This death was arid/ There was no groan, no sorrowing at the wake—/ Only curses . . .") and elsewhere the word-twisting wit of Dylan Thomas ("The meeting is called/ To odium . . ."), but comparisons with other poets fail to do Soyinka justice, for the wit, the words and the rhythms are in any final account distinctly his own. Yet for all the praise this collection deserves, it must be noted that Soyinka's tendency to be obscure is here exaggerated beyond anything he has previously written. In several of the poems the images are so personal and abstract that communication between poet and reader simply breaks down. Despite the great demands Soyinka makes of his audience, and very often because of these demands, anyone who enjoys good poetry will surely be rewarded by reading *A Shuttle in the Crypt*.

Richard Priebe. *Books Abroad*. Spring 1973, p. 407

The news that Wole Soyinka was following up his recent spate of activity in drama, poetry and polemical prose with a second novel must have stirred expectations of another work as complex and richly textured as *The Interpreters*. *Season of Anomy* is not that

book; it belongs, rather, with his other post-prison writings in its narrower margin of hope, its determination to face and master the dragon of terror, its more direct use of allegory and representative character. These qualities associate it in particular with his last play, *Madmen and Specialists*.

The system of *The Interpreters* was a kind of mythologized realism, which offered characters highly individuated in their daily aspects, yet drawn towards a universal harmony through the divine, eternal aspects which they shared with the gods. In *Season of Anomy* the treatment of both character and incident is allegorical throughout. The characters hardly take on individual life and there are none of the metaphysical subtleties which made his earlier novel so difficult, yet so rewarding. The rewards of *Season of Anomy* are of a kind we have come recently to expect from Mr. Soyinka—an unrelenting determination to count the cost of Nigeria's tragic years, to show us how near the human spirit came to extinction or despair. The generalized power of his allegory is all the greater because it is not precisely located in time; it has elements of the situation before, during and after the civil war.

*Times Literary Supplement*. December 14, 1973, p. 1529

*A Dance of the Forests*, [Soyinka's] most ambitious play, attempts a fantastic unification of both the living and the dead and of men and gods, a theme which derives from the West African mythic system in which gods, men, the dead, and the living exist in a unified world. This world of the play is established, as in Tutuola's work, within the forest, the primeval landscape inhabited by all the combined forces of the universe. This forest is also a mirror of the real world, even though it also serves as the world of countless spirits. The town dwellers mingle freely with the forest dwellers who are the elemental spirits representing universal attributes. The action of the play enables a long intercourse between the town dwellers and the forest dwellers.

The effectiveness of *A Dance of the Forests* lies in its elaborate use of a significant segment of the Yoruba pantheon for the purpose of seeking a unity between men and gods and between the living and the dead. . . .

Soyinka is perhpas the most eclectic of the African writers writing in English today. His absorption of the Western idiom is complete, and at times takes over entirely his artistic direction. His freshness is in his return to his Yoruba sources, to its poetry and ideas for language and themes that dramatize his concern for fusion for the new African.

Kofi Awoonor. *The Breast of the Earth* (Garden City, New York: Doubleday, 1975), pp. 318, 327–28

The Nigerian Civil War, which was the culminating point of the series of political crises in that country since 1962, has provided some of the Nigerian poets with the opportunity of manifesting through art the nature of their feelings about life and human values. . . .

Wole Soyinka looks at war from a general point of view in "Idanre." In this poem, war is shown to be a two-sided sword cutting its owner as well as his enemy. The central character in this poem is Ogun, the ambivalent Yoruba god of creation and destruction, who indeed is himself a true symbol of the ambivalent nature of war as Soyinka sees it. Thus when men invited this god to lead them in a war against their enemies, he spared the enemies and destroyed his clients. . . . Because of this Soyinka feels he is "a guest no one / Can recall," just as war is an event no sane people can wish to experience twice. . . .

It is in his later poems, however, that Soyinka deals specifically with the Nigerian Civil War, which he feels was completely irrational. Thus in "When Seasons Change" the present generation made up of the organizers of the war is shown to have blindly refused to heed the lessons of the past (i.e., history). The ghosts of war ("Time's specters") "evade guardianship of predecessors" and come to the earth bringing with them old hints and old truths "up-held in mirrors of the hour." Instead of heeding these hints and truths, the "mind" remains "banked upon the bankrupt flow / of wisdom new." It becomes "a noble slave airborne on the cross" of two contradictory forces: its knowledge of the "futility" of "far ideas and urgent action" on one hand, and "fate" which compels response to the "present call" to war on the other. . . .

In another of his poems, "And what of it if thus he died?," Soyinka paints a picture of the wicked hearts of some fellow human beings. The victim of the hatred delineated in the poem is the artist, Soyinka himself or any artist of the same spirit, who refused to "be still" (against the orders of the sadists) "while winds of terror tore out shutters / Of his neighbor's home." For him "the wrongs of day / And cries of night burnt red fissures / In chambers of his mind." He endeavors to provide "a compass for bewildered minds," strives "to bring / Fleeting messages of time / To tall expression," and wishes to "regulate the turn of hours." Little does he know he is "seeking that whose plenitude / Would answer calls of hate and terror." For the reaction of the calloused hearts is of course: "What of it if thus he died / Burnt offering on the altar of fears?"

Because of Soyinka's outspoken advice for brotherly love instead of brotherly hate, for temperance instead of extremity, for reason instead of unreason, it would have mattered little to many "if thus he died." If he had "thus died" he would have been a mere victim of the fear that he might not have had good intentions for his nation. But from the evidence in his poem, he was genuinely concerned about the fate of his country and her values. The motivating force of his utterances has been a deep-rooted humanity which imbues his work with transcendent qualities.

R. N. Egudu. *Modern African Poetry and the African Predicament* (New York: Barnes & Noble, 1978), pp. 104–5, 108–9

When Soyinka's first novel, *The Interpreters*, was published in 1965, practically all the early reviews were favorable, and some were downright adulatory. But critical opinion quickly settled against the novel; and although it is still sometimes mentioned, it is rarely read, even in the universities. How is one to explain this sudden decline in the fortune of a book which was once proclaimed as the African novel of the future? Virtually all the participants at a symposium on "The Novel and Reality in Africa and America," in Lagos in 1973, seemed to have agreed with Michael Echeruo that it was because Soyinka did not respond to the climate of opinion around him. "Nobody is bothered, I am afraid, by *The Interpreters*," Echeruo scorned. "It has not disturbed anybody as far as I know. It does not address itself to a general emotion." . . .

*The Interpreters* attempts to maintain a proper historic viewpoint. Egbo, the most "authorial" character, is most intimately

connected with the past because of the choice he has to make between taking over the inheritance of his father's kingdom in the delta or becoming a bureaucrat in Lagos. Instead of being nostalgic, he is resentful of his traditional past, as he complains to Bandele and Sekoni: "If the dead are not strong enough to be ever-present in our being, should they not be as they are, dead?" When Sekoni replies that to make such distinctions would disrupt the dome of continuity, which is what life is, Egbo acknowledges that the past cannot be ignored, although it is tempting to do so, for "the present, equally futile, distinguishes itself only by a particularly abject lack of courage." So, where would morality come from? Egbo replies firmly: "A man's gift of life should be separate, an unrelated thing. All choice must come from within him, not from promptings of his past."

The contemporary reality which Soyinka dealt with in *The Interpreters* was highlighted in a paper on "modern black African theater," which he delivered at the First World Festival of Negro Arts in Dakar in 1966. The paper, subtitled "The Nigerian Scene, a Study of Tyranny and Individual Suppression," sums up the first five years of Nigerian political independence, 1960 to 1965. . . . *The Interpreters* deals with the problems of the intellectuals in the emerging African nations, a question of individual sensibility at war with the claims of society. The interpreters, the novel's composite "hero," are young intellectuals all of whom have had their visions frustrated by their society. . . .

*Season of Anomy*, unlike *The Interpreters*, is truly a political novel. It analyzes political motives, actions, and their consequences. However, because it deals with the world of action, where ideas as well as personalities become both polarized and simplified, it is inevitably less complex than *The Interpreters*. Clearly Soyinka means to subjugate art to social purpose. Here, he carries the war to his enemies. For it is Ofeyi who imbues the men of Aiyero (who constitute the progressive forces in the story) with his revolutionary ideas, and thereby initiates the fight against the Cartel which later provokes the massacre from the reactionary forces. But soon Ofeyi is forced to yield leadership of the progressive forces to the Dentist (Demakin), the apostle of violence whose morality is summed up by the professional ethics to extract the tooth of evil before it infects others. True, Ofeyi himself is not averse to violence. But the Dentist, the "selective assassinator," goes beyond Ofeyi's stated objective, the "need to protect the young seedling" of the revolution, and justifies the use of violence as a means of seizing the initiative from the Cartel, whose more efficient system of creating violence threatens to annihilate the Aiyero ideal. As the full dimension of the wanton destruction wrought by the Cartel becomes known, [the Dentist] wrests from Ofeyi the task of leading Aiyero against the Cartel. . . .

In the "season of anomy," violence becomes an inevitable prelude to political emancipation. But it remains only a means, to be used to achieve that higher ideal which it is the business of the man of vision to define. The Dentist himself acknowledges as much to Ofeyi: "Don't ask me what I envisage. Beyond the elimination of men I know to be destructively evil, I envisage nothing. What happens after is up to people like you."

Kolawole Ogungbesan. *New West African Literature* (London: Heinemann, 1979), pp. 1–3, 6–7

During the Nigerian Civil War Soyinka was imprisoned in 1967 and held in solitary confinement for nearly two years by the government, which claimed that he had aided the Biafran secessionist movement. Much of his subsequent writing has treated of his experiences during these years or, by allusion, of the events connected with them. *The Man Died* is an autobiographical account of his arrest and imprisonment. Shortly after his arrest Soyinka is interrogated by Mallam D. ''When the government has already laid down a policy, what makes you think you know better? You are intellectuals living in a dream world, yet you think you know better than men who have weighed out so many factors and come to a decision.''. . .

Soyinka has claimed that his African mythic perspective provides a unified view of reality which has been lost to the West as a result of fragmentation proceeding from rationalist and materialistic thought. The power of his writing results from the obsessive vision permeating his work regardless of its explicit subject matter. In his prison poems, *A Shuttle in the Crypt*, the sequence ''Chimes of Silence'' in compressed form makes use of the analogy found in *The Man Died* between Ogun's passing through chaos and the author's will to survive imprisonment. Hezzy Maduakor has said: ''Ogun's trials in the abyss of disintegration have their parallels in the private experience of every individual. Man must pass through the crucibles of experience like Ogun, and one's manhood is proven by the degree to which he summons the inner resources of his being to dare and overcome the abyss of dissolution.'' The early poems in the sequence both locate the experience in the prison and show the fatality of those who attempt to survive by prayer, compliance, or acceptance. ''Purgatory'' shows the absurdity of law with its supposed function of restoring man to society through punishment. Those who punish are themselves villains or perverts; the imprisoned include ''the mad,'' ''the damned'': ''Epileptics, seers and visionaries,'' all ''Trudging the life-long road to a dread / Judicial sentence.'' Seeing the pain suffered by those who hope for reprieve, ''The mind retreats behind a calloused shelter / Of walls, self-censor on the freedom of remembrance.'' The emasculation of hope and desire brings the ''comfort of a gelded sanity.'' Where will such loneliness end? ''Recession (*Mahapralaya*)'' tells of the dissolution of the self from relationship with the world. Such negation or destruction is necessary before there can be liberation and renewal. Soyinka's footnote to *Mahapralaya* reads: ''In Hindu Metaphysics, the return of the universe to its womb; here, expressed as the consoling experience of man in the moment of death, the freeing of his being from the death of the world.'' The poems that follow speak of psychic renewal. Noah and the Dove are invoked in ''Space'': ''His mind was boundless when out / He flew.'' Rebirth in ''Seed'' is suggested by ''Roll away the stone,'' the reference to Lazarus, the images of ''splitting wood-grains'' and ''gentle rain.''

> Bruce King. *The New English Literatures: Cultural Nationalism in a Changing World* (New York: St. Martin's Press, 1980), pp. 93–95

In *Season of Anomy*, Soyinka portrays a mythical community of Aiyéró as a foil to the anomic ''Illosa'' and ''Cross-River'' countries that are controlled by a cocoa cartel and characterized by brutality and slaughter, a carnage directed specifically toward an unnamed tribal group. Illosa and Cross-River, though undoubtedly universal in their implications, are clearly symbolic of Nigeria, the

slaughter reminiscent of the historical events that led up to the Biafran secession and civil war, the unnamed tribal group its Igbo victims. Aiyéró, in contrast to the Illosa and Cross-River areas, is an idyllic community. . . .

In this portrayal of Aiyéró, Soyinka offers the traditional African spiritual-political ideal. Survival and spiritual continuity are inextricable. At the same time, the Religion of the Grain is not passive or pacifistic: Ogun is the god of gunmakers. It becomes obvious in *Season of Anomy* that the celebration of the past is not a retreat from political problems, but rather a potential source of strength in political battle. . . .

The power of Soyinka's myth derives from a specifically African circumstance and the affirmation of a traditional African concept of the sacred continuum. Simultaneously, however, Soyinka echoes the Western myth of Orpheus. Ofeyi, the musician, rescues his wife after crossing a river to the underworld of Cross-River, clearly divided into an outer Erebus and the Tartarus of the inner prison. He is guided toward the inner recesses of the prison by a deformed Charonlike guide who demands more than pennies for his pay. The prison is guarded by a mute who is consistently described in images of a monstrous Cerberus-like dog. Strengthening this parallel is the Yoruba echo of the names of these characters' Greek counterparts. Orpheus becomes Ofeyi; Eurydice becomes Iriyise. Charon becomes Karaun, and Cerberus, Subaru.

It is insufficient to note that Soyinka has Africanized a motif of Western literature. In a narrative that equates evil with the influence of the West, Soyinka's African analogue of a Western myth is used as a weapon, one that has been symbolically seized from the intruders and used against them. To see the analogue without simultaneously perceiving this irony is to falsify Soyinka's achievement.

> Bonnie J. Barthold. *Black Time: Fiction of Africa, the Caribbean, and the United States* (New Haven: Yale University Press, 1981), pp. 185–87, 194–95

Wole Soyinka is a leading writer in Nigeria, his own country, as well as in the rest of Africa, Europe, and America. Into his work he has integrated most facets of the African experience. Between the poles of tradition and change, he searches for essential human values, which he tries to make universally recognizable from an African perspective. Because he has most convincingly succeeded, and because interest in his work is growing throughout the world, it seems logical to give special attention to this playwright. . . .

Soyinka's work is filled with ideas from his African cultural heritage. He stands close to the ''return to the sources'' to which [Léopold Sédar] Senghor refers in his Négritude philosophy. According to the Senegalese poet, Négritude is the basis of the cultural heritage, values, and spirit of African civilization. The Négritude movement originated in reaction to colonial cultural domination. . . .

Soyinka kept a distance between himself and the Négritude writers, especially the French African writers. In his now famous dictum, he is as little concerned with meditating on his Africanness or his Négritude as the tiger has the need to talk about his ''tigritude.'' In a discussion with American students at the University of Washington, he explained his point of view. He said that Négritude was the cause of a group of alienated people who had practically no contact with their own culture: Négritude is part of a

European philosophy, which explains why intellectuals like [Jean-Paul] Sartre were enthusiastic about it. Essentially its concern is to place the African personality within a European frame of reference.

> Mineke Schipper. *Theatre and Society in Africa* (Johannes-burg: Ravan Press, 1982), pp. 136, 142–43

Critics have claimed Soyinka's nonalignment to any specific ideology, but in *Season of Anomy* Soyinka comes very close to a commitment to socialist ideals. The author may not consider himself committed to socialism, but his work can certainly be given a socialist interpretation. . . . In *Season of Anomy* there is a definite antithesis between monopoly capitalism and repression on the one hand, and progressive communalism on the other. Monopoly capitalism is represented by the Cartel Corporation and the Mining Trust; and since monopoly capitalism must protect itself against the wrath of the exploited masses, we see an unholy alliance coming into existence, an alliance between "the purse and the gun." The regime running the affairs of the country (which could be Nigeria or any other African state) is a military regime. The Cartel itself is propped up by four distinguished personages: Chief Batoki, Chief Biga, Zaki Amuri, and the Commandant-in-Chief who declares that the hope for "national stability" is in "the alliance of the purse and the gun." The forces of progress are represented at the most elementary level by the communalist ideals of Aiyéró and on a higher level by Ofeyi's idea of a community of workers breaking down the artificial frontiers of tribe and region and undermining the exploitative activities of the Cartel. The idea is summarized in the following sentence: "The goals were clear enough, the dream a new concept of laboring hands across artificial frontiers, the concrete, affective presence of Aiyéró throughout the land, under-mining the Cartel's superstructure of robbery, indignities and murder, ending the new phase of slavery." Ofeyi would like to work with the men of Aiyéró because "they live by an idea." Ofeyi's idea eventually merges with that of Demakin, the Dentist, who believes in the systematic elimination of the chief members of the group of exploiters. . . .

Soyinka's novel is stylistically difficult. It is not easy for the average reader to penetrate the complexities of symbol and verbal structure which characterize the novel. These difficulties will prevent many readers from enjoying one of Soyinka's most impor-tant artistic creations to date: *Season of Anomy* is not only a very accomplished novel, but it also marks a significant turning point in Soyinka's [career] as a writer. The theme of the novel is based on the dialectical relationship between exploitation and revolution, and Soyinka points to the inevitability of violence as a method of bringing about justice to the oppressed peoples of Africa. For thinking people like Ofeyi, the prevailing social conditions present a serious challenge. But the challenge applies no less to Soyinka than it does to Ofeyi, for Soyinka is certainly becoming a militant writer. . . . This recent commitment on the part of Soyinka is clearly stated in his introduction to *Ch'Indaba*, a journal of which he is the editor. There he expresses the view that it is not in the nature of man to sit idly while political events "roll over him."

> Emmanuel Ngara. *Stylistic Criticism and the African Novel* (London: Heinemann, 1982), pp. 99, 115

To enter the world of *Aké: The Years of Childhood* is to enter an enchanted world, [Léopold Sédar] Senghor's "Kingdom of Child-hood," sometimes charmingly recreated by the adult Soyinka in some of his best prose to date. One of the most charming features of the work is the image of the boy which comes across—a preco-cious, mischievous but clever boy who is only too ready to become physically aggressive in an expression of an as yet unreached manhood: a denial of his inevitable youthful weakness. Another element is the child's perspective from which people, things, and events are seen and described. Soyinka is able to convey a child's sense of the magic and wonder of life—wonder at the incompre-hensible world around him as in the early recapitulations, and the magic world of imagined demons and spirits, or "creatures," which people the world of children. Most charming and amusing of all is the child's sense of himself which Soyinka, the narrator, through his tongue-in-cheek prose, evokes admirably. This sense of self is very meaningful and serious for the child while it is only quixotic to adults. Hence the general indulgence of the boy, although this is partly due to his being male and a first-born son. Going to school, being choosy of women when he hasn't even reached puberty, his concern with his "wife," Mrs. Odufuwa—all these incidents come across humorously from the child's perspec-tive so acutely presented in the older Soyinka's mocking tone. . . .

Soyinka succeeds in recreating the past from a child's perspec-tive by his handling of focus—in an almost cinematic but verbal and structural way. It is best exemplified by the first chapter, in particular in the evocation of Bishop Ajayi Crowther. In Soyinka's past work, these characteristic techniques, employed in *The Inter-preters*, and to our chagrin, in *A Dance of the Forests* and in parts of *Idanre [& Other Poems]* have aroused the cry of "obscurity" and "difficulty" among his readers. But in *Aké* these techniques are perfectly suited to the handling of a child's incomplete, imagina-tive and often surrealist view of life.

> 'Molara Ogundipe-Leslie. In Eldred Durosimi Jones, ed. *African Literature Today*. 14 (1984), pp. 141, 143

Recent attacks on the writings of Wole Soyinka sound very similar to the earlier criticism of [Camara] Laye's *Dark Child*. . . . The critics involved may at first seem bothered by questions of obscuri-ty in Soyinka's work, but what really angers them is their percep-tion that Soyinka is a colonial writer. He does not deal directly with political issues, does not show any clear commitment to the problem of building Africa, politically and culturally, and thus sanctions a negative ideology. If these critics have had trouble with Soyinka's other works to date, they will undoubtedly find even mores to complain about in *Aké: The Years of Childhood*. After all, this work is not just a piece of literature; it is history. It chronicles the life of Soyinka from when he was two through roughly his eleventh year. These years corresponded with a significant era of colonialism, from the late 1930s through the mid-1940s; but only at the end do we see or hear about the colonial presence in any direct way. As is true of any piece of literature, it can be subjected to multiple readings (or deconstructive "misreadings"); and yet any close examination of rhetoric should reveal a definite ideological load and a very strong statement about a society in transition. . . .

*Aké* is not a work in which we can locate a clearly fixed center, or point to a single unified structure. One way of reading this work is to see it as a very nostalgic piece about lost innocence. We merely need to follow the chronological structure and the shape of the images. In the beginning, Aké is the child's world, physically and spiritually secure. If there are external threats such as the *àbikú*, the *iwin* and the *óró*, they serve only to give definition to boundaries and make the child more secure in his knowledge that he is within the safe area. But he must venture out, and he learns in his first experience of getting lost, that all compounds are not clearly connected with his own. Later he will have to come to terms with his mother's fear of his being poisoned outside the home, and he will learn to redefine snake as food. He will also be ritually treated by his grandfather. The treatment, a kind of initiation, is to insure he will be safe from the threatening powers of the outside world. All of this has to do with order versus disorder, apparently a central conflict in the work. Change always threatens one's ordered view of the world, and the young Soyinka discovers this is not just a matter of venturing away from one's compound. Change intrudes even inside the house in the form of a birth or a death, the rearrangement of furniture, the appearance of a "new" relative, the coming of electricity. Change, in a manner reminiscent of [Amos] Tutuola is made a palpable presence, personified and given capital letters: "Change often acted inconsistently . . . I had believed that change was something that one or more of the household caught, then discarded—like Temperature." . . .

In the remainder of *Aké* [after chapter ten], we see the child moving out into the world, gaining in social awareness. His immediate concern, and the concern of his family, is with his formal education; and we see him enter Abeokuta Grammar School. At the end, he is about to go off to Government College, Ibadan. There is, however, another education he gets as he watches his mother and some other women become increasingly involved in a woman's movement. At first the women are only interested in helping women who are "socially backward," African women, for example, who do not know how to dress or act when they marry in a Christian/Western ceremony. There is, of course, no awareness on their part, or the young Soyinka observing them, that they are all engaged in "the depressing attempt to impose an outward covering—and an alien one—on a ceremony that lacked heart or love or indeed, identity." The women soon expand their area of "do gooding" to include women outside their elite economic and social circle, market women and farm women who are illiterate. At this point they become aware of problems they have never confronted before, and as a result become part of a much larger movement across the land. They see women exploited by a corrupt system of taxation, and they literally move to confront those traditional leaders immediately involved. Indirectly, they find themselves pitted against the entire colonial system. They are, through their action and experience, transformed from a ladies' social club to the Egba Woman's Union: "At some point, much later, we heard of the formation of the Nigerian Women's Union. The movement . . . begun over cups of tea and sandwiches to resolve the problem of newlyweds who lacked the necessary social graces, was becoming popular and nationwide. And it became all tangled in the move to put an end to the rule of white men in the country." In the final pages we see the mother developing a global awareness of the problems they face when she is on the phone verbally attacking the District Officer for the Western decision to drop atomic bombs on Japan. The racism in the decision is clear to her. More immediately, for the young Soyinka, that racism is somehow tied to even his

clothing as he listens to his uncle on the subject of his not wearing shoes or having pockets in his shorts in secondary school. Moving out into the world has meant a progressive move from order to disorder, from the garden to the atomic bomb; and the tension of living in transition and change has intensified. The child at eleven feels "the oppressive weight of [his] years."

In these chapters subsequent to chapter ten we can see a very progressive view of Africa moving through the crisis of cultural and political transition. The position argues a way out for Africans from Western class stratification through their functional involvement in community education and political action. . . . [There] is little direct interpretation of events in these chapters. We merely see them through the eyes of the child trying to order his world.

Richard Priebe. In Stephen Arnold, ed. *African Literature Studies: The Present State/L'État présent* (Washington, D. C.: Three Continents Press, 1985), pp. 127, 130–33

As early as *A Dance of the Forests*, Soyinka had created Rola, who we learn had callously sent a stream of lovers to their deaths. It is here that the image of the femme fatale is set, and she reappears with amazing frequency in succeeding works. For the purposes of our discussion, Simi of *The Interpreters* is the first of these mysterious, quasi-mythical courtesans. Simi is a woman living and moving in the real world, but she is imbued with the characteristics of the river goddess. Simi is excessively beautiful, the "goddess of serenity" with the "skin of light pastel earth, Kano soil in the air." But there is a quality of danger and hypnotism in this beauty, for she is the "Queen Bee" who destroys the drones who are nevertheless attracted to her. . . .

Similarly, Segi of *Kongi's Harvest* is so beautiful, so alluring that she is, like Simi, the subject of praise songs. She too has hypnotic eyes (a physical feature which seems to fascinate the author) to which praises are sung, and nipples as "violent as thorns." She too is the "Mammy Watta" who "frolics by the sea at night." But this quality of danger is heightened in the description of Segi, for there is a beauty with viciousness expressed in the image of *agbadu* "the coiled black glistening snake."

Segi, Kongi's sometimes mistress, is by far Soyinka's most dangerous woman, but at least in this play her venom has a practical use. As the play climaxes and Daoudu is unable to carry through with the overthrow of Kongi, Segi resourcefully seizes the time and valorously sends the head of her executed father to Kongi. . . .

The depiction of Iriyise in *Season of Anomy* seems to take the positive woman's image created in Segi several steps backwards, as the characterization moves from woman as subject to woman as object [of] quest. Iriyise again has the characteristics of the goddess, the image of exceptional beauty that defines the Soyinka woman. She is "Celestial," "Iridescent," "the Cocoa Princess." But she can be moody and "bitchy" and one never knows if she is going to prepare breakfast for him or chase him with a stick. Iriyise is also the "Queen Bee" who actually lives in what the author explicitly describes as "a cell in a deep hive." Animal imagery again surrounds her portrayal. "Once in a while she unleashed the caged tigress in her at some trivial or imagined provocation . . .".

Iriyise is mysterious too. She disappears and reappears at will without giving plausible explanations for her absence. Indeed her act as the Cocoa Princess involves her disappearance into the pod and reappearance as the new shoot. In this context, there is a definitive positive quality about her as expressed in her immersion into the life of Aiyéró, a context in which Ofeyi felt he knew little of her. Yet this quality of Iriyise is never developed by the author. Instead, her sexual attributes dominate as Ofeyi is caught in a trance admiring her beauty. . . .

Throughout Soyinka's works, one finds the kernel of positive portrayal of the female image which is never fully realized. The energy of Sadiku's victory song/dance [in *The Lion and the Jewel*] and Sidi's fire, Segi's organization of the prostitutes, the challenges of the chorus of women and the young girls in *Death and the King's Horsemen*, and Iriyise's brief involvement in Aiyéró, all provide the basis for a balanced image of women in this literature. But the author continuously abandons these potentially positive female characters or characteristics. Dehinwa, a realistic, modern African woman, is never developed in *The Interpreters*, for example. Instead, we find the idealization of physical attributes of women or the quest for the ideal, which limits the author's development of plausible female characters.

> Carole Boyce Davies. In Kofi Anyidoho, Abioseh M. Porter, Daniel L. Racine, and Janice Spleth, eds. *Interdisciplinary Dimensions of African Literature* (Washington, D. C.: Three Continents Press, 1985), pp. 94–97

Soyinka has a primed sense of engagement and an abiding youthfulness of spirit. He has a wide range of imaginative sympathies. Those who see his initials as one of a few points of comparison with Shakespeare are right in the sense that . . . he has cast his dreams into the mold of a vast range of characters. And his writing is shot through with a rich inimitable poetry. Since Soyinka is a man of unique sensibilities, his circle of friends in Nigeria affectionately call him Kongi after one of his roguish creations. . . .

His versatility and sophistication [are] astounding. He has wrestled with almost every literary form, has written two novels, countless plays, sketches, reviews, has produced a film, and released an album of satiric songs, and published four volumes of poetry. Wole Soyinka represents to the younger generation of African writers the necessity of realizing the full potential of one's gifts and abilities. It is a remarkable living heritage. And it is more striking when one takes into consideration the fact that when he started he had no models. He represents imaginative fecundity, the ceaseless creation of self in constant interaction with the world. And the reason he can be like this is because he will not accept that there is only one mode of being. Existence, in his world, is necessarily creative. People cannot survive without myth, without religion. His desire to bring together, to reconcile the social with the mythic, the comic with the tragic, the condemnatory with the celebratory, makes of the corpus of his works something irreducible. Soyinka speaks of the creative process as a stream. In an interview I had with him two years ago, I asked if he had any influences or models. "No models," he said, pointedly. "My work has taken the form of creative experience and that includes not just the literary world. It could be, for instance, traditional art, music, architecture, pottery, cloth dyeing. I think people should learn to look at literature as extracts and summations of various aesthetic experiences, rather than looking in terms of direct models." . . .

Wole Soyinka has brought the center to Africa and it is fairly certain that there will be an explosion in our literature. The writers will have to rise to the challenge, and take the literary explorations farther on down the unending road. We have no choice but to have a larger vision of ourselves than we have shown over the last couple of years. Blaze open the arguments, debate not in rhetoric but in works of art, widen the range of our dialogues. We cannot afford to write as if we are in a corner, when in fact we inhabit one of the richest areas in the world in terms of literature. Pass me the casket of wine, brother; Wole Soyinka has inflamed us with joy.

> Ben Okri. *West Africa.* October 27, 1986, pp. 2249–50

As in his collection of poems, *Idanre*, the authorial presence in *The Swamp Dwellers* and *The Strong Breed* [in *The Trials of Brother Jero, and The Strong Breed*] is clearly prophetic. Both plays, however, are rather straightforward, interesting in the evolution of Soyinka's dramatic talent, but lacking the force that the prophetic voice carries in the poetry. The origins of Soyinka's genius lie in Yoruba ritual and myth and none of these early plays demonstrates this so fully as *The Trials of Brother Jero*. More than anything else, Soyinka failed to endow the other two short plays with a sense of life, and above all Jero, that archetypal fantasist, is such an overwhelming success on stage because he is so entirely alive. To find the origins then is not enough; we must also see Soyinka's particular genius at work. He never again returned to the forms he experimented with in the three short plays, but he apparently learned that his forte is comedy. Though his interest is in "serious" writing, he must have found that his prophetic voice in drama was too sharp and brittle, that only by mellowing this voice with the fantastic could he achieve a roundness and suppleness in his plays.

Relatively little critical attention has been given to *Brother Jero* despite the fact that much of the action is generally considered quite successful as comedy. The play is usually dismissed as a rather conventional farce, saved somewhat by the effective interplay of Pidgin and conventional speech, but ruined by a weak ending.

Nevertheless, with the theater public, both in Nigeria and abroad, the play has proven to be one of the most popular Soyinka has written and possibly the most frequently produced. As an audience we become active participants in Jero's trials. The play opens with Jero speaking directly to us, telling us about himself. We learn that he is "a prophet by birth and by inclination" and has worked his way up against a lot of competition from others in his field as well as the modern diversions which keep his "wealthier patrons at home." In short, he tells us that he views his work as a profession that happens to be his chosen one by virtue of his extraordinary ability to gain money and power through his practice of it. Three of the five scenes in the play begin in a similar fashion with Jero addressing us and confiding in us secrets of his business. Since Brother Jero has told us much more than he would dare tell any of his usual patrons, this does more than merely set the point of view from which we are going to view the rest of the action. We are conned into letting him lead us through a day in his life, and even into conspiring with him as he moves his other pawns around. . . .

The question remains, how serious is Jero? Because he is such a perfect chameleon, it is difficult to say; but therein also lies our answer. He shifts from one role to another with ease, and as he does so we laugh with him. Nevertheless, there is more ambiguity here than just his role shifting. There are glimpses of Jero being absolutely serious in his desire to control the politician at the end of the play. In using a trickster figure as the central character in the play, Soyinka introduced a mechanism for controlling the temperature of the satire. Throughout, the satire stays at a mild level, never getting so hot that we are unable to laugh at the folly that we ourselves have become involved in. Yet it is, after all, this folly that has resulted in Chume's being led off to an insane asylum; and despite our intimate association with Jero, we see too much of ourselves in Chume to rest comfortably in our laughter.

Richard K. Priebe. *Myth, Realism, and the West African Writer* (Trenton, New Jersey: Africa World Press, 1988), pp. 129–30, 137

It should never be said that Wole Soyinka is unresponsive to criticism. Attacked by [the Nigerian critic] Chinweizu and others as a Eurocentric modernist out of touch with Africa, Soyinka responded with *Aké: The Years of Childhood*, a memoir that clarified his African roots and cultural allegiances. Attacked by the same critics for overly difficult and esoteric poetry, Soyinka now responds with *Mandela's Earth [and Other Poems]*, a new volume of poetry much less enigmatic than his earlier verse and overtly Africanist in its political commitments. However, not all responses are created equal, and though *Aké* is a superb work, possibly Soyinka's greatest achievement, *Mandela's Earth* is not nearly so successful. Soyinka is a great prose writer and dramatist, whether working in an esoteric or exoteric mode, but I have never found his poetry as powerful. *Mandela's Earth*, despite its greater directness, does not make me change my mind.

The volume opens with the sequence that gives it its title, and though the political sentiments expressed there are irreproachable, irreproachable political sentiments do not necessarily make for great poetry. The problem is that [Nelson] Mandela has been in prison for so long that for Soyinka he has become almost completely a symbol and affords nothing concrete for the poet to come to grips with. The only part of the sequence that rises above the tone of unexceptionable sentiments is "Like Rudolf Hess, the Man Said!," which takes off from Pik Botha's statement that "we keep Mandela for the same reason the Allied Powers are holding Rudolf Hess" into a fantasy that Mandela is really Hess or even [Joseph] Mengele in disguise. Here is the real Soyinka, superb at turning the rhetoric of dictators against themselves in savage and funny ways. However, as if thinking that he might be misunderstood, he retreats from this satire into the tepid pieties of the rest of the sequence.

Reed Way Dasenbrock. *World Literature Today.* 63, 3 (summer 1989), pp. 524–25

*Isarà[: A Voyage around Essay]* stands in a particularly close relationship to *Aké*, but it is not in any usual sense a sequel or even a predecessor to that work. The times in which the volumes are set overlap. Soyinka was born in 1934, and *Aké* treats his early childhood, whereas *Isarà* ends in 1940 during World War II. Soyinka himself, moreover, is not a character in *Isarà* and is not at all an agent or object of narration. This constitutes the major difference between the two memoirs. Though Soyinka assures us that elements in both are fictional, *Aké* seems like a book based directly on childhood memories; *Isarà*, in contrast, is an attempt to imagine how the author's father must actually have been as a young

man, how—for instance—he must have seemed to his coevals, not to his young son. . . .

Still, the greatest interest of *Isarà* for me is in how it thematically continues the project of *Aké*, not how it may generically contrast with it. *Aké* was in large measure a response to those critics, such as Chinweizu, who have attacked Soyinka as a Euromodernist without African roots, and its dense evocation of the author's childhood worked to show how little there was to that criticism. *Isarà* takes the discussion a stage further. Soyinka's father is portrayed throughout the book as the kind of modernizing intellectual Soyinka is attacked as being; but the climactic action concerns his involvement in the struggle over the appointing of a new king for Isarà, and a new face of "Teacher Soditan" is shown. Here the modernizing intellectual seems like a traditionalist, for he becomes intensely involved in the struggle, despite being told by a friend that such a kingship is outmoded in modern Nigeria. Soyinka's real point—here as elsewhere—is that these are falsely dichotomized choices. If African traditions are to survive, then they must also be transformed. However, as he tells his friend, there is no reason why the kingship of Isarà is an outmoded survival if the kingship of England is not. Those pretending to uphold African traditions do [themselves] a disservice by insisting that they have no connection to the modern world.

Reed Way Dasenbrock. *World Literature Today.* 64, 3 (summer 1990), pp. 517–18

A Nobel prizewinner and a dramatist to be reckoned with on three continents, Wole Soyinka remains the subject of intense debate. Is he fundamentally a satirist? Or a tragedian? A Yoruba traditionalist? Or a romantic individualist or modernist who appeals to a foreign bourgeoisie? There is some truth in each of these views. Against the satirical emphases of many plays—*The Lion and the Jewel, The Trials of Brother Jero, Kongi's Harvest, Madmen and Specialists, Jero's Metamorphosis, Opera Wonyosi, Requiem for a Futurologist,* and *A Play of Giants*—we can set the tragic emphases of others: *The Swamp Dwellers, A Dance of the Forests, The Strong Breed, The Bacchae of Euripides,* and *Death and the King's Horsemen.* In each of those plays, however, and especially in *The Road,* the satirical and the tragic are complementary. Nor can we separate Soyinka's traditionalism from his romantic modernism. The expressionist and absurdist strategies of *Madmen and Specialists* pay tribute to Yoruba folklore. The ritual pattern of *Death and the King's Horsemen* consorts with an Ibsenite realism. The revision of Euripides' *The Bacchae* into a post-Christian communion rite and the translation of [Bertolt] Brecht's *Threepenny Opera* into the Nigerian satire of *Opera Wonyosi* are exercises in yet bolder eclecticism. Soyinka's plays are so various in mode and style that they elude assessment from any narrow point of view.

Such variety also characterizes his work in other genres: the volumes of poetry from *Idanre* through *Ogun Abibimang*; the two novels, *The Interpreters* and *Season of Anomy*; the autobiographical works, *Aké: The Years of Childhood* and *Isarà: A Voyage around Essay*; and the lectures and essays in *Myth, Literature and the African World* and *Art, Dialogue and Outrage.* The eclecticism results from an evident belief that all peoples are now coming into a single conversation. But it also results from an imagination that, as Biodun Jeifo has noted in his introduction to *Art, Dialogue and*

*Outrage*, is itself antinomic or dialectical. An early essay, "The Fourth Stage," pits the regenerative "will" against the tragic "abyss." A more recent essay finds in Aristophanes's *Lysistrata* both a satirical verve and an "idiom of fertility rites," and behind both a "Life impulse" that can be manifested in both comedy and tragedy. Such opposites inform Soyinka's own work. Indeed, the generative center of his most important plays can be described as a multiform "abyss" or field of transformation that promises both destruction and recreation.

> Thomas R. Whitaker. In Bruce King, ed. *Post-Colonial English Drama: Commonwealth Drama since 1960* (New York: St. Martin's Press, 1992), pp. 200–1

*From Zia with Love* is both a painful cry and a warning to those who perpetuate military buffoonery and selfishness in the Nigeria of the present and the very recent past. As is usual with Soyinka, especially since *A Play of Giants*, the main dramatic characters here are based on ousted military leaders—Generals Buhari and Idiagbon—and the event which is dramatized is the most topical in Nigeria's recent history. The central action is the macabre display of arrogance and the unbridled power show that culminated in the killing of several drug peddlers in the mid-1980s following the enactment of a retroactive decree. What is implicit in Soyinka's handling of this "national disgrace," as some have termed it, is not so much the killing of these "cocaine peddlers" as the absolute neglect of human rights which military dictatorships have brought on this country.

The story of *From Zia with Love* is simple enough. A group of megalomaniacs takes over power in Nigeria. This group transforms the nation's complex cultures into a massive cell for everyone, issues Draconian decrees, and converts the political system into a fascist outfit. This is only a facade, however, a show purely for public consumption. In "a session in the court of the commandant," with the dramatic dexterity for which he is known, and using music and satire, Soyinka dramatizes the childishness of these "leaders" as they prattle over unserious matters only to issue outrageous decrees. He portrays such characters as laughable, idiotic, and bloodthirsty shadow-chasers. The metaphor of Zia al-Haq, the late Pakistani leader, is clear, representing the misuse of power and the inevitable consequences of such misdeeds.

From the evidence of things seen, Soyinka has produced a living text, beautifully constructed around the *danse macabre* and the drama of Nigeria's recent past. It takes a Soyinka to produce a work such as this. On a very significant level, *From Zia with Love* furthers Soyinka's discourse of power and coloniality.

> Onookome Okome. *World Literature Today*. 67, 2 (spring 1993), p. 432

Soyinka's latest non-fiction book is less impressive, and seemingly less carefully crafted, than its immediate predecessor on the Nigerian crisis, *The Open Sore of a Continent* (1996). Indeed its two halves—the first more directly political, musing on the ideas of reconciliation, reparations, forgiveness, truth and memory in the aftermath of tyranny; the second a more literary reflection on the legacy of the "negritude" poets—are only loosely articulated,

with the South African example the connecting thread. The text veers between acute insights and portentous generalisations.

Soyinka arouses passions, especially among his fellow Nigerians, as strong as those he expresses himself. The pro-government Nigerian press has recently been filled with unpleasant and, if even a quarter true, damaging stories about Soyinka's behavior. That's only to be expected, and could easily be dismissed were it not that some of the same accusations are repeated by more independent-minded critics, and are circulating widely among the global Nigerian Internet community.

Soyinka brings to his political writings the same taste for polemic and satire that make his plays so compelling. He is a forceful, scathingly funny critic of his literary and political opponents; but he is not a discriminating or magnanimous one. He may not be the "tribalist" that some enemies have called him but he can refer, gratuitously, to people's ethnic origins, and his justified pride in the cultural achievements of his own Yoruba tradition sometimes shades towards chauvinism. And he couldn't be called a consistent political thinker. In some places he warns solemnly and movingly against the desire for revenge that so often follows the fall of dictatorship and which South Africa has so far impressively avoided. It is clear, though, that Soyinka himself cannot resist the impulse to vengeance.

Wole Soyinka aspires, it seems, to become Nigeria's Vaclav Havel: a philosopher-president overseeing the country's passage back to democracy. He certainly has the intellectual standing and courage for the role. It remains to be seen whether he can achieve the generosity of spirit—the capacity to bring people together—of a Havel, Nelson Mandela or Tutu. Despite being a country of such potential wealth and creativity, Nigeria remains mired in autocracy, corruption and factional violence. Soyinka may be too volatile, too much the angry old man, to attain the required qualities to lead the country back to democratic health.

> Stephen Howe. *New Statesman and Society*. 128, 4422 (February 5, 1999), pp. 48–49

BIBLIOGRAPHY

"Salutations to the Gut," 1962; *A Dance of the Forests*, 1963; *The Lion and the Jewel*, 1963; *The Strong Breed*, 1963; *The Swamp Dwellers*, 1963; *Three Plays*, 1963; *The Trials of Brother Jero*, 1963; *The Interpreters*, 1965; *The Road*, 1965; "Idanre", 1967; *Idanre and Other Poems*, 1967; *Kongi's Harvest*, 1967; *Poems from Prison*, 1969; *Madmen and Specialists*, 1971; *The Man Died*, 1972; *A Shuttle in the Crypt*, 1972; *The Bacchae of Euripides*, 1973; *Season of Anomy*, 1973; *Jero's Metamorphosis*, 1974; *Death and the King's Horsemen*, 1975; *Myth, Literature, and the African World*, 1976; *Ogun Abibimang*, 1976; *Opera Wonyosi*, 1981; *Aké: The Years of Childhood*, 1981; *A Play of Giants*, 1984; *Requiem for a Futurologist*, 1985; *Art, Dialogue, and Outrage*, 1988; *Mandela's Earth, and Other Poems*, 1988; *Isarà: A Voyage around Essay*, 1989; *The Soyinka Reader*, 1991; *The Credo of Being and Nothingness: First in the Series of Olufosoye Annual Lectures on Religions*, 1991; *From Zia with Love*, 1992; *The Blackman and the Veil*, 1993; *Ibadan: The Penkelemes Years: A Memoir, 1946-1965*, 1994; *The Open Sore of a Continent: A Personal Narrative of the Nigerian Crisis*, 1996; *The Beatification of Area Boy: A Lagosian Kaleidoscope*, 1995; *Early Poems*, 1998; *The Burden of Memory, the Muse of Forgiveness*, 1999

# ST. OMER, Garth (1931–)

St. Lucia

The structure of [Garth St. Omer's] novellas is largely fragmentary, consisting of incidents, memories, flashbacks in time, letters, dialogue, present and past thoughts, and similar devices which create rather mood and reflection than sequential, linear plot development. The general style is of concise economy, understatement, and episodes which are related by association rather than cause and effect. The focus of the narratives is more on the inner consciousness and observing the sensibility of the individual than on externalities. There is little action, few events; the focus rarely shifts from the consciousness of the characters, whose memories make up most of the narrative. Even dialogue seems observed rather than in itself dramatic. It is difficult to piece events together into a chronological sequence. Individual chapters begin with imprecise emotions, the object of which is not clear until later when some previous event is mentioned.

There is disillusionment, despair, introspection, and haunting immobility; often the main characters are unlikable, being in themselves both victims and exploiters. The effect is of carefully constructed, sensitive, artfully shaped brooding over memories rather than of story. This characteristic of guilty meditation is strengthened by the various characters and stories being analogous so that parts of the novellas could be moved to another book without seeming out of place....

*A Room on the Hill* tells of the death of John Lestrade's mother, the long estrangement between mother and father, the death of a beautiful young woman, and the insanity of a local priest who has returned to the island. The central events are the suicide of Stephen, John's best friend, whose money to escape from the island was wasted by a callous father, and the rejection of John by Stephen's girlfriend. It is a record of isolation, drifting, lives without purpose, the young dying in accidents, heavy drinking, and premature aging....

"The Lights on the Hill," the first of the two narratives [collected] in *Shades of Grey*, concerns Stephenson, [a] twenty-eight-year-old drifter, who, ironically, because of favoritism given those from the smaller, backward islands, finds himself on a scholarship at the then University College of the West Indies. Despite his escape from the small island, Stephenson's life seems a continuation of John Lestrade's brooding aimlessness.

The central event of the novella is Eddie's death by lightning, an incident which in its effect parallels the suicide of Stephen in the previous novel. Stephenson had envied Eddie as someone who, unlike himself, can achieve, but the arbitrariness of death makes him realize that achievement in itself cannot be a goal: "human effort, in the end, if it did not benefit others, was futile." This realization depresses him further. He feels he has no special talents and is merely a spectator.

"Another Place Another Time," the second narrative in *Shades of Grey*, is somewhat more sociological in purpose. Derek (the name is also that of one of John's friends in *A Room on the Hill*) is another emotional cripple produced by history. Although the island is changing—elections, black faces replacing mulattos and whites at the college—his family is too poor to enjoy the benefits. Education is his only means upward in society. His mother, with whom he no longer can speak, works endlessly to pay for his schooling as that is the "only thing to save us poor people." He

feels he should work to relieve her sufferings and he is guilty of losing contact with his childhood friends, but he must continue his education if his mother's efforts are not to be wasted. Although he does not want it and has no personal ambition, he must leave the island for further schooling. After winning the island scholarship to study abroad, he refuses to accept a teaching position at the local school, despite the headmaster's claim that Derek could help others of his race, as this would end his advancement.

St. Omer's third book, *Nor Any Country*, describes a successful young West Indian who, after being educated abroad, returns to his island feeling uprooted and alienated. He can no longer speak with his family; beyond exchanging memories, they have nothing in common. His father feels threatened both by Peter's achievement and by his brother's failure to succeed in a career. We learn that Peter had been trapped into a loveless marriage eight years before. If the marriage allowed his wife to escape from her family—she was an illegitimate child—Europe was Peter's escape from her.... The repetitive nature of the situation is shown when Peter makes his unloved wife pregnant again and, trying to be responsible, reluctantly takes her with him to his new job teaching at the university on a different island.

The fourth book, *J—, Black Bam and the Masqueraders*, is both a further development and a commentary on *Nor Any Country*. Here we see Peter's souring life as a lecturer at the university and his brother Paul's comments on his own, and implicitly Peter's, experience. The two lives, although apparently so different, are similar products of the same culture.

Bruce King. *Commonwealth Essays and Studies*. 3 (1977–78), pp. 56–58

It is, of course, true that his Catholic background is a central force in St. Omer's novels. The sin-guilt-punishment syndrome operates throughout the work and, though St. Omer does not preach, as [St. Lucian poet Robert] Lee puts it, "His tone is that of the confessional...." In *A Room on the Hill*, as in all the novels, this air of the confessional pervades. It achieves its greatest heights in *J—, Black Bam and the Masqueraders*, where chapters headed "Paul" are confessions of one brother. There are also, of course, the Catholic Brothers who often appear in his work: successful as well as failed priests. One of the white characters—the headmaster—in part two of *Shades of Grey* is described as "a picture of colonial seediness," reminding Derek, the hero, of "Graham Greene's novels of expatriates in Africa and America."...

Within this framework, the theme of personal sin and public expiation (giving, as it were, a religious twist to the conflict between private sensibility and public function), St. Omer's characters are very tightly linked. In fact, characters in early books reappear (often in greater depth) in the later ones. We first meet Derek Charles, briefly, in *A Room on the Hill*. In part two of *Shades of Grey*, he is the main character. In part one of the same book, Dr. Peter Breville and his wife Phyllis and their violently unhappy marriage are mentioned peripherally. In *Nor Any Country* their relationship and Peter's sense of despair, of panic on his return to the island, are the central elements. His relationship with his brother Paul, who—"trapped on the island"—is becoming mentally unbalanced, is introduced. In *J—, Black Bam and the Masqueraders* the relationship between Peter and Paul is central; and Paul's voice, his own point of view, is more insistent. It is as if St.

Omer is considering a particular group of characters—indeed a particular relationship between the homecoming intellectual and his less fortunate trapped brethren—in greater and greater depth. From a general, almost aerial survey of a society caught in the colonial mesh of poverty, guilt, and self-contempt (the world of "Syrop") St. Omer focuses, in successive novels, on the nature of the educated individual's relationship to his society and (with *J—, Black Bam and the Masqueraders*) on the divided intellectual's relationship with friend, brother, and finally, with himself. Exile, escape from a restricting, uncreative society leads to the inevitable return. But, if in St. Omer's work exile is seen primarily as a need to break out of the psychological prison of guilt and self-contempt, then the return—at its deepest level—suggests the equally vital need to live with the confusion and pain and frustration that a genuine at-one-ment involves.

> Michael Gilkes. *The West Indian Novel* (Boston: Twayne, 1981), pp. 106–7

There is one representative figure behind St. Omer's four interlinked works of fiction, *A Room on the Hill, Shades of Grey, Nor Any Country*, and *J—, Black Bam, and the Masqueraders*. He is one of the first generation in his small island to make a breakthrough by way of secondary education and a scholarship which enables him to study abroad, and he is returning as the educated professional to take his "place" in the society. [*A Room on the Hill*] presents its protagonist, John Lestrade, prior to departure, in a kind of anticipatory disillusionment with the prospect of achievement; and in "Another Place Another Time," one of the two novellas in *Shades*, we go further back to the college days of Derek Charles to trace the growth of the single-minded determination to "escape" through education. Essentially these stories function as flashbacks in the total scheme, projecting the predestined course of one essential crisis—that of the professional returning home. The implicit effort to reconnect with his past environment is balked at every turn, and he returns to a sense of acute exile at home. From this condition of isolation, he assumes the role of spectator, this twofold motif being expressed in the first title, "room on the hill."

Thus, he becomes enmeshed in a close network of family relationships, friendships, past associations. He moves in the flesh, incapable of quite cutting himself off from the ties that bind; but in spirit he lives and inclines elsewhere. From his position as spectator, however, the St. Omer persona surveys the "several postures" of his small island with a clinical precision, which Gordon Rohlehr has aptly compared to [James] Joyce's "scrupulous meanness."

St. Omer has the rare novelistic skill of deploying an introspective drama through a texture of sheer, stark, social realism. He presents a full portrait of the social, cultural, moral condition of the St. Lucian environment, though the island is in fact never named. We get a close-up view of the small, cramped community of Castries, sharing its few, spare essentials—school, church and its various observances; of its narrow range of occupations, small vendors/domestics, civil servants, teachers. The milieu is pervaded by a sense of privation. The one cultural force binding all classes together is conformism to religious custom, the norms and codes of Christian morality—which makes for a prevailing atmosphere of constraint.

> Patricia Ismond. *Carolina Quarterly*. 28, 1–2 (1982), pp. 34–35

There can be little comfort in the utter despondency, the seemingly banal void with which Garth St. Omer concludes *J—, Black Bam and the Masqueraders* and, to a large extent, the quartet of which it is more the nadir than the climax. The petrification of both individual and society, the ceaseless repetition implicit in the novel's ending, these can go no further. This is not to say, however, that the characters have reached the end, since to have done so would at least be some consolation, and St. Omer's characters are not that fortunate! They remain, on the contrary, totally unable to control either their social or psychological worlds, condemned to a common, endless, often directionless search for identity, the victims of both their society and their lucidity.

We face, in the world created by St. Omer, the individual's struggle for self-awareness and, as a seemingly inevitable corollary, his inability to fit into his society—or, perhaps more precisely, the inability of that society to integrate meaningfully the individual because it is itself static, chaotic, apparently meaningless. Little wonder, then, that St. Omer's protagonists are unable to define themselves in terms of a positive existence when their every legitimate demand (career, personal relationships, intellectual and spiritual quest) is thwarted.

St. Omer's analysis goes beyond this, however, and through the socio-cultural dimension he nudges his reader towards a growing awareness of the universal existential dilemma which, equally bleakly, accompanies it.

> Peter Dunwoodie. *Carolina Quarterly*. 29, 2 (June 1983), p. 30

From his earliest published novella, "Syrop," to his most recent, *J—, Black Bam and the Masqueraders*, St. Omer's works reveal a familiar complex of themes, conflicts, and even characters, consistently developed, elaborated upon, modified, and deepened effectively through an ever-increasing technical control and formal sophistication. Organized in a manner comparable to the connected narratives of [William] Faulkner, [James] Joyce, [Marcel] Proust, and [Thomas] Mann, his works constitute a trenchant, interrelated, multivolumed commentary on the existential dilemmas inherent in colonial and postcolonial life in the West Indies. Progressing in a style which tends to replace chronology and external reference with duplication and internal associations as formal determinants, these slim volumes continue uniquely to mine the fundamental themes of exile, identity, and alienation implicit in the entire body of Caribbean writing.

"Syrop" is St. Omer's earliest novella and the first work to be published outside the Caribbean. This story, with its classical overtones of man's untimely but inevitable meeting with fate, is chronologically, stylistically, and thematically the best introduction to St. Omer's art. It contains many motifs employed by the writer in later (and longer) works: madness, sibling rivalry, intergenerational conflict, religion, illegitimacy and its social responses, exile and return, success, and responsibility for oneself and others. Graced by a subtly symbolic pattern of imagery, highly descriptive language, and an astute manipulation of point of view and temporal sequence, "Syrop" dramatizes the brief and ironic passage of a young boy into manhood, achieved on the very day of his death. In this tale of a divided house in which rejection, guilt, and the explosive violence of internalized frustrations characterize family and social relationships, life as imprisonment and death as a release are pervasive elements. . . .

The organizational method employed by St. Omer in his novellas reflects an attempt to evoke an awareness of the whole in each narrative. It is a compositional conception which, in its intention of totality, establishes an organic relationship between individual volumes; that is, each novella becomes "associated" with those that precede and those that follow. This is achieved through the repetitions mentioned above (i.e., characters, themes, locales, imagery, and even tone). The protagonists of St. Omer's fiction, for example, are usually presented with psychological "doubles" (in order to emphasize how the characters are invaded from both the outside and the inside) and are presented as if fully developed. Since we have seen them before, it avoids the necessity for "overlaboration of individual character" found in the conventional narrative genres. In this way, St. Omer approximates the kind of "epic and revolutionary novel of associations" described by Wilson Harris, whereby the "characters are related within a personal capacity which works in a poetic and serial way so that a strange jigsaw is set in motion."

The correspondence between perspective and form is further reinforced by the open-ended nature of the plots. With this method of concluding his narratives, St. Omer emphasizes the ambiguity and inconclusiveness of life and also underscores the interconnectedness of the novellas; that is, the sense of inconclusiveness, the absence of a definite or certain resolution of conflict(s), functions as narrative interstices of a multivolumed work and also helps to sustain the anticipation of future installments. Moreover, along with the use of duplication and internal associations, this characteristic ending effects a style in which internal elements assume a greater importance than chronology and external reference.

> Roland E. Bush. In Daryl Cumber Dance, ed. *Fifty Caribbean Writers* (Westport, Connecticut: Greenwood Press, 1986), pp. 406, 414

The large-scale tragedy of "Syrop," the experimentations in existential anti-heroism of "The Lights on the Hill," the social realities in "Another Place Another Time," the concern over Catholicism found in *A Room on the Hill* are all ingredients welded together in *Nor Any Country.*

While it would be extreme to call *Nor Any Country* a work of reconciliation, the novella leaves the St. Omer reader with the impression that the author has finally gained control over his topic, his style, and his hero. Peter is the familiar educated West Indian who has left his island for England and who returns home with the potential for ordering his values.

St. Omer does not provide his reader with any forewarning that this time he is creating an existential antihero with a difference. Peter is like his predecessors in many ways: he exploits the women with whom he lives, he watches others rather like a scientist collecting specimens, he is generally self-indulgent. He takes a greater interest in the member of his family, however, and his accounts of his father, his mother, his brother, and his wife are more sympathetic than hitherto. Finally, Peter is able to listen to the fears and worries of a Roman Catholic clergyman. He allows Father Thomas time to explain his own sense of alienation as a dark-skinned clergyman assigned to labor among parishioners on his home island. In short, Peter has outgrown his solipsism enough to hear another's anxieties.

Peter's ability to open himself to Father Thomas's anxieties might well be the crack through which compassion for Phyllis enters. Once able to accept her love and to recognize her need for her husband, Peter is also able to extend his compassion to include Michael, his brother's little son. Peter, still a man of few words, may appear to be a stereotypic antihero, but he has grown beyond the protagonists of St. Omer's earlier works. He has redefined tragedy to include the angst of those who share his world.

Having achieved the ability to participate in the angst of those around him, Peter in *J—, Black Bam and the Masqueraders* is able to empathize with his brother's world view. Paul, not unlike Hamlet, declares himself mad. Paul's antic disposition enables him to countenance the disappointing turn his life has taken. An earlier Peter would have been too self-centered to share so much as bookspace with his brother. . . .

[John] Thieme believes that *J—, Black Bam and the Masqueraders* is St. Omer's most successful novel because the author is able to sustain the two parallel but separate points of view that Peter and Paul present. The point of view St. Omer elects is an interesting variant of the omniscient narrator. The St. Omer reader is so conditioned to accept the existential antihero's self-absorption that he or she assumes that Paul's narration is filtered through Peter's sensibility. In fact, it is not. Double, each narrative line is nevertheless distinct, enabling both Peter and Paul to delineate the details of their personal tragedies.

Whereas *Nor Any Country* offers promise of reconciliation, St. Omer's final West Indian novel plunges the reader back into the depths of modern alienation. This time, however, the degree of alienation is compounded by the doubling. Not one but two promising West Indians have succumbed to disillusionment and despair.

> Elaine Campbell. In A. L. McLeod, ed., *Subjects Worthy Fame* (New Delhi: Sterling Publishers, 1989), pp. 7–9

[St. Omer's novels] explore one single subject: the dilemma of the educated native son, returning home to take his place and make a contribution to his society. He finds this purpose thwarted by a society still trapped in the dearth of persisting poverty and alien religious values. He comes to face instead, his own personal paralysis and psychic disability. In a sensitive response to St. Omer's theme, [Derek] Walcott has described this dilemma as "homecomings without home." The St. Omer persona, who appears in all the various protagonists, sums up the problem thus: "From his memory he had exhumed corpses of his old self, probing them with the scalpel of his new awareness. . . . But the timidity and fear his discovery of himself had instilled and the paralysis they induced made any reconstruction in the future too daring for him to contemplate." Inclined toward self-withdrawal, he remains intimately enmeshed in the reality of . . . society, experiencing his past and continuing ties with it. He therefore reflects the predicament of the society in analyzing his own. . . .

What stands out especially in the community St. Omer presents is the rigid system of orthodox morality, which closely regulated its life. It dictated the prevailing codes, sanctions, and mores of the society. Among these, the most formidable was the sanction against illegitimacy. It imposed all kinds of double standards and constrains in a largely underprivileged class where the traditional pattern of unmarried mothers and fatherless homes obtained. Most expressive of the kind of authoritarianism the Church stood for was its policy for enforcing this sanction. Young men and women involved in pregnancies outside marriage had the choice of either getting married or losing their jobs in the teaching service and similar educational opportunities. . . .

One thing becomes quite clear about the society St. Omer recaptures: there were glaring gaps between its prescribed norms and its actual practices. . . . Most critically, its pressures and strains backfired to cause total disarray within the most private areas of human relationship. Family, married, and sexual life were all strangely disordered. Most of St. Omer's characters are casualties of one type or another of these abnormal relationships; and his final, most penetrating focus is on the toll in damaged psyches and ruined lives.

In his culminating novel, *J—, Black Bam and the Masqueraders*, St. Omer describes a situation that highlights the extreme reaches of just these violations. The novel juxtaposes the stories of two St. Lucian brothers, Paul and Peter Breville. Paul, the older brother who remained on the island, has ended up mad; Peter, who left the island on a scholarship, has just returned to a university post in one of "the larger islands to the north." The technique of the novel is both functional and thematic. Paul's letters to his brother, a desperate outpouring of his memories, alternate with snapshots of Peter's present life [on] the other island. The two brothers, in fact, emerge as alternate sides of the same coin: Paul, a victim of madness; Peter trapped in a violent, destructive marriage to a St. Lucian girl from his past. It is as if, in other words, neither had "escaped."

Behind their two contrasting circumstances lay two opposite choices. Both brothers had found themselves faced with the same problem, common enough: to conform to the Church's policy on extramarital pregnancies or lose their chances of a future through education. Paul, always confident of his own brilliance, had preferred to defy the system rather than enter into a marriage he did not want. Peter had married Phyllis, whom he later suspects of having deliberately trapped him, to preserve his chance of pursuing a career. To survive [on] the island, where he is doomed to remain, Paul dons a pose of madness. He is seduced into the role by egomaniac delusions of his own apartness, and contempt for his mean surroundings. The pose of madness becomes all too real. Peter, on the other side, pays an equally high price for his convenient conformism. His life with Phyllis is a mutually destructive affair, now down to a level of raw brutality and violence. He has nothing in common with the wife who had actually waited eight years in his mother's house during his absence. (Peter had left to take up the scholarship soon after marrying her). Phyllis embodies some of the worst hangovers of the past. She is devoid of ambition and is inarticulate, driven solely by her ambition to find her own salvation in someone, like Peter, who had achieved success. . . .

St. Omer singles out a portrait of St. Lucia which obviously has some personal urgency for him. Though there are other faces besides the one he shows, he does sound some of the key notes of the St. Lucian sensibility, and evokes strains and postures which also appear in Walcott. His images point to an authentic pull between two opposite strains of the sensibility—the one repressed, the other charged with a spirit and energy that will not stay harnessed.

Patricia Ismond. *World Literature Written in English*. 29, 2 (autumn 1989), pp. 107–10

*Nor Any Country* (1969) marks the full maturing of St. Omer's prose. Clive Jordan in the *New Statesman* said of this novella, "The quiet, flat honesty of his style tends to mislead. Its impact is

frequently delayed . . . and it hides latent warmths." Honesty is a good word to apply to St. Omer's fourth novella. In it, the hero's posturings no longer dominate the story, although Peter remains remote and relatively dispassionate toward those around him—especially his wife, Phyllis, whom he has left behind for eight years while furthering his career in England. But Peter, in the last chapter, confronts his social responsibilities. All the while intending to leave Phyllis behind again after a week's visit to his Caribbean island, Peter surprises the reader and himself by deciding to take Phyllis back to England with him along with his orphaned nephew Michael. He reaches this decision with few histrionic statements.

This closeness to reality was prepared for by all St. Omer's preceding fiction. The largescale tragedy of "Syrop," the experimentations in existential antiheroism of *The Lights on the Hill*, the social realities in *Another Time Another Place*, and the concern over Catholicism found in *A Room on the Hill* are all ingredients melded together in *Nor Any Country*. While it would be extreme to call *Nor Any Country* a work of reconciliation, the novella probably leaves the St. Omer reader with the impression that the author has finally gained control over his topic, his style, and his hero.

Peter is the familiar educated West Indian who has left his island for England and who returns home with the potential for reordering his values. St. Omer does not provide the reader with any forewarning that, this time, he is creating an existential antihero with a difference. Peter is like his predecessors in many ways. He exploits the women with whom he lives; he watches others, rather like a scientist collecting specimens; and he is generally self-indulgent. He takes a greater interest in the members of his family, however, and his accounts of his father, his mother, his brother, and his wife are more sympathetic. Finally, Peter is able to listen to the fears and worries of a Roman Catholic clergyman. He allows Father Thomas to explain his own sense of alienation as a dark-skinned clergyman assigned to labor among parishioners on his home island. In short, Peter has outgrown his solipsism enough to hear another's anxieties.

Peter's ability to open himself to Father Thomas's anxieties might well be the crack through which compassion for Phyllis enters. Once he is able to accept her love and to recognize her need for him, Peter is able to extend his compassion to include Michael, his brother's little son. While Peter appears to be a stereotypical antihero, he has grown beyond the protagonists of St. Omer's earlier works. He has redefined tragedy to include the angst of those who share his world.

Having achieved the ability to participate in the angst of those around him, Peter in *J—, Black Bam and the Masqueraders* (1972) is able to empathize with his brother Paul's worldview. Paul, not unlike Hamlet, declares himself mad. Paul's antic disposition enables him to countenance the disappointing turn his life has taken. An earlier Peter would have been too self-centered to share space with his brother. Now, he and his brother become, as John Thieme notes, "fully-fledged doubles in the Dostoevskyan or Conradian sense."

Thieme believes that *J—, Black Bam and the Masqueraders* is St. Omer's most successful novel because the author is able to sustain the two parallel-but-separate points of view that Peter and Paul present. The point of view St. Omer elects is an interesting variant of the omniscient narrator. The St. Omer reader is so conditioned to accept the existential antihero's self-absorption that he assumes Paul's narration is filtered through Peter's sensibility.

In fact, it is not. Each narrative line is distinct, enabling both Peter and Paul to delineate the details of their personal tragedies.

Whereas *Nor Any Country* offers the promise of reconciliation, St. Omer's *J—, Black Bam and the Masqueraders* plunges the reader back into the depths of modern alienation. This time, however, the degree of alienation is compounded by the doubling. Not one, but two promising young West Indians have succumbed to disillusionment and despair.

> Elaine Campbell. In Bernth Lindfors, and Reinhard Sander, eds. *Dictionary of Literary Biography,* Volume 117: *Twentieth-Century Caribbean and Black African Writers* (Detroit: Gale Research, 1992), pp. 278–283

BIBLIOGRAPHY

*A Room on the Hill*, 1968; *Shades of Grey*, 1968; *Nor Any Country*, 1969; *J—, Black Bam and the Masqueraders*, 1972

# SUTHERLAND, Efua (1924–)

## Ghana

Efua Sutherland founded the Ghana Drama Studio in Accra . . . and did much in the late 1950s and early 1960s to encourage experimental work in drama. Through her post in African literature and drama in the University of Ghana, she has been influential in the training of young dramatists and actors; and her own research on Ghanaian music theater and concert parties is of importance. In addition to her three major plays, *Foriwa, Edufa* and *The Marriage of Anansewa*, Efua Sutherland has written several plays for children. *The Marriage of Anansewa*, a play which uses music and dance to decorate and guide the action, is a witty and lighthearted story of a man who attempts to marry his daughter to several rich chiefs all at the same time, in order to raise money from them. When they all converge on his home together it takes all his ingenuity to resolve the situation. *Edufa*, by contrast, is the story of a man who gives his wife's life in place of his own. Edufa, a rich and successful businessman, respected in his hometown and greatly loved by his wife, learns from an oracle that he will die and that the only way to escape death is to find someone willing to die for him. To his horror, instead of being able to trap his old father into saying that he loves him well enough to die for him, his wife Ampoma states her affection for him in those terms, and is consequently made the victim of the charm Edufa has bought to save himself. The similarities to Euripides's *Alcestis* are acknowledged; but the play often seems rather static in construction and in dialogue, and the full impact of the story may be hindered by this.

*Foriwa*, however, has a lightness and a charm about it that make it probably Sutherland's most effective play. It is a simple moral tale, perhaps almost didactic in some ways, but not restricted by its morality and didacticism in any way. The play is set in a Ghanaian town, Kyerefaso, which is crumbling into dust through the neglect and inactivity of the elders. It takes a "stranger" (a Hausaman from northern Ghana) to come to Kyerefaso and revitalize it, helped by the Queen Mother of the town and her beautiful daughter Foriwa. The stranger, Labaran, clearly represents the new spirit of Ghana. He is a graduate, and yet lives simply and without ostentation. He is a stranger in the town, and yet makes the point that he is a

Ghanaian, and though of different tribe is of the same nation. He represents the forces and the virtues of self-help—a respect for the tradition of the elders tempered by an awareness that tradition should be a creative force and not simply an exercise in placid nostalgia. Where others talk, Labaran acts. Often he attracts attention to himself not because of what he does, but of the way in which he does it. As he says: "If you want people to listen to you, do something that astounds them. They weren't astonished because I carried rubbish. It was because I wore a suit for the job." Labaran's first ambition is to build a bookshop in the town, and this he does through encouraging the local postmaster to extend his shop for this purpose. The symbol is obvious, and the care that Labaran takes to make his schemes seem to be the idea of the local people themselves is also quite clearly intended as a subtle lesson to the audience. Foriwa, who previously turned her back on her hometown because of its bickering and inertia, resolves to stay to support Labaran. All this takes place in the context of the town celebrating its annual festival. The elders see it as merely a ritual, devoid of meaning, simply perpetuating old ways. The Queen Mother, inspired perhaps by Labaran and Foriwa, challenges the elders and the townspeople to turn their thoughts to more positive ways and to hold their festival as a sign of regeneration. . . . The play ends on an optimistic note, and the moral is nicely made. This play has a charm and a functional quality about it, and is a good example of the conscious use of the drama in a social context.

> Martin Banham and Clive Wake. *African Theatre Today* (London: Pitman, 1976), pp. 52–54

In a discussion of the theater in Ghana, Efua Sutherland once declared that a truly vital theater should heed the example of oral literature by dealing directly with contemporary experience. Oral literature, she pointed out, "uses . . . experience artistically." By a similar token, a national theater should look at and utilize the repositories of a culture's experience, it should avoid the merely imitative art of "performing plays just because they exist in books already," and it therefore should depend on the willingness of the artist to create forms which can communicate both the contemporary experience and the historical process out of which it grew. In this sense, theater becomes a kind of immediate cultural exploration: "There are all sorts of exciting things to venture and I take a deep breath and venture forth . . . I'm on a journey of discovery. I'm discovering my own people." Sutherland's views and practice find a ready supporter in Ama Ata Aidoo: "What she conceives," Aidoo observes of Sutherland, "is that you take the narration—the traditional narration of a folktale. In the course of the narration, you get a whole lot of dramatic behavior which one should use, in writing plays even in English. . . . I believe with her that in order for African drama to be valid, it has to derive lots of its impetus, its strength, from traditional African dramatic forms.". . .

As writer, producer, and teacher, Sutherland has always been personally involved in the mechanics of theater, as well as the art of dramatic writing itself. Her career has enabled her to experiment with approaches to Ghanaian theater that explore the possible relevance of European models and the continuing vitality of indigenous folk drama and folktales. She has adapted Western drama (including her own adaptation of *Everyman*) to a Ghanaian context. At the same time, she has also been adapting Ghanaian tales to her contemporary theater. In fact, her career has been a ''journey of discovery,'' to borrow her own words—a journey that has taken her from the adaptation of classical Greek drama, to the distinctive milieu of rural life in modern Ghana, to the reliance on indigenous folk forms. . . . Her other works [include *Odasani, Nyamekye*, and children's plays (*The Pineapple Child, Ananse and the Dwarf Brigade*, and *Vulture! Vulture!* and *Tahinta: Two Rhythm Plays*)]. But her three major, published plays exemplify at its best her continuing quest for certain dramatic forms—specifically, those forms which are analogous to the theme of sexual role-playing in the plays themselves.

> Lloyd W. Brown. *Women Writers in Black Africa* (Westport, Connecticut: Greenwood Press, 1981), pp. 61, 65

*Edufa*, Efua Sutherland's adaptation of the Greek play *Alcestis*, is a study of the cultural conflicts of the transitional African who is torn between the differing values of the traditional tribal society and the modern industrialized world. But her play is also a folk art form which engages the mythic elements of Sutherland's Ghanaian society. It therefore relies on the oral tradition—folk art forms of song, language, and image—which plays an elemental role in an African historical past. Sutherland's adaptation of Greek classical forms establishes analogies between sexual and cultural conflicts in her society with those in Euripides's Greece. Both plays question the validity of certain social roles—the duties of husband, wife, parent, and citizen. From a broader thematic perspective, Euripides's complex, feminist-oriented portrait of Alcestis as woman, wife, and mother provides a functional backdrop for Sutherland's examination of the similarities of women's roles in various cultures: the limited role of women in society, entrenched male social privileges, and the vulnerability of women in relation of men. On an equally fundamental level, *Edufa* endeavors to express the tragic implications of African cultural rootlessness and the anxiety of assimilation. . . .

Sutherland explores Edufa's conflict of identity through the form of Greek drama because of its rootedness in the folklore that serves as the fundamental origin of Western cultural values. His African rootlessness stands in ironic contrast with the sense of roots represented by the Greek drama apropos of the West. The classical form in *Edufa*, with the prologue and choral mode as a representation of social mores, ironically contrast with a return to traditional African values. But the play also incorporates African modes, such as the emphasis on communal values exemplified by Kankam's family ethic. Sutherland's use of Western dramatic forms and African modes amounts to an Afro-Western synthesis which draws upon the strengths of Western and African traditional values. This ideal synthesis is utilized successfully by Senchi, Sutherland's alter ego, in the guise of the Afro-Western intellectual/philosopher/poet. . . . This ideal synthesis, however, is external to a rootless African like Edufa. . . . His conflict as a transitional individual arises because of his own unresolved relationship to African cultural values. By manipulating the social conventions of the Greek cultural tradition, embodied by the chorus, Sutherland touches upon the brutalizing effects of Western influence and the exacting price inflicted upon the weak individual. Hence, on an equally fundamental level, the Afro-Western elements in *Edufa* function as signs of disorienting social transition.

> Linda Lee Talbert. *World Literature Written in English*. 22, 2 (autumn 1983), pp. 183, 188–89

The reputation of Efua Sutherland rests perhaps most firmly on her contribution to African theater. Since the 1950s, she has been involved with the theater as playwright, theater director, and founder of Ghana's foremost and most notable experimental theater group. Her emphasis on artistic dramatic form has been rightly noted. At times this emphasis seems so accomplished that the critic is misled into assuming that Sutherland's plays sacrifice thematic profundity for stylistic innovation. Her theatrical embellishment and inventiveness which comprise an overt use of stage props, the use of the Akan language and an emphasis on audience participation do not exclude authentic meanings for the reader or the audience. Sutherland's thematic concerns in her most popular plays, *Edufa, Foriwa*, and *The Marriage of Anansewa* range from an indictment of unscrupulous materialism to ideas on rural development, the uses of tradition, and an inquiry into the essence of true love. In all these plays, which are directed primarily towards Ghanaians, Sutherland's aims have been consistently didactic: teaching readers and audiences about the moralities of life, and how best to cope with their environment. She uses tradition and popular culture as the foundations of her plays, and through the dramatic process attempts to redefine and refine such traditions and cultures. Her plays reflect a conviction that through the play, the writer can actually monitor as well as influence a nation's cultural direction and taste. . . .

The theme of commitment and giving to others is the main concern in . . . *Foriwa*. In this play the theme is expanded into the conception of group self-help. *Foriwa* tells the story of a village, Kyerefaso, and its backward-looking and complacent people. The traditional ruler of the village, the Queen Mother, is herself progressive, but her ideas are always opposed by the more conservative elements of her council. This trend continues until Labaran, a visitor from the northern part of the country, throws in his lot with the Queen Mother and Foriwa, her daughter. The playwright's motive seems twofold: to show that group effort is the only really worthwhile way of achieving progress, and to demonstrate the true meaning of progress based on the proper use of tradition. She achieves the first by using not one, but three characters to advance the dramatic movement of the play. She makes the form of her play—the use of group protagonists in the persons of the Queen Mother, Labaran, and Foriwa—complement her main thematic concern—the need for group leadership and collective participation in societal development. In order to deal with the second issue of the appropriate approach to tradition and the past, Sutherland adopts and overly realistic mode in which her protagonists as simulated people are used to deliver her sermon. . . .

In *Foriwa*, Sutherland's idea of theater is fully realized. The play's structure is successfully integrated with the dominant themes of rebirth and communal involvement. Most of the play's action takes place in the vicinity of the four-branched god-tree. The tree, a symbol of vitality and change, dominates the town square, and thus indicates the vital role it has to play in the life of the village. The tree also imposes its presence on the language of the play—''the scattering of seeds like forest trees, and the picking of fruit from living branches.'' In addition, this tree of life is presented as related to the question of agricultural self-sufficiency and food for the sustenance of life, one of Labaran's major interests. The play achieves a similar synthesis with its other themes. The idea of the necessity to merge the old with the new, and the need to incorporate African values with Western ones for a rounded development, as well as the need for men and women from various tribes to work together are suggested formally through character representation. The Queen Mother, by virtue of her role as traditional ruler, belongs to the African past. Foriwa and Labaran, on the other hand, represent the new as well as the Western. In addition, Foriwa, a girl educated in Western values, represents emancipated woman. Labaran, being a university graduate, depicts the educated male elite with access to modern Western technology. Labaran is also used to represent the outsider from another ethnic group in the country. These characters who are not typical, but rather exemplary members of the class they represent, are used to demonstrate how the best from the old and the new, from Africa and the West can be utilized to achieve formidable progress. By using three characters of equal importance to carry her message, Sutherland uses the form of collective heroism to depict the idea of group leadership and participation of the community. The Queen Mother, Foriwa, and Labaran all start working for the good of Kyerefaso on an individual basis with little success. They begin to achieve real success when they team up with one another and with the entire village of Kyerefaso.

> Adetokunbo Pearce. In Eldred Durosimi Jones, ed. *Women in African Literature Today* (Trenton, New Jersey: Africa World Press, 1987), pp. 71, 75–77

Efua Sutherland . . . is well known as one of Ghana's most active voices in utilizing traditional modes of theater to promote social change. Her goal has been to acknowledge traditional oral drama performed in villages, stimulate modern dramatic activities, and set up community theaters in rural areas. Moreover, she has been instrumental in fostering indigenous drama in both her concept of theater groups and her plays. Sutherland's plays have been integral to her concept of theater as a means of revitalizing rural life in African communities, and her impact has been felt through her plays for children as well as for adults. Sutherland's best-known works, *Edufa*, *Foriwa*, and *The Marriage of Anansewa*, are all directed toward reconciling the conflict of Western and African cultural values in modern-day African society; the latter two plays also satisfy her objective that written drama serve the community as the oral tradition has done. . . .

Sutherland's play *Foriwa* is a later version of a short, allegorical tale called "New Life in Kyerefaso." Both pieces are based on the transformation of an African folktale used by mothers to warn their daughters away from unknown, handsome men. The folktale tells of a beautiful and proud girl who refuses to marry any young man chosen by her family but decides instead to marry a handsome stranger. Whether the man turns into a python, a spirit, or a skull, the moral taught is that young women who disobey their families and do not listen to the wisdom of their elders will eventually meet disaster. This folktale has been reworked by numerous West African writers, yet Sutherland is unique in that the moral of the folktale in *Foriwa* is a positive one. The choice of a stranger brings "new life" to the town of Kyerefaso rather than devastation, altering the meaning of the old tale. In this way Sutherland expands the message of the folktale to illustrate a different dilemma: how to build a nation out of the different ethnic groups in Ghana. . . .

In *Foriwa*, as in *The Marriage of Anansewa*, what is of real value is not necessarily material. The grandmother gives Anansewa advice in the form of a riddle, an aspect of the oral tradition. Moreover, her values come from the traditional culture that has been distorted, in the present generation, by Western materialistic

values, illustrated by the trickery of her son, Ananse. So when the Queen Mother asks Foriwa why she wants to refuse the present suitor, a man who "has salvaged his life from this decrepitude" by making a great success of his life materially, Foriwa answers that she will not join her life with a man who is interested merely in personal gain. She shudders at the kind of society he represents by ameliorating his own life at the expense of the community. She responds instead by approaching the subject of the town's deterioration and the Queen Mother's fights with the elders who care more for the words of the traditions than for what those words convey. . . .

In her three published plays for adults, Sutherland's aim has been to focus on the kinds of values that are being passed on the children: What will become of traditional culture, weakened by colonial domination, if the present generation does not continue their oral traditions and reform them to fit modern Ghanaian society? *Foriwa* works toward the resolution of these cultural conflicts by utilizing orature and literature as vehicles for the revitalization of rural communities. Sutherland's emphasis on women's role in "minding the culture" and bringing new life into old traditions, mirrors her own concern for and active participation in strengthening the bonds between the African past and future generations. Her performances and productions, her village education for children, and her plays themselves illustrate a playwright tied not only to the traditions and customs of the African continuum but secure in her place as an African woman passing on the values of her foremothers to the children.

> Gay Wilentz. *Research of African Literatures*. 19, 2 (summer 1988), pp. 182–85, 194

An autobiographical strain is discernible in *Foriwa* if one considers the Queen Mother as an alter ego for Sutherland, while Foriwa might represent Sutherland's eldest daughter, Esi Sutherland-Addy, who has followed in her mother's footsteps somewhat by working in the Institute of African Studies, and by being recently chosen by the Jerry Rawlings government to help in nation building. The mother-daughter bonding is well developed in *Foriwa* with its emphasis on female and communal solidarity. The Queen Mother and Foriwa are independent and dynamic, traits that benefit the society. The play was first performed in the Akan language in 1962 and comments fearlessly on the five years of little progress after Ghanaian independence in 1957. The play accentuates the women's voice to show what women can do to contribute to national development.

"Kyerefaso has long been asleep," the audience is told by Labaran, a new arrival in the country. (Kyerefaso represents Ghana in the play.) The outsider's interest and involvement reflect Ghana's ideological contacts, especially with African-Americans. (Labaran could represent Sutherland's husband). In the play, Kyerefaso needs a prince and a princess (Labaran and Foriwa) to wake it up. The foundation on which they are to build has already been laid by their predecessors. In the play, Sutherland proposes that all the people—men and women, old and young, educated and illiterate, traditionally oriented and technologically minded, indigene and stranger—should be involved in community development. This play appeals for national unity, discarding gender, ethnic, and ideological differences.

To convey the idea of the social malaise, images of decadence proliferate. There is the foundation of a building that has not been completed; the ''dilapidated royal house'' a symbol of the condition of the country; the ''camp'' with its temporary nature; the ''depressed condition'' of the bookstore, which should help to disseminate knowledge; and vultures, those ''birds of death.'' With Kyerefaso/Ghana in this terrible state, the sensitive Queen Mother calls for rethinking and for renewed commitment on the part of the people. The Queen Mother's unprecedented request for a rehearsal of the festival is not fortuitous. She uses the occasion to express herself before the entire population, thus giving them a new sense of direction. Her speech is a challenge to the people: the chauvinists such as Sintim; the idlers, including the draughts players; and the uncommitted.

Foriwa rejects the marriage proposal of the ''fly,'' Mr. Anipare, and accepts Labaran, the new man. This acceptance is indicative of the desired fusion of different parts of Ghana—Hausa and Akan, North and South—for the building of the nation. Some of Foriwa's friends' marriages have failed, a sign of the fragmentation of the society, but Foriwa's marriage will (symbolically) cement and improve relationships needed for growth.

*The Magic of Dreams*, an old book in the local bookstore, shows the dreams the Queen Mother and her supporters have for transforming their world. Foriwa, the symbol of the new woman, joins her mother; so also does Labaran, the man of the future with his technology, tape-recording present events as a catalyst for the future. Akan rather than English is spoken because the Scholar's Union finds English difficult, and one's own language should serve as the basis for scholarship. The Head Priest throws white powder in a ritual to cleanse the village. Thereafter the quarrelsome Sintim undergoes a change and provides the lamb that will be sacrificed to usher in a new era.

The radical mother and daughter thus unite on the occasion of the festival to effect a revival. Sutherland revises the source of the play, a folktale about a fussy girl who ends up with a horror for a husband. Foriwa, the so-called choosy bride, chooses propitiously by accepting Labaran, with whom she can build a home on a solid foundation. Foriwa, exquisitely dressed like a butterfly, represents social cross-pollination. She dances into the future, following in her mother's footsteps. The punctuation of the play with songs shows that Sutherland believes in the efficacy of the oral tradition.

The tragedy *Edufa* dramatizes the tensions in a sexist society in which women are assigned subservient roles. The audience sees the actions of Abena, Edufa's sister; Seguwa, a female member of Edufa's household; the chorus of women singing Edufa's praise; and, most important, Ampoma, Edufa's wife, who works herself to death so that Edufa might have life more abundantly. Sutherland depicts gender inequalities in a sexist Ghanaian society where women serve men for a pittance.

Chikwenye Okonjo Ogunyemi. In Bernth Lindfors, and Reinhard Sander, eds. *Dictionary of Literary Biography, Volume 117: Twentieth-Century Caribbean and Black African Writers* (Detroit: Gale Research, 1992), pp. 284–90

BIBLIOGRAPHY

*Edufa*, 1967; *Foriwa*, 1967; *Vulture! Vulture!!*, 1968; *Anansegoro: Story-telling Drama in Ghana*, 1975; *The Marriage of Anansewa*, 1975; *The Voice in the Forest*, 1983

# T

## TABAN LO LIYONG (1939–)
### Uganda

Taban lo Liyong is an East African writer and critic who genuflects before no idols—European, Nigerian, or local—and who proves that he is right to exercise the prerogatives of genius. With this slim book of essays [*The Last Word*] he introduces himself as a powerful voice, a spectacular and audacious intelligence.

Finely and broadly educated but no pedant, [Taban] lo Liyong does not wear his learning on his sleeve. Instead, it is most visible where one is accustomed to its absence: at the business end of a set of brass knuckles. He writes with passion and a sense of humor, with a merciless contempt for cant and the wit and will to be devastating. His work is contentious, irreverent, and exciting. He writes on what interests him—and that, often, is what angers him: American arrogance, African self-indulgence, intellectual slackness, pettiness. He writes his own version of English, and, in a sentence of concentrated irony, has advised compatriots seeking a viable medium that "a domesticated East African English should be an obedient servant.". . .

He has no respect for the view that African writers should not be judged on the same scale as Homer and Shakespeare. He damns, equally, self-indulgent evaluations by Africans and the flattery of Africans by Europeans who may want to be encouraging but are in effect patronizing. He wants an African literature—above all an East African literature—which will move nobody to pat it on the head and say, "You're really very nice." In his view of writing, it is good *that* it's African (and he exhorts African schools to give encouragement of writing a high priority), but it's never good *because* it's African.

Basil Busacca. *Africa Report*. 15, 8 (November 1970), p. 34

It is as hard to write about Taban lo Liyong as it is to write about Amos Tutuola, for these two writers are Africa's greatest eccentrics. If, in Taban's phrase, the Yoruba writer is the true son of Zinjanthropus, then he himself is his delinquent nephew. Faced with either case, literary criticism is not sure where to start; and Taban's career . . . is deliberately designed to ensure that no critic ever will finally get at the truth about him. What Taban is or represents, what he wants to be or appears to be—these are as hard as deciding . . . into which pigeonhole his work should be squeezed. Teacher, researcher, marathon walker, polymath, eater of library books (and shelves), born cynic, utopian, bibliographer extraordinary, reformer, journalist, essayist, professional devil's advocate, catalyst, midwife, prophet, dabbler in riddles, poet, pop philosopher, brother to Ocol (secret lover of Lawino), Voltaire to [Okot p'Bitek's] Frederick the Great, Whitmanesque gadfly, modernist, traditionalist, sociologist, individualist, iconoclast, sententious elder of thirty-six. Which of all these is he, at heart? In which role would he like to be remembered? Chris Wanjala has rightly noted that "his works are full of the proud and grateful consciousness that he is a synthetic being," and perhaps this is as good a description as one could find. But whatever the answer, there is no doubt that

Taban is the most chameleonlike figure in East Africa today. But of course all the critics say this, and it would be a relief simply to leave it there and get on with Ngugi [wa Thiong'o] or [Leonard] Kibera. Yet Taban's impact on the modern scene has been too great for so brief a dismissal: it won't do simply to label him as some weirdly synthetic chameleon. . . .

Like a prophet emerging from the desert, Taban returned home [from the United States] determined to do all in his power—by cajolery, coercion, provocation, and intellectual freedom-fighting—to transform East Africa and end its literary drought. After dipping his head deep into many wells of modern thought, he would, furthermore, return with no fixed position visible to readers, colleagues, or critics. His choice of a confessional strain, a stream-of-conscious-tell-it-all mode suggesting an honest mind's encounter with a myriad [of] viewpoints, looks like a quirk of temperament; but it was also a preferred way of releasing the maximum latent energy in the home scene and of placing before his community the widest possible range of ideas on which planning for the future might be based. Hence the persistent and deliberate contradictions; hence the love of paradox and Swiftian lists. Certainly East Africa's current position as the matrix of the continent's fiercest and most creative debates can be ascribed in generous measure to Taban's influence. His arrival from Iowa changed the local scene like magic. The words began to pour, essays, letters, poems, longer poems. Then books. First *The Last Word*, perversely titled because it was his first word (in book form) on African problems. Then came *Fixions [& Other Stories]*, comprising work arising from research into oral tradition; *Eating Chiefs*, more work in oral literature; then *Frantz Fanon's Uneven Ribs*, a book of verse; and most recently, still more verse, *Another Nigger Dead*, and a potpourri, *Thirteen Offensives against Our Enemies*.

Initial response to Taban's writing mixed astonishment with disbelief. Astonishment at the jesting freshness of it all, disbelief at the violence of Taban's attacks on a herd of sacred cows including Négritude. There was a problem of appropriate response to writing whose viewpoint always shifted, never settling long enough to be pinned down or explained. The show kept moving at speed, and masks worn during the early period were thrown from the caravans as the circus headed up the road to a new pitch. A show over, what it had offered had to take its chance, either to live or die. The new reality, the current show, mattered most. Audience and disciples, gathering in droves, faced an impossible task trying to keep up and understand.

What emerges from behind the masks, and from writing that runs simultaneously in a dozen different directions, is a mind of Olympian independence, which refuses to be reduced to a formula, together with a comic attitude that cries plague on everyone's house, including the writer's own which he is just about to burn down. In the guessing game Taban's work sparked, it was fashionable to blame it all on [Friedrich] Nietzsche, especially when an adulatory Goethe Institute lecture by the author coincided with published work revealing dream visions of a supermodern Africa, a new economic and military giant. But it is not in Taban's nature to be the prisoner of one influence. A fuller picture emerges from seeing him partly as a gifted (and highly assimilative) child of Nietzsche, and partly as a child of an ancient tradition of world satire. The lineage is familiar enough. Beginning with Menippus, it comes down through [Francois] Rabelais, [John] Skelton, [Miguel] Cervantes, [Samuel] Butler, [Jonathan] Swift, [Alexander] Pope, [Laurence] Sterne . . . Voltaire, and [Thomas] Carlyle. Writers in this tradition often serve up satire in a narrative framework, despise—or appear to despise—formal principles, rejoice in rollicking wit, cock a snook at orthodox style, love exaggeration, delight in the grotesque and caricature, and work from values very hard to fix. It is the mad world of Jolly Rutterkin, Martinus Scriblerus, Gulliver, Tristram and Uncle Toby, Candide, and Professor Teufelsdrockh, a world where anything goes, or seems to go, except orthodoxy and stuffy conventionality.

> Adrian Roscoe. *Uhuru's Fire: African Literature East to South* (Cambridge: Cambridge University Press, 1977), pp. 114–16

Taban lo Liyong . . . in his poem "bless the African coups" blesses (ironically) the African coups, for according to him, "tragedy now means a thing." But it is with regard to tragedy as a physical and negative experience that it means something to the Africans. . . . To the extent that African coups bring about suffering and death and suppression of the "best ideas," they constitute a tragedy; but they fail to attain the overall status of tragedy because they do not effect spiritual regeneration or rebirth, and that knowledge and new awareness gained through experience.

For tragedy is like the fire that "burns the phoenix," from which it will emerge renewed; and is like the stage on which Proteus changes from shape to shape for more effective self-preservation. Tragedy is also like the process of reincarnation or metempsychosis in Hindu philosophy, whereby at death the soul leaves the body and finds a new and higher level of existence elsewhere; and is like the death of Jesus Christ which resulted in his resurrection and heavenly glorification. After establishing these parallels, [Taban lo] Liyong fervently prays that our own tragedy (the coups) may "also save us," teach us "that we are not the Lords of this world," make us "know our place in this world," teach us "final humility," open for us "the door by mistakes," and grant us "the tragic character's last self awareness."

> R.N. Egudu. *Modern African Poetry and the African Predicament* (New York: Barnes and Noble, 1978), pp. 95–96

The writings of Taban lo Liyong raise in an acute form the question of what poetry is. If poetry were solely lyrical, concerned with the songlike expression of emotions, then Taban would not be a poet, for his verse is made of gnomic philosophical utterances, rhetorical shouts, and repetitive lists. Where the Cameroonian poet Mbelle Sonne Dipoko will alter, and in particular condense, his prose utterances before presenting them as verse, Taban, who writes highly rhythmical prose, sometimes seems merely to divide it into lines or strophes and call it poetry. Where the Ghanaian poet Atukwei Okai seems aware of the danger of endlessly repeating a refrain or a structural formula of words in a rhetorical poem, Taban's tolerance of repetition sometimes knows no bounds.

Like Mazisi Kunene, Taban is a philosophical poet, prepared to make poetry directly out of belief. But his combination of substance (largely from Friedrich Nietzsche) and form (reminiscent of Heraclitean fragments, [William] Blake's gnomic sentences,

Wyndham Lewis's "blasts," and, indeed, Nietzsche's own aphoristic style in *Human, All-Too-Human* and *Thus Spake Zarathustra*) is unique. His advocacy of Nietzsche's concepts of progress through the fusion of opposing tendencies (Taban's "syntheism"), the nature of frenzied creative energy, the elite Übermensch or Superman, and the dangers of rationalism (including orderly form) have made him an outsider to many literary circles. He is a person admired for his intellect and warmth of personality, but often deeply suspect because of his alien and uncongenial ideas. African poets in English are often expected to develop political ideas within a fairly narrow band of liberal or left-wing orthodoxy, whereas Taban conforms to no expectations, not even his own.

The cult of the Superman has made him quite shameless in talking about himself and his family in both prose and verse. He examines the meaning of his father's life and death, castigates his wife for infidelity, laments his loss of custody of his two sons, and discusses his own personal and literary ambitions. If the Freudian notion of creativity being the attempt to sublimate neurosis or the Jungian notion of it as an anodyne for inner distress and tension have any plausibility, it is in the work of people like Taban. And as an outstandingly intelligent and introspective person, he is aware of this. *Meditations [of Taban lo Liyong]* is "Dedicated to people with strong complexes of one kind or another"; and in it he justifies neurosis because it "lifts people up to another level, beyond society, *ahead* of society." He notes that "Somewhere in my make up, I share epicycles with the mad" and "It is madness of a sort." But it is not only in madness that he feels an affinity with Nietzsche; he also suggests that "Without syphilis, without malignant derangement, can a man ever amount to anything?" and announces that, in this sense, "Ladies and gentlemen, I have syphilis."

The short-breathed forms adopted by Taban allow him to try out propositions, even the most outrageous and shocking, to see where they lead. Because his senses of fact and of fiction are so intermingled, he sees no inconsistency between, for instance, advocating physical suicide, advocating metaphorical suicide by the cessation of writing, or advocating fortitude and resistance to depression. Each is a possibility, each an idea worth entertaining. As a result, when he seriously advocates practical policies (as, for instance, in *Thirteen Offensives against Our Enemies*) he is likely to be treated as a jester, prankster, impossible idealist, or self-appointed irritant rather than as an imaginative thinker of the unconventional and even the unthinkable.

> K.L. Goodwin. *Understanding African Poetry* (London: Heinemann, 1982), pp. 78–79

Taban lo Liyong is a unique figure in East African literature both in his thought and work. A highly individualistic poet, critic, short-story and folk literature writer, he draws his material from both traditional and modern life. The many facets of his character and work leave his critics and reviewers hiding behind such epithets as "stimulating," "prolific," and "controversial." However, his short stories fail to provoke much reaction and are all too often passed over as trivia in comparison with the longer, philosophical poems.

The short stories in Taban's two volumes, *Fixions* and *The Uniformed Man*, fall into three classes. There are the modern stories such as "A Traveller's Tale" and traditional tales like "Ododo pa Apwoyo Gin ki Lyech." Many of the stories, though, overlap into a third category in which a traditional story is brought up to date or a modern tale is told in the manner of a *lucak wer*, the traditional oral artist.

    Elizabeth Knight. In Eldred Durosimi Jones, ed. *African Literature Today*. 12 (1982), p. 104

There is no apparent consistency in the form of Taban's books. *Another Nigger Dead* is supposed to be a book of poems, but the last item, ''Batsiary in Sanigraland,'' is a dissertation which could have fitted into *The Last Word*. *Fixions* is a book of short stories but most of the items in it are fables, which would have been in place in *Eating Chiefs*, a collection of folktales. *Thirteen Offensives against Our Enemies* is supposedly a program for development but contains some poems. *The Last Word* is meant to be literary criticism but contains autobiography. It is not that Taban cannot be a good critic. He shows profound insight into Ngugi [wa Thiong'o] when he says, before Ngugi wrote *Petals of Blood*, ''This is a man who thinks (or used to think) in terms of 'Moses,' in terms of universalism, in terms of ideals: categorical imperatives. Obviously the whole Mau Mau war made him look at the Kikuyus as the oppressed children of Israel . . . When the Messianic Path was lost, James also got lost. . . . But that side of Ngugi which he had donated to the messiah to fulfill still yearned for actualization.''

What Taban is doing is to deliberately break what he calls ''categorical imperatives,'' linking together the apparently irreconcilable (for example, the American one-liner, Greek philosophy, television) because they unite in his consciousness. By breaking forms, Taban upsets our expectations. *Ballads of Underdevelopment* has in its table of contents not the conventional titles or first lines but several lines, even the complete poems we find in the text. In contrast, *Meditations in Limbo* has no table of contents. It is the uniform, the outward structure stifling the inner content, that Taban is seeking to smash: the Platonic vision of humanity and art is the enemy. For Plato, only content is fluid, while form is permanent; for Taban, form is changeable. For Plato, the good life is an escape from the world of the body; for Taban, the world is patently body, hence the numerous descriptions of his sexual escapades with ''real'' people.

*Meditations in Limbo* is Taban's most integrated work because it has the consistency of inconsistency. . . . Taban says, ''In a sense, this is a novel.'' The antinovel as novel. The Taban ''author'' goes through many changes, sometimes becoming an all-seeing, timeless self, at other times earthbound; sometimes a critic, at other times a defendant. There is a shaping tension in this work: the changes are bounced off his father's expectations of him (tribal, success through monolithic education) and Plato's world-view (only content is fluid while form is permanent). Plato too is a character, just like Ngugi. . . .

*The Uniformed Man*, published shortly after, is an epilogue to the antinovel, equally successful, with Taban as author, hyperactive student, character, critic, and teller of folktales, bouncing off his father and Plato. Taban uses different forms and mixes forms. ''The Education of Taban lo Liyong'' is a counterpoint in a class of literature between the monovisioned professor and the multifarious, complex consciousness of the student, yoking disparate elements together. ''Project X'' . . . is a brief, do-it-yourself story, like something by Julio Cortázar of Argentina. The story that follows, ''Asu the Great,'' is like a folktale, interrupted by philosophic one-line questions of historic and mythic figures, followed by an animal fable in which Shark talks to Monkey, the twist being that the shark has postgraduate degrees. Genres are deliberately mixed—*deus ex machinas* swoop in at the author's will, creating what Paul Holz calls metafiction. In ''A Prescription for Idleness,'' there is a folktale within a folktale. The book ends with a chapter . . . containing a critique of Plato and his father, concluding with an episode of graphic, mindless violence whose meaning we must figure out, if there is one.

    Peter Nazareth. In G.D. Killam, ed. *The Writing of East and Central Africa* (London: Heinemann, 1984), pp. 171–73

Taban lo Liyong is an exciting African avant-garde writer who refuses to be tied to any traditional literary models. Although he acknowledges his indebtedness to both [Amos] Tutuola and African oral literature from which he claims he draws inspiration, his attitude toward these sources is not slavish but creative. Basil Busacca aptly identifies the freedom of his creative spirit when he describes [Taban lo Liyong] as a writer who ''genuflects before no idols—European, Nigerian or local—and who proves that he is right to exercise the prerogative of genius.'' Like most avant-garde artists, [Taban lo Liyong] proceeds in his writing from the premise that literary models existing before him are no longer adequate to express the reality of his time. An artist who accepts without question existing artistic traditions is not likely to create anything new. . . .

Among African writers Taban lo Liyong is perhaps the one who best understands the challenge of ''a living literature.'' He perpetually experiments by synthesizing old and new methods with the hope of creating a style that is uniquely suited to his themes. In a story called ''Sages and Wages,'' for example, there is a sentence with an unusual syntax covering sixteen lines. We may note here that this kind of experiment with syntax has been equalled and surpassed by the American writer, Donald Barthelme, whose story ''Sentence'' is a one-sentence story covering eight pages. What is important, however, is that, given [Taban's] independent approach to writing and his taste for avant-garde experimentation, it is only to be expected that he would explore the exciting artistic possibilities of the mode of the absurd. . . .

The title story in Taban lo Liyong's collection *Fixions* . . . paints a picture wherein a president of an African country receives in his secret chambers an envoy of a foreign nation in the middle of the night. This president had requested aid to build a road and a bridge to his home. The envoy now comes to report that the money for the project has arrived. The president concludes arrangements for the money to be diverted into his personal bank account. He is overjoyed for, as he says, ''It will earn me quite a bit of interest.'' The envoy then proceeds in a studied fashion to inquire about the state of the president's national security. Thereafter the envoy discloses that a coup d'état is secretly being hatched by the leader of the opposition in collaboration with the deputy president and that the plotters aim to kill the president. Before departing, the envoy succeeds in putting the president in a state of seething rage. The story ends as the president is about to unleash a bloodthirsty, insane revenge on the supposed plotters.

All along the story strongly suggests that nobody is actually plotting a coup. Instead the calculated lie is told with the aim of destabilizing the African country. Furthermore, the reader is aware that the malicious envoy succeeds only because he is not dealing with an African leader of worth but with this greedy fool of a president, who appears to be even more gullible, and more naive than a child. This president is indeed no better than an animated cartoon being manipulated according to the wishes of the foreign envoy, his master. When a person—the more so a president—becomes a mere puppet, his life loses meaning. It becomes absurd. This story is an obvious satire on African heads of state. Furthermore, the situation which makes the reign of such ignorant, unpatriotic characters possible is exposed for its absurdity.

> F. Odun Balogun. *African Studies Review.* 27, 1 (March 1984), pp. 46–47, 50

[Taban lo Liyong] perceives black consciousness as part of the themes worth exploring in his poetry. Although his views have baffled numerous critics, he possesses that distinguishing mark of commitment required to create relevant works. He feels that English should be tamed and naturalized "so that it echoes local sentiments and figures of speech." The emergent synthesis does not, however, appear palatable, and he is given an original nomenclature as the creator of "Tabanic genre" that has no predecessor and [is] unlikely to possess a successor due to the frequency of its highly poetic variations. . . .

It appears that Taban poses a problem to critics, but that does not mean that he wraps his poetry in miscellaneous garbs of nonsense. It is, rather, a difficulty generated by an avidity for style due to the kind of books he read as a student. The style notwithstanding, his poetry gives the impression of a subject matter polished with digested ideas. One of these ideas is black consciousness, which indicates his concern with the nature of the black man in the world. . . .

The rousing call in this poetry is that the theme of black consciousness should be made substantial and practical. The black man must eliminate mouthing irrelevant slogans and assert his presence in world affairs. This is why the poet's preoccupation is the analysis of the collective experience of all black peoples. It appears that the message which this theme wishes to make persuasive to the reader is that the black man must and should solve his problems without waiting for international racial structures to be dismantled by liberating members of the dominating races.

> Ezenwa-Ohaeto. *Presence Africaine.* 140 (1986), pp. 12, 16

The seven stories in *The Uniformed Man* are a coordinated study in the cause and nature of violence as a pervasive reality of human existence. There is a deliberate plan in which our knowledge about the cause and nature of violence is gradually deepened by each successive story either by showing an increasingly intensified level of violence through a correspondingly intensified symbolism, or by demonstrating the pervasiveness of violence through an expanding variety of human participation. Also, each story is in itself a complete artistic unit that reveals three aspects of violence, namely, the personal, the societal, and the universal. . . .

It is obvious from the stories in this cycle that Taban lo Liyong has no illusions about human nature. Man, he correctly observes, "is not axiomatically human" and one cannot but agree with him when he says, "Pity, humanism, reverence for human life are not inherent in man: these are acquired characteristics." Human acts of gratuitous violence, the violence induced by selfishness, and the role of society in promoting robotism through mental enslavement—all of which are shown in this story cycle—reflect [Taban's]

attempt to make us realize how much we have failed to transform ourselves from the "animal man" to the humane man. This is not pessimism but realism. If strong emphasis is laid throughout this cycle on the negative role of social institutions such as education, marriage, religion, and the army in promoting mental enslavement, robotism, and violence, we should not be misled into thinking that [Taban] is advocating nihilist individualism and anarchy. Clearly, [Taban's] objective is to alert us to the imperfections and negative characteristics of the institutions we operate so that we can better be able to organize a more humane, less violent society. This is a timely warning for Africa, his immediate audience, where violence has become a common feature, thanks to the aberrations of some of its leaders and the inhumanity of apartheid. It is similarly a timely warning for the world at large engulfed as it is in daily regional violence, any of which, unfortunately, might develop someday into the holocaust of a Third World War in spite of the periodic rapprochement of the superpowers (which are short-lived in any case) and in spite of, or perhaps because of, the even less frequent redrawing of the political map of the world.

> F. Odun Balogun. *Tradition and Modernity in the African Short Story: An Introduction to a Literature in Search of Critics* (New York: Greenwood Press, 1991), pp. 150–51, 158–59

*Another Last Word* is profound, provocative, humorous, sarcastic, relaxed, anti-ideological, anticolonial, anti-Négritude, antistereotype, antifailure, the work of a gadfly. Only Taban could begin a book, "Good wine matures with age. So do good essays like these ones." Only Taban could say, "There was brooding James Ngugi, the committed Christian, who has now diversified into committed Christian Socialism. There was the publicly extroverted Okot p'Bitek, who, in private, was rather shy. And there was me; and this book is me." Yes, it is Taban, and it provides evidence that my interpretation . . . was right. I said that Taban is a transitional figure; Taban says, "There is something called transition." He adds that there were a "variety of styles" in his early books and wonders whether readers found that out. I did.

So, does the new book only confirm what I knew? Yes and no. There is a center to the work: "I regard this book as an essay in establishing a base for all our endeavors." This is a complex endeavor; there are many traps, one of which is mythifying other writers, particularly Ngugi [wa Thiong'o], whose socialism he finds dangerous because it is attractive to East African intellectuals who do not want to think. He is referring to Ngugi when he concludes, "Kuku is my tribe. Others have had their homecoming in Limuru. I had mine in Kajokaji." "Most of us entertain the false notion that our country needs us," Taban writes. "Some of us are needed, that's true. Some of us are also feared and hated. For others of us nobody really cares. The sooner we disabused ourselves of the sense of our self-importance, the better. Where your path is blocked at home, open up another elsewhere and fulfill yourself. Otherwise you might drink your talents to death, develop ulcers and cancer and neurosis." He then charges: "When the coups came through the barrels of the guns, we danced like little children for a day and cried thereafter. African so-called intellectual servants have been the blindest creatures among their peers in the world." A price must be paid for the blindness: exile, for "what we could not see at home because it was too immediate we might have the hindsight created by distance to put it in the proper perspective. And design better alternatives for the future." *Another Last Word* contains old steps, but the dance is new.

Peter Nazareth. *World Literature Today.* 65, 2 (Spring 1991), pp. 354–55

[With *The Cows of Shambat*] Taban Lo Liyong remains an iconoclast, only a little more measured than before. His latest collection threads together public and private experiences that show a poet at once enraged and cynical about the mistreatment of Africa by the developed West and its institutions and at the same time relishing his personal experiences as he turns fifty.

The poet begins with the fantastical and symbolic in the title poem "The Cows of Shambat." In the section titled "Underdevelopment in Africa" Lo Liyong condemns colonialism and the bad influence of the West on Africans. In the rather prosaic yet interesting "Open Letter to a Distant Friend" the poet in a lighthearted but highly critical style condemns the West for attempting to impose family planning on Africans. He also condemns both the World Bank for its relations with Africa and Canada for linking aid to the "awakening women" of Africa. He exposes the contradiction and hypocrisy of Westerners in belonging to the Green Party, whose members advocate the natural yet do not want children.

As the poet condemns the West, he creates a persona who stands for justice, as in "The Case of Rwachkaro." He is critical of what he considers to be false accusations leveled against the Cuban hero of the Angolan war, General Ochoa, by the Castro government. The poet professes admiration for Muammar al-Qaddafi. He rails against oppression and victimization in such poems as "See Me Lakayana—Again." The poet remains human, with his own individual experiences ranging from his lament of being "born / After the main event," to his suffering in the Sudanese civil war in Juba, to his love life in "Master of Hearts." Both "The Hathors Foretell Rwachkaro's Fate Through His Passion" and "Master of Hearts" tell the fate of the artist such as the poet.

The collection is highly indebted to Lo Liyong's knowledge of traditional African folklore. Women used to die when delivering their babies "Till one day Dog felt pity on us / And coached a pregnant woman to squat like her." The poet uses the legend of the Marakwet elders of Kenya, who in times of famine committed suicide so as to bequeath "scarce resources to their children.". . .

Time and again, the poet is lighthearted and humorous as he condemns what threatens his people, as in "Come, Sit with Me My Love in Videoland" and "An Open Letter to a Distant Friend." There are allusions to the Bible, literature, and history. References to Aristotle, Plato, Archimedes, Odysseus, Noah, and Paul Gauguin illustrate the wide field of the poet's imagination. There is topicality in subtle references to the civil war in Sudan and other contemporary issues.

I find "An Open Letter to a Distant Friend," the Rwachkaro poems, and "Circumspect Penelope Regards Ragged Odysseus" most appealing. A poem like "Tongue-Twister" is too long without any redeeming features. "Ka" is too obvious in its teaching. Generally the poet's lexicon is close to prose and is not sufficiently imagistic. His language may be defended as attempting to reflect African orature, but there is too much of the speaking voice and no mediation with the poetic in images. Still, these are minor shortcomings in an interesting collection. In *The Cows of*

*Shambat* Taban Lo Liyong speaks with a more mature and moderate voice than in his other poetry collections.

Tanure Ojaide. *World Literature Today.* 68, 3 (Summer 1994), p. 625.

A postmodern nomad, the Ugandan-born [Taban Lo Liyong] has traveled so extensively that one can barely keep count of his numerous abodes: China, England, Ghana, Japan, Papua New Guinea, the Philippines, Singapore, South Africa, and the United States, among others. These 223 "courting songs" for the Japanese lady with whom he fell in love have made memorable his two-month intense sojourn in Japan. *Words That Melt a Mountain* carries the poet's experience in a specific place (Japan) and time (mainly January and February 1994). There is reference to the Tokyo Olympic Games of 1964. The poet who feels lonely in a new cultural environment seeks social intercourse that he nurtures into sexual intercourse.

So passionate and excited are his feelings for his Japanese lady friend, called Nihokosan, that the black African poet already espouses mixed blood. Liyong's inaugural lecture in South Africa calls for the expansion of African studies, an idea that corresponds to his poetic theme of desiring mulatto children. The series of poems are for and about the poet's lover, to "melt" her into intimate relationship. Each poem is a vignette, with occasional digressions about past loves, travels, family, and ancestry to put the main story in perspective. The portrait of Nihokosan shows her to be small, young, sweet, fresh, and with eyes and face frequently praised for their unique beauty. Compared to her, the male poet is older and considerably more experienced, with several earlier mistresses and a wife.

The poet unabashedly exposes himself as an adulterer and a flirt. Could a married African woman poet have the nerve to write about her affairs with men? None has done so yet. Many feminists might quarrel with the poet for making Nihokosan a sexual commodity and for such lines as "It is man's happiness when he's loved by two [women]" and "Iteso women insist on being beaten, / to show that their husbands love them." However, one of the many strengths of *Words That Melt a Mountain* is the poet's frankness. Love, with its physical overtones in the *carpe diem* tradition, makes him and his beloved behave like kids. The poet is metaphysical and Donne-like in poem 110. As is common in such verse, the lady is placed on a lofty pedestal through exaggerated metaphors and images. The poet is never obscene but instead is subtle and indirect, even when he uses such erotic images as "arrow," "barb," and "flower opening out." The references to fruit are very sensuous.

Though love is central to the poems here, the poet also touches on such subjects as computers and television (modern technology), religion, philosophy, feminism/freedom, and Western art, literature, and music. Believing that art should "clarify," Liyong writes in a very simple yet moving style. He uses a speaking voice, sometimes addressing the lady he loves and at other times addressing the reader, thereby creating a lively rhetorical style that engages the reader. Occasionally, poems are internal monologues, as the love-struck poet wonders what to do. The language is rich in wordplay, puns, and humor, as the poet "dribbles" his woman friend: "I was a tea-totaller when I came to Japan / having totalled tea since 1981." Elsewhere, Japan "yens for yen." He also puns with "lie" and talks of "West-eastian."

*Words That Melt a Mountain* is a major contribution to modern African poetry in two main respects. First, in these poems simplicity is a strength, as the poet imbues his language with an array of metaphors, allusions, and images which reflect his passionate love. The verse is fluid and belies the public mistrust of modern African poetry as academic, dry, and rigid. Second, love poetry, is very rare in modern Africa, and this collection by a mature, philosophical lover highlights this area of human experience, which tends to be hidden. Retaining many of the iconoclastic features of his earlier poetry and opening new technical and thematic frontiers, *Words That Melt a Mountain* is a moving testimony of one individual's emotional turmoil and the process of seeking love in a culturally alien society. It is a work that will satisfy many who love poetry.

> Tanure Ojaide. *World Literature Today.* 71, 3 (Summer 1997), pp. 641–42.

BIBLIOGRAPHY

*Fixions & Other Stories*, 1969; *The Last Word*, 1969; *Eating Chiefs*, 1970; *Meditations in Limbo*, 1970; *Frantz Fanon's Uneven Ribs*, 1971; *The Uniformed Man*, 1971; *Another Nigger Dead*, 1972; *Thirteen Offensives against Our Enemies*, 1973; *Ballads of Underdevelopment*, 1976; *Meditations of Taban lo Liyong*, 1978; *Another Last Word*, 1990; *Culture is Rutan*, 1991; *The Cows of Shambat: Sudanese Poems*, 1992; *Words That Melt a Mountain*, 1996; *Carrying Knowledge Up a Palm Tree*, 1997; *Homage to Onyame: An African God*, 1997

# TATI-LOUTARD, Jean-Baptiste (1938–)

Congo

[Jean-Baptiste] Tati-Loutard's *Anthologie de la littérature congolaise d'expression française* is a well-conceived, well-constructed book of modern Congolese writing. Tati-Loutard is quite aware that other, more intensive, and more specialized anthologies will be needed as the literary activity of the Congo develops and expands, but he wisely sees that the present need is for the kind of book he has produced. His book introduces the reader to the lives and the thought and style of eighteen writers of the past quarter-century who have managed to have some of their work published. Most of the items included (except for a few tales and some short poems) are excerpts and can therefore only partially suggest their authors' literary virtues. Tati-Loutard's introductory comments for each writer cited, however, do much to overcome this limitation and help the reader to know whether he should look for the total work from which the excerpt has been made.

> David K. Bruner. *World Literature Today.* 52, 1 (Winter 1978), p. 162

Throughout nearly a dozen novels, Tati-Loutard illustrates with simplicity the fragility of man, but also his strength when faced with death. Each character has the privilege of escaping the present and being able to look at his life "du dehors." Thus emerge the memories, the joys, the deceptions . . . all that one calls a past, and

which is nothing other than the path that one should have traveled to know how to live the present. For each person, it is a parenthesis which opens; and when it closes, one is no longer quite the same, without anything really being different in appearance in the meantime.

It is the theme of missed meetings which is most prominent in several novels. In *La Rendez-vous de la retraite*, Kotodi, crazy about his Peugeot 204, meets death on the road while getting ready to pick up his friend at the station. It is not only his friend that he missed, but also "les joies d'une retraite qu'il avait longtemps et soigneusement preparée" [the joys of retirement that he had meticulously planned for a long time]. A missed meeting, exactly like Alphonsine's, who at twenty-seven years had known nothing but pain and weariness. [One] Sunday, a car ride with a foreign diplomat made her see that life can be something other than the moments of terror spent with her brutal and unfaithful husband. But even when she is going to take advantage of this opportunity that she knows is unique, Alphonsine sees this parenthesis of her life close. In "le refuge," Matembélé, former political person-in-charge destroyed by prison, does not find his wife on his return home: after four years of solitude, she had asked for a divorce. . . .

Why don't these paths cross, why do these routes close, which have barely opened? The author does not bring any response to these questions; the reader, whoever he might be, will recognize this anxiety and will look for the answer in his own life.

The meetings of friendship, love, life . . . often fail in narratives filled with nostalgia; death, on the other hand, is present and points out to men their helplessness. . . .

Through all these nothings of existence, one begins to think that in the Congo or elsewhere, man has a need to think about his life, to meditate, and to judge that path that has been traveled.

> Françoise Bureau. *Presence Africaine.* 116 (1980), p. 220

*La Tradition du songe* is Tati Loutard's last collection. It comprises three parts, and one could catalogue each one as follows: poetry, poetic prose, and "pensées" or reflections. Besides, the collection is literally divided into three parts: "Force et declin," "Force et destin," "Histoire," plus an appendix titled "Elements d'une vie poétique," which comprises essentially what we have named "pensées.". . .

In general, the texts are made up of reflections from the poet's own condition and reminiscences of friends who have disappeared, or of regions transfigured, not by dreams this time! . . .

At the level of language, what characterizes this collection is . . . the way in which the poet uses the natural elements of the African continent: fauna, flora, etc. What is also new is the entrance of the proverb, in a surreptitious manner, into poetry: "Le chacal vibre encore / Dans le chien" [The jackal still resonates / In the dog].

> Willy Alante-Lima. *Presence Africaine.* 142 (1987), pp. 179, 182.

The masculine/feminine opposition . . . which is part of an archaic, traditional perception of the world is . . . one of the major principles which structure Tati-Loutard's poetry. . . . One finds it in the contrast between the sidereal immobility and fluidity of the night, between the constellations and the darkness, and between the sand and the sea. The sun, being from the beginning an element of male domination like fire, is seen in opposition to the feminine water although a distinction is imposed between the maternal sea and the gentle water which gives birth to the lover.

Man's environment is constituted by some great oppositions: sun/rain, afternoon/morning or evening, sea/land. These contrasts cover a more fundamental opposition between masculine and feminine principles or between paternal and maternal principles. . . .

The violence of the geographical and cosmic oppositions marks the imaginary world of the poet. Sun and rain, like day and night, alternate and follow each other, concretizing the cycle of time. The antithetical elements evoked suggest the dawn of life and a renaissance, the fruit of a transformation celebrated by the poet as the synthesis of extremes. But let us first envisage the elements in their divided opposition.

The sun, whose attributes are light and drought, is in opposition to both the moist night and the feminine rain. This dichotomy, from the first poems . . . to the most recent ones, reveals itself to be loaded with mythical significance, corresponding to the antithesis between sterility ("soleil de midi, étrange calvitie" [noonday sun, strange baldness]) and fertility. This image, the origin of which is linked to agrarian civilizations, has social connotations signifying economic misery as opposed to the desired prosperity. Light is experienced as an aggressive roughness, the sun rays in contrast to the softness ("la morbidezza") of the humid shade, the star opposing the nocturnal darkness, which is attractive, "inspiring," and rich in hidden life.

The tension is suggested in *Poèmes de la mer, Les Racines congolaises*, the collection written on the return to the country after studies in Europe. At the time of readaptation to local realities, this opposition becomes more noticeable. This opposition reaffirms itself with *L'Envers du soleil* and *Les Normes du temps*. Opposing the blinding and destructive solar values are the feminized night propitious to human flourishing, as well as the rain, the gentle water which has the same power. The place for the gestation of life is maternal like the warm and humid night and like the ground drenched by showers.

The harshness of the sun leads the prodigal son to refuse the seductiveness of African nature in order to turn his interest to human beings and their difficulties. The poet opposes a nostalgic romanticism of natural beauties with a humanism and social spirit: "Retourne vers l'homme, poète . . . l'homme d'une renaissante Afrique" [Return to man, poet . . . man of an Africa reborn]. Denouncing the "horror" of the sun is a way of turning away from the ideology of Négritude and from the themes that have become conventional with African poets from a certain time.

Arlette Chemain. *Presence Africaine.* 145 (1988), pp. 117–19

Jean-Baptiste Tati-Loutard has already distinguished himself as one of the foremost poets in the Congo. He is now being acclaimed as a master of the prose narrative. In fact, his is an exquisite poetic prose which maintains the originality and, to a degree, the high quality of his prizewinning *Le Récit de la mort*. The narrative's hero, Touazock, shares the author's preoccupation with death, "la lutte désespérée de son esprit contre le silence absolu" [the desparate struggle of his mind against absolute silence]. Death, as a central character in the book, is a capricious being which does not respect age, beauty, or intelligence and brings along with it at times a scandalous reminder of physical frailty, an acknowledgment of intellectual disappointment, or a shameful surrender to political

disgrace. In his turn, the author informs us that death offers unsuspected traps in thousands of places and situations.

In addition to the protagonist's constant obsession with death as a lethal element against life, the author presents a number of disparate subjects, skillfully adjusting them to the somewhat dejected general theme of his narrative: the haunted citizens of contemporary Africa; revolution and torture; public health; national education; corruption and theft of public funds; the role of African women in society and politics; and allusions to recent African history, especially that of the Congo and Burkina-Faso. As an appropriate ending to the narrative, the last third of the book, entitled "Le Grand Exilé," is a text written by the hero, in which he introduces a study of the psychological trauma of a fallen ruler who is allowed to live in guarded exile: "L'homme n'est-il pas déjà mort à partir du moment où il ne peut plus former de projets?" [Isn't a man already dead from the moment he can no longer conceive?]. *Le Récit de la mort* is not a particularly fascinating story; however, the author seems to understand literature, and his storytelling craft makes the narrative more illuminating than depressing.

Robert P. Smith, Jr. *World Literature Today.* 63, 1 (Winter 1989), p. 157

BIBLIOGRAPHY
*Les Racines congolaise* (The Congolese Roots), 1968; *Poémes de la mer* (Poems of the Sea), 1968; *L'Envers du soleil* (The Wrong Side of the Sun, 1970; *Les Normes du temps* (The Norms of Time), 1974; *Nouvelles Chroniques congolaises*, 1980; *Le Dialogue des Plateaux*, 1982; *La Tradition du songe*, 1985; *Le Récit de la mort*, 1987; *Le Rendez-vous de la retraite*, 1990; *Fantasmagories*, 1998

# TCHICAYA U TAM'SI (1931–1988)
## Congo

Tchicaya U Tam'si is not only the most prolific of Africa's modern poets, but the one whose work displays the most sustained energy and intensity. He has been steadily engaged with development of his art for a period of nearly thirty years, during which he has published seven major collections of poetry. . . .

[His] initial move to France, no doubt well-intended on his father's part, left the deepest possible mark on his early poetry, which is charged with an overwhelming sense of loss. Whether literally or metaphorically, he feels deprived of his country, a mother, and even of a genealogical identity. These are some of the recurrent themes throughout the first collection, *Le Mauvais Sang*, [which he] published in 1955 at the age of twenty-four. All his poetry, however, is haunted by the figure of this "mère inconnue," and he reverts continually to the idea of something strange and alienated in his parentage. . . . Tchicaya had in fact been brought up in ignorance of his mother's identity, and even of her continued existence. The figure of the father in his poetry is also enigmatical, charged with tension and perhaps a sense of opposition. This is the father who brought the poet to Paris at the age of fifteen and who thus both connects him with Africa (by his existence) and separates him from it (by his action). . . . Tchicaya's second and third collections, *Feu de brousse* and *À triche-coeur*, are haunted by the figure of "the child" or "the orphan," who wanders everywhere seeking the tree or root of his origin, the source of his very being. . . .

The sense of isolation grows still deeper in *Epitomé*, when feelings in the West began to run high over the Congo tragedy, but in a direction absolutely contrary to those of any radical, informed African—more especially, any Congolese African. But these earlier lines give us already a powerful impression of the poet's inner exploration of a body, a physical "presence," which is his only link with the landscape and people of his own country. And since death is above all the process by which we mingle our elements with those from which we came, it is this process which dominates the opening stanza of the poem. But the impression is far from deathly, for the imagery of "breath of sperm," of "yeast" and of "rich suns" stresses that the path is more one of renewal than of disappearance. . . .

The poems in the main sequence of *Epitomé* each carry a superscription identifying them with particular phases or events of the struggle which raged on the banks of the Congo in 1959–1961. . . . The first part of *Epitomé* reads like a poetic diary of these events, in which their initial impact is recreated, their meaning sought in the deeper perspective of all other events suffered by the same or other colonized peoples. The vision nurtured during those perilous but heady days in Kinshasa was something very different from the American-dominated dictatorship which later rose upon the wrack of Lumumbist hopes. It could even be dreamed, as Tchicaya dreamed in some of those poems, that the Congo's five centuries of anguish since the Portuguese arrival might be resolved at last into freedom and unity for its peoples. The poet taunts Christ to share to the full the specific agony and division of his people, wrought by such "Christian" enslavers, colonizers, and intriguers. . . .

[The] poetry of *Epitomé* and *Le Ventre* is on the whole more public in its concerns than the intensely self-communing volumes that preceded it. And this more public orientation is matched, particularly in *Le Ventre*, by a slight simplification of style. A more stanzaic form reappears on the page, after the boiling cascades of images which pour through *Feu de brousse* or *À triche-coeur*, and there is a return to a limited use of punctuation, capitalization, and closed sentences within each poem.

Tchicaya continues to search for the tree of his origins, he pummels and dissects his own belly to find the meaning of rebirth within the giant fact of death in the Congo of those years; the great river flows as ever through his pages, carrying, changing and delivering up the burden of a tragic historic experience. Thus all the elements of continuity are present; only the poet's preoccupations begin to take on a more representative character; he is both literally and imaginatively closer to the experience of his people than the brilliant young Parisian poet of the 1950s.

Gerald Moore. *Twelve African Poets* (Bloomington: Indiana University Press, 1980), pp. 147–49, 154, 157–58, 162

The first novel which the poet and playwright Tchicaya U Tam'si agreed to publish [*Les Cancrelats*] can definitely be stated as a combination of depth and density. From the start, the narrative introduces us to the heart of a world so close and so troubled that no reader can remain indifferent to it. One is caught up in the web of a writing that mobilizes the symbols of a great richness and in the meanderings of so profound a story that one follows it as if it were a return to the origins. . . .

The narration introduces, into a world of mystery and darkness and into the depths of a being and his culture, the functioning of societies and of the human psyche at an obscure level. . . .

The novel gives us a cross-section of life, "tranche de vie," under colonial rule, in the region neighboring Loango, of a people with a touch of foreign culture, embedded in its traditions, hunted down in everyday life by the militia, and progressing toward an evolution of the situation in 1946, with the "pétition," title of the last chapter—which will lead to the elections.

But the novel, without concession to stereotypes, is much more than just a historic reconstruction.

The narration offers some chronological references, some landmarks which permit us to reconstruct the sequence of facts out of the multiple anachronisms, the flashbacks, the narrations within the narration and the "métalepses." The narration winds around itself even as it moves forward.

Two grids will help the reader to reestablish the logic from this dense romanesque fabric, a fabric inextricable from symbolic notations and allusions.

A family tree spreads its branches throughout the narration. It is opportunely summed up periodically in a way which complicates it further.

Ndundu, who followed his white employer to France in 1880, returns to the Congo twelve years later, with two children born in Grand-Bassan, where he had put into port and tried to found a family.

The novel focuses on the two—not the husband and wife but the brother and sister with symbolic names: Sophie, the wise, and Prosper, promise of prosperity—at the time of a second marriage. . . .

The other grid concerns dates and temporal references. . . .

The novel begins with the narration of the difficulty the steamboat experienced docking on the wharf. Past events are recaptured in an internal monologue.

Arlette Chemain. *Presence africaine.* 115 (1980), pp. 211–13†

Tchicaya's short stories [in *La Main sèche*], published the same year as his first novel, *Les Cancrelats*, have the same triple thrust as that novel. First, there is the surreal and fascinating style; second, there is the blend of Western Christianity and African tradition; and third, there is the proverbial tone to the diction. Particularly salient in these tales is the fascinating blend of Christian elements and the personal African optics of the narrator. A black baby who takes the place of the papier-mâché Jesus in a crèche has been abandoned by its mother. Or are we actually witnessing the Second Coming? In another story a talking mouth ("noire et lippue, bien sûr") retraces the evolution from sea organism to Homo sapiens.

Tchicaya has often been assimilated into the surrealist movement because of his unusual imagery and his interest in [Arthur] Rimbaud. Now, with the stories of *La Main sèche*, Tchicaya reinforces that association, especially in the oneiric passages of "Rebours" and on the plotless urgency of several other stories. These tales are not slices of life but rather slices of consciousness lent a palpable dimension. The major coordinates of Tchicaya's world are African and French conventions. If Tchicaya *is* a "surrealist," it his on his own terms. His devotion to the Rimbaudian tradition of the *hallucination simple* is embraced somewhat cynically, and his prime world-view remains African—namely natural rather than supernatural. Tchicaya brilliantly reverses one of Europe's most famous existentialist quotations when he speaks of people entering a judge's chambers, including "un certain Pascal qui, dit-on, enseignait aux arbres la mauvaise foi des humains" [a certain Pascal, who, it is said, taught trees the dishonesty of humans]. In this reversal lies the clue to the fundamental difference between European surrealism and African surreality.

Eric Sellin. *World Literature Today.* 56, 1 (Winter 1982), pp. 162–63

In Tchicaya U Tam'si's second and last published play, *Le Destin glorieux du Maréchal Nnikon . . .* political satire in drama attains a level of originality and achievement only rarely seen in modern black francophone African theater. Central to the play is a poetic dislocation of nightmare and reality or of nightmare as reality. Within these unstable boundaries, Tchicaya transforms political oppression into a surrealistic vision whose semantic underpinning is supported by satire and its attendant ironies. This study examines the rhetorical devices of satire in *Destin* and how they function to demystify the archetype of the African tyrant and expand the text's literal meaning. Ultimately, the satirical mode serves to destabilize fixed conception and involves the audience in the cathartic deposing of the self-appointed "supreme guide", and president-dictator for life.

Katheryn Wright. *Ufahamu.* 19, 2–3 (1991), p. 80

Firmly convinced of the necessity, for Africa, to preserve its identity in a world that tends towards uniformization under the influence of the industrial culture of the masses, Tchicaya U Tam'si promoted the intelligent return to the original expressions of African theater. He saw in it one of the suitable means for the safeguarding, in our continent, of an art of living and simply of an art that achieves a syncretic harmony between tradition and modernity.

In an article published by *Le Monde diplomatique* and dealing with "the sacred origins of our theater," Tchicaya recognizes that "amongst the arts of speech," the theater, is "the one that is the greatest collection of the founding myths." The judgment that he gives on "neo-theater africain" objectively takes things into account. On the one hand, he criticizes those who, under the pretext of originality for the sake of originality denature the entire theater; they present it "as a poor and strange juxtaposition of dance tracks (with uninspired choreography), of words and farces, the entire thing stuffed with the weight of a doubtful folklorism." On the other hand, he recognizes that this "neo-theater" is capable of "authentic successes" when the "most demanding" of its creators know how to make use of the recourse "to the sources of ritual (among others)." . . .

Tchicaya U Tam'si was "born"—perhaps without himself having complete awareness of the exceptional richness of all the registers of his dramatic range—for the theater. His poetic work has brought to his work as playwright an inestimable source of sensitivity and of images with which his characters are endowed. For example, some of his poetic collections (*Epitomé, Le Ventre*) are composed like funeral operas traversed by cries and tears causing alternately lulls and storms. *Epitomé*, a dramatic poem par excellence, which marks the passage of time through the breathless succession of the editions of the press, is a work that can be directly transposed onto the stage. Three characters—Lumumba, Christ,

and the author himself confuse their silhouettes in a hallucinating superimpression—portray in it, in the strongest sense, Passion. Roger Godard, who has worked on Congolese poetry, has emphasized in Tchicaya U Tam'si the permanence of his poetic themes in his dramatic work.

Sylvain Bemba. *Europe.* 69, 750 (October 1991), pp. 124–26†

The death of Tchicaya U Tam'si on April 22, 1988, at the age of fifty-seven sent shock waves through the world of African literature. Tchicaya, the oldest of a generation of important Congolese writers, is one of the few whose reputation has reached beyond the confines of francophone Africa and France. During his lifetime, however, he never reached the wide audience that he deserved, not only as a poet, but also as novelist and playwright. . . . While recognizing him as one of the leading contemporary African poets, critics and readers remain strangely reserved. In a recent publication Théophile Obenga puts his finger on one of the main reasons for this reticence: "U Tam'si n'est l'héritiére de personne et de rien: à souhait, et non sans belle ironie" (U Tam'si inherits from nobody and nothing: by choice and not without beautiful irony). Tchicaya's writing defies classification. His intensely personal world view and poetic expression create his own individual mythology, which sets him apart from all neat literary categories. His poetry is often described as hermetic, which is, in reality, the literary critic's terminology for admitting that it is not easily understood. At the same time the poet's obvious mastery of his medium precludes his being dismissed as obscure or unintelligible. . . .

It is important to read [Tchicaya's] oeuvre not only as a whole but also chronologically, in the order of composition. His novels illustrate this very well; the first three . . . form a trilogy that paints a vast human and sociopolitical fresco of the Congo, although spanning only fifty-some years in the life of the main protagonists, Sophie and Prosper. In fact, it was conceived of as a single narrative and was divided into three in order to satisfy the editors. Thus, although each novel may be read and enjoyed in isolation, characters and events in one of the three may be alluded to in another or may reappear without explanation, with the result that the full significance is lost on the reader. Similarly, certain recurrent images become key symbols, an understanding of which is essential in order to release the full meaning of the text. One such image-symbol is that of the *cancrelat* or cockroach, which lends its name to the first novel, *Les Cancrelats*. The word first appears in the enigmatic proverb which introduces the novel: "Le cancrelat alla plaider une cause au tribunal des poules!" (The cockroach went to plead its cause before the hens' court). Both the proverb and the cockroach image reappear at significant points in the first and last of the three novels, illuminating the meaning of the text and themselves acquiring new connotative dimensions. . . .

In [Tchicaya's] writing, repetition and rhythm are not only semiological but also structurally significant. The collection *Le Ventre* represents one of the most striking illustrations of this. . . . [It] is important to consider the *ventre* symbol in the context of the collection as a whole in order to appreciate how the contradictions and contrasts make up a synthetic unity. Space does not allow for the required detailed study of this high-frequency word. However, a chronological reading of the poems in the collection would reveal how the development of the referential value of the *ventre* symbol mirrors the organically integrated structure of the whole. This rhythmic pattern is a constant in [Tchicaya's] writing, a structural technique which can be found in his first collections of poems and which is developed to a striking degree in his later works. For example, repeated semiological and linguistic elements link the poems in *Le Mauvais sang*, and key recurrent images such as blood, water, the woman/mother/Africa, and the Christ are introduced. In later volumes the title of a poem is often anticipated in the preceding poem, thus reinforcing the sense of pattern in ideas and sounds. This repetition is not static; each reappearance of an image brings to it a new dimension, and its development can be traced through [Tchicaya's] work as a whole. It is significant that many of the key images in his verse are important signifiers in his prose. . . .

[Tchicaya's] work is of particular interest in this respect, for his highly integrated poetic universe reflects a holistic world view that stands in sharp contrast to the Manichean Western world-view. [Tchicaya's] thought processes are firmly rooted in a sense of rhythmic pattern, the cycles of life, and man's collective identity. His poetic discourse is strongly individualistic in terms of image and language, yet his concern is for understanding the meaning of "existential anguish," not for the individual as part of a corporate body—past, present, and future. His poetry is the concrete expression of his conception of the poet-prophet, whose role in the life of society is as important as that of the mason or the carpenter: "The poet is above all a man, a man in the full meaning of the word, a conscious man. A conscious man is he who dreams, and the dream is only a projection into the future of what can be realized." The poet, like Christ and the political martyr, lays himself open to the conflicting forces of life. [Tchicaya's] creative writing constitutes the commitment of a life to this task.

> Betty O'Grady. *World Literature Today*. 65, 1 (Winter 1991), pp. 29–34

Very few Africans have had the courage to express their outrage at the stifling African traditions with the vigor and consistency of U Tam'Si. The break with the tube, the ethnic group, and Africa is an expression of his anger and frustration at himself as reflected in the practices this society.

In fact, self-criticism is a major theme in Tchicaya's work as he strives to build a dynamic identity through a dynamic writing style. A dynamic identity changes with time and it is directed toward the future as opposed to static identity, which is concerned with only the past. The former is an attempt to live the present, an opening up of self to reality and the necessities of life. The latter is an attempt to escape reality in order to swim in the stagnant waters of an idyllic past.

U Tam'Si's attempt to face up to the present, to confront it in order to change it, permeates all his work as he tries to teach and educate his readers about the danger of a return to a mythic past:. . . .

[In order to understand his position better] it is imperative to place him and his work in historical context. Born before the independence of Africa, he grew to witness and experience colonization and the struggle for independence in his native Congo. As a matter of fact, he worked closely with Patrice Lumumba to gain political independence for the country. Thus, his personality as a writer must have grown out of those difficult moments in the history of the continent, and one should expect his work to reflect his personal take of the events.

In addition to the political events, Tchicaya could not ignore the literary activities of his contemporaries. He had to communicate with them in one way or the other since each writer is the product of his or her epoch. In this respect, Négritude was one important literary event he could not circumvent. Founded in Paris in the thirties by Léopold Sédar Senghor, Aimé Césaire and Léon G. Damas, it was then their attempt to create an image for and about Africa with which they could identify with a sense of pride.

[U Tam Si's] break with Africa is not a total rejection of his roots or an absolute refusal to keep usable elements of the past. On the contrary, it is an attempt to build a cultured identity from within, that is, an identity geared toward the future. Such an identity has to be informed not by literary patterns imposed from without, but by pages of African history. Seen from that perspective, his break with ethnic can be interpreted as an effort to break free from the chains of ethnicity in order to reach out to and accommodate the other.

As a matter of fact, Africa is now coming to grips with post cold war problems such as famine and civil unrests that contrast with the peace in [Senghor's] "Night of Sine" and further complicate divisions along ethnic lines. In this respect, Tchicaya's verbal construction of reality carries some dose of nationalist concerns and his self-criticism is just the other side of the dream of fraternity.

It is unfortunate that he has received so little attention from critics of African literatures. Whether their relative silence is the result of his position vis-à-vis the stifling African traditions and Négritude or of the difficulty in penetrating work is uncertain. But there is no doubt that he is one of most modern African writers, as George Lang (1985) has already noted, and one of the greatest as well.

Tchicaya wants everyone to face their world as it is, to look at themselves critically in order to see their reality. His self-criticism has cost him his credibility in the eyes of many people in Africa. Yet as Emil Magel (1980) claims, Tchicaya is critical of both Europeans and Africans. His criticism of them in the process of the search for the truth has been seen as unfaithful, treacherous, and disloyal. Despite his awareness of the criticism, U Tam'Si persists against what Magel calls the normative rules of the game. They consist of the unspoken prohibition against providing ammunition to racist enemies by exposing the ugliness of Africa.

But for Tchicaya, the search for the truth is more important than whatever the searcher happens to find. Thus in *Les Cancrelats*, Damien, whose daughter is murdered, goes to search for the killer. In the process, he makes important discoveries about himself and the conditions of his life. The authorial voice comments:

> La révolte, née de cette recherche, l'aurait conduit à l'avant vers un acte. Qu'importe quel acte? Chaque acte étant l'affirmation d'une liberté!

> The revolt, born of this search, would lead him forward toward an act. Does it matter what kind of act? Each act being the affirmation of a liberty!

The search is therefore essential in U Tam'Si's philosophy and it should be considered as such. To his counterparts who undertook the search for their identity in a remote past, he warns that the search ought to be exhaustive as well as objective. . . .

> Chaibou Elhadji Oumarou. *Studies in Twentieth-Century Literature*. Summer 1995, pp. 223–37

BIBLIOGRAPHY

*Le Mauvais Sang*, 1955; *Feu de brousse: Poeme parle en 17 visions*, 1957; *A triche-coeur*, 1958; *Epitomé: Les Mots de tete pour le sommaire d'une passion*, 1962; *Le Ventre: Le Pain ou la cendre*, 1964; *L'Arc musical*, 1970; *Selected Poems*, 1970; *La Veste d'interieur; Notes de veille*, 1977; *Le Zulu; Vwene le fondateur*, 1977; *Le Destin glorieux du marechel Nnikon Nniku, prince qu'on sort: Comedie-farce-sinistre*, 1979; *Les Cancrelats*, 1980; *La Main seche*, 1980; *Soleil sans lendemains*, 1981; *Les Meduses ou les orties de mer*, 1982; *Ces fruits si doux de l'arbre a pain*, 1987

# THOBY-MARCELIN, Philippe (1904–1975) and Marcelin, Pierre (1908–)

Haiti

You [Thoby-Marcelin] could write prose poems or stories dealing with the local or provincial life of your country, works in which you would have the characters speak the delightful French of the Caribbean, which seems to me to be so full of resources. John-Antoine Nau (have you read him?) tried his hand at it, but in the genre of the animated and the grotesque; there is room, alongside his works, for scenes in prose that would be both poetic and sentimental. A transplanted Frenchman cannot write those works. They have to come from your land. . . .

A danger for the poet is facility. You should be very sparing with your words; use them parsimoniously, as if they were very costly. That is half the secret; the other half is incommunicable. But reading poets, especially ancient poets, greatly helps the poetry that is within us to free itself and express itself forcefully. I believe I see the influence of the prosody of Jules Romains and Jean Cocteau in your poems; is that true? But the *personal tone*, the essence, is in the lines and stanzas that I have indicated to you, and you can be satisfied with them. [July 29, 1925]

> Larbaud. Quoted in *Haïti-Journal*. December 1943, pp. 5, 7†

The winner of the Second Latin American Literary Prize Competition is important for more reasons than the excellence—which is high—of its literary structure. *Canapé-Vert* is a pioneer, a pilgrim, in fact, walking among us with a story to tell and a lesson to teach. It is the first novel to appear in English giving a picture of Haitian life from the viewpoint of the Haitians themselves—it was written by two Haitians, brothers; it is a ''regional'' novel of native life on the Caribbean islands; it is a treatise on voodoo which gives a sensible and completely understandable picture of this over-glamorized remnant of the mystery religions. . . .

Haiti offers a study of the Negro in transition. He is freed of the negative, smothering tribal influence which made change impossible in Africa. He is surrounded at all times with the opportunity to ''progress.'' But the opportunity is not pressed; he can take it or leave it. Thus advancement, or change, or evolution, however you may wish to name it, proceeds naturally. And it is the natural change, this subtle development from an unself-conscious member of a group to a self-assured, self-directing individual which is illustrated in *Canapé-Vert*.

Aladin, Florina, Grande Da, Tonton Bossa, Judge Dor, Sor Cicie, all the characters of the story, believe in the pantheon of the Vodun cult. . . . They are convinced that in all matters of importance these *loas and mystères* are concerned, and that they are vitally interested and will take action within a short time. . . . The characters in *Canapé-Vert* are at the same stage as those in the Greek and Shakespearian tragedies. They determine to express their personal opinions and satisfy their desires in the face of certain anger on the part of the gods. Swiftly they are pursued and relentlessly they are punished. . . .

The story is beautifully told. The brothers who wrote it are poets, and they have written about the peasants of their country in lean, rhythmic prose that never uses ten words where one will do the trick. The picture they paint is full and detailed, but the fulness and detail are trapped in adverbial phrases and quick sentences that blossom into a dozen meanings when slowly read. The repressed and the sentimental may find the violence and simplicity of the book's action hard to take, but any mature person will thoroughly enjoy it, and find matter for contemplation when he considers that these Haitian peasants are the same people as our American Negroes, from whom we are inclined to expect a great deal of cultural advancement in return for a limited attempt to understand a basic evolutionary problem.

There have been some fine novels by and about American Negroes, but none will teach the white reader as much about the soul of his black brother as this brief, simple tragedy of Haitian peasant life.

> Thomas Sugrue. *Saturday Review.* March 25, 1944, p. 13

Writing with a hard pencil in thin strokes, the Marcelin brothers of Haiti, in the third of their short novels to be published in the United States, deal in the macabre materials of illicit sex and unhappy voodoo as they eventually affect a large portion of the population of Saint-Marc. This is a charming Caribbean seacoast town which had, when I was last there, one of the loveliest flower-strewn beaches I have ever seen. Little did I suspect that this sleepy Haitian village might harbor such goings-on as are revealed in *The Pencil of God*.

The Marcelins make their tormented little tale of desire and guilt come to life in a surface kind of way, in terms of passion and conjure, without the reader ever getting to know any of the characters very well or really caring about anyone.

Though fate and the furies are leading characters, the writing has, particularly in the earlier chapters of the book, a tongue-in-cheek quality. This seems out of keeping with the kind of story being told, as though rather quaint puppets are being described instead of human beings. Like pretty scenes in a smart musical revue . . . the love affair of a middle-aged married Diogène with a 16-year-old girl is told with frequent humor and the lightness of a Ronald Firbank. . . .

The story travels fast, is never dull, but the people are almost like comic-book figures. You know *who* they are but you never know *them*, except as you might know rather exotic neighbors from occasionally seeing them out the window or gossiping about them with the servants.

> Langston Hughes. *New York Times Book Review*. February 4, 1951, p. 5

[*The Pencil of God*] sets out to explore a problem which the Yorubas claim to have solved with *magun*. *Magun*, a magic charm, is believed to have the power of paralysing the gallant male who must carry his amorous adventures into the forbidden territory of other people's wives. . . .

The story is told in a simple direct style remarkable for its economy. The characters are boldly drawn and clear-cut. Tonton Georges, the seventy-year-old man who "had made women his principal concern in life" and still "pursued them" is probably the most amusing, the most active tale bearer in a community where gossip and tale bearing are the rule; where a small story, passing between new pairs of lips all the time, becomes distorted into terrifying proportions.

In about half the length of the normal novel, the writers have succeeded in conveying the philosophy and mode of life of a people living a type of life not unlike that of many parts of West Africa. Certainly one need not seek far among West African proverbs to find an equivalent for that which gave them the theme of their book: "The pencil of God has no eraser."

> C. O. D. Ekwensi. *West African Review.* July 1952, pp. 713, 715

*Canapé-Vert* and *The Beast of Musseau*, void of logical action, try to imitate life in the disorder of the specific adventures that fill them. Each individual is treated with fresh interest, and each one enters the structure of the novel (especially in *Canapé-Vert*) as an important element. There are no secondary characters or elementary facts: everything receives equal weight. And in the confusion of these equivalent destinies, it is difficult to single out the novels' objective.

The main observation to be made about the writing of the Marcelins is that these works try to be precisely as meaningless and aimless as life itself. The writers take as much care as possible not to take sides or to isolate individual actions and pursue them to a logical outcome. The writers' concern seems to be to exploit facts drawn from experience and observation; and the abundance of narratives and popular tales suggests the methods of the naturalists.

How much their vision reminds me of Zola's! The Marcelins' penchant for writing about alcoholics, the mentally deficient, murderers, and women of easy virtue is not new. Moreover, there is also a dryness in their narratives and a lack of psychological analysis! Surely the truth is powerful, and the reader begins to admire the Marcelins for having simplified superstitious practices and for attempting to explain them rationally. But why, while claiming to intervene on behalf of morality, do they systematically apply arbitrary conclusions? The plot always ends, as in the theater, with the death of the protagonists.

> Ghislain Gouraige. *Histoire de la littérature haïtienne* (Port-au-Prince: Imprimerie H. A. Théodore, 1960), pp. 277–78

[After the success of *The Pencil of God*] the brothers, who had always worked together, were now to be condemned to an enforced separation. M. Philippe Thoby-Marcelin came to work in the Pan American Union in Washington and married an American wife, while his brother remained in Haiti. Eventually the two collaborators effected a partial rapprochement. Pierre arranges to spend his summers in the United States with Philippe, and they have now

written another novel, which seems to me, to date, their masterpiece. It is in some ways rather different from its predecessors. It covers a good deal more ground, involving a greater variety of social types, and its tone is somewhat different. The earlier novels of the Marcelins had something of the fresh excitement of the relatively recent discovery by sophisticated city-dwellers, brought up in the Catholic religion and the tradition of French culture, of the more or less fantastic life in a kind of visionary world of the African denizens of the hinterland. Their new novel, *All Men Are Mad*, is drier and more objective. It is based on, though it does not follow literally, a real episode in Haitian history. In 1942, there was a special effort on the part of the Catholic Church to redeem the vodou worshippers for Christianity. . . .

[The material] is presented by the Marcelins in a style of unemphasized irony that belongs to the French tradition of Maupassant and Anatole France. There is almost no overt comment; the criticism is all implied. And though what happens, if viewed in an ironic light, is often extremely funny, what is suggested is also pathetic. It is sad that human beings should be living with such delusions and in such limitations; should be talking such inflated nonsense, suffering helplessly from such wretched diseases, be intimidated and dominated by such outlandish superstitions. The vodouists and the Roman Catholics are equally inept and mistaken. Here again the special plight of the Haitians is made to extend a perspective to the miseries and the futilities of the whole human race, to our bitter "ideological" conflicts and our apparently pointless ambitions. *All Men Are Mad* is a very entertaining but also a troubling book, and it is a most distinguished work of literature.

> Edmund Wilson. Introduction to Philippe Thoby-Marcelin and Pierre Marcelin, *All Men Are Mad* (New York: Farrar, Straus & Giroux, 1970), pp. ix–xii

BIBLIOGRAPHY
*Canapé-Vert*, 1944; *La bête de Musseau* (The Beast of the Haitian Hills), 1946; *Le crayon de Dieu* (The Pencil of God), 1951; *Tous les hommes sont fous* (All Men Are Mad), 1970; *Contes et legendes d'Haiti* (The Singing Turtle, and Other Tales from Haiti), 1971

# THURMAN, Wallace (1902–1934)
## United States

The new Negro play, *Harlem*, written by William Jourdan Rapp and Wallace Thurman, and sub-titled "An Episode of Life in New York's Black Belt," has plenty of comedy of a distinctly low order. A few critics admitted that certain scenes needed toning down, and even intimated that the police authorities would probably attend to that aspect before the play had worn out its welcome. But none of them, so far as I know, raised a voice to protest against the particular way in which this melodrama exploits the worst features of the Negro and depends for its effects solely on the explosions of lust and sensuality. The "good" characters are hopelessly ineffectual, and all the rest are either worthless hypocrites, like the father who uses his home as a centre for debauched parties in order to pay the rent, or criminals of the worst type. Anyone given to prejudice or haphazard judgments would come away from this play with the impression that Harlem is a den of black filth where animal passions run riot and where the few Negroes with higher ideas or ideals are hopelessly snowed under by black flakes from a sodden sky. . . .

The offense to the Negro, as I see it, is not lessened by the fact that the entire cast, with the exception of one white detective, is Negro. It only doubles the irony of the exploitation. The Negro is apparently a natural-born actor, unspoiled as yet by self-consciousness. We have had enough examples of his work in the last few years to realize that, given legitimate opportunity, he is as capable at creating illusion and the feeling of deep sincerity as the best of our white actors. But to purchase his talent in order to turn it to the public degradation of his own race, to use his very powers as an actor to discredit him as a man—this, I believe, is the cheapest and most contemptible form of exploitation of which the American whites have yet been guilty.

R. Dana Skinner. *Commonweal.* March 6, 1929, p. 514

Wallace Thurman, a young Negro, who has recently come out of the West, apparently has joined the ranks of the successful. And yet one wonders whether it is a success of artistic achievement or a success consummated because Mr. Thurman has become a devotee of the most fashionable of American literary cults, that dedicated to the exploitation of the vices of the Negro of the lowest stratum of society and to the mental debauching of Negroes in general.

*The Blacker the Berry* is a story of a girl, possessed on her mother's side of the best sort of lineage that the American Negro knows, but with a despised black skin, a legacy from a roving black father. Merely tolerated at home in Idaho among her lighter kin, she seeks a happier and fuller life at the University of Southern California where again her ambitions for comradeship are thwarted because of her ebony hue. She abandons her college work and eventually arrives in Harlem where once more color prejudice forces her downward in the social scheme of things until the end of the book leaves her economically adjusted as a school teacher but bitter, disillusioned and alone, an emotional derelict.

In spite of Emmy Lou Morgan's easy virtue and lack of fastidiousness all that the author can do fails to make her vicious. Nor does he even succeed in making her indiscretions exciting. He simply has created an incredibly stupid character. The moral that evidently is intended to adorn this tale is to the effect that young women who are black are doomed to a rather difficult existence should they aspire to anything but life in its most humdrum and sordid forms. But somehow it seems that were she as fair as a lily, a young woman, at once so dominated by the urge of sex and so stupid, would succeed in being exploited by the gentlemen of her acquaintance in one way or another.

Eunice Hunton Carter.*Opportunity.* May 1929, p. 162

Wallace Thurman wanted to be a great writer, but none of his own work ever made him happy. *The Blacker the Berry*, his first book, was an important novel on a subject little dwelt upon in Negro fiction—the plight of the very dark Negro woman, who encounters in some communities a double wall of color prejudice within and without the race. His play, *Harlem*, considerably distorted for box office purposes, was, nevertheless, a compelling study—and the

only one in the theater—of the impact of Harlem on a Negro family fresh from the South. And his *Infants of the Spring*, a superb and bitter study of the bohemian fringe of Harlem's literary and artistic life, is a compelling book.

But none of these things pleased Wallace Thurman. He wanted to be a *very* great writer, like Gorki or Thomas Mann, and he felt that he was merely a journalistic writer. His critical mind, comparing his pages to the thousands of other pages he had read, by Proust, Melville, Tolstoy, Galsworthy, Dostoyevski, Henry James, Sainte-Beuve, Taine, Anatole France, found his own pages vastly wanting. So he contented himself by writing a great deal for money, laughing bitterly at his fabulously concocted "true stories," creating two bad motion pictures of the "Adults Only" type for Hollywood, drinking more and more gin, and then threatening to jump out of windows at people's parties and kill himself.

Langston Hughes. *The Big Sea* (New York: Alfred A. Knopf, 1940), pp. 234–35

Perhaps the most interesting sections of *Infants of the Spring* are those containing satirical comments on the Negro Renascence. Though the so-called "New Negro" was acclaimed and patronized throughout the United States as a phenomenon in art, Thurman observes that very little "was being done to substantiate the current fad, to make it the foundation for something truly epochal.". . .

In *Infants of the Spring* Thurman had an unusual opportunity to produce a competent satire upon the young libertines of upper Manhattan and the participants in the Negro Renascence. He himself was a member of the Harlem literary coterie, and his home was a favorite meeting place for certain bohemians of black Manhattan and Greenwich Village. In practice, however, Thurman showed himself unable to master this rich literary material. *Infants of the Spring* reveals an author morbid in outlook, diffuse in thinking, and destructive in purpose. Nowhere do we find the spontaneous humor which characterizes George Schuyler's *Black No More*. Every indication suggests that Thurman had not settled in his own mind the many issues that he introduces helter-skelter in the book. More than any other novel, therefore, *Infants of the Spring* illustrates the decadence of the [Carl] Van Vechten Vogue which, like the Elizabethan tragedy and the Restoration heroic play, spent itself in excesses and exaggerations.

Hugh M. Gloster. *Negro Voices in American Fiction* (Chapel Hill: University of North Carolina Press, 1948), pp. 170–72

One might say that [Thurman], of all the Harlem literati, contained within him the paradoxes of Negro art. Robert A. Bone, whose book on the Negro novel is often faulty, is nowhere less perceptive than in his treatment of Thurman. Bone dismisses *Infants of the Spring* perfunctorily as the vehicle of Thurman's personal bitterness, self-hatred, and suicidal impulses directed to the critical destruction of the entire renaissance generation. "No one who has read *The Blacker the Berry* will doubt that the source of this self-hatred was his dark complexion." Actually, Thurman was critical of the renaissance because it was naïve, innocent, optimistic, and engaged in the promotion of art. After all the talking was over, Thurman knew that it would take a lot of hard work and skill to write good novels and short stories and poems. And he knew that little truly good art had come from that theorizing. . . .

It is on this ground that Thurman satirized the Harlem Renaissance in *Infants of the Spring*. It was not merely bohemianism which was at fault, but the very self-conscious promotion of art and culture typified by Alain Locke and the "New Negro." He knew, or at least some part of him knew, that artistic production was an extremely personal, individualistic thing, not to be turned on or off by nationalism of any kind. And as he looked over the results of a decade of Negro art, his perhaps too critical mind could find very little to applaud, his own work included. So he wrote *Infants of the Spring*, one of the best written and most readable novels of the period, to bury the renaissance once and for all.

Nathan Irvin Huggins. *Harlem Renaissance* (New York: Oxford University Press, 1971), pp. 239–41

*Infants of the Spring* was Thurman's second novel. In 1929, he had published *The Blacker the Berry*, a novel concerned with middle-class racial self-hatred. Although critics generally applauded his choice of subject, they panned his performance. They were quite right. Thurman could not even bring his main character to life. He was too obsessed with her hatred of her black skin to give her the human dimensions so important in skillful characterization.

*Infants of the Spring* was no improvement. It is warped by Thurman's bitterness over the failure of the Renaissance and, perhaps, over his own failure as an artist. Devoid of plot, the novel chronicles the aimless lives of the inhabitants of Niggeratti Manor—the Harlem intelligentsia and would-be intelligentsia who just seem to drift from party to party and drink to drink. The novel is flawed by the interminable discussions of these characters. The only two men who possess any real talent, Raymond and Paul, pontificate upon various issues of large import. They are little more than obvious mouthpieces for Thurman. In fact, Thurman is so overly concerned that each of his characters should reflect certain points of view that he never lifts them above stereotype. . . .

He never put himself at a great enough distance to look at them with some objectivity and wider perspective. One suspects that in writing of the failure of the Renaissance, he was really more concerned with his own.

James O. Young. *Black Writers of the Thirties* (Baton Rouge: Louisiana State University Press, 1973), pp. 210, 212

BIBLIOGRAPHY
*The Blacker the Berry*, 1929; *Harlem* (with William Jourdan Rapp), 1929; *Infants of the Spring*, 1932; *The Interne* (with A. L. Furman), 1932; *Tomorrow's Children*, 1934; *High School Girl*, 1935

# TLALI, Miriam (1933–)
## South Africa

*Muriel at Metropolitan* is largely autobiographical, based on [Miriam] Tlali's experiences in a hire purchase firm in Johannesburg. . . . [However], it has a theme which goes beyond the beginning and end of the contents.

Metropolitan, the H.P. firm, is a microcosm of South African life, with its variety of people and their relationship to each other.

Muriel is unhappy there, not so much because of the way she is treated by the white staff but because she has to become part of the system of charging unduly high interest rates to black purchasers who can ill afford it. She hates having to ask for their particulars and passes and thus becoming identified with the establishment. Muriel is never in doubt, of course, where her loyalty lies. She would not defraud the firm herself and refuses to cooperate with another black employee who is doing so, but she would not dream of giving him away. Muriel's inner tensions increase. While she "knew the laws of this country" and did not want to "stage a one-man protest against them," the constant insults also tell on her eventually. Since the white clerical workers will not sit in the same office with Muriel, a workshop in the attic is cleared for her. Later she is moved downstairs into a section of the general office, separated from her white colleagues by cabinets and steel mesh wires. When the white women object to her using the same toilet, the boss promises to repair an outside toilet for her, but this never happens so she takes a leisurely stroll to the nearest public convenience.

Muriel needs the money, so she resigns only when she finds another job. This is with a garage concern, but ironically she later finds she cannot accept it after all, because the owner, an Italian immigrant, is less adept than her Jewish boss in bribing the authorities not to implement the apartheid laws governing the employment of blacks and therefore cannot obtain the necessary permission.

Irony is the moving force in the story. It sets the tone in which the absurd situations forming the action are told, and it underlies the description of the characters. It provides the humor with a sharp and serious undertone. The boss, Larry Bloch, is completely believable. Although we see only his business face, we can easily assume the rest to form a rounded picture. He is pleasant, he makes no bones about the fact that money is his god. Muriel looks on with amused tolerance. She accepts his brand of morality and never blames him for his system of doing business, only herself for being part of it. The three white women and the black characters also come to life. They are not an anonymous and interchangeable set of people identified by their color only. . . .

Miriam Tlali's second novel, *Amandla*, meaning "Power," was published by Ravan Press in 1980. The censors probably did not go further than the title and the picture of the clenched fist on the cover, both symbols of the struggle for freedom, before banning it. *Amandla* is a very different novel from *Muriel at Metropolitan* in every respect. Gone is most of the easy humor, the ironic approach, the tolerance. . . . [The] bitterness of . . . earlier writers and the hope which was emerging from it has given way to rage, frustration, and confrontation. The characters in *Amandla* and their creator have experienced the Soweto uprisings, and it has altered their outlook. Muriel did not want to stage a one-man protest. In *Amandla* almost all the characters know that they must be part of a combined protest against the system. The struggle is a hard and ruthless one, and it has transformed their lives. . . .

The racial ideas in *Amandla* concern the events in Soweto when school-children rebelled against their inferior education, boycotted the schools, and were confronted by the police. The events are seen through the eyes of members of a family whom these events affect in various ways. Pholoso is a nineteen-year-old matriculated student. One of his friends is shot during a demonstration, which affects Pholoso enormously. He becomes a protest leader. Later he is arrested, tortured, and put into solitary confinement. While being transferred he manages to escape; as he is wandering from place to place evading further arrest, he and others organize large-scale demonstrations in Soweto and elsewhere. Eventually, when arrest seems inevitable, he leaves the country in secret. Pholoso is the central character around whom the events in the novel are built, but there are many others, members of his extended family and their friends; all their lives are disrupted by the events in Soweto.

In the course of the narrative we learn about every aspect of life in black townships in a period of crisis: how the students organize demonstrations and strikes, meeting literally underground (in a bunker under a church) and swearing oaths of secrecy based on traditional initiation formulas. We see the mourners at the graveside of children killed in confrontation with the police. There is fear, but the dominant mood is one of defiance. The liberation of women, in the black South African context, means that women must play their part and this they do courageously. The melodrama of violence . . . now comes to a head, and again it is the melodrama of real events. For art and psychology, and anything extraneous to the events, Tlali can find no place in literature; there is no place for it in life at such a time. At the end of the novel Pholoso's girlfriend, Felleng, has come to say farewell; and they are waiting for his transport across the border. He is telling her of an incident during the crisis when he tried in vain to protect a white man who had been taken hostage. The young couple only have a short while left together and Pholoso tries to change the subject: "Let us talk about more pleasant things, Felleng. Let us talk about ourselves." The girl replies: "But we are talking about ourselves, Pholoso. Talking about this land is talking about ourselves."

> Ursula A. Barnett. *A Vision of Order* (London: Sinclair Browne, 1983), pp. 157–58, 161–63

[Tlali] displays an incisive knowledge of the application of the vicious doctrine of apartheid to the blacks in South Africa. Her two novels concentrate on the inhumanity and cruelty of this system, the complete denial of human rights to the blacks, and the consequences of such a denial as manifested in the Soweto riots of 1976. She describes in detail the institutional arrangements which are designed to make the blacks second-class citizens in their own country and discusses the effectiveness of some of the measures Africans are taking to fight the obnoxious laws of apartheid. . . .

*Muriel at Metropolitan* discusses in great detail the depressing situation in South Africa where the system of apartheid has poisoned relations between the white and black communities, and made the achievement of racial harmony difficult. The policy of separate development for the two races is used as a smoke-screen to oppress the blacks and keep them in perpetual bondage. The blacks cannot fend for themselves and have to depend on the whites for their livelihood. They are treated as second-class citizens and are prevented from benefitting from an economy to which they make so much contribution. For the blacks South Africa is a place of physical and mental torture; for the whites it is a paradise. Yet without the sweat and labor of the black proletariat, the Republic cannot survive economically. It is to the hard work and perseverance of the blacks that "the Republic owes her phenomenal industrial development." A situation in which the white minority oppress the black majority is manifestly unjust. A political arrangement which proclaims the superiority of one culture to another is untenable. An attitude of mind which undermines a black man's ability and performance because of the color of his skin only helps

to produce resentment and discontent. It kills initiative and destroys any sense of loyalty to the state. . . .

It is to this organized injustice, of which the blacks are the victims, that the author directs her attention in the novel. Attention is focused on the Metropolitan Radio to show how it reflects in [its] staff policy, methods of operation and attitude to customers the system of apartheid. Muriel is made to play a substantial part in the work of the company and react with the staff and customers in order to reveal the weaknesses in concept and organizational structure which exist in the establishment. . . .

In *Amandla* the author continues her assault on the iniquitous system of apartheid in South Africa. This is a more ample work than the previous novel. She brings in more details and uses these effectively by concentrating them on the Soweto riots of June 16, 1976. The riots are presented as the unavoidable outcome of the flagrant denial of human rights to the blacks. When oppression assumes the monstrous proportions that one reads about in this novel, then the reaction is bound to be violent.

> Oladele Taiwo. *Female Novelists of Modern Africa* (New York: St. Martin's Press, 1984), pp. 163, 175–76, 180

Miriam Tlali's most recent publication, *Mihloti* in many ways fits into the same generic pattern as [her] autobiographical works but with a variation in format. It is a collection of interviews, travelogues, an autobiographical account of her detention, and her classic story "Point of No Return." . . . The author's prefatory remarks locate the text's purpose. *Mihloti* means "teardrops" and each piece she writes presents various shades of the pain, grief, strength, and struggle that is black South African life. There are many painful pieces. Her "Detour into Detention," for example, reveals all the pathos connected to Steve Biko's death and the mass arrest and brutal treatment of people who were attempting to journey to the funeral. "Point of No Return," which anchors the collection, provides a dialogue on the need for self-sacrifice and commitment to a larger struggle than to individual satisfaction. Her first work, *Muriel at Metropolitan*, had detailed the experiences of a South African woman as she works in a store which is portrayed as a microcosm of the South African apartheid system. It is an autobiographical novel, and Tlali takes us through Muriel's unwitting collaboration with the dehumanizing system because of her work. Her position as a clerk in this department store places her in the uncomfortable position of being caught between her people and the Jewish owner and staff. Not only is her relationship with them a challenge, but she has to participate in a system which exploits. She constantly describes herself as feeling like a traitor; but except for a few outbursts, continues throughout her career at Metropolitan to do her job well. Muriel's final decision to leave Metropolitan is not an assertive resolution to abandon the system but is prompted by the fact that she is offered a higher-paying job with better conditions elsewhere. She discovers unfortunately that she is not immune from apartheid's machinations as even in the promised new position, the question of the African woman's place recurs. Interestingly, the "toilet" metaphor figures prominently at the close of the novel as if to underline her ambiguous position. Earlier in the text and at Metropolitan, the white female co-workers had expressed indignation at her using their toilet facilities, and she had been instructed to use one down the street. Her job at Continental Scooter Repairs is delayed because a special toilet has to be constructed for her.

*Amandla*, her second novel, describes the activities of Soweto youth in their struggle against the system. We see the resourcefulness of the youth who are now engaging in guerrilla warfare. The burning of an administrative building and the ceremony for the raising of a grandfather's tombstone, provide the forum for ongoing debate and dialogue (largely by men) on the mode of dismantling apartheid. The work provides a vast canvas of characters and activities which seems to mirror the turmoil of South African life.

Carole Boyce Davies. *Ufahumu*. 15, 1–2 (1986–1987), pp. 124–25

*Muriel at Metropolitan* is very largely autobiographical; it is, however, devoid of all reference to the private life of the author beyond her work in the secretarial office of a white-owned firm in Johannesburg, Metropolitan Radio. In spite of its name, the firm sells a bit of everything: radios and electrical appliances certainly, but also the kind of coal-fired stove currently used by blacks in the townships, carpets, and furniture such as sofas, tables, and armchairs. The boss, Mr. Bloch, employs—apart from his own sister, Ms. Kuhn—a second white woman, Ms. Stein, who is an Afrikaner, as well as some white and colored mechanics and a number of black delivery men and [truck] drivers, who also function as retrievers of merchandise. . . .

Muriel/Miriam depicts her own feelings and the small world which gravitates around her with considerable verve and sensibility. The minor occurrences of everyday life reveal the characters in all their complexity, which she portrays, whoever they are, without Manichaeism. Reflections of a political nature, when they appear, are not laid on thick in an artificial manner: Miriam Tlali does not seek to convince, to ''get a message across,'' but simply to show human relationships as truthfully as possible as she sees them around her. Her book is a sociological document of the first importance, not only because the milieu portrayed lies at the point where the worlds of white and black meet, but also, as far as the latter are concerned, because they form part of a culture going through a process of change. *Muriel at Metropolitan* is no less a full-fledged literary work for that. One has difficulty in accepting the affirmation made by the author/narrator as early as the fourth page of the text that she is not a writer and has no pretensions to authority in the study or the representation of human behavior—the opposite is the case.

Jacques Alvarez-Pereyre. *Matatu*. 2, 3–4 (1988), pp. 112–14

*Amandla* is constructed as an account of the lives of Soweto dwellers in the year after the uprising. The use of dialogue and the interweaving of several human-interest stories allows Tlali to present a number of areas of black discontent. . . .

After a brief prelude during the Israeli Embassy siege in Johannesburg in 1975, *Amandla* describes the events of the uprising mainly through the experiences and conversations of an extended family living in the Moroka area of Soweto. The love affair of Felleng and Pholoso, a high school student who becomes the leader of the Soweto Student Representative Council until his arrest, is one of the main areas of attention of the novel: *Amandla* ends with their parting and his departure into exile. Several other stories are interwoven with this: the death and funeral of Dumisani, shot by the police in the first clash between police and students; the

attempts of Pholoso's grandmother, Mrs. Moeng (Gramsy), to save enough money to erect a tombstone on her husband's grave in Braamfontein Cemetery; the difficulties her niece Agnes experiences in her marriage to a drunk husband; the effect the dislocations of the Soweto uprisings have on her other niece, Nana, and her politically articulate husband, Moremi; an adulterous affair featuring a black policeman, Nicodemus; the political organization undertaken by a group of students under Pholoso; Pholoso's capture and escape from imprisonment and his subsequent exile. Into this web of familial experience Tlali places a number of other figures, historical events, and issues of discontent and political debate in Soweto at the time.

Kelwyn Sole. *Research in African Literatures*. 19, 1 (Spring 1988), pp. 66–67

Muriel [in *Muriel at Metropolitan*] is undisguisedly Miriam [Tlali] herself. It is Tlali's experience in the white job market that concerns her. Her offense at the apartheid regime is personal. She makes the point about how unfair the system is to her as a black woman over and over again. She complains bitterly about how she is paid far less for often more work than her white female counterparts. But her personal offense against the racist and capitalist job market becomes a concerted economic analysis of the position of black labor, which is controlled entirely by white interests.

Muriel works in a white Afrikaans radio shop with a predominantly black clientele. When she first joins the establishment one of her black colleagues tells her: ''the only thing I am not happy about is the rate of interest at this place. It's killing our people. Every time I introduce a person here, I know he'll pay and pay and pay. It makes me feel guilty, like I've brought him to be slaughtered.'' These conditions of extremely high interest exist only for the black consumer who makes one-third less in a comparable job than the white consumer does. These conditions are part of the economic system which first forced black people into urban communities by annexing their land through high taxation and then keeps them at the lowest economic level by mercilessly charging high interest for common household commodities.

There is something else which Tlali documents in her first . . . novel. This involves her stories of Western women as well. For those of us who cherish ''a dream of a common language,'' Tlali bursts the illusion of the universal sisterhood of women. Muriel records how colonialism and capitalism (both phenomena occurring at the same time) have eroded the possibility of a joint struggle. The very fact . . . that white Western women have economically benefited and are benefiting from the colonies precludes spontaneous cross-cultural solidarity between First-and Third-World women. As we all know, this problem was expressed in the split between black and white feminists in this country. In South Africa, as Tlali tells us, the split is very clear.

In Metropolitan Radio, the two white women, Mrs. Kuhn and Stein, are not only allowed to have better working space and conditions, but if Muriel is given more privileged work by the boss, they are up in arms against her: ''Just because she knows a bit of English . . . she thinks she is like us, you know.''. . . As long as Muriel has kept to the place prescribed for her by the Afrikaan women, the pretense of friendship could continue unhindered. This aspect of Third-World women's herstories is rooted in the actual betrayal by First-World women, and indeed places these personal testimonies in their political context.

Huma Ibrahim. In Carol Ramelb, ed. *Biography East and West* (Honolulu: University of Hawaii Press, 1989), pp. 123–24

*Amandla* certainly captures the immediacy of events and draws the reader into the confused apprehensions which must be the lot of many of the participants in such a period of social turmoil. She allows the reader to stumble on events, on connections between characters, and on sequences of cause and effect in much the same state of bewildered ignorance as must have been the lot of many of the citizens of Soweto. This could have welded itself into a brilliant artistic play to draw the reader into significant experience of the action of the novel. But somehow it never does: it remains accident rather than design. The writer's rejection of Western structural devices may have been as deliberate as it was necessary; nevertheless the confusion of the action merely seems to reflect a confusion in the mind of the writer which is never resolved. It may be that the black South African reader, familiar with township relationships and interconnections, is less at a disadvantage here than the Western reader. And, after all, the novel is aimed at the black South African reader. However, there seems a low level of organizational awareness even on the part of the central characters, though their prototypes in the real event obviously constructed some loose organizational framework to control their activities and their destiny as much as they could in the teeth of accelerating events. Thus even for the black South African reader, there is a failure to transmit an important element of revolutionary consciousness.

Jane Watts. *Black Writers from South Africa* (New York: St. Martin's Press, 1989), p. 222

Miriam Tlali is an African writer working within a Third-World context, and her aim is to represent her people and their aspirations. Her project is primarily political and humanistic, rather than aesthetic or formal. Tlali rejects what she terms ''intellectualism'' and in her writing often shows little respect for traditional generic categories of ''novel'' and ''short story.'' In the case of *Muriel at Metropolitan* and *Amandla*, for example, she presents her texts as ''novels'' but interjects discursive and often seemingly tangential elements of history and social commentary. The result is not a well-crafted artifact, but rather a loosely woven rendering of the fabric of black experience from the perspective of a black woman. Her most recent offering, *Mihloti*, is a disparate collection of prose pieces that reflect on the lives of black women under apartheid. Any critical approach that aims to do justice to the character of her work must take into account that her purpose as a writer is to use her art as a weapon in a continuing political struggle. As Rebecca Matlou observes: ''Her literature reflects life and it responds to the realities of the situation around her. She is committing her art to the needs of the people.'' Form, therefore, is determined by the imperatives of her project, which is didactic in nature, as she herself notes in an interview in 1981: ''I regard the raising of the level of consciousness of blacks as my prime responsibility, I am personally committed to doing this . . . I must go deeper into them, their feelings, try to make them understand their hopes, desires and aspirations as a people.''

Tlali's work has developed across the period of what is known as the ''renaissance'' of black writing, the 1970s and 1980s, and reflects the temper of the times by offering first social protest (in *Muriel at Metropolitan*) and then political resistance (in *Amandla*), always from a black woman's perspective. In the 1980s her interest in women's issues has intensified and *Mihloti* adds a feminist voice to the black writing in English. . . .

The writing of Miriam Tlali spans a period of almost twenty years. The fabric of black experience that she presents includes threads of history, both personal and communal; and her work covers the history of her people from Sophiatown in the 1950s, Sharpeville in the 1960s, Soweto in the 1970s and continuing into the early 1980s. She is shortly to edit an anthology of writing by black women in South Africa and also to publish her first collection of short stories with a British publishing house. She travels frequently to Europe and America to talk about her work, yet is not widely known here. Surely it is in the context of the developing critical interest in South African women writers . . . that Miriam Tlali deserves to be given wider recognition.

Cecily Lockett. In Cherry Clayton, ed. *Women and Writing in South Africa: A Critical Anthology* (London: Heinemann, 1989), pp. 276–77, 285

For Miriam Tlali's Muriel, an accountant/clerk in *Muriel at Metropolitan*, it is a sense of guilt which prompts her to her act of resistance. Her ambivalence is evident when she laughs with her white co-workers about the 'funny first names' of other blacks yet she feels strongly the inequities of the society:

> You shudder at the thought of bringing into this world children to be in the same unnatural plight as yourself, your parents and your grandparents before you—passing on a heritage of serfdom from one generation to another. You are not human. Everything is a mockery.

While representing herself in terms of her Christian values and moral superiority, Muriel in turning a blind eye on the scam being perpetrated by Douglas and the postman who steal radios from Douglas and Muriel's employers, feels no sense of guilt, even though she recognises that her silence constitutes her as an accomplice; rather, 'what [she] feared most was what [she] knew would happen to Douglas and his family if he was found out'. The tension for Muriel lies between the sense of moral equivocalness and political outrage:

> Taking those portables from a man like Mr Bloch who had all the laws in his favour to protect him and his descendants for all time, and to provide for their security, well-being and comfort, would never compare with the suffering which was reflected all over Douglas's face even as he stood there trying to force a smile.

Although Muriel feels strongly the inequities experienced by blacks, she is not incapable of alignment along class lines and across race lines; perhaps surprisingly, she feels a sense of sympathy for her white coworkers whose racism she encounters daily, and she empathises with their professional dissatisfaction. She conceptualises it, however, as a fight on a 'different battlefield':

> For the whites, the struggle was that of human beings trying to better themselves. For the blacks it was that of the

underdogs, voiceless and down-trodden. In addition to the difficult task of making a living we still had to labour under the effects of a rigid apartheid system supported by our own colleagues. Yet we had the same problems. We were all under the thumb of a demanding boss, who was unyielding in many ways, giving little consideration to the fact that we had private lives of our own, homes and dependants to look after. (163)

If 'non-racial working-class consciousness' is unusual in South Africa, it is not unknown. In the novel, this intersection of race and class is short lived, for Muriel immediately foregrounds white rejection of this sense of a common ground: 'as long as the system granted them certain privileges that the other racial groups did not enjoy, then they were contented. If they were treated the same, they grew resentful'. For Muriel, there is no intrinsic difference between the workers who are subjected to inconsideration on the job by their common employer; for whites, however, the sense of substantive difference needs to be retained.

Ultimately, Muriel's sense of complicity in the exploitation of her fellow Africans overwhelms her and she resigns. As well as feeling vulnerable because of the nature of her job, particularly when issuing summonses for the retrieval of electrical goods bought on hire purchase—'I dreaded to think what would happen to me and my family in Soweto (where taking life means nothing), if it were known that I was responsible for the letters'—she also feels a sense of solidarity: 'I would never again place myself in a position in which I had to ask for pass-books or be "loyal to the firm" at my own people's expense'. Muriel shifts from a sense of assimilation to one of a hard won politicisation. She struggles with the will to enact her feelings and resign, since this would place hardship on her own family: 'perhaps it is high time we, too, went on our knees and prayed God to grant us that boldness, unintimidated by fear, to stand up against those things that we believe are not right—and to suffer the consequences'. . . .

A sense of limitations placed on female involvement is also evident in Miriam Tlali's *Amandla* (1980) which documents responses to the 1976 Soweto students' resistance to the attempted imposition by the apartheid regime of Afrikaans as the medium for instruction. Indeed, Pholoso, a male student leader, endorses conservative values about male and female involvement in a key speech which is both patronising and contradictory. There is considerable tension between his rationalisation of women's limited participation as dependent on constraints on the social mobility of women, an argument used in the action against passes in the 1950s, and his exhortations that women should be freed from subservient roles. This implies a struggle between Tlali's need to construct a strong black male in a positive role and the more radical implied authorial ideology which sees that black women's social roles are circumscribed. It seems apparent that Tlali, too, feels the tension of 'prov[ing] her blackness.' Pholoso says:

I am surprised that no-one has asked why there are no women in this innermost core. The reason is that it is very difficult for them to move about easily from one point to another without the risk of being molested in some way. As you know we have very active women who are indispensable to the cause. In many instances, they are our "feelers." They do a lot of conscientising by engaging in the many women's organizations which attract large numbers, in the church, for instance.

His subsequent endorsement of the liberation of women is undercut, first, because it is authorised by a male and, second, because a chief strategy is intended to be the criticism of women who do not conform to this new mandate:

Our girls and women can accomplish a lot if we let them. Let us avoid the pitfalls of the past when women were confined to the kitchen, and were never allowed to read. Literature is for everyone. . . . The women were brainwashed into believing that the only thing they could do was to wait on us and be at our disposal. . . . Criticise them and make them feel inadequate because they are not reading politics and newspapers. . . . I know of women who complain that their menfolk don't want them to read books. . . . Let us liberate ourselves from this destructive kind of thinking. (89)

Answering a question from Lockett about the fact that she seems, in *Amandla*, to be suggesting that women must play a 'supportive role to men in the struggle,' Tlali confirms this is 'because they are not allowed to come to the forefront. If they were allowed by the system—and by the men—they would. Many women protect their husband's egos by playing up the fact that they are merely supportive, and they really know they are the very ones who are behind the forceful nature of the men.'

Margaret Miller. *Hecate*. 24, 1 (May 1998), pp. 118–44

BIBLIOGRAPHY
*Muriel at Metropolitan*, 1975; *Amandla*, 1980; *Mihloti*, 1984; *Footprints in the Quag*, 1989

# TOLSON, Melvin B. (1900–1966)
## United States

It is fitting that Dodd, Mead and Company, publishers of Dunbar's poems forty years ago, should bring out *Rendezvous with America*, a volume of poems from the pen of Melvin B. Tolson, one of the most articulate Negro poets of the present generation. Dunbar was the poet-interpreter of a people still somewhat primitive but struggling to throw off the thwarting effects of years of slavery. Tolson is the full-throated voice of a folk that feels its power surging up and that has come to demand its place in a country it helps to make great and free. Much of the promise indicated in the best of the formal English poems of Dunbar reaches its fulfillment in the poetry of Professor Tolson. . . .

Professor Tolson in his two sustained poetic efforts, "Rendezvous with America" and "Dark Symphony," catches the full and free rhythmic swing and the shifting tempo of the verses of Walt Whitman—or of the late Stephen Vincent Benét. Both poems exhibit genuine poetic feeling, facility of expression, and vividness. The title poem, which is especially strong in imagery, is so apt an interpretation of and challenge to America that it deserves a lasting place in the anthologies of American literature. . . .

Some readers will doubtless find a few of the poems difficult reading in spots, for, as a teacher of English, Tolson is fairly well saturated with literary allusions; and, occasionally, his vocabulary naturally has a tendency to be learned. But most of the poems in the present collection can be understood and enjoyed by a wide public; and they deserve a wide public. For here is poetry with pleasing melody and rhythm, maturity of expression and imagery, and personal depth and universal interest. *Rendezvous with America* establishes Tolson as a substantial American poet.

Nathaniel Tillman. *Phylon.* 5, 4, 1944, pp. 389–91

What influence [*Libretto for the Republic of Liberia*] will have upon Negro poetry in the United States one awaits with curiosity. For the first time, it seems to me, a Negro poet has assimilated completely the full poetic language of his time and, by implication, the language of the Anglo-American poetic tradition. I do not wish to be understood as saying that Negro poets have hitherto been incapable of this assimilation; there has been perhaps rather a resistance to it on the part of those Negroes who supposed that their peculiar genius lay in "folk" idiom or in the romantic creation of a "new" language within the English language. In these directions interesting and even distinguished work has been done, notably by Langston Hughes and Gwendolyn Brooks. But there are two disadvantages to this approach: first, the "folk" and "new" languages are not very different from those that White poets can write; secondly, the distinguishing Negro quality is not in the language but in the subject-matter, which is usually the plight of the Negro segregated in a White culture. The plight is real and often tragic; but I cannot think that, *from the literary point of view*, the tragic aggressiveness of the modern Negro poet offers wider poetic possibilities than the resigned pathos of Paul Laurence Dunbar, who was only a "White" *poète manqué.* Both attitudes have limited the Negro poet to a provincial mediocrity in which one's feelings about one's difficulties become more important than poetry itself.

It seems to me only common sense to assume that the main thing is the poetry, if one is a poet, whatever one's color may be. I think that Mr. Tolson has assumed this; and the assumption, I gather, has made him not less but more intensely *Negro* in his apprehension of the world than any of his contemporaries, or any that I have read. But by becoming more intensely Negro he seems to me to dismiss the entire problem, so far as poetry is concerned, by putting it in its properly subordinate place. In the end I found that I was reading *Libretto for the Republic of Liberia* not because Mr. Tolson is a Negro but because he is a poet, not because the poem has a "Negro subject" but because it is about the world of all men. And this subject is not merely asserted; it is embodied in a rich and complex language, and realized in terms of the poetic imagination.

Allen Tate. *Poetry.* July 1950, pp. 217–18

Tolson's *Libretto for the Republic of Liberia*, commissioned by the first African republic, has in its American publication an introduction by Allen Tate. Mr. Tate is a Confederate of the old school who has no use for Negroes but who will salute an exception to the race. . . . But in trying to assert that Tolson has been assimilated by the Anglo-American tradition, he puts Tolson in quarantine and destroys the value of the poem—possibly this critic's conscious intention. Thus it took a Southern intellectual and poet, an anti-Negro poet, to introduce Tolson's *Libretto for the Republic of Liberia.* That was the only possible literary context for a great Negro poet ten or fifteen years ago: he must in that context be captured and returned to colonization, to that Tradition which had enslaved his ancestors, and would continue to do so if it could manage it.

The refusal to see that Tolson's significance lies in his language, Negro, and that only that language can express the poetic sensibility of the Negro at the door of freedom, is a final desperate maneuver to contain the Negro within the traditional culture. And for that it is too late. The Tradition is already antebellum.

The falsification I speak of is that of trying to assimilate Tolson into the tradition when he was doing the opposite. The fact that Tolson's *Libretto for the Republic of Liberia* is unknown by white traditionalists gives the lie to the critic's assertion that Tolson has risen above Negro experience to become an "artist." The facts are that Tolson is a dedicated revolutionist who revolutionizes modern poetry in a language of American Negritude. The forms of the *Libretto for the Republic of Liberia* and of *Harlem Gallery,* far from being "traditional," are the Negro satire upon the poetic tradition of the Eliots and Tates. The tradition cannot stand being satirized and lampooned and so tries to kick an authentic poet upstairs into the oblivion of acceptance. But the Negro artist won't stay in the attic anymore than he stayed in the cellar.

Karl Shapiro. *Wilson Library Bulletin.* June 1965, p. 853

Melvin Tolson offers [*Harlem Gallery*] as preface to a comprehensive Harlem epic. Its roots are in the Twenties, but they extend to the present, and very strong here are the spirit and symbols of the African heritage the poet acknowledges and reverences. He is as skillful a language fancier as the ablest "Academician." But his language startles more, agitates more—because it is informed by the meanings of an inheritance both hellish and glorious.

You will find in this book a much embroidered concern with Art; many little scheduled and cleverly twisted echoes from known poetry ("with a wild surmise," "a Xanthippe bereft of sonnets from the Portuguese," "a mute swan not at Coole," "a paltry thing with varicose veins," etc.); a reliance on clue-things, the thing-familiar; Harlemites of various "levels" and categories; humor and wit that effectively highlight the seriousness of his communiques. . . .

Although this excellent poet's "news" certainly addresses today, it is very rich and intricate news indeed, and I believe that it will receive the careful, painstaking attention it needs and deserves when contemporary howl and preoccupation are diminished.

Gwendolyn Brooks. *Negro Digest.* September 1965, pp. 51–52

One admires Tolson's big-hearted mind, but his verse too obviously comes *via* Eliot and Pound in the classroom. It also comes boosted in public by a willing suspension of critical disbelief among American reviewers towards a Negro who has made the "modern" grade in poetry. Encyclopedic erudition, world-shaking utterances, sardonic epigrams fill out *Libretto for the Republic of Liberia.* What is missing is the inner world of poetry, a story and rhythm for it all. "Possibly," writes Karl Shapiro, "it is too early for the assimilation of such a poem, even by poets." And possibly it will always be so.

Tolson is at present Director of the Dust Bowl Theatre, Langston University, and Professor of Creative Literature. *Harlem Gallery* shows he knows his America well. He writes as an academic gone under-ground. The subterranean and gothic dimension of American life that the White Negro mind has been exploring for the past ten years is here explored once again, but this time by a real Negro mind in a kind of Menippean satire and with an overall equanimity of tone. . . .

*Harlem Gallery*, as a sign of its universal sweep, lists its poems ''Alpha,'' ''Beta,'' ''Gamma,'' down through ''Omega,'' and the writing simply teems with names. Fortunately, there are no notes. Even more fortunately, none are needed as the best quality of the poems is the humor with which these strange but simple people make their entrances and exits as incidents in Tolson's mind. There is a passive, droll, detached manner about this American Anti-Dream.

James Tulip. *Poetry Australia*. June 1966, pp. 38–39

When Tolson had completed *Libretto for the Republic of Liberia*, he felt as if he had put the best of himself into the long ode. In only a matter of months, however, he began to think of the old manuscript of Harlem portraits which he had scrapped several years before. At first, he toyed with the problem of how to weave the characters into a story; then he conceived the idea of a great epic work which would narrate the story of the black man in America from the early 1600's to the present. He envisioned a five-volume work: *Harlem Gallery: Book I, The Curator; Book II, Egypt Land; Book III, The Red Sea; Book IV, The Wilderness*; and *Book V, The Promised Land*. This undertaking was unique and ambitious, and Tolson was an artist who refused to be hurried. He spent the next eleven years writing and polishing *Harlem Gallery: Book I, The Curator* while he was completing his teaching career at Langston University. . . . The illness which cut short Tolson's work struck without warning. . . .

In *Harlem Gallery*, he succeeded in creating, through representative types, dramatic scenes, and philosophical discussions, a community of black Americans who offer an education to all who meet them in the one hundred and seventy-three pages of their existence. In this book, his style is somewhat relaxed in comparison with *Libretto for the Republic of Liberia*—though it is also intellectually stimulating and challenging. In much of *Harlem Gallery* he employs the dramatic scene, which he enjoyed writing and wrote effectively. A former dramatist, Tolson, like Frost, had ''a great love of people and of talk.'' Tolson ranges easily from the level of intellectual word play on down. The allusions and special learning are still there, but the sometimes strained quality of *Libretto for the Republic of Liberia* is gone. In this work, Tolson truly found his voice as he juxtaposed the literary and literal worlds in which he lived.

Joy Flasch. *Melvin B. Tolson* (New York: Twayne, 1972), pp. 38, 147

*Libretto for the Republic of Liberia* is not only one of the great odes in the English language, it is in many respects one of the finest poems of any kind published in the English language during the twentieth century, so far as my acquaintance goes. Allen Tate's minor caveats are meaningless to me in the presence of Tolson's afflatus and Jovian humor. I get carried away. And the ''irony,'' which Tate comments on, that an American government has never, could never have, commissioned such an official poem to be read in Washington, only reminds me that I agree with Tolson that ''these truths,'' of which Jefferson wrote, are bearing and will bear fruits for which white Americans must yet acquire the taste. Imagine if you can the humor of this black Pindar of a Mark Twain celebrating

the dignity of the small African republic founded by American ex-slaves with a poem at once so everyday American and yet so arcane, abstruse, and allusive that even with the author's notes it files largely over the highbrow heads, not merely in his Liberian audience but of his fellow countrymen, white or black, literati suckled on Eliot and Pound for a quarter century! . . .

It is not [Eliot's] *The Waste Land* or *Four Quartets*, I think, which limn the present or light the future with the past so well that scholars salvaging libraries of this era may someday guess what manner of men were we. Nor is it even Sandburg's *The People, Yes*, nor William Carlos Williams' *Paterson*, but Tolson's *Harlem Gallery*, rather, where the heart of blackness with the heart of whiteness lies revealed. Man, *what* do you think you are is not the white man's question but the black man's rhetorical answer to the white man's question. No poet in the English language, I think, has brought larger scope of mind to greater depth of heart than Melvin Tolson in his unfinished song to the soul of humanity.

Roy P. Basler. *New Letters*. Spring 1973, pp. 67, 73

Throughout *Harlem Gallery*, Tolson uses couplets (though usually not in the metrically identical lines of ''Alpha'') to suggest thematic connections that he then revises in an ongoing process of individual and communal call and response. Placing couplets at the end of only two poems—''Alpha'' and the bitterly ironic ''Nu''—Tolson implicitly subverts their traditional use for thematic resolution. Rather, he presents all resolutions as strictly provisional. Connections such as those implied by the ''plain-brain'' rhyme in ''Alpha'' or the ''mouth-South'' rhyme in ''Psi'' emerge as momentary points of reference but are quickly withdrawn or revised. Frequently, subsequent use of a rhyme sound from a couplet explicitly redefines the provisional resolution, as in the following stanza from ''Phi'':

> Beneath the sun
> as he clutched the bars of a barracoon
> beneath the moon
> of a blind and deaf-mute Sky
> my forebears heard a Cameroon
> chief, in the language of the King James Bible, cry,
> ''O Absalom, my son, my son!''

The stanza is a virtuosic prosodic performance, drawing on both visual and oral techniques. The couplet rhyming ''barracoon'' and ''moon'' stresses the slave's alienation. Almost immediately, however, Tolson redefines the tentative resolution with the rhyme of ''Cameroon,'' directing attention to the African heritage that belies the New World definition of blacks as slaves. The off-rhymes of ''sun'' and ''son'' with ''moon-barracoon-Cameroon'' emphasize the underlying tension, as does Tolson's manipulation of the iambic-anapestic metrical base to create thematically significant clusters of stressed syllables. The clusters on ''deaf-mute Sky,'' ''forebears heard,'' and ''King James Bible'' suggest the Euro-American attack on the African sense of an animate universe implied by the capitalization of ''Sky.'' It seems particularly significant that the African's alienation involves the destruction of aural/oral connections; the deafness of the Sky cuts off the call and response between human beings and the world they live in, a basic modernist dilemma. Similarly, the allusion to the biblical Absalom both reflects the shift in Afro-American religious sensibility from spirit (the sun) to Jesus (the son) and invokes Faulkner's literary meditation on the absurdity and destructiveness of America's racial dichotomies.

Distrusting all resolutions, questioning all definitions, Tolson commits himself to an artistic process that envisions a world in which the artist can express all sides of his/her sensibility, whether in the Zulu Club, the Gallery, or the anthologies of world literature. The problem with such a commitment, as for all synthetic artists, is that most actual audiences continue to perceive art in a frame of mind conditioned by belief in the reality of the dichotomies. Only a small segment of the modernist/Euro-American/visual arts audience understands the populist/Afro-American/oral aesthetic as a serious encounter with the central problems of contemporary consciousness. Conversely, most audience members who are aware of black cultural traditions view the modernist tradition as irrelevant to Afro-American concerns. The question then becomes: how can the artist conscious of aesthetic and social interrelationship, actual or potential, help create an audience not bound to the dichotomies? In *Harlem Gallery*, Tolson suggests that if the artist can establish contact with the members of a particular audience through the use of techniques and themes already familiar to it, then he/she can use that contact to initiate the audience into new aesthetic and social experiences. In theory, Tolson's mastery of irony and Euro-American modernist aesthetics should enable him to communicate something of the blues sensibility to an audience comfortable with the performances of Pound and Eliot. His familiarity with call and response and the details of Afro-American experience should enable him to communicate the value of the high modernist tradition to an audience that associates it primarily with an oppressive social system. To date, this approach has attained at best limited success. Most readers of the Euro-American modernists simply ignore Tolson while most members of the Afro-American audience prefer music to literature and, on the occasions when they turn to poetry, respond more readily to the relatively direct calls of Hughes or Gwendolyn Brooks. A blues irony, which Tolson would certainly have recognized, adheres to the situation. Public and private, racial and modern, Tolson's Afro-modernist blues suite remains ironically enmeshed in the dichotomies it so eloquently and thoroughly discredits.

> Craig Hansen Werner. *Playing the Changes: From Afro-Modernism to the Jazz Impulse* (Urbana: University of Illinois Press, 1994), pp. 178–80

BIBLIOGRAPHY
*Rendezvous with America*, 1944; *Fire in the Flint*, 1952; *Libretto for the Republic of Liberia*, 1953; *Harlem Gallery*, 1965; *Caviar and Cabbage: Selected Columns by Melvin B. Tolson from the Washington Tribune, 1937-1944*, 1982

# TOOMER, Jean (1894–1967)
## United States

Reading [*Cane*], I had the vision of a land, heretofore sunk in the mists of muteness, suddenly rising up into the eminence of song. Innumerable books have been written about the South; some good

books have been written in the South. This book *is* the South. I do not mean that *Cane* covers the South or is the South's full voice. Merely this: a poet has arisen among our American youth who has known how to turn the essences and materials of his Southland into the essences and materials of literature. A poet has arisen in that land who writes, not as a Southerner, not as a rebel against Southerners, not as a Negro, not as apologist or priest or critic: who writes as a *poet*. The fashioning of beauty is ever foremost in his inspiration: not forcedly but simply, and because these ultimate aspects of his world are to him more real than all its specific problems. He has made songs and lovely stories of his land . . . not of its yesterday, but of its immediate life. And that has been enough.

> Waldo Frank. Foreword to Jean Toomer, *Cane* (New York: Boni and Liveright, 1923), p. vii

*Cane* does not remotely resemble any of the familiar, superficial views of the South on which we have been brought up. On the contrary, Mr. Toomer's view is unfamiliar and bafflingly subterranean, the vision of a poet far more than the account of things seen by a novelist—lyric, symbolic, oblique, seldom actual. . . .

*Cane* is sharply divided into two parts. The first is a series of sketches, almost poetic in form and feeling, revolving about a character which emerges with very different degrees of clarity. The second half is a longish short story, "Kabnis," quite distinct from the sketches, and peculiarly interesting. In this Mr. Toomer shows a genuine gift for character portrayal and dialogue. In the sketches, the poet is uppermost. Many of them begin with three or four lines of verse, and end with the same lines, slightly changed. The construction here is musical, too often a little artificially so. The body of the sketch tends to poetry, and to a pattern which begins to lose its effectiveness as soon as one guesses how it is coming out. . . .

It isn't necessary to know exactly what [a passage] means in order to find pleasure in reading it. Which is one way of defining poetry. And once we begin to regard Mr. Toomer's shorter sketches as poetry, many objections to the obscurer symbolism and obliqueness of them disappear. There remains, however, a strong objection to their staccato beat. The sentences fall like small shot from a high tower. They pass from poetry into prose, and from there into Western Union.

"Kabnis," the longest piece in the book, is far the most direct and most living, perhaps because it seems to have grown so much more than been consciously made. There is no pattern in it, and very little effort at poetry. And Mr. Toomer makes his Negroes talk like very real people, almost, in spots, as if he had taken down their words as they came. A strange contrast to the lyric expressionism of the shorter pieces. A real peek into the mind of the South, which, like nearly all such genuinely intimate glimpses, leaves one puzzled, and—fortunately—unable to generalize.

> Robert Littell. *New Republic*. December 26, 1923, p. 126

The world of black folk will some day arise and point to Jean Toomer as a writer who first dared to emancipate the colored world from the conventions of sex. It is quite impossible for most Americans to realize how straight-laced and conventional thought is within the Negro World, despite the very unconventional acts of the group. Yet this contradiction is true. And Jean Toomer is the first of our writers to hurl his pen across the very face of our sex conventionality. In *Cane*, one has only to take his women characters *seriatim* to realize this: Here is Karintha, an innocent prostitute; Becky, a fallen white woman; Carma, a tender Amazon of unbridled desire; Fern, an unconscious wanton; Esther, a woman who looks age and bastardy in the face and flees in despair; Louise, with a white and a black lover; Avey, unfeeling and unmoral; and Doris, the cheap chorus girl. These are his women, painted with a frankness that is going to make his black readers shrink and criticize; and yet they are done with a certain splendid, careless truth.

Toomer does not impress me as one who knows his Georgia but he does know human beings; and, from the background which he has seen slightly and heard of all his life through the lips of others, he paints things that are true, not with Dutch exactness, but rather with an impressionist's sweep of color. He is an artist with words but a conscious artist who offends often by his apparently undue striving for effect. . . .

All of these essays and stories, even when I do not understand them, have their strange flashes of power, their numerous messages and numberless reasons for being. But still for me they are partially spoiled. Toomer strikes me as a man who has written a powerful book but who is still watching for the fullness of his strength and for that calm certainty of his art which will undoubtedly come with years.

W. E. B. Du Bois. *Crisis*. February 1924, pp. 161–62

In Jean Toomer, the author of *Cane*, we come upon the very first artist of the race, who with all an artist's passion and sympathy for life, its hurts, its sympathies, its desires, its joys, its defeats and strange yearnings, can write about the Negro without the surrender or compromise of the artist's vision. So objective is it, that we feel that it is a mere accident that birth or association has thrown him into contact with the life he has written about. He would write just as well, just as poignantly, just as transmutingly, about the peasants of Russia, or the peasants of Ireland, had experience brought him in touch with their existence. *Cane* is a book of gold and bronze, of dusk and flame, of ecstasy and pain, and Jean Toomer is a bright morning star of a new day of the race in literature.

William Stanley Braithwaite. In Alain Locke, ed., *The New Negro* (New York: Albert and Charles Boni, 1925), p. 44

In writing about Toomer, one is discussing a man who has been poetically quiet for the past eight years. His importance lies in this fact, gainsaid only by J. W. Johnson, since he neglects to include him in his *Second Book of American Negro Verse*—that whether or not he has written anything recently, he remains one of the more important Negro poets. . . .

There is ample enough poetry as poetry in his one book for him to be included in any select niche of poetical art. . . .

In *Cane* raving critics and poetasters recognized a naturalism of such a distinctive kind that the applause was deafening. This novel element in his poetry was distinctive because first of all, here was a Negro who composed not as a Negro, but as an artist, and secondly because there was not in his poetry any obsession of race. At first, the critics could not understand that a Negro could write poetry that did not reek with rebellion and propaganda. Toomer wrote as a poet, never as an apologist. Reading the turbulent and rebellious

poetry of the McKay of that time, this poetry of Toomer's came upon the poetic horizon as a breath of sweet, cool air.

Eugene Holmes. *Opportunity*. August 1932, p. 252

One of the most talented of the Negro writers, Jean Toomer, went to Paris to become a follower and disciple of [the Russian founder of Unitism, George] Gurdjieff's at Fontainebleau, where Katherine Mansfield died. He returned to Harlem, having achieved awareness, to impart his precepts to the literati. . . .

But the trouble with such a life-pattern in Harlem was that practically everybody had to work all day to make a living, and the cult of Gurdjieff demanded not only study and application, but a large amount of inner observation and silent concentration as well. So while some of Mr. Toomer's best disciples were sitting long hours concentrating, unaware of time, unfortunately they lost their jobs, and could no longer pay the handsome young teacher for his instructions. Others had so little time to concentrate, if they wanted to live and eat, that their advance toward cosmic consciousness was slow and their hope of achieving awareness distant indeed. So Jean Toomer shortly left his Harlem group and went downtown to drop the seeds of Gurdjieff in less dark and poverty-stricken fields. . . . From downtown New York, Toomer carried Gurdjieff to Chicago's Gold Coast—and the Negroes lost one of the most talented of all their writers—the author of the beautiful book of prose and verse, *Cane*.

The next thing Harlem heard of Jean Toomer was that he had married Margery Latimer, a talented white novelist, and maintained to the newspapers that he was no more colored than white—as certainly his complexion indicated. When the late James Weldon Johnson wrote him for permission to use some of his poems in *The Book of American Negro Poetry*, Mr. Johnson reported that the poet, who, a few years before, was ''caroling softly souls of slavery'' now refused to permit his poems to appear in an anthology of *Negro* verse—which put all the critics, white and colored, in a great dilemma. How should they class the author of *Cane* in their lists and summaries? With Dubose Heyward and Julia Peterkin? Or with Claude McKay and Countee Cullen? Nobody knew exactly, it being a case of black blood and white blood having met and the individual deciding, after Paris and Gurdjieff, to be merely American.

One can't blame him for that. Certainly nobody in Harlem could afford to pay for Gurdjieff. And very few there have evolved souls.

Now Mr. Toomer is married to a lady of means—his second wife—of New York and Santa Fe, and is never seen on Lenox Avenue any more. Harlem is sorry he stopped writing. He was a fine American writer.

Langston Hughes. *The Big Sea* (New York: Alfred A. Knopf, 1940), pp. 241–43

Jean Toomer's *Cane* is an important American novel. By far the most impressive product of the Negro Renaissance, it ranks with Richard Wright's *Native Son* and Ralph Ellison's *Invisible Man* as a measure of the Negro novelist's highest achievement. Jean Toomer belongs to that first rank of writers who use words almost as a plastic medium, shaping new meanings from an original and highly personal style. Since stylistic innovation requires great technical dexterity, Toomer displays a concern for technique which is fully two decades in advance of the period. While his contemporaries of the Harlem School were still experimenting with a crude literary realism, Toomer had progressed beyond the naturalistic novel to "the higher realism of the emotions," to symbol, and to myth. . . .

Toomer's symbols reflect the profound humanism which forms the base of his philosophical position. Man's essential goodness, he would contend, his sense of brotherhood, and his creative instincts have been crushed and buried by modern industrial society. Toomer's positive values, therefore, are associated with the soil, the cane, and the harvest; with Christian charity, and with giving oneself in love. On the other side of the equation is a series of burial or confinement symbols (houses, alleys, machines, theaters, nightclubs, newspapers) which limit man's growth and act as barriers to his soul. Words are useless in piercing this barrier; Toomer's intellectualizing males are tragic figures because they value talking above feeling. Songs, dreams, dancing, and love itself (being instinctive in nature) may afford access to "the simple beauty of another's soul." The eyes, in particular, are avenues through which we can discover "the truth that people bury in their hearts."

> Robert A. Bone. *The Negro Novel in America* (New Haven: Yale University Press, 1958), pp. 81, 84

Now that the Jean Toomer papers have found a home at the Fisk University library it is no longer necessary to speculate as to why Toomer ceased to write after he published *Cane* in 1923. In fact, he did not cease to write. He continued to write, and write voluminously; but to no avail—he could find no publisher. The story of Toomer's literary efforts after 1923 is a story of frustration, despair and failure—this after what was surely one of the most promising beginnings in the history of American literature. Toomer's story is one of a young man caught up in the tangled skein of race relations in America. But it goes beyond even that. For a time, at least, it was the story of modern man; the story of a search for identity—for an absolute in a world that had dissolved into flux. It is a story of success—at the age of thirty-one his search for an identity-giving absolute was over. It is a story of tragedy. As long as he was searching he was a fine creative artist; when the search ended, so did his creative powers. So long as he was searching, his work was the cry of one caught in the modern human condition; it expressed modern man's lostness, his isolation. Once Toomer found an identity-giving absolute, his voice ceased to be the cry of modern man and became the voice of the schoolmaster complacently pointing out the way—his way.

> S.P. Fullinwider. *Phylon.* Winter 1966, p. 396

Jean Toomer may have considered 1933 a year of new beginnings after ten years of fruitlessness, ten years of wandering. . . .

Toomer regarded *Eight Day World* as "a revelation of the psyche of a single man or woman," an explanation of the meaning of this terrestrial and cosmic journey. He felt that for once he had expressed all the details. He was correct only that the book represented a new Toomer, with all of the flaws and few of the virtues of the old. . . .

He could not return to the style and thought of *Cane*. He refused to recognize his major limitations—inability to develop a dramatic plot, inability to write about himself effectively, and refusal to

write about anyone else. He could not free his art from his dogma. To understand his work, one needed to comprehend and to believe his philosophy that the only meaningful life is a continuous growth toward Being, a process requiring the separate and total development of mind, soul, and body. Beyond that philosophy, nothing existed. Toomer could sketch, lyrically or realistically, the people whom he knew. His talent was perhaps restricted in range, but it approached genius within its limits. But the engraver wanted to paint murals and could not.

> Darwin T. Turner. *In a Minor Chord: Three Afro-American Writers and Their Search for Identity* (Carbondale: Southern Illinois University Press, 1971), pp. 52–53, 56

When Jean Toomer's *Cane* was published in 1923, it was noticed by only a very few reviewers and critics, most of them black, and it sold around five hundred copies. It seemed that, as Thomas Bailey Aldrich said of an early volume of Emily Dickinson's poems, "Oblivion lingers in the immediate neighborhood." It is now known that Toomer continued to write, but after *Cane* he published only a few pieces in "little" magazines, a play *Balo*, and a privately printed collection of epigrams and aphorisms called *Essentials*. The rest was silence—and mystery. To all intents and purposes, Jean Toomer vanished. In efforts to see him, people like Allen Tate made appointments for meetings, but when the time came Toomer failed to appear. . . .At his death in 1967 he was apparently almost forgotten, and his masterwork had been out of print for nearly half a century. . . .

Finally, in 1969, two years after Toomer's death, Harper & Row brought out a new paperback edition of *Cane* in their Perennial Classic series. It found a receptive audience among both scholars and general readers, and already stories and poems by Toomer, often from *Cane* itself, are being included in anthologies of American literature.

The story of Jean Toomer and *Cane*, then, follows the archetypal pattern of birth, death, and resurrection, on a smaller scale perhaps, but similar to the stories of the reputations of Herman Melville, Henry James, F. Scott Fitzgerald, and other American writers who have experienced oblivion and rehabilitation.

> Frank Durham. Preface to Frank Durham, ed., *The Merrill Studies in Cane* (Columbus, Ohio: Charles E. Merrill, 1971), pp. iii–iv

Toomer's answer to the quest for Negro identity [in *Cane*] is to find one's roots in the homeland, the South, and to claim it as one's own. It is to look into the fullness of the past without shame or fear. To be, and to relive the slave and the peasant and never be separated from that reality. It is to know Father John, the black, gnarled, ugly, brutalized slave. To know and to accept slavery: the horror of it, the pain of it, the humiliation of it. To absorb it all, this living and dying past, as part of blood and breath. The Negro has to embrace the slave and the dwarf in himself. He, like a son, despite all, must learn to love his father—flesh of his flesh, blood of his blood—to be a man. . . .

The real power of Jean Toomer's conception and its superiority to the romanticisms of McKay and Cullen was that *Cane*, though symbolic and mystical, dealt with the past as a palpable reality. It faced the fact of the South and slavery. The final, and perhaps supreme, irony of the primitives was that they were, in their quest for Africa, in their fancy of Timbuctoo and Alexandria, forsaking their actual past. They were in effect denying that which was immediate, personal, and discernible for something which was vague, distant, half-myth. Toomer asked to embrace the slave father, while Countee Cullen fancied ''spicy grove and cinnamon tree.''

Nathan Irvin Huggins. *Harlem Renaissance* (New York: Oxford University Press, 1971), pp. 186–87, 189

''I am of no particular race. I am of the human race, a man at large in this human world, preparing a new race. I am of no specific region, I am of earth'' [writes Toomer in *Essentials*]. Walt Whitman himself would have subscribed to this declaration of identity, which bears witness to the transcendence and sublimation of race, not to its repudiation. We will see the new race emerge in that great poetic upsurge, ''Blue Meridian,'' which still, more than a quarter-century after publication, unfortunately remains almost unknown. In this long poem, Toomer reaches the last stage of a spiritual experiment whose point of departure was *Cane*, and which aims at the reconstruction of man. . . .

The fundamental thesis of ''Blue Meridian'' is the need for a regenerated America, to be achieved through the regeneration of each individual and each community composing it, of an America once more united around the spiritual dream of its founders. . . .

The ultimate driving force behind the whole body of Jean Toomer's work is his ardent longing for unity at the highest level of the spirit. Setting out from the immediate data of racial difference, he rapidly soars above them—too rapidly for the taste of those who, unable to imagine any universe not black and white, were not internally ready to join him in his pursuit of the Blue Meridian. They had expected him to be a poet of his race, but he resolved to be purely the poet of man. Did this provide sufficient reason for the accusation that he had repudiated his origins and abandoned his own people? One can scarcely believe that Jean Toomer, with a mind so tempered and with a soul so generous, could have toyed even fleetingly with the notion of treason. Quite to the contrary: it would seem that we must count him among the very great for having refused, for his own part and on behalf of his fellows, the shackles that are worn by men divided. [1963]

Jean Wagner. *Black Poets of the United States* (Urbana: University of Illinois Press, 1973), pp. 264, 274, 281

It may come as a surprise to many of his new admirers, but Jean Toomer viewed himself as a cultural aristocrat, not a cultural nationalist. Recalling how the discovery of [Johann Wolfgang von] Goethe's *Wilhelm Meister* helped him to pull together the scattered pieces of his life, he wrote in 1918:

I was lifted into and shown my real world. It was the world of the aristocrat—but not the social aristocrat; the aristocrat of culture, of spirit and character, of ideas, of true nobility. And for the first time in years and years I breathed the air of my land. . . . I resolved to devote myself to the making of myself such a person as I caught glimpses of in the pages of *Wilhelm Meister*. For my specialized work, I would write.

More like the avant-garde of the Lost Generation than the vanguard of the Harlem Renaissance, Toomer was deeply involved in creating a synthesis of new forms and themes. In the wake of World War I he completely devoted himself to the task of learning the craft of writing. During this period he confessed to being strongly influenced by two approaches to literature. First, he was attracted to those American writers and works that used regional materials in a poetic manner, especially Walt Whitman, Robert Frost, and Sherwood Anderson. Secondly, he was impressed by the Imagists. ''Their insistence on fresh vision and on the perfect clean economical line,'' he wrote, ''was just what I had been looking for. I began feeling that I had in my hands the tools for my creation.'' The artistic fusion in *Cane* (1923) of symbols of the Black American's African and Southern experience and the Afro-American tradition of music bears witness to this influence and establishes the book as a landmark in modern American literature.

Following the publication of *Cane*, Toomer, convinced by personal experience and extensive reading that, ''the parts of man—is mind, emotions, and body—were radically out of harmony with each other,'' discovered the method for unifying these three centers of being in the teachings of George Ivanovitch Gurdjieff, the ''rascal sage.'' A synthesis of Western science and Eastern mysticism, Gurdjieff's system was a rigorous discipline that taught self-development and cosmic consciousness through self-awareness, sacred exercises, temple dances, and various psychic feats. In 1934 Toomer began making annual retreats to the Institute for the Harmonious Development of Man, Gurdjieff's headquarters in Fontainebleau-Avon, France. He returned as a Gurdjieffian prophet to spread the gospel in Harlem—where his sessions included such talented artists as Aaron Douglass, Wallace Thurman, Harold Jackman, Nella Larsen, and Dorothy Peterson—and in Chicago. He also continued writing voluminously, but most of these writings, which repudiate racial classifications and celebrate a Gurdjieffian vision of life, were rejected by publishers.

The most significant exception is ''Blue Meridian,'' a long Whitmanesque poem. ''Blue Meridian'' is the poetic zenith of Toomer's quest for identity. It represents the resolution of a long process of agonizing emotional and intellectual turmoil over the problems of race and aesthetics as viewed through the prism of his own personal crisis. Toomer began grappling with the question of race in high school and began the first draft of the poem, then entitled ''The First American,'' in the early 1920s. Completed in 1930, a section of the poem appeared as ''Brown River, Smile'' the following year in The Adelphi. But the entire poem was not published until 1936, when it appeared in Kreymborg, Mumford, and Rosenfeld's The New Caravan.

Toomer the poet/prophet sings exultantly of a new world order in ''Blue Meridian.'' Neither Black nor white, Eastern nor Western, the new order of man is ''The blue man, the purple man''; the new people are the ''race called the Americans,'' and the new society is America, ''spiritualized by each new American.'' Through evolution the regenerated American is also the harmoniously developed, universal man, free of definitions and classifications that restrict or confine the vitality of his being. For Toomer, as for Whitman, America was, in Whitman's exuberant words, ''the greatest poem,'' ''a teeming nation of nations,'' and ''the race of races.''

''Art,'' writes Toomer (in *Essentials*), ''is a means of communicating high-rate vibrations,'' and the artist is he ''who can combine opposing forms and forces in significant unity.'' Toomer splendidly fulfills both the letter and spirit of these definitions in "Blue Meridian." As with Cane, the chief symbol of "Blue Meridian" is implicit in its title. In the context of the poem, the meridian, which generally denotes the highest point of prosperity, splendor, and power, symbolizes the Spirit of mankind. On the geographical and astronomical planes it also represents the imaginary circles which connect both geophysical poles and the circle passing through the celestial poles. Other important symbols relating to the spiritual power of the new American include the Mississippi River, a pod, a grain of wheat, a waterwheel, crocks (i.e., earthenware receptacles), and the cross. The title of the poem thus generates a series of symbols which reinforce the themes of potential wholeness, evolution, and cosmic consciousness. So intricate is the symbolic pattern that the color progression of the meridian from black to white to blue corresponds to the movement of the poem through different stages of man's historical and organic development to a higher form.

Retracing the stages of man's development and the process by which the new American was born, Toomer invokes the primeval forces of life waiting to energize select men to a higher form of being. In the first section of the poem primal darkness is upon the face of the deep:

> Black Meridian, black light,
> Dynamic atom-aggregate,
> Lay sleeping in an inland lake.

In order to elevate himself man must let the "Big Light" in to awaken his dormant potential. Neither Christian nor mystical in the traditional sense, the genesis is an eclectic yet harmonious blend of Darwinian evolution and Gurdjieffian mysticism. The poet invokes the "Radiant Incorporal,/The I of earth of mankind" to crash through confining barriers, across the continent and spiral on into the cosmos:

> Beyond plants are animals,
> Beyond animals is man,
> Beyond man is the universe.

At this stage the Mississippi River, sister of the Ganges and main artery of the Western world, has the potential for becoming a sacred river, a potential which is realized in the White Meridian section of the poem. Similarly, each form that appears in the first section, the Black Meridian stage, contains the seed for its future growth. For, since Adam, man has been in a state of becoming, ready to unite parts and reconcile opposites into a moving whole of total body and soul:

> Men of the East, men of the West
> Men in life, men in death,
> Americans and all countrymen—
> Growth is by admixture from less to more,
> Preserving the great granary intact,
> Through cycles of death and life,
> Each stage a pod,
> Perpetuating and perfecting
> An essence identical in all,
> Obeying the same laws, unto the same goal,
> The far distant objective,
> By ways both down and up,
> Down years ago, now struggling up.

The poet is firm in the conviction that the capacity for growth is common to all men and has always been present in America. Past generations, however, have not fully realized their human potential and, by extension, the promise of the nation and the universe.

Toomer's purpose, then, is not the glorification of the common man but the celebration of "A million men, or twelve men," the result of a long process of natural selection and self-realization. Elitist in nature, Toomer's view of modern man in "Blue Meridian" is essentially Gurdjieffian. Comparing man to an acorn, Gurdjieff says (in Fritz Peters's *Boyhood with Gurdjieff*; 1964):

> Nature make many acorns, but possibility to become tree exist for only few acorns. Same with man—many men born, but only few grow. People think this waste, think Nature waste. Not so. Rest become fertilizer, go back into earth and create possibility for more acorns, more men, once in while more tree more real man. Nature always give—but only give possibility. To become real oak, or real man, must make effort.

For both Gurdjieff and Toomer, the real man, the new man, must manifest Understanding, Conscience, and Ability. Defective men—those who lack or fail to acquire these three attributes—become the fertilizer for perpetuating the promise of eternally awake souls. . . .

At the end of *Cane*, the apparent analog for the *Black Meridian* section of the poem, Toomer left us with only the promise of self-realization. In "Blue Meridian" he moved beyond race to become the prophet of a new order of man known as the American. But rather than a betrayal of race for a cheap chauvinism, Toomer's poetic resolution of his private and public quest for identity represents a genuine effort to cast off all classifications that enslave human beings and inhibit the free play of intelligence and goodwill in the world.

> Bernard W. Bell. *Black American Literature Forum*. 14, 2 (summer 1980), pp. 77–80

An aura of melancholy surrounds Jean Toomer, an aura traceable to the writer's failure to reconcile a debilitating inner conflict involving his intellectual prowess, his artistic sensibility, his racially mixed African-European-American ancestry, and his familial circumstances. A mulatto who could pass for white, and the grandson of the Honorable P.B.S. Pinchback, the first and only Afro-American to serve as governor of a state (initially lieutenant governor, then acting governor of Louisiana during the Reconstruction era), Toomer nevertheless suffered intellectual and artistic frustration as a result of his ethnic marginality.

Had Toomer dealt more directly with these circumstances, rather than escaping into philosophical idealism in quest of a universal man—whose prototype he ultimately proclaimed himself to be—we might have been spared the tediously ingenuous "spiritualizing of experience" he undertook in his writings, to the detriment of his poetry in particular. Had he followed the course he set in the poems he wrote between 1919 and 1923, some written specifically for inclusion in his highly successful experimental novel *Cane*, Toomer would have left not only a more aesthetically viable poetic legacy but a more voluminous body of poetry and fiction as well. Instead, he ended up as the essentially one-book author he is likely to remain even if everything he left behind were to be published, judging from the qualitative description we have so far of his papers in the Yale Library.

*Cane*, indisputably an American classic, is a striking melange of prose sketches, poems, etc. in which Toomer both celebrates and bids farewell to his African-American heritage. It was in the creative atmosphere of Cane that Toomer produced the poems coeditors Robert B. Jones and Margery Toomer Latimer, Toomer's daughter, assign to what they call Toomer's ''Ancestral Consciousness Period (1921–1923).'' Relatively early in his long life (1894–1967), Toomer began to repudiate his African-American identity. Partly for this reason, and despite Cynthia Earl Kerman and Richard Eldridge's excellent biographical study of him in *The Lives of Jean Toomer: A Hunger for Wholeness* (1987), Toomer remains pretty much a figure of myth. And it is essentially his mythopoeic attraction that invests Toomer's collected poems with an extra-aesthetic appeal, perhaps to the point of inviting excuses for their aesthetic flaws.

It is Toomer's early poems that we find most aesthetically viable, most acceptable to our contemporary sensibility in their concreteness and existentiality—an experiential existentiality, rather than the philosophical one coeditor Robert B. Jones attributes to the later ''Christian Existential'' poems written out of Toomer's Quaker experience. . . . [Among these are the apprentice poems he wrote] under the influence of Orientalism, French and American symbolism, and Imagism (1919–1921), and those written under the same aesthetic impetus but with an African-American consciousness (1921–1923), the poems that appear in *Cane*. After these early periods, a deleterious abstractionism begins to creep into Toomer's poems, although in many of those written later (1924–1955) there remain traces of Toomer's recognition of the value of concrete representation.

Toomer's metaphysical, abstractionist tendency first appears in the poem ''As Eagles Soar'' and intensifies in the lengthy, rhetorically derivative Whitmanesque ''The Blue Meridian,'' which Jones calls ''minor classic of American literature.'' That it may well be, but for reasons other than aesthetic. A much shorter poem of the same period, ''It Is Everywhere,'' better accomplishes a similar philosophical purpose, in less detail but with such felicitous lines as: ''And what comes down goes up again/Within the view of purple hills.''. . .

The short poem ''The Chase'' exemplifies Toomer's increasing tendency in his later poems to yoke poetry and rhetoric to the detriment of the former. The two-stanza poem opens in concrete description but virtually self-destructs in a sudden rhetorical shift in the second half of the second stanza, a pattern that marks subsequent poems in the book and Toomer's poetry generally. The first half of the second stanza, extending though markedly diluting the concrete descriptiveness of the first, works fine: ''As the white bird leaves the dirty nest,/Flashes in the dazzling sky,/And merges in the blue.'' But then an aesthetically numbing metaphysical application rushes the poem toward its meaning: ''May my spirit quit me,/And fly the beam straight/Into thy power and thy glory.''

As an archetypal victim of the American color caste system, Jean Toomer stands with the likes of Beat poet Bob Kaufman. Toomer's poems, poetic prose, and critical commentary invite the speculation that under more equitable conditions he would have become a truly outstanding American Modernist, ranking with the likes of T. S. Eliot, Ezra Pound, and William Carlos Williams as a shaper of our modern and contemporary poetic sensibilities.

Alvin Aubert. *The American Book Review*. 10, 6 (January-February 1989), pp. 12, 21

BIBLIOGRAPHY
*Cane*, 1923; *Balo*, 1927; *Essentials: Definitions and Aphorisms*, 1931; *The Flavor of Man*, 1949; *The Wayward and the Seeking: A Miscellany of Writings*, 1978; *Jean Toomer: Selected Essays And Literary Criticism*, 1996

# TUTUOLA, Amos (1920–1997)
## Nigeria

Technical faults notwithstanding, *The Palm-Wine Drinkard and His Dead Palm-Wine Tapster in the Deads' Town* is a valuable contribution to West African Literature, both as an exciting story told with characteristic African brevity and symbolism, and as an anthropological study.

Here may be encountered much that is familiar in the folk-lore of West Africa, and much that has never, to my knowledge, been recorded before and is peculiar to the Yorubas. Of the familiar ideas may be mentioned the impersonation of death, the conception of the spirit world, and the symbolic tale of the ever-recurring stranger (*the complete gentleman*) who seduces a maiden who has resisted the local lads, but is in reality no more than a cheap glitter of borrowed limbs. Disillusioned far away from home, the maiden is too broken hearted to think clearly of a way out and is completely helpless. We find this theme in the story of Onwuero and Ogilisi in the Ibo, and I have no doubt that other tribes record similar stories, though perhaps with slight variations.

But new are the explanations for the universal existence of death, of famine, and the impersonation of ''Drum, Song, and Dance,'' which permit Mr. Tutuola to play delightfully upon words: ''Nobody in the world could beat a drum as drum himself could beat, nobody could dance as dance himself, and nobody could sing as song himself could sing.'' And, in the stories of the Red men, and the man who did not know the meaning of the word ''poor,'' one can only wonder whether a warning finger is not being pointed at the present-day Western World, and the ultimate goal to which it is drifting.

C.O.D. Ekwensi. *African Affairs*. July 1952, p. 258

[*The Palm-Wine Drinkard*] is the brief, thronged, grisly and bewitching story, or series of stories, written in young English by a West African, about the journey of an expert and devoted palm-wine drinkard through a nightmare of indescribable adventures, all simply and carefully described in the spirit-bristling bush. . . .

Luckily the drinkard found a fine wife on his travels, and she bore him a child from her thumb; but the child turned out to be abnormal, a pyromaniac, a smasher to death of domestic animals, and a bigger drinkard than its father, who was forced to burn it to ashes. And out of the ashes appeared a half-bodied child, talking with ''a lower voice like telephone.'' There are many other convenient features of modern civilized life that crop up in the black and ancient midst of these fierce folk-legends, including bombs and aeroplanes, high-heel shoes, cameras, cigarettes, guns, broken bottles, policemen. There is, later, one harmonious interlude in the Faithful Mother's house, or magical, techni-colour nightclub in a tree that takes photographs; and one beautiful moment of rejoicing, when Drum, Song, and Dance, three tree fellows, perform upon themselves, and the dead arise, and animals, snakes, and spirits of the bush dance together. But mostly it's hard and haunted going until the drinkard and his wife reach Deads' Town. . . .

The writing is nearly always terse and direct, strong, wry, flat and savoury; the big, and often comic, terrors are as near and understandable as the numerous small details of price, size, and number; and nothing is too prodigious or too trivial to put down in this tall, devilish story.

> Dylan Thomas. *Observer.* July 6, 1952, p. 7

The important thing in Tutuola is his power to set down the collusion of dream and person. The startled critic will find [in *My Life in the Bush of Ghosts*] moments of *Alice in Wonderland*, Bunyan and the Bible, in the story-telling and a groping, Christian jubilation. His ghosts are apocalyptical yet local. He is carried off by a "smelling ghost" to be eaten alive by him. Obscene as a cesspit, crawling with insects and snakes, smeared with urine and rank blood, this thing carries the child off and turns him into a horse. The story goes from one repulsive terror to another, from city after city of the dead, where river ghosts, insect ghosts, burglar ghosts, the ghosts of the Nameless town and the Hopeless town conspire to punish him or to eat him. In each episode the narrator is enslaved and beaten, in one buried alive, in another half roasted on a fire, in others crushed or bitten by snakes. . . .

This would be intolerable because preposterous reading but for two things: the dramatic idea of compulsion in an animistic culture. The boy cannot move, for example, "because the bush wanted me to be in one place"; at another point he is betrayed in his flight by "the talking land," which speaks as he runs over it and so exposes him to his enemies. These inventions are poetic and alarming. The barbarous fantasy is not free, but is ruled by the dreadful conspiracy of primitive belief and sensibility. The other strength of the story is simply its seriousness. The marvellous is domesticated. . . .

Tutuola's fancy is endless; yet it is controlled by the tribal folklore. It discernibly expresses the unconscious of a race and even moments of the nightmare element in our own unconscious. The slimy or electric movements of nightmare, its sickening logic, its hypnotising visual quality, its dreadful meaningfulness, are put down by an earnest and ingenious story-teller. One feels one has been taken back thousands of years to the first terrors of human nature. A book like this disposes at once of the illusions, so useful to settlers, that "the African is a child." Tutuola's voice is like the beginning of man on earth, man emerging, wounded and growing. He is not the specimen of the folklorist and anthropologist, but a man living out a recognisable human and moral ordeal.

> V.S. Pritchett. *New Statesman and Nation.* March 6, 1954, p. 291

Mr. Tutuola's work which I have seen belongs to the world of fantasy and it may seem here a little ironic to consider that the social situation of the Negro in some places belongs to the world of a fantastic and concrete brutality. It is, in a sense, a great relief to come upon *The Palm-Wine Drinkard*. And it is not only the wine that helps us. Mr. Tutuola has magic.

This novel appears to have a certain continuity which satisfies a conventional and respectable requirement of the novel; but on closer inspection, it is made up of a series of episodes which seem to be parts and even fragments of different legends. That is true. The effect of incantation on the reader is also true. But what I want to mention now, which has been passed on as a fact, is the writer's method. It has been said that these episodes were the man's recollection of his mother's or grandmother's stories, rearranged and organised to suit his purpose. If this is true, there is something of the Homeric fable in the undertaking.

The English response to this has been one of surprise, a double surprise. On one level, it is a surprise at the material itself, and on another it is the surprise at Mr. Tutuola's capacity for a certain sustained invention. This surprise may be described as the unasked question: Is it really true? And when one considers that Mr. Tutuola has always been very near, for all I know at the very centre of, what is almost wholly an oral tradition of story-telling, this surprise is understandable. And what is true of Mr. Tutuola, from the point of view of the Other's attitude would, I believe, be equally true, of Mr. Ekwensi, or any other African imaginative writer, although their methods and concerns might vary enormously.

> George Lamming. *Presence africaine.* June-November 1956, pp. 319–20

Tutuola published a third book, *Simbi and the Satyr of the Dark Jungle*, in 1955. Here the heroic figure is a young girl, born with great advantages of every kind, who comes to feel that these must ultimately be paid for by comparable abasement and suffering. This is a theme as universal in literature and myth as that of the deliberate quest; in reality the quest and the ordeal are simply two different ways of expressing the same life-renewing, regenerating experience. The belief that expense must some-how be balanced by equivalent earning or sacrifice, by a "storing-up," may perhaps be described as the mythic "Law of the Conservation of Energy." But in myth it is seen that *man himself*, by heroic action or sacrifice, must renew the energy of his world and keep it in equipoise. As in [*My Life in the Bush of Ghosts*], however, Tutuola seems to be only fitfully aware of this overall theme and he does not succeed in relating Simbi's adventures to it in any significant way. . . .

A much more definite decline is evident in the latest book, *The Brave African Huntress*, which was published in 1958 with illustrations by Ben Enwonwu. This is a workmanlike narrative of a young huntress who sets out for the Jungle of the Pigmies to rescue her four lost brothers. The theme is like that of a simple fairy tale, whereas *The Palm-Wine Drinkard*, a book of comparable length, displayed the close form and episodic richness of a complete heroic cycle, in which events full of terror or grotesque comedy crowded along the pages. In that book, Tutuola casts an incantatory spell over his reader with the very first page. We know at once that a whole new world of the imagination is opening before us.

> Gerald Moore. *Seven African Writers* (London: Oxford University Press, 1962), pp. 51, 54

[Tutuola is] a storyteller in the best Yoruba tradition, pushing the bounds of credibility higher and higher and sustaining it by sheer adroitness, by a juxtaposition of analogous experience from the familiar. It is typical that even the last war should spill onto *The Palm-Wine Drinkard*. The hyperbole of the bomb and the Complete Gentleman—''. . . and if bombers saw him in a town which was to be bombed, they would not throw bombs on his presence, and if they did throw it, the bomb itself would not explode until this gentleman would leave that town, because of his beauty''—is not a rupture in the even traditionalism of Amos Tutuola. It is only writers with less confidence who scrupulously avoid such foreign bodies in their vision of the traditional back cloth. The result in Tutuola is a largeness that comes from an acceptance of life in all its manifestations; where other writers conceive of man's initiation only in terms of photographic rites, Tutuola goes through it as a major fact of a concurrent life cycle, as a progression from physical insufficiency, through the quest into the very psyche of Nature. *The Palm-Wine Drinkard*, as with [D. O.] Fagunwa's *Ogboju Ode* and universal myth, is the epic of man's eternal restlessness, symbolized as always in a Search. Between the author's own exorcism and the evidence of his immediate environment, we may continue our own presumptuous search for meaning.

If however we elect to return, like Tutuola's hero, wise *only* from the stress of experience, it will not have been a totally valueless journey. For Tutuola involves us in a coordination of the spiritual and the physical, and this is the truth of his people's concept of life. The accessories of day-to-day existence only become drawn into this cosmic embrace; they do not invalidate it. Questioning at the end what Tutuola's reality is, we find only a tight web enmeshing the two levels of perception. In his other books, strain becomes evident, effect for the sake of effect; the involved storyteller has yielded to the temptations of the extraneously bizarre, a dictation of his early outsider admirers who thus diffused his unified sensibility. Tutuola is not a primitive writer. With this objection removed, it is possible that the audience for which Tutuola wrote primarily (not that he thought consciously at first of any audience) would come to recognize him for what his talents offer—the contemporary imagination in a storytelling tradition.

Wole Soyinka. *American Scholar*. Summer 1963, pp. 391–92

The conclusion of *The Palm-Wine Drinkard* has its sources in a Yoruba myth. In one version of the Yoruba tale it is the vulture, despised by all other birds, who volunteers to take the sacrifice to Heaven, but when he returns he finds that he is still shunned and outcast. In Tutuola's much more moving version, it is a slave who ''took the sacrifice to heaven for Heaven who was senior to Land . . .'' and when he returns and seeks shelter from the rain which has now begun to fall, no one will permit him into their houses lest he carry them off to Heaven as he did the sacrifice.

Gerald Moore sees the slave as a human sacrifice, and he believes that the return of the slave is really the return of a ghost. He also sees the seniority of Heaven as an indication that ''. . . from henceforth the supreme deity will be the male Sky God and not the old female Earth Goddess, protectress of matriarchy'' (*Seven African Writers*). Anne Tibble, in her *African/English Literature: A Survey and Anthology*, points out that this interpretation will not quite do, because Tutuola specifically refers to Land as ''he,'' so that the deity of Heaven and the deity of Earth are both male. It is

true that Tutuola does refer to Land as male; nevertheless, Moore's interpretation seems basically to be the right one. The Yoruba myth is paralleled in the myths of many cultures, for it represents a transfer of affiliation which did in fact take place in innumerable religions at one time or another—the decision that the heavenly deity was superior to the gods of earth. In many places this change took the form of a rendering of chief homage to a male deity—Our Father which art in heaven—instead of the earth mother with which most religions began, and this shift in emphasis often paralleled a similar social move away from matriarchy.

Whatever the ending contains, intentionally or unintentionally, Tutuola has completed his story not as a theologian but as an artist, with a strong sense of calm after a perilous journey.

Margaret Laurence. *Long Drums and Cannons* (London: Macmillan, 1968), pp. 131–32

[*The Palm-Wine Drinkard*] bowled the English critics completely over. The fascination it held for Dylan Thomas can now be better understood against a background of the man's own belief in the bizarre magic and mesh of language as revealed in his poetry and recently published letters. But unlike Thomas or the much greater Joyce, Mr. Tutuola did not consciously set out to probe further into the depths of man by re-organising afresh the language he knew too well to be exhausted to accept again as an efficient tool to record, explore and extend experience. He in fact provides a concrete case of the ''natural'' performing in the one style known to him. Later when he grows self-conscious and avails himself of the services of a post-tutorial course in English, we can see the results for what they really are as in his *Feather Woman of the Jungle*. . . .

Here is no original language as such but one to be found everywhere in Nigeria in the letters and ''compositions'' written among a vast group of people who for various reasons have not proceeded beyond a certain stage of school. It is a level of English considered ''vulgar,'' half-illiterate by all sections of Nigerian society, and it is for this reason parents disapprove of their children reading Tutuola. . . .

''Naïveté,'' made so much of by the adulators of Mr. Tutuola and incidentally by the followers of the Onitsha market novelette, is not enough; language has to be ''moulded'' by the artist with skill and consciousness. Mr. Tutuola who lacks both of these qualities in his early work sacrifices something of his natural charm and power by trying to acquire them in his later works. It is as if the Onitsha market novelist were to aspire to the equipment of an Achebe. . . .

Nor is his disposition of words Yoruba as Milton's was said to be Tuscan. Rather he adheres to the practice of his adopted language, and it is because he suffers open handicaps here that his is said to be no language for others to imitate but essentially a tour de force or possibly a hoax.

J. P. Clark. *Black Orpheus*. February 1968, pp. 36–37

*Ajaiyi and His Inherited Poverty* is not different from the usual Tutuola stories. It is the story of poverty and search. The search is for wealth which, it is believed, can grant happiness to the searcher. . . .

The prose here captures the freshness and the startling originality of *The Palm-Wine Drinkard*. But Tutuola seems to have become exhausted, and the language of *Ajaiyi and His Inherited Poverty* has the tedium and pathetic boredom of almost all his later work. It seems he has begun to labour to create the old effect. And it just doesn't come off. It would perhaps be rewarding to examine the obvious ''improvement'' which Tutuola's language has undergone; he consults his dictionary and has begun to grasp basic English syntax. Then one gets the impression that the quaintness and the odd usage here and there are put on for effect.

Tutuola, perhaps alone among present day African writers, invites very antagonistic criticism from Africans. He is accused of illiteracy, lack of talent, and of an immensely damaging naïveté which is objectionable to the African élite and their literary spokesmen.

But Tutuola is essentially a story-teller with a remarkable genius for ordering traditional folk material into a readable form. Sadly it seems he could only do this once with *The Palm-Wine Drinkard*; his late works limp along struggling for effect and ending up as brilliant exercises in boredom. One may ask what else can he write after the ghosts, goblins, devils and the fantasy world of dreams and magic? Perhaps nothing.

George Awoonor-Williams. *West Africa*. April 27, 1968, pp. 490–91

*Ajaiyi and His Inherited Poverty*, like Tutuola's other tales, is not traditionally Yoruba, but rather an imaginative narrative that blends tradition with contemporary life. Fantasy creatures like the Witch-Mother and Devil-Doctor live in a money economy, just as Ajaiyi and his townsmen do. As in all Tutuola's tales, both real and fantasy characters are obsessed with counting. They count their wealth in pounds, shillings and pence; they measure their fields in acres and specify the number of miles they travel; they precisely name the time of day at which action takes place; and when the wealth, distance or time exceeds the limits of imagination, it simply becomes ''uncountable.''. . .

Although no one would have difficulty in identifying the author of *Ajaiyi and His Inherited Poverty*, this book is different from the others. The world of fantasy which dominates *The Palm-Wine Drinkard, Simbi and the Satyr of the Dark Jungle, My Life In the Bush of Ghosts*, and *Feather Woman of the Jungle* still exists, but in *Ajaiyi and His Inherited Poverty* it is secondary. More scenes take place in the real world in *Ajaiyi and His Inherited Poverty* and human characters other than the hero are important in these scenes, especially Ajaiyi's sister Aina, and his companions, Ojo and Alabi. Ajaiyi acts in terms of contemporary values, like seeking monetary wealth for himself, and he evaluates the action of his fellow human beings, as well as the actions of the creatures of the fantasy world, in terms of the Christian ethic. . . .

The contemporary world has intruded into the composite imagery of all Tutuola's tales in many ways other than those associated with religion and the desire for large sums of money. However, Tutuola has formerly appeared to be neutral towards the cultural influences of the contemporary world. At least if he was critical of them, his criticism was sufficiently subtle or so clothed in Yoruba symbolism that it was not obvious to a non-Nigerian reader. In *Ajaiyi and His Inherited Poverty* Tutuola takes a definite stand in

reference to some aspects of contemporary Nigerian life, namely, religion, kinship ties and politics.

Nancy J. Schmidt. *Africa Today*. June-July 1968, pp. 22–24

In Tutuola's fiction the imaginatively conceived monsters, the fanciful transformations, and other marvels of oral literature are somehow intellectually refreshing, like brainstorming sessions, utopian thinking, and the wild absurdities of *risqué* jokes. It would seem that our minds are in danger of getting petty and stuffy if we feed too regularly on commonplace reality (perhaps the ''fairy tales'' of science also keep minds less stodgy).

Tutuola's work is of course jampacked with monsters and marvels to give us this sort of mental fillip. What reader, no matter how badly given over to the ''mimetic fallacy,'' could fail to be stimulated by such matters as the self-beating drum that sounds like the efforts of fifty drummers, the free-loaders' hostelry-cum-mission-hospital in the huge white tree, the exhibition of smells, the woman-hill with noisy hydra heads and fire-flashing eyes, the stumpy, weepy-eyed, ulcerous Television-handed Lady, and the concert hall of birds with a guard company of white-shoed ostriches? . . .

Even those critics and readers who do not care for Tutuola's work are likely to admit that he has one characteristic strength—his self-assurance, his literary aplomb, or composure. In spite of the junior clerk English with its distracting nonstandard syntax and vocabulary, in spite of the oddities of typography, in spite of the wildly mythical mode of fiction, Tutuola's authorial voice is magnificently composed, compellingly assured, like some oracle in the heyday of oracles, or like the passionate speech of a man speaking from lifetime convictions. . . .

Another of Tutuola's distinctive literary qualities, the memorability of his incidents, may be partly due to this verve and assurance, this sort of impetuous aplomb, and to his downright, no-nonsense style. Many of his incidents lodge fast in our consciousness; they stick like burrs in the memory. . . .

Although Tutuola is devoted to the mythical mode of thought, his works are full of graphic touches, clear and lively descriptions showing striking imaginative power, that should make the most inveterate partisans of realism lend momentary belief to his magical world.

Harold R. Collins. *Amos Tutuola* (New York: Twayne, 1969), pp. 117–19

In the kaleidoscopic world of Amos Tutuola's novels, all realms flow together, all varying manifestations of reality merge and coalesce. Yoruba myths, customs, and manners synchronize with Western artifacts, bringing about a concretization of concepts and a tautness of imagery. All details are foreground, illuminated by the author's total experience. There is no inherent clash of cultures, for all cultures are his domain and from all of them he derives his material. This material is transmuted through the author's imagination, and the fusion gives to reality a sense of otherness and to myth a veracity.

Much in Tutuola is mythic and folkloric, but much springs from ordinary, everyday, lived reality. Only after being fortified by juju and prepared by sacrifice do his heroes cross over into an imaginary realm contiguous to their own real world to pursue their searches and go on their wanderings. Indeed, Tutuola's novels are the ultimate expression of return to acceptance of tradition in all its varying manifestations. All things flow together, movement away leads to movement back, return follows exile, a new day follows the agony of night.

> Wilfred Cartey. In John Paden and Edward Soja, eds., *The African Experience* (Evanston: Northwestern University Press, 1970), Vol. I, p. 590

The difficulties we face in dealing critically with Tutuola are legion. His works are as difficult to pin down as the monsters he writes about. In talking about the form of these stories, we have no label we can easily use. For convenience it is commonly referred to as the novel, but arguments have also been advanced that the form is that of the extended folktale, the prose epic, or the romance. The structure no less than the language of these works is often confusing, the characters as well as the settings are more often than not fantastic, and the situations we and the characters are presented with are always problematical. While there is a great deal of disagreement over the assessment he should be accorded, it is clear that the words, images and even the sense of what Tutuola is saying more often than not violate our prevailing notions of propriety, Western or African.

This sense of propriety being violated points to a rather significant aspect of Tutuola's work that has not yet been fully explored, namely the rhetorical stance of the author and the relationship between the authorial voice in these works and the audience. The rhetoric, of course, has been touched on by the critics who have recognized that Tutuola is more like a fireside raconteur than a conscious literary artist, but the implications have not been pursued. His rhetoric is that of a riddler; he generates confusion, transgresses propriety, and inverts our normal perceptions of the real, physical world, leaving us with the sheer joy we derive out of participating in that confusion as well as the astonishment we get on emerging from fictional chaos and finding the world reordered.

> Richard Priebe. In Bernth Lindfors, ed., *Critical Perspectives on Amos Tutuola* (Washington, D.C.: Three Continents, 1975), p. 266

The African writer should aim to use English in a way that brings out his message best without altering the language to the extent that its value as a medium of international exchange will be lost. He should aim at fashioning out an English which is at once universal and able to carry his peculiar experience. I have in mind here the writer who has something new, something different to say. The nondescript writer has little to tell us, anyway, so he might as well tell it in conventional language and get it over with. If I may use an extravagant simile, he is like a man offering a small, nondescript routine sacrifice for which a chick, or less, will do. A serious writer must look for an animal whose blood can match the power of his offering.

In this respect Amos Tutuola is a natural. A good instinct has turned his apparent limitation in language into a weapon of great

strength—a half-strange dialect that serves him perfectly in the evocation of his bizarre world. His last book, and to my mind, his finest, is proof enough that one can make even an imperfectly learned second language do amazing things. In this book, *Feather Woman of the Jungle*, Tutuola's superb storytelling is at last cast in the episodic form which he handles best instead of being painfully stretched on the rack of the novel. [1964]

> Chinua Achebe. *Morning Yet on Creation Day* (Garden City, New York: Doubleday, 1975), pp. 100–101

Tutuola was one of the first African writers I ever read (Alan Paton and Laurens van der Post, both white South Africans, were probably the first). This was long before I had the opportunity to study African or even African American literature. I still have my old Grove Press paperback of *The Palm Wine Drinkard* (price, $1.45!), with a quote from Dylan Thomas on the front cover: "a grisly and bewitching story of indescribable adventures." And one of my proudest possessions is a Faber and Faber paperback of *My Life in the Bush of Ghosts* (purchased on the Ife campus for 1.50 naira), personally autographed by Mr. Tutuola on 11 December 1979.

For the record, I think Dylan Thomas's *Drinkard* blurb (perhaps inevitably) mischaracterizes Tutuola's novel. I find Tutuola's writings fascinating, not "grisly," and one of the main features of this fascination is the manner in which Tutuola describes supposedly "indescribable" adventures. His English is certainly not imperial English, nor is it (as some have supposed) wannabe English; rather, it's an English possessed by Yoruba as a vehicle for conveying its own particular magic to the world—in short, an English perfectly appropriate to the material. Thomas is correct, though, when he calls this tale "bewitching." Tutuola definitely had some potent creative juju; the mojo of his imagination was workin' overtime.

Ugandan author Taban lo Liyong called Tutuola "a genius" and dubbed him "the Father of Modern African literature". Though the title of the essay in which he issues this judgment, "Tutuola, Son of Zinjinthropus," seems to suggest that Baba Amos was African literature's primitive ancestor, a sort of aesthetic missing link, it's actually a highly ironic nod to those misguided critics of Tutuola's work who disparaged his achievement and were embarrassed by his success. Tutuola's admirers, though, always outnumbered his detractors, even if we admit that there may have been a dubious basis for some of the early admiration. But "the seduction of the exotic" notwithstanding, time has proven the celebration of Tutuola's work to be justified. He isn't the son of Zinjinthropus, but he certainly is the legitimate son of Oduduwa.

Tutuola also may be an unrepeatable phenomenon, but that doesn't mean that his work is merely a curiosity or a "dead-end" for African writing. To take one prominent, instructive example: despite his advanced education, sophistication, and artistic self-consciousness, there is a profoundly Tutuolan element in the work of Ben Okri, especially in the story "What the Tapster Saw" (from *Stars of the New Curfew*) and the novels *The Famished Road* and *Songs of Enchantment*. . . .

Amos Tutuola passed away in June of 1997 at the age of seventy-seven. Whatever else may be said about his work, it undeniably is part of the foundation of African writing—that part which is sunk most deeply in the substratum and psyche of African culture and imagination. However high and wide the African literary edifice grows, we'll keep coming back to Tutuola, not just as an historically important entity, but as a necessary counterpoint to other developments. Tutuola has become, and as time passes, will continue to become, less exotic and more inevitable as a contributor to the realm of African lit/orature. While we mourn his death, let us celebrate the life of his writings.

Robert Elliot Fox. *Research in African Literatures.* 29, 3 (Fall 1998), pp. 203–8

BIBLIOGRAPHY

*The Palm-Wine Drinkard and His Dead Palm-Wine Tapster in the Dead's Town*, 1952; *My Life in the Bush of Ghosts*, 1954; *Simbi and the Satyr of the Dark Jungle*, 1955; *The Brave African Huntress*, 1958; *The Feather Woman of the Jungle*,1962; *Ajaiyi and His Inherited Poverty*, 1967; *The Witch-Herbalist of the Remote Town*, 1981; *The Wild Hunter in the Bush of the Ghosts*, 1982; *Pauper, Brawler, and Slanderer*, 1987; *The Village Witch Doctor and Other Stories*, 1990

# V

## VILAKAZI, B. W. (1906–1947)

South Africa

Mr. Vilakazi in the richness of his Zulu vocabulary, in the truly African flavor of his imagery and in the exuberant extravagance of some of his descriptions [in *Zulu Songs*] is a true descendant of the *imbongi* [tribal bards]. But the background of his thought is not that of the *imbongi*. He is not much concerned with warlike prowess. Aggrey [the Gold Coast scholar] is a greater hero to him than Shaka [the early-nineteenth-century Zulu chief]. The clay pot family heirloom, the song of the lark, the train that dashes by in the night, leaving him vainly waiting—all the little incidents of daily life serve as starting points for the flow of his verse. He is the human poet rather than the Zulu poet also in the attention he pays to his own emotions and those he observes in others. It is the *imbongi* come to consciousness of the abstract and of the inner self, through contact with the work of other poets and through the unconscious influence of education and European culture.

His technique also is not that of the pagan *imbongi*. He attempts rhyme, but with limited success, as Zulu syllables, invariably ending in vowels, do not present the variety of sound and tone that makes successful rhyming possible. Even the forms of English rhythm that he uses do not supply a perfect medium, for Zulu accents and stresses refuse to be bent into conformity with the beat of the music. But Mr. Vilakazi is an experimenter in a new field and is to be congratulated on the large measure of his success, rather than criticized for small failures. He will perhaps, as he grows surer in his art, develop a technique more indigenous and more pliable to the Zulu words. The Zulu in which the poems are written will be the delight of the linguist and the despair of the tyro. His sensitiveness to words is remarkable and he has gathered a vocabulary which must enrich the Zulu speech. But it is when one turns to the emotional content of the poems that the real talent of the author is revealed and a new respect must be felt for the capacity of the Zulu mind and heart.

J. Dexter Taylor. *Bantu Studies.* June 1935, p. 164

[Vilakazi] began with fiction in a story called *For Ever*. The scene is laid at the mission station of Groutville in the days of [the Zulu king] Mpande. A girl, who as a child was a refugee from Zululand, gives a promise to a boy, who is going off to work in Durban, to wait for him "for ever." The fortunes of both are told in an interesting way. . . .

Dr. Vilakazi is the only Zulu who has attempted to write poetry on any scale, and his first collection of poems was published in the "Bantu Treasury" series under the title of *Zulu Songs*. . . . He afterwards wrote another book of poems, *Zulu Horizons*, and a novel, *Truly, Indeed*, both of which show an advance upon his previous work. The poems are concerned largely with social questions of the day as they affect the Zulu people.

D. Malcolm. *Africa.* January 1949, pp. 37–38

[Vilakazi] believed that Bantu literature would make a notable contribution to the literature of the world. He believed that his people were capable of rising high in intellectual achievement and he devoted his energies, not only to himself, but to the self-effacing and unselfish end of encouraging and advising many a budding Bantu author. . . .

By whatever standards he is judged, there can be no question that he was a poet of high merit. He revealed possibilities in the Zulu language. Even in translation his poetry has vitality and no ordinary beauty. Dr. Dexter Taylor's translation of Vilakazi's poem on the Victoria Falls ["The Victoria Falls"] came as a revelation to English readers of the powers of observation and expression which the latter possessed. He had a large vocabulary which his sensitive spirit and trained intellect used with notable dexterity.

To the African people he remains a shining example of what perseverance and pluck can accomplish, when in the charge of a disciplined mind and spirit. The early years with their remoteness from such means of culture as libraries; that unflagging determination to study by sun or candle-light; that fight with poverty which could not get him down; that refusal to be daunted however towering seemed the summit which he had to climb—these things make one of his rich legacies to his people.

R. H. W. Shepherd. *Bantu Literature and Life* (Lovedale, South Africa: Lovedale Press, 1955), p. 124

Among the Zulus Vilakazi is remembered more as a poet than as a prose writer. I think the main reason for this is that he was mainly responsible for developing poetry whose form departed radically from the traditional Izibongo (or praises). Instead of adopting the style and pattern of the Izibongo, he experimented with European forms. He divided his poems into regular stanzas. He also experimented with rhyme. Many of the poems contained in the first book of poems, *Zulu Songs*, employ rhyme. If the poems in the second book of poems entitled *Zulu Horizons* are any guide, Vilakazi was not happy with the results of his experiment because in *Zulu Horizons* he discarded rhyme almost completely. In only one poem out of a total of twenty did he employ rhyme. I am inclined to think that even in that one poem he employed rhyme because it was a sequel to a poem appearing in the first book in which he had used rhyme.

Those of you who know Zulu will realise just what it means to attempt rhyme in that language. In Zulu only five endings are possible—in the vowels, a, e, i, o, u because Zulu has open syllables. Any rhyming scheme is confined to these endings. English on the other hand uses not only open syllables but closed syllables, that is, syllables ending in consonants. The English poet is, therefore, not hampered in the same way as is a Zulu poet. A Zulu poet who attempts rhyme might have on paper something which looks like rhyme but which does not produce the desired effect on the ear. I believe that rhyme is for the ear more than for the eye. The controversy still rages as to whether or not Zulu is a suitable medium in which to attempt rhyme.

> C. L. S. Nyembezi. *A Review of Zulu Literature* (Pietermaritzburg, South Africa: University of Natal Press, 1961), pp. 7–8

The main direction in Vilakazi's development . . . lay in ever deeper reverence for the Zulu tradition. Many of the poems in [*Zulu Horizons*] deal once more with the great events and figures of the past, the beauty of the Natal landscape, the cult of the ancestors, African respect for the wisdom of old age, or the mission of the poet in Zulu society. The writer's technique also demonstrates that he was not happy with his experiments in the earlier collection [*Zulu Songs*]. He now discards rhyme almost completely, thus rallying to the views expressed by [J. Dexter] Taylor and [Herbert I.E.] Dhlomo. . . .

Although Vilakazi did not engage actively in politics, it is clear that his experience of township life in Johannesburg, because of the contrast it offered with the sheltered seclusion of Natal mission schools and with the comparative humaneness of life in Durban, prompted him toward more explicit protest through his chosen medium. This second orientation reached its climax in what is commonly considered his best poem, ''In the Gold Mines,'' which deals with the black laborer's life on the Rand. Vilakazi's mood and attitude are very close to those of Dhlomo in *The Valley of a Thousand Hills*. The main difference is that Dhlomo, writing in Durban, found his symbols of oppression in the ''commercial dells'' of the modern mercenary city, whereas Vilakazi, writing in Johannesburg, found apt emblems of man's inhumanity to man in the industrial society and in the roaring machines. . . .

> Albert S. Gérard. *Four African Literatures* (Berkeley: University of California Press, 1971), pp. 251, 253–54

Vilakazi began his activities at the end of the 1920's when racist legislation was just starting to be applied in his country. He wrote in Zulu, and could not—and did not want to—give up his mother tongue. He wrote for his fellows with whom he had spent his youth at Groutville and during his twelve years' teaching at Mariannhill. Vilakazi felt immense respect for the culture of his nation which had been deliberately humiliated by the colonizers. As a scholar, he understood that a people's true national literature, and especially their poetry, is closely connected with the language and history of their nation.

Vilakazi's poetry is the truthful statement of a courageous man; his protest against racial oppression, it is also his emotionally expressed appeal to struggle. . . . Vilakazi sees the only path to liberation as struggle, a cruel fight which, the poet firmly believes, will be victorious. Each of Vilakazi's poems includes his central idea of the fight for freedom, stimulating and encouraging its readers and listeners. The poet admits the difficult fate of the black man and shows the need for a patient waiting for the time of victory. . . .

Vilakazi died too young. Although his life was hard in the country of racism and segregation, he succeeded in overcoming poverty and humiliation thanks to his persistence, courage, belief in his own powers and love of work. As a scholar, poet and novelist, he greatly contributed to the development of South African vernacular writing in the Bantu languages.

> Karel František Růžička. In Vladimír Klíma, Karel František Růžička, and Petr Zima, *Black Africa: Literature and Language* (Dordrecht, Netherlands: D. Reidel, 1976), pp. 236–37

BIBLIOGRAPHY

*Noma Nini*, 1935; *Inkondlo kaZulu* (Zulu Songs), 1935; ''Ezinkomponi,'' 1945; *Nje Nempela*, 1949; *Zulu Horizons*, 1962

# WALCOTT, Derek (1930–)

## St. Lucia

*In a Green Night*, by the West Indian poet Derek Walcott, is a striking first collection. His writing belongs to the pleasure band of the spectrum; it is full of summery melancholy, fresh and stinging colours, luscious melody and intense awareness of place—"like entering a Renoir," to quote himself. He puts all this to a purpose, however. His joyful apprehension of the immediate physical world serves to focus the other things he has to say, to give substance to conflicting loyalties. He uses a metaphysic of natural mutability and renewal—the "green yet ageing orange tree" of Marvell's *Bermudas*—to come to terms with the immutable historic wrongs of his people. His favourite personal symbols are of himself as a ribbed vessel, condemned to migrancy and shipwreck, and of his heart as a coal—the repository of forces stored up long ago but ready to burst into flame again.

He is an intensely and innocently literary poet—his volume hums with echoes of Villon and Dante, Catullus and the metaphysicals—but there is a kind of aptness in this, since history has made him a citizen of the world. Certainly the literariness is not a substitute for feeling, and his poems have immense freshness and verve.

> P.N. Furbank. *Listener.* July 5, 1962, p. 33

Robert Graves notes that [Walcott] "handles English with a closer understanding of its inner magic than most (if not any) of his English-born contemporaries." Graves's favorites have always been odd; the oddest thing here is that of all the poets who have influenced Walcott (and there are many), Graves has made the slightest impact. Walcott lingers over his language like a lover; he employs orotund, mellifluously spun lines. He is, as they say, "on stage," and certainly his poems read aloud are more rewarding. In any case, these characteristics alone set him apart from his English-born contemporaries, most of whom in the manner of the Movement write wry, inelegant miniatures, the new emblem of the Welfare State.

But Walcott is an exotic (his descriptions are drenched with the "sea-music and sea-light" of his islands), and he is also *engagé* (factors of race and repression are the backwash beneath every breaker). His world is almost a continual surge of scenic delights and/or degradations, all of which he uses for dramatic effect, sometimes in the symbolist mode, sometimes as a sort of pictorial choreography, and sometimes as a violently-charged reverie, or as a declamation. . . .

His preoccupation with the Self, with the solitary figure against the horizon, with something vague and minatory, rings down the curtain too often, and Walcott's lush melancholy, that itch to be impressive, strikes me, after a while, as a bore. But Walcott has special gifts, which as has already been observed are not much evident in younger poets, whether English or American: his textures are musical, he has a painter's eye, his craftsmanship is adventurous, and his moral or imaginative responses aren't shabby.

When these qualities triumph as they do in about a half-dozen poems, primarily "In a Green Night," "Return to D'Ennery," "Rain," and "Crusoe's Island," then the full force of his personality, the personality of *place*, the troubled beauty of his Antillean land, comes strikingly to the surface.

> Robert Mazzocco. *New York Review of Books.* December 31, 1964, pp. 18–19

Some of Derek Walcott's most quoted poems have probed aspects of regional identity. His new volume [*The Castaway*] worries the matter further, but the predicament of isolation in which he has sometimes found himself has now become more subjective, less geographical. The castaway of his recent poems may indeed wear the expression of Crusoe, with "that sun-cracked, bearded face," and his intelligence is certainly West Indian, but his confinement appears to be on an exotic island located in time. . . . It is a lonely environment compounded of approaching middle age, of lost roots ("some grill of light clanged shut on us in bondage"), of a greater ease in unburdening to the dead than to the living, and of the absence of a consoling faith or a compelling fear. . . .

A visit to New York provides no alleviation. Snow and cold are the most sensational of Northern experiences ("I thought winter would never end"), and at times they assume the proportions of a personal ice age ("since that winter I have learnt to gaze on life indifferently as through a pane of glass"). Indeed, isolation sometimes becomes a universal condition, and all men become castaways. . . .

The excitement of thought and technique is often at variance with the withdrawn mood and the absorbed self-reference. The imagery is intense and sometimes violent. Rhyme and metrical patterns are set only to be broken in a sudden racing of the poetic mechanism. The result is occasionally an inconclusiveness: images and ideas may be stranded, like unfinished remarks left hanging in conversation. But the best poems are an important and unique achievement, and of these "The Almond Trees" stands out remarkably. It accomplishes a sensitive commentary on landscape and identity, of vivid suggestion and careful structural unity.

> Kevin Ireland. *Journal of Commonwealth Literature.* December, 1966, pp. 157–158

[Walcott] began as a precocious, imitative writer of great promise and has weathered successfully the sirens and becalmings apt at some stage to do in a poet's voyage through youth. His problem, as with so many writers in English-speaking, ex-English possessions, has been the provincialism of his background. He himself has stuck to the West Indies, though growing fame has given him the opportunity for travel—to England, to North and South America. The theme of his new book [*The Gulf, and Other Poems*], is the journey from and back to provincialism, and whatever crabs one may have about its details there is no doubt that he has abundantly succeeded in the difficult talk of lifting his situation on to an interesting and, indeed, universal plane. "There are homecomings without home,'' he says memorably, and his view of his native islands is refined and sharpened by his returning sense of significant history and life happening elsewhere. . . .

The title poem, a meditation, in an aircraft flying over the Gulf of Mexico, on racial violence, seems to me entirely successful, a poem of vision and compassion, with just the right amount of concrete detail to make effective the rhetoric and imaginative use of vocabulary that have always been Walcott's strength. In some other poems (e.g. ''Mass Man'') I feel that the fuss and the language is not quite justified by the donnée, and there is often an inexplicitness that seems less a studied effect than a failure to grasp. One does not expect from a poet like Walcott a directness of irony or satire but the clotted bits of this collection arise equally from a syntactical clumsiness as from the obscurity of the attitude and situation.

Roy Fuller. *London.* November 1969, pp. 89–90

Derek Walcott's brooding allegorical drama, *Dream on Monkey Mountain* . . . [is] a very extended work, too long and sometimes structurally unsteady. Too many words. Yet an engrossing study, exercising its fascination upon us, designed within a lengthy framework that regularly compels. . . .

The play is rich and complex; the author's use of fable interwoven with a stark elaboration of historical evidence of oppression illuminates his work, lends it an arresting weight and texture. Walcott's characters are drawn with bold, sometimes extravagant strokes and, prodded by the author, they have an inclination to talk a bit too much. But the play also achieves a lush depiction of the many moods implicit in the ritual and realistic aspects of Caribbean Black life. . . .

Walcott is a writer who obviously loves the sound of the language he uses in his work. This affection is not always requited, the theater being an essentially visual arena. (And anyway, Walcott's ideas seem sturdy enough to reach us in a less verbally overdressed manner.) But what he has to say is extremely important at a time when, in America, Black people are regularly challenging the more basic concepts of governmental and cultural ''normalcy.'' The thesis, as proposed in *Dream on Monkey Mountain,* is that the West cannot—nor should it—exist forever, given its deplorable record of racist exploitation and butchery throughout the world.

Clayton Riley. *New York Times Book Review.* April 4, 1971, p. 3

There is a lot in this long poem [*Another Life*] by Derek Walcott that I do not understand. It seems to me too long, too choked with people, places, and things, and there is too much foreign talk and far too much British style. Even as the poet repudiates the intrusion of European ''culture'' into Black West Indian life, he proves at the same time that he can write a poem in which very little that is recognizably Black West Indian survives.

Perhaps this is unfair. Perhaps there is no such thing as a Black West Indian sensibility, that quality of *difference* that, in the United States, informs the work of even the most academic black poets. I do not know. What I do know is that Walcott writes an English line that can at times rise to perfection, and that his mastery of language and expression—though occasionally rendered with a 19th century twist—is complete and beautiful to see. He is a fine, mature, often brilliant and moving poet, which makes it harder than ever to determine exactly what it is that is missing.

What it is, I think for me, is a view of Mr. Walcott's West Indies that escapes the camouflage of an essentially European interpretation. Eager to know Mr. Walcott's West Indies, *his* island, *his* people, *his* greenness, *his* sea, I am disappointed that what he chooses to tell me comes hidden behind names from Greek myths I only half remember, or written in Latin I never studied, or so sprinkled with the ''glories'' of English empire days that I, finally, can recognize nothing without a debilitating struggle; but must pick my way laboriously from page to page, choosing bits and pieces that speak to me and leaving the rest for the dons of Oxford.

Alice Walker. *Village Voice.* April 11, 1974, p. 26

With the years, Walcott has evolved from the wary self-affirmation of one who ''had entered the house of literature as a houseboy'' to open-hearted self-evaluation. This is the honesty of the wise man who feels he has nothing to hide because he has discovered in all men the same frailty which used to make him ashamed. What appeals to me in the man as in his poetry is not so much the denseness and intensity as the kindness and frailty at the core, not the polished perdurable lines but the humanity with its doubts and loves, not the classicist but the tempered romantic. Or rather, it is the tension between the smile and the anger, the lamb and the lion.

It has been repeated that Walcott's verse is universal, that his cultural heritage makes him a ''citizen of the world.'' Indeed, there is in his lines a high degree of universality. Such universality should not be mistaken, however, for the sort of colorless common denominator often defined by Western humanism. Walcott's universality does not lie in the so-called ''ageless nature of mankind'' but in his own precise, circumscribed and deeply-rooted experience, in the small-village culture of Castries [in St. Lucia] with its unique mixture of contrasting traditions. Walcott can look fruitfully on the ''other life'' of his childhood and youth because he is ready to accept its particulars and because he now sees himself as a native of St. Lucia first, a ''citizen of the world'' second.

He is thus beginning to achieve a solution to the dilemma of the Third World artist which he had described as ''the natural terror of losing touch with the tribal truth and the natural ambition for universal recognition.'' After rendering in prose (dramatic or otherwise), in *Dream on Monkey Mountain,* the very *tone* of his people's experience, he has succeeded, in *Another Life,* in creating a poetic language which is deeply attuned with his personal growth and yet immediately universal. This is a more important achievement than restoring dialect as the only authentic alternative to classical English. It proposes an original strategy towards the development of literature as global cultural synthesis; it opens a path which is not remote from the prophetic vision that it takes another Caribbean genius, Wilson Harris, to create.

Michel Fabre. *New Leader.* Fall 1974, pp. 106–7

Derek Walcott is a poet of great verbal resources and skills engaged in a complex struggle to render his native Caribbean culture, the new world, first successor to Eden. For the past 28 years, as a poet and playwright, he has continually returned to the themes of that new world, locked in an ''ancient war between obsession and responsibility,'' and it is one of the touchstones of his gift that he has remained attentive to the diversity and reality of the West Indies without surrendering its symbolic resonances and possibilities. Now in his sixth book of poems, *Sea Grapes*, we see him returning to his first concerns but with a new intensity, a deep, well-sharpened focus.

The 46 poems detail the sensibility of a passionate man circling an endlessly complex subject in a range of compelling voices—bitter, violent, desperate, learned, tender. . . .

The title poem marks the emotional tenor of what literature can and cannot do with a conclusive "The classics can console. But not enough."

Derek Walcott is one of the most incisive poets writing in English today. His poems do comfort and console, though, finally, as *Sea Grapes* teaches, not even the classics can rescue us from our perpetual struggle to recreate the world.

> Edward Hirsch. *New York Times Book Review.* October 31, 1976, p. 38

While often concerned to define his identification with a specific region or a particular historical condition, Derek Walcott has always, in theory and in practice, been willing to draw on the total heritage available to him as an alert and inquiring human being. He was born in Castries, St. Lucia, on January 23, 1930, and he is racially mixed: "Mongrel as I am," he has written, "something prickles in me when I see the word Ashanti as with the word Warwickshire, both separately intimating my grandfathers' roots, both baptizing this neither proud nor ashamed bastard, this hybrid, this West Indian." But as a writer he has a wider ancestry than that; the whole world is his family, and he has argued that "maturity is the assimilation of the features of every ancestor.". . .

Walcott will draw on anything, and in discussion of his own work is often conscious of his attempt to fuse elements drawn from differing sources. "I am a kind of split writer: I have one tradition inside me going one way, and another tradition going another. The mimetic, the narrative, and dance element is strong on one side, and the literary, the classical tradition is strong on the other." With the Trinidad Theater Workshop which he formed in 1959 (and left in 1976), he tried to create "a theater where someone can do Shakespeare or sing Calypso with equal conviction."

Walcott has been consistently hostile to any force which seeks to limit his creativity or restrict access to anything which might feed it. "Most black writers," he has said, "cripple themselves by their separatism. You can't be a poet and believe in the division of man." Although so much of his own writing explores and dramatizes divisions within himself, the thrust is usually towards reconciliation, acceptance, compassion. Aware of history and the manifold cruelties it records, he has in recent years sought ways to avoid its uncreative traps. He has argued that "The truly tough aesthetic of the New World neither explains nor forgives history. It refuses to recognize it as a creative or culpable force." He finds in poets such as [Pablo] Neruda, [Aimé] Césaire, and [Saint-John] Perse an "awe of the numinous," the "elemental privilege of naming the new world which annihilates history. . . . They reject ethnic ancestry for faith in elemental man."

[*In a Green Night*] includes versions of six poems from Walcott's first book, *25 Poems*, and one from *Poems*, two volumes which, like *Epitaph for the Young*, were privately published. *In a Green Night* was followed by *Selected Poems* which has a selection from *In a Green Night* and a number of new poems. . . .

In the later Walcott, from *The Castaway [and Other Poems]* on, it is difficult to make a distinction between influence and allusion. Not so in the earlier books, where the poet is less confident in voice, trying on the manner of others. "Other men's voices, / other men's lives and lines."

> Mervyn Morris. In Bruce King, ed. *West Indian Literature* (Hamden, Connecticut: Archon Books, 1979), pp. 144–47

Walcott's poems in *The Castaway* use the myth of [Robinson] Crusoe to suggest that the New World is a new beginning, a new Eden. Both white and black have been shipwrecked and, while those of African descent suffer an amnesia of their racial past, it is from such forgetfulness that a new culture began. Walcott sees himself in the line of such poets of the Americas as [Walt] Whitman, [Pablo] Neruda and [Saint-John] Perse. Art will give form and self-awareness to this new society. But in "Crusoe's Island" Walcott admits the limitations of art replacing belief. . . . Walcott has become increasingly conscious of the life of the St. Lucian community which he has left. Where others have sought their roots in Africa, or have identified with the black urban slum dweller, Walcott sees the poor, French-influenced, Catholic black community of St. Lucia as his home.

"What the Twilight Says: An Overture," which prefaces *Dream on Monkey Mountain and Other Plays*, is partly an analysis of West Indian culture from the period preceding independence until the Black Power Movement of the late 1960s. . . . The Black Power intellectuals mimic foreign revolutions in urging the people "to acquire pride which meant abandoning their individual dignity"; even the fury of the intellectual was "artificially generated" by an imitation of foreign "metropolitan anger." Thus Walcott angrily attacks politicians and intellectuals in *The Gulf [and Other Poems]* and *Sea Grapes*.

> Bruce King. *The New English Literatures: Cultural Nationalism in a Changing World* (New York: St. Martin's Press, 1980), pp. 124–25

For those awakening to the nightmare of history, revenge—Walcott has conceded—can be a kind of vision, yet he himself is not vengeful. Nor is he simply a patient singer of the tears of things. His intelligence is fierce but it is literary. He assumes that art is a power and to be visited by it is to be endangered; but he also knows that works of art endanger nobody else, that they are benign. From the beginning he has never simplified or sold short. Africa and England beat messages along his blood. The humanist voices of his education and the voices from his elemental inarticulate place keep insisting on their full claims, pulling him in two different directions. He always had the capacity to write with the elegance of a [Philip] Larkin and make himself a ventriloquist's doll to the English tradition which he inherited, though that of course would have been an attenuation of his gifts, for he also has the capacity to write with the murky voluptuousness of a [Pablo] Neruda and make himself a romantic tongue, licking poetic good things off his islands. He did neither, but made a theme of the choice and the impossibility of choosing. And now [in *The Star-Apple Kingdom*] he has embodied the theme in the person of Shabine, the poor mulatto sailor of [the poem "The Schooner *Flight*"], a kind of democratic West Indian Ulysses, his mind full of wind and poetry and women. Indeed, when Walcott lets the sea breeze freshen in his imagination, the result is a poetry as spacious and heartlifting as the sea weather at the opening of [James] Joyce's *Ulysses*, a poetry that comes from no easy evocation of mood but from stored sensations of the actual. . . .

Walcott's poetry has passed the stage of self-questioning, self-exposure, self-healing to become a common resource. He is no propagandist. What he would propagate is magnanimity and courage, and I am sure that he would agree with [Gerard Manley] Hopkins's affirmation that feeling, and in particular love, is the great power and spring of verse. This book is awash with love of people and places and language: love as knowledge, love as longing, love as consummation, at one time the Sermon on the Mount, at another *Antony and Cleopatra*. . . . There is something risky about such large appropriations, but they are legitimate because Walcott's Caribbean and Cleopatra's Nile have the same sweltering awareness of the cynicism and brutality of political adventurers. He is not going beyond the field of his own imagery; he is appropriating Shakespeare, not expropriating him—the unkindest postcolonial cut of all.

> Seamus Heaney. *Parnassus*. 8, 1 (Fall-Winter 1980), pp. 6, 9–10

*Dream on Monkey Mountain* and *Ti-Jean and His Brothers* mark the climax of Derek Walcott's mature, professional achievement as a dramatist. He makes, in these plays, his definitive statement on the seminal questions of West Indian liberation and identity. Subsequently (broadly speaking), his drama enters a new phase distinguished by certain interesting new trends, both in content and style. *The Joker of Seville* and *O Babylon!* . . . present various transitional features. . . .

*The Joker* and *O Babylon!*, the two musicals heading the post-*Dream* output, provide a useful introduction to these later developments. Each presents contrasts which serve to highlight the new trends. *The Joker*, outstanding in sheer theatrical scope, is in fact the culminating point of the characteristic style developed in *Dream*. Walcott's adaptation of the musical form grows organically out of the ritual structure employed in *Dream* and preserves its essential dynamic. That is, characters still function primarily as emblems, the action turns upon an internalized, metaphorical conception of theme, inner experience finds expression in physical enactment, and setting is essentially stylized.

Walcott is adapting, in this play, the story of the legendary seducer, Don Juan. In the Spanish original, he is the libertine who defies the codes of chastity and honor to make the most of it this side of the grave. Walcott's own portrait stresses the principle of moral freedom which Juan embodies. In satisfying the forbidden lusts of his women, he serves to release libido, denied by the prescribed norms of order and decorum. He frees them thereby to face the burden of choice. Walcott heightens the meaning of this quality of freedom in identifying it with the muse of the local Creole stick-fighter in whose guise the indigenized Juan appears. The watchword of the stick-fighting tradition, *sans humanité*, is thus adopted to affirm the principle of unflinching courage and affirmative purpose in strife. So that Walcott's Juan comes to personify, above all, that spirit which ''can change to elation each grave situation,'' in the words of the theme song.

The focal point here is that the action materializes out of just this kind of ideation and mythicizing. Juan, although a vibrant personality in the play, is more of an animated force than a character, and action is realized in ritual modes. The plot thus moves through a series of major musical sequences, which present what are essentially moments of spiritual confrontation and recognition. They are enacted in powerful orchestrations of choral and physical performance. Juan's climactic triumph over the dead system represented by the statue-like Don Gonzalo, for example, is extended in a ritual performance of the stick-fight.

*O Babylon!*, his next venture into a full-scale musical, is not so successful. It presents here the interesting case of a work uneasily strung between the two phases, which partly accounts for its weaknesses. On the one hand, the musical form links it with the preceding phase; on the other, it introduces the preoccupation with the current political, social climate, more subtly explored in *Pantomime* and *Remembrance*. This is, in fact, the only play of Walcott's explicitly and wholly devoted to public protest. The play presents the situation of the Rastafarian sect of Jamaica, oppressed by the corruption of the materialistic Establishment, and in rebellion against it. Walcott is on very solid, topical ground in speaking through a group that has emerged as the rallying point of militant anti-establishment posture, and with the equally strong appeal of an ideology aimed at a radical break with the Western value system. The Rastafarians are presented in a situation which shows a sympathetic engagement with both their crisis and their revolutionary cause. They face the threat of eviction from their area, which has been earmarked for a hotel construction site by the local politicians, who serve American big business. They appear, in the meantime, in a harmonious communal setting, practicing their pieties of brotherhood, love, and peace.

The play fails, however, for several related reasons. Many of the flaws show up in the plot itself: a number of issues, not sufficiently centered, seem to be going different ways. The Rastafarians are engaged in resisting the major threat of eviction; they are equally intent on pursuing the latest promise of African repatriation. When eviction comes, they retreat into a mountain hermitage to rebuild their ideal community—a fate which virtually obviates the revolutionary motive, and indeed protest. At the same time, Walcott allows one individual member of the community, his central figure Aaron, a symbolic gesture of rebellion against Babylon. Earl Lovelace, commenting on the play, sees Walcott's Rastas as a powerless bunch, with no clear, constructive direction.

> Patricia Ismond. *Ariel*. 16, 3 (July 1985), pp. 89–91

Walcott had been drawn to art early by being ''more deeply moved by the sight of works of art than by that of the things which they portray,'' as [André] Malraux wrote of Giotto. Walcott used Malraux's anecdote as an epigraph in *Another Life*, in which he wrote of his discovering art as if he were Saul, blinded with revelation of the true religion. His will alone could ''transfigure'' the mountain shacks of the poor into a ''cinquecento fragment in gilt frame.'' He felt the power of art to re-create the world, to transcend the poverty of those shacks, to redeem his dispossessed people and their history. The task was as immense as that of Adam standing before his unnamed world, though Walcott had this advantage: in the books of his father's library, he had inherited the work of centuries of European masters.

The West Indian reverence for ancestors became for Walcott a need to assimilate tradition, to assume its features, to make it part of his visual vocabulary. He believed that his knowledge of tradition would augment his treatment of the island's watercolor seas, its vegetation ripe for oils. But where [Dunstan] St. Omer painted "with the linear leation of an eel," Walcott's own hand was "crabbed by that style, / this epoch, that school / or the next." Tradition proved too powerful a master; he was its sunstruck Caliban. . . .

The connection between poet and painter in Walcott lies deeper than eye level, being rooted in his early, most basic experience of the world. *Another Life* is the autobiography of his life as a young artist, an intimate odyssey in which he first experiences the primal facts of life and death through art. He undertakes the conventional epic journey to the underworld, the land of the dead, which he finds in books of paintings by the European masters. . . . Among the relics of art, he recognizes his father, who is not his natural father (also a painter, but who had died young) and not the liturgical Our-Father-who-art-in-heaven, but "Our father, / who floated in the vaults of Michelangelo." His spiritual father could be accessible only through art, wherein Walcott collects his true heritage and recognizes his future.

> Robert Bensen. *Literary Review.* 29, 3 (Spring 1986), p. 257–58

Derek Walcott's recent poetry is one of traveling and mapping where history becomes the knowledge only places can give. "North and South," the central poem of his *The Fortunate Traveller* (a collection which, not incidentally, is divided into three sections, where two sections titled "North" straddle the central "South"), describes the tensions between the two poles. History becomes defined by the dialectic of these two places. Walcott foresees no resulting synthesis, except the holocaustic. The "white glare / of the white rose of inferno" merges the imagogical mystery of Dante's celestial white rose with imminent extinction. Yet, if the "North," with its history of colonialism and exploitation, is "sown with salt" and marked for a prefigured destruction, the "South" and Walcott's role as the voice of the place, is ambiguous: "I accept my function / as a colonial upstart at the end of an empire, / a single, circling, homeless satellite." The poetic process calls into question perceptions and the common assumptions that attend our perceptions. . . .

*Midsummer*, Walcott's most recent collection of poems, moves fully into the "South": "the sea glares like zinc. / Then, in the door light: not Nike loosening her sandal, / but a girl slapping sand from her foot, one hand on the frame." Walcott's line has expanded, usually carrying twelve or thirteen syllables, which extends even beyond the sustained pentameter of "The Spoiler's Return." Walcott's more expansive and traveled line, which is sustained throughout *Midsummer*, suggests another form of rupture or ambivalence toward the traditional poetics of the language he writes in, which is his mirror and map. Walcott increasingly seeks to site himself and history in the present, not to deconstruct or depoliticize the present, but to map its tensions traced in language. Yet, as Walcott creates a poetry of self-definition, he ironically moves away from any political recognition of the language used by the marginal, the exploited, or the other—the patois or demotic forms

and tonal ranges. Earlier poems such as "Sainte Lucie" began to explore these possibilities; however, this was transformed into the more decorous mode of dramatic monologues or narrative poems such as "The Schooner *Flight*" and "The Spoiler's Return," where the language, like the narrator, is masked and thus mediated.

The poems of *Midsummer* arguably acquiesce to the conventions and poetics of the language of the colonialists in the rejection of the patois. One wonders if Walcott does not then become a "North" American poet rather than an Antillean poet. In turn, in what ways does the more personal (and self-defining) poetry of *Midsummer* abrogate the very process of self-definition in the acquisition and maintenance of the conventions of a colonialist's culture? One may ask for whom Walcott's maps are intended. Walcott may move geographically to the "South" in a poem like "Tropic Zone"; however, he has become not a resident but a displaced person, the radical version of the traveler.

> James McCorkle. *Ariel.* 17, 2 (April 1986), pp. 3–4, 10–11

Derek Walcott's massive *Collected Poems, 1948–1984* has an edge of defiance, as if to say, "Dismiss me if you can." But who would want to dismiss him? Walcott's poems stand out from the wash of contemporary American poetry (so much of it so *mild*, like half-whispered, devious apologies) because they are so boldly eloquent. The writing is some of the most exquisite in the English language, resembling the Caribbean in its many voices—sometimes crisp, sometimes tough, sometimes sweetly lyrical, or clear and treacherous as water in a stream. The syntax is often elaborate, frustrating yet seductive in the way it both reveals and obscures. When a Walcott poem fails, the writing is rarely at fault.

A true Renaissance man, Walcott has consistently resisted being cubby-holed. He has rejected neither his Caribbean heritage nor his British education. Although in recent years he divides his time between Trinidad and Boston, for a while he lived exclusively in the West Indies as director of the Trinidad Theater Workshop. Although St. Lucia, his birthplace, forms his primary subject matter, he has also written about Manhattan and Mandelstam. In the eyes of the public, however, his unique position as the first English-speaking Caribbean poet of international renown threatens to make him ". . . a man no more / but the fervor and intelligence / of a whole country." And so the girth of this *Collected Poems* is also a demand to consider the whole man—not just his skin or age or prosody or heart or mind.

> Rita Dove. *Parnassus.* 14, 1 (1987), pp. 49–50

*A Branch of the Blue Nile*, the most recent published play by Derek Walcott, the St. Lucian-born poet and playwright, wonderfully exemplifies [Mikhail] Bakhtin's notion of "heteroglossia." In the play Walcott draws upon his rich African, patois, French, English, and classical Latin linguistic legacy, his St. Lucian and Trinidadian heritage, and his long experience in the United States, to bring his mastery of heteroglotic language to a peak. He continues the sort of black/white, colonizer/colonized cultural reversals that he played with in his earlier drama, *Pantomime*, by means of his Crusoe/ Friday role shifts. He also compounds his fascination with the Antony and Cleopatra legend, which configured several of his major poems, such as "Egypt, Tobago." Intertextual and intercultural references, woven through much of Walcott's poetry and drama, multiply exponentially in *A Branch of the Blue Nile*.

Stephen P. Breslow. *World Literature Today*. 63, 1 (Winter 1989), p. 36

Derek Walcott has said, "schizoids, in a perverse way, have more personality than the normal person, and it is this conflict of our racial psyche that by irritation and a sense of loss continues to create artists." He further asserts in the same article that we are "deprived of what we cannot remember, or what, when we visit its origins never existed the way we imagined, or where we remain strangers, contemptible cousins, the children of indentured servants and slaves." The picaro in *The Fortunate Traveller* portrays this kind of "tormented ambiguity," to borrow a term from James Livingston. Because the term "ambiguity" is usually associated with meaning rather than with personal attitude, as intended here, "ambivalence" is chosen as the operative word for the purpose of this study.

Poet and persona share this ambivalence, and the artistic process which brings them together is marked by image patterns which map out a journey that simultaneously regresses to the past and advances inevitably into the future. History and memory frequently yield precedence to forward-moving time which eventually becomes apocalyptic vision. A brief consideration of the poet in relation to his consciousness of history, and a sketch of his artistic and psychological involvement with his persona should lead to a more informed analysis of Walcott's artistry in *The Fortunate Traveller*, an artistry that carries the imprint of the author's ambivalence expressed in the poem through a pattern of dual, ambiguous and paradoxical elements integrated by the complex personality of the traveler himself.

Despite Walcott's objections to the "masochistic recollection" of poets who look to the brutal history of the West Indies for inspiration, he presents in his main persona a quester who is ironically forced to confront his origins and the events of his past in the mirrored reflections of the present. His journey from the old to the new merely provides an unrelenting satire on the evils of the old. Put another way, in *The Fortunate Traveller*, a journey through the modern world of American and European civilization represented, among other things, by the passage across the Mason-Dixon line, is merely a repetition of the old order of victim and victimizer, conquered and conqueror, native dweller and foreign intruder. Walcott, consciously or unconsciously, is negating the statement made in "Laventville": "The middle passage never guessed its end." Instead, *The Fortunate Traveller* illustrates the counterclaim of [Edward Kamau] Brathwaite that the passage has guessed its end. Its end is inextricably bound up in its beginning. The process of the journey and of the quest is not only constructed from the racial memories of the past, but the outcome is shaped by and mirrored in this process.

Clement H. Wyke. *Ariel*. 20, 3 (July 1989), pp. 55–56

In writing a play where white characters are so much to the forefront and so sympathetically rendered, Walcott is certainly rare among his generation of West Indian writers. *The Last Carnival* is a revision of an earlier unpublished play *In a Fine Castle*. *In a Fine Castle*, written after *Dream on Monkey Mountain* and *Ti-Jean* and before *The Joker of Seville* and *O Babylon!*, shows Walcott already engaging in exploration of crises of identity among the educated and the urban. Issues of racial confrontation persist but are rendered so differently from the myth and symbol-laden *Dream*. *In a Fine Castle* too has leading roles for whites, which as Walcott had anticipated, drew him the ire of many local critics. But the center of focus is still the divided consciousness of Brown whose name captures his mixed racial inheritance. The white characters are sympathetically rendered, but Walcott's rendering of their predicament is somewhat hackneyed and melodramatic. . . .

Walcott's development as a playwright is in a sense his exploration of the many strategies that will allow him to most fully possess his environment in all its elements. First there is the matter of language. English has been the language of the master; Walcott wishes to claim it as his own. At the outset, for the young poet in love with the English language, come the heady imitations of blank verse. Walcott's great eloquence, his high English, is, however, at odds with the consciousness of characters he now chooses to represent. "You proffered silently the clarity of a language they could not speak, until your suffering, like the language, felt superior, estranged." In imitating [John Millington] Synge [in *The Sea at Dauphin*], he is also looking at Synge's rich poetic idiom crafted out of the dialect of his islands. He sets out to forge a "language that went beyond mimicry," that transformed his gift of English into something uniquely West Indian. The result is the moving poetic prose of this first volume—eloquent, accessible, yet clearly reflecting the idioms of West Indian speech. . . .

In *Omeros*, the playwright and poet come together in creating a narrative poem with characters as alive and vibrant as in any play. "Homeros" means hostage and, like the blind poet, Walcott too is in a sense a hostage of the past. We all are, but as survivors of this past we must learn to live with memories, all of them. The memories that Walcott appropriates in his work are not of one race but many races. The central characters of his poem—Helen, Achille, Hector—are ordinary people of St. Lucia, but in their lives are captured and renewed and refashioned many dimensions of the past. The poet's mind ranges from Antilles now to Greece of antiquity, to Africa of slavery, to the British Empire, to the America of the Indians, to America of today. The literary references are equally wide-ranging. There is nothing false about Walcott acknowledging Homer as his master or seeing Homer's song in the chants of the shaman: "I have always heard / your voice in that sea, master, it was the same song / of the desert shaman." In an interview with Robert Hamner, Walcott had said, "The more particular you get, the more universal you become." In writing about his Antillean characters and their particular experiences imagined with great temporal specificity, Walcott is also writing about the human condition. And like Homer, in this song about St. Lucia, London, Athens, and Boston, Walcott sings about what happened both to Trojans and to Greeks, to those who lost and those who won, to those who are black and those who are white. Experience of all is rendered with equal sympathy and understanding. This is how we can remember the past without becoming hostage to it.

Renu Juneja. In Bruce King, ed. *Post-Colonial English Drama: Commonwealth Drama Since 1960* (New York: St. Martin's Press, 1992), pp. 239, 247, 264

[In *Omeros*] Walcott aims for a Homeric scope of human conflict and visionary experience and, obviously, raises expectations for his language and characterization by comparing himself to such an illustrious predecessor. But *Omeros* is also ambitious in a second sense; for by raising the question of his relationship to Homer, Walcott defines himself against a primary Western paradigm of originality and mimetic power, and re-evaluates that paradigm as well as his own poetry. The "basic impulse of the Homeric style," as [Erich] Auerbach observes, is "to represent phenomena in a fully externalized form, visible and palpable in all their parts, and completely fixed in their spatial and temporal relations." Walcott's mimicry of Homer thus confronts mimesis at what we usually think of as both its root and its apex. Further, the series of parallels upon which *Omeros*, like [James] Joyce's *Ulysses*, stands presses us toward our own confrontations with mimesis. Our first impulse may be to compare Walcott's Helen to Homer's, Achille to Achilles, Philocte to Philoctetes, and so on. But the continuous process of doing so will likely cause us to question our impulse to perceive, and hence to create, likenesses—especially when such questioning becomes an overt theme of the poem itself. When, for example, both Major Plunkett (a British veteran and colonist) and the persona of the poet struggle to grasp the St. Lucian Helen and then fail to determine her relation (if any) to her Greek counterpart, the validity of similitude falls into doubt.

Likewise, because Homer stands at or slightly before the beginning of Western poetic genealogy—at a distance at which genealogy evades the grasp—Walcott's rapprochement with Homer means a rapprochement with not just *a* poetic ancestor but with poetic ancestry. Walcott highlights this, too, first by making Omeros a character in the drama and casting his own persona as Omeros's poetic heir, and second by several times retelling the Odysseus-Telemachos story—a story that can be read as a parable of paternal, hence genealogical, mystery.

*Omeros's* two tiers of reference—Walcottian and Homeric—also complicate mimicry in new ways. I suggested at the outset that mimicry points to its own nonoriginality as well as to that of its model. *Omeros* does do this, in that "life" mimics "art" within the fiction of the poem. That is, the St. Lucian characters are ostensibly "real people" who yet appear to recall Homeric or other literary models. The character of Warwick Walcott, for example, the poet's father—who died of an ear infection at an early age—notices that his past echoes parts of Shakespeare's plays. . . . Walcott once again places literary models, representations—albeit tentatively—in positions usually reserved for originals. But given two fictional tiers, one will likely shine at the expense of the other. Odds are that figures in a painting gazing at another painting gain the appearance of verisimilitude in comparison to other figures inside the painting at which they gaze. Similarly, the rhetorical effects of Walcott's references to Homer's more distant poems is to vivify his own poem. By appearing to model "real" St. Lucians upon fictional Greeks, Walcott suggests that "life" imitates "art"—and thereby distracts the reader from the fact that what he calls "life" imitates "art"—and thereby distracts the reader from the fact that what he calls "life" is already "art." In this sense *Omeros* actually *disguises* its own status as representation. If elsewhere in Walcott's work we learn that mimicry haunts mimesis, in *Omeros* a trompe-l'oeil mimesis returns to haunt mimicry.

Rei Terada. *Derek Walcott's Poetry: American Mimicry* (Boston: Northeastern University Press, 1992), pp. 183–85

Walcott's poetry draws much of its energy from his uneasiness, his unrest, the hovering and hesitation that he characterizes as the stance of the poet—a detachment from the natural (men acting as men—though there is ambiguity in the word *acting*) and an acceptance of the artifice of another life, another way of seeing the world, a new frame for the familiar. His unease derives partly from his recognition of the ambivalences that define his being, not simply racial and historical but more profoundly imaginative, with allegiances both to piety and power, to the Old World and the New, to the condition of insider and outsider, to the particular and the universal, to the world as it is and the world as it might be. But partly also Walcott's unease comes from a deeper contradiction. "Where then is the nigger's home?" asks [Edward Kamau] Brathwaite. Like Odysseus, Walcott might answer—it is where I am going, which is where once I came from; but it is also where I am, for I am a wanderer, and have been one from the start. My cunning and good humor mask a sorrow that I must name; and then I will find peace. . . .

*Omeros* represents a new kind of achievement, for despite its affiliations with the epic it does not come out [of] the literature and history of Europe; and despite its acceptance of the heritage of slavery it does not come out of Africa either. Rather, it emerges unmistakably from a West Indian literary tradition, one that Walcott has played a major role in shaping but that now has a broad reach and deep roots. *Omeros* would not be possible outside that tradition.

Set in St. Lucia—called Iounalao, "where the iguana is found," by the Arawaks—it is a story about storytelling, contemplating the relationships between individual and collective histories, invoking figures of fact and fiction, proposing rhymes and half-rhymes across centuries and oceans and peoples and verse forms, a dense weave of metaphors and metonymys . . . and puns, for like all good poems it takes pleasure in its outrageousness and it takes liberties with its readers. *Omeros* is underwritten by a belief in the power of the imagination, and in real continuities—between the Mediterranean and the Caribbean, between suffering then and now, between all the experiences of men and women, even those that are shadowed by stereotypes. The territory of the poem is, in Walcott's phrase, a "reversible world," with the pun on verse being one of the least ostentatious in a poem whose exuberance is sometimes close to over-whelming. One of its most disconcerting extravagances is the number of voices and varieties of language in the poem—not untypical for Walcott, but developed with such irrepressible enthusiasm that ultimately the play becomes the thing and the parts are taken by whoever is next in line. And as so often in West Indian poetry, who is speaking is not nearly as important as who is listening.

J. Edward Chamberlin. *Come Back to Me My Language: Poetry and the West Indies* (Urbana: University of Illinois Press, 1993), pp. 167, 174–75

Walcott's epic perspective on history provides him with the necessary neutrality to perceive that glory does not necessarily follow from revolution, that all change is a mixed blessing. In his more recent poetry, in many poems from *The Fortunate Traveller, The Arkansas Testament,* and *Omeros,* Walcott has turned his attention often to the corruption and demise of the empire itself; and he links the waning of power of England and the United States to the final histories of Rome, Tyre, and Alexandria. From a cosmic or epic perspective, all civilizations follow many of the same patterns of rise, decline, and fall; the struggles of different peoples frequently resemble one another within the vast and ancient currents of human life around the world: "Albion too was once / A colony like ours."...

The Caribbean, as Walcott is so painfully and acutely aware, will forever remain quixotic among the world's annals. As a region, it may form the paradigm for postcolonial "antihistory," for the overturning of long-cherished myths and the brutal new chronicling of oppression, racism, and genocide. Its cultural history, which Walcott traces so accurately in the complex designs of his heteroglottic "multitexts," provides one of the world's richest models for true multiculturalism—a dense crossroads of human differences, sometimes tragic and sometimes hilarious in their juxtapositions and interrelationships.

If we are entering an era in which multiculturalism is our central ideology, Derek Walcott must be acclaimed as one of our greatest cultural leaders. He repeatedly demonstrates, in dozens of his plays and volumes of verse, the true meaning of "many cultures coexisting in dialogue" within the work of a single writer. His multiple voices with Joycean brilliance range not only among the numerous dialects and speech genres of the English-and French-patois-speaking Caribbean, but also move to the widest limits of our entire treasure house of Judeo-Christian, Greco-Roman, and European cultures. We may detect in Walcott's microcosmic Caribbean a paradigm for the most tolerant, mutually enriching coexistence of all the world's voices. Most wonderful of all, Walcott thoroughly exemplifies a "both/and" global political and cultural philosophy rather than an "either/or" divisive one. The Swedish Academy has certainly perceived this, and my congratulations go to its members for their choice, as well as to this profoundly accomplished, inspirational author whom they have lauded [as the 1992 Nobel Laureate in literature].

Stephen P. Breslow. *World Literature Today.* 67, 2 (Spring 1993), p. 271

"There is a force of exultation, a celebration of luck, when a writer finds himself a witness to the early morning of a culture that is defining itself, branch by branch, leaf by leaf, in that self-defining dawn," Derek Walcott says in his Nobel Prize lecture for 1992. That force of exultation and celebration of luck, along with a sense of benediction and obligation, a continuous effort of memory and excavation, and a "frightening duty" to "a fresh language and a fresh people," have defined Walcott's project for the past four-and-a-half decades. He has always been a poet of great verbal resources and skills engaged in a complex struggle to render his native Caribbean culture: the New World—not Eden but a successor to Eden, a polyglot place, an archipelago determined to survive—a world he calls "a ferment without a history, like heaven . . . a writer's heaven.". . .

Walcott has repeatedly sought to give voice to the inlets and beaches, the hills, promontories, and mountains of his native country. His birthplace of St. Lucia is one of the four Windward Island in the eastern Caribbean, a small craggy place that faces the Atlantic Ocean on one side and the Caribbean Sea on the other. The sea—or what he has called "the theater of the sea"—is an inescapable presence in his work and has fundamentally affected his sense of being an islander, a poet of a floating new world surrounded by water. "The sea was my privilege / And a fresh

people," he writes in *Omeros*, where he also defines the ocean as "an epic where every line was erased / yet freshly written in sheets of exploding surf." At the same time Walcott has been a determined advocate of pan-Caribbean literature and culture, considering each island an integral piece of one larger historical unit. He thus defines himself as part of a constellation of writers—among them St.-John Perse; Aimé Césaire, and C. L. R. James—who have created one literature in several different languages, and he belongs to a generation who have often described their sense of excitement and creative possession at writing about places for the first time, defining their role in terms of what Alejo Carpentier calls "Adam's task of giving things their names."

Walcott is a writer who exults in nouns and verbs, in the tang of vernacular speech, in the salty, sea-drenched sounds of words themselves. He has one of the finest ears of any poet writing in English since Hart Crane or Dylan Thomas. It is as if the very vowels and consonants of his vocabulary had been saturated in the sea. ("When I write / this poem, each phrase go be soaked in salt," the seaman-poet Shabine declares in "The Schooner *Flight*.")...

There is a quality of earthly prayer in the way Walcott luxuriates in sounds and savors letters, turning over the words, holding up the names. A sacred sense of vocation informs his high eloquence and powerful commitment to articulating his native realm, calling out "the litany of islands, / The rosary of archipelagoes" and "the amen of calm waters."...

Walcott has always been attracted to writing "soaked in salt," testing the richness of his own linguistic impulses against the simple clarities of the natural world, seeking a transparent and gritty style "crisp as sand, clear as sunlight, / Cold as the curled wave, ordinary / As a tumbler of island water" ("Islands"). He grew up speaking English, English patois, and French patois, but in his early work he mostly bifurcated those languages, mining the resources of English in his poems and exploring the possibilities of patois in his plays. In such groundbreaking dramatic works as *The Sea at Dauphin, Ti-Jean and His Brothers*, and *Malcochon*, he used a Creole-inflected language, still a mostly uncharted territory for West Indian literature, and turned outward to render the landscape and life of West Indian foresters and fishermen.

The language of Walcott's boyhood bubbles to the surface in his autobiographical work *Another Life*, which fixes in place his childhood and youth in St. Lucia and tells the story of the growth of a poet's mind, of how "he fell in love with art, / and life began." There is also a key moment in *Sea Grapes* when he brings his multiple linguistic heritages together in his poems. (Significantly, *Sea Grapes* is the first book to contain a large number of poems about being away from the West Indies.) The moment takes place in the poem "Sainte Lucie," a lyric infused with homesickness, when the speaker suddenly cries out "Come back to me, / my language," and calls up the French patois of his childhood: "C'est la moi sorti," he says, "is there that I born." Thereafter, Walcott has often imported dialect into his poetry. He has called himself "a mulatto of style" (a phrase borrowed from Senghor) and explored the different registers of speech in a series of dramatic monologues as well as in his epic poem *Omeros*. And he has thereby given a place in his poems to the contending languages—contending cultures—at work inside him. The Odyssean figure of Shabine undoubtedly speaks for his creator when he uses the demotic and turns the language of colonial scorn into a source of pride:

I'm just a red nigger who love the sea,
I had a sound colonial education,

I have Dutch, nigger, and English in me,
and either I'm nobody, or I'm a nation. . .

One way to view Walcott's work is as an energizing struggle to reconcile a divided heritage. His pact with his island, his first commitment to describing the world around him, was balanced by a sense of self-division and estrangement. He grew up as a "divided child"—a Methodist in an overwhelmingly Catholic place, a developing artist with a middle-class background and a mixed African, English, and Dutch ancestry coming of age in a mostly black world, a backwater of poverty. Some of the dramatic tension in his work comes from the gap he has always had to cross to describe the people with whom he shared an island. At the same time, his "sound colonial education" was accompanied by a rueful awareness that "the dream of reason / had produced its monster; / a prodigy of the wrong age and colour." In a sense, Walcott's real work began with his dual commitment to the English literary tradition and to the untouched country he wanted to re-create in his writing. From the beginning he was faced with the precocious burden of his choices, pulled between mimicry and originality, between the Old and New Worlds. . . .

Throughout his work Walcott has delineated the enigmas, paradoxes, and dilemmas of the Antillean artist trying to shoulder—and shoulder aside—the burdens of a colonial heritage. Robinson Crusoe was his first, and indeed his most persistent, symbolic figure for the West Indian artist. In his early and middle work Walcott returned often to the Crusoe story ("our first book, our profane genesis") because it represented for him the double nature of working out one's destiny on a small island. Walcott's Crusoe despairs at being shipwrecked and alone—the very titles of *The Castaway* and *The Gulf* suggest the burdens of artistic isolation—but he is also exhilarated at being the monarch of his island. He is Adamic man, "the first inhabitant of a second paradise," a resilient chronicler of an unspoiled surrounding. Crusoe also enacts the process of colonization, since he saves Friday but then transforms him into a servile figure. The poet himself is both Crusoe and Friday, a castaway forging the tools for a new culture.

The figure of the castaway has slowly shifted in Walcott's work to the figure of the exile, the wayward but fortunate traveler. "I accept my function / as a colonial upstart at the end of an empire," he says wryly in the poem "North and South," "a single, circling, homeless satellite." In each of his books since *Sea Grapes* Walcott has written poems set in both the Caribbean and abroad, moving between cultures, setting up a dialogue between the emblematic "North" (metropolitan countries) and "South" (the Caribbean). *The Fortunate Traveller*, for example, has three sections: "North," "South" and "North"; *The Arkansas Testament* is divided into two parts, "Here" (St. Lucia, the Caribbean, the anchor "home") and "Elsewhere" (which stands for all other foreign landscapes but most especially America and the American South). His increasing cosmopolitanism and range, expressing a global vision of empire, have been accompanied by an equivalent restlessness, a greater feeling of distance from his origins. Throughout his life Walcott has written poems of painful self-awareness and homecoming, among them "Homecoming: Anse la Raye," "Return to D'Ennery, Rain," the final chapter of *Another Life*, "The Lighthouse," and "The Light of the World." These take up the subject of how far he has grown from his provincial past, of "homecomings without home." The fear that he has abandoned the people around him ("I, who could never solidify my shadow / to be one of

their shadows") becomes the prelude to a renewed commitment to the making of an Antillean art. . . .

Walcott is ultimately a poet of affirmations, a writer who believes that the task of art is to transcend history and rename the world. As he says in "The Antilles: Fragments of Epic Memory," "For every poet it is always morning in the world. History a forgotten, insomniac night; History and elemental awe are always our early beginning, because the fate of poetry is to fall in love with the world, in spite of History." In the end and the beginning, the poet's enterprise is a redemptive one, a joyous calling. Derek Walcott's lifework is a grand testament to the visionary powers of language and to the freshening wonders of a world that is always starting over again despite History, a world that is always startling and new.

Edward Hirsch. *Georgia Review*. XLIXI (Spring 1995), pp. 307–13

Reading Derek Walcott can be like listening to some grand cathedral music that's all tangled up in its own echoes: it's lovely, most definitely, but it can sometimes be tough to tell one note from the next. I know several people who find him too "gorgeous," who sense a hollowness in the high rhetoric. To my mind, the criticism reveals less about Walcott's work than it does about typical American taste in contemporary poetry. . . .

[Though] it surprises me to say it, because so few poets sustain their creative capacities into their later years, *The Bounty* is among Walcott's best work.

There is little in [*The Bounty*] that won't be familiar to readers of Walcott's earlier poetry. There are the same island landscapes; the same literary allusiveness; the same tidal lines that seem always almost too much for the iambic measure that periodically reclaims them; the same density of texture that is occasionally decorative and occluding, but mostly wonderful. . . .

Poets revive their work in various ways, but one of the most ruthlessly consistent truths about poetry is the part death so frequently plays in that revival. As teeming and "bountiful" as this book is, there is also something of Dickinson's "sumptuous destitution" to it, a sense that all of the inventiveness and linguistic fertility, all of this grand sound, is being offered up in the face of voids more immense than any poem can fill. It is, quite literally, a book of endings, elegiac not only in its subject matter, but also, in a way, in its forms.

You can feel these poems moving ineluctably toward their final lines, toward "closure," and it is notable how often the endings of the poems are the points at which the writing is best, as if those echoes were trailing off, everything coming clear. What prevents these endings from seeming forcibly imposed upon the poems, merely artful evasions of the actual death that is the poems' subject, is the sense they retain of their own inadequacy and limits, that utter absence underlying their crafted permanence. The effect is like that of a bell whose vibrations continue to trouble the air when the sound is gone, life at once completed and ramifying. . . .

Yes, the descriptions sometimes sag under a heavy adjectival weight; yes, there is occasionally a note of self-importance in Walcott's frequent references to his own "gift"; and yes, it sometimes seems that every line has been burnished to the same unseeable sheen. But in its imaginative abundance; in the immediacy and intensity of its passions and its achievement of a voice which is so much more than merely personal; in the evidence it gives of a craft that is wholly mastered and yet still vulnerable to living experience; and in its music—above all in its abiding music—*The Bounty* seems to me a great book.

Christian Wiman. *Poetry*. 172, 5 (August 1998), pp. 279–81

BIBLIOGRAPHY
*Twenty-Five Poems*, 1948; *Epitaph for the Young: A Poem in XII Cantos*, 1949; *Henri Christophe: A Chronicle in Seven Scenes*, 1950; *Harry Dernier: A Play for Radio Production*, 1951; *Poems*, 1953; *Wine of the Country*, 1953; *The Sea at Dauphin: A Play in One Act*, 1953; *Ione: A Play with Music*, 1957; *Drums and Colours: An Epic Drama*, 1958; *Ti-Jean and His Brothers*, 1958; *Malcochon; or, Six in the Rain*, 1959; *In a Green Night: Poems, 1948-1960*, 1962; *Selected Poems*, 1964; *The Castaway and Other Poems*, 1965; *Dream on Monkey Mountain*, 1967; *The Gulf and Other Poems*, 1969; *Dream on Monkey Mountain and Other Plays*, 1970; *In a Fine Castle*, 1970; *Another Life*, 1973; *The Joker of Seville*, 1974; *The Charlatan*, 1974; *O Babylon!*, 1976; *Sea Grapes*, 1976; *Selected Verse*, 1976; *Remembrance*, 1977; *Pantomime*, 1978; *The Star-Apple Kingdom*, 1979; *The Fortunate Traveller*, 1981; *Selected Poetry*, 1981; *The Isle Is Full of Noises*, 1982; *Midsummer*, 1984; *Collected Poems, 1948-1984*, 1986; *The Arkansas Testament*, 1987; *Omeros*, 1989; *The Poet in the Theatre*, 1990; *Steel*, 1991; *Odyssey: A Stage Version*, 1993; *Antilles: Fragments of Epic Memory*, 1993; *Homage to Frost* (with Seamus Heaney and Joseph Brodsky), 1996; *The Bounty*, 1997; *The Capeman: A Musical* (with Paul Simon), 1998; *What the Twilight Says: Essays*, 1998

# WALKER, Alice (1944– )
## United States

Miss Walker's poems [in *Once*] lack little in poetic quality, in the traditional, *i.e.*, white sense. I was frequently reminded of Emily Dickinson while I read her. Miss Walker has the tight tongue, the precise wordings, the subtle, unexpected twists, the reversal of the anticipated order of words and understatements for plus emphasis, or the shifting of emotions. . . .

Her poetry is dignified, unobtrusive, almost, at times, matter-of-fact. There is a lack of celebration or affirmation that one finds so exhilarating and so often in today's black literature. Her poetry is timid thunder. Black people are explosions of love, hate, fear, joy, sorrow, *Life*. Their literature should be that way.

The reader will hear a soft hum; a lovely delicate melody will brush him and he will think, "I want to hear more." He will re-read, lean closer and strain to touch, or be pulled by the magnetic isness of a lovely sound. He will wait and search and wait for the melody to break forth into some wildly glorious song which will roll and roll and roll like a chorus of thunder, under him, through him, swelling him, so that he too might burst forth, join in and sing. Though the song might be terrible, the notes our Black life's blood. But our singer does not here sing. In *Once*, she hums a haunting, poignant, yet certain, distinctive song.

Carolyn M. Rodgers. *Negro Digest*. September-October 1968, pp. 52, 12–13

[*The Third Life of Grange Copeland*] is an ambitious novel, for [Alice Walker's] attention is focused on a man wavering between the traditional poverty in Georgia and the glimpse of freedom that can never be his. Uprooted, he goes north, only to be disappointed by the confusing life of New York and the bitter cold. He returns to Georgia to find that his son has grown up, but little else has changed: The son, Brownfield, is satanic, methodically brutalizing his wife and children in a way which appalls even Grange, who is no angel. . . .

The violent scenes are numerous, but the arguments between husband and wife, father and son, are if anything more harrowing than the shotgun murders. It is hardly an idealized portrait of three generations of a black family, but the passions are enacted against a landscape which is carefully drawn: Baker County, the cotton fields, the ramshackle houses pitched in misery. Mrs. Walker has no lack of compassion, but has an essential detachment and so avoids being racially tendentious: She records skillfully the fakery and guilt of the cracker and the cotton picker, the awakening of Grange to his corrosive self-pity.

If the novel fails in parts it is because it attempts too much—too many years, too many characters. The movement is occasionally ponderous; elsewhere the years skip glibly by leaving the reader breathless. At times Mrs. Walker clumsily stitches episode to episode. Her strength is in her control of character rather than all the "business" that goes on in a family chronicle.

Paul Theroux. *Book World*. September 13, 1970, p. 2

*Revolutionary Petunias*, Alice Walker's second book of poetry, is a major achievement by a poet who deserves more critical attention than she has received. The promising seeds she planted in *Once* have blossomed into poems of extraordinary grace, wisdom, and strength.

What especially recommends this volume to readers, makers, and scholars of poetry is Miss Walker's sensitive and intelligent use of black Southern roots, the primal sources of much that gives definition and tone to Afro-American writing. Unlike poets who, in the words of Eugene Redmond, "dismiss the legacy and anger of their ancestors by practicing various forms of heresy and sacrilege," she celebrates the legacy, probes it to find practical methods for handling contemporary problems. Her preface tells us the "poems are about Revolutionaries and Lovers; and about the loss of compassion, trust, and the ability to expand in love that marks the end of hopeful strategy." Yet the poems are hopeful strategies for recapturing one's humanity. And from the gifts and lore of ethnic heritage the poet draws strength to love and to be fully human amidst the crises of twentieth-century American life. It is a sure understanding of how to apply ancestral wisdom that informs these precise, lucid and skillfully crafted poems.

Jerry W. Ward. *CLA Journal*. September 1973, pp. 127–28

My initial reaction to the first several stories of *In Love & Trouble* was negative. Miss Walker's search for ways to be new and different struck me as too willful and strained. I felt the same way about her earlier novel, *The Third Life of Grange Copeland*, whose style seemed too fine for the rough subject—the way two black men, a son and a father, try to degrade and destroy each other. But as I read on through these thirteen stories, I was soon absorbed by the density of reality they convey. They contain the familiar themes and situations of conventional black political and sociological fiction. There are black revolutionaries who read books and meet in small study groups, radical lady poets who read before black student audiences shouting "Right on!," and sharecroppers victimized by white landlords. But we see all these from genuinely new angles, from the point of view of the black woman or man totally absorbed in the pains of their inner life rather than the point of view of the protester or the newspaper headline.

The subtitle of the collection, *Stories of Black Women*, is probably an attempt by the publisher to exploit not only black subjects but feminine ones. There is nothing feminist about these stories, however. Neurosis and insanity, hatred and love, emptiness and indifference, violence and deceit—that is what they are about.

Jerry H. Bryant. *Nation*. November 12, 1973, pp. 501–2

[*In Love & Trouble*] would be an extraordinary literary work, if its only virtue were the fact that the author sets out consciously to explore with honesty the textures and terrors of black women's lives. Attempts to penetrate the myths surrounding black women's experiences are so pitifully rare in black, feminist, or American writing that each shred of truth about these experiences constitutes a breakthrough. The fact that Walker's perceptions, style, and artistry are also consistently high makes her work a treasure, particularly for those of us whom her writing describes.

Blood and violence seem the everyday backdrop to her characters' lives—a violence all the more chilling because it is so understated. It affects the 10-year-old girl who discovered a lynched man's headless body just as surely and ruinously as it destroys the middle-aged wife trapped in a loveless marriage or the ancient black woman ousted from a white house of worship.

Even as a black woman, I found the cumulative impact of these stories devastating. I questioned the quantity of pain in these sisters' lives and also wondered why none of the men and women were able to love each other. Women love their men, but they are neither loved or understood in return. The affective relationships are between mother and child or between black woman and black woman. The only successful "romance" is in "To Hell with Dying"; it flowers between the young girl narrator and the lonely, grandfatherly Mr. Sweet.

I soon realized, however, that the reason these stories saddened me so much was because of their truthfulness. For everyone of Walker's fictional women I knew or had heard of a real woman whose fate was all too similar. Harsh as these stories seem, they described the kind of pain that can be described only by one who has shared it and has recognized its victims as real. Because Walker tells each story from the point of view of the character herself, we share the inner life of persons who have been dismissed as superdominant matriarchs or bitches by both white sociologists and together "revolutionary" brothers like.

Barbara Smith. *Ms.* February 1974, p. 43

*Meridian*, Alice Walker's second novel, is the story of Meridian Hill, a young Southern black woman, from her early childhood on through her thirties. Set in the South, Meridian's story also invokes the impact of the Civil Rights movement, its major psychological and social stresses, as borne out in the lives of the three main characters, Meridian, Truman Held, a black artist and activist, and Lynne, his white wife, also a civil rights organizer.

Written in a clear, almost incandescent prose that sings and sears, there is great breadth and depth to Ms. Walker's imagination that ranges, in *Meridian*, from treatment of earlier vestiges of African and Indian life, back woods poverty, a college for black girls named Saxon (formerly a slave plantation) on to the grim confrontations of the Civil Rights era. It is an extraordinarily fine novel. . . .

In this novel as in her other works, one is aware of the very considerable size of Alice Walker's talent, the ease with which she handles language, her ability to see the essence of life in all things and take joy in it in an almost pantheistic fashion reminiscent of Tolstoy or Shakespeare.

One senses here, too, a dialectical tension between the values and practices of the black Christian tradition on the one hand and the black secular tradition of militant struggle on the other. While *Meridian* embodies one resolution of this tension, one anticipates future development of this theme, by this very talented writer, who is emerging as one of the major humanistic voices of our time.

Robert Chrisman. *Black Scholar*. April 1976, p. 3

[Alice] Walker ends *The Third Life of Grange Copeland* with a focus on the voting-rights marches in Grange's town, but in *Meridian* she joins some of the younger black writers who came to prominence in the 1960s and who participated in the Civil Rights Movement; she makes the movement her primary subject. *Meridian* is perhaps the most memorable of the works in this vein; it depicts the involvement of the title character in civil rights activity both during the heyday of the movement and when it was no longer fashionable. Walker draws upon her own experiences as a worker in voter registration and other activities in Mississippi and Georgia in the 1960s to portray Meridian's intense involvement in marches, voter registration, and desegregation of public facilities. Having deserted her child and husband to commit herself, paradoxically, to a life of improving conditions for black people, Meridian finds it hard to give up that pledge once the fervor of the movement has subsided. She therefore continues her solitary crusade against white Southern sheriffs and others who would stand in the way of progress. Strangely effective, indeed almost "touched in the head" in the manner of Harriet Tubman, Meridian not only has her small triumphs but succeeds in inspiring those who would prefer not to be inspired to follow in her footsteps. An exploration of the dissolution of the Civil Rights Movement, the novel is no less an exploration of its psychological impact upon a particular kind of committed individual. The movement, from one perspective, may have destroyed Meridian's homelife, but it represents the only fulfillment she finds in life; when it slows down, her dogged continuance successfully conveys Walker's point that the future in the South is possible only through constant vigilance.

Trudier Harris. In Louis D. Rubin, Jr, et al., eds. *The History of Southern Literature* (Baton Rouge: Louisiana State University Press, 1985), pp. 569–70

Alice Walker, in both short stories and novels, makes much more explicit use of history than [Toni Cade] Bambara, but ironically, she has a greater tendency to construct political solutions that run counter to the thrust of that very folk history. This history takes public and private forms. Whether re-creating the rural black South of the 1930s or the Civil Rights Movement of the 1960s, Walker seeks to place her narrative within the framework of the sociopolitical history of blacks in America. On the other hand, she gives her characters a very strong sense of their own pasts; in many cases, they are haunted by what has happened to them. Since she is, like Bambara, primarily concerned with black women, she writes stories that show these doubly oppressed figures searching for their own voices in the context of social and psychological conditioning that would deny them expression.

In her first novel, *The Third Life of Grange Copeland*, Walker's overt concern does not immediately seem to be with female characters. After all, the title character and his son Brownfield occupy center stage. Their development and inevitable conflict form the focus of the novel. In this sense the story resembles those by Ernest [J.] Gaines, who even in *The Autobiography of Miss Jane Pittman* concentrates on males. Walker, however, insists on testing the meaning of male development by its impact on female characters. The achievement of self-consciousness or identity is thus doubly dialectical: it occurs in relation to both race and gender. In shaping the narrative, Walker uses folklore on both these subjects in showing the operation of the dialectical patterns.

The characterizations of both Grange and Brownfield draw on folk figures, principally the bad man and the moral hard man. Brownfield lives out the selfish, violent, malevolent existence with which his father begins. In addition to being sexually promiscuous, he mistreats his wife and ultimately kills her, and he puts his newborn albino son outside on a winter night so that he will freeze to death. When his wife goes against his wishes in trying to create a more decent life for the family, he patiently and coldly calculates his revenge; he succeeds in returning the family to the barely human conditions from which they sought to rise. In all this, his attitudes resemble those of the bad man of black legend: the Great McDaddy, Billy Dupree, Stagolee. . . .

The stories in *In Love and Trouble* repeat the tension between folk wisdom and conventional systems of order. And again . . . black as well as white characters must be shown the limits and oppressiveness of those systems. "Strong Horse Tea," "The Revenge of Hannah Kemhuff," and "Everyday Use" provide the best examples of the working out of this theme. In each case a strong folk female figure must deal with the unbelief of a woman who has, either consciously or unconsciously, adopted an antifolk system of values. The validity of that system must be called into question and then the folk alternative given primacy. . . .

*Meridian* is Walker's most impressive effort to incorporate history, folk forms, and the conditions of women into fiction. While the time frame in which it operates is not extended, taking in only the period just before and during the Civil Rights Movement, the use of legends and folk tales adds historical depth in matters of race and gender. In addition, the technique of repetition moves it into the realm of cyclical time. As in *The Third Life of Grange Copeland*, the tension is between those who see that time as changelessness, which reduces people to ciphers, and those who see it as the pattern of growth and individuation. In *Meridian* . . . the powerful have a reductive, mechanistic vision, which is opposed by those who have or seek some connection with the folk in order to achieve an individual voice. The conflict in Walker's novel operates on three levels: gender, sexual politics, and race. These are

not mutually exclusive categories, but rather dynamically related aspects of the basic quest for expression and, through it, power. . . .

*The Color Purple*, Walker's award-winning and much-praised novel, has achieved immense popularity. In part, this success can be explained because the book is, in essence, a "womanist" fairy tale. Like Snow White, Celie is poisoned (psychologically in the novel) by an evil stepparent; like Cinderella, she is the ugly, abused daughter who ultimately becomes the princess; like Sleeping Beauty, she is awakened from her death-in-life by the kiss of a beloved; and like them all, she and her companions, after great travails, live happily ever after. Moreover, the fairy-tale quality is more than metaphoric, since major plot elements are worked out with fairy-tale devices. The story is generated out of what Vladimir Propp calls interdiction and violation of interdiction. Celie is told by her evil stepfather, after he rapes her, that she must tell no one but God what he has done; she chooses to write her story, which . . . makes it a public text. Transformation from a life of shame to one of self-esteem occurs when Celie receives the physical embrace of the regal Shug Avery. Finally, the plot is resolved and the characters reunited through the exposure of villainy and the death of the primary villain, an event which reverses the dispossession of Celie and her sister Nettie.

Keith E. Byerman. *Fingering the Jagged Grain: Tradition and Form in Recent Black Fiction* (Athens: University of Georgia Press, 1985), pp. 128–29, 138, 146, 161

Possibly the most famous study of the interaction between the factors of gender, class, and race by a black woman writer is Alice Walker's *The Color Purple*. Despite the public acclaim the novel has received, certain of its features have proved highly controversial. Criticism has been leveled at Walker's treatment of the "unitary self"; at her celebratory depiction of the family unit (albeit an extended family and one which is not exclusively heterosexual); and at the element of "utopian fantasy" apparent in the novel's design. The plot, as Rachel Bowlby observes, is structured on a series of fortunate coincidences which provide the central character Celie with both personal fulfillment and economic security. Commenting on this particular feature of the novel, Bowlby complains that: "Rather than posing residual problems that thwart her growing aspirations, Celie's world falls into place to meet them, presenting her as in the best commercials with a dream house and a successful small business." The novel does have, however, a number of defenders. Anselma Jackson, replying to the criticism that Walker models her characters on the humanist concept of the unitary self, points to the strongly *collective* focus which she nonetheless achieves. Jackson claims, rightly in my view, that "the autobiographical element that informs the text is not one of individual singularity, but that of the black Western Woman." And, in response to the accusation that Walker fails adequately to address the "determinants of patriarchy and capitalism as they work within the United States," she draws attention to her description of the cruelties of rape, incest, and forced marriage which the female characters suffer. These are, of course, crimes perpetrated by men—and the major part they play in the novel indicates Walker's interest in investigating the structures of male power. Her treatment of the theme is illuminated by [Audre] Lorde's analysis of the brutalizing effect which racial oppression has on black masculinity: "Exacerbated by racism and the pressures of powerlessness, violence against black women and children often becomes a standard within our communities, one by which manliness can be measured.'' Lorde's comments have obvious relevance to Walker's representation of the violent behavior of the male protagonists in the early stages of the novel. As Sofia laconically remarks: ''A girl child in't safe in a family of men.''

Paulina Palmer. *Contemporary Women's Fiction: Narrative Practice and Feminist Theory* (Jackson: University Press of Mississippi, 1989), pp. 82–83

The publication of *The Color Purple* transformed Alice Walker from an indubitably serious black writer whose fiction belonged to a tradition of gritty, if occasionally ''magical,'' realism into a popular novelist, with all the perquisites and drawbacks attendant on that position. Unlike either *The Third Life of Grange Copeland* or *Meridian*, *The Color Purple* gained immediate and widespread public acceptance, winning both the Pulitzer Prize and the American Book Award for 1982–1983. At the same time, however, it generated immediate and widespread critical unease over what appeared to be manifest flaws in its composition. Robert Towers, writing in the *New York Review of Books*, concluded that on the evidence of *The Color Purple* ''Alice Walker still has a lot to learn about plotting and structuring what is clearly intended to be a realistic novel,'' and his opinion was shared by many reviewers, who pointed out variously that in the last third of the book the narrator-protagonist Celie and her friends are propelled toward a fairy-tale happy ending with more velocity than credibility; that the letters from Nettie, with their disconcertingly literate depictions of life in an African village, intrude into the middle of the main action with little apparent motivation or warrant; and that the device of the letters to God is especially unrealistic inasmuch as it forgoes the concretizing details that traditionally have given the epistolary form its peculiar verisimilitude: the secret writing place, the cache, the ruses to enable posting letters, and especially the letters received in return.

Indeed, the violations of realist convention are so flagrant that they might well call into question whether *The Color Purple* ''is clearly intended to be a realistic novel,'' especially as there are indications that at least some of those aspects of the novel discounted by reviewers as flaws may constitute its links to modes of writing other than Anglo-American nineteenth-century realism. For example, Henry Louis Gates, Jr., has recently located the letters to God within an Afro-American tradition deriving from slave narrative, a tradition in which the act of writing is linked to a powerful deity who ''speaks'' through scripture and bestows literacy as an act of grace. . . .

Gates's paradigm suggests how misleading it may be to assume that mainstream realist criteria are appropriate for evaluating *The Color Purple*. But the Afro-American preoccupation with voice as a primary element unifying both the speaking subject and the text as a whole does not deal with many of the more disquieting structural features of Walker's novel. For instance, while the letters from Nettie clearly illustrate Nettie's parallel acquisition of her own voice, a process that enables her to arrive at conclusions very like Celie's under very different circumstances, the Afro-American tradition sheds little light on the central *place* that these letters occupy in the narrative or on why the plot takes this sudden jump into geographically and culturally removed surroundings. And Gates's subtle explication of the ramifications of ''voice'' once Walker has reconstrued the term to designate a *written* discourse

does not attempt to address the problematic ending, in which the disparate members of Celie's extended family come together, as if drawn by a cosmic magnet—and as if in defiance of the most minimal demands of narrative probability.

Molly Hite. In Henry Louis Gates, Jr., ed. *Reading Black, Reading Feminist* (New York: Meridian, 1990), pp. 431–32

The context for Walker's meditations on the spirit is principally female and Afro-American: these are the chief elements in her cosmology, the chief sources of her inspiration. Although this interest in the particular doings of a particular group may strike some as insular, those who perceive this as a fault would do well to remember that it is Walker's intention to tell all of our stories, or some part of them, by recounting the adventures, mistakes, and triumphs of Afro-American women. We see our faces in the faces of Mem and Ruth Brownfield; we hear our voices in the voices of Meridian Hill and Celie. As indicated by my examples, I am principally interested in Walker's novels—*The Third Life of Grange Copeland*, *Meridian*, [and] *The Color Purple*—for it is in this narrative form that her commitment to spirituality, to our spiritual survival, is most apparent. It is here that she gives us her most instructive and most potent models.

*The Third Life of Grange Copeland* is, for many of us, an extremely difficult novel to read. The difficulty does not stem from Walker's selection and manipulation of language for she has consistently proven herself at least equal to the trials of the word. Nor does the difficulty stem from a young writer's—*The Third Life of Grange Copeland* is her first novel—mishandling of a deceptively facile, extremely complex form. The difficulty, and even the pain that we as readers initially avoid and then, perforce, face, stems from Walker's capacity to make us, in the spirit of Joseph Conrad, see the good and evil in ourselves. Plainly, Walker believes that truth is the best medicine for an ailing spirit; but the truth is sometimes, since confabulations are often more appealing than facts, hard to bear. . . .

The Civil Rights Movement of the 1960s is the subject of Walker's second novel, *Meridian*. Here in a work that deserves a larger audience, Walker travels much farther than other novelists who have aided us in our re-examination of this important period in American history. Although [Ernest J.] Gaines's *The Autobiography of Miss Jane Pittman* and *In My Father's House*, powerful works in their own right, bring us to a point where we are able to engage the spirit of that volatile time, we do so only for a moment. In these novels Gaines's concerns are not defined by the Civil Rights Movement—this is not a flaw—but more by events that precede it, or by developments that occur alongside it. *Armies of the Night*, by Norman Mailer—another work of the imagination, although there is some debate about whether it is a novel—also treats the Civil Rights Movement. But Mailer seems more interested in documenting his own role in the events of history than in analyzing the events themselves. What sets *Meridian* apart from these texts is that the Civil Rights Movement is the subject, not an episode, backdrop, or mirror. The events of the time and the people who are caught in their pull are the poles between which an imagined, symbolic conflict achieves its resolution. . . .

In *The Third Life of Grange Copeland* the context for Walker's meditations on the spirit—on our spiritual survival and possibilities—is the home and the family. In *Meridian* her context is chiefly political and we are asked to consider the various ways in which we can assure the survival of that larger, greater family of which we are all members. In *The Color Purple*, her most controversial and most highly acclaimed novel, Walker returns to the home and to the family, for it is here that our first spiritual battles are fought. It is here that the spirit is most under siege. It is here that the spirit, when not respected and nurtured, is most in danger of being weakened and trivialized. . . .

The novels of Alice Walker contain the things of this world: pain and consolation, betrayal and reconciliation, love and transformation. They also contain the very thing we need to live in this world: models. It seems that Walker has always known what is essential for our survival because as a writer, as a womanist, and as an *artist* she has never failed to provide us with this vital resource. For Walker, models are essential spiritual aids with revelatory properties. Models reveal many things about ourselves and the world, but most importantly they reveal truth. This is why Walker shares with us situations in literature that are grounded in truth. Although we may sometimes wish to reject these situations, to dismiss them . . . as womanist propaganda, the force and purity of these situations, as well as our own knowledge of history and of human behaviour, make such dismissals and rejections—if we love the truth—the greatest self-deception. But Walker's models reveal more than truth; they also reveal direction. Truth without direction is an oppression of the spirit. Without direction we flounder and agonize, but with it we apprehend not just a means of escape, but relief from spiritual suffering and an awareness not only of our fallibility but of our potentiality as well. In *The Third Life of Grange Copeland*, *Meridian*, and *The Color Purple*, Walker forces us, through her artful use of models, to face the truth; but she also, through these same models, provides direction. We celebrate Grange's transformation, Meridian's commitment, and Celie's triumph because each reveals what is true and possible.

> Rudolph P. Byrd. In Joanne M. Braxton and Andrée Nicola McLaughlin, eds. *Wild Women in the Whirlwind: Afro-American Culture and the Contemporary Literary Renaissance* (New Brunswick: Rutgers University Press, 1990), pp. 364–65, 367, 373–74, 376–77

In *Meridian*, the individual experience of black motherhood within the context of historical black motherhood obliterates the souls of women and damages their children in an ever more serious cycle of destruction. Many critics have commented on this striking theme since Barbara Christian drew attention to it in *Black Women Novelists*. Gloria Wade-Gayles, for example, considers this resistance to motherhood as the sole defining element of black women's worthiness to be *Meridian*'s most original point. Christian explores contradictory social definitions of motherhood's paramount value and of black children as worthless, merely evidence of black women's promiscuity. Examining this issue further, Susan Willis proposes that, under these circumstances, mothers' impulses toward murder of their children or suicide "are the emotional articulation of social realities." In addition, *Meridian* "is less an indication of future possibilities and more a critique of the way heterosexual relationships have individualized a woman's relationship to *her* children, making them *her* property." *Meridian* simultaneously critiques traditional definitions of motherhood and implies more widely shared responsibility for children. In almost their only act of self-assertion, Saxon students riot when the college administration refuses to allow them to claim the Wild Child as one

of their own. In focusing on the novel's opening scene—Meridian leading a "children's crusade" past a tank to desegregate a freak Show—critics like Christian and Willis point to a politicized ideal of communal responsibility for children as central to Walker's vision in *Meridian*.

Accurate in itself, this critical focus has obscured another equally crucial component of the novel: the necessity for this rather abstract relationship of community and children to be manifested in an individual mother surrogate who provides emotional nurturance that the traditional role both demands and prevents. *Meridian* consistently focuses on both issues, on oppressive social structures and on the individual's capacity to resist them. Throughout, the novel emphasizes the power of individual example to rally opposition to injustice. The bereaved father testifying in church to the worth of his dead son's life, the minister who consciously imitates Martin Luther King, Jr.'s voice, Truman's inheritance of Meridian's role—all of these make a claim for the individual's power and worth. Both the harm done by oppressive institutions and the effectiveness of specific strategies of resistance are measured by their consequences for particular individuals. *Meridian* does not adopt a purely "quantitative" approach toward social change; that is, while continually emphasizing the need for social change, it values the rescue of each individual life, not only for its potential contributions toward social change, but in itself. With individuality such a strong underlying value, then, *Meridian* pushes beyond an abstract commitment of adults to the community's children and insists on one-to-one mothering nurturance for survival.

> Missy Dehn Kubitschek. *Claiming the Heritage: African-American Women Novelists and History* (Jackson: University Press of Mississippi, 1991), pp. 158–59

From the predominately Gothic vision in *The Third Life of Grange Copeland*, to the somewhat Camusian vision in *Meridian*, to the vision of the great gender divide-and-conquer in *The Color Purple*, Walker moves into *The Temple of My Familiar* and creates a salutary vision, which points toward a monistic idealism in which humans, animals, and the whole ecological order coexist in a unique dynamic of pancosmic symbiosis.

Evidently, Walker must have been leery of the danger posed to her imagination by fragmentation—hence the urgency in the novel toward an ideal of the unity—the unity of culture, moral truth, and imaginative thought and emotion. The best summation of this unity in *The Temple of My Familiar* is Lissie's long, moving story about the spirit of mutual dependence between humans and their animal cousins and Suwelo's reflections on its moral . . . and cultural implications, both for himself as well as for those with whom he has come in contact. . . .

With this vision clearly set before her, Walker proceeds to construct *The Temple of My Familiar* into six major parts, each consisting of diverse vignettes that project iconographic narrative movement (iconographic because Alice Walker not only tells a story in each movement, but also conveys its underlying metaphysical meaning by a carefully selected icon or mythic image, pretty much in the convention of African cosmological art and iconography). Behind the insistent particularity of each individual story is a serious quest, albeit unconscious, for the demonstrable values of oneness, wholeness, and unity as opposed to dialectical tension, exclusivity, and separateness. Insistently and consistently, characters in the novel are in motion, even when it appears they are in conflict, toward an underlying kinship that binds them with one another and with forces beyond themselves. For Walker this act of seeking means a basic freedom, which only a bird can enjoy, to range over all time, to employ any subtheme, to consecrate a limitless range of subject matter, to begin where she pleases, and to stop where she wishes.

The basic intent is to trace human life in its pancosmic and mythical dimensions through all its protean turns and twists, all its recesses, all its races and peoples. The watchwork throughout the novel is communion, a communion forged through three distinct metaphysical contexts: Time, Nature, and Self.

Ikenna Dieke. *African American Review*. 26, 3 (Fall 1992), pp. 507–8

In 1989, while living part of the time in London, I reported on a series of cases of young girls who had been kidnapped and sexually mutilated in and around the city. But unlike other sex crimes I had reported on, these attacks were not at the hands of strangers. Each of these young girls had been mutilated at the request of her family.

I had been aware of the practice of so-called female circumcision since college when it had been a primary focus of the first International Tribunal on Crimes Against Women. But before the girls in London, I had never seen the face of genital mutilation close-up. And until I spoke with a Somali woman gynecologist at a London clinic, I never truly understood what was being done to these young girls in London and how their lives were forever altered.

Reading *Warrior Marks* created the same sense of horror and rage I felt in that London clinic. Alice Walker and Pratibha Parmar, a Pulitzer Prize-winning African-AmerIndian writer and internationally known Indian lesbian filmmaker, embarked on a joint project to document female genital mutilation in Africa.

*Warrior Marks* is a record of that process and the making of Parmar's film. Letters, diary entries, poems, interviews and photographs from both women all combine to provide an indelible image of the mutilation of millions of the world's women and girls. . . .

Walker and Parmar present very different commentary, both mesmerizing. Walker ties the practice to the range of mutilations women across the globe suffer at the hands of patriarchal influence. Parmar's responses are less poetic, less intellectualized than Walker's—she is simply raw with the images. Both women, in very different ways, discuss how fragile they are made by their experience. Both of them (and most of the women on their crew) end up getting injured and/or sick; Parmar has nightmares, Walker, insomnia. Walker talks about nearly going off her head from the horror, Parmar calls her lover in London and cries to her.

The images are cataclysmic, oppressive, dramatic, insufferable. Walker's feminism pours out on the page like a kind of healing salve for these tortured girls. Parmar, whose films have spoken eloquently of the oppressions of Indian women, and lesbians and gay men, worries that she won't be able to get the images she needs to tell the story properly.

*Warrior Marks* is as chilling as it is visionary. Walker and Parmar lead us like brave guides into the charnel house. But they show us not only the terrible horrors. . . .

They also show us the valiant women (and some men) struggling to eradicate the ritual through education and political movements, the faces of the youngest girls who may possibly escape, the words of mothers who insist they will not allow their daughters to be mutilated.

Female genital mutilation has been allowed to continue under the rubric of "culture." But as Walker so simply and astutely notes, "there is a difference between torture and culture." Lesbian and gay men have been tormented under the same guise of heterosexual "culture." *Warrior Marks* provides valuable insight for the queer community, as Walker and Parmar each explore the reasons this mutilation and others are allowed to thrive. Female genital mutilation is the most primal form of sexual oppression. *Warrior Marks* is a book every queer must read.

Victoria A. Brownworth. *Lambda Book Report*. 4, 6 (September-October), 1994, p. 37

[*Possessing the Secret of Joy*] functions as an example of revolutionary action against the oppression of those colonized by the imperialist gaze. The female body and the African body are exposed as sites of colonization by power elites; the ritual of female genital mutilation and the AIDS epidemic are both imaged as means to oppression. However, in Walker's text these bodies also become sites of resistance to domination by power elites. In addition, the power relations in this text are not simplistically demarcated in a binary of colonized versus colonizer/good versus evil. Walker posits a complex system of power relations in which those oppressed themselves become oppressors through hegemonic systems.

The female body is revealed as a site of male and national colonization through the ritual clitoridectomy and infibulation that the protagonist, Tashi/Evelyn Johnson, undergoes. Walker bases the experience of her fictional character upon fact. Genital mutilation impacts upon approximately 100 million women worldwide; this is a procedure generally covered by the comparatively innocuous term "female circumcision." . . .

[Examples] of genital mutilation are given to the reader to underscore the prevalence and pain of this practice: that of Dura, Tashi's older sister, and that of M'Lissa, the tsunga. Dura's experience is key as it forms part of Tashi's post-ritual madness. A hemophiliac, Dura died as a result of the ritual performed at M'Lissa's hands. After this traumatic occurrence, Tashi experiences a sort of amnesia related to her ensuing madness; when she overcomes this amnesia, a vital part of her cure is effected. This part of the cure entails naming her and her sister's oppression; Dura's death is named a murder which, in addition to the traumatic effects of the ritual upon Tashi, must be revenged. And the person upon whom vengeance must be visited is the one who performed the ceremony and the one praised as a national treasure: M'Lissa.

M'Lissa is also a victim of genital mutilation. She drags her left leg behind her, as the tendons were severed during the operation. M'Lissa's mother (the tsunga at the time) had attempted to simply knick M'Lissa's clitoris; the male witch doctor, however, was vigilant and, perceiving a violation of the ceremony, performed a thorough clitoridectomy and infibulation himself. As M'Lissa bucked under the razor-sharp stone, he also cut the tendons in her left leg.

Although M'Lissa is a victim, the reader is not persuaded to empathize with her plight. Although her body is marked and experienced as a site of male domination, she becomes the next tsunga and thus becomes complicitous with the patriarchy. She learns to stop feeling and becomes callous in the performance of her "duty." As this ritual is her livelihood, she decides to ensure her own autonomy at the expense of other women, women whom she sees as fools. She believes the women themselves to be the agents of their own domination; in her eyes, if women are stupid enough to obey this tradition, then they deserve everything they get as a result. Tashi puts this sort of belief as follows, describing its consequences: "'If you lie to yourself about your own pain, you will be killed by those who will claim you enjoyed it.'"

In looking at the female body as a site of colonization in this text, then, a few points are clear. First, those who are colonized may also act as colonizers. This is true of both the tribal leaders who encourage genital mutilation and the tsunga M'Lissa. As the leaders are subordinated to English colonial authority, so, too, do they subordinate women to their own authority, limited as it may be. As Audre Lorde writes, genital mutilation "is not a cultural affair as the late Jomo Kenyatta insisted. It is a crime against black women." Nationalism does not excuse oppression.

Second, Walker avoids easy binary oppositions of male/female, colonizer/colonized, white/black, European/African, and good/evil. This second point is further developed through the use of Adam and his sister, Olivia. While Adam and Olivia are both black Americans and, thus, victims of oppression themselves, they are also agents of colonization. As part of a missionary family (their mother, father, and aunt acted as missionaries to the Olinkans until the village was destroyed), they are seen as outsiders and, more importantly, as cultural TNT by the Olinkans. The mores (concerning religion, clothing, education, sexuality, beauty, et cetera) that Adam and Olivia's family had brought to the tribe are seen as the means to colonization that they are. Tashi phrases this discourse in the following way in a conversation with Olivia before she leaves for the ritual:

> They are right, I said to her from my great height astride the donkey, who say you and your family are the white people's wedge. . . . All I care about now is the struggle for our people, I said. You are a foreigner. Any day you like, you and your family can ship yourselves back home. . . . Who are you and your people never to accept us as we are? Never to imitate any of our ways? It is always we who have to change. . . . You are black, but you are not like us. We look at you and your people with pity, I said. You barely have your own black skin, and it is fading. . . . You don't even know what you've lost! And the nerve of you, to bring us a God someone else chose for you!

In this quote we can see the complexities of both intranational and international colonization for both America and Africa. Here we have two African-Americans who have accepted a religion, foreign to their ancestry, that was once used as a justification for slavery; in turn, they are asking Africans to replace their beliefs with this same religion. We have a woman who comes from and represents a patriarchal background, in religious as well as other American ideologies, begging another woman not to submit to a patriarchal tradition. And we have a woman who, in asserting and celebrating her tribal identity, is victimized by that tribal belief system.

Walker also complicates the male/female binary. For example, the character of Adam provides further complexities. As a colonizer, Adam acts as religious, male, and American figures of domination. The moment at which Tashi spiritually left their relationship, she tells us, is when Adam, a progressive minister, refused to give a sermon on female suffering as evidenced in Tashi's mutilation; he

had lectured on the suffering of Christ, and Tashi believed he should lecture on the suffering of women like herself as well. . . .

Not only does Walker image the body as victim, as a site of colonization, but she shows how the status of victim and Other can be transcended to that of agent and subject. Relations of oppression are also complexly imaged. In unmasking systems of domination, many authors are accused of not taking the next logical step and proposing a new solution; this is not the case with Walker. Her text acts as a revolutionary manifesto for dismantling systems of domination. As such, her text is that of a radical. To simply strive for social and economic equality with white men or to simply combat racism is not enough, although liberal and conservative ideology might propose these as solutions for sexism, racism, and classism. Instead, the complete system must be overturned. And the first step is overcoming the silence that empowers dominant groups; this is part of an overall resistance that might very well be the key to the secret of joy.

Alyson R. Buckman. *Journal of American Culture*. 18, 2 (Summer, 1995), pp. 89–94

BIBLIOGRAPHY

*Once: Poems*, 1968; *The Third Life of Grange Copeland*, 1970; *Five Poems*, 1972; *Revolutionary Petunias and Other Poems*, 1973; *In Love and Trouble: Stories of Black Women*, 1973; *Meridian*, 1976; *Goodnight, Willie Lee, I'll See You in the Morning*, 1979; *You Can't Keep a Good Woman Down*, 1981; *The Color Purple*, 1982; *In Search of Our Mothers' Gardens: Womanist Prose*, 1983; *Horses Make a Landscape Look More Beautiful*, 1984; *Living by the Word: Selected Writings, 1973-1987*, 1988; *The Temple of My Familiar*, 1989; *Her Blue Body Everything We Know: Earthling Poems, 1965-1990 Complete*, 1991; *Possessing the Secret of Joy*, 1992; *Warrior Marks: Female Genital Mutilation and the Sexual Blinding of Women* (with Pratibha Parmar), 1993; *Alice Walker Banned*, 1996; *Anything We Love Can Be Saved: A Writer's Activism*, 1997

# WALKER, Margaret (1915–)
## United States

Straightforwardness, directness, reality are good things to find in a young poet. It is rarer to find them combined with a controlled intensity of emotion and a language that, at times, even when it is most modern, has something of the surge of biblical poetry. And it is obvious that Miss Walker uses that language because it comes naturally to her and is part of her inheritance. A contemporary writer, living in a contemporary world, when she speaks of and for her people older voices are mixed with hers—the voices of Methodist forebears and preachers who preached the Word, the anonymous voices of many who lived and were forgotten and yet out of bondage and hope made a lasting music. Miss Walker is not merely a sounding-board for these voices—I do not mean that. Nor do I mean that [*For My People*] is interesting and moving poetry because it was written by a Negro. It is too late in the day for that sort of meaningless patronage—and poetry must exist in its own right. These poems keep on talking to you after the book is shut because, out of deep feeling, Miss Walker has made living and passionate speech.

> Stephen Vincent Benét. Foreward to Margaret Walker, *For My People* (New Haven: Yale University Press, 1942), pp. 5–6

Miss Walker's poems [in *For My People*], though they are songs and portraits of American Negroes of today, are suffused with the prayers and hopes of the submerged and semi-submerged of all times. . . .

Miss Walker's poems for her people everywhere show that she has thought long and felt deeply about the sorrow laden past and present of the American Negro. Out of a rich experience in the lower Mississippi Valley and in Black Chicago at the head of that valley she has seen the substance of poetry in the blind struggle of her people. The Yale Series of Younger Poets, whose choice she is this year, has here launched a career indeed. Miss Walker's poems are not new to *Opportunity* readers, for several of them have appeared in these pages, but the intensity of her sustained effort may come as a surprise to those who know only her shorter pieces. Her symbols, the South, the "L," the delta, the white gods, cotton, 1619, are familiar, but her use of them is with new strength.

A full pride in the past and a healthy view of the present give her poems distinction. She is no mournful weeper wearing her pen out over the twin literary tragedies of lynching and color. Her sorrow and her pride find themselves in more tangible and commonplace symbols: the grandmothers who were strong and full of memories, the money-gods who take life away, the strange contradiction of beauty in the bitter low cotton country. Her hearty portraits of Molly Means, Stagolee, Kissie Lee . . . and of Gus the Lineman are not, fortunately, of the how-I-have-loved-thee school of feminine poets. Perhaps Miss Walker's volume marks the end of a school of Negro women poets; she is more struck by the fact that "We with/our blood have watered these fields/and they belong to us" than she is in the crenellated visions of archaic sorrow so freely indulged in by the "lady poets" in their small black and gold veined volumes. *For My People* contains some of our strongest recent verse. "Sorrow Home" is a dirge of real power.

> Ulysses Lee. *Opportunity*. December 1942, pp. 379–80

To appreciate the extent of innovation *Jubilee* brings to a thoroughly quarried, frequently hackneyed genre of writing, it is only necessary to recall that the Civil War novel has been the source of some of the crudest stereotypes of Negro characters in American fiction. As Robert A. Lively pointed out in *Fiction Fights the Civil War*: "the Negro is rarely a central figure in Civil War novels—he only hovers near the white heroes and heroines, to whom space and interest is given." Margaret Walker has reversed the picture completely. With a fidelity to fact and detail, she presents the little-known everyday life of the slaves, their modes of behavior, patterns and rhythms of speech, emotions, frustrations, and aspirations. Never done on such a scale before, this is the strength of her novel. As it unfolds one sees plantation life as it was seen by Negro slaves, feels the texture of American history as it was felt by Negro slaves: the Civil War with the hopes it aroused, its sordid and grim

realities; the participation of the Negroes in the fight against slavery; the ugly and frustrating rise of the Ku Klux Klan; the postwar waves of terror in the South to keep the Negro down and prevent emancipation from becoming a reality.

The author is so intent on presenting her historical data as accurately as possible, on correcting the distortions which have crept into so many Civil War novels, that at times she fails to transform her raw material into accomplished literary form. There are passages of very pedestrian prose. Fortunately, the colorful and musical speech of the Negro characters in the novel transcends the stilted prose of the narrator. . . .

And there is Vyry, the heroine of the novel, who distills out of her life as a slave, and the trials of the Civil War, and the frustrated hopes of the Reconstruction years, a hard realism, a fierce spiritual force and hope. . . .

> Abraham Chapman. *Saturday Review*. September 24, 1966, pp. 43–44

[*Jubilee*] serves especially well as a response to white "nostalgia" fiction about the antebellum and Reconstruction South—especially Margaret Mitchell's poor but popular *Gone with the Wind*. One cannot read one of these novels without repeatedly contrasting it with the other. On dialect: Miss Walker's is thoroughly researched and linguistically accurate; Miss Mitchell's ranges from rather accurate to absurd. On the role of blacks: Miss Walker reveals the various levels of black mentality, as well as the devotion of some slaves to, and the intense hatred of others for, their masters; Miss Mitchell presents blacks before the Civil War as happy darkies completely devoted to "missy" and "massa." On "social controls": Miss Walker portrays vividly the savagery of white vigilante repression; Miss Mitchell portrays the Ku Klux Klan as an organization of noble and dedicated men with the highest moral objectives. In short, the novels make for an interesting and enlightening companion study—a study of painful historical reality and romanticized self-deception.

> Roger Whitlow. *Black American Literature* (Chicago: Nelson-Hall, 1973), pp. 138–39

After a lapse of twenty-eight years Margaret Walker has brought out a new volume of verse. Entitled *Prophets for a New Day*, it was printed by the Broadside Press. Though a very thin volume (it contains only 32 pages), the work is impressive. It is the best poetical comment to come from the civil rights movement—the movement which came to a climax with the march on Washington and which began thereafter to change into a more militant type of liberation effort.

In *Prophets for a New Day* Miss Walker, with poems like "Street Demonstration," "Girl Held without Bail," and "Sit-Ins," catches the spirit of the civil rights age, when young blacks gladly went to jail for the cause of freedom. "The Ballad of the Free," another liberation poem, treats as kindred souls Nat Turner, Gabriel Prosser, Denmark Vesey, Toussaint L'Ouverture, and John Brown. The inclusion of the last name shows that Miss Walker, though much "blacker" now in her thinking than she was in her early works, has not lost her respect for men of good will, whether black or white. Unlike most present-day Negro writers, she is willing to honor not only abolition heroes like John Brown but white martyrs of the civil rights movement as well. . . .

Arthur P. Davis. *From the Dark Tower* (Washington, D.C.: Howard University Press, 1974), pp. 184–85

Since, quite often, there are misconceptions about the definition of folklore or "fakelore" (a term coined by Richard Dorson [in *American Folklore*] in 1950, which means the falsifying of the raw data for capitalistic gain rather than totalitarian conquest), it is necessary to establish some ground rules for exploring folklore in literature. Three tests that can be used to see if an author has used folklore follow:

1. There must be biographical evidence; we should be able to establish that the author knew of and was part of the oral tradition.

2. From reading the story, we should be able to establish that the author gives an accurate description of the folk group and their customs—in other words, he has observed the group firsthand.

3. We must be able to show that the folk motifs can be found in the Motif Index and that the folk material has had oral circulation before the author included it in his story. [David Laubach, *Introduction to Folklore*]

Couple the above three-faceted test set forth by Dorson with a four-part test by Laubach—(1) Folklore is oral; (2) folklore is traditional within a certain group; (3) folklore must exist in different versions; and (4) folklore is anonymous—and one readily observes that Walker definitely utilizes the folk tradition. . . . [A] close examination of any number of Walker's poems reveals just how deeply steeped she is in the folkloric traditions of black people.

"Ballad of the Hoppy-Toad" is an example of Walker's masterful usage of folklore elements. Surface-wise, this poem is about a protagonist's concern about an evil spell cast upon her by "the goofer man" or the "root worker." No reason is given for this act, but the spell is reversed and the caster is ultimately the victim of his own evil deed. On the surface, also, is the tall tale told in ballad form. Structurally, the poem follows most of the conventions of the traditional ballad. Each stanza consists of four lines with four beats or stresses in the first line, three in the second, four in the third, and three in the fourth. The second and fourth lines rhyme; the first and the third do not. Thus, if the word "Ballad" were not included in the title, one could merely scan the poem and identify its form. . . .

Like a number of ballads, also, the "Ballad of the Hoppy-Toad" has many of the properties of a full-blown short story: setting, plot, characters. This story takes place on a Saturday on Market Street, wherever, U.S.A. While the street may mean some place specific to Walker, her description leads the reader to a vivid description of the Southern Saturday marketing day, washing day, and fighting and drinking day. Thus, she gives a time, background, and place for the oncoming story. Her characters, likewise, are well established: The narrator or protagonist, the goopher man or antagonist, and Sis Avery. The rise in action begins with "the night I seen the goopher man / Throw dust around my door," and continues throughout the narrator's seeking Sis Avery's assistance in curtailing the spell. The climax of this dramatic piece is the changing of the horse to a toad with the dénouement being the toad and goopher man dying simultaneously.

In addition to the traits previously listed, the "Ballad" abounds in other folklore elements. There is, for example, the constant mentioning of various animals, and the animal stories are very much a part of folklore tradition. The reader is introduced to the toad, via inference, of course, in the first stanza: "When the Saturday crowd went stomping / Down the Johnny-jumping road." In the second stanza, the deacon's daughter is "lurching / Like a drunken alley goat"; the "root-worker" is a dog that needs to behave; and the charging horse is reduced to the ultimate "hoppy-toad." . . .

Another element that authenticates this ballad as folklore is Walker's use of the conjurer or conjurers, when one considers Sis Avery. The use of magic, ju ju, mojo, voodoo, hoodoo, etc., has long been a part of the black heritage. . . .

One final observation about the "Ballad" is that it conforms to the Dorson test of folklore in literature: (1) it is definitely an outgrowth of the oral tradition since the story was told to Walker by someone (anonymous) from the North Carolina area; (2) the storyteller / narrator gives a very detailed account of the characters, as noted, and their customs (any reader would recognize the description of the typical Souther-Saturday and Saturday-night episodes); and (3) the fire or prayer to ward off evil spirits, the reversal of spells or duper being duped, and the animal lore are representative folk motifs that can be found in the Motif Index.

Equally as compacted with similar folkloric elements of the "Ballad of the Hoppy-Toad" in content is Walker's "Molly Means." There is good and evil (the innocent bride and evil conjurer); there is the spell casting and its reversal; there is the animal emphasis, and the animals in "Molly Means" are a dog and hog. Yet Molly has all the charm of a snake. Further comparison/ contrast of these two works reveals a male goopher man in the "Ballad" and a female witch in "Molly Means," with both becoming victims of their own evil doings. Additionally, Walker, in "Molly Means," tells how the witch gets her powers:

Some say she was born with a veil on her face
So she could look through unnatchal space
Through the future and through the past
And charm a body or an evil place. . . .

Yet the reader is not privy to such information in the "Ballad's" root worker. This particular idiom of a person's being born with a veil has been catalogued, and the belief is still widespread among the black community; however, it does not always indicate evilness. Rather, a child born with a veil (in actuality the placenta) is born for good luck and has the gift of being able to see into the future.

There is the lack of religious impetus to counteract the evil spirit in "Molly Means," and the reader gets the implication that religion is replaced by the devout love of the husband for his young bride. As with the religion that does not work in the "Ballad," the husband has to contact a conjurer, "who said he could move the spell / and cause the awful thing to dwell / On Molly Means. . . ." Details of how the conjurer accomplishes this feat are not as explicit as in the "Ballad," but the resulting deaths of the evildoers are evident. While nothing remains of the "Hoppy Toad," the ghost of Molly Means remains whining, crying, cackling, moaning, and, of course, barking, thus iterating that her demise, too, is somehow affiliated with an animal, more specifically, a dog. The return of a person in the form of a ghost or an animal can be found in the Motif Index, although the reasons for returning differ.

Two other folklore elements of note found in "Molly Means" are the use of numbers and the refrain structure. In folklore, especially modern lore, each number represents something in particular. Numbers have been catalogued, and usually the odd numbers (3, 7, 11) used by Walker indicate good luck; but these seem to mean the opposite in ''Molly Means'': ''Imp at three and wench at 'leben / she counted her husbands to the number seben.''

The second point of note is that the structure of ''Molly Means'' is a variation of the traditional folk ballad; some ballads repeat the last line of each stanza, and some repeat a particular refrain. Walker thus makes use of incremented repetition in ''Molly Means'' which ''involves repeating the basic structure of a line but changing it slightly (the increment) in order to move the story forward; sometimes this technique has striking dramatic effects.'' The first line of the refrain that follows each stanza is basically the same— ''O Molly, Molly, Molly Means''—with the exception of stanzas two, three, and six, where the ''O'' is replaced with ''Old.'' So the balladeer refers to Molly as ''old'' when describing her evilness, her ''black-hand arts,'' and her death. The first two words of the second line of the refrain are also changed slightly to denote progression: ''There goes the ghost of Molly Means''; ''Dark is . . .''; ''Cold is. . . .''; ''Where is . . .''; ''Sharp is . . .''; ''This is . . .''; ''Lean is. . . .'' The only time Walker asks a question is before the husband goes in search of the witch, thus suggesting a change in the action of the story.

While the ''Ballad of the Hoppy-Toad'' is structurally much like the traditional ballad, ''Molly Means'' has more dissimilarities than similarities. It is, however, of the oral tradition, about a particular group of people and their customs and about a specific event. Walker is like the traditional balladeer in ''Molly Means'' because this poem is more objective; she ''reports the news of the day in a very impersonal way'' and ''refuses to condemn.'' On the other hand, in the ''Ballad,'' she is author/narrator/protagonist, making judgments about the townspeople and even calling the goopher man a dog. With this subjectivity, too, comes more dialogue, particularly between the narrator and Sis Avery and between Sis Avery and the goopher man. . . .

Walker's folk heroes come in different sizes and shapes, and she celebrates the good heroes in *Prophets for a New Day* and the more diversified ones in the second section of *For My People*. Most of her prophets are fighters for civil rights, with special attention being given to Michah and Amos, Medgar Evers, and Martin Luther King. In this collection, she calls on numerous Biblical figures and images to describe her heroes; and if one considers the folklore inherent in the Bible, he need not test any of these poems for elements of lore. . . .

In conclusion, Walker's poetry is definitive proof that she is a poet of the people, her people. The folkways, customs, beliefs, or superstitions embodied in lines, even words, of her poetry reveal that she is a folklorist and, indeed, a folk poet.

Dilla Buckner. *CLA Journal*. XXXIII, 3, (March 1990), pp. 367–77

*Jubilee,* properly considered, is a work that was much ahead of its time, a fiction that recalls the truth of what was too long silenced and overlooked in the annals of both American history and American fiction. *Jubilee* is a revolutionary celebration of African American women's lives. Ironically, the work achieves its aims in the very terms that white southern culture tended to reserve for its own self-expression: folklore, history, and the literature of memory.

*Jubilee* tells the story of Vyry, from her days as a young child living under slavery in the Deep South through the Civil War and Reconstruction. Walker's story, as is well known, attempts on one level to recover the struggles and triumphs of her own great-grandmother's life as preserved in family tradition. But Walker's historical and folkloric research and the long struggle to get the story told gave her project another dimension. In different but difficult times and circumstances, and with ambitions to learn, to write, and to teach, Walker herself approximated Vyry in ways that she could not have anticipated when she first developed the ambition to tell the story. Vyry's trials come in the rural slave-holding South, on a small plantation and later at meager farms or in unhospitable small towns, in times of explicit danger for ambitious African Americans. Walker's struggles took place in the Jim Crow South, and her intellectual and creative project was carried out in the restricted atmosphere of segregated education and the exclusively white territory of state historical collections. With Vyry she shared an ambitious mind and heart, and she too bore children, cared for a family, and maintained a household. ''But then,'' she says, ''it's always been hard for women writers—not just in my lifetime.''

It should not surprise us, then, that through Vyry's struggles and hardships, Walker portrays not only the story of her grandmother but also the values she developed as she relieved Vyry's struggle in her own terms, in her own time. Telling this story in literary terms put her into a great tradition, as she has said. In ''The Humanistic Tradition of Afro-American Literature,'' Walker writes, ''At its best it [literature] reflects the ultimate of the Black experience . . . a people oppressed who refuse to be suppressed; a people who refused to be dehumanized or made into machines . . . a people who have had to develop compassion out of suffering and who are passionately tied to all that is earthy, natural, and emotionally free.'' Rather than becoming embittered by the stories she knew or the ones she lived, however, through Vyry's character Walker ''calls for Christian love and spiritual wholeness, the inner peace that sees Vyry through and leads eventually to her transcendence over oppression.''

*Jubilee* is more than a family narrative turned to fiction or an experience of Walker's humanism. The historical significance of Walker's *Jubilee* can be summed up in a recent correspondence from John Hope Franklin, the twentieth-century dean of African American historians. Franklin notes that Walker ''immersed herself in the entire sweep of nineteenth-century history and consequently delivers a work that is as faithful to historical fact as any work of fiction can be.'' Reflecting on the tripartite structure of *Jubilee*, Franklin writes, ''I have always liked the first section— dealing with the antebellum years—better than the other two sections. Perhaps this is because the antebellum years are traditionally romanticized and glorified—if such is possible—more even than the Civil War and Reconstruction years. Margaret Walker will have none of this, however, and even before the historians began to 'revise' the antebellum years, she had done so in Jubilee.''

Presenting the historical setting of her novel with accuracy and authenticity, Walker does equally well in researching and recording the folk traditions dramatized in *Jubilee*. . . .

Walker's reader learns of these traditions and folklore genres of the African American through Walker's characters as they reveal their customs, habits, beliefs, and ways of life. Walker's use of folklore in literature is a combination of the three distinct relationships that Paul L. Bennett discusses in ''Folklore and the Literature to Come.'' Bennett suggests that folklore is used in literature directly as itself. It may be part of the realist strain of a novel in which folklife is important; it may be a modified form of literature—that is, transformed into what we think of as literary, rather than everyday, expression; or it may be a plane of reference in the production of literature, one of the schema on which more sophisticated expression may be based. In *Jubilee*, Walker does not transfer her grandmother's oral history directly to the printed page: the passage of time and the filtering of the story through family tradition alone would militate against that. Her poetic talent and her thorough research make her account far removed from a simple expression of the folk voice. Nevertheless, she privileges folklore in her treatment of love and birth and death and the family.

> Jacqueline Miller Carmichael. *Trumpeting a Fiery Sound: History and Folklore in Margaret Walker's 'Jubilee'* (Athens: University of Georgia Press, 1998), pp. 1–5

BIBLIOGRAPHY
*For My People*, 1942; *Ballad of the Free*, 1966; *Prophets for a New Day*, 1970; *October Journey*, 1973; *This Is My Century*, 1989; *Jubilee*, 1965; *How I Wrote Jubilee*, 1972; *Richard Wright: Daemonic Genius*, 1987; *On Being Female, Black, and Free: Essays by Margaret Walker, 1932-1992*, 1997

# WARNER-VIEYRA, Myriam (1939–)
## Guadeloupe

[*Le Quimboiseur l'avait dit*, translated as *As The Sorcerer Said*] is a short and touching first novel by a Guadeloupean woman. Myriam Warner-Vieyra ably raises the dilemma: is today's adolescent from the islands fated to a life of alienation and anguish in her search for education and a better life?

The author presents this dilemma through the literary device of the flashback. Zetou first appears in a state of shock, in a Parisian hospital ward for emotionally disturbed children. She is sixteen. Her plight and medical incarceration are explained as she relives in intervals of psychic, nostalgic retreat within herself the security of her island youth, her love of school successes, her hope to rise above the traditional life of the illiterate fisherman and their families. She remembers her idyllic dream of uniting with her first love, a bright neighbor boy, hoping that they might work together to benefit society. . . .

The exploitation of the promising child, rather than the themes of parental egoism and incestuous domination, provides the pathos and the originality of this novel. Certainly familiar elements appear: racial bigotry, hypocrisy in Parisian fringe societies, the irony of these islanders who are legally French but factually second-class citizens, escaping home poverty to survive abroad. The thrust, however, is a more universalized dilemma. Does the bright, industrious Antillean adolescent of today have a chance for a better life? Or, in today's developing and fluctuating social milieu, is she doomed, as the sorcerer said, to rejection and alienation, or even psychic disorientation?

> Charlotte H. Bruner. *World Literature Today*. 57, 2 (Spring 1983), p. 337

If one were simply interested in showing that [Warner-Vieyra's second novel] *Juletane* belongs to a certain genre of black African literature in Western languages, a summary of the novel would be sufficient to reveal what it has in common with other neo-African literary texts such as Ama Ata Aidoo's *The Dilemma of a Ghost* and Mariama Bâ's *Un Chant écarlate*: each one of them deals with the problem of a foreign woman who cannot fit well into her African husband's family. . . .

To dwell only on this point, however, would be to run the risk of missing the most striking feature of Warner-Vieyra's story: its insistent highlighting of the ways in which narrators and narratees relate to one another and how this, in turn, makes the text define "in quite specific and explicit terms its narrative situation and [describe] the conditions in which . . . it makes sense." This helps confirm the view that "every literary work *faces outward away from itself*" through narratees, toward real, flesh and blood listeners or readers, depending on whether we are in the oral or the written tradition. And to the extent that it does that, the text anticipates possible reactions to itself. As readers then we cannot help but come to a recognition that reading "is steered by two main structural components within the text: first, a repertoire of familiar literary patterns and recurrent literary themes, together with allusions to familiar social and historical contexts; second, techniques or strategies used to set the familiar against the unfamiliar." It is this second component that is of primary importance in the present essay. . . .

Narratees do play key roles in structuring the plurality of narratives in *Juletane*: they number at least three in a total of two narratives involving two different narrators. And insofar as two of the narratees are fictional characters themselves, they are internal to the stories under consideration and are easily identifiable. The overall structure of *Juletane* involves the embedding of a first-person narrative (by and essentially about the main character who gives her name to the novel) into a third-person narrative, and both of them are, in turn, prefaced by the authorial dedication and an epigraph on the same page. The third narratee, who is also the narratee of the novel as a whole, is external to the stories and is, in this respect, closer to actual readers of the text. The narrator of the third-person narrative is external to the events it relates and whereas its focus is on a female character who emerges as an unexpected reader of the first-person narrative, the author's function in writing the dedication is, as it were, to help provide the frame that makes it possible to contextualize the events of the novel.

> Jonathan Ngate. *Callaloo*. 9, 4 (Fall 1986), pp. 553–55

*Juletane* is a frame-story narrative of cross-cultural marriage and tragedy. One Guadeloupean woman, Hélène, supposedly reads the diary of another, Juletane, and finds her heart touched and her sensibilities reawakened. Juletane wrote the diary in a month's time in 1961, but told in it the events of the last five years of her life. Orphaned early, she had left her island home to stay with her godmother in Paris. There she met a Senegalese charmer, Mamadou, whom she married. When she accompanied him to Africa, to her dismay she discovered that he already had a wife and child. She is only temporarily appeased when he promises to send his first wife, Awa, back to the village. Juletane keeps postponing her resolution to leave Mamadou and go back home. When she discovers she is pregnant, her husband avows his love for her, promising to live with her alone and to divorce Awa. An accident terminates the pregnancy, however, and saps Juletane's will. She begins to doubt her sanity. From that time on, a succession of frustrations (betrayals as she sees them) brings on her increasingly frequent periods of disorientation. Mamadou brings Awa back. Later Awa bears more children. Mamadou takes a cold, arrogant third wife who scorns Juletane and calls her a *toubabesse* (white woman). Juletane finally revenges herself on both wives and dies in a hospital for the criminally insane. . . .

When Juletane's story ends, Hélène closes the diary and weeps with compassion. Even Hélène's goal, however, is a conventional and not a radical one. Although she is a Paris career woman and expects to dominate her future husband, she is still marrying him in order to have a child. She believes she can find [in] motherhood the necessary fulfillment for her past life, which she now sees as empty. Perhaps the most insightful section of the novel, and the most original, is the gradual waning of Juletane's resolution to go home and reject a polygamous life. For many who wonder how a Western woman can accept the constraints of polygamy, *Juletane* provides some clues.

> Charlotte H. Bruner. *World Literature Today*. 62, 2 (Spring 1988), p. 323

A desire for oneness moves the feminine figures [in Warner-Vieyra's fiction] although they fail to define themselves. They seek refuge in madness, suicide, or symbolic self-annihilation. Zetou, the tragic character of Myriam Warner-Vieyra's *Le Quimboiseur l'avait dit*, recounts her tale of slow disintegration from her small Caribbean village of Karura to the psychiatric asylum in France where she has been committed. Uprooted, living under the constant fear of imminent catastrophe, Zetou, an adolescent abused by a cynical mother and her lover, unleashes her insane rage against the irrational order of life as she experiences it. . . . [*Juletane*] is in the form of an intimate diary. It recounts the "passion" in the sense of suffering and martyrdom of a Caribbean woman in Africa. Juletane, the protagonist, is married to an African whom she met in Paris and, when she arrives in Africa, she must share conjugal life with her husband's two other wives. The novel is a dark tale of the exile, solitude, and despair of a woman for whom madness becomes the principle of liberation and survival. She is known in the African community as "the mad one," and she herself dreams of "waking up in another world where insane people are not insane, but wise people who defend justice."

> Marie-Denise Shelton. In Selwyn R. Cudjoe, ed. *Caribbean Women Writers* (Wellesley: Calaloux Publications, 1990), pp. 350–51

Suzette and Juletane, the antiheroines of Miriam Warner-Vieyra's two companion novels (*Le Quimboiseur l'avait dit* and *Juletane*) are figures of dislocation, isolation, and alienation, victims of misguided efforts to escape from their initial restricted situations. Both are associated with closed spaces, severely circumscribed worlds. Suzette, a young West Indian girl, confined to her room in an insane asylum in Paris, looks back nostalgically to her island and what had once seemed to be a restricted environment comes to be in retrospect an idyllic paradise. Suzette's selective memory evokes an image of simple, communal life in a tiny village on an island "as big as two coconuts." In terms of the fate of woman's ambitions

[Warner-Vieyra's] novels are pessimistic. Suzette affirms that she ought never to have left her village. The journeys to Europe [in *Le Quimboiseur l'avait dit*] and to Africa [in *Juletane*], attempts at self-actualization and escape, end in catastrophe. The woman who is not content to limit herself or to "be satisfied with the known domestic world," Suzette seems to suggest, is doomed to failure, to a last state worse than the first, partly because of her society's taboos, but also because of false, misplaced ambition. Juletane in Africa goes mad because she has been betrayed by her husband but also because she is unable to accept and be content with the sort of life typified by her husband's first wife, for whom "the entire universe was limited to a mat under a tree and three children around her."

> Elizabeth Wilson. In Carole Boyce Davies and Elaine Savory Fido, eds. *Out of the Kumbla: Caribbean Women and Literature* (Trenton, New Jersey: Africa World Press, 1990), pp. 48–49

*Femmes échouées* is a collection of nine stories by the Guadeloupean-born writer Myriam Warner-Vieyra, who has made Senegal her home for the last twenty years. The book is her third following the two novels *Le Quimboiseur l'avait dit* and *Juletane*. The stories are set in Guadeloupe, that beautiful French-speaking Caribbean island, and the rich mixture of its cultures permeates the stories with an exotic flavor, either through the local variety of the "fruit of passion" or through the lifestyles of its inhabitants.

The protagonist in each selection is a woman. A black servant girl dreams of winning the first prize at a Paris music academy when her gift for music is discovered by her (female) employers ("Premier Prix"); a married woman finds herself slowly dying from marriage to a cool, indifferent, uninterested husband, whom she calls "Wall" ("Le Mur, ou les charmes d'une vie conjugale"); a wheelchair-bound wife castrates her husband when she learns that their young maid is expecting his child ("Sidonie"). All the stories are written in a wholly realistic style except "Heure unique" (Unique Hour), in which the burial of a loved one triggers impressions of a revival of the love affair.

> Nadezda Obradović. *World Literature Today*. 64, 1 (Winter 1990), pp. 185–86

*Juletane* relies heavily on the principle of doubling, on both the levels of theme and structure. The text constructs a dialogue between Juletane's diary and Hélène's reading: it is thanks to the personal narrative of a fellow Guadeloupean that Hélène recognizes her own "face," and her own predicament in the mirror of the story. Doubling also occurs among the three co-wives, Juletane, Ndèye, and Awa, in a way that is suggestive of the echoing patterns of disfiguration, death, and castration that are at the center of Warner-Vieyra's works.

Feeling exiled in an inhospitable land, Juletane progressively loses her ability to function in the family compound that she shares with Awa and Ndèye, and literally shuts herself off from the community, depriving herself of food, and gradually sinking into mental illness: "Je restai enfermée dans notre chambre, sans boire ni manger" [I remain locked in our room without eating or drinking]. After a nervous breakdown and a violent outburst caused by her inability to adapt to her husband's polygamous culture, she spends time in a mental hospital, then has a miscarriage as a consequence of an accident, becomes sterile, and thus alienates herself completely from the household: ''J'ai définitivement enterrétout ce qui se passe en dehors de cette maison. Ma vie se déroule dans une chambre de cinq pas sur quatre et sous le manguier de la cour où je prends mes repas'' [I have buried once and for all everything that goes on outside this house. My life unfolds in a room five paces by four and under the mango tree in the yard where I eat my meals]. This ''manguier stérile'' [barren tree] is significant: it does not bear any fruit, and planted in the middle of the courtyard, it is a nagging reminder of Juletane's own ''short-comings'' as a sterile wife. She begins to think of suicide, goes for days without food, shaves her head, begins to see Mamadou as a *monstre*, and displaces her fears onto every other human face she sees: ''Je regardais les êtres humains qui m'entouraient; c'étaient des géants terrifiants, au visage monstrueux'' [I looked at the people who surrounded me; they were frightful giants, with monstrous faces]. She even harbors thoughts of murder against Mamadou: ''Pour me venger, je l'imaginais mort, une belle dépouille de crapule puante sur laquelle je crachais'' [To get revenge, I imagined him dead, nothing but a fine stinking corpse, on which I spat]. Her conflicts with Ndèye escalate to the point where the latter, calling her a *toubabesse* denies her the very identity she had come to Africa to claim: that of a black woman. Ndèye destroys Juletane's recording of Beethoven's Ninth Symphony, and violently slaps her face, propelling Juletane on a violent course of her own: ''Cette gifle n'est que la goutte d'eau qui fait déborder ma coupe de passivité et transforme ma patience en torrent impétueux'' [That slap in the face was the last drop that made my cup of passivity overflow and transformed my patience into a raging torrent]. Awa's children are found dead the following morning, and a week later, she literally disfigures Ndèye by pouring hot oil on her face, an incident that occurs after she had spent some time imagining herself sharpening the long kitchen knife, stabbing Ndèye to death, and watching her face become ''un masque hieux aux yeux vitreux'' [a hideous death mask, her eyes . . . glassy]. After being confined to a mental hospital, she dreams of visiting a cemetery with her father and seeing her own grave stone, with no name on it. Feeling ever more like a ''zombie'' from the Caribbean, she has the impression ''d'être à la fois au-dessus et en dessu'' [of being inside and outside the grave], of being a traveler between the world of the living and that of the dead. Narrative closure is finally provided by her actual death three months later in the hospital, a death that appears to redeem Hélène, the reader in the text, from her own coldness and unfeeling existence as a displaced Guadeloupean. . . .

If, as [Hélène] Cixous argues, the disfiguration and decapitation to which patriarchy subjects women is a displacement of male castration anxiety, then Myriam Warner-Vieyra's works constitute an interesting attempt to work out this problematic in structural as well as thematic terms. In her short story ''Sidonie'' [in *Femmes échouées*] there is a double crime which links both castration and disfiguration. The castrated husband musters enough strength to strangle his invalid wife, who is confined to a wheelchair. Here, it is Sidonie's brother, Septime, whose perspective dominates the third-person narrative. Warner-Vieyra uses free indirect discourse to enter the minds of all the protagonists. But it is Septime's interior monologue that frames the beginning and the end of the tale. His self-centered concerns for his personal loss at the death of his sister reveal a shallowness and a callousness, which are damning. There is an unequal and dissymmetrical presentation of perspectives

which mirrors the relative power of the characters. Each character's interior monologue allows the reader some insight into Sidonie's life and feelings, into her reasons for writing: her jealous nature, her relationship with Bernard, the car accident that paralyzed her, and her feelings toward the young woman her husband has gotten pregnant. But we are never allowed into her own consciousness, and it is truly her silence that is resounding here. No one really knows her. She writes, but the reader does not have access to her notebooks. . . .

[There] is no interpretation of Bernard's own actions and reactions: only Sidonie's unruly behavior gets the benefit of each character's speculations and judgement. If the surface coherence of the texts thus strongly implies that Sidonie has gone mad, there is however an equally powerful countercoherence that emerges from the radical and disruptive force of the uninterpreted events of the story: it is up to the reader to examine these structural dissymmetries, and to understand the unstated social inequalities in the vision of each character. Sidonie is perhaps a ''victim'' gone mad, but, as with Juletane whose delusions make it hard to determine what degree of agency she is capable of having, it becomes clear that the very notion of agency needs to be redefined to accommodate those situations where extreme pain is *the* condition of subjectivity, of a ''radical subjectivity'' that imprisons humans in an utterly incommunicable experience. Juletane and Sidonie are locked in a private and painful world that remains largely inarticulate, and eruptions of violence are their only means of acting out their pain.

Thematically and textually, narrative closure is reached in death: the death of the title character. This is a very traditional way to provide closure and to restore order to the community. One might argue, then, that Warner-Vieyra's texts equivocate, that is, that they disown on a constructural level what they embrace on an ideological one. Since Juletane regrets that Mamadou has died before being able to read her journal, she appears to have reached a state of ''rationality'' and accommodation that allows her final reentry into the symbolic realm of patriarchal culture. She no longer wants to live . . . and it is suggested that Hélène becomes a more gentle, tender, accommodating, and ''feminine'' woman after reading the diary. In effect, the structure of the work reinforces traditional notions of femininity in the end, despite the strong ideological critique of female alienation it contains. Warner-Vieyra seems to want to do an about-face that will not antagonize traditional readers who constitute the majority of literate Africans capable of reading her works. . . . It is even clearer in ''Sidonie'' since Septime's point of view is more sympathetic to Bernard's awful ''mutilation'' than to his sister's crippled body and death. Male solidarity triumphs over female hysteria, and the social order remains intact.

Françoise Lionnet. *Callaloo*. 16, 1 (Winter 1993), pp. 139–43

In the novel *Juletane*, by Myriam Warner-Vieyra, we find the narratives of two extremely different Caribbean women, Juletane and Hélène. Geographically, they followed the same migratory patterns of retour and *détour* that are common to Caribbean narratives. They both were born in the Francophone Caribbean, then lived and studied in Paris, and finally moved to Africa as adults. However, their adaptation to their new cultural environments are diametrically opposed—Juletane went into isolation from the world and became labelled a mad woman by her village in

Africa, while Hélène became a professionally successful social worker and an emotionally icy, modern woman. In spite of the differences that separate them, my contention here is that these women both set out to recover or discover the creole identity that has been either suppressed or discarded from their lives. . . .

To begin with our analysis of the main protagonist, Juletane, we find that initially she begins the diary to pass the long hours of boredom and depression. She also claims that she is writing for her husband Mamadou, with the hope that once he has read her thoughts, he will understand her pain, and will then abandon his other wives and return to her and to their life as it was at the beginning of their marriage. The most debilitating problem for Juletane has become her inability to communicate: she cannot talk with the women around her, first because they do not speak French at all, or very little. Furthermore, even after she tries to learn their language, the understanding and acceptance remain difficult because of cultural and moral differences, and the process of creolization begins to stagnate for Juletane in Sénégal. She has no community in Sénégal with whom she may share her language—neither the Senegalese women's groups nor her husband's semi-westernized male friends will accept her particular cultural discourse. Thus, the writing is not practiced solely for the benefit of her estranged husband nor to pass the time. As she continues to make her daily entries, Juletane gradually begins to realize the healing effects that the writing has for her. . . .

When Juletane writes about losing those qualities that she had believed were essential to her identity, she begins to problematize her previous conception of self and to define a new position for herself in opposition to those surrounding her. She thus reconstitutes the boundaries of her identity with a more complex notion of self and enters the second stage in the process of creolization.

Juletane's story at first appears to follow typical patterns in Caribbean women writers' fiction, as she unconsciously voyages along the paths enunciated by Edouard Glissant in *Le Discours antillais*. Africa had beckoned her at first, symbolizing the "mystical return to origins" that haunted the fragmented and painful history of her ancestors. However, the unfortunate sequence of events and the resulting cultural oppression that Juletane encountered when she first arrived in Sénégal worked together to betray Juletane's romantic dreams about the Return: the retour ended up being nothing but a *détour* that finally turned out to be a dead-end situation. Yet as Glissant has argued, the desire for a return to origins is too strongly internalized in uprooted and de-historicized peoples to be easily dismissed or forgotten. Juletane does not capitulate to her dead-end situation of exile in Sénégal, but begins to dream of yet another mystical return to another space and time in the Past. It is at this point that Juletane's plot diverges from typical patterns of antillean discourse.

I would argue that Juletane's decision to write a confessional-style journal may be considered symptomatic of her desire to make a return to an idyllic past in the métropole. The long-standing tradition of confessional writing in white, male, European literary history definitely places Juletane in a long line with other writers of the métropole: Montaigne, Rousseau, and others. One of the women whom she meets in a mental hospital late in the novel actually tells Juletane that she refuses to write a personal diary, because it is "une histoire de Blancs". Juletane, in contrast, actually finds pleasure in remembering to follow the structured path of certain formal French grammar rules, probably ones that she learned in a Parisian collège or lycée. Furthermore, she

indulges in carefully obeying the forms of penmanship that she had learned many years earlier in school, even though her writing instruments are rudimentary and her setting (an unlit, roach-infested bedroom) is not conducive to writing for style and form. None of these writing details are necessary for a healing of the self or for communication with Mamadou, yet they do point to a desire to recapture the structure and form of the West, learned during her schooling in Paris. I do not interpret this desire to return, formally and through writing, to Paris and the West as a desire to become white. On the contrary, when Juletane was in Paris, she lived with her godmother, her only surviving Caribbean relative who could take care of her. Her desire to return to the métropole via her writing is thus merely another detour, this time for reconnection and community with her Caribbean past.

It must be admitted, however, that to view Juletane's diary writing only as a positive, healing gesture for new growth and reconnection would be misleading, to say the least. Although the diary writing may help Juletane to reconcile the Other within herself, it eventually sets the wheels in motion for her acts of murderous revenge and destruction. We see here the beginnings of the third phase of creolization which is one of direct contact and confrontation. Once Juletane has begun to analyze her pain and the causes for it, she launches upon a series of destructive and deadly acts. The first crime, that of poisoning her first co-wife's children, is committed unconsciously, denied to such an extent that she cannot even remember having performed the act. The second crime, that of defacing her second co-wife with boiling oil, is committed as a conscious act. It is a crime that Juletane considers more cruel and more appropriate than murder, because, of course, the co-wife will continue to live, but as a hideously disfigured woman.

The violent anger and deadly actions are difficult to reconcile with the supposedly positive aspects of coming to speech and writing. However, the third stage of the process of creolization will not necessarily be one that results in productive or comfortable hybridity. While Westernized versions of hybridity feature a "jouissance" of "différence," postcolonial expressions of hybridity are often based in pain and frustrating dislocation. Ketu Katrak explains the necessary use of violence in Fanonian terms, "Given the colonizer's initial violence, the native in the decolonization process must use violence in order to establish his human identity". Although Juletane is not fighting a "colonizer" in the traditional sense of the term, she is overcoming those forces that have led to her years of oppression, namely a combination of patriarchy, capitalism, and religious and cultural traditions in Sénégal. Through this confrontation we can hope that the new, syncretic subject position will offer a more complex and polemical sense of creole identity.

The secondary narrative that I mentioned at the beginning of the paper also moves through the three stages of the process of creolization for Hélène, who is reading Juletane's notebook many years after Juletane's death. However, the stages manifest themselves in different forms than those of Juletane, due to Hélène's position in society and the ways in which she has become separated from her creole identity. We find several contradictions in Hélène's character. For example, she is the most empowered woman in the novel, holding an advanced degree from Paris, an important position as a social worker, and a certain amount of wealth and cultural capital. However, she has the weakest and most mediated voice. We have only indirect contact with Hélène's thoughts via the third-person omniscient narrator who always speaks for her, while

Juletane's thoughts are always narrated directly to us, in the first person singular. Hélène's relationship to the Caribbean is also different from Juletane's, because she has purposefully given up her past and her ties to her Antilles homeland, except for the money that she sends to her family and occasional visits to the summer villa that she has had built for herself there. This conscious severing of ties is partially due to the fact that she is absorbed in her career and cannot make the trip back home very often. But for emotional reasons, as well, she remains far away from her homeland.

As Hélène reads of Juletane's suffering, she begins to realize that she has also suffered and that she too has silenced an important part of her creole identity. The silencing is doubled, because it is tied to the love that she had to renounce and to her compatriot from the Antilles who betrayed her for a white woman. Thus the act of reading about Juletane's life forces Hélène to question some of the assumptions that she made, about herself as an independent professional woman. Her self-definition had been based on rejection and refusal, not only of the Caribbean but also of a specific man. Through reading Juletane's diary, Hélène realizes that she must reexamine the choices she has made for her own life and search for new ways to reinscribe her identity. At the beginning of the novel, Hélène's original plans for her upcoming marriage to the young Ousmane were viewed as a convenient arrangement: she wants to have a legitimate child and yet not fall into a relationship with a husband who might dominate her. However, at the midpoint of her all-night reading session, she begins to see the emptiness of such a plan. . . .

The self-inquiries that Hélène makes are important, as they begin the second stage in the process of creolization—the process of redefinition and new growth for her. But even stronger are the spiritual bonds that form between Juletane and herself. As an unspoken yet recognizable sentiment of cultural community develops, Hélène comes to terms with her own hybrid position as an Antillean woman living in Africa, and with her connection to her oppressed compatriots of the Third World.

Because of Hélène's position, the third stage in the process of building a woman's creole identity, the moment of confrontation, is not an overtly violent or destructive act directed against others. Instead, the third stage occurs on an internal basis for Hélène. Her action is one of release. . . .

These two women, although diametrically opposed in their social positions and their personal lives, both struggle through the same processes in order to build a women's creole identity. They achieve this identity through different actions and reflections, but both work through the colonial and the patriarchal oppressions that alienate them from their cultural heritage. While Juletane's process ends in destruction and death, the written documents that she leaves behind enable Hélène to begin her own process of creolization. Thus both are able to rebuild or rediscover their creole identity through reading, writing, and recovering.

Juliette M. Regers. *French Review*. 69, 4 (March 1996), pp. 595–6

Myriam Warner-Vieyra, born in Guadeloupe but currently residing in Senegal, has been concerned throughout her works with the sense of alienation and fragmented identity experienced by women who are in exile from their communities and/or their countries of origin, and who are subsequently forced to adapt to the constructs of an "other" society. *Juletane*, Warner-Vieyra's second novel, and "Sidonie," a short story from her collection entitled *Femmes échouées*, narrate the experiences of Antillean women who, displaced from their homelands and alienated from the indigènes in the respective societies in which they are undergoing their exile, find themselves crossing the border which separates sanity from madness. The protagonists' profound alienation—stemming from physical, cultural and linguistic differences—often reduces them to silence. . . .

Warner-Vieyra's texts illustrate the precarious position of women who refuse to conform to sanctioned female roles in a patriarchal society. In response to the repressive circumstances which lead to their silencing, both Juletane and Sidonie will ultimately reveal "une violence qu'on n'aurait pas soupçonnée", a violence which ends in tragedy in both cases.

In both of Warner-Vieyra's fictional renderings, the protagonists' failure to enunciate indicates a lack of agency, an inability to become the subject of one's own narrative, and functions as a sign of female oppression. The attempt to "speak" their difference is rendered all the more formidable in light of the fact that, in psycholinguistic theory, women themselves occupy a position of silence.

The conditions which lead to the silencing of the protagonists are strikingly similar in both narratives. Both protagonists are extrinsic figures who have to recast themselves in response to the geographical and psychological displacement they experience. First, the two women have been displaced from Guadeloupe, their motherland. Sidonie, who had abandoned her own studies in order to support those of her brother, Septime, follows him to France after the death of their parents. Juletane, after an initial expatriation to France following the death of her father, undergoes a second and more painful exile, as she marries a West African student named Mamadou and returns to his village with him. . . .

The act of writing becomes an enabling gesture, affording both women the opportunity to establish control and to exert authority in at least one area of their lives, and providing them access to a dimension other than that of the physical space in which they exist. In *Juletane*, the protagonist's journal entries are reproduced in the text, complete with dates and times. Juletane makes it clear that she is engaged in the act of writing her story in a notebook, and that she herself will serve as primary narratee; this is a move which denotes the cathartic value of the journal as well as its substantive role in opening up an imaginative space for the protagonist. These entries are framed and destabilized by the third-person narrative, printed in italics, of another displaced Antillean woman. Hélène is a social worker living in France who had been given the journal by one of the staff members at the psychiatric institution in which Juletane had been confined during the final few months of her life. Hélène will appropriate her compatriot's story, using it to explore her own solitary existence. She realizes the subversive nature of Juletane's text: "A-t-elle commencé la lecture de ce journal au moment opportun? Elle sent confusément que cette lecture changera sa vie".

While Juletane comments on the autobiographical nature of her text, Sidonie chooses to fictionalize her life, creating a heroine who emblematizes her own emergence as subject. It is through the consciousness of Sidonie's sister-in-law, Nicaise, that we discover Sidonie's literary production. Again, Sidonie's words are mediated—we know of her writing only through the observations of others: "Nicaise espérait que cette activité la libérerait de ses chimères: l'histoire qu'elle racontait ressemblait étrangement à sa propre vie. . . . C'était sa propre souffrance, ses sentiments de frustration, de solitude, de femme incomprise, qu'elle laissait entrevoir dans ce récit''.

Unfortunately for the protagonists, textualizing their anger does not result in a liberating transformation. This salutary strategy will not fulfill the protagonists' expectations or allow them to sufficiently express their anger. Sidonie, after the revelation of her husband's unfaithfulness, abandons her writing and stops speaking. Bernard's inability to comprehend Sidonie increases her suffering and reduces her options for self-preservation: ''Il ne savait quelle attitude adopter devant le comportement bizarre de sa femme. Il préférait de loin quand elle criait et le menaçait, car il finissait toujours par la calmer. Son mutisme du moment le déroutait. Pourquoi brûlait-elle des papiers?''.

The stage is set for the violence to follow. Renewal has begun too late for these women, both of whom have suppressed their anger—along with their words—for many years; they become engulfed by violent impulses, nourishing plans for the retribution they will enact upon those who have exploited their passivity. Their acts of vengeance will be horrific. . . .

Myriam Warner-Vieyra's texts do not depict violence as an answer to silence, but rather show it as a consequence of repression and a potential subversive gesture. In *Juletane* and ''Sidonie,'' both protagonists felt victimized by acts of oppression related to gender-role expectations, and both lashed out with acts of ''unspeakable'' violence against what each considered to be the oppressive force in her life.

> Patrice J. Proulx. I *French Review*. 70, 8 (April 1997), pp. 698

BIBLIOGRAPHY

*Le Quimboiseur l'avait dit* (As the Sorcerer Said), 1980; *Juletane*, 1982; *Femmes échouées*, 1988

# WIDEMAN, John Edgar (1941–)
## United States

In this hypnotic and deeply lyrical novel [*Sent for You Yesterday*], Mr. Wideman again returns to the ghetto where he was raised and transforms it into a magical location infused with poetry and pathos.

The book's title announces both the tone and the action. ''Sent for you yesterday, and here you come today.'' The elegiac outcry of this old Jimmy Rushing blues suggests the urgent need, apparent loss and ironic recovery that characterizes the novel's beautiful first-person narrative. The narrator, his speech laden with news and the blues, is a character who has appeared in Mr. Wideman's fiction before. His is the voice in ''Across the Wide Missouri'', one of the stories in *Damballah*. Like Mr. Wideman, he is a young black writer who has moved to Wyoming and spends only vacation time in his native Pittsburgh; but he has returned to Homewood to take on the roles of both son and father in mind and feelings. The narration here makes it clear that both as a molder of language and a builder of plots, Mr. Wideman has come into his full powers. He is a literary artist with whom any reader who admires ambitious fiction must sooner or later reckon.

As his last two books demonstrated, he has the gift of making ''ordinary'' folks memorable. And many of the engaging characters from *Damballah* and *Hiding Place* tumble onstage to assist in the recreation of Homewood's communal life from the wild and vital 1920's through the drugged and debilitated 70's.

The man who affects the destinies of [the book's many characters], . . . the daring, dangerous but gifted Albert Wilkes, arrives early in a swirl of piano blues and departs early in a storm of police bullets. His music evokes ''a moody correspondence between what his fingers shape and what happens to the sky, the stars, the moon.'' Through Wilkes's presence, Mr. Wideman establishes a mythological and symbolic link between character and landscape, language and plot, that in the hands of a less visionary writer might be little more than stale sociology. At one point in the novel, Albert Wilkes's ghost apparently inspires Brother Tate's otherwise unsupple hands to play at the Homewood Elks hall. The narrator, although he has a great deal of talent to begin with, appears to be equally inspired throughout the book.

Doot Brother Tate dubs him when he is only a boy, employing one of the sounds of scat singing, the only sounds that Brother makes after his son's death. The nickname seems appropriate, since Doot continually turns the barest descriptive passages into his own form of verbal music.

He can take what the normal eye might perceive as an ordinary scene . . . and spin out images over a page or more as part of a moving evocation of ghetto dreaming. He can show us rows of ''wooden shanties built to hold the flood of black immigrants up from the South'' and transmute them into ''islands, arks, life teeming but enclosed or surrounded or exiled to arbitrary boundaries.'' And he can reveal the city beyond these bounded streets as he has his grandfather, John French, perceive it, with its steel mills along the river belching clouds of smoke. ''If you didn't know the smoke could kill you, if you didn't think of it as an iron cloud pressing the breath out your body, the dirt and the soot and gas coloring the sky made a beautiful sight.''

That is the view from Homewood—a place that, thanks to John Edgar Wideman, we have now lived and died in.

> Alan Cheuse, *New York Times Book Review*, May 15, 1983, pp. 13, 41

''Do not look for straightforward, linear steps from book to book,'' wrote John Edgar Wideman in the 1985 preface to his Homewood Trilogy. ''Think rather of circles within circles within circles, a stone dropped into a still pool, ripples and wavemotions.'' In *Fever*, Wideman has troubled the water again, refining his already elliptical and dense prose; in the process he has reinvented black English and (re)made it, elegant, suave, as elastic as ever: ''Ball be swishing with that good backspin, that good arch bringing it back, blip, blip, blip, three bounces and it's coming right back to Doc's hands like he got a string on the pill,'' he writes in ''Doc's Story,'' a story about stories, a nigh-fantastical tale of a blind man and the man who inexplicably watches him and ponders over lost love.

Wideman began evolving the style evidenced in these stories in his *Homewood Trilogy*, most markedly in the 1983 PEN/Faulkner award-winning *Sent for You Yesterday* and further still in 1987's *Reuben*. It is his own patented stream of consciousness, sliding easily through tense and point of view; and, when it works, its power has the force of the most righteous prayer. It is as if he wrote his stories and then compressed them to a third of their original size. Eschewing quotation marks, Wideman has his speakers shift and shift and at times meld—as if into one mind, one voice.

The word haunting best describes the result. In each story some dim memory, some deep urge, some knowledge, some inescapable prophecy reaches through time or space. Voices whisper across voids; calls float over oceans.

These voices he often finds—like a child picking up pebbles on the beach—in fragments of history, news items, his own novels, even Bobby Short! Valaida Snow, the legendary trumpeter of the Jazz Era to whom the Queen of Denmark gave a golden trumpet, supplies perhaps the most chilling voice in ''Valaida.'' ''Tell him,'' she speaks from the grave, ''they loved me at home too, a down-home girl from Chattanooga, Tennessee, who turned out the Apollo, not a mumbling word from wino heaven till they were on their feet hollering and clapping for more with the rest of the audience. . . . Yesteryears, yesterhours.'' But the story turns into a What If: What if Valaida Snow, who was interned in a Nazi concentration camp for over a year, what if she had saved the life of a 13-year-old boy who would become a survivor? Cut then within the same story to an old man disgusted and indifferent toward life trying to tell the remarkable tale of how he had one day been saved by a ''colored woman'' to his equally disgusted and indifferent black cleaning woman who ''has put on flesh for protection. To soften blows. To ease around corners.'' The ironies do not merely abound, they cluster, almost fester—he, a Jew, tells her, a black woman, the story on Christmas Eve.

For irony is the tool Wideman is forever honing, sharpening, working with surgical precision. ''Hostages,'' the story of a woman whose husband is a captive of Arab terrorists, becomes an unraveling, a debunking of the concept of ''prisoner.'' Suddenly everything is to be viewed in a new light—marriage, sickness, materialism—and to be seen as imprisoning. An immigrant in a new land; to be black in America; to be a child in the care of parents: Mostly trouble haunts these characters, trouble as in tension between black and white, Arab and Jew, men and women. Wideman manages to transmute that trouble into some of his most challenging and powerful prose yet, in which everything is subject to ridicule to doubt.

Even his own fiction is fair game, as in ''Surfiction,'' where he takes on his own opaque, relentless, spiderwebby prose. It is a parody that is oddly more than a parody, a question within a question, a sly illumination—or is it yet more nasty tricks on the ever-gullible, at times contemptible, reader? He ponders: ''Without authors whose last names begin with B, surfiction might not exist. B for Beckett, Barth, Burroughs, Barthes, Borges, Brautigan, Barthelme.'' But even in his high-minded meta-play, amid the (de) analysis of fragments of Charles Chestnutt and his own journal, we get a nugget of the old tensions and ironies, for ultimately in this quagmire of twisted logic he slips in a story as old-fashioned as *Gilgamesh*, about a couple fighting over a diary.

And though it may seem like wordplay, ''Surfiction,'' offers insights into some of Wideman's less opaque motives:

All goes swimmingly until a voice from the watermelon patch intrudes. . . . Recall your own reflection in the fun house mirror and the moment of doubt when you turn away and it turns away and you lose sight of it and it naturally enough loses sight of you and you wonder where it's going and where you're going in the wrinkling reflecting plate still laughing behind your back at someone.

Time and Space. Like present-day cosmologists, Wideman seems to have in mind not merely a blurring of the two concepts but their elimination. He meta-jokes about our Western cultural bias toward ''clock time, calendar time,'' to time ''acting on us rather than through us'' and ''that tames space by manmade structures and with the I as center defines other people and other things by nature of their relationship to I rather than by the independent integrity of the order they may represent.'' Wideman's true mission appears to be to replace the I at the center of all his stories, to make it subject to an internal order of things rather than to external structures and limitations. Unlike Ishmael Reed, his humor does not slice to the bone to the truth; Wideman's humor is sparse if not (at times) nonexistent. And unlike Amiri Baraka, his rage is far from militant; it is sublimated, almost repressed.

Nowhere in this collection is this more evident than in the title story. More a meditation than an eyewitness account, ''Fever'' centers around Philadelphia's yellow fever epidemic of the late eighteenth century. Snatching up bits and pieces of history here and there, he brilliantly creates an organism, like a New Age psychic channeler, that transports the suffers from the 1700s to the present, and takes us back in time as well. Its scenes bring to mind images from Herzog's *Nosferatu* of a plague-ridden town debilitated, full of coffins, corpses, rats and decay: ''A large woman, bloated into an even more cumbersome package by gases and liquids seething inside her body, had slipped from his grasp. . . . Catching against a rail, her body had slammed down and burst, spraying Wilcox like a fountain.'' Yet without warning the story shifts to the present, to the aftermath of the 1985 MOVE massacre, to the voice of a black hospital orderly. It is as if Wideman is again playing games with us, forcing us to see the past and the present as one; how we are affected by what has gone before, not only in our thinking but in our acting and in our soul-deep believing. Science (knowledge) becomes a metaphor for understanding hate; disease, a euphemism for the plague visited upon the wrongs of the unholy.

And the voices. Wideman leads us to believe the main character of ''Fever'' to be none other than Richard Allen, who founded the African Methodist Episcopal Church. His voice, initially eighteenth-century and pious, merges with a chorus of victims, singing of guilt, of racism, of ignorance. Ultimately the voices question Allen—a freedman—for staying in Philadelphia, abandoning his wife and children, risking his life by working with the virus-infected, practically enslaving himself to strange, clueless physicians. And Allen can articulate no reason for staying to combat the ''unpleasantness from Egypt.''

Not all of these stories sing as clearly. ''The Statue of Liberty'' seems particularly peculiar, a gratuitous walk on the prurient side, whose only purpose seems to be to shock for shock's sake. ''Presents,'' though powerful in spots, slips too close to cliche for comfort. Based on a song by rhythm and blues holy man Solomon Burke, it is a grandmother's prophecy of a child's rise to fame and fortune through music and his eventual, inevitable decline; an all-too-familiar story with no new insights. ''The Tambourine Lady,'' a light / dark-hearted play on the children's ditty ''Step on a crack / break your mama's back,'' amuses but does not linger. ''Rock River,'' on the other hand, returns once again to the conceit of the voice of the dead reaching back, this time after a husband's suicide while his best friend attempts to console the stolid widow. In the end pleasant, life-affirming memories overtake us, but leave us with more questions than resolutions.

More successful is "Little Brother," a biography of a dog in the form of a conversation between two old characters from *Homewood*, Geraldine and Penny, a discourse that encompasses the here and the gone, man and animal alike. In "Concert" a jazzman's meditations on his mother's death become an elegant musical riff. And "When it's Time to Go" calls up once again the all-too-easy symbol of blindness, but this time Wideman lets loose the language like a snake in a cage of rats: "Light was just singing to me, Mama, telling me I didn't need no eyes. Wasn't no such thing as eyes less you call your knees and hands and shoulders eyes cause everything you got can hear the light, or touch it and everything you got is something to see with." This tale of a blind boy whose witch mother cannot save him is also a thrice-told tale, but the language, the concentration, the shifting viewpoints, lift it above the mere or the hackneyed, transforming it into a story full of the incantatory power of a Zora Neale Hurston or a Virginia Woolf; a haunting yarn of magic and ways of being in the world.

> Randall Kenan. *The Nation*. 250, 1, (January 1, 1990), pp. 25–7

Thematically and structurally, [John Edgar Wideman's works published between 1967 and 1992] reflect the author's evolution from one who is dominated by the history, culture, and language of Europe to one who accepts and appreciates African history, culture, and language. *A Glance Away* and *Hurry Home*, Wideman's first two novels, are the products of an African writer who is immersed in the western literary tradition. *Hurry Home*, for example, chronicles the life of an African male who has been so influenced by European culture that he begins to see with the eyes of a European, looking at the demeaning and hard work of a shoeshine boy as "romantic." Structurally too it reflects an author whose audience is European and whose interest is in impressing that audience. Major parts of the novel are inscribed with "foreign" quotes (the inscription for the first part of the novel reads "muertries / De la langueur goutee a ce mal d'etre deux'''). These quotes are obstruse in their meaning and relevance to the African community. *Philadelphia Fire*, one of Wideman's last major works to date, is significantly different from the early ones, both thematically and structurally. It reflects the writing of an author who appreciates, respects, and embraces African life and culture and who has concern for African people. The title of the novel itself—reflecting the circumstances surrounding the bombing of a house occupied by members of an activist African organization—is sufficient proof. Structurally, Wideman sees the need to burn down the western literary standards that have ghettoized his works up to this point. Using narrative techniques such as the triple-voiced narrator to reflect the collective voice represented in traditional African societies, Wideman imbues his text with meaning and structure relevant to the African community. . . .

[Wideman's early] writings record the history of an author who has been taught to hate his culture, taught to hate himself and all those who look like him. Wideman now acknowledges his early self-hatred and attributes his Eurocentric view to the education he received at the University of Pennsylvania:

> At Penn I became a better player, but I paid a steep price for that. . . . Teachers, coaches, nearly everyone important in the white university environment, urged me to bury my past. I learned to stake too much of who I was on what I would

become, lived for the day I could look back, look down on Reds and everybody else in Melton Park, in Homewood. (*Brothers and Keepers*)

There is, however, evidence within Wideman's own works that his Eurocentric perspective began much earlier than his University experience. Seemingly, his family's own rejection of "hard core" African features and African ways tenderized and seasoned him for the non-Afrocentric education he subsequently received at Penn.

One of the best insights into the forging of Wideman's non-Afrocentric view is *Brothers and Keepers*, a work in which Wideman attempts to explain how his brother Robby's path to prison for armed robbery was laid out for him by the race and class reality of U.S. society. But more important for this study, *Brothers and Keepers* is a book "about a writer who goes to prison to interview his brother but comes away with his own story." . . .

Not knowing his history made him divorce himself totally from his identity, culture, and family. Perhaps it also played a decisive role in his choice of female companionship, for Judy, his wife, is a European, and his relationship with and marriage to her occurs in this early, Eurocentric phase of his life. During this stage, with Wideman's limited knowledge of his heritage, he chose to be as much like the European as possible. . . .

Wideman's ability in *Brothers and Keepers* to analyze himself is made possible by the re-education process that he undergoes. It is a detoxification process that enables him to shed his old European-centered frame of reference and reclaim his African personality. This he is able to do only after immersing himself in his culture, including discovering his family history and studying the literature of African people.

> Doreatha D. Mbalia. *John Edgar Wideman. Reclaiming the Africa Personality*. (Cranbury, New Jersey: Associated University Presses, Inc., 1995), pp. 15–18

In Wideman's first novel, *A Glance Away* (1967), the protagonist, Eddie Lawson, returns to Pittsburgh where an embittered, crippled mother poisons the air with her incendiary anger, and the youth leaves the home for a stroll with his best friend, Brother, through Bum's Forest. The place assaults his memory and his senses. . . .

This place is a site of his utter alienation, an antipode as far removed as the moon, a dwelling that invokes his visceral disgust, yet he seeks to dominate his primal fear of this place of rejection, for ". . . if I sing too, will I be less afraid?"

*A Glance Away*, although published in 1967, is already an expression of class alienation, of distancing and of difference, which ripens until its flowering in *Brothers and Keepers*, a work published some 17 years later. In his latter work, Wideman's first overtly written non-fiction, the voice of alienation is clear, and undisguised behind characterization. Here John Edgar Wideman speaks of his hegira from the city of his familial youth.

> Most of what I felt was guilt. I'd made my choices. I was running from Pittsburgh, from poverty, from Blackness. To get ahead, to make something of myself, college had seemed a logical, necessary step; my exile, my flight from home began with good grades, with good English, with setting myself apart long before I'd earned a scholarship and a train ticket over them mountains to Philadelphia. With that willed alienation behind me, between us, guilt was a predictable.

One measure of my success was the distance I'd put between us.

This is the voice of one who knowingly, spatially, and temporally, left some of his own behind.

Nor is Wideman alone in this phenomenon, for he came of age during the civil rights movement's ascendancy, and therefore was among the first generation of African Americans allowed to pursue legal and social integration, which opened doors to educational, employment, and housing opportunity.

For Wideman, and for a generation of black thinkers, this very integration became a virtual recipe for estrangement — for this new, emergent generation, sprung from a people one generation out of peasantry, and two generations from legal chattel slavery, became a people who were misfits in traditional black culture and in white culture — folks who were, in the words of Harold Cruse, ''[a] rootless class of displaced person.'' They represent the generation not quite at home in the midst of two cultures, and often, two classes, a generational migration from poverty to the middle class, a distance as measurable in miles as in dollars.

For Wideman, this alienation would be assuaged by making it the centerpiece of his art. He would return home sporadically and intermittently, but his fiction, drawn like tracings from the original prints of life, would return there, settle there, and live in the house of alienation. . . .

Few would doubt the oppressed, caste-like status of American-born blacks, yet the flight to mysticism, or a magical escape, is not present in the fiction of John Edgar Wideman. Wideman's work is, in its earlier expressions, at least, a fiction drawn from a close, almost microscopic, study of the vagaries of black life, unmitigated by mystic release. His fiction is funky, real, which represents the inner life of a people who still possess echoes of ancient, primeval magic, yet who are nitty-gritty in their pragmatism. I call Wideman's work ''fictive realism,'' for although it utilizes all of the forms of fiction, narrative, characterization, settings and moods, the plot lines are drawn from lives lived within the marrow and memories of the novelist.

Wideman's voice for dialogue is so acute it seems to be transcribed from the real life rap sessions that folks hold in bars, in the streets and in one's home. And rather than resort to mysticism, Wideman, even in his first novel, crafted a dialogue that crackles with a realness that spits fire from a reality of conflict. . . .

The Rosetta Stone of Wideman's fiction is in his non-fiction work, *Brothers* and *Keepers*, the haunting telling of John's brother, Robert, whom readers will recognize as Tommy in both *Damballah* and *Hiding Place*. Indeed, *Brothers and Keepers* is the matrix through which the vast majority of the characters that populate the fictional universe may be known, for in the frontispiece of *Damballah* and *Hiding Place* there is illustrated a family tree, and upon the tree are both real folks and fictional composites. The tall, light-skinned John French who drank liberally and battled on the streets of *Damballah* and *Hiding Place* really was John Edgar's and Robby's grandfather, named John French.

If *Damballah* and *Hiding Place* provide insights into John Edgar Wideman's Homewood roots, *Hurry Home* and *The Lynchers* give us insight into Wideman abroad and in Philadelphia, respectively. Even abroad, Wideman's American experience is one of alienation. . . .

John Edgar Wideman's works speak to that pervasive sense of estrangement, and the restorative power of family. He especially melds these elements in *Brothers and Keepers* where fiction is

abandoned to an introspective exposition into the powerful undertows of class, and the even more powerful call of blood, across space and time. It seeks to create the consciousness that may have opened a door for the fallen younger brother, and by so doing enters a literature of love.

Mamia Abu-Jamal. *The Black Scholar*. 28, 1 (Spring 1998), pp. 75–79

Textual tropes of urban community often clarify the difficulty of imagining a discrete community that might lend literature the instrumental value it bears in nationalist aesthetic theories. Because contemporary literary readerships are highly specialized and restricted as well as racially and culturally mixed, and are certainly not coextensive with ''the black community'', several contemporary African-American novels are unable to invest literature with clear-cut social and political uses. The ambivalence toward literature consistently manifested in such novels might be read as symptomatic of a post-nationalist crisis of urban literary representation. . . .

[John Edgar Wideman's 1990 novel *Philadelphia Fire*] takes as its point of departure an actual urban crisis that took place in Philadelphia in 1985—the confrontation between MOVE, a predominantly African-American back-to-nature cult, and the city administration, which culminated in a police bombing that destroyed sixty-one houses and killed eleven people. In *Philadelphia Fire*, this particular disaster is presented as part of a larger upheaval in economic, political, and social order brought about by a number of interlocking structural transformations that have occurred in American cities since the 1970s. In what follows, I examine Wideman's endeavor, in Philadelphia Fire, to make sense of recent changes in American urban order and to test the viability of imaginary alternatives to the dystopia brought about by these changes. A sacred text written by the leader of MOVE as well as a book about MOVE projected by the novel's narrator help to focus Wideman's double-edged evaluation of contemporary urban order and of pastoral and primitivist reactions to this order. Wideman uses these books-within-his-book to assess the writer's role in mediating urban crisis and to explore different ways of constructing knowable urban communities in literature. *Philadelphia Fire* forcefully rejects organic notions of community, and gropes instead for more complex ways of representing urban communities as ''concrete abstractions'' rather than as self-contained units of social experience and value. In the course of this endeavor, *Philadelphia Fire* obliquely tries out a variety of nationalist resolutions to problems of urban literary representation, and ultimately arrives at deeply conflicted conclusions about the social roles possible for black writers in present-day cities. . . .

Among the reasons that urban redevelopment projects are so scathingly criticized in *Philadelphia Fire* is that these projects exemplify the fetishistic ways in which ideologies of consumption serve to legitimize contemporary urban order. The urban renewal projects initiated during the 1970s transformed cities organized around declining industrial production into luminous centers of privatized cultural consumption. In *Philadelphia Fire*, the renovated Philadelphia downtown is described as an enticing ''circus of lights,'' a site of lavish consumption where everything, including time, can be ''bought and sold''. But waste and scarcity are the necessary offshoots of the progress achieved by the city of conspicuous consumption: ''At the same time over in the north and in the west where people from here [are] forced to move, what's growing is garbage dumps''. This is one sense in which the ideologies of consumption that underwrite urban renewal projects work fetishistically—by repressing the structural interdependence between the renovated city centers and their adjoining urban wastelands. These ''garbage dumps'' are peopled by the poor and homeless, whose expulsion enables the creation of the city as a ''consumption artifact''. (David Harvey, *The Urban Experience*). . . .

By means of frequent parallels between Philadelphia and ''Third World'' cities, *Philadelphia Fire* locates American urban spaces such as the renovated Philadelphia downtown within a global structure of uneven development. The novel thus offers a ''way of seeing that unmasks the fetishisms'' promoted by the capitalist production of urban space—fetishisms which, as David Harvey argues, treat the spatial text of the city as a self-contained object. In order to resist this kind of myopic vision, Cudjoe resolves that ''he must always write about many places at once. No choice . . . . First step is always . . . toward the word or sound or image that is everywhere at once, that connects. . . . Always moving,'' the contemporary writer must ''travel through those other places'' because no place contains its own meaning. *Philadelphia Fire* treats social space as an asymmetrical global system of interconnected locales whose meaning is ''always everywhere at once.'' It is no wonder, then, that one of the narrators of *Philadelphia Fire* is the homeless man, JB, who ''inhabits many places, no place''.

Mobility and simultaneous occupation of several places are necessary conditions of contemporary urban writing because no places remains still long enough to permit a stable spatial or temporal perspective. When Cudjoe first returns to Philadelphia after a nearly decade-long absence, he searches for the old urban places preserved in his childhood memories. ''I have places, almost like stage sets, in my mind. I've been trying to find them since I've been back but they're gone,'' they have been ''urban-removed''. Cudjoe couches his longing for durable places is pastoral terms, as, for example, when he describes Clark Park, where he played as a child, as a ''green oasis''. However, Wideman is suspicious of the nostalgic yearnings that often fuel pastoral reactions to urban conditions: ''Oh, it [the city] must have been beautiful once. Walking barefoot in green grass, the sky a blue haven, the deep woods full of life. Now the grit of old dogshit,'' along with drugs and guns, attests to the decay of the green ideal in the city. . . .

Further illustrating this effect, Cudjoe reaches back to one of the earliest Western pastoral images, the Garden of Eden, and imagines Adam and Eve ''missing the good ole days, how things used to be, and they ain't been in the garden five minutes''.

But the novel's assessment of pastoral responses to urban conditions is far more complex and ambivalent than the simple mockery of the preceding passages might suggest. *Philadelphia Fire* remains deeply sympathetic to the pastoral when it operates not as a mode of imaginary escape from the city but as a means of imaginative engagement and transformation. The novel's epigraph, quoting William Penn, governor of Pennsylvania and founder of Philadelphia, offers one instance of the pastoral mode used to envision an ideal urban order: ''Let every house be placed, if the Person pleases, in the middle of its platt . . . so there may be ground on each side, for Gardens or Orchards or fields, that it may be a greene Country Towne, which will never be burnt, and always be whol[e]some.'' Despite its urban rather than agrarian setting,

Penn's vision of a garden city is in keeping with a traditionally American pastoral ideal which Leo Marx has characterized as a cultivated landscape located in the ''middle ground'' between nature and culture.

The garden city ideal presented in the epigraph is qualified by the novel's action, which centers around the conflict between the city of Philadelphia and the MOVE community and ends in the sort of calamity Penn wished to preempt—the burning of sixty-one houses. In addition to this particular incident, the novel emphasizes the city's failure to live up to Penn's garden ideal by means of numerous references to green areas reduced to smoke and ashes. Fire, in Penn's vision, as well as in the various actual and hallucinatory images of people and places burning in Wideman's fictional Philadelphia, appears as a uniquely urban symbol of destruction and disorder counterpoised to the fertility and ordered cultivation of the pastoral ideal. Although *Philadelphia Fire* stresses the gap between Penn's garden ideal and the realities of late-twentieth-century Philadelphia, as an ideal the garden image remains imaginatively compelling to the novel's narrator, even if only as a means of measuring the magnitude of contemporary urban decay.

> Madhu Dubey. *African American Review*. 32, 4 (Winter 1998), pp. 579–95

BIBLIOGRAPHY

*A Glance Away*, 1967; *Hurry Home*, 1969; *The Lynchers*, 1973; *Damballah*, 1981; *Sent for You Yesterday*, 1983; *Brothers and Keepers*, 1984; *Hiding Place*, 1984; *Reuben*, 1987; *Fever*, 1989; *Philadelphia Fire*, 1990; *The Homewood Books*, 1992; *The Stories of John Edgar Wideman*, 1992; *Fatheralong*, 1994; *Live from Death Row, with Mumia Abu-Jamal*, 1995; *The Cattle Killing*, 1996; *Conversations with John Edgar Wideman*, 1998; *Two Cities*, 1998

# WILLIAMS, John A. (1925–)
**United States**

Though it is certainly conceivable that *Night Song* will appeal to the deep neurotic strain in a far-out section of the reading public, this reviewer is in conscience bound to report that he does not dig this novel about a mewing mess of real-gone cats whose emotions are poured from bottles and squirted from syringes, and whose brains, such as they are, are in their gonads. It's crazy, man. Real crazy! And crazy never did add up to truth. . . .

[His] characters, who are about as viable as a row of wooden dolls, meet and join on a theatrical level of action and reaction that is maudlin, morbid and mad. The Beats may be flattered by this group portrait of themselves, but they will scarcely believe the flattery.

Yet there is one matter with which a reader's sympathies may become engaged; and that matter is the author's serious intention. He wants to say something important about bi-racial love, and about the life of art and artists, and about loss and pain and grief, and one can sympathize with his desire to say important things. But the mischief of it is that a sort of sickly sentimentalism takes over, and one gets the feeling that John A. Williams is playing around with values he does not understand.

Saunders Redding. *New York Herald Tribune Books*. November 26, 1961, p. 14

John A. Williams is the author of the earlier *Night Song*, a novel about jazz. In his new work, *Sissie*, he draws in part on his authoritative knowledge of that world, but this novel is far richer and cuts deeper than most books about jazz. For *Sissie* is a chronicle of Negro life in transition, and it unites, as few novels do, the experience of the brutalized older generation of Negroes with that of the sophisticated young, who, one way or another, have made it in American life. As such, it is full of vivid contrasts, and it conveys memorably an image of the double war that Negroes wage—against their white oppressors on the one hand, and generation against generation on the other. . . .

[Sissie] may well be the authoritative portrait of the Negro mother in America, that *Machtweib* who has given the beleaguered Negro family whatever strength and stability it has. Williams depicts Sissie with stunning fidelity—her capacity to endure, her cunning, and her abiding strength, at once supportive and disabling. For what *Sissie* is really about is the effort of her children to emancipate themselves from this Big Mama who in nurturing them almost destroyed them. . . .

Inevitably, this novel invites comparison with James Baldwin's *Another Country*. *Sissie* is by far the better work. For all his platform polemics, Baldwin does not seem to possess the grasp of the Negro *milieu* that Williams displays. And where *Another Country* is shrill and noisy, Sissie is permeated by a quiet anger that builds and builds inexorably. John A. Williams may well be a front-runner in a new surge of Negro creativity.

David Boroff. *Saturday Review*. March 30, 1963, p. 49

As with black music, black literature continues to grow, extend, and ceases to be invisible. Our literature now cuts and you do bleed. Mr. Williams' latest book [*The Man Who Cried I Am*] is this type of work; a blood bringer, causing you to hurt and forcing you to redefine your relationship with your surroundings. It makes you open your eyes and enables you to see much more than what is in front of you. While reading this book, we see through mirrors, across continents, into other cultures, and unconsciously we feel—that is, if we are capable of feeling. John A. Williams has written an extensively handsome and dangerous novel.

Jean-Paul Sartre said, "It is true that all art is false." He lied, or he was talking about white Western art. The book in question is a work of Art. That is, if art, among other things, is a creative effort that others can identify with, an accent on a particular life-style, communication, a bringer of knowledge, a mind wakener, movable prose which is esthetically pleasing and meaningful and, in essence, one artist's comment on life as he views it. The work is *The Man Who Cried I Am* and the artist is John A. Williams. . . .

No doubt about it, Mr. Williams can write; he proved that with *Night Song* and *Sissie*; but the Williams of this novel transcends the artist and becomes the seer, the prophet.

Don L. Lee. *Negro Digest*. March 1968, pp. 51–52, 79

If you have an ambitious theme, you just have to go on being ambitious with it till you get to the end. Mr. Williams [in *Sons of Darkness, Sons of Light*] has the theme: the beginnings of a race war some time in the 1970s, told from everybody's point of view. The characters are treated as independent agents of history, crisscrossing like ants on separate errands, forming a pattern that none of themselves can see.

Nor does the ambition stop there. Williams has made serious overtures at understanding each of his ants in turn: the beady-eyed black businessman, the Israeli gunman who has slipped into killing out of habit, even, with a sour face, the Irish cop who starts the ball rolling by shooting a black boy.

So there we are—intricate design and compassion to burn. And there we stay. Because the author is too modest. He has decided to use his materials for a conventional fast-paced adventure yarn. The Hegelian interconnections of history, by which poisons grown in the Middle East can cause death in America, become simple plot devices, as trivial as the coincidental collisions of characters that Williams also favors. As trivial, but also as entertaining. . . .

It is a good design for a novel, and the combustible climax is not, like most such prophecies, too silly to contemplate. But a novel that winds up so many themes and characters cannot put them all to rest in 279 pages. The characters bustle about but do not grow in complexity. Nor does the background fill up: the performers always seem to be the only people in New York that day.

John Williams has a notable, attractive author's voice and an impressive range of sympathy, but this time he has been content to do a skin job.

Wilfrid Sheed. *Book World*. June 29, 1969, p. 5

By all rights, John A. William's *Captain Blackman* should have been much worse than it is. Its method is documentary, its aim is consciousness raising, not the loftiest of fictional ways and goals. Williams has, apparently, gone over every inch of ground where, at any time in American history, black soldiers have fought. As he did so, he tried to imagine not only the men he knew had been there but also a binding single figure, a soldier named Abraham Blackman, who fought in all the battles, from Lexington to New Orleans to Petersburg to Fort Sill in the Indian wars, to San Juan Hill, to France, Spain, Italy, Korea, and Vietnam. As the novel opens Blackman is wounded in Vietnam trying to shield some of his company from slaughter, and the rest is his dreams and hallucinations of his role in all the earlier battles.

As a novel the book doesn't begin to count. Blackman himself may not be superhuman, but he is strictly a fantasy figure: huge, strong, brave, serious, always right, always able to speak the deeper ironies. His women, most of whom are named Mimosa Rogers, are always strong, sexy, eager, and tough-minded. The episodes, though many and varied, always carry the same message: whites are always willing to use blacks in battle, always afraid of the power blacks might have if properly rewarded for their service, always willing to find ways to ignore, degrade, or simply kill black soldiers who become a problem. So Williams has given himself practically no fictional room to move in. The coins have to keep falling exactly as Williams calls them. But, given this, *Captain Blackman* is not without merit. . . .

If Williams's fictional device is clumsy, and many of his attempts to flesh out history are vulgar, the central vision is one worth reading. It may not matter much that we learn about this or that incident that we've never heard of, but the grim joke that is our racial history does need to be told over, and over, and the very sameness of the joke in each of Williams's many episodes is necessarily part of the telling, the irony, the joke.

Roger Sale. *New York Review of Books.* October 5, 1972, p. 34

[Williams'] first two works, *The Angry Ones* and *Night Song,* apprentice works at best, are defeated by many of the structural and stylistic problems so few novice writers are able to surmount. Where they do surprise, though, is in their failure to exhibit any of those saving moments of raw talent or unmistakable power that suggest promising later careers. They suffer from a welter of extraneous details, descriptions, and asides which interrupt irreparably the narrative flow, and from a conspicuous absence of dramatic tension. Not so much shown or revealed, the novels are explained; where one expects drama, he receives the didactic, a telling and invariably fatal substitution. Unable to attract serious critical attention on their own intrinsic merits, they obtain our interest now because they contain the characters, conflicts and themes that characterize Williams' later work and because they embody in embryo form the controlling myth of his fiction. . . .

*Sissie* represents a considerable advance over the earlier novels, an advance that can best be appreciated perhaps by recognizing what Williams does *not* do. In *Night Song* he becomes lost in the myth of the tragic black genius. In *Sissie* the same opportunity offers itself in the figure of the dominant black matriarch. But Sissie is an individual, strong, willful, childish, destructive, bewildered. We come not so much to admire her achievement as to respect it, aware as we are every moment of all she is willing to sacrifice in order to earn her "right to live."

Ronald Walcott. *CLA Journal.* December 1972, pp. 202, 213

John A. Williams' *The Man Who Cried I Am* has attracted considerable attention among the general public not so much for its literary excellence but because in the last pages of the novel its protagonist, Max Reddick, discovers a monstrous plot—code named "King Alfred"—to eradicate the black population of the United States. The plot, similar in many ways to Nazi Germany's "final solution," employs enough facts from everyday life to give the reader an uneasy feeling that perhaps this section of the book is not pure fiction. . . .

This feature of the novel is not to be ignored. By suggesting the logical extension of America's past and present treatment of black people, the novel, hopefully, may jolt the conscience of the nation and influence its future policies. However, Williams deserves credit for the art of the novel as well as its message. The King Alfred extermination plan is only one item in a series of nightmarish elements which Williams uses to dramatize not only the psychological problems of the main character but also the frightening social conditions which foster them. Like most nightmares, these particular elements of the novel evoke emotions of fear and repugnance and often a frantic refusal to accept what is detestable or unbelievable. As in a nightmare, the seemingly impossible happens, and evil or death is manifested in peculiarly horrifying

ways; perversion, savagery, and hatred may threaten one's humanity, reason, or life itself. Employing these gothic elements with considerable artistic success, Williams frees himself from the naturalistic protest format which for a time seemed the sole métier of the black novelist.

Robert E. Fleming. *Contemporary Literature.* Spring 1973, pp. 186–87

After *Night Song,* Williams discovered that the writer was master of time in the novel; that time was never static but an ever-changing reality. To merge history and fiction, therefore, necessitated that the writer exercise great control over time; that he prepare to break it up—change endings into beginnings and vice versa. Flashbacks are used to accomplish this feat in *The Man Who Cried I Am* and, as a result, Reddick moves quickly and easily across three continents. In *Captain Blackman,* the manipulation of time occurs through dream sequences and stream of consciousness. Blackman, therefore, appears simultaneously as a wanderer through history and a patient on an operating table in Vietnam. Williams, however, has not completely mastered the usage of time in either novel, and, thus, both are flawed by confusion. Past and present incidents are thrust upon the reader so quickly that sometimes it is difficult to distinguish between the two. When the technique works well, however, more often in the latter than the former novel, Williams comes close to mastering the form of the historical novel.

This is no small achievement. More important is Williams' determination to explore black life realistically, to search for paradigms of the distant past, to search out images, symbols, and metaphors relevant to the present. Thus the close parallel between past and present, shown specifically in *Captain Blackman,* between characters and incidents is neither artificial nor contrived. Those who appear in Blackman's Odyssey in the sixteen hundreds, eighteen hundreds, nineteen hundreds have their mirror images in those who appear in the nineteen sixties. In other words, the men who struggled in the distant past, who met the test of manhood, differ little from those who act accordingly in the twentieth century. . . .

Addison Gayle, Jr. *The Way of the New World* (Garden City, New York: Doubleday, 1975), p. 346

Obviously Williams didn't intend [*Mothersill and the Foxes*] as a serious novel, and when compared to his previous works (most notably *The Man Who Cried I Am,* a story of existential proportions about a black reporter dying of rectal cancer) it would appear that this represents an unnecessary departure for Williams. But in reading *Mothersill and the Foxes,* one gets the impression that Williams wrote it with the intention of confronting looming shadows. Unquestionably his intention was to write about sex, but more important, it appears Williams sought to break from the strictures black writers have often imposed on themselves when it comes to dealing with the whole subject of sex. In the past the choice has been either not to write about it at all, or at best, not to write too lustfully about it lest they add fuel to the prevailing myth. The myth, of course, being that of potent black male sexuality.

And though this is not to imply that Williams believes in the myth, or that he sought to dispel or even exploit it, still his characterization of Mothersill seems to have been written with a high level of consciousness. So carefully balanced between extremities, Mothersill never quite comes off as the sexual character Williams intended him to be. And this perhaps is due to a fear Williams himself has as to what the myth implies: that whether true or not, it still carries a tinge of undesirable, painful smells about it. Thus the character Odell Mothersill, a character so vulgarly successful outside the realm of sex that not only is he not the average black man, but also eons removed from those causes giving rise to the myth in the first place; he is the black man without problems who has passed through the matrix unscathed by the usual pitfalls which often hurl black men toward undesirable, self-destructive ends.

Stated quite simply, then, Mothersill is a man who loves sex and women undoubtedly for the same reason that men climb mountains, but in order to be that, and be a black man as well, Williams has deemed it necessary to shroud him with credentials and high purpose. He comes off as the proverbial over-qualified black. The subject of sex is wasted on him.

James T. Lampley. *Black Scholar.* January—February 1976, pp. 43–44

John A. Williams is a black writer, the way the crocus is a spring flower. *The Junior Bachelor Society*, his latest novel, is the story of nine middle-aged black men and what their lives have become in the more than three decades gone by since they played ball together, and grew up together, in Central City, in upstate New York. . . .

Along with the lives of the nine principals, rendered in loving detail, Williams also fleshes out their wives, and the marital relationships, as well as the intricate crosscurrents prevailing when they all get back together. . . .

Williams not only manages it all, combines and orchestrates it all, but gives the reader (as the best novelists have always done) the sense of still *more* interconnected life out there, still *more* books out there, already written and yet to come, than what is here so brilliantly encompassed.

Ivan Gold. *New York Times Book Review.* July 11, 1976, pp. 32–33

[John A. Williams's] first three novels—*The Angry Ones* (1960), *Night Song* (1961), and *Sissie* (1963)—deal with racism in the world of music and literature. *Sissie* is the best of the three, showing how a black playwright finally accepts the truth of his situation by concluding that his paranoia is not pathological but practical, a rational response to the reality of life in America. By 1967, with the heating up of the civil rights movement and the advent of the Black Power concept, Williams was evidently no longer content to dramatize the process of discrimination. Like those of many other black intellectuals, Williams's frustrations led him to consider theoretical violence, and he used *The Man Who Cried I Am* and *Sons of Darkness* as laboratories for his investigation.

*The Man Who Cried I Am* is one of those works of fiction in which a writer's special abilities happen to fuse with his best themes in a harmony that seems as much chance as plan. This is the story of Williams's own intellectual and racial life as well as a history of the period the novel covers, 1940–66. It is also the story of the black writer's life during the years of Wright, Baldwin, Chester Himes, and of how white racism affects their emotions, their attitudes, and their writing. Africa breaks its colonial bonds; black Americans discover their beauty and their political power; the status of the black writer improves. But the gains are only external. Underneath, white supremacy remains as the foundation and prevents any real progress toward eliminating those racial barriers that can be perceived only by an African American. One of Williams's main convictions is that African Americans must, in order to survive, acknowledge the full truth of their place in the white scheme of things and understand with absolute clarity the true nature of white prejudice. They must, like Ralph Ellison's Invisible Man, achieve a higher consciousness, which will function not to reform the system but to provide psychological liberation. Much of "true" white prejudice is bound up in people's mannerisms, the inability to uncouple their unconscious belief in black inferiority from the artistic judgments they make of blacks' artistic work. This produces a tacit conspiracy to keep black writers or painters or musicians out of the main media of dissemination, the refusal to accept black intellectuals on their own ground.

To give all this an economical form, Williams devises a clever metaphor. European racism is embodied in an "Alliance Blanc," in which the white nations of Europe agree secretly to prevent black Africa from taking charge of its own destiny and enjoying the profits of its own resources. The American arm of the Alliance Blanc is the "King Alfred Plan," which white authorities have developed for use "in the event of widespread and continuing coordinated racial disturbances." The plan calls for the mobilization of all federal, state, and local law enforcement units to detain, imprison, or contain as necessary any black person thought to pose a danger to whites in an armed insurrection. The lives of the characters in the novel illustrate that such a plan has always existed in America, that it is simply a codification in writing of the measures that whites have always used in their suppression of African Americans. The experience of the protagonist, Max Reddick, is a movement toward a discovery of the actual existence of this plan, developed step by step as he moves through white America and Europe in the novel's action.

In the hours before he is killed, ironically by two black CIA agents, novelist Reddick reads a long letter from his fellow novelist, Harry Ames, a Richard Wright figure. Harry's letter documents the existence of the Alliance Blanc and the King Alfred Plan. As he reads, Max relives his own life, moving back and forth from the present to the past. As the letter unfolds the information about the King Alfred Plan, flashbacks unfold the course of Reddick's life and his fragment of African American history. Thus the evidence exposing white racism accumulates on two parallel tracks, the past and the present, which reflect each other. In the end, Max reads the letter straight through. By then, with a knowledge of the past in his mind, the reader realizes, and so does Max, that the King Alfred Plan is a logical extension of historical American policy. Even so, it is suddenly and vividly illuminating. "I'd spent so much of my life writing about the evil machinations of Mr. Charlie," writes Harry, "without really knowing the truth, as this material made me know it". That Williams puts this knowledge into the hands of two novelists indicates his conviction that the role of the black writer is first to perceive and then to articulate the truth about the white world as they see it. *The Man Who Cried I Am*, as a novel, does what its characters do in the story.

Max himself is not a violent man, nor are any of Williams's intellectuals. But Williams suggests that the white world surrounds them with violence to suppress them, and this forces them eventually into violence themselves. Whites preach nonviolence and human rights but forcefully repress attempts by unauthorized groups to exercise those rights. The black person who would discover and then disclose the truth about America endangers himself. In *The Man Who Cried I Am*, every statesman or artist who exposes the elaborate institutional framework by which whites rationalize their crimes is killed, either literally or figuratively. Knowledge is a terminal disease, a "pain in the ass," as Max calls the rectal cancer from which he is dying. The cancer commences at the same point that Max begins to learn the truth, a few hemorrhoids, some irritating discomfort, a bloody stool or two. It develops slowly, until the time Max starts reading Harry's letter with only a little while to live. As the African American rises toward the goal of existence, understanding, he also moves toward death—and not a natural death, either. This is the fatal illness of being black in America. Max moves through his last hours in a cloud of pain, able to cut it only in the classical way that many black men have used to cut the agony of their lucidity, through liquor and dope.

Williams identifies too closely with the activist spirit of the decade, however, to leave it at this. Understanding may be a worthwhile goal in itself, but there are things to be done and a world to be changed, and finally it is the question of how change may be achieved that confronts Max Reddick in the final pages of the novel. It is impossible not to write a political novel in these years. But Williams addresses the question with skill and a writer's sensitivity. *The Man Who Cried I Am* is not an opportunistic exploitation of a chic market fashion, nor is it a puerile fantasy. It is an attempt to make meaning out of a set of events that Williams would rather not have to face. He attacks the problem on the personal and the political levels. Max Reddick is the man who cries "I am," asserting both his personal existence and a political determination to act as a catalyst of change. To act in this way is to exist. His political act is to make public the King Alfred Plan before he himself is killed for possessing his knowledge. He makes the decision reluctantly, for he knows it will begin a civil war, a suggestion that requires a weakening bit of melodramatic fudging by Williams. Yet, in the uncertain atmosphere of those times of riot, the possibility did not seem all that remote. Black people, Williams suggests, have always been resourceful in finding reasons for not acting. The voice of those reasons is "Saminone," Max's other side, who appears to him at critical times in his life. Saminone is all the Uncle Toms and cynical hipsters wrapped into one. To Max's desperate "I am," Saminone counters with a sardonic and bitter humor: "You am whut, you piece of crap? Turd." Max's assertion defies the white man's negation of the black. Saminone finds in that defiance a contemptibleness that causes him to laugh bitterly, as well as a little nervously. You are only a black man, he says in effect to Max, believing in his own inferiority. What can a black man expect to do to the forces arrayed against him? Saminone is the profoundly fatalistic strain in the black character, and Max struggles to defeat it. His decision to disclose Harry's information is another way of saying "I am." To discover and then reveal the truth is to assert one's black existence. To the tradition of black rebels like Josh Green and Perigua, Williams brings a humanizing depth and discloses another aspect to the heroic but desperate logic of "if we must die" poetry. Not to

act, though the act will inevitably bring Max's own death and the death of others, is to place no value on his own and other blacks' lives, to allow whites to make what they will: a Saminone who has internalized a paralyzing cynicism and pessimism. To fight, and to accept death as a probable consequence—even if nothing is gained by it—is to create one's own value. No white value system can supersede that.

*The Man Who Cried I Am* is Williams's adaptation of the rhetoric of Black Power. It is a gloss upon a sentence in his *This Is My Country Too*: "Today the strength of the contemporary Negro is in being ready to die." There is no stereotypical black militancy in this novel, however. Williams does not resort to simple reversal or get any vindictive pleasure in imagining the deaths of whites or the superior ability of blacks to kill. Melancholy pervades this novel, not heroic anger or righteous resentment or revolutionary fervor. The violent ending, in which Max is gunned down after he has made a civil war in America certain, cannot erase the sorrow that dominates every scene, a sadness over the tarnishing of America's promise. And after the political implications in the failure of whites to live up to their professed creed comes yet another discovery that makes the novel so complex and effective. African Americans can be as petty and self-serving, grasping and self-centered, as anyone else. Like America itself, every relationship carries with it warm human possibility, and every promise dissipates in the air of human frailty and the deficiency of conditions. No motive is pure, no act untainted with bias. Blacks as well as whites display greed, jealousy, duplicity, opportunism. Even the authenticity of Max's decision to risk death by exposing the King Alfred Plan is undercut by the fact that he is already dying of cancer.

But no more than many other black writers can Williams relinquish all hope. The civil war that Max's disclosure makes inevitable implies a violent revolt of blacks as they set about defending themselves against King Alfred. No black commandos are introduced to stand in glorious silhouette against the flames of a burning America. This is an apocalypse of pain and loss, but one in which some future lies. The issue is not the right to kill; it is whether America is worth the agony of this rebellion.

Max's successor in *Sons of Darkness*, Gene Browning, also believes that America is worth saving, and he also concludes, only with reluctance, that violent confrontation is necessary. Blacks have exhausted every other recourse and want desperately to make their country healthy, to heal the division between races. Violence is like the shock treatment one authorizes for a beloved relative. That it is his country is a conviction from which Williams never wavers; the problems of the African American can only be solved in America, and only violence, reluctantly used, can solve them.

Jerry H. Bryant. *Victims and Heroes: Racial Violence in the African American Novel* (Amherst: University of Massachusetts Press, 1997), pp. 251–57

BIBLIOGRAPHY

*The Angry Ones*, 1960; *Night Song*, 1961; *Sissie, Farrar*, 1963; *The Man Who Cried I Am*, 1967; *Sons of Darkness, Sons of Light: A Novel of Some Probability*, 1969; *Captain Blackman*, 1972; *Mothersill and the Foxes*, 1975; *The Junior Bachelor Society*, 1976; *Click Song*, 1982; *The Berhama Account*, 1985; *Jacob's Ladder*, 1987

# WILSON, August (1945– )
## United States

[If] August Wilson has wanted anything in his career as a play-wright, it is to be recognized by the people of the ghetto as their voice, their bard. Wilson gives words to trumpeters and trash men, cabbies and conjurers, boarders and land-ladies, all joined by a heritage of slavery. Their patois is his poetry; their dreams are his dramas. And while Wilson's inspiration is contained—a few sloping blocks in Pittsburgh—his aspiration seems boundless. He intends to write a play about black Americans in every decade of this century, and he has already completed six of the projected ten.

*Fences*, a drama set in the 1950s . . . is the second of the cycle to reach Broadway. It was preceded by *Ma Rainey's Black Bottom*, which won the New York Drama Critics Circle Award as the best play of the 1984–85 season and . . . it established Wilson as "a major find for the American theater," a writer of "compassion, raucous humor and penetrating wisdom."

Fecundity, too, can be added to the list. *Joe Turner's Come and Gone*, written after *Fences* . . . may come to New York next season. *The Piano Lesson*, Wilson's most recent work, is on the 1987–88 schedule of the Yale Repertory. . . . It adds up to the most auspicious arrival of an American playwright since that of David Mamet some fifteen years ago.

*Fences* may prove the most accessible of Wilson's plays, faster-moving than *Ma Rainey* and less mystical than *Joe Turner*. Several critics have likened this family drama to Arthur Miller's *Death of a Salesman*, centering as it does on a proud, embittered patriarch, Troy Maxson, and his teenage son, Cory. Their immediate conflict is kindled when Cory is recruited to play college football and Troy, once a baseball star barred from the segregated big leagues, demands he turn down the scholarship because he cannot believe times have truly changed. Behind the narrative looms Wilson's concern with legacy. As Cory Maxson almost grudgingly discovers the value in his father's flawed life, he accepts his part in a continuum that runs from Pittsburgh to the antebellum South and finally to Mother Africa. . . .

Most of Wilson's plays concern the conflict between those who embrace their African past and those who deny it. "You don't see me running around in no jungle with no bone between my nose," boasts one character in *Ma Rainey*. Wilson's answer is that Africa remains a pervasive force, a kind of psychic balm available to twentieth-century blacks through blues songs, communal dances, tall tales. Wilson the mythologist coexists with Wilson the social realist. There is a broad historical truth to his characters—to Levee, the jazz musician who naively sells off his compositions to a white record company executive; to Troy Maxson, whose job prospects go no further than becoming the first black truck driver in the Pittsburgh Sanitation Department.

Samuel G. Freedman. *New York Times Magazine*. March 15, 1987, pp. 36, 40

Every culture generates its own myths and superstitions, taboos and rituals of exorcism. To secure a glorious afterlife, Egyptians embalmed their deceased rulers. Ancient Greeks went to Delphi to worship divine wisdom and to learn about their fates. Most Chinese people still follow elaborate burial rites which commemorate the dead for forty-nine days with chants and incantation. Being a black

American, August Wilson's heritage goes back to African traditions which are based on similar pantheistic views of celestial order ruling both the living and the dead. From *Joe Turner's Come and Gone*, through *Fences* to his present work *The Piano Lesson*, a seamless blend of Christianity with the inherent African cosmology defines the spiritual landscape within which the characters suffer and rejoice.

Set in small-scaled domestic environments, the three plays are immersed in a sense of mystery that transgresses the confinements of rigid realism. Wilson's central characters are all marvelous storytellers. In their fantastic tales, daily life takes on a subliminal cloak, transforming mundane facts into allegorical rituals.

Mei-Ling Ching. *Theater*. 19, 3 (Summer 1988), p. 70

The center of African-American playwright August Wilson's growing theatrical universe is conspicuously occupied by African-American men. They are the thinkers, the doers, the dreamers. Revolving around them in seemingly expendable supporting roles are wives, mistresses, sisters, children, and other relatives. As characters such as Levee [in *Ma Rainey's Black Bottom*], Troy Maxson [in *Fences*], Herald Loomis [in *Joe Turner's Come and Gone*], and Boy Willie [in *The Piano Lesson*], impose their authority, they overshadow the concerns of others. Most noticeable in their blind quest for omnipotence and wealth is that they place no stock in Christian dogma, adapting instead a purely secular ideology. Consequently, what emerges from their abandonment of Christianity is a more convenient, self-serving religion—one totally unaligned with the cultural reservoir provided by what many African-Americans have traditionally referred to as "good old-fashioned religion." While this good old-fashioned religion has, for centuries, provided inspiration, strength and moral principles for African-Americans, Wilson's men affirm that it has not and will not suit their needs. Therefore, they demonstrate their disavowal by challenging and withdrawing from the religion of their ancestors.

August Wilson has apparently chosen to focus on the African-American man's oppression in this country to symbolize the collective struggles of all African-Americans. Since the early 1980s, Wilson has committed himself to writing ten plays chroni-cling the history of his people in each decade of their existence in the United States. Often depicted on the verge of an emotional breakdown, Levee, Herald Loomis, Troy Maxson, and Boy Willie dominate center stage and become Wilson's primary spokesmen. Although the African-American woman appears in various sup-porting roles—devoted wife and mother, cranky blues singer, docile sex object, stubborn sister, etc.—the actions of the African-American man clearly convey the themes of each of the four plays Wilson has completed toward his ten-play mission. . . .

With a foreboding resonance, each of Wilson's four published plays addresses the difficulties the African-American man has had in accepting Christianity as a moral frame of reference. Levee, Herald Loomis, Troy Maxson, and Boy Willie do not stop short of lambasting white society for their misfortunes. They blaspheme against Christianity with ease and run roughshod over any obstacle to their respective ambitions. But they are not above acknowledg-ing themselves as villains. Having conceded this, they choose to pass over Christianity as practiced by fellow African-Americans in favor of less restrictive adaptations of their own brand of survival. Consequently, the language and actions associated with their makeshift ideals reflect a new means of compensating for their previously unquestioned belief in God.

Quite unlike the sorely tried though patient Job of the Old Testament, Wilson's African-American men have given up on their God. No longer content to "wait on the Lord," they make impetuous, often foolhardy decisions about their lives. They are no longer so easily appeased by spewing profanity and threats at white America or by finding solace in the word of God. Neither are they intimidated by the moral consequences of their infidelity. Where once the sanctity of Christianity may have been reinforced by a heavy hand like that extended by [Lorraine] Hansberry's uncompromising Lena Younger [in *A Raisin in the Sun*]: "In my mother's house there is still God," its ethics are being either challenged or totally ignored. Consigned to a life of subjugation, the African-American men who dominate Wilson's plays discard Christianity in favor of more flexible, manmade commandments.

> Sandra G. Shannon. *MELUS*. 16, 3 (Fall 1989), pp. 127, 141–42

All of Wilson's plays spring from specific inspirations with widespread cultural implications; the genesis of [*Ma Rainey's Black Bottom*] was the first blues—a Bessie Smith record—he heard as a youth. He listened to the record twenty-two consecutive times, feeling that someone was speaking directly to him and that he understood instantly and emotionally. He came to see the blues as part of blacks' oral tradition: a way of passing on information that was given an emotional reference by music. The information Wilson received was that there was a nobility and beauty to blacks he hadn't seen.

This nobility and beauty he conveys in his plays in a style and tone that could be likened to a combination of Sophocles and Aristophanes: hauntingly poetic and raucously humorous, inexorable and irrepressible. Though Wilson's settings are realistic, his protagonists are larger than life; they are very much themselves and something more. His recurring themes and the stories embodying them (both those dramatized and those told by the characters) raise the black experience in America to epic stature. The dialogue, inspired by Wilson's longtime observation of black speech, is evocative stage poetry in what is said and not said. The pressure of characters struggling with a fate that is both within their own natures and a legacy of being black in America, the threat of being pushed beyond endurance into violence, gives the plays a sense of danger, dramatic tension and high theatricality. . . .

Though Wilson did not set out intending to write a cycle of plays, as *Fences* (set in 1957), *Joe Turner's Come and Gone* (set in 1911) and *The Piano Lesson* (set in 1936) were in various stages of development, he realized that he was creating a play for each decade of the [twentieth] century: "I'm taking each decade and looking at one of the most important questions that blacks confronted in that decade and writing a play about it. Put them all together and you have a history."

*Fences* began with the image of a man holding a baby in his arms—it was Wilson's reaction against the stereotype of the irresponsible black man. His protagonist, Troy Maxson, tries to hold closely what is his and keep out whatever threatens his control—he builds real and psychological fences in the play. . . .

The grandeur of Wilson's vision is most evident in *Joe Turner's Come and Gone*. The play's setting is a Pittsburgh boarding house in 1911, inspired by black artist Romare Bearden's painting of a boarding house scene that includes an abject man in a coat and hat. Wilson wondered why the man was so abject, and created the character of Herald Loomis—"Herald, because he's a herald. Loomis, because he's luminous," the playwright told a *New York Post* interviewer. Loomis is an ominous figure in a black coat and hat, a former church deacon pressed into seven years' labor by Joe Turner, whose villainous history W. C. Handy made into the blues song that is the play's title. . . .

August Wilson is a demanding playwright; the fabric of his plays is densely woven and speaks to attentive audiences. In the first scene of *Joe Turner*, Bynum describes a cleansing ritual that preceded his finding his song. That ritual is unwittingly repeated by Herald upon himself, and not only frees him from the past and sends him out to sing his own song, but gives Bynum the sanction of his life, for the last line of the play is "Herald Loomis, you shining! You shining like new money!" Wilson's language is incantatory, his story at once a spiritual allegory and a social document.

> Holly Hill. In Bruce King, ed. *Contemporary American Theatre* (New York: St. Martin's Press, 1991), pp. 88, 91, 93–94

His 1984 play *Ma Rainey's Black Bottom* is a disturbing look at the consequences of waiting, especially as it relates to the precarious lot of black musicians during the pre-Depression era. Although the play features a still shot in the lives of several members of Ma Rainey's 1920s band, it is also suggestive of the many and varied oppressive forces under which the entire Afro-American population labored at that time. From education to employment, blacks got the smallest share of the American pie, while clinging to an often self-destructive ideology of tolerance. Through the actions and the dialogue of three crucial characters—the blues singer Ma Rainey, her piano player Toledo, and her trumpet player Levee—Wilson conveys the damage that prolonged periods of waiting have caused the Afro-American artist. . . .

While Ma Rainey tries the patience of her two promoters, her musicians waiting in the basement band room, all of whom are black males, bicker and taunt each other in deceptively simple repartee. Their conversations, which slip from the correct spelling of *music* to an existentialist discussion of black history, gradually intensify and unexpectedly erupt in a fatal stabbing. The self-made philosopher and pianist, Toledo, inadvertently steps on the new Florsheim shoes of the ambitious though disgruntled trumpet player Levee. In a gradual chain of events, this otherwise commonplace incident leads to murder. Apparently still angered by the recent refusal of one of Ma Rainey's promoters to launch his musical career, Levee, during several moments of extreme anger, stabs Toledo in the back. . . .

Because of the blatant image of a stabbing death, an unsympathetic viewer might perceive Levee's action to be monstrous. However, his conversations throughout the play give various reasons for a pre-existing cynicism. He brings with him to the recording session a history of negativism which spans his entire life. For example, as an eight-year-old, he watched white men rape his mother. In addition, his business arrangement with Sturdyvant is not proceeding as he had hoped. After agreeing to purchase lyrics Levee has composed, Sturdyvant squashes the trumpet player's ambitions to start a band of his own so that he can play his more upbeat, avant-garde arrangements. Added to these setbacks is

Levee's incompatibility with Ma Rainey. He cannot yield his ambitious nature to the strict control that she exerts over her band and her promoters. He constantly rebels against the sovereignty that Ma Rainey has over what and how the band plays. Inevitably, because of their irreconcilable differences, Ma Rainey has no choice but to fire him. . . .

Despite Levee's genuine ambition to excel in the music industry, he is sucked under by the swirling vortex of oppression. If isolated and studied strictly in terms of his sociological relevance, Levee might easily serve as the basis for a viable case study on the root causes of black-on-black crime in the United States. His character mirrors the all-too-familiar results of the black male's battle to survive in a white-dominated society. No longer convinced that the Christian's God is the black man's ally, Levee resorts to annihilating members of his own race to appease his frustrations at having to wait for others in order to actualize his ambitions. Thus, Levee, like many one-time-ambitious, creative young black hopefuls, becomes disillusioned, self-defeating, and ultimately violent.

Each of August Wilson's four completed plays emphasizes "the choices that we as blacks in America have made." However, the playwright is also concerned about the oppressive forces which have precluded many of those choices. To this end, *Ma Rainey's Black Bottom* provides a provocative look into the world of several black musicians who have little or no control in determining the course of their professional lives. Even as they create and enjoy their music, the origins of which may be traced to their own African ancestry, they are forced to yield their primary rights of ownership to whites, who prey upon them. Waiting becomes the sedative that allows such predators to keep the personal aspirations of these black musicians forever in the balance. Waiting also stifles their "warrior spirit," the absence of which leads to noticeably neurotic compensations in their characters. Waiting becomes a dominant motif in the play, affecting each member of the band, as well as Ma Rainey, in some awkward manifestation. In addition to Ma Rainey's unrefined and boisterous personality, the extraordinary behavior of her pianist and her trumpet player suggests latent reactions to figurative roadblocks placed before them.

> Sandra G. Shannon. *Black American Literature Forum.* 25, 1 (Spring 1991), pp. 135–36, 143–45

The question of self-identity seems to be the major force in [Wilson's] plays. In *Ma Rainey's Black Bottom* the play centers on black musicians who are exploited by white managers and record producers. . . . In a dispute over the arrangement of the music the blacks cease to argue only when the white manager Sturdyvant says what he wants. The piano player chides the others, saying, "As long as the colored man look to white folks to put the crown on what he say . . . as long as he looks to white folks for approval . . . then he ain't never gonna find who he is and what he's about." The title of the play is a type of pun: the Black Bottom was a dance popularized by Ma Rainey's song, but, of course, Ma Rainey also has a black bottom. The action of the play is very simple: the black musicians and the white managers are waiting for the arrival of the famous singer Ma Rainey. When she finally arrives she initially refuses to make the records, then finally agrees. She makes it clear throughout the play that she feels used by the white men who run the business. Saying that they care nothing about her, she concludes, "As soon as they get my voice down on them recording machines, then it's just like if I'd be some whore and they roll over and put their pants on.". . .

In *Fences* Wilson is dealing with the polarities of loving and dying. In *Beyond the Pleasure Principle* [Sigmund] Freud noted Eros and the death wish as the elementary powers whose counterpoint governs all the puzzles of life. Wilson establishes these two forces as the governing factors in the life of the protagonist. *Fences* deals with the failed dreams of Troy Maxson, a black ball player who played in the minority black leagues, but was barred from the major (all white) leagues because of his race. Wilson wrote the play to show the indignities which blacks in that generation suffered, but hid from their children. Set in the 1950s, the play presents conflicts familiar to blacks in the audience—indeed, one critic wrote that he was moved to tears because he seemed to see his own life on stage. . . .

In Wilson's next play, *Joe Turner's Come and Gone*, the question of identity is central. Into a boarding house in Pittsburgh comes a strange, lost man with a child, seeking his wife. Almost everyone in the play is seeking someone, and they appeal for assistance to two wondrously mythic types . . . the People Finder and the Binder of What Clings. The white man Selig is in a line of People Finders; but in contrast to his father who found runaway slaves for the plantation bosses, he is a beneficent figure who finds black people displaced after the end of slavery and reunites families. Bynum is in a line of African conjure men and works spells. He, however, is in search of his own song: in a vision his father revealed to him that if he could find a "shiny man"—a man who is One Who Goes Before and Shows the Way—"I would know that my song had been accepted and worked its full power in the world and I could lay down and die a happy man." In the course of the play it is revealed that the stranger, Loomis, was entrapped into seven years of indentured servitude by the notorious Joe Turner (an actual historical figure), and thereby lost not only his wife, but his whole sense of the world and his place in it. . . .

Wilson's latest play to open in New York has, like his others, first been performed at Yale, and then in a number of other cities. . . . *The Piano Lesson* is set in 1936. A group of blacks living in Pittsburgh are displaced from their roots and their acquaintances in Mississippi. Doaker and his niece Berneice are surprised by the unexpected arrival of Berneice's brother, the high-spirited Boy Willie, and his friend Lymon who have driven from Mississippi with a load of watermelons. Boy Willie hopes to make a large amount of money from the watermelons, so he will have part of the money he needs to buy a farm. He also hopes to persuade his sister Berneice to sell the family piano so that he can get the rest of the money he needs. The play becomes a struggle over the family inheritance, an elaborately decorated piano with pictures of family members carved on the legs. . . .

In a time when many American playwrights write about transitory problems, petty characters, and minor themes. Wilson seeks the great themes. . . . Although he feels very passionate about "the historical treatment of blacks in American society," his characters speak to both whites and blacks because they relate to archetypal themes and questions: What is true freedom? What is it to be a man? How does a family relate? What is the nature of responsibility? What, ultimately, is the purpose of life, and how does one "find one's own song?" How does one become (or find) a shiny man? In plays filled with poetic images, Wilson explores these questions.

> Yvonne Shafer. *Zeitschrift fur Anglistik und Amerikanistik.* 39, 1 (1991), pp. 20–26

In his newest play, *Two Trains Running*, August Wilson summons up . . . people and circumstances . . . from his own memory, reclaiming stories from the obscurity into which so much of the oral storytelling tradition has passed. The audience enters into the intimacy of the routine of these characters—stopping by for their morning coffee, checking on the numbers, commenting on the events of the street—just as Sterling Johnson, newly released from prison, breaks into the closed circle of the restaurant and provokes new performances of the stories and debates shared by Memphis and Holloway. . . .

The insistent rhythm of time and mortality pulses through the play. The restaurant is across the street from Lutz's Meat Market and West's Funeral Home—the characters travel between these three primitive sites of slaughter, consumption, and decay. People speculate about the last days of the world. The block the restaurant is on is scheduled to be levelled. West, the undertaker, goes about the ancient rituals of preparing the dead for the afterlife. He is a modern high priest officiating over the ceremonies of grief and valediction. Yet an impulse towards action emerges out of this desolation. Risa, Holloway, Sterling, and Memphis try to find their own ways to envisage a future through consulting prophets and oracles, playing with chance. Wolf, the numbers runner, offers new lives and different endings for the price of a ticket.

Playing the numbers is a way to try to control fate and get enough money to get ahead. There is no logic to the world: getting ahead happens only through a lucky number or a sudden contract. Working, particularly working according to standards imposed by white America, yields up only a slight variant on slavery. The real battle is revealed to be one not of language or attitude but of economics. Wilson tells stories of people inadequately recompensed for the work they've done, legal clauses written so a property owner can be bought out for a fraction of the price he paid, even lottery winnings that are cut in half. The only way to recover what has been lost or stolen is by following the dominant culture's tactics: robbery, burning buildings for insurance, carrying guns to assert power. But these people are arrested and imprisoned for actions that in the marketplace would be considered shrewd business. Wilson's characters are not innocent: they have already tried to make their lives work as the world dictates and lost. Their need to reclaim what has been taken from them, either in actual or symbolic terms—Herald Loomis's lost wife in *Joe Turner's Come and Gone*, the piano bought with a father's blood in *The Piano Lesson*, Memphis' farm—becomes the truest form of revolution and affirmation.

Lisa Wilde. *Theater.* 22 (Fall 1991), pp. 73–74

African American folkloric traditions have taken on many recognizable forms, ranging from the Brer Rabbit and John the Slave trickster tales to the blues, from legends and folktales to spirituals and gospels, from folk beliefs and ghostlore to preaching and folk expressions. Scholars studying such patterns have garnered their categorizations of the lore from a variety of collected sources, such as Zora Neale Hurston's *Mules and Men* and the seven-volume *Frank C. Brown Collection of North Carolina Folklore*. Patterns in the lore reflect patterns in African American history, including strategies for survival, ways of manipulating a hostile Anglo American environment, and a world view that posited the potential for goodness prevailing in spite of the harshness of American racism and the exclusion of blacks from American democracy and the American dream. African American folklore, as Ralph Ellison astutely pointed out, revealed the willingness of blacks to trust their own sense of reality instead of allowing the crucial parts of their existence to be defined by others.

In turning to examine August Wilson's plays and where they fit into this historical conception of African American folklore, it becomes clear that there is overlap as well as extension. Wilson's use of African American folk traditions approximates that of Henry Dumas and Toni Morrison. Certainly, he includes recognizable patterns of the lore in his dramas, but he is also about the business of expanding—within established patterns—what African American folklore means and what it does. Like Dumas and Morrison, he is as much a mythmaker as he is a reflector of the cultural strands of the lore he uses. His conception of "the shiny man" in *Joe Turner's Come and Gone* (1988) will serve to illustrate the point. "The shiny man" is an extranatural guide/seer who leads Bynum, one of the central characters, to discovery of the song that defines his being; his purpose in life, and his relationships with others. While there is no specific "shiny man" who can be documented in Hurston's work or any other collections of African American folklore, there are certainly references to unusual encounters with extra-or supernatural phenomena. Wilson adapts that pattern of human encountering otherworldly being from historical folklore; then, he riffs on the established pattern by naming the phenomenon "the shiny man." In imaginatively expanding traditional forms of the lore, Wilson shares kinship with Morrison, who also takes traditional forms, gives them new shapes, and bends them to her imaginative will throughout her novels. Wilson's creation in *Joe Turner* of "the shiny man" and of powerful songs that define the essence of human significance and his creation in *The Piano Lesson* of a piano that evokes ghostly presences link him to the same creative folkloristic vein as Dumas and Morrison.

The references to "the shiny man" begin Wilson's transformation of traditional supernatural and religious phenomena into African American folkloristic phenomena. Jesus is obviously the supernatural being usually slotted into black folk religious encounters, yet Wilson argues that "the shiny man" serves the same purpose of rebirth or conversion. He will similarly reclaim rituals, such as baptism, for the African American folk tradition, for it is by resorting to rituals informed by their own culture and history that black people can save themselves. Songs, which play a large role in traditional conversion processes, become equally important for Wilson in relocating the power of conversion within Afrocentric forms. The process Wilson employs constantly encourages a rewriting of history and folklore as it relocates religious expectations and patterns firmly within folkloric traditions.

Wilson creates folklore, therefore, that is recognizable even in its surface unfamiliarity. It writes the history of a people tied to the South, to racism and repression, but simultaneously to a strength that transcends those limiting categories. Like Morrison, Wilson encourages a willing suspension of disbelief about the nature of the lore he presents. He does not establish the possibility of the existence of certain phenomena; he simply writes as if they are givens. We might say that his plays begin "in medias res." A world exists; Wilson invites viewers into it. Instead of going to meet the audience by trying to *prove* belief in supernatural phenomena, Wilson unapologetically invites the audience to come into his world, to rise to his level of belief. Wilson's willingness to receive black cultural phenomena into his creative imagination is reflected in his characters' willing immersion in those same traditions and in the power they have to influence audience participation in the worlds in which they live.

Trudier Harris. "August Wilson's Folk Traditions," in *August Wilson: A Case book*, edited by Marilyn Elkins. Garland, 1994

Success in the theatre business—especially on Broadway—hinges upon immediately visible and tangible results; that means large audiences, cash profits, and a production's overall staying power. This being the case, Wilson is undoubtedly a ringing success story. Yet evaluating the product of his dramatic vision is not nearly as simple as counting dollars and cents; something else is needed to describe the full ramifications of Wilson's decade-long efforts in the theatre. Since his project attempts to alter attitudes among black Americans, measuring success in his own terms becomes virtually impossible. One can only observe an audience's reactions or gather individual testimony to assess the impact of his plays.

Having avoided the label of the "one-play playwright" that stigmatized fellow black dramatists such as Ntozake Shange, Charles Fuller, and Joseph Walker, Wilson has set for himself the more long-term goal of putting the importance of culture back onto black America's agenda. In an afterword to *August Wilson: Three Plays*, Paul Carter Harrison observes, "Wilson's plays arguably represent the culmination of political, social, and aesthetic objectives presaged by the Harlem Renaissance in the twenties and the Black Arts Movement of the sixties". Working through the medium of his writing, Wilson advocates cultural pride, responsible action, and self-determination: "I think there are some questions of aesthetics and questions of exactly how writers can contribute to the development of the culture, not contribute to anyone's polemic, not contribute to anyone's idea about what we should not be doing, but to the thing that remains the basis of our culture. This is our culture. How can we contribute? How can we develop it?" (interviewed by the author). In the tradition of collagist Romare Bearden, cultural nationalist Amiri Baraka, novelist Toni Morrison, blues singer Ma Rainey, and poet Sterling Brown, Wilson's history chronicles teem with black cultural referents. Indeed, taken together the seven plays from *Jitney!* to *Seven Guitars* can provide a course in black culture, demonstrating the history of black achievements and setbacks.

The teacher/critic in Wilson is particularly concerned that his work reach a black audience, although his dramatic texts are open to any reader. He attempts to communicate blackness as a positive force whose continued health is linked to blacks reestablishing emotional links with the past, particularly with Africa. He is bothered that Africa and slavery have become sources of pain for some and embarrassment for others. Thus he attempts to represent Africa in his plays as an emotional balm—usually the wiser choice between the frenzy of modern life and the symbolic refuge of the motherland. Wilson is uneasy about widespread cultural apathy among modern blacks. He sees the need for blacks to celebrate Juneteenth, for example, with as much resolve as is shown in commemorating the atrocities of slavery.

As a staunch advocate of sustaining one's cultural ties, Wilson is apprehensive about blacks who cast culture to the wind in favor of assimilation. He argues that political and economic equality in America does not have to mean giving up one's distinct attributes:

"Blacks have been all too willing and anxious to say that we are the same as whites, meaning that we should be treated the same, that we should enjoy the same opportunities in society as whites. That part is fine . . . but blacks are different, and they should be aware of their differences".

Wilson hails cultural differences as sources of pride rather than as evidence of inferiority. He is well aware that black people do things differently from whites and demonstrates in his plays in both subtle and more obvious ways a host of cultural distinctions. Even in the least conspicuous of the daily rituals of blacks, Wilson finds their cultural signature: in the way they decorate their houses, in the way they bury their dead, in the way they talk, in the way they worship, and so on. In each play, he constructs a black world, drawing from as many aspects of the culture as possible: folk customs and beliefs, music, religion, work, language, food, clothing, and so on. Black Ensemble director Jackie Taylor notes, "The African-American community has always struggled to preserve its stories, to reach into history's bag and bring out something accurate and honest. Wilson intensifies that search and brings it to a much larger market".

Wilson's typical play represents an infusion of a number of recognizable signs of blackness peculiar to a particular decade; some are immediately obvious, while others operate on the level of the collective unconscious. For example, in *Joe Turner's Come and Gone*—set some fifty years after slavery—Herald Loomis's frightening vision of bones rising to the water's surface is a not-so-subtle reference to the thousands of slaves captured or bought in Africa who perished during the Middle Passage to America. Similarly the ghost of Robert Sutter in *The Piano Lesson* suggests more than what meets the eye: on one level the white man's ghost demonstrates a long-standing belief among blacks in the supernatural; on another his ghost exemplifies the looming threat of the white power structure. Collectively Wilson's plays provide a veritable museum of black cultural artifacts ranging from the ever-present narrative tradition to the prevalence of the blues aesthetic and the signifying trickster.

By highlighting the black experience, August Wilson's on-going ten-play chronicle challenges the exclusionary tradition of white America's history. Like recreations of history envisioned by Shakespeare, O'Neill, and Fuller, Wilson's project transcends the limitations imposed by past events and sets the black experience within a more positive context. . . .

To suit his dramatic vision, August Wilson alters the motions of history. The mission of this modern-day mythmaker is not so much to assail the wrongs of the past but to bring them into focus to show how African Americans addressed them and emerged from them. So far, in plays set in 1911, 1927, 1936, 1948, 1957, 1969, and 1971, he challenges today's African Americans to see themselves on stage participating in an historical dialectic intended to teach them to avoid the mistakes of previous generations. His plays are to be used as means of communicating and empowering. Despite the seemingly insurmountable odds against characters such as Troy Maxson, Ma Rainey, or Memphis Lee, they endure oppression with relative grace and heroism. The decisions that they make in terms of their private lives may seem controversial, but these choices merely confirm that they are human. Looking past these details and considering the context of their times, one can admire how each stands up to his or her persecutors while continuing to work under near unbearable circumstances. Some, like Troy, die having never realized their life's dream; others, like Memphis and Ma Rainey, thrive financially and gain the respect of their peers for their willingness to confront their oppressors.

However, Wilson's plays do not portray blacks exclusively as victims of racism. Like the Revolutionary Theatre of the 1960s, Wilson's theatre holds racism accountable for lowering the quality of life for black Americans. He de-emphasizes racism, however, as a primary cause for oppression and gives it a less pronounced presence in his work. While Revolutionary Theatre typically featured black men whose warrior spirit manifested itself as the ever-present urge to eradicate white oppression (as well as the oppressor), Wilson peoples his plays with black men and women who grapple with *themselves* within the racist scheme of things. They spend a good deal of their rhetoric and energy reacting to their own unfulfilled lives, their own wrong decisions, their own missed opportunities.

While the plays largely internalize conflict within the characters, Wilson structures them with an unmistakable awareness of the role that racism plays in the black man or black woman's condition. For example, Troy Maxson simmers with discontent about his unfulfilled life. He recognizes how racism has destroyed his dreams of playing professional baseball and how it continues to plague him on his job as a garbage collector. Yet Troy does not address his discontent as, say, a typical LeRoi Jones-style revolutionary hero would. Instead of hurling curses and other threats of bodily harm against whites, Troy handles his frustration on a more personal level and thereby allows a more intimate look at the indirect human costs of racism. To be sure, he confronts his white oppressors without fear, but the resulting promotion from garbage hauler to dump truck driver is hardly a cure-all for other injustices he experiences daily both on and off his job. His despair over the band-aid treatment of his complaints finds its way to the surface in the form of numerous eloquent speeches, a brief wrestling match with his younger son, and an affair with "one of them Florida gals". Likewise, Ma Rainey realizes that she is no better than a prostitute to the white men who essentially steal her singing talent. However, with every fiber of her being she rejects the label "victim." Like Troy she confronts her oppressors at every turn. As a result, she commands and gets respect from them and enjoys a relatively heroic stature. Wilson allows his characters to confront their persecutors, not with intent of bodily harm or annihilation but with an honor that comes with simply knowing the rules of their games.

Sandra Garrett Shannon. *The Dramatic Vision of August Wilson*. Washington: Howard University Press, 1995

The backdrop for Wilson's theater is permeated with images of trains, tracks and roads. "(We) come from all over. Whichever way the road take us that's the way we go," says Loomis in *Joe Turner's Come and Gone*, in effect summarizing the entire experience of the Wilson hero. Railways, and trains in particular, are an obsessive theme in Wilson's work. They are endowed with a voice and an independent will in *The Piano Lesson*, and they figure in the very title of *Two Trains Running*. In *Fences*, references to them are more discreetly limited to songs, but in *Ma Rainey's Black Bottom*, the semantics of railroads penetrate to the heart of impassioned revelry: the lovers groan like the midnight train from Alabama when it crosses the Mason-Dixon Line.

In African American thought, trains are an integral part of everyday life as well as of legend. The means par excellence to flee

the South and to gain freedom in the North, the train embodies hope and even life itself. Nonetheless the idea of flight implies a more general idea of danger, underscored in this instance by the actual history of slaves whose attempts to escape often ended in capture and death. This negative aspect of the train, unquestionably specific to the African American experience, is juxtaposed to the other traditional aspects. As the courser whose speed surpasses human possibilities, the train is a modern equivalent of the mythical Greek horse, an image of man's anxiety faced with the passage of time symbolized by a sudden and thunderous change in death.

This train, charged with life and hope but also with fear and death, cannot help but to impregnate the elements which are contiguous to it with the same ambiguity. This is especially true for images of the road which bear the iron horse on its way. Wilson thus imprints the networks of both railways and highways with undertones which have their origins in several different cultural traditions.

When one of his characters takes the road to hunt down another, the image evoked is that of the spider trapping a prey in its web. This terrifying and destructive spider is the one conceived of by European tradition and calls to mind the tragic Arachnea and the fearsome weavers and spinners of Greek mythology Philomela, Athena and the Fates.

Not surprisingly the role of hunter/spider is often assigned to a white man, most often the sheriff or some other kind of policeman. In Joe Turner's *Come and Gone*, he is successively a slave trader, a hunter of runaway slaves, a smuggler of freed blacks and a carpetbagging informer. But, in *Two Trains Running*, Holloway reminds us that although the railways and roads are owned by European Americans, they were built by African Americans, who as a result know all their secrets. The roles of the hunter and of the hunted can sometimes be reversed as in *The Piano Lesson* where Sutter, a white man, tracks down Boy Charles, an African American, with the intent to kill him. Burned alive, Boy Charles returns to haunt Sutter's footsteps and finally drives him to throw himself down a well. Sutter's ghost then pursues Boy Charles'son, Boy Willie, who once more reverses the roles by attacking the phantom. . . .

Regardless of how the roles are cast, whenever highways and railways form the threads of the web which lead the characters into the presence of death, Arachnea is its spinner.

In the African tradition the spider can be tricky, but it can also be well meaning. Its name is Ananse and he is hybrid. As a spider, he is suspended between heaven and earth. As a human, he lives on the edge of society. One of his principal functions is that of a half-terrestrial, half-celestial guide existing beyond time and human passion. He is the omnipotent and benevolent master of paths and especially of their crossings. He has the power to draw men's steps and to help them pass over even the most difficult of obstacles. As the interpreter of the will of the gods, he can alter men's destinies simply by revealing part of their future to them. Although most often represented as male, Ananse is also sometimes given a female or hermaphroditic form in accordance with his role as the reconciler of opposites. An infirmity often indicates that he belongs partially to the world of the invisible having one leg longer than the other, as he is sometimes described, is a sign that he has one foot on earth

Ananse the spider, as he is known to the Ashanti, is called Elegbara by the Fon and Esu by the Yoruba. Is it any wonder then that the character of the wise man takes on so many different identities in Wilson's work?

Ananse-Elegbara-Esu is presented as Toledo in *Ma Rainey*, Bono in *Fences*, Bynum in *Joe Turner* and Doaker in *Two Trains*. Gabriel in *Fences* and Hambone in *Two Trains*, who are missing part of their brains, are his incarnations as invalid. Aunt Ester in *Two Trains* is a feminine representation. In all cases, age and experience have tempered the passions of these characters; Bono, Toledo and Doaker are over fifty, Bynum probably somewhat older, and Aunt Ester is exactly three hundred forty-nine years old.

In his role as spiritual guide, Ananse is selflessly devoted to the service of others. At the intersections of roads and of tracks, at the points where contradictory emotions clash, the unenlightened characters in Wilson's plays are torn by internal conflicts. The resulting tension is such that they experience a feeling dislocation. This stressful state reaches its extreme with Loomis (*Joe Turner*) who is overwhelmed by a vision of walking bones. At a crossroads, the choice of direction appears on the surface to be a matter of personal preference but has in fact been predetermined by a divergence of cultural imperatives. In *Fences*, Troy finds self-fulfillment impossible with a single woman (perhaps a manifestation of the African tradition of polygamy), but maintaining several households does not fully satisfy him either, and he blames himself for the suffering of his legal wife, the only legitimate one in terms of Western social conventions. . . .

Only the benevolence of the wise man is capable of illuminating these contradictory emotions expressed by the novice. Troy dies after having rejected the advice of Bono by sending Gabriel to an institution. Levee is left alone in his torment because he killed Toledo. On the brink of insanity, Loomis is saved because he listened to Bynum. As the screeching of the rails grows louder with the approach of a train speeding to the switching point where he is waiting, Wining Boy (*The Piano Lesson*) suddenly becomes taller than the looming locomotive. Bynum acquires wisdom and becomes a spiritual guide only after having encountered a turning in the road an apparition whose enormous mouth covers his entire face. The apparition makes him the present of a song and Bynum becomes capable of directing the steps of others towards the discovery of their own internal music.

Mostly grave and serious, Wilson's wise man is also capable of humor and even risqué jollity, reminding us that the role of spiritual guide is only one side of Ananse-Esu-Elegbara, the other side being that of the trickster and mystifier who transgresses all family, social and economic laws. In Africa the trickster appears where least expected, laughingly sowing confusion and perpetrating the most frustrating practical jokes, but always with enough skill, style and humor to insure his pardon. Ananse-the-trickster is selfish and lazy, a liar, a thief and a seducer, but he nonetheless invariably manages to extricate himself from the most hopeless situations. The moral basis for his actions is doubtful at best, but very often has a salutary effect by opening new horizons to his victims, by obliging them to confront the unimaginable, to question their most firmly anchored principles, and thus to progress in their spiritual development.

Whereas this mischievous practical joker is recognized in Africa as an integral part of Ananse-Esu-Elegbara, he seems to lead a life of his own in the US. Having become a purely African American phenomenon and liberated from the principle of the mediation of opposites, the trickster barely resembles except perhaps in his extraordinary verbal skills the wise (and often feminine or handicapped) Esu. Rechristened the Signifying Monkey or Brer Rabbit, this incomparable egotist ceaselessly plays

on his masculinity, his mad audacity and his physical and mental dexterity.

Wilson's hero seems to oscillate between the African Mystifier and the American Signifying Monkey, and the trickster becomes whole only when he accepts the advice of the wise man. In *Fences* and *The Piano Lesson*, the trickster's role is successively given to Troy and to Wining Boy. In *Ma Rainey* and Joe Turner, he appears in the characters of Levee, Jeremy and partially in Loomis. . . .

At the same time, the entire African American world can be contained within an instrument of music. The role played by the piano in *The Piano Lesson* is eloquent in this respect. The Sutters, plantation owners, trade a slave mother and her child for a piano. Her husband, the father of her child, carves likenesses of their faces into the wood of the piano, and one of his sons subsequently steals it from the planter. The son is killed for his crime, but the white assassin himself dies. The young Maretha, the great-granddaughter of the slave couple, is finally the only one who can play this piano which is haunted by the spirits of both African and European Americans. The family's story, contained within the piano, traces the entire history of the African American experience: the cruelty of slavery, the wanton murders following abolition, the rebellions, the knitting of family and community relations through artistic endeavor, the desire to reappropriate one's own history. . . .

Even though all of the characters in Wilson's drama are not blessed with Maretha's musical gifts or Ma Rainey's talent, each carries within in him a song; a song which is simultaneously collective and individual. Bynum's father has one which heals the sick, Bynum's song (his name is a contraction of bind them) brings together those elements that need to be united. Bynum, just like glue, sticks together not only members of the families but also diverse facets of people's spirituality.

His song is the identifying mark of the African American and the discovery of this internal music is the object of each character's quest. A fellow forget that (his song) and he forget who he is, states Bynum. Once again, music seems to be a manifestation of the Yoruba Esu; Anybody who does not have an Esu in his body cannot exist, even to know that he is alive . . . individual Esu is an immense power to be summoned, a medicine of supernatural power. The importance of the relationship between African American music and the sacred does not go unnoticed by Wilson. The planter, Joe Turner, captures Loomis for the express purpose of stealing his song; Ma Rainey is afraid of entrusting her voice to the radio; Berniece (*The Piano Lesson*) refuses to sell her piano to a white person, and the pastor in *Ma Rainey* must be forced to dance for hoodlums.

These particular characters are striving to preserve the sacredness of their music. Others, it is true, could scarcely care less: Levee, Troy, Jeremy and Boy Willie would eagerly sell their souls and their music to the highest bidder. But even if they have forsaken Esu, he has not forgotten them. The walking blues is also Esu.

Alice Mills. *Black Scholar*. 25, 2 (Spring 1995), pp. 30–5

## BIBLIOGRAPHY

*The Homecoming*, 1979; *The Coldest Day of the Year*, 1979; *Fullerton Street*, 1980; *Black Bart and the Sacred Hills*, 1981; *Jitney*, 1982; *The Mill Hand's Lunch Bucket*, 1983; *Ma Rainey's*

*Black Bottom*, 1984; *Fences*, 1985; *Joe Turner's Come and Gone*, 1986; *The Piano Lesson*, 1987; *Two Trains Running*, 1990; *Seven Guitars*, 1995

# WRIGHT, Richard (1908–1960)

**United States**

[*Uncle Tom's Children*] is a book about hatreds. Mr. Wright serves notice by his title that he speaks of people in revolt, and his stories are so grim that the Dismal Swamp of race hatred must be where they live. Not one act of understanding and sympathy comes to pass in the entire work.

But some bright new lines to remember come flashing from the author's pen. Some of his sentences have the shocking-power of a fortyfour. That means that he knows his way around among words. With his facility, one wonders what he would have done had he dealt with plots that touched the broader and more fundamental phases of Negro life instead of confining himself to the spectacular. For, though he has handled himself well, numerous Negro writers, published and unpublished, have written of this same kind of incident. It is the favorite Negro theme just as how the stenographer or some other poor girl won the boss or the boss's son is the favorite white theme. What is new in the four novelettes included in Mr. Wright's book is the wish-fulfillment theme. In each story the hero suffers but he gets his man.

In the first story, ''Big Boy Leaves Home,'' the hero, Big Boy, takes the gun away from a white soldier after he has shot two of his chums and kills the white man. . . . In the other three stories the reader sees the picture of the South that the communists have been passing around of late. A dismal, hopeless section ruled by brutish hatred and nothing else. Mr. Wright's author's solution, is the solution of the PARTY—state responsibility for everything and individual responsibility for nothing, not even feeding one's self. And march!

Since the author himself is a Negro, his dialect is a puzzling thing. One wonders how he arrived at it. Certainly he does not write by ear unless he is tone-deaf. But aside from the broken speech of his characters, the book contains some beautiful writing. One hopes that Mr. Wright will find in Negro life a vehicle for his talents.

Zora Neale Hurston. *Saturday Review.* April 2, 1938, p. 32

*Uncle Tom's Children* has its full share of violence and brutality; violent deaths occur in three stories and the mob goes to work in all four. Violence has long been an important element in fiction about Negroes, just as it is in their life. But where Julia Peterkin in her pastorals and Roark Bradford in his levee farces show violence to be the reaction of primitives unadjusted to modern civilization, Richard Wright shows it as the way in which civilization keeps the Negro in his place. And he knows what he is writing about.

Some of the tragedies may seem too coincidentally contrived, may seem to concentrate too much upon the victims, but the book has its great importance in spite of this. The essential quality of certain phases of Negro life in the South is handled here vigorously, authentically, and with flashes of genuine poetry. Here are characters seen from the inside: Big Boy, alert, full of animal spirits,

suddenly turned into a hounded fugitive; the perplexed preacher with a stake in keeping quiet and orderly, and a bitter knowledge of what his people suffer; the farmer who has labored for a home that a white man casually disrupts. In these little shacks, overburdened with poverty, the first mention of trouble with the white folks brings paralyzed fear and a conniving that is pitifully feeble. The people show a wisdom brewed of suffering, not the artless philosophy endeared to Southern mythologists. And finally there are those who are not only aware of what is being done to them but determined to do something about it, resolutely muttering: ''Ah'll go ef the nex' one goes!'' and ''Ah ain' got but *one* time t'die.'' The South that Mr. Wright renders so vividly is recognizable and true, and it has not often been within the covers of a book.

Sterling A. Brown. *Nation.* April 16, 1938, p. 448

The skeleton of [*Native Son*] can be found in the police records of Chicago. The art of this novelist breathes upon the dead bones: they quicken, become flesh and blood, and indict our civilization. . . .

Bigger Thomas suggests Dmitry Karamazov in [Dostoyevski's] *The Brothers Karamazov* and Clyde Griffiths in [Dreiser's] *An American Tragedy*. Dmitry and Clyde and Bigger are bungled jobs from the mangled hand of Society the Potter. Wright's business with Bigger approximates a Shakespearean obsession. In his haste to get at the centrality of Bigger's reactions, he leaves the black cosmos of the South Side amorphous; minor characters, without physical differentiae and psychological entity, scarcely emerge from the shadows. Dreiser, with bedeviling assiduity, draws the details of character and environment; his story goes forward like a huge, prehistoric animal in labor. Antithetically, as Bigger moves through crescendos of violence and hysteria to a vitalizing sense of release and affirmation of life, his creator is sucked by the immediacy of the things that Bigger sees and hears and feels. Wright's is a midnight nether-world where diagnostics of character and environment gain essentiality only as they affect Bigger. From a Marxian *bema* in the lower depths Bigger's lawyer hurls nitroglycerin philippics at Society the Potter. Mr. Max plays the role of a dialectic Edgar Bergen to Bigger's fated Charlie McCarthy.

A study of the artistic styles of Hemingway and Wright reveals illuminatingly antipodal contrasts. Hemingway's characters are exteriorized; Wright's, interiorized. The works of both contain an almost Nietzschean flair for the accents of violence, ''the hideous trampling march of lust and disease, brutality and death.'' Hemingway's uncerebral characters act; Wright's not only act but try to put together the jigsaw-puzzle reasons for their actions. Essentially, the approach of Hemingway is that of the behaviorist; that of Wright, the psycho-analyst. Thus Wright places upon himself a heavier artistic burden, since he is unwilling to let dialogue and action be the *raison d'être* of his characters. In this he is like the recent Steinbeck.

M.B. Tolson. *Modern Quarterly.* Winter 1939, pp. 22–24

Year by year, we have been noticing the rising tide of realism, with its accompanying boon of social honesty and artistic integrity. . . . It is to Richard Wright's everlasting credit to have hung the portrait of Bigger Thomas alongside in this gallery of stark contemporary realism. There was artistic courage and integrity of the first order in his decision to ignore both the squeamishness of the Negro minority and the deprecating bias of the prejudiced majority, full knowing that one side would like to ignore the fact that there are other Negroes like Bigger and the other like to think that Bigger is the prototype of all. Eventually, of course, this must involve the clarifying recognition that there is no one type of Negro, and that Bigger's type has the right to its day in the literary calendar, not only for what it might add in its own right to Negro portraiture, but for what it could say about America.

In fact Wright's portrait of Bigger Thomas says more about America than it does about the Negro, for he is the native son of the black city ghetto, with its tensions, frustrations and resentments. The brunt of the action and the tragedy involves social forces rather than persons; it is in the first instance a Zolaesque *J'accuse* pointing to the danger symptoms of a self-frustrating democracy. Warping prejudice, short-sighted exploitation, impotent philanthropy, aggravating sympathy, inconsistent human relations, doctrinaire reform, equally impotent punishment stand behind the figures of Bigger, the Daltons, Mary, Jan and Max, as the real protagonists of the conflict. This is timely and incisive analysis of the core dilemmas of the situation of race and American democracy. Indeed in the present crisis, the social import of *Native Son*, with its bold warnings and its clear lessons, temporarily overshadows its artistic significance. Its vivid and vital revelations should be a considerable factor in awakening a social sense and conscience willing at last, after much evasion and self-deception, to face the basic issues realistically and constructively.

Alain Locke. *Opportunity*. January 1941, pp. 4–5

The vogue of such a novel as Richard Wright's *Native Son* may suggest that the novel of "social significance" had at last entered into the thinking of the middle class, that the people who read it with bated breath or applauded it on the stage felt a deep compassion for, and even some solidarity with, the oppressed Negro masses; but that is an illusion. It is precisely because Wright himself was so passionately honest and desired to represent the sufferings of his race as forcefully as possible that the unconscious slickness of *Native Son*, its manipulation of terror in a period fascinated by terror, seems so sinister. For Wright was only the child of his generation, and his resources no different in kind from the resources of naturalism and the left-wing conception of life and literature to which, like many Negro writers, he surrendered his thinking because of the general indifference or hostility to Negroes and Negro writing. If he chose to write the story of Bigger Thomas as a grotesque crime story, it is because his own indignation and the sickness of the age combined to make him dependent on violence and shock, to astonish the reader by torrential scenes of cruelty, hunger, rape, murder, and flight and then enlighten him by crude Stalinist homilies. Bigger Thomas "found" himself in jail as Wright "found" himself, after much personal suffering and confusion, in the Communist party; what did it matter that Bigger's self-discovery was mechanical and unconvincing, or that Wright— from the highest possible motives—had written "one of those books in which everything is undertaken with seriousness except the writing" [R.P. Blackmur]?

Alfred Kazin. *On Native Grounds* (New York: Harcourt, Brace, 1942), pp. 386–87

In the South the sensibilities of both blacks and whites are inhibited by the rigidly defined environment. For the Negro there is relative safety as long as the impulse toward individuality is suppressed. (Lynchings have occurred because Negroes painted their homes.) . . . The pre-individualistic black community discourages individuality out of self-defense. Having learned through experience that the whole group is punished for the actions of the single member, it has worked out efficient techniques of behavior control. . . .

Within the ambit of the black family this takes the form of training the child away from curiosity and adventure, against reaching out for those activities lying beyond the borders of the black community. And when the child resists, the parent discourages him; first with the formula, "That there's for white folks. Colored can't have it," and finally with a beating.

It is not, then, the family and communal violence described by *Black Boy* that is unusual, but that Wright *recognized* and made no peace with its essential cruelty. . . .

Nowhere in America today is there social or political action based upon the solid realities of Negro life depicted in *Black Boy*; perhaps that is why, with its refusal to offer solutions, it is like the blues. Yet in it thousands of Negroes will for the first time see their destiny in public print. Freed here of fear and the threat of violence, their lives have at last been organized, scaled down to possessable proportions. And in this lies Wright's most important achievement: He has converted the American Negro impulse toward self-annihilation and "going-under-ground" into a will to confront the world, to evaluate his experience honestly and throw his findings unashamedly into the guilty conscience of America. [Summer, 1945]

Ralph Ellison. *Shadow and Act* (New York: Random House, 1964), pp. 89–91, 94

*Black Boy*, the story of his own youth in the South by Richard Wright, the enormously talented young Negro who also wrote *Native Son*, has been greeted by several placidly busy white reviewers and by a couple of agitated Negro reviewers as betraying too much "emotion," too much "bitterness."

Now this is the story of a colored boy who, just yesterday, found in his native community not merely that he was penalized for having the same qualities that in a white boy would have warmed his neighbors to universal praise—the qualities of courage, energy, curiosity, refusal to be subservient, the impulse to record life in words—but that he was in danger of disapproval, then of beatings, then of being killed, for these qualities, for being "uppity." Not bitterness but fear charges the book, and how this young crusader can be expected to look back only a few years to the quiet torture with anything except hatred is beyond me.

When we have a successful comedy by an ex-prisoner about the kindness and humor of the warders in a German concentration camp, then I shall expect Mr. Wright to mellow and to speak amiably of the teachers who flattened him, his colored neighbors and relatives who denounced him, the merchants who cheated him, the white fellow-mechanics who threatened him for wanting to learn their skills, and the librarian who suspected him—quite rightly—of reading that militant and bewhiskered Bolshevik, that polluter of temples and Chambers of Commerce, Comrade H.L. Mencken.

Sinclair Lewis. *Esquire*. June 1945, p. 76

There is another book which should be taken off the book racks of the Nation; it should be removed from the book stores; its sale should be stopped. It is the recent book of the month, which has had such a great sale. Senators can understand why it has had such a sale if they will read it. It is entitled *Black Boy* by Richard Wright. Richard Wright is a Mississippian. He was born and reared near Natchez, Miss. He went from Natchez to Jackson, from Jackson to Memphis, from Memphis to Chicago, and from Chicago to Brooklyn, N.Y., where he is married to a white woman and is living happily, he says. He wrote the book *Black Boy* ostensibly as the story of his life. Actually it is a damnable lie from beginning to end. It is practically all fiction. There is just enough truth to it to enable him to build his fabulous lies about his experiences in the South and his description of the people of the South and the culture, education, and life of the southern people.

The purpose of the book is to plant the seeds of hate in every Negro in America against the white men of the South or against the white race anywhere, for that matter. That is the purpose. Its purpose is to plant the seeds of devilment and trouble-breeding in the days to come in the mind and heart of every American Negro. Read the book if you do not believe what I am telling you. It is the dirtiest, filthiest, lousiest, most obscene piece of writing that I have ever seen in print. I would hate to have a son or daughter of mine be permitted to read it; it is so filthy and so dirty. But it comes from a Negro, and you cannot expect any better from a person of his type.

Senator Theodore Bilbo [of Mississippi]. *Congressional Record—Senate.* June 27, 1945, p. 6808

To whom does Richard Wright address himself? Certainly not to the universal man. The essential characteristic of the notion of the universal man is that he is not involved in any particular age, and that he is no more and no less moved by the lot of the negroes of Louisiana than by that of the Roman slaves in the time of Spartacus. The universal man can think of nothing but universal values. He is a pure and abstract affirmation of the inalienable right of man. But neither can Wright think of intending his books for the white racists of Virginia or South Carolina whose minds are made up in advance and who will not open them. Nor to the black peasants of the bayous who can not read. And if he seems to be happy about the reception his books have had in Europe, still it is obvious that at the beginning he had not the slightest idea of writing for the European public. Europe is far away. Its indignation is ineffectual and hypocritical. Not much is to be expected from the nations which have enslaved the Indies, Indo-China, and negro Africa. These considerations are enough to define his readers. He is addressing himself to the cultivated negroes of the North and the white Americans of good-will (intellectuals, democrats of the left, radicals, C.I.O. workers). . . .

Each work of Wright contains what Baudelaire would have called ''a double simultaneous postulation''; each word refers to two contexts; two forces are applied simultaneously to each phrase and determine the incomparable tension of his tale. Had he spoken to the whites alone, he might have turned out to be more prolix, more didactic, and more abusive; to the negroes alone, still more elliptical, more of a confederate, and more elegiac. In the first case, his work might have come close to satire; in the second, to prophetic lamentations. Jeremiah spoke only to the Jews. But Wright, a writer for a split public, has been able both to maintain

and go beyond this split. He has made it the pretext for a work of art. [March, 1947]

Jean-Paul Sartre. *What Is Literature?* (New York: Harper & Row, 1965), pp. 72, 74

A writer of brutal power, scornful alike of Bohemianism and finicky art, Wright still stands as the most typical as well as the most famous example of the depression-bred WPA writer. To begin with, he was angry and resentful. He was poor, kicked-around and discriminated against, and he hated it. When he was finally given a turn at a typewriter in the offices of the Illinois Writers' Project on Erie Street, he was so steamed up he immediately began turning out rugged, fighting poems and thudding, belly-punching stories between project assignments. His aim was to tear the living hearts out of his gasping readers, not even allowing them, as he later admitted, ''the consolation of tears.'' And he came pretty close to accomplishing it. A couple of years later a group of these stories won him a prize in a competition open to all U.S. writers on WPA, led to his first book *Uncle Tom's Children* and launched the most impressive literary career yet achieved by a Negro American.

Arna Bontemps. *Negro Digest.* June 1950, pp. 44–45

The idea of Bigger's monstrosity [in *Native Son*] can be presented without fear of contradiction, since no American has the knowledge or authority to contest it and no Negro has the voice. It is an idea, which, in the framework of the novel, is dignified by the possibility it promptly affords of presenting Bigger as the herald of disaster, the danger signal of a more bitter time to come when not Bigger alone but all his kindred will rise, in the name of the many thousands who have perished in fire and flood and by rope and torture, to demand their rightful vengeance.

But it is not quite fair, it seems to me, to exploit the national innocence in this way. The idea of Bigger as a warning boomerangs not only because it is quite beyond the limit of probability that Negroes in America will ever achieve the means of wreaking vengeance upon the state but also because it cannot be said that they have any desire to do so. . . .

Negroes are Americans and their destiny is the country's destiny. They have no other experience besides their experience on this continent and it is an experience which cannot be rejected, which yet remains to be embraced. If, as I believe, no American Negro exists who does not have his private Bigger Thomas living in the skull, then what most significantly fails to be illuminated here is the paradoxical adjustment which is perpetually made, the Negro being compelled to accept the fact that this dark and dangerous and unloved stranger is part of himself forever. [Nov.-Dec., 1951]

James Baldwin. *Notes of a Native Son* (Boston: Beacon, 1955), pp. 41–42

Richard Wright's new book, *The Outsider* . . . is something very close to a Dostoevskian novel. Lonely, puzzled but constantly brooding, warm-hearted but impelled into savage hostilities, his hero lives and dies as a rebel against traditional morality, against social distinctions and divisions, against friendship and love, against organized law and organized rebellion, and against relig-ion. His aim is to be free. He becomes an anarchic individualist. To all who love him and many who hate him he brings suffering and death; he dies alone, yet still not free, tormented by solitude and remorse. It is a moving story, for the most part expertly told. America (particularly colored America) is full of these lonesome wanderers, sad and dangerous men. Faulkner created another of them, the hero of *Light in August*; and we remember the book that opens ''Call me Ishmael.''

Still, the novel has one major defect. . . . His hero (when we meet him first) is a distracted, debt-ridden, heavy-drinking, lustful postal clerk, desperate to escape from the disasters his own lack of self-control has brought upon him. When the opportunity of escape is created by a terrible accident, he seizes it with astonishment and relief and goes on his way, killing and dodging like a rat caught in a henroost. We watch his agonies with understanding and even with sympathy, wishing he would sober up and straighten out; but when—only a week or two later—he emerges as a cool philosopher with his head full of Nietzsche and the answers to Lenin, we find the transition impossible to believe. It looks, in fact, as though Mr. Wright had written two different tales and then tried to blend them: one, the story of a poor incontinent man haunted by drink and desire until he would welcome any disaster as a relief; the other, an account of the adventures of a dispassionate intellectual who was educated into violence by the brutality and treachery of the Communist party until he revolted against it and became an existentialist. Both men are solitary and rebellious; the same man could have led both lives; but not in the same short space of time.

Gilbert Highet. *Harper.* May 1953, pp. 96, 98

Wright's heavy-handed, morose approach to everything racial is the exact antithesis of his original sponsor in France, the late Gertrude Stein, who arranged with the French government official-ly to invite him to France, when he had trouble getting an American passport. I met the famed American author in her Paris flat several years before her death and we talked at length about Wright, who she told me was ''without question the best master of English prose in America since myself. That's fairly high praise coming from me.''. . .

She had never heard of Wright until her return to Paris after its liberation from the Nazis. Her books *Wars I Have Seen* was published soon after that, and among the reviews she saw was a laudatory one by Wright in *PM*. Asking a G.I. friend who this admirer of hers was, she was given a copy of *Black Boy* from the Army library.

''I was very excited and wrote for the rest of his stuff,'' she told me. ''I found Wright was the best American writer today. Only one or two creative writers like him come along in a generation. Every time he says something it is a distinct revelation.''

Ben Burns. *Reporter.* March 8, 1956, pp. 22–23

I thought of Richard Wright, with whom I had had breakfast that morning [in 1953]. This was his first visit to any part of Africa and he seemed to find it bewildering. . . .

What Wright did not understand, what his whole background and training had made difficult for him to understand, was that being black did not of itself qualify one for acceptance in tribal

Africa. But how could he, when there are thousands of urban-bred Africans up and down the vast continent who do not themselves understand this? The more perceptive of the urban Africans are only now beginning to comprehend, but slowly. . . .

Richard Wright was surprised that even educated Africans, racially conscious literate people, had not heard of him and were skeptical of a grown man earning his living by writing. They could not understand what kind of writing brought a man enough money to support a family. Wright really wanted to understand the African, but—''I found the African an oblique, a hard-to-know man.''

My sympathies were all with Wright.

Peter Abrahams. *Holiday.* April, 1959, p. 75

When I saw Richard Wright at his apartment in Paris three days before he died, he did not look ill. He looked perfectly all right—except that it appeared he was freshly laid out for dead. I had not seen Wright for many years. When I rang his doorbell, his charming teen-age daughter, Julia, said, ''Daddy is in the bed-room,'' and she escorted me there. The foot of the bed faced the door. Fully clothed in a gray suit and tie, but two-thirds covered by a quilt, Wright lay all dressed up flat on his back on the bed. The effect was startling—as if he were on a bier. I stopped short in the door. Without thinking, my words came out even before I greeted him. ''Man,'' I said, ''you look like you are ready to go to glory!''

We both laughed as Wright, while we shook hands, explained to me he was waiting for a car to come at any moment to take him to the hospital, that was why he already had his jacket and tie on. Periodically, he said, he needed routine treatments for an old stomach ailment he had picked up in Africa. He felt fine, he told me as he offered me a cigarette, except that he had been unable to eat anything much for three days. The medicine he had taken, he grinned, upset him worse than the ailment. As he talked, he seemed and looked very much like the young Dick Wright I had known in Chicago before he became famous—vigorous, questioning, very much alive, and with a big warm smile. He wanted to know the happenings in the states. ''How is Harlem these days? I'd like to see it again.''. . .

Three days later in London, I learned that Richard Wright was dead. I was his last visitor at home.

Langston Hughes. *Ebony.* February 1961, p. 94

In *Native Son* Richard Wright jolted the American literary scene with Bigger Thomas, a hapless, bitter, damned, ignorant, brutal, ghetto-condemned black Negro, who would have whipped half to death any one of Hemingway's soldiers and he-men on a southside Chicago street corner. Bigger was not romantic like Queequeg in *Moby Dick*, nor was he legendary like John Henry. He was no Stepin Fetchit or Mantan Moreland. He was none of the shadow, soft and unobtrusive, mysterious, that we find in our literature. He was a Negro that few white people ever believed they would meet face to face, and yet, they faced him every day. He was real.

If Theodore Dreiser took his place in American literature by telling us of the damned relationship between American love and the American dollar in *An American Tragedy*; if Upton Sinclair and Frank Norris achieved their positions by giving us the first full-blown stink of the bottomside of capitalism in *The Jungle* and *The Pit*; if Sinclair Lewis could name the emptiness of America *Babbit*;

then Richard Wright deserves a place beside them because he gave us a stunning view of the economic and spiritual poverty of millions of people. He deserves to be included among the American authors college students find in their literature books because he brought an entirely new dimension to American letters—a dimension that we have come to accept, after so long a time, as real.

John A. Williams. Introduction to Richard Wright, *White Man, Listen*! (Garden City, New York: Doubleday, 1964), pp. x-xi

Of all black American novelists, and indeed of all American novelists of any hue, Richard Wright reigns supreme for his profound political, economic, and social reference. Wright had the ability, like Dreiser, of harnessing the gigantic, overwhelming environmental forces and focusing them, with pinpoint sharpness, on individuals and their acts as they are caught up in the whirlwind of the savage, anarchistic sweep of life, love, death, and hate, pain, hope, pleasure, and despair across the face of a nation and the world. . . . Wright's forte, it seems to me, was in reflecting the intricate mechanisms of a social organization, its functioning as a unit. [1967]

Eldridge Cleaver. *Soul on Ice* (New York: McGraw-Hill, 1968), pp. 108–9

Richard differed from the [French] existentialists in that they understood modern life through philosophical contemplation. In the black American fear led to dread, then anger, then self-hatred and ended in a sense of emptiness and meaninglessness—the ennui and malaise of Sartre's characters. But it was more than philosophy to the black man; it was life itself. He knew that his own unbearable times of futility arose when he was confronted by the abysmal ignorance and stupidity of the white man who could not understand what a Negro was saying. And his preoccupation with self-hate and anguish was an examination of a reality, not philosophy. . . .

*The Outsider* despaired that white Americans could liberate themselves from their fears, panic and terror when they confronted black men striving for liberation from irrational ties. Cross Damon, an intellectual black man, awakened in a society which could not contain such a giant. In an immoral society, a man conditioned, shaped and molded by that society attempted to form his own morality and failed.

Perhaps we should define freedom negatively, by showing what it is not, Richard had told Jean-Paul Sartre. And the anti-hero of *The Outsider*, a rebel without a set of values, finds an uncreative freedom because it is in a vacuum. Richard used elements from existentialist thought, picked up the philosophy as if it were a dark coat, plucked out the threads he needed and then threw it aside. Just like the French existentialists Richard knew, Damon was driven by an emotional compulsion, religious in its intensity, to feel and weigh the worth of himself. He longed for an experience deeply felt enough to remove or transform his eternal sense of dread. But at the edge of doom Damon drew back and repudiated a dead-end philosophy. Struggling to still an exploding ball of fire that leaped white-hot in his chest, he warned: the search cannot be done alone; never alone; alone a man was nothing. A bridge between man and

man had to be made. Tell others not to come down this road, he forced through dying lips.

Constance Webb. *Richard Wright: A Biography* (New York: G.P. Putnam's Sons, 1968), pp. 280, 310

*Lawd Today*, Richard Wright's first novel (published posthumously in 1963), is in some ways more sophisticated than his second, the more sensational *Native Son*, which established his popularity, and to a large extent his reputation. It is ironic that this should be so in view of the fact that *Native Son* has subsequently come to be regarded as a brilliant but erratic work by an author who was perhaps ignorant of modern experimental techniques in prose fiction. For had *Lawd Today* been published when Wright completed it, such an impression might never have gained acceptance.

If the novel reveals anything about its author, it indicates that Wright had learned his Joyce, his Dos Passos, his James T. Farrell, his Gertrude Stein only too well. It is not that *Lawd Today* is a hodgepodge of the styles of the above authors—actually, Wright is usually in good control of his material—but that Wright here appears as much interested in craftsmanship, form and technique, as he is in making explicit social comment. Indeed, social comment derives from the way Wright structures the novel—twenty-four hours in the life of a Negro postal worker—and the theme does not confine itself to Negro oppression but says something about the very quality of life in urban America. Moreover, Wright uses here for the first time a Negro anti-hero: Jake Jackson is a loutish, heavy-handed, narrow, frustrated, and prejudiced petit bourgeois who, though unable to cope with his environment, refuses to reject it—and is incapable of dreaming of a life different from the kind he knows. Yet, for all his limitations, Wright invests him with a sense of life that simmers just below the surface of his dreary existence.

Here then lies the crux of Wright's success, for despite the huge indebtedness to other modern authors, the book is distinctly Wright's and the life and times he evokes are as immediate and as crushingly felt as his more popular radical fiction.

Edward Margolies. *The Art of Richard Wright* (Carbondale: Southern Illinois University Press, 1969), pp. 90–91

There was a brief, wonderful trip to Paris in 1946, a return to New York in November, and in the following July the Wrights returned to Paris for good. . . .

The native son, the black boy from Mississippi, spent the rest of his life as an adopted citizen of France. And the work in exile, book after book, was voluminous. But as he sent these new books back across the seas, critics began to feel that the serenity he had chosen for himself had severely damaged his writing. While the man was surviving in peace, the tight hard center of the talent was getting unwound. If there are no second acts in the dramas of American writers' lives, the work of Richard Wright in France seemed to prove the rule in his case. Reviewing *The Long Dream* for the New York *Times* (October 26, 1958), Saunders Redding would speak of Wright as if he were already dead, calling (rather cruelly) in the last line: ''Come back, Dick Wright, to life again!''. . .

Robert A. Bone has said that the last novel in exile, *The Long Dream*, is ''a still more disastrous performance'' than *The Outsider*. It is a strange verdict; while *The Long Dream* is a retreat to old ground, it is ground Wright knows well and can cover with considerable authority. . . .

The novel is a *Bildungsroman*, the story of a black boy's gradual discovery of what the Southern community means and the illness that it endures. If that is its strength, it was essentially the same strength of *Black Boy. The Long Dream* does not really take us into any new territory; it re-establishes Wright's claim to the old. . . .

The trouble with the new version was that it was not so cleanly written a book as was *Black Boy*, nor is it so consistently alert in its moral attention; Fishbelly's story is overlong, full of speeches, infected with Wright's late tendency to insert pat Freudian symbols, where too often the characters suddenly blurt into spokesmen for the author's message. Where it is good, *The Long Dream* is very good, conveying the harsh dirty world of the South as a surrealistic nightmare, yet Wright is not altogether sure of himself, and pads the narrative, falls into old errors.

> Dan McCall. *The Example of Richard Wright* (New York: Harcourt Brace Jovanovich, 1969), pp. 138, 140, 155, 159–60

During the first week in June, 1938, I received in rapid succession two airmail special delivery letters. I answered one at once but before he could receive my answer he wrote again in great excitement. He said, "I have just learned of a case in Chicago that has broken there and is exactly like the story I am starting to write. See if you can get the newspaper clippings and send them to me." The case was that of a young black boy named Nixon who had been accused of rape, and when the police captured him they forced a confession of five major crimes, of which rape was only one.

I went at once to the offices of the five daily Chicago newspapers to get all the back issues; and I began what lasted a year, sending Wright every clipping published in the newspapers on the Nixon case. Frankly, there were times when the clippings were so lurid I recoiled from the headlines, and the details in the stories were worse. They called Nixon a big black baboon. When I went into news offices or bought papers on the stands, I listened to jeers and ugly insults about all black people. . . .

[In November] Wright explained a little about the new book and told about the clippings. He said he had enough to spread all over his nine by twelve bedroom floor and he was using them in the same way Dreiser had done in *An American Tragedy*. He would spread them all out and read them over and over again and then take off from there in his own imagination. The major portion of *Native Son* is built on information and action of those clippings. . . .

We went to the Library and checked out on my library card two books we found on the Loeb-Leopold case and on Clarence Darrow, their lawyer. The lawyer's defense of Bigger in *Native Son* was modeled after Darrow's defense. Wright was so long sending those books back that I wrote him a hot letter reminding him that I had not borrowed those books permanently! He finished the book early in the Spring of 1939 and he wrote that he had never worked so hard before in all his life.

> Margaret Walker Alexander. In David Ray and Robert M. Farnsworth, eds., *Richard Wright: Impressions and Perspectives* (Ann Arbor: University of Michigan Press, 1973), pp. 58–61

Like the period 1947–52, the last years of Wright's life could have merely corresponded to a pessimistic phase. His close friends and relatives all testify that he did not at the time suffer from even the slightest mental illness, and his work is certainly confirmation of this. The evidence, in fact, betrays nothing more than intense physical exhaustion due to recurring disease, combined with a nervous reaction to the numerous "slings and arrows of outrageous fortune." Wright's heart attack, then, can be characterized as an indirect consequence of the tensions which he suffered throughout his life, as well as the more immediate result of his recent illness and anxiety, and was not hastened or heralded by any sort of mental derangement.

Answering this last question is important in evaluating Wright's literary career because it enables us to consider whether, as some American critics claim, Wright's death may be interpreted as the natural conclusion to a period of artistic decline due to his living abroad, or, rather, as the abrupt interruption of a cyclic process of development. Even admitting that the best of Wright's fiction was written in the early forties, I am in favor of the second interpretation and would rather say that death caught him in a period of evolution. . . .

It seems unfair, therefore, to limit Wright's literary achievements to two books just because critics are right in hailing them as his best. *Black Boy* and *Native Son* do not represent the extent of Wright's accomplishment and critics should beware of claiming that Wright could never find literary salvation outside of the Old South and the ghetto.

> Michel Fabre. *The Unfinished Quest of Richard Wright* (New York: William Morrow, 1973), pp. 525, 527

Like the autobiographies of Gertrude Stein and Sherwood Anderson, Richard Wright's *Black Boy*, published in 1945, has confused readers because of its generic ambiguity. For many readers, the book is particularly honest, sincere, open, convincing, and accurate. But for others, *Black Boy* leaves a feeling of inauthenticity, a sense that the story or its author is not to be trusted. These conflicting reactions are best illustrated by the following representative observations by Ralph K. White and W. E. B. Du Bois. White, a psychologist, has identified [in *Black Boy*] "ruthless honesty" as "the outstanding quality which made the book not only moving but also intellectually satisfying." But Du Bois notes [in "Richard Wright Looks Back"] that although "nothing that Richard Wright says is in itself unbelievable or impossible; it is the total picture that is not convincing." Attempting to reconcile these opposing views, I wish to argue that both sides are correct; that the book is an especially truthful account of the black experience in America, even though the protagonist's story often does not ring true; and that this inability to tell the truth is Wright's major metaphor of self. A repeated pattern of misrepresentation becomes the author's way of making us believe that his personality, his family, his race—his whole childhood and youth—conspired to prevent him from hearing the truth, speaking the truth, or even being believed unless he lied.

For most readers, worries about *Black Boy's* trustworthiness stem from questions of genre. Although the book was clearly not called "The Autobiography of Richard Wright," its subtitle—"A Record of Childhood and Youth"—does suggest autobiography with some claim to documentary accuracy. The following descriptions of Black Boy reflect the confusion of readers: biography, autobiographical story, fictionalized biography, masterpiece of romanced facts, sort of autobiography, pseudoautobiography, part-fiction/part-truth autobiography, autobiography with the quality of fiction, and case history. . . .

Although Wright seemed unsure of his book's generic identity, he never referred to *Black Boy* as autobiography. His original title, *American Hunger*, later used for the portion of his life story that began after leaving Memphis for Chicago, came after he had rejected *The Empty Box, Days of Famine. The Empty Houses, The Assassin, Bread and Water*, and *Black Confession*, all of which sound like titles for novels. When his literary agent suggested the subtitle ''The Biography of a Courageous Negro,'' Wright responded with ''The Biography of an American Negro,'' then with eight other possibilities including ''Coming of Age in the Black South,'' ''A Record in Anguish,'' ''A Study in Anguish,'' and ''A Chronicle of Anxiety.'' Such titles indicate his feeling that the book he had written was less personal, more documentary—a study, a record, a chronicle, or even a biography—than autobiography. Constance Webb reports [in *Richard Wright*] that Wright was uneasy with the word autobiography, both because of ''an inner distaste for revealing in first person instead of through a fictitious character the dread and life'' and because he realized that he would write his story using ''portions of his own childhood, stories told him by friends, things he had observed happening to others,'' and fictional techniques.

Although some readers believe Wright gave in to the ''strong desire to alter facts'' and ''to dress up'' his feelings, the book's tendency to intermix fiction and facts is clearly part of both Wright's personal literary history and the Afro-American literary tradition in which he was writing. The form of *Black Boy* in part imitates the traditional slave narrative, a literary type that allowed for a high degree of fictionality in the cause of abolition. A number of major works of literature by black Americans, such as Du Bois's *The Souls of Black Folks*, Toomer's *Cane*, and Johnson's *The Autobiography of an Ex-Coloured Man*, feature mixtures of genres; and Wright, simultaneously a poet, novelist, essayist, journalist, playwright, and actor, often used the same material in different genres. For example, ''The Ethics of Living Jim Crow'' first appeared as an essay and was later attached to the stories of Uncle Tom's Children, one of which, ''Bright and Morning Star,'' is retold in *Black Boy* as a tale that held the protagonist in thrall, even though he ''did not know if the story was factually true or not.'' When ''black boy'' says that the story is emotionally true, he reflects exactly the kind of truth Wright wants his readers to respond to in *Black Boy*. Some of the characters in Black Boy have been given fictional names, whereas Bigger Thomas, the central character in the fictional *Native Son*, is the real name of one of Wright's acquaintances. That he used real names in fiction and fictional names in nonfiction is typical of Richard Wright, who further confounded the usual distinctions between author and persona by playing the role of Bigger Thomas in the first film version of Native Son.

Richard Wright makes clear that *Black Boy* is not meant as a traditional autobiography by presenting much of the story in the form of dialogue marked with quotation marks, a technique that suggests the unusual degree of fiction within the story. Although critics often point to Wright's first novel, *Native Son* (1940), as the other half of *Black Boy*, another model for this autobiographical work was his more recently completed *Twelve Million Black Voices: A Folk History of the American Negro in the United States*

(1941). Writing *Black Boy* in the spirit of folk history seemed a reasonable thing to do, and Wright apparently saw no hypocrisy in omitting personal details that did not contribute to what he was simultaneously thinking of as his own story and the story of millions of others. Wright's claim to be composing the autobiography of a generic black child is reinforced by the narrator's particular reaction to racism: ''The things that influenced my conduct as a Negro did not have to happen to me directly; I needed but to hear of them to feel their full effects in the deepest layers of my consciousness.''

[Most] of the omission in *Black Boy* is designed not to make the persona appear admirable but to make Richard Wright into ''black boy,'' to underplay his own family's middle-class ways and more positive values. Wright does not mention that his mother was a successful school teacher and that many of his friends were children of college faculty members; he omits most of his father's family background and his own sexual experiences. Also mainly left out are reactions from sensitive southern whites, including those of the Wall family to whom, we learn from Michel Fabre's biography [*The Unfinished Quest of Richard Wright*], ''he sometimes submitted his problems and plans . . . and soon considered their house a second home where he met with more understanding than from his own family.''

In addition to omissions, name changes, poetic interludes, and extensive dialogue, *Black Boy* is replete with questionable events that biographical research has revealed to be exaggerated, inaccurate, mistaken, or invented. The section of Fabre's biography dealing with the *Black Boy* years is characterized by constant disclaimers about the factuality of the story. Some omissions can be explained because the urbane ex-Communist who began Black Boy ''wanted to see himself as a child of the proletariat,'' through ''in reality he attached greater importance to the honorable position of his grandparents in their town than he did to his peasant background.'' Although these distortions are acceptable to many, especially in light of Wright's intention of using his life to show the effects of racism, numerous other manipulations are less acceptable because they are more self-serving.

Most of these incidents are relatively minor and might be judged unimportant; however, the misrepresentations in two of the book's most important episodes—the high school graduation speech and the story of Uncle Hoskins and the Mississippi River—might be less acceptable. ''*Black Boy's*'' refusal to deliver the principal's graduation speech rather than his own is apparently based on truth, but the version in *Black Boy* leaves out the important fact that Wright rewrote his speech, cutting out more volatile passages, as a compromise. The story of Uncle Hoskins does not ring true, for how could a boy whose life had been so violent to that point be scared of his uncle's relatively harmless trick? He says of his Uncle Hoskins, ''I never trusted him after that. Whenever I saw his face the memory of my terror upon the river would come back, vivid and strong, and it stood as a barrier between us.'' One reason the tale feels false is that the whole story—complete with the above revelations about Uncle Hoskins—actually happened to Ralph Ellison, who told it to Richard Wright [see Webb, p. 419].

Black Boy should not be read as historical truth, which strives to report those incontrovertible facts that can be somehow corroborated, but as narrative truth. The story that Richard Wright creates in *Black Boy*, whatever its value as an exact historical record, is important both in telling us how the author remembers life in the pre-Depression South and in showing us what kind of person the author was in order to have written his story as he did. Although he is often deliberately false to historical truth, he seldom deviates from narrative truth. In *Black Boy*, Wright has made both the horrifyingly dramatic and the ordinary events of his life fit into a pattern, shaped by a consistent, metaphoric use of lying.

Timothy Dow Adams. *Telling Lies in Modern American Autobiography* (Chapel Hill: The University of North Carolina Press, 1990), pp. 69–83

Arnold Rampersad and the editors of the Library of America have given us not the original [*Native Son*] published version of 1940, but the text of the bound galleys that lay, for weeks during the fall of 1939, on the submission desk at the Book-of-the-Month Club, while the directors fretted over whether they could tolerate Bigger masturbating in a movie theater, or Mary Dalton moving her ''hips . . . in a hard and veritable grind'' against his black body. Richard Wright was a young writer tasting his first chance for fame, and so when the verdict came in that these scenes had to be cut if the Club was to select his novel, he agreed. At last, with the deletions now restored, we have, as Rampersad says, ''the words of the book as Wright wanted them to be read.''

It is always a tricky business to disqualify a text that a living author has at least tacitly approved. A few years ago a group of scholars, working on the premise that Theodore Dreiser had been bullied into making changes in the text of *Sister Carrie* just before it went to press, put forward a new text based on his typescript, and the Library of America wisely refrained from following suit. This time the Library has rejected the text in which an American classic has been known for half a century. The publication of this new edition is not just an editorial innovation, it is a major event in American literary history.

There can be no doubt that the book is better for the restorations. For one thing, the restored text solves some consistency problems, as when the State's Attorney tells Bigger that ''I knew about that dirty trick you and your friend Jack pulled off in the Regal Theatre''—a statement that floats without antecedent in the 1940 text, but, in the intact version, refers to Bigger's ''polishing his night stick'' in the movie house. More important than such textual repairs is their total effect: we now have the first book in our literary history that represented the full, urgent sexuality of a young black man. . . .

*Native Son* is a book about the imperatives of the body—about Bigger's panic-sweat beading on his skin; about his convulsive stomach pain when he gulps water after parched days on the run; about his struggle to will his erection to subside while a white woman and man have sex on the car seat behind him. There are brilliant descriptions of Bigger forcing a street crony to lick the blade of his knife in an act of public submission, and of his chewing frantically his first loaf of bread in days, until it bulges his cheeks like a trumpeter's and coaxes the scarce saliva from his tongue. The book has an almost brutal immediacy, which the newly restored text not only confirms, but heightens. I have never been able to drive past the severe houses of Hyde Park, or through the tangent black neighborhoods, without seeing Bigger huddled against a steamed window in a passing streetcar, or seeing the snow fall softly, as if flake by flake, onto the Daltons' blue Buick that he has left parked in their gated driveway. One feels pushed by the wind off the lake toward the edge of the plains; one peers with Bigger

through the ''gauzelike curtain of snow'' at the streetlights that taunt him with the promise of warmth—''street lamps covered with thick coatings of snow, gleaming like huge frosted moons above his head.''. . .

Though he had broken with the Chicago Communist Party in 1937, he did not leave the national party until 1942, and was still trying to construct *Native Son* within the framework of a class analysis. He had been active in the '30s in the John Reed Club, a largely white literary organization sponsored by the Communists, and later became Harlem editor of The Daily Worker. His early novel *Lawd Today*! (published posthumously) is largely an evocation of soul-deadening labor; its central character, like Wright himself (who held jobs during these years as a ditch-digger, delivery boy, dishwasher, hospital worker), is a postal clerk whose body becomes a mechanical extension of the canceling machine, and whose mind can only accommodate ''images [that] would flit [in] . . . and then aimlessly out again, like stray cats.'' The early stories, collected in *Uncle, Tom's Children* (1938), look back to the South, and are concerned with the gathering desperation of rural blacks, whose inarticulate rage against a world owned by white men was beginning to take the form of apocalyptic expectation.

This implicit Communist criticism of capitalist society is still at work in *Native Son*, in which Wright gives Bigger an incipient proletarian consciousness, a desire to ''merge himself with others and be a part of this world, to lose himself in it so he could find himself, to be allowed a chance to live like others, even though he was black.'' As part of the same allegory of class conflict, Wright draws the kindly Mr. Dalton as a stock figure from agitprop fiction—a giver to causes who sends his servants to night school even as he rakes in the rent from black tenants who live five to a rat-infested room (a contradiction of which ''in a sullen way Bigger was conscious''). And if Dalton keeps a human screen of ''house niggers'' between him and the brutal reality of the plantation, he has an overseer to do his dirty work—Britten, the thick-necked security man, who studies Bigger to see if he waves his hands about and if his voice rises at the ends of sentences, clues that would clinch his theory that he has been fraternizing with Jews).

Here, under rough interrogation, Bigger begins to see the futility of his plan to blame Mary's murder on Jan, her Communist boyfriend: ''Britten loosened his fingers from Bigger's collar and shrugged his shoulders. Bigger ''relaxed, still standing, his head resting against the wall, aching. He had not thought that anyone would dare think that he, a black Negro, would be Jan's partner.'' This remarkable phrase, ''black Negro,'' is not a tautology, but a clue that the concept of ''Negro'' is, for Wright, not fundamentally a racial idea. ''Negro'' is a generic word for hopelessness and degradation. The early pages on Bigger—his portrait as a gang leader who compensates with cruelty for his sense of exile from the world of satisfactions—are almost indistinguishable in social content from James T. Farrell's portrait of the Irish thug in Studs Lonigan (1932–35).

But a ''black Negro'' is something quite different—something for which Bigger hates himself more than he hates his oppressor. A ''black Negro'' is worse, he knows, than the refuse of the white world, since he is a creature held by whites of every class (from coons to vigilantes, they all close ranks in his pursuit) to be not only low and incorrigible, but foul and poisonous. A wall stands between Bigger and the sensations he craves. He finds himself smacked back like a dog that lifts its head to the table rather than wait for the white man's scraps to fall to the floor. Not merely exploited, he is despised; and Native Son, almost in spite of itself, is a book about this distinction.

It is, in other words, a book about self-hatred—about a young man who loathes his own color and physiognomy and dialect and all the features of his irreparable social ugliness. Bigger is not so much an autonomous consciousness as he is the projection of the white imagination, a figure whose closest precursors in American fiction come not from previous black writers, but from racist white writers (such as Thomas Dixon, author of The Clansman, 1905) for whom black men were nothing more than clothed apes. Earlier black writers had certainly remarked the "peculiar sensation," as W. E. B. DuBois famously put it, of a "double-consciousness, this sense of always looking at one's self through the eyes of others, of measuring one's soul by the tape of a world that looks on in amused contempt and pity." But before Wright, black novelists had tended to approach this psychological dilemma from a connoisseur's distance and with Jamesian finesse—as in the tradition of the mulatto novel, which dramatized the mixed relief and guilt of light-skinned blacks who tried to solve the problem of double-consciousness by obliterating their black identity altogether. . . .

For Wright, the resurrection of his senses was a liberating event, benign and even gentle, evoked in almost pantheistic terms borrowed from Walt Whitman. For Bigger, it was the discovery that he had the power to damage and destroy white lives.

In 1940 Bigger's was an almost unwritable violence. Explosive, indiscriminate, he finds that he has a taste for killing: hours after burning Mary Dalton's body in the furnace he crushes Bessie's head with a brick, this black woman whom he both loves for her tenderness and hates for her despair. Wright's editors and sponsors worried that this squalid story might prove unreadable. They were wrong. Native Son sold 215,000 copies in three weeks-in a world poised on the verge of a conflagration in which the human capacity for systematic and spontaneous violence would be proved larger than anyone dreamed.

Wright had invented a young black man who awakens to himself by discovering his capacity for rage, by punching through the racial wall into moments of bodily contact (carnal and lethal) that confirm the aliveness of his body. In the autobiography that he wrote five years later, Wright makes it clear that he, too, had found salvation in the life of the body. . . .

In the mid-1940s Wright moved to Paris (a city of refuge," he called it) and became part of the literary circle including Gertrude Stein (whose "Melanctha" had been an early influence) and André Gide, as well as leading intellectuals of the "Negritude" movement—Leopold Senghor, Aime Cesaire, and others. Wright, in turn, gave encouragement and patronage to younger black American writers like James Baldwin and Chester Himes. In the later 40s and early 50s he devoted himself to a new novel, The Outsider (1953)—the story of a black intellectual who begins life with a new identity after being presumed dead in a train wreck. Wright composed this novel, whose theme is the exhilarating loss of a burdensome self, under the personal influence of Sartre and de Beauvoir, and after considerable reading in Heidegger and Husserl. Like the second section of his autobiography (which he had agreed to drop, again at the behest of the Book-of-the-Month Club, and which was published after his death under the original title of the whole work, American Hunger), The Outsider contained a bitter attack on the Communist Party as a purveyor of false messianic hope.

Along with the second part of the mutilated autobiography (now reattached to Black Boy in the Library of America edition),

The Outsider is a candid record of Wright's disillusionment with the Communist promise. Blaming the Party for intervening with friends at the Book Club to drop the offending section of his memoir, he again acceded to the pressure, but went on to publish some of the deleted chapters separately—including one long section, "I Tried to be a Communist," that appeared in The Atlantic and was widely read in Richard Crossman's notable book, The God That Failed (1950).

"Shattering" is a critical word that has been properly consigned to service as an adjective in blurbs. But there is a class of books for which this word, or some synonym that conveys the idea that a book can do real violence to the mind, is indispensable. Not all great books work by this kind of assault, but some do, and thereby they are fatal to whatever mental structure the reader inhabits when he sits down to read them. Native Son is such a book. It is all the more remarkable because it achieves its destructive power not by exposing the inadequacies of conventional thinking, but by dramatizing conventional ideas in such a way that they can never be held casually again. Native Son was indeed the book Wright swore to write so that "no one would weep over it," the book that would be so hard and deep" that it would deny its readers "the consolation of tears." It was the first book that forced Americans to take their racial fears seriously, and it did so by turning their most vicious thoughts against themselves.

It is a profound irony that the arc of Wright's career moved downward after Native Son because of his refusal to be imprisoned by the thematics of race. His move to France, where he partook of the prestige attached to the man of color in exile from crass America, did not enlarge him as a writer. He became, perhaps, a more cosmopolitan artist. Still, as Baldwin said, speaking from within the same paradox, Paris would not have been a city of refuge for us if we had not been armed with American passports," and "it did not seem worthwhile to me to have fled the native fantasy only to embrace a foreign one."

In his moving eulogy, Baldwin reflected that Wright was "one of the most illustrious victims" of "the war in the breast between blackness and whiteness." Writing in the heady atmosphere of postcolonial possibility, Baldwin added that "it is no longer important to be white—thank heaven—the white face is no longer invested with the power of this world; and it is devoutly to be hoped that it will soon no longer be important to be black." Such a dissolution of difference was Wright's hope, too. All his work was a plea that racial identity be submerged in the colorless fact of being human. But his enduring greatness as an artist will be owed, I think, to his unprecedented ability to convey the horror of being black in America. What he wished for was to lose his subject. After reading Native Son, no one can doubt his willingness to make the sacrifice.

Andrew Delbanco. The New Republic. 206, 13 (March 30, 1992), 28–32

BIBLIOGRAPHY

Uncle Tom's Children: Four Novellas, 1938; Native Son, 1940; Twelve Million Black Voices: A Folk History of the Negro in the U.S., 1941; Black Boy: A Record of Childhood and Youth, 1945; The Outsider, 1953; Savage Holiday, 1954; Black Power: A Record of Reactions in a Land of Pathos, 1954; The Color Curtain: A Report on the Bandung Conference, 1956; Pagan Spain: A Report of a Journey into the Past, 1957; White Man, Listen!, 1957;

*The Long Dream*, 1958; *Eight Men*, 1961; *Lawd Today*, 1963; *The Man Who Lived Underground*, 1971; *American Hunger*, 1977

# WYNTER, Sylvia (1928–)

Jamaica

Sylvia Wynter's *The Hills of Hebron* documents the wide range of cults in the islands, including a Pocomania cult (corresponding to the Haitian voodoo worshippers): ''the Believers'' (corresponding to the Afro-Baptist cults which Philip Curtin and Orlando Patterson describe as having first formed themselves in the 1860s); and the ''New Believers'' (a cult invented from two related creeds—Marcus Garvey's Black God religion and the Jamaican Rastafarians' belief in the divinity of the Emperor of Ethiopia). When the Believers' movement collapses with the ignominious failure of their leader to take flight to heaven, some of the brethren join the orthodox Christian Church: ''There was something atavistic about their singing as though they were shouting to recall lost gods from the primeval forests of Africa. And at times their singing stirred up secret urges in the Reverend's own heart which had been slumbering through centuries of civilization.'' Reverend Brooke's disturbance at his flock's hearts of darkness corresponds with the uneasiness of nineteenth-century missionaries at the incursions of rhythmic singing and other ''African'' manifestations into the orthodox Church.

Wynter comically deflates the cults depicted in her novel. A good illustration of the method used is Moses' confession to his first convert of how the Lord inspired him in a vision: ''It was just a day like any other, Sister Edwards. No sign to mark it as different. I was watering the flowers. I came to a rhododendron bush that stood alone by itself. As I poured out water at the root, I see the whole bush light up with fire before my eyes. I step back, I stand still, I watch. The bush flamed orange and green fire. The presence of God was all round about me. I fall on my knees, I bow my head to the earth. I make to take off my shoes but as it wasn't Sunday I wasn't wearing any. And the ground on which I was standing, Sister Edwards, was holy, holy ground.''

But the author does not simply make fun of her cultists. The novel shows a passionate concern about the void in the lives of the socially depressed cultists, and sees part of the solution as lying in socioeconomic adjustments. The socioeconomic leaning is given emphasis by Wynter's allowing Moses to become unnerved when a labor leader rouses the people to take stock of ''the extent of their misery, the hopelessness of their poverty, the lack of any future for their children.'' He advises them to have nothing to do with churches (''All that is finished and done''); rather, they should believe in organized labor, and Man. The weight of the presentation leads the reader to think that this is Wynter's advice too.

> Kenneth Ramchand. *The West Indian Novel and Its Background* (London: Heinemann, 1983), pp. 127–29

[Wynter's] criticism alone would ensure her a place in the history of West Indian writing. Beginning in 1967, she published a series of articles and book reviews that would open, in her own words, ''a new dimension for criticism.''

In 1968 and 1969 she had published in two parts the monumentally titled ''We Must Learn to Sit Down Together and Talk about a Little Culture: Reflections on West Indian Writing and Criticism.'' This was occasioned by her desire to express her disagreement with several works of criticism emerging from the university and to articulate what she saw as the radical difference between what she termed ''acquiescent'' criticism versus ''challenging'' criticism. For her, the ''acquiescent'' critic pretended to take an objective stance outside of the historical process which has molded his point of view. This ''pretended objectivity and detachment'' in fact resulted in a distorted perspective which merely served to bolster the status quo. The ''challenging'' critic, on the other hand, accepted and was aware that his point of view was molded by this historical process, and this awareness—Wynter felt—could lead to creative insights that could help to initiate conscious change. She expanded further on this in 1973, when in a note on her critique ''Creole Criticism,'' she wrote, ''Creole criticism . . . is merely literary criticism rehashed in brown or black face.'' Her attacks were wide-ranging and, at times, savage, aimed particularly at the work of W. I. Carr and Louis James (then lecturers in the Department of English at Mona) as well as at the work of Wayne Brown, John Hearne, Cameron King, and Mervyn Morris. As far as Wynter was concerned, all critics were too quick to come to terms with the ''brilliant myth'' of Europe as the ''super culture which embraces all other cultures, and obliterates as it absorbs.'' In being enchained by this cultural myth, such ''acquiescent'' critics reflected and paralleled ''the inauthenticity of the University and its society.'' Worse yet, since these critics were also the educators, Wynter felt that ''the hostility that the West Indian writer meets with from university students comes directly from the concept of literature sold to them by [such] educators.'' Moreover, what she found is that the critics she examined almost all failed to understand that ''when the creative instinct is stifled or driven into exile the critical faculty can survive only as maggots do—feeding on the decaying corpse of that which gives it a brief predatory life.'' The writing of criticism in the university had become like a ''branch plant'' industry, with the interpreter replacing the writer and the critic displacing the creator.

Sylvia Wynter's second major piece of literary criticism, ''Creole Criticism: A Critique,'' reflected her belief that the folk culture represents ''the only living tradition in the Caribbean'' and that it is only by ''drawing from, by feeding from [the West Indian peasant] that a truly national literature could begin.'' Indeed, it was that personality through ''the reinvention of its culture against impossible odds, that made the West Indian novel possible.'' She also saw the culture of the folk as a kind of ''guerrilla resistance against the market economy,'' and she posited the existence of a pervasive ''African heritage which has been the crucible of the cultural deposits of the immigrant peoples.'' It was this recognition which motivated, in large measure, her attack on Kenneth Ramchand because she saw his mission as being ''to negate, destroy, diminish, disguise the African centrality in the cultural dynamic of the Caribbean peoples.'' In opposition to this, she celebrated and emphasized the importance of the folk culture in such essays as ''Jonkonnu in Jamaica,'' ''Novel and History: Plot and Plantation,'' and ''One Love: Aspects of Afro-Jamaicanism.'' In ''Jonkonnu,'' for instance, she set out to prove the existence of ''a pervasive African-descended folk culture in Jamaica, one that had . . . acted as a principle of revolt and a form of cultural resistance to the cultural superstructure brought by the colonizer.''

From the viewpoint of the 1980s, when we have such magisterial and insightful criticism as Gordon Rohlehr's book on [Edward

Kamau] Brathwaite's poetry, *Pathfinder*, and Bruce King's collection of critical essays on *West Indian Literature*, the controversy and heat generated by Wynter's articles in the 1970s, seem out of proportion. But her work was crucial because she was the first to articulate, and focus on, the problem, and she was ideally suited for it, being a creative writer herself, academically trained in literary criticism, and educated in the metropole. She was also an agitator, a stimulating lecturer, and a polemical writer who presented papers at numerous conferences expressing her point of view.

Whether West Indian criticism would have inevitably come of age and shed its dependent role is difficult to say. There is little doubt, however, that she helped to hasten the process by her provocative and stimulating articles.

Victor L. Chang. In Daryl Cumber Dance, ed. *Fifty Caribbean Writers* (Westport, Connecticut: Greenwood Press, 1986), pp. 500–2

Where many Caribbean novels . . . indeed romanticize the image of woman as mother, in at least one Caribbean novel this very real mother-as-victim syndrome is dealt with. Jamaican Sylvia Wynter, as the first black woman novelist from the English-speaking Caribbean, creates, in her only novel, *The Hills of Hebron*, an indomitable woman figure, in the form of Gatha Randall Barton. But it is Gatha who falls desperately into the throes of this self-sacrificing motherdom. Like the mothering situation itself, Miss Gatha is a paradox. She is an ideal as a Caribbean black mother, the self-sacrificing, self-effacing woman parent to a young self-centered, ungrateful, partially crippled man-child. At the same time, Gatha Randall Barton, within the Hebron settlement, becomes an anomaly, a woman who is a pillar of fortitude, resourcefulness, and wisdom as the community's efficient leader. For most Caribbean women, the former role would certainly be the narrow enclosure from which there would be no easy means of escape, while the latter would not even be within the realm of consideration. Although for Miss Gatha both experiences are personal realities, she is caught fast in her narrow enclosure. Even with community acknowledgement, acceptance, and approval of her "more masculine" leadership attributes, Gatha, having so completely internalized her function as mother, never attempts to escape or even to obvert this most sacred of women-roles. Instead, this function becomes a prime motivation for everything else in her life; her every accomplishment rests on the fragile relationship she has with her son, Isaac, and her desire to see him as Hebron's leader. Gatha can never be an independent and individuated personality herself because of her almost fanatical commitment to her son's destiny which serves to entrap her in society's small enclosure of motherdom. This, indeed, is the tragic flaw in an otherwise self-assured Caribbean woman.

The primary thematic concern of *The Hills of Hebron* is certainly not with women, although women, as in nearly every facet of Caribbean life, play significant roles in the communication of the novel's theme. The rites of passage of a black community in the 1940s from postslavery oppression and poverty towards physical, psychological, and spiritual freedom is the basic concern of the novel. It is actually the story of Prophet Moses Barton, Gatha's husband, opportunist and visionary who, like the biblical Moses, leads his people out of a physical and psychological bondage. His

Egypt is a small, decadent village called Cockpit Center. His exodus is to the hillside: to a landscape called Hebron where he will settle his Church of the New Believers of Hebron. Moses Barton, although depicted by Wynter with some farcical humor, is a forerunner of Jamaican "deliverers." Wynter tells us this; thus, we are never really expected to believe that Moses Barton's black God, whom he promises "would be on their side forever," will actually deliver the Hebronites from inequity. Through the brief glimpses of a young labor leader, the author hints to us that the movement to liberation which Moses Barton inspires will be evolutionary.

Janice Lee Liddell. In Carole Boyce Davies and Elaine Savory Fido, eds. *Out of the Kumbla: Caribbean Women and Literature* (Trenton, New Jersey: Africa World Press, 1990), pp. 322–23

With *The Hills of Hebron* we enter the era of Black Power, black pride, and the quest for self-government. The novel heralds a time of radical reorientation, seemingly linking us with our past and taking us back where we began. For if, as Wynter suggests, slavery involved "the cutting off of a memory of the past, the denial of any indigenous history, and a kind of intellectual alienation from the self and society," *The Hills of Hebron* argues for the repossession of that past and the finding of a voice to express that denial and absence. And if, as Wynter insists, Caribbean people were oppressed first as natives, then as blacks, before the question of gender arose, the relative importance of gender has to be considered in that light. And even though Miss Gatha emerges as a powerful voice in the novel, she is powerful not so much because she is a woman but because of her status as a colonial person anxious to articulate this private sense of dispossession. . . .

In this novel, Wynter captures the vital instinct of Caribbean people to survive and to create. Although the novel may be much too long in parts and somewhat overbearing in its didacticism, it captures the sense of restlessness with the past and the need to break out of discourses and practices that are designed to keep us coffined within an alien ideology and culture. Structured in the anticolonialist struggle of the 1950s and 1960s, *The Hills of Hebron* brings to a closure the story of Mary Prince, coffined on her slave plantation and subjected to the brutality of the slave master, offered in 1831. *The Hills of Hebron* almost seems a response to Prince's plea for the recognition of her humanity. As she asked: "How can slaves be happy when they have the halter round their neck, and the whip upon their back? and are disgraced and thought nothing more of than beasts?—and are separated from their mothers, and husbands, and children, and sisters, just as cattle are sold and separated? Is it happiness for a driver in the field to take down his wife or sister or child, and strip them, and whip them in such a disgraceful manner?—women that have had children exposed in the open field to shame!"

Certainly, *The Hills of Hebron* reflects the movement toward the creation of a new day, a movement from the symbol of "the halter round their neck[s] and the whip upon their back[s]." Here, indeed, the spirits of the ancestors meet and ask that libation be given to soothe the transition from the old to the new, from the past to the present, from the public to the private sphere of discourse. The women writers of the contemporary era would explore new areas of concern, different continents of sensibility and feelings, and varied ways of speaking about their relationships with each

other and with their men. Much of the work would be influenced by
the Black Power, Rastafarian, and women's movements.

Selwyn R. Cudjoe. *Caribbean Women Writers* (Wellesley,
Massachusetts: Calaloux Publications, 1990), pp. 42–43

BIBLIOGRAPHY
*The University of Hunger* (with Jan Carew), 1961; *Ssh . . . It's a
Wedding*, 1961; *Miracle in Lime Lane* (with Jan Carew), 1962; *The
Hills of Hebron: A Jamaican Novel*, 1962; *Black Midas*, 1970;
*Jamaica's National Heroes*, 1971; *Rody and Rena, The Sea Star
Readers* (with Annemarie Isachsen), 1975

# Z

## ZADI ZAOUROU, Bernard (1938–)
### Cote D'ivoire

[Bernard] Zadi Zaourou has advocated a rehabilitation of African languages as the most valid vehicles for African thought and expression; in [his play] *L'Oeil*, he has moved in this direction in significant ways. There are four linguistic forms of expression: standard French, the language of officialdom and of the intellectuals (students); French slang, the language of intermediaries such as Django and Gringo; Pidgin French, a dialect of the People; African languages—principally Bambara, and several exclamations in Malinké. A fifth "language" of the play is that of the talking drum, the *attoungblan*, which uses a transcoded language, the mediated word. These linguistic codes dominate. Nonetheless, the author's use of mime must also be taken into account inasmuch as it represents a decision not to use language in favor of a form of non-verbal expression. . . .

Standard French is the dominant language of *L'Oeil*. It is dominant because the dramatic structure privileging the goal of the Ruling Class is dominant. Of the eighteen brief tableaux, eight are exclusively in standard French, and six contain varying combinations of standard French and other aforementioned forms of expression. In other words, government officials, and those like Djédjé who are aspiring to join them, speak standard French, both in public and private discourse. Students, whose sympathies are with the workers and the unemployed, speak standard French as well, accounting for two of the linguistically mixed tableaux.

Slang, essentially French, with American and Pidgin French traces, is used consistently by Django and Gringo, the two "strong-arm" men employed by Sôgôma Sangui.

The nameless workers and the unemployed, who are presented principally as a social class . . . speak what Zadi Zaourou calls Pidgin French. It does, in fact, conform to Webster's definition of the term: "a form of speech that usually has a simplified grammar and a limited often mixed vocabulary and is used principally for intergroup communication." The working class's use of Pidgin is not artificial (beyond the given fiction of a literary and scenic work). While [Côte d'Ivoire] is nowhere named, using the country of the author as a referent, there are sixty-odd African languages spoken within its borders. It is important to note, however, that in the three tableaux in which Pidgin is used, standard French occurs as well and often reiterates part of the discourse of the workers.

Finally, there are African languages called for, but *not* encoded, in the text in two sequences. This could conceivably have to do with the present state of linguistic research and the development of orthographies. But, based on [an] interview with Zadi Zaourou, it would appear that the lack of precise dialogue is linked to his concept of performance, specifically, a preference for improvisation in those sequences that call for group interaction, whether in a traditional or modern setting. One of the sequences in question is the meeting between the *marabout* (the Holy Man) and Sôgôma Sangui. The general theme of the tableau is developed in a dialogue in Pidgin and standard French, but Zadi Zaourou specifies that "ce tableau gagnerait à être joué en bambara. Ce texte n'est qu'indicatif du thème à traiter" [this scene would gain by being played in Bambara. The text is merely indicative of how to treat the theme]. And in the final tableau, when The People invade the home of the Governor General and confront his colleagues and guests, the unspecified slogans and cries of the crowd are called for 'en langue du pays."

There are two sequences that are basically non-verbal: the arrest of Sôgôma Sangui, a brief pantomime, and the final tableau, where language is minimal and mime is the medium. This all-important dénouement, dominated by mime, symbolic decor (the panoply), and the transcoded word—the talking drum that transmits a call to action—furnishes a network of signs that communicates a message of mythological or epic portent. . . .

[It] is quite evident from a reading of *L'Oeil* that the political and cultural conflict is greatly heightened by the clash of linguistic codes, which are the most crucial ones for the reader. Should this direction of linguistic authenticity lead eventually to a modern theater in the major languages of Africa (or the major languages of individual African countries), then, the Western spectator and/or reader of African theater has the challenge of learning a new language (or languages), if he/she is to follow. What is more, this is the goal of many African writers today, who recognize that other potential African authors are paralyzed by the historically imposed dilemma of creating works in an alienating linguistic form.

Louise M. Jefferson. *French Review.* 55, 6 (May 1982), pp. 831–33

Zadi [Zaourou], who has been involved with the theater since he was a student, has developed in fairly characteristic fashion. After his return to the Ivory Coast in 1971, he continued to write plays on the classical model—for example, *Les Sofas*. But, in the light of the debates of the period, and perhaps encouraged by the experiments of La Griotique, he began to question his own approach. . . . The break began with *L'Oeil et la tignasse*. Zadi said he would henceforth base his writing on three principal elements: symbolism, rhythm, and narrative. Through them, he wanted to attack the evils bedeviling his country. He therefore opted for a political theater expressing itself in a host of symbols. The fact that his new company was called "Didiga" was no chance, and his latest play is an example of his new conception of the theater. The word *didiga* has, in fact, a symbolic origin. According to the author himself, it is a concept of hunting among the Bété people. It is the term used to refer to a kind of adventure story without an end which always features the same hero, Djergbeugbeu, the ideal hunter whom his more fallible brethren seek to emulate. As in most Bété legends and stories, the vision of the world portrayed by the *didiga* defies ordinary logic. The hunter stops on the bank of a river and starts to fish to amuse himself, intending to continue his hunting later. He casts a hook into the water, but instead of catching a large fish, he is surprised to pull up a wild guinea-fowl. It is the illogical aspect of this mystical world to which Zadi returns as the basis of his new approach to the theater. It is further enriched by the theoretical ideas developed by Aboubacar Touré.

His starting point is the use of symbolism. It works through the language of music (especially percussion), through bodily expression, and through the discourse of silence and the unspoken. The objects and animals he uses have an anthropomorphic quality, for among the Bété the panther, the elephant, and the buffalo are considered to be human beings. The hunter who kills them commits homicide and must undergo the ordeal of expiation. At this level, we enter the domain of ritual. These are all cultural elements deriving from the concept of *didiga.*

Unfortunately, in *La Termitière*, the spoken word is used sparingly, whereas the music, dance, and symbolic gesture which tell the story of a society in crisis are clearly dominant. But, while the gestures are transformed into ritual acts, the latter do not have any effective power; they are purely symbolic. . . .

[Although] Zadi is much more concerned with the theater as an art form, his discourse can fail to reach the listener as he does not always use the symbols present in the collective consciousness; or, when he does use symbols rooted in the culture, he sometimes detaches them from their context. This has led, for instance, to criticism over his giving a mask to a young girl to wear. Among the Dan, as well as among the Gouro and the Wê, women are forbidden to wear masks; not only does he, therefore, commit an error on the anthropological level, but he also goes against the rules of plausibility.

Barthélémy Kotchy. *Theatre Research International.* 9, 3, (1983–84), pp. 239–40

In Bété culture, the *didiga* is the art of the unthinkable, relating the adventures of an imaginary named Djerabeugbeu. It is by extension every narration, behavior, or act defying logic and physical laws.

The *didiga* creates a certain kind of relationship between beings, phenomena, and things, giving rise to the unusual and to a break in order to create a new consciousness. This technique suits a group who wish to defend a political or aesthetic notion of the theater by producing the constants of the African word: the symbolic, the poetry, and the rhythm. . . .

Zadi, in his dissertation "La Parole poétique dans la poésie africaine" favors this traditional form of African speech and has strived to present it in his theater, with all its dramatic force. This speech expresses itself by adopting the contours of melodic and rhythmic lines contrasted in a particular way in African languages, because of the varied and complex play of the tones.

The first speaker, master of the word, transmits a powerful and educative speech. A second speaker is composed of two elements: a musical instrument, a talking instrument like the musical bow [l'arc musical] or the "pédou," and the actor with the memory of the first speaker. Thereby results a new message thanks to the association of the actor and the talking instrument. The receiver of the message then needs a preliminary initiation.

Thus mediated speech can be conceived of as an instrumental language aimed at the reproduction of spoken sentences.

In Zadi's modern *didiga*, the mediated speech is translated by symbolic dances like the talking dance, through talking instruments like the musical bow, the tambour, the "pédou" and the double bell and finally through a "masked" language that the director introduces into the very structure of his plays. . . .

In *La Termitière*, the bow is especially well used and assures the intensity of the dramatic progression. Due to the fact that the bow has a sorrowful tone, it is used to transmit to the spectators a part of the anguish expressed. In the scene of the "jeu de la graine," the

bow calls a musician with a "bissa" who undertakes the search of the hidden seed following the indications of the bow. It is the voice of the bow that tells the player if he is on the right track or not. The bow replies "oui" or "non" to the player's questions and the bow speaks so well that the player succeeds in finding the grain with the warm congratulations of his comrades.

The bow appears then as a character with a complete part who leads the whole scene. . . .

The songs are obviously accompanied by instruments. Just as the *didiga* does not require the public to decode the language of the musical arc, it does not demand that one understand the meaning of the words of its songs. One only expects from the public an emotional reaction on hearing the song, preceded naturally by a presentation and psychological preparation. The songs are never neutral, mere fillers, but portray a certain behavior, reinforce the depth of a certain character.

The poetic speech of Zadi Zaourou's *didiga* thus expresses itself under the most diverse forms, it is danced, proffered, sung, makes use of symbols, creates beauty from all angles. This speech enacted for the pleasure of the eyes and the ears, to promote awareness, is molded and molds in its turn by producing the richest images (rhythmic, melodic, visual). These word-spectacles which act upon our senses, present man under different aspects in order to help the spectator to understand the often contradictory situations and behavior. The poet, says Dibéro, is born with a "strong shadow" and the strength of that shadow is what gives strength to his words.

Zadi as a poet has been able to free, thanks to the theater, this poetic African speech, shackled today by writing; he knew how to draw from his cultural origin (orality) all the benefits that it could provide from the point of view of stylistic and dramatic rendition.

It is in pursuing the perfection of different possibilities of this speech that the theater of Zadi Zaourou will attain its originality and African specificity.

Marie-José Hourantier. *Notre Librairie.* 86 (1987), pp. 84–89†

As a specific imaginary structure, as a *significant human reality*, the *didiga* indicates at the outset, in the Bété cultural space of Zadi Zaourou, the art of the hunters in the form of oral narratives, relating to the accompaniment of a musical bow the strange experiences, mysterious, marvelous, and dangerous of the hunt, perceived as a singular experience—an experience which goes well beyond a simple work process, or routine economic activity.

In its nature and substance, the ancient *didiga* is a practice in which the process of signification is identical or homologous to literary art. It is the same way of constructing the signification as is practiced by poetic speech. . . .

The modern *didiga*, that of Zadi Zaourou, brings about a displacement, a transfer, a profound distortion in order to take the form and substance of a game, or a dramatic spectacle: the *didiga* becomes a spectacular ceremony of great amplitude, of a ludic, aesthetic, and secular nature. . . .

In the modern *didiga*, not only the constituent forces of the play and the sudden changes in fortune, but also the lighting, the colors—in one word, the dramatic apparatus—function as a universe, structured by a new subjective impetus. Instead of incitement to the esoteric initiation, it is a question hence-forth of introducing indirectly through the play the compassion and objectivity of the public to the level of comprehension and detection of political and ideological mechanisms which regulate the functioning of today's societies. It is about our societies which, one knows, are characterized by new forms of domination, oppression, and surveillance, in a perspective that is at once dialectic and Freudian. In theatrical writing, as well as in the spectacle, this perspective is continuously illustrated by the articulation "Répression-Résistance" in its reversals and complex modalities.

Koudou Aiko. *Imprévue*. 1 (1990), pp. 71–72

BIBLIOGRAPHY
*L'Oeil*, 1975; *Les Sofas*, 1975; *L'Oeil et la tignasse*, 1981; *La Termitière*, 1984

# ZOBEL, Joseph (1915–)
## Martinique

[Joseph] Zobel wishes to distinguish himself clearly from other black writers for whom the link between politics and art is both necessary and vital in the Third-World context. And behind this distinction lies the refusal to "sacrifice his individuality" and the possible suggestion that he be placed in a special category and judged by different standards. Zobel seems to be making a discreet appeal for consideration as "un artiste tout court," fearing that classification as a disciple of Négritude might obscure the purely artistic qualities of his work. . . .

[In *Diab'là*, *La Rue cases-nègres*, and *La Fête à Paris*, one of Zobel's] chief preoccupations is the creation of heroes who symbolize the Negro's triumph over his destiny and the resultant pride in the black race. It is in this sense that we consider him to be a Négritude writer, aiming at black consciousness and black liberation. The picture of the Negro that eventually emerges from an overall examination of the novels in question is quite unlike the one usually painted by white Europeans. Against a background of misery, social injustice and suffering, the Negro stands out as a resourceful human being, an individual of dignity and honor, equal if not superior in status to his oppressors. In short, the myth of Negro inferiority is exploded by a display of qualities whose existence the European has refused to acknowledge, and which consequently the Negro does not easily recognize in himself. . . .

The simplicity of style and structure in Zobel's first novel, *Diab'là*, is in keeping with the simple nature of life in a small fishing village near Le Diamant on the Martinican South Coast. The story concerns the arrival of Diab'là, a peasant from a hillside village, Morne-Vent, and the use of his skill in agriculture not only to earn a living but to establish himself in the community as a leader and awaken in the inhabitants a spirit of cooperation and self-reliance. In essence, Diab'là's role is very similar to the one played by Manuel in [Jacques] Roumain's *Gouverneurs de la Rosée*, with the obvious difference that the former is a complete stranger to the scene of his operations. Zobel succeeds in capturing the frankness and simplicity of everyday life in rural Martinique through the use of a modified form of Creole dialogue and a direct, uncomplicated narrative style. He examines in great detail, and with considerable charm and appeal, the manners of the people, to the extent that in the early stages of the novel, we are tempted to place it in the category of the exotic novel devoted to "local color." As the story

progresses, however, it becomes clear that the role of Diab'là and of his older, more experienced counterpart, Capitain'là, is to promote the interests of the underprivileged black Martinican and to serve as examples of the Negro's hope for the future emancipation of his race.

The real significance of Diab'là's achievements can be appreciated only in the light of the difficulties with which he is faced in the village of his adoption and his response to these pressures. He wins the early admiration of the villagers for his refusal to continue to place his services at the disposal of the white plantation owners and for his decision to rely on his own talents and initiative to attain a position of dignity. . . .

To experience the hardships of colonialist oppression is one thing. To fully appreciate its complex nature and draw up an effective plan for the liberation of the colonized Negro is a task which demands a careful analysis of the problems confronting the black man in his native society as well as in the "Mother" country. This is the task to which Zobel, after firing his first salvo in *Diab'là*, addresses himself in *La Rue cases-nègres* and *La Fête à Paris*. Together, the novels form a single unit in the sense that they trace the history and development of one character, José Hassam, from the period of his early childhood in a depressed rural area in Martinique to the time of his graduation from the Sorbonne. There is one real motivating force in José's itinerary, it is clear that Zobel considers education to be the key to the Negro's emancipation, the basic tool he needs to carve out for himself a new and meaningful destiny. For Zobel, however, the Negro's education ought not to be limited to the formal European-oriented type but must include an awareness of his relationship to the society and the development of an ability to apprehend and come to terms with his environment. On the other hand, it is in the very nature of the colonizer to wish to safeguard his position by perpetuating the status quo. To this end, he seeks to keep the colonized in a state of abject poverty and dependent on him for their survival. What is more, he provides limited opportunities for education and, whenever school places are made available, he ensures that the type of education offered is designed in such a way as to create individuals whose thinking and values are identical to his own. That is how the colonialist system operates. And what we see in *La Rue cases-nègres* and *La Fête à Paris* is an attempt to defeat the system.

Randolph Hezekiah. *Black Images*. 4, 3–4 (1975), pp. 44–45, 48–49

[*La Rue cases-nègres*, translated as *Black Shack Alley*] is divided into three almost equal sections. Part one deals with the early life of the narrator, José, as he grows up on the plantation and sees him through to the start of his primary school years. It is to the author's credit that he has avoided the pitfall of allowing the adult that is writing to filter through to the narrative of the young child. As a result, José's descriptions sound genuine and authentic, truly in keeping with the type a child would give and not at all inconsistent with the fact that beyond these it is the adult that is analyzing in retrospect.

It would, for example, be somewhat artificial to have the young José make certain telling comments on the state of the society—these are introduced gradually as José matures over the length of the novel—so these are put into the mouths of other characters. In this respect, Médouze's account of his father's troubles in the postslavery period is typical. In fact, it is this account that brings out one of the rare impulses to violence that we see in José: ''I had this maddening desire to hit the first *béké* I set my eyes on,''he concludes.

Part two shows José in primary school and takes us up to his preparation for and success in the examination that sends him to secondary school, the *lycée*. In order to take better care of him during this period, his grandmother, M'man Tine eventually leaves Petit Morne, and Zobel uses this occasion to introduce us to a wide variety of pen portraits of the typical plantation society in Martinique prior to World War II. José once more looks on at the adult world with eyes of innocence, allowing events to make, in a way, their own commentary. However, we witness the gradual awakening of the young narrator to the complexities of class distinctions and other social inequalities, an awakening that comes full circle in part three.

In this section, José is shown in the urban environment of Fort-de-France, where he is reunited with his mother Délia as he works his way up to the *baccalauréat*. It is a new type of life that José and his companions see in this setting. Contemporary Fort-de-France is shown in its vivid realism, one that comes from an eye for significant detail which Zobel obviously possesses. . . .

Inevitably, comparisons will be made with other novels of the same type. One of the more striking resemblances has to be with George Lamming's *In the Castle of My Skin*, set in Barbados and published in 1953. Lamming's novel is also about life in a village in colonial times, about poverty, about class and color, and about growth and change in a West Indian society. It too has an appeal that is both contemporary and universal.

Another comparison can be made with Camara Laye's *L'Enfant noir*, also published in 1953. The genesis of both novels is remarkably similar: the author alone in France, having problems of re-adaptation and thinking of his homeland, of his childhood and his loved ones. Since Zobel also wrote his novel while working in France . . . one can be tempted to ask the same question that some critics have asked with respect to Laye's novel: Does the author tailor what he says to suit the tastes of the French among whom and possibly for whom he was writing? In all fairness to Zobel, it does not appear so. And, of course, the *béké* was a different breed altogether, with a different sociopolitical background, so that the metropolitan white could easily divorce himself from Zobel's portrayals.

Zobel's impact in this novel can best be summed up by referring to the old saying that we can best know where we are going once we know where we have been. Zobel helps us see more clearly where we have been. In this respect, the novel takes its place alongside many of the fine autobiographical works that have made their mark on the West Indian literary landscape.

Keith Q. Warner. Introduction to Joseph Zobel, *Black Shack Alley* (London: Heinemann, 1980), n. p.

[Zobel's] best known work, *La Rue cases-nègres*, is autobiographical; it describes the childhood of a young boy living alone first with his grandmother, who cuts cane six days a week and is prematurely old at age forty, then with his mother, who works as a servant in Fort-de-France. The child/grandmother or child/mother relationship is the seminal one in the life of many of Zobel's characters and seemingly in his own life. This relationship is rich and human, warm and loving, but is also seen as a kind of alienation—still one

upon which the protagonist looks back with nostalgia. This key event seems to color all other aspects of Zobel's novelistic world: ''Cet enfant s'est retranché dans une méfiance toujours en éveil sous une inébranlable placidité. . . . Ses joies les plus vraies lui viennent-elles de tout ce qu'il découvre dans ses livres. . . . Et sa revanche et son bonheur sont d'être presque invariablement le premier de sa classe. Ce que les autres ne lui pardonnent guère.'' [The child took refuge in an ever-alert mistrust, under an unflappable calmness. . . . His truest joys came from what he discovered in books. . . . And his revenge and his happiness were that he was almost always head of his class, for which the others scarcely forgave him.] This description of Mapiam in *Laghia de la mort* may be analogous to the author's own character. Mapiam gets by in an alienated world, feeling like an outsider but making his way into productive and responsible levels of society. Zobel apparently prefers to play a supporting role in the drama of Third-World development; he and his characters are not leaders, presidents, mayors, though they may be key social figures in the village (especially Cocotte in *Les Mains pleines d'oiseaux*). He and they do not present an abrupt alternative to the status quo; they seem to believe that progress in the condition of blacks and other Third-World peoples will be gradual and evolutionary. They are down-to-earth, practical, pragmatic people who seek solutions in a humanistic understanding of the problem, in return to smaller, decentralized structures (the village, etc.), in education, and in the development of pride and self-confidence. It seems that Zobel himself was slow in developing both as a writer and as a person, but he has put his great breadth of experience in many jobs and roles to good use in describing the world of formerly colonized peoples. His personal choices and his contribution to Third-World development are now clear; only his literary works remain to be better known. . . .

The alienation of the individual character becomes something of a symbol for the situation of the whole race. Alienation and disalienation are key themes in Zobel's novelistic world, where the psychological descriptions of the characters produce very true-to-life people, not ideal types. At first reading, the rather strong, obvious introversion of most of the male characters seems gratuitous and somewhat out of place. Then we see that this is meant as another documentary fact, and we see the objective correlations with other facts in the social milieu being described. . . .

Zobel is not a romantic spirit and practices a rather staid prose style based on the nineteenth-century novel. He offers neither the polemical fireworks of Négritude nor the magic of avant-garde formal experimentation or of ''marvelous realism.'' Romantic love is not a concern. Zobel is not a revolutionary, another kind of romanticism. He preaches gradual reform and liberation, rooted in the understanding of the other and of foreign societies. Reform must be based on education and personal and social disalienation and the acceptance of responsibility.

Hal Wylie. *World Literature Today*. 56, 1 (Winter 1982), pp. 62–64

[Zobel's] superb talent as a *conteur* . . . is revealed . . . in this delightful collection of short stories under the title of *Et si la mer n'était pas bleue*, which may have been neglected by reviewers at the time of publication.

It is the last story of the five, ''Nardal,'' a type of postscript, which attracted me mostly to this book. ''Nardal'' is a panegyrical statement intended as a public compliment to the Nardal family of Martinique, especially to Paulette Nardal, who has been referred to as the godmother of Négritude. Zobel speaks of this family's love of knowledge and excellence and its pride of blackness. The title story, ''Et si la mer n'était pas bleue,'' tells of a whole new world opened up to a young peasant boy during his first visit on foot to the seaside from his remote village, in the company of a mysterious aunt Oberline. In the second story, ''Le Cahier d'Edouard Tanasio,'' the narrator gives an amusing account of his admiration for two childhood classmates, Eugène Tanasio for his macho image and Edouard Tanasio for his beautiful handwriting. In ''Le Retour de Mamzelle Annette,'' the longest of the five stories, an industrious and obliging little peasant girl gives a child's view of the amorous and irreligious affair between Monsieur Ernest, the town barber, and his longtime housekeeper Mamzelle Annette. This third story also offers a quick look at the repugnant caste system based on the color of one's skin which has long plagued the French Antilles. The fourth story, ''Le Cousin,'' gives credence to the old saying that it is often unwise and unsafe to judge a book by its cover. The ''cousin,'' a fashionable young white gentleman, is none other than a relative of ''Monsieur,'' a wealthy black man who, because he spurns ostentation, performs menial tasks and loves to work in his flower garden, is often mistaken for a lowly servant by those who happen to see him in action or visit his mansion.

Robert P. Smith, Jr. *World Literature Today.* 57, 4 (Autumn 1983), p. 679

Zobel's *Black Shack Alley* is centered on an estate village in Martinique between the two world wars. . . . In Zobel's novel it is the black child José, born on the estate but too young at first to understand the frustration of the laborers and the quality of their despair, whose eyes are gradually opened to the interaction of color and class, first in rural Martinique and later in the Route Didier of the capital. This street with its rich *béké* villas and appendage of domestics' shacks mimics the contrast of the master's *grand' case* and the slaves' *cases-nègres* on the plantations, as the Rue Cases-Nègres itself, where José first lives—the ''street of Negro huts'' which gives the novel its French title—reminds the reader, by its very name, of the inequalities and injustices of slavery. . . .

The child narrator of Zobel's *Black Shack Alley* is largely unaware, during his first seven years, of the subtle class and color distinctions which are the heritage of plantation society. The divisions within José's own community are simpler, though no less rigidly hierarchical. On the one hand, there is the small and uniform group of black estate workers among whom he lives with his grandmother, M'man Tine, the canefield weeder. On the other hand, there are a few remote figures of authority whose power, in the child's eyes, derives principally from their adult status and their occupation on the estate. Their race is irrelevant to him; it is only in passing that he mentions that the overseer is a mulatto, and the care which he and his fellow urchins exercise in avoiding this man's attention during their forages into the canefields is due above all to their fear of parental punishment if they get into any trouble. In José's mind the distance between the management and the laborers is to be measured principally by the visible evidence of their

dwelling places: the latter live in some three dozen ramshackle wooden huts perched on a hillside above the canefields; higher up the hill is the overseer's house; and at the very top stands the manager's larger house, tile-roofed and majestic, presiding over the *cases-nègres* and the great expanse of cane beyond them.

Beverley Ormerod. *An Introduction to the French Caribbean Novel* (London: Heinemann, 1985), pp. 64–65

[*La Rue cases-nègres* is] based on myth. The child-hero leaves the bosom of his family and his closed world in order to go away little by little—towards the schools and villages and cities further and further away. Age, the degrees that he accumulates, and even the distance he travels are the ironic measures of his success because this road is also the road of separation from the ones he loves.

This is because the novel marches to two beats: that of an actual blocked sociohistorical state, where any progress seems impossible; and the personal one of the child who by nature moves, evolves, and develops progressively his vision and comprehension of the exterior world. It is this confrontation between the fixed and the dynamic, anchored in the characters of José and M'man Tine that appears to structure the reality of *La Rue cases-nègres*.

In the initial period it is the world of childhood that dominates. . . . *La Rue cases-nègres* poses the problem of an adult narrator who is at the same time the child subject. Zobel chooses to respect the progressive development of his character without distantiation and this results in the poetry of the novel. . . .

If the world of the child lends itself to the poetic language of the adult narrator because of its elementary temporality and happiness, it is also because of its subjectivity. This point of view which dominates the first part of the narration is also its subject because that which impresses the most is the sensitivity and emotion of the child viewing the colored frescoes that pass in front of his eyes, the meaning of which he is unable to decipher. The reader then is interested as much in childhood as in the real world in which the child lives. . . .

The first part of the narration is marked by the intimacy, mystery, and unique vision that is childhood. . . . In the second and third parts of the story, this vision gives way to another one of the cities. Life there is more noisy and varied; one finds there a cacophony of voices and personalities. Although this society also passes through the eyes and thoughts of José, one no longer has the impression of regularity, stability, or harmony of the first part because the child himself notes the counter-currents, the tensions of social forces, the movement and the changing faces of the actors. The poetry of mystery and naïveté is exchanged for the poetry of the modern, dynamic, and vital swarming city. . . .

The principal agent of this progressive structuring of reality in *La Rue cases-nègres* is M'man Tine, who reflects the real world and structure in the imagination and nascent understanding of the child. She dominates the narration, because it is through her that José learns to see the world. It is thus that throughout the story M'man Tine lives this unfortunate reality and rejects it. The child, still very young, realizes this truth. M'man Tine is the reason of his success and also of his story. She is part of the real world and the mythical world, because she is the object of a closed society and yet she alone is capable of assuring the progress of the child. . . .

But, in José's text, M'man Tine is especially a narrative and poetic solution. She is the symbol of determination and of the will of metamorphosis.

Is it not the same metamorphosis that is carried out on the textual level? José's life is explained through literary forms such as the puzzles, the imaginary tales of Victor and Médouze, and by the fairy tales that help him see and understand his grandmother better. Literature nurtures his life and this metamorphosis is double because José, following the example of his grandmother, transforms the sad destiny of his grandmother and of the Cases-Nègres street into a novel of vision and poetic power.

Eileen Julien. *French Review.* 60, 6 (1987), pp. 781–84, 786†

BIBLIOGRAPHY
*Diab'là*, 1946; *Laghia de la mort*, 1946; *La Rue cases-nègres*, 1950; *La Fête à Paris*, 1953; *Les Mains pleines d'oiseaux*, 1978; *Et si la mer n'était pas bleue*, 1982

# ACKNOWLEDGMENTS

Peter Abrahams. For excerpt from article on Wright in *Holiday*.

Timothy Dow Adams. From *Telling Lies in Modern American Autobiography*. The University of North Carolina Press, 1990. Copyright © 1990 The University of North Carolina Press. All rights reserved. Used by permission of the publisher.

Opal Palmer Adisa. From *Caribbean Women Writers: Essays from the First International Conference*. Edited by Selwyn R. Cudjoe. University of Massachusetts Press, 1990. Copyright © 1990 by Calaloux Publications. All rights reserved. Reproduced by permission of the University of Massachusetts Press.

Africa Quarterly. For excerpts from article by Yashoda Ramamoorthy on Rubadiri. Reprinted with permission of the Indian Council for Cultural Relations.

Africa Report. For excerpts from articles by Charles R. Larson on Soyinka; Taban lo Liyong on Ngugi; Lewis Nkosi on Peters. For excerpts from article by Basil Busacca on Taban lo Liyong. Reprinted with permission of *Africa Report*. Copyright © 1970 by the African-American Institute.

Africa Today. For excerpts from article by Juliet I. Okonkwo on Farah. For excerpts from articles by Charles R. Larson on Armah; Bernth Lindfors on Aluko, Ekwensi; Nancy J. Schmidt on Tutuola.

Africa World Press. For excerpts from articles by Irène Assiba d'Almeida on Bâ in Carole Boyce Davies and Anne Adams Graves, eds., *Ngambika: Studies of Women in African Literature* (1986); Muyiwa P. Awodiya on Osofisan in Eldred Durosimi, ed., *Orature in African Literature Today* (1992); Aderemi Bamikunle on Osundare in Eldred Durosimi, ed., *Orature in African Literature Today* (1992); Brenda F. Berrian on Sembène Ousmane in Carole Boyce Davies and Anne Adams Graves, eds., *Ngambika: Studies of Women in African Literature* (1986); Abena P. A. Busia on Schwarz-Bart in Carole Boyce Davies and Elaine Savory Fido, eds., *Out of the Kumbla: Caribbean Women and Literature* (1990); Abena P. A. Busia on Armah in Carole Boyce Davies and Anne Adams Graves, eds., *Ngambika: Studies of Women in African Literature* (1986); Rhonda Cobham on Bennett in Carole Boyce Davies and Elaine Savory Fido, eds., *Out of the Kumbla: Caribbean Women and Literature* (1990); Carolyn Cooper on Brodber in Carole Boyce Davies and Elaine Savory Fido, eds., *Out of the Kumbla: Caribbean Women and Literature* (1990); Giovanna Covi on Kincaid in Carole Boyce Davies and Elaine Savory Fido, eds., *Out of the Kumbla: Caribbean Women and Literature* (1990); Carole Boyce Davies on Cliff, Kincaid, Lorde in Carole Boyce Davies and Elaine Savory Fido, eds., *Out of the Kumbla: Caribbean Women and Literature* (1990); Chris Dunton on Osofisan in Eldred Durosimi, ed., *The Question of Language in African Literature Today* (1991); Jennifer Evans on Ngugi wa Thiong'o in Eldred Durosimi Jones, ed., *Women in African Literature Today* (1987); Ezenwa-Ohaeto on Osundare in Eldred Durosimi, ed., *The Question of Language in African Literature Today* (1991); Elaine Savory Fido on Goodison, Senior in Carole Boyce Davies and Elaine Savory Fido, eds., *Out of the Kumbla: Caribbean Women and Literature* (1990); Anne Adams Graves on Lopes in Carole Boyce Davies and Anne Adams Graves, eds., *Ngambika: Studies of Women in African Literature* (1986); Tobe Levin on Ngugi wa Thiong'o in Carole Boyce Davies and Anne Adams Graves, eds., *Ngambika: Studies of Women in African Literature* (1986); Janice Lee Liddell on Wynter in Carole Boyce Davies and Elaine Savory Fido, eds., *Out of the Kumbla: Caribbean Women and Literature* (1990); Edris Makward on Bâ in Carole Boyce Davies and Anne Adams Graves, eds., *Ngambika: Studies of Women in African Literature* (1986); Chimalum Nwankwo on Aidoo in Carole Boyce Davies and Anne Adams Graves, eds., *Ngambika: Studies of Women in African Literature* (1986); Adetokunbo Pearce on Sutherland in Eldred Durosimi Jones, ed., *Women in African Literature Today* (1987); Richard K. Priebe, *Myth, Realism, and the West African Writer*, (1988) (Achebe, Armah, Awoonor, Soyinka); Charles Ponnuthurai Sarvan on Head in Eldred Durosimi Jones, ed., *Women in African Literature Today* (1987); Marie Linton Umeh on Emecheta in Carole Boyce Davies and Anne Adams Graves, eds., *Ngambika: Studies of Women in African Literature* (1986); Elizabeth Wilson on Condé, Schwarz-Bart, Warner-Vieyra in Carole Boyce Davies and Elaine Savory Fido, eds., *Out of the Kumbla: Caribbean Women and Literature* (1990).

African Affairs. For excerpts from articles by C. O. D. Ekwensi on Tutuola; Mercedes Mackay on Achebe.

African American Review. For excerpts from articles by John F. Callahan on Harper. Reprinted from *African American Review*, Volume 13, Number 3, (Winter 1979). Copyright 1979 by Indiana State University; Sandra Hollin Flowers on Shange. Reprinted from *African American Review*, Volume 15, Number 2 (Summer 1981). Copyright 1981 by Indiana State University; Trudier Harris on Childress. Reprinted from *African American Review*, Volume 14, Number 1 (Spring 1980). Copyright 1980 by Indiana State University; Mary Jane Lupton on Fauset. Reprinted from *African American Review*, Volume 20, Number 4 (Winter 1986). Copyright 1986 by Indiana State University; Elinor S. Miller on Juminer. Reprinted from *African American Review*, Volume 11, Number 1 (Spring 1977). Copyright 1977 by Indiana State University; Carol E. Neubauer on Angelou. Reprinted from *African American Review*, Volume 17, Number 3 (1983). Copyright 1983 by Indiana State University; Sandra L. Richards on Shange. Reprinted from *African American Review*, Volume 17, Number 2 (Summer 1983). Copyright 1983 by Indiana State University; John W. Roberts on Gaines. Reprinted from *African American Review*, Volume 18, Number 3 (Fall 1984). Copyright 1984 by Indiana State University; Claudia C. Tate on Jones. Reprinted from *African American Review*, Volume 13, Number 4 (Winter 1979). Copyright 1979 by Indiana State University; v. 27, 1933 for "Albert Murray: Literary Reconstruction of the Vernacular Community" by Warren Carson; v. 26, Fall, 1992 for "A Distaff Dream Deferred? Ann Petry and the Art of Subversion"by Keith Clark; v. 27, Spring, 1993 for "Yusef Komunyakaa: The Unified Vision-- Canonization and Humanity" by Alvin Aubert; v. 28, Summer, 1994 for "'Would You Really Rather Die than Bear My Young?': The Construction of Gender, Race, and Species in Octavia E. Butler's 'Bloodchild'" by ElyceRae Helford; v. 30, Summer, 1996 for "Femininity, Publicity, and the Class Division of Cultural Labor: Jessie Redmon Fauset's There Is Confusion"by Nina Miller; v. 31, Summer, 1997 for "'The Black Dick': Race, Sexuality, and Discourse in the L. A. Novels of Walter Mosley"by Roger A. Berger; v. 32, Winter, 1998 for "Michelle Cliff and the 'Tragic Mulatta' Tradition" by Suzanne Bost; v. 32, Winter, 1998 for "Literature and Urban Crisis: John Edgar Wideman's 'Philadelphia Fire'" by Madhu Dubey; v. 32, Spring, 1998 for a review of "Flying Home and Other Stories" by Robert J. Butler; v. 33, 1999 for a review of "The Blue Devils of Nada: A Contemporary American Approach to Aesthetic Statement" by Carolyn M. Jones; v. 33, Spring, 1999 for a review of "Longer Views" by Robert Elliot Fox. Copyright 1933, © 1992, 1993, 1994, 1996, 1997, 1998, 1999 by the respective authors. All reproduced by permission of the respective authors.

African Arts. For excerpt reprinted from *The Works of Thomas Mofolo* by Daniel P. Kunene, Occasional Paper No. 2, 1967. African Studies Center, University of California, Los Angeles; unsigned article on Mphahlele reprinted from *African Arts*, Volume II, No. 2, 1969.

The African Communist. For excerpt from article by Langa Mokwena on Kunene.

African Publishing Company. For excerpts from essay by Christopher Heywood on Abrahams in *Perspectives on African Literature*, Christopher Heywood, ed.; G. D. Killam, *The Novels of Chinua Achebe*; Gerald Moore, *Wole Soyinka*; Ezekiel Mphahlele's Introduction to *Climbié* by Bernard Dadié; Eustace Palmer, *An Introduction to the African Novel* (Amadi, Armah, Ngugi).

African Studies Review. For excerpts from articles by F. Odun Balogun on Taban lo Liyong; Charlotte [H.] Bruner on Emecheta; Chimalum Nwankwo on Cheney-Coker. For excerpt from article by J. Dennis Delaney on Aluko.

Tyohdzuah Akosu. From *The Writing of Ezekiel Mphahlele, South African Writer: Literature, Culture, and Politics*. The Edwin Mellen Press, 1995. Copyright © 1995 The Edwin Mellen Press. All rights reserved. Reproduced by permission.

Ala Bulletin. For excerpts from article by Ezenwa-Ohaeto on Marechera.

J.B. Alston. From *Yoruba Drama in English: Interpretation and Production*. The Edwin Mellen Press, 1989. © 1989 The Edwin Mellen Press. Reproduced by permission.

Nora M. Alter. From *Alteratives*. French Forum Publishers, 1993. Reproduced by permission.

Jacques Alvarez-Pereyre. For excerpts from *The Poetry of Commitment in South Africa* (Brutus, Kunene, Mtshali, Sepamla, Serote).

America. For excerpt from article by James Finn Cotter on Hayden. Reprinted with permission of *America*. All rights reserved. © 1976 by America Press, 106 W. 56 Street, New York, N.Y. 10019; v. 175, July 29, 1996. © 1996 All rights reserved. Reproduced with permission of America Press, Inc.,106 West 56th Street, New York, NY 10019.

American Imago. For excerpts from "David Bradley's *The Chaneysville Incident*: The Belly of the Text" by Martin J. Gliserman. Reprinted from *American Imago*. Volume 43, Number 2, Summer 1986. Reprinted by permission of The Johns Hopkins University Press.

The American Book Review, v. 10, January-February, 1989; v. 17, February-March, 1996. © 1989, 1996 by The American Book Review. Both reproduced by permission.

The American Poetry Review, v. 7, July-August, 1978 for "Stomping the Blues: Ritual in Black Music and Speech" by John Wideman; v. 22, November-December, 1993, for "Lucille Clifton" by Alicia Ostriker. Copyright © 1978, 1993 by World Poetry, Inc. Both reproduced by permission of the respective authors.

The American Scholar. For excerpts from "From a Common Back Cloth: A Reassessment of the African Literary Image" by Wole Soyinka. Reprinted from *The American Scholar*, Volume 32, Number 3, Summer, 1963. Copyright © 1963 by the United Chapters of Phi Beta Kappa. By permission of the publishers (Achebe, Beti, Camara, Tutuola); "Charles W. Chesnutt: The Marrow of Tradition" by John Wideman. Reprinted from *The American Scholar*, Volume 42, Number 1, Winter, 1972–73. Copyright © 1972 by the United Chapters of Phi Beta Kappa. By permission of the publisher; v. 67, Spring 1998. Copyright © 1998 by the United Chapters of the Phi Beta Kappa Society. Reproduced by permission of the publishers.

Debra L. Anderson. From *Decolonizing the Text: Glissantian Readings in Caribbean and African-American Literatures*. Peter Lang Publishing, Inc., 1995. © 1995 by Peter Lang Publishing, Inc. All rights reserved. Reproduced by permission.

Applause Books. For excerpts from article by Shelby Steele on Baraka in Errol Hill, ed., *The Theatre of Black Americans* (1987).

Ariel. For excerpts from articles by Brian Crow on Mugo, Copyright © 1983, The Board of Governors, The University of Calgary; Lorna Down on Edgell, Copyright © 1987, The Board of Governors, The University of Calgary; Jean-Pierre Durix on Harris, Copyright © 1984, The Board of Governors, The University of Calgary; Simon Gikandi on Hodge, Copyright © 1989, The Board of Governors, The University of Calgary; John Haynes on Kunene, Copyright © 1987, The Board of Governors, The University of Calgary; Patricia Ismond on Walcott, Copyright © 1985, The Board of Governors, The University of Calgary; Anthony Kellman on Baraka, Copyright © 1990, The Board of Governors, The University of Calgary; Maria Helena Lima on Collins, Copyright © 1993, The Board of Governors, The University of Calgary; Mbulelo Vizikhungo Mzamane on Rive, Copyright © 1985, The Board of Governors, The University of Calgary; James McCorkle on Walcott, Copyright © 1986, The Board of Governors, The University of Calgary; Chikwenye Okonjo Ogunyemi on Brutus, Copyright © 1982, The Board of Governors, The University of Calgary; Tanure Ojaide on Brutus, Copyright © 1986, The Board of Governors, The University of Calgary; Virginia U. Ola on Head, Copyright © 1986, The Board of Governors, The University of Calgary; Richard F. Patteson on Senior, Copyright © 1993, The Board of Governors, The University of Calgary; Shalini Puri on Brodber, Copyright © 1993, The Board of Governors, The University of Calgary; Stephen Slemon on Harris, Copyright © 1988, The Board of Governors, The University of Calgary; Colin Style on Marechera, Copyright © 1985, The Board of Governors, The University of Calgary; Clement H. Wyke on Walcott, Copyright © 1989, The Board of Governors, The University of Calgary; A. Rasheed Yesufu on Ntiru, Copyright © 1987, The Board of Governors, The University of Calgary; v. 24, January, 1993 for "Revolutionary Developments: Michelle Cliff's 'No Telephone to Heaven' and Merle Collins 'Angel'"by Maria Helena Lima; v. 27, October, 1996 for "'Her Words Are Like Fire': The Storytelling Magic of Dionne Brand" by Kathleen J. Renk; v. 28, April, 1997 for "George Lamming's 'In The Castle of My Skin': A Modern West Indian Novel" by Viney Kirpal; v. 28, July, 1997 for "Trapped and Troping: Allegories of the Transnational Intellectual in Tsitsi Dangarembga's 'Nervous Conditions'" by Biman Basu. Copyright © 1993, 1996, 1997 The Board of Governors, The University of Calgary. All reproduced by permission of the publisher and the respective authors.

Associated University Presses. For excerpts from articles by John Timpane on Shange; Catherine Wiley on Childress in *Modern American Drama: The Female Canon* (1990), June Schlueter, ed..

Association Pour La Diffusion De La Pensée Française. For excerpts from article by Roger Mercier on Maran in *Tendances*.

The Atlantic Monthly. For excerpt from article by Peter Davison on Brooks; v. 234, December, 1974 for "The View from the Chinaberry Tree" by James Alan McPherson. Copyright 1974 by The Atlantic Monthly Company, Boston, MA. Reproduced by permission of the author.

Éditions Aubier-Montaigne. For excerpts from Sunday O. Anozie, *Sociologie du roman africain* (Bhêly-Quénum, Kane).

Houston A. Baker, Jr. For excerpt from article on Johnson in *The Virginia Quarterly Review*.

Baobab Books. For excerpts from articles by Anthony Chennells on La Guma; Ismael Mbise on Okot p'Bitek in *Literature, Language and the Nation* (1989), Emmanuel Ngara and Andrew Morrison, eds.

Amiri Baraka. From *'A Raisin in the Sun' and The Sign in Sidney Brustein's Window*. By Lorraine Hansberry. Edited by Robert Nemiroff. New American Library, 1987. Copyright Amiri Baraka. Reproduced by permission of Sterling Lord Literistic, Inc.

Barnes and Noble. For excerpts from R. N. Egudu. *Modern African Poetry and the African Predicament* (Brutus, Soyinka, Taban lo Liyong).

Bonnie J. Barthold. From *Black Time: Fiction of Africa, the Caribbean, and the United States*. Yale University Press, 1981. Copyright © 1981 by Yale University Press. All rights reserved. Reproduced by permission.

Beacon Press. For excerpts from *Diving Deep and Surfacing: Women Writers on Spiritual Quest* by Carol P. Christ (Shange). Copyright © 1980 by Carol P. Christ. Reprinted by permission of Beacon Press. For excerpt from James Baldwin, *Notes of a Native Son*. Copyright © 1951, 1955 by James Baldwin. Reprinted by permission of Beacon Press (Wright).

Herman Beavers. From *Wrestling Angels into Song: The Fictions of Ernest J. Gaines and James Allan McPherson*. University of Pennsylvania Press, 1995. Copyright © 1995 by the University of Pennsylvania Press. All rights reserved. Reproduced by permission.

Belles Lettres: A Review of Books by Women, v. 10, Fall, 1994. Reproduced by permission.

Robert Bensen. For excerpts from article on Walcott in *The Literary Review*.

Olympe Bhêly-Quénum. For excerpt from article on Camara in *L'Afrique actuelle* 28, Avenue Émile Zola, 78300 Poissy, France.

Bim. For excerpts from article by Harold Barratt on Anthony. For excerpts from articles by Edward Brathwaite on Harris, Lamming.

Black American Literature Forum. For excerpt from article by Robert J. Willis on Hansberry in *Negro American Literature Forum*; v. 14, Summer, 1980 for "Archetypal Victim" by Bernard W. Bell. Copyright © 1980 by the author. Reproduced by permission of the publisher and Bernard W. Bell.

Black Issues in Higher Education, v. 15, December 10, 1998. Reproduced by permission.

Black Orpheus. For excerpts from articles by Akanji on Camara; Ulli Beier on Clark, Okigbo, Sembène; J.P. Clark on Tutuola; Martin Esslin on Soyinka; Gerald Moore on U Tam'si; Lewis Nkosi on La Guma, Mphahlele; Paul Theroux on Awoonor, Brutus.

The Black Scholar. For excerpts from articles by Robert Chrisman on A. Walker; James T. Lampley on Williams; v. 28, Spring, 1998. Copyright 1998 by The Black Scholar. Reproduced by permission.

The Bobbs-Merrill Company, Inc. For excerpt from *Nikki Giovanni, Gemini* (Chesnutt).

Robert Bone. From *The Negro Novel in America*. Revised edition. Yale University Press, 1965. Copyright © 1965 by Yale University. Copyright renewed by Robert A. Bone in 1985. All rights reserved. Reproduced by permission of the author.

Book World--The Washington Post, May 5, 1996. © 1996, Washington Post Book World Service/ Washington Post Writers Group. Reproduced by permission of Liesl Schillinger./ August 20, 1995 for "Living in Blues" by Julius Lester. © 1995, Washington Post Book World Service/Washington Post Writers Group. Reproduced by permission of the author.

James Booth. From *Writers and Politics in Nigeria*. Africana Publishing Company, 1981. Copyright © 1981 James Booth. Reproduced with permission.

Georges Borchardt, Inc. For excerpts from Franck Jotterand, *Le nouveau théâtre américain* (Bullins). Léopold Sédar Senghor, *Liberte I: Négritude et humanisme* (Abrahams, Camara, Césaire, U Tam'si).

The Boston Globe, July 19, 1995. Reproduced by permission.

Bowling Green State University Popular Press. For excerpts from articles by Angelita Reyes on Marshall; David Lionel Smith on Baraka in *Politics and the Muse: Studies in the Politics of Recent American Literature* (1989), Adam J. Sorkin, ed.

Anthony Boxill. For excerpt from article on Lamming in *World Literature Written in English*.

Edward Brathwaite. For excerpts from articles on Harris, Lamming in *Bim*.

The British Council. For excerpt from article by Martin Banham on Ekwensi in *A Review of English Literature*.

Broadside Press. For excerpts from Gwendolyn Brooks, *Report from Part One*. Copyright © 1972 by Gwendolyn Brooks (Baraka); Addison Gayle, Jr., *Claude McKay: The Black Poet at War*. Copyright © 1972 by Addison Gayle, Jr.; Don L. Lee's Preface to *Report from Part One* by Gwendolyn Brooks.

Pierre Brodin. For excerpt from *Présences contemporaines* (Ellison).

Curtis Brown, Ltd. For excerpt from article by Fannie Hurst on Hurston in *Yale University Library Gazette*.

Lloyd W. Brown. For excerpts from *West Indian Poetry* on Bennett, Brathwaite.

Jerry H. Bryant. For excerpt from article on Gaines in *The Southern Review*. From *Victims and Heroes: Racial Violence in the African American Novel*. The University of Massachusetts Press, 1997. Copyright © 1997 by The University of Massachusetts Press. All rights reserved. Reproduced by permission.

Diana Brydon. For excerpts from article on Clarke in *Canadian Literature*.

Robert Butler. From *Contemporary African American Fiction*. Associated University Presses, 1998. © 1998 by Associated University Presses, Inc. All rights reserved. Reproduced by permission.

Stephen Butterfield. For excerpts from *Black Autobiography in America* (Angelou).

Callaloo. For excerpts from "To Write in a New Language: Werewere Liking's Adaptation of Ritual to the Novel" by Anne Adams. Reprinted from *Callaloo*. Volume 16, Number 1, Winter 1993; "Chronicling Everyday Travails and Triumphs" by Michael Awkward on McMillan. Reprinted from *Callaloo*. Volume 11, Number 3, Summer 1988; "Their Long Scars Touch Ours: A Reflection on the Poetry of Michael Harper" by Joseph A. Brown, SJ. Reprinted from *Callaloo*. Volume 9, Number 1, Winter 1986; "Debrouya pa peche, or il y a toujours moyen de moyenner: Patterns of Opposition in the Fiction of Patrick

Chamoiseau" by Richard D. E. Burton. Reprinted from *Callaloo*. Volume 16, Number 2, Spring 1993; "Reflections on Maryse Condé's *Traversée de la Mangrove*" by Patrick Chamoiseau. Reprinted from *Callaloo*. Volume 14, Number 2, Spring 1991; "Revisioning Our Kumblas: Transforming Feminist and Nationalist Agendas in Three Caribbean Women's Texts" by Rhonda Cobham on Hodge. Reprinted from *Callaloo*. Volume 16, Number 1, Winter 1993; "Scars and Wings: Rita Dove's *Grace Notes*" by Bonnie Costello. Reprinted from *Callaloo*. Volume 14, Number 2, Spring 1991; "Engagement, Exile and Errance: Some Trends in Haitian Poetry 1946–1986" by J. Michael Dash on Depestre and Phelps. Reprinted from *Callaloo*. Volume 15, Number 3, Summer 1992; "Race, Privilege, and the Politics of (Re) Writing History: An Analysis of the Novels of Michelle Cliff" by Belinda Edmondson. Reprinted from *Callaloo*. Volume 16, Number 1, Winter 1993; "Fictionalizing History: David Bradley's *The Chaneysville Incident*" by Klaus Ensslen. Reprinted from *Callaloo*. Volume 11, Number 2, Spring 1988; "Maximin's *L'Isolé Soleil* and Caliban's Curse" by John D. Erickson. Reprinted from *Callaloo*. Volume 15, Number 1, Winter 1992; "Rita Dove: Crossing Boundaries" by Ekaterini Georgoudaki. Reprinted from *Callaloo*. Volume 14, Number 2, Spring 1991; "Geographies of Pain: Captive Bodies and Violent Acts in the Fictions of Myriam Warner-Vieyra, Gayl Jones, and Bessie Head" by Françoise Lionnet on Warner-Vieyra. Reprinted from *Callaloo*. Volume 16, Number 1, Winter 1993; "The Assembling Vision of Rita Dove" by Robert [E.] McDowell. Reprinted from *Callaloo*. Volume 9, Number 1, Winter 1986; "Reading Warner-Vieyra's *Juletane*" by Jonathan Ngate. Reprinted from *Callaloo*. Volume 9, Number 4, Fall 1986; "Poetic Viewpoint: Okot p'Bitek and His Personae" by Tanure Ojaide. Reprinted from *Callaloo*. Volume 9, Number 2, Spring 1986; "An Introduction to the Poetry and Fiction of Olive Senior" by Velma Pollard. Reprinted from *Callaloo*. Volume 11, Number 3, Summer 1988; "The Poems of Rita Dove" by Arnold Rampersad. Reprinted from *Callaloo*. Volume 9, Number 2, Winter 1986; "A Shift Toward the Inner Voice and Créolité in the French Caribbean Novel" by Ann Armstrong Scarboro on Maximin. Reprinted from *Callaloo*. Volume 15, Number 1, Winter 1992; "Patrick Chamoiseau, *Solibo Magnifique*: From the Escheat of Speech to the Emergence of Language" by Marie-Agnès Sourieau. Reprinted from *Callaloo*. Volume 15, Number 1, Winter 1992; "Cold Hearts and (Foreign) Tongues: Recitation and the Reclamation of the Female Body in the Works of Erna Brodber and Jamaica Kincaid" by Helen Tiffin on Kincaid. Reprinted from *Callaloo*. Volume 16, Number 3, Fall 1993. Reprinted by permission of The Johns Hopkins University Press; v. 16, Fall, 1993; v. 18, 1995; v. 29, 1996. Copyright © 1993, 1995, 1996 by Charles H. Rowell. All reproduced by permission of The Johns Hopkins University Press.

Calaloux Publications. For excerpts from articles by Selwyn R. Cudjoe on Bennett; Daryl Cumber Dance on Brodber; Laura Niesen de Abruna on Hodge, Kincaid; Marie-Denise Shelton on Schwarz-Bart, Warner-Vieyra; Ena V. Thomas on Hodge in *Caribbean Women Writers*, Selwyn R. Cudjoe, ed.

Cambridge University Press. For excerpts from Dorothy S. Blair, *African Literature in French: A History of Writing in French from West and Equatorial Africa* (Badian, Bebey, Kourouma, Ndao, Ouologuem). Reprinted with the permission of Cambridge University Press; Robert Fraser, *West African Poetry* (Anyidoho, Awoonor, Rabéarivelo). Reprinted with the permission of Cambridge University Press; "Ethnos and the Beat Poets," by Steve Harney on Baraka, in *Journal of American Studies*, Vol. 25, No. 3 (1991). Reprinted with the permission of Cambridge University Press; Adrian Roscoe, *Uhuru's Fire: African Literature East to South* (Ntiru, Serumaga, Taban lo Liyong). Reprinted with the permission of Cambridge University Press; Wole Soyinka, *Myth, Literature and the African World* (Rive). Reprinted with the permission of Cambridge University Press. For excerpts from Adrian A. Roscoe, *Mother Is Gold* (Clark, Okara).

Canadian Literature, v. 151, Winter, 1996 for "Disturbing the Peace" by Geoffrey V. Davis; v. 154, Fall, 1997 for "Caribbean Word Power" by Brenda Carr. Both reproduced by permission of the respective authors.

Katie G. Cannon. From a conclusion to *Katie's Canon: Womanism and the Soul of the Black Community*. The Continuum Publishing Company, 1995. Copyright © 1995 by Katie Geneva Cannon. All rights reserved. Reproduced by permission.

Caribbean Quarterly. For excerpts from articles by Selwyn R. Cudjoe on Juminer; Peter Dunwoodie on St. Omer; Patricia Ismond on St. Omer; Consuelo Lopez Springfield on James.

Jacqueline Miller Carmichael. From an introduction to *Trumpeting a Fiery Sound: History and Folklore in Margaret Walker's Jubilee*. University of Georgia Press, 1998. © 1988 by the University of Georgia Press. All rights reserved. Reproduced by permission.

Carribbean Studies. For excerpt from Book Review by Sylvia Wynter of publications: *Green Days by the River*, and *The Games Were Coming*, by Michael Anthony in *Caribbean Studies* 9, No. 4 (January 1970): 114–18. Reprinted by permission of the Author and The Institute of Caribbean Studies. Copyright 1970 by The Institute of Caribbean Studies, University of Puerto Rico, Río Piedras, Puerto Rico.

Wilfred Cartey. For excerpt from article on La Guma in *African Forum*.

Thomas Cassirer. For excerpt from article on Bhêly-Quénum in *African Forum*.

Edward J. Chamerlin. From *Come Back to Me My Language: Poetry and the West Indies*. © 1993 by the Board of Trustees of the University of Illinois. Reproduced by permission.

Myriam J. A. Chancy. From *Searching for Safe Spaces: Afro-Caribbean Women Writers in Exile*. Temple University Press, 1977. Copyright © 1997 by Temple University. All rights reserved. Reproduced by permission.

Balasubramanyam Chandramohan. From *A Study in Trans-ethnicity in Modern South Africa: the Writings of Alex la Guma*. Mellen Research University Press, 1992. © 1992 Mellen Research University Press. Reproduced by permission.

Chicago Tribune. For excerpts from articles by Wilfrid Sheed on Williams; Paul Theroux on A. Walker in *Book World*.

Choice. For excerpt from unsigned article on Jordan.

Barbara Christian. From an introduction to *Bake-Face and Other Guava Stories*. Kelsey St. Press, 1986. Copyright © 1986 Opal Palmer Adisa. All rights reserved. Reproduced by permission.

The Christian Science Monitor. For excerpt from article by Roderick Nordell on Reed. Reprinted by permission from The Christian Science Monitor. © 1976 The Christian Science Publishing Society. All rights reserved.

Citadel Press, Inc. For excerpt from Carl Milton Hughes, *The Negro Novelist* (Attaway).

CLA Journal. For excerpts from articles by Houston A. Baker, Jr., on Brooks; Arthur P. Davis on Brooks; W. Edward Farrison on Brown, Hansberry; Kennell Jackson, Jr., on Bullins; Maurice O'Sullivan, Jr., on Hayden; Robert P. Smith on Beti; Ronald Walcott on Williams; Jerry W. Ward on Walker; Jill Weyant on Kelly; from essay by Harry L. Jones in *Langston Hughes: Black Genius*, Therman B. O'Daniel, ed.; v. 32, September, 1988; v. 33, March, 1990; v. 34, September, 1990; v.36, December, 1992; v. 38, March, 1995; v. XL, March 1997; v. 41, September 1997; v. 41, June, 1998; Copyright © 1988, 1990, 1992, 1995, 1997, 1998 by The College Language Association. All used by permission of The College Language Association.

VèVè A. Clark. From "Talking Shop: A Comparative Feminist Approach to Carribean Literature by Women" in *Borderwork: Feminist Engagements with Comparative Literature*. Edited by Margaret R. Higonnet. Cornell University Press, 1994. Copyright © 1994 by Cornell University. Used by permission of the publisher, Cornell University Press.

College Literature. For excerpts from article by Elizabeth Ammons on Fauset.

Harold R. Collins. For excerpt from article on Armah in *World Literature Written in English*.

Columbia University Press. For excerpt from Vernon Loggins, *The Negro Author* (Dunbar).

Commentary. For excerpts from articles by Saul Bellow on Ellison; Steven Marcus on Baldwin; Robert Penn Warren on Ellison.

Commonweal. For excerpts from articles by Michele Murray on Kelley; R. Dana Skinner on Thurman; Gerald Weales on Hansberry.

Commonwealth Essays & Studies. For excerpts from articles by Chidi Amuta on Iyayi; Aderemi Bamikunle on Osofisan; Alfred Kiema on Amadi; Bruce King on St. Omer; Ayo Mamudu on Okri; Alastair Niven on Anthony; J. O. J. Nwachukwu-Agbada on Okot p'Bitek; Roydon Salick on Gilroy; A. Rasheed Yesufu on Ntiru.

Commonwealth: Novel in English, v. 7 & 8, 1997-98. Reproduced by permission.

Comparative Literature Studies. For excerpts from Josie P. Campbell, "To Sing the Song, to Tell the Tale: A Study of Toni Morrison and Simone Schwarz-Bart" on Schwarz-Bart, *Comparative Literature Studies*, Volume 22, Number 3, pp. 394–412. Copyright 1985 by The Pennsylvania State University. Reproduced by permission of The Pennsylvania State University Press; v. 32, Summer, 1995. Copyright © 1995 by The Pennsylvania State University. Reproduced by permission of The Pennsylvania State University Press.

Contemporary Literature. For excerpts from articles by Henry Louis Gates, Jr. on Naylor; Catherine C. Ward on Naylor. Reprinted by permission of The University of Wisconsin Press; v. 39, Winter, 1998; v. 39, Summer, 1998. © 1998 by the Board of Regents of the University of Wisconsin. Both reproduced by permission of The University of Wisconsin Press.

Contributions in Black Studies, October, 1993 for "Aesthetics, Ideology, and Social Commitment in the Prose Fiction" by Frederick Ivor Case. Reproduced by permission of the author.

Cornell University Press. For excerpts from Simon Gikandi, *Writing in Limbo: Modernism and Caribbean Literature* (Cliff, Edgell, James, Lamming, Marshall). Copyright © 1992 by Cornell University. Used by permission of the publisher, Cornell University Press.

Carl Cowl. For excerpt from Claude McKay, *Harlem: Negro Metropolis* (Johnson).

The Crisis. For excerpts from articles by Cedric Dover on Hayden; W. E. B. Du Bois on Bontemps, McKay, Toomer; Saunders Redding on Baraka, Hansberry; Henry F. Winslow on Brooks, Killens.

Critique: Studies in Contemporary Fiction, v. XVI, Winter, 1974; v. 35, Spring, 1994; v. 38, Spring, 1997. Copyright © 1974, 1994, 1997 Helen Dwight Reid Educational Foundation. All reproduced with permission of the Helen Dwight Reid Educational Foundation, published by Heldref Publications, 1319 18th Street, NW, Washington, DC 20036-1802.

Cuadernos Americanos. For excerpt from article by Rémy Bastien on Roumain.

David Daiches. For excerpt from article on Hughes in *New York Herald Tribune Book Section*.

J. Michael Dash. From an introduction to *Eduoard Glissant*. Cambridge University Press, 1995. © Cambridge University Press 1995. Reproduced with the permission of Cambridge University Press and the author.

Charles T. Davis. For excerpt from essay in *Modern Black Poets*, Donald B. Gibson, ed. (Hayden).

Gregson Davis. From *Aimé Césaire*. Cambridge University Press, 1997. © Cambridge University Press 1997. Reproduced with the permission of Cambridge University Press and the author.

Thulani Davis. For excerpt from article on McMillan in *The Village Voice*.

Claire L. Dehon. From "Fate in Mongo Beti's Novels" in *Critical Perspectives on Mongo Beti*. Edited by Stephen H. Arnold. Lynne Rienner Publishers, Inc., 1998. © 1998 by Lynne Rienner Publishers, Inc. All rights reserved. Reproduced by permission of the author.

Maison Henri Deschamps. For excerpt from *Manuel illustré d'histoire de la littérature haïtienne* (Alexis).

The Dial Press. For excerpts from Sherley Anne Williams, *Give Birth to Brightness* (Baraka, Gaines). Copyright © 1972 by Sherley Anne Williams. Reprinted by permission of The Dial Press.

Les Éditeurs Français Réunis. For excerpt from Jacques-Stéphen Alexis's Preface to *La montagne ensorcelée* by Jacques Roumain.

Educational Ministries. For excerpt by Edward A. Jones on Damas in *Voices of Négritude*, Edward A. Jones, ed., published by The Judson Press. Used by permission.

Romanus N. Egudu. From"Christopher Okigbo and the Growth of Poetry" in *European-Language Writing in Sub-Saharan Africa, Vol. 2*. Edited by Albert S. Gerard. Akadmiaié Kiad ©, 1986. Reproduced by permission.

Cyprian Ekwensi. For excerpts from articles on Abrahams, Thoby-Marcelin and Marcelin in *West African Review*.

Isaac Irabor Elimimian. From *Theme and Style in African Poetry*. The Edwin Mellen Press, 1991. Copyright © 1991 Isaac I. Elimimian. All rights reserved. Reproduced by permission.

The English Academy Review. For excerpts from Es'kia (Ezekiel) Mphahlele, "Mongane Serote's Odyssey: The Path that Breaks the Heels." *The English Academy Review*. Volume 3, 1985. The English Academy of Southern Africa. pp. 67–68.

Betsy Erkkila. From *The Wicked Sisters: Women Poets, Literary History, and Discord*. Oxford University, 1992. Copyright © 1992 by Oxford University Press. Used by permission of Oxford University Press, Inc.

L'Esprit Createur. For excerpts from articles by Christopher L. Miller on Ouologuem; Mildred Mortimer on Glissant. For excerpts from articles by Thomas Cassirer on Beti; Frederick Ivor Case on Césaire; Enid H. Rhodes on D. Diop; Austin J. Shelton on Camara, Dadié.

David Estes. From *Critical Reflections on the Fiction of Ernest J. Gaines*. University of Georgia Press, 1994. © 1994 by the University of Georgia Press. All rights reserved. Reproduced by permission.

Esquire. For excerpt from article by Sinclair Lewis on Wright.

Europe. For excerpts from articles by Pierre Gamarra on Roumain, Sembène; Gérard Pierre-Charles on Alexis; Claude Souffrant on Alexis.

M. Evans and Company, Inc. For excerpt from Fern Marja Eckman, *The Furious Passage of James Baldwin*. Copyright © 1966 by Fern Marja Eckman. Reprinted by permission of the publisher, M. Evans and Company, Inc. New York, N.Y. 10017.

Evans Brothers Limited. For excerpts from Sunday O. Anozie, *Christopher Okigbo: Creative Rhetoric*; essays by Dan Izevbaye on Clark, Douglas Killam on Ekwensi, Paul Theroux on Okigbo in *Introduction to Nigerian Literature*, Bruce King, ed.; Gerald Moore, *Wole Soyinka*; Michael Wade, *Peter Abrahams*.

Everett/Edwards, Inc. For excerpts from Dan Jaffe on Brooks, Jordan Y. Miller on Hansberry, Mike Thelwell on Baldwin in *The Black American Writer*, C. W. E. Bigsby, ed. Reprinted by permission of Everett/Edwards, Inc., DeLand, Florida.

The Explicator, v. 56, Winter, 1998; v. 57. Copyright 1998 by Helen Dwight Reid Educational Foundation. Both reproduced with permission of the Helen Dwight Reid Educational Foundation, published by Heldref Publications, 1319 18th Street, NW, Washington, DC 20036-1802.

Extrapolation, v. 23, Spring, 1982. Copyright © 1982 by The Kent State University Press. Reproduced by permission.

Faber and Faber Ltd. For excerpts from Ezekiel Mphahlele, *The African Image* (Kunene, Plattje); Kenneth Ramchand, *The West Indian Novel and Its Background* (Anthony, Harris, Lamming, McKay). Reprinted by permission of Faber and Faber Ltd.

Michel Fabre. For excerpt from article on Walcott in *New Letters*.

Farrar, Straus & Giroux, Inc. For excerpts from Ezekiel Mphahlele, *Voices in the Whirlwind*. Copyright ©
1967, 1969, 1972 by Ezekiel Mphahlele (Baraka, Brutus); Norman Podhoretz, *Doings and Undoings*.
Copyright © 1953, 1954, 1955, 1956, 1957, 1958, 1959, 1962, 1963, 1964 by Norman Podhoretz
(Baldwin); Philippe Thoby-Marcelin's Introduction to *The Dark Child* by Camara Laye. Copyright ©
1954 by Camara Laye. Edmund Wilson's Introduction to *All Men Are Mad* by Philippe Thoby-Marcelin
and Pierre Marcelin. Copyright © 1970 by Farrar, Straus, Inc. Reprinted with permission of Farrar, Straus
& Giroux, Inc.

Feminist Studies. For excerpts from article by Sagri Dhairyam on Lorde. This article is reprinted in part
from *Feminist Studies*, Volume 18, Number 2 (Spring 1992): 229–56, by permission of the publisher,
*Feminist Studies*, Inc., c/o Women's Studies Program, University of Maryland, College Park, MD 20742.

Moira Ferguson. From a conclusion to *Jamaica Kincaid: Where the Land Meets the Body*. The University
Press of Virginia, 1994. Copyright © 1994 by the Rector and Visitors of the University of Virginia.
Reproduced by permission.

Katherine Fishburn. From *Reading Buchi Emecheta: Cross-Cultural Conversations*. Greenwood Press,
1995. Copyright © 1995 by Katherine Fishburn. All rights reserved. Reproduced by permission of
Greenwood Publishing Group, Inc., Westport, CT.

Jeanie Forte. From "Kennedy's Body Politic: The Mulatta, Menses, and the Medusa" in *Intersecting
Boundaries: The Theatre of Adrienne Kennedy*. Edited by Paul K. Bryant-Jackson and Lois More
Overbeck. University of Minnesota, 1992. Copyright © 1992 by the Regents of the University of
Minnesota. All rights reserved. Reproduced by permission.

Margery Foster-Davis. For excerpt from article on Mittelholzer in *Caribbean Quarterly*.

Foundation, March, 1975 for "Cultural Invention and Metaphor in the Novels of Samuel R. Delany" by
Douglas Barbour. Reproduced by permission of the author.

Freedomways. For excerpts from articles by Ossie Davis on Hansberry; Ruby Dee on Morrison; John
Henry Jones on Killens; Julian Mayfield on Baldwin; Cynthia J. Smith on Kelley. Reprinted from
*Freedomways* Magazine published at 799 Broadway, New York City.

The French Review. For excerpts from articles by JoAnne Cornwell on Beti; Joan Dayan on Depestre;
Arthur Flannigan on Condé; Louise M. Jefferson on Zadi Zaourou; Louise Fiber Luce on Labou Tansi;
Kitzie McKinney on Schwarz-Bart; Rosemary G. Schikora on Kourouma; Arlette M. Smith on Condé. For
excerpts from articles by Mercer Cook on Maran, Roumain; Edward Allen Jones on Senghor; Richard
Regosin on Césaire; v. 67, March, 1994; v. 69, March, 1996; v. 70, April, 1997; v, 70, May 6, 1997.
Copyright 1994, 1996, 1997 by the American Association of Teachers of French. All reproduced by
permission.

P. N. Furbank. For excerpt from article on Walcott in *The Listener*.

Edwin Fussell. For excerpts from article on Harper in *Parnassus*.

Roger Gaillard. For excerpt from *L'univers romanesque de Jacques Roumain*.

David Galler. For excerpts from article on Hayden in *Poetry*.

Éditions Gallimard. For excerpt from Jean-Paul Sartre, *Black Orpheus*. Copyright © 1949 by Éditions
Gallimard (Césaire).

The Gar. For excerpts from article by Charlotte H. Bruner on Phelps.

Susan Gardiner. For excerpts from article on Head in Cherry Clayton, ed., *Women and Writing in South
Africa*.

The Georgia Review, v. XLIXI, Spring, 1995; v. 50, Summer, 1996. Copyright, 1995, 1996, by the
University of Georgia. Both reproduced by permission.

Judith Gleason. For excerpt from article on Bhêly-Quénum in *African Forum*.

William Gleason. For excerpts from article on Johnson in *Black American Literature Forum* (now *African American Review*).

Martin J. Gliserman. From *Psychoanalysis, Language and the Body of the Text*. University Press of Florida, 1996. © 1996 by the Board of Regents of the State of Florida. All rights reserved. Reproduced with the permission of the University Press of Florida.

Nadine Gordimer. From "Soyinka the Tiger" in *Wole Soyinka*. Heinemann Educational Publishers, 1994. Essays © Individual Contributors. Reproduced by permission. Also excerpts from articles on Abrahams, Achebe in *TLS*; La Guma, Ngugi in *The Michigan Quarterly Review*.

Sanford J. Greenburger Associates. For excerpt from Jean-Paul Sartre, *What Is Literature?* Copyright © 1949 by Philosophical Library, Inc. Reprinted by permission of Philosophical Library (Wright).

Greenwood Press. For excerpt from Margaret Perry, *A Bio-Bibliography of Countee P. Cullen, 1903–1946*. Used with the permission of the original publishers, Greenwood Press.

Greenwood Publishing Group. For excerpts from F. Odun Balogun, *Tradition and Modernity in the African Short Story: An Introduction to a Literature in Search of Critics* (Taban lo Liyong), reprinted with permission of Greenwood Publishing Group, Inc., Westport, CT. Copyright © 1991; Lloyd W. Brown, *Women Writers in Black Africa* (Aidoo, Emecheta, Head, Nwapa, Sutherland), reprinted with permission of Greenwood Publishing Group, Inc., Westport, CT. Copyright © 1981; article by Roland E. Bush on St. Omer in *Fifty Caribbean Writers*, Daryl Cumber Dance, ed., reprinted with permission of Greenwood Publishing Group, Inc., Westport, CT. Copyright © 1986; article by Victor L. Chang on Wynter in *Fifty Caribbean Writers*, Daryl Cumber Dance, ed., reprinted with permission of Greenwood Publishing Group, Inc., Westport, CT. Copyright © 1986; article by Eugenia Collier on James in *Fifty Caribbean Writers*, Daryl Cumber Dance, ed., reprinted with permission of Greenwood Publishing Group, Inc., Westport, CT. Copyright © 1986; article by Daryl Cumber Dance on Reid in *Fifty Caribbean Writers*, Daryl Cumber Dance, ed., reprinted with permission of Greenwood Publishing Group, Inc., Westport, CT. Copyright © 1986; article by David Ingledew on Hearne in *Fifty Caribbean Writers*, Daryl Cumber Dance, ed., reprinted with permission of Greenwood Publishing Group, Inc., Westport, CT. Copyright © 1986; Margaret Paul Joseph, *Caliban in Exile: The Outsider in Caribbean Fiction* on Lamming, reprinted with permission of Greenwood Publishing Group, Inc., Westport, CT. Copyright © 1992; article by Mark A. McWatt on Heath in *Fifty Caribbean Writers*, Daryl Cumber Dance, ed., reprinted with permission of Greenwood Publishing Group, Inc., Westport, CT. Copyright © 1986; article by Mervyn Morris on Bennett in *Fifty Caribbean Writers*, Daryl Cumber Dance, ed., reprinted with permission of Greenwood Publishing Group, Inc., Westport, CT. Copyright © 1986; article by Evelyn O'Callaghan on Brodber in *Fifty Caribbean Writers*, Daryl Cumber Dance, ed., reprinted with permission of Greenwood Publishing Group, Inc., Westport, CT. Copyright © 1986; Richard K. Priebe, *Ghanaian Literatures* on Aidoo, reprinted with permission of Greenwood Publishing Group, Inc., Westport, CT. Copyright © 1988; article by Juris Silenieks on Glissant, Phelps in *Voices from Under: Black Narrative in Latin America and the Caribbean*, William Luis, ed, reprinted with permission of Greenwood Publishing Group, Inc., Westport, CT. Copyright © 1984; H. Nigel Thomas, *From Folklore to Fiction: A Study of Folk Heroes and Rituals in the Black American Novel* on Baldwin, reprinted with permission of Greenwood Publishing Group, Inc., Westport, CT. Copyright © 1988.

Gurleen Grewal. From an introduction to *Circles of Sorrow, Lines of Struggle: The Novels of Toni Morrison*. Louisiana State University Press, 1998. Copyright © 1998 by Louisiana State University Press. All rights reserved. Reproduced by permission of Louisiana State University Press.

Kyle Grimes. For excerpts from article on Harper in *Black American Literature Forum* (now *African American Review*).

The Griot. For excerpts from "Poetry, Humanism and Apartheid: A Study of Mazisi Kunene's *Zulu Poems*" by Chidi Maduka. Reprinted from *The Griot*. 4, 1–2 (1985), pp. 60–61, 70–71.

Giselle Von Grunebaum. For excerpt from G. E. von Grunebaum, *French African Literature: Some Cultural Implications* (Senghor).

Gunter Narr Verlag. For excerpts from articles by Richard Bjornson on Bebey; Jeanne N. Dingome on Liking; Hena Maes-Jelinek on Harris; Clive Wake on Beti in *Semper Aliquid Novi: Literature Comparée et Literatures d'Afrique* (1990), Janos Riesz and Alain Ricard, eds.

Dorian Haarhoff. For excerpts from article on Mphahlele in *English in Africa*.

Harcourt Brace Jovanovich, Inc. For excerpts from James Weldon Johnson's Introduction to *Southern Road* by Sterling A. Brown; James Weldon Johnson's Preface to *The Book of American Negro Poetry*, James Weldon Johnson, ed. (Dunbar, McKay); Alfred Kazin, *On Native Grounds* (Wright); Dan McCall, *The Example of Richard Wright*; Claude McKay, *Harlem: Negro Metropolis* (Johnson).

Harper & Row, Publishers, Inc. For excerpt from Gerald Moore, *The Chosen Tongue* (Brathwaite, Harris, Okigbo).

Wilson Harris. For excerpt from *Tradition, the Writer and Society* (Lamming).

Karelisa Hartigan. For excerpts from article by Rosemary K. Curb on Sanchez in Karelisa Hartigan, ed., *The Many Forms of Drama*.

Harvard University Press. For excerpts from Gayl Jones, *Liberating Voices: Oral Tradition in African American Literature* (Baraka, Harper). Cambridge, Mass.: Harvard University Press, Copyright © 1991 by the President and Fellows of Harvard College. Reprinted by permission of the publishers.

Harvester Wheatsheaf. For excerpts from Paulina Palmer. *Contemporary Women's Fiction: Narrative Practice and Feminist Theory* (1989) (Walker).

Jennifer Hayward. For excerpts from article on Johnson in *Black American Literature Forum* (now *African American Review*).

Hecate, v. 24, May, 1998. Reproduced by permission.

Heinemann Educational Books Ltd. For excerpts from essay by Christopher Heywood on Abrahams in *Perspectives on African Literature*, Christopher Heywood, ed.; G. D. Killam, *The Novels of Chinua Achebe*; Ezekiel Mphahlele's Introduction to *Climbié* by Bernard Dadié; Ngugi wa Thiong'o, *Homecoming* (Achebe, Lamming, Mittelholzer, p'Bitek, Soyinka); Eustace Palmer, *An Introduction to the African Novel* (Amadi, Armah, Ngugi); essay by Peter Young on Okara in *The Critical Evaluation of African Literature*, Edgar Wright, ed.

Heinemann Publishers, Ltd. For excerpts from Gillian Stead Eilersen's Introduction to *Tales of Tenderness and Power* by Bessie Head; Craig MacKenzie's Introduction to *A Woman Alone* by Bessie Head; Emmanuel Ngara, *Art and Ideology in the African Novel: A Study of the Influence of Marxism in African Writing* (Achebe, Armah, Maillu, Ngugi wa Thiong'o, Sembène Ousamane); Kenneth Ramchand's Introduction to *The Schoolmaster* by Earl Lovelace.

Calvin C. Hernton. For excerpts from essay on Kelley, Reed in *Amistad 1*, John A. Williams and Charles F. Harris, eds.

Gilbert Highet. For excerpt from article on Wright in *Harper's Magazine*.

Lawrence Hill & Co. Publishers, Inc. For excerpts from Ngugi wa Thiong'o, *Homecoming* (Achebe, Lamming, Mittelholzer, p'Bitek, Soyinka).

Alice Baur Hodges. For excerpt from article by George H. Dillon on Cullen in *Poetry*.

Holiday. For excerpt from article by Peter Abrahams on Wright. Reprinted with permission of Holiday Magazine. © 1959 The Curtis Publishing Company.

Karla F. C. Holloway. From *Moorings and Metaphors: Figures of Culture and Gender in Black Women's Literature*. Copyright © 1992 by Karla F. Holloway. All rights reserved. Reproduced by permission of Rutgers, The State University.

Howard University Press. For excerpts from *From the Dark Tower: Afro-American Writers 1900–1960* by Arthur P. Davis. Reprinted by permission of Howard University Press. Copyright © 1974 by Arthur P. Davis (Bontemps, Hayden, Hughes, Hurston, McKay, M. Walker).

Irving Howe. For excerpts from articles on Baldwin, Redd in *Harper's Magazine*.

The Hudson Review. For excerpt from review by Hayden Carruth of Brathwaite. Reprinted by permission from The Hudson Review, Vol. XXVII, No. 2 (Summer, 1974). Copyright © 1974 by The Hudson Review, Inc.

Max Hueber Verlag. For excerpts from essay by Wolfgang Klooss on Achebe in *Essays on Contemporary Post-Colonial Fiction*, Hedwig Bock and Albert Wertheim, eds.; Werner Sollors on Baraka in *Essays on Contemporary American Drama*, Hedwig Bock and Albert Wertheim, eds. Reprinted by permission of Max Hueber Verlag, 85737 IsmAning Germany.

Ibadan University Press. For excerpts from articles by Arthur D. Drayton on Aluko; M. M. Mahood on Soyinka; Ben Obumselu on Achebe; Wole Soyinka on Clark in *Ibadan*.

Huma Ibrahim. From a conclusion to *Bessie Head: Subversive Identities in Exile*. University Press of Virginia, 1996. © 1996 by the Rector and Visitors of the University of Virginia. Reproduced by permission.

Indiana University Press. For excerpts from Charles R. Larson, *The Emergence of African Fiction* (Abrahams, Peters); Webster Smalley's Introduction to *Five Plays by Langston Hughes*. For excerpts from articles in *Research in African Literatures* by Bernadette Cailler on Mudimbe; Rhonda Cobham on Farah; Chris Dunton on Aidoo; Azubike F. Iloeje on Munonye; Eileen Julien on Labou Tansi; Nina D. Lyakhovskaya on Bemba; Guy Ossito Midiohouan on Kourouma; Mildred [P.] Mortimer on Kourouma; Fírinne Ní Chréacháin on Iyayi; Charles Okumu on Okot p'Bitek; Nidra Poller on Kourouma; Dieter Riemenschneider on Marechera; Kelwyn Sole on Sepamla, Tlali; Florence Stratton on Bâ, Emecheta; Clive Wake on Serote; Gay Wilentz on Sutherland.

Inscape. For excerpt from Peter Young's essay on Okara in *The Critical Evaluation of African Literature*, Edgar Wright, ed.

International African Institute. For excerpts from articles by G. A. Gollock on Mofolo; D. McK. Malcolm on Vilakazi in *Africa*. All Rights Reserved.

The International Fiction Review. For excerpts from articles by Dexter Noël on Anthony; Julius N. Ogu on Munonye; v. 23, 1996. © copyright 1996 International Fiction Association. Reproduced by permission.

The Iowa Review. For excerpts from Darwin T. Turner, "Visions of Love and Manliness in a Blackening World," in *The Iowa Review*, Volume 6, Number 2, © 1975 by The University of Iowa (Bullins).

Abiola Irele. From *The African Experience in Literature and Ideology*. Heinemann Educational Books Ltd., 1981. © Abiola Irele 1981. Reproduced by permission.

Jamaica Journal. For excerpts from article by Pamela Mordecai on Goodison.

Louis James. For excerpt from article on Harris in *TLS*.

Dianne Johnson-Feelings. For excerpt from article on Clifton in *The Children's Literature Association Quarterly*.

Johnson Publishing Company, Inc. For excerpts from articles by Langston Hughes on Wright in *Ebony*. Reprinted by permission of *Ebony* Magazine, copyright 1961 by Johnson Publishing Company; Arna Bontemps on Wright; Gwendolyn Brooks on Tolson; Don L. Lee on Williams; Carolyn M. Rodgers on A. Walker in *Negro Digest*. Reprinted by permission of *Negro Digest* Magazine, copyright 1950, 1965, 1968 by Johnson Publishing Co.; Sterling A. Brown on Bontemps; Ellen Conroy Kennedy on Damas; Ishmael Reed on Himes; John A. Williams on Ellison in *Black World*. Reprinted by permission of *Black World* Magazine, copyright 1970, 1972, 1973 by Johnson Publishing Company.

D. A. N. Jones. For excerpt from article on Bullins in *The Listener*.

Eldred Jones. For excerpt from article on Aidoo in *The Bulletin of the Association for African Literature in English*.

Edward A. Jones. For excerpt from article on Senghor in *The French Review*.

Michael Joseph Ltd. For excerpt from James Baldwin, *Notes of a Native Son* (Wright).

Journal of American Culture. For excerpts from articles by Emmanuel S. Nelson on Brathwaite; Jean Strandness on Shange; v. 18, Summer, 1995; v. 16, Fall,1998. Copyright © 1995, 1998 by Ray B. Browne. Both reproduced by permission.

Journal of Black Studies, December, 1994. Copyright © 1994 by Sage Publications, Inc. Reproduced with permission of Sage Publications, Inc.

Journal of Caribbean Studies and O. R. Dathorne. For excerpts from article by Evelyn O'Callaghan on Senior.

The Journal of Commonwealth Literature. For excerpts from articles by Joyce Adler on Harris; Martin Banham on Clark; Frank Birbalsingh on Mittelholzer: David Cook on p'Bitek; Kevin Ireland on Walcott; Eldred Jones on Achebe; M. Macmillan on Anthony; David Rabkin on La Guma; John Reed on Ngugi; v. 33, Winter, 1981; v. 63, Spring, 1998; v. 31, 1996. All reproduced with the kind permission of Bowker-Saur, a part of Reed Business Information Ltd.

Journal of West Indian Literature. For excerpts from articles by Steven R. Carter on Anthony; Michael G. Cooke on Brodber; Joyce Walker-Johnson on Brodber.

The Journal of Modern Africa, v. 34, 1996 for "Returning Voyagers: the Ghanaian Novel in the Nineties" by Derek Wright. © 1996 Cambridge University Press. Reproduced with the permission of Cambridge University Press and the author.

Journal of Popular Culture, v, 32, Summer, 1998. Copyright © 1998 by Ray B. Browne. Reproduced by permission.

Mohamadou Kane. For excerpt from *Les contes d'Amadou Coumba* (B. Diop).

Ana Louise Keating. From *Women Reading Women Writing: Self-Invention in Paula Gunn Allen, Gloria Anzaldua, and Audre Lorde*. Temple University Press, 1996. Copyright © 1996 by Temple University. All rights reserved. Reproduced by permission.

G. D. Killam. For excerpt from article on Nzekwu in *African Literature Today*. For excerpts from *An Introduction to the Writings of Ngugi* (Mugo, Ngugi wa Thiong'o); article on Ngugi wa Thiong'o in *The Writing of East and Central Africa*; article by Jacqueline Bardolph on Mwangi in *The Writing of East and Central Africa*; article by Angus Calder on Mwangi in *The Writing of East and Central Africa*; article by D. R. Ewen on Farah in *The Writing of East and Central Africa*; articles by [K. L.] Goodwin on Ntiru and Rubadiri in *The Writing of East and Central Africa*; article by Bernth Lindfors on Okot p'Bitek in *The Writing of East and Central Africa*; article by T. O. McLoughlin on Marechera in *The Writing of East and Central Africa*; articles by Peter Nazareth on Serumaga and Taban lo Liyong in *The Writing of East and Central Africa*.

Adele King. From "A Portrait and Conclusion" in *The Writings of Camara Laye*. Heinemann Educational Books Ltd., 1983. Reproduced by permission.

William Kluback. From a conclusion to *Léopold Sédar Senghor: From Politics to Poetry*. Peter Lang Publishing, Inc., 1997. © 1997 Peter Lang Publishing, Inc. All rights reserved. Reproduced by permission.

Jan Knappert. For excerpt from *Four Centuries of Swahili Verse*.

Daniel P. Kunene. For excerpt from *The Works of Thomas Mofolo*.

Alex La Guma. For excerpt from Brian Bunting's Foreword to *And a Threefold Cord* by Alex La Guma.

Lambda Book Report, v. 4, September-October, 1994 for a review of "Warrior Marks" by Victoria A. Brownworth. Reproduced by permission of the author.

Peter Lang. For excerpts from Evelyn J. Hawthorne on Mais, *The Writer in Transition: Roger Mais and the Decolonization of Caribbean Culture* (1989); Dolly A. McPherson on Angelou, *Order Out of Chaos: The Autobiographical Works of Maya Angelou* (1990).

Language Quarterly. For excerpts from article by Elerius Edet John on Bebey.

Hank Lazer. For excerpt from article on Clifton in *The Southern Review*.

Legon Journal of the Humanities. For excerpts from article by J. Bekunuru Kubayanda on Anyidoho.

Neal A. Lester. For excerpts from article on Shange in *African American Review*.

Libra Publishers, Inc. For excerpts from Stephen H. Bronz, *Roots of Negro Racial Consciousness* (Cullen, McKay).

Laurence Lieberman. For excerpt from article on Hughes in *Poetry*.

Bernth Lindfors. For excerpt from article on Achebe in *African Literature Today*.

J. B. Lippincott Company. For excerpts from *Selected Letters of Malcolm Lowry*, edited by Harvey Breit and Margerie Bonner Lowry. Copyright © 1965 by Margerie Bonner Lowry. Reprinted by permission of J. B. Lippincott Company (Ellison); from *Native Sons* by Edward Margolies. Copyright © 1968 by Edward Margolies. Reprinted by permission of J. B. Lippincott Company (Attaway, Demby, Himes).

The Literary Criterion. For excerpts from articles by Aderemi Bamikunle on Osundare; Ebele Keo on Amadi; Hank Okazaki on Phillips; Jasper A. Onuekwusi on Brutus.

The Literary Half-Yearly. For excerpts from articles by David Olusegun Agbaje on Mtshali; Isaac I. Elimimian on Brutus; Andrew Horn on Serumaga. For excerpts from articles by A. D. Drayton on Anthony; Michael Gilkes on Harris; G. Rohlehr on Brathwaite.

The Literary Review, v. 38, Spring, 1998 for "Genre to the Rear, Race and Gender to the Fore: The Novels of Octavia E. Butler"by Burton Raffel. Copyright © 1998 by Fairleigh Dickinson University. Reproduced by permission of the author.

Little, Brown and Company. For excerpt from Alfred Kazin, *Contemporaries* (Baldwin).

Liveright Publishing Corporation. For excerpts from William Stanley Braithwaite on Toomer in *The New Negro*, Alain Locke, ed.; Waldo Frank's Foreword to *Cane* by Jean Toomer.

Cecily Lockett. For excerpts from article on Tlali in Cherry Clayton, ed., *Women and Writing in South Africa*.

The London Magazine. For excerpts from articles by Roy Fuller on Walcott; Frank McGuiness on Anthony; Alan Ross on Brathwaite.

Longman Group Limited. For excerpts from Gerald Moore, *The Chosen Tongue* (Brathwaite, Harris, Okigbo).

Longman Publishing Group. For excerpts from article by Mbulelo Vizikhungo Mzamane on Serote in *Literature and Society in South Africa*, White and Couzens, eds.

Los Angeles Times Book Review, June 5, 1994. Copyright, 1994, Los Angeles Times. Reproduced by permission.

The Sterling Lord Agency, Inc. For excerpt from article by LeRoi Jones on Clark in *Poetry*.

Louisiana State University Press. For excerpts by Blyden Jackson on Brooks, Cullen, Hughes in Blyden Jackson and Louis D. Rubin, Jr., *Black Poetry in America*; Olga M. Vickery's essay on Baraka in *The Shaken Realist*, Malvin J. Friedman and John B. Vickery, eds.; James O. Young, *Black Writers of the Thirties* (Thurman). For excerpts from article by Blyden Jackson on Gaines in *American Letters and the Historical Consciousness: Essays in Honor of Lewis P. Simpson*, edited by J. Gerald Kennedy and Daniel Mark Fogel. Copyright © 1987 by Louisiana State University Press. Used with permission; article by Trudier Harris on Walker in *The History of Southern Literature*, edited by Louis D. Rubin, Jr. Copyright © 1985 by Louisiana State University Press. Used with permission; article by Theodore R. Hudson on Gaines in *The History of Southern Literature*, edited by Louis D. Rubin, Jr. Copyright © 1985 by Louisiana State University Press. Used with permission.

The Lovedale Press. For excerpt from R. H. W. Shepherd, *Bantu Literature and Life* (Vilakazi).

Gordon K. MacDonald. For excerpt from Benjamin Brawley, *The Negro in Literature and Art* (Chesnutt).

Macmillan Publishing Co., Inc. For excerpts from Christina Ama Ata Aidoo's Introduction to *Beautyful Ones Are Not Yet Born* by Ayi Kwei Armah. Introduction Copyright © 1970 by Macmillan Publishing Co., Inc.; Wilfred Cartey's Introduction to *Tell Freedom* by Peter Abrahams. Introduction Copyright © 1970 by Macmillan Publishing Co., Inc.; Edris Makward's Introduction to *Boy!* by Ferdinand Oyono. Introduction Copyright © by Macmillan Publishing Co., Inc.; William Targ, *Indecent Pleasures*. Copyright © 1975 by William Targ (Himes); Martin Tucker's Introduction to *Weep Not, Child* by James Ngugi. Introduction Copyright © 1969 by Macmillan Publishing Co., Inc. For excerpts from Dorothy S. Blair, *Senegalese Literature: A Critical History* (Bâ, Diallo, Ndao, Sembène Ousmane, Sow Fall); Lloyd W. Brown, *West Indian Poetry* (Bennett, Brathwaite); Michael Gilkes, *The West Indian Novel* (Harris, James, Lamming, Mais, St. Omer); article by Deborah E. McDowell on Fauset in *Modern American Women Writers*, consulting editor, Elaine Showalter. Lea Baechler and A. Walton Litz, general editors. Copyright © 1991, Charles Scribner's Sons.

MacMillan South Africa, Publishers, Ltd. For excerpt from John L. Comaroff's Introduction to *The Boer War Diary of Sol T. Plaatje*.

Marabout S. A. For excerpts by Lilyan Kesteloot on Kane, Roumain in *Anthologie ñegro-africaine*, Lilyan Kesteloot, ed. © 1967, Gérard & Co., Verviers.

Marion Boyars. For excerpts from Gareth Griffiths on Mais. *A Double Exile: African and West Indian Writing between Two Cultures*.

Massachusetts Review. For excerpt from article by William C. Fischer on Baraka. Reprinted from *The Massachusetts Review* © 1973 by The Massachusetts Review, Inc. For excerpts from articles by Andrea Benton Rushing on Shange. Reprinted from *The Massachusetts Review*, Copyright © 1976, The Massachusetts Review, Inc.; Robert B. Stepto on Harper. Reprinted from *The Massachusetts Review*, Copyright © 1981, The Massachusetts Review, Inc.

Matatu. For excerpts from articles by Cecil Abrahams on Serote; Jacques Alvarez-Pereyre on Tlali; Arlene A. Elder on Mugo.

Harold Matson Company, Inc. For excerpt by Malcolm Lowry on Ellison in *Selected Letters of Malcolm Lowry*, Harvey Breit and Margerie Bonner Lowry, eds.

Jill L. Matus. For excerpts from article on Naylor in *Black American Literature Forum* (now *African American Review*).

Doreatha D. Mbalia. From *John Edgar Wideman: Reclaiming the African Personality*. Associated University Presses, 1995. © 1995 Associated University Presses, Inc. All rights reserved. Reproduced by permission.

McGraw-Hill Book Company. For excerpts from Eldridge Cleaver, *Soul on Ice*, copyright © 1968 by Eldridge Cleaver. Used with permission of McGraw-Hill Book Company (Baldwin, Wright).

McIntosh And Otis, Inc. For excerpt from Fern Marja Eckman, *The Furious Passage of James Baldwin*.

David McKay Company, Inc. For excerpt from Ellen Tarry, *The Third Door*. Copyright © 1955 by Ellen Tarry. Published by David McKay Company, Inc. Reprinted by permission of the publisher (McKay).

Joanne Megna-Wallace. From *Understanding "I Know Why The Caged Bird Sings": A Student Casebook to Issues, Sources, and Historical Documents*. Greenwood Press, 1998. Copyright © 1988 by Joanne Megna-Wallace. Copyright © 1998 by Joanne Megna-Wallace. All rights reserved. Reproduced by permission of Greenwood Publishing Group, Inc., Westport, CT.

Melus, v. 21, Fall, 1996. Copyright, MELUS: The Society for the Study of Multi-Ethnic Literature of the United States, 1996. Reproduced by permission.

MEP Publications. For excerpts from "Negritude and Surrealism, Marxism and Mallarmé: Ideological Confusion in the Works of Aimé Césaire" by April Ane Knutson in *Ideology and Independence in the Americas*, April Ane Knutson, ed. Used by permission of MEP Publications, 116 Church St. SE., Minneapolis, MN 55455-0112.

Scott Meredith Literary Agency. For excerpts from Norman Mailer, *Cannibals and Christians*, copyright © 1966 by Norman Mailer (Baldwin); Norman Mailer, *Advertisements for Myself*, © 1959 by Norman Mailer (Ellison). Reprinted by permission of the author and the author's agents, Scott Meredith Literary Agency, Inc., 846 Third Avenue, New York, N.Y. 10022.

Charles E. Merrill Publishing Co. For excerpt from Frank Durham's Preface to *The Merrill Studies in Cane*, Frank Durham, ed. (Toomer).

Michigan Quarterly Review. For excerpts from an article by Lisa M. Steinman on Dove.

The Midwest Quarterly, v. XXXVIII, Autumn, 1996. Copyright © 1996 by The Midwest Quarterly, Pittsburgh State University. Reproduced by permission.

The Mississippi Quarterly, v. 49, Fall, 1996. Copyright 1996 Mississippi State University. Reproduced by permission.

MIT Press Journals. For excerpts from *October*, 55, Manthia Diawara, "Reading Africa through Foucault: V. Y. Mudimbe's Reaffirmation of the Subject." Reprinted by permission of the MIT Press, Cambridge, Massachusetts, Copyright, © 1990.

Edgar Mittelholzer and V.S. Reid in *"The Novel as History" in Historical Thought and Literary Representation in West Indian Literature*. Edited by Nana Wilson-Tagoe. University of Florida Press, 1998. Copyright 1998 by the Board of Regents of the State of Florida. All rights reserved. Reproduced with the permission of the University Press of Florida.

Modern Drama. For excerpts from article by Martin Banham on Rotimi; v. XL, Spring, 1997. © 1997 University of Toronto, Graduate Centre for Study of Drama. Reproduced by permission.

Modern Fiction Studies. For excerpts from articles by J. O. J. Nwachukwu-Agbada on Bâ; Maxine Sample on Amadi; Charles Ponnuthurai Sarvan on Bâ, *Modern Fiction Studies*, copyright 1970, by Purdue Research Foundation, West Lafayette, Indiana 47907. Reprinted with permission; v. 44, Spring, 1998. Copyright © 1988 by Purdue Research Foundation, West Lafayette, IN 47907. All rights reserved. Reproduced by permission of The Johns Hopkins University.

Le Monde. For excerpts from articles by Jacques Chevrier on U Tam'si; Bertrand Poirot-Delpech on Baraka; Pierre-Henri Simon on Kane.

Gerald Moore. For excerpt from article on p'Bitek in *TLS*.

William Morris Agency, Inc. For excerpts from James Baldwin's preface, "Sweet Lorraine," to *To Be Young, Gifted and Black* by Lorraine Hansberry. Copyright © 1969 by James Baldwin. Reprinted by permission of William Morris Agency, Inc.; Ralph Ellison, *Shadow and Act*. Copyright © 1964 by Ralph

Ellison. Reprinted by permission of Ralph Ellison (Baraka, Wright); article by Ralph Ellison on Attaway in *The Negro Quarterly*. Copyright © 1942 (renewed) by Ralph Ellison. Reprinted by permission of Ralph Ellison; article by William Melvin Kelley on Ngugi in *African Forum*.

William Morrow and Company. For excerpts from Harold Cruse, *The Crisis of the Negro Intellectual* (Hansberry); Michel Fabre, *The Unfinished Quest of Richard Wright*.

Frederic Morton. For excerpt from article on Himes in the *New York Herald Tribune Book Section*.

Mosaic. For excerpts from "Ndebele's *Fools*: A Challenge to the Theory of 'Multiple Meaning'" by K. J. Phillips. An earlier version of this chapter originally appeared in *Mosaic*, Volume 23/4 (Fall 1990), pp. 87–102/ v. 23, Fall, 1990. © Mosaic 1990. Acknowledgment of previous publication is herewith made.

Ezekiel Mphahlele. For excerpts from *Voices in the Whirlwind* (Baraka, Brutus); Introduction to *Night of My Blood* by Kofi Awoonor.

Ms. For excerpts from articles by Margo Jefferson on Morrison; Barbara Smith on A. Walker. Copyright © 1974 Ms. Magazine, Corp. Reprinted with permission.

Romanus Okey Muoneke. From a conclusion to *Art, Rebellion and Redemption: A Reading of the Novels of Chinua Achebe*. Peter Lang Publishing, Inc., 1994. © Peter Lang Publishing, Inc., 1994. All rights reserved. Reproduced by permission.

Carol Muske. For excerpts from article on Clifton in *Parnassus*.

Editions Naaman. For excerpts from Rodney E. Harris, *L'humanisme dans le théâtre d'Aimé Césaire*.

Supriya Nair. From *Caliban's Curse: George Lamming and the Revisioning of History*. University of Michigan Press, 1996. Copyright © by the University of Michigan 1996. All rights reserved. Reproduced by permission.

Wilson-Tagoe Nana. From *Historical Thought and Literary Representation in West Indian Literature*. University Press of Florida, 1998. Copyright © 1998 by the Board of Regents of the State of Florida. All rights reserved. Reproduced with the permission of the University Press of Florida.

Susheila Nasta. For excerpts from articles by Elleke Boehmer on Nwapa; Carolyn Cooper on Brodber; Elaine Savory Fido on Emecheta; Anna R. Morris and Margaret M. Dunn on Cliff; Laura Niesen de Abruna on Kincaid in *Motherlands*, Susheila Nasta, ed., first published by The Women's Press Ltd., 1991, 34 Great Sutton Street, London, EC1V 0DX.

Nathan. For excerpts from S. M. Battestini, *Littérature africaine, Seydou Badian*.

Fernand Nathan Éditeur. For excerpts from Roger Mercier and M. and S. Battestini, *Mongo Beti*; Roger Mercier and M. and S. Battestini, *Olympe Bhêly-Quénum*; Roger Mercier and M. and S. Battestini, *Bernard Dadié*; Roger Mercier and M. and S. Battestini, *Ferdinand Oyono*.

The Nation. For excerpts from articles by Gwendolyn Brooks on Hughes; Sterling Brown on Hurston, Wright; Jerry H. Bryant on Bullins, Morrison, Reed, A. Walker; Ernest Jones on Demby; Denise Levertov on Baraka; Philip Blair Rice on Cullen; New York, v. 250, January 1, 1990; April 27, 1998; November 16, 1998. © 1990, 1998 The Nation magazine/The Nation Company, Inc. All reproduced by permission.

National Publications Centre. For excerpt from article by Mary Ellen Brooks on Bullins in *Literature & Ideology*.

National Urban League, Inc. For excerpts from articles by William Stanley Braithwaite on Johnson; Sterling A. Brown on McKay; Eunice Hunton Carter on Thurman; Countee Cullen on Hughes; William Harrison on Hayden; Eugene Holmes on Toomer; Ulysses Lee on M. Walker; Alain Locke on Wright in *Opportunity*. Reprinted with permission of the National Urban League.

Thomas Nelson & Sons Limited. For excerpts from Oladele Taiwo, *An Introduction to West African Literature* (Clark, Ekwensi).

Nelson–Hall. For excerpts from Roger Whitlow, *Black American Literature* (Demby, M. Walker).

The New African. For excerpts from articles by Mofolo Bulane on Kunene; Alfred Hutchinson on Aluko; Mazisi Kunene on Soyinka; Lewis Nkosi on Ngugi. For excerpts from article by Flora [Veit-] Wild on Marechera. New African, published by IC Publications, London.

The New Leader. For excerpts from articles by James Baldwin on Himes; Albert Bermel on Bullins. Reprinted with permission from *The New Leader*. Copyright © 1947, 1968 The American Labor Conference on International Affairs, Inc.

New Letters. For excerpts from articles by Roy P. Basler on Tolson; Michel Fabre on Walcott; from essay by Margaret Walker Alexander in *Richard Wright: Impressions and Perspectives*, David Ray and Robert Farnsworth, eds., originally published in *New Letters*, Winter 1971.

New Literary History. For excerpts from "Appropriate(d) Discourse: Plagiarism and Decolonization" by Marilyn Randall on Ouologuem. Reprinted from *New Literary History*. Volume 22, 1991. Reprinted by permission of The Johns Hopkins University Press.

The New Republic. For excerpts from articles by Tom F. Driver on Hansberry; William Esty on Baldwin; Robert Littell on Toomer; Barbara Smith on Reed; Martin Tucker on Armah; Richard Wright on Hughes; v. 204, April 8, 1991; v. 206, March 30, 1992; v. 209, September 6, 1993; v. 216, April, 1997. © 1991, 1992, 1993, 1997 The New Republic, Inc. All reproduced by permission of The New Republic.

New Statesman. For excerpts from articles by A. Alvarez on Hansberry; Cyril Connolly on McKay; Janice Elliot on Gaines; Dan Jacobson on Ellison; V. S. Naipaul on Lamming; William Plomer on Mphahlele; V. S. Pritchett on Tutuola; Maurice Richardson on Ekwensi; Keith Waterhouse on Achebe; Chris Waters on Anthony.

New Statesman & Society. For excerpts from article by Suzanne Cronje on Okri; v. 125, July 12, 1996; v. 125, September 27, 1996; v.128, February 5, 1999. © 1996, 1999 The Statesman & Nation Publishing Co. Ltd. All reproduced by permission.

New Statesman and Society, v. 1, July 22, 1988. © 1988 Statesman & Nation Publishing Company Limited. Reproduced by permission.

New Trends & Generations in African Literature Today, Alt 20, 1996. James Curry Ltd., London, African World Press, New Jersey. Reproduced by permission.

New York, Magazine, November 20, 1995. Copyright © 1995 PRIMEDIA Magazine Corporation. All rights reserved. Reproduced with the permission of New York Magazine.

New York Post. For excerpt from article by Langston Hughes on Baraka. Reprinted by permission of the New York Post. © 1965, New York Post Corporation.

The New York Review of Books. For excerpts from articles by Thomas R. Edwards on Reed; D. A. N. Jones on Soyinka; Robert Mazzocco on Walcott; Philip Roth on Baldwin, Baraka; Roger Sale on Williams; John Thompson on Awoonor; Michael Wood on Kelley. Reprinted with permission from *The New York Review of Books*. Copyright © 1964, 1969, 1971, 1972 Nyrev, Inc. For excerpts from articles by Milan Kundera on Chamoiseau. Reprinted with permission from *The New York Review of Books*. Copyright 1991 Nyrev, Inc.; Michael Wood on Morrison. Reprinted with permission from *The New York Review of Books*. Copyright 1992 Nyrev, Inc.; v. XXXVI, March 16, 1989; November 4, 1993. Copyright © 1989, 1993 NYREV, Inc. Both reproduced with permission from The New York Review of Books.

The New York Times. For excerpts from numerous reviews and articles, copyright © 1951, 1952, 1956, 1959, 1967, 1970, 1971, 1972, 1973, 1975, 1976 by The New York Times Company; from article by Dylan Thomas on Tutuola. © 1952 by London Observer/The New York Times Company. Reprinted by permission. For excerpts from "Charles Johnson's Tale of Slaving, Seafaring and Philosophizing" by

Eleanor Blau on Johnson (January 2, 1991); "Slaves to Fate" by Janet Burroway on Phillips (January 30, 1994); "A Voice From The Streets" by Samuel G. Freedman on Wilson (March 15, 1987); "Separate Prisons" by George Garrett on Phillips (February 16, 1992); "Women Together" by Annie Gottlieb on Naylor (August 22, 1982); "Chilling Out in Phoenix" by Susan Isaacs on McMillan (May 31, 1992); "McMillan's Millions" by Daniel Max on McMillan (August 9, 1992); "An Affair of Convenience" by Reginald McKnight on Mudimbe (April 30, 1989); "In Short" by Tom Nolan on Phillips (April 29, 1990); "Abandoned for Their Own Good" by Elizabeth Nunez-Harrell on Cliff (September 23, 1990); "Nothing Succeeds Like Virginia" by Geoff Ryman on Dove (October 11, 1992); "Someone to Walk Over Me" by Valerie Sayers on McMillan (August 6, 1989); "Dying Like a Man" by Carl Senna on Gaines (August 9, 1993). Copyright © 1982, 1987, 1989, 1990, 1991, 1992, 1993, 1994 by The New York Times Company. Reprinted by permission; November 22, 1991. Copyright © 1991 by The New York Times Company. Reproduced by permission.

The New York Times Book Review, May 15, 1983; June 24, 1984; February 10, 1985; July 16, 1995; August 13, 1995; May 11, 1997; January 4, 1998; February 8, 1998; September 27, 1998; April 11, 1999. Copyright © 1983, 1984,1985, 1995, 1997, 1998, 1999 by The New York Times Company. All reproduced by permission.

The New Yorker, v. XLVI, October 17, 1970 for "Human Nature Is Finer"by Robert Coles. © 1970 by The New Yorker Magazine, Inc. All rights reserved. Reproduced by permission of the author.

Newsweek. For excerpt from article by Richard Gilman on Hansberry. Copyright 1964 by Newsweek, Inc. All rights reserved. Reprinted by permission.

Emmanuel Ngara. For excerpts from *Stylistic Criticism and the African Novel* (Ngugi wa Thiong'o, Soyinka).

Northeastern University Press. For excerpts from the foreword by Mae G. Henderson in the 1991 edition of *White Rat* by Gayl Jones. Reprinted with the permission of Northeastern University Press; *Derek Walcott's Poetry: American Mimicry* by Rei Terada. Copyright © 1992 by Rei Terada. Reprinted with the permission of Northeastern University Press, Boston.

Northwestern University Press. For excerpts from Wilfred Cartey's essay in *The African Experience*, John Paden and Edward Soja, eds. (Tutuola); Judith Illsley Gleason, *This Africa* (Achebe, Ekwensi, Mofolo, Nzekwu).

Richard C. Ntiru. For excerpt from article on p'Bitek in *Mawazo*.

Harold Ober Associates. For excerpts from Chinua Achebe, *Morning Yet on Creation Day*. Reprinted by permission of Harold Ober Associates, Inc. Copyright © 1975 by Chinua Achebe (Armah, Okigbo, Tutuola); Langston Hughes, *The Big Sea*. Reprinted by permission of Harold Ober Associates, Inc. Copyright © 1963 by Langston Hughes (Hurston, Thurman, Toomer); article by Langston Hughes on Brooks in *Voices*. Reprinted by permission of Harold Ober Associates, Inc. Copyright © 1950 by Langston Hughes.

Emmanuel Obiechina. For excerpt from article on Demby in *African Forum*; on Okara in *Nigeria Magazine*.

Octagon Books. For excerpts from Suzanne Juhasz, *Naked and Fiery Forms: Modern American Poetry by Women* (Brooks, Giovanni).

October. For excerpts from article by Manthia Diawara on Mudimbe. Reprinted with permission of MIT Press.

Vincent O. Odamtten. From "Reviewing Gloria Naylor: Toward A Neo-African Critique" in *Of Dreams Deferred, Dead or Alive: African Perspectives on African-American Writers*. Edited by Femi Ojo-Ade. Greenwood Press, 1996. Copyright © 1996 by Fermi Ojo-Ade. All rights reserved. Reproduced by permission of Greenwood Publishing Group, Inc., Westport, CT.

Kolawole Ogungbesan. From *The Writings of Peter Abrahams*. Africana Publishing Company, 1979. Copyright © 1979 K. Ogungbesan. Reproduced with permission.

The Ohio Review, v. 52. 1994. Copyright © 1994 by the Editors of The Ohio Review. Reproduced by permission.

Ohio University Press. For excerpts from articles by Martin Trump on Ndebele in Martin Trump, ed. *Rendering Things Visible: Essays on South African Literay Culture*, (1990); Michael Vaughan on Ndebele in Martin Trump, ed. *Rendering Things Visible: Essays on South African Literary Culture* (1990).

Okike. For excerpt from article by Chinweizu on Awoonor.

Tejumola Olaniyan. From *Scars of Conquest/Masks of Resistance: The Invention of Cultural Identities in African, African-American, and Caribbean Drama*. Oxford University Press, Inc., 1995. Copyright © 1995 by Tejumola Olaniyan. All rights reserved. Used by permissjon of Oxford University Press, Inc.

Beverley Ormerod. For excerpts from *An Introduction to the French Caribbean Novel* (Glissant, Schwarz-Bart, Zobel).

Oxford University Press, Inc. (New York). For excerpts from Nathan Irvin Huggins, *Harlem Renaissance*. Copyright © 1971 by Oxford University Press, Inc. Reprinted by permission (Hughes, Thurman, Toomer). For excerpts from articles by Barthélémy Kotchy on Zadi Zaourou in *Theatre Research International*; Mineke Schipper on Bemba, Liking, in *Theatre Research International*; Gary Warner on Ndao in *Theatre Research International*; Harold A. Waters on Ndao in *Theatre Research International*.

Oxford University Press, Oxford.For excerpts from Dorothy S. Blair's Foreword to *Tales of Amadou Koumba* by Birago Diop. Copyright 1966 by Oxford University Press; essay by John Hearne on Harris in *The Islands in Between*, Louis James, ed. Copyright © 1968 by Oxford University Press; Gerald Moore, *Seven African Writers*. Copyright © 1962 by Oxford University Press (Achebe, Beti, D. Diop, Mphahlele, Senghor, Tutuola).

Parnassus, v. 18, 1993-94. Copyright © 1993 Poetry in Review Foundation, NY. Reproduced by permission.

Partisan Review. For excerpts from articles by Stephen Spender on Baldwin, Copyright 1963 by *Partisan Review*; Richard Wright on Bontemps, Copyright 1936 by *Partisan Review and Anvil*.

Penguin Books Ltd. For excerpts from Mazisi Kunene's Introduction to *Return to My Native Land* by Aimé Césaire, translated by John Berger and Anna Bostock (1969). Copyright © Mazisi Kunene, 1969.

Jeanne Martha Perreault. From *Writing Selves: Contemporary Feminist Autography*. University of Minnesota Press, 1995. Copyright © 1995 by the Regents of the University of Minnesota. All rights reserved. Reproduced by permission of the publisher and the author.

Peters Fraser & Dunlop. For excerpts from Gerald Moore, *The Chosen Tongue* (Hearne, Mais, Reid, Salkey). Reprinted by permission of the Peters Fraser & Dunlop Group Ltd.

Ann Petry. For excerpts from article on Killens in *New York Herald Tribune Book Section*.

Joyce Owens Pettis. From *Toward Wholeness in Paule Marshall's Fiction*. The University Press of Virginia, 1995. © 1995 by the Rector and Visitors of the University of Virginia. Reproduced by permission.

Marlene Nourbese Philip. From "Managing the Unmanageable" in *Caribbean Women Writers: Essays From the First International Conference*. Edited by Selwyn R. Cudjoe. University of Massachusetts Press, 1990. Copyright © 1990 by Calaloux Publications. All rights reserved. Reproduced by permission of the University of Massachusetts Press.

Phylon. For excerpts from articles by Anna Bontemps on Hayden; Eugenia W. Collier on Johnson; Arthur P. Davis on Cullen; S. P. Fullinwider on Toomer; Nick Aaron Ford on Kelley; Blyden Jackson on

Abrahams; Miles M. Jackson on Gaines; George E. Kent on Brooks, Gaines, Killens, Reed; Ulysses Lee on Brown; Alain Locke on Ellison; Robert A. Smith on McKay; Nathaniel Tillman on Tolson; Margaret Walker on Brooks.

René Piquion. For excerpts from *Ébène* (B. Diop); *Langston Hughes: Un Chant nouveau.*

Players. For excerpts from article by James R. Giles on Bullins.

Ploughshares, Spring, 1997 for a profile of Yusef Komunyakaa by Susan Conley. Reproduced by permission of the author.

Poetry. For excerpts from articles by George H. Dillon on Cullen, copyright 1926 by The Modern Poetry Association; David Galler on Hayden, copyright © 1967 by The Modern Poetry Association; LeRoi Jones on Clark, copyright 1964 by The Modern Poetry Association; Laurence Lieberman on Hughes, copyright © 1968 by The Modern Poetry Association; Allen Tate on Tolson, copyright 1950 by The Modern Poetry Association; Amos N. Wilder on Brooks, copyright 1945 by The Modern Poetry Association. Reprinted by permission of the Editor of *Poetry*; v. 163, March, 1994 for a review of "The Book of Light" by Calvin Bedient; v. 167, March, 1996 in a review of "Mother Love" and "The Darker Face of the Earth" by Ben Howard; v. 172, August, 1998 for a review of "The Bounty" by Christian Wiman. © 1994, 1996, 1998 by the Modern Poetry Association. All reproduced by permission of the Editor of *Poetry* and the respective authors.

Poetry Australia. For excerpt from article by James Tulip on Tolson.

John Povey. For excerpt from article on Brutus in *Journal of the New African Literature and the Arts.*

Prager Publishers, Inc. For excerpts from Margaret Laurence, *Long Drums and Cannons* (Aluko, Amadi, Nzekwu, Okara, Soyinka, Tutuola); Ezekiel Mphahlele, *The African Image* (Kunene, Plaatje).

PrXsence Africaine. For excerpts from Hubert Juin, *Aimé Césaire, poète noir*; Thomas Melone, *Mongo Béti: L'homme et le destin*; C. Quillateau, *Bernard Binlin Dadié: L'homme et l'œure*; Léopold Sédar Senghor's Preface to *Les nouveaux contes d'Amadou Koumba* by Birago Diop; Léopold Sédar Senghor's essay in *Hommage à René Maran*; Paulin Soumanou Vieyra, *Ousmane Sembène, cinéaste;* from articles by Olympe Bhêly-Quénum on B. Diop; Joseph Miezan Bognini on Dadié; Andrée Clair on Bhêly-Quénum; Gerald Moore on Oyono; anon. on D. Diop in *Présence africaine* (English edition); Mongo Beti on Camara; Maryse Conde on Amadi; Luc Decaunes on Mofolo; René Depestre on Dadié, D. Diop; Lamine Diakhaté on Sembène; David Diop on Beti, Oyono; Nicolás Guillen on Hughes; Barthélemy Kotchy on Maran; Georges Lamming on Tutuola; A. U. Ohaegbu on Sembène; Magdeleine Paz on B. Diop in *Présence africaine.*

Princeton University Press. For excerpts from James Olney, *Tell Me Africa: An Approach to African Literature* (copyright © 1973 by Princeton University Press), pp. 126–127, 202–203, 280–281, and 283–284. Reprinted by permission of Princeton University Press (Achebe, Camara, Mphahlele. Ngugi); from a 1982 essay. Reproduced by permission.

The Progressive. For excerpt from article by Nora Sayre on Bullins. Reprinted by permission from *The Progressive*, 408 W. Gorham St., Madison, Wisc. 53703. Copyright © 1969, The Progressive, Inc.

Publishers Weekly, v. 244, April 28, 1997; v. 245, August 17, 1998. Copyright 1997, 1998 by Reed Publishing USA. Both reproduced from Publishers Weekly, published by the Bowker Magazine Group of Cahners Publishing Co., a division of Reed Publishing USA., by permission.

G. P. Putnam's Sons. For excerpts from Norman Mailer, *Advertisements for Myself* (Ellison); Constance Webb, *Richard Wright: A Biography.*

Quagga Press. For excerpt from Tim Couzens's Introduction to *Mhudi* by Sol. T. Plaatje.

Kenneth Ramchand. For excerpts from *The West Indian Novel and Its Background* (Clarke, James, Reid, Wynter).

Arnold Rampersad. From *The Harlem Renaissance: Revaluations*. Edited by Amritjit Singh, William S. Shriver and Stanley Brodwin. Garland Publishing, 1989. Copyright © 1989 Amritjit Singh, William S. Shriver and Stanley Brodwin. Reproduced by permission.

Random House, Inc. For excerpts from Wilfred Cartey, *Whispers from a Continent* (Ekwensi); Ralph Ellison, *Shadow and Act*. Copyright © 1945 by Ralph Ellison. Reprinted by permission of Random House, Inc. (Baraka, Wright); John Simon, *Uneasy Stages* (Bullins); John Updike, *Picked-Up Pieces*. Copyright © 1971, 1974 by John Updike. Reprinted by permission of Alfred A. Knopf, Inc. Originally appeared in *The New Yorker* (Amadi, Awoonor, La Guma, Mphahlele); Carl Van Vechten's Introduction to *The Autobiography of an Ex-Coloured Man* by James Weldon Johnson.

Random House UK Limited. For excerpts from Edward [Kamau] Brathwaite's Introduction to *Brother Man* by Roger Mais. Jonathan Cape, publisher; Jean D'Costa's Introduction to *Black Lightning* by Roger Mais. Jonathan Cape, publisher.

Ravan Press. For excerpts from Mineke Schipper, *Theatre and Society in Africa* (Soyinka).

Arthur Ravenscroft. For excerpt from *Chinua Achebe*.

C. J. Rea. For excerpt from article on Aidoo in *African Forum*.

J. Saunders Redding. For excerpts from articles on Achebe, Killens in *African Forum*; on Baldwin, Williams in *New York Herald Tribune Book Section*.

Research in African Literature, v. 23, Spring, 1992; v. 23, Fall, 1992; v. 24, Winter, 1993; v. 24, Spring, 1993; v. 27, Summer, 1994; v. 26, Winter, 1995; v. 27, Summer, 1996; Spring, 1997; v. 28, Summer, 1997; v. 29, Winter, 1998; v. 29, Spring, 1998; v. 29, Summer, 1998; v. 29, Fall 1998. Copyright © 1992, 1993, 1994, 1995, 1996, 1997, 1998 Indiana University Press. All reproduced by permission.

Review of Contemporary Fiction. For excerpts from articles by Jack Byrne on Reed; Laura Frost on Cliff; v. 16, Fall, 1996; v. 17, Summer, 1997; v. 17, Fall, 1997, Copyright, 1996, 1997, by John O'Brien. All reproduced by permission.

Review of National Literatures. For excerpts from articles by Lyndon Harries on Robert; Bernth Lindfors on Serumaga; J. Mbelolo Ya Mpiku on Ouologuem; Clive Wake on Rabéarivelo.

Revista/Review Interamericana. For excerpts from article by Henry Cohen on Depestre.

Paul R. Reynolds, Inc. For excerpts from John A. Williams's Introduction to *White Man, Listen!* by Richard Wright; Richard Wright's Introduction to *In the Castle of My Skin* by George Lamming; from articles by Richard Wright on Bontemps in *Partisan Review and Anvil*; on Himes in *PM*.

Alfred Rice. For excerpt from article by Ernest M. Hemingway on Maran in *Toronto Star Weekly*.

Rodopi. For excerpts from articles by Lucia Nankoe and Essa Reijmers on Marshall; Joseph Swann on Achebe in *Crisis and Creativity in the New Literatures in English*, Geoffrey V. Davis and Hena Maes-Jelinek, eds.

Howard Rosenstone. For excerpt by Ed Bullins in *New Plays from the Black Theatre*, Ed Bullins, ed. (Baraka).

Rothco Cartoons Inc. For excerpt from article by David Pryce-Jones on Reed in *Punch*.

Routledge & Kegan Paul. For excerpts from Henry Louis Gates, Jr., ed., *Black Literature and Literary Theory* (Brooks, Morrison, Reed); article by Douglas Killam on Ogot in *Literatures of the World in English*, Bruce King, ed.

Charles H. Rowell. For excerpts from article on Gaines in *The Southern Review*.

Ashraf H. A. Rushdy. For excerpts from article on Johnson in *African American Review*.

Russell & Volkening, Inc. For excerpts from articles by Nadine Gordimer on Abrahams, Achebe in *TLS*; on La Guma, Ngugi in *The Michigan Quarterly Review*. Reprinted by permission of Nadine Gordimer. Copyright © 1961, 1970, 1975 by Nadine Gordimer.

Rutgers University Press. For excerpts from article by Abena P. A. Busia on Marshall in *Changing Our Own Words*, Cheryl A. Wall, ed.; Karla F. C. Holloway, *Moorings & Metaphors: Figures of Culture and Gender in Black Women's Literature* (Naylor); article by [Akasha] Gloria T. Hull on Lorde in *Changing Our Own Words*, Cheryl A. Wall, ed.; article by Toni Morrison on Bambara in *Literature and the Urban Experience*, Michael C. Jaye and Ann Chalmers Watts, eds.; articles by Barbara Smith on Naylor and Lorde in *Wild Women in the Whirlwind: Afra-American Culture and the Contemporary Literary Renaissance*, Joanne M. Braxton and Andrée Nicola McLaughlin, eds.; article by Susan Willis on Morrison in *Changing Our Own Words*, Cheryl A. Wall, ed.

St. Martin's Press. For excerpts from article by Pierrette M. Frickey on Lovelace in Bruce King, ed. *Post-Colonial English Drama: Commonwealth Drama since 1960*. Copyright © 1992 Bruce King. Reprinted with permission of St. Martin's Press, Incorporated; article by Holly Hill on Wilson in Bruce King, ed. *Contemporary American Theatre*. Copyright © 1991 Bruce King. Reprinted with permission of St. Martin's Press, Incorporated; article by Renu Juneja on Walcott in Bruce King, ed. *Post-Colonial English Drama: Commonwealth Drama since 1960*. Copyright © 1992 Bruce King. Reprinted with permission of St. Martin's Press, Incorporated; Bruce King, ed. *The New English Literatures: Cultural Nationalism in a Changing World* (Brathwaite, Harris, Soyinka, Walcott). Copyright © 1980 Bruce King. Reprinted with permission of St. Martin's Press, Incorporated; article by George Lamming on Hearne in Edward Baugh, ed. *Critics on Caribbean Literature*. Copyright © 1978 Edward Baugh. Reprinted with permission of St. Martin's Press, Incorporated; article by Mervyn Morris on Bennett in Edward Baugh, ed. *Critics on Caribbean Literature*. Copyright © 1978 Edward Baugh. Reprinted with permission of St. Martin's Press, Incorporated; Oladele Taiwo. *Female Novelists of Modern Africa* (Head, Nwapa, Ogot, Tlali). Copyright © 1984 Oladele Taiwo. Reprinted with permission of St. Martin's Press, Incorporated; Jane Watts. *Black Writers from South Africa: Towards a Discourse of Liberation* (La Guma, Mphahlele, Rive, Tlali). Copyright © 1989 Jane Watts. Reprinted with permission of St. Martin's Press, Incorporated; article by Thomas R. Whitaker on Soyinka in Bruce King, ed. *Post-Colonial English Drama: Commonwealth Drama since 1960*. Copyright © 1992 Bruce King. Reprinted with permission of St. Martin's Press, Incorporated; article by Bruce Woodcock on Goodison in Gina Wisker, ed. *Black Women's Writing*. Copyright © 1993 Gina Wisker. Reprinted with permission of St. Martin's Press, Incorporated.

Saturday Review. For excerpts from articles by John W. Aldridge on Baldwin; Arna Bontemps on Cullen, Hughes; David Boroff on Williams; Abraham Chapman on M. Walker; John Howard Griffin on Killens; Zora Neale Hurston on Wright; Alain Locke on Hughes; Charles Miller on Armah; Thomas Sugrue on Thoby-Marcelin and Marcelin in *Saturday Review*; Conor Cruise O'Brien on Soyinka in *World*. Copyright © 1927, 1938, 1944, 1952, 1963, 1966, 1968, 1973, 1974 by The Saturday Review, Inc.

The Scarecrow Press, Inc. For excerpt from Jacqueline Covo, *The Blinking Eye* (Ellison).

Schocken Books Inc. For excerpt from Wayne F. Cooper's Introduction to *The Passion of Claude McKay*. Copyright © 1973 by Wayne F. Cooper and Hope McKay Virtue.

Martin Secker & Warburg Limited. For excerpt from Alfred Kazin, *Contemporaries* (Baldwin).

Éditions Seghers. For excerpts from François Dodat, *Langston Hughes*; Lilyan Kesteloot, *Aimé Césaire*.

The Sewanee Review, v. CVII, Winter, 1999 for "A Witness to Culture" by Bruce King. Copyright © 1999 by the author. Reproduced with permission of the editor and the author.

A. J. Seymour. For excerpt from *Edgar Mittelholzer: The Man and His Work*.

Sandra G. Shannon. For excerpts from article on Wilson in *Black American Literature Forum* (now *African American Review*).

Karl Shapiro. For excerpt from article on Tolson in *Wilson Library Bulletin*.

Theodore F. Sheckels. From *The Lion on the Freeway: A Thematic Introduction to Contemporary South African Literature in English*. Peter Lang Publishing, Inc., 1996. © 1996 Peter Lang Publishing, Inc. All rights reserved. Reproduced by permission.

The Shoe String Press, Inc. For excerpts from Donald C. Dickinson, *A. Bio-Bibliography of Langston Hughes, 1902–1967*; J. Noel Heermance, *Charles W. Chesnutt: America's First Great Black Novelist*. Reprinted by permission of Archon Books, The Shoe String Press, Inc., Hamden, Connecticut.

Robert E. Skinner. From a conclusion to *Two Guns From Harlem: The Detective Fiction of Chester Himes*. Bowling Green State University Popular Press, 1989. Copyright © 1989 by Bowling Green State University Popular Press. Reproduced by permission.

South African Outlook. For excerpts from articles by A. C. Jordan on Mqhayi; I. Oldjohn on Jordan; M. S. S. on Plaatje.

Southern Humanities Review. For excerpts from article by Sidonie Ann Smith on Angelou. Copyright *Southern Humanities Review*, 7.4 (1973): 367–68, 374–75. Published by Auburn University.

Southern Illinois University Press. For excerpts from *The Art of Richard Wright* by Edward Margolies. Copyright © 1969 by Southern Illinois University Press. Reprinted by permission of Southern Illinois University Press; *In a Minor Chord* by Darwin T. Turner. Copyright © 1971 by Southern Illinois University Press. Reprinted by permission of Southern Illinois University Press (Cullen, Hurston, Toomer).

Southern Literary Journal, v. XXVII, Spring, 1995. Copyright 1995 by the Department of English, University of North Carolina at Chapel Hill. Reproduced by permission.

The Southern Quarterly. For excerpts from "Alice Childress: Black Woman Playwright as Feminist Critic" by Gayle Austin. Reprinted from *The Southern Quarterly*, Volume 25, Number 3, Spring, 1987, pp. 53–65.

Southwest Review. For excerpt from article by James Presley on Hughes.

Wole Soyinka. For excerpt from article on Okara in *African Forum*.

The Spectator. For excerpts from articles by Anthony Burgess on Harris; Peter Cohen on Anthony; Geoffrey Grigson on Lamming; Auberon Waugh on Achebe.

Stephen Spender. For excerpt from article on Baldwin in *Partisan Review*; on Ellison in *The Listener*.

Hortense J. Spillers. For excerpts from article on Brooks in Henry Louis Gates, Jr., ed. *Reading Black, Reading Feminist*.

Standpunte. For excerpt from article by R. H. W. Shepherd on Jordan.

Robert B. Stepto. For excerpts from article on Lorde in *Parnassus*.

Studies in American Fiction. For excerpts from article by Jonathan Little on Johnson.

Studies in Black Literature. For excerpts from articles by Joan Bischoff on Morrison; Donald Bayer Burness on Aidoo; v. 4, 1973 for "The Poetry of Christopher Okigbo: Its Evolution and Significance" by Omolara Leslie. Copyright 1973 by the editor. Reproduced by permission.

Studies in Short Fiction. For excerpts from Raymond A. Mazurek, "Gordimer's 'Something Out There' and Ndebele's *Fools and Other Stories*: The Politics of Literary Form." *Studies in Short Fiction*. 26 (1989): 71–79. Copyright © 1989 by Newberry College; v. 32, Spring 1995. Copyright 1995 by Newberry College. Reproduced by permission.

Studies in the Novel, v. 29, Fall, 1997; v. 30, Winter, 1998. Copyright 1997, 1998 by North Texas State University. Both reproduced by permission.

Studies in Twentieth-Century Literature. For excerpts from articles by Janis L. Pallister on Neto; W. Curtis Schade on Bebey; Janice Spleth on Mudimbe; v. 19, Summer, 1995. Copyright © 1995 by Studies in Twentieth Century Literature. Reprinted by permission of the publisher.

Gunther Stuhlmann. For excerpts from Edward Margolies, *Native Sons* (Attaway, Demby, Himes).

Roslyn Targ Literary Agency. For excerpts from Chester Himes, *The Quality of Hurt* (Baldwin); William Targ, *Indecent Pleasures* (Himes).

Ellen Tarry. For excerpt from *The Third Door* (McKay).

Allen Tate. For excerpt from article on Tolson in *Poetry*.

Theatre Journal. For excerpts from "Nigerian Independence Onstage: Responses from 'Second Generation' Playwrights," by Sandra L. Richards on Osofisan. Reprinted from *Theatre Journal*. Volume 39, Number 2, 1987. Reprinted by permission of The Johns Hopkins University Press.

Theater Magazine. For excerpts from articles by Mei-Ling Ching on Wilson. *Theater Magazine*, Vol. 19; Lisa Wilde on Wilson. *Theater Magazine*, Vol. 22. Used by permission of *Theater Magazine*, Yale School of Drama.

Theatre Research International, v. 21, Fall 1996 for "Werewere Liking: Pan/Artist and Pan-Africanism in the Theatre," by Judith G. Miller; v. 21, Fall 1996 for "L'engagement dans le théâtre haïtien: l'oeuvre dramatique de Jean Métellus," by Ginette Adamson. Both reproduced by permission of the publisher and respective authors./ v. 23, Autumn, 1998. Reproduced by permission of the publisher and Judith Miller.

Third World Quarterly. For excerpts from article by Michael Gilkes on Gilroy.

Three Continents Press. For excerpt from Richard Priebe's essay in *Critical Perspectives on Amos Tutuola*, Bernth Lindfors, ed. For excerpts from article by Sandra Barkan on Ouologuem in *Interdisciplinary Dimensions of African Literature*, Kofi Anyidoho, Abioseh M. Porter, Daniel [L.] Racine, and Janice Spleth, eds.; article by Charlotte H. Bruner on Head in *When the Drumbeat Changes*, Carolyn A. Parker and Stephen H. Arnold, eds.; Donald Burness, *Fire: Six Writers from Angola, Mozambique, and Cape Verde* (Neto); article by Carole Boyce Davies on Soyinka in *Interdisciplinary Dimensions of African Literature*, Kofi Anyidoho, Abioseh M. Porter, Daniel [L.] Racine, and Janice Spleth, eds.; Albert S. Gerard, *African Language Literatures: An Introduction to the Literary History of Sub-Saharan Africa* (Robert); article by Thomas A. Hale on Césaire in *When the Drumbeat Changes*, Carolyn A. Parker and Stephen H. Arnold, eds.; article by Kenneth [W.] Harrow on Mudimbe in *African Literature Studies: the Present State/L'État présent*, Stephen Arnold, ed.; article by Kenneth [W.] Harrow on Mudimbe in *Literature of Africa and the African Continuum*, Jonathan A. Peters, Mildred P. Mortimer, and Russell V. Linneman, eds.; article by Mildred A. Hill-Lubin on Baldwin in *Interdisciplinary Dimensions of African Literature*, Kofi Anyidoho, Abioseh M. Porter, Daniel [L.] Racine, and Janice Spleth, eds.; article by Ingeborg Kohn on Juminer in *Literature of Africa and the African Continuum*, Jonathan A. Peters, Mildred P. Mortimer, and Russell V. Linnemann, eds.; article by Thomas R. Knipp on Awoonor in *African Literature in Its Social and Political Dimensions*, Eileen Julien, Mildred [P.] Mortimer, and Curtis Schade, eds.; article by Virginia U. Ola on Achebe in *Literature of Africa and the African Continuum*, Jonathan A. Peters, Mildred P. Mortimer, and Russell V. Linnemann, eds.; article by Jonathan A. Peters on Sembène Ousmane in *African Literature in Its Social and Political Dimensions*, Eileen Julien, Mildred [P.] Mortimer, and Curtis Schade, eds.; article by Richard [K.] Priebe on Soyinka in *African Literature Studies: the Present State/L'État présent*, Stephen Arnold, ed.; article by Ahmed Saber on Armah in *Literature of Africa and the African Continuum*, Jonathan A. Peters, Mildred P. Mortimer, and Russell V. Linnemann, eds.; article by W. Curtis Schade on Bebey in *When the Drumbeat Changes*, Carolyn A. Parker and Stephen H. Arnold, eds.; article by F. E. M. K. Senkoro on Robert in *Design and Intent in African Literature*, David F. Dorsey, Phanuel A. Egejuru and Stephen H. Arnold, eds.; article by [H.] Nigel Thomas on Césaire in *Literature of Africa and the African Continuum*, Jonathan A. Peters, Mildred P. Mortimer, and Russell V. Linnemann, eds.; Paul L. Thompson's Introduction to *Bozambo's Revenge* by Bertène Juminer; article by Hal Wylie on Depestre in *When the Drumbeat Changes*, Carolyn A. Parker and Stephen H. Arnold, eds.; article by Hal Wylie on Depestre in *Interdisciplinary Dimensions of African Literature*, Kofi Anyidoho, Abioseh M. Porter, Daniel [L.] Racine, and Janice Spleth, eds.

827

Edwin Thumboo. For excerpts from articles on Brutus in *Joliso*; on Peters in *African Literature Today*.

Thunder's Mouth Press. For excerpts from the book, *The Negritude Poets* by Ellen Conroy Kennedy. Copyright © 1975 by Ellen Conroy Kennedy. Foreword © 1989 by Maya Angelou. All Rights Reserved.

Times Literary Supplement. For excerpts from articles by Louise Doughty on Cliff; Frances Stead Sellers on McMillan; n. 4980, September 11, 1998. © The Times Supplements Limited 1998. Reproduced from The Times Literary Supplement by permission.

Times Newspapers Limited. For excerpts from articles by C.P. Snow on Abrahams in *The Sunday Times*; anon. on Abrahams, Himes, Mittelholzer, Mofolo, Nzekwu, Soyinka in *The Times Literary Supplement*.

Ruth S. Tolson. For excerpts from articles by Melvin B. Tolson on Peters in *African Forum*; on Wright in *The Modern Quarterly*.

Transition. For excerpts from articles by Daniel Abasiekong on Brutus; Chinua Achebe on Awoonor; John Pepper Clark on Okara, Okigbo; David Cook on Soyinka; David Rubadiri on Abrahams; Austin J. Shelton on Achebe.

Clara Tsabedze. From *African Independence From Francophone and Anglophone Voices: A Comparative Study of the Post-independence Novels by Ngugi and Sembène*. Peter Lang Publishing, 1994. © Peter Lang Publishing, Inc. All rights reserved. Reproduced by permission.

Twayne Publishers, Inc. For excerpts from Harold E. Collins, *Amos Tutuola*; Joy Flasch, *Melvin B. Tolson*.

Twentieth Century Literature. For excerpt from article by Neil Schmitz on Reed.

Ufahumu. For excerpts from articles by J. Ndukaku Amankulor on Badian; A. R. Brás on Neto; Carole Boyce Davies on Tlali; Kandioura Dramé on Beti; Kalu Ogbaa on Maillu; John Povey on Mtshali; Katheryn Wright on Tchicaya U Tam'si.

UNESCO Courier, December, 1997; March, 1999. Both reproduced by permission.

University of California Press. For excerpts from Albert S. Gérard, *Four African Literatures: Xhosa, Sotho, Zulu, Amharic*. Copyright © 1971 by Regents of the University of California. Reprinted by permission of the University of California Press (Jordan, Mofolo, Mqhayi, Vilakazi); from article by Lyle Pearson on Sembène in *Film Quarterly*.

The University of Chicago Magazine. For excerpt from article by Ralph Ellison On Baldwin. Reprinted with permission from the April, 1962 *University of Chicago Magazine*.

The University of Chicago Press. For excerpt from Eugene Levy, *James Weldon Johnson: Black Leaders, Black Voice*. Copyright © 1973 by The University of Chicago Press.

The University of Georgia Press. For excerpts from Keith E. Byerman, *Fingering the Jagged Grain* (Bambara, Gaines, Jones, Reed, Walker). Copyright © 1985 by the University of Georgia Press.

University of Hawaii at Manoa. For excerpts from "The Autobiographical Content in the Works of South African Women Writers: The Personal and the Political" (Tlali) by Huma Ibrahim in *Biography East and West*, Carol Remelb, ed.

University of Illinois Press. For excerpts from article by Houston A. Baker, Jr. In *A Life Distilled: Gwendolyn Brooks, Her Poetry and Fiction*, Maria K. Mootry and Gary Smith, eds.; J. Edward Chamberlin, *Come Back to Me My Language: Poetry and the West Indies* (Bennett, Goodison, Senior, Walcott); article by Maria K. Mootry in *A Life Distilled: Gwendolyn Brooks, Her Poetry and Fiction*, Maria K. Mootry and Gary Smith, eds.

The University of Massachusetts Press. For excerpts from Ursula A. Barnett, *A Vision of Order: A Study of Black South African Literature in English (1914–1980)* (Head, Kunene, Mphahlele, Mtshali, Rive, Sepamla, Serote, Tlali). Reprinted from *A Vision of Order: A Study of Black South African Literature in*

*English (1914–1980)*, by Ursula A. Barnett (Amherst: University of Massachusetts Press, 1983), copyright © 1983 by Ursula Barnett; Bernard W. Bell, *The Afro-American Novel and Its Tradition* (Baldwin, Fauset, Morrison, Reed) (Amherst: The University of Massachusetts Press, 1987), copyright © 1987 by the University of Massachusetts Press; Joan Dayan's Introduction to *A Rainbow for the Christian West*, by René Depestre.

The University of Michigan Press. For excerpt from Robert M. Farnsworth's Introduction to *The Conjure Woman* by Charles W. Chesnutt. For excerpts from "Lucille Clifton: A Changing Voice for Changing Times" by Andrea Benton Rushing in *Coming to Light*. Diane Wood Middlebrook and Marilyn Yalom, eds. (Ann Arbor: The University of Michigan Press, 1985).

The University of Minnesota Press. For excerpts from O. R. Dathorne, *The Black Mind* (Aluko, Damas, Mofolo, Mqhayi, Okara, Okigbo, U Tam'si).For excerpts from article by Françoise Lionnet on Cliff in *De/ Colonizing the Subject*, Sidonie Smith and Julia Watson, eds. Copyright 1992 by the Regents of the University of Minnesota. Published by the University of Minnesota Press.

University of Missouri Press. For excerpts from Terry Otten, *The Crime of Innocence in the Fiction of Toni Morrison*.

University of Natal Press. For excerpt from C. L. S. Nyembezi, *A Review of Zulu Literature* (Vilakazi). For excerpts from "Mongane Serote: Humanist and Revolutionary" by Dorian Barboure in *Momentum: On Recent South African Writing*. M. J. Daymond, J. U. Jacobs, and Margaret Lenta, eds. (1984).

The University of North Carolina Press. For excerpts from Benjamin Brawley, *Paul Lawrence Dunbar*; Hugh Gloster, *Negro Voices in American Fiction* (Bontemps, Chesnutt, Dunbar, Johnson, Thurman); J. Saunders Redding, *To Make a Poet Black* (Chesnutt, Cullen, Dunbar). For excerpts from Elizabeth Fox-Genovese on Giovanni, "My Statue, My Self: Autobiographical Writings of Afro-American Women," in *The Private Self: Theory and Practice of Women's Autobiographical Writings*, edited by Shari Benstock. Copyright © 1988 by The University of North Carolina Press. Used by permission of the author and publisher. Reprinted in Henry Louis Gates, Jr., ed. *Reading Black, Reading Feminist* (1990).

University of Oklahoma Press. For excerpts from articles by Martin Banham on La Guma; David Dorsey on Brutus; Robert E. Morsberger on Peters; C. E. Nelson On Damas; Richard Priebe on Aluko, Armah, Soyinka; Edwin Thumboo on Clark; C. H. Wake on Senghor in *Books Abroad* (now *World Literature Today*).

University of Pennsylvania Press. For excerpts from articles by Mary K. DeShazer on Lorde; Estella Lauter on Lorde in *Writing the Women Artist: Essays on Poetics, Politics, and Portraiture*, Suzanne W. Jones, ed.

University of South Carolina Press. For excerpts from article by Elinor S. Miller of Sow Fall in *French Literature Series*.

University of Tennessee Press. For excerpts from Jane Campbell, *Mythic Black Fiction: The Transformation of History* (Baldwin, Bradley).

University of Toronto Quarterly, v. 62, Winter, 1992-93. © University of Toronto Press 1992. Reproduced by permission of University of Toronto Press Incorporated.

The University of Wisconsin Press. For excerpt from Robert E. Fleming, "The Nightmare Level of *The Man Who Cried I Am*," in *Contemporary Literature*, © 1973 by the Regents of the University of Wisconsin (Williams). For excerpts from Houston A. Baker, Jr. In *Afro-American Poetics* on Baraka.

University Press of Kentucky. For excerpts from D. H. Melhem on Brooks. Reprinted from D. H. Melhem, *Gwendolyn Brooks: Poetry and the Heroic Voice*, copyright © 1987 by D. H. Melhem, by permission of the publishers; D. H. Melhem on Sanchez and Baraka. Reprinted from D. H. Melhem, *Heroism in the New Black Poetry*, copyright © 1990 by D. H. Melhem, by permission of the publishers; Martha M. Vertreace on Bambara. Reprinted from Mickey Pearlman, ed., *American Women Writing Fiction: Memory, Identity, Family, Space*, copyright © 1989 by The University Press of Kentucky, by permission of the publishers.

University Press of Mississippi. For excerpts from Missy Dehn Kubitschek, *Claiming the Heritage: African American Women Novelists and History* (Marshall, Morrison, Walker); Paulina Palmer, *Contemporary Women's Fiction: Narrative Practice and Feminist Theory* (Walker).

University Press of Virginia. For excerpts from Angela Y. Davis's Foreword to *I Tituba, Black Witch of Salem* by Condé.

The Viking Press Inc. For excerpts from Eric Bentley, *Theatre of War*, copyright © 1972 by Eric Bentley (Baraka); Ellen Conroy Kennedy in *The Négritude Poets*, Ellen Conroy Kennedy, ed., copyright © 1975 by Ellen Conroy Kennedy (Senghor); David Littlejohn, *Black on White*, copyright © 1966 by David Littlejohn, reprinted by permission of Grossman Publishers (Dunbar, Killens).

The Village Voice. For excerpt from article by Alice Walker on Walcott. Reprinted by permission of *The Village Voice*. Copyright © The Village Voice, Inc., 1974.

The Virginia Quarterly Review. For excerpts from articles by Houston A. Baker, Jr., on Johnson; Raymond Nelson on Himes. For excerpts from article by Peter Harris on Dove.

Hope McKay Virtue. For excerpt from Claude McKay. *Harlem: Negro Metropolis* (Johnson).

VLS, June, 1993 for a review of "Neon Vernacular: New and Selected Poems" by Robyn Selman. Copyright © V. V. Publishing Corporation. Reproduced by permission of the author./ October, 1992. Copyright © V. V. Publishing Corporation. Reproduced by permission of The Village Voice.

Jean Wagner. For excerpts from *Black Poets of the United States* (Brown, Cullen, Dunbar, Johnson, McKay, Toomer).

Keith Q. Warner. From *Critical Perspectives on Léon-Gontran Damas*. Three Continents Press, 1988. © Three Continents Press 1988. All rights reserved. Reproduced by permission of the author.

A. P. Watt & Son. For excerpts from Margaret Laurence, *Long Drums and Cannons* (Aluko, Amadi, Nzekwu, Okara, Soyinka, Tutuola).

Craig Hansen Werner. From *Playing the Changes: From Afro-Modernism to the Jazz Impulse*. University of Illinois Press, 1994. © 1994 by the Board of Trustees of the University of Illinois. Reproduced by permission.

West Africa. For excerpts from articles by Ama Ata Aidoo on Brathwaite, Soyinka; George Awoonor-Williams on Tutuola; D. B. on Amadi; K. W. on Aidoo.

Amos N. Wilder. For excerpt from article on Brooks in *Poetry*.

Gay Wilentz. For excerpts from article on Naylor in *Women's Review of Books*.

Catherine Wiley. From *Modern American Drama: The Female Canon*. Edited by June Schlueter. Fairleigh Dickinson University Press, 1990. Reproduced by permission.

Brian William. From *Sol Plaatje: South African Nationalist, 1876-1932*. Lovedale, 1930. Reproduced by permission.

Pontheolla Williams. From *A Critical Analysis of the Poetry of Robert Hayden, 1940-78*. University of Illinois Press, 1987. © 1987 by the Board of Trustees of the University of Illinois. Reproduced by permission.

Witwatersrand University Press. For excerpts from D. D. T. Jabavu's review of *Inzuzo* by S. E. K. Mqhayi (2, 3, 1943); John Riordan, "The Wrath of the Ancestral Spirits" (20, 1, 1961) (Jordan, Mqhayi) in *African Studies*; J. Dexter Taylor, "*Ikondlo ka Zulu*: An Appreciation" (9, 2, 1935) in *Bantu Studies* (Vilakazi).

Women in African Literature Today, Alt 15, 1987. African World Press, New Jersey, 1996. James Curry Ltd., London. Reproduced by permission.

The Women's Review of Books, v. V, October, 1987 for "Revolutions on Stag" by Rachel Koenig; v. XVI, March, 1999 for "The Whole Story" by Deborah McDowell. Copyright © 1987, 1999. All rights reserved. Both reproduced by permission of the respective authors.

Women's Studies: An Interdisciplinary Journal, v. 25, September, 1996. © Gordon and Breach Science Publishers, Inc. 1996. Reproduced by permission.

Bruce Woodcock. From "Long Memoried Women: Caribbean Women Poets" in *Black Women's Writing*. Edited by Gina Wisker. St. Martin's Press, 1993. © Editorial Board, Lumière (Co-operative) Press Ltd. 1993. Copyright © Gina Wisker. All rights reserved. Reproduced by permission of Macmillan, London and Basingstoke. In North America by St. Martin's Press, Incorporated.

World Literature Today. For excerpts from articles by Kofi Anyidoho on Rive; Ursula A. Barnett on Mapanje; Richard F. Bauerle on Awoonor, Cheney-Coker; Robert L. Berner on Rive; Stephen P. Breslow on Walcott; Charlotte H. Bruner on Bebey, Condé, Phelps, Warner-Vieyra; David K. Bruner on Condé, Emecheta, Tati-Loutard; Danielle Chavy Cooper on Métellus; Cyril Dabydeen on Brathwaite; Diva Barbaro Damato on Glissant; Reed Way Dasenbrock on Soyinka; Priska Degras on Glissant; Jean-Pierre Durix on Harris; Wendy Dutton on Kincaid; [R.] N. Egudu on Ogot; Ezenwa-Ohaeto on Sepamla; Samba Gadjigo on Sow Fall; Kenneth [W.] Harrow on Labou Tansi; Evelyn J. Hawthorne on Kincaid; Jidlaph Kamoche on Ngugi wa Thiong'o; Renée Larrier on Schwarz-Bart; Charles R. Larson on Mtshali; Fernando Martinho on Neto; Robert E. McDowell on Heath; A. L. McLeod on Heath; Fredric Michelman on Labou Tansi; Peter Nazareth on Head, Reed, Salkey, Taban lo Liyong; A. S. Newson on Gilroy; Philip A. Noss on Lopes; Nadezda Obradović on Condé, Warner-Vieyra; Ode S. Ogede on Armah; Tanure Ojaide on Osundare; Chinyere G. Okafor on Rotimi; Onookome Okome on Soyinka; [Juliet] I. Okonkwo on Farah; Pamela J. Olubunmi Smith on Cheney-Coker; Daniel L. Racine on Glissant, Métellus; Wilbert J. Roget on Schwarz-Bart; Andrew Salkey on Gilroy, Goodison, Lovelace, Phillips; Reinhard Sander on Harrish; Charles [Ponnuthurai] Sarvan on Phillips; Eric Sellin on Tchicaya U Tam'si; Juris Silenieks on Césaire, Chamoiseau; Robert P. Smith, Jr. on Tati-Loutard, Zobel; Thomas C. Spear on Condé Michael Thorpe on Osofisan; Melvin B. Tolson, Jr. on Sembène Ousmane; Satoru Tsuchiya on Mwangi; Hal Wylie on Bemba, Beti, Depestre, Métellus, Salkey, Zobel. Copyright *World Literature Today*. Reprinted with permission of the Editor; v. 70, Fall, 1986; v. 64, Winter 1990; v. 66, Summer, 1992; v. 68, Spring, 1994; v, 68, Summer, 1994; v. 69, Summer, 1995; v. 61, v. 69, Winter, 1995; v. 70, Winter, 1996; v. 70, Spring, 1996; Winter, 1997; v. 71, Spring, 1997; v. 71, Summer, 1997; v. 72, Winter, 1998; v. 72, Spring 1998; v. 72, Summer 1998. Copyright © 1986, 1990, 1992, 1994, 1995, 1996, 1997, 1998 by the University of Oklahoma Press. All reproduced by permission.

World Literature Written in English. For excerpts from articles by Anthony Boxill on Lamming; Harold R. Collins on Armah; R. Langenkamp on Clark; v. 27, Autumn, 1987. © Copyright 1987 WLWE-World Literature Written in English. Reproduced by permission of the publisher.

Kent Worcester. From an introduction to *C. L. R. James: A Political Biography*. State University of New York Press, 1996. © 1996 State University of New York. All rights reserved. Reproduced by permission of the State University of New York Press.

Yale French Studies. For excerpts from "France Reads Haiti" by Joan Dayan on Depestre; "The Unknown Voice of Yambo Ouologuem" by Eric Sellin.

The Yale Review. For excerpts from articles by Louis O. Coxe on Abrahams; Babette Deutsch on Brooks. Copyright © 1950, 1955 by Yale University.

Yale University Library. For excerpt from article by Fannie Hurst on Hurston in *The Yale University Library Gazette*.

Yale University Press. For excerpts from Stephen Vincent Benét's Foreword to *For My People* by Margaret Walker; Kimberly W. Benston, *Baraka: The Renegade and the Mask*; Robert A. Bone, *The Negro Novel in America* (Attaway, Bontemps, Demby, Himes, Hughes, Hurston, McKay, Toomer).

Zaïre-Afrique. For excerpt from article by Christophe Gudijiga on Camara in *Congo-Afrique*. For excerpts from Bonnie J. Barthold, *Black Time: Fiction of Africa, the Caribbean and the United States* (Jones, Soyinka). Copyright © 1981 by Yale University Press; Michael G. Cooke, *Afro-American Literature in the*

*Twentieth Century: The Achievement of Intimacy* (Baldwin, Bradley, Harper). Copyright © 1984 by Yale University Press; Neil Lazarus, *Resistance in Postcolonial African Fiction* (Ngugi wa Thiong'o, Sembène Ousmane). Copyright © 1990 by Yale University Press.

Zambezia. For excerpts from article by Flora Veit-Wild on Marechera. University of Zimbabwe Publications (Publisher).

Zed Books. For excerpts from *The Theory of African Literature* by Chidi Amuta on Neto; *Words Unchained* by Chris Searle on Collins; *A People's Voice* by Piniel Viriri Shava on Mtshali, Serote.

Zeitschrift for Anglistik Und Amerikanistik. For excerpts from article by Yvonne Shafer on Wilson.

Zora Neale Hurston Forum. For excerpts from articles by Enid Bogle on Edgell; Brenda DoHarris on Collins.

# CRITIC INDEX

Gold, Ivan
  Williams, 774

Gollock, G. A.
  Mofolo, 479

Goodwin, K. L.
  Awoonor, 53; Brutus, 137; Kunene,
  396; Ntiru, 554; Rubadiri, 642; Taban
  Lo Liyong, 710

Gordimer, Nadine
  Abrahams, 2; Achebe, 9; Mtshali, 503;
  Ngugi Wa Thiong'o, 545

Gottlieb, Annie
  Naylor, 527

Gould, Jean
  Giovanni, 280

Gouraige, Ghislain
  Alexis, 27; Thoby-Marcelin, 720

Gratiant, Isabelle
  Juminer, 368

Grewal, Gurleen
  Morrison, 490

Griffin, John Howard
  Killens, 377

Griffiths, Gareth
  Mais, 441

Grigson, Geoffrey
  Lamming, 412

Grimes, Kyle
  Harper, 299

Gros, Léon Gabriel
  Damas, 204

Gruesser, John C.
  Angelou, 35

Grunebaum, G. E. von
  Senghor, 667

Gudijiga, Christophe
  Camara, 149

Guillén, Nicolás
  Hughes, 338

Haarhoff, Dorian
  Mphahlele, 500

Hale, Thomas A.
  Césaire, 154

Harney, Steve
  Baraka, 83

Harries, Lyndon
  Robert, 634

Harris, Peter
  Dove, 236

Harris, Rodney E.
  Césaire, 154

Harris, Trudier
  Childress, 169; Walker, A., 753;
  Wilson, 780

Harris, Wilson
  Lamming, 412; Mais, 441

Harrison, William
  Hayden, 310

Harrow, Kenneth
  Labou Tansi, 402; Mudimbe, 506,
  508, 510

Hassan, Ihab
  Baraka, 79; Ellison, 253

Hawthorne, Evelyn J.
  Kincaid, 380; Mais, 442

Haynes, John
  Kunene, 397

Hayward, Jennifer
  Johnson, J., 355

Heaney, Seamus
  Walcott, 746

Hearne, John
  Harris, 301

Hébert, Kimberly
  Danticat, 212

Heermance, J. Noel
  Chesnutt, 169

Hefferman, Teresa
  Morrison, 488

Helford, Elyce Rae
  Butler, 145

Hemingway, Ernest
  Maran, 448

Henderson, Mae G.
  Jones, 362

Herd, David
  Okri, 576

Hernton, Calvin C.
  Kelley, 371; Reed, 620

Heron, G. A.
  p'Bitek, 596

Heywood, Christopher
  Abrahams, 3

Hezekiah, Randolph
  Zobel, 797

Highet, Gilbert
  Wright, 786

Hill, Holly
  Wilson, 777

Hill-Lubin, Mildred A.
  Aidoo, 22; Baldwin, 69

Himes, Chester
  Baldwin, 68

Hirsch, Edward
  Walcott, 745, 751

Hite, Molly
  Walker, A., 755

Hofmeyr, Isabel
  Marechera, 456

Holladay, Hilary
  Petry, 603

Holloway, Karla F. C.
  Emecheta, 259; Naylor, 530; Nwapa,
  559; Shange, 686

Holmes, Eugene
  Toomer, 730

Hopkinson, Amanda
  Lopes, 424

Horn, Andrew
  Serumaga, 680, 681

Horne, Naana Banyiwa
  Aidoo, 25

Tucker, Martin
Armah, 42; Camara, 150; Ngugi Wa Thiong'o, 544; Plaatje, 614

Tulip, James
Tolson, 728

Turner, Darwin T.
Bullins, 142; Cullen, 198; Hurston, 343; Toomer, 731

Umeh, Marie Linton
Emecheta, 255, 256

Upchurch, Michael
Danticat, 213

Updike, John
Amadi, 31; Awoonor, 53; Mphahlele, 498

Vail, Leroy and White, Landeg
Mapanje, 445

Valdés, Ildefonso Pereda
Brown, 132

Valéry Larbaud
Thoby-Marcelin, 719

Van Sertima, Ivan
Hearne, 320; Mais, 439

Van Vechten, Carl
Johnson, J., 358

Vaughan, Michael
Ndebele, 539

Vavilov, V.
Okara, 567

Veit-Wild, Flora
Marechera, 452, 453

Vertreace, Martha M.
Bambara, 73

Vickery, Olga W.
Baraka, 78

Vieyra, Paulin Soumanou
Sembène, 659

Vinson, Audrey L.
Gaines, 273

Wade, Michael
Abrahams, 4

Wagner, Jean
Brown, 132; Cullen, 198; Dunbar, 243; Johnson, J., 360; Mckay, 468; Toomer, 732

Wake, Clive
Beti, 100; Rabéarivelo, 617, 618; Senghor, 666; Serote, 677

Walcott, Ronald
Williams, 773

Walker, Alice
Gaines, 269; Walcott, 744

Walker, Margaret
Brooks, 125

Walker-Johnson, Joyce
Brodber, 121

Wallenstein, Barry
Baraka, 85

Wangusa, Timothy
Ntiru, 553

Waniek, Marilyn Nelson
Marshall, 456

Ward, Catherine C.
Naylor, 527

Ward, Jerry W.
Walker, A., 752

Warner, Gary
Ndao, 535

Warner, Keith Q.
Damas, 208; Zobel, 798

Warren, Robert Penn
Ellison, 252

Washington, Mary Helen
Brooks, 128

Waterhouse, Keith
Achebe, 6

Waters, Chris
Anthony, 38

Waters, Harold A.
Ndao, 535; Onwueme, 578

Watson, Julia
Diallo, 230

Watts, Jane
La Guma, 406; Mphahlele, 500; Rive, 632; Tlali, 725

Waugh, Auberon
Achebe, 8

Weales, Gerald
Hansberry, 295

Webb, Constance
Wright, 787

Weedman, Jane
Delany, 216

Werner, Craig Hansen
Kennedy, 375; Tolson, 729

Weyant, Jill
Kelley, 372

Whitaker, Thomas R.
Soyinka, 700

White, Emily
Marshall, 459

White, Mark Bernard
Clifton, 189

Whitlow, Roger
Demby, 220; Walker, M., 759

Wideman, John
Chesnutt, 168

Wilde, Lisa
Wilson, 779

Wilder, Amos N.
Brooks, 124

Wilentz, Gay
Naylor, 530; Nwapa, 558; Sutherland, 707

Wiley, Catherine
Childress, 171

Willan, Brian
Plaatje, 616

Williams, 'Bayo
Munonye, 516